To: Sandy
"Happy 50th Birthday"
March 2001
Love
Travis,
Denise &
Chantal

ANATOMICA

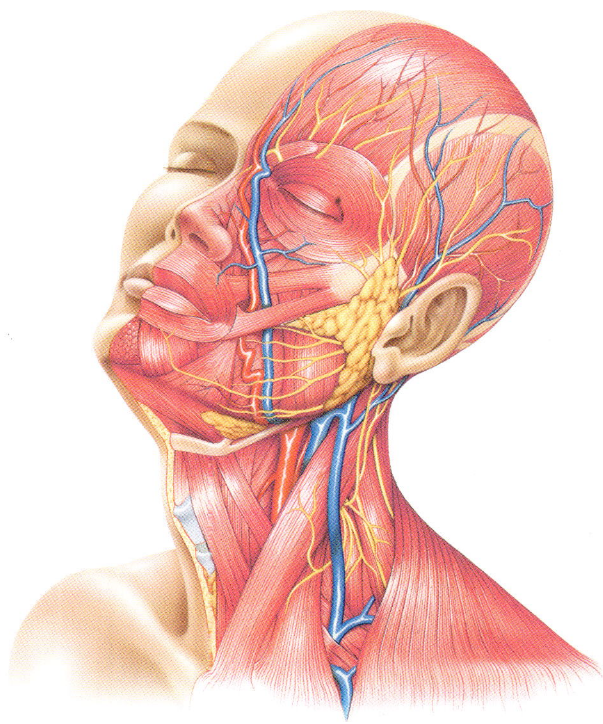

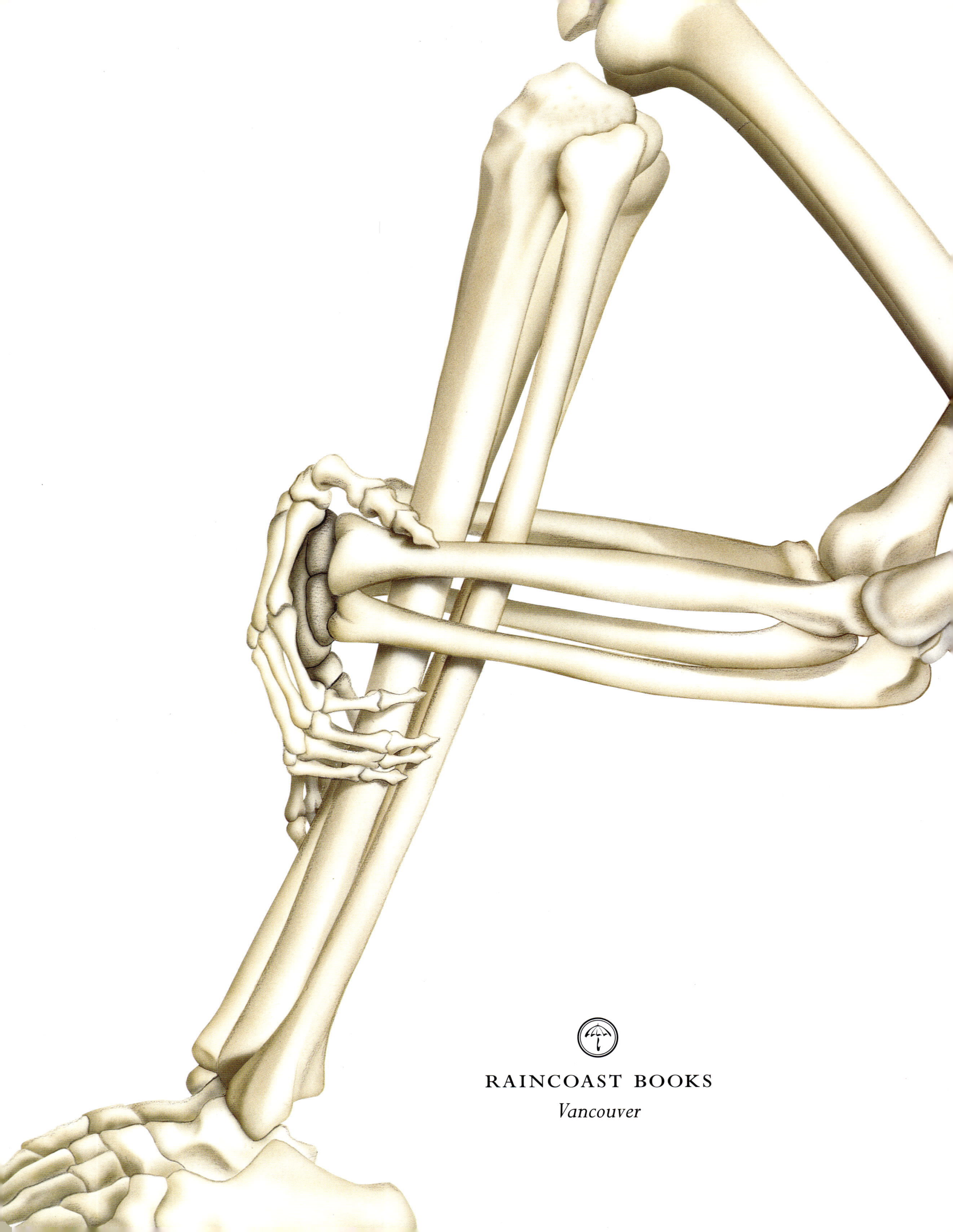

RAINCOAST BOOKS
Vancouver

ANATOMICA

The Complete Medical Encyclopedia

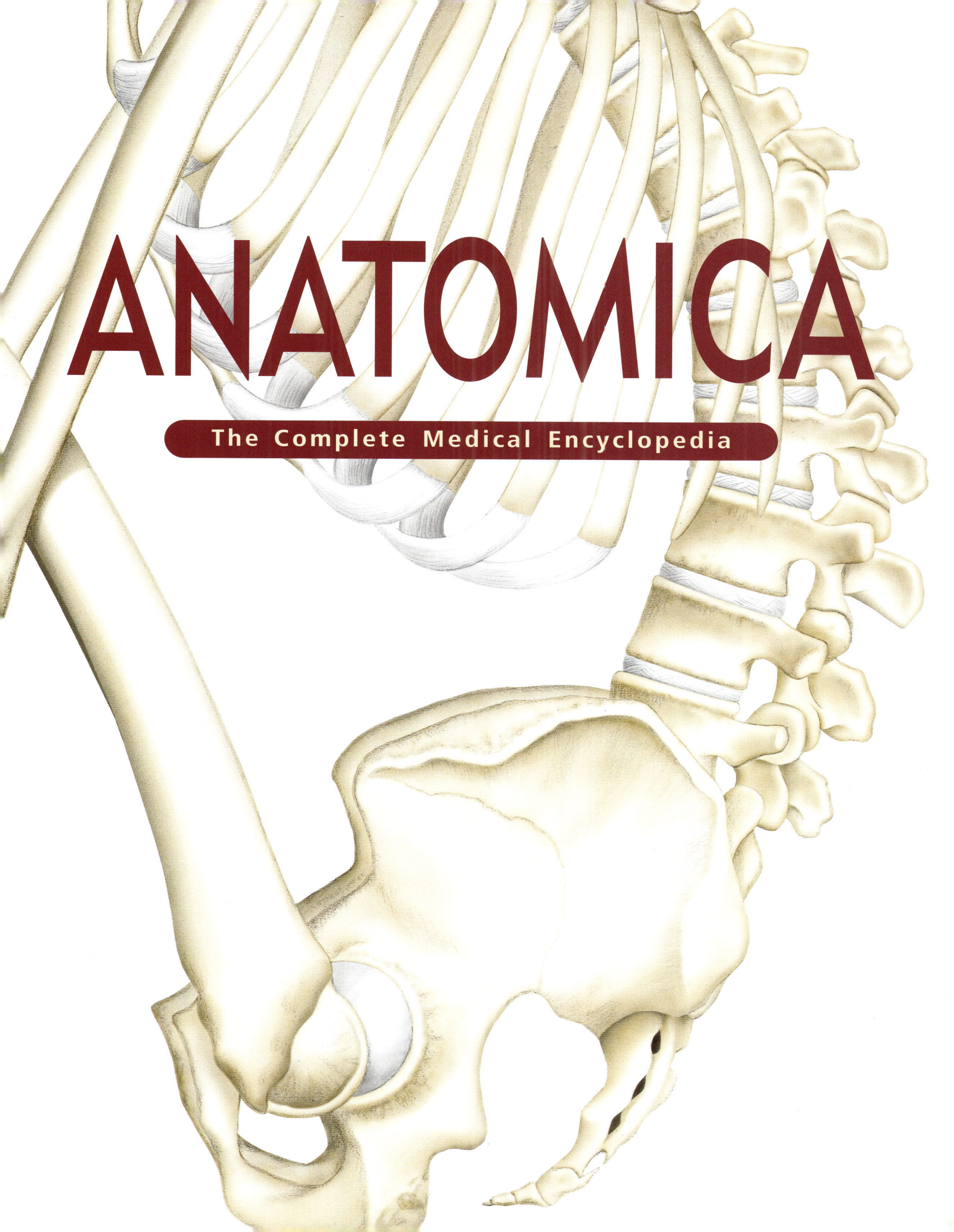

Publisher **Gordon Cheers**

Associate publisher **Margaret Olds**

Text managing editor **Kate Etherington**

Illustration managing editor **Anna Cheifetz**

Chief illustration consultant **Dzung Vu** MD MBBS DipAnat CertHEd

Illustration consultants **John Frith** MBBS BSc(Med) DipEd MCH
David Jackson MBBS BSc (Med)

Symptoms table text **Jenni Harman**
Melanie George MBBS DipPaed
Annette Kifley MBBS
Robyn McCooey BAppSci (Speech & Hearing)
Sue Markham BAppSci (Phty)

First aid information provided by **St John Ambulance Australia**

Illustrators
David Carroll
Peter Child
Deborah Clarke
Geoff Cook
Marcus Cremonese
Beth Croce
Wendy de Paauw
Levant Efe
Hans De Haas
Mike Golding
Jeff Lang
Alex Lavroff
Ulrich Lehmann
Ruth Lindsay
Annabel Milne
Tony Pyrzakowski
Oliver Rennert
Caroline Rodrigues
Otto Schmidinger
Bob Seal
Vicky Short
Graeme Tavendale
Jonathan Tidball
Paul Tresnan
Valentin Varetsa
Veronica Varetsa
Glen Vause
Spike Wademan
Trevor Weekes
Paul Williams
David Wood

Senior editor **Denise Imwold**

Text editors
Michael Wall
Anne Savage
Heather Jackson
Margaret Malone
Diana Marks
Dannielle Doggett
Michael Roberts

Illustration editors
Janet Parker
Heather McNamara
Alan Edwards
Jan Watson
Louise Buchanan
Kavita Enjeti
Barry Grossman
Bernard Roberts

Labels
Thao Vu
Jin-Oh Ree

First published in Canada in 2000 by
Raincoast Books
9050 Shaughnessy Street
Vancouver, B.C.
V6P 6E5
604 323 7100
www.raincoast.com

Produced by Global Book Publishing Pty Ltd
1/181 High Street, Willoughby, NSW Australia 2068
Phone 61 2 9967 3100 fax 61 2 9967 5891

Canadian Cataloguing in Publication data:

Main entry under title:
Anatomica

Includes index.
ISBN 1-55192-357-2

1. Medicine, Popular–Encyclopedías. 2. Human anatomy–Popular works. 3. Human physiology–Popular works. 4. Health. I. Currie, William. II. Baume, Peter, 1935- III. Tracey, David J.
QM26.A49 2000 610í.3 C00-910738-X

Printed in Hong Kong by Sing Cheong Printing Co. Ltd
Film separation Pica Colour Overseas, Singapore

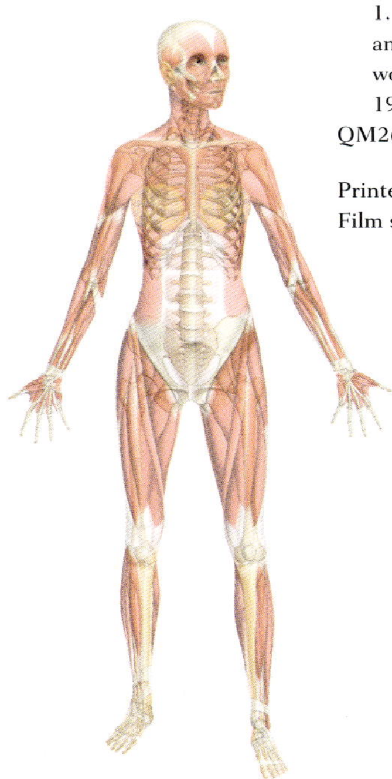

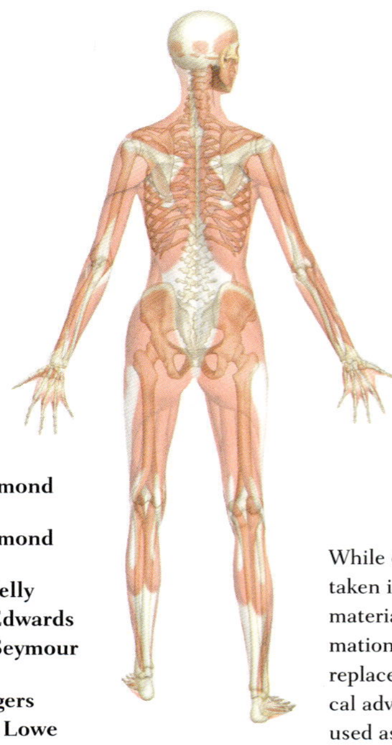

Art director **Stan Lamond**

Cover design **Stan Lamond**

Page layout **Paula Kelly**
Claire Edwards
Emma Seymour

Typesetting **Dee Rogers**
Deanne Lowe

Index **Michael Wall**

International rights **Sarah Sherlock**

Publishing assistant **Erin King**

Production assistant **Rosemary Barry**

CONSULTANTS

CHIEF CONSULTANTS

Dr R. William Currie BSA, MSc, PhD is Professor of Anatomy and Neurobiology in the Faculty of Medicine at Dalhousie University, Halifax, Nova Scotia, Canada. In his academic career, Dr Currie has taught all aspects of gross anatomy to medical, dental and health professional students. He is a pioneer and leader in his research on the protective role of heat shock proteins in the heart and the brain. He is a founding member of the editorial board of *Cell Stress and Chaperones*.

David Tracey BSc, PhD studied for his PhD in neuroscience at Stanford University and has worked as a neuroscientist in Munich, Paris, Melbourne and Canberra. In 1982 he joined the School of Anatomy at the University of New South Wales, where he teaches musculoskeletal anatomy.

He became Professor of Anatomy there in 1995 and is Head of Department. His research has included work on the anatomy and physiology of the spinal cord, and currently focuses on mechanisms of pain following nerve injury. He is a board member of the Federation of Australian Scientific and Technological Societies.

The Honorable Emeritus Professor Peter Baume AO, MD, BS (Syd), HonDLitt (USQ), FRACP, FRACGP, FAFPHM has been a professor since 1991. He was Head of the School of Community Medicine at the University of New South Wales until May 2000, and is currently with the Social Policy Research Centre within the University of New South Wales. He is Chancellor of the Australian National University.

He is a physician who holds a doctorate and several fellowships. He has been a consultant physician, a Senator for New South Wales (1974-91), Minister for Aboriginal Affairs, Minister for Health, Minister for Education and a Minister in Cabinet.

He is a Past President of the Public Health Association (New South Wales Branch), Chair of the Drug Offensive Council of New South Wales, a member of the Minister for Health Advisory Committee in New South Wales. He has published widely and was made an Officer in the Order of Australia in 1992. He is married with two children.

SENIOR CONSULTANT

John Frith, MB, BS, BSc(Med), GradDipEd, MCH, RFD is a general practitioner and lecturer in general practice at the School of Community Medicine, University of New South Wales, Sydney. He graduated from the University of New South Wales in 1973, 1976 and 1994, and Sydney College of Advanced Education in 1988. His experience is in clinical and academic general practice and community health. Professional memberships include Member of the Royal Australian College of General Practitioners and medical officer in the Royal Australian Naval Reserve. Other committee memberships include drug and alcohol education and prevention, health and safety in child care, and motor accidents compensation scheme. He lectures in undergraduate general practice and medical ethics and law, and postgraduate primary health care, public health, and environmental health.

Dr Frith has contributed to publications and books on general practice and on public health.

CONSULTANTS

Kurt H. Albertine PhD is Professor of Pediatrics (Neonatology), as well as Adjunct Professor of Medicine (Pulmonary) and Neurobiology and Anatomy at the University of Utah School of Medicine in Salt Lake City, Utah, USA.

Dr Albertine received a bachelor's degree in biology from Lawrence University and a doctoral degree in human anatomy from the University of Chicago, Stritch School of Medicine. He received postdoctoral training at the University of California, San Francisco, Cardiovascular Research Institute. He has taught human gross anatomy for twenty-five years, and is currently the course director for gross anatomy at the University of Utah. One of his current scholarly projects is developing radiographic holograms for learning 3-dimensional human anatomy.

Laurence Garey MA, DPhil, BM, BCh, recently the Professor of Anatomy at the University of London, in the Division of Neuroscience of Imperial College School of Medicine at Charing Cross Hospital, London, is now the Professor of Anatomy in the Faculty of Medicine and Health Sciences at the United Arab Emirates University, Al Ain.

He qualified in medicine at Worcester College, Oxford, and St Thomas' Hospital, London, and obtained a doctorate in Oxford, based on research on the mammalian visual system. He worked in neuroanatomical research in Oxford, Berkeley, Lausanne and Singapore, before returning to London in 1990.

His research interest is on the structure, development and pathology of the human brain, especially the cerebral cortex. For some years he has been active in research on the pathophysiological basis of schizophrenia.

He has contributed to the *Oxford Companion to the Body*, and translated a number of biomedical science books from French, including *Neuronal Man* by Jean-Pierre Changeux (1985), *The Population Alternative* by Jacques Ruffié (1986), and *The Paradox of Sleep* by Michel Jouvet (1999). He has also translated (1994) from the German the famous *Localisation in the Cerebral Cortex* by Korbinian Brodmann, written in 1909.

Gareth Jones BSc (Hons), MB, BS (Lond), DSc (Univ West Aust), CBiol, FIBiol is the Professor and Head of the Department of Anatomy and Structural Biology, University of Otago, Dunedin, New Zealand. His main specialties are neurobiology—the organization and plasticity of synaptic connections in the brain; bioethics—issues related to the human body and human tissue; and anatomical education. His recent book projects include *Medical Ethics*; *Speaking for the Dead*; *Universities as Critic and Conscience of Society*; and (forthcoming) *Synapses in the Central Nervous System*.

CONTRIBUTORS

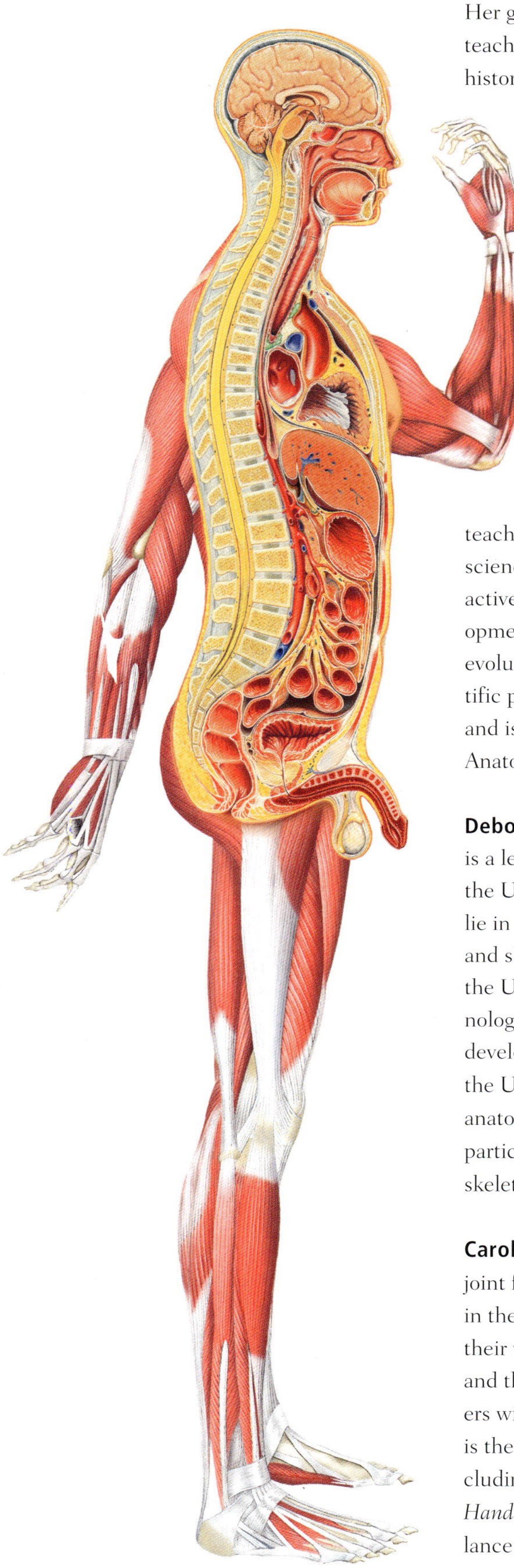

Robin Arnold **MSc** is a lecturer in the Department of Anatomy at the University of Sydney. Her general professional interests include teaching gross anatomy, microscopy, medical history and dental histology. In the area of research her main interests lie in comparative mammalian female reproduction and atherosclerosis.

Ken Ashwell **BMedSc, MB, BS, PhD** graduated in medicine from the University of New South Wales in 1983. After a short time in clinical medicine he returned to research and teaching, undertaking a PhD studying processes in abnormal brain development and graduating from the University of Sydney in 1988. He has been teaching anatomy to medical, chiropractic and science students since 1984 and maintains an active involvement in research on brain development (both normal and abnormal) and brain evolution. He is the author of over fifty scientific papers, two books and two book chapters and is currently Associate Professor in Anatomy.

Deborah Bryce **BSc, MScQual, MChiro, GrCertHEd** is a lecturer in the Department of Anatomy at the University of Sydney. Her special interests lie in teaching and learning in higher education and she has completed studies in this area at the University of NSW and University of Technology, Sydney. She has been central in the development of online teaching resources at the University of Sydney, including an online anatomy museum and anatomy glossary. Her particular area of teaching interest is musculoskeletal anatomy and the vertebral column.

Carol Fallows **BA** and **Martin Fallows** are joint founders of several consumer magazines in the areas of health and parenting. Both began their writing careers in the magazine industry and they share a passion for providing consumers with accurate up-to-date information. Carol is the author of several books on parenting including *The Australian Baby & Child Care Handbook* and *Having a Baby*. Martin is a freelance editor and publishing consultant.

John Gallo **MB, BS (Hons), FRACP, FRCPA** is a Senior Staff Hematologist at South Western Area Pathology Service and Liverpool Hospital, Sydney, Australia. He graduated in medicine from the University of Sydney in 1976 and, as part of his post-graduate training, was a Research Fellow at the University of Maryland Cancer Center in Baltimore, USA, in 1982–1983. His research interests were in the fields of chromosomal abnormalities in leukemia, and the cell cycle. After completing his specialist training he was in private clinical hematology practice in Sydney for 10 years. His main clinical interests are in Hodgkin's lymphoma and bone marrow disorders of the elderly.

Brian Gaynor **MB, BS, FRACP, FRACGP, MRCGP (UK) DCH** is a retired general pediatrician who is currently enjoying life as a part-time family doctor and part-time columnist on the internet. His experience in pediatrics has covered many aspects including hospital consultant, staff specialist in community pediatrics, superintendent of a large home for intellectually handicapped children, plus stints in remote areas, including Fiji, Iraq and Papua New Guinea. His writing career began as part of a midlife crisis when he started as a columnist for a Sydney daily newspaper, then progressed to being a feature writer for different newspapers, magazines and other publications.

Sally Gillespie **BA, DipHerb** has been in private practice in Sydney since 1983, working as a natural therapist and a dream and sandplay therapist. She is the author of *Living the Dream* and *The Book of Dreaming* and the co-author of *The Knot of Time*. In her work as a freelance writer she has contributed articles to *New Woman, Family Circle* and *Nature and Health* magazines.

Jenni Harman **BVSc, BA (Hons I)** is a freelance medical writer specializing in medical education. She trained and worked as a veterinary surgeon before completing an arts degree and working as a research assistant in a university education faculty. As a medical writer, she has specialized in continuing medical education for primary care physicians and specialists, as well as newspaper journalism. Her recent projects include the development of small-group discussion-based educational programs for doctors on asthma, cardiovascular disease and psychiatry, teaching resources for specialists, and fact sheets for patients.

Rakesh Kumar MB, BS, PhD graduated in medicine from the All-India Institute of Medical Sciences, New Delhi, and took up an appointment at the University of New South Wales, Sydney in 1977. He subsequently completed a PhD at the University of New South Wales and is now Associate Professor of Pathology. He is an enthusiastic teacher and is involved in courses for both medical and science students. He has a long-standing interest in chronic lung disease and his research focuses on mechanisms of inflammation of the airways in asthma.

Peter Lavelle MB, BS graduated in medicine from Sydney University in 1983 and practiced as a primary care physician for several years before becoming a full-time medical writer. He contributes regularly to the *Age* and *Sydney Morning Herald* newspapers, the *Australian Doctor* and the *Medical Observer*.

Lesley Lopes BA Communications (Journalism) is a journalist and editor who began her career in publishing as a cadet newspaper reporter 15 years ago. She edited photographic and home entertainment magazines in Sydney for six years before working for a London publishing firm developing a range of children's and lifestyle publications. Lesley recently held the position of Features Editor of Australia's *Better Homes and Gardens* magazine.

Karen McGhee BSc is a Sydney-based freelance journalist. Her work has focused on the areas of science and the environment for more than a decade. She has written for newspapers (including the *Sydney Morning Herald*), magazines (ranging from *Time* to *Australian Geographic*), books and television documentaries for both Australian and overseas audiences.

Emeritus Professor Frederick Rost BSc (Med), MB, BS, PhD, DCP (London), DipRMS was born in London in 1934 and arrived in Australia in 1937. He was Professor of Anatomy at the University of New South Wales from 1974–95. Retired, Fred is now a freelance author, photographer and artist, and has honorary appointments at the University of New South Wales and Macquarie University. He is currently writing his fifth major book. His interests include cosmology.

Elizabeth Tancred BSc, PhD is a Senior Lecturer in Anatomy at the University of New South Wales, with more than 20 years experience in teaching anatomy. Following a BSc with honours in anatomy, she completed a PhD in neuroanatomy in 1983. Her early research was in the area of visual neuroscience but she is now focused on the role of information technology in medical education. She is the author of several software packages for teaching neuroanatomy and cross-sectional anatomy, most notably, "BrainStorm: Interactive Neuroanatomy" which is used widely in universities throughout the world.

Dzung Vu MD, MB, BS, DipAnat., GradCertHEd is an orthopedic surgeon and clinical anatomist. He teaches clinical anatomy to medical students and candidates of specialist degrees, and is the author of many teaching videotapes and computer-assisted learning programs in anatomy. He was the recipient of the Vice Chancellor's Award for Excellence in Teaching at the University of New South Wales in 1992 and is an examiner of the Royal Australian College of Ophthalmologists. He is also a gifted medical illustrator and belongs to the Australian Institute of Medical and Biological Illustration, among many other national and international professional associations.

Phil Waite BSc (Hons), MBChB, CertHEd, PhD obtained a BSc in physiology followed by a PhD in sensory neurophysiology at University College, London. After emigrating to Australia, she held teaching and research positions at Monash University, Melbourne, and then at the University of Otago in New Zealand. She later graduated in medicine at Otago University and is now a Professor of Anatomy at the University of New South Wales, working on brain development and the effects of injury.

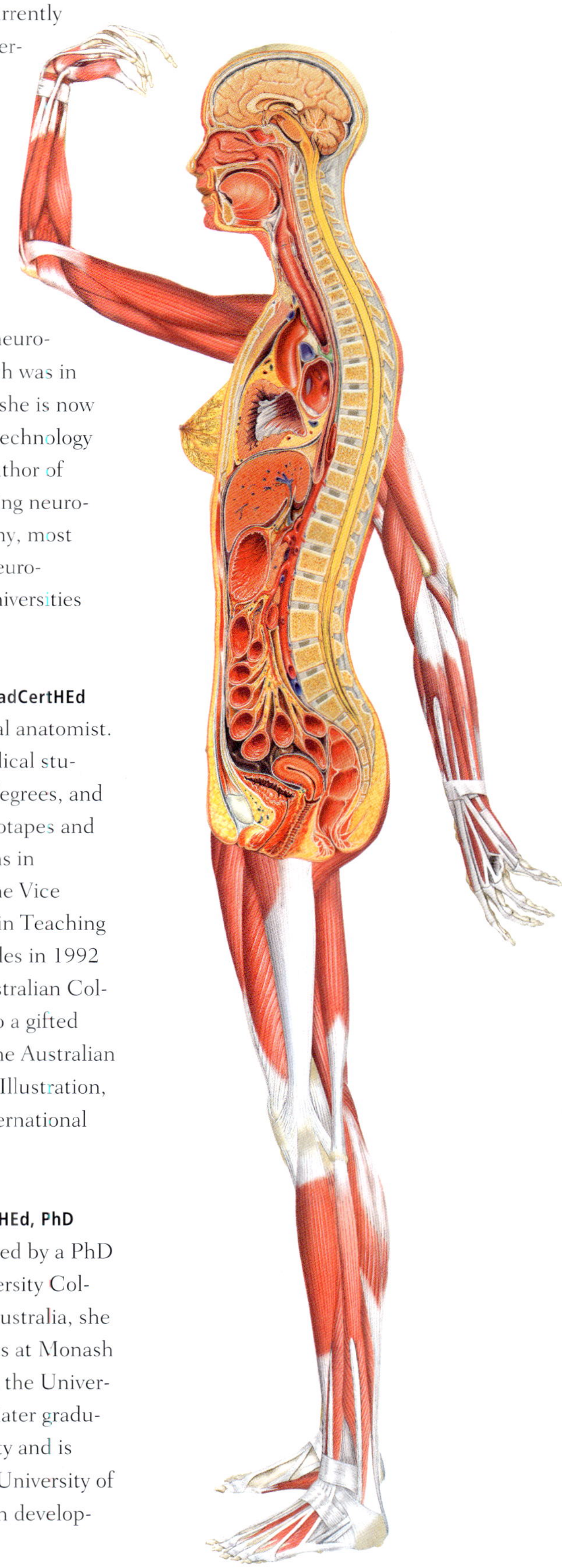

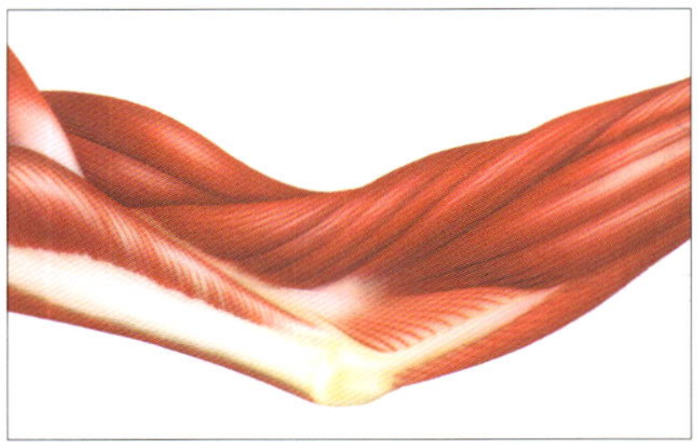

C O N T

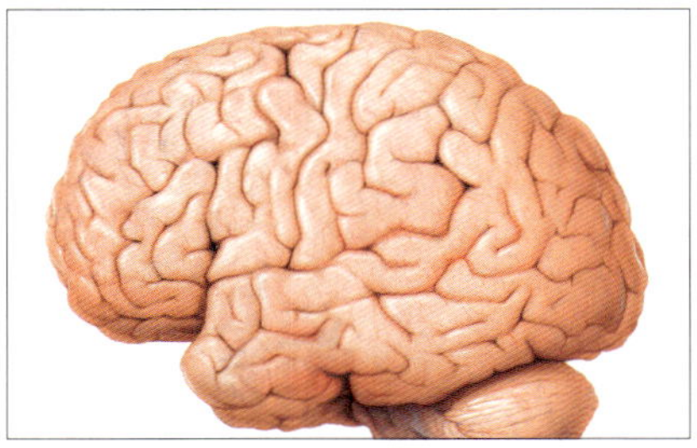

How This Book Works 10

Foreword 12

BODY SYSTEMS 14

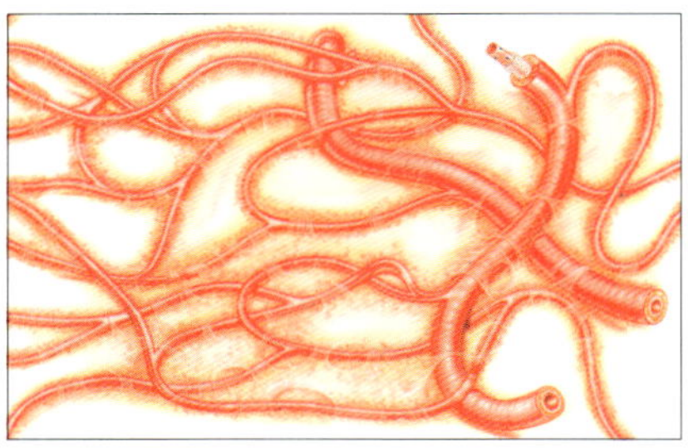

A to Z ENCYCLOPEDIA

Abdomen *to* Ayurvedic medicine **50**

Back *to* Buteyko breathing technique **112**

Caffeine *to* Cytotoxic drugs **152**

Dacrocystitis *to* Dysuria **206**

Ear *to* Eyelids **242**

Face *to* Fragile X syndrome **280**

Gallbladder *to* Gums **306**

Hair *to* Hysteroscopy **330**

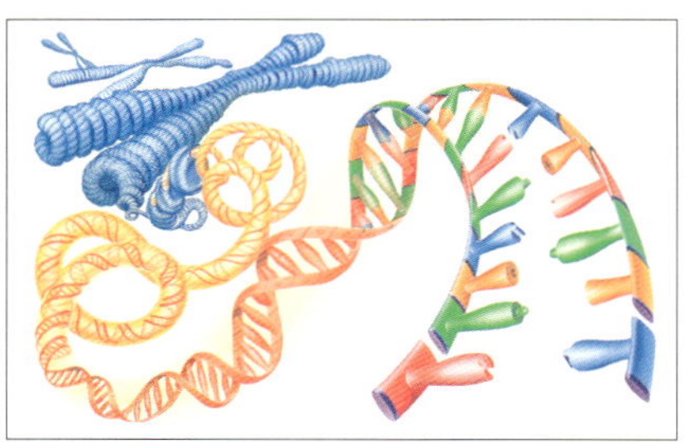

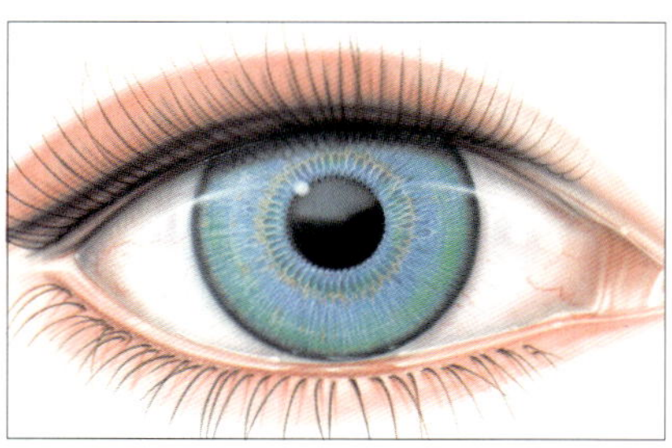

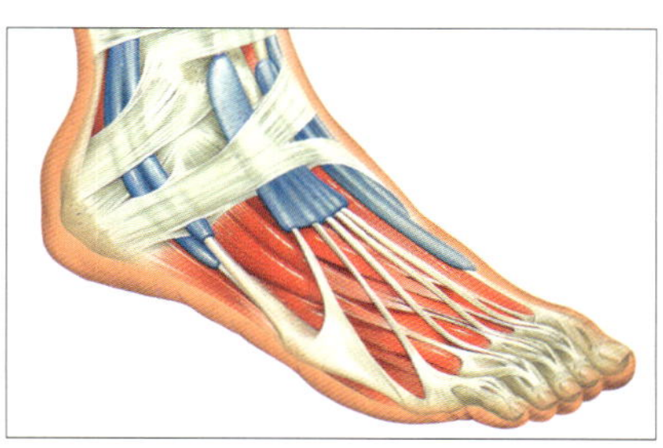

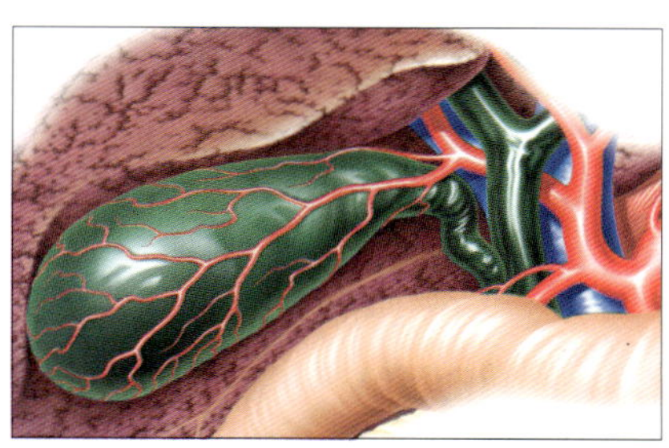

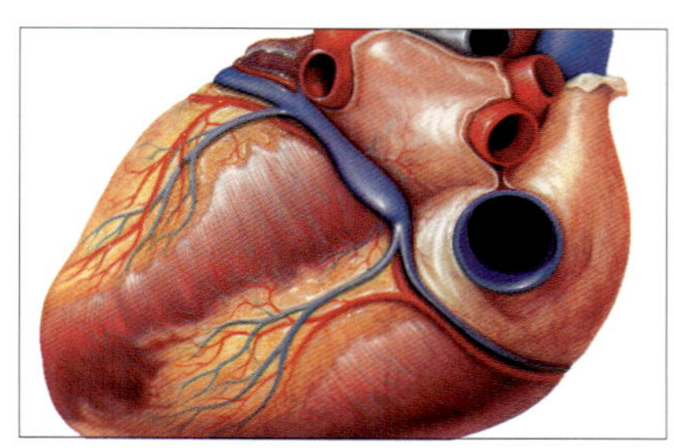

E N T S

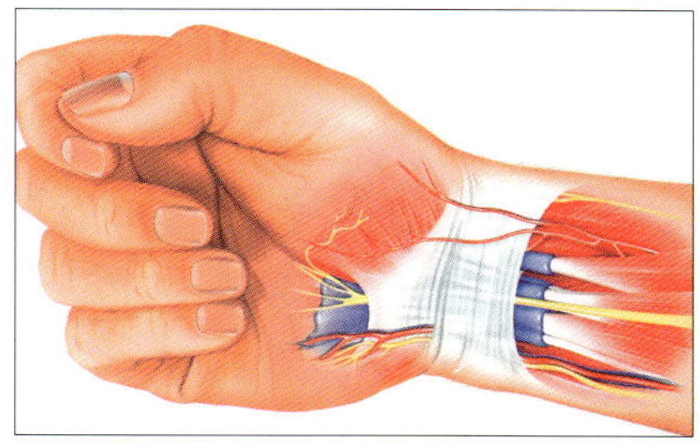

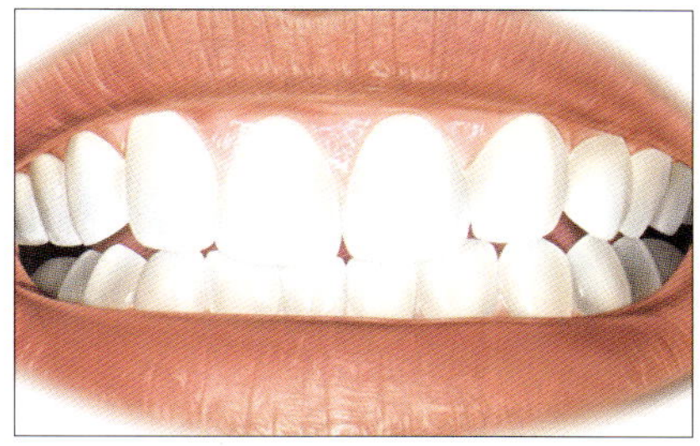

Iatrogenic disease *to* Kyphosis **380**

Labyrinthitis *to* Lymphogranuloma venereum **418**

Macular degeneration *to* Myxedema **450**

Nails *to* Oxytocin **490**

Pacemaker *to* Pylorus **530**

Q fever *to* Rubella **588**

Sacroiliac joint *to* Syphilis **612**

T cells *to* Typhus **690**

Ulcer *to* Zygote **736**

FIRST AID 768

SYMPTOMS TABLES 785

THE TIME OF YOUR LIFE 882

Index 886

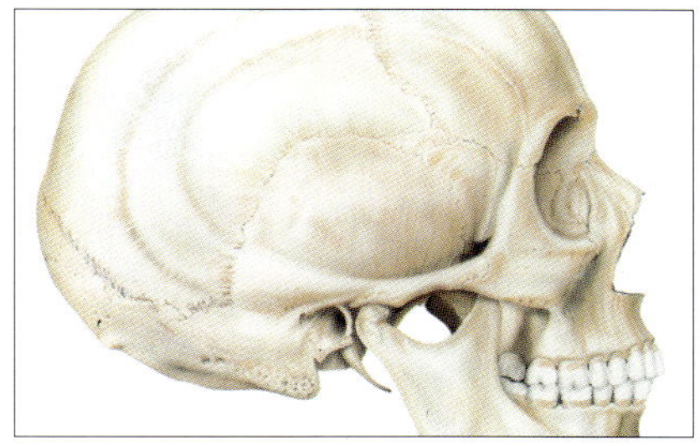

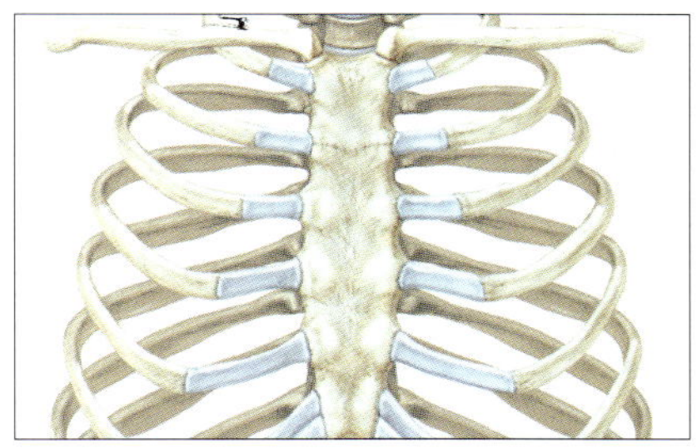

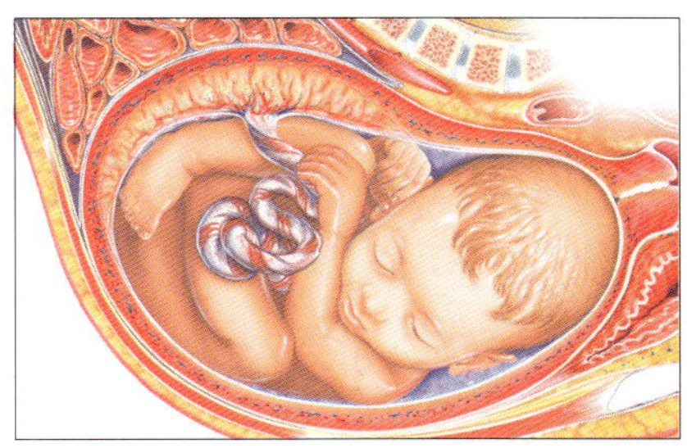

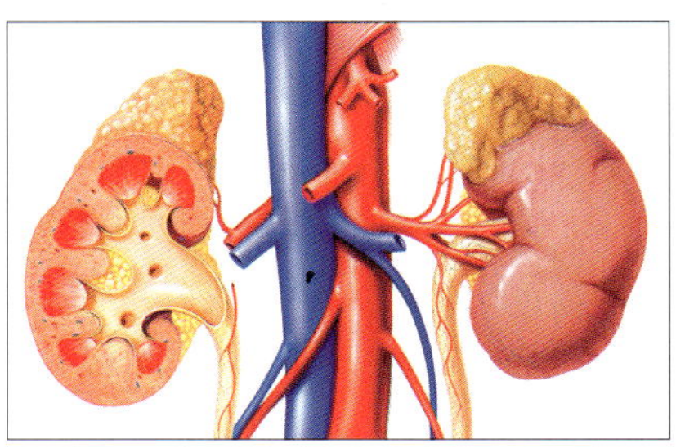

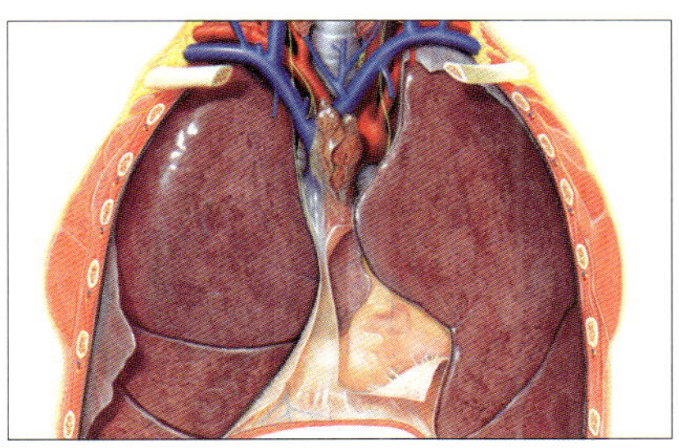

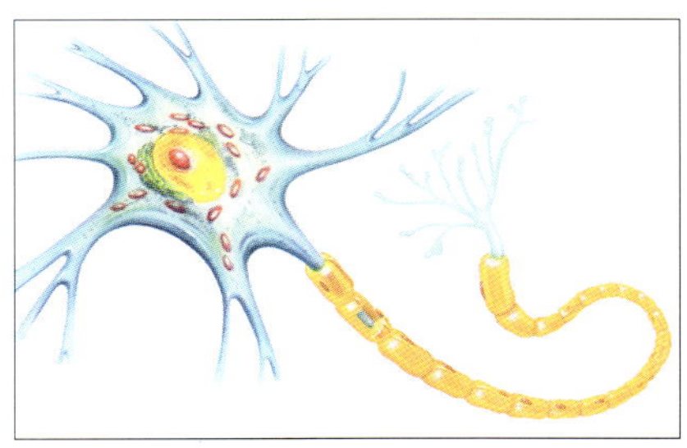

HOW THIS BOOK WORKS

Anatomica is a complete illustrated reference to the human body. However, it is not just a book on anatomy; *Anatomica* is also a comprehensive and authoritative family medical encyclopedia.

The book is divided into several sections. The first section contains the major body systems (Circulatory, Digestive, Endocrine, Lymphatic/Immune, Muscular, Nervous, Reproductive, Respiratory, Skeletal and Urinary) and provides a clear overview of the workings of the body.

The second, and largest section, is an alphabetical listing of entries. It includes descriptions of the various organs and parts of the body, such as the heart, lungs, head and spine. It also contains listings for a large variety of diseases, conditions and injuries—for example, measles, acne, asthma, fractures, hypertension and glaucoma. There are listings for procedures, techniques and diagnostic tests (biopsy, electrocardiograph and CAT scan, to name but a few), and entries for various types of medication, such as anticonvulsants, anti-inflammatory drugs and sedatives.

The A–Z section also contains entries dealing with every stage of life: pregnancy, infancy, childhood, adolescence, menopause, ageing, geriatric medicine and palliative care. There are articles pertaining to aspects of preventive medicine, such as nutrition, diet, exercise and immunization. *Anatomica* recognizes that a person is not simply a physical entity, but also a complex, mental, emotional and social being, and to that end, discusses such topics as alcoholism, domestic violence, grief, sexuality, stress and personality disorders. The book also includes a wide range of alternative therapies, from acupuncture to yoga.

The last part of the book has a chapter on First Aid, which covers every type of emergency. There is also an informative Symptoms Table, which looks at symptoms ranging from abdominal pain to rashes, and advises when to see a doctor. The final section, The Time of Your Life, highlights developmental milestones and preventive health issues for men and women. An extensive index completes the volume.

The detailed illustrations are a visual connection and complement to the text, facilitating understanding. The corresponding captions and labels are relevant and instructive. In some instances, the illustration has removed one part of the body so another may be viewed more clearly; for example, in some of the illustrations of the abdominal organs the liver has been peeled back to show the gallbladder. This is also true of some of the lung illustrations. Many illustrations are supplemented by a locator diagram, which indicates where the organ is in relation to the rest of the body. The appearance of an organ depends on the angle from which it is viewed, and for this reason some of the locators (for example, the uterus) may appear slightly different from the main illustration.

For each alphabetical entry there is a heading, and if there is an illustration, it will include a caption and labels. The SEE ALSOs refer the reader to other relevant A–Z entries; where the cross reference is to a body system, for example, Respiratory system, the reader will need to go to the appropriate section in the front of the book.

For ready reference, colored alphabetical tabs (margin markers) are printed on the margins of the A–Z section and move down the pages to help readers find the entry they are looking for.

Because of the nature of *Anatomica*, technical terms are unavoidable, but we have tried as much as possible to make the language and style interesting and accessible.

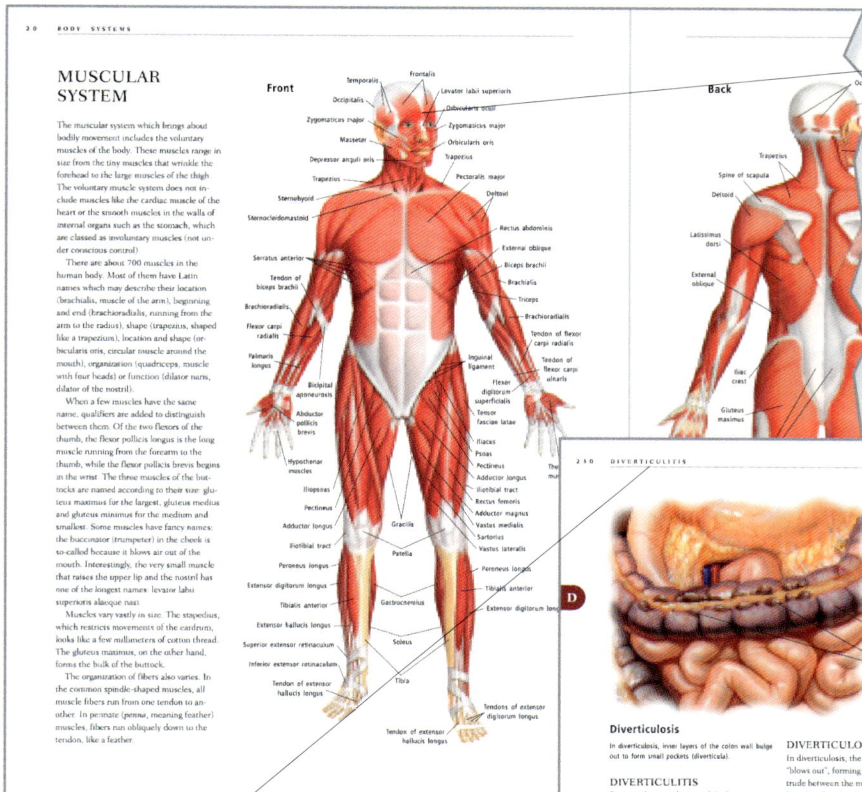

Illustrations

Illustrations show what is described in the text. They may show a whole body system, a single organ, microstructure, or the effects of damage or disease on a particular part of the body.

Locator diagrams

Locator diagrams are included to give an indication of where a body part is located in relation to the rest of the body.

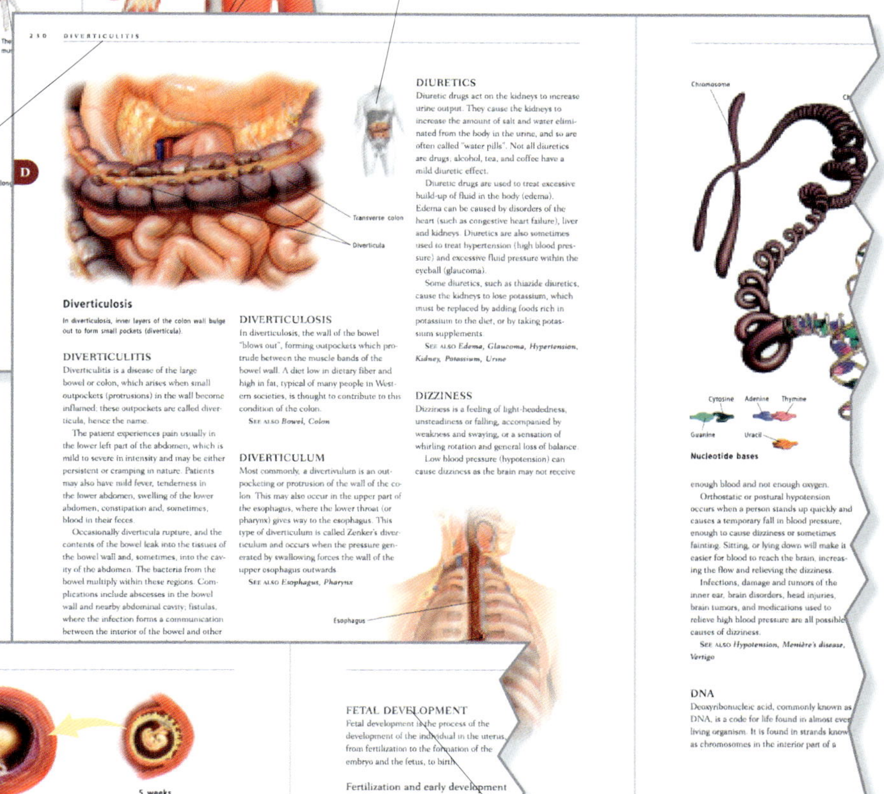

Page headings

Page headings on each spread give the name of the first new entry on the left-hand page and the last entry on the right-hand page to make it easy to find the entry you are looking for in the A–Z section.

Margin markers

Colored tabs on the edges of the pages help you find your way to the section you want.

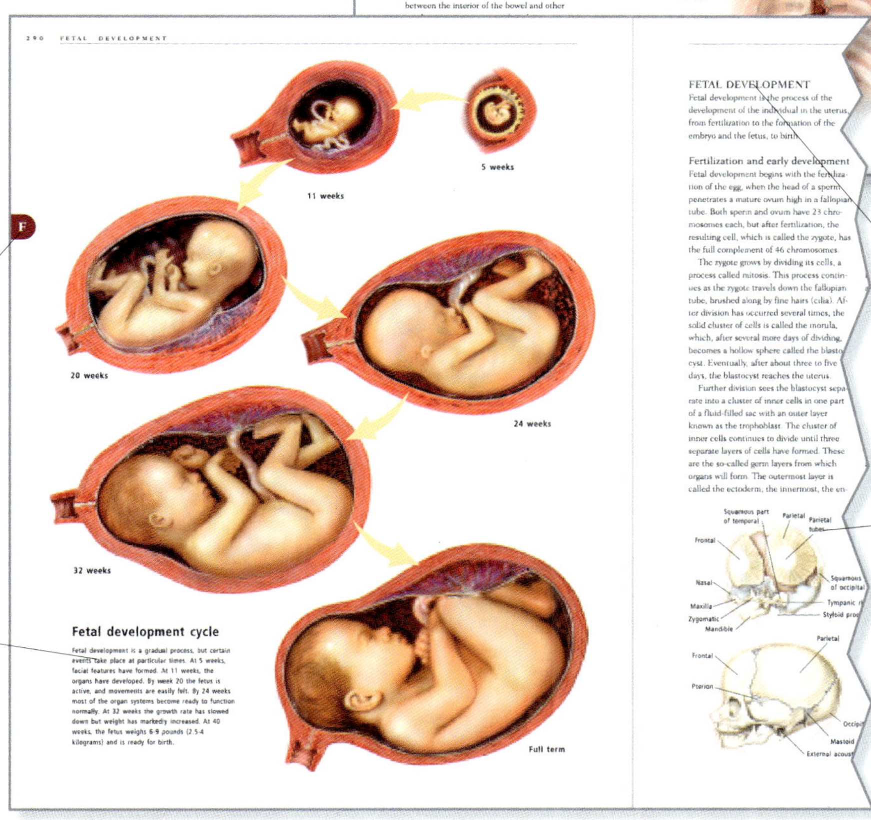

Headings

The entries run in alphabetical order, with a heading marking the beginning of the entry.

Labels

The labels on each illustration label particular elements that are relevant to the purpose of that illustration.

Captions

The captions to the illustrations make it easy to understand what the illustration is showing.

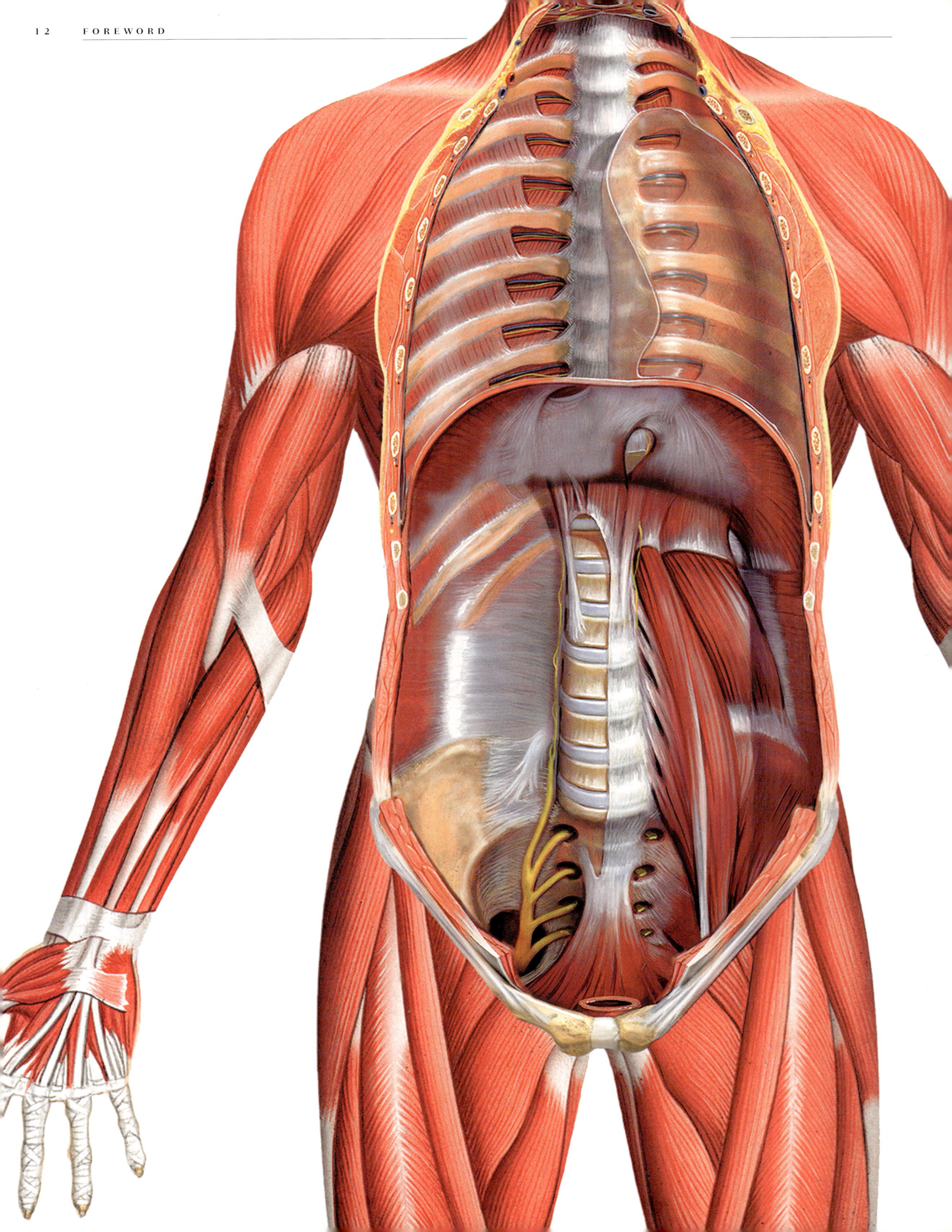

FOREWORD

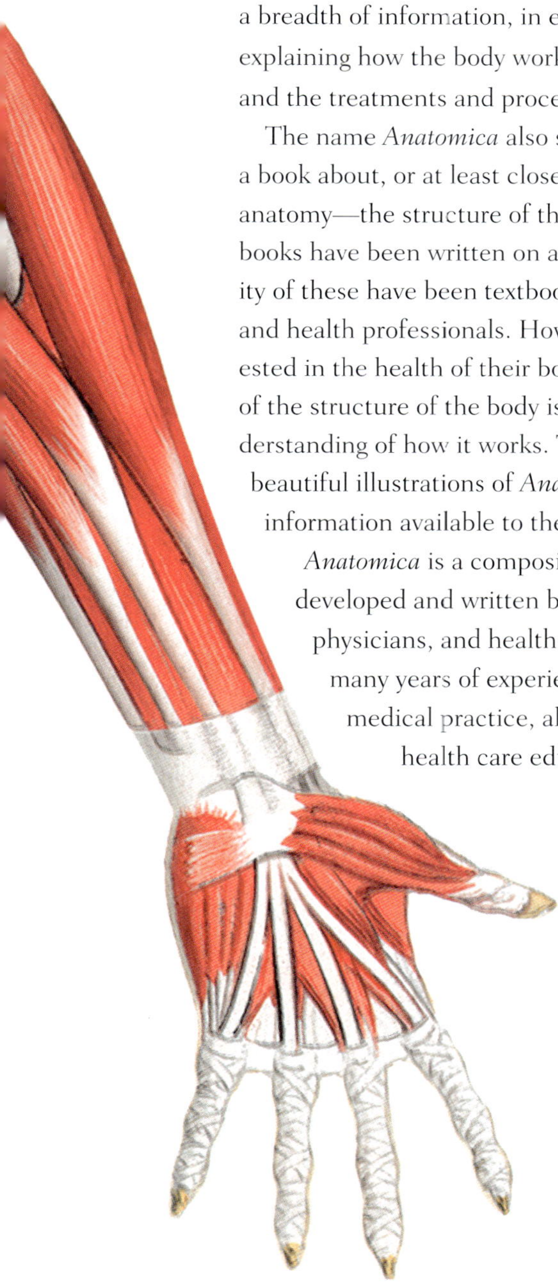

Today we must remember that our current knowledge of the human body, how it works and how we care for it has been generated over many centuries and that truly massive amounts of information have been learned. There is now an abundance of this medical, pharmaceutical and health care information freely available on the Internet. One can quickly become overwhelmed trying to find details about a health care problem and then frustrated trying to understand medical terminology. The value and importance of *Anatomica* is that it brings together a breadth of information, in easy-to-read language, explaining how the body works, what can go wrong, and the treatments and procedures that are available.

The name *Anatomica* also suggests that this is a book about, or at least closely associated with anatomy—the structure of the human body. Many books have been written on anatomy, but the majority of these have been textbooks for medical students and health professionals. However for anyone interested in the health of their body, an understanding of the structure of the body is fundamental to an understanding of how it works. The text and many beautiful illustrations of *Anatomica* now make this information available to the general public.

Anatomica is a composite reference book developed and written by senior academics, physicians, and health care practitioners with many years of experience in their areas of medical practice, alternative therapies and health care education, and by journalists specializing in health care writing. Thus *Anatomica* represents the best efforts of the authors to provide a clear synopsis of a broad range of commonly used health care terms, conditions, and treatments as well as clear explanations of specialist terms for therapies and medications. The inclusion of conventional medical therapies is complemented by coverage of alternative therapies, showing how they may fit into the wide array of health care offerings available today.

We tend to pay minimal attention to the structure and function of our bodies while they are young and working perfectly, but as we age or as soon as something goes wrong most of us would like to understand the ageing process or the problems that have arisen and how they can be treated. *Anatomica* provides a guide to the normal and damaged or diseased body through all aspects of our life cycle.

It is important to remember, however, that health care and individual diseases often affect more than one part of the body, and one or more treatments may be available for specific problems. Similarly, no one form of therapy is likely to cure all the problems of the body. The reader should appreciate the continuity of health care through all aspects of life.

Anatomica is intended to help health-conscious readers understand their bodies and to know what sorts of solutions are available to treat the body's ills. Think of *Anatomica* as the "owner's manual" for the human body. It is not intended as a do-it-yourself guide, or as a substitute for the advice and expertise of health professionals.

Professor R. William Currie

DEPARTMENT OF ANATOMY AND NEUROBIOLOGY
FACULTY OF MEDICINE
DALHOUSIE UNIVERSITY
HALIFAX, NOVA SCOTIA

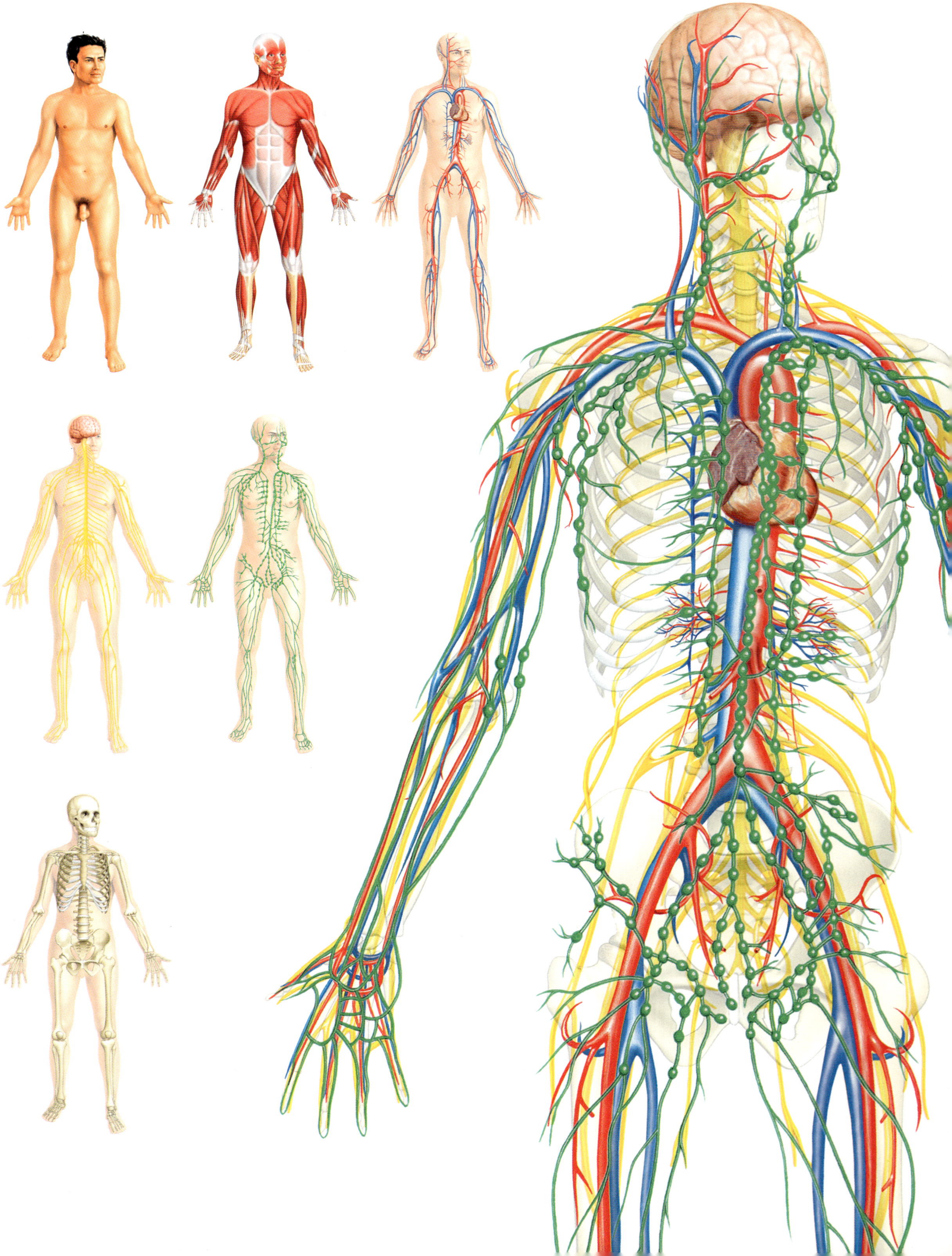

BODY SYSTEMS

When considering the structural and functional organization of the body, it is usual to divide the body into various systems. Actually, body systems collectively make up just one level of structural organization. The most basic structural unit of the body is the cell. Cells group together to make tissues, which in turn are grouped together to make organs. Organs work together to make body systems and these systems cooperate to form a complete human being.

The systems of the body are each concerned with a particular function or a group of related functions. To understand how they work together to produce a complete person, we need to briefly consider the function of each system. The skeletal system is composed of the bones, and the cartilage and ligamentous structures associated with them. It protects and supports soft tissues and provides scaffolding for muscle attachment. The muscular system produces movement and is composed of muscles, tendons and sheaths around muscles and lubricating sacs called bursae. The nervous system collects and analyzes information about the environment and internal body function and controls and coordinates body function. The nervous system consists of the central nervous system (brain and spinal cord); the peripheral nervous system, which includes all the nerves outside the brain and spinal cord; and the autonomic nervous system, which controls the automatic internal function of the body and partially overlaps with the peripheral and central nervous systems. Another system which is also concerned with control of the internal body function is the endocrine system, which uses circulating chemical messengers called hormones to exert its effects. The circulatory system consists of the heart and all the blood vessels (arteries, veins and capillaries) and is responsible for moving nutrients, waste and some special proteins (for example hormones) and cells around the body. The lymphatic system is also an important transport system for the body, moving excess tissue fluid back to the veins and transporting fat from the gut to the bloodstream. Its other important role is the defense of the body, and for this reason some elements of the lymphatic system are referred to as the immune system. The respiratory system is concerned with gas exchange and the intake of oxygen, needed by all the body's tissues and cells. The digestive system is concerned with the ingestion, processing and absorption of nutrients, as well as the elimination of some types of waste. The urinary system controls fluid and salt balance in the body and excretes nitrogen waste. The reproductive system is concerned with production of the next generation and is linked during fetal development with the developing urinary system.

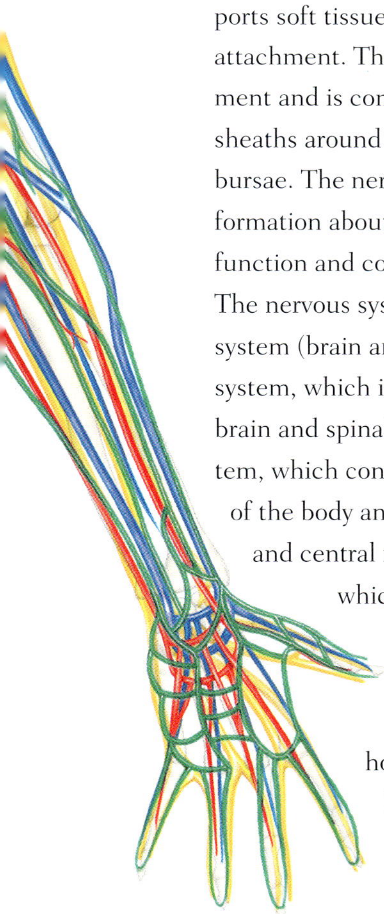

Apart from responding to changes in the external environment, producing the activity which outside observers see as human behavior, the body must also act to produce a relatively constant internal environment. This process is called homeostasis and involves many facets of internal function, including maintaining constant body temperature, relatively constant blood sugar levels, blood pressure and blood calcium levels. Homeostasis is achieved by the coordinated action of the autonomic nervous and endocrine systems on the other systems in the body. The hormones produced by the glands of the endocrine system often stimulate the production of other hormones in the target organs. These secondary hormones act on the gland that produced the first hormone, thereby reducing its production. This type of negative feedback system brings about the constant balancing of internal body function.

SKELETAL SYSTEM

The skeleton is the framework of the body and is usually described in two parts, the axial skeleton and the appendicular skeleton.

The axial skeleton

The axis of the body is formed by the skull, the vertebral column (backbone) and the thoracic cage (chest).

The skull

The skull forms the skeleton of the head. It consists of the cranium, the mandible (lower jawbone) and the hyoid bone at the base of the tongue. The top part of the skull (the cranial cavity) houses and protects the brain and part of the brain stem. The facial skeleton is the lower part of the skull that underlies the face. The upper jaw is fixed and formed by two bones called the maxillae.

Where the cranial cavity meets the facial skeleton, there are two orbits, or sockets, for the eyes. Underlying the nose is the nasal aperture of the skull that leads to the nasal cavity.

The base of the skull articulates with the first bone of the spine: the atlas vertebra. This joint allows the head to flex and extend (as in nodding) and to move sideways.

Many bones of the skull are hollow. The cavities inside them are called sinuses. They lessen the weight of the bone and give resonance to the voice.

The vertebral column

The vertebral column (backbone or spine) is a stack of small bones known as vertebrae. There are 7 vertebrae in the neck, 12 in the thorax (the chest region), and 5 in the lumbar region (the small of the back, behind the abdomen). The last two bones of the vertebral column, the sacrum and the coccyx, are formed by vertebrae which fuse after puberty (5 in the sacrum, 4 in the coccyx).

Vertebrae articulate with one another on intervertebral disks. These are flexible pads of cartilage that separate one vertebra from another. Each vertebra can only move a few degrees at its intervertebral disk, but the sum of all these individual movements gives great mobility to the vertebral column.

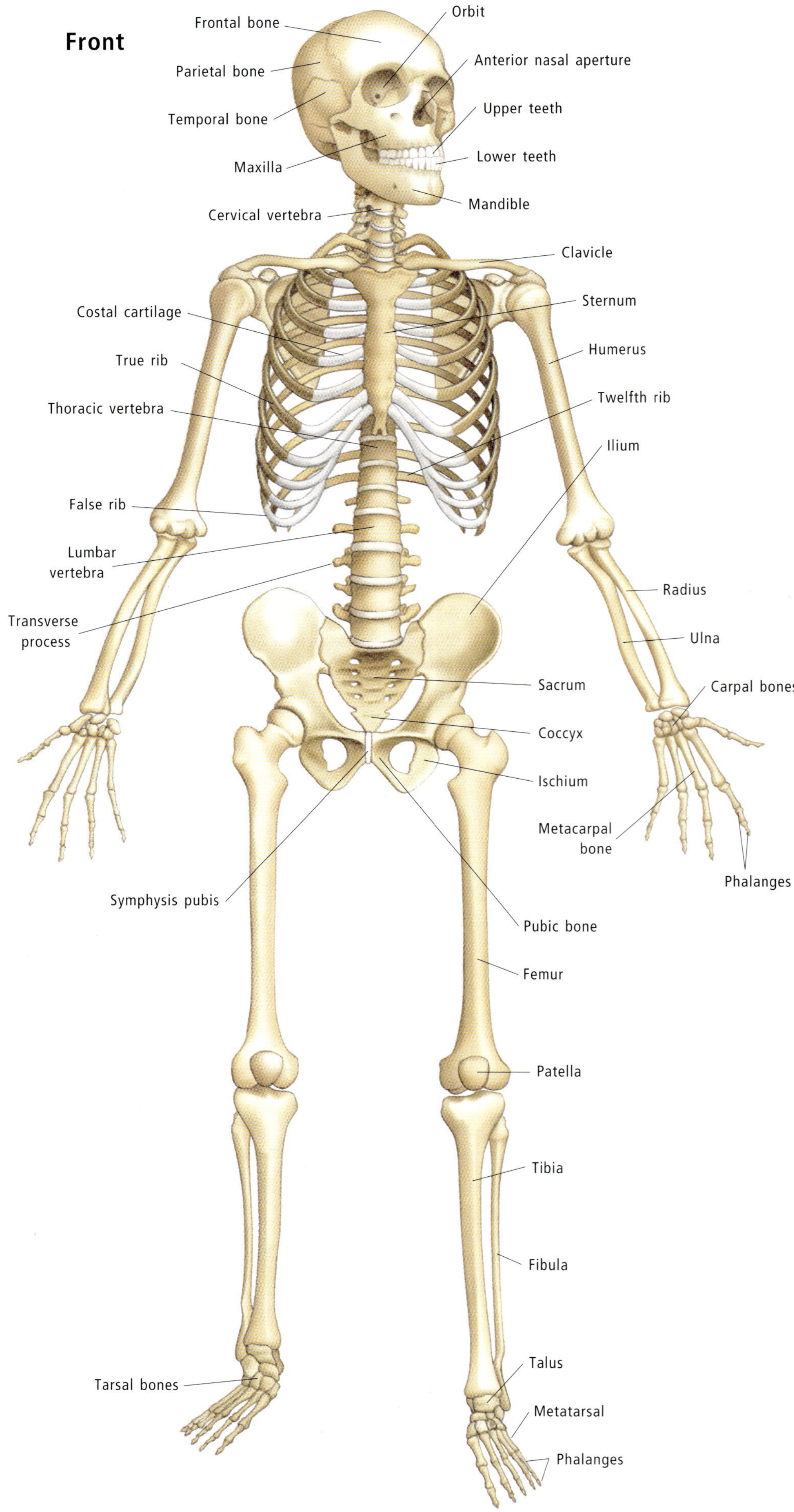

Back

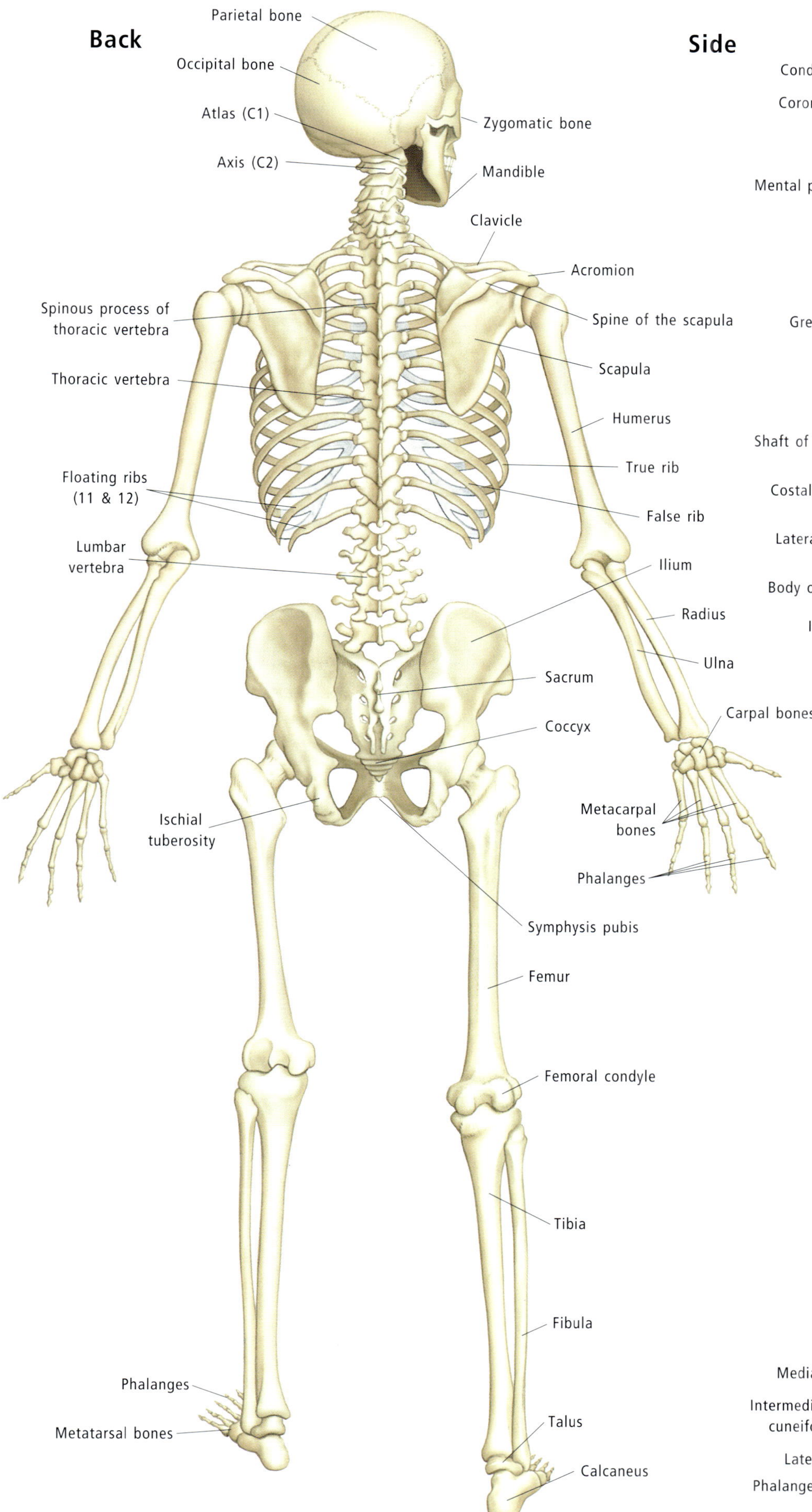
Parietal bone
Occipital bone
Atlas (C1)
Axis (C2)
Zygomatic bone
Mandible
Clavicle
Acromion
Spinous process of thoracic vertebra
Spine of the scapula
Scapula
Thoracic vertebra
Humerus
True rib
Floating ribs (11 & 12)
False rib
Lumbar vertebra
Ilium
Radius
Ulna
Sacrum
Carpal bones
Coccyx
Metacarpal bones
Ischial tuberosity
Phalanges
Symphysis pubis
Femur
Femoral condyle
Tibia
Fibula
Phalanges
Metatarsal bones
Talus
Calcaneus

Side

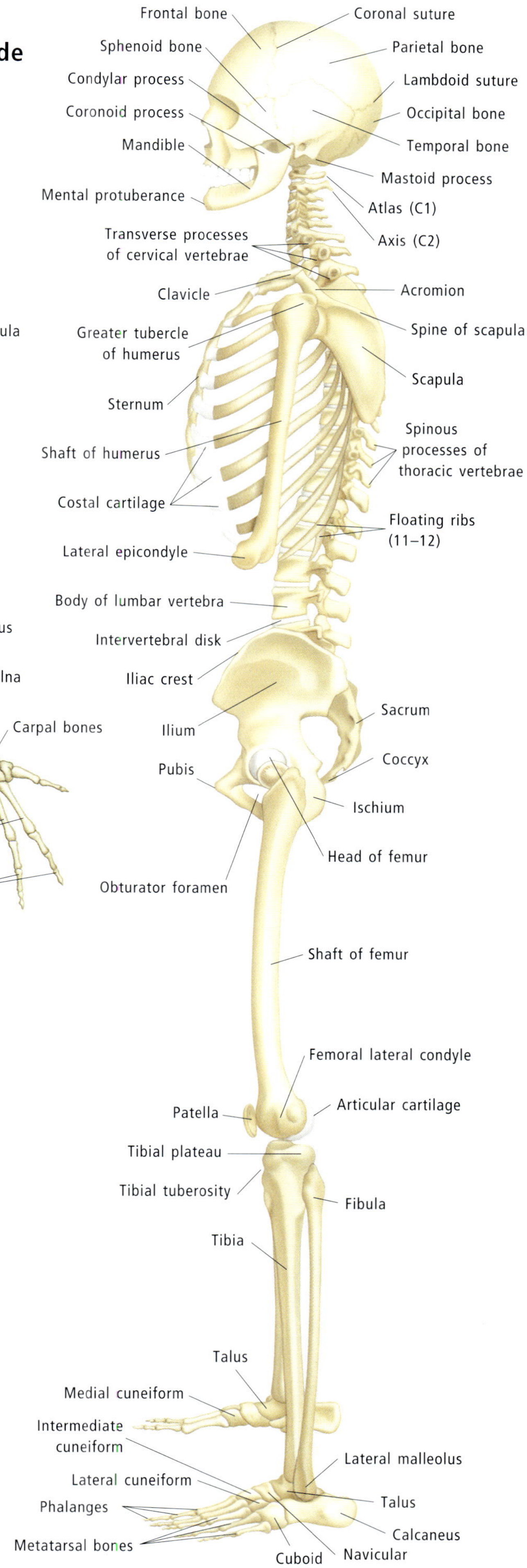
Frontal bone
Coronal suture
Sphenoid bone
Parietal bone
Condylar process
Lambdoid suture
Coronoid process
Occipital bone
Mandible
Temporal bone
Mastoid process
Mental protuberance
Atlas (C1)
Transverse processes of cervical vertebrae
Axis (C2)
Clavicle
Acromion
Greater tubercle of humerus
Spine of scapula
Scapula
Sternum
Spinous processes of thoracic vertebrae
Shaft of humerus
Costal cartilage
Floating ribs (11–12)
Lateral epicondyle
Body of lumbar vertebra
Intervertebral disk
Iliac crest
Sacrum
Ilium
Coccyx
Pubis
Ischium
Head of femur
Obturator foramen
Shaft of femur
Femoral lateral condyle
Patella
Articular cartilage
Tibial plateau
Tibial tuberosity
Fibula
Tibia
Talus
Medial cuneiform
Intermediate cuneiform
Lateral malleolus
Lateral cuneiform
Talus
Phalanges
Calcaneus
Metatarsal bones
Cuboid
Navicular

When you carry a heavy weight, the vertebral column is turned into a rigid pillar by the contraction of muscles at the back of the column. When you bend forward to lift a load, the force applied to the intervertebral disk can be large enough to damage the disk.

The thoracic cage

The thoracic cage, or chest, is made up of the 12 thoracic vertebrae, the ribs and the sternum. The top 7 true ribs extend from the vertebrae at the back and curve around the front to the sternum and connect to it by extensions of cartilage, the costal cartilages. The next 3 ribs, the false ribs, do not extend all the way around—their costal cartilage fuses onto the cartilage of the last true rib. The final 2 ribs, the floating ribs, do not reach the front. The rib cage protects the heart and lungs. The ribs, moved by the intercostal muscles, are involved in breathing.

Appendicular skeleton

The appendicular skeleton consists of the bones of the limbs and the shoulder and pelvic girdles, the bones that support and attach the limbs to the axial skeleton. The upper and lower limbs are similar in their composition. The shoulder girdle of the upper limb corresponds to the hip or pelvic girdle in the lower limb. The long bone of the upper arm is the humerus; in the lower limb the long bone is known as the femur. The forearm and the lower leg both have 2 long bones; the wrist has 8 bones, the ankle has 7. There are 5 bones in both the palm of the hand and the sole of the foot, with 14 bones making up the digits of both the hand and the foot.

The lower limb has to support the body weight and therefore is less flexible than the upper limb. The scapula (shoulder blade) can slide freely on the rib cage because it is attached to it by muscles. It is only stabilized at the front, by a strut known as the clavicle (collar bone). By contrast, the pelvic girdle is fixed to the axial skeleton where the 2 hip bones articulate with the sacrum at the base of the vertebral column. In front, the 2 hip bones join at the symphysis pubis. Each hip has an acetabulum, a deep socket that accommodates the head of the femur.

Structure and function of bone

Bone tissue is formed by a matrix of connective tissue with a heavy deposition of calcium salts. In addition to its obvious functions such as the support and protection of vital organs, the skeleton is thus a reservoir of mineral salts, especially calcium, and plays an important role in calcium metabolism.

Although skeletons in museums give the impression that bones are brittle, living bones are much stronger than dry bones. Their structure is designed to best serve their mechanical functions and is continually remodeled throughout a lifetime.

The role of the bones in body movement is best seen in the limbs. The limb bones act as levers which are moved by the muscles attached to them in much the same way that the arms of a crane are activated by motors. The femur must be mechanically strong enough to bear the weight of a person's body but light enough to minimize the muscle force required to move that weight. A metal tube is much stronger against bending than a solid rod made out of the same amount of metal. Similarly, the shaft of a long bone, such as the femur, is made up of a cylinder of compact bone. In the center of the femur is spongy bone formed by bands of bone called trabeculae. The spaces between the trabeculae are filled up with bone marrow. This cylindrical arrangement is repeated within the compact bone, which is made up of tiny cylinders formed by concentric layers of bone surrounding blood vessels and nerves. The gaps between these microscopic cylinders are packed with thin plates of bone (laminae) running in all directions.

At the ends of the long bones, the trabeculae are aligned along the lines of stress applied to the bone. The body weight received by the head of each femur is transmitted down the neck of the bone to the shaft; the trabeculae there form arches along the lines of stress just like arches under a bridge.

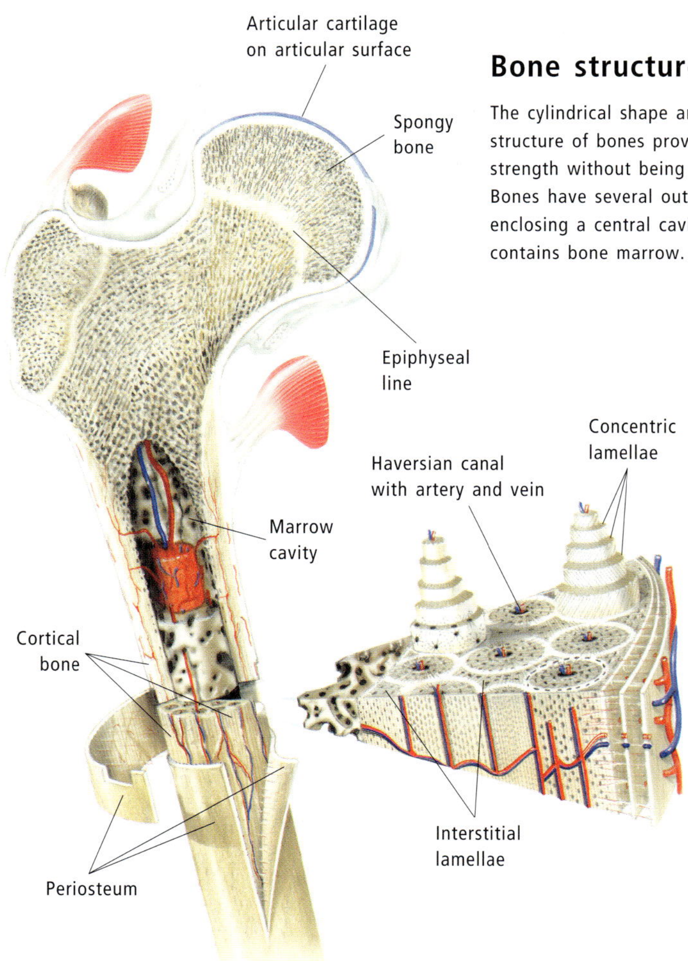

Bone structure

The cylindrical shape and internal structure of bones provides maximum strength without being too heavy. Bones have several outer layers enclosing a central cavity which contains bone marrow.

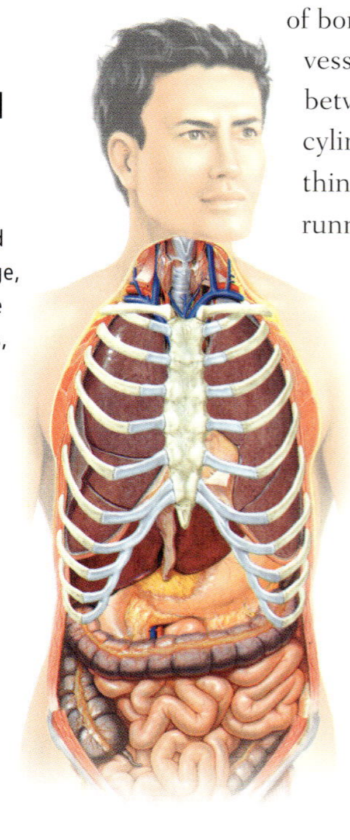

Protection for internal organs

The heart and the lungs are protected by the thoracic cage, a structure of bone comprising the ribs, sternum and the vertebral column.

The structure of a bone changes according to the stress applied to it. Exercise strengthens bones, while a prolonged state of inactivity weakens bone structure. When new bone is formed to bridge over a fracture, the trabeculae are rearranged along the line of stress. Weight bearing is therefore recommended during bone healing to promote the optimal development of new trabeculae.

The joints

Wherever two bones come into contact with each other, there is a joint: this is known as articulation. The bones may be separated by cartilage and often fluid. Not all joints are mobile. There is no perceptible movement at the sutures of the skull, for example, where the serrated edges of the skull bones interlock. There is only a small amount of movement at joints such as the symphysis pubis where the bones are connected to one another by cartilage. The most mobile joints are the synovial joints, found in the appendicular skeleton.

The articular surfaces of a joint never fit together perfectly. The better the bones fit together, the more stable the joint becomes. Looser joints are more mobile but less stable.

The hip joint must be stable to support the body weight, so the acetabulum is deep and fits snugly on the head of the femur. For the same reason the hip bones are fixed to the vertebral column, and the thigh has limited movement.

By contrast, the articular surface of the scapula is smaller and does not fit well with the head of the humerus. The shoulder joint is thus very mobile but not stable; it dislocates easily. Free sliding of the scapula on the rib cage further increases the range of movement of the arm.

Where there is a series of joints, the total range of movement is the sum of the movements of the individual joints. The vertebral column is one such example of a chain of joints. The 8 carpal bones of the wrist allow a wide range of movement of the hand. The 7 tarsal bones of the ankle allow the foot to be tilted in many directions to negotiate uneven ground.

Synovial joint

In a synovial joint, the ends of the bones are smooth, and covered by articular cartilage with an extremely low coefficient of friction.

The two bones are bound together by a capsule of fibrous tissue. The fibrous capsule is lined on the inside by a synovial membrane that secretes synovial fluid to lubricate the joint and nourish the cartilage.

The joint is reinforced by ligaments. Some ligaments are just thickened areas of the capsule itself, while others are attached to the bones. The cruciate ligaments of the knee joint, for example, are very strong fibrous cords that are separate from the capsule of the knee joint.

Capsules and ligaments are both made up of fibers of connective tissue. While the fibers in capsules are randomly arranged, those in ligaments are densely packed and run parallel in one direction. This arrangement gives ligaments a shiny appearance and great tensile strength in the direction of the fibers. In some injuries, bones break before ligaments rupture.

When a synovial joint is injured, it becomes swollen either because of bleeding into the joint or as a result of increased secretion of synovial fluid. Inflammation of the joint is called arthritis and can be caused by either infection or diseases of the synovial membrane or cartilage.

When a joint is sprained, the ligaments may be stretched or ruptured. When a joint is immobilized for a long period of time, such as in a cast, the capsule and ligaments contract and become stiff, reducing the range of movement of the joint when the cast is removed. Physical therapy and stretching exercises often help the joint regain its mobility.

SEE ALSO *Ankle, Arm, Arthritis, Back, Bones, Cartilage, Collar bone, Connective tissue, Disk, intervertebral, Femur, Hand, Hip, Humerus, Joints, Knee, Leg, Ligaments, Pelvis, Ribs, Shoulder, Skull, Spine, Sternum, Synovial fluid, Synovial membrane, Vertebrae, Wrist*

Tissue types in a synovial joint

In a synovial joint, cartilage acts as a cushion between the bones. Ligaments reinforce the joint. Spongy bone tissue, containing air pockets, forms most of the bone with compact bone underlying the cartilage. Hyaline cartilage is made up of connective tissue and is flexible and elastic. Ligaments also comprise connective tissue, but the tissue fibers are densely packed and run parallel in one direction to provide great tensile strength.

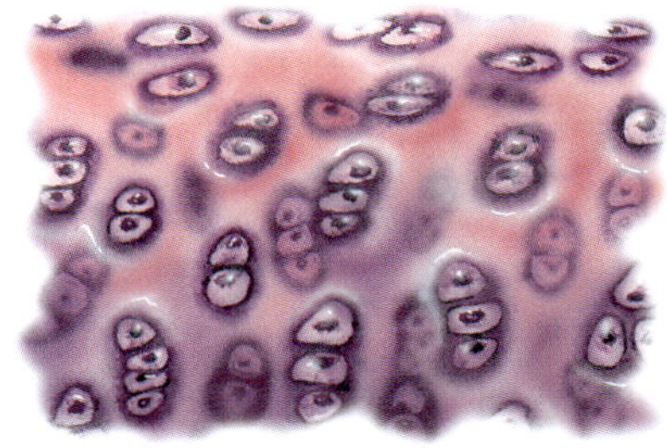

Hyaline cartilage

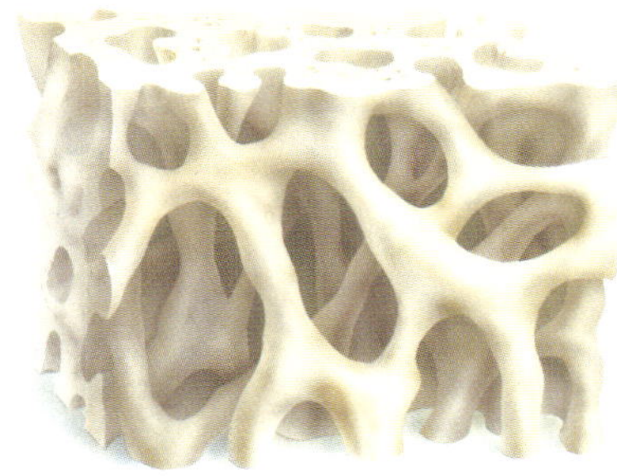

Spongy bone tissue

Ligament

Movement of joints

A joint is more mobile if the articular surfaces are not a perfect fit. The shoulder joint has the widest range of movement of all the joints, because the articular surface of the scapula does not fit exactly with the head of the humerus bone.

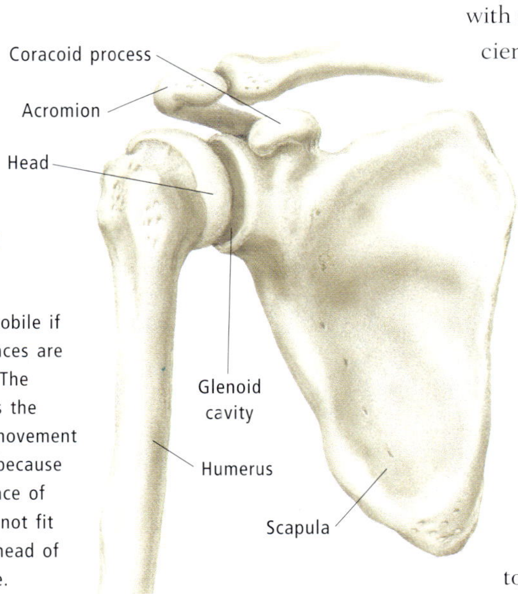

MUSCULAR SYSTEM

The muscular system which brings about bodily movement includes the voluntary muscles of the body. These muscles range in size from the tiny muscles that wrinkle the forehead to the large muscles of the thigh. The voluntary muscle system does not include muscles like the cardiac muscle of the heart or the smooth muscles in the walls of internal organs such as the stomach, which are classed as involuntary muscles (not under conscious control).

There are about 700 muscles in the human body. Most of them have Latin names which may describe their location (brachialis, muscle of the arm), beginning and end (brachioradialis, running from the arm to the radius), shape (trapezius, shaped like a trapezium), location and shape (orbicularis oris, circular muscle around the mouth), organization (quadriceps, muscle with four heads) or function (dilator naris, dilator of the nostril).

When a few muscles have the same name, qualifiers are added to distinguish between them. Of the two flexors of the thumb, the flexor pollicis longus is the long muscle running from the forearm to the thumb, while the flexor pollicis brevis begins in the wrist. The three muscles of the buttocks are named according to their size: gluteus maximus for the largest, gluteus medius and gluteus minimus for the medium and smallest. Some muscles have fancy names; the buccinator (trumpeter) in the cheek is so-called because it blows air out of the mouth. Interestingly, the very small muscle that raises the upper lip and the nostril has one of the longest names: levator labii superioris alaeque nasi.

Muscles vary greatly in size. The stapedius, which restricts movements of the eardrum, looks like a few millimeters of cotton thread. The gluteus maximus, on the other hand, forms the bulk of the buttock.

The organization of fibers also varies. In the common spindle-shaped muscles, all muscle fibers run from one tendon to another. In pennate (*penna*, meaning feather) muscles, fibers run obliquely down to the tendon, like a feather.

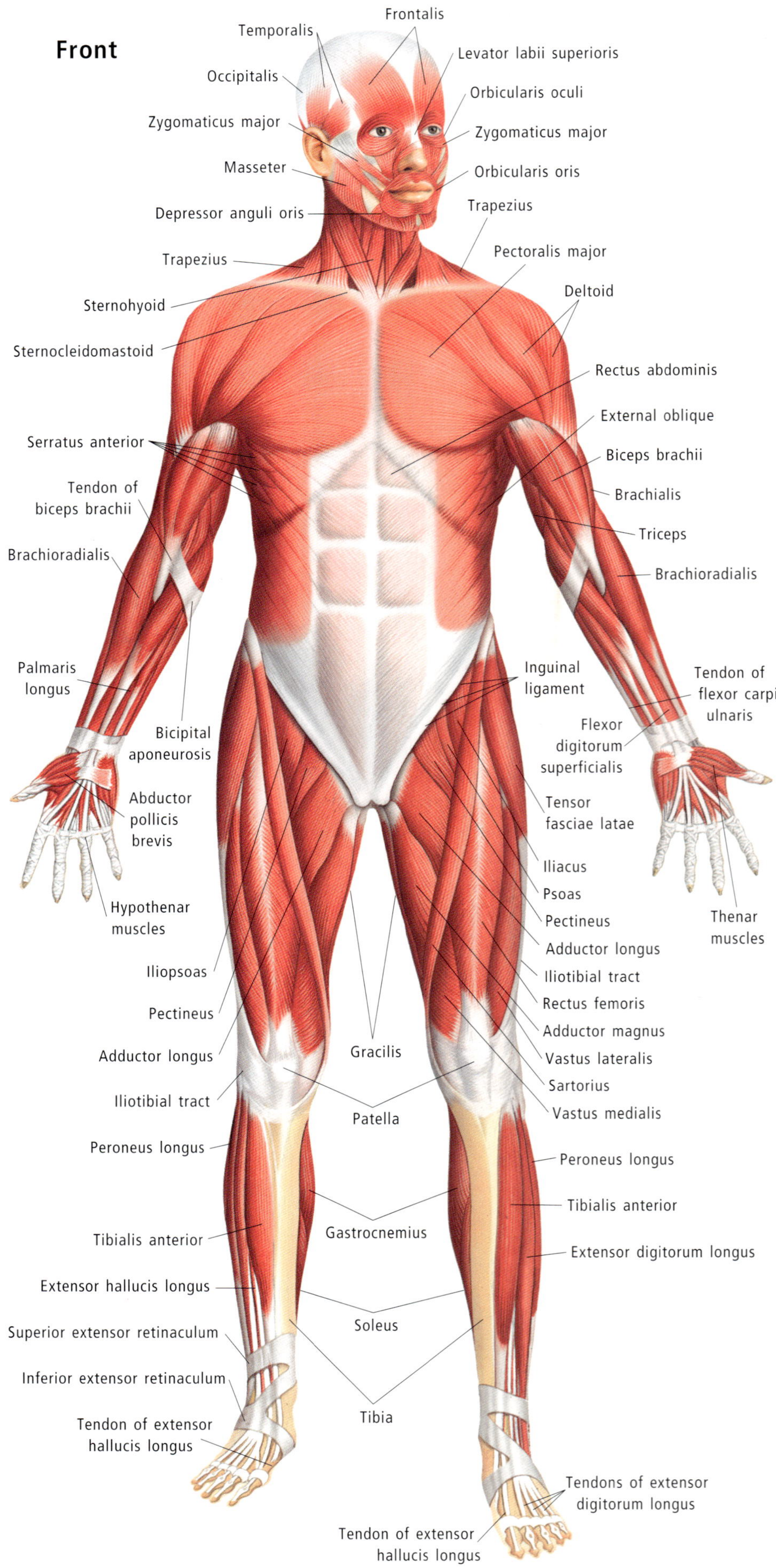

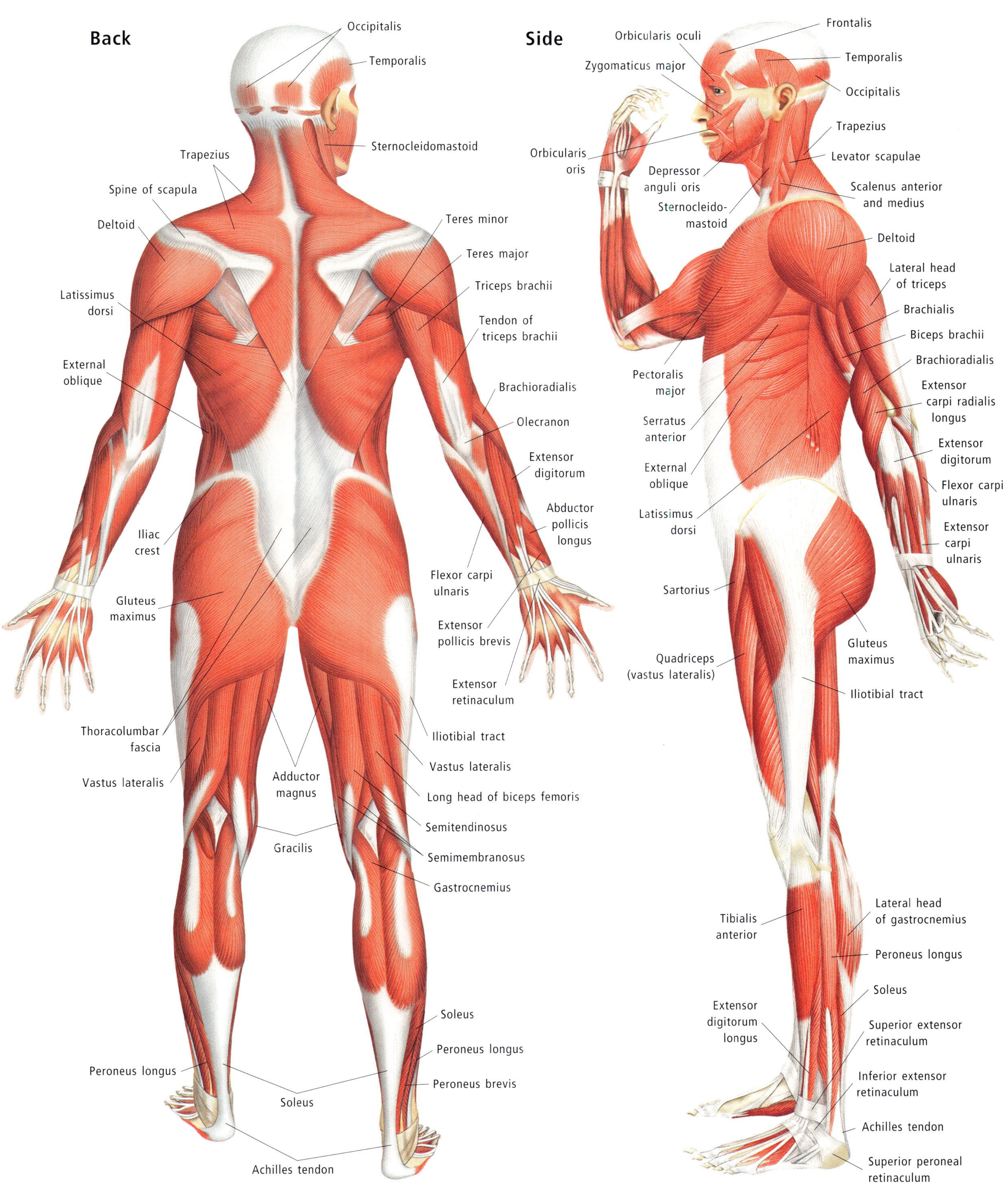
Back
Occipitalis
Temporalis
Sternocleidomastoid
Trapezius
Spine of scapula
Deltoid
Teres minor
Teres major
Triceps brachii
Latissimus dorsi
Tendon of triceps brachii
External oblique
Brachioradialis
Olecranon
Extensor digitorum
Abductor pollicis longus
Iliac crest
Flexor carpi ulnaris
Gluteus maximus
Extensor pollicis brevis
Extensor retinaculum
Thoracolumbar fascia
Iliotibial tract
Vastus lateralis
Adductor magnus
Vastus lateralis
Long head of biceps femoris
Semitendinosus
Gracilis
Semimembranosus
Gastrocnemius
Soleus
Peroneus longus
Peroneus longus
Soleus
Peroneus brevis
Achilles tendon
Side
Frontalis
Orbicularis oculi
Temporalis
Zygomaticus major
Occipitalis
Trapezius
Orbicularis oris
Levator scapulae
Depressor anguli oris
Scalenus anterior and medius
Sternocleido-mastoid
Deltoid
Lateral head of triceps
Brachialis
Biceps brachii
Brachioradialis
Pectoralis major
Extensor carpi radialis longus
Serratus anterior
Extensor digitorum
External oblique
Flexor carpi ulnaris
Latissimus dorsi
Extensor carpi ulnaris
Sartorius
Gluteus maximus
Quadriceps (vastus lateralis)
Iliotibial tract
Lateral head of gastrocnemius
Tibialis anterior
Peroneus longus
Soleus
Extensor digitorum longus
Superior extensor retinaculum
Inferior extensor retinaculum
Achilles tendon
Superior peroneal retinaculum

Some muscles have several tendons at one end—for example, two in the biceps, three in the triceps and four in the quadriceps.

Muscle fibers attach either directly to a bone, or to a tendon which is fixed to a bone. The force produced by the contraction of the muscle fibers is transmitted to the bone by the tendon. Tendons are made up mainly of strong collagen fibers that run parallel in one direction and are tightly packed together to give maximum strength in the line of force of the muscle.

Structure of muscles

The contracting part of a muscle consists of bundles of muscle fibers which themselves are made up of myofibrils.

Each myofibril is made up of thousands of thin actin filaments and thicker myosin filaments, which overlap. Where they overlap they are linked by connections (cross-bridges), which change shape to draw one set of fibers towards the other, thus shortening the muscle.

There are two main classes of muscle fibers, called fast twitch (F) and slow twitch (S) fibers. F fibers generate more power and contract faster, but fatigue more quickly than S fibers. The relative proportion of the two types of fiber varies in different individuals and in different muscles. People tend to excel in sports that are suited to their predominant fiber type. For example, 95 percent of fibers in the gastrocnemius muscles in the legs of marathon champions are S fibers, compared to only 25 percent in champion sprinters.

Muscle contraction

When a muscle contracts, it shortens and exerts a pull on the muscle attachment. The action of a muscle depends on its position in relation to the joint it works on. The tibialis anterior, for example, crosses in front of the ankle and moves the foot upwards.

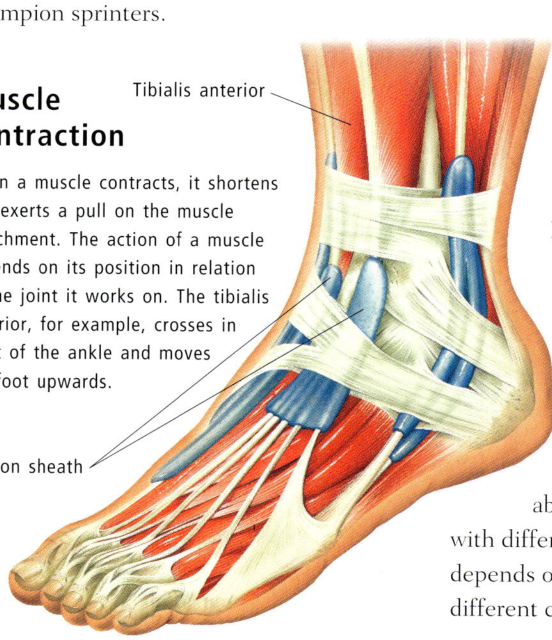

Movement and support

The muscles of the shoulder joint, known as the rotator cuff muscles, provide important support for the joint, while allowing a wide range of movement.

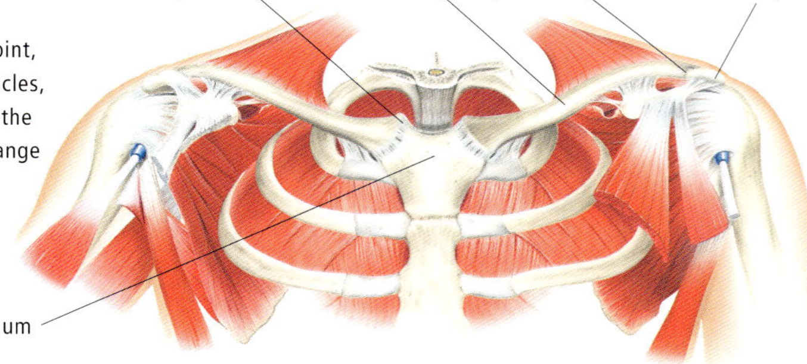

Actions of muscles

Usually a muscle shortens when it is activated (or "contracts"), but not always. When holding a camera up in front of the eyes, for example, the muscles of the arm generate force against gravity to prevent the camera from falling, but do not change length. This kind of "contraction" is called isometric (meaning "same length") contraction. In the action of putting the camera down on a desk, the muscles that bend the elbow generate a force which is smaller than the pull of gravity on the camera. In this case the muscles of the arm are lengthened by the force of gravity and work to slow down the fall of the camera. Sometimes "contraction" is a poor term to describe muscle action.

The action of a muscle depends on its position in relation to the joint it works on. The biceps, crossing in front of the elbow, flexes the elbow; the triceps tendon crossing the back of the elbow straightens it.

The deltoid on the outside of the shoulder brings the arm out, away from the body (abducts the arm). The pectoralis major, running from the upper part of the arm towards the breastbone (sternum) pulls the arm in (adducts the arm).

However, most muscle actions are not as simple as these examples. The upper part of the pectoralis major, which runs from the clavicle to the arm, tends to raise the arm from a position of rest at the side of the body. Its lower part, which runs downwards to the lower ribs, tends to pull the arm down when it is above the head. In muscles like this with different parts, the resulting movement depends on different levels of activity of different components.

Coordination of muscles

Each movement of a limb, however simple, is the result of a number of muscles working together. In kicking a football, the quadriceps is the prime mover, or agonist muscle. Its attachment on the femur is stabilized by muscles of the hip. The hamstring muscles, which have the opposite action to the quadriceps, begin to contract as the leg picks up momentum to control the force of the kick. The contraction of these muscles, which are called antagonist muscles, is maximal at the end of the kick to stop the movement.

The cooperation of the muscles in this example must be well orchestrated, each muscle having to contribute the right force at the right time. If the antagonist muscles contract too early, before the leg has gained enough momentum, the kick will be too weak. If they come in too late, the leg will extend too far and damage the knee joint.

The cerebellum of the brain is important in fine muscle (motor) control. Just watch a very young child attempting to throw a ball. The young cerebellum has not learned to program muscle actions. The arm flings out too far and the hand does not release the ball at the right time. Even movements that we take for granted, such as walking and running, are only possible after much training in the first years of life. More sophisticated muscle coordination, such as dancing, requires years of intensive training. When the cerebellum fails to work properly, either temporarily in a drunk person, or permanently in cerebellar diseases, even walking becomes difficult.

When a muscle is used repeatedly in lifting weight, it develops more strength and also enlarges because of the increase in diameter of individual muscle fibers. The best exercises to increase muscle bulk are those that make the muscles lengthen while they contract, such as slowing the fall of a weight.

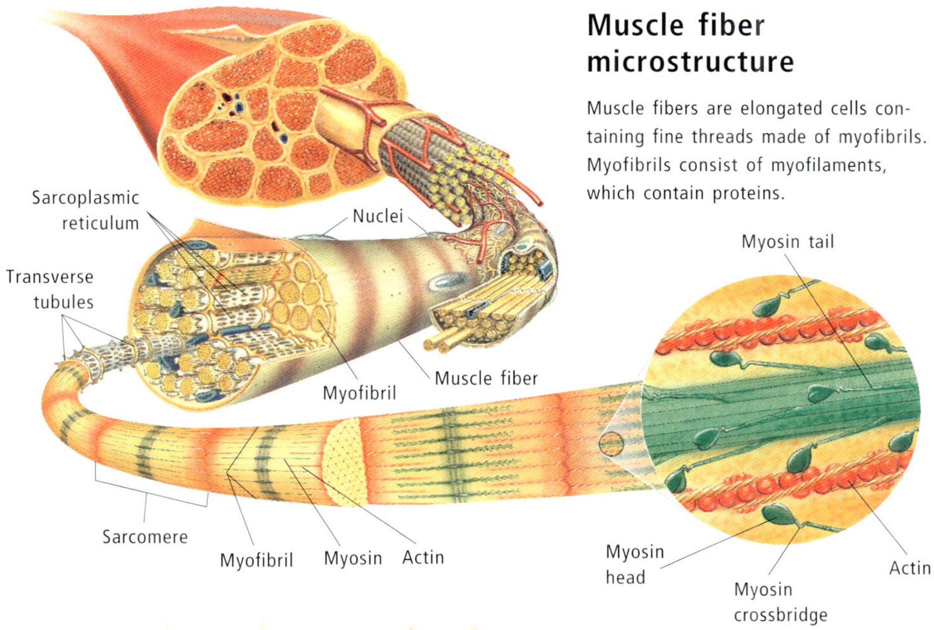

Muscle fiber microstructure

Muscle fibers are elongated cells containing fine threads made of myofibrils. Myofibrils consist of myofilaments, which contain proteins.

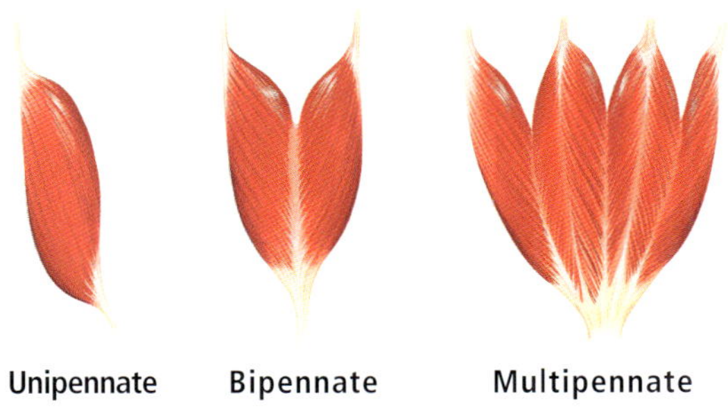

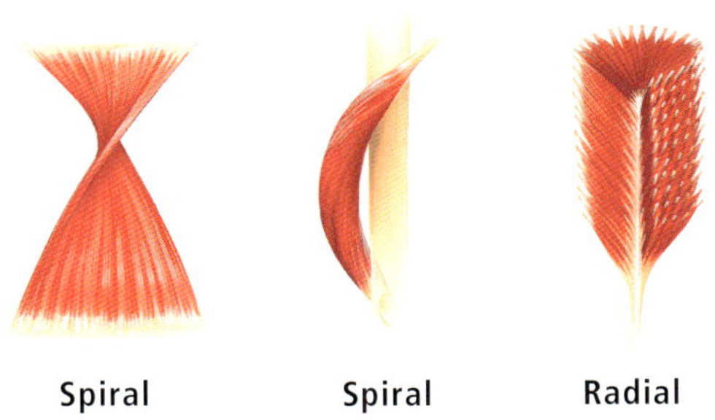

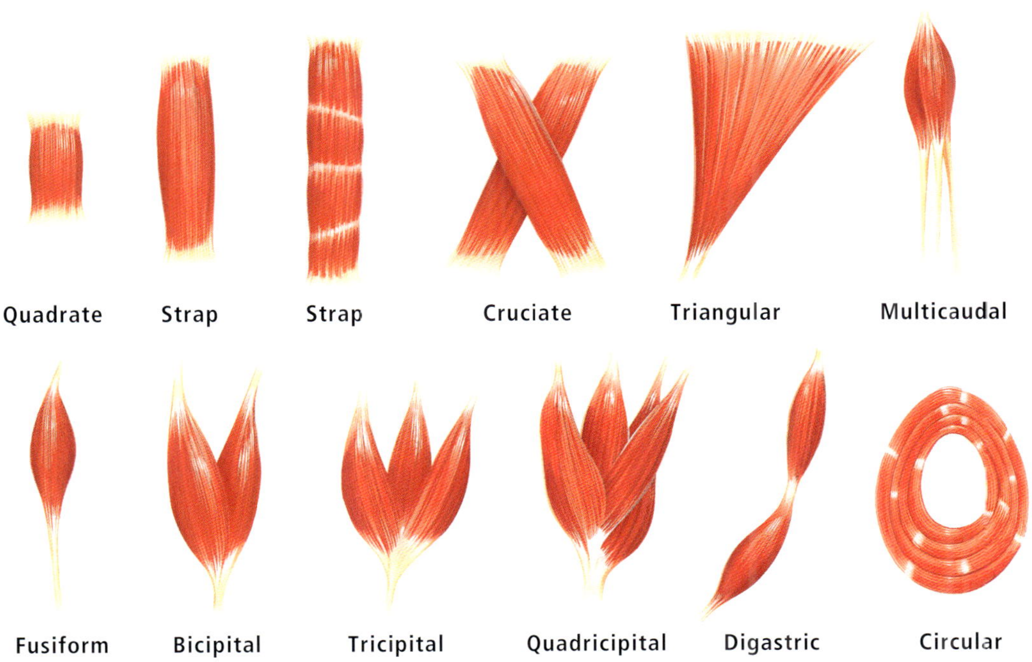

Muscle fibers

Muscles consist of bundles of fibers which can be organized in different ways according the function of the muscle. The force exerted by a muscle depends on its cross-sectional area.

When muscles are inactive, they decrease in both size and strength and their tendons become weaker. Muscle wasting (atrophy) is most obvious when the muscles are completely paralyzed by nerve injury; it is also seen in some congenital or metabolic diseases of muscle such as muscular dystrophy. Our knowledge of muscles and their actions has advanced tremendously as a result of recent physiological and biomechanical studies and has had far-reaching applications in many different fields, from sports medicine to engineering and robotics.

Involuntary muscles

Skeletal muscle is under conscious control and is therefore called voluntary muscle. In contrast, the cardiac muscle of the heart is controlled by nerve impulses produced by a natural pacemaker called the sinoatrial node, the rate of which is controlled by the autonomic nervous system. Smooth muscle is found in the digestive system, reproductive system, major blood vessels, the skin and internal organs, and is also controlled by the autonomic nervous system.

SEE ALSO *Hamstring muscles, Muscle, Muscular dystrophy, Quadriceps muscle, Tendons, Trapezius muscle*

Cardiac muscle tissue

Muscle in the heart (cardiac muscle) is similar to striated or voluntary muscle but its contractions are controlled by the heart's pacemaker.

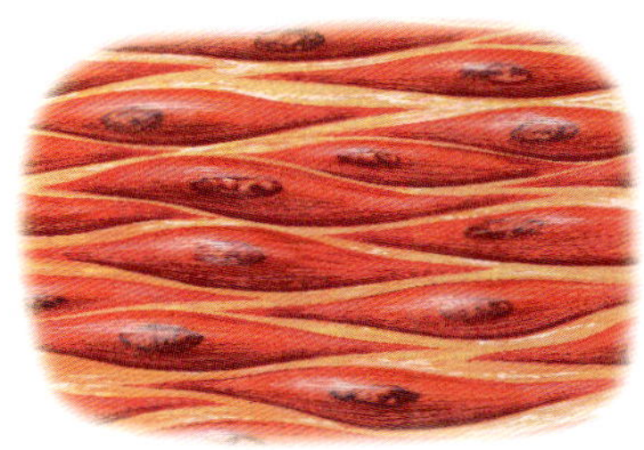

Smooth muscle tissue

Smooth muscle is found in the skin, major blood vessels, and the reproductive and digestive systems. It is controlled by the autonomic nervous system.

NERVOUS SYSTEM

Along with the endocrine and the immune systems, the nervous system is one of three systems concerned with coordinating the activities of the body. The nervous system receives information about the outside world and internal organs, determines the appropriate response to changes in both domains and responds rapidly. Information is processed and transferred by means of nerve cells firing electrical signals called action potentials, which can move along nerve fibers at speeds of up to 320 feet (100 meters) per second. The endocrine and immune systems respond more slowly because they depend on chemicals or cells released into the blood to communicate responses.

Divisions of the nervous system

The nervous system is divided into a central nervous system (CNS) and a peripheral nervous system. The CNS is made up of the brain and spinal cord, while the peripheral nervous system consists of all the nerves distributed throughout the rest of the body. The parts of the peripheral nervous system concerned with controlling aspects of body function over which we have no voluntary control are called the autonomic nervous system. Although most of the constituent nerve cells of the autonomic nervous system are located peripherally, some are also located in the CNS. The autonomic nervous system is also under the control of parts of the brain such as the hypothalamus.

There are also many nerve cells located in the wall of the gastrointestinal tract (stomach and intestine) that coordinate and control the movement of the gut and the secretions of the gut glands, and also transport sensory information about conditions in the gut. Gut nerve cells may actually outnumber those in the spinal cord.

The brain and spinal cord consist of nerve cells and their processes, along with bundles of nerve fibers. Gray matter refers to the parts of the CNS where nerve cell bodies are concentrated; white matter refers to parts with very few cells and many nerve fibers.

A typical nerve cell has a cell body with a nucleus and a number of branching processes (dendrites), which receive incoming information, and an outgoing fiber (axon),

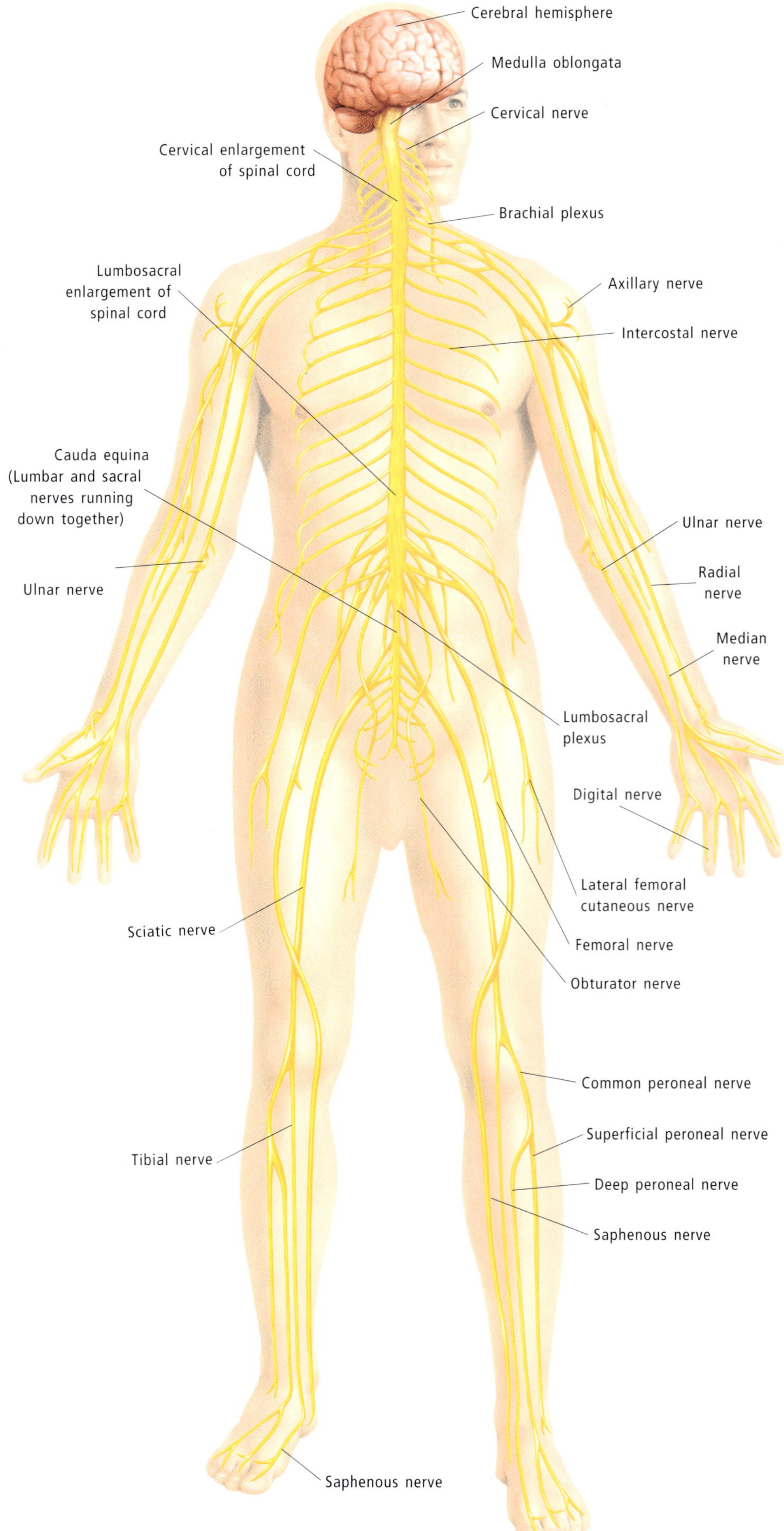

which carries information away from the nerve cell body. The dendrites are quite short, usually less than 1/16 inch (1–1.5 millimeters), while the axon may be very long, anywhere from 1/16–36 inches (1 millimeter to 1 meter). Many axons are coated in layers of a fatty material (myelin), essential for the rapid transmission of nerve impulses (action potentials) along the axon. In diseases such as multiple sclerosis, where the myelin sheath is damaged, the transmission of nerve impulses is severely impaired. Nerve cells communicate with each other by releasing chemicals (neurotransmitters) at sites where the processes of two or more cells meet (synapses).

The CNS also contains many cells called glia. These fulfill diverse roles such as the formation of myelin, maintaining the correct concentrations of salts and chemicals in the spaces between the nerve cells, and providing surveillance against invading microorganisms.

Central nervous system

From a functional viewpoint the CNS can be divided into parts concerned with interpreting sensory information (sensory systems), with controlling the function of the body (motor systems), and with higher brain functions, such as memory, language and social behavior. In practice, a few brain regions may combine all three functions.

Sensory systems are concerned not just with the senses of vision, touch, hearing, smell and taste, but with many other senses of which we are not usually aware, such as the sense of up and down, feelings of rotation or acceleration, bladder fullness, stomach distension, joint position and blood pressure. Motor (effector) systems are concerned not just with controlling our muscles and movement, but also with controlling many automatic functions, including sweating, blood pressure and gut movements.

Anatomy of the brain

Anatomically, the brain is divided into three main regions—the forebrain, midbrain and hindbrain. The forebrain contains most of the brain substance and is capped by the highly folded cerebral cortex. The midbrain and hindbrain carry many fiber bundles that convey information to and from the upper parts of the brain. The hindbrain can be further divided into the pons, medulla and cerebellum. The midbrain, pons and medulla, collectively called the brain stem, contain many nerve cell groups that control the muscles of the face and head and process information about touch on the face, taste and hearing.

Other important functions of the brain stem are the control of breathing, blood pressure and heart function.

The forebrain is a very complex and important region. At its surface, the cerebral cortex is broadly organized into the frontal lobe, the occipital lobe at the back, the parietal lobe in the middle and the temporal lobe below. Each lobe contains many different areas concerned with particular functions.

At the very front of the frontal lobe, the prefrontal area is concerned with the control of social behavior, motivation and planning.

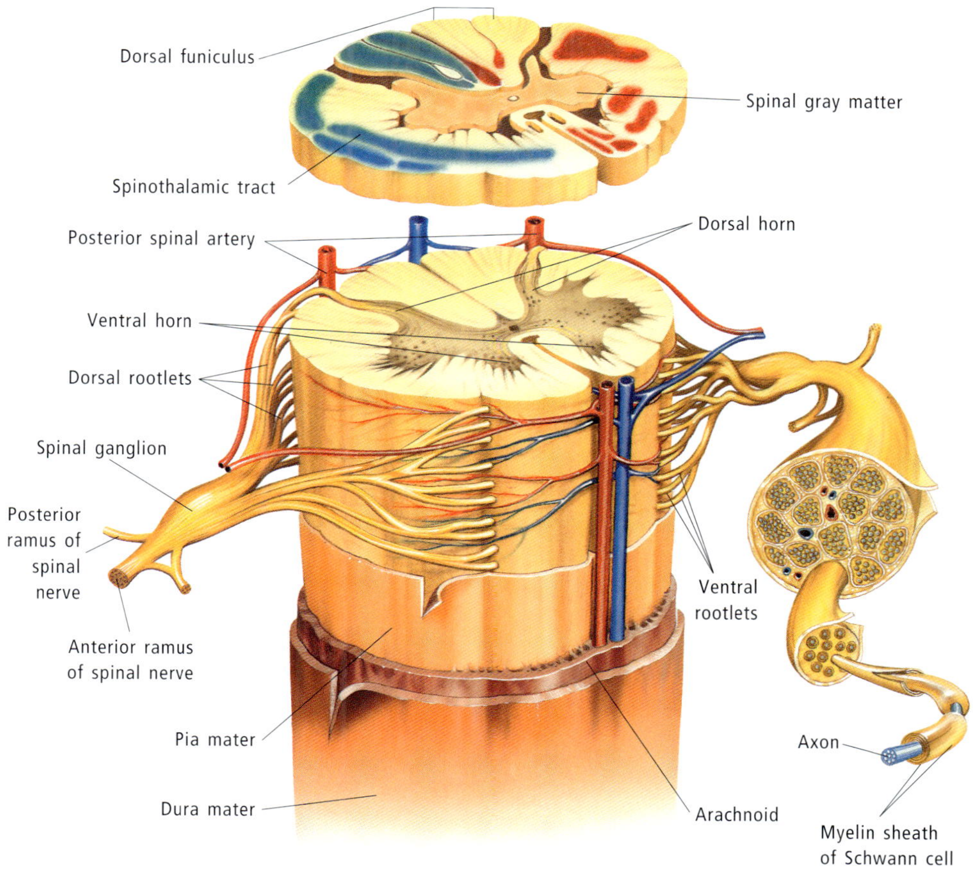

Spinal cord cross-section

The spinal cord is part of the central nervous system that runs down the vertebral canal. The central core of gray matter receives and processes sensory information, and sends signals to the muscles. The surrounding layer of white matter contains axons which communicate between the brain and spinal cord.

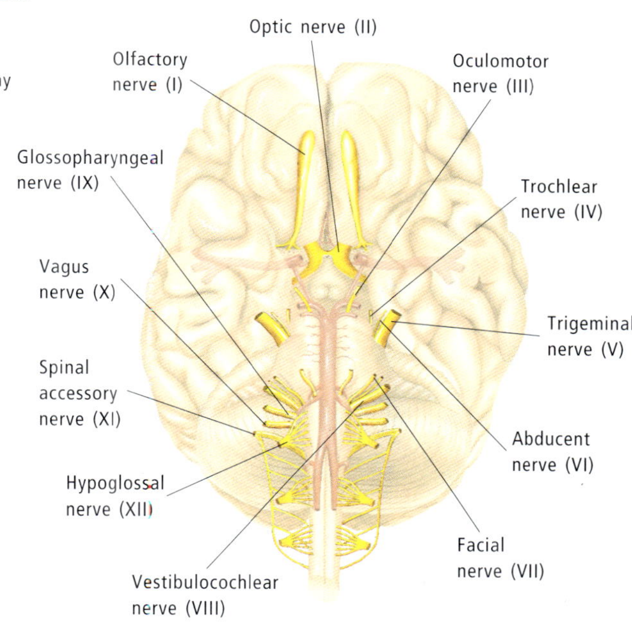

Nerves in the brain

There are 12 cranial nerves which are visible at the base of the brain. In addition to their motor and sensory functions, the cranial nerves serve the 5 systems for special senses.

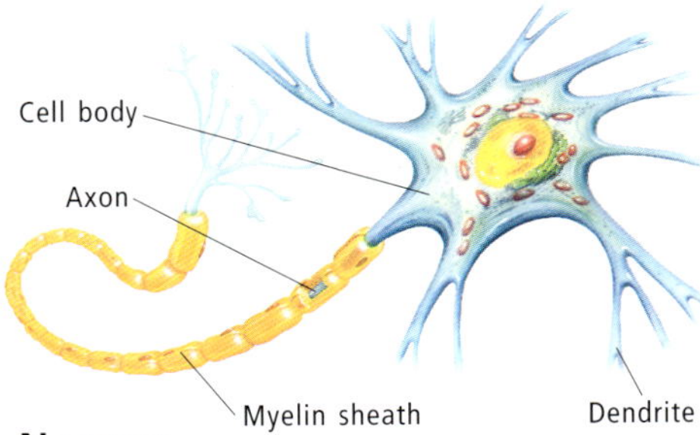

Neuron

Neurons are nerve cells that are specially designed to conduct nerve impulses to and from all parts of the body.

Behind the prefrontal area lie the premotor cortex, which plans motor actions, and the primary motor cortex, which sets those motor commands into action. The lower part of the left frontal lobe contains Broca's area, concerned with the expression of language. The occipital lobe contains a series of visual areas. The parietal lobe contains a primary somatosensory area, concerned with processing sensory information about touch, pain and joint position from the body and face. Further back in the parietal lobe lies a region that generates our sense of the spatial organization of the outside world. The temporal lobe contains areas concerned with hearing, smell and memory. At the junction of the temporal and parietal lobes lies Wernicke's area, concerned with understanding language. Deep inside the forebrain are groups of nerve cells called the basal ganglia, which are primarily concerned with motor control, but may also be involved in some higher functions like language and thought. The forebrain also contains the thalamus, which is primarily concerned with relaying sensory information to the cerebral cortex and controlling motor activity. Below the thalamus lies the hypothalamus, which serves as the interface between the brain and the autonomic nervous system and controls food and water intake, sexual function and body temperature, among other functions.

The spinal cord

The spinal cord acts as an intermediary between the peripheral nervous system and the brain. It extends from the base of the skull to a point about two-thirds of the way down the back, running through the vertebral canal. The spinal cord has many nerve fibers attached to it, arranged in sets and named according to their level on the cord. The cord itself has a central region of gray matter, which is divided into posterior (dorsal) and anterior (ventral) horns and an intermediate region. The gray matter is surrounded by white matter carrying ascending and descending fiber tracts.

At each level, the spinal cord receives sensory nerves, which convey information about touch, pain, temperature, muscle tension and joint position. This information may be used at the level at which it enters the spinal cord to control muscle tension or stimulate reflex responses, such as withdrawing a hand from a hot object, or it may be transmitted up the white matter of the cord to the brain for conscious appreciation of the information.

The spinal cord also gives rise to motor and autonomic nerve fibers, which control muscles and affect internal organs, respectively. The brain sends controlling signals down through the white matter of the spinal cord to spinal motor neurons, so that we can consciously control our muscles.

Peripheral nervous system

The peripheral nervous system consists of nerve fibers or axons that control muscle activity or carry sensory information back to the spinal cord or brain stem. The motor axons come from cell bodies located in the anterior horn of the spinal cord, while the sensory axons arise from cell bodies located in clumps or ganglia alongside the spinal cord. Many axons in the peripheral nervous system are coated with myelin (much like axons in the central nervous system) produced by Schwann cells.

An important difference between the peripheral and central nervous systems is that peripheral nerves have the ability to repair and regenerate, where central axons do not. This difference may be partly due to the behavior of Schwann cells after nerve injury.

Diseases of the nervous system can be considered by category. Probably the two most important types of central nervous system disease in Western society are trauma and vascular disease. Motor vehicle, diving and other accidents may cause injury to the spinal cord, resulting in either complete or partial separation of the fiber tracts joining the brain to the lower spinal cord. Depending on the level of the injury, the patient may be paralyzed in the lower limbs (paraplegia) or all four limbs (quadriplegia). Vascular diseases of the brain can involve bleeding into the brain from ruptured vessels or death of brain tissue due to the obstruction of brain arteries. Tumors may spread to the brain from tumors in other parts of the body or arise in the brain itself, usually from glial cells. Degenerative diseases of the brain include Alzheimer's disease and Huntington's disease.

SEE ALSO *Alzheimer's disease, Autonomic nervous system, Brain, Cerebellum, Endocrine system, Huntington's disease, Hypothalamus, Lymphatic/Immune system, Multiple sclerosis, Spinal cord*

Reflexes

A reflex is a response to a stimulus, in which sensory information triggers an automatic response in muscles or glands. The response usually involves nerve cells in the spinal cord and does not involve a conscious reaction.

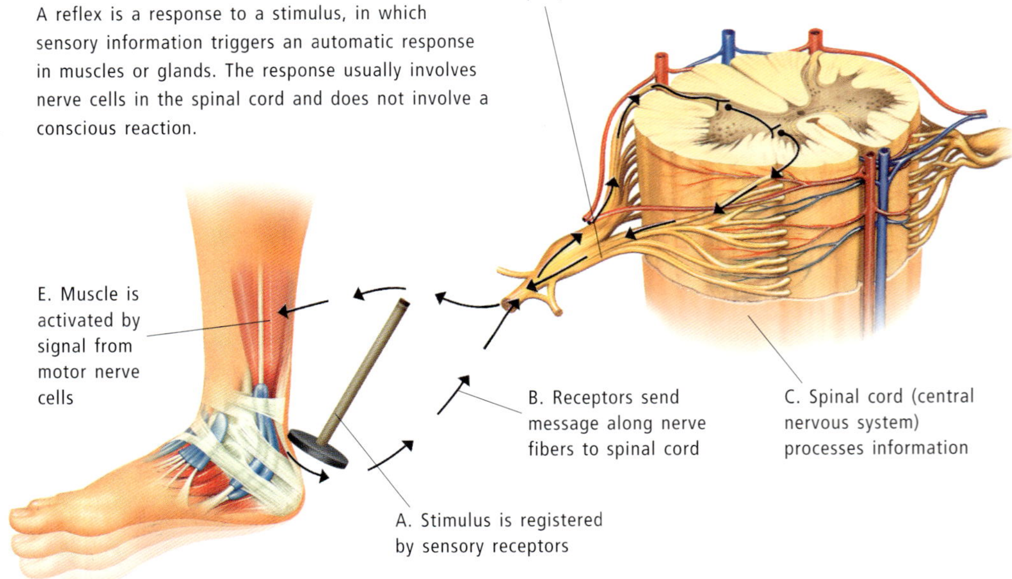

AUTONOMIC NERVOUS SYSTEM

The autonomic nervous system is the part of the nervous system concerned with controlling relatively automatic bodily functions. The body's tendency to maintain a constant internal environment and a constant heart rate and blood pressure, is called homeo-0stasis. While many body systems contribute to homeostasis, the autonomic nervous system is probably the most important.

Most of the activities of the autonomic nervous system occur without our being aware of them, and so the system could also be called the involuntary nervous system. Nevertheless, some bodily functions can be influenced by conscious activity—the effect of relaxation therapy on blood pressure is an example of this.

While most of the activities of the autonomic nervous system are actions on body organs and tissues (for example, motor functions) there are also many sensory nerves accompanying the autonomic motor nerves. These sensory nerves relay information about internal organs (such as the tension in the wall of a full stomach or blood pressure in parts of the cardiovascular system) back to the central nervous system (CNS).

This information is important for keeping the brain and spinal cord informed about changes in the body, and allows appropriate control procedures to be carried out to keep conditions in the body's interior in a relatively constant state.

Structure

The autonomic nervous system consists of some nerve cells (neurons) in the brain and spinal cord, their fibers which leave the central nervous system, collections of nerve cells in the various body cavities, and nerve fibers which are distributed in the internal organs.

Collections of nerve cells in the body cavities are called ganglia. These ganglia are often embedded in networks of nerve fibers called plexuses, which are located near the heart and lungs, in front of the aorta in the abdomen, and in front of the sacral bone in the pelvis.

The autonomic nervous system differs in a number of ways from the somatic nervous system, which is concerned with voluntary control of the body's muscles. The autonomic nervous system has a series of two or more nerve cells between the CNS and the organ that is being controlled, while the somatic nervous system has only one nerve cell between the CNS and the muscle being controlled.

The somatic nervous system neurons have their cell bodies in the brain or spinal cord and axons or nerve fibers that run directly to the muscle being controlled. Those autonomic nervous system neurons whose cell bodies lie inside the spinal cord or brain stem are called preganglionic nerve cells, while those neurons whose cell bodies lie in ganglia are called postganglionic nerve cells.

While both the somatic and autonomic nervous systems may use acetylcholine as a neurotransmitter, the sympathetic part of the autonomic nervous system also uses the chemical norepinephrine (noradrenaline), which is released from the postganglionic nerve cells onto smooth muscle and other target tissues.

Another difference between the somatic and autonomic nervous systems is that all the nerve fibers controlling voluntary muscles in the somatic nervous system have thick myelin sheaths, while usually only the preganglionic nerve cells of the autonomic nervous system have myelin sheaths. Since myelin sheaths around nerve fibers contribute to the rapid conduction of nerve impulses, it follows that the somatic or voluntary nervous system usually acts on the muscles much more rapidly than the autonomic nervous system can influence the internal organs.

Divisions of the autonomic nervous system

Traditionally, the autonomic nervous system is divided into a sympathetic and a parasympathetic division. The two divisions are considered to be anatomically and functionally separate, but there are several places in the body (such as the nerve supply of the pelvic organs) where the two may overlap.

Sympathetic division

The sympathetic division is often referred to as the "fight-or-flight" system. It comes into play during emergency situations when our bodies need extra energy to avoid or overcome danger. During emergencies we experience a pounding heartbeat, cold sweaty skin, rapid breathing and enlarged pupils—all produced by activation of the sympathetic nervous system. In addition, the sympathetic nervous system can cause changes such as increased blood pressure, a dry mouth, increased blood sugar levels, and dilation of the small airways of the lung. The sympathetic nervous system also increases the flow of blood to muscles and diverts blood away from the gastrointestinal tract. All of these effects increase the individual's ability to cope with the emergency.

The sympathetic nervous system also has an important effect on the control of body temperature. Some sympathetic nerve cells stimulate the activity of sweat glands in the skin to increase sweat production and lower body temperature by the evaporation of perspiration. Other sympathetic nerve cells control tiny smooth muscles in the skin, which when stimulated pull on the hairs of the skin causing them to stand up. This change is commonly called "goose bumps" and keeps a layer of relatively still air close to the skin to minimize heat loss.

In the eye, the sympathetic nervous system causes enlargement of the pupil to increase the amount of light reaching the sensitive retina at the back of the eye.

Anatomically, the sympathetic nervous system consists of nerve cells in the thoracic and lumbar levels of the spinal cord as well as a long chain of nerve cells which lies alongside the backbone. This long chain is called the sympathetic trunk and gives off nerves to other plexuses and internal organs. Some sympathetic nerve fibers go to the adrenal medulla, which is part of the endocrine system.

These nerve fibers stimulate the adrenal medulla, which contains modified nerve cells, to release epinephrine (adrenaline) and norepinephrine (noradrenaline) into the bloodstream. These hormones are released in emergency situations where energy reserves need to be rapidly mobilized.

Parasympathetic division

The parasympathetic division is most active when the body is not under threat and when

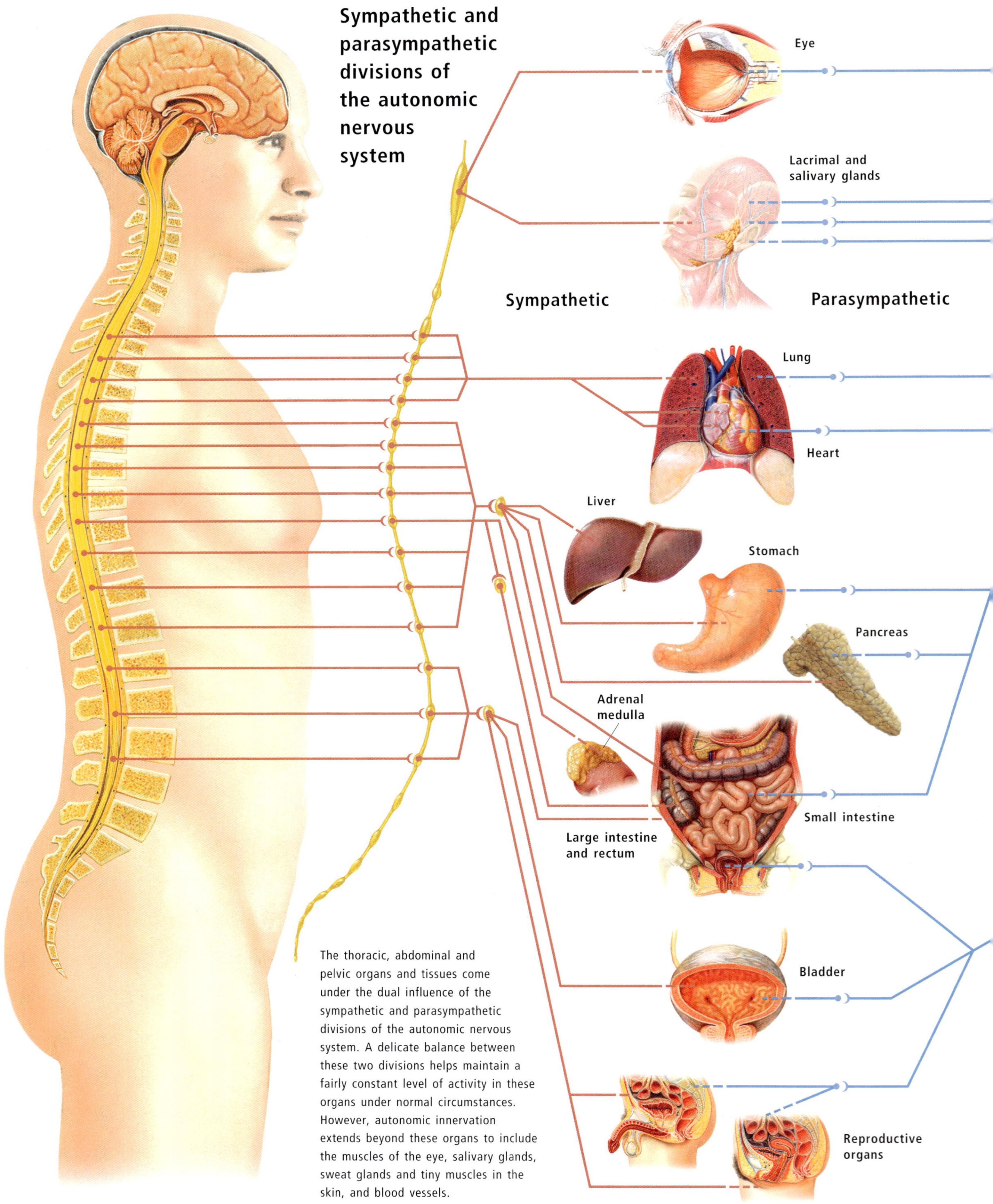

The thoracic, abdominal and pelvic organs and tissues come under the dual influence of the sympathetic and parasympathetic divisions of the autonomic nervous system. A delicate balance between these two divisions helps maintain a fairly constant level of activity in these organs under normal circumstances. However, autonomic innervation extends beyond these organs to include the muscles of the eye, salivary glands, sweat glands and tiny muscles in the skin, and blood vessels.

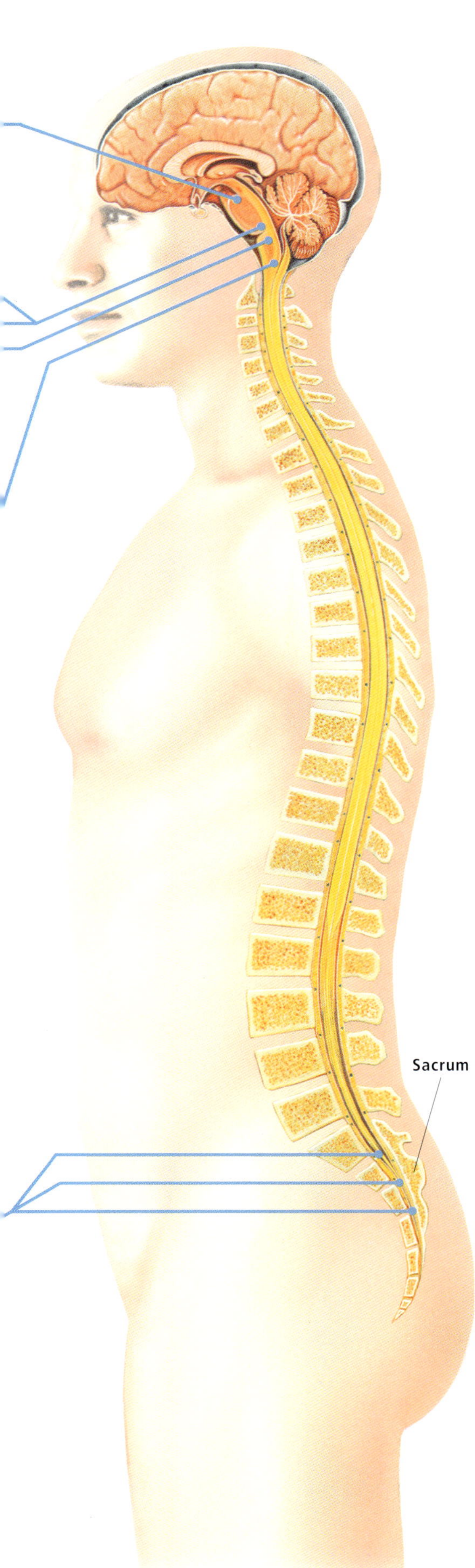

the person is largely at rest. Its main function is to conserve energy, restoring the internal body state to normal by promoting digestion and eliminating urine and feces from the body.

In the head, for example, the parasympathetic nervous system increases the production of saliva by the salivary glands, while in the stomach and intestines it increases the activity of the smooth muscle and glands. The increased activity of the smooth muscle in the gut increases the movement called peristalsis, which helps to move food along the gut and break it up into a more readily digestible consistency. The increased activity of glands in the gut will increase the production of digestive enzymes to break down food, and the production of mucus and other fluid to promote the absorption and movement of food along the gut.

In the cardiovascular system, the parasympathetic nervous system lowers the heart rate and blood pressure and diverts blood from muscles to the gut to assist with digestion.

In the lungs, it causes constriction of the small airways and increases the activity of the small glands in the airways, which will increase the amount of secretions.

In the eye, the parasympathetic nervous system closes down the pupil of the eye, decreasing the amount of light reaching the retina, and stimulates contraction of the ciliary muscle, which leads to bulging of the lens of the eye for close vision.

Involvement with the urinary and reproductive organs

The sympathetic and parasympathetic nervous systems have important complementary actions in the urinary and reproductive organs. The release of urine from the bladder is stimulated by the parasympathetic nervous system, which relaxes the sphincter muscle at the outlet from the urinary bladder and causes contraction of bladder wall muscle. Urination is inhibited by the sympathetic nervous system, which constricts the sphincter muscles around the outlet from the urinary bladder. In the male reproductive organs, the parasympathetic nervous system causes erection of the penis by increasing the flow of blood into the cavernous spaces of the penis.

The system is also involved in ejaculation, the process of expulsion of semen from the penis. If a man experiences anxiety about his ability to perform sexually, then the sympathetic nervous system will be more active. This may cause difficulty in obtaining and maintaining an erection—a problem called impotence or erectile difficulty—and/or a too-rapid progression from arousal to ejaculation, known as premature ejaculation. This type of sexual dysfunction is often responsible for sexual problems in younger men, but in older men impotence is more likely to be due to vascular problems and diabetic damage to pelvic nerves.

Diseases and disorders

The autonomic nervous system can be affected in a variety of diseases. In Raynaud's phenomenon, patients experience episodes of pallor and blue coloration of the ends of the fingers and toes. The phenomenon may occur in young women with no apparent cause (Raynaud's disease), or it may accompany connective tissue disease or occupations involving the use of vibrating tools. Patients with this problem may develop ulcers on their fingertips and, in severe cases, develop skin infections. Treatment consists of keeping the hands and feet warm, but if this is not effective, surgically cutting sympathetic nerves to the fingers may be of assistance.

Deliberate destruction of part of the sympathetic nervous system may also be helpful in some other conditions such as arterial obstruction due to atherosclerosis, excessive sweating, and frostbite.

Patients with diabetes mellitus may experience problems as a result of damage to the autonomic nervous system. Male patients may develop impotence, while both sexes may suffer from nocturnal diarrhea, problems maintaining adequate blood pressure when standing, and occasionally problems of retention of urine in the bladder with urine overflow.

SEE ALSO *Atherosclerosis, Brain, Diabetes, Endocrine system, Epinephrine, Eye, Ganglion, Nerves, Nervous system, Neurons, Peristalsis, Raynaud's disease, Reproductive systems, Retina, Sexual dysfunction, Spinal cord, Sympathetic nervous system, Urinary systems*

LYMPHATIC/ IMMUNE SYSTEM

The lymphatic system is a network of vessels, aggregates of lymphoid tissue (lymph nodes) and lymphoid organs, and has two main functions. Apart from bringing back to the heart much of the interstitial fluid which bathes all cells of the body, it is also loaded with specialized white blood cells (lymphocytes) and macrophages, which sweep up foreign bodies or invaders, such as bacteria, viruses, and cancer cells.

Lymph vessels

Unlike the complete circle of the circulatory system, the lymphatic system is a one-way system, which begins with a capillary network of blind-ended tubes. These capillaries absorb large molecules and particles (foreign bodies and nutritional elements), and converge to form gradually larger lymphatic vessels that carry the lymph towards the heart. Lymph vessels have valves to ensure one-way flow. Along the lymph vessels are found collections of lymphoid tissue or lymph nodes (frequently and colloquially called lymph glands).

Lymph nodes and lymphoid tissue

The lymph nodes are small pea-sized organs located in groups at the confluence of lymphatic vessels. Each node is connected to incoming and outgoing lymphatic vessels. Incoming lymph spreads throughout the node to pass through aggregations of lymphocytes and macrophages. Debris or foreign matter and cancer cells are engulfed by macrophages and specialized lymphocytes called killer cells. Invaders such as bacteria are also digested by the macrophages, which extract essential and unique parts of the bacteria (antigens) to present to nearby lymphocytes. Activated by the contact with the antigens, these lymphocytes produce antibodies (antidotes for particular antigens). This type of lymphocyte proliferates as necessary to step up the production of required antibodies. Thus lymph nodes not only filter out and destroy foreign bodies before they get into the circulation, they also activate the cloning of lymphocytes to produce specific antibodies, which is part of the immune response.

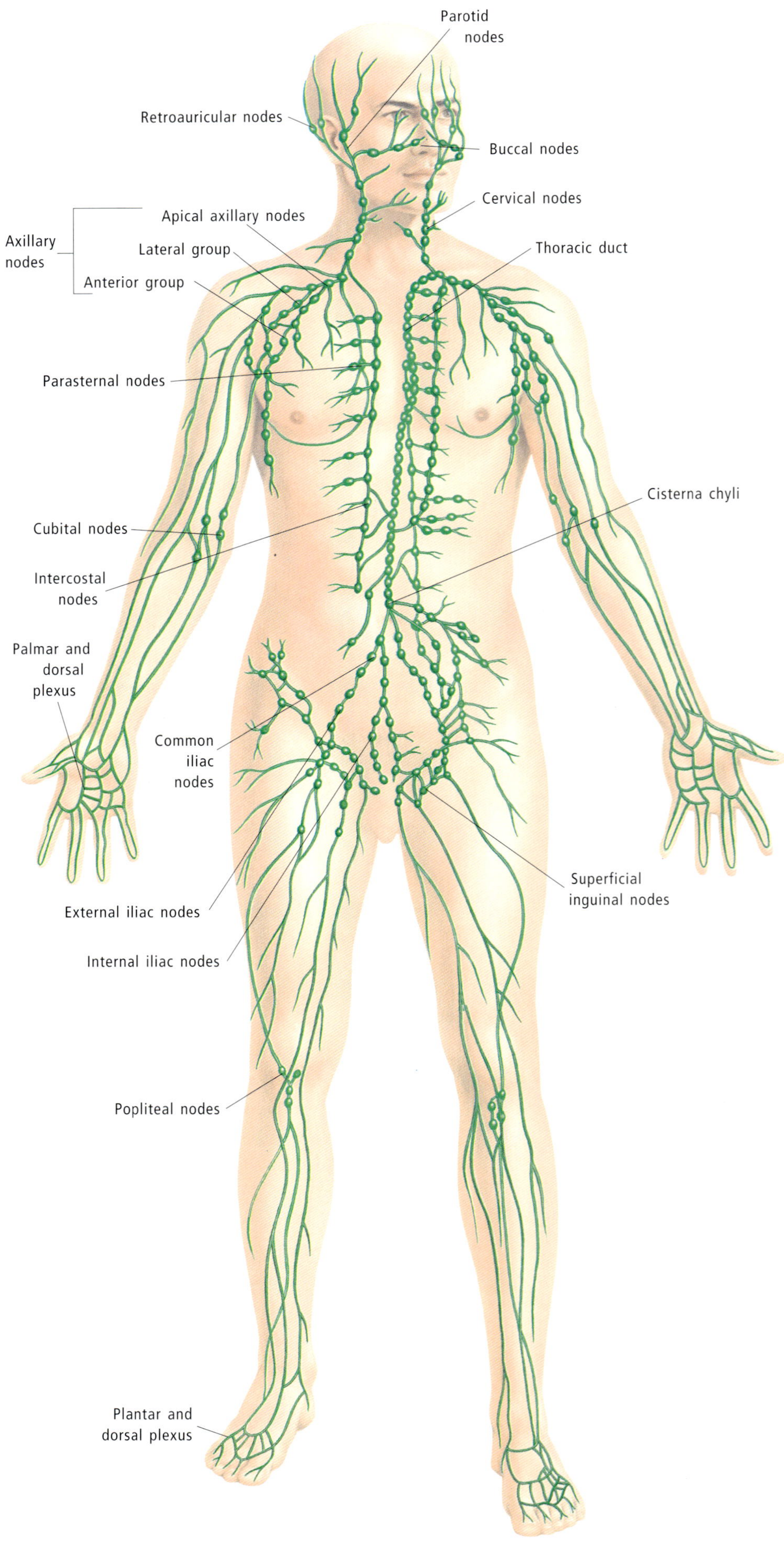

Lymph nodes can be compared to outlying fortresses along the main highway into a city. The battle against invaders begins in the outermost fortress. If the first fortress fails to contain the invasion, fighting will continue along the highway, fire and smoke progressing to fortresses closer in. In a similar fashion, inflammation traveling along major lymph vessels is sometimes visible as red streaks under the skin (lymphangitis). Inflammatory reaction to bacteria in lymph nodes results in swollen, red and painful nodes. When cancer cells colonize the nodes, they become swollen and hard, but not painful, because the enlargement is more gradual. The track of enlarged lymph nodes (lymphadenopathy) gives clues to the origin of infection or the progress of cancer cells.

The tonsils at the back of the oral cavity and the so-called adenoids at the roof of the throat are aggregates of lymphoid tissue.

How lymph returns to the general circulation

The peripheral lymph vessels converge into large lymphatic trunks, which link up in turn to the right lymphatic duct and the thoracic duct, which empty into the large veins at the base of the neck. An overwhelming infection can thus spread along lymph vessels into the general circulation causing "blood infection" (septicemia), which can be fatal.

Lacteals are lymphatic vessels in the walls of the digestive system, which collect large molecules and lipids (chyle) extracted from food. They play a major role in the absorption of fats. They engorge after a meal and become visible as fine whitish streaks in the mesentery. The lacteals empty into the cisterna chyli, a sac located below the diaphragm.

Lymphatic vessels from the head and neck pass through a collar of lymph nodes under the lower jaw, to end in chains of nodes along the internal jugular veins. Cancer of the tip of the tongue spreads first to the nodes under the chin, then to cervical nodes. Some lymph nodes in the lower part of the neck (jugulodigastric nodes) are called tonsillar nodes because they become enlarged in tonsillitis.

Lymphatic vessels of the upper limb ascend from the hand to the armpit (axilla). The nodes in the axilla, which can be felt along the upper arm and against the upper part of the rib cage, also receive lymph from the chest wall, back and the breast. They become enlarged in breast cancer.

Lymph node

A lymph node consists of a mass of lymphatic tissue that is surrounded by a fibrous capsule. Each lymph node is connected to an incoming and outgoing lymph vessel.

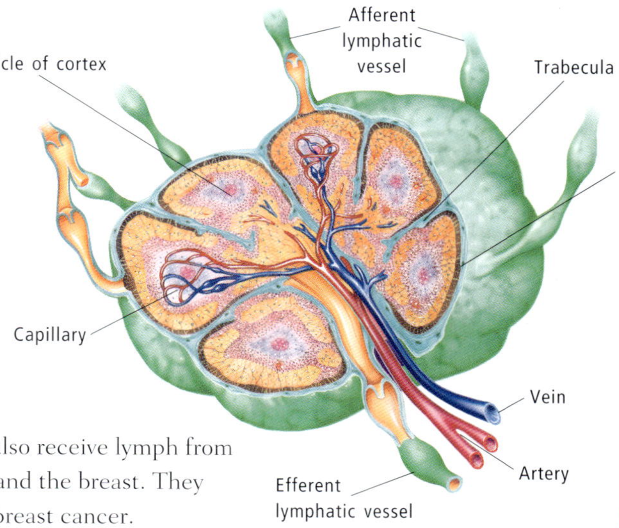

Lymphatic vessels of the lower limb ascend from the foot to the inguinal lymph nodes in the groin. These nodes also drain the buttocks, the back and parts of the genitalia, and empty into the cisterna chyli.

Lymph from the internal organs of the thorax and abdomen drains into chains of lymph nodes along major arteries and the aorta. Lymph nodes draining the lungs are located around the bronchi and trachea. Enlargement of these nodes in lung cancer (bronchogenic carcinoma) can be seen on chest x-rays. Lymph from the abdominal and pelvic viscera drains into lymph nodes along the iliac arteries and the aorta, and eventually into the cisterna chyli. These deep nodes, when enlarged, are visible on CAT scans and magnetic resonance imaging (MRI) scans. They can be visualized through radiography after injecting radiopaque dye into the lymphatic vessels (lymphangiography).

The cisterna chyli empties into the thoracic duct, which ascends through the thorax into the neck and empties into the junction of the left internal jugular and subclavian veins. The thoracic duct also collects the lymph from the thoracic organs, from the left upper limb and left half of the head and neck.

Lymph from the right half of the head, neck, and thorax, and the right upper limb, converges in a short right lymphatic duct which empties into the junction of the right internal jugular and subclavian veins.

Lymphoid organs

The lymphoid organs include the thymus, the spleen, and mucosa-associated lymphoid tissue.

Lymph vessel

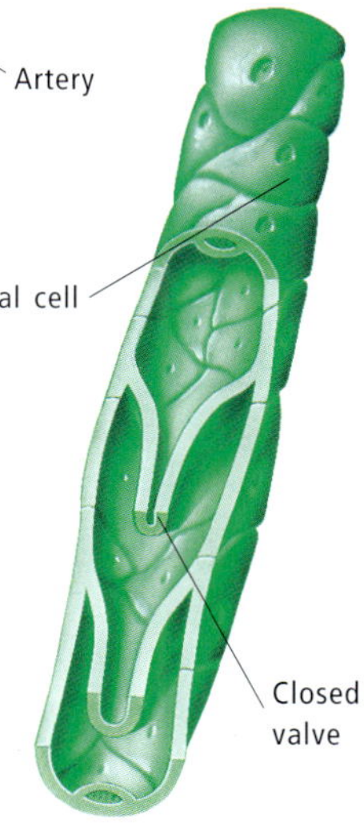

Lymph circulation

The lymph vessels contain numerous valves which prevent the backflow of lymph. The lymph is returned to the general circulation by two large lymphatic vessels which empty into the large veins at the base of the neck.

Thymus

The thymus lies in the upper part of the thorax, between the heart and the sternum. It is the first lymphoid organ to develop in the embryo, and reaches 1–1½ ounces (30–40 grams) at puberty. It is gradually replaced by fat and fibrous tissue to become unrecognizable in old age.

Lymphocytes, which are manufactured in the lymph nodes and bone marrow, mature as they are pushed from the outer cortex of the thymus into the central part (medulla), and from there enter the circulation. Most of the lymphocytes in the thymus are T lymphocytes, which are able to recognize foreign-body antigens. B lymphocytes recognize only the body's own cells and antigens. The thymus also secretes hormones that regulate T cell production and function. When the thymus regresses after puberty, T cells continue to proliferate, thus maintaining an adequate number throughout life.

Spleen

The spleen lies under the left ninth, tenth and eleventh ribs, near the end of the pan-

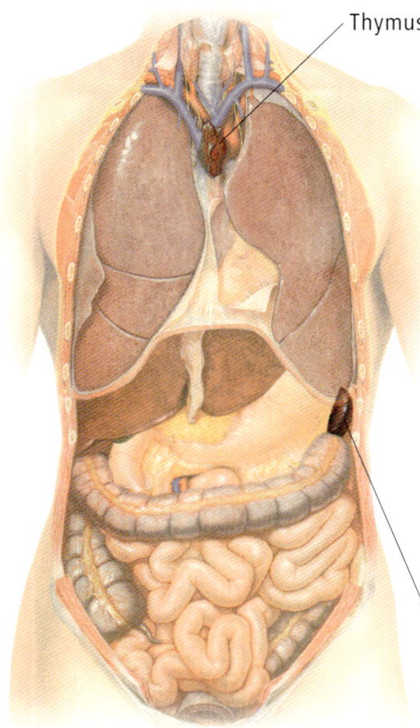

Organs of the lymph system

The thymus gland is an important lymphatic organ in infancy, but gradually regresses after puberty. The spleen is the largest concentration of lymphatic tissue in the body; other concentrations of lymphatic tissue are found in the lymphatic nodules of the gut, and in the tonsils.

Lymphatic tissue

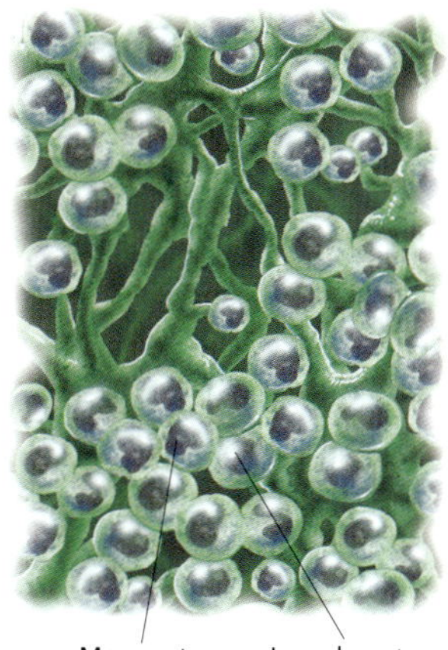

creas. It normally weighs about 5 ounces (150 grams) but can become extremely enlarged in conditions such as malaria and leukemia. It has a rich network of blood capillaries and sinusoids, called the red pulp, and aggregates of lymphocytes around branching arteries, called the white pulp.

The spleen removes particles and aged red blood cells from the circulation. Old red blood cells have rigid membranes and break when they squeeze through the narrow spaces between reticular cells of the spleen.

The spleen also plays an important role in building the immune response, functioning in a similar way to lymph nodes.

Mucosa-associated lymphoid tissue

Masses of lymphoid tissue are found in the linings (mucosa) of the respiratory system, urogenital tract and digestive tract. These mucosa-associated lymphoid tissues contain B and T lymphocytes and serve the same protective function as lymph nodes in the cavities of the body exposed to the external environment.

Lymphocytes and the immune response

Lymphocytes play a central role in the body's immune system. There are three major types of lymphocytes: natural killer cells (NK cells), B lymphocytes and T lymphocytes.

NK cells do not react to specific antigens like T lymphocytes, but kill a variety of target cells, including cancer cells.

T lymphocytes derived from the thymus can be either effector or regulator cells. Each effector T cell recognizes and is activated by one antigen. Activated T cells present antigen to antibody-producing cells to stimulate production of antibody to the particular antigen. Regulator T cells include T helper cells and T suppressor cells, which either facilitate or inhibit the immune response.

B lymphocytes, which come from bone marrow, produce specific antibodies. Each B cell is specialized in producing immunoglobulins or Ig (antibody) to a single antigen. There are five general classes of immunoglobulins: IgG, which is the most important serum globulin; IgM, which is the first antibody to appear in response to infection; IgA, which is found in secretions such as tears or saliva; IgE, which initiates allergic and hypersensitivity reaction; and IgD, which is found on the surface of B cells to help in binding antigens.

When a specific set of T and B cells are activated by an antigen, they multiply to increase production of the appropriate antibody as long as infection lasts. Some T and B cells, called memory cells, remain after the infection is over to ensure a quick response the next time the body is exposed to the same antigen.

Immune disorders

Allergy happens when a substance (allergen), which is not generally harmful to the body, triggers an inappropriate and exaggerated immune response. The immunoglobulin responsible is IgE. The binding of allergen with IgE on mast cells causes them to release histamine and other chemical mediators which initiate a series of reactions: red eyes, urticaria, constriction of the bronchi due to smooth muscle contraction, and mucus secretion in the nasal glands causing sneezing and runny nose. Antihistamine drugs such as phenergan can block these reactions. Common allergic conditions are asthma, allergic rhinitis, allergic conjunctivitis and dermatitis.

Anaphylaxis is an extremely quick overreaction to an antigen caused by widespread activation of mast cells in the body. Extreme cases lead to the potentially fatal anaphylactic shock, when there is a sudden drop in blood pressure. Anaphylactic reaction to penicillin is a well-known example.

Autoimmune disease results when the immune system reacts to the normal cells and antigens of the body, producing autoantibodies which damage or destroy normal tissues. Common examples are psoriasis, rheumatoid arthritis, thyroiditis and systemic lupus erythematosus.

Immunodeficiency diseases can be acquired when the production of immunoglobulin and/or T lymphocytes is inadequate to protect the body from even the most benign infections. Acquired immunodeficiency syndrome (AIDS) is caused by the human immunodeficiency virus (HIV), which binds to CD4 membrane proteins on the surface of T helper cells. When enough infected T helper cells are destroyed, the immune system collapses. Microorganisms that do not affect individuals with a normal immune system can cause lethal opportunistic infections in HIV-infected patients. A marker used to follow the progress of HIV infection is the number of CD4 helper cells in the blood. To date, all efforts to find a vaccine or cure for AIDS have been unsuccessful.

SEE ALSO *Adenoids, AIDS, Allergies, Autoimmune disease, Immunity, Immunodeficiency, Immunosuppression, Lymph, Lymph glands, Lymphatic vessels, Lymphocytes, Spleen, T cells, Thymus, Tonsils*

Lymphocytes

A lymphocyte is a type of white blood cell that plays an important role in the immune response. There are several types, including B cells, T cells and natural killer cells.

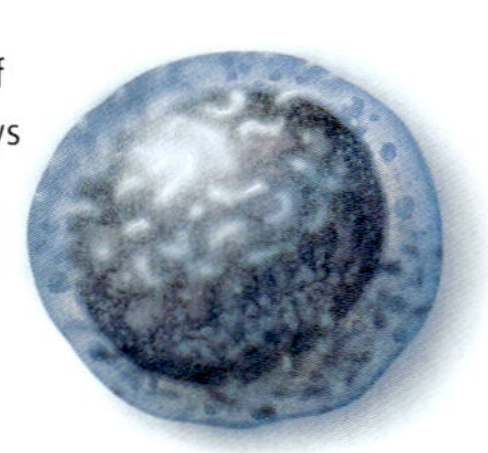

CIRCULATORY SYSTEM

The circulatory system includes the heart and blood vessels, which form a closed ring. The heart has four chambers. It pumps blood out from its two pumps—the left and right ventricles—and collects returned blood into its left and right atria. Blood is pumped out of the ventricles through arteries into a distribution network of tiny vessels, invisible to the naked eye, called the capillaries. After exchanging gases and nutrients with surrounding tissues, blood returns to the atria by the veins.

There are two separate circulations in the circulatory system, which are connected in series. Blood from the left ventricle is distributed to the capillaries throughout the body to deliver oxygen and nutrients to the entire body, and returns to the right atrium. This is the systemic circulation. Blood returning to the right atrium is depleted of oxygen and loaded with carbon dioxide. It then flows into the right ventricle where it is pumped into the capillary network in the lungs, from where, after exchanging carbon dioxide for new oxygen, blood returns to the left atrium. This is the pulmonary circulation. From the left atrium, blood flows to the left ventricle and the cycle continues.

The phase of the heart cycle when both ventricles contract is known as ventricular systole. The ventricles dilate during diastole to receive blood from the atria. In the last part of diastole, the atria contract to squeeze their contents into the ventricles.

Anatomy of the heart

The heart lies in the midline of the thorax, between the lung, surrounded by a double-layered membrane called the pericardium. The heart looks like a pyramid lying on one of its sides, with the apex pointing forward and to the left side. The right and left atria are located at the back, and the right and left ventricles at the front. A septum divides right and left atria, and right and left ventricles. Abnormal development of this septum in the embryo results in "holes in the heart", either between the atria (atrial septal defect), or between the ventricles (ventricular septal defect). Each atrium opens into a

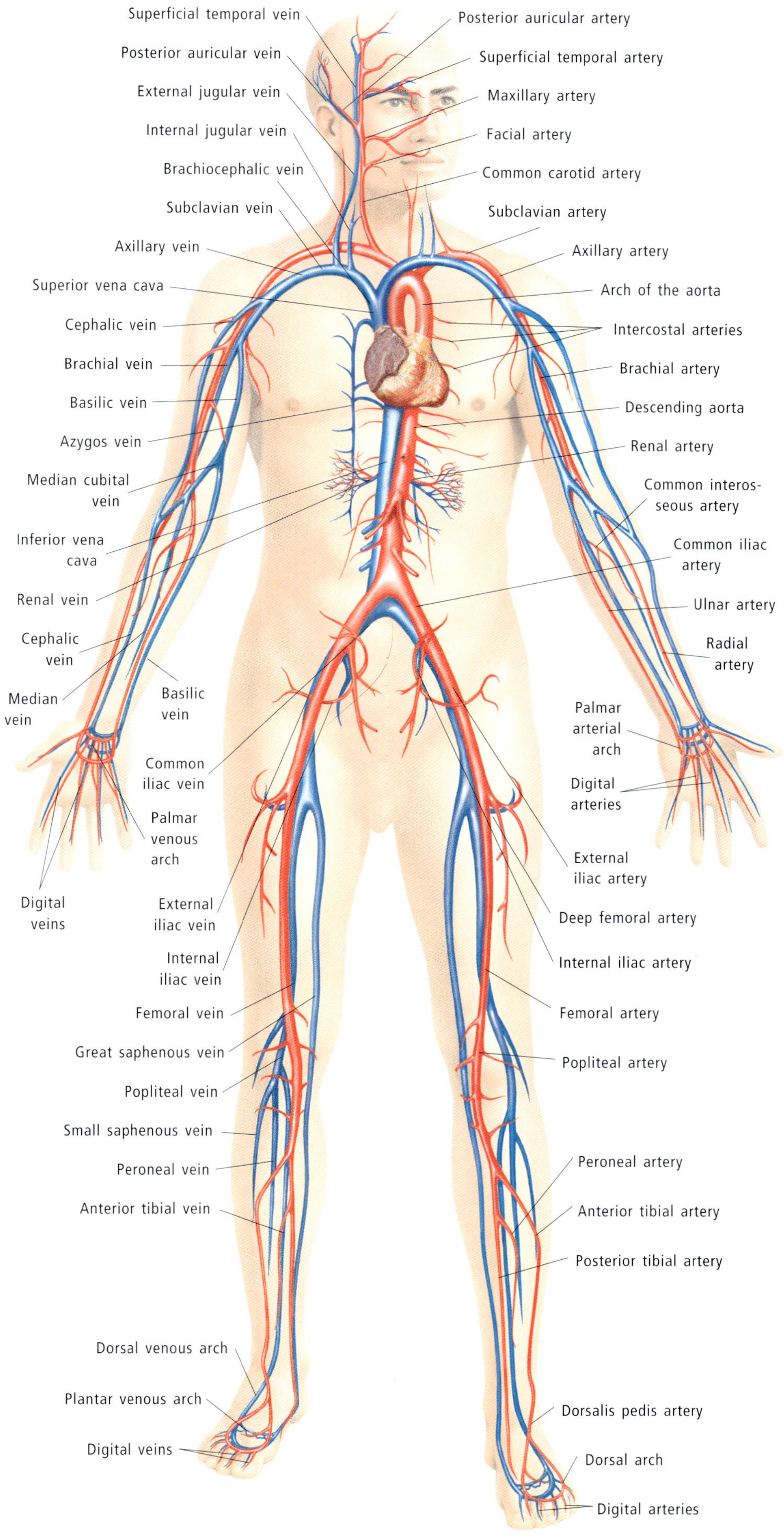

ventricle by an atrioventricular orifice, which is guarded by a valve to ensure that blood flows only in that direction. The valves consist of leaflets (cusps) located in the ventricles and attached to the rim of the orifice. Blood can flow unimpeded into the ventricle, but when it tries to run backwards into the atrium, it pushes the leaflets back towards the rim and closes down the orifice. The right atrioventricular valve has three cusps and is called the tricuspid valve. The left atrioventricular valve is called the mitral valve because its two leaflets look like the split top of a bishop's mitre.

The aortic and pulmonary valves, which prevent reflux of blood back into the ventricles, are formed by three pockets attached to the inside wall of the aortic and pulmonary arteries. They are squashed against the arterial wall by outgoing blood and present no resistance to blood flow, but blood trying to return to the heart will fill up the pockets and close down the opening.

When any of these valves fail to close completely, blood is forced back, causing damage to the heart chamber behind them. In mitral valve incompetence, for example, the left atrium and the pulmonary circulation become overloaded. When the cusps of a valve stick together, the opening is narrowed down (stenosed). In aortic stenosis, the left ventricle is enlarged (hypertrophied) because it has to pump blood against increased resistance. Valvular diseases can be treated by open heart surgery, which is now commonplace.

The end stage of most heart problems is cardiac failure, when the "pump" fails. The common causes are damage to the heart muscle due to a heart attack (myocardial infarction) or valve problems, or diseases of the heart muscle itself (cardiomyopathy).

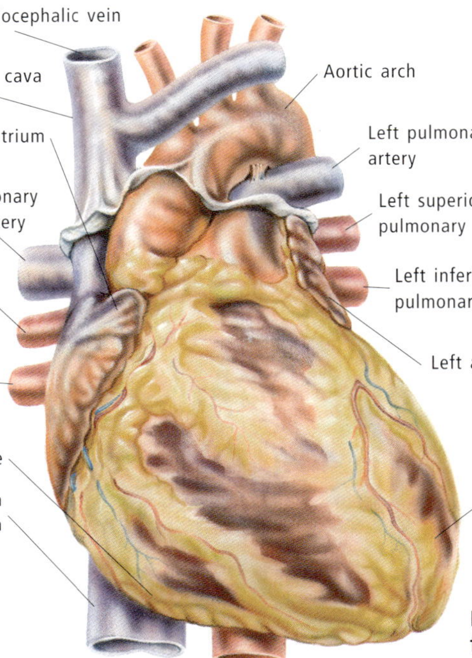

Heart front

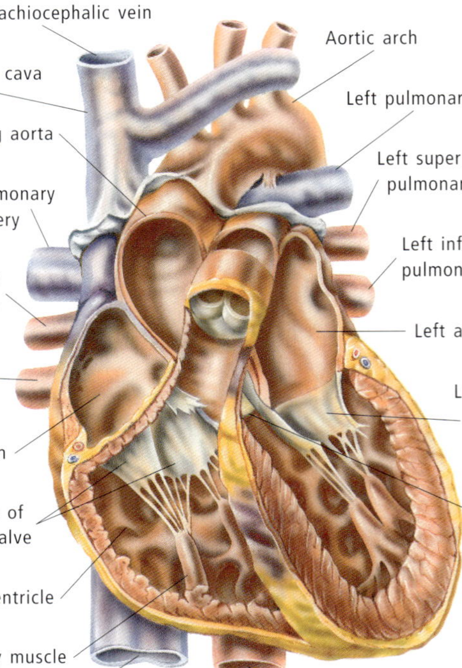

Heart front—cross-section

Heart function

The ventricles of the heart pump blood around the body. Blood from the left ventricle delivers oxygen and nutrients to the whole body via the systemic circulation. Blood from the right ventricle collects oxygen from the lungs via the pulmonary circulation.

Heart valves

During ventricular systole (when the ventricles contract), the aortic and pulmonary valves open to allow blood to be pumped into the pulmonary and general circulatory system, while the mitral and tricuspid valves remain closed. During ventricular diastole (when the ventricles dilate), the aortic and pulmonary valves close while the tricuspid and mitral valves open to allow blood to pass from the atria into the ventricles.

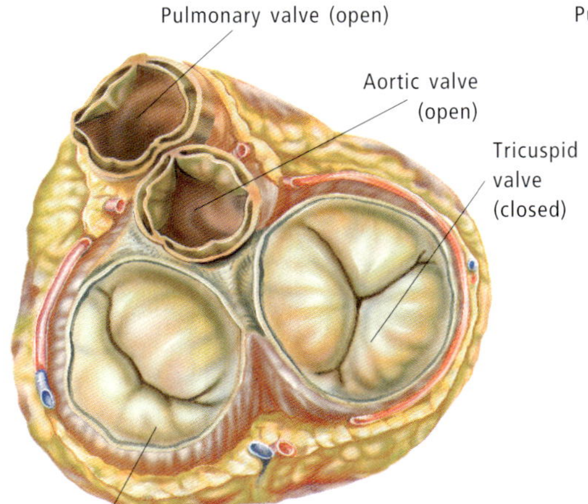

Ventricular diastole

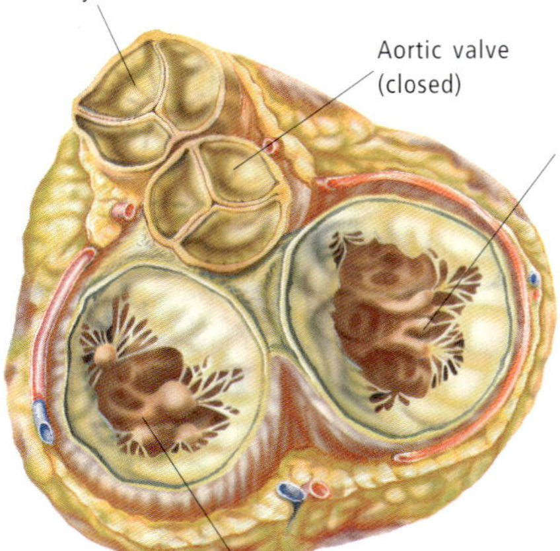

Ventricular systole

Coronary arteries

The heart is only the size of the human fist, yet it is responsible for about 8 percent of the body's total oxygen consumption.

Blood supply to the heart comes from the right and left coronary arteries, so-called because they wrap around the heart like a crown.

The right coronary artery runs in the groove between the right atrium and the right ventricle to the back of the heart, where it turns 90 degrees to run in the groove corresponding to the interventricular septum. The left coronary artery divides shortly after its beginning into the anterior interventricular artery, which runs in the groove of the interventricular septum at the front of the heart, and the circumflex artery, which runs in the groove between the left atrium and left ventricle.

Deposits (plaques) inside the arteries can reduce blood flow. If this happens in a coronary artery, part of the heart will not receive adequate blood supply. With moderate blockage, blood supply becomes inadequate when the heart has to pump harder to cope with physical exertion or mental stress. This lack of blood supply, called ischemia, causes sensations of pain and pressure over the chest known as angina pectoris. When blockage is complete, an area of heart muscle dies, resulting in a heart attack.

Nerve supply

The heart can continue beating when taken out of the body because it has a built-in nerve supply. The sinoatrial node, located in the right atrium, is the pacemaker triggering the contraction of the right and left ventricles. The autonomic nervous system, by way of the cardiac plexus, modifies the intrinsic heart rhythm and adjusts heart rate and contraction power to the requirements of the body. In some cases, when the innervation of the heart malfunctions, an artificial pacemaker must be connected to drive the heart.

In the condition known as arrhythmia, the heart rhythm is disturbed: it may be too fast (tachycardia), too slow (bradycardia), or have added beats or skipped beats.

Blood vessels

The major arteries of the systemic circulation are derived from the aorta: these are the carotid arteries for the head and neck, the axillary arteries for the upper limbs, and the iliac arteries for the pelvis and lower limbs.

Arteries can be blocked by plaque deposits, or become stiff, resulting in raised blood pressure (hypertension). This is usually associated with a high cholesterol level in the blood (hypercholesterolemia).

There are two main systemic veins, the superior vena cava, which returns blood from the head and upper limbs, and the inferior vena cava, which returns blood from the lower limbs. The four pulmonary veins return oxygenated blood to the left atria. The systemic veins form a storage system for blood.

The deep veins of the legs are often the site of the formation of a blood clot, or deep vein thrombosis, when blood flow is sluggish due to prolonged immobilization. This condition can be fatal. Disorders of the superficial veins are not as serious. If veins are dilated, as in varicose veins, they can be removed by surgery.

Many diseases of the circulatory system are the result of smoking, poor eating habits and lack of exercise, and in many cases can be alleviated (or prevented) by adopting a healthier lifestyle. Heart disease is the greatest cause of death in Western countries.

SEE ALSO *Angina pectoris, Aorta, Arteries, Blood vessels, Cardiomyopathy, Coronary arteries, Heart, Hypertension, Ischemia, Mitral valve, Myocardial infarction, Pericardium, Stenosis, Thrombosis, Tricuspid valve, Veins, Ventricle*

Blood vessels

The three types of blood vessels are arteries, veins and capillaries. The arteries carry the blood from the heart to the capillaries, where oxygen and other nutrients are exchanged with surrounding tissues. The veins then carry the blood from the capillaries back to the heart.

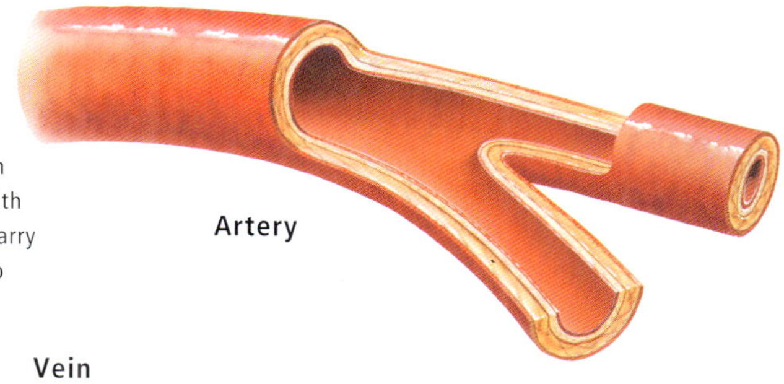

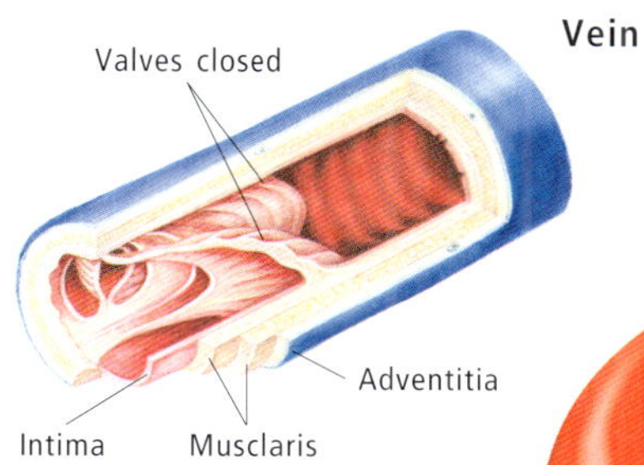

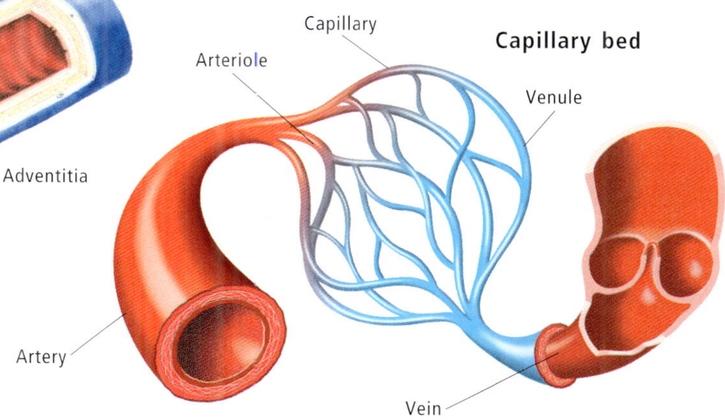

Blood composition

The blood is composed of red cells, white cells (leukocytes), platelets and plasma. Red blood cells carry oxygen to the tissues while plasma carries essential nutrients to the tissues. This illustration shows all the components of blood and is only representational in its proportions.

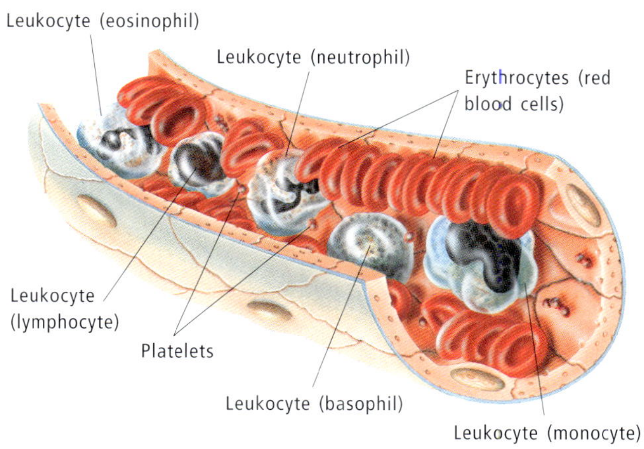

RESPIRATORY SYSTEM

In the process of metabolism, the human body consumes oxygen and produces carbon dioxide as a waste product. The respiratory system is designed to exchange the carbon dioxide accumulated in the blood for oxygen in the airways, which enters the lungs as air from the surrounding atmosphere. This air is breathed into the airways via the nose, pharynx, larynx, trachea and bronchi.

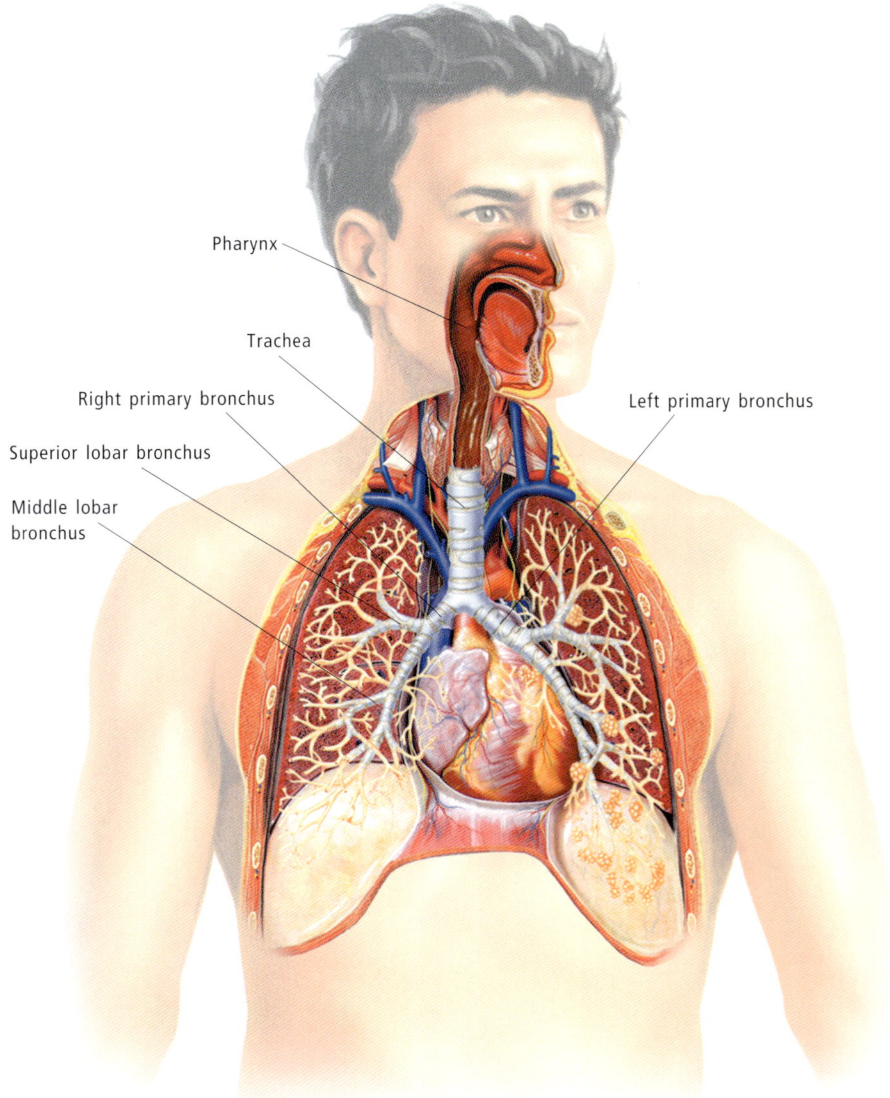

NB: The top two-thirds of the lungs have been removed to show the heart and bronchial tree.

Nose

The visible part of the nose is supported by cartilage and is only the front opening of the nasal cavity. The nasal septum divides the nasal cavity through the middle, and is formed by septal cartilage at the tip and by bone closer to the skull. When the septal cartilage is curved in septal deviation, half of the nasal cavity may be narrowed although the external nose still looks symmetrical.

The inner surface of the nostril is covered by skin with coarse hairs that trap dust from air that has been drawn in (inspired). The remainder of the nasal cavity is lined by mucous membrane with many blood vessels and mucus-secreting glands. Blood heat warms up inhaled air, while the moist sticky mucus traps more dust. Three curved structures known as conchae, jutting out from each side wall into the nasal cavity, increase the surface area for warming up inspired air. In the common cold, the nose is blocked by swollen mucous membrane and increased secretion of mucus.

A small area in the roof of the nasal cavity is supplied (innervated) by the olfactory nerve for smell.

Pharynx

The pharynx lies behind the nasal cavity, oral cavity and larynx and ends in the esophagus. Located in each side wall of the pharynx, just behind the nasal cavity, is the opening of the auditory tube, which connects the pharynx with the middle ear cavity. It equalizes pressure of the ear cavity with atmospheric pressure. When the pharynx is inflamed as the result of a common cold, the opening of the auditory tube is blocked, the eardrum cannot vibrate freely because of the pressure difference, and sounds are muffled.

The larynx and speech

The larynx is a tube located in front of the pharynx and made up of a membrane reinforced by muscles. It begins with a cartilage—the epiglottis—which closes the entry into the larynx when we swallow to prevent food from passing into the airway. This tube has two segments separated from each other by a small gap. The top segment begins at the upper edge of the epiglottis and ends below it at the vestibular folds or "false vocal cords". The lower segment begins at the vocal cords and ends where it is attached to the cricoid cartilage. The cricoid cartilage is attached to the trachea below. The vocal cords are attached to the thyroid cartilage at the front and to the arytenoid cartilage at the back of the larynx.

We speak by blowing air from the lungs into the larynx, which vibrates the vocal cords. The arytenoids spin around a vertical axis, bringing the vocal cords close together or further apart. The thyroid cartilage tilts on the cricoid to control the tension of the vocal cords and the frequency of the vibration. The vibrations of the cords are converted into the different sounds of speech by the position of the tongue and lips.

When the larynx is surgically removed due to cancer, a device similar to an electric razor held against the throat can be used to transmit a pure vibration to the column of air breathed out (expired). Movements of the tongue and lips turn the vibration into robot-like speech which is not as clear as normal speech and lacks inflection but is still intelligible.

The thyroid cartilage protects the front of the larynx. It has two plates (laminae) joined together at an angle, like the spine of an open book. The upper end of the angle is more prominent in males and known as the "Adam's apple". The thyroid cartilage is connected by membrane to the hyoid bone above and cricoid cartilage below. The larynx moves up and down when we swallow or when we want to sing with a vibrato effect.

Trachea, bronchi and lungs

The trachea is a stack of 15–20 C-shaped cartilages, connected to each other by fibrous tissue, forming a vertical gutter opening at the back. The trachealis muscle connects the ends of the Cs, closes up the gutter and turns it into a tube.

Food passing down the esophagus bulges into the trachea through the trachealis. A large mass of food (bolus) stuck in the esophagus can block the air passage and choke the victim to death. If the larynx is obstructed by edema (swelling), as in smoke inhalation, tracheostomy may save life by creating a temporary opening in the trachea at the root of the neck.

The trachea ends by dividing into the right and left main bronchi for the right and left lungs. The left lung is divided into upper and lower lobes by an oblique fissure. An additional horizontal fissure divides the right lung into three lobes, the upper, middle and lower lobes.

Inside each lung, the main bronchus divides first into lobar bronchi, then into smaller and smaller bronchi (bronchioles). The lining (epithelium) of the trachea and bronchi has hairlike structures known as cilia and contains many goblet cells and mucous glands that secrete mucus to trap dust. Dust trapped in mucus is moved upwards by the cilia. The bronchial epithelium also contains lymphoid tissue which secretes antibody IgA. The bronchioles are entirely muscular and have no cartilage in their walls. During asthma attacks, the channels of the bronchioles are narrowed by edema of the mucous membrane, by increased mucus secretion, and by spasm of the smooth muscle in their walls.

The bronchial tree ends in the air sacs, or alveoli, that branch out of the terminal bronchioles like bunches of grapes. Alveoli are separated from one another by interalveolar septa which greatly increase the surface area available for gas exchange.

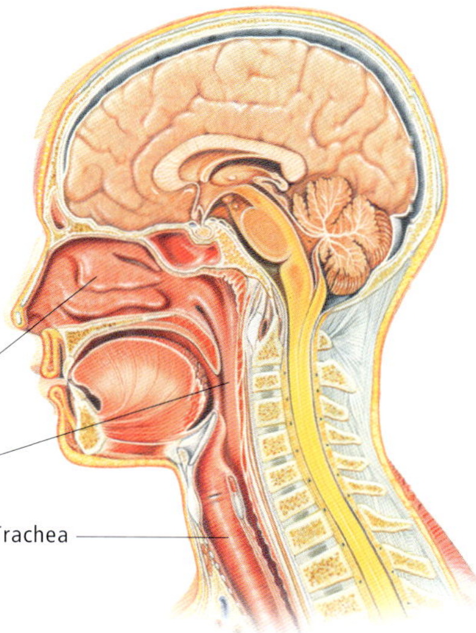

When interalveolar septa are destroyed in emphysema, the architecture of the alveoli is destroyed and gas exchange is compromised. The walls of the alveoli are thin and contain a network of capillaries. Blood coming from the pulmonary artery is depleted of oxygen and rich in carbon dioxide, while inspired air is full of oxygen and low in carbon dioxide. Gases move across the alveolar membrane: carbon dioxide passes into the alveolar air, and oxygen passes into the blood. The blood leaving the alveoli is again saturated with oxygen, and carbon dioxide in the alveoli is expelled into the atmosphere with expired air.

The alveolar walls also contain cells that secrete surfactant, a substance that reduces surface tension of the alveolar wall, enabling the alveoli to expand in inspiration and preventing alveolar collapse during expiration. In infantile respiratory distress syndrome, the alveoli collapse because they are deficient in surfactant. Lying on the inner surface of the alveolar wall are macrophages which engulf inhaled bacteria, dust or carbon particles.

Pleura

Each lung is surrounded by a double-layered membrane called the pleura. Just imagine a slightly inflated balloon containing a teaspoonful of oil. Wrap the balloon around the lung, stretching it until it reaches the entrance of blood vessels and bronchus, and you have an image of the pleura. The half of the balloon in contact with the lung corresponds to the "visceral layer" of the pleura,

Upper section of the respiratory system

The upper part of the respiratory system consists of the nose, the nasal cavity and the pharynx. The pharynx is shared by the respiratory and digestive systems.

Muscles used for breathing

The diaphragm and intercostal muscles are involved in breathing. During inspiration these muscles contract to increase the front to back, side to side, and vertical size of the rib cage. Expiration is a passive process involving the recoil of the ribs and the return of the diaphragm to its normal position.

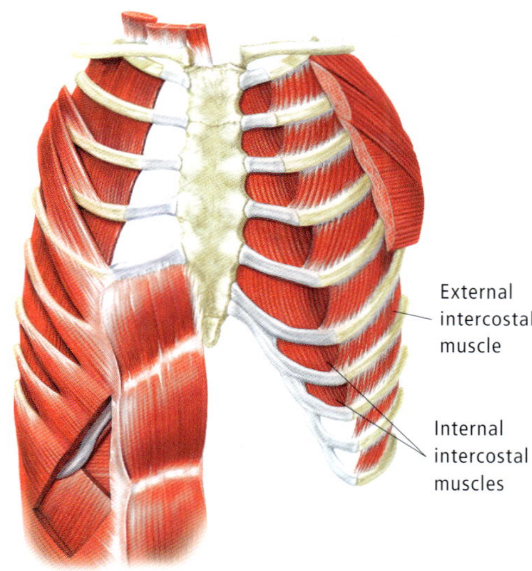

the other half visible from outside corresponds to the "parietal layer" of the pleura. The parietal layer is attached to the inside of the rib cage. The small amount of fluid in the pleura allows frictionless movements of the lung against the ribcage.

The common term "pleurisy" refers to accumulation of fluid in the pleura. A large collection of fluid in the pleura—such as serum in some cases of viral infection or blood caused by stab wounds to the chest—must be aspirated out. Expansion of the lung is also hampered by the presence of air in the pleural cavity (pneumothorax). Pneumothorax may be caused by a chest wound or it may be spontaneous in some young, tall and lean individuals. Exposure to asbestos is a common cause for mesothelioma, a cancer of the pleura.

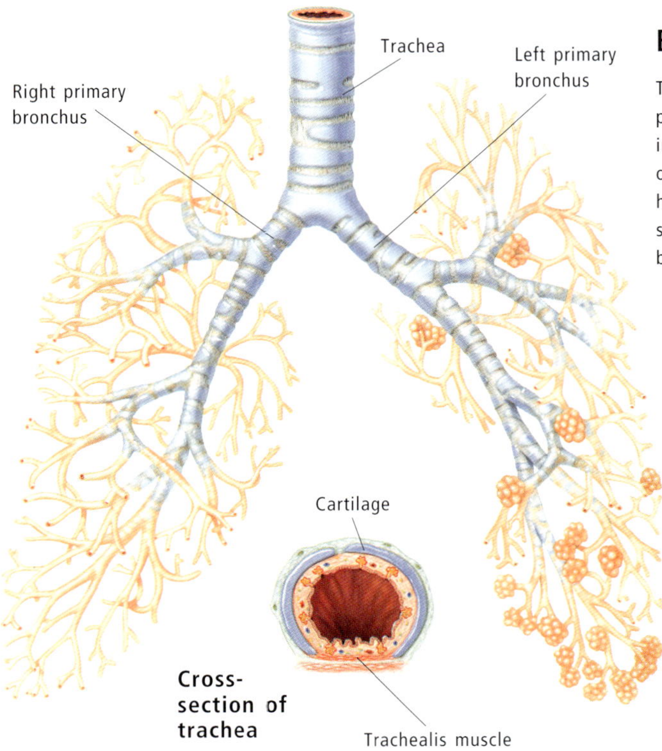

Cross-section of trachea

Bronchial tree

The bronchial tree provides a passageway for inspired air to pass into the alveoli where gas exchange occurs. Bronchi contain cilia (small hair-like structures) and mucus-secreting glands, which ensure the bronchial airways remain clear.

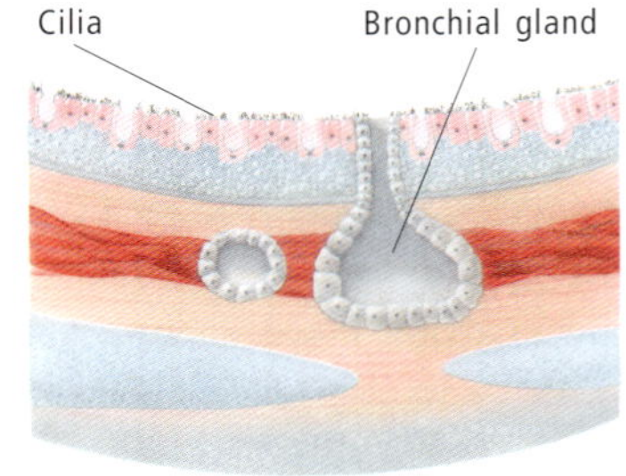

Cross-section of bronchi

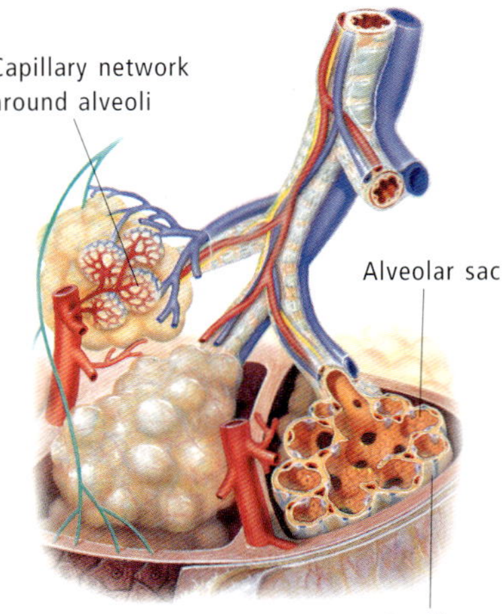

Gas exchange in the alveoli

The smallest bronchioles end in alveoli (air sacs). The sac walls are surrounded by small blood vessels which allow oxygen from the air to enter the bloodstream and carbon dioxide accumulated in the blood to pass into the alveoli to be breathed out.

Blood and nerve supply

Deoxygenated blood from the body is pumped by the right ventricle of the heart through the pulmonary arteries into the lungs. Branches of the pulmonary arteries follow the bronchial tree and end in the capillaries that surround the alveoli, where gas exchange occurs. Reoxygenated blood is collected by venules that converge into two pulmonary veins for each lung, and returns to the left atrium of the heart so that it can be pumped back around the body.

In mitral stenosis, the narrowed mitral valve increases resistance to bloodflow from the left atrium to the left ventricle. The increased pressure is transmitted back to the capillary system in the lungs, making the lungs stiffer and breathing difficult. If the pressure is high enough, serum leaks out of the capillaries causing pulmonary edema, capillaries burst into the alveoli and the patient coughs up blood—this is known as hemoptysis.

The airway and lungs receive oxygen and nutrients from the small bronchial arteries. Deoxygenated blood returns to the heart via the pulmonary veins.

Lymphatic vessels from the lungs eventually empty into the thoracic duct. The lymph nodes are located in the root of the lungs (where vessels and bronchi enter the lungs) and around the bronchi and trachea. When they are enlarged in lung cancer, they become visible even on standard chest x-rays.

How do we breathe?

The rib cage is an airtight cylinder, with the diaphragm as its base, and the root of the neck as its top lid. The wall is made up of the ribs running from the thoracic vertebrae to the sternum, and connected together by three layers of intercostal muscles. When we breathe in, the ribs rotate around their vertebral articulations, and the sternum at their front ends is raised, increasing the front-to-back as well as the side-to-side diameters of the rib cage. The diaphragm moves down, increasing the vertical size of the rib cage. The capacity of the thoracic cavity increases, resulting in a decrease in intrathoracic pressure to a value below atmospheric pressure. The air is sucked into the lungs through the airway. This mechanism fails if there is a large wound in the rib cage equalizing the intrathoracic pressure with atmospheric pressure.

Breathing out is a passive process—the recoil of the ribs and the lungs and the return of the diaphragm to a higher position squeeze the air out. In asthma attacks, resistance in the airway causes more trouble in the expiratory phase of breathing. Patients have to make an effort to squeeze air out of the body, and the wheezing noise of breathing is more prominent in expiration. To overcome the resistance, patients often have to sit up, grasp a fixed object like the bed post, and use "accessory respiratory muscles" in the neck to generate extra pull on the first rib and sternum. When airflow is severely reduced, for example when movements of the ribs are hindered in a bedridden patient, stagnation of air and secretion in the lungs increases the risk of respiratory infection (pneumonia). Physical therapy of the chest is vital for the prevention of pneumonia in bed-bound, chronically ill patients.

Lung cancer

Lung cancer is actually cancer of the airway and properly called "bronchogenic carcinoma". Smoking causes constant irritation and infection of the bronchi (chronic bronchitis), and is also a proven cause of lung cancer. Lung cancer can be more dangerous than other cancers because it is insidious, and unlike skin or breast tumors, it gives no external visible sign. Lung cancer is often already well developed by the time it is suspected or diagnosed.

See also Asthma, Breathing, Bronchus, Common cold, Epiglottis, Larynx, Lung cancer, Lungs, Mesothelioma, Metabolism, Mitral valve, Mucous membranes, Nose, Pharynx, Pleurisy, Pneumothorax, Pulmonary edema, Ribs, Speech, Trachea, Vocal cords

URINARY SYSTEM

The urinary system is essential to life. It excretes the waste products of metabolism and maintains the balance of water and electrolytes in the blood.

Blood and the internal environment

All cells and tissues of the body consume oxygen and nutrients and produce carbon dioxide and waste products. The respiratory system removes carbon dioxide from the body. Waste products are filtered out of the blood by the kidneys and excreted in the urine.

An inorganic compound such as salt (sodium chloride) breaks down into sodium and chloride ions when dissolved in water. These ions allow the solution to conduct electricity and so are called electrolytes.

The cells of the body contain intracellular fluid and are surrounded by extracellular fluid that includes serum from the blood. All chemical reactions in the body and the functions of the nervous system depend on a constant concentration of electrolytes inside the cells and in the extracellular fluid. Sodium is the main electrolyte in extracellular fluid; potassium is the main electrolyte in intracellular fluid.

Changes in the proportions of ions in intracellular and extracellular fluid can have serious consequences. A high concentration of potassium in extracellular fluid can cause cardiac arrest; a low concentration may result in muscle paralysis. Hydrogen ions and bicarbonate ions determine the acidity of the blood, which influences the conduction of impulses in the nervous system and metabolic reactions of the body. The kidney is one of the main regulators of the balance of electrolytes and acids.

Kidneys

The kidneys are located on the back wall of the abdomen on either side of the vertebrae, enveloped by a renal capsule and enclosed in perirenal fat. Their position, below the last rib, explains why some kidney diseases cause pain at the angle between the lumbar vertebrae and the twelfth rib.

The right kidney lies behind the duodenum and is slightly lower than the left, which lies behind the pancreas and the stomach. The ends of the transverse colon, where it joins the ascending and descending colon, are located in front of the two kidneys. The adrenal glands cap the upper tip of each kidney.

Internal structure of the kidney

Each kidney has an outer part (cortex) and an inner part (medulla). The cortex contains filtration units (glomeruli and tubules). The medulla is made up of about a dozen renal pyramids, so-called because of their shape. The major component of each pyramid is a bundle of collecting tubules which collect the urine produced by the filtration units in the cortex.

The tips of the pyramids project into the sinus as small papillae, each of which is capped by a small cup-like minor calyx. Minor calices join to form major calices which empty into the renal pelvis; this joins with the ureter.

Each renal artery branches off the aorta and divides into branches that enter the renal sinus to reach the medulla and cortex of the kidney. The veins accompany the arteries and end in the inferior vena cava.

The functions of the kidney

The kidney performs both excretory and endocrine functions.

Excretory function: the kidney filters the blood, removing metabolic waste products such as urea and any other unwanted substances. It maintains the balance of electrolytes in the blood and the water content of the body.

Diuretic drugs, which increase the excretion of water by the kidneys, are often prescribed in cases of mild hypertension to reduce the amount of water circulating in the body, and to treat mild heart failure by reducing the load on the heart.

Each kidney has about a million microscopic functional units called renal tubules or nephrons. Each nephron begins with a glomerulus that is made up of a tuft of capillaries surrounded by the Bowman's capsule (a filtration membrane that is tightly wrapped around the capillaries of the glomerulus). Filtrate from the blood leaves the capsule and passes through the proximal and distal convoluted tubules of the nephron, where vitamins and various electrolytes are reabsorbed.

A part of the nephron (the loop of Henle) dips into the medulla of the kidney, and plays an important role in the reabsorption of water, sodium and potassium ions. Reabsorbed water and electrolytes enter the networks formed by the capillaries that leave the Bowman's capsule. Waste products and toxic substances are either not reabsorbed or are actively secreted into the urine.

The last part of the nephron, the collecting duct, is also the site of the reabsorption of water and electrolytes and plays an important role in adjusting the concentration of urine. The collecting ducts are bundled in the pyramids and open at the papillae.

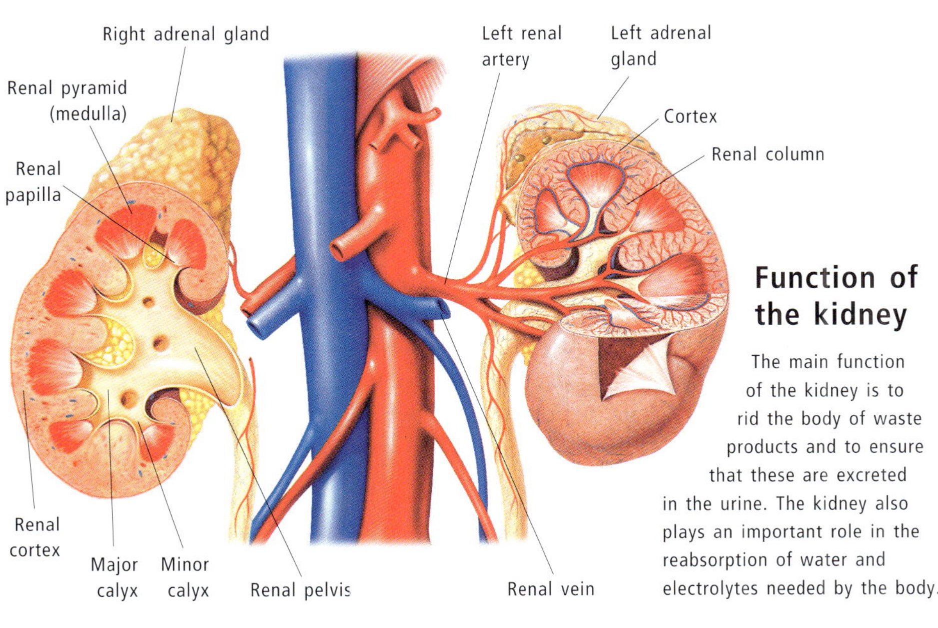

Function of the kidney

The main function of the kidney is to rid the body of waste products and to ensure that these are excreted in the urine. The kidney also plays an important role in the reabsorption of water and electrolytes needed by the body.

The average urine output in the adult is about 1–1½ quarts (1–1.5 liters) a day. The amount and concentration of urine varies according to fluid intake and fluid loss through respiration, perspiration and fecal elimination. When the body is dehydrated only a small amount of very concentrated urine is produced.

People prone to urinary tract infections or kidney stones should maintain an adequate urine output to avoid the recurrence of infection or stone formation.

The filtration membrane in the renal glomerulus is a complex structure that can be damaged by the body's own immune reaction in glomerulonephritis. This disorder often develops after streptococcal infections or in some autoimmune diseases. In diabetes mellitus, thickening of the basement membrane of capillaries in the glomeruli disturbs the function of the glomeruli and causes renal failure.

The abuse of painkillers (analgesics) may cause severe damage to renal tubules. The tubules can also be blocked by hemoglobin released from muscles that have been destroyed by massive crush injury or excessive overheating in marathon runners. Damage to the renal tubules results in drastic changes in the composition of extracellular fluid. Renal failure may be fatal because concentration of some ions, such as potassium, can rise to lethal levels.

In late-stage kidney disease, life may be sustained by dialysis or artificial kidneys, both requiring close monitoring and constant intervention by a renal physician.

The function of the kidney extends far beyond simple filtration of the blood. Infection of the kidney is a common complication which used to result in death for bedridden patients. Even with recent advances in medicine, kidney failure is still an end stage of many general medical conditions.

Endocrine function: the kidney's endocrine function involves the release of hormones into the blood: erythropoietin affects blood formation and hydroxycholecalciferol is involved in calcium metabolism.

Where the distal convoluted tubule joins the capillary in the glomerulus, specialized epithelium can sense blood concentration and endocrine secretion. This setup (the juxtaglomerular apparatus) also senses reductions in sodium concentration in the blood and responds by releasing renin, an enzyme that triggers a chain reaction to reestablish electrolyte balance.

Renin converts angiotensinogen in the blood into angiotensin I, which is converted into angiotensin II by the lungs. Angiotensin II stimulates the adrenal cortex to secrete aldosterone, which acts on the nephron to increase the reabsorption of salt. This increases the output of diluted urine, restores the concentration of salt in body fluids, and raises blood pressure.

Many antihypertensive drugs work by suppressing this renin-angiotensin-aldosterone system.

Ureter

The renal pelvis continues into the ureter, a muscular tube that carries urine to the bladder. Small kidney stones originating from the renal pelvis may become lodged in the ureter, especially where it is slightly constricted, such as at the junction with the renal pelvis. The smooth muscles above the blockage contract violently as they try to push the stone through the ureter, causing intense waves of pain (renal colic).

The first line of treatment is simply loading the body with water to increase urine flow, and using a muscle relaxant to relax the ureter and facilitate the passage of the stone. The stones can either be removed by surgery or destroyed by ultrasound.

The ureter descends almost vertically along the line of the tips of the transverse processes of the lumbar vertebrae. At the hip bone it turns backwards to enter the back of the bladder near the midline. The ureter is narrowest when it pierces the bladder wall. It runs obliquely for about ¾ inch (2 centimeters) in the bladder before opening to a slit-like aperture.

When the bladder is full, the increased pressure compresses the part of the ureter inside the bladder wall, preventing reflux of urine back to the renal pelvis. When there are bacteria in the bladder, reflux can spread infection to the kidney (pyelonephritis). If the ureter runs perpendicularly through the bladder wall because of defective development, this "flap-valve" mechanism does not operate and kidney infection by reflux occurs frequently.

The urinary bladder

Urine is continuously produced by the kidney and stored in the bladder, a muscular sac that resembles an inverted pyramid. The urethra emerges from the neck (apex) of the bladder, which is located just behind the symphysis pubis. The rear surface of the bladder is in front of the rectum and receives the ureters. The openings of the two ureters and the urethra form the three corners of the triangular trigone.

The bladder is behind the pubis when empty; when full, it rises above the symphysis pubis and can be ruptured by a direct blow above the pubis. In males, the bladder rests on the prostate and is anchored to the pubis and to the side walls of the pelvis by ligaments attached to its neck.

The male urethra

The prostate, located below the apex of the bladder, rests on the pelvic floor, which is reinforced by a layer of muscles—the urogenital diaphragm. The urethra leaves the neck of the bladder and passes through the prostate and the membrane formed by the muscle layers before reaching the penis; it is usually divided into prostatic, membranous and penile parts.

The male urethra is the common passage for sperm as well as urine and is closely related to the reproductive system.

The urethra is a muscular tube reinforced by muscle fibers that extend like slings from the bladder around the upper part of the prostatic urethra. An enlarged prostate distorts the geometry of this sphincter and interferes with the mechanism that closes the urethra after voiding (micturition). This sphincter is under autonomic control. Among the muscles of the urogenital diaphragm is another sphincter, which is under conscious control.

The full bladder sends a message to the reflex center in the sacral part of the spinal cord where it triggers a reflex contraction of the muscle of the bladder and causes the neck of the bladder to relax. This reflex is suppressed until there is an opportunity to relieve the bladder. Voluntary control is lost (incontinence) when the reflex center in the spinal cord is damaged and the bladder overflows when filled to capacity. Incontinence also occurs when the pathway for inhibition

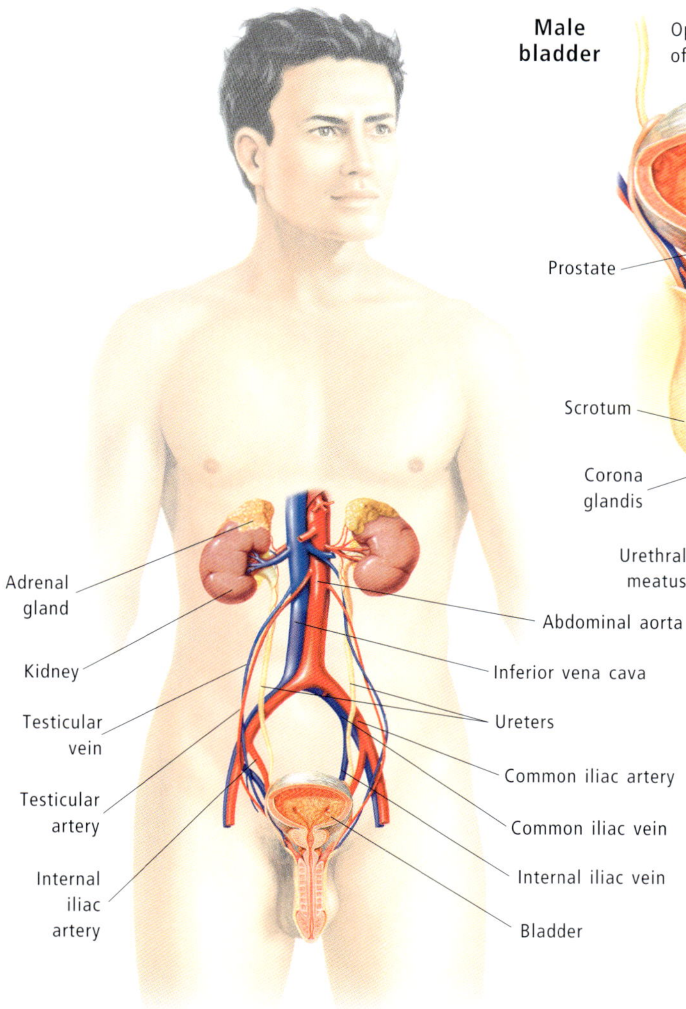

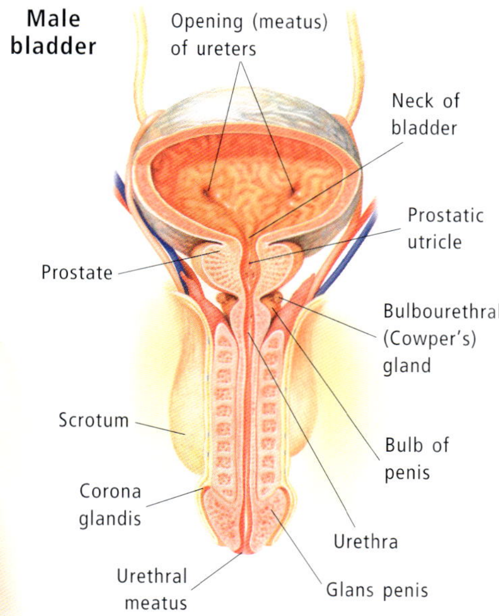

Control of the closure of the urethra is less efficient in the female than in the male. Distortion of the muscle floor of the pelvis, or damage to the sphincters of the urethra by several pregnancies, often results in stress incontinence. Urine may leak with the slight raise in intra-abdominal pressure caused by a simple cough, for example.

The short urethra allows easy examination of the inside of the bladder using a cystoscope, but also provides an easy route of entry for bacteria. Thus infection of the lower portion of the urinary system (called urinary tract infection) is more common in females than in males, especially in young girls who have an even shorter and straighter urethra than adult women.

SEE ALSO *Adrenal glands, Bladder, Cystitis, Cystoscopy, Diuretics, Electrolytes, Glomerulonephritis, Hypertension, Kidney, Potassium, Reproductive systems, Sodium, Urethra, Urinary incontinence, Urinary tract*

Male urinary system

The urinary system comprises the kidneys, the ureters, the bladder and the urethra. The male urethra is the passage for both sperm and urine.

from the brain is damaged by spinal injury and the bladder empties automatically.

Female urinary system

The structure and organization of the urinary system is similar in both sexes from the kidney down to the bladder. However, the position of the ureter within the pelvis is slightly different. One example is the close proximity of the female ureter to the artery that supplies the uterus. During removal of the uterus (hysterectomy), surgeons have to be careful not to accidentally damage the ureter when they clamp and cut the artery.

Female bladder and urethra

The vagina lies between the rectum and the rear surface of the bladder, with the uterus lying on the top of the bladder. The urethra passes directly through the pelvic floor. As the female urethra is not involved in the reproductive system, it is very short and opens out in front of the entrance of the vagina.

Female urinary system

The female urinary system is essentially the same as the male, except that the female urethra is much shorter. This provides bacteria with an easy route into the body, and is the reason why urinary tract infections are far more common in women than men.

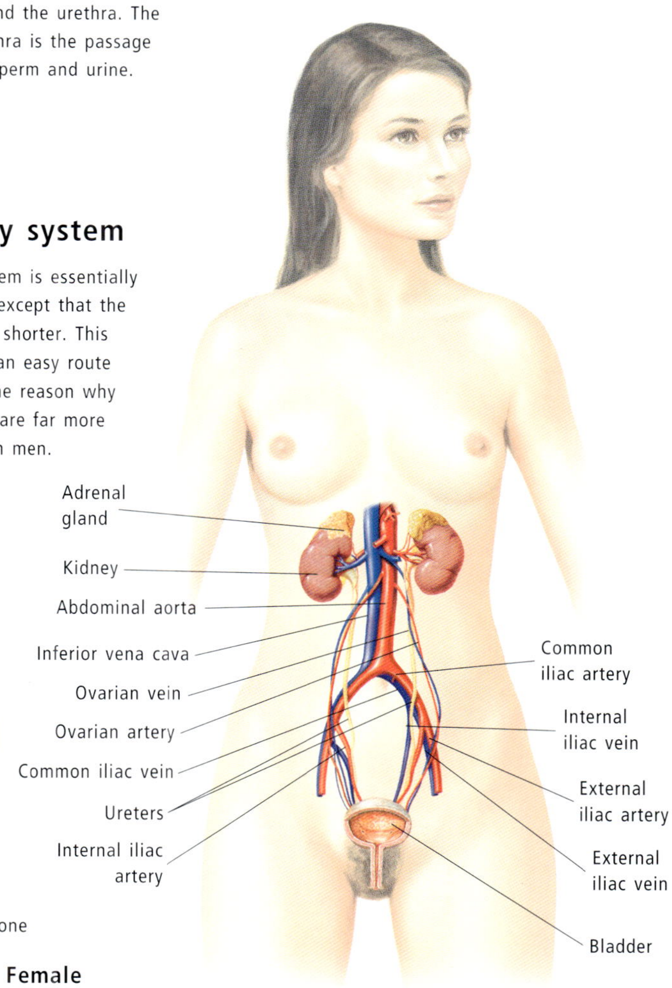

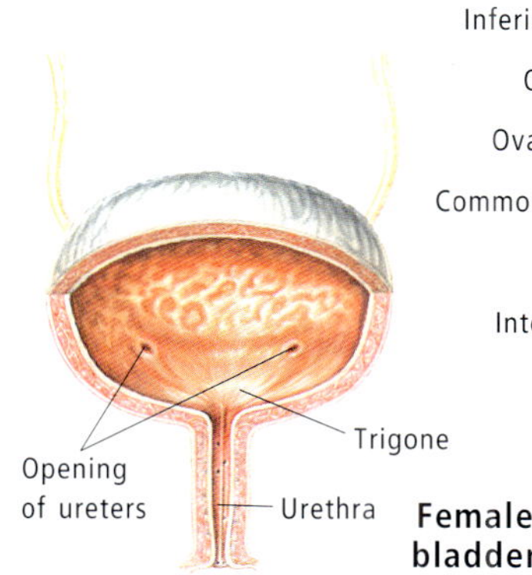

DIGESTIVE SYSTEM

The process of digestion breaks down foods into small, simple molecules for absorption and use as building blocks for human cells.

The design of the digestive system

The mechanical action of the digestive tract optimizes the chemical actions of enzymes. The entire tract is made up of smooth muscle fibers running in circular and longitudinal directions. In some places, the circular fibers are condensed into a thick ring (sphincter), which contracts to close down the cavity (lumen) within the tract. The circular fibers can contract sequentially along the tract (peristalsis) in order to knead the contents with digestive enzymes or to squeeze it along.

Digestive enzymes split the three main groups of food into their components: carbohydrates into glucose, proteins into amino acids, and lipids into glycerol and fatty acids. There are more than two dozen amino acids, most of which are common to all animal species. For example, human proteins are made up amino acids that are derived from meat proteins.

The digestive tract and glands

Food is bitten into mouthfuls by the incisor teeth, shredded by the canines, and ground by the premolars and molars. It is pushed around in the mouth and held between the molars by the tongue and the buccinator muscles in the cheeks. The top surface of the tongue is rough due to the presence of papillae which carry taste receptors.

Saliva in the mouth comes from three pairs of salivary glands. The largest, the parotid glands, are located just below the ears. The submandibular and sublingual glands are under the floor of the mouth. Saliva wets the food to facilitate chewing and swallowing. It also contains the enzyme amylase, which digests carbohydrates, and antibodies to help resist infection.

Inadequate production of saliva (as seen in Sjögren's syndrome) makes speaking and swallowing very difficult.

At the beginning of swallowing, food is rolled into a round mass (bolus) which is pushed to the back of the mouth by the tongue. Muscles of the pharynx then push the food bolus down the esophagus.

The esophagus runs vertically down behind the windpipe (trachea), passing through the diaphragm to end in the stomach. The opening of the stomach into the small intestine (the duodenum) is controlled by a thick bundle of circular muscle fibers, the pylorus. Food is retained in the stomach where proteins are digested by hydrochloric acid and pepsin secreted by gastric glands. At intervals, the pylorus relaxes to empty the gastric content, now a half-digested mix known as chyme, into the duodenum.

The small intestine has three parts: the duodenum, jejunum and ileum. The lining of the duodenum and jejunum has many transverse folds called plicae circulares (circular folds). On each fold are numerous tiny projections called intestinal villi, giving the lining a velvety appearance. The plicae and villi greatly increase the surface area available for the absorption of nutrients. Glands at the root of the villi and in the submucosal layer secrete intestinal juice that protects the lining against acidity and digestive enzymes.

Most of the digestive process occurs in the duodenum due to the action of pancreatic enzymes. The pancreas is an elongated gland lying behind the stomach. Its large head is framed by the C-shaped loop of the duodenum, while its tail ends near the spleen. Pancreatic secretions are collected by the main pancreatic duct which, together with the bile duct, enters the duodenum at a common opening, the duodenal ampulla.

The pancreatic juice contains inactive proenzymes that are converted by the duodenal hormone (enterokinase) into active enzymes that digest carbohydrates, proteins, nucleic acids, and lipids. In pancreatitis, the proenzymes are activated inside the pancreas and thus cause massive destruction of the gland.

One of the many functions of the liver is bile production. The bile duct passes through the head of the pancreas to open at the duodenal ampulla.

Cancer of the pancreas can constrict or block the bile duct. The resulting raised bile concentration in the blood is one cause of jaundice, in which the skin and the white of the eyes take on a yellow tinge.

The gallbladder is located under the liver and connected to the bile duct. It concentrates and stores bile to be discharged into the duodenum when chyme containing fat enters from the stomach. Bile emulsifies the fat to facilitate digestion by the pancreatic enzyme lipase. Gallstones are formed by the precipitation of components of bile in the gallbladder; these irritate the lining, causing inflammation (cholecystitis). Gallstones migrating down the bile duct can cause severe pain or block the duodenal ampulla.

As the chyme reaches the jejunum, the products of digestion are ready for absorption. Small molecules enter the blood capillaries of the villi. Larger molecules enter small lymphatic channels in the villi (lacteals), and flow along the mesenteric lymph vessels into the general circulation. Vitamin B_{12} is absorbed in the last portion of the ileum in the presence of intrinsic factor, a protein secreted by the stomach.

The ileum joins the large intestine, which consists of the cecum, colon, and rectum. The cecum—the blind-ended pouch of the colon—and the ileum meet at the ileocecal valve. Near the valve is the appendix which can become inflamed in the condition called appendicitis. The contents become feces as they move along the parts of the large intestine: the ascending, transverse, descending, and sigmoid colon. The colon absorbs water and bile salts, and contains bacteria that synthesize some vitamins such as vitamin K and biotin. The epithelium (the lining) of the colon here contains numerous goblet cells and mucus-secreting glands to facilitate the movement of the feces. When peristalsis of the colon is reduced in aged people, more water is absorbed and the feces become dry and impacted, causing severe constipation. When the balance between normal colonic flora and pathogenic bacteria is disturbed by some antibiotics, pathogenic bacteria may prevail causing diarrhea.

The last parts of the large intestine are the rectum and anal canal, situated just in front of the sacrum. The anus is closed by an involuntary and a voluntary sphincter, which open up during defecation. When the rectum is distended by feces, the defecation reflex is initiated if the voluntary anal sphincter is intentionally relaxed. Fecal incontinence results when the sphincters or

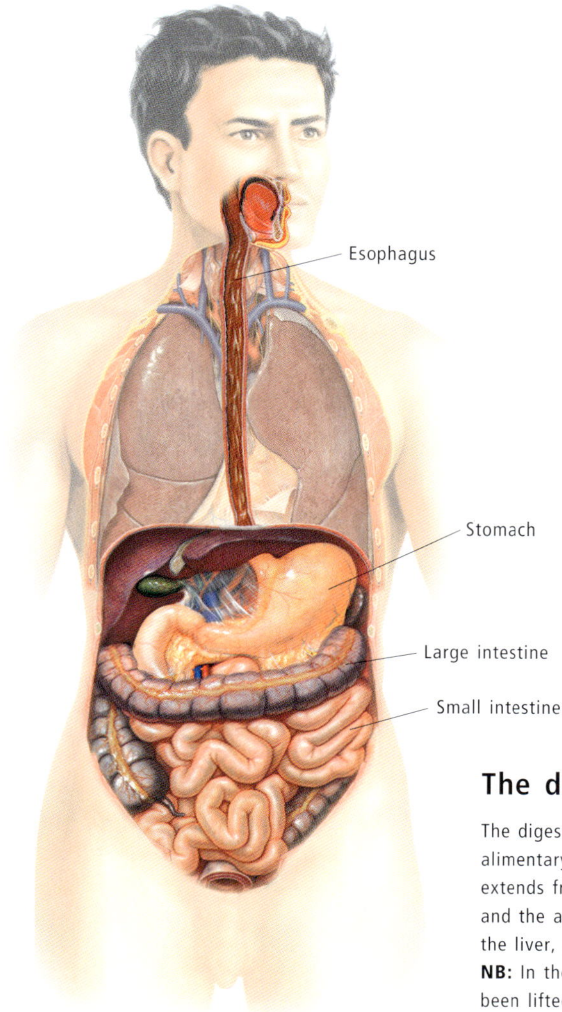

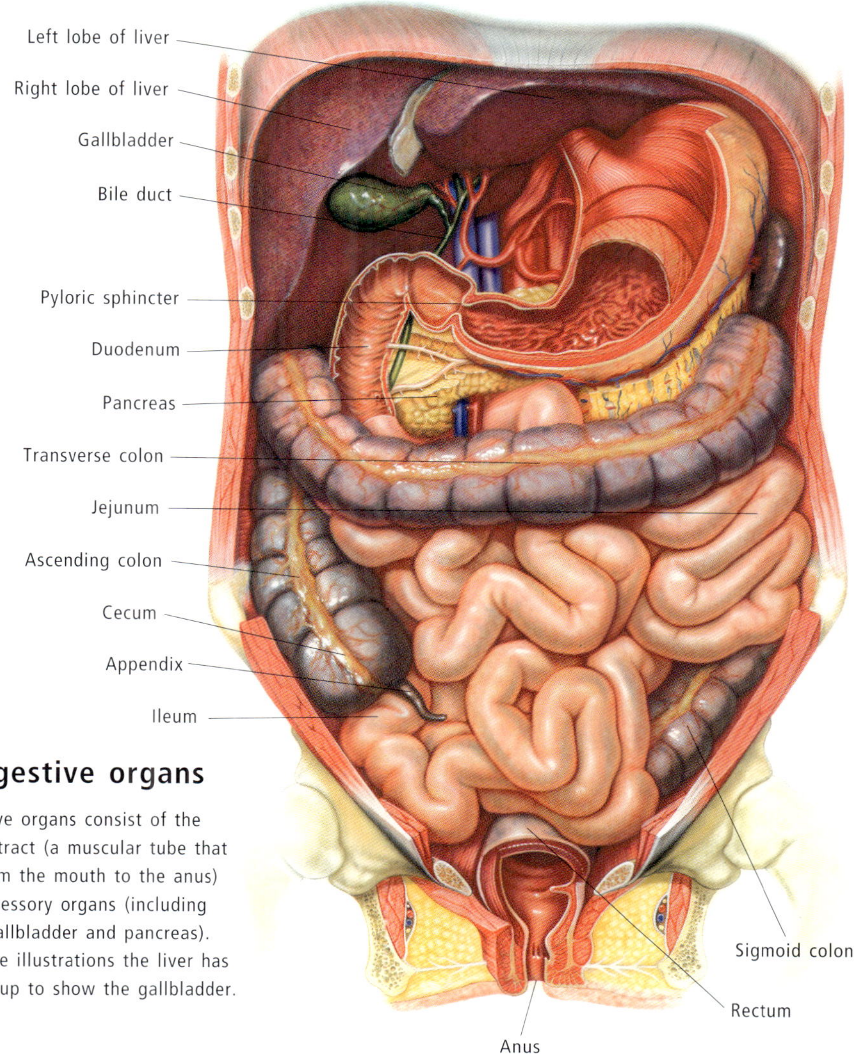

The digestive organs

The digestive organs consist of the alimentary tract (a muscular tube that extends from the mouth to the anus) and the accessory organs (including the liver, gallbladder and pancreas). **NB:** In these illustrations the liver has been lifted up to show the gallbladder.

the neural mechanism controlling them are defective. A network of veins in the lining of the rectum and anal canal facilitates the passage of feces. When these veins are dilated, they become hemorrhoids and may protrude from the anus during defecation, and may bleed. Cancer of the colon is common in Western countries, and involves the rectum in 50 percent of cases.

Control of the activities of the digestive system

The mechanical and secretory activities of the digestive tract and its glands are controlled by neural and hormonal mechanisms. The autonomic nervous system sets the general level of activity of the digestive system; the parasympathetic system increases the contraction of the gastrointestinal wall and the secretion of the digestive glands. There are networks (plexuses) of autonomic nerves in the intestinal wall which coordinate muscle contraction, and the secretion of gastric acid may be initiated by the central nervous system via the vagus nerve.

A system of "local" hormones ensures that secretions begin and end at the right time. When the stomach is distended by food, its lower part secretes more gastrin which increases the secretion of acid by gastric glands. The arrival of chyme in the duodenum initiates the release of hormones which inhibit gastric secretion and stimulate secretion of bile and pancreatic enzymes.

When treating stomach ulcers, the stimuli for acid secretion can be reduced by surgically resecting the endings of the vagus nerve on the stomach (vagotomy), or the gastrin-secreting portion of the stomach (gastrectomy).

SEE ALSO *Bowel cancer, Cholecystitis, Colon, Constipation, Duodenum, Gallbladder, Gastrectomy, Ileum, Intestines, Jejunum, Liver, Pancreas, Peristalsis, Rectum, Saliva, Stomach, Teeth*

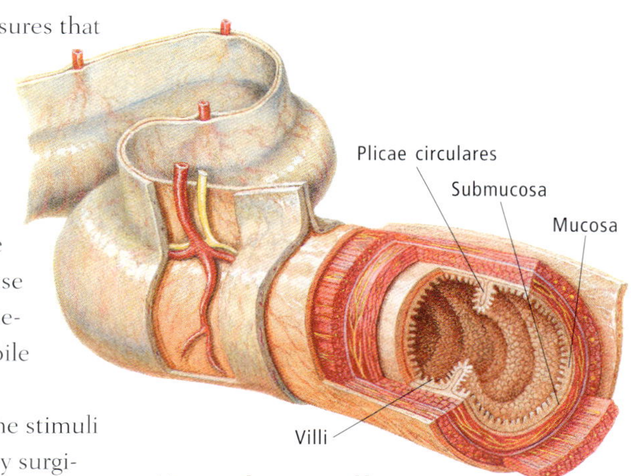

How the small intestines function

The vast majority of digestion and absorption takes place in the small intestine. The lining of the small intestine has many small transverse folds (plicae circulares) and numerous tiny finger-like projections called villi. The plicae and villi greatly increase the surface area available for the absorption of nutrients.

FEMALE REPRODUCTIVE SYSTEM

The reproductive system of the female includes two ovaries that produce ova (eggs) and female hormones, two fallopian (uterine) tubes that convey eggs to the uterus, the uterus itself, and the vagina, which is connected to the external genitalia.

Ovaries

The ovaries are almond-shaped organs in the side wall of the pelvis, situated just below the division of the common iliac artery. They are slightly flattened sideways, with a vertical axis measuring about $1^1/_2$ inches (3.5 centimeters). All the ovary's blood vessels and lymphatics enter its upper part. Its lower part is bound to the corner of the uterus by a band of connective tissue, the ligament of the ovary.

The ovary is enveloped by peritoneum, the membrane that surrounds all organs in the abdomen. Inside its covering epithelium is a shell of cortex which encloses the medulla at its core. The bulk of the ovary is the supporting structure called the stroma. The cortex contains ova at different stages of development.

Unlike the testis, which produces sperm continuously, the ovary is endowed in embryonic life with a fixed number of ova. By birth, each ovary has about a million ova; by puberty, the number has been reduced to about a quarter of a million.

The ova begin as primordial oocytes, surrounded by a layer of flat cells called granulosa cells. With the onset of puberty, hormones from the pituitary gland stimulate the development of more mature primary and secondary follicles. The granulosa cells multiply and form the multilayered theca interna that secretes estrogens; the surrounding stromal cells form the theca externa. A split appears in the theca interna and expands to form a fluid-filled cavity that pushes the oocyte to one side; the follicle is now a tertiary or Graafian follicle, which is visible as a small blister on the surface of the ovary. Ovulation takes place in the middle of each menstrual cycle—a Graafian follicle ruptures to release its ovum, which enters the fallopian tube.

The empty follicle fills with blood and regresses into a corpus luteum ("yellow body"); the yellow color is caused by the lipid-rich granulosa cells. If the ovum is fertilized, the corpus luteum will persist and continue secreting progesterone to maintain pregnancy. If not, it shrinks into a small mass of collagenous tissue (the corpus albicans).

Fallopian tubes

The fallopian tubes, or uterine tubes, are small tubes that begin as funnel-shaped passages with many finger-like projections called fimbriae. The ovum released from a burst Graafian follicle is "captured" by one of the fimbriae and moved along to the uterine cavity by the action of cilia of the epithelium and the contraction of the tube. Fertilization happens in the outer third of the fallopian tube if a sperm penetrates the ovum and its nuclear material fuses with that of the ovum. If the ovum is fertilized it will implant in the uterus and begin to develop into an embryo.

A constriction of the tube may block the progress of the fertilized ovum, resulting in an ectopic pregnancy in which the ovum implants and develops in the tube. As the tube can only be dilated to slightly more than an inch (a few centimeters) in diameter, it will burst after a few weeks of pregnancy, causing torrential bleeding which can only be controlled by emergency surgery.

Uterus

The uterus looks like a slightly flattened, upside-down pear, with a slight constriction dividing it into two parts. The upper two-thirds is the body, the lower third is the cervix. The body rests on the bladder and has a very thick wall of smooth muscle. The uterus is flattened from the front to the back. The uterine tubes open into the two top angles and the angle below opens into the lumen of the cervix.

The cervix is a cylindrical muscular tube that protrudes into the vagina. The lumen of the cervix is a spindle-shaped cervical canal.

The epithelium of the cervical canal secretes mucus that becomes thick, scanty and more acid after ovulation, a characteristic that can be used to determine the time of ovulation. The secretion is also thick during pregnancy, and forms the "mucus plug" which closes the cervical canal.

The epithelium at the vaginal end of the cervix is the most common site of cancer of the cervix, detectable by a Pap smear.

The inner lining of the uterus, the endometrium, is highly vascular and contains numerous tubular glands. It is shed at the end of each menstrual cycle. When the ovum is fertilized, the endometrium persists, and its glands secrete mucus rich in glycogen in preparation for implantation of the fertilized ovum. The part of the endometrium surrounding the developing embryo develops into the placenta.

Endometriosis is a condition in which islands of functioning endometrial tissue are found outside the uterine cavity, on the surface of abdominal or pelvic organs. They can cause bleeding or the formation of an abnormal mass.

During pregnancy, the uterus is distended to accommodate the developing fetus, extending beyond the umbilicus at full term. The muscular wall expels the fetus during labor and compresses the blood vessels to stop bleeding after expulsion of the placenta.

The uterus is fixed in place by connective tissue which runs inwards from the pelvic wall together with vessels and nerves destined for the vagina and uterus. Weakness of the pelvic floor may result in prolapse of the uterus. In extreme cases, the cervix protrudes from the vulva.

Vagina

The vagina is a fibromuscular tube that runs from the cervix to the vestibule of the vulva. Normally, its front and back walls lie close together, but it is capable of much distension and elongation. The epithelium of the vagina is thin before the menarche (onset of puberty), becoming thicker and undergoing cyclical changes during the menstrual cycle. With the cessation of hormonal stimulation after the menopause, it becomes thin and atrophic. This can be reversed by hormone replacement therapy (HRT) or by applying hormone cream directly to the vagina.

External genitalia

The external genitalia can also be called the pudendum or vulva. The lower end of the vagina continues into the labia minora. At their junction is a thin fibrous membrane called the hymen which, even when intact, allows the passage of menstrual blood. The labia minora may be pigmented and are devoid of hair. The space between them, the vestibule, receives the openings of the greater vestibular glands (Bartholin's glands).

The erectile bodies are comparable to those in the male genitalia. The equivalent of the corpus spongiosum is split into two masses flanking the vaginal opening. The corpora cavernosa occupy the same position as in the male. Corresponding to the penis is the clitoris, which also has a prepuce, a small hood formed by the junction of the labia minora.

The skin outside the vaginal opening is thickly padded with subcutaneous fat and forms the labia majora. They join and continue over the symphysis as the mons pubis (mons veneris), a small mound raised by a thick underlying pad of fat. The mons pubis and labia majora are covered by hair, the distribution of which is controlled by female hormones.

Menstrual cycle

After puberty, the endocrine system has reached maturity, and the menstrual cycle becomes regular.

The menstrual cycle begins from the first day of bleeding. Under the influence of follicle stimulating hormone (FSH) from the pituitary gland, one or more follicles in the ovary mature, releasing estrogen into the blood, and stimulating the proliferation of the endometrium and its glands. At midcycle, about day 14, the surge of luteinizing hormone (LH) from the pituitary gland triggers ovulation and initiates the development of the corpus luteum, which secretes progesterone, maintaining the proliferation of the endometrium in anticipation of implantation of the fertilized ovum. Without fertilization, LH and FSH secretion ceases, the corpus luteum breaks down, and the levels of estrogen and progesterone drop. The endometrium then degenerates, dies, and sloughs off, causing menstrual bleeding which usually lasts about four days.

The pituitary gland, the master gland controlling the menstrual cycle, is under the influence of the hypothalamus and the limbic system, the part of the brain that controls emotions. Menstrual cycles can be disturbed in times of emotional distress.

Irregularity and abnormality of the menstrual cycle are common problems, including absence of menstruation (amenorrhea), painful menstruation (dysmenorrhea), and excessive menstrual bleeding (menorrhagia). The cycle often becomes erratic near the menopause. It is important to seek medical advice for abnormal bleeding, as it may be an early warning sign of cancers of the reproductive system.

SEE ALSO *Cervix, Clitoris, Contraception, Endometriosis, Endometrium, Estrogens, Fallopian tubes, Graafian follicles, Hormones, Menopause, Menstruation, Ovaries, Ovulation, Ovum, Pap smear, Pituitary gland, Placenta, Pregnancy, Progesterone, Retroversion of uterus, Sexual intercourse, Urethra, Uterus, Vagina, Vulva*

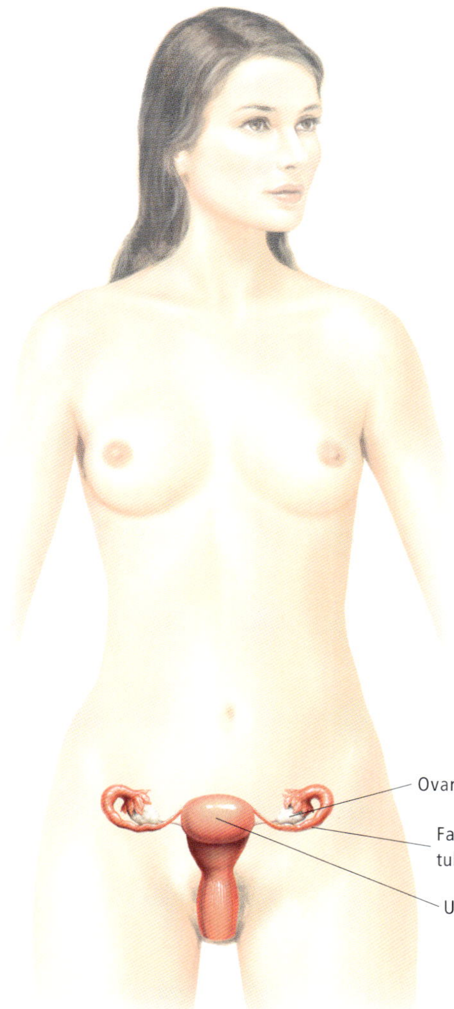

Female reproductive system—cross-section

The uterus is located behind the bladder and in front of the rectum. The upper two-thirds of the uterus is known as the body while the lower third is known as the cervix. The vagina is a long fibromuscular tube that extends from the cervix to the vulva.

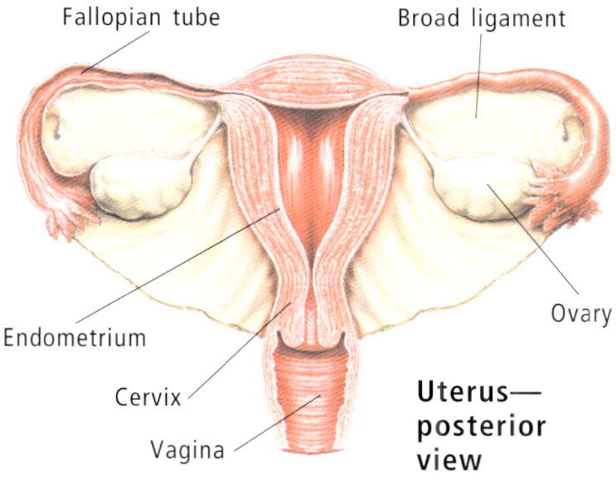

Uterus—posterior view

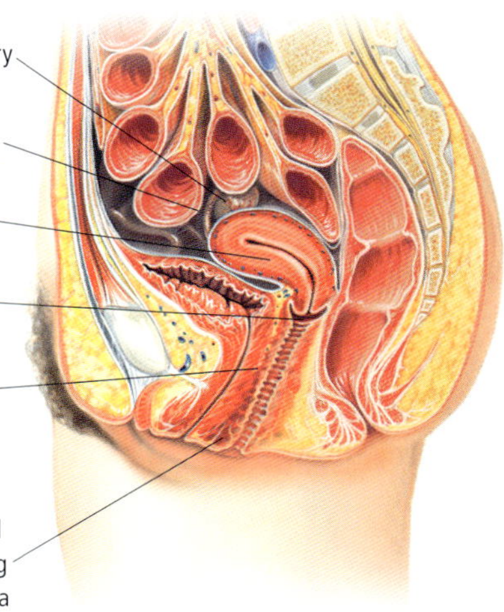

Female reproduction

During each menstrual cycle the ovary produces an oocyte (ovum) which enters the fallopian tube and travels towards the uterus. Fertilization (if it occurs) normally takes place in the outer third of the fallopian tube, and the fertilized ovum then implants into the inner lining of the uterus and develops into an embryo.

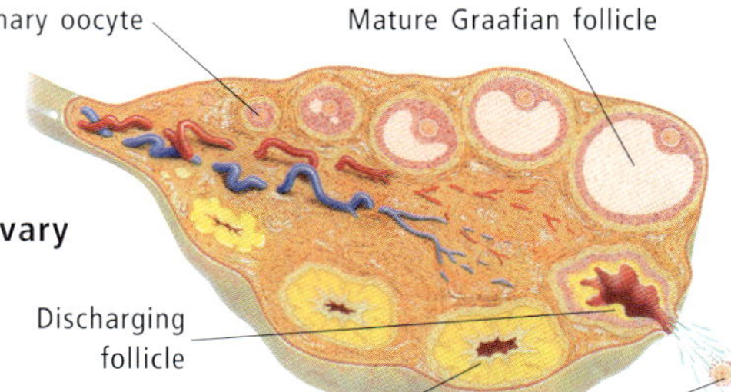

MALE REPRODUCTIVE SYSTEM

The reproductive system of the male includes two testes which produce spermatozoa (sperm) and male hormones, a system of ducts which convey sperm, glands which contribute secretions to semen, and the external genitalia, the scrotum and penis.

Testes

The testes are two oval organs contained in the scrotum, the right one usually higher than the left by nearly $^1/_2$ inch (about 1 centimeter). At the back, the testis is capped by the epididymis. The epididymis has a large head at the top, tapers towards its lower end, then makes a sharp turn back to become the ductus deferens (or vas deferens, hence the term vasectomy).

The testes are separated by a central partition. Surrounding each testis is a double-layered membrane, the tunica vaginalis. Each testis has a tough inelastic fibrous wall called the tunica albuginea which sends partitions inwards to divide it into about 300 lobules. Each lobule contains coiled seminiferous tubules that produce sperm, and converge into a network which sends about 20 small ducts through the tunica albuginea into the epididymis. The ducts become larger and convoluted, forming the head of the epididymis, and gradually fuse into the ductus deferens, which runs back up towards the inguinal canal in the groin.

The tunica vaginalis is an extension of the peritoneal cavity in the embryo, and later separates. If the closure is not complete, a painless swelling known as a hydrocele develops, caused by a collection of fluid above the testis.

Squeezing the testes and epididymis causes a peculiar painful sensation. This tenderness not only makes the testes a vulnerable area to be protected in contact sports, but is also used to roughly assess the functional status of the testes. In old age or in severe liver failure, when the testes are no longer active, they are not tender to pressure. Because of the inelastic tunica albuginea, inflammation of the testes results in an increase in pressure and extreme pain.

The germ cells in the seminiferous tubules—the spermatogonia—undergo division (meiosis) to become spermatids. Spermatids mature into sperm that have a head and a long tail.

The head is capped by an acrosome which releases enzymes to help the sperm penetrate the ovum (egg). The tail propels the sperm like the tail of a tadpole. The spaces between the seminiferous tubules contain clumps of endocrine cells called interstitial cells or Leydig cells.

These interstitial cells synthesize the male hormone testosterone, responsible for the development of sexual characteristics in the adolescent male and the functioning of the reproductive system.

Ductus deferens

The ductus deferens (or vas deferens), is a thick-walled muscular tube, which can be felt above the testis through the loose part of the scrotum. This is where a vasectomy is performed. The ductus deferens is surrounded by the testicular artery, lymphatic vessels, autonomic nerve fibers and a plexus of veins called the pampiniform plexus. All these structures, enveloped by layers of connective tissue and muscle fibers, form the spermatic cord.

The spermatic cord runs upwards to the level of the pubic tubercle on the pubic bone, passes through the inguinal canal, then turns sharply to enter the pelvic cavity. The ductus deferens then heads towards the back of the prostate where it expands into an ampulla, and joins the duct of the seminal vesicle to form the ejaculatory duct.

The muscle fibers in the spermatic cord (cremasteric muscle) pull the testes up in cold weather to maintain an optimal temperature for sperm formation. The pampiniform plexus fuses into a testicular vein that empties into the inferior vena cava on the right side, and the renal vein on the left side. When the plexus is dilated, which more often happens on the left side, it is known as a varicocele.

In a condition called torsion of the testis, the testis can be twisted around the spermatic cord, causing severe pain. Torsion of the testis is a surgical emergency because the arteries become obstructed by the torsion, resulting in "death" of the testis.

Seminal vesicle

The seminal vesicle is a single tube coiled upon itself into a pyramidal organ. It lies on the outer side of the ductus deferens. The fusion of its duct with the ductus deferens forms the ejaculatory duct, which penetrates the prostate gland to open into the prostatic urethra.

Secretion from the seminal vesicle makes up about 60 percent of semen.

Prostate

The prostate is shaped like an inverted pyramid and lies under the bladder, with the apex pointing downwards. The urethra emerging from the neck of the bladder runs vertically through the prostate, leaving it just in front of its apex.

The prostate has two major groups of glands. The central zone surrounding the urethra contains periurethral glands and is the site of benign prostatic enlargement. The peripheral zone containing the main glands is usually the site of prostate cancer. All the glands open into the prostatic urethra and secrete the enzyme acid phosphatase, fibrinolysin, and some other proteins. Prostatic secretion makes up about 25 percent of semen.

The prostate is commonly enlarged in old age (a condition called benign prostatic hypertrophy) and blocks the urethra. It can be removed by inserting a cutting instrument through the urethra, in an operation known as transurethral resection of the prostate (TURP). Because the prostate lies just in front of the rectum, prostate cancer can easily be detected by a digital rectal examination.

After leaving the prostate, the urethra runs through the muscles of the urogenital diaphragm, and enters the penis. Here it receives the ducts of the paired bulbourethral glands. The secretion of these glands precedes the emission of semen and perhaps has a lubricating function.

Penis

The penis is the organ of copulation and is made up of three cylinders of erectile tissue. The midline cylinder is the corpus spongiosum (the spongy body) which contains the urethra. Its front end flares out into the bulbous glans penis, which has in its center the opening of the urethra. On each side of the corpus spongiosum runs a corpus cavernosum (the cavernous body). All three cylinders are enveloped in a thick cylinder of tough connective tissue. The glans is covered by a hood of loose skin called the prepuce, or foreskin. The foreskin can be retracted to the base of the glans. If the prepuce cannot be retracted past the glans, in a condition called phimosis, it can be removed by circumcision.

The three cylinders are structured like a sponge, the interconnecting spaces containing blood.

When the blood flows through them, they are flaccid. When the outflow of blood is prevented by closure of the veins, these cylinders become engorged with blood, thereby causing an erection. The connective tissue around the cylinders helps to build up pressure.

The mechanism of erection is controlled by the parasympathetic component of the autonomic nervous system and is the result of a very intricate interplay of many neurotransmitters. Thus erection is not under voluntary control, and can fail when the autonomic system is disturbed in psychological conditions such as depression or anxiety.

Erection can also fail when the arteries delivering blood to the penis are blocked by vascular diseases such as atherosclerosis or diabetes.

Implanted devices, including pump-up cylinders, can be inserted into the corpora cavernosa to give rigidity to the penis. Knowledge of the chemical mediators of the erection mechanism has led to the development of drugs that can induce or improve erection. The drugs can be mixtures to inject into the penis, pellets to insert into the urethra, or oral tablets.

Erection facilitates the entry of the penis into the vagina. When stimulation during intercourse reaches a threshold, the sympathetic system triggers a powerful emission of semen (this is known as ejaculation). The ejaculate, although it measures only about a teaspoon (5 milliliters), contains a few million sperm.

Fertility depends on the number of normal, healthy, motile sperm that is present in the ejaculate.

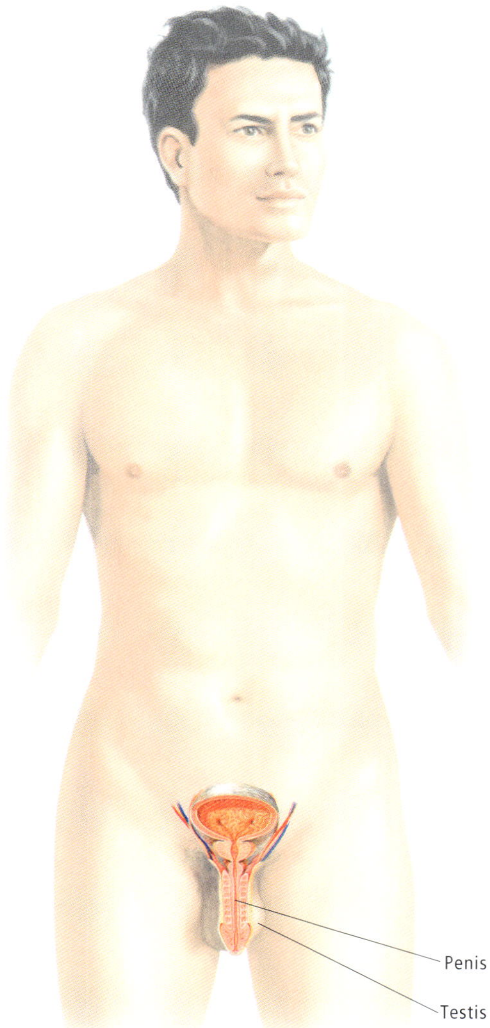

Descent of the testes

During the development of the fetus, the testis moves down from its original position on the side of the upper lumbar vertebrae to the scrotum, carrying with it an extension of the peritoneum which is later pinched off into the tunica vaginalis. If the descent is not complete, the testis may be stuck in the inguinal canal, hidden from sight (this condition is known as cryptorchidism).

If the body temperature is too high for production of sperm, the man with a cryptorchidism is usually infertile; he also has greater risk of developing cancer of the testis. The lymph nodes of the testis are next to the aorta in the lumbar region. Cancer of the testis spreads first to these aortic lymph nodes.

SEE ALSO *Bladder, Circumcision, Epididymis, Erection, Fertility, Glans, Hormones, Hydrocele, Impotence, Penis, Premature ejaculation, Prostate cancer, Prostate gland, Scrotum, Semen, Sexual intercourse, Sperm, Testes, Testosterone, Urethra, Variocele, Vasectomy*

Organs of male reproduction

Sperm is formed in the testes, then passes along the ductus deferens which joins the duct of the seminal vesicle to form the ejaculatory duct. During ejaculation the sperm combine with secretions from the prostate and seminal vesicles to form the seminal fluid.

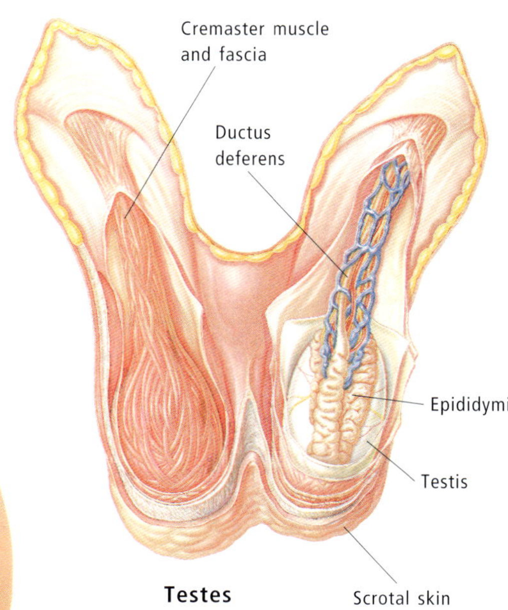

Testes

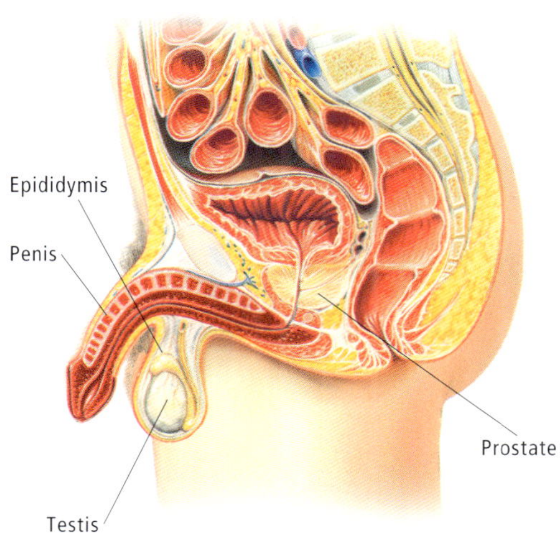

Male reproductive system—cross-section

The male reproductive system consists of the testes, the ductus deferens, the seminal vesicle, the prostate and the penis.

ENDOCRINE SYSTEM

The endocrine system, involved in coordinating the activities of tissues throughout the body, acts by means of organic chemicals called hormones. Hormones, made of amino acids or steroids, are released from endocrine cells at specific times and in precise amounts to act on target organs often at some distance from their site of release. Hormones usually act by combining with special receptor sites on or inside target cells.

Endocrine organs (often called endocrine glands), secrete only into the bloodstream or body cavities, unlike exocrine glands which usually secrete their products onto the skin surface or the linings of the digestive and respiratory systems.

Endocrine hormones affect the nervous system and many endocrine organs are stimulated or inhibited by nerve cells. The hypothalamus of the brain has an intimate connection with the chief organ of the endocrine system, the pituitary. This means that the endocrine and nervous systems share control of body functions: the nervous system usually controls activities occurring rapidly or in the short term, while the endocrine system controls slow or long-term changes.

The endocrine system (pineal, thymus, thyroid, parathyroids, adrenals, pancreatic islets, ovaries and testes) acts under the control of the pituitary gland. The ovaries and testes also function as endocrine glands, producing hormones which control sexual function and secondary sexual characteristics.

The pituitary, the central coordinator of the endocrine system, lies immediately below the hypothalamus of the brain and is closely controlled by it. The pituitary is divided into anterior and posterior lobes. The anterior lobe contains many different types of cells, which produce growth hormone, prolactin, follicle-stimulating hormone, luteinizing hormone, thyroid-stimulating hormone, adrenocorticotrophic hormone and melanocyte-stimulating hormone. The posterior lobe contains oxytocin and antidiuretic hormones, produced in the hypothalamus and transported to the pituitary within nerve fibers.

Growth hormone stimulates the growth of long bones, and is particularly important during childhood and early adolescence.

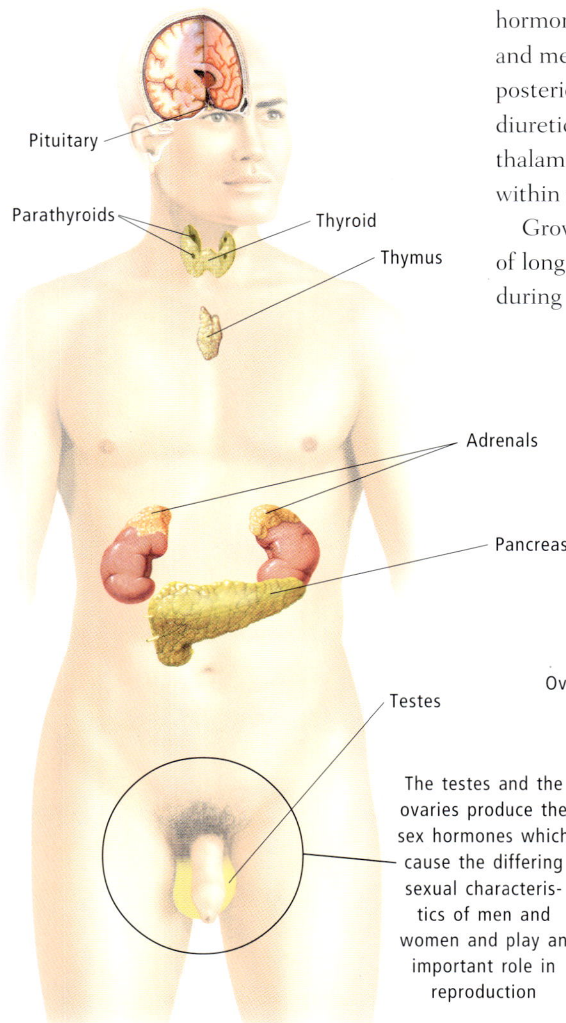

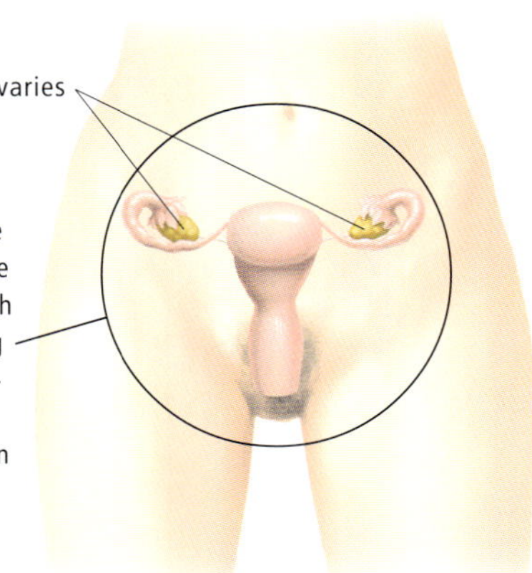

Endocrine glands

The endocrine glands secrete hormones that regulate growth, metabolism, sexual maturation and other important body functions.

Prolactin or lactogenic hormone acts on the mammary glands of the breast to stimulate and maintain the production of milk. Follicle-stimulating hormone (FSH) stimulates the production of eggs in women and sperm in men. Luteinizing hormone stimulates the release of eggs and the production of the hormone progesterone in women, and the secretion of testosterone in men. Thyroid-stimulating hormone (TSH) stimulates the production of thyroid hormone and promotes its release into the bloodstream. Adrenocorticotrophic hormone stimulates the production of corticosteroid hormone by the adrenal gland. Oxytocin promotes contraction of the smooth muscle cells in the uterus and around the milk glands in the breasts. Antidiuretic hormone, or vasopressin, promotes the reabsorption of water from the urine in the kidney, thereby helping to control the concentration of salts in the blood.

The thyroid gland, under the influence of TSH from the pituitary, produces thyroxine and triiodothyronine, which act on cells throughout the body to increase energy production. Thyroid hormones also affect the developing brain; insufficient thyroid hormone during prenatal development can lead to mental deficiency (cretinism). Parafollicular cells or C cells, also found in the thyroid, produce calcitonin, responsible for reducing the concentration of calcium in the blood.

The parathyroid glands produce parathyroid hormone, which acts to raise the concentration of calcium in the blood and reduce the concentration of phosphate ions.

The adrenal glands lie on the upper end of each kidney. Each has an inner part (medulla) and an outer part (cortex). The adrenal medulla contains many modified nerve cells, which produce the hormones epinephrine and norepinephrine (adrenaline and noradrenaline). Epinephrine and norepinephrine are released in bursts during emergency situations or accompanying intense emotion (such as fright). These two hormones act to increase the strength and rate of heart contraction, raise the blood sugar level and elevate blood pressure.

The adrenal cortex produces three main types of hormone: glucocorticoids, mineralocorticoids and sex steroids. Glucocorticoids, produced and released under the control of adrenocorticotrophic hormone (ACTH)

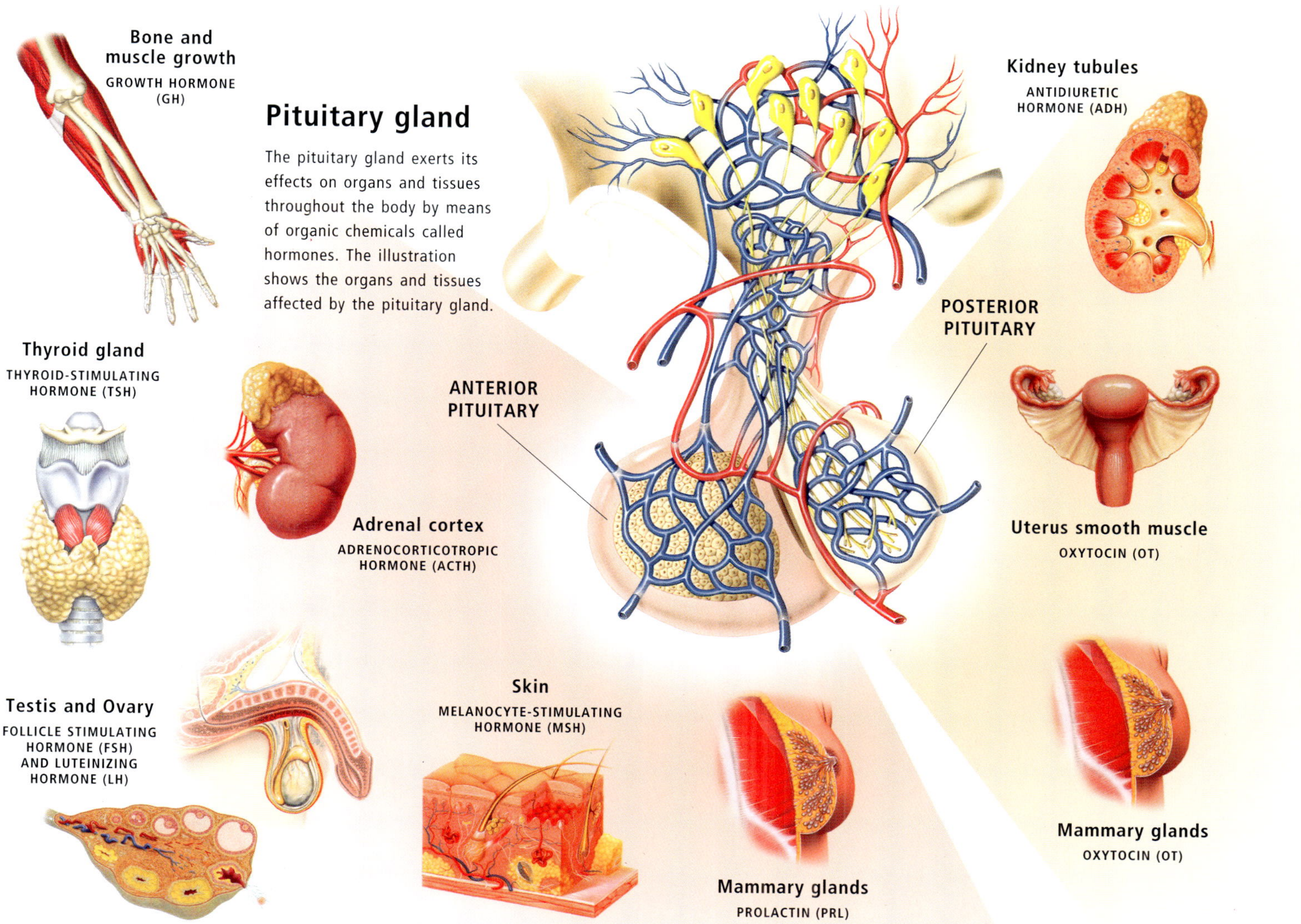

Pituitary gland

The pituitary gland exerts its effects on organs and tissues throughout the body by means of organic chemicals called hormones. The illustration shows the organs and tissues affected by the pituitary gland.

from the pituitary, influence the metabolism of fat, protein and carbohydrates, promoting the breakdown of protein and the release of fat and sugars into the blood stream. Mineralocorticoids, such as aldosterone, stimulate the absorption of sodium in the kidney. The sex steroid produced by the adrenal cortex, dehydroepiandrosterone, has masculinizing effects if secreted in large amounts. Excessive amounts of glucocorticoids in the blood, usually due to medical treatment with high doses of the hormone, causes a condition known as Cushing's syndrome, in which the patient develops a moon-shaped face and obesity around the trunk. Insufficient production of corticosteroids produces Addison's disease, a condition in which patients experience weight loss, dehydration and low blood pressure. Excessive production of dihydroepiandrosterone in boys results in early puberty, while girls may develop an enlarged clitoris, and may be mistakenly raised as boys if clitoral enlargement occurs before birth.

The pancreatic islets (the islets of Langerhans) are located within the pancreas, an abdominal organ mainly concerned with producing digestive enzymes for the gastrointestinal tract. The islets produce hormones responsible for controlling blood sugar level. Insulin acts to lower blood glucose concentration, while glucagon acts to raise it.

The small pineal body is located inside the skull cavity, surrounded by the brain. It produces melatonin, whose concentration varies in tune with the 24-hour cycle of the day (the circadian rhythm). The pineal gland probably has an effect on the ovaries and testes and may influence mood; its precise role is uncertain.

The ovaries produce estrogen and progesterone. Estrogen causes growth of the breasts and reproductive organs, among other functions; progesterone maintains the lining of the uterus in a state suitable to receive a fertilized ovum. Estrogen and progesterone undergo cyclical changes in level every 28 days under the influence of FSH and luteinizing hormone from the pituitary.

During pregnancy, the placenta acts as an endocrine organ, producing a hormone to sustain the pregnancy (human chorionic gonadotrophin). The placenta also produces estrogen, progesterone and relaxin (which relaxes the pelvic ligaments), along with human placental lactogen, which promotes milk production and fetal growth.

The production and release of hormones by glands such as the thyroid and adrenals is constantly regulated by a mechanism called feedback inhibition, in which high levels of the hormone suppress its further production. Other glands, such as the pancreatic islets and the C cells of the thyroid, detect changes in blood concentrations of sugars or calcium respectively, and modify their hormone production accordingly.

SEE ALSO *Adrenal glands, Ovaries, Pancreas, Parathyroid glands, Pituitary gland, Testes, Thymus gland, Thyroid gland*

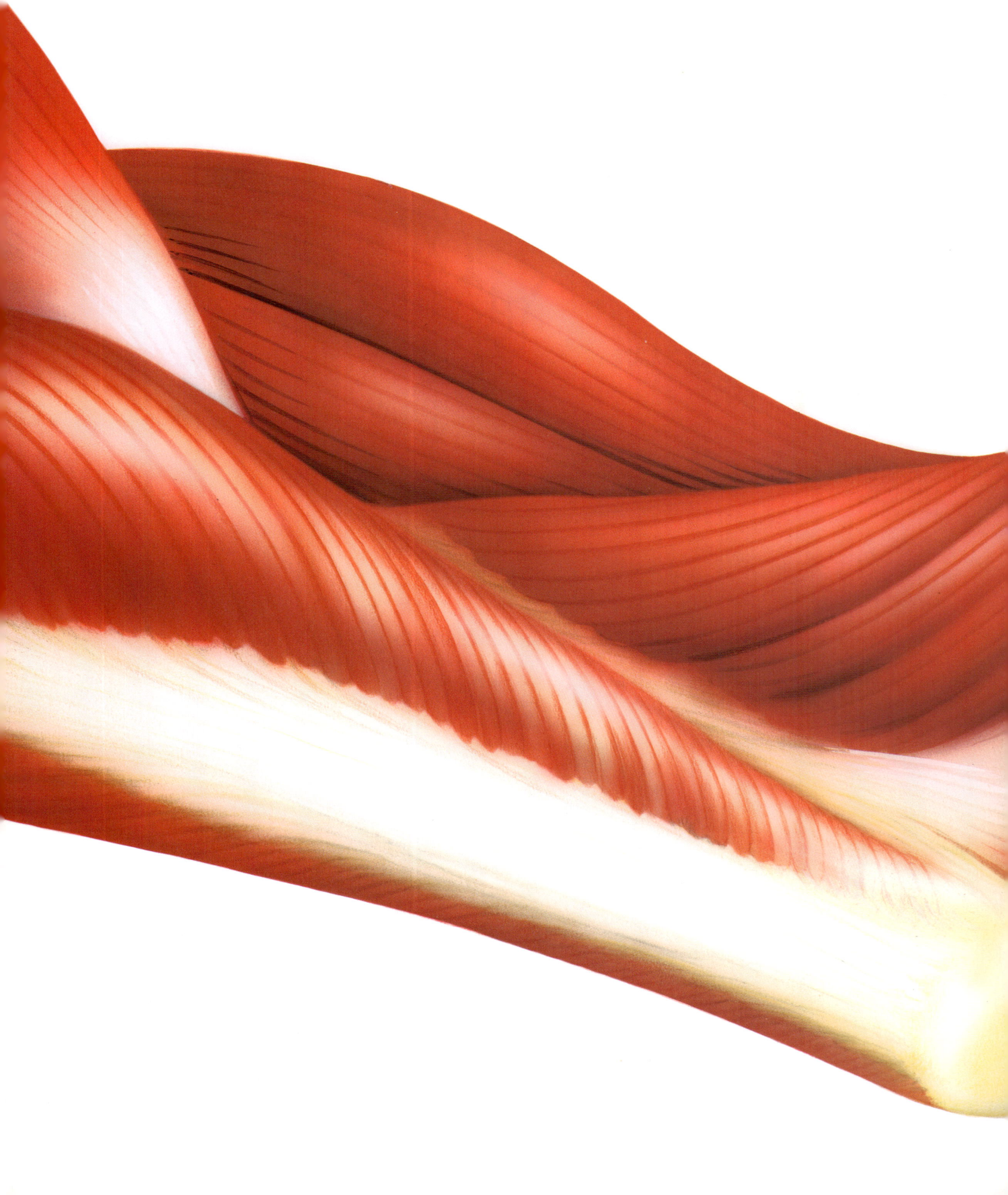

A

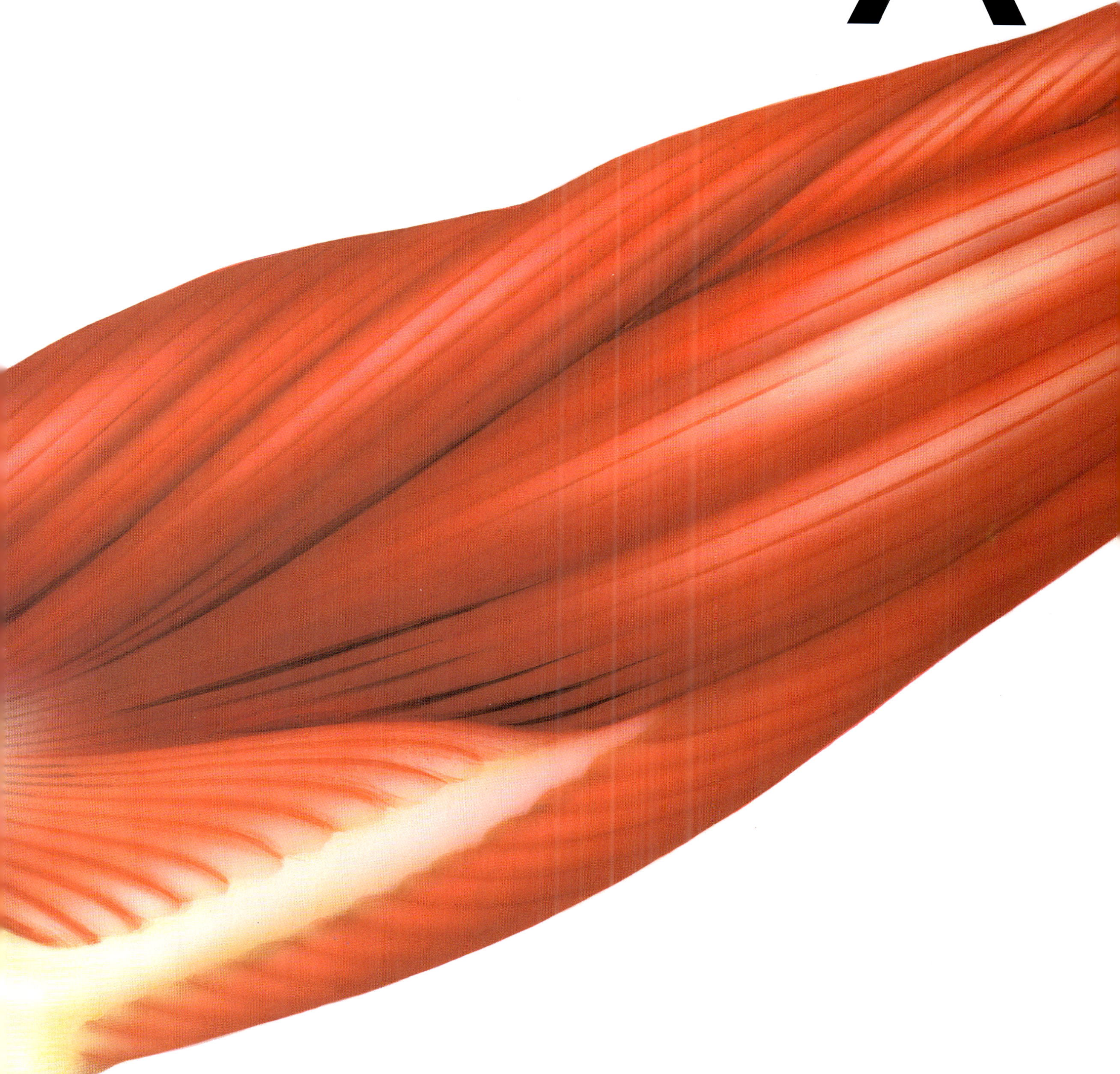

A

ABDOMEN

Situated between the thorax and the pelvis, the abdomen is the larger of the body's two major cavities (the other is the thorax, or chest). The abdomen contains some of the body's most important organs—those organs associated with digestion (the stomach, small and large intestine, liver, gallbladder and pancreas), elimination (kidneys, ureters and bladder) and, in females, reproduction (ovaries and uterus).

Parts of the abdomen

The sides (the lateral walls) and the front (the anterior wall) of the abdomen are made up of layers of muscle covered by fat and skin. When they contract, the muscles raise the pressure in the abdomen to aid breathing and passing of feces. The back (or posterior wall) of the abdominal cavity is formed by the vertebral bones of the spinal column and by the muscles that run up and down them. The roof of the abdominal cavity is formed by the diaphragm, a dome-shaped sheet of muscle separating the abdomen from the thorax. When the diaphragm contracts, it raises the pressure in the abdominal cavity and assists breathing.

The pelvic cavity is usually also considered to be part of the abdomen (though some consider it separately, while others refer to both the pelvic cavity and the abdominopelvic cavity). The pelvic cavity contains the bladder, rectum, and, in females, the uterus and the ovaries. The floor of the pelvic cavity is formed by muscles and bones.

Lining the abdominal cavity, and also extending out into the cavity to cover the organs within, is a thin lubricating membrane, the peritoneum. Folds of the peritoneum attach the organs to the back of the abdominal cavity, while allowing the intestines to move relatively freely, in order to aid movement of food down the alimentary canal. Other folds of the peritoneum, called mesenteries and omenta, supply the organs with nerves, blood vessels and lymph channels.

To make it easier to identify internal organs, and to help locate where abdominal pain is coming from, health professionals divide the abdomen into four quadrants: right upper, right lower, left upper and left lower.

Abdominal disorders

Because the abdomen contains a large number of important organs, it is not surprising that abdominal disorders are common. Symptoms of abdominal disease include heartburn, pain, cramps, constipation, diarrhea, vomiting and nausea. Indigestion (known as dyspepsia), food poisoning and gastroenteritis are common maladies that can be treated at home or by a primary care physician (general practitioner).

More serious conditions, which will require some sort of treatment by a specialist physician or surgeon, include a gastric or duodenal ulcer, hepatitis (inflammation of the liver), colitis (inflammation of the large bowel), as well as cancers of the stomach, liver and large bowel.

An abdominal illness can be an emergency. An acute abdominal infection such as peritonitis, appendicitis, cholecystitis (inflammation of the gallbladder) or salpingitis (inflammation of the fallopian tube) can be serious and life threatening. A perforated gastric or duodenal ulcer and injury from trauma are other common abdominal emergencies. "Acute abdomen" is the term health professionals use to refer to an abdominal emergency.

SEE ALSO *Bladder, Gallbladder, Intestines, Kidneys, Liver, Ovaries, Pancreas, Stomach, Ureter, Uterus*

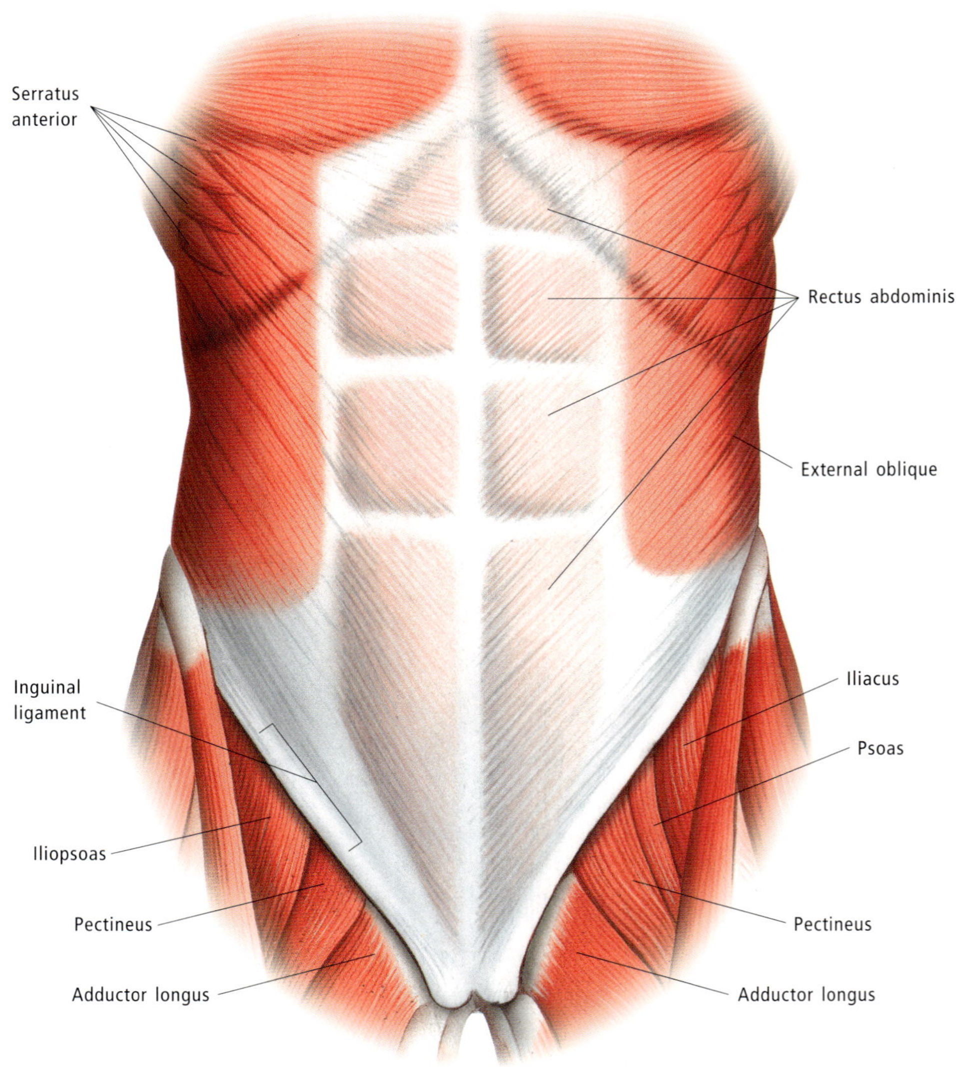

Muscles of the abdomen

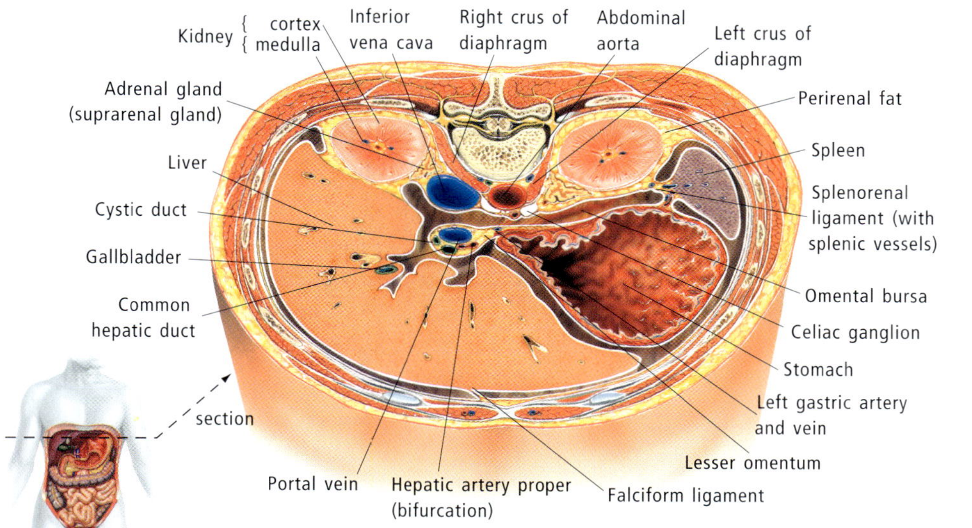

Cross-section of the abdomen

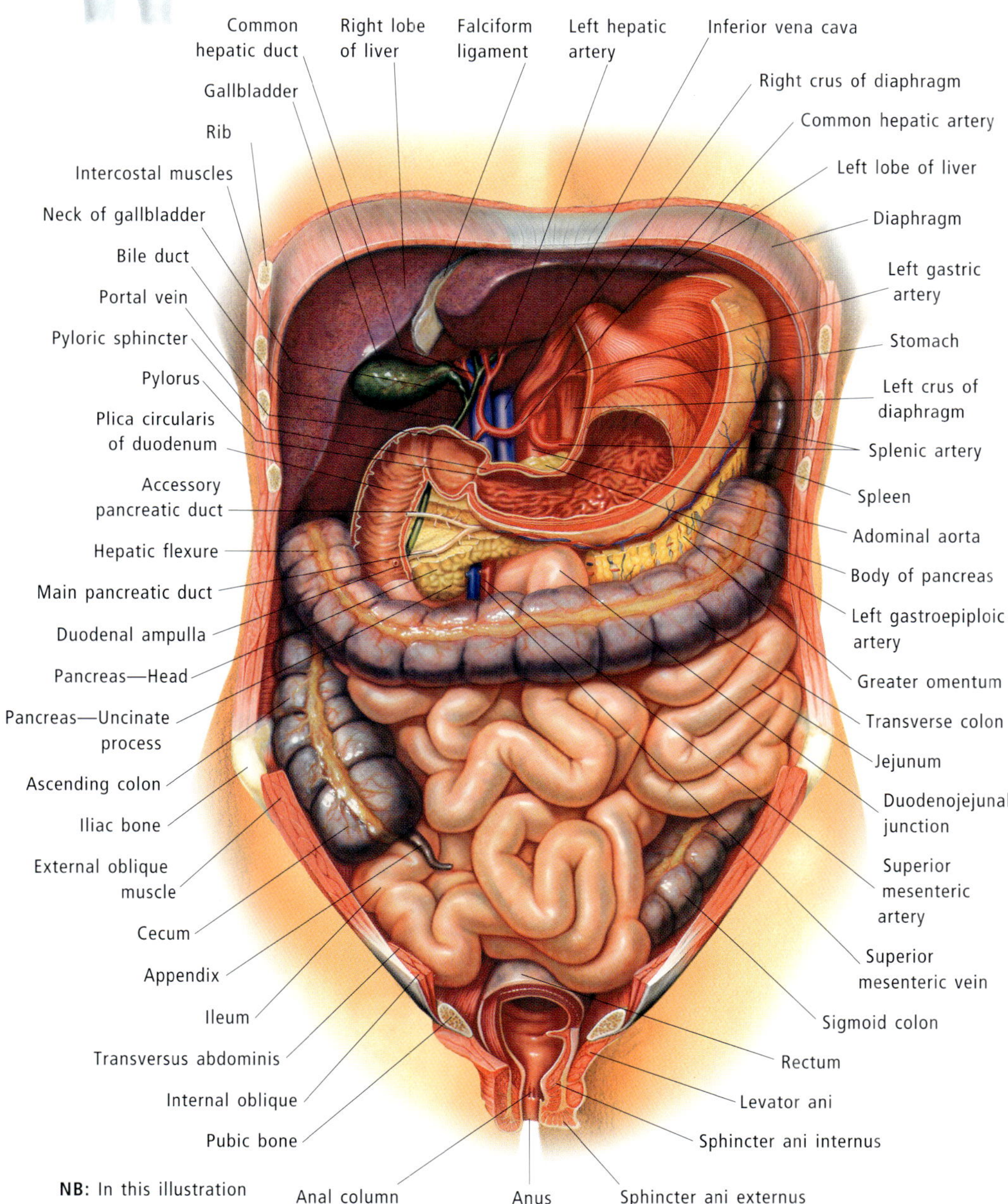

NB: In this illustration the liver has been pulled back to reveal the other abdominal organs

Organs of the abdomen

ABORTION

An abortion is a pregnancy that ends prematurely with the loss of the embryo or fetus, either spontaneously or by artificial induction. In common speech, the word "abortion" refers to artificial induction, while a spontaneous abortion is generally known as a miscarriage.

Abortion is an issue that raises strong passions. Those supporting abortion argue that it should be made legally available to women who choose to have it, and that refusing to do so often leads to women trying various unsafe ways of aborting the fetus themselves. Those against abortion argue that it as soon as an embryo is conceived it is a life, and that to abort it is to take this life.

The decision to have an abortion is never free of conflict, and counseling is very important. When antenatal testing reveals that the fetus has a lethal abnormality such as anencephaly, or a defect which can be a major disability such as spina bifida with hydrocephalus, termination is acceptable to many parents. Some women choose not to have an antenatal test if their beliefs would not allow them to have an abortion; or they may decide not to abort a fetus even if it has a high risk of a birth defect. In any situation, difficulties can arise and counseling is advisable, and imperative when defects with less predictable outcomes are detected.

History

It could be said that since the beginning of humanity people have tried to terminate unwanted pregnancies, using either external or internal methods. External methods included hot sitz baths, binding the abdomen, jumping from high places, punching or pummelling the abdomen, and abdominal massage. Of these, only the last one is thought to have been at all successful, and most were highly dangerous.

Internal methods included herbal concoctions which attempted to induce menstruation, strong purgatives (some containing lead and mercury compounds) and instruments such as knitting needles, bottles and syringes. Again, these methods had mixed results and were often dangerous.

Not until the nineteenth century were civil laws passed in most Western countries making abortion a criminal offence. It was in 1869 that Pope Pius IX decreed that abortion was murder. What followed was legislation against the procedure, which, it is frequently argued, led to a "back-street" abortion industry, the continued use of unsafe practices and considerable loss of life.

In the late 1960s and early 1970s Western countries began to pass more liberal legislation relating to abortion. Today abortion laws and their enforcement vary from country to country, and continue to generate passionate debate and even violent protests.

Types of abortions

There are several methods of performing an abortion. The method used generally depends on how far the pregnancy is advanced, with the duration of the pregnancy being calculated from the date of the woman's last menstrual period.

Surgical evacuation—removing the contents of the uterus through the vagina—is the method used in over 95 percent of abortions and almost always for pregnancies of less than 12 weeks. The technique is known as suction aspiration or suction curetting. The cervix is dilated and the lining of the uterus, containing the embryo, is drawn out by suction. A curette may also be used to scrape the uterine walls. This takes up to two minutes. If the cervix needs to be dilated more widely (this can be used for a pregnancy of seven weeks or more) then laminaria (strips of a special seaweed which expand as they absorb moisture) are inserted a few hours before the procedure, or even the night before.

For pregnancies over 12 weeks and under 20 weeks, dilation and evacuation (D&E) is used. When the cervix is dilated enough, forceps and a combination of suction and curettage remove the fetus. This can be done under general or local anesthetic.

A hysterotomy, the cutting open of the uterus to remove the embryo or fetus, is the same procedure as a cesarean delivery and is used only when the pregnancy must be terminated quickly in order to save the mother or when other methods are impossible.

Drugs such as mifepristone (RU-486) and prostaglandins are used in some cases, especially after 16 weeks of pregnancy, though mifepristone may be used shortly after conception. Taken as a tablet, it is followed 48 hours later with a prostaglandin and the abortion starts soon after this. In over 95 percent of cases it is completed quickly with minimal blood loss. If it is not successful, surgical termination is necessary.

High dose oral contraceptives (known as the "morning after pill") are sometimes prescribed to prevent conception after people have had unprotected intercourse.

Complications

Induced abortion before the twelfth week of the pregnancy and performed by a skilled doctor in a safe environment is a safe procedure. However, as with any surgical procedure, there are possible complications and some risks. The probability of complications increases with the duration of the pregnancy.

Complications include: infection (many clinics routinely prescribe antibiotics to reduce this risk and women are advised of the symptoms, as immediate medical attention is needed); incomplete abortion (this will require a further curettage); hemorrhage; perforation of the uterus (a rare complication when the operation is performed by a skilled doctor); and tearing of the cervix (which will require stitching). Occasionally, the abortion is unsuccessful and the pregnancy continues.

Bleeding, similar to a menstrual period, is normal within a few days of the abortion and a checkup is part of the normal procedure.

Many women find an abortion can have psychological repercussions. These are less common when counseling is part of the procedure. They are more likely to occur if the abortion was performed late in the pregnancy, the pregnancy was terminated for medical reasons, or there are psychiatric problems.

As well as psychological counseling, women often choose to seek advice about reliable forms of contraception, and find out which one may be most suitable for them.

SEE ALSO *Congenital abnormalities, Contraception, Dilation and evacuation, Pregnancy*

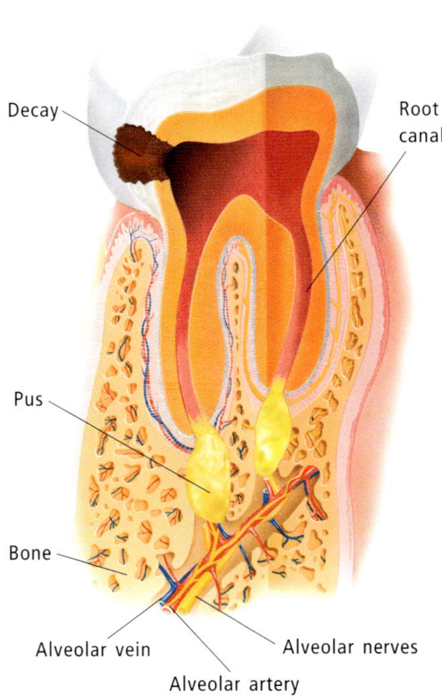

Tooth abscess (advanced)

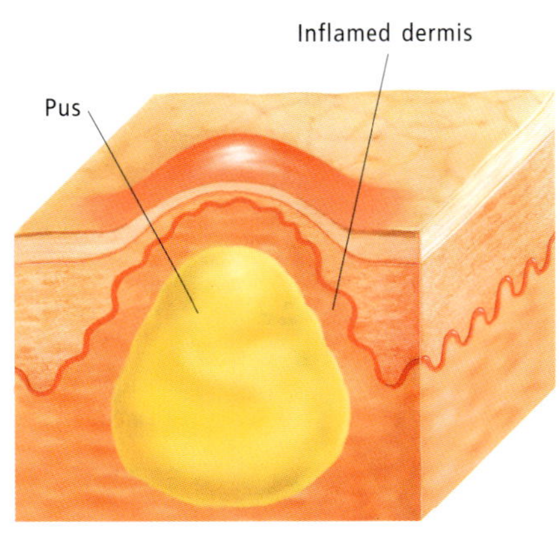

Skin abscess

Abscess

An abscess is an infection that contains pus and causes inflammation of the tissues. Abscesses are common on the skin and teeth but also occur on internal organs such as the liver, lung or brain. In teeth, the pulp and nerves break down in the root canal. Treatment involves antibiotics and proceeding with root canal therapy.

ABSCESS

An abscess is a collection of pus. The pus is made up of dead white blood cells, destroyed tissue and cells, and dead and live microorganisms (usually bacteria) which are all by-products of inflammation and infection. It can form in an internal organ such as the large intestine, lung, liver or brain, when it is often the result of another debilitating disease, for example AIDS. Most abscesses are bacterial or fungal in origin, although they are sometimes caused by ameba (especially in the liver) or by the tuberculosis bacillus. These are carried to the internal organs through the bloodstream and once there cause inflammation and infection.

In healthy people abscesses more often occur in the soft tissues beneath the skin. The invading organism finds its way through the skin via an infected wound or bite, or the abscess may begin in a hair follicle, when it is known as a boil. Boils are most common in hairy sites such as the nostrils, the armpits, the back of the neck and between the legs and buttocks. An abscess below the skin is usually very painful, looks swollen and red, and feels hot to the touch. An abscess may also cause fever, sweating, tachycardia (rapid pulse rate) and malaise.

Antibiotics are often given, usually intravenously, although their usefulness is limited, as drugs do not readily penetrate past the abscess lining into the abscess.

The mainstay of treatment is surgical drainage. This involves making a cut into the abscess and providing a drainage route either through a drainage tube or by leaving the abscess open to the skin (though an abscess will often burst through the skin by itself). A dressing is then applied daily until the wound and infection have healed.

SEE ALSO *Bacteria, Boil*

ACHALASIA

Achalasia is a disease of the esophagus and prevents normal swallowing (peristaltic action) that allows food to pass from the mouth to the stomach. The esophagus is a muscular tube connecting the throat (pharynx) to the stomach. It can expand and contract at its upper and lower ends using circular muscles called sphincters. The upper sphincter relaxes to accept food from the pharynx, and the food is moved by muscular contractions to the lower sphincter, which relaxes to let food enter the stomach. It then closes to prevent gastric reflux (return flow).

In achalasia, nerve damage prevents the lower sphincter from relaxing and food cannot pass. The cause is not known, although tension may be a contributing factor. Treatment involves muscle-relaxing drugs, or in more extreme cases, surgery may be used.

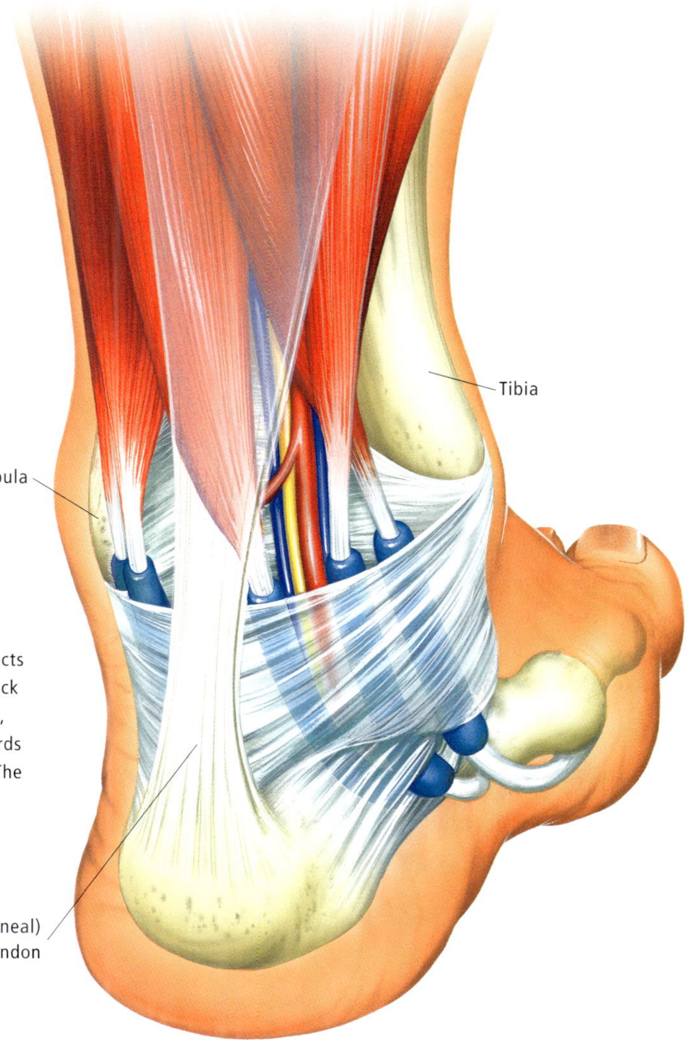

Achilles tendon

The Achilles tendon connects the calf muscles to the back of the heel bone. Running, jumping or pushing forwards suddenly may rupture it. The ruptured tendon will take six weeks to heal in a plaster cast.

ACHILLES TENDON

The Achilles tendon is a band of fibrous tissue that connects the calf muscles to the back of the heel bone. It is named after the legendary Greek hero of the Trojan Wars whose body was invincible except for the heels (he was beaten only after the tendons were cut). When you stand on tiptoes, your calf muscles contract, pulling the heel up via the Achilles tendon.

Rupture of the tendon

The Achilles tendon is a weak spot and if subjected to sudden stress—running, jumping, pushing forwards—it may snap. This most commonly occurs in sportspeople and middle-aged men. When it happens, there is a snapping sensation and immediate pain in the heel or the back of the leg. Flexing the foot downwards becomes difficult.

To treat an Achilles rupture, the doctor usually puts the back of the patient's foot, ankle and the lower part of the leg into a plaster cast, with the toes pointing downwards, so that the two ends of the tendon are close and can heal. The patient uses crutches, keeping weight off the foot, for six weeks. After removal of the plaster, physical therapy is needed to restore the function of the calf muscles and ankle joint. It usually takes about six months to return to normal.

Another option is surgery. Under general anesthetic, the two ends of the ruptured tendon are sewn together by a surgeon, and the foot goes into plaster for six weeks, followed by months of physical therapy.

Achilles tendinitis

Achilles tendinitis—inflammation of the Achilles tendon—can develop if the tendon suffers too much wear and tear. It happens most often after strenuous activity, especially by those not used to exercise. Wearing shoes with high heels or with worn heels, both of which place abnormal stresses on the tendon, may also cause inflammation.

A

Sufferers feel pain in the affected tendon, which gets worse with activity. The Achilles tendon may become thicker than it normally is and be painful or tender when it is touched. An inflamed Achilles tendon is susceptible to rupture.

The treatment for Achilles tendinitis is rest, analgesics and anti-inflammatory drugs, which relieve the symptoms but do not cure the condition, which tends to recur. In rare cases, the tendon can be removed under anesthetic by an orthopedic surgeon and replaced with artificial or natural tissues.

The best treatment, though, is prevention. Warming up before exercise, leg and calf muscle stretching before and after running, and the wearing of proper shoes during exercise will help prevent the condition from developing.

SEE ALSO *Ankle, Foot, Leg*

ACHONDROPLASIA

Achondroplasia is a genetic defect that prevents cartilage from forming properly during the body's development, which in turn prevents the formation of bones. The bones—especially the limbs—become shorter and thicker than in normal development.

The most common cause of dwarfism, achondroplasia occurs about once in every 10,000 births. The condition is a dominant genetic trait, which means that there is no such thing as a carrier—anyone carrying the genetic trait will show the symptoms. This also means a parent with the disorder has a 50 percent chance of passing it to a child. However, most sufferers do not inherit the condition; it develops as a genetic mutation in the uterus. It is diagnosed at birth from the characteristic appearance of the infant.

Persons with achondroplasia have abnormally short arms and legs. The trunk and head are normal-sized, but the head often appears large because of the smaller arms. The forehead is prominent; there is an exaggerated curvature in the lower back; and the bridge of the nose has a scooped-out appearance.

Unfortunately there is no treatment for achondroplasia. But many of the complications—which include bowed legs, nerve compression in the spine, hydrocephalus and, in children, middle ear infection, which can result in hearing loss—can be treated. Achondroplasia does not interfere with the capacity to reproduce nor does it affect mental capacity. Most people with achondroplasia can remain in good health and have a normal life span.

SEE ALSO *Growth disorders*

ACIDOSIS

Acidosis is an excess of acid in the body's fluids. Body metabolism works best in a narrow pH range—between 7.35 and 7.45 (pH is a measure of acidity). It is the job of the lungs, kidneys and chemical buffers in the blood (such as bicarbonate) to keep the pH at this level. But in illness, the pH can fall, causing acidosis. If uncorrected, it can lead to death.

There are two types of acidosis. Where the excess acid is produced by a metabolic process, it is known as metabolic acidosis. Diabetes, kidney failure, loss of bicarbonate from the body, diarrhea, drug overdose or abnormal metabolic states can cause this. If due to hypoventilation, or inadequate respiratory effort, it is known as respiratory acidosis. Cardiac arrest, asthma or other obstructive lung disease and drug overdose can cause respiratory acidosis.

In mild cases of acidosis the symptoms are agitation, headache and tachycardia (abnormally fast heartbeat). In more serious cases it causes lethargy, confusion, seizures, stupor and coma.

The treatment of acidosis is, if possible, to correct the underlying cause. If the acidosis is severe, the patient is given sodium bicarbonate intravenously.

SEE ALSO *Alkalosis, Metabolism*

ACNE

Acne (cystic acne, acne vulgaris) is a skin condition that commonly occurs in adolescence. It can start at puberty and continue as a problem into adulthood.

The hormones active at puberty stimulate the sebaceous (oil-producing) glands, and the excess oil produced makes a fertile breeding ground for bacteria. Bacterial infection creates debris and waste matter (pus) that blocks the gland. The area becomes red and inflamed and a whitehead appears, developing into a pimple—this may become a blackhead, or develop further into a painful cyst or boil. The most commonly affected areas are those that are naturally greasy, including the forehead, face, nose, chin, chest and back.

Acne affects adult men and women as well as adolescents. Polycystic ovaries can be a cause of continuing acne for women. An excess of the hormone androgen in adulthood can be another cause. Contrary to popular belief, the cause of acne is not poor hygiene and probably is little affected by particular foods. Acne is a skin disease, although it is not infectious, and taking good care of the skin can help to control the symptoms and lessen the chance of scarring.

Severe acne, acne vulgaris, will require medical treatment. Medication may be prescribed to fight the acne bacillus, usually antibiotics such as tetracycline or retinoic acid, which is derived from vitamin A.

Skin care routine

- Wash the face and other affected areas gently twice each day. Use a mild soap or special cleansing lotion, to degrease the skin and dissolve blackheads.
- Wash the hair each day and tie it back away from facial skin. Use only non-greasy hair gels.
- Do not squeeze pimples—this can lead to infection and scarring.
- Keep makeup away from pimples. Do not use any preparation that could block the oil glands.

There are several skin cleansers available that are recommended for acne. Some may contain benzoyl peroxide, which induces peeling in the skin's surface layer; they may also contain retinoic acid, which dissolves blackheads—but this is not to be used during pregnancy.

Medical treatments

See the doctor if acne persists, particularly if there is no improvement four to six weeks after onset, if there are cysts or boils, or if the condition is causing distress.

Antibiotics work but may not be a long-term cure. The most common prescription treatments are erythromycin applied in a lotion and tetracyclines taken in tablet form.

The absorption of tetracyclines can be reduced by milk in the diet. Minocycline is an alternative that has the advantage of not being affected by milk consumption, but which carries some risk of arthritis. Women may treat acne with a contraceptive pill that contains the sex hormone cyproterone. A moderate amount of sunlight (UV light) can aid treatment and reduce the occurrence of acne.

Isotretinoin is used to treat recurrent acne. It is similar in structure to vitamin A but acts differently, reducing the oil content of the skin. It also inhibits the growth of bacteria in the skin that are the cause of inflammation and the pus associated with acne. There are some significant side effects with this substance, including dry skin and possible liver upsets. Isotretinoin is harmful to a fetus so is not to be taken if you are pregnant, or for a certain time before conceiving a baby—seek the advice of your doctor.

Acne

Right: Acne affects the skin, with inflammation, pustules (pimples) and plugs (blackheads). Here some of the pustules have broken through the skin. Below: Overproduction of sebum may block the outlet of a sebaceous gland and its hair follicle, forming a blackhead. Later, the area becomes inflamed and pus may form under the skin, producing a pustule.

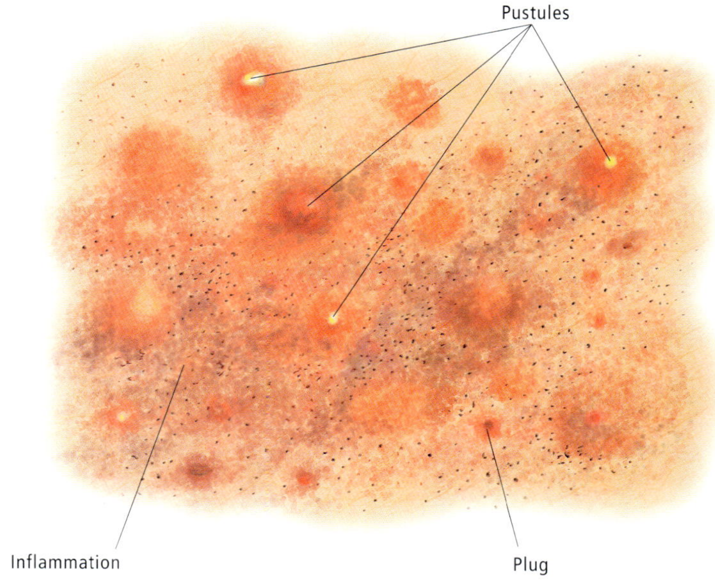

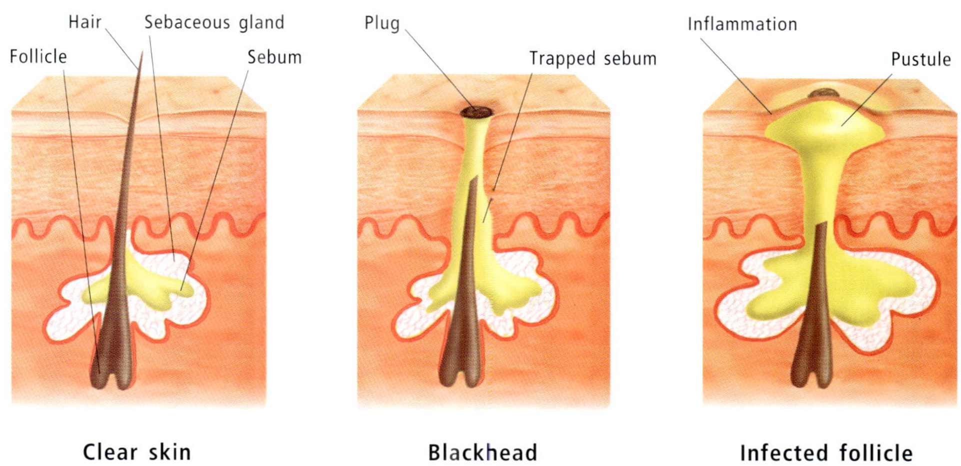

ACNE ROSACEA

Acne rosacea, also called rosacea, is an inflammation of the skin of the face. It is more common in males, especially alcoholics.

Unsightly red, thickened excess skin tissue forms on the nose, cheeks and forehead, associated with changes in the hair follicles, sebaceous glands and surrounding connective tissue. The exact cause of acne rosacea is unknown, though it sometimes results from an overuse of steroid creams on the face.

Antibiotics are taken orally or applied in a cream or lotion on the affected area to treat this condition. The excess tissue may be removed with a scalpel or laser.

ACROCYANOSIS

This is a harmless, often painless, but annoying discoloration of the extremities, brought about usually by cold but sometimes by emotional states.

Mostly a disease of women, it starts sometime before the age of 30. The hands are most often affected, but the feet may be affected also. They turn blue, cold and sweaty. Warming the hands or feet restores their former pink color.

The cause is thought to be overreaction of the sympathetic nervous system, which controls nerves to the arterioles (small arteries) of the hands and feet. The arterioles contract, restricting the supply of oxygen to the hands and feet; enough oxygen gets through the constricted arteries to keep the tissues of the extremities alive, but not enough to give them their normal healthy pink color. Despite this, there is no permanent damage to the tissues or to the skin of the hands and feet.

Sufferers are advised to dress warmly and avoid exposure to the cold to keep the symptoms at bay. Gloves are a good idea. Rarely, in very troublesome cases, drug treatments are prescribed. Surgery, which consists of cutting the sympathetic nerve supply to the arterioles, is also an option.

SEE ALSO *Arteries*

ACROMEGALY

Affecting only about 1 in every 20,000 people, acromegaly is a rare hormonal disease that causes overgrowth of the body's bones, muscles and other tissues. It is caused by overproduction of an essential hormone called growth hormone (GH) by the pituitary gland.

In young children this can cause abnormal growth of long bones in the limbs. The condition is then called gigantism. If it happens in older children or in adulthood, the disorder is called acromegaly.

Acromegaly can cause the affected person's hands and feet to grow. The facial features coarsen; the jaw line, nose and forehead grow; the tongue grows larger and teeth get more widely spaced as the jaw grows larger. The voice gets deeper because of swelling of the larynx.

The cause of the overproduction of GH is usually a small benign tumor in the pituitary called a pituitary adenoma. As it grows, the tumor may also press on surrounding structures, especially the optic nerve nearby, so that vision may be affected. Changes to the menstrual cycle and abnormal production of breast milk are also common. Growth hormone can also have other unwanted metabolic effects, including diabetes, high blood pressure, gallstones and kidney stones.

Treatment is surgical removal of all or part of the pituitary adenoma. Drugs such as bromocriptine and octreotide, which suppress growth hormone production by the pituitary, are often used as well.

SEE ALSO *Gigantism, Growth disorders*

ACROPHOBIA

Acrophobia is a fear of heights. Acrophobics will feel anxiety or distress when in a high place or when just imagining themselves to be. This excessive fear is termed a phobia because it is an irrational and unrealistic perception of the danger of being in the imagined situation. Research has shown that acrophobics imagine that far greater injuries would result through falls from a given height than would really be the case.

Their level of fear is well above that of a normally cautious person; it can prevent them from climbing ladders or going up a flight of stairs, and can be associated with aerophobia, a fear of flying. Recent studies have questioned previous views that phobics know their fears are unreal. In many cases sufferers believe themselves to be in mortal danger, and, whether they are reacting to fear of the danger or are apprehensive about the possibility of a panic attack, their feelings are real and the effects are debilitating.

With treatment, many phobics can lead normal lives. Medications may help them control and manage their fears, and therapy (including self-help groups) can also be used; these are often used in combination.

SEE ALSO *Anxiety, Panic attacks, Phobias*

ACUPRESSURE

Acupressure, or *tui na*, is a form of traditional Chinese massage where pressure is applied to acupuncture points by the practitioner's fingers, and occasionally their elbows or feet. The depth and duration of pressure is an important aspect of the treatment.

The practitioner diagnoses which points to use by taking a case history and pulse readings (six in each wrist) and by physical examination. Acupressure can be practised on someone in a sitting or lying position and can be performed through clothing. It is also possible to do acupressure on oneself. Acupressure is used to strengthen overall health and to relieve pain and discomfort.

ACUPUNCTURE

Acupuncture is a major branch of traditional Chinese medicine, a healing system that dates back to about 1000 BC. Its earliest text is the *Huang Ti Nei-Ching* or the *Yellow Emperor's Manual of Internal Medicine*, thought to have been written about 200 BC. This text included a systematic approach to acupuncture treatment that provided a foundation for all later developments. By the time of the Tang dynasty (AD 618–907) the Imperial Medical College taught acupuncture and medical theory based on Taoist philosophies in which the notions of harmony, balance and energy flow were applied to the treatment of illnesses.

In modern China, acupuncture continues to be an essential part of the medical system alongside Western medical practices. Acupuncture in the West has spread rapidly in the twentieth century. It is practised by both traditional Chinese medicine practitioners and by medical doctors who are not necessarily trained in all aspects of traditional Chinese medicine.

Philosophy

Acupuncture, along with all other types of traditional Chinese medicine, is based upon the principle that optimum health is achieved and maintained by balancing the flow of life energy through the body. This life energy flow, which is known as *ch'i* or *qi*, is seen to be made up of two polarities: the *yin*, which is passive, internal, contracting and cold, and the *yang*, which is active, external, expanding and warm. For good health to be maintained, the theory is that *yin* and *yang* need to be in constant interplay—flowing, balancing and moving between each other. If either *yin* or *yang* energy becomes excessive in the body, it automatically creates a deficiency state in the other which, if not corrected, will lead to ill health. For example, an infectious disease where there is fever is seen as an excess *yang* condition while chronic fatigue syndrome, where there is pallor, is seen as an excess *yin* condition.

The theory is that *ch'i* travels through the body along twelve pathways known as meridians, each corresponding to a particular body organ or system. The twelve meridians are the gallbladder, liver, lung, large intestine, stomach, spleen/pancreas, heart, small

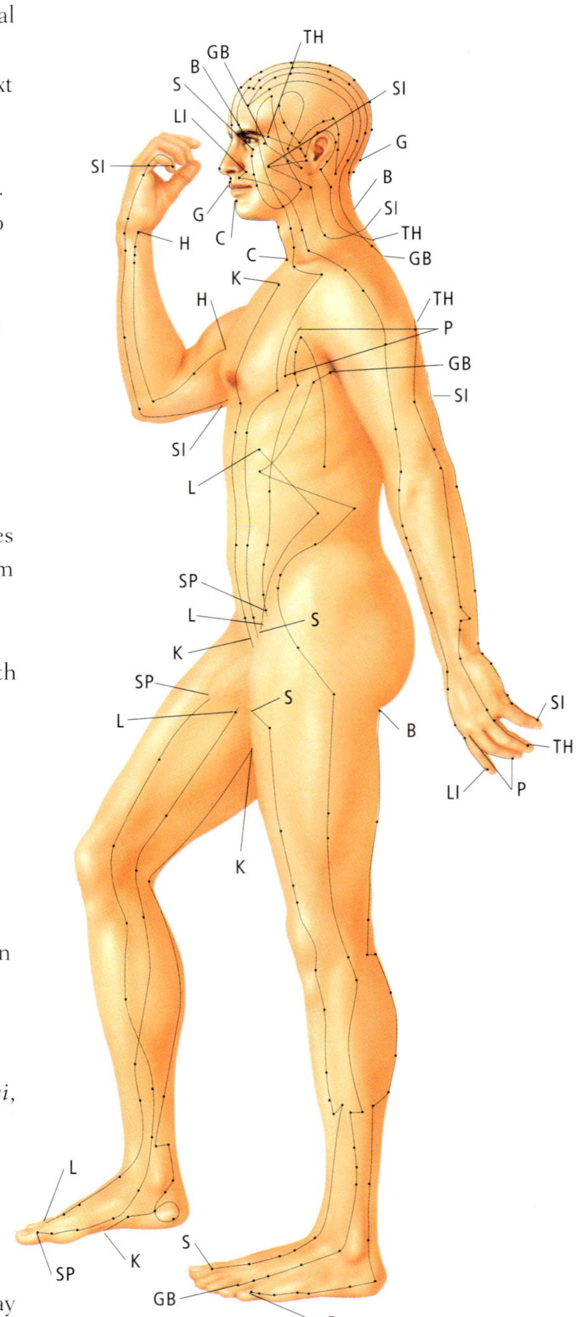

Side view

intestine, bladder, kidney, pericardium (which controls circulation and is important in sexual activity) and triple heater (which controls the endocrine system). Two extra meridians, the governor and the conception, run up the midline of the body. The meridians overlap with the circulatory and nervous systems but are separate to them. Some modern research supports the idea of meridians, suggesting their flows may relate to fluctuations in the body's electromagnetic field.

Acupuncture works through points, or gates, located along the meridians. Traditional acupuncture identifies 365 points; modern charts show up to 2,000 points. Each meridian has a point of entry and a point of exit. Diagnosis takes into account the way *ch'i* acts in relation to all the parts of the body. Treatment involves regulating *ch'i*, drawing it in or dispersing it.

To further understand the flow of energy through the body, traditional Chinese medicine aligns the body with the five elements of nature. Each of the five elements is associated with major organs of the body: fire (heart, small intestine); earth (stomach, spleen); metal (lungs, colon); water (kidneys, bladder); and wood (gallbladder, liver). The elements are seen to work cyclically through the body; an understanding of these cycles forms a vital part of acupuncture diagnosis and treatment.

Diagnosis

Traditional acupuncturists diagnose a patient's condition through observing their voice, tongue, eyes, complexion, hair texture, body language and physical symptoms. Lifestyle, sleep patterns and food preferences are also taken into account. The acupuncturist puts light pressure with the fingers on the patient's twelve pulses, six

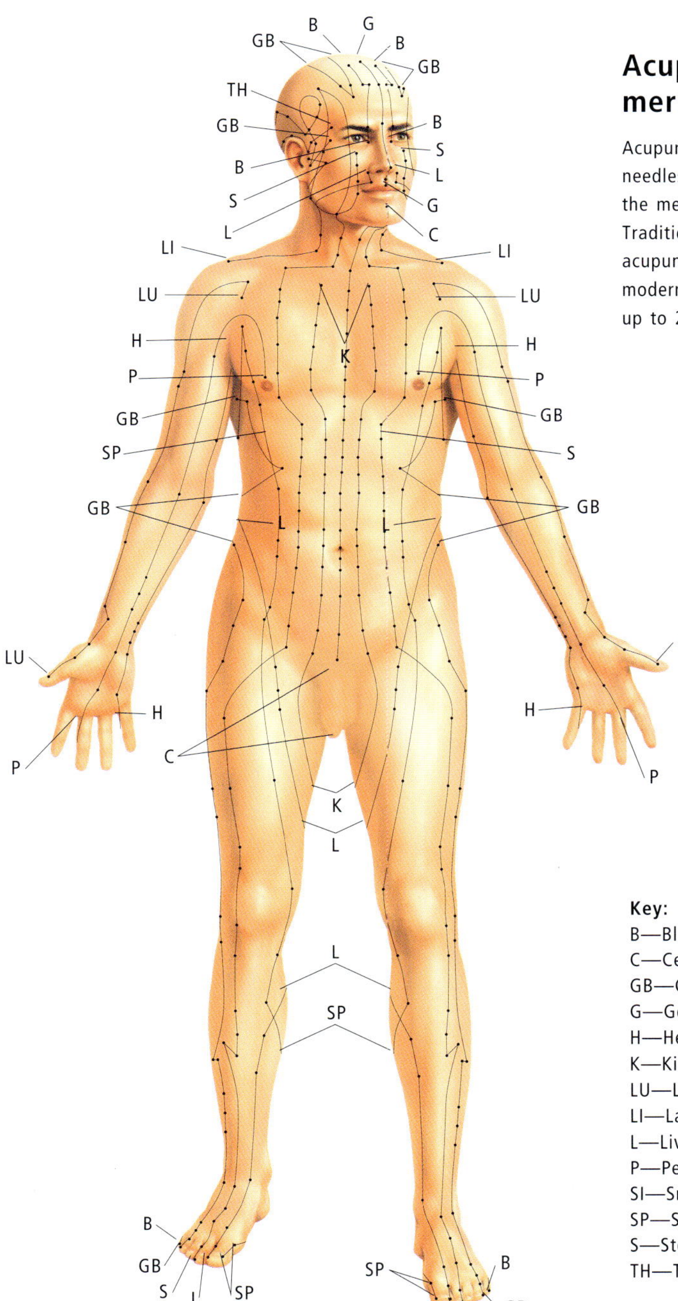

Front view

Acupuncture meridians

Acupuncture works by placing needles at special points on the meridians of the body. Traditionally there were 365 acupuncture points but in modern practice there are up to 2,000 points.

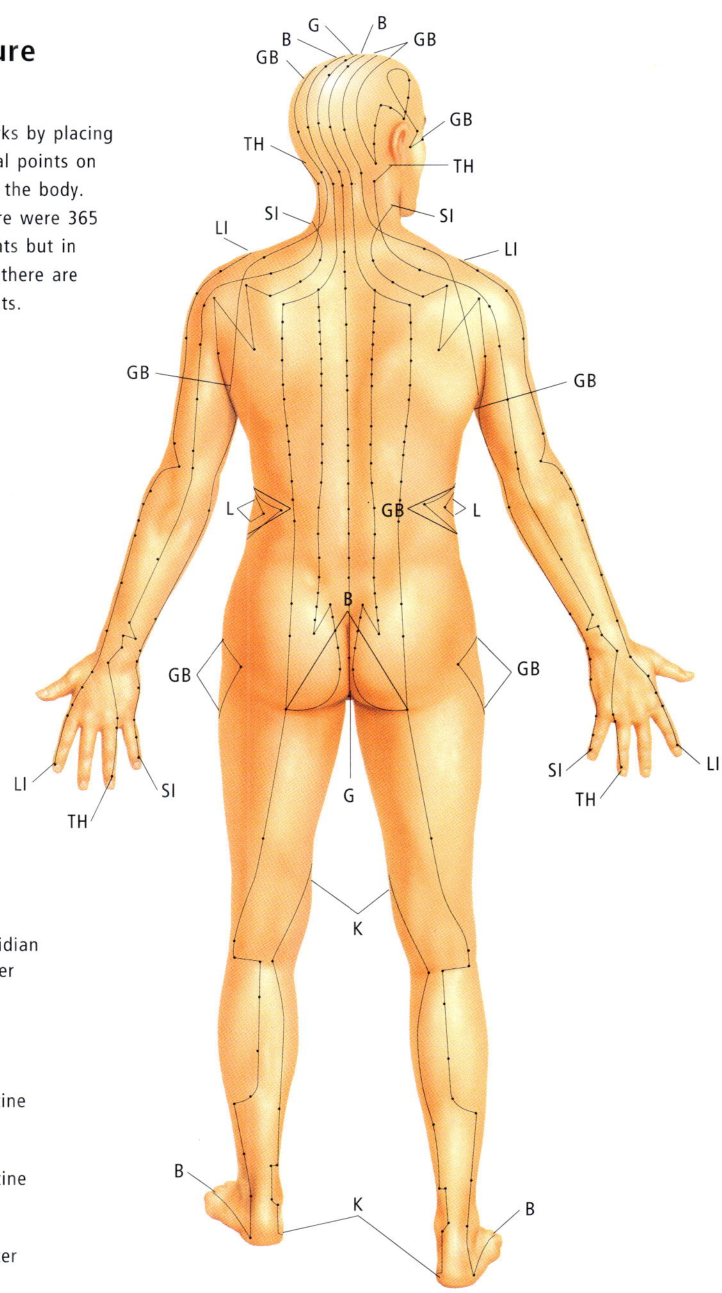

Back view

Key:
B—Bladder
C—Central Meridian
GB—Gall Bladder
G—Governor
H—Heart
K—Kidney
LU—Lung
LI—Large Intestine
L—Liver
P—Pericardium
SI—Small Intestine
SP—Spleen
S—Stomach
TH—Triple Heater

A

in each wrist, to measure the flow of *ch'i* through the organs. Diagnosis aims to understand the imbalances in the body which underlie the illness. This understanding forms the basis of an individualized treatment for the patient which goes beyond mere symptom relief.

Treatment

In the most common form of acupuncture treatment, the surface of the skin is pierced by very fine stainless steel needles on specific points. The depth to which the needle is inserted varies according to both the patient and the point used. The needles are left in for varying lengths of time up to about 45 minutes. The acupuncturist may briefly manipulate the needles with slight touches during this time. The number of needles used varies considerably, depending on the acupuncturist's technique and the patient's condition. Acupuncture treatment usually takes place at regular intervals over a few months, depending on the condition that is being treated.

Acupuncture should not be a painful procedure, as long as it is done with precision and expertise. Usually there is no more than an awareness of a pinprick when the needle is first inserted. This can be followed by a tingling sensation, a sensation of dull heaviness around the needle, or a warm spreading feeling. Often in the course of the session the patient becomes very relaxed.

Modern developments

There have been several modern developments in acupuncture treatment.

Ear acupuncture is a procedure in which needles are applied to points on the outer ear. Studs (small stainless steel plugs) are also inserted over the points and left in for some days. In the West, ear acupuncture has been used in drug and alcohol detoxification programs to help relieve anxiety.

In electro-acupuncture, electrical stimulators delivering small regular pulses are attached to the needles. The stronger stimulation of the needles means that fewer needles than normal are required.

Laser acupuncture utilizes laser-light emitted from a hand-held wand to stimulate the acupuncture points.

Uses of acupuncture

Acupuncture treatment based on the principles of traditional Chinese medicine is said to have a wide application, including boosting the immune function, normalizing circulation, assisting the female reproductive system, relieving headaches, migraines and musculoskeletal pain, and treating respiratory and digestive disorders. In China it is also used in conjunction with, or as a substitute for, surgical anesthesia.

ACUTE RESPIRATORY DISTRESS SYNDROME

Acute respiratory distress syndrome (ARDS), sometimes called adult respiratory distress syndrome, is a name given to several conditions in which fluid leaks out of the blood vessels and into the alveoli of the lung, causing pulmonary edema, respiratory failure, and in some cases death. The syndrome, also known as pump lung, stiff lung or white lung, may be caused by a number of conditions, including shock, fluid overload, narcotic overdose, disseminated intravascular coagulation and massive trauma or burns.

Clinical signs include breathlessness, rapid heartbeat, cyanosis (a bluish discoloration) and hypoxia (lack of oxygen). A lung x-ray shows evidence of interstitial and alveolar edema.

The condition is treated with mechanical ventilation. Diuretics such as frusemide may be used to decrease the amount of fluid in the lung, and antibiotics may be needed to combat lung infection. If the underlying condition is treatable the prognosis is good.

SEE ALSO *Blood vessels, Cyanosis, Lung, Pulmonary edema*

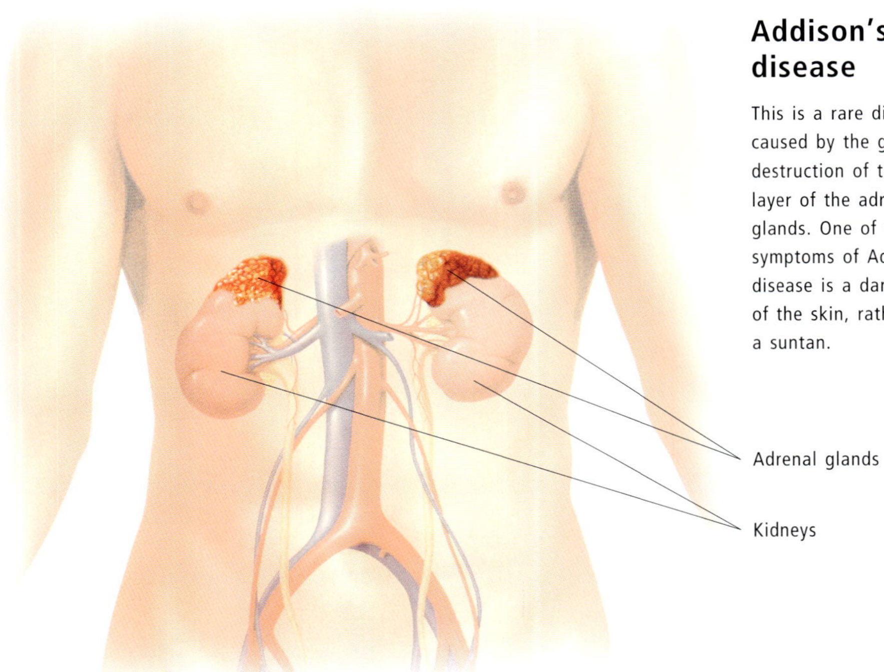

Addison's disease

This is a rare disease caused by the gradual destruction of the outer layer of the adrenal glands. One of the symptoms of Addison's disease is a darkening of the skin, rather like a suntan.

ADDISON'S DISEASE

This rare disease mainly affects people between 30 and 50 years of age. It is caused by the gradual destruction of parts of the adrenal glands. An adrenal gland is situated on the top of each kidney. The glands produce steroids such as hydrocortisone (cortisol) which are vital to the body's metabolism. In Addison's disease, the adrenal cortex, or outer layer, is destroyed and the adrenal glands can't produce enough hydrocortisone for the body's needs.

The usual cause of the destruction is an autoimmune process in which the body destroys its own cells. Diagnosis is made after a blood test shows low hydrocortisone levels.

The early symptoms are loss of appetite and weight, and a feeling of increased tiredness and weakness. There may be abdominal symptoms, such as diarrhea or constipation, and mild indigestion with nausea and vomiting. Usually the skin becomes darker. If untreated, the condition leads to acute adrenal failure and coma, requiring emergency treatment in hospital.

The treatment of Addison's disease is replacement hydrocortisone hormones in the form of tablets which need to be taken daily and continued for life. Affected people who take their tablets regularly will lead a normal, healthy life.

SEE ALSO *Adrenal glands*

ADDUCTION AND ABDUCTION

Abduction is a movement in a direction away from the center line of the body. For example, if you are standing and then lift your right leg off the floor to the right side, you are abducting it.

Adduction is the movement in the opposite direction, back towards the center line of the body. For example, if you return your leg to the original standing position so that the foot once again rests on the floor, you are adducting it.

With the fingers, the midline of the middle digit serves as the reference point, with the palms facing forward; abduction is defined as movement away from this point and adduction movement towards it. In the case of the toes, the midline of the second toe represents the point of reference.

Some muscles in the body are named after their ability to abduct or adduct limbs or other parts of the body. For example, abductor pollicis longus is the long muscle that abducts the thumb.

SEE ALSO *Muscle, Muscular system*

ADENOIDS

The adenoids are two glandular swellings at the back of the throat, above the tonsils, usually present in children before the onset of adolescence. Composed of lymphatic tissue, the adenoids are thought to assist the body in fighting throat infections. They are one of the first barriers against microscopic invaders entering the body via the nose and mouth.

Enlargement

Normally, adenoids grow slowly in size from the age of three until the age of five, when they shrink again, disappearing around puberty. But in some children who suffer repeated throat infections, they keep growing, becoming swollen and painful. The tonsils often also become enlarged. Eventually the adenoids may block the space between the nasal passages and the throat. Inflammation of the mucous membrane of the nose (rhinitis) and of the air sinuses behind the nose (sinusitis) may follow.

The adenoids can also block the opening of the narrow eustachian tube that connects the middle ear to the throat. When this happens, bacteria grow inside the middle ear and infection (otitis media) can develop. Repeated infections in the ear can turn into a chronic (long-term) condition known as "glue ear" and can cause deafness.

A child with enlarged adenoids tends to breathe through the mouth, snores at night, and speaks with a nasal-sounding voice. The child suffers repeated blocked or runny nose, a cough (especially at night) and painful ear infections. The child may do poorly at school or show other signs of deafness.

The diagnosis is made by a pediatrician or primary care physician, who will examine the back of the child's throat, using a mirror with a light attached. Hearing should be tested and an x-ray of the sinuses may be required. Usually the adenoids themselves don't need to be treated, as they decrease in size around puberty. Any infections that arise must be treated with antibiotics.

If infections are very frequent or persist in spite of antibiotic treatment, then an operation to remove the adenoids may be necessary. This procedure is called an adenoidectomy and is performed by an ear, nose and throat or pediatric surgeon in hospital, under general anesthetic. Removal of the tonsils (tonsillectomy) is often performed at the same time. The child is in hospital for about three days and usually recovers rapidly.

SEE ALSO *Otitis media, Rhinitis, Sinusitis, Tonsils*

ADENOMA

An adenoma is a benign tumor of glandular tissue. Adenomas can occur in specialized glandular tissues such as the thyroid, pancreas or pituitary, or in organs and tissues that contain glandular tissue. They are common in the breast, ovaries and uterus, where glandular tissues are stimulated by hormones throughout a woman's reproductive life, and can also occur in the colon.

As long as it remains benign, an adenoma poses no problems and needs no treatment. Occasionally it may press on surrounding structures and cause pain or other symptoms. If this happens, or if it becomes unsightly, it may need to be removed by a surgeon under local or general anesthetic. In some cases an adenoma can become cancerous. It is then known as an adenocarcinoma, and surgical removal is advised.

Adenomas of endocrine glands (those which produce hormones, such as the pituitary gland, thyroid gland, adrenal glands and pancreas) can cause excessive hormone

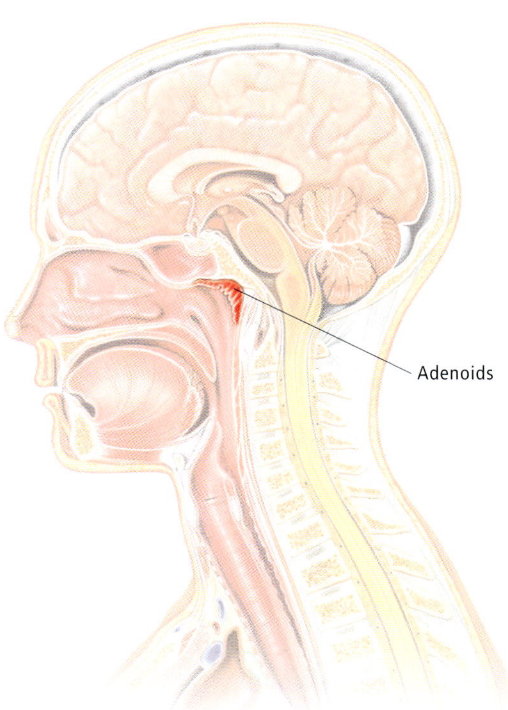

Adenoids

The adenoids are glands children have at the back of the throat, and which tend to disappear at puberty. It is thought they fight throat infections, but sometimes they can swell, which can lead to infection and difficulty with swallowing, breathing and hearing.

Adenoma

An adenoma is a benign (mild) tumor that can grow in the lining of the colon (as in this picture) or in other glandular tissue, such as the thyroid, pancreas or pituitary. In a woman, they can occur in the breast, ovaries or uterus throughout her reproductive life.

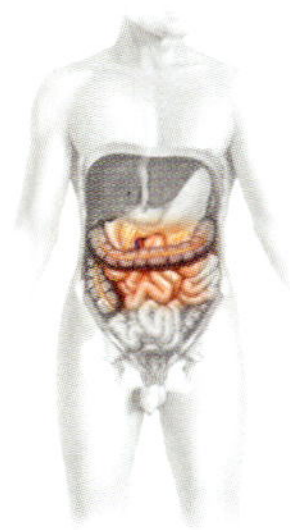

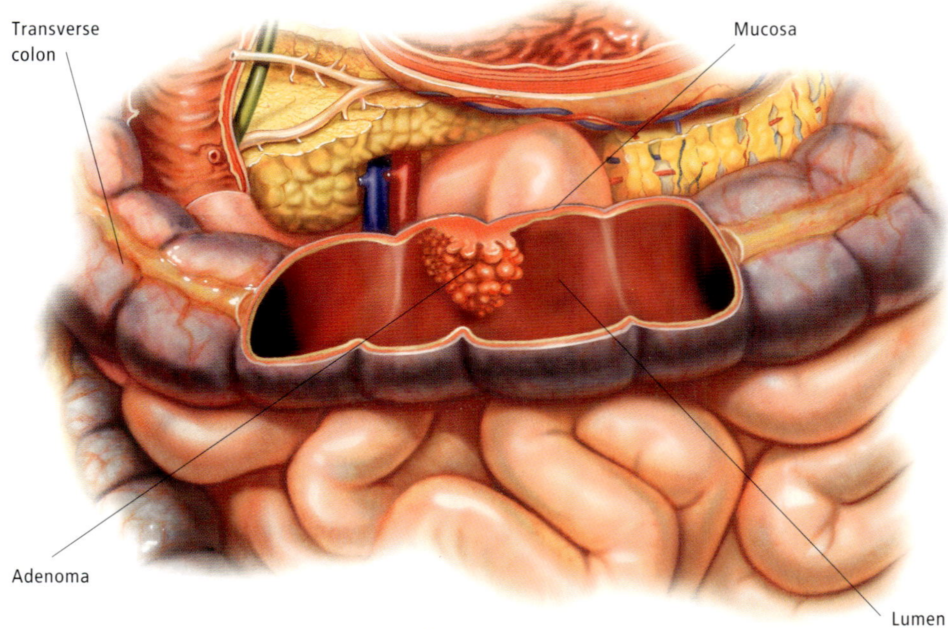

production, leading to disease. Pituitary adenomas, for example, can result in acromegaly or Cushing's syndrome. If two or more different endocrine glands are involved, the condition is called adenomatosis.

SEE ALSO *Acromegaly, Cushing's syndrome, Endocrine glands*

ADENOVIRUS

Adenoviruses are a group of DNA viruses that mainly cause diseases of the upper respiratory tract. They most commonly affect infants and children, particularly between autumn and spring, when they cause an acute upper respiratory tract infection, with sore throat, fever and swollen lymph glands in the neck, sometimes with bronchiolitis and pneumonia. They may also cause a condition called pharyngoconjunctivitis (sore throat and fever with inflammation of the conjunctiva) often seen in children on summer camps. Adenoviruses can cause an acute diarrheal illness in children, and in immunosuppressed people, such as those with AIDS, may cause severe pneumonia.

There are no effective treatments for adenoviruses. However the course of the infection is usually mild and the child makes a good recovery. Vaccines for some adenoviruses have been developed but their use is currently limited.

SEE ALSO *Conjunctivitis, DNA, Pneumonia, Viruses*

ADHESIONS

Adhesions are thin bands of scar tissue that form in a body cavity after an operation or a severe infection. They occur most commonly in the abdomen. Though adhesions are painless, they may restrict movement and function of surrounding organs. For example, the intestines may become pinched or entangled by them. When this happens, the normal movement of food material through the intestines may be prevented—abdominal obstruction, vomiting, abdominal swelling and pain can occur. If untreated a bowel obstruction can lead to death.

Treatment is by surgery. While the patient is under general anesthetic, the surgeon opens the abdomen, locates the adhesion(s) and cuts them, releasing the trapped bowel. Unfortunately they have a tendency to grow back after the operation. Some sufferers undergo multiple operations.

ADOLESCENCE

The period between childhood and adulthood, adolescence roughly corresponds to the teenage years. It coincides with and overlaps with puberty, when the secondary sexual characteristics appear, marking the onset of physical and sexual maturity. Adolescence begins with the onset of puberty and lasts until about 18 years of age.

Changes in personality

Adolescence is a time of great change, both for the individual and the family. Adolescents must control and direct sexual drives, begin an occupation and career orientation, develop a mature set of values with responsible self-direction, and learn to modify behavior in response to expectations from an adult world. And they must still rely on adults for emotional and financial support. It can be a confusing and disorienting time.

Particularly if the bonding in childhood has been poor, adolescents may rebel against parental standards and expectations. They frequently adopt outrageous modes of dress and behavior. They may not readily be able to control aggressive drives, which can end up in outbursts of temper or antisocial behavior. An adolescent may take persons outside the family as role models—often sports stars or pop stars. It could be argued that there is greater chance of psychological and behavioral problems if an adolescent comes from a disturbed or deprived home environment, but even in a relatively stable home environment most adolescents go through a stage of rebellion.

Physical and sexual changes

Adolescents must come to terms with changing body shape and self image. Between the ages of 12 and 18, muscle mass, strength, fat distribution and secondary sexual characteristics develop rapidly. In a girl, breasts develop and menstruation begins between 11 and 14, pubic hair from 10 to 14, and by 16 menstruation is usually occurring regularly. In boys, the testes and penis begin to enlarge from around the age of 12, body hair develops from around 13, and from 14 to 15 the voice deepens.

Accompanying these physical changes is anxiety about sexual attraction, and preoccupation with physical appearance, especially skin, hair and weight. Conditions such as acne and eating disorders are more prevalent in adolescence than at any other time of life.

Sexual experimentation inevitably takes place during adolescence. Many adolescents question their own gender; homosexual feelings are normal in this period, though they often do not last. Masturbation usually begins during this time.

If sexual intercourse takes place in adolescence, it tends to occur later rather than earlier. There are also the risks of sexually transmitted diseases and unwanted pregnancy. These can be avoided if the adolescent has access to helpful information, which can be provided by parents or carers only if the communication lines are open and the relationship is built on mutual trust.

Experimentation

The desire to experiment, and peer group pressure, among other factors, can lead to adolescents using drugs and alcohol for the first time. The use of "soft" drugs—cannabis, alcohol and tobacco—is common. Drugs and alcohol may also be a means to relieve anxiety and depression. A factor in managing drug and alcohol use is to make sure the adolescent fully understands the health problems and risks associated with drug and alcohol consumption. Parents can help by not smoking, and drinking in moderation.

Managing adolescence

Adolescents are often referred to doctors and psychologists because parents or teachers are worried about their behavior. But only a small percentage need psychiatric treatment. However, problems should be taken seriously and never dismissed.

Good communication remains the key to managing adolescence. It can encourage self-confidence and responsibility and so prepare an adolescent to cope with life. This may take some flexibility on the part of parents. Presenting a united front, parents should emphasize those issues which affect the adolescent's health and safety. Rules such as informing parents of their whereabouts, never driving a motor vehicle after drinking alcohol and so on may be considered important, whereas other issues such as dress may not be so important.

After the age of about 18, having left school, joined the workforce or gone to higher education, young people are more willing to compromise and accept advice, and tend to become more constructive and sensitive in dealings with others.

SEE ALSO *Acne, Eating disorders, Puberty*

Adolescence

Change, both physical and emotional, is the characteristic feature of adolescence, a period that begins with puberty and continues through the teenage years.

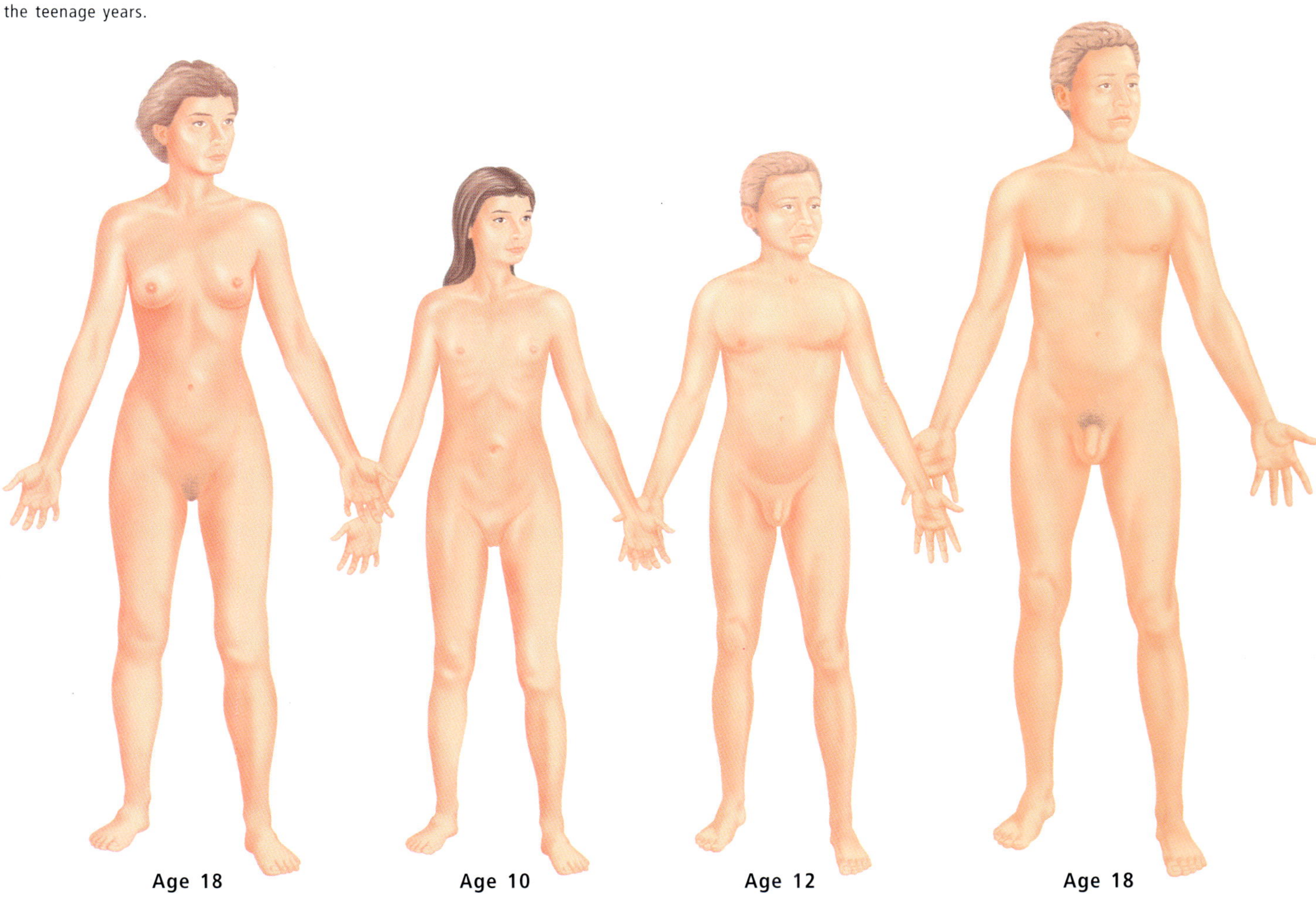

A

ADRENAL GLANDS

The two adrenal (or suprarenal) glands lie one on top of each kidney at the back of the abdomen. Each adrenal gland is 1–2 inches (3–5 centimeters) long, somewhat triangular in shape and yellowish brown in color. Each gland has two parts, an outer region, the adrenal cortex, and a core, the medulla. Both produce and secrete hormones but differ in structure, function and development.

Hormones

Hormones are chemicals produced by certain glands (called endocrine glands, which include the adrenals) and secreted into the tissues and blood vessels. They act by changing the activity of specific cells, which can be localized or widespread, and may be some distance from the endocrine gland. The adrenal glands release several hormones from both the cortex and medulla.

The adrenal cortical (cortex) hormones are produced from cholesterol and are called steroids. They are divided into glucocorticoids such as cortisol, mineralocorticoids such as aldosterone, and androgens, which are similar to sex hormones.

Glucocorticoids are involved in the metabolism of glucose and the response of the body to injury. One of the effects of glucocorticoids is to reduce the body's immune response. This has led to their use in treating tissue rejection after organ transplants, and in reducing allergic responses.

Aldosterone is the most important of the mineralocorticoids. It increases the retention of sodium in the kidneys and other tissues such as the sweat and salivary glands; it also causes secretion of potassium. The effect of aldosterone on sodium retention is important in controlling blood volume. If there is a decrease in blood flow or blood volume in the kidney, renin is released from the kidney and acts on a second hormone, angiotensin, to increase aldosterone levels. This helps conserve sodium and hence to restore blood volume.

Androgens contribute to the development of male sexual characteristics. Excess production in women causes masculinization.

The amount of glucocorticoids and androgens secreted by the adrenal glands is controlled by adrenocorticotropic hormone (ACTH). This is a hormone secreted by the front (anterior) lobe of the pituitary (the hypophysis). ACTH then travels via the bloodstream to the adrenal gland to stimulate the release of the glucocorticoids and sex steroids from the adrenal cortex. ACTH secretion is regulated by the hypothalamus, which secretes corticotrophin-releasing hormone (CRH), which stimulates ACTH secretion. Cortisol acts to control both CRH and ACTH, by a mechanism known as a negative feedback loop, in which an increase in cortisol leads to a decrease in CRH and ACTH and vice versa.

The adrenal medulla is derived from neural (nerve) tissue and is concerned with production and secretion of epinephrine (adrenaline) and norepinephrine (noradrenaline). These hormones can cause increased heart rate, widening of the airways, and breakdown of glycogen to glucose for energy. All of these make the body more equipped to handle emergency situations.

Adrenal disorders

If the levels of the hormones produced by the adrenal glands fall below or increase to above normal, various disorders will result.

Adrenal hyperplasia

Adrenal hyperplasia is an enlargement of the adrenal gland and affects the outer region, the cortex. It can be caused by overproduction of ACTH from the pituitary, such as can occur with pituitary tumors. The excess ACTH leads to excess stimulation of the adrenals, with enlargement (hyperplasia) and excess production of cortisol and androgens. The hyperplasia may also be caused by a defect in cortisol production. High ACTH leads to masculinization in women, including excess facial hair, deepening of the voice and loss of menstrual periods. If the cortisol defect is present in a fetus, the baby can be born with congenital adrenal hyperplasia (this is the condition known as adrenogenital syndrome).

Addison's disease

Addison's disease is caused by insufficient adrenal cortical hormones. Symptoms include tiredness, weakness, loss of appetite and vomiting, and a brownish pigmentation of the skin. Treatment involves lifelong steroid therapy.

Cushing's syndrome

Cushing's syndrome occurs when there is an excess, or prolonged use, of cortisol. Symptoms of Cushing's syndrome include weight gain, muscle weakness, high blood pressure, a "moon" face and facial hair. Diagnosis is based on symptoms, with blood and urine tests to confirm increased cortisol levels and magnetic resonance imaging (MRI) or CAT scan to reveal any tumors.

Pheochromocytoma

Pheochromocytoma is a tumor involving the medulla of the adrenal gland or associated tissues. It causes the excess production of epinephrine (adrenaline) and norepinephrine (noradrenaline). These tumors are most common in young and mid-adult life and are generally not malignant. Symptoms include severe headache, rapid heart rate and palpitations, sweating, abdominal pain, nervousness, irritability, increased appetite and loss of weight. Patients generally have high blood pressure, and diagnosis is based on raised hormone levels in the blood or urine. Treatment can be by medication to block the hormones, or may involve removal of the tumor.

SEE ALSO *Addison's disease, Androgens, Cushing's syndrome, Endocrine glands, Hormones, Pituitary gland*

ADRENOGENITAL SYNDROME

Adrenogenital syndromes are an inherited group of disorders, present from birth, in which there are enzyme deficiencies. Depending on which enzyme is reduced, the effects can be masculinization of women, or more rarely feminization of men, or early sexual development of children. In some severe forms, metabolic changes due to the lack of a hormone called aldosterone can cause vomiting, dehydration, electrolyte changes and cardiac arrhythmias in the newborn, which can lead to death if untreated.

These conditions are caused by a lack of an enzyme needed by the adrenal gland to make the steroid cortisol. The pituitary gland secretes a hormone called adrenocorticotropic hormone (ACTH) that stimulates the adrenal gland, causing the overproduction of male hormones (androgens) but without causing any increase in cortisol. This causes females to be born with an enlarged clitoris and male-like genitalia, though the ovaries, uterus and fallopian tubes are normal. As a girl grows, masculine features (deepening of voice, facial hair) appear, and she fails to menstruate at puberty.

No obvious abnormality is present in the male newborn, but secondary sexual characteristics such as deepening of the voice, enlargement of the penis and appearance of pubic hair appear well before puberty. At puberty, the testes are small.

The condition can be diagnosed by blood and urine tests which show abnormally low levels of cortisol and aldosterone, and abnormally high levels of androgens. Treatment involves replacement therapy with steroid hormones. Medication must be given daily and continued for life. Reconstructive surgery is usually performed in the first few years of life in girls with masculine external genitalia. Prospective parents with a family history of adrenogenital syndrome should have genetic counseling.

SEE ALSO *Adrenal glands, Androgens, Congenital abnormalities, Feminization, Genetic counseling, Hormones, Pituitary gland, Steroids, Virilization*

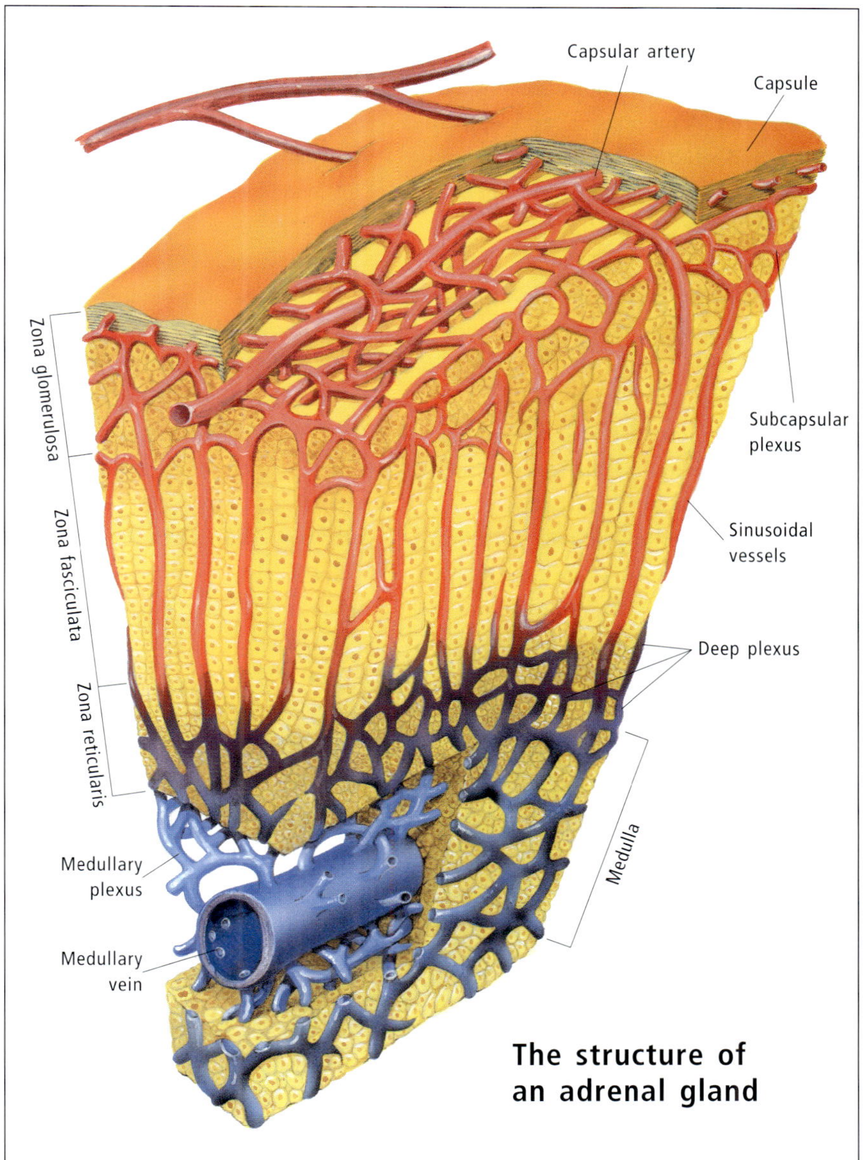

The structure of an adrenal gland

Adrenal glands

These tiny glands are just as essential to our health as the much larger organs all around them. They secrete steroids, which deal with glucose, help the body respond to injuries, keep the volume of blood at the right level, and, in males, contribute to the development of sexual characteristics.

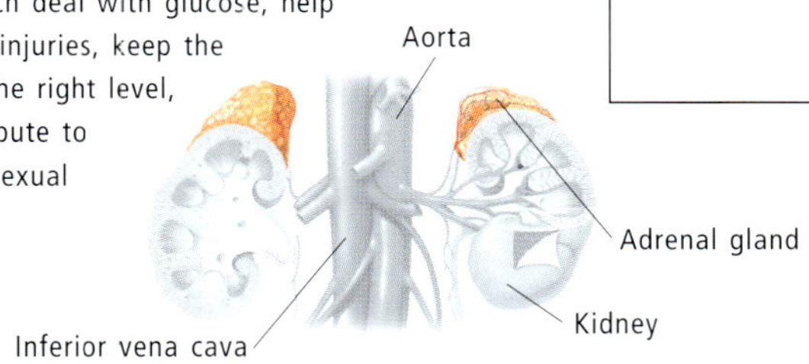

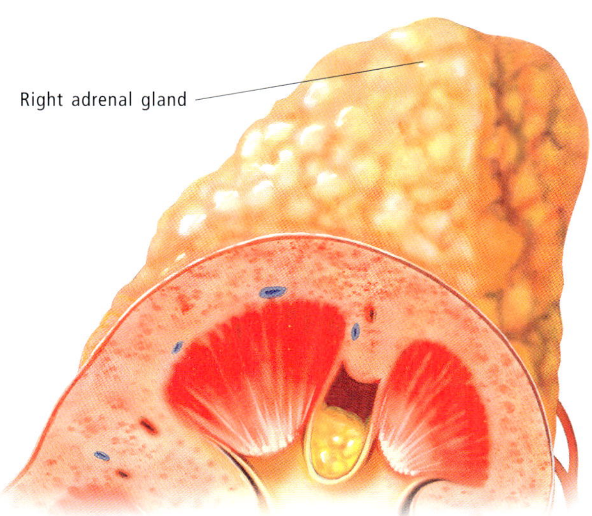

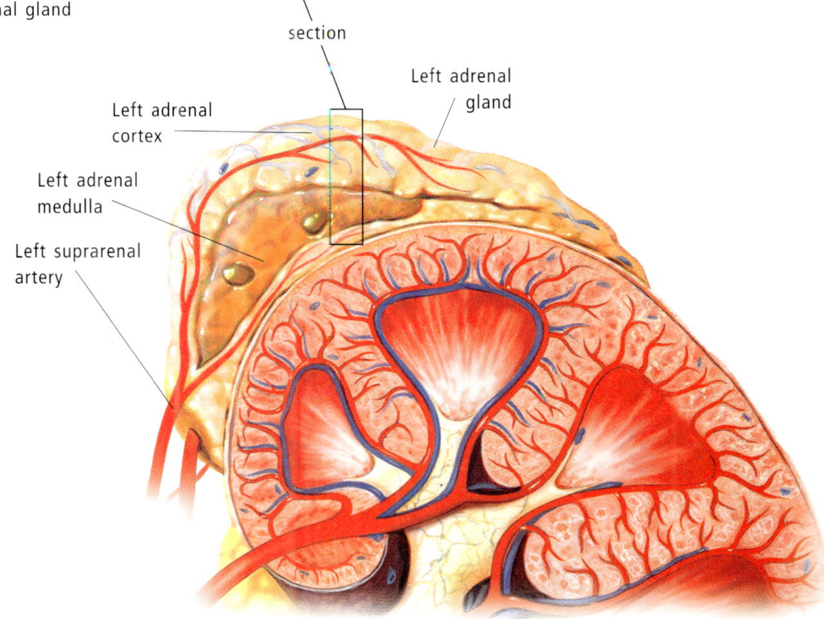

AGEING

A human develops through the stages of infancy, childhood and adolescence to become an adult. After physical development peaks by mid-adulthood, the ageing process begins and continues until death. There is no fixed or universal time frame, but the periods in the human life span are characterized by changes in outward structure and in the function of body systems.

Childhood

Childhood begins after the first year of infancy and ends with the changes of puberty. A child is not an adult in miniature. A baby's head at birth makes up about a quarter of the baby's total length; however the eyes are relatively large because they have almost reached their adult size. Fat cells increase in both size and number in the first two years of life, then change very little after that, except in severely obese children.

Children's bones of the arms and legs still have cartilage at the ends. Growth of the cartilage plates causes bone to lengthen. During the first 12 years of life, ossification (bone-forming) centers appear in the heads of long bones (epiphyses) and bone gradually replaces the cartilage.

The first set of teeth appears in the first two years, then from the sixth year they are shed and replaced by permanent teeth.

X-rays of the ossification centers and the appearance of teeth are used to assess age and physical maturity. The *Factory Act* in England, which was passed in the early nineteenth century with the aim of preventing exploitation of young children, only allowed children with second molar teeth to work in factories.

The brain grows rapidly in childhood: from half the adult size at two years of age to about 90 percent of adult size at age six. By a process called myelination, nerve fibers are progressively coated in myelin, a substance that improves conduction of nerve signals. The cortex of the brain is almost fully myelinated by age seven, when children can use language effectively and can think logically about concrete things that they experience in everyday life.

Adolescence

Adolescence is the stage characterized by structural, physiological and psychological changes that occur when a boy or girl undergoes puberty. The most noticeable structural change is the growth spurt that begins at about the age of 10 or 11 years in girls and about two years later in boys. Height typically increases by 3 inches (8 centimeters) or more each year, and the body proportion becomes more like an adult's. The growth spurt of muscles results in a dramatic increase in physical strength and endurance.

The appearance of pubic hair is followed by underarm hair one to two years later, and facial hair a year after that. However, growth of fat under the skin layer slows down and the lymphatic system, especially the thymus, even regresses. The sebaceous and sweat glands of the skin are more active, making acne a common problem of puberty.

The key event of puberty is the maturation of the reproductive system. In girls, the onset of menstruation (menarche) usually occurs somewhere between 11 and 14 years of age. The uterus develops its adult shape

How women grow and age

At about 10 years of age, girls have a growth spurt, and pubic hair and underarm hair start to grow a year or two later. Soon the reproductive system develops, with the first period arriving around the age of 13. By 18 the body is approaching maturity and from there it continues to change, but not grow. From 35 the production of eggs and sex hormones decreases, culminating in menopause. Without the hormonal effects, the breasts and skin lose firmness, fat distribution changes, bones thin and height decreases.

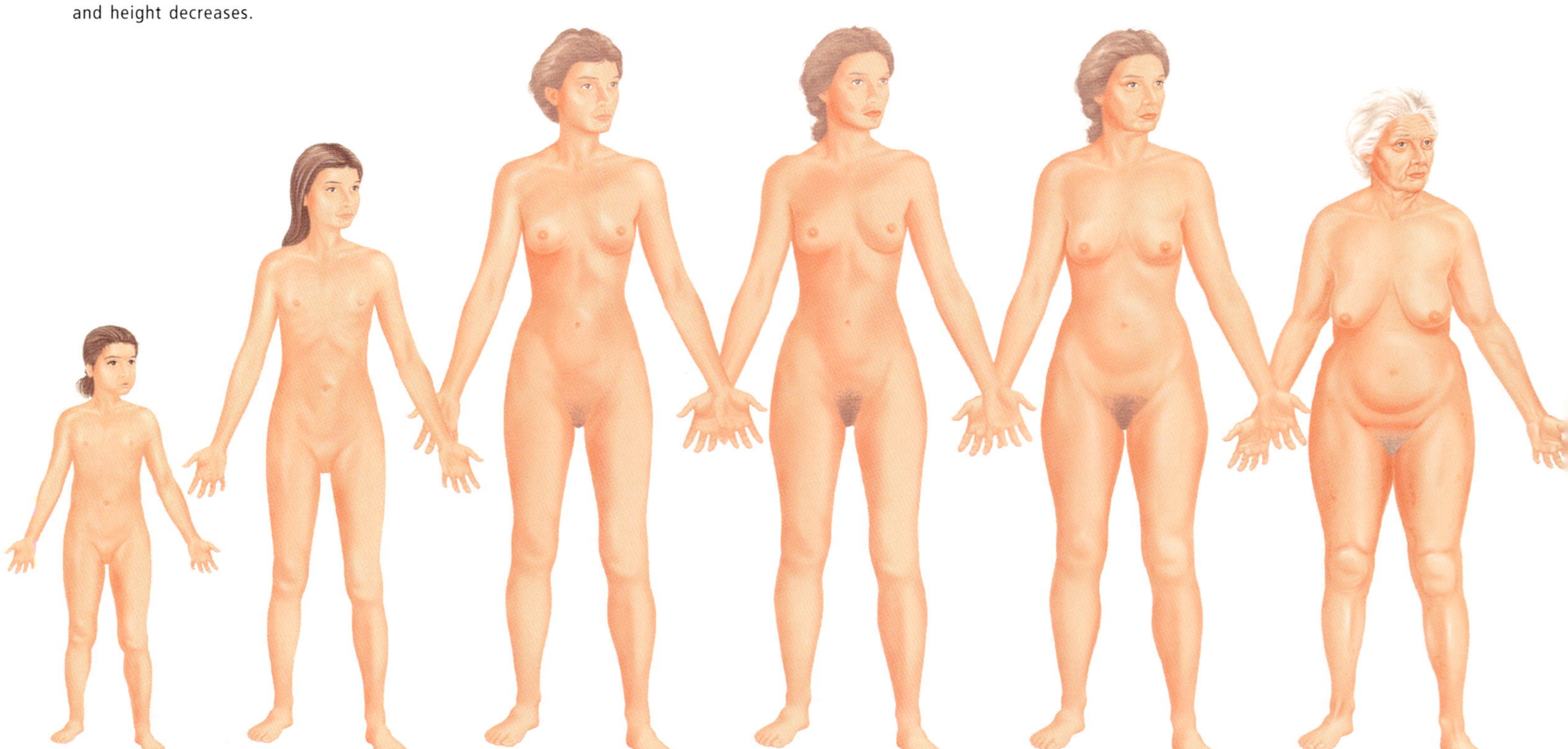

Age 5 | Age 10 | Age 18 | Age 30 | Age 45 | Age 70

and the first period occurs. Increased secretion of sex hormones by the ovaries leads to development of breasts and female pattern of pubic hair. The external genitalia also mature, with a thickening of the fat pad over the pubic bone and enlargement of the labia majora and clitoris.

In boys, the testes grow rapidly and begin to secrete testosterone and produce sperm. The first ejaculation usually occurs around age 14 or 15 but may not contain sperm. Testosterone is responsible for secondary sex characteristics such as facial and pubic hair. The scrotum grows, and its skin becomes darker and wrinkled. The penis increases in length and girth, and develops a glans at its tip. Compared to girls, boys have broader shoulders, narrower hips and smaller buttocks; also the cartilage of the larynx (voice box) is more prominent (making what is known as the "Adam's apple") and the voice is deeper as the vocal cords are longer. The voice begins to break at about age 14 and this process is complete after about a year.

Puberty also brings about cognitive changes. Adolescents progress beyond the concrete thinking of childhood to develop more abstract and conceptual thinking. But they can often see only their own point of view, and have difficulty in appreciating views of others. This transition from childhood to adulthood is a critical time and carries with it risks of emotional problems, as adolescents have to develop a personal identity, of which sexual identity is an important part.

Adulthood and senescence

There is no definite age for the beginning of adulthood, although in most Western societies it is legally set at 18 or 21 years of age. Adulthood can be understood as the stage in which the individual has reached full anatomical, physiological and sexual maturity.

The bones have ceased to grow because the cartilage growth plates have been entirely replaced by bone. All the body systems are now fully functioning. However, the body continues to change in response to environmental changes, and to physical as well as emotional trauma. The bones, for example, heal after fractures and are continually remodeled to adapt to pressure applied to them. The processes of adaptation and repair are vital for survival of the individual. However, adaptation and repair are not always completely successful. The genetic coding which controls them is altered by external influences such as radiation, or by errors introduced by cell division over the years. This decline in function is called the ageing process. Although old age (senescence) is said to begin at age 65, the ageing process has already begun much earlier.

The structural changes of ageing are well known. The skin becomes thin, fragile and wrinkled. On the face, the skin sags and forms bags under the eyes and a double chin. Dark "age spots" become more and more numerous. Baldness begins as hair loss exceeds replacement rate. Poor function of melanocytes (cells which produce the dark pigment melanin) causes hair to go gray. Muscle mass is reduced and muscle tone declines. Bones become more porous and weak because of loss of bone substance and minerals, especially calcium, and osteoporosis may develop. Spongy bones such as vertebrae partially collapse, reducing height.

How men grow and age

Boys' growth spurt occurs at around 13 or 14 years of age. Muscles begin to bulk up and body hair grows. The testes grow and produce sperm, and the voice deepens. As men mature the body reaches full muscular development, then starts to decline. The production of male hormones and sperm reduces. The skin and muscles become softer, fat may increase, the prostate enlarges, production of male hormones and sperm reduces, and hair loss occurs.

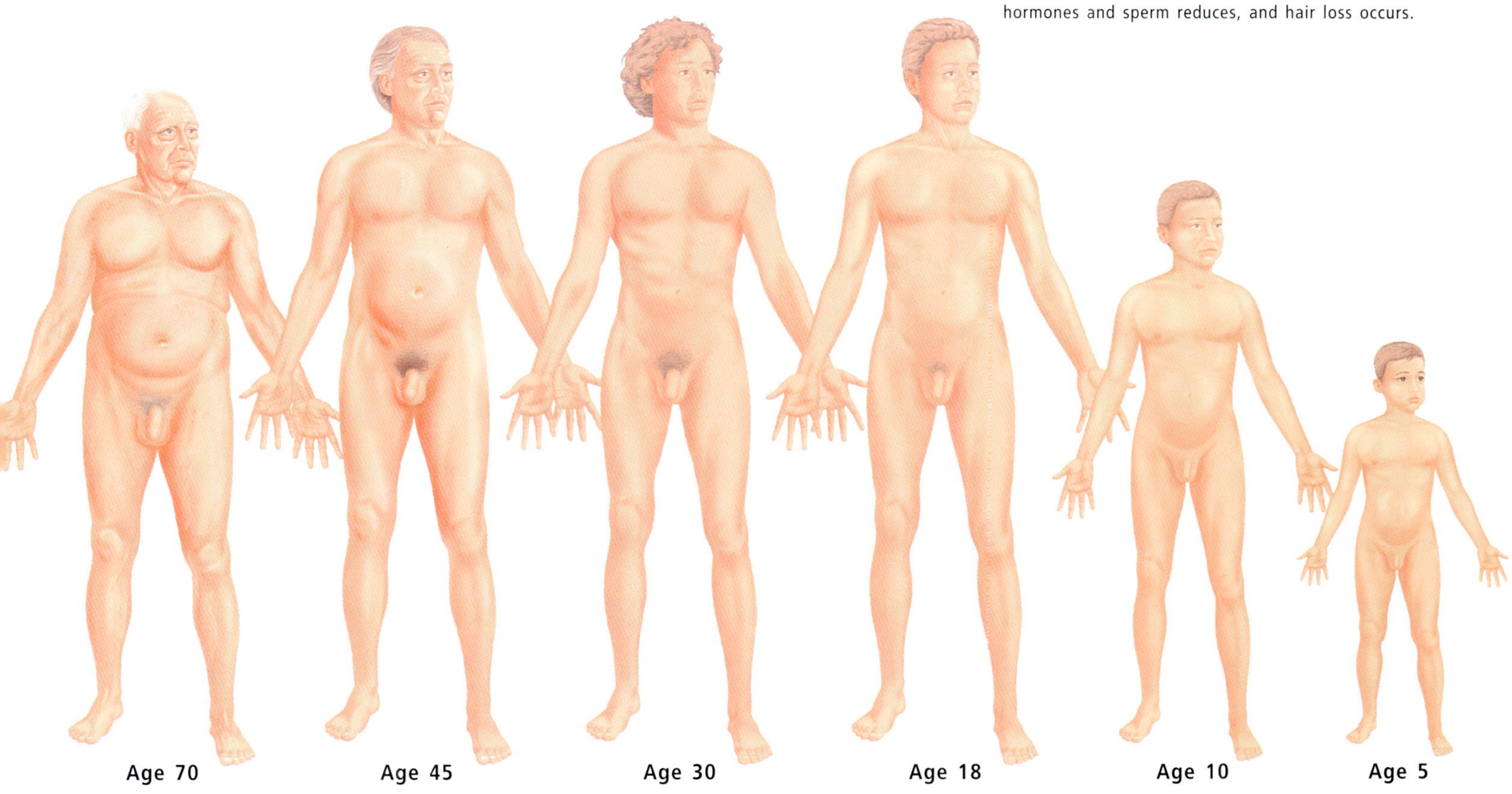

A

Hip and wrist fractures are common. Wear and tear of joints leads to osteoarthritis.

All body systems deteriorate. For many, by 50 years of age, hearing is reduced and the lens of the eye loses some elasticity, making small print difficult to read. For some the lens may also become clouded by a cataract. The immune response is reduced because of the decline in the activation of both T and B lymphocytes, which fight infection. Thus people over the age of 60 should be immunized against common infections such as influenza in winter. The arteries become thicker and less elastic, predisposing the elderly to hypertension. The heart is less efficient as a pump. The lungs begin to lose their elasticity, making breathing more laborious and oxygen exchange less efficient. Digestion becomes slightly less efficient because of reduced secretion of digestive enzymes. Absorption of some important molecules extracted from food, such as calcium and vitamin B_{12}, is impaired. Vitamin B_{12} deficiency leads to impaired nerve function and anemia.

The kidneys shrink and their filtering function declines, resulting in the build-up of waste products like urea. The bladder which collects urine from the kidney and contracts to empty its contents now does not expand and contract as effectively, resulting in more frequent trips to the bathroom. In males, the prostate, which is located under the neck of the bladder and encircles the urethra (the tube conducting the urine out from the bladder), frequently becomes enlarged, constricting the urethra.

The reproductive system undergoes dramatic changes. At the climacteric (the male equivalent of menopause), the production of testosterone and sperm in the testes are reduced. The sperm count may be low, but is still adequate in some instances to produce offspring until a very old age. Semen volume is also reduced. Erection is more difficult to obtain and to maintain, even in the absence of problems in the blood vessels of the penis. Research is progressing in this field.

In females, the production of eggs and sex hormones by the ovaries is reduced. From the mid-thirties, the risk of chromosomal abnormalities such as Down syndrome increases sharply because the eggs may be more genetically defective. The complex balance of sex hormones begins to be disturbed by the fourth or fifth decade, resulting in irregular menstruation, hot flashes and mood swings. Without the stimulation of the hormone estrogen, the breasts lose their firmness, distribution of fat in the body changes, and pubic hair becomes sparse. The external genitalia become wrinkled because of loss of pubic fat, the vagina is less elastic and its lining thins, making sexual intercourse potentially painful. Loss of the protective effects of estrogen results in a higher risk of cardiovascular diseases. Hormone replacement relieves many of these changes but, according to some authorities, may carry a small potential risk of breast cancer. Isoflavones extracted from plants such as soy beans may be a safer alternative.

As the nervous system ages, cognitive function begins to decline. The brain shows increasing atrophy with age, and loss of nerve cells is more localized in some special areas. Attention is not affected by age, but loss of neurons (nerve cells) in the hippocampus results in impaired memory function. Older people take longer to learn new information or a new skill, but can retain the knowledge for as long as younger people. The ability to form new concepts also declines with age, as does performance in intelligence tests, although this only drops significantly after 70 years of age. Dementia is also a problem in the ageing population; Alzheimer's disease and incidents causing lack of oxygen in the brain.

The cellular basis of ageing

Scientists have been studying bacteria and single human cells to find out the cellular basis of ageing, with a strong focus on proteins and genes. Proteins are important structural and functional molecules in cells. The synthesis of each protein is controlled by a gene, a segment of a DNA molecule of a chromosome. Each DNA molecule is a string of genes. Some genes control protein synthesis, some turn other genes on or off. Scientists are making progress in mapping all the genes of the human chromosomes and have formulated a number of hypotheses to explain how and why cells age.

We can think of chromosomes as the hard disk which contains all the programs that can run on a computer. A free demonstration program may have a code built into it so that it will be deactivated at the end of the 30-day trial period. The "programmed cell death" hypothesis holds that some genes will initiate cell death at the end of the cell's life span. These "suicide" genes have been isolated. Other genes have been discovered that can rescue the cell from the action of the death genes. Scientists have succeeded in using these rescue genes to extend the life span of cells.

Another hypothesis can also be explained using our computer analogy. Every now and then the computer crashes, either because of an error in reading the file from disk, or some instability of the power line. The computer can automatically search the corrupted file and repair the errors. DNA molecules can be damaged either by spontaneous changes (mutation), by environmental agents such as radiation, by accumulation of toxic waste products in the cell, or simply by errors introduced during copying of the genes. DNA can repair these damages, but when the repair is imperfect, abnormalities in DNA will accumulate and may contribute to the ageing process or lead to cancer. This is the "error accumulation" hypothesis.

One group of potentially damaging chemicals produced by cells is "free radicals". Normally oxygen molecules take up those free electrons which are products of chemical reaction in the cells, then combine with hydrogen atoms to form harmless water. When this process fails, excess electrons will join up with other molecules, forming free radicals, which can damage DNA molecules. (Fruit flies do not have enzymes which can destroy free radicals. When the genes for these enzymes were inserted into embryonic fruit flies, they could produce these enzymes and their life span was increased.) In addition to enzymes, cells also fight free radical damage with antioxidants.

Current research in cell and molecular biology has unlocked some of the secrets of ageing and even prolonged the life of some simple organisms. However, studies suggest that regular activity, a healthy diet and mental stimulation may help abate the deterioration of ageing.

SEE ALSO: *Adolescence, Childhood, DNA, Geriatric medicine, Menopause, Puberty, Reproductive systems*

AGORAPHOBIA

Agoraphobia (the word is derived from the Greek word for marketplace, *agora*) is a fear of being in open spaces or in crowded places. It can cause people to stay only within familiar surroundings, avoiding public places and gradually restricting themselves to areas closer to home. Symptoms may continue to increase in severity to the point where sufferers are unable to go out without experiencing symptoms of panic.

Associated with agoraphobia are feelings of helplessness, depression, fear of being alone, dependence on others, fear of losing control in public, and depersonalization or loss of identity. Women are more usually afflicted than men, and the disorder often has its root cause in a previous incident or a panic attack suffered in a public place. Agoraphobia may then be a way of attempting to prevent the embarrassment of that incident from recurring. When severely affected, people may be housebound for years and be quite cut off from normal relationships.

Specialist treatment is essential and is aimed at enabling the person to function normally. Prescribed medications can overcome anxiety and depression, but there is a risk that the person can become dependent on these if a cure is not achieved.

SEE ALSO *Anxiety, Panic attacks, Phobias*

AGRANULOCYTOSIS

This rare condition, occurring in one person in every 100,000, is a disorder of neutrophil production in the body's bone marrow. Neutrophils are a type of white blood cell whose purpose is to fight bacteria and other invading organisms. They are formed in the bone marrow and released into the blood to fight infection.

In agranulocytosis, production of neutrophils in the bone marrow slows or stops altogether, usually as a side effect of certain drugs. If the production of red blood cells and platelets is also affected, this is called pancytopenia. If there are not enough neutrophils circulating through the blood, the body becomes susceptible to opportunistic infections. These may range from mild illnesses, such as a sore throat or mouth ulcer, to serious and life-threatening illnesses, such as pneumonia.

The diagnosis is made by the primary care physician (general practitioner) after a physical examination and a blood test which shows a lower than normal neutrophil count. A specialist physician or hematologist will then do a bone marrow biopsy in order to confirm the diagnosis. It is generally recommended that the patient discontinue the drug that is causing the problems. The bone marrow should then recover naturally. Any infection should be treated with antibiotics. In rare cases where the bone marrow does not respond, drugs that stimulate the bone marrow may be given. The disease may recur in a mild form, but most people have no further problems.

SEE ALSO *Bone marrow biopsy, Opportunistic infections, White blood cells*

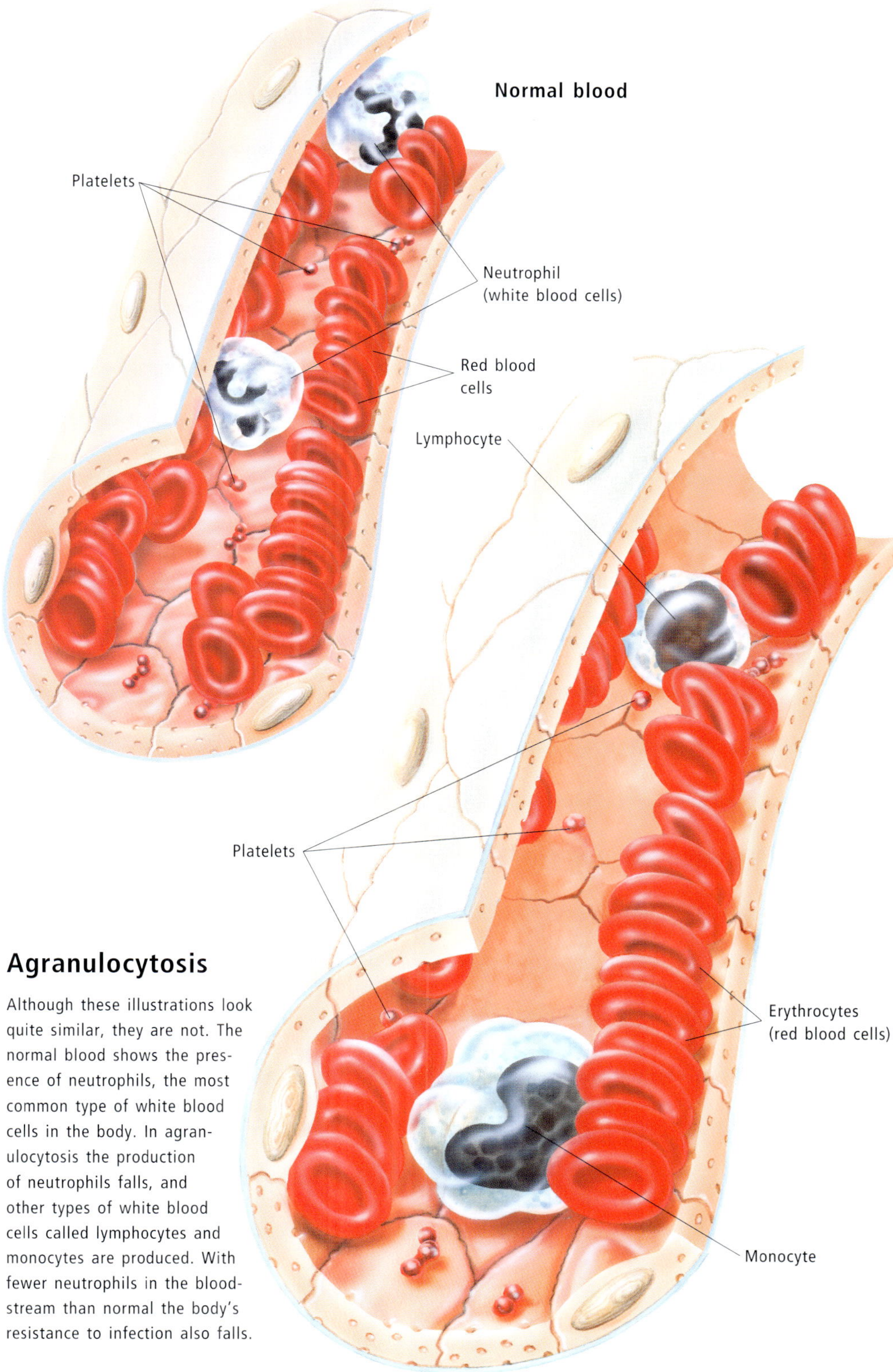

Agranulocytosis

Although these illustrations look quite similar, they are not. The normal blood shows the presence of neutrophils, the most common type of white blood cells in the body. In agranulocytosis the production of neutrophils falls, and other types of white blood cells called lymphocytes and monocytes are produced. With fewer neutrophils in the blood-stream than normal the body's resistance to infection also falls.

A

AIDS

AIDS stands for acquired immune deficiency syndrome. It is caused by the HIV (human immmunodeficiency virus). AIDS is the final and most serious stage of HIV disease. The illness is characterized by severe immune deficiency, leaving the body vulnerable to life-threatening illnesses.

The HIV attacks and destroys certain types of white blood cells called T4 lymphocytes (also known as CD4 or T helper lymphocytes), which are responsible for patrolling the body and destroying foreign invaders. Because the HIV destroys these cells, they are no longer available to fight common bacteria, yeast and viruses which normally would not cause disease. The body's lowered defenses, then, leave it susceptible to these invaders which cause opportunistic infections.

It is these infections, not the HIV, that eventually cause the death of AIDS sufferers. First recognized in the USA in 1981, the disease has grown rapidly to become one of the world's major health problems. The World Health Organization estimates there are more than 20 million cases of HIV infection worldwide and most of these are in the developing countries of Africa and Asia.

Transmission

The HIV virus is transmitted, among other ways, through sexual contact (including oral, vaginal and anal sex). It is also transmitted via blood through transfusions, needle sharing or accidental needlestick injury. It is possible for a pregnant woman to pass the virus to the fetus, and a nursing mother can infect her baby through her milk. The infection is not spread by touching and hugging, or by contact with inanimate objects.

High-risk behaviors include promiscuity, especially when involving anal intercourse, and intravenous drug use with shared needles. Others at high-risk include infants born to mothers with HIV, the sexual partners of those exhibiting high-risk behavior and people who received blood transfusions before screening for the virus was introduced (around the mid-1980s). Contrary to some popular perceptions, AIDS is not a "homosexual disease"; in Africa and other developing regions, in particular, transmission is predominantly through heterosexual contact.

Development of the illness

The initial illness resembles a mild flu, with fever, headache, fatigue, loss of appetite, swollen lymph nodes and skin rashes. The symptoms appear within two to four weeks of exposure. The illness can then lie dormant for as long as ten years. During this time there may be no symptoms at all.

Then the sufferer may develop low-grade fever, chronic tiredness and weakness, appetite loss and loss of weight, with swollen lymph nodes especially in the neck, jaw, groin and armpits. Diarrhea, malnutrition and minor infections such as oral thrush are common. This stage is sometimes known as AIDS-related complex, or ARC.

In a small percentage (between 1 and 10 percent) of those infected with HIV, the illness doesn't progress any further. But in the great majority, immunity levels eventually fall off to below critical levels and infections become more serious and life threatening. These include *Pneumocystis carinii* pneumonia, toxoplasmosis, tuberculosis and a range of viruses, including cytomegalovirus, herpes simplex virus, varicella zoster and Epstein-Barr viruses. This stage represents full-blown AIDS; people with full-blown AIDS may die within two years if not treated.

AIDS-related cancers

Lymphocytes play an important role in the body's fight against cancer. When T4 cell function is damaged, cancers may develop. Kaposi's sarcoma is the most common form of AIDS-related cancer. Lymphomas (tumors of the lymphatic system) are also frequent.

Diagnosis

HIV infection is confirmed by an HIV antibody test, which looks for HIV antibodies in the blood formed in response to infection with HIV. If the test is positive, a follow-up is always performed to confirm it. The test becomes positive within three months of exposure. Someone who has been recently exposed, yet has a negative result, should be tested again three months after exposure. Progress of the disease can be monitored by regularly measuring the T4 cell count in the blood. The lower the count, the further the disease has progressed. Serious infections are likely to develop at counts of below 200 cells per cubic millimeter.

Herpes simplex virus
Genital herpes, mouth ulcers and cold sores are caused by the herpes simplex virus which is common in AIDS patients with severely compromised immunity.

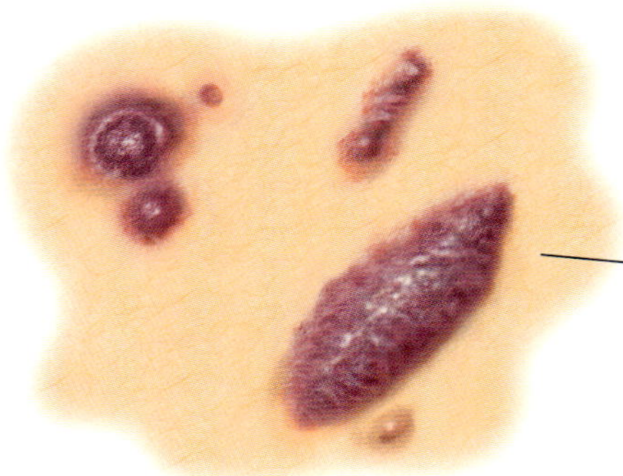

Kaposi's sarcoma
The most frequently occurring cancer in AIDS sufferers, Kaposi's sarcoma produces raised, purple-brown skin lesions. In late stage of the disease it may also affect the lungs and other internal organs.

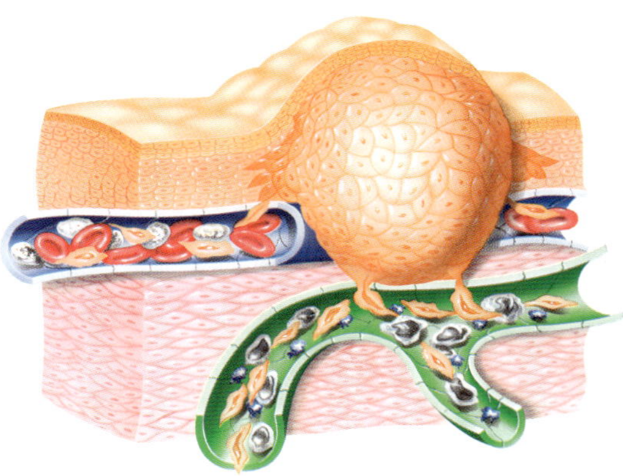

Lymphoma
Low T4 cell counts in AIDS result in increased cancer incidence. Non-Hodgkins lymphoma, which spreads through the lymphatic system, may develop.

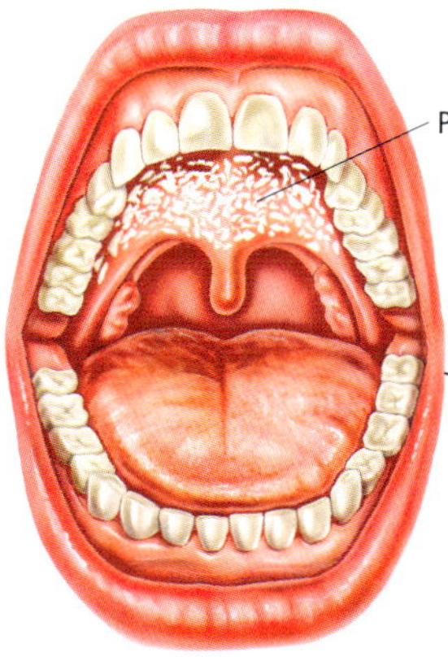

Candidiasis

Fungal infections are common in HIV infection. This picture shows flat white patches of *Candida albicans* in the soft palate of the oral cavity.

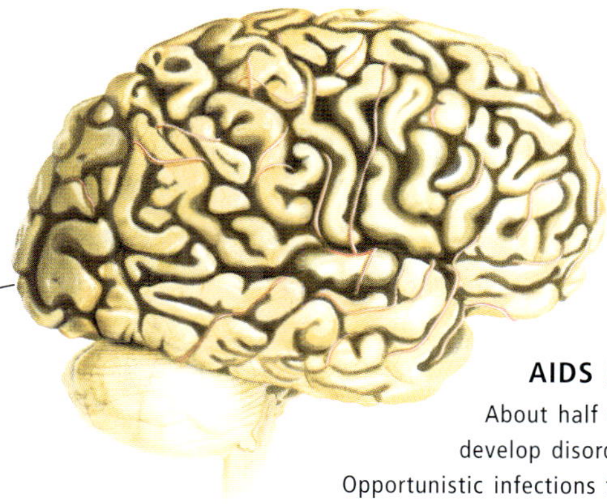

AIDS Dementia

About half of all AIDS patients develop disorders of the brain. Opportunistic infections from viruses and other organisms are common. So is dementia, a condition in which concentration and memory fail. This brain shows the atrophy (shrinking in size) that occurs in AIDS dementia.

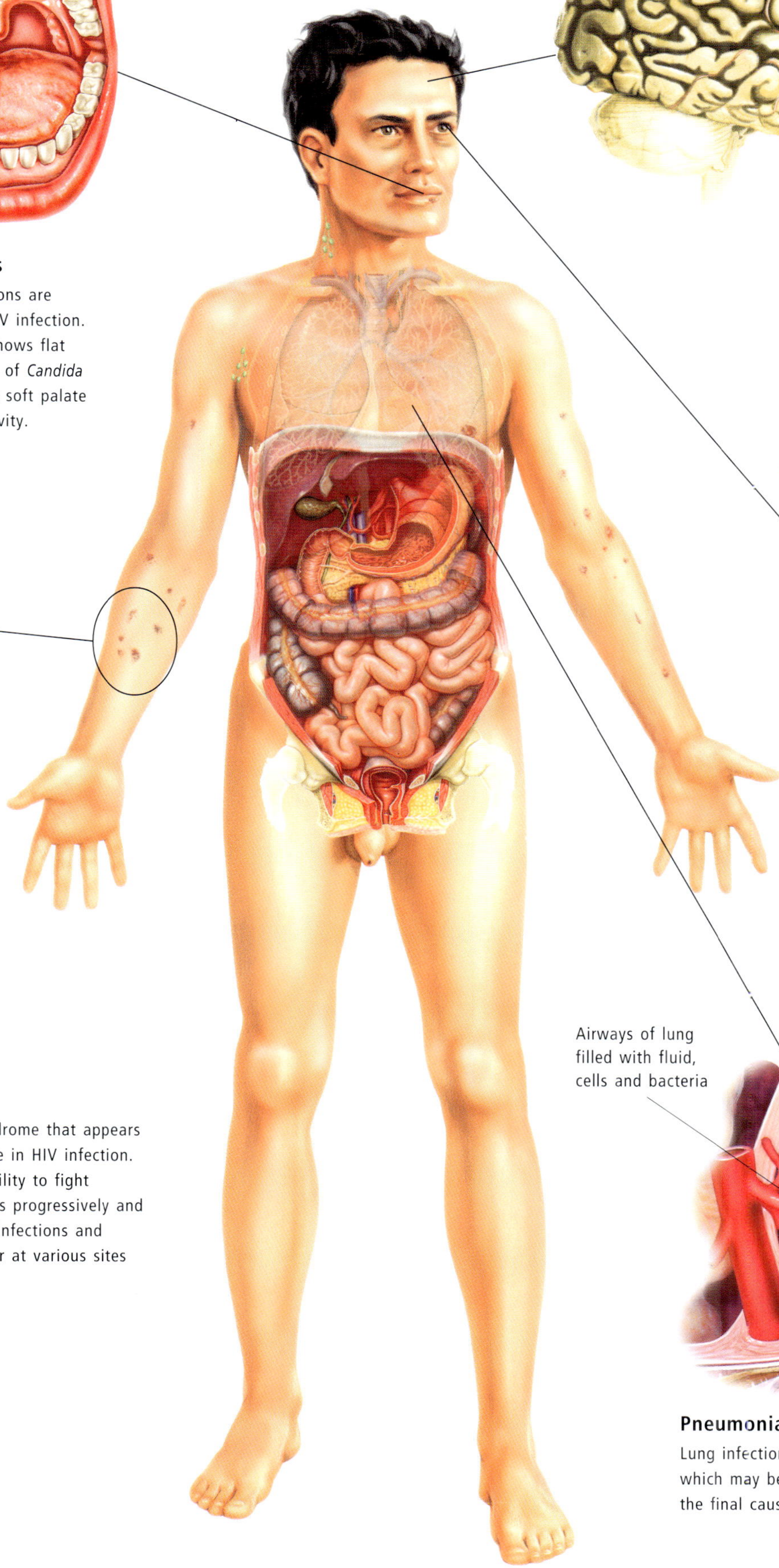

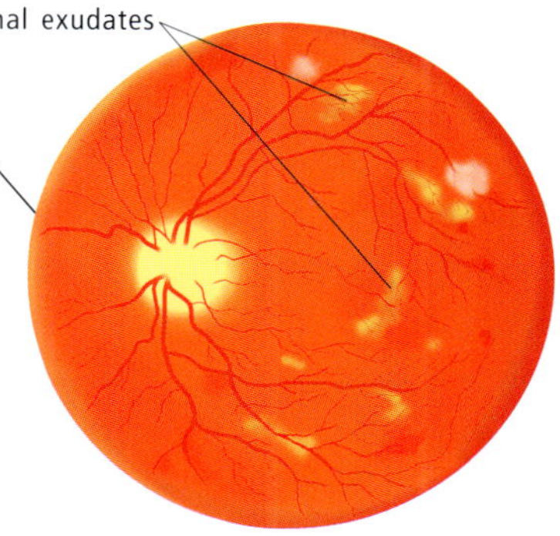

Retinopathy

AIDS can cause eye disorders such as retinopathy, which can result in loss of vision.

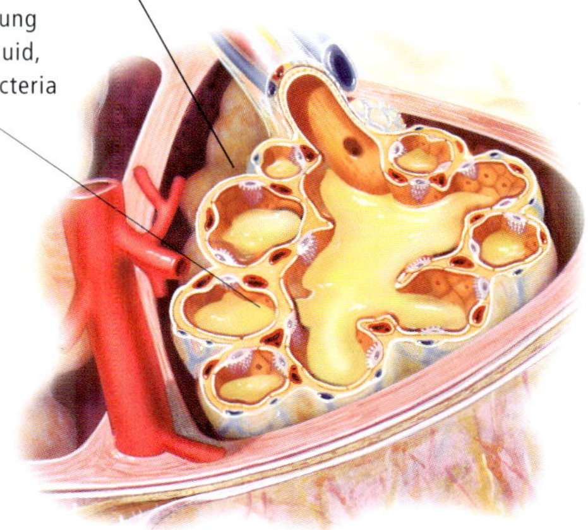

Pneumonia

Lung infections may progress to pneumonia which may be difficult to cure and is often the final cause of death in late stage AIDS.

AIDS

AIDS is a syndrome that appears at a late stage in HIV infection. The body's ability to fight disease lessens progressively and opportunistic infections and cancers appear at various sites in the body.

Treatment

AIDS and HIV are treated by a primary care physician (general practitioner) or by a specialist physician in an outpatient department or hospital clinic. In the later stages of the illness, when serious infections develop, the condition must be treated in hospital.

No cure exists for HIV infection itself. Until recently, the only treatment for HIV was to treat the opportunistic infections with antibiotic and antiviral drugs. However, over the past few years, antiviral drugs such as AZT and acyclovir have been developed to try and slow down the body's loss of immune function and susceptibility to disease.

These drugs suppress the HIV virus replicating itself in the body and so effectively arrest the progress of the disease. They are often used in combination. They are expensive, and they may not be well tolerated by the sufferer. Nevertheless, when used with conventional treatment of opportunistic infections, it is thought they can prolong life indefinitely. Prior to combination antiviral therapy, the mortality from full-blown AIDS was generally thought to be 100 percent.

Still, prevention remains the major tool in combating HIV and AIDS. Practising safe sex and using condoms (which have the added advantage of protecting against other sexually transmitted diseases such as chlamydia and gonorrhea) are the most effective means of stopping HIV transmission. Intravenous drug users should never share needles. Before entering into a sexual relationship with anyone who is at risk of having or contracting HIV, it is wise to find out about their HIV status first.

Thanks to AIDS awareness and safe sex campaigns, rates of new HIV infections are falling, at least in the developed world. Unfortunately, however, because of the cost of combination therapy drugs, widespread use of them in developing countries is impractical. Management of AIDS and HIV in these countries depends on public awareness campaigns and on the hope of finding a cheap and effective method of immunization.

SEE ALSO *HIV, Kaposi's sarcoma, Opportunistic infections, T cells*

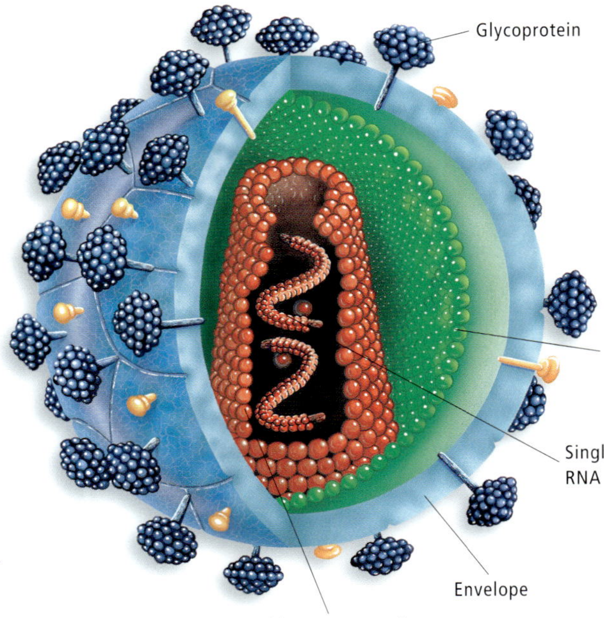

HIV

The human immunodeficiency virus (HIV) is a type of virus called a retrovirus. It is unusual in that its genetic material is RNA rather than DNA, like most other viruses.

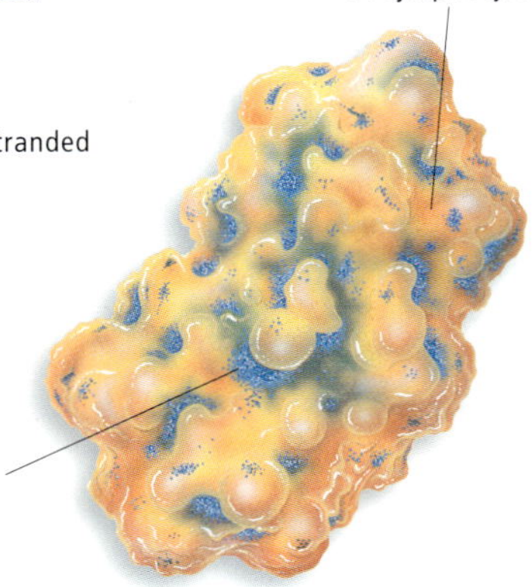

T4 lymphocyte

HIV attacks and destroys a certain type of lymphocyte called a T4 lymphocyte. T lymphocytes are white blood cells that defend the body against viral and bacterial infection.

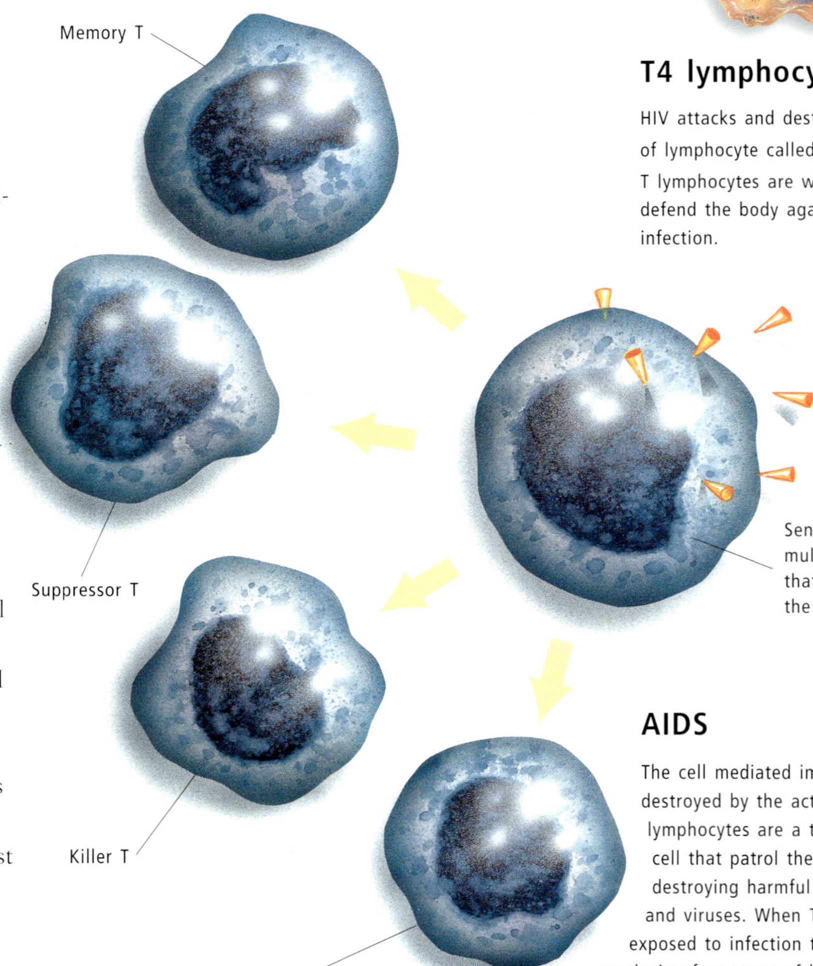

AIDS

The cell mediated immune reponse is destroyed by the action of HIV. T lymphocytes are a type of white blood cell that patrol the body identifying and destroying harmful invaders like bacteria and viruses. When T lymphocytes are first exposed to infection they multiply, producing four types of lymphocytes: memory cells, suppressor cells, killer cells and helper (T4) cells, each of which play an important role in the body's immune system. Helper (T4) lymphocytes direct our immune response by identifying foreign invaders and calling other lymphocytes to attack. These helper Ts are destroyed by HIV leaving the body with lowered immunity and vulnerable to opportunistic infections such as pneumonia.

ALCOHOLISM

Alcoholism is a progressive disease marked by a physical, mental and emotional dependence on alcohol. It affects all ethnic, socioeconomic and age groups. In recent years, the number of female and teenage alcoholics has markedly increased.

Alcohol and its effects

Alcohol (ethanol, ethyl alcohol) is present in beers, liqueurs, spirits and wines, and also in many common medications. Because alcohol is a potentially dangerous yet widely available drug, its use is restricted by law in certain situations. Health authorities generally recognize that men can safely consume up to two standard drinks per day, and women one standard drink (the specified quantity is lower for women because of their lower body weight). During pregnancy, abstinence is the wisest course. Abnormalities in the developing fetus have been linked with regular consumption of only two standard drinks per day.

Alcohol acts as a sedative on the brain. A small amount will slightly reduce a person's inhibitions, helping them to overcome shyness and relax in social situations.

Moderate social drinking is generally accepted in Western societies. Most adults can maintain their alcohol intake at an acceptable level. Greater amounts can suppress internal controls and lead to socially unacceptable behavior. Continued drinking may affect muscle control. People who have consumed a large amount of alcohol may slur their words, stagger, lose concentration and eventually lapse into unconsciousness. All heavy or persistent drinkers place their general health at risk. A single bout of alcohol abuse can severely damage health and even cause death. Inexperienced drinkers are very much at risk because they have no tolerance to alcohol and do not know their own limits or what is safe.

Who is an alcoholic?

Alcoholism may, like diabetes or asthma, have genetic causes. Social environment and peer group influences are also triggers in susceptible people. Alcoholics do not conform to just one type; rather, they seem to fall into several categories. Professor E. Jellinek, an American specialist, grouped alcoholics into five different types, according to their various drinking patterns. Some alcoholics may fit more than one category.

Type I alcoholics are depressed, anxious people who drink to elevate their mood and to feel "normal".

The Type II alcoholics do not suffer from the mental obsession with alcohol to the extent that the other types do, but their excessive drinking causes serious physical damage such as pancreatitis or cirrhosis.

Often known as "periodic", "bender" or "binge" drinkers, Type III alcoholics can go for days or weeks without drinking, but once they start they lose the power of choice over when to stop. As the disease progresses, the benders become closer and more severe.

Type IV alcoholics don't often get falling-down drunk, but are usually never sober either. They will "top up" with small portions of alcohol through the day and night.

Type V is similar to Type III, but the binges are more intense, yet further apart.

Behavior problems

Alcoholics can suffer from a wide range of physical and behavioral symptoms. They experience a physical craving for alcohol, usually combined with a mental obsession. When alcohol is not taken, withdrawal symptoms can include nausea, sweating, shakiness, distress and fits. Alcoholics often develop an increasing tolerance for drink, so that greater amounts are needed to get the desired effect. Conversely, as the disease progresses, tolerance may decrease, and one or two drinks will be enough to make the person drunk or sick.

Alcoholics may behave totally out of character when under the influence, and are described as having "Dr Jekyll and Mr Hyde" personalities. They become deceitful and secretive about their drinking, as well as feeling guilt, shame and remorse. Blackouts may occur—these are lapses of consciousness that can last for minutes or up to many hours, and afterwards the person cannot remember what happened during that period.

Needless to say, alcoholics have unmanageable and chaotic lives. They may become unable to fulfil work or school commitments, often losing jobs and failing courses. They may cause injury to themselves and others, becoming involved in dangerous situations such as driving or operating machinery when drunk, and continuing to drink despite a worsening effect on health, finances, and sexual and personal relationships. Alcohol is a common factor in traffic accidents and crimes of violence.

Health problems

Alcoholism can cause many serious disorders of the body and mind. Poor nutrition is commonly associated with long-term alcohol abuse, as consumption of alcohol reduces appetite. The alcohol replaces food but does not supply the protein, minerals and vitamins the body needs.

Alcohol can also cause pancreatitis, in which the pancreas becomes inflamed and results in abdominal pain. Chronic pancreatitis is due to the small ducts in the pancreas narrowing and becoming clogged. It may damage the cells which make insulin and so lead to diabetes. Acute pancreatitis follows when ducts are completely blocked, and this can result from an alcoholic binge. It causes severe persistent pain just below the breastbone, with accelerated heartbeat and shallow breathing. Blood pressure may fall and bring on shock. This is a life-threatening condition requiring emergency treatment.

Liver damage is common in the later stages of alcoholism. This can be an accumulation of fat, producing no symptoms or only mild tenderness and enlargement. Inflammation, also called alcoholic hepatitis, can produce greater enlargement, pain, fever and jaundice. Cirrhosis scars liver tissue, making it hard and inefficient. This damage is permanent, but can be stopped as long as drinking is halted.

Polyneuropathy (also known as peripheral neuritis or polyneuritis) is an inflammation of the peripheral nerves, producing muscle weakness and numbness, particularly in the hands and feet. Physical therapy and vitamin B_1 (thiamine) can relieve symptoms.

Dementia is an organic brain disease marked by loss of memory and reasoning power and can be a consequence of alcoholism. The symptoms are confusion, disorientation and apathy.

Delirium tremens causes confusion and mental disorder; it is induced by the withdrawal of alcohol after a period of severe intoxication. Symptoms include trembling, hallucinations, delusions, fever, dilated pupils, sweating and very rapid heartbeat.

Wernicke-Korsakoff syndrome is a brain disease caused by a deficiency in vitamin B_1 (thiamine); this can occur because alcoholics replace food with alcohol and become malnourished. Symptoms include confusion, memory loss, and lack of muscular coordination, which produces twitching and random movements, particularly of the eyes, and a staggering walk. Brain damage may be permanent with this disease.

Treatment

The first step in treatment is acceptance by the drinker that there is a problem, as alcoholism has been termed "the disease of denial". Medical treatment can include admission to a hospital detoxification unit. The alcoholic may be given drugs such as tranquilizers to aid withdrawal from alcohol, naltrexone to help with physical cravings, or disulfiram, which causes nausea when alcohol is taken. Vitamin B injections are also beneficial.

Once the alcoholic has physically detoxified, the next challenge is to learn how to live without drinking. Unfortunately, the percentage of alcoholics who stop drinking and then remain sober is very low. Some clinics offer controlled drinking programs, which aim to teach the alcoholic how to drink socially through behavior modification. However, many experts believe that no alcoholic is ever able to drink again with safety, and recommend total abstinence.

Alcoholics have a much greater chance of long-term recovery if they go to a treatment or rehabilitation center. These centers offer residential programs, usually lasting three to eight weeks, and provide psychological counseling, education, group therapy and nutritional guidance. Recovery is likely to be more successful if treatment is followed up by further counseling (particularly if there is an underlying depressive illness) and regular attendance at Alcoholics Anonymous (AA) meetings. AA is a self-help program founded in 1935 by two alcoholics: Bill Wilson, a New York stockbroker, and Dr Bob Smith from Akron, Ohio. They believed that no one can help or understand an alcoholic as well as a fellow sufferer can. AA now has a membership of hundreds of thousands of men and women around the world. In AA meetings, people share their stories and support each other in leading healthy and productive lives.

SEE ALSO *Cirrhosis of the liver, Delirium tremens, Detoxification, Drug dependence, Fetal alcohol syndrome, Pancreatitis, Wernicke-Korsakoff syndrome*

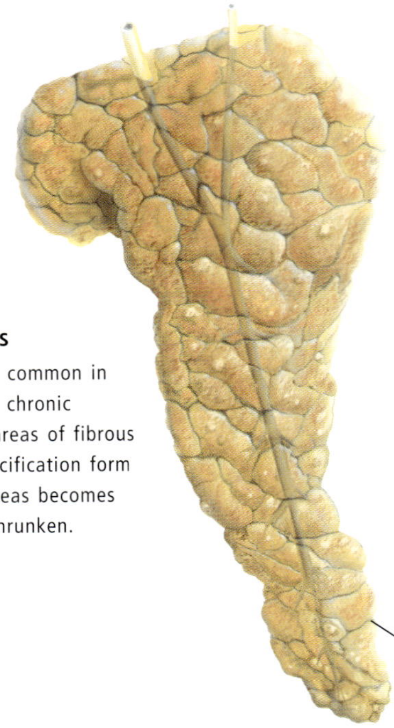

Pancreatitis
Pancreatitis is common in alcoholism. In chronic pancreatitis, areas of fibrous tissue and calcification form and the pancreas becomes scarred and shrunken.

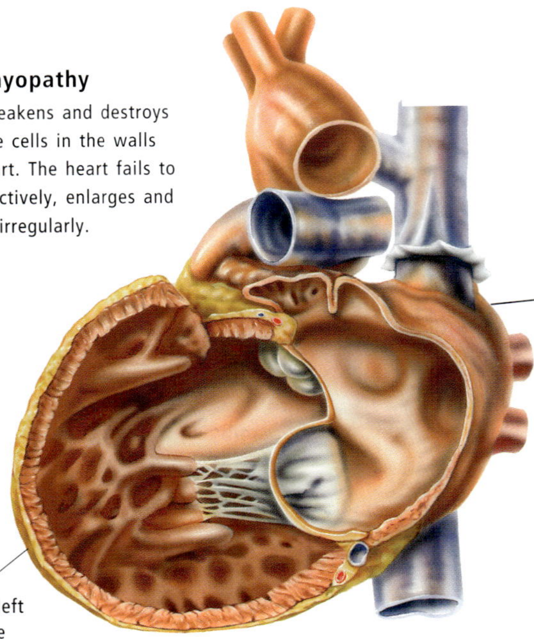

Cardiomyopathy
Alcohol weakens and destroys the muscle cells in the walls of the heart. The heart fails to pump effectively, enlarges and may beat irregularly.

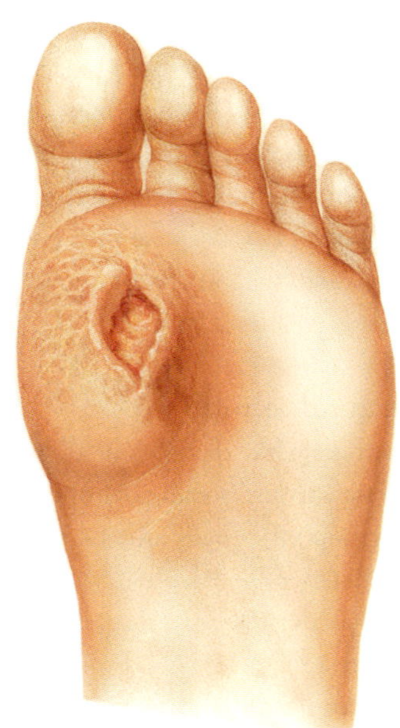

Neuritis
Alcoholism can cause damage to peripheral nerves (peripheral neuritis) which can lead to foot ulcers.

Alcoholism

In small or moderate amounts, alcohol does no permanent damage to the body. But if used in excessive amounts over a long period of time it can damage many organs. Chronic alcoholics suffer disorders of the heart, the muscles, the alimentary tract, brain, spinal cord and nerves.

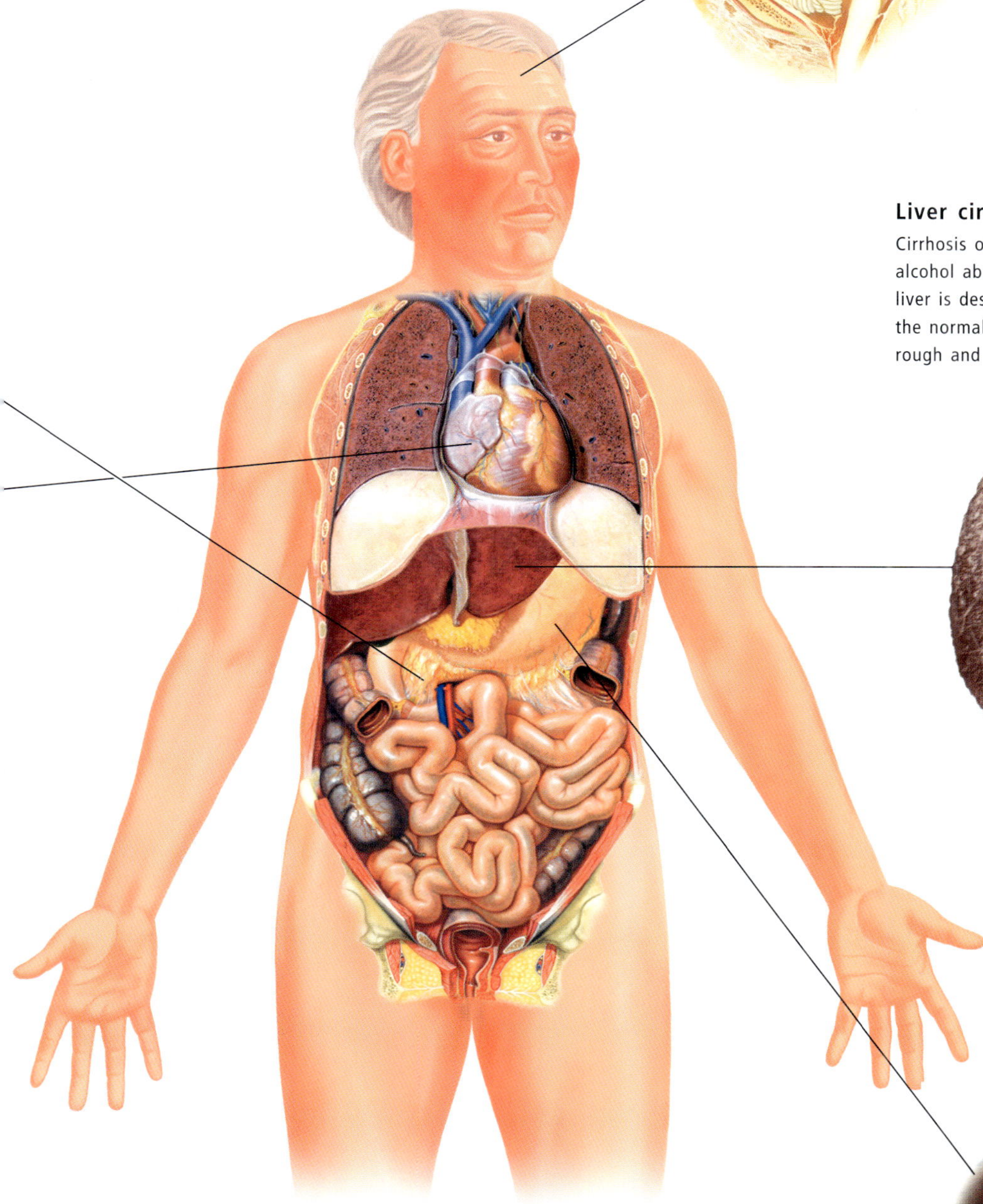

Esophageal disorders

Chronic alcoholism can cause disorders such as esophageal reflux, which produces irritation and heartburn. Cancer is a possible outcome of long-term damage.

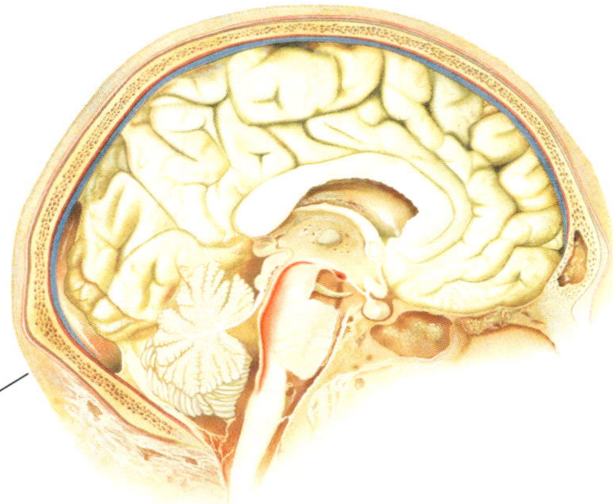

Wernicke's encephalopathy

This is a brain syndrome suffered by chronic alcoholics. It is caused by a deficiency of thiamine (Vitamin B_1) in the diet. The lack of this vitamin causes damage to certain areas in the brain stem, resulting in confusion, drowsiness, an unsteady gait, and paralysis of the eye muscles.

Liver cirrhosis

Cirrhosis of the liver occurs in longstanding alcohol abuse. The lobular architecture of the liver is destroyed by bands of fibrous tissue and the normally smooth surface of the liver appears rough and nodular.

Gastric ulcer

A gastric ulcer is a hole in the lining (mucosa) of the stomach. It is more common in alcoholics than in the general population.

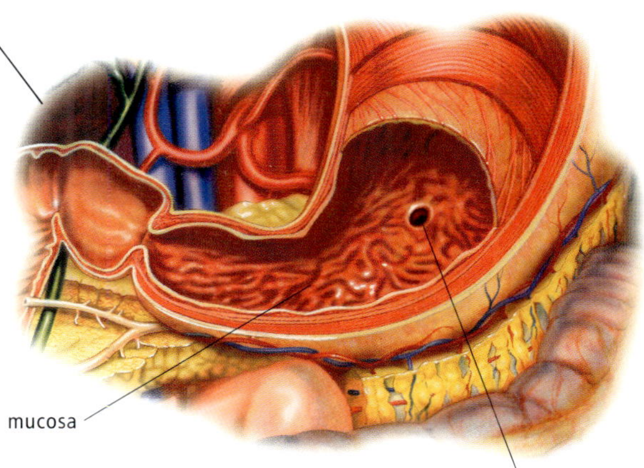

A

ALEXANDER TECHNIQUE

The founder of the Alexander technique was the Australian-born actor Frederick Matthias Alexander (1869–1955). He developed his technique as a consequence of regularly losing his voice during his recitals. Finding no relief from medicine, Alexander began to study himself declaiming in front of carefully positioned mirrors. He observed that he was in the habit of pulling his head back and tightening the area around the larynx. Convinced that this was the cause of his problem, he painstakingly retrained himself to lift his head vertically and free his neck. Not only did he find that his voice problems disappeared, he also felt healthier and more self-confident.

This experiment inspired Alexander to make a lifelong study of posture and to devise his technique to retrain the muscle system, focusing particularly on the relationship between the head, neck and torso.

In 1904 Alexander traveled to England to teach his technique, and then to the USA, attracting a following among actors, writers and educators. His most famous book *The Use of Self* was published in 1932. Today the Alexander technique is claimed as having health benefits, particularly for those suffering from back pain, repetitive strain injury, breathing problems, high blood pressure and stress-related illnesses.

Learning the technique

Alexander believed that most adults needed to relearn the correct way to stand, sit, walk, lift objects and breathe. His technique is based upon posture, corrective exercise and balance, all combining to realign the body so that it can function more efficiently. Alexander's dictum is "let the neck be free to let the head be forward and up, and the back widen and lengthen". This fundamental realignment of the head and upper torso is known as the "primary control". One way to regain primary control is to visualize a cord coming out of the top of your head pulling you gently towards the sky, counterbalancing the effects of gravity.

The Alexander technique teaches you to observe and "unlearn" your habitual responses through focusing awareness on the body. The technique is learnt from a teacher in individual sessions or classes. The first step is for the teacher to observe how you habitually stand, sit, walk, move and breathe. From that point the teacher helps you to gain an experience of what it will mean to make these movements in a more natural way. You are asked to focus on the means of movement rather than on the end result. Using touch, the teacher guides your body into its correct balance as you sit, stand and lie down.

The experience of the benefits of a more coordinated body in a lesson becomes the incentive to develop a greater awareness of your body and its means in daily life. Practice and self-discipline are required to prevent the body falling back into its bad habits. The technique takes some time to establish itself in a person's mind and body and a series of lessons is required to support the change.

ALIMENTARY CANAL

The alimentary canal (otherwise known as the digestive tract) is a long muscular tube (about 30 feet, or 9 meters) extending from the mouth to the anus. It is made up of layers of circular muscles which contract and move the food in waves along the tract; this process is known as peristalsis. Its function

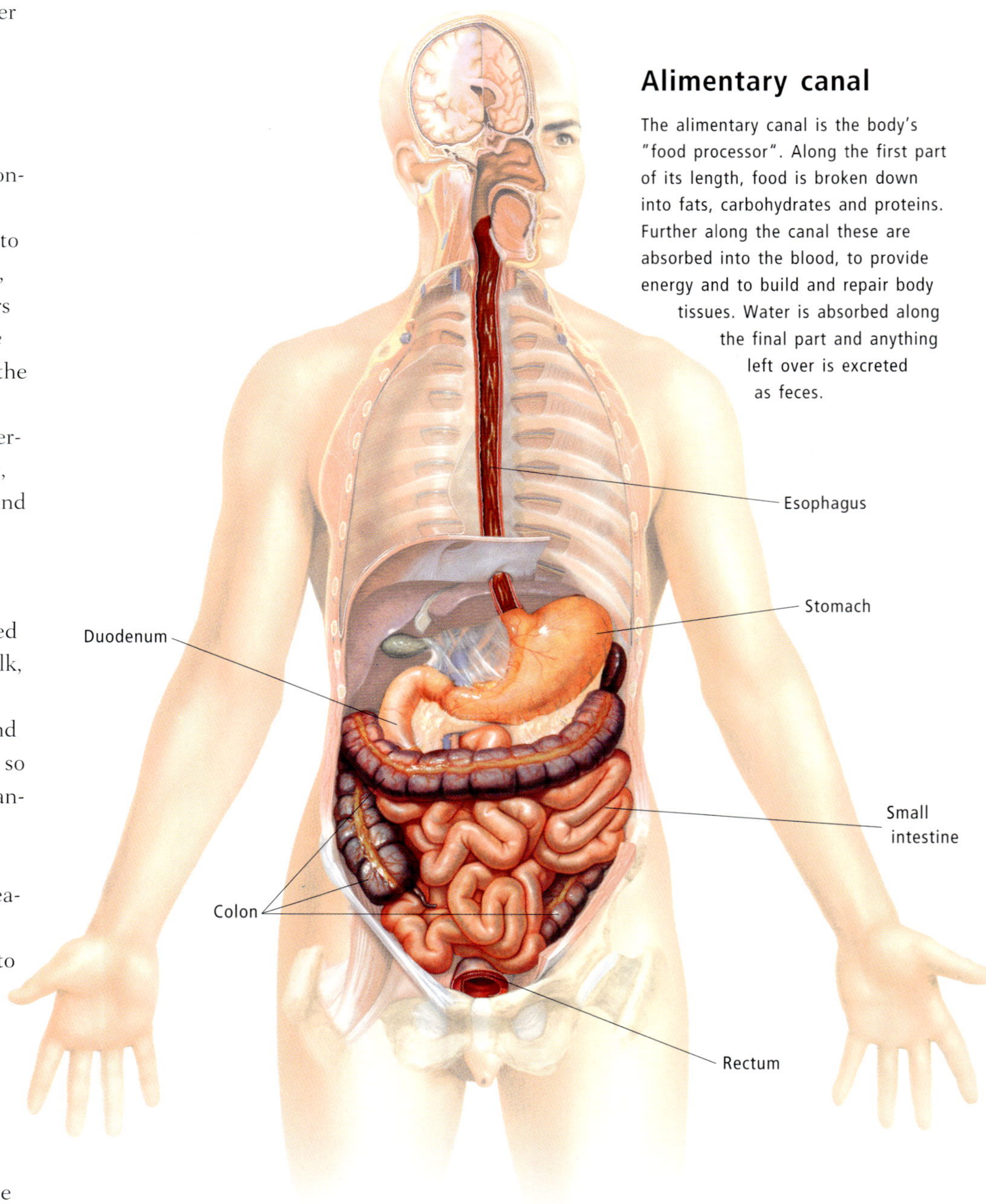

Alimentary canal

The alimentary canal is the body's "food processor". Along the first part of its length, food is broken down into fats, carbohydrates and proteins. Further along the canal these are absorbed into the blood, to provide energy and to build and repair body tissues. Water is absorbed along the final part and anything left over is excreted as feces.

is to break food down into smaller and smaller particles, absorb the nutrients along the way and expel the rest as waste. Different parts of the tract have different functions.

Food enters through the mouth, or oral cavity. Jaws, tongue and teeth work to mash and mix the food into smaller pieces. Saliva, secreted from the salivary glands placed around the oral cavity, moistens the food to make it easier to transport, and contains enzymes (digestive proteins) that begin the process of breaking down the food.

From the mouth, food passes down a muscular tube called the esophagus into an acid-rich pouch—the stomach. In the stomach, the food is gradually broken down by pepsin, an enzyme, into a semi-liquid stew of food, acid and digestive juices.

Next, the mixture passes into the duodenum, which is the first part of the small intestine. More digestive juices are added to the mix: bile from the liver and digestive enzymes from the pancreas. As the food particles move further down the intestine they are reduced to smaller and smaller constituents—carbohydrates, proteins, fats, vitamins and water. These are absorbed through the lining of the small intestine and pass into the bloodstream. They are stored in the liver to be used in the body's metabolic processes.

Two other organs are essential in this process. One is the liver, which, as well as storing nutrients, also produces bile. Via the gallbladder and bile ducts, bile travels into the small intestine where it aids in the absorption of fats and fat-soluble vitamins. Then there is the pancreas, which makes the amylase, protease and lipase enzymes needed to break down carbohydrates, proteins and fats in the small intestine.

Once food has reached the end of the small intestine, what's left is essentially waste material. The waste enters the large intestine, or colon—a tube that is wider but shorter than the small intestine. As it travels along the colon, water is reabsorbed, the waste hardens and becomes feces. The fecal material is then stored in the last part of the large intestine, the rectum, before being expelled through the anus.

As the digestive tract is located within the abdominal cavity, it can be difficult for medical professionals to visualize the tract. Gastroenterologists use methods such as ultrasound, x-ray and endoscopy to "see" various organs. Endoscopy is an examination using a flexible fiberoptic rod which is inserted through the mouth or via the anus. The endoscope has a lens and camera attached, allowing a detailed view of the interior of the alimentary canal. A separate attachment can be used to take a biopsy if necessary.

SEE ALSO *Colon, Digestive system, Endoscopy, Intestines, Liver, Pancreas, Peristalsis, Stomach*

ALKALOSIS

Alkalosis is an excess of alkali in the blood and other body fluids. Normally, the body's regulatory mechanisms keep the pH of the blood slightly alkaline, within the range of 7.35 and 7.45 (pH is a measure of acidity). But certain conditions cause it to rise above this level, causing alkalosis.

There are two types of alkalosis. Metabolic alkalosis occurs when there is a loss of acid from the body fluids. This can happen during kidney failure, vomiting and intestinal obstruction, or due to the effect of some drugs. Metabolic alkalosis can also occur if there is excess absorption of alkali, as occurs sometimes after a blood transfusion or excess ingestion of bicarbonate in drug preparations.

The other type is respiratory alkalosis. This is caused by hyperventilation (rapid breathing) that results in excessive loss of carbon dioxide. Respiratory alkalosis can also be caused by head injury, lung disease, liver failure and salicylate (aspirin) poisoning.

Symptoms of alkalosis include tingling skin, muscle weakness and muscle cramps. The condition is confirmed by a blood test which shows changes in blood pH, bicarbonate and oxygen and carbon dioxide levels.

Alkalosis is a serious condition. Hospitalization is necessary to correct the underlying cause and to facilitate replacement of lost body fluids. In some cases, intravenous administration of acidic compounds will be needed to restore the pH to normal levels.

SEE ALSO *Acidosis, Metabolism*

ALLERGIES

An allergy is a physical reaction to certain substances. In the allergic person, the immune system mistakenly identifies a substance as being harmful and mounts a defense against it. This unnecessary defense reaction is often excessively vigorous, and the antibodies manufactured to fight the substance have irritating or harmful effects, which constitute an allergic reaction.

Allergies tend to run in families but are also affected by environmental factors. They develop through exposure to substances, and a process called sensitization that can occur on first contact, or over a brief period or even through repeated exposure over several years. During this period, the immune system is activated to react against what is usually a relatively harmless substance.

Allergies can show up at any age but they often appear first in childhood, particularly contact allergies that are a reaction on first contact with the allergenic substance.

Asthma and hay fever, allergic rhinitis and sinusitis, cows' milk allergy and various other food allergies are well-known conditions. If you are a sufferer, contact with the offending substance will trigger a variety of unpleasant symptoms that could include skin rashes, itching or swellings, red and swollen eyes, runny nose, severe nasal inflammation, wheezing and shortness of breath. Sometimes a severe reaction can require immediate emergency treatment.

Allergens

Any substance that will produce an allergic reaction is an allergen. Contact with an allergen is the event that triggers the allergic reaction. The substance may be quite harmless to others, but to a person with a specific allergy it will be a substance to avoid.

Common respiratory allergens are grass pollen, mold spores, nettles (in Europe), poison ivy (in North America), the house dust mite and its droppings, dandruff and animal hairs and fur.

Pet allergy is a reaction to contact with animal fur or dander (minute particles of skin) and can build up over a period of regular contact. Cat hairs are a very common trigger for asthma as well as hay-fever-type allergic reactions and it is advisable to avoid potential problems in susceptible people rather than have to get rid of a loved pet.

Allergies to drugs can arise even after previous treatments with the same drug

A

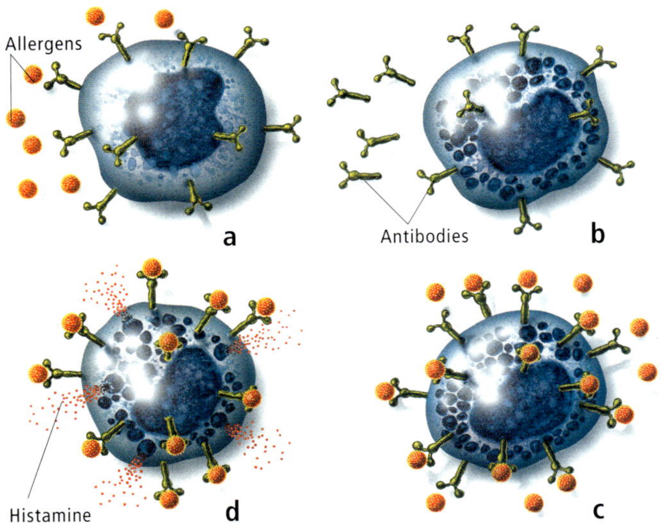

Allergic reaction

An allergic response is a reaction by the body to foreign irritants called allergens. The four-step process involves specialized cells and a chemical called histamine.

(a) Allergens enter the body and stimulate plasma cells to produce antibodies

(b) These antibodies attach to mast cells

(c) The next time allergens enter the body they bind to the antibodies on the surface of the mast cells

(d) Mast cells release histamine which produces the irritating effects of the allergy

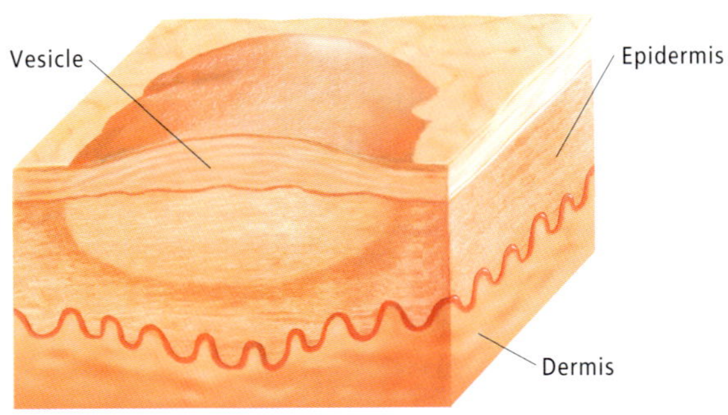

Urticaria

When allergens enter the body they stimulate the release of histamine, which can produce itchy, slightly elevated skin wheals known as urticaria or hives.

produced no adverse reaction, and can be triggered by very small amounts. Reactions can be mild or severe, even including anaphylactic shock, which is life-threatening, and people known to be at risk should wear medical bracelets or carry information cards.

Serum sickness is an allergic reaction that occurs eight to twelve days after a vaccination and may produce a skin rash or swellings, enlarged lymph glands and fever.

Foods can also be allergens, with cows' milk, eggs, peanuts, strawberries, wheat and wheat flour, shellfish and seafood all possibilities. Insect bites, chemicals, drugs and dyes can all cause allergy problems. Milk can cause allergies to milk proteins or drugs such as penicillin in the milk. However, lactose intolerance is not the result of an allergy; it occurs when the enzyme responsible for breaking down lactose is lacking.

Bee stings can produce a severe allergic reaction. Latex, a component of rubber, has caused allergies to develop through repeated exposure over time in many adults. Sunlight can also be responsible. Solar urticaria is a condition where exposure to ultraviolet light produces wheals on the skin.

The physical effect of exposure to an allergen is that the body will produce antibodies, normally manufactured in the body to fight invading germs. In an allergic reaction, allergens and antibodies act together to cause the release of histamine that then acts on capillaries, mucous glands and muscles of the stomach and internal organs, stimulating them into excessive, and often harmful, activity. Every time an allergic person is exposed to a particular allergen it is likely that the same response will result, and the reaction may become more severe over time. The level of exposure to the substance at which an allergic reaction will be triggered is the person's allergic threshold.

Allergic reactions

Allergic reactions can take many forms, from mild (involving minor discomfort such as a rash or indigestion) to severe (involving extreme irritation of skin or mucous membranes, respiratory distress or anaphylactic shock). In rare cases an allergic reaction may prove to be fatal.

Allergic reactions can be divided into four types: immediate, where the allergen is inhaled or ingested, as in most of the common allergies; reactions against foreign substances in the bloodstream, which occur for example in mismatched blood transfusions; autoimmune diseases, where the body's defenses attack its own tissue; and delayed reactions caused by repeated exposure, such as contact dermatitis produced by metals in jewelry.

It is not known to what extent allergic reactions are controlled by the nervous system; stress and emotional problems may increase their probability and severity.

Allergic reactions can appear on the skin as a rash. Respiratory allergens may affect breathing and the respiratory system, as in asthma, with a narrowing of the airways of the lungs and a feeling of tightness in the chest; or they may cause sneezing, as in hay fever; or even more severe irritation and inflammation of the mucus membranes of the nose as in chronic rhinitis. They also may cause skin rashes, dermatitis and swellings and nasal polyps (swollen tissue in the nose) that can obstruct the airway.

Food allergies and gastrointestinal allergies, thought to be caused by the protein component of certain foods, can also affect respiration but more usually symptoms include vomiting, diarrhea, skin rashes or swellings, swellings inside the mouth and, rarely, anaphylactic shock. Reaction follows swiftly after contact with (touching or eating) the food.

Sensitivity to certain foods may not necessarily be an allergy. Food intolerance is a term used to differentiate between suffering side effects from certain components or ingredients of foods and the more severe allergic reactions. Food intolerance is quite common and can produce a range of symptoms similar to those of allergies. And because food sensitivity—a term covering both allergy and intolerance—is a complex condition with many possible causes and symptoms, specialist diagnosis is essential.

Anaphylaxis, or anaphylactic shock, is an extreme allergic reaction where histamine and other chemicals are released within the body. This is a medical emergency.

Diagnosis and treatment

Diagnosis may be a lengthy process, unless the allergic reaction is immediate and the allergen can be identified beyond doubt. A medical examination may be done while the patient is suffering an allergic reaction and will take account of blood pressure, pulse rate, skin condition, breathing and general mental condition.

Antigen tests aim to find the substance (the antigen) in the blood of the allergic person that results from contact with the allergen—the food or chemical in the environment or diet. It is the allergen that starts the reaction, and the antigen that combines with antibodies in the blood to produce the physical effects of the allergic reaction.

A medical specialist will do antigen tests as part of a course of treatment. First, the presence of an allergy must be diagnosed to establish that what has happened before is not just an isolated reaction. Then tests are undertaken to find the allergens in the diet or environment of the allergic person so that contact with them can be avoided or completely eliminated. There may be skin or blood tests, or more long-term procedures where contact with all substances suspected of causing problems is eliminated. Controlled dieting is an elimination method used to detect digestive food allergies. Foods that commonly cause allergies are removed from the diet, then returned one at a time to see if the allergy also returns.

There is no complete cure for allergies: they can be identified and the causes revealed, but the allergy remains. The benefits of correct diagnosis and treatment are that the allergy can be managed, and life can go on as normally as possible in the circumstances. Untreated allergies tend to become worse. Treatment may mean strict avoidance of the allergens responsible or may require medication to control the allergic reaction. Antihistamines and steroids are the most commonly used medications in cases of respiratory allergies; for digestive allergies, other drugs (known as H2 antagonists) may be prescribed.

SEE ALSO *Anaphylaxis, Antibodies, Antigen tests, Antihistamines, Asthma, Autoimmune disease, Conjunctivitis, Dermatitis, Desensitization, Eczema, Hay fever, Lactose intolerance, Photosensitivity, Urticaria*

ALVEOLUS

An alveolus, also known as a pulmonary alveolus, is one of the tiny air spaces in the lung where blood exchanges carbon dioxide for oxygen. There are about 300 million alveoli in each human lung, grouped in grape-like clusters (alveolar sacs).

Inhaled air enters through the mouth or nose, travels through the throat, larynx and windpipe (trachea) and via the left and right bronchial tube to the lungs. The bronchial tubes (bronchioles) narrow and divide into alveolar ducts, ending in the alveolar sacs.

Alveoli give the lungs their huge surface area, estimated to be 1,000 square feet (93 square meters), and the thin-walled blood vessels in each provide the means for gases—carbon dioxide and oxygen—to be exchanged by diffusion.

ALZHEIMER'S DISEASE

Alzheimer's disease is a common brain disease which results in dementia (confusion and loss of intellectual function). It usually occurs in elderly people but may occasionally appear in middle age.

This is the most common (but not the only) cause of senile dementia. After a person reaches the age of 65, the risk of Alzheimer's disease doubles with each five years of age. As the average life expectancy of the world population continues to rise, the number of those affected will continue to increase.

The symptoms of Alzheimer's disease appear very gradually, followed by a progressive deterioration over a period of five to ten years. Its major feature is increasing forgetfulness—initially forgetfulness of the

Alveoli

The small air spaces at the end of the air passageways of the lungs are called alveoli. Each lung contains millions of these tiny sacs. In an alveolus, oxygen is absorbed into the blood and carbon dioxide passes from the blood into the alveolus, to be breathed out by the lungs.

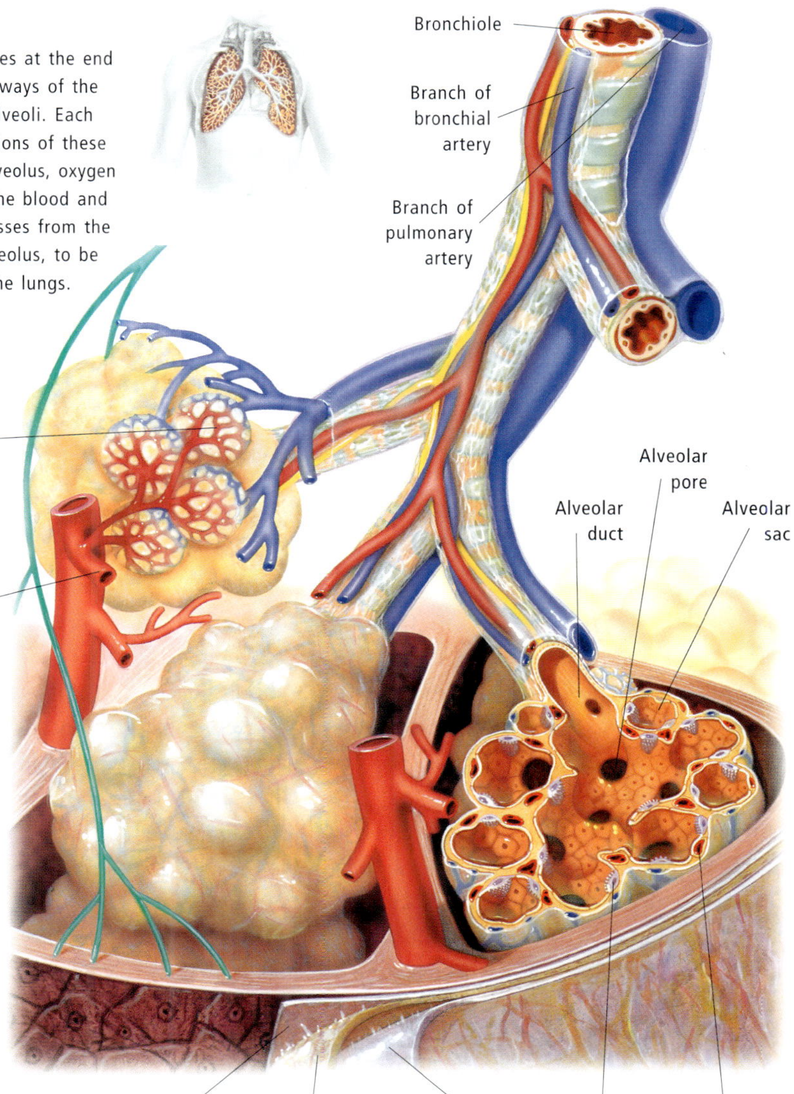

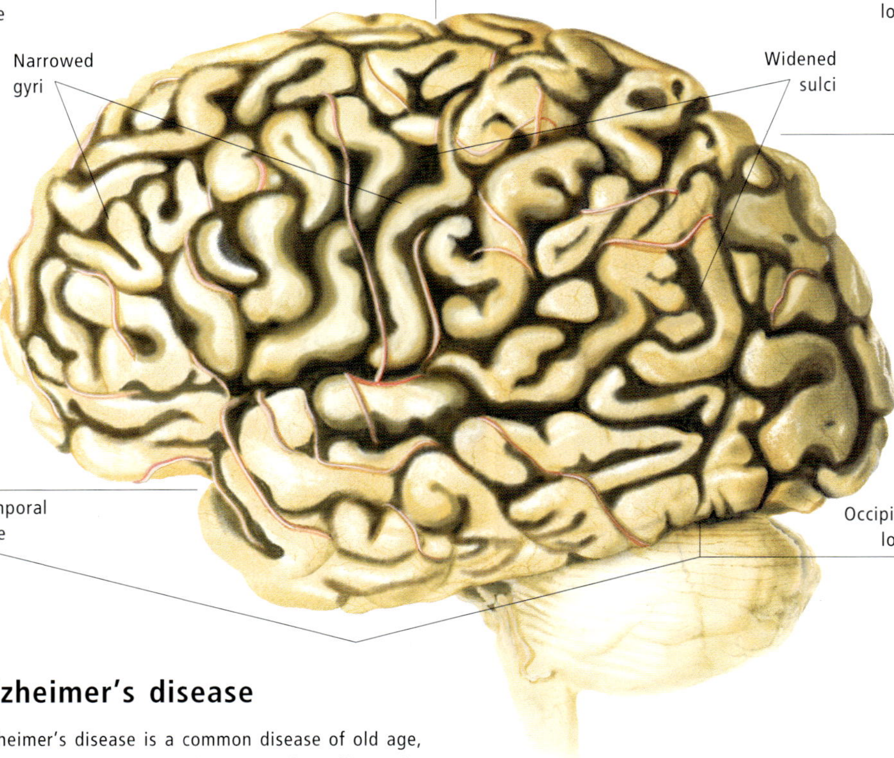

Alzheimer's disease

Alzheimer's disease is a common disease of old age, affecting the memory. In this brain of a sufferer, the brain has shrunken slightly and the gaps between brain matter have widened. Nobody knows exactly what causes the changes.

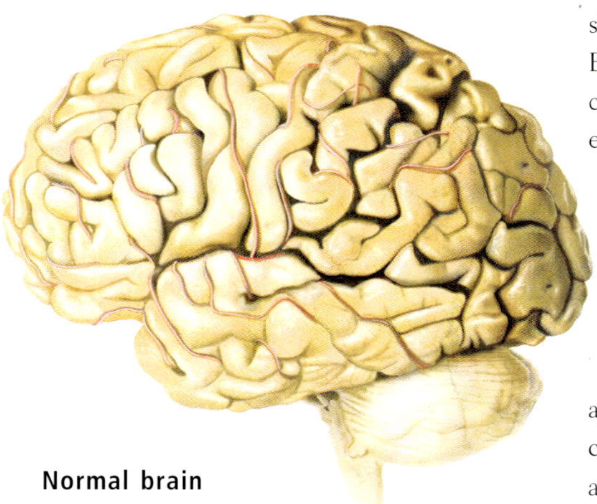

Normal brain

names of objects, people and places as well as day-to-day events. The person begins to miss appointments and lose possessions. One of the most striking features in the early stages of the disease is that, although sufferers can't remember recent events, they may be able to describe in great detail incidents or people from early in their life. Unfortunately the ability to recall even old memories fades as the disease progresses.

Affected people gradually become more and more disorientated and confused, frequently getting lost or forgetting how to do simple tasks such as getting dressed or setting the table. Their intellectual capacity diminishes—reading, writing, mathematical skills and decision-making are all affected. Eventually they undergo personality changes, neglecting personal hygiene and exhibiting uncharacteristic and sometimes bizarre patterns of behavior, such as paranoia or sexual indiscretions. They gradually become immobile, bedridden and susceptible to infections.

The development of Alzheimer's disease is not considered a normal consequence of ageing—it is a real disease in which there are characteristic changes in both the structure and chemistry of the brain.

Alzheimer's sufferers lose up to 20 percent of their normal brain volume, with the shrinkage (cell death) occurring mainly in parts of the temporal, frontal and parietal lobes of the brain. These are the areas which are responsible for creating and storing memory and for intellectual processing. Parts of the brain dealing with motor and sensory functions (vision, touch and hearing) seem relatively unaffected. Examination of affected tissue under a microscope shows three main characteristics: large spaces formed by dying cells; abnormal protein deposits, called senile plaques; and twisted, knotted bundles of fibers, known as tangles.

What causes these changes in the brain is not yet understood. Less than 5 percent of cases have a proven genetic basis and these are almost invariably cases which have an early age of onset. For the vast majority it appears likely that the disease results from long-term exposure of genetically susceptible individuals to a combination of (as yet unidentified) environmental factors.

At present there is no known cure for the disease. Several drugs are currently being trialed but at best they only slow down the intellectual decline—they cannot stop the progression of the disease.

SEE ALSO *Confusion, Dementia, Memory*

AMINO ACIDS

Amino acids are the building blocks of proteins. The body needs proteins in order to build cells and grow, and to maintain its metabolic functions. To make proteins, it needs amino acids.

There are two groups of amino acids: non-essential (if we don't include them in our diet the body itself can make them) and essential (they must be included in the diet if we are to stay healthy).

Lack of essential amino acids in the diet can lead to malnutrition and protein deficiency disorders such as kwashiorkor. These are common in the developing world where protein in the diet is scarce. Rich sources of amino acids include meat, fish, poultry, egg white, milk, cheese, peas and beans.

SEE ALSO *Kwashiorkor, Malnutrition*

AMNESIA

Amnesia is partial or complete loss of memory. It is usually caused by brain damage due to trauma or disease, though it can sometimes be caused by psychological trauma. Memory loss is usually temporary and selective, being confined to one part of the affected person's experience, such as memory of recent events.

Causes of amnesia include Alzheimer's disease, head trauma or injury, seizures, general anesthetics, alcoholism, stroke or transient ischemic attack (TIA), drugs such as barbiturates or benzodiazepines, electroconvulsive therapy (especially if prolonged) and brain surgery.

There are various types of amnesia. Anterograde amnesia involves the loss of one's ability to form new memories. The affected person has difficulty remembering ongoing day-to-day events following an injury to the head, although they remember events prior to this. It may also affect alcoholics and usually leads to dementia.

In retrograde amnesia, the affected person has difficulty recalling events prior to an episode of head injury. Part or all of the memory loss may return in the days, weeks or months following the trauma.

In a condition called transient global amnesia (TGA), the affected person, who is usually elderly, suddenly forgets how they came to be where they are. Their name and the names of family and friends can be recalled, but not the events leading up to the attack. The condition is thought to be caused by unusual electrical activity in the temporal lobe of the brain. Recovery usually takes place in four to six hours. The condition does not cause permanent damage and requires no medical treatment.

In Wernicke-Korsakoff syndrome, memory loss is caused by a thiamine deficiency due to alcohol abuse. The affected person will have normal short-term memory, but will have difficulty acquiring new information and in remembering events that happened before the illness. It is a progressive disorder, usually accompanied by neurological problems such as uncoordinated movements and loss of feeling in fingers and toes.

Hysterical amnesia (also known as fugue amnesia) is usually temporary and is triggered by a traumatic event that the mind of the affected person cannot cope with. Usually the memory returns after a few days, though the memory of the traumatic event may remain incomplete.

The treatment of amnesia is to reverse the underlying cause if possible. Support of the family is important. The family may need to orientate the affected person by providing familiar music, objects or photos, and relearning programs are also helpful. Medication schedules should be written down so they are not forgotten and lost. Nursing home and other extended care facilities may be needed if safety, nutrition or other basic needs are at risk.

SEE ALSO *Alcoholism, Alzheimer's disease, Convulsions, Dementia, Electroconvulsive therapy, Memory, Psychotropic drugs, Stroke, Trauma, Wernicke-Korsakoff syndrome*

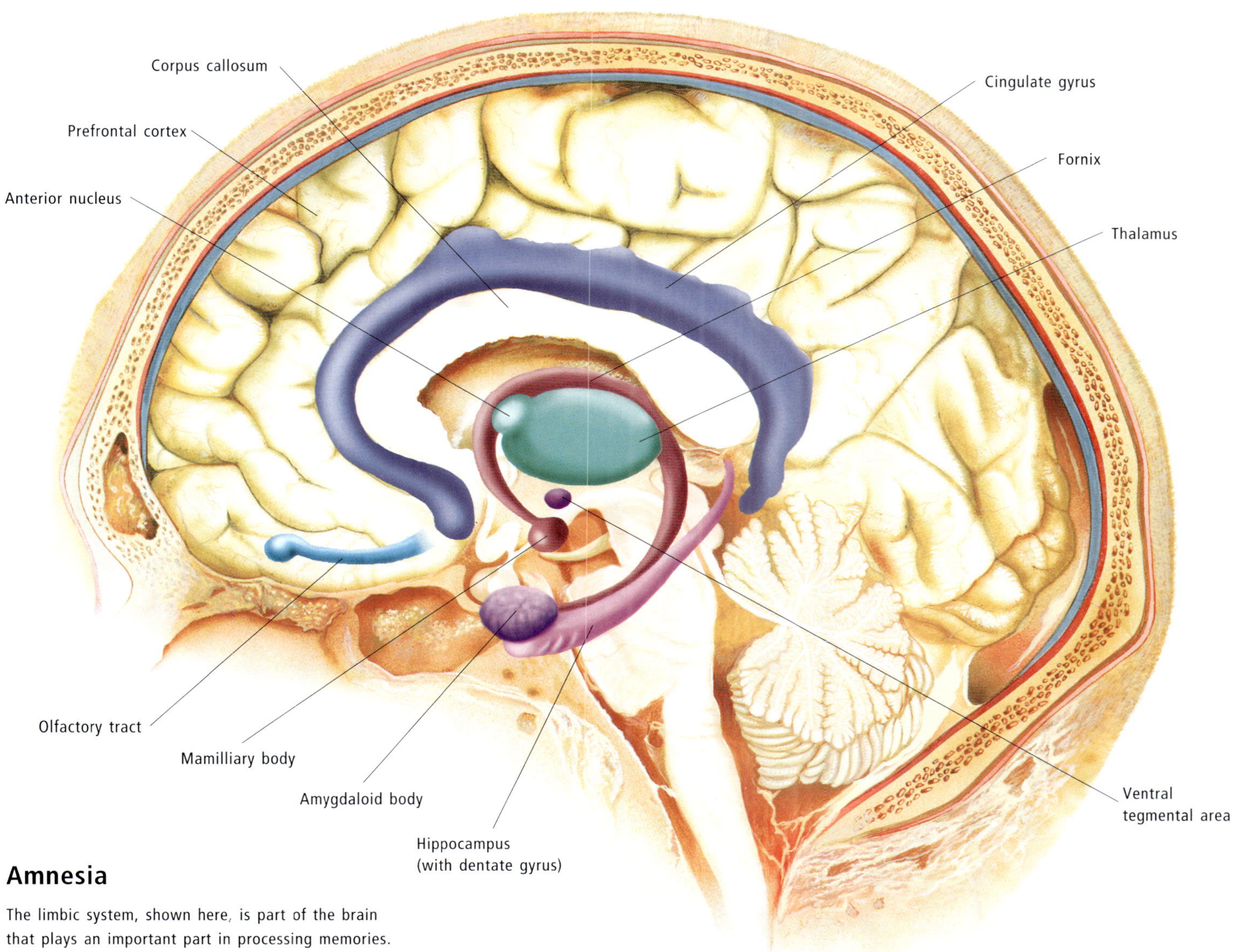

Amnesia

The limbic system, shown here, is part of the brain that plays an important part in processing memories. Injury to the limbic system can cause amnesia.

AMNIOCENTESIS

Amniocentesis involves a sample of amniotic fluid being taken from the amniotic sac. A hollow needle is inserted into the mother's uterus through the abdominal wall, using ultrasound to determine the needle's position. The fluid is cultured in a laboratory, a process that can take up to four weeks. Women found to be carrying a baby with an abnormality are usually offered an abortion.

Amniocentesis is performed between the 14th and 18th week of a pregnancy on women deemed to be at high risk of having a baby with physical defects of the central nervous system (such as spina bifida or anencephaly) or genetic abnormalities (such as Down syndrome). Those at greater risk are usually women whose family history indicates there may be a problem, or women over 35 years of age. Counseling should be offered to the woman and her partner before the procedure takes place, as well as after the procedure if an abnormality is detected.

Amniocentesis is sometimes performed late in the pregnancy where there is a risk of placenta previa (in which the placenta obstructs the birth) or premature birth.

There is a risk of miscarriage with amniocentesis of between 1 and 2 percent. There is also a 0.5 percent risk that the baby will be born with a very low birth weight.

SEE ALSO *Chromosomal abnormalities, Congenital abnormalities, Pregnancy*

AMPHETAMINES

Amphetamines are stimulants, and are used in the treatment of uncontrollable attacks of sleep or drowsiness (narcolepsy). In children over the age of three years, however, they are prescribed for hyperactivity disorders.

Side effects of taking amphetamines include restlessness, insomnia, dryness of the mouth, twitching and loss of appetite. Overdose may cause coma and death. Treatment for overdose is to induce vomiting (in order to prevent further absorption).

Amphetamines should be used only under medical supervision. There is a danger of dependency with long-term use. Use of amphetamines is prohibited in competitive sports.

SEE ALSO *Attention deficit hyperactivity disorder, Drug dependence, Stimulants*

AMYOTROPHIC LATERAL SCLEROSIS

Amyotrophic lateral sclerosis (ALS) is a progressive, fatal disorder resulting in the loss of the use and control of muscles. Also called Lou Gehrig's disease (after the American baseball hero who suffered from it), ALS is a member of the class of disorders known as motor neuron diseases.

The condition is caused by gradual degeneration of nerve cells in the brain and spinal cord that control voluntary movement. As neurons shrink and disappear, the muscles under their control weaken and waste away. Symptoms include poor coordination, paralysis of hands and arms, twitching and cramping of muscles, and difficulty in speaking, swallowing and breathing. Symptoms usually do not develop until well into adulthood, often not until after 50 years of age. Mental faculties remain unaffected.

The condition is confirmed by electromyography (EMG), which shows the nerve and muscle degeneration. There is no cure for ALS, although one drug, riluzole, has been shown to prolong the survival of people with the condition. Physical therapy, rehabilitation and use of appliances such as braces or a wheelchair will assist the affected person to stay mobile as long as possible.

ALS is usually fatal within five years after symptoms appear. The condition may run in families; if so, genetic counseling is advisable.

SEE ALSO *Muscles, Rehabilitation, Spinal cord*

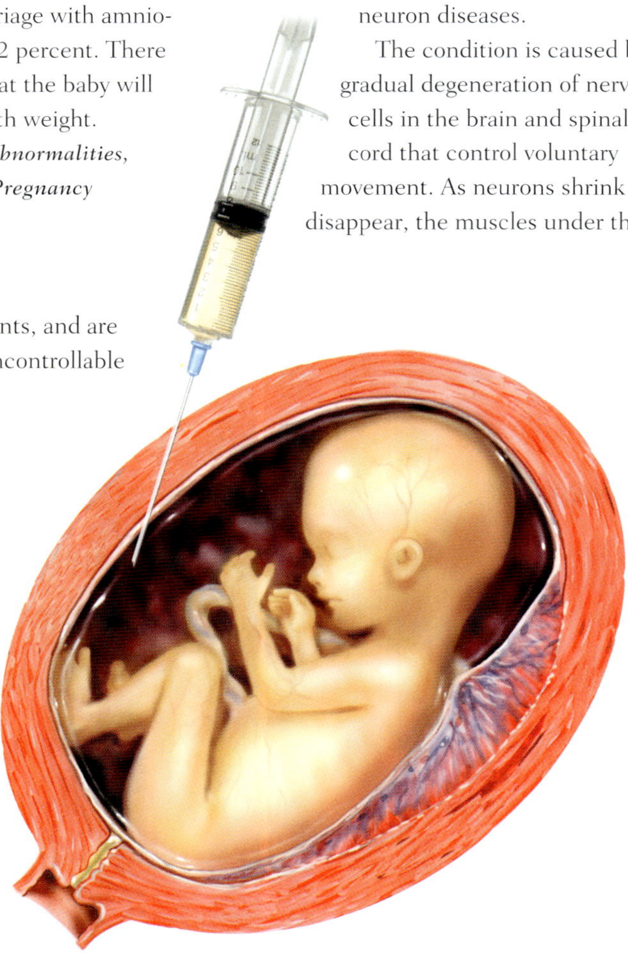

Amniocentesis

Amniocentesis can detect over 40 different types of inherited fetal disorders. The technique samples skin cells and biochemical substances in the amniotic fluid that have come from the fetus.

ANABOLIC STEROIDS

Some naturally occurring steroids produced by the body, for example testosterone, have anabolic (muscle-building) effects. Increasingly, and controversially, synthetic anabolic steroids are being used, especially by athletes, to enhance muscle strength and power. Similar to testosterone, these drugs have been shown to increase strength and muscle mass when combined with exercise.

But they can also be dangerous. To be effective they must be used in dosages that are 10 to 40 times greater than those normally found in the body. As well as being anabolic, they are androgenic (they enhance male sexual characteristics) which in females can result in masculinization. Anabolic steroids have also been known to cause liver failure, arteriosclerosis, acne, baldness and blood lipid disorders. Their use can also lead to increased aggression, known as "roid rage". Increasingly, their use is being banned from organized sport.

SEE ALSO *Testosterone*

ANALGESICS

An analgesic is a drug that reduces or eliminates pain without loss of consciousness. Aspirin (acetylsalicylic acid) is the oldest

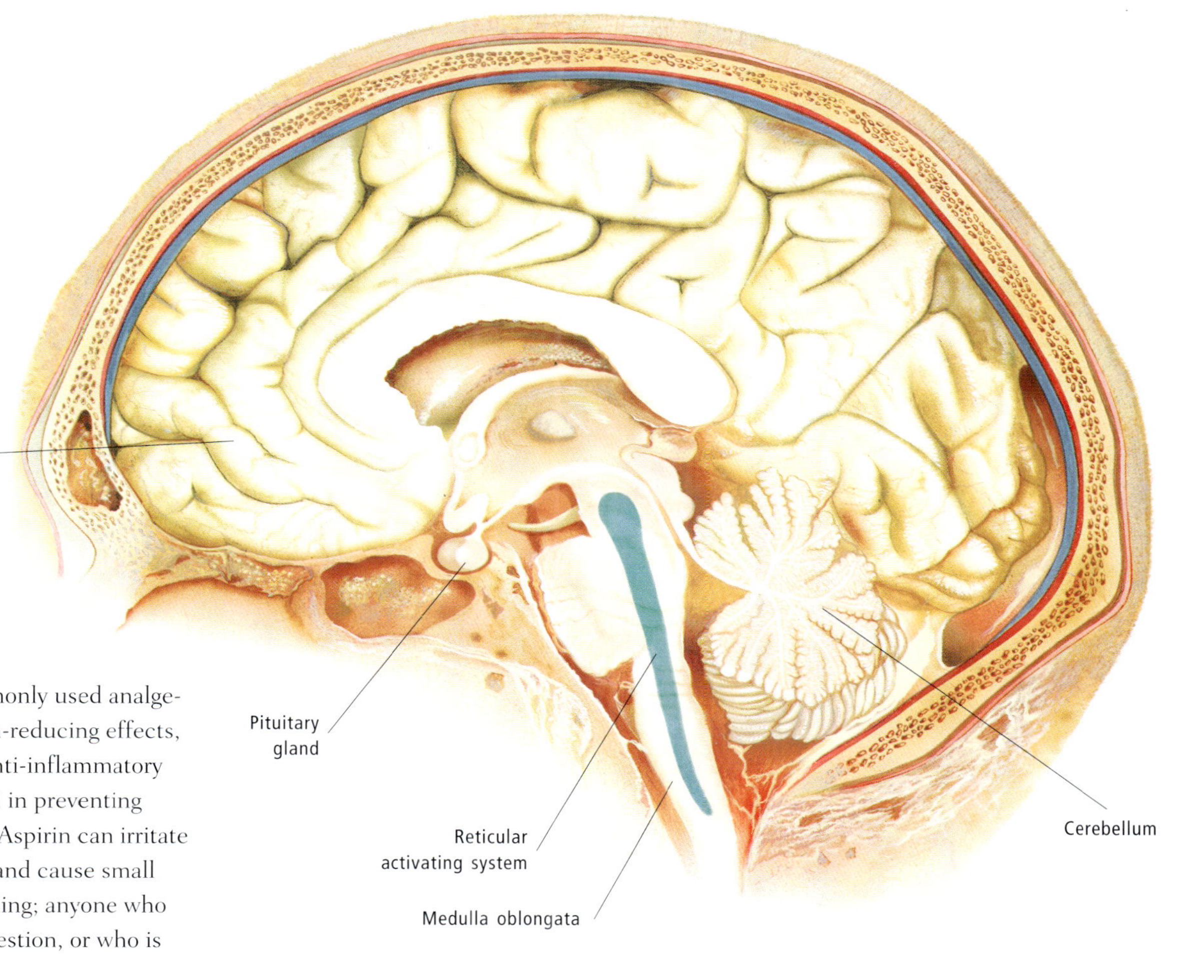

Amphetamines

Amphetamines are thought to work by acting on the cerebral cortex and the reticular activating system.

and one of the most commonly used analgesics. In addition to its pain-reducing effects, it reduces fever and has anti-inflammatory properties. It is also useful in preventing strokes and heart attacks. Aspirin can irritate the lining of the stomach and cause small amounts of stomach bleeding; anyone who has a peptic ulcer or indigestion, or who is taking anticoagulants, should use another analgesic such as acetaminophen (paracetamol). Aspirin should not be given to children, as it may cause Reye's syndrome.

Acetaminophen relieves pain and reduces fever. It is often used in its own right, or as a substitute for aspirin. It doesn't reduce inflammation, so it is not as useful as aspirin in treating inflammatory conditions such as arthritis. Side effects are not very common, but an overdose may cause liver or kidney damage.

Codeine is an opium derivative that is used for stronger pain. It is also used as a cough suppressant and a treatment for diarrhea. Prolonged use of large quantities of codeine may produce dependency. Codeine is often combined with aspirin or acetaminophen in analgesic preparation.

Other narcotic analgesics, such as morphine and its derivatives, are used for severe pain. They can also produce drowsiness, constipation and nausea. Prolonged use of these may be habit-forming, and an overdose can lead to death.

SEE ALSO *Morphine, Narcotics, Pain, Reye's syndrome*

ANAPHYLAXIS

Anaphylaxis is an immediate and violent reaction brought on by hypersensitivity to a particular substance. It is an extreme allergic response that occurs when a person comes into contact with a substance—an antigen—to which they are already allergic.

Antigens stimulate the body's immune system to fight them with specific antibodies and the release of histamine. The histamine within the body triggers the violent response known as anaphylactic shock. Capillaries enlarge and leak fluid into surrounding tissues; blood pressure collapses; the brain's oxygen supply is reduced; airways narrow and breathing is restricted; skin is pale and damp; there may be nausea and vomiting; there is a risk of heart failure and death. Anaphylaxis is often associated with insect bites or certain medications, such as penicillin.

Treatment often involves the injection of epinephrine (adrenaline) to restore blood pressure, and of other drugs such as steroids and antihistamines. People at risk often wear bracelets inscribed with their personal medical information and may even carry their own adrenaline injection kits. First aid is the same as required for a person who is in shock, and medical assistance is essential in all cases.

SEE ALSO *Allergies, Antihistamines, Epinephrine, Steroids*

ANDROGENS

Androgens are steroid hormones that produce male sex characteristics. The two main androgens are androsterone and testosterone. In men, they are secreted into the bloodstream by the testes (and to a lesser extent the adrenal glands) under stimulation from the pituitary gland. In women, smaller amounts are secreted by the ovaries and adrenals.

At the onset of puberty, production of testosterone in boys increases; facial and pubic hair develops, the larynx enlarges (so that the voice deepens), the penis and testes enlarge and there is an increase in body muscle strength. Virilism is the appearance of masculine characteristics in women or children, caused by excessive secretion of testosterone by the adrenal glands. In women, a male body hair pattern develops, the voice deepens, acne and baldness may develop, and menstrual periods may cease. In boys, it precipitates early puberty.

SEE ALSO *Pituitary gland, Puberty, Testes, Testosterone, Virilization*

ANEMIA

Anemia is a condition in which the red blood cells fail to provide sufficient oxygen supplies to the tissues of the body. It can be caused by decreased amounts of hemoglobin in red blood cells, or decreased numbers of red cells in the blood. Signs of anemia include tiredness and weakness, pallor (especially in the hands and eyelids), fainting, breathlessness and rapid heartbeat. To diagnose anemia, a physician takes a small sample of blood from the patient and counts the number of red blood cells and the concentration of hemoglobin in the sample. Normal levels of hemoglobin in the blood are approximately 14–17 grams per 100 milliliters (deciliter) for males and 12–15 grams per 100 milliliters for females.

The size and shape of the red blood cells can give a clue as to the cause of anemia. In pernicious anemia, for example, the red blood cells are larger than normal, whereas in iron deficiency anemia they are often smaller and paler than normal.

There are several causes of anemia. Iron deficiency anemia is caused by decreased absorption of iron, loss of iron from the body (usually from bleeding), or an increased need for iron. Malabsorption and/or poor nutrition may result in decreased absorption of iron and iron deficiency anemia. Premature babies often have low stores of iron at birth. Heavy menstrual bleeding or gastro-intestinal disease with bleeding (such as bowel cancer) may deplete the body's iron stores. Pregnancy or rapid growth may place too much demand on the body's iron reserves. Treatment is to maintain an adequate iron intake through a well-balanced diet or supplements, and to correct the underlying cause.

Pernicious anemia is the result of inadequate absorption of vitamin B_{12}, normally found in meat, fish and dairy products. It is

Androgens

The pituitary gland produces the hormones that trigger the release of androgens (androsterone and testosterone) by the adrenal glands and testes in men. These hormones are also produced in small amounts by the adrenals and ovaries in women. Androgens increase muscle mass and strength when combined with exercise. They are sometimes used by body builders to build muscle bulk.

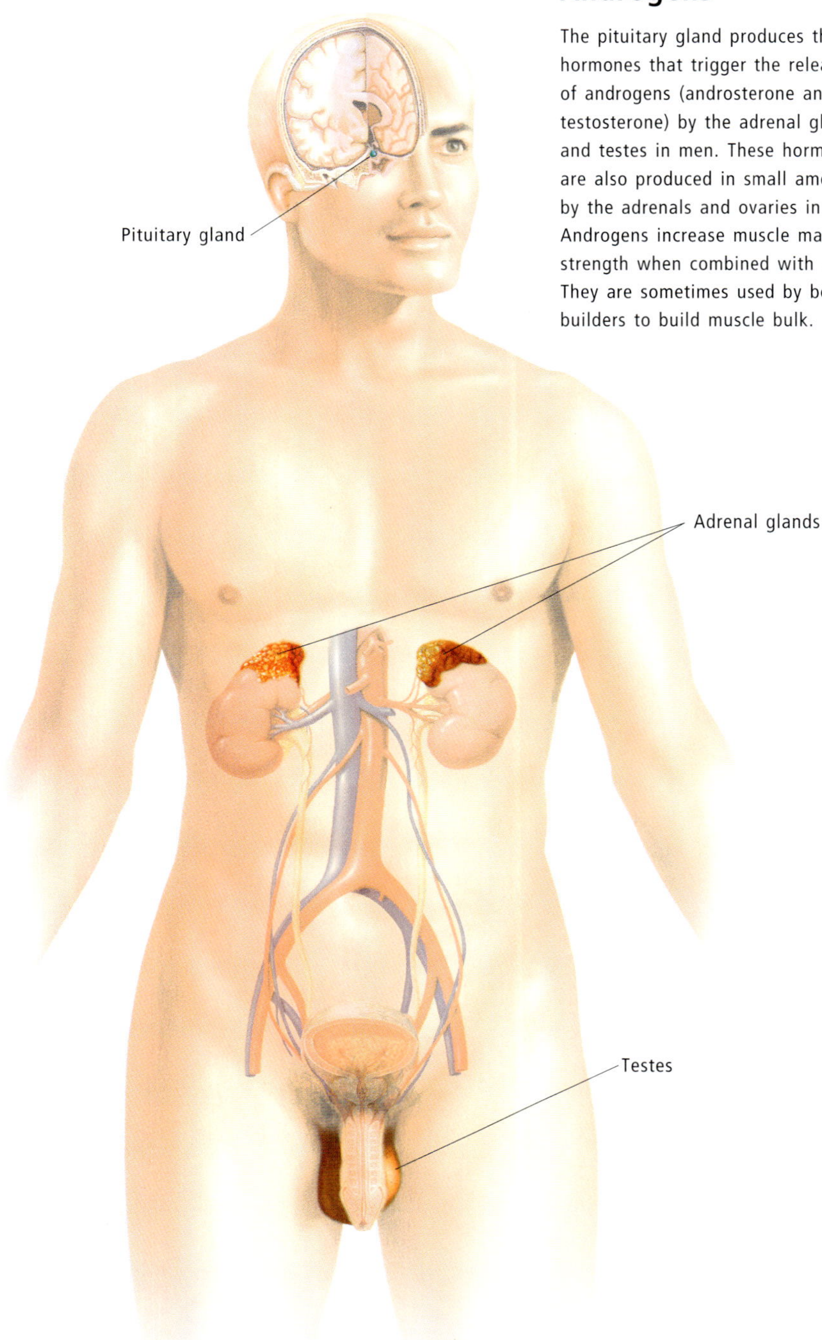

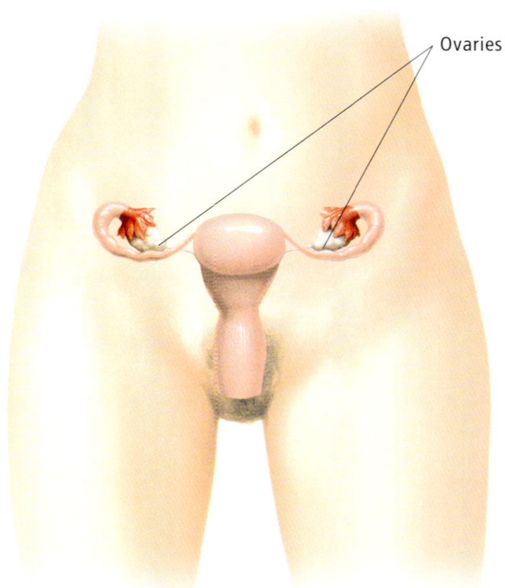

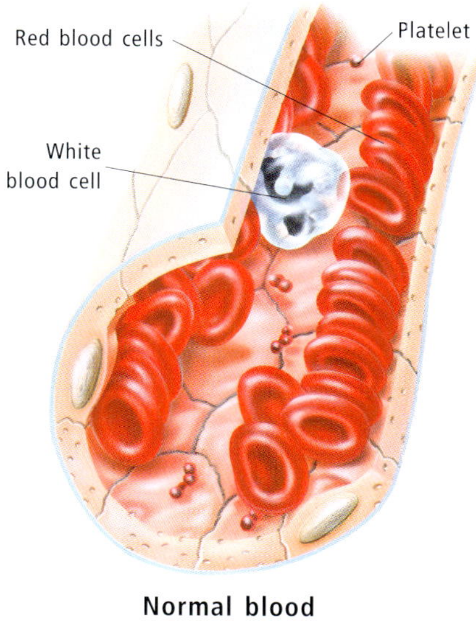

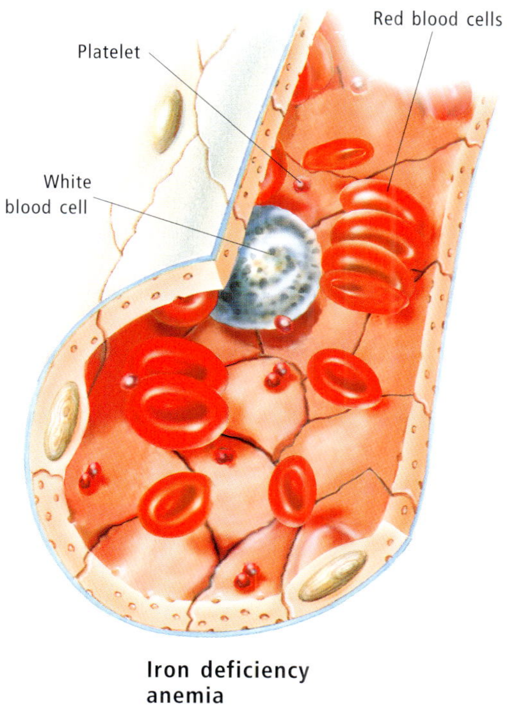

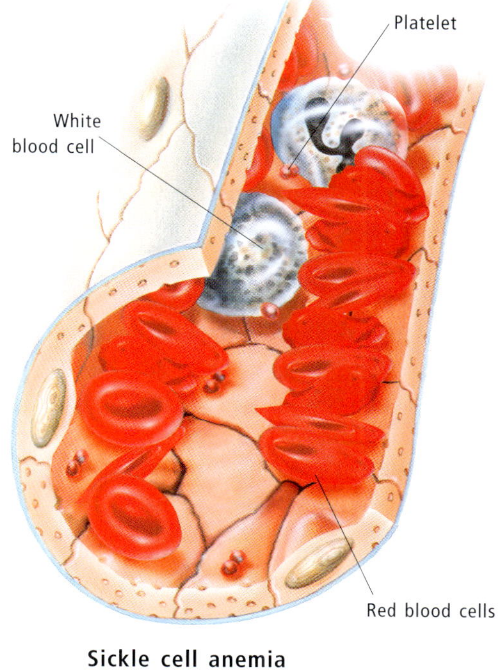

Anemia

In iron deficiency anemia the red blood cells (as shown here in a capillary) are smaller and paler than normal; in sickle cell anemia they are shaped liked a sickle.

caused by the absence of intrinsic factor, a chemical secreted by the stomach's lining which assists in the absorption of vitamin B_{12}. It may occur as an autoimmune disease or after stomach surgery. Pernicious anemia cannot be cured, but symptoms can be controlled with regular injections of vitamin B_{12}. Treatment needs to be continued for life.

Aplastic anemia is caused by decreased bone marrow production of red blood cells. Platelet and white blood cell production is also diminished so that, as well as anemia symptoms, the patient suffers abnormal bleeding and reduced resistance to infections. The condition is most often caused by drugs, especially immunosuppressant drugs, anti-cancer drugs, chloramphenicol or chemicals such as benzene. It may also be caused by immunodeficiency or severe illness. The patient should be isolated in hospital to avoid infection, and may receive blood transfusions and bone marrow transplantation.

Hemolytic anemia is caused by hemolysis, the premature destruction of red blood cells. The cells may be destroyed because they are abnormal or because of antibodies that attack them; bone marrow cannot produce red blood cells fast enough to compensate. Along with other symptoms, there may be jaundice (yellow skin and eyes, dark urine) and an enlarged spleen (splenomegaly).

The condition may be inherited (as in hereditary spherocytosis, sickle cell disease or thalassemia) or acquired, from blood transfusions or drugs. Acquired hemolytic anemia is treated by removing the cause. Immunosuppressant drugs may also be needed. Inherited forms of the condition are incurable, though symptoms can be controlled. Splenectomy (removal of the spleen) is sometimes needed.

SEE ALSO *Hemoglobin, Hemolytic anemia, Iron, Red blood cells, Sickle cell disease, Thalassemia*

ANESTHESIA

Anesthesia is loss of sensation, particularly to pain. Anesthetics are drugs which halt the sensation of pain through the body's nervous system. The nervous system is made up of neurons (nerve cells) which send information to the brain. The brain then processes this information and relays it to the muscles via motor neurons. Anesthetics act in various ways, such as affecting certain parts of nerves (called axons) and interfering with transmission between neurons.

History

Before anesthetics were available, surgery was a frighteningly painful ordeal. The practice of surgery was changed when in 1846, William Thomas Morton, in front of a group of physicians at Massachusetts General Hospital in Boston, demonstrated that ether could be used as a general anesthetic in an operation. Before that a British chemist had suggested that nitrous oxide (laughing gas) could be used but no-one tried this until an American dentist extracted his own tooth using it in 1844.

Four years later a Scottish physician, Sir James Simpson, gave chloroform to women in childbirth and Britain's Queen Victoria was among the first to promote it.

Both ether and chloroform had all kinds of ill effects, including death of the patient. As they were administered using simple devices made of glass or metal containing sponges soaked in the anesthetic, there was no control of the dosage given. Modern inhalation anesthetics such as trichlorethylene and halothane are administered by a machine which the anesthetist can control precisely.

Before today's extremely effective local anesthetics, many different substances were used to relieve the pain of surgery—cannabis, opium and rum being among the most common. Cocaine was the first generally used local anesthetic and since then it has become the convention to end the names given to local anesthetics with "caine", for example procaine, lidocaine, and tetracaine.

A

Types of anesthetics

There are three types of drug-induced anesthesia: local anesthesia, which involves the numbing of a local nerve and can be administered in the form of a cream, injection or eye drops; regional anesthesia, which is the numbing of larger areas, for example a limb, and is done by a series of local anesthetic injections around a nerve or number of nerves; and general anesthesia, which renders the person totally unconscious and involves the inhalation of gas, the injection of drugs into the bloodstream or a combination of both.

When local anesthetics are applied directly to mucous membranes they are known as topical anesthetics—teething gels being an example. When a local anesthetic is injected into the space just outside the membranous sheath of the lumbar spinal cord (dura), it removes sensation from the lower part of the body, either partially or completely. This form of regional anesthesia is known as a lumbar epidural injection or epidural anesthesia and is commonly used in childbirth. Spinal anesthesia, which is rarely used because of complications, is an injection into the cerebrospinal fluid in the lower spine.

Acupuncture, which uses fine needles inserted into key areas of the body to stimulate lines of energy, provides relief for many, though how it works is still poorly understood. Hypnosis can also be used to reduce the amount of pain a person is experiencing. Rather than actually anesthetizing, hypnosis is most useful in relaxing the patient prior to anesthesia and in improving the effect of the drugs, as well as reducing the dosage required. Both acupuncture and hypnosis have been found to reduce the need for other forms of analgesia in childbirth. In the treatment of intractable pain, hypnosis is a useful tool and it is also sometimes used in dental treatment.

TENS (transcutaneous electrical nerve stimulation) is a method which involves the application of a gentle current to the surface of the skin. It is a form of pain relief which is used for back, neck and joint pain, as well as arthritis, migraines and the pain of childbirth.

SEE ALSO *Acupuncture, Cocaine, Epidural anesthesia, Hypnotherapy, Pain, Synapses*

ANEURYSM

An aneurysm is an abnormal dilatation of a blood vessel, usually an artery, caused by weakness in the vessel's wall.

An aneurysm of the aorta, the major artery connecting the heart to other arteries of the body, typically occurs in an older person and is usually caused by arteriosclerosis. Often it has no symptoms for many years, then eventually ruptures, resulting in profuse bleeding into the chest or abdomen. Symptoms are searing chest pain, shortness of breath, collapse with low blood pressure (hypotension) and shock from blood loss.

A rapidly expanding or ruptured aortic aneurysm is a medical emergency requiring resuscitation, hospitalization and surgery. Death occurs in 50 percent of cases. However, if the aneurysm occurs in the abdominal aorta and is detected early, allowing surgery before rupture occurs, chances are better.

An aneurysm can also occur in the large arteries at the base of the brain (berry aneurysm). It is usually congenital and hereditary. Bleeding from the aneurysm into the subarachnoid space in the brain is known as subarachnoid hemorrhage; this causes severe headache and stroke with paralysis and coma. Emergency surgery may be life saving, but the mortality rate is high.

SEE ALSO *Aorta, Arteries, Arteriosclerosis, Blood vessels, Subarachnoid hemorrhage*

ANGINA PECTORIS

Angina pectoris is the name given to chest pain caused by lack of oxygen to the heart, due to arteriosclerosis in the coronary (heart) arteries. It is usually brought on by exercise. In severe arteriosclerosis, the pain may be felt at rest, when it is known as unstable angina. The pain is felt across the chest and may also be felt in the neck, between the shoulder blades and in the arms. In severe cases sufferers describe the pain as "crushing", and may also feel cold, sweaty and anxious, and have difficulty breathing.

Angina pectoris can be confirmed by an electrocardiogram (EKG), which shows certain changes while the pain is present. If pain is not present, changes can be demonstrated while the patient is undergoing exercise (stress test). Other tests include cardiac angiography and perfusion scanning.

The condition is commonly treated with drugs that dilate the coronary arteries and increase the blood flow to the heart muscle. These include nitroglycerin tablets, which can be taken under the tongue (they usually relieve pain within seconds and confirm the diagnosis of angina). Nitrates can also be given as tablets or skin patches. Beta-blockers and calcium antagonists (channel blockers) are also used to treat angina. Balloon angioplasty and bypass surgery are other options.

Angina can be treated at home if it responds to drug treatment. If not, or there is unstable angina (pain at rest), hospitalization may be necessary, as the angina may then be a sign of myocardial infarction (heart attack).

SEE ALSO *Arteriosclerosis, Beta-blockers, Coronary artery disease, Electrocardiogram, Heart*

ANGIOEDEMA

Angioedema is a severe allergic reaction, similar in many ways to urticaria. The chief difference is that urticaria affects the surface layers of the skin while angioedema affects the deeper layers. It may occur with or without urticaria. Like urticaria, angioedema is caused by an allergic trigger. This may be an insect bite or sting, food (shellfish, nuts, food additives or strawberries), exposure to animals or pollen, or a reaction to a drug such as penicillin.

While the hives and wheals of urticaria are annoying, they are not dangerous. In angioedema, however, the eyes, lips and skin around the eyes may swell markedly. If the swelling spreads to the throat, suffocation may occur. As with urticaria, mild cases of angioedema can be treated with antihistamine tablets. In more serious cases an intravenous injection of hydrocortisone or epinephrine (adrenaline) is given to reduce the swelling and remove the risk of suffocation. Any trigger factors known to bring on the condition should be avoided.

SEE ALSO *Allergies, Urticaria*

ANGIOGRAPHY

Angiography is an investigative x-ray technique that is used to show the nature and extent of disease in arteries, veins and lymph vessels. It involves insertion of a catheter,

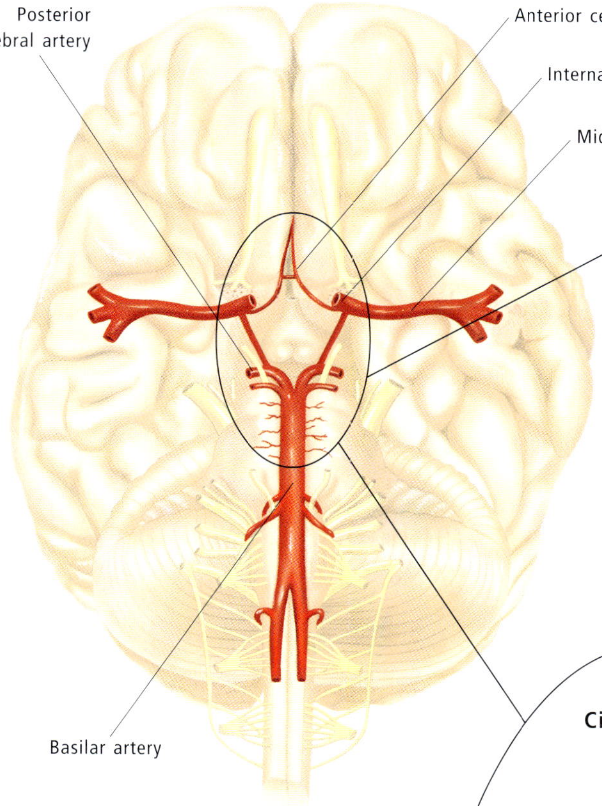

Underside of the brain

Circle of Willis

The circle of Willis is a circuit of arteries at the base of the brain. It is the most common site for a berry aneurysm to form. A berry aneurysm is a type of small congenital aneurysm that forms in the brain and may cause a fatal stroke.

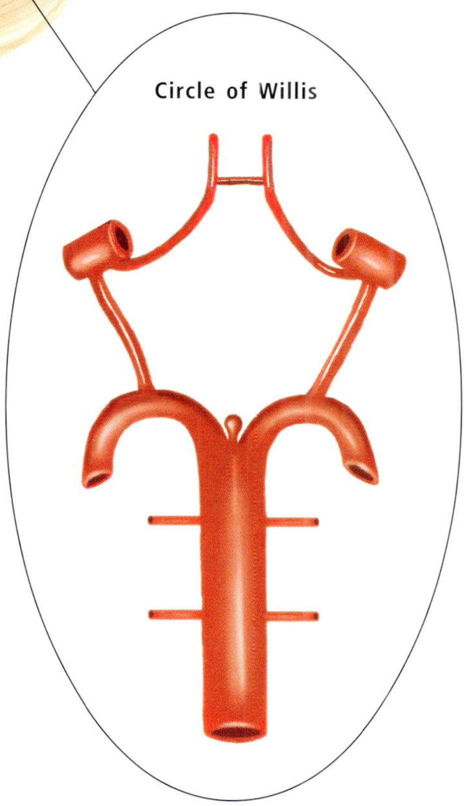

followed by the injection into the artery of a dye that is opaque to x-rays. X-rays are taken, and any areas of abnormal blood flow or blockages of arteries are highlighted by the dye. Angiography is used by the physician or surgeon to decide if arterial disease is present, and, if so, which arteries to treat.

Arteries commonly examined this way include femoral (thigh) arteries and the coronary arteries of the heart. It is commonly used before heart surgery. In the great majority of cases, the procedure is very safe and is performed with the patient sedated but conscious. A few patients are allergic to the dye and may develop hives or, in more serious cases, anaphylactic shock. Hence, the procedure is carried out in hospital with resuscitation facilities nearby. Treatment of shock is with intravenous epinephrine (adrenaline). Allergic people are treated with steroids before the procedure to prevent an allergic reaction.

SEE ALSO *Angioplasty, Arteries, Arteriosclerosis*

ANGIOMA

An angioma is an abnormal, though benign (non-cancerous), growth of small blood vessels. It may occur internally, or as a soft, purplish or reddish mark on the skin. Cherry angioma, spider angioma and strawberry nevus are common examples.

Treatment may not be necessary if the disfigurement can be concealed by cosmetics. If treatment is required, a small angioma in the skin may be burned or cauterized, but larger ones need plastic surgery.

An angioma in the brain may bleed, causing subarachnoid hemorrhage or a stroke. An angioma that bleeds in the digestive tract may cause anemia, black stools (melena), or vomiting of blood.

SEE ALSO *Anemia, Blood vessels, Stroke, Subarachnoid hemorrhage*

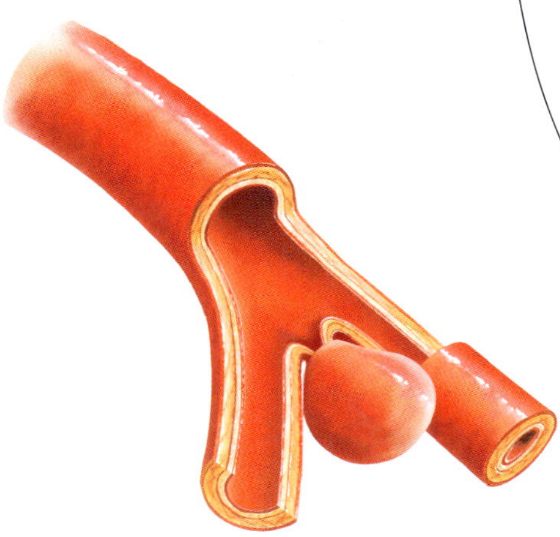

Berry aneurysm

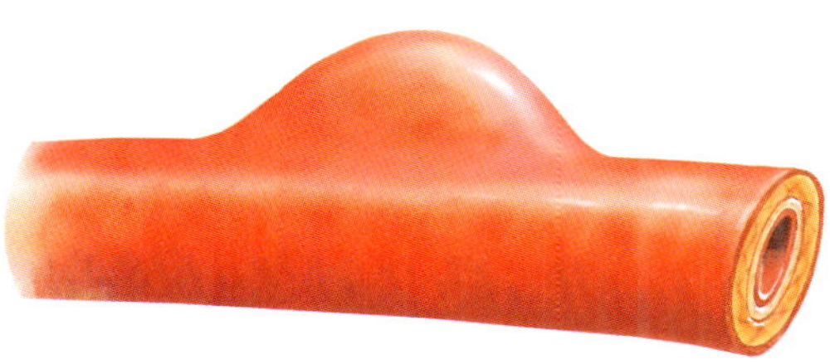

Aneurysm

Aneurysm

When an artery wall is weakened by a disease such as arteriosclerosis, blood pressure may force the walls of the artery out. This ballooning of an artery is called an aneurysm.

A

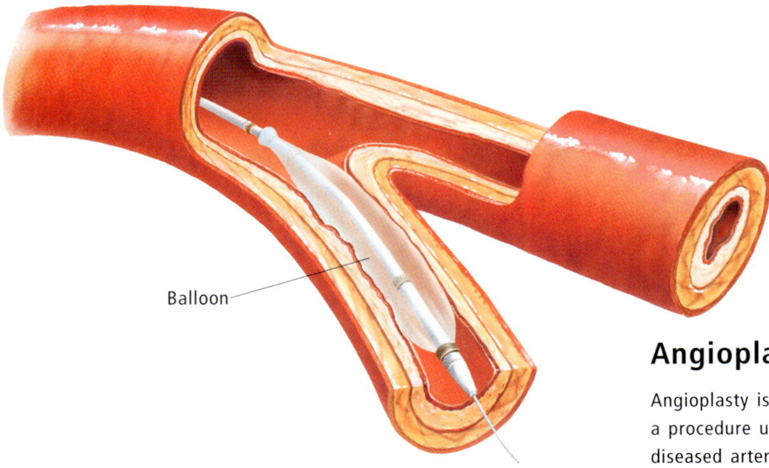

Angioplasty

Angioplasty is the name for a procedure used to repair a diseased artery. One technique uses an inflatable balloon on the end of a catheter which is inserted into the artery. The balloon expands and compresses the blockage.

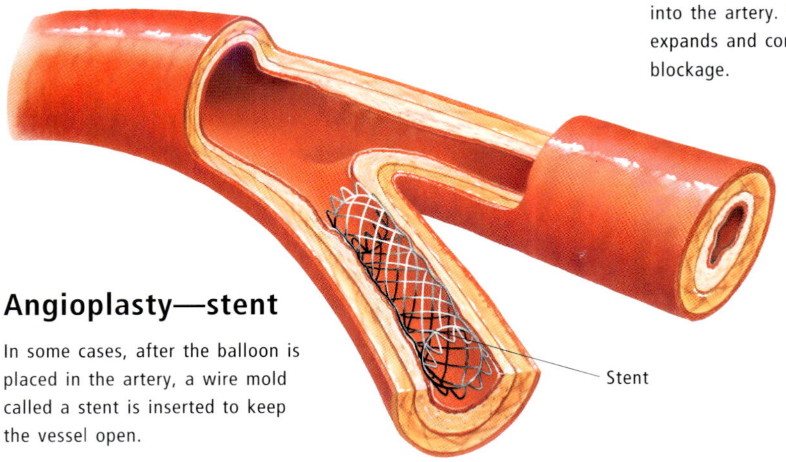

Angioplasty—stent

In some cases, after the balloon is placed in the artery, a wire mold called a stent is inserted to keep the vessel open.

ANGIOPLASTY

Angioplasty is the repair of blood vessels affected by disease (usually atherosclerosis). It may be performed in the blood vessels supplying the heart or in the arteries of the limbs, brain or kidney.

Angioplasty may be surgical or non-surgical. In surgical angioplasty, segments of the affected artery are removed and replaced with tissue from a vein from elsewhere in the body, or synthetic tissue. This procedure provides an alternative to bypass surgery.

Balloon angioplasty is a non-surgical method of removing atherosclerotic plaque, the fibrous and fatty deposits on the walls of blocked arteries. A catheter with a balloon-like tip is threaded up from the arm or groin through the artery until it reaches the blocked area. The balloon is then inflated many times, flattening the plaque and widening the blood vessel; the balloon is then removed. Often a wire mold called a stent is then inserted into the vessel to keep the vessel open. This technique is especially suitable when only one vessel is blocked.

Laser angioplasty involves a similar technique, except that the catheter has a camera lens on its tip connected to a screen, allowing the physician to spot areas of plaque build-up. A laser fixed to the tip is used to destroy the plaque.

SEE ALSO *Arteries, Atherosclerosis, Blood vessels*

ANKLE

The ankle is the region where the lower leg joins the foot. The ankle attaches the bones of the lower leg, the tibia and fibula, to the talus, one of the bones of the foot. The ankle joint is what's known as a synovial hinge joint and is fairly stable. It allows the heel to be raised from the ground, as in pointing one's toes (plantarflexion) and for the upper surface of the foot to be brought closer to the front of the leg (dorsiflexion). Prominent features of the ankle joint include the medial malleolus, a bony protrusion on the end of the tibia and the lateral malleolus, a similar bony landmark at the lower end of the fibula. The two malleoli, together with a part of the tibia, form a socket in which the talus can move. Because the talus is wider at the front, the joint is most stable when the heel is raised, where the fit between the talus and socket is tightest.

Several ligaments help to make the ankle joint stronger and more stable. The deltoid or medial ligament is a broad, strong, triangular-shaped ligament which connects the medial malleolus to three of the tarsal bones (talus, navicular and calcaneus). On the outside of the ankle there are three cord-like ligaments that attach the lateral malleolus to the talus and calcaneus. These cords are not as strong as the deltoid ligament so they can be more easily damaged. Ligaments between the tibia and fibula also help ankle joint stability by strengthening the socket.

The main muscles producing dorsiflexion of the ankle lie at the front of the lower leg while the main muscles producing plantarflexion are at the back of the lower leg (calf muscles).

Sprain

A sprain is an over-stretching or tearing of ligaments; sprains are particularly common around the ankle joint. A frequent injury, referred to as "twisting the ankle", occurs when the foot is forcefully turned inward. This usually occurs as a result of a fall on an uneven surface and leads to tearing of the ligaments on the outside of the ankle. This will cause pain and swelling in front and below the lateral malleolus and can make the ankle joint quite unstable.

As for most sprain injuries, ice packs, rest and elevation will reduce swelling and aid healing. Injuries to the deltoid ligaments (when the sole of the foot is turned outwards) can also occur but are less common, because these ligaments are stronger.

Fractures

Fractures of the ankle are fairly common, and include breaking of the lateral malleolus and an injury known as Pott's fracture. Pott's fracture occurs when the foot is forcefully

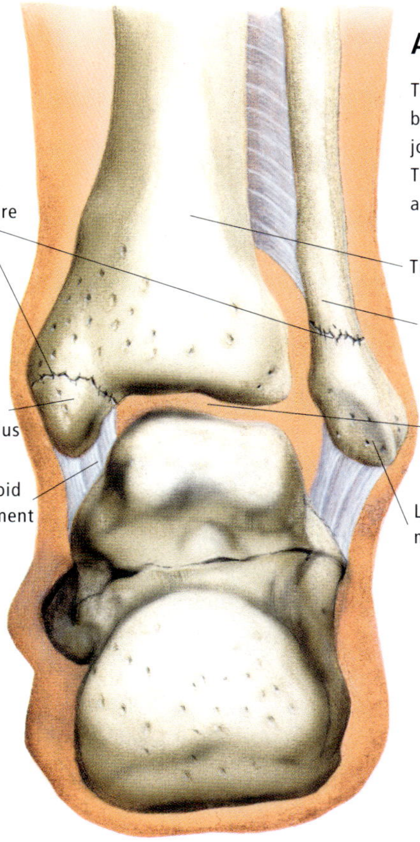

Ankle fracture

The ankle bones are prone to fracture because the ankle is a weight-bearing joint and is easily put under stress. The ankle fracture shown here is called a Pott's fracture.

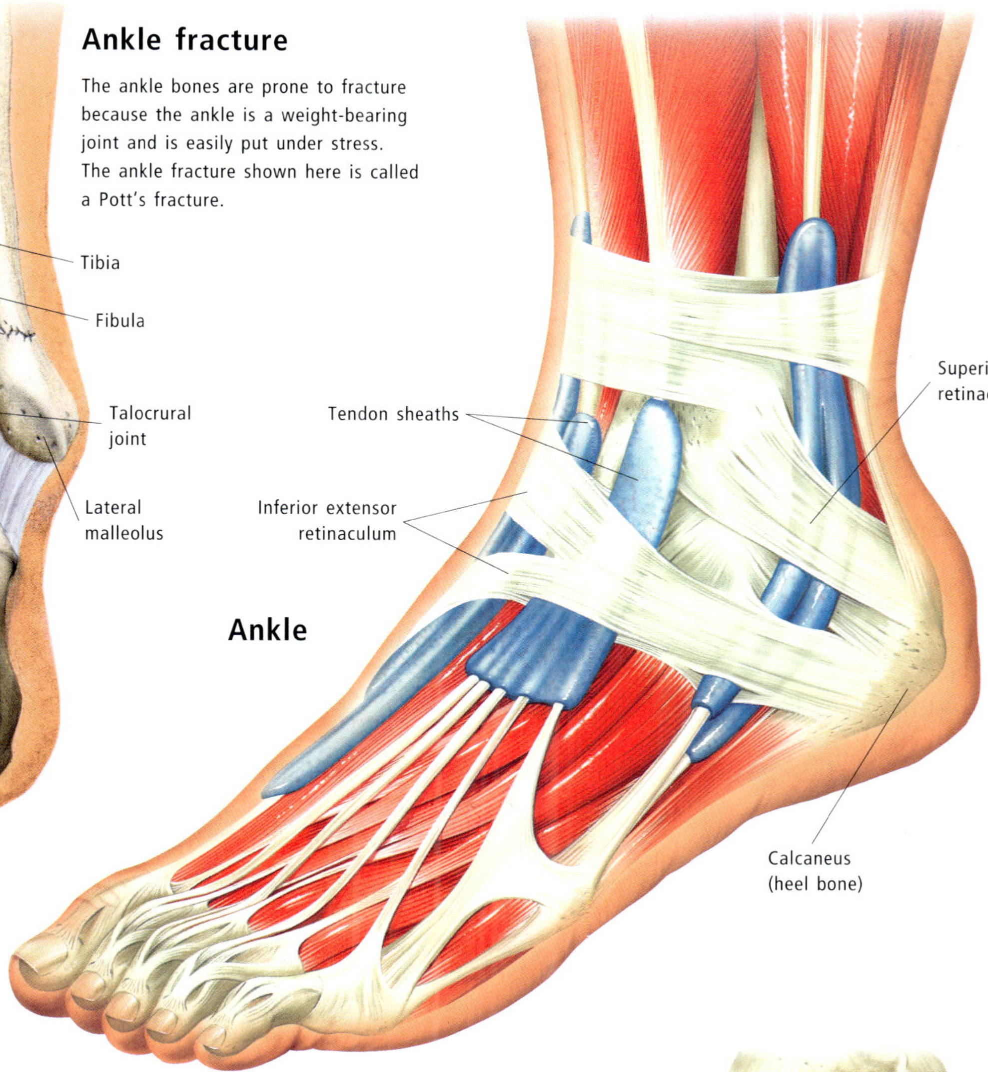

Ankle

turned outward. The medial malleolus is broken and there is also an associated fracture of the fibula, either at the lateral malleolus or higher, on the shaft of the bone.

SEE ALSO *Foot, Fractures, Leg, Sprain*

ANKYLOSING SPONDYLITIS

Ankylosing spondylitis is a form of arthritis affecting young men between 15 and 40 years of age. It involves the spine, the sacro-iliac joints in the pelvis, the hip and the shoulder. Over the years these joints gradually become inflamed and eventually stiff and immovable. The cause is unknown, though the disease tends to be inherited and to run in families.

The first sign of the illness is often low back pain and stiffness, which is worse in the morning, gets better during the day with exercise, but occurs again at night, often waking the sufferer from sleep. As the disease progresses, back pain and stiffness

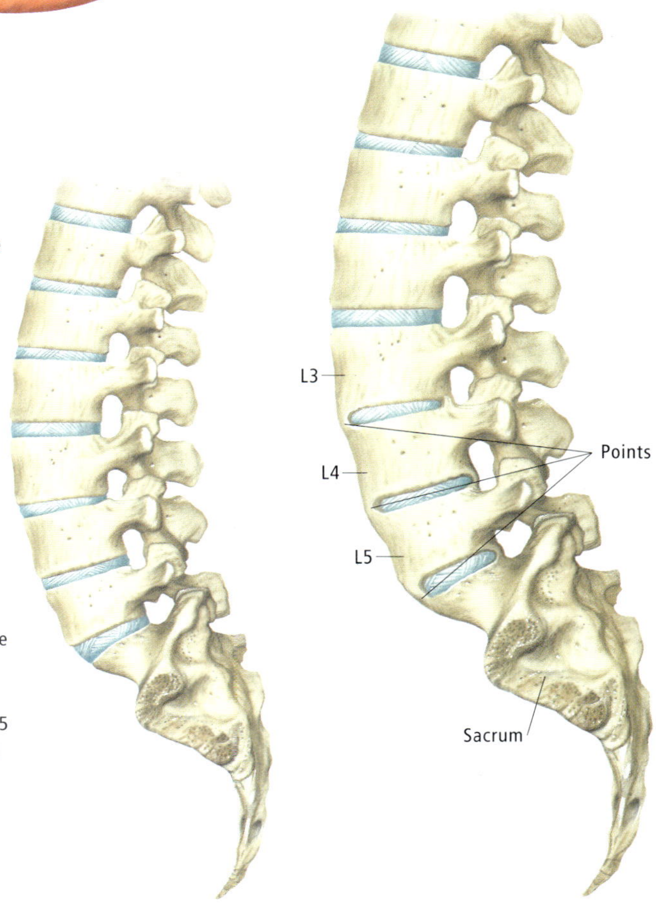

Normal spine

Ankylosing spondylitis

In long-standing cases of ankylosing spondylitis, the vertebral bones of the spine may fuse together. In this example, the bodies of lumbar vertebrae 3, 4 and 5 and the sacrum have fused together.

A

eventually affect the upper part of the spine and sometimes the neck. The vertebrae in the spine may become fused, creating an abnormal curve in the upper spine. Hips and shoulders are affected in a third of cases. A quarter of cases develop uveitis, or inflammation of the front part of the eye.

There is no cure for ankylosing spondylitis, but some measures can lessen the effects of the disease. Breathing exercises, and exercises to maintain posture, help with the curvature of the upper spine. Analgesics and anti-inflammatory drugs are commonly prescribed. Surgery, for example hip replacement, may be required in severe cases.

SEE ALSO *Arthritis*

ANTHRAX

Anthrax is an infectious disease caused by the bacterium *Bacillus anthracis*, rarely seen in the Western world today, but which still exists in Africa, Asia and the Middle East. The infection is transmitted to humans most commonly by farm animals such as sheep, cattle, horses, goats and swine, and is transmitted through a break in the skin.

Symptoms include nausea, fever and the occurrence of a skin boil that forms a dark scab. The boil forms slowly and may spread to form other boils.

In another (rarer) form, anthrax spores are inhaled and cause a rapidly fatal pneumonia—hence experimentation by some governments with anthrax as a biological weapon.

Immediate treatment with penicillin or tetracycline is usually effective in treating the skin form of anthrax. A vaccine is available for travelers at risk of exposure to animals or animal products in affected areas.

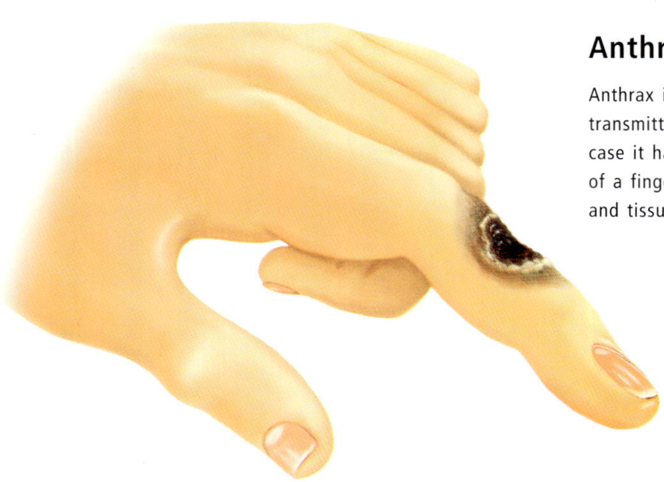

Anthrax

Anthrax is an infectious disease transmitted from farm animals. In this case it has caused an ulcer on the skin of a finger. The dark area is dead skin and tissue.

ANTHROPOSOPHICAL MEDICINE

Rudolf Steiner, the Austrian philosopher and scientist, pioneered anthroposophical medicine in the early twentieth century. At the heart of its approach is the belief that a person is more than just a body, and that medical treatment needs to integrate the physical and spiritual components of being.

Natural and creative therapies are favored, including herbal and homeopathic preparations, art therapy, music therapy and massage. Best known of the anthroposophical treatments is the mistletoe (*Viscum album*) remedy, given intravenously to cancer patients, and believed to have an anti-tumor action through its immune stimulating effects. Anthroposophical medicine is officially recognized throughout continental Europe.

ANTIARRHYTHMIC DRUGS

Antiarrhythmic drugs control irregularities of the heartbeat. The oldest antiarrhythmics are digitalis and quinidine, both of which were originally plant extracts. Modern antiarrhythmics include beta-blockers, calcium antagonists and disopyramide. Digitalis medications (digoxin and digitoxin) help control the rate of contractions and regulate the rhythm of the heart. If the dose is too high, digitalis toxicity can occur, producing unusual visual effects, nausea and vomiting; blood tests need to be done regularly to monitor blood levels. Beta-blockers such as propanalol, atenolol and pindolol decrease heart rate by affecting conduction in the heart. Beta-blockers can cause asthma attacks, so are not suitable for asthmatics.

SEE ALSO *Heartbeat*

ANTIBIOTICS

Antibiotics are drugs that fight bacterial infection. They work either by preventing an infection from growing (bacteriostatic antibiotics) or by destroying an existing infection (bactericidal antibiotics). Some are effective against a broad range of bacteria (broad-spectrum antibiotics), while others are only effective against certain types of bacteria.

Antibiotics are produced either from a mold or a fungus, or are produced synthetically. Common forms include aminoglycosides, macrolides, penicillins, tetracyclines and cephalosporins. They may be given orally, or via intravenous or intramuscular routes in more serious infections.

The modern trend is against using antibiotics indiscriminately or for the wrong reasons—for example, in treating viral illnesses (on which they have no effect).

A course of antibiotics must be finished to prevent bacteria re-establishing infection and developing immunity against the drug.

Side effects may include rashes, nausea, diarrhea and secondary infections such as thrush. In rare cases, anaphylaxis may occur. Tetracyclines should not be administered during pregnancy, or given to young children as they may discolor developing teeth. Aminoglycosides such as gentamicin, amikacin and tobramycin can cause damage to the auditory nerves and to the kidney.

SEE ALSO *Bacteria, Penicillins*

ANTIBODIES

An antibody forms part of the body's defense against infection. When an invader (antigen) such as a virus or bacterium enters the body during an infection, specialized white blood cells known as lymphocytes react by making proteins called antibodies. These combine with the invader and neutralize it. The presence of antibodies indicates past exposure to a disease. Many blood tests for diseases work by identifying antibodies in the blood.

Antibodies can be created artificially in the body by immunization. This involves exposing the body to a weakened or killed form of virus or other invader. It causes the body to manufacture antibodies, so that if later exposed to the real disease, it can launch a prompt and effective immune response.

SEE ALSO *Immunization*

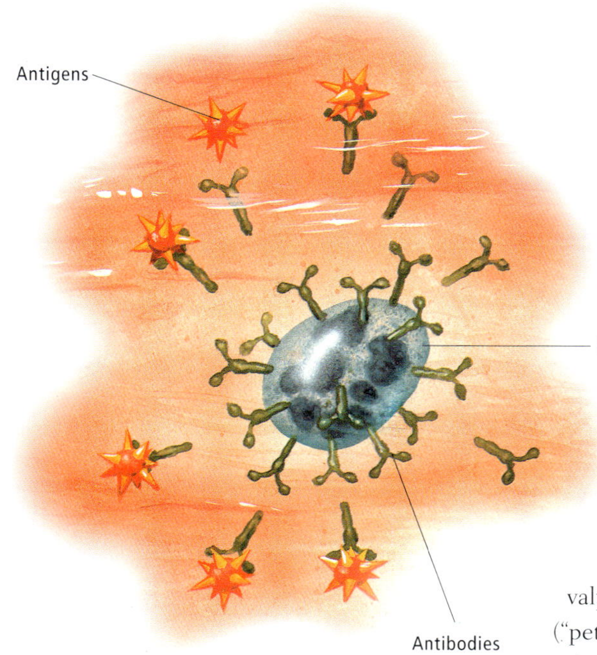

Antibodies

Once the body recognizes a foreign substance (antigen) has entered the body, B lymphocytes are activated, become plasma cells and begin producing antibodies. The antibodies attach to the antigens, which are eventually neutralized.

ANTICOAGULANTS

Anticoagulants are drugs that interfere with the normal clotting of blood. They are used in myocardial infarction (heart attack), strokes, embolism and during surgery in order to prevent blood clotting (thrombosis). Warfarin is an oral preparation suitable for long-term therapy. Heparin is a quick-acting intravenous or intramuscular preparation used over shorter periods, for example in a hospital setting. Low-dose aspirin is taken by many people as a low-grade anticoagulant.

As too much anticoagulant can cause bleeding, people taking them require regular blood tests to ensure correct dosage. They should also carry a card or wear a bracelet identifying the drug and dose in case of accident. Some medications affect the action of anticoagulants—check with your doctor.

SEE ALSO *Blood*

ANTICONVULSANTS

Anticonvulsant drugs prevent epileptic attacks by depressing the activity of the brain. Some are more suited to particular types of seizures and not to other types. They are often used in combination. Anticonvulsants need to be taken for the long term: years, or even for life. However, once the sufferer has been free of seizures for several years, the dose can be reduced or the drugs stopped. Commonly used anticonvulsants include carbamazepine, phenytoin, lamotrigine, gabapentin, topiramate and valproate for generalized ("grand mal") seizures; and valproate or ethosuximide for smaller ("petit mal") seizures. Possible side effects include drowsiness, rashes, dizziness, headache, nausea and indigestion.

SEE ALSO *Convulsions, Epilepsy*

ANTIDEPRESSANTS

Antidepressants are drugs that alleviate depression. They work by correcting the biochemical imbalance in the brain that is thought to be the cause of depression.

The oldest are the tricyclic antidepressants such as amitriptyline and imipramine, which elevate the levels of the neurotransmitters serotonin and norepinephrine (noradrenaline) in the brain. Side effects may include dry mouth, blurred vision, sweating, constipation, urinary problems and impotence (in males).

The monamine-oxidase (MAO) inhibitors are less popular as they interact dangerously with foods such as cheese, some meats, alcohol and yeast extracts. They are usually used only if other antidepressants fail.

The newest category of antidepressants are the serotonin-specific reuptake inhibitors (SSRI). As they work quickly and have few side effects, they are the most commonly prescribed nowadays. Examples include fluoxetine (Prozac) and paroxetine.

It takes from two to six weeks for an antidepressant to begin to work. The initial dose is usually kept low to minimize side effects and is increased over time until the desired result is reached. Most side effects disappear in a few days or weeks.

SEE ALSO *Depression, Psychotropic drugs*

ANTIDIARRHEALS

Antidiarrheals are drugs used for the relief of symptoms of diarrhea. Some are simple absorbent substances such as kaolin, chalk or charcoal. They absorb water and help harden the feces. Others, such as diphenoxylate (often used in combination with atropine), slow down the contractions of the bowel muscle so that the contents are propelled more slowly and more water is

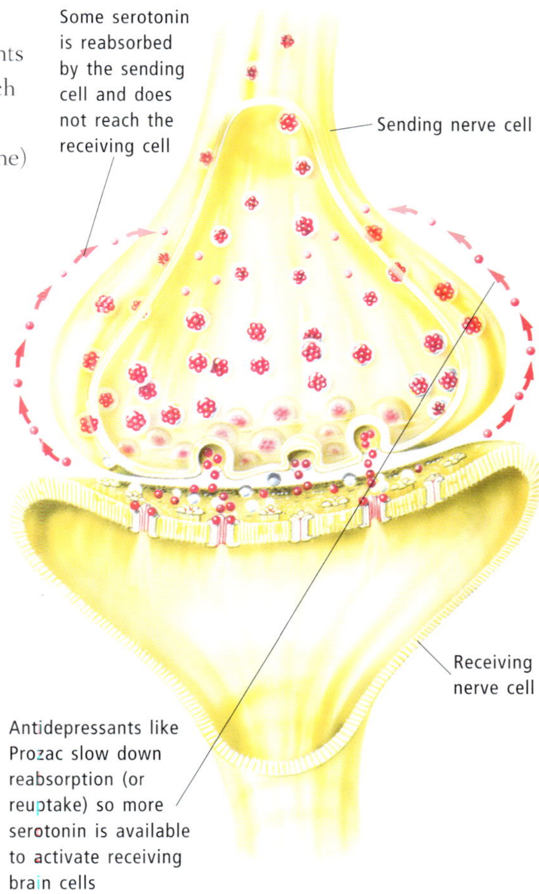

Antidepressants

Serotonin is a neurotransmitter which activates nerve cells in the brain. Sending cells pass serotonin across the synapse to receiving cells but also reabsorb a certain amount. Depression may occur when too much serotonin is reabsorbed by the sending cells and does not reach the receiving cells. Antidepressant drugs called serotonin-specific reuptake inhibitors work by slowing down this reabsorption process, allowing more serotonin to reach receiving cells.

absorbed by the bowel. Overtreatment with anti-diarrhea drugs can cause constipation and abdominal cramps, so excessive or extended use is not recommended. Codeine, an analgesic, also relieves diarrhea, though prolonged use may cause addiction.

SEE ALSO *Diarrhea*

ANTIEMETIC DRUGS

Antiemetic drugs are used to treat the symptoms of nausea and vomiting. Phenothiazines, a type of major tranquilizer, are the most potent antiemetics, but they also have the greatest number of side effects, including drowsiness, hypotension (low blood pressure) and movement disorders.

Antihistamines (usually used to treat allergies) are also useful in treating nausea, especially when it is associated with motion sickness. Antihistamines may produce drowsiness, so people who take them should not drink alcohol, drive automobiles or operate machinery.

Anticholinergics, which slow the actions of the smooth muscle in the bowel, are often used in the relief of nausea and vomiting associated with vertigo and motion sickness. Side effects of these drugs can include blurred vision, dry mouth and tachycardia (rapid heart rate). They should not be used for treatment of people with glaucoma and urinary retention as they worsen these conditions.

SEE ALSO *Antihistamines, Nausea, Vomiting*

ANTIFUNGALS

Antifungals are used to treat infections such as ringworm, candidiasis and athlete's foot (tinea pedis). Those commonly used include clotrimazole, miconazole and ketoconazole.

Since fungi tend to be more resistant to treatment than other microorganisms, a lengthy duration of treatment is usually required to cure a fungal infection.

Antifungals may be taken in tablet form or applied as creams, ointments or pessaries. Serious internal fungal infections such as actinomycosis, blastomycosis and histoplasmosis may be treated by antifungal injections.

SEE ALSO *Candidiasis, Ringworm, Tinea*

ANTIGEN TESTS

The immune system responds to molecules that are recognized as foreign: these are called antigens and are carried by bacteria (e.g. salmonella), viruses (e.g. hepatitis B), toxins and other substances such as allergens. Antigen tests are used to detect which foreign substance is causing illness or other reactions in the affected person.

It is possible to test for the development of different types of immune responses to an antigen in a number of ways, but an important group of antigen tests is that used to detect responses to allergens in the environment. These allergens include, for example, cat and dog fur; feathers; house dust mites; cockroaches; various molds; and pollens of grasses, weeds or trees. Testing for an allergic response involves introducing small amounts of antigen into the superficial layers of the skin by a prick or scratch, then measuring the resulting zone of redness and wheal formation 30 to 60 minutes later. Multiple antigens are usually tested at once. People predisposed to developing allergic responses often react to several antigens.

SEE ALSO *Allergies*

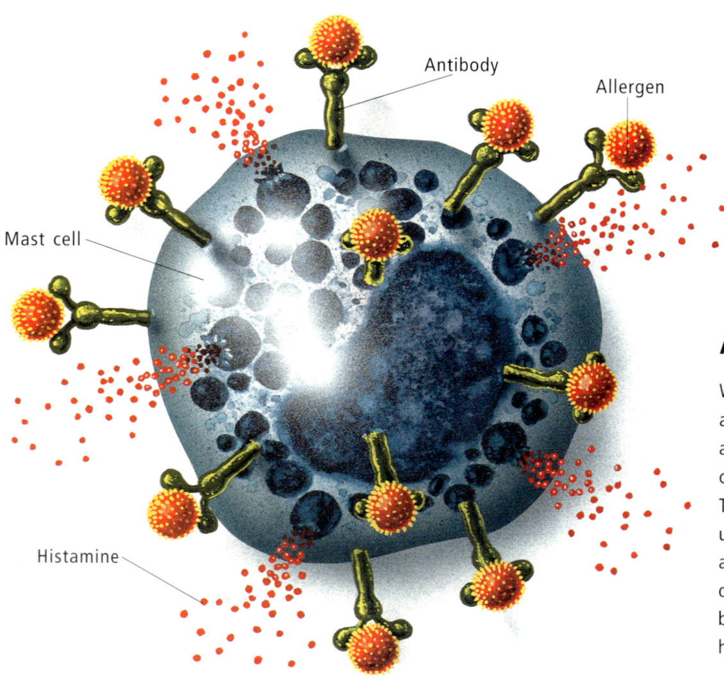

Antihistamines

When mast cells are activated by invading allergens they release a chemical called histamine. This is responsible for the unpleasant effects of allergies like hay fever or hives. Antihistamines block the release of histamine.

ANTIHISTAMINES

Antihistamines form the main group of medicines used in treatment and control of allergies. They work by blocking the action of histamine, a chemical produced in the body as part of an allergic reaction. They can also fight nausea and so can be used to counter travel sickness. The side effect of most antihistamines is drowsiness (though some newer types are less sedating), so they should not be taken before driving or operating machinery, and it is not safe to drink alcohol while on the medication. They are often used at night, and their sedative effect can be useful for treating insomnia.

SEE ALSO *Allergies*

ANTIHYPERTENSIVES

Antihypertensives are drugs used to treat high blood pressure (hypertension). They may be given orally or by injection for rapid effect, and may be used alone or in combination.

Beta-blockers decrease heart rate and cause relaxation of small peripheral blood vessels, lowering blood pressure. They are not suitable for asthmatics as they may cause an asthma attack. Thiazide diuretics relax small blood vessels and also cause the kidneys to increase the amount of salt and water eliminated in the urine. Potassium levels may drop, so doctors also commonly prescribe a potassium supplement.

Calcium channel blockers influence the movement of calcium ions into the cells of the heart and blood vessels, lowering blood pressure and decreasing the heart work load. Alpha-adrenergic blockers and angiotensin-converting enzyme (ACE) inhibitors act by dilating blood vessels. There is evidence that antihypertensive treatment reduces vascular and organ complications (such as to eyes and kidneys).

Because there are often no symptoms, people with high blood pressure may feel normal whether or not they take their medication. But medication should be taken according to the doctor's instructions; treatment may need to be continued for life. Since some medications have annoying side effects, non-compliance with treatment becomes an increasing problem over time.

SEE ALSO *Beta-blockers, Hypertension*

ANTI-INFLAMMATORY DRUGS

Anti-inflammatory drugs reduce inflammation, and are used in conditions such as rheumatoid arthritis, osteoarthritis and connective tissue disorders. They do not cure these disorders, just control the symptoms.

Aspirin is one of the most popular over-the-counter anti-inflammatory drugs. Side effects include irritation of, and bleeding from, the lining of the stomach. The drug should not be given to children, as it may cause Reye's syndrome.

Nonsteroidal anti-inflammatory drugs (NSAIDs) cause fewer digestive problems than aspirin and are often used to treat headache and menstrual cramps. Ibuprofen and naproxen are two common NSAIDs.

To control more serious inflammatory disorders, corticosteroids such as hydrocortisone (cortisol) are often used. However, because of potential side effects such as bruising, osteoporosis, infections, diabetes and high blood pressure, their use is limited to short courses when other therapies fail.

SEE ALSO *Arthritis, Corticosteroids, Nonsteroidal anti-inflammatory drugs, Reye's syndrome*

ANTIOXIDANTS

Antioxidants are substances that deactivate free radicals, protecting cells from damage. Free radicals are oxygen byproducts that are produced both in our bodies and in the environment by factors such as cigarette smoke. They can severely damage human cells, allowing diseases such as cancer to develop.

Vitamins C and E are the most important antioxidants. They appear to prevent carcinogenic (cancer producing) compounds from forming in the stomach, and help prevent atherosclerosis (hardening of arteries).

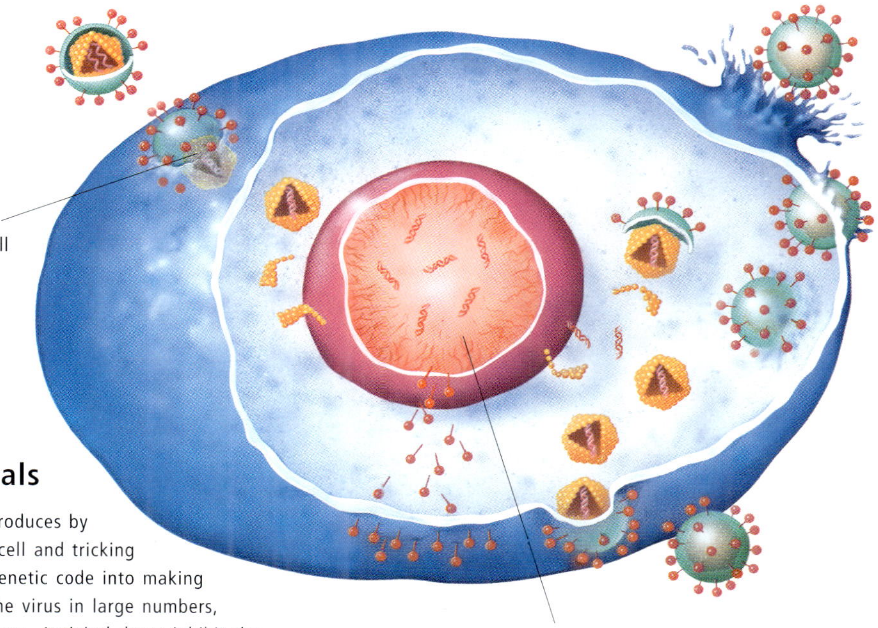

Antivirals

A virus reproduces by entering a cell and tricking the cell's genetic code into making copies of the virus in large numbers, as shown here. Antiviral drugs inhibit the process by preventing the virus from entering the cell; or preventing the cell from making new viruses.

Nutritionists recommend eating a balanced diet that includes at least five to six servings daily of fruits and vegetables, which are high in antioxidants.

SEE ALSO *Atherosclerosis, Nutrition, Vitamins*

ANTIPSYCHOTICS

Also known as "major tranquilizers", antipsychotic drugs (neuroleptics) reduce many of the symptoms of schizophrenia. They do not cure the disorder, but reduce such symptoms as agitation, confusion, hallucinations, distortions and delusions. They allow the sufferer to think more clearly and make better-informed decisions. Response to an antipsychotic can vary. Most schizophrenic patients show improvement, some will experience little or no effect, and others don't need them at all.

In most people, the side effects of antipsychotics are mild. These include drowsiness, rapid heartbeat, dizziness when changing position, weight gain, decrease in sexual ability or interest, menstrual problems, skin rashes or increased susceptibility to sunburn. More serious side effects include muscle spasms of the neck, eye or back, a slowing down of movement and speech, and a shuffling walk.

Tardive dyskinesia is a disorder characterized by involuntary movements affecting the mouth, lips and tongue. These symptoms are usually seen in long-term treatment with older antipsychotics such as haloperidol or chlorpromazine. Most of them can be controlled with an anticholinergic medication. Several new antipsychotic drugs have been introduced, including clozapine, risperidone and olanzapine. They are better tolerated and safer than the older drugs.

SEE ALSO *Schizophrenia, Tranquilizers*

ANTIVIRALS

Antivirals are drugs used to treat viral infections or to prevent them from developing. Usually they work for only one kind of virus infection. Many viruses, including the common cold, don't respond yet to antiviral drugs. Those that do include herpes simplex (cold sores) and herpes zoster (shingles). Treatment with antiviral drugs must be started early if they are to work.

Acyclovir is used to treat the symptoms of chickenpox, shingles and herpes virus infections of the genitals, skin, brain, lips and mouth. It is also used to prevent recurrent genital herpes infections. Although it doesn't cure herpes, it helps relieve pain and discomfort and promotes healing of the sores. Idoxuridine is an antiviral drug that is commonly used to treat viral infections of the eye.

SEE ALSO *Chickenpox, Genital herpes, Herpes simplex, Shingles, Viruses*

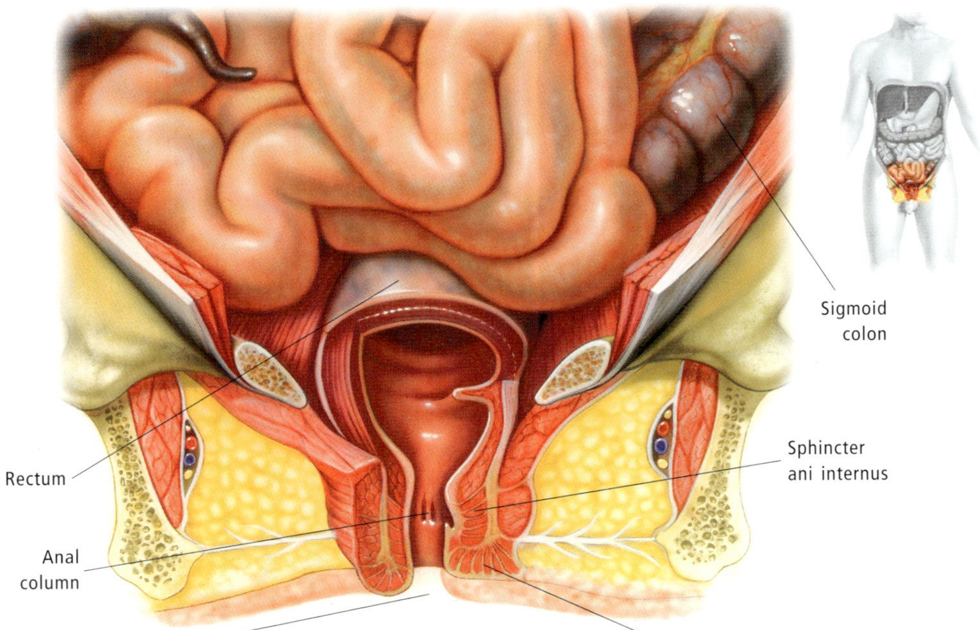

The anus

ANUS

The anus is a short tube about $1\frac{1}{2}$ inches (3–4 centimeters) long leading from the rectum through the anal sphincter to the anal orifice, through which feces are expelled.

Anal fissure

An anal fissure is a slit or tear in the mucosa (or lining) of the anus that produces a tearing pain when feces are passed. Bright red bleeding from the fissure is common. The best treatment is a high-fiber diet and anti-inflammatory ointments. A chronic fissure may result in anal spasm or stenosis (narrowing), requiring minor surgery.

Anal itching (pruritus ani)

Anal itching is caused by irritation of the anal skin. It can be caused by diarrhea, infections (especially yeast infections), skin diseases, or other problems such as hemorrhoids or tearing of the anal skin. Treatment is to clean and dry the area thoroughly. Cortisone cream applied to the anal skin relieves the symptoms.

Hemorrhoids

Hemorrhoids are varicose veins in the lower portion of the rectum or anus. They are common in pregnancy. Symptoms include anal itching and pain during bowel movements. A high-fiber diet helps, and ointment can relieve pain. Ligation (tying off), surgery and injections can also be used.

SEE ALSO *Hemorrhoids*

ANXIETY

Anxiety is an emotional state characterized by feelings of tension, apprehension and uncertainty brought about by anticipation of a real or imagined threat. It is a basic emotion and can be experienced from early childhood.

Most people will experience feelings of anxiety from time to time, and in the mentally healthy these will be manageable. Some measure of anxiety is normal for anyone who has responsibilities or is under pressure. Tensions may even be constructive sometimes, stimulating action. But when fears and worries dominate daily life, particularly when there is no obvious cause and no apparent problem, then anxiety becomes a disorder and needs treatment.

Where anxiety becomes severe it can make normal life, work and relationships impossible. If fears are related to specific situations, such as high places (acrophobia) or spiders (arachnophobia), then the disorder is termed a phobia. When there is no such specific relationship, a generalized anxiety disorder or anxiety neurosis may exist. Anxiety neurosis is thought to arise through repression of emotional issues.

Withdrawal of antidepressants can cause anxiety with symptoms of agitation, irritability, vertigo, light-headedness and fever. These drugs should be started and discontinued only under medical supervision.

Anxiety disorders can be mild or severe, with excessive worry building insidiously to destroy relaxation and lower energy. Sufferers will feel edgy and may startle easily. They may be so obsessed with their worries they cannot wind down, and this may lead them to rely on drugs such as alcohol. Despite constant anxiety, at this stage they may be coping and might not seek help.

A more severe level of anxiety may show up as an anxiety attack (panic attack). Anxiety attacks can occur without warning, even while relaxing in a seemingly friendly environment, and with no apparent reason. An anxiety attack consists of intense feelings of impending death or physical collapse, panic or crisis. The symptoms can be irregular heartbeat (tachycardia), palpitations, sweating, disturbed breathing, trembling, paralysis and mental confusion. Constant anxiety can be harmful, physically and mentally. Physical symptoms can include irritability, muscle tension and sleeplessness. Over a long period this may lead to depression.

Treatment of anxiety disorders can use a combination of medication and therapy. Various types of tranquilizers such as benzodiazepines and antidepressants can give short-term relief. Other treatments include relaxation techniques, psychotherapy and biofeedback. If there are lifestyle factors that can be changed for the better, this will help to achieve long-term success.

SEE ALSO *Agoraphobia, Biofeedback, Depression, Panic attacks, Phobias, Psychotherapy, Relaxation techniques, Tranquilizers*

ANXIOLYTICS

Anxiolytics (also known as mild tranquilizers) are drugs that reduce anxiety; they include barbiturates, benzodiazepines and buspirone hydrochloride. They provide relief from anxiety and muscle spasm and can be used in treatment of alcohol withdrawal and epileptic fits. Anxiolytics are sometimes given to patients prior to surgery.

People using these drugs will be drowsy and less alert than normal. More rare side effects can include trembling, lack of coordination, rash, low blood pressure, nausea, muscle weakness and jaundice. There is a danger of dependency with extended use, so supervision is needed.

SEE ALSO *Anxiety, Barbiturates, Drug dependence, Psychotropic drugs, Tranquilizers*

AORTA

The aorta, a thick elastic tube, is the largest artery in the body. It arises from the left ventricle of the heart, arches upward, backward and to the left, then down the back of the thorax through the diaphragm and into the abdomen. From the thoracic aorta, arteries arise that supply the heart, head, neck and arms. From the abdominal aorta, arteries supply the abdominal organs, pelvis and legs.

Aortic aneurysm is the abnormal stretching of the walls of the aorta. It is often caused by arteriosclerosis (hardening of the arteries), which usually occurs in older people. It can lead to symptoms such as chest pain and shortness of breath, and can worsen to be a medical emergency requiring hospitalization.

Aortic stenosis is narrowing of the aortic valve, caused by valvular heart disease such as rheumatic fever. The narrowing causes an additional strain on the heart that may lead to angina and heart failure. Surgical replacement with an artificial valve is usually the preferred treatment.

SEE ALSO *Aneurysm, Arteries, Heart*

Aorta

The aorta is the biggest artery in the body. It receives blood from the heart and channels it to the other major arteries of the body.

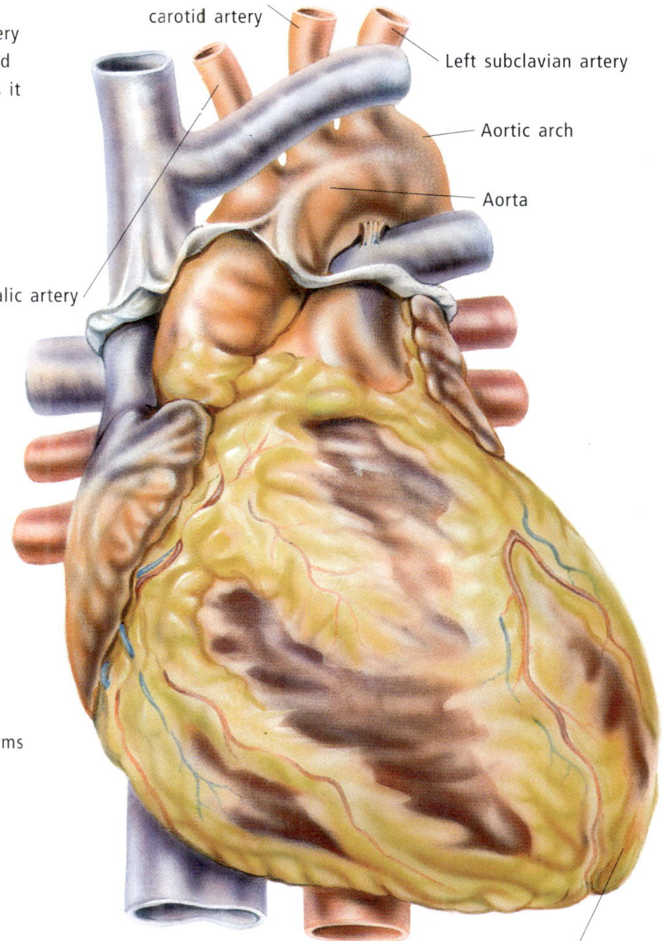

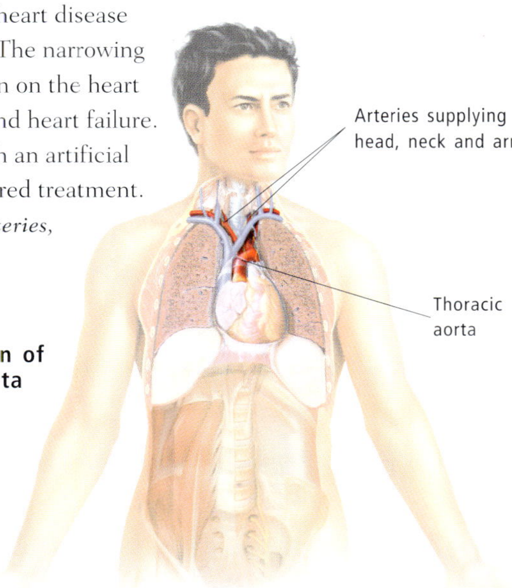

Location of the aorta

Disorders of the aortic valves

Normally the aortic and pulmonary valves open and close at the same time, allowing the heart to pump blood out into the large arteries. In a heart with an incompetent aortic valve, blood will leak back from the aorta into the heart after a pumping action. In a heart with a stenosed (narrowed) aortic valve, the heart will have trouble pumping blood through the valve into the aorta.

Incompetent valve

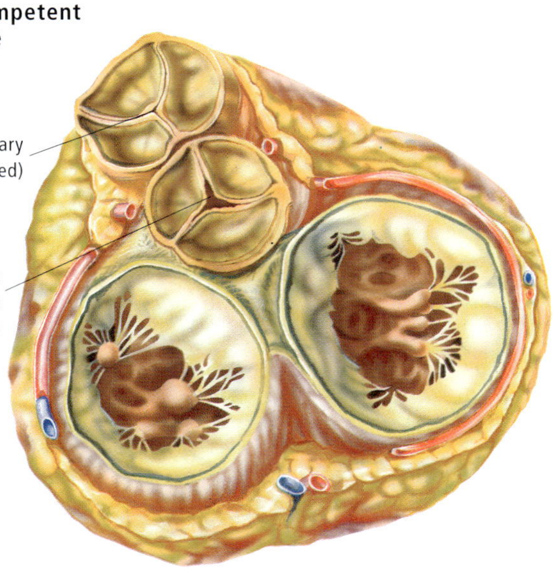

Stenosis of valve

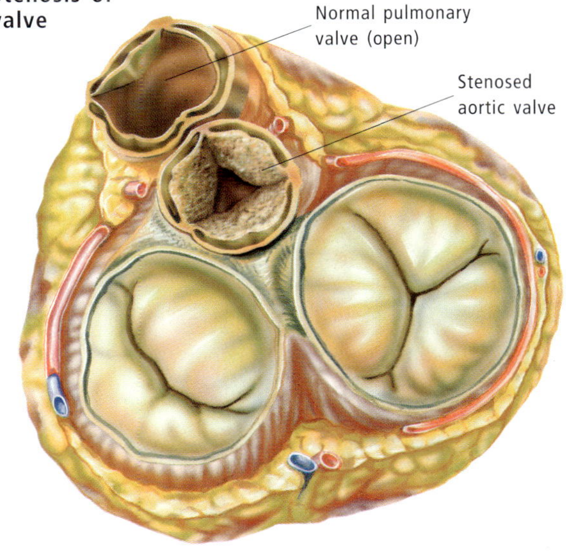

A

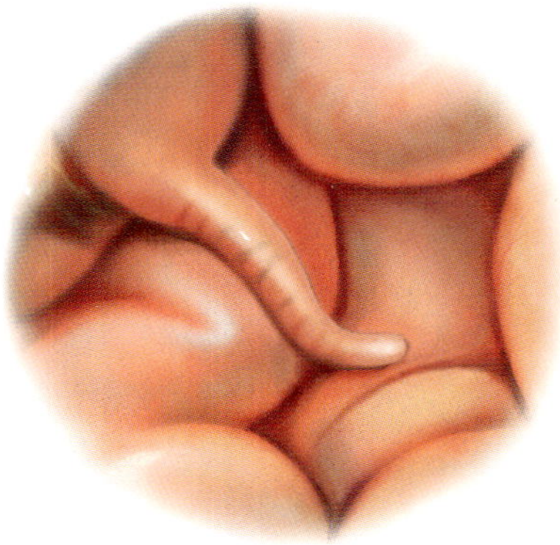

Normal appendix

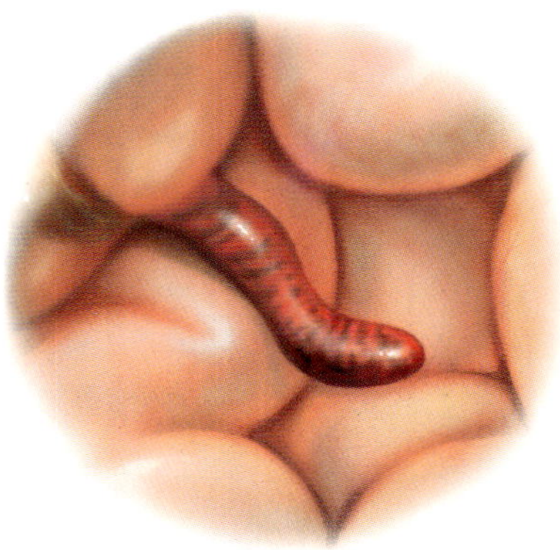

Inflamed appendix

Appendix

The appendix is a redundant organ which is attached to a part of the large bowel. In children especially, it may become inflamed and if so, will need to be surgically removed in hospital. The term for an inflamed appendix is appendicitis.

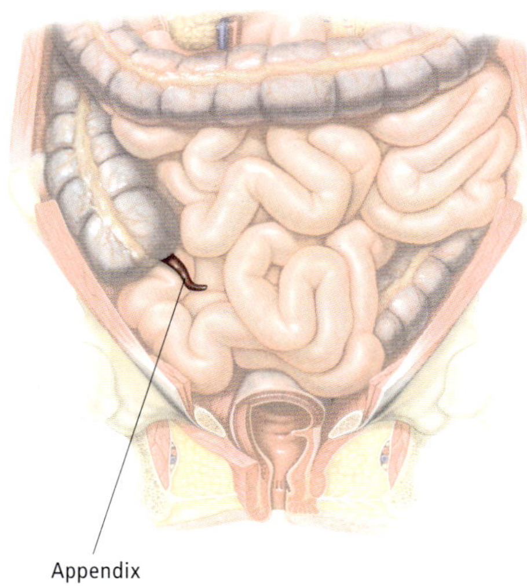

APHASIA

Aphasia is a brain disorder resulting in the loss of speech or ability to understand language, including the ability to read and write. It is usually caused by brain disease, stroke or injury affecting the speech areas of the cerebral cortex. An aphasic seizure is a brain disturbance causing temporary speech loss.

APPENDIX

A thin, worm-shaped pouch, 3½ inches (9 centimeters) long, the appendix is attached to the first part of the colon (large intestine). It has no function and appears to be a relic of evolution. When it becomes inflamed, the condition is known as appendicitis.

Appendicitis

Appendicitis is thought to be caused by an obstruction of the opening into the appendix, possibly by feces or lymph tissue; inflammation of the appendix follows. Pain develops in the lower right side of the abdomen, which is spasmodic at first, but then becomes constant. Other symptoms include fever, nausea and vomiting. In some cases, the inflammation can turn into an abscess which can burst, causing peritonitis.

Appendicitis is treated by urgent surgery. The surgeon removes the appendix through an incision in the lower right side of the abdomen. Recovery from appendectomy takes about a week, and usually there are no further problems.

SEE ALSO *Peritonitis*

APPETITE

Appetite is a general term to express the body's desire for a substance or stimulus. Appetite is most often associated with the need for food or drink, but it can also express the need for sexual intercourse, or for other bodily cravings such as substances to which the body is addicted, including cigarettes, alcohol or drugs.

The need for food or drink is signalled by hunger, a strong and sometimes unpleasant sensation that may result in pain felt in the abdomen or stomach area. The normal response is to seek food or drink and to eat until a feeling of being full overcomes the hunger. The level of glucose in the blood rises as the food is digested and signals that further eating is unnecessary. An area in the hypothalamus of the brain can detect low levels of glucose in the blood and produces the sensation of hunger.

Appetite may disappear temporarily during illness but usually responds to the gradual reintroduction of foods. Anorexics will deliberately choose to ignore hunger pains to exert control over their appetite.

In societies where people generally have enough food to sustain healthy life, personal appetites may regulate dietary habits and people will eat what they like rather than what they actually need; the sensations of deprivation produced by true hunger will rarely be experienced. Research shows that high-fat foods may not generate a feeling of fullness that is the signal to stop eating.

Exercise lowers the blood sugar level and, when taken regularly, can help to regulate the appetite so that food intake matches the body's energy needs. Insulin, a hormone produced by the pancreas and missing in diabetics, lowers blood sugar levels and can stimulate appetite by inducing hunger.

When food intake is not properly regulated a person may easily eat more, or less, than is necessary for health. They become overweight or obese through overeating and suffer related physical problems. Undereating will cause weight loss plus a range of additional problems resulting from the lack of proper nutrients in the diet.

Appetites change when people from one culture go to live in another. Traditional foods may not be available, or new foods may be more attractive or be seen as more socially acceptable. Regulating the appetite may be difficult with new foods to choose from. This trend is seen in Japan where imported dairy foods and meat are widely eaten, replacing traditional foods which are relatively low in protein.

Appetite suppressants are drugs sometimes used to reduce hunger and make it easier to follow a weight reduction diet. Their effect is temporary and they carry a risk of dependency or addiction plus worrying side effects such as increased blood pressure, restlessness and insomnia.

SEE ALSO *Diet, Nutrition, Obesity*

ARM

The arm, or upper limb, extends from the shoulder, where it is attached to the trunk, to the wrist, where it joins the hand. It has two parts: the upper arm, the section between the shoulder and elbow, and the forearm which extends from the elbow to the wrist. The whole limb is designed for mobility. It gives the hand such a range of motion that it can reach most regions of the body and manipulate external objects.

The upper arm

The upper arm contains one bone, the humerus, which joins the shoulder blade (scapula) at the shoulder joint. This is a ball and socket joint, in which the head of the humerus engages with a shallow socket on the shoulder blade. The shape of the joint gives mobility to the upper arm.

The shoulder joint is strengthened by ligaments and by the long tendon of the biceps muscle, which passes through the joint cavity. Important muscles involved in shoulder movements include the deltoid, which makes the rounded contour over the upper surface of the arm and shoulder, and a group of four muscles known as the rotator cuff muscles. These help to raise and rotate the arm, and also contribute to

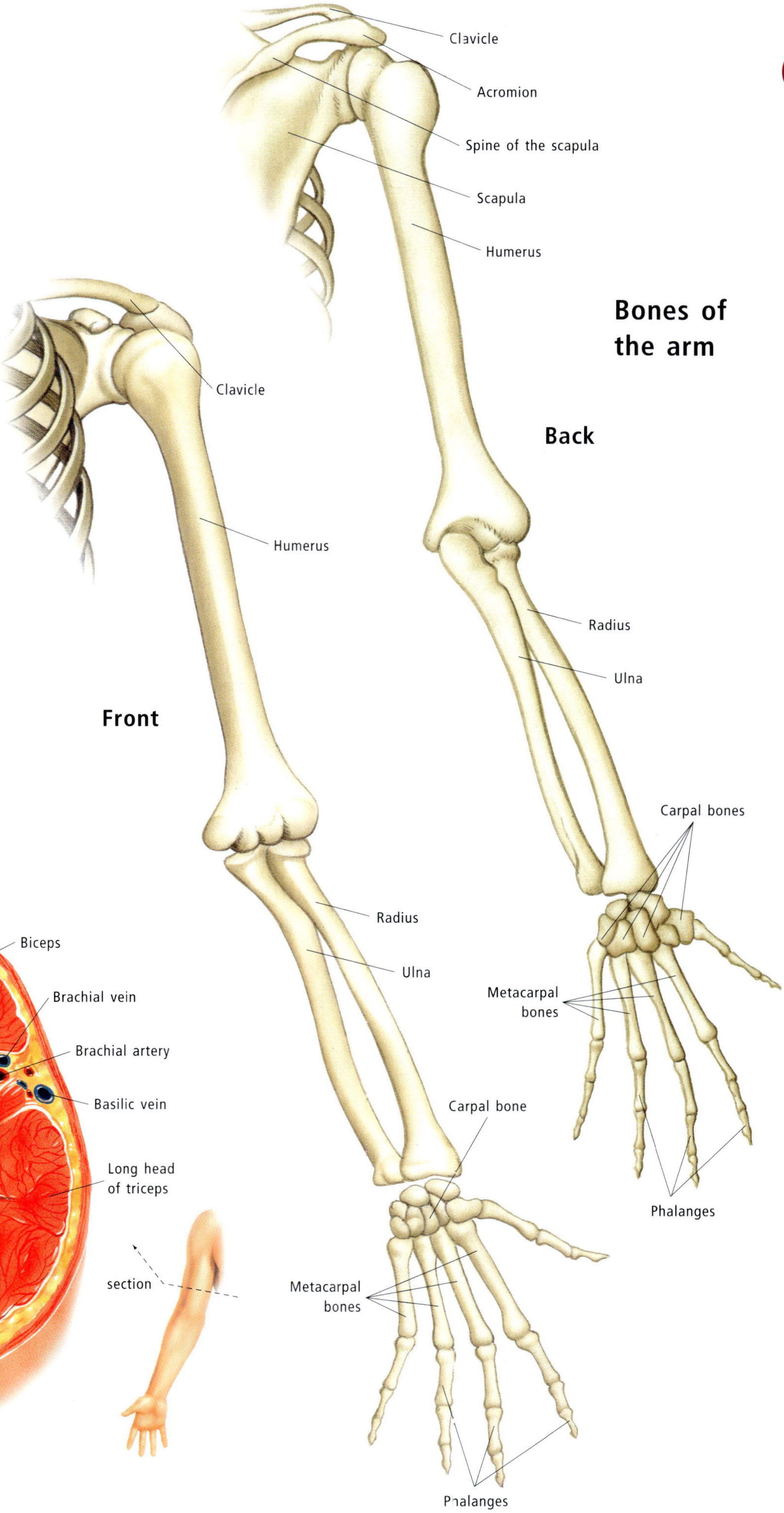

Cross-section of the arm

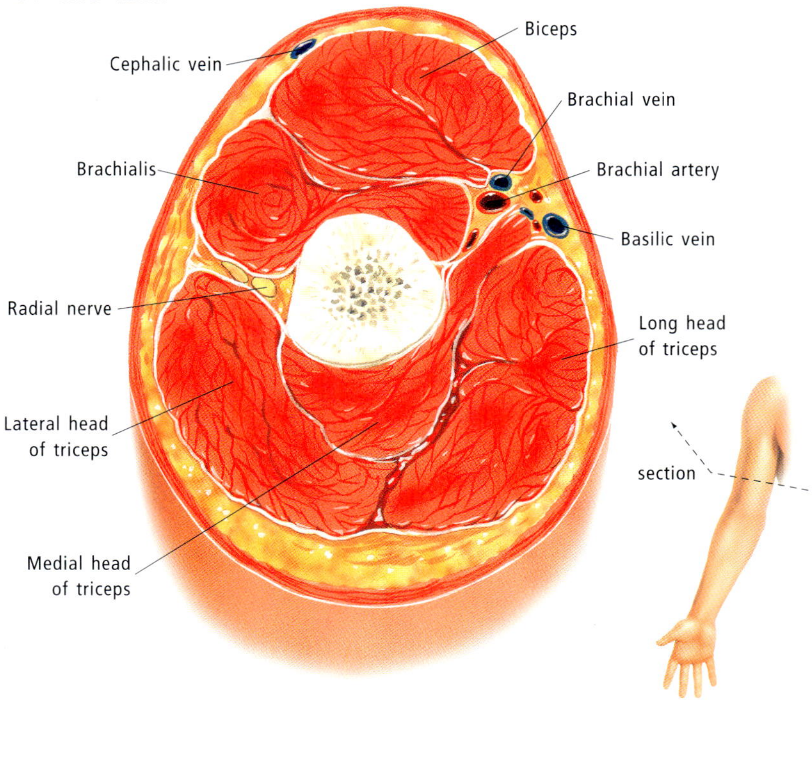

A

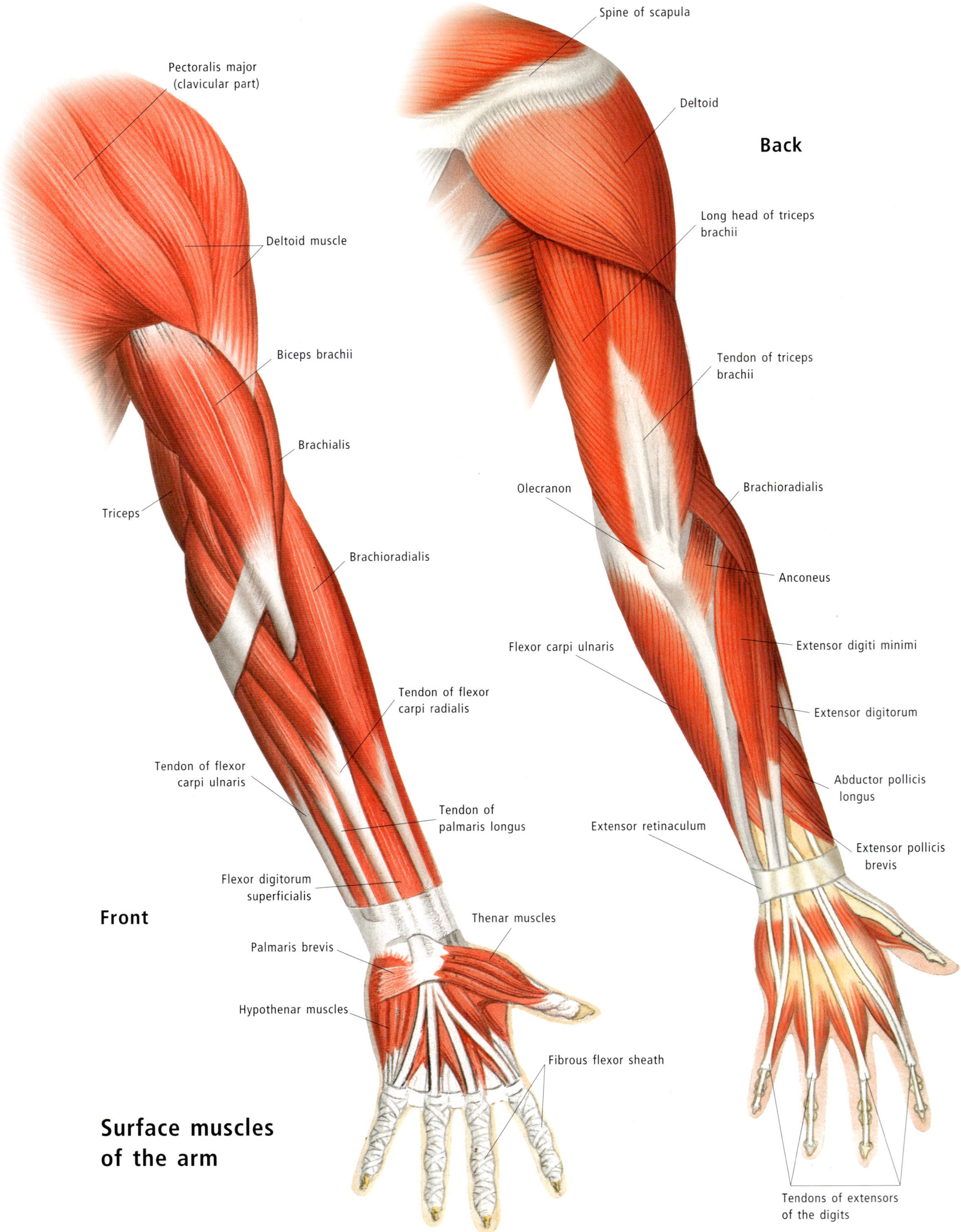

Surface muscles of the arm

Deep muscles of the arm

NB: Labels in brackets are included to show context

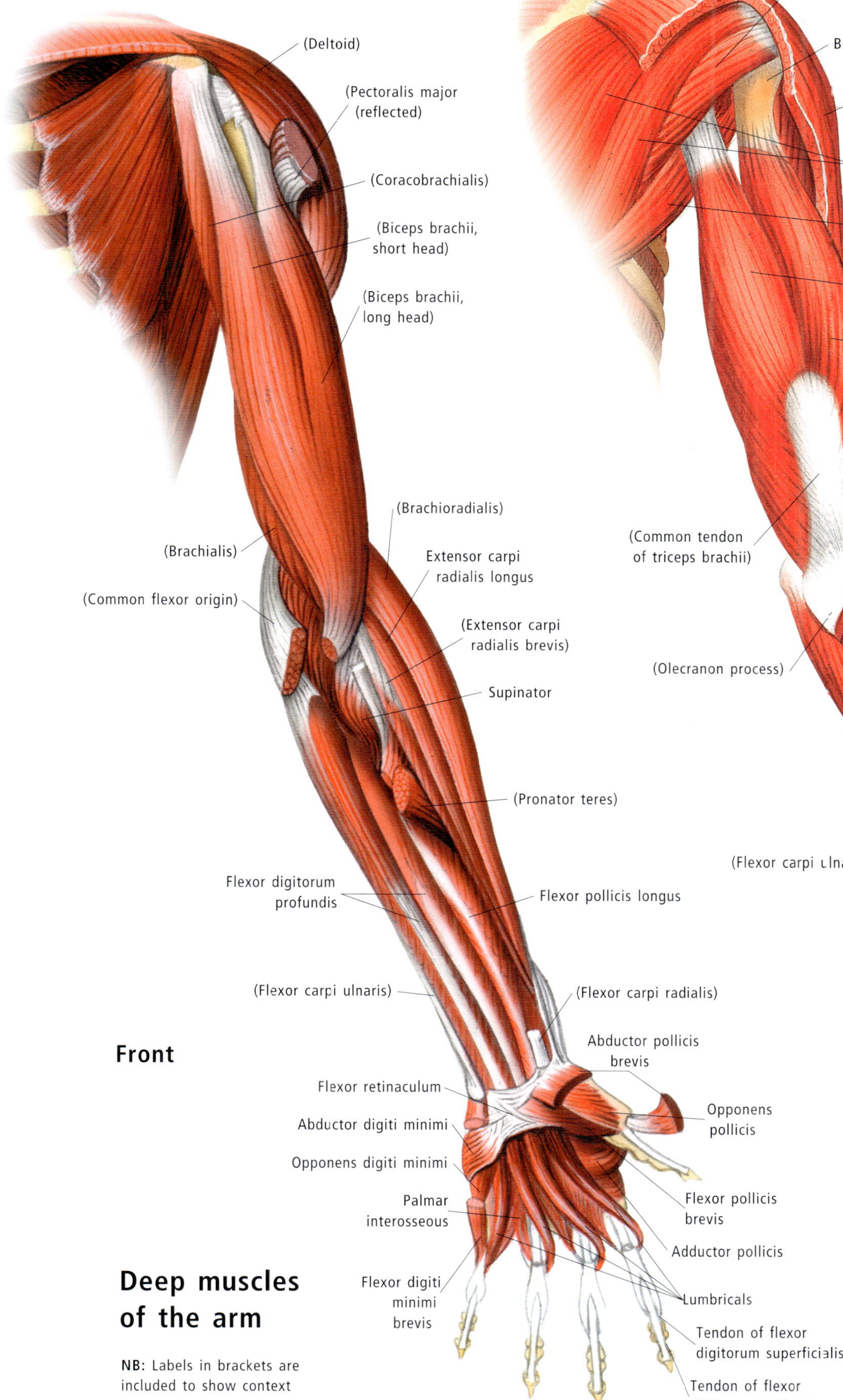

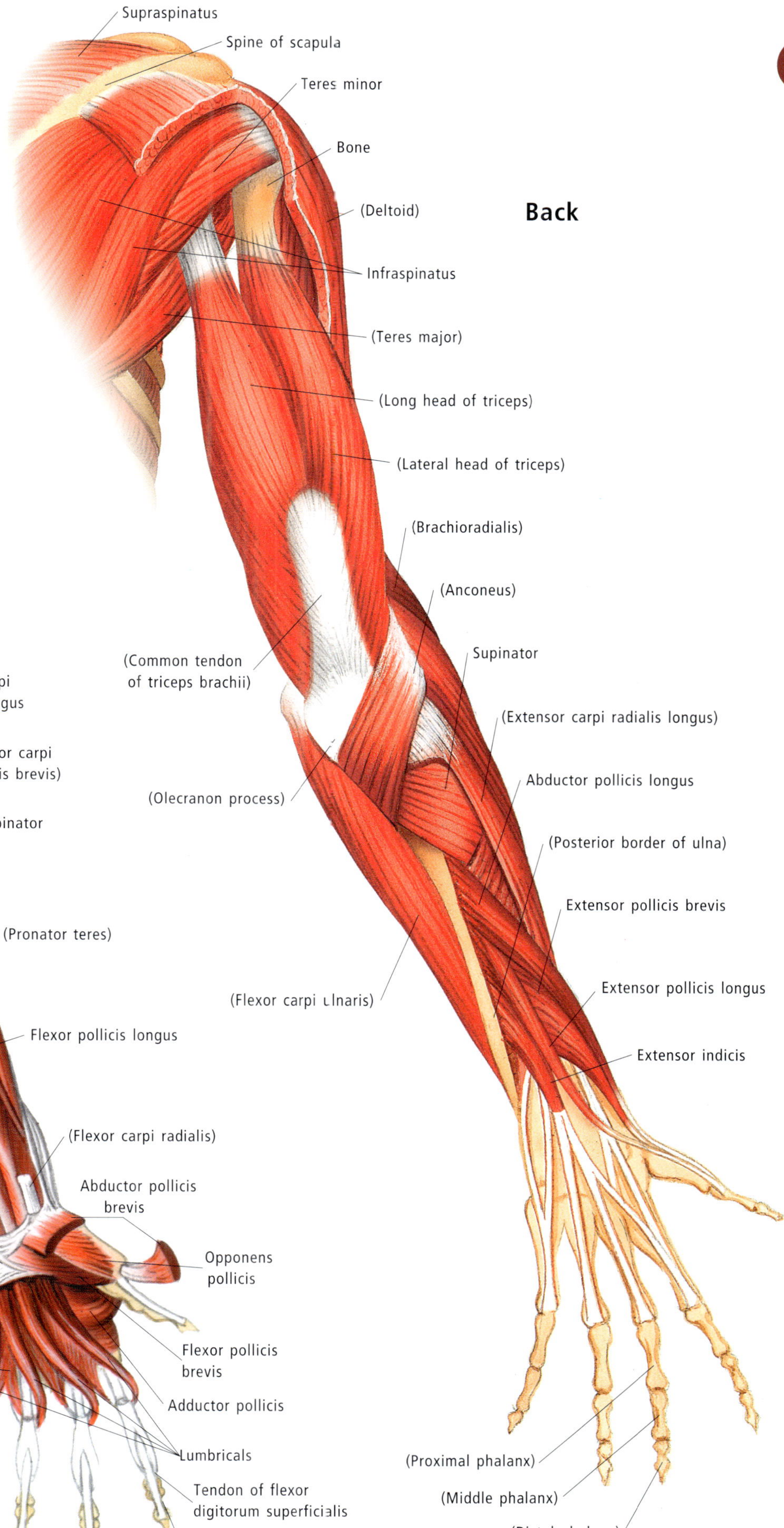

shoulder joint stability. The tendon of the supraspinatus, one of the rotator cuff muscles, can become inflamed as it passes under a bony projection of the shoulder blade. This can cause pain when the arm is raised to a certain position, a condition known as a painful arc. The shoulder joint is relatively unstable and can dislocate downward fairly easily, by a direct blow to the shoulder, for instance, as in sports injuries.

The region just below the shoulder, between the trunk and upper arm, is known as the armpit or axilla. Blood vessels and nerves supplying the arm travel through this region. The armpit also contains lymph nodes which drain the arm, hand and breast. These nodes can become swollen, as a result of an infection in the hand, for instance. They can also become sites of secondary growths in breast cancer. Their removal in a radical mastectomy can lead to a swollen arm.

The major artery of the arm, the brachial artery, starts at the top of the arm and passes down the inside of the arm to the front of the elbow. Fractures to the shaft of the humerus can damage the brachial artery, or the radial nerve, which winds around the back of the humerus.

The elbow

The elbow joint separates the humerus from the two forearm bones, the radius and the ulna. This is a synovial hinge joint, which is a relatively stable joint. It allows the arm to flex (bend) and extend. Important muscles for flexion include the biceps and brachialis, while the main extensor muscle is the triceps. The sharp point of the elbow is due to a projection of the ulnar bone called the olecranon. The olecranon is covered by a sac, or bursa, which can become swollen and inflamed, leading to a condition commonly known as bursitis.

At the elbow, the brachial artery divides into two branches, the radial and ulnar, and these arteries supply the forearm and hand. Veins lying close to the surface of the inside (front) of the elbow region are a common site for taking blood samples.

Three major nerves—the ulnar, median and radial—also pass through the elbow region. These three nerves control the feeling and movement of the forearm and hand. The ulnar nerve is particularly vulnerable where it passes behind the elbow joint, just under the skin. A sharp tap on the elbow in this region—hitting the "funny bone"—activates the ulnar nerve and sends a shooting pain down the side of the arm.

The forearm

The two bones of the forearm, the ulna and the radius, extend from the elbow to the wrist. Joints between these bones at both the elbow and wrist allow the forearm to be rotated, from the palm held upwards (supination) to the palm held downwards (pronation). These are the movements that are used when you are undoing a screw top bottle (supination) or tightening a screw (pronation). In these movement the radius pivots around the ulna. Occasionally in young children the joint between the radius and ulna closest to the elbow can dislocate when the child is forcefully lifted or pulled forward. This can normally be treated quite easily by a doctor.

The forearm contains many of the muscles involved in hand movements. Most of the powerful muscles for gripping an object or making a fist (the flexor muscles) lie in the inside (front) of the forearm. Similarly the extensor muscles which are used for straightening the fingers lie on the outside (back) of the forearm. Extensive use of these muscles can cause pain: pain in the extensors is known as "tennis elbow", while for the flexors it is "golfer's elbow". Both can be helped by rest and physical therapy. The long tendons of these finger flexors and extensors have to pass across the wrist joint and hand to reach the fingers. They can therefore be damaged by cuts or inflamed by overuse, as can occur with prolonged typing.

The forearm is supplied by two arteries, the ulnar and radial. The pulse can be felt easily in either of these vessels if they are pressed against the underlying bone at the end of the forearm, close to the wrist.

The forearm is the site of one of the commonest fractures, known as Colles' fracture. It usually occurs when someone falls and lands on an outstretched arm. The deformity is described as "dinner-fork", with the broken part of the radius closest to the wrist pushed behind the remaining part. Treatment includes repositioning the bone and immobilizing the wrist and elbow.

SEE ALSO *Elbow, Shoulder*

Colles' fracture

A Colles' fracture is often caused by a fall on the outstretched arm. The broken fragments must be realigned and held in place by a plaster cast covering the wrist and elbow until healed.

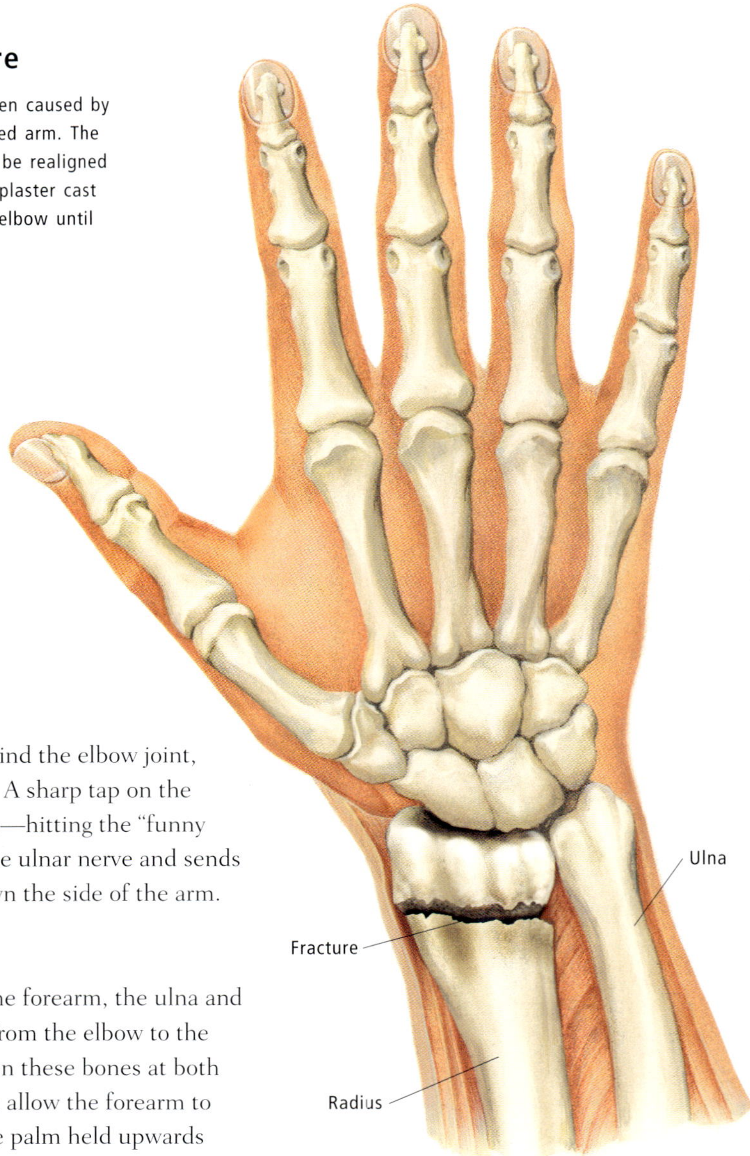

AROMATHERAPY

Aromatherapy is based on the principles of holistic health. It consists of the use of natural aromatic essences extracted from plants for therapeutic purposes. Aromatherapists believe that the actions of the oils maintain and restore the natural life force which supports the body's own healing mechanisms. The oils are said to have both physiological and psychological actions, the latter operating via the sense of smell. Physiologically the oils are believed to work by being absorbed in minute amounts through the skin and mucous membranes into the bloodstream, affecting the entire body's organs and systems.

Aromatherapists most frequently employ therapeutic massage to administer oils, using in addition a variety of techniques that may include shiatsu and reflexology. Individual blends of oils are made up for each patient, taking into account the volatility of the oils, the therapeutic effects of each oil and the patient's preferred smells. Aromatherapy has also become popular for home use, especially in baths and oil burners.

History

The history of aromatherapy dates back at least 4,000 years in the Middle East and in China. Scented oils were widely used as perfumes, bath and massage oils by ancient Greek and Roman physicians. The production of essential oils through distillation was mastered by the Arabian physician Avicenna in the late tenth century and their use was spread to Europe by the returning Crusaders.

By medieval times, these oils were an important part of the physician's dispensary. They were universally acknowledged for their antiseptic properties; it was believed that perfumers were rarely affected by cholera and other illnesses.

With the advent of modern medicine in the nineteenth century, the medical use of essential oils declined. However, in the early twentieth century, French and Italian physicians and biochemists, most notably Rene Gattefosse, utilized scientific research and advanced distillation techniques to build up a modern system of aromatherapy which these days is becoming increasingly popular worldwide.

Essential oils

Essential oils, also known as volatile oils, are the odorous extract of plants. They differ from fixed oils (e.g. olive, sunflower) in two ways: they can be distilled; and they do not leave a permanent grease mark on paper. Essential oils readily evaporate at room temperature when exposed to air and, like fixed oils, are not readily soluble in water.

Essential oils are compounds whose many constituents unite to produce their unique therapeutic and aromatic signature. The most common constituents belong to chemical families including alcohols, aldehydes, esters, phenols, nitrogen compounds and sulphur compounds. However it is not so much the individual constituents which are considered by aromatherapists to be therapeutic as the effect of their combined action. For this reason the oils are extracted from the whole plant (including bark, flowers, seeds, leaves or roots) with maximum preservation of all of their constituents.

The quality of essential oils varies considerably, depending on the time of day and year in which the plant was harvested and its soil conditions and climate. The amount of oil present in plants varies quite considerably, between approximately .01 percent and 10 percent.

There is a variety of methods for extracting essential oils. The main methods are distillation (open-fire, steam or vacuum), maceration (softening by soaking) in vegetable oils or fats, dissolving by volatile solvents, and pressing. The cost of oils varies enormously depending on their quality, availability and method of harvesting and extraction. Only essential oils that are 100 percent pure are considered suitable for therapeutic use.

Aromatherapists classify essential oils according to their various therapeutic properties. Many essential oils are antiseptic.

Aromatherapists also classify oils by their volatility, classifying them into one of the three following groups.

Top notes are fast-acting oils which are the most stimulating and uplifting to body and mind (e.g. bergamot, lemon and eucalyptus).

Middle notes are moderately volatile oils that work on the body's functions (e.g. chamomile, lavender and peppermint).

Base notes evaporate slowly, and have relaxing and sedating qualities (e.g. sandalwood, patchouli and ylang ylang).

Methods and uses

Aromatherapy utilizes the essential oils therapeutically through a number of different methods. These include the following.

Baths (full body, sitz, hand or feet) are considered useful for insomnia, muscular disorders, circulation problems, vaginal infections, rheumatism and arthritis. A few drops of oil are added to a full warm bath.

Burners and diffusers scent a room. The soothing vapors may help in respiratory disorders, anxiety and depression.

Compresses soaked in warm water with oils added may relieve bruises, muscular problems and headaches.

Inhalations are recommended by aromatherapists for respiratory disorders and skin conditions. A bowl of hot water with oil added or a handkerchief sprinkled with oil are the suggested methods of inhalation.

Internally, oils can be taken in very small doses added to sugar, honey and water, wine or tea (though see the warning following about ingestion of these oils). This method is used for digestive disorders, cystitis and dysmenorrhea.

Massage is recommended for muscular problems, rheumatism, arthritis, circulation problems, skin conditions, depression, anxiety and headaches. Essential oils are added to a fixed carrier oil such as cold-pressed apricot kernel, sweet almond or grape seed. Small amounts of wheatgerm oil or vitamin E oil are added to prevent oxidation.

The most commonly prescribed essential oils include the following.

Lavender is a versatile oil, used for treatment of insomnia, headaches, depression, anxiety, burns, wounds, heat exhaustion and insect stings.

Eucalyptus is used for treating respiratory infections, fevers, exhaustion, cramps, wounds and skin ulcers.

Rosemary is said to relieve poor circulation, headaches, general debility, poor memory, muscular aches and pains.

Tea tree can be used for respiratory infections, skin conditions, fungal conditions, wounds and insect bites.

A

Peppermint is often used for digestive disorders, headaches, influenza and colds.

Chamomile is used for digestive disorders, balancing the female reproductive system, headaches, muscular and rheumatic pain, nervous tension and insomnia.

Jasmine is used for the treatment of dysmenorrhea, nervous debility, depression, apathy and poor libido.

Sandalwood is used to treat urogenital infections, respiratory infections and skin inflammation.

Clary sage is used to balance the female reproductive system, and may help with debility, depression and nervous conditions.

Warning

Essential oils should be used with caution as some are highly toxic and irritating to the skin. For safe use, always observe the following guidelines:

- Do not take internally unless prescribed by a qualified practitioner.
- Use only under professional guidance if you are pregnant, suffering from blood pressure disorders or epilepsy.
- Before using any oil on the skin, patch test on the skin, using a diluted amount of the oil, to check for allergic reactions.
- Always use in dilution.
- Do not use for prolonged periods.
- If your symptoms are not relieved by aromatherapy, consult a primary health physician (general practitioner).

ARRHYTHMIA

An arrhythmia (also known as a dysrhythmia) is a variation in heartbeat from the normal rhythm. An arrhythmia may be a normal variation in the heartbeat, or it may be due to disease that has damaged the heart muscle and caused irregularities in nerve conduction and muscle contraction. Certain drugs, including caffeine, cocaine, psychotropics, and sympathomimetics, can also cause arrhythmias.

Not all arrhythmias are dangerous. In sinus arrhythmia, a normal occurrence in children, the pulse rate increases or decreases with breathing. Sinus arrhythmia usually does not require treatment.

Some other arrhythmias (varying in their degrees of danger) include atrial fibrillation, paroxysmal supraventricular tachycardia, sinus tachycardia, sinus bradycardia, bradycardia associated with heart block, sick sinus syndrome and ectopic heartbeat.

Certain types of arrythmia can be life-threatening. Ventricular fibrillation and ventricular tachycardia, for example, can cause cardiac arrest and severe decrease in blood flow to tissues and organs.

Symptoms of arrhythmia include noticeable changes to the rhythm or pattern of the pulse, a sensation of awareness of the heartbeat (palpitations), chest pain, shortness of breath, light-headedness, dizziness or unconsciousness. In ventricular fibrillation, the first symptom may be loss of heartbeat; sudden death can occur in this situation.

To confirm and diagnose an arrhythmia, tests such as an electrocardiogram (EKG) and 24-hour Holter monitoring are often performed. An echocardiogram and coronary angiography could show heart disease that may be producing an arrhythmia.

Arrhythmias are usually treated with drugs; either traditional antiarrhythmic drugs such as digitalis and quinidine, or more modern antiarrhythmics such as beta-blockers, calcium antagonists and disopyramide. Some arrhythmias are treated by electrical destruction of diseased tissue, and sometimes a surgical implant is inserted.

SEE ALSO *Angiography, Antiarrhythmic drugs, Echocardiogram, Electrocardiogram, Fibrillation, Heart, Heartbeat, Holter monitor, Tachycardia*

ART THERAPY

Although artwork created by patients had been studied by psychiatrists such as Jung and Freud from around the turn of the twentieth century, it was not until after World War II that art therapy gained widespread acceptance in both the UK and the USA when it was used to treat traumatized veterans.

In art therapy, patients are encouraged to express themselves through drawing, painting, sculpting and other art media. The focus of the therapy is not on creating a masterpiece but on the actual process of art making, and the sharing with the therapist of the thoughts and feelings that arise out of this. Interpretations of the art come from the patient rather than the therapist.

Art therapy has been found to be valuable in its ability to provide a safe place for the release of painful and potentially destructive feelings. The patient is able to express unconscious concerns, thus helping resolve old issues that have been repressed or new issues that may be only just arising.

Art therapy is used in mental health programs with people of all ages, and in children's hospitals, rehabilitation centers and in private practice. Sessions can be undertaken individually or in couples, families or groups.

ARTERIES

Arteries are flexible, thick-walled, tube-shaped blood vessels that carry blood away from the heart to the rest of the body.

The largest artery is the aorta, which channels blood from the heart to other arteries, and to the body's organs and other structures. Two small branches of the aorta, the coronary arteries, supply the blood to the heart muscle itself. The right and left carotid arteries carry blood to the two sides of the neck and head. Blood flows to the shoulders and arms through the right and left subclavian arteries. In the abdomen, the aorta divides into two large branches, the left and right iliac, supplying blood to the pelvic region. The iliac arteries then continue into the legs, where they are called the femoral arteries.

From the arteries, blood passes into very small blood vessels called capillaries, and from there to veins and then back to the heart. The heart pumps the blood through the pulmonary artery to the lungs, where it becomes oxygenated. The blood is then returned to the heart, where it is once again pumped out through the aorta.

Arteriosclerosis

Arteriosclerosis is a disease in which the arteries thicken and lose their elasticity. It is often referred to as "hardening of the arteries". The most common cause of arteriosclerosis is a process called atherosclerosis (also known as atheroma) in which fatty deposits called plaques are deposited within the endothelium (the inner lining of the arteries). The plaques make the blood vessels narrower, restricting blood supply.

A

Angiography

Angiography is an investigative x-ray technique that is used to show the nature and extent of disease in arteries, veins and lymph vessels. It is often used prior to surgery. If angiography shows extensive disease, a vascular surgeon may perform endarterectomy (removal of the deposits in the arteries) or angioplasty (repair of the affected arteries) or may bypass the diseased section.

Vasculitis

Vasculitis (angiitis) is a general term for a group of autoimmune diseases which feature inflammation of the blood vessels. Polyarteritis nodosa, for example, affects arteries in the muscles, joints, intestines, nerves, kidneys and skin. Diagnosis of polyarteritis nodosa is confirmed by a biopsy of the relevant tissue. Other examples of vasculitis include Kawasaki disease, Behçet's disease, Wegener's granulomatosis, Churg-Strauss syndrome, Takayasu's arteritis, giant cell arteritis (temporal arteritis) and Henoch Schönlein purpura. Vasculitis is treated with corticosteroids and other immunosuppressant drugs.

SEE ALSO *Angiography, Angioplasty, Aorta, Arteriosclerosis, Blood vessels, Hypertension, Ischemia, Raynaud's disease, Stroke, Vasculitis*

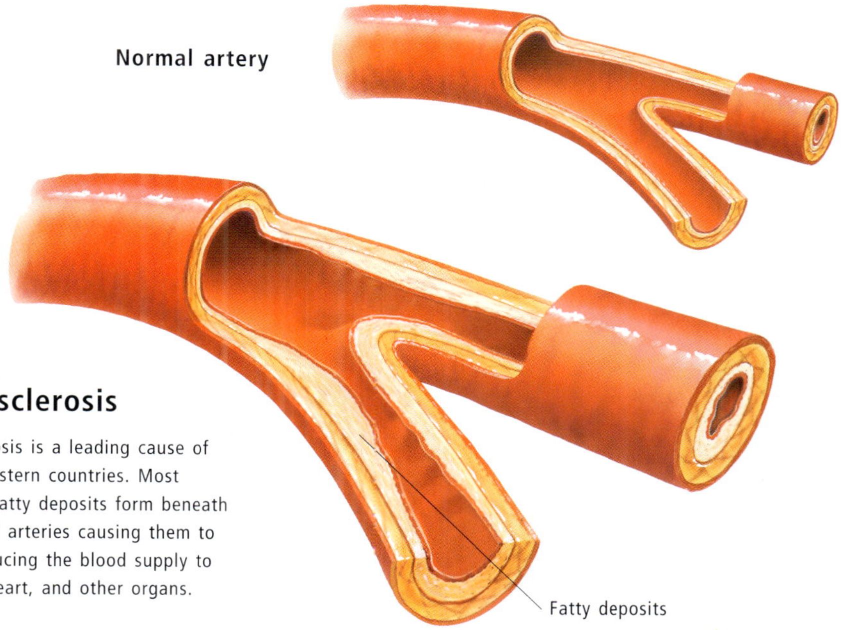

Arteriosclerosis

Arteriosclerosis is a leading cause of death in Western countries. Most commonly, fatty deposits form beneath the lining of arteries causing them to narrow, reducing the blood supply to the brain, heart, and other organs.

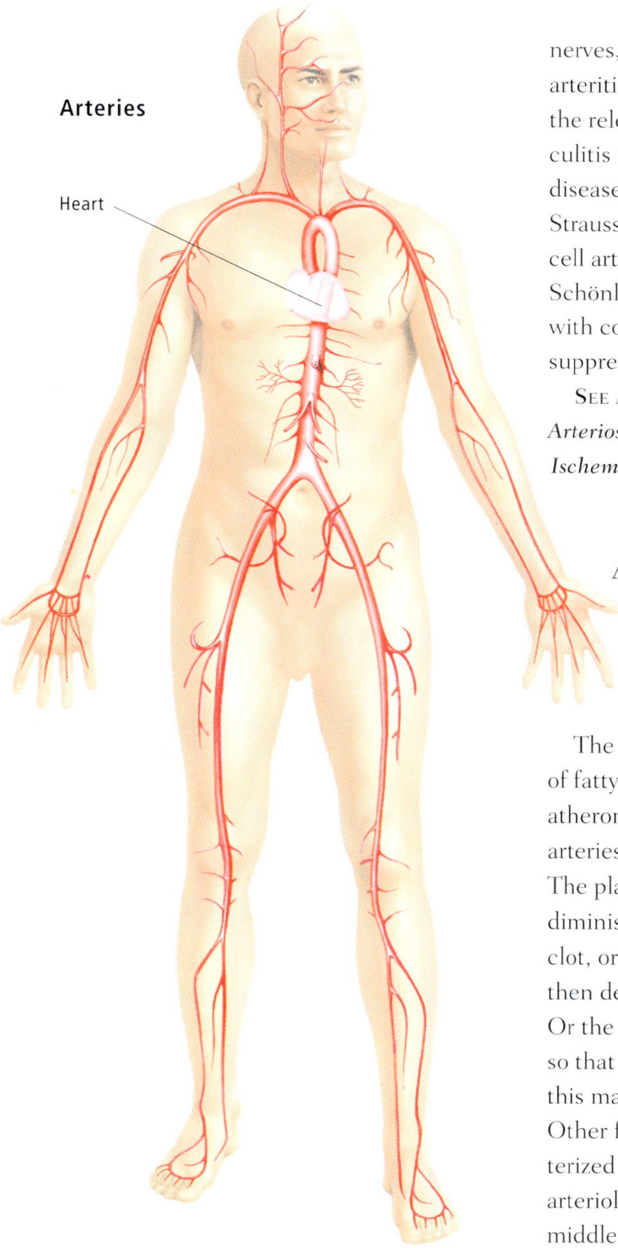

ARTERIOSCLEROSIS

The major cause of death in the developed world, arteriosclerosis is commonly referred to as "hardening of the arteries".

The most common cause is the formation of fatty deposits (plaques, also known as atheromas) within the inner lining of the arteries, a process called atherosclerosis. The plaques narrow the blood vessel and diminish the blood supply to the tissues. A clot, or embolism, may form at the plaque, then detach and lodge further downstream. Or the plaque may weaken the artery wall so that it balloons out, forming an aneurysm; this may burst and cause a hemorrhage. Other forms of arteriosclerosis are characterized by thickening of the walls of the arterioles (small arteries) or damage to the middle layer of the arteries.

When arteriosclerosis develops in the coronary arteries it can cause angina, cardiac ischemia or myocardial infarction (heart attack). In the cerebral arteries it can cause cerebrovascular accidents or strokes. In the arteries of the leg it can cause intermittent lameness, pain or gangrene. Arteriosclerosis can also cause kidney and eye damage.

The disease has no single known cause, but risk factors include high blood pressure (hypertension), cigarette smoking, obesity and elevated levels of cholesterol in the blood. Physical inactivity and a family predisposition are also risk factors. In advanced cases, surgery may be necessary, involving removal of the deposits in the arteries (endarterectomy) or replacement of the affected arteries (angioplasty).

SEE ALSO *Angioplasty, Arteries, Atherosclerosis, Cholesterol, Hypertension, Myocardial infarction, Stroke*

ARTHRITIS

Arthritis is inflammation of one or more joints, causing redness, swelling, pain and sometimes loss of joint mobility. There are many different kinds of arthritis. Arthritis may result from wear and tear on the joints (osteoarthritis) or from active joint diseases such as gout or rheumatoid arthritis. It may also be a symptom of a generalized disease, such as connective tissue disease. Symptoms of arthritis include joint pain (arthralgia), joint swelling, early morning stiffness and reduced joint movement. There may be warmth and redness of the skin around a joint, and more general symptoms such as unexplained weight loss and fever. Swelling is often due to a fluid collection called an effusion. The joint may be tender, and painful when moved. Treatment depends on the underlying cause. Rest and exercise, physical therapy, drug treatments and surgery all play a role in managing it.

Osteoarthritis

Osteoarthritis is a chronic disease causing deterioration of the weight-bearing joints of the knees, hips and spine in older people. It may also affect the hands. The sufferer notices the gradual onset of aching joint pain, which becomes worse after exercise or weight bearing, and is often relieved by rest. The joint becomes stiff, and movement becomes painful and grating. X-rays of the joints in the affected areas will show degenerative changes.

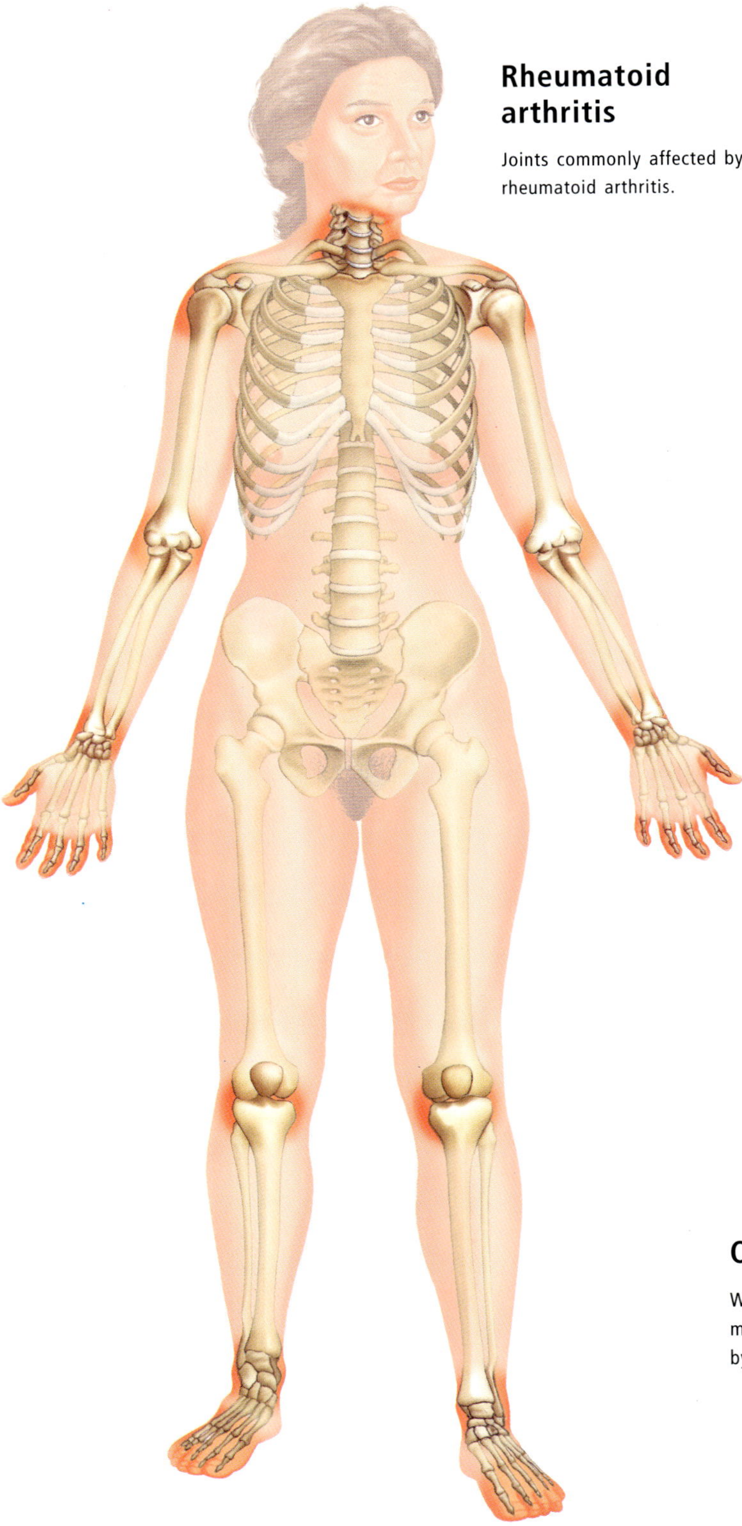

Rheumatoid arthritis

Joints commonly affected by rheumatoid arthritis.

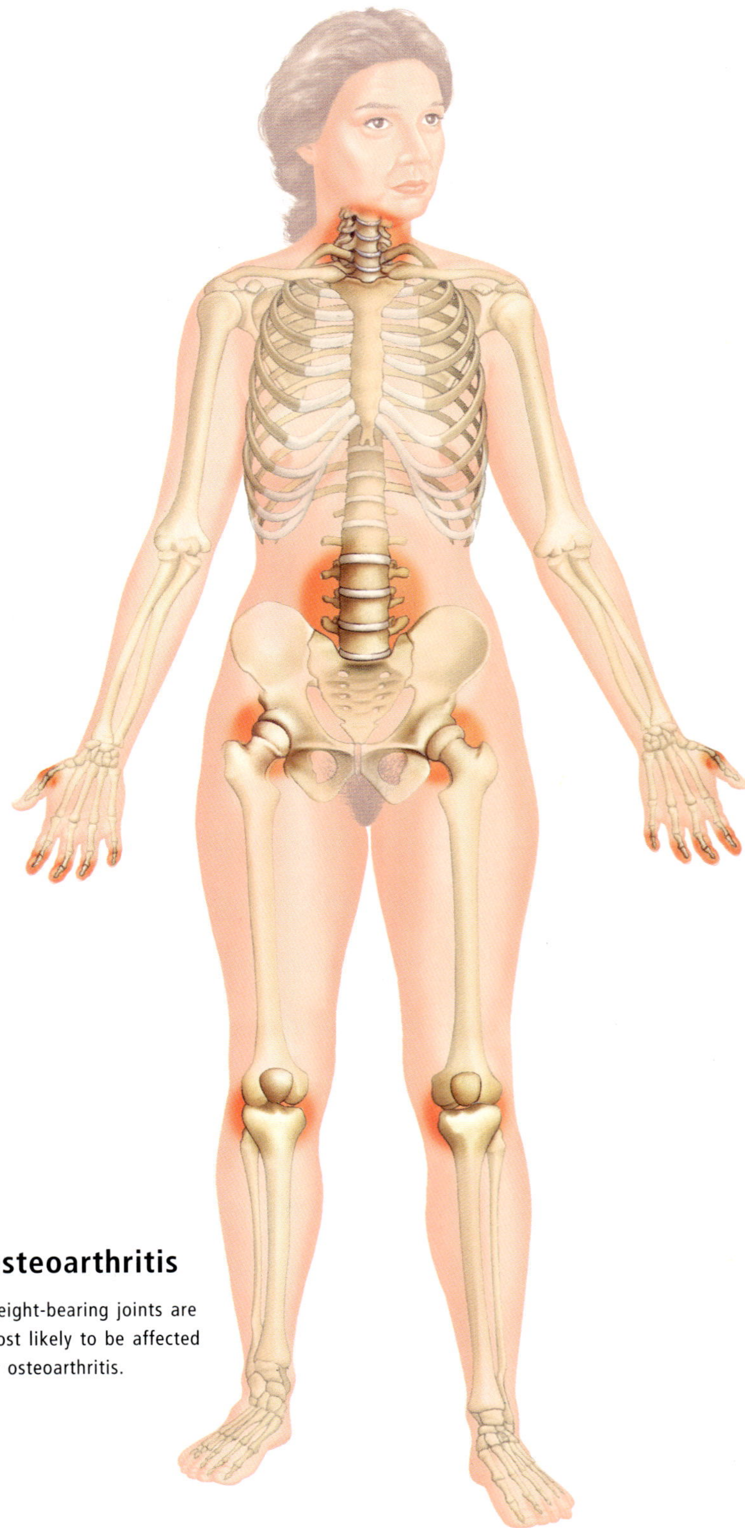

Osteoarthritis

Weight-bearing joints are most likely to be affected by osteoarthritis.

Osteoarthritis cannot be reversed, but the symptoms can be relieved. Weight loss reduces the risk of developing knee osteoarthritis, especially in women. Treatment includes exercises, physical therapy and medications, which include a variety of nonsteroidal anti-inflammatory drugs (NSAIDs). Corticosteroids, which are injected directly into the joint, may also be used. Surgical treatment to replace or repair damaged joints may be needed in severe, debilitating disease. Surgery options include arthroplasty (total or partial replacement of the deteriorated joint with an artificial joint) and arthrodesis (surgical fusion of bones, usually in the spine).

Rheumatoid arthritis

A chronic inflammatory disease, rheumatoid arthritis affects the joints and surrounding tissues. Hands, wrists, elbows, shoulders, knees and ankles are the most frequently affected. In about a quarter of cases, painless hard round nodules called rheumatoid nodules appear under the skin, usually on pressure points such as the elbow or Achilles tendon. Unlike osteoarthritis, rheumatoid arthritis can cause damage throughout the body in the skin, muscles, blood vessels, eyes or lungs. The cause is unknown. It can occur at any age, but typically begins between 25 and 55 years of age. Women are affected three times more often than men.

Rheumatoid arthritis has no known cure. Treatment, which needs to be lifelong, can relieve many of the symptoms, however. Drug treatment will usually consist of aspirin or anti-inflammatory drugs such as naproxen or sulindac. Injections of gold salts, D-penicillamine and chloroquine are sometimes used. Use of corticosteroid drugs can dramatically improve symptoms, but side effects can be a problem. These include bruising, osteoporosis (thinning of the bones), cataracts, susceptibility to infections, diabetes and high blood pressure. Occasionally, surgery is needed for severely affected joints.

SEE ALSO ***Anti-inflammatory drugs, Autoimmune disease, Connective tissue, Corticosteroids, Non-steroidal anti-inflammatory drugs, Osteoarthritis, Rheumatoid arthritis***

ARTHROSCOPY

Arthroscopy is a surgical procedure in which a small telescope known as an arthroscope is inserted into the cavity of a joint through a small incision to allow examination of joints for damage or disease. Surgical instruments have been devised for use in arthroscopy, and operations conducted in this way generally heal more quickly because of the small incision made.

ARTIFICIAL INSEMINATION

The introduction of semen into the vagina or cervix of a female by any method other than sexual intercourse is known as artificial insemination. It is a procedure used as a solution to infertility to impregnate women whose partners are sterile or impotent; it is also used in animal breeding.

Developed in the early part of the twentieth century in Russia for use in animals, its use spread internationally in the 1930s. In animals it has the advantage of passing on the desired characteristics of a bull or other male livestock animal to the offspring and producing more offspring than would be possible in the natural course of events. In humans, apart from sterility or impotence problems in the male, artificial insemination can also be an option when the female's cervical mucus is unreceptive, or when the infertility is unexplained.

Semen may be freshly obtained or it may be frozen. It may be from the partner (if he is not impotent) or from some other male donor (if the partner is sterile), in which case it may be described as donor insemination. If freshly obtained from the partner, he needs to masturbate and ejaculate in the hour before the insemination is scheduled to take place. If it is to be frozen then it is drawn into plastic straws before storing in liquid nitrogen. Frozen sperm can be kept for long periods and used, for example, if the partner is about to undergo medical treatment, often for cancer, which could render him infertile.

At around the time of ovulation, determined by checking her temperature or cervical mucus, the woman goes through a simple procedure in which the sperm is introduced by a syringe into her vagina or cervix. The technique has been reasonably successful, with 50 to 65 percent achieving conception and pregnancy. Where insemination is by donor the legal and emotional aspects are complex. Counseling is essential. Although the father is the social and birth father, he is not the genetic father. The mother is the genetic, birth and social parent.

Surrogate motherhood occurs when a woman (the surrogate mother) bears a child for a couple unable to produce children in the usual way, usually because the woman is infertile or unable to undertake a pregnancy for medical reasons. Surrogacy can take two forms: one in which the surrogate mother is impregnated using artificial insemination and the father's sperm; the other in which the woman's egg (ova) and the man's sperm are joined in the process of in vitro fertilization. When an embryo results it is implanted in the surrogate mother. Usually the surrogate mother gives up all legal rights, though this has been legally challenged.

SEE ALSO ***Infertility***

ASBESTOSIS

Asbestosis is a disease in which the lungs become inflamed through the inhalation of asbestos particles. It can develop into asbestos cancer (mesothelioma), which is a malignant tumor of the lining of the lung, chest or abdominal cavity.

Asbestos is an extremely poor conductor of heat and so was used industrially as an insulating material for many years. It is fibrous, and the fibers are easily shed and inhaled with air. The fibers can then accumulate in tissues of the airways and lungs and inhibit the exchange of oxygen between inhaled air and blood. Asbestos is no longer used because of its harmful effects; removing it from old installations requires special breathing apparatus and protective suits.

SEE ALSO ***Cancer, Mesothelioma***

ASCARIASIS

Ascariasis is an infection caused by the parasitic roundworm *Ascaris lumbricoides*. Inadequate sanitation and poor personal hygiene are major contributing factors behind the spread of ascariasis. The worm's microscopic eggs are spread in soil, water, on the hands, and on vegetables and fruit

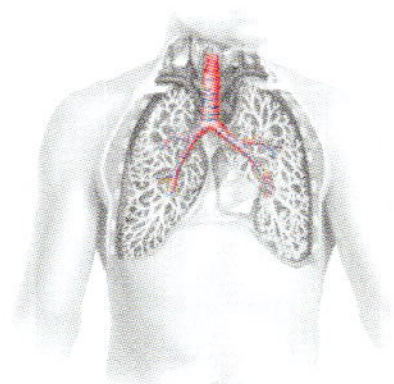

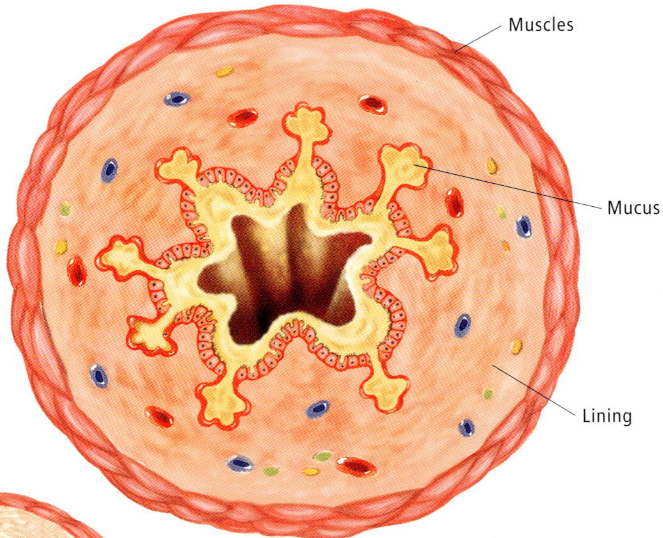

Normal bronchus

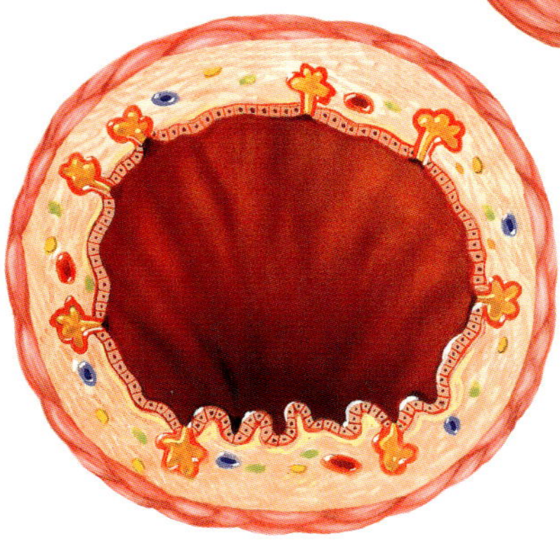

Asthma

In asthma, the lining of the bronchi become inflamed and swollen. The smooth muscles of the bronchial walls go into spasm, and the bronchi produce excessive mucus.

fertilized with untreated sewage. Early signs of infection include irritability, poor appetite, fatigue and weight fluctuations. Adult worms live in the intestine and, when infestations become heavy, can cause abdominal discomfort, obstructions and malnutrition. As part of their life-cycle, larval worms migrate through the lungs of the host, producing a cough and discomfort while breathing. Effective medications are available. Surgery is sometimes needed to clear internal blockages.

SEE ALSO *Roundworms*

ASCITES

Ascites is an abnormal accumulation of fluid around the tissues and organs of the abdominal cavity. It can indicate a range of disorders, but cirrhosis of the liver, cancer or heart failure are among the most common causes. If enough fluid is present, ascites can cause the abdomen to become distended and painful.

Ultrasonography is one of the best ways to confirm the condition, particularly in overweight patients. The cause of ascites is indicated by its appearance and chemical content. Collection of the fluid for analysis is done using a medical procedure called paracentesis. This may also be used to drain fluid to relieve discomfort. Treatment of ascites usually targets the underlying cause.

SEE ALSO *Paracentesis*

ASTHMA

Asthma is a disease of the bronchi (or air passages) of the lung, characterized by periodic attacks of wheezing alternating with periods of normal breathing. The muscles of the bronchi contract, reducing airflow and producing shortness of breath, coughing and wheezing. Mucus production increases and the lining of the bronchi becomes inflamed.

In industrial countries, asthma currently affects one in twenty people, and the number of sufferers is rising. Asthma is more prevalent in children than adults, affecting one in ten children; by adulthood, many children seem to have outgrown it. The disorder is more common if there is family history of asthma, eczema or allergies. In some cases asthma does not develop until adulthood. Commonly an adult asthmatic is short of breath early in the morning. Cough is less frequent than in childhood asthma. Adult asthma is often associated with cigarette smoking or chronic (long-term) lung diseases such as chronic bronchitis.

Asthma attacks typically come and go. There may be intervals of days, months or years between attacks, or there may be attacks every day. Symptoms can occur spontaneously or can be set off by trigger factors. The most common form of asthma (allergic bronchial asthma) is caused by an allergic reaction. Many pollens, molds, dusts (especially house dust and wood dust), cigarette smoke, feathers and animal hair can cause allergic-type asthma attacks. Asthma is sometimes associated with hay fever.

Respiratory infections, exposure to cold, industrial fumes and certain emotional and psychological states can trigger an asthma attack. Drugs such as aspirin, anti-inflammatory drugs and beta-blockers are other precipitating factors. Asthma from these causes may occur in people who have no history of allergic reactions, as well as in those who do. Exercise may trigger asthma; symptoms of exercise-induced asthma (coughing, wheezing, chest tightness lasting several minutes to an hour or more) are different from the deep and rapid breathing that quickly returns to normal after exercise.

In a mild attack, wheezing may be barely audible and the wheezing occurs only during exhalation. As the attack worsens, wheezing becomes louder and may also be present with inhalation; the sufferer breathes rapidly, gasps for breath, and becomes agitated. In a severe asthma attack, if the bronchioles become totally blocked, airflow may diminish and wheezing may stop. In children especially, this is a sign of serious trouble. An attack of asthma may be prolonged and may not respond to treatment. This condition is called status asthmaticus. An attack of status asthmaticus requires hospitalization and urgent treatment.

Diagnosis and tests

Usually it is not difficult for a physician to diagnose an asthma attack, especially if the sufferer is already known to be asthmatic. Wheezing sounds, audible through a stethoscope, and rapid improvement of symptoms after treatment confirm the diagnosis. Breathing tests such as spirometry show reduced airflow across the airways during attacks, which improves after treatment.

Chest x-rays are usually normal. In some asthmatic people, eosinophils (white cells associated with allergies) are found in the blood and sputum.

Other conditions that can cause shortness of breath or other lung problems may need to be ruled out with further tests. These conditions include blood clots in the lung, lung cancer, heart failure, cystic fibrosis, emphysema and chronic bronchitis.

Management of asthma

Unlike other lung diseases such as emphysema or chronic bronchitis, asthma is usually a reversible condition; the narrowing of the airways caused by bronchospasm improves spontaneously or in response to medications.

Several simple measures can reduce the risk of attack. Trigger factors such as pollens, animal furs and foods known to cause asthma should be avoided. A person with allergic asthma should sleep in a room without carpets or rugs. Blankets and pillows of synthetic fiber reduce the risk of house dust and mites. Asthmatics should not smoke, nor should others smoke in the same house. Asthma medication should be taken prior to events known to trigger an episode—before exercise, for example.

Several different medications are available for use in treating acute attacks, and for the long-term prevention of asthma. Often they are used in combination. Bronchodilators dilate the bronchial wall, allowing air through and relieving the symptoms of asthma. Some of these are "beta agonists", so called because they act on the beta adrenoreceptor of bronchial wall muscle, which results in bronchodilation. Others, known as anticholinergic agents, also act on the bronchi, though using a different mechanism to relax and open the airway passages. Both types of bronchodilator may be used together. Side effects of bronchodilators include nervousness, restlessness, insomnia and headache. Elderly patients and children may be more sensitive to the effects of bronchodilators.

When symptoms of asthma are frequent and difficult to control with bronchodilators, preventive medications are used. These medications do not cure an attack of asthma once it has begun. Instead, they prevent attacks from recurring. Physicians believe that long-term damage to the bronchi is minimized by using preventive medications.

Commonly, bronchodilators and preventive medications are used together—the bronchodilators to treat the symptoms of an attack and the preventive medication to stop attacks from occurring. Corticosteroids are the most commonly used preventive medications. They reduce bronchial inflammation and airway obstruction and improve lung function. Sodium cromoglycate is another preventive medication; it stops the release of chemicals such as histamine into the bronchi, which can cause asthma. Sodium cromoglycate is useful for asthma triggered by exercise, cold air and allergies, such as to cat fur.

In the treatment of asthma, inhaled medications are generally preferred over tablet or liquid medicines. Inhaled medications act directly on the surface of the airways; absorption into the rest of the body is minimal so side effects are fewer compared with oral medications. Inhaled medications include beta-agonists (metaproterenol, albuterol and terbutaline sulfate); anticholinergics (ipratropium bromide); corticosteroids (beclomethasone dipropionate, triamcinolone acetonide and flunisolide) and sodium cromoglycate.

Inhaled medications are administered via a metered dose inhaler, or a puffer. In children who have difficulty with inhalers or puffers, or in adults with a more severe attack, asthma medications can be given by nebulizer, which administers the medication in the form of a fine mist inhaled through a mouth mask. Some people may experience minor side effects of hoarseness and thrush (a fungal infection of the mouth and throat) from using corticosteroid inhalers. These and other problems can be minimized by rinsing the mouth and using a spacer device, which reduces the amount of medication residue left in the mouth and the throat.

Oral corticosteroids, such as prednisone, methylprednisone and hydrocortisone, may be used as preventive medications. However, they have more side effects than inhaled corticosteroids, so long-term use is not recommended, except when other treatments have failed to restore normal lung function and the risks of uncontrolled asthma are greater than the side effects of the steroids. Corticosteroids may also be given intravenously in severe attacks requiring hospitalization, for example in status asthmaticus. Intravenous epinephrine (adrenaline) and oxygen may also be needed during a life-threatening attack.

Asthma plan

As the severity of an asthma attack varies so much from person to person, it is helpful for an asthmatic to have an individual management plan in case of an attack. The plan should be made available to carers, teachers, nurses, parents and anyone else who has responsibility for that person.

In the event of an asthma attack, follow the asthma plan and help the sufferer to take the medication as directed in the plan. Get emergency help if the person fails to improve or if those symptoms listed on the plan as emergency indicators are present.

A simple device called a peak flow meter, which measures how well air moves out of the airways, can be used regularly at home to measure lung function. Monitoring peak flow helps an asthma sufferer monitor changes and to adjust the medication dosage up or down as needed. Each person has a personal-best peak flow reading, which should be noted in the asthma plan. A peak flow reading less than 80 percent of the personal best indicates the need for action.

An asthmatic patient should seek medical advice promptly when suffering from a respiratory infection. Generally, any infection producing green or yellow sputum should be treated with antibiotics quickly. Some asthmatics may benefit from breathing exercises. These help the lungs to function more effectively and give the sufferer a psychological boost during an attack. Asthmatics whose symptoms are triggered by allergies may benefit from a course of desensitizing allergy injections, though benefits are variable and may not last.

SEE ALSO *Allergies, Bronchitis, Bronchodilators, Corticosteroids, Emphysema, Lungs*

ASTIGMATISM

An astigmatism is a lack of symmetry in the curvature of the cornea of the eye (the cornea is the transparent wall in front of the pupil and iris). It can also be a lack of symmetry in the crystalline lens. The result is that the patient sees an image which is blurred or smeared in one direction, either vertically, horizontally or obliquely.

The cause is not known, though some types of astigmatism may run in families. Astigmatism is rarely serious, and corrective lenses can be used if necessary. Surgery and laser treatment are used in some cases. The first contact lens, developed by Adolf Fick in 1887, was made of glass and designed to correct astigmatism.

SEE ALSO *Cornea, Eye*

ATELECTASIS

A partial or complete collapse of a lung is know medically as atelectasis. It is most often caused by a blockage in a bronchus or bronchioles, the air tubes leading to the lungs. Obstructions can include tumors, inhaled objects, or thick mucus from infections or a disease such as cystic fibrosis. A form of atelectasis can also occur as a post-operative complication caused by the effects of surgery.

Acute atelectasis can lead to a sudden and major collapse accompanied by chest pain, rapid and uncomfortable breathing, dizziness and shock. Alternatively, the signs of atelectasis may include a less dramatic, more gradual collapse, cough, shortness of breath and a fever.

Atelectasis is not normally fatal and the affected lung usually reinflates once any obstruction has been extracted or dislodged. A procedure called a bronchoscopy may be required to remove a blockage. Pneumonia and permanent scarring of lung tissue are potential complications of atelectasis.

SEE ALSO *Bronchoscopy, Lungs, Pneumonia, Respiratory system*

ATHEROSCLEROSIS

Atherosclerosis is a disease of the major arteries in which fatty deposits called plaques collect on the interior walls, leading to narrowing and obstruction of blood flow. This build-up is a contributing factor in cardiovascular disease which causes heart attack. Calcium accumulates in the fatty material as part of a process known as arteriosclerosis, or "hardening of the arteries".

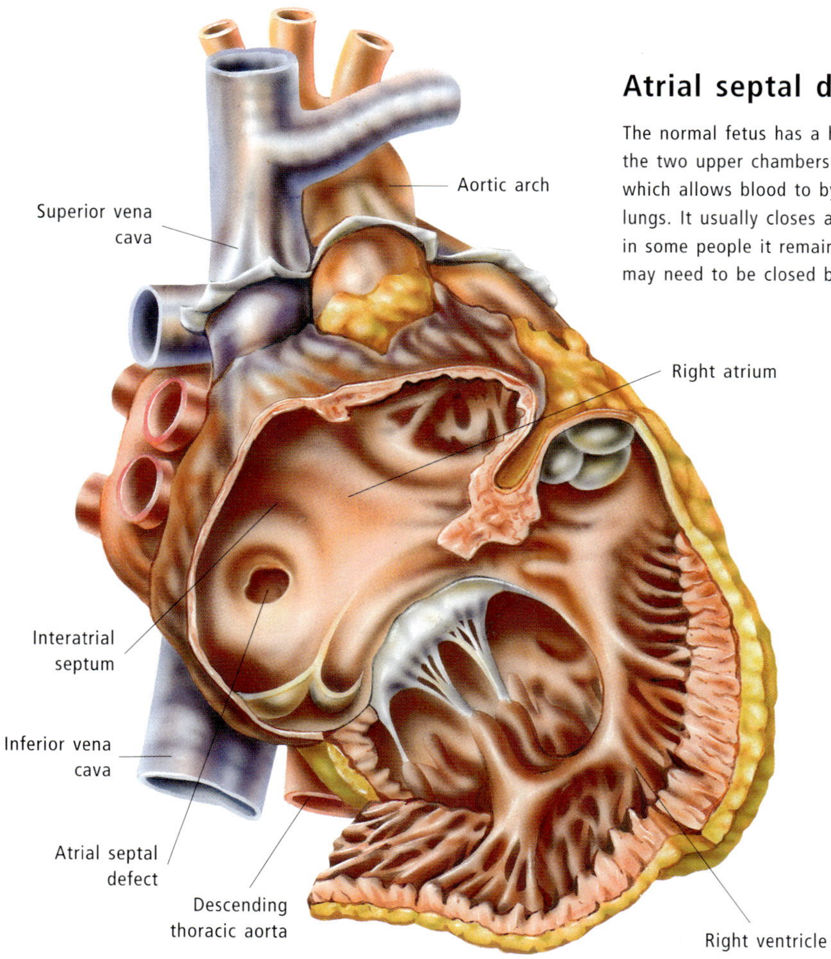

Atrial septal defect

The normal fetus has a hole between the two upper chambers of the heart, which allows blood to bypass the lungs. It usually closes at birth, but in some people it remains open and may need to be closed by surgery.

Severe heart attack and perhaps death can occur as a result of sudden arterial blockage. This may be due to plaques rupturing and releasing fatty deposits, or a blood clot attaching to the plaque. Smoking, obesity and high cholesterol may be contributing factors, along with high blood pressure, excess fat intake and a family history of heart disease.

Atherosclerosis can occur in the carotid and vertebral arteries leading to the head and brain, as well as in the coronary arteries. It generally has no symptoms until complications set in. When blood flow in the heart is severely restricted it may cause chest pain. Stroke and damage to the body's organs are also possible results of blockage.

Treatment includes the inflation of a balloon-tipped catheter in the artery to clear blockages, or surgical bypass of blockages in the heart using veins from the legs. A cold laser can destroy plaques with ultraviolet light, or a drill-tipped catheter may be used. Certain drugs can reduce cholesterol and fats in the blood, and anticoagulants such as aspirin reduce the chance of clotting.

SEE ALSO *Angioplasty, Arteries, Arteriosclerosis*

ATHETOSIS

Athetosis is involuntary slow and twisting movements of the head, limbs, trunk or neck, creating abnormal and often grotesque postures. The symptoms typically improve or disappear during sleep but worsen during exercise (such as walking) and emotional stress. Athetosis is caused by a disorder of certain nerve pathways in the brain, and is seen in a number of conditions, including cerebral palsy, encephalitis and Huntington's disease. It can be a side effect of certain drugs. Treatment (if any) depends on correcting the underlying cause.

ATRIAL SEPTAL DEFECT

Atrial septal defect (ASD) is a congenital "hole in the heart" between the two upper chambers of the heart (the atria). In the fetus, this opening is normal, and allows blood to bypass the lungs (which are not in use).

At birth, this opening usually closes to allow blood to be pumped into the lungs once breathing starts. In persons with ASD, the hole doesn't close. Most people with ASD don't have symptoms, but if the opening is large enough there may be symptoms of shortness of breath and irregular heartbeats (palpitations). These symptoms often don't develop until adulthood.

Through the stethoscope, a physician may hear abnormal heart sounds in a person with ASD. An ultrasound of the heart or an echocardiogram will show the hole. An EKG (electrocardiogram) may also be abnormal, as the hole interferes with the normal conduction of the heartbeat through the heart.

No treatment is necessary if there are no symptoms; if there are symptoms or the hole is large, surgical closure of the defect may be needed. People affected with ASD will need to take antibiotics during dental and surgical procedures, as they are at increased risk of developing bacterial endocarditis.

SEE ALSO *Endocarditis, Heart*

ATROPHIC VAGINITIS

Atrophic vaginitis is a skin condition of the vagina caused by a lack of estrogen in the body. It occurs most commonly in women after the menopause, or following surgical removal of the ovaries. The lining of the vagina becomes thin and easily damaged, giving rise to vaginal itching. Urinary symptoms such as burning and greater frequency and urgency are common.

Treatment is with estrogen replacement therapy. This is prescribed as a pill or skin patch, or as an estrogen cream or pessary which can be applied to the vagina.

SEE ALSO *Vaginitis, Vulvitis*

ATTENTION DEFICIT HYPERACTIVITY DISORDER

Attention deficit hyperactivity disorder (ADHD), formerly known as hyperactivity, is a behavioral disorder which shows itself in an inability to concentrate and in excessive restless, impulsive, destructive, disruptive behavior often coupled with irritability and aggression. Attention deficit disorder (ADD) is a similar condition without the hyperactivity and is less common. Children with either of these conditions find it difficult to make friends.

Statistics differ between countries; for example, in the USA between 10 and 15 percent of young males are diagnosed with ADHD or ADD, and in Australia the figure is between 2 and 6 percent. Boys are more likely to be affected and it usually manifests itself once school starts, though a very small number of children seem to be hyperactive from birth. These babies are often described as "high need" rather than as having ADHD. It is thought to be mainly a biological condition with family, environmental, genetic and social factors coming into the equation.

Diagnosis and misdiagnosis

ADHD can be incorrectly diagnosed, so a thorough, wide-ranging investigation is necessary. Criteria for the diagnosis of ADHD include fidgeting and squirming, difficulty staying seated, and difficulty in taking turns and following instructions. Also, the child is noisy and talks incessantly, does not seem to be listening, loses things, and gets involved in physically dangerous activities without considering consequences.

Parents, teachers, psychologists and doctors should be involved, and other possibilities such as learning difficulties investigated. Children who do not relate to their school curriculum or who have learning difficulties may be seen to have ADHD.

Some professionals doubt that it is a real condition and others believe that hyperactivity is a subjective assessment, as all adults perceive children's behavior differently. Between 12 and 20 percent of children suffer from a range of learning difficulties, with 2 to 4 percent suffering quite severely. If children are having difficulty with listening, speaking, reading, writing, mathematical or reasoning skills, they are seen as not being able to give proper attention to tasks at hand and may be misdiagnosed. Therefore assessment for learning difficulties should precede diagnosis of ADHD.

Depression can also be confused with ADHD as depressed children have low self-esteem. Between 1 and 3 percent of children suffer depression, and it is hard to detect. Sleep problems have also been suggested as causing ADHD. Early diagnosis is important in treating antisocial behavior.

Treatment

Treatment includes short-term medication together with behavioral and educational strategies and family counseling. Dietary restrictions or interventions have not been proven to work and are no longer considered appropriate. Adequate nutrition is important for growth and many diets intended to address the problem of hyperactivity were severely restrictive.

There are dangers with long-term use of brain stimulant drugs which are often used to treat the condition, as some research suggests it could lead later to cocaine addiction.

The management of ADHD is never simple. Many people need to be involved if treatment is to succeed. As children grow older some of the behaviors improve, but often many of their difficulties continue into adulthood. ADHD has been diagnosed in adults, though this is controversial.

SEE ALSO *Amphetamines, Behavioral problems, Learning disorders*

AUDIOMETRY

Audiometry is a very precise method of measuring a person's ability to hear. In normal hearing, sound reaches the eardrum and inner ear through the air and through the mastoid bone behind each ear. An instrument called an audiometer electronically produces pure tones at a specific pitch and volume; it is used to test each ear, with different tests for measuring air conduction and bone conduction hearing. In both tests the volume of each tone is reduced to the point at which the person can no longer hear it. These sound thresholds are charted or graphed to produce an audiogram.

Audiometry can also measure the speech threshold to show how words are heard and understood at specific volumes. This involves listening to a series of words and repeating each one as it is heard. A separate speech test measures the ability to discriminate between similar-sounding words.

Tympanometry is a test used to establish the cause of hearing loss, particularly in children. It can differentiate between problems caused by a blocked eustachian tube, fluid in the middle ear and malfunction of the bones of the middle ear.

SEE ALSO *Ear, Hearing*

AUTISM

Autism is part of the spectrum of conditions called pervasive developmental disorder (PDD). It involves problems with social interaction and communication. This developmental disorder usually becomes apparent by the time the child is three years old; signs include self-absorption, lack of reaction to other people, and a quite narrow range of activites and interests.

Evidence suggests autism is a problem of the nerve system that can be caused by genetic disorders, brain injury (either before or after birth), metabolic disorders, viral infections or diseases. Four times as many boys as girls suffer from this condition.

There are varying degrees of autism. Children with mild autism, also called high functioning autism, can be high achievers; children with the most severe form avoid eye contact as well as physical contact and show no understanding of other creatures, including people and their own family. Behavioral patterns, such as hand flapping, will be repetitive. Autism can be confused with intellectual disability.

Autistic children can be affectionate, though on their own terms. Routine is paramount and any changes can cause a major upset. Autism affects the capacity to make sense of the environment. For an autistic child the world is chaos. In autistic children language is either non-existent or very poorly developed. They do not attempt to communicate, make gestures or imitate sounds, or show other signs that are part of normal language development. Persistent, purposeless and seemingly involuntary repetition of certain sounds or phrases, known as echolalia, is also a symptom.

There is no cure or prevention for autism, but early intervention can have great benefits. The child needs to be assessed by an experienced child psychologist or psychiatrist. Treatment is very specialized and labor intensive. From about age three, children can be enrolled in programs that have the ultimate aim of integrating them into school and the community. No medications have been found to make a difference to autism.

AUTOIMMUNE DISEASE

Autoimmune diseases develop when the body's immune system fails to recognize normal body tissues and attacks and destroys them as if they were foreign. The cause isn't fully understood, but in some cases is thought to be triggered by exposure to microorganisms and drugs, especially in people with a genetic predisposition to the disorder. A single organ or multiple organs and tissues may be affected.

Examples of autoimmune diseases and the tissues they attack include: Hashimoto's thyroiditis (thyroid); pernicious anemia (blood); Addison's disease (adrenal cortex); diabetes mellitus (pancreas); rheumatoid arthritis (joints); systemic lupus erythematosus and dermatomyositis (connective tissues); and myasthenia gravis (muscles).

Symptoms of autoimmune disease are related to the lack of function of the organ or tissue involved. In addition, generalized symptoms common to all autoimmune disorders include tiredness and fatigue, dizziness, malaise and low-grade fever. The diagnosis is made from blood tests and other tests which indicate the degree of loss of function in the organ system involved. A blood cell count may show increased numbers of white blood cells. Levels of certain immuno-globulins and other proteins in the blood may be higher than normal.

There is no cure for an autoimmune disorder. Thyroid supplements, insulin injections or other supplements may be required to alleviate the symptoms, depending on the specific disease. Disorders that affect the blood components may require blood

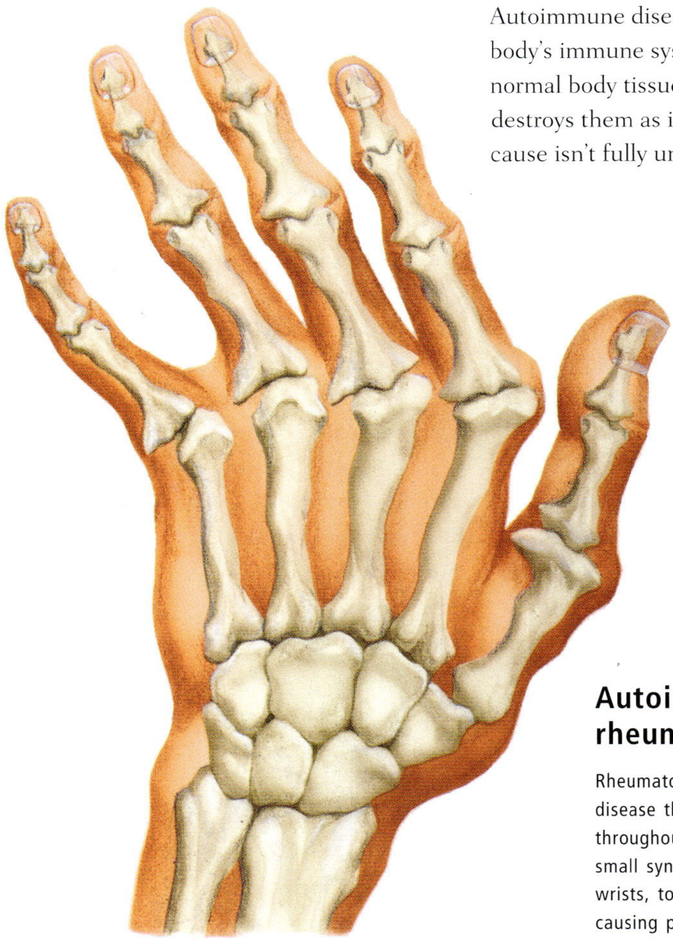

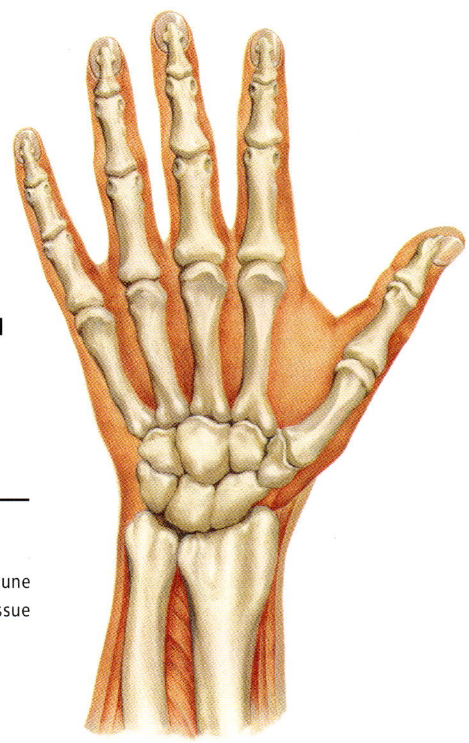

Autoimmune disease—rheumatoid arthritis

Rheumatoid arthritis is an autoimmune disease that inflames connective tissue throughout the body. It affects the small synovial joints of the fingers, wrists, toes, ankles and elbows, causing pain and swelling.

transfusions. Measures to assist mobility or other functions are sometimes needed for disorders that affect the bones, joints, or muscles. Symptoms can often be controlled by corticosteroids. However, side effects such as osteoporosis (thinning of the bones), bruising, susceptibility to infections, diabetes and high blood pressure are common. Immunosuppressants (drugs that suppress the immune system) such as cyclophosphamide or azathioprine may also be used.

Lupus erythematosus is an autoimmune disease that affects connective tissue. There are two forms of the disorder: discoid lupus erythematosus (DLE) and systemic lupus erythematosus (SLE). Both conditions affect the skin. SLE involves other tissues and organs as well.

Rheumatoid arthritis is one of the more common autoimmune diseases, affecting the joints; typically the hands, wrists, elbows, shoulders, knees and ankles. Skin, muscles, blood vessels, eyes and lungs can also be involved. There is no cure, but treatment, which usually needs to be lifelong, can relieve many of the symptoms. Drug treatment consists of anti-inflammatory drugs and injections of gold salts. Oral corticosteroid drugs are also used, but have side effects. Occasionally, surgery is needed for severely affected joints.

Vasculitis (angiitis) is a general term for a group of uncommon autoimmune diseases which cause inflammation of the blood vessels. Examples of vasculitis include Kawasaki disease, Behçet's disease, Takayasu's arteritis, Churg-Strauss syndrome, giant cell arteritis (temporal arteritis) and Henoch Schönlein purpura. Polyarteritis nodosa affects the arteries in muscles, joints, intestines, nerves, kidneys and skin. Diagnosis of polyarteritis nodosa is confirmed by a biopsy of the relevant tissue. Anti-inflammatory and immunosuppressant drugs are used in treatment.

SEE ALSO *Addison's disease, Connective tissue, Dermatomyositis, Diabetes, Hashimoto's disease, Lupus erythematosus, Myasthenia gravis, Rheumatoid arthritis, Vasculitis*

AYURVEDIC MEDICINE

The term Ayurveda comes from the Sanskrit words *ayur* meaning life, and *veda*, meaning knowledge or science.

Ayurveda is the basis of the traditional health system in India, tracing its history back to the ancient Hindu texts of the *Rig Veda*. Within this system an individual is seen to be a microcosm of the larger macrocosm of the earth.

In Ayurveda everything in the universe is divided up into five elements: *prithvi* (earth), *ap* (water), *teja* (light, fire or heat), *vayu* (air) and *akasha* (space or ether). Food is composed of these elements and different foods are seen to work either with or against the elemental balance in the body. Ruling everything are the three basic forces, known as the *doshas*. *Vata* is equated with the wind and governs the central nervous system; *pitta* is like the sun and governs the digestive system and biochemical processes; and *kapha* is like the moon and governs cell growth and the fluid balance of the tissues.

In dealing with the body, the Ayurvedic practitioner is interested in the *dhatus*, or the seven basic constituents of the body: *rasa* (food), *rakta* (blood), *mamsa* (bone), *meda* (fat and perspiration), *asthi* (bone marrow), *majya* (viscidity) and *shukra* (satisfying movements).

In Ayurveda the health of an individual depends on the balance between the life-giving energies which flow through the various organs and systems of the body. Illnesses are seen as the result of imbalance, and are classified under four groupings: accidental, physical, natural and mental. The physician's task is to assess the balance of the various elements at play in the body and to prescribe treatment which will bring the body back into harmony. The primary emphasis is on prevention rather than cure. Where illness has already developed, the emphasis is on treating the source of the disease, not the symptoms.

The Ayurvedic practitioner aims to identify the innate disposition/constitution of each patient, which is believed to be determined at the time of conception. Personal lifestyle, diet, work and life stage are all taken into account, along with a physical examination of the urine, stools, sweat, skin, nails, eyes, tongue and voice.

Treatments prescribed can include dietary changes, fasts, exposure to the sun, massage, baths, inhalations, enemas and homeopathic and herbal medicines. Yoga and yogic breathing techniques are considered particularly important in their ability to control the mind through the physical discipline of the body, which in turn can strengthen the mind's ability to influence the overall health of the body. Meditation is also valued for its ability to reduce stress and tension.

Ayurvedic medicine is still widely practised and taught in India, often in conjunction with orthodox Western medicine. It was initially popularized in Western countries by the Maharishi Mahesh Yogi, and more recently through the work of Dr Deepak Chopra, whose work places a strong emphasis on the role of consciousness in medical therapy.

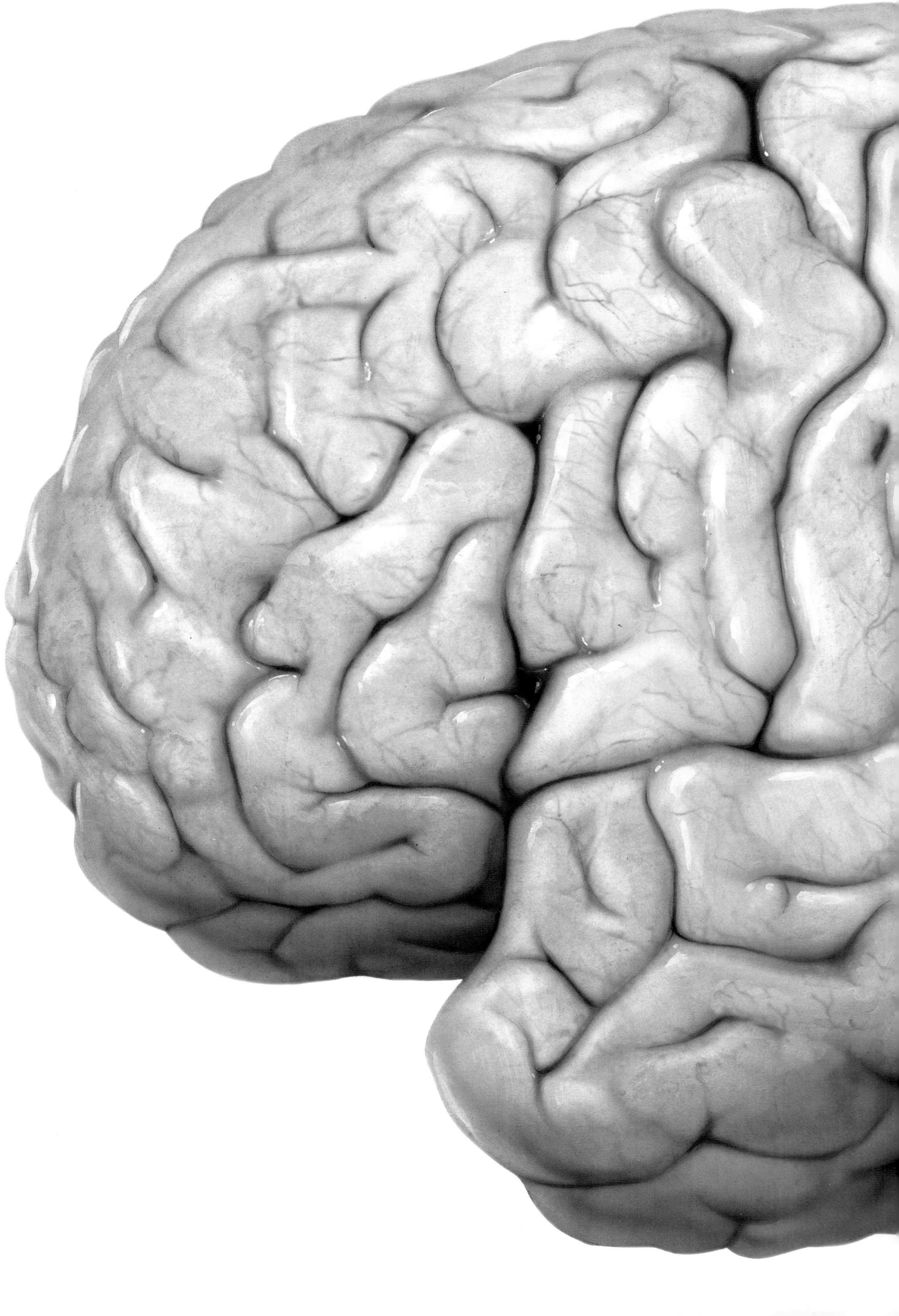

B

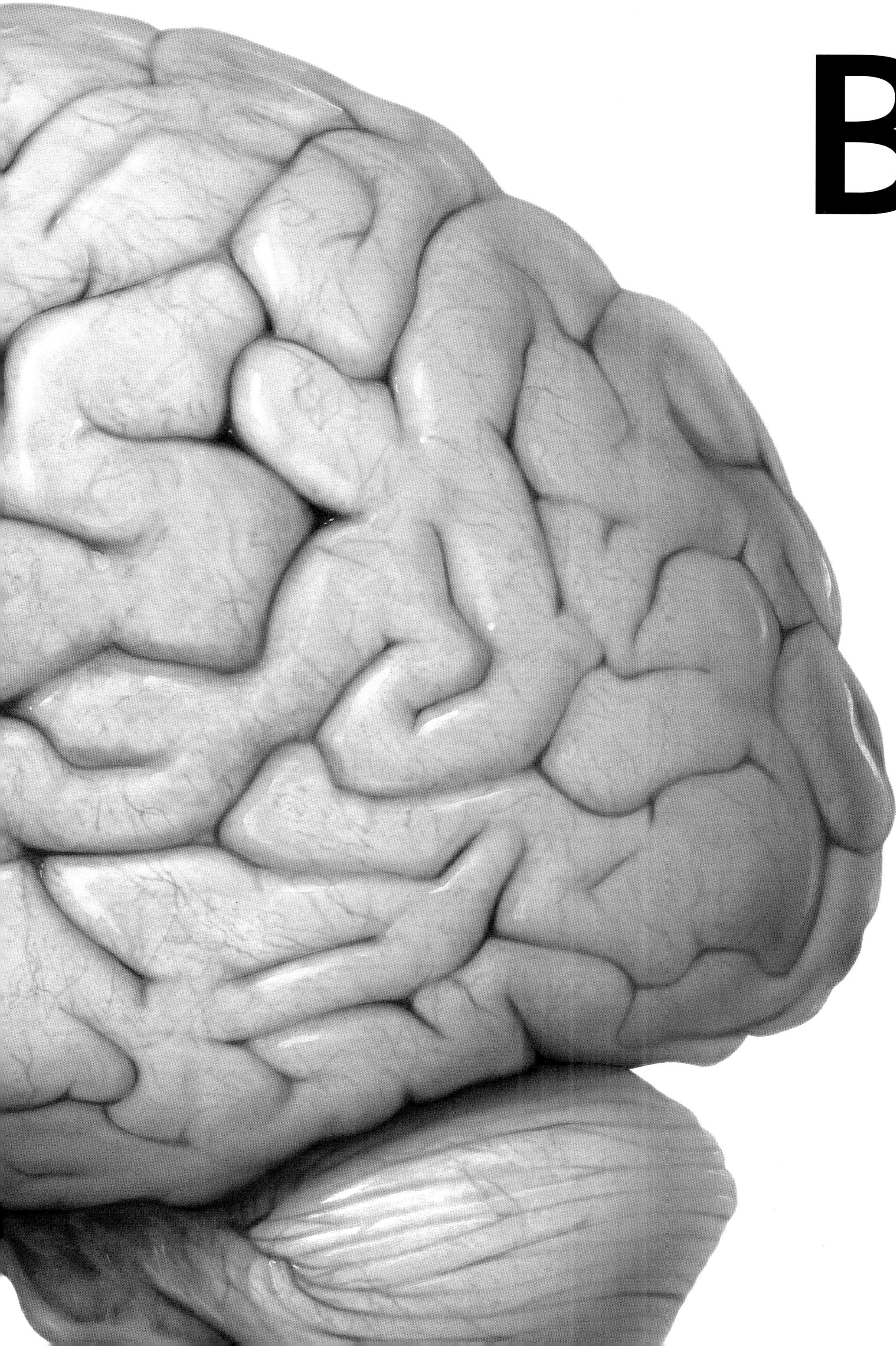

BACK

The back is the part of the human body from below the neck to the lower end of the spine, just above the buttocks. The bones of the spine are known as the vertebrae and are joined to each other by disks (invertebral disks) and joints (facet joints) to form the vertebral column; the spinal cord runs through a canal formed by the vertebrae. The spinal cord is composed of nerve tissue, and nerves branch off through spaces between vertebrae.

The vertebrae are separated from each other and cushioned by the invertebral disks, which are flexible. The disks are designed to bear weight and to cushion the surfaces of the vertebrae as the spine moves.

The vertebral column protects the spinal cord and spinal nerves, supports the weight of the body and head, and anchors the rib cage. It plays a major role in movement and posture, and provides an attachment point for muscles of the trunk, arms and legs.

Moving down from the head, there are 24 separate vertebrae: 7 cervical (C), 12 thoracic (T) and 5 lumbar (L). A further 5 are fused together and form the sacrum, then another 4, the smallest vertebrae, are fused to form the coccyx (the tail bone). The normal number of vertebrae is 33, but there may be one more (this most often occurs in males) or one less (mostly in females). The largest are the lumbar vertebrae, which bear the most weight. It is the fifth lumbar vertebra (L5) that carries the weight of the whole upper body and transfers it to the sacrum.

Paget's disease—in which bones enlarge and soften—can cause the spine to weaken and deform. Height is lost and the deformity may pinch nerves, causing pain or paralysis.

The arteries that supply blood to the brain stem travel up the cervical vertebrae. When bloodflow through them is reduced, as may happen when one has arteriosclerosis, turning the head can produce a feeling of dizziness.

Anesthetics are sometimes injected directly into the epidural space in the spinal column for operations on the lower trunk and legs, and during childbirth and delivery by cesarean section.

Injuries and diseases

The spine may be deformed by forward curvature or hunching (kyphosis), hollowed or sway back (lordosis), being curved to one side (scoliosis), or being both hunched and curved (kyphoscoliosis).

Abnormalities can be caused by injury or muscular weakness, habitually poor posture, deformities at birth, or inherited disease such as ankylosing spondylitis. This disease affects connective tissue, inflaming the spine and large joints such as hips, shoulders and knees, producing pain and stiffness and a tendency to stoop. Many back problems are correctable without surgery. Considerable improvements can be made by developing strong back and abdominal muscles to counter poor posture.

The disks can be damaged by violent movement (such as in accidents or sporting collisions), by lifting very heavy weights, or by poor posture. They may be squashed or deformed, causing one or more to protrude, the classic condition known as a slipped disk. This may cause back pain and often will occur at the fourth or fifth lumbar vertebra (L4 or L5).

This type of injury becomes more common with increasing age as the disks lose their water content and become less flexible. They also become thinner, which results in the loss of height seen in old age. Damaged disks may impinge on the spinal nerves which form the sciatic nerve, resulting in sciatica—pain down the back of the thigh and into the leg. There may also be muscular spasm (an involuntary contraction of a muscle group), which is a protective mechanism.The muscles in spasm act as a splint to prevent further damage, and they are associated with pain, distortion of normal movement and a twisted, unnatural posture.

Whiplash injury can damage the cervical vertebrae. It is often caused by accidents in motor vehicles and contact sports where the head moves backwards (hyperextension) and forwards (hyperflexion) violently and farther than normal. This movement can cause vertebrae to fracture or, more often, injure the ligaments which connect the vertebrae. Dislocated vertebrae can damage the spinal cord.

Falls on the head or sporting injuries involving head-on collisions can result in fractured vertebrae or ruptured disks. Fractured vertebrae can injure the spinal cord and cause paralysis or death. Disks that rupture will bulge out from between the vertebrae above and below, causing pain as they touch and compress the spinal nerves.

Strains and sprains are less severe injuries to muscles that result from extreme rotations or extensions of the spine. Adequate warm-up routines and stretches can help to prevent back strain injuries.

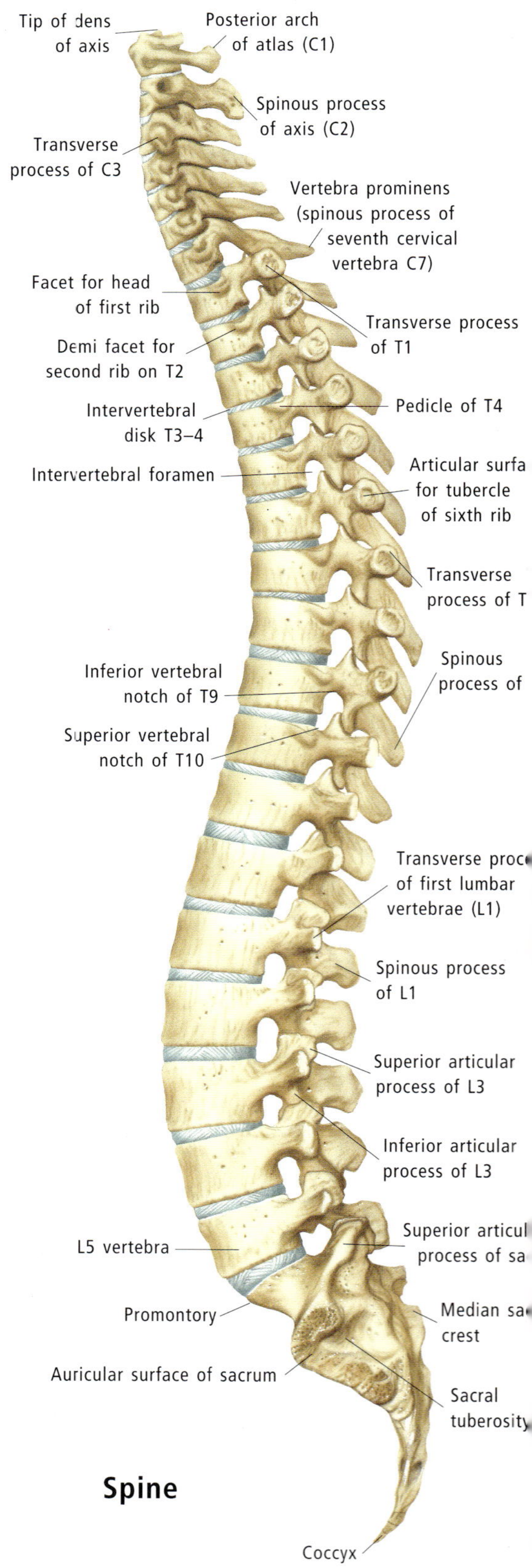

Spine

Spinal cord injuries may cause shock and paralysis below the injury site. This could result in paraplegia (paralysis in both legs and the lower body) if the injury is in the lumbar spine, and quadriplegia (paralysis in all four limbs) if the injury is above the fifth cervical vertebra. If spinal injury is suspected, the person should only be moved by trained paramedical workers. If inappropriate movements are made, this could result in further injury and even paralysis.

Osteoporosis, a degenerative bone disease, is especially disabling and painful when it affects the spine. Loss of minerals from bones causes them to become more porous, and therefore brittle, than normal. Vertebrae become weak and may collapse or fracture, causing pain and immobility or paralysis. Bone cancer can also be a cause of pain but symptoms are usually felt elsewhere in the body.

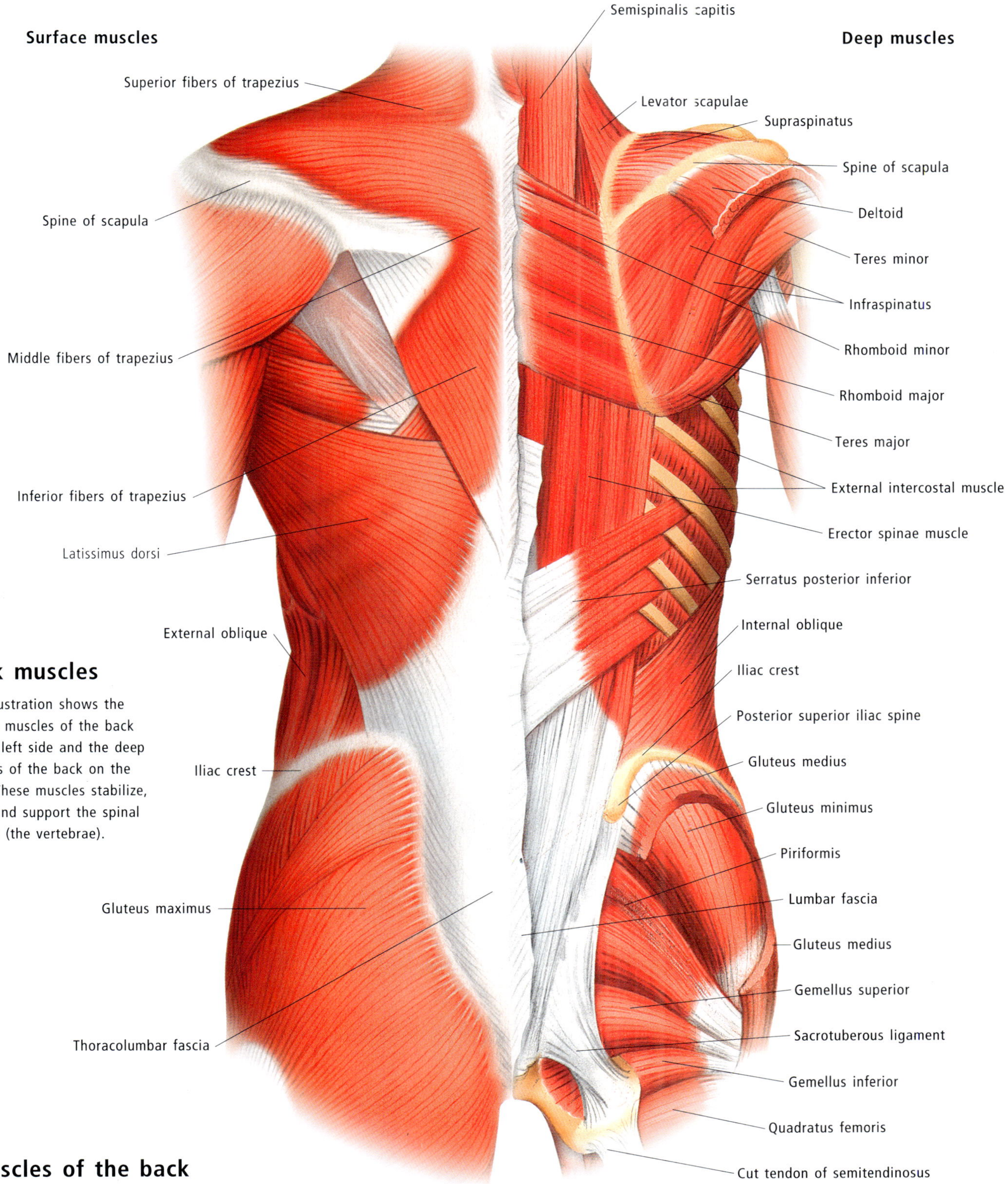

Back muscles

This illustration shows the surface muscles of the back on the left side and the deep muscles of the back on the right. These muscles stabilize, move and support the spinal column (the vertebrae).

Muscles of the back

Causes of back pain

Low back pain is a very common complaint in many societies because of the increasingly sedentary nature of daily work. Symptoms can be pain or numbness in the lower back and surrounding areas, commonly called lumbago. When pain extends down the buttocks and into the upper legs it is associated with pressure on spinal nerves which form the sciatic nerve and is known as sciatica. Factors which place people at risk of back strain injury and low back pain include the following.

Poor physical condition. Good muscle tone in the abdomen and deep muscles which support the spinal column is essential to allow the full range of movement without displacing the disks. Poor muscle tone does not of itself cause back pain, but it brings a greater risk of injury if you are lifting, bending or rotating when the spine is under load.

Loading unprepared muscles. Starting any sporting activity or lifting any significant weight without warming up is dangerous. It is important to prepare for such exertion with stretching, gentle flexing and extension of the muscle groups to be worked. This applies to manual work as well as to sports.

Poor posture. Forward bending of the back compresses the disks at their front edges, and they tend to bulge to the rear. This causes the disk protrusion known commonly as slipped disk and causes pain when the surrounding muscles go into spasm and the disk aggravates spinal nerve roots.

Lifting heavy weights. The knees should be bent when lifting weights from low places, and the back kept as straight as possible. The weight should be kept close to the body as reaching out or up high for a heavy load brings a greater risk of injury. Lifting should be a smooth action as jerking can strain the back. The load should not be too heavy for the lifter. Injuries are common when people do not respect their limitations. Back belts and trusses are poor insurance against injury compared to good muscle tone and common sense.

Care of the back

Back care starts with good posture, whether sitting, standing or working. Good muscle condition plays a very large part, as poor posture often results in muscle weakness. It is important to maintain muscular strength in both abdominal muscles and in the deep muscles that act directly on the spinal column. If working at a desk, it is important to be in a comfortable posture with the seat backrest supporting the back. Having frequent breaks is a good preventive measure.

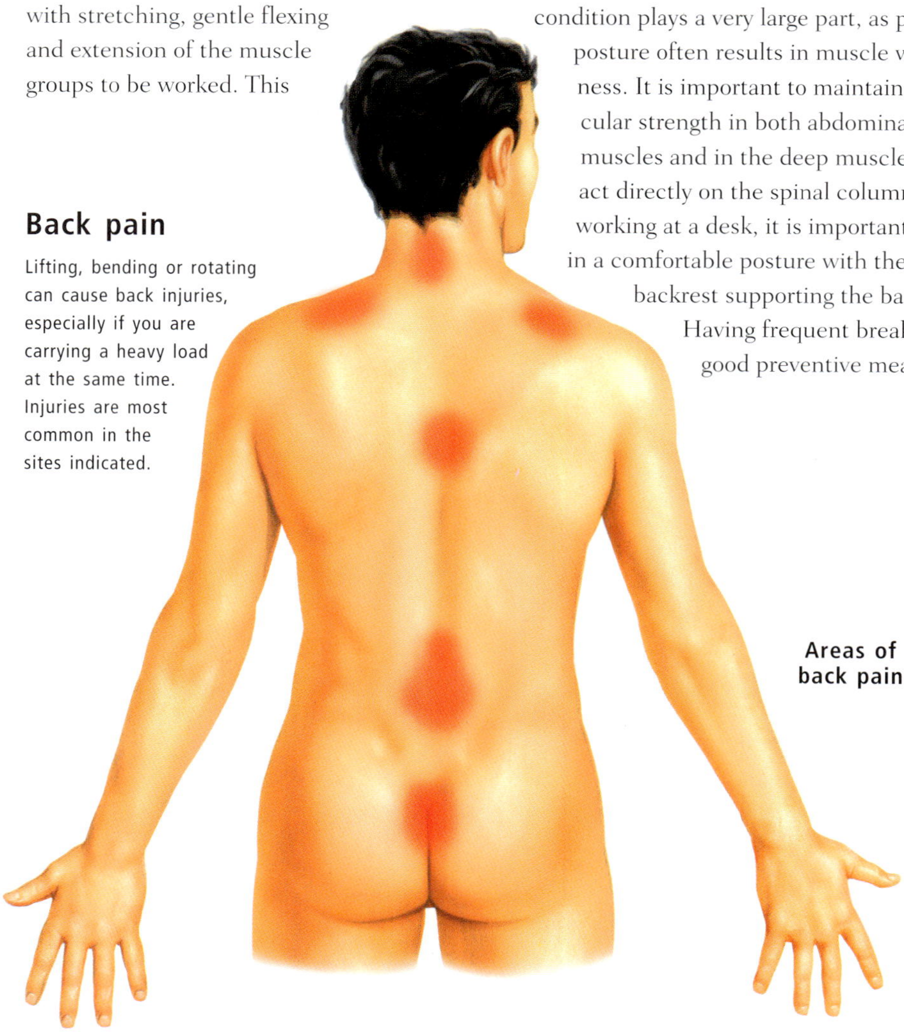

Back pain

Lifting, bending or rotating can cause back injuries, especially if you are carrying a heavy load at the same time. Injuries are most common in the sites indicated.

Good back care is essential in pregnancy when changes in weight affect posture and when tendons and ligaments are softer due to the action of the hormone progesterone. Low back pain can be due to poor posture, or the growing baby may cause the uterus to press on the sciatic nerve.

When pain or discomfort occur, good diagnosis is essential to establish whether muscular strain or spasm are responsible, or whether there is more serious injury involving the structure of the spinal column. X-rays may be taken, or a back specialist may make a diagnosis after extensive observation and examination of symptoms. Muscles may be in spasm if there is underlying damage to disks. Traction may be used to relieve the pressure on compressed disks and help them regain normal shape. Later treatment may involve exercise to strengthen underused muscles.

There are a number of alternative therapies that may help to alleviate the symptoms of back pain. Acupuncture may relieve acute spasm and muscle tension, easing back pain sufficiently for massage or manipulation to be given. Aromatherapy massage and baths with essential oils such as lavender, rosemary and peppermint are said to be useful in treating muscle spasm and tension. Massage eases chronic pain associated with postural imbalance, occupational strain or muscle fatigue. Chiropractic manipulation may relieve pain through restoring normal movement to the joints of the back. Osteopathy may provide relief from pain with gentle manipulation and massage of spine and surrounding soft tissue. Postural therapies such as Alexander technique, Feldenkrais method, Pilates, tai chi and yoga may correct postural imbalance and reduce stress.

Exercise can help prevent back problems by correcting poor posture and strengthening vital supporting muscles. However, some back conditions can be made worse by the wrong type of exercise. Specialist advice is essential if you have an injury or an existing back problem.

SEE ALSO *Ankylosing spondylitis, Coccyx, Epidural anesthesia, Exercise, Kyphosis, Lordosis, Lumbago, Osteoarthritis, Osteoporosis, Paget's disease of the bone, Sciatica, Scoliosis, Skeletal system, Spina bifida, Vertebrae, Whiplash injury*

Bacteria

Streptococcus

Meningococcus

Gonococcus

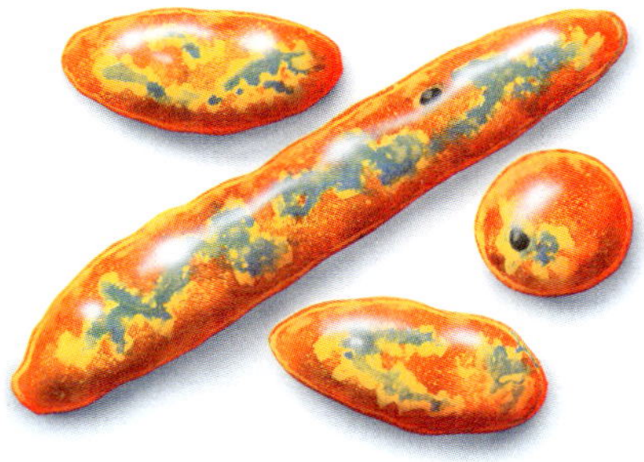

Legionella bacillus

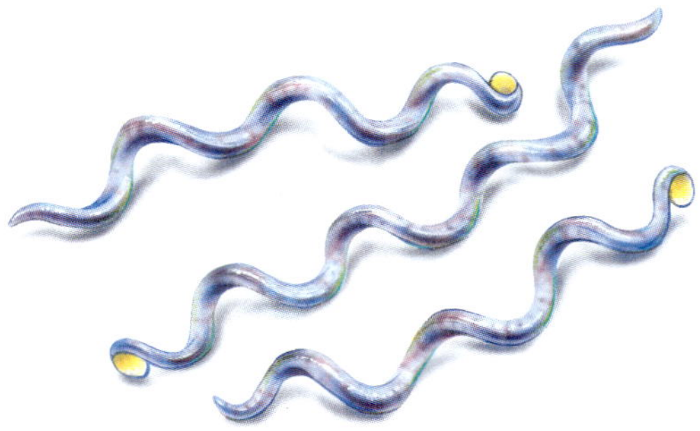

Syphilis spirochete

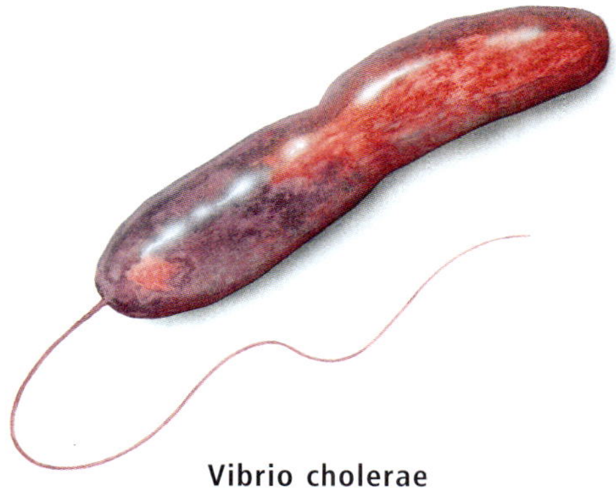

Vibrio cholerae

Bacteria
Bacteria are classified according to their shape; usually they are either spherical (coccus), rod-shaped (bacillus), coil-shaped (spirochete) or comma-shaped (vibrio).

BACTERIA

Bacteria are simple organisms of microscopic size and were one of the early forms of life to evolve. Many are beneficial and live in harmony with humans—in the digestive system aiding the breakdown and absorption of food, and in soil and water breaking down dead matter and animal wastes, a process which maintains conditions for life on our planet. Some are harmful and can cause and spread infections such as cholera, pneumonia, tuberculosis and whooping cough, or release deadly toxins that cause illness or death. Botulism, a serious type of food poisoning, results from bacterial growth in food stored without proper sterilization.

Immunization is a way of stimulating the body to make antibodies to a specific disease without first catching the infection. Public health authorities in most countries now recommend immunization for all citizens against the most common diseases of childhood. Widespread immunization has been very successful in preventing the spread of many once devastating bacterial (as well as viral) diseases. Antibiotics are drugs commonly prescribed to fight bacterial infections.

Immunization and the use of antibiotics have controlled many serious bacterial diseases within human society and eradicated smallpox. Unfortunately, antibiotics may eliminate beneficial as well as harmful bacteria; this can be a cause of digestive disorders and secondary infections. Overuse of antibiotics may be the reason that some bacteria, notably *Staphylococcus aureus*, are resisting treatment.

Shape is a major feature used in the classification of bacteria. There are four main forms: spheres (cocci), rods (bacilli), coils (spirochetes) and commas (vibrios). Within these groups, there is much variation. Rods, for example, can be thick or thin, long or short, and have pointed or rounded ends. Bacteria may also occur as single cells or in groups such as chains, pairs or clusters.

SEE ALSO *Antibiotics, Immunization*

BALANCE

Changes in body position are detected by different sensory receptors in the semicircular canals and otolith organs of the inner ear, the eyes, and the sensors in the joints and muscles that send messages to the brain. These organs, together with the nerves and muscles that control motor coordination and movement, maintain the body's balance.

Any disruption to these organs and pathways can lead to disturbances of balance. Inner ear infection (labyrinthitis) can affect the semicircular canals, causing disturbance of balance. Vertigo, in which balance is so severely affected that the room seems to be spinning around, may be a symptom of Menière's disease or some other ear disorder.

Lack of an adequate blood supply, and thus oxygen to the brain, may disrupt balance. Anemia, heart disease and circulatory disorders may cause dizziness, faintness and loss of balance.

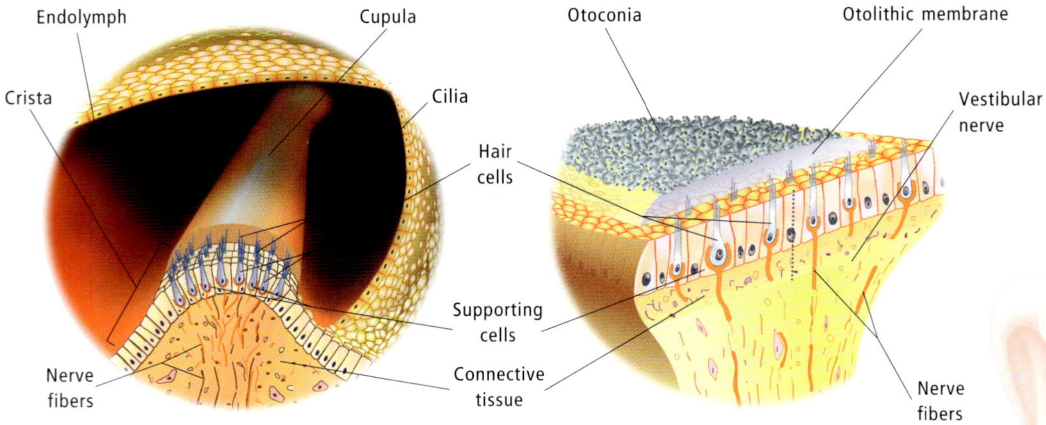

Ampulla of semicircular canal

Macula of otolith organ

Balance

Specialized organs in the inner ear known as the semicircular canals and the otolith organs contain tiny hairs that are sensitive to the body's position in space. Changes in position excite the hairs which send nerve signals via the vestibular nerve to the brain. The brain uses this information to help balance the body.

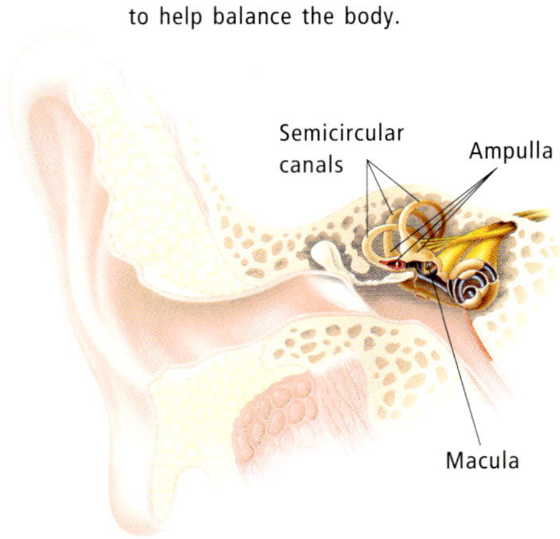

Balance mechanism in the ear

Motion sickness is discomfort caused by repeated movements in cars, boats, airplanes and amusement rides such as carousels and roller coasters. Symptoms include nausea and vomiting. More common in children, motion sickness often disappears with age as the semicircular canals in the ear become less sensitive to movement.

SEE ALSO *Ear, Menière's disease, Motion sickness, Otitis media, Semicircular canals, Vertigo*

BALDNESS

The most common cause of loss of hair (alopecia) is male hormones. Hair loss can take several forms, but the most common, androgenetic alopecia (male pattern baldness) occurs in both sexes and is an inherited condition associated with sexual development. It is characterized by a receding hairline, progressing to leave only a peripheral rim of hair. Another type is alopecia areata, a non-scarring, inflammatory hair loss disease which gives the hair a patchy, moth-eaten look, and is thought to be an autoimmune disorder that can affect men, women and children.

Common among people of the European and Australian races—in Australian Aborigines alopecia is often accompanied by balding of the calves of the legs—baldness is less common in native Americans, Africans and Asians. It affects between 50–80 percent of Caucasian men and between 20–40 percent of women. In men it is age related, affecting around 30 percent of men in their thirties, 40 percent in their forties, and so on; it is not age related in women.

Temporary hair loss can be caused by illnesses that are accompanied by high fever, but can also be caused by pregnancy, chemotherapy, x-rays, ingestion of metals, malnutrition, some skin diseases, endocrine disorders, chronic wasting diseases and trauma such as chemical damage to the hair.

Not all hair loss needs treatment. If it is caused by illness, trauma or pregnancy, regrowth will take place within three to four months. There are three treatments: hair transplantation from an area where hair is growing; the drug minoxidil, which stimulates regrowth and is applied to the scalp; and the drug finasteride, which may promote growth. If hair loss is not hereditary, tests for thyroid disease, autoimmune conditions and anemia should be done.

SEE ALSO *Androgens, Anemia, Autoimmune disease, Hair, Hormones, Thyroid gland*

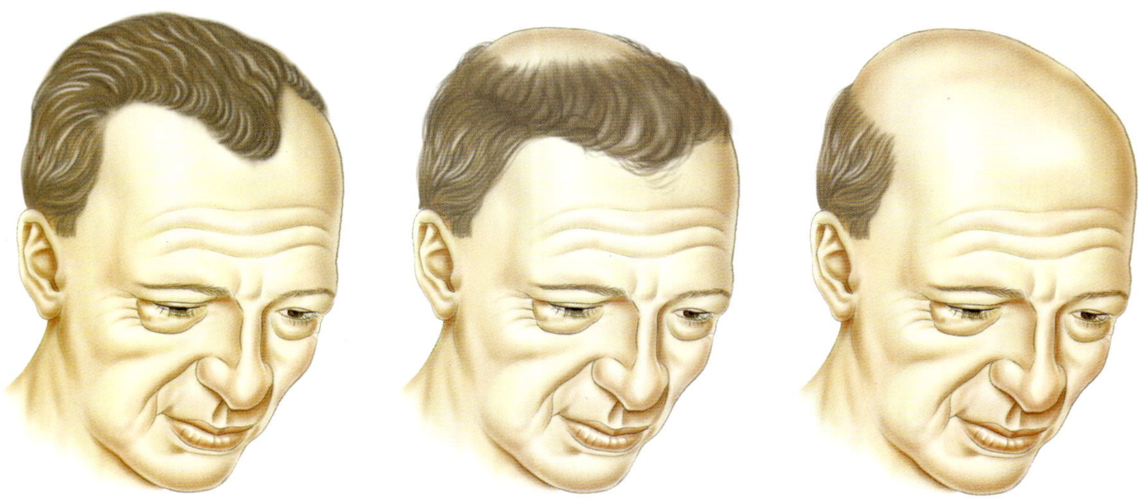

Male pattern baldness

Hair loss follows a typical sequence in male pattern baldness. It begins at the temples, continues at the top and back of the head until finally, in severe cases, hair grows only at the sides of the head.

BARBITURATES

Barbiturates are sedative and sleep-inducing drugs derived from barbituric acid. They act by depressing the central nervous system. In larger doses, they lower the blood pressure and slow down breathing. Once commonly prescribed for insomnia and anxiety, they have fallen from favor in recent years because they are habit-forming and, in larger doses, especially if taken with alcohol or other drugs, can result in a fatal overdose.

They have largely been superseded by safer, more modern drugs. However, barbiturates are still used in the treatment of epilepsy, and in intravenous form as anesthetics. Barbiturates commonly used as anticonvulsants for the treatment of epilepsy and seizures include mephobarbital, metharbital and pentobarbital. Those used as anesthetics include sodium pentothal.

SEE ALSO *Anticonvulsants, Anxiolytics, Drug dependence, Epilepsy, Psychotropic drugs*

Barium meal

Also called a barium swallow, a barium meal gives the doctor an idea of the condition of the esophagus and stomach (pictured), and how well foods and liquids travel through them.

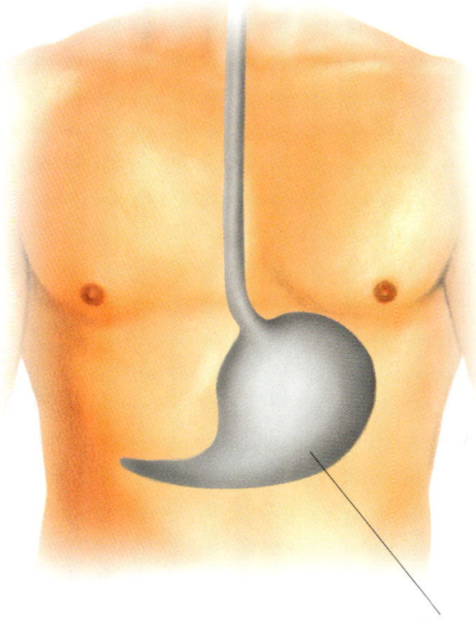

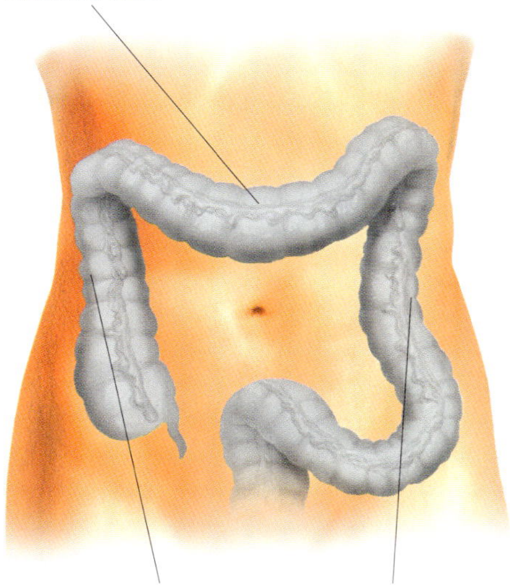

Barium enema

In a barium enema, a white-colored liquid called barium is introduced into the rectum and moved around the colon (shown at left) by a radiologist. Bowel movements may be white or lighter colored in the days following the test.

BARIUM ENEMA

Barium enema is a procedure used to examine the large intestine. The patient's bowel is emptied, and an enema tube containing a solution of barium sulfate is inserted through the anus and into the colon. Barium is opaque to x-rays and lines the bowel so that if polyps, cancers or other such features are present, they will show up.

Used in conjunction with sigmoidoscopy, barium enema is almost as effective as colonoscopy in detecting abnormalities.

SEE ALSO *Colon, Contrast x-ray, Intestines*

BARIUM MEAL

Barium meal is a procedure used to examine the upper gastrointestinal tract. The patient swallows a solution of barium sulfate, then its course is followed by x-ray down the esophagus (gullet) into the stomach.

Largely superseded by endoscopic direct viewing into the stomach, barium meal remains useful for diagnosing hiatus hernia when narrowing of the esophagus prevents endoscopy, and when checking the wave forms of the esophagus during swallowing.

SEE ALSO *Contrast x-ray, Endoscopy, Esophagus, Hiatus hernia*

BARTHOLIN'S GLAND

Bartholin's glands are lubricating glands located on either side of the vaginal opening at the innermost part of the labia.

Blockage of the opening of a Bartholin's gland may cause the gland to swell, forming a Bartholin's cyst. Symptoms include a feeling of vaginal stretching and discomfort, particularly during intercourse. The gland may become infected and form a painful abscess (Bartholin's abscess).

If treatment is considered necessary because of discomfort or infection, the gland can be surgically removed. The procedure can be done under local anesthesia in a doctor's office.

SEE ALSO *Vagina*

Bartholin's gland

Normally Bartholin's glands cannot be detected. But if one becomes blocked, a Bartholin's gland may form a cyst.

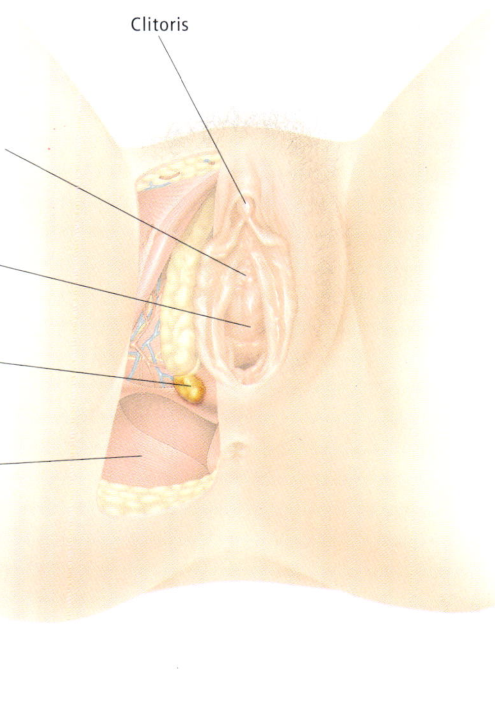

B

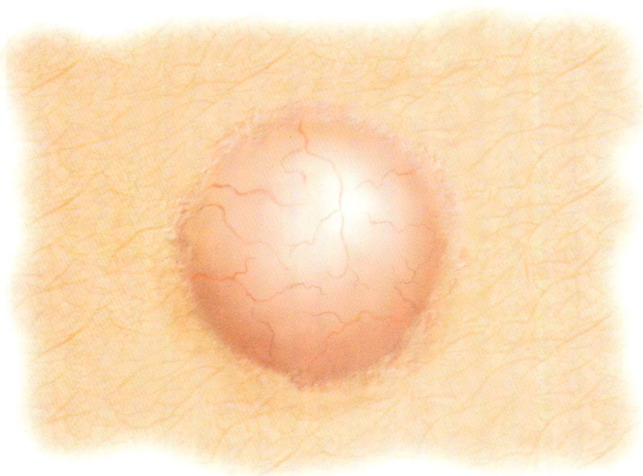

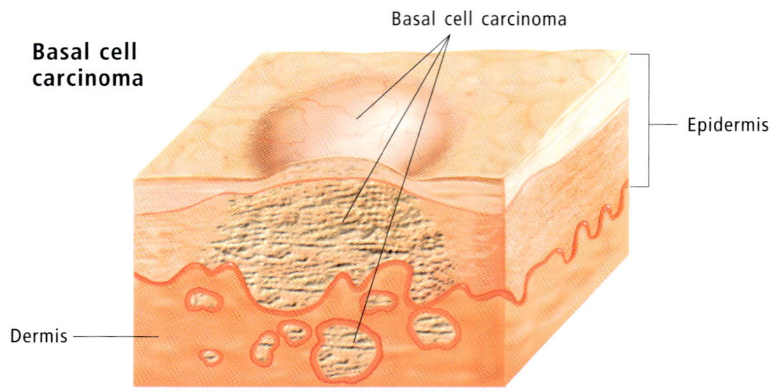

Basal cell carcinoma

A basal cell carcinoma, as it appears on the skin and in cross section. The best treatment is prevention; anyone who spends a lot of time outdoors, and in particular children, should wear sunscreen and a hat and avoid exposure to direct sunlight.

BASAL CELL CARCINOMA

Basal cell carcinoma (BCC) is a common form of skin cancer. It usually appears on the face, and is caused by excessive exposure to sunlight over the years. At first, the sore appears as a small, pear-like nodule, which slowly grows and ulcerates in the center to form a small scab. Basal cell carcinoma is treated with cautery (application of heat or electric current), liquid nitrogen, or low-dose radiation therapy. Larger tumors will need to be removed surgically. Early treatment achieves a cure rate of more than 95 percent. Ongoing checkups should be carried out, as once a basal cell carcinoma has occurred, the chance of getting further basal cell carcinomas is increased.

SEE ALSO *Skin cancer*

BED-WETTING

Also known as enuresis, bed-wetting commonly refers to involuntary discharge of urine, usually during sleep at night. Children can only be said to be bed-wetting if they are still unable to control urination during sleep at the age of five. Even at this age, however, it is still quite common. In extreme cases, enuresis can continue into adulthood unless treatment is sought.

Causes

There are three main factors which affect bed-wetting. The first factor is heredity—if both parents were bed-wetters then there is a three-out-of-four chance their child will experience similar problems. The second factor is the ability, or inability, of the bladder to send a signal to the brain strong enough to wake the sleeping person. The third is over-productive kidneys—in some cases the kidneys produce the same quantity of urine at night as they do during the day.

It is usually recommended that parents wait until a child is seven or eight years old before seeking assistance; however, if the problem is causing a great deal of distress to the child or family, or if the child suddenly starts to wet the bed after being dry, then help should be sought. The first step should be a medical checkup to make sure that the cause of the bed-wetting is not organic, such as developmental or physical problems or infections of the urinary tract.

Treatment

The usual forms of treatment are counseling with behavior therapy, use of alarms, and drug therapy. Counseling is usually the first course of action; it involves both parents and child and is best sought from a continence specialist. It will include behavioral modification programs. Bed-wetting alarms, used on the bed or the body, and under specialist supervision, are usually successful. Bladder training programs also have a good record of success. Medication is usually the last resort and needs to be prescribed by a specialist. Punishment for wetting, limiting the amount a child drinks, and waking the child to go to the toilet during the night are not helpful.

Bladder control

Bladder control develops in the following stages. When the child is up to one year old the bladder empties automatically when it is full. At one to two years of age an awareness of when the bladder is full develops. At three, the ability to hold urine grows as the bladder becomes able to contain larger quantities. At four, the ability to stop urine at will is fully developed. Most children are dry at night by this age. By the age of six, the ability to pass urine on command is possible.

SEE ALSO *Behavior therapy, Bladder, Kidney*

BEHAVIOR THERAPY

Behavior therapy is also known as behavior modification and it uses counseling, or group interaction and support, to change behavior that is unwanted, potentially harmful or unacceptable. It can also be used to treat habits such as cigarette smoking, overeating, alcoholism, stress-induced conditions, and stuttering and tantrums in children.

Developed in the 1950s and '60s, the techniques of behavior therapy are based on theories derived from the work of Ivan Pavlov, John Broadus Watson and B. F. Skinner. Watson, who started work in 1915 as an animal psychologist following in the footsteps of Pavlov, is credited as being the American psychologist who established behaviorism as a therapy. He believed that, if correctly conditioned, babies would grow up to be socially competent, emotionally healthy individuals. Skinner saw human behavior in terms of physiological responses to the environment.

Behavior therapy is based on the idea that human behavior is a result of a stimulus–response interaction and that observable behavior can be modified. The stimulus–response interaction says that all complex types of behavior, including reasoning, emotional reactions and habits, are made up of simple stimulus–response events, which can be measured. Once the stimulus and the response it elicits are identified, an individual's behavior can be predicted. Then, if the stimulus is controlled, the individual's behavior can be controlled.

There are two possible kinds of response: elicited—the response that occurred in the presence of the stimulus; and emitted—the response that occurred not in reaction to a stimulus but was emitted by the organism.

There are also two forms of conditioning: respondent or classical conditioning (the theory developed by Pavlov), which is a learned response that can be evoked by a new stimulus—for example, a kangaroo that flees as soon as it smells a dog; and operant or instrumental conditioning, in which a new response is learned as a result of satisfying a need, for example milking cows coming to the milking sheds at the same time each day because they have a need to be milked as well as fed.

With application, most people can use behavior modification to change their own behavior.The techniques they use include changing the stimuli in their environment, monitoring their behavior (keeping records), making commitments, and setting up consequences for their behavior.

The critics of behaviorism say that it oversimplifies human behavior and that the human being has a free will and is not an automaton. However, behaviorism can solve behavior-related problems and it has had, and will continue to have, an important role in learning.

SEE ALSO *Counseling, Psychotherapy*

BEHAVIORAL AND EMOTIONAL PROBLEMS

Adults, teenagers and children can suffer from disorders that affect their behavior and emotions. Some have a physical cause involving the chemistry of the brain; others are caused by an individual's response to stressful experiences or circumstances.

In most instances, professional help should be sought, initially from a primary care physician. A patient can then be advised of the different types of therapy availalable.

SEE ALSO *Alcoholism, Anxiety, Bipolar disorder, Depression, Drug dependence, Eating disorders, Obsessive-compulsive disorder, Panic attacks, Personality disorders, Phobias, Posttraumatic stress disorder, Schizophrenia, Seasonal affective disorder, Smoking*

BELL'S PALSY

Bell's palsy is a paralysis caused by a swelling or cutting of the facial nerve; it affects one side of the face. The sufferer is unable to close the eye on that side, or to contract the muscles controlling the forehead, mouth or cheek. The mouth droops and the face is distorted. The unaffected side retains normal function. The disorder may appear after a short period of pain and there may be loss of the sense of taste on the tongue. Treatment is with steroids and antiviral drugs. Most sufferers will recover, but a few will remain permanently impaired.

SEE ALSO *Paralysis*

BETA-BLOCKERS

Beta-blockers are drugs that block the effects of epinephrine (adrenaline) in the heart cells and blood vessels. Beta-blockers slow the heart down and reduce the heart's need for oxygen. They are used to treat angina (chest pain), some arrhythmias (irregular heart rhythms) and hypertension (high blood pressure). They can also be used to treat migraine headaches, hyperthyroidism and glaucoma.

Beta-blockers are not suitable for asthmatics, as they tend to constrict breathing passages. They should not be used by people with heart failure, bradycardia (slow heart rate) or heart block. Patients with diabetes mellitus should take beta-blockers with caution. Side effects include drowsiness, sleep disturbances, weakness, dizziness and shortness of breath.

SEE ALSO *Angina pectoris, Arrhythmia, Epinephrine, Glaucoma, Heart, Hypertension, Hyperthyroidism, Migraine*

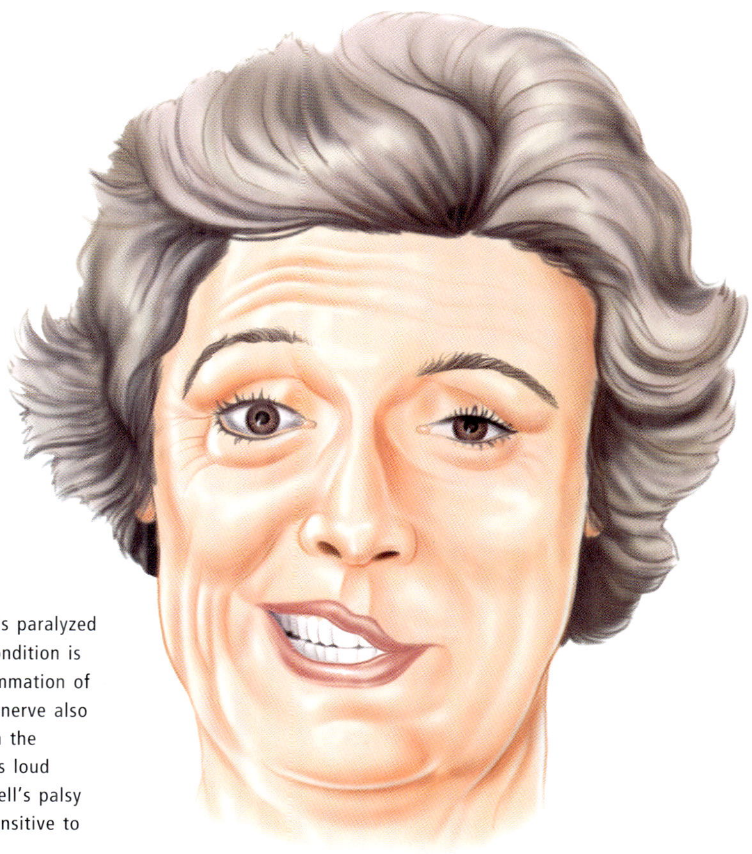

Bell's palsy

One side of the face is paralyzed in Bell's palsy. The condition is due to injury or inflammation of the facial nerve. This nerve also controls the muscle in the eardrum that dampens loud noises; people with Bell's palsy may be abnormally sensitive to loud sounds.

BILE DUCTS

The bile ducts (sometimes collectively called the biliary tree) are the narrow tubes through which bile flows in the liver. They are found in various parts of the body, but work together as a system. The hepatic ducts transport bile from the liver (where it is made) to the rest of the biliary system. The hepatic ducts join to form the common bile duct, which transports bile to the duodenum (the first part of the small intestine). The cystic duct transports bile from the gallbladder (where bile is stored) to the common bile duct.

Bile ducts can be blocked by gallstones or cancers, or may become inflamed. Endoscopic retrograde cholangio-pancreatography (ERCP) is an x-ray procedure in which a physician inserts an instrument called an endoscope into the duodenum and uses it to inject dye that is opaque to x-rays into the common bile duct in order to demonstrate any blockage of the hepatic, cystic, or common bile ducts.

SEE ALSO *Cholangitis, Duodenum, Gallbladder, Gallstones, Liver*

BIOCHEMIC TISSUE SALTS

Dr W. H. Schuessler, a nineteenth-century homeopath and chemist, maintained that there are twelve mineral salts vital for the healthy functioning of the cells in the body. He recorded the action of each salt and the symptoms caused by a lack of each. To remedy mineral salt deficiencies, he developed his twelve biochemic tissue salts, also known as cell salts, which he prepared in a homeopathic 6x potency for easy assimilation.

Schuessler did not regard his remedies as homeopathic because they do not follow the "like cures like" philosophy of homeopathy; his belief was that they cure symptoms that result from a deficiency.

SEE ALSO *Homeopathy*

BIOFEEDBACK

Biofeedback is the process of measuring body and mind activity using electronic machines and using these signals to modify behavior or body functions. The machines use detectors attached to the patient's skin which pick up changes that relate to the body's heart rate, skin temperature, muscle tension, brain waves, pulse rate and breathing. This feedback is relayed by the machine in the form of electronic beeps or flashing lights, which can then be interpreted.

With the use of biofeedback machines, researchers have discovered that it is possible for a person to train themselves to control their so-called "involuntary functions", such as their heart beat or pulse rate. Patients can learn to recognize the fluctuations in the body's responses/functions by following the flashes or beeps from the machine. They then learn how to positively affect their involuntary functions through the use of techniques such as concentration, meditation, visualization or breathing exercises.

The ability to recognize and alter body functions has been found to be particularly helpful for people suffering from chronic anxiety states, and related illnesses such as migraine and hypertension. Biofeedback machines have also been used to assist people with epilepsy and cerebral palsy.

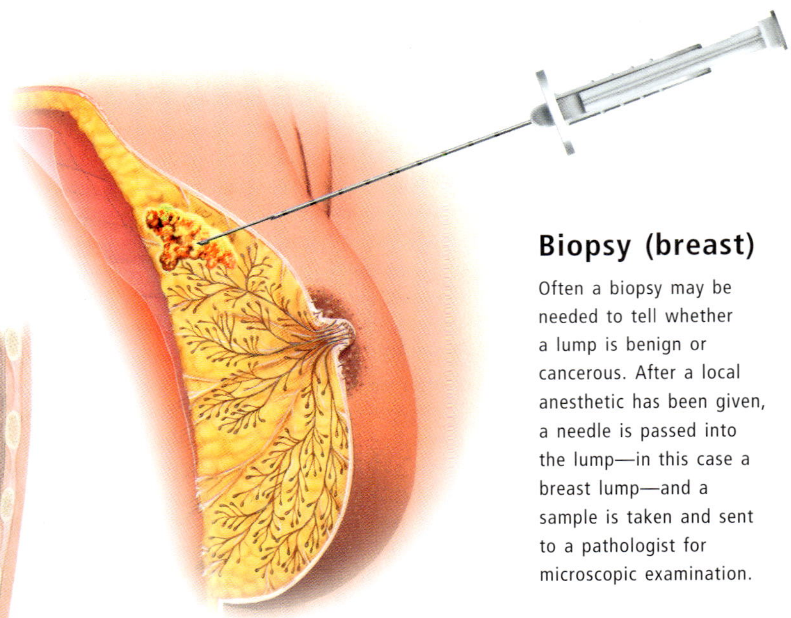

Biopsy (breast)

Often a biopsy may be needed to tell whether a lump is benign or cancerous. After a local anesthetic has been given, a needle is passed into the lump—in this case a breast lump—and a sample is taken and sent to a pathologist for microscopic examination.

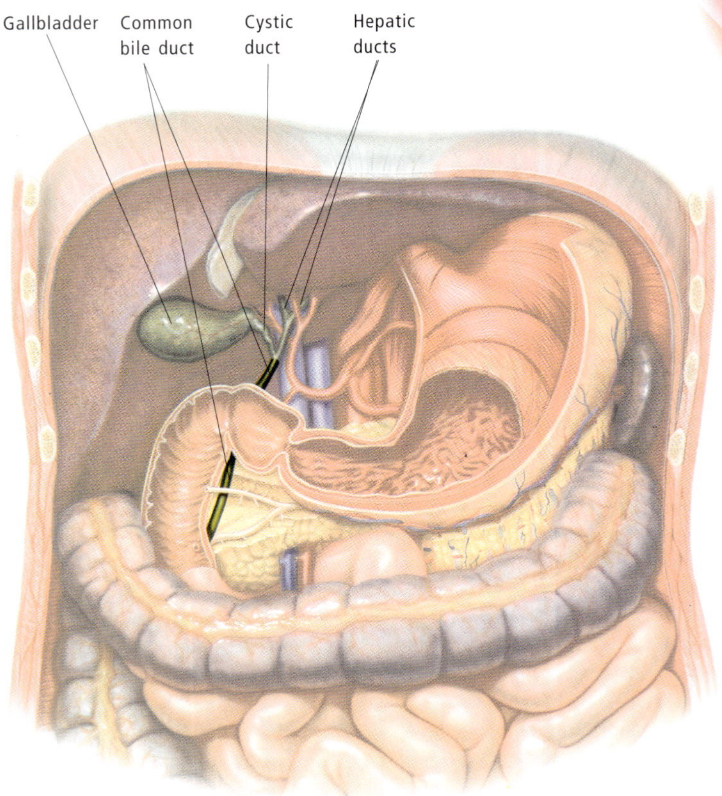

Bile ducts

The gallbladder is a storage pouch that receives bile from the liver via the hepatic ducts. When the gallbladder contracts during a meal, bile is expelled into the cystic duct. It travels along the bile duct through the pancreas and enters the duodenum where it helps digest fats.

B

Bipolar disorder

The changes in mood that people with bipolar disorder experience are thought to be caused by biochemical changes in the limbic system of the brain, shown here.

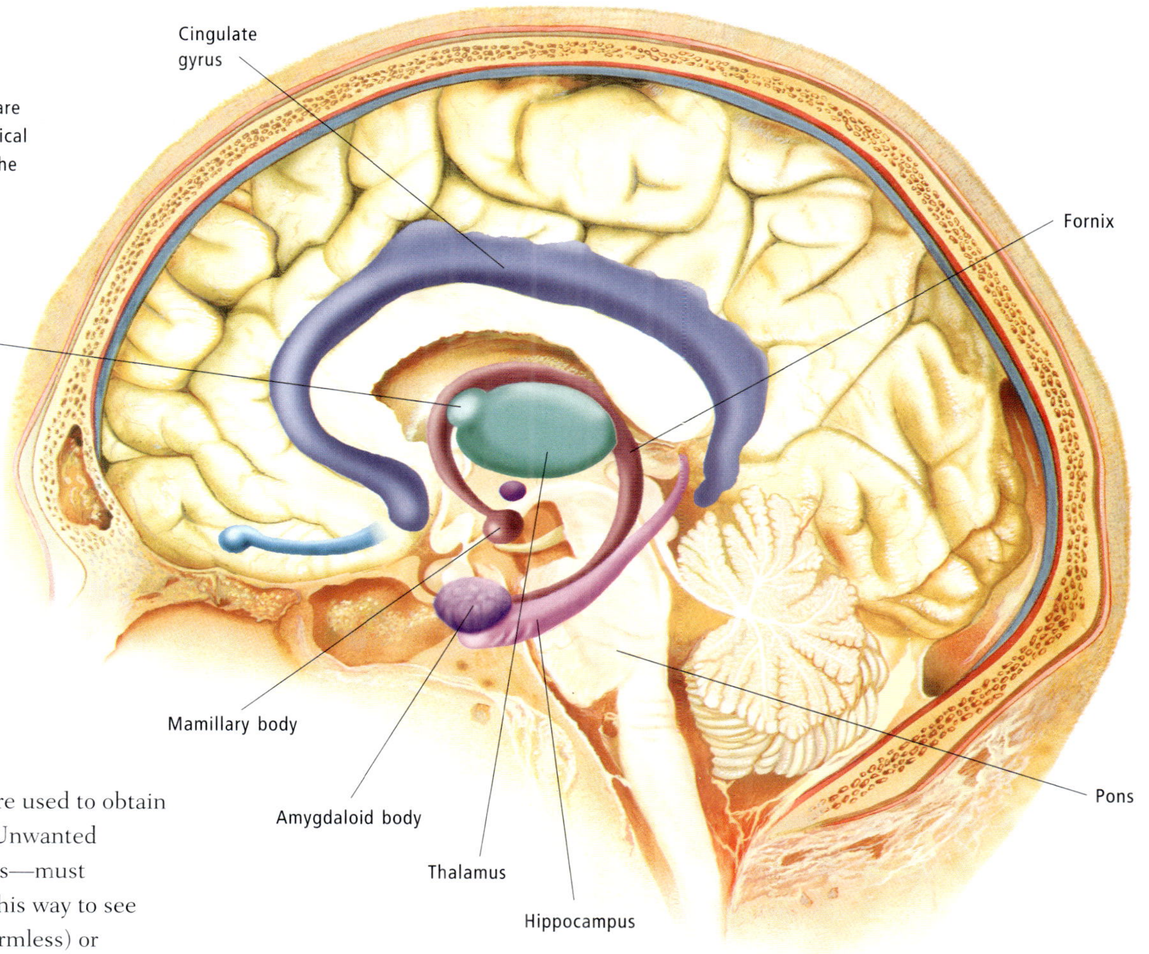

BIOPSY

Biopsy is a medical procedure used to obtain live tissue for examination. Unwanted growths in the body—tumors—must sometimes be examined in this way to see whether they are benign (harmless) or malignant (cancerous). Under anesthetic a small piece of tissue is surgically removed and sent to a laboratory for examination.

Biopsy can aid diagnosis of various diseases. A small sample of tissue or cells from lymph nodes, internal organs such as the liver, or from bones, can be obtained simply for intensive examination and the correct diagnosis made without unnecessary surgery.

SEE ALSO *Tumors*

BIORHYTHMS

Scientists in the early part of the twentieth century identified three energy cycles, or internal body clocks. The theory holds that a physical cycle of around 23 days governs resistance to disease, strength, vitality and sex drive; an emotional cycle of 28 days is linked to sensitivity, moods, perceptions and mental balance; and an intellectual cycle of around 33 days is linked to decision-making, memory and alertness. Because these cycles are of varying lengths, their "highs" and "lows" rarely coincide.

A computer can calculate individual biorhythm charts; these charts may be used by a natural health practitioner to detect swings in behavior and mood, and their effects on their patient's health.

BIPOLAR DISORDER

Bipolar disorder, also known as manic-depressive illness, is a mental illness which is characterized by episodes of mania ("highs"), followed by depression ("lows"). Moods swing from one extreme to the other, with relatively normal moods between.

In the manic phase, which may last from several days to months, the person feels elated and hyperactive, talks rapidly, has inflated self-esteem, is easily distracted and has no desire for sleep. Uncharacteristically poor judgment, increased sexual drive and intrusive or aggressive behavior are common.

Feelings of guilt, worthlessness, sadness and low self-esteem are symptoms of the depressive phase. The sufferer loses interest in ordinary activities, including sex, and may feel suicidal. In both high and low phases, dependence on alcohol and drugs such as cocaine or sleeping medications is common.

Bipolar disorder can have devastating consequences, including marital breakups, job loss, alcohol and drug abuse and suicide. Gambling, sexual promiscuity and poor decision-making are some of the behaviors that can affect the sufferer, spouse, friends, employers and family.

Symptoms of bipolar disorder begin between 15 and 25 years of age, affecting men and women equally. There is no known cause, although a chemical imbalance in the brain is thought to be involved. It also tends to run in families and may be inherited. The condition may occur in younger children, when it is often confused with attention deficit hyperactivity disorder (ADHD).

Treatment

In severe forms of the disorder, hospitalization is necessary, particularly during the depression that follows a manic phase, when the danger of suicide is high.

Lithium carbonate, a drug with complex effects on the nervous system, is generally effective in controlling the symptoms and preventing future episodes. Lithium's effects usually begin within one week of starting treatment, and the full effect is seen after two to three weeks.

However, side effects of lithium deter some sufferers from taking it. These include fine hand tremor, dry mouth, weight gain, increased thirst, increased frequency of urination, mild nausea or vomiting, impotence, decreased libido, diarrhea and kidney abnormalities, among other things. Non-compliance with a medication schedule can sometimes be a problem.

The anticonvulsants carbamazepine and valproate are also useful as mood stabilizers, and they are often combined with lithium. Antidepressants may also be used to treat the depression.

Psychotherapy is often helpful and sufferers may benefit from belonging to a support group. Children and adolescents with bipolar disorder are generally treated with lithium, but carbamazepine and valproate are also used. If severe bipolar disorder does not respond to drugs, electroconvulsive therapy (ECT) may be used.

Because manic-depressive illness is recurrent, treatment must be long term and, in some cases, permanent.

SEE ALSO *Anticonvulsants, Antidepressants, Depression, Electroconvulsive therapy, Mania, Psychotherapy*

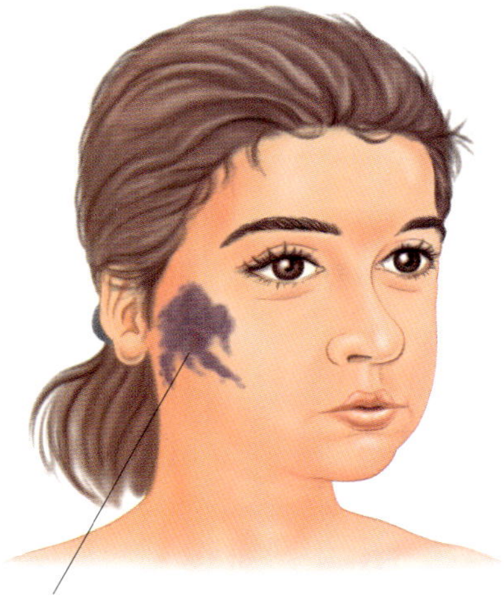

Port-wine stain

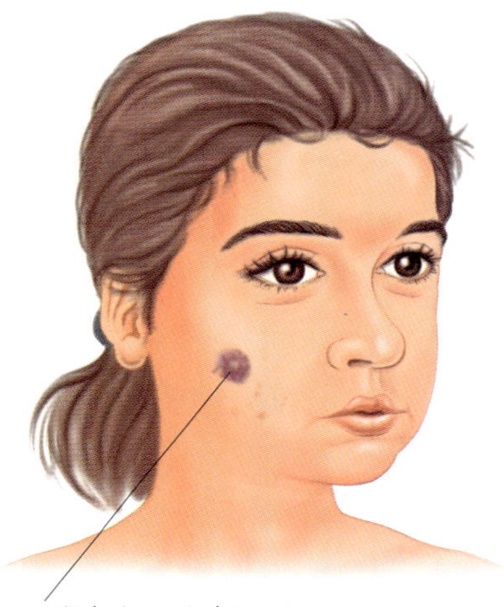

Congenital pigmented nevus

Birthmarks

Although most birthmarks are harmless, they may be regarded as a problem and some may be unsightly. They may be hidden by cosmetics or treated by plastic surgery, laser surgery, cautery (electric current) or cryosurgery (freezing). Some birthmarks disappear of their own accord. Their cause is unknown.

BIRTHMARKS

Babies are sometimes born with marks, spots or patches on their skin, known as birthmarks. These marks remain, unlike bruises that are caused by the trauma of birth. The most common birthmarks include the following.

Mongolian blue spots are blue-colored "bruises" or nevi. These are common on dark-skinned and Asian babies. These spots are harmless and they will disappear during childhood.

Salmon patches are red marks on the eyelids, nose or back of head. Formerly called "stork bites", they are very common and will usually disappear over time. They are a type of hemanigoma.

Port-wine stains are also a type of hemangioma. They are reddish purple-brown lesions that do not fade but can be treated with surgery.

Cafe au lait spots appear as coffee-colored patches on the skin. They are quite common and will not disappear.

Congenital pigmented nevi are moles which vary in color from light brown to black and which may have hairs. They are usually surgically removed.

SEE ALSO *Hemangioma*

BISEXUALITY

Bisexuality means being sexually attracted to both sexes. The development of sexuality is a complex process and often involves experimentation with members of the same sex, which doesn't necessarily indicate a preference for homosexuality. Similarly, a person may live as a heterosexual within a traditional family yet maintain their preference for sexual partners of the same sex. Bisexuals are physically normal and may give no outward sign of their bisexuality.

SEE ALSO *Homosexuality, Sexuality*

BLADDER

Found in the pelvic cavity, the bladder is the part of the urinary tract that collects and stores urine via the ureters from the kidneys. When the bladder is full it empties, expelling urine from the body through the urethra. In most adults, the bladder holds about one pint (475 milliliters) of urine when full. It passes from 24–68 fluid ounces (700–2000 milliliters) of urine a day.

There are several conditions affecting the bladder. Cystitis or inflammation of the bladder, usually from bacterial infection, is the most common. The symptoms are frequent, painful urination, and blood in the urine. Cystitis is confirmed by a urine test, which identifies the bacterium that is causing the infection. Treatment is with antibiotics and fluids by mouth. Drinking unsweetened cranberry juice may help to reduce the number and severity of bacterial infections, although the reason behind this is not clear.

Stones, or calculi, may form in the bladder. Composed mainly of salts, cholesterol and some protein, calculi may grow in the bladder slowly without causing symptoms. When they grow to a certain size, they may block the outlet to the urethra and cause urinary obstruction. Cystitis often accompanies calculi. Treatment is usually surgical. This may mean lithotomy—an operation to remove a stone through a surgical incision. Alternatively, the stone may be destroyed by lithotripsy, a procedure in which an instrument called a lithotrite is passed through the urethra into the bladder and used to crush the stone or shatter it with an electrical spark. Ultrasonic lithotripsy is similar except that high-frequency sound waves are used to destroy the stone without inserting any instruments into the body. The crushed fragments of the stone can then be passed out of the body.

Bladder cancers usually arise from cells lining the bladder. The most common form of bladder cancer is a papilloma—a slow-growing wart-like growth, or tumor, attached to a stalk. Tumors other than papillomas are less common but have a poorer prognosis, spreading by penetrating the bladder muscle, infiltrating surrounding fat and tissue, and eventually invading the bloodstream and lymphatic system. In its early stages, bladder cancer may not have obvious symptoms; later symptoms may include blood in the urine, frequent urinary tract infections, frequent and painful urination, abdominal or back pain, persistent low-grade fever and anemia.

Male bladder

Urine is stored in the bladder and expelled through the urethra, which passes through the prostate gland and travels the length of the penis. In old age an enlarged prostate can obstruct the flow of urine at the outlet of the bladder and surgery may be required.

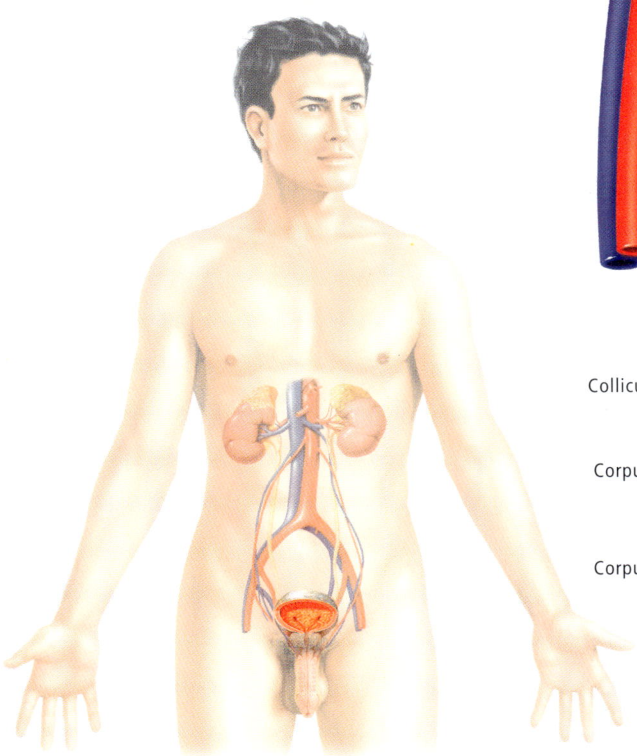

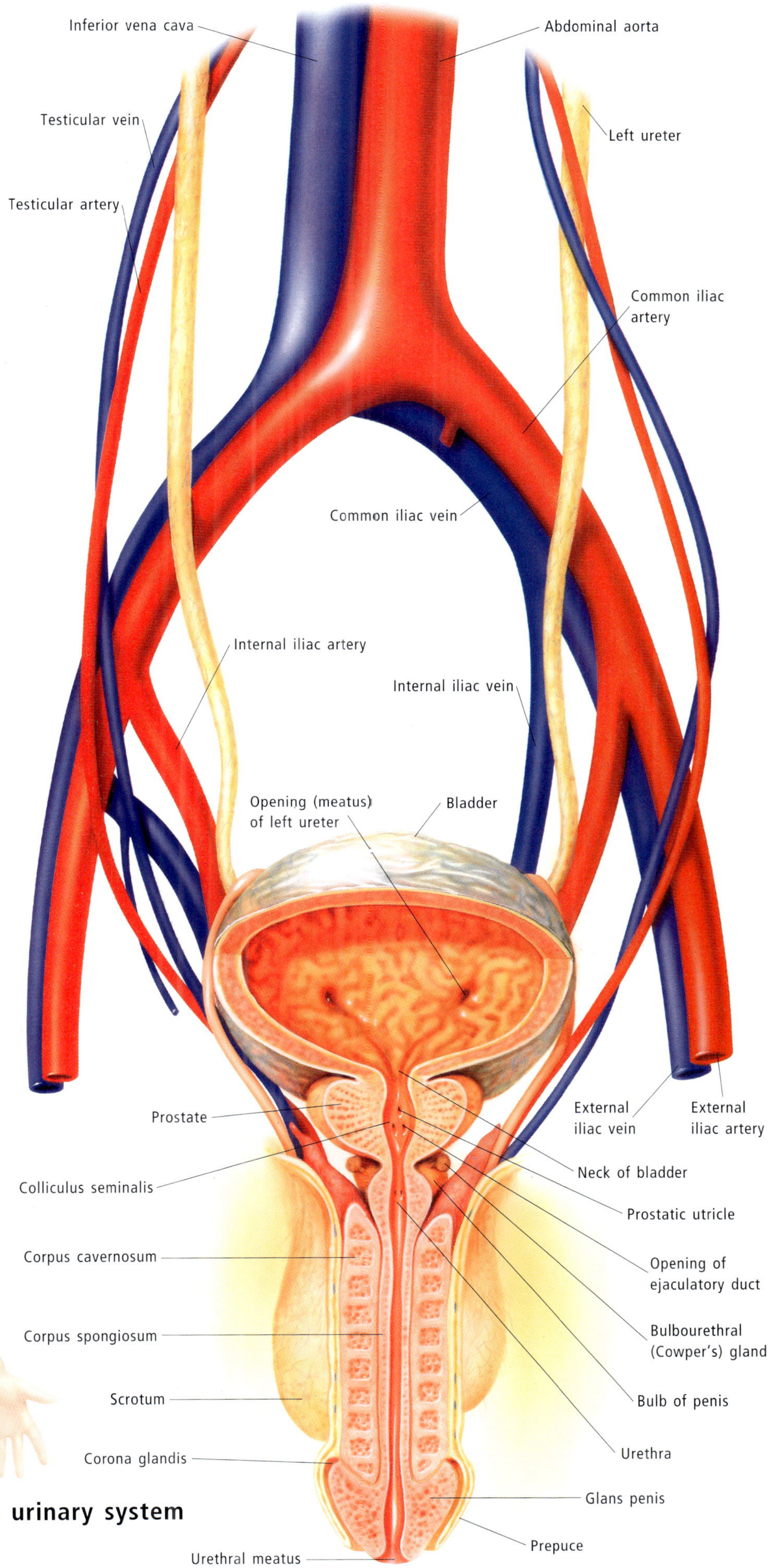

Male urinary system

Bladder cancer has no known cause. However, it has been firmly linked to exposure to cancer-promoting chemicals (carcinogens). Cigarette smokers, painters, truckers, leatherworkers, machinists and metalworkers, rubber and textile workers, and people exposed to industrial dyes are at increased risk. It is more common over the age of 40. If detected early, papillomas can usually be treated successfully by transurethral resection (TUR). In this procedure the urosurgeon inserts a small tube into the bladder and removes or cauterizes the tumor. It may be combined with chemotherapy or radiation therapy. Larger, more invasive cancers require radical cystectomy (bladder removal) and construction of an artificial storage organ.

Obstruction of the outlet of the bladder may cause urinary retention, particularly in older men, due to benign prostatic hypertrophy (enlargement of the prostate). TUR of a part of the prostate usually relieves the obstruction.

Calculi, cancers and other bladder disorders can be identified using x-ray, ultrasound, computerized axial tomography (CAT) scan or magnetic resonance imaging (MRI). The urologist can also view the bladder through a fiberoptic tube known as a cystoscope, which can also be used to take a biopsy. A cystogram is an x-ray taken of the bladder after dye that is opaque to x-rays is injected into a vein. Filtered out by the kidneys, the dye passes into the bladder, showing stones, papillomas, cancers and other conditions.

SEE ALSO *Biopsy, Cystitis, Cystogram, Cystoscopy, Kidney, Prostate gland, Urinary systems*

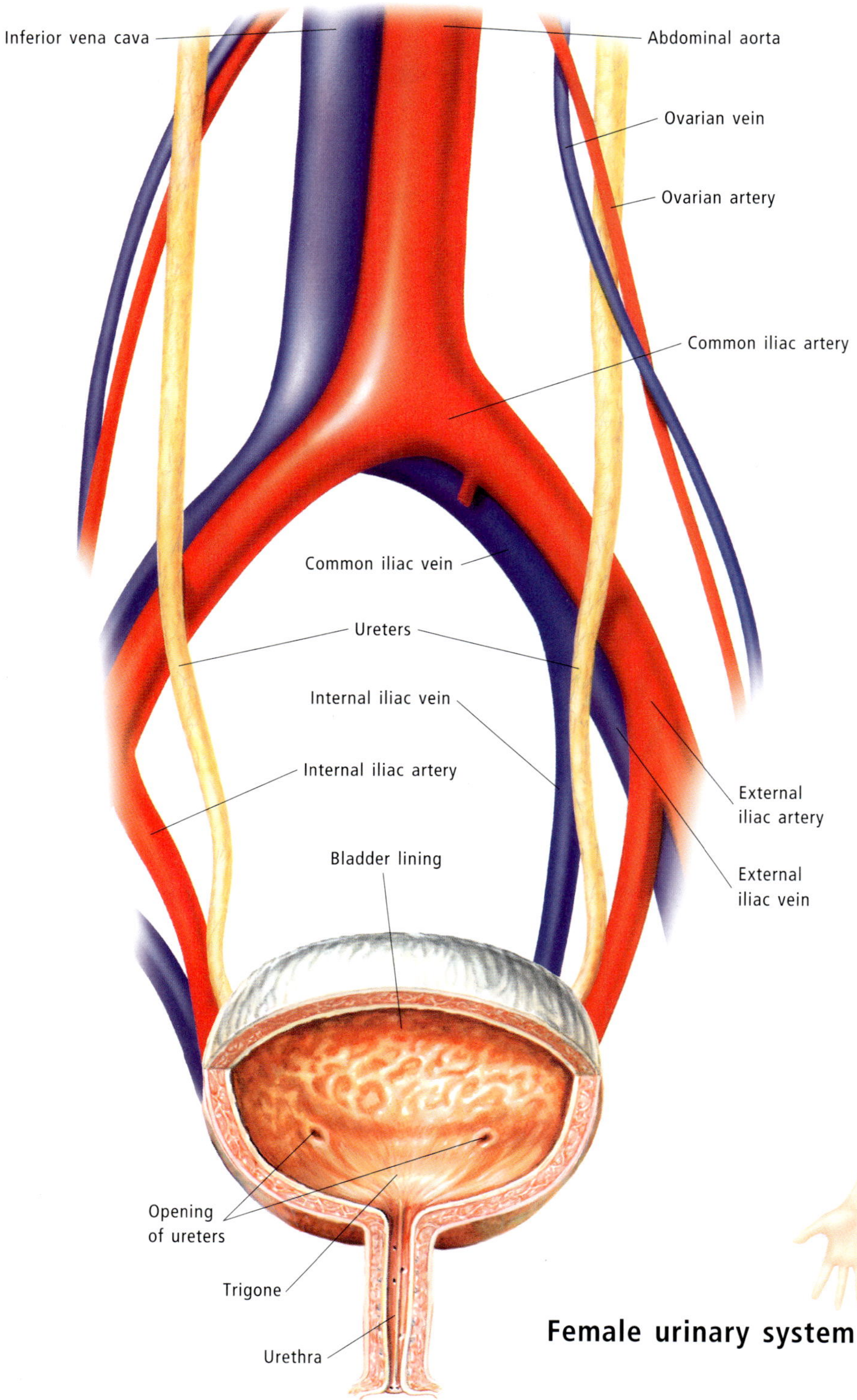

Female bladder

In the female, the urethra is much shorter than in the male. The shorter urethra makes it easier for bacteria from outside the body to enter the bladder and cause cystitis (inflammation of the bladder). As a result, cystitis is more common in women than in men.

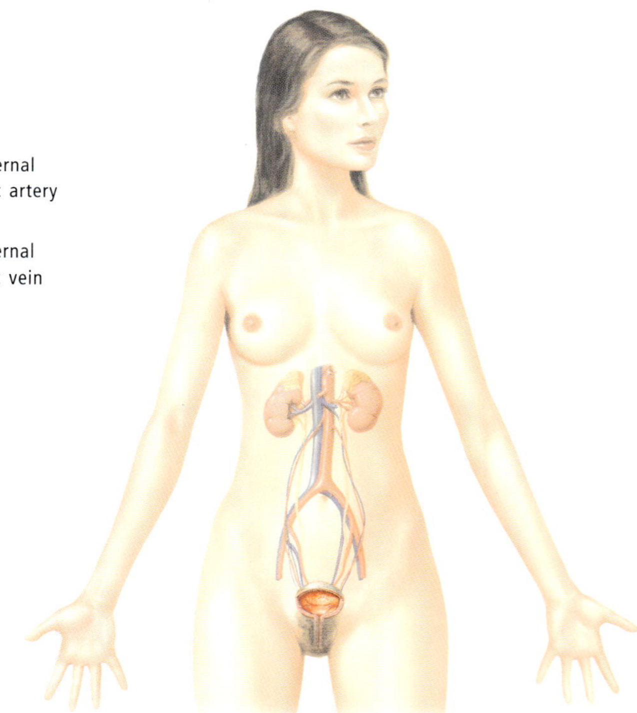

Female urinary system

Bladder transitional cell carcinoma

Bladder cancers such as this one are often caused by cancer producing chemicals such as cigarette smoke, dyes, paint and rubber. Most can be easily cured by removal or cauterization (burning) with an instrument that is passed through the urethra and into the bladder.

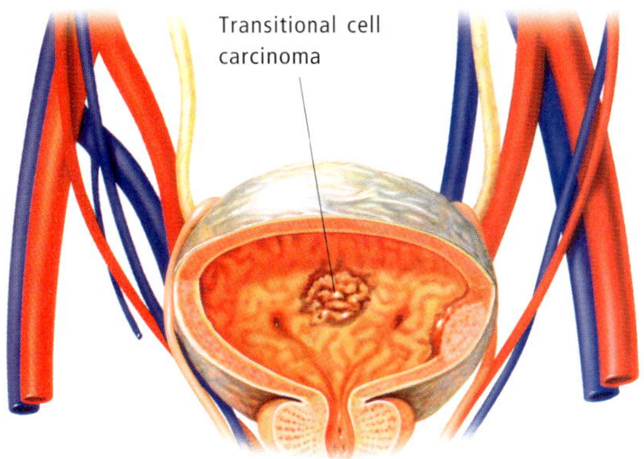

Bladder stones

Bladder stones grow slowly and often cause no symptoms until they are large. They may block the outlet of the bladder, or cause bladder infections. These (from left, mulberries, jackstones and gravel) are shown at their actual size.

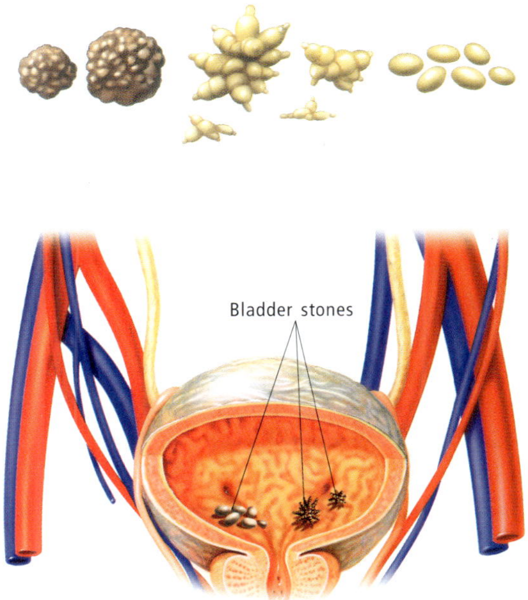

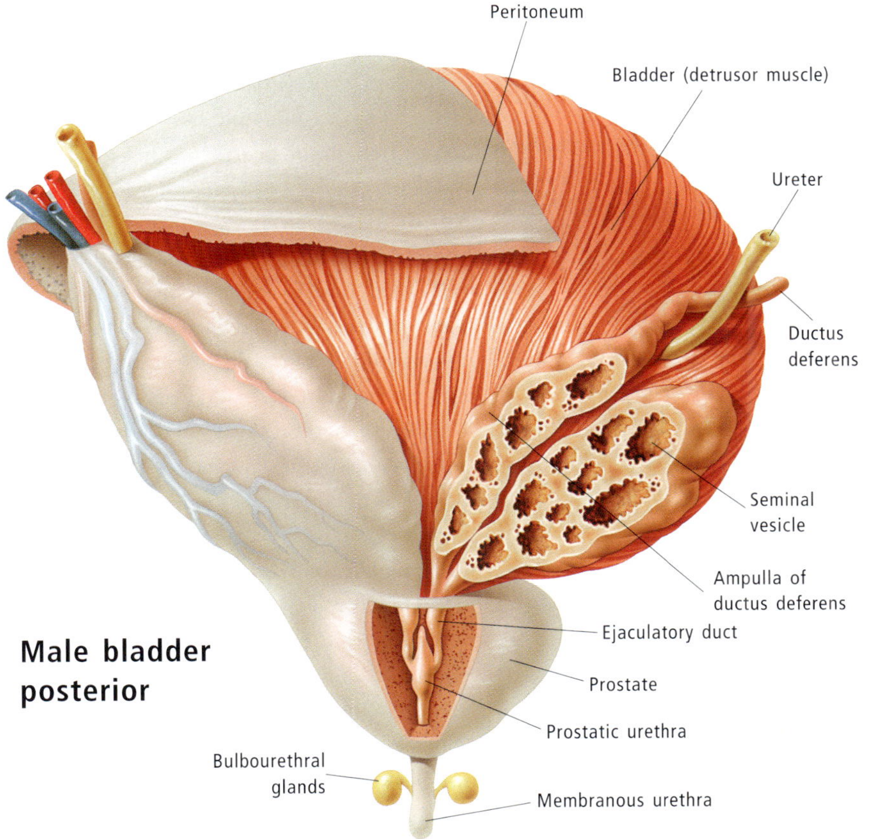

Male bladder posterior

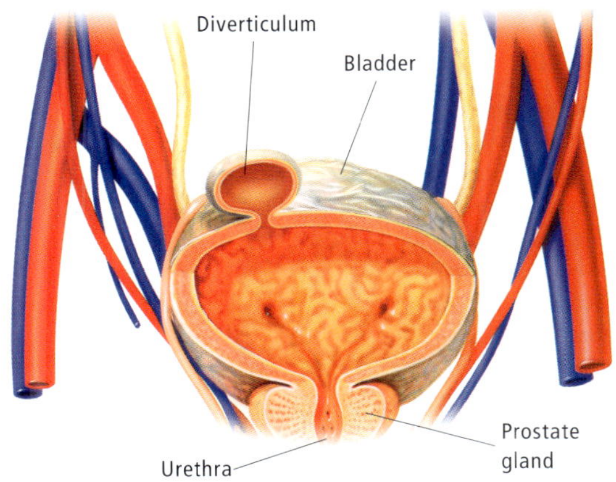

Bladder diverticulum

A bladder diverticulum is an abnormal pouch of the wall of the bladder, usually caused by a weakness in the wall. If untreated it may cause recurrent bouts of cystitis (inflammation of the bladder). It can be repaired by surgery.

BLINDNESS

Blindness can be a total or partial inability to see. Total blindness means the inability to distinguish darkness from light. Partial blindness means having some sight in one or both eyes. A person may have partial sight but still be declared blind—that is, blind according to a definition in law. This may be important in establishing a right to benefits, or training or employment allowances.

Blindness may be congenital, that is, present at birth, or may be acquired through illness or injury.

Industrial accidents are common causes of eye injury. Infections after injury can also cause permanent sight loss. A violent blow or accident can cause the retina to be detached from the inner layer of the eye called the choroid, with loss of sight. In snow blindness, vision is lost due to corneal damage caused by the sun's bright ultraviolet rays reflecting on the snow. Color blindness is the inability to see, or at least differentiate between, specific colors.

Complete or partial blindness may also be due to injury to the neural pathways from the retina to the visual cortex.

SEE ALSO *Cataracts, Color blindness, Diabetes, Macular degeneration, Night blindness*

BLOOD

Blood is a suspension of red and white blood cells, platelets, proteins and chemicals in a straw-colored fluid called plasma. It is the means by which oxygen and essential nutrients are transported from the lungs and digestive tract to other parts of the body.

Blood transfers waste products to organs such as the kidneys and lungs, which eliminate them. It transports antibodies and white blood cells to the sites where they are needed to fight infection. And it transports heat from inner parts of the body to the skin to keep body temperature body stable. A normal-sized adult has about 10 pints (nearly 5 liters) of blood. At rest, the heart pumps all of it around the body in about one minute.

The disk-shaped red blood cells (also called erythrocytes) are the body's means of transporting oxygen to the body's tissues. In a healthy person, each cubic millimeter (0.006 cubic inches) of blood contains between four and six million red blood cells. The oxygen is carried by an iron-containing compound in the red blood cells called hemoglobin. When oxygenated, hemoglobin appears red—hence the red appearance of blood in the arteries. Once the red blood cells reach the tissues, the oxygen is exchanged for carbon dioxide, which the hemoglobin then carries back to the lungs, where it is exhaled.

White blood cells (also known as leukocytes) are the agents of the body's immune system, traveling via the blood to sites of injury and infection. Some types of white cells, called neutrophils and monocytes, engulf invading bacteria and small particles. Others, called lymphocytes, produce antibodies which destroy foreign organisms and are responsible for establishing ongoing immunity. A healthy person has between 4,000 and 10,000 white blood cells per cubic millimeter (0.006 cubic inches) of blood.

Platelets (or thrombocytes) are small fragments of cells responsible for clotting. Clotting is the normal way the body stops bleeding and begins the healing process following injury. It involves complex chemical reactions between many substances that are present in the blood plasma.

In order to deliver oxygen and remove waste products, blood must reach the tissues. In the so-called systemic circulation, oxygenated blood is pumped from the heart through arteries to capillaries in tissues where the oxygen is removed, and then back to the heart via the veins. In the pulmonary circulation, deoxygenated blood flows from the heart to the lungs and then returns, oxygen-rich, to the heart.

Blood

Blood is composed of red blood cells, various types of white blood cells (leukocytes) and platelets in a solution of water, electrolytes, and proteins called plasma. About 40 percent (by volume) of blood is red blood cells. This illustration shows all the different types of blood cell—it does not accurately represent the proportions present in the blood.

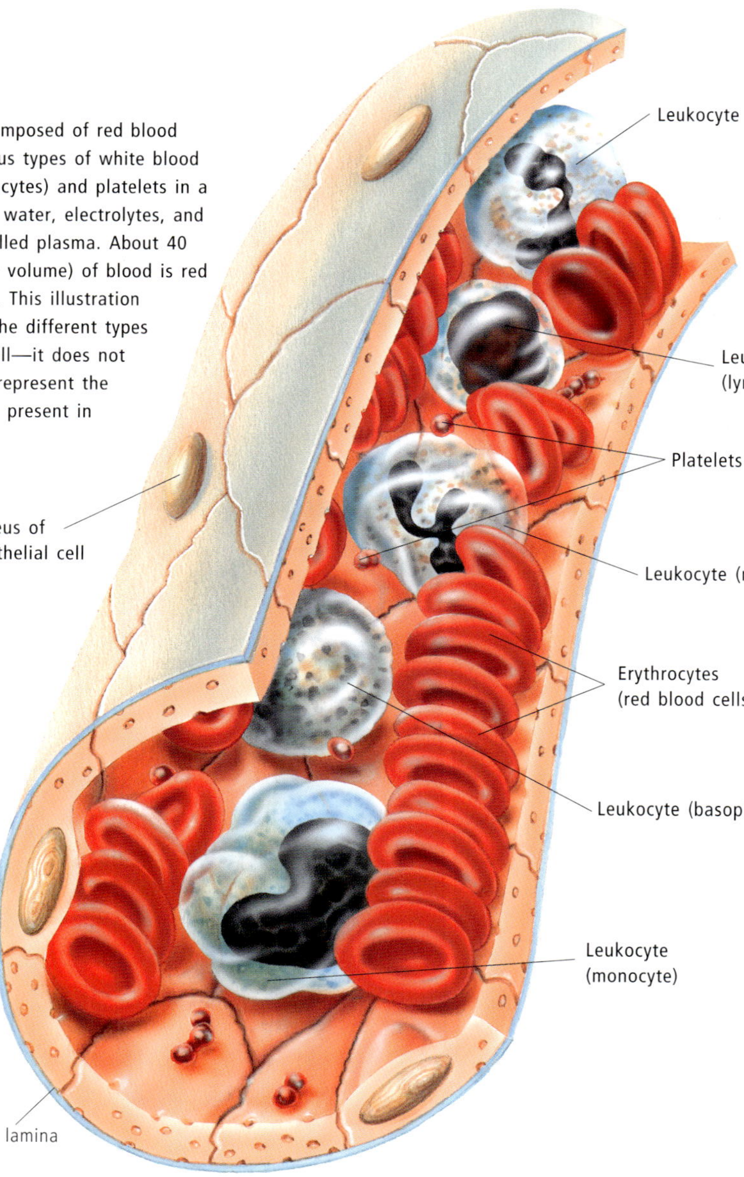

Anemia

Anemia is the failure of the red blood cells to provide enough oxygen to body tissues. It may be caused by a decreased number of red blood cells or a decreased amount of hemoglobin in red blood cells.

There are several causes of anemia. Blood cells may be too few in number because of blood loss or abnormally rapid destruction of circulating blood cells by the body. There may be inadequate amounts of hemoglobin in red blood cells because vital compounds needed to make hemoglobin are missing, as in iron deficiency and vitamin B_{12} deficiency anemias. Or hemoglobin levels in red blood cells may be normal but the hemoglobin may be defective, as in sickle cell disease and thalassemia.

Physicians diagnose anemia by taking a small sample of blood from the patient and counting the number of red blood cells, as well as measuring the concentration of hemoglobin, in the sample. Normal levels of hemoglobin in the blood are approximately 14–17 grams per 100 milliliters (deciliter) for males and 12–15 grams per 100 milliliters (deciliter) for females. In order to treat anemia, the cause must be reversed. Iron or B_{12} supplements, corticosteroid drugs, blood transfusions, or surgery to correct blood loss may be required, depending on the cause.

In some conditions there are too many red cells. This may occur as a compensatory mechanism in chronic lung disease. It may also occur because of an abnormal increase in red blood cell production by the bone marrow, such as in polycythemia vera.

Clotting

Normal blood clotting, or coagulation, is a complex process involving as many as 20 different plasma proteins known as coagulation factors. These factors interact to form a reaction that leads to the production of fibrin, a protein that stops bleeding. In bleeding disorders, certain coagulation factors are deficient or missing. Such a disorder may be hereditary, such as hemophilia. Abnormal bleeding may also be caused by vitamin K deficiency, severe liver disease or prolonged treatment with anticoagulants.

A clot within a blood vessel is called a thrombus. Thrombi can form on damaged blood vessel walls; hence they are more likely in people with arteriosclerosis. A slower than normal flow of blood through the veins can also cause clotting, for example in varicose veins and in people who require prolonged bed rest. Smoking and some birth control pills can also cause blood clots.

A thrombus can block an artery and cause tissues downstream to die from lack of oxygen; it can also block a vein. If it occurs in an artery to the brain, it can cause a stroke. The blood clot may dislodge and travel further upstream, causing ischemia (lack of blood) where it lodges. It is then an embolus. A thrombus can form in a leg or pelvic vein, then detach and lodge in the lung.

Blood clot

This picture of a blood clot as seen by an electron microscope shows red blood cells trapped in a network of fibrin fibers.

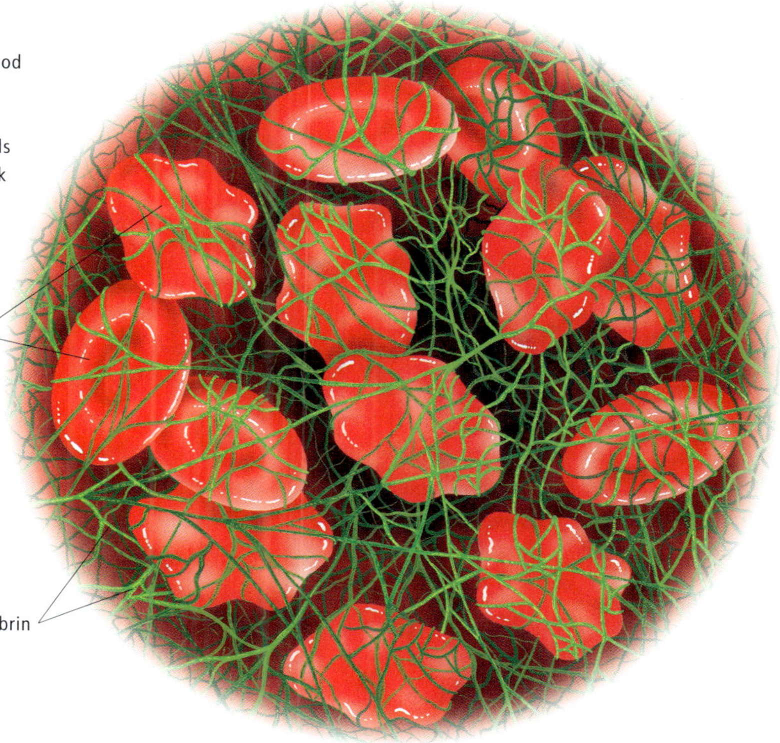

Bacteremia and septicemia

Bacteremia and septicemia (also called blood poisoning) occur when bacterial infection has entered the bloodstream. Once infection has spread to the blood, it may be carried to other parts of the body. Symptoms include high fever, sweating, malaise and chills.

The difference between bacteremia and septicemia is one of degree; septicemia is more serious and usually indicates that the bacteria are multiplying in the blood and causing serious illness. In extreme cases of septicemia, abscesses may form in internal organs such as the liver or brain. Severe blood poisoning may be fatal. The condition requires urgent treatment with intravenous antibiotics in hospital.

SEE ALSO *Anemia, Arteriosclerosis, Embolism, Hemoglobin, Ischemia, Plasma, Platelets, Red blood cells, Septicemia, White blood cells*

Blood clotting

Blood clots in three stages:

a. When a blood vessel is damaged, platelets and red blood cells spill into the damaged tissues.

b. Platelets increase in number and begin to attach to damaged surfaces. Strands of a protein called fibrin are formed.

c. Blood cells, platelets and strands of fibrin become enmeshed in a fibrous tangle called a clot.

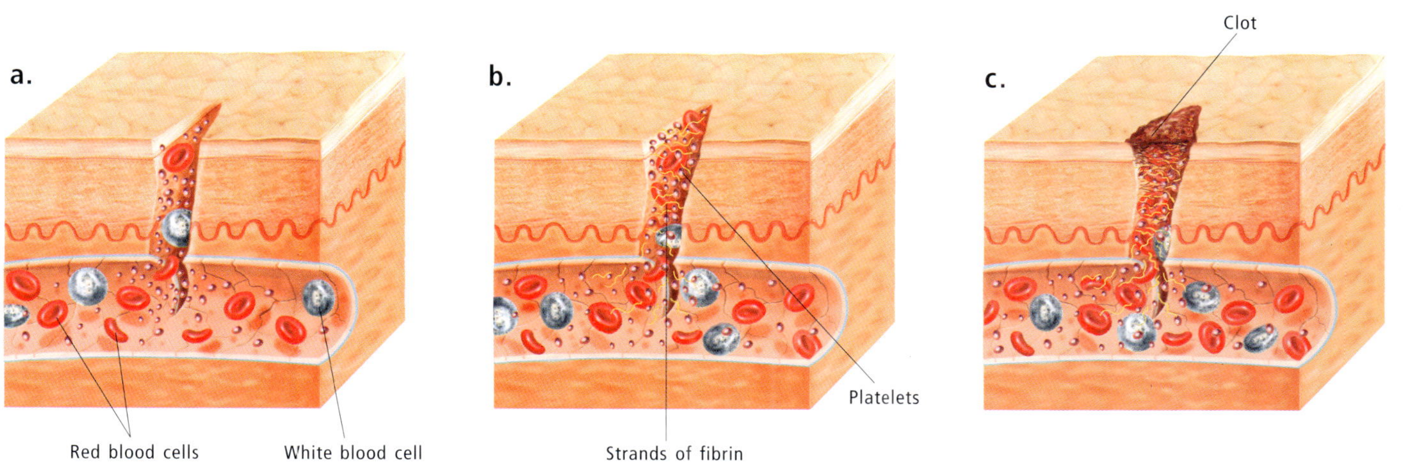

B

BLOOD COUNT

A blood count is a test to establish the number of red cells, white cells, platelets and hemoglobin in the blood. A blood sample is taken and then the number of blood cells counted electronically, or visually using a microscope.

Other laboratory tests determine the hemoglobin level and the percentage of red and white cells in the sample. Some infections can be suspected if the white cell count is too high, while too few white cells could indicate damage to bone marrow.

SEE ALSO *Blood, Hemoglobin, Platelets, Red blood cells, White blood cells*

BLOOD GAS ANALYSIS

Blood gas analysis is a test done on arterial and venous blood to measure oxygen and carbon dioxide levels and hydrogen ion concentration (pH).

The sample can be taken from an appropriate artery or vein. The levels will show how well carbon dioxide is being removed from the blood and how efficiently the lungs are working to re-oxygenate it. Gas analysis of arterial blood also gives a correct measure of the blood's acidity.

SEE ALSO *Acidosis, Alkalosis*

BLOOD GROUPS

Blood is classified into groups, or types, based on antigens (substances which produce immune responses) found on the red blood cells. The main blood groups are A, B, AB and O. In any of these groups individuals can be either Rh positive or, more rarely, Rh negative. In pregnancy, Rh incompatibility will cause the mother to generate antibodies against the fetus' red blood cells, and in later pregnancies a fetus may suffer anemia or jaundice, or not survive.

Blood typing is vital for safe blood transfusions. Mixing incompatible blood types will cause the red cells to clump together, blocking blood vessels and even causing death. Blood typing, as well as a test called cross-matching, performed prior to transfusion, ensures that blood of donor and host are compatible.

SEE ALSO *Blood transfusion, Rhesus (Rh) factor*

BLOOD PRESSURE

Blood pressure is the pressure blood exerts against the walls of the arteries. The amount of pressure depends upon the strength and the rate of the heart's contraction, the volume of blood in the circulatory system and the elasticity of the arteries.

Normal blood pressure varies from person to person, but usually normal blood pressure at rest is about 120/80 mm Hg. It is lower in children. Systolic blood pressure, the top number, represents the maximum pressure in the arteries as the heart contracts and ejects blood into the circulation. Diastolic pressure, the bottom number, represents the minimum blood pressure as the heart relaxes following a contraction.

Blood pressure is measured using an instrument called a sphygmomanometer. A single blood pressure reading, unless it is very high or very low, should not be considered abnormal. Usually, several readings are taken on different days and the results are then compared.

High blood pressure (hypertension) is a major disorder that requires treatment. Untreated, it can damage the heart, blood vessels and kidneys. Low blood pressure (hypotension) is often just normal for a particular person. It may, however, indicate disease such as vasovagal syncope or hypoaldosteronism. It is sometimes a side effect of drugs, particularly antidepressants.

SEE ALSO *Hypertension, Hypotension*

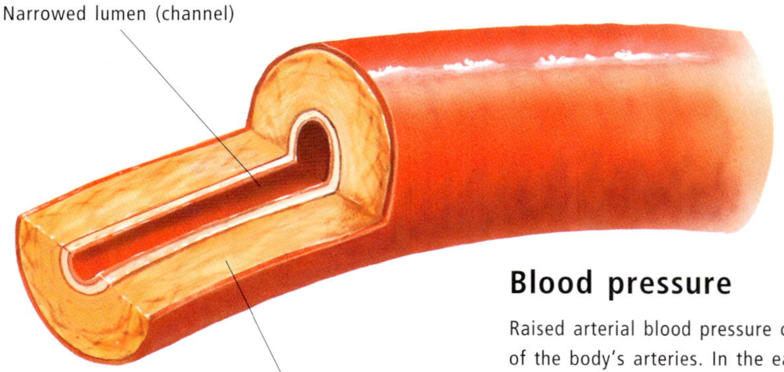

Blood pressure

Raised arterial blood pressure can damage the wall of the body's arteries. In the early stages, the artery wall becomes thickened, as shown here. Later, fatty patches known as atherosclerotic plaques form in the wall and further reduce the flow of blood through the artery.

BLOOD SUGAR TESTS

Blood sugar tests determine the level of glucose in the blood. Glucose is a simple sugar obtained from digesting carbohydrates in food, and is needed to nourish cells throughout the body. It circulates in the blood. If sugar is present in the urine this will indicate a high level in the blood, and a blood sugar test may then be done in order to confirm this.

A person with a low blood sugar level (hypoglycemia) will feel hungry, weak and tired, may have a headache, be sweating and feel faint, and may even lapse into a coma. A high blood sugar level (hyperglycemia) means the body is not properly controlling the absorption of glucose; this can be a symptom of diabetes.

SEE ALSO *Diabetes, Hyperglycemia, Hypoglycemia*

BLOOD TRANSFUSION

Blood transfusion is the transfer of blood from one person to another. A transfusion may be required in serious cases of anemia, either as a result of disease or from a loss of blood, or it may be part of the treatment of acute shock. Blood for transfusion usually comes from a donor and is stored in a blood bank (though the bank may store your own blood to be given back to you later for elective surgery). The donor's blood is screened for HIV and other viruses prior to the transfusion. Blood is cross-matched by the bank to prevent incompatibility between the donor's and the recipient's blood. Incompatibility can cause a transfusion reaction, which in severe cases can be fatal.

An exchange transfusion is the complete replacement of a person's blood. It is sometimes necessary in newborn babies or for people suffering severe poisoning.

SEE ALSO *Blood*

BLOOD VESSELS

Blood vessels form an intricate system through which the blood circulates in a continuous cycle. The heart pumps blood into the aorta, a large elastic artery, which sends off branches to supply the head and arms, the internal organs and the lower limbs. Repeated branchings form thin-walled capillaries, across which oxygen and nutrients are transferred to all body cells and through which carbon dioxide is transferred away from the same cells. Specialized capillaries in the kidneys, known as glomeruli, allow waste to leave the body as urine.

After leaving the limbs and organs, blood is channeled into veins of increasing size, returning eventually to the heart to repeat the cycle.

SEE ALSO *Aorta, Arteries, Blood, Capillaries, Heart, Kidney, Veins*

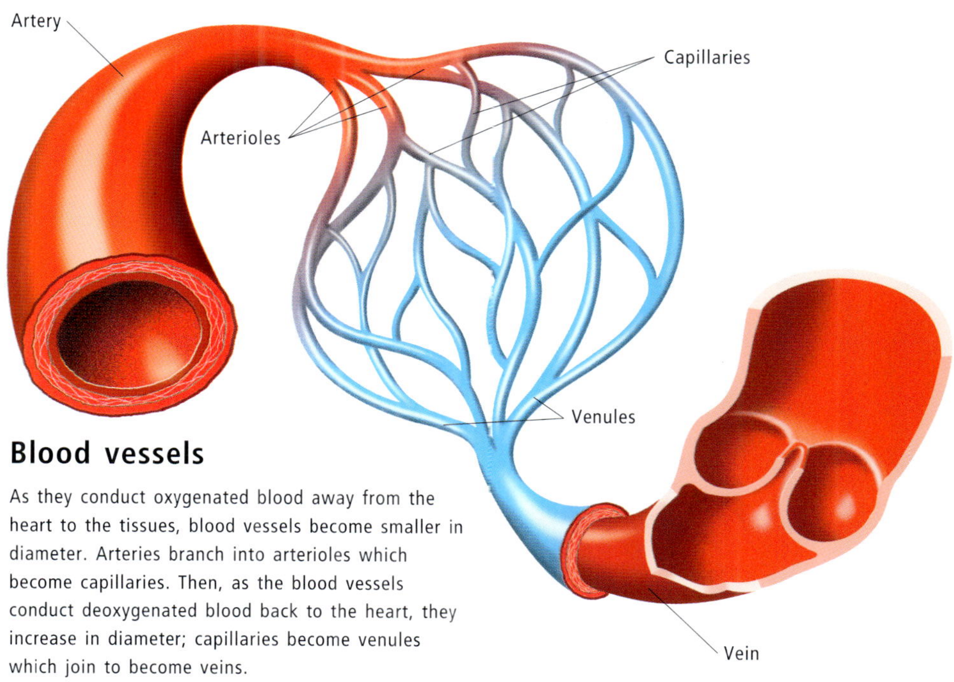

Blood vessels

As they conduct oxygenated blood away from the heart to the tissues, blood vessels become smaller in diameter. Arteries branch into arterioles which become capillaries. Then, as the blood vessels conduct deoxygenated blood back to the heart, they increase in diameter; capillaries become venules which join to become veins.

BODY LANGUAGE

The means by which humans exchange information can be categorized as verbal and non-verbal communication. When newborn babies gaze directly into their mothers' or carers' eyes, they are using the skills for non-verbal communication that humans possess at birth. From the very beginning, a baby must draw a loving response from a mother or carer that will ensure the baby is fed and cared for. Smiling develops within the first six weeks of a baby's life and is important in strengthening the bond between baby and carer. The ability to smile is shown by children born without sight.

The messages conveyed by body language in every face-to-face encounter between humans are estimated to convey more than half the communication—making the body language more important than what is actually said. Signals, signs and gestures are the components of non-verbal communication. Some are present at birth; some are cultural, that is, they are in common use and thus are learned from the family along with spoken language; and some may be genetic, innate to the species and sex.

Studying body language

Actors and dancers know that movement and gesture alone can be powerful tools for communication, and they use a rich vocabulary of body language for expression and communication in their art. The modern study of body language started in the 1950s when an American anthropologist analyzed the behavior of people during conversations recorded on film. To establish meaning, postures, eye movements, facial expressions and gestures with hands and arms were related to the context and the culture in which they occurred.

Cultural differences

Some deliberately used signs and gestures seem to be common to all human cultures. Smiling generally indicates friendliness or welcome. A snarl, or baring the teeth and flaring the nostrils, are strong signals of anger and hostility.

Other gestures may have one meaning in one culture and a completely different meaning in another. In the UK, the "V" sign, made by holding up the straightened index and second fingers in the shape of the letter V, means "victory" (palm facing out towards the recipient) or an obscene gesture of defiance (palm facing in), but in Europe generally both versions would mean either "victory" or simply the number "two", and a completely different gesture is used for the disdainful insult.

Personal space

The definition of personal space—the clear area needed around a person to make each individual feel comfortable—is a vital component of body language. Personal space requirements are dictated by relationship, status, intentions, the culture and the occasion, and will be different for each instance. Standing close during conversation may be normal for one person, but may invade the personal space of another and thus convey completely the wrong message. Depending on the sex of each person, this could merely cause discomfort or else it could wrongly signal either hostility or sexual attraction.

Using body language

Knowledge of everyday body language is particularly useful in situations of face-to-face communication such as interviews, introductions, personal relationships, sales meetings and negotiations.

Participants in a negotiation or business meeting can observe the body language of the other parties to read signs that may reinforce or run counter to what is being said. Posture is important: it can indicate openness and acceptance or the opposite, distrust or disbelief. Hand gestures and

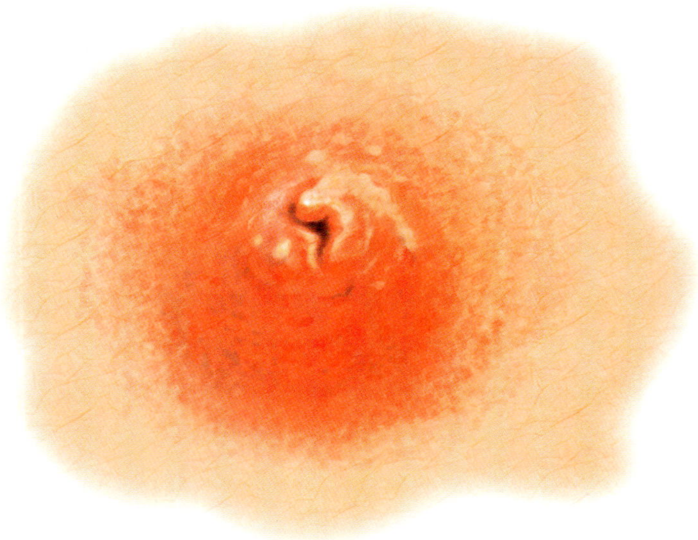

Boil

A boil is a bacterial infection of a hair follicle. This boil has burst through the skin and is discharging pus.

positions can reveal a state of mind or attitude which is unspoken: a hand on the chin may show thoughtful consideration, while a hand over the mouth may indicate disbelief or discomfort with what is being said. Posture can also have meaning. Crossing legs or ankles can convey a defensive attitude, while sitting with legs splayed could indicate boredom, or indifference, or a desire to dominate the proceedings.

BODY MASS INDEX

Body mass index (BMI) is a figure used to determine whether an individual is of healthy, normal weight in proportion to height. It is more useful than using a standard "weight for height" chart and more meaningful to the individual who wants to know whether they are overweight or underweight, and how far they are outside the range of what is considered healthy.

The BMI is calculated according to the following formula: BMI = weight (in kilograms) divided by height (in meters) squared. For example, a man weighing 220 pounds (100 kilograms) and measuring 6 feet (1.8 meters) in height would have a BMI of 30.9 (100 divided by 1.8^2).

A BMI of 20–24 is accepted as normal for men, while for women a range of 19–24 is accepted as normal. A figure higher than this suggests a person is a bit overweight, with the term obesity being used when the BMI is above 30.

Overweight people who wish to reduce their weight can use the BMI to set a target weight range. A person's target BMI will be a weight within the normal range where they feel comfortable, and may be at the higher or lower end of that range.

SEE ALSO *Nutrition, Obesity*

BODY SHAPE

Human bodies are categorized into three body shapes (somatotypes): endomorphic—soft, rounded body shape, and with a tendency to store fat; mesomorphic—strongly framed, muscular and evenly proportioned; and ectomorphic—lean, angular in shape, fragile in appearance and rather low in fat.

Neither overeating nor dieting will change a person's body type, but can change the shape superficially by altering the amount of fat stored. The majority of dieters are women, whose shape is affected by fat stores at hips, thighs, abdomen and breasts. When overweight, fat deposits at these places will be greatly increased.

Fluid retention, which may occur with menstruation in women, and in either sex as a result of illness, can affect body shape. Exercise can affect body shape when it tightens slack muscles, aids loss of excess weight by reducing fat stores, or improves posture. But it will not change a person's somatotype. Cosmetic surgery may offer a solution (rather drastic though it may be) for people who wish to change their body shape.

Body image is the individual's perception of their own shape. This may be distorted, as in sufferers from eating disorders who may see themselves as grossly overweight when they are emaciated and starving. Perceptions of body shape are, to a great extent, dictated by fashion. Adolescent girls often have a distorted body image, and they are the main group at risk of dieting to excess in an effort to conform to a certain standard.

SEE ALSO *Cosmetic surgery, Eating disorders, Obesity*

BODY TEMPERATURE

In adults the normal temperature, taken orally, is 98.6°F (37°C). When taken under the armpit, it is about 1°F (0.5°C) lower than the oral temperature. The rectal temperature is about 1°F (0.5°C) higher. In the elderly, the body temperature tends to be slightly lower. In a child, it varies more than in an adult, so a moderate temperature increase in a child is usually of less significance.

SEE ALSO *Fever, Heatstroke*

BOIL

A boil, also known as a furuncle or carbuncle, is a bacterial infection of a hair follicle. It appears as a painful, swollen red lump, most commonly on the face, neck, armpit, buttocks or thigh. A boil contains pus, a thick yellow fluid that is a byproduct of inflammation, made up of white blood cells, dead tissue matter and bacteria. Boils may heal spontaneously, or they may grow in size, burst, drain and then heal. Most boils must be drained surgically by a primary care physician (general practitioner).

BONE MARROW BIOPSY

This is a procedure in which a needle is inserted into a bone to obtain a sample of the cells of the bone marrow—a process known as aspiration. Bone marrow biopsy can also involve removing a piece of bone tissue, including the marrow; this is correctly termed biopsy. Bone marrow samples are usually taken from the sternum (breastbone) or iliac crest (hip bone), under local anesthetic.

Bone marrow biopsy is valuable for establishing a specific diagnosis for several groups of diseases of the blood and bone marrow such as anemia, leukemia and lymphoma.

SEE ALSO *Anemia, Biopsy, Leukemia*

Body shapes

Ectomorph female

Mesomorph female

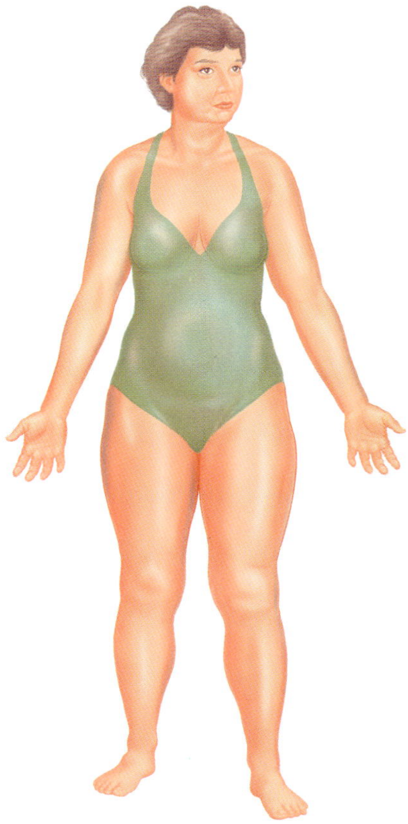

Endomorph female

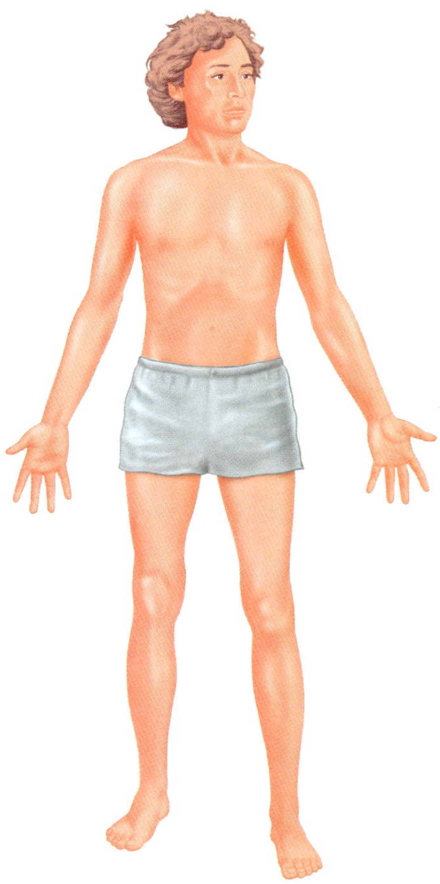

Ectomorph male

Mesomorph male

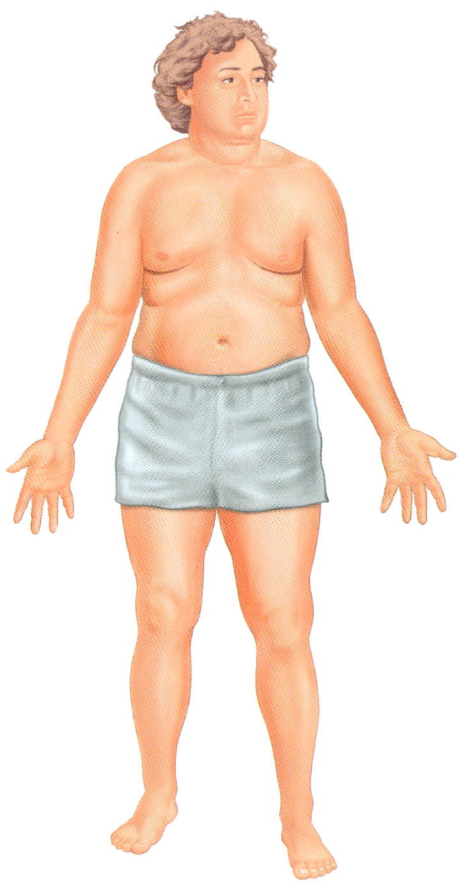

Endomorph male

B

Bone

Bone is made up of different layers, the outermost of which is the periosteum. Beneath this is the compact or cortical bone which surrounds the spongy or cancellous bone. At the core is the bone marrow.

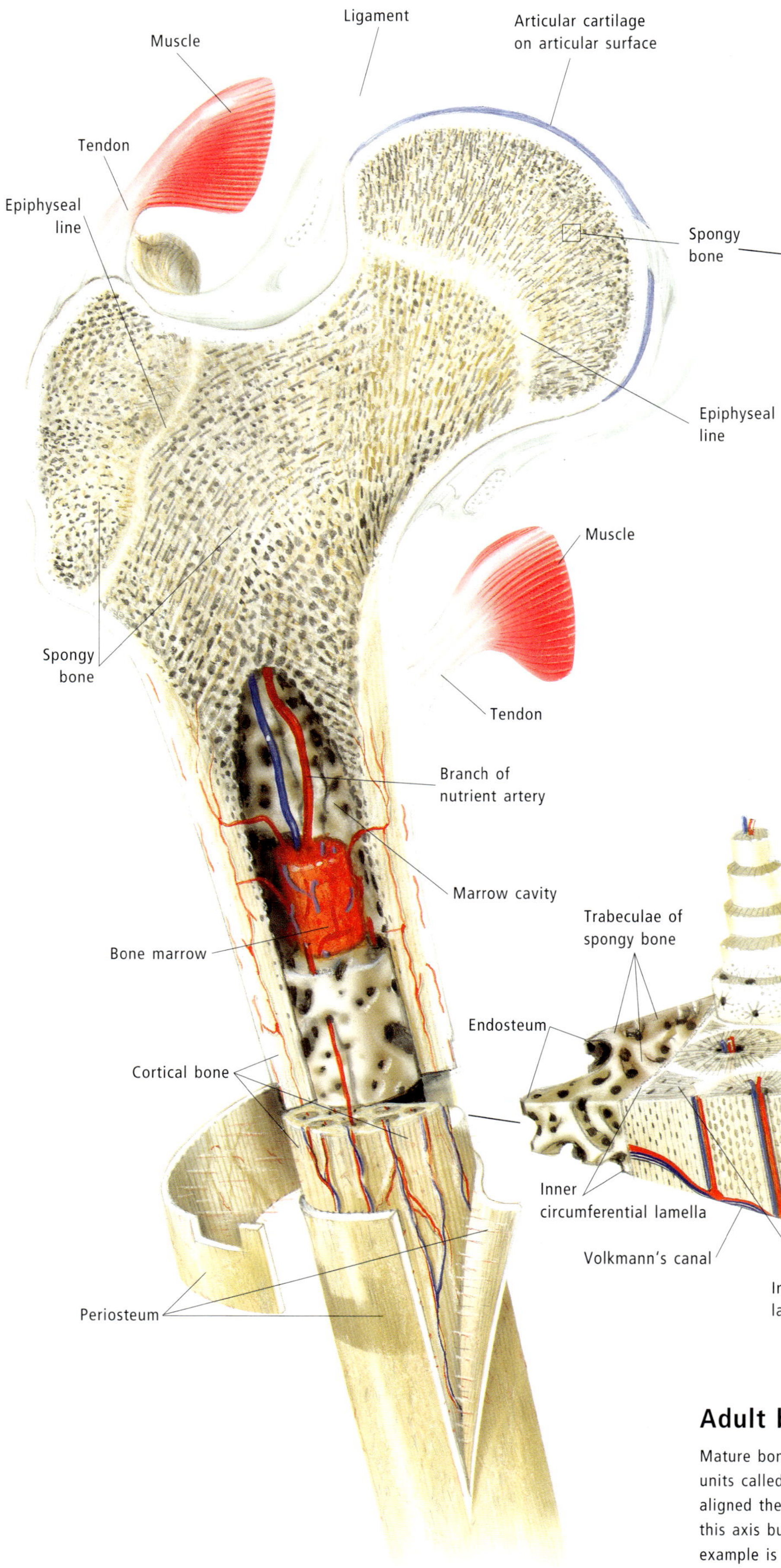

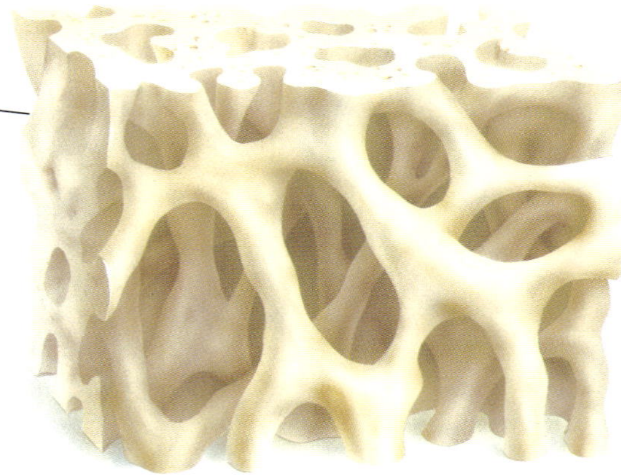

Spongy (cancellous) bone

Spongy or cancellous bone consists of a lattice work system of bony spikes called trabeculae, arranged in different directions. It is light and strong enough to withstand stress from many directions. An example is the head of the femur.

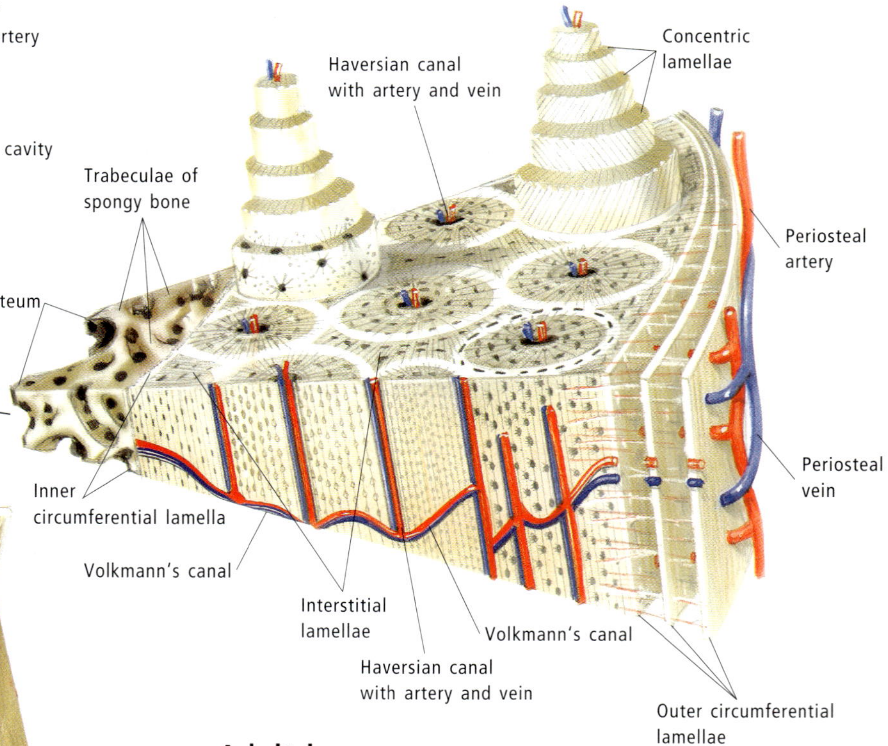

Adult bone

Mature bone consists of densely packed rod-shaped units called osteons (or Haversian systems) all aligned the same way. Cortical bone is strong along this axis but weak in any other direction. An example is the outer part of the shaft of the femur.

B

BONES

Bone is the rigid, calcified tissue that makes up the skeleton. It supports the body and surrounds and protects its internal structures. It acts as a store of calcium, and houses the bone marrow in which blood cells are manufactured. Bones provide an attachment for muscles, which contract, allowing the body to move. There are 206 bones in the body in all.

Being connective tissue, bone is composed of cells in a matrix. The major components of the matrix include mineral salts (mainly calcium phosphate), which provide hardness, and collagen fibers, which give strength.

Four types of cell are present: osteoprogenitor cells, osteoblasts, osteocytes and osteoclasts. Osteoprogenitor cells develop into osteoblasts, which form bone tissue. Osteoblasts mature into osteocytes, which maintain bone tissue. Osteoclasts, which occur on bone surfaces, are involved in the reabsorption of the matrix, required for bone development, growth and repair.

A typical mature long bone has a central shaft—the diaphysis—and ends known as epiphyses. Inside the diaphysis is the medulla, which contains yellow bone marrow, and is lined by the endosteum, a layer rich in osteoprogenitor cells and osteoclasts. The diaphysis meets the epiphysis at the metaphysis. This is the location, in an immature bone, of the cartilage layer from which length-wise growth occurs. Most of the bone is protected and nourished by the periosteum, a membrane served by nerves and blood vessels that enter the bone.

Bone fractures and diseases

A break in a bone is called a fracture. Any bone in the body can be fractured, but some bones, because of their vulnerable positions (for example, the long bones of the arms and legs), tend to fracture more often than others. Most fractures occur as the result of injury or accident. Sometimes, a bone breaks following repeated minor strains. Some bones have a tendency to fracture easily because they are weak from a disease, osteoporosis for example. Treatment for all fractures is to place the broken ends of the bone as close together as possible, in the original position, and to hold them there until new bone has had time to heal the break. This can be done with a plaster of Paris or fiberglass cast, or with screws, metal plates, thick pins or wires. Healing can take from three weeks to three months or more.

Osteomyelitis is an infection of the bone, usually caused by bacteria. The bacterial infection reaches the bone via the bloodstream from another area of infection—a septic tooth or a boil for example. Or it may reach the bone through an injury, such as an open fracture. Symptoms are pain, fever and tenderness at the site of infection. Swelling occurs and the skin becomes red. X-rays are normal at first, but a bone scan will reveal the infection. Large doses of antibiotics are given intravenously in hospital. If there is an abscess it is surgically drained.

Osteoporosis is a condition which is characterized by the progressive loss of bone density and thinning of bone tissue, resulting in brittle, fragile bones that are subject to fractures. It occurs in older age groups, especially women after the menopause. It can be prevented by exercise and maintaining a healthy diet which includes a sufficient

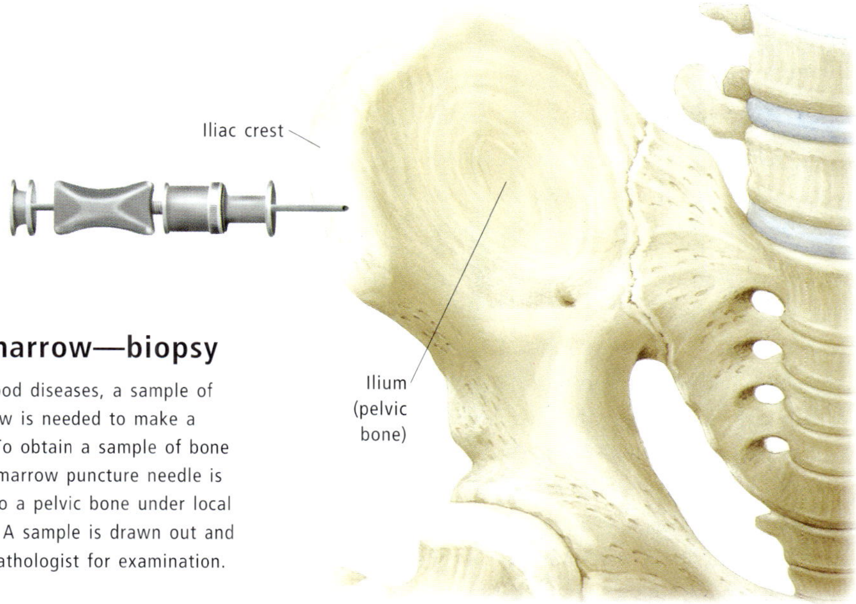

Bone marrow—biopsy

In some blood diseases, a sample of bone marrow is needed to make a diagnosis. To obtain a sample of bone marrow, a marrow puncture needle is inserted into a pelvic bone under local anesthesia. A sample is drawn out and sent to a pathologist for examination.

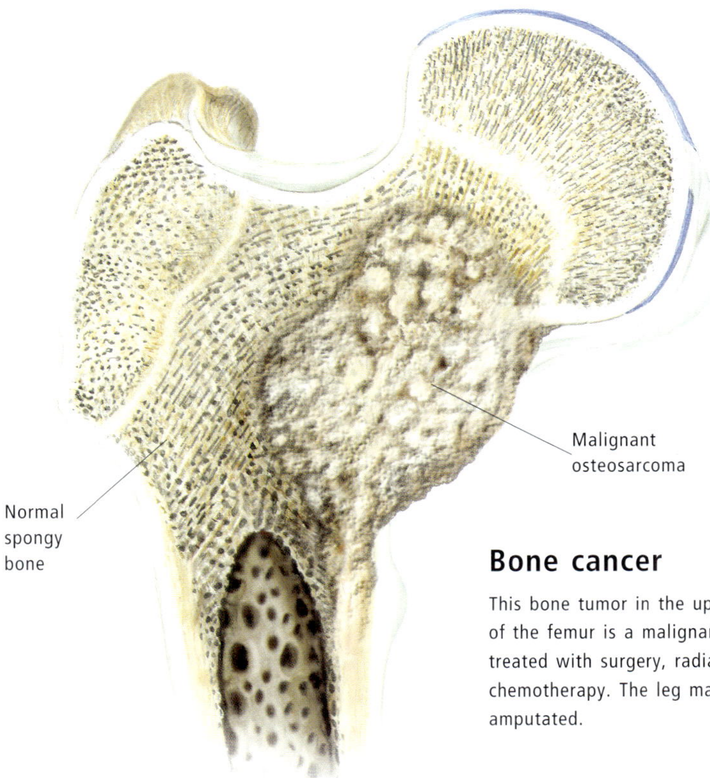

Bone cancer

This bone tumor in the upper part of the shaft of the femur is a malignant osteosarcoma. It is treated with surgery, radiation therapy and chemotherapy. The leg may need to be amputated.

amount of calcium, phosphorous and vitamin D. Postmenopausal women with osteoporosis may be treated with estrogen replacement therapy.

Bone tumors (cancers) may be benign or malignant. Benign tumors include osteochondromas (the most common) and osteomas. They usually do not require treatment but can be removed for cosmetic reasons. Malignant bone tumors usually arise from primary cancers of the breast, lung, prostate, kidney or thyroid. Primary malignant bone tumors are rare and are more common in young men. These include osteosarcomas, Ewing's sarcoma, fibrosarcoma and chondrosarcoma. They require surgical removal followed by radiation therapy and chemotherapy. Often, an affected limb may need to be amputated.

Tests

There are several tests for bone disease. Blood tests can show abnormally high or low levels of calcium, phosphorus and bone enzymes such as alkaline phosphatase. An x-ray can be used to detect fractures, tumors or degenerative conditions of the bone. A bone scan is a test that detects areas of increases or decreases in bone metabolism. This is done by determining how a radioactive isotope collects in the bone. It can be used to identify tumors or bone infection. Bone marrow biopsy uses a needle to extract bone marrow for examination. This test is used to diagnose leukemia, secondary bone tumors, anemia and infections.

SEE ALSO *Calcium, Ewing's sarcoma, Fractures, Muscle, Osteomyelitis, Osteoporosis, Skeletal system*

BOTTLE FEEDING

Breast milk is ideal food for babies, particularly in the first weeks of life. However, for some mothers, breast feeding can be physically and emotionally demanding, and they may choose not to breast feed. Others may have difficulties such as sore nipples which can make feeding painful. Occasionally babies do not thrive on breast milk alone.

Bottle feeding is the feeding of babies (human and animal) with a bottle containing artificial baby milk (for humans it is usually called infant formula) and a teat. Artificial baby milk consists of a powder which, when made according to directions, makes a liquid which resembles human milk; it is nutritionally complete but does not contain all the properties of breast milk.

Bottle feeding requires a number of sterile bottles and teats, infant formula and boiled water. It is essential that the formula is mixed accurately, according to directions given, and that the water in which it is mixed is sterile. It is also important that the equipment used to feed the baby is kept sterile. This can be done chemically with sterilizing solution, or by boiling. Diarrhea, dehydration and malnutrition can be caused by unsafe bottle feeding, but these problems rarely occur in societies with a good standard of hygiene. It is best to serve the milk at body temperature.

If correct methods are followed, bottle feeding can be a positive and rewarding experience. The mother needs to hold the baby close to her body, so they can both enjoy the warmth of physical contact. It is not safe to let babies feed themselves. Bottle feeding also gives other members of the family a chance to feed and bond with the baby.

SEE ALSO *Breast feeding, Infancy, Newborn*

BOWEL

The bowel consists of two parts: the small bowel (or small intestine) and the large bowel (or large intestine). The small bowel (containing the duodenum, jejunum and ileum) is mainly concerned with the final stages of digestion, and absorption of nutrients from food. The large bowel (colon and rectum) is concerned with absorption of water and salts. Generally speaking, the bowel occupies the lower two thirds of the abdominal cavity.

SEE ALSO *Colon, Duodenum, Ileum, Intestines, Jejunum, Rectum*

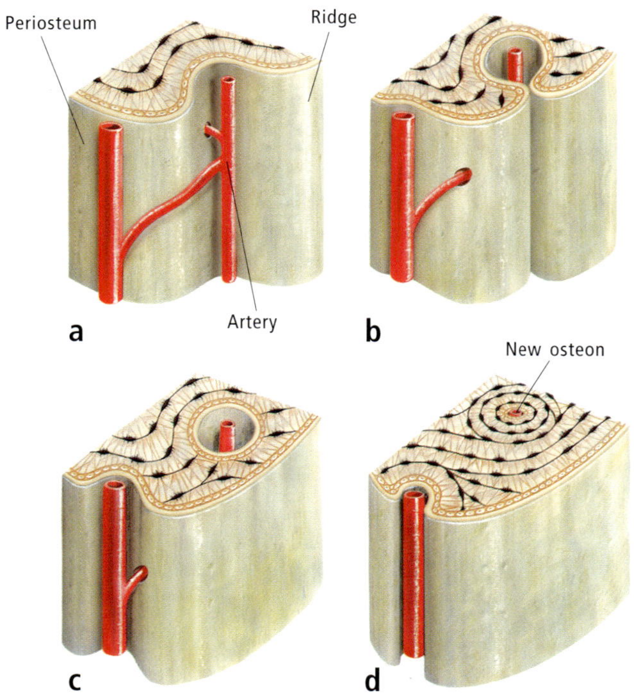

Bone formation

Bone grows in width as new bone is laid down in ridges (a) either side of a blood vessel. The ridges grow together and fuse, enclosing the vessel (b). More bone is laid down, diminishing the space around the vessel (c), and eventually an osteon is formed. The process continues, enclosing parallel blood vessels and causing the bone to become thicker (d).

BOWEL CANCER

Bowel cancer almost always arises from the layer of cells lining the inside of the large intestine (which includes the colon and rectum); it is also known as colorectal cancer. In the economically developed nations of the world, it is one of the three most common cancers (the others being lung cancer and either prostate cancer in men or breast cancer in women) and is a major cause of death from cancer.

Causes

Dietary factors appear to play an important role in the development of bowel cancer. In particular, diets low in fiber and high in fat are associated with an increased risk, though it is not known exactly why this is.

There is good evidence that for most bowel cancers a sequence of abnormal

Bowel cancer

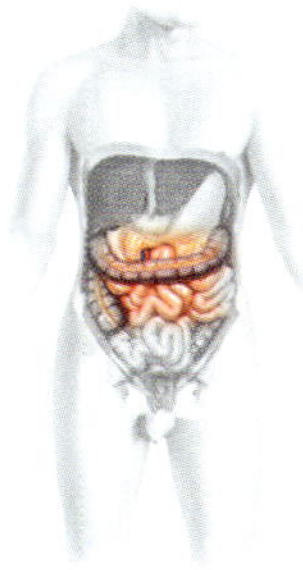

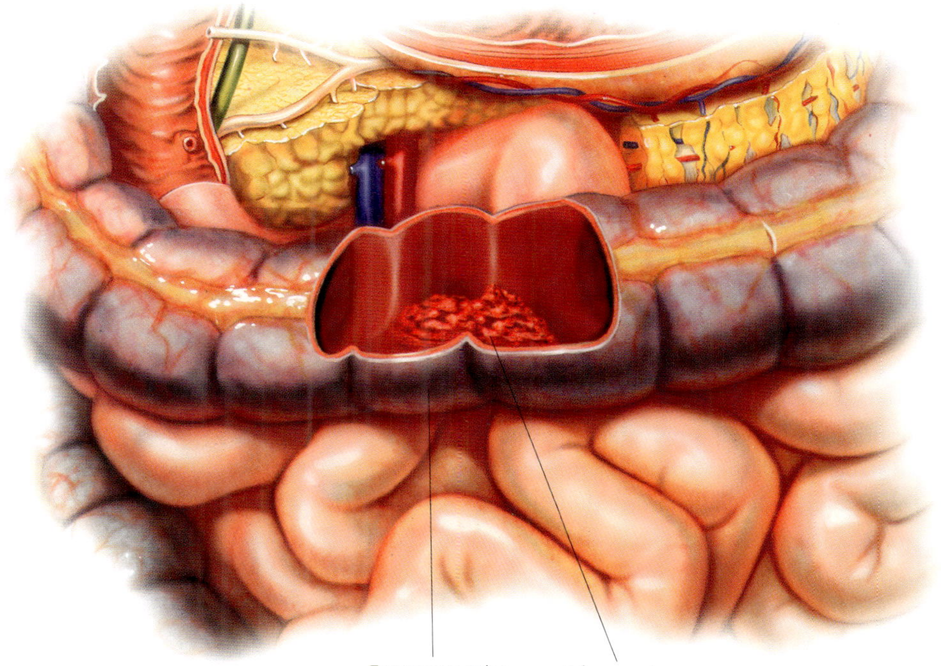

This bowel cancer is growing out from the wall of the transverse colon. It will need to be surgically removed, along with some surrounding bowel and nearby lymph nodes. If the cancer has not spread beyond the walls of the bowel, the prospects for long-term survival are very good.

changes in the bowel wall precedes the emergence of a cancer. One of these is the development of pre-cancerous polyps (outgrowths of the lining of the bowel), although not all polyps are pre-cancerous. Several inherited disorders that lead to the formation of multiple colorectal polyps have been identified. There are other inherited conditions associated with bowel cancer but without polyp formation. Also, there is an increased risk of bowel cancer in patients with long-term inflammatory bowel diseases, such as ulcerative colitis or Crohn's disease.

Symptoms

Cancer of the large intestine usually develops in persons aged 50 or older. It is somewhat more common in men. The symptoms are variable and often vague. Pain is unusual at first. Cancers cause bleeding from the lining of the bowel, but in the upper part of the large bowel this blood is mixed with the liquid intestinal contents so that no blood is evident in the feces and may not be detected until the tumor is far advanced, when the patient becomes pale, weak and easily tired because of anemia.

About half of all large bowel cancers develop in the lower third of the colon or the rectum. Bleeding from these tumors may be visible, but often goes unnoticed. Such cancers may produce crampy abdominal pain, constipation, or alternating constipation and diarrhea.

How bowel cancer develops

Bowel cancers grow relatively slowly, so early recognition of symptoms by the patient and prompt diagnosis of the disease by the doctor has enormous potential to save lives. Blood screening of feces can also help recognize the disease early. Diagnosis is by barium enema (an x-ray investigation), colonoscopy (using a flexible fiberoptic instrument) and sampling of blood for a chemical released by cancer cells—the carcinoembryonic antigen (CEA). Many bowel cancers are, however, not diagnosed until the tumor has spread.

The spread of bowel cancer is initially through the wall of the bowel, then by lymphatics to the nearby draining lymph nodes and later via the blood to the bones, liver, lungs and other organs. As is true for many cancers, the extent of spread of the cancer at the time of diagnosis is the most important factor that determines the course of the disease and the patient's chances of survival.

Treatment

Treatment of bowel cancer is by surgery, removing the tumor and surrounding bowel and lymph nodes, and sometimes radiation therapy for those patients for whom major surgery may be too risky. If caught early, when the cancer is limited to the inner lining of the bowel, the likelihood of the patient surviving at least five years from the time of diagnosis is almost 100 percent. If it spreads through the wall and to nearby lymph nodes, this figure falls sharply.

As early diagnosis is the key to surgical cure, a screening procedure for bowel cancer would be extremely useful, but at present there is no inexpensive reliable test for the disease at an early stage. However, because bowel cancers usually bleed, testing for blood in the feces has some value. Colonoscopy with biopsy is the most effective method of early diagnosis currently available.

SEE ALSO *Anemia, Barium enema, Bowel, Cancer, Colon, Colonoscopy, Crohn's disease, Intestines, Rectum, Ulcerative colitis*

BRACES

Braces are orthodontic devices used in the correction of protruding or crooked teeth and misaligned jaws.

Designed to improve appearance, function and dental health, they usually consist of stainless steel or clear ceramic brackets that are fitted over each tooth or cemented to them. These are connected by wires which are adjusted at regular intervals over a period of up to three years to slowly change the position of the teeth. Springs, rubber bands or appliances which fit to the teeth may also be attached to the braces to generate the necessary tension and to speed the straightening process.

Braces are commonly worn in adolescence, when the teeth and jaw are easier to manipulate, but have become more popular with adults in recent years. They are fitted by an orthodontist, who assesses each dental problem with the help of x-rays and plaster molds of the teeth. Some teeth may need to be removed before braces are fitted.

B

BRAIN

The brain is the headquarters of the nervous system. As well as providing overall control of vital body functions, it enables us to perceive and respond to incoming sensory information, to think, speak and make decisions, and to carry out a whole range of purposeful, coordinated movements.

Its average weight is around 3 pounds (1.4 kilograms) and it lies mostly within the cranial cavity of the skull. It is made up of billions of nerve cells (neurons) and supporting cells (glia). Messages are transmitted from one part of the neuron to another electrically, and from one neuron to another by the release of chemicals. The complexity of the connections between different neurons in the brain is almost incomprehensible, with some neurons commonly making 10,000 or more connections with other neurons. In the nervous system, neuronal cell bodies group together as gray matter and their processes group together as white matter.

The human brain can be divided into four main parts: the cerebrum, diencephalon, brain stem and cerebellum.

The cerebrum

The largest part of the brain is the cerebrum. This is formed by the cerebral hemispheres that are joined together by a massive bundle of white matter called the corpus callosum and covered by the cerebral cortex. This is a sheet of gray matter (1.5–4 millimeters thick). The cerebral cortex is the site where the highest level of neural processing takes place, including language, memory and cognitive function.

The cortex makes up about 40 percent of the total brain mass, its surface area being so great in humans (just over 1 square yard, or approximately 1 square meter) that it is thrown into numerous folds in order to fit inside the cranial cavity. The basic pattern formed by these folds is similar in all humans, but the size and shape of some folds varies between individuals. The cortex covers the frontal, parietal, temporal and occipital lobes.

We know from studies on patients who have sustained damage to the cortex that the results of damage depend on which part of the cortex is affected. For example, the occipital lobe is involved in the perception of vision, the temporal lobe in memory, and the parietal lobe in the perception of touch and the comprehension of speech. The fron-

The limbic system

The components of the limbic system govern emotional states and behavioral drives. They are the link between the cerebral cortex and the unconscious functions of the brain stem. The limbic system also helps store and retrieve memories.

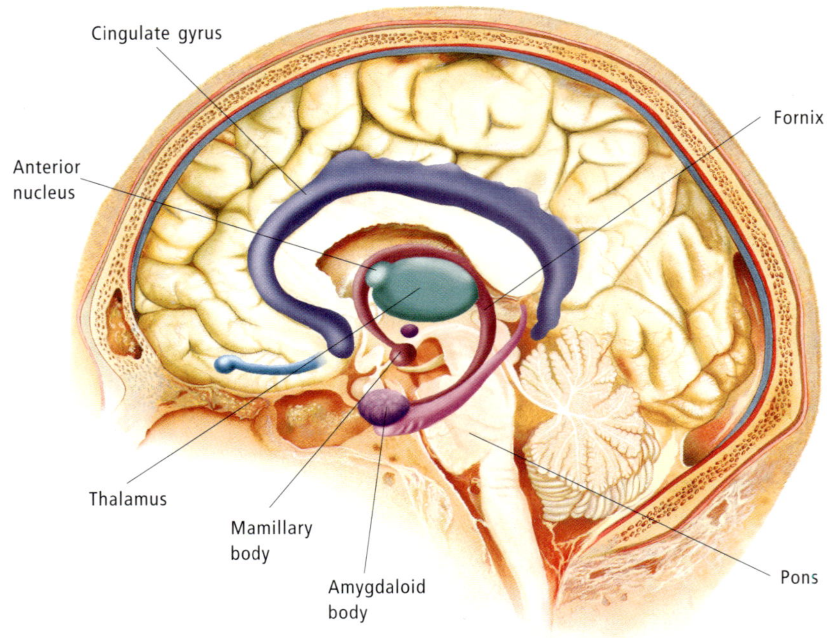

Brain ventricles

The ventricles of the brain contain cerebro-spinal fluid. They connect via passageways (called foramina and aqueducts) and with the space surrounding the outside of the brain (the subarachnoid space). The cerebro-spinal fluid acts as a shock absorber, cushioning the brain from mechanical forces.

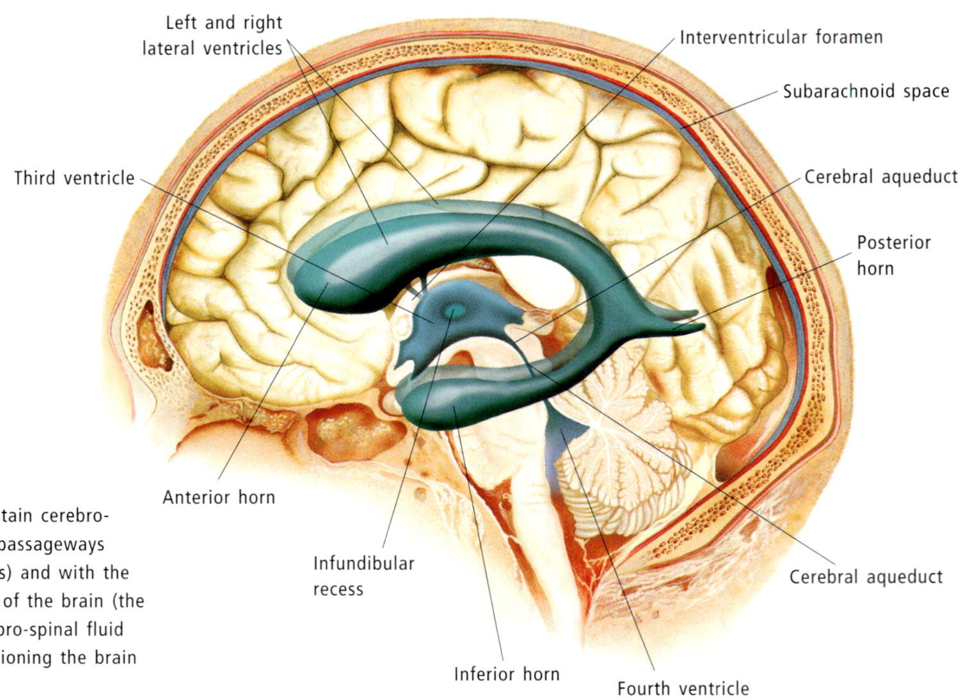

tal lobe is not only important in movement but also has a large area devoted to thinking, behavior and personality. The overall patterns of electrical activity in the cortex can be measured in an electroencephalogram (EEG), which is obtained by recording responses from electrodes placed on the scalp.

Beneath the gray matter of the cerebral cortex is a thick mass of white matter, formed by fibers, which transmits information between different parts of the cortex or between the cortex and other parts of the brain. Embedded within the white matter of each hemisphere are some islands of gray matter known as the basal ganglia, which play a role in the control of movement and are affected in disorders such as Parkinson's disease or cerebral palsy.

The diencephalon

The diencephalon lies beneath the cerebral hemispheres and has two main structures, the thalamus and the hypothalamus. The thalamus, which is about the size of a walnut, is an important relay station, distributing sensory information from the periphery to different regions of the cortex. The hypothalamus lies on the underside of the thalamus and is surprisingly small, considering its importance as the control center for body functions such as eating, drinking, defence and reproduction. It also plays a role in behavior, particularly in the expression of emotions, such as fear and anger.

The brain stem

The brain stem, which is continuous with the spinal cord below it, consists of the midbrain, pons and medulla. Passing through the brain stem are ascending pathways, carrying sensory information from the spinal cord to the brain, and descending pathways, carrying motor commands down to the spinal cord. The brain stem contains many important reflex centers which control vital functions such as heartbeat and respiration. It is also important in regulating levels of consciousness—injury to the brain stem can result in prolonged loss of consciousness or death.

The cerebellum

The cerebellum (Latin for "little brain") is attached to the brain stem and resembles a cauliflower in appearance. Like the cerebrum, its surface is formed by a highly folded cortex. The cerebellum is important in the control of movement, particularly in the coordination of voluntary muscle activity and in the maintenance of balance and equilibrium. It is particularly sensitive to excess alcohol, and the effects of severe drunkenness (poor balance and coordination) to some degree mimic cerebellar disease.

Damage to the brain

In the adult brain there are structures called ventricles (derived from parts of the embryonic brain). These ventricles contain a watery substance called cerebrospinal fluid (CSF), which provides buoyancy and protection. Under certain conditions the volume of the CSF may be increased, causing a rise in pressure and hence damage to adjacent brain structures. This is known as "water on the brain" (hydrocephalus).

Although the brain only makes up 2 percent of the average body weight it uses 20

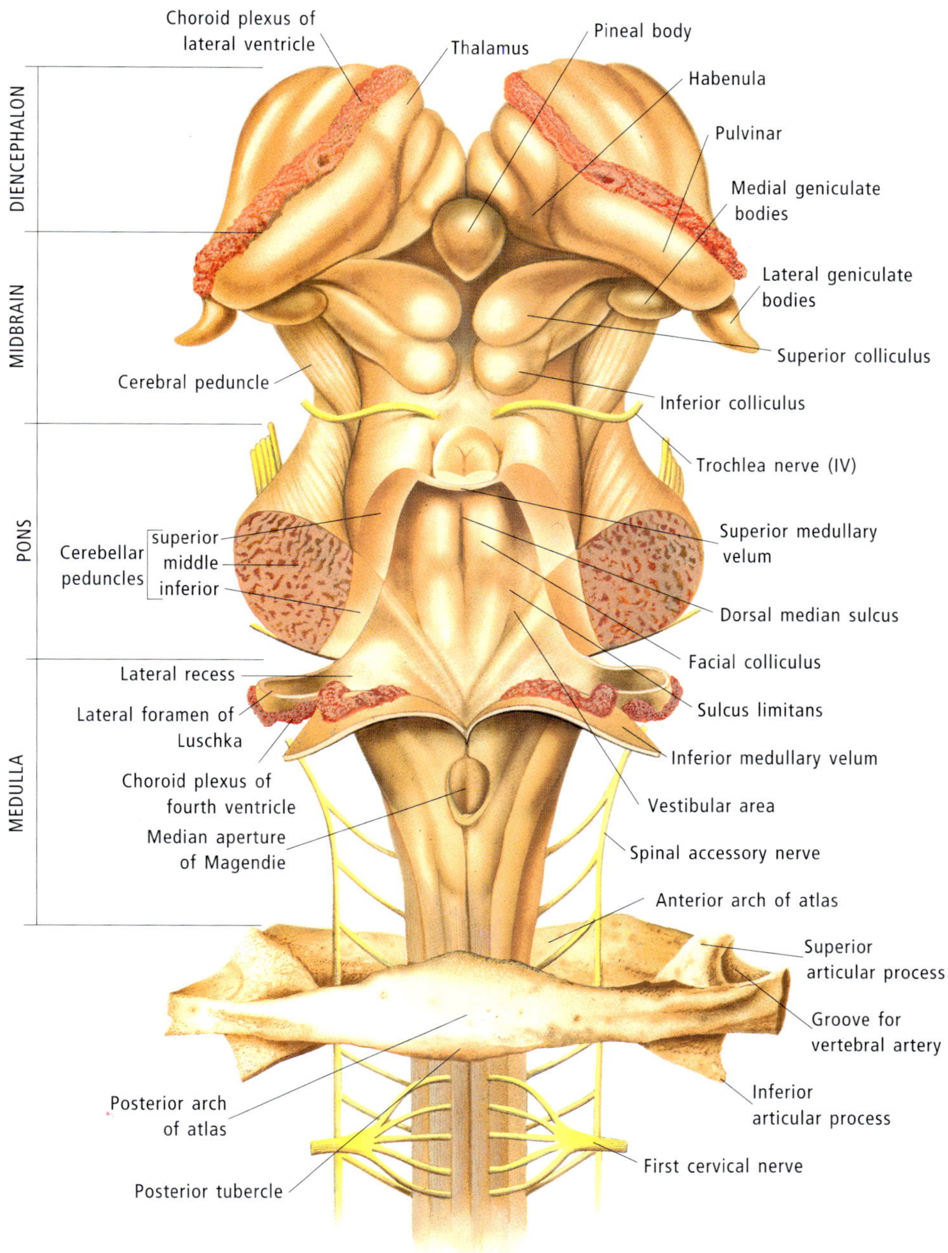

Brain stem

Centers in the brain stem regulate many vital functions including breathing, heartbeat and blood pressure. Damage to it from stroke or other injury may result in death.

percent of the available oxygen, and its cells will start to die if they are deprived of oxygen (via blood) for only a few minutes. This could result from cessation of breathing (as in drowning) or from a stroke, in which brain tissue is damaged due to lack of blood.

The effects will depend on the size of the affected blood vessel and the location of the damaged cells. Occasionally a small floating body (embolus) lodges briefly in a brain artery then frees itself, causing a transient ischemic attack (TIA), lasting a few minutes.

SEE ALSO *Brain wave activity, Cerebellum, Cerebral palsy, Electroencephalogram, Hydrocephalus, Neurons, Parkinson's disease, Stroke, Thalamus, Transient ischemic attack*

BRAIN WAVE ACTIVITY

Because nervous impulses are transmitted electrically, it is possible to record the activity of cells in the brain by placing electrodes on the scalp. The resulting graph, the electroencephalogram (EEG), shows wavelike patterns of activity, known as brain waves, which vary with different states of consciousness. Alpha waves indicate a relaxed awake state, beta waves are typical when we are mentally alert, theta waves are common in children but not adults, and delta waves appear during sleep. Brain wave activity becomes intensified during epileptic seizures. Prolonged absence of brain wave activity is an indication of brain death.

SEE ALSO *Brain, Electroencephalogram*

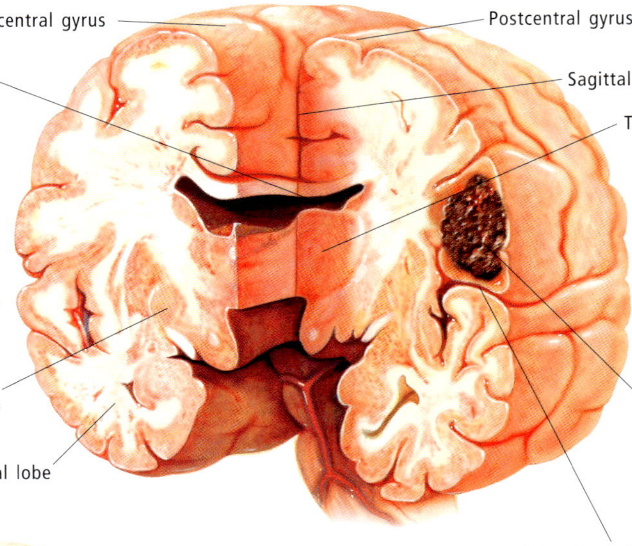

Brain tumor

A tumor of the brain tissue may be benign or malignant. Symptoms include headache, vomiting, speech defects and muscle paralysis. Brain tumors are treated by surgery and radiation therapy.

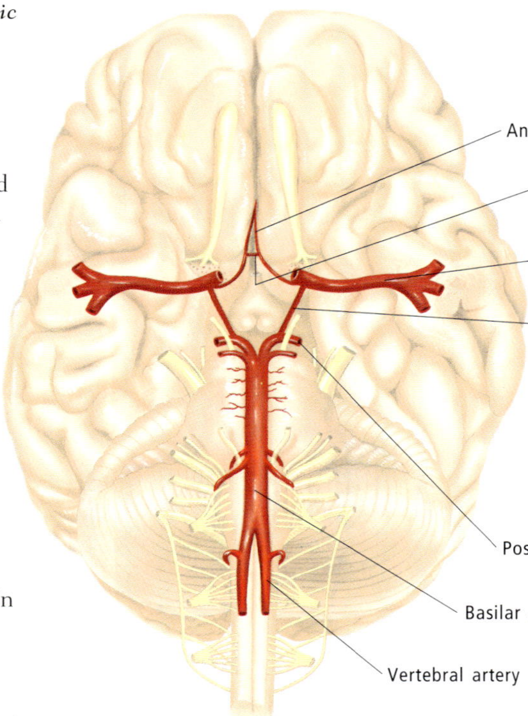

Arteries of the base of the brain

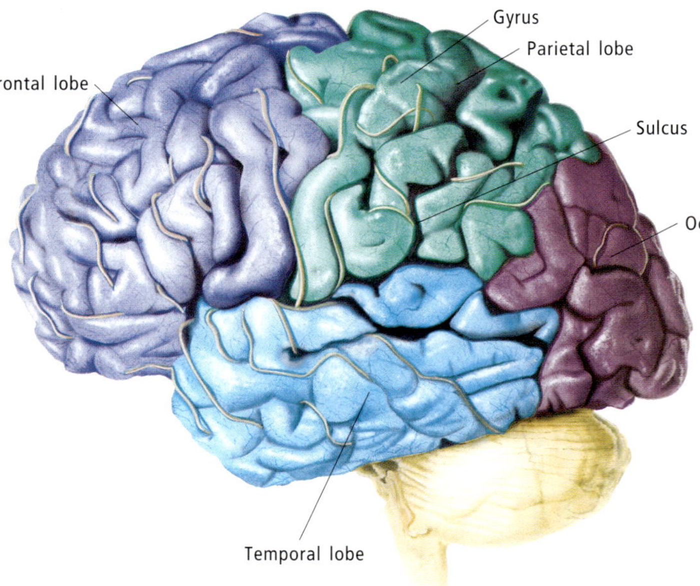

Lobes of the brain

The surface of the cerebral cortex (also called the cerebrum) is heavily folded. A ridge on the surface of the cortex is called a gyrus. A groove is called a sulcus if shallow, or a fissure if deep. Fissures and sulci divide the cortex into separate functional areas called lobes.

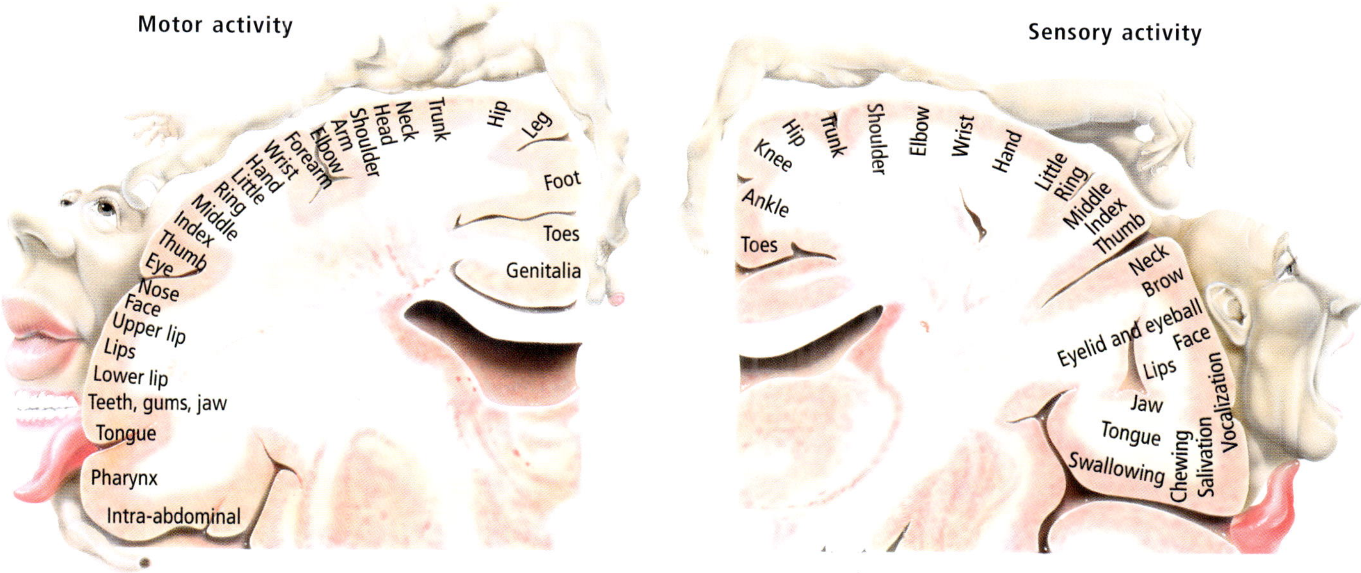

Organization of the motor and sensory areas of the cerebral cortex

The varying sizes of the body parts (top left) show the proportions of the precentral gyrus involved in motor activity in particular parts of the body, and (top right) the proportions of the postcentral gyrus involved in sensory activity in particular parts of the body.

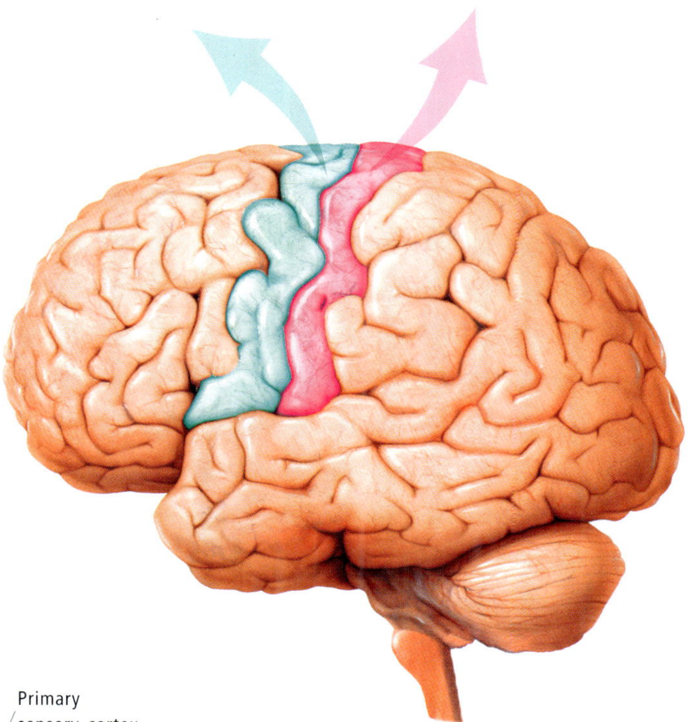

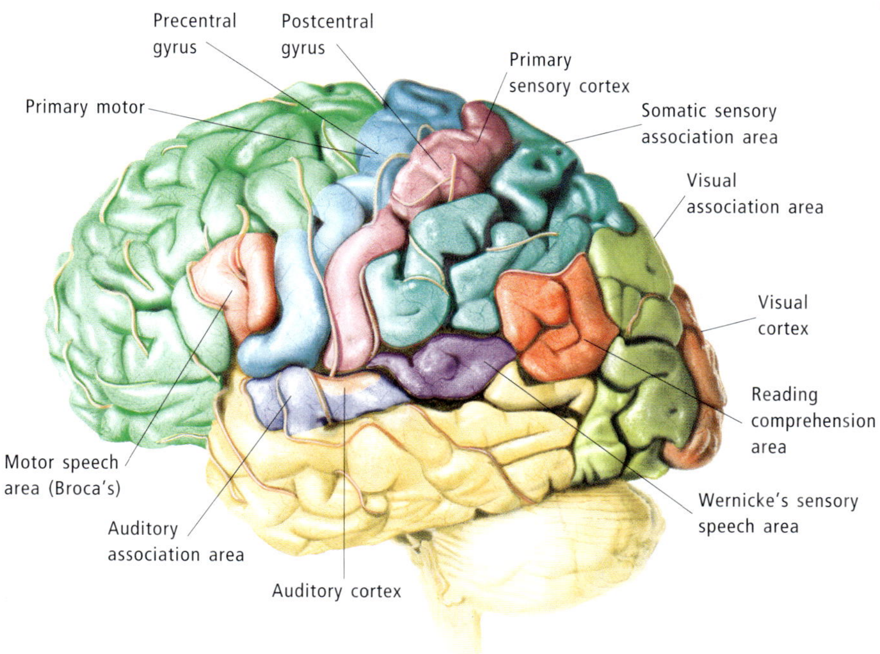

Functional areas

Particular regions of the cerebral cortex are associated with certain functions. For example, the precentral gyrus (motor cortex) is associated with the voluntary control of skeletal muscles, while the postcentral gyrus (sensory cortex) is associated with sensations from skin, muscles and joints.

B

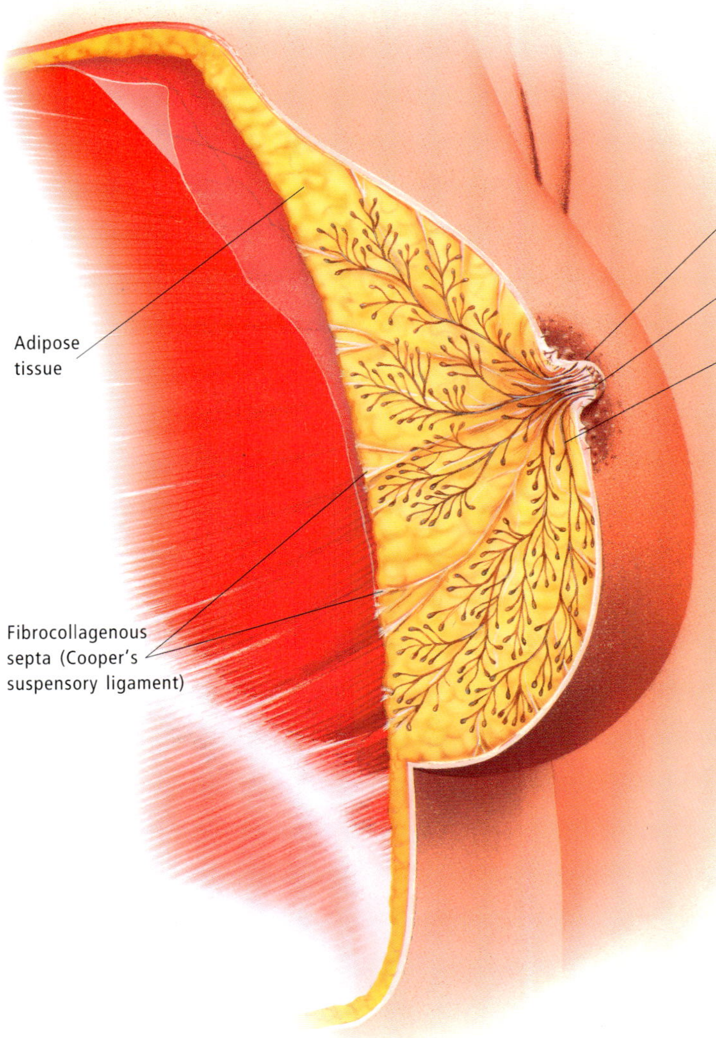

Normal breast

The development of breast tissue is governed by hormones, in particular the sex hormone estrogen. Towards the end of each menstrual cycle the breasts tend to swell and may become painful, but after menstruation, return to their normal size. After the menopause, the breasts usually shrink in size.

Breast abscess

A red, swollen, painful lump in the breast is usually a sign of a breast abscess. It often occurs if the nipples are cracked or inflamed, as bacteria can more easily enter the breast tissue.

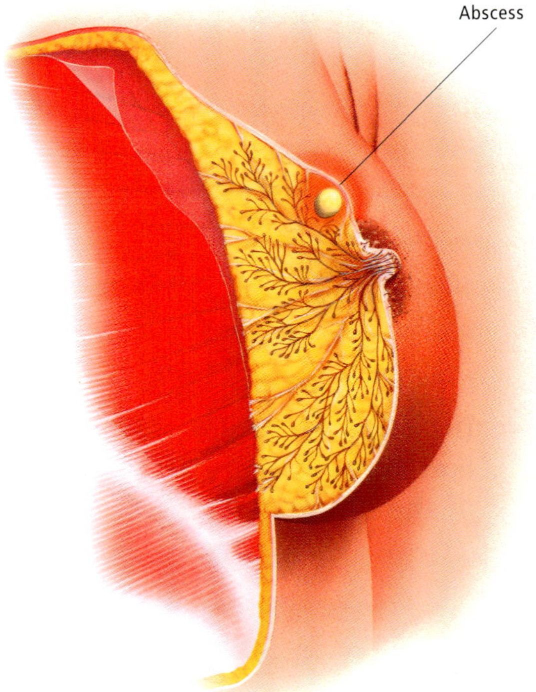

BRANCHIAL CYST

A branchial cyst is an abnormal cyst that lies just in front of one of the muscles (the sternocleidomastoid) in one side of the neck. It is caused by defective embryonic development of the second branchial cleft in the neck. Though present at birth, it is often not recognized until adolescence, when it tends to enlarge and become more noticeable. It may be left alone if it causes no symptoms, but if it makes an opening in the skin it may become infected or cause mucus to drain, so should be removed surgically.

BREAST

The breasts, or mammary glands, are two milk-producing organs situated on the chest. Normally only functional in the female, they are composed mainly of fat cells (cells capable of storing fat) interspersed with sac-like structures called lobules. These lobules are glands that can produce milk in females when stimulated by certain hormones such as prolactin. The lobules empty into a network of ducts (channels) that transport milk from the lobules to the nipple.

Differences in breast size and shape are largely due to inherited factors; also, being overweight increases the amount of fatty tissue in the breasts and hence their size. During puberty, the sex hormone estrogen causes the breasts to grow in size, due to the laying down of fat deposits. The breasts also get larger during pregnancy under the influence of estrogen. In pregnancy, the breasts grow in size by the same amount, regardless of whether the woman is normally small- or large-breasted.

Every woman should examine her breasts every month to check for any unusual lumps or other changes that might indicate cancer. It is best carried out a few days after menstruation, when the breasts are least swollen by estrogen. A woman who detects a lump should see her physician immediately.

Most breast lumps are not cancer, but are either solid fibroadenomas or fluid-filled cysts. Multiple cysts are often more prominent just before menstruation and are known as fibrocystic disease. A malignant (cancerous) lump feels hard, may be fixed to surrounding breast tissue, and may cause retraction of the skin or nipple. There may be a nipple discharge or bleeding. Lymph nodes under the armpit (axilla) on the same side may be enlarged and hard. Investigations, such as needle biopsy, mammography, ultrasonography and thermography, will confirm whether a lump is malignant or not.

Cancer and other conditions

The cause of breast malignancy is unknown. Risk factors include having a family history of breast cancer, early menarche (starting menstruation before age 12), late menopause (after age 55), never being pregnant, or having a first pregnancy after 30 years of age. Treatments may include lumpectomy, mastectomy (partial, total, or radical, i.e. extending to the armpit) and radiation therapy. Chemotherapy and hormonal therapy with antiestrogen drugs such as tamoxifen may also be used. After the procedure, except in the case of radical mastectomy, a breast implant or prosthesis may be inserted.

Reconstructive breast surgery is also used to enlarge or reshape breasts for cosmetic purposes. Breast implants consist of a silicone envelope with additional silicone gel or saline. While implants are not thought to cause autoimmune or connective tissue diseases as has been claimed, there are risks involved, including breast scarring, pain and misshapen breasts.

Mastitis is an inflammation of the breast. Acute mastitis is caused by a bacterial infection, which usually enters through a cracked nipple after childbirth, when the breast is swollen with milk. The breast feels hot, swollen and tender and the woman may have a fever. Treatment is with antibiotic drugs and analgesics. Breast feeding should continue if possible, as this keeps the breast ducts clear. Mastitis may progress to a breast abscess, in which case breast feeding should be stopped and the abscess treated.

Gynecomastia is the appearance of an enlarged breast or breasts in a male, usually occurring at puberty. It disappears naturally after six to twelve months, so needs no treatment. In older men, gynecomastia may be due to treatment with estrogens or steroids.

SEE ALSO *Breast cancer, Breast feeding, Estrogens, Fibroadenoma, Fibrocystic disease of the breast, Mammary glands, Mastectomy, Mastitis, Nipple, Pregnancy, Puberty*

BREAST CANCER

Cancer of the breast is the most important malignant tumor in women. It is by far the most common cancer in women in the economically developed nations of the world, where approximately one woman in ten will develop the disease. (Cancer of the cervix is almost as common in many developing nations.) Breast cancer is also one of the leading causes of cancer death in women (the other is lung cancer). Men can develop breast cancer, but this is approximately 100 times less common than in women.

Causes

Except during pregnancy and breast feeding, there are no functional milk-producing glands in the breast. There are, however, branching tubes called ducts which radiate out from the nipple and subdivide into smaller and smaller ducts. It is the layer of cells lining these small ducts that gives rise to almost all breast cancers. As is the case for most cancers, not enough is understood about how breast cancers develop, but two influences do seem to be important. Firstly, the growth and division of the lining cells of the ducts is controlled by hormones (especially estrogen), and stimulation of cell growth by a relative excess of estrogen (without a counterbalancing effect of progesterone) may create an environment in which breast cancer is more likely to develop. This could explain why breast cancer is often associated with other non-cancerous lumps in the breast. It could also account for the greater risk of breast cancer later in life, in association with early onset of menstruation and late menopause, in women who have not had children and in women whose first child was born relatively late.

Secondly, some breast cancers arise because of genetic factors. Genes associated with a familial risk of developing breast cancer have been identified. Despite this, environmental influences are probably much more important in causing breast cancer, but we have very little knowledge about exactly which factors play a role or how they affect an individual's risk of developing the tumor.

How breast cancer develops

Most breast cancers develop in women aged over 30 years and arise either in the upper outer part of the breast (which includes tissue that extends into the armpit) or in tissue immediately underlying the nipple. At first, the tumor cells grow entirely within the ducts of the breast, but later they invade through the walls of the ducts and into the surrounding fat and connective tissue. Still later, breast cancer cells enter the lymphatic vessels and spread to the nearest groups of lymph nodes which include nodes present in the connective tissue of the armpit and nodes in the area above the collar bone. At about the same time, the cells may enter blood vessels and thus spread to the lungs, or throughout the body.

Early diagnosis is critical to the outcome of breast cancer. Some of these tumors are more rapidly growing than others and more likely to spread. However, the stage at which a breast cancer is diagnosed is the single most important factor that determines the course of the disease and the patient's chances of survival. Tumors diagnosed at the stage where the cancer cells are still confined to the walls of the ducts can be treated very effectively. In such cases, the likelihood of the patient surviving at least five years from the time of diagnosis is over

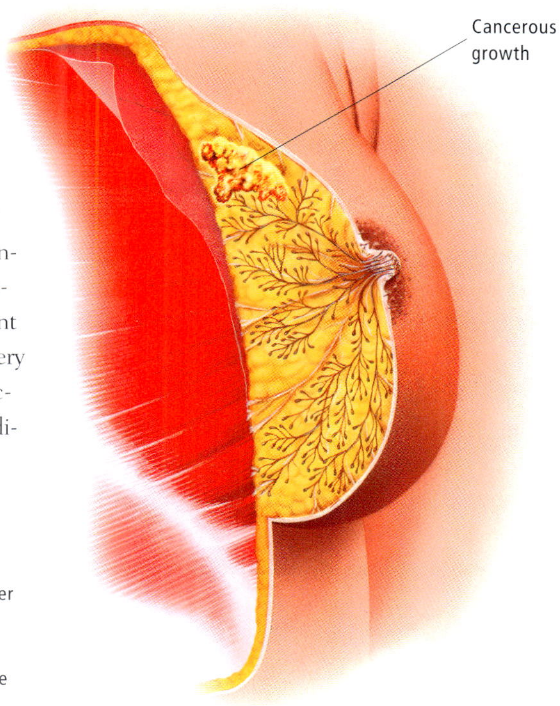

Breast cancer

The most common indication of a breast cancer is a hard lump in the breast that is often immovable. The skin over the lump may look dimpled, the nipple may turn inward and there may be lumps under the arm.

90 percent. Once the cancer cells have spread to nearby lymph nodes, the survival figure drops considerably. When tumors are diagnosed at the stage when secondary cancer is widespread, the five-year survival rate is less than 15 percent.

Unfortunately, breast cancers may not produce obvious symptoms until relatively late, by which time they may have spread too far for effective treatment. Therefore, an active effort to identify them at an early stage must be made. Two useful approaches to achieving early identification are self-examination for the presence of a lump, and screening by mammography. To make a reliable diagnosis, any mass that is detected must be sampled for microscopic examination. This may involve removal of cells using a fine needle, removal of a core of tissue using a biopsy needle, or complete removal of the lump. The pathologist can provide information about the likely behavior of an individual cancer based on the appearance of the cells.

Current treatment for breast cancer involves much less removal of tissue by surgery than was the case 20 or 30 years ago. Radiation therapy, chemotherapy and hormonal therapy all have a place in modern management. Newer treatments being tested include drugs and antibodies that can block signals to cancer cells.

SEE ALSO *Biopsy, Breast, Cancer, Lumpectomy, Mammography, Mastectomy*

BREAST FEEDING

Breast feeding means feeding a baby with milk directly from the mother's breast. Within each breast are about 15 to 20 milk glands, or lobules, in clusters. It is here that the milk is produced. From the alveoli, canals called ductules lead into larger canals called milk ducts and the milk flows through these to pools which lie under the areola, the brown circle around the nipple. The baby takes the whole of the nipple into its mouth and milks the breast by pressing and pumping the milk from these pools.

One of the first actions of the healthy human baby after birth is to seek its mother's nipple. The first "milk" is actually a nutrient- and antibody-rich yellowish substance known as colostrum. Only after two or three days will real milk start to appear. This will provide all the nourishment, both food and drink, which the baby will need for the next four to six months. Ideally, babies should be breast fed for six to twelve months, but even just a few weeks of breast feeding will get them off to a good start.

Breast feeding is a learned skill for both mother and baby, and without some family support and knowledgeable advice many mothers encounter difficulties. However, many more mothers have no problems and find breast feeding a very pleasurable and rewarding experience. Breast milk is a unique, constantly changing substance containing antibodies, hormones, enzymes, growth factors and immunoglobulins, as well

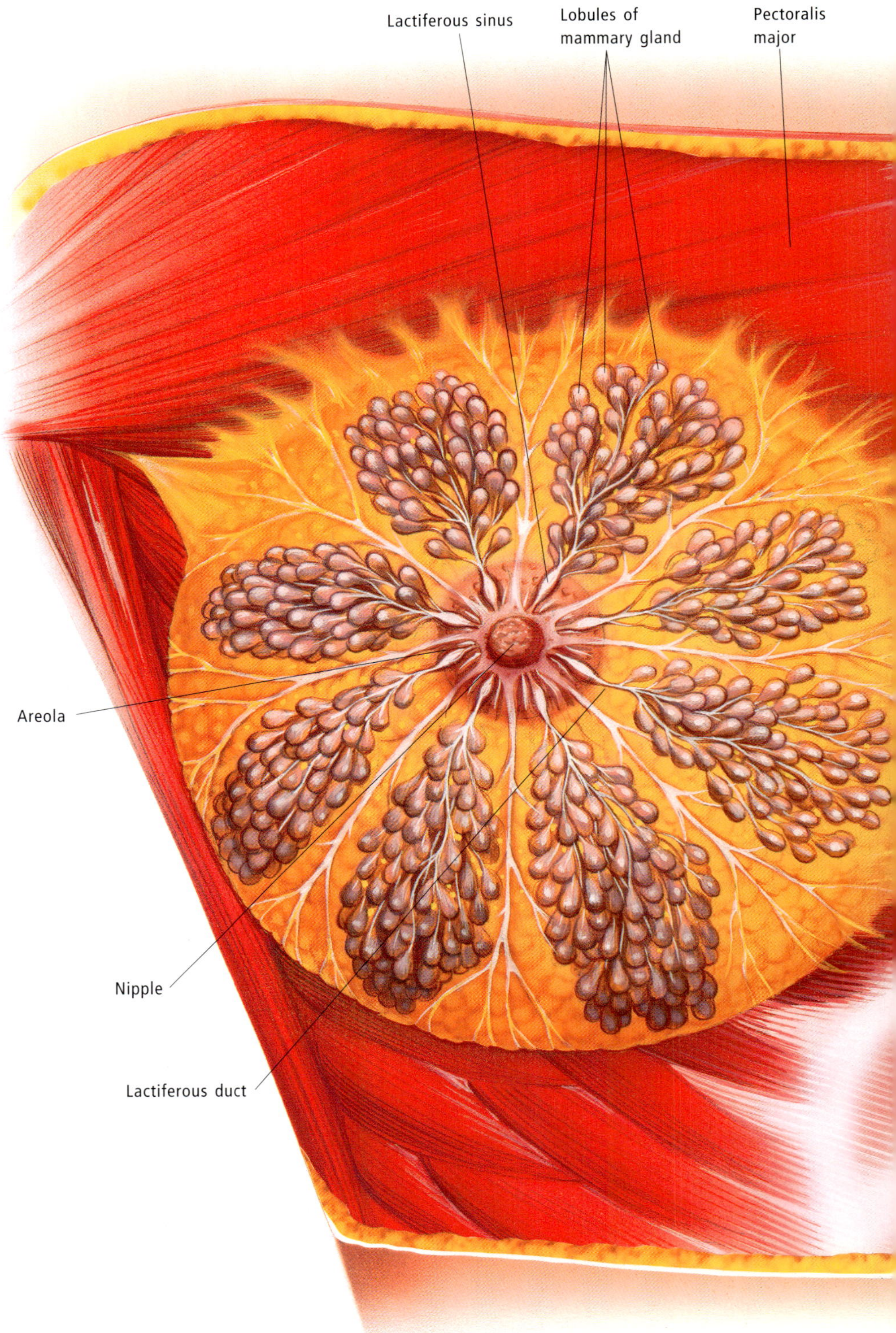

as vital nutrients. The keys to successful breast feeding are correct positioning of the baby—chest to chest and chin to breast—in a relaxed and comfortable environment, allowing the baby to feed for as long and often as necessary, understanding how the human body produces milk and how it is released, and having the support and advice of someone who understands how to breast feed. The breast feeding mother knows her baby is getting enough milk if the baby wets six to eight diapers a day, has pale yellow urine, is bright-eyed, grows steadily and feeds well at the breast.

One of the most common reasons women stop breast feeding is reduced milk supply: very few women are actually unable to breast feed. The only way to increase the amount of breast milk available is to breast feed. Supplementing a baby's feeds with artificial baby milk will decrease the demand for breast milk and result in a subsequent drop in supply. To keep up her milk supply, it is important that the mother drinks plenty of water, gets as much rest as possible, and eats healthy, nutritious food. Women also stop breast feeding because of sore, cracked nipples or breast infection (mastitis). However, these problems can be remedied with medical treatment.

Breast milk can be "expressed" (pumped) by hand or by using a hand-operated or electric pump. This milk, if stored correctly, can then be fed to the baby in a bottle, or for sick or premature (pre-term) babies via a tube. Expressing milk allows the mother some time away from her baby, which is important if she must return to the workforce. Many companies in industrialized countries now make provisions for women to continue to breast feed their babies after they return to work.

Artificial baby milks, if mixed according to directions, can be bottle fed to babies if breast feeding is unsuccessful or not desirable. They are nutritionally complete but they do not contain all the properties of breast milk. The woman who breast feeds has a lower risk of breast and ovarian cancer, osteoporosis and heart disease. Breast feeding is convenient, costs little or nothing and helps the mother's body to return to its pre-pregnant shape. Both mother and baby benefit from the intimacy of the close physical contact, which is an important part of the bonding process.

SEE ALSO *Breast, Bottle feeding, Infancy, Mastitis, Newborn, Nipple, Nutrition*

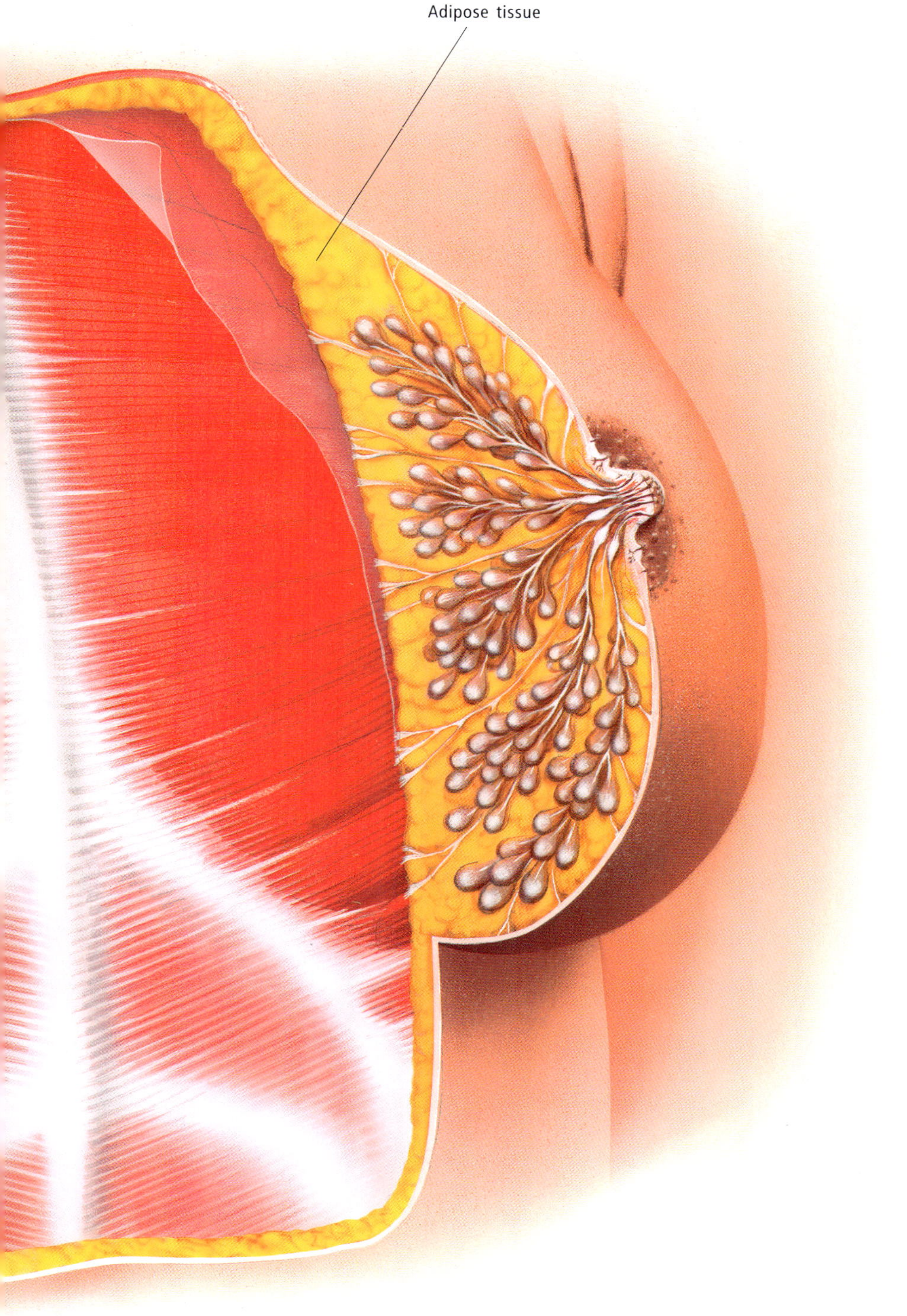

Breast feeding

In the days following childbirth the alveoli and ducts of the mammary glands fill with milk, a process controlled by a pituitary hormone called prolactin. When the baby sucks at the nipple another pituitary hormone, oxytocin, causes cells in the lactiferous ducts and sinuses to contract, ejecting milk.

B

BREATHING

Breathing—also known as respiration or ventilation—is the inspiration and expiration of air into and out of the lungs, by the contraction and relaxation of the diaphragm, the chest wall and abdominal wall. Breathing is the means by which a person absorbs oxygen from the air through the lungs into the bloodstream, and exhales carbon dioxide from the bloodstream through the lungs into the air.

At rest, the average person (at sea level) breathes 10 to 15 times a minute. In times of stress, or during exercise or other physical activity, the demand for oxygen by tissues is greater, and breathing is deeper and faster. Respiration is more labored at higher altitudes (unless the person is acclimatized) and during the later stages of pregnancy. Lung disorders such as asthma, chronic bronchitis, pneumonia or cancer may interfere with breathing and cause shortness of breath (dyspnea). An inhaled foreign body in the lung can also cause dyspnea. Breathing may also be slowed or may cease (apnea) in brain damage, poisoning, drug overdose or cardiac arrest. If breathing stops, oxygenation of the blood ceases, and irreversible brain damage or even death may occur in four to six minutes.

Breathing problems

In some situations, a person may breathe too fast. Rapid breathing (hyperventilation) is most commonly caused by anxiety, and produces dizziness, lightheadedness, a sense of unsteadiness and tingling around the mouth and fingertips. Symptoms subside when the person breathes in and out of a paper bag (to increase carbon dioxide levels in the blood). Hyperventilation can also occur in a condition known as metabolic acidosis, associated with diabetes, kidney disorders or starvation.

Cheyne-Stokes respiration is an abnormal breathing pattern with shallow, infrequent breathing that progresses to deep rapid breathing and then back to shallow breathing. It is seen in seriously ill patients with brain or heart disorders or during sleep.

Tests are available that can measure whether ventilation is adequate. Spirometry is a test using an instrument called a spirometer, which measures how well the lungs take in air, how much air they hold, and how well the lungs exhale air. A peak flow meter is a smaller device that measures resistance to breathing seen in disorders such as asthma and bronchitis. Both tests can be performed in the doctor's office. In cases of severe dyspnea, a blood test can determine oxygen and carbon dioxide levels in the blood.

Resuscitation

Artificial respiration (mouth-to-mouth or mouth-to-nose resuscitation) is a lifesaving method used to restore breathing to a person whose breathing has stopped, usually because they have almost drowned or have suffered a cardiac arrest. It may also be used in cases of poisoning, stroke, smoke inhalation, electrocution, suffocation and coma.

Mechanical ventilation is the use of a machine called a ventilator (or respirator) to introduce air into the airways. The patient is connected to the ventilator by a tube passed through the nose or mouth into the trachea (windpipe). The tube is sometimes inserted through an opening made in the trachea.

SEE ALSO *Asthma, Bronchitis, Dyspnea, Lungs, Respiratory system, Tracheostomy*

Moving oxygen around the body

Blood travels continuously through two different types of circulatory systems: the pulmonary (lung) and the systemic (body) circulations. The heart pumps deoxygenated blood from the veins of the systemic circulation into the arteries of the pulmonary circulation. This blood is oxygenated by the lungs and then flows back to the heart to be pumped into the arteries of the systemic circulation. Once the oxygen has been extracted by the body's tissues, the blood flows back to the heart and is pumped again into the pulmonary circulation.

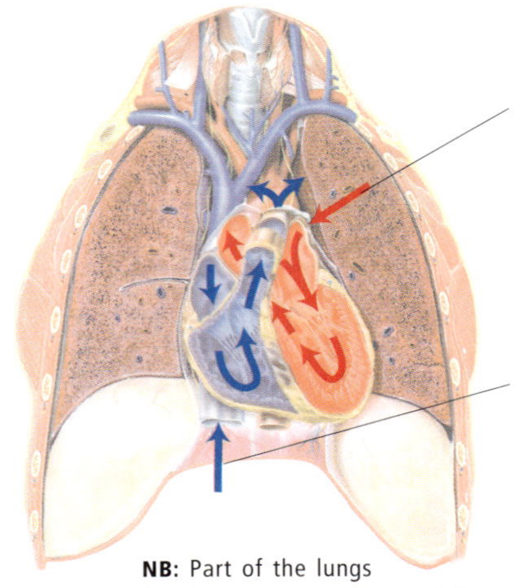

NB: Part of the lungs has been removed to reveal the pleura covering the diaphragm

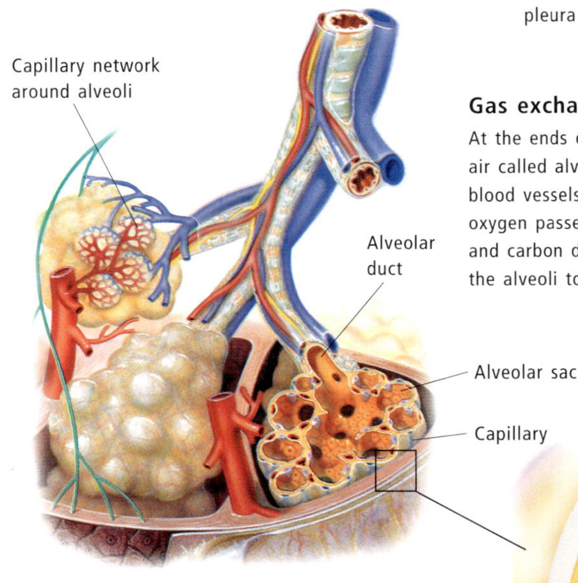

Gas exchange in the alveoli

At the ends of the airways are tiny sacs full of air called alveoli. They are surrounded by small blood vessels called capillaries. It is here that oxygen passes from the air into the bloodstream and carbon dioxide passes from the blood into the alveoli to be breathed out.

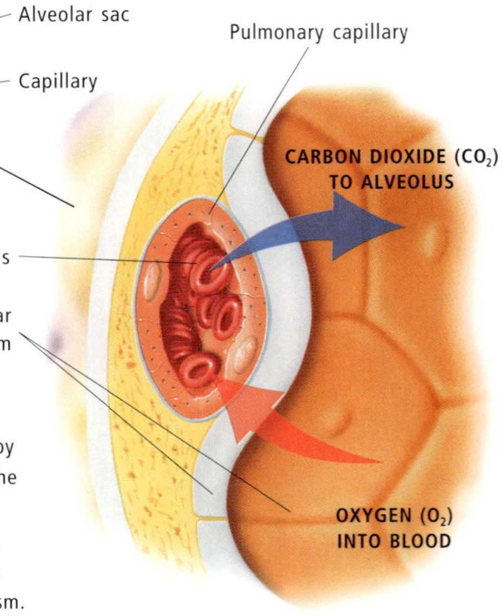

Oxygenation at cell level

Red blood cells carry oxygen into the bloodstream by combining it with a protein called hemoglobin. In the alveoli, red blood cells carry oxygen away to the tissues and pass carbon dioxide back to the alveoli. When it reaches the tissues, the oxygen is released, absorbed by the cells and used in cellular metabolism.

B

Breathing

Respiration is the name given to the act of breathing. It also refers to the transfer of oxygen from the lungs to the body's tissues, and of carbon dioxide from the tissues to the lungs.

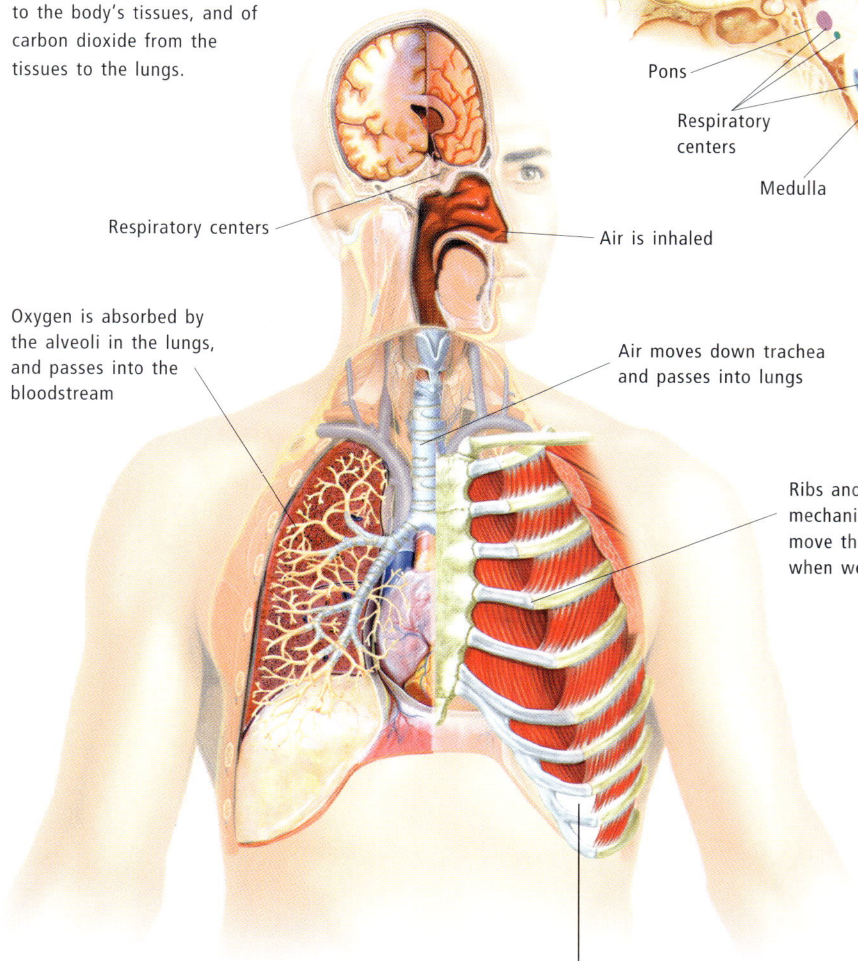

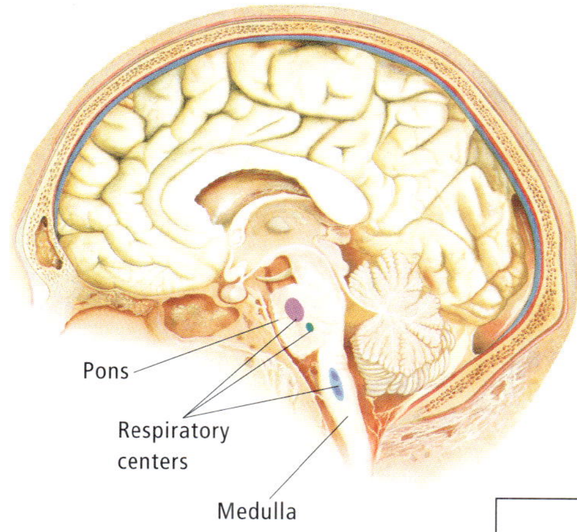

Respiratory centers in the brain

Specialized areas in the pons and the medulla receive information about blood carbon dioxide and blood oxygen levels from monitors elsewhere in the body. These respiratory centers send messages to the respiratory muscles to increase or decrease the rate and depth of breathing.

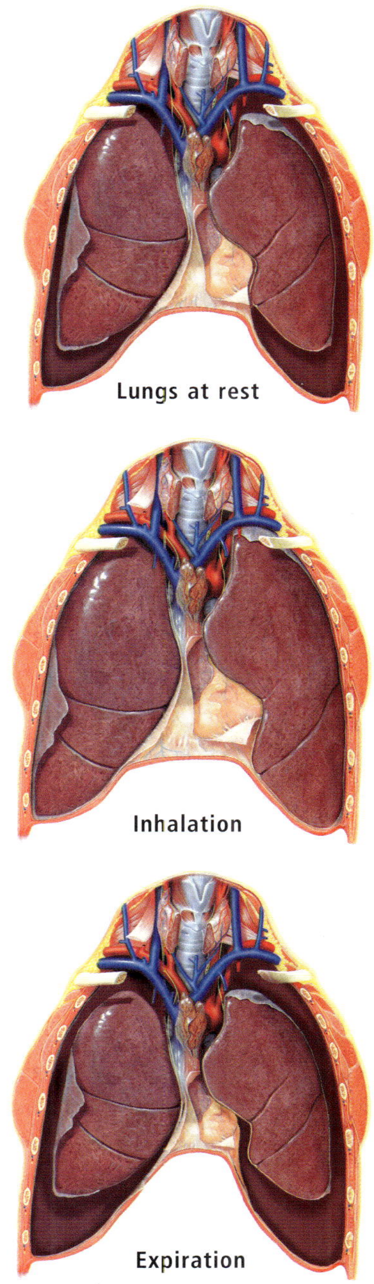

When we breathe in, the intercostal muscles move the ribs upwards and outwards and the diaphragm pushes downwards. This draws air into the expanded lungs.

Breathing muscles

Breathing is caused by the actions of the intercostal muscles (the muscles between the ribs) and the diaphragm, a muscular dome that separates the abdomen from the chest.

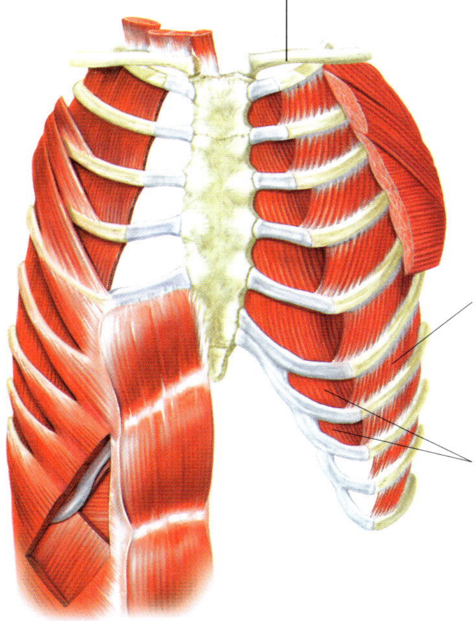

B

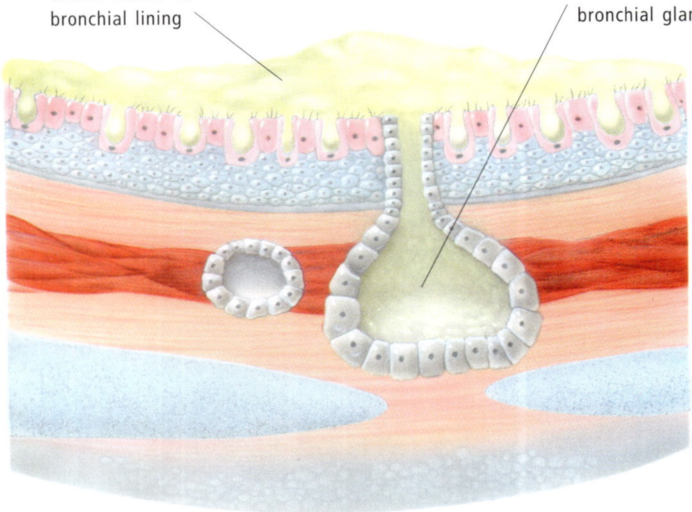

Bronchitis

In bronchitis, the walls of the airways (the bronchi) become inflamed. The glands then secrete excessive amounts of mucus, which may be coughed up as sputum. Bacterial bronchitis produces thick, yellow or greenish sputum; in viral bronchitis the sputum is thin and clear.

BRONCHITIS

This term bronchitis literally refers to inflammation of the large airways (bronchi). In practice, it is used to describe two quite separate disease processes.

Acute bronchitis is an inflammation of the major airways, usually following upper respiratory infection by a virus such as influenza, causing cough and production of sputum. It generally clears up by itself, unless a bacterial infection also occurs, in which case the sputum usually becomes thick and yellow. Because acute bacterial bronchitis can lead to the development of pneumonia, especially in elderly patients, treatment with antibiotics is advisable.

Chronic bronchitis results from inhalation of airborne irritants over a long period. By far the most common cause of this disease process is cigarette smoking, although it can also be triggered by repeated exposure to high levels of dusts, irritant gases or other pollutants. In the early stages of chronic bronchitis (simple chronic bronchitis) the main change in the large airways is not inflammation, but rather an increase in mucus secretion by cells lining the airways and glands within the airway walls. This leads to cough and the production of white or clear sputum (mucus secretion). There is often also bacterial infection and inflammation, which may cause coughing up of yellowish or greenish sputum that is a mixture of mucus and pus (mucopurulent bronchitis).

In some people, continuing exposure to the inhaled irritant leads to progressive involvement of smaller airways. This is an important complication because it causes widespread inflammation and scarring of the walls of these airways, leading to narrowing which limits the flow of air (chronic obstructive bronchitis). The person becomes increasingly breathless. To make matters even worse, the damage is usually not limited to the airways. The irritants that trigger chronic bronchitis usually also damage and destroy the alveoli of the lung in parallel, leading to the development of emphysema, which causes even more breathlessness.

The combination of chronic bronchitis and emphysema, which is referred to by terms such as chronic obstructive lung disease and chronic airflow limitation, may also overlap with asthma (asthmatic bronchitis). Eventually, these forms of chronic respiratory disease may be complicated by development of heart failure. They are major causes of chronic disability and death.

Because damage to the small airways and the lungs is difficult or impossible to reverse, stopping smoking or avoiding exposure to other inhaled irritants is by far the most important step a person can take to ensure that severe disease does not develop. In the early stages of chronic bronchitis, stopping smoking can lead to complete disappearance of symptoms. In the late stages, treatment with antibiotics, anti-inflammatory agents, bronchodilators and oxygen may be required.

SEE ALSO *Asthma, Bronchus, Cough, Emphysema, Pneumonia, Smoking*

BRONCHODILATORS

These are drugs used for treatment of asthma. Following inhalation, they provide rapid relief of breathlessness by relaxing the smooth muscle that surrounds the airways. Most bronchodilators are short-acting and are used for temporary relief of acute symptoms—more than one dose may be necessary. These drugs do not treat the airway inflammation that is the basis of asthma and so should be used in combination with anti-inflammatory agents.

Long-acting bronchodilators are also used but they are not rapidly effective, and therefore are not useful for treating an acute attack of asthma. They can, however, be used in combination with anti-inflammatory drugs.

SEE ALSO *Anti-inflammatory drugs, Asthma*

BRONCHOSCOPY

In bronchoscopy, the patient is anesthetized and the airways are examined by insertion of a tube called a bronchoscope. Modern bronchoscopes are flexible and equipped with a fiberoptic illumination system.

Tissue and cell samples can be obtained from the major airways and, by infusing and removing fluid, from the more peripheral parts of the lung as well. This makes the bronchoscope a valuable tool for the diagnosis of a variety of diseases of the airways and lungs, especially lung cancer. In addition, foreign bodies or other causes of obstruction of the airway tube can be removed using this instrument.

SEE ALSO *Lungs*

BRONCHUS

The trachea, or windpipe, branches at its lower end into two large (primary) air tubes—the right primary bronchus leading into the right lung, and the left primary bronchus serving the left lung. The route from the trachea through the right primary bronchus is more vertical, wider and shorter than it is to the left, and so inhaled objects are more likely to end up in the right lung.

The outer wall of each bronchus is supported by cartilage. The interior is lined with mucous membrane and many microscopic, mobile, hair-like projections called cilia that shift mucus and trapped particles upwards. An inflammation of the mucous membrane of a bronchus is called bronchitis.

At the lung's entrance, the primary bronchus branches into smaller (secondary) bronchi. These are also called lobar bronchi because one of them serves each lung lobe, of which there are usually three in the right lung and two in the left.

Each secondary bronchus divides into smaller (tertiary) bronchi. These split into bronchioles that separate into hair-like terminal bronchioles (of which there are about 64,000) ending at microscopic bubbles known as alveoli, where the exchange of carbon dioxide for oxygen occurs.

Together, all these branching air passages are referred to as the bronchial tree.

SEE ALSO *Alveolus, Bronchitis, Lungs, Trachea*

BRUCELLOSIS

Common in Spain, Mexico and South America but rare elsewhere, brucellosis is caused by contact with farm animals carrying the *Brucella* bacterium—usually cattle, goats, dogs or pigs.

Transmission to humans occurs through swallowing unpasteurized milk or other dairy products, or meat products, or by farm workers coming into contact with the placenta of an infected animal. Symptoms are mild fever, chills, sweating, muscle aches, tiredness and aching joints. Typically, the fever peaks every afternoon; hence the name "undulant fever". The disease may relapse and last for years.

Treatment is with antibiotics such as tetracycline or an aminoglycoside, often in combination. Pasteurization of dairy products and preventive measures for farm workers (such as vaccination of cattle and wearing of protective clothing) will generally prevent the disease.

BRUISE

A bruise (or contusion) is a discoloration of the skin. It occurs when blood vessels are damaged or broken as the result of a blow to the skin, such as bumping against something. The discoloration is caused by blood leaking out from damaged vessels into the skin. It first appears reddish, then, one or two days later, blue or purple. By day six, the color changes to green and after a week or so, the bruise will appear yellowish-brown. The skin color will return to normal in two to three weeks.

Bruising is usually more extensive in older persons, because of the greater fragility of blood vessels in older age groups. Some medications, especially those that cause bleeding such as aspirin and anticoagulants, make bruising more likely. Cortisone medications such as prednisone, clotting disorders like hemophilia, or liver diseases can also cause serious bruising and bleeding.

To prevent or minimize bruising after an injury, apply ice to the affected area. Apply pressure by hand or with a bandage, but do not use a tourniquet.

Bronchus

A bronchus is a tube that conducts air from the trachea to the lung tissue. The two main bronchi divide several times into smaller branches until they give rise to thin, delicate airways called bronchioles. These connect to small air sacs known as alveoli.

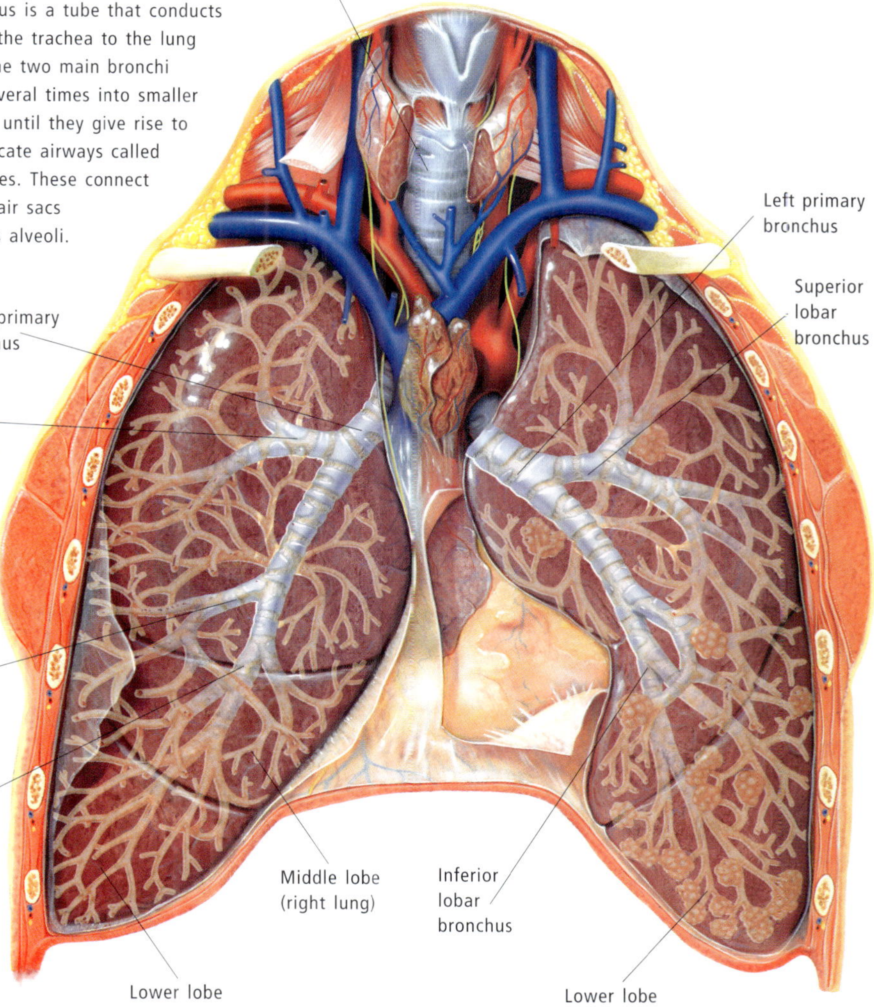

Bruise

Bruising is a discoloration of the skin that takes place after an injury. If bruising occurs frequently, for no apparent reason, it may indicate an underlying bleeding disorder.

B

B

BUNION

A bunion is a solid growth that forms a lump at the base of the big toe, or hallux. The lump results from friction and distortion of the first metatarsal bone, plus fluid and bony growths, where the bone meets the base of the big toe.

Although susceptibility to bunions is often inherited, there is no precise cause. They usually develop in middle age. Bunions can be tolerated and are not usually painful unless cramped by badly fitting footwear. Over-tight shoes will cause pain but have not been proven to actually cause bunions. Treatment is by surgery and is usually successful but recovery can be painful.

SEE ALSO *Foot*

Bunion

A bunion is a lump at the base of the big toe. If painful, it can be treated by wearing properly fitted shoes. If that does not ease the pain, surgery may be required.

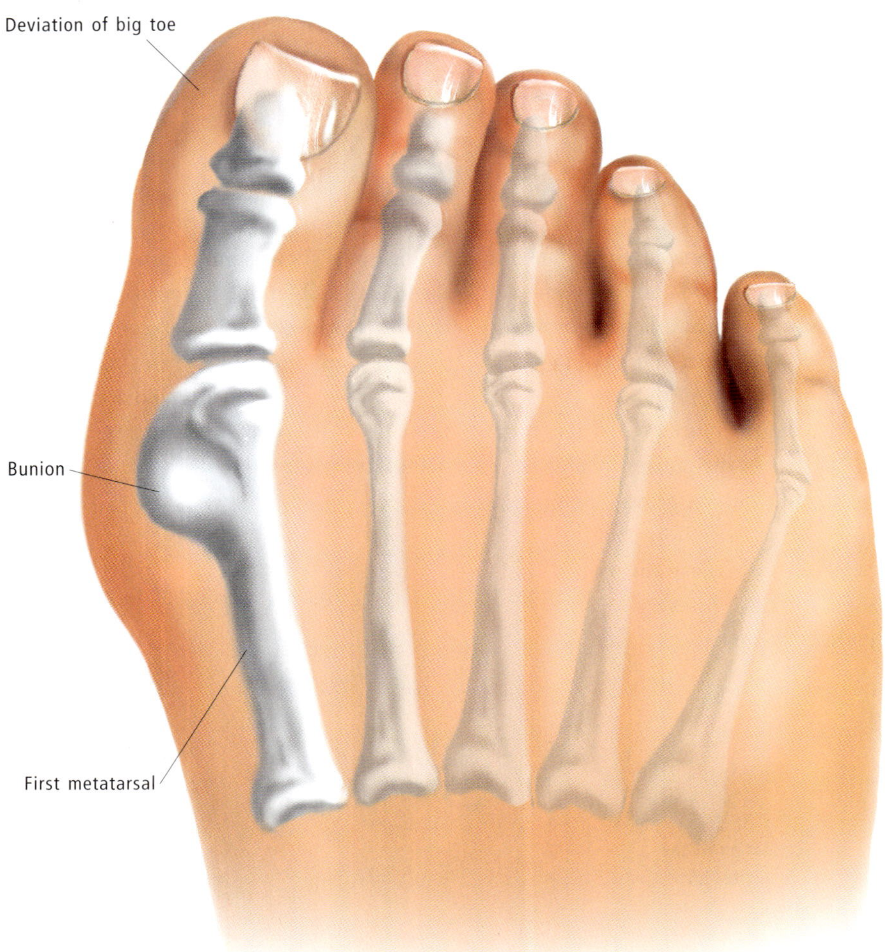

BURKITT'S LYMPHOMA

Burkitt's lymphoma, also known as B cell lymphoma, is a tumor of the lymph glands. It arises from a type of white blood cell called a B lymphocyte, although it is a different type of lymphoma from a Hodgkin's lymphoma. It is often associated with the Epstein-Barr virus (EBV), which causes infectious mononucleosis (glandular fever).

Burkitt's lymphoma is usually first noticed as a painless but rapid swelling of the lymph nodes in the neck or below the jaw (though lymph nodes in other areas may be affected). The diagnosis can be confirmed by biopsy of the node. Treatment involves a combination of radiation therapy and chemotherapy. The disease is often curable if it is treated in the early stages.

SEE ALSO *Biopsy, Infectious mononucleosis, Lymph nodes, Lymphocytes, White blood cells*

BURSITIS

A bursa is a small, fluid-filled sac-like structure, found mainly around joints, that protects bones and tendons from friction. Bursitis is inflammation of a bursa.

Bursitis often occurs in the shoulder, but it may also affect the knee (infrapatellar bursitis), elbow (olecranon bursitis), the back of heel (retrocalcaneal bursitis) or other areas. In most cases the cause is unknown, but it can be caused by injury, infection and repeated friction. Repeated attacks of bursitis or injury can cause chronic inflammation. Symptoms are pain and swelling over the area involved. Nearby joints are tender.

Bursitis is treated by rest, alternating cold and heat treatments and oral anti-inflammatory drugs. Occasionally, fluid may need to be aspirated from, and corticosteroids injected into, the bursa. Surgery is rarely required. If bursitis is caused by bacterial infection, it must be treated with antibiotics and surgical drainage of the infected bursa. As the pain eases, exercises are needed to build strength and increase mobility, especially if disuse or prolonged immobility has caused muscle wasting.

SEE ALSO *Joints*

BUTEYKO BREATHING TECHNIQUE

The Buteyko breathing technique was developed in the 1950s by Konstantin Buteyko, a Russian medical scientist, to treat asthma. This technique is based on the premise that asthma is the result of over-breathing (hyperventilation), which causes an activation of the defence mechanisms of the body in an attempt to constrict the abnormal breathing patterns. Asthmatic patients are therefore taught to recognize their own hyperventilation patterns and to return their breathing levels to normal. In encouraging nasal breathing the Buteyko technique also reduces inhalation of allergens. The technique is taught in a consecutive five-day course, and it is claimed that results can be achieved within the first three days.

SEE ALSO *Asthma, Breathing*

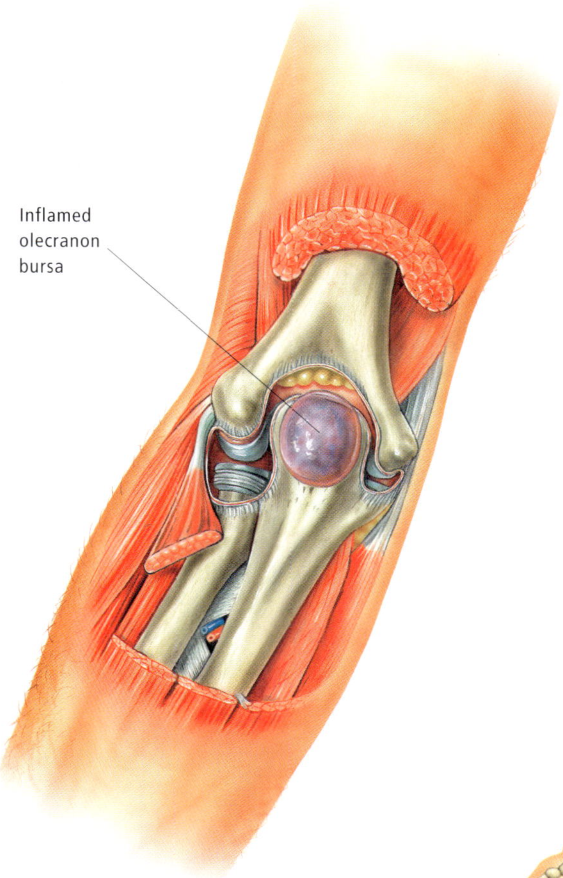

Bursitis

Bursitis in the elbow is called olecranon bursitis (the olecranon is the prominence at the upper part of the ulna where the bursa is situated). The bursa becomes hot, red and filled with fluid, which may need to be drawn out with a needle.

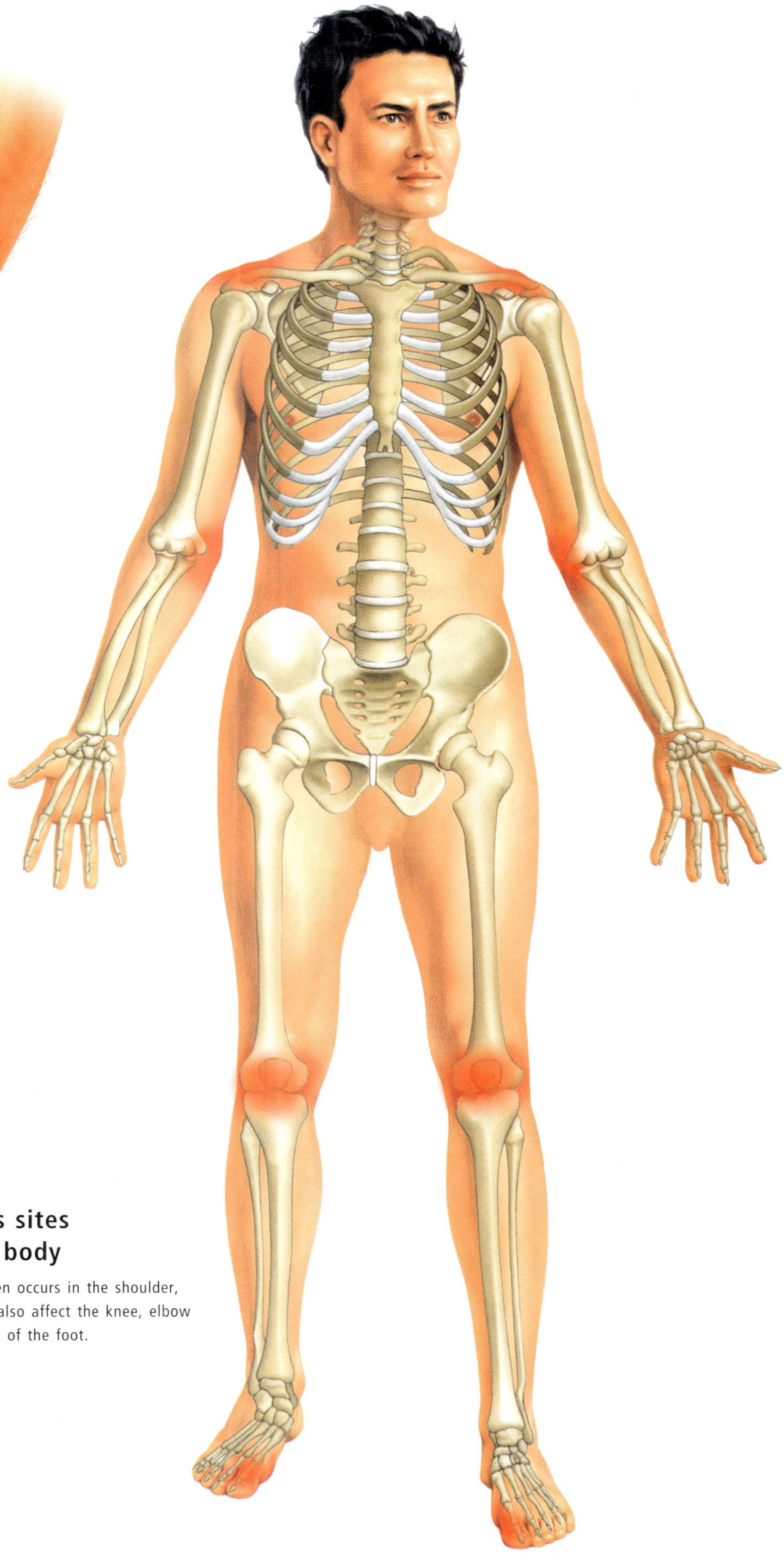

Bursitis sites on the body

Bursitis often occurs in the shoulder, but it may also affect the knee, elbow or the parts of the foot.

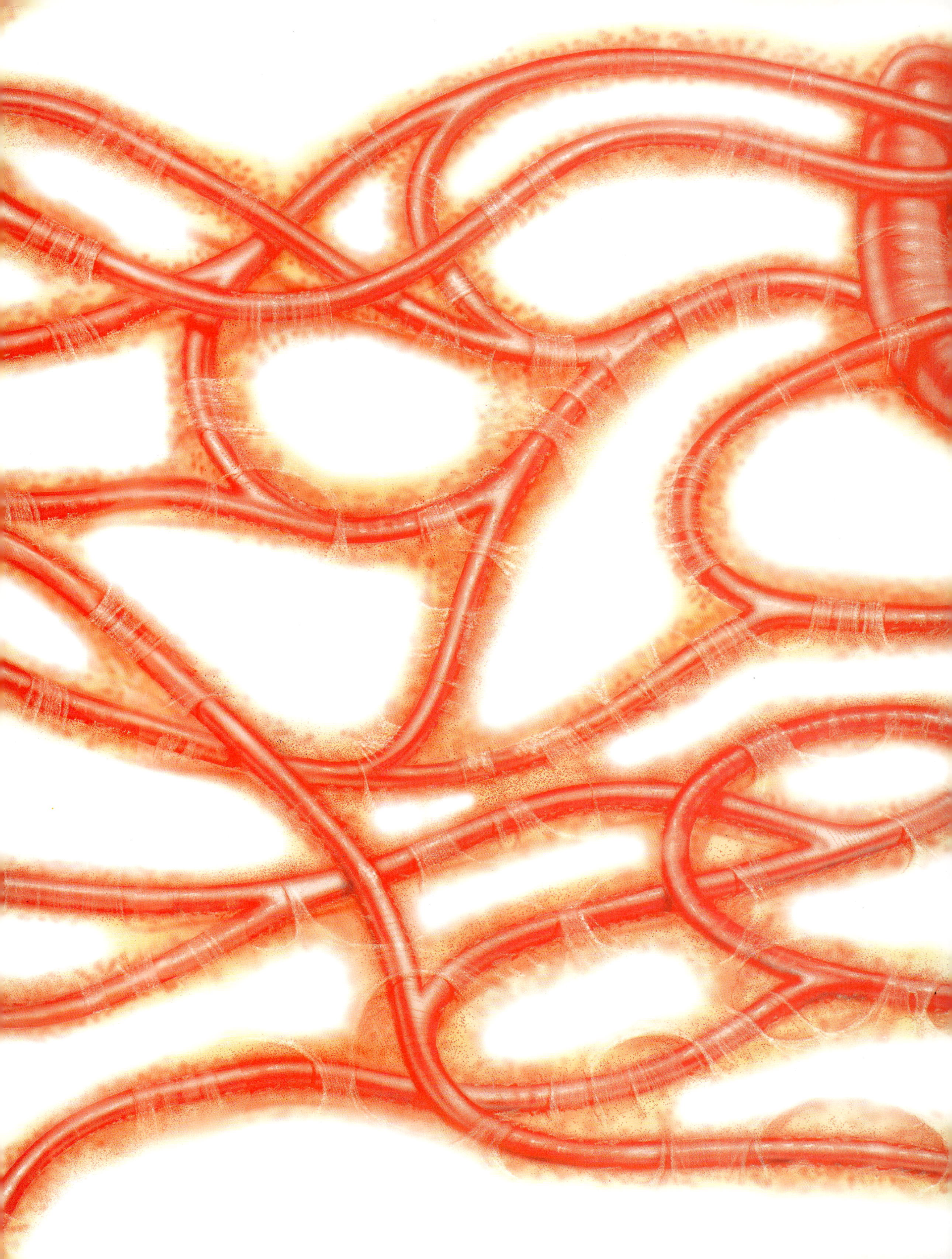

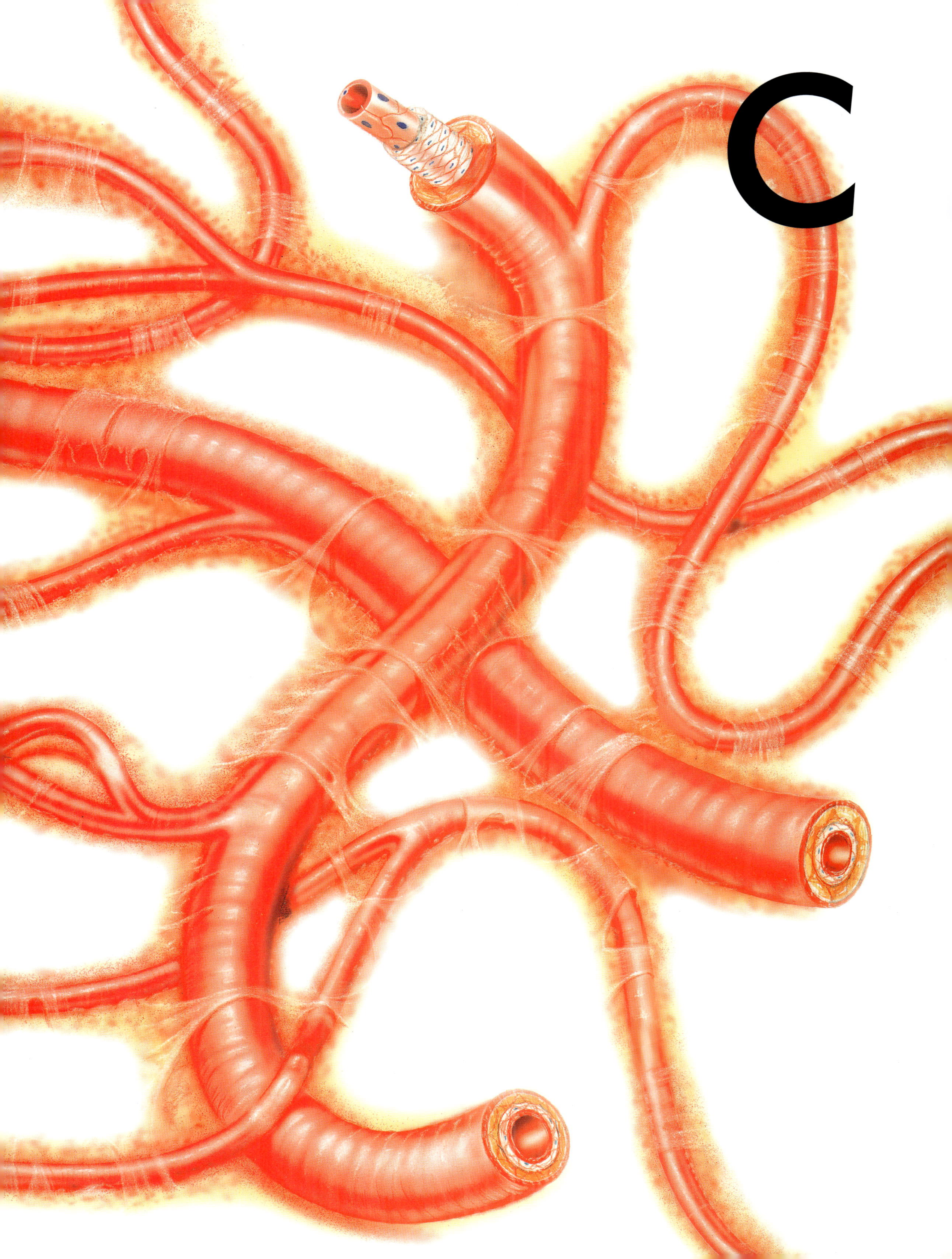
C

C

CAFFEINE

Caffeine tops the list of the world's most widely consumed drugs. It is a component of many foods and drinks, including coffee, tea, soft drinks (particularly colas), chocolate and guarana. Caffeine is also an ingredient in an extensive array of over-the-counter medications, such as treatments for allergies, headaches, migraines, muscle tension and colds. In some preparations it is designed to help people diet or stay awake.

Chemically, caffeine is an alkaloid—an organic compound containing nitrogen and derived from plants. Medically, it is regarded as a mild stimulant of the central nervous system. The physiological effects of caffeine include raised blood pressure and heart and respiration rates. It also increases the need to urinate.

A cup of coffee usually contains between 65 milligrams and 115 milligrams of caffeine. Behavioral impacts of low to moderate daily consumption of between 50 milligrams and 300 milligrams of caffeine are elevated alertness, energy and concentration levels. At higher doses, caffeine can cause adverse health effects such as anxiety, depression and insomnia. It is also possible to overdose on caffeine. A dose of about 10 grams of caffeine (equivalent to about 100 cups of strong coffee) would be fatal to most people.

Caffeine is widely considered within the medical profession to be a drug of both physical and psychological dependence. Like most addictive chemicals, people can develop tolerance to it and may suffer from withdrawal symptoms when they cease to use it. Physiological and behavioral reactions to caffeine withdrawal may include drowsiness, headaches, irritability, nausea, vomiting and depression.

SEE ALSO *Stimulants, Withdrawal*

CALCIUM

Calcium is found in bones and teeth, where it provides strength and rigidity. It is also found (in much smaller amounts) circulating in the blood and the cells, where it performs several important functions, including the regulation of the heartbeat, the transmission of nerve impulses, the contraction of muscles and the clotting of blood. Calcium occurs naturally in dairy products such as milk, cheese and yoghurt, leafy green vegetables such as broccoli, and fish such as salmon and sardines.

The absorption of calcium from the intestine is dependent on the presence in the body of sufficient quantities of vitamin D. The absorption and incorporation of calcium into bone from the bloodstream is regulated by parathyroid hormones, secreted by the parathyroid glands, and calcitonin, secreted by the thyroid gland.

Too little calcium in the blood (hypocalcemia) is usually caused by a parathyroid hormone deficiency or a vitamin D deficiency (rickets) in the body. Hypocalcemia causes muscle spasms (tetany), twitching or cramps, numbness and tingling in the extremities, seizures, and irregular heartbeat. Over the longer term, hypocalcemia causes thinning of the bones (osteoporosis) or the softening of bones (osteomalacia). The treatment is calcium and vitamin D supplements.

Too much calcium in the blood (hypercalcemia) can be caused by over-secretion of parathyroid hormones (hyperparathyroidism); by excessive ingestion of vitamin D; or by failure of the kidneys to secrete calcium (kidney failure). Symptoms of hypercalcemia are lethargy, delirium, and seizures. Over time, hypercalcemia may cause calcium deposits in soft tissues of the body, kidney stones, and hardening of the blood vessels. The treatment is to correct the underlying condition.

SEE ALSO *Bones, Hypocalcemia, Kidney, Nutrition, Osteomalacia, Osteoporosis, Parathyroid glands, Rickets, Teeth, Thyroid gland*

CALCIUM CHANNEL BLOCKERS

Calcium channel blockers (CCBs) are a group of prescription medications commonly used in the treatment of a range of heart and vascular (blood vessel) disorders. These include hypertension (high blood pressure), angina (chest pain caused by lack of oxygen to heart muscles) and certain types of arrhythmias (abnormal heart rhythms). They are also sometimes effective in treating certain types of migraines. CCBs work by obstructing the flow of calcium ions into vascular and heart muscle cells. This causes the muscle cells to relax. As a result the arteries dilate, which improves blood flow to the heart and leads to a drop in blood pressure. The heart rate is also slowed by some CCBs. There can be side effects associated with certain CCBs. These vary according to the drug used but may include swelling in the legs and dizziness.

SEE ALSO *Angina, Arrythmia, Arteries, Blood vessels, Heart, Hypertension, Migraine*

CANCER

Cancer (also called malignancy) is a disease in which normal cells become abnormal and grow uncontrollably, often metastasizing (spreading from the site of origin to other sites). A leading cause of death in many countries, only diseases of the heart and blood vessels kill more people than cancer in developed countries. It affects people of any age but is more common in middle and old age. There are over a hundred forms of cancer; most are named for the type of cell or the organ in which they arise. Almost any tissue in the body may become malignant, but the skin, the digestive organs, the lungs and the female breasts are particularly prone to cancer.

There are three main classifications of cancer. Carcinoma is cancer of the epithelial tissue that forms the skin and the linings of the internal organs. Sarcoma is cancer of connective tissue, such as cartilage, muscle or bone. Cancers of the bloodstream (leukemia) and the lymph system (lymphoma) are a third category.

A cancer by definition is malignant, that is, capable of spreading beyond its site of origin. (A benign tumor does not spread and is not malignant.) Cancer spreads by infiltrating the tissue around it, or by distant spread to other parts of the body via blood or lymph vessels, or both. Frequently it spreads to the lymph nodes that drain the tissues in which the tumor has arisen; breast cancer, for example, tends to spread to the lymph nodes in the axilla (armpit). When a cancer spreads beyond the tissue of origin to a distant site and forms a tumor, the new tumor is called a metastasis. Metastases are common in the liver, lung, bone and brain. They generally indicate a poorer expectancy or prognosis. Most cancers, if left alone, are fatal. However, advances in diagnosing and treating cancer have improved greatly over the past few decades. About one-third of all persons treated for cancer now recover completely (defined as surviving five years) or live much longer than they would have lived without treatment.

Skin cancer (including melanoma) is the most common type of cancer for both men and women in developed countries. The next most common type among men is prostate cancer; among women, it is breast cancer. Lung cancer is the leading cause of death from cancer for both men and women. Brain cancer and leukemia are the most common cancers in children and young adults.

The causes of cancer are not fully understood. Some cancers (including melanoma and cancers of the breast, ovary, and colon) tend to run in families. Others are known to be associated with certain risk factors; tobacco smoking is known to cause oral cancer and cancers of the larynx, lung, esophagus, pancreas, bladder, kidney, and cervix. Passive smoking, or exposure to smoke in the environment, increases the risk of lung cancer for non-smokers. A deficient diet may make cancer more likely. A high-fat diet may contribute to cancer of the breast, colon, uterus, and prostate. Obesity is associated with increased rates of cancer of the prostate, pancreas, uterus, colon and ovary, as well as increased rates of breast cancer in older women. Ultraviolet radiation from the sun and from other sources (such as sunlamps and tanning booths) may cause skin cancer, especially in those people with fair skin. Excess alcohol consumption may cause cancer of the mouth, throat, esophagus, larynx and liver. Chemicals and other substances in the workplace can cause cancer. Asbestos, nickel, cadmium, uranium, radon, vinyl chloride and benzene are examples of occupational carcinogens (cancer-causing substances). Radiation from medical x-rays can increase the risk of cancer.

In general, the sooner cancer is diagnosed and treated, the better the chance of survival. Regular medical checkups and self-examination of organs such as skin, testicles (in men) and breasts (in women) will increase the chance of early detection. Depending on age and gender, screening tests may be advised. These include Pap tests (a smear taken of cells of the cervix), mammograms (x-rays of the breast) and sigmoidoscopy (examination of the sigmoid colon). If there are signs and symptoms that suggest the possibility of cancer, the physician may order tests such as x-rays, ultrasound, MRI or CAT scans, endoscopy, and blood tests. A biopsy may be taken for examination by a pathologist. The tests will allow a cancer to be "staged", that is, rated according to how far it has spread. Local lymph node involvement or distant metastases indicate more advanced disease, with a correspondingly poorer outlook.

There are several approaches to treating cancer, which may be used alone or in combination with each other, depending on the type and location of the cancer, the stage of the disease, the person's age and general health. Surgery is frequently used to remove a primary tumor. The tissue around the

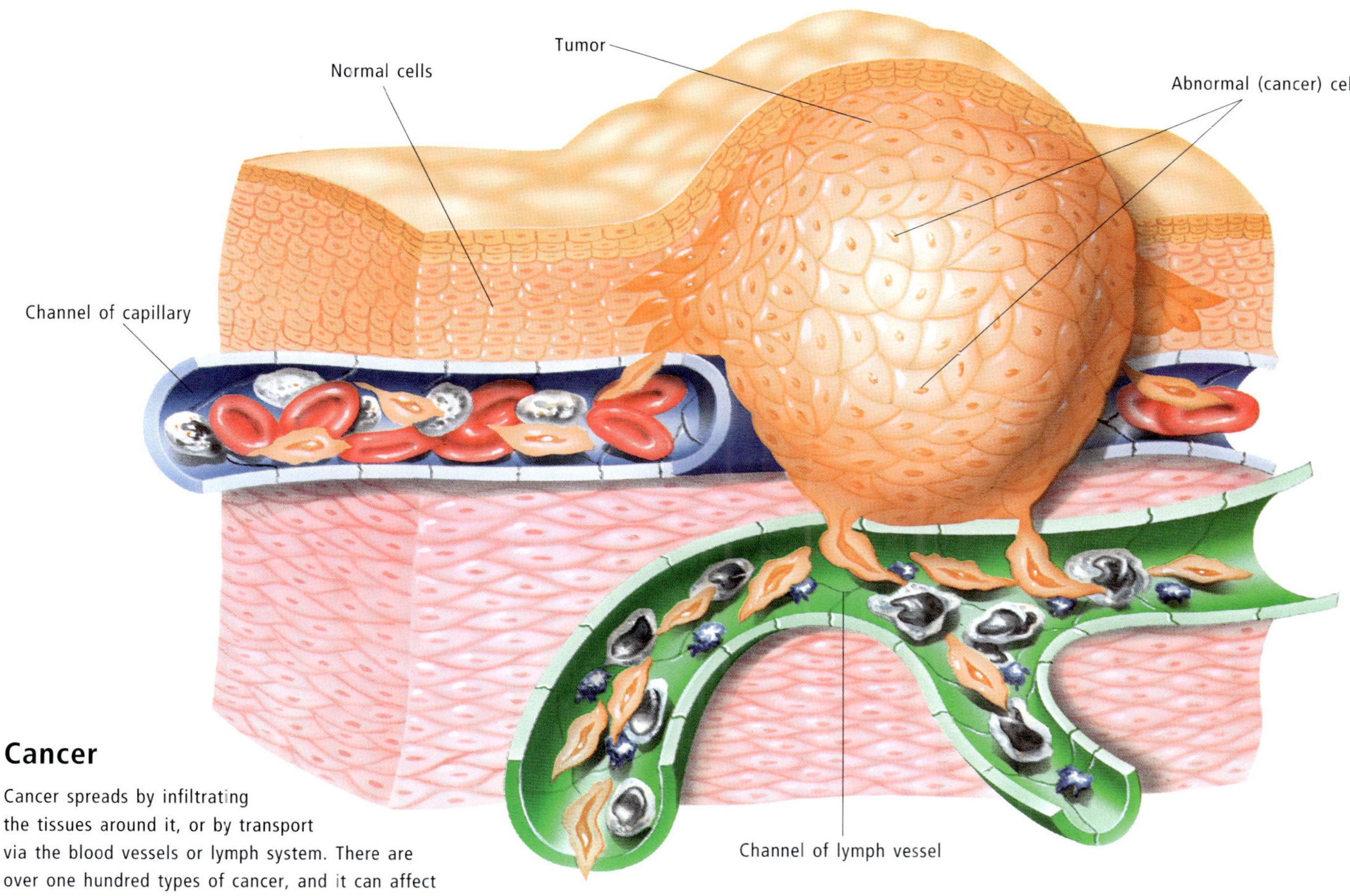

Cancer

Cancer spreads by infiltrating the tissues around it, or by transport via the blood vessels or lymph system. There are over one hundred types of cancer, and it can affect almost any site in the body. Cancer is more likely to develop when the immune system is not functioning normally.

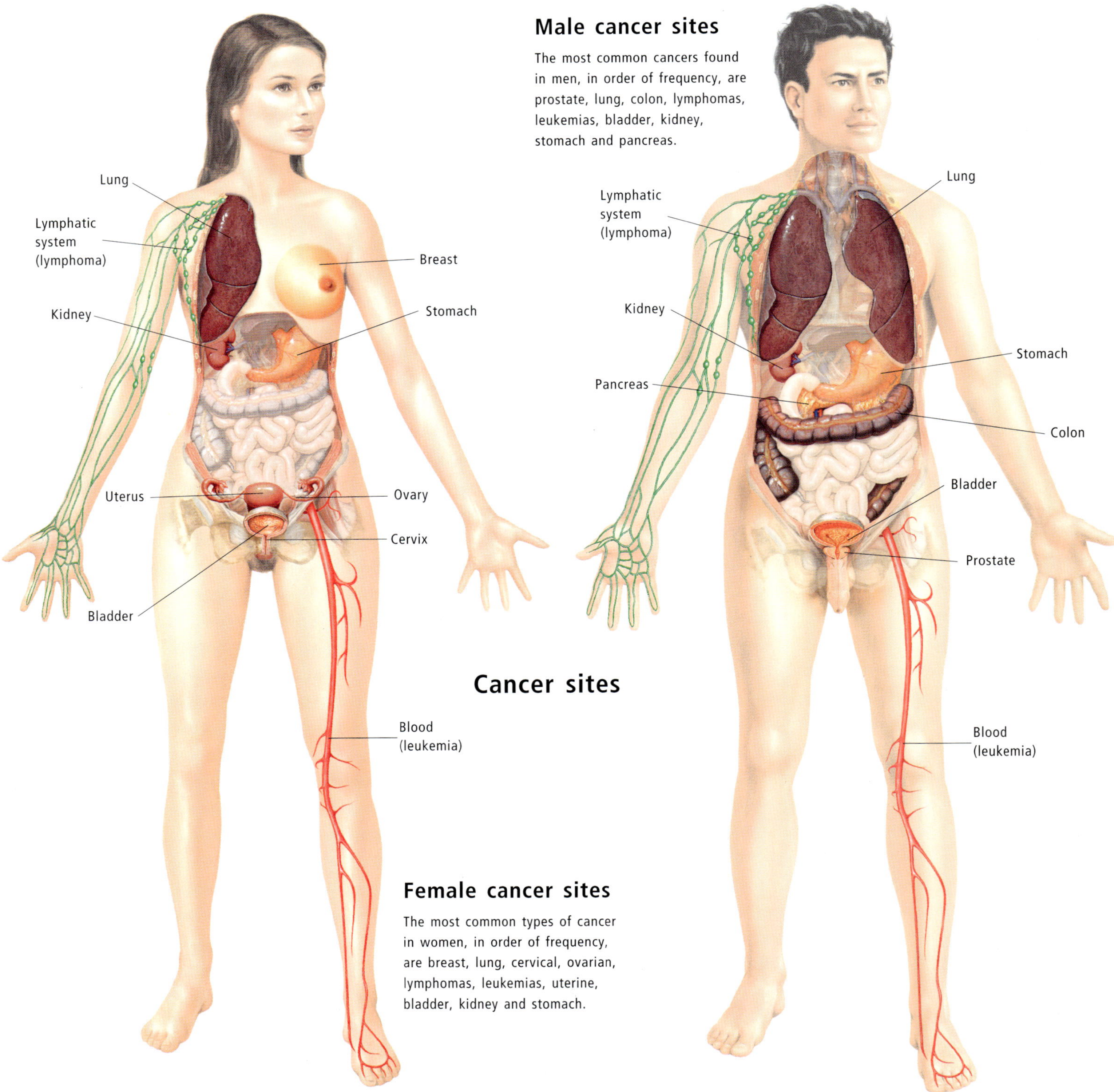

Cancer sites

Male cancer sites

The most common cancers found in men, in order of frequency, are prostate, lung, colon, lymphomas, leukemias, bladder, kidney, stomach and pancreas.

Female cancer sites

The most common types of cancer in women, in order of frequency, are breast, lung, cervical, ovarian, lymphomas, leukemias, uterine, bladder, kidney and stomach.

tumor and nearby lymph nodes may also be removed during the operation. Radiation therapy (radiotherapy) involves high-energy rays used to directly destroy or slow the growth of cancer cells. Chemotherapy is treatment with cytotoxic (cell-killing) drugs, introduced either directly into the tumor, or via the bloodstream. Hormone therapy and immunotherapy are used in certain cancers sensitive to these treatments. As cancer treatments affect normal cells as well as cancer cells, they often cause unpleasant side effects such as nausea, skin rashes, loss of hair, and bone marrow suppression.

Prevention is important in managing cancer. Physicians recommend giving up smoking and avoiding smoke and other environmental carcinogens. A good diet will include foods that are low in fat, rich in vitamins A and C and high in fiber such as whole-grain cereals, fruits, and vegetables. Alcoholic beverages should be taken in moderation, and overexposure to the sun avoided, particularly by fair-skinned people.

SEE ALSO *Bowel cancer, Breast cancer, Chemotherapy, Leukemia, Lung cancer, Melanoma, Metastasis, Prostate cancer, Radiation therapy, Skin cancer; information on cancers of other parts of the body is included in the entry for the body part*

CANDIDIASIS

Candidiasis, also called moniliasis, is an infection caused by the candida fungus (usually *Candida albicans*). This organism normally grows harmlessly in the intestinal tract, mouth and the vagina, but under certain conditions it can proliferate and cause infection. These conditions include damaged skin, moisture and warmth. A person is also more susceptible to candidiasis during pregnancy, when taking antibiotics or corticosteroids, or when the immune system is weakened as in AIDS.

In the mouth and the vagina, candidiasis appears as small, white patches on a red, inflamed background. In the skin, candida forms moist, bright red flat patches with poorly defined borders. These occur usually in the groin, around the anus, beneath the breasts (particularly in overweight women with pendulous breasts), in folds of skin of obese people, and in the armpits. In babies, they may occur as diaper rash.

It is important to keep the affected areas cool, dry and exposed to sunlight where possible. Eating yoghurt, buttermilk or sour cream, or taking acidophilus helps prevent candidiasis. A physician may prescribe antifungal topical medications such as nystatin, haloprigin, miconazole, or clotrimazole. These drugs are also available as vaginal pessaries and creams, and as suppositories.

SEE ALSO *Antifungals, Diaper rash, Opportunistic infection, Vaginitis*

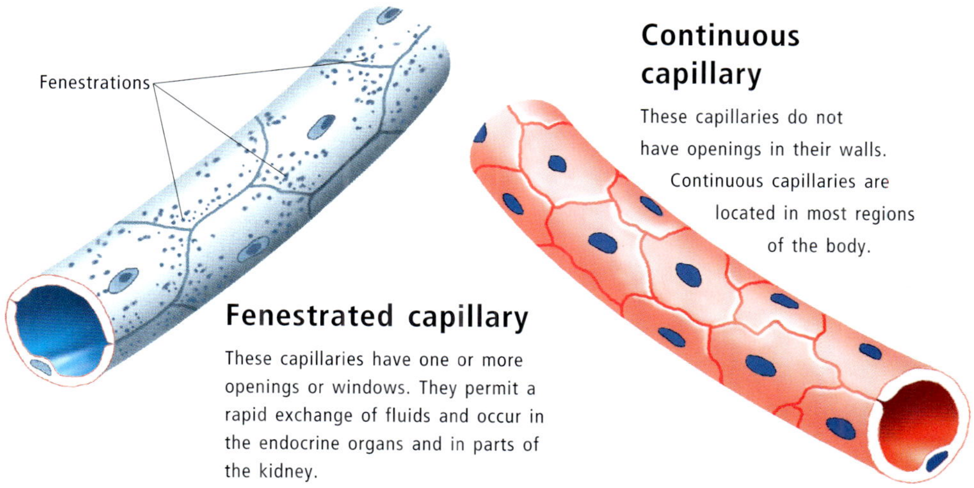

Fenestrated capillary

These capillaries have one or more openings or windows. They permit a rapid exchange of fluids and occur in the endocrine organs and in parts of the kidney.

Continuous capillary

These capillaries do not have openings in their walls. Continuous capillaries are located in most regions of the body.

CAPILLARIES

A capillary is the smallest type of blood vessel in the vascular system. Capillaries connect the smallest arteries with the smallest veins; most are so narrow they have the same diameter as a single blood cell. The function of capillaries is to carry oxygen-rich blood to the tissues, to pass food substances to tissue cells, and to carry away waste products, such as carbon dioxide and nitrates, back to the lungs and kidneys for elimination from the body.

During inflammation of body tissues, the capillaries become more permeable. They allow white blood cells and proteins into the tissues to fight infections and stimulate inflammation. Capillaries can also become more permeable as a result of some allergic reactions. In serious reactions, such as anaphylaxis, the blood can lose volume and the person can go into shock.

Microangiopathy is a term used to describe a disorder of capillaries in which the capillary walls become so thick and weak that they bleed, leak protein, and slow the flow of blood. For example, diabetics may develop microangiopathy with thickening of capillaries in the eye and the kidney.

SEE ALSO *Arteries, Blood vessels, Circulatory system, Veins*

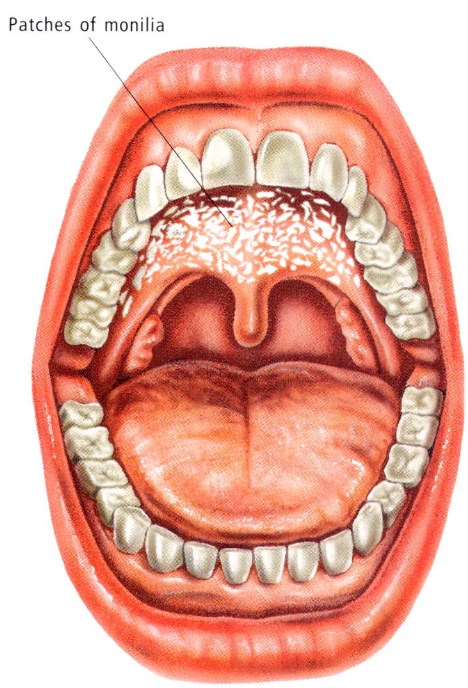

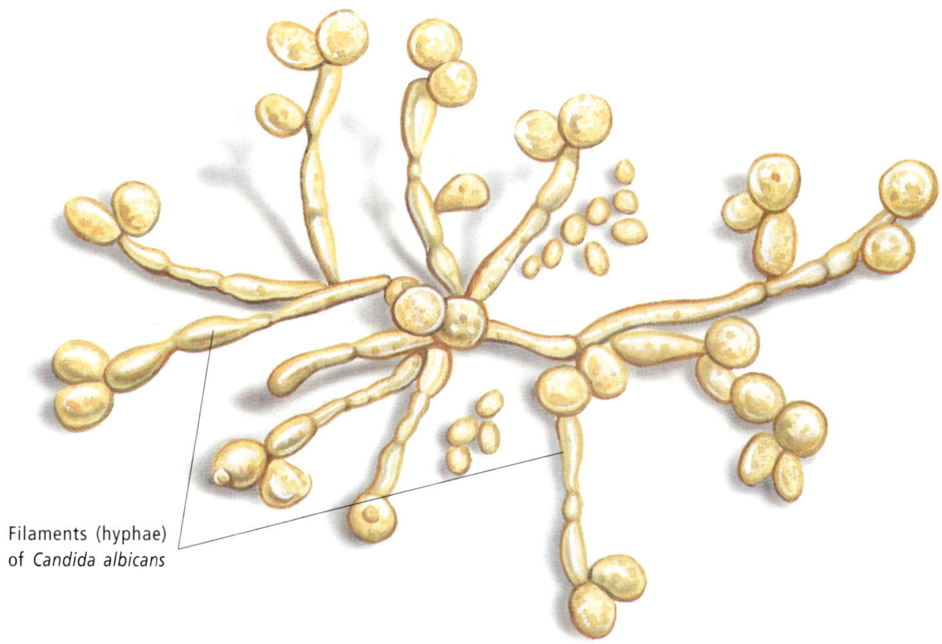

Candidiasis

Candidiasis is a fungal infection that affects the mucous membranes of the body. Infection of the mouth (thrush) causes red, inflamed areas and creamy, white, painful patches to form inside the mouth. It can be treated by applying antifungal drugs directly to the area or by taking medications orally.

C

Cardiac hypertrophy

Cardiac hypertrophy is the term for enlargement of the heart. The heart muscle cells become enlarged because of an increased demand for the heart to work harder.

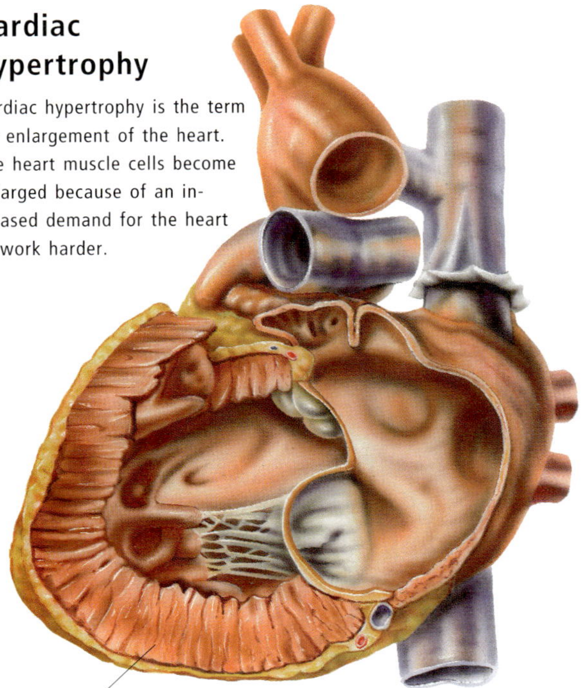

Cardiomyopathy

Cardiomyopathy is a disease that alters the structure or function of muscular wall of the heart ventricles (lower chambers). The diseased heart becomes enlarged, weak, and has trouble pumping blood effectively. The heart rhythm may also become abnormal.

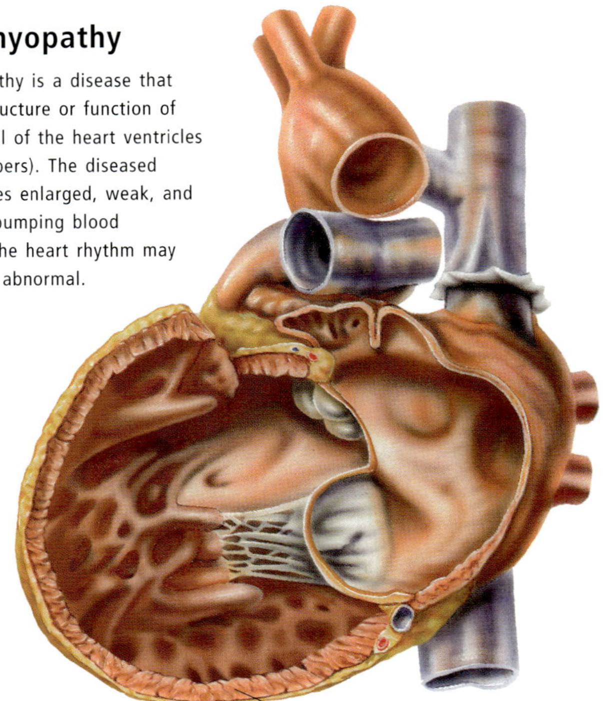

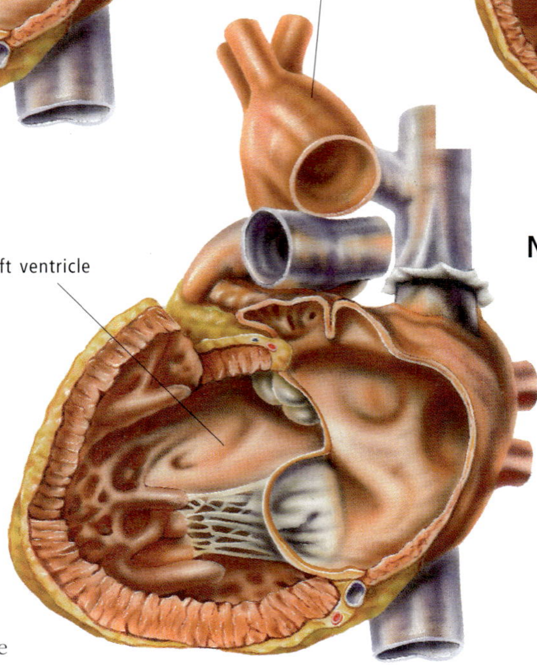

Normal heart

CARDIAC HYPERTROPHY

Cardiac hypertrophy is enlargement of the heart. It is caused by enlargement of heart muscle cells in response to a need for the heart to pump harder over months or years, in conditions such as hypertension or restricted flow of blood from the heart to the aorta (aortic stenosis). Because the heart must work harder, it requires more oxygen than normal; therefore, someone with cardiac hypertrophy is more vulnerable to conditions such as angina and myocardial infarction. It is necessary to treat the underlying cause.

Hypertrophic cardiomyopathy (formerly known as hypertrophic subaortic stenosis) is a group of diseases in which the cardiac muscle enlarges for no apparent reason. About half the cases are inherited and the disease affects mainly young adults. Symptoms are breathlessness, tiredness, fainting and chest pain. The condition is treated with beta adrenergic and calcium channel blocking drugs. In severe cases, an operation to cut or excise the muscle may be required.

SEE ALSO *Angina pectoris, Calcium channel blockers, Cardiomyopathy, Heart, Hypertension, Myocardial infarction*

CARDIAC TAMPONADE

Cardiac tamponade (also called pericardial tamponade) is a potentially life-threatening condition in which blood or fluid accumulates in the pericardium (the sac enclosing the heart), causing pressure on the heart. This prevents the ventricles from expanding fully, so they cannot adequately fill or pump out the blood.

The condition may result from a wound which ruptures blood vessels in the heart muscle, from bacterial or viral inflammation of the pericardium (pericarditis), or from cancer invading the pericardial sac. It may also be caused by radiation therapy to the chest, hypothyroidism, or systemic lupus erythematosus (SLE).

Symptoms involve chest pain radiating to the neck, shoulder, back or abdomen, difficulty in breathing, a weak or absent pulse, and low blood pressure. A chest x-ray, echocardiogram or CAT or MRI scans of the chest may show blood or fluid in the pericardium if there is any.

Cardiac tamponade is a medical emergency. Treatment is aimed at stabilizing the patient, removing the fluid by means of a needle with a suction syringe inserted through a surgical puncture, and correcting the underlying cause.

SEE ALSO *Heart, Pericarditis, Pericardium*

CARDIOMYOPATHY

Cardiomyopathy is a general term for diseases of the muscle of the heart (the myocardium). As cardiomyopathy progresses, the heart becomes weakened, enlarged and beats irregularly. In the terminal stages, the heart fails and the person may require a heart transplant. The condition may be caused by chronic diseases such as coronary atherosclerosis, excessive alcohol intake, infection due to viruses, or beriberi and other vitamin B deficiency disorders. In less common cases it is caused by the inflammation of heart muscle due to rheumatic fever or other immune disorders.

To begin with, the person notices a shortness of breath (dyspnea) and a decreasing ability to tolerate physical exertion. Chest pain, fainting (syncope), and palpitations (a sensation of feeling the heart beat) may be present. When the heart fails, swelling of the ankles and abdomen may occur.

Tests such as a chest x-ray, echocardiogram, coronary angiography, chest CAT or MRI scan will show the extent of the condition. Blood tests and a biopsy of the heart muscle may be needed to find the cause. Treatment is aimed at correcting the underlying cause. Medication will relieve the workload of the heart and stabilize the patient's condition. Rest and oxygen (given by mask) will reduce the workload of the damaged heart muscles. Hospitalization is advised if symptoms of severe heart failure are present. A heart transplant may be necessary if the patient is suitable and a donor is available.

SEE ALSO *Cardiac hypertrophy, Heart*

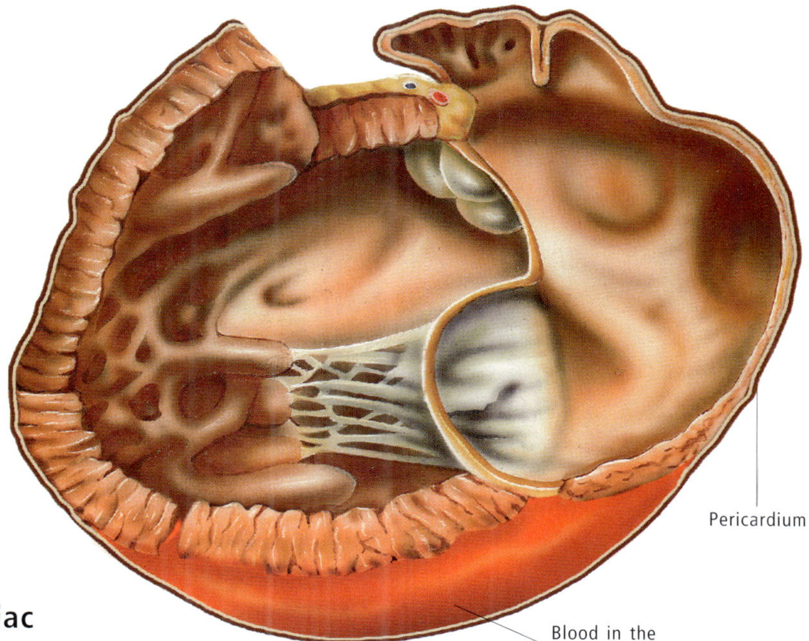

Cardiac tamponade

Cardiac tamponade is a condition in which blood or fluid accumulates in the area surrounding the heart (the pericardium). The flu d puts pressure on the heart and interferes with its ability to pump blood efficiently. This is a serious condition requiring urgent treatment.

CARDIOVASCULAR ISOTOPE SCANNING

Using a small amount of radioactive tracer injected into the circulation, an image of the blood flow through the chambers of the heart, or through the heart muscle, can be recorded with a highly sensitive scanning camera. This technique is used to define an area of heart muscle which does not receive adequate blood flow, as well as to measure cardiac performance.

SEE ALSO *Heart*

CARPAL TUNNEL SYNDROME

This is a syndrome resulting from compression of the median nerve in the carpal tunnel in the wrist. The carpal tunnel is a gap formed by the wrist bones (called the carpal bones) and the tough ligament that forms the roof of the tunnel (the flexor retinaculum). The passageway is rigid, so swelling of any of the tissues in this area can cause compression of the nerve, causing a numbness or pain in the wrist, hand, and fingers (except the little finger). The symptoms are usually worse at night.

Carpal tunnel syndrome is most commonly found in middle-aged women. It may occur during pregnancy, before the menstrual period, or during menopause. The condition is also found in diseases such as rheumatoid arthritis, acromegaly and hypothyroidism, or following injury or trauma to the area.

Treatment consists of splinting the wrist to immobilize it for several weeks. Anti-inflammatory drugs may help to improve the condition. If these fail, a physician may inject a corticosteroid drug into the ligament. In severe cases, surgical excising (resection) of the flexor retinaculum may be needed to relieve the pressure on the nerve.

SEE ALSO *Wrist*

CAROTID ARTERY

The carotid arteries are the main arteries of the neck. The right and left carotid arteries are situated on either side of the neck and carry blood from the aorta to both sides of the neck, head and brain. Stenosis (narrowing) of the carotid artery caused by atherosclerosis can result in transient ischemic attacks (TIAs)—passing symptoms of a restricted blood flow to the brain—and stroke if the narrowing is severe.

SEE ALSO *Arteries, Cerebrovascular disorders, Stroke, Transient ischemic attack*

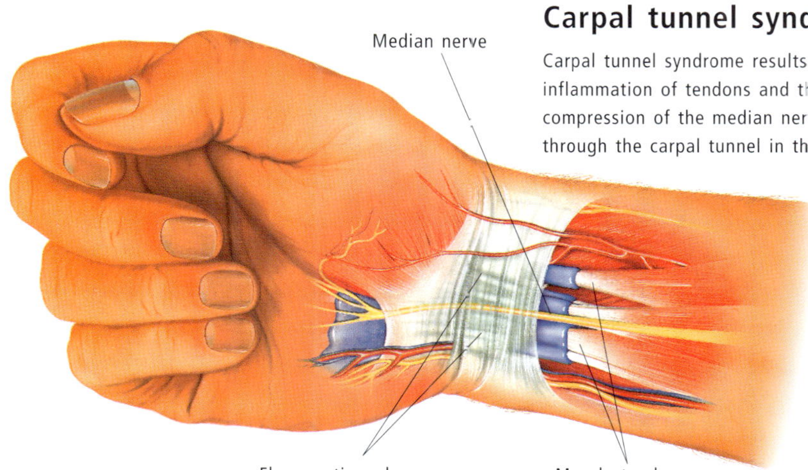

Carpal tunnel syndrome

Carpal tunnel syndrome results from inflammation of tendons and the resulting compression of the median nerve as it travels through the carpal tunnel in the wrist.

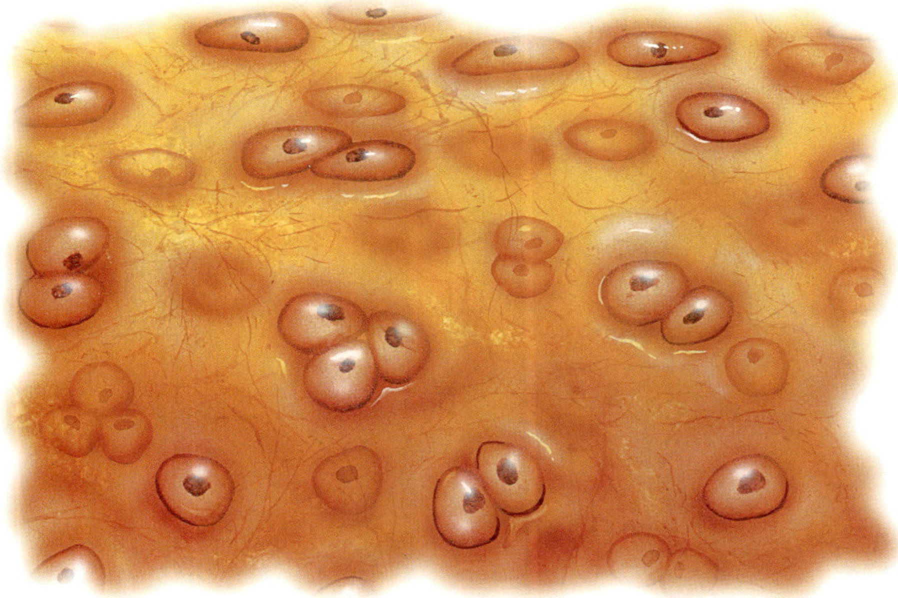

Elastic cartilage

Elastic cartilage is strong but supple cartilage containing proteins called elastin and collagen embedded in ground substance. Elastin gives it a distinctive yellow color. Elastic cartilage makes up the springy part of the outer ear, and also forms the epiglottis (the flap of tissue in the throat that prevents food from entering the airways).

Fibrocartilage

Fibrocartilage contains large amounts of collagen, making it both resilient and able to withstand compression. It is found between the bones of the spinal column, hip and pelvis.

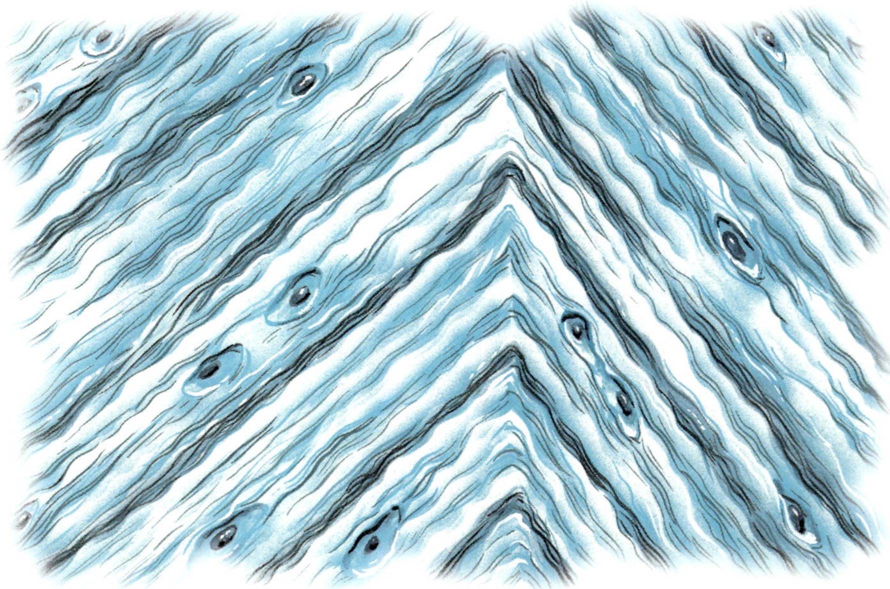

Hyaline cartilage

Hyaline cartilage is a tissue which contains collagen fibers. It forms the skeleton in the embryo and remains as a thin layer on the end of bones which form joints. It also forms the end of the nose, and the stiff rings around the windpipe. It is found on the ends of the ribs and supports the larynx.

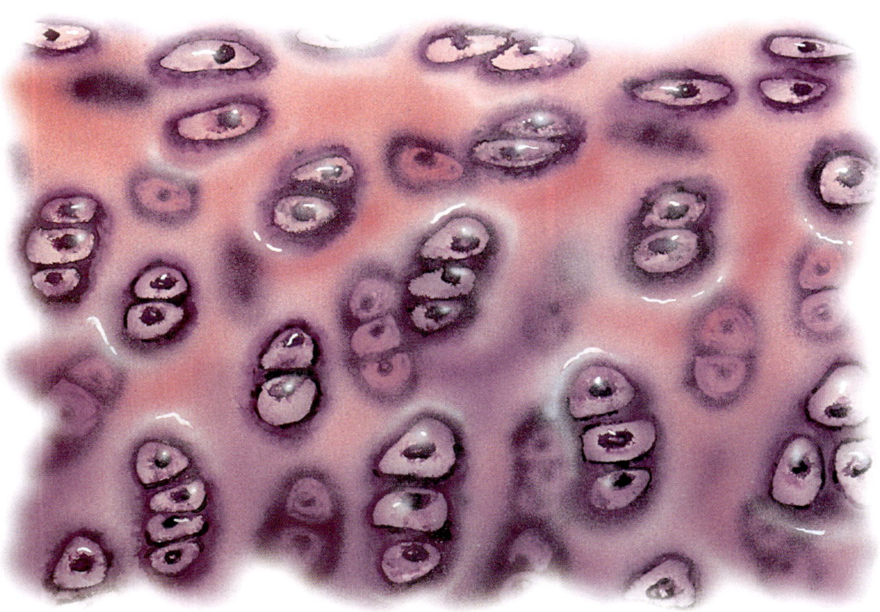

CARTILAGE

Cartilage is a tough, semi-transparent, elastic, flexible connective tissue consisting of cartilage cells (chondrocytes and chondroblasts) scattered through a glycoprotein material strengthened by collagen fibers. The exterior part of cartilage is covered by a dense fibrous membrane called the perichondrium. There are no nerves or blood vessels in cartilage, and when damaged it does not heal readily.

Cartilage has several functions. It covers the surfaces of joints, allowing bones to slide over one another, thus reducing friction and preventing damage; it also acts as a shock absorber. It forms part of the structure of the skeleton in the ribs, where it joins them to the breastbone (sternum). Cartilage is found in the tip of the nose, in the external ear, in the walls of the windpipe (trachea) and the voice box (larynx) where it provides support and maintains shape. In an embryo, the skeleton is formed of cartilage which is gradually replaced by bone as the embryo grows. Cartilage is known as elastic cartilage, fibrocartilage or hyaline cartilage, depending on its different physical properties.

A "torn cartilage" commonly refers to a disorder of the knee. A section of cartilage pad inside the knee joint known as the meniscus tears, and may move around in the knee joint, causing pain, swelling, and preventing weight being placed on that knee. A minor tear can be treated effectively with rest and a firm bandage around the knee. More serious tears require the surgical removal of part or all of the cartilage. This can often be done through an arthroscope—a tube that is passed into the knee joint, allowing visualization of the interior of the joint. Osteoarthritis later in life is a common complication of a torn meniscus.

Costochondritis (Tietze's syndrome) is a painful inflammation of the cartilage of the ribs (commonly the third or fourth rib). It causes pain in the chest wall, which may be mistaken for cardiac pain. The cause is often unknown, though it may be the result of trauma (such as a blow to the chest), unusual physical activity or an upper respiratory infection. It usually clears up in a short time with rest and mild anti-inflammatory medications such as aspirin, acetaminophen (paracetamol) or ibuprofen.

Chondrosarcoma is an uncommon cancer that may arise from cartilage associated with bone or outside of bone. The affected person notices a painful lump, usually in the long bones of the limb, pelvis or ribs. The diagnosis is confirmed with x-ray, CAT or MRI scans, biopsy and laboratory examination. The treatment is surgical removal of the tumor. If the tumor is slow growing and detected and treated early, the chances of survival are good.

SEE ALSO *Connective tissue, Joints, Knee, Osteoarthritis*

CAT SCAN

CAT or CT scan (computerized axial tomography) is an x-ray technique that can produce a three-dimensional image of a body part. The patient is placed inside a cylindrical-shaped scanner, around which an x-ray tube revolves. From multiple pictures taken from many angles, a computerized image is formed. The contrast resolution is much better than that displayed by conventional x-ray.

CAT scanning has revolutionized the diagnosis of many diseases. Tumors and other brain disorders can be delineated accurately, although a contrast fluid may occasionally still be required to outline the associated blood vessels. Lung cancers may be discovered earlier, making surgery more successful. The small coronary arteries of the heart can be checked closely for the degree of blockage when considering bypass surgery. In the abdomen, sometimes in conjunction with contrast solutions in the bowel or stomach, pathology or other abnormalities can be more accurately diagnosed without need of a major operation.

Bone disorders such as fractures (especially stress fractures of the small bones of the feet and the scaphoid bone in the wrist) can be checked more quickly and accurately than with conventional x-ray. Bone disease and spinal pathology such as slipped disks are also more clearly depicted. However, soft tissues such as muscles, ligaments and cartilages are more easily demonstrated by using the newer magnetic resonance imaging (MRI) machines.

SEE ALSO *Contrast x-ray, Magnetic resonance imaging, X-ray*

CAT-SCRATCH FEVER

Cat-scratch fever is a mild infectious disease, common in children, and caused by a small bacterium, *Bartonella henselae* (or CSD bacillus). The bacterium is carried on the claws or in the saliva of a healthy cat (usually a kitten) and transmitted by a scratch or bite.

Between three days and two weeks after the scratch or bite, a lump develops at the site of the injury and the person feels unwell with fatigue, headache and a mild fever. Lymph nodes draining the area swell, and although the lump soon disappears, the lymph nodes may remain swollen for several months. No specific treatment is necessary.

CATARACTS

Cataracts are cloudy spots which develop in the lens of the eye, sometimes due to injury but more often to age. As the cloudiness gradually increases, vision becomes hazy and a halo may be seen around bright objects. As the cataract grows, vision worsens to the point where it is severely restricted and surgery is needed. Cataracts are very common—about 20 percent of people over 60 will be subject to them—but they are not painful. During surgery the cloudy lens is removed and a plastic or silicone lens implant inserted. Certain types of cataract may respond to medication that dilates the pupil.

SEE ALSO *Eye*

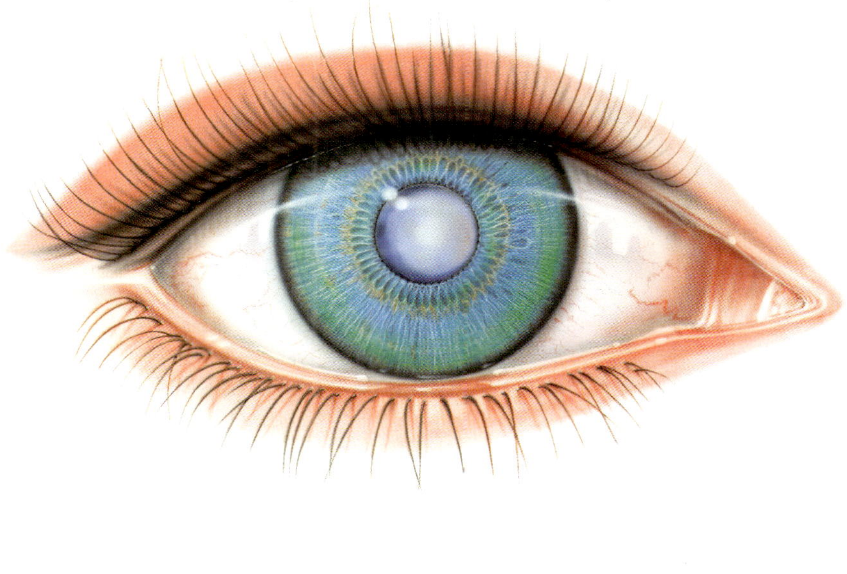

Cataracts

A cataract is a cloudiness (opacity) in the lens of the eye that produces a progressive, painless loss of vision. It causes the lens to look like a misty pane of glass. A cataract impairs vision by reducing the amount of light that reaches the lens of the eye and distorting the light being focused onto the retina. Cataracts are more common in older people because the lens becomes thicker, less resilient, and less transparent with ageing.

C

CATARRH

Catarrh is a term used for an inflamed mucous membrane, usually in the nose or throat, which causes a discharge of mucus. It occurs as a symptom of various upper respiratory tract infections such as hay fever, rhinitis, laryngitis, or the common cold.

SEE ALSO *Common cold, Hay fever, Laryngitis, Rhinitis*

CATATONIA

Catatonia, or catatonic motor behavior, is seen in people afflicted with catatonic schizophrenia. It is characterized by total immobility, holding unnatural postures for long periods, failure or refusal to speak, and sometimes by meaningless physical activity. Schizophrenia is treatable with drugs and psychotherapy, and about a third of cases achieve a lasting improvement.

SEE ALSO *Schizophrenia*

CATHETERIZATION

A catheter is a flexible, hollow tube that is introduced into a cavity through a narrow opening, in order to discharge the fluid in the cavity or to unblock a vessel. It may be made of glass, metal, hard or soft rubber, rubberized silk, or plastic. A catheter may be inserted into the bladder temporarily during an operation, or permanently after a brain or spinal injury to relieve an underactive or overactive bladder, or because of paralysis.

A catheter may also be inserted into an artery or vein or directly into the heart in order to inject drugs, to measure blood flow or pressure, to use in the diagnosis of congenital heart disease, to explore narrow passages, or to pass electrodes into the heart so that the heartbeat can be restored or made regular.

SEE ALSO *Bladder, Heart*

CELIAC DISEASE

Celiac disease, also known as nontropical sprue, is a true allergic reaction to gluten in the diet. This hypersensitivity results in the destruction of the food-absorbing surface of the jejunum in the small intestine; only rarely is the cecum involved. Gluten is a protein found in many grains, especially wheat, rye, barley and oats. Normally the immune system cells, known as T lymphocytes, protect the body against invaders, but in celiac disease they attack gluten, thus inflaming the small intestine lining and resulting in inefficient absorption of nutrients.

Celiac disease is considered to be inherited, though the actual cause is not known. It is rare in non-Caucasians but affects 1 in 1,500 to 2,000 Caucasians, being particularly common in people of western Irish descent, of whom it affects around 1 in 300. About half of those suffering from the disease are diagnosed during childhood. It usually manifests itself between the ages of 6 and 21 months, often following an infection. Symptoms in children are diarrhea, failure to thrive (stunted growth) and weight loss. Teenagers can suffer delayed puberty and loss of some hair (alopecia areata). In adults, symptoms include flatulence, chronic diarrhea (which does not respond to treatment), weight-loss and chronic fatigue. Vitamin deficiency can also result and produce symptoms including scaly skin, bruising, blood in the urine, tingling and numbness, muscle spasms and bone pain. It is usually diagnosed through screening blood tests. Osteoporosis is a serious illness which often occurs in people with celiac disease and symptoms can include night-time bone pain. Five percent of adults with celiac disease will also have anemia, and lactose intolerance is a common feature of celiac disease at all ages.

Once the disease is diagnosed, gluten must be totally eliminated from the diet. This is not easy as gluten is found in a surprising number of prepared foods, including canned foods, peanut butter, dips, luncheon meats, candy and yoghurt, among others. It is important to read the labels on all prepared foods to ensure they do not contain gluten. The diet needs to be under the supervision of a specialist who will suggest certain strategies and there are support groups offering valuable resources, and cookbooks that feature gluten-free products. In young babies, breast feeding and postponing the introduction of foods containing gluten can offer some protection.

Celiac disease can go into spontaneous remission in children at about the age of five years and in others, strict adherence to the diet can heal the intestine. However, for most people it will be necessary to stay on a gluten-free diet for the rest of their lives.

SEE ALSO *Anemia, Baldness, Intestines, Osteoporosis, Sprue*

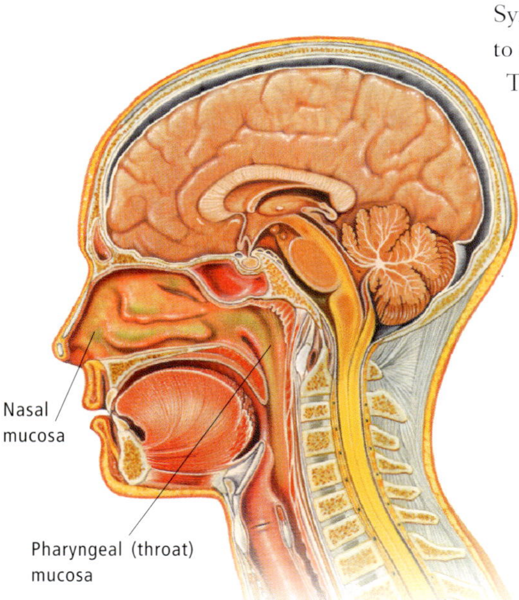

Catarrh

Catarrh is a term used to describe inflammation of the mucous membranes of the nose or throat, leading to an increased discharge of mucus (runny nose, mucus in the throat).

CELLS

Cells are the basic structural units that make up all living organisms. Cells are organized into tissues, and tissues into organs. Typical cells are surrounded by a cell membrane. Within the cell membrane lies the cell's cytoplasm, which is a fluid containing many important structural units called organelles. Some organelles are concerned with the manufacture of protein (rough endoplasmic reticulum), the generation of energy (mitochondria), the packaging of manufactured products (Golgi apparatus) and the process of cell division (centrioles). The control of the cell's function is directed by the nucleus, which contains genetic information in the form of DNA. In larger and more complex cells, the nucleus is separate from the cytoplasm.

Cell division

Many (but not all) types of cells undergo a process called mitosis, or cell division, by which a mother cell divides into two daughter cells. This is particularly well seen in the cells lining the gut and the skin. In these sites, cells are continually being shed and must therefore be replaced. When cells are dividing continuously, they pass through a series of stages called the cell cycle. This cycle consists of four individual stages: a growth stage (G1), a synthetic stage (S), another growth stage (G2) and a cell division stage (M).

When cell division runs out of control and the daughter cells invade other tissues, a cancer results. Cancers usually arise in sites where cell division is already occurring rapidly, such as the skin, gut and airway lining. Most cells are formed through this process of cell division.

In sexual reproduction, sex cells (the egg and sperm) are produced by a different type of cell division. This process is called meiosis. At fertilization, the sperm and egg unite (fuse) to form a zygote.

Specialized cells

Many cells are specialized to perform particular functions. For example, blood is made up of two broad types of cells (red and white blood cells) and specialized cell fragments called platelets.

Red blood cells develop in the red bone marrow of bones such as the sternum and hip. During their development, red blood cells lose their nucleus and their cytoplasm becomes filled with a protein called hemoglobin, which carries oxygen and carbon dioxide.

White blood cells can be of several types. Granulocytes are so called because their cytoplasm contains granules. Another type of white blood cell is the agranulocyte, which has no granule in its cytoplasm.

Agranulocytes include lymphocytes and monocytes. Lymphocytes are further divided into T and B types. T lymphocytes (T cells) are involved in the so-called cell-mediated immune response, which is a defence reaction of the body against viruses and cancer cells. B lymphocytes (B cells) are involved in the humoral immune response, which is directed mainly against bacteria.

Another type of defense cell, which travels through the blood, but also can enter and move through the tissue outside the blood stream is the macrophage (phagocytic or scavenger cells). These cells have the ability to engulf foreign material (bacteria, inorganic foreign bodies) and either destroy the bacteria or prevent escape of the invaders to the rest of the body.

Other specialized types of cells include nerve cells (neurons), which are electrically active and transmit information to other

Celiac disease

Celiac disease is an inherited disorder in which an allergic intolerance to gluten in the diet causes changes in the small intestine. This results in difficulties in the absorption of food.

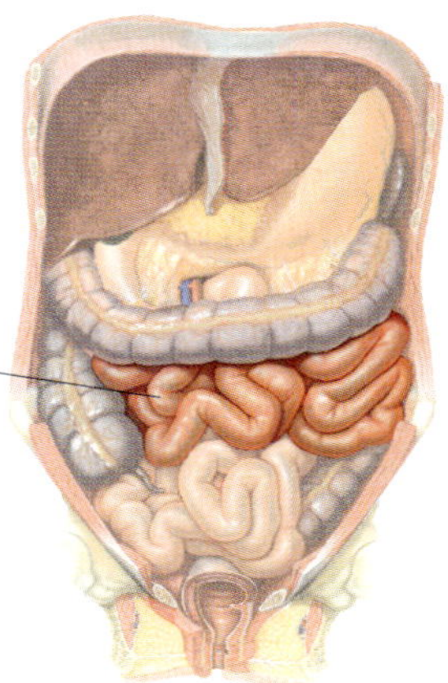

Villi

In the small intestine, tiny, finger-like projections, known as villi, stand out from the lining to increase the surface area available for absorption of nutrients. In celiac disease, the villi in the jejunum in the small intestine are flattened, making it harder for the nutrients in food to be absorbed.

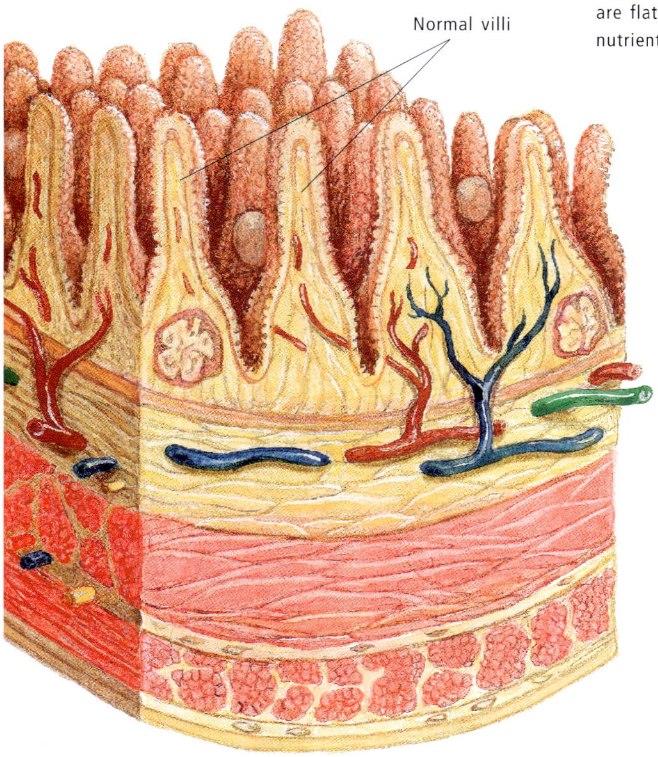

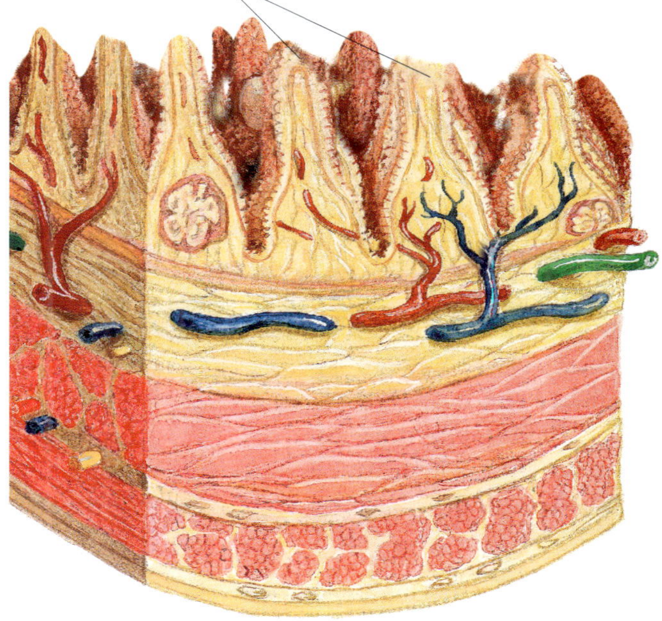

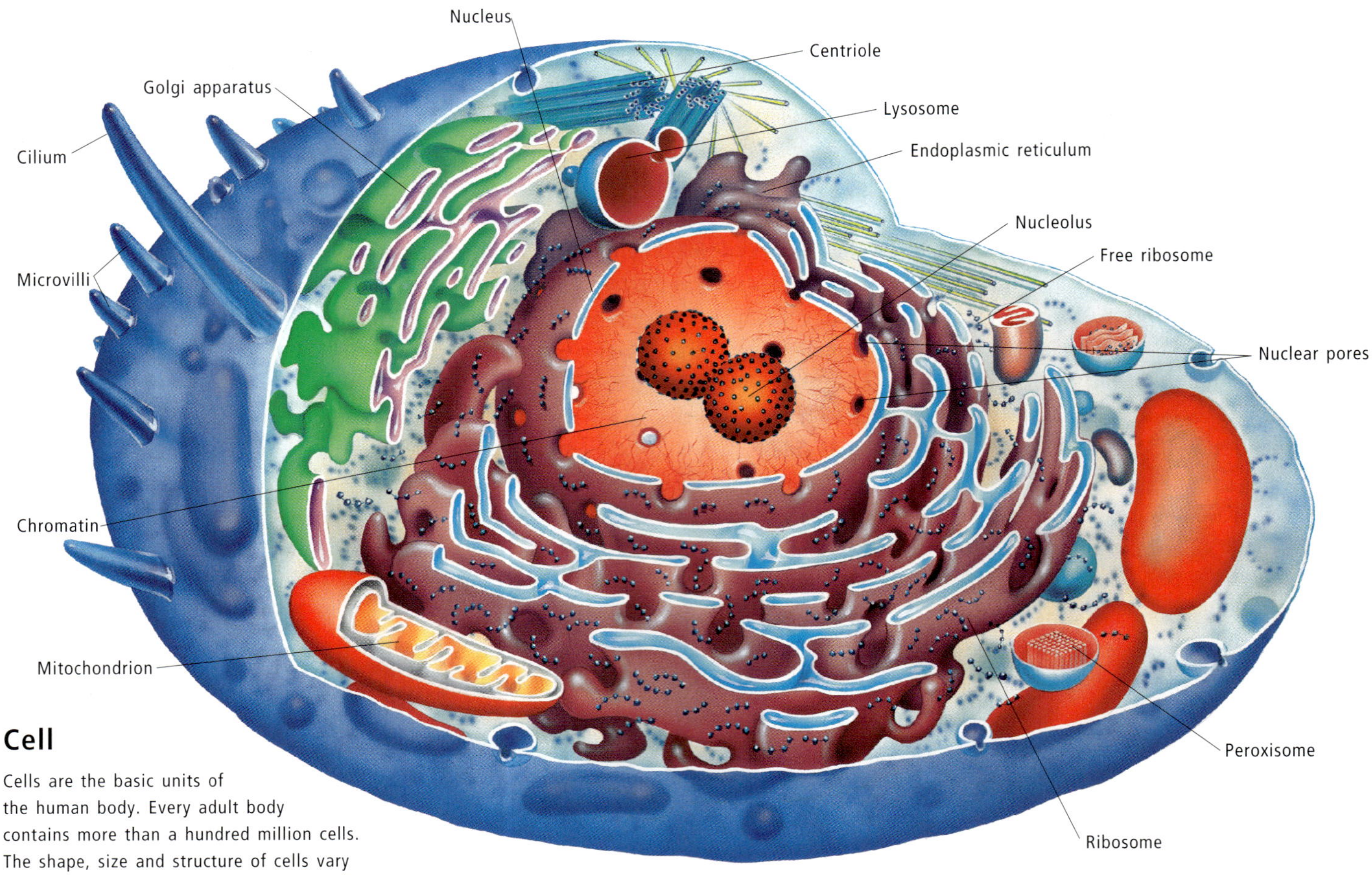

Cell

Cells are the basic units of the human body. Every adult body contains more than a hundred million cells. The shape, size and structure of cells vary according to their functions within the body.

nerve cells across special junctions called synapses. Another type of electrically active cell is the muscle cell, which contracts in response to nervous or hormonal stimulus.

Skin cells are also highly specific. They are designed to be progressively shed, because they are continuously exposed to the damaging effects of the harsh external environment with its ultraviolet radiation, physical wear and tear, extremes of temperature and low humidity. To replace shed cells, the lower layer of the skin contains cells that divide rapidly.

SEE ALSO *Blood, DNA, Skin, Tissues*

CELLULITE

Cellulite is a popular (non-medical) term for the fatty tissue that puckers and dimples just beneath the skin. The dimpling indicates that fat cells are not being strongly supported by the connective framework of the adipose (fatty) tissue. Weight reduction may not improve the appearance of cellulite and in some cases cosmetic surgery is effective.

SEE ALSO *Cosmetic surgery*

CELLULITIS

Cellulitis is a bacterial (usually streptococcal) infection of the skin and underlying tissues. Cellulitis can arise after dermatitis, ulcers, injury or animal bites. The symptoms are redness, swelling and tenderness of the skin, swollen lymph nodes which may be accompanied by fever, chills and rapid heartbeat. Medical assistance should be sought.

SEE ALSO *Streptococcal infections*

CEREBELLUM

The cerebellum (Latin for "little brain") is a cauliflower-shaped structure that lies at the back of the brain and is important in the control of movement. It coordinates movement by regulating the timing, direction and force of muscle contractions, and it regulates muscle activity in order to maintain balance and posture.

SEE ALSO *Brain*

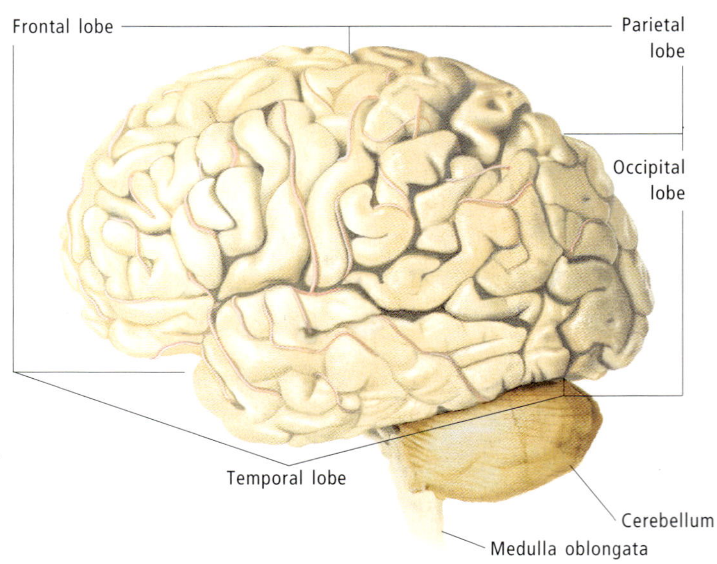

Cerebellum

The cerebellum is the part of the brain that coordinates the movements of the body and helps to maintain balance. It is situated at the back of the skull, beneath the cerebrum (largest part of the brain).

CEREBRAL ARTERIES

The cerebral arteries are blood vessels in the head that transport blood (containing oxygen and other nutrients) to the cells of the hemispheres of the brain. Three cerebral arteries on each side arise near the base of the brain and give branches to deep structures before supplying the cerebral cortex.

SEE ALSO *Brain, Cerebral cortex*

CEREBRAL CORTEX

The cerebral cortex in the human brain is a highly folded sheet of nerve cells (neurons) that forms the outer surface of the hemispheres of the brain. It enables a person to store memories, think, make decisions, speak and carry out voluntary movements, and to consciously perceive and understand sensations, such as vision, hearing and touch.

SEE ALSO *Brain, Neurons*

CEREBRAL HEMORRHAGE

A cerebral hemorrhage is a form of stroke which occurs when a blood vessel in the brain suddenly ruptures, releasing blood into the brain. Within a few minutes the patient will experience decreased consciousness, headache and vomiting. Other symptoms depend on which part of the brain is affected.

SEE ALSO *Brain, Stroke*

Cerebral arteries

The brain is supplied by a network of arteries (cerebral arteries). The carotid arteries supply the front and middle of the brain; the vertebral and basilar arteries supply the back of the brain, cerebellum and brain stem. The vertebral arteries join up at the back of the head and become the basilar artery. The three cerebral arteries are linked by communicating arteries to form the circle of Willis.

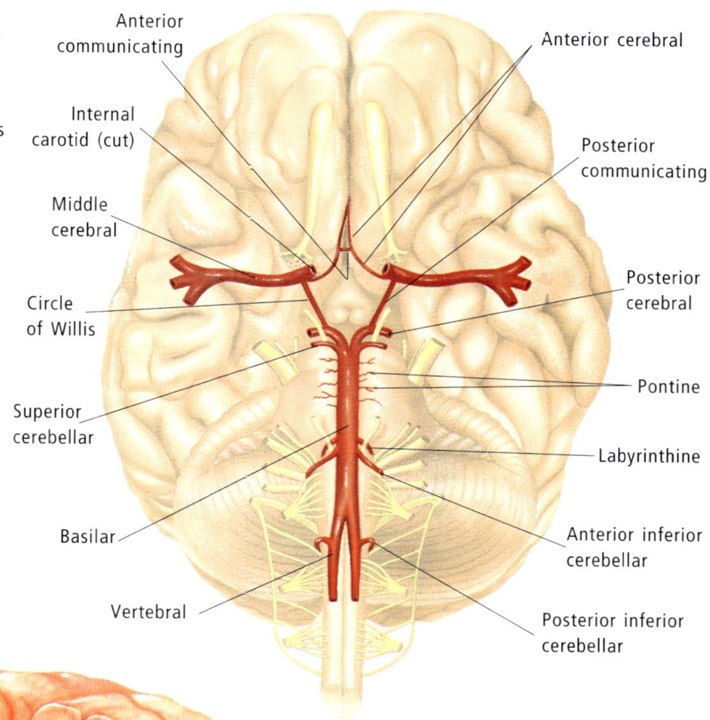

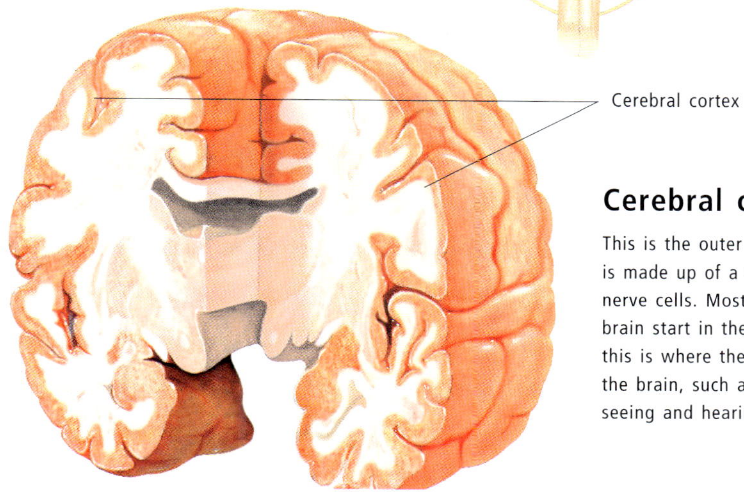

Cerebral cortex

This is the outer layer of the brain; it is made up of a vast network of nerve cells. Most messages from the brain start in the cerebral cortex, and this is where the higher functions of the brain, such as thinking, talking, seeing and hearing occur.

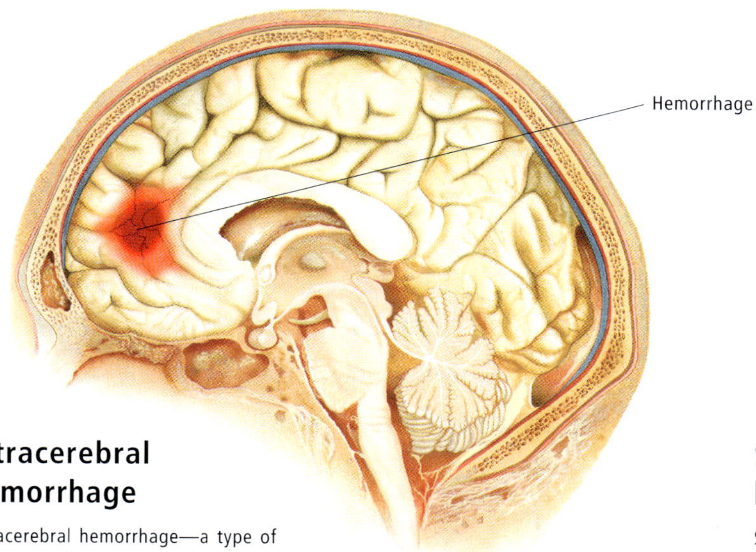

Intracerebral hemorrhage

Intracerebral hemorrhage—a type of stroke—is caused by bleeding inside the brain. It is the most dangerous type of stroke because the hemorrhage is usually large. The symptoms begin abruptly with a headache, followed by steadily worsening neurological problems, such as weakness, paralysis, loss of speech or vision. Loss of consciousness and seizures are common.

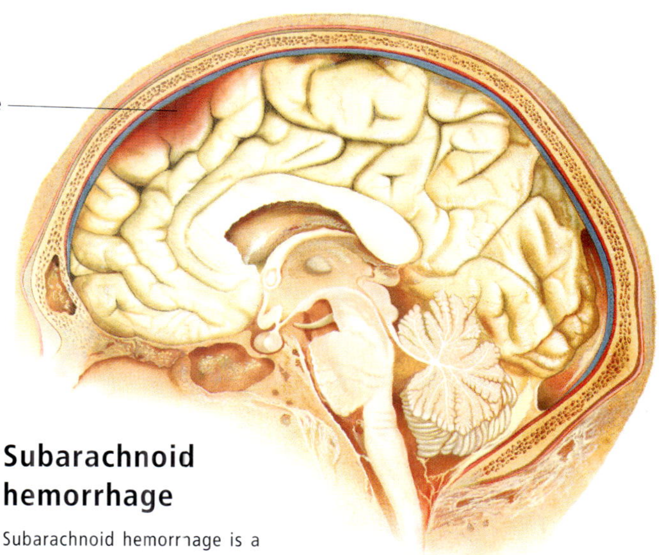

Subarachnoid hemorrhage

Subarachnoid hemorrhage is a sudden bleed into the space between the brain and its covering (meninges). The usual cause is a weak blood vessel that suddenly ruptures. The rupture usually produces a sudden, severe headache followed by a loss of consciousness. Surgery is usually necessary to repair the damaged vessel.

Cervical rib

Occasionally, a small extra rib is formed, attaching to the seventh cervical vertebra in the neck. This so-called cervical rib can compress the nerves in the neck, causing tingling, pain, weakness or numbness on the affected side of the neck and arm.

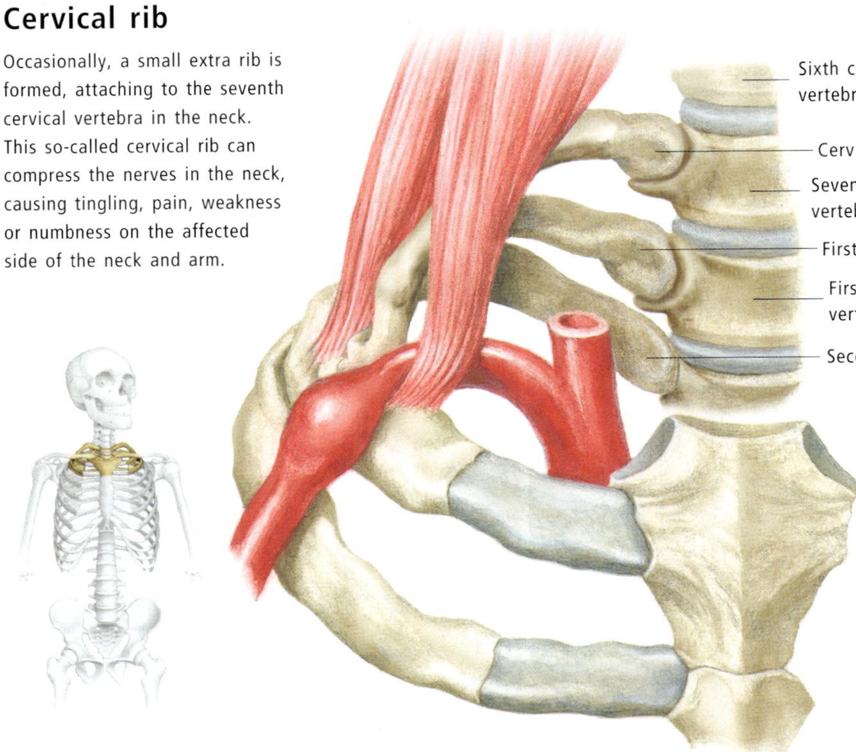

CEREBRAL PALSY

Cerebral palsy is a general term used to describe a group of disorders in which there is faulty development or damage to motor areas in the brain, which impair the brain's ability to adequately control movement and posture. The damage may result from disease, faulty growth, or injury, which may occur before, during, or shortly after birth. Rubella (German measles) in pregnancy, premature birth and brain damage due to a difficult delivery are common causes. Often, the cause is never found. The condition is never inherited.

The symptoms differ from one person to the next. Someone with cerebral palsy may have difficulty with fine motor tasks, have trouble maintaining balance and walking, or be affected by involuntary movements such as uncontrollable writhing motion of the hands, or drooling. In some persons, there is also intellectual disability, learning difficulties, slow growth, seizures, and hearing and vision problems. Usually, the condition is not apparent until the child is between one and two years old.

There is no cure for cerebral palsy. Treatment is aimed at helping affected people make best use of their abilities and may include physical therapy, speech therapy, and psychological support. Drugs to help control seizures and muscle spasms, special braces to compensate for muscle imbalance, and other mechanical aids may be required. The earlier treatment begins, the better a child will do. Many people with cerebral palsy can enjoy near-normal lives if their problems are properly managed.

CEREBROVASCULAR ACCIDENTS

Cerebrovascular accidents (strokes) are caused by damage to the arteries which supply oxygenated blood to the brain and are characterized by a sudden loss of neurological function.

There are two main types of cerebrovascular accident. The first involves occlusion or blockage of an artery, resulting in a lack of oxygen (ischemia) and consequent death (infarction) of the brain tissue supplied by that artery. Occlusion of an artery results from either a thickening of the arterial wall (arteriosclerosis) or, more commonly, from blockage by a floating body. The functional loss experienced by the patient will depend on which region of the brain is damaged. Sometimes the blockage is only temporary and the effects pass after a few minutes or hours; the patient is said to have suffered a transient ischemic attack (TIA).

The second and more common type of cerebrovascular disorder involves a sudden rupture (hemorrhage) of one of the brain's arteries, causing large quantities of blood to accumulate in the brain tissue (cerebral hemorrhage) or in the space surrounding the brain (subarachnoid hemorrhage). This leads to a sudden increase in pressure within the skull, causing severe headache, decreased consciousness and vomiting. Other signs, which vary in their severity, depend on the specific location of the rupture.

SEE ALSO *Brain, Cerebral hemorrhage, Ischemia, Stroke, Subarachnoid hemorrhage, Transient ischemic attack*

CERVICAL RIB SYNDROME

Some people are born with a small extra rib known as a cervical rib, which is an appendage to the seventh cervical vertebra in the neck. It generally causes no problems, but in some cases it can compress the nerves in the neck, causing pain, numbness and tingling in the neck, shoulders, arms and hands and weakness in the arms and fingers. If these symptoms occur, the rib should be surgically removed. The condition is sometimes called thoracic outlet obstruction syndrome. A similar disorder may be caused by an injury to the neck (often while someone is unconscious or asleep). That disorder can be treated with physical therapy.

SEE ALSO *Neck, Vertebrae*

CERVIX

The cervix is the lower part of the uterus. It is situated between the body of the uterus and the vagina. It has a centrally placed cervical canal, which leads into the cavity of the uterine body at one end and opens to the vagina at the other.

Sperm must pass through the cervix on their way to the uterine body, and menstrual blood passes down the cervix to the external environment. In labor, the cervix must dilate as much as 4 inches (10 centimeters) during the passage of the baby's head down the birth canal. The sensitive surface tissue of the cervix is in contact with the external environment, especially during sexual intercourse when the penis may introduce viruses and bacteria to the vagina. Two viruses of particular concern are the human papilloma virus (HPV) and the herpes simplex type II virus. HPV may cause warts to grow on the vaginal and cervical tissue. Herpes simplex type II is believed to cause cervical cancer (carcinoma), by inducing changes in the cells of the cervix.

Cervical cancer is the second most common cancer affecting women, accounting for almost 10 percent of cancers in females in developed countries. The incidence of the disease is more common in those women who have frequent intercourse with many different partners and is also more common in women who have given birth. During the early stages the cancer may be confined to the cervical tissue and can be easily removed by cutting out a cone-shaped block of tissue. For this reason early detection, by regular use of the Papanicolou ("Pap") smear test, is very important.

Cervical polyps are small tear-shaped structures that protrude through the vaginal opening of the cervical canal. They are composed of tissue derived from the inner lining of the cervical canal. They can cause bleeding and may be removed surgically.

Colposcopy is the medical term for the examination of the upper vagina and cervical opening. Colposcopy is used principally for diagnosis, whereby samples of cervical tissue and fluid are taken for further examination.

Cervical incompetence is a condition where the fetus is in danger of being lost during pregnancy because the cervix is not tight enough to hold the fetus and its membranes inside the uterus. This problem is more common in women who have had many surgical terminations of pregnancy (abortions). Damage to the cervix during abortions may stretch or tear the fibers that help to hold the cervix closed.

In some women, the fluid of the cervix (cervical mucus) may be resistant to the penetration of sperm cells. This may be because the mucus is too thick or because it contains antibodies (biological defence chemicals), which bind to the sperm and interfere with their movement or survival. This will lead to infertility (an inability to conceive a child) and may require sperm to be artificially introduced higher up.

SEE ALSO *Miscarriage, Pap smear, Reproductive systems*

CHALAZION

A chalazion (also known as a meibomian or tarsal cyst) is a small cyst that forms when a meibomian gland (a gland which secretes oils that lubricate the eyelids) becomes blocked with oil secretion. It is harmless, but can be surgically removed if it becomes painful or unsightly.

SEE ALSO *Eyelids*

CHANCROID

Chancroid, or soft chancre, is a sexually transmitted disease (STD) most common in tropical regions. Shallow painful ulcers appear in the infected areas, usually the genitals, three to five days after exposure through sexual contact. They are caused by the bacterium *Haemophilus ducreyi* and can be mistaken for the first symptoms of syphilis, in which similar but hard and painless chancres appear. In chancroid, localized swelling and inflammation of lymph glands follow the appearance of ulcers. The disease is often associated with HIV transmission.

Chancroid can be treated successfully with sulfonamides, or the antibiotics azithromycin and erythromycin, although the ulcers may leave scars.

SEE ALSO *Sexually transmitted diseases, Syphilis*

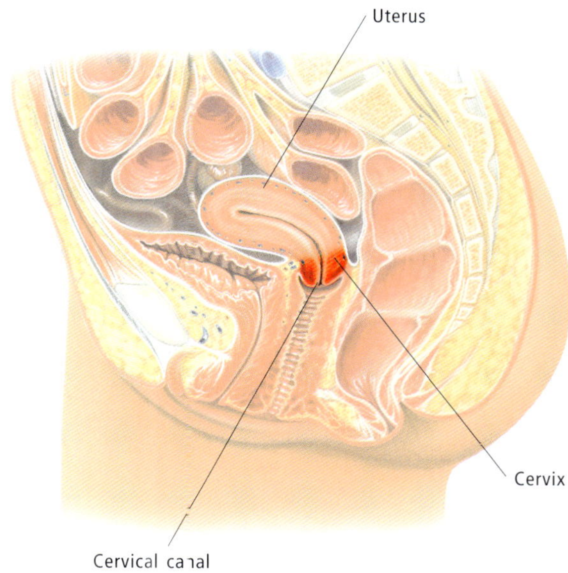

Cervical canal

The cervical canal is located in the center of the cervix, and leads into the cavity of the uterus at one end and the vagina at the other.

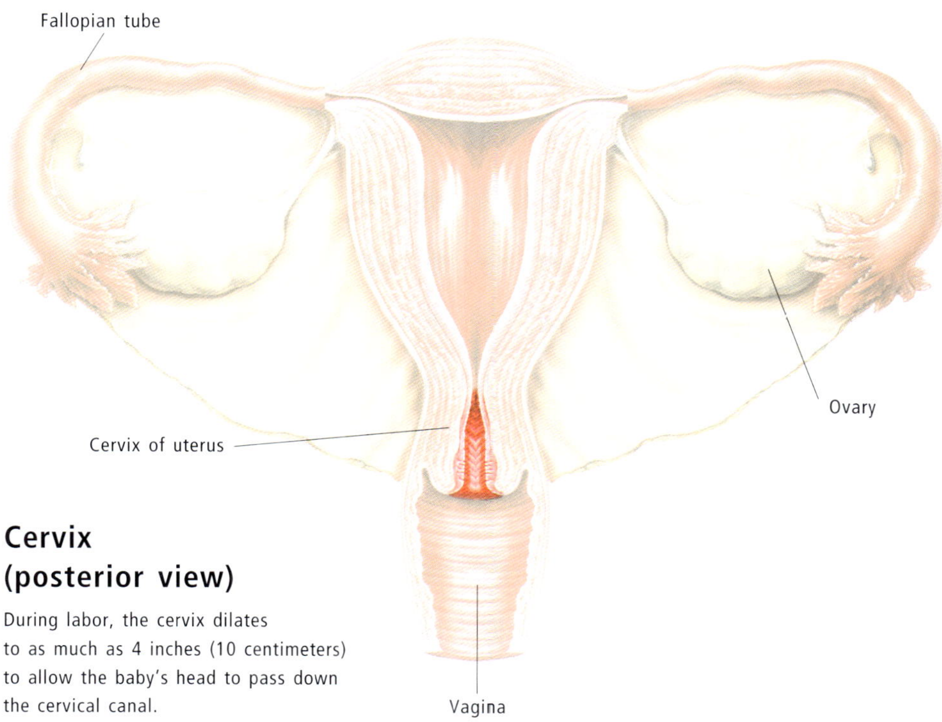

Cervix (posterior view)

During labor, the cervix dilates to as much as 4 inches (10 centimeters) to allow the baby's head to pass down the cervical canal.

C

CHEMOTHERAPY

Chemotherapy is the use of chemicals to kill cancer cells. There are many different anti-cancer drugs; some are given by mouth and some are injected. There is no drug yet available which is 100 percent effective in killing cancer cells, nor is there one which does not potentially harm healthy cells.

Research is constant, and treatment methods are improving to minimize the harmful effects. Chemotherapy may be given over a brief period, or may extend over several years; it can be given in hospital, outpatient clinics, at a doctor's rooms or even at home. There are many different courses of treatment and all are being improved through sharing scientific knowledge and by international trials of new drugs and procedures.

The drugs used in chemotherapy are basically poisons, some of which developed out of research into chemical warfare. Standard combinations, or cocktails, of drugs have been set for treating most forms of cancer. After starting treatment and observing the patient's response, the combinations and doses are adjusted. This has made chemotherapy less unpleasant and more effective as cancer treatment skills improve.

Hormone therapy can be used to restrict the growth of certain cancers. Immunotherapy uses substances such as interferon to attack specific tumors. Combination therapy uses surgery or radiation as well as chemotherapy to fight cancer: surgery or radiation to treat the cancer directly, chemotherapy to wipe out cancer cells that have spread to other parts of the body.

Anti-cancer drugs attack all fast-dividing cells, so that normal, healthy fast-dividing cells are killed along with the cancer cells. Most of the side effects are due to the killing of healthy cells. The major side effects of chemotherapy include the following.

Nausea and vomiting are common, but are now less severe than in the past since drug doses are constantly adjusted to a patient's responses. Vomiting can often be controlled with drugs called anti-emetics. Sometimes eating small quantities at a time and avoiding any foods which cause upset can help.

Hair loss is also common, and some cancer patients choose to shave their heads before hair loss occurs, or wear a wig. Hair usually grows back after chemotherapy.

Low blood cell count (cytopenia) does not always need treatment but, if it is thought necessary, red blood cell deficiencies can be corrected by transfusion, and the production of white blood cells can be stimulated if needed.

Damage to liver and kidneys can be caused by anti-cancer drugs and is minimized by adjustment of dosages.

Mouth ulcers and digestive disorders occur because the cells of the mucous membranes which line the mouth and the digestive tract are fast-dividing cells. Painful mouth ulcers or diarrhea can occur during treatment and can cause nutritional deficiencies when patients do not eat or the food is not properly absorbed.

Infertility and fetal abnormalities can be caused by chemotherapy, so birth control is essential while taking the drugs. Some treatments can cause permanent infertility in men and women.

Chemotherapy today involves careful monitoring of patients, including regular blood tests. As a result, problems are quickly detected and drug doses can be adjusted and other treatments given to minimize any side effects and discomfort. Success in this has meant many people now have chemotherapy as outpatients, and do not require a stay in hospital.

SEE ALSO *Cancer, Radiation therapy*

CHEST X-RAY

Early detection and diagnosis of lung disease relies initially on chest imaging by x-ray. This will also reveal an outline of the heart and major blood vessels, but as x-rays pass easily through soft tissues they show only gross abnormalities and enlargements of these organs. Conditions such as pneumonia, tumors of the lung, and emphysema can be detected, and where abnormalities are suspected, the x-ray results will help physicians to decide which further examinations and tests will be needed. Identification of a condition is increased by the use of a contrast medium such as iodine.

X-ray examinations expose subjects to very low dosages of radiation. In some countries, levels are limited to the equivalent of the amount received from natural exposure to sunlight and radio waves over six months.

SEE ALSO *X-ray*

CHICKENPOX

Chickenpox (varicella) is a highly contagious, airborne viral disease. It is most common among school-age children, though it can occur at any age, and one attack usually protects a person for life, unless it is very mild.

The main symptom, which usually appears 13–17 days after contact, is a rash which is at first apparent on the trunk and then spreads over the body. This rash has three stages: little red itchy bumps, followed by a clear blister on each bump and finally crusts or scabs. The infection lasts until all bumps have crusted, which takes seven to ten days from when the rash first appears. Headache and cold symptoms can also accompany chickenpox but these usually occur before the rash appears.

Treatment revolves around relieving the itching, as scratching of the scabs can lead to life-long scarring. A lukewarm bath with cornflour or an oatmeal preparation added can provide relief. Calamine lotion can also be applied and the fingernails should be kept very short. Some children may need antihistamines, but these should only be taken on medical advice. Acetaminophen (paracetamol) may reduce fever, but aspirin must never be given as it can lead to the complication of Reye's syndrome.

Anyone who is pregnant, has a chronic illness or weak immune system should seek medical advice if they have been in contact with someone with chickenpox. After chicken pox clears, the virus which causes the disease may lie dormant and later cause shingles.

SEE ALSO *Infections, Reye's syndrome, Shingles*

CHILBLAIN

Chilblain is an inflammation of the skin, usually occurring on the ears, face, toes or fingers. The inflammation is due to cold, damp weather that can damage small blood vessels and nerves in the skin. The condition causes pain, itching, swelling, redness, and sometimes blistering and ulceration of the skin. People with poor circulation are more susceptible to chilblains. Treatment is to gently warm the affected areas and provide warm, protective clothing.

Chickenpox areas

Chickenpox is a contagious viral illness that produces a characteristic itchy rash. The trunk is usually affected first (and most severely), and spots then spread to the arms, face, and legs.

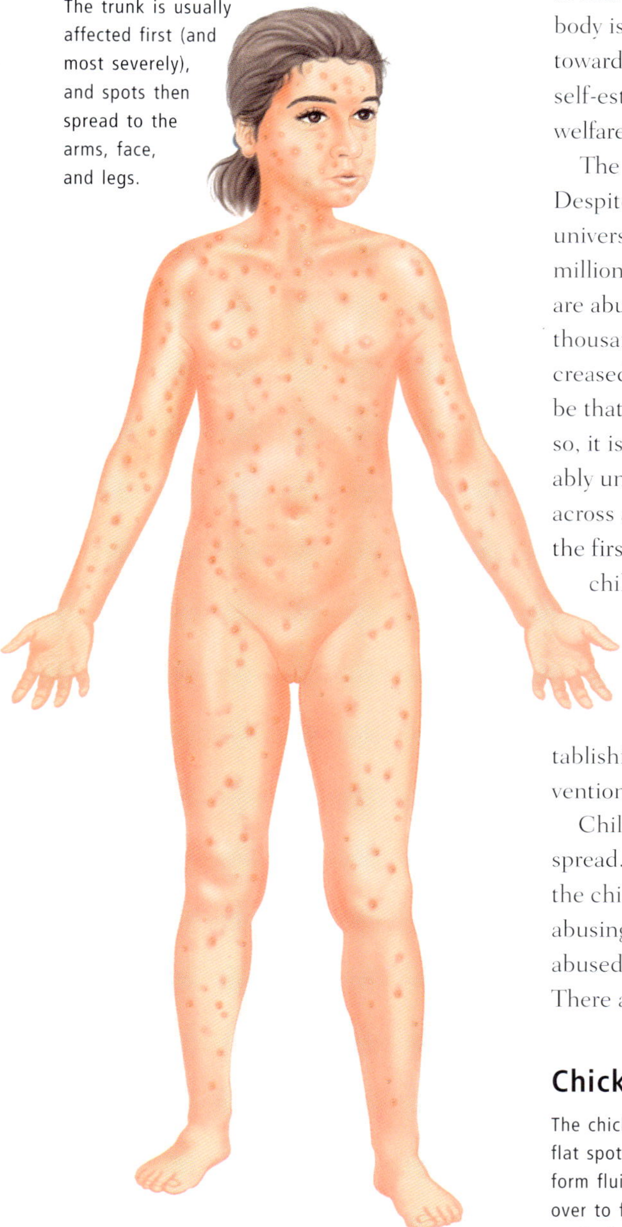

CHILD ABUSE

Child abuse is the non-accidental harming of a child by an adult. This can be in one of four ways: physically, when the child's body is injured; emotionally, when behavior towards the child damages or destroys self-esteem; through neglect of the child's welfare and health; and through sexual abuse.

The statistics on child abuse are alarming. Despite the fact that child abuse is almost universally condemned by criminal statutes, millions of children throughout the world are abused and neglected each year, with thousands dying. Child abuse could have increased in recent times, or it could simply be that more cases are being reported; even so, it is believed that it is generally considerably under-reported. Child abuse occurs across all social and economic strata. One of the first countries to adopt laws to protect children was the USA where the state of New York legislated for their protection in 1875. National laws to protect children from cruelty were passed in Great Britain in 1884, establishing the National Society for the Prevention of Cruelty to Children.

Child abuse, in all its forms, is widespread. In many cases it is not detected until the child reaches adulthood and becomes an abusing parent. Without proper treatment, abused children can be damaged for life. There are a number of signs that may indicate a child is being abused, including: physical signs such as bruises, burns, broken bones or damaged organs; poor self-image; inability to trust other people; aggressive, disruptive behavior; anger; self-destructive or abusive behavior, including suicide; withdrawal; fear of new activities or relationships; school problems; symptoms of depression; nightmares; and drug and alcohol abuse.

Abusers have not necessarily been abused themselves; they can be grandparents, older siblings, other relatives, neighbors, teachers, church or sporting group leaders, child care workers or baby-sitters. Those who abuse children often do not see themselves as abusers. Some even consider that what they were doing was for the child's benefit—parents especially often say this.

Child abuse occurs for many reasons: inadequacies in the adult, which may be stress- or tension- related (an inability to cope with the caring of their children together with complications in their own lives); too high expectations often coupled with a misunderstanding of the mental and physical development of the child; a belief in physical punishment as a method of discipline; sexual attraction to children; pedophilia (knowingly seeking to perform sexual acts with children for self gratification); and being abused themselves as children. Children who are disabled are considered to be at greater risk. Babies, because they are unable to communicate on an adult level, can be abused—babies can suffer severe damage as a result of being shaken. Shaking a baby can stretch the skull and move the brain so that blood vessels between the brain and skull shear off, bleed, swell and eventually atrophy, causing damage and even leading to death.

People in the community have a moral duty to report any serious suspicions they have to the appropriate authority. Managing child abuse involves a multi-disciplinary team working with the family, identifying the causes and helping the family to deal with the issues. If a parent suspects their child is being abused it is important for them to realize that it is never too late to protect their child. Children need to be valued, spoken to respectfully, listened to, taken seriously, and made to feel safe.

Chickenpox

The chickenpox rash usually begins as small flat spots, which then become raised and form fluid-filled blisters. These then crust over to form scabs. The virus is contagious until all spots have crusted over.

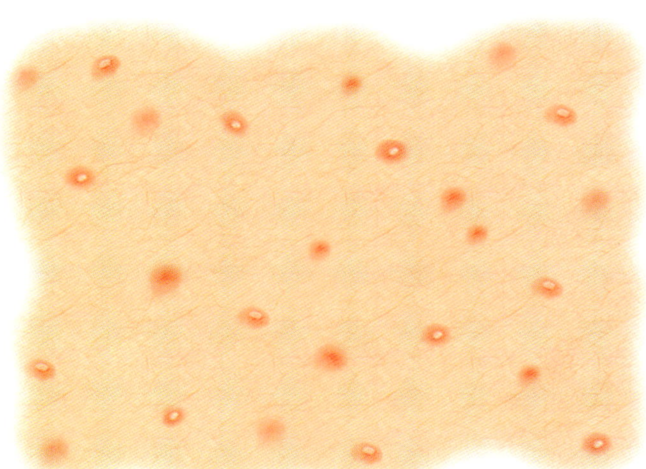

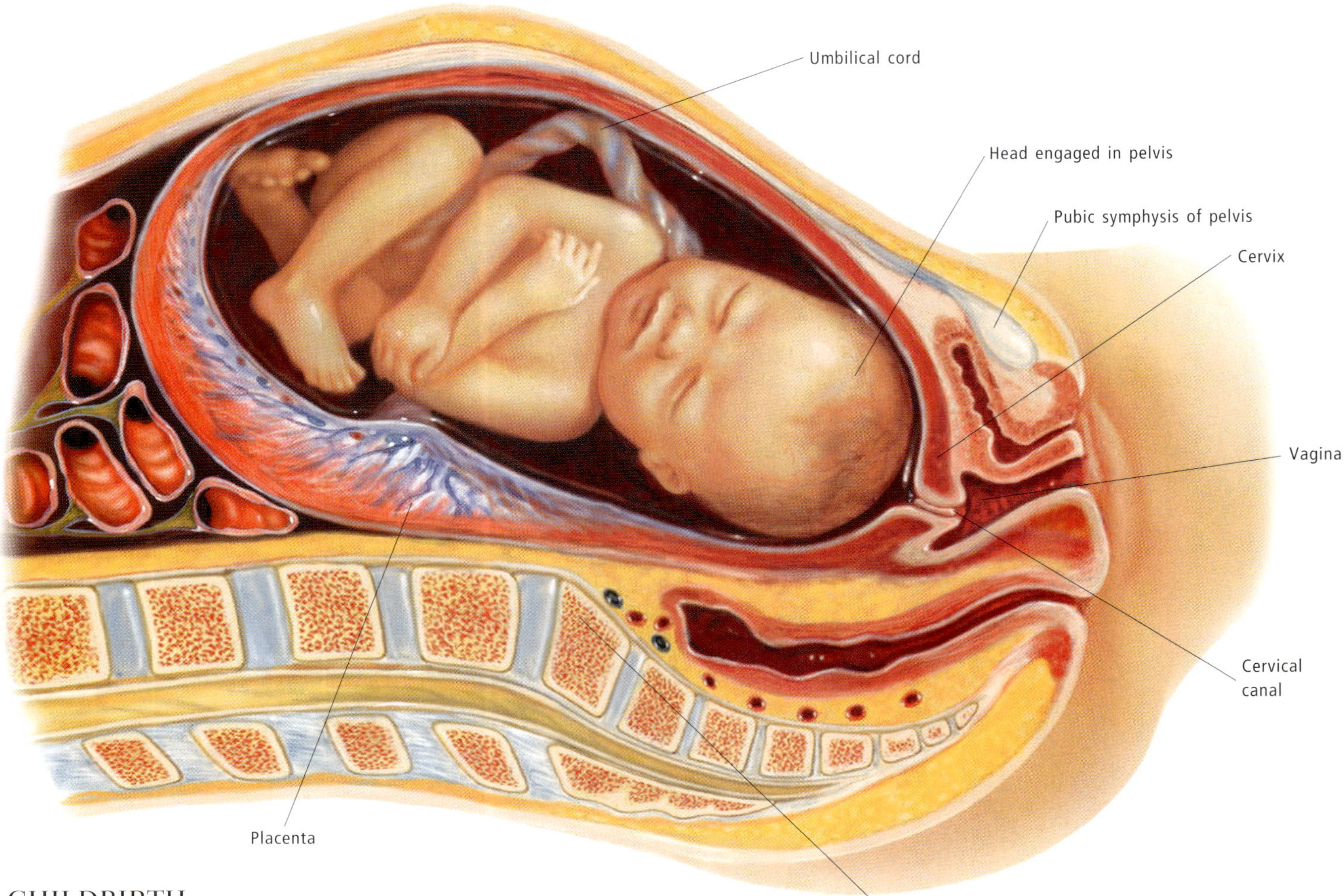

Full term

CHILDBIRTH

Childbirth is the act of giving birth to a baby, and can be done with varying degrees of assistance and intervention. Most babies born in industrialized societies are born in hospitals, under the direction of the medical profession. This has been associated with huge drops in maternal death rates. The rate of maternal death is 5 per 100,000 births for normal vaginal delivery; for cesarean section it is approximately 40 per 100,000 births. In many countries, home birth is also an option. In the Netherlands, for example, a country where home birth has always been an option for all women, about a third of births occur at home.

Home birth has a very low rate of medical intervention (a priority of many women) and a low rate of complications and hospital transfers. If a mother is prepared, and informed and supported by qualified carers, home birth can be a good choice. Many women choose home birth not just because of the familiar environment but also because they are able to have other members of the family present and can create an environment which helps them to feel relaxed.

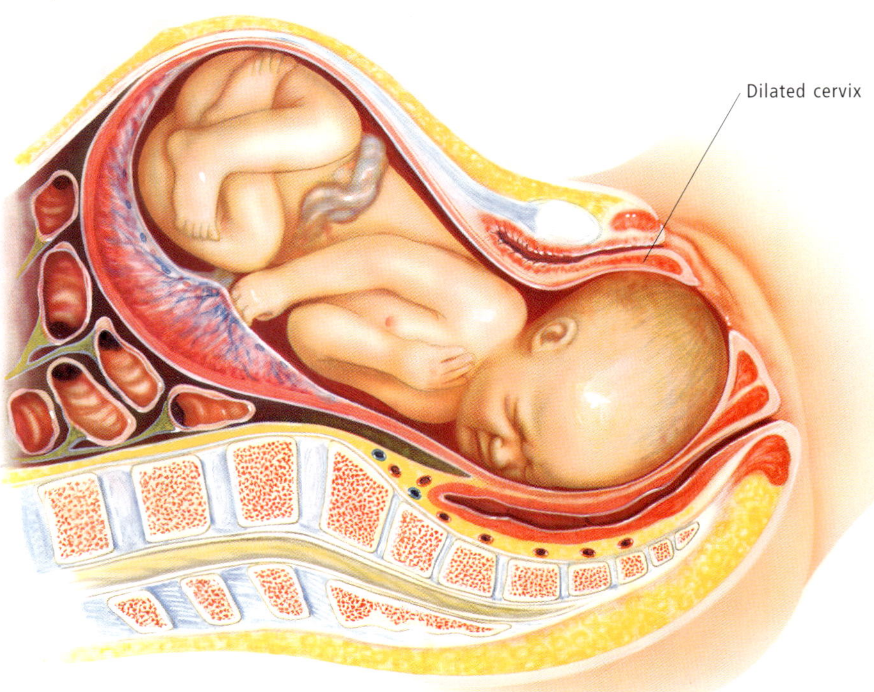

Dilation

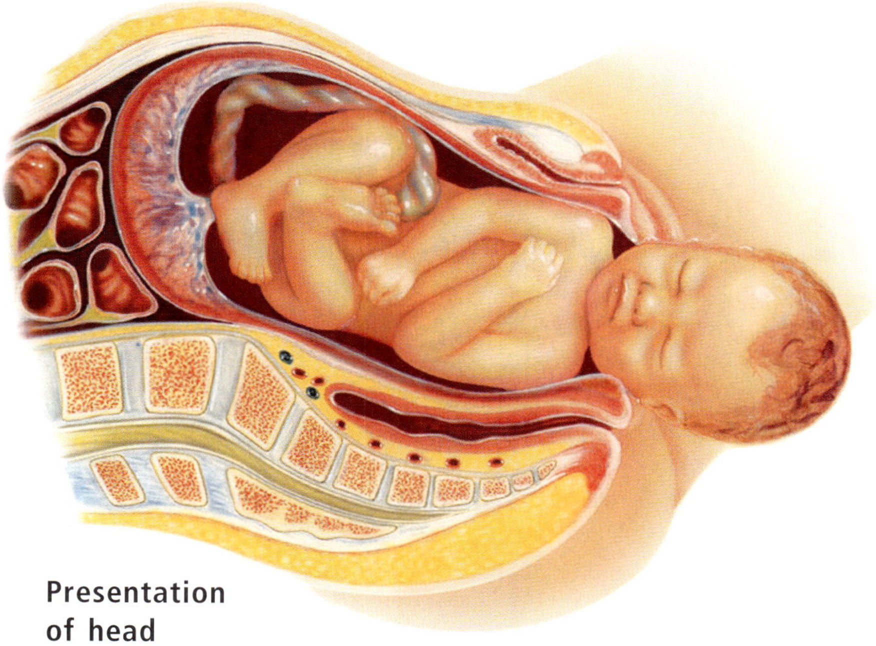

Presentation of head

There are, however, medical reasons why a home birth may not be possible—or sensible—and these include complications such as toxemia or sudden unpredictable hemorrhage, medical problems such as heart disease, and fetal problems such as the baby presenting in transverse (across the uterus) position.

Some mothers favor a water birth, which is often only possible in the home environment. For those women who want to go through labor and give birth in water, some birth centers and hospitals will provide a large enough bath. As soaking in a warm bath can relieve pain, many institutions have a protocol which allows laboring in water, but not birthing. However, around half the women who labor in water will also give birth in water. When this occurs, the baby is lifted straight from the birth canal, out of the water and into a warmed room where both mother and baby are kept warm.

In the 1970s, in industrialized countries, fathers-to-be first began to attend the births of their babies, and this is now accepted in most birth centers. The man who has attended antenatal classes with his partner and learnt how he can support her during the birth is a valuable companion. A woman who is knowledgeable and supportive also makes an excellent birth companion for the mother; in some countries these women are known as *doulas*. Research has shown that the presence of a trained female support person can reduce medical intervention in the birth process and enable the birthing woman to have a more satisfying experience. Some families choose to have their baby at home or in a birth center so the baby's siblings can be present during the birth. Preparing the children for the experience, and supporting them, helps ensure it will be a rewarding experience for all.

Labor

Labor—the process of giving birth—is described in three stages. The first stage is actual labor, during which the cervix is thinned and dilated, and is followed by a period known as transition; the second stage is the birth of the baby; and the third stage is the expulsion of the placenta, which nourished the baby during the pregnancy.

During the first stage of labor, the cervix must dilate fully to allow the baby to move into the birth canal. The endocrine signal that the baby sends to the placenta stimulates the production of estrogen. The uterus then produces prostaglandins and contracts more strongly and more frequently as it works to shorten and soften (efface) the cervix by pressing the baby's head against it. This effacement and stretching of the cervix then triggers the posterior pituitary gland to produce oxytocin; the contractions become stronger, working the uterus to stretch and dilate the cervix.

Once the cervix is fully dilated the baby can move into the birth canal. This stage of labor can be very short or last as long as 36 or more hours. In many hospitals, labor is augmented and accelerated after 12 hours.

The second stage of labor begins when the mother feels an urgent need to bear down and push the baby into the birth canal. This stage is much shorter than the first, with an average three to five "pushes" before the baby's head presents at the opening to the vagina. This is known as the "crowning". The baby's head then passes beneath the pelvic bone, with the face

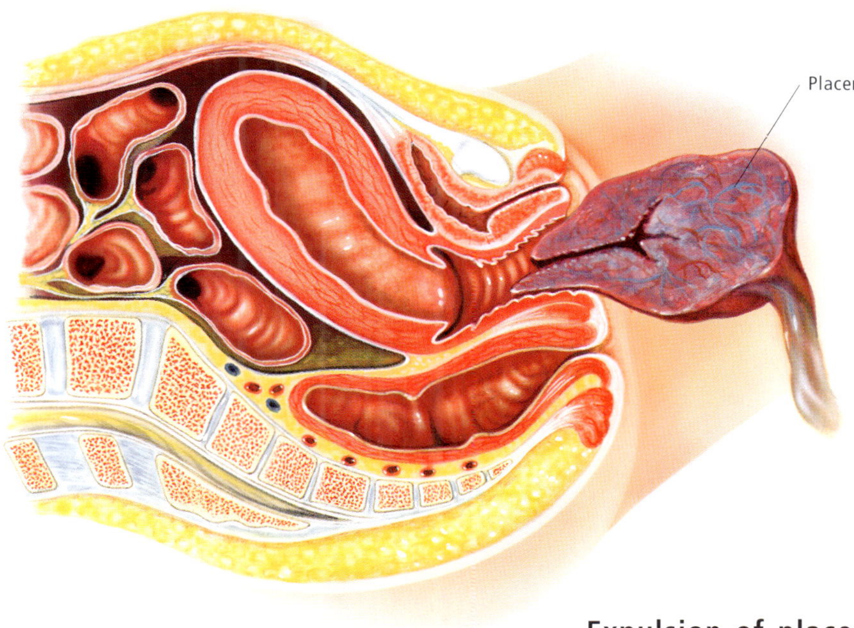

Expulsion of placenta

C

towards the mother's spine. The shoulders will quickly follow the head and the baby will soon be born.

The third stage of labor is the expulsion of the placenta. Once the baby is born the uterus continues to contract and there is a rush of oxytocin that prompts the placenta to separate from the uterus in a peeling action. The umbilical cord will still be joined to the placenta and may still be attached to the baby at this stage. Once the placenta has separated from the uterus it will slide down the birth canal of its own accord.

Labor, though it can be circumvented with a cesarean birth, is beneficial for the wellbeing of the baby. Stress hormones, known as catecholamines, surge through the baby's system during a vaginal delivery in response to the contractions of the uterus and the baby's head being squeezed. This surge both protects the baby from asphyxia and prepares the baby for the environment outside the uterus. It also clears the baby's lungs and prepares them to breathe, and sends a rich supply of blood to the baby's heart and brain.

Position

Advocates of natural childbirth encourage women to labor in an upright position, either standing supported by others (partner, support person such as a midwife) or squatting. Lying prone, often with legs in stirrups, is known to slow the birth and increase the likelihood of the baby's delivery by instrument (forceps or vacuum extraction). The upright position, with the woman responding to her body's signals, leads to a lower incidence of episiotomy.

Though women are given an estimated date of confinement or delivery calculated from the date of their last menstrual period, and often confirmed by the use of ultrasound, only 4 percent of babies are actually born naturally on this day.

Signs of labor

Signs of labor include: the show, which is the expulsion of a mucous plug at the mouth of the uterus (the cervix) and which can appear as many as two or three weeks before actual labor; contractions, which can be regular or irregular but which indicate labor when they become stronger and more painful as they progress; and the waters breaking, which means the amniotic sac which is holding the baby has broken.

Pain control

Labor is a painful experience and many women in industrialized societies who have little or no experience of pain use medication to help them cope with it. Epidural anesthesia is a very common form of pain relief, as are nitrous oxide gas and pethidine (a narcotic). Less invasive methods include acupuncture, aromatherapy, hypnosis, massage, relaxation, transcutaneous electrical nerve stimulation, nipple stimulation, and warm baths and showers.

Assisted births

Some obstetricians believe in active management of labor which involves breaking the waters (amniotomy), the use of synthetic oxytocin to speed up labor and continuous monitoring of the labor's progress. This can involve electronic fetal monitoring, an epidural anesthetic, episiotomy (an incision in the perineum to facilitate the delivery of the baby's head and shoulders) and instrument delivery either with forceps or by vacuum extraction. In an episiotomy the woman's perineum is cut under local anesthetic, ostensibly to give the baby an easier passage and to prevent tearing. The World Health Organization says the systematic use of episiotomy is unjustified and advises protecting the perineum in other ways. When labor is allowed to progress naturally and the woman gives birth in an upright position (squatting, sitting or standing), a tear is less likely and gravity helps the birth of the baby.

Problems and complications

The most common position (85 percent of births) for a baby to be born in is the occipito anterior position (head down, facing the mother's spine). However, babies can also be born in various positions, including: occipito posterior (with the spine against the mother's, a position which causes long backache during labor); breech (bottom first); or transverse (lying across the uterus). Breech babies can be buttocks first or have a foot presenting; this is known as footling breech. Breech babies are sometimes turned in the uterus by the obstetrician or midwife or by using natural therapies prior to the birth; they are then born by cesarean section or born naturally.

Even a baby in the most natural position for birth can present problems that require medical help. Cesareans are life-saving in an emergency and are often used with breech babies, though this is not always justified. Other methods, such as forceps and vacuum extraction, can assist the delivery of a baby. Forceps (two instruments shaped like large flat spoons that fit over the baby's head) are often used when the mother's blood pressure rises and the baby needs to be delivered, or when there are signs of fetal distress, or when the baby is in an unusual position. Vacuum extraction is used in similar situations. It involves using a suction instrument to guide the head down the canal.

Despite all the best intentions and most sophisticated calculations, babies are still born unexpectedly. When this happens it is important to make the environment as warm as possible, to support the laboring woman both physically and emotionally, and to be ready to assist if necessary. This can involve gently unlooping the cord from around the newborn baby's neck and making sure there is no membrane over the baby's face preventing breathing. It may also involve keeping both mother and baby warm and comfortable until assistance arrives. It is not vital to clamp and cut the cord which attaches the baby to the placenta; so long as the placenta detaches from the wall of the uterus during the third stage of labor without problems. The placenta can remain attached to the baby for some time. However, if the placenta does not detach then hemorrhage can result.

In the normal progress of labor, the expulsion of the placenta occurs in the third stage, often passing almost unnoticed. The uterus continues to contract, the placenta separates from the lining, the contractions of the uterus prevent excess bleeding, and the placenta slides out. Some attendants will pull on the cord to help the placenta to separate and in other situations the woman will be given an intravenous injection of ergotamine to induce powerful contractions and help the placenta separate. This, however, is considered a controversial treatment.

C

Breech birth

By the end of gestation, the fetus has usually rotated within the uterus, with its head towards the birth canal and face towards the mother's sacrum. If the fetus faces the mother's pubis instead (6 percent of deliveries) and the legs and buttocks enter the vaginal canal first, then this is called a breech birth.

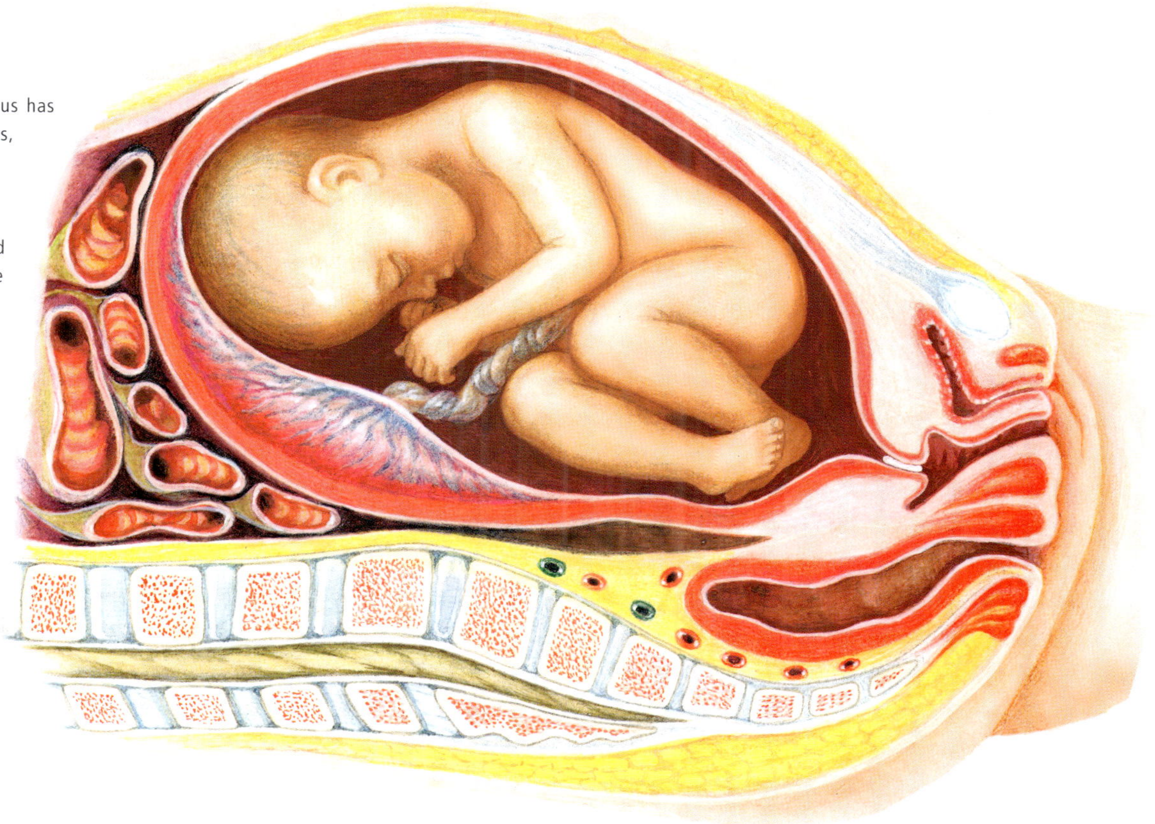

Hemorrhage is still a major cause of maternal disease and death, and a retained placenta may need manual removal. Clamping the cord early has not been found to have any effect on blood loss or hemorrhage.

Cesarean section

Cesarean section, the delivery of the baby through an incision made across the abdomen, in a line just below the pubic hair line, is the surgical alternative to vaginal birth. In many industrialized countries the cesarean rate has risen due to fear of litigation (about deaths of babies born vaginally). The World Health Organization has found that cesarean rates should not be higher than 10–15 percent, but in many industrialized countries, apart from the Scandinavian countries, the rate is climbing through the 20s, and this climb is attributed to clinical practice. Cesarean birth is a major operation. The potential benefits are great when done appropriately, but there are also substantial risks for both mother and baby. Cesareans are often used for the delivery of multiple pregnancy though the indications have not been properly established.

Premature and overdue births

Nearly half of all multiple births will occur prematurely. Other causes of prematurity are maternal illness or placental problems, such as placenta previa, smoking, anxiety, distress or excess tension, and poor nutrition. However, many premature births have no known cause. Around 6 percent of babies are born underweight and the majority of these are premature—the rest are termed small-for-dates. Prematurity is defined by the baby's gestational age (the time the baby has been in the uterus), not by birth weight.

It is unreasonable to expect all babies to spend 280 days *in utero;* just as some are premature, some will naturally be overdue. Only around 5 percent of babies are born on the estimated date of delivery or estimated date of confinement. With ultrasound, pregnancies can be closely monitored and a pregnancy can be allowed to go two or more weeks past the due date through the use of this technology, which can monitor the baby and the uterine environment. Babies born overdue are termed postmature.

After giving birth

During the labor and birth the woman's hormones help her to cope physically and emotionally with the whole experience. Once the baby is born, if there have been no drugs, she is usually in a state of euphoria. She can cuddle, caress and gaze into her baby's eyes as she grows accustomed to holding this little person she has been carrying *in utero* for nine months. This euphoria can continue for some time and in some women it buoys them along through the early days and weeks of motherhood. For others there is an emotional drop in mood sometime in the first week, which is often called the "baby blues", and for a few there is the trauma of postnatal depression. A hospital environment is not conducive to maternal–infant bonding and often restrictive hospital practices will not allow the mother to spend precious time with her baby, thus interfering with the establishment of breast feeding and the forming of this bond. This, together with the hormonal changes and a new mother's lack of experience with babies, can lead to postnatal depression. Postnatal psychosis is a rare mental illness that needs medical treatment.

The postpartum period is the first days after the delivery of a baby. In this time a woman's body will change again as it returns to the non-pregnant state. Excess fluid will be excreted and muscle tone will begin to return. The body will also adapt to its new role of feeding the baby. Women who are supported by friends and others find that coping with being a new mother is easier.

SEE ALSO *Bottle feeding, Breast feeding, Episiotomy, Infancy, Labor, Newborn, Placenta, Postnatal depression, Pregnancy*

C

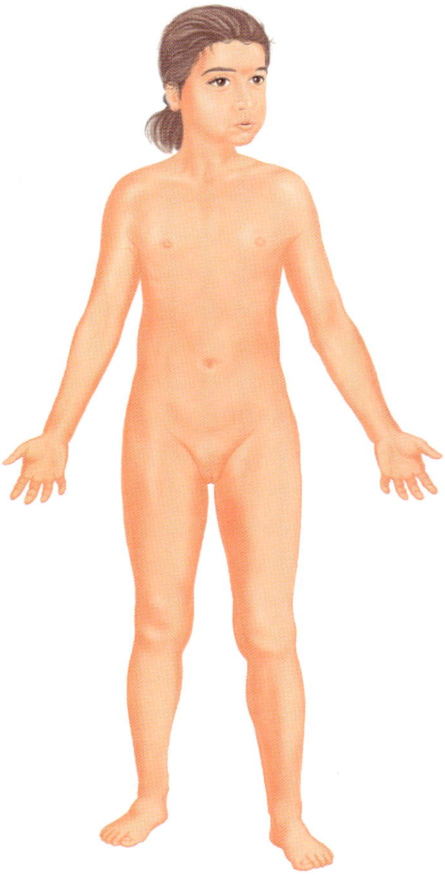

5-year-old girl

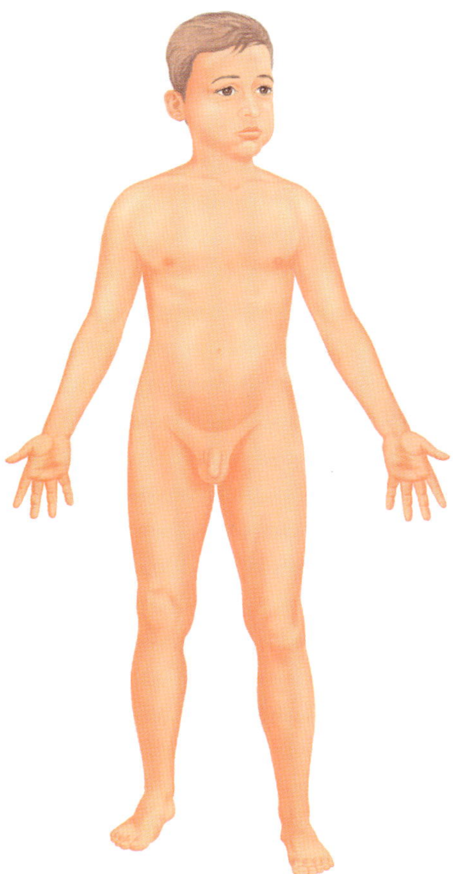

5-year-old boy

CHILDHOOD

Childhood is regarded as the period between infancy and puberty. It is the beginning of the journey towards full independence, a period of fast physical and mental growth during which education and experience build a foundation for adulthood. Childhood ends in the teenage years when growing sexual maturity brings a marked change in appearance, attitude and interests.

Each child is an individual and will develop as determined by genetic inheritance, familial traits and environmental input. Physical, emotional, social and spiritual developments will impact on each other, and, though highly complex, the changes a child undergoes are ordered and specific.

In most children growth occurs in irregular spurts. Some children will be larger or smaller than their peers. Build is a factor in growth, and overweight children may appear to grow slowly in height compared to their weight; adolescents who reach puberty later than their peers usually catch up eventually.

At 12 months old a child will be able to sit without support, crawl or move around, come up to a standing position, smile and babble, and say words which have meaning, or appear to. In the second year a child will learn to walk alone, drink from a cup, wave goodbye, understand simple commands and questions, and combine words.

By around the age of 3 or 4 years, most children will have mastered the major physical tasks, including walking, jumping, running, climbing stairs, grasping and manipulating objects. By the third year, the child will able to use sentences containing 5 or 6 words, and can understand grammar and meaning by 6 years old. At the age of 3 or 4, the child will have a vocabulary of several hundred words. Between 2 and 6 years of age the child develops cognitive skills such as knowing how to perceive, think, recognize, and remember. There is growing awareness of the child's own emotions as well as empathy with feelings and perspectives of others.

Overall, growth is a steady process, with weeks or months of slightly slower growth alternating with mini "growth spurts". After the first year, a baby's growth slows considerably, and by 2 years, growth usually continues at a fairly steady rate of approximately 2½ inches (6 centimeters) per year until adolescence.

Boys grow slightly faster than girls at birth but at about 7 months growth rates are even after which girls grows faster until about 4 years. From then until adolescence growth rates are the same. On average girls are slightly shorter than boys until adolescence and weigh less than boys until about the age of 8, after which they are heavier until about 14 years of age.

By the time a child is 6 years of age all the primary teeth will have appeared and the secondary teeth are starting to emerge. The primary (baby) teeth appear in a pattern from as early as 6 months old until around 3 years. Likewise, the secondary teeth erupt in a pattern, gradually replacing the primary teeth.

During childhood the long bones, such as those in the arm and leg, start as cartilage "models" which are then gradually converted into bone (ossified). The centers of ossification are the shaft (diaphysis) and regions near the ends of the bone (epiphyses). Between the diaphysis and epiphyses is a growth plate where increase in length of the bone takes place. By the age of about 20, ossification reaches and includes the growth plate, at which time growth stops.

Similarly the skull has certain bones which develop directly from the soft connective tissue membrane through the process of ossification. Other parts of the skull are derived from pre-existing cartilage. As the brain grows, the flat bones of the skull enlarge by expansion at the margins. The brain (along with the skull, the eyes and the ears) develops earlier than other parts of the body. At birth the brain is already 25 percent of its adult weight, at age 5 about 90 percent, and at age 10, about 95 percent. Other internal organs such as the liver, the spleen, and the kidneys grow in line with the child's general increase in height.

The different bones of the wrist ossify at known times during development, so that x-rays of a child's wrist are used as a measure of a child's growth compared to chronological age. These can also be used to estimate the expected height of a child during investigation of height problems.

Normal growth depends on a sufficient intake of nutrients and vitamins, exercise

Bone formation during childhood

Long bones begin as cartilage in the embryo. By birth, ossification (development of bone) has reached almost to the ends of the cartilage models. New centers for bone growth then develop at either end of the bone. A plate of cartilage (growth plate) develops between these two areas of bone, and is where the increase in bone length occurs. The growth plate moves steadily away from the center of the bone towards the ends until all cartilage has ossified. Growth in bone length is then complete. Long bones are modeled to be wider at the ends than the middle, providing extra support at the joints where it is needed.

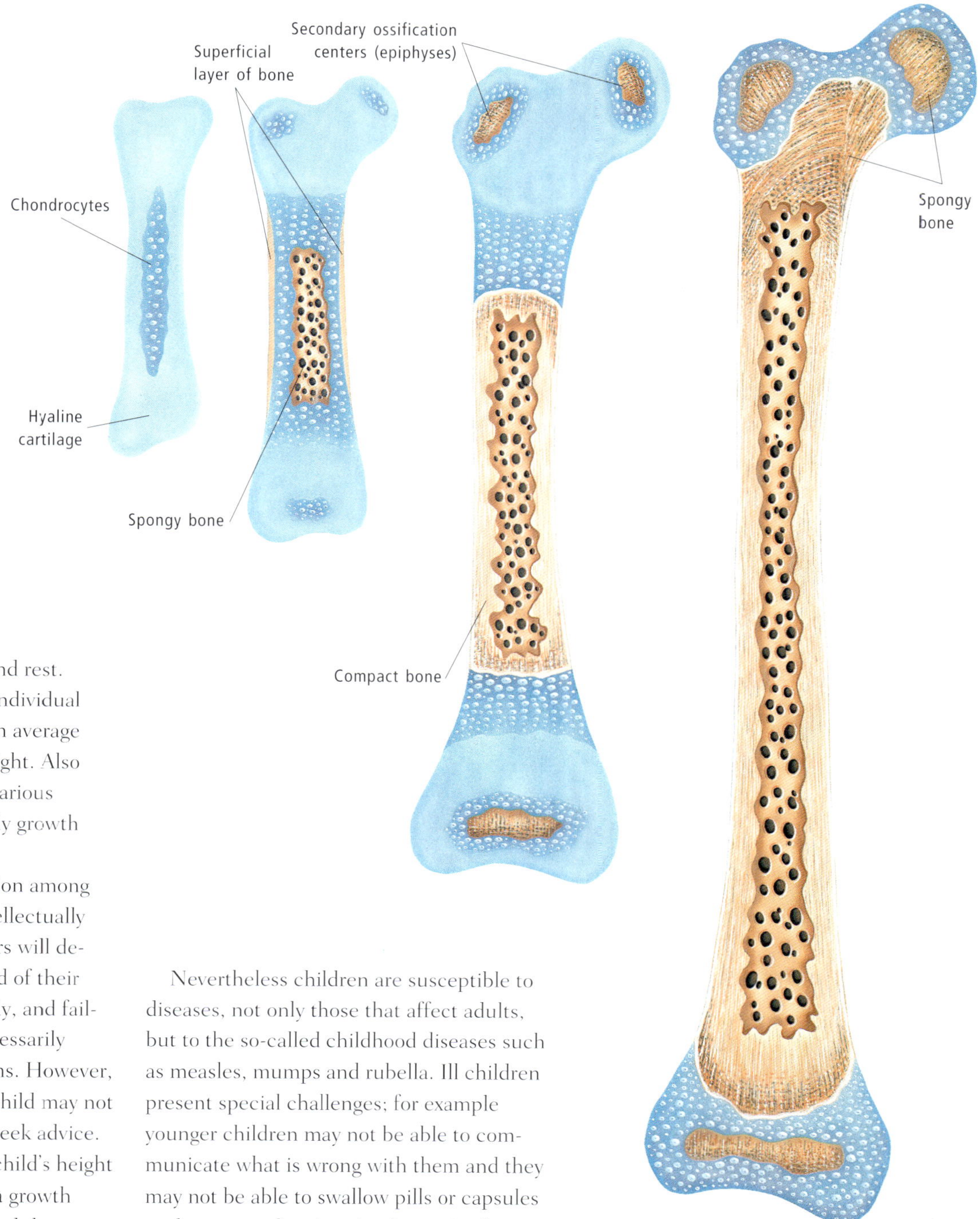

(which helps prevent obesity) and rest. Sleep patterns vary by age and individual child, but most children need an average of 10 to 12 hours of sleep per night. Also important is the production of various hormones by the body, especially growth hormone.

There is a great deal of variation among children. Some will develop intellectually ahead of their peers, while others will develop physically or socially ahead of their peers. Milestones are guides only, and failure to match them does not necessarily mean that there are any problems. However, parents who suspect that their child may not be developing normally should seek advice. During visits to the doctor, the child's height and weight can be recorded on a growth chart. This enables the doctor and the child's parents to compare the child's height and weight compared with that of other children the same age, and determine whether the child is growing at an appropriate rate. Most children who are short or delayed in development are healthy and normal.

Childhood health

Infant and childhood mortality rates over the past decades have declined dramatically, thanks to preventive measures such as better maternal nutrition and obstetrical care, and improved housing, water supply, and sewage disposal.

Nevertheless children are susceptible to diseases, not only those that affect adults, but to the so-called childhood diseases such as measles, mumps and rubella. Ill children present special challenges; for example younger children may not be able to communicate what is wrong with them and they may not be able to swallow pills or capsules so drugs must be given in alternative forms. Fortunately, because they are still growing, children tend to recover faster than adults from many conditions. Bone fractures for example tend to heal better because in childhood bone is still being remodelled and reshaped.

Behavioral problems

Although behavioral problems cause parents to worry they are not usually serious, and unless there are severe underlying emotional disorders, the children will usually grow out of them. However, counseling may be needed in some cases.

Aggression

When children play together some aggressive behavior is normal until they learn from the adults in whose care they are how to get on with others, when to stand up for themselves, when to wait and how to share. Children who grow up in a violent family environment often grow up into violent adults who are unable to solve their problems, except in an aggressive manner. Adults who never learn these skills usually carry on with their aggressive physical behavior of hitting, fighting or being unable to share. By the time children reach school age they should be able to control aggressive behavior; if it is still a problem then it is wise to seek skilled advice from a counselor.

Biting

Children who bite others do so for differing reasons, perhaps out of frustration because they feel powerless, as an experiment, or because they are feeling stressed. In the first two instances if they get a response, or the biting gives them a sense of power, they may do it again. If the action seems to be an experiment, such as when they are breast feeding, they must be prevented from biting and told "no" firmly. If they are biting because of stress, that stress must be eased. Whatever the circumstances, the biter needs to know that such behavior is inappropriate and that there are no rewards.

Bullying

Being bullied is not just a problem among children. The deliberate act of hurting other people—frightening them with words or deeds—can be practised by adults, teenagers and children. Bullying is a problem for both the victim and the perpetrator. People who bully will choose a victim who seems to be easy to hurt, and being bullied can destroy someone's self-esteem. At the same time, research has found that it is people who already have low self-esteem who are the targets of bullies. Strategies which help to avoid bullying include learning empowerment. Adults should be involved in the case of a bullied child. Bullies have also been found to have low self-esteem and low self-confidence and likewise need strategies—usually from professional counselors—to help them find ways of being accepted.

Lying

In order for an untruth to be told, the difference between fact and fantasy must be understood. Young children, especially children who have not yet started school, cannot do this. They are unable to make moral judgments: to them, getting caught is wrong, getting out of trouble is right. Even up to the age of eight or nine some children have trouble grasping such concepts—pleasing adults is important, telling lies is not. Once children understand what telling an untruth is, they may lie in many different situations: if they are afraid of being punished or of affection being withheld; if they have low self-esteem and want attention; if they want to impress their peers; if people they look up to tell lies; or if they need to feel independent—this last circumstance is especially the case with adolescents. To help reduce the telling of lies, mistakes should be dealt with without harsh punishments; the difference between fantasy and truth should be taught; and an understanding shown that some lies are really heart-felt wishes. Children need to be taught why it is important to tell the truth, and praising children who tell the truth and giving adolescents some privacy will contribute to minimizing the telling of lies.

Tattle (tale) telling

When someone tattle tells it is important to decide what is behind the telling. Is it jealousy, meanness or is there a real danger? Having assessed the situation, it can either be sorted out by dealing with the cause of the jealousy or by offering the tattle-teller strategies to cope with whatever is causing the unhappiness. If there is danger involved, then the situation should be resolved and the informer's helpfulness acknowledged.

Tantrums

These are not just the province of toddlers. Tantrums are thrown by people—adults, teenagers as well as children—who have no other outlet for their frustration or stress. The frustration can be mixed with other emotions such as jealousy or feeling unwanted and these can add to the fury. Tantrums in young children can be dealt with by an adult who stays in control, is ready to come to the child's assistance, and who does not give in to the demands. With older children the causes and consequences of their behavior should be discussed. Tantrums in adults generally are the sign of deeper problems and may need counseling.

Whining

On the whole, it is unhappy children who whine. Causes can be tiredness, ill health, boredom, frustration or a feeling of insecurity. Reacting swiftly to deal with the cause of the problem and not giving in to the demands of the person who exhibits this behavior, together with providing a secure emotional environment, will help to avoid any whining.

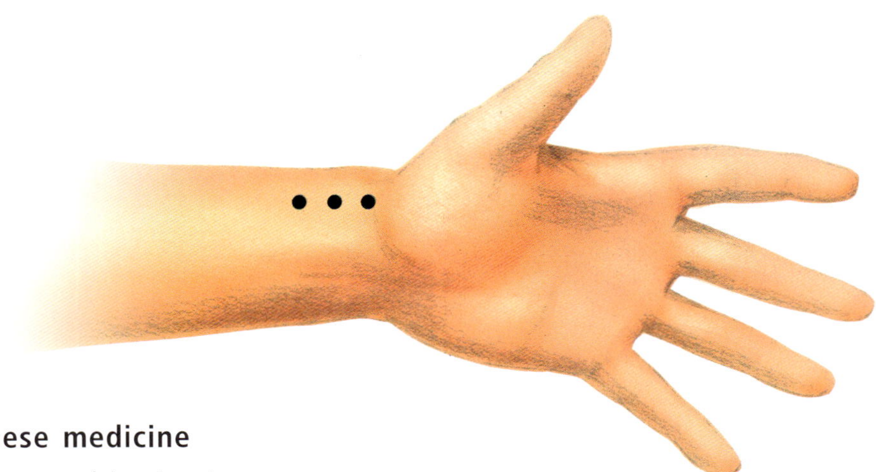

Chinese medicine

These are some of the pulse points measured by herbalists to check the balance of yin and yang.

CHINESE HERBALISM

Chinese herbalism, also known as Chinese internal medicine, is an important aspect of traditional Chinese medicine. The history of Chinese herbal medicine is believed to date back at least 5,000 years to a time when medicine was practised by shamans. The first written records date back to 1500 BC, when medicine was largely a matter of magic and superstition.

A major advance had taken place by around 200 BC when the *Huang Ti Nei-Ching*, or the *Yellow Emperor's Manual of Internal Medicine* was written. Written records, experiment and observation are emphasized; diagnosis distinguishes between the "root" of a disease and its manifestation. By the seventh century AD there were over 800 remedies classified in Chinese herbals. Today there are over 5,000 remedies, many of which have attracted interest from both Western herbalists and medical researchers. Chinese herbalism is still widely practised in China, and is gaining popularity in the West.

Philosophy

Traditional Chinese medicine is based on the Taoist philosophy that emphasizes the importance of balance in life. Herbs are used in this system to help establish and maintain the body's internal balance. *Qi* or *ch'i* refers to the life energy or force which is thought to circulate throughout the body and its organs. This energy is composed of the *yin* and the *yang*—polarities which counterbalance each other while being in a constant state of movement.

Illness is seen as a result of imbalance where overall blockages and deficiencies have developed in the flow of *ch'i*, and hence in the balance between *yin* and *yang*. These "patterns of disharmony" are said to manifest in the body's organs resulting in a particular set of physical, mental and emotional symptoms.

Herbs

Chinese herbs are drawn from a wide range of plant, mineral and animal substances. Great care is given to the correct method of growing, harvesting and processing of each herb to maximize its healing properties. Chinese herbalists classify herbs according to their nature (e.g. warming, cooling or neutral), their taste, their appearance and their properties (e.g. dispersing, consolidating, nourishing, or toning). Herbalists therefore believe they understand not only how the herb may affect a symptom (e.g. diarrhea), but also how it will address the underlying pattern of disharmony (e.g. strengthening the spleen and clearing "damp").

Diagnosis

Chinese herbalists assess a patient's condition by studying the patient's medical history, lifestyle and appearance, particularly of the eyes, skin, hair and tongue. Twelve pulses, six in either wrist, are felt, to measure the flow of *ch'i* through the organs. This gives the herbalist a picture of the underlying disharmony beneath the presenting symptom. The same symptoms may stem from a completely different imbalance within the body; for example, a headache may be caused by an imbalance of either the liver or the stomach.

After diagnosis, the Chinese herbalist prescribes a combination of herbs that may come in the form of powders, pills or raw herbs. The latter are mixed specifically for the client who then makes a decoction out of them by simmering them for between 20–40 minutes, preferably in a traditional Chinese clay pot. Usually a few courses of treatment over weeks or even months, are required to firmly rebalance the body's *ch'i*.

Chinese herbalism is said to be suitable both for general health maintenance and for treatment of specific conditions. It is particularly recommended for chronic conditions such as skin problems, migraine, chronic fatigue syndrome, respiratory and digestive disorders, arthritis, and disorders of the reproductive system.

Chiropractic

Chiropractic is a system of treating musculoskeletal and other ailments based on the manipulation of the spinal joints.

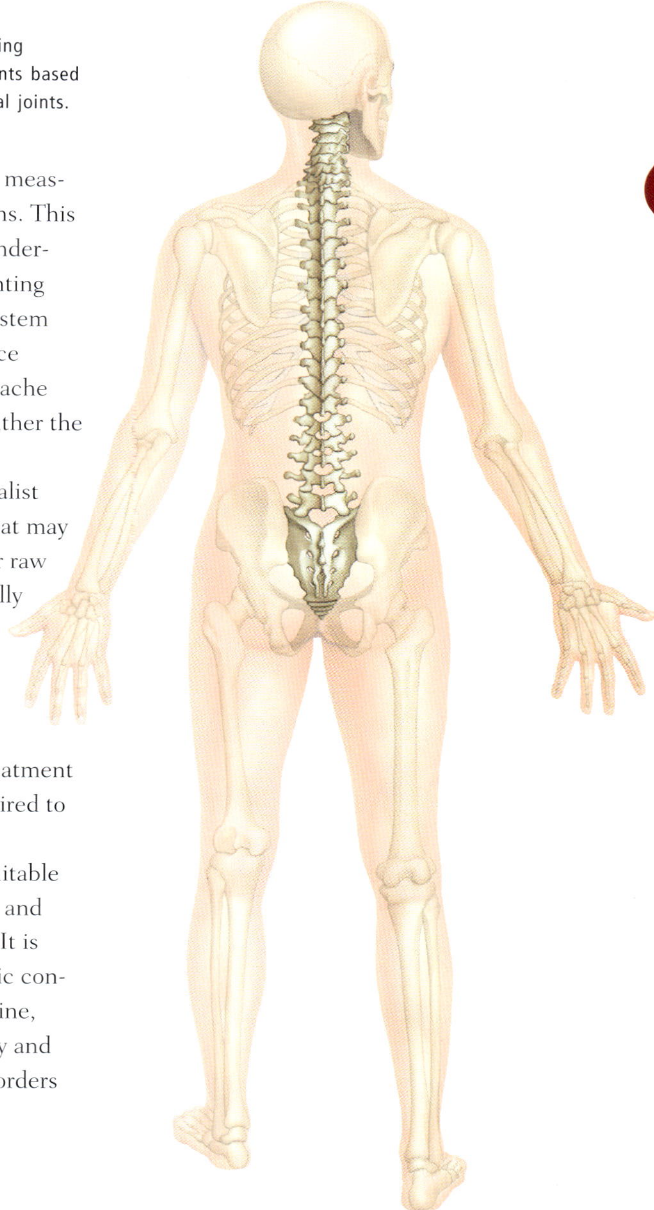

CHIROPRACTIC

Chiropractic is a system of healing based upon the manipulation of the spine and joints. It was pioneered by Daniel David Palmer (1845–1913), an American healer, who developed the premise that illness is essentially due to malfunction in the spine which affects the body's nervous system and organ function, a premise made after he cured a patient's deafness with spinal adjustments in 1895. Palmer coined the word chiropractic from the Greek *cheiro*, (hand) and *praktikos* (to do), meaning "done" by hands, and in 1897 he founded the Palmer Institute and Chiropractic Infirmary to teach his skills. Since that time chiropractic has spread rapidly, and gained acceptance for its therapeutic benefits. It is the second largest health care system in the USA.

Principles

Chiropractic works from the principle that modern life produces abnormalities in the musculoskeletal system, most especially the spine, as a result of trauma, ageing, physical and mental stress and tension. A spinal displacement which upsets the nervous system is known as subluxation; this is said to reduce neural signals and inhibits the body's natural healing ability. Chiropractors work to locate and adjust variations along the spine in order to free up the nervous system's pathways to the brain which govern the function, repair and regeneration of the body's tissues. Chiropractic care is said to enhance the body's function resulting in an improved immune response and resistance to diseases.

Diagnosis

Before any treatment is given the chiropractor needs to have a full picture of the spine's state of function. This is done through a combination of medical history, physical examination (including tissue and organ palpation), postural analysis, muscle testing and spinal x-rays. Where there is a chronic health problem a series of treatments is usually prescribed.

Treatment

Chiropractic adjustment involves changing the position of the vertebrae by specific direct force in a way that causes the vertebrae to move normally with both the vertebrae above and below. The adjustment is delivered with a controlled speed, depth and force, and requires considerable practice and training; treatment should only ever be undertaken by a qualified professional.

The most common forms of chiropractic adjustment are mobilization and manipulation. Mobilization encourages movement by rotation, stretching and pressure to the extent which is possible for the patient without causing discomfort or pain. In manipulation, movement is forced beyond the limit of normal range by a sudden thrust, often accompanied by "clicking" sounds.

Some chiropractors choose to follow a more conservative philosophy of limiting their treatment solely to spinal manipulation. But most chiropractors combine spinal manipulations with various other treatment methods such as soft tissue manipulation, acupressure, heat, and breathing and postural exercises. Many chiropractors employ massage therapists to loosen and warm the back's soft tissue before making any adjustments.

Chiropractors are most commonly consulted for specific musculoskeletal ailments such as back pain, repetitive strain and sports injuries, sciatica, arthritis, rheumatism, and whiplash, as well as migraines and tension headaches. In addition, chiropractic treatment can be used to treat asthma, digestive disorders, menstrual problems and muscular tension where postural problems and spinal misalignments are involved.

SEE ALSO *Massage, Nervous system, Skeletal system, Spine, Vertebrae*

Chlamydia bacteria

CHLAMYDIA

Chlamydia is a genus of three bacterial parasites: *Chlamydia psittaci*, which causes psittacosis; *Chlamydia trachomatis*, which causes trachoma, conjunctivitis and a variety of sexually transmitted diseases; and *Chlamydia pneumoniae*, which causes respiratory tract infections.

It is estimated that up to 30 percent of sexually active women have had a sexually transmitted chlamydial infection, which is six times as common as genital herpes and thirty times as common as syphilis. There may be no symptoms, or mild ones: women may suffer urethritis, slight menstrual-like discomfort and vaginal discharge; men may notice a frequent urge to urinate, a whitish yellow discharge and redness at the tip of the penis. The relative absence of symptoms increases the possibility of unknowingly passing the disease to others. Chlamydia has been linked with pelvic inflammatory disease, ectopic and premature birth, conjunctivitis in babies or pneumonia. A test for chlamydia in those planning a baby is wise.

Chlamydia pneumonia, which was identified as a separate species in the 1980s, causes a mild atypical pneumonia with fever, cough and sore throat.

Fortunately, most forms of chlamydia infection are easily treated with antibiotics.

SEE ALSO *Pelvic inflammatory disease, Pneumonia, Psittacosis, Trachoma, Urethritis*

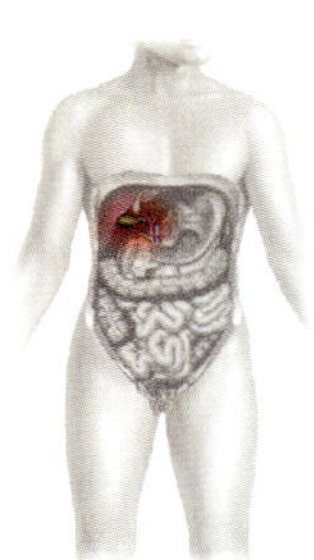

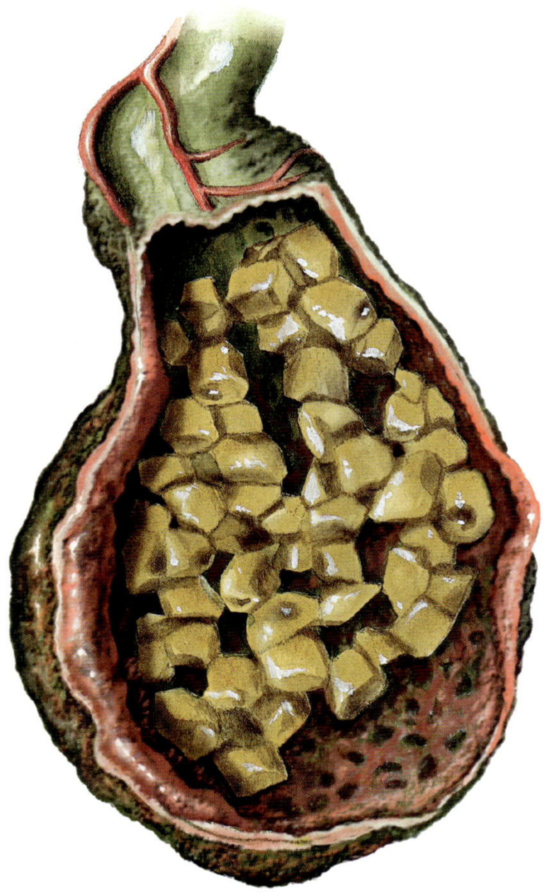

Cholecystitis

Cholecystitis is inflammation of the gallbladder, resulting in attacks of severe, sharp abdominal pain. It is usually caused by gallstones, which will be visible on ultrasound examination.

CHOLANGIOGRAPHY

A cholangiogram is an x-ray of the gallbladder and bile ducts used to identify the presence of gallstones. It involves injection into the body of a dye that is opaque to x-rays; the dye becomes concentrated in the gallbladder and bile ducts, outlining the gallstones. The dye can be injected into a vein (intravenous cholangiogram) or into the hepatic ducts (bile ducts around the liver) though the skin (transhepatic cholangiogram). Alternatively, it may be injected via an endoscope into the opening where the bile duct joins the duodenum (endoscopic retrograde cholangiography).

SEE ALSO *Endoscopy, Gallbladder, Gallstones*

CHOLANGITIS

Cholangitis is inflammation of the bile ducts. It is usually caused by an obstruction of the duct that transports bile from the gallbladder to the small intestine. The obstruction is usually caused by gallstones or a tumor in the pancreas. Pain in the upper abdomen is accompanied by a high fever and chills, often with vomiting and jaundice. The urine may be dark and the feces pale. Treatment with antibiotics may cure the condition, but a severe obstruction may require surgical removal of the gallstones. Sclerosing cholangitis is a chronic disorder of the liver in which the bile ducts become inflamed, thickened, scarred (sclerotic) and obstructed, leading to cirrhosis of the liver. It is fatal without a transplant.

SEE ALSO *Cirrhosis of the liver, Gallbladder, Gallstones, Liver, Pancreas*

CHOLECYSTECTOMY

Cholecystectomy is the surgical removal of the gallbladder. It is a common treatment in severe cases of pain due to gallstones or acute cholecystitis.

Traditionally, cholecystectomy involved removal of the gallbladder through a surgical incision in the abdomen under general anesthesia. However, laparoscopic cholecystectomy has now largely replaced it. In this procedure, the gallbladder is surgically removed through a small incision in the abdomen with the aid of a fiberoptic tube called a laparoscope. It can be performed under local anesthetic, and greatly reduces the hospital stay and recovery time, although there can often be more complications.

SEE ALSO *Cholecystitis, Gallbladder, Gallstones, Laparoscopy*

CHOLECYSTITIS

Cholecystitis is an inflammation of the gallbladder. It is usually caused by gallstones obstructing the outlet of the gallbladder into the cystic duct, which empties into the bile duct system. It may be chronic (long term), or acute (sudden) when there is often accompanying bacterial infection of the gallbladder. Cholecystitis occurs in middle-aged people, especially women who are overweight and who are on the contraceptive pill. The condition causes severe pain in the right upper abdomen with nausea, chills, vomiting and high fever. Ultrasound shows gallstones in the gallbladder and cystic duct.

Treatment is with antibiotics and intravenous fluids in hospital. If the inflammation does not settle down, surgical removal of the gallbladder (cholecystectomy) is required.

SEE ALSO *Cholecystectomy, Gallbladder, Gallstones*

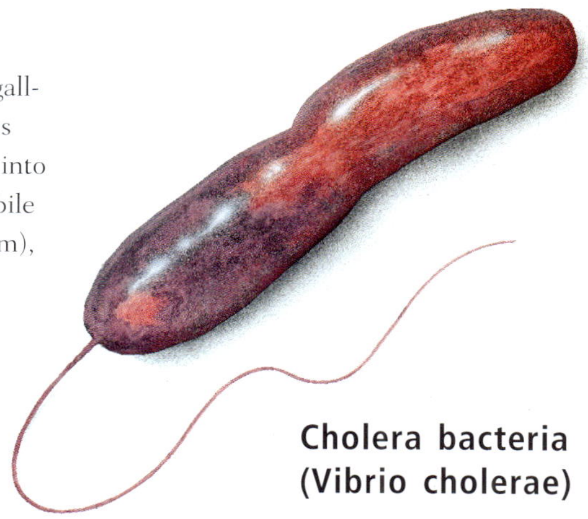

Cholera bacteria (Vibrio cholerae)

CHOLERA

Cholera is a bacterial infection of the intestines. It is spread in contaminated water supplies, in contaminated food and, rarely, by person-to-person contact. The disease occurs one to five days after ingesting the vibrio cholerae bacteria. The sufferer passes large volumes of pale watery diarrhea, and this can quickly lead to dehydration and to death if not treated. Cholera is particularly dangerous to young children whose relatively small body mass results in a more rapid onset of dehydration. Treatment is oral rehydration through salt solutions by mouth, or drip, which may be combined with antibiotics.

SEE ALSO *Dehydration, Diarrhea, Infectious diseases, Intestines*

CHOLESTEROL

Cholesterol is a fatty substance manufactured in the body and also absorbed from foods. It circulates in the blood in substances called lipoproteins. A high level of low-density lipoprotein (LDL) is linked to atherosclerosis—a condition where cholesterol sticks to the inside walls of arteries and

Cholesterol and lipoprotein

Cholesterol travels around the body in lipoprotein as free cholesterol and cholesteryl esters.

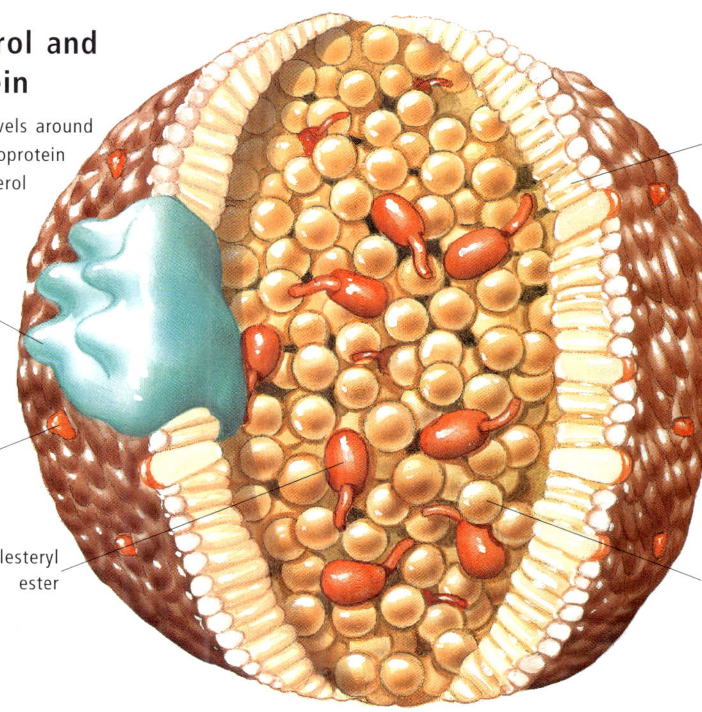

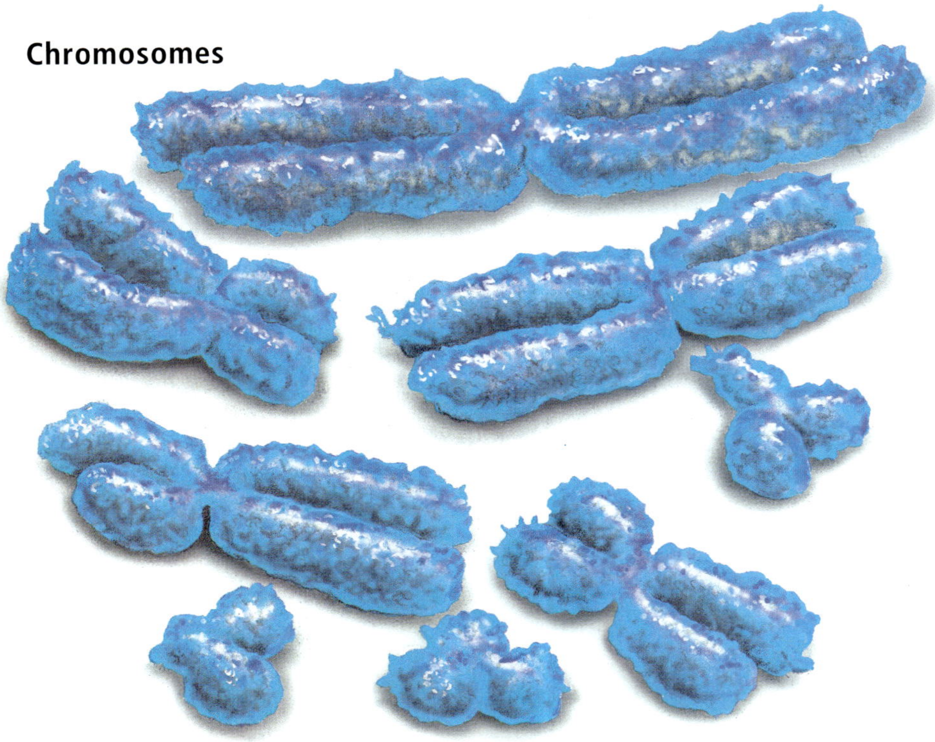

restricts blood flow. Arteries can become completely blocked, and where this happens in the arteries inside the heart the person will suffer myocardial infarction (heart attack). If arteries to the brain are blocked, a cerebral infarction (stroke) may result.

High-density lipoprotein (HDL) is believed to help remove cholesterol from the body by carrying it to the liver for processing and excretion.

International guidelines suggest that levels of LDL cholesterol in the blood should be below 200 milligrams per 100 milliliter (deciliter)—but levels differ with personal profile. In a small number of people, high cholesterol levels can be genetically inherited and the family's history plus a full medical examination will allow a doctor to consider all factors. Modifying the diet to exclude foods high in saturated fats can reduce levels of cholesterol in the blood.

This means eating less meat, butter and other dairy foods and eating more fruit, vegetables and cereals. Other risk factors, such as smoking, high blood pressure, being overweight, and not taking regular exercise need to be considered, as they further increase the chance of a heart attack.

As well as the dietary changes already mentioned, naturopaths suggest adding fish, onions, garlic, oat, barley and rice bran and vegetable proteins, especially soy products and dried legumes. Coffee, especially percolated, is to be avoided. Naturopaths recommend filtered water, as well as supplements of fish oil, nicotinic acid, calcium, vitamins C and E, lecithin and brewers' yeast.

SEE ALSO *Arteries, Diet, Fats, Heart, Myocardial infarction, Nutrition*

CHORIOCARCINOMA

Choriocarcinoma is a malignant, rapidly growing tumor that develops from embryonic tissue and may metastasize (spread to distant sites in the body). The tumor develops from the outer layer of the membrane (chorion) that had surrounded an embryo in an earlier pregnancy. It is most commonly seen after hydatidiform moles (molar pregnancies). Occasionally it appears in males in the testes.

A rare condition, choriocarcinoma tends to occur in women over the age of 40. The symptoms are irregular vaginal bleeding and discharge. It is often diagnosed by measuring levels of human chorionic gonadotropin (HCG) in the blood. Biopsy and laboratory examination confirms the diagnosis.

Choriocarcinomas are treated with chemotherapy (alone or in conjunction with radiation therapy) and prognosis is generally good. Hysterectomy is not usually needed.

SEE ALSO *Cancer, Hydatidiform mole, Pregnancy, Tumors*

CHORIONIC VILLUS SAMPLING

Chorionic villus sampling (CVS) is a prenatal test used to diagnose genetic defects in the fetus. Prenatal testing is recommended for mothers over 35, as they are at increased risk of having a child with a chromosomal abnormality such as Down syndrome. CVS has an advantage over amniocentesis in that it can detect problems much earlier in the pregnancy, but it has a slightly higher incidence of miscarriages due to the procedure (about 1.5 percent) and has been associated with limb deformities.

The procedure involves inserting a catheter through the cervix and into the uterus and sampling the chorion, a membrane that forms around the embryo in early stages of pregnancy before the placenta forms. The catheter is guided by abdominal ultrasound.

SEE ALSO *Amniocentesis, Chromosomal abnormalities, Congenital abnormalities*

CHROMOSOMAL ABNORMALITIES

Chromosomal abnormalities may arise through mutation of chromosomes during sperm production or ovum (egg) fertilization, or they may be genetically inherited. Most chromosomal abnormalities cause premature death of the fetus in the uterus, leading to spontaneous abortion (miscarriage). Some abnormalities are compatible with life, though physical or metabolic abnormalities may shorten or affect quality of life. In trisomy 21, for example, there are three number 21 chromosomes instead of two. This causes Down syndrome, a condition in which the child survives into adulthood but with developmental defects.

Suspected chromosomal abnormalities can be detected during pregnancy by amniocentesis, a procedure in which a small amount of amniotic fluid is removed from the amniotic sac around the fetus, which is then tested for specific defects in fetal cells. It is usually performed between the fifteenth and eighteenth weeks of pregnancy. It is recommended for some pregnant women known to be at risk, for example those with a family history of the abnormality or women over 35 years of age. Chorionic villus sampling (CVS) is another technique used during the first trimester of pregnancy; a tissue sample is taken from the placenta and analyzed for evidence of genetic defects in the fetus. If parents are concerned about possible chromosomal abnormalities in an unborn child—if there is a family history, or if an abnormality has occurred in a previous child—they should seek genetic counseling.

SEE ALSO *Amniocentesis, Chorionic villus sampling, Chromosomes, Down syndrome, Genetic counseling*

CHROMOSOMES

A chromosome is a threadlike structure in the nucleus of a cell. Every chromosome consists of a double strand of deoxyribonucleic acid (DNA), arranged in a helical shape. Each chromosome contains many hundreds of genes.

The nucleus of every cell in the normal human body cell contains 46 chromosomes arranged as 23 pairs. The exceptions are the ova (eggs) and sperm cells, which have only 23 single chromosomes. At fertilization, the two sex cells fuse to form an embryo cell with 23 pairs of chromosomes. One pair of the 23 pairs of chromosomes are the sex chromosomes. In males, one of the two sex chromosomes is shorter and contains fewer genes than the other; this is the Y chromosome. The other, longer, sex chromosome is the X chromosome. Males have an X and a Y sex chromosome, while females have two X sex chromosomes.

Chromosomal abnormalities may arise through mutation of chromosomes or may be inherited. Some abnormalities are compatible with life, though usually the affected person has physical or metabolic abnormalities that may be severe. Trisomy 21, in which there are three number 21 chromosomes, not two, causes Down syndrome.

SEE ALSO *Cells, Chromosomal abnormalities, DNA, Down syndrome*

CHRONIC FATIGUE SYNDROME

Chronic fatigue syndrome (CFS), also known as myalgic encephalo-myelitis (ME) or Tapanui flu (and also "yuppie flu"), is not fully understood. There is much debate as to whether this is a disease, but general agreement is that the syndrome does exist and the cause is unknown.

CFS may begin suddenly after an illness similar to flu or following surgery, accident, or bereavement. It affects the immune system and strikes more women than men. Said to exist where a person suffers chronic tiredness over at least six months and cannot gain relief through rest, the symptoms must be severe enough to prevent normal functioning at home and at work. Pain in muscles and abdomen, painful lymph nodes, and mild mental confusion are among the symptoms. Sufferers may develop sensitivity to certain foods, and to medications. Diagnosis is made after excluding pre-existing conditions such as psychiatric illness, depression, eating disorders, substance abuse and physical abnormalities.

Research has not found a cause, nor a cure, but stress seems to trigger the disease and worsen the symptoms. CFS can last for several years and some people never get better, although others recover in under a year. Treatment includes bed rest, avoiding stress, and prescription medications which help to alleviate anxiety.

There are a number of alternative therapies that may help to ease the symptoms of CFS. Acupuncture is thought to restore life energy known as *ch'i* and treats energy imbalance contributing to symptoms such as digestive weakness, muscle aches and mental cloudiness. It may also boost the immune system. Chinese herbs can also be given. Counseling or psychotherapy are often suggested to treat the depression that frequently accompanies chronic fatigue. Herbalism aims to boost the immune system with echinacea, garlic, and digestive tonics such as dandelion and chamomile. Ginkgo biloba may improve brain function and St John's wort may relieve depression. Homeopathy prescribes individual remedies, based on the patient's physical, mental and emotional profile, intending to facilitate a long-term healing process. Naturopathy treats with a detoxification diet, eliminating food additives and pesticides. An anti-candida diet may also be suggested. Patients are tested for food allergies and advised to avoid exposure to chemicals and perfumes. Various vitamins and minerals are prescribed along with exercise.

CIRCUMCISION

The operation of cutting away all or part of the foreskin of the penis is called circumcision. The operation of removing part or all of the female genitalia is known as female circumcision, clitoridectomy or female genital mutilation.

Circumcision of boys is done before or at puberty or, in some Arab peoples, just before marriage. A rite since the time of the ancient Egyptians, circumcision is today an important religious ritual in Islamic and Jew-

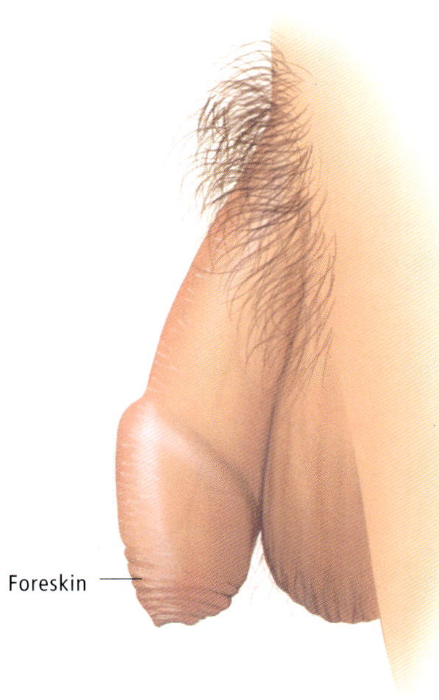

Uncircumcised penis

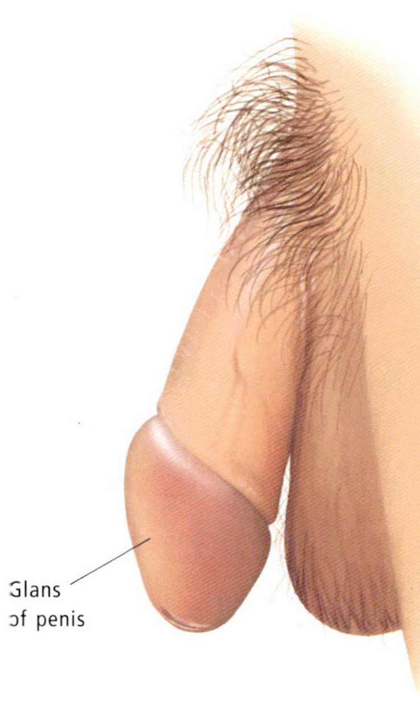

Circumcised penis

ish communities worldwide. It became popular in many industrialized cultures in the early 1900s in the belief that it promoted good hygiene and also discouraged masturbation. Generally, the arguments in favor of circumcision are that there is less likelihood of penile cancer, urinary tract infections or sexually transmitted diseases; the penis is easier to clean; the rest of the males in the family are circumcised; or problems with the foreskin. The arguments against are that it is an unnecessary, painful operation with the possibility of complications, the sensation at the tip of the penis (the glans) is diminished, it is just as easy to clean under a foreskin as without, and that problems with the foreskin are most often caused by adults forcibly attempting to retract it in a young boy before it is ready.

Female circumcision has been performed for centuries in parts of Africa, the Middle East and Southeast Asia with the purpose of preserving virginity, improving hygiene or as a religious ritual. It is usually performed by non-medical practitioners in non-medical settings and has a high risk of complications and long-term consequences including sterility. The procedure can involve infibulation which is the removal of the clitoris, the labia minora and the anterior two-thirds of the labia majora with a join made leaving a small opening. It can also involve the introduction of corrosive substances to cause bleeding for the purpose of narrowing the vagina; or any or all of the above. Even when the wounds heal normally, urination and sexual intercourse can be painful and unreleased menstrual blood can cause problems. In societies where clitoridectomy is practised, male circumcision is usually also practised and it is considered to be an important religious ritual or ethnic tradition.

The World Health Organization, the United Nations Population Fund and the United Nations Children's Fund have drawn up a plan to reduce female genital mutilation, with the aim of eliminating it completely. Strong lobby groups against female genital mutilation exist in many industrialized countries who view it not only as a major health risk but also as the subjugation of women so that they will never enjoy sexual relations.

SEE ALSO *Clitoris, Glans, Penis*

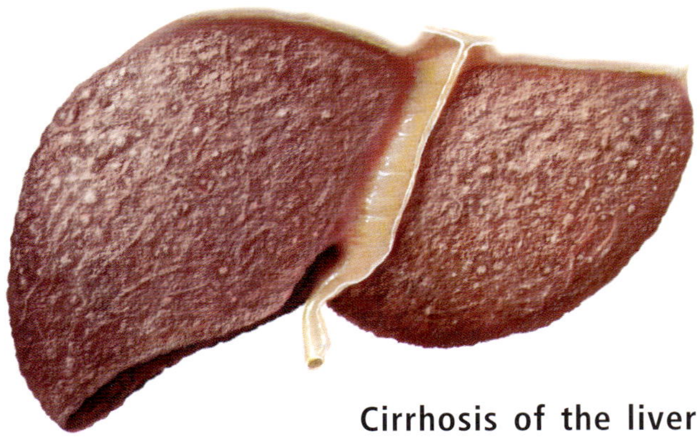

Cirrhosis of the liver

Cirrhosis is the destruction of normal liver tissue. The liver becomes shrunken and filled with fibrous tissue. It functions poorly, and the flow of blood through the liver may become restricted. Eventually, a liver transplant may be needed.

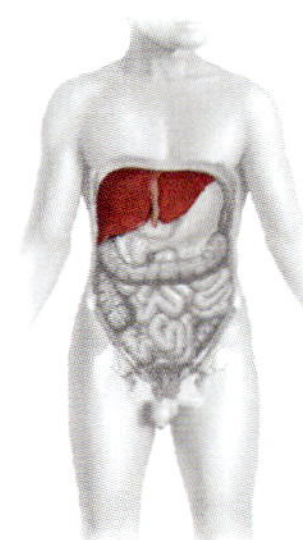

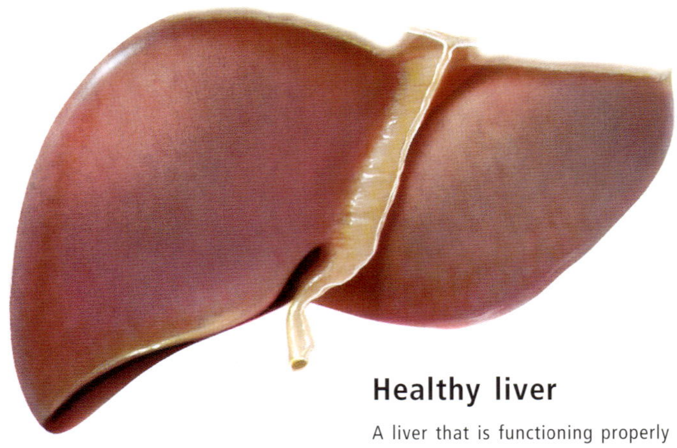

Healthy liver

A liver that is functioning properly has a number of important tasks to perform for the body, including filtering the blood, secreting bile, and converting sugars into glycogen.

Cirrhosis and liver cells

Cirrhosis disrupts the regular microstructure of the liver. Scarring of the liver occurs when cells become misshapen and form nodules, and the bands of tissue that divide the lobules become fibrous or fatty. As the structure of the lobule breaks down, the blood vessels may become blocked, leading to increased blood pressure and hypertension.

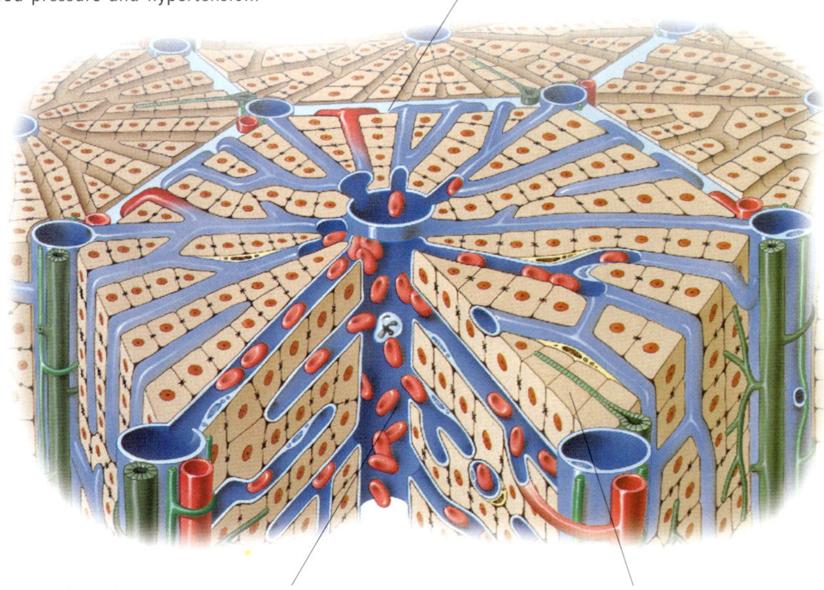

CIRRHOSIS OF THE LIVER

Cirrhosis of the liver is a disease in which there is death of liver cells followed by production of fibrous tissue and regeneration of liver cells in lumps or nodules. The nodules distort the normal structure of the liver and prevent the easy flow of blood through the liver. Cirrhosis may be caused by excessive and prolonged consumption of alcohol. In this case the damage to the liver cells is probably due to the direct toxic effects of alcohol, although a poor diet may also contribute. Patients with alcoholic cirrhosis may also show Dupuytren's contracture, a contraction of connective tissue in the hand, deterioration of the brain, heart problems and enlargement of the parotid salivary gland in the cheek. Men may develop breast enlargement (gynecomastia) and wasting of the testes. Other causes include problems with the storage of iron (hemochromatosis) and an inherited disease to do with copper metabolism (Wilson's disease).

Complications which may arise from cirrhosis include vomiting blood from the esophagus, swelling of the abdomen and ankles, drowsiness, confusion and unconsciousness. About 20 percent of patients with cirrhosis will develop liver cancer.

Treatment of cirrhosis will depend on the cause of liver damage. Alcoholics must abstain from alcohol. Hemochromatosis is treated by removal of blood, while Wilson's disease is treated by drugs which serve to bind the excess copper.

SEE ALSO *Alcoholism, Dupuytren's contracture, Hemochromatosis, Liver, Wilson's disease*

CLAUSTROPHOBIA

Claustrophobia is a specific type of anxiety disorder—an unrealistic and extreme fear of closed places or of being confined. The thought of confinement, or a memory of a confined place, may be all that is needed to trigger the symptoms, which can be physically debilitating. Symptoms include nausea, vomiting, racing heartbeat, diarrhea, and throat constriction. A fear becomes a phobia when the condition interferes with the ability to lead a normal life. Sufferers may know that their reactions are irrational and out of proportion, but whether they are conscious of this or not, the fears are real and must be treated as such.

SEE ALSO *Anxiety, Anxiolytics, Phobias*

CLEFT PALATE AND CLEFT LIP

Cleft palate is a congenital abnormality, in which there is an abnormal opening in the roof of the mouth. Normally as the fetus develops, separate tissues from either side of the mouth fuse together to form the palate, upper lip and upper jaw. If the tissues do not fuse, an abnormal gap connecting the nasal passages with the mouth is the result. The gap is called a cleft palate; it can be closed by surgery, but a series of operations is often required.

Often, a cleft palate is accompanied by a similar gap in the upper lip—this is known as a cleft lip, or harelip. Cleft lip may occur on its own or with cleft palate. Normally, both sides of the upper lip should fuse in the first 35 days in the uterus. If it fails to fuse, a cleft lip is the result. The cleft may vary in size from a notch to a fissure that extends across the whole lip. Usually, it extends from the mouth up into the nostril. It can be on one side only (unilateral) or on both sides (bilateral). The treatment for cleft lip is surgery, usually when the infant is about 10 weeks old or weighs 10 pounds (4.5 kilograms).

Both cleft palate and cleft lip affect females more often than males and sometimes run in families. A cleft palate may occur in combination with heart defects, and an abnormal face, and also learning problems in the congenital disorder known as Shprintzen syndrome (also called the velo-cardio-facial syndrome).

SEE ALSO *Lip, Mouth*

CLITORIS

The clitoris is part of the external female genitals. The shaft of the clitoris is about half an inch (approximately 1 centimeter) in length. The clitoris lies about ½–1 inch (1–2 centimeters) in front of the external opening of the urethra, which carries urine from the bladder. The tip of the clitoris has a glans or head, usually hidden within a fold of thin skin known as the prepuce. The prepuce of the clitoris is a forward extension of the hairless folds of skin (labia minora) which lie on each side of the vagina. Much like the penis, the clitoris is extremely sensitive to sexual stimuli.

SEE ALSO *Reproductive systems, Vulva*

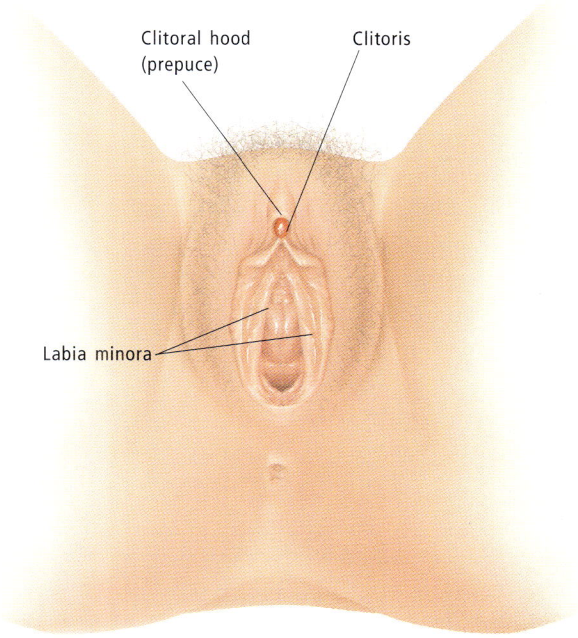

Clitoris

The clitoris is a small protrusion that is very sensitive to stimulation. When a woman becomes aroused, the clitoris fills with blood, enlarges and becomes erect.

COCAINE

Cocaine is a stimulant drug illegal in most countries. Extracted from the leaves of the coca plant, it is processed into cocaine hydrochloride, a white powder that can be inhaled or injected. Crack is a modified form of cocaine that can be smoked. Historically, cocaine was used for medicinal purposes as an anesthetic for surgery of mucous membranes.

Cocaine speeds up the central nervous system producing a faster heartbeat, a rise in temperature, feelings of exhilaration, anxiety, or even panic, loss of concentration, and unpredictable or violent behavior. Large quantities can cause paranoia, heart attack and even death. Likewise, long-term use can induce paranoia and hallucinations, repeated injections can block and inflame blood vessels, and inhalation can damage the lining of the nose and the septum (the barrier between the nostrils).

SEE ALSO *Anesthesia, Drug dependence, Stimulants*

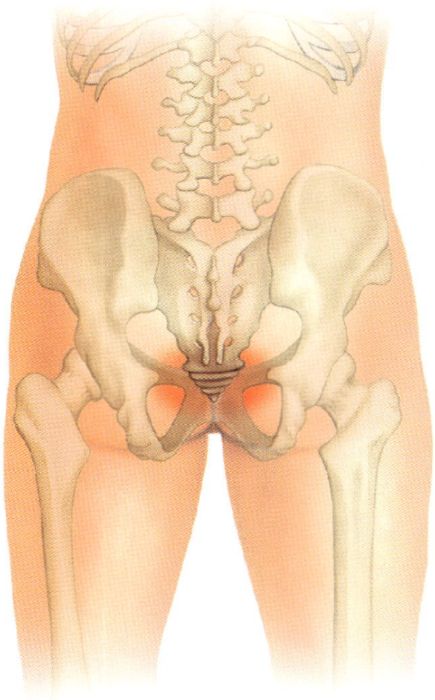

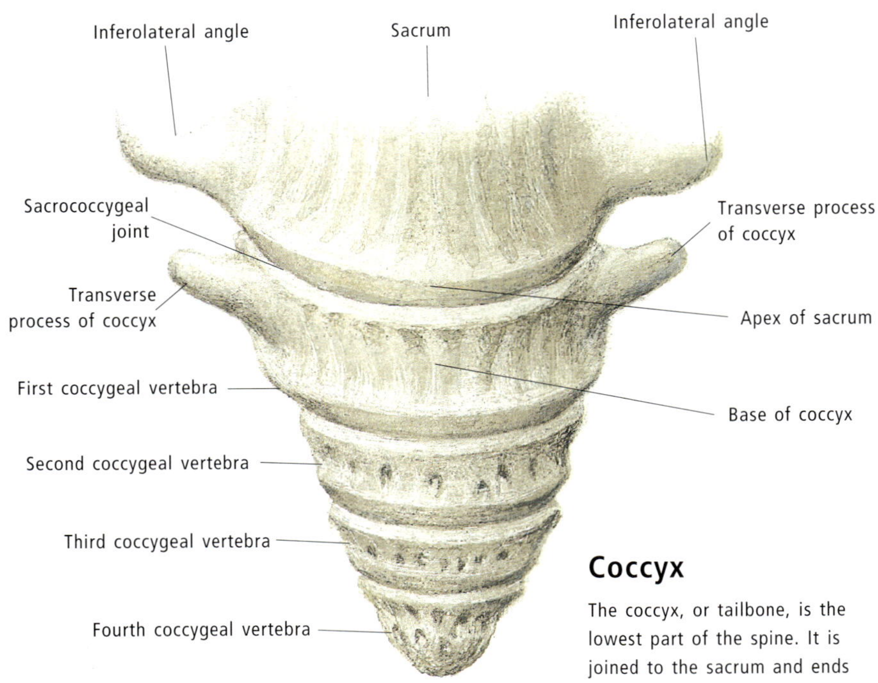

Coccyx

The coccyx, or tailbone, is the lowest part of the spine. It is joined to the sacrum and ends just above the level of the anus.

Coccygodynia

Coccygodynia is a painful inflammation of the coccyx (tailbone) that usually occurs following a direct fall onto the area. Treatment with anti-inflammatory drugs may be necessary to relieve the symptoms.

COCCYGODYNIA

Coccygodynia (also called tailbone pain) is inflammation of the bony area (tailbone or coccyx) located at the lowest part of the spine. It may occur for no apparent reason, but more usually follows an injury to the coccyx—for example when someone falls heavily backward in a sitting position. The pain is worse when sitting or passing feces, but goes when the person stands.

Treatment with anti-inflammatory and analgesic drugs can relieve the symptoms. People with coccygodynia should avoid long periods of sitting and when they do sit, they should use a padded cushion or seat. Persistent coccygodynia can be treated with cortisone injected into the area. In severe cases that don't respond to other treatments, the coccyx can be surgically removed.

SEE ALSO *Coccyx, Spine*

COCCYX

The coccyx is the lowest bone of the spine. Situated just above the anus, it is formed from three to five rudimentary vertebrae, which are fused and joined to the sacrum above. The coccyx is also called the tailbone. The word "coccygeal" derives from the Greek *kokkyx* meaning "cuckoo bird" as the coccyx was thought to look like a cuckoo's bill.

Coccygodynia is persistent, severe pain in the coccyx. It usually follows an injury to the coccyx. Treatment with analgesic and anti-inflammatory drugs can ease the symptoms on many cases.

SEE ALSO *Coccygodynia, Spine*

COCHLEA

The cochlea is a small, spiral-shaped structure in the inner ear containing fluid and special hair cells which serve as sound sensors.

Sound waves entering the ear set up a chain of vibrations, beginning with the eardrum (tympanic membrane). These continue with the middle ear bones (ossicles), which transmit vibrations to the cochlea, where they cause waves to form in the cochlear fluid. The waves in turn stimulate tiny hair cells in the cochlea, which transform vibrations into nerve impulses for transmission to the brain. These are recognized by the brain as sounds.

A cochlear implant (also known as a bionic ear) is a system of tiny electrodes which is surgically inserted into the inner ear and which transmits sound vibrations to the auditory nerve. It restores hearing to a person whose cochlea has been damaged, for example by trauma, drug toxicity or infection.

SEE ALSO *Ear, Hearing*

COGNITIVE THERAPY

Cognitive therapy is a widely practised form of psychotherapy used to treat emotional and behavioral disorders, particularly depression and anxiety. The word cognize, from which the term cognitive comes, means "to know or perceive".

A simple interpretation of the underlying basis of cognitive therapy is that thoughts affect a person's behavior and emotions. Practitioners using this treatment help patients turn around their way of thinking from being negative, destructive and sometimes harmful to being positive and constructive. As fundamental as it may sound, changing the way someone thinks about events can, however, be a complex process.

Patients with depression or anxiety often fail to understand that thoughts which enter their mind in response to experiences in their lives may be based on errors in reasoning—that is, cognitive errors or distortions. They may, for example, place all blame for a relationship breakdown on themselves or believe they are personally responsible for a tragedy beyond their control. A fundamental component of cognitive therapy involves helping patients recognize and modify cognitive distortions.

Another aspect of this form of therapy is aimed at modifying, when necessary, a patient's core beliefs or "schemas". These are regarded as the basic rules the mind uses for interpreting information.

Frequently, cognitive therapy involves the use of intervention techniques for dysfunctional behaviors, in the belief that what patients do reinforces the way they think, as well as the other way around.

SEE ALSO *Anxiety, Behavioral therapy, Counseling, Depression, Psychotherapy*

COLD SORES

A cold sore, also known as herpes simplex type 1 or HSV-1, results from a viral infection. It attacks the skin and nervous system producing small, sometimes painful, fluid-filled blisters around the mouth and nose. After a first infection the virus will continue to live in the nerve system in a dormant state from which it can be reactivated by a trigger. These triggers may include sunlight, physical or emotional stress, hormonal changes, certain foods or drugs. The trigger can also be unknown.

An attack begins with a tingling sensation at the spot where the sore will erupt, followed by a rash, then blisters or spots. These can come in clusters, fill with fluid, rupture and form crusts. Cold sores can take up to three weeks to disappear and are highly contagious until healed. Anyone with a cold sore must be diligent about washing hands and scrubbing fingernails, and avoid kissing and other oral contact. It is important not to touch the eye after touching a sore as this can cause an infection or corneal ulceration.

While cold sores are unpleasant to look at, they are not a serious risk to general health. Most cold sores will clear up without treatment; however, acyclovir, an anti-viral drug, can be prescribed. It is most effective if used at the first signs of a sore. Aromatherapists recommend neat lavender oil.

Once the herpes virus has entered the system it stays with the person for life, though attacks usually diminish and often disappear over time. From 10 to 15 percent of cases of genital herpes are caused by the cold sore virus (herpes simplex type 1) and it is possible to sexually transmit cold sores to the genitalia.

SEE ALSO *Genital herpes, Herpes simplex*

COLIC

Colic is pain resulting from the distension of a hollow internal organ, usually the intestine. Babies and children are especially prone, but adults can suffer too. Typically colic in babies begins at two to four weeks and lasts until around three months. Symptoms are excessive crying (three hours or more a day, three days a week is excessive) and curling up the legs. Older children complain of pain. One common cause is wind that has passed into the stomach or intestine rather than being released through a burp. Colic can also be caused by a groin hernia.

There is no safe medicine for babies with colic. Aromatherapy and osteopathy are said to help. If the baby is being breast fed, this should be continued as ceasing will not solve the problem. If the baby's crying is causing tension in the mother and it affects her breast feeding, then relaxation and reassurance that the colic will pass may help. Making sure the baby has a routine and learning what the baby's cries mean can also help. It is also important that the mother of a colicky baby has regular breaks herself and is offered support.

SEE ALSO *Breast feeding, Infancy, Newborn*

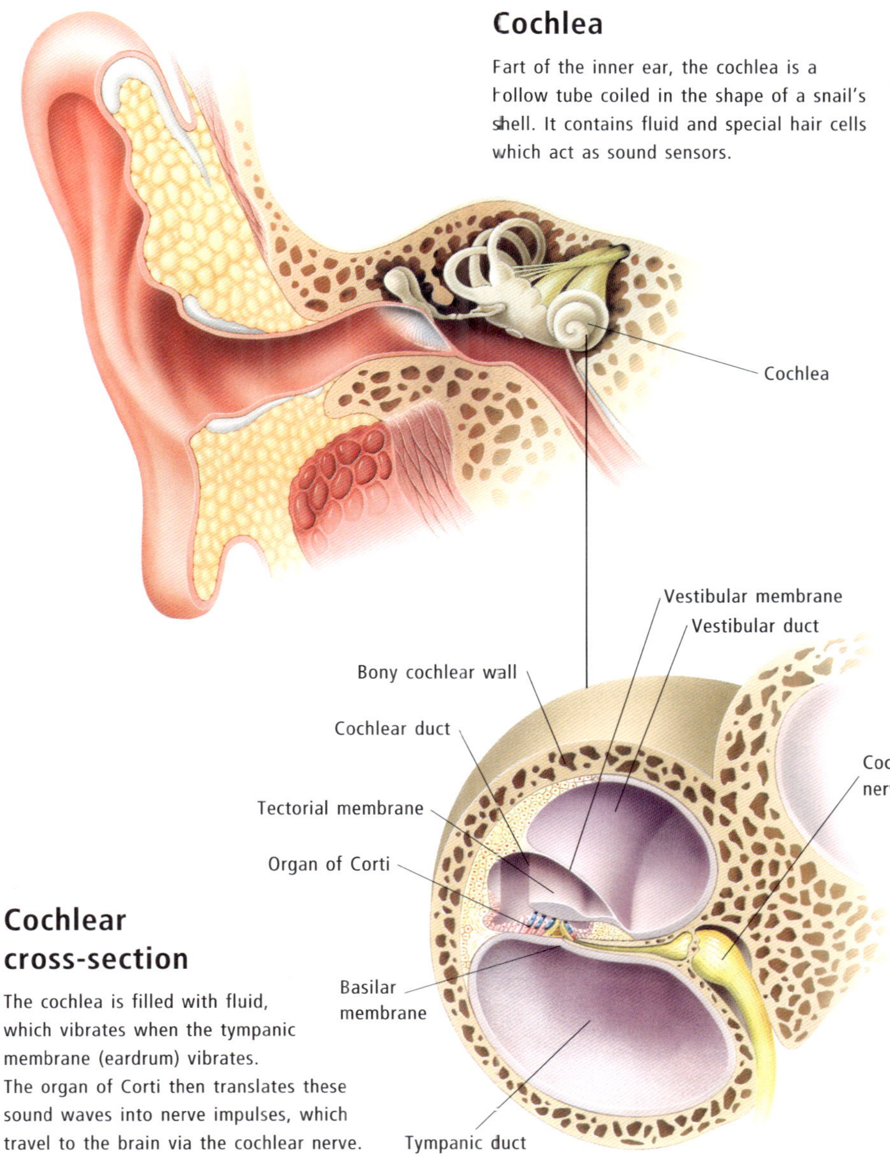

Cochlea

Part of the inner ear, the cochlea is a hollow tube coiled in the shape of a snail's shell. It contains fluid and special hair cells which act as sound sensors.

Cochlear cross-section

The cochlea is filled with fluid, which vibrates when the tympanic membrane (eardrum) vibrates. The organ of Corti then translates these sound waves into nerve impulses, which travel to the brain via the cochlear nerve.

a

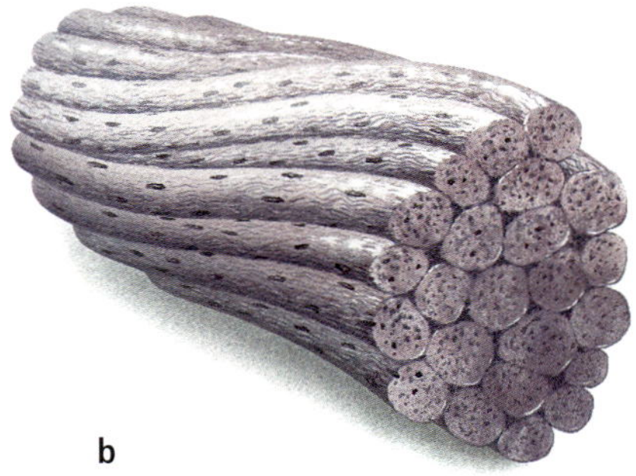

b

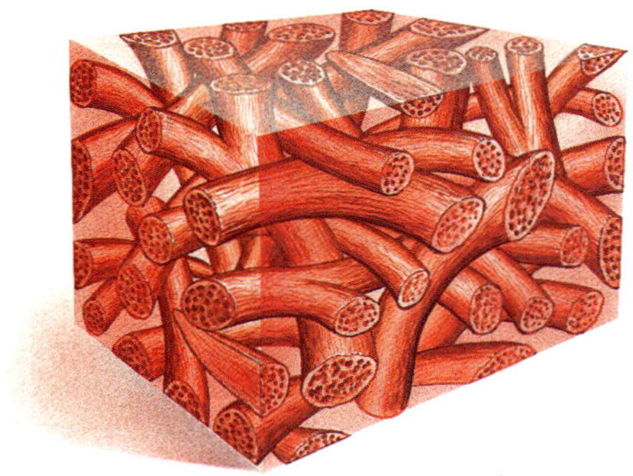

c

Collagen

Collagen is a tough, flexible protein, found in different arrangements, in structures such as ligaments (a), tendons (b), and the supporting capsules of internal organs (c).

COLITIS

Colitis is inflammation of the large intestine (colon). It may be mild or it may be more serious with severe symptoms, as in ulcerative colitis or Crohn's disease. Symptoms of colitis tend to come and go unpredictably. They can include diarrhea, fever, and crampy abdominal pain. In Crohn's disease or ulcerative colitis there may be intermittent bleeding from the rectum.

Diagnosis is confirmed by a barium enema, or better still, direct viewing by sigmoidoscopy or colonoscopy, which allows a sample of the lining of the large bowel to be taken for laboratory analysis.

Crohn's disease can involve both the colon and small intestine, whereas ulcerative colitis usually involves only the colon. Both are thought to be autoimmune diseases. Crohn's disease may cause ulcers in the lining of the colon, causing scarring, narrowing of the bowel, obstruction, perforation and peritonitis. It is treated with anti-inflammatory, immune suppressant and antibiotic drugs.

Ulcerative colitis can also be associated with inflammation in the joints, spine, skin, eyes, liver and bile ducts. Long-standing ulcerative colitis increases the risk of colon cancer. Mild attacks are usually treated with drugs, a low-fiber diet and rest.

SEE ALSO *Barium enema, Bowel, Crohn's disease, Colon, Intestines, Irritable bowel syndrome, Ulcerative colitis*

COLLAGEN

Collagen is an important structural protein in the body. It is made up of chains of amino acids, with glycine, proline and hydroxyproline being the most common. Collagen is often organized in long parallel bundles of fibers, forming connective tissue, which has a very high tensile strength (for example ligaments and tendons). Collagen may also be formed into sheets (such as mesenteries of the abdominal cavity).

Collagen diseases are a group of diseases (also known as connective tissue diseases), in which there is an attack by the body's immune system on the structural protein of the patient's body. One example is systemic lupus erythematosus.

SEE ALSO *Autoimmune disease, Connective tissue*

COLLAR BONE

The collar bones, or clavicles, are a pair of short horizontal bones above the rib cage. They are attached to the breast bone (sternum), and the two shoulder blades (scapulas) on either side. The function of the collar bones is to stabilize the shoulders.

A fracture of the collar bone is common in childhood. It is usually caused by a fall onto an outstretched hand or the point of a shoulder. Following the fall, the arm on the injured side is limp, and a lump or deformity can be felt or seen over the fracture site.

Treatment involves stabilizing the clavicle with a figure-of-eight splint, which holds the shoulders back and allows the two broken ends of the clavicle to knit and heal.

Collar bone

The collar bone, or clavicle, helps to stabilize the shoulder joint. It is attached to the scapula (shoulder blade) at one end and the sternum (breastbone) at the other.

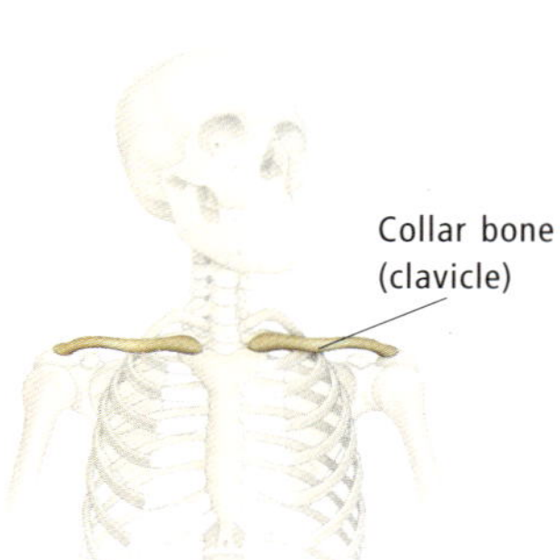

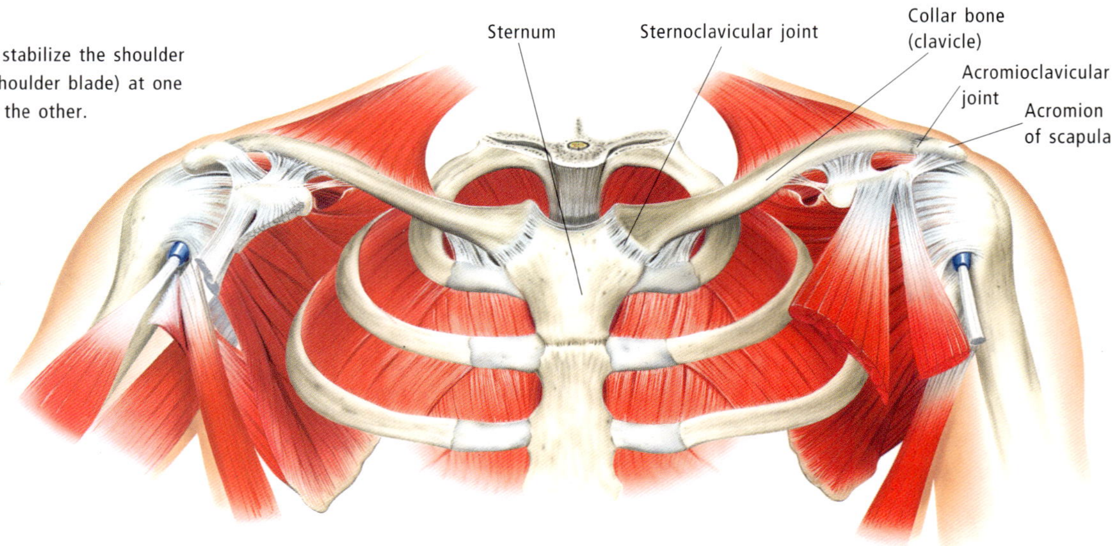

To heal completely takes eight to twelve weeks. Fracture of the clavicle is especially common in the newborn infant. It is prone to breakage so as to allow the infant's shoulders to pass through the narrow birth canal. No treatment is needed as the fracture heals by itself in a few weeks.

SEE ALSO *Ribs, Scapula, Shoulder*

COLON

The colon is part of the large intestine and moves waste material to the anus, absorbing salt and water. It is composed of various organs: the cecum, ascending colon, transverse colon, descending colon and sigmoid colon. The appendix is attached to the cecum.

Ulcerative colitis is a disease that can affect the colon. It occurs in the 15 to 20 age group, or in people over fifty. Patients present with rectal bleeding and diarrhea. They may have frequent discharges of watery stools mixed with pus, blood and mucus. Many patients have cramping abdominal pain, fever, vomiting and weight loss. The disease may have a family history, but is thought to involve some infective or toxic agent interfering with the immune system function in the bowel, causing the body's own defence cells to attack the lining of the colon. Complications include anal problems, perforation of the colon, bleeding from the colon and an increased risk of cancer of the colon.

Hirschsprung's disease is a congenital condition in which the nerve cells controlling the large bowel are missing. The bowel is unable to propel feces along its length, so that obstruction results.

Polyposis of the colon is a rare genetic condition. Patients develop multiple polyps (mushroom-shaped lumps which usually have a stalk, by which they attached to the bowel lining) in the large intestine. Polyps develop in other conditions, but not as many as seen in polyposis. The danger is that each polyp has a chance of cancer developing within it; the more polyps there are, the greater the chance of cancer. This means that patients with polyposis are almost certain to develop cancer within their lifetime. The only cure is to completely remove the colon.

Common investigations of the colon include barium enema and colonoscopy. In a barium enema, the colon is filled with a barium compund which is opaque to x-rays. An x-ray is taken both while the colon is full of barium and after evacuation, and can detect abnomalities of the colon lining. Colonoscopy involves the insertion of a fiberoptic or electronic instrument into the colon to inspect its interior.

SEE ALSO *Barium enema, Colitis, Colonoscopy, Hirschsprung's disease, Intestines*

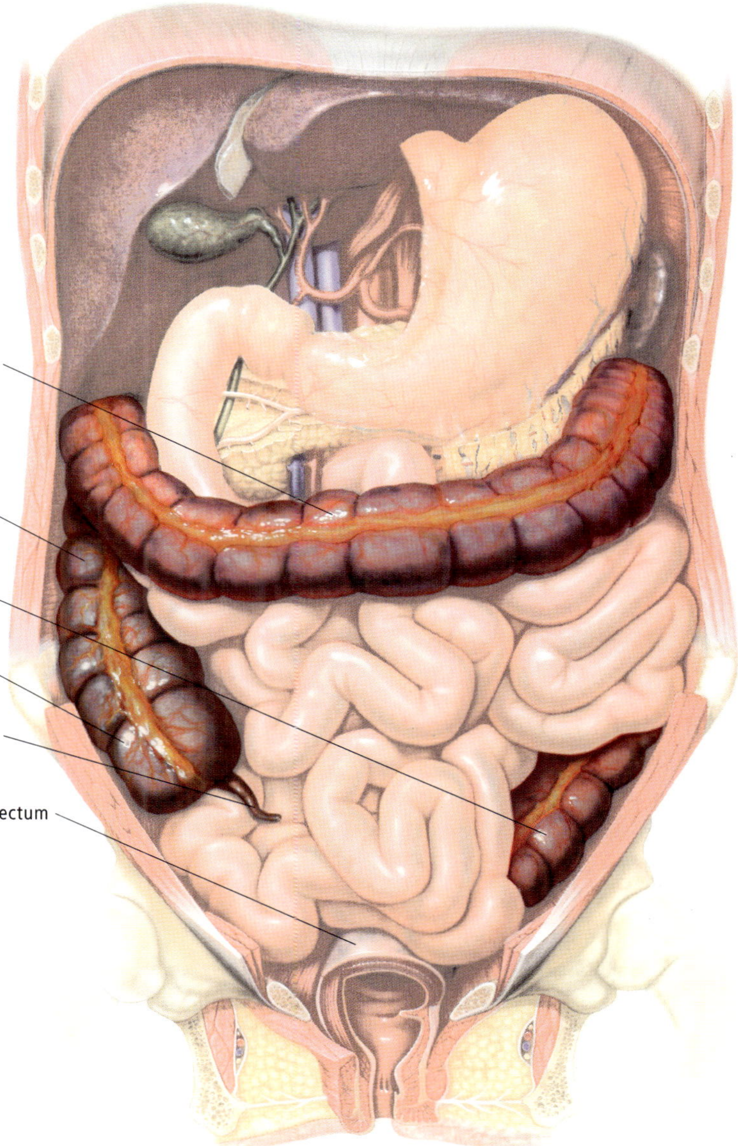

Colon

The colon is part of the large intestine. It stretches from the end of the small intestine through to the rectum and is made up of several parts. The function of the colon is to move solid material to the anus and to absorb salt and water remaining after passage through the small intestine.

COLONIC IRRIGATION

Colonic irrigation is a detoxification technique recommended by some natural therapists. It involves cleansing the large intestine with purified water introduced through the anus via plastic or rubber tubing.

During this procedure the patient lies in a knee-to-chest position on a specially designed table for the 30–40 minutes it takes for the irrigation to take place either manually or by machine. To be safe, this procedure must be performed by qualified staff using sterilized equipment. It is prescribed for chronic bowel conditions and digestive discomfort. Colonic irrigation is considered to help restore the bowel's muscle tone and circulation.

SEE ALSO *Bowel, Colon, Intestines*

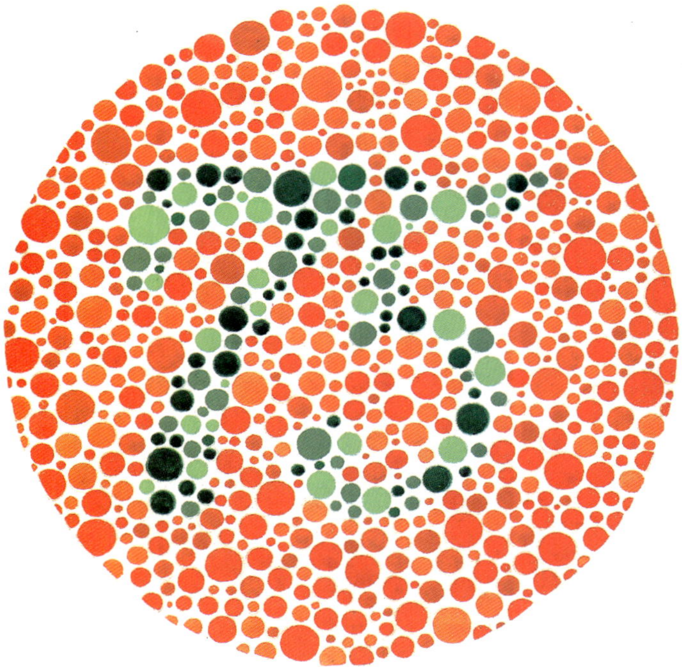

Color blindness

This is a classic test for color blindness. Those with red-green color blindness would not be able to see the number in this image. Tests like this are known as Ishihara tests.

COLOR BLINDNESS

Color blindness is an inability to distinguish between certain colors. A total inability to see color—achromatic vision, where everything appears as black, white or shades of gray—is rare in humans, although about 10 percent of males are believed to have impaired color vision.

The ability to distinguish colors is the job of cone cells in the retina of the eye. There are three types of cone cells, each absorbing different wavelengths. When one type is missing it may cause red blindness, with difficulty telling red from green, or blue blindness where it is difficult to distinguish between blue and yellow, or there may be various grades of difficulty, depending on the impairment.

Color blindness is primarily an inherited condition, caused by a gene linked to the Y (male) chromosome. The gene can be carried by both males and females, but is more likely to be inherited by male children. Another factor is age—the lens darkens with age and colors become more difficult to distinguish. Some medications and various eye diseases can also affect color vision.

Children having learning difficulties at school, and anyone with a family tendency, should be tested for color blindness. People are often ignorant of their impairment until tested. There are no cures for color blindness and sufferers will be unable to perform certain jobs where normal color vision is vital.

COLOSTOMY

A colostomy is a surgical procedure in which the interior of the bowel is opened and brought to the surface of the body. The resulting opening is called a stoma. Colostomies may be used to relieve pressure in an obstructed bowel, to divert the stream of feces in preparation of the bowel for surgery, to allow for removal of feces from the lower bowel when a portion is removed, and to protect surgically repaired bowel further down the gut. Colostomies may be temporary or permanent and may be performed by opening either the side of the bowel, or one end of the bowel, onto the skin surface. The most common type of permanent colostomy involves the sigmoid part of the colon, which is located in the pelvis. This is usually performed at the time of removal of the rectum for cancer. Usually patients can eat the same types of food which they enjoyed before colostomy, except that fruits may cause diarrhea.

SEE ALSO *Bowel, Colon, Intestines*

COMA

Coma is a deep, often prolonged, state of unconsciousness. It may be caused by a disease (such as diabetes), liver or kidney failure, head injury, stroke, reaction to drugs or alcohol, or an epileptic seizure. It differs from sleep in that the subject cannot be roused by external stimulation.

Anyone found to be unconscious should be laid on their side in the so-called recovery position. Emergency services should be called at once, as the comatose person will need to be hospitalized, where treatment will be aimed at reversing whatever is causing the coma. In the meantime, airways must be kept open, and artificial respiration and cardiopulmonary resuscitation started if pulse and breathing are absent.

SEE ALSO *Unconsciousness*

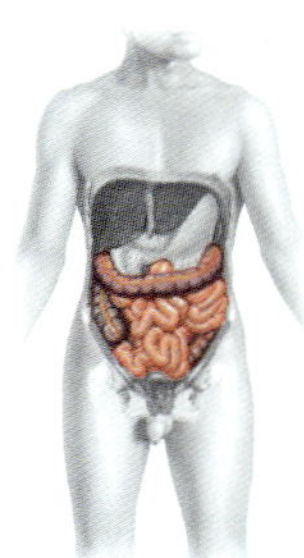

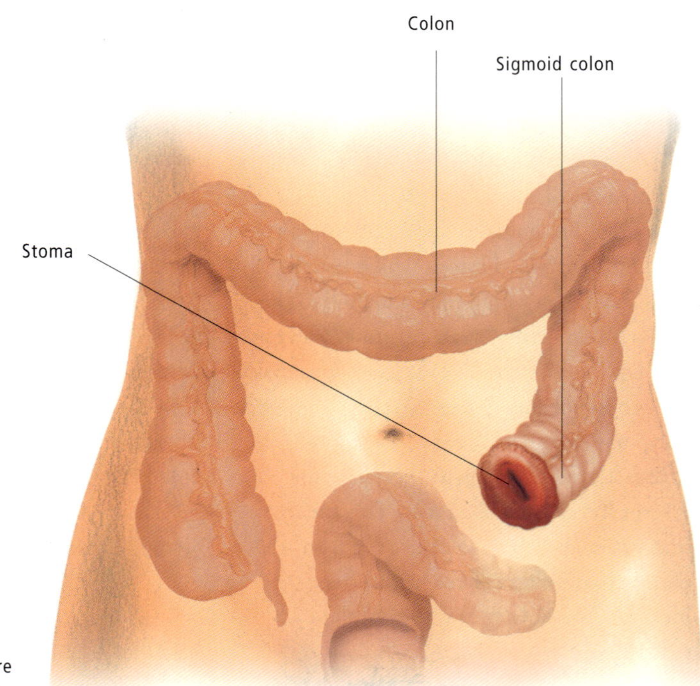

Colostomy

A colostomy is the surgical creation of an opening between the large intestine and abdominal wall. A removable colostomy bag is attached to the opening where the colon meets the skin. This opening is known as a stoma.

COMMON COLD

The common cold can be caused by one of five viral families that, between them, encompass a couple of hundred unique viral strains. Most typical of these are the rhinoviruses and coronaviruses, which affect the upper respiratory tract. Secondary infections may occur in the eye or middle ear, particularly in children. Adults may also suffer from inflamed sinuses. The main difference between the common cold and other respiratory infections, including the flu, is the absence of fever (except in children), as well as the general mildness of the symptoms.

Because the viral strains are sufficiently different from one another it is possible to catch one and later be infected by another. So children are particularly susceptible, especially if they mix socially with large numbers of people; they can have between four and ten colds in a year, or more if they suffer asthma attacks. The cold is spread by contact between people, which is thought to be the reason why colds are more prevalent in winter when people spend more time indoors and in contact with each other. Colds are transmitted by droplets breathed, coughed or sneezed onto another person. The incubation period is short—between one and four days. First symptoms can be a sore throat, feeling tired, nasal discharge and/or aching muscles followed by sneezing, coughing, headaches, a chill and nasal discharge. Cold symptoms will vary from person to person, but will usually take from seven to ten days from start to finish.

Treatment consists of easing the symptoms; plenty of fluids and acetaminophen (paracetamol) or ibuprofen may help. Children should never be given aspirin because of the possibility of Reye's syndrome, which can be fatal. Antibiotics are of no value against a virus, though they may be prescribed for an infectious complication. Over-the-counter preparations are plentiful for treatment of cold symptoms. Some contain drugs to constrict the blood vessels, others contain antihistamine which relieves stuffiness and can help induce sleep. There have been over sixty trials of vitamin C and its effects on the common cold, with different and confusing results. The majority, however, show that taking vitamin C has little effect on reducing the incidence of colds.

The reason it is difficult for researchers to come up with a cure is the number of different viruses. An additional factor is that the cold is only common to humans, which makes it difficult to test possible cures.

Although there is no cure, precautions can be taken: these include a nutritious diet with plenty of fruit, vegetables and legumes; regular exercise; avoiding smoky environments; getting enough sleep; staying away from people with colds and other illnesses; washing hands frequently and teaching children to do likewise, particularly after touching the nose or mouth; keeping warm and dry; and avoiding crowds.

There are a number of alternative therapies that may help to alleviate the symptoms of the common cold. Acupuncture is said to speed recovery and boost the immune system in cases of repeated bouts of cold. Aromatherapy uses decongestant oils such as eucalyptus or peppermint in inhalations, baths or oil burners. Herbalism prescribes anti-inflammatory and antiviral herbs such as echinacea, garlic and astralagus, as well as ginger and cayenne for warming. Sweating is encouraged with diaphoretic herbs such as peppermint or yarrow. Naturopathy views colds as a natural detoxification process which should not be suppressed. To ease the severity of a cold, naturopaths recommend vitamin C and zinc along with a light cleansing diet, plenty of fluids and rest.

SEE ALSO *Asthma, Viruses, Respiratory system, Reye's syndrome*

Cold virus

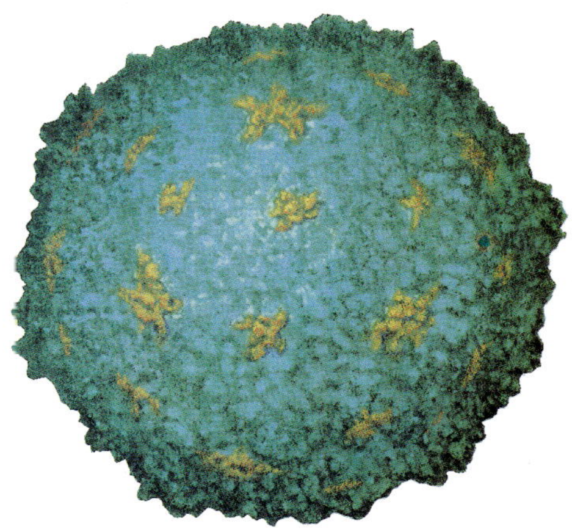

Viral attack at cell level

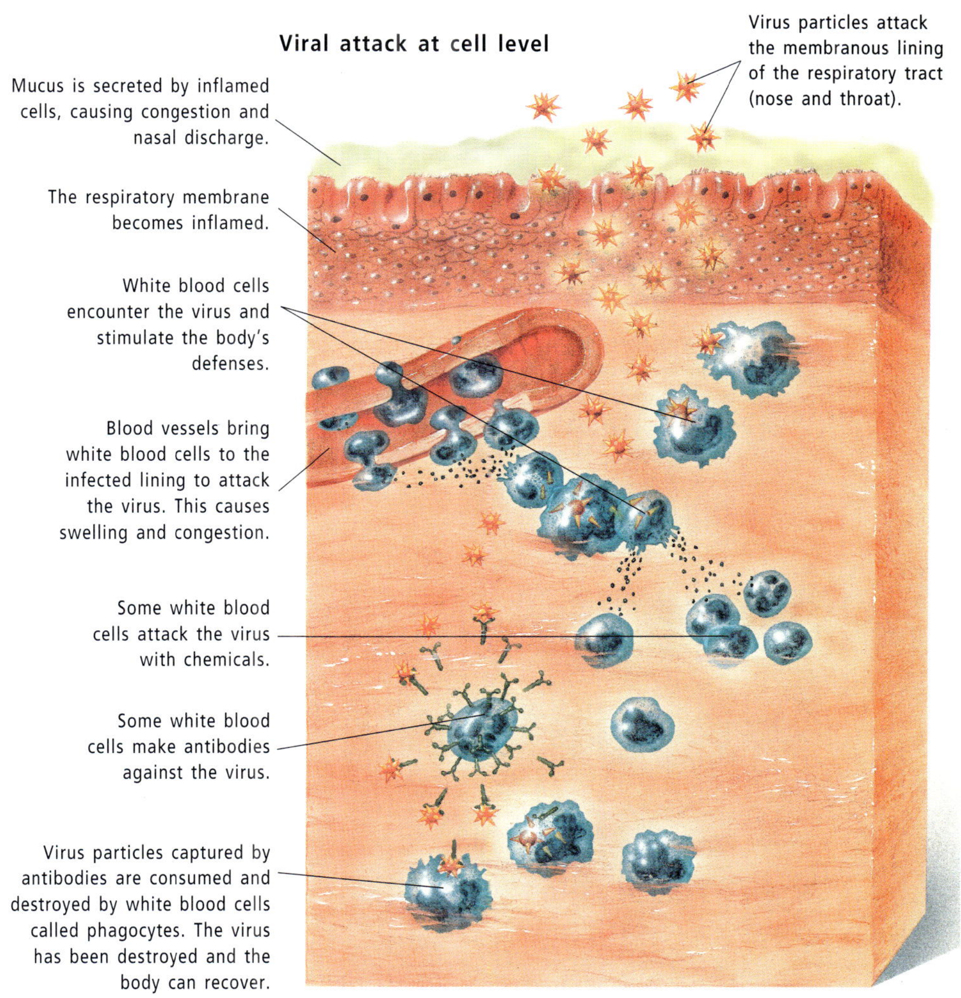

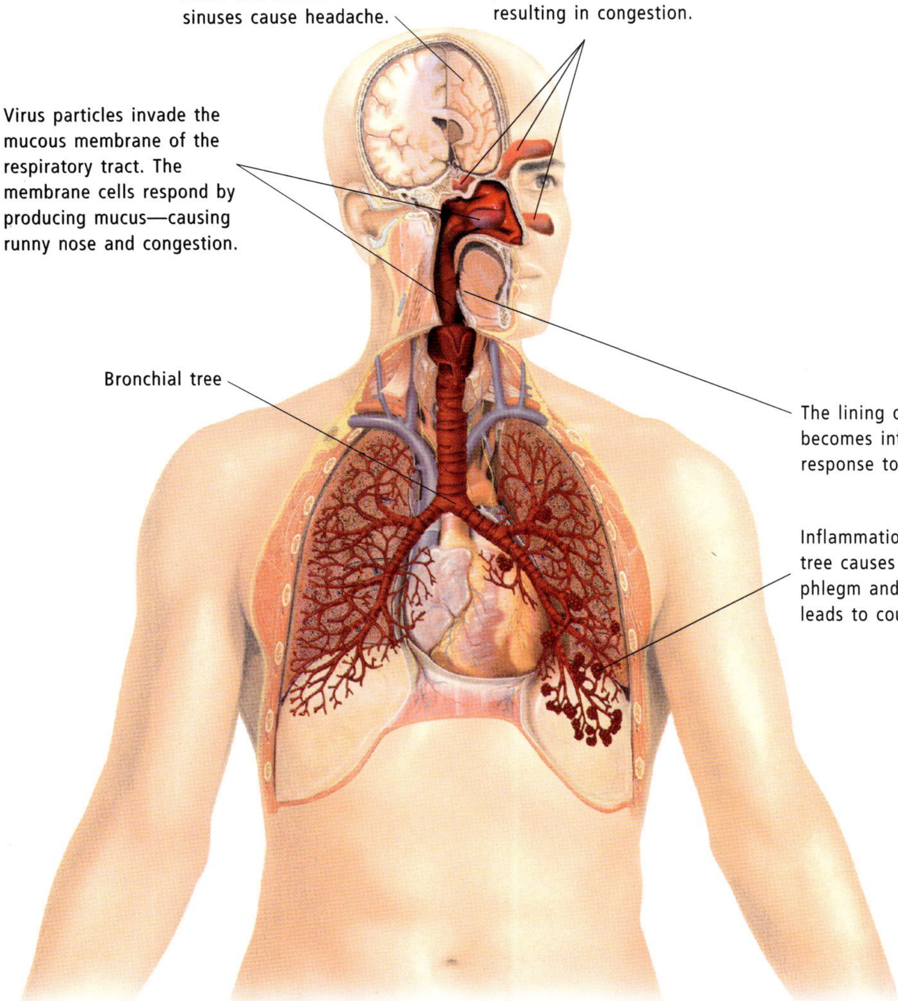

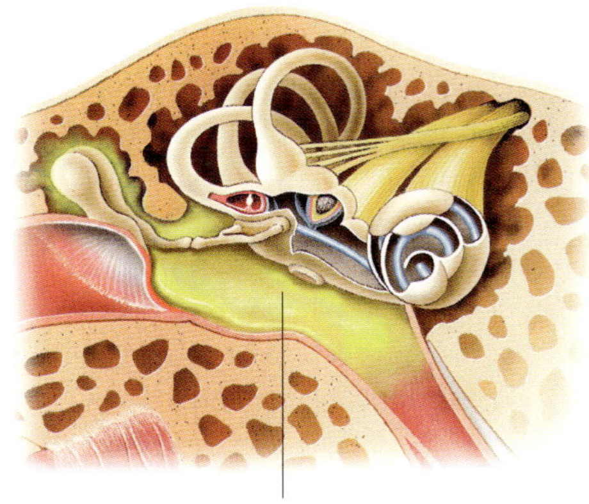

Ear infection

Virus particles traveling into the middle ear cause infection, leading to swelling and accumulation of fluid. This causes earache.

Cold

The common cold is caused by one of many viruses. Millions of cold viruses are easily transmitted via infected droplets that are coughed or sneezed into the air. When a droplet is inhaled, the virus attacks the lining of the upper respiratory tract, causing cold symptoms to develop.

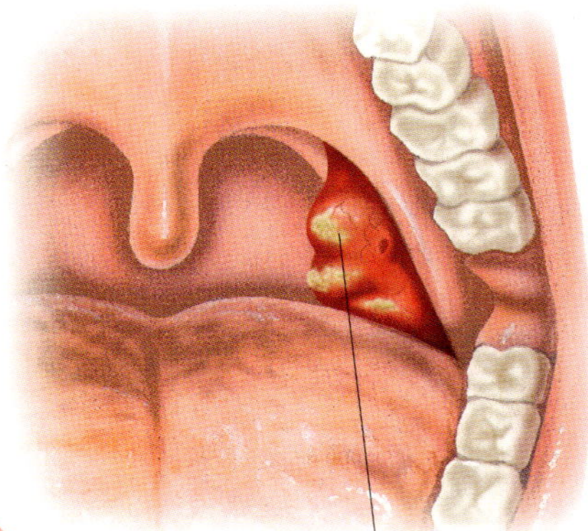

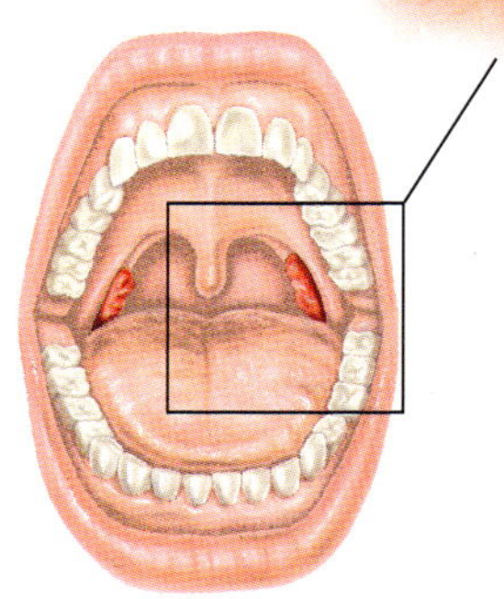

Tonsillitis

The tonsils protect the membrane of the mouth and throat from invading cold viruses. They become swollen and inflamed as part of the body's defense system to stop infection moving from the exterior to the interior of the body.

Throat and mouth

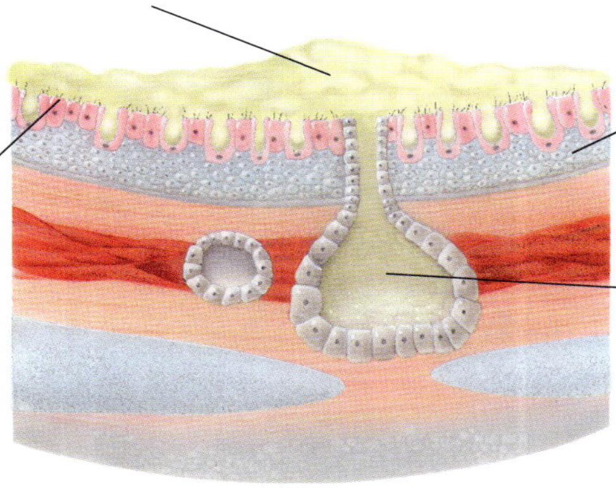

Lungs and bronchial tree

The cold virus attacks the tiny hairs (cilia) and cells on the lining of the bronchial tree in severe cases of cold. The tissue swells and glands produce mucus, resulting in coughing.

COMPARTMENT SYNDROME

The muscles of a limb are grouped into compartments, separated by connective tissue (intermuscular septum). In a muscle injury or strain, these compartments can become swollen with blood and fluid leaking from blood vessels. The rising pressure in the compartment compresses blood vessels; nerves and muscles may become ischemic (deprived of oxygen) and rapidly die. Treatment is surgical relief of the pressure inside the compartment, often by cutting the fibrous connective tissue.

SEE ALSO *Muscle*

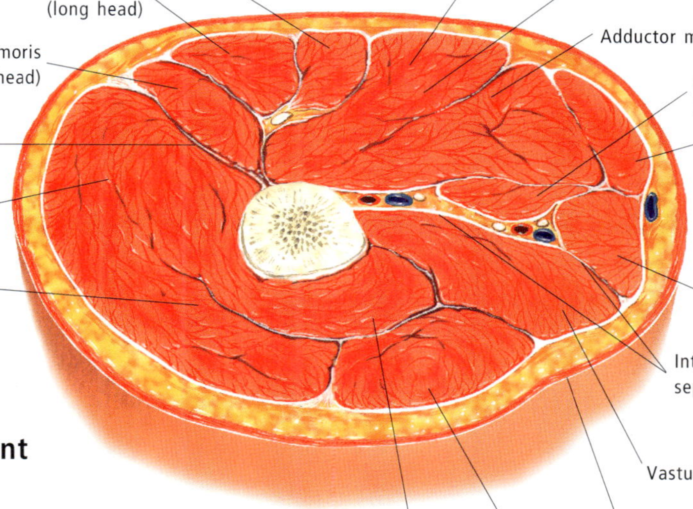

Compartment syndrome

Muscle compartments can become swollen and inflamed after injury. Pressure can build up inside the compartment, causing compression of blood vessels and nerves, and depriving the muscles of oxygen. This illustration shows the compartments in the thigh.

CONCUSSION

Concussion is a sudden alteration in levels of brain function following a blow to the head, often resulting in unconsciousness. It may be caused by a fall in which the head strikes against an object, or by a moving object striking the head. It frequently occurs in contact sports, and in auto, motorcycle or bike racing. Often, the injured person may not be aware of the problem; it may be teammates or observers who notice the confusion and disorientation. The injured person must be made to abandon the sport or activity, especially if there has been loss of consciousness.

Following the injury, the sufferer may have temporary retrograde amnesia; that is, for a time there will be no memory of events preceding the injury. There also may be headache, difficulty in concentrating and focusing, nausea, vomiting, and depression.

Usually concussion is temporary and causes no permanent brain damage. However, if the concussion is severe, there may be prolonged unconsciousness and persistent confusion. The level of consciousness is the single most important indicator of the severity of a brain injury; the more severe the concussion, the longer the period of unconsciousness. In more serious cases, there may be convulsions, vomiting, a weakness of the muscles, and permanent brain damage, depending on the extent of the injury. Loss of memory of events following the concussion (anterograde memory loss) also signifies a more serious concussion.

Concussed persons should seek medical treatment. A physician or neurologist will order x-rays of the head and neck to rule out the possibility of a skull fracture, and a CAT scan of the head if internal bleeding is suspected. If the injured person recovers and there are no signs of complications, rest at home and analegsics may be sufficient treatment. However, serious after-effects may be delayed and can appear 48 to 72 hours after injury, so a responsible person must watch the patient for serious symptoms. The first 24 hours are the most critical. Danger signs include repetitive vomiting, unequal pupils, confused mental state or varying levels of consciousness, seizures, or the inability to wake up (coma). If these signs are present, urgent medical advice should be sought.

If there are no further signs or symptoms, the patient can rest in bed for a few days, after which time, normal activity may be resumed. However, sporting and athletic activities should be avoided for three months. A second or subsequent concussion is particularly dangerous, especially if it occurs before the symptoms of the earlier concussion have cleared. Even though the second injury may be milder than the first, together they have a compounding effect that may cause acute brain swelling and rapid death.

To prevent concussion, protective head gear such as helmets should be worn when engaging in contact sports or any other activity that may result in head injury.

SEE ALSO *Amnesia, Unconsciousness*

CONFUSION

Confusion is a mental state in which a person is unsure of time, place or identity. A confused person is easily bewildered and has trouble making decisions and thinking in an orderly way. The condition is more common in elderly people, especially at night, when there are fewer stimuli to provide orientation. Confusion often occurs in hospitalized patients. It may come on suddenly (as in acute confusion or delirium) or gradually over time. The condition may be temporary, or permanent and irreversible, depending on the cause. It is often a symptom of physical illness.

Common causes of confusion include alcohol intoxication or withdrawal, low blood sugar, head trauma or head injury, concussion, fluid and electrolyte imbalance, nutritional deficiencies (such as niacin, thiamine, vitamin C or vitamin B_{12} deficiency), hyperthermia (fever), hypothermia (a drop in body temperature), hypoxia (inadequate oxygenation of the blood as seen, for example, in lung diseases), heat stroke, drugs (such as atropine or central nervous system depressants), and withdrawal from narcotics and barbiturates.

Acute confusion, or delirium, develops over a few hours or days. Delirious people may be confused about where they are or what time of day or year it is; they have a poor attention span and become easily distracted. Memory may be poor and there may be trouble speaking or understanding what others say. There may also be impaired concentration, restless excitement, senseless activity, hallucinations and fragmented delusions. Older people with delirium sometimes have mood swings and can become frightened and may try to run away.

Common causes of delirium include severe infections and high fevers (especially in the elderly or very young), drugs, alcohol, or prescription medications, dehydration, seizures, hypoxia (lack of oxygen) and head injury. Delirium can occur in the period immediately after surgery.

If a person becomes confused or delirious, medical advice should be sought. A physician may examine brain and nervous system function and may order investigations such as CAT scan, blood tests, x-rays and other tests, depending on the likely cause. Hospitalization may be necessary if the underlying condition is serious or is not easily reversible. The treatment of confusion is to correct the underlying cause, if possible. Sedatives or tranquilizers may be useful in the short term. A friend or relative should stay close by to prevent the patient from coming to any harm. Familiar surroundings, and conversation about familiar things in a calm voice will reassure the confused person. Visitors should always identify and introduce themselves. A calendar and clock can help with orientation. In order to ensure the patient's safety, physical restraints are recommended in some situations.

A permanently confused patient could be suffering from dementia, a mental deterioration due to age or from gradual changes in the brain tissue resulting from disease.

SEE ALSO ***Delirium, Dementia, Memory***

CONGENITAL ABNORMALITIES

A congenital abnormality is one that is present at, and usually before, birth. It arises from the faulty development of a fetus in the uterus. The abnormality may be caused by a genetic disorder, so that it is inherited, or it may be acquired while the fetus is growing in the uterus, due to exposure to an agent that causes abnormal development. Though they are generally rare, the range of possible congenital abnormalities is wide. Limbs or organs may be absent, duplicated or malformed. Organs may fail to move to the correct place, as in cryptorchidism (undescended testes), they may fail to open properly as in imperforate anus, or may fail to close at the correct time, as in patent ductus arteriosus. Congenital abnormalities may be obvious at birth, or they may take months or years to become evident, as in the case of Huntington's disease, which does not manifest itself until middle age.

Inherited congenital anomalies are caused by abnormal genes. There are over 2,000 known inherited congenital anomalies. Some are common, for example achondroplasia (a form of dwarfism), hemolytic disease of the newborn, sickle-cell disease, Down syndrome, and cleft palate. Others, such as phenylketonuria, an inherited metabolic disorder, are very rare.

Children with genetic abnormalities can be born to normal parents if the condition is caused by an abnormal recessive (nondominant) gene, and both parents have that recessive gene—in other words, they are both carriers. In this case there is a one in four chance that the child will inherit both genes and so manifest the disorder. Hemophilia is an example of such a condition.

Sometimes, genetic abnormalities occur if there is a spontaneous mutation of the parental genes, which may take place during sperm production or egg fertilization. In this case the affected child also has normal parents. Acquired congenital abnormalities can be caused by a variety of agents that affect the fetus in the uterus, including drugs, infections and toxins. Infection in the mother is a common cause of congenital abnormality. Rubella (German measles) contracted in the first three months of pregnancy may cause deafness, cataracts, heart disease, jaundice, or other abnormalities. Cytomegalovirus and toxoplasmosis are two other organisms that cause congenital anomalies.

Some drugs taken by a woman during pregnancy are responsible for abnormalities in the child. Corticosteroids, anticonvulsants, anti-cancer drugs, narcotics, sedatives, tranquilizers, antidepressants, antibacterials,

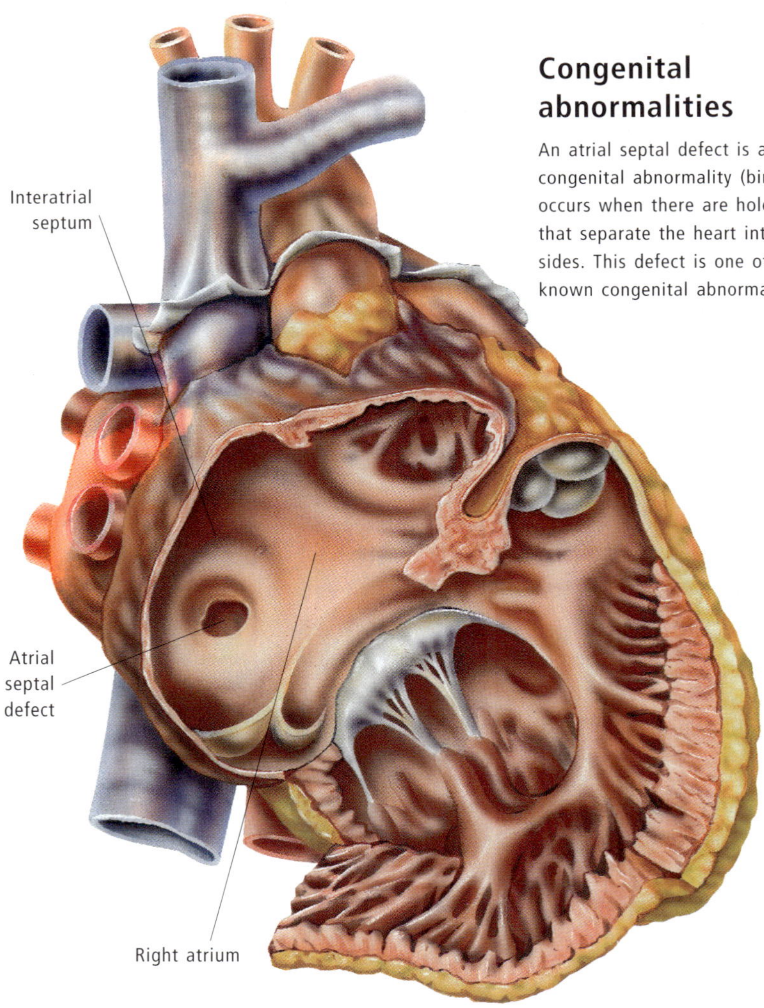

Congenital abnormalities

An atrial septal defect is an example of a congenital abnormality (birth defect) that occurs when there are holes in the walls that separate the heart into right and left sides. This defect is one of over 2,000 known congenital abnormalities.

(especially tetracycline), anticoagulants, and drugs prescribed to treat cardiac conditions and hypertension can all cause congenital defects. A pregnant woman should avoid taking any medication without first obtaining medical advice as to whether it is safe to take in pregnancy. Environmental toxins, x-rays, or injury to the fetus (for example from an intrauterine device), may cause an abnormality in the fetus. The age of the mother may be a factor (with Down syndrome, for example). Congenital abnormalities cannot be reversed, but can often be successfully treated with surgery, hormone treatment, diet, and physical therapy, depending on the condition and its severity.

If there is a known or suspected risk of a congenital abnormality developing, it can often be detected during pregnancy by a screening procedure. The most reliable procedure is to examine a sample of fluid from the amniotic sac obtained by amniocentesis between the fifteenth and eighteenth week of pregnancy. Microscopic examination of the cells in the fluid then reveals possible abnormalities in the chromosomes. The amniotic fluid can be tested for abnormal substances, for example alpha-fetoprotein, abnormally high levels of which are found in anencephaly or spina bifida. Chorionic villus sampling (CVS) is a technique used in the first trimester of pregnancy in which a tissue sample is taken from the placenta and analyzed for genetic defects in the fetus.

Termination of pregnancy (abortion) may be considered if fetal disorders are found early in a pregnancy. The decision to abort rests with the parents and is taken after they have been made aware of the nature of the disorder and the consequences of abortion. Genetic counseling should be considered by anyone who has a history of chromosomal abnormalities and all pregnant women aged 35 and over. There may be a higher risk than normal of congenital abnormality in a second child if the first is born with an abnormality; parents should have genetic counseling if they want another child.

SEE ALSO *Achondroplasia, Amniocentesis, Chromosomal abnormalities, Cleft palate and lip, Down syndrome, Genetic counseling, Hemolytic disease of the newborn, Huntington's disease, Phenylketonuria, Sickle cell disease*

CONJUNCTIVITIS

The conjunctivum is the membrane that lines the inner part of the eyelids and covers the whites of the eyes. Conjunctivitis, also called "pinkeye", is inflammation of the conjunctivum. The eye looks red and is painful and itchy with a watery discharge. The condition is common in childhood. Acute conjunctivitis may be caused by bacterial or viral infection, allergy or irritation. In bacterial conjunctivitis, the discharge from the eye is a yellow or greenish color. It accumulates during sleep, so the person wakes with the eyelids "stuck together". A warm wash-cloth applied to the eyes will remove the discharge. Antibiotic eye drops prescribed by a physician will cure the condition.

Viral pinkeye is usually associated with a more watery discharge and other viral "cold-like" symptoms. There is no treatment for viral conjunctivitis, though decongestant drops will help relieve the symptoms.

Allergic conjunctivitis is frequently seasonal, occurring in the spring and summer, and the sufferer has typical allergy symptoms such as sneezing and runny nose. The eye is intensely itchy and the conjunctiva is swollen. Decongestant, antihistamine or corticosteroid eye drops will bring relief.

Conjunctivitis may be caused by irritation—for example by dust, cosmetics, or smoke. Prompt, thorough washing of the eyes with large amounts of water will relieve the symptoms. If conjunctivitis is caused by a bacteria or virus, do not to rub the eye because the infection may be transmitted to the other eye. Anyone with conjunctivitis should wash their hands often and use their own towel so as not to transmit the disease.

Conjunctivitis may also be caused by the eye disorder trachoma or by other rare conditions such as rheumatic diseases and some inflammatory bowel diseases.

SEE ALSO *Allergies, Eye, Eyelids, Trachoma*

Allergic conjunctivitis

In allergic conjunctivitis, the eye becomes intensely itchy and the conjunctiva are swollen. This condition is typically seen in conjuction with other allergy symptoms such as sneezing and runny nose.

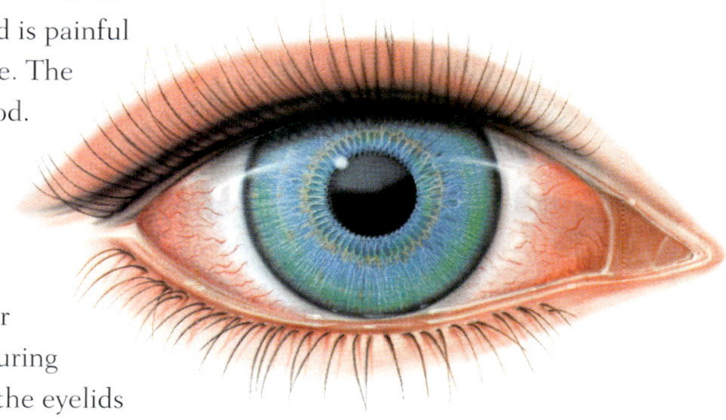

Bacterial conjunctivitis

Bacterial conjunctivitis causes a yellow or green discharge from the eye that builds up when the eyes are closed. This often causes the eyelids to stick together upon waking.

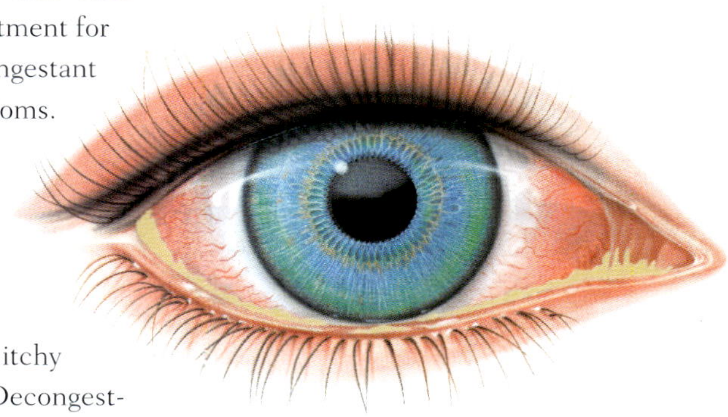

CONNECTIVE TISSUE

Connective tissue is tissue made up of cells and protein fibers arranged in a framework which provides support for other body tissues and holds them together. It is composed of two major structural proteins, collagen and elastin. Collagen is the principal protein of tendons, cartilage, bone and other connective tissue. Elastin is a protein which can stretch and return to its original length.

Connective tissue diseases attack the collagen or other components of connective tissue. Some are genetically inherited, such as Marfan's syndrome and Ehlers-Danlos syndrome. Others are part of the group of diseases known as autoimmune diseases, in which the body's defence mechanisms attack its own tissues. Autoimmune diseases include systemic lupus erythematosus, rheumatoid arthritis, scleroderma, polymyositis and dermatomyositis. A malignant (cancerous) tumor formed from connective tissue is called a sarcoma. The usual treatment for sarcoma is surgical removal, which is often followed by the use of radiation therapy.

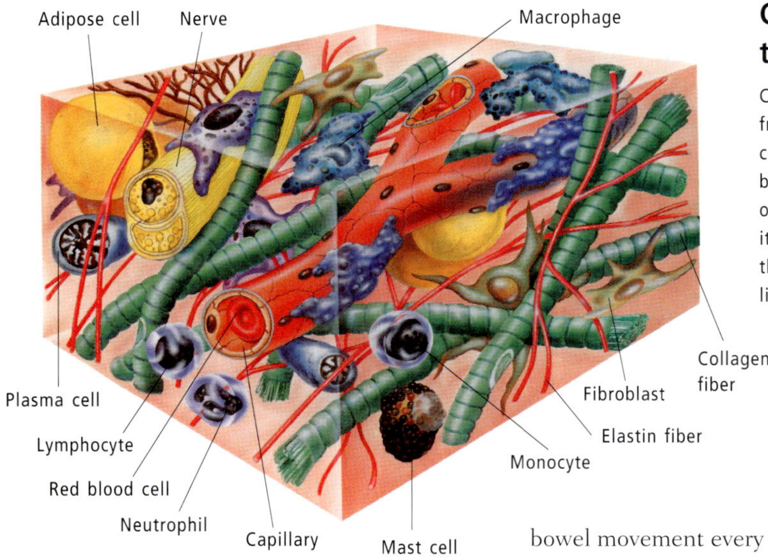

Connective tissue

Connective tissue is the framework that supports, connects and fills out body structures. Made up of collagen and elastin, it is found throughout the body. Tendons and ligaments are examples.

Vitamin C (ascorbic acid) is essential for connective tissues to function properly. Lack of vitamin C causes scurvy, with a weakening of the blood capillaries and bleeding, and bone defects. Scurvy can be prevented by eating fresh vegetables and fruits regularly.

SEE ALSO *Autoimmune disease, Collagen, Dermatomyositis, Lupus erythematosus, Polymyositis, Rheumatoid arthritis, Scleroderma, Scurvy*

CONSTIPATION

Constipation is a condition in which a person will have hard feces and infrequent bowel movements. The bowel contents do not move and excess fluid is absorbed, leaving hard feces that are difficult to pass. They gradually dry out more and more until eventually the bowel opens through sheer weight of the material, usually leaving the sufferer feeling that the rectum is still full.

Many people think a daily bowel movement is necessary; however, this is not the case. For some, two or three movements a day are normal; for others one every two or three days. Constipation is often the result of a low-fiber diet with not enough consumption of water. Stress, anxiety or lack of exercise contribute to the problem. Constipation can also be a feature of irritable bowel syndrome.

Often a problem during pregnancy, constipation can be avoided with a high-fiber diet and plenty of water (around eight glasses a day). In breast-fed babies, constipation is rare and a baby may go from one bowel movement every few days to four a five in a day. Babies who are fed artificial baby milks can become constipated; professional help may be advisable in this situation.

Among the other causes are diseases of the central nervous system or typhoid, the taking of drugs such as codeine or morphine, and the overuse of laxatives. People who are bedridden and who have suffered a head or spinal injury can also suffer from constipation. Occasionally it is a symptom of a problem such as a bowel obstruction. It can also occur temporarily when lifestyle is changed such as when travelling.

Changes to diet will often fix the problem, especially increasing fluid intake. Laxatives and enemas are only temporary solutions.

SEE ALSO *Bowel, Intestines, Irritable bowel syndrome, Laxatives*

CONTACT LENSES

Contact lenses are artificial lenses worn on the eyes' surface to correct vision defects, commonly astigmatism, aphakia (absence of the eye's crystalline lens) and myopia (short or near sightedness). They are a popular alternative to glasses because in many cases they provide better vision, and some people think they are more attractive. Today's lenses are also comfortable and easy to wear and care for. However, they are not suitable for everyone: elderly people and those with arthritis often find them difficult to use.

The first lenses were made of glass in 1887, but today's lenses are made of plastic. They were originally made on a mold taken from an impression of the eye; now a measurement of the curvature of the cornea is made and the plastic lens sits on a cushion of tears covering the iris and the pupil. They need to be individually prescribed and must be disinfected and cleaned regularly. Those who wear the lenses need more frequent eye examinations than those who wear glasses.

There are two types of plastic lenses available: soft, which are the most common, and rigid. Soft lenses can be tinted and are quickly adapted to and comfortable to wear. They include disposable lenses, which are designed to be replaced every two to four weeks, and extended wear lenses which can be kept in the eye for up to thirty days. These are specially designed to allow a large amount of oxygen to pass to the eye and are not suitable for all. Rigid lenses, while they give the wearer better vision, require more adaptation and are typically less comfortable. On the other hand, they last longer.

SEE ALSO *Astigmatism, Cornea, Eye, Myopia, Sight*

CONTRACEPTION

Contraception (birth control) is, quite simply, any action taken to avoid conception. The only sure guarantee against pregnancy is to avoid vaginal intercourse. For conception to occur, the female's egg (ovum) must be met by sperm-loaded semen from the male. In natural conception the semen is deposited in the vagina. It then travels through the cervix and uterus to fertilize the egg. This egg must then implant itself into the lining of the uterus (endometrium).

Written details of birth control—a term first used by the reformer Margaret Sanger in 1915—date back to 1550 BC in Egypt. Classical writers such as Pliny the Elder and Soranus of Ephesus wrote about methods like washing the vagina after intercourse. A major advance came with the condom, which was first made from animal intestines. Vaginal barriers such as diaphragms and caps were mentioned in 1823 by the German physician F. A. Wilde. Vasectomy was used in the nineteenth century and the first documented female sterilization was performed in 1881. An Australian couple, the Billings, first used the monitoring of changes in cervical mucus to determine fertile times in the

1960s, about the same time as the first contraceptive pills became available.

Contraception should be discussed with qualified medical professionals in order to determine which method should be used, according to current lifestyle, medical history and future plans.

Intrauterine device

This is a small device inserted into the uterus to prevent conception. It is still not sure how it works but it seems that almost any foreign body in the uterus will prevent conception. Made of plastic, metal or other material, and inserted under sterile conditions by a trained professional, intrauterine devices (IUDs) have a failure rate of between 1 and 6 pregnancies per 100 women.

Barrier methods

These are the condom (for both males and females), the diaphragm and the cap.

The male condom, which is a penile sheath, acts by catching and collecting the semen so it does not get into the vagina. The female condom is a thin silicone membrane which partly or completely covers the outside of the female genitals, acting as a barrier.

Diaphragms and caps are placed inside the vagina to cover the entrance to the uterus and stop sperm getting into the womb. They come in a range of sizes and must be fitted to the user by a trained health professional. Many family planning clinics and doctors recommend the use of a spermicide (which kills the sperm) at the same time. When used carefully, barrier methods have about the same effectiveness as IUDs.

Fertility awareness methods

Not having sexual intercourse at a fertile time is the basis of the methods variously described as fertility awareness, periodic abstinence, the Billings method, the rhythm method and the temperature method.

Changes in a woman's body during the menstrual cycle can be interpreted to indicate fertility. The cervical mucus changes under the influence of estrogen and at the time a woman is most fertile is plentiful, clear and sticky. The woman's basal body temperature, taken with a special thermometer, also rises slightly for around three days. Most women have cycles which can be documented so that they can work out when they are most likely to be fertile. There is a wide range of pregnancy rates depending on the method used and the couple involved.

Hormonal contraceptives

More than 70 million women around the world use this method which involves taking an oral contraceptive pill regularly and diligently, or using slow-release implants under the skin, injections into the muscle, or using devices such as IUDs which contain hormones. Combination pills contain estrogen and progestin (progestogen); mini-pills contain progestin only. The combination pill prevents the release of an egg and both types of pill thicken the cervical mucus to prevent the sperm from reaching the egg. They can also prevent fertilized eggs from implanting. The combination pill, when taken as directed, is more than 99 percent effective in preventing pregnancy. The mini-pill has higher rates of failure.

Injections of progestin work by stopping ovulation and theoretically they are the most effective way to prevent pregnancy apart from abstinence from intercourse. Contraceptive implants, which are not available in all industrialized countries, are also highly effective and can be removed at any time, as can hormone-releasing vaginal rings and IUDs. The male pills and contraceptive injections are still being studied and researched.

The emergency pill (also called the morning-after pill) is a short course of hormones which must be started within 72 hours of unprotected intercourse. These hormones delay ovulation and change the lining of the uterus. Fewer than 5 in 100 will conceive when this method is used correctly. Emergency IUD insertion or copper IUD insertion, if done within five days of unprotected sex, will prevent conception and also provide on-going contraception.

Spermicide

This kills or immobilizes sperm. The spermicide should be inserted into the vagina at least 15 minutes before intercourse and can be a foam, cream, jelly, film or suppository. It can also be a sponge which carries the spermicide. Spermicides can be used together with a barrier method or on their own when they have about a 30 percent failure rate.

Coitus interruptus or withdrawal

This is the act of withdrawing the penis during sexual intercourse before ejaculation takes place. It has a high failure rate and is not a recommended method.

Breast feeding

Another "method" with a high failure rate is breast feeding. Thought by many to be a natural way to plan families, it is only likely to work if the baby is being breast fed at least 5 times in a 24-hour period and is not being fed solid foods, and the woman has not started to menstruate.

Female sterilization and vasectomy

Permanent contraception methods such as sterilization and vasectomy continue to be popular. A woman is sterilized by blocking both fallopian tubes (through which sperm reach the egg). This tubal ligation is

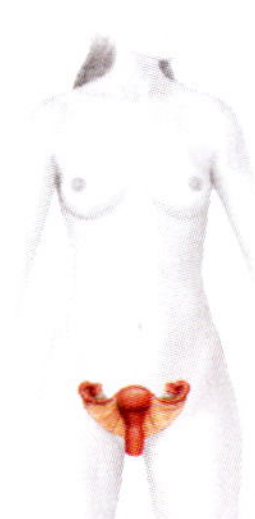

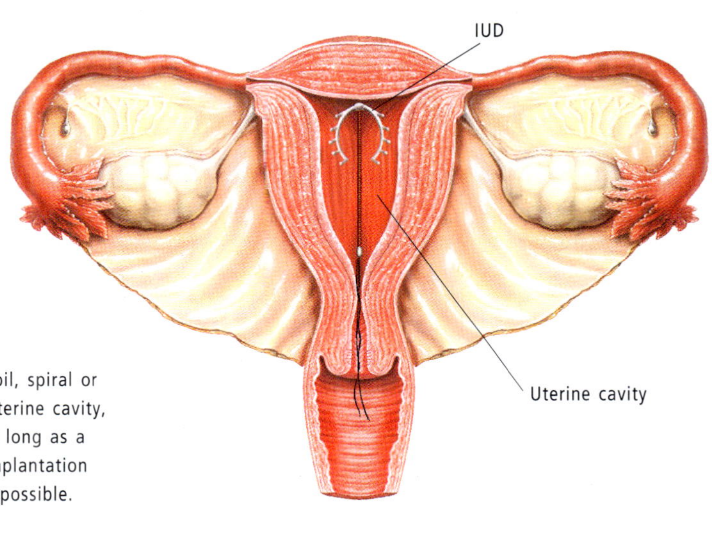

Contraception

An IUD consists of a ring, coil, spiral or loop. Once inserted in the uterine cavity, it can be left in place for as long as a year. Its presence renders implantation of a fertilized egg almost impossible.

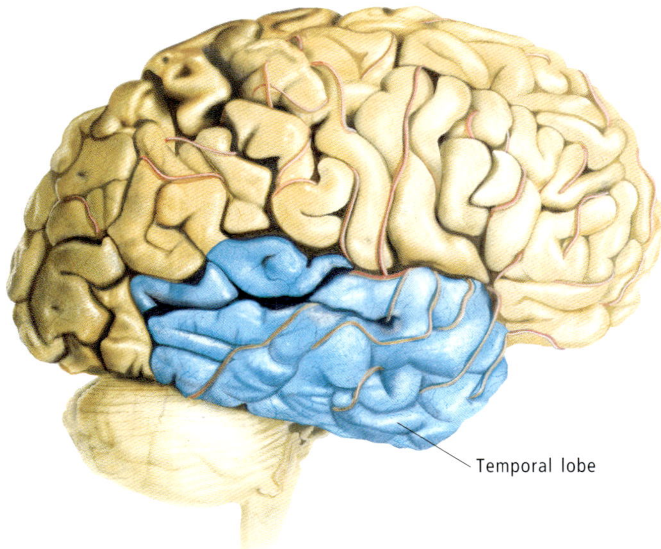

Convulsions

Convulsions, or seizures, are the result of abnormal electrical discharges in the brain. Anything that irritates the brain can cause a convulsion. Temporal lobe epilepsy is a condition that causes recurrent convulsions that may be triggered by flashing lights, repetitive sounds or even touching certain parts of the body.

a surgical procedure which is now commonly carried out by endoscopy using an optical instrument through an abdominal incision. A vasectomy blocks the tube (the vas deferens) which carry the sperm from the testis to the semen. This is a simple operation done via a small incision in the front of the scrotum.

While the success rate in reversing these methods can be as high as 70 percent, they are not recommended birth control methods for people who may want children one day.

SEE ALSO *Breast feeding, Oral contraceptives, Reproductive systems, Sterilization, Tubal sterilization, Vasectomy*

CONTRAST X-RAY

Contrast x-ray is a diagnostic technique which can outline organs and blood vessels, and reveal abnormalities of anatomy. The x-rays are obtained after injecting a solution that is opaque to x-rays into blood vessels, introducing it by means of an enema tube, or by giving the patient a solution of barium sulfate to swallow. Contrast x-ray is useful in demonstrating the function of various organs, such as the peristaltic waves of the esophagus when swallowing, or the emptying of the gallbladder and kidney.

When the solution is injected into the blood vessels of the brain, aneurysms or blow-outs of the arteries can be identified, as can shifting of the blood vessels by tumors. The physician is able to assess the degree of narrowing of coronary arteries when considering bypass operations. Barium is sometimes used during CAT scanning to allow separation of bowel shadows from associated tumors.

SEE ALSO *Barium enema, Barium meal, CAT scan*

CONVULSIONS

Convulsions—fits, epileptic attacks or seizures—are characterized by abnormal, often violent and uncontrolled spasmodic contractions and relaxations of the voluntary muscles. The eyes may roll, the teeth clench and the sufferer will twitch and shake. Convulsions can be a symptom of a disease and vary in severity, in some cases being accompanied by a loss of consciousness. Around 1 in 100 people will have a convulsion of some kind during their lifetime and about half of these will occur during childhood, most commonly between the ages of 3 months and 5 years. Seizures, particularly the first one, can be particularly worrying to parents of young children; however, they are rarely harmful.

Simple febrile convulsions (convulsions caused by a high fever) usually last less than a minute and are not repeated, though the child does have a slightly increased chance over children who never have a seizure of having subsequent attacks not associated with fever. Complicated febrile convulsions will last longer than 15 minutes and recur 2 or more times in 24 hours. Children who suffer from these have a greater risk of subsequent attacks and around 25 percent of cases will have a family history of seizures.

When people have convulsions, the most important thing is to make sure they do not injure themselves. They should be placed on a flat surface with the head to one side. It is not appropriate to put anything in the sufferer's mouth: it is more likely to cause harm. It is also not appropriate to attempt expired air resuscitation if children hold their breath in the early stages as this too can cause damage. When the convulsion has passed, medical help should be sought immediately.

Reducing and controlling fever with tepid sponge baths and acetaminophen (paracetamol) or ibuprofen—never aspirin—may prevent a convulsion. A child who suffers convulsions may be prescribed anticonvulsant medicine; however, such medication can affect a child's ability to learn so it is prescribed with care. Most children outgrow febrile convulsions.

There are a number of other types of convulsion. They can occur because of scarred brain tissue after a head injury, or can be triggered by flashing lights. They can be partial, only affecting one part of the body, or general, involving the entire body. Petit mal convulsions are not violent and show as a sudden cessation of activities. Epilepsy is diagnosed when an electroencephalogram (EEG) shows more than one convulsion. Prevention of these types of convulsion depends on the cause, and requires specialist advice.

SEE ALSO *Electroencephalogram, Epilepsy, Fevers*

COR PULMONALE

Cor pulmonale is a condition in which the right side of the heart enlarges, weakens and may fail. It is caused by high blood pressure in the pulmonary (lung) circulation, which forces the right ventricle (which pumps blood into the lungs) to overwork. Usually the high blood pressure in the pulmonary circulation is caused by lung diseases such as chronic bronchitis or emphysema.

Cor pulmonale is usually chronic (long term) and incurable, though affected people may live 10 or 15 years with the condition. In the meantime, symptoms can be relieved or controlled with medications such as diuretics, digitalis, antibiotics, and vasodilators. Plenty of rest and a low-salt diet are recommended. Oxygen (inhaled using a mask) may be needed in later stages of development. Ultimately, only a lung transplant will cure the condition.

SEE ALSO *Bronchitis, Circulatory system, Emphysema, Heart, Hypertension, Lung*

CORNEA

Lying at the front of the eye, the cornea is the transparent part of the outer layer of the eyeball. The cornea is responsible for most of the bending of light which enters the eye, but as it cannot change its shape readily, the focusing of the image on the retina is achieved by the lens. The surface of the cornea may be ulcerated through injury by foreign bodies or by infection with bacteria (*Streptococcus pneumoniae, Pseudomonas aeruginosa*) or viruses (*herpes simplex*). Corneal ulcers will impair sight and may require corneal transplantation. Examination of the inner parts of the eye is made through the cornea with the aid of an instrument known as an ophthalmoscope.

SEE ALSO *Eye, Sight*

CORONARY ARTERIES

Coronary arteries are the arteries that supply the heart with oxygenated blood. The right and left coronary arteries arise from the aorta and branch out into smaller arteries supplying the right and left sides of the heart. Arteriosclerosis, or hardening of the arteries, may result in stenosis (narrowing) of the coronary arteries and ischemic heart disease.

SEE ALSO *Arteriosclerosis, Coronary artery disease, Heart*

CORONARY ARTERY ANGIOGRAPHY

Coronary artery angiography is an x-ray technique used to show the nature and extent of disease in coronary arteries. Dye that is opaque to x-rays is injected through a thin flexible tube (or catheter) placed into the aorta or the heart. A succession of x-rays is taken to view the flow of the dye through the coronary arteries. Any sections that are narrowed (stenosed) can be clearly seen.

SEE ALSO *Coronary arteries, Coronary artery disease*

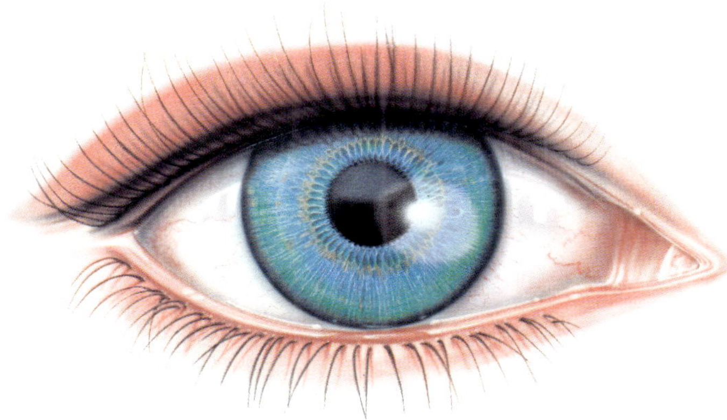

Corneal ulcer

A corneal ulcer is a sore or break in the surface layer of the cornea. It causes pain, redness, and sensitivity to light as well as blurred vision.

CORONARY ARTERY DISEASE

Coronary artery disease is a disease in which the walls of the coronary arteries thicken, cutting off blood and oxygen to the heart muscle and causing angina, arrhythmias, myocardial infarction, heart failure, or cardiac arrest. The disease is caused by atherosclerosis (also known as arteriosclerosis) in which fatty deposits called plaques are deposited within the endothelium (the inner lining) of blood vessels, including the arteries of the heart. Risk factors include smoking, hypertension, high blood cholesterol and obesity. The affected person suffers a range of cardiac symptoms such as chest pain on exertion or at rest, sweating, palpitations, breathlessness, fainting or even sudden death.

Investigations include chest x-ray, electrocardiogram (EKG), stress test, ultrasound (echocardiography) and nuclear scanning. Coronary angiography, in which a series of x-rays of the heart is taken after dye is injected into the coronary arteries, is useful in showing the extent of the disease.

Coronary artery disease—damage to heart tissue

Heart attack (myocardial infarction) occurs when some of the heart's blood supply is suddenly severely restricted or cut off. This causes part of the heart muscle to die from lack of oxygen.

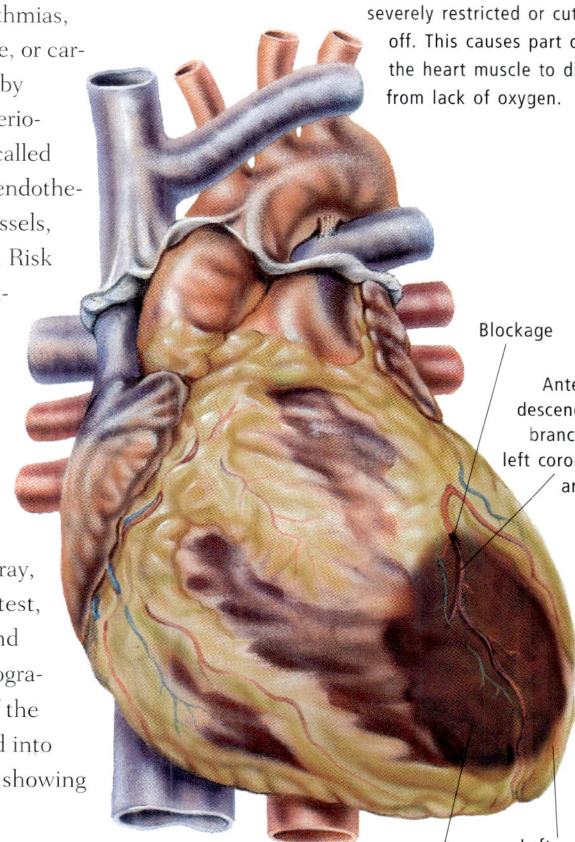

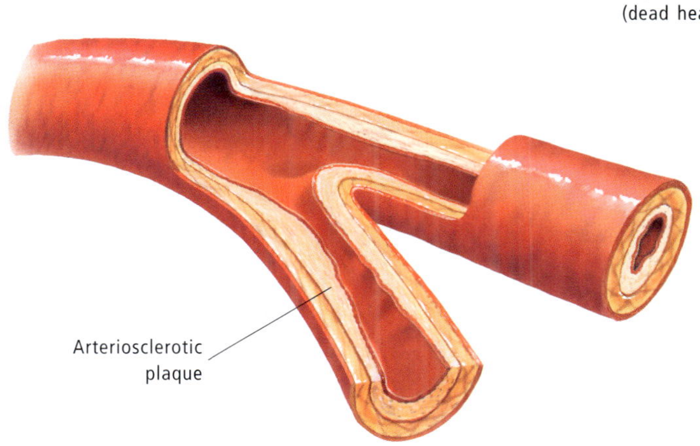

Coronary heart disease—damage to arteries

Fatty deposits (plaques) are deposited within the lining of the blood vessels. The flow of blood through the vessels is restricted, which may decrease the blood supply to vital organs.

The effects of angina can be relieved with medications such as nitrates (nitroglycerin), beta-blockers or calcium channel blockers. If one or more arteries are severely blocked, coronary bypass surgery may be needed to relieve blockages of the blood vessels of the heart muscle. The disease may be prevented by exercise, a low-fat diet, cessation of smoking and control of blood pressure with medications.

SEE ALSO *Angina pectoris, Arrythmia, Arteriosclerosis, Cholesterol, Coronary arteries, Heart, Hypertension, Myocardial infarction, Obesity, Smoking*

CORONARY THROMBOSIS

Thrombosis is the presence of a blood clot (thrombus) in an artery or vein. Coronary thrombosis is due to a blood clot blocking a coronary artery, often resulting in myocardial infarction and/or cardiac arrest (heart attack) and death. The condition is usually seen in people whose coronary arteries have been damaged by atherosclerosis. A thrombus forms at the site of the damaged arterial wall, cutting off the blood supply to the heart muscle. The affected person may feel crushing chest pain, palpitations (awareness of heart beat), abnormal heart rhythms, dizziness and sweating. The person may die suddenly.

Coronary thrombosis is an emergency and may require resuscitation, immediate transport to hospital and treatment in a cardiac unit. Treatment is with oxygen, pain relief, drugs called thrombolytics that activate natural clot-dissolving processes in the blood, and anticoagulant drugs such as heparin which prevent further clot formation. If the person is well enough, coronary bypass surgery may be needed to bypass the blockage and restore adequate blood flow to the heart muscle.

SEE ALSO *Arteries, Coronary arteries, Heart, Myocardial infarction, Veins*

CORTICOSTEROIDS

Corticosteroids, or corticoids, are steroid hormones produced in the outer layer (cortex) of the adrenal glands. The most important steroid hormones are aldosterone, which regulates the excretion of sodium and potassium salts through the kidney, and cortisol (hydrocortisone), which promotes the synthesis and storage of glucose and regulates fat distribution within the body. The production of the hormones is controlled by the pituitary gland via the hormone ACTH. Insufficient production of corticosteroid by the adrenal gland causes Addison's disease, while excessive production causes Cushing's syndrome. The term corticosteroid is also used for a number of synthetic derivatives with similar properties to naturally occurring corticosteroids, used to treat allergies, rheumatic disorders and inflammation.

SEE ALSO *Addison's disease, Adrenal glands, Cushing's syndrome, Pituitary gland*

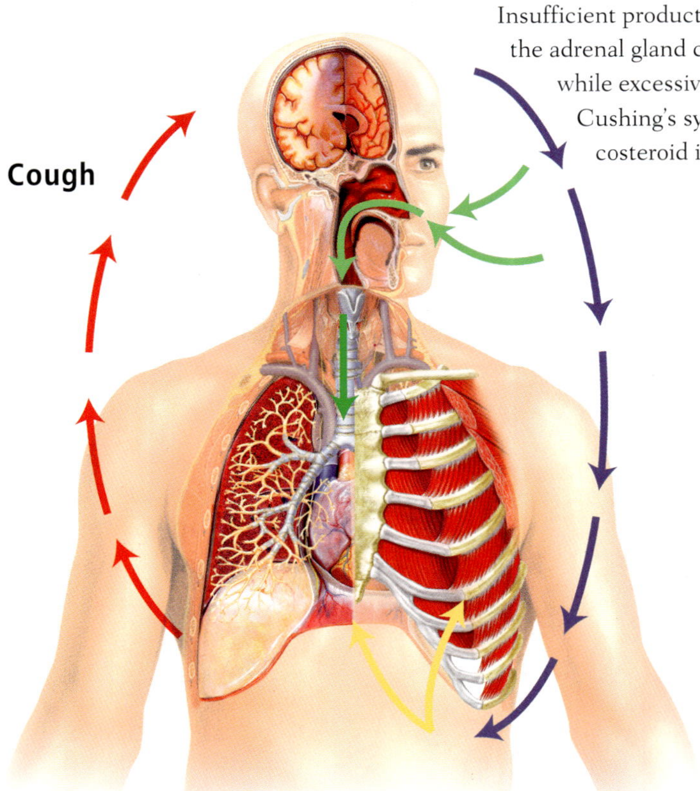

COSMETIC SURGERY

Cosmetic surgery is undertaken in order to reshape normal parts of the body with the intention of improving the patient's appearance and usually self-esteem. It is generally not covered by health insurance because it is elective, though some countries accept psychological stress as a sufficient reason for an insurance claim.

Cosmetic surgery makes up around 10 percent of plastic surgery, a specialty which also treats cancers, reconstructs damage after trauma such as hand injury or burns, and repairs congenital abnormalities such as cleft palate.

Some common cosmetic surgery procedures are rhinoplasty, which involves changing the shape of the nose via the nostrils or the tip so that no external scars are obvious; face lift, which is quite a complicated procedure as it can involve the whole facial structure; breast reduction; breast augmentation or reconstruction which can be complicated procedures depending on whether artificial implants or body fat are used; hair transplants; and liposuction. The latter consists of smashing the fat cells with a steel bar which is stuck into the area to be suctioned, and the fat is then sucked out. Other procedures involve lasers and heat.

Face lifts have become fairly common operations and are usually carried out on women between 40–60 years of age. Technically known as rhytidectomy, the procedure involves simple scalpeling and reshaping of the fat and the skin, or more sophisticated laser techniques which remove layers of wrinkled skin. Other facial reconstructions are ear reduction (ostoplasty), and the removal of fatty tissue and skin from and around the eyelids (blepharoplasty).

The essence of effective cosmetic surgery is in the planning of the incisions—so that they are in the line of where the skin folds naturally—and in the appropriate way of closing the wound. The use of fine material to suture and the early removal of exposed stitches so that the wound is kept closed by hidden sutures aid the healing with minimal scarring. Techniques which can be used in both cosmetic and plastic surgery include chemosurgery, electrosurgery, laser surgery and dermabrasion.

These procedures are not without risk of complications which can include scars and swelling, hematoma (blood clots requiring removal under anesthetic), and nerve damage, which will result in loss of feeling.

SEE ALSO *Plastic surgery*

COUGH

A cough is one of the most common symptoms of lung irritation or disease; almost any lung disease will cause a cough. A cough is a reflex action resulting in contraction and a sharp expiration of the diaphragm to expel something that is causing irritation to the lining of the bronchi (airways). It may be provoked by irritants such as smoke, allergens, viral or bacterial infection or other inflammation, foreign bodies or a growth in the bronchi.

In children and adults, a cough is commonly caused by bronchitis (inflammation of the airways). This commonly follows an upper respiratory tract infection such as the common cold or a viral throat infection. A bacterial bronchitis may result, especially in those with asthma or other lung disease. In adults, smoker's cough may be due to emphysema and chronic bronchitis, conditions caused by damage to the airways and connective tissue of the lung as the result of smoking. A cough may also be a symptom of lung cancer, or pulmonary fibrosis, and seen in a variety of lung disorders and connective tissue diseases.

If a cough lasts longer than a few weeks, the physician may wish to investigate further, with x-rays, CAT scans and MRI scans of the lung. Sputum can be collected and sent to the laboratory for microbial analysis. To cure a cough, the underlying cause must be treated. Cough symptoms can usually be suppressed by medications such as codeine. Often a cough suppressant will be combined with anti-flu preparations for greater effectiveness.

SEE ALSO *Bronchitis, Common cold, Emphysema, Lung*

COUNSELING

While the knowledge of the healing virtues of a good talk with an understanding person is as old as humanity, the professional practice of counseling is very much a twentieth-century phenomenon. Much of contemporary counseling theory and technique has its foundation in the work of the American psychiatrist Carl Rogers, who pioneered the "client-centered" approach.

Counseling usually takes place over a number of sessions. The general aim of counseling is to help clients review problematical situations in their lives and to explore the options they have to deal with them. Counselors aim to facilitate their clients' insight into themselves and their problems, not to direct or manage their clients' lives.

In a counseling session, clients are able to talk freely about themselves and their difficulties. The counselor listens and responds to the client with a sensitive receptivity. Fundamental to the success of the counseling relationship is the counselor's ability to be empathetic and non-judgmental.

There is no standard form of counseling. Many counselors today augment their basic counseling skills with a wide range of psychotherapeutic techniques such as Gestalt therapy, transactional analysis, art therapy, hypnotherapy, somatic (body) awareness and visualization methods. The various techniques are secondary to the basic requirement which is that counselors treat their clients with dignity and respect.

Basic counseling skills are increasingly being taught to a wide range of health professionals who can utilize them during their consultations. Alternatively, medical practitioners may refer their patients to a counselor if they feel the health condition of the patient could be improved by psychological support and insight. Counselors can help people identify and deal with any psychological issues contributing to their illness, as well as with emotional challenges posed by having the illness.

Counseling can be useful in managing stress-related illnesses, depression, alcohol and drug addictions, chronically debilitating conditions and life-threatening illnesses. In the case of the latter two categories, carers as well as patients may be helped by being involved with the counseling.

When looking for a counselor, it is a good idea to seek recommendations and talk to a few different ones before making a decision. The client should consider who they would feel most comfortable with and would be able to trust, as well as the amount of compassion and insight the counselor is able to offer.

SEE ALSO *Behavior therapy, Psychotherapy*

CRADLE CAP

Cradle cap, a skin condition that can occur on a baby's scalp, looks unpleasant, especially if it is yellow and crusty. However it is not infectious. It is a form of seborrheic dermatitis and occurs if a baby's head is not cleaned properly, usually because the parents are concerned that they may damage the soft spot (fontanelle) on the baby's head. Sebum, which is secreted from the sebaceous glands, forms in layers on the scalp, creating patches or a "cap" on the head.

Treatment is simple and usually effective if carried out when the crusts first appear: the affected areas should be rubbed with a little olive oil or paraffin in the evening. The next morning the area should be washed gently with soap and warm water and the scales should lift off easily. This should be repeated until the crusts disappear.

Careful shampooing will prevent cradle cap from returning. Persistent cases may require a special preparation available from a pharmacist or prescribed by a doctor.

SEE ALSO *Seborrheic dermatitis*

CRAMP

Cramp is a painful, involuntary contraction or spasm of muscles that can affect healthy people. It can involve any muscles and may occur suddenly while awake or asleep.

Poor circulation can be responsible, especially in the elderly, as can taking exercise without a warm-up. Swimmers can get cramps in cold water. Heavy work in hot conditions can induce heat cramps. Contraction of the uterus during or prior to menstruation is responsible for menstrual cramp (dysmenorrhea). Spasm of muscles controlling the stomach and large intestine can produce abdominal cramps. Repetitive use of muscles can cause cramps. Abdomi-

Cranial nerves

There are 12 cranial nerves that lead directly from the brain to various parts of the head. They control movements of the face, tongue, eyes and throat, and receive sensory input from the organs of hearing, sight, smell and taste.

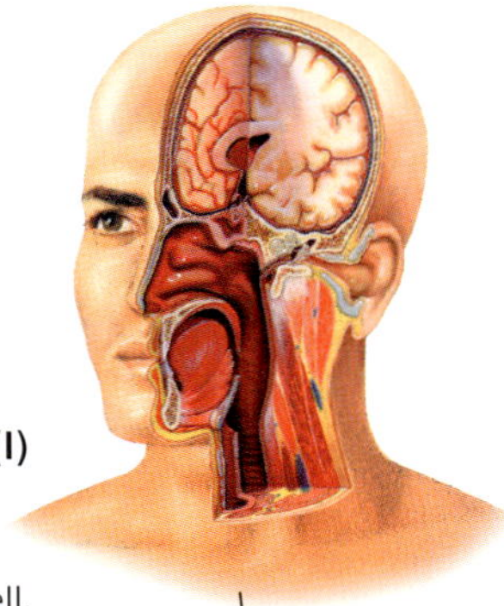

Olfactory nerve (I)

The first cranial nerve is concerned with the sense of smell. Nerve fibers starting in the mucous membranes of the nose carry messages to the cerebrum.

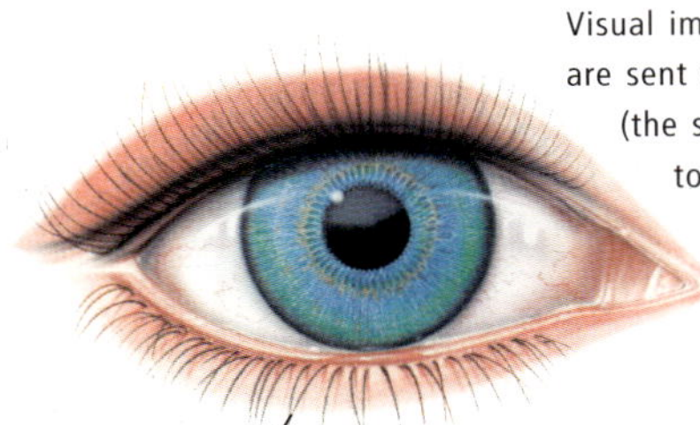

Optic nerve (II)

Visual impulses from the retina are sent along the optic nerve (the second cranial nerve) to the brain.

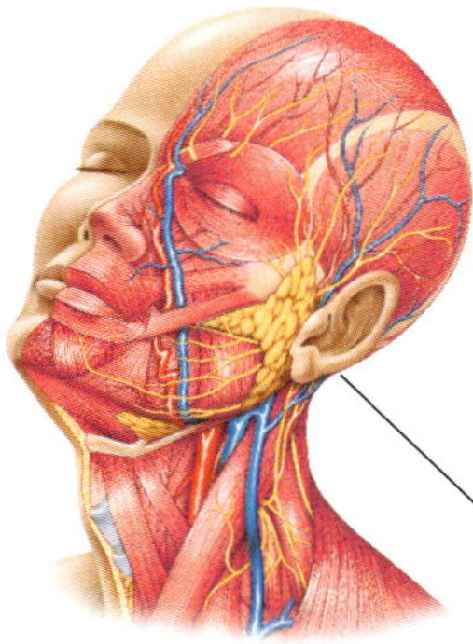

Trigeminal nerve (V)

The trigeminal nerve (fifth cranial nerve) has three sections: the ophthalmic, maxillary and mandibular divisions. They supply sensory fibers to areas such as the forehead, skin of the cheek and the muscles used for chewing.

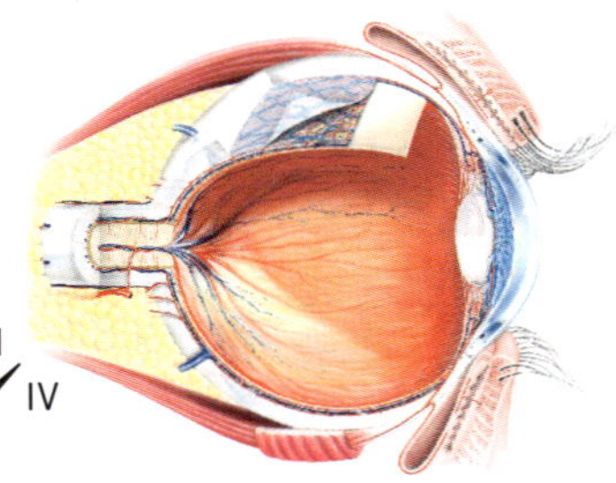

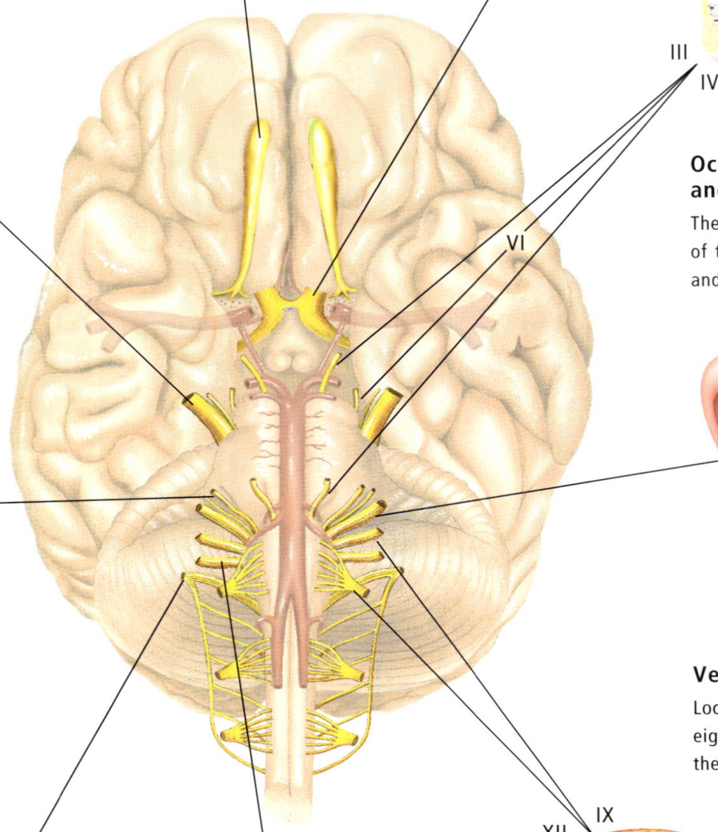

Oculomotor (III), trochlear (IV) and abducent (VI) nerves

These cranial nerves control movement of the muscle which moves the eyeball and eyelids, and allows focusing.

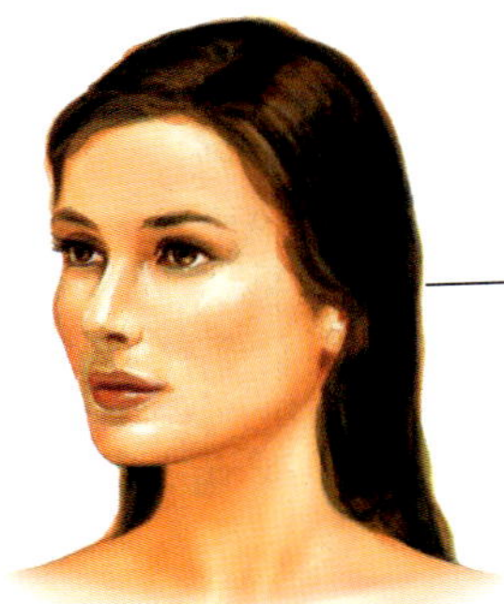

Facial nerve (VII)

The facial nerve is the seventh cranial nerve. It provides the motor fibers for facial expression. It is also responsible for the sensation of taste in the front part of the tongue.

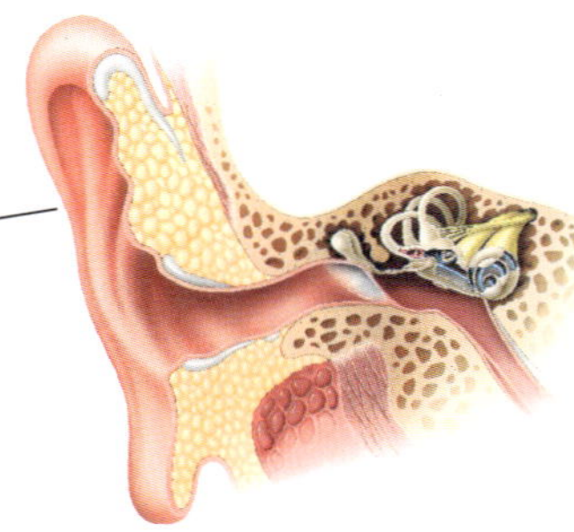

Vestibulocochlear nerve (VIII)

Located behind the facial nerve, the eighth cranial nerve carries impulses for the sense of balance.

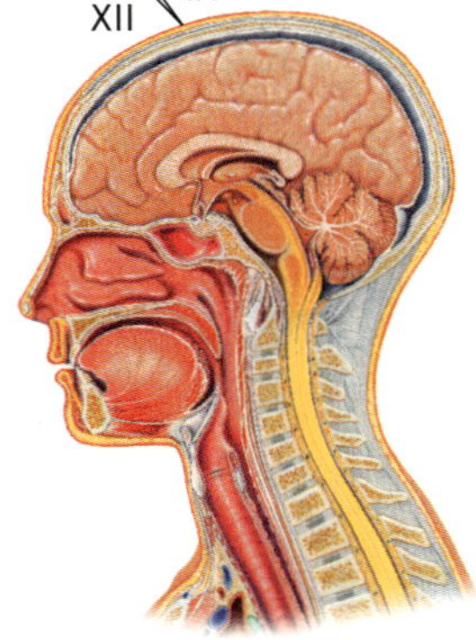

Glossopharyngeal (IX) and hypoglossal (XII) nerves

Supplying the carotid sinus, the ninth cranial nerve is responsible for the reflex control of the heart. It also supplies the back part of the tongue and the soft palate. The twelfth controls movement of the tongue.

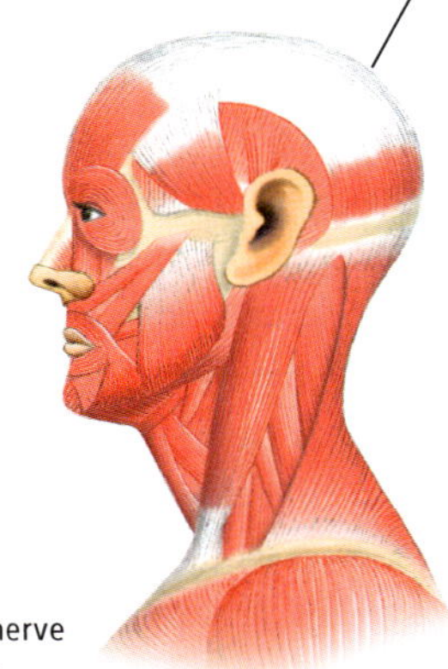

Spinal accessory nerve (XI)

The eleventh cranial nerve is primarily responsible for movement of the muscles of the upper shoulders, head, neck, and larynx and pharynx.

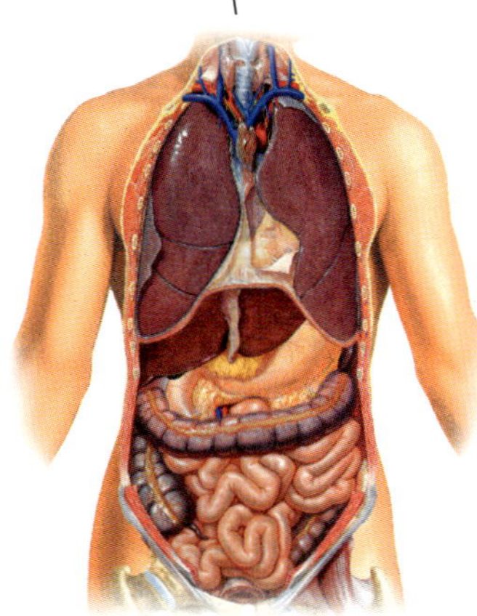

Vagus nerve (X)

The tenth cranial nerve is involved with functions such as coughing, sneezing, swallowing, speaking, secretions from the glands of the stomach, as well as the sensation of hunger.

nal cramps are common in pregnancy. Those occurring in the first 20 weeks may precede miscarriage. Light, irregular cramps later in a pregnancy (Braxton-Hicks contractions) may be mistaken for true labor.

Cramps can be prevented by stretching muscles before strenuous work or exercise, and by having adequate fluid in order to prevent dehydration. Cramps may be relieved by massaging and stretching the muscle, or by applying warmth from a safe source, such as a covered hot water bottle. Salt tablets (to replace salt lost in sweat) may ease cramps associated with exertion.

SEE ALSO *Muscle*

CRANIAL NERVES

The cranial nerves provide innervation (distribution of nerves) to the muscles and sensory structures of the head and neck (including skin, membranes, eyes and ears). They also distribute nerves to the organs of the chest (trachea, bronchi, lungs and heart) and the upper part of the gastrointestinal tract. The twelve pairs of cranial nerves arise mainly from the brain stem.

SEE ALSO *Brain, Nerves*

CRETINISM

Cretinism is a metabolic disorder that results from inadequate secretion of thyroid hormones during early life. It is characterized by a low metabolic rate with retarded growth and mental development. It occurs most commonly in populations whose diet is iodine deficient, and is preventable by administering iodine to pregnant mothers. Lack of thyroid hormones must be detected and treated as soon as possible after birth to prevent permanent brain damage.

SEE ALSO *Iodine deficiency, Thyroid gland*

CREUTZFELDT-JAKOB DISEASE

Creutzfeldt-Jakob disease is a rare, degenerative, invariably fatal brain disorder that causes movement abnormalities and a rapid decrease of mental function. The disorder first appears about age 60 and progresses rapidly to loss of brain function similar to that of Alzheimer's disease. There may be muscle tremors, rigid posture and changes in coordination. It may occur spontaneously with no known cause. In a small number of cases the disease is hereditary. In rare instances, it is acquired through exposure fo brain or nervous system tissue during medical procedures; it is thought to be transmitted via a viral-like protein called a prion. Adolescents who have received growth hormone derived from cadavers have contracted the disease; the use of synthetically manufactured growth hormone has meant contagion is no longer a problem. The disorder is fatal in a short time, usually within a year.

SEE ALSO *Alzheimer's disease*

CROHN'S DISEASE

Crohn's disease is a long-term, progressive disease that may involve both the small and large intestine. Most patients develop the disease in their twenties or early thirties. The disease involves swelling of lymphoid (immune system) tissue in the wall of the gut. This leads to ulcers on the inner lining of the bowel and cracks or fissures in the wall itself. Patients complain of diarrhea, lower abdominal pain, weakness, weight loss and fever. Many patients develop anemia (defined as reduced number, size and/or hemoglobin content of red blood cells in the blood) due to iron or vitamin B_{12} deficiency. Complications include bowel obstruction, abscesses in the bowel wall and bleeding from the bowel.

SEE ALSO *Anemia, Autoimmune disease, Bowel, Intestines*

CROUP

Difficulty inhaling, combined with making a noise like a barking seal (known as stridor), is the most obvious symptom of croup. It can be caused by bacterial or viral infections and in the early stages is contagious. Occasionally stridor is caused by a more serious condition known as epiglottitis which is caused by a bacterium and is life threatening. If the child is very distressed, sits bolt upright and has a high fever, emergency medical attention should be sought. Usually associated with a cold, croup is normally worse at night and upsets the child.

If the child has difficulty breathing and is distressed, then medical attention should be sought; otherwise, the usual treatment is a session in a steamy room, such as a bathroom. This can be created by turning on the hot water. Ideally the child should be sitting up on an adult's lap. Caution with hot water is important. Nothing can be done to prevent a child getting croup, although using a humidifier or vaporizer may help.

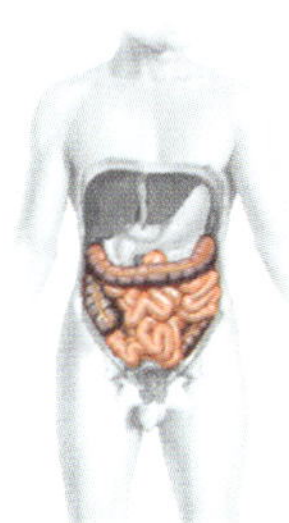

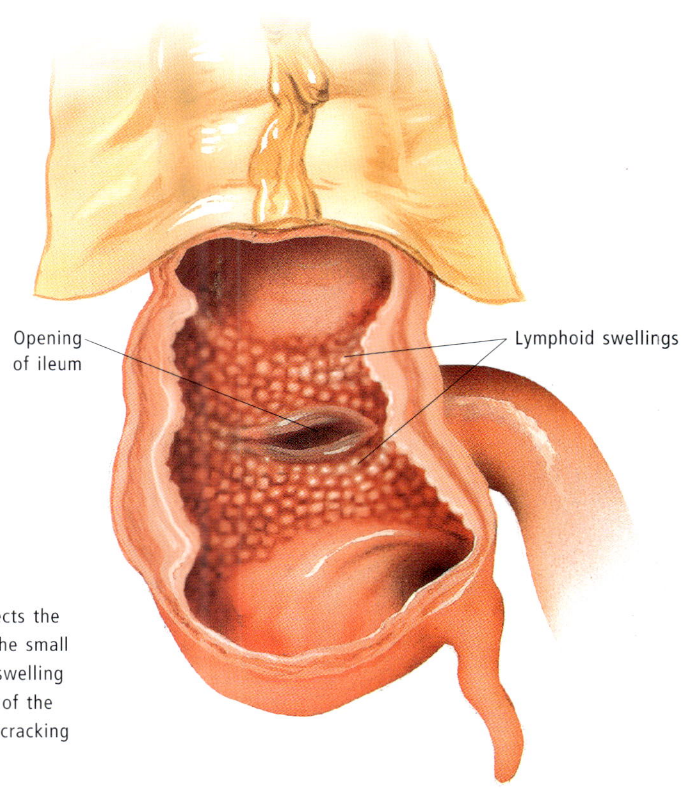

Crohn's disease

Crohn's disease commonly affects the colon and the lowest part of the small intestine (ileum). It results in swelling of lymphoid tissue in the wall of the gut. This swelling can lead to cracking and fissures in this area.

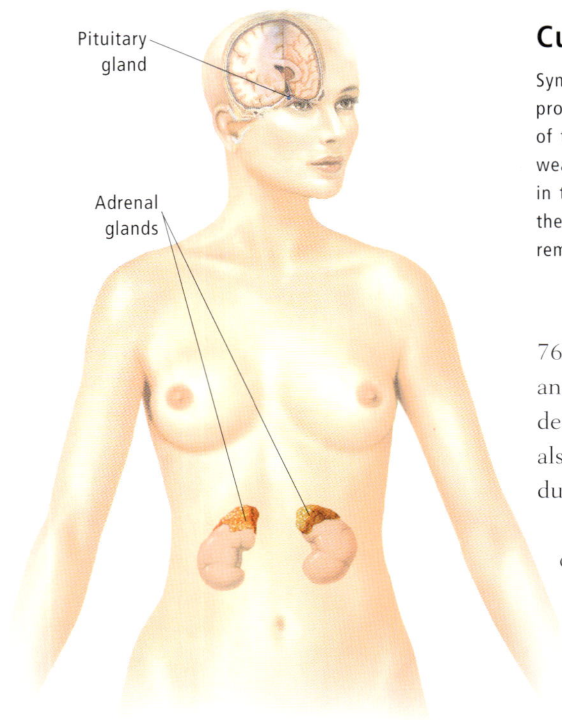

Cushing's syndrome

Symptoms produced by an excessive production of cortisol include fatty swellings of the face and trunk, and general weakness. It is usually a result of a tumor in the pituitary gland, which overstimulates the adrenal glands. The tumor may be removed surgically to cure the condition.

CROWN AND BRIDGE

These are two dental procedures, often used in combination, to fill a space created by one or more missing teeth. A crown is an artificial tooth or covering for the remains of a natural tooth, made of metal or porcelain. The teeth either side of a gap may be crowned in order to act as an anchor for a bridge. A bridge consists of false teeth on a mounting, and is often made of gold or porcelain on gold. It functions as normal teeth would and may prevent adjacent teeth from moving into an empty space. The crowns and bridge become one solid piece designed to look like individual natural teeth.

SEE ALSO *Teeth*

CRYOSURGERY

Cryosurgery is a medical technique in which extreme cold is used to destroy tissue. A part of the body is rapidly cooled to minus 76°F (-60°C) . The targeted tissue freezes and ice crystals form, breaking up and destroying the cell structure. Freezing can also stimulate the immune system to produce antibodies which attack diseased cells.

Cryosurgery is used to destroy skin cancers, warts, hemorrhoids, cataracts and difficult-to-reach internal tumors (such as in the kidney or brain). It is less invasive, less traumatic and involves less blood loss than traditional surgery. When treating growths on internal organs, liquid nitrogen is delivered through a small incision, thus avoiding major surgery.

CRYPTOSPORIDIOSIS

Cryptosporidium is a parasite of domestic and wild animals. In people with normal immune systems, it causes no illness or only mild symptoms. In people with deficient immune systems, for example those with AIDS or those on long-term corticosteroid or immunosuppressive medication, it may cause severe diarrhea, abdominal pain, malnutrition, dehydration, weight loss, and, occasionally, death. The organism is transmitted by the oral–fecal route, by person-to-person contact or through ingestion of contaminated water. Treatment for people suffering from the condition includes rehydration and antidiarrheal medications. There is no effective drug treatment for cryptosporidiosis.

CUSHING'S SYNDROME

Cushing's syndrome is a rare hormonal disorder caused by excessive production of cortisol. It is usually the result of a tumor in the pituitary gland which overstimulates the adrenal glands, but may be a side effect of corticosteroid drugs.

The affected person has fatty swellings on the back of the neck, a characteristic "moon face", fatigue, weakness, obesity of the trunk (while the limbs remain thin), and skin discoloration with pink streaks. In addition, there may be diabetes mellitus, hypertension, excessive hair growth and reduced sex drive in men; in women, menstruation may cease. The diagnosis can be confirmed by means of blood and urine tests for glucose and cortisol. Surgical removal of the pituitary tumor will cure the condition.

SEE ALSO *Adrenal glands, Pituitary gland*

CUTICLE

At the point on a finger or toe where skin meets nail, the skin grows back underneath itself, creating a fold. The topmost, visible tissue of this fold is the eponychium, commonly called the cuticle. The "true cuticle", however, is the non-living, unseen part of the fold underneath that seals off the site of new nail growth to protect it from infection.

SEE ALSO *Nails*

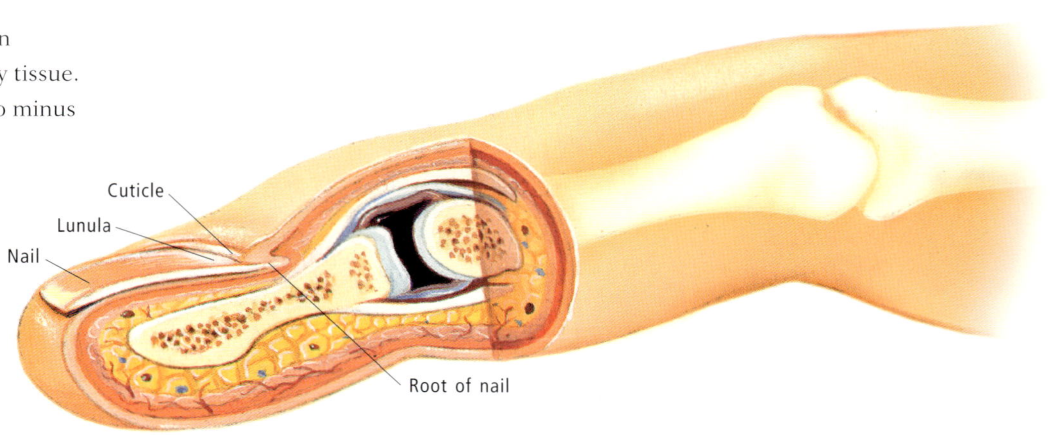

Cuticle

The cuticle is the fold of skin where the nail meets the skin. The top layer is visible, while the unseen bottom layer seals off the site of new nail growth to prevent infection.

CYANOSIS

Cyanosis is a bluish discoloration of the skin and mucous membranes (such as the lips). It is a sign that arterial blood is inadequately oxygenated. When it occurs in the whole of the body (central cyanosis) it is usually due to heart or lung disease.

Cyanosis often occurs in the terminal phases of a cardiac arrest, drug overdose, drowning or pneumonia, in fact whenever oxygenation of blood is not occurring. In rare cases it can be caused by abnormal hemoglobin (such as methemoglobinemia) and toxins such as cyanide.

Cyanosis of an area of the body, such as the feet or hands, can be caused by arterial disease. Arterial spasm in cold environments may cause cyanosis, which clears when the extremities are warmed. Arteriosclerosis may cause ischemia and cyanosis of extremities; angioplasty or amputation may be needed.

Cystic fibrosis

Signs of cystic fibrosis begin to appear between infancy and childhood. Life expectancy is short. Thick mucus is formed in the alveoli in the lungs, which can block the airways. Mucus can also block the ducts of the liver and pancreas.

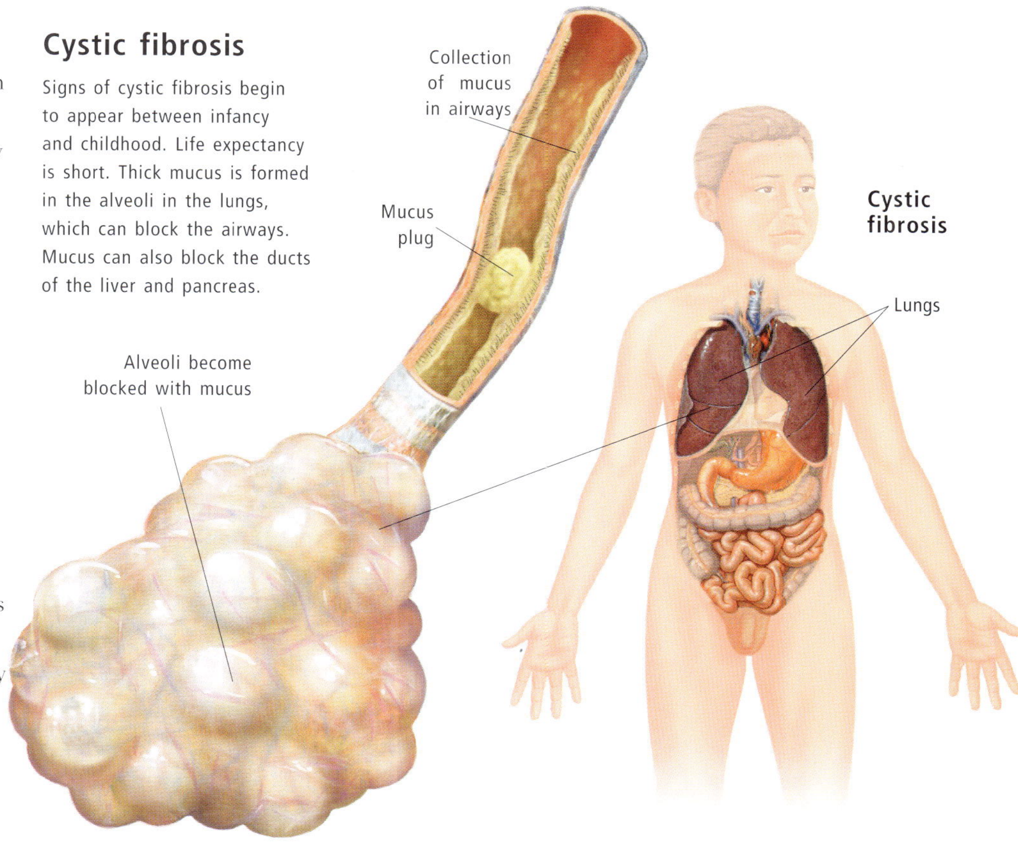

CYST

A cyst is an abnormal swelling that is sac-like in structure, with an outer wall of cells or fibrous tissue enclosing liquid or semi-liquid material. Cysts may contain a range of substances including blood, fat, pus or parasites. They are very common and can occur virtually anywhere in the body but are most often noticed in the skin, ovaries, breasts or kidneys.

Although usually benign, cysts can sometimes create complications. For example, symptoms caused by ovarian cysts (fluid-filled lumps on the ovaries) can include abdominal pain, abnormally heavy and irregular menstrual periods and increased growth of facial and body hair. If ovarian cysts rupture, they can cause severe pain, nausea, vomiting and shock. These cysts are usually benign in women during their reproductive years, but frequently are found to be malignant when they occur in young girls or post-menopausal women.

A cyst in the kidney may sound ominous, but more than 50 percent of people aged over 50 are thought to have these usually harmless and symptomless lesions. Only occasionally do cysts impair kidney function and require treatment. Likewise, cysts in the breasts are very common and mostly benign, although it is extremely important that each and every breast lump is assessed medically before being dismissed as harmless. Breast cysts can be as small as pin heads or as large as walnuts. They feel hard and round and move easily when touched.

Hydatid cysts are formed by the larvae of the dog tapeworm. In humans they occur most often in the liver and tend to be more common where people have close associations with dogs and sheep. They can survive for many years growing very slowly without major consequences, but they have the potential to cause serious illness. They are usually treated with potent medications or removed surgically.

SEE ALSO *Fibrocystic disease of the breast, Hydatid disease, Ovarian cysts, Tumors*

CYSTIC FIBROSIS

Cystic fibrosis is an inherited disorder, caused by a defective gene. In cystic fibrosis, mucous secretions in several organs become thick and sticky, and interfere with normal functioning. Thick mucus is formed in the lung airways which predisposes the person to chronic lung infections. Mucus can also block the ducts of the liver and the pancreas, causing inadequate absorption of nutrients from the intestinal tract (malabsorption) and malnutrition.

Cystic fibrosis affects about 1 in 2,500 people, although 1 in 25 people are carriers. Most affected people are born healthy, but begin showing signs of the disorder between infancy and adolescence. They gradually develop a chronic cough, persistent wheezing and recurrent respiratory infections. Their feces becomes greasy and foul-smelling and they fail to gain weight or thrive.

There is no known cure for cystic fibrosis. Treatment usually involves relieving and treating symptoms. Antibiotics, postural drainage, chest percussion and other breathing treatments will help fight infection in the lungs. Digestion can be improved with special diet and enzyme supplements. Advances in genetic engineering may one day provide a cure for cystic fibrosis. But for now the prognosis is poor; only about 50 percent of children with cystic fibrosis live beyond age 20 and few live beyond 35 years of age. Death usually occurs from lung complications. Screening of family members of a cystic fibrosis sufferer may detect the cystic fibrosis gene in up to 75 percent of carriers.

SEE ALSO *Genetic counseling, Liver, Lungs, Malnutrition, Pancreas*

CYSTINOSIS

About 2,000 people in the world are thought to suffer from cystinosis, a very rare inherited disorder in which abnormal levels of the amino acid cysteine accumulate and crystallize in the cells. Potentially, every organ may be affected but kidney and eye functions tend to be impaired first.

Of the three forms of the disease, infantile nephropathic cystinosis, which affects young children, is the most severe. Babies often appear normal at birth but tell-tale symptoms, such as excessive thirst and urination, usually appear by about 10 months. Growth and development are affected and death by the age of 10 years due to kidney failure was once inevitable. These days, kidney transplants and other treatments may prolong life.

In late-onset nephropathic cystinosis, symptoms first appear between the ages of 2 and 26 years and most commonly in the early teens. Without a transplant, death due to kidney failure commonly occurs within a few years of diagnosis.

In the third and mildest form of this disease, known as benign non-nephropathic cystinosis, symptoms often don't appear until middle age and do not include the kidney dysfunction that characterizes the other forms of cystinosis.

SEE ALSO *Amino acids, Kidney*

CYSTITIS

Cystitis is inflammation of the bladder, usually from bacterial infection. Bladder infections cause the sufferer to urinate more frequently than normal. Urination is accompanied by a burning or stinging sensation and there may be blood in the urine. If the infection spreads upstream to the kidneys, inflammation of the kidneys (pyelonephritis) may occur, with fever and back pain.

Cystitis is usually caused by bacteria gaining entry into the bladder via the urethra. Because the urethra is shorter in women than in men, cystitis is more common in females. It sometimes occurs in women after sexual intercourse. Any abnormality in the bladder makes cystitis more likely. A tumor or stones in the bladder, an enlarged prostate, or a distended uterus during pregnancy may obstruct the normal flow of urine and cause the disorder.

Cystitis is confirmed by a urine test which isolates the bacteria responsible and determines which antibiotic(s) will be the most effective. A short course of the correct antibiotic usually clears up the infection. The patient should drink copious amounts of water to help flush the bacteria out of the urinary tract. Should another attack of cystitis occur, it may be because of an abnormality, in which case the bladder should be more fully investigated. This may involve blood tests, an intravenous pyelogram (IVP) and cystoscopy.

There are a number of alternative therapies that may help to alleviate the symptoms of cystitis. Aromatherapy uses urinary antiseptic oils such as sandalwood and juniper in baths or massage. Herbalism dispenses urinary antiseptic herbs (uva ursi, buchu); antibacterial herbs (echinacea, goldenseal); demulcent herbs (marshmallow, cornsilk) to treat cystitis. Naturopathy advises eliminating sugar, coffee, tea, alcohol and acidic fruits while keeping to a low-protein whole-food diet. Fluids should be increased, including water, vegetable broth, barley water and cranberry juice. Sodium bicarbonate, non-acidic vitamin C, vitamin A and zinc are commonly prescribed as are alternating hot and cold sitz baths. An allergy-free diet or anti-candida diet may be prescribed for recurring urinary tract infections.

SEE ALSO *Bladder, Pyelonephritis, Urinary systems*

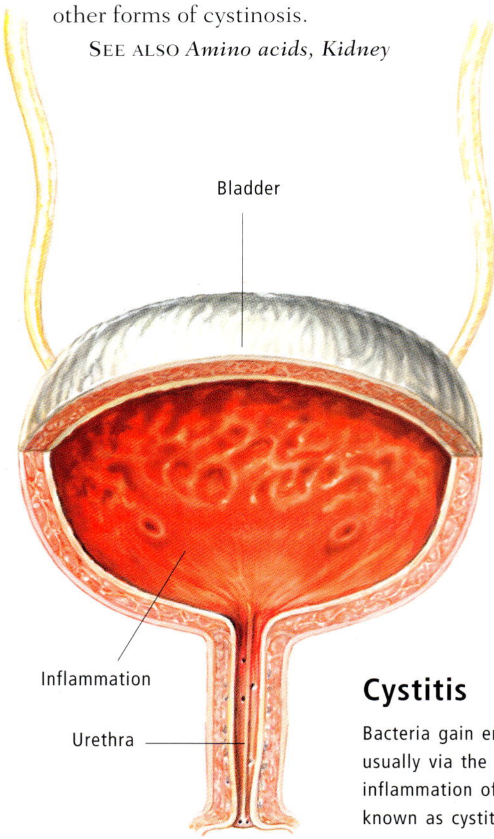

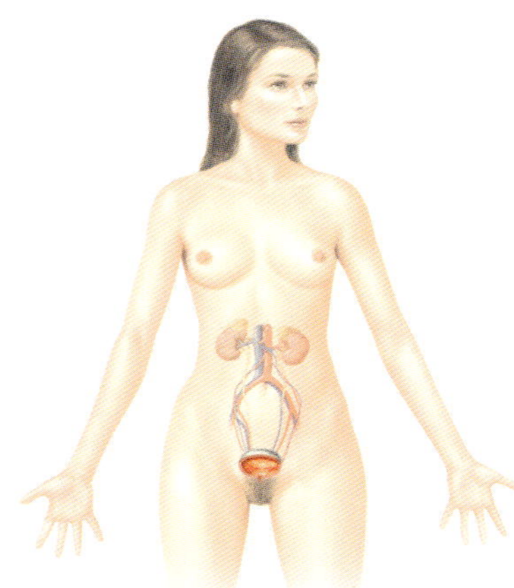

Cystitis

Bacteria gain entry to the bladder, usually via the urethra, leading to inflammation of the bladder–this is known as cystitis.

CYSTOCELE

A cystocele may occur in post-menopausal women who have lost hormonal support of the pelvic floor tissues. The pelvic floor becomes weak and the base of the urinary bladder pushes the front wall of the vagina backwards and downwards, making a urine-filled pocket bulging from the front wall of the vagina. It is sometimes associated with rectocele, which is a similar condition involving the posterior vaginal wall and the rectum. Patients are advised to do pelvic floor exercises; however, in more severe cases, surgery to repair the bladder may be considered necessary.

SEE ALSO *Bladder, Urinary incontinence, Urinary systems*

CYSTOGRAPHY

A cystogram is an x-ray taken of the bladder after radiopaque dye has been injected into a vein. The dye is filtered out by the kidneys into the bladder, where it outlines calculi (stones), papillomas (benign tumors), cancers and other problems.

SEE ALSO *Bladder, Kidneys*

CYSTOMETOGRAPHY

Cystometography is a medical procedure used to assess bladder function in people who are experiencing problems with urination. It is also commonly known as filling cystometography.

The patient normally lies down and remains as relaxed as possible while the bladder is filled with sterile water. Abdominal pressure is also applied to the bladder via the rectum. Throughout the procedure the patient reports on the sensations that they are feeling, and bladder pressure is monitored continuously.

SEE ALSO *Bladder*

CYSTOSCOPY

Cystoscopy is the examination of the bladder with a cystoscope, a special fiberoptic tube equipped with a lens and a light. The cystoscope is introduced through the urethra into the bladder. Through it, a surgeon or urologist can visualize the interior of the bladder. Special attachments can be used to crush stones, take a biopsy of a tumor, or to cauterize diseased tissue.

SEE ALSO *Bladder, Urethra*

Cytomegalovirus

Cytomegalovirus causes many illnesses, including retinitis, an inflammation of the retina in the eye, which can result in loss of vision if untreated.

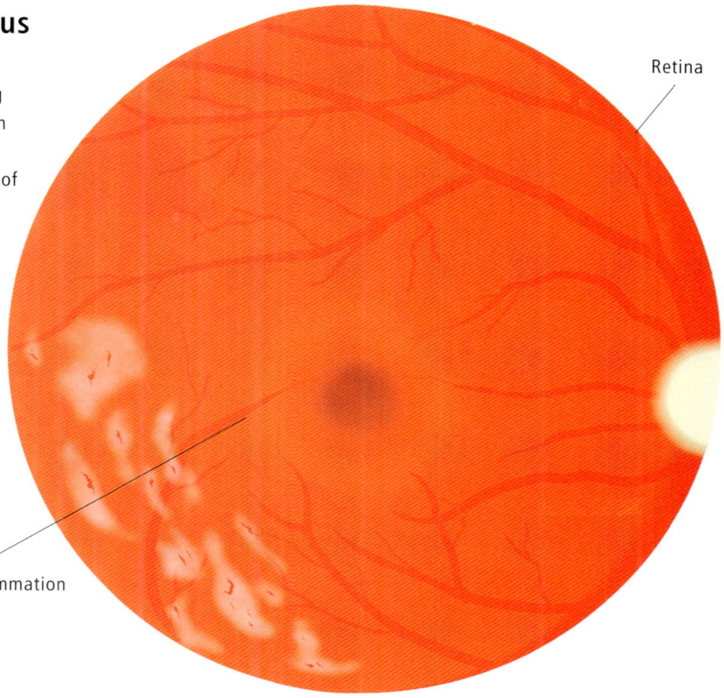

CYTOMEGALOVIRUS

The human cytomegalovirus (CMV), a member of the herpes family of viruses, causes cytomegalic inclusion disease. This is an extremely common virus and some 90 percent of people in the over-70s population have antibodies to CMV in their blood.

Infants commonly acquire the virus from their mother in the uterus, during birth or through breast feeding. It can be spread by close contact later in life and can be reactivated in adults after a period of dormancy.

Most healthy people do not develop any significant symptoms to CMV, though it may a cause a flu-like illness lasting a few weeks. However, people with suppressed immune systems (such as those on immunosuppressive drugs or with AIDS) who become infected with CMV may develop serious diseases such as pneumonia, hepatitis, encephalitis (brain inflammation), colitis, and retinitis (inflammation of the eye). They may need to be hospitalized and receive treatment with antiviral drugs.

Congenital cytomegalovirus is caused when an infected mother passes the CMV virus to the fetus through the placenta. In a fetus, it can cause a range of defects and may result in miscarriage. The baby may eventually develop minor impairments affecting hearing, vision or mental capacity. A small percentage are born with severe neurologic damage, causing intellectual disability or profound hearing loss. There is no specific treatment.

SEE ALSO *Immunity, Viruses*

CYTOTOXIC DRUGS

Cytotoxic drugs destroy cells or prevent their multiplication. Penicillins or other antibiotics used in the treatment of bacterial infections are cytotoxic, but the term usually refers to drugs used in the treatment of cancer, such as methotrexate and cyclophosphamide. They are sometimes used to treat other disorders such as rheumatoid arthritis.

Cytotoxic drugs affect not only cancer cells but also other cells, especially those that grow rapidly such as cells of the skin, gastrointestinal tract and bone marrow. They may cause side effects such as serious blood disorders, hair loss (alopecia) and reduced resistance to infection. Dosages and side effects of cytotoxic drugs need to be carefully monitored by the physician.

SEE ALSO *Cancer, Cells*

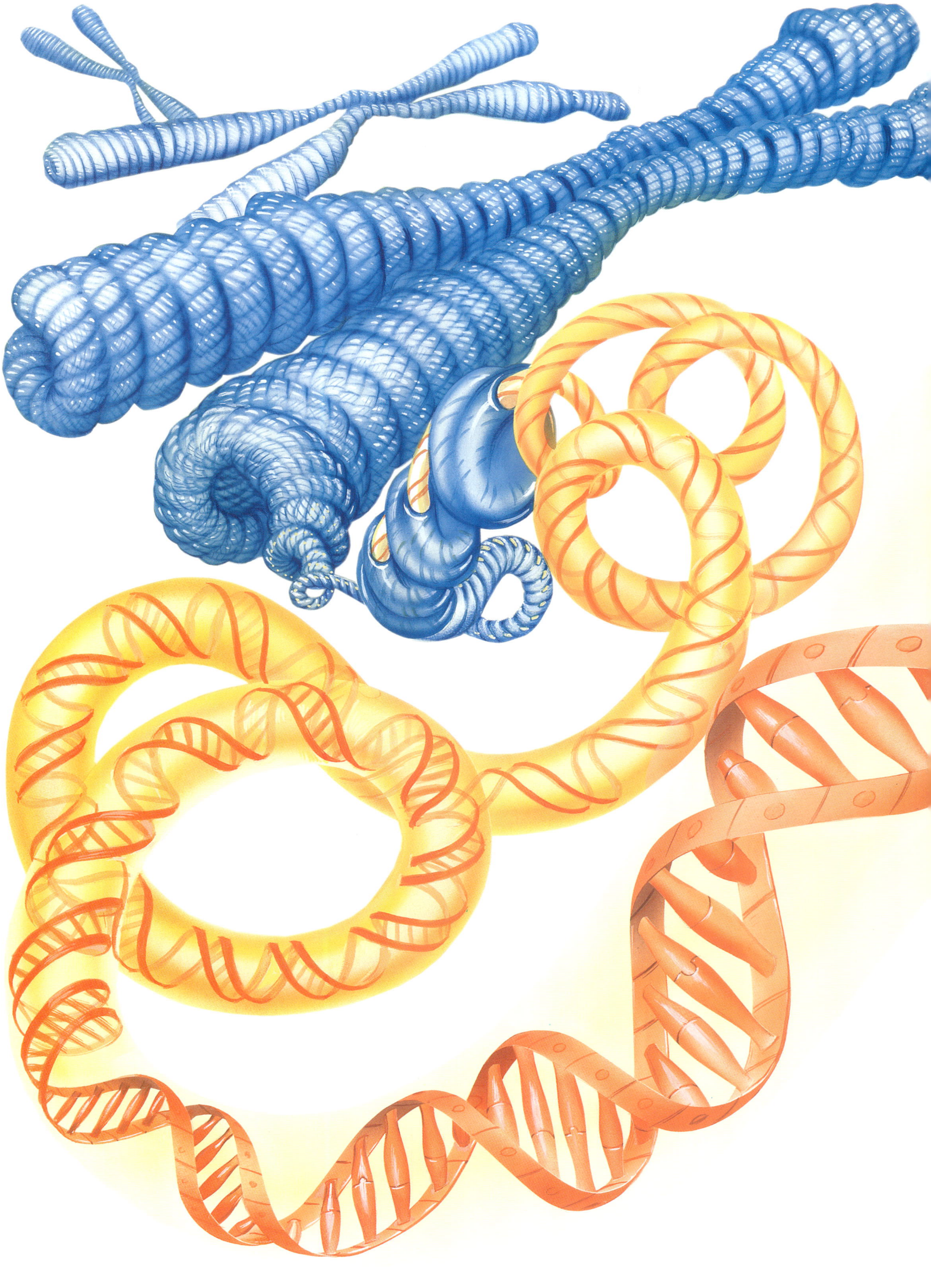

D

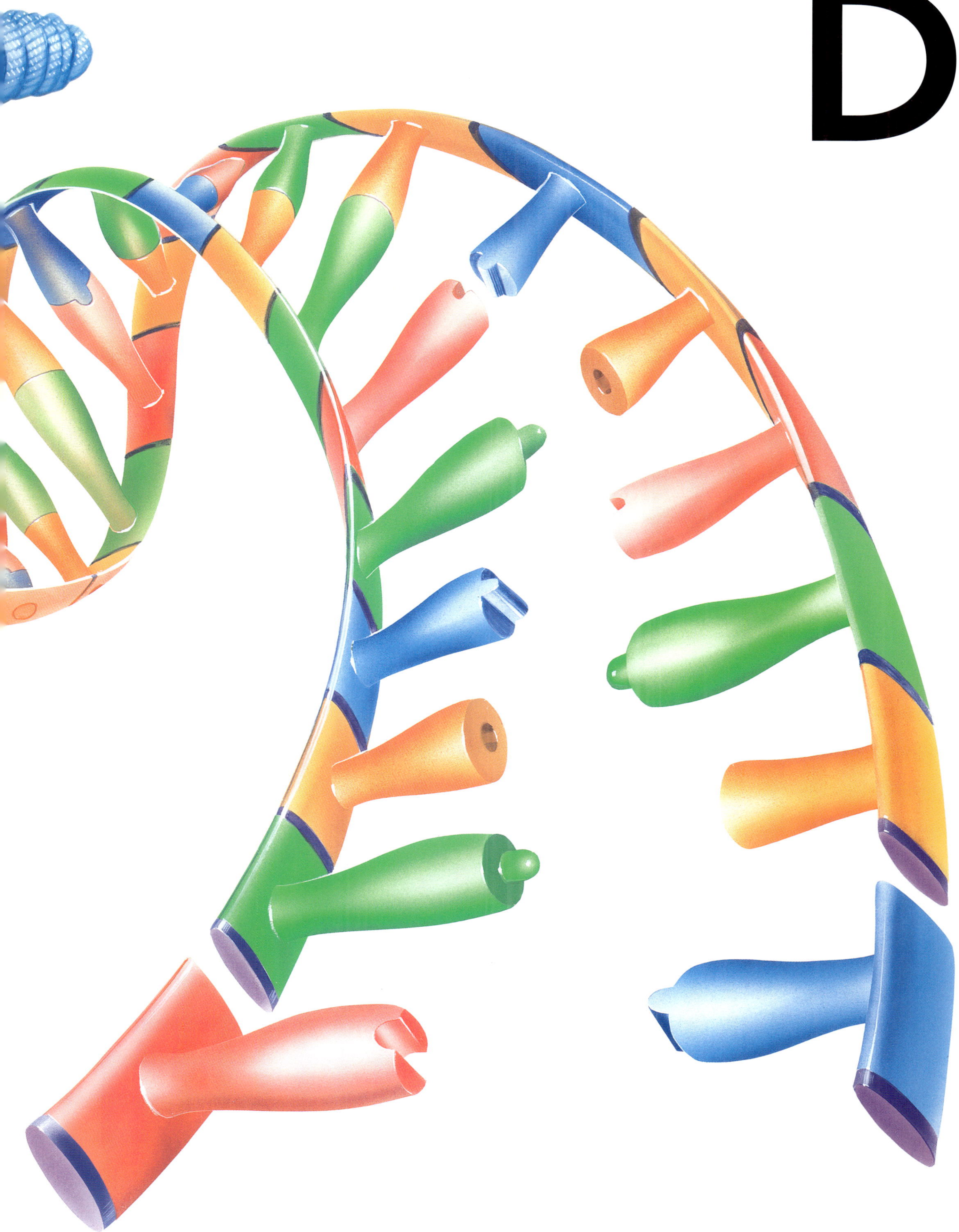

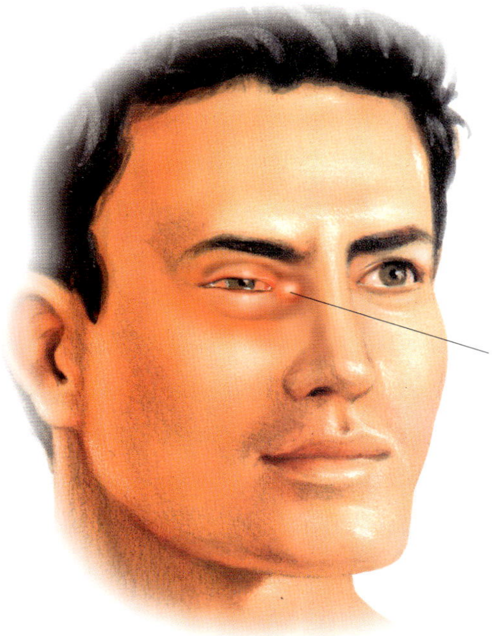

Dacryocystitis

Infection of the lacrimal sac usually results from blockage of the lacrimal duct. The area around the sac becomes red, swollen, and painful. The eye becomes red and watery and oozes fluid. An abscess may develop in which the lacrimal sac is swollen and filled with pus.

DACRYOADENITIS

Dacryoadenitis is inflammation of the lacrimal gland, which is situated above the eye. It is usually caused by bacteria from other infection such as conjunctivitis or upper respiratory tract infection, resulting in a blockage of the lacrimal duct, the duct that drains tears from the eye into the nasal cavity. It often occurs along with dacryocystitis. The eye is red, and the lacrimal gland is swollen and tender. The condition is treated with oral antibiotics.

SEE ALSO *Conjunctivitis, Dacryocystitis, Eye, Lacrimal glands*

DACRYOCYSTITIS

Dacryocystitis is inflammation of the tear (lacrimal) sac, caused by a blockage of the lacrimal duct, which normally drains tears from the eye into the nasal cavity. It is most common in children, and may follow sinus or nasal infection, nasal polyps, eye injury or infection, especially conjunctivitis. It may also occur as an inherited condition, usually appearing in infants at 3 to 12 weeks of age.

The symptoms of dacryocystitis are pain, swelling and tenderness in the corner of the eye, with a discharge of pus and tears. Treatment is required to prevent infection spreading to the cornea, or permanent scarring of the tear duct (dacryostenosis). Irrigation of the infected ducts, massage of the tear duct and the application of antibiotic ointments will usually cure the condition.

Severe cases may require surgery to dilate and probe the tear duct canal to clear the infection and prevent recurrences. Complete obstruction may require a surgical opening from the eye into the nasal passage.

SEE ALSO *Eye, Lacrimal glands*

DANCE MOVEMENT THERAPY

In many ancient cultures illness is seen to be caused by a loss of soul and dance is viewed as an important way of bringing people who are sick back to themselves and their life energy.

In modern Western culture, Isadora Duncan became a pioneer of early dance movement therapy by championing dance as a spontaneous form of emotional expression. Also in the USA around the 1920s there was another contributor to the beginnings of dance therapy, Rudolph van Laban. A dancer and a theoretician, he explored the space and dynamics of movement, offering a movement-based model for human wholeness that reflected both conscious and unconscious processes.

In the aftermath of World War II the need to deal with large groups of traumatized veterans led to the development of a number of creative therapies suited to group work. In Washington DC, Marian Chace used dance in her work with psychiatric patients, finding it particularly helpful for encouraging withdrawn patients back into the present. Chace's view was that dance is a form of communication that fulfils a basic human need. She recognized that both dancers and psychotic patients used symbolic body movements to communicate emotions and ideas. Chace moved with her patients using rhythm as an ordering principle, and the circle as a means of containment. She also made a study of the movement patterns of different diagnostic categories.

Another early dance therapist pioneer, Mary Starks Whitehouse, was inspired by the psychiatrist Carl Jung who believed that all psychological complexes have a physical component. She encouraged patients to find their "authentic movement".

Practice

Dance movement therapy is based on the assumption that body and mind are inter-related. In practice dance is used psychotherapeutically to bring about changes in feelings, behavior, cognition and physical functioning. Everyday and creative movement are used through processes that help patients learn more about themselves and their interaction with others.

How dance therapy is actually practised varies widely. Generally the emphasis is on exploring and expanding movements as patients discover and express their own resources and feelings. Patients may also be encouraged to find individual movements to themes and music given by the therapist.

There is no stress on competence or experience nor do patients have to be fit or fully physically able. Some of the benefits of dance movement therapy include the development of a positive body awareness and self-image, anger management, improved communication skills and the stimulation of creativity and playfulness. This is a particularly effective therapy for children especially those with behavioral or learning problems or with physical disabilities.

Dance movement therapy is used in psychiatric hospitals, mental health care clinics, rehabilitation facilities and special schools as well as in private practice. Practitioners believe it can help with severe emotional disorders, autism, cognitive delays, neurological disorders, the elderly, those suffering trauma from physical or sexual abuse, or those in substance abuse recovery programs. Preventive health schemes also make use of dance movement therapy to relieve stress and assist movement function. It is most commonly practised in groups.

SEE ALSO *Alexander technique, Feldenkrais method, Music therapy*

DANDRUFF

Dandruff is the everyday term for mild seborrheic dermatitis of the scalp. It is related to cradle cap in infants, and in adults, manifests as greasy or dry, white scales that are shed from the scalp. Other areas may also be affected, including eyebrows, forehead, and behind the ears.

Dandruff is also sometime associated with excessive production of grease or oil from the sebaceous glands, and sufferers tend to have oily skin. The cause is unknown, but it tends to be worse in hot, humid weather or cold, dry weather and in periods of stress and fatigue.

Dandruff is a chronic condition with periods of improvement followed by deterioration. It is not dangerous, but it can be annoying and socially embarrassing. Shampooing should be frequent (daily), prolonged (at least 5 minutes) and vigorous enough so that the scales are loosened with the fingernails. As well, a non-prescription dandruff shampoo containing selenium sulfide or zinc pyrithione should be used at least once a week. If the condition worsens, a doctor should be consulted, as corticosteroid creams or ointments may be needed.

SEE ALSO *Cradle cap, Dermatitis, Scalp*

DEAFNESS

Deafness can be simply defined as an inability to hear. It can be partial, in which a person has an inability to hear in one ear, or inability to hear sounds at a certain frequency or below a certain volume (intensity). Or it can be profound, meaning a total inability to hear.

Unlike partially deaf people, people with a profound deafness have a hearing loss so severe that a hearing aid is useless. About 10 percent of people with deafness are profoundly deaf.

There are two main types of hearing loss: conductive hearing loss and sensorineural hearing loss.

Conductive hearing loss occurs when sound is not properly transmitted to the cochlea (a small, spiral-shaped structure in the inner ear) because of a blockage, disease or disorder of the middle ear. A person with a conductive hearing loss can generally benefit from a hearing aid.

Sensorineural hearing loss is caused by damage to the cochlea or auditory nerves. This type of deafness occurs, for example, when the tiny hair cells of the cochlea in the inner ear become damaged, with the result that sound reaching the cochlea is not adequately processed, and faulty nerve signals are sent to the brain. A hearing aid is often of no use to a person with a sensorineural loss.

Some experts recognize two other categories of deafness. Mixed hearing loss is caused by illness or injury in both the outer or middle ear and the inner ear. Central hearing loss is caused by damage to the neural pathways or parts of the brain concerned with hearing.

Factors affecting hearing loss

Babies will respond to sound soon after birth and speech begins to develop at two to three months, words following from eight to twelve months. If these developments do not occur, a hearing problem may be the reason.

Hearing problems can appear at any age but they are particularly serious in childhood as the ability to hear affects the development of speech. Hearing enables the reception of sounds and recognition of language, and allows self-monitoring when those sounds are imitated, which is an essential part of the learning process.

Birth defects causing loss of hearing can be inherited, or are the result of injury or disease. Lack of oxygen or Rh disease (Rh incompatibility) can damage the auditory nerve and inner ear. The likelihood of a child suffering birth defects that affect hear-

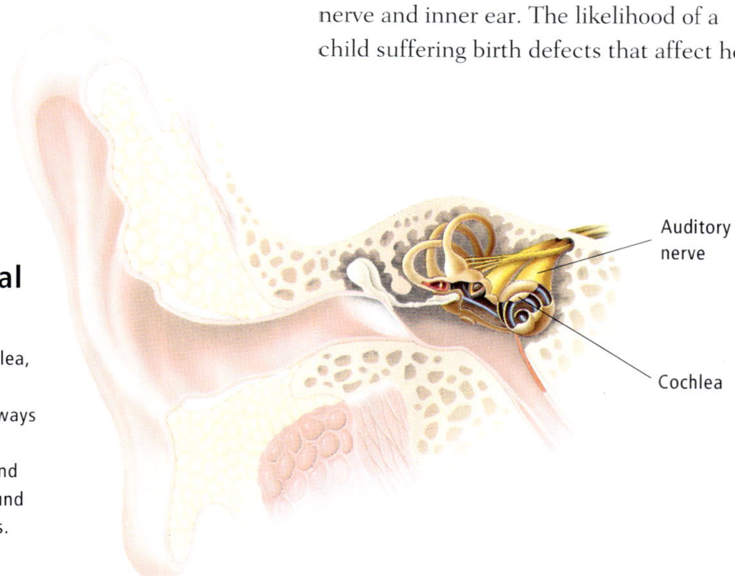

Sensorineural deafness

Damage to the cochlea, auditory nerve or auditory nerve pathways interferes with the brain's perception and interpretation of sound resulting in deafness.

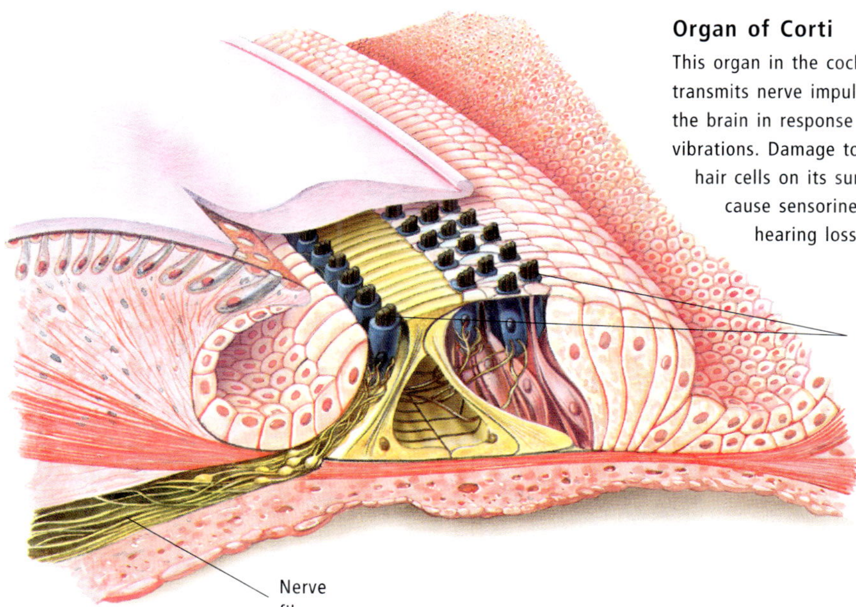

Organ of Corti

This organ in the cochlea transmits nerve impulses to the brain in response to sound vibrations. Damage to the tiny hair cells on its surface cause sensorineural hearing loss.

ing is greater where other family members were born with hearing defects or where there is exposure before birth to infection by toxoplasmosis, syphilis, rubella, herpes or cytomegalovirus.

Down syndrome and other genetic problems can result in impaired hearing, as can exposure of the mother to certain antibiotics, quinine or radiation during pregnancy. Risk factors at birth are greater for babies with a low birth weight; those who need to spend more than ten days on a ventilator; those with an Apgar score below three; and those with high levels of bilirubin, indicating possible liver dysfunction.

Childhood illnesses including measles, mumps, meningitis and ear infections—all of which can cause scarring that restricts the movement of the ossicles—can permanently impair hearing. Head injury, exposure to very loud noises and side-effects of certain antibiotics are all possible causes of hearing loss.

Normal hearing can be affected temporarily in children by a blockage in the ear canal, which can be due to excessive ear wax, or a foreign body such as a bead or piece of food. Ear infections can infect or block the eustachian tube very easily in children as the tube is narrow. Hearing can also be lost temporarily after exposure to loud noise.

Injuries to the head, blows, sudden pressure changes (for example when divers rise too quickly to the surface) and extremely loud noises (such as explosions) can rupture the eardrum and damage the bones of the middle ear or the delicate inner ear. Repeated exposure to loud noise can also produce gradual hearing loss. Noise intensity greater than 85 decibels can destroy hair cells in the inner ear. Damage is permanent and may be accompanied by tinnitus, a high-pitched noise heard in one or both ears.

Age-related hearing loss (presbycusis) can begin in early adulthood and usually diminishes ability to hear high frequency sounds first. It can advance to profound deafness and affects men more often than women.

Sudden attacks of vertigo, nausea and vomiting, possibly preceded by hearing loss and tinnitus may indicate Menière's disease, which is a chronic disease of the inner ear. There may be pressure in one or both ears, and hearing ability gradually diminishes. The cause is unknown, but vertigo can be

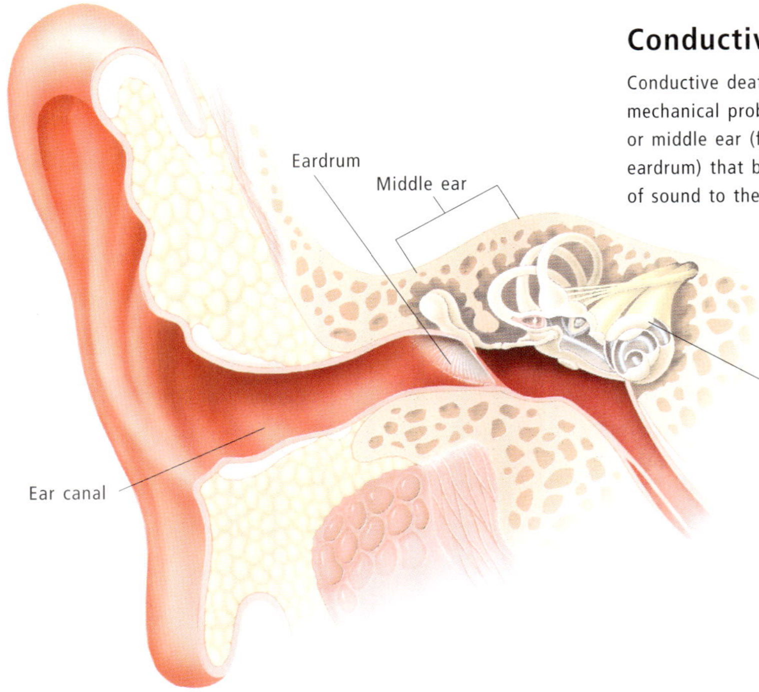

Conductive deafness

Conductive deafness is caused by a mechanical problem in the ear canal or middle ear (for example, a perforated eardrum) that blocks the transmission of sound to the inner ear (cochlea).

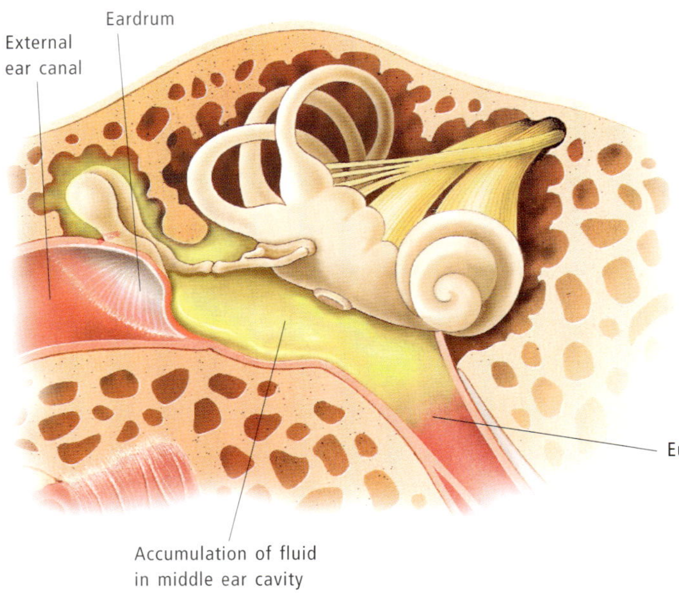

Temporary blockages

Ear infections can block the eustachian tube and can result in temporary deafness. This occurs especially in children where the tube is narrow.

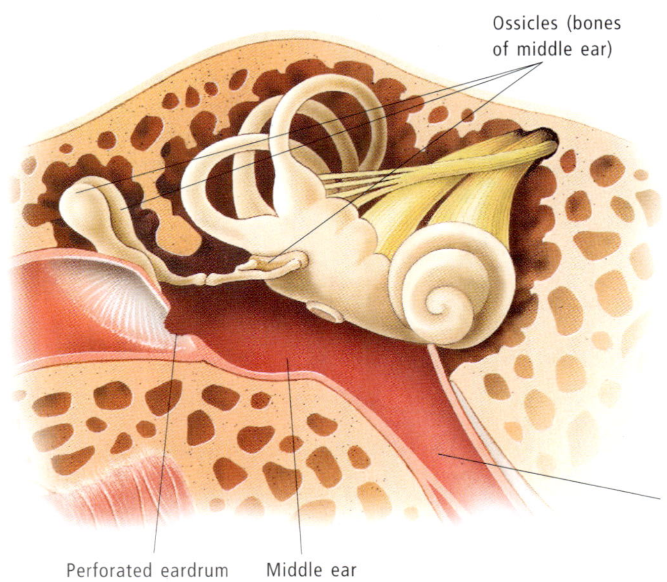

Middle ear damage

Injuries to the head, sudden pressure changes and extremely loud noises can rupture the eardrum or damage the bones of the middle ear.

treated temporarily with drugs, or more permanently, by surgery to the nerves of the inner ear.

Hearing tests

Hearing tests can show the intensity (in decibels) at which various frequencies can be heard, and at which speech is correctly understood. Testing for deafness seeks to determine whether the loss is conductive or sensory, temporary or permanent, and congenital or acquired later in life. The ears can also be checked for blockages or structural abnormalities.

Bone-conduction hearing tests include tuning-fork tests where the vibrating tuning fork is held against the mastoid process, which is part of the skull. The patient reports how long a sound is heard for, then the test is repeated with the tuning fork held close to the ear canal. If the first part of the test registers a longer audible period, conductive hearing loss is suspected.

Audiometry testing usually includes a separate test that involves a calibrated bone-conduction vibrator. The test aims to reveal any loss in hearing ability by comparing what is heard by bone conduction alone with the hearing of airborne sounds through the middle ear.

Deafness is treated by specially trained physicians called otolaryngologists (ear, nose and throat specialists). Their approach to treating deafness is to correct the underlying condition if possible. For example, infections can be treated with antibiotics, and wax can be removed by ear syringing. However, many causes of deafness are irreversible or degenerative and cannot be treated. In these cases the aim is to augment hearing with electronic devices where possible.

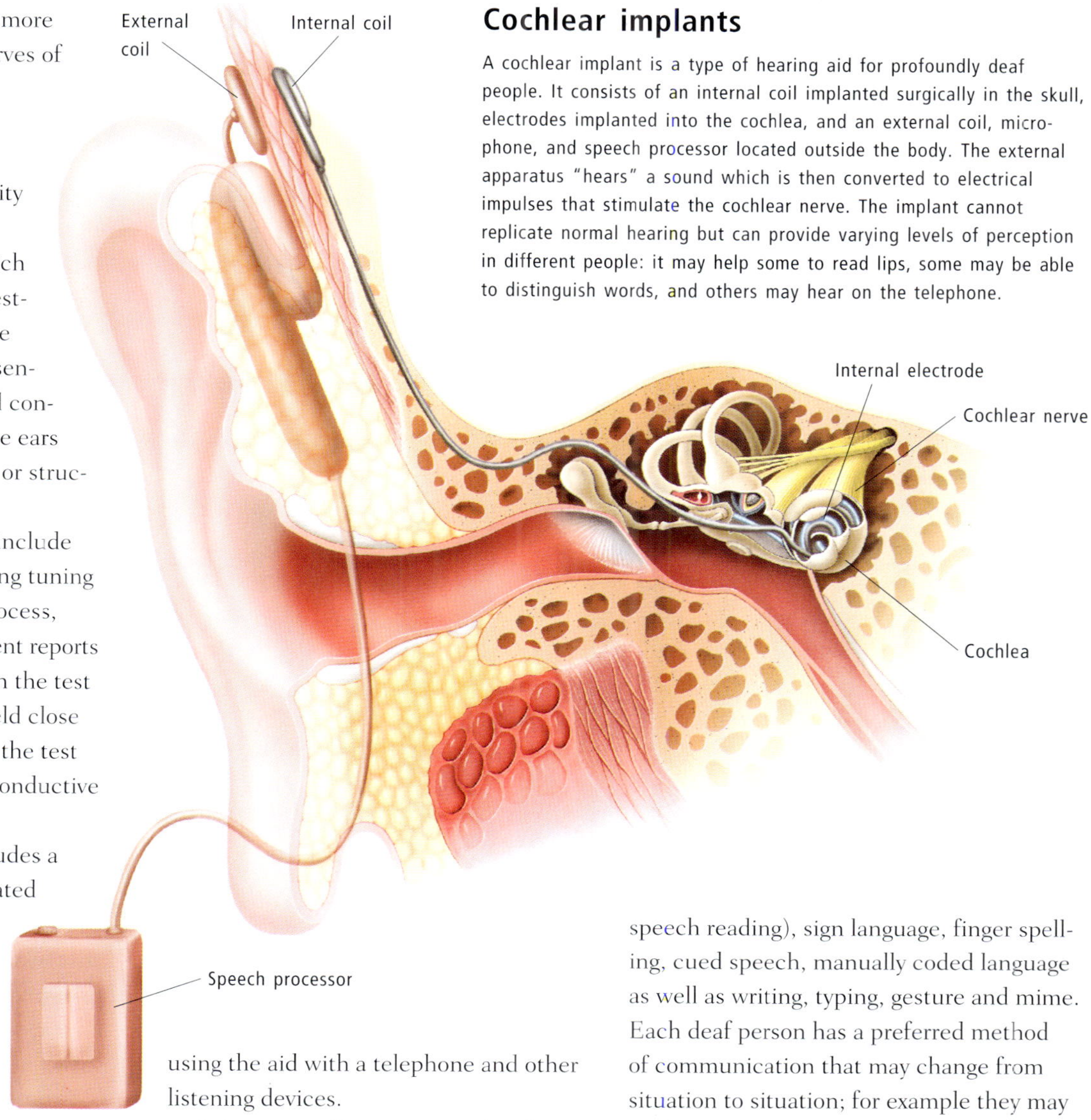

Cochlear implants

A cochlear implant is a type of hearing aid for profoundly deaf people. It consists of an internal coil implanted surgically in the skull, electrodes implanted into the cochlea, and an external coil, microphone, and speech processor located outside the body. The external apparatus "hears" a sound which is then converted to electrical impulses that stimulate the cochlear nerve. The implant cannot replicate normal hearing but can provide varying levels of perception in different people: it may help some to read lips, some may be able to distinguish words, and others may hear on the telephone.

Hearing aids

A hearing aid is an electronic device that improves hearing. It consists of a microphone, amplifier, receiver and power source (usually batteries). It is adjustable for pitch (frequency response) and volume (saturation response) by the prescribing audiologist. Some aids have external volume controls which the user can adjust, and switches for when using the aid with a telephone and other listening devices.

Aids are usually miniaturized to fit in or behind the ear or wholly within the ear canal. Where those aids are unsuitable or the most powerful amplification is needed, larger aids using a microphone and power pack worn on the chest can be used.

The cochlear implant is a recently developed aid that is surgically implanted in profoundly deaf people. It converts sounds to electrical impulses that are sent to electrodes implanted in the cochlea and thence to the brain.

A bone-conduction hearing aid is mounted on a headband which holds it securely in contact with the head for the greatest possible sound conduction through the skull bone.

Treatment

Profoundly deaf people must communicate by means other than spoken language. There are several ways in which this can be accomplished, including lip reading (known also as speech reading), sign language, finger spelling, cued speech, manually coded language as well as writing, typing, gesture and mime. Each deaf person has a preferred method of communication that may change from situation to situation; for example they may prefer lip reading with some persons but not with others.

Deaf people face unique problems. Unemployment or underemployment is higher than in the general population and they may be discriminated against in the workplace. However, deaf people are employed in almost every type of job, and increasingly employers are hiring deaf people and adapting the workplace to accommodate them, for example by providing sign language interpreters. Deafness does not affect a person's intellect or learning ability. However, deafness may make the learning of language more difficult. Consequently, a hearing-impaired child's progress at school may be slower than that of a child who can hear. However the hearing-impaired child who is taught lip reading and sign language at an early age is more likely to do well.

SEE ALSO *Cochlea, Ear, Hearing, Menière's disease, Newborn, Speech, Tinnitus*

D

DEATH

Death is the inevitable end for all living organisms, the final and permanent shutdown of all the functions and processes that maintain life.

In past centuries identifying death was reckoned to be an easy task. A container of water balanced on the chest, or a feather held before the lips or nostrils were standard aids to show that heartbeat and breathing had stopped. If further proof was needed, bodies were allowed to lie for several days before burial to let putrefaction provide its evidence. Absence of circulation was another observable fact taken as proof of death, and a finger might be cut off to show that blood had ceased to flow. Such observations were the only tools available, and the more extreme measures allayed widespread fears of people being buried alive.

In the absence of movement, heartbeat and breathing, life was pronounced extinct. But in the last century, with the knowledge that signs of life might reappear in people apparently dead, and with medical technology evolving to sustain vital processes well beyond the point of irreversible brain death, a more exact description and definition of the moment of death were needed.

A definition was provided in 1966 by the National Academy of Medicine in France, stating that death could be certified when the brain was no longer able to take control of the body's vital functions and the brain had shown no signs of activity as measured by electroencephalogram for 48 hours. The concept of death as irreparable and irreversible loss of function and reflexes in the brain stem was accepted and enshrined in medical practice and in law in the USA, the UK and generally throughout the world.

The test for brain stem death is applied to people who have lapsed into apnea coma; that is, they are unconscious, normal breathing has stopped and they are on a ventilator. A senior medical specialist normally carries out this type of examination and, for ethical reasons, would not be in any way concerned with use of the person's organs for transplants after death.

In this process the cause of the coma is established, the presence of irreversible brain damage is confirmed, all possible curable or reversible causes (such as drug overdose, intoxication or hypothermia) are eliminated and no brain stem reflexes can be detected. After these inquiries, a series of tests is applied to stimulate the reflexes of the eyes and airways, and of the responses that induce breathing.

Diagnosis of brain stem death made in this manner is generally accepted and has been proven reliable. It is a vital step before any decision can be made to cease using a life support system.

A diagnosis of brain stem death will raise moral, ethical, religious and legal questions for everyone involved in treatment. The decision must be taken to continue or refrain from further treatment, including those measures that mechanically support life. The issues are complex and difficult to resolve. The rights of the patient must always be considered.

After death, the body is treated according to law and the wishes of the deceased. Permission may have been given for organs to be donated for transplants, in which case the organs are removed from the donor as speedily as possible after death has been certified. Arrangements may have been made for the cadaver to be used for medical research or teaching.

After death

After death, the skin becomes pale and loses elasticity, and the muscles lose their tone and flatten where they are pressed, particularly under the body's weight. Breathing and pulse stop. The body cools down and its rate of cooling can be predicted, allowing forensic pathology to determine the approximate time of death. A postmortem examination, or autopsy, may be made to establish the cause of death, if unknown.

After a few hours, muscles stiffen in rigor mortis, then relax again after three to four days. Blood clotting and the death of individual cells in the body begin within a few hours of death. Decomposition starts within 48 hours, depending on the surrounding temperature, as bacteria in the gut multiply and consume dead cells. In low temperatures this process may not start and bodies can be preserved in ice or peat bogs for centuries. In high temperatures and dry atmosphere bodies may dessicate, shrivel and mummify.

Preparation for dying

When a terminal disease is diagnosed it is now accepted practice to inform the patient of the diagnosis. The medical profession has in the past shied away from sharing this information with patients, but now the benefits of informing them are acknowledged. Despite the initial pain, truthful communication allows the sharing of grief and the full expression of emotions between loved ones, and gives patients time to put their affairs in order, not only financialy but emotionally as well.

Acceptance of approaching death does not always come immediately, but knowledge and time may help terminally ill people to find peace, which may be denied them if they are not told the truth.

The period before death can also be used to make important decisions on organ donation, disposal of assets and any other matters of concern. The dying person may choose to prepare a living will, where power is conferred on relatives to make decisions such as when to remove life support in case of coma prior to death.

The question of the "right to die" may arise, where terminally ill patients can decide to be put painlessly to death; this is known as euthanasia, or mercy killing, which is an illegal act in most of the countries of the world.

Attitudes to death vary widely, as many people in the industrialized nations have little knowledge of or familiarity with it. The death of an elderly person may be readily accepted, whereas that of a child may be seen as unjust and cause untold grief. Counseling can aid acceptance and assist the natural process of grieving.

DECOMPRESSION SICKNESS

Decompression sickness, also called the bends or caisson disease, is a disorder caused by bubbles of nitrogen gas coming out of solution in the bodily fluids and tissues, due to a sudden drop in environmental pressure. It is usually seen in divers who surface too quickly, or in people in a nonpressurized aircraft that climbs too rapidly.

The bubbles of nitrogen gas block arteries and cause loss of blood (ischemia) and death (infarction) of tissues. The person experiences joint pain (especially in the

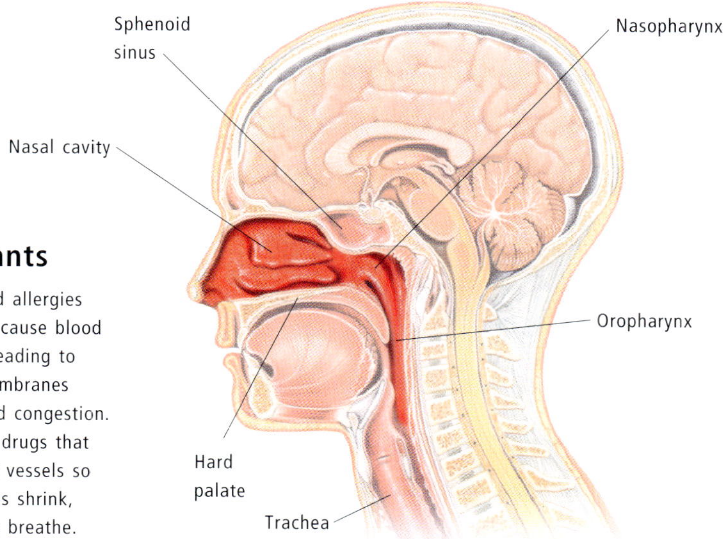

Decongestants

Viral infections and allergies affecting the nose cause blood vessels to dilate, leading to swelling of the membranes inside the nose and congestion. Decongestants are drugs that constrict the blood vessels so that the membranes shrink, making it easier to breathe.

elbow, shoulder, hip and knee), vomiting, giddiness, abdominal pain, and visual disturbances. Convulsions, paralysis and death may follow in severe cases.

Treatment involves placing the affected person into the high-pressure atmosphere of a decompression chamber. The nitrogen bubbles dissolve into the blood, and as the pressure is gradually lowered in the chamber, are safely breathed out as nitrogen gas via the lungs.

DECONGESTANTS

Decongestants are drugs that shrink swollen membranes in the nose and make it easier to breathe. They are useful in relieving the symptoms of a stuffy or runny nose in cold and flu infections, sinusitis and nasal allergies. Decongestants can be taken orally or by nasal spray.

Oral medications usually contain pseudoephedrine and phenylpropanolamine; they are effective, but may cause insomnia. People who suffer from high blood pressure (hypertension) should seek advice from a medical practitioner before taking oral decongestants, as they may cause an increase in blood pressure.

Many decongestant nasal sprays have a rebound effect if used for along time, resulting in irritation and inflammation of the nasal membranes when the treatment is stopped. A doctor's advice should be sought if treatment with a nasal decongestant is to be continued for more than five days.

SEE ALSO *Allergies, Common cold, Sinusitis*

DEEP VENOUS THROMBOSIS

Deep venous thrombosis is clotting in a deep vein, usually in the leg or pelvis. It may occur after surgery or periods of prolonged bed rest. It is more common in the elderly, people with arterial disease or diabetes, and women on some types of contraceptive pill. The calf of the leg may be swollen, warm, red and tender.

Complication occurs if a piece of the blood clot breaks off to form an embolus which can lodge in the vessels of the heart or lungs; this is potentially fatal. Treatment involves intravenous anticoagulant drugs in hospital, followed by oral anticoagulants for several months or permanently.

SEE ALSO *Anticoagulants, Embolism, Thrombosis, Vein*

DEFIBRILLATION

Fibrillation is rapid, irregular twitching of muscle fibers. In the heart it may be caused by heart disease, such as coronary artery disease, by drugs (such as digitalis), or by electrocution. Defibrillation is the term used for stopping fibrillation of the heart muscle.

If fibrillation affects the lower chambers (ventricles) of the heart, it causes cardiac arrest, which will rapidly lead to death because a heart that is fibrillating will pump little or no blood around the body's circulatory system.

Sometimes, normal heart contractions can be restored by electric shocks from a machine called a cardiac defibrillator. Cardiac defibrillation is an emergency procedure, and is combined with cardiopulmonary resuscitation (CPR). If cardiac arrest and defibrillation occur in a hospital, the survival rate is high; elsewhere it is very low. Defibrillation must occur within about five to seven minutes to be successful.

There are three types of defibrillators: the manual defibrillator; the automated external defibrillator (AED), which can read a patient's heart rhythm and deliver the shock automatically; and implantable cardiac defibrillators (ICDs), which are surgically implanted and are suitable for people with recurrent fibrillation.

SEE ALSO *Coronary artery disease, Fibrillation, Heart, Ventricle*

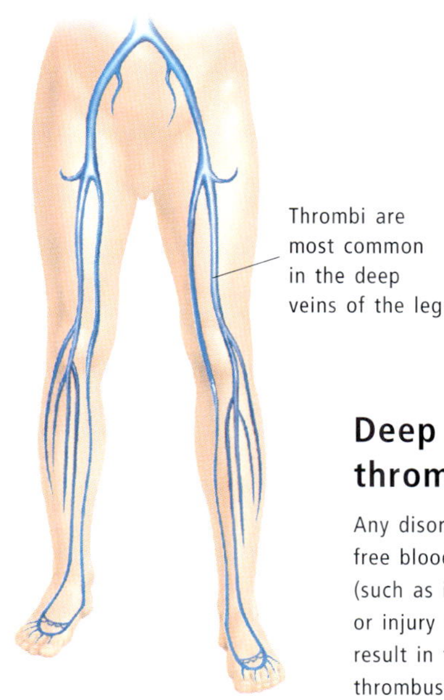

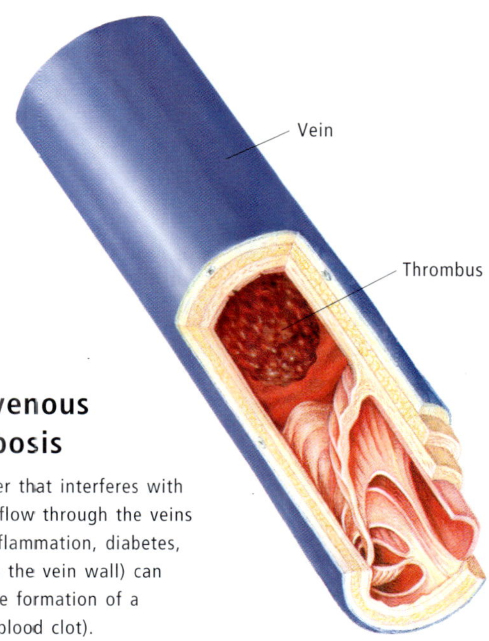

Deep venous thrombosis

Any disorder that interferes with free blood flow through the veins (such as inflammation, diabetes, or injury to the vein wall) can result in the formation of a thrombus (blood clot).

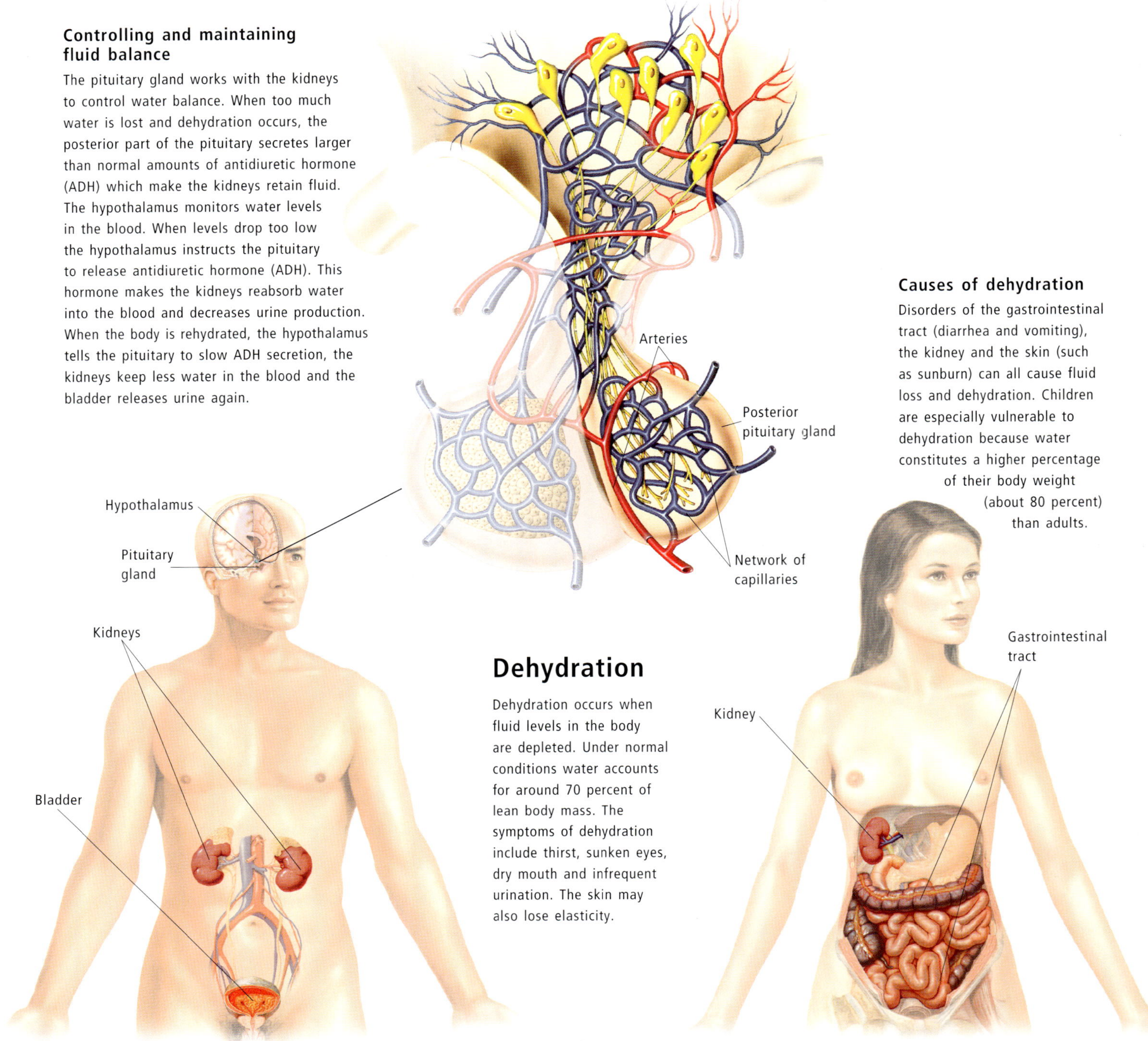

Controlling and maintaining fluid balance

The pituitary gland works with the kidneys to control water balance. When too much water is lost and dehydration occurs, the posterior part of the pituitary secretes larger than normal amounts of antidiuretic hormone (ADH) which make the kidneys retain fluid. The hypothalamus monitors water levels in the blood. When levels drop too low the hypothalamus instructs the pituitary to release antidiuretic hormone (ADH). This hormone makes the kidneys reabsorb water into the blood and decreases urine production. When the body is rehydrated, the hypothalamus tells the pituitary to slow ADH secretion, the kidneys keep less water in the blood and the bladder releases urine again.

Causes of dehydration

Disorders of the gastrointestinal tract (diarrhea and vomiting), the kidney and the skin (such as sunburn) can all cause fluid loss and dehydration. Children are especially vulnerable to dehydration because water constitutes a higher percentage of their body weight (about 80 percent) than adults.

Dehydration

Dehydration occurs when fluid levels in the body are depleted. Under normal conditions water accounts for around 70 percent of lean body mass. The symptoms of dehydration include thirst, sunken eyes, dry mouth and infrequent urination. The skin may also lose elasticity.

DEHYDRATION

Dehydration—the depletion of the body's water content—is a life-threatening condition. Babies and small children, who need more fluid relative to their body weight than adults, can become dehydrated—and be rehydrated—more easily.

The most common causes of dehydration are not drinking enough liquid (the deprivation of water is even more serious than the deprivation of food), vomiting, diarrhea (commonly associated with gastroenteritis), the use of diuretics which cause the kidneys to excrete excess water and salt, overheating and fever. Dehydration as a result of diarrhea is a major cause of death in children of developing countries. Some diseases such as diabetes mellitus and Addison's disease can also lead to dehydration.

Overheating or heat stress can cause severe problems, even death in the elderly, babies and young children who are not protected against high temperatures. People in conditions where the heat is severe and there is little or no water can dehydrate quickly. Babies and children die every year when they are left in cars in the summer sun.

On average the human body loses around 2.5 percent of its total body water each day, which is equal to $2\frac{1}{2}$ pints (1.2 liters) in urine, expired air, perspiration and from the gastrointestinal tract. Drinking plenty of water before, during and after exercise helps prevent dehydration.

Symptoms of dehydration include thirst (which the most obvious), eyes that look sunken and dark (in a baby the fontanelle will also look sunken), dry mouth, infrequent dark urination (fewer wet diapers), lethargy and irritability. Skin tone will deteriorate so that when the skin is pinched it will not spring back as normal skin does. Blood in the stools, a high fever, extreme weakness or collapse are a medical emergency and require immediate treatment.

Since dehydration is almost invariably associated with some loss of salt (sodium chloride), rehydration also requires the restoration of the normal concentration of salt within the body fluid. Mild cases can be treated with an oral rehydration fluid. However, more severe cases need to be under medical supervision so that the correct amounts of salts and water are given to restore the normal osmotic relationships between cells, allowing the kidneys to once again begin to work properly.

SEE ALSO *Addison's disease, Diarrhea, Diabetes, Diuretics, Gastroenteritis, Heatstroke, Kidney*

DELIRIUM

Delirium is a mental disorder marked by confusion and disorientation. A mental abnormality with a sudden onset, sometimes confused with dementia, delirium is not a disease and is potentially reversible.

The common symptom is confusion. People who are delirious may suffer hallucinations, be drowsy, be gripped by imaginary fears or impelled by sudden visions of catastrophe. They may be unable to recognize their surroundings, their speech may ramble and their memory of recent events may be poor or completely missing. They will have trouble concentrating and be unable to take in new information.

Delirium can result from a number of conditions or disorders. These include injury, intoxication, drug overdose, abrupt cessation of drug taking, dehydration and disease. It is common to find the person has deteriorated physically prior to the onset of delirium.

The most common causes are alcohol, illegal drugs and poisons, high fever, stroke, brain injuries and disorders, or severe physical injury. Treatment will be dictated by diagnosis of the exact cause. If delirious people seem likely to injure themselves through physical agitation, they may have movement restricted with padded restraints.

SEE ALSO *Alcoholism, Confusion, Delirium tremens, Drug dependence*

DELIRIUM TREMENS

Delirium tremens (DTs) is a severe effect of alcohol withdrawal and is evidence of acute alcoholic dependency. It can occur after heavy bouts of drinking or several days after alcohol intake ceases.

Symptoms include sweating, shaking, nausea and anxiety and may worsen to confusion, sleeplessness and fever. Pulse rate may increase and there may be increasing tremors affecting the hands or the whole body. Movement becomes uncoordinated. There is a strong craving for alcohol. Hallucinations and disorientation may occur, inducing terror. If left untreated, the physical disorders underlying delirium tremens can be fatal.

Alcoholics who suffer DTs treat their own symptoms by drinking. Sometimes alcohol tolerance will be so high that relief is not possible. Seeking medical assistance may mean the person has taken a decision to stop drinking or that the symptoms have become too severe to endure.

Treatment will aim first to control the high fever and anxiety, then to restore nutritional and fluid balance. Alcoholics are often dehydrated and suffer thiamine deficiency and other nutritional deficiencies that can cause brain disorders. These must also be remedied to save life and minimize chances of permanent damage to the brain and nervous system.

Lastly, a process of detoxification as well as a program of alcoholic rehabilitation must be undertaken in order to treat the alcohol dependence.

SEE ALSO *Alcoholism, Delirium*

DELTOID MUSCLE

The deltoid muscle is situated on top of the shoulder joint and upper arm. This powerful, triangular muscle serves to lift the arm away from the side of the body, as well as allowing forward, backward and sideways movement of the upper arm.

The muscle is comprised of three divisions—lateral (top), anterior (front) and posterior (rear)—which all work to give the arm movement in different directions. The muscle stems from the upper part of the collar bone at the front and from the shoulder blade at the back, and attaches to the middle of the outer side of the arm bone. Underneath the muscle is a fluid-filled cavity which is designed to reduce friction between the muscle and shoulder joint.

SEE ALSO *Arm, Collar bone, Muscle, Shoulder*

DELUSIONS

Delusions are a feature of mental disorders where irrational and bizarre false beliefs are held with absolute conviction. People so affected may believe they are a queen or president, or that they are being persecuted. Delusions occur in paranoia, schizophrenia, major depressive illnesses, and in various types of psychosis.

SEE ALSO *Paranoia, Psychosis, Schizophrenia*

DEMENTIA

Dementia is a condition in which there is a long-term loss of intellectual function, with little or no disturbance of consciousness or perception. It involves a deterioration of memory and reasoning ability and changes in personality, and usually results from degeneration of cells in the cerebral cortex of the brain.

Dementia generally occurs in elderly people and is becoming more common as the life-expectancy of the population increases. In the USA, about 1 in 15 people over the age of 65, and 1 in 3 people over the age of 85 suffer from dementia. It is, however, not an inevitable consequence of ageing, as was previously thought. (The majority of people will not develop dementia in their old age.) Rather, it is a condition which develops in association with some diseases which happen to be more common in old age.

By far the most common cause of dementia is Alzheimer's disease, which accounts for up to 70 percent of dementia cases and currently affects approximately 2 million Americans. The onset and progression of this form of dementia (also known as senile dementia) is very gradual, usually extending over a period of 5–10 years.

The affected person becomes increasingly forgetful, disoriented and confused, and intellectual functions, such as reading, writing and decision-making, gradually diminish. As the disease progresses the person may also undergo a personality change, becoming aggressive, paranoid or depressed.

Alzheimer's disease can be distinguished from other forms of dementia by characteristic changes which occur in the cerebral cortex, in particular the presence of dying cells, abnormal protein deposits (plaques), knotted fibers (tangles), and degenerate neurons.

At present the cause of Alzheimer's disease is not well understood but it is thought to be the result of a combination of genetic and as yet unidentified environmental factors. Although it is a very active area of research, no treatment has been found.

The second major type of dementia, multi-infarct or arteriosclerotic dementia, is caused by numerous episodes in which tiny blood vessels supplying the frontal and temporal lobes of the cerebral cortex become blocked due to cardiovascular disease, resulting in death of nerve cells (neurons) in these areas because of the lack of oxygen.

These episodes (mini-strokes) may go undetected at the time but they have a cumulative effect on the cortex and make up for 10–15 percent of dementia cases. The symptoms are sometimes difficult to distinguish from those seen in Alzheimer's disease, but they often tend to appear in a more step-by-step fashion (as the mini-strokes occur).

Other causes of dementia are numerous and include chronic alcoholism, degenerative diseases such as Huntington's disease and AIDS, nutritional and metabolic disorders, infections and tumors. Some of these disorders are treatable and recovery from the dementia can be expected but in most cases dementia is a chronic ongoing condition.

When a person suffers a temporary loss of intellectual function, such as may occur when they have a very high fever or are withdrawing from alcoholism, they are said to be suffering from delirium, not dementia.

SEE ALSO *Alcoholism, Alzheimer's disease, Confusion, Memory, Stroke*

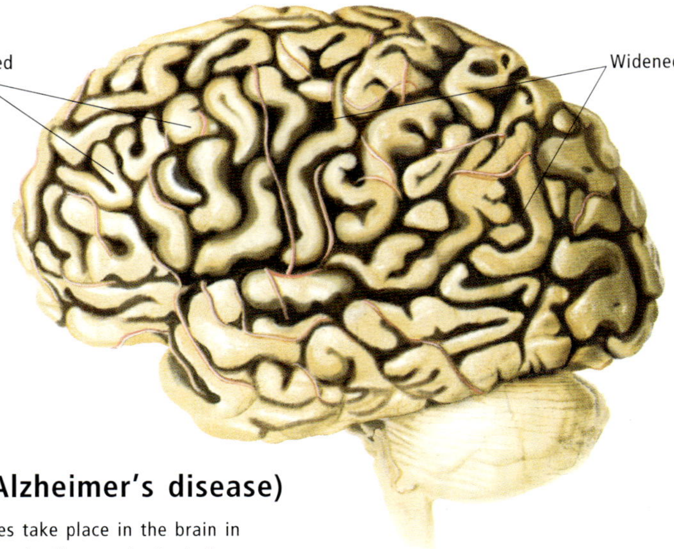

Dementia (Alzheimer's disease)

Degenerative changes take place in the brain in dementia. In Alzheimer's disease, the brain has shrunk slightly and the gaps between the folds of the cerebral cortex have widened.

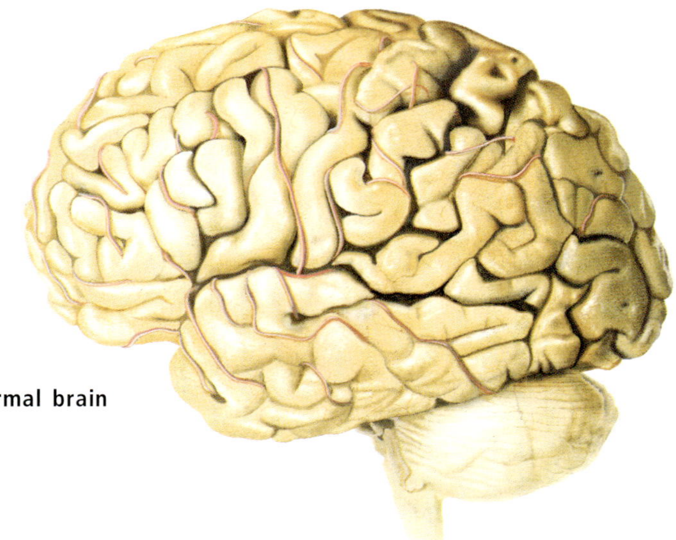

Normal brain

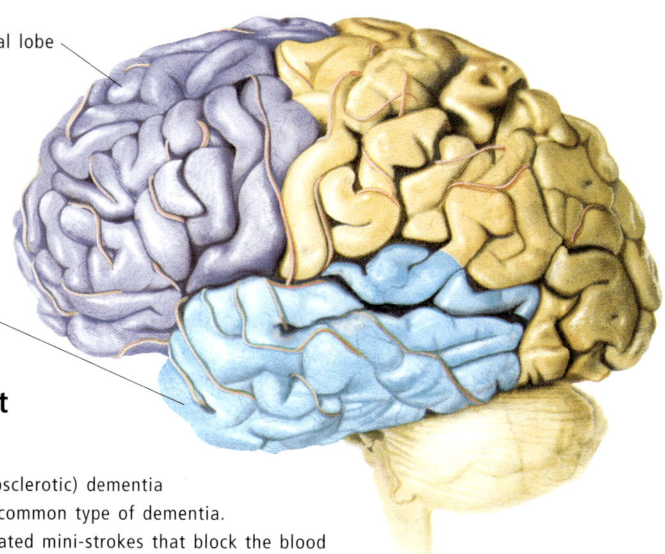

Multi-infarct dementia

Multi-infarct (arteriosclerotic) dementia is the second most common type of dementia. It is caused by repeated mini-strokes that block the blood supply to parts of the brain, eventually destroying brain tissue. The frontal and temporal lobes are most commonly affected.

DENGUE

Dengue fever is an acute viral infection of the body, transmitted by mosquitoes. It is similar to malaria in that it is a very common cause for hospitalization of children in tropical countries. It is spread from animals to humans by mosquito bites. There are two types of this disease— ordinary dengue fever (DF), which is usually a mild disease with no serious complications, and hemorrhagic dengue fever (HDF), which is a much more virulent form.

The incubation period from the mosquito bite to the appearance of the first symptoms is about 5 to 6 days. In DF, the symptoms are headache, fever, vomiting, muscle pain, joint pain, and enlarged lymph nodes. The fever rises and falls in cycles of 1 to 2 days, and the illness usually lasts about 10 days.

HDF is mostly only common in Southeast Asia. This form causes the capillaries in the skin and body organs to rupture resulting in a petechial rash (hemorrhaging in the skin), bleeding from the nose, bowels and kidneys, and can lead to serious and even fatal complications. Treatment for DF is symptomatic—analgesic for the fever, and rest and fluid replacement. There is no vaccine and the most important advice for travelers is to prevent being bitten by mosquitoes.

SEE ALSO *Infections, Viruses*

DENTURES

Dentures, also known as plates or false teeth, are composite artificial replacements of teeth and gums. A complete denture is required when all the teeth in the upper or lower jaw have been removed. Partial dentures are used to replace one or more missing teeth. Complete dentures are usually removable; partial dentures may be removable or fixed. An overdenture is a partial denture that takes support from any remaining teeth roots and gum near the missing teeth.

Titanium implants can be surgically inserted into the jawbone; replacement teeth are attached later which provide a fixed denture. This process helps to prevent resorption, which is shrinkage of the jawbone with loss of nerve and surrounding tissue, a common situation where all the teeth have been removed.

SEE ALSO *Gums, Teeth*

DEPRESSION

Depression (also known as clinical depression) affects thoughts, feelings, physical health and behaviors. Depression is not just feeling sad, it is a medical disorder, like high blood pressure.

Depression is not the same as grief— though extreme grief can bring on depression in susceptible people. Depression can be caused by many things, including genetic inheritance, an illness, certain medicines, drugs, alcohol and other psychiatric conditions. A major trauma or loss during childhood is also thought to increase a person's vulnerability to depression. There are also biochemical causes, the main one being the defective regulation of the release of naturally occurring monoamines (neurotransmitters) in the brain.

Someone suffering from depression will experience one or more of these symptoms: sadness or hopelessness, low self-esteem, an inability to enjoy daily life, low energy, lethargy, loss of appetite, or sleep problems.

This is the most common psychiatric complaint and for centuries was known as melancholia. More common in women than men, it occurs most often in the 35 to 45 age group. Many people mistakenly believe depression is normal for certain people including the elderly, teenagers, pregnant women, new mothers and the chronically ill.

While mood swings are common during pregnancy and in the early days of mothering, depression is not normal. Depression during pregnancy can occur in the last trimester as the woman begins to feel tired and apprehensive about her forthcoming role as a mother. It is important to seek advice and support if the low mood does not lift as it can carry over into the postpartum period when it can also affect the newborn child.

Postnatal depression is not the "baby blues" which frequently affects new mothers when the hormone surge their bodies experienced during the pregnancy and birth drops. Postnatal (or postpartum) depression has been found to be more common in single women who lack support, women with an unwanted pregnancy, and professional women with unrealistic expectations of how they will cope. It can also occur in women who lack emotional and physical support systems.

Research has found that both parents need help and guidance in the early days of parenting and that where the father is supportive, the mother is less likely to suffer real depression. In industrialized societies where women have little experience of mothering (apart from how they were mothered) some women suffer feelings of inadequacy at this time.

Bipolar depression or disorder, when moods swing from extreme mania to depression, is also known as manic-depressive illness. This condition requires psychiatric care and also hospitalization at certain times; bipolar disorder responds well to salts of lithium. Winter depression or seasonal affective disorder (SAD) has only recently been recognized as the cause of depression directly related to the loss of natural light.

Depression often goes untreated because people do not recognize the symptoms, are too embarrassed to seek treatment or think they can cure it themselves. Major depression can often lead to suicide.

Over 80 percent of sufferers can be treated successfully by a qualified health professional. There are three forms of treatment: psychotherapy, which seeks to resolve underlying problems which may be causing the depression as well as providing support; antidepressant drugs which affect the chemistry of the brain; and electroconvulsive therapy (ECT) which is a brief application of an electric stimulus which produces a generalized seizure. ECT is normally used for severe cases, in combination with psychotherapy and/or drug therapy.

There are a number of alternative therapies that may help to alleviate the symptoms of depression. Acupuncture practitioners regard some depressions as "liver" disorders and treat with appropriate points to release "stagnant" energy. Aromatherapists prescribe oils such as basil, clary sage, jasmine or rose. Herbalists principally prescribe St John's wort (*Hypericum*), as well as tonics such as oats, vervain or rosemary. Naturopaths will often prescribe vitamin B complex with extra B_3 (niacinamide) and magnesium. Flower essences, such as the Bach flower remedies, may be used. Counseling, exercise and a detoxifying diet are sometimes recommended.

SEE ALSO *Antidepressants, Bipolar disorder, Counseling, Electroconvulsive therapy, Emotions, Postnatal depression, Psychotherapy, Seasonal affective disorder*

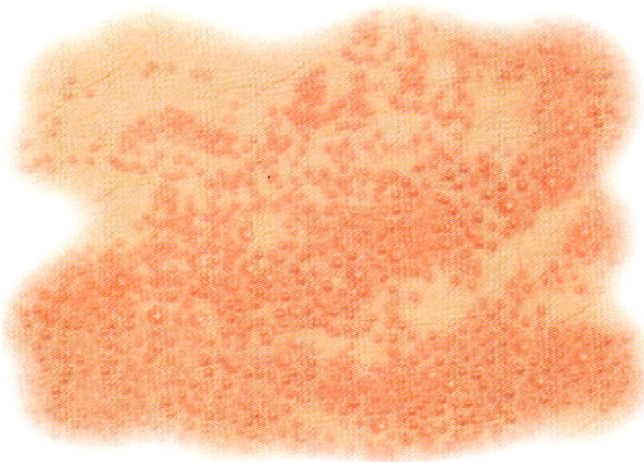

Atopic dermatitis

Seborrheic dermatitis

Dermatitis

Symptoms of atopic dermatitis include itching rash and dry thickened skin. Seborrheic dermatitis mainly appears on the head and trunk. Skin becomes greasy or dry and red patches appear topped by white scales.

DERMATITIS

Dermatitis means inflammation of the skin. Though dermatitis is not contagious, and not usually life threatening, it can be debilitating as it tends to recur and become chronic (a long-term problem).

There are many different types of dermatitis. Seborrheic dermatitis is characterized by greasy or dry, white scales over reddish patches that form on the skin of the scalp, eyebrows, forehead, face, behind the ears, or on the trunk.

Dandruff and cradle cap are both forms of seborrheic dermatitis. Both sexes and all ages are affected; the cause is unknown and the condition is usually chronic. Treatment is a steroid cream for the affected skin. Dandruff can be controlled with frequent shampooing with preparations containing selenium sulfide or zinc pyrithione. If the condition does not improve, shampoos that contain coal tar or scalp creams that contain cortisone may be used.

Atopic dermatitis affects mostly children, and is often associated with asthma or hay fever. It causes an itching rash and dry, thickened skin in the creases of elbows, knees, neck, face, hands, feet, and groin. The cause is unknown though it tends to run in families. It may disappear with age. Sufferers are advised to wear loose-fitting cotton clothing. Petroleum- or lanolin-based ointments and topical steroids or coal-tar creams relieve the itching. Scratching must be avoided, because it causes secondary bacterial infection.

Contact dermatitis is caused by contact with an irritating substance that damages the skin, causing itching, redness, cracks and fissures and in severe cases, bright red, weeping areas. The hands, feet and groin are commonly affected.

Many substances can cause contact dermatitis, including topical drugs, cosmetics, chemicals, soaps, detergents, bleaches, metal cleaners and paint removers. Treatment is to avoid contact with the irritant, wear protective gloves and other protective clothing, bathe in lukewarm water, and apply topical creams, ointments or lotions. These may include lubricants to preserve moisture, or steroid preparations to reduce inflammation. Contact dermatitis usually clears up within two or three weeks.

Stasis dermatitis is the result of fluid build-up under the skin. It is caused by varicose veins, poor circulation, and other conditions that cause swelling of the extremities, especially the feet and ankles (peripheral edema). The swelling causes surrounding tissue to become fragile; the skin darkens and becomes thin and inflamed. Ulcers may form and are slow to heal. Itching and scratching of the area may cause the skin to thicken. Elevation of the affected limbs, the wearing of elastic stockings and gentle exercise such as walking will help relieve the swelling. The underlying condition must be controlled, which may involve surgical correction of varicose veins, and diuretics in order to remove excess fluid.

SEE ALSO *Cradle cap, Dandruff, Eczema, Seborrheic dermatitis, Varicose veins*

DERMATOMES

Each of the 31 segments of the spinal cord gives rise to a pair of spinal nerves, which carry messages into and out of the central nervous system. These nerves branch into and service particular areas of the body. Ultimately, each ends up innervating a different region of the skin called a dermatome.

The location of dermatomes across the body forms a pattern that is significant when

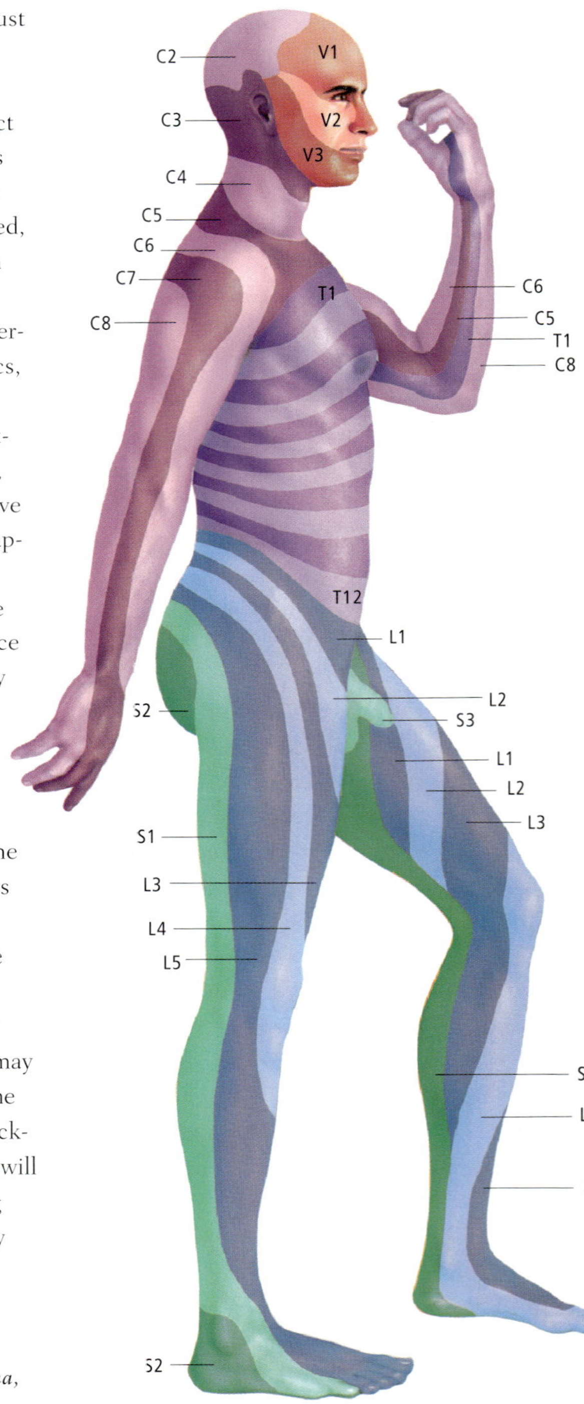

certain parts of the body require anesthesia. It indicates specific nerves that need to be blocked to cut sensations in a region. It is also of relevance in spinal cord injuries—identifying dermatomes with abnormal or no sensations helps isolate the location of damage to spinal nerves or the spinal cord.

SEE ALSO *Nervous system, Spinal cord, Spinal nerves*

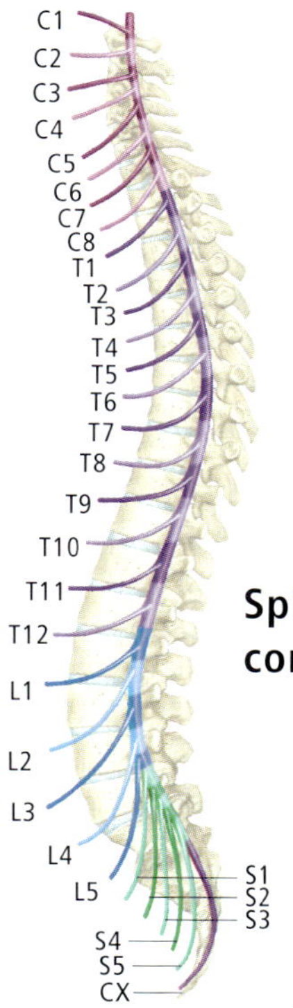

Spinal cord

Nerve to skin link

The spinal nerves are numbered and correspond closely to the spinal vertebrae. Each pair of nerves supplies a specific dermatome (skin area) of the body. The face is supplied by branches of the trigeminal nerve (V1, V2, and V3).

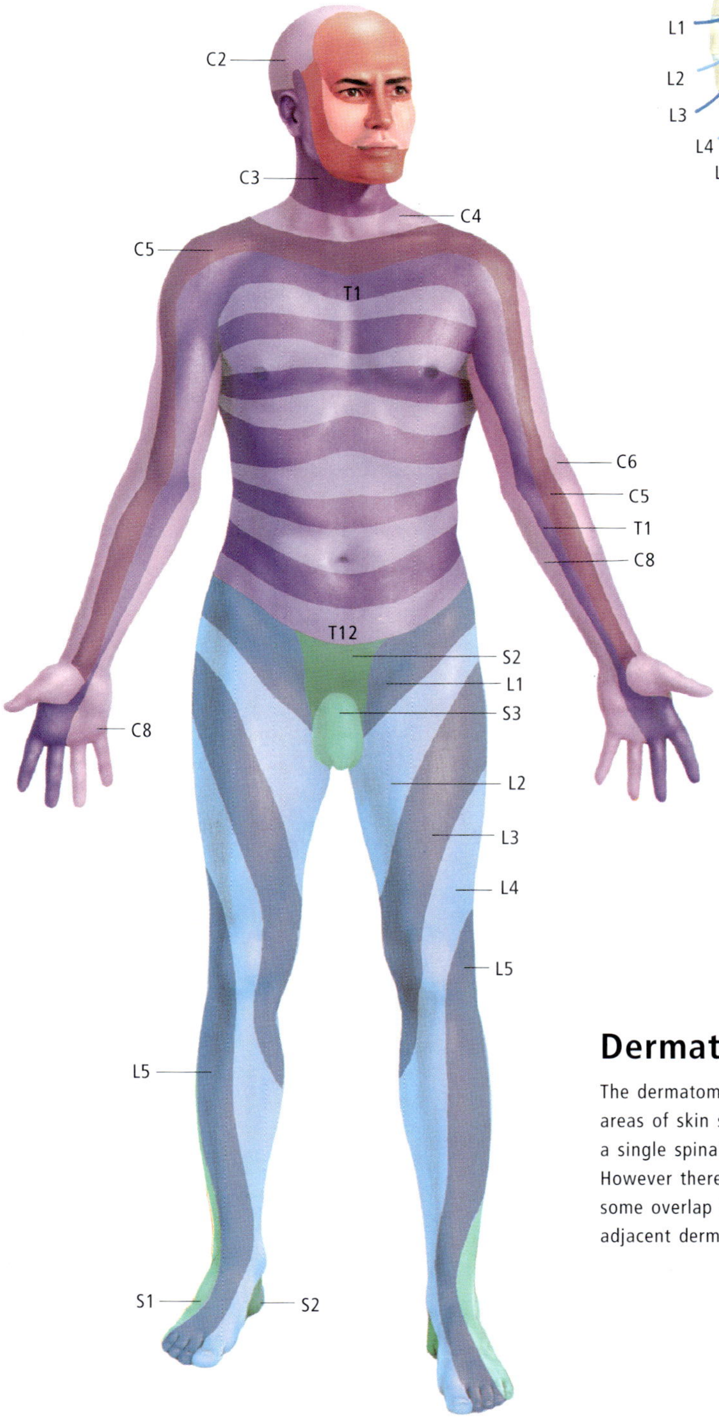

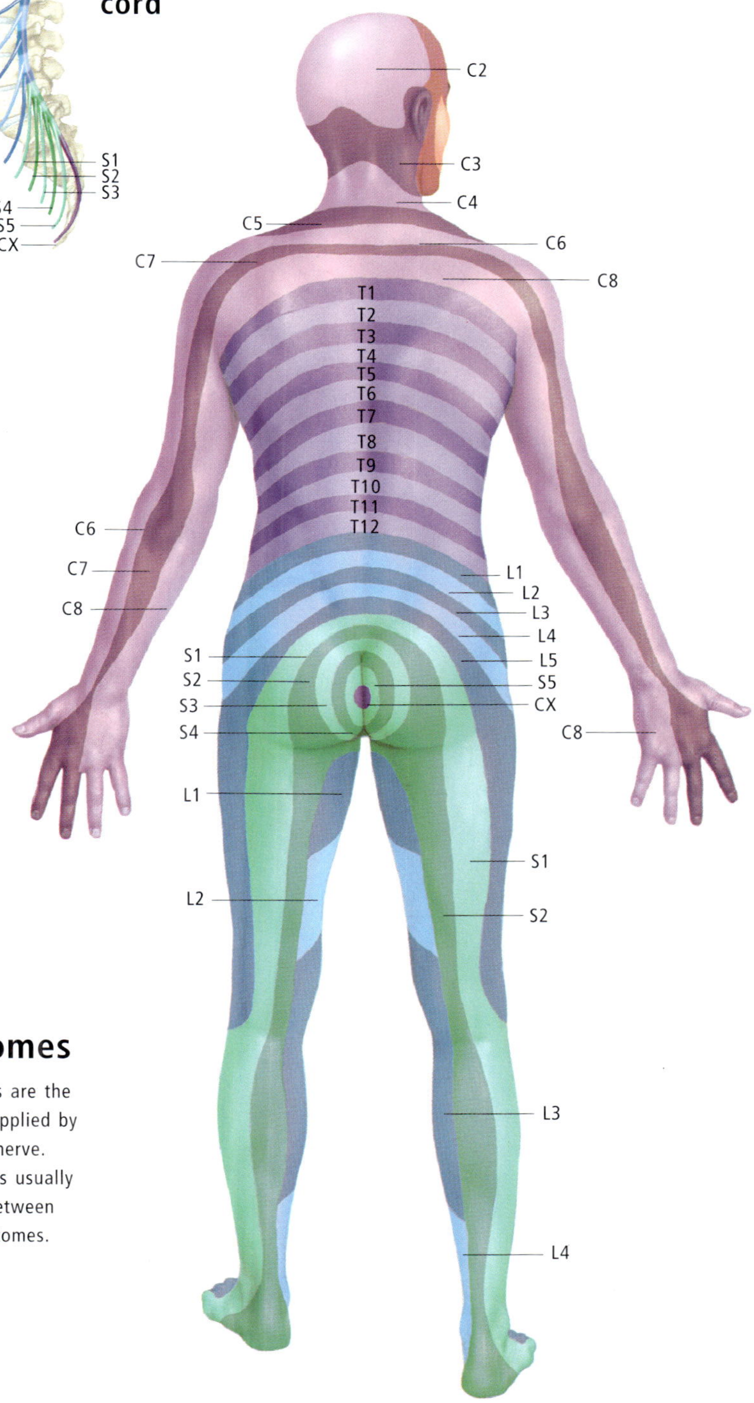

Dermatomes

The dermatomes are the areas of skin supplied by a single spinal nerve. However there is usually some overlap between adjacent dermatomes.

D

DERMATOMYOSITIS

Dermatomyositis is a rare connective tissue disease that is characterized by inflammation and degeneration of the skin and the muscles throughout the body. It causes muscle weakness and a dusky red rash over the face, neck, shoulders, upper chest and back. Joint, heart and lung disease may occur. Treatment may include physical therapy and prednisone (a steroid hormone) or immunosuppressant drugs such as azathioprine and methotrexate.

SEE ALSO *Autoimmune disease, Connective tissue*

DESENSITIZATION

Desensitization is a method of treating allergies by attempting to reduce the sufferer's allergic reaction. This is done after establishing exactly which allergen is causing the reaction. The sufferer is exposed to a minute quantity of the substance; exposure may take the form of a regular injection of small quantities of the allergen over a period of perhaps a month or two. The injected dose is increased gradually to a point where the body produces specific antibodies to block the effect of the allergens. The goal is to block enough of the allergens till a point is reached where they do not provoke the allergic reaction. Desensitization attempts to reverse the process of sensitization that originally created the allergy.

SEE ALSO *Allergies, Antigen tests*

DETACHED RETINA

Retinal detachment occurs when the retina of the eye, which contains light-sensitive cells, becomes separated from the choroid, or middle layer of the eyeball. Separation may be partial or complete. The detachment usually occurs without any obvious cause, but some cases may be due to trauma, such as a blow to the head. The patient usually complains of progressively blurred vision.

Many of the nerve cells in the separated retina will die if they remain detached from the choroid, so it is important to reattach the retina as soon as possible. Patients must rest in a position such that gravity will encourage reattachment. Surgical treatments include draining fluid below the retina, fusing the retina to the choroid with lasers, electrical diathermy or very cold probes.

SEE ALSO *Blindness, Eye, Retina, Sight*

DETOXIFICATION

Detoxification is the removal of toxins from the body. Drug taking causes toxins (poisons) to accumulate in the body tissues. When a drug-dependent person enters withdrawal, and ceases to use the substance of dependence, detoxification begins.

Dependency is an overwhelming craving for something, which is felt after a period of non-use. The most common drugs of dependency are alcohol, nicotine, amphetamines, opiates and barbiturates.

Detoxification is usually undertaken as a program managed by medical and psychological professionals.

The success of the program depends on a high level of commitment from the drug user. Withdrawal of drugs of any kind should only be started, and continued, under medical supervision.

The symptoms of detoxification vary according to the substance of dependency, and can be quite severe.

Alcohol withdrawal starts within 48 hours after alcohol intake stops. The symptoms include shaking, sweating and nausea, seizures and hallucinations. If physical effects are acute they can lead to death if not treated.

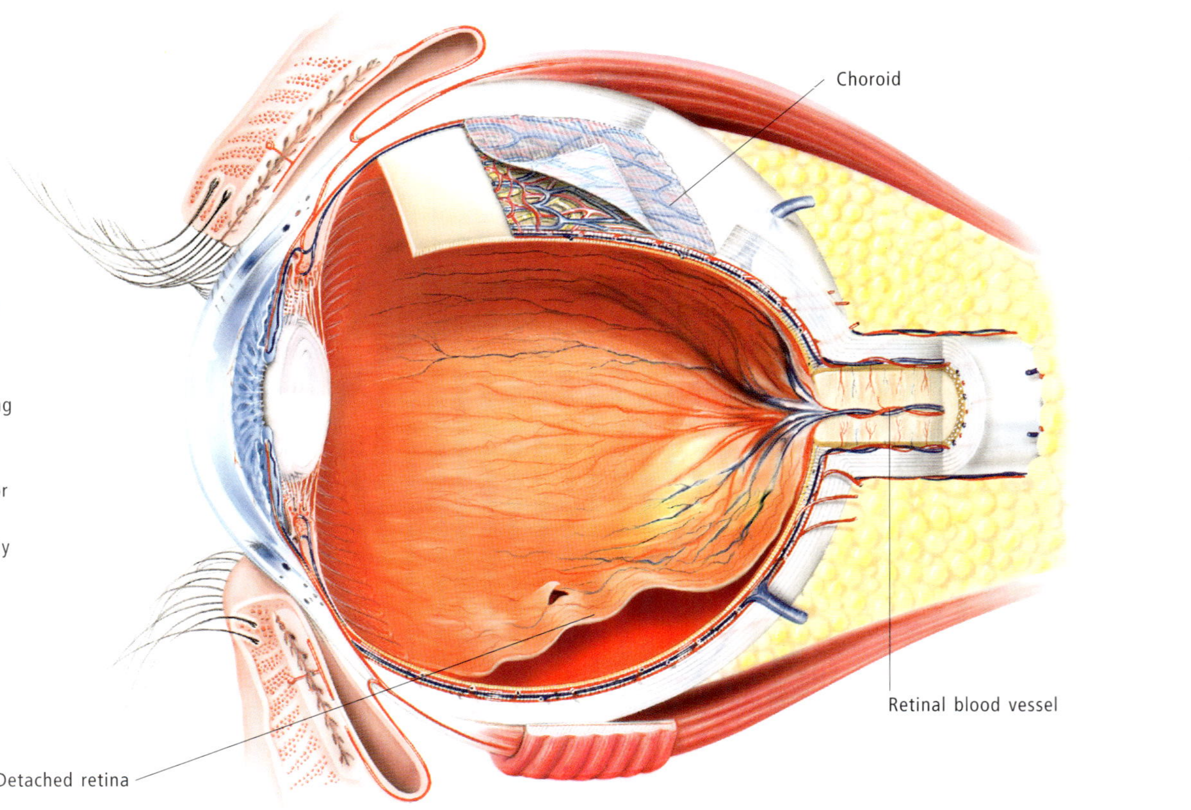

Detached retina

A detached retina occurs when the retina of the eye separates from its underlying support (choroid). It is painless, but can create images of floating shapes or flashes of light. Vision will usually become progressively more blurry.

Amphetamine withdrawal may bring on severe drowsiness or accentuate symptoms of depression that may have existed before taking the drugs. Chronically depressed users may attempt suicide and should be under close medical supervision while in detoxification.

Anti-anxiety drugs (anxiolytics, barbiturates, tranquilizers) can cause physical and psychological dependence, decreasing or depressing bodily functions and activity as well as slowing down thought processes. Abruptly stopping use can bring on symptoms of nervousness, shaking and weakness within 24 hours. Symptoms can worsen over the following three or four weeks to include seizures, delirium, sleeplessness, confusion and hallucinations.

Cocaine withdrawal will produce reactions opposite to those induced by taking the drug. Users can become extremely tired, depressed and suicidal, and may be given antidepressant drugs.

Marijuana can induce psychological dependency, and detoxification may induce insomnia in heavy users. It may take up to a year to overcome psychological dependence on the drug.

Narcotics such as morphine and heroin are pain relievers that may induce a sense of relaxation and well-being. Long-term users who withdraw may very quickly experience the opposite effects, including a falsely heightened sense of alertness, fast heartbeat, fever and rapid breathing. Dilated pupils, runny nose and stomach cramps are other common symptoms.

Nicotine withdrawal is characterized by feelings of anger and irritability. Some people increase their intake of food and drink as oral substitutes for smoking. Nicotine gum or patches, used in gradually decreasing doses, may lessen the severity of the symptoms.

Measures that help in detoxification are drinking plenty of water, taking exercise, following a balanced diet, and gaining the support of family and friends. Supportive therapies such as massage and acupuncture may be helpful.

Physical detoxification is only the first step in treatment, since psychological dependency is a major factor in substance abuse. The alcoholic or drug-dependent person needs to learn how to live without drinking or using. Many specialists believe that detoxification needs to be followed up with long-term rehabilitation, which includes spending time in a treatment center, follow-up counseling, and regular attendance at self-help groups such as Alcoholics Anonymous and Narcotics Anonymous.

SEE ALSO *Alcoholism, Anxiolytics, Barbiturates, Cocaine, Drug dependence, Hallucinogens, Heroin, Hypnotics, Marijuana, Methadone, Morphine, Narcotics, Nicotine, Psychosis, Psychotropic drugs, Sedatives, Stimulants, Tranquilizers, Withdrawal*

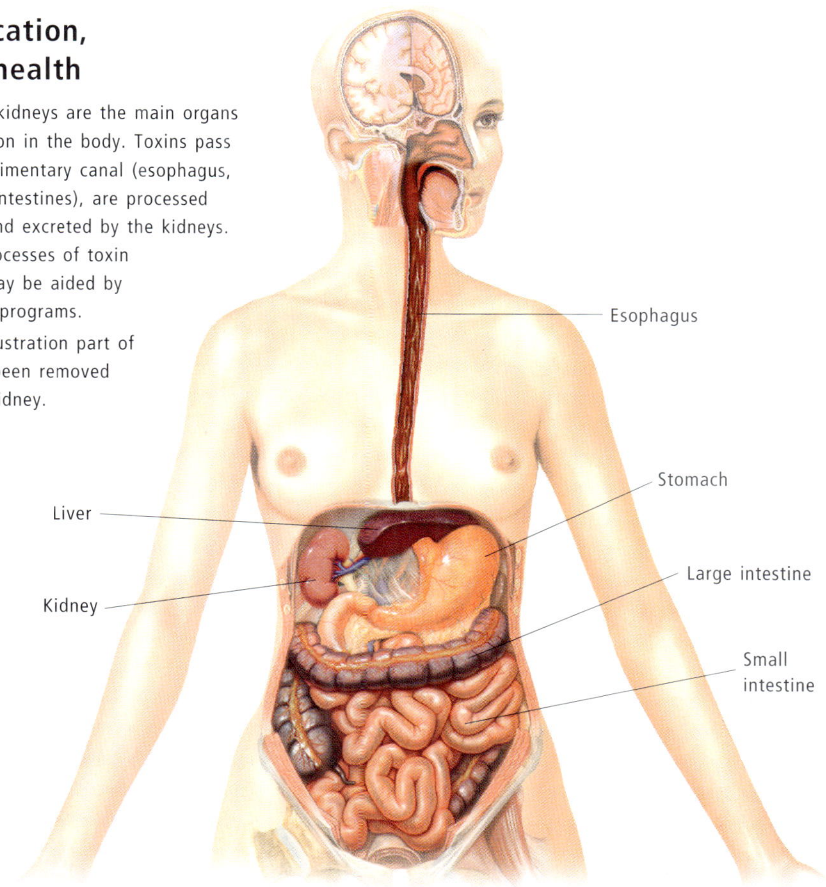

Detoxification, natural health

The liver and kidneys are the main organs of detoxification in the body. Toxins pass through the alimentary canal (esophagus, stomach and intestines), are processed in the liver, and excreted by the kidneys. The body's processes of toxin metabolism may be aided by detoxification programs.

NB: In this illustration part of the liver has been removed to show the kidney.

DETOXIFICATION, NATURAL HEALTH

Many of the natural therapies incorporate the belief that a process of detoxification of the body is of great benefit in the attaining and maintaining of good health. It is considered that the increasing level of pollutants, chemicals and food additives encountered by anyone living in an industrialized society can create a toxic overload in the body which can lead, in turn, to disturbances in metabolism, the immune system, respiratory function and mental outlook.

Natural therapists prescribe a range of detoxifying treatments, the most favored being fasting. Abstaining from solid foods for a set period of time is believed to give the body an opportunity to cleanse itself of toxins. Juice fasts are most commonly advised, and like any fast should only be undertaken under professional guidance. Patients are warned to expect some initial symptoms of detoxification such as headaches and bad breath. Enemas are often prescribed to help clear the bowel of toxins.

Other means of detoxification prescribed by natural therapists include colonic irrigation, mono diets (e.g. grapes only or rice only), dry brush massage, saunas, hydrotherapy, and liver/gallbladder flushes with olive oil and lemon juice. Regular detoxification is considered to be very important in Ayurvedic medicine where specific hatha yoga techniques are used to cleanse the entire intestinal tract.

SEE ALSO *Ayurvedic medicine, Colonic irrigation, Hydrotherapy, Naturopathy*

D

DIABETES

Diabetes mellitus is a disorder caused by decreased production of insulin by the pancreas, or by a decreased ability on the part of the body to use insulin. It is a serious, sometimes fatal, disorder and remains a leading cause of death in Western societies. The cause of diabetes mellitus is not known, though it may run in families and is more common in obese individuals.

Normally, food digested in the body releases glucose, a form of sugar, into the blood. This in turn causes certain cells called beta cells in the pancreas to release insulin into the bloodstream. The insulin aids in transporting glucose from the blood into storage in liver and muscle cells; it can be later released from these cells into the blood and used in metabolism.

However, if the pancreas is producing insufficient amounts of insulin, or if there is a failure of the mechanism of transporting glucose into the cells (so-called "insulin resistance") then diabetes results.

Types of diabetes

There are two types of diabetes. Type I, sometimes called insulin-dependent or juvenile-type diabetes, is caused by insufficient amounts of insulin being produced by the pancreas. It is usually found in persons under 25 years of age. Type II, sometimes called non insulin-dependent, maturity onset or adult-type diabetes, is more common. It is found in persons over age 40, and is usually caused by insulin resistance.

In both types, there is excess sugar in the blood (hyperglycemia) which then needs to be removed by the kidneys. Symptoms of excessive thirst, frequent urination, and hunger develop. The metabolism of carbohydrates, fats, and proteins is altered. Fatty acids released from tissue throughout the body are converted by the liver into chemical compounds called ketones which enter the bloodstream causing the blood to become dangerously acidic (ketoacidosis). Especially in juvenile Type I diabetes, this can lead to diabetic coma and, if untreated, to death. Diabetic coma is a medical emergency requiring urgent treatment in hospital.

A physician can diagnose diabetes by testing for sugar in urine and blood. A glucose tolerance test determines how well the body uses and stores sugar, by measuring blood glucose levels periodically for up to six hours after the patient swallows a glucose solution.

Regulation of diabetes

Type I diabetics need daily injections of insulin (the hormone is not available in an oral form). Most diabetics self-administer their insulin by subcutaneous injection (below the skin) from one to four times per day, though some diabetics use a portable pump that delivers insulin directly to the body through an implanted cannula.

Careful regulation of activity and a strict diet are important to keep the levels of insulin and sugar in the blood within as normal a range as possible. Both the physician and the diabetic when at home should monitor their blood glucose levels regularly to make sure the dosage of insulin is correct. During periods of stress, such as surgery and infection, the insulin dosage may need to be temporarily increased.

Type II diabetes is usually easier to control than Type I. Type II diabetes is usually treated with diet alone, or with diet plus oral antidiabetic drugs. In some cases, insulin treatment is needed. Weight control and regular exercise are also important.

Imbalance of insulin and glucose

Too much insulin or too little glucose in the diet causes hypoglycemia, or insulin shock. The signs of hypoglycemia are mild hunger, dizziness, sweating, and heart palpitations followed by mental confusion and coma. Diabetics can stop hypoglycemia by eating sugar, sweets or candy, or by injecting glucagon, a hormone that raises blood sugar.

Diabetics should be familiar with the symptoms of both hypoglycemia and hyperglycemia so as to be able to treat themselves or seek help to prevent the onset of coma. They should wear an identification card, tag or bracelet in case they need emergency care.

Diabetes and pregnancy

Diabetes can be aggravated by pregnancy, so good management during pregnancy and labor is essential. Infants of women with poorly controlled diabetes are at risk for birth defects, but if the condition is well controlled, the risk is the same as for a non-diabetic mother.

Glaucoma

Glaucoma often occurs in diabetes. In glaucoma, pressure inside the eyeball rises, damaging the retina and causing loss of vision.

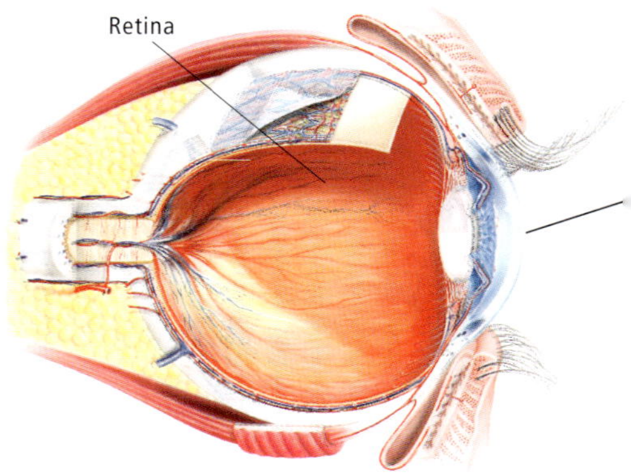

Diabetic nephropathy

Diabetic nephropathy damages the glomeruli and small blood vessels of the kidneys, due to high levels of blood glucose. This results in the loss of necessary proteins through the urine, swelling of body tissues and eventually renal failure.

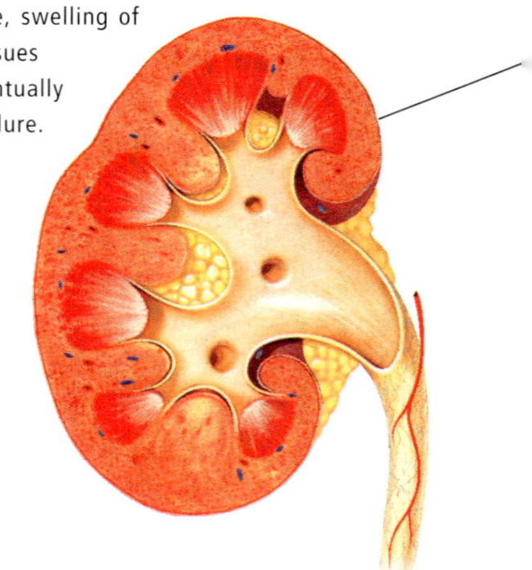

Foot ulcer

Diabetes slows the healing of body tissues and also causes degeneration of the peripheral nerves (neuropathy). These two factors act together to cause foot ulcers in diabetics.

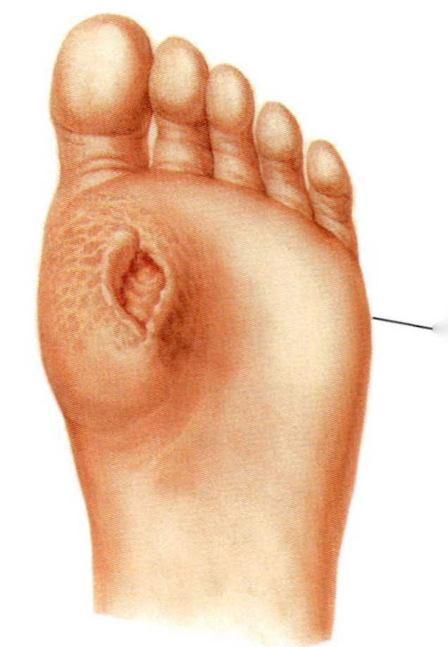

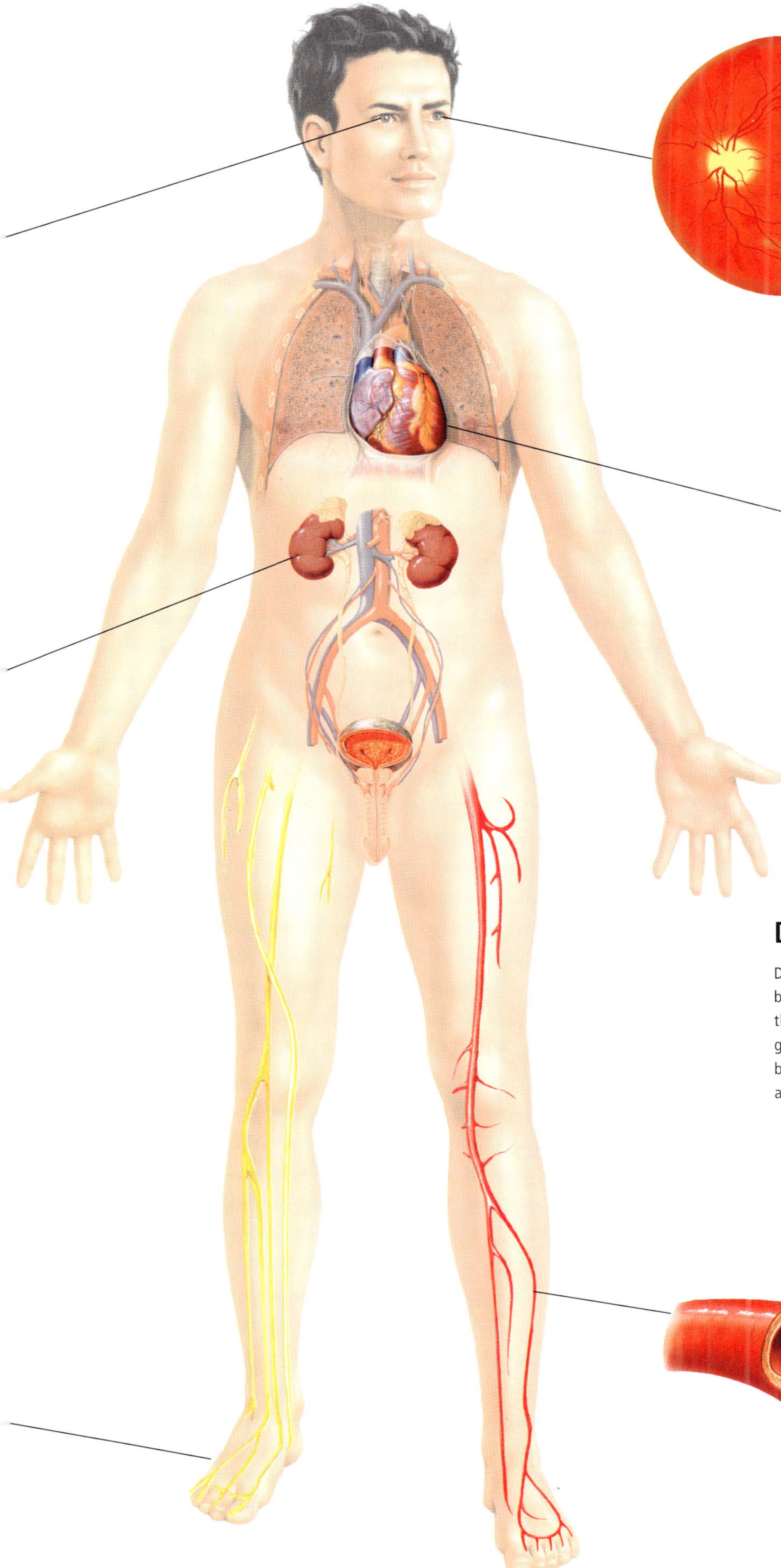

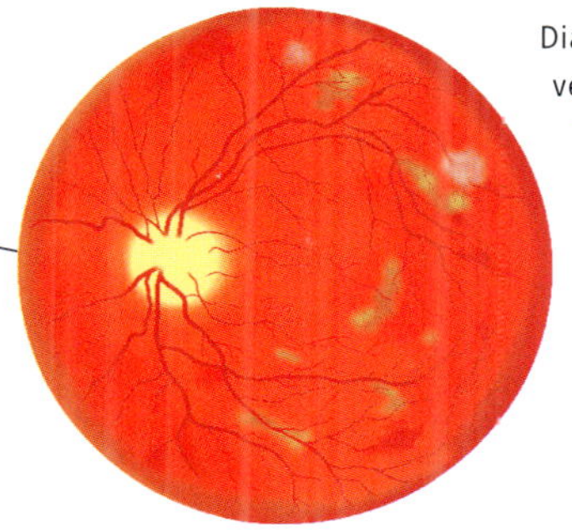

Diabetic retinopathy

Diabetes damages the small blood vessels in the retina of the eye. The damaged vessels can bleed, causing hemorrhages, or they can cause areas of retina to die, resulting in loss of vision.

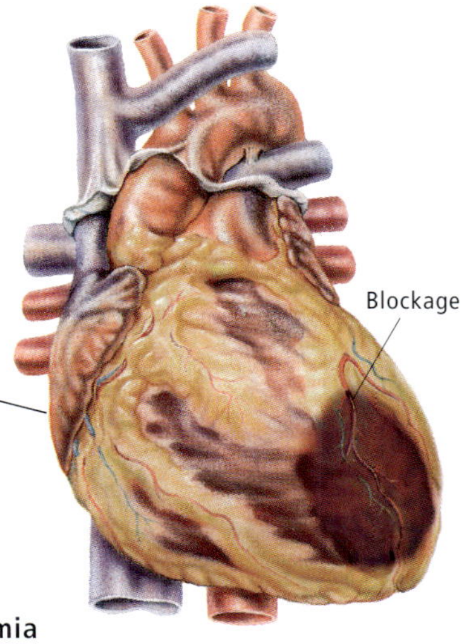

Ischemia

Diabetes can cause coronary artery disease, which in turn can cause death of cardiac tissue known as myocardial infarction.

Diabetes

Diabetes mellitus is caused by a disruption in the body's processing of glucose. Instead of reaching the body tissues and cells that need it, excess glucose circulates in the bloodstream upsetting the body's chemical balance. Over time, this can cause a variety of disorders.

Atherosclerosis

Diabetes is one of the risk factors for atherosclerosis, a disease in which fatty deposits build up under the lining of the artery and block off its blood flow.

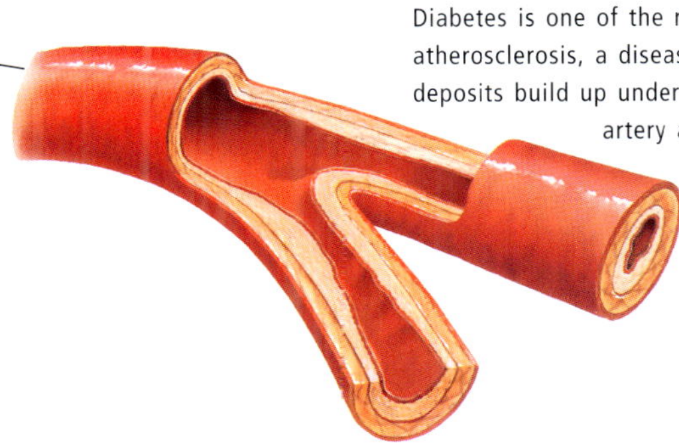

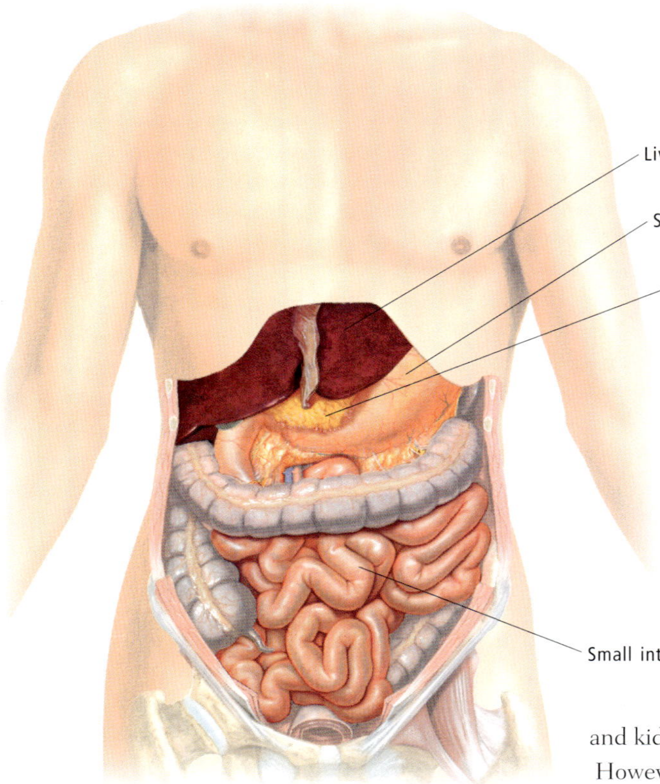

Diabetes and glucose metabolism

The hormone insulin helps the body process glucose—the sugar needed for energy by all body cells. In normal insulin production:

(a) Carbohydrates are broken down in the stomach and small intestine and converted into glucose.

(b) Glucose travels in the blood from the intestine to the liver, which releases it to body tissues for energy when needed.

(c) The pancreas controls how much glucose is stored in the liver and how much is released into tissues. When the pancreas registers increased levels of glucose in the blood it secretes insulin. Insulin instructs the liver and other tissues to absorb more glucose, lowering blood sugar levels. n Type I diabetes, insufficient amounts of insulin are produced by the pancreas. In Type II diabetes, the body either produces too little insulin, or insulin receptors in liver cells and other tissues do not respond to the hormone. In both forms of diabetes too much glucose circulates in the blood, a condition known as hyperglycemia.

Gestational diabetes is diabetes that only appears during pregnancy. It usually becomes apparent during the weeks 24–28. In many cases, the blood glucose level returns to normal after delivery. However, there is a risk the mother may develop full-blown diabetes in the future.

Long-term complications

Diabetes mellitus has long-term complications as well. Generally, the longer the diabetic condition exists, the greater the complications. Atherosclerosis is the most serious, damaging small and large blood vessels especially in the retina of the eye (diabetic retinopathy) and in the kidney (diabetic nephropathy), causing eventual blindness and kidney failure. Nerve degeneration resulting in loss of sensation in peripheral nerves, and reduced resistance to infections are other common complications.

People with diabetes are prone to foot problems because of complications caused by damage to large and small blood vessels, damage to nerves, and decreased ability to fight infection, so diabetics need to learn the techniques of foot care.

With good diabetic control, the onset of complications such as retinopathy and kidney disease can be delayed. However, they cannot be prevented, especially in the case of Type I diabetes and long-standing Type II diabetes.

SEE ALSO *Blood sugar tests, Hyperglycemia, Hypoglycemia, Insulin, Pancreas*

DIABETES INSIPIDUS

Diabetes insipidus is a rare condition causing pronounced thirst and the passage of large quantities of dilute urine. It is unrelated to diabetes mellitus.

The most common type is so-called "central" diabetes insipidus, which is caused by a lack of antidiuretic hormone (ADH or vasopressin). This hormone is produced in the hypothalamus of the brain and controls the way the kidneys filter blood to make urine. Lack of this hormone (or failure of the kidneys to respond to the hormone), allows too much fluid to pass through the kidneys.

A person with diabetes insipidus must drink large quantities of water to compensate for the fluid loss in order to avoid dehydration. The lack of ADH secretion can be caused by damage to the hypothalamus as a result of surgery, infection, tumor or head injury. There is no cure for the condition; however, synthetic ADH injections will correct the hormone deficiency. ADH is also

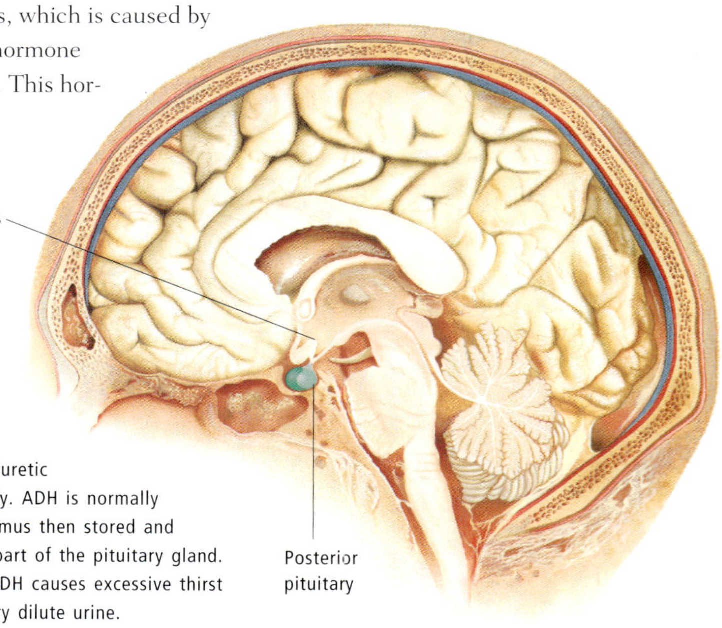

Diabetes insipidus

Diabetes insipidus is a disorder resulting from insufficient levels of antidiuretic hormone (ADH) in the body. ADH is normally produced in the hypothalamus then stored and released by the posterior part of the pituitary gland. Decreased production of ADH causes excessive thirst and large quantities of very dilute urine.

available as a nasal spray.

Diabetes insipidus can also be caused by a rare hereditary defect in the tubules of the kidney. The condition is called nephrogenic diabetes insipidus and produces symptoms similar to those of central diabetes insipidus. It may be treated with diuretic drugs.

SEE ALSO *Diuretics, Hypothalamus, Kidney*

DIALYSIS

Dialysis is a method of removing toxic substances (impurities or wastes) from the blood when the kidneys cannot do so. This is usually because of kidney disease, but dialysis may sometimes be used to quickly remove drugs or poisons from the bloodstream in people who have been poisoned or who have overdosed on drugs.

If the kidneys are unable to fulfil more than 10 percent of their normal function, this situation is considered end-stage kidney disease and dialysis is necessary. There are two types of dialysis: peritoneal dialysis and hemodialysis.

Peritoneal dialysis uses the person's abdominal peritoneal membrane to act as a dialysis mechanism. It involves filling the abdominal cavity (via a catheter) with a special solution, using the peritoneal membrane inside the abdomen as the semipermeable membrane. The fluid is allowed to absorb wastes for several hours, and then the waste-filled fluid is exchanged for a fresh batch of solution.

Hemodialysis involves filtering the blood slowly through an artificial kidney machine called a dialyzer. Inside the dialyzer, blood is run through tubes with semipermeable membranes, and the tubes are bathed with solutions that will remove small soluble molecules (such as urea) from the blood. The purified blood is then fed back into one of the patient's veins.

For hemodialysis to be successful, there must be adequate access to the circulation. A normal vein is not big enough to carry a wide bore IV (intravenous) line, so special types of arterial and venous access have to be constructed. A common method is to surgically join an artery and vein together under the skin; this is called an AV (arteriovenous) fistula. The increased blood volume stretches the elastic vein to allow a larger volume of blood flow into which a wide bore IV line can be inserted.

In people whose veins are not suitable for an AV fistula, a graft from an artery to a vein may be used. The graft may come from the person's own saphenous vein (in the leg), or it may be a synthetic graft.

Usually, dialysis needs to be performed three times a week for periods of four to six hours. Dialysis may take place in a hospital, at a special dialysis center, or at the patient's home. It needs to be continued until the kidneys recover their normal function. In chronic renal failure, this usually means for the rest of the person's life or until a kidney transplant is performed.

SEE ALSO *Hemodialysis, Kidney, Peritoneal dialysis*

DIAPER RASH

Diaper rash (nappy rash) is a common inflammation of the skin in babies mainly due to wetness and heat beneath the diaper, resulting in red blotches, spots or lesions. It can also be caused by contact friction, chemical allergies and the blockage of sweat glands and may be exacerbated by the interaction of the skin with feces and the ammonia in urine. The rash tends to be worse in the creases of the skin.

Diaper rash can be treated or prevented by keeping the skin as dry as possible, changing diapers frequently, air drying between changes and leaving the diaper off for as long as is practical each day. Plastic pants used to cover diapers can make the condition worse, and wipes containing potential irritants such as alcohol should be avoided. Simply cleanse with mild soap, water and a soft cloth. Ointments containing zinc oxide are helpful for reducing any friction between the diaper and the baby's skin.

Secondary infections can be caused by fungi (such as *Candida*) or bacteria (such as *Staphylococcus* or *Streptococcus*) which are normally found in the skin and which thrive in damaged areas. These infections can be treated with topical antibiotics.

Diaper rash is also known as baby rash, miliaria, diaper dermatitis and nappy rash.

SEE ALSO *Candidiasis, Staphylococcal infections, Streptococcal infections*

DIAPHRAGM

The diaphragm is a muscular layer which separates the chest cavity from the abdominal cavity. It is attached at the back to the vertebral column (spine), to the ribs along the side of the chest, and to the sternum at the front of the chest. The diaphragm is essential for life because it is the main muscle used for breathing.

When the diaphragm is at rest (i.e. not contracting) it forms a high dome; when the diaphragm contracts, this dome descends, thus increasing the height of the chest cavity. Increasing the height of the chest cavity in turn draws air into the lungs within the chest. This means that the diaphragm is the main muscle for inspiration (drawing air into the lungs).

Expiration, or the passage of air out of the chest cavity, is usually passive, i.e. it occurs because of the relaxation of tension in the soft and hard tissues of the chest and abdomen. The diaphragm does not play any active part in expiration.

The phrenic nerves controlling the diaphragm come from the upper parts of the spinal cord in the neck. If the nerve cells which control the diaphragm are separated from the brain stem control centers for breathing (e.g. by a high spinal cord injury), then the patient will be unable to breathe without assistance from a ventilator. High spinal injuries can occur if someone dives into a too-shallow pool, falls onto the crown of the head from a height, or experiences a violent whiplash injury in a car accident.

The diaphragm is pierced by several structures which pass between the chest and abdominal cavities. The three largest of these are the esophagus, carrying food to the stomach; the aorta, carrying oxygenated blood from the heart to the lower body; and the inferior vena cava, a large vein which carries deoxygenated blood from the lower body back to the heart. Several other nerves and lymphatic channels also pass through the diaphragm.

The central part of the diaphragm is called the central tendon. It is fibrous rather than muscular and has the pericardial sac, which surrounds the heart, firmly attached to its upper surface. The central tendon descends with every inspiration.

The stomach and abdominal part of the esophagus may be forced through the esophageal opening of the diaphragm and into the chest cavity—this is known as hiatus hernia. This condition may cause discomfort after meals, reflux of stomach acid into the chest part of the esophagus (gastroesophageal reflux) leading to heartburn, and a sense of pressure in the lower chest. Medical treatment could include antacids, change of diet, and maintaining upright posture. Surgical treatment involves fixing the esophagus and stomach firmly into the abdominal cavity with sutures.

SEE ALSO *Abdomen, Aorta, Breathing, Esophagus, Hiatus hernia, Gastroesophageal reflux, Lungs, Ribs, Spinal cord, Spine, Stomach*

DIARRHEA

When food reaches the intestinal tract it is a liquid mush with a volume of around 1 gallon (almost 4 liters) per day. The water content is reabsorbed in the large intestine, making the feces solid or semi-solid. When the bowel fails to reabsorb fluid the feces are liquid, and this condition is known as diarrhea. It may be accompanied by abdominal cramps, low-grade fever, vomiting, blood in the stools and dehydration.

In developing countries diarrhea caused by the unsanitary preparation of artificial baby milk kills more than a million babies annually. In total, diarrhea that is caused by an infection kills nearly 8 million children under 5 years of age, worldwide. Chronic diarrhea causes an abnormal loss of essential nutrients which results in malnutrition.

Less severe forms of diarrhea, which can be caused by having too much fiber in the diet (especially unprocessed bran), lactose intolerance, or artificial sweeteners such as sorbitol or mannitol, does not require specific treatment.

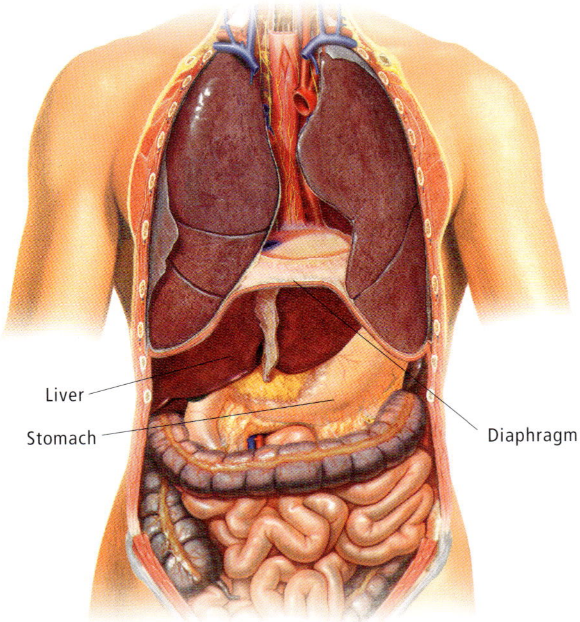

Diaphragm

The diaphragm is the muscular layer that separates the chest cavity from the abdominal cavity. It is the main muscle used for breathing.

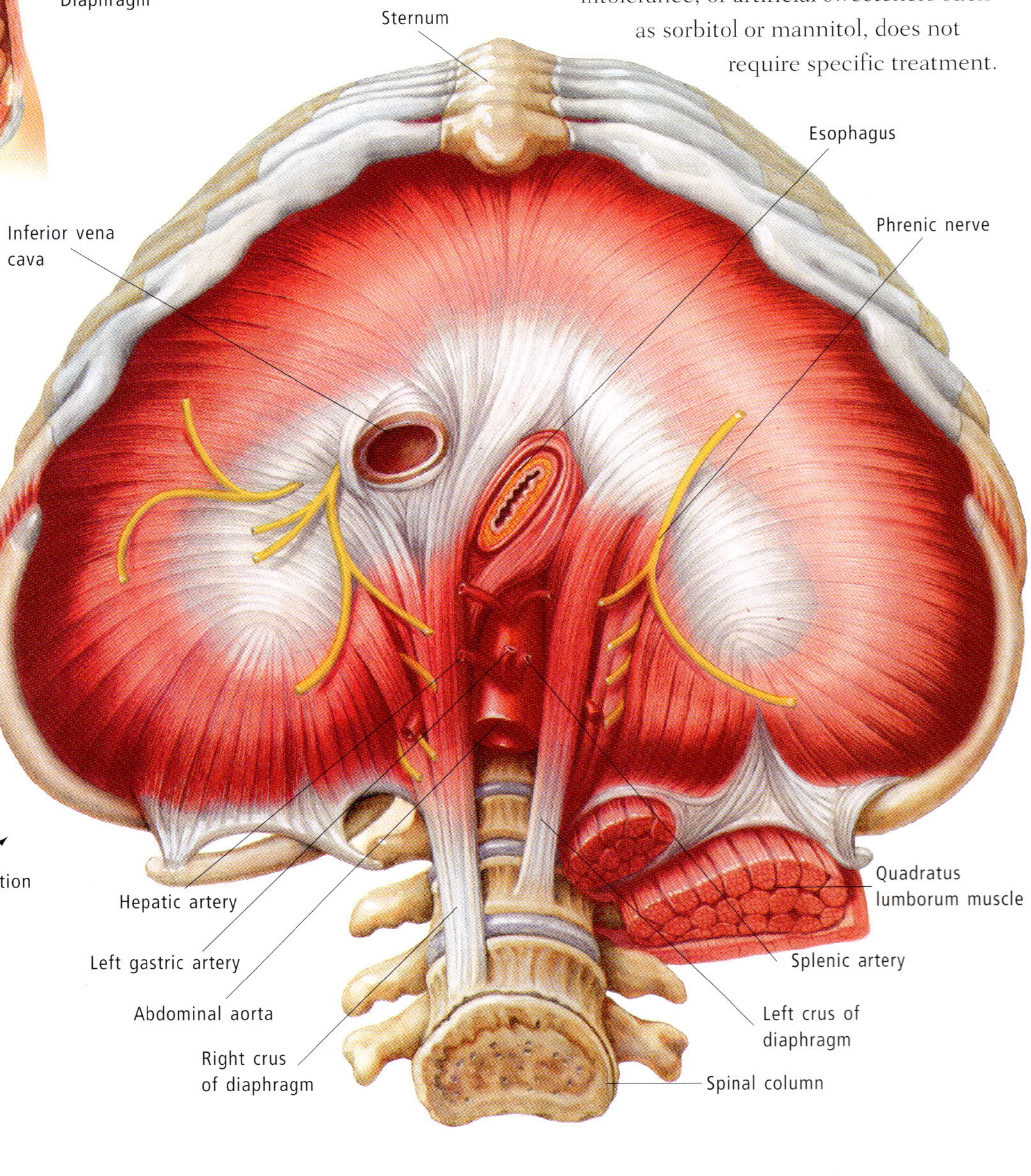

Diaphragm

The heart and the lungs rest on the upper convex surface of this muscle. The lower concave surface forms the roof of the abdominal cavity, lying over the stomach on the left and the liver on the right. This illustration shows the diaphragm as seen from below.

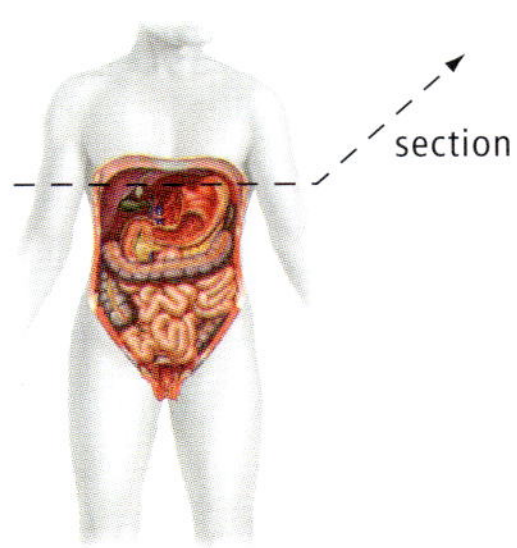

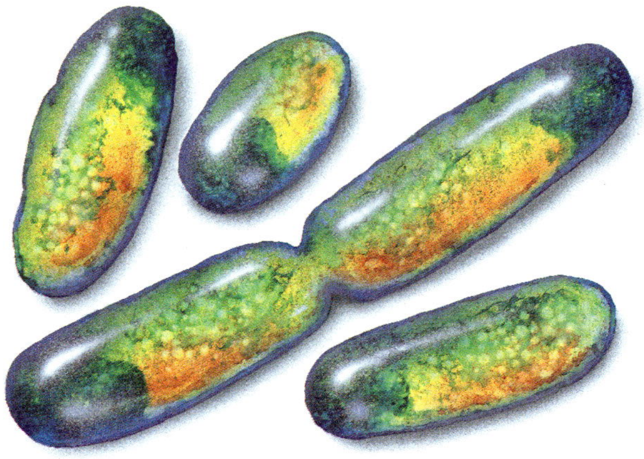

Diarrhea

The bacterium *Escherichia coli* shown here is a common cause of diarrhea in children. It can also lead to other infections such as urinary tract infections and conjunctivitis.

Causes of more severe diarrhea can be a temporary inflammation brought on by common viruses (this is especially common in children); food poisoning; infections (bacterial, viral or parasitic); eating highly spiced food; drinking large quantities of alcohol; emotional stress; poisons such as arsenic or mercury bichloride; gastroenteritis; medications such as laxatives, antibiotics and antacids; diseases such as dysentery or cholera (unusual in the industrialized world); and benign or cancerous growths in the bowel.

Diarrhea is also a symptom of conditions such as celiac disease and colitis. It is also the main cause of illness among travelers when it occurs as a result of a bacterial infection from the unsanitary handling of food and eating utensils.

Babies and children with diarrhea need medical attention if the condition does not resolve within 24 hours or if they are showing signs of dehydration, have bloody or slimy bowel movements (feces), an extremely high temperature, or are aged under six months. Treatment includes a diet of clear liquids and oral rehydration fluids which replace the lost electrolytes.

SEE ALSO *Celiac disease, Cholera, Colitis, Constipation, Dysentery, Dehydration, Gastroenteritis, Giardiasis, Irritable bowel syndrome, Lactose intolerance, Malnutrition*

DIET

Diet is a person's regular nutrition: it represents the total intake of food and drink. A balanced or normal diet is one that will maintain good health. In Western societies this means eating foods from each of the four main food groups: cereals, fruits and vegetables, protein foods, and dairy products, in proportions laid down in generally agreed dietary guidelines.

Governments around the world have recognized the links between diet and health, and many have issued guidelines to inform people as to what constitutes a healthy diet, and the benefits of good eating habits. The quantities recommended will differ according to the age, general health and energy requirements of the person.

An unbalanced diet, for example one high in fat, will have a negative effect on health, increasing weight or bringing a greater risk of dietary disorders such as diabetes.

Individual diets are influenced by cultural factors as well as by what is locally or seasonally available. People tend to eat the foods they were brought up on. Migrants from dissimilar cultures may find their preferred foods are not available in their adopted country and will have to choose unfamiliar manufactured foods with many hidden ingredients. They may unwittingly change the balance of nutrients in their diet, increasing the amounts of salt, sugar or fats they eat, with harmful effects on weight and health.

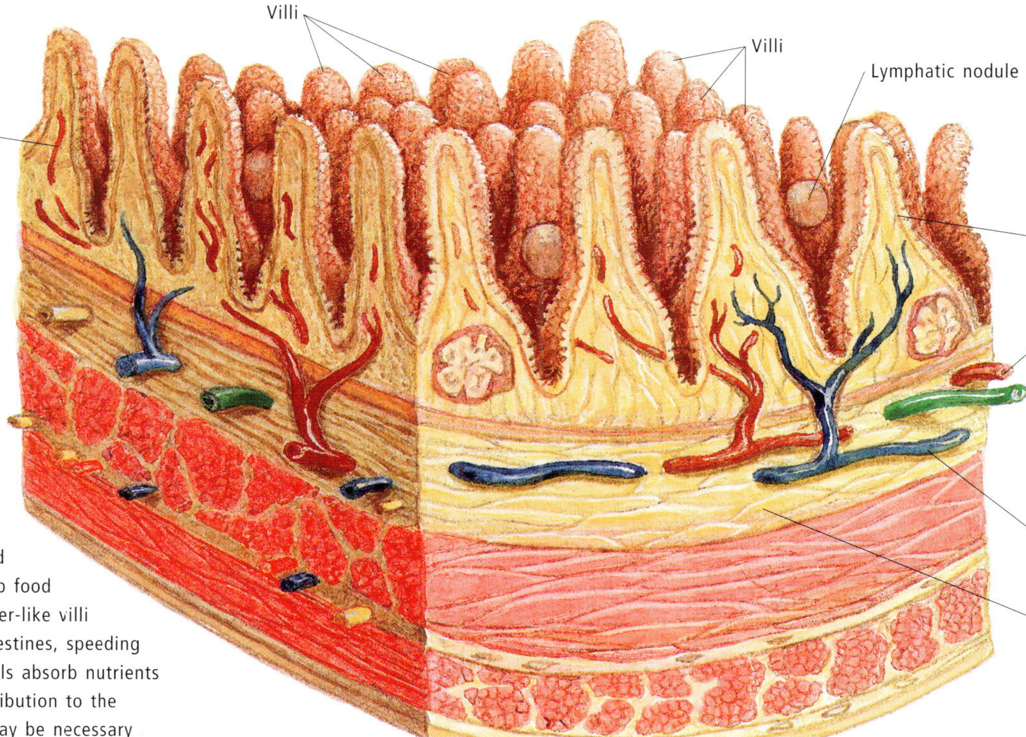

Diet—food processing

The mucosal lining (epithelium) of the intestine is specially designed to help the body process and absorb food and its nutrients. Thousands of finger-like villi increase the surface area of the intestines, speeding absorption of nutrients. Blood vessels absorb nutrients and carry them to the liver for distribution to the rest of the body. Changes in diet may be necessary if the intestinal lining is damaged by disease.

Special diets are those prescribed by a dietitian to meet the needs of a particular condition or illness; to prepare for a surgical procedure; to reduce weight; to lower the cholesterol levels of the blood; to eliminate foods which might trigger an allergic reaction; to improve digestion; or to improve health in a poorly fed person.

D

Diet and obesity

As lifestyles in industrialized societies have become less active, daily energy requirements have fallen. Because individuals walk less and perform less manual labor, food intake should be correspondingly lower, but where food is more affordable and more plentiful, and with many foods being dense energy sources, overeating is common.

The result is that many people are overweight, suffer poor health and increased incidences of weight-related diseases such as diabetes mellitus, high blood pressure, and heart disease.

The energy provided by food is measured in kilocalories or kilojoules—1 kilocalorie is equal to 4.2 kilojoules. Women who are overweight may adjust their diet by limiting the total energy value of their foods to approximately 1,500 kilocalories (equal to 6,300 kilojoules) per day and most will lose excess weight at this level of intake. Men may lose weight with a higher energy intake of 1,800 kilocalories (equal to 7,560 kilojoules) per day.

Fiber in diet

Diets that are lacking in fiber and high in fat have been linked with digestive diseases and certain types of cancer. Cereal foods are the major source of dietary fiber in Western societies except where fiber is removed by the refining process. This fact has been recognized in many countries and minimum requirements have been set for dietary fiber intake.

Elimination diet

An elimination diet is a therapy for suspected food allergies. Foods suspected of causing the allergic reaction are first excluded, then re-introduced one by one. When the food that triggers the reaction is identified, it can be avoided by following an exclusion diet, which allows all foods to be eaten except those containing this particular substance.

SEE ALSO *Allergies, Appetite, Celiac disease, Constipation, Diabetes, Nutrition, Obesity*

DILATION AND CURETTAGE

Often called D & C, dilation and curettage is the most commonly performed gynecological procedure. It involves the surgical opening (dilation) of the cervix (the neck of the uterus), and the removal of the contents of the uterus with a curette, an instrument with a long handle and an end shaped like a spoon. This is used to obtain tissue from the uterus lining (endometrium) for examination or to remove fragments of placenta after a miscarriage. The procedure can be performed under a general or a local anesthetic and has few side or after effects.

SEE ALSO *Abortion, Dilation and evacuation, Miscarriage*

DILATION AND EVACUATION

This procedure is used in abortions when the pregnancy is into the second trimester, or from 12 to 20 weeks, and is usually done under a general anesthetic. It involves dilating the cervix more widely than for a dilation and curettage to allow the removal of fetal parts. The fetus is removed with suction, a curette and forceps.

SEE ALSO *Abortion, Dilation and curettage*

DIPHTHERIA

Diphtheria is an acute infectious disease of the larynx, tonsils, and throat, caused by the bacterium *Corynebacterium diphtheriae*. As a result of widespread immunization against diphtheria over many years, this disease is now rare and usually seen in non-immunized children, under ten.

Diphtheria is transmitted from person to person by airborne droplets from infected persons or asymptomatic carriers, that is, people who carry the disease but do not show symptoms. The illness develops after a period of one to four days after exposure to the bacterium. The child feels weak and unwell with fever and a sore throat, and may find the lymph nodes in the neck will become swollen.

A toxin produced by the infection damages the lining of the throat, causing a tough, fibrous gray or greenish yellow membrane to form at the back of the throat, which may obstruct breathing. The toxin may enter the bloodstream and cause damage to the heart, kidneys and nervous system. Treatment involves bed rest in hospital and administration of diphtheria antitoxin and antibiotics such as penicillin or erythromycin.

Diphtheria immunization is usually carried out in the first year of life. It is usually combined with pertussis and tetanus immunization (DPT). Falling childhood immunization rates in some Western countries have led to a resurgence of the disease.

SEE ALSO *Immunization, Infectious diseases, Larynx, Throat, Tonsils*

DISK, INTERVERTEBRAL

The intervertebral disks are flexible, cartilaginous structures, which lie between adjacent vertebrae and make up approximately 25 percent of the length of the vertebral column in a young person. Intervertebral disks form joints between the bodies of the vertebrae, which serve both to unite adjacent vertebrae and to permit movement between them. They also play a role as shock absorbers when force is transmitted along the vertebral column during standing and movement.

Each disk is formed of two parts, a central mass called the nucleus pulposus (soft center), and a surrounding fibrous layer (the annulus fibrosus). The nucleus pulposus has a semi-fluid, gelatinous consistency which allows it to become deformed when pressure is placed upon it, enabling the disk to change shape as the vertebral column moves.

The surrounding annulus fibrosus is formed by concentric layers of fibers which are firmly attached to the adjacent vertebrae. These fibers pass in an oblique direction between the vertebrae and are arranged in such a way as to resist excessive movement in almost any direction. The joints formed by the intervertebral disks are reinforced in front and behind by ligaments, which pass along the length of the vertebral column.

The thickness and shape of the disks varies in different parts of the vertebral column. They are relatively thin and flat in the chest (thoracic) region, thicker in the neck (cervical) region and thickest and wedge-shaped in the lower back (lumbar) region.

Intervertebral disks in young people have a high water content (80–90 percent). This gradually reduces during the day because water is squeezed out of each disk as it bears weight during standing and movement. The lost water is however reabsorbed into the disk during sleep when lying down. The average young adult is around ¾ inch (2 centimeters) taller upon waking than at the end of the day. As a person ages, the ability to replace this water gradually reduces and the disks become drier and thinner. This partly explains why people lose height, or appear to shrink, as they get older.

The fibers of the fibrous annulus become more fragile with age and may be torn by excessive force on the joint, such as sudden twisting or flexion, causing the nucleus to protrude into or through the damaged part of the annulus. Because the annulus is thinner and weaker behind, the damaged disk usually bulges in this direction and may compress nearby spinal nerves. This condition is commonly known as a herniated disk, or slipped disk.

Herniation of the disk can occur in part of the vertebral column but is most common in the lumbar region where the nerves to the lower limbs originate. When herniation is mild and only irritates local structures, it causes pain in the lower back and buttocks ("lumbago"). If the herniation is severe enough to press on the spinal nerve roots as they emerge from the spinal cord and pass over the herniated disk, this will cause sciatica, which is pain, numbness, "pins and needles", or muscle weakness down the leg.

Treatment is usually conservative (anti-inflammatory drugs, rest, physical therapy) but in severe cases surgery may be necessary to release pressure on the nerve.

SEE ALSO *Back, Sciatica, Spine, Vertebrae*

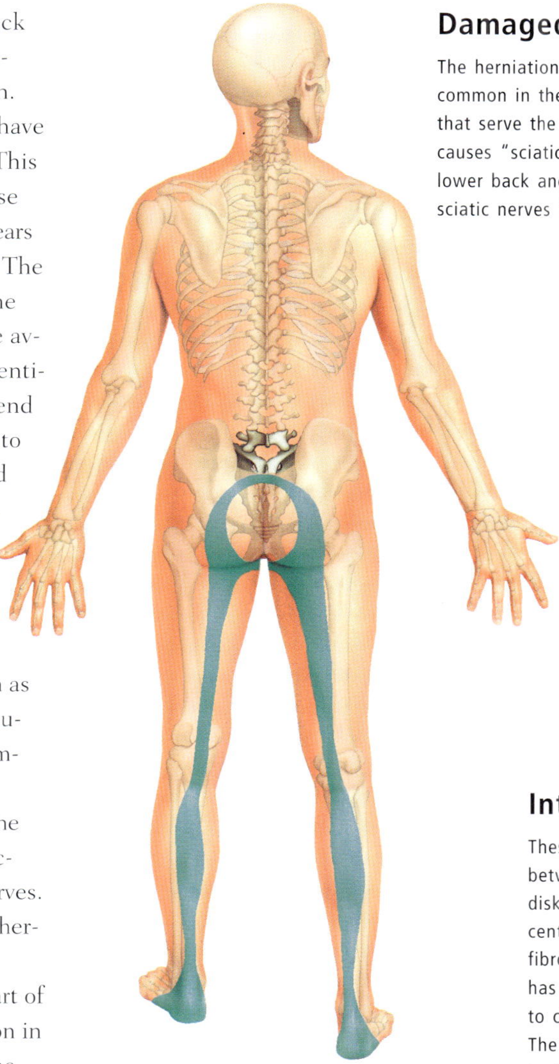

Damaged lumbar disks

The herniation of intervertebral disks is most common in the lumbar region where the nerves that serve the lower limbs are situated. This causes "sciatica"—a sharp pain in the lower back and along the route of the sciatic nerves in the legs.

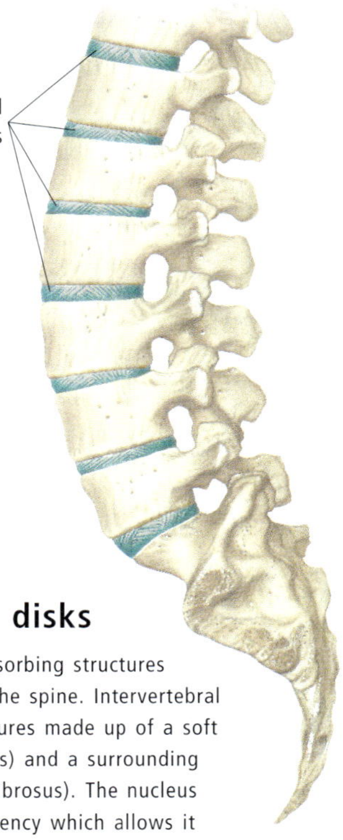

Intervertebral disks

These are the shock-absorbing structures between the bones of the spine. Intervertebral disks are flexible structures made up of a soft center (nucleus pulposus) and a surrounding fibrous layer (annulus fibrosus). The nucleus has a semi-fluid consistency which allows it to change shape when placed under pressure. The surrounding annulus fibrosus is attached to the bones (vertebrae) of the spine.

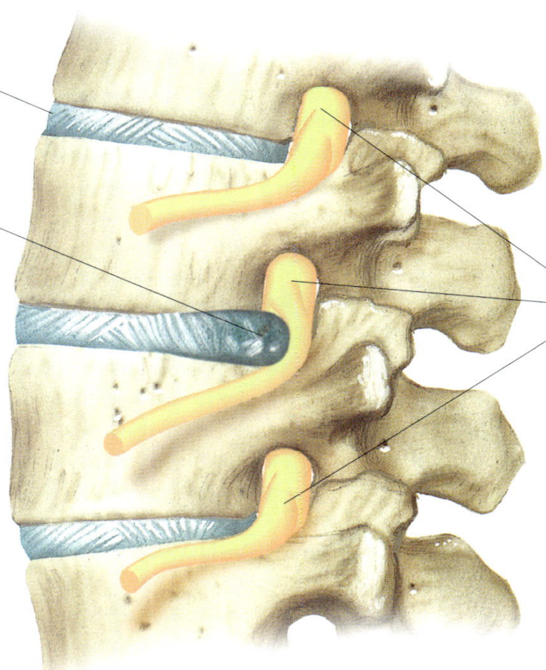

Herniated disk

Invertebral disks comprise a soft nucleus and a fibrous outer casing (annulus) that holds the disk in place. If the annulus is weakened by age or injury, the disk may bulge into the vertebral canal compressing nearby spinal nerves, referred to as a "slipped" or herniated disk.

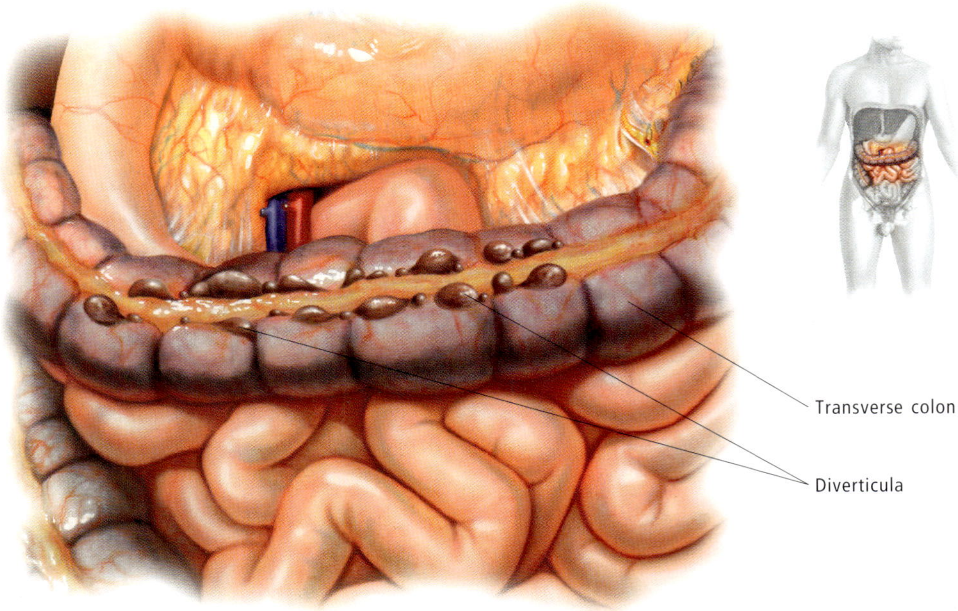

Diverticulosis

In diverticulosis, inner layers of the colon wall bulge out to form small pockets (diverticula).

DIVERTICULITIS

Diverticulitis is a disease of the large bowel or colon, which arises when small outpockets (protrusions) in the wall become inflamed; these outpockets are called diverticula, hence the name.

The patient experiences pain usually in the lower left part of the abdomen, which is mild to severe in intensity and may be either persistent or cramping in nature. Patients may also have mild fever, tenderness in the lower abdomen, swelling of the lower abdomen, constipation and, sometimes, blood in their feces.

Occasionally diverticula rupture, and the contents of the bowel leak into the tissues of the bowel wall and, sometimes, into the cavity of the abdomen. The bacteria from the bowel multiply within these regions. Complications include abscesses in the bowel wall and nearby abdominal cavity; fistulas, where the infection forms a communication between the interior of the bowel and other nearby organs; peritonitis, where bacteria spread freely through the abdominal cavity; and obstruction of the bowel.

About one-quarter of patients with acute diverticulitis require surgical treatment to either drain or remove abscesses, relieve obstruction or close fistulas.

SEE ALSO *Bowel, Colon, Diverticulosis, Peritonitis*

DIVERTICULOSIS

In diverticulosis, the wall of the bowel "blows out", forming outpockets which protrude between the muscle bands of the bowel wall. A diet low in dietary fiber and high in fat, typical of many people in Western societies, is thought to contribute to this condition of the colon.

SEE ALSO *Bowel, Colon*

DIVERTICULUM

Most commonly, a divertivulum is an outpocketing or protrusion of the wall of the colon. This may also occur in the upper part of the esophagus, where the lower throat (or pharynx) gives way to the esophagus. This type of diverticulum is called Zenker's diverticulum and occurs when the pressure generated by swallowing forces the wall of the upper esophagus outwards.

SEE ALSO *Esophagus, Pharynx*

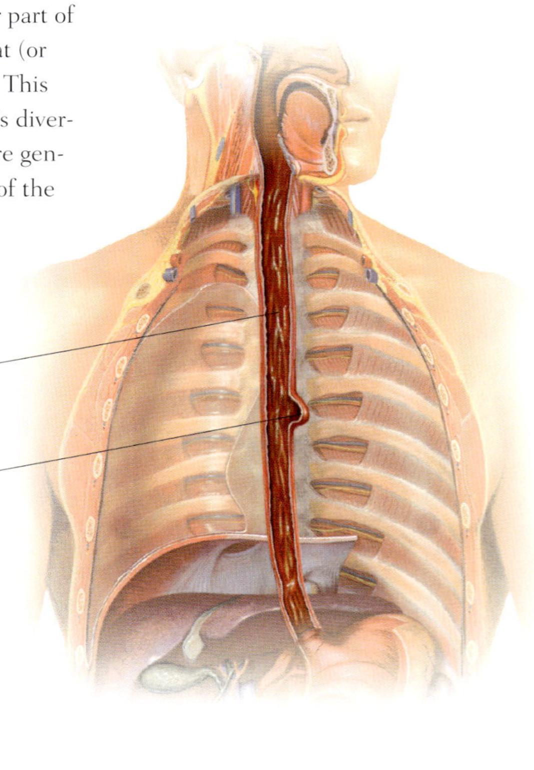

Diverticulum

A diverticulum is the formation of a small pouch or protrusion in the wall of a mucous membrane. It often occurs in the esophagus or colon.

DIURETICS

Diuretic drugs act on the kidneys to increase urine output. They cause the kidneys to increase the amount of salt and water eliminated from the body in the urine, and so are often called "water pills". Alcohol, tea and coffee also have a mild diuretic effect.

Diuretics are used to treat excessive buildup of fluid in the body (edema) or the lungs (pulmonary edema). Edema can be caused by disorders of the heart (such as congestive heart failure or heart attack), liver dysfunction (by not producing protein) or kidney dysfunction (by leaking protein). Diuretics are used to treat hypertension (high blood pressure), congestive heart failure and also high fluid pressure within the eye (glaucoma).

Some diuretics, such as thiazide diuretics, cause the kidneys to lose potassium, which must be replaced by adding foods rich in it to the diet, or by taking potassium supplements.

SEE ALSO *Edema, Glaucoma, Hypertension, Kidney, Potassium, Urinary systems*

DIZZINESS

Dizziness is a feeling of light-headedness, unsteadiness or falling, accompanied by weakness and swaying, or a sensation of whirling rotation and general loss of balance.

Low blood pressure (hypotension) can cause dizziness as the brain may not receive enough blood and not enough oxygen.

Orthostatic or postural hypotension occurs when a person stands up quickly and causes a temporary fall in blood pressure, enough to cause dizziness or sometimes fainting. Sitting, or lying down will make it easier for blood to reach the brain, increasing the flow and relieving the dizziness.

Infections, damage and tumors of the inner ear, brain disorders, head injuries, brain tumors, and medications used to relieve high blood pressure are all possible causes of dizziness.

SEE ALSO *Hypotension, Menière's disease, Vertigo*

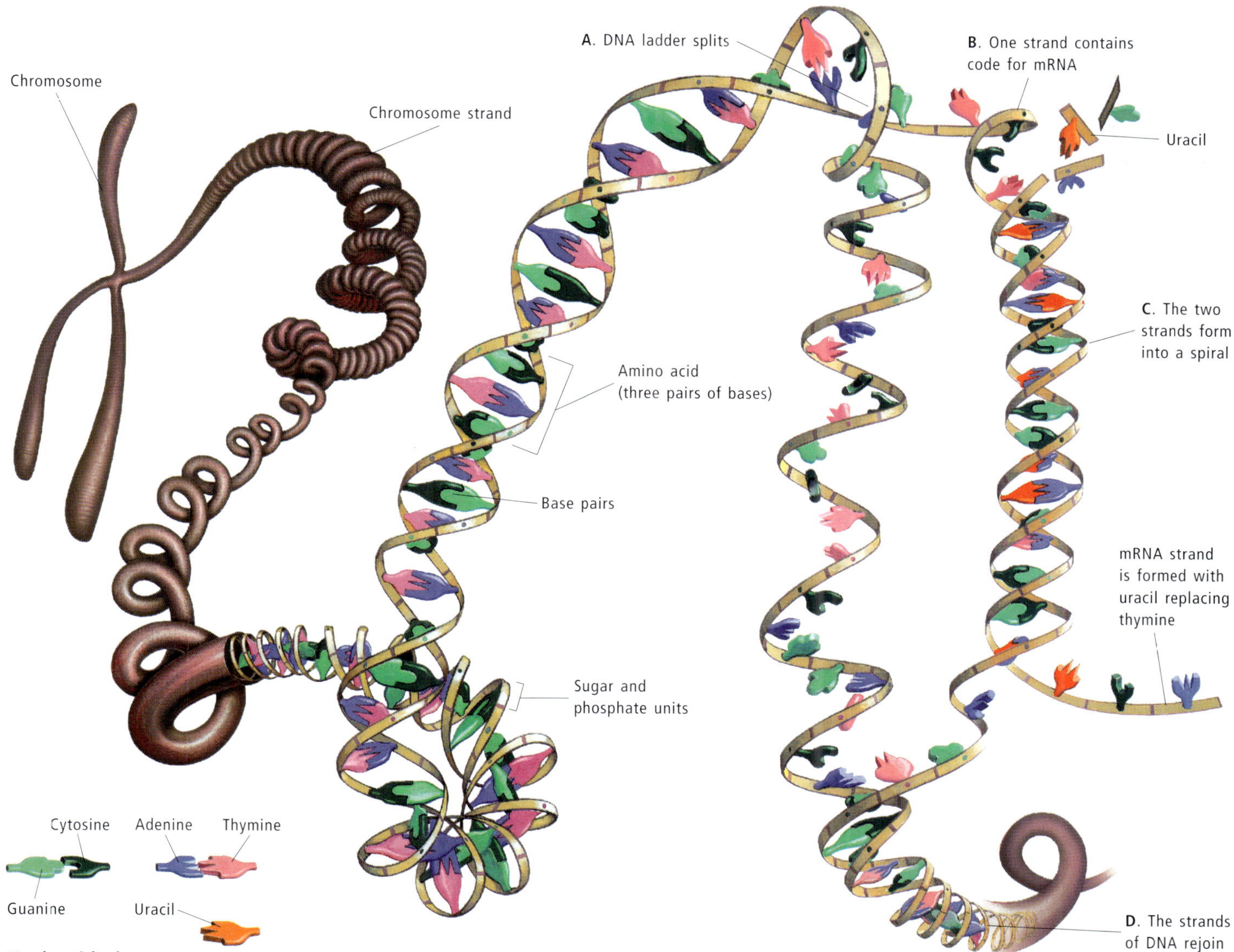

Nucleotide bases

DNA

Deoxyribonucleic acid (DNA) molecules, found in the chromosomes in the nucleus of every cell, carry the genetic information that determines inherited traits (such as hair and skin color and body function). This information dictates the formation of proteins used by the body for growth and chemical processes.

Unravelling a chromosome shows that DNA comprises a spiral ladder consisting of two chains of phosphate and sugar units attached to nitrogenous bases. The chains are joined together at the bases—like the rungs in a ladder. There are four bases in DNA—adenine, thymine, cytosine and guanine—which bind together in limited combinations (adenine always binds with thymine; cytosine always binds with guanine). Proteins are made up of chains of amino acids. DNA passes on its information to protein factories (ribosomes) in the cytoplasm of the cell by creating a messenger acid—messenger ribonucleic acid (mRNA).

A. To make mRNA, the DNA ladder separates lengthwise, separating the bases of each strand.

B. One of the newly separated DNA strands is used as a template to make an mRNA strand.

C. The mRNA strand contains the bases of DNA, but thymine is replaced with a new base: uracil. mRNA leaves the nucleus of the cell and passes into the cytoplasm where it gives the ribosomes the information they need to produce proteins.

D. The two chains of DNA now join back together to form a spiral ladder once more.

DNA

Deoxyribonucleic acid, commonly known as DNA, is a code for life found in almost every living organism. It is found in strands known as chromosomes in the interior part of a cell—the nucleus. Each chromosome contains genes, which are blueprints of genetic information and are made up of segments of DNA. DNA also contains the blueprints for making proteins and for replicating itself.

The structure of DNA was discovered in 1953 by Francis Crick and James Watson, who were awarded the Nobel prize for medicine in 1962 for their discovery.

The DNA molecule is a double helix, resembling a spiral ladder. The sides of the ladder are made up by alternating units of phosphate and a sugar, deoxyribose. Attached to the sugar units are the rungs of the ladder, which are made up of combinations of bases. There are four bases: adenine, cytosine, guanine and thymine (A, C, G, and T).

Each rung in the ladder consists of two bases. Because of chemical attractions, only a few combinations of bases are possible: A–T, T–A, C–G, or G–C. Lengthwise up and down the ladder, the bases form different patterns, for example ATCGAT. Three of these bases together form a codon which encodes a single amino acid of a protein. The order of the bases in one strand (half) of the ladder determines the order of the bases in the other strand. For example, if the bases in one strand are ATCGAT, the bases in the opposite strand would be TAGCTA.

Before a cell divides, the DNA duplicates. The ladder splits lengthwise, separating the bases of each strand. Then, with the help of special enzymes, the bases in each half ladder pick up their matching mates. The As attach to Ts, the Ts to As, the Gs to Cs, and the Cs to Gs. In this way, each new ladder becomes a duplicate of the original ladder. When the cell divides, the two new cells have identical DNA molecules.

DNA also determines the proteins a cell makes. It does this by encoding a messenger ribonucleic acid (mRNA) with information needed to make proteins in "cell factories" called ribosomes in the cytoplasm of the cell. The amino acid structure of each protein made by a ribosome corresponds to a particular sequence of bases in the DNA.

If there is a mistake made during DNA replication and a sequence is altered (known as a mutation) the composition of a protein may be also be changed. The result may be a genetic disorder. There are an estimated 4,200 diseases caused by genetic defects.

The Human Genome Project is mapping the entire genetic code of DNA. It will be completed early in the twenty-first century, holding out the promise of an understanding, and possibly a cure, for inherited disorders.

SEE ALSO *Cells, Chromosomes, Genes*

DOMESTIC VIOLENCE

Any abuse in a relationship situation can be described as domestic violence. The abuse is most commonly perpetrated by a male towards his female partner. It can be physical assault, rape or other sexual assault, and emotional or psychological abuse such as demeaning and making threats. Very often the abuse is a combination of these.It occurs in all socioeconomic, cultural and educational backgrounds.

Domestic violence is the major cause of injury to women in the 15 to 44 age group in the US; 15- to 24-year-olds are most commonly the victims of sexual assault and domestic violence is the cause of one-third of the murders of women. It was not until the women's movement of the 1970s that domestic violence became a matter for the courts.

Experts believe that it is widely under-reported because family matters are still thought of by many as private, even when they include violence. There is often an element of denial of the situation, and those involved are frightened of the legal consequences. Some research indicates that nearly 30 percent of relationships are believed to have suffered from violence at some stage.

Men can also experience domestic violence. Because they are more likely to report it than women are, it can seem that the percentage of men who suffer from domestic violence is higher than the actual incidence of abuse. However, data indicate that women are six times more likely to be victims than men.

Historically women have been regarded as the property of men, and wife-beating was acceptable and even considered necessary in medieval times. Patriarchal (male-dominated) societies with traditions which allow husbands to punish wives physically and afford women a lower socioeconomic status than men still exist in many parts of the world, and where these traditional laws have been replaced there are still vestiges of male proprietorial rights over the women and children in their family.

There is usually more than one reason why violence occurs in a relationship. Causes include low income, alcohol or substance abuse, growing up in a violent family, unemployment and low job satisfaction, sexual difficulties, and not knowing other ways to cope or behave. The age of the couple involved can also be a factor: violence is more common in couples under 30 years of age.

The effects of domestic violence are both physical and emotional. Physical injuries include bruises, cuts, burns, stab wounds, broken bones and miscarriage. Consequent emotional problems include eating disorders, alcohol and substance abuse, psychological disturbances, anxiety and depression.

A woman who wants to leave an abusive relationship, particularly if she comes from a lower socioeconomic background, may often have to choose between the abuse or living on the streets. Shelters and refuges which have been established for women and children in this situation are frequently filled to capacity. This situation can add to the woman's dilemma. Victims will often leave a violent relationship and then return because of the economic, emotional, cultural and social difficulties which they encounter when they leave.

Escaping from a violent situation is the best course of action when children are involved. Research reveals that in the US domestic violence is the crime which is increasing the fastest. It also indicates that children who come from violent homes where they are either the witnesses to domestic violence, or the victims of it, or both, are likely to grow up to become violent adolescents and adults.

Once a woman, with or without children, has found a place in a shelter or refuge she will then have access to a number of different programs, including legal aid and counseling. There is also an increasing number of treatment programs being established to which courts may send offenders.

SEE ALSO *Child abuse*

DOPPLER ULTRASONOGRAPHY

Named after Christian Doppler (Austrian physicist, 1803–1853), Doppler ultrasound is used to measure the flow of a liquid, usually blood flow. It is based on the principle that when a source of sound or light moves rapidly the pitch of sound appears to get higher as the object approaches and lower as the object recedes. It can measure the rate and quantity of the flow and therefore highlight any abnormalities or obstructions in the circulatory system.

SEE ALSO *Ultrasound*

DOUBLE VISION

Double vision, known clinically as diplopia, occurs when the movements of the two eyes are not properly coordinated. The eyes are moved by a number of "extraocular" muscles in the bony cavity known as the orbit. Normally when we choose to view an object, both eyes are directed towards the object. If the muscles moving one eye are weakened or paralyzed the patient will not be able to turn that eye in the correct direction. Consequently, the good eye looks at the object, the bad eye looks elsewhere, causing two quite different images to reach the brain which results in double vision.

SEE ALSO *Eye, Sight*

DOWN SYNDROME

Down syndrome, or trisomy 21, is a congenital defect: a person with Down syndrome has three number 21 chromosomes instead of two. An affected person survives into adulthood, but with a range of physical and mental abnormalities.

There are several characteristic physical features of Down syndrome. The head is round, flat and may be smaller than normal (microcephaly). The ears are small and low-set, the nose is flattened and the eyes slant upwards (Mongolian slant). The inner corner of the eyes may have a rounded fold of skin rather than coming to a point. The hands are broad with short fingers and often have a single palmar crease (simian crease). Normal growth and development is retarded; most Down syndrome children never reach average adult height.

The most significant feature of the condition is that intellectual development is retarded; an affected child will have an IQ (intelligence quotient) of about 60 although some are borderline retarded or have low average range IQs. Adult Down sufferers have an average mental age of about eight years. Nearly all Down syndrome adults will develop Alzheimer's disease and become prematurely senile.

Down syndrome is often associated with other congenital disorders such as heart and intestinal defects, chronic respiratory and ear infections, and visual problems. About half of Down syndrome children are born with a heart defect, often a hole between the two sides of the heart. Hirschsprung's disease (congenital aganglionic megacolon), which can cause intestinal obstruction, occurs more frequently in Down syndrome. Children with Down syndrome also have a higher than average incidence of acute lymphocytic leukemia.

The older a woman becomes, the greater her chance of having a Down syndrome child. Between the ages of 35 and 39, a mother has a 1.5 percent chance of having a child with Down syndrome; over the age of 40 she has a 5 percent chance. Down syndrome can be detected in the first few months of pregnancy by examination of fetal chromosomes from a sample of the fluid surrounding the fetus obtained by amniocentesis. Chorionic villus sampling (CVS) can provide the same information. If Down syndrome is detected, the woman may then be offered the chance to terminate the pregnancy.

There is no cure for Down syndrome. But with specialized education and training, most affected children can learn to look after themselves and to lead useful lives. Heart and gastrointestinal defects may require surgical correction. Down syndrome can be inherited, so the mother of a child with Down syndrome could be at increased risk of having another. However, inherited Down syndrome is rare: in most cases, subsequent children will be normal. It is advisable for parents to seek genetic counseling before they begin another pregnancy.

SEE ALSO *Amniocentesis, Chorionic villus sampling, Chromosomal abnormalities, Chromosomes, Genetic counseling, Intellectual disability*

Down syndrome

The physical features of Down syndrome are easily recognizable. The head is round and flat, eyes slant upwards and the nose is flat. The hands are broad with short fingers.

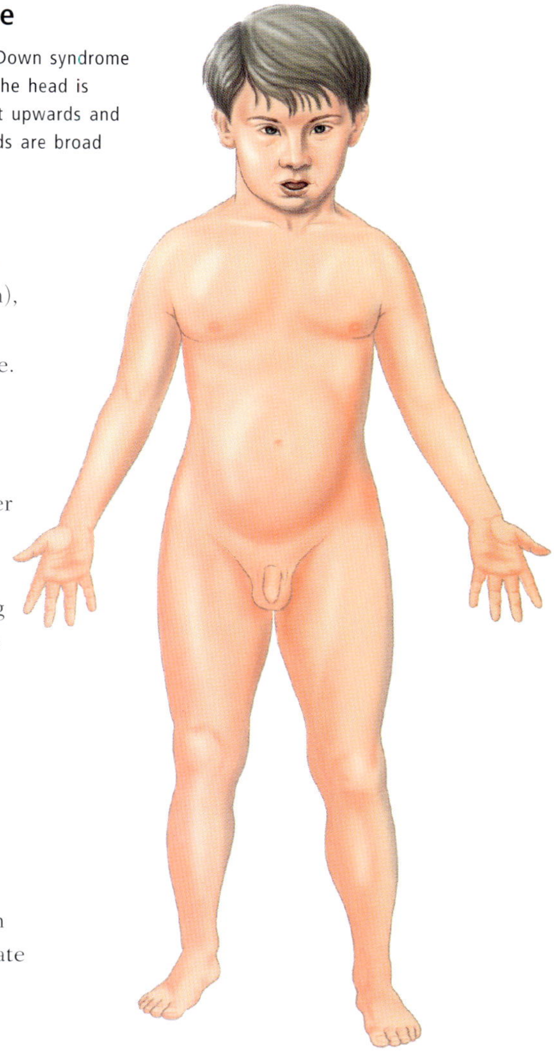

DRUG DEPENDENCE

The use of drugs in a harmful way is described as "drug abuse". Many substances can be abused, from prescription drugs to petroleum vapors inhaled to gain a "high". Drug abusers may be habitual users without being dependent, or addicted ("dependence" is currently the term used instead of "addiction", and a dependent person is a drug "user" rather than an "addict"). Dependence is usually considered to involve both psychological and physical dependency. Often a description includes the name of the drug, e.g. "morphine type" drug dependence.

Physical dependence arises as the user's body adapts to the repeated use of the drug. Tolerance to the drug is high (meaning there is a need to continually increase the dose to obtain the original effect). Psychological dependence is present when users believe they cannot cope without the drug. This compulsion can be extremely strong and may be due to underlying emotional issues.

Drug dependence is characterized by loss of control over the use of a drug. The voluntary decision to take a drug is replaced by a craving that arises as the effects of the last intake wear off. The craving can be so great

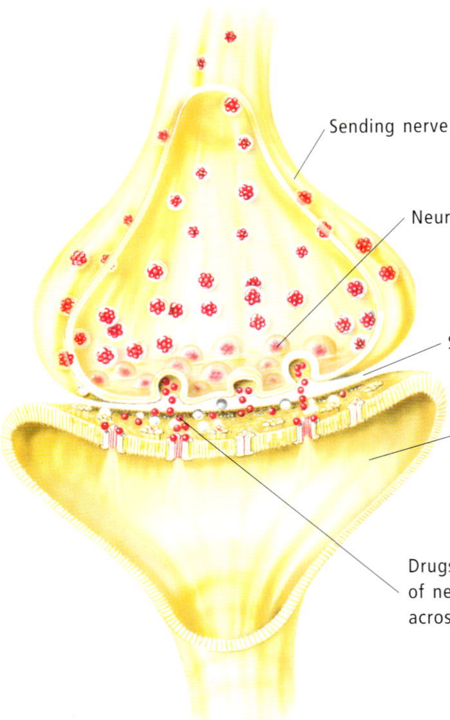

Drug mechanisms

Drugs act on the body in a number of different ways. Some work by blocking the action of neurotransmitters, which carry chemical signals between nerves. These drugs prevent an impulse from traveling from one nerve to another. Drugs that work in this way include some anesthetics and cardiovascular drugs, antihypertensives and antipsychotics.

Drug dependence

With frequent and prolonged use of many drugs, tolerance develops and the user must take more of the drug to get the required effect. In the case of some depressants, such as narcotics, increased doses may depress the respiratory centers in the brain stem, ultimately causing overdose and death.

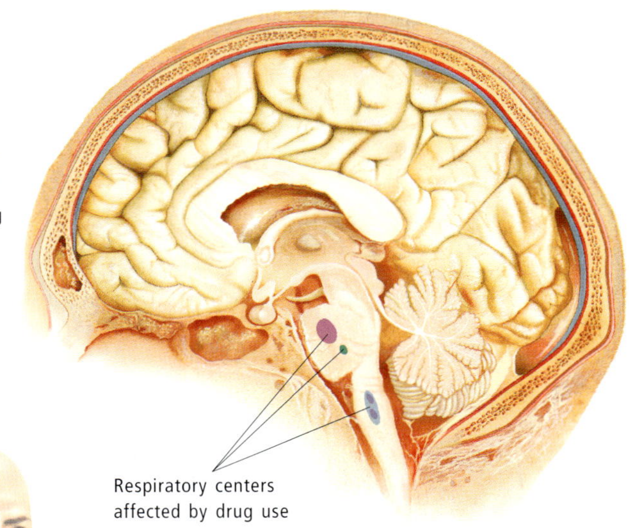

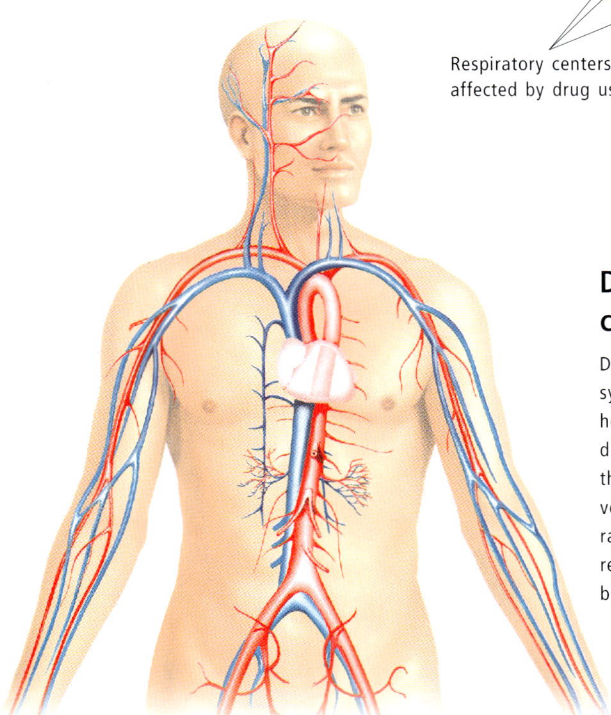

Drugs and the cardiovascular system

Drugs that act on the cardiovascular system are used to treat hypertension, heart disease and peripheral vascular disease. They usually work by acting on the muscle in the heart and the blood vessels, for example by slowing the heart rate, making the heart pump harder, or by relaxing the blood vessels and lowering the blood pressure in the circulatory system.

that the user's thoughts and activities are directed solely toward getting more of the drug. This is destructive of other facets of life.

Dependence may dramatically alter behavior. Work, social responsibilities and personal hygiene may be neglected as more time is spent under the influence of drugs or in chasing further supplies. Drug users often lose jobs, families and friends this way. Health will suffer if drugs replace normal food intake. The person may suffer nutritional disorders or acquire diseases from contaminated syringes. Dependence is often a route to crime and prostitution, since drugs, especially street drugs, are very costly.

Personality problems, social pressures, inability to deal with relationships, and life crises all may provide impetus to use drugs.

Types of drugs and their effects

Drugs of dependence can be grouped as depressants, stimulants and hallucinogens.

Depressants include alcohol, opiates (morphine, heroin, methadone, codeine, pethidine), barbiturates, tranquilizers, anxiolytics, hypnotics and inhalants such as petroleum, glue, paint thinners and lighter fluid. Effects vary from mild (relaxation, euphoria) to extreme (slurred speech, uncoordinated movement, reduced breathing and heart rate) with large doses causing nausea, vomiting and occasionally death.

Stimulants are drugs that affect the nervous system. Depending on the strength and type of the particular substance, stimulants generally make you more alert and active, help you stay awake, reduce hunger and elevate mood. Legal stimulants include caffeine and nicotine, and ephedrine, which is an ingredient in some medicines used for respiratory conditions. Illegal stimulants include Ecstasy, amphetamines and cocaine.

Hallucinogenic drugs include lysergic acid diethylamide (LSD), mescaline and psilocybin. Marijuana also has hallucinogenic properties. All of these drugs can produce psychological dependency and offer an altered perception of reality, providing complete, if temporary, escape. Hallucinogens can be the cause of psychosis in certain people.

How dependence develops

Just as there are many different types of drugs, there are many different types and patterns of dependence, as well as a variety of causes. Explanations put forward suggest that users display personalities that make them more vulnerable to dependence. Certain types of dependence seem to be inherited and are described as familial because no clear genetic cause has yet been found.

There is no such thing as instant dependence, although the period of use before becoming dependent may be very short. With many drugs, but not all, the user develops a rising level of tolerance to the drug. This may result in the person using an increasing quantity of the drug each time.

Detoxification and treatment

Repeated drug use causes the level of substances derived from the drug in body tissues and bloodstream to rise. When use stops, these substances are excreted and blood levels fall. This is the process of detoxification, which is the body's natural process of breakdown and excretion of waste products. But in the drug-dependent person, this fall in toxin levels triggers craving and often results in severely unpleasant physical and psychological withdrawal symptoms. These can include nausea, cramps, sweating, restlessness, seizures, insomnia, headaches, tremors, delirium, depression and suicidal impulses—all varying with the particular drug and its quantity and strength.

It is extremely dangerous to come off any drug of dependence without professional help. Sometimes heroin users are given methadone under medical supervision as a substitute for heroin. Although methadone is a drug of dependence, it is safer than heroin and users are able to live relatively normal lives. Medical treatment can also include admission to a hospital detoxification unit. The patient may be given drugs such as mild tranquilizers to aid withdrawal, and naltrexone to help stop the physical cravings. Patients who are dependent on tranquilizers or anxiolytics are given gradually decreasing doses before complete withdrawal happens.

Physical detoxification is only the first step—the next challenge is to learn how to live without drugs. Many experts believe that no dependent person is ever able to use again with safety, and recommend total abstinence from all drugs, including alcohol. There is a much greater chance of long-term recovery if detoxification is followed by several weeks in a treatment or rehabilitation center. These centers offer residential programs and provide psychological counseling, education, group therapy and nutritional guidance. Sometimes extended rehabilitation (six months to a year) in a long-term center or halfway house is advised.

Recovery is likely to be more successful if treatment is followed up by further counseling (particularly if there are underlying mental and emotional disorders), and regular attendance at Narcotics Anonymous (NA) meetings. NA is a self-help program run along similar lines to Alcoholics Anonymous. At NA meetings, recovering drug users share their stories, and support each other in leading healthy, fulfilling lives.

Social consequences

Drug dependence is a social problem imposing massive personal and social costs. It is perpetuated by a constant supply of illegal drugs which has become a worldwide industry fueled by criminal activity in drug agriculture and manufacturing, the transfer of huge sums of money between countries, and the distribution to users. The huge illegal rewards of this trade provide funds and opportunity for corruption of officials at every stage. The cost to nations is increased medical care, loss of productivity, street crime and violence.

SEE ALSO *Alcoholism, Anxiolytics, Barbiturates, Cocaine, Detoxification, Hallucinogens, Heroin, Marijuana, Methadone, Morphine, Narcotics, Nicotine, Psychosis, Psychotropic drugs, Sedatives, Solvent sniffing, Stimulants, Tranquilizers, Withdrawal*

DRUG INTERACTIONS

Drugs can interact with other chemicals in the body, and these include other drugs. Chemical interactions between drugs may change the make-up of those drugs and render them ineffective, less (or more) effective, or toxic (poisonous).

The risk of adverse drug interactions is higher in older people, because their vital organs process drugs less easily and because they tend to have more diseases and take more drugs than younger persons.

The following types of drugs commonly interact with other medications: antibiotics, anticoagulants, anticonvulsants, antidepressants, antihypertensives, decongestants, and sedatives. Common antibiotics (such as ampicillin, amoxycillin, neomycin and tetracycline) and anticonvulsants can interfere with the effect of oral contraceptives (birth control pills), and increase the risk of pregnancy.

Special care should be taken with heart drugs. The combination of beta-blockers and calcium channel blockers, for example, may slow the heart rate excessively or cause heart failure. Beta-blockers can aggravate asthma and prevent diabetic patients from recognizing the signs of low blood pressure due to an insulin reaction. The combination of calcium channel blockers and digoxin can also slow the heart rate. Angiotensin-converting enzyme (ACE) inhibitors can cause dangerously high potassium levels in people who use potassium supplements. Diuretics combined with digoxin can cause dangerously low potassium or magnesium levels, which can cause heart arrhythmias.

Certain foods or beverages can interfere with drugs as well. Foods most likely to interfere with medications include dairy products, alcohol, caffeine, salt, and fruit juices. For instance, some antidepressants (those known as MAO inhibitors) are dangerous when consumed with anything containing tyramine (such as red wine, cheese and beer). It is advisable not to take over the counter drugs with other medications. Many common medications contain the same antihistamines as anti-cold preparations; you can get an unexpected double dose by taking an allergy drug along with some cold remedies.

Harmful interactions can also occur between herbal products and drugs. Warfarin taken with ginseng, garlic, ginkgo, ginger and feverfew may result in bleeding. Echinacea and zinc may negate the effects of cyclosporine. Ginseng may interfere with digoxin. It may also cause headaches, trembling, or manic episodes if taken with phenelzine sulfate. Saint John's wort and saw palmetto may inhibit anemia drugs. Drugs can also interact with alcohol and tobacco; smoking reduces the effectiveness of many medications.

Always ask your physician or pharmacist if the drug you have been prescribed can interact with any foods, other medications, or herbal remedies you may be taking.

SEE ALSO *Antibiotics, Anticoagulants, Anticonvulsants, Antidepressants, Antihistamines, Beta-blockers, Diuretics, Sedatives*

D

DRUGS

A drug (also called a medication or a pharmaceutical) is a compound that is introduced into the body for a therapeutic effect, to cure a disease or to relieve or control the symptoms of a disease. There are thousands of drugs available. Common types of drugs include antibiotics, vaccines, antiserums and immunoglobulins, cardiovascular drugs, analgesics, anesthetics, sedatives, hypnotics, diuretics, hormones and vitamins.

Some drugs are available only with a prescription from a physician, while others are available "over the counter" from a drugstore, pharmacy or other outlet. Drugs may be sold under a particular brand name, or they may be "generic"; that is, sold unbranded. Generic drugs are often cheaper than branded drugs. Drugs (for example, antibiotics) may need to be taken for a short period, e.g. an acute chest infection, or they may need to be continued for life, for example insulin for certain diabetics.

Administering drugs

Drugs are usually administered either orally or by injection. Oral medications can be taken as syrup, capsules or tablets. They are absorbed in the small intestine along with food. Injected drugs can be administered via intramuscular or intravenous routes; drugs administered intravenously begin acting almost immediately, while those administered intramuscularly can take minutes or hours to take effect, depending on the drug.

Occasionally a drug many be given subcutaneously, that is, injected into the tissue below the skin. Some drugs can be inhaled, such as asthma medications. Others can be administered as suppositories, placed into and absorbed via the rectum.

Side effects

Drugs may have side effects, which differ from person to person. Some are minor and can be tolerated; nausea and a skin rash, for example, are common to many drugs. In other cases side effects can cause serious illness. If side effects are not outweighed by the medical benefits of taking the drug, the drug should be discontinued. Drugs may produce allergic reactions in some people.

Allergic reactions may range from a slight rash to a fatal shock. It is not possible to predict whether someone will have an allergic reaction to a prescribed drug, though they are more common in older persons. One of the biggest risk factors is a previous reaction to a drug, since drug-induced immune responses may persist for years. A drug that causes an allergic reaction should be discontinued. The reaction may require antihistamines or corticosteroids.

Some medications can cause birth defects, especially when taken early on in pregnancy. A physician should always be consulted before taking a drug during pregnancy. In general, physicians are reluctant to prescribe drugs unless necessary, though some believe reluctance to take drugs during pregnancy does more harm than good.

Drug resistance

Drug resistance has emerged as a major problem in recent years, particularly in the case of antibiotics. Increasingly, disease-causing organisms are able to resist eradication, making infections more difficult to treat. To avoid resistance, antibiotics should only be used against microorganisms sensitive to them (and not against viruses, for example). Inadequate duration of treatment also leads to resistance, so the full course of antibiotics should always be completed.

SEE ALSO *Allergies, Analgesics, Anesthesia, Antihistamines, Corticosteroids, Diuretics, Hormones, Hypnotics, Immunization, Insulin, Sedatives, Vitamins*

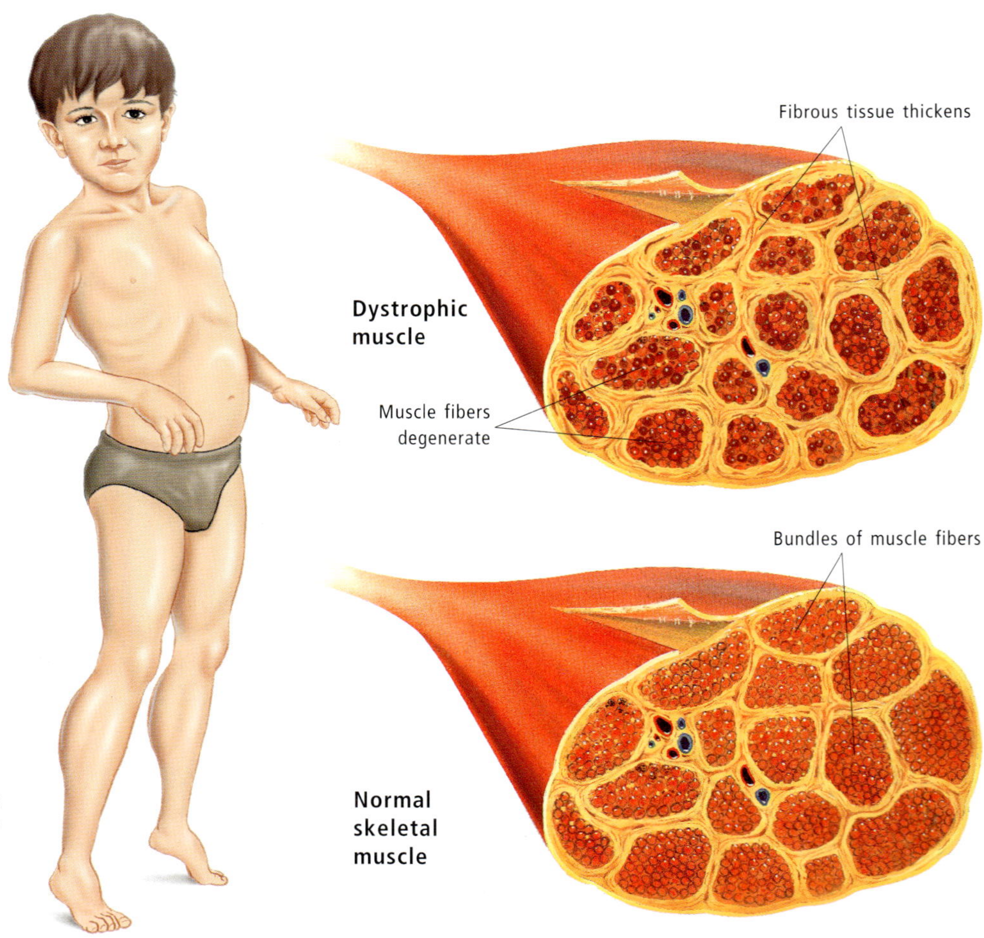

Duchenne muscular dystrophy

This disease affects young boys, and usually presents as muscle weakness in and around the pelvis. The weakness spreads to the limbs and as muscles weaken they also enlarge. Progressive muscle wasting and weakness occurs in Duchenne muscular dystrophy when the normal structure of skeletal muscle deteriorates. Individual muscle fibers degenerate, while the tissue that surrounds them thickens.

D

DUCHENNE MUSCULAR DYSTROPHY

This is a rare inherited disorder caused by an abnormal gene that causes rapidly progressing weakness of the muscles. It is the most serious of the muscular dystrophies, a group of disorders that cause malfunction and degeneration of voluntary muscles.

Duchenne muscular dystrophy occurs in boys from infancy to age six. There is progressive muscle weakness and wasting of muscles, especially in the legs and pelvis. Heart muscle is damaged and the bones of the chest become malformed, causing respiratory difficulty. By their teens, most sufferers are confined to a wheelchair. There is no known cure, and sufferers usually die by their mid-teens. The disorder can be detected in the fetus by genetic studies performed during pregnancy.

SEE ALSO *Congenital abnormalities, Genetic counseling, Muscle, Muscular dystrophy*

DUMPING SYNDROME

Dumping syndrome is a digestion disorder that occurs in a patient who has had an operation to remove part or all of the stomach. Most patients experience the problem to a minor degree for one to six months after the surgery, but in about 1–2 percent of cases, symptoms persist. The cause of dumping syndrome is not fully understood; however the symptoms result from the remnants of the stomach "dumping" its contents too quickly into the small intestine after a meal. The affected person experiences explosive diarrhea, abdominal cramps, belching and vomiting. There may also be headache, dizziness and sweating.

The condition can be relieved by eating several small meals instead of one or two large ones per day. The meals should be low in carbohydrates and high in fat and protein. Most affected persons recover spontaneously within a few months to a year.

SEE ALSO *Diarrhea, Digestive system, Intestines, Stomach*

DUODENAL ULCERS

The duodenum is that part of the gut immediately beyond the stomach. Ulcers are formed when the mucus and internal epithelium (lining) of the gut are broken down, e.g. by aspirin-like drugs or the *Helicobacter* bacterium, thus exposing the deeper layers of the gut wall. Duodenal ulcers belong to a group of diseases of the gut called peptic ulcers. These peptic ulcers arise when the highly damaging stomach juices, which contain acid and enzymes designed to break down protein, erode the surface of the stomach or duodenum.

Patients with duodenal ulcers often complain of pain in the upper abdomen, which is usually relieved by food, milk or antacid preparations. They may also be tender in the upper abdomen and may occasionally experience vomiting. Complications of duodenal ulcers include heavy bleeding, obstruction of the duodenum, or perforation of the duodenal wall with spilling of the duodenal contents into the abdominal cavity. The last complication may cause life-threatening peritonitis, or inflammation of the tissues of the abdominal cavity.

SEE ALSO *Duodenum, Peptic ulcers, Stomach*

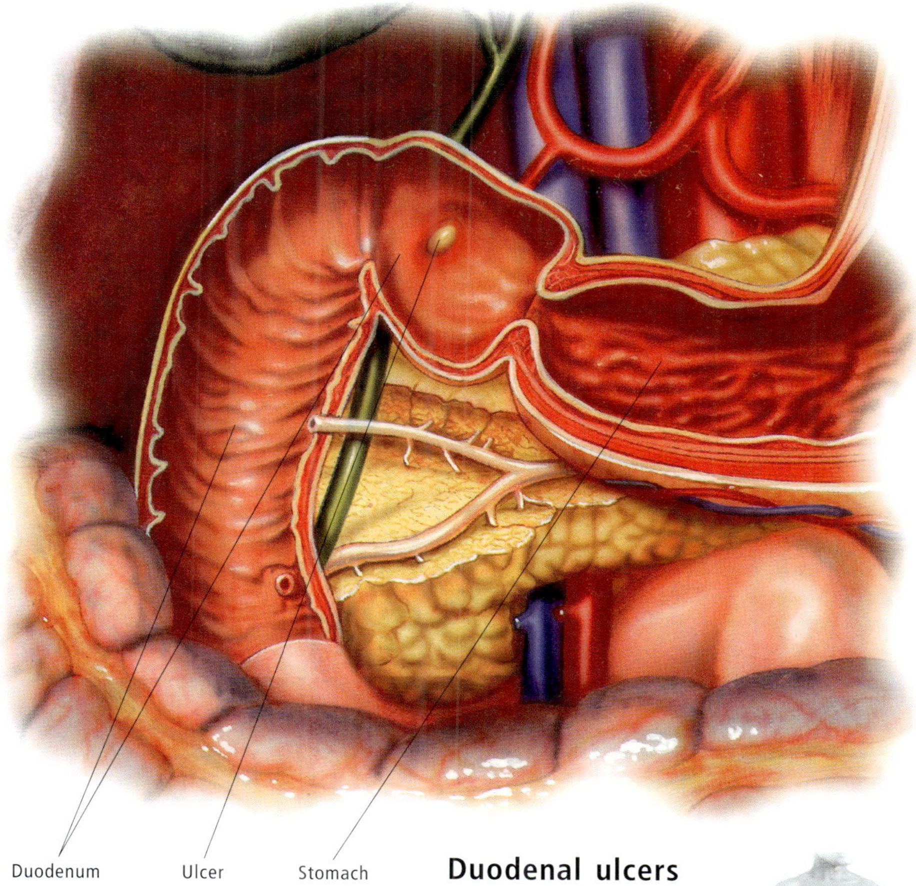

Duodenal ulcers

A round or oval sore is formed when the lining of the duodenum is eroded by stomach juices. These ulcers are the most common type of peptic ulcer.

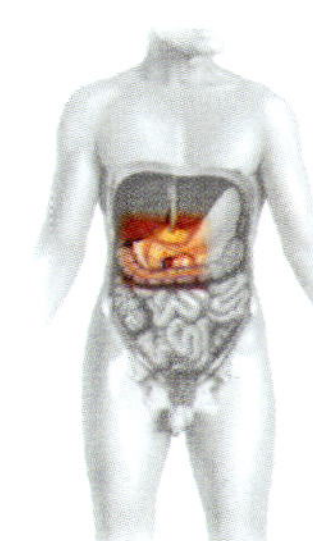

DUODENUM

The duodenum is the part of the gut directly beyond the stomach and is the first part of the small intestine. It has a "C" shape, with the curvature of the "C" encircling the head of the pancreas. The duodenum receives the contents of the stomach once the stomach has added digestive enzymes and acid to the food and begun the digestion of protein. This means that the duodenum must be able to withstand periodic exposure to the highly acid stomach contents. The duodenum is also the site where bile, from the liver and gallbladder, and pancreatic enzymes, from the pancreas, are brought into contact with food.

The interior of the duodenum has a folded surface, which increases the available surface area for absorption of sugars, fats and amino acids. While some of the absorp-

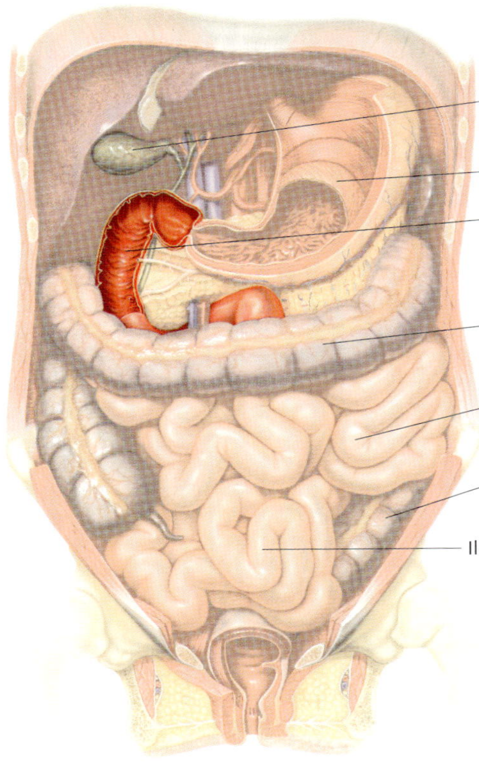

Duodenum

The first 10 inches (25 centimeters) of the small intestine is known as the duodenum. It receives the contents of the stomach, including digestive enzymes and acid, and is the site where bile is brought into contact with food.

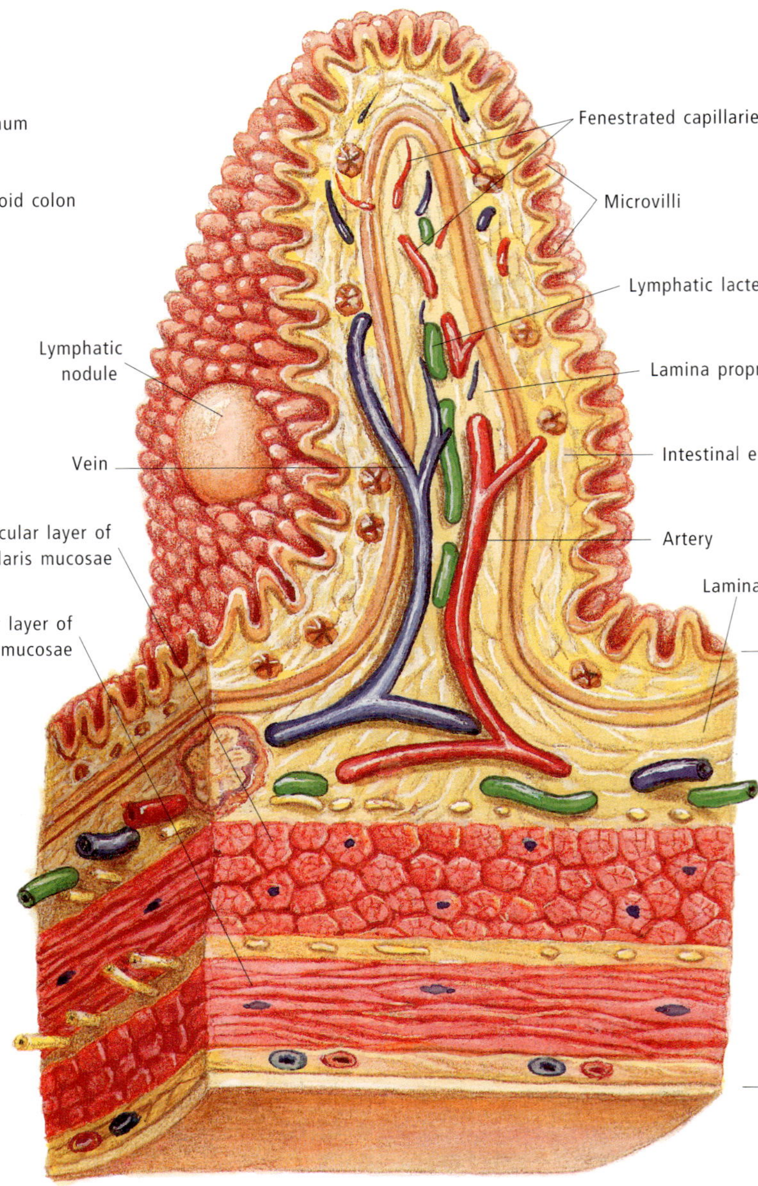

Duodenal lining

The wall of the duodenum has folds covered in tiny finger-like villi which increase the surface area available for the absorption of sugars, fats and amino acids. Fat and lipids are absorbed by the lymphatic nodules; sugars and amino acids are absorbed into the bloodstream through the arteries.

tion of these nutrients will begin in the duodenum, the other parts of the small intestine, the jejunum and ileum, will continue the process.

The duodenum is a common place for ulcers to occur because of its periodic exposure to stomach juices. It is only very rarely the primary site of malignant disease (cancer).

SEE ALSO *Duodenal ulcers, Gallbladder, Ileum, Intestines, Liver, Pancreas*

DUPUYTREN'S CONTRACTURE

Dupuytren's contracture is a painless thickening and contracture of the connective tissue beneath the skin on the palm of the hand. A small, painless nodule eventually develops into a cord-like band, which prevents the fingers from straightening. The fourth and fifth fingers are the most affected. In advanced cases, the hand looks like a claw. One or both hands may be affected. Sometimes it can affect the soles of the feet as well.

The cause is not known, but it may be inherited. It is more common in men over the age of forty, and in alcoholics and persons with diabetes or epilepsy. Treatment may involve an operation to remove the thickened fibrous tissue and release the ligaments, followed by physical therapy. This usually restores normal movement of the fingers.

SEE ALSO *Connective tissue, Finger, Hand*

DWARFISM

Dwarfism is the condition of being abnormally small in physical stature. A dwarf may be born normal, but growth is arrested during the childhood years because of malnutrition, chronic illness or growth hormone deficiency. The affected person (also known as a midget) has normal body proportions but is smaller than normal.

So-called "true" or genetic dwarfism is congenital (present at birth) and results in abnormal body proportions, that is, disproportionate stunting. Achondroplasia, in which growth of the bones of the limbs is retarded, is the most common form of congenital dwarfism. An achondroplastic dwarf has a normal-sized head and trunk, but proportionally short arms and legs.

SEE ALSO *Achondroplasia, Growth disorders, Pituitary gland*

DYSARTHRIA

Dysarthria is difficulty in speaking. It differs from dysphasia (aphasia) in that in dysarthria, the speech impediment is due to inability to articulate speech rather than inability to recognize and formulate speech.

Dysarthria may be caused by poorly fitting dentures, alcohol intoxication, stroke affecting the part of the cortex which controls face or larynx muscles, or damage to the nerves that supply those muscles. It may be temporary and reversible as in alcohol intoxication, or permanent as in nerve injury. In irreversible cases, speech therapy may improve the symptoms.

SEE ALSO *Aphasia, Dysphasia, Speech*

DYSENTERY

Dysentery is an inflammatory disease of the large bowel, common in tropical areas where living conditions are crowded and sanitation is poor. In areas of Africa, Latin America, Southeast Asia and India, it is endemic.

In humans there are two main forms: bacterial dysentery (caused by the bacterium *Shigella sonnei*), and amebic dysentery (caused by an ameba, *Entamoeba histolytica*). Both forms are transmitted by fecally contaminated drinking water or food, or hand to hand contact. Amebic dysentery is also spread by flies and cockroaches.

Dysentery

There are two main forms of dysentery: bacillary, caused by *Shigella* bacteria (shown here) and amebic, caused by *Entamoeba histolytica*.

Both forms of dysentery cause severe diarrhea often with blood and mucus in the stools, abdominal pain and sometimes contracting spasms of the anus with a persistent desire to empty the bowels. The infection may spread through the blood to the liver, lungs, brain or other organs.

Shigella infections are mild and usually curable in a week or so with antibiotics such as ampicillin or trimethoprim. However, in a severe attack, excessive dehydration can be fatal (especially in infants and young children); serious cases require hospital care and intravenous fluid supplements.

Amebic dysentery causes attacks that come and go for months before the diagnosis is made, and which may be complicated by abscesses, particularly liver abscesses. Drugs such as metronidazole or idoquinol are usually successful in treating the condition. In tropical areas where food or water may be contaminated, one should avoid eating uncooked foods and ensure that foods are hygienically prepared. Drinking water should be boiled and foods covered to prevent flies from contaminating them.

SEE ALSO *Bacteria, Bowel, Dehydration, Diarrhea, Intestines*

DYSKINESIA

Dyskinesia is a syndrome in which there are dysfunctional involuntary movements of various body parts. These abnormal movements usually occur as side effects of medications taken to treat psychiatric or neurological conditions such as schizophrenia or Parkinson's disease. They may manifest as writhing, wriggling or jerking of body parts such as the body trunk, legs, arms, fingers, mouth, lips, or tongue. There may be facial tics, grimacing, eye blinking, lip smacking, tongue thrusting, moving one's head back or to the side, foot tapping, ankle movements, shuffled gait, and head nodding. As well as being socially embarrassing, these abnormal movements may cause difficulty walking and standing, eating and breathing. There are various forms of dyskinesia, including acute dystonia, tardive dyskinesia, akathisia and Parkinsonian syndrome. The most common is tardive dyskinesia, which is associated with long-term use of antipsychotic medications such as haldoperidol, fluphenazine, and chlorpromazine. Tardive dyskinesia may appear anywhere from three months to several years after initial use of these medications, and withdrawal from these drugs often makes the symptoms worse. If dyskinesia appears, the drug(s) which caused the symptoms must be discontinued.

Medications such as propanalol, amantadine, bromocriptine and diazepam can be given to counteract the symptoms of dykinesia but their effect is variable. The dosage of antipsychotic drugs and other medications that may cause dyskinesia should be kept as low as possible to prevent the syndrome from developing.

SEE ALSO *Antipsychotics, Parkinson's disease, Schizophrenia*

DYSLEXIA

Dyslexia is a disability which makes learning to read difficult. It can affect both children and adults despite a normal intellect and satisfactory education. Originally a catchword which covered various disorders, the term dyslexia came to refer to all types of reading, writing and spelling problems.

There is currently no internationally agreed definition of dyslexia and for that reason not all educators and psychologists will use the term. Dyslexia, as it is now generally understood, refers to its key feature: a substantial difficulty in gaining effective reading skills. Dyslexia was originally thought of a as a disability produced by poor sight, but it is now seen as result of abnormal brain function. There is no proven genetic basis for the condition, but current research into families with many affected members suggests that it may be inherited. The degree of intellectual ability plays no part, as dyslexia sufferers often score above average in non-language based intelligence tests. Unlike the ability to speak, which is innate in humans, reading skills are learned.

Children with normal vision learn to read after a gradual acquisition of pre-reading skills—the ability to follow a sequence of characters, the development of a vocabulary of language, the identification of sounds, and the recognition that sounds can be represented by letters.

This last process is one which dyslexic children are unable to develop. They are unable to decode speech into the individual sound components (phonemes) used to build words. There are 40 or more phonemes in the English language. The word pit, for example, is a combination of three sounds: "puh", "ih" and "tuh". It is essential to understand this and be able to associate the individual letters *p*, *i* and *t* with the sounds they represent before one can recognize the written word. Where the brain cannot hear the individual sounds it cannot make the association between sounds and letters, and reading skills will not properly develop.

Dyslexia is suspected when reading skills fail to match a child's intellectual level, with the key indicator being the inability to decode phonemes. This inability may affect one child in five severely enough to persist into adulthood, and at this level it may not improve with time or instruction, causing academic standards to fall gradually behind.

Identification

Before confirming a diagnosis of dyslexia it is important to investigate other possible reasons for delayed reading development, including poor hearing, poor sight, emotional disorders, environmental or family problems and poor teaching. Dyslexia produces poor readers and writers in children who are otherwise intellectually able, even above average. It has been identified in other cultures with written languages different in form and structure from English, notably Chinese, and it can affect speech.

Although dyslexia has previously been identified more in boys than girls, recent research indicates that both sexes may be represented equally and that girls with problems are simply not being identified.

Treatment

Treatment should always be attempted. It will usually take the form of special instruction aimed at developing awareness of phonemes before moving on to improving word recognition, pronunciation and reading comprehension. With early identification and special instruction it is possible to make dramatic improvements in reading ability in most affected children. Without help, problems may become extremely difficult to fix, with devastating effects on academic achievement, adult life and future employment. Specialist remedial help should always be considered to minimize the possibility of problems extending into adulthood, when they may be considerably more difficult to alleviate.

Famous people with dyslexia include screen actor Tom Cruise, and US decathlon athlete and 1996 Olympic gold medallist, Dan O'Brien.

DYSPHAGIA

Dysphagia refers to difficulty when swallowing. This constant or recurring condition can be caused by a throat disorder, lack of muscle coordination, anxiety disorder, esophageal spasm, or radiation treatment. Medications for treating other illnesses may be a trigger, as can neurological disorders such as stroke, or infections such as diphtheria. Dysphagia can also be an early symptom of cancer of the esophagus or stomach.

Dysphagia often affects elderly people and can cause chronic dehydration and malnutrition if not diagnosed and monitored. It may also cause aspiration pneumonia due

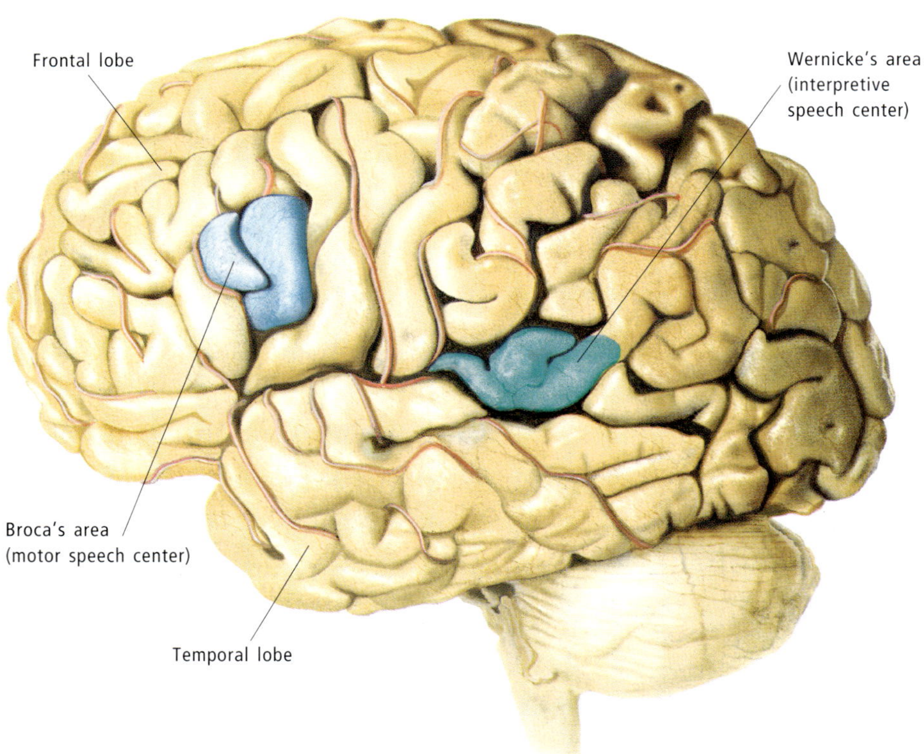

Dysphasia

Damage to the temporal and frontal lobes of the brain can result in impaired speech, known as dysphasia. The type of dysphasia varies depending on which part of the cortex is affected. Damage to Broca's area, for example, causes problems in the formation of words as this area controls motor function. Damage to Wernicke's area affects speech comprehension.

to the inhalation of food, drink, vomit or saliva into the airway. Treatment depends on the cause, though eating slowly and chewing food thoroughly may help.

SEE ALSO *Esophagus, Throat*

DYSPHASIA

Dysphasia is an impairment of speech due to damage to the brain (usually the temporal or frontal lobes). It differs from dysarthria in that the speech impediment in dysphasia is due to damage to the parts of the brain that recognize and formulate speech, whereas dysarthria is an inability to articulate speech.

Dysphasia may be caused by stroke, transient ischemic attack (TIA), head trauma or Alzheimer's disease. The impairment may vary according to which part of the brain is affected. Damage to Wernicke's area in the temporal lobe (the interpretative center) results in trouble understanding speech and the written word. Damage to Broca's area in the frontal lobe (the motor speech area) results in difficulty in mentally constructing written and spoken language. In total dysphasia, both comprehension and language formation are impaired. Speech therapy may improve the symptoms.

SEE ALSO *Aphasia, Dysarthria, Speech, Stroke*

DYSPNEA

Dyspnea is the medical term for the sensation of breathlessness or shortness of breath. The word comes from the Greek "dys-", difficulty + "pnoia", breathing. It may be a normal reaction to greater than usual exertion, such as vigorous physical exercise. However, if shortness of breath occurs without undue physical exertion, it may a sign of serious disease of the airways, lungs, or heart requiring medical attention.

See also Breathing, Lungs

DYSURIA

Dysuria is a medical term for painful or difficult urination. Dysuria is most often a symptom of urinary disorders such as cystitis or stones in the bladder. It may indicate that there is prostate disease such as prostatitis or enlarged prostate. In males, dysuria can be a symptom of gonococcal urethritis or other sexually transmitted diseases.

SEE ALSO *Bladder, Cystitis, Prostate, Urethritis, Urinary systems*

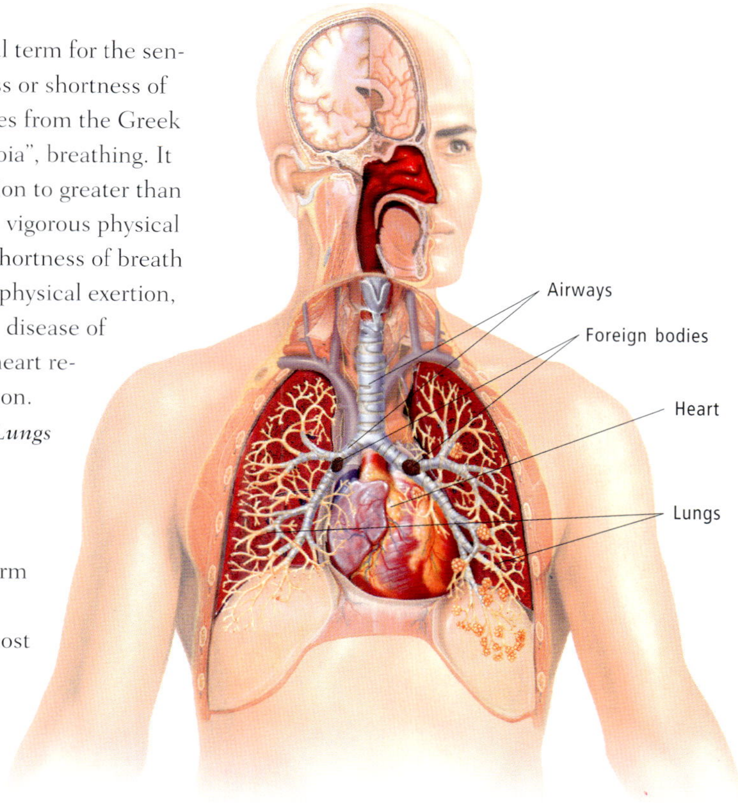

Dyspnea

Shortness of breath may be a sign of disease of the airways, lungs or heart, or obstruction of an airway by a foreign body.

D

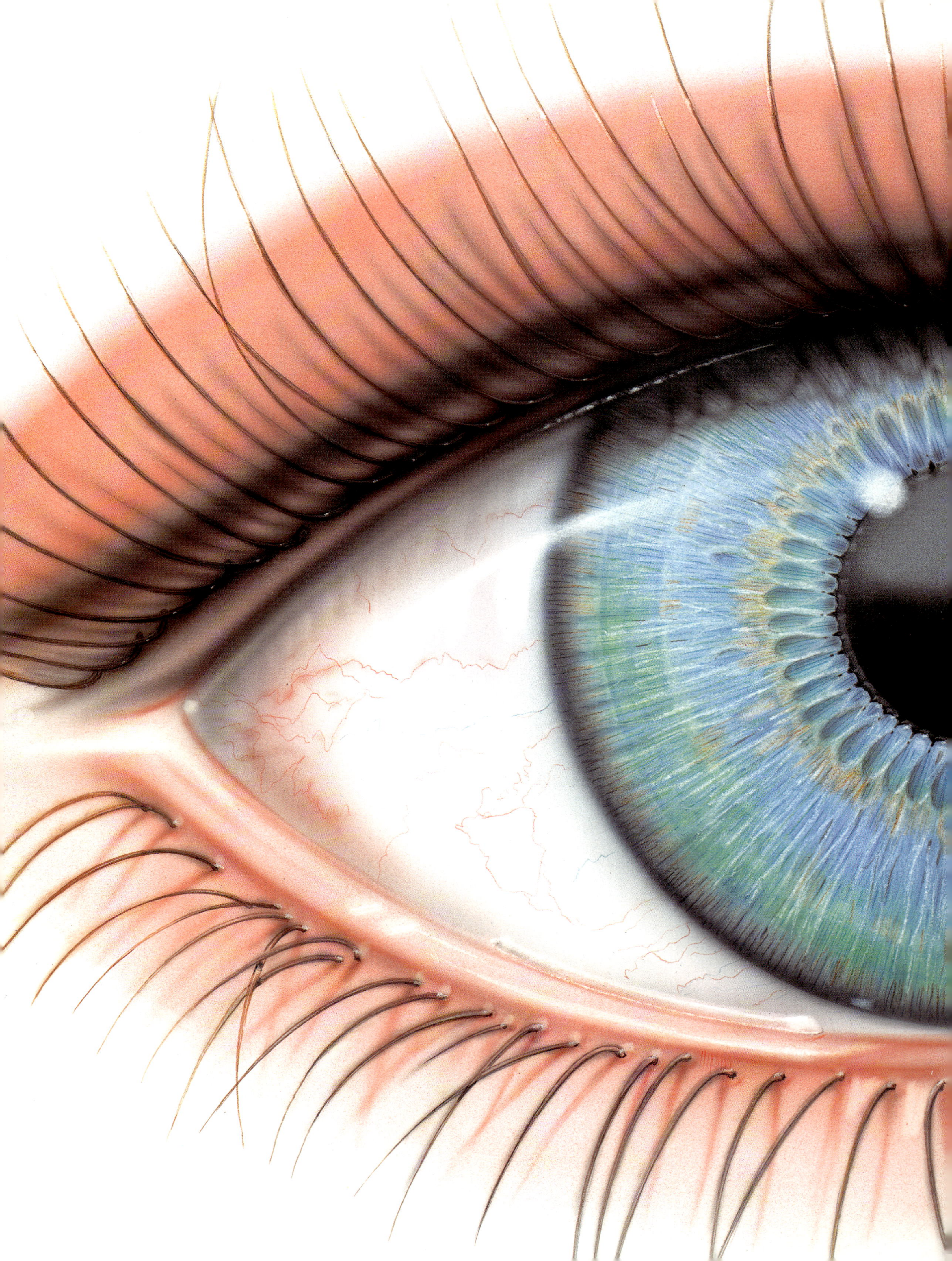

E

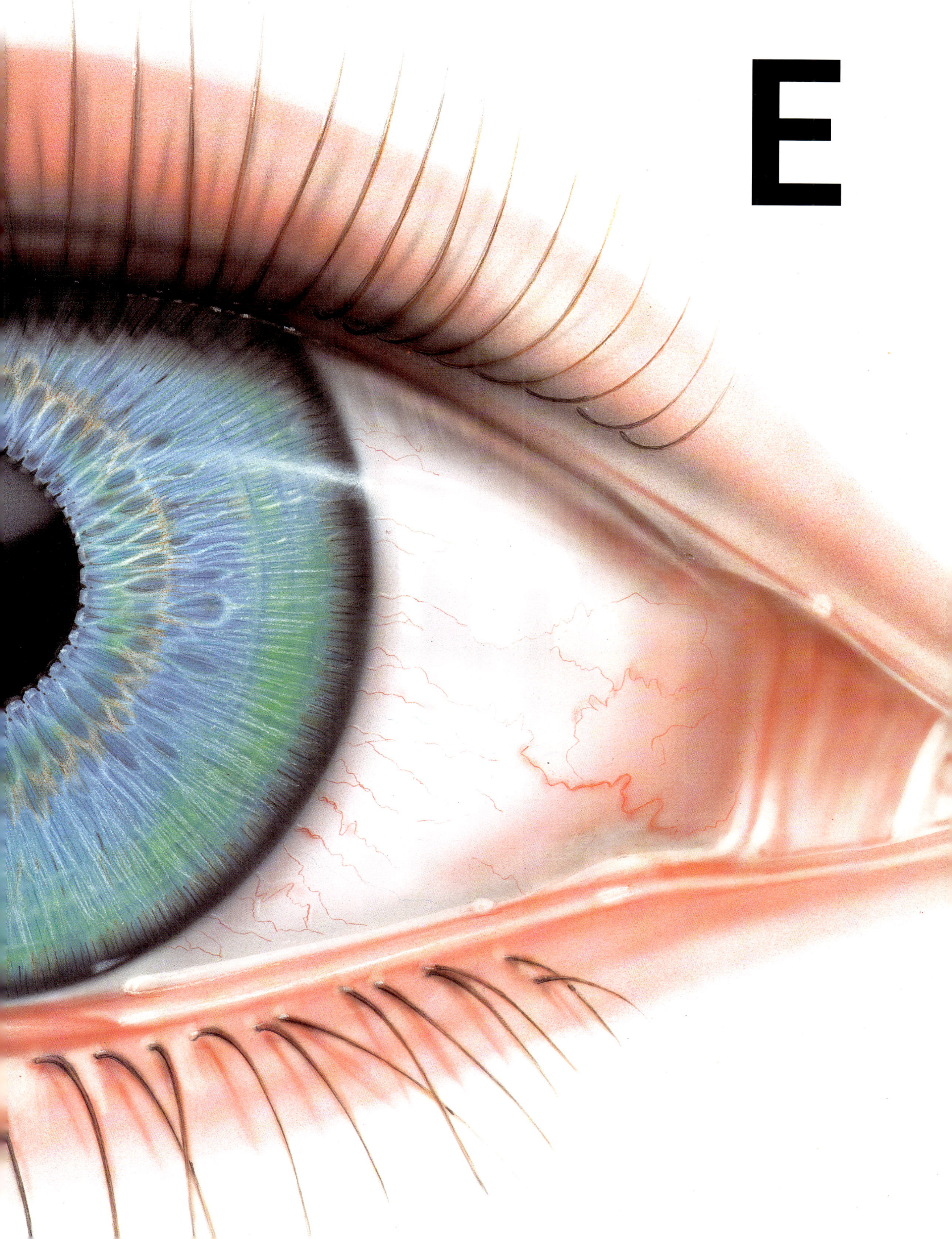

E

EAR

The ear is the organ of hearing and balance. It receives sound waves traveling through the air and changes them first into mechanical vibrations and then into electrical nerve impulses which are sent to the brain and interpreted as sounds. The ear also senses the body's position relative to gravity, sending information to the brain that allows the body to maintain postural equilibrium.

Structure and function

The ear is positioned in a hollow space in the temporal bone of the skull. It is comprised of three separate sections: the outer ear; the middle ear; and the inner ear. Each section has its own function.

The purpose of the outer ear is to collect sound waves and guide them to the tympanic membrane (the eardrum). The outer ear has three parts. The auricle (also called the pinna) funnels sound waves into the external acoustic meatus (or ear canal), a narrow canal that leads to the eardrum.

The eardrum, or tympanic membrane, is a thin, semitransparent membrane, approximately ⅓ inch (9 millimeters) in diameter. It separates the external ear from the middle ear. Wax (also called cerumen) is secreted by glands lining the auditory canal, protecting the eardrum from damage by trapping dust and dirt.

The middle ear is an irregular-shaped, air-filled space, about ¾ inch (19 millimeters) high and ⅕ inch (5 millimeters) wide. It is spanned by three tiny bones: the malleus (hammer); the incus (anvil); and the stapes (stirrup), collectively known as the ossicles.

When sound waves strike the outer surface of the eardrum, they cause the tympanic membrane to vibrate. These vibrations are mechanically transmitted through the middle ear by the ossicles, which relay them to a membrane that covers the opening into the inner ear. This opening is called the oval window.

Connecting the middle ear to the throat is a short narrow passage called the eustachian tube, which helps to ensure equal air pressure on both sides of the eardrum.

The function of the inner ear is to turn the mechanical vibrations received from the ossicles of the middle ear into nerve impulses. The inner ear contains a structure

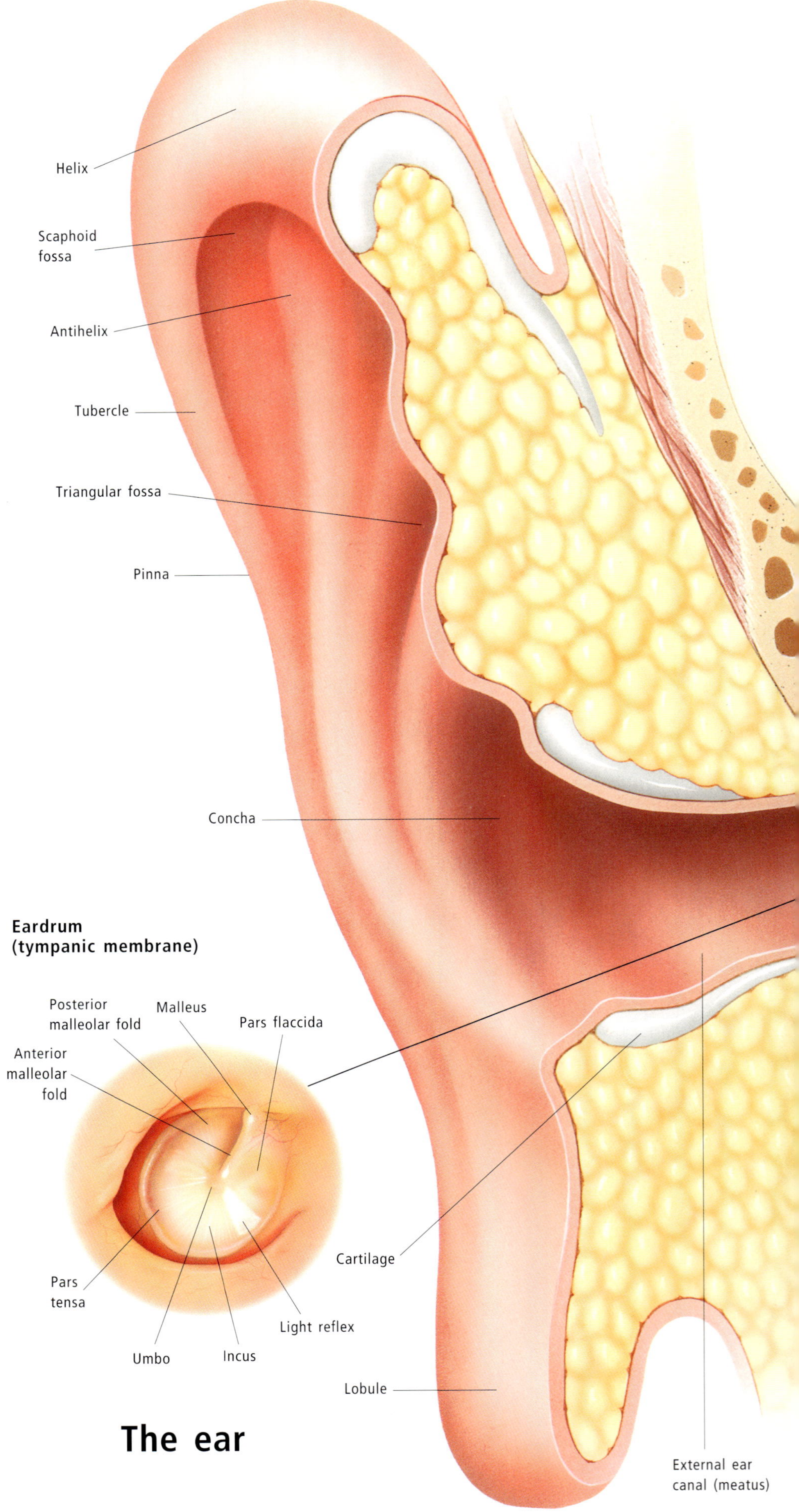

The ear

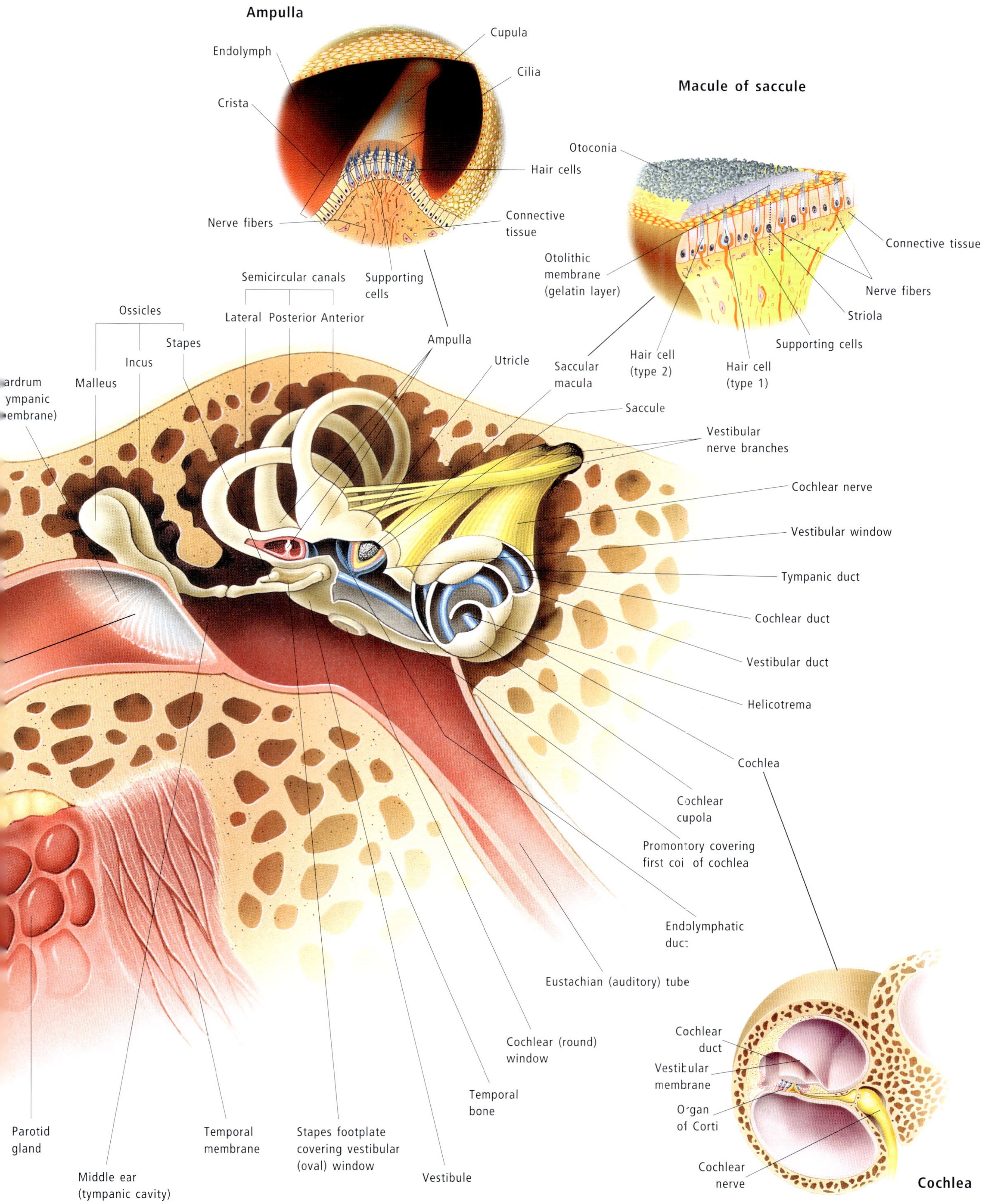

Ampulla
Endolymph
Cupula
Cilia
Crista
Hair cells
Nerve fibers
Connective tissue
Supporting cells
Macule of saccule
Otoconia
Connective tissue
Otolithic membrane (gelatin layer)
Nerve fibers
Striola
Supporting cells
Hair cell (type 2)
Hair cell (type 1)
Semicircular canals
Lateral
Posterior
Anterior
Ossicles
Stapes
Incus
Malleus
ardrum
ympanic
embrane)
Ampulla
Utricle
Saccular macula
Saccule
Vestibular nerve branches
Cochlear nerve
Vestibular window
Tympanic duct
Cochlear duct
Vestibular duct
Helicotrema
Cochlea
Cochlear cupola
Promontory covering first coil of cochlea
Endolymphatic duct
Eustachian (auditory) tube
Cochlear (round) window
Temporal bone
Parotid gland
Temporal membrane
Stapes footplate covering vestibular (oval) window
Vestibule
Middle ear (tympanic cavity)
Cochlear duct
Vestibular membrane
Organ of Corti
Cochlear nerve
Cochlea

called the cochlea, a small, spiral-shaped structure containing fluid and special hairs which serve as sound sensors.

The vibrations of the membrane covering the oval window cause waves to form in the cochlear fluid. These vibrations are picked up by the organ of Corti, the hearing organ housed in the cochlea. The organ of Corti contains tiny hairlike nerve endings anchored in a membrane that extends the length of the cochlea.

These nerve endings are highly specialized endings of the eighth cranial nerve, also called the vestibulocochlear nerve. When vibrations in the fluid reach them, these nerve endings fire off electrical impulses, which are sent along the nerve to the brain to be interpreted as sounds.

The inner ear is also the organ of equilibrium, or balance. It contains tiny organs that sense the body's relationship to gravity. A person knows which way is up because these organs send information to the brain about the body's position. Comprised of the utricle, the saccule and the three semicircular canals, they are collectively known as the vestibular organs.

Both the utricle and the saccule are hollow sacs filled with a gelatinous fluid called endolymph. Fixed into the inner surface of each of them are tiny, hair-like structures, the free ends of which project into the hollow space. Crystals of calcium carbonate, known as otoliths, lie over the hair cells; when the head is tilted, the otoliths change position. In shifting, they pass over the hair cells, which in turn generate impulses which are sent to the brain. The brain then triggers the body's reflex mechanisms to correct the position of the body.

The three semicircular canals act in a similar way. Fluid-filled tubes, they are placed at right angles to each other. They connect with the utricle and contain hair cells in the ampulla. When the head turns, fluid flows through the canals, stimulating the hair cells to send signals to the brain about the position of the body.

Diseases of the ear

The three parts of the ear are affected by disease or injury in different ways. Disorders of the outer ear are mainly related to disorders of the skin, glands and hair follicles in the outer ear canal. Infection and inflammation can affect the middle ear and (rarely) the inner ear.

Inflammation of the outer ear is called otitis externa and is usually caused by a bacterial or fungal infection, most commonly from swimming in polluted water. Symptoms are itching and pain and a slight discharge from the ear. The condition is treated with antibiotic ear drops in the affected ear.

Some people may experience some degree of hardened wax build-up in the ear. Wax in the outer part of the ear can be removed by wiping it away with a clean, damp washcloth. Never try to reach the wax in the ear canal with a cotton swab or a finger, as you may push the wax deeper into the ear canal. Instead, the wax must be removed by a physician who will syringe it out with warm water. The wax may be softened first with a warm solution of olive oil, bicarbonate of soda, or an over-the-counter solution for softening earwax.

After swimming or washing the hair, water may be trapped in the ear canal if there is wax in it, causing temporary deafness. If this happens, tip your head to one side and gently pull the external ear forward. The water will then flow out of the ear.

Children commonly push small objects into the ear. Parents should never try to remove anything lodged in the ear, but instead should seek professional aid. Similarly, if an insect lodges in the ear, see a physician.

A perforated or "burst" eardrum is a painful injury which can lead to partial hearing loss and discharge of fluid or blood from the

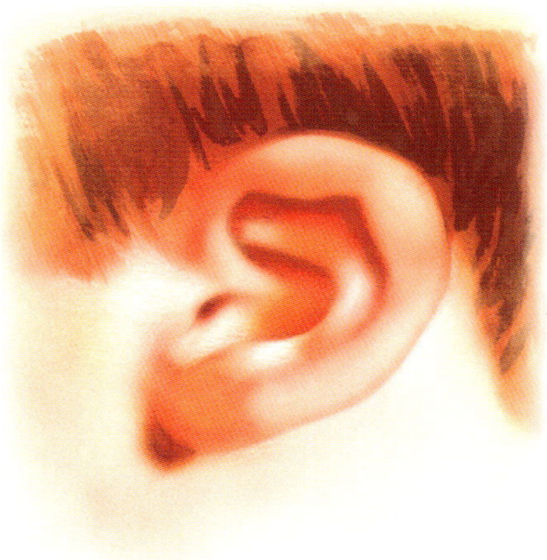

Child

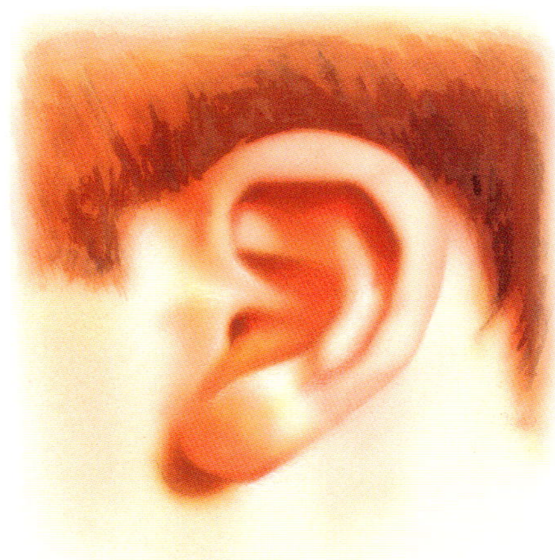

Adolescent

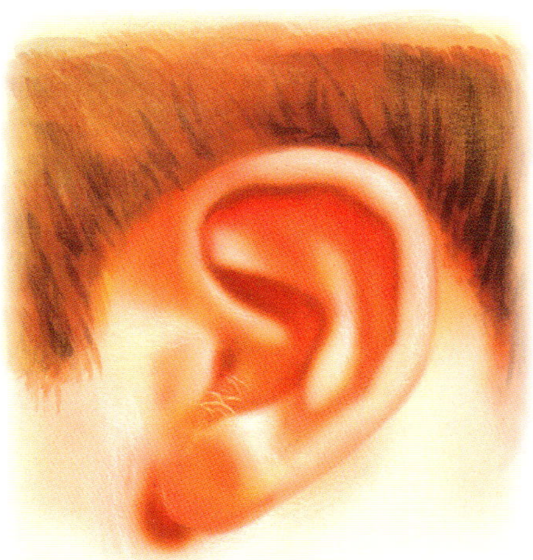

Adult

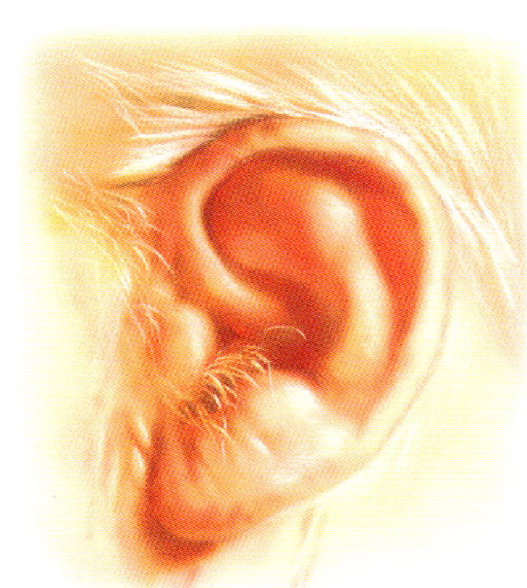

Elderly

Ageing of the ear

As the ear ages, the lobe becomes fleshier and longer. Hairs begin to grow on the lobes and in the ear canal. The skin becomes dryer, thinner and wrinkled. Brown age spots may appear. The ear is one of the few body organs that can continue to grow throughout the body's lifetime.

ear. It is caused by a sudden inward pressure on the eardrum such as that from an explosion, a foreign object being pushed into the ear, a slap or diving too deep when scuba diving. If left alone, the eardrum is often able to repair itself, but sometimes surgery may be required if it does not heal. Those with a perforated eardrum can expect to have their hearing restored in one to two weeks, but in some cases healing may take up to two months.

Many conditions of the outer ear are treated with ear drops. Warm the drops by placing the container in a bowl of warm water (though antibiotic drops should not be warmed). Lie the person on their side with the affected ear uppermost. Pull back the earlobe to create as large an opening into the canal as possible. Rest the end of the dropper over the ear opening and allow the drops to trickle gently into the ear. Place a small plug of cotton in the outer ear to prevent the drops from leaking out. The person should continue to lie in this position for about five minutes.

Unless the physician advises otherwise, do not administer ear drops if the eardrum is perforated or if a child has plastic tubes in the ears.

The most common disease of the middle ear is bacterial infection. The medical term for inflammation of the middle ear is otitis media. This condition is very common in children and is most commonly caused by the spread of bacteria from the throat into the middle ear via the eustachian tube (which is shorter in childhood). Usually there is an associated infection of the throat.

Otitis media causes fever, sometimes deafness in the affected ear, and earache that may be severe or mild, due to an accumulation of pus in the middle ear which continues to accumulate until it may rupture the eardrum. Treatment with painkillers and antibiotics cures the condition.

However, some children experience recurrent attacks of otitis media; in others the condition may become persistent (chronic). This is known as glue ear, and it may cause deafness. This is a very common in some populations, and can have a detrimental effect on children's learning and development. Treatment is with antibiotics and the insertion of a small plastic tube (grommet) into the affected ear(s) to allow pus to drain.

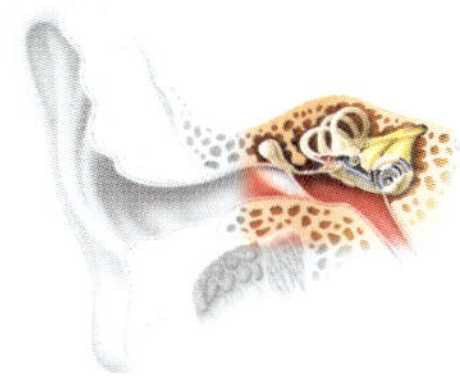

Glue ear

When children have glue ear (persistent otitis media), a grommet is inserted to allow drainage.

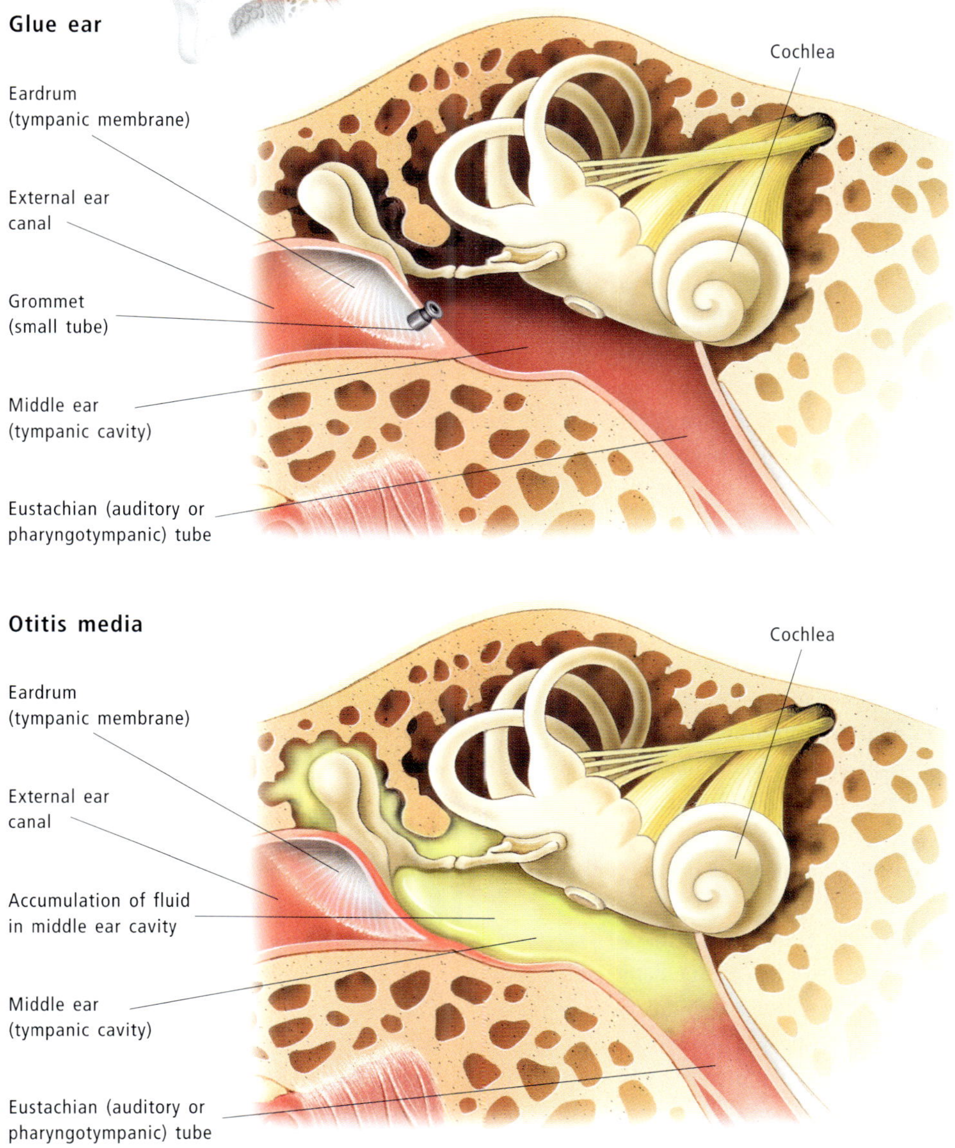

In some cases, an acute infection in the middle ear may spread to the mastoid bone, located behind the ear (mastoiditis). The symptoms include fever and a throbbing earache. The mastoid bone may be tender, and the ear may discharge pus. Treatment with antibiotic drugs cures most cases, but if treatment has been delayed and there is necrosis (death) of bone, surgical removal of part of the mastoid bone may be necessary.

Otosclerosis is a disorder of the middle ear in which there is a gradual build-up of abnormal spongy bone tissue around the footplate of the stapes (one of the ossicles), impeding their function and causing gradual deafness. It is most commonly seen in women between the ages of 15 to 30, and may be triggered by pregnancy. A family history of the condition is common, though the exact cause is unknown. It is treated by surgical replacement of most of the rigid stapes bone with a prosthesis (stapedectomy).

Diseases affecting the inner ear may cause deafness, tinnitus (ringing in the ear) and vertigo (the sensation that one's self or surroundings are spinning). A common inner ear disease is congenital nerve deafness, which is caused by a defect of the hearing nerves in the cochlea. This may be present at birth or may develop during, or soon after, birth. Usually both inner ears are affected, causing (often severe) deafness.

Some drugs, such as aspirin and some antibiotics, can cause damage to the hair cells in the inner ear, which may be permanent. Exposure to loud noise may also cause temporary or permanent hearing damage. A single loud noise such as an explosion may produce severe and permanent deafness. Repeated exposures to sounds that reach more than 80–90 decibels (for example, listening to rock bands) may cause a more gradual loss of hearing. Anyone who is likely to be exposed to noise levels greater than this should wear earplugs or ear protectors.

Labyrinthitis is inflammation of the labyrinth (another term for the inner ear). It is usually caused by a virus and is accompanied by vertigo, nausea and vomiting. Menière's disease is a disorder of the inner ear arising from changes in the pressure of fluid within the vestibular organs. Symptoms include attacks of severe dizziness, nausea, vomiting, tinnitus and fluctuating hearing loss in the affected ear. The cause is not known.

Both labyrinthitis and Menière's disease usually clear up spontaneously in one to six weeks, but Menière's disease may recur. The symptoms can be treated with antihistamines and antinausea drugs.

Hearing tests and aids

Hearing disorders can be detected by a physician using a tuning fork. Audiometry is a more sophisticated technique that demonstrates the extent of hearing loss, and determines whether it has occurred in the upper or lower frequencies.

Abnormal hearing can frequently be improved by hearing-aid devices. If hearing loss is permanent and disabling, the use of sign-language and lip-reading may also become necessary.

A cochlear implant is a system of tiny electrodes which are surgically inserted into the inner ear and which transmit sound vibrations to the auditory nerve. It restores hearing to a person whose cochlea has been impaired by congenital deafness, trauma, drug toxicity or infection.

SEE ALSO *Audiometry, Balance, Cochlea, Deafness, Hearing, Labyrinthitis, Mastoiditis, Menière's disease, Otitis externa, Otitis media, Otosclerosis, Semicircular canals, Tinnitus, Vertigo*

EATING DISORDERS

An eating disorder exists where there is persistent abnormal behavior related to meals, specific foods or the intake of food. Eating disorders are always serious because they will almost certainly lead to malnourishment and poor health, and have been the cause of death. People of any age, male or female, can suffer from an eating disorder, but young women seem to be particularly at risk.

When there is strong pressure to conform to the looks and body shapes dictated by fashion, this can set up unrealistic goals and expectations. Dissatisfaction with looks, body shape or weight can cause an obsession with dieting or exercise and a quest for the perfect body. There may be no real need to lose weight, and no possibility of changing basic body shape.

Although friends and family may clearly see that the weight loss is unnecessary and excessive, the person affected may persist, perhaps in secret to avoid interference or criticism, to the point where health is at risk. Before this point is reached, an eating disorder may be suspected.

Diagnosis

It is necessary to differentiate between an eating disorder and what may only be a temporary change in habits. Eating habits may change, especially during periods of physical illness, and this makes it very important to have an accurate diagnosis from a medical practitioner.

Severe under-nourishment will almost certainly require specialized medical help, and a person with an eating disorder may also need counseling or closely supervised psychiatric treatment and dietary re-education in order to establish healthy eating habits.

The most serious and most widely known eating disorders are anorexia nervosa and bulimia nervosa. The disorders have also been associated with severely low self-esteem, obsessive-compulsive disorder and other mental and emotional problems.

Anorexia nervosa

Consciously deciding not to eat, anorexia sufferers are deliberately starving. Refusing food while still feeling hunger, they may be constantly thinking of food but are terrified of gaining weight. The self-image may be distorted: sufferers will persist in believing themselves to be overweight despite a painfully thin appearance. The fear of becoming fat may cause anorexics to deny the pain of hunger, to be excessively choosy about which foods they will eat, and to exercise obsessively. Adolescent girls are the most likely sufferers, but boys, adults, even athletes, can become anorexic.

The causes are widely thought to be cultural—that is, the pressure from society and peer groups to conform to what is currently thought fashionable or beautiful. This pressure is felt strongly by young adults who may become obsessive dieters, reducing weight well below healthy levels.

Anorexics often feel that they are not in charge of their own lives—losing weight is one way of achieving control. Anorexia may also follow weight loss dieting or can result from weight loss after illness.

It is also thought that there may be a biological component to anorexia nervosa, stemming from hormonal or metabolic disorders.

Bulimia nervosa

Overeating or binge eating followed by self-induced vomiting or by purging with laxatives is known as bulimia nervosa. Bulimia sufferers may be of normal weight but are afraid of becoming overweight. Rather than simply starving themselves, they may eat uncontrollably, consuming a large amount of food in a short time. They may then purge themselves by vomiting or taking laxatives, exercise excessively or deny themselves food. They may do one or all these things in secret.

The behavior of bulimia sufferers is out of their control. The cycle of binge eating, followed by purging, then fasting, is a hard one to break. Not being in control may produce feelings of shame, guilt and self-hatred; many sufferers may become depressed and even suicidal.

Either anorexia or bulimia can cause severe weight loss: anorexia because the food intake is too low for the body's needs, and bulimia because the food is ejected before the nutrients can be absorbed by the body. People can suffer from anorexia at some stages in their lives, and bulimia at other stages.

Symptoms

Symptoms of eating disorders may include obsession with eating, exercise or weight loss, and obvious and continuing weight loss below normal levels. The person may become excessively picky about food; could have unusual rituals or quirky behavior around foods or meals; or will not be eating regular meals or will be eating unusually small amounts. The person appears to be eating well but is losing weight, perhaps by secretly vomiting after meals or by constant use of laxatives. Other symptoms include refusal to eat with the family, inability to concentrate and constant tiredness. Girls may cease menstruation—note that starvation in puberty can stop proper physical development, including the start of periods. Feelings of guilt, anxiety or depression may accompany these behavior patterns.

Effects

The effects of eating disorders may include excessive weight loss, weakness, dry skin, and fine hair growth all over the body. Some cases result in death, either from excessive starvation or by suicide due to depression.

The lack of vital nutrients in the body produces the same effects as plain starvation: poor health, dry skin, hair loss and brittle nails are early signs. With constant vomiting, tooth enamel is eroded. Purging through constant use of laxatives can cause stomach cramps—this is common with senna-based laxatives.

Treatment

Early diagnosis of anorexia or bulimia is vital. Specialist treatment can then be considered. The first priority is to remedy the damage from unhealthy eating, then to correct problems that have caused the disorder.

People who suffer eating disorders generally recover under treatment, but are likely to have continuing problems or adverse health effects throughout their lives. Early diagnosis and treatment will minimize the damage. A stay in hospital or treatment as an outpatient may be needed. Group therapy or self-help programs can be beneficial.

The prospect of recovery is good if the person receives specialized help and is willing to work hard. Adolescents can recover spontaneously, but it is important to seek medical assistance early and to recognize that it can take time to get well.

It is always wise to seek the advice and supervision of a qualified medical practitioner or dietitian before modifying the diet of a child, adolescent, pregnant or lactating woman, or when aiming to significantly reduce food intake for weight loss.

SEE ALSO *Diet, Laxatives, Malnutrition, Nutrition*

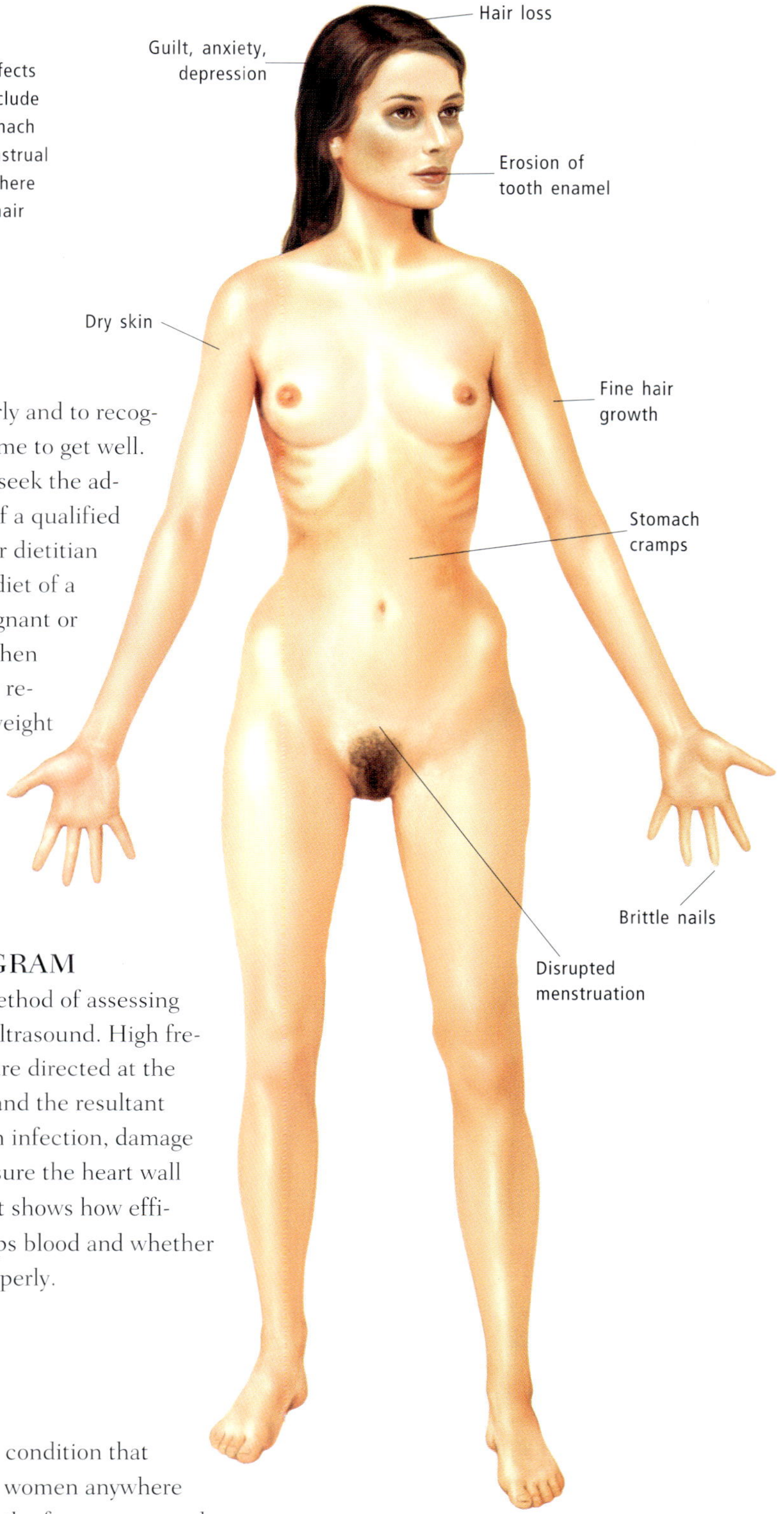

Eating disorder

As well as weight loss, effects of eating disorders can include dry skin, brittle nails, stomach cramps and hair loss. Menstrual periods often cease, and there may be a fine growth of hair over the body.

ECHOCARDIOGRAM

This is a diagnostic method of assessing cardiac health using ultrasound. High frequency sound waves are directed at the heart wall and valves and the resultant echo used to detect an infection, damage or tumors and to measure the heart wall and chamber. The test shows how efficiently the heart pumps blood and whether valves are working properly.

SEE ALSO *Heart*

ECLAMPSIA

Eclampsia is a serious condition that can occur in pregnant women anywhere between the fifth month of pregnancy and the end of the first week after delivery. It is characterized by headaches, high blood pressure, visual disturbances, irritability, abdominal pain and convulsions.

In the most severe cases eclampsia causes coma and death. It is one of the most dangerous complications of pregnancy, and the best treatment is prevention. Regular measuring of blood pressure and testing of urine during pregnancy is used to detect pregnancy-induced hypertension (PIH).

If detected and treated early, complications can be prevented. When eclampsia does occur, expert hospital care is absolutely essential as the sufferer will need heavy sedation. Any woman who suffers from preeclampsia is at risk of eclampsia.

SEE ALSO *Hypertension, Preeclampsia, Pregnancy*

E

Eczema

Eczema is an allergic condition that most commonly affects the face, scalp, neck, hands and feet, and the creases of the trunk, elbows and knees.

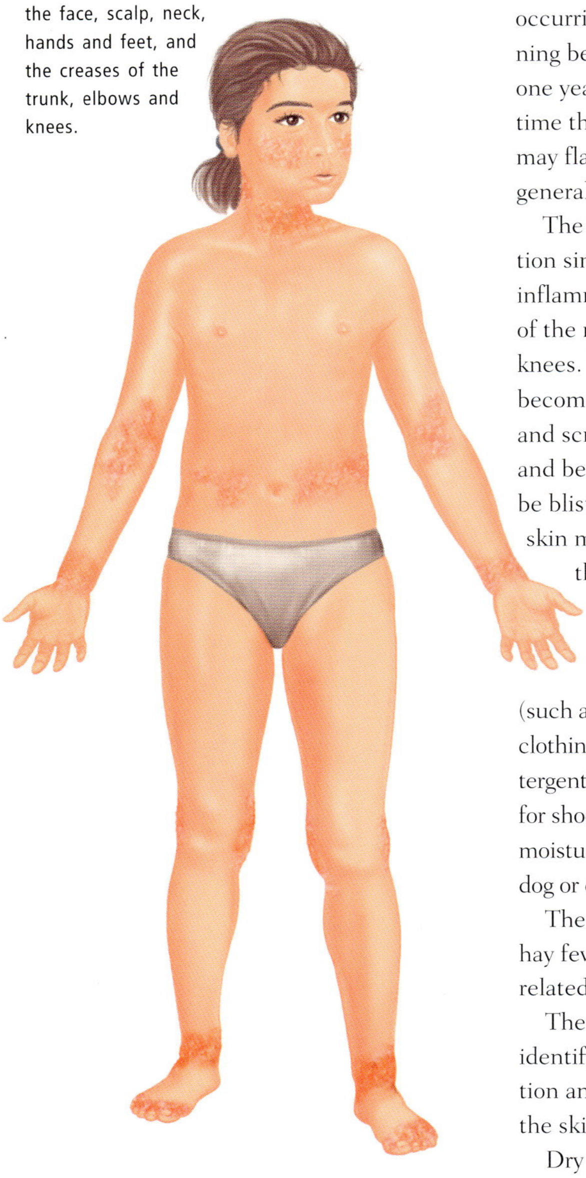

Atopic eczema

Eczema is characterized by itching, redness, blisters, oozing and crusting. Scratching can cause further irritation.

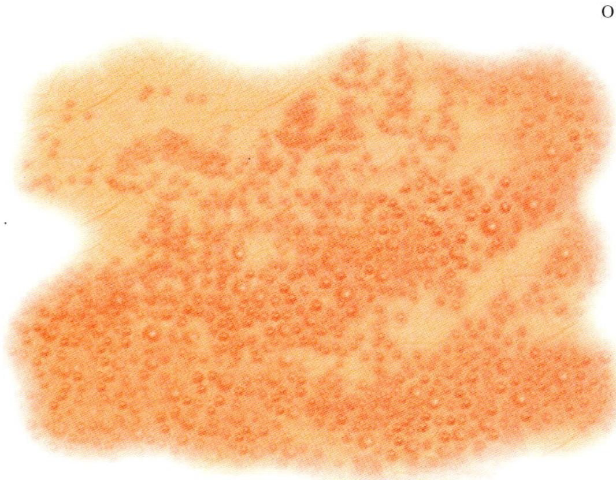

ECZEMA

Also known as atopic dermatitis, eczema is a chronic (long term) allergic skin disorder, occurring most commonly in infants, beginning between the ages of one month and one year. Most infants will outgrow it by the time they are two to three years old, but it may flare up again at any age. In adults, it is generally a chronic or recurring condition.

The condition is a hypersensitivity reaction similar to an allergy, causing chronic inflammation of the hands, scalp, face, back of the neck or skin creases of elbows and knees. The inflammation causes the skin to become itchy and scaly. Chronic irritation and scratching can cause the skin to thicken and become leathery-textured. There may be blisters with oozing and crusting, and the skin may become secondarily infected through scratching.

Eczema may occur for no known reason, or as an allergic reaction to a wide variety of things including foods (such as eggs, wheat, milk or seafood), woolen clothing, skin lotions and ointments, soaps, detergents, cleansers, plants, tanning agents used for shoe leather, dyes, topical medications, moisture, overheating, common house dust, dog or cat dander, cigarette smoke and stress.

There is often a family history of asthma, hay fever, eczema, psoriasis or other allergy-related disorders.

The first step in treating eczema is to identify whatever it is that causes the reaction and if possible remove or avoid it. Next, the skin itself should be cared for.

Dry skin makes the condition worse, so to keep the skin healthy, reduce the frequency of bathing to once or twice a week in lukewarm water, and use a small amount of very mild soap (or better still, use no soap at all). Bath oils and soap substitutes are often recommended. Apply a moisturizing lotion to the affected areas as least twice a day and after bathing; this keeps the skin moist and protects it from other irritants.

If this doesn't improve the condition, a physician may prescribe mild cortisone cream or ointment; for example, 1 percent hydrocortisone cream. The physician may also prescribe antihistamines to reduce itching (in rare cases, sedatives or tranquilizers may be needed). Keep nails short and wear soft gloves at night to minimize scratching. Sometimes exposure to sunlight helps heal the rash.

Chronically thickened areas may be treated with ointments or creams that contain tar compounds, or medium-to very high-potency steroid creams. In very severe cases, corticosteroids by mouth may be needed. Antibiotics may be prescribed for areas of infection. These measures are usually successful in controlling the disorder.

There are a number of alternative therapies that may help to alleviate the symptoms of eczema. Ayurvedic and traditional Chinese medicine prescribe herbs and a change of diet. Counseling, hypnotherapy or psychotherapy may be of use if there are emotional or stress-related factors. Herbalism prescribes alterative herbs such as burdock, nettle and red clover to cleanse and boost the lymphatic system, and liver tonics, such as dandelion, to aid in the detoxification process. Homeopathy views eczema as a constitutional illness and prescribes remedies to match the patient's overall constitution, as well as to treat individual symptoms. Naturopathy prescribes evening primrose oil, flaxseed oil, zinc and a range of vitamins. Patients are advised on eliminating allergens, additives and colorings from their diet and a supervised fast may be suggested (not for children). Oatmeal or Epsom salt baths are traditional home remedies used to ease symptoms. Reflexology treats eczema by massaging skin and liver zones, and by helping the patient to relax.

SEE ALSO *Allergies, Dermatitis*

EDEMA

Edema is swelling caused by the build-up of fluid in the tissues. It can be localized (limited to a part of the body), or generalized (occurring throughout the body).

Localized edema may result from injury or infection, sunburn or varicose veins. Slight edema of the legs commonly occurs in warm summer months and during pregnancy.

More generalized edema can be caused by heart failure or by a lack of protein in the blood from cirrhosis of the liver, chronic nephritis or malnutrition. It can also occur as a result of toxemia of pregnancy (preeclampsia).

Edema is treated by correcting the underlying cause. Diuretic drugs, which make the kidneys eliminate excess salt and water, are often used to relieve the symptoms. Elastic stockings will help prevent edema caused by pregnancy, failure of lymphatic drainage, or varicose veins.

Pulmonary edema is a complication of heart disease in which the failing heart allows fluid to accumulate in the lungs, which eventually seeps into the air spaces (alveoli). This interferes with the exchange of oxygen and carbon dioxide, causing severe breathlessness. Pulmonary edema is a medical emergency, requiring immediate hospitalization and treatment with oxygen, diuretics, morphine and drugs for the underlying heart failure.

SEE ALSO *Diuretics, Pulmonary edema*

ELBOW

The elbow is the joint between the expanded lower end of the bone of the upper arm (the humerus) and the two bones of the forearm (the radius and ulna). The radius is on the thumb side of the arm and the ulna on the side of the little finger. When the arms are placed by the side with the palms facing forwards, the ulna is closest to the body (medial) and the radius is away from the body (lateral).

The radius and ulna articulate with the expanded end of the humerus. There are bony swellings on the humerus, either side of the joint, called the lateral and medial epicondyles. These bony protrusions can be felt through the skin on either side of the elbow.

The brachial artery is the main artery of the upper arm, which runs down the medial side of the humerus and across the inside surface of the elbow, below which it divides into radial and ulnar arteries. The brachial artery is compressed against the humerus by means of a cuff when blood pressure is checked using a sphygmomanometer and stethoscope.

A number of superficial veins cross the front of the elbow (the cubital fossa). These vary considerably in arrangement but their position just under the skin makes them suitable for obtaining a sample of blood or for cardioangiography. This involves insert-

Elbow, back

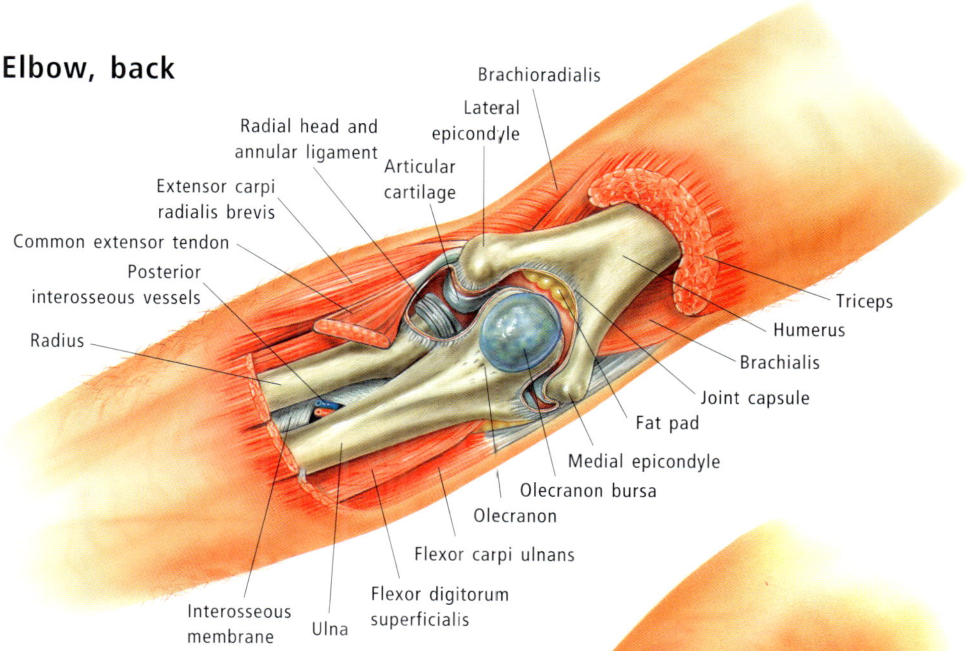

Elbow, front

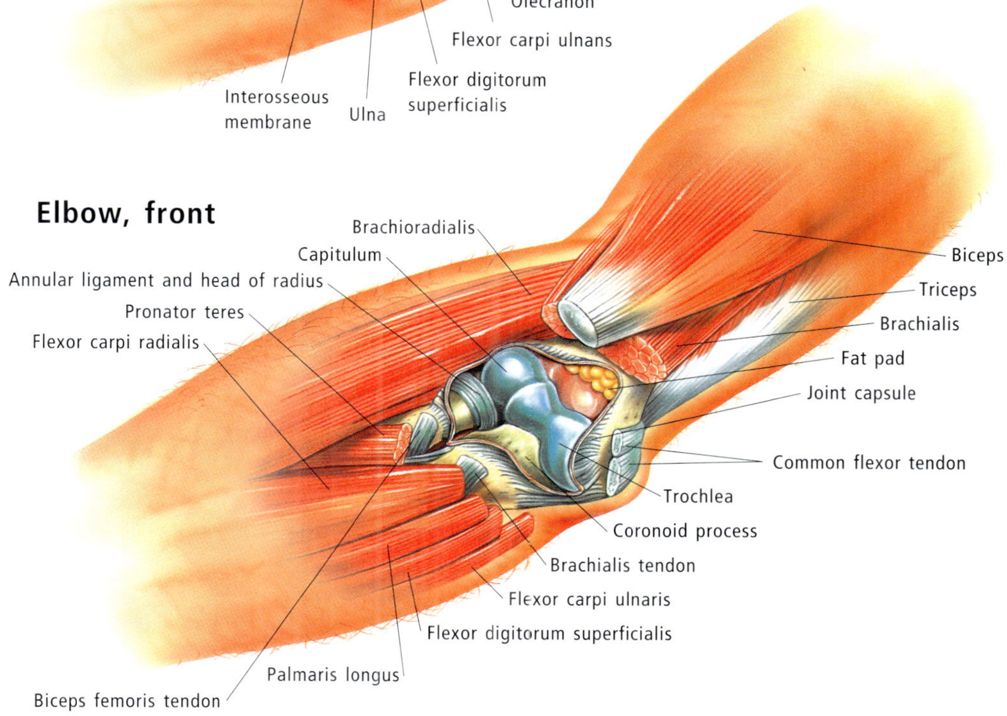

Elbow, articular

Cross-sectional view of the elbow joint.

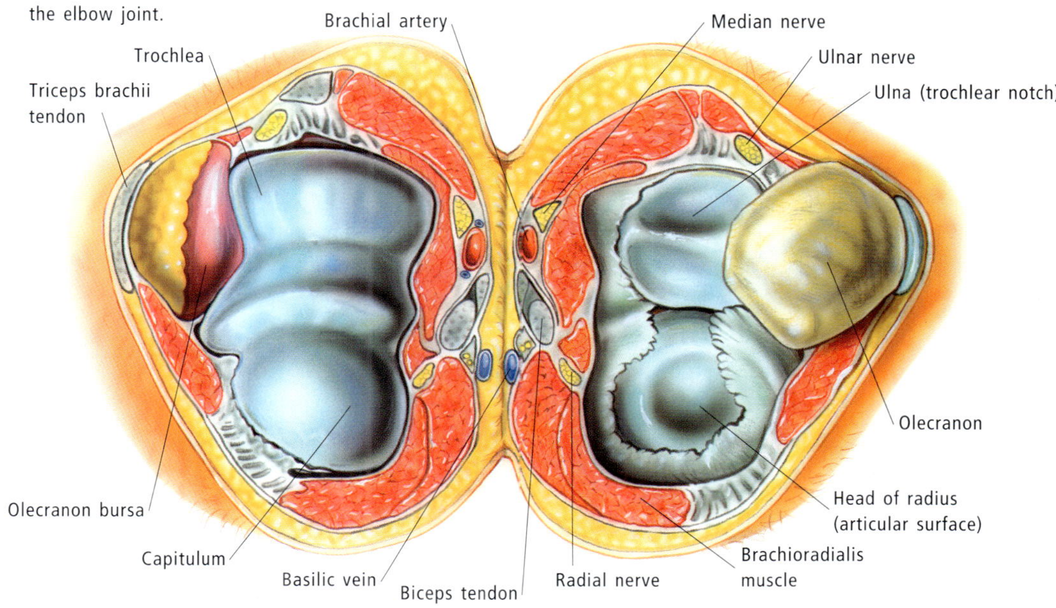

ing a fine tube (catheter) into the vein and threading it through the vessels of the arm and ultimately into the heart where blood samples can be taken or an opaque dye injected prior to taking an x-ray.

Elbows are prone to certain types of sports injuries, commonly called "tennis elbow" and "golfer's elbow".

Tennis elbow is a painful sensation in the vicinity of the lateral epicondyle (lateral epicondylitis). The pain may also radiate down the forearm. Some of the muscles which extend (straighten) the wrist attach to the lateral epicondyle and it is thought that repetitive wrist movements cause strain or damage to this attachment.

Golfer's elbow is pain in the vicinity of the medial epicondyle where some of the muscles which flex (bend) the wrist attach. Repetitive movements of the wrist are believed to place stress on this part of the elbow. A similar condition can arise from excessive throwing using poor technique.

Despite the common names for the two conditions, tennis and golf can affect either epicondyle, and epicondylitis can also result from other sports requiring repetitive wrist or forearm movements, including bowling, gymnastics, baseball, fencing, swimming and karate. Epicondylitis does not usually resolve without some sort of treatment.

Therapies include laser treatments, injections of botulinum toxin or steroids, oral or topical non-steroidal anti-inflammatory agents, elbow support bands, remedial exercise and acupuncture. Some of these remedies seem to give relief in many cases.

There is no universal agreement as to which method is best, nor do there seem to have been any clinical trials which satisfy the majority of practitioners treating these conditions.

SEE ALSO *Arm, Humerus, Radius, Tennis elbow, Ulna*

ELECTROCARDIOGRAM

The activity of the heart can be measured through minute electrical impulses from the cardiac muscle that reach the skin surface.

This electrical activity can be detected through the taping of electrodes to the skin in positions dictated by the information required. The ankles, wrists and the chest wall are the standard sites for applying the electrodes. Electrical signals are amplified and the details are recorded on an electrocardiogram, a chart scribed on a moving strip of paper.

Results show the efficiency of the heart's ability to transmit the electrical impulses that control the cardiac cycle, and its rate and rhythm. In a person with a normal heart, the EKG tracing has a characteristic pattern, showing upward and downward deflections. The first upwards deflection, called a P wave, is known as the atrial complex and is due to the electrical activity associated with the contraction of the upper chambers (atria) of the heart. A further series of deflections, the Q, R, S and T waves, are the ventricular complexes and are due to the electrical activity associated with the contraction of the lower chambers (ventricles). Delayed transmission of electrical impulses, abnormally-shaped complexes and abnormal rhythms in the EKG tracing may indicate heart disease.

Some EKG changes only become apparent when the subject is exercising. An EKG carried out in a physician's office when a person is exercising vigorously is called a stress test. Other abnormal electrical activity in the heart may occur intermittently and may not be present when an EKG is performed. A Holter monitor is a device that makes a 24-hour EKG recording which can be used to detect sporadic arrhythmias.

SEE ALSO *Arrythmia, Heart, Heartbeat*

ELECTROCONVULSIVE THERAPY

Electroconvulsive therapy (ECT) is a psychiatric treatment that involves bringing on a seizure by administering an electric shock to the brain. The patient is first anesthetized and given a muscle relaxant, then an electrode is placed on each temple and an electric current is passed through the brain between the two electrodes.

The patient usually experiences some memory disturbance immediately after treatment, but this usually passes with time. Exactly how or why ECT works is still unclear but it is known to be effective in the treatment of certain types of depression.

ECT is probably the most controversial psychiatric treatment in use today, the controversy revolving around its effectiveness versus its side effects. The major side effect is the risk of prolonged memory loss and confusion in some patients.

Although ECT was widely used in the 1940s and 50s to treat cases of severe psychiatric illness, it was subsequently found to be relatively ineffective in many cases, particularly those involving psychosis. Today its use is more limited but it is still being used, usually in conjunction with medication, to successfully treat cases of severe depression and sometimes to interrupt manic episodes. Generally, a number of treatments are required over a period of several weeks for ECT to be effective.

SEE ALSO *Bipolar disorder, Depression, Psychosis*

ELECTROENCEPHALOGRAM

An electroencephalogram (EEG) is a record of the overall activity occurring in the cerebral cortex of the brain. It is obtained by recording electrical signals from electrodes placed at various points on the surface of the head and appears as a series of spikes on a graph. These spikes, known as brain waves, can be classified according to their frequency into four groups known as alpha, beta, theta and delta waves. Their pattern varies during different types of brain activity such as rest, sleep and mental concentration.

In certain brain conditions the EEG reading is found to be abnormal. An EEG can be used in the diagnosis of epilepsy (the test will help determine the type of epilepsy), brain injuries, abscesses, meningitis, encephalitis and brain tumors. The procedure is usually carried out in a hospital clinic or a doctor's office. A sleep encephalogram, performed on a person after they have been kept awake the previous night, can help evaluate some types of sleep disorders.

Absence of electrical activity in an EEG is sometimes used as legal proof of brain death in a person who is in a coma and is being kept alive only by artificial means.

SEE ALSO *Brain wave activity, Coma, Epilepsy*

ELECTROLYTES

Electrolytes are ions in solution in the blood and other body fluids. They play an essential role in all body functions. The major electrolytes are sodium, potassium, calcium, phosphate, chloride and bicarbonate. Derived from food, their concentration in the blood is regulated mostly by the kidneys and lungs and can be measured by laboratory studies of serum (the clear liquid in plasma).

Different fluids in the body have different concentrations of electrolytes. For example, the concentration of sodium in serum is 142 millimoles/liter whereas the potassium concentration is only 4 millimoles/liter. Inside the cell, the concentration of sodium is 10 millimoles/liter while the concentration of potassium is 160 millimoles/liter. This difference in concentration is maintained by special ion pumps in cell membranes which continuously move sodium ions out of the cell and potassium ions into the cell. The difference in concentration of electrolytes in different fluids is important for some metabolic processes, for example, the conduction of electrical impulses along nerve fibers.

The concentration of electrolytes in body fluids depends on an adequate intake of electrolytes in the diet, adequate absorption from the intestine, and proper functioning of the kidneys and lung, which also regulate electrolyte concentration in body fluids. Diseases that interfere with these processes can cause disturbances of electrolyte concentration. For example, kidney disease may cause the body to retain too much sodium, chloride, bicarbonate and calcium. Electrolyte concentrations in the body are also controlled by hormones, and diseases which affect the production of these hormones also cause electrolyte disturbances, which can have severe effects on the body's metabolism.

Different electrolytes play different roles in the body's metabolism. Sodium helps regulate the body's water balance, and maintains normal heart rhythm, blood pressure and blood volume. Increased intake of sodium may contribute to high blood pressure, so people with high blood pressure may be advised to reduce their sodium intake. Sodium also plays a part in the conduction of nerve impulses and muscle contraction.

Too much sodium in the blood and body fluids (hypernatremia) or too little sodium (hyponatremia) can cause confusion, restlessness, anxiety, weakness, muscle cramps, edema and, in severe cases, stupor or coma.

Potassium assists in the regulation of the acid-base and water balance in the blood and the body tissues. It assists in protein synthesis from amino acids and in carbohydrate metabolism. It is necessary for the building of muscle and for normal body growth. Along with sodium and calcium, it maintains normal heart rhythm, regulates the body's water balance and is responsible for muscle contractions and nerve impulses.

Tissue cells usually have a high concentration of potassium, while blood usually has a low concentration. Too much or too little potassium in the blood can cause weakness and paralysis and affect the heartbeat.

Sodium and potassium levels in the blood and body fluids are regulated by aldosterone, a hormone secreted by the adrenal gland, which increases sodium resorption from the kidneys and promotes potassium loss by the kidneys. A tumor of the adrenal gland may cause excess secretion of aldosterone (hyperaldosteronism), leading to hypernatremia, hypokalemia and fluid imbalance.

Calcium is a mineral component of blood which, along with phosphate, forms bone and teeth. Calcium also helps in the regulation of the heartbeat, transmission of nerve impulses, contraction of muscles and clotting of blood. Calcium and phosphate levels in the blood are regulated by parathormone, a hormone secreted by the parathyroid gland, which requires vitamin D to function. Calcium levels are also regulated by calcitonin, a hormone secreted by the thyroid gland. Too much calcium causes lethargy, delirium and seizures; too little causes muscle spasms, twitching, cramps, numbness and tingling in extremities, seizures and irregular heartbeat.

Chloride is necessary in the maintenance of the body's acid-base and fluid balance. It is an essential component of the secretions of the stomach, aiding in digestion. Fluid loss due to excessive sweating, vomiting or diarrhea can cause a deficiency of chloride, resulting in excessive alkalinity of body fluids (alkalosis), low fluid volume (dehydration) and loss of potassium in the urine.

Bicarbonate acts as a buffer in blood and body fluids, keeping the pH (acidity) to within a narrow range of 7.35–7.45. The concentration of bicarbonate is regulated by the kidney and the lungs.

SEE ALSO *Adrenal glands, Calcium, Kidney, Potassium, Sodium*

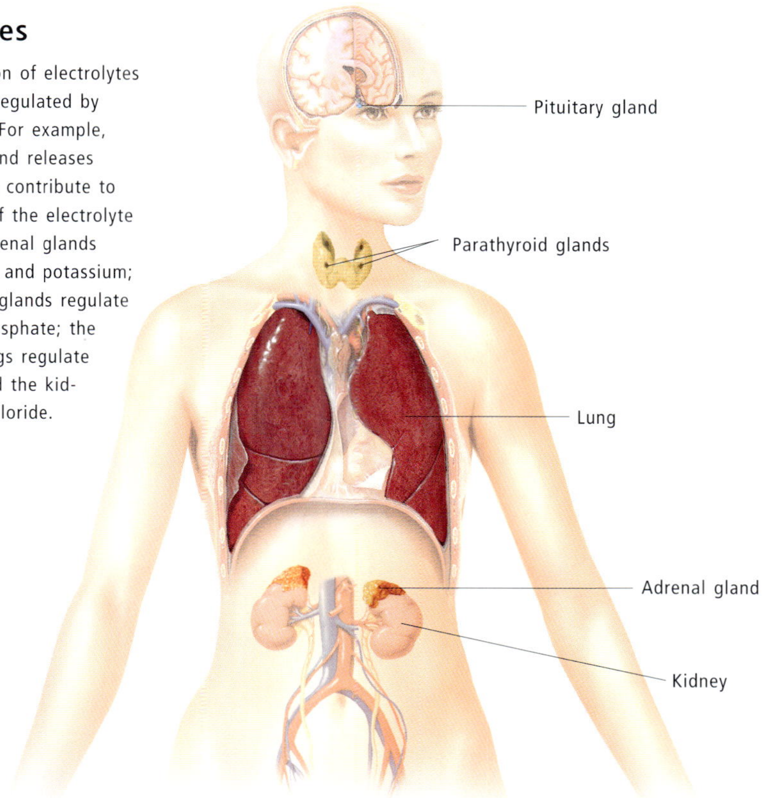

Electrolytes

The concentration of electrolytes in the blood is regulated by various organs. For example, the pituitary gland releases hormones which contribute to the regulation of the electrolyte balance; the adrenal glands regulate sodium and potassium; the parathyroid glands regulate calcium and phosphate; the kidneys and lungs regulate bicarbonate; and the kidney regulates chloride.

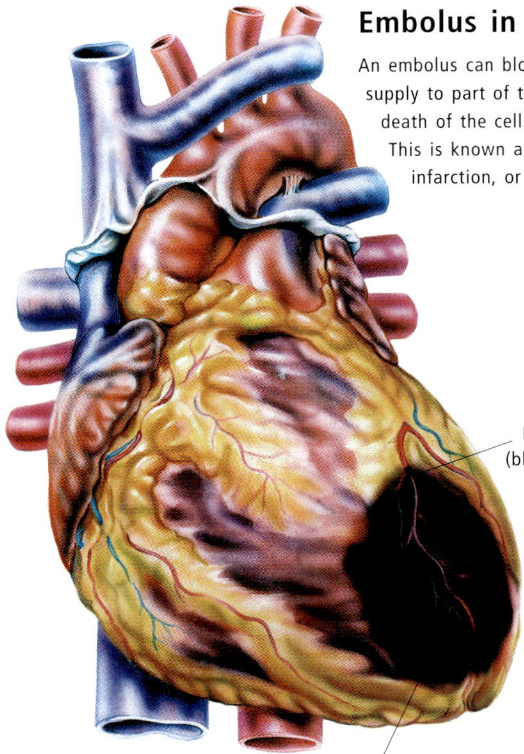

Embolus in the heart

An embolus can block off the blood supply to part of the heart, resulting in death of the cells of the heart muscle. This is known as myocardial infarction, or heart attack.

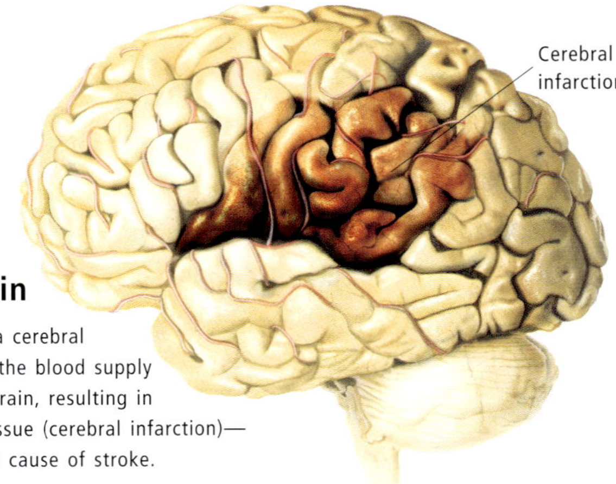

Embolus in the brain

An embolism in a cerebral artery can block the blood supply to areas of the brain, resulting in death of brain tissue (cerebral infarction)—this is a common cause of stroke.

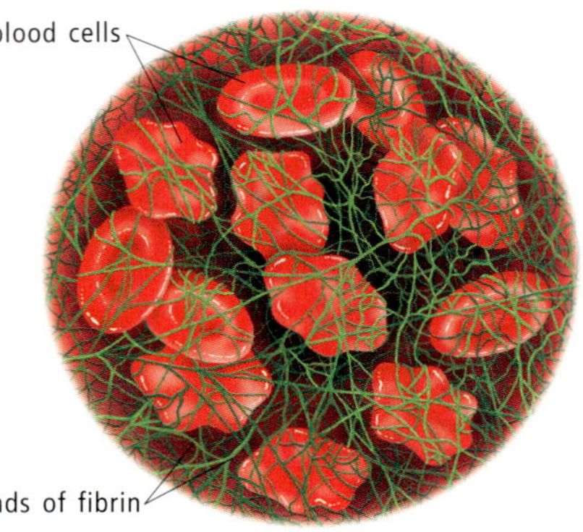

Embolus

Emboli are usually clots composed of strands of fibrin and red blood cells (erythrocytes). They form most commonly in the arteries of the brain, heart, kidney, legs and intestines.

ELECTROMYOGRAPHY

Electromyography is a method of diagnosing the health of muscle tissue by measuring its electrical activity. At rest, muscles are electrically silent, producing no electrical impulses, but when stimulated or voluntarily contracted they generate an electrical current. These impulses are recorded on a cathode ray tube by continuous tracing in the form of a wave and monitored as a sound through a loudspeaker.

The visual tracing or electromyogram records the electrical impulses, and these can be interpreted to evaluate the health of the muscle, to reveal any weakness or wasting indicating impairment of nerve functions or muscle disease.

SEE ALSO *Muscle*

ELECTROSURGERY

Electrosurgery is the use of electrical current to destroy healthy or diseased tissue. It is used to make incisions in healthy tissue (for example, to excise skin lesions), to destroy diseased tissue such as tumors, or to coagulate bleeding blood vessels during surgery. There are several electrosurgery techniques, all of which use the principle that as electrical current is converted into heat by tissue resistance, it destroys tissue.

Electrosurgery has largely been replaced by laser surgery, which is more accurate and can be used in areas where electrosurgery cannot, for example in eye surgery.

ELEPHANTIASIS

Elephantiasis is a condition associated with infectious disorders known collectively as filariasis. The filarial worm in tropical and subtropical regions is transmitted to humans as larvae by mosquitoes. After about a year the larvae mature into nematodes which live in lymph nodes and vessels, mainly those draining the legs and genital regions, where they impair circulation and induce allergic reactions in surrounding tissues.

The disease progresses as attacks with fever and increasing swelling, usually of the legs. Over time, gross hardening and enlargement give the skin an appearance similar to elephant hide, hence the name of the condition. Treatment may kill the worms but drugs and surgery are the only recourse for advanced symptoms. The disease is not curable.

SEE ALSO *Filariasis*

EMBOLISM

Embolism is the sudden obstruction of blood flow to an organ or body part by an embolus. Usually the embolus is a blood clot that has formed in an artery and has traveled in the blood and lodged in a smaller artery downstream.

An embolus may sometimes be composed of fat globules from the site of a bone fracture (fat embolus), infected material from an abscess, cancer cells, or an air bubble (air embolus).

The effect of an embolus is to block off the blood supply and cause ischemia (damage caused by lack of oxygen) to the organ supplied by that artery.

An embolus may cause myocardial infarction (in the heart), stroke (in the brain) or leg pain and ulcers.

Treatment for embolism depends on the size, nature, and location of the embolus. An embolus in one of the major organs, such as the heart, lung or brain, will require emergency treatment at a hospital. Surgery or drug treatment with thrombolytics and anticoagulants may considered to be necessary.

SEE ALSO *Anticoagulants, Ischemia, Myocardial infarction, Stroke*

EMBRYO

The term "embryo" covers the time from fertilization to the end of week 8 of gestation. After this, the term "fetus" is used. During the first eight weeks the embryo grows from a single cell to a complex multicellular organism. The placenta and fetal membranes develop and all the major organ systems are acquired, although not necessarily in functional form. External features are sufficiently developed by the end of week 8 that the fetus has a recognizably human form, including head, arms and legs.

Fertilization results in a single-celled embryo called a zygote. This divides rapidly as it passes down the fallopian tube. When it reaches the uterus a cavity forms with an inner mass of cells on one side of the cavity, which will become the embryo and the embryonic membranes. The cells on the outside will form the placenta. Implantation begins on about day 7.

Formation of embryo and amnion

The inner mass of cells undergoes rearrangement to form a flat elongated sheet covered by a hollow balloon-like structure (rather like a gondola under a hot air balloon). The hollow structure will form the amnion, a fluid-filled sac in which the embryo will eventually float, connected to the placenta by the umbilical cord. The flat sheet of cells will become the embryo. The amnion does not form part of the embryo's body but its normal functioning is important in development. If the amniotic sac is punctured prematurely, loss of amniotic fluid may lead to miscarriage or infection.

Damage to the amniotic membrane may cause the formation of strands of tissue (amniotic bands) within the sac. If one of these becomes wrapped around a developing body part it may cause constriction of its blood supply and distortion or loss of the part. Amniotic bands can be detected by ultrasound in some cases.

If there is insufficient amniotic fluid the loss of its cushioning effect can also result in pressure damage to the developing embryo; this mostly results in spontaneous abortion (miscarriage). A sample of amniotic fluid (obtained by amniocentesis, a common test for fetal abnormalities) contains molecules and cells shed from the embryo which can be used to detect some abnormalities such as Down syndrome and spina bifida. It is difficult prior to week 14 to

E

Embryo

Three days after conception, the fertilized egg (zygote) begins its journey down the fallopian tube. On entering the uterus, the zygote sheds its protective, jelly-like covering before implanting itself in the uterine lining. In just 8 weeks, the embryo will have transformed from a single cell to a tiny (1 inch/2.5 centimeter) yet recognizably human entity with limbs, facial features and all the major organ systems.

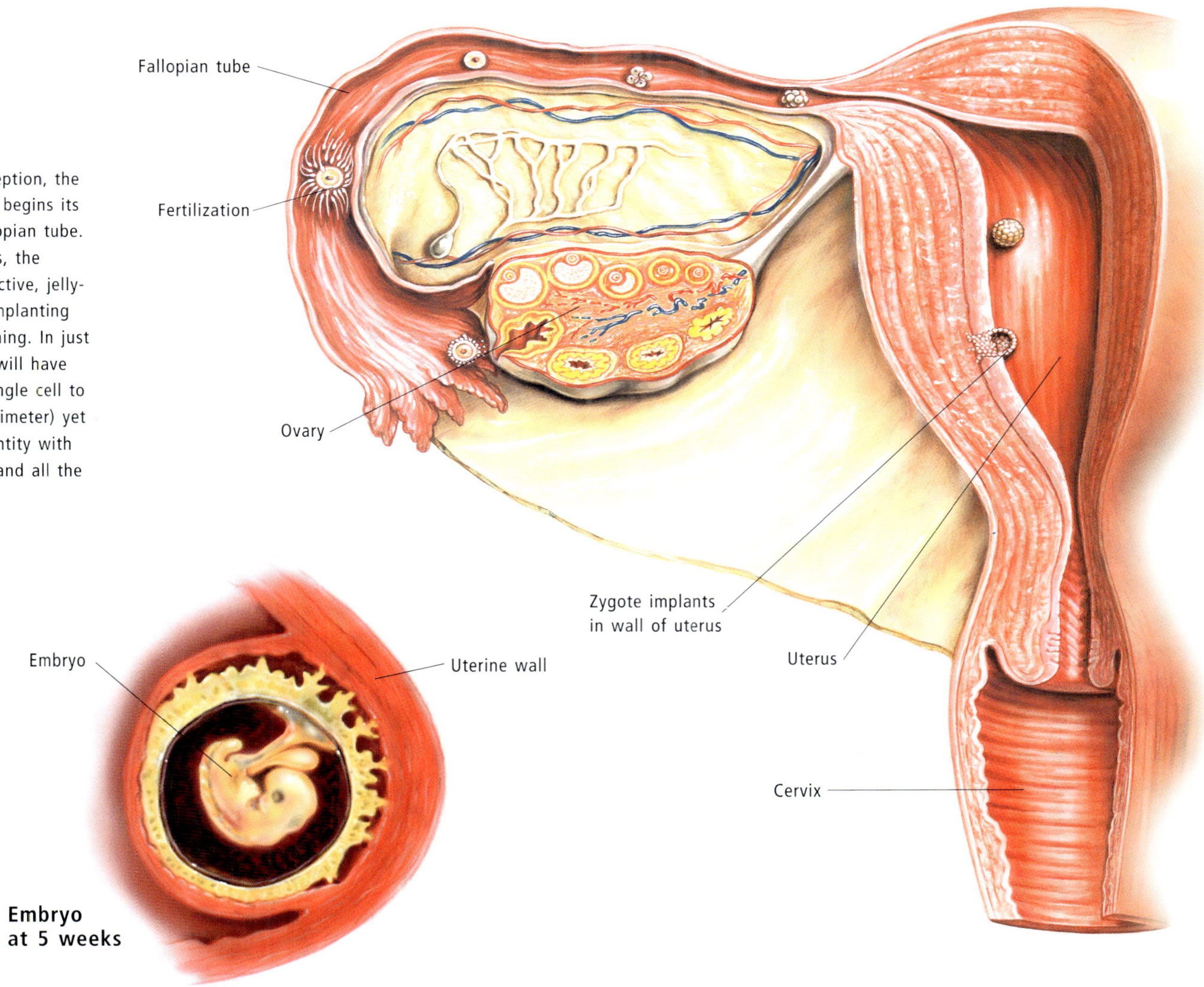

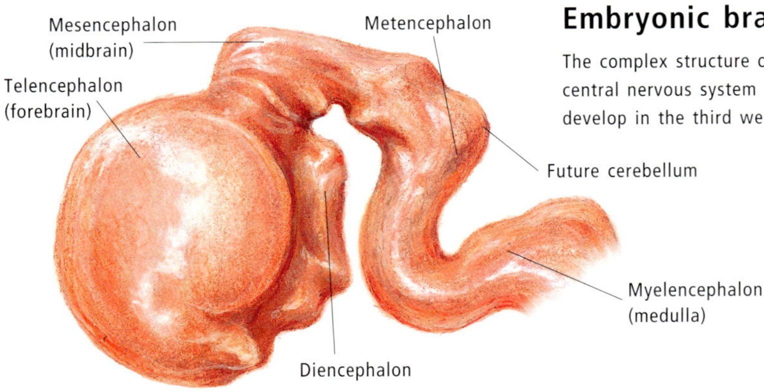

Embryonic brain

The complex structure of the brain and central nervous system (CNS) begins to develop in the third week of gestation.

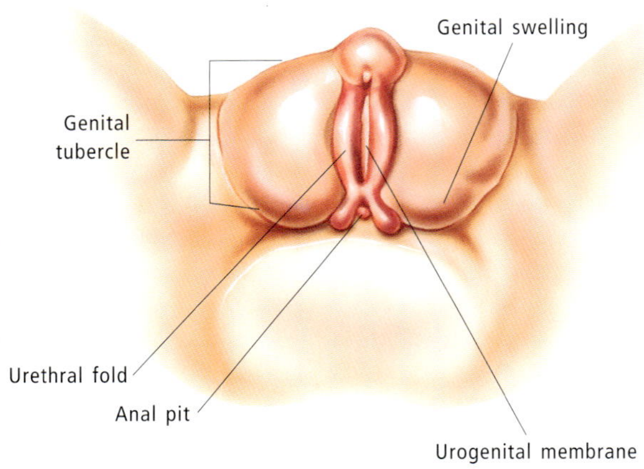

Gender difference

In the first few weeks of life the sex organs are undifferentiated. As the embryo develops, the genital tubercle will become part of the penis (the glans) if the embryo is male, and the clitoris if it is female.

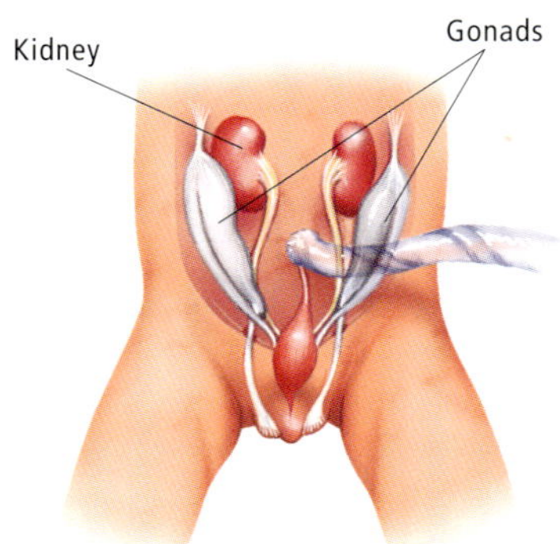

Development of testes

As the gonads (the sex glands) develop in the embryo, it is possible to distinguish between ovaries and testes as early as week 7. The testes start to form in the body cavity near the kidneys, gradually descending into the scrotum during fetal development.

safely remove enough amniotic fluid for diagnosis, so this is not done during the embryonic period.

Organ development

Considerable rearrangement is required for a flat sheet of cells to become a recognizably human embryo. Folding and growth during week 3 results in a rolling under of the sides, head and rear of the embryo so that it becomes a hollow tube with the gut suspended inside it. This coincides with the start of formation of many of the organ systems. The diaphragm and the compartments in the chest cavity which contain the lungs and heart begin to develop just after folding. These are important for normal postnatal function and in embryonic development. For example, if the diaphragm fails to form completely there may be herniation of abdominal organs into one of the pleural (lung) cavities and these may compress the lung and prevent its proper development.

Heart and blood vessels

The heart and blood vessels are the first organs to function. This is important as even a small embryo is so functionally active that it requires a good blood supply.

During week 3, groups of blood vessels form throughout the embryo and, as they grow, join and form a network. This network communicates with the heart which develops separately. The heart then starts to beat. Heartbeat can be detected by ultrasound during week 5 of gestation. The heart is initially a simple tube; the partitions which will convert it into a 4-chambered structure develop later. If one of these partitions is incomplete a "hole in the heart" (septal defect) results, which will misdirect the flow of blood through the postnatal heart. These defects can usually be corrected surgically.

Brain and spinal cord

Development of the brain and spinal cord (the central nervous system or CNS) is initiated during the third week when a shallow groove forms along the back of the embryonic disk. This groove becomes deeper and the edges fuse together to form a tube. The fusion starts in the region of the neck and extends forwards and backwards to fully enclose the tube by the end of week 4 of gestation. Sometimes an abnormal opening remains at one or, rarely, both ends.

If the tube fails to close at the end which should form the brain, then normal brain and skull do not form and there is either a portion of brain protruding from an opening in the skull or, in extreme cases, an open undeveloped structure where the brain and cranium should have been. This is called anencephaly. A defect in the closure of the rear end of the neural tube leads to spina bifida.

After closure of the tube, there is extensive further growth and development of the CNS which continues during the first two years of postnatal life. It is important to realize that the CNS is prone to abnormal development in the embryonic period due to extensive cell division. A common cause of CNS malformations is heat stress, which can be caused by infections or strenuous exercise in early pregnancy. The hollow center of the neural tube remains and becomes filled with cerebrospinal fluid. The vertebrae and skull form around the developing CNS.

Continuing growth of the CNS is possible after bone formation because of remodeling, i.e. resorption of old bone from the inside and laying down of new bone on the outside, which results in a larger structure of the same shape. In the case of the developing brain, the fontanelles and the flat bones of the skull also play a role in permitting growth.

Some nerves grow out from the CNS to innervate muscles and organs of the body. Other nerves, including those carrying sensory information, develop separately and later make communication with the appropriate parts of the CNS.

Digestive system

The digestive system starts as a simple tube, formed when the underside of the flat embryo is rolled inwards during folding. The upper part becomes the esophagus and this joins to the mouth when it develops. The part of the tube below the diaphragm expands to form the stomach. Outgrowths from this region will also form the liver, gallbladder and pancreas. The rest undergoes enormous change to form the intestines.

The growth of the intestines is so considerable that they temporarily herniate into the body cavity in the umbilical cord during weeks 6 to 10. After this the abdominal cavity has enlarged sufficiently to permit return of the intestines to their normal position. This procedure occasionally fails and the infant is born with a type of umbilical hernia.

Respiratory system

The respiratory system arises at the end of week 4 as a tubular outgrowth from the front of the upper digestive tract. The first part of the respiratory system remains unbranched and forms the larynx and trachea. Development of the other respiratory structures involves a process of repeated branching and later differentiation. The first branches are the main lower airways (bronchi). Later branching forms the smaller airways and the alveoli where, in postnatal life, oxygen is supplied to the blood.

The lungs are immature until around 32 weeks of gestation; an infant born before this has a reduced chance of survival, though with sophisticated treatment some do survive from as early as 23 weeks. The lungs develop slowly because the embryo lives in a fluid rather than a gaseous environment, and the lungs are non-functional before birth, oxygen being obtained from the placenta via the umbilical arteries.

Face and jaws

The face and jaws start to develop during week 4, arising from a series of thickenings on either side of the developing head, which fuse in the midline and rearrange to form small but recognizable jaws, mouth and nose by the end of the embryonic period.

The main problem encountered with this process is the formation of a cleft lip or palate, resulting from failure of fusion of the thickenings which would normally form these structures.

The eyes and the ears

The retina of each eye starts as an outgrowth of the brain, which elongates towards the surface of the head. As the retina develops, it assumes a shape rather like a cup on the end of a stalk. The cup becomes the retina and part of the iris, and the stalk becomes the optic nerve. The presence of the developing retina induces superficial structures of the head to form lens, cornea and eyelid. Final maturation of the retina takes place after birth as a result of exposure to light.

The inner, middle and external ears all develop from surface structures on the side of the developing head. The precursor to the inner ear (which contains the organs of hearing and balance) starts as a hollow vesicle which sinks into the underlying tissues, undergoes profound development and connects to nerves from the brain during weeks 5 to 7 of gestation. The middle ear is filled with air and contains three tiny bones (the ossicles), which transmit sound from the external ear to the organ of hearing. These bones develop near a tubular outgrowth from the pharynx, which will become the eustachian tube. The external ear grows inwards to make contact with part of the middle ear to form the eardrum.

Many noxious influences, such as rubella (German measles) or heat stress, can disrupt the normal development of these complex organs. Rubella or heat stress during the embryonic period can cause congenital cataract (lens opacity) and deafness.

Limbs

Limbs start as small protrusions from the surface of the embryo during week 4. The ends of the limb buds become paddle-shaped and during week 6 develop thickenings where the fingers and toes will develop.

Controlled (or programmed) cell death is an important mechanism in many parts of the embryo for disposing of tissue which is no longer required. The skeletal support of both the limbs and digits is initially cartilage, which is replaced by bone from week 7. It is not known what determines the development of an arm rather than a leg or why particular fingers or toes form where they do.

Limb abnormalities are common and most are caused by genetic factors. Drugs such as thalidomide can be involved as well. The most critical time is during weeks 5 to 7, when the basic pattern of the limbs is being structured.

Kidneys

Three successive sets of kidneys develop in intrauterine life. The first is rudimentary and the second, the mesonephros, functions from weeks 4 to 9, being gradually replaced by the final pair of kidneys, the metanephrons. Renal function is important in intrauterine life as the urine helps to maintain the correct volume of the amniotic fluid.

Reproductive system

The gonads develop at about the same time and in the same region of the posterior body wall as the mesonephros. By week 7 it is possible to distinguish ovaries from testes. Most of the development of the gonads and other reproductive organs takes place during fetal life, including relocation of the ovaries into the pelvis and testes into the scrotum.

Chemical factors and development

The process of embryonic development as a whole is a highly coordinated affair. Much of the early embryo consists of cells which can develop along one of many lines rather than being committed to form a particular organ from the very beginning. This flexibility only lasts while the tissue is primitive and is lost once development is initiated.

As the tissues develop they either produce a chemical signal or modify their surrounding environment. These signals attract cells from other parts of the body. These cells in turn start to develop and produce their own chemical factors, and so on. In many cases the critical time during which normal development of a particular structure is determined is only a matter of a few days.

SEE ALSO ***Amniocentesis, Fertilization, Fetal development, Placenta, Pregnancy***

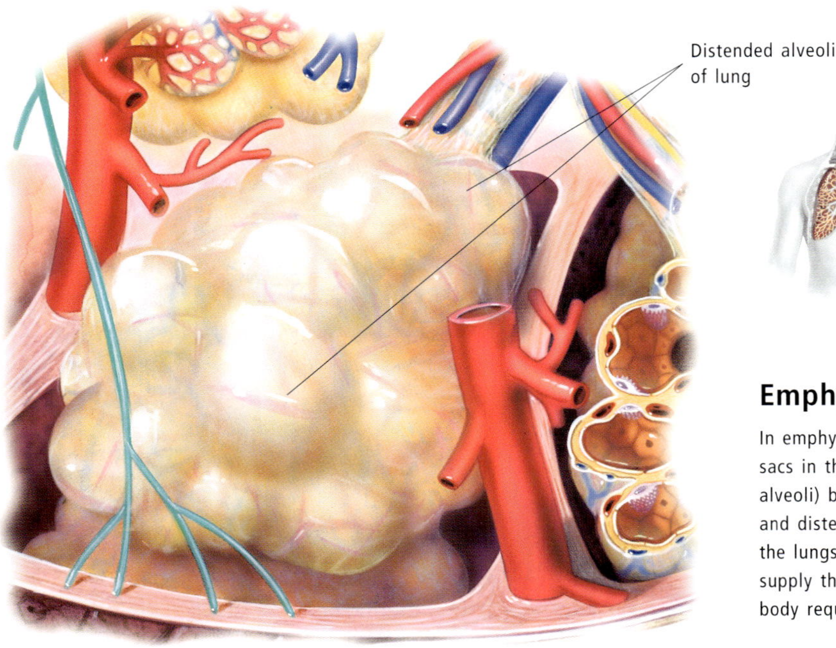

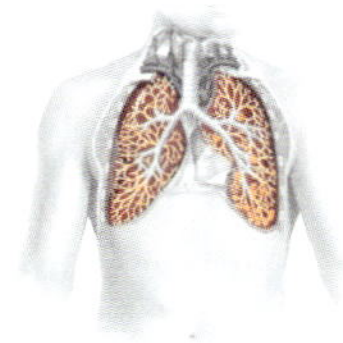

Emphysema

In emphysema, the air sacs in the lungs (the alveoli) become damaged and distended. As a result, the lungs are less able to supply the oxygen that the body requires.

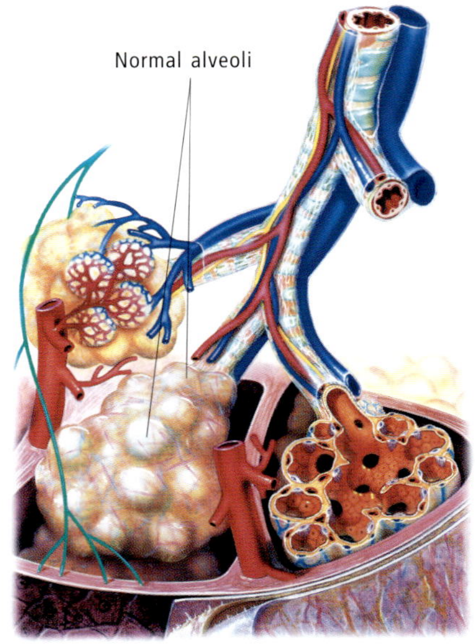

EMBRYOSCOPY

Using the same high-resolution fiberoptic equipment as employed in fetoscopy, embryoscopy allows surgeons to see the embryo and fetus (two stages of a growing baby) in early pregnancy in order to identify abnormalities. Fetal blood sampling can also be performed using this technique, known as embryofetoscopy.

SEE ALSO *Embryo, Fetoscopy*

EMOTIONS

Emotions or feelings influence the way humans react to and interpret the world they live in; they affect thoughts, words, actions and bodily functions. The basic emotions are anxiety, fear, anger, happiness and sadness. Emotions are activated by neural processes, bodily changes and mental activity. They may or may not be reflected by a person's outward appearance.

Anxiety and fear are the ways our body signals that something is wrong and that action is needed to alleviate those feelings. Usually, a person experiencing fear can identify the source; anxiety, however, may be felt only as vague uneasiness. Both emotions may be rational or irrational, which can cause psychological and bodily tension in anticipation of something which is not really a threat.

Anger, which can be caused by external or internal events, can vary from intense fury to mild irritation and, like other emotions, is accompanied by physiological and biological changes. Heart rate and blood pressure go up, as does the level of the energy hormones epinephrine (adrenaline) and norepinephrine (noradrenaline).

Sorrow or grief can often encompass other emotions such as anger and fear. Triggered by a loss the feelings can, depending on the cause, last for a long period. Happiness, together with love, is a complex emotion, which may be triggered by many factors. The causes underlying most complex emotions, such as joy, grief and anxiety, are not known.

Mood refers to a sustained emotional state; for example, elation or depression. Mood disorders are a cluster of mental disorders outside the normal emotions of sadness or elation, and are characterized by excessive depression or mania.

SEE ALSO *Anxiety, Body language, Depression, Grief, Mania*

EMPHYSEMA

Emphysema or pulmonary emphysema is a chronic obstructive lung disease marked by wheezing, breathlessness and increasing loss of lung function. The disease occurs most commonly in smokers and people exposed to polluted air and airborne dust or similar irritants, but can also affect children who suffer asthma or bronchitis.

In the early stages of emphysema the lining of the lung's airways, the bronchi and bronchioles, is stimulated by irritation of smoke or other pollutants to produce abnormal quantities of mucus. Mucus is produced in the lungs to trap dust and it is normally removed by the movement of specialized cells. Over time, the greater quantity of mucus leads to persistent coughing, "smoker's cough", and a greater susceptibility to colds, which can lead to chest infections.

The early symptoms are similar to those of bronchitis: coughing and bringing up mucus combined with asthmatic wheezing as the airways narrow. In emphysema, there is the added complication that the alveoli decay. Alveoli are the tiny sacs at the end of the bronchioles where blood gives up carbon dioxide and takes on fresh oxygen from inhaled air.

As the alveoli become less efficient, air is trapped in the lungs and the lung tissue decays. The trapped air decreases the volume of fresh air that can be inhaled and the lungs may expand permanently in the effort to counter this, resulting in a permanently expanded chest and a "barrel-chested" appearance that is characteristic of the disease. The lungs are unable to supply the oxygen the body needs, and the smallest exertion may produce severe breathlessness.

In addition to breathlessness, the symptoms of emphysema include a bluish tinge to the skin, a build-up of carbon dioxide caused by inefficient reoxygenation of the blood, loss of weight, swelling in hands and feet, tightness in the chest and increased respiratory distress in cold or smoky air. Reduced oxygen intake causes the heart to pump faster, and the strain can lead to heart failure. Bullous emphysema is a condition in which the alveoli distend and form cysts on the lungs that may rupture causing lung collapse.

The exact cause of emphysema is not known, but it is commonly associated with cigarette smoking and long-term exposure to air pollutants in mining and industrial processes. A deficiency in a protein in the liver (alpha$_1$-antitrypsin) has been found in some sufferers. Antitrypsin counteracts trypsin, an enzyme produced by many types of bacteria that decays tissue.

When emphysema is diagnosed it is essential to stop further damage by giving up smoking and avoiding exposure to pollutants and dust. No treatment can reverse the lung damage but existing lung function can be improved with the use of drugs such as bronchodilators, which relax muscles that restrict the airways, and by supplying oxygen to the sufferer for inhalation at home. Steroids can reduce lung inflammation and antibiotics are used to clear up infections. A more recent development is the surgical removal of damaged lung tissue to allow the functioning tissue room to expand and work better. Lung transplantation is also an option.

SEE ALSO *Asthma, Breathing, Bronchitis, Lungs, Respiratory system, Smoking, Wheezing*

ENCEPHALITIS

Encephalitis is inflammation of the brain, causing swelling of brain tissue (cerebral edema), bleeding within the brain (intracerebral hemorrhage) and, sometimes, brain damage. Encephalitis is usually caused by one of a number of viruses. A virus may be transmitted to humans by mosquitoes or ticks, especially in rural areas. It can also follow other viral disorders such as measles, mumps, chickenpox, rubella, infectious mononucleosis (glandular fever) and coxsackievirus illnesses. Symptoms range from a mild illness with fever and tiredness to headache, stiff neck, vomiting and, in more serious cases, seizures, paralysis and drowsiness progressing to coma.

A laboratory analysis of blood and cerebrospinal fluid (taken via lumbar puncture) will confirm the presence of the virus. Electroencephalography, cranial magnetic resonance imaging (MRI) or a CAT scan of the head may be needed to determine the extent of the infection.

Mild viral encephalitis is common and often requires no treatment other than bed rest and painkillers (analgesics). Severe cases are uncommon and usually require hospitalization and treatment with antiviral drugs such as acyclovir or amantadine, corticosteroids and drugs to control seizures, if needed.

Most cases make a full recovery within two to three weeks. A small percentage of cases suffer permanent brain damage—usually infants or the elderly.

SEE ALSO *Brain, Lumbar puncture, Viruses*

ENCEPHALOMYELITIS

Encephalomyelitis is an inflammation of the brain and the spinal cord, usually caused by a viral infection. It is closely related to encephalitis, which is an acute inflammatory disease of the brain, but without involvement of the spinal cord. Causes, symptoms, treatment and prognosis are the same as for encephalitis.

SEE ALSO *Brain, Encephalitis, Spinal cord*

ENDOCARDITIS

Endocarditis is inflammation of the smooth inner lining of the heart (the endocardium). It is caused by bacteria or fungi that enter the blood and infect and damage the endocardium of the heart chamber as well as the

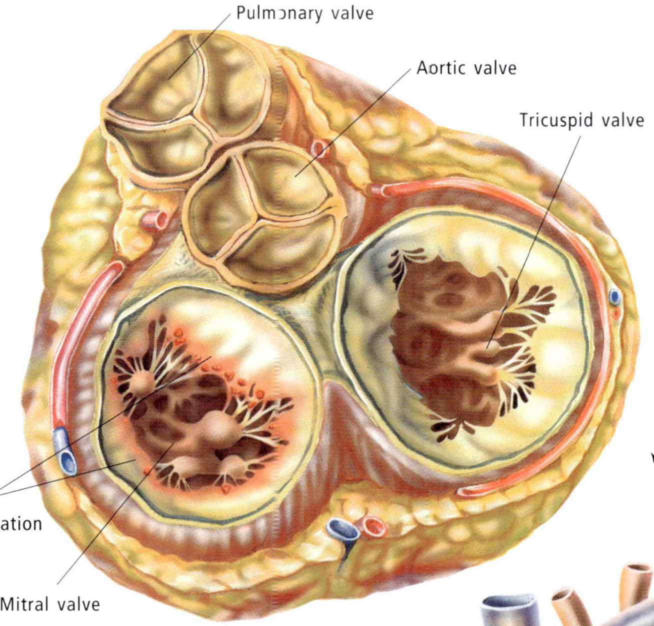

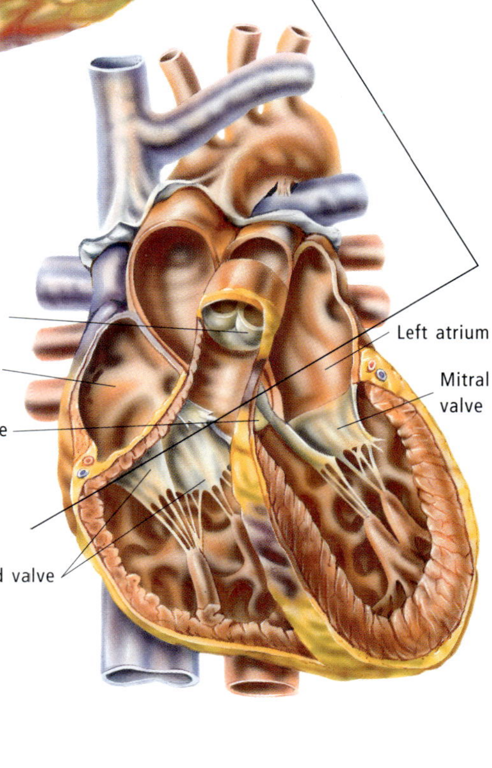

Endocarditis

Endocarditis is a bacterial or fungal infection that affects the inner lining of the heart, as well as the valves and muscle. The picture above shows diseased heart valves; the one on the right shows the location of the valves in the heart.

E

valves and the heart muscle itself. Endocarditis is more likely if there is pre-existing damage to the heart such as a congenital heart deformity, an artificial heart valve, or rheumatic heart disease. It may follow the delivery of a baby, surgery or dental work, or the use of intravenous drugs, all of which may introduce organisms into the bloodstream.

Symptoms begin gradually with fatigue, chills, aching joints and intermittent fever. Blood culture of the bacterium or fungus confirms the diagnosis. Treatment is with antibiotics which may be given intravenously. If untreated, death from heart failure is usual, but, with early treatment, most patients survive. Persons who have pre-existing heart valve disease should take antibiotic drugs before any dental or surgical procedure.

SEE ALSO *Heart*

ENDOCRINE GLANDS

The endocrine glands secrete hormones into the blood which determine growth and structure of many organs (such as during growth and maturation). They also control many vital body functions. The endocrine glands include the anterior and posterior pituitary gland, the pineal gland, thyroid and parathyroid glands, pancreas, adrenal glands, ovaries (in women) and testes (in men).

The pituitary gland is often considered the master controller, regulating the function of the thyroid, adrenal glands, pancreas, ovaries and testes. Over- or under-production of hormones from any of these glands is associated with many different types of disease. Disorders of the pituitary include dwarfism, acromegaly, diabetes, gigantism and diabetes insipidus.

Disorders of the thyroid include cretinism, myxedema, goiter and thyrotoxicosis. Disorders of the adrenal glands can cause Addison's disease, adrenogenital syndrome, Cushing's syndrome or pheochromocytoma, while disorders of the parathyroid glands cause tetany, kidney stones (renal calculi) and abnormal loss of minerals from bone. Disorders of the pancreas include diabetes mellitus and hypoglycemia.

Underproduction of sex hormones by the testes and ovaries causes lack of sex development. Underproduction of hormone is usually treated by hormone replacement therapy. Overproduction may be treated with surgery, radiation therapy or medications which suppress production of hormone by the gland.

SEE ALSO *Adrenal glands, Endocrine system, Hormones, Ovaries, Pancreas, Pituitary gland, Testes, Thyroid gland*

ENDOMETRIAL BIOPSY

During an endometrial biopsy a sample of tissue is removed from the uterine wall for testing in a laboratory. This is usually done to determine the cause of abnormal bleeding. A small tube is passed through the cervix and into the uterus and the sample taken from the uterine lining, the endometrium.

If the purpose of the test is to exclude the likelihood of endometrial cancer, a curette may be preferred. This is a different procedure which requires anesthetic, usually general, and involves removing tissue by scraping the wall with a curette. A biopsy can be performed with no anesthetic.

SEE ALSO *Biopsy, Dilation and curettage, Endometrium*

Endocrine glands

The endocrine glands produce hormones that regulate growth, sexual development and other important body functions.

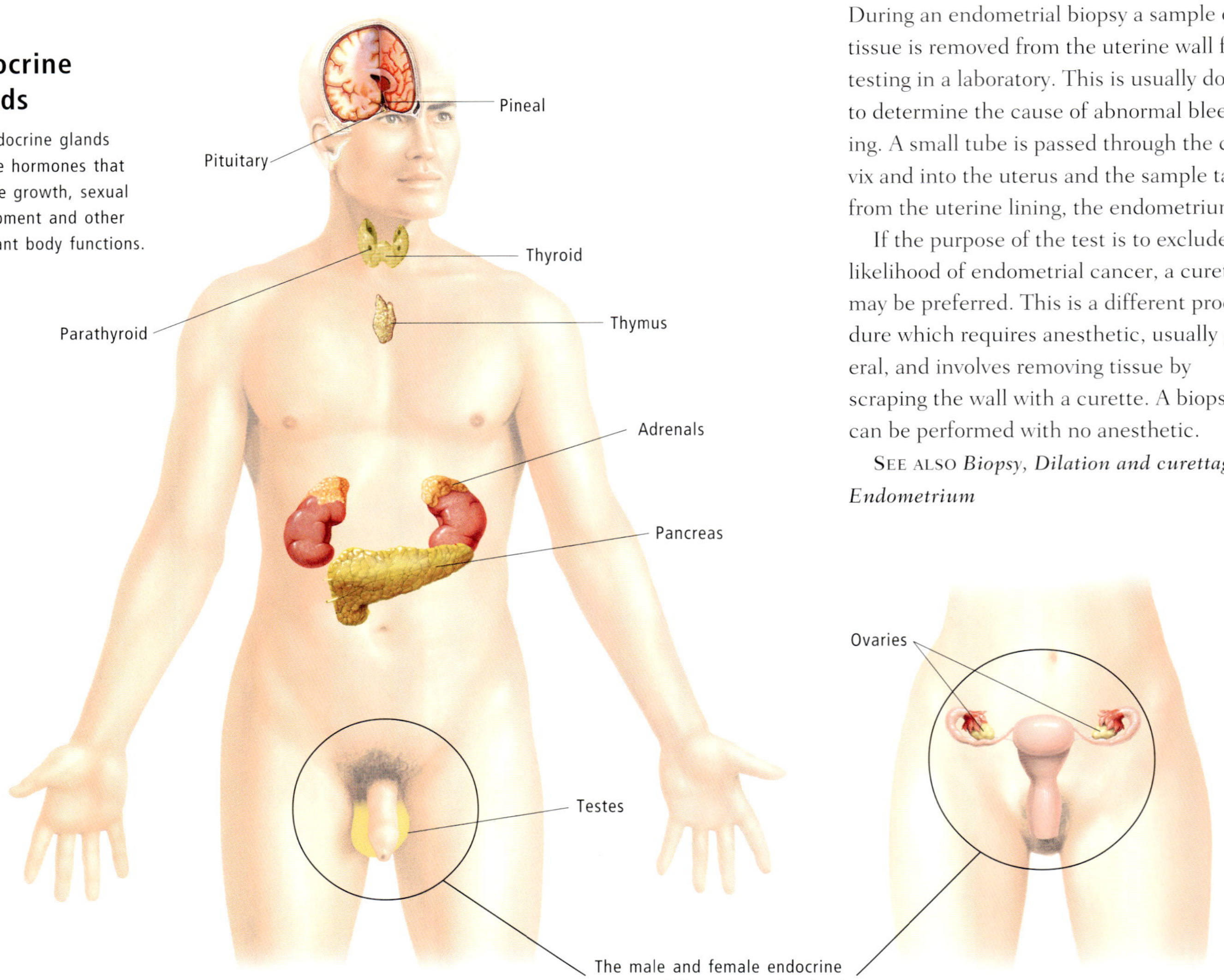

The male and female endocrine systems differ only in the glands producing the sex hormones

ENDOMETRIOSIS

Endometriosis is a condition in which tissue normally found on the lining of the uterus grows in other parts of the body such as the pelvic cavity, ovaries, bowel, bladder and rectum. This tissue (called the endometrium) acts in the same way as it would in the uterus, swelling before each period as if to prepare for nourishing a fertilized egg and then bleeding. The result is scarring and adhesions (clusters of endometrial cells) which may implant in the ovaries and fallopian tubes and obstruct the passage of the ovum.

Symptoms include increasingly painful and abnormal periods, lower back pain, pelvic cramps, pain during intercourse, abdominal pain before or during menstruation, blood in the urine, fatigue, bloating, diarrhea and constipation. Some women may experience no pain at all. Serious side effects include blood cysts in the ovaries and infertility.

The cause of endometriosis is not known, though women whose mother or sisters have had the condition have a greater chance of suffering from it. Mild cases are treated with painkillers. Symptoms may be reduced by creating a state of pseudo-pregnancy or menopause using hormonal drugs or oral contraceptives. Where pregnancy is not desired, options include removal of the ovaries or a hysterectomy. Scar tissue and adhesions may be surgically removed in some cases. Pregnancy has been known to cure the condition.

SEE ALSO *Adhesions, Endometrium, Hysterectomy, Menstruation, Reproductive systems, Uterus*

Endometriosis

In this condition, endometrial tissue is found outside of the uterus in other parts of the body, for example the fallopian tubes, cervix, ovaries, rectum, bladder and bowel.

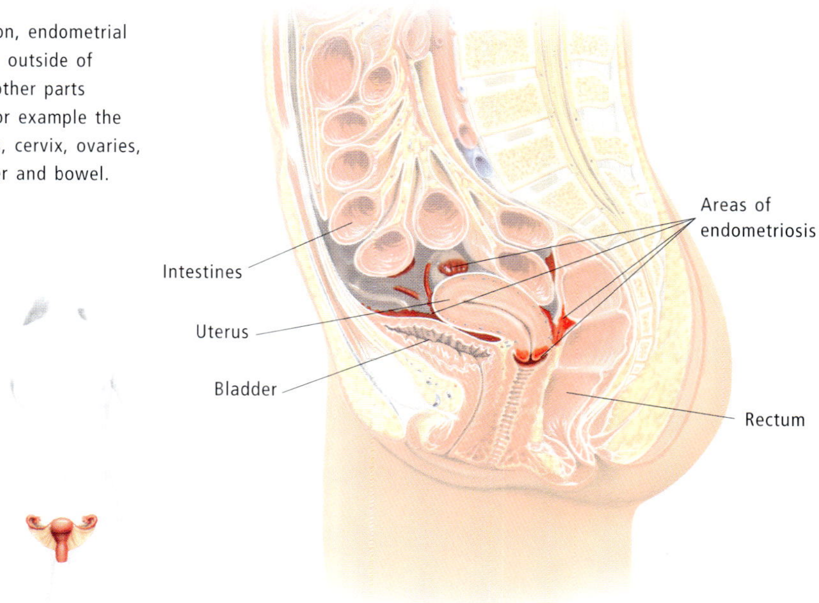

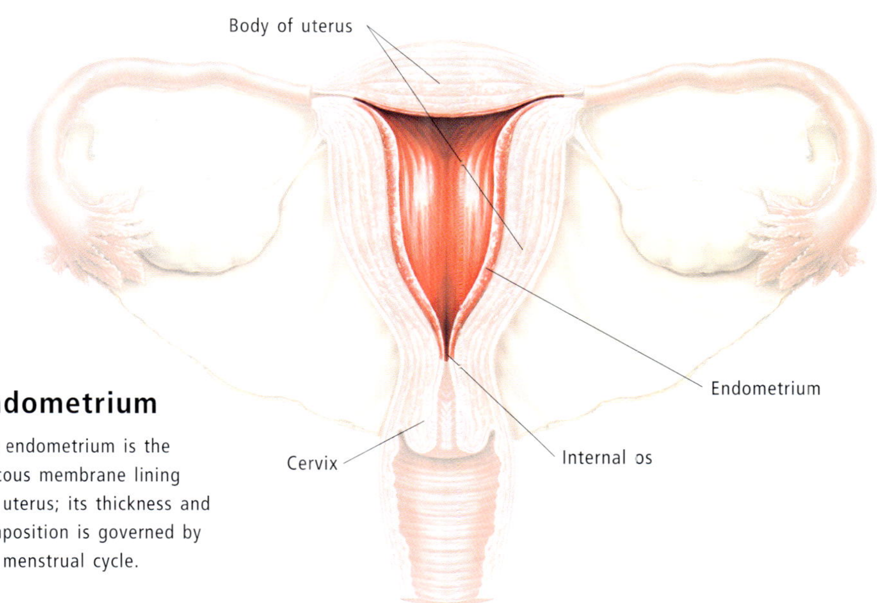

Endometrium

The endometrium is the mucous membrane lining the uterus; its thickness and composition is governed by the menstrual cycle.

ENDOMETRIUM

The endometrium is the inner glandular layer of the uterus. It consists of simple, tubular-shaped glands overlying a layer of connective tissue called the lamina propria. In a woman of reproductive age (approximately 13 to 50 years), the endometrium undergoes cyclical changes in its thickness and composition as part of the 28-day menstrual cycle.

During the first part of the cycle (the proliferative phase—lasting from 5 to 14 days after the appearance of menstrual blood), estrogen from the ovaries makes the endometrium thicker by inducing the multiplication of gland cells.

The second part of the cycle (the secretory or luteal phase—from 15–28 days after the appearance of menstrual blood) starts after the release of the egg from the ovary and the formation of the corpus luteum, which secretes progesterone. Progesterone makes the glands of the endometrium secrete and blood vessels of the endometrium be more coiled.

The final stage is the menstrual phase, which begins at the end of the secretory phase, lasts 4 days, and ends when the proliferative phase of the next cycle begins. The menstrual phase occurs only if the egg is not fertilized and no embryo embeds in the endometrium. During the menstrual phase, hormonal support for the endometrium is lost and the endometrium breaks down with bleeding. Blood and discarded endometrium are expelled from the cervix into the vagina as menstrual fluid.

The effect of oral contraceptives is to inhibit secretion of the pituitary hormone (follicle stimulating hormone, or FSH) which stimulates the maturation of eggs in the ovary. Oral contraceptives also produce cyclical changes in the endometrium.

The endometrium is also where the embryo will implant to continue its development into a fetus during pregnancy. It is the tissue of the endometrium that contributes blood vessels to the maternal part of the placenta, supplying the fetus with nutrient-rich blood.

After menstrual cycles have ceased (usually at about 50 years of age—a stage of a woman's life called menopause), the hormonal support of the endometrium is lost and the endometrium becomes thinner, less vascular and not prone to cyclical changes.

Cancer of the endometrium is usually seen only in post-menopausal women. The most common symptom is bleeding after menopause. In fact, about 40 percent of women who have vaginal bleeding after menopause have a cancer of the reproductive tract. Pain is not a common symptom, but mild uterine cramping may occur.

Diagnosis is made by taking a scraping of the uterus wall (curetting) after cervical canal dilation, and examining the tissue under a microscope. Treatment consists of removal of the uterus (hysterectomy), which is curative if the cancer is confined to the uterus, or radiation therapy combined with hormone therapy and surgery, if some spread has occurred to areas outside the uterus.

SEE ALSO *Endometriosis, Hormone replacement therapy, Menopause, Menstruation, Oral contraceptives, Placenta, Pregnancy, Reproductive systems, Uterus*

ENDORPHINS

Endorphins are a group of naturally occurring opiates with pain-relieving properties found in the brain. They are related to painkilling opiates such as opium, morphine and heroin; the word "endorphin" comes from the word "endogenous" (meaning "produced within the body") and the word "morphine".

Endorphins were discovered in 1973, following the discovery of receptors in the brain that morphine binds to. This led to the belief that the body must contain its own naturally occurring opiates; since then, several related molecules called enkephalins have also been discovered.

Endorphins and enkephalins are released into the circulation during vigorous physical exercise, such as running and jogging, and are believed to account for the painkilling (analgesic) and euphoric effect which exercise can produce in people (the "runner's high'), especially if they are mildly depressed or anxious. (Acupuncture is also thought to work by stimulating the production of endorphins.)

Dependence on and tolerance to morphine and other narcotic analgesics is thought perhaps to be caused by suppression of the body's normal production of endorphins by these opiates. When the effects of morphine wear off, it is thought that withdrawal symptoms occur because the body lacks endorphins.

SEE ALSO *Acupuncture, Exercise, Heroin, Morphine, Narcotics*

ENDOSCOPY

An endoscopy involves looking inside the body through an endoscope to investigate suspected abnormalities. Endoscopes are narrow tubes containing optical fibers and lights, and are extremely flexible. Many can also remove tissue samples or destroy abnormal tissue.

Endoscopy is used to examine the esophagus (esophagoscopy), the stomach

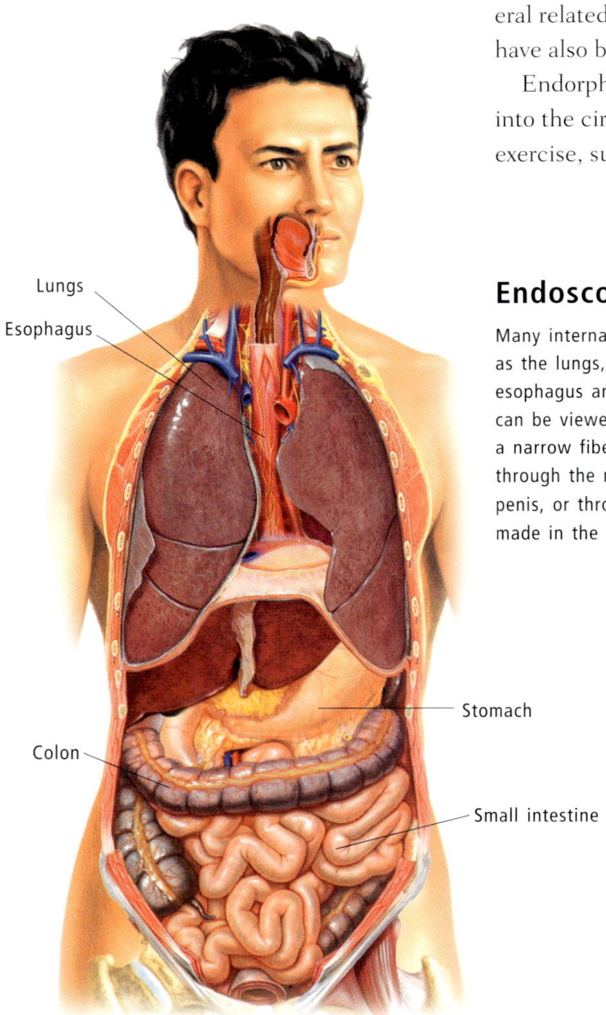

Endoscopy

Many internal organs, such as the lungs, stomach, esophagus and intestine, can be viewed by passing a narrow fiberoptic tube through the mouth, anus or penis, or through a small cut made in the abdominal wall.

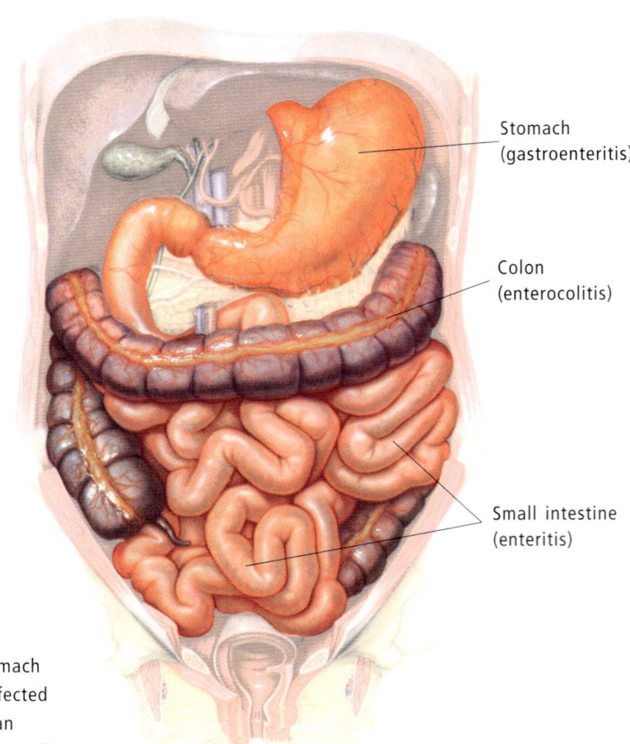

Enteritis

The small intestine, stomach and colon can all be affected by a form of enteritis, an inflammatory condition usually caused by bacterial or viral infection.

(gastroscopy), the lungs (bronchoscopy), the small intestine (upper gastrointestinal endoscopy), the lower portion of the large intestine (sigmoidoscopy), and all the large intestine (colonoscopy). Some conditions can also be treated during an endoscopy.

The use of the endoscope has simplified diagnosis and treatment of a number of problems which in the past required barium meals and enemas, though these are still used. Complications from an endoscopy are rare.

SEE ALSO *Barium enema, Barium meal, Bronchoscopy, Colonoscopy, Gastroscopy*

ENEMA

Enema is the injection of fluid into the rectum via the anus to expel the rectum's contents. Enemas were once routine for pregnant women but are more commonly used to treat cases of constipation or colonic inertia that have caused fecal impaction—the compaction of hard stools in the rectum which can cause painful cramps and block normal defecation. Enema fluids may be a saline solution or contain an oil such as olive oil.

A barium enema is given to outline the lower portion of the large intestine in x-ray procedures. It is expelled by taking a mild laxative.

SEE ALSO *Barium enema, Colonic irrigation, Constipation*

ENTERITIS

Enteritis is inflammation of the small intestine, caused by a bacterial or viral contamination of ingested food or liquids. The stomach is often also involved; the condition is then known as gastroenteritis. If the colon is involved, it is called enterocolitis. Symptoms of abdominal pain, diarrhea, fever and dehydration can begin as soon as four hours or as late as 72 hours after exposure.

Mild cases usually need no treatment and clear up in one to three days. Clear fluids such as apple juice or broth are recommended, and milk should be avoided. Anti-diarrheal medications may be useful in relieving symptoms. Diarrhea can cause rapid and extreme dehydration in infants and in such cases medical advice should be sought immediately.

SEE ALSO *Dehydration, Diarrhea, Gastroenteritis, Intestines*

ENZYME DEFICIENCIES

An enzyme is a protein produced by a living cell that speeds up chemical reactions. There are hundreds of them in the human body. Some release energy to make the heart beat and the lungs expand and contract. Many help convert sugar and foods in the digestive tract into simpler compounds so they can be absorbed and used to build tissue, replace dead cells and release energy to move muscles.

There are many diseases caused by deficiencies of enzymes. Most of them are genetic and most are rare. Two examples of enzyme-deficiency diseases are phenylketonuria (PKU) and lactose intolerance.

Phenylketonuria is caused by the absence of the enzyme phenylalanine hydroxylase, which prevents the build-up of the amino acid phenylalanine by converting it to tyrosine. If this does not happen, intellectual disability and seizures can eventuate. The enzyme deficiency can be detected at birth by a PKU test (Guthrie's test). The treatment is a diet that limits the intake of phenylalanine.

Lactose intolerance is caused by deficiency or absence of the enzyme lactase. Lactase breaks down lactose, the main sugar in milk. Without lactase, the stools become foamy and loose, with nausea and abdominal cramps and bloating. The disorder usually develops in adulthood, and can be diagnosed by examination of the stools and a lactose-tolerance test. Though not curable, the condition can be controlled with a milk-free diet.

SEE ALSO *Lactose intolerance, Phenylketonuria*

ENZYME-LINKED IMMUNOSORBENT ASSAY

Enzyme-linked immunosorbent assay (ELISA) is a family of very versatile immunologic techniques which rely on the binding of an antibody or antibodies to their corresponding antigen. An enzyme linked to one of the antibodies (either directly or indirectly) is used to generate a reaction product, usually colored, and measurement of this product allows the amount of bound antibody to be determined. Uses of ELISA techniques include detection of antibodies in blood serum, which is valuable in the diagnosis of infections, and measurement of minute amounts of circulating proteins or drugs.

SEE ALSO *Antibodies*

EPIDERMIS

The skin has three layers of tissue: epidermis, the outermost layer; dermis, the middle layer; and subcutaneous tissue, the innermost layer. The epidermis is made up of five sublayers, each with its own function. As cells in the

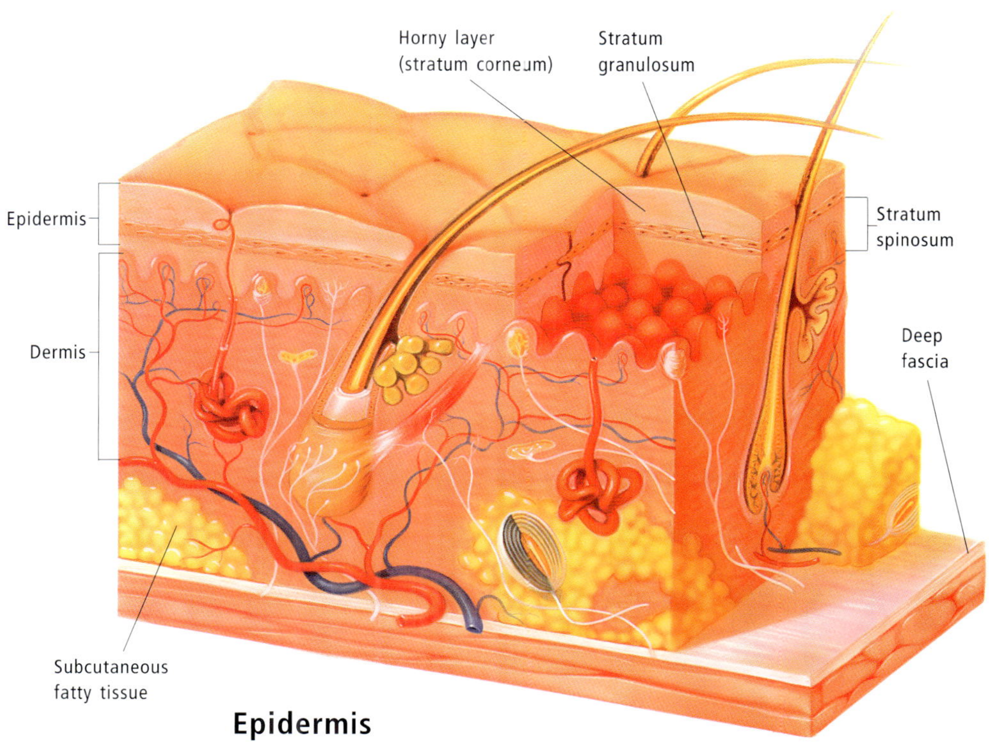

Epidermis

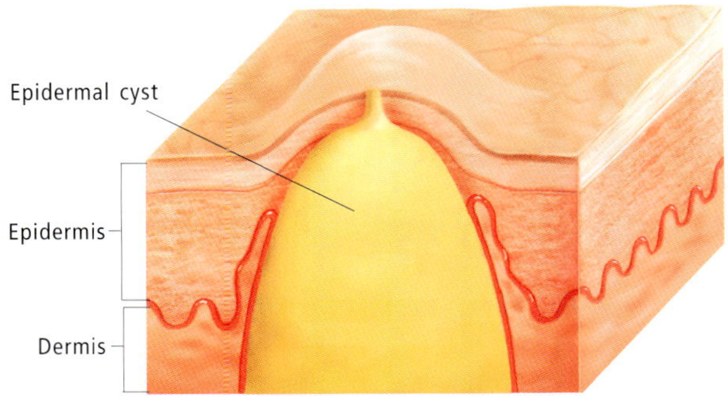

Epidermal cyst

Epidermal cysts (also known as sebaceous cysts) contain the fatty secretions of the sebaceous gland, and most commonly occur on the scalp, neck, face and trunk.

keritanous material. They occur from adolescence onwards, most commonly on the trunk, face, neck and scalp. They may become infected, turning bright red and painful. Symptomless cysts may be left alone, but if they become a source of infection or are unsightly, medical advice should be sought.

SEE ALSO *Dermatitis, Keratin, Sebaceous cyst, Skin*

top layer die and are sloughed off, they are continually replaced by cells from the lower layers. It takes approximately four weeks for cells formed in the bottom layer to reach and replace those in the top layer.

The bottom layer of the epidermis is the basal layer (*stratum basale* or *stratum germinativum*). This layer is three to five cells thick; cell mitosis, or cell reproduction, occurs here, and it is also the layer in which pigment-producing cells called melanocytes are found. They produce the pigment melanin, responsible for absorbing dangerous ultraviolet light and for giving skin its dark appearance in dark-skinned races.

Sunlight stimulates the production of melanin, resulting in a tanned appearance following prolonged exposure to sunlight.

On top of the basal layer lies the spiny layer (*stratum spinosum*), which is eight to ten cells thick and is made up of flattened cells with spiny projections. Above this is the grainy layer (*stratum granulosum*). This layer is three to five cells thick; cells in this layer produce keratin, a waxy substance that forms a tough surface layer in the outermost epithelial cells.

Next is the clear layer (*stratum lucidum*), a thin, clear, keratin-rich layer three to four cells thick, which is thickest on areas subjected to heavy wear and tear, such as the palms of the hands and the soles of the feet.

The outermost layer is the horny layer (*stratum corneum*). Most of the cells in this layer (25–30 cells thick) are dead; it takes about two weeks for cells to reach the surface, where they are sloughed off. Thus, the skin is in a constant process of renewal. The stratum corneum is the main barrier to skin infection; if a bacterium, virus or fungus manages to penetrate this layer, dermatitis (inflammation of the skin) may follow.

Epidermal cysts, also called sebaceous cysts, are benign cysts containing fatty or

EPIDIDYMITIS

Epididymitis is inflammation of the epididymis, an oblong structure attached to the upper part of each testis in the male. The inflammation causes the epididymis to become swollen and painful. The condition may be caused by the spread of a bladder infection (cystitis), or it may be a complication of a sexually transmitted disease.

The affected person experiences pain when urinating and increased frequency of urination. The scrotum may be painful, enlarged and tender. Treatment with antibiotic drugs and painkillers (analgesics) is usually effective.

SEE ALSO *Cystitis, Sexually transmitted diseases, Testes, Urinary systems*

EPIDURAL ANESTHESIA

Epidural anesthesia is used to eliminate pain in childbirth and involves the administration of an anesthetic near the base of the spinal cord. It numbs the lower part of the body, either completely or partially, and allows the woman to remain conscious. An epidural may be used on request or on the advice of the doctor or other caregiver; an epidural is sometimes to lower high blood pressure (hypertension).

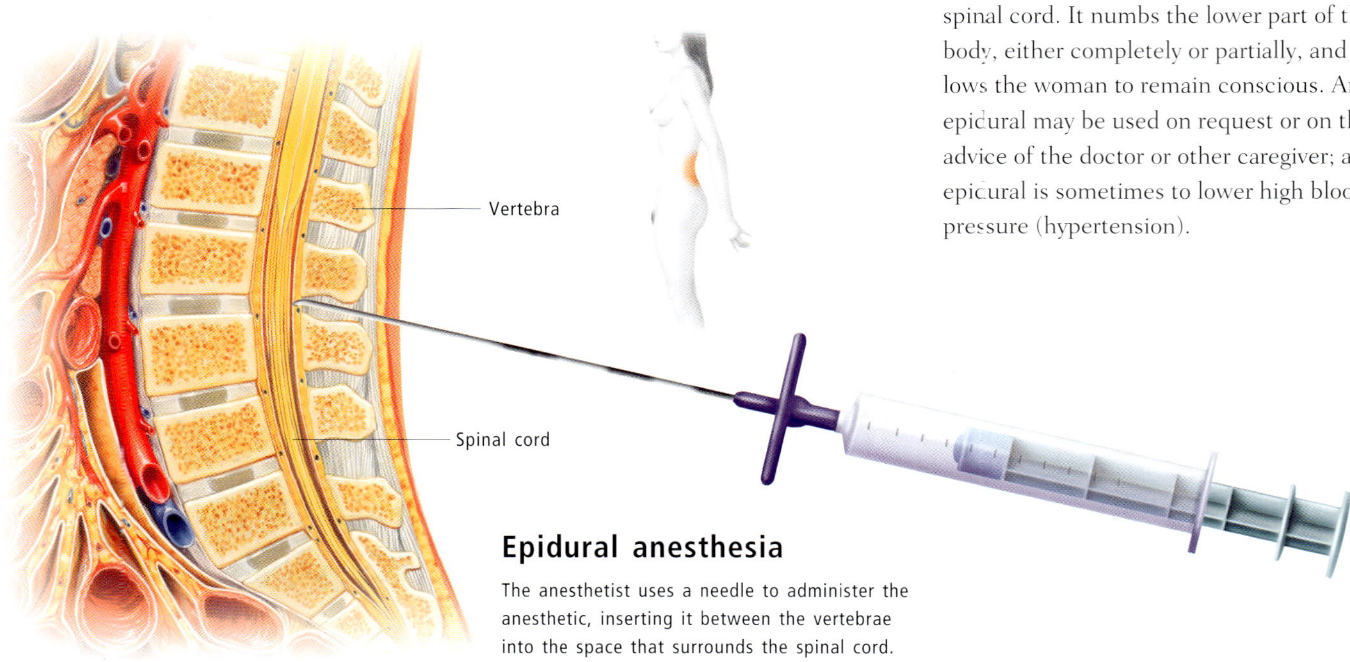

Epidural anesthesia

The anesthetist uses a needle to administer the anesthetic, inserting it between the vertebrae into the space that surrounds the spinal cord.

It is a more effective method of pain relief than the alternatives but carries with it an increased likelihood of cesarean section and, if used in the second stage of labor, an increased likelihood of instrumental delivery. There is little data available on its effects on the baby or long-term effects on the mother.

SEE ALSO *Anesthesia, Childbirth*

EPIGLOTTIS

The epiglottis is a leaf-shaped flap of tissue in the throat that lies just behind the base of the tongue and over the opening of the voice box (larynx) and windpipe (trachea). It closes off the trachea when swallowing, preventing food and liquids from accidentally passing into the trachea, directing them instead into the esophagus.

Epiglottitis is inflammation of the epiglottis. It is most common in children between two and six years old and is usually caused by the bacterium *Hemophilus influenzae*, although it may be caused by other bacteria or viruses. It begins with a high fever and sore throat, followed by rapid swelling of the epiglottis and difficulty swallowing. The swollen epiglottis can obstruct breathing and very quickly becomes a medical emergency. No attempt should be made to look in the throat if epiglottitis is suspected. Emergency medical help should be sought immediately.

The condition is treated in intensive care in hospital with antibiotics and oxygen therapy. Surgery may be needed to make a temporary opening in the trachea or to place a tube in the trachea to allow breathing until the condition improves, which may take up to a week or ten days.

SEE ALSO *Esophagus, Larynx, Trachea*

EPILEPSY

Epilepsy is disturbance in the normal electrical functions of the brain, causing seizures that may range from brief attacks of unusual behavior, a change in consciousness, erratic movements, or major seizures involving loss of consciousness. The condition affects between 0.5–1 percent of people in Western countries, and usually begins between two and fourteen years of age.

The cause is usually unknown, though there is often a family history of seizure dis-

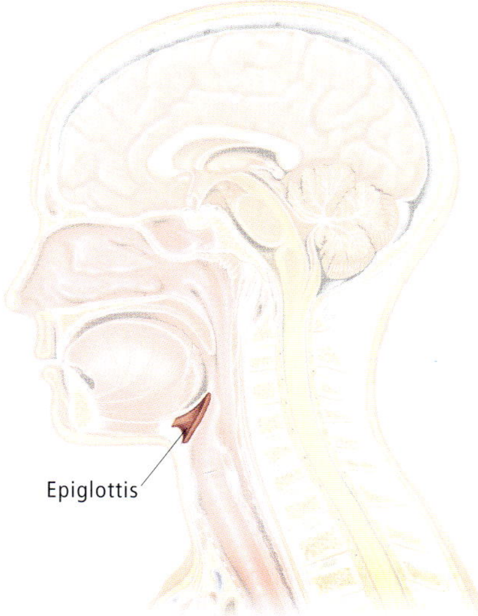

Closed epiglottis

The epiglottis is a lid made from cartilage that covers the entrance to the larynx and trachea.

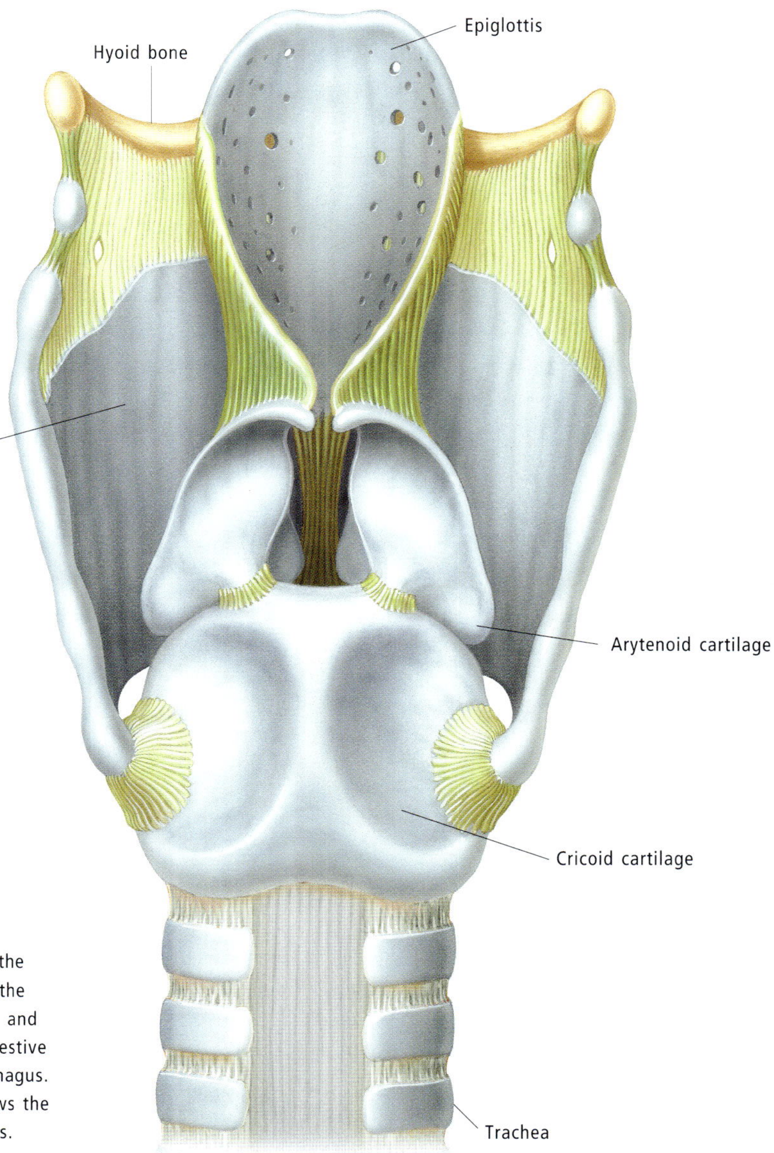

Epiglottis

When you swallow, the epiglottis closes off the trachea so that food and liquids enter the digestive system via the esophagus. This illustration shows the back of the epiglottis.

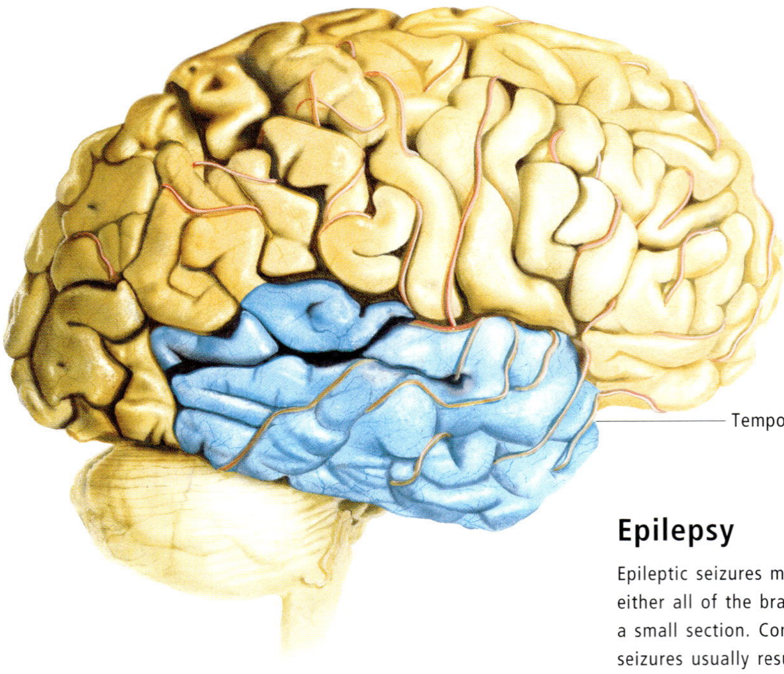

Epilepsy

Epileptic seizures may affect either all of the brain, or only a small section. Complex partial seizures usually result from a disturbance in the temporal lobe.

orders. In about a quarter of cases, there is an organic brain disorder such as a head injury, brain tumor, cerebral palsy, meningitis or encephalitis.

Seizures may occur in a generalized form (affecting all or most of the brain) or in a partial form (affecting only a portion of the brain). Generalized seizures cause loss of consciousness and include grand mal or tonic-clonic seizures (major seizures) and petit mal (minor) seizures (which occur mostly in children). Partial seizures that are termed focal result from a disturbance in the cortex; there may be abnormal movements or sensations, but the sufferer usually remains conscious. Complex partial seizures most commonly result from a disturbance in the temporal lobe.

Generalized tonic-clonic seizures begin with a sudden loss of consciousness. The person falls and the muscles become rigid (the tonic phase). As the abdominal muscles contract, forcing air from the lungs through the larynx, the person may give a shrill scream. Respiration ceases briefly, and the skin may turn blue. The lower limbs become extended and the upper limbs flexed. After about a minute, the clonic phase follows, consisting of jerking contractual movements of muscles in all four limbs. Breathing starts again, but is heavy and irregular, with frothing of saliva at the mouth. Incontinence (loss of bowel and bladder control) is common and the tongue may be bitten. Recovery occurs after 3–5 minutes. A period of confusion follows, when the person feels sleepy and may have a headache. Afterwards, there is no recollection of the seizure or the period of confusion after it.

A petit mal seizure is much shorter than a grand mal seizure. It generally lasts less than 15 seconds and is characterized by loss of consciousness, but there are no involuntary movements and the person does not fall over. After the seizure, the person is alert and can resume their previous activity.

Other symptoms and signs may accompany the seizures; including headache, changes in mood or energy level, dizziness, fainting, confusion and memory loss. An aura (a sensation such as a peculiar smell, vision or other sensation) may occur just before a generalized seizure. In some people, seizures may be triggered by hormone changes such as pregnancy or menstruation, illness, or by sensory stimuli such as lights, sounds and touch.

An electroencephalogram (EEG) which measures electrical activity in the brain will confirm the diagnosis; it shows abnormal patterns of electrical activity and may show where the seizure is emanating from. A CAT or MRI scan of the brain may help to rule out an organic cause. Unless there is a reversible cause, epilepsy is considered a chronic, incurable condition. Nevertheless, anticonvulsant drugs can prevent most seizures and allow a near-normal life.

Grand mal seizures are usually treated with phenytoin, carbamazepine, valproic acid, phenobarbital or primidone. Petit mal seizures usually respond best to valproic acid, ethosuximide or clonazepam. Focal seizures or partial complex seizures are treated with phenytoin or carbamazepine.

If the sufferer has been free of seizures for a period (usually some years), the medications may be withdrawn gradually; many sufferers (especially children) will then stay free of seizures without medication.

Any circumstance that has triggered a seizure should be avoided and sufferers should wear a bracelet or pendant that identifies the condition. If someone has a seizure, clear the area of objects that might get in the way. Do not attempt to restrain the person. Turn the person onto the side if vomiting occurs. When the seizure is over, keep the person on their side as they sleep.

Epilepsy is a serious, potentially life-threatening condition, usually defined as recurrent major convulsions that last for more than twenty minutes. Permanent brain damage or death can result if the seizure is not treated effectively; the longer the seizure lasts, the greater the danger. Treatment with intravenous anticonvulsants should be given as soon as possible.

SEE ALSO *Anticonvulsants, Brain, Cerebral palsy, Electroencephalogram, Encephalitis, Meningitis*

EPINEPHRINE

The hormone epinephrine (adrenaline) is released by the central part (medulla) of the adrenal glands in response to stress. Epinephrine increases heart rate, blood pressure, and flow of blood to the muscles. It causes the liver to release glucose into the blood. These changes enable the body to perform under conditions of stress and danger.

Epinephrine can be produced chemically and used as a drug to treat shock, allergy attacks, anaphylaxis and asthma. It is used in surgery to decrease bleeding or prolong the effect of local anesthetics, and can be given as a heart stimulant during cardiac arrest.

Pheochromocytoma is a tumor of the adrenal medulla which secretes abnormally high amounts of epinephrine and norepinephrine. It causes headaches, palpitations, anxiety and high blood pressure. The treatment is surgical removal of the tumor.

SEE ALSO *Adrenal glands, Anaphylaxis, Allergies, Asthma*

EPISCLERITIS

Episcleritis is inflammation of the episclera, a thin layer of loose connective material that covers the sclera (the white of the eye). The cause is unknown, but is often associated with diseases such as rheumatoid arthritis, Sjögren's syndrome and herpes zoster. The affected eye is sensitive to light, and is painful and bloodshot.

Episcleritis clears up in one to two weeks without treatment, sometimes sooner with corticosteroid eyedrops.

SEE ALSO *Eye, Rheumatoid arthritis, Sjögren's syndrome*

EPISPADIAS

Epispadias is a congenital defect of the penis. The urethra—the duct connecting the bladder to the tip of the penis—opens abnormally on the top of the penis, either in the head or along the entire length. The result is abnormal leakage of urine (incontinence) and sexual dysfunction. Reconstructive surgery usually cures the defect.

SEE ALSO *Bladder, Hypospadias, Incontinence, Penis, Urethra, Urinary systems*

ERECTION

Erection is a state in which the erectile tissue of an organ or body part has become distended and rigid by the accumulation of blood. Though the nipple and clitoris contain erectile tissue, the term usually refers to the distension of the penis.

The penis is comprised primarily of two cylinders of sponge-like vascular tissue. (A third cylinder contains the urethra, a tube that carries the urine and the ejaculate.) After physical or psychological sexual stimulation, the cylinders become engorged with blood and the penis becomes erect and hard. This enables the male to insert the erect penis into the female's vagina during sexual intercourse. The blood is unable to drain out through the veins because they are temporarily closed by pressure from arterial blood in the spongy tissue of the penis.

Inability to produce or maintain an erection of the penis is called impotence. It is more common in older men and can be caused by psychological problems, alcohol, drugs, surgery, or disorders such as diabetes and stroke. Depending on the cause it can be successfully treated with sex therapy, penile implants, needle injection therapy, vacuum cup devices or medications such as sildenafil (Viagra).

Peyronie's disease (curvature of the penis) is a bend in the penis that occurs during erection. It cannot be cured but it can be helped with hormone (corticosteroid) injections into the penis.

SEE ALSO *Impotence, Penis, Peyronie's disease, Reproductive systems*

EROGENOUS ZONES

An erogenous zone is any part of the body that, when stimulated, can produce sexual arousal or pleasure.

In the mid-twentieth century, the American researcher Alfred Charles Kinsey found that there is no part of the human body that is not able to bring about sexual arousal in some individuals. He estimated that in about half of all females the breasts and nipples were erotically sensitive enough for stimulation to result in orgasm. Conversely, his research found about 2 percent of females had never found themselves to be sexually aroused under any conditions.

Obvious erogenous zones in men are the external sex organs: the penis, particularly the glans which is the sensitive head above the shaft; the skin of the scrotum and inner thighs; the buttocks and external skin around the anus; and in some men, the nipples. In women the clitoris, vulva, nipples, areolae, breasts and inner thighs are the main areas sexually responsive to stimulation.

Every part of the body can be sexually aware, and respond to stimulation, as our experience of sexual pleasure is largely mental. When injury or disablement affects the touch-receptive nerve endings in one area, new areas can replace them, and relocate the traditional erogenous zones.

The hypothalamus, the part of the brain that regulates the autonomic nervous system, receives nerve impulses generated by manual stimulation of the nipples and genitalia. It responds to sexual desire by releasing hormones that increase heart rate, blood circulation and respiration rates and dilate the pupils of the eyes, bringing about a state of sexual arousal or readiness for sexual intercourse.

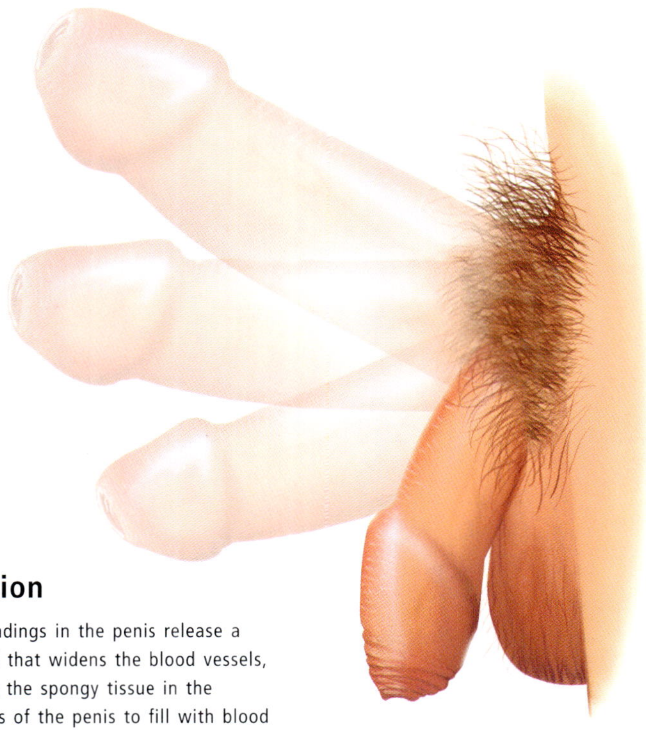

Erection

Nerve endings in the penis release a chemical that widens the blood vessels, enabling the spongy tissue in the chambers of the penis to fill with blood and enlarge, thus producing an erection.

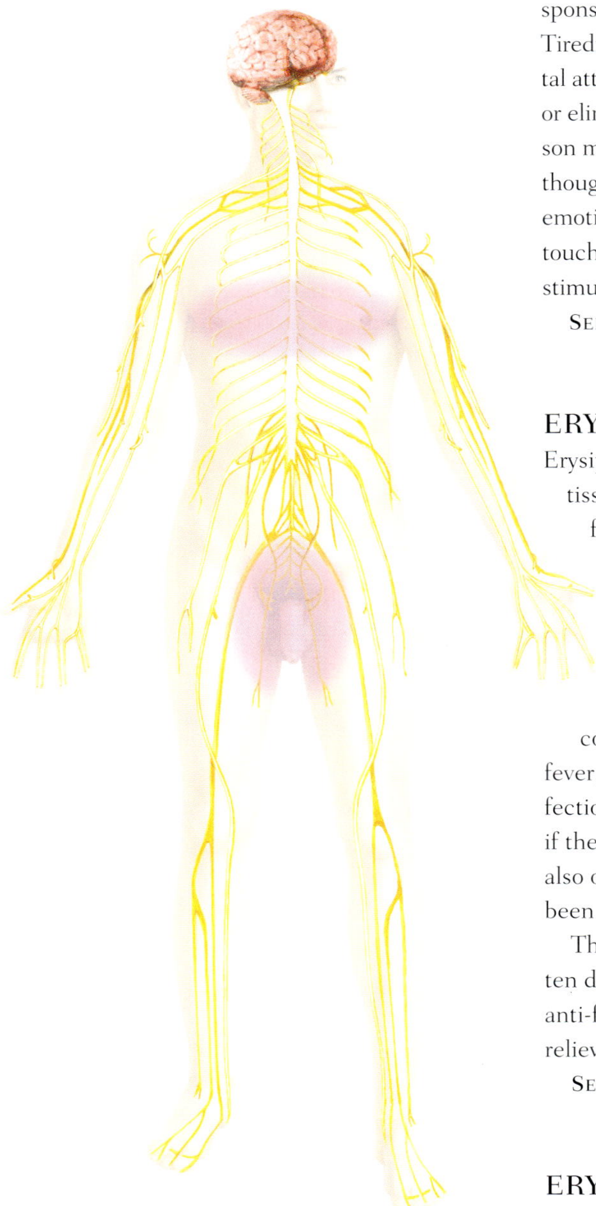

Erogenous zones

Although any part of the body can be an erogenous zone, the main areas for both men and women include the genitals, inner thighs, buttocks, breasts and nipples.

Sexual arousal is a complex emotional and physical response to stimulation of the senses—sight, smell, hearing and touch. What a person finds stimulating will be a combination of individual preferences, personal history, memories and influences from culture and conditioning. A person's response at any one time can be influenced by their physical and emotional condition.

Under stress, such as financial pressures or relationship problems, sexual drive and response to normal stimulus may be very low. Tiredness, physical disorders and pain, mental attitudes and conditioning can also reduce or eliminate normal sexual arousal. The person may have no interest in sexual contact, although they may still need the physical and emotional reassurance given by the loving touch of a partner. Under these conditions, stimulation may not produce sexual arousal.

SEE ALSO *Sexual activity, Sexuality*

ERYSIPELAS

Erysipelas is an acute inflammation of the tissues below the skin, usually on the face, caused by infection by *Streptococcus* bacteria. The bacteria enter via a break in the skin, often following a respiratory infection such as a cold. A bright red spot appears on the nose or cheeks, enlarges and becomes hot and painful, accompanied by fever, chills, muscle pains and malaise. Infection of the blood (septicemia) may follow if the condition is not treated. Erysipelas can also occur in the legs, where veins have been cut.

The inflammation subsides over a week or ten days with antibiotics. Painkillers and anti-febrile medications (antipyretics) help relieve the symptoms.

SEE ALSO *Septicemia*

ERYTHEMA

Erythema is a condition in which there is reddish discoloration of the skin or mucous membrane. Blushing and mild sunburn are examples of erythema. More serious forms of erythema are associated with inflammation, and include erythema nodosum and erythema multiforme.

Erythema multiforme

Erythema multiforme is a type of hypersensitivity (allergic) reaction that occurs usually in children and young adults. It is caused by infection (especially with the herpes simplex virus), drug sensitivity or other allergic reactions. Spots, pimples or vesicles appear on the face, hands and legs, caused by damage to the blood vessels of the skin and to underlying skin tissues.

Usually the condition subsides in two to three weeks with oral corticosteroid treatment and skin dressings. In one variant, Stevens-Johnson syndrome, lesions are extensive, involving multiple body areas and requiring treatment in a burns unit in hospital.

Erythema nodosum

In erythema nodosum, painful, red, oval nodules appear on the skin, usually on the shins. The nodules turn purple, then brown, and disappear after several weeks. Fever and malaise are accompanying symptoms.

The condition usually follows a streptococcal throat infection, but may be associated with diseases such as tuberculosis or ulcerative colitis. Certain drugs such as penicillin, salicylates and birth control pills may also cause the condition. Treatment is with oral hormones (corticosteroids), bed rest and aspirin; topical creams have no effect on the nodules.

SEE ALSO *Corticosteroids, Herpes simplex, Stevens-Johnson syndrome, Tuberculosis, Ulcerative colitis*

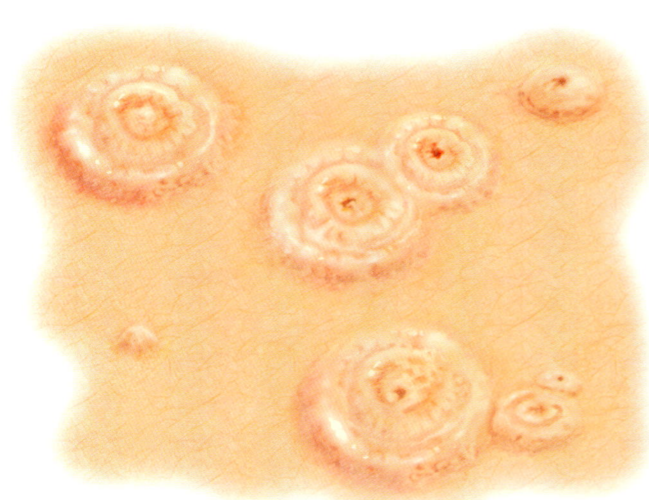

Erythema multiforme

Erythema multiforme is characterized by spots, pimples or blisters that usually appear on the face, hands and legs.

ERYTHRASMA

Erythrasma is a chronic, slowly spreading skin infection. It occurs mostly in adolescents, in overweight people and in those with diabetes, especially in hot areas like the tropics. Reddish-brown, slightly scaly patches with sharp borders appear in moist areas such as the groin, axilla and skin folds, and between the toes. They resemble a fungal infection, but in fact are caused by a bacterium, *Corynebacterium minutissimum*.

Antibacterial soaps and oral antibiotics (such as eythromycin or tetracycline) clear the infection, but it tends to recur.

SEE ALSO *Intertrigo*

Erythema nodosum

Erythema nodosum is a painful condition in which red nodules appear, usually on the shins, fading to bruise-like patches that disappear after several weeks.

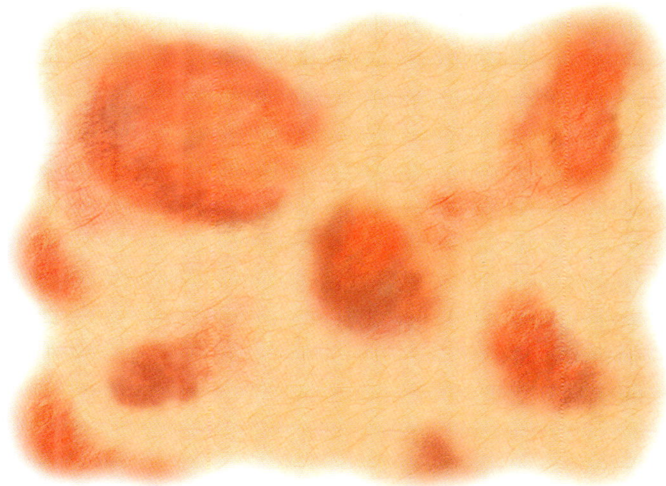

ERYTHROCYTE SEDIMENTATION RATE

A commonly requested pathology test, erythrocyte sedimentation rate (ESR) is a measure of the rate at which red cells settle in a column of blood standing in a thin tube.

Infections, anemia, certain rheumatic diseases and other autoimmune disorders are all associated with a rapid rate compared to normal ESR (1–20 millimeters/hour). Certain cancers such as multiple myeloma can also, though not invariably, produce a high ESR reading.

The efficacy of treatment of infections can be monitored over a period until cure—judged by a normal ESR—has occurred. Therapy for tuberculosis and bone infections is checked in this way.

SEE ALSO *Red blood cells*

ESOPHAGITIS

Esophagitis literally means inflammation of the esophagus, the tube connecting the back of the throat (pharynx) with the stomach. An inflammation of the esophagus usually damages the inner, or epithelial, lining most of all. It may be due to the accidental swallowing of corrosive chemicals such as caustic soda or concentrated acid (corrosive esophagitis), or due to reflux of acidic stomach juices into the lower esophagus (reflux esophagitis). The latter may occur in sliding hiatus hernia when the mechanism which keeps stomach juices in the stomach, is impaired.

Reflux esophagitis is a serious disease and may be accompanied by heartburn and regurgitation. In severe cases, surgery to treat the sliding hiatus hernia may be necessary.

SEE ALSO *Esophagus, Hiatus hernia*

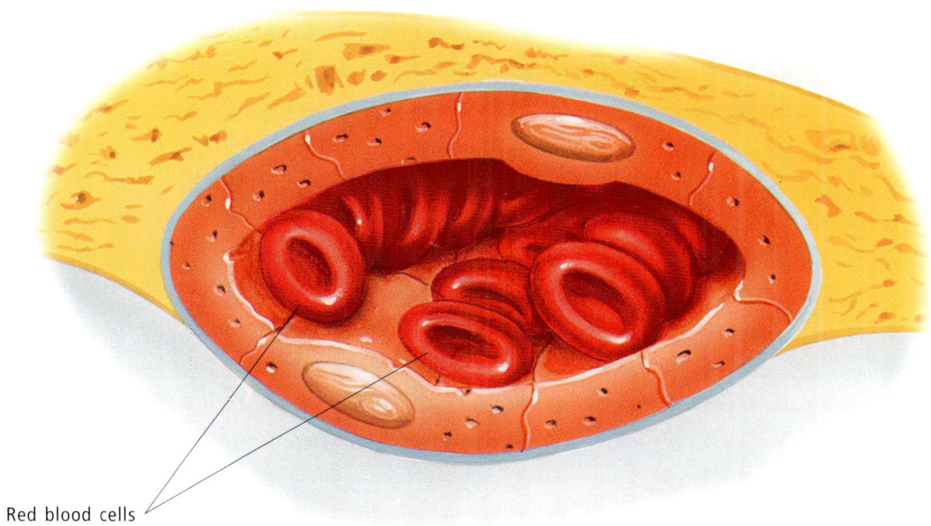

ESOPHAGUS

The esophagus is a muscular tube that allows food to be transported from the throat (pharynx) to the stomach. It passes through the neck and chest and into the abdomen, with the portion through the chest being the longest. The esophagus must pass through the diaphragm on its way to the stomach.

Three areas of the esophagus are relatively narrow and may be sites where swallowed corrosive substances (such as caustic soda or sulfuric acid) are slowed up and may cause major damage. These sites of narrowing are at the beginning of the esophagus, where the esophagus crosses the arch of the aorta just above the heart, and where the esophagus passes through the diaphragm.

Sometimes the esophagus does not form properly during development and may be obstructed; this condition is known as esophageal atresia. The infant has great difficulty in swallowing milk; the regurgitated milk may be inhaled, causing pneumonia.

Achalasia of the esophagus is a condition in which nervous control of the esophageal muscle is impaired, due to degeneration of nerve cells in the esophageal wall. It results in difficulty in swallowing (dysphagia), retention of food in the esophagus and dilation of the esophagus.

Erythrocyte sedimentation rate

Erythrocyte sedimentation rate (ESR) measures the rate at which red blood cells (erythrocytes) settle in a column of blood standing in a tube. It is a test used to help diagnose many illnesses.

Cancer of the esophagus is a relatively rare, but serious, condition, usually involving the malignant growth of the cells lining the esophagus. The patient complains of progressive difficulty in swallowing, beginning with solids and eventually involving liquids. There can be progressive weight loss and, occasionally, bleeding. Complications of the disease include fatal bleeding, pneumonia, obstruction of the trachea and problems with heart rhythm.

Infection of the esophagus itself is rare, but infection by yeast cells (candidiasis) can affect the esophagus. This is more common in those patients whose immune defenses against fungus are impaired.

As already mentioned, the esophagus may be damaged by swallowed corrosive substances such as strong acids or caustic soda (corrosive esophagitis). These substances cause chemical burns to the lining of the esophagus, which may cause perforation of the esophagus with spilling of food into the chest cavity, bleeding from esophageal ulcers and constriction (esophageal strictures) when scar tissue forms several weeks after injury.

A diverticulum or out-pocketing of the esophagus may occur when the esophagus "blows out" between strands of encircling muscle. This usually occurs in the upper part of the esophagus.

The esophagus leads into the stomach. In some situations, stomach juices may regurgitate from the stomach into the lower esophagus (gastroesophageal reflux). This usually occurs when part of the stomach slides through the diaphragm into the chest cavity (sliding hiatus hernia), thus interfering with the ability of the diaphragm to prevent reflux of stomach juices into the esophagus.

In cirrhosis of the liver, often caused by chronic alcoholism or viral hepatitis, small veins in the lower end of the esophagus may become enlarged (esophageal varices). These varices protrude through the inner surface lining of the esophagus and may rupture, discharging large amounts of blood into the lower esophagus. This blood is either vomited (hematemesis), or passed out through the anus as a dark, black, tarry stool. This is a very serious condition, because most patients who have massive bleeding from esophageal varices die as a result of the initial bleed.

SEE ALSO *Achalasia, Candidiasis, Cirrhosis of the liver, Diaphragm, Digestive system, Dysphagia, Gastroesophageal reflux, Hiatus hernia, Pharynx, Stomach*

ESTROGENS

Estrogens are a group of steroid hormones produced in the ovaries and, in lesser amounts, by other organs such as the adrenal glands. Steroid hormones are fatty substances derived from cholesterol and are taken up from the blood. The conversion of cholesterol to estrogens takes place via a series of steps, each of which is controlled by an enzyme. Intermediate substances in the pathway include both progesterone and testosterone; if one of the enzymes is deficient or inactive, testosterone may be secreted instead of estrogen.

The estrogens produced in the ovary are estradiol and a related substance, estrone. These are both released into the circulation

Esophageal diverticulum

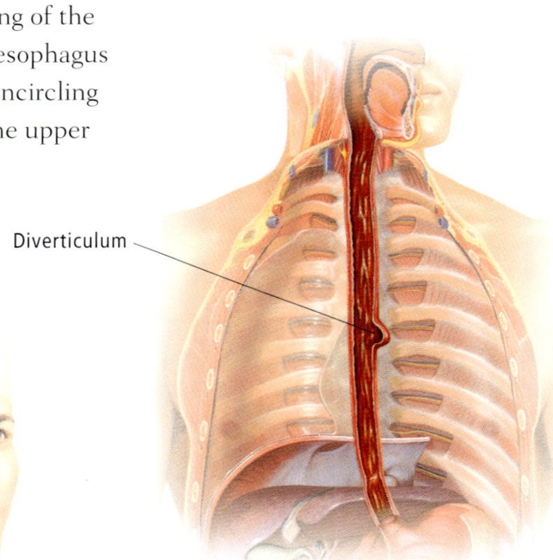

Achalasia

In achalasia, a constriction of the lower sphincter impedes the passage of food, dilating the esophagus above it.

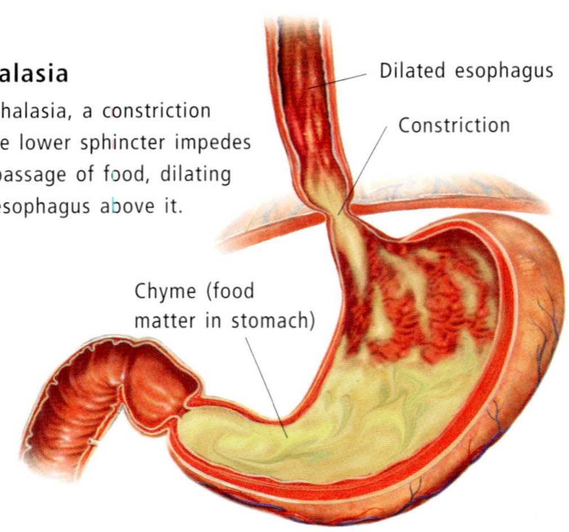

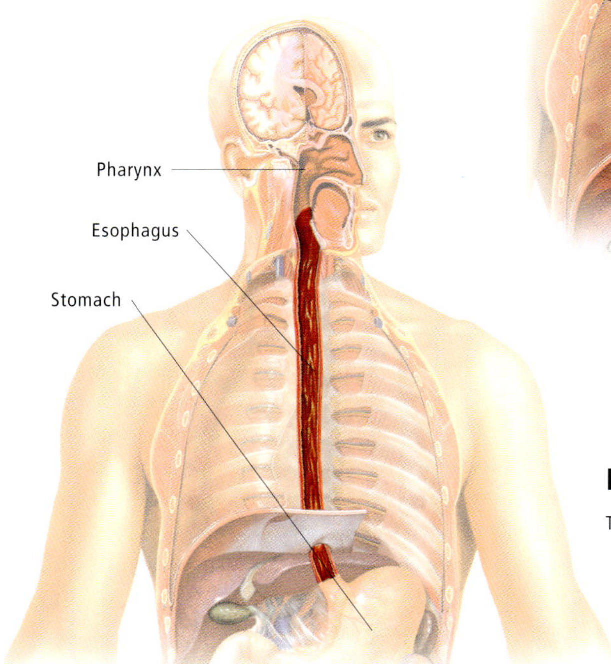

Esophagus

The esophagus is the muscular passage extending from the pharynx to the stomach. When the esophagus "blows out" between strands of encircling muscle, a diverticulum may occur.

Hiatus hernia

Part of the stomach protrudes through the esophageal opening in the diaphragm.

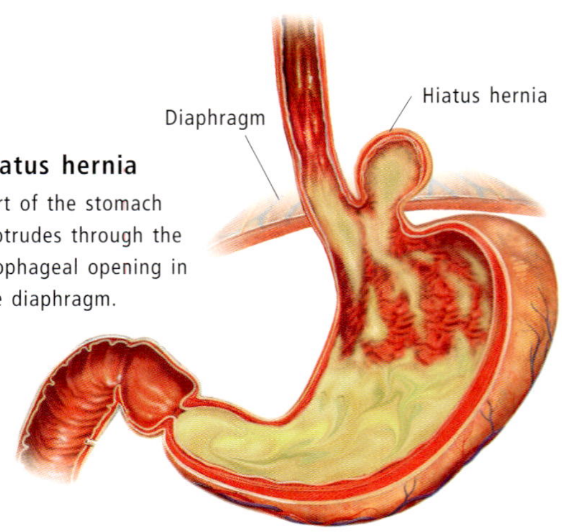

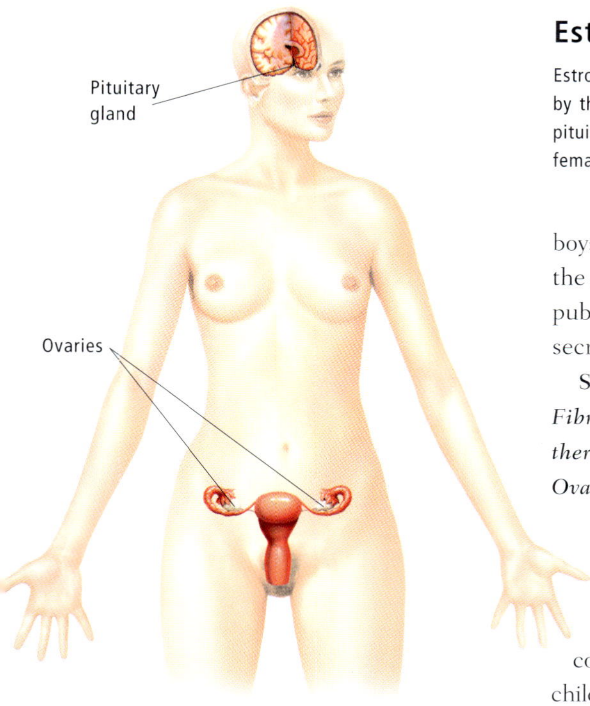

Estrogens

Estrogens are female sex hormones produced mainly by the ovaries. Their production is controlled by the pituitary gland. They control the development of the female sex characteristics and reproductive system.

and are broken down in the liver to form estriol, found in urine. The ability of target organs, such as the uterus, to respond to estrogens and other hormones is determined by whether the cells of that organ have receptors for the hormone on their surfaces.

Estrogens are secreted in high quantities in pregnancy. The placenta and the fetal and maternal adrenal glands are all involved. Estrogen levels fall a few days after giving birth. Estrogen production declines before and during menopause, and its loss may cause thinning of the lining of the vagina, vulvitis, osteoporosis and increased risk of cardiovascular disease. Hormone replacement therapy, using a combination of estrogen and progesterone, reduces or eliminates these effects.

Estrogens are involved in the development of fibroids (benign tumors in the muscle wall of the uterus and the most common pelvic tumor in women). Fibroids tend to grow rapidly during pregnancy when estrogen levels are high and may cause complications or miscarriage. Fibroids decrease in size following menopause.

Abnormally early breast development (gynecomastia) can result from ovarian tumors, which produce large amounts of estrogens, or from estrogens in oral contraceptives mistakenly ingested by young children. Gynecomastia may also occur in boys because of the transient increase in the amount of estrogens produced during puberty. It disappears when testosterone secretion is established in normal amounts.

SEE ALSO *Adrenal glands, Cholesterol, Fibroids, Hormones, Hormone replacement therapy, Menopause, Oral contraceptives, Ovaries, Pregnancy, Testosterone*

EWING'S SARCOMA

Ewing's sarcoma is the second most common type of bone cancer. It occurs in children and adolescents (usually Caucasians) between 10 and 20 years of age. A person will experience pain and sometimes swelling at the tumor site, usually in the long bones of the arms and legs (especially the femur), or the pelvis or ribs. The tumor grows quickly and spreads to other bones and the lungs.

Treatment involves a combination of intensive radiation therapy and chemotherapy, and (in some patients) surgical removal. If treated before it has spread, 60 percent of children with the tumor will survive.

SEE ALSO *Cancer, Metastasis*

EXERCISE

Exercise is physical activity undertaken to develop, maintain or improve physical fitness. People need exercise because humankind evolved leading a much more active life than is normal in industrialized societies today.

The nomadic existence of hunters was a necessity as they traveled to follow their food supplies, migratory animal herds and wild food sources that waxed and waned with the seasons. As agricultural societies evolved, a life of physical exertion and manual labor was normal for most. Only since the Industrial Revolution has the less active lifestyle largely become the norm, and this has made regular exercise a necessity to maintain good physical condition.

The mechanics of exercise

All exercise involves tension or contraction of muscles. Because muscles can only actively contract (shorten) they can only pull in one direction. They are arranged in opposing pairs to enable active extension and flexion, as in the biceps and triceps that contract to bend and straighten the elbow.

Energy for muscular contraction comes from glycogen, a form of the sugar glucose, stored in muscle tissue. When the stored energy is required, the glycogen reacts with oxygen in the blood to metabolize its energy. If oxygen is not present, which can happen during heavy workouts, the glycogen can still be metabolized, but this process creates an oxygen debt and a build-up of lactic acid in the muscles being worked. The oxygen

Exercising muscles

Muscles are arranged in antagonistic pairs to allow opposing movements such as flexion of a joint in one direction and extension in another. For example, the biceps controls flexion of the elbow, while the triceps controls elbow extension.

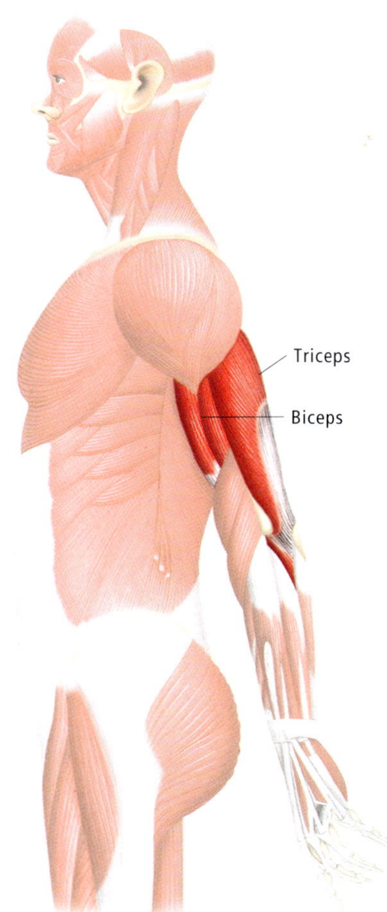

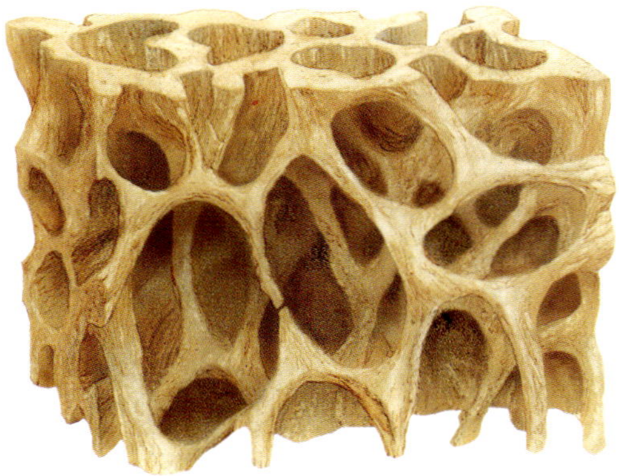

Osteoporotic bone

It is important to maintain exercise levels in later life to prevent diseases such as osteoporosis—a progressive bone disease in which bone density decreases, causing weakness and a greater likelihood of fracture.

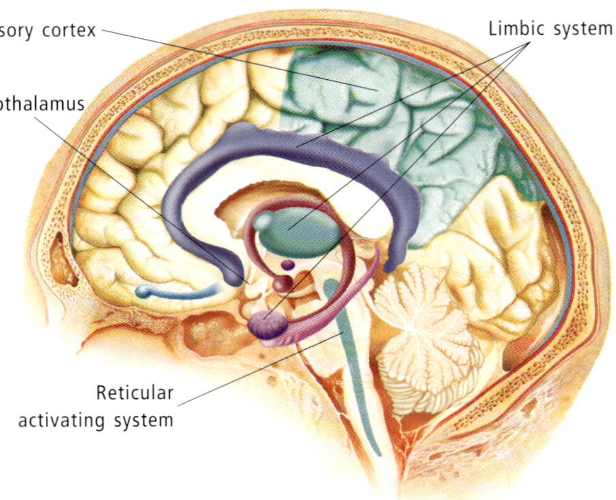

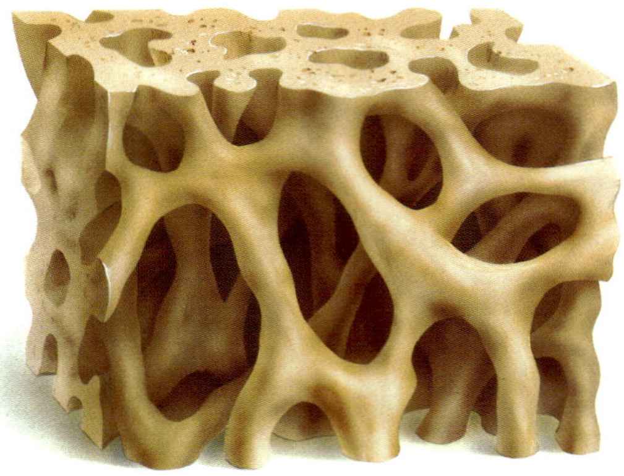

Normal bone

Exercise, particularly weight-bearing exercise, can help to maintain or increase bone density.

Role of the brain in exercise

Endorphins are found in the hypothalamus, limbic system and reticular formation. The hypothalamus influences the blood supply to muscles through the autonomic system and spinal nerves. Endorphin release increases during exercise. These neurotransmitters inhibit the conduction of pain impulses to the sensory cortex and their release can induce a feeling of well-being.

debt is repaid when oxygen becomes available. The lactic acid build-up may lead to muscle soreness.

Exercise programs are directed specifically at a performance task, or at improving flexibility, strength or endurance. The type of exercise must relate to the outcome required. Progression is another feature of exercise. A sedentary person just beginning a fitness walking program needs to start at a very modest, easily achievable level of activity, then aiming to cover a few hundred yards (meters) more every day until a goal distance is reached.

Exercise relies for improvement on continually increasing the demands put upon the muscles being exercised. Weightlifters make heavier lifts and sprinters aim to shave tenths of seconds from their timed runs.

Warming up and cooling down are vital steps in an exercise session. A gradual start allows the body's various systems to adjust to the higher demands being made: heart rate increases, pumping more blood around the body and muscle temperatures rise.

As the session draws to a close, it is important to let activity tail off and reduce intensity. This lets the heart rate slow and avoids complications such as lowered blood pressure which can cause fainting or even cardiac arrest. Target heart rate for the cool-down period is 120 to 100 beats per minute, depending on age and fitness level.

To be effective, exercise must be frequent. A minimum level of frequency is generally agreed to be three times a week or every second day. While exercising every day may be the goal for some, others may find this excessive.

Effect on health

Exercise changes the body's composition to increase the proportion of lean muscle tissue and proportionally reduce fat.

A recent study has found a marked difference in body composition with significantly lower levels of visceral fat (fat around the trunk and internal organs) between those whose daily routine included walking 7,500 paces—approximately 2½ miles (4 kilometers)—each day and those who did less. It was not important whether the walking was planned as exercise or part of their daily living routine, the effect was the same. This research, although not yet scientifically proven, seems to confirm that a sedentary lifestyle is the greatest enemy of health.

Babies, from the moment they are born, begin to exercise their muscles. As they play and experiment they are learning how to use their muscles until they can crawl, walk and run. Children also exercise when they are involved in activities such as running and bicycle riding. Obesity is a major problem for children today as the time spent on sedentary tasks has reduced the time exercising in active play. Exercise and sport need to be a natural part of childhood and adolescence, both for physical and emotional well-being and to protect against diseases in later life such as osteoporosis.

Adults who continue to exercise as they grow older will continue to benefit. Women can continue to exercise during and after pregnancy: it is wise to consult a doctor about exercise when pregnant, but most forms can usually be adapted for pregnancy. Exercises that help the woman's body to return to its pre-pregnant state are often taught during the early postpartum period and most forms of exercise can be resumed from around six weeks after the birth.

Kegel or pelvic floor exercises will often be taught to women at this time in order to strengthen pelvic floor muscles and prevent urinary incontinence, which can occur when the hormones of pregnancy relax these muscles. Women can practice these exercises throughout their adult life to help prevent urinary incontinence, which can also occur in menopause.

In later life both men and women will benefit from continuing weight-bearing types of exercise, either in daily life by walking as much as possible or by involving themselves in an activity such as swimming, cycling, golf, dancing, yoga or bowling. Exercise is important to general well-being—it can elevate mood, relieve anxiety, improve sleep and enhance mental alertness.

Aerobic exercises

Such exercises include activities like walking and jogging which involve moving muscles throughout their full range over a relatively long period, during which rates of respiration and heart rate increase, building to a desired maximum level and sustaining that for 15 to 20 minutes. This type of exercise is used to improve cardiovascular fitness, which increases blood flow and transport of oxygen to the muscles, and has a beneficial effect on general health.

Aerobic exercise programs are planned to improve heart–lung capacity by raising heart rate to about 70 percent of its maximum, which is calculated as 220 minus the person's age in years. Thus at 45 years of age, the heart should be capable of 175 beats per minute and should be 120 during exercise.

Anaerobic exercises

These are the body-builders' methods of adding bulk and involve high-intensity activity by a small group of muscles and a limited range of movement over short periods of time. Weightlifting is an example where the energy demand on muscles outstrips the body's ability to aerobically metabolize glycogen and creates an oxygen debt. Anaerobic activities increase muscle mass and strength but deliver little benefit to heart, lungs and overall health.

Beginning an exercise program

When undertaking exercise, beginners should ideally be supervised as they must initially be made aware of potential strains on the heart and circulatory system. Loading muscles to the point of pain or exhaustion is dangerous, and where heart health is already poor this can bring on collapse or cardiac arrest.

In the beginning, even moderate exercise will require effort and create an oxygen debt. After a few weeks or months, heart and lung function may improve, allowing more efficient conversion of glycogen to muscle energy and increasing capacity for sustained effort.

Regular exercise is a necessity for everyone and particularly important for those whose daily lives include little physical effort. Starting an exercise program for the first time or after a period without regular exercise should be done cautiously to lessen risks of injury.

SEE ALSO *Heart, Muscle, Muscular system, Obesity, Osteoporosis, Pilates, Respiratory system, Sports medicine, T'ai chi ch'uan, Yoga*

EXOPHTHALMOS

Exophthalmos is abnormal protrusion or bulging of one or both eyeballs. It may be accompanied by double vision and eye pain. The condition is usually a symptom of an overactive thyroid gland (hyperthyroidism), but may have other causes, such as a tumor or blood clot behind the eye. It improves after the underlying cause is corrected; surgical correction may be necessary.

SEE ALSO *Eye, Hyperthyroidism*

EXPECTORANTS

Expectorants are compounds used in cough and cold products to help loosen phlegm and make coughing more productive. They can be bought over-the-counter without a doctor's prescription. Guaifenesin is the most widely used expectorant and is found in a range of over-the-counter preparations.

Expectorants cause mucus and other substances blocking the airways to become thinner, so they are easier to cough up. Coughing becomes easier and less irritating, and chest congestion is relieved. For example, someone with pneumonia may find an expectorant helps clear the airway of mucus, making breathing easier.

Some medical professionals question whether using an expectorant speeds recovery or really does relieve symptoms of respiratory illness. Some compounds commonly sold as expectorants do not in fact have expectorant properties at all; these include ammonium chloride, a bitter plant extract called horehound, pine tar and spirits of turpentine. Moreover, if the cough does not produce mucus, then an expectorant is of no use. In this case, a cough suppressant may be more appropriate because it allows the sufferer to cough less, feel more comfortable and sleep better.

It is important to follow label instructions on cough suppressants to avoid over-use and possible side effects. If a cough persists, medical advice should be sought.

SEE ALSO *Cough*

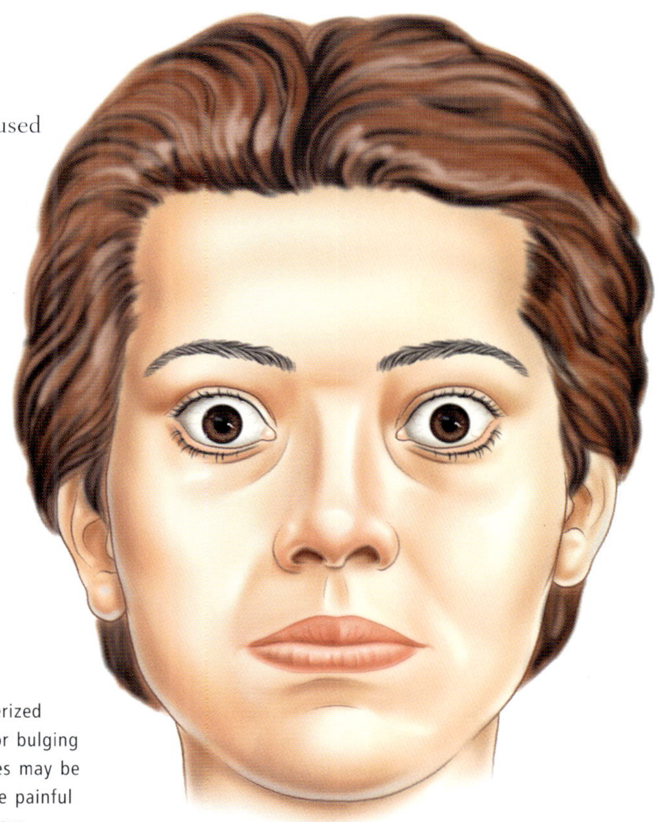

Exophthalmos

This condition is characterized by abnormal protruding or bulging eyeballs. One or both eyes may be affected. The eyes may be painful and double vision can occur.

E

EYE

The eye is the organ of sight: a complex, versatile and delicate structure.

Eyeball

Every time we look at a scene, an image is formed on the retina of the eye and sent to the brain for analysis. The eyeball can be compared to a camera. A camera has three main parts: the camera body, the lens and the film.

The eyeball is made up of three layers. The outer layer consists of the sclera and cornea, the middle layer is the uvea and lens, and the inner layer is the retina.

Sclera and cornea

The eyeball is a sphere formed by a white layer called the sclera. The front part of this sphere is cut off and replaced by a section of a smaller sphere. This section is more curved and formed by a transparent layer called the cornea.

The sclera gives the eyeball its shape and maintains a constant distance between the cornea and the retina at the back of the eye. It serves the same function as the camera body. When the eye is focused on infinity, the image should fall on the back of the eye. If the sphere of the sclera is slightly too large, images of close objects will fall exactly on the back of the eye but distant objects will not, and so the eye can only clearly see close objects, a condition known as near-sightedness or myopia.

The opposite condition is far-sightedness or presbyopia, occurring when the scleral sphere is too small.

The sclera has a hole near the posterior pole of the eyeball through which the optic nerve, which connects the retina to the visual area of the brain, passes.

The cornea is transparent because its fibers and cells are organized in a very orderly fashion. Opacity results when this arrangement is disrupted by injuries and scarring.

Just like the camera lens, the cornea must have a perfect and adequate curvature, because it is the front element of the optic system of the eye. The cornea bends the light and works together with the lens to form an image on the retina. Vision is very poor in the condition called keratoconus (the cornea, *kerato-*, is shaped like a cone, *conus*). In this condition, the image is distorted because the cornea does not have the profile of a sphere but is more pointed at the center.

In astigmatism, the image on the retina is distorted because the cornea is not exactly spherical.

The cornea is very sensitive to pain and temperature. We all experience that pain when a tiny speck of dust gets in our eyes.

The junction between the sclera and the cornea is called the limbus (meaning the rim) and contains Schlemm's canal, a circular channel which drains the fluid from the front part of the eye. Its significance is discussed below.

Uvea and lens

The uvea is the middle layer of the eye and has three parts: the choroid, ciliary body and iris.

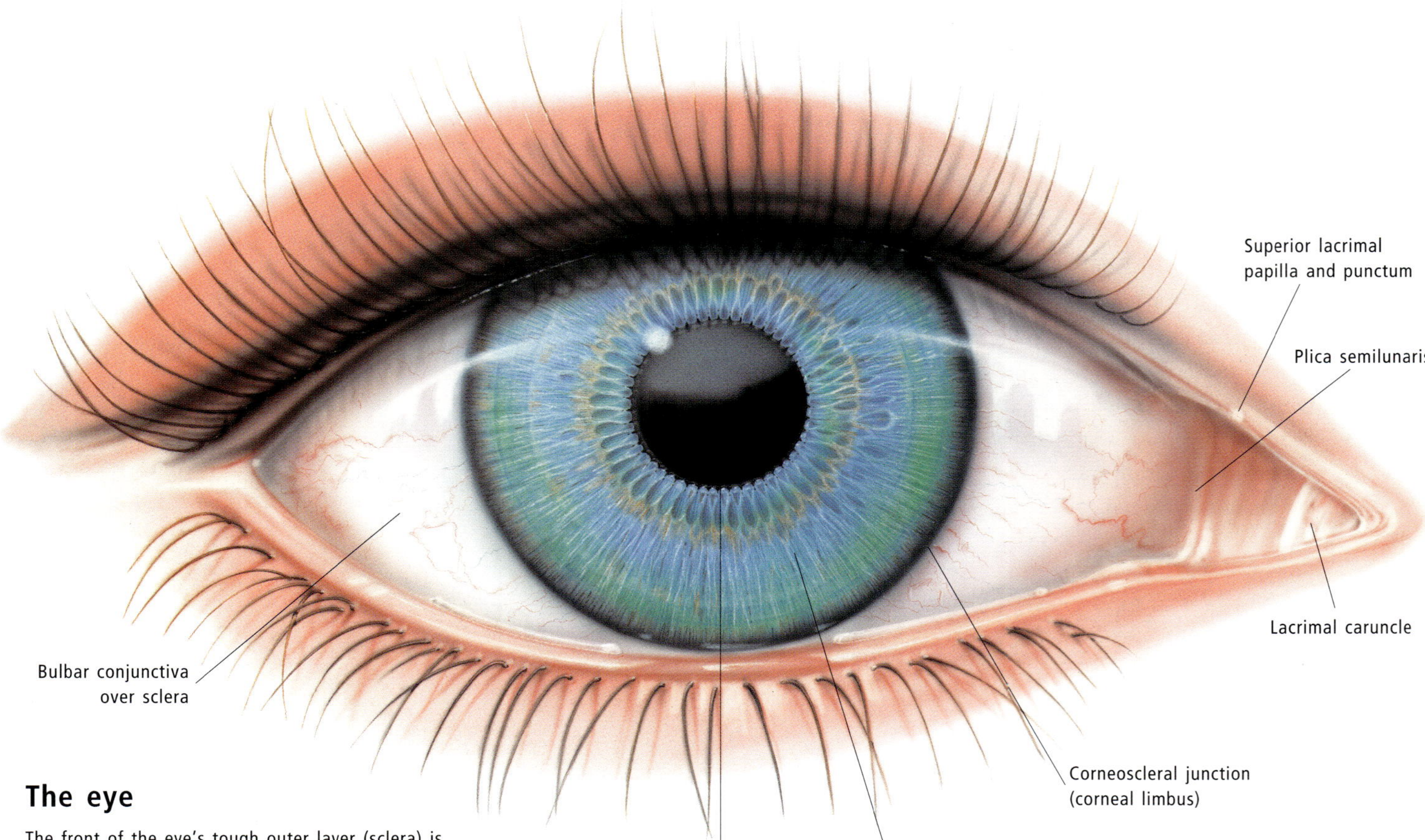

The eye

The front of the eye's tough outer layer (sclera) is covered by a thin membrane (conjunctiva). Light enters the eye through the cornea, which is a transparent dome on the surface of the eye. The cornea helps to protect the eye and transmits light to the retina at the back of the eye.

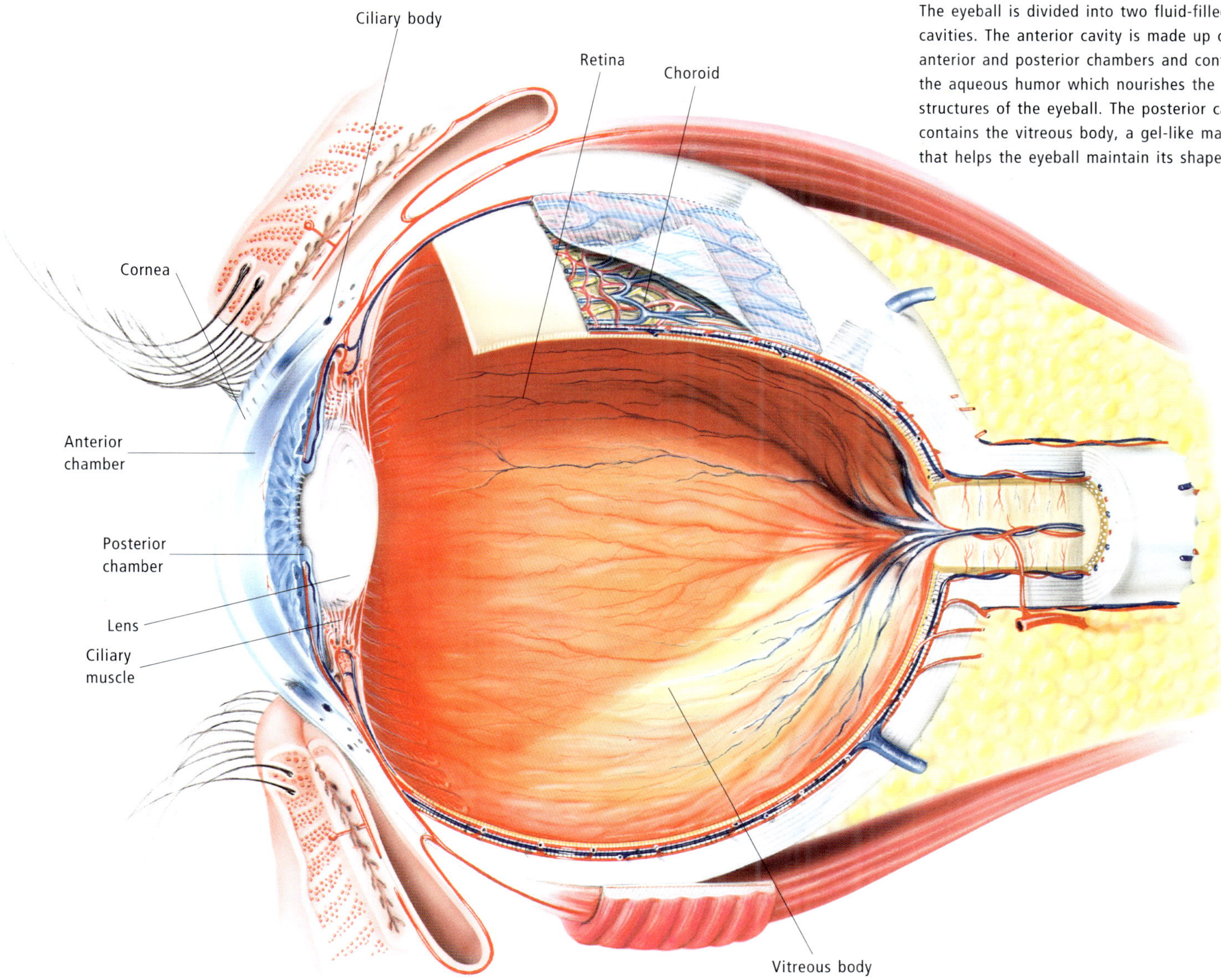

Eyeball

The eyeball is divided into two fluid-filled cavities. The anterior cavity is made up of the anterior and posterior chambers and contains the aqueous humor which nourishes the internal structures of the eyeball. The posterior cavity contains the vitreous body, a gel-like material that helps the eyeball maintain its shape.

The choroid is the back part of the uvea. It contains many blood vessels and gives passage to nerves going to the cornea, ciliary body and iris.

The choroid continues forwards as the ciliary body. If you were to cut the eye in two and look at the inside of the front half, you would see the ciliary body as a dark ring which gradually becomes thicker at the front. When the lens is removed, one can see that the ciliary body joins a flat ring that stretches down in front of the lens, the iris. The hole in the center of the iris is the pupil.

The ciliary body contains ciliary muscles. Tiny fibers that look like nylon strings run from the ciliary body to a ring near the equator of the lens. They form a suspension mechanism for the lens called the zonule.

The lens is a clear structure that looks and works as a magnifying glass. It does not bend the light as much as the cornea (i.e. its refractive power is not as great), but it can change its curvature. When the lens is in place in a normal eye which is looking into the distance, it is stretched and flattened by the pull of the zonule.

An experiment with a magnifying glass will help us understand how the eye focuses. Point the magnifying glass towards a tree far away outside a window and collect the inverted image on a piece of white cardboard. Move the cardboard back and forth until the tree looks sharp. The image of the window frame (which is nearer to us) is blurred. To get a sharp image of the window, we must either move the lens slowly further from the cardboard or add another lens in front of it to increase its refractive power.

The first conclusion is that the image of a close object is further from the lens than that of a distant object. That is why someone whose eyeball is slightly too large will not be able to see distant objects—their images fall in front of the retina. Corrective glasses must be concave to effectively reduce the refractive power of the lens of the eye to bring the image further back, onto the retina.

The second conclusion is that when we want to get a sharp image of a nearer object without moving the lens, we have to increase the thickness of the lens. This is achieved in the eyeball by the action of the ciliary muscles. The ciliary muscles contract, causing a movement of the ciliary body, which slackens the tension on the zonule. The lens shrinks back by its elasticity, becomes thicker (more rounded) and the image of the object is pulled back to the retina. As we age, the lens loses its elasticity and fails to achieve the thickness required. We can no longer focus on a near object and need reading glasses to add refractive power to our lenses.

If you have used manual cameras, you will be familiar with the diaphragm which controls the amount of light entering the lens. You will also know that when the opening of the diaphragm is small, depth of field is increased— objects closer to and further from the distance set on the lens will be acceptably sharp in the photograph. Photographers always use a small diaphragm opening to photograph close objects.

The iris works as the camera's diaphragm. It is heavily pigmented to block the light. It has circular muscle fibers around the pupil which contract in bright light to constrict the pupil. The iris also has contractile cells radiating out from the pupil. In darkness, these cells contract and the pupil is dilated.

The adjustment of pupil size and actions of the ciliary muscles is controlled by the autonomic nervous system, the part of our nervous system that operates without conscious effort. If this system is disrupted, the pupils will not constrict when a light is shone on the eyes.

Retina

The retina lines the inside of the back part of the eyeball. It receives and converts the image cast on it by the eye's optic system into neural signals. The retina develops the same way in the embryo. The outside layer is pigmented to reduce light reflection just like the black paint inside a camera. The inside layer is light sensitive like film in a camera.

A blow to the eyeball may result in a "retinal detachment" (this may also occur from no obvious cause); the two layers are separated from each other and vision is lost at the detached area.

The optical axis of the eye is a straight line between the center of the lens and the center of its image on the retina. The point where all the nerve fibers from the retina converge into the optic nerve is called the optic disk.

Photoreceptors

Light is converted into neural impulses by specialized cells called photoreceptors. These are classified into two types based on their shape: rods and cones. Cone receptors are not as sensitive to light as the rods but they can detect colors. Signals from individual cones are not mixed together much because only a few cones are connected together before the signal is sent to the brain. They are therefore responsible for detailed vision.

According to the laws of optics, the image made by a lens is sharpest around the optical axis of the lens. The area of the retina around the optical axis is designed for high resolution perception with a high concentration of cones. At the central point, each cone is connected by one optic nerve fiber to one point on the cortex of the brain. This point-to-point projection to the brain ensures the highest resolution possible. When you read this page, you really only see clearly the words in the center of your visual field. You cannot recognize the words on the rest of the page.

Rod photoreceptors are more sensitive to light, but a large number of them are connected together before the sum of signals is sent to the brain. Thus they are good for sensing brightness and movement, not for color or detailed vision. The rods are almost nonexistent around the optical center of the retina, but they are the only type of photoreceptor in the periphery of the retina. That is why we can only see movements of a friend from the "corner of the eye", not the facial expression.

There is no light detection at the optic disk where there are no photoreceptors. Light falling on the optic disk it will not be perceived by that eye, it is in the "blind spot".

When the photoreceptors are exposed to light, they lose an amount of a light-sensitive pigment called rhodopsin which has to be replaced by synthesis in the cell. After staring at a bright light, the eye is blinded for a short while because the photoreceptors are depleted of their rhodopsin.

Central artery of the retina

The central artery of the retina enters the eyeball by running in the center of the optic nerve. As it emerges from the optic disk it fans out into four main branches accompanied by their veins. These branches run on the inside of the retina and spread out into a capillary network.

Observation of these blood vessels through an ophthalmoscope is not only important for the diagnosis of disorders of the eye but also tells the doctor much about the general condition of arteries in diseases such as high blood pressure or diabetes.

Vitreous body

The cavity behind the lens and its zonule is filled up by a viscoelastic gel which is called the "vitreous body" because it is as clear as glass. In old age, tiny particles may form in the vitreous body and these are visible as floating spots in the visual field because they cast shadows on the retina.

Anterior and posterior chambers

The space in front of the lens and zonule is divided by the iris into the anterior and posterior chambers. The ciliary body secretes into the posterior chamber a fluid called aqueous humor which passes through the pupil into the anterior chamber.

The lens and cornea do not receive any blood vessels and rely entirely on aqueous humour for nutrition. Aqueous humor is drained into Schlemm's canal, located in the anterior chamber, and from there into the veins.

The pressure in the eye, the intraocular pressure, depends on the balance between the rate of production and drainage of aqueous humor. This pressure is often measured when you have your eyes examined by your doctor or optometrist. Excess intraocular pressure is seen with glaucoma, which can lead to blindness.

Appendages of the eye

The eyeball is moved by extraocular muscles and is protected by the eyelids and the lacrimal apparatus.

Movements of the eyeball

We move our eyes to look around us or to follow a moving object. Movement must be precise because the eye turns only a tiny angle to fixate on a person walking across the visual field a hundred yards (or meters) away. Moreover, movement of both eyes have to be coordinated to maintain stereoscopic vision.

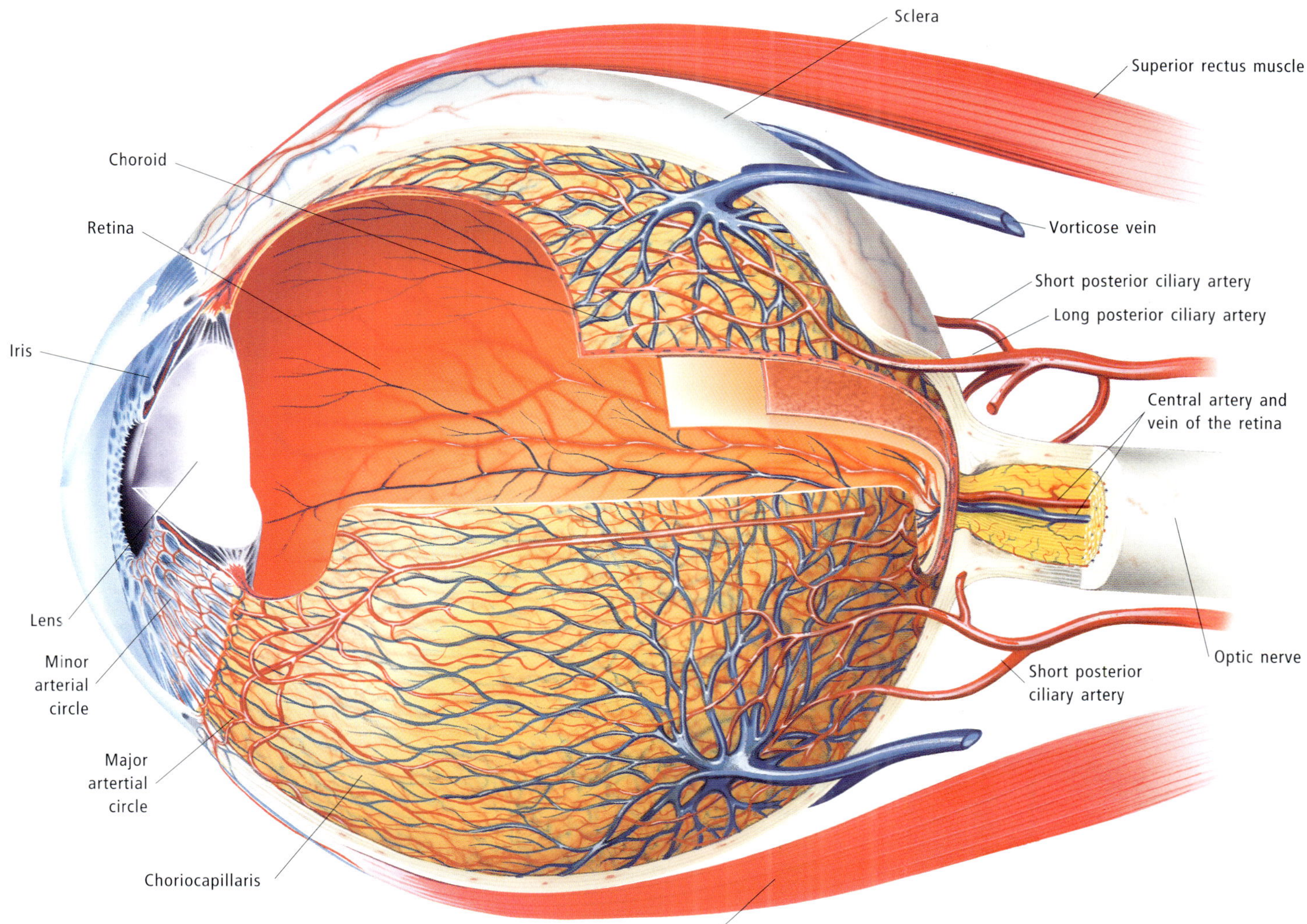

Arteries of the eye

The central artery of the retina enters the eye through the center of the optic nerve. It fans out into four main branches, each accompanied by veins. These arteries spread out to form a capillary network within the eye. The arteries can be adversely affected by conditions such as high blood pressure or diabetes.

Blind spot

Cover your right eye and focus on the red cross with your eyes at about 12 inches (30 centimeters) from this page. You can vaguely see the black dot in the periphery of your visual field. Move the page slowly closer, still focusing on the cross. At a certain distance, the black dot will disappear (when its image falls on the blind spot). With both eyes open, we see no blind spot as objects falling on the blind spot of one eye do not fall on the blind spot of the other eye.

The eyeball in its resting position is suspended by six muscles that run from the bones of the orbit (the cavity of the skull which accommodates the eyeball) to the eyeball. To simplify their actions, we can think of them as working in pairs to move the eyeball. For example, when the right eye looks to the right, the lateral rectus on the right side of that eye contracts and the medial rectus on the left side of the same eye relaxes to allow for the movement. In actual fact every movement of the eyeball involves actions of all six muscle. The neural mechanism of control is thus extremely complex.

If one muscle is too long (take the example above, the lateral rectus of the right eye), the eye is deviated to the opposite side (the left) by the pull of the unopposed muscle of the pair (the medial rectus) and this eye does not move in harmony with the other eye. This squint is known by the medical term strabismus. It can be repaired surgically by shortening the muscle or moving its attachment on the eyeball.

Eyelids

The eyelids are shutters that protect the eyes. The framework of each eyelid is a plate of connective tissue called the tarsus which is covered on the outside by the skin and on the inside by conjunctiva. The eyelid margin carries a few rows of eyelashes and has openings of numerous glands. Inflammation of these glands is the cause of chalazion while a stye (hordoleum) is caused by their infection. Inflammation of the conjunctiva is called conjunctivitis.

Disorders of the eye

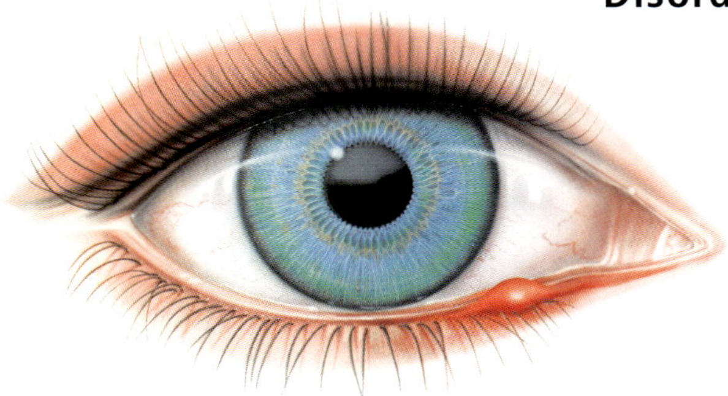

Stye

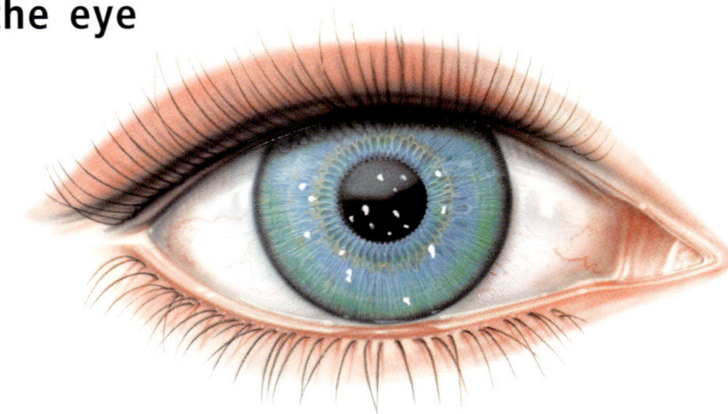

Punctate keratitis

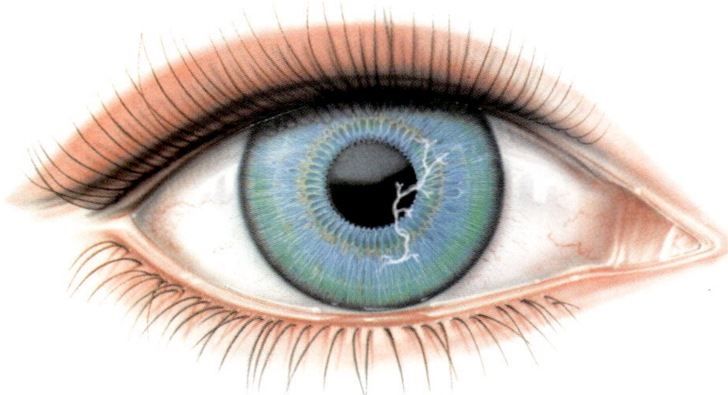

Dendritic keratitis

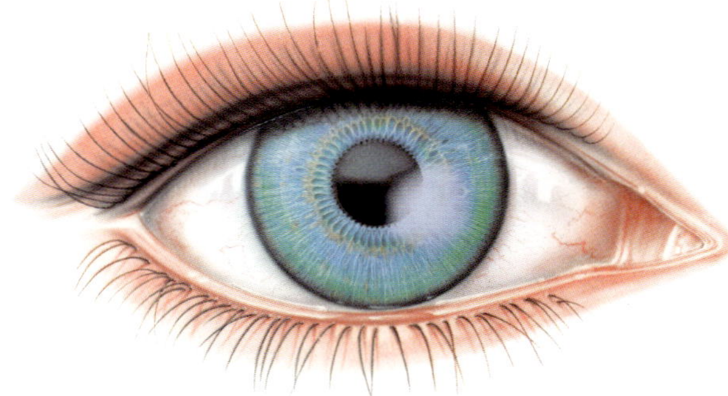

Diskiform keratitis

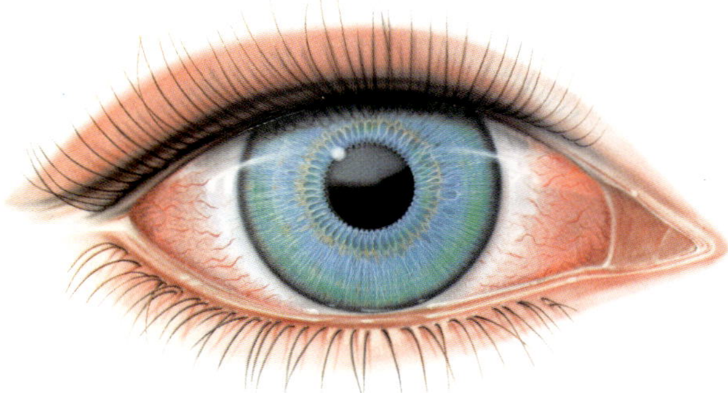

Allergic conjunctivitis

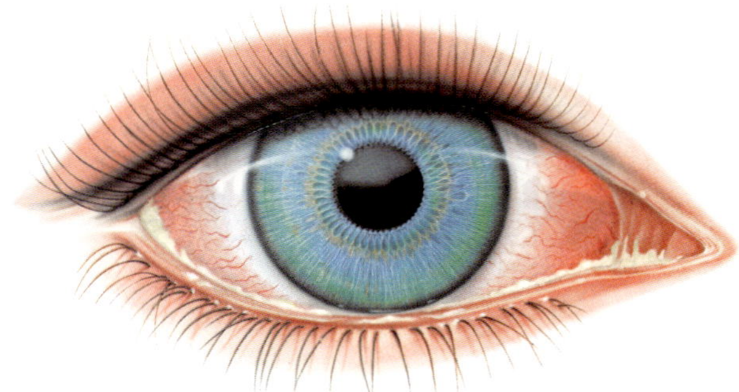

Bacterial conjunctivitis

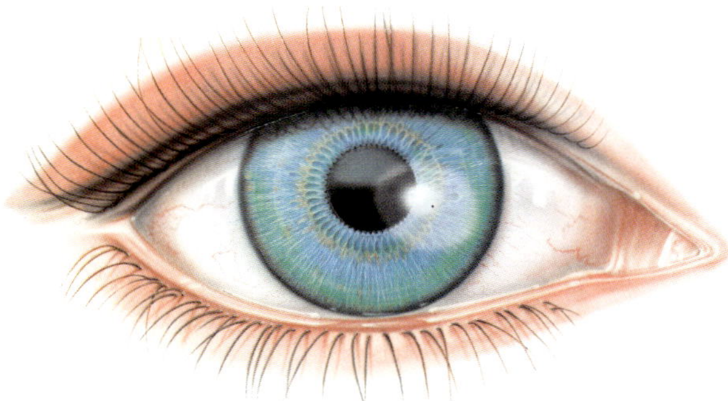

Corneal ulcer

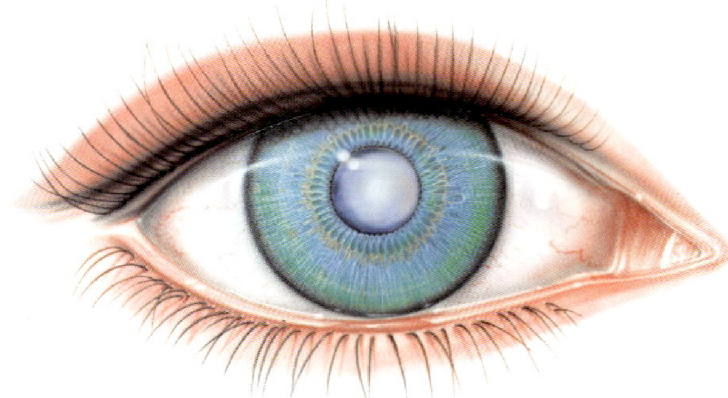

Cataract

Lacrimal apparatus

Tears keep the eye moist as well as providing lubrication and protection against infection. They are secreted by the lacrimal gland which is located at the upper outer corner of the orbit.

Tears form a film over the eye and flow down across the cornea towards the inner corner of the eye to be collected by two tiny canals which open near the inner end of each eyelid. Tears go from these canals into the lacrimal sac and flow down the nasolacrimal duct, a small tube which opens into the nose. This is why we can taste bitter eye drops—they get into the nose and drip onto the back of the tongue.

Movement of tears is facilitated by blinking. Tears overflow when we cry, when we have hay fever or when smoke gets into our eyes, because their production exceeds the draining mechanism.

Tears are essential in maintaining the integrity of the eye. The cornea may be ulcerated if it is dry. When their production is deficient, in conditions such as Sjögren's syndrome, patients have to instil artificial tears every few hours.

Eye disorders

The eye is subject to infection, inflammation, structural disorders and tumors. Some disorders are illustrated here, but more information is to be found under their specific entries.

SEE ALSO *Autonomic nervous system, Blindness, Cataracts, Chalazion, Color blindness, Conjunctivitis, Cornea, Eyelashes, Eyelids, Glaucoma, Iris, Keratitis, Lacrimal glands, Myopia, Pupil of eye, Retina, Sclera, Sight, Sjögren's syndrome, Squint, Stye*

EYELASHES

The eyelashes are hairs that extend out from the eyelids. They have a protective as well as a cosmetic function. Trichiasis is a condition in which the eyelashes grow inward and rub against the cornea of the eye, causing irritation, watering of the eyes, and a feeling of a foreign body in the eye. It is usually caused by entropion, in which the eyelids curl inward. It is treated by removing the inturned eyelash or by surgical correction.

SEE ALSO *Cornea, Eyelids*

EYELIDS

Eyelids are folds of skin that protect the front of each eyeball. When the eye is open, the upper eyelids retract above the eyeball; when closed, both upper and lower eyelids cover the visible area of the eye. The margins of the eyelids contain meibomian glands which secrete oils that lubricate the eyelids. The conjunctiva, a mucous membrane covering the surface of the eyeball, also extends to cover the undersurface of the eyelids.

Eyelid disorders include black (bruised) eye, blepharitis, chalazion, conjunctivitis, ectropion, entropion, ptosis and stye. The skin of the eyelids is also affected by skin disorders such as eczema.

Blepharitis is a disorder caused by an increased oil secretion from, or infection of, the meibomian glands. The eyelids become red and inflamed; the treatment is to cleanse the eyelids regularly with a warm solution of salt water.

A chalazion, or meibomian or tarsal cyst, is a small cyst formed when a meibomian gland becomes blocked with oil secretion. Chalazions are harmless but can be surgically removed if painful or unsightly.

Ectropion of an eyelid is a condition where the eyelid (usually the lower eyelid) turns outwards instead of remaining close to the eyeball. Common among the elderly, it is usually caused by the degeneration of the muscles of the eyelid.

Entropion of the eyelids is the opposite of ectropion: the eyelid curls inward toward the eye and may rub against the cornea, causing pain and redness of the eye. Both of these conditions can be corrected with minor surgery.

A stye is a small abscess of hair-follicle glands in the eyelid caused by a bacterial infection. The symptoms include swelling, redness and pain. Eventually the stye bursts and the symptoms subside. Treatment is to bathe the stye repeatedly with warm water. Antibiotic drops and ointments may also be prescribed.

SEE ALSO *Chalazion, Conjunctivitis, Eye, Stye*

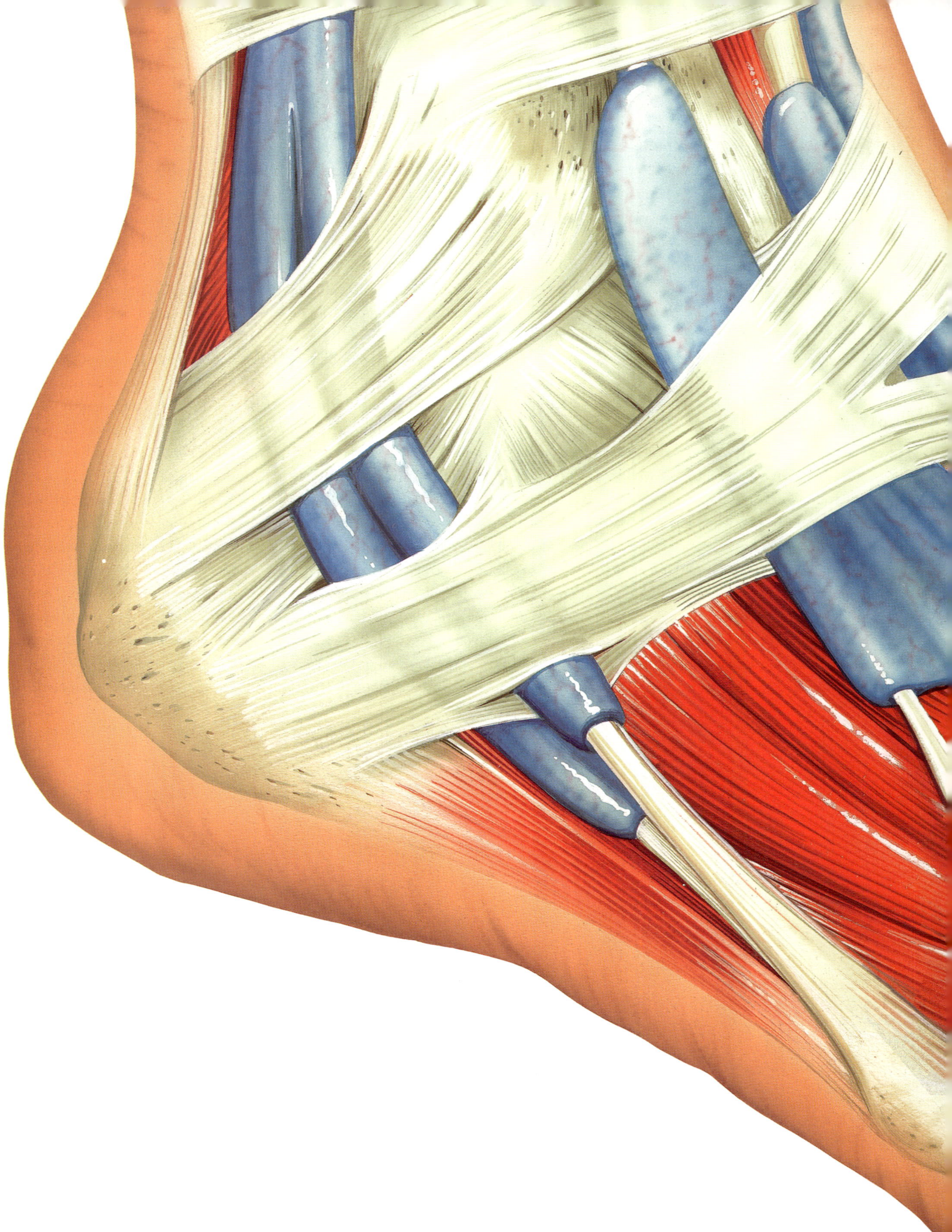

F

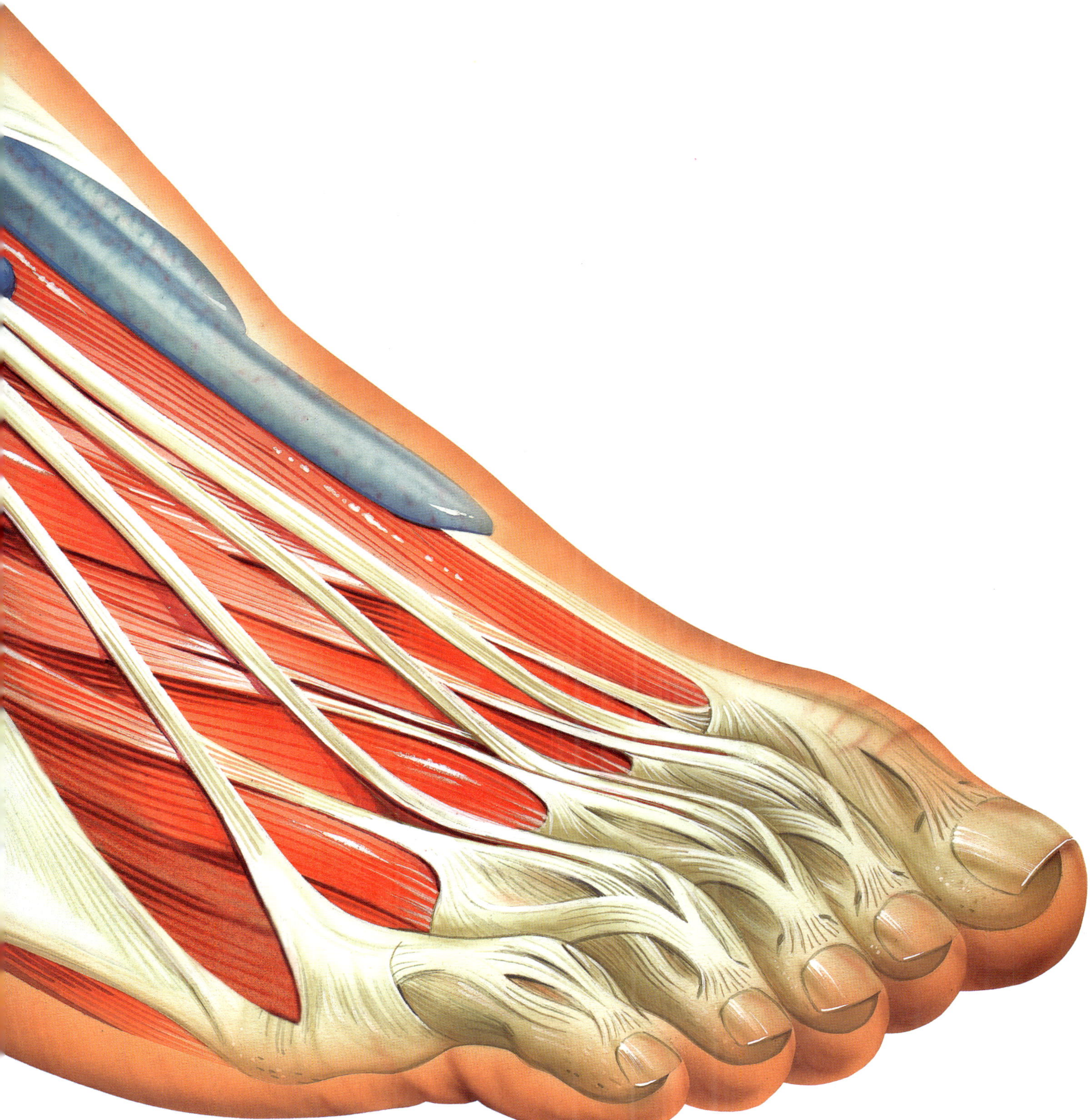

F

FACE

The face is made up of facial bones, muscles, skin, eyes, nose, jaws, cheeks and chin, as well as the nerves and blood vessels supplying these structures. The facial bones are covered with muscles and skin. Variations in these features account for our individual appearance; thanks to these variations we can recognize each other and tell one another apart. Much of what we think and feel is expressed in the face.

Evolution and development

During evolution from the prehuman *Australopithecus* to modern human *(Homo sapiens)*, the face became smaller compared to the overall size of the head. The brain and the cranium (braincase) tripled in volume, but the jaws became shorter and the teeth smaller. In consequence, the face receded beneath the forehead. As a result, the modern human face exhibits an essentially vertical profile, in marked contrast to the protruding facial muzzle of the gorilla and the chimpanzee. As the jaws receded, they left the distinctive modern human features of a prominent nose and a sharply defined chin.

By the age of six years, the brain and the cranium have reached 90 percent of their adult size. But the face grows more slowly; at birth it is less than one-fifth the size of the braincase; by adulthood it has increased to nearly half. Facial dimensions increase most in depth, next in height (length), and least in width. Facial musculature increases and the nasal sinuses enlarge during adolescence, especially in males.

Parts of the face

The facial skeleton is made up of 14 bones. The frontal bone forms part of the forehead. The facial bones include the two nasal bones, forming the upper portion of the bridge of the nose; two lacrimal bones, which are located in each eye socket (orbit) next to the nose and close to the tear ducts; two maxillary bones (upper jaw); the mandible (lower jaw); the two palatine bones of the hard palate; the vomer, which, with a part of the ethmoid bone, makes up the nasal septum; and the two inferior turbinates of the nose.

The eyes are the organs of sight. Shaped like a ball, with a slight bulge at the front, each eye lies within a bony socket of the skull, protected from glare and dust by the eyelids, lashes and eyebrows. When the eyelids are closed as in sleep, the surface of the eye is covered; when awake, the eyelids blink roughly once every six seconds, washing the eye with salty secretions from the lacrimal (tear) glands, which are situated at the outer corner of the eye behind the upper eyelid. These secretions drain through the tear duct at the inner corner of the eye and into the nose; in certain emotional states, secretions from the lacrimal glands overwhelm the ducts and tears spill out over the eyelids. If an object suddenly moves too close to the eye, the eyelids automatically close.

The nose is a protuberance consisting of two cavities around a wall of cartilage called the nasal septum. The skeleton of the nose is cartilage at the tip, but bony closer to the skull. The nose functions as part of the breathing apparatus—filtering, warming, and moistening incoming air on its way to the lungs. The nose also contains olfactory nerve endings that detect smells. Just inside the nostrils grow short, coarse hairs which filter dust particles from the incoming air.

There are also a number of muscles in the face. There is a circular muscle around the mouth and one around each eye. Other muscles spread out over from the face from the edge of the circular muscles.

The mouth is the opening between the maxillae and the lower jaw. It is used for ingesting food, breathing air and for making sounds, especially speech. Lips, which form the mouth's muscular opening, contribute to formation of words during speech and also help hold food in the mouth. They also help form facial expressions, such as smiling and frowning. The sides of the mouth are formed by the cheeks. These are composed of muscle tissue covered on the outside by skin and on the inside of the mouth by mucous membrane. The cheeks also play an important

Bones of the face

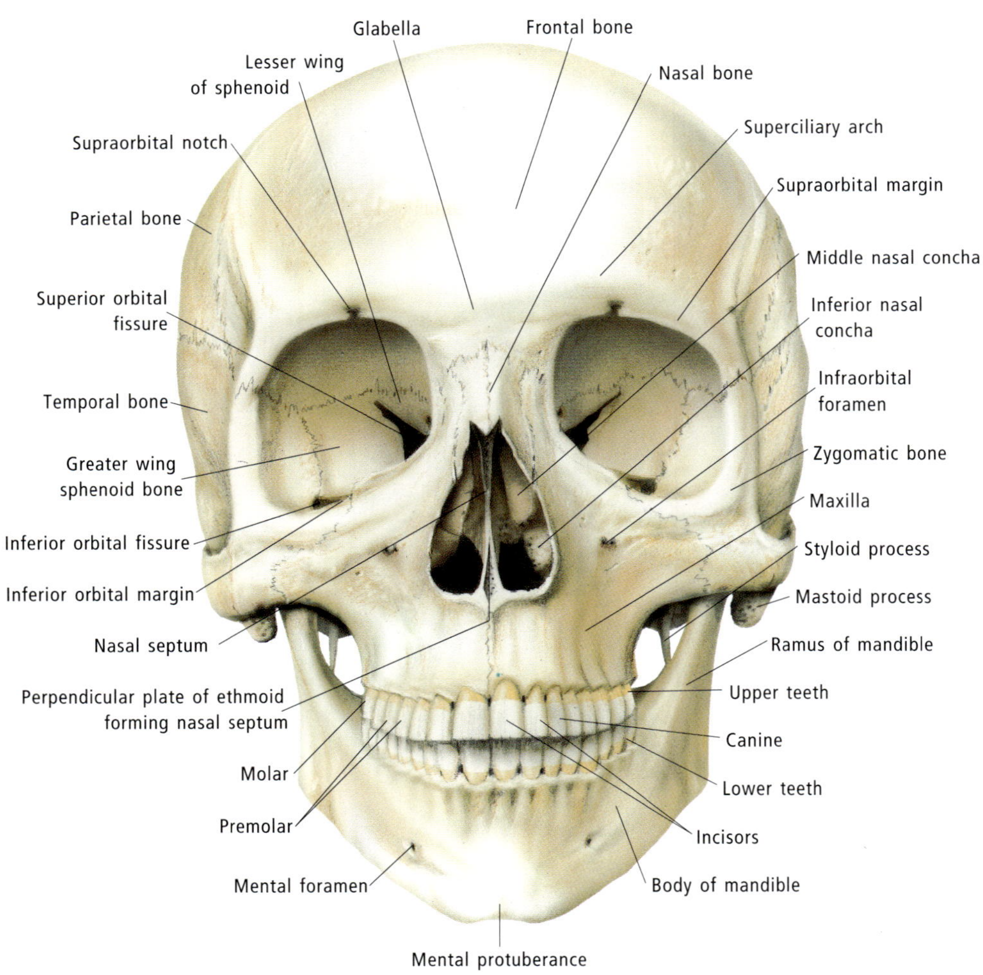

Face

A complex range of thoughts and emotions is expressed in the face—this requires an intricate system of muscles and nerves. The special sense organs (eyes, nose, ears and tongue) are all part of the facial structure.

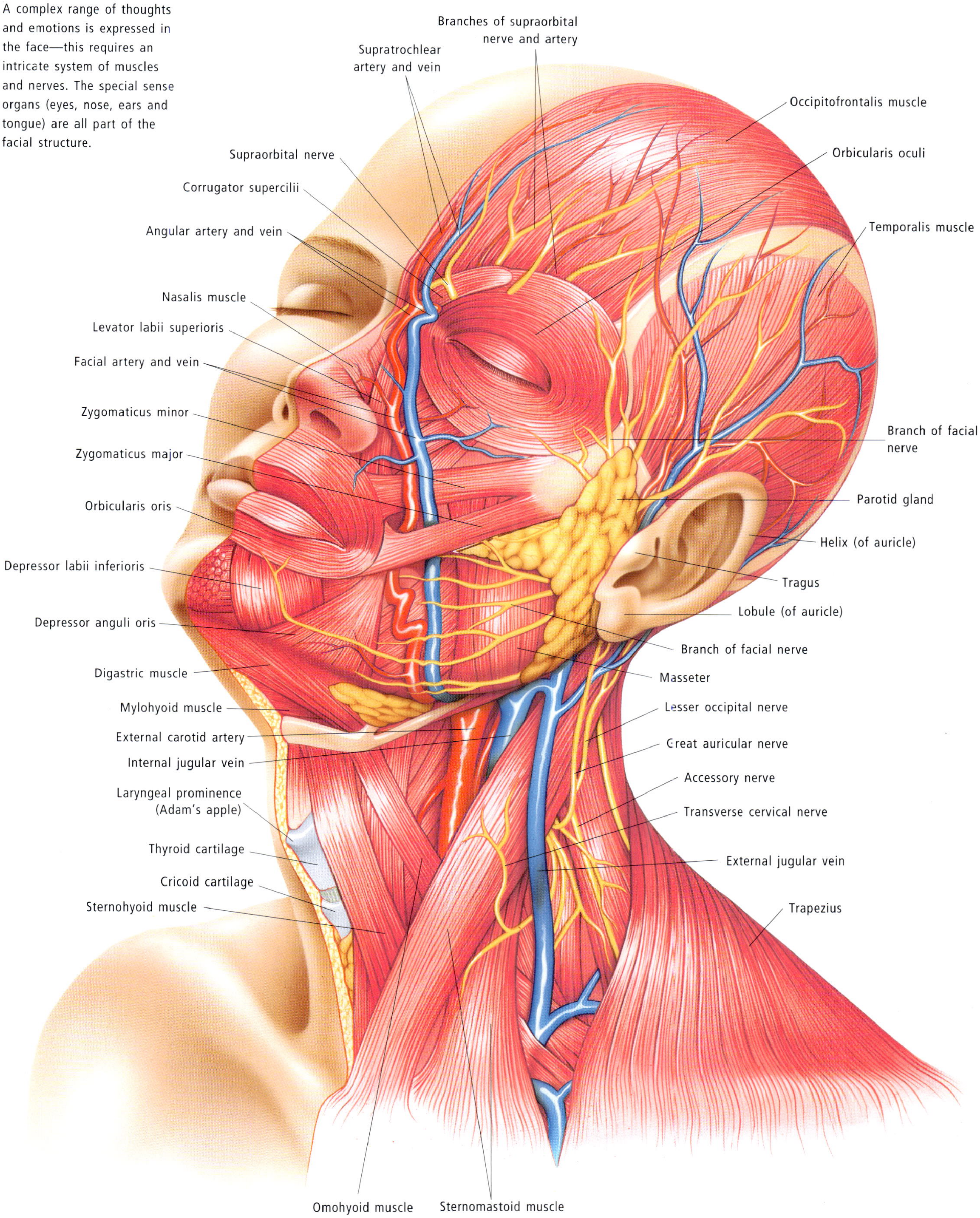

F

role in speech and help hold food as it is chewed and then swallowed.

The jaws are three bones making up the bony framework of the mouth. The two upper jaw bones (maxillae) are fixed, while the lower jaw (mandible) is moveable. By moving in opposition to each other, jaws can bite and chew food to prepare it for swallowing.

Fixed to the bottom of the maxillae and the top of the mandible are the teeth, which are used for biting into and chewing food. Children have 20 primary teeth, which first appear about age six months and are replaced at the age of about six years by the 32 permanent teeth.

Problems

The face can be affected by a variety of problems. Diseases including infections of the skin such as herpes zoster (shingles), herpes simplex, tinea and impetigo can affect the face. Conditions of inflammation of the skin (dermatitis), such as eczema and psoriasis, can also occur. Acne may occur, especially in adolescence, and can cause unsightly scarring. Cancers of the skin such as squamous cell carcinoma, basal cell carcinoma and melanoma commonly occur on the face. Many systemic (generalized) diseases affect the face. Endocrine diseases such as Graves' disease, hypothyroidism, Cushing's disease or acromegaly may affect the features by altering the soft tissues or bones of the face. Muscle movements and facial expressions may be affected in neurological diseases such as myasthenia gravis, Parkinson's disease and Bell's palsy. Infections such as tuberculosis, leprosy and cellulitis can damage the tissues of the face and its features.

A number of conditions can cause facial pain. Inflammation of the joint in the jaw (the temporomandibular joint) can cause aching pain over or around the jaw. Infection around a tooth can cause a throbbing pain on one side of face that worsens at night, when eating, or when touching a particular tooth. Sinus infection can cause pain or tenderness around the eyes and cheekbones which worsens when bending the head forward. It commonly follows a recent cold or nasal allergy. Headache may be caused by migraine, tension or stress, meningitis, or high blood pressure (hypertension). Herpes zoster may also cause severe facial pain.

Fractures of the facial bones are common, and are usually due to a sporting injury or a blow to the face. The facial bones that most commonly fracture are those of the upper jaw, the cheekbones, the bones that form the eye sockets, and the nose. There is severe pain at the injury site, swelling and bruising of soft tissue around the fracture (including black eyes), and deformity if the fracture is complete and bone fragments separate enough. Often no treatment is needed, as the fracture heals spontaneously within six weeks. If there has been displacement of bones, surgery may be needed to realign fractured bones and reconstruct normal facial contours. Fractures to facial bone can often be avoided by wearing protective face masks and headgear when playing contact sports.

Hairs are particularly numerous in the skin of the face, especially in males. A condition called folliculitis, or infection of the hair follicles with staphylococcus bacteria (also known as beard rash), is common on the face. Characteristic yellow-white pustules surrounded by reddish rings form on areas of beard. The condition is treated by avoiding hot moist conditions, using an antibacterial cream on affected areas, and, if the infection is severe, antibiotics which are taken orally.

Cosmetic surgery

Cosmetic procedures can be performed by a plastic or cosmetic surgeon to alter the features of a person's face. Rhinoplasty (nose surgery) can correct or alter a nose; otoplasty (ear surgery) can be used to correct protruding ears; blepharoplasty can remove excess fat and skin from the eyelids. So-called "face-lifts" can eliminate skin wrinkles; the surgeon makes an incision in the scalp and behind the ears, then pulls the skin taut to remove the wrinkles.

SEE ALSO *Acne, Acromegaly, Basal cell carcinoma, Bell's palsy, Brain, Cellulitis, Cosmetic surgery, Cushing's syndrome, Dermatitis, Eye, Facial nerves, Folliculitis, Graves' disease, Head, Headache, Herpes simplex, Hypothroidism, Impetigo, Jaw, Lacrimal glands, Leprosy, Lip, Melanoma, Migraine, Mouth, Myasthenia gravis, Nose, Parkinson's disease, Plastic surgery, Shingles, Sinusitis, Squamous cell carcinoma, Teeth, Tuberculosis*

FACIAL NERVES

The facial nerves, one on either side of the face, are the nerves that control the muscles of the face. They also supply the salivary glands below the mouth and the lacrimal glands in the eye, and carry taste sensations from the front two-thirds of the tongue. They are the seventh pair of the twelve pairs of cranial nerves. The facial nerves emerge from the brain stem, pass through the temporal bone in the skull (which houses the middle and inner ears), exit the skull through a small hole called the stylomastoid foramen, and then fan out over each side of the face anterior to (forward of) the ear.

Disorders of the facial nerves may be caused by fractures of the base of the skull, injuries to the face or middle ear, and birth or surgical trauma. The result is paralysis, weakness, or twitching of the face on the affected side; also, facial features lose their symmetrical arrangement, the mouth droops at one corner, the eyelid may not close properly, and there may be dryness of the eye or mouth and loss of taste. When the condition occurs with no known cause it is called Bell's palsy. This condition may come on suddenly or develop over several days; often there is a preceding condition such as stress, fatigue or the common cold. In most cases it improves by itself over a few months. Prompt treatment with corticosteroid drugs will help recovery.

SEE ALSO *Bell's palsy, Cranial nerves, Face*

FAINTING

Fainting (syncope) is usually triggered by severe deep-seated pain, or sudden shock or grief. It can often follow a period of acute anxiety. Fainting may also be caused by prolonged standing, particularly in a crowd and especially if the person has not eaten before going out. Early pregnancy may be a contributing factor.

Sudden blood loss can cause a fall in blood pressure followed by a fainting episode, as can the sight of severe trauma in others.

The experience of fainting can include a sudden drop in blood pressure, slowing of the heart, and pooling of blood in the extremities due to reflex dilation of their blood vessels. The person usually feels anxious, becomes clammy, and then falls unconscious to the ground. If the person is

Activating the face

The brain controls the motor and sensory activity of the body from different parts of the cerebral cortex. The sensory activities associated with the skin and muscles of the face are processed by the postcentral gyrus and the motor activities associated with the voluntary muscles, such as smiling, are processed by the precentral gyrus.

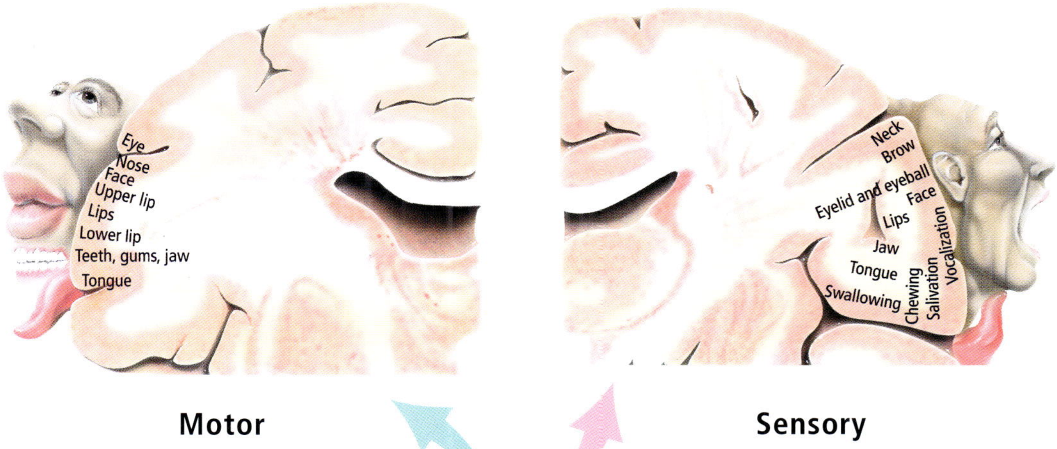

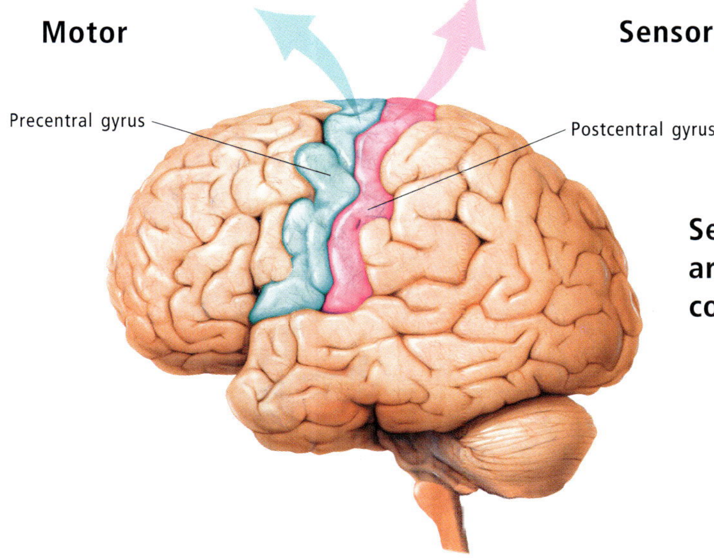

Sensorimotor areas of cortex

surrounded by a crowd of people and is not able to fall over, the brain becomes starved of sufficient blood supply and a seizure might occur.

Once the head is at or below the level of the heart, consciousness rapidly returns. Lying the patient flat and elevating the legs hastens the process. Traditionally a fainting person would be given spirits of ammonia to inhale. However, by the time anyone can find a bottle of ammonia these days, the patient will have already returned to consciousness (also, ammonia can be very dangerous if inhaled).

SEE ALSO *Blood pressure, Hypotension, Unconsciousness*

FALLOPIAN TUBES

Each of the two fallopian (uterine) tubes leads from its corresponding ovary, which lies on the lateral wall of the pelvis, to the body of the uterus. They are shaped a little like an alpine or medieval trumpet, with a narrow end joined to the uterus and a broad, flared end next to the ovary. In fact, the anatomical term for them is *salpinx*, which is Latin for trumpet.

The fallopian tubes convey the woman's egg (ovum) to the uterus. Also, shortly after sexual intercourse, sperm cells may reach the fallopian tubes, travelling in the opposite direction. In fact, the fallopian tubes are a common site for

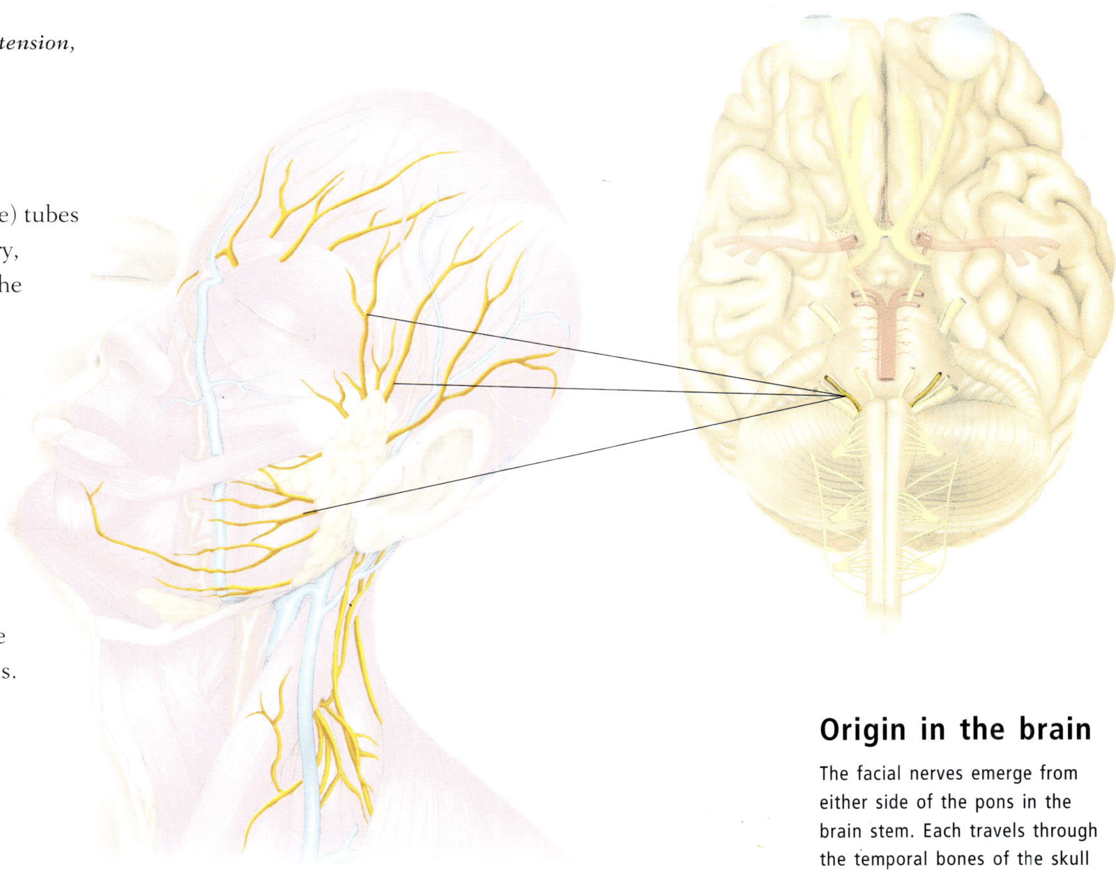

Origin in the brain

The facial nerves emerge from either side of the pons in the brain stem. Each travels through the temporal bones of the skull before giving off branches which fan out across the face.

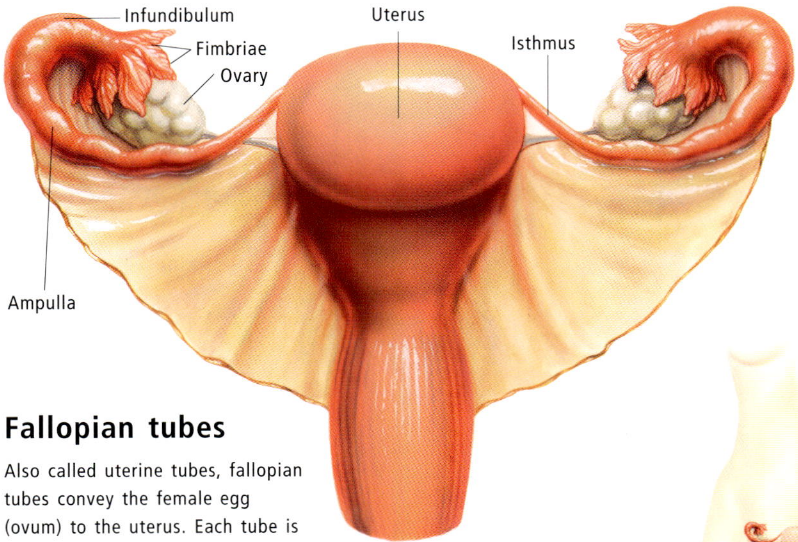

Fallopian tubes

Also called uterine tubes, fallopian tubes convey the female egg (ovum) to the uterus. Each tube is about 5 inches (13 centimeters) in length. It usually takes 3–4 days for an ovum to travel the length of the tube to the uterine cavity.

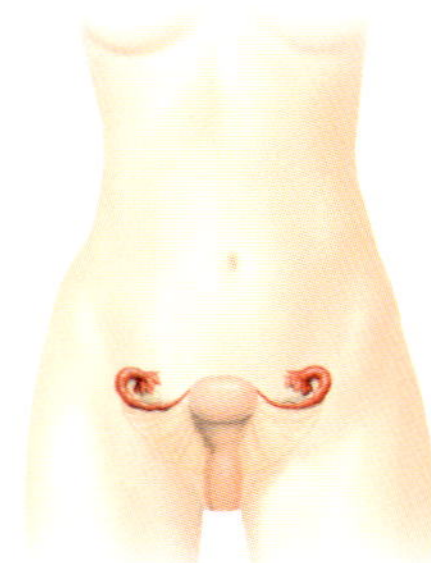

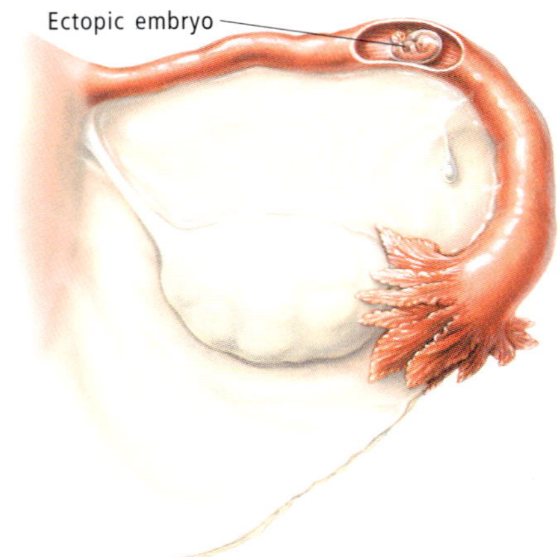

Ectopic pregnancy

An ectopic pregnancy occurs when a fertilized egg implants in the wall of the fallopian tube instead of in the wall of the uterus. At first it feels like a normal pregnancy until severe pelvic pain and vaginal bleeding occur. If not quickly treated, the condition can turn into a life-threatening medical emergency.

fertilization (the junction of the egg and sperm) to occur. The fertilized egg becomes an embryo, and moves down the tube and implants in the wall of the uterus.

Occasionally the embryo may implant in the wall of the tube itself, a type of ectopic pregnancy. Ectopic pregnancies are unable to proceed to full term, because the embryo quickly outgrows the available blood supply and may rupture the tube. The mother's life may also be at risk when this happens, because profuse bleeding into the mother's abdominal cavity may occur, leading to potentially fatal blood loss. Surgery to remove the damaged tube may be required. Fortunately, this procedure normally leaves the other tube intact and capable of performing its reproductive function.

SEE ALSO *Embryo, Fertilization, Ovaries, Ovum, Pregnancy, Reproductive systems, Salpingitis, Sperm, Uterus*

FAMILY HISTORY

A doctor will, during a first consultation, take a record of the patient's family medical history in order to form an overall picture of their state of health. It is an essential tool, as many illnesses, such as heart disease, run in families.

A family history is necessary before certain procedures take place. For instance, adverse reactions to anesthetics can run in families. These reactions may only become apparent when a family member needs surgery. Two such rare conditions are pseudocholinesterase deficiency, which is a reaction to a muscle relaxant; and malignant hyperthermia, which affects people who have a defective gene. When there is a possibility of a genetic abnormality, family history is also important. For an accurate assessment, the family history of three generations is required.

SEE ALSO *Genetic counseling*

FARMER'S LUNG

This condition is a hypersensitivity reaction to a mold-like bacterium found dwelling in hay. The reaction causes inflammation or irritation of the lungs (pneumonitis). The hay handler, usually a farmer, initially feels generally unwell then develops a fever, chills, breathlessness and a cough within the next four hours. Up to 5 percent of farmers in the United Kingdom develop this condition, generally during the wet part of the summer months. Though the condition is mostly self-limiting (tends to run its own course for a limited time without need for treatment), occasionally steroids, to be taken orally or inhaled, may be required.

SEE ALSO *Lungs*

FATS

Fats (also called lipids) are an extremely rich source of energy that can be used by the body as an alternative to carbohydrates. Fats are ingested in food and stored in layers of fatty (adipose) tissue under the skin, in the liver and around internal organs. Fats are broken down in the small intestine by lipases (fat enzymes) and are transported, stored and utilized in the body as triglycerides, cholesterol, lipoproteins and other fatty molecules.

Food high in animal fats (such as red meat, dairy products and eggs) can produce high levels of cholesterol and triglycerides in the blood, which may lead to various disorders including atherosclerosis, a common cause of heart disease and stroke. Some lipoproteins have also been linked to heart disease in recent years, especially high-density lipoproteins (HDL) and low-density lipoproteins (LDL). A low HDL to LDL ratio has been shown to protect against developing heart disease. People who exercise regularly and eat less animal fats are more likely to have a low HDL to LDL ratio.

A lipoma is a benign (non-cancerous) tumor made up of fat cells. Lipomas commonly occur in the limbs, abdomen or breasts, and feel like soft swellings under the skin. They seldom cause problems but may be surgically removed if preferred.

SEE ALSO *Atherosclerosis, Cholesterol, Lipoma*

FELDENKRAIS METHOD

Dr Moshe Feldenkrais (1904–1984) was a Russian-born Israeli physicist and Judo master who devoted more than 40 years to developing his method of movement education. His system of learning through movement, the Feldenkrais method, focuses on conscious thinking, moving, sensing and feeling. It is a gentle form of physical training which works the mind as much as the body.

The method is taught through two processes. The first process is a series of lessons called "awareness through movement". In these lessons, students are talked through a series of "movement explorations" that aim to increase awareness of habitual movement patterns (that is, patterns they use, and which may be inappropriate, but are unaware of) and develop more efficient and appropriate options. These explorations are achieved by having students focusing their attention on subtle differences in movement and by experiencing the interconnectedness of body movements.

In the second process, known as "functional integration", the practitioner helps the student to move through postures and exercises that benefit the nervous system and the skeletal structure. The goal is for the student to instinctively find postures and movements that require less energy and improve flexibility. Feldenkrais taught that developing body awareness enables the brain's signals to change, facilitating a shift away from rigid patterns of behavior, thought and movement.

Supporters of the Feldenkrais method recommended it particularly for people who suffer from recurring injuries, breathing disorders, chronic pain or anxiety.

SEE ALSO *Alexander technique, Pilates method*

FEMINIZATION

Feminization, the normal sexual development of females, occurs during puberty. It is a process which is governed by the sex hormones estrogen and progesterone. Under the influence of the sex hormones, the breasts develop, the hips widen, hair appears on the underarms and around the vulva, the uterus grows, and menstruation begins. Feminization can be delayed in certain circumstances, or be absent if the female is suffering from certain diseases, such as Turner's syndrome and hypopituitarism.

Testicular feminization syndrome is the development of female sex characteristics in a male, giving rise to a genetic male with the appearance of a female. It is caused by lack of response of tissues to male hormones produced by the testes.

SEE ALSO *Estrogens, Hormones, Turner's syndrome*

FEMORAL ARTERY

Most of the blood supplied to the legs travels from the aorta to the external iliac artery. This becomes the femoral artery as it enters the thigh by passing deep to the ligament (known as the inguinal ligament) at the groin. A major branch of the femoral artery, called the profunda femoris artery, supplies blood to much of the thigh.

The femoral pulse is one of four pulses that can be felt in the leg. It can be felt in the groin at the mid-inguinal point, that is, midway between the uppermost part of the pubic symphysis (joint) and the anterior limit of the ilium (a pelvic bone).

SEE ALSO *Aorta, Arteries*

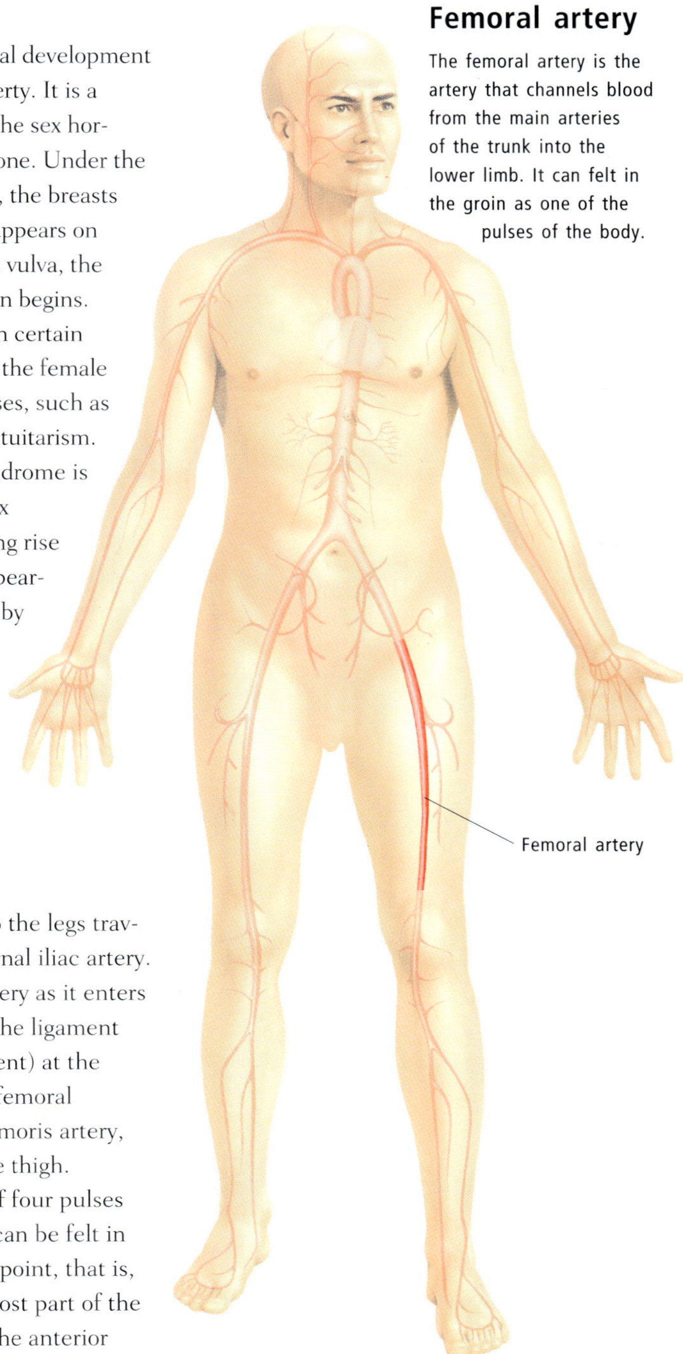

Femoral artery

The femoral artery is the artery that channels blood from the main arteries of the trunk into the lower limb. It can felt in the groin as one of the pulses of the body.

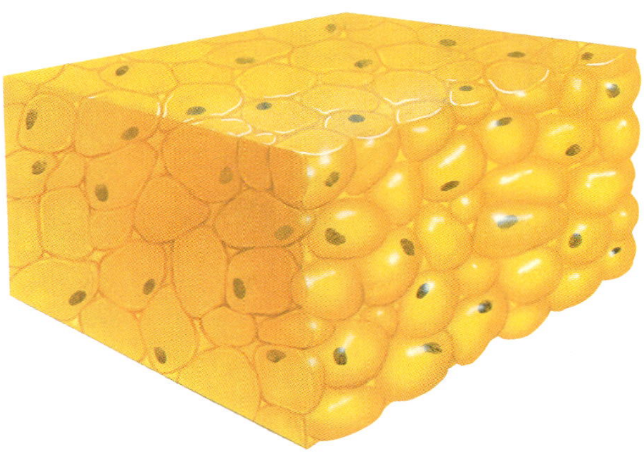

Fat

Fatty (adipose) tissue is found just under the skin, in the liver and around the internal organs. It helps to insulate the body from extremes of temperature, and serves as an energy store.

FEMUR

Extending from the hip to the knee, the femur (thighbone) is the longest and strongest bone in the body. It articulates (joins with) the hip bones above, and the tibia (shinbone) and patella (kneecap) below. The tendons of the powerful muscles that move the leg are attached to the femur.

Fracture of the neck of the femur (hip fracture) often follows a fall, and is common in the elderly, especially those with osteoporosis. Surgery followed by physical therapy is the recommended treatment. Fracture of the shaft of the femur is caused

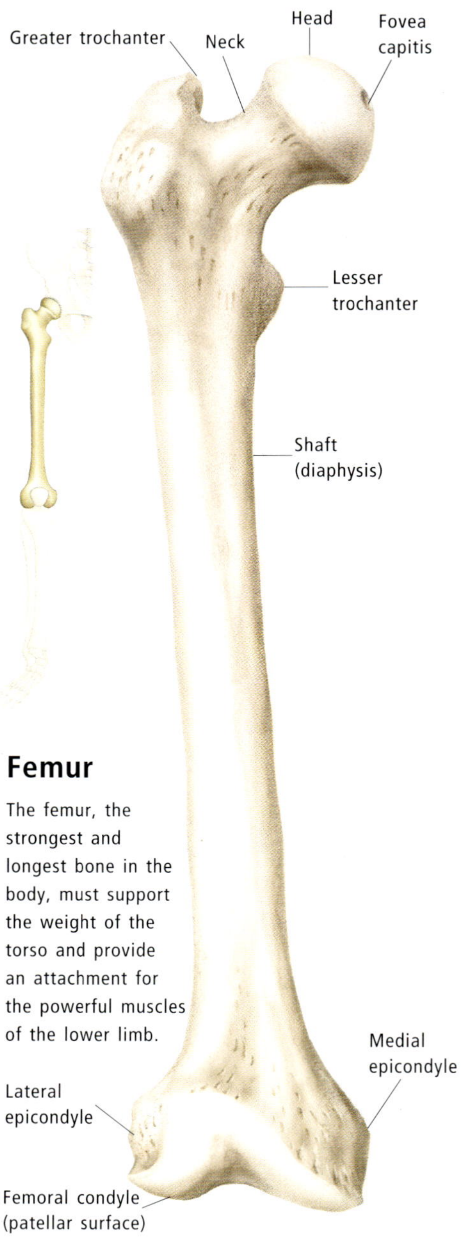

Femur

The femur, the strongest and longest bone in the body, must support the weight of the torso and provide an attachment for the powerful muscles of the lower limb.

by a blow to or a fall on the knee or leg, for example in a sporting injury. The fracture must be re-aligned under anesthesia and then held by traction, a splint, or surgical device (such as a nail inserted into the bone) while healing takes place.

SEE ALSO *Hip, Knee, Tibia*

FERTILITY

Fertility is the ability to conceive a child; it depends on several factors in both male and female reproductive function.

Males must have an adequate number of vigorous sperm cells. Normal human semen has a volume of approximately 0.1 fluid ounces (3 milliliters) per ejaculate, with 60 to 100 million sperm per milliliter. At least 50 percent of sperm should be moving four hours after ejaculation and at least 60 percent of sperm should be normal in shape.

In women, the vagina must be hospitable to the sperm and the mucus of the cervix must be thin enough for the sperm cells to penetrate. The interior of the uterus and uterine tube must allow movement of sperm to the egg. Egg production depends on many factors, including the normal cyclical production of sex hormones by the hypothalamus of the brain and normal production of eggs by the ovary. Once the egg has been fertilized, there must be a favorable environment for implantation of the early embryo into the wall of the uterus; infections and tumors in the uterus may prevent the early embryo developing.

Subfertility is defined as the failure to conceive after a year of normal intercourse. Of 100 women wanting to become pregnant, 70 will usually do so within a year, and 85 within two years. If a woman has never conceived then the problem is said to be one of primary subfertility. If she has conceived before, the problem is one of secondary subfertility. A common factor reducing fertility is blockage of the fallopian tube, which is caused by pelvic inflammatory disease.

Fertility tests include an examination of a sample of the man's ejaculate, looking at the percentage of sperm with normal shape and movement as well as the absolute number; a hysterosalpingogram and/or a laparoscopic examination of the woman to ensure that the fallopian tubes will allow the passage of sperm cells and fertilized egg; a cervical mucus sperm penetration test to determine if the cervical mucus is hostile to the sperm cells; and analysis of blood levels of the woman's pituitary hormones and progesterone to check for normal hormonal control of egg production and evidence of ovulation. It is also thought to be advisable for a woman to prepare a body temperature chart to help identify times of egg release.

SEE ALSO *Cervix, Embryo, Fallopian tubes, Hormones, Ovum, Pelvic inflammatory disease, Reproductive systems, Semen, Sperm, Uterus, Vagina*

FERTILIZATION

Fertilization is the fusion of ovum and sperm to form a zygote, which is essentially a one-celled embryo. This usually takes place in the ampulla (middle region) of the fallopian tube.

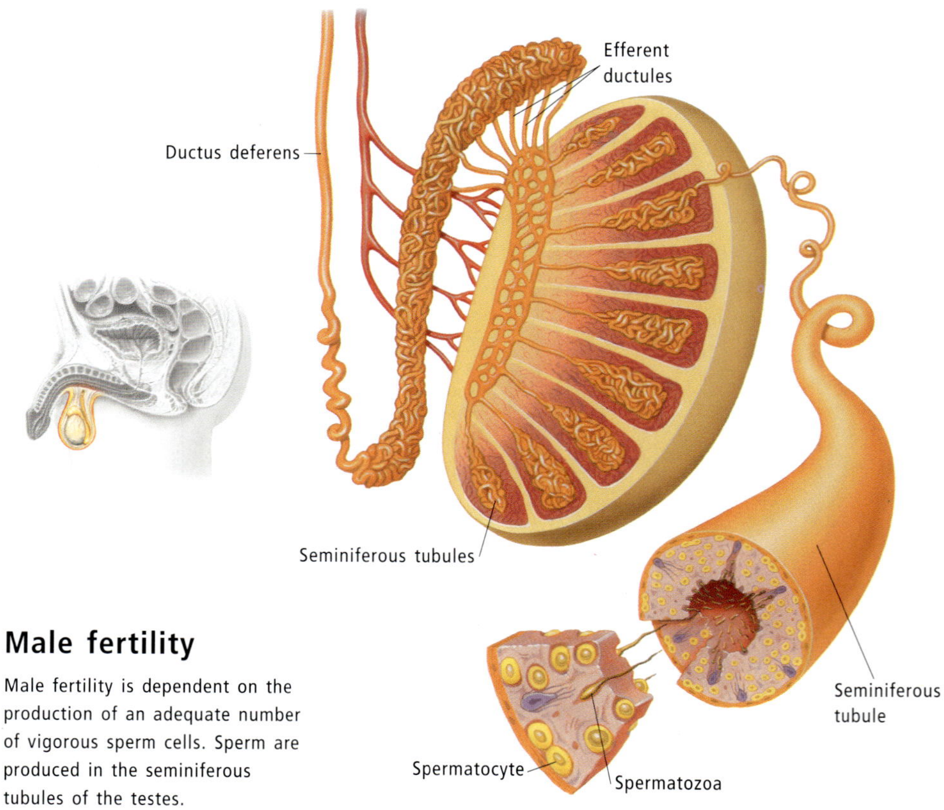

Male fertility

Male fertility is dependent on the production of an adequate number of vigorous sperm cells. Sperm are produced in the seminiferous tubules of the testes.

The ovum is released from the ovary along with two important coverings: a thin non-cellular membrane called the zona pellucida, which forms around the ovum while it is still in the ovary and, outside this, some of the cells from the outer wall of the ovarian follicle. The unfertilized ovum can remain in the ampulla for only two days, after which it degenerates.

At ejaculation, 60 to 100 million sperm are deposited in the vagina, but only a few of these travel through the female reproductive tract, with just 200 or so sperms reaching the ampulla. A major barrier to sperm travel for most of the menstrual cycle is the cervical mucus, but this becomes watery and readily penetrable around the time of ovulation. If this does not happen, or if the original number of sperm in the ejaculate is abnormally low, fertilization is unlikely to occur. Sperm motility is also an important factor, as transport to the ampulla is dependent on sperm movement, as well as on contractions of the muscular walls of the female reproductive tract.

Sperm undergo some maturation in the male reproductive tract and a process called capacitation in the female reproductive tract completes maturation. Capacitation takes about seven hours and is induced by secretions produced in the uterus and fallopian tube. The process is mainly concerned with changes in the outer surface of the sperm which will allow it to penetrate the ovum. Most sperm remain viable for only two days in the female reproductive tract.

Fertilization includes safeguards which ensure that just one sperm penetrates the ovum. The first barrier is the layer of cells adhering to the ovum. A few of the sperm which pass through these cells will adhere to the zona pellucida, the layer covering the egg. The first sperm to release enzymes allowing it to penetrate the zona pellucida will trigger an immediate reaction which makes the zona impenetrable to other sperm. The sperm thus selected then fuses with the ovum, and the chromosomes of ovum and sperm blend to form the nucleus of a new cell, the zygote. This starts dividing almost immediately and begins to move down the fallopian tube towards the uterus.

Penetration of the ovum by two sperm occasionally happens. The resulting embryo has 69 chromosomes in each of its body cells instead of the normal 46 and has severe development problems which in almost all cases lead to early spontaneous abortion (miscarriage). Occasionally, infants with this problem are born alive but all die very shortly after birth.

Fertilization with the combination of genetic material from two different individuals has the advantage of providing genetic variability in the embryo. This is enhanced by the rearrangement of genes on both maternal and paternal chromosomes during meiosis. It also allows for both male and female individuals. Development of a new individual from an ovum alone is called parthenogenesis and occurs naturally in certain insects and a few reptiles, and can also be induced artificially, using chemicals. The offspring are always female. Parthenogenesis has never been verified in humans.

SEE ALSO *Embryo, Fallopian tubes, Genes, Reproductive systems, Ovaries, Ovum, Sperm, Uterus*

Female fertility

Egg production and a favorable uterine environment are the key factors in female fertility. Once an egg has been produced successfully in the ovaries it moves down the fallopian tubes where it may be fertilized.

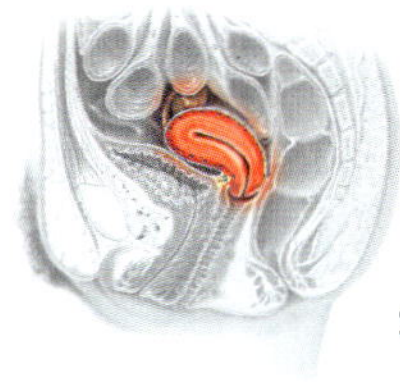

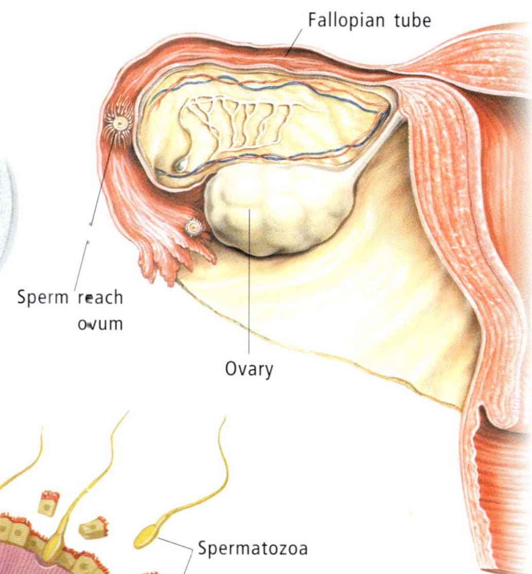

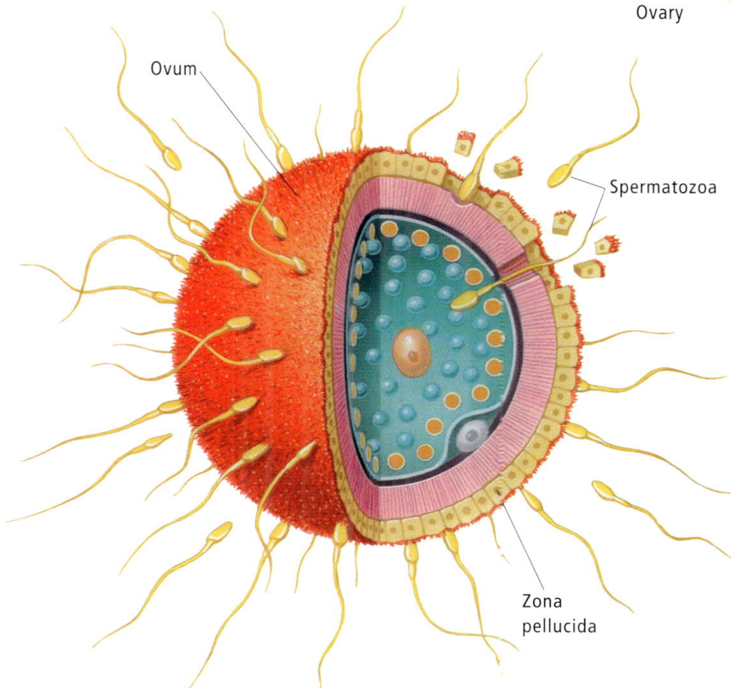

Fertilization

For successful fertilization to take place, millions of tiny sperm must be deposited in the female vagina after ejaculation. They dissolve the coating of the ovum allowing only one sperm to finally penetrate the outer surface, fertilize the ovum and join with it to produce a zygote.

FETAL ALCOHOL SYNDROME

Fetal alcohol syndrome (FAS) is the name given to a group of symptoms characterized by physical and mental abnormalities in an infant, and linked to alcohol consumption by the mother during pregnancy.

Opinions differ as to how much alcohol is too much, and many doctors recommend abstinence for this reason. It is known that binge drinking, particularly in the first trimester (12 weeks) of the pregnancy, is potentially dangerous and the baby may be born with varying degrees of fetal alcohol syndrome.

A baby born with the most severe form of FAS will suffer from intellectual disability, growth deficiencies (most babies with FAS are shorter and weigh less than normal babies), and facial abnormalities, such as narrow eyes, low nasal bridges and thin upper lip. Heart and joint abnormalities are also likely. The child will not recover from these defects.

SEE ALSO *Alcoholism, Fetal development*

F

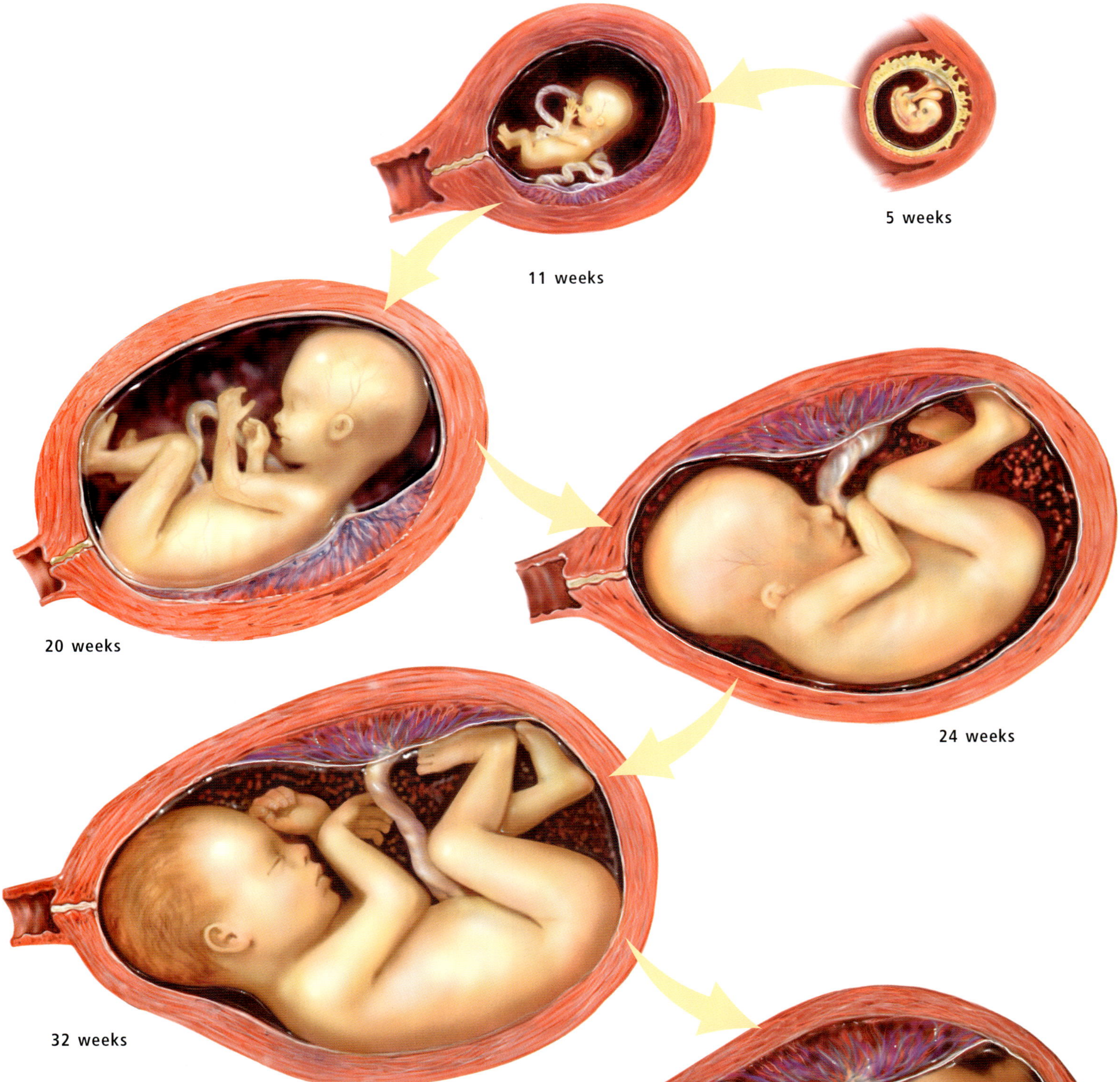

Fetal development cycle

Fetal development is a gradual process, but certain events take place at particular times. At 5 weeks, facial features have formed. At 11 weeks, the organs have developed. By week 20 the fetus is active, and movements are easily felt. By 24 weeks most of the organ systems become ready to function normally. At 32 weeks the growth rate has slowed down but weight has markedly increased. At 40 weeks, the fetus weighs 6–9 pounds (2.5–4 kilograms) and is ready for birth.

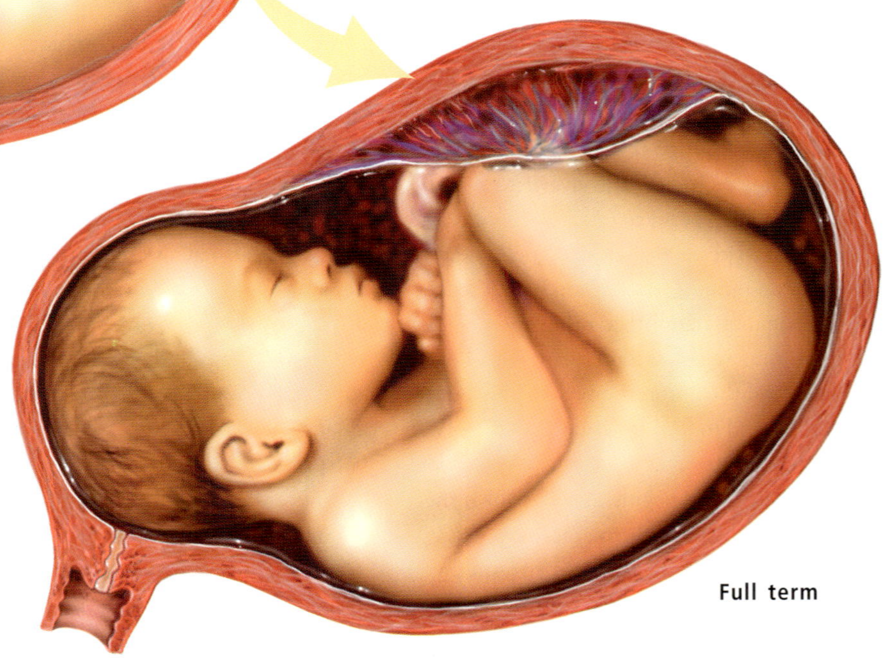

FETAL DEVELOPMENT

Fetal development is the process of the development of the individual in the uterus, from fertilization to the formation of the embryo and the fetus, to birth.

Fertilization and early development

Fetal development begins with the fertilization of the egg, when the head of a sperm penetrates a mature ovum high in a fallopian tube. Both sperm and ovum have 23 chromosomes each, but after fertilization, the resulting cell, which is called the zygote, has the full complement of 46 chromosomes.

The zygote grows by dividing its cells, a process called mitosis. This process continues as the zygote travels down the fallopian tube, brushed along by fine hairs (cilia). After division has occurred several times, the solid cluster of cells is called the morula, which, after several more days of dividing, becomes a hollow sphere called the blastocyst. Eventually, after about three to five days, the blastocyst reaches the uterus.

Further division sees the blastocyst separate into a cluster of inner cells in one part of a fluid-filled sac with an outer layer known as the trophoblast. The cluster of inner cells continues to divide until three separate layers of cells have formed. These are the so-called germ layers from which organs will form. The outermost layer is called the ectoderm; the innermost, the endoderm. Between these two layers develops a third layer, the mesoderm.

Now the blastocyst implants itself in the lining of the uterus (endometrium) until, about ten days after fertilization, it is completely buried. By this time, from the germ cells, unique tissues and organs begin to take shape. From the mesoderm, bone, muscle, heart, connective tissue, blood cells and vessels begin to grow. From the endoderm, digestive and respiratory tracts form, and from the ectoderm, skin, hair, and the tissues of the central nervous system. A cavity forms between the layers of germ cells and the outer trophoblast; this is the amniotic cavity, and it is filled with amniotic fluid.

Development of the embryo

The embryo grows inside the amniotic cavity, floating in the amniotic fluid, which acts as a water cushion, absorbing jolts and allowing the embryo to change posture. About two weeks after fertilization, blood vessels begin to develop within the embryo. At the same time, tiny extensions from the outer trophoblast layer of the blastocyst reach out into the endometrium and become blood vessels, joining with the mother's circulation. They develop into an organ called the placenta.

Across the placenta, separated by only a few layers of cells, the mother's circulation and that of the embryo come into close proximity. Across this barrier, oxygen, nutrients and antibodies (infection-fighting proteins) are able to pass from mother to embryo and waste products can pass from embryo to mother. The placenta also secretes hormones that help maintain the endometrium.

Securely floating within the amniotic fluid, and nurtured by the placenta, the embryo's cells continue to divide. By the third week, a closed tube called the neural tube has formed, which will become the brain and spinal cord. The front part of the neural tube enlarges; this enlargement will become the brain; the rest will be the spinal cord.

The brain itself forms into three separate parts: the prosencephalon, the mesencephalon, and the rhombencephalon. These areas will differentiate into the various parts of the mature brain. The relative positions of these areas of the brain to each other will change over time, as the brain flexes and doubles up on itself.

Meanwhile, as the alimentary canal is forming, another tube is developing into the heart. The embryo forms a circulation system different from that of an adult, as it includes short circuits which bypass the liver and lungs (these organs are not needed as their function is being performed by the placenta). At birth, these circuits will close.

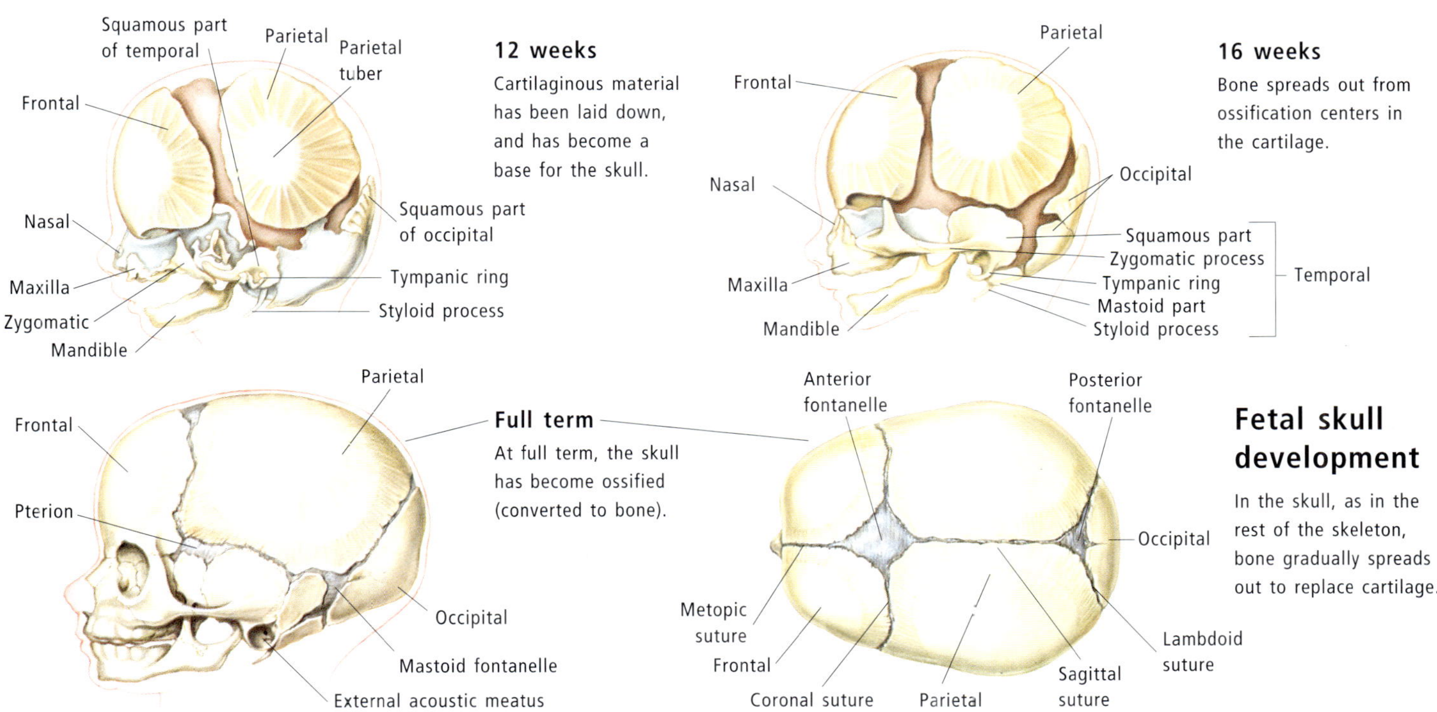

12 weeks
Cartilaginous material has been laid down, and has become a base for the skull.

16 weeks
Bone spreads out from ossification centers in the cartilage.

Full term
At full term, the skull has become ossified (converted to bone).

Fetal skull development
In the skull, as in the rest of the skeleton, bone gradually spreads out to replace cartilage.

At the start of its fourth week, the embryo has the beginnings of eyes and ears. Early in the second month, the major internal organs begin to take shape, and at about week six, bones and muscles begin to form. The buds of the arms and legs appear in week six; by week seven they are well defined.

Development of the fetus

From eight weeks, the embryo is described as a fetus. It is only tiny, at 1 inch (2.5 centimeters) long, and weighing about 1 gram, but all the human features are present. Limbs, eyes, ears, nose, mouth can all be seen, and the internal organs such as the heart, kidneys, liver, lungs, brain and digestive tract have formed. The limbs have begun to move (though the movements are not discernible by the mother until the twentieth week). From now on the main changes will be in size. Growth becomes more rapid; from now on it grows at about $\frac{1}{20}$ inch (1.5 millimeters) each day.

During the embryonic stage, material (either cartilage or membrane derived from mesenchyme) is laid down, becoming a template for the skull. The base of the skull develops from cartilage, which gradually becomes ossified (bony) as bone spreads out from ossification centers in the cartilage.

The rest of the skeleton develops in a similar way. Gradually, bone spreads out and replaces the cartilage until, by birth, much of the skeleton is fully ossified.

The genital organs begin to develop in the second month, but there is no difference in appearance between the sexes until about the seventh week. After this the sex glands develop differently, becoming the testes in the male and ovaries in the female. Both the testes and the ovaries gradually move to lower positions in the body, with the testes coming to lie in the scrotum by the end of the eighth month. In the male, a pair of tubules form which join up to the testes, and then open into the urethra; pouches in the ducts become the seminal vesicles. In the female, a pair of ducts also develops; one end of these ducts comes to lie alongside the ovaries, while the other end fuses into a common tube that becomes the uterus and vagina.

In both sexes, the external genital organs develop from a genital tubercle, along with a pair of urogenital folds with genital swellings on either side of the fold. At twelve weeks these differentiate into external male or female genitalia; in the male the tubercle and the united urogenital folds become the penis and the genital swellings fuse together and become the scrotum, while in the female, the tubercle becomes the clitoris and the urogenital folds and genital swellings become the lesser and greater lips of the vulva.

By twelve weeks, the fetus has a definite face with discernible facial expressions, though the head is disproportionately large because of development of the brain. In the eleventh or twelfth week the external geni-

Fetal brain development

Over a period of 9 months, the primitive neural tube forms into the prosencephalon, the mesencephalon and the rhombencephalon, which in turn develop into the various sections of the mature brain. By 4 weeks the prosencephalon has become the telencephalon and the diencephalon, and the rhombencephalon has become the myelencephalon and the metencephalon. The telencephalon develops into the cerebral hemispheres. At full term, all the surface features of the adult brain are already present.

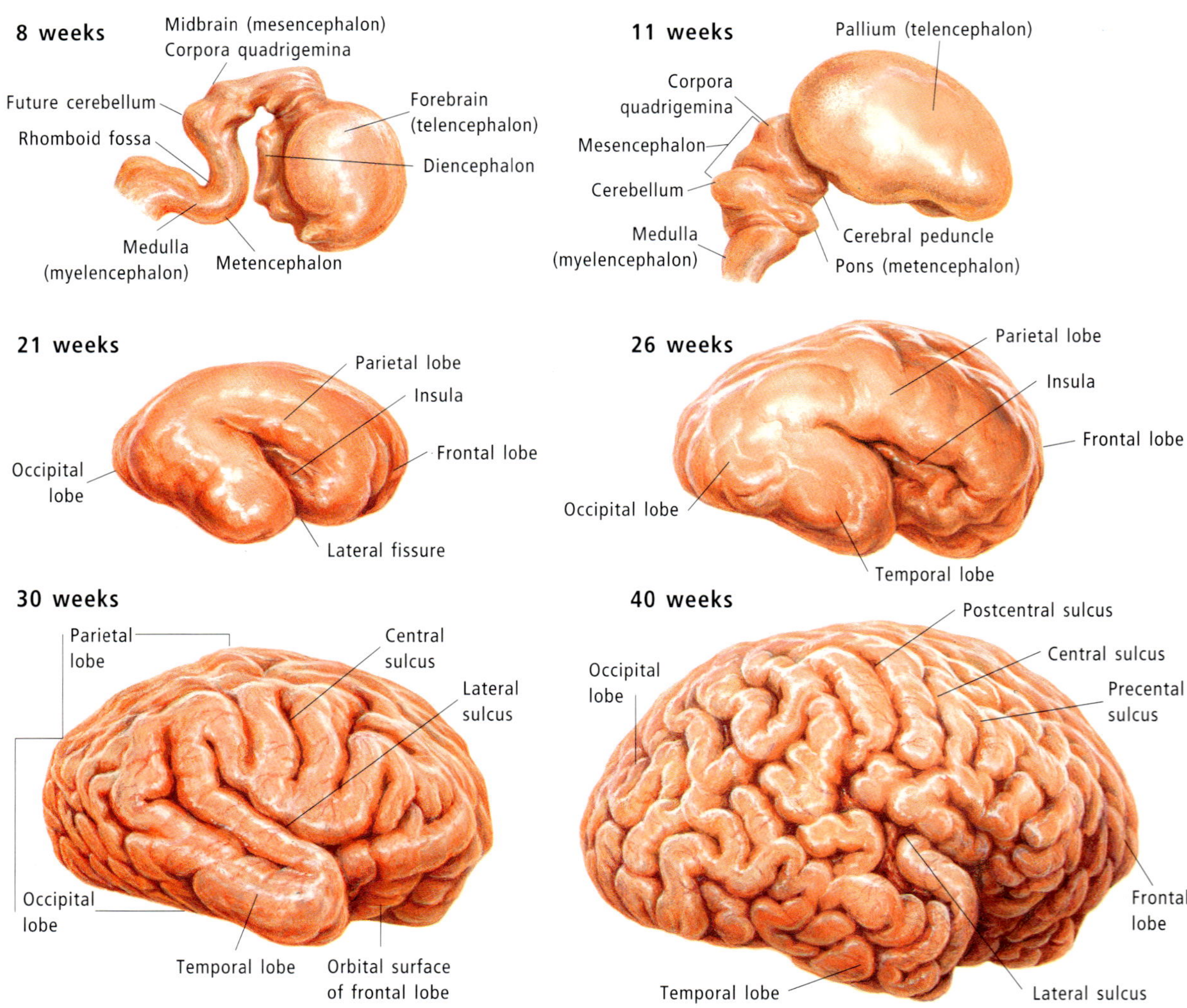

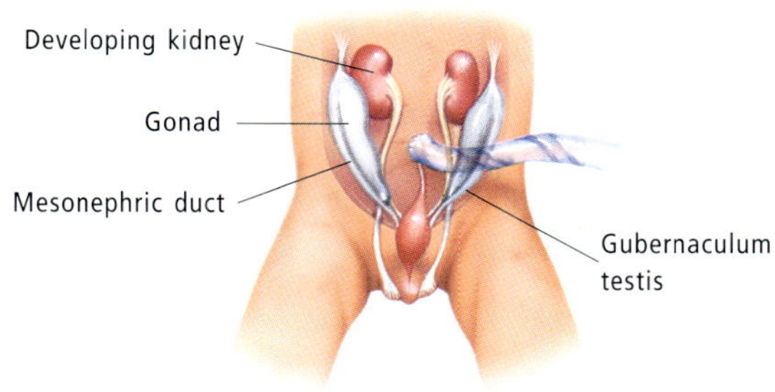

7 weeks

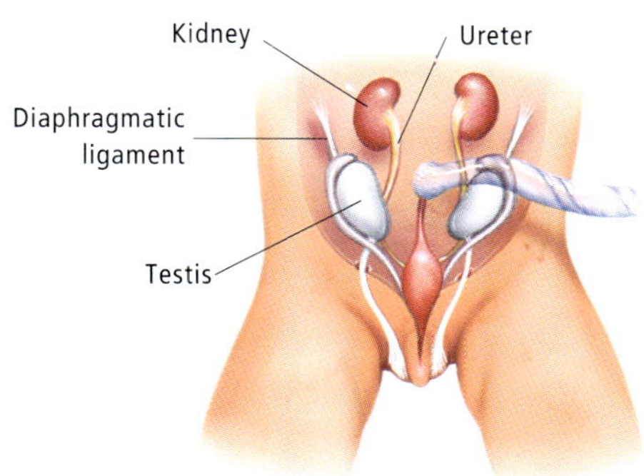

16 weeks

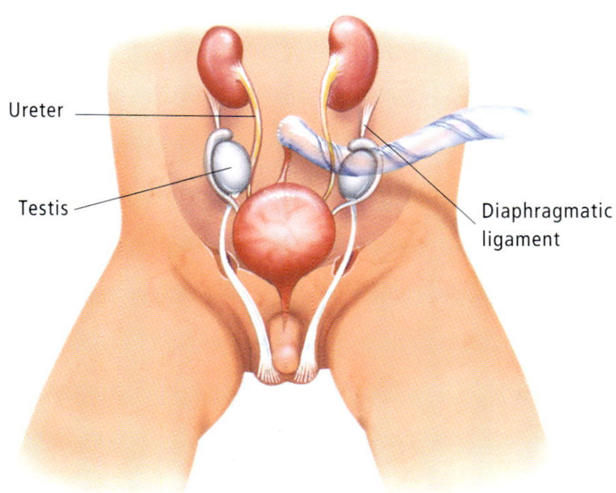

30 weeks

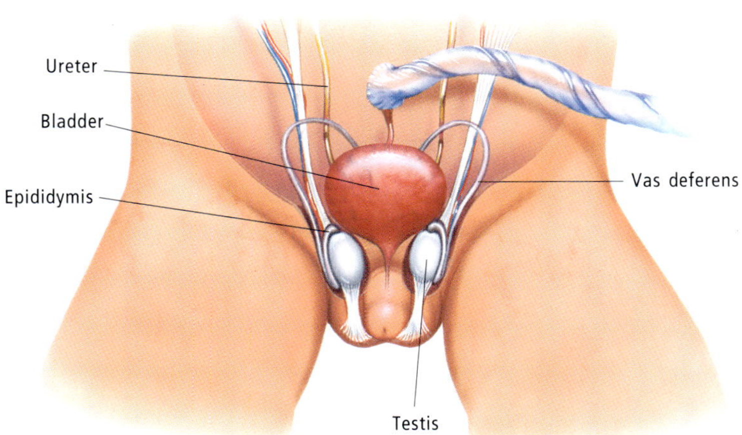

Fully developed

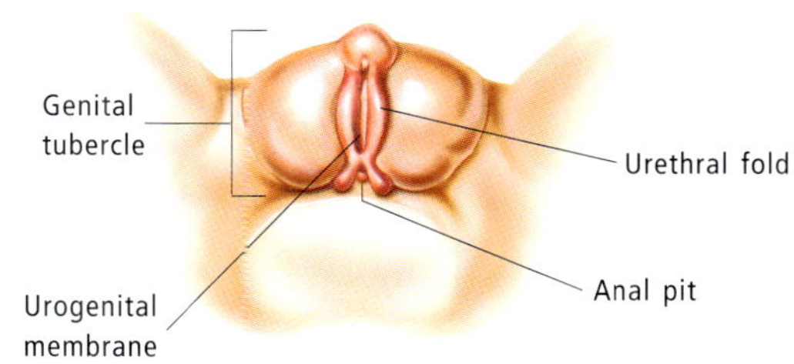

Undifferentiated

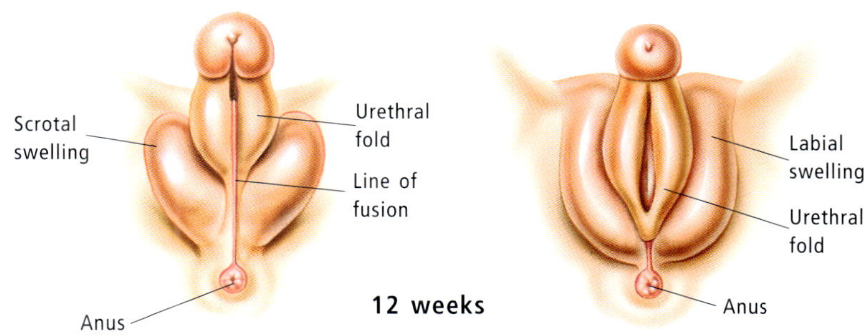

12 weeks

Male

Female

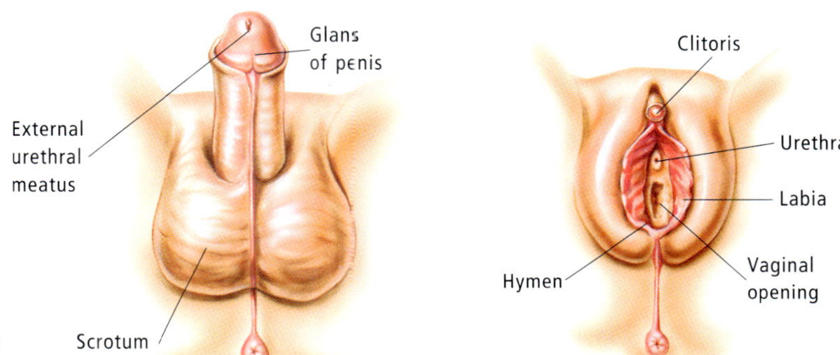

Fully developed

Fetal sex differentiation (above)

Up to 12 weeks, there is no difference between the male and female external genital organs, which consist of a genital tubercle, a urogenital membrane, a pair of urogenital folds and a genital swelling. After 12 weeks, these differentiate into the penis and scrotum in the male, and the clitoris and vulva in the female.

Descent of testes (left)

The testes (male gonads) form in the embryo from a piece of tissue at the back of the abdomen, near the kidneys. When they are fully developed at about 30 weeks, the testes make their way down the inguinal canal, reaching the scrotum as the time of birth approaches.

tals become evident, and by the fourth month the fetus is clearly recognizable as human. By twelve weeks, tiny nails are growing on its fingers and toes. The external ears, the eyelids (which will remain fused until the sixth month or so), and 32 permanent teeth buds have formed.

During the fourth month, simple reflexes have developed, and the mother first becomes aware of the movements of the fetus. The fetus will now respond to stimuli, such as a loud noise or a change in the mother's position, by moving vigorously. During the fifth and sixth months a downy covering (lanugo) develops on the body, and the body becomes increasingly larger in proportion to the head.

Weight gain begins during the seventh month, when fat is deposited under the skin all over the body. In the last few weeks before birth a special type of fat called brown fat will also be deposited in the upper part of the body. During the seventh month the skin, which is red and wrinkled, is covered with a creamy white substance known as vernix, manufactured by glands under the skin. This keeps the fetus waterproof. At 40 weeks, the fetus weighs 6–9 pounds (2.5–4 kilograms), is about 20 inches (50 centimeters) long, and is mature and ready for birth.

The physician or the obstetrician will monitor fetal development in various ways —through measurements of the mother's weight and abdominal girth, by listening to the fetal heartbeat through a special stethoscope, and by ultrasound, which is performed routinely during pregnancy.

Fetal abnormalities

Several factors can cause delayed growth of an otherwise normal fetus. These include poor nutrition, heart disease or high blood pressure, smoking, drug dependence, multiple pregnancies, heart disease in the mother, preeclampsia or eclampsia, and high altitude. Babies born to these mothers may be below normal weight. The general outlook for the development of these infants is poorer than for normal weight children.

Sometimes the fetus may develop abnormally. A disorder of development while the fetus is growing in the uterus is known as a congenital abnormality. It may be caused by a genetic disorder, so that the abnormality is inherited, or it may be acquired while the fetus is growing, due to exposure to an agent that is teratogenic, that is, causes abnormal development. Though they are generally rare, the range of possible congenital abnormalities is wide. Limbs or organs may be absent, duplicated or malformed. Organs may fail to move to the correct place, as in undescended testes (cryptorchidism); they may fail to open properly, as in imperforate anus, or fail to close at the correct time, as in patent ductus arteriosus (when the channel bypassing the lungs does not close).

Congenital abnormalities may be obvious at birth, or they may take months or years to become evident, as in the case of Huntington's disease (a degenerative brain disease), which doesn't manifest until middle age.

Inherited congenital anomalies are caused by abnormal genes. There are over 2,000 known inherited congenital anomalies; some are common, for example sickle cell disease, Down syndrome, and cleft palate, while others such as phenylketonuria, an inherited metabolic disorder, are rare.

Sometimes genetic abnormalities may occur if there is a spontaneous mutation of the parental genes, which may happen during sperm production or egg formation. Severe mutations are not compatible with life and result in miscarriage. Others allow the fetus to survive to birth but it may not live long. Other abnormalities, such as Down syndrome, are compatible with life well into adulthood, but the affected person may have disabilities.

Acquired congenital abnormalities can be caused by a variety of agents that affect the fetus in the uterus, including drugs, infections and toxins. Infection in the mother is a common cause of acquired congenital abnormality. Rubella (German measles) contracted in the first three months of pregnancy may cause deafness, cataracts, heart disease, jaundice or other abnormalities in the child. Cytomegalovirus (CMV) and *Toxoplasma* are two organisms that cause congenital anomalies.

Some drugs taken by a woman during pregnancy are responsible for abnormalities in the child. Corticosteroids, anticonvulsants, anti-cancer drugs, narcotics, sedatives, tranquilizers, antidepressants, antibacterials (especially tetracycline), anticoagulants, and drugs prescribed to treat cardiac conditions and hypertension can all cause congenital defects in a few cases. A pregnant woman should avoid taking any medication without first obtaining medical advice.

Environmental toxins, x-rays, or injury to the fetus may cause an abnormality in the fetus. The age of the mother may also be a factor. Down syndrome (trisomy 21), for example, occurs more frequently when conception takes place after about 35 years of age.

Congenital abnormalities cannot be reversed, but they can often be successfully treated with surgery, hormone treatment, diet and physical therapy, depending on the condition and its severity. In the future, gene therapy may provide a treatment.

If there is a known or suspected risk of a congenital abnormality developing, it can often be detected during pregnancy by screening procedures. The most reliable procedure is to examine a sample of fluid obtained by amniocentesis from the amniotic sac between the fifteenth and eighteenth week of pregnancy. Chorionic villus sampling (CVS) is a technique used in the first trimester of pregnancy in which a tissue sample is taken from the placenta and analyzed for evidence of genetic defects in the fetus. Ultrasound can also reveal some abnormalities.

Termination of pregnancy (abortion) may be considered if fetal disorders are found early in a pregnancy. The decision to abort rests with the parents and should be taken after they are made fully aware by their physician of the nature of the disorder and the consequences of abortion.

Genetic counseling should be considered by anyone who has a history of chromosomal abnormalities, and by all pregnant women over 35 years of age. There may be a higher risk than normal of congenital abnormality in a second child if the first is born with an abnormality; parents in this situation should undergo genetic counseling if they wish to have another child.

SEE ALSO *Amniocentesis, Chorionic villus sampling, Congenital abnormalities, Embryo, Fertilization, Genetic counseling, Lanugo, Miscarriage, Ovum, Placenta, Sperm, Ultrasound, Uterus*

FETOSCOPY

Fetoscopy is the use of high-resolution fiberoptic equipment in surgery on a pregnant woman. It is used when performing operations on the growing baby (fetus) or its environment, in the first and early second trimester of the pregnancy. The surgery is performed through a small incision in the abdomen and uterus. It is sometimes referred to as embryofetoscopy.

SEE ALSO *Embryoscopy, Fetal development*

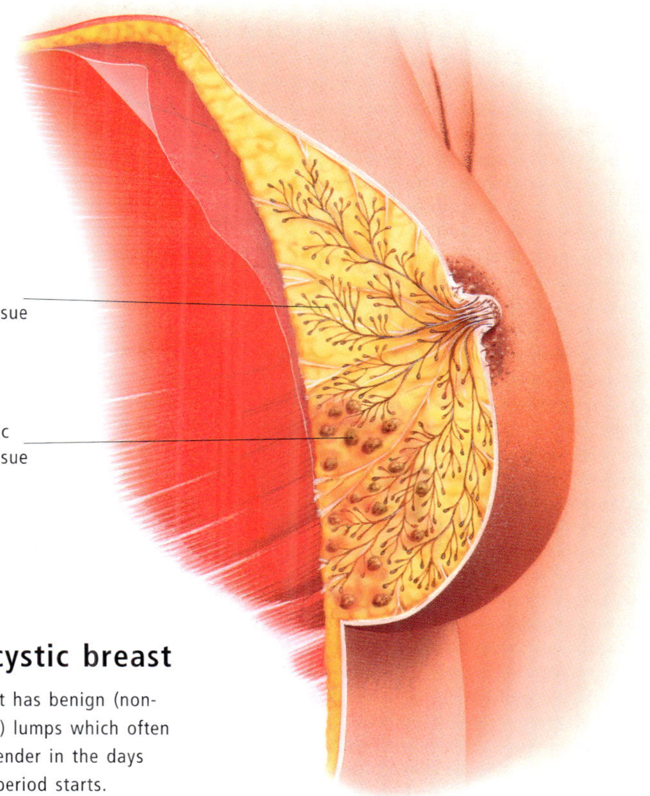

Fibrocystic breast

The breast has benign (noncancerous) lumps which often become tender in the days before a period starts.

FEVER

Fever is an abnormal increase in body temperature. Normal temperature, taken orally, is 98.6°F (37°C). Someone with fever has a temperature at least 0.5°F (about 0.3°C) above normal, on two recordings taken at least two hours apart to be certain. Fever can occur in otherwise healthy people through exercise or dehydration, or following childhood immunizations. Usually fever is a symptom of illness, particularly viral or bacterial infection. It may be accompanied by shivering, sweating, headache, restlessness, weakness and loss of appetite. An overactive thyroid gland, certain cancers and connective tissue disorders can be responsible for prolonged fever.

If the fever is less than 24 hours old, and the temperature is less than 102°F (39°C), it is recommended that the patient drink plenty of fluids and take an oral antipyretic drug like acetaminophen (paracetamol) or ibuprofen every four hours. Children under the age of 16 should not take aspirin.

If the fever persists, if there is mental confusion or disorientation, if the temperature rises above 102°F (39°C) or if there is vomiting or diarrhea, consult a physician. In very young children, fevers above 102°F (39°C) may trigger a febrile convulsion, requiring immediate medical attention.

SEE ALSO *Body temperature, Viruses*

FIBRILLATION

Fibrillation is irregular electrical activity of the heart muscle, with the result that the heart muscle cannot contract effectively. It may occur in either the atria or ventricles of the heart. Atrial fibrillation may be due to disease of the mitral valve, myocardial infarction, infections or thyroid disease. The great danger of atrial fibrillation is that stagnant blood in parts of the atrium may coagulate. Small fragments of coagulated blood may then break off and become lodged in the arteries of the brain or kidneys. Ventricular fibrillation is even more serious, because the ventricles are unable to pump blood while fibrillating. Patients with ventricular fibrillation will have no pulse and will die in minutes unless resuscitation and electrical defibrillation are used.

SEE ALSO *Arteries, Defibrillation, Heart, Mitral valve, Myocardial infarction, Ventricle*

FIBROADENOMA

A fibroadenoma is a benign tumor formed from glandular tissue. It occurs most commonly in the female breast, most often among women who are in their reproductive years. Fibroadenomas are not usually tender. However, they generally need to be surgically removed to confirm they are benign, and because they can continue to grow and cause an unsightly lump. Usually a fibroadenoma can be removed under local anesthesia.

SEE ALSO *Breast, Tumors*

FIBROCYSTIC DISEASE

Fibrocystic disease is a very common condition of women in their reproductive years. It is characterized by a number of small cysts (fluid filled sacs surrounded by fibrous tissue) that give the breast a dense, irregular and bumpy consistency. Usually both breasts are involved.

The breasts become enlarged and tender just before the menstrual period, with symptoms improving after the period finishes. The condition improves after menopause and often after commencing the contraceptive pill. No treatment is required, though any single lump that stands out should be investigated by a physician.

SEE ALSO *Breast, Menopause, Menstruation, Oral contraceptives*

FIBROIDS

Leiomyomata uteri, known colloquially as fibroids, are benign (non-malignant) tumors of the uterus which are believed to arise from smooth muscle cells of the wall of the uterus. They are extremely common, occurring in 20 percent of Caucasian women and 50 percent of African-American women.

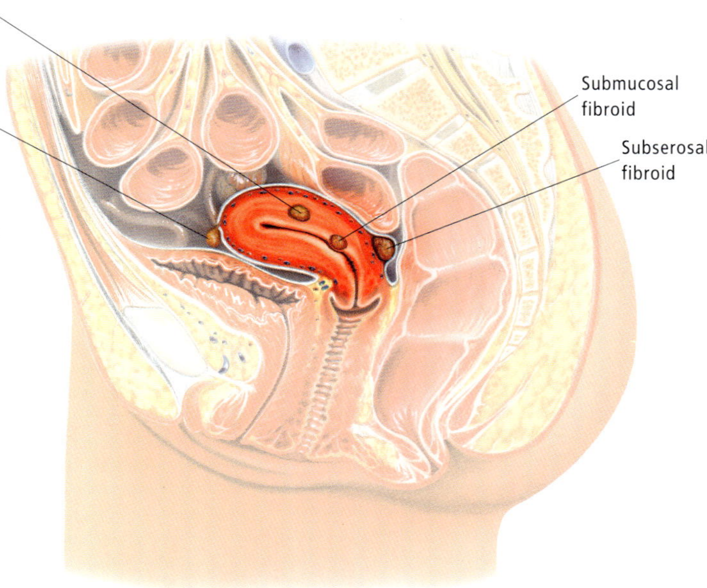

Fibroids

Fibroids are non-malignant tumors that occur in the uterus. Intramural fibroids grow in the muscular tissue in the uterus wall. Submucosal fibroids grow in the endometrial layer. Subserosal fibroids occur just under the surface of the uterine wall. Pedunculated fibroids develop a stalk which can protude from the uterus or cervix.

The cause is unknown and most tumors have no symptoms. Where symptoms do occur, they include abdominal distension (swelling), abdominal discomfort, constipation, heavy periods (hypermenorrhea), increased frequency of urination, and bleeding between periods.

Pregnancy may occur in women with fibroids, but complications may arise, such as miscarriage, premature labor, prolonged labor and excess bleeding after birth (postpartum hemorrhage). Some patients with fibroids may suffer from anemia (reduced hemoglobin in the blood) due to excessive blood loss associated with the heavy menstrual periods.

Treatment of fibroids is not necessary where there are no symptoms, but such tumors should be carefully watched to determine the rate of growth. If the woman is experiencing symptoms, the uterus may be removed (hysterectomy) or the individual lump cut out (myomectomy). Myomectomy is used in younger women who wish to retain the ability to have children. Unfortunately, myomectomy is usually less effective than hysterectomy and fibroids may recur.

SEE ALSO *Anemia, Hysterectomy, Menstruation, Tumors, Uterus*

FIBROMYALGIA

Fibromyalgia is a common rheumatic condition consisting of painful muscles, body aches and pains, and sleep disorders. The cause is unknown; the muscles themselves are not weak, nor is there any sign of inflammation or disease in them. Fibromyalgia is usually mild and improves with treatment in the form of stretching exercises, application of heat and/or gentle massage, and taking of anti-inflammatory drugs, and, in some cases, antidepressant drugs.

SEE ALSO *Anti-inflammatory drugs, Antidepressants, Massage, Muscle, Rheumatism*

FIBROSIS

Fibrosis is the formation of fibrous scar tissue. It normally follows after infection, injury and inflammation. Too much scarring can cause a disorder, such as adhesions in the peritoneum following peritonitis, or keloid tissue, an overgrowth of scar tissue at the site of a skin injury. Scarring can also be a result of chronic inflammatory diseases such as interstitial lung disorders (a group of disorders characterized by scarring and thickening of the deep lung tissues) and hepatitis, which can cause cirrhosis, or scarring of the liver.

SEE ALSO *Adhesions, Cirrhosis of the liver, Hepatitis, Keloid, Peritonitis*

FIBULA

The fibula is the long, slender bone on the outside of the lower leg. It extends from just below the knee to the ankle, where its lower end forms the outer side of the ankle joint.

Fibula

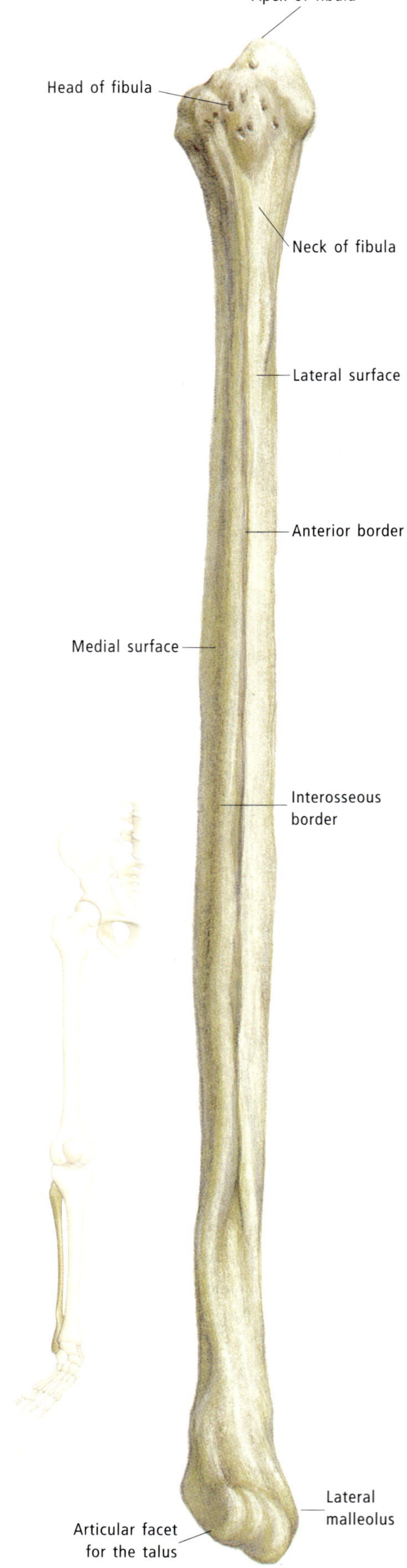

It does not bear weight like the shinbone (tibia), but instead serves as an attachment for some of the leg muscles. Fracture of the fibula is common, especially in children, often occurring in contact sports such as football or hockey. It can occur with an ankle sprain. In most cases fractures are not serious, and setting is usually unnecessary; surgery is occasionally necessary.

SEE ALSO *Ankle, Knee, Leg, Tibia*

FILARIASIS

Characterized by irregular swinging fevers, and swelling and inflammation of lymph nodes and vessels, this tropical disease is due to infection by the larvae of the nematode *Wuchereria bancrofti*.

Monkeys, cats and human beings may be infected by the bites of mosquitoes, after which the larvae develop into adult worms, which may grow up to 3 inches (8 centimeters). Over time the adult worms invade the lymph nodes and vessels causing both inflammation and obstruction. Massive swelling of legs, arms, breasts and scrotum can occur (known as elephantiasis).

In the early stages, antibiotics may be required for secondary infection. While drugs can suppress, if not always cure, the disease, surgery may be required when swelling or elephantiasis occurs.

SEE ALSO *Elephantiasis, Lymphatic vessels*

FILLINGS

Fillings are metal, porcelain or plastic material used to replace decayed parts of teeth and to halt the growth of dental cavities. The process of filling a tooth may begin by drilling into the cavity to remove the decayed matter. Smaller cavities may not require drilling. The hole is then filled with gold, silver alloy, porcelain or plastic, depending on the desired effect. Plastic and porcelain look more like the natural tooth and may be preferred for fillings in front teeth. Metal fillings are usually stronger. Fillings may be done with the aid of local or general anesthetic, or nitrous oxide gas.

SEE ALSO *Teeth*

FINGER

A finger is any of the digits of the hand. Each finger has three bones (phalanges), separated by joints, except the thumb, which has only two phalanges.

Powerful movements of the fingers and thumb are carried out by muscles in the forearm, whose long tendons run in front of and behind the wrist and along the front and back of the phalanges, where they attach. Precision movements of the fingers and thumb are made by small muscles in the hand.

Finger joint sprains and dislocations are common in sporting injuries. They are usually treated by splinting the broken finger to an adjacent finger. If the fracture is unstable or cannot be reduced, then surgery may be felt to be necessary. "Mallet finger" results from damage to the tendon attaching to the tip of the finger, resulting in an inability to straighten the fingertip. It is usually treated with a special splint for six to nine weeks.

SEE ALSO *Hand*

FISSURE

A fissure is a crack or a groove in the skin or the surface of an internal organ. It may be a normal feature, or it may result from an injury or disease and be abnormal.

The most common pathological (abnormal) fissure is an anal fissure, which occurs when skin around the anus is torn when passing hard feces. Most common in infants and children, the condition is very painful, and there may be bleeding while passing feces.

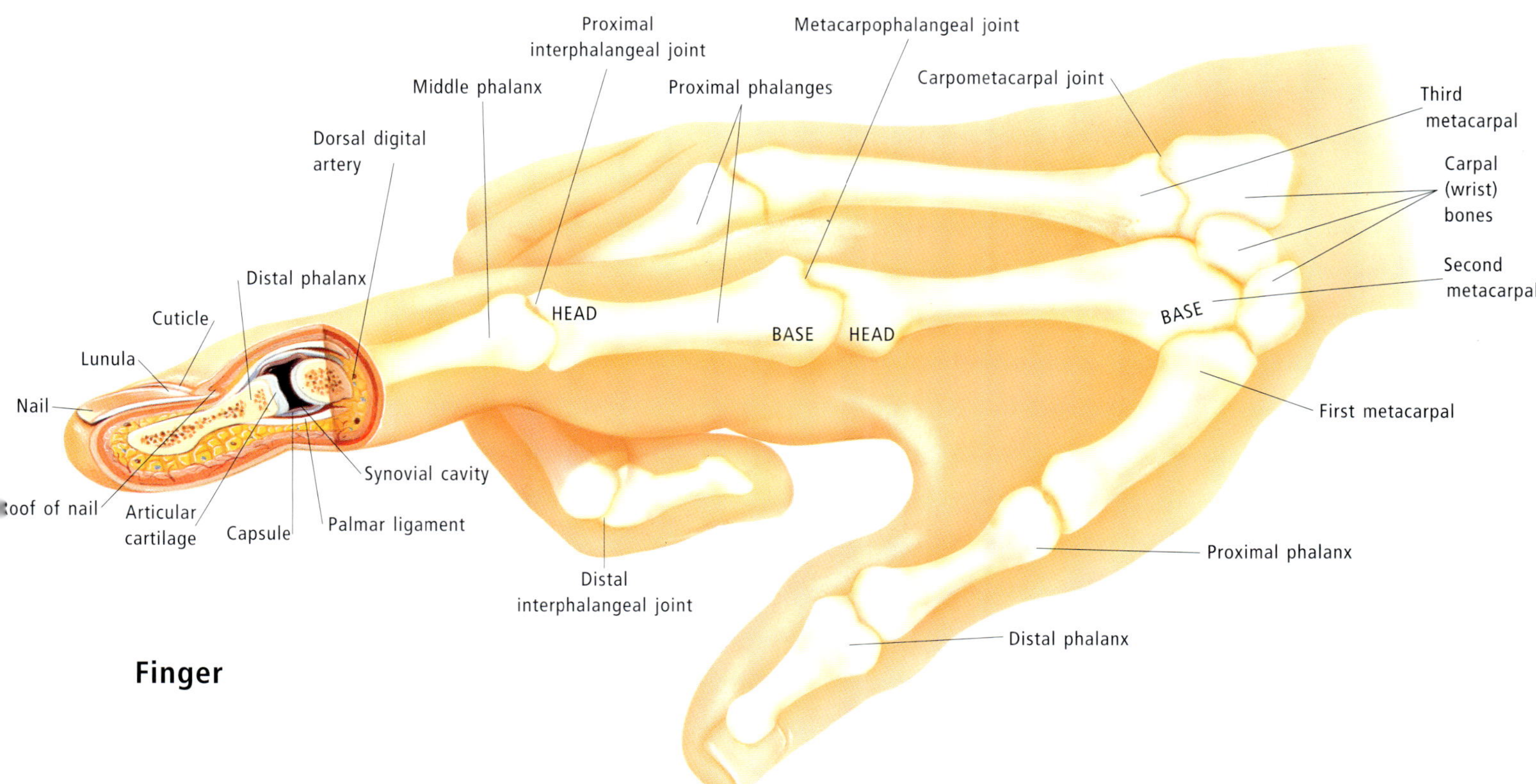

Finger

Fissure

A fissure is a split or crack in the skin or on the surface of an organ, often resulting from disease or injury.

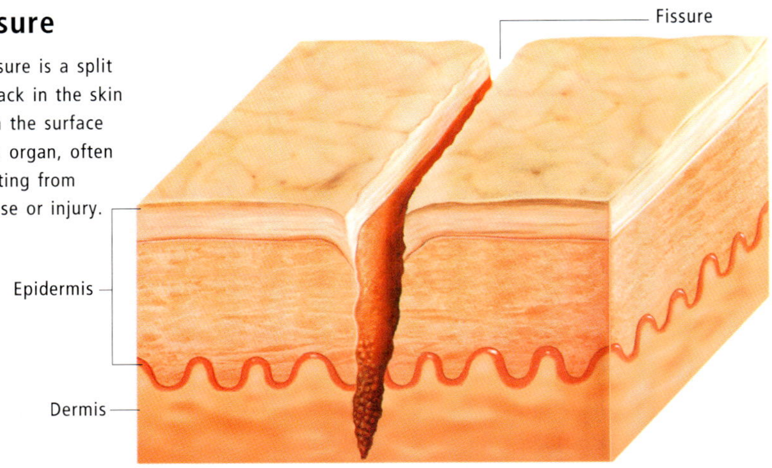

Anal fissures usually heal after several days when the constipation ceases. A laxative may help constipation. An anesthetic ointment applied to the anus will help relieve pain. If the fissure does not heal by itself, surgery may be needed.

SEE ALSO *Anus*

FISTULA

A fistula results from an abnormal communication between the inner surface linings of two adjacent organs. It may occur, for example, between the rectum and the bladder, where urine may pass from the bladder to the rectum, or between the rectum and the vagina, which can lead to feces passing into the vagina. A fistula may be caused by malignant (cancerous) tumors, inflammation or infection. Treatment is by the use of surgery.

Anorectal fistula

Anorectal fistula (or "fistula in ano") is a condition in which there is an abnormal passage between the inner surface of the anus and the surface of the skin around the anus. It is due to infection on the anus, usually by pus-causing bacteria that results in a break in the wall of the anal canal or rectum. Other cases may be due to cancer of the anus and rectum, Crohn's disease or diverticulitis. An untreated anorectal fistula may lead to bacterial infection throughout the body, and some may become the sites of origin of cancers. Small anorectal fistulas may repair themselves, but for larger ones the site of infection should be removed and the fistula opened to allow pus to drain.

SEE ALSO *Anus, Bladder, Crohn's disease, Diverticulitis, Rectum*

FLAT FEET

"Flat feet" is a musculoskeletal disorder characterized by loss of the arches of the feet.

Normally, the arches of the feet are formed by the arrangement of the tarsal and metatarsal bones and are flexible to assist weightbearing and shock-absorbency. The head of the talus bone is the keystone of the arch and is supported by a ligament. The plantar or longitudinal arch runs from the ball of the foot to the heel; the metatarsal arch runs across the ball. Under load, the arches may flatten slightly.

Flat feet can occur in adolescence or adulthood and may result from abnormally stretched ligaments, a condition that can be caused by standing for long periods. The head of the talus bone is unsupported and rotates excessively, flattening the arch. When weight is taken off the foot the arch may become visible again.

At birth, a newborn's feet appear to be flat, but this is simply the appearance produced by thick pads of fat under the skin layer in the soles of the feet, and does not indicate flat feet. The arches will be visible a few months after the child begins walking.

Diagnosis of flat feet will consider stress fractures and arthritis as possible causes. Treatment for flat feet in children used to be to wear arch supports inside the shoes but this is now considered of little value, though adults may wear them to reduce shoe wear.

SEE ALSO *Foot*

FLATULENCE

Flatulence is excessive build-up of gas in the gastrointestinal tract. It may produce a bloated feeling and is expelled through the mouth or through the anus. Air can be swallowed when eating or gas can be ingested with foods that have a high gas content, such as fizzy drinks. Also gases, such as hydrogen, methane and carbon dioxide, can be

Fistula

For a woman, a problematic labor may lead to the formation of a fistula between the rectum and the vagina, which can lead to feces passing into the vagina.

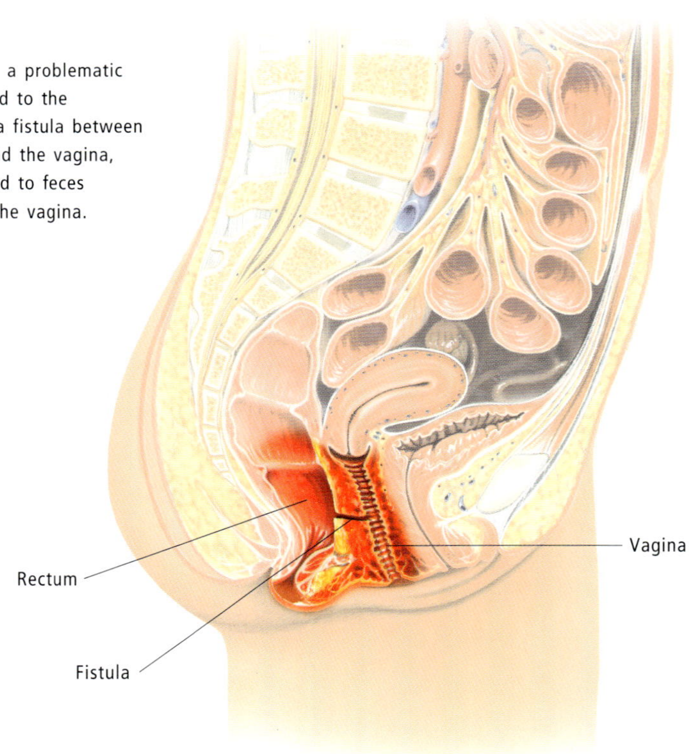

produced by the various bacteria in the colon or the lower part of the large intestine.

Intestinal gas may have an offensive smell, or be odorless, depending on the bacteria, and the volume produced can be affected by the foods eaten. Beans, cabbage, unprocessed wheat bran and other foods high in dietary fiber may produce large quantities of gas, while an inability to digest foods, such as milk products, may also produce gas.

SEE ALSO *Colon, Digestive system, Intestines, Lactose intolerance*

FLOATERS

Also known as muscae volitantes or "spots before the eyes", floaters appear as small shadows that seem to float over the fields of vision. Most common among the aged, they are caused by anything that breaks into the jellylike portion (vitreous humor) of the eyeball. Such breaks may be due to a few blood cells floating away from a broken capillary at the back of the eye, degenerative deposits, escaped fluid from blood vessels (exudates), and contraction of the vitreous gel and its detachment from the retina. These agents cause shadows to fall on the retina, characteristically perceived by the patient as tiny shadows, usually trailing just behind the center of vision. They are most often noted while reading across a page. A sudden shower of floaters may indicate detachment of the retina (the inner lining of the eyeball), which may result in flashing lights and disturbed vision.

The majority of floaters are not overly serious and generally occur when the patient is tired. A major problem, however, can be the cause and early referral to an eye specialist is required to ensure that this is not the case.

SEE ALSO *Eye*

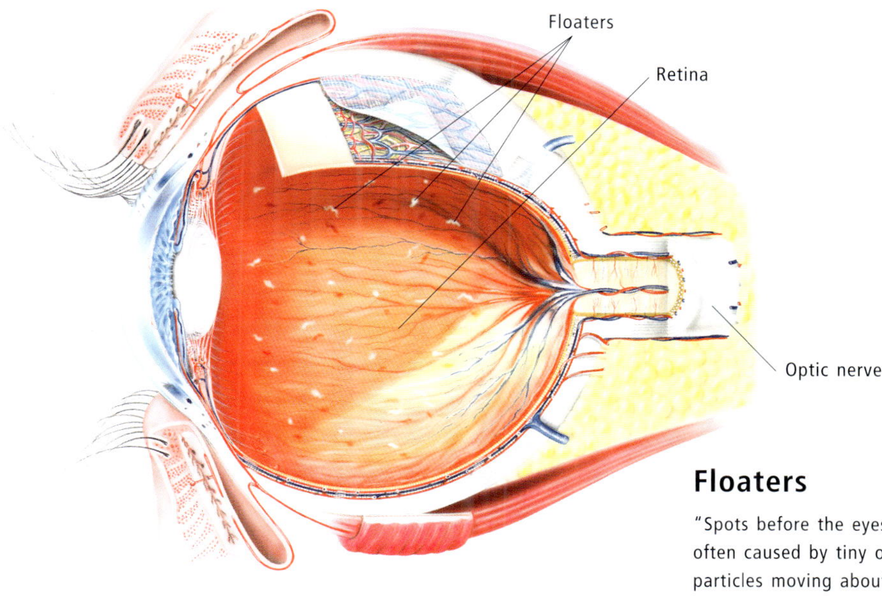

Floaters

"Spots before the eyes" are often caused by tiny organic particles moving about in the vitreous humor of the eye.

FLOTATION THERAPY

The purpose of flotation therapy, also known as restricted environmental stimulation therapy (REST), is to introduce patients to states of deep mental and physical relaxation. In this therapy, patients float for 30 to 60 minutes on very salty water heated to around 94°F (34°C) in a tank a little larger than a bathtub. Alternatively, in dry flotation systems, a membrane separates the patient from the fluid underneath. There may be no lighting or sound, or there may be dim lights and relaxation music or guided visualizations. Practitioners consider flotation therapy to be effective for stress-related disorders and for the management of chronic pain.

SEE ALSO *Relaxation techniques*

FLOWER REMEDIES AND ESSENCES

The original flower remedies were the work of the English physician Dr Edward Bach (1880–1936). A distinguished Harley Street doctor and bacteriologist, Bach became disillusioned with orthodox medicine, believing that it treated symptoms rather than causes of illness. He became interested in homeopathy and worked at the London Homeopathic Hospital for many years.

Bach believed in treating a person's temperament rather than their physical symptoms. He urged his patients to search within themselves for the emotional and psychological origins of their illness, and to address them. At the same time Bach sought natural healing remedies that would facilitate emotional shifts to bring increased vitality and inner peace.

Bach devoted the final six years of his life to walking the countryside in search of his healing flower remedies. He believed that the essence of a plant was concentrated in a flower before it seeded. Holding a flower in his hands he would intuitively sense its essence and the effect it had on him. From his observations he identified 38 flower remedies which he believed could heal through releasing their particular qualities, thereby bringing about a change of outlook.

Rescue remedy

The best known of all the Bach flower remedies is the combination rescue remedy, which is thought to relieve the effects of any kind of trauma, from physical shock to mental anxiety. It has often been noted that it is particularly effective when given to children and animals. Rescue remedy consists of: star of Bethlehem for shock, rock rose for panic and terror, impatiens for mental stress, cherry plum for fear of losing control and clematis for feeling "out of the body".

Remedy preparation

Bach believed that his remedies worked on a vibrational level and devised a method of preparation to release the flower's vibrational essence. Wild flowers are placed in a bowl of spring water and left in the sun for three hours to transfer their essence to the water. This water then becomes the concentrated remedy, or stock, with the addition of brandy to stabilize it. The stock is further diluted to make up an individual remedy, often containing several remedies. This is taken a few times a day in drop doses.

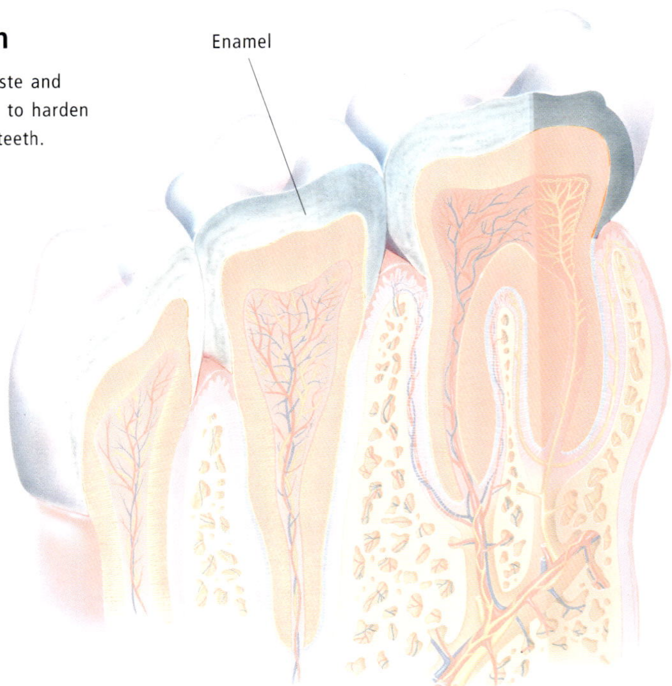

Fluoridation

Fluoride in toothpaste and water supplies acts to harden the enamel of the teeth.

The use of flower remedies has spread worldwide, although there is as yet no scientific explanation as to how they work. Researchers in more than 50 countries have followed the work of Bach in making flower essences from their native wildflowers. Flower remedies and essences can be self-prescribed, or may be prescribed by natural therapists, counselors or psychotherapists in conjunction with other treatments.

FLUID RETENTION

Fluid retention is the abnormal accumulation of the fluid that surrounds cells and is a symptom of an underlying disorder of kidney function and fluid balance.

The balance of fluid in the body is regulated by the hypothalamus, which triggers the release of hormones to control the functions of the kidneys and bladder. Normal fluid balance can be upset by excessive blood loss, and by various disorders, including kidney malfunction, which can cause an excess of sodium in the blood. When sodium levels rise the blood volume also rises and the excess fluid results in edema and swelling in the feet and legs. Dietary salts can aggravate fluid retention, and heart patients particularly are advised to follow low-sodium diets. Hormonal changes during the menstrual cycle may cause retention of sodium and fluid and produce a bloated feeling. Heart, liver or kidney failure may also cause fluid retention.

In pregnancy, swelling caused by fluid retention is common and can usually be relieved by resting with the legs up; if it is severe it can also be a sign of a more serious condition and a doctor should be advised.

Other causes include certain drugs used in the treatment of heart disease (notably calcium channel blockers), head injuries, stroke, and any surgery or disorder that interferes with normal drainage of lymphatic fluid and its return to the blood.

Diuretic drugs may be prescribed to increase urine output and decrease fluid volume throughout the body. They are prescribed with care since they cause dilation of blood vessels and loss of potassium.

SEE ALSO *Angioedema, Edema, Hypothyroidism, Myxedema, Papilledema, Preeclampsia, Pulmonary edema, Varicose veins*

FLUORIDATION

Fluoride is an inorganic ion found in seawater and in most fresh groundwater. It is added to water, foods or toothpaste to increase dietary intake to levels at which it is known to reduce tooth decay.

Numerous studies throughout the world have shown that fluoridation of water supplies significantly reduces tooth decay or dental cavities. Fluoride, added to water as sodium fluoride, or to toothpaste as stannous fluoride, increases the ability of tooth enamel to replace minerals lost when the teeth are attacked by the bacterial acids that produce decay.

Public health authorities in many countries have acted on this information. Fluoride is applied by dentists or added to foods such as salt, or to mouthwash. The most effective, and most economical, method of distribution is through water supplies. Fluoridated water is supplied to over half the population of the USA and Canada, and to two in every three people in Australia, reducing the need for dental treatment and particularly benefiting people who are less able to afford preventive treatment. Fluoridation of water supplies also reduces the needs for restorative work later in life. Concerns about fluoride added to the water supply are usually related to water purity and freedom of choice.

The role of fluoride

When teeth are being formed, fluoride in the diet of the mother-to-be will be incorporated into the developing baby's tooth enamel, improving its structure and making it less vulnerable to acid dissolution. From birth, and up to adolescence as teeth continue to develop, fluoride in saliva, from water, toothpaste, or when applied as part of dental treatment, has been shown to increase resistance to acids, help teeth to repair themselves by remineralization after attack by acids, and reduce the formation of acids by the bacteria which promote decay. In adults, these benefits continue to apply as the presence of fluoride in saliva reduces decay on exposed root surfaces of teeth. High concentrations of fluoride are used to inhibit the growth of decay-causing bacteria.

SEE ALSO *Minerals, Teeth*

FOLLICLE STIMULATING HORMONE

This is one of two hormones produced by the pituitary gland which are collectively called gonadotropins and which stimulate the sex glands (the gonads). In females, FSH stimulates the development of ovarian follicles up to the time of ovulation. The other gonadotropic hormone, luteinising hormone (LH), is involved in ovulation. In males, FSH is one of the hormones stimulating the production of sperm while LH induces testosterone production.

SEE ALSO *Hormones, Ovulation, Pituitary gland*

FOLLICULAR CYST

Following degeneration of an ovum (egg), the unruptured Graafian follicle enclosing the ovum begins to secrete fluid from its lining cells. This leads to the formation of a cyst in the ovary, which may grow to up to 2 inches (5 centimeters) in diameter. When this happens, the menstrual cycles sometimes become longer and excessive menstrual bleeding can ensue. Multiple cysts (Stein-Leventhal syndrome) may also be associated with obesity, hirsutism, infertility and lack of periods. If the cyst is larger than 2 inches (5 centimeters) in diameter, it needs to be surgically removed.

SEE ALSO *Menstruation, Ovaries, Ovum, Stein-Leventhal syndrome*

FOLLICULITIS

Folliculitis is a bacterial or fungal infection of the hair follicles. It can occur anywhere on the body and often arises when follicles are damaged by shaving or wearing tight clothing. The condition is marked by itching, reddened skin, a rash and pustules around the follicles that may dry out and crust over. It is treated with antiseptic creams and antibiotics.

SEE ALSO *Hair*

FONTANELLE

Known as the "soft spot" on a newborn baby's skull, the fontanelle is a gap between the bones due to the normal delay in the joining together of several flat bones making up the skull. (There are actually two—one at the top of the skull and a smaller one at the back—with the one at the top known as "the fontanelle".) Examined with the baby sitting quietly, the fontanelle shows a slight depression in the skull, but when the baby cries, or if infection or hemmorhage has occurred, the fontanelle will bulge.

Normal closure of the gap occurs by about one year. If the fontanelle appears closed at birth or shortly thereafter, it may indicate failure of underlying brain growth (craniosynostosis). Craniosynostosis can not only distort the shape of the skull and limit its growth, but can also lead to intellectual disability and deafness. Surgery to reopen the closed gaps is imperative.

Delayed closing of the fontanelle is occasionally associated with thyroid gland deficiency (cretinism).

SEE ALSO *Cretinism, Newborn, Skull*

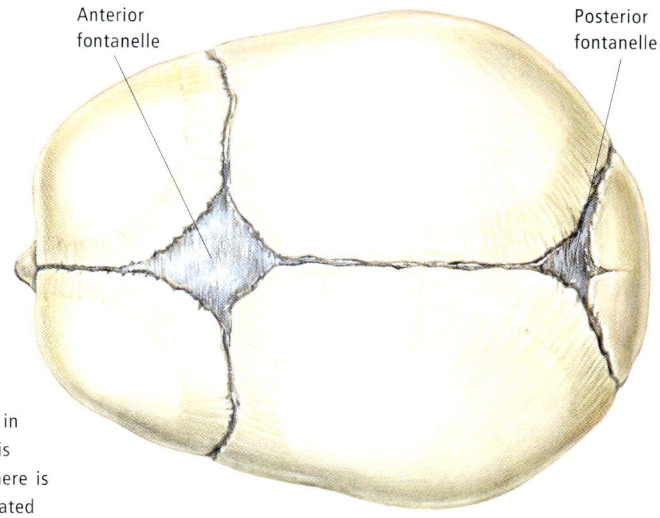

Fontanelle

The soft spot or depression in the top of the baby's skull is known as the fontanelle. There is also a second soft spot, located at the back of the skull.

FOOD ADDITIVES AND PRESERVATIVES

Food additives and preservatives have been known and used in human society for thousands of years. As humans formed fixed settlements and cultivated their food they gave up their nomadic existence and learned to live with the extremes of seasons in one location. This produced the necessity for preservatives to help in storing food for use during the winter months or in unproductive seasons.

Microorganisms such as *Lactobacillus bulgaricus* were used to produce yoghurt, and wild yeasts were used to make beer and bread. Common salt is one of the oldest food additives and has been used widely for thousands of years in cooking for flavor enhancement and as a preservative. It reduces the availability of water to bacteria and fungi. Drying, smoking and pickling in brine are also traditional techniques of preserving food. Smoking is an effective preserving technique because it reduces the water content (minimizing bacterial growth) and deposits chemicals toxic to bacteria on the food surface. Honey, spices and vinegar also have a long history of use as food additives and preservatives.

Today there are over 2,500 additives used in food manufacture. There are substances that preserve foods against deterioration during storage and distribution; add flavor or color to enhance appetite appeal; improve

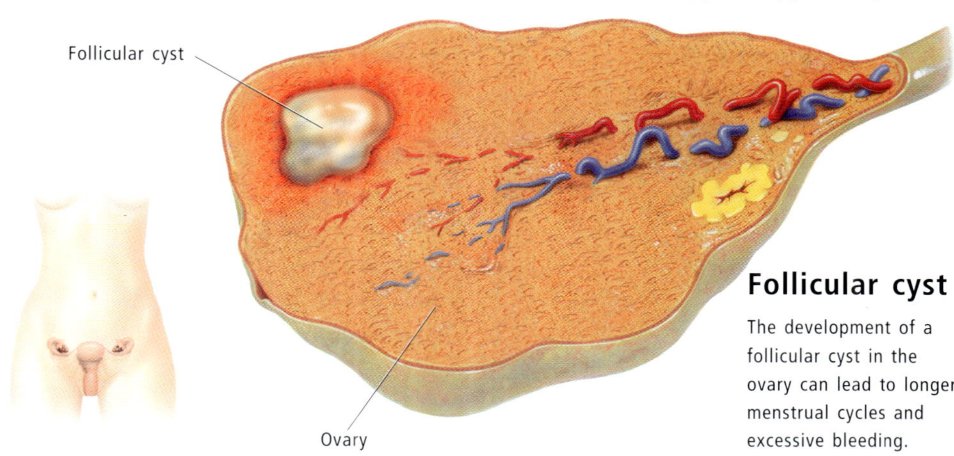

Follicular cyst

The development of a follicular cyst in the ovary can lead to longer menstrual cycles and excessive bleeding.

F

nutritional content; and assist in processing. Their use is subject, in the industrialized countries, to stringent tests before approval, and to close regulation when incorporated into foods. But there is no completely harmless substance—only safe quantities. Many individuals and consumer groups keep a watch on what they see as a threat to nutritional standards and to possible sources of nutritional deficiencies and allergy problems.

Processing additives may be: emulsifiers, which help to maintain a mixture that might otherwise separate, such as oil and water; stabilizers and thickeners, which make products more viscous, or foamy, or stop ice crystals forming; propellants, such as those used in pressurized foods; and chelating agents, which protect foods from enzyme action which would cause deterioration.

Preservatives can be antioxidants or antimicrobials. Antioxidants, such as ascorbic acid (vitamin C), citric acid and sulfite compounds, prevent food spoilage due to oxidation and enzyme action that causes browning on cut surfaces. Antimicrobials, such as common salt, nitrites, acetic acid, sulfites and preservatives produced by microorganisms, prevent or inhibit the growth of bacteria, molds and yeasts that spoil food.

Coloring directly influences perceptions of taste as well as quality and visual appeal. Processing foods often diminishes their natural colorings, so colorant additives, which may be natural (derived from plant sources) or synthetic, are then included to achieve the desired appearance. Bleaching agents remove unwanted coloring, as in the manufacture of white flour.

Sweeteners as additives are either nutritive or non-nutritive. Nutritive sweeteners, such as glucose, fructose, corn syrup and sucrose, provide energy in the form of carbohydrates or as sugar alcohols. Non-nutritive sweeteners are used in low-calorie foods suitable for dieters or for diabetics, or in sweet foods to reduce tooth decay. They include aspartame and saccharine.

SEE ALSO *Nutrition, Food poisoning*

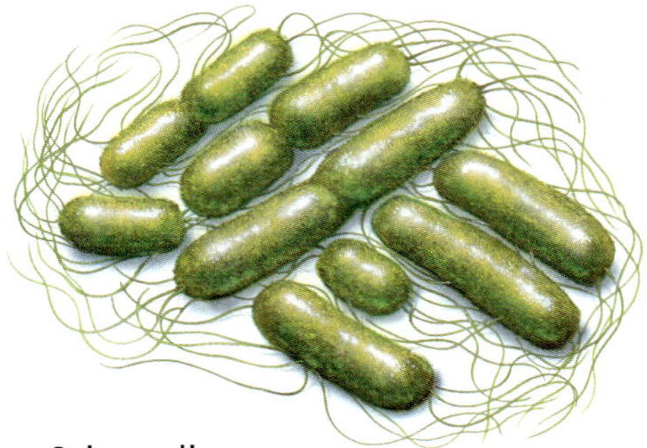
Salmonella

Shigella

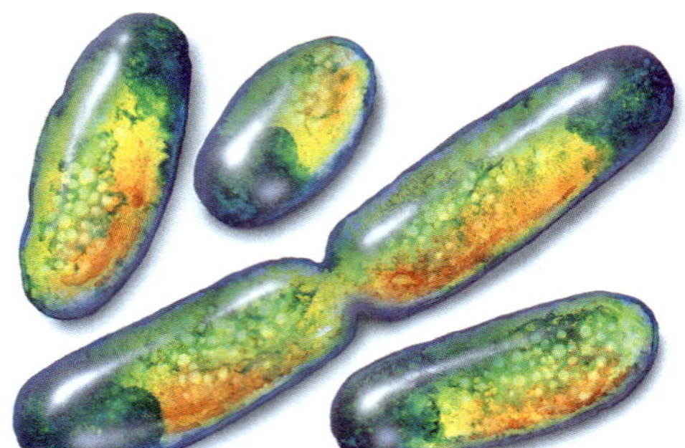
E. coli

Food poisoning

Bacteria such as these can cause food poisoning, producing vomiting, abdominal pain, headache and diarrhea.

FOOD POISONING

Food poisoning is an acute gastroenteritis caused by eating contaminated or poisonous food. Though not common in the Western world thanks to health regulations governing food vendors, it still occurs when food preparation is poor or when food is reheated or partly refrigerated. Food poisoning can be caused by bacteria (*Salmonella*, *Shigella* or *E. coli*, for example) which survive in poorly cooked or unrefrigerated meats. The bacteria are swallowed and produce toxins which affect the gut. *Staphylococcus* bacteria, for example, can be transmitted from someone who has a boil, abscess or other infection. These bacteria produce a toxin which may survive the cooking process.

One to eight hours after ingesting the contaminated food, the patient experiences nausea, followed by vomiting, abdominal cramping, and sometimes diarrhea, along with general symptoms such as fever and chills, weakness and headache. Other people who ate the same food may be similarly affected. Children, the elderly, and those with poor immune systems (for example, with HIV infection) are worst affected.

Fortunately, food poisoning is rarely fatal (with the exception of botulism) and recovery usually takes place after about 6–24 hours. Affected people should avoid dehydration by drinking electrolyte solutions to replace fluids lost by diarrhea. Those unable to take oral fluids due to nausea, and young children who can dehydrate very rapidly, may need intravenous fluids administered in hospital.

Food poisoning is best prevented in the first place by storing and preparing food carefully and cooking it thoroughly. It is advisable to wash all uncooked fruits and vegetables and refrigerate them. Picnic coolers containing cold or frozen food should be packed with ice packs on top. On a hot day, eat perishables or refrigerate them within an hour. It is best not to buy seafood that is not on ice.

Botulism is a dangerous form of food poisoning caused by a toxin that affects the nervous system. The toxin is produced by *Clostridium botulinum,* a bacterium found in contaminated or incompletely cooked canned foods (such as home-canned vegetables and fruits), undercooked sausage, smoked meats, and fish. Eighteen to 36 hours after eating the contaminated food, vomiting and diarrhea occur, which is then followed by signs of nervous system damage such as blurred or double vision, drooping eyelids, dry mouth, slurred speech, weakness of the arms and legs, and paralysis. The condition is a medical emergency requiring treatment in hospital with intravenous fluids and injections of the botulism antitoxin. Botulism has a 10–25 percent mortality rate.

SEE ALSO *Diarrhea, Gastroenteritis*

FOOT

The foot is designed to support the body weight and to act as a lever to propel the body forwards during walking. Rather than being just one rigid bone, its skeleton is segmented, allowing it to adapt to the shape of any surface and to enhance its propulsive effect during running.

Bones and tissues of the foot

The back half of the foot (the tarsus) is formed by seven irregularly shaped tarsal bones. One of these, the talus, fits into a socket formed by the bones of the leg to form the hinge-like ankle joint. The talus sits on top of the largest tarsal bone, the calcaneus, which forms the heel and has the

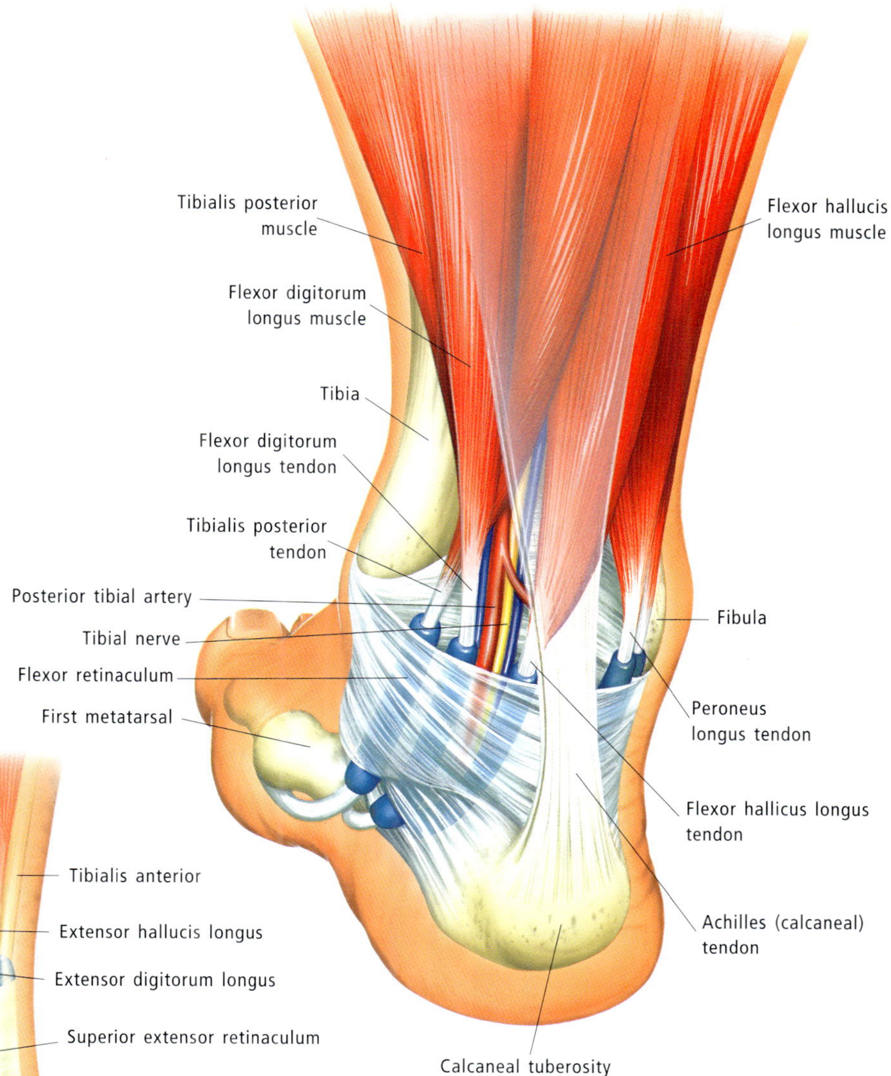

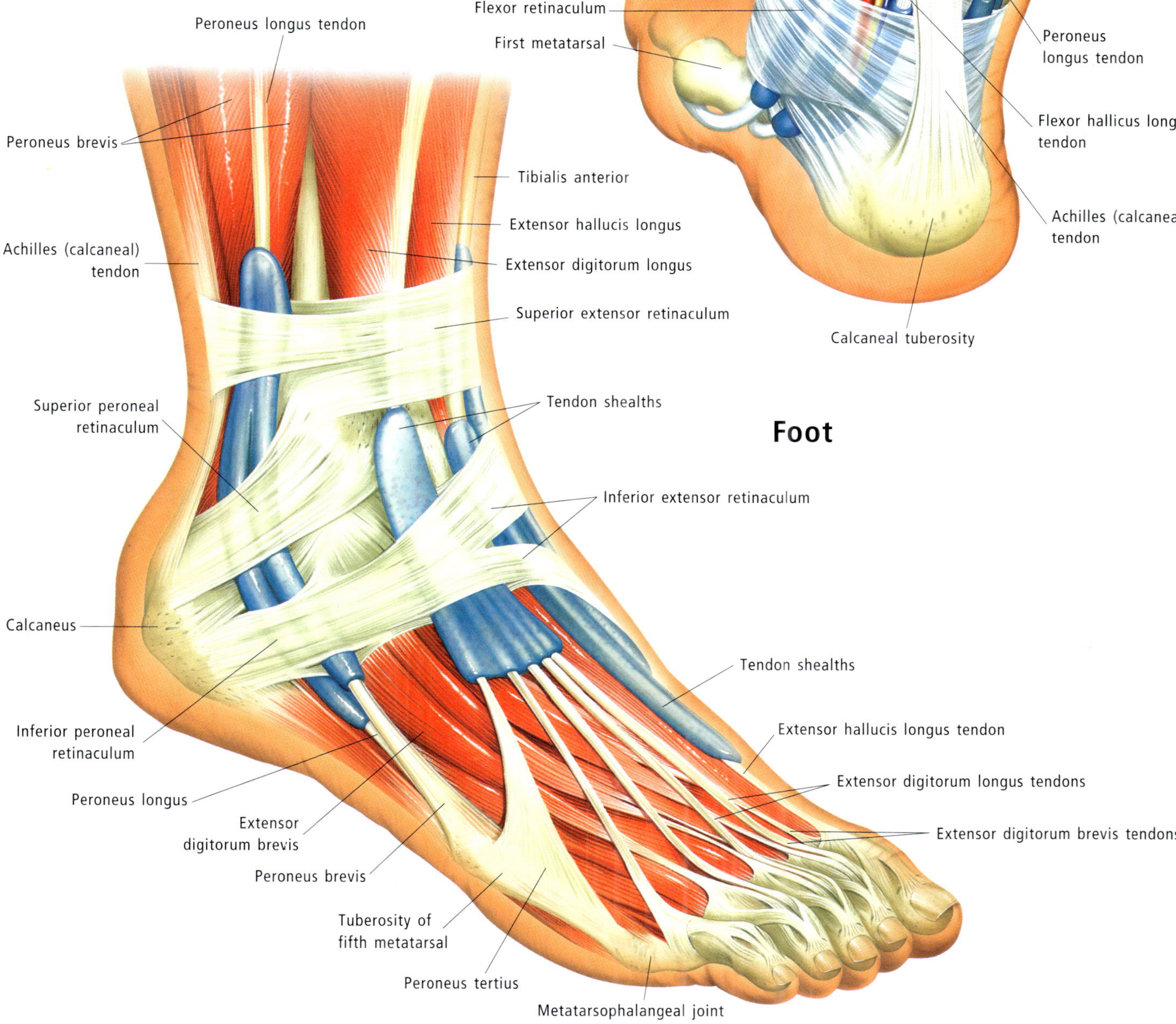

Foot

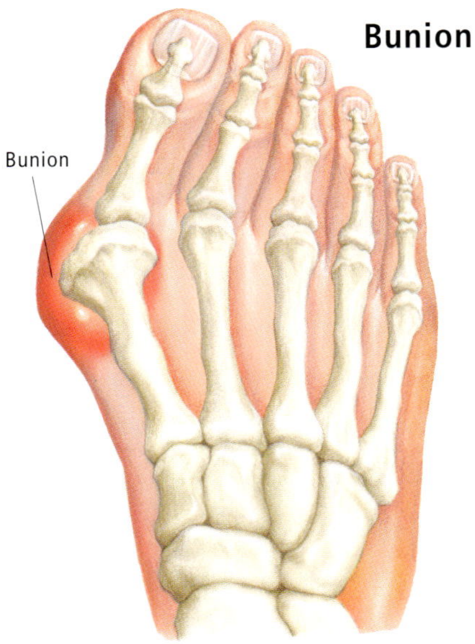

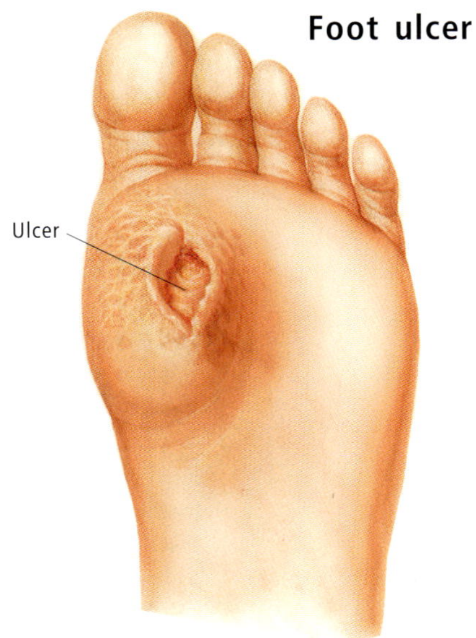

Achilles tendon attached to it. The other tarsal bones are the navicular, the cuboid and the three cuneiform bones. The bones of the tarsus are separated from each other by joints, which allow gliding movements to occur between them.

The skeleton of the front of the foot is formed by the metatarsals and phalanges. The metatarsals are long bones which form joints behind with the tarsus, and in front with the phalanges, or toe bones. The big toe has only two phalanges, the other toes have three phalanges each.

The upper surface of the foot is formed by thin skin, which overlies tendons extending from the front of the leg to the tarsus and toes. In contrast, the sole of the foot is covered by thick skin which is separated from the underlying tissues by fat pads. Fibrous tissue extends longitudinally along the sole, deep into the fat pads, from the calcaneus to the toes. It is important in binding the overlying skin and fat firmly to the deeper bones and ligaments of the foot, so it does not slip around during walking. The plantar fascia, which also acts like a bowstring to maintain the longitudinal arches of the foot, becomes stretched when the foot is flattened after the heel hits the ground. Repeated excessive stretching of this structure, which may occur in dancers, athletes or obese people, causes it to become inflamed, resulting in heel pain, especially in the mornings or at the commencement of exercise.

The sole of the foot contains long tendons and a number of small muscles which are arranged in four layers. Unlike on the hand, the big toe is prevented from coming into contact with the other toes. However, the toes do have the potential to be used for grasping; this can be seen in people born without arms, who can learn to write, draw and manipulate objects with their feet.

Problems

Arthritis or tight-fitting shoes can deform the metatarsophalangeal joint of the big toe, causing the toe to be forced against the other toes and the head of the metatarsal to protrude onto the medial side of the foot, forming a lump known as a bunion. Ill-fitting footwear can also cause bunions on the outside of the foot, as well as deformities of the toe joints, or thickening of the skin (corns). Deformities of the toe joints, usually caused by shoes which are too short, include hammer toe and mallet toe.

Clubfoot is a relatively common condition in which the foot is turned so that the sole faces inward, the toes point downwards (inverted and plantarflexed) and the foot cannot be straightened. It usually occurs in newborn babies as a result of genetic factors or, more commonly, from the developing foot being forced into an abnormal position in the uterus. If treated early, clubfoot is curable by gradually straightening the foot over time using a series of plaster casts.

Movement

Movements of the foot can be defined as dorsiflexion (feet point upwards), plantarflexion (feet point down), inversion or supination (sole faces inwards) and eversion or pronation (sole faces outwards). The ankle joint, between the talus and the bones of the leg, is the most commonly injured joint in the body, with injury usually resulting from a fall which forces the ankle into a position of excessive inversion. This causes damage to the ligaments which reinforce the outside of the ankle (ankle sprain) and swelling around the joint. More severe sprains may also involve fractures of the fibula or base of the fifth metatarsal.

SEE ALSO *Achilles tendon, Ankle, Bunion, Flat feet, Heel spur, Joints*

FRACTURES

A fracture is a break in a bone, usually caused by excessive stress being applied to the bone.

There are several types of fractures. In a complete fracture, the two parts of the bone are completely separated. In an incomplete fracture, the two parts are partially separated. An incomplete fracture in a long bone in a child is often called a greenstick fracture. If there are more than two bone fragments at the fracture site, it is called a comminuted fracture. If the fractured bone has broken the skin and is exposed to the air, it is a compound or open fracture; if it hasn't broken the skin, it is a simple, or closed fracture. In an impacted, or compression fracture, the break occurs from extreme pressure on the bone. A stress fracture is a crack in a bone caused by repetitive and prolonged pressure on the bone, usually from exercise. A pathologic fracture is one that occurs in bone that is weakened or destroyed by disease such as osteoporosis or a tumor; the injury itself may be minor. A compression fracture is an example of this.

The symptoms and signs of a fracture are pain, swelling and deformity at the fracture site, weakness of movement, and inability to bear weight on the affected parts. The arteries around the fracture may be damaged, causing bleeding or bruising at the site. In a limb especially, there may be loss of pulse, with cold white extremities. Nerves around the fracture sometimes become damaged; there may be numbness, tingling or paralysis in the extremity below the fracture.

A fracture can usually be seen clearly in an x-ray. The treatment of a fracture is to reduce (realign) the bone back into its normal position, then immobilize the bone fragments to prevent movement and so they can join back together. Immobilization can be achieved by means of a plaster cast, traction (usually in hospital), or surgical insertion of rods, plates or screws. After the bones have healed (which may take from six weeks to six months), physical therapy and rehabilitation are required.

First aid is vital in the treatment of fracture. Follow the procedure for bleeding, and cover any open wounds. Do not move the person—especially if the injury is to the hip, pelvis, or upper leg—unless necessary. Do not try to straighten a bone or change its position, or give the person anything by mouth. Arrange emergency transport to the hospital immediately.

SEE ALSO *Bones*

FRAGILE X SYNDROME

The fragile X syndrome is the most common cause of inherited intellectual disability and is due to a defect involving a gene called the FMR1 gene. The syndrome most often involves males, although females may also be affected. The abnormality occurs in the X chromosome, of which females have two and males only one. Boys with the defective chromosome will be intellectually disabled; women with only one damaged X chromosome will be carriers of the disease, with the chance of having intellectually disabled boys. If parents are at risk of having boys with this disease, the fragile X mutation can be detected by prenatal sampling of fetal tissue, and abortion may be offered.

SEE ALSO *Chromosomes, Congenital abnormalities, Genes, Genetic counseling, Intellectual disability*

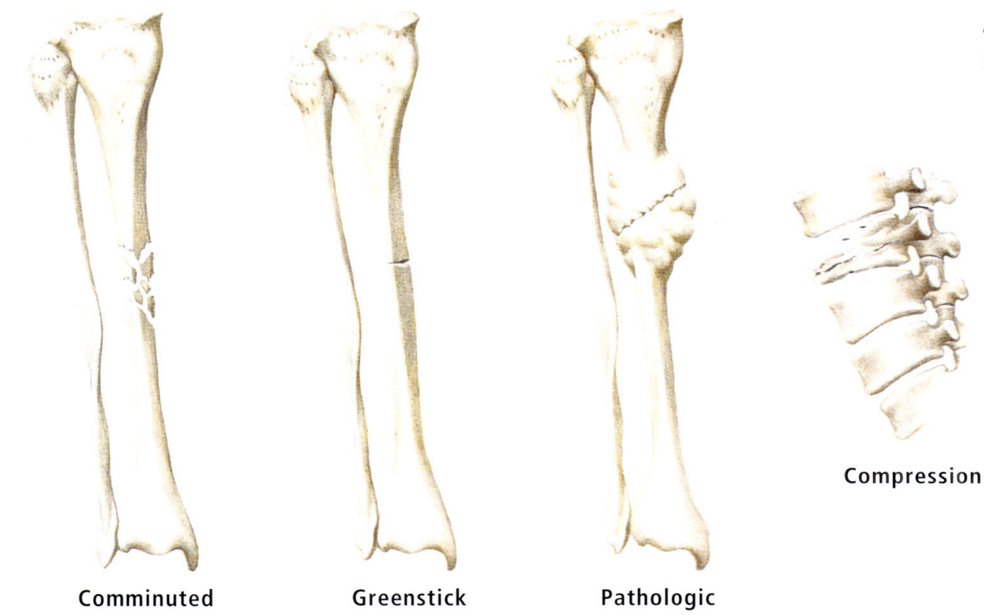

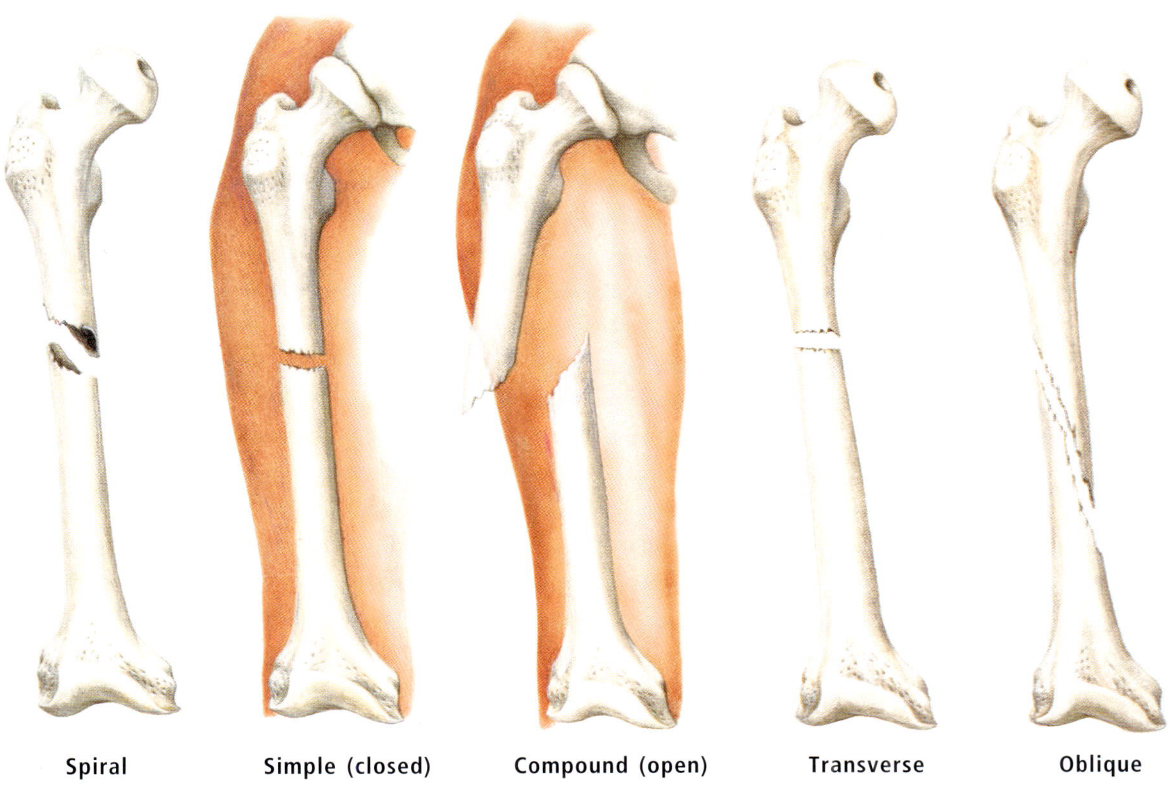

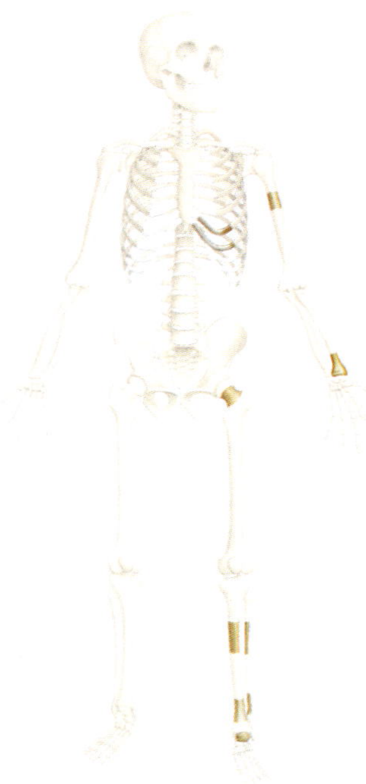

Common fracture sites

Common fracture sites include the arm, wrist, hip, leg and ankle.

Bone fractures

Fractures are named according to their appearance and characteristics.

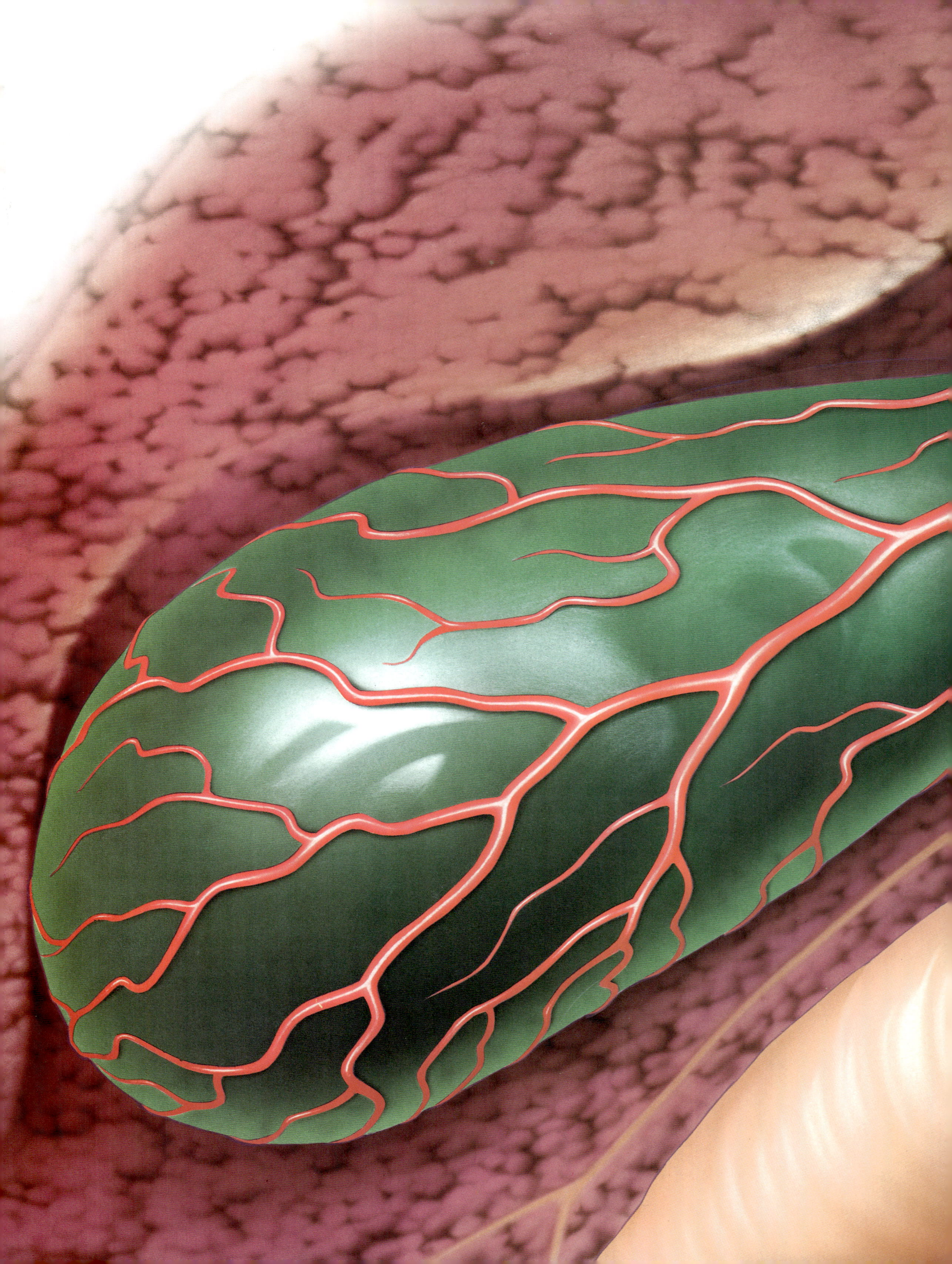

G

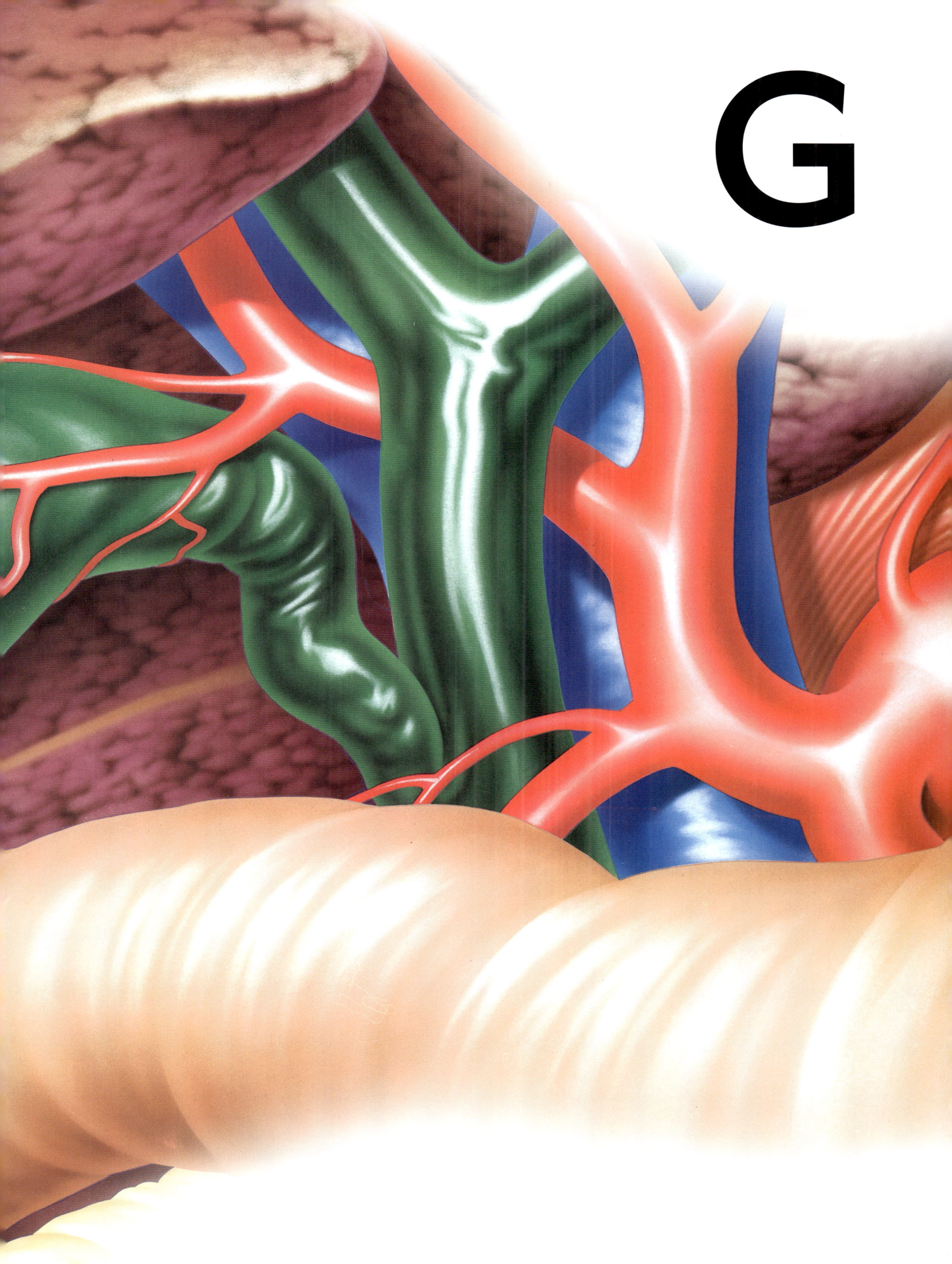

G

GALACTOSEMIA

Galactosemia is an uncommon inherited disorder, caused by a deficiency of an enzyme in the intestine that breaks down galactose, a sugar normally found in milk. It is seen mainly in newborn infants in whom the condition is not yet diagnosed.

The infant feeds poorly, vomits, and fails to thrive or gain weight. If milk feeding continues, the infant may develop jaundice, cirrhosis, cataracts and brain damage.

The condition is confirmed by special blood and urine tests that show the lack of the enzyme. Treatment consists of eliminating all milk and milk-containing products from the diet for life, using milk substitutes such as soy formula instead. If the diet is modified, life expectancy is normal. A potential parent with a family history of galactosemia may need to seek genetic counseling before having children.

SEE ALSO *Genetic counseling*

GALLBLADDER

The gallbladder is a sac-shaped organ that stores and concentrates bile prior to its release into the small intestine. It is part of the biliary tree, a series of ducts that conveys and stores bile. The gallbladder is usually firmly attached to the lower surface of the liver and lies on the right side of the abdomen just below the ribs at the front.

Bile is a body fluid which contains pigments, lecithin and bile salts. The pigments are made from cholesterol and bilirubin, and give the bile fluids a yellow to orange color during life. Bile is very important because, when it is released into the small intestine, it serves to break down relatively large globules of fat into smaller droplets, thus increasing the available surface area of the fat particles so as to improve their digestion and absorption.

Bile is produced by liver cells, then passes along the bile ducts, and is stored and concentrated in the gallbladder before being released into the initial part of the small intestine, known as the duodenum. Once digestion and absorption of fats has taken place, the bile is reabsorbed in the end of the small intestine, carried back to the liver by a group of veins known as the portal system, and there re-excreted into the bile ducts to begin the process again. This is known as the enterohepatic biliary circulation.

The gallbladder is joined to the bile duct by the cystic duct. The bile duct passes from the junction with the cystic duct down through the head of the pancreas to drain bile into the duodenum. Just before it enters the duodenum, the bile duct is joined by the main duct of the pancreas. The passage of the bile duct through the pancreas means that a tumor (cancer or, more correctly, carcinoma) in this pancreatic head can obstruct the lower bile duct and cause a build-up of bile in the biliary tree. This back-up eventually reaches as far up the biliary tree as the gallbladder and liver, causing an enlarged gallbladder and leading to jaundice, when the bile salts reach the blood.

Another more common disease of the biliary tree is cholelithiasis, or gallstones. This condition commonly affects women in their reproductive years who are fair-skinned and overweight, but it may affect men and women of all ages. Gallstones are formed when bile chemicals come out of solution to form crystals in the gallbladder. These stones may irritate the inner lining of the gallbladder, causing a condition known as cholecystitis.

The gallbladder does not usually enlarge in cholecystitis, because the inflammation causes the formation of fibrous tissue in the gallbladder wall. Sometimes gallstones may enter the cystic and bile ducts and be passed down to the duodenum. The pain that results when the smooth muscle of the bile duct attempts to squeeze the stones along the duct is known as biliary colic. Characteristically, the pain is severe, located on the upper right side or in the upper middle parts of the abdomen, and occurs minutes after eating a meal, particularly one with a high fat content. The pain may subside over 12–18 hours, only to recur after a subsequent meal. Other common symptoms include fever, nausea, vomiting, chills and shaking. Sometimes a stone does not give rise to pain but silently obstructs the bile ducts, causing jaundice.

Certain x-ray examinations help to diagnose disorders of the biliary tree. During these examinations, the patient swallows a chemical similar in structure to normal bile constituents, and one that is also opaque to x-rays. The chemical is absorbed from the small intestine and transported to the liver by the portal system. It is subsequently excreted into the biliary tree and concentrated in the gallbladder. X-rays taken at this stage will reveal the ducts of the biliary tree (cholangiography) and gallbladder (cholecystography) standing out against the darker upper abdominal contents.

Further investigations include ultrasound and retrograde cholangiography, which involves back-filling the biliary tree from the duodenum with a chemical opaque to x-rays. This test requires the insertion of an endoscope, a device for viewing the interior of the gut. The endoscope is inserted through the stomach and into the duodenum, in order to place a catheter into the lower bile duct.

Removal of the gallbladder is known as cholecystectomy—this may be done by open surgery or by laparoscopy, a technique whereby instruments are inserted into the abdomen through small punctures in its wall. Laparoscopic surgery results in a shorter hopsital stay and faster recovery, as the abdominal scar is much smaller than with surgery via the open method. Gallbladder disease can be prevented or minimized by losing weight and reducing one's intake of fatty foods.

SEE ALSO *Bile duct, Cholangiography, Gallstones, Intestines, Jaundice, Liver, Pancreas*

GALLSTONES

These are very common—as many as 7 percent of adults in the USA have gallstones (cholelithiasis) in their gallbladders. Each year in the USA approximately 350,000 people have operations for gallstones, and as many as 6,000 people die from associated complications. Gallstones are more common in women in the 40–65 years age group than any other group in the community, suggesting a hormonal link. In fact, taking the contraceptive pill contributes to formation of gallstones in susceptible women.

About 75 percent of gallstones are made of cholesterol, while the remainder are composed of bile pigments. Problems arise when cholesterol or bile pigments come out of solution in the bile fluids concentrated in the gallbladder. This means that gallstones are usually encountered in the gallbladder

Gallstones

Gallstones have different shapes and sizes. They can be multifaceted or round, and vary in color from yellow to brown to black. Small black gallstones are made of calcium bilirubinate. Yellow-brownish gallstones are made from cholesterol and can range from about $\frac{1}{2}$–$1\frac{1}{2}$ inches (1–4 centimeters) in size. A single gallstone can grow large enough to fill the gallbladder. These illustrations are all actual size.

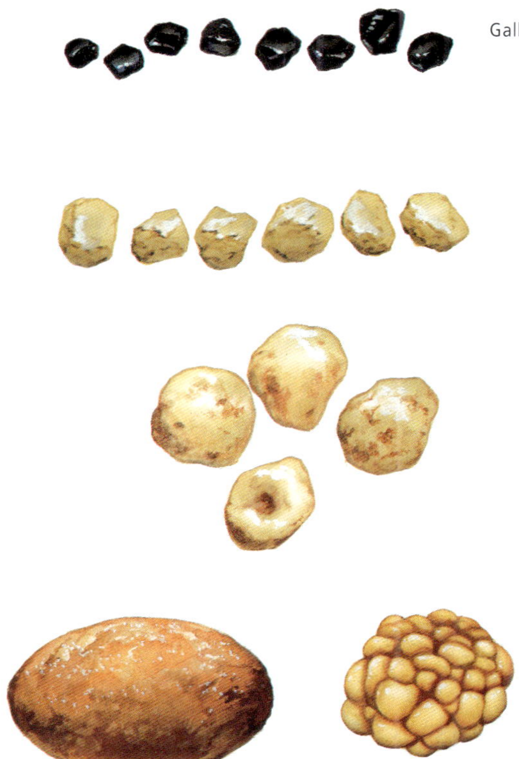

itself, where they may cause chronic inflammation of the gallbladder lining (chronic cholecystitis). Occasionally the gallstones may leave the gallbladder and become lodged in the bile duct, where they can cause obstruction to bile flow. Jaundice results as bile builds up in the liver and eventually the bloodstream.

Actually, 70 percent of people with gallstones never require surgery, but several problems can arise. Chronic cholecystitis is the most common form of gallbladder disease. Patients experience episodes of abdominal pain (biliary colic) whenever the gallstones cause transient obstruction of the cystic duct, which leads out of the gallbladder. This pain is usually felt in the upper right part of the abdomen and is sometimes accompanied by nausea and vomiting.

Patients may not be able to tolerate fatty foods, and may complain of indigestion, heartburn and flatulence.

If the impaction of the gallstone in the cystic duct leads to inflammation, the abdominal pain may become more severe and persistent. The pain may be accompanied by fever and increased numbers of white blood cells in the blood. This is known as acute cholecystitis. Resulting complications include gangrene of the gallbladder, formation of pus in the gallbladder (empyema, or suppurative cholecystitis), perforation of the gallbladder with spilling of infected contents into the abdominal cavity, or the formation of abscesses around the gallbladder.

Gallstones may pass through the cystic duct into the bile duct. In this situation, known as choledocholithiasis, patients experience biliary colic pain accompanied by moderate to severe jaundice, chills and fever. The pancreas may become inflamed (pancreatitis).

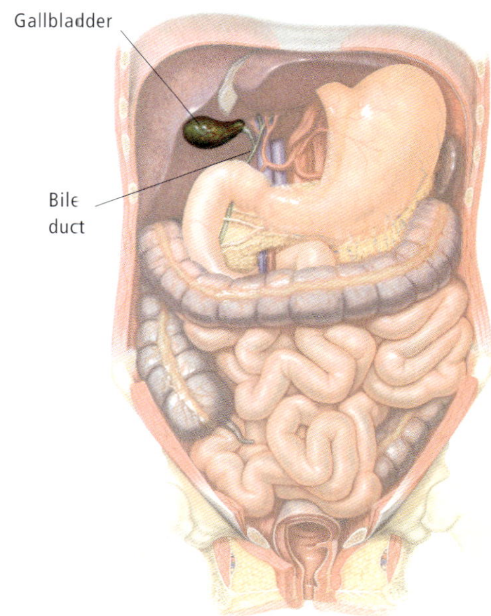

Gallbladder

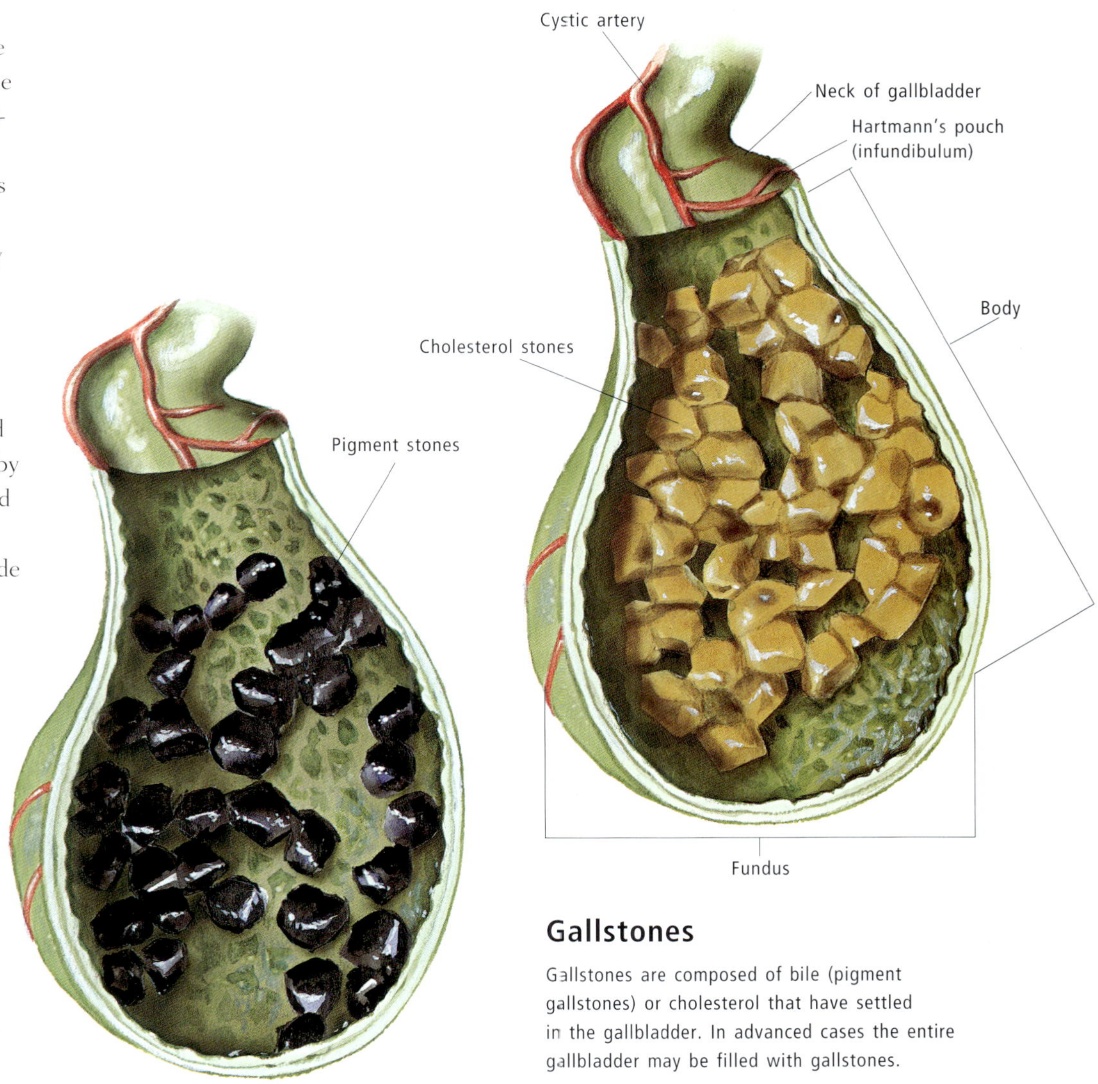

Gallstones

Gallstones are composed of bile (pigment gallstones) or cholesterol that have settled in the gallbladder. In advanced cases the entire gallbladder may be filled with gallstones.

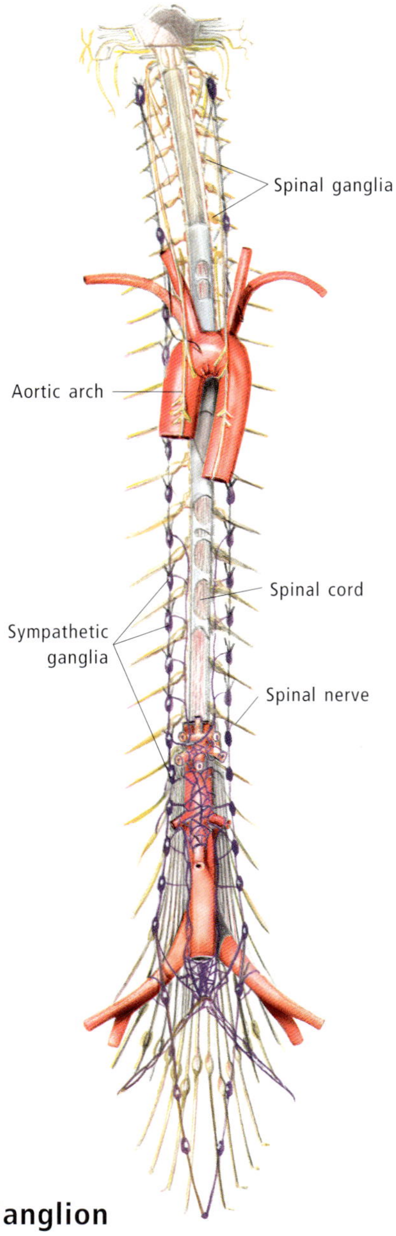

Ganglion

A ganglion (plural ganglia) is a cluster of nerve cell bodies found in the peripheral nervous system. Spinal ganglia contain the cell bodies of sensory nerve fibers in the peripheral nerves. Sympathetic ganglia are part of the autonomic nervous system.

Gallstone disease is detected in a number of ways. During an oral cholecystogram, the patient is given a chemical that is opaque to x-rays and is excreted by the liver into the gallbladder and bile duct. Ultrasound is a technique whereby sound waves are used to form an image of the gallbladder and the stones within. Retrograde cholangiography is an investigation in which an endoscope is used to insert a catheter into the lower bile duct and back-fill the biliary tree from the duodenum.

The symptoms of gallstones can be prevented or minimized by losing weight and reducing one's intake of fatty foods. However if symptoms persist then the gallstones (along with the gallbladder) should be surgically removed, either by open abdominal operation or through a laparoscope. Laparoscopic surgery is the preferred method for most people as it results in a shorter hospital stay and faster recovery.

If there is bacterial infection of the gallbladder (for example cholecystitis) urgent treatment in hospital with intravenous antibiotics is necessary; after the inflammation has subsided, the gallbladder can be removed at a convenient time in the subsequent weeks or months.

SEE ALSO *Cholecystitis, Gallbladder, Liver, Pancreas, Pancreatitis*

GANGLION

The word "ganglion" refers to two different things. Firstly, a ganglion is a group of nerve cell bodies outside the central nervous system. For example, a spinal ganglion is a cluster of sensory nerve cell bodies found along the spinal cord at the root of a spinal nerve. Secondly, a ganglion is a cyst in or around a tendon or joint, especially in the hands, wrists and feet. Ganglion cysts can be treated with ice packs applied directly to the affected area, together with oral medication for pain. A ganglion cyst may be removed by a ganglionectomy or cyst aspiration.

SEE ALSO *Nerves, Nervous system, Spinal cord*

GANGRENE

This term refers to death of tissue, with secondary growth of bacteria that derive their nutrition by breaking down the dead tissue. In practice, gangrene is often used to refer to death of a large area of tissue (frequently as a result of loss of blood supply or in wounds infected by anaerobic bacteria), whether or not it has undergone significant bacterial decomposition.

Gangrene occurs most often in the extremities, for example in the foot or toe resulting from blockage of an artery, though it can also involve internal organs, such as with hernias. Fever, pain, darkening of the skin and unpleasant odor are common symptoms. Correcting the initial causes, medication and surgery may be required.

SEE ALSO *Bacteria, Circulatory system*

GAS GANGRENE

In this form of gangrene, dead tissue is invaded by bacteria called *Clostridium welchii* which break it down and in the process release bubbles of gas into the tissue. Bacteria are frequently found in soil and include a variety of organisms that are able to secrete very powerful toxins. For example, the bacteria causing tetanus and the serious food poisoning known as botulism are members of this group. Despite its name, it is the toxins and the tissue-destroying enzymes released by the bacteria, not the gas bubbles, that make gas gangrene so dangerous. Progressive breakdown of tissue, damage to blood cells and other effects of the toxins can eventually kill the patient.

Clostridia prefer a low-oxygen environment and therefore grow well in deep wounds with considerable tissue damage, especially if contaminated by soil and dirt. This is why gas gangrene is such a feared complication of wounds during war. It may also develop after injury in an accident or after surgery. Attention to wound care is essential to prevent the onset of gas gangrene.

SEE ALSO *Bacteria, Food poisoning, Gangrene*

GASTRECTOMY

Gastrectomy is the surgical removal of part or (very rarely) all of the stomach. It is used for treatment of gastric cancer, and gastric ulcers that do not respond to medical treatment. Partial gastrectomy involves removal of the lower parts of the stomach, while keeping other parts (the fundus and cardiac parts) intact.

SEE ALSO *Gastric ulcer, Stomach*

GASTRIC ULCER

Gastric ulcers involve the loss of the inner lining (mucous layer) of the stomach to produce a lesion (wound). Most patients with gastric ulcers are aged 40 to 60 years, about 10 years older than patients who develop duodenal ulcers. Most gastric ulcers develop on the inner surface of the right edge of the stomach, usually within a few inches (5–6 centimeters) of the last part of the stomach (pylorus). Some gastric ulcers are associated with duodenal ulcers, but most appear separately. Some gastric ulcers develop in conjunction with gastric cancers and it is of the utmost importance that these are identified early to improve the patient's chance of survival.

Causes vary, but environmental and genetic factors play important roles. Gastric ulcers can be related to a number of drugs (aspirin, non-steroidal anti-inflammatory drugs and steroids) and dietary and personal factors. It is now recognized that infection of the stomach with acid-resistant bacteria (*Helicobacter pylori*) is an important contributing factor in the development of gastric ulcers. Also, people with a family history of gastric ulcers are at greater risk.

Patients with gastric ulcers usually complain of experiencing pain in the upper abdomen within 30 minutes of eating a meal. With duodenal ulcers, the pain usually comes on more than one hour after meals.

The severity and duration of attacks of pain from the gastric ulcer are usually more severe than that from duodenal ulcers, but in both cases food and antacids often temporarily relieve the pain. Some patients with gastric ulcers experience vomiting, loss of interest in (or aversion to) eating, and pain aggravated by meals. Treatment is by antibiotics, antacids or surgery.

SEE ALSO *Duodenal ulcer, Stomach*

Gastric ulcer

When the mucous lining of the stomach wall is damaged, the acid in the stomach erodes the wall and an ulcer forms.

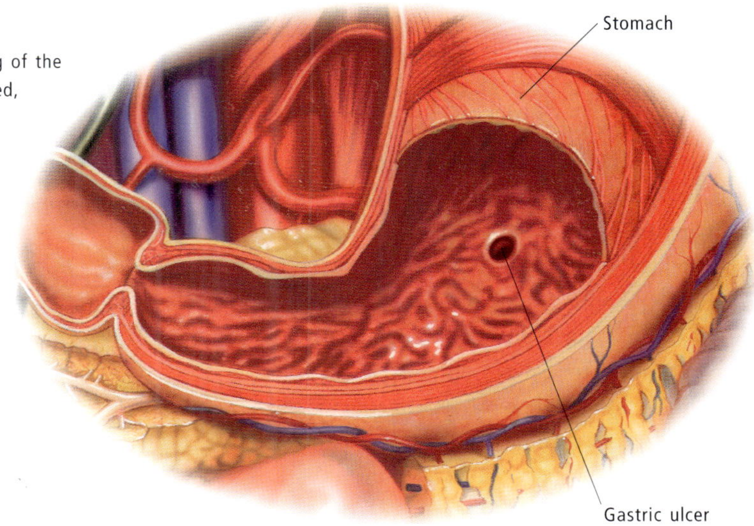

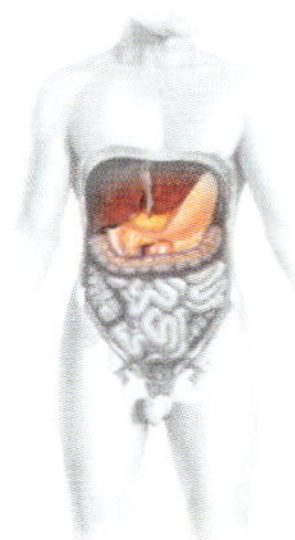

Gastritis

Inflammation of the stomach (gastritis) is a common disorder. It often manifests as a sudden pain resulting from the irritation of the stomach wall.

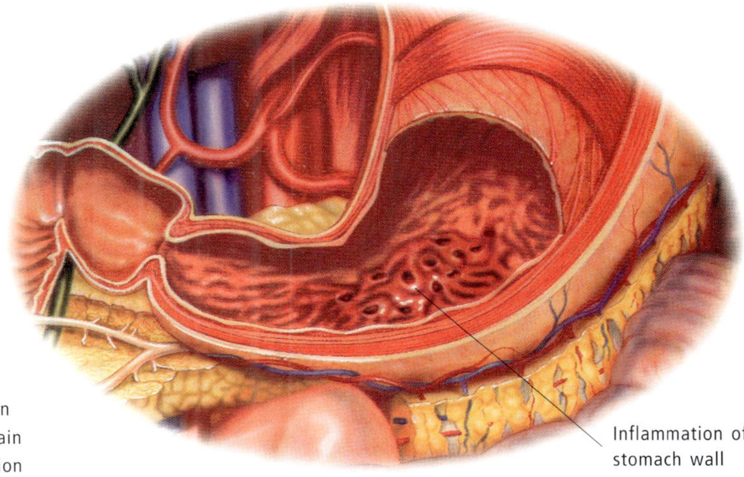

GASTRITIS

Gastritis is an inflammation of the stomach lining. It tends to become more prevalent with age and can appear as a short-lived acute (sudden onset) condition or may be ongoing and chronic (long term).

Depending on the cause and type of gastritis, symptoms can range from mild stomach aches and cramps, burping, diarrhea, a swollen abdomen, chest pain, loss of appetite and an unpleasant (often acidic) taste in the mouth due to vomiting. Although gastritis is a common and usually minor ailment, signs that may indicate the need for medical attention include black tarry feces (melena) due to bleeding in the stomach, vomit containing blood, a fever and severe pain.

Potential causes of acute gastritis include alcohol, caffeine, nicotine, overeating, medications that irritate the stomach lining (such as aspirin and non-steroidal anti-inflammatory drugs), physiological stress brought on by another illness or major surgery, food allergies and bacterial or viral infections.

Treatment depends on the cause, but the symptoms of acute gastritis usually disappear within a few days with rest and avoidance of drugs or food that irritate the stomach. Over-the-counter antacid medications usually provide short-term relief of symptoms. The use of aspirin or related drugs should be avoided but, if painkillers are required, alternatives such as acetaminophen (paracetamol) may help.

The only definitive way to identify the cause (and sometimes, to confirm the presence) of chronic gastritis is through medical tests such as endoscopy and biopsy. An endoscopy involves passing a long, thin, flexible tube down the esophagus into the stomach to view and often photograph the appearance of the stomach wall. A biopsy, taking a small piece of the stomach wall for analysis, is often performed with an endoscopy. The two procedures normally require the patient to be mildly sedated.

These days, one of the most common causes of chronic gastritis is widely acknowledged to be a bacterium called *Helicobacter pylori,* first described in the medical literature in the 1980s by two Western Australian medical researchers. Not all people infected with these bacteria develop symptoms. Many people become infected in childhood and live normal lives without ever developing any complications. However, *H. pylori* infections (which are readily treated with antibiotics) are now understood to be a major cause of stomach ulcers and cancers.

Chronic gastritis can also be due to an autoimmune disorder in which the cells in the stomach lining are attacked by the body's own immune system. This causes a loss of stomach cells and a reduction in a person's ability to absorb vitamin B_{12}, which leads to a condition known as pernicious anemia. The gastritis itself may not cause any symptoms but may be identified when causes of the anemia are investigated.

Another type of chronic gastritis is hypertrophic gastritis, in which the folds of the stomach wall become enlarged and inflamed. Ménétrier's disease, a rare form of this condition, is most often seen in elderly patients; protein loss is a common complication. Drug treatments are available but, if they fail, surgery may be required.

SEE ALSO ***Anemia, Autoimmune disease, Biopsy, Digestive system, Endoscopy, Stomach***

Gastroesophageal reflux

The backflow of acid fluid from the stomach (gastroesophageal reflux) may damage the lining of the lower esophagus.

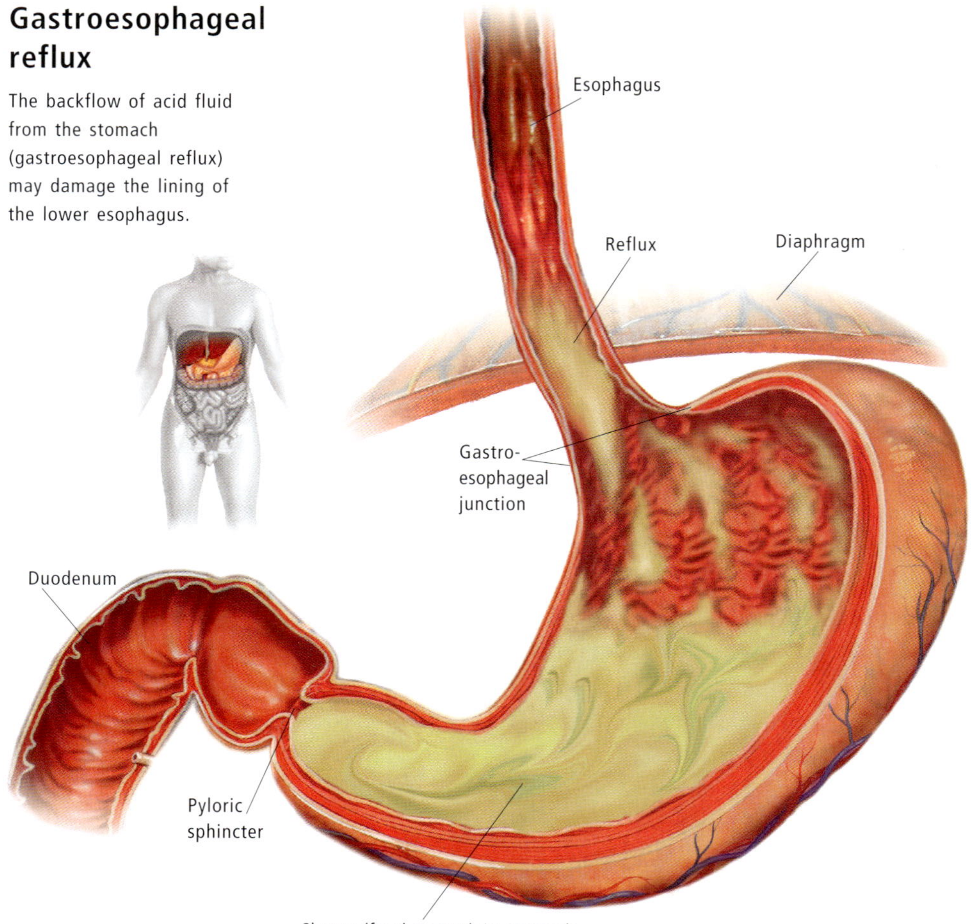

GASTROENTERITIS

Gastroenteritis is characterized by infection—usually of the entire gastrointestinal tract—and diarrhea is the hallmark, generally with associated nausea and often vomiting.

Death from gastroenteritis is greatest among young children and the old or debilitated, particularly in developing countries. Rotavirus and certain forms of *Escherichia coli* (*E. coli*) are the main causes, closely followed by cholera and amebic dysentery. The major problem lies in dirty food handling or inadequate sewerage management, particularly when polluted river water or well water is not boiled before use. Like the toxin of *E. coli*, rotavirus can produce watery diarrhea, rapidly leading to dehydration and death. Fluid replacement, either orally or intravenously, may be required, particularly if vomiting is a feature. If dehydration is present, as characterized by sunken eyes, diminished skin tone and sunken fontanelle (in babies), similar urgent fluid and electrolyte replacement is required.

Frequent causes of diarrhea among travelers are giardiasis and amebic dysentery. Giardiasis is caused usually by swallowing water contaminated by animal feces, and produces nausea and foul-smelling, pale, frothy and bulky stools, that usually float. Diarrhea may persist for many weeks but is neither watery nor likely to cause dehydration. Due to a flagellate protozoa (*Giardia lamblia*) in the small intestine, giardiasis is diagnosed by either small bowel biopsy via endoscopy or else from the presence of the flagellate in the stools. Because of the difficulty of diagnosing giardiasis, the physician will often presume its presence, based on symptoms, and prescribe medication accordingly.

Amebic dysentery is caused by a protozoan (*Entamoeba hystolytica*), usually passed on from an infected carrier. The condition develops slowly, leading to frequent sloppy bowel movements with a foul odor. Blood is occasionally seen in the stool. The illness can be debilitating but is rarely overwhelming. Liver abscess can be a complication and must always be considered. Treatment is with metronidazole, while liver abscesses also respond to chloroquine (a drug used for malaria).

Shigella infections, that can cause dysentery, range from mild to severe and are characterized by high fever, severe colic and bloody diarrhea. Nausea is the usual accompaniment. The condition is normally short lived, generally lasting no more than three or four days following a short incubation period. Rarely fatal, the condition usually responds rapidly to medication. If the infection is severe, intravenous fluids may be necessary.

Cholera remains a major problem, with epidemics occurring in developing countries and sporadically elsewhere, particularly where there has been strife and war. Poor hygiene and inadequate sewerage are the major factors. Sufferers dehydrate extremely rapidly and can die within hours unless intravenous replacement fluids are given immediately.

Helicobacter infection can cause acute gastroenteritis and is commonly reputed to occur after eating undercooked chicken. Nausea and colic are usual symptoms, together with foul-smelling bowel movements. The infection is mostly self-righting after two or three days, but occasionally an antibiotic is required for cure.

Many viruses have associated diarrhea. However, the gastroenteritis with these infections tends to be a minor part of the illness overall and usually subsides spontaneously within a day or so.

SEE ALSO *Cholera, Dehydration, Dysentery, Food poisoning, Giardiasis*

GASTROESOPHAGEAL REFLUX

Gastroesophageal reflux is the movement of stomach fluid up into the lower esophagus. It occurs quite normally during the waking hours, especially after meals. In some people, however, reflux of stomach acids is excessive and causes symptoms. Usually in these people the band of muscle fibers that closes off the esophagus from the stomach (called the lower esophageal sphincter) is incompetent.

This happens most commonly in pregnancy, obesity, or with a hiatus hernia (when part of the somach has moved up into the chest).

The symptoms are heartburn (pain felt under the breastbone, or sternum) which is made worse by bending, stooping, or eating, and is relieved by milk or antacids. There may be other symptoms such as belching, nausea, vomiting, and difficulty swallowing.

A specialist physcian will usally confirm the diagnosis by performing an endoscopy (a tube placed down into the esophagus to enable it to be visualized), which will show inflammation and possibly ulceration of the esophagus lining due to stomach acid. A barium swallow may show the reflux occurring.

Other specialized tests may demonstrate that stomach acids are in the esophagus, and that the sphincter is incompetent.

In most cases the symptoms improve after simple preventive measures have been taken. These include losing weight, avoiding lying down after a meal, and avoiding foods like fat, chocolate, caffeine, alcohol and tobacco, which seem to make the condition worse. When sleeping, the head of the bed should be elevated.

Medications such as antacids (taken after meals and at bedtime) and histamine H2 receptor blockers will relieve the symptoms. In a small percentage of cases, surgery to correct the sphincter is needed.

Recurrent gastresophageal reflux may cause a pre-cancerous condition of the lower esophagus called Barrett's syndrome.

SEE ALSO *Esophagus, Heartburn, Hiatus hernia, Stomach*

GASTROSCOPY

Gastroscopy is one of a number of tests that use fiberoptic tubes called endoscopes to see inside the body and perform minor procedures such as taking samples or destroying diseased or abnormal tissue. The tubes are flexible, carry a light, and can also be fitted with small surgical instruments. This technique is used to examine the stomach. Patients are required to fast for several hours before endoscopy to ensure that food does not obstruct the internal examination. Endoscopy can cause irritation and minor internal bleeding, and in rare instances may damage the bowel.

SEE ALSO *Endoscopy*

GENES

Genes are the units of genetic information, passed from parent to offspring and found on chromosomes in the nucleus of each cell. Humans have 23 pairs of chromosomes, and at conception each parent contributes one chromosome of each pair. These chromosomes are then copied into each cell in the body.

Chromosomes consist of deoxyribonucleic acid (DNA), with each gene being a section of DNA that instructs the cell how to make a particular protein. (Proteins are extremely important functional and structural molecules in cells.)

The instruction is contained in the order, or sequence, of nucleotide bases (adenine, guanine, cytosine and thymine) of the DNA, which codes the sequence of amino acids in the protein.

Humans have approximately 100,000 genes, with each of us having different combinations giving us our unique characteristics. Not all genes are active at any one time; gene expression can be inhibited or induced, depending on the function of the cell and the body's needs.

Because each person has a unique genetic makeup, DNA analysis ("DNA fingerprinting") can be used to identify individuals, as in forensic medicine.

Since we inherit half our genetic makeup from each parent, the DNA of close family members contains more similarities than that of unrelated people. This can be used to establish relationships, in paternity cases for instance.

Mutations

Mutations occur when there is a change in one or more nucleotides in the DNA molecule in a cell. Mutations can occur if the DNA is damaged, for instance by excess radiation or by harmful chemicals, such as those in cigarette smoke. The change in the DNA sequence in a gene may result in a change in the amino acids in the protein that the gene encodes.

Mutations are relatively rare and may be beneficial, but are more often harmful. Sickle cell disease, for example, is due to a change in one base in the gene that controls hemoglobin, the protein that carries oxygen in red blood cells. This causes a change in one amino acid in the hemoglobin, leading to poor oxygen transport. Mutations can also occur when DNA is copied, as in cell

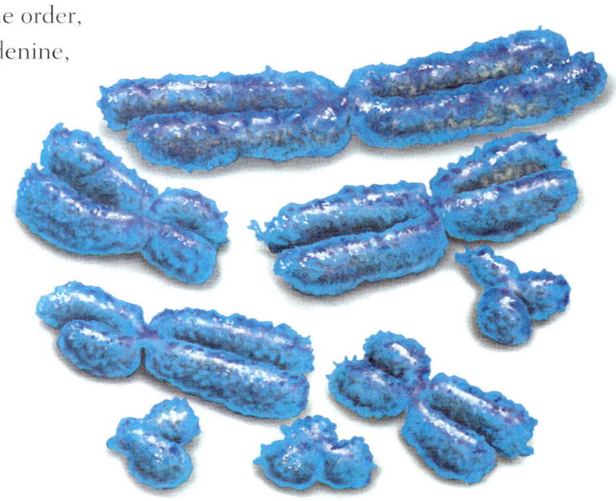

Chromosomes

There are about 100,000 separate genes in the human genome (or genetic blueprint), spread across 23 pairs of chromosomes (coiled, double stranded DNA material of varying lengths). In the gamete (sperm or egg), these are separated into 23 single chromosomes through a process called meiosis. Once an egg is fertilized by a sperm new pairs of chromosomes are formed.

division. Cells have mechanisms to repair damaged DNA, but some degree of mutation is desirable since it may produce new proteins and useful variability.

If harmful mutations occur in the germ cells (ova and sperm), they may be passed to the offspring. If that offspring survives and reproduces again, the mutation may be passed onto the next generation, and so on, to eventually become established in the population.

Many disorders are inherited. Some disorders run in families but occur irregularly. Environment, diet, smoking and other factors are often as important as genetic influences in causing a number of diseases.

However, there are over 3,500 diseases that are known to be linked to a defect in a single gene and are strictly genetically inherited. In some of these diseases, the defective gene is "dominant"—only one parent needs to pass on the gene to give their offspring the disease, for example, myotonic dystrophy, a type of muscular dystrophy associated with muscle wasting and loss of muscle tone. In others, the defective gene is "recessive", requiring the gene from both parents for the disease to be genetically expressed, for example, cystic fibrosis, a disease of the exocrine glands of the lung, skin and pancreas.

Other defective genes are "X-linked", (also called sex-linked); that is, they are located on the X chromosome. This means that usually only males get the disease; women have two X chromosomes and X-linked diseases are usually recessive, so the disease is not expressed. The women become carriers, however. Hemophilia is an X-linked disease.

Prospective parents with a genetic disorder in the family may not want to risk passing it on to their future offspring. Genetic counseling for the parents may be valuable so that they can discuss the genetic risks and possible options. For some inheritable disorders such as Down syndrome, screening during pregnancy can provide a prenatal diagnosis, and allow the parents to consider terminating the pregnancy.

Gene sequencing

Each nucleotide base interlocks with a specific partner to form a base pair. Three base pairs form a codon and code for one amino acid. The order in which the bases are carried on a DNA strand determines the information contained in that strand.

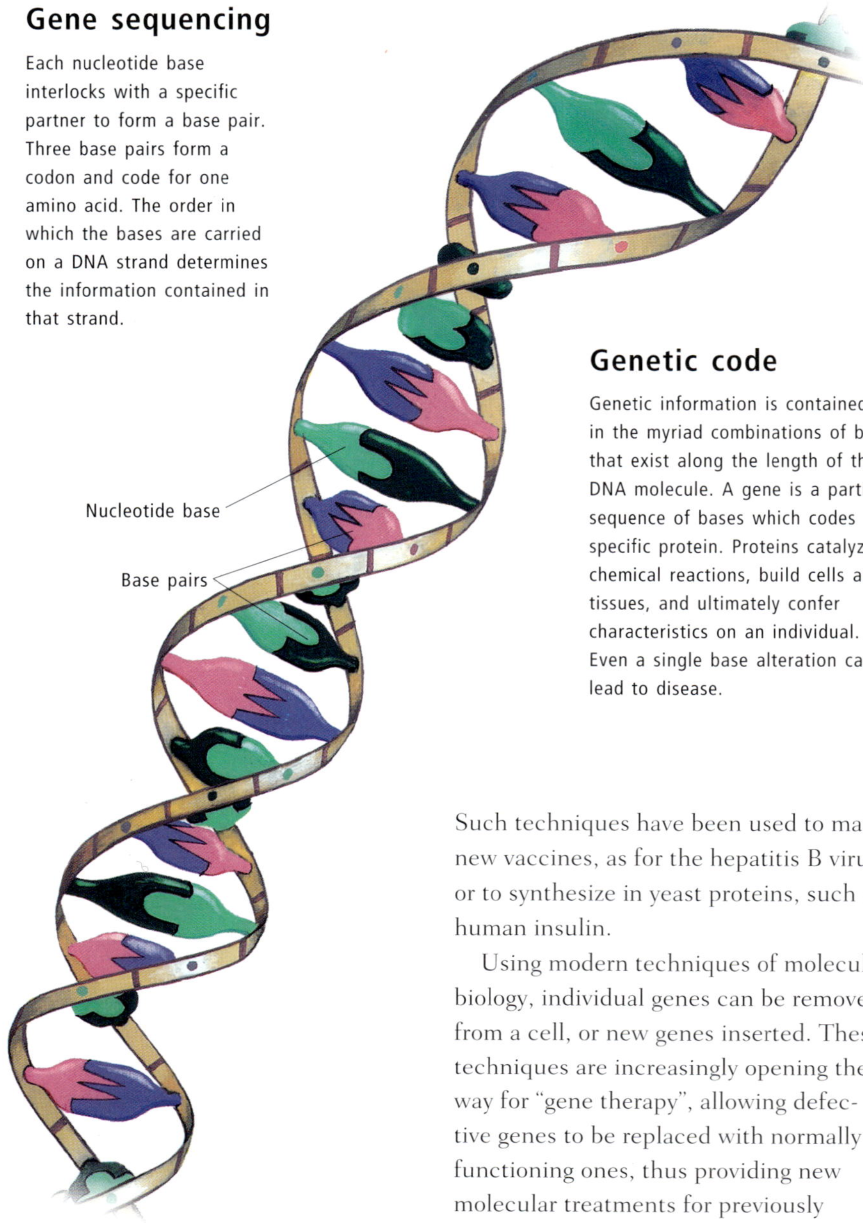

Genetic code

Genetic information is contained in the myriad combinations of bases that exist along the length of the DNA molecule. A gene is a particular sequence of bases which codes for a specific protein. Proteins catalyze chemical reactions, build cells and tissues, and ultimately confer characteristics on an individual. Even a single base alteration can lead to disease.

Gene mapping

Gene mapping refers to the sequence and spacing of genes along a chromosome. Genes that are close together on a chromosome are more likely to be passed to the offspring together, and are referred to as "linked genes". However, linkages can change. Sections of chromosomes can break apart and groups of genes can "cross over" to other chromosomes or recombine in different sequences. An exciting international initiative in recent years has been the Human Genome Project, which has mapped all the genes in the human body.

Genetic engineering

Genetic engineering refers to our ability to manipulate DNA, for instance to sequence a gene and recombine it to make the code for a new or modified protein. Such techniques have been used to make new vaccines, as for the hepatitis B virus, or to synthesize in yeast proteins, such as human insulin.

Using modern techniques of molecular biology, individual genes can be removed from a cell, or new genes inserted. These techniques are increasingly opening the way for "gene therapy", allowing defective genes to be replaced with normally functioning ones, thus providing new molecular treatments for previously incurable diseases.

Advances in genetic engineering also makes possible the cloning of organisms, that is, the manufacture of a organism from a single body cell of its parent which is genetically identical to it. Cloning has been known to agriculture since ancient times, but because of their greater biodiversity, cloning of animals has proved more difficult.

A breakthrough came in 1996 when researchers were able to produce a cloned lamb called "Dolly" using DNA from an adult sheep. The possibility exists that humans beings may also one day be cloned, a prospect raising many ethical and moral dilemmas.

SEE ALSO *Chromosomes, Congenital abnormalities, DNA, Down syndrome, Genetic counseling, Heredity, Sickle cell disease*

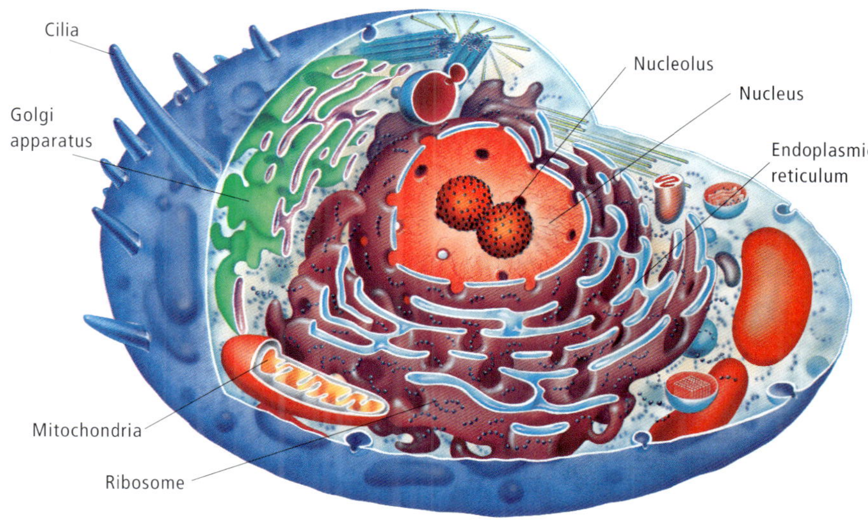

Passing on genetic information

DNA, containing genetic information, is found within the nucleus of the cell. It is transcribed to mRNA within the nucleolus of the cell. The genetic information is then translated, by ribosomes in the endoplasmic reticulum, into a sequence of amino acids which form a protein. The proteins are then incorporated by the Golgi apparatus into small packets (vesicles) and released at the cell membrane.

GENETIC COUNSELING

Genetic counseling is the education of individuals (and the community) about inherited disorders. It usually stems from an inquiry from a couple about whether a given disease is likely to recur in a planned family. Genetic counseling usually involves a session in which a medical practitioner will explain to prospective parents the probability of producing a child with a disorder. They can then make responsible and informed decisions from a range of options. One option might be for example to accept the risk and take a chance that the baby will be unaffected or the condition will be treatable. Alternatively the parents may decide against conceiving and adopt a baby instead. The aim of counseling is to educate, not advise.

Couples with a genetic disease in their family history, or who are first cousins, or in which the woman is over 35, may seek genetic counseling before they attempt pregnancy. Cousins share 25 percent of the same gene pool, and older women have a greater risk of a chromosomal disorder, the risk rising with age.

Women who have had three or more miscarriages may also benefit from genetic counseling. Genetic counseling is also available for pregnant women; where tests discover an abnormality in the fetus, abortion may be discussed.

SEE ALSO *Chromosomes, Genes*

GENITAL HERPES

Genital herpes is a virus infection of the genitals by one of two types of herpes simplex virus. The type that usually causes genital herpes is called herpes simplex type 2, and it is most often transmitted by sexual intercourse (including oral sex).

The initial infection usually follows contact with a partner who has an active herpes lesion. An itching and irritation of the skin follows, which reddens. Multiple vesicles (blisters) then appear, filled with a clear straw-colored fluid. The blisters break, leaving shallow painful ulcers which eventually crust over and slowly heal over a period of one to two weeks. The vaginal lips or penis, less commonly the thigh and buttocks, are affected. During the acute stage, there may be a fever, and the lymph nodes in the groin may be swollen. The infection then goes into a latent stage with the virus lying dormant in nerve cells in the skin. At any time—but most often in times of stress, menopause, sunburn, or following another illness—the lesions erupt again. Recurrent attacks may be rare or be so frequent that the symptoms seem continuous. In some people they can last many years. Fortunately, attacks tend to get milder and less frequent over time.

Recurrent herpes is a diffucult condition to treat. Oral acyclovir (an antiviral medication) reduces the duration and severity of the attacks, but it doesn't cure the infection, which persists for life.

Genital herpes may increase the risk of cervical cancer, and it can be a traumatic and psychologically damaging condition.

The best cure is prevention. Avoid sexual intercourse if either partner has blisters or sores. Use a condom if either has had herpes lesions in the past. Condoms are a barrier to transmission of the virus.

Pregnant woman need to tell their physician about previous herpes infection as a cesarean delivery may be advised to prevent infection of the baby.

SEE ALSO *Herpes simplex, Sexually transmitted diseases*

GENITAL WARTS

Genital warts are a sexually transmitted infection, caused by the human papilloma virus. The warts occur on the penis and on the vulva, vagina and cervix. They are also common in the anal region in homosexual men. The warts have a cauliflower-like appearance. They can be removed surgically or by laser or cryotherapy. In women, follow-up treatment is particularly important, as genital warts can lead to cervical cancer.

SEE ALSO *Sexually transmitted diseases, Warts*

Genital herpes

Genital herpes is caused by the herpes simplex virus which invades nerve cells. Mostly spread by sexual intercourse, it is highly contagious. There is no known cure.

GERIATRIC MEDICINE

Geriatric medicine, or geriatrics, is an area of medical specialization that deals with health care of the elderly, and the disorders and diseases that arise with age. It is not to be confused with gerontology, which is the study of the ageing process and its social effects.

Industrialized countries have experienced a change in their population structure throughout the last century. As standards of nutrition and public health have improved, life expectancy for men and women has also improved, and the proportion of aged persons has increased. People over 70 years make up an increasing percentage of the population in Western countries.

Although people in the industrialized nations are living longer, they still experience the declines associated with ageing, and many diseases requiring full-time or nursing home care are becoming more common. In the UK, one-third of all hospital beds are occupied by people over age 65, about half of those being psychiatric patients. Aged patients often have more than one disorder, and more often suffer from chronic (long term) or incurable conditions, meaning they require proportionately more specialized attention. Women tend to live longer than men and constitute over half of the aged population. Geriatric medicine is increasingly concerned with disorders affecting women.

Complicating the provision of health care to elderly people are factors such as unreported illness, multiple disorders, loneliness and potential loss of independence. As infirmity grows, people may be reluctant to visit their doctor with what seem only minor symptoms. These may grow to become major problems by the time they are reported and may be complicated by other disorders that have arisen in the meantime. If mobility or normal dexterity is affected, elderly persons may be unable to care for themselves or to leave the home alone. This can result in depression, which may require treatment as well as the underlying causes. Care may therefore involve a team of health professionals as well as the family doctor.

Geriatric medicine developed in response to the special health needs of the elderly and infirm. Fast help in emergencies, a thorough

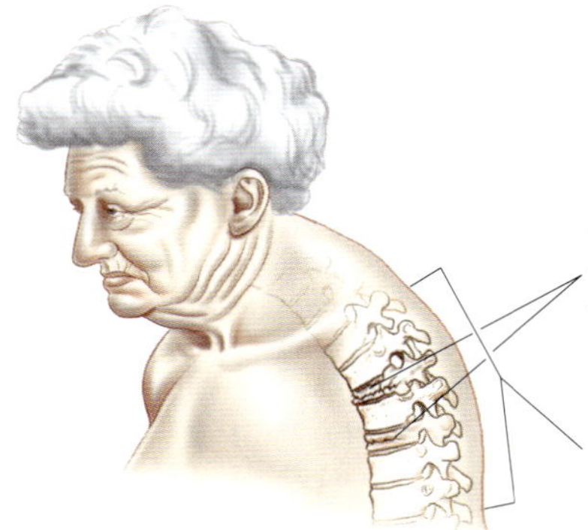

Dowager's hump
Older women with severe osteoporosis may develop dowager's hump. The vertebrae in the spine compress and become distorted, leading to a forward curvature of the thoracic spine which may worsen progressively.

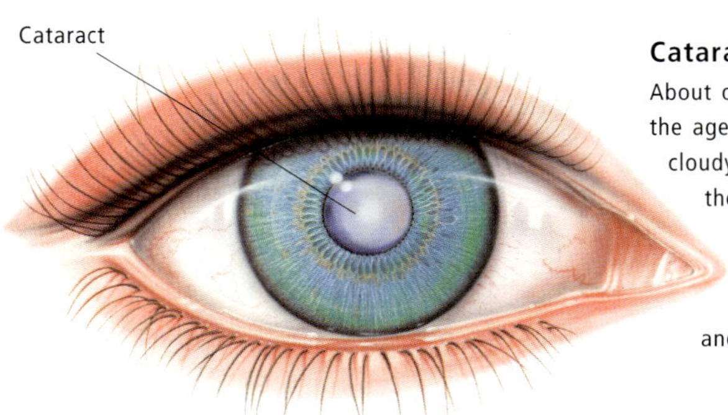

Cataracts
About one in five people over the age of 60 will develop cloudy spots in the lens of the eye. Cataracts are more common in older people because, as we age, the lens may deteriorate and become less transparent.

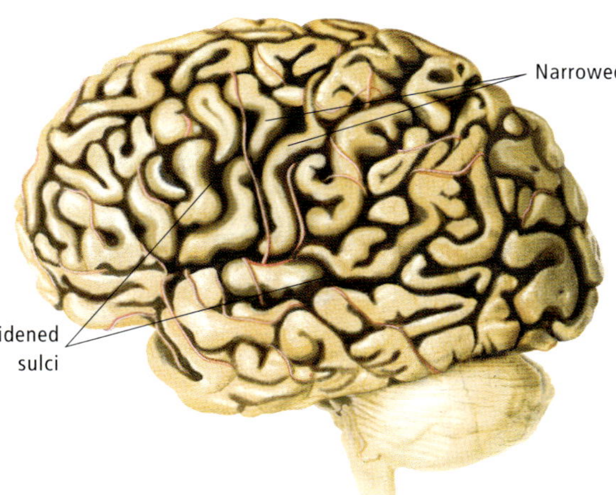

Alzheimer's disease
After the age of 65, the risk of developing Alzheimer's disease doubles every 5 years. Signs of this form of dementia include increasing forgetfulness, diminished intellectual capacity, personality changes and loss of motor skills and coordination.

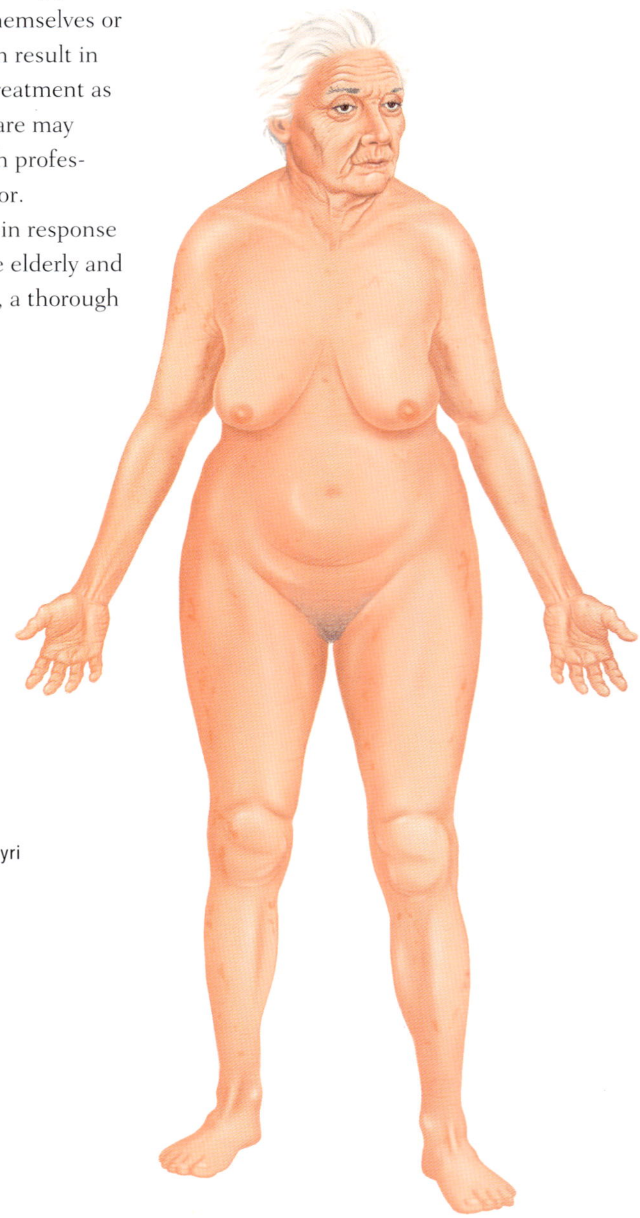

Elderly woman

Geriatrics

As people grow older their bodies become less flexible and more inefficient. There is a loss of height—women shrink more than men—and muscle tone is reduced and fat deposits increase.

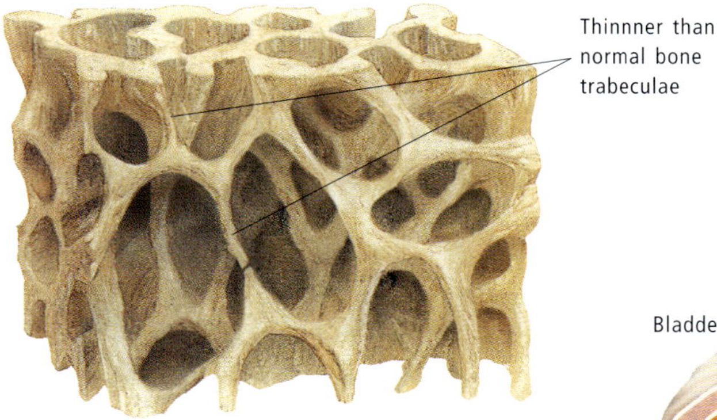

Osteoporosis

Both elderly men and women can suffer from osteoporosis. As we age, new bone growth no longer replaces old bone as quickly as it used to, so the bones become porous and brittle.

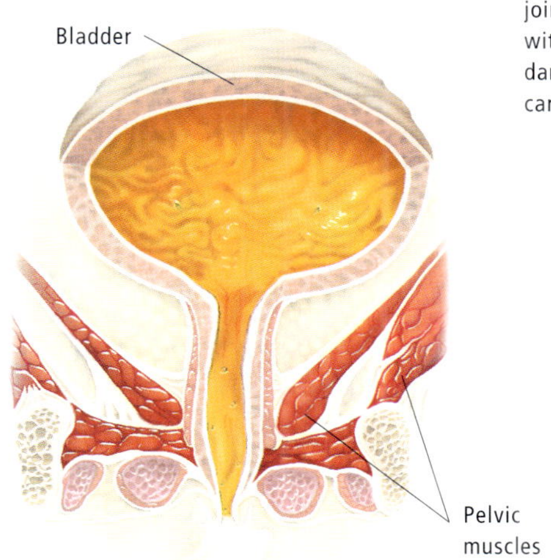

Incontinence

In the elderly, incontinence can be caused by a number of different factors. The muscles that support the bladder and floor of the pelvis can weaken with age, or incontinence may be associated with disorders such as senility, stroke or diabetes mellitus.

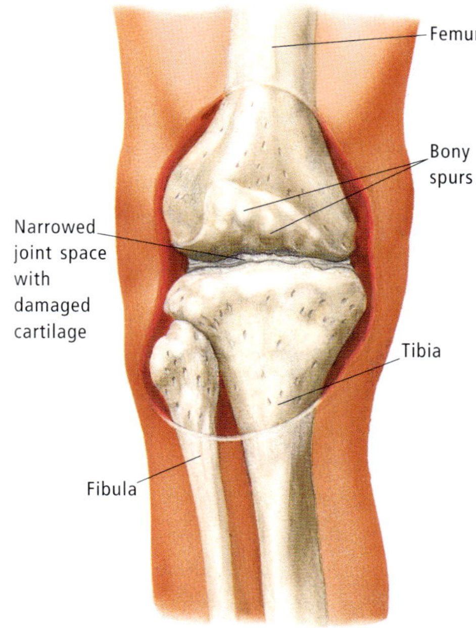

Osteoarthritis

As part of the ageing process, the cartilage that covers the ends of the bones begins to disintegrate, and the bones themselves may wear down. Symptoms of osteoarthritis include pain, stiffness and discomfort in joints such as fingers, knees, hips, toes and the spine.

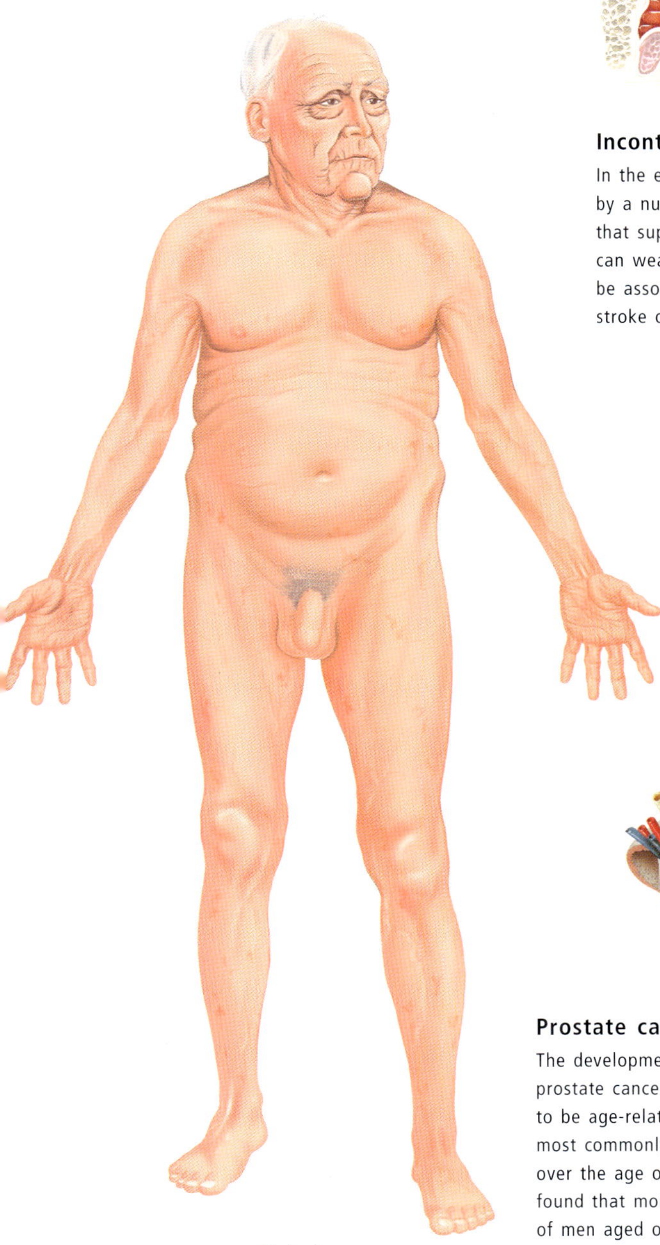

Elderly man

Ankle fracture

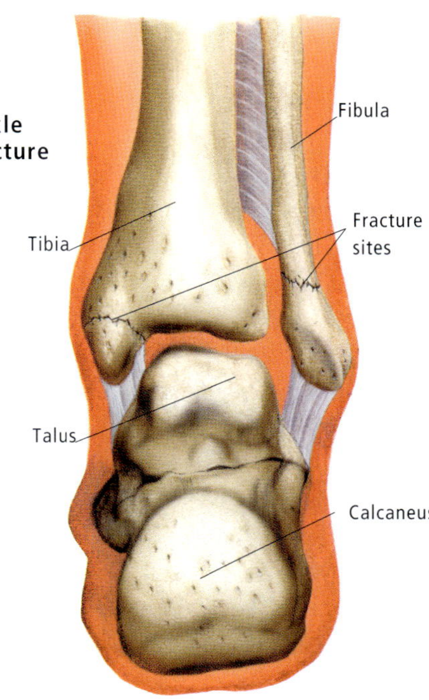

Fractures

In older age groups, especially women after menopause and people suffering from osteoporosis, bones lose calcium and phosphate and become less dense. Consequently they become weak and prone to fracture. Wrist, humerus, ankle, hip and vertebral fractures as a result of falling are particularly common.

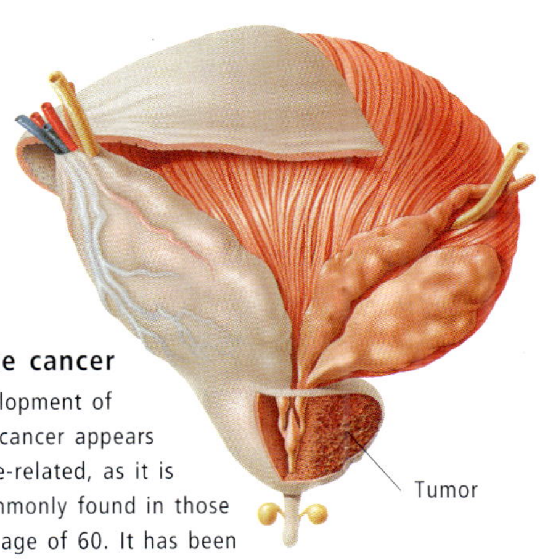

Prostate cancer

The development of prostate cancer appears to be age-related, as it is most commonly found in those over the age of 60. It has been found that more than 50 percent of men aged over 80 years have latent tumors of the prostate.

G

assessment of each patient's needs, comprehensive treatment aimed to reduce disability (or minimize its effects) and assistance in keeping patients in their homes while addressing the needs of their caregivers are all elements of this medical specialty. The practice of geriatric medicine is based on acceptance that medical disorders in elderly people are not necessarily curable. Treatments prescribed may be different than in general medicine. The emphasis is on retaining quality of life for patients, rather than solely achieving a cure. The aims and expected outcomes of any treatment must be clearly defined.

Physicians and health professionals dealing with the elderly aim to relieve discomfort and treat symptoms, no matter what the predicted outcome or the nearness or apparent certainty of death. Disorders or their effects are kept under control in order to allow patients to live as well as possible and maintain physical mobility and independence for as long as possible. It is important to maintain access to all medical services in order to fulfil these aims.

Central to geriatric medicine is the provision of care in the home. This relieves the pressure on hospital beds and in many cases retains the quality of life that comes from familiar surroundings and maintenance of domestic routines. In financial terms it is less costly to provide or subsidize a range of services aimed at maintaining elderly people in their homes than to create places in hospitals and attempt to provide services in that environment. Home care includes nursing, many forms of therapy, counseling, providing special equipment, rehabilitation, personal care services, preparation or delivery of meals, and even making modifications to the home.

Palliative care for the terminally ill and bereavement counseling for relatives are also part of a web of services which support health workers in geriatric medicine.

Ageing is an inescapable fact of life, and a process that begins at conception. Cells mature, die and are replaced. Life expectancy and general health are products of our genetic heritage, from parents, grandparents and their parents, and of our environment, particularly nutritional standards in childhood years, and health care.

As age advances, soft tissues become less flexible and the internal organs lose their efficiency. Sharpness of the senses is lost or gradually declines. Eyes lose their ability to focus on close objects and reading glasses become necessary. Hearing high-pitched tones becomes more difficult, taking some of the impact and enjoyment out of listening to music and affecting how speech is heard and understood.

Statistically, humans grow fatter with age. Fat becomes a greater proportion of body weight and is distributed differently, subcutaneous fat decreasing while abdominal fat and fat around internal organs increases—but these changes are statistical observations and may only tell us what is happening in society, rather than what should happen as we age. There is ample reason to suppose that an active lifestyle and balanced nutrition can maintain good health and physical abilities well into old age.

Although the effects of age can be reduced, delayed and deferred, they cannot be eliminated. As the body ages, circulatory and respiratory ailments become more common. Blood flow to the liver, kidneys and brain is reduced, affecting the clearance of waste products from the bloodstream. Lung capacity decreases, reducing the effective reoxygenation of blood and leaving increasing amounts of unexpired air in the lungs. Intellectual impairment is a common problem in the elderly and is a serious problem, affecting many aspects of an elderly person's life, including the ability to live independently, manage financial affairs, or drive a vehicle. About 10 percent of persons over the age of 65 years have some degree of mental impairment. It may be due to irreversible conditions, such as Alzheimer's disease or multiple small strokes, or it may be treatable, as in diseases of the thyroid gland, sleep disorders, or depression.

Decreasing mobility is also a feature of old age. Decreased balance, poor gait, muscle weakness, poor coordination and arthritis in the joints may also restrict movement. Basic functions such as bathing and dressing become more difficult and there is an increased incidence of falls and injuries. As elderly people become more sedentary, medical problems may develop; those who are bed- or chair-bound may develop edema, contractures, incontinence or pressure sores.

As a person ages, the senses deteriorate. Most older adults have at least some degenerative disease of the eye; 16 percent of those aged 75 to 84, and 27 percent of those older than 85 are blind in both eyes. Visual impairment reduces the ability to drive, read, shop, and even walk.

Hearing loss affects one-third of 65 year olds, two-thirds of those over age 70, and three-quarters of those 80 years of age and older. Typically, elderly people have difficulty hearing sounds in the higher frequencies. Visual and hearing losses increase their sense of alienation and loneliness and are often a contributing factor in falls and injuries.

Maintaining adequate nutrition is essential in the elderly, who are often malnourished because of poverty, social isolation, depression, dementia, pain or immobility. As a consequence of malnourishment, they tend to suffer pressure sores and take longer to recover from illnesses.

As a rule, elderly people tend to take too many medications. It has been estimated that an elderly person over the age of 65 takes on average 13 different medications in a year. These may interact, with toxic effects. To make matters worse, the kidneys don't function as well in old age, so toxic levels of the drugs may build up.

The immune system functions more poorly in old age, making elderly people more susceptible to cancers and infections. Progressive diseases also tend to become more severe in old age. Other diseases that are common in the elderly include fracture, (hip, ankle); heart attack; incontinence; kidney disorders; osteoarthritis (painful degenerative disease of the joints); osteoporosis (decalcification of bones, making them fragile and prone to fracture); Parkinson's disease; prostate problems (cancer or enlargement of the prostate gland); shingles (painful skin rash); and stroke.

Geriatric medicine can now ensure a comfortable and functional independent life for sufferers of some chronic conditions that previously resulted in death or disability.

SEE ALSO *Ageing, Cataracts, Diabetes, Glaucoma, Incontinence, Kidney, Osteoarthritis, Osteoporosis, Palliative care, Parkinson's disease, Prostate cancer, Shingles*

GIARDIASIS

Caused by the flagellate protozoa (*Giardia lamblia*) that is found in contaminated water, giardiasis is a common infection of the small intestine. It is characterized by stomach ache and large, bad-smelling, frothy stools containing mucus. It is infectious and is usually transmitted as cysts through oral-fecal contact or by ingesting food or water contaminated by feces.

Giardia is one of the most common intestinal parasites, and it is estimated that up to 20 percent of the world's population is infected with it at any one time. It is most common in tropical regions and in developing countries with poor sanitary conditions, inadequate water quality control and overcrowding.

Children are more likely to be affected than adults, and families with young children who attend preschool or day care centers, as well as homosexual men and women, and anyone who drinks untreated water from creeks or rivers, are at most risk.

The period from infection to the onset of acute symptoms ranges from several days up to two weeks, distinguishing it from food poisoning. Without treatment, the disease can go on for months, with recurrent mild symptoms, such as digestive troubles, intermittent diarrhea, and weight loss. Diagnosed by laboratory testing of fecal matter, giardiasis is treated with drugs.

SEE ALSO *Diarrhea, Intestines*

GIGANTISM

Gigantism is a rare condition of bone, muscle and organ overgrowth in childhood, caused by overproduction of growth hormone (GH), usually due to an overactive pituitary gland. The result is an adult of excessive size and stature. If the hyperpituitarism begins after puberty, the condition is known as acromegaly, and is characterized by excessive enlargement of the jaw, hands and feet.

Gigantism is treated with combinations of surgery, radiation therapy and the drug bromocriptine. Hormone replacement therapy with pituitary hormones may be needed after surgery. Early diagnosis in childhood is essential for successful treatment.

SEE ALSO *Acromegaly, Growth disorders, Pituitary gland*

Gingivitis

The accumulation of food particles in the crevices between teeth and gums can cause gingivitis (inflammation of the gums). Symptoms include gum bleeding and swelling.

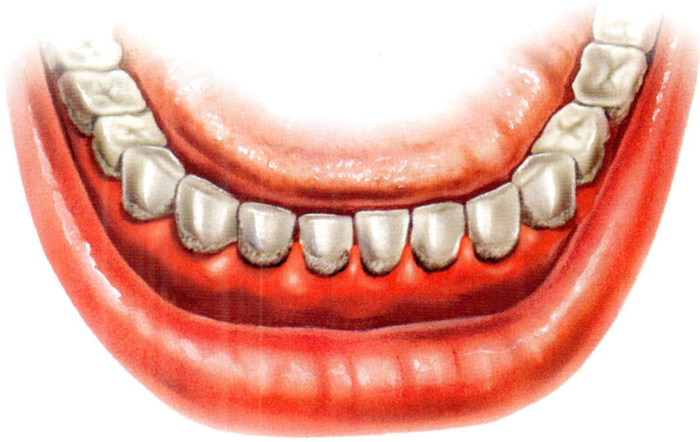

GINGIVITIS

Gingivitis is an inflammation of the gums. It commonly occurs when small particles of food get trapped between the tooth and gum, causing the build-up of bacteria in these areas. The gums become swollen and red, and bleed easily.

Chronic gingivitis is often the result of poor oral and dental hygiene, with build-up of debris and plaque (tartar) around the teeth, although it may also occur with poorly fitting dentures, or with tooth decay or abscesses.

If left untreated, gingivitis can lead to periodontitis, where the infection spreads to deeper tissues such as the tooth socket and bone. This causes bone loss, and leads to enlarging of the tooth socket, so that teeth become loose and may eventually fall out. Regular visits to the dentist and improved tooth brushing, with flossing between teeth, are recommended.

Acute ulcerative necrotizing gingivitis is a more severe inflammation caused by a gum infection. The infected areas bleed heavily and are very painful and ulcerated, and the breath smells foul. Again the inflammation can spread to deeper tissues and eventually inflammation will lead to the destruction of periodontal tissues and tooth loss. An urgent dental referral is recommended.

SEE ALSO *Gums, Periodontitis, Teeth*

GLANDS

Glands are a type of tissue that is made up of cells specialized for the production of a fluid secretion. These special secretions may contain mineral salts, protein, fats or complexes of carbohydrates and proteins.

There are two broad types of glands: exocrine glands, which drain their secretions to the surface of the body or the interior of the gut, lungs or reproductive organs; and endocrine glands, which release their secretions directly into the blood stream or tissue spaces for circulation to other places in the body.

Exocrine glands have a secretory part, which makes the secretory product, and a tubular duct, which carries the secretion to the body or the gut surface. It is the presence of the duct that distinguishes these glands from endocrine glands. In some types of exocrine glands, the cells release their secretion without any loss of cellular material, while in other types the entire cell becomes filled with the secretory product and is completely shed with the secretion.

Examples of exocrine glands include the sweat and sebaceous glands of the skin. Sweat glands are responsible for helping in the control of body temperature, while the fats of sebaceous gland secretions (sebum) prevent water loss from the skin and help to control the growth of microorganisms like bacteria and fungi.

Mammary glands, found only in mammals, are a modified type of sweat gland. They produce milk, which is rich in many secretory products (protein, fats, carbohydrates, immune system proteins and vitamins).

Other types of exocrine glands include: the salivary glands of the oral cavity; the exocrine part of the pancreas, which produces digestive enzymes; the mucus-secreting cells of the lining of the gut and respiratory tract; enzyme secreting cells of the stomach and small intestine; and secretory cells lining the uterus. The pancreas is unique in that it contains both exocrine and endocrine glands.

Endocrine glands, or ductless glands, produce hormones which travel to all tissues of the body via the bloodstream. The main endocrine gland is the pituitary, located immediately below the brain and receiving commands from the hypothalamus in the brain by special nerve pathways and blood channels. The pituitary gland produces a number of important hormones with diverse functions. These include growth hormone (GH), which controls the growth of bones by affecting the cartilage at growth plates; thyroid stimulating hormone (TSH), which controls the production of thyroid hormones by the thyroid gland; follicle stimulating hormone (FSH); luteinizing hormone (LH); adrenocorticotropic hormone (ACTH); and prolactin.

Other endocrine glands are scattered throughout the body (such as the adrenal glands, thyroid gland, parathyroid glands, ovaries and testes). The adrenal gland is divided into two parts: an outer cortex and an inner medulla. The outer cortex produces corticosteroids, which control carbohydrate, lipid and protein metabolism, mineralocorticoids, which control the resorption of sodium in the kidney, and sex steroids, which play a minor role under normal conditions. The adrenal medulla produces epinephrine and norepinephrine (adrenaline and noradrenaline), released in times of acute physical or emotional stress. The parathyroid gland produces a hormone that controls blood calcium. The ovaries and testes produce sex hormones (estrogen and testosterone), responsible for the bodily changes associated with sexual maturity (for example, growth of pubic hair, development of sexual organs and breasts). The placenta is also an endocrine gland, secreting chorionic gonadotropin.

The thymus is often called a gland, but is more accurately described as a lymphoid organ. During early childhood it produces a type of white blood cell known as the "T" lymphocyte. These cells are later distributed throughout the body, going to lymph glands (lymph nodes), the spleen and the gut wall.

The lymph glands are positioned along the lymphatic vessels—on both sides of the neck, in both armpits and on both sides of the groin, as well as the internal body cavities. They act as filters, inhibiting the spread of infection.

During a reaction to infection, the cells in a lymph gland multiply, and the gland becomes large and painful.

SEE ALSO *Adrenal glands, Endocrine glands, Estrogens, Hypothalamus, Lymph glands, Mammary glands, Ovaries, Parathyroid glands, Pituitary gland, Sebaceous glands, Sweat glands, Testes, Testosterone, Thymus gland, Thyroid gland*

Glands

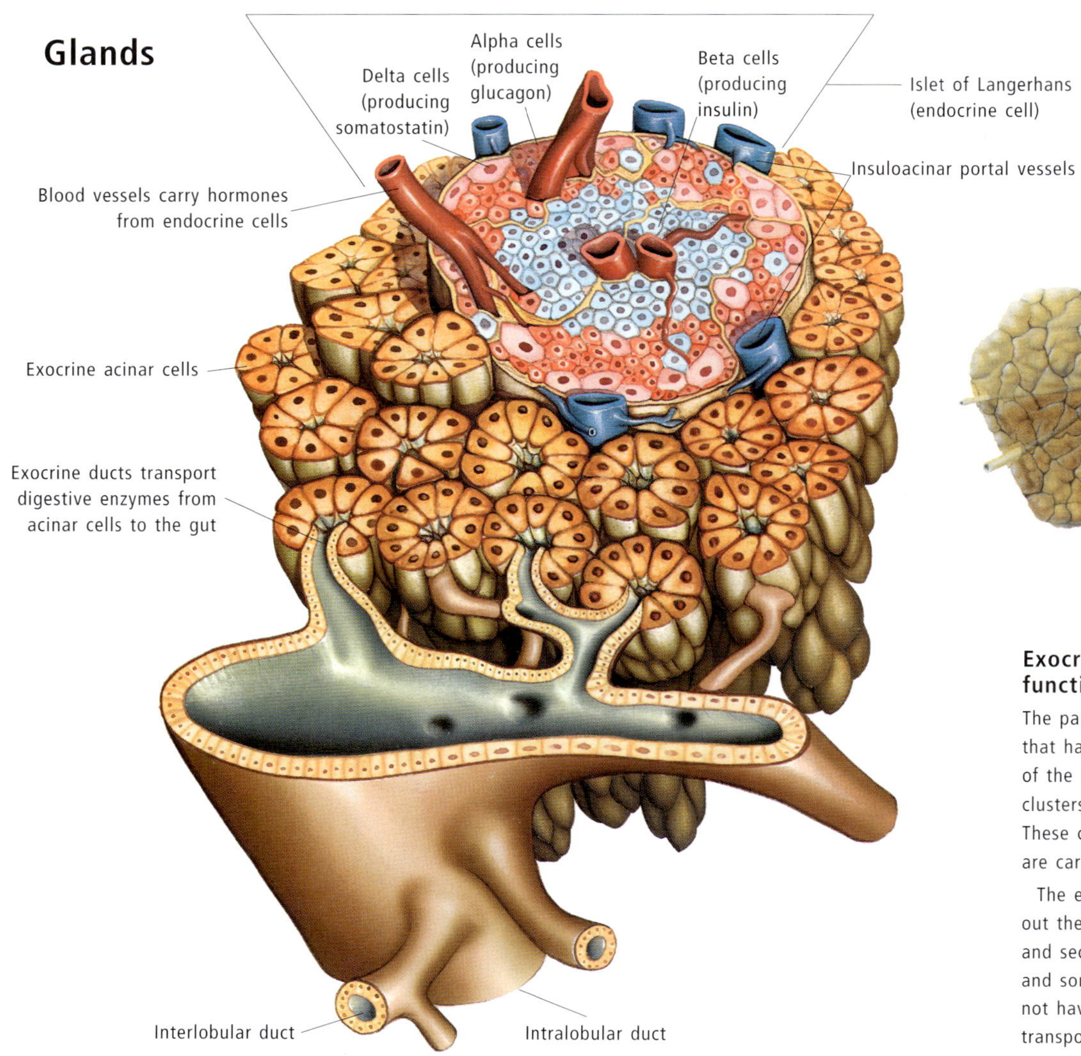

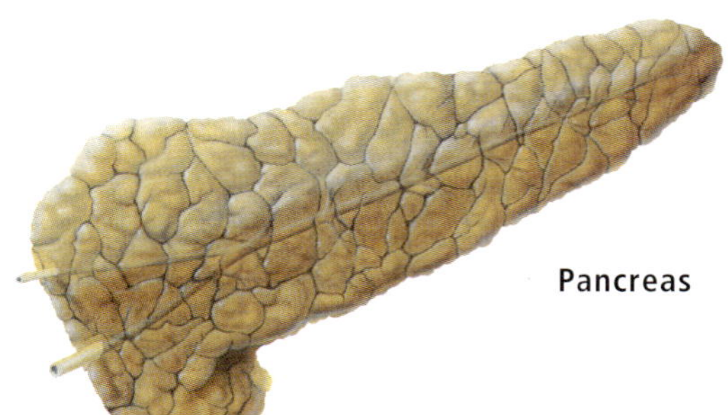

Pancreas

Exocrine and endocrine function—the pancreas

The pancreas is the only glandular organ that has endocrine and exocrine parts. Most of the organ is an exocrine gland comprising clusters of acinar cells with attached ducts. These cells produce digestive enzymes which are carried by the ducts to the gut.

The endocrine cells are scattered throughout the pancreas. They are located in islets and secrete the hormones glucagon, insulin and somatostatin. As endocrine glands do not have ducts, a network of blood vessels transports the hormones out of the pancreas.

Glands

Exocrine glands

These glands drain their secretions to the surface of the body or into the gut, lungs or reproductive organs. They are comprised of secretory cells and ducts which carry the secretion to the body or gut surface. They include sweat and mammary glands and part of the pancreas.

Mammary glands (exocrine)

The mammary glands (breasts) are modified sweat glands. They produce milk when stimulated by the hormone oxytocin, secreted by the pituitary gland. The mammary lobules secrete into the lactiferous ducts, which carry milk through a wider tube (the lactiferous sinus) to the nipple.

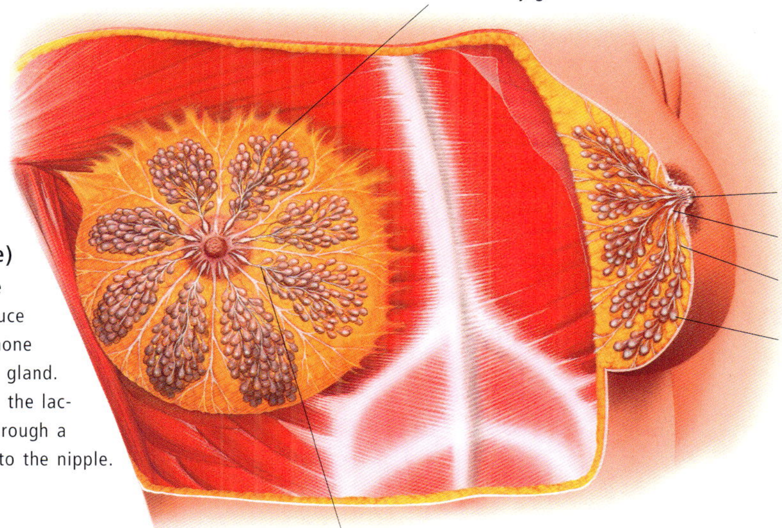

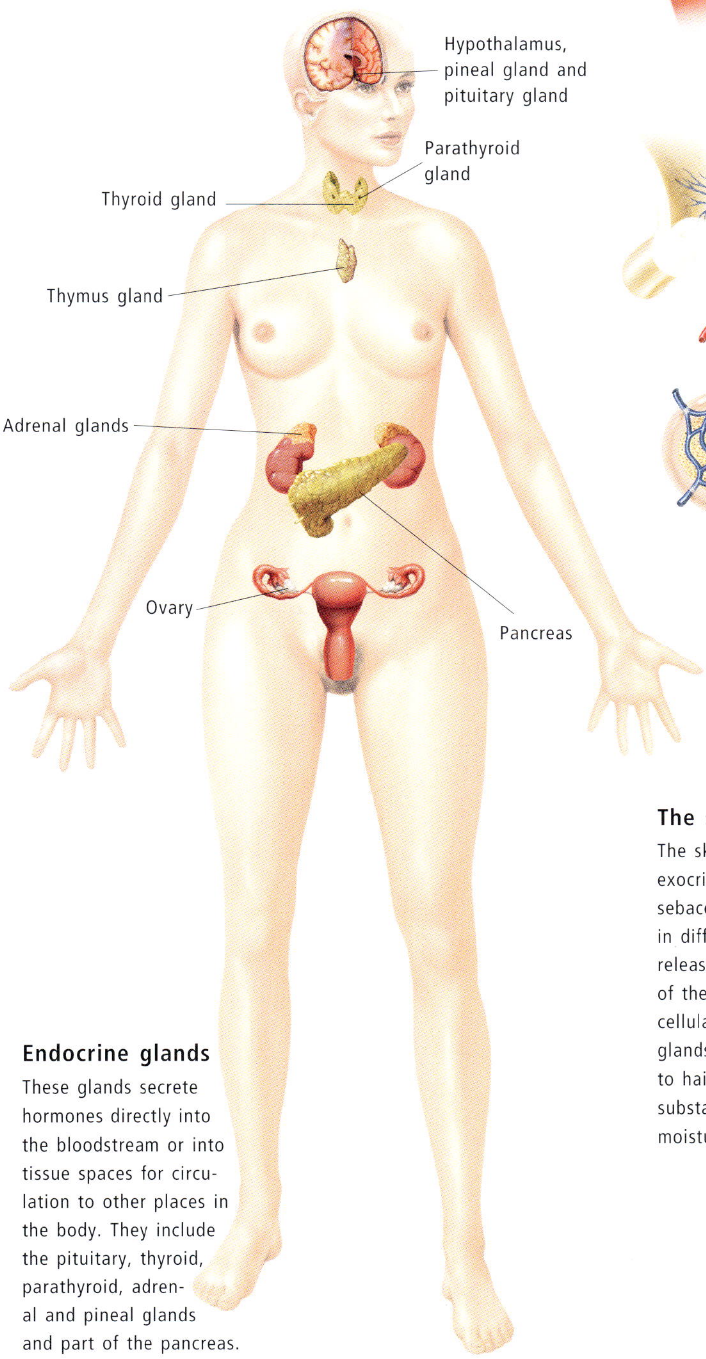

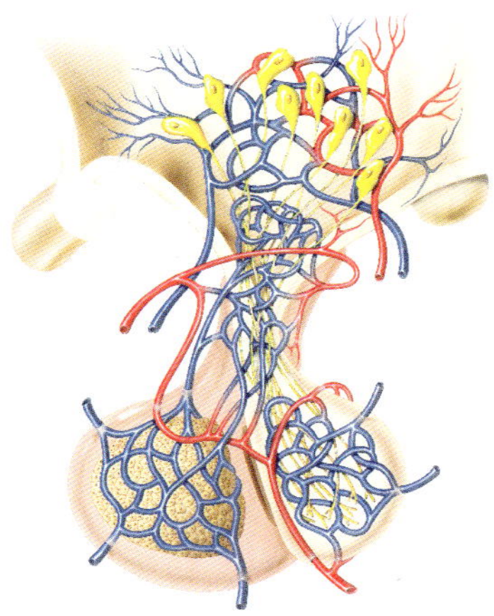

Pituitary gland (endocrine)

The pituitary is the main endocrine gland.

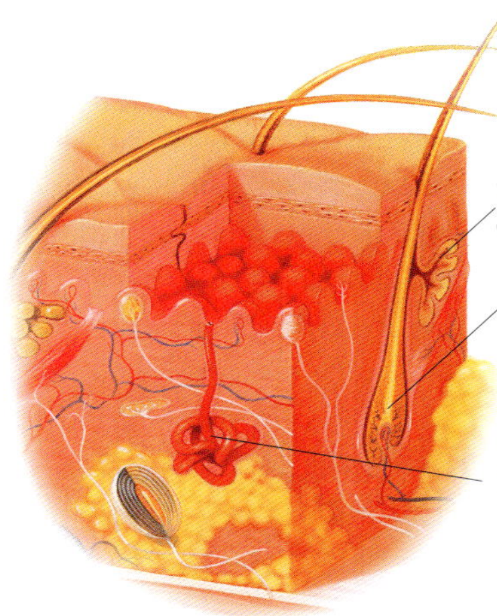

Sweat and sebaceous glands (exocrine)

The sweat and sebaceous glands of the skin are two examples of exocrine glands.

The skin (exocrine)

The skin contains two types of exocrine glands—the sweat and sebaceous glands—that secrete in different ways. Sweat glands release perspiration to the surface of the skin without losing any cellular material. The sebaceous glands which are mostly attached to hair follicles release an oily substance called sebum which moisturizes the skin and hair.

Endocrine glands

These glands secrete hormones directly into the bloodstream or into tissue spaces for circulation to other places in the body. They include the pituitary, thyroid, parathyroid, adrenal and pineal glands and part of the pancreas.

GLANS

The glans is a small mass of erectile tissue found in both the female and male genitals. In women it is known as the glans clitoris, and is located at the tip of the clitoris.
In men the glans penis is the smooth, expanded end of the penis. The glans penis is usually partly covered by the foreskin and contains the slit-like opening of the urethra, the tube carrying the urine and sperm. In both sexes the glans is composed of tissue that can engorge with blood when sexually aroused. It is highly sensitive to physical stimulation, since it contains many sensory nerve endings.

SEE ALSO *Clitoris, Penis, Urethra*

G

GLAUCOMA

This is a group of eye diseases that can cause damage to the optic nerve. Glaucoma is typically, although not invariably, associated with increased pressure within the eyeball. If untreated, it causes progressive loss of vision and may ultimately lead to blindness. Glaucoma ranks with diabetic eye disease, macular degeneration and cataracts as a major cause of blindness today.

Of the various forms of glaucoma, the most common is known as open-angle glaucoma. In this form of the disease, the angle between the iris and the cornea, through which the nutrient fluid (the aqueous humor) drains, remains open. Despite the open angle, drainage of the fluid (into an area called the canal of Schlemm) is inadequate, for reasons that remain unknown. The resulting tendency towards accumulation of fluid within the eye causes pressure (known as the intraocular pressure) to rise above the normal range of 12–21 millimeters of mercury. However, increased intraocular pressure is not synonymous with glaucoma and the pressure may be normal in some forms of glaucoma.

In its early stages, open-angle glaucoma produces few symptoms and may not be recognized or treated. Over time the increased pressure causes death of the photoreceptor (light-receiving) cells within the retina and their nerve fibers. This change first affects the peripheral (side) vision so that the patient progressively develops what is termed tunnel vision, but eventually sight may be completely lost. The exact mechanism by which elevation of intraocular pressure damages the retinal nerve cells is not yet well understood.

In closed-angle glaucoma, a blockage between the iris and cornea prevents the drainage of aqueous humor. Intraocular pressure increases rapidly and sharply and may result in severe pain. Other less common forms of glaucoma, such as congenital glaucoma and glaucoma secondary to injuries or other eye diseases, are also usually associated with noticeable symptoms.

Although glaucoma is not yet curable, it can be controlled by a variety of measures, including drug treatment, laser surgery to increase drainage through the angle, and conventional surgery to establish a new pathway for drainage. For control of the disease to be effective, it is essential that the diagnosis is made as early as possible. This can be achieved by regular eye examination, especially for individuals at risk, such as persons over 60 and those with a family history of the disease. Measurement of intraocular pressure, known as tonometry, is part of such an examination. Examination of visual sharpness, changes in the visual fields and changes in the optic disk viewed through a dilated pupil are very helpful in determining whether significant damage to the eye has occurred.

SEE ALSO *Cornea, Eye, Iris, Retina, Sight, Tonometry*

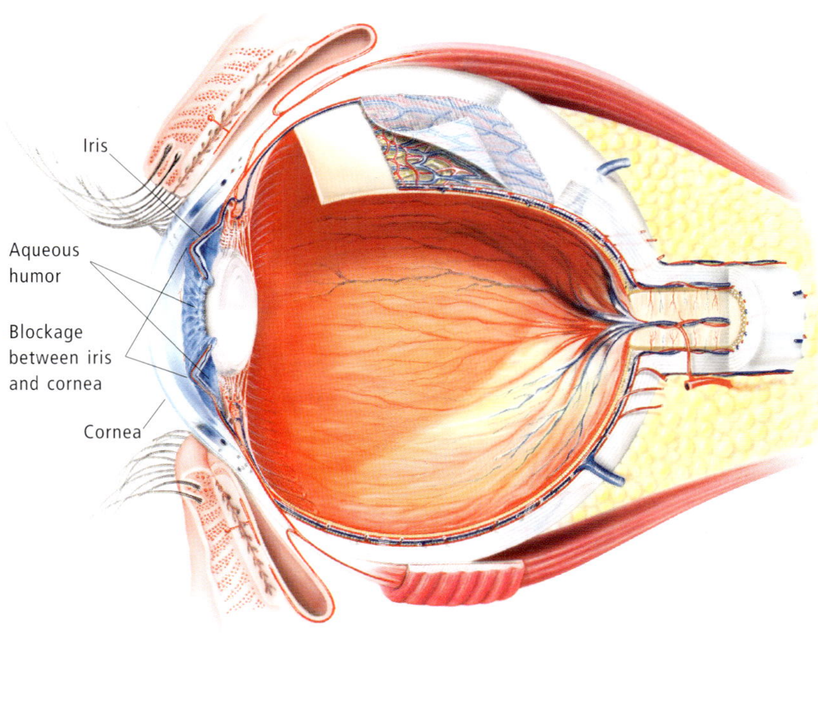

Glaucoma

The buildup of pressure in the eye may result in the loss of side vision, blurred or fogged vision and the appearance of colored rings or halos around bright objects. In closed angle glaucoma, the drainage of aqueous humor from the chamber in front of the lens is disrupted by the narrowing of the exit channel at the angle between the iris and cornea.

GLOBULINS

Globulin is one of two types of proteins in the blood plasma, the other being albumin. Globulins can be divided into alpha, beta, and gamma subgroups. Alpha and beta globulins include fibrous and contractile proteins, transport proteins, and enzymes. Gamma globulins play a vital role in natural and acquired immunity to infection; they are manufactured by the immune system to help destroy or neutralize infection-causing bacteria. Gamma globulin (also known as antibodies) derived from blood of other humans can be used to induce temporary immunity to some diseases, for example hepatitis A.

SEE ALSO *Immunity, Plasma*

GLOMERULONEPHRITIS

Glomerulonephritis is inflammation of the glomeruli, the clusters of tiny blood vessels in the kidney that filter waste products from the bloodstream to form urine. Damaged glomeruli cannot filter these waste products, leading to serious kidney complications. The disease may be caused by specific problems with the body's immune system, but the precise cause of most cases is unknown. There are two types; acute and chronic.

Acute (sudden) glomerulonephritis sometimes follows a sore throat caused by a streptococcal infection and is more common in children than in adults. A few weeks after the onset of infection, the affected person notices smoky or slightly red urine, puffy eyes and ankles, a general ill feeling, drowsiness, nausea or vomiting, and headaches. Blood tests for kidney function reveal biochemical abnormalities in the blood, and the urine is found to have blood and protein in it. Mild cases are treated with bed rest, and by restricting salt and fluid intake.

Sometimes, and especially in adults, kidney dialysis is necessary until the kidneys recover.

Chronic glomerulonephritis develops slowly, and may not be detected until the kidneys fail, which may take 20–30 years. Because symptoms develop gradually, the disorder may only be discovered during a medical examination for some other problem. Or it may be discovered as an unexplained cause of hypertension. In other cases, there are symptoms, such as blood in the urine, or unexplained weight loss, nausea, vomiting, a general ill feeling, fatigue, headache, muscle cramps, seizures, increased skin pigmentation, bruising, confusion, or delirium. There may be signs of chronic renal failure such as edema and fluid overload.

The diagnosis can be confirmed with blood tests that show reduced kidney function, and a urine test that may show blood and proteins in the urine. Abdominal ultrasound, CAT scan, or intravenous pyelography may show scarred, shrunken kidneys. A kidney biopsy will reveal inflammation of the glomeruli.

In some cases of glomerulonephritis there is spontaneous remission. In other cases, treatment with corticosteroid or immunosuppressive drugs will bring about an improvement. However, many cases cannot be cured so the goal will be to manage symptoms for as long as possible.

Glomerulonephritis

Due to the inflammation of the capillary loops in the glomeruli, the kidneys are unable to filter waste products from the blood. This may lead to fluid retention in the legs, face and arms.

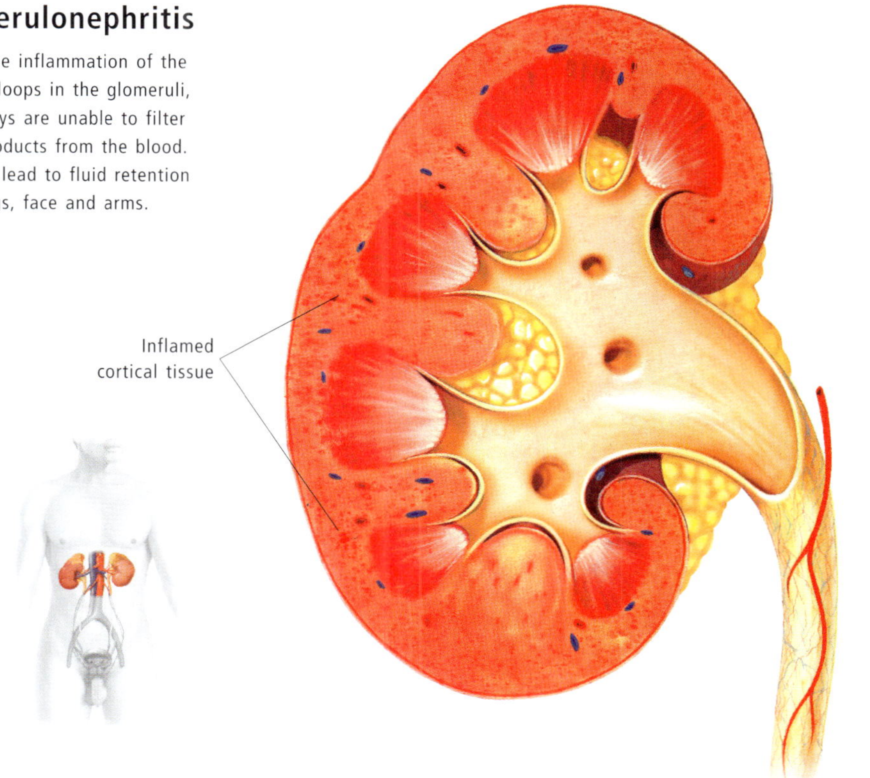

Various antihypertensive medications may be used to control high blood pressure along with dietary restrictions on salt, fluids and protein. In the end stages, regular kidney dialysis or kidney transplantation may be necessary.

SEE ALSO *Dialysis, Hypertension, Kidney, Urinary systems*

GLOSSITIS

Glossitis is inflammation of the tongue. Acute (sudden) glossitis often occurs in children; symptoms of acute glossitis include a painful, bright red, swollen tongue, which is sometimes ulcerated. There may be difficulty in swallowing, and the child may complain of an unpleasant taste in the mouth. Other mouth disorders such as gingivitis (inflammation of the gums) and stomatitis (inflammation of the mouth) may be present. Acute glossitis is treated with antiseptic mouthwashes and an anesthetic solution to reduce pain.

Chronic (long term) glossitis is associated in an adult with chronic ill health, anemia, poor nutrition, vitamin deficiencies, tooth infections, smoking, alcohol consumption, and occasionally as a side effect of antibiotic drugs. Chronic glossitis is treated by correcting the underlying cause.

SEE ALSO *Gingivitis, Tongue*

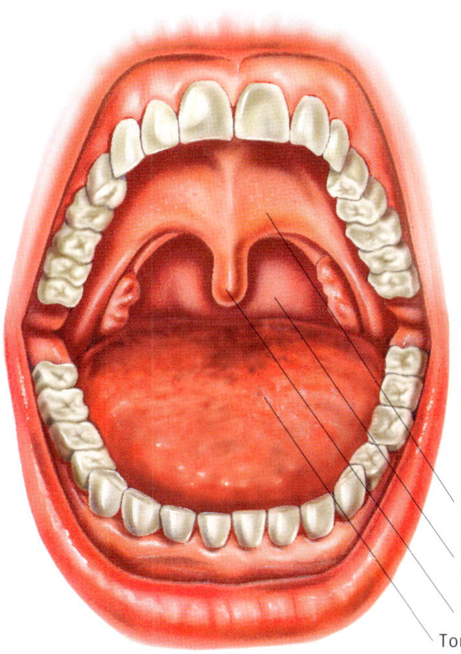

Glossitis

In glossitis the tongue becomes bright red and swollen.

GOITER

Goiter is an enlargement of the thyroid gland, which is located in the front of the neck. The thyroid gland makes the hormone thyroxine, that regulates the body's metabolism. Goiters can be associated with high, low and sometimes even normal thyroxine levels. Symptoms of goiter depend on thyroxine levels (too much leading to thyrotoxicosis; too little leading to myxedema); the goiter itself is only a problem if it affects breathing or swallowing.

The amount of thyroxine produced is regulated by a hormone from the pituitary gland called the thyroid stimulating hormone (TSH). If there is insufficient thyroxine, TSH will be released to stimulate the thyroid to produce more, and this can lead to enlargement of the gland (goiter). A common cause of goiter is a lack of iodine in the diet. With insufficient iodine, and low thyroxine levels, TSH production will increase to stimulate

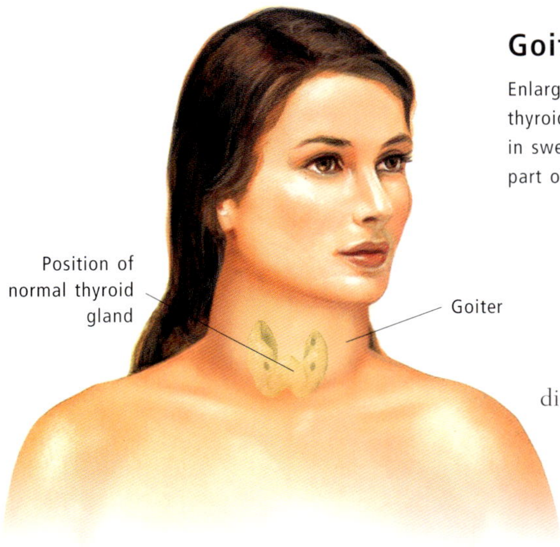

Goiter

Enlargement of the thyroid gland may result in swelling of the front part of the neck.

the thyroid to make more thyroxine. This type of goiter can be treated by addition of iodine to the diet.

Goiter can be caused by excess stimulation of the thyroid gland from other causes, such as abnormally high levels of TSH ocurring with pituitary tumors. Similarly, excess thyroid stimulation occurs in Graves' disease, an autoimmune disorder in which abnormal antibodies are produced that mimic TSH. Treatment can include medication, radioactive iodine, or surgery. Another autoimmune disorder, Hashimoto's disease, is associated with inflammation of the gland, goiter and low thyroxine levels.

SEE ALSO *Graves' disease, Hashimoto's disease, Myxedema, Thyroid gland, Thyrotoxicosis*

Gonorrhea bacteria

GONORRHEA

Gonorrhea is a common sexually transmitted disease caused by a bacterial infection (*Neisseria gonorrhoeae*). It is frequently transmitted during sexual intercourse, including both oral and anal sex.

Gonorrhea is most common in people aged 15–30 years. Risk of infection increases with multiple partners, partners with a history of infection, and unprotected intercourse.

In women the infection usually involves the cervix, although it may also spread to the vulva and vagina, urethra and fallopian tubes. Signs of infection include a vaginal discharge and pain on urinating although, in about half the cases, no symptoms may be noted. In some cases the rectum may become infected, causing discomfort in the anal region. Throat infections can occur following oral sex. Symptoms start 1–3 weeks after infection.

If the bacteria spread to the fallopian tubes (as happens in 10–15 percent of untreated cases) the condition is termed pelvic inflammatory disease (PID). PID can cause abdominal pain and may lead to blocked fallopian tubes and infertility. Approximately 50 percent of women will be unaware they have the disease and therefore may pass it on to unsuspecting sexual partners. On rare occasions the disease may be transmitted from mother to baby during childbirth, and may result in infection of the baby's eyes.

In males, gonorrhea usually affects the urethra and is associated with a discharge and pain on urinating. In homosexuals, infections of the throat, anus and rectum are common. In men the infection can spread to other regions of the reproductive tract, such as the epididymis and the prostate. In both sexes gonorrhea can occasionally (in about 1 percent of cases) lead to more widespread infection of the peritoneum, joints and blood, with abdominal pain, arthritis and fever.

Gonorrhea

Gonorrhea in men

A painful burning sensation during urination is an early sign of disease.

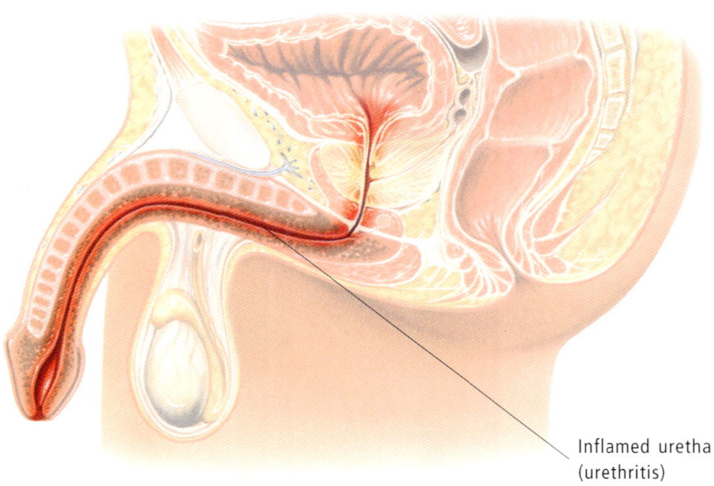

Gonorrhea in women

Women may experience no early symptoms, making gonorrhea difficult to diagnose.

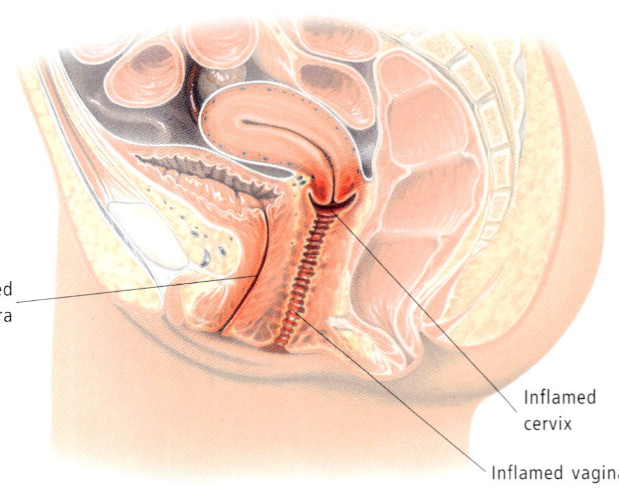

Diagnosis of gonorrhea is made by identifying the bacteria in the discharge, for example from the cervix, urethra or rectum. As many strains of gonorrhea have become resistant to common antibiotics, specific antibiotic courses are used. If the disease is treated early the prognosis is good. Gonorrhea is often associated with other sexually transmitted infections, including HIV, which should also be tested for. Patients should be advised to abstain from sexual contact until treatment for gonorrhea has been successfully completed. Also, all sexual contacts should be traced and tested for infection.

SEE ALSO *Pelvic inflammatory disease, Sexually transmitted diseases*

GOODPASTURE'S SYNDROME

Goodpasture's syndrome is a form of rapidly progressive inflammation of the kidney (glomerulonephritis) which results in progressive decrease in kidney function. The alveoli of the lung are also involved, producing a cough with bloody sputum. It is an autoimmune disorder, triggered in some cases by a viral illness or by sniffing glue or inhaling gasoline, resulting in the formation of antibodies by the body's immune system, which are deposited in the glomeruli of the kidneys and in lung tissue, damaging them. It is a rare disorder, seen most often in men ages 16–60, usually around 20 years old. It may develop after a recent viral respiratory infection, and smoking is known to increase the risk of developing the disorder.

The symptoms are blood in urine, poor urinary output, cough with blood in the sputum, difficulty breathing after exertion, and weakness and weight loss. As kidney function deteriorates there may be signs of kidney failure such as edema and fluid overload.

A blood test may show antibodies to the kidney and lung tissue. Lung and kidney biopsies will show the deposits in the lung and kidney tissue. Treatment is with corticosteroids, electrophoresis dialysis (a procedure by which blood plasma, which contains antibodies, is replaced with plasma free of antibodies), and kidney transplant. The prognosis is variable but is better if the condition is diagnosed and treated early.

SEE ALSO *Autoimmune disease, Glomerulonephritis, Kidney*

GOUT

Gout is an inflammation of the joints that is usually accompanied by the presence of excess uric acid (one of the body's waste products) in tissues in the body. If the uric acid level gets sufficiently high, needle-shaped crystals develop within a joint, leading to an inflammatory response in the joint. Gout most commonly occurs in the joint at the base of the big toe but it can affect other joints such as the hands, wrist, elbow and ankle. The attack usually starts suddenly, often at night, with the joint becoming red, swollen and very painful.

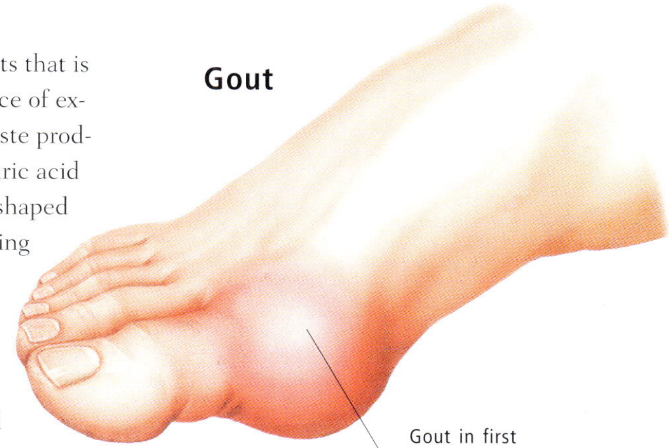

Gout is most common in middle-aged men, but can occur in women after menopause. The high levels of uric acid are basically due to either its overproduction or to not excreting enough, or a combination of both. Uric acid is formed from the breakdown of purines in the diet, which particularly come from offal, shellfish and some vegetables and fruits. Gout can also be aggravated by too much alcohol, which inhibits the excretion of uric acid by the kidneys. In rare cases, the overproduction of uric acid can be due to an inherited disorder of protein synthesis or to diseases which increase cell turnover.

The most common finding is reduced excretion of uric acid in the urine. Although the cause is often unclear, it can be aggravated by some drugs, such as diuretics, commonly used in the treatment of high blood pressure, and aspirin.

Besides being deposited in joints, crystals of urate may also be deposited in tissues around the joints and under the skin, for instance in the hands, elbows and around the ear. These deposits are called tophi; those under the skin can be felt as hard nodules. The presence of tophi in the joints, which can be seen on x-rays, can lead to arthritis and joint erosion. Crystals can also be deposited in the kidneys, where they are known as kidney stones. These may cause kidney damage, obstruction of urine flow, or painful renal colic as the stones are passed out of the body.

The diagnosis of gout can be made by measuring the uric acid levels in the blood, and by finding urate crystals within a joint. Gout is treated by anti-inflammatory drugs to reduce the pain and joint inflammation. Aspirin should not be used because it actually inhibits uric acid excretion. After the acute attack passes, long-term medication with drugs such as allopurinol can reduce the production of the uric acid. This can help to prevent future attacks, and if uric acid levels can be lowered sufficiently, may lead to resorption of some tophi and therefore prevent further joint destruction. High fluid intake is also helpful, especially for patients with kidney stones. If uric acid levels are untreated attacks usually become more common, and can lead to permanent joint damage and deformity.

SEE ALSO *Arthritis, Joints*

GRAAFIAN FOLLICLE

At puberty the average woman has about 300,000 egg cells (ova) lying dormant within her ovaries. When she becomes sexually reproductive, some 20 ova (each contained within its own sac-like structure known as a follicle) begin to ripen at the beginning of each menstrual cycle. Usually just one follicle becomes dominant and continues development while the others, and the eggs they contain, shrivel up. This remaining follicle ultimately matures into a Graafian follicle, named after the seventeenth-century Dutch physician Reijnier de Graaf.

The Graafian follicle has a diameter of about $^{1}/_{2}$ inch (12 millimeters), is composed of an outer wall three to four cells thick surrounding follicular fluid, and a mature ovum; it produces the hormone estrogen which prepares the uterus for pregnancy. During ovulation it ruptures, releasing the ovum which is then swept into the

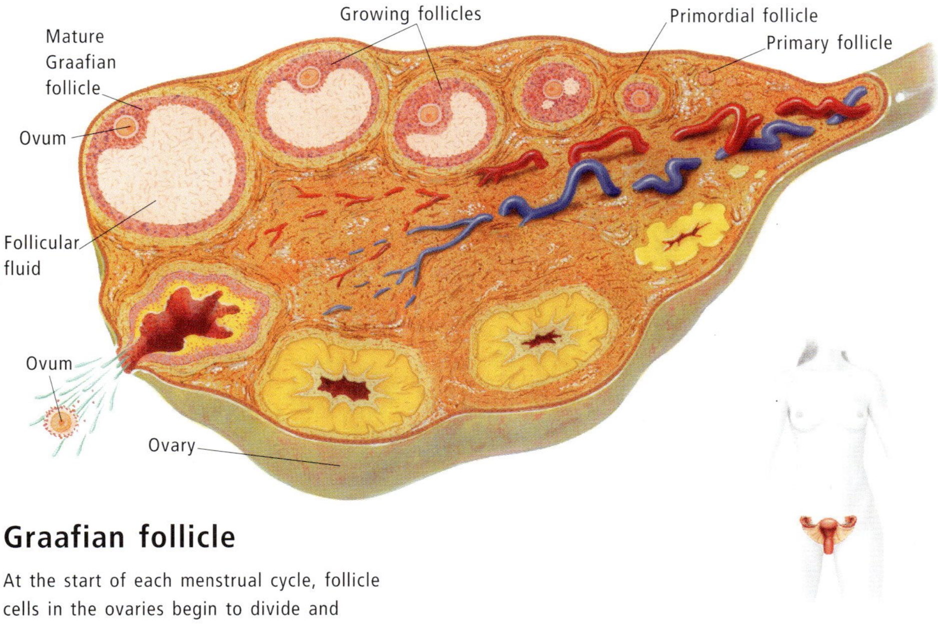

Graafian follicle

At the start of each menstrual cycle, follicle cells in the ovaries begin to divide and produce the hormone estrogen which prepares the uterus for pregnancy and stimulates an ovum (egg) to mature. By days 8–10 one follicle is dominant and develops into a Graafian follicle—a sac-like structure containing a mature ovum. The follicle releases its ovum into the fallopian tube during ovulation, then collapses.

fallopian tubes where it may be fertilized by a sperm. The remaining follicle collapses on itself, its cells enlarge and the structure develops into the corpus luteum, or yellow body, which produces the hormones progesterone and estradiol.

If conception fails to take place, the corpus luteum ceases development after about 14 days and degenerates. If, however, the ovum is fertilized, the corpus luteum continues development and plays an important role during pregnancy.

SEE ALSO *Fertilization, Menstruation, Ovaries, Ovulation, Ovum, Pregnancy, Reproductive systems*

GRAFTING

Grafting is a medical procedure used to repair or replace damaged, defective or diseased parts of the body. It usually involves isolating and removing living tissue and joining it to other living tissue in either the same or a different person. (In some cases, the grafted tissue may come from an animal or it may be produced synthetically.)

Grafts, which are also known as transplants, may be portions of tissue such as skin, bone, nerves, blood vessels or muscle, or they may be complete organs, such as the heart, liver or kidneys. When a graft is intended as a permanent transplant it should grow and fuse with other tissues at its new location and ultimately function as normal.

There are several different types of grafts. In an autograft, tissue is taken from the body of an individual and relocated to another area on the same person. Skin, bone and cartilage are tissues commonly used in autografts. An allograft or homograft is tissue removed from one person (known as the donor) and implanted in another person (the recipient). Some organs used as allografts can be provided by living people. These include bone marrow and kidneys. But organs such as the heart and corneas (in the eyes) can only be used after a person has died.

Whenever tissue is taken from one person and grafted into another, there is always a risk the recipient's immune system will treat the donated material as foreign and trigger a serious response known as rejection. This often occurs between 4 and 15 days after a graft, though it may not appear for a year or more. Rejection is characterized by fever, and pain and function loss in the grafted area. A system of cross-matching the tissues of donors and recipients, similar to blood typing, helps reduce the severity of rejection. Powerful immunosuppressive drugs are also used to reduce rejection reactions.

SEE ALSO *Immunosuppression, Lymphatic/Immune system, Transplant surgery*

GRANULOMA INGUINALE

Granuloma inguinale is a sexually transmitted disease (STD) marked by the appearance of painless red ulcers on or close to the genitals that appear within 60 days of infectious contact. Lymph nodes are not affected but the ulcers will bleed easily on contact. They may also be subject to futher infection.

Rare in industrialized nations, granuloma inguinale is a bacterial infection caused by *Calymmatobacterium granulomatis* and is found mainly in tropical areas, including India, Africa and Papua New Guinea. Treatment with streptomycin and broad spectrum antibiotics is usually successful although relapse can occur any time from 6–18 months later.

SEE ALSO *Sexually transmitted diseases*

GRAVES' DISEASE

Graves' disease is associated with overactivity of the thyroid gland. The thyroid gland secretes thyroid hormones important for the control of body metabolism. The thyroid gland is regulated by the pituitary gland, which secretes thyroid stimulating

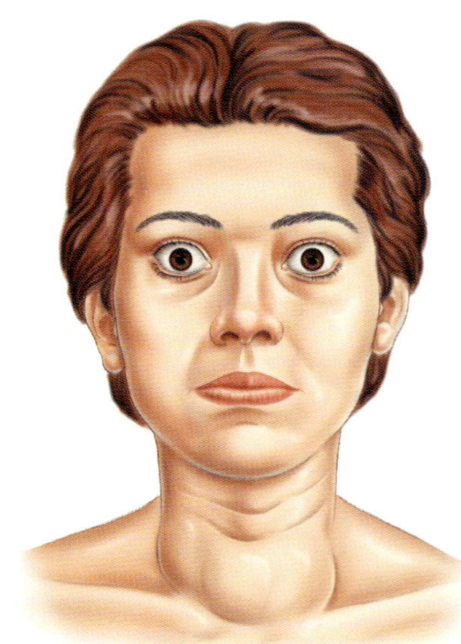

Graves' disease

Exophthalmos (abnormally protruding eyes, as if staring) is a common feature of this disease.

hormone (TSH). Graves' disease is due to the body producing antibodies which mimic TSH and stimulate the thyroid gland to secrete large amounts of thyroid hormone. The thyroid gland enlarges (causing a goiter) and symptoms include feeling hot, and having increased sweating, weight loss and muscle weakness, rapid heart rate and palpitations, frequent bowel movements, nervousness and anxiety. Exophthalmos (abnormally protruding eyes, as if staring) is another common feature of this disease.

Graves' disease can be treated with antithyroid drugs, radioactive iodine or surgery to remove a portion of the thyroid gland.

SEE ALSO *Exophthalmos, Goiter, Pituitary gland, Thyroid gland*

GRIEF

Grief is an intense basic emotion, described as a feeling of sharp sorrow at a potential or real loss. Grief may be felt for many reasons, such as the loss of a loved one, job, possessions, home, or body part or function. Each person experiences grief differently, but there are reactions which most experience.

The initial reaction is usually shock at the loss. Sometimes, in the case of death, if the loved one has died from a prolonged illness, the shock will be less as people will have had time to prepare themselves for the loss.

Emotional release through crying is a healthy expression of grief and a beneficial release of tension. Depression, loneliness and a feeling of isolation may also accompany feelings of grief. This can be particularly true for someone who has lost their life partner. Physical reactions to a severe loss such as death may also be experienced. This can include loss of appetite, overeating, sleeplessness and sexual difficulties. Panic may follow. It is important to avoid using drugs and alcohol at this time as not only is there a risk of dependence, but the substances may also hinder the necessary grieving process.

Guilt, real or imagined, is another common reaction. Feelings of "if only" may be thought or expressed. Anger, which, like guilt, needs to be expressed and worked through, is another common reaction. Some find that they are unable to return to usual activities. In most cases, however, the person will start to heal, with a gradual regaining of hope and acceptance as they adjust their lives to the reality of their loss.

Children experience grief differently to adults. Although they may feel the loss acutely, they commonly show it in less direct ways than adults do and can move in and out of grieving—sometimes showing what seems like a callous disregard for the loss. Very young children do not understand that death is permanent. Children in the early years of school will likewise not understand the permanency and may worry about their own situation and ask lots of questions. By the time they are ten, children will be able to understand the permanency of death. Their strong sense of right and wrong will be challenged and they may be interested in religious explanations. Children need careful attention and support when they are grieving; just because they appear not to be suffering does not mean they are not feeling the loss.

Groin

This is the name given to the junctional region between abdomen and thigh. Groin strain occurs in this area when the muscles are overextended.

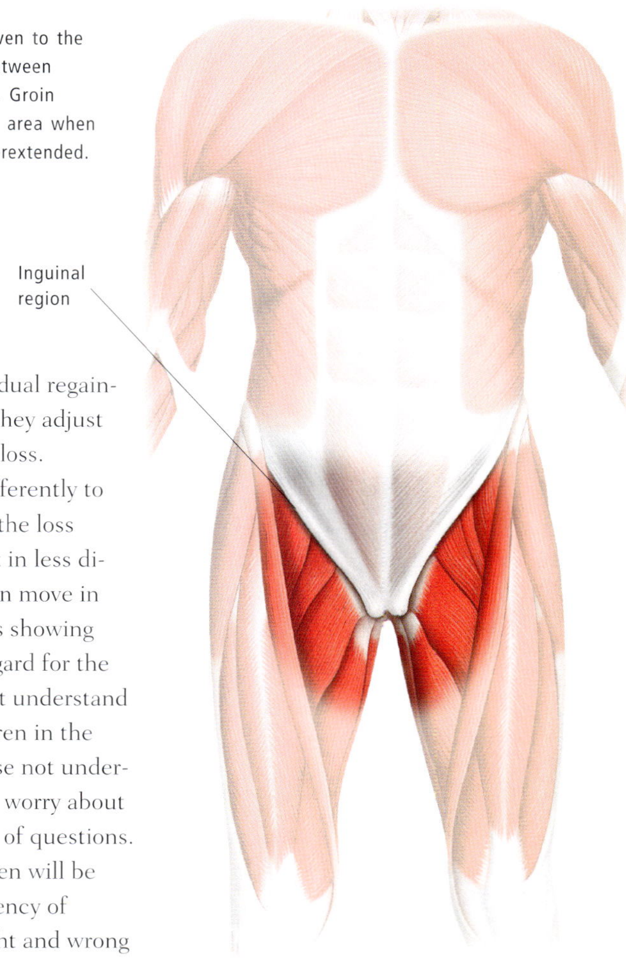

GROIN

The groin (inguinal region) is where the abdomen joins the front of the thigh. Groin strain occurs when muscles in this region are pulled. Groin swellings may be the result of a hernia, which occurs when part of the gut is forced into the front of the thigh under pressure through a weakness in the abdominal wall in the region of the inguinal canal. If painful, medical advice should be sought, because the gut may become damaged. The groin also contains lymph nodes (also known as lymph glands), and these can swell if inflamed, for instance with infections in the leg. Tinea cruris (jock itch) is a fungal infection that occurs in the groin, particularly in men.

SEE ALSO *Hernia, Lymph glands*

GROWTH

Growth is the process by which the body and its various parts increase in size and reach maturity. It is largely controlled by hormones, the secretion of which is influenced by a large number of interrelated factors, ranging from genetics and nutrition to environment, hygiene and disease.

Most people continue to grow in height until the long bones of the body cease expanding, which usually occurs around the age of 18 years. Although the rate and times at which individuals grow vary considerably, most people experience two significant periods of accelerated growth en route to reaching adulthood. The first of these periods occurs during the 12 months after birth. On average, a healthy baby triples its birth weight by the age of one year, while increasing its height by about 50 percent. The other notable growth spurt occurs during puberty, in the early to mid-teens, when most people shoot upwards by about 20 percent of their final adult height. Growth rates for boys during this period can reach as much as $3\frac{1}{2}$ inches (9 centimeters) a year.

Among the many hormones affecting growth in the body, the most significant is human growth hormone (hGH) which is released by the pituitary gland in the brain. Too little hGH during childhood and adolescent development leads to dwarfism. Too much causes gigantism.

SEE ALSO *Dwarfism, Gigantism, Growth disorders, Hormones, Infancy, Pituitary gland, Puberty*

GROWTH DISORDERS

Human growth is controlled by hormones, especially growth hormone. Excessive production of growth hormone by the anterior part of the pituitary gland in adulthood causes acromegaly, a disorder in which the bones in the arms and legs, hands, feet, jaw, and skull get thicker and longer. Facial features become coarser, and the voice may become deeper. If the condition occurs before puberty, it results in gigantism, causing excessive size and stature. Treatment is surgery or radiation therapy on the pituitary gland.

A deficiency of growth hormone causes dwarfism. The affected person has normal body proportions but is smaller than normal. Administration of growth hormone to patients with pituitary dwarfism may induce skeletal growth. Dwarfism may also be caused by malnutrition and chronic illness.

SEE ALSO *Achondroplasia, Acromegaly, Dwarfism, Gigantism*

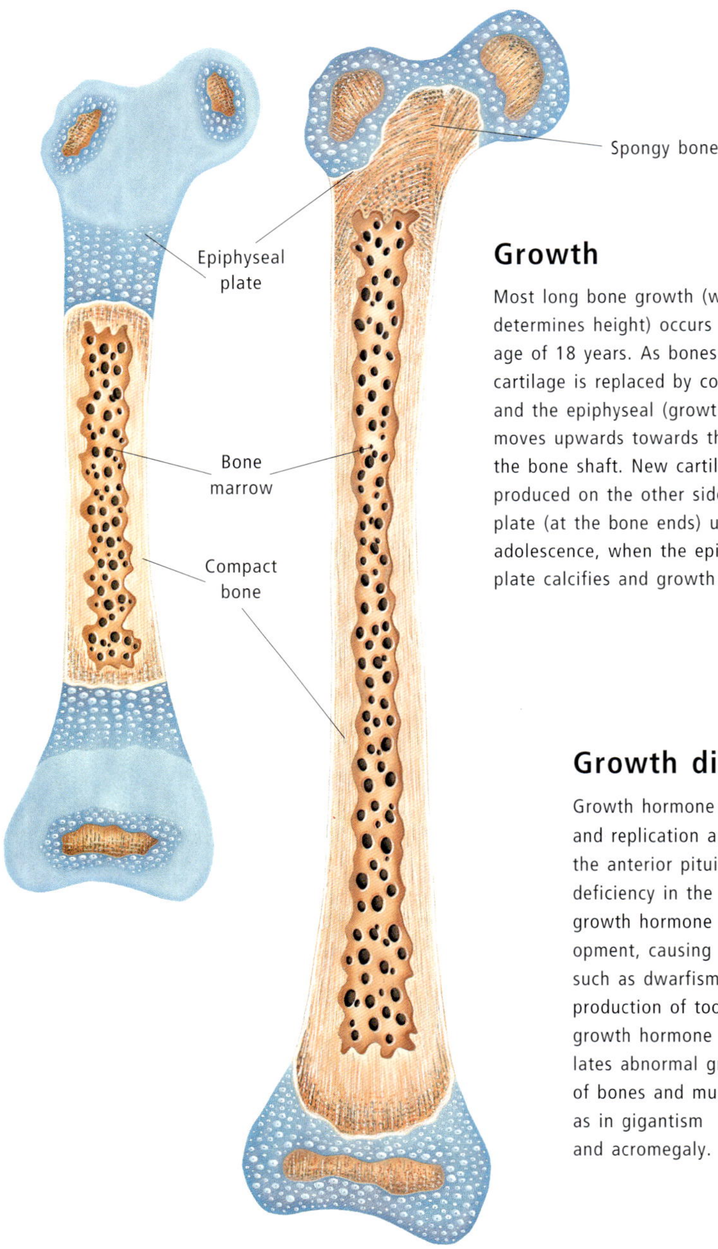

Growth

Most long bone growth (which determines height) occurs before the age of 18 years. As bones elongate, cartilage is replaced by compact bone and the epiphyseal (growth) plate moves upwards towards the end of the bone shaft. New cartilage is produced on the other side of the plate (at the bone ends) until late adolescence, when the epiphyseal plate calcifies and growth ceases.

GUILLAIN-BARRÉ SYNDROME

Guillain-Barré syndrome (also called acute inflammatory polyneuropathy) is an inflammatory disorder of the peripheral nerves. It starts suddenly (usually over days) with muscle weakness in the legs and arms, associated with numbness in the feet and hands. The weakness may spread to muscles in the face and trunk, and there may be difficulty swallowing or breathing. The syndrome usually follows an infectious illness and is thought to involve an autoimmune attack on the nerves. Damage to the nerves involves loss of the myelin sheath surrounding nerve fibers. This results in the loss of signals going along the nerves to control the muscles or provide sensation.

Guillain-Barré syndrome can be diagnosed by observing the rapid onset of weakness and the loss of reflexes and sensation on both sides of the body. Diagnosis is confirmed by lumbar puncture, from which cerebrospinal fluid is withdrawn for protein analysis; increased protein concentration indicates disease. If the disease progresses rapidly with serious complications, patients need to be hospitalized and monitored constantly. The airway must be kept clear and respiration supported artificially if necessary. Treatment may involve exchanging the patient's blood plasma for normal plasma, or replacing albumin and blood cells. Most patients recover but some may be left with muscle weakness and may require physical therapy and rehabilitation. If symptoms are relieved within three weeks of their onset the outcome is usually good.

SEE ALSO *Nerves, Neuropathy*

Growth disorders

Growth hormone controls cell growth and replication and is produced by the anterior pituitary gland. A deficiency in the production of growth hormone inhibits development, causing disorders such as dwarfism. The production of too much growth hormone stimulates abnormal growth of bones and muscles as in gigantism and acromegaly.

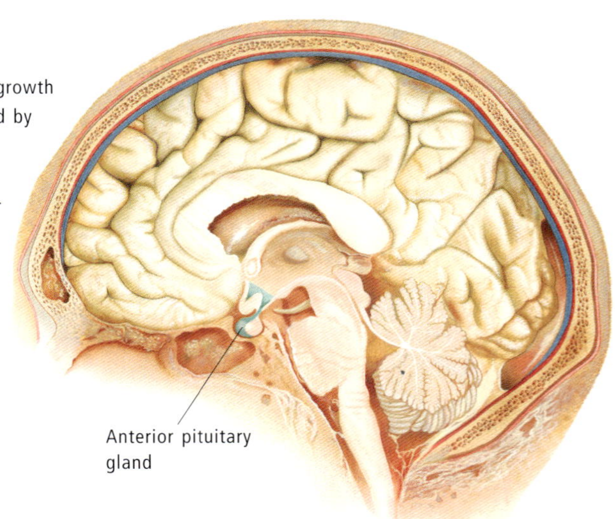

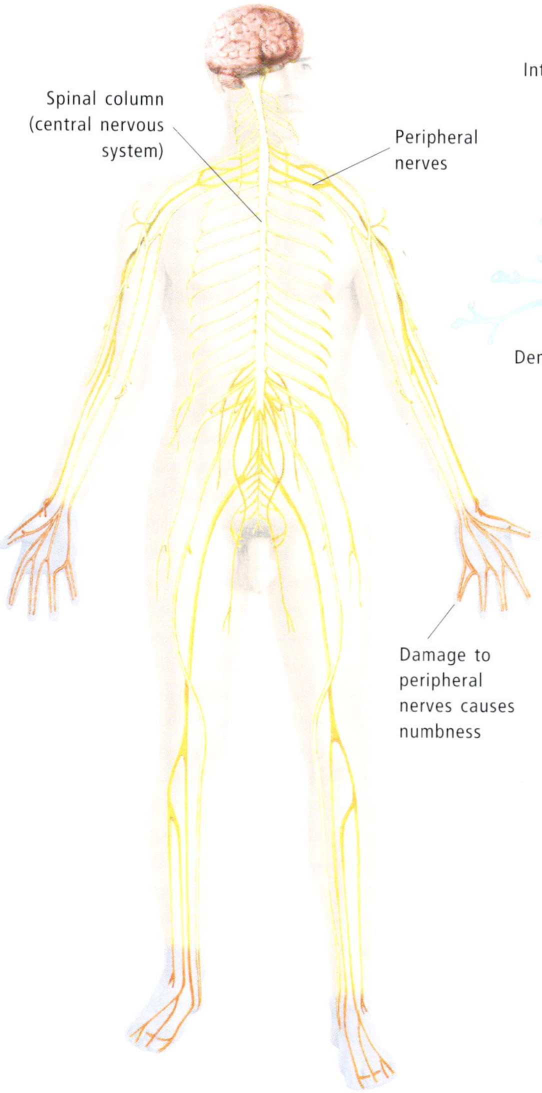

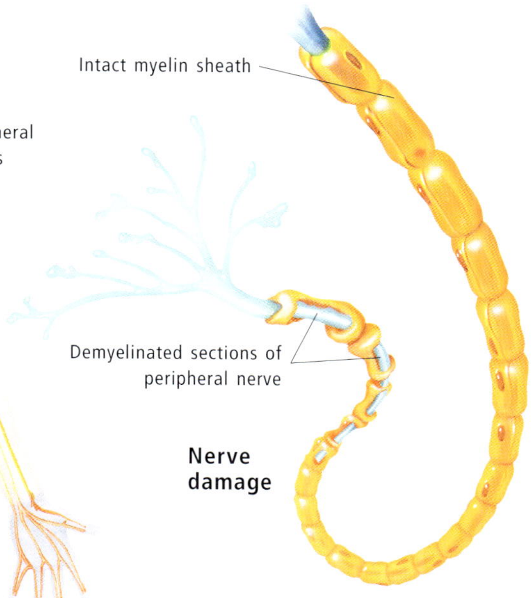

Guillain-Barré syndrome

Demyelination (loss of the myelin sheath surrounding nerve fibers) in this disorder results in numbness in the feet and hands and muscle weakness in the legs and arms. If weakness spreads to muscles in the face and trunk it may be difficult to breathe or eat.

GUMS

The gums (gingivae) are the soft tissue covering the upper and lower jaws, inside the mouth. They extend from inside the lips, around and between the teeth, to the floor of the mouth (lower jaw) and the palate (upper jaw). The gums are kept moist by saliva and receive sensory nerves, similar to the skin. The gums are attached around the neck of the teeth, where food particles can become lodged and cause gum inflammation (gingivitis). Swelling, ulcers or discoloration of the gums may indicate more widespread disease and should be investigated. Severe lack of vitamin C (scurvy) also leads to swollen and bleeding gums and loose teeth.

SEE ALSO *Gingivitis, Teeth*

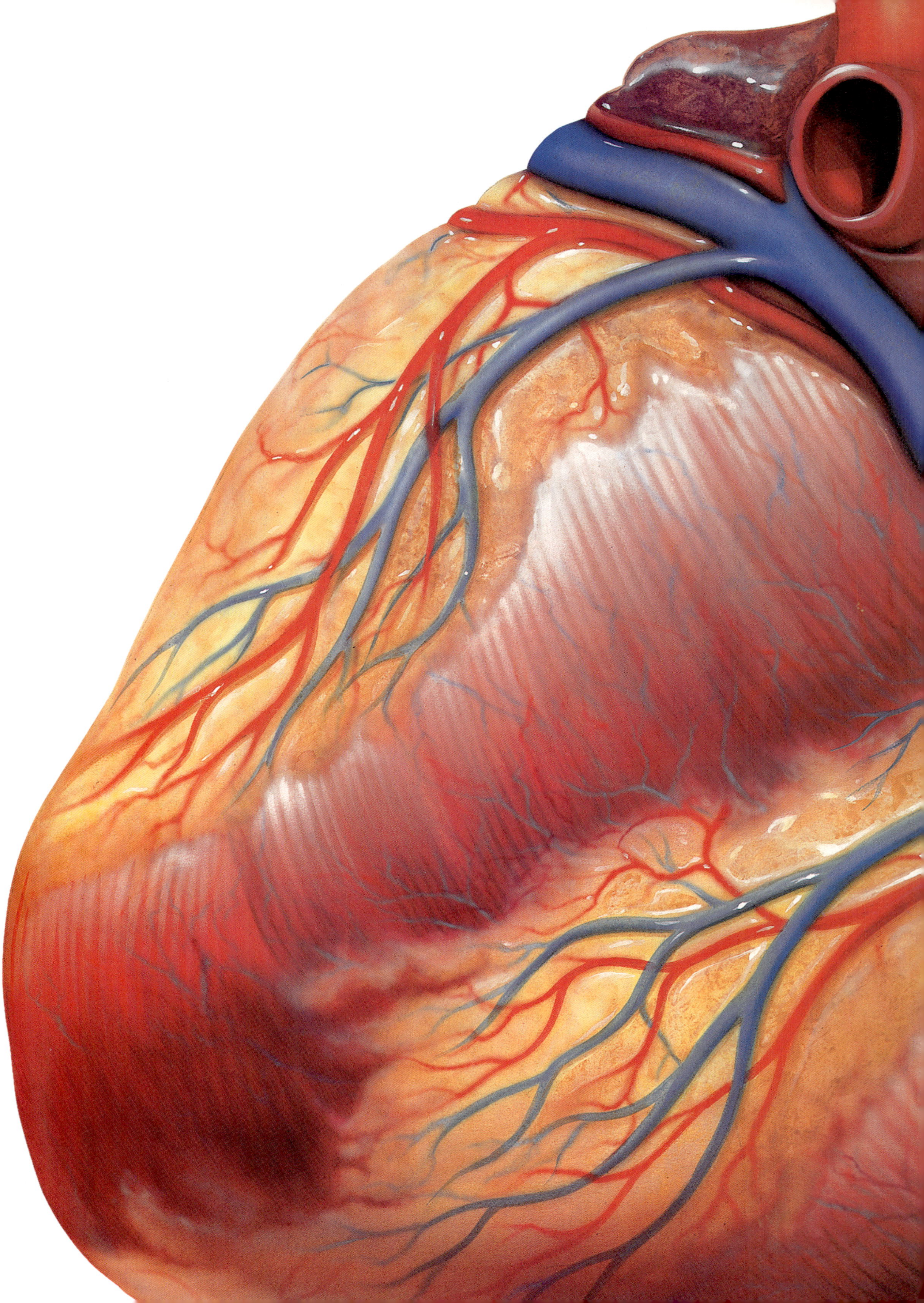

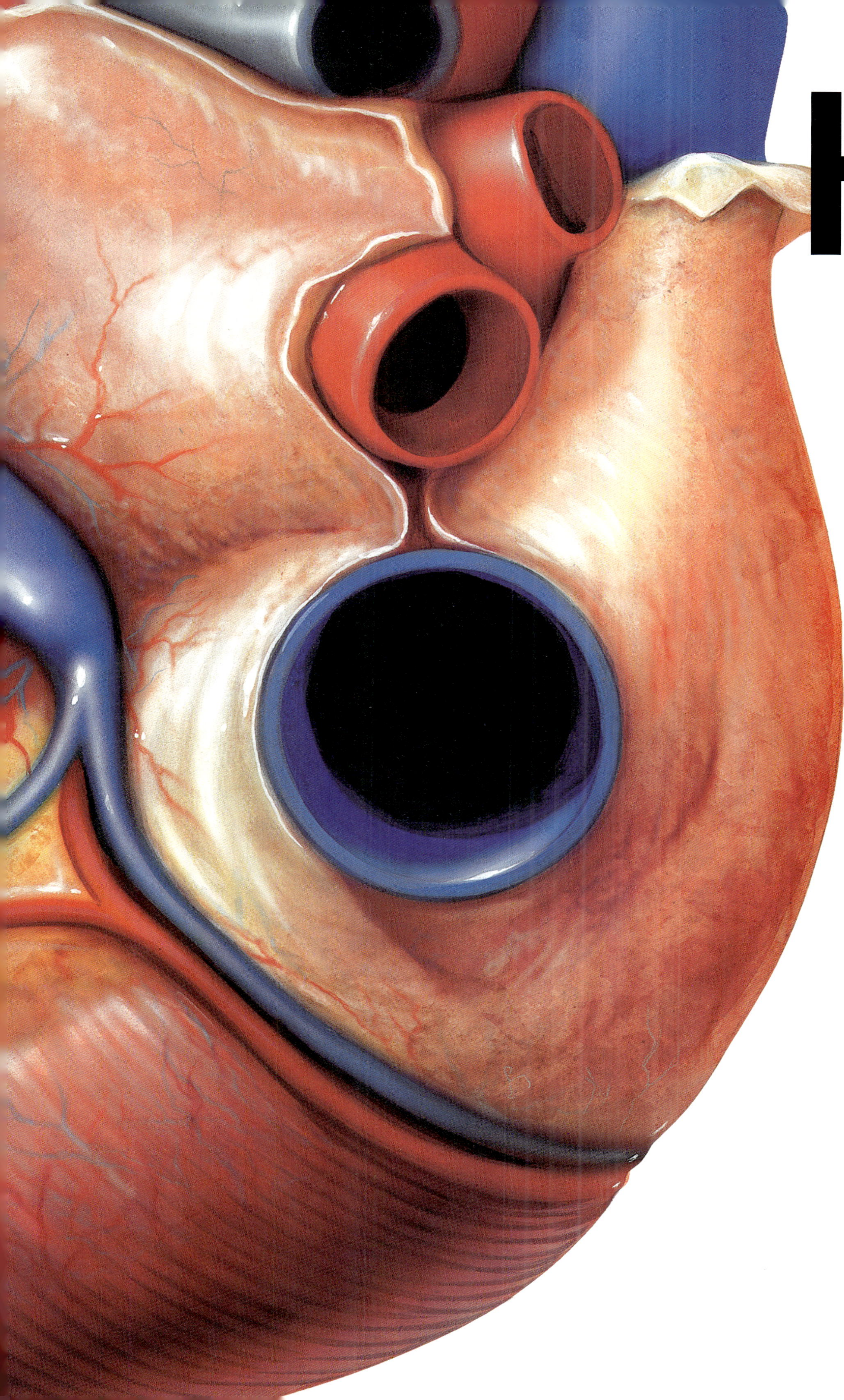

H

HAIR

Hair is a fine, threadlike structure, made of a tough protein called keratin. It is produced only by mammals and is an identifying character of that group of animals. Hair consists of a root, embedded in the skin, and a shaft, projecting from the skin surface. The root ends in a soft, whitish enlargement, the hair bulb, which is lodged in an elongated pit in the skin, called the follicle.

The hair grows upwards from the base of the follicle at the rate of about ⅓ millimeter a day. Blood vessels arranged in a small protrusion known as a papilla extend up into the follicle and the root of the hair and nourish it. Attached to each hair follicle is a tiny muscle called the erector pili. This muscle is under the control of the autonomic nervous system and under certain conditions, for example in the cold, it contracts to make the hair stand on end.

Individual hairs are composed of dead epithelial cells containing keratin, arranged in columns around a central core. The cells also contain varying amounts of the dark pigment melanin, which is responsible for the color of the hair. With age, less pigment is deposited into these cells, so hairs tend to become white.

Hair has a protective function. Hair around the eyes, ears and nose serves to prevent dust, insects and other matter from entering these organs. The eyebrows decrease the amount of light that is reflected into the eyes.

Hair color is genetically determined. Dark hair color usually dominates over light hair color. For example, if a child has one parent with black or brown hair and one with red or blond hair, the child's hair is likely to be dark.

Hair loss

All body hair falls out gradually and is replaced by new hair. Baldness (alopecia) results when hair replacement fails to keep up with hair loss. It may have several causes, including ageing and genetic factors. It occurs more frequently in men than in

Hair follicle

The shaft of the hair projects from the skin's surface. The root is embedded in the skin—it ends in a bulb, which is lodged in a pit known as the follicle.

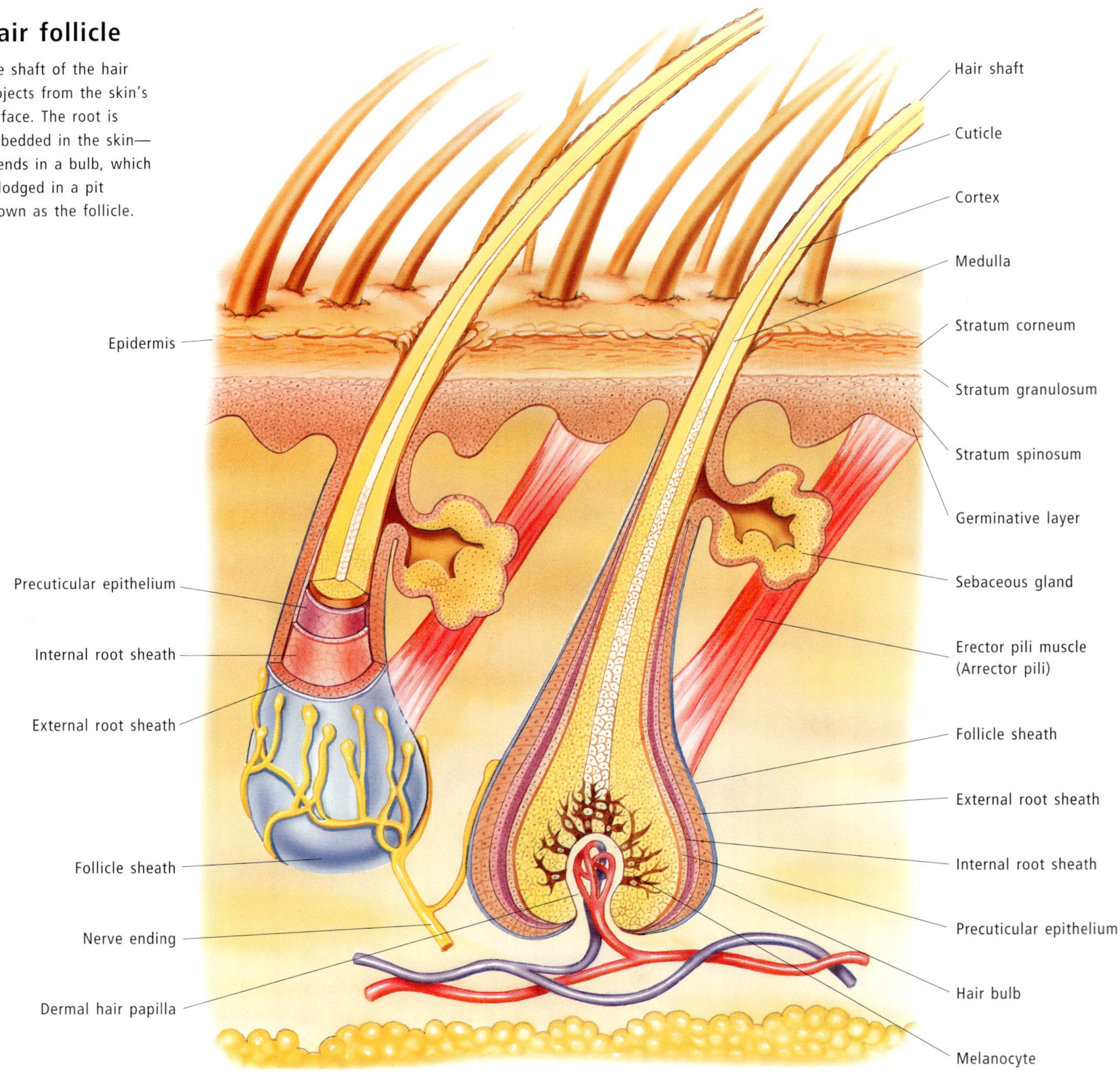

women. Partial hair loss may affect women after menopause. Sometimes hair loss occurs after a severe emotional shock, a severe illness, or childbirth.

Some medications, such as Minoxidil, may slow or prevent hair loss. Minoxidil must be used continually, as hair loss resumes when the drug is stopped. A hair transplant involves surgically replacing non-productive hair follicles with productive follicles from another area of the scalp. The procedure is expensive and the results vary.

SEE ALSO *Baldness*

HALITOSIS

Halitosis is an unpleasant, disagreeable or offensive breath odor. Poor oral hygiene is the leading cause of halitosis, though it may also be due to eating smelly foods such as onion or garlic, or to smoking. It may be a symptom of an underlying illness, such as alcoholism, throat infection, sinusitis, lung infection, gum disease (gingivitis), tooth abscess, or a foreign body in the nose (usually in children). Occasionally it may be due to more serious disease such as acute renal failure, chronic renal failure or bowel obstruction.

The condition is treated by improving oral hygiene (brushing teeth more frequently, rinsing with a mouth rinse, and visiting a dentist regularly) and by treating any underlying disorder.

SEE ALSO *Gingivitis, Gums, Teeth*

HALLUCINATION

A hallucination is a false perception of vision, sound, taste, smell or touch. Though the person experiences the sensation as real, no stimulus actually exists. Visual hallucinations are the most common type. Hallucinations may occur in a variety of states of altered consciousness such as prolonged wakefulness, while under hypnosis, in delirium, or after taking mind-altering drugs such as marijuana, mescaline or lysergic acid diethylamide (LSD). Alcoholics can also experience hallucinations.

Auditory hallucinations may occur in schizophrenia, in which a sufferer hears what are believed to be "voices". These hallucinations may lead to panic attacks or even suicide.

The exact cause of hallucinations is unknown, but it is thought that, like dreams, they may be unconscious expressions of memories that erupt when the normal attention mechanisms of the brain are diminished.

SEE ALSO *Alcoholism, Delirium, Hallucinogens, Schizophrenia*

HALLUCINOGENS

An hallucinogen, or hallucinogenic drug, sometimes called a psychedelic or mind-expanding drug, temporarily changes the functioning of the brain.

Hallucinogens affect the senses, emotions, and reasoning, distorting the perception of self and surroundings.

In Western countries, laws prohibit the manufacture, distribution and possession of these drugs, except in government-approved research. Nevertheless, hallucinogens such as LSD are available on black markets, sold as "trips". Less widely available are hallucinogens derived from plants, for example, peyote and mescaline.

Some drug users claim that, during a trip, they have gained a new understanding of themselves. Others have "bad trips"—acute panic or paranoid reactions which may resemble schizophrenia.

Some users of hallucinogens afterwards suffer "flashbacks", which can last for months or years.

SEE ALSO *Drug dependence*

HAMMER TOE

A hammer toe is a deformity in which the toe is bent in the shape of a hammer. Although any toe may be affected, it usually affects the second toe.

The condition may be congenital or it may be acquired, occurring most often in children who have outgrown their shoes. In older people it may be caused by pressure from a bunion.

Hammer toe is best prevented by making sure footwear fits correctly. A physician can treat mild cases by manipulating the toe and then splinting it. Corns can be treated with corn pads. In severe cases, surgery may be needed to straighten the joint.

SEE ALSO *Foot*

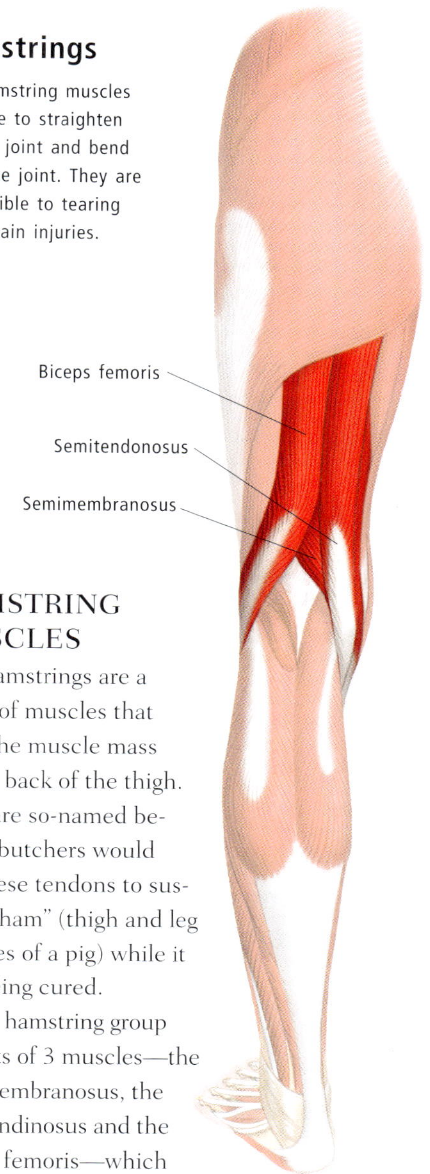

Hamstrings

The hamstring muscles are able to straighten the hip joint and bend the knee joint. They are susceptible to tearing and sprain injuries.

HAMSTRING MUSCLES

The hamstrings are a group of muscles that form the muscle mass on the back of the thigh. They are so-named because butchers would use these tendons to suspend "ham" (thigh and leg muscles of a pig) while it was being cured.

The hamstring group consists of 3 muscles—the semimembranosus, the semitendinosus and the biceps femoris—which are all attached above to the ischium (part of the pelvis). In the middle of the thigh they separate so the biceps femoris tendon passes behind the outside of the knee to reach the fibula, and the semimembranosus and semitendinosus tendons pass behind the inside of the knee to reach the tibia. These tendons can be easily felt on either side, just behind the knee when it is bent.

Because the hamstrings pass behind both the hip and knee joints they are able to cause movements at both joints but they are also more vulnerable to injury (tearing). The hamstrings function to extend (straighten) the hip joint and flex (bend) the knee joint.

A hamstring muscle may be torn or strained when it is suddenly and forcefully contracted, usually when it is either not properly warmed up, or fatigued.

SEE ALSO *Fibula, Hip, Knee, Tibia*

HAND

The hand is designed to grasp and manipulate objects. It consists of the palm, or front of the hand, the dorsum or back, and the thumb and fingers. Between the wrist bones (carpals) and finger bones (phalanges) are five metacarpal bones. The metacarpals join the bones of the fingers, the phalanges ("phalanx" is the term for a single one) in the metacarpophalangeal (MCP) joints.

The metacarpal bones can be easily felt through the skin over the back of the hand. The first metacarpal, between the wrist and thumb, is particularly mobile, allowing the thumb a wide range of movements. The fifth metacarpal can be fractured relatively easily. Between the metacarpals and the dorsal skin of the back of the hand are long tendons which pull the fingers and thumb backwards (extension) and a network of veins draining blood from the fingers and hand.

The palm has a slightly hollowed surface, that helps with gripping objects, and it is covered by thick skin which is tightly bound to the tissue below. The creases on the skin of the palm are the result of flexing the thumb and fingers and their joints. The palm also contains tendons, which bend the fingers forward (flexion), and two soft bulges due to the thenar and hypothenar muscles.

The thenar muscles form the fleshy prominence between the wrist and the thumb and contribute to thumb movements. These include the important movement of opposition by which the thumb can be touched to the tips of the fingers.

The hypothenar group lies along the side of the palm, between the wrist and little finger. The interosseus muscles lie between each of the metacarpal bones and move the fingers apart (abduction) and back together (adduction), as well as helping with flexion of the MCP joints and extension of the fingers. The thumb has a separate adductor muscle to move it towards the palm.

Besides these muscle groups there are four thin, worm-like muscles, the lumbricals, which connect between the long flexor tendons and the fingers and also assist with MCP flexion and finger extension.

Sheets of connective tissue, known as septa, separate the palm into compartments: the thenar and hypothenar compartments; a central compartment containing the long flexor tendons, blood vessels and nerves; and an adductor compartment for the thumb adductor. These compartments can become infected, but can also help to contain infections within their boundaries. Treatment with antibiotics is needed.

The long tendons are surrounded by synovial sheaths containing fluid which lubricates the tendons. These sheaths can become inflamed (tenosynovitis) through injury or excess use (in repetitive strain injury, for example). Treatment is by immobilization of the limb.

The four fingers are referred to as the index, middle, ring and little finger. They each contain three bones or phalanges, with hinge joints between them. The thumb has only two bones, the proximal and distal phalanx, again with a hinge joint between. The fingers contain no muscles, and are moved by tendons connected to muscles in the palm or forearm. Their tips are protected by nails on the dorsal (back) surface.

The fingertips are covered in a unique

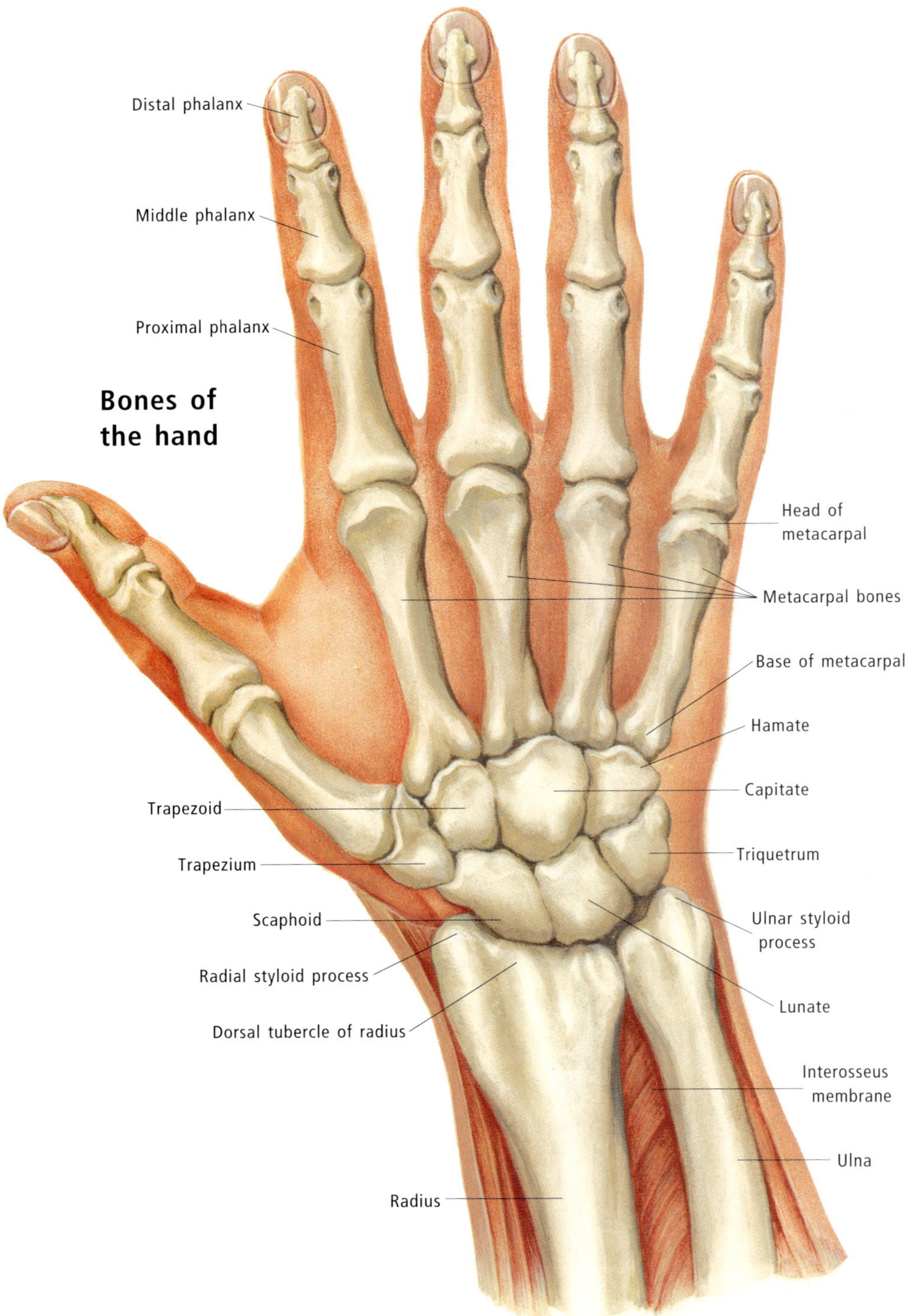

Bones of the hand

pattern of skin ridges, and these ridges give us our fingerprints.

The hand is supplied by two arteries, the radial artery on the same side as the thumb, and the ulnar artery on the other side. These two arteries join to form two arches in the palm. The digital arteries branch off from these arches and run down each side of the fingers.

Three large nerves—the ulnar, median and radial—supply the muscles and skin of the hand. The ulnar nerve supplies the hypothenar, interosseus muscles, the thumb adductor and two of the lumbricals, as well as the skin over the little finger and the adjacent side of the ring finger. The median nerve supplies the thenar muscles and the remaining two lumbricals, together with the skin of the palm, thumb, index, middle and adjacent side of the ring finger.

The sensory nerve supply (innervation) of the fingertips is particularly rich, providing for sensitive, delicate tactile discrimination. The radial nerve does not supply any hand muscles, but innervates the skin over most of the back (dorsum) of the hand and the back of the thumb.

The hand is involved in holding objects in two rather different ways, referred to as the power grip and precision grip.

In the power grip, used for carrying heavy bags or for holding tight to a support, objects are grasped in the palm, with much of the muscle power coming from flexor muscles in the forearm. Long flexor tendons run from the forearm to the fingers and thumb, so that the digits can be held tightly around the object. Muscles within the hand may also be active but the large forearm flexors are particularly important.

The precision grip is used for delicate manipulation of an object, for example, when writing, sewing or drawing. The thumb is opposed to one or more of the fingertips, involving the thenar and adductor muscles. Precision grip particularly involves muscles within the hand, most of which are controlled by the ulnar nerve, except for the thenar muscles of the thumb, controlled by the median nerve.

Injury to any of the hand nerves causes a unique group of problems. Damage to the ulnar nerve causes loss of abduction and adduction movements of the fingers, and loss of sensation in the little finger. The hand develops a deformity called clawhand in which the fourth and fifth MCP joints are extended and the fingers flexed.

The median nerve can be damaged by cuts to the wrist or by compression, such as in carpal tunnel syndrome. This causes weakness or loss of opposition of the thumb, and loss of sensation in the thumb and fingertips.

Radial nerve injury in the hand only affects sensation over the back of the hand. However, radial nerve injury in the arm leads to inability to extend the hand, and the hand flexes at the wrist (wrist drop). Since it is not possible to have a firm power grip when the wrist is flexed, wrist drop makes it difficult to hold implements (knife, fork, hairbrush, etc). This can be helped by a brace which holds the wrist in a slightly extended position.

SEE ALSO *Adduction and abduction, Arteries, Carpal tunnel syndrome, Finger, Muscle, Nerves, Radial nerve, Skeletal system, Tenosynovitis, Ulnar nerve, Wrist*

Muscles and tendons of the hand

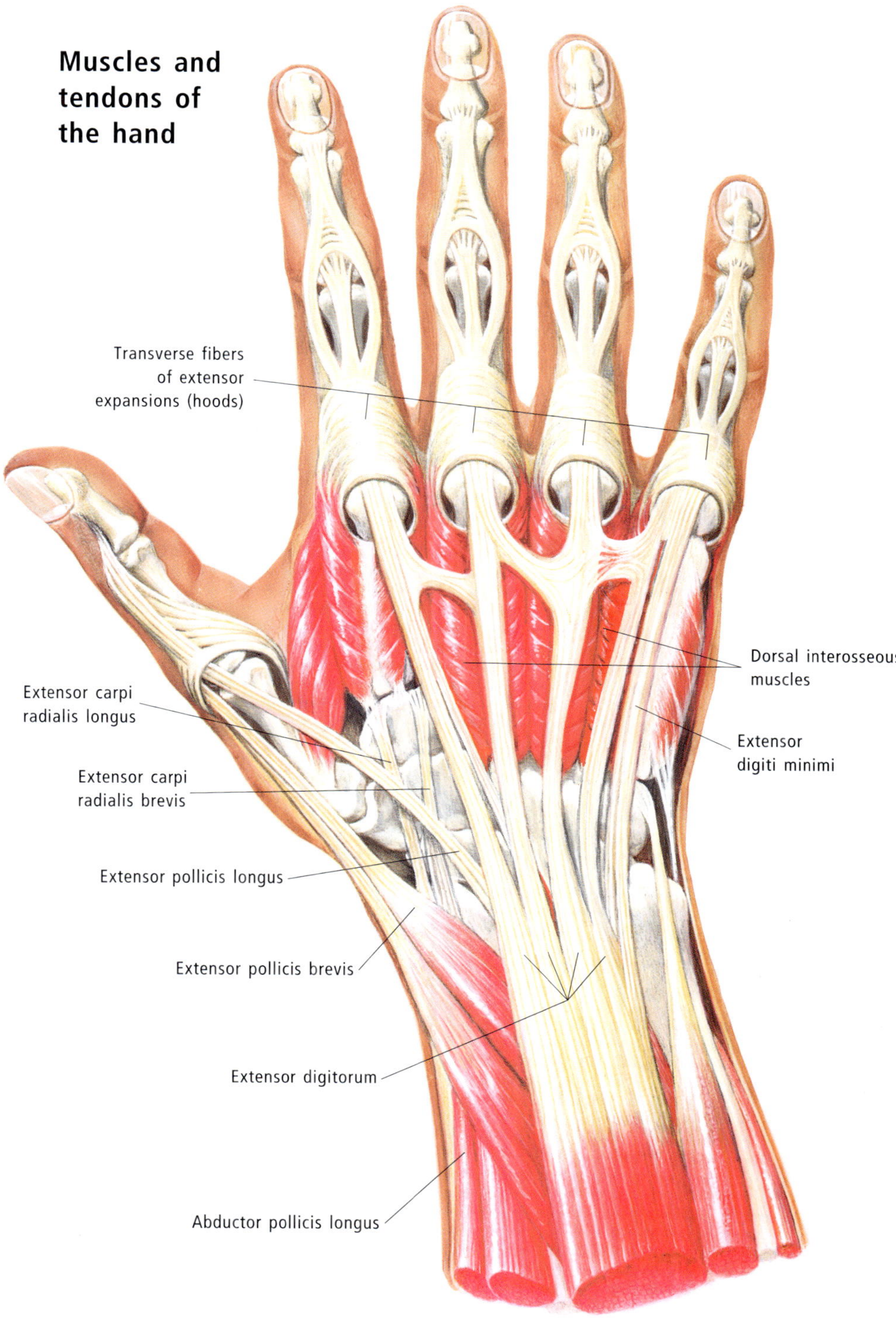

Hay fever

Sensitivity to pollen in the air, particularly during spring, triggers an allergic reaction in those who suffer from hay fever. This often results in blocked sinuses, a runny nose, red eyes and sneezing.

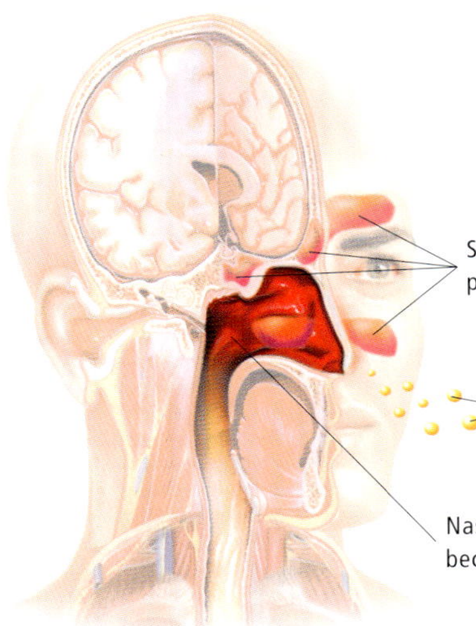

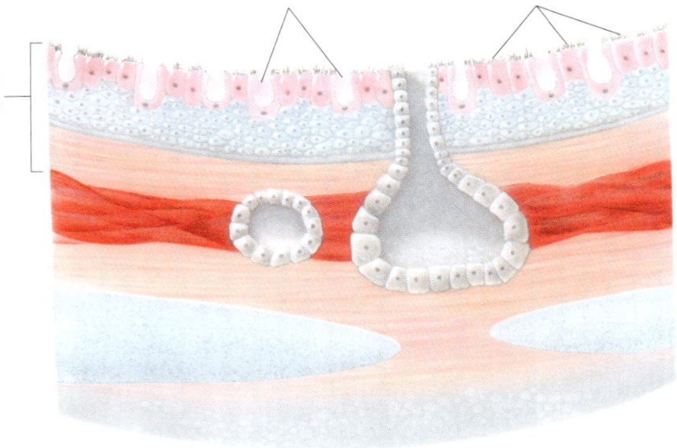

Mucous membrane

The lining of the nasal passages, trachea and lungs is covered in a sensitive mucosal lining that intercepts airborne particles. When pollen is inhaled and trapped in this lining it can trigger an allergic reaction—causing inflammation and mucus production.

Allergic response

Each time pollens (allergens) enter the body of a hay fever sufferer, they are captured by antibodies attached to mast cells. These cells release histamine—an inflammatory substance which produces the symptoms of hay fever.

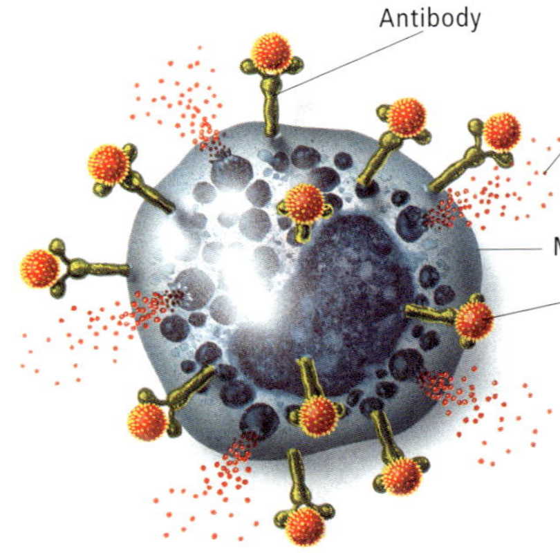

HASHIMOTO'S DISEASE

Hashimoto's disease is a destructive inflammation of the thyroid gland, most commonly affecting women, which is believed to be the result of autoimmunity and may be associated with other autoimmune disorders. Initially, it causes painless enlargement of the thyroid, but the loss of functioning thyroid tissue eventually leads to hypothyroidism, requiring treatment with thyroxine.

SEE ALSO *Autoimmune disease, Hypothyroidism, Thyroid gland*

HAY FEVER

Hay fever or seasonal allergic rhinitis (also sometimes called pollinosis) is caused by extreme sensitivity to airborne pollen, and is common through spring and summer. Hay fever may affect up to 10 percent of the population and tends to run in families, as do many allergies. It can develop at any age.

Pollen is the fine powdery yellow dust that is the fertilizing agent of plants. Airborne pollen from grasses, weeds and trees is the major cause of hay fever. In the USA and Australia, the pollen of common ragweed is well known as a hay fever allergen. Russian thistle, another plant known to cause allergic reactions, is widespread in mid-western USA, while ryegrass is a common source in Europe. A combination of pollen with pollution from vehicle exhaust gases can produce irritation similar to hay fever.

There are many airborne substances that can trigger hay fever. Besides pollen, molds and fungal spores can cause or worsen seasonal symptoms, and most are light enough to be carried hundreds of miles if the wind is right. This is what makes airborne allergens almost impossible to avoid. If you suffer from hay fever it helps to know which substances you are most sensitive to, and this can be established by observation and through specialized tests.

It is almost impossible to eliminate contact with airborne allergens in your local area, but avoiding heavy concentrations of whatever you are most sensitive to will certainly limit the amount of the allergens you are exposed to, which can decrease the severity of your allergic reaction.

In some countries the pollen count is often broadcast by local radio stations. This can alert sufferers to take medication before the onset of symptoms. The pollen count is a figure that expresses the number of pollen grains per cubic yard (cubic meter) of air and is highest in the spring and summer months. But pollens from different plants can be airborne and present even in winter and still produce symptoms at low concentrations.

When pollen or dust is inhaled, it is trapped in the lining of the trachea (windpipe). This triggers a reaction in a sensitized or allergic person. The release of histamine then causes the typical signs of hay fever: a runny nose, red and swollen mucous membranes in the nose and eyes, and sneezing. Symptoms present at times when pollens are not may be caused by sensitivity to household dust mites, or animal hairs. This condition is called perennial rhinitis.

Antihistamines, the medication most often used to control hay fever, block the action of histamine, which is responsible for the runny nose and other symptoms. Possible side effects are drowsiness, nausea and dryness of the mouth. Some of the newer antihistamines do not cause drowsiness; these can be used for daytime medication, under medical supervision.

SEE ALSO *Allergies, Antigen tests, Antihistamines, Asthma, Desensitization, Respiratory system, Rhinitis*

HEAD

The head contains the brain, encased in the cranium within the skull. There are five special senses in the head associated with cranial nerves: smell, vision, taste, hearing and balance (semicircular canals, inner ear).

The tongue is contained in the oral cavity (mouth). At the back of the oral cavity is the pharynx, which allows food to pass to the esophagus and air to pass into the trachea. Muscles in the neck allow the head to be flexed, extended and partially rotated.

Skull

The skull is the most complex bony structure in the body. With the exception of the lower jaw (mandible), the numerous bones of the skull are joined to each other by fibrous joints called sutures. Many of the skull bones develop separately from a membrane which covers the embryonic head.

At birth a significant amount of this membrane is still present between the partially formed bones, allowing them to slide over each other as the head passes through the birth canal. This means the bones are not crushed during the birth process. For descriptive purposes the skull is divided into two parts, the cranium and the face.

Cranium

The cranium surrounds and protects the brain. It is formed, from front to back, by the frontal bone, the paired parietal and temporal bones and the occipital bone with the sphenoid bone also forming part of the cranial joint. The lobes of the cerebral hemispheres of the brain are named according to the bone which overlies them—the frontal, parietal, temporal and occipital lobes. The temporal bone contains a system of spaces within it, which form the middle and inner parts of the ear (see below). Each bone (except the parietal) also contributes to the floor of the cranium, which is divided into three terraces known as the anterior, middle and posterior cranial fossae.

The anterior fossa is occupied by the frontal lobes of the brain, the middle one by the temporal lobes and the posterior one by the cerebellum and brain stem. The floor of the cranium contains many holes (foramina) through which the spinal cord, cranial nerves and blood vessels enter or leave.

The brain is separated from the skull by three layers of membrane, which are known as the meninges. The outermost layer, the dura mater, is a tough, fibrous membrane which adheres to the inner surface of the skull. The middle layer, the arachnoid mater, lines the inner surface of the dura, to which it is loosely attached. The innermost layer, the pia mater, adheres to the brain and follows its contours. Between the arachnoid and pial layers is the fluid-filled subarachnoid space, which forms a cushion around the brain, providing buoyancy and protection.

Arteries which supply the skull and meninges, and veins draining blood from the brain, lie between the dura and the skull. An extradural hemorrhage occurs when these vessels are torn (usually in association with a skull fracture) and blood rapidly accumulates between the dura and the skull, putting pressure on the underlying brain. This is a potentially fatal condition which must be treated quickly, usually by making a hole in the skull to release the pressure.

Subdural hemorrhage occurs when veins are ruptured as they pass through the dura mater, causing blood to accumulate between the dural and arachnoid layers. This can occur from a bump on the head but is not as serious as an extradural hemorrhage because the blood accumulates at a much slower rate. The major arteries supplying the brain run through the subarachnoid space before entering the brain. A sudden increase in blood pressure in patients with cardiovascular disease can cause these arteries to rupture, causing blood to accumulate in the subarachnoid space (subarachnoid hemorrhage).

Face

The bones of the front of the skull constitute the face. The frontal bone forms the forehead, the zygoma forms the cheek bone, the maxilla forms the upper jaw, palate and outer walls of the nasal cavity, and the mandible forms the lower jaw.

Unlike most other parts of the body, the skin of the face, lips and scalp contains numerous small muscles, known as the muscles of facial expression, which enable us to open and close the mouth, smile, blink and frown. The skin of the face and scalp is extremely sensitive to touch and pain and is also very vascular, so that while wounds may bleed profusely they also heal quickly.

Temporomandibular joints

Each side of the mandible has a head which fits into a socket on the base of the skull, forming the temporomandibular joints. These joints, located just below and in front of each ear, permit both the hinge-like and gliding movements of the mandible that occur during eating and speech. When the mouth is forced open beyond its normal range the joints can dislocate forwards, becoming locked in the open position.

Orbit

Each eye and its associated structures (muscles, nerves and blood vessels) occupies a cavity on the front of the skull known as the orbit. The walls of the orbit are relatively thin and fragile and can be easily fractured if a small object is inadvertently poked into the orbit, or by a blow to the front of the eye. The outer margin of the orbit, however, is thick and strong, protecting the eye from damage by larger objects. The eyelids function to protect and lubricate the eye. The lacrimal gland, which produces tears, is located just behind the upper eyelid.

Nose (nasal cavity)

The walls of the nasal cavity are formed by bone at the back and by the nasal cartilages at the front; the cartilages surround the nostrils. The cavity is divided into halves by the nasal septum and its floor is formed by the palate, which is also the roof of the mouth.

The inner lining of the nostrils is formed by hairy skin; the membrane at the roof of the nasal cavity contains specialized olfactory cells, which are responsible for detecting smells. The remainder of the nasal cavity has a specialized lining called respiratory epithelium, which has a very rich blood supply and numerous mucous glands to warm and moisten the air as we breathe.

In order to maximize the available surface area for this epithelium, the walls of the nasal cavity contain coiled inward-projecting bones, known as conchae or turbinate bones. The nasal cavities open behind into a space known as the pharynx, through which air passes on its way down to the lungs.

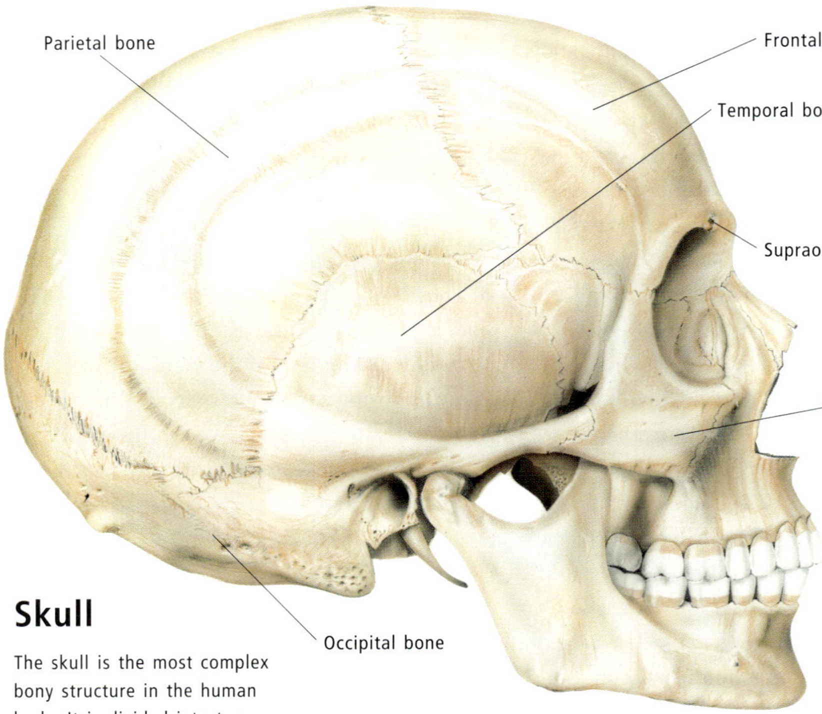

Bones of the cranium

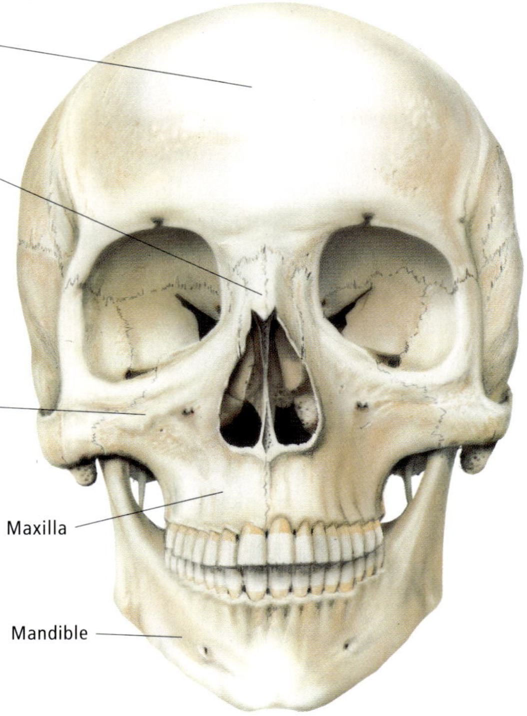

Bones of the face

Skull

The skull is the most complex bony structure in the human body. It is divided into two parts—the cranium and the face.

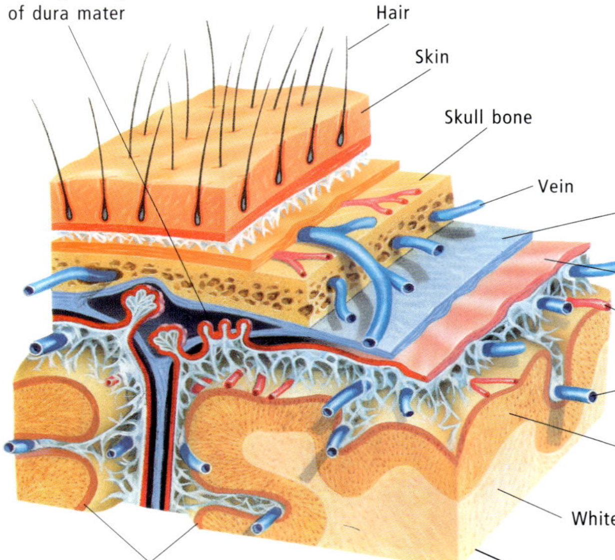

Protecting the brain

Between the skull and the brain there are three membranes which serve to cushion and protect the brain: the dura mater, the arachnoid and the pia mater.

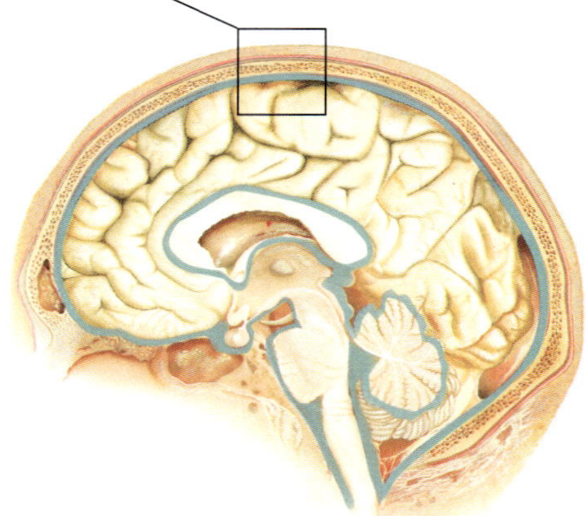

Paranasal sinuses

The nasal cavity also communicates with spaces known as the paranasal sinuses, which occupy the major bones adjacent to the nasal cavity (the maxillary, frontal, ethmoid and sphenoid sinuses, named after the bones in which they are located). These sinuses are also lined by respiratory epithelium and infection can spread to them easily from the nose, causing congestion and pain (sinusitis).

The maxillary sinuses, which lie to the sides of the nose, are the largest and most susceptible to infection, from either the nose or the upper teeth.

Oral cavity (mouth)

The oral cavity or mouth extends from the lips at the front to the throat (pharynx) behind, and is bounded at the sides by the cheeks. Its roof is formed in front by the hard (bony) palate and behind by the soft (muscular) palate. Its floor is formed by muscle. Its major contents are the teeth and the tongue.

There are a total of 20 baby (deciduous) teeth, which usually appear between the ages of 6 and 24 months. From approximately 6 years of age onwards, the deciduous teeth are gradually replaced by permanent or adult teeth. The mature adult has a total of 32 teeth. Each jaw contains 4 incisors (for cutting), 2 canines (for tearing), 4 premolars and 6 molars (for grinding). The third molars, or wisdom teeth, are the last to appear and cause problems in people whose jaws are not long enough to fit them comfortably.

The tongue is a muscular organ essential for normal swallowing and speech. It is also a very important sensory organ; it is extremely sensitive to touch and contains taste buds, special cells which detect different tastes.

The tongue, which is attached below to a small bone in the neck called the hyoid bone, consists of a root (in the throat), dorsum (the main part in the mouth) and an apex or tip. It is formed by numerous muscle fibers which lie in different planes, allowing it to change shape and move in almost any direction.

The sides and upper surface of the dorsum and apex are rough because they contain numerous tiny projections called papillae, which enable the tongue to grip food and move it around during chewing. Taste buds are located on the sides of the papillae. The root of the tongue has a smooth, slippery surface so food can slide freely over it as it passes down the throat during swallowing.

Pharynx (throat)

The pharynx (throat) is a muscular tube, which is suspended from the base of the skull. It is a common passageway for both food and air, being continuous at the front with the nasal and oral cavities, and below with the trachea or windpipe (for air) and esophagus (for food and liquids). During swallowing, the muscular walls of the pharynx contract to force food down to the esophagus. At the same time the soft palate is pulled upwards to prevent food passing into the nasal cavity, and the epiglottic cartilage flips down like a lid to prevent food entering the larynx and trachea.

The walls of the upper part of the pharynx contain the palatine tonsils and the adenoid tonsils. These are islands of lymphatic tissue which are important in the immune system, particularly in children.

Inflammation of the palatine tonsils is known as tonsillitis, and is usually treatable by antibiotics or, in recurring cases, surgical removal. Inflammation of the adenoid tonsils can block off the nasal cavity, causing breathing difficulties and snoring. They may also be surgically removed.

Ear

The ear contains sensory organs necessary for both hearing and balance. It consists of outer, middle and inner parts.

The outer ear is located on the side of the skull and consists of the auricle and ear canal. The auricle directs the sound waves down the ear canal where they cause vibration of the tympanic membrane.

The middle ear is an air-filled cavity in the temporal bone. It is separated from the outer ear by the tympanic membrane. The middle ear contains a chain of three tiny bones or ossicles (hammer, anvil and stirrup) extending across the cavity from the tympanic membrane to the oval window. Vibration of the tympanic membrane causes movement of the ossicles, which is then transmitted to the inner ear through the oval window.

The inner ear is filled with a fluid called perilymph. Suspended in this fluid is a system of membrane-covered ducts which are filled with a different fluid (endolymph). These ducts include the cochlear and semicircular ducts, and the utricle and saccule. Specialized receptors in the cochlear duct respond to vibrations of the fluid (caused by the stirrup vibrating in the oval window) and enable us to detect different frequencies and intensities of sound. Receptors in the semicircular ducts detect the direction of head movements and those in the utricle and saccule can detect head position, even when the head is not moving.

Some viral infections, as well as alcohol, can change the pressure of the fluid, causing abnormal stimulation of the receptors and consequent dizziness and nausea, as well as ringing in the ear (tinnitus).

SEE ALSO *Brain, Ear, Esophagus, Eye, Face, Lacrimal glands, Nose, Pharynx, Sinuses, Sinusitis, Skull, Subarachnoid hemorrhage, Teeth, Throat, Tinnitus, Tongue, Trachea*

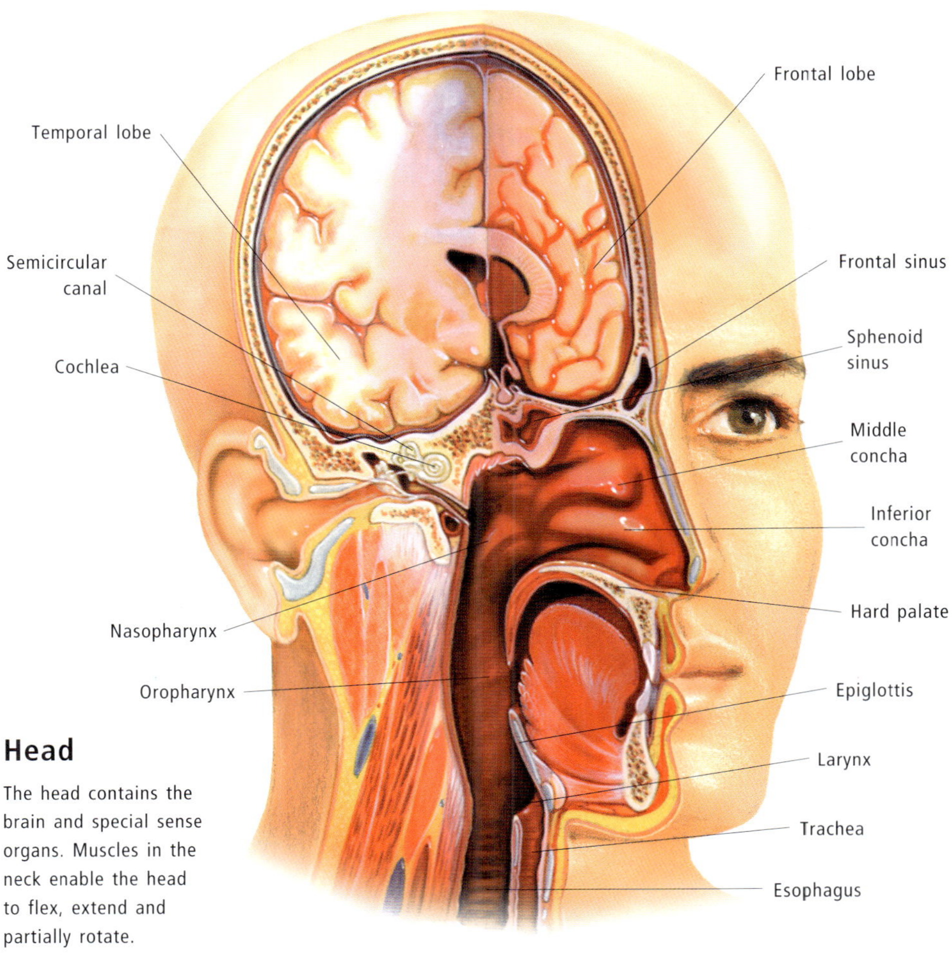

Head

The head contains the brain and special sense organs. Muscles in the neck enable the head to flex, extend and partially rotate.

HEAD LICE

Tiny wingless insects that live on the scalp and suck blood, head lice are spread through direct contact and by sharing hats and combs. Though anyone can have them, young children, particularly those who attend preschool, school or child care, are more likely to suffer because of the contact they have with other children. Lice are attracted to clean rather than dirty hair, and are very common (parents should not feel that their children having head lice is a sign of neglect).

Head lice cause itching. Their presence can be confirmed by a fine black powder of louse feces or pale flecks on the pillow, by the lice themselves, and by their eggs (nits—white specks stuck to hairs, near their roots).

Head lice can be eradicated by the use of special shampoos, which everyone in the household should use. Wash the hair, then have the sufferer sit in the sunlight. Check behind the ears and the back of the neck, then comb the hair carefully using a special lice comb, rinsing or wiping the comb between strokes. Dry the hair with a hair dryer, as the heat will also help to eradicate the pest. Daily combing is important once you are sure the lice have been eradicated. Hair brushes, combs, pillow cases, hair accessories and hats should also be washed.

SEE ALSO *Lice*

HEADACHE

Headache is a very common problem which can seriously interfere with a person's normal activities. It is not usually the result of another, more serious, underlying disease but severe or persistent headache, especially in children, requires medical investigation to exclude the presence of any such disorder.

By far the most common headaches are those referred to as tension headaches. Most persons experience occasional headaches of this type, often related to emotional stress or fatigue, but not necessarily triggered by tension. Tension headaches can also be triggered by caffeine, alcohol, certain foods, stress, fatigue, and skipping meals. The precise mechanics behind the development of these common headaches remain unclear. There can be associated tightening and tenderness of the muscles of the scalp, neck or jaw. Pain is usually moderate but may be severe with a sensation of the head being "gripped in a vise."

Episodic tension headaches usually respond to over-the-counter analgesics such as acetaminophen (paracetamol) or aspirin. Chronic tension headache can be associated with depression, anxiety, insomnia or other medical problems. Chronic or severe tension headaches should be investigated by a primary care physician, as they can be due to another cause, and there are other treatments that are available.

Vascular headaches make up a second large and important group, in which there is an associated dilation of the blood vessels supplying the head. The specific mechanisms involved are again poorly understood.

Migraine and its many variants are in cluded in this category. Most migraine sufferers develop pain that usually affects one half of the head and lasts for several hours, often with throbbing and sometimes accompanied by nausea and vomiting. A number of precipitating factors for migraine headaches are

Headache

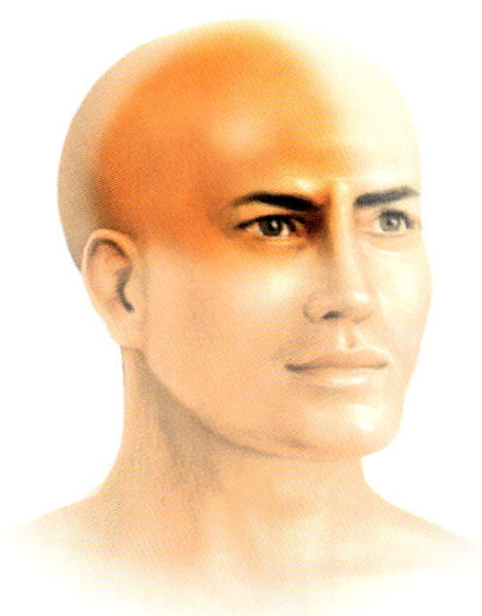

Headache—migraine

A migraine headache is characterized by severe, throbbing pain, usually on one side of the head.

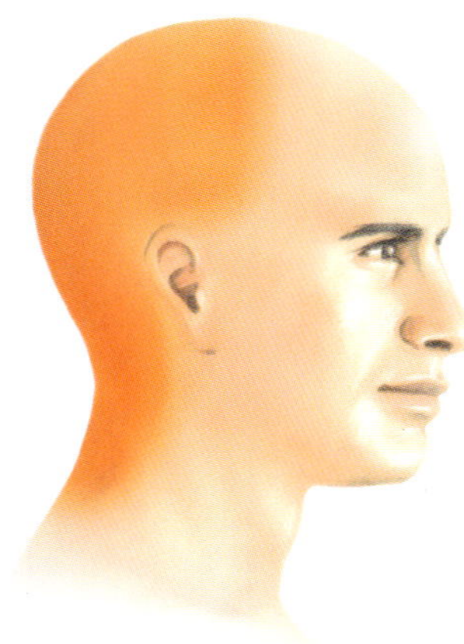

Headache—occipital neuralgia

Occipital neuralgia is a painful, stabbing sensation in the back part of the head (occiput).

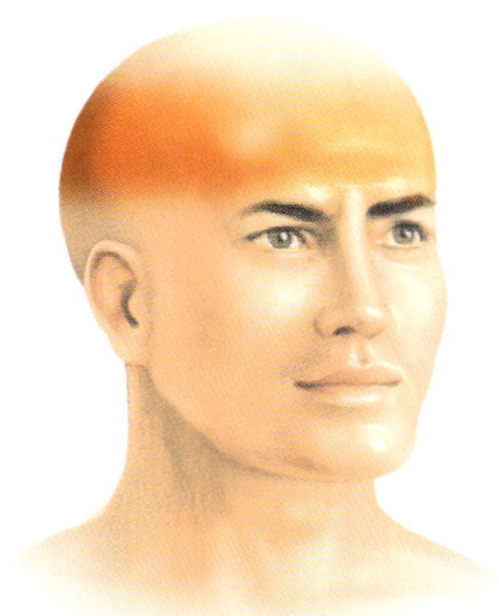

Headache—tension

A tension headache usually occurs in the front part of the head and is often accompanied by tightness in the muscles of the scalp, neck and jaw.

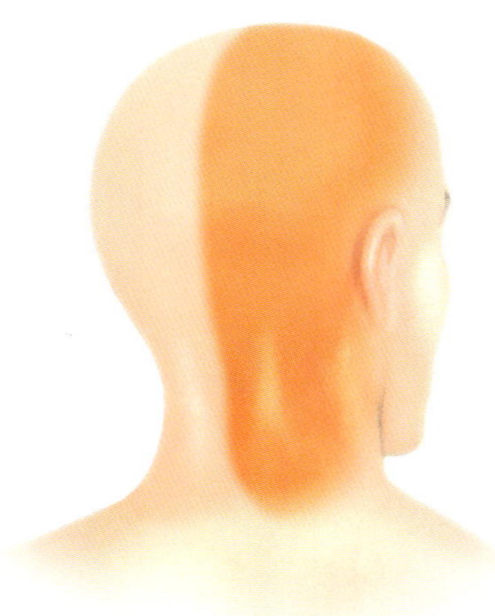

Occipital neuralgia—back view

recognized and several types of migraine can be distinguished. So-called hormonal headaches, associated with menstruation, pregnancy, oral contraceptive therapy and menopause, are forms of migraine headache.

Another important, although much less common, type of vascular headache is known as cluster headache. They are of relatively short duration, but very severe attacks occur in clusters over periods of several weeks.

Headache is sometimes a manifestation of an underlying disease, although such headaches occur much less commonly than either tension or vascular headaches. Among the specific disease processes that may initially appear as headache are: inflammation of the blood vessels supplying the head and neck (known as cranial or temporal arteritis), which is of particular concern in older persons; pain originating from inflamed nasal sinuses, inflamed teeth, osteoarthritis of the vertebrae in the neck, or injured or inflamed nerves; inflammation of the meninges covering the brain; very high blood pressure; and pain caused by masses within the cranium, including various brain tumors.

Excessive self-medication for headaches can cause further headache, sometimes referred to as rebound headache. This is especially true of overuse of analgesics such as aspirin and acetaminophen (paracetamol).

The varieties of headaches that develop in children are similar to those in adults; both tension headaches and migraines commonly occur. Children's headaches can frequently be the first sign of underlying diseases (such as inflammation of eyes, ears, nose, head trauma, meningitis, and brain tumors), so severe or recurrent headaches should always be investigated by the family doctor.

SEE ALSO *Brain, Depression, Hypertension, Meningitis, Migraine, Osteoarthritis, Sinusitis*

HEALING

Healing is the restoration of structure and function of damaged tissues. Different processes are involved depending on the nature and extent of the injury, and the type of body tissue involved.

Inflammation

Inflammation is the body's natural response to tissue damage. It takes place after infections, burns, frostbite, or radiation exposure. The process begins with dilation of blood vessels and increased blood flow to the area. The vessels become more permeable, allowing plasma to escape from the blood into the extracellular fluid. This produces swelling of the affected region. Leukocytes (white blood cells) also escape from blood vessels in the region, and release chemicals that may cause pain. These changes together produce the classic signs of inflammation: heat, redness, swelling, and pain and tenderness.

As inflammation progresses, leukocytes migrate in increased numbers from the bloodstream into the injured area. The inflammatory response proceeds until the dead tissue and invading organisms have been removed. The inflammation then resolves—the excess fluid is drained from the area by the lymphatics, the blood vessels constrict and become less permeable, and the swelling, heat and redness subside.

If there has been damage of the tissue as well, then healing also involves regeneration of tissue—that is, the repeated division of surviving tissue cells to take the place of those damaged. Not all tissue can regenerate, however (e.g. brain and nerve cells). Moreover, if the damage is extensive, it may not be possible for regeneration to occur.

Surgical intervention sometimes may be necessary to aid the healing process. In some cases, dead bacteria, cells and tissue may collect to form pus, which may collect and form an abscess. This may need to be drained. If there are large areas of dead tissue, the dead tissue needs to be removed.

Wound healing

If an injury causes a wound such as a laceration, then healing takes place by a different mechanism. If the edges of the wound are close together, wound healing takes place by "primary intention". A blood clot forms in the wound which contracts, bringing the edges still closer together. From the edges, fibroblasts produce granulation tissue, which is gradually replaced with connective tissue. Meanwhile, epithelial tissues grow over the surface of the wound. If the edges of the wound are far apart, healing takes place by "secondary intention". Granulation tissue forms at the base and sides of the wound and "fills up" the wound until it reaches the level of the skin. The granulation tissue is gradually replaced with (often unsightly) scar tissue.

Healing

For a wound to heal, leukocytes (white blood cells) must first migrate from blood vessels to the injured tissues in order to remove dead cells and invading organisms. A blood clot comprising fibrin strands, platelets and red and white blood cells then forms to bring the edges of the wound together. Finally, fibroblasts produce new granulation tissue.

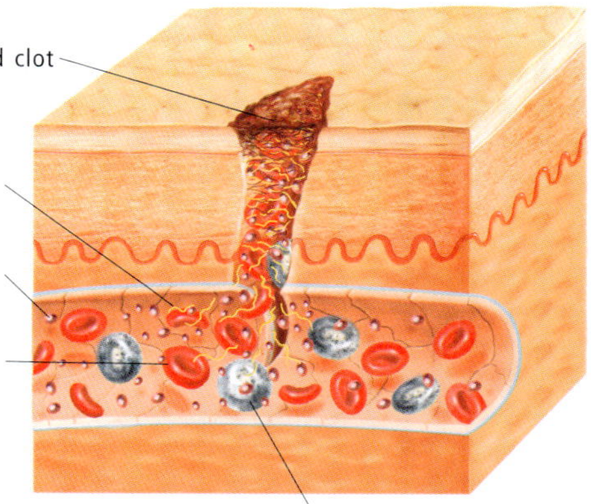

Bone healing

Healing of bone is similar to that of other injured tissue, but uses specialized cells and materials. Immediately after a fracture, bone forming cells called osteoblasts begin to produce a tough binding material called callus, which knits the bones together. Once this is accomplished, the bone is remodeled as the callus is absorbed and replaced by true bone, which is gradually remodeled into its previous shape.

The process of bone healing is greatly helped if displacement of the ends of the fractured bone is minimal. Several general factors can influence the healing process. The younger the person is, the faster healing takes place. Someone who is in good general health will heal faster than someone in poor general health or who is malnourished. Sufferers from liver or kidney disease or diabetes do not heal as well as healthy individuals. Someone who is immunosuppressed or on cytotoxic, immunosuppressant or corticosteroid drugs may take longer to heal. Poor blood supply to damaged tissues also slows or prevents healing.

HEARING

Hearing is the ability to perceive sound vibrations, which are transmitted in waves through gas, water or solid matter. Sounds can vary in frequency (be pitched high or low) and in intensity. Frequency is measured in hertz (cycles per second); sounds are audible from a low frequency of about 50 hertz to a high frequency of about 16,000 hertz. Intensity is measured in decibels, ranging from inaudible at zero to the devastatingly loud (above 140 decibels). Sound is conducted to the brain through the delicate and complicated mechanisms of the ear. Binaural hearing (i.e. with both ears) gives information about direction and distance of the source of sound.

The ear contains the sensory organ that perceives the sound through a process called audition, and converts the mechanical energy of the sound wave into nerve impulses which are transmitted to the brain and interpreted. Hearing is present before birth, the inner ear developing in the fetus at around 9 weeks.

The ear has three parts—the outer, middle and inner ear—each of which plays a special role in the hearing process.

The outer or external ear consists of the pinna or auricle and the auditory canal, a tubular passage lined with fine hairs and glands which secrete earwax (cerumen). The passage connects the external ear to the eardrum.

The middle ear includes the eardrum and the chain of three bones, the ossicles, whose individual names are derived from the Latin for hammer, anvil, and stirrup (malleus, incus and stapes, respectively) which connect across the tympanic cavity to the oval window, in the cochlea.

The eustachian or auditory tube connects the air space of the tympanic cavity with the pharynx and allows air pressure in the middle ear to be equalized with atmospheric pressure. The tube is lined with mucous membrane and can be blocked by swelling due to head colds or similar viral infections. This can cause discomfort and pain in the ear on changes of pressure, such as when flying, and hearing can be severely reduced. Swallowing or chewing can help unblock the tube and equalize pressure.

The inner ear (labyrinth) contains the major organ of hearing, the fluid-filled cochlea, and the semicircular canals, the organs of balance.

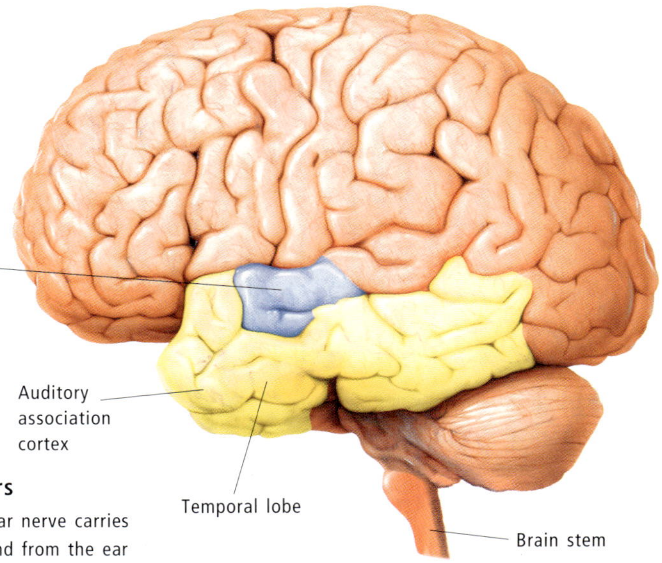

Auditory centers

The vestibulocochlear nerve carries information on sound from the ear into the brain stem. From here, the information passes through the midbrain and on to the auditory cortex in the temporal lobe of the brain. This is where we recognize and interpret sounds. High frequency sounds activate one part of the cortex, low frequency sounds activate another part.

How we hear (opposite page)

(a) Sound waves enter the ear canal and hit the eardrum. **(b)** The eardrum vibrates and passes vibrations to the ossicles (three tiny bones in the middle ear). **(c)** The ossicles intensify the pressure of the sound waves and transmit vibrations to the oval window (a membrane that covers the entrance to the cochlea). **(d)** The vibrations pass into the cochlear spiral where fluid displaces tiny hair-like receptor cells in the organ of Corti. **(e)** These cells send nerve impulses along the cochlear nerve to the brain stem, midbrain, then the hearing center in the temporal lobe of the brain where sounds are interpreted.

Airborne sounds or sound waves are captured by the auricle (outer ear), which directs them through the auditory canal to the eardrum (in the middle ear). From here waves are relayed by vibration of the ossicles to the organ of Corti, which is in the cochlea (the inner ear). There they disturb the cochlear fluid, exciting thousands of tiny hair cells which transduce mechanical energy to electrical impulses that are relayed via the cochlear nerve to the brain. Different hair cells relay high- and low-pitched sounds, those in the deepest part of the cochlea receiving the lowest pitches.

Conductive hearing is the reception of sound through the bones of the skull and is the main transmission route for one's own voice. Sound waves go direct to the cochlea, bypassing the middle ear.

The loudness of sound is measured in decibels, and the lowest sound of a certain pitch that can be heard is expressed as the hearing threshold for that pitch. Sounds below 10 decibels (dB), the volume of a whisper, are difficult to hear, and those above 140 dB will cause actual pain. Constant or regular exposure to sounds above 70 dB in volume can accelerate hearing loss, and those above 100 dB may inflict permanent damage on a single exposure.

Hearing sensitivity has some protection from the acoustic reflex which, in response to loud noise, stiffens the chain of bones, the ossicles, in the middle ear to diminish the strength of vibrations transmitted to the inner ear. This protection, however, is not enough to prevent damage caused by repeated exposure, which permanently destroys hair cells in the cochlea.

SEE ALSO *Deafness, Ear*

Hearing

Auditory ossicles

The ossicles in the inner ear (the malleus, incus and stapes) are three tiny bones that act as an amplifier by magnifying the movement of the eardrum. This allows us to hear even very faint sounds. The malleus is attached to the eardrum; when the eardrum vibrates the malleus vibrates the incus which in turn vibrates the stapes. The base of the stapes covers the oval window, a membrane that passes vibrations into the spiral of the cochlea.

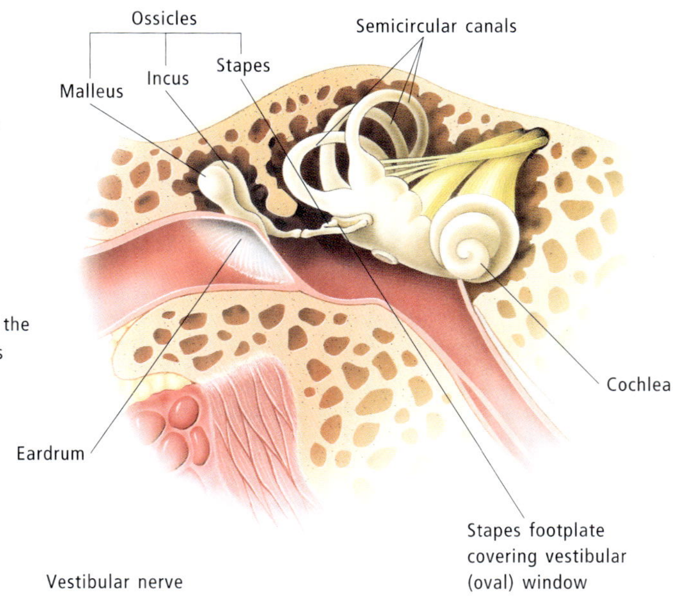

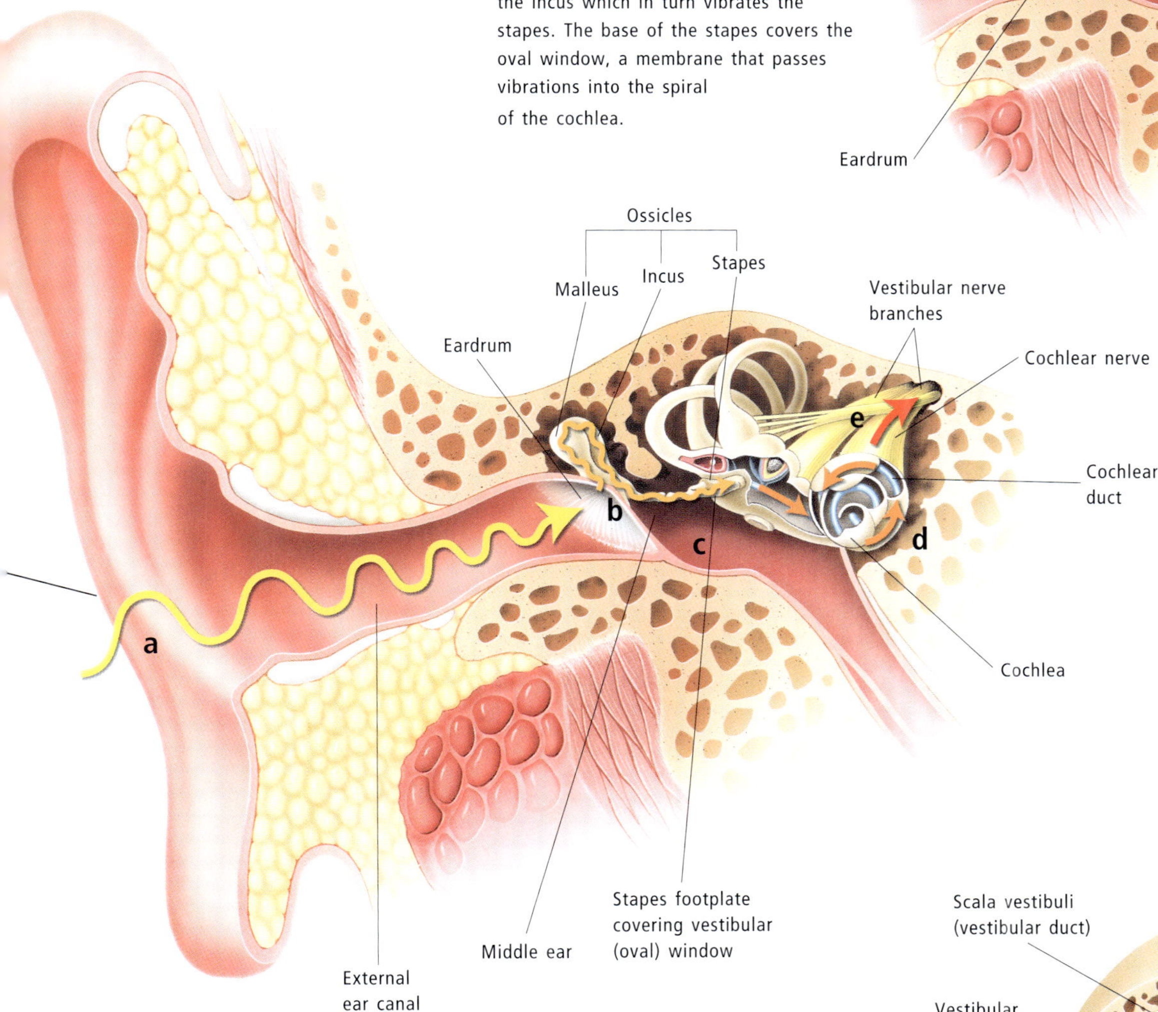

Inside the cochlea

Three channels run through the spiral of the cochlea. Inside the central channel—the cochlear duct (scala media)—lies the organ of Corti. When fluid in the central channel pulses with sound waves, it moves the membrane and hairs of the organ of Corti which send signals to the cochlear nerve and on to the brain.

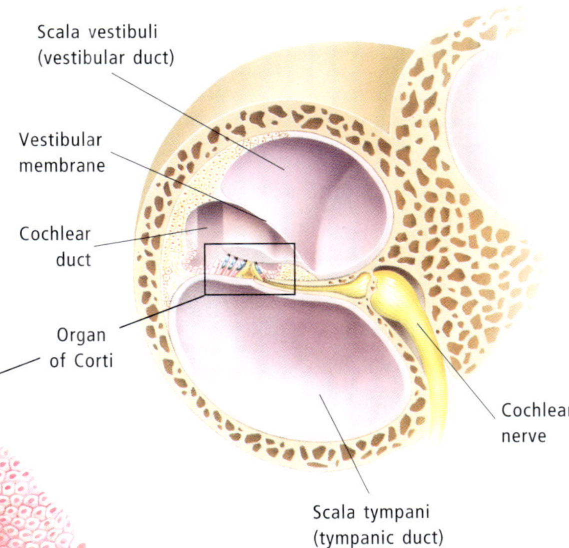

Organ of Corti

The organ of Corti consists of rows of cells with fine hair-like projections under a layer of membrane. Movement of the hairs provides the brain with information on the volume or intensity of sound. Soft sounds stimulate only a few cells; loud sounds stimulate cells in many of the rows. The cells stimulate the cochlear branch of the vestibular nerve which carries information to the brain.

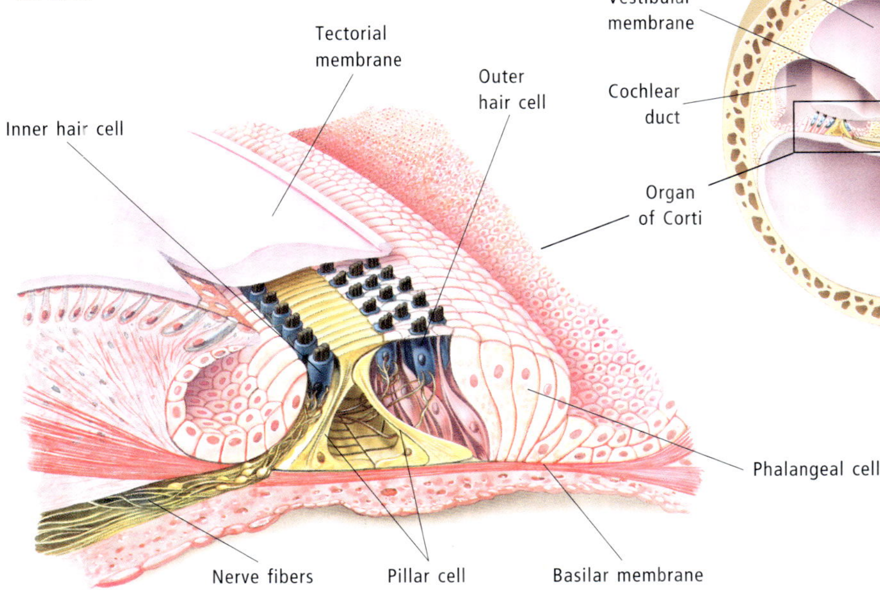

HEART

The heart is essentially a muscular pump, which is responsible for moving blood around the vessels of the body. It is made up of two halves, separated by the septum, a thick muscular wall. Each half is again divided into an upper and lower chamber.

The two chambers on the left side of the heart (left atrium and ventricle) are responsible for receiving oxygen-rich blood from the lungs and pumping it out to the body along its largest artery, the aorta. The two chambers on the right side of the heart (right atrium and ventricle) are responsible for receiving relatively deoxygenated blood from the body and distributing it via the pulmonary trunk to the lungs for gas exchange to occur. These two circuits of blood flow are called systemic and pulmonary circulations respectively.

Within the heart there are four valves that ensure blood flows in one direction: from atrium to ventricle and out through its appropriate artery. The two atrioventricular valves are located between the atria and ventricles on each side of the heart. Between the right atrium and right ventricle lies the tricuspid valve, while the mitral valve lies between the left atrium and left ventricle. The function of atrioventricular valves is to prevent backflow of blood from the ventricles to the atria during ventricular contraction.

The other two cardiac valves (semilunar valves) are located at the outlets from the ventricles: the pulmonary valve lies at the point where the right ventricle expels blood to the pulmonary trunk, while the aortic valve lies at the outlet of the left ventricle. The role of semilunar valves is to prevent backflow of blood from the aorta and pulmonary trunk into their respective ventricles when the ventricles relax.

The heart muscle receives a rich blood supply from the coronary arteries, which branch from the aorta. Cardiac blood is returned to the right atrium by the cardiac veins.

The pumping action

The heart has a system of specialized cells, which either set the rhythm of cardiac contraction or allow for rapid spread of electrical impulses through the heart.

The sinoatrial node, in the right atrium, is a specialized tissue that acts as the heart's pacemaker; it controls the frequency of the heart's rhythmic contractions. Electrical impulses are then transmitted through the atria to the atrioventricular node, which then passes the impulse down the atrioventricular bundle, resulting in coordinated contractions of the ventricles.

Although divided into a left and right side, with distinct functions, the heart is organized in such a way that its pumping action serves both sides at once. In the relaxation phase (diastole) blood pours from the left and right atrium into its corresponding ventricle. In the next contraction phase (systole) the blood is forced from the left and right ventricles into the aorta and the pulmonary artery, respectively. The valves control the direction of blood flow. At the beginning of each contraction, the atrioventricular valves close and the pulmonary and aortic valves open. At the end of each contraction the aortic and pulmonary valves close and the atrioventricular valves open.

Diseases of the heart

Heart disease can be congenital (existing from birth), or can develop later in life.

Diseases of the coronary arteries

Disease of the coronary arteries usually leads to narrowing and reduced blood supply to the cardiac muscle. The most common type of coronary artery disease is due to atherosclerosis, which involves the accumulation of fats (atheroma) within the vessel wall leading to the formation of fatty/fibrous plaques and deposition of calcium. This disease may also occur in arteries of the neck, legs and abdomen, but is particularly dangerous in the brain and coronary arteries. Lifestyle factors, such as smoking and a diet rich in saturated fats, increase the risk of atherosclerosis. High blood pressure is also an important contributing factor.

The interior of a vessel may be blocked by fatty plaques, which cause thickening and loss of elasticity in the wall. Plaques may also lose their surface, with the result that blood coagulates on them (thrombus formation) which also contributes to obstruction of coronary arteries (coronary heart disease).

Partial obstruction of the coronary artery may severely limit the patient's ability to perform physical activity. Such patients will complain of chest pain that has a crushing feeling and is usually located in the center of the chest (angina pectoris). Angina pectoris is usually felt when the patient is climbing stairs or walking up a hill. It will pass in a few minutes once the patient stops to rest.

Complete obstruction of a coronary artery (coronary thrombosis) will lead to the death of the heart muscle supplied by that artery (myocardial infarction). This is commonly known as a "heart attack" or "coronary". In this case the patient will experience a crushing pain in the center of the chest which does not pass with rest and may last for several hours. The pain may spread into other parts of the body such as the left arm, neck, back and upper abdomen. The patient may also experience severe breathlessness. If the death of cardiac muscle causes abnormal electrical activity then the remaining heart muscle may not be able to contract effectively (ventricular fibrillation).

Obstruction of the coronary arteries may be treated before too much damage has occurred by several techniques. Partial or mild obstructions may be treated by dilating the blocked segment with a balloon, removing the obstructing matter (plaque) with laser pulses, or inserting a "stent" to hold the artery open. These are all methods of angioplasty. More severe obstructions may be bypassed surgically by grafting a piece of leg vein or chest wall artery alongside the obstructed segment (coronary artery bypass).

If the death of cardiac muscle occurs slowly, the patient may develop congestive cardiac failure. In such cases, the heart is unable to move blood around the body effectively, so that blood accumulates in the veins of the legs, abdomen or lungs. This leads to swelling of the ankles or swollen liver due to pooling of fluid in the tissue spaces of those sites. Pooling of fluid in the lungs will cause shortness of breath. Treatment of congestive cardiac failure is usually aimed at improving the strength of the heart and removing excess fluid from the body by increasing the output of urine.

Electrical abnormalities

Problems with the conducting and pacemaking tissues of the heart may lead to abnormalities of the cardiac rhythm (cardiac arrhythmias) or delayed and ineffective contraction of cardiac muscle (bundle branch

The heart

Heart—front

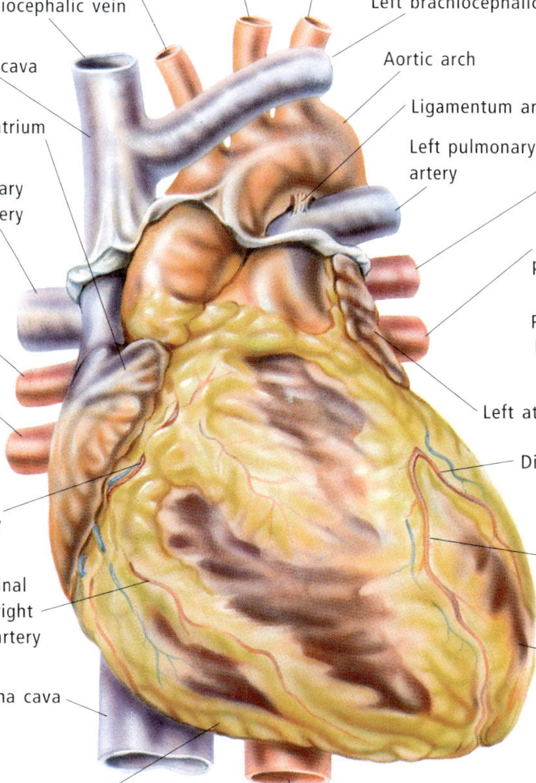

Heart—back

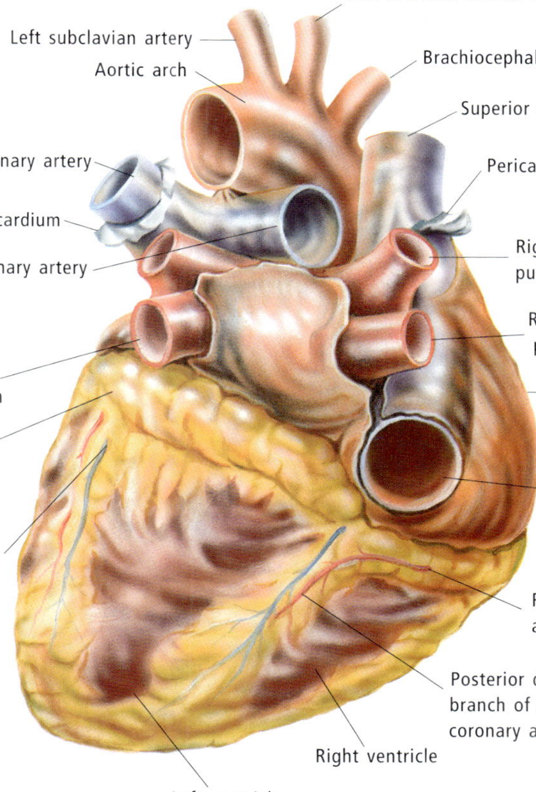

Heart—section
showing all four chambers

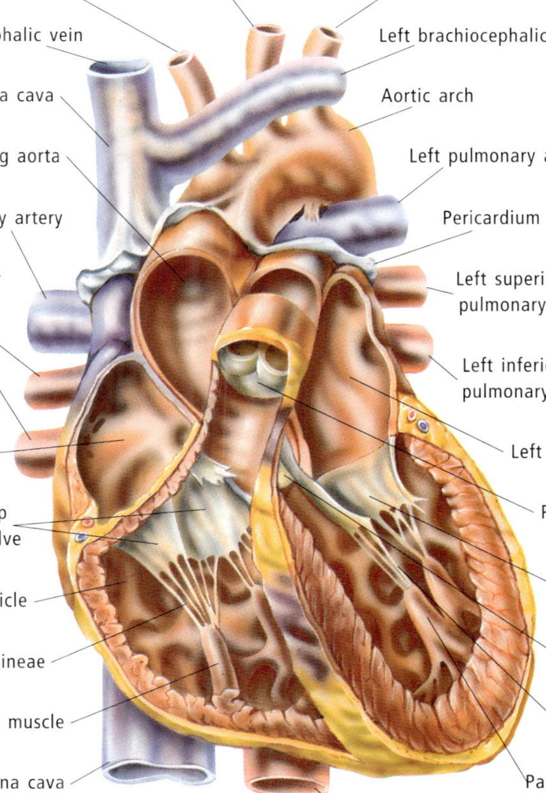

blocks or heart block). Cardiac arrhythmias may affect the atria (atrial tachycardia, atrial fibrillation) or the ventricle (ventricular tachycardia, ventricular fibrillation). Many electrical abnormalities are linked with problems with the coronary arteries, although some can be caused by rheumatic heart disease, fever, excess thyroid hormone, coffee and alcohol.

Ventricular fibrillation is a particularly serious cardiac arrhythmia. It often arises shortly after myocardial infarction and is a common immediate cause of death. In ventricular fibrillation chaotic electrical activity in the ventricles prevents effective pumping of blood to the body. The patient will have no pulse, breathing will stop and loss of consciousness will occur. The patient will die within minutes unless the normal rhythm is re-established.

This can often be achieved by delivering a powerful electrical current across the chest cavity (cardioversion or defibrillation). If a

Heart cycle

In the cardiac cycle, the chambers of the heart pass through a relaxation phase (diastole) and a contraction phase (systole).

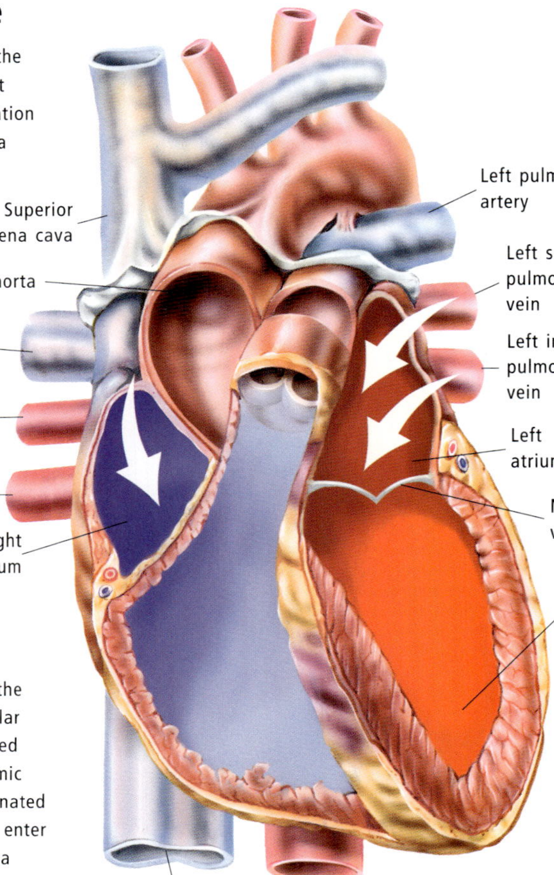

Heart cycle 1

In atrial diastole (at the beginning of ventricular diastole), deoxygenated blood from the systemic circulation and oxygenated blood from the lungs enter the left and right atria (upper chambers) of the heart.

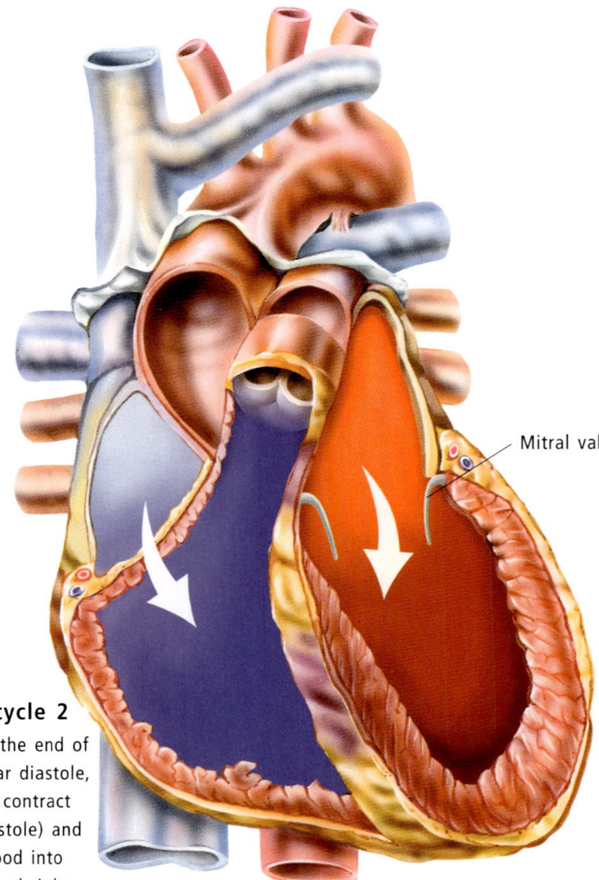

Heart cycle 2

Towards the end of ventricular diastole, the atria contract (atrial systole) and pump blood into the left and right ventricles.

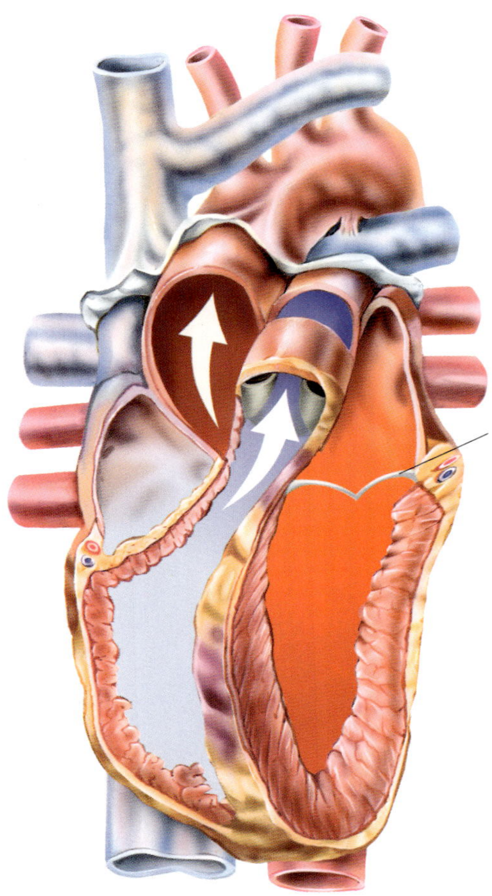

Heart cycle 3

In ventricular systole, the right and left ventricles contract and eject blood into the aorta and pulmonary arteries.

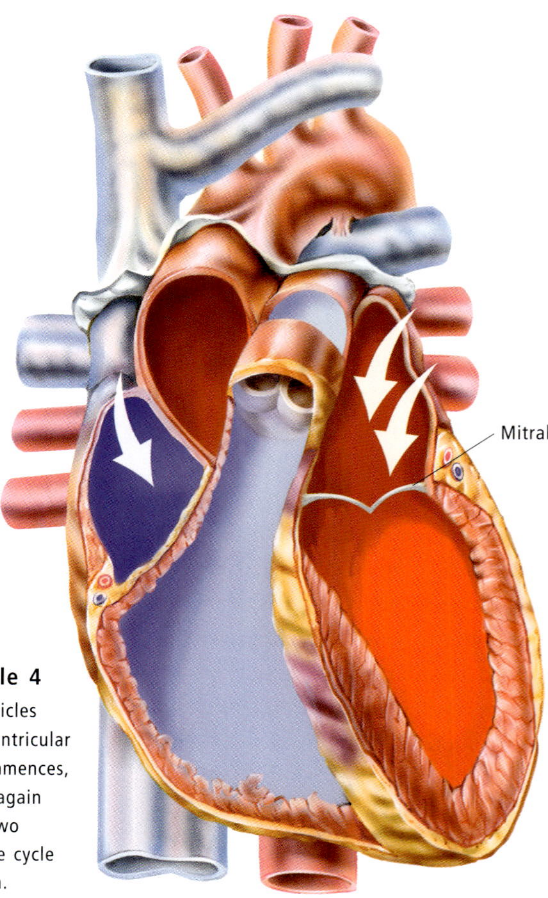

Heart cycle 4

As the ventricles relax and ventricular diastole commences, blood once again enters the two atria and the cycle begins again.

Heart in ventricular systole

The ventricles of the heart contract, pushing oxygenated blood into the aorta (for circulation around the body) and deoxygenated blood into the pulmonary artery (to be sent to the lungs).

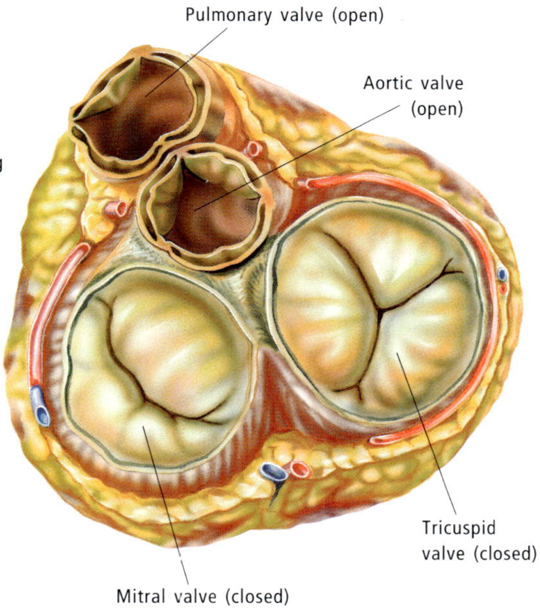

Heart in ventricular diastole

After a contraction the mitral and tricuspid valves open, allowing blood to fill the left and right ventricles of the heart.

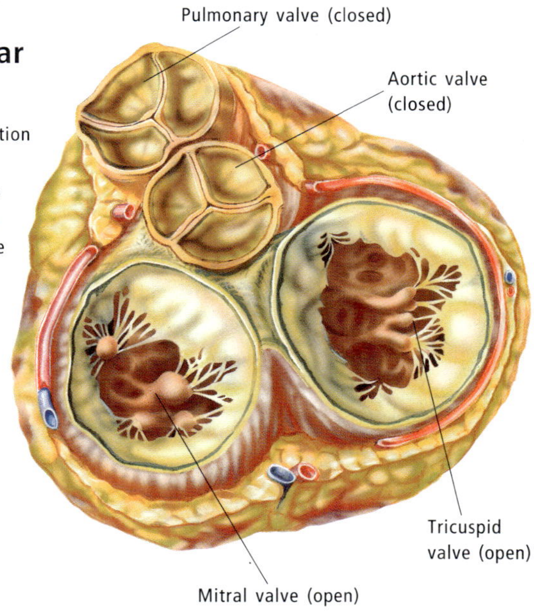

defibrillator is not available, the patient may be kept alive for a short time by compressing the heart between the breastbone and the vertebral column (external cardiac massage) and breathing into the patient's mouth (expired air ventilation). Together these techniques are called cardiopulmonary resuscitation (CPR). In abnormalities of the conducting and pacemaking tissues of the heart, the condition may be treated using drugs or by use of an artificial pacemaker).

Congenital heart diseases

Congenital heart diseases arise before birth, and affect about 1 in every 100 babies born in developed countries. About half of all babies born with a congenital abnormality of the heart will die during the first year of life. Often there is no known cause, but some may be due to abnormal genes, viruses (rubella) or drugs (thalidomide). Congenital heart disease may accompany other congenital abnormalities.

Congenital heart disease is usually due to one (or a combination) of the following defects: abnormal openings between the two sides of the heart (atrial or ventricular septal defect), blockage of large arteries or valves (coarctation of the aorta, pulmonary stenosis), or abnormal positioning of heart chambers or vessels.

Another type of congenital heart disease is patent ductus arteriosus. The ductus arteriosus is a normal opening between the aorta and pulmonary trunk in unborn babies. It usually closes shortly after birth, but in patent ductus arteriosus it remains open into adult life; it can be connected surgically.

Diseases of the valves

The valves of the heart may be involved in disease. The valve openings may become narrowed (valvular stenosis) with the result that blood does not readily flow through; or be unable to prevent the backward flow or regurgitation of blood (valvular incompetence or insufficiency).

Many valve diseases give rise to murmurs—sounds produced by the turbulent flow of blood across roughened valve surfaces, or the excessive movement of blood through normal valves. These may be heard with the aid of a stethoscope, or if loud enough, the vibrations may be felt on the chest wall. Often the presence of a heart murmur may not indicate serious disease, but any murmur should be investigated.

Rheumatic heart disease

Rheumatic heart disease is a condition which follows throat infection with a particular type of bacteria (group A streptococci). The patient's body mounts an immune reaction which damages connective tissues in the heart and joints.

Other heart diseases

Most disease of the heart muscle is due to blockage of the coronary arteries, but there are some rare but serious heart diseases that primarily affect the heart muscle itself. One of these, myocarditis, involves infection or toxic damage of the heart muscle, usually as a result of viral or parasitic infections or toxins from infectious agents, such as diptheria toxin.

Cardiomyopathy is a term used for diseases of the heart muscle of unknown origin. Some cardiomyopathies appear to be caused by alcohol or genetic disorders.

Endocarditis is inflammation of the inner lining of the heart (endocardium). It may occur in rheumatic heart disease and in some connective tissue diseases. It may also be due to infection by bacteria, fungi or viruses.

Pericarditis is an inflammation of the membranes that enclose the heart (the pericardium). If fluid or blood accumulates in the pericardium the heart may be unable to pump effectively (pericardial tamponade). If the pericardium contracts as it heals, the heart may be squeezed (constrictive pericarditis). There are many forms of pericarditis, and it can often be the result of some other disease, such as renal failure.

SEE ALSO *Angina pectoris, Aorta, Arteries, Arrhythmia, Atherosclerosis, Atrial septal defect, Cardiomyopathy, Circulatory system, Coronary arteries, Coronary artery disease, Coronary thrombosis, Endocarditis, Fibrillation, Heartbeat, Hypertension, Myocardial infarction, Myocarditis, Pacemaker, Pericarditis, Rheumatic fever, Stenosis, Tachycardia, Ventricle, Ventricular septal defect*

HEARTBEAT

The beating of the heart against the chest wall is known as the apex beat. It results from the contraction of the ventricles of the heart and can be felt on the lower left side of the chest, immediately below the left nipple. The rate and rhythm of the contraction of the heart can also be assessed by feeling the pulse, a pressure wave conducted down the main arteries of the body with each beat of the heart. The pulse is usually felt at the wrist (radial artery pulse), the neck (common carotid artery pulse), the groin (femoral artery pulse) or the back of the knee (popliteal artery pulse).

The rate and rhythm of contraction of the heart chambers is normally determined by the sinoatrial node, located near the entrance of the superior vena cava into the right atrium. The sinoatrial node is known as the pacemaker of the heart, as the regular electrical impulses it sends out produce the orderly contraction of the heart chambers. It, in turn, is under the influence of sympathetic and parasympathetic nerves, which tend to increase or reduce the heart rate, respectively, and is also influenced by circulating hormones like epinephrine (adrenaline).

Disorders of the rhythm of the heart are called arrhythmias. Abnormalities of heart rhythm can range in severity from mildly annoying to life-threatening. A quite common type of minor arrhythmia is the ventricular ectopic beat (ventricular extrasystole). These occur when an abnormal focus of electrical activity in the ventricles causes a premature contraction. This may occur in healthy people, particularly if they are tired or have consumed a lot of caffeine. The patient may feel nothing or may notice the occasional heavy heartbeat.

More serious types of arrhythmia include atrial fibrillation, in which irregular electrical impulses in the atria cause an uncoordinated contraction of the atria; or ventricular tachycardia in which an abnormal electrical focus in the ventricles drives the heart rate up to 140–220 beats per minute. Atrial fibrillation may arise as a result of mitral valve disease and can have serious consequences. Blood may coagulate (thrombose) in the left atrium and throw off small fragments (thrombotic emboli) that can become lodged in arteries to the brain or legs. Ventricular tachycardia usually accompanies serious heart disease and often causes a feeling of breathlessness and chest pain. The most serious arrhythmia, however, is ventricular fibrillation, which may occur after electrocution, drowning or the death of heart muscle (myocardial infarction). Ventricular fibrillation causes chaotic, uncoordinated and ineffectual contraction of the ventricles. Patients will die within minutes unless cardiopulmonary resuscitation (CPR) is commenced immediately. If available, an electrical defibrillator may be used to reset the heart rhythm (cardioversion).

Another type of disorder involving electrical conduction in the heart is heart block. In this condition the conduction of electrical impulses from the atria to the ventricles is blocked (AV block) so that the atria beat at a faster rate than the ventricles. Conduction blocks may also occur within the conduction pathways of the ventricle.

Many drugs are now available that can help control arrhythmias. These drugs may act to stabilize the electrically excitable membranes of heart cells (such as with quinidine, procainamide, lignocaine, disopyramide and phenytoin), slow the rate of ventricular response to atrial arrhythmias (for example, digitalis) or block the effects of circulating sympathetic substances on the rate and excitability of heart tissue (beta-blocking drugs).

SEE ALSO *Antiarrhythmic drugs, Arrythmia, Beta-blockers, Fibrillation, Heart, Mitral valve, Pacemaker, Pulse, Tachycardia*

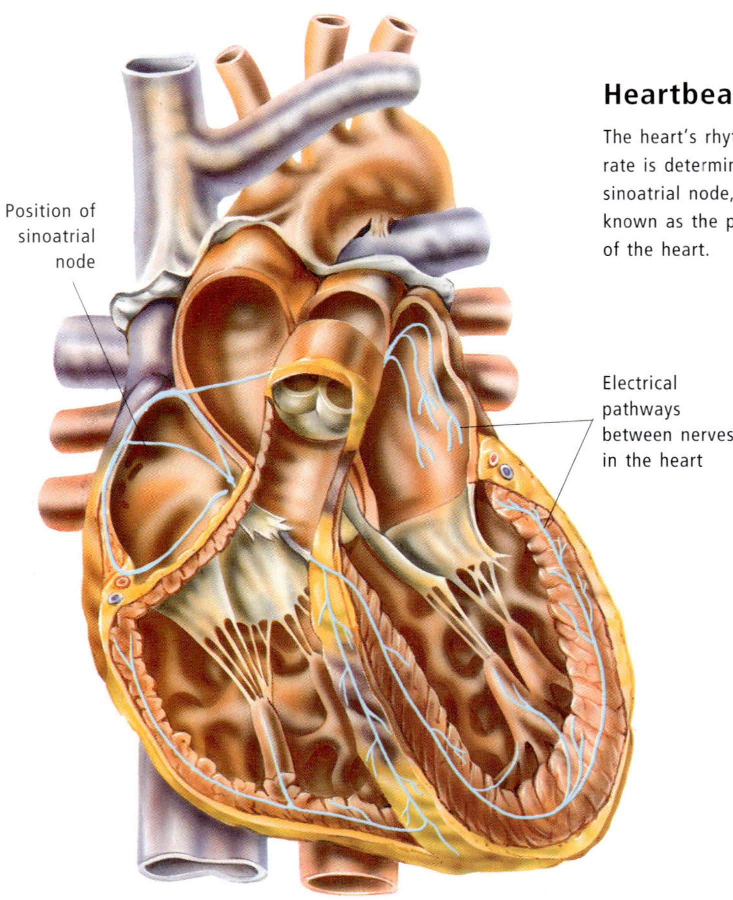

Heartbeat

The heart's rhythm and rate is determined by the sinoatrial node, which is known as the pacemaker of the heart.

HEARTBURN

Heartburn is a feeling of burning pain in the chest behind the breastbone combined with a sour or bitter taste at the back of the throat. These symptoms are caused by the regurgitation (reflux) of stomach contents, a mixture of food and digestive acids which flows back up the esophagus causing pain and irritation. Gastroesophageal reflux is common in otherwise healthy people although it can also be a symptom of an underlying disorder.

Chronic cases of heartburn are termed GERD (gastroesophageal reflux disease) and may be associated with intestinal disorders.

Chronic exposure of the esophegeal lining to stomach acids can lead to a number of complications such as ulceration of the esophagus, scarring and narrowing (strictures), and changes in the lining (epithelium) that can lead to cancer.

Relaxation of the lower esophageal sphincter, a muscle which closes after allowing swallowed food to pass to the stomach, is the cause of reflux. The sphincter may be weakened, or may react to stimulus from certain foods, alcohol or tobacco, or may open under pressure from the stomach that results from overeating or from sitting, lying or taking up activity too soon after eating.

Heartburn is common in the overweight, can be caused by hiatus (hiatal) hernia, and is also common in pregnancy through the displacement of the stomach by the developing baby and the hormonal changes which reduce the tone of all muscles, including the stomach and esophageal sphincters.

The symptoms are usually treated with antacids or, for more severe cases, anti-ulcer drugs. It is also important to reduce or avoid coffee, very spicy foods and curries, give up smoking, lose weight, eat smaller and less-rich meals, reduce alcohol, not lie down or bend over until food is digested. Certain drugs such as aspirin, anti-inflammatory or anti-arthritic drugs should be avoided. Raising the head of the bed when you sleep may help avoid heartburn at night.

There are a number of alternative therapies that may help to alleviate the symptoms of heartburn. Acupuncture treats heartburn at points that are believed to improve gastric function, relieve pain and reduce feelings of stress and anxiety. Herbalism prescribes alfalfa and meadowsweet to alkalize stomach acids, marshmallow and licorice to soothe mucous membranes and chamomile for dyspepsia associated with nervous tension.

Naturopathy suggests a low acid, non-spicy wholefood diet of frequent, small meals, eaten in a calm environment. Possible food allergens such as gluten need to be eliminated and smoking, coffee, citrus or alcohol should be avoided. Slippery elm or barley water taken before eating may help soothe the stomach. The biochemic tissue salt Nat Phos may reduce acidity and relieve nausea.

SEE ALSO *Esophagus, Gastroesophageal reflux, Hiatus hernia, Intestines, Pregnancy*

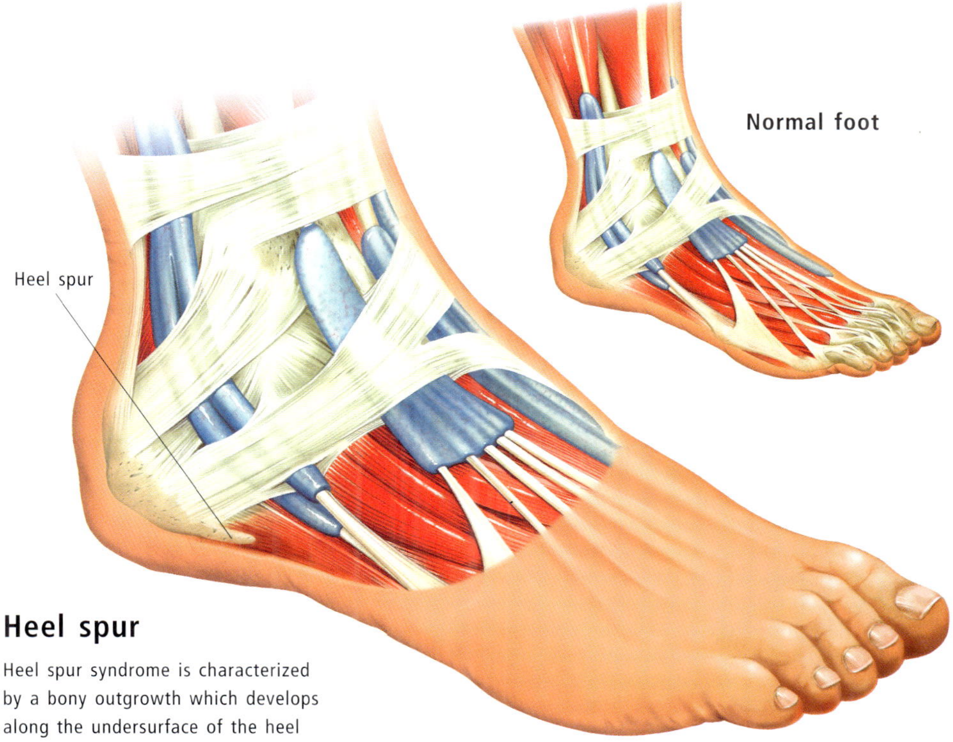

Heel spur

Heel spur syndrome is characterized by a bony outgrowth which develops along the undersurface of the heel bone, causing inflammation.

HEAT RASH

Also known as miliaria or prickly heat, heat rash consists of tiny blisters at the site of sweat pores. When the sweat ducts become blocked, the sweat escapes into other levels of the skin and the blisters result. Extremely hot weather is usually the cause. In newborn babies the sweat glands are not fully developed and will become blocked if the baby is overheated. Babies may also suffer heat rash when they have a fever.

Treatment for babies is a tepid bath, fresh air and lightweight clothing; sometimes calamine lotion may also be necessary. The rash usually disappears in a couple of days, if not then check with a health professional.

Other types of heat rash include miliaria crystallina, seen in people who have a fever or are suffering from sunburn. These blisters are tiny and dewdrop shaped. Miliaria rubra, commonly called prickly heat, is the most common form of heat rash and produces dense, itchy red papules (solid cone-shaped lumps), which appear on the trunk. Miliaria pustules are blisters filled with pus, and miliaria profunda are firm papules found in the vascular layer of the skin.

Treatment for heat rash concentrates on reducing heat, minimizing sweating, and avoiding irritants such as tight clothing.

SEE ALSO *Newborn, Rash, Skin*

HEATSTROKE

Heatstroke, or sunstroke, is a potentially fatal reaction to heat caused by the body's inability to regulate its own temperature. Its onset may be gradual or sudden with headache, weakness and nausea followed by mental confusion and high body temperature around 104–115°F (40–46°C). Shock, convulsions, brain damage, coma and death may follow.

Treatment is to reduce the temperature below 102°F (39°C) by moving the person to a cooler place, removing clothing where possible, and cooling with fans and ice packs to the head, neck, armpits and groin.

SEE ALSO *Body temperature, Fever*

HEEL SPUR

A painful condition, heel spur syndrome is often most severe upon standing after a period of rest. It is typically associated with development of a spur-like projection from the bone of the heel, visible on x-ray

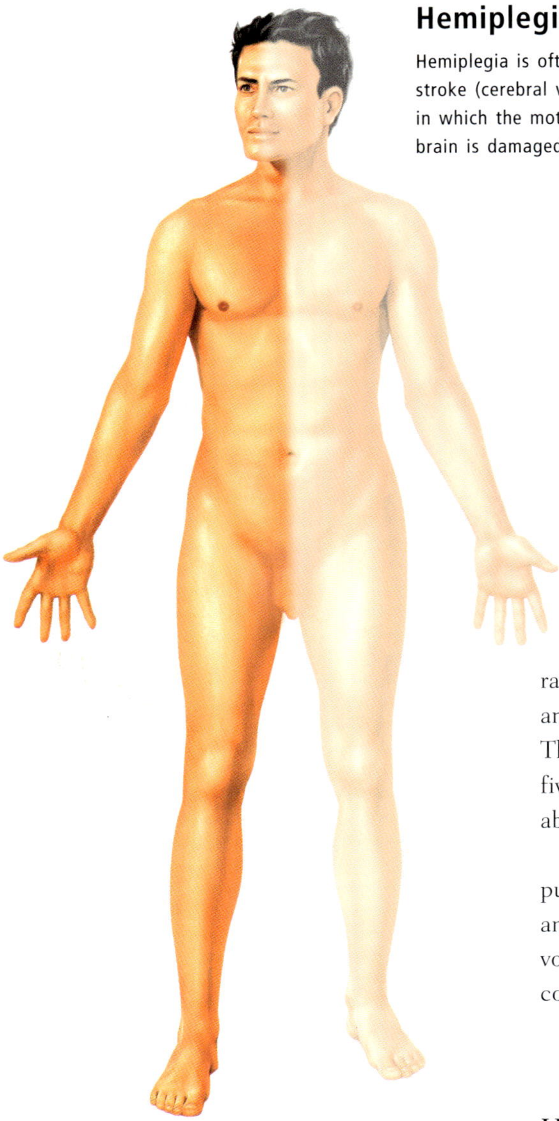

Hemiplegia

Hemiplegia is often the result of stroke (cerebral vascular accident) in which the motor area of the brain is damaged.

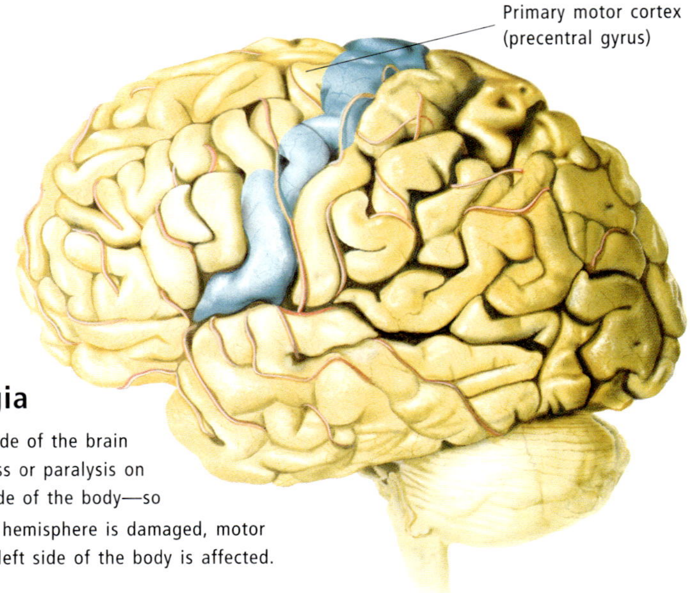

Hemiplegia

Injury to one side of the brain causes weakness or paralysis on the opposite side of the body—so when the right hemisphere is damaged, motor control on the left side of the body is affected.

examination. The spur itself is not the cause of the pain—it is usually secondary to injury or inflammation of the plantar fascia (a ligament that extends from the heel bone across the sole of the foot) which becomes calcified to form the visible spur. Other causes of heel pain include stress fractures and bursitis.

Treatment of the heel spur syndrome may involve providing suitable physical support to the heel, anti-inflammatory drugs or injections, or surgery.

SEE ALSO *Bursitis, Foot, Fractures*

HEMANGIOMA

A hemangioma is a benign, congenital tumor consisting of a cluster of blood vessels. There are two main types: capillary and cavernous.

Capillary (strawberry) hemangiomas are raised red lumps that look like strawberries and are caused by dilated blood vessels. They usually disappear between the ages of five and ten but laser treatment is also available if it is considered necessary.

Cavernous hemangiomas are raised large purple or dark red patches, which can occur anywhere on the body. Treatment may involve surgical removal or, for children, corticosteroids.

SEE ALSO *Birthmarks*

HEMIPLEGIA

Paralysis of two limbs on the same side of the body is known as hemiplegia. When it is the result of a stroke (cerebral vascular accident), the weakness or paralysis occurs on the side of the body opposite to the side of the brain which has been injured by the stroke. Hemiplegia can make it difficult for the affected person to sit, walk or stand, even when their muscles are strong enough.

Acute alternating hemiplegia in children is a rare disorder which occurs before the age of 18 months. The disorder is identified by frequent attacks of paralysis on alternate sides of the body. These paralysis attacks are treated with drugs.

SEE ALSO *Paralysis, Stroke*

HEMOCHROMATOSIS

Hemochromatosis is a disease state characterized by excessive retention of iron within the body, most commonly the result of a recessive genetic disorder associated with increased iron absorption. It can lead to liver damage, pancreatic injury leading to diabetes, and skin pigmentation. Treatment requires repeated bleeding of the patient to deplete body iron stores.

SEE ALSO *Iron*

HEMODIALYSIS

Also known as kidney dialysis, hemodialysis is the filtration of the blood through semi-permeable membranes to remove waste materials in patients lacking renal function (renal failure). Blood from an artery is pumped through the artificial kidney, known as a dialyzer, and then returned to the body via a vein. Intermittent dialysis has kept some patients alive for nearly 20 years and though it is mostly carried out in hospitals, some patients, using automatic equipment, can carry out the procedure at home.

SEE ALSO *Dialysis, Kidney*

HEMOGLOBIN

Hemoglobin is a compound found in red blood cells. It consists of an iron-containing pigment, called heme, which combines with the protein globin to form hemoglobin. Oxygen combines readily with hemoglobin: so-called oxyhemoglobin looks bright red, while deoxygenated hemoglobin looks much darker. The role of hemoglobin is to carry oxygen in the blood from the lungs to the body tissues and transport carbon dioxide back to the lungs. Hence hemoglobin is essential to metabolism.

Normal levels of hemoglobin in the blood are approximately 14–17 grams per 100 milliliters (deciliter) for males and 12–15 grams per 100 milliliters for females.

People with anemia have lower than normal levels of hemoglobin. They feel tired and weak and look pale. Anemia may be due to blood loss, inadequate manufacture of hemoglobin in the bone marrow, or the production of abnormal hemoglobin. Sickle cell disease and thalassemia, for example, are genetic diseases caused by different, abnormal forms of hemoglobin.

SEE ALSO *Anemia, Red blood cells, Sickle cell disease*

HEMOLYTIC ANEMIA

Hemolytic anemia is a condition in which red blood cells (erythrocytes) are rapidly destroyed in the blood (a process called hemolysis). It can happen in hereditary conditions where red blood cells are abnormal, such as in sickle cell disease, hereditary spherocytosis or thalassemia. Hemolysis may be caused by antibodies, for example after a mismatched blood transfusion, or it may be a side effect of some drugs.

Treatment for hemolytic anemia involves replacing the blood with blood transfusions and correction of the cause if possible. Sometimes splenectomy (surgical removal of the spleen) is required.

SEE ALSO *Red blood cells, Sickle cell disease, Spleen, Thalassemia*

Hemoglobin

Hemoglobin consists of four molecules of heme, each of which contain an iron ion, and strands of the protein globin.

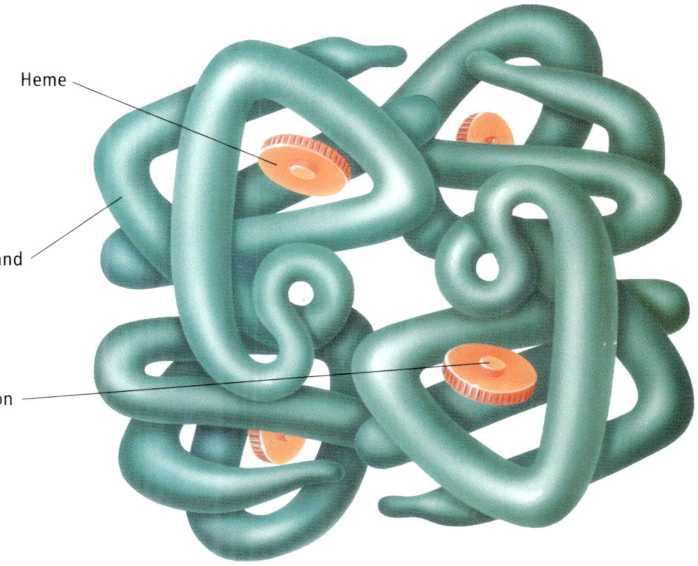

Hemolytic anemia

Hereditary spherocytosis is an inherited form of hemolytic anemia in which 50 percent or more of red blood cells are replaced by abnormal, small round spherocytes.

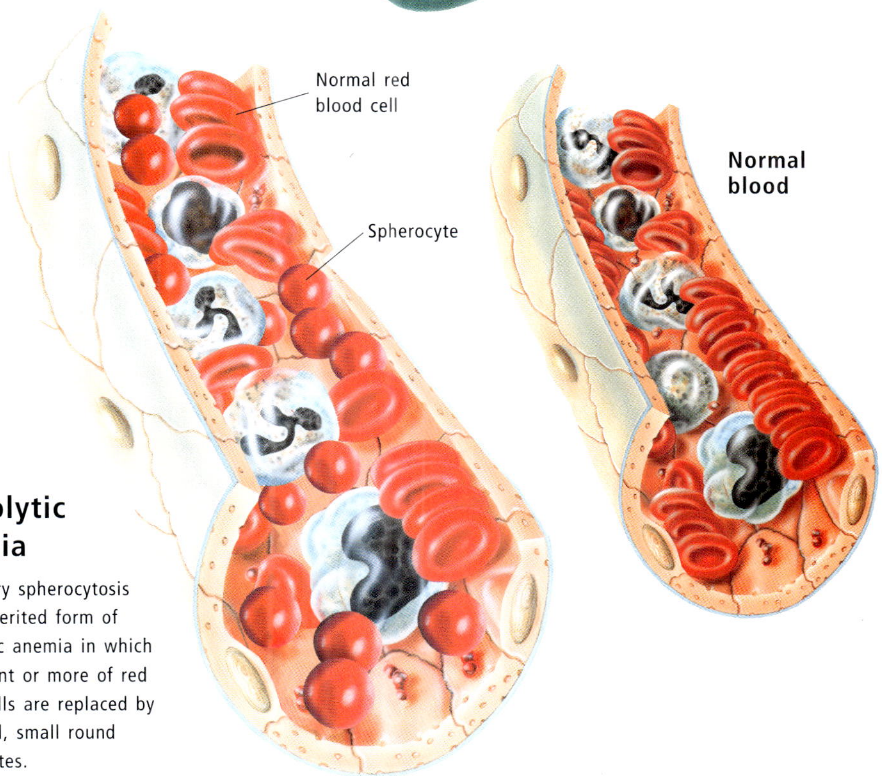

Hemoglobin and oxygen transport

Hemoglobin is the main component of the red blood cell and serves as the oxygen-carrying protein. In the lungs, hemoglobin carries oxygen from the alveoli (air sacs) to the body tissues and transports carbon dioxide back to the alveoli.

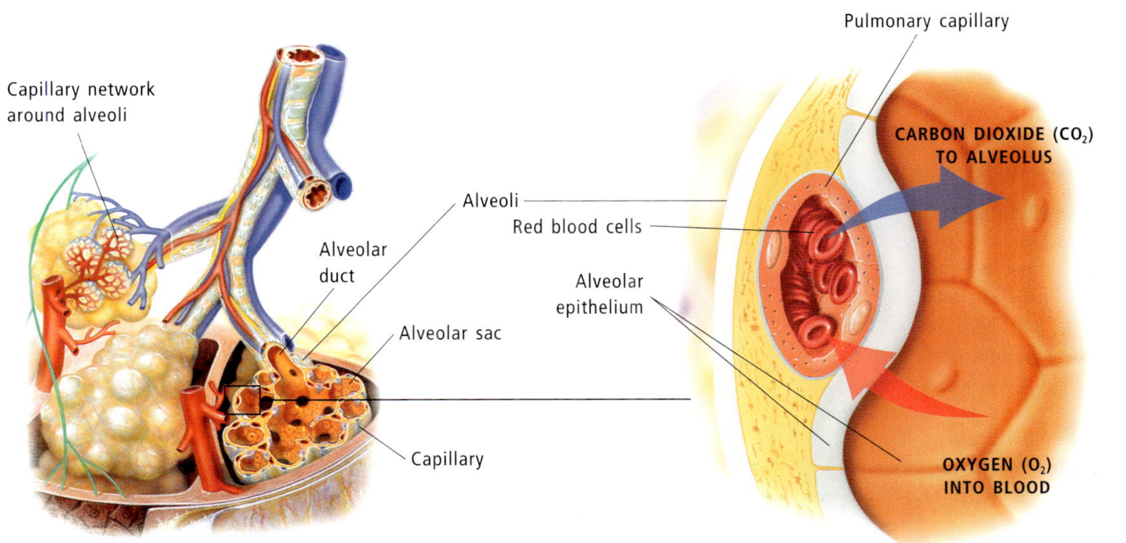

HEMOLYTIC DISEASE OF THE NEWBORN

Also called erythroblastosis fetalis, hemolytic disease of the newborn is a condition that develops in an unborn infant when there is an incompatibility between the mother's blood type and the baby's.

As a result of the incompatibility (usually of the Rh blood factor), antibodies that are formed in the mother's blood attack the red blood cells of the fetus. The incompatibility of the blood cells usually leaves the first child unharmed, affecting subsequent pregnancies. It can still affect the first pregnancy if the mother has formed antibodies from a previous blood transfusion. The child may be born with anemia (because of the destruction of fetal blood), jaundice (because the yellow pigment bilirubin is released when the red blood cells break down), an enlarged liver and/or spleen, and generalized swelling (edema).

If too much bilirubin is released, brain and nerve damage (kernicterus) may result. If there is too much edema, fatal heart failure may result (hydrops fetalis).

The condition can be prevented by screening the mother with a blood test during pregnancy. If she is Rh negative, and if the father is Rh positive (meaning there is a chance of an Rh positive fetus and hence incompatibility), then an injection of gamma globulin should be given to the mother during the pregnancy and within a few days of delivery. These injections prevent the development of maternal antibodies against the fetal blood. Babies born with hemolytic anemia may need to be given blood transfusions after delivery.

SEE ALSO *Antibodies, Rhesus (Rh) factor*

HEMOPHILIA

Hemophilia refers to a group of inherited disorders which can result in severe bleeding. An abnormal gene is carried on an X chromosome of unaffected females and produces the bleeding disorder in their affected male children, who have no additional normal X chromosome. Affected males cannot transmit hemophilia to their sons. Fifty percent of the sons of carrier females will be affected, and 50 percent of daughters of carrier females and affected males will be carriers.

In about a quarter of cases, hemophilia develops in a male without a family history of it, due to a new abnormal gene. The abnormal gene can result in decreased production of factor VIII (classical hemophilia) or factor IX (Christmas disease).

Hemophilia varies in severity, depending on the level of the clotting factor involved. If severe, it may cause bleeding in the newborn, from the umbilical cord or at circumcision. More often it appears when the boy starts to walk, causing painful bleeding into joints, especially the knee joint. Milder forms may not be detected until surgery, or until a major injury results in large bruises in the muscles.

The treatment of hemophilia involves preventing excess bleeding when injury occurs by giving the person an infusion of clotting factors obtained from normal blood donors. In the past, giving clotting factor transfusions (and blood transfusions in general) was complicated by the transmission of hepatitis B and HIV (the AIDS virus). In most countries plasma is now treated to destroy viruses and the risk of this is very small, and factor VII can be produced synthetically.

SEE ALSO *Chromosomes, Congenital abnormalities, Genes*

HEMORRHAGE

Hemorrhage is the technical term for bleeding. Bleeding can be a normal process, as with menstrual bleeding, but it is usually abnormal. The commonest cause of bleeding is trauma, such as from a cut. Bleeding is often a sign of damage to a blood vessel. This may be due to minor trauma, such as most nosebleeds; trauma can also cause subconjunctival hemorrhage under the white part of the eye.

Damaged blood vessels may be due to infection; cystitis, for example, can produce blood in the urine, and bronchitis can cause blood to appear in the sputum. Erosion of the vessel wall by acid can cause bleeding from peptic ulcers. Sometimes damage to the blood vessel is the result of a more serious disease, such as inflammation of the blood vessel (vasculitis) or a tumor invading it.

Bleeding can result from increased pressure in veins or arteries. An example of the former is bleeding from hemorrhoids and of the latter is subarachnoid hemorrhage, which is bleeding on the surface of the brain; this is often associated with high blood pressure.

Some types of bleeding can have serious or life-threatening effects, due either to the volume of blood lost or the site of the hemorrhage. Massive blood loss can result from major trauma, such as a car accident or, less often, from deficiencies of platelets or clotting factors. Bleeding that can be serious due to its location includes cerebral hemorrhage and bleeding before (antepartum), during (intrapartum) or just after (postpartum) childbirth.

SEE ALSO *Blood vessels, Bronchitis, Cystitis, Hemorrhoids, Peptic ulcer, Platelets, Subarachnoid hemorrhage, Vasculitis*

Hemophilia

In hemophilia, an important clotting factor in blood, known as factor VIII, is missing due to an abnormal gene. The first stage of clotting (a), in which platelets, leukocytes (white blood cells) and red blood cells spill into the damaged tissues, occurs normally, but in the second stage (b), coagulation between fibrin strands and blood cells fails to occur. This means that the normal formation of a clot cannot occur and bleeding continues instead.

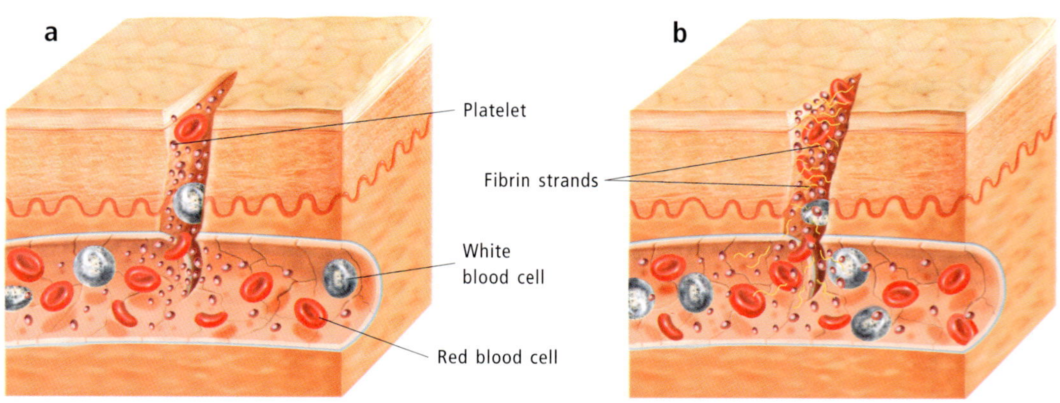

HEMORRHOIDS

Often known as piles, hemorrhoids are enlarged veins in the lower portion of the rectum and anus, which become swollen due to straining when passing feces. They occur frequently in people who suffer constipation and those who sit down for prolonged periods.

Hemorrhoids are common, affecting 1 in every 500 persons. They are especially common during pregnancy, after childbirth and in hepatic hypertension, caused by tumors or cirrhosis. Though not dangerous, they can cause irritation by bleeding or passing through the anus. Symptoms include bright red blood in the stool, anal itching and pain during bowel movements. Painful thrombosis (clotting of blood in the veins) sometimes occurs.

The diagnosis is usually made by a primary care physician (general practitioner), who may use a small tube called an anoscope or proctoscope to visualize the hemorrhoids in the anal canal. More serious conditions such as colonic or rectal polyps and cancer, which can also cause bleeding, must be ruled out.

Hemorrhoids are treated with a high-fiber diet, topical steroid ointment, and surgery in troublesome cases. Surgical techniques include rubber band ligation, cryosurgery and hemorrhoidectomy. These treatments are usually effective, but the condition may recur unless preventive measures—treatment of constipation and a more active lifestyle—are adopted.

SEE ALSO *Anus, Constipation, Rectum, Thrombosis, Veins*

Hemorrhoids

Hemorrhoids are swollen veins in the lower part of the rectum or anus, often due to constipation or prolonged periods of sitting.

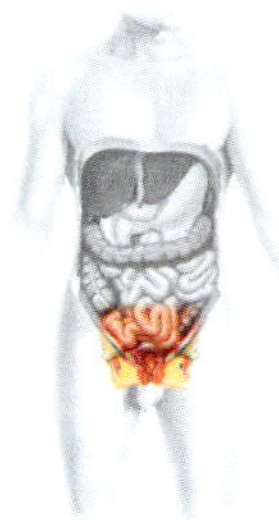

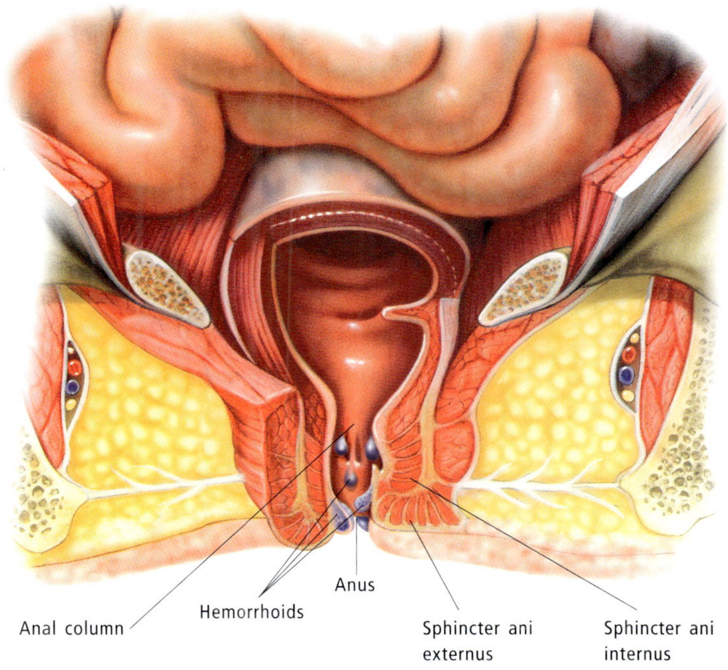

HEPATIC ARTERY

The hepatic artery supplies 30 percent of the liver's blood supply, the rest coming from the portal vein. The common hepatic artery divides into right and left hepatic arteries to supply both sides of the liver with oxygenated blood. The portal vein delivers venous blood from the gut.

SEE ALSO *Liver*

HEPATIC ENPHALOPATHY

Hepatic encephalopathy is an acute complication of liver disorders in which the nitrogen wastes such as urea and other toxins build up in the body and affect the brain and nervous systems.

When liver cells are damaged due to conditions such as alcoholic cirrhosis or hepatitis they cannot effectively do their job of cleansing the body of toxins. This causes metabolic abnormalities marked by symptoms ranging from confusion and memory loss to muscular tremors and speech impairment.

Hepatic encephalopathy may be chronic, leading to dementia, coma and death. It is due to liver failure as a result of diseases like hepatitis, alcoholic cirrhosis, some medications, and cancer, or eating too much protein when you have those diseases.

Treatment involves addressing contributing causes and may include removing toxins from the intestinal tract, preventing ammonia absorption from the intestines, adopting a reduced-protein diet and avoiding medications that are normally metabolized by the liver. Those who are suffering from hepatic encephalopathy may require hospitalization with respiratory and cardiovascular support.

SEE ALSO *Cirrhosis of the liver, Hepatitis, Liver, Nervous system*

Hepatic artery

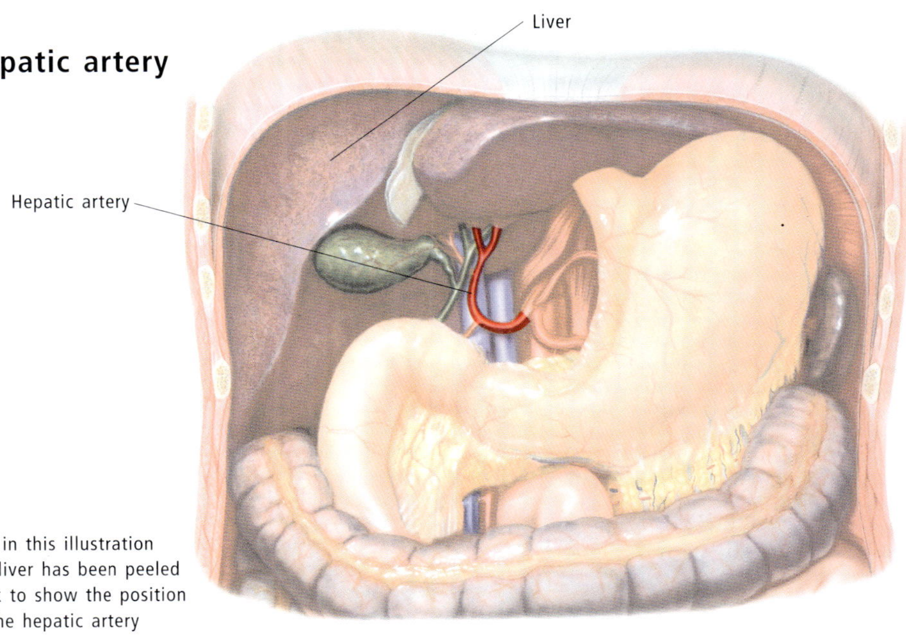

NB: in this illustration the liver has been peeled back to show the position of the hepatic artery

H

HEPATITIS

Hepatitis is an inflammation of the liver which reduces its ability to function. It can be infectious, when caused by viruses and parasites, or non-infectious, when caused by alcohol, certain drugs and toxic agents such as chemicals found in aerosol sprays and paint thinners. Alcoholic hepatitis is the result of sustained consumption of excessive quantities of alcohol. If caught early enough it can be reversed, if not, it leads to alcoholic cirrhosis.

Hepatitis can also be caused by an autoimmune disorder when the body mistakenly fights its own healthy tissue with its own cells, and can be associated with some illnesses such as Wilson's disease. Most cases are caused by a viral infection.

Some cases of hepatitis are difficult to recognize, but when symptoms are present there may be general weariness, loss of appetite, fever, vomiting, abdominal pain and jaundice (a yellowing of the skin and eyes). This yellowing is a result of the damage the virus inflicts on the liver cells. Viral hepatitis in its acute phase usually lasts from a few days to several weeks. In about 5 percent of cases the symptoms will subside into chronic hepatitis, which can continue for years.

There are seven known hepatitis viruses, labeled A, B, C, D, E, F and G. Hepatitis A (HAV), the most common form worldwide, is spread through oral–fecal transmission. For example, it can be spread via an infected person with fecal matter on their hands handling food that is to be eaten by non-infected people. This virus can also be transmitted in drinking water, or water in contact with food which is infected with raw sewage. Time between exposure and developing symptoms is around 28 days. Treatment is usually bed rest and adequate intake of fluids and most patients recover completely. A vaccine against the disease (made from inactivated hepatitis A virus) is available to those considered at risk. This provides at least ten years protection. Otherwise, good personal hygiene and avoiding raw seafood in areas where hepatitis A is prevalent is recommended.

Hepatitis B (HBV), though not as common as HAV, is becoming increasingly frequent. Spread through blood transfusions, intravenous drug use or unprotected sexual intercourse, this virus remains in the body for many years. Babies born to a mother with HBV have a 95 percent chance of being infected. A more serious disease than hepatitis A, it can become chronic and can lead to permanent liver damage such as cirrhosis or liver cancer. Symptoms appear between 40 days to six months after exposure, and include fatigue, abdominal pain, loss of appetite, nausea, diarrhea, dark urine and jaundice. Treatment is bed rest. A vaccine is available which provides protection for at least 5 years.

Hepatitis C (HCV) was first identified in the 1980s and initially was known as non-A or non-B. It is spread through blood, most commonly through sharing needles among intravenous drug users, occasionally during sexual acts or from an infected mother to her baby. It can also spread through sharing toothbrushes or razors. Symptoms are rarely acute and may be similar to HBV. Of 100 people infected with HCV about 20 will find the virus has cleared up of its own accord after about six weeks, the other 80 will suffer chronically. Treatment is via interferon formulations, which are effective in about 30 percent of patients. In many countries blood and sperm donors are screened for HCV. There is no vaccine.

Hepatitis D (HDV), also known as delta agent, is a parasite of HBV using the B virus to survive and can therefore occur only at the same time as HBV. Transmitted only through infected blood, it has similar symptoms to HBV. Between 70 and 80 percent of those infected will develop cirrhosis. It can be prevented with the same vaccine used against HBV and treatment is with alpha interferon, though this is not always effective.

Hepatitis E (HEV) is similar to HAV. Transmitted in the same way, via feces and oral ingestion, it is found mostly in countries where sanitation is poor or among travelers returning from high-risk areas. It is particularly dangerous for pregnant women, in whom infection can prove fatal. The symptoms of fatigue, abdominal pain, loss of appetite, nausea, diarrhea, dark urine and jaundice are similar to HAV. There are few chronic cases and treatment is rest for two weeks.

Hepatitis F (HFV), was first reported in 1994 and is spread in the same way as HAV and HEV.

Hepatitis G (HGV) is thought to be the cause of large numbers of sexually transmitted and blood-borne cases of hepatitis. Symptoms are not yet fully determined though it does cause both acute and chronic forms of the disease and can infect a person already infected with HCV. There is no vaccine and treatment is rest.

When symptoms associated with hepatitis are present, tests will be conducted on liver function to determine whether the illness is hepatitis or some other problem, such as gallstones, or even cancer. Laboratory tests, including a biopsy, may be necessary.

Anyone who is wanting to travel to areas where hepatitis is a risk needs to consider vaccination and to be aware of the need for good hygiene practices. People who are working in high-risk professions, such as physicians, nurses and dentists, also need to consider vaccination. In some countries, immunization is also advised for newborns and adolescents.

SEE ALSO *Alcoholism, Cirrhosis of the liver, Jaundice, Liver, Viruses, Wilson's disease*

HEPATOMA

Hepatoma, or hepatocellular carcinoma, is a malignant tumor of the liver. It is a primary tumor, that is, originating in the liver rather than spreading to the liver from another site. It is usually associated with an underlying liver disease such as alcoholic cirrhosis or by hepatitis B or C infection, and it is especially common in South Africa and Southeast Asia.

The symptoms are a hard mass in the right upper abdomen, unexplained weight loss and appetite loss, abdominal aches and pains and sometimes jaundice with yellow skin. Blood tests for liver function, an abdominal CAT scan and a liver biopsy may be used by the physician to confirm the diagnosis.

Treatment is not usually successful; in only about 25 percent of cases can the tumor be fully removed and it tends to spread to other organs such as lungs and bones. It is usually considered incurable.

SEE ALSO *Cancer, Cirrhosis of the liver, Hepatitis, Liver*

Cirrhotic liver

If it is not treated, chronic hepatitis can lead to cirrhosis of the liver. When this occurs, nodular, fibrous tissue replaces damaged liver cells and connective tissue in the liver, distorting its smooth surface and internal microstructure.

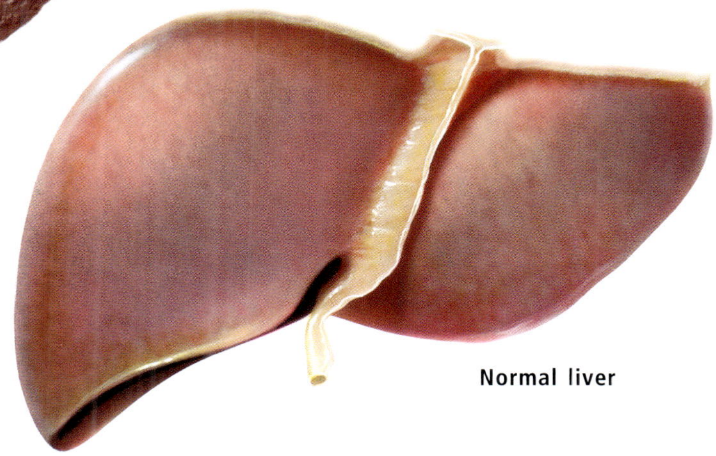

Normal liver

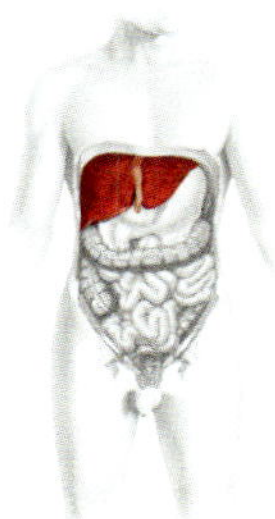

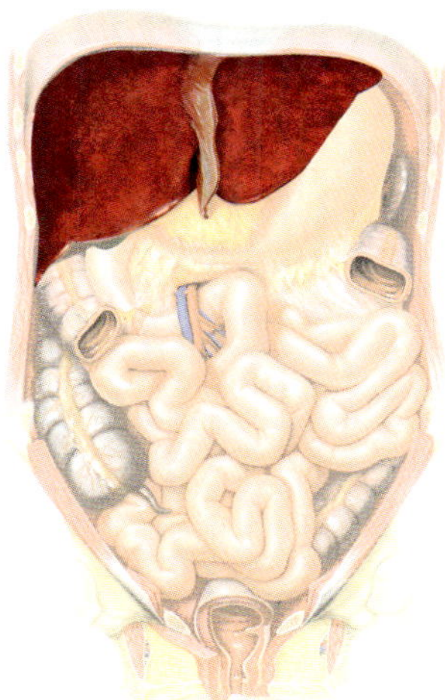

Hepatitis virus

Hepatitis is inflammation of the liver. When caused by a virus, it is called viral or infectious hepatitis. Sometimes viral hepatitis can be transmitted in drinking water.

Damaged liver microstructure

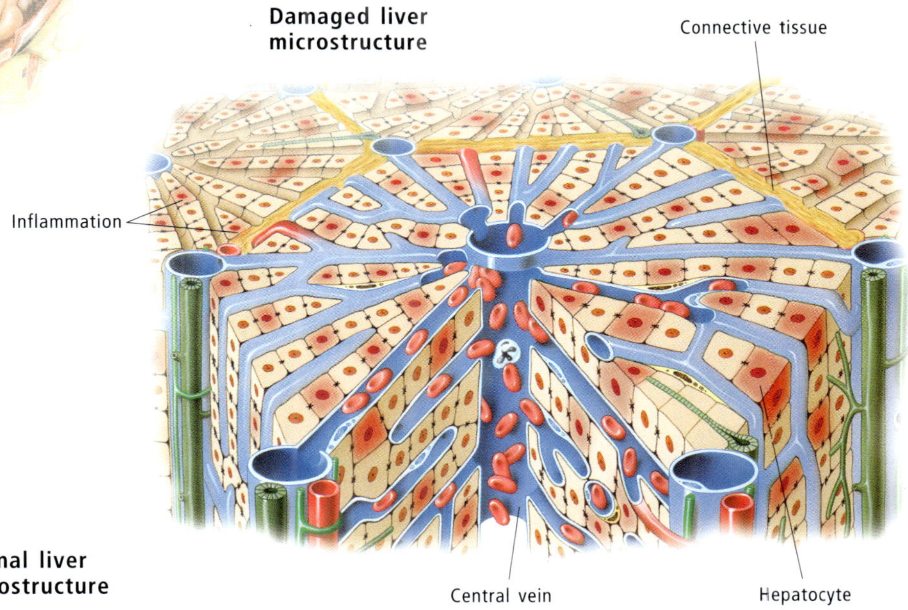

Normal liver microstructure

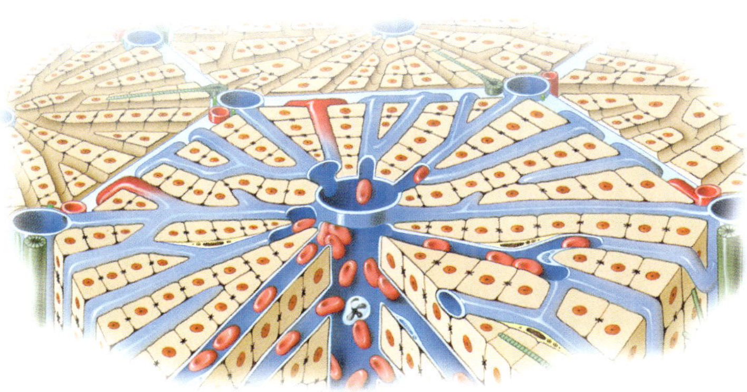

Scarring of the liver microstructure

Chronic hepatitis causes cirrhosis, a disease in which the normal microscopic lobular architecture of the liver is destroyed. Scarring and distortion of the hepatocytes (liver cells) and connective tissue that form each hexagonal lobule can disrupt the flow of blood through the liver.

HEPATORENAL SYNDROME

This is a syndrome that occurs when a person who has liver dysfunction undergoes a decrease in kidney function as well. The cause is unknown but is thought to involve a reduction of blood flow to the kidney. As in acute renal failure, there is decreased urine production and abdominal swelling. Nitrogenous wastes build up in the bloodstream, causing nausea, dementia, delirium, confusion, and jerky muscle movements.

Hepatorenal syndrome is diagnosed when other causes of kidney failure are ruled out. The treatment is the same as for other types of renal failure and dialysis may be necessary. The underlying liver disease must be corrected and liver transplantation may be necessary.

Despite failing, the kidney itself remains normal in structure and if the liver disease is corrected, or following liver transplantation, kidney function improves. More often, though, the syndrome is a terminal stage of liver failure, cirrhosis, or alcoholic hepatitis, and death occurs from secondary infections or internal bleeding.

SEE ALSO ***Cirrhosis of the liver, Hepatitis, Kidney, Liver***

HERBALISM

The use of herbal medicine is as old and as widespread as humanity. Paleontologists have found bunches of medicinal herbs among the fossilized remains of our Neanderthal ancestors. In traditional societies knowledge of the healing properties of plants, probably originating from an intuitive animal instinct and then continuously tested and evaluated, has been passed down through the millennia.

The earliest written records of herbal medicine, found in the Middle East, India and China, date back over 3,500 years. From these beginnings herbal treatment developed into an important branch of Traditional Chinese Medicine, still widely practiced today, and Ayurvedic medicine in India also makes use of an extensive herbal dispensary.

Traditional European herbalism developed under the ancient Greeks, most particularly Hippocrates (460–380 BC) who emphasized careful diagnosis, minimalist intervention and the use of simple herbal drugs. During the Dark Ages, Greek medicine was kept alive in monasteries, and developed by Arab physicians, most notably Avicenna (AD 979–1037), whose research influenced the practice of herbal medicine from India to Europe for many centuries.

In Renaissance Europe herbalism was augmented by herbs brought from the New World where native Americans had an impressive knowledge of plant remedies. The printing press led to the publication of many self-help herbals; the best known of these, the seventeenth century's Nicholas Culpeper's *Complete Herbal,* is still in print today.

With the Industrial Revolution people lost touch with their herbal folklore as they moved into the cities, turning to herbally based pharmaceutical preparations. In the nineteenth century a number of traditional herbs, such as the quinine-containing Peruvian bark, were analyzed and their active ingredients extracted to make potent drugs.

Professional herbal associations and colleges have sprung up in the twentieth century to pass on the traditions of herbal medicine and to bring them up to date. In Europe the term herbalism has been replaced by "phytotherapy", from the Greek *phyton* (plant) and *therapeuein* (to heal). This renaming reflects a shift by medically-orientated herbalists towards the scientific proof of their plant-based medicines. In Western societies there has been a huge revival of interest in herbal medicine by both people seeking alternatives to drug therapy and by pharmaceutical researchers investigating the active principles of plants for new medicines. In the less industrialized nations locally produced herbs continue to be used as the main source of medicine.

Philosophy

Herbalists use plant-based medicines to encourage the body to make its own corrective healing processes. They favor the use of the whole herb as medicine, rather than its isolated active ingredients, arguing that this provides a gentler, safer and more natural form of treatment than pharmaceutical drugs do.

Where herbalism is based on a holistic philosophy, such as in Traditional Chinese Medicine or Ayurveda, illness is viewed as a result of imbalance and the herbal remedies are given to restore overall harmony within the body. Western herbalists usually work from a dual understanding of both naturopathic principles and orthodox medical diagnosis. They prescribe herbal remedies by matching their therapeutic properties with the patient's symptoms, as well as by seeking to strengthen the body's systems that are under-functioning.

In order to make the right choice of herbs for their patient's condition, professional herbalists undertake a comprehensive assessment of the patient's medical history, lifestyle and physical and psychological symptoms.

Herbal constituents and actions

A herbal medicine may comprise whole plant, part of a plant (root or flower) or an extract of a plant, such as a tincture or oil. Chemical analysis of herbs show up a range of active principles, the most common being tannins, glycoside and alkaloids. Other chemicals are produced as plant hormones, volatile oils, gums or resins. Herbs also contain vitamins, minerals and enzymes in small amounts.

Herbs are classified medicinally according to their specific actions. There are many herbs that may be used, but the main ones include the following.

Alterative herbs are believed to restore healthy function and stimulate the body's nutrition and elimination processes, e.g. yellow dock (*Rumex crispus*), red clover (*Trifolium pratense*).

Antiseptic herbs aim to prevent or reduce infection, e.g. echinacea (*Echinacea angustifolia*), garlic (*Allium sativum*).

Antispasmodic herbs are prescribed to ease muscle tension and spasm, e.g. passion flower (*Passiflora incarnata*), cramp bark (*Viburnum opulus*).

Astringent herbs are said to bind the proteins of the skin and mucous membranes, reducing inflammation, e.g. witch hazel (*Hamamelis virginiana*), sage (*Salvia officianalis*).

Bitter herbs may help to stimulate saliva and gastric juices, aiding digestion and appetite, e.g. dandelion (*Taraxacum officinale*), gentian (*Gentian lutea*).

Nervine herbs

It is thought that some herbs can affect the body's nervous system, restoring harmony and balance. Herbs such as lavender and St John's wort may have a calming effect, whereas other herbs, such as oats, may be stimulating.

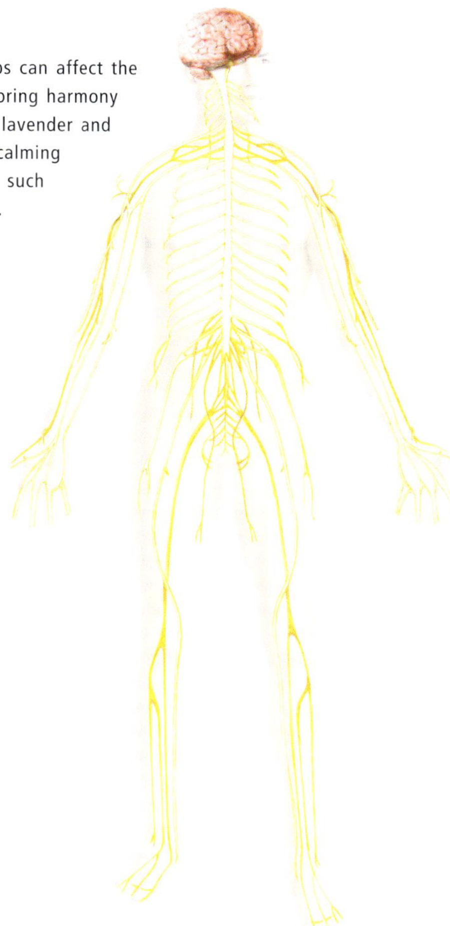

Muscle health

Herbalists prescribe damiana and goldenseal to nourish muscle and tissue. Antispasmodic herbs such as passion flower and cramp bark may help ease muscle spasm.

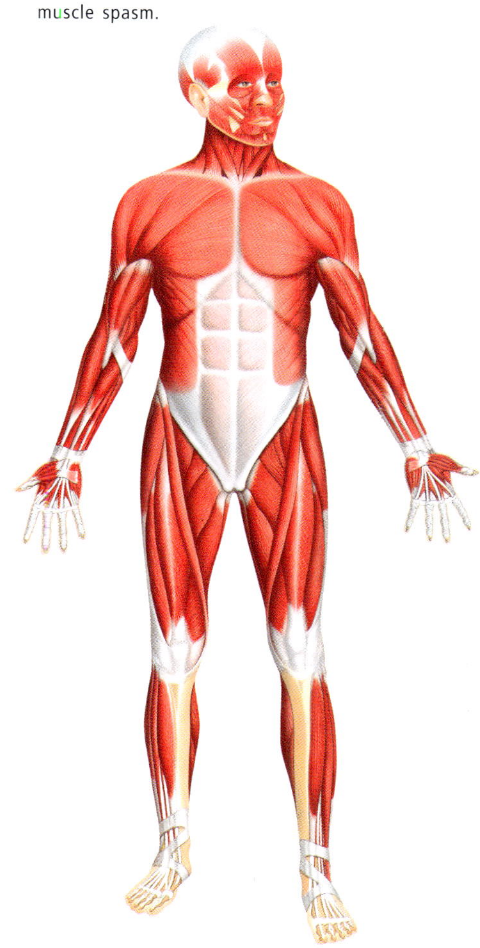

Herbs and digestive disorders

Practitioners of herbal medicine treat disorders of the digestive system with herbs such as red clover, peppermint, fennel and senna. These alterative, carminative and laxative herbs are thought to stimulate the body's nutrition and waste elimination processes.

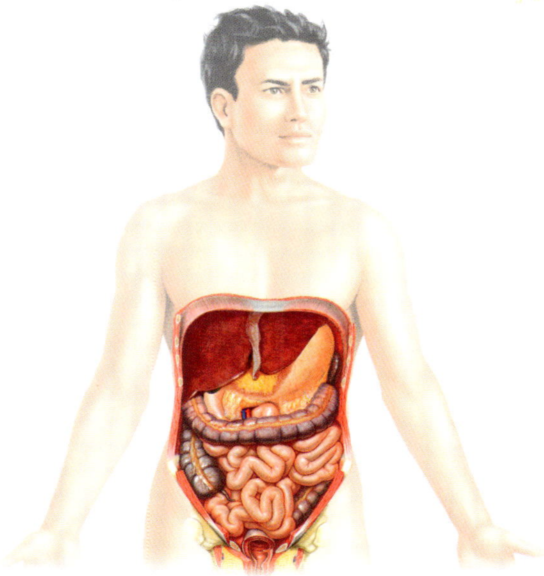

Herbalism

Carminative herbs may relieve digestive pain and flatulence, e.g. peppermint (*Mentha piperita*), fennel (*Foeniculum vulgare*).

Demulcent herbs are said to form a soothing and protective coating over mucous membranes, e.g. slippery elm (*Ulmus fulva*), marshmallow (*Althaea officinalis*).

Diuretic herbs are thought to promote excretion of urine, e.g. parsley (*Petroselinum crispum*), nettle (*Urtica dioica*).

Expectorant herbs may aid the softening and expulsion of lung secretions, e.g. licorice (*Glycyrrhiza glabra*), horehound (*Marrubium vulgare*).

Laxative herbs may help to promote bowel movements when constipation is a problem, e.g. senna leaves (*Cassia angustifolia*), aloe vera (*Aloe vera*).

Nervine herbs aim to soothe and restore the nervous system, and may be sedating, e.g. lavender (*Lavendula officianalis*), or stimulating, e.g. oats (*Avena sativa*).

Nutritive herbs may assist assimilation and nourish and build tissues, e.g. alfalfa (*Medicago sativa*), fenugreek (*Trigonella foenum-graecum*).

Stimulant herbs are used to temporarily raise the energy level of organs, e.g. chilli (*Capsicum minimum*), ginger (*Zingiber officinalis*).

Tonic herbs can help restore and nourish muscle and tissue tone and build energy, e.g. damiana (*Turnera diffusa*), goldenseal (*Hydrastis canadensis*).

Herbal preparations

Preparation begins with the correct cultivation and harvesting of a plant to maximize its healing properties. The choice of preparation depends on both the type of active ingredients in a plant and the purpose of the medicine. A herbal medicine may consist of one plant, known as a simple, or it may consist of a combination of herbs. The most common herbal preparations are infusions, decoctions, tinctures, powders and ointments.

Infusions are fresh or dried herbs steeped in boiling water in a pot covered with a lid. Decoctions are usually used for the tougher parts of the herb, such as the root, which is brought to the boil in water and simmered slowly. In a tincture, the herb is steeped in a solvent, usually alcohol or gycerol, and strained off. Powders are pulverized dried herbs mixed in water or put into capsules. Ointments are made with fresh or dried herbs, or tinctures in an oily base.

SEE ALSO ***Ayurvedic medicine, Chinese herbalism, Naturopathy***

HEREDITY

Heredity is the genetic transmission of biological traits from one generation to the next. Millions of traits, ranging from eye color and facial features to information the body needs to develop organs and tissues, are transmitted via heredity.

Heredity operates via structures in the nucleus of the cell known as chromosomes, of which there are 46 in humans. The chromosomes contain deoxyribonucleic acid, or DNA, a complex molecule capable of duplicating itself exactly. The chromosomes carry thousands of units of DNA called genes, which contain the hereditary "code". These codes cover the physical, biochemical and physiological traits of a person. For example, some genes govern the development of tissues and organs. Others govern certain traits such as straight or curly hair, color vision and blood type.

Chromosomes are found in pairs, that is, 23 pairs of chromosomes, or 46 in all. When a normal body cell divides, each chromosome produces a duplicate of itself. In this way, newly formed cells have the same DNA, contained in 23 paired chromosomes with the same genes, as the other cells in the body. Sex cells, the male sperm cells and female ova (egg cells), however, have only 23 single chromosomes rather than pairs.

During fertilization a sperm cell and an ovum unite to form a fertilized ovum, or zygote, with the full number of chromosomes. The zygote then begins to reproduce itself by the normal process of cell division, mitosis. As the genetic material in the original cell has come from different parents, it will be a new, unique individual, developing with traits from both parents.

The expression of some traits in the new individual depends on how the parents' genes interact. Some genes are dominant, while others are recessive. The presence of one or two dominant genes results in expression of the dominant trait; for example, the gene for brown eyes in humans is dominant over the gene for blue eyes. To exhibit a recessive trait, such as blue eyes, both genes, one from each parent, must be recessive.

Many characteristics are influenced by more than one gene; skin color, for example, is controlled by several genes. Some depend on other input besides the genes. Although intelligence may be genetically influenced, it is also determined by environmental influences. Sex-linked traits refer to those hereditary traits that are carried on the X chromosome, such as color blindness.

Genetic defects, passed on by heredity from one generation to the next, are the cause of many human diseases and disorders. There may a single defective gene as in muscular dystrophy, phenylketonuria and sickle cell disease, or there may be a predisposition in the genetic make-up for a certain condition, such as arteriosclerosis or some types of cancers. More and more diseases, for example hypertension, are now thought to be made much more likely by particular combinations of genes.

Many genes that cause disease have now been identified, allowing parents the option of genetic counseling and testing during pregnancy. Advances in DNA mapping hold out the promise of one day eliminating or curing many hereditary diseases.

SEE ALSO *Chromosomes, Congenital abnormalities, DNA, Genes, Genetic counseling*

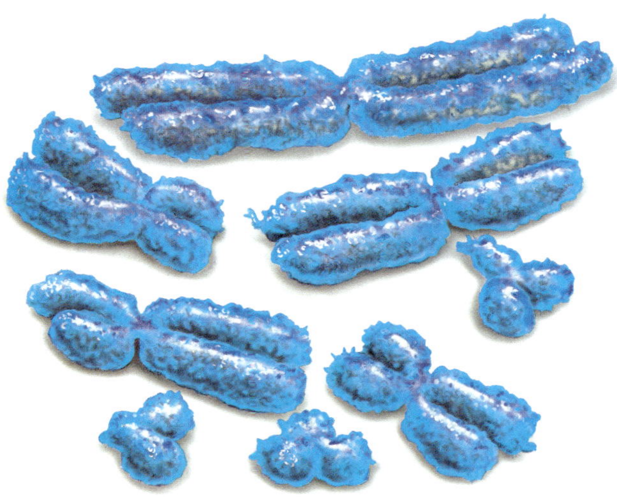

Chromosomes

Chromosomes consist of genes which carry the hereditary code that determines a person's physical and psychological make-up. We all have 46 chromosomes arranged as 23 pairs; one of these pairs is the sex chromosomes. Women have two X chromosomes and men have an X chromosome and a Y chromosome which carries the male features. One sex chromosome from each parent determines the sex of a baby—the embryo inherits an X chromosome from the mother; if it inherits the X chromosome from the father it is a girl, and if it inherits the Y, it is a boy.

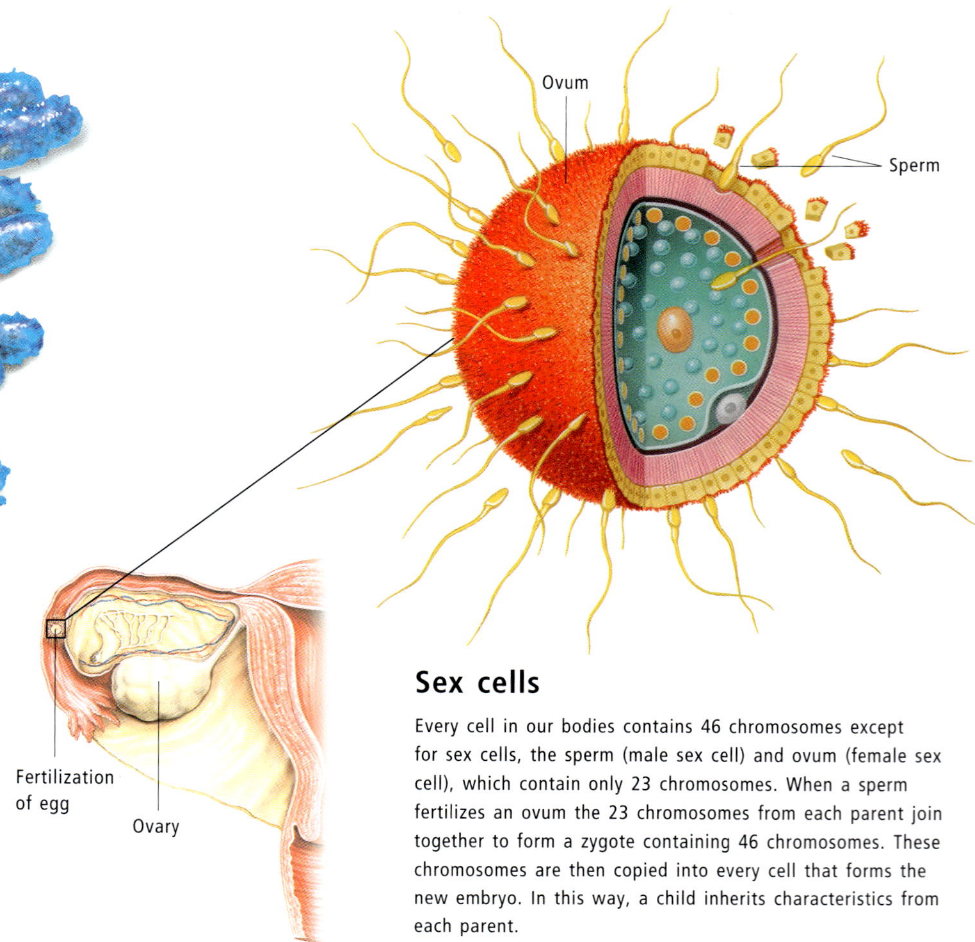

Sex cells

Every cell in our bodies contains 46 chromosomes except for sex cells, the sperm (male sex cell) and ovum (female sex cell), which contain only 23 chromosomes. When a sperm fertilizes an ovum the 23 chromosomes from each parent join together to form a zygote containing 46 chromosomes. These chromosomes are then copied into every cell that forms the new embryo. In this way, a child inherits characteristics from each parent.

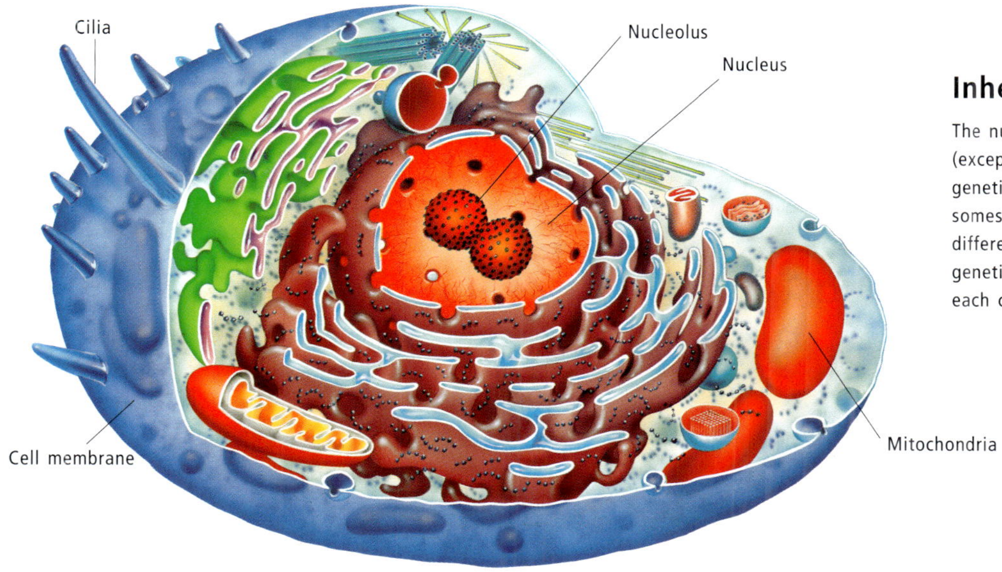

Inherited information

The nucleus of every body cell (except the sex cells) contains genetic information on 46 chromosomes. When cells replicate to form different body parts and organs this genetic information is copied into each cell structure.

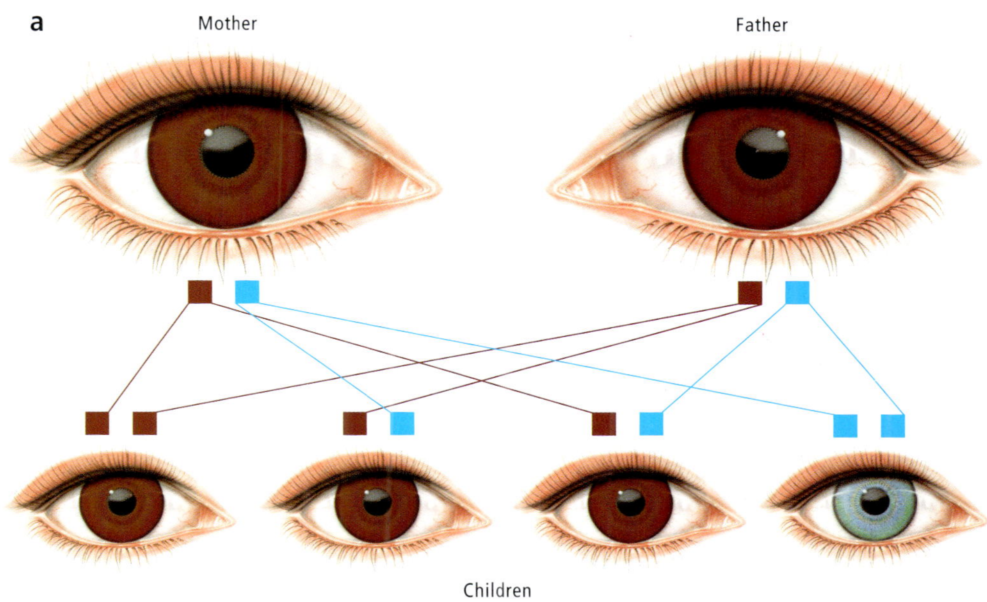

Dominant and recessive genes

Most characteristics result from a mixture of two sets of genetic instructions contained in one or more gene pairs, but some features, such as eye color, are determined by a single gene. This dominant gene overrides the instructions of the other recessive gene. A recessive trait can only emerge when two recessive genes for that trait are inherited. The gene for brown eyes is dominant over the recessive gene for blue eyes. This means that two parents with brown eyes can only have a child with blue eyes if the child inherits a recessive blue gene from each parent (a). If one parent with brown eyes has two dominant brown-eye genes, all children will inherit at least one dominant gene (even if one parent is blue eyed) and will all have brown eyes (b). If both parents have blue eyes, neither will have the dominant gene and all children will have blue eyes.

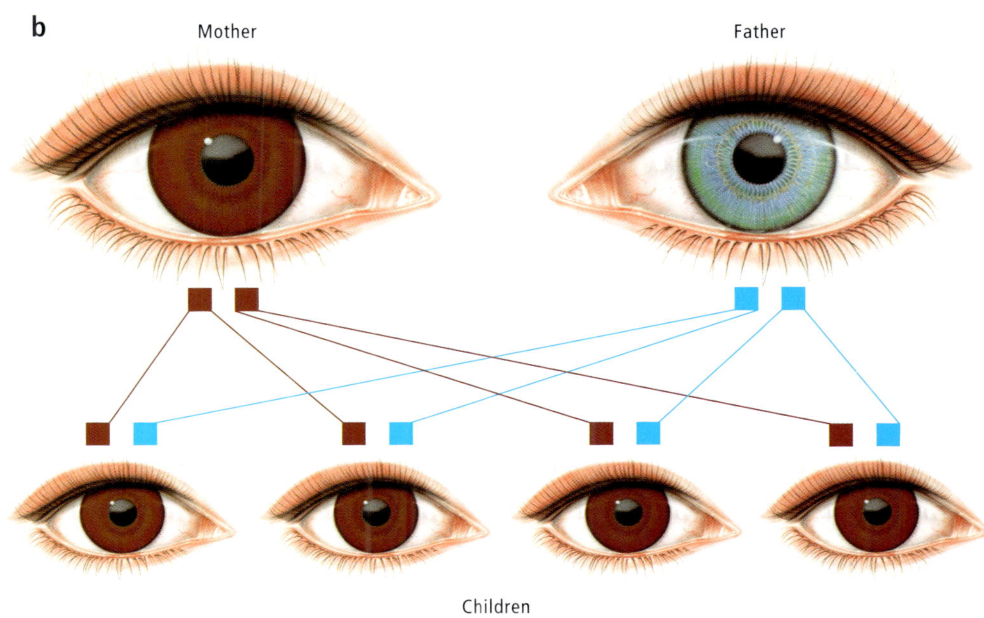

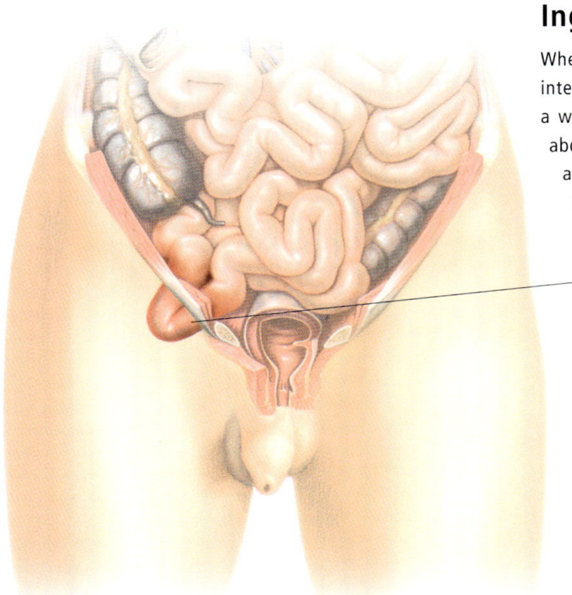

Inguinal hernia

When a hernia occurs, the intestine protrudes through a weakened muscle in the abdominal wall, causing a lump under the skin of the groin.

HERNIA

A hernia is a protrusion of tissue or an organ through an abnormal opening. A hernia may be acquired or congenital, and may occur in various parts of the body, though most hernias involve the abdomen. They occur most often when pressure in the abdomen, during coughing or lifting a heavy weight, for example, forces the soft abdominal tissue through a weakness in the muscles of the abdominal wall.

The most common types of hernia are inguinal and femoral hernia. Both involve protrusion of the small intestine from the abdomen into the groin. Inguinal hernias are more common than femoral, and more common in men than women, as the hernia can enter the inguinal canal more easily. Femoral hernias occur below the inguinal canal at the top of the thigh. Hiatus hernia, in which the stomach protrudes through the diaphragm muscle into the chest, is also common. An incisional hernia is one where tissue has protruded through the site of a previous surgical operation. An umbilical hernia is usually seen in newborn infants and involves protrusion of tissues through the navel.

Some hernias are reducible—they can be pushed back into the abdomen. A hernia which cannot be pushed back is called irreducible, and such a hernia may become pinched ("strangulated"). If the blood supply is cut off, the hernia may become gangrenous and cause death. If there is intestine caught in the hernia, intestinal obstruction, infection and gangrene may follow. These conditions require emergency surgery. Nonurgent treatment of a hernia depends on where it is located. In an infant, an umbilical hernia will usually disappear by itself by the age of about four; if not it can be surgically corrected. An inguinal, femoral or incisional hernia is treated with an operation called a hernia repair, in which a surgeon closes the weakness in the abdominal wall under general or local anesthesia. Hernias in the midline of the abdomen usually do not need treatment. If a person with an inguinal hernia is too old or too unwell for an operation, wearing a truss will sometimes help.

SEE ALSO *Abdomen, Groin, Hiatus hernia*

HEROIN

Heroin (diacetylmorphine) is a drug developed from morphine and was used in the late nineteenth century as a painkiller. When it was found to be highly addictive, its use was prohibited, and it is now illegal in most countries.

Heroin can be inhaled or injected, intravenous injection producing the most rapid uptake. The early effect is a warm feeling known as a "rush". This is followed by a range of reactions that can include drowsiness, relaxation, poor concentration, restlessness, nausea and depression. A heroin "habit" is dangerous to health, is expensive and also has social and legal risks. A heroin dependent person often has to inject several times a day, and can die from contaminated drugs or overdose, or may contract hepatitis B or C, or HIV (AIDS virus) from sharing infected needles.

SEE ALSO *Detoxification, Drug dependence, Hepatitis, Morphine, Narcotics*

HERPES SIMPLEX

The family of herpes viruses includes the herpes simplex viruses (two closely related types) as well as the viruses responsible for chickenpox and for infectious mononucleosis (glandular fever). All these viruses may produce symptoms at the time of initial infection, but in 50 percent of people they persist indefinitely in a dormant form in the sensory nerve cells of an infected person, with later reactivation and recurrent disease.

Herpes simplex virus types 1 and 2 (HSV-1 and HSV-2) infect the skin and mucous membranes. Transmission requires close personal contact, but the initial infection is often inapparent. Both HSV-1 and HSV-2 infect the cells of the nerves that supply the infected area and persist in these cells. Reactivation of herpes simplex virus infections may be triggered by stress, menstruation, exposure to sunlight or by other illnesses. Severe disease may develop if reactivation follows suppression of the immune response.

Most initial infection by HSV-1 occurs in children and is symptomless, although it may be associated with fever, a sore throat, or ulceration of the mouth. Because infection with HSV-1 usually involves the skin and mucous membrane of the mouth, recurrences are manifested as "cold sores" that typically develop on the lip margins.

In contrast, HSV-2 is mainly spread by sexual transmission and thus produces genital herpes, although some 10–15 percent of cases of genital herpes are due to HSV-1. The initial infection usually produces small blisters which burst and turn into sores that are often painful or itchy. These involve the genital area, buttocks and thighs, and can be accompanied by

Herpes virus

fever, headache and a flu-like illness. Recurrences are associated with similar skin and mucous membrane changes and may be preceded by flu-like symptoms.

Diagnosis of the common forms of herpes virus infection is largely based on medical history and physical examination; in addition, various laboratory tests are available. While there is no treatment available that will eliminate the infection, it can be quite effectively controlled using different antiviral drugs, which need to be administered as early as possible in the course of the primary infection or episode of recurrence.

Severe forms of infection are uncommon but include inflammation/ulceration of the cornea of the eye (mostly HSV-1); encephalitis (brain inflammation and tissue destruction) (also mostly HSV-1); and disseminated infection in the newborn (mostly HSV-2) and in individuals with HIV (AIDS).

There are a number of alternative therapies that may help to alleviate the symptoms of herpes. Acupuncture may help to relieve the symptoms and may also strengthen the immune system against the virus, reducing the frequency and intensity of subsequent attacks. Herbalism prescribes echinacea and garlic internally, and aloe vera gel, St John's wort (*Hypericum*) or calendula externally to soothe pain and itching. Homeopathy prescribes specific remedies according to the patient's symptom picture. Naturopathy prescribes vitamins B and C, zinc, lactobacillus acidophilus, lauric acid and lysine during an attack to weaken the virus. Dietary measures include fruits, vegetables and foods high in protein, and avoidance of chocolate, coconut, peanuts, wheat, soy beans and peas. One can bathe or wash in warm salty water and apply zinc cream to the affected areas.

SEE ALSO *Antiviral drugs, Chickenpox, Cold sores, Infectious mononucleosis, Viruses*

HIATUS HERNIA

Hiatus (hiatal) hernia is a condition in which part of the stomach protrudes through the opening through which the esophagus passes, through the diaphragm, into the chest cavity. There are two types of hiatus hernia: sliding and rolling.

Sliding hiatus hernia is the most common (about 90 percent) and involves the sliding of the upper stomach (cardiac part and cardioesophageal junction) through the esophageal opening in the diaphragm.

Patients complain of heartburn, a burning pain in the lower front of the chest and the upper abdomen, particularly after meals and when lying down. They may also experience regurgitation of bitter or sour-tasting fluid (waterbrash) as far as the throat and mouth, particularly at night. Difficulty in swallowing may also occur due to swelling of the lining of the lower esophagus. Continued regurgitation of stomach juices into the esophagus can result in reflux esophagitis.

Sufferers are often advised to take antacids, eat smaller meals more frequently, elevate the head of the bed and avoid lying down after meals. Surgical treatment of sliding hernias is aimed at anchoring the gastroesophageal junction in the abdomen and tightening the esophageal opening through the diaphragm. Most patients will experience a good outcome from surgical treatment.

Rolling hiatus hernia is also known as paraesophageal hiatus hernia. The cardioesophageal junction, where the esophagus and stomach join, stays within the abdominal cavity; it is usually the fundus of the stomach which protrudes into the thorax. Patients complain of gaseous eructations (burping), a sense of pressure in the lower chest and, occasionally, irregular heartbeat.

Rolling hiatus hernia is usually treated by the use of surgery which aims to fix the part of the stomach which herniates to the back of the anterior abdominal wall.

SEE ALSO *Diaphragm, Esophagitis, Esophagus, Heartburn, Hernia, Stomach*

HICCUPS

Hiccups are spasmodic involuntary contractions of the diaphragm that cause a disturbance in the rhythm of breathing. They develop when some stimulus, such as rapid eating, triggers a sudden spasm of the diaphragm. The irregular rhythm causes a sudden closure of the vocal cords, resulting in the characteristic hiccup noise.

Hiccups are most likely to occur after a meal when the stomach is stretched. They usually begin without warning and stop in the same way. There are dozens of folk remedies—from taking a tablespoon of sugar to drinking from a glass of water backwards—but most do not work and the hiccups disappear of their own accord. Remedies which do work involve increasing the carbon dioxide in the blood, and include holding the breath, and breathing into a paper bag (though this is not advised as it is dangerous). Persistent hiccups may require medication.

Far less commonly, hiccups may also be caused by irritation of the diaphragm during pneumonia, or after surgery; or from harmful substances in the blood, such as those which result from kidney failure; or from interference with the part of the brain that controls the breathing, due to a stroke.

SEE ALSO *Breathing, Diaphragm*

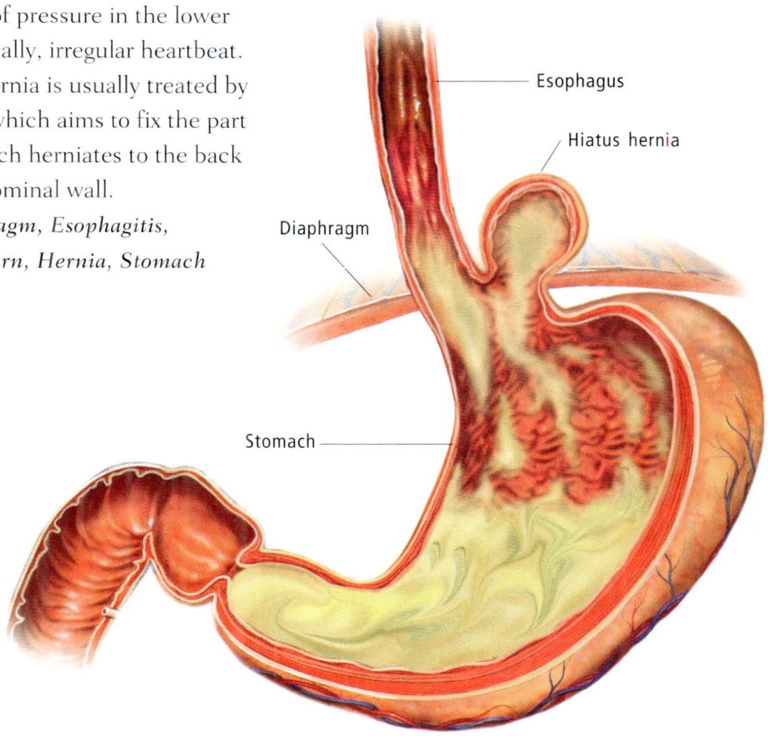

Hiatus hernia (rolling type)

The stomach bulges out of the weakest part of the diaphragm, through which the esophagus passes. Sufferers can experience heartburn and indigestion.

HIP

The hip (coxal or innominate) bone is made up of three bones: the ilium, ischium and pubis. The three bones fuse with each other at the acetabulum (part of the hip joint) at 14–16 years of age.

The crest of the ilium is found at the waist, laterally, below the ribs. The tuberosities of the two ischia are the bony knobs that we sit on. The pubic bones are at the front at the lower limit of the soft anterior abdominal wall. The left and right hip bones and the sacrum form the bony pelvis. The hip joint is formed by the acetabulum, a cup-shaped socket and the rounded head of the femur.

The head of the femur is covered with cartilage and lubricated by synovial fluid. The whole joint is enclosed in a fibrous capsule which is loose enough to permit free movement yet strong enough to hold the femoral head securely in place. The muscles of the hip joint are large and powerful to hold the joint firm and to move the thigh for walking and running. They include the gluteus maximus and the gluteus medius at the back, and the rectus femoris at the front.

More than half the round head of the femur is held within the acetabulum and surrounding cartilage, making the hip joint extremely stable and strong, with capability of rotation second only to the shoulder joint and limited only by the flexibility of its supporting ligaments. The hip transmits the entire weight of the upper body to the head and neck of each femur and is at its most solid during weight-bearing activities.

The strength and flexibility of the pelvis and hip allows the femur to descend vertically while bearing the body's full weight, an ability vital for the development of standing, running and jumping.

Blood supply to the hip joint is from the femoral arteries. Several nerves supply the hip joint and pain in the hip can be misleading as it may be generated from the spinal column. Loss of blood supply due to accident or dislocation can result in pain which radiates to the knee.

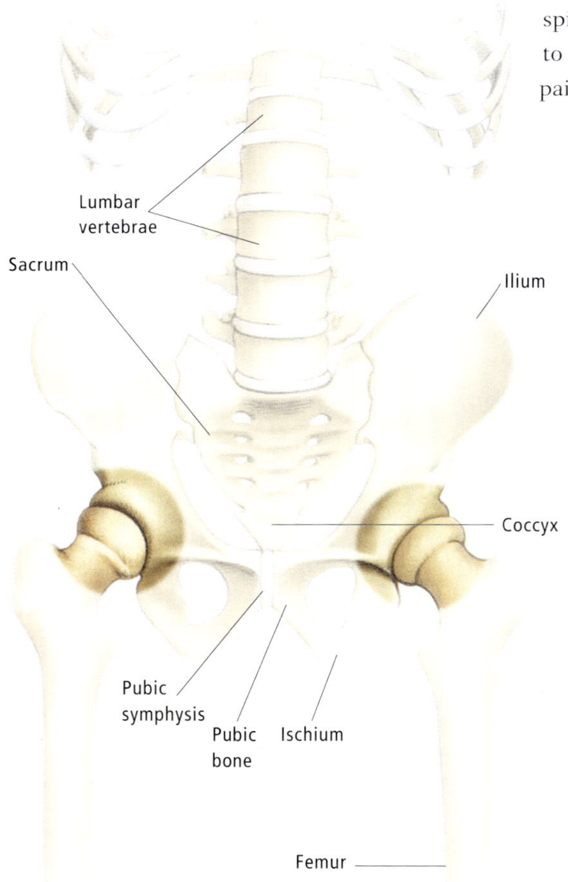

Hip bone and joint

The hip is a ball-and-socket joint formed at the point where the thigh bone (femur) meets the pelvis. The rounded end of the thigh bone fits into the cup-shaped socket.

Disorders

Joint abnormalities, deformities or malalignments are revealed by radiography or, in newborns, by observation. Congenital dislocation of the hip is found in approximately 15 babies per 10,000 births and may affect one or both joints. It is eight times as common in girls as boys. In such cases, the end of the femur is not properly located in the socket (acetabulum).

To test for congenital dislocations of the hip, the baby is laid face upwards and the thighs are moved sideways to see if movement produces a clunk as the head of the femur enters the pelvic socket. Instability of the joint at this stage can right itself but if present after five days, treatment will usually be recommended. The pelvic harness, which holds the thighs so that the head of the femur is securely in its socket, is worn for a few months, until radiography reveals that the abnormality has been corrected.

If further treatment is required, the baby may wear abduction splints for a further few months. Clicks or noises heard on moving a baby's hips should always be investigated as untreated abnormalities can lead to limping and permanent deformity.

Disorders affecting growth of bones during childhood, such as rickets, can affect the formation of the head of the femur and the joint. Slipped epiphysis of the femur may occur in late childhood and adolescence and is a dislocation of the growing head (epiphysis) of the femur from the femoral neck. Perthe's disease also occurs around this age. Symptoms are increasing discomfort at the hip with pain referred to the knee.

Osteoarthritis is a degenerative disorder common in adults of middle age, which involves the abrasion and loss of cartilage at the surfaces of joints with outgrowths of bony ridges at abraded surfaces.

Osteoarthritis of the hip joint may be secondary to a structural abnormality, or of a primary nature, involving no underlying abnormality. One underlying cause is congenital dysplasia, dislocation or subluxation of the hip, where the head of the femur and socket fit badly, which can arise in infancy due to genetic factors or swaddling, which leaves the thighs extended. This delays development of the hip joint, which can become deformed once the child begins to walk.

Osteoarthritis of the hip joint in people under age 40 often follows from disease or disorder and may require surgery to correct it. This may involve osteotomy, reshaping the end of the femur, or removal of diseased tissue and replacement with an artificial hip. As age advances, degenerative diseases and hip replacements become more common.

Injuries

Trauma or violent stresses can result in dislocation or fracture of the hip bone or fracture of the neck of the femur. Such injuries commonly result from falls onto hard surfaces in sports such as ice-skating or athletics. Automobile accidents are also a common cause because of the high velocity of secondary impacts, such as when the knee strikes the dashboard. This type of stress can dislodge the head of the femur from its socket, causing dislocation with injury to surrounding tissues. Where there is greater force, or in persons with osteoporosis, the neck of the femur may fracture with far greater damage to surrounding tissues.

Persons over 60 are at risk of serious fracture from even trivial falls, because their bones and supporting tissue structures are likely to be weaker than those of younger persons, especially if the person has osteoporosis. The femur is the largest bone in the body and its fracture is one of the most serious, sometimes taking a year to heal.

Hip replacement

This is an increasingly common and successful option in instances where a joint has deteriorated through rheumatoid arthritis, osteoarthritis or osteoporosis. The materials used are constantly improving, extending the useful life of replacement joints and reducing the possibility of an adverse response from the body's tissues. Stainless steel in early artificial joints has been replaced by titanium alloys, which are usually lighter and more stable.

The artificial hip usually consists of a highly polished metal (cobalt-chromium) ball, which replaces the head of the femur, and a cup made of extremely tough polyethylene, to replace the socket (acetabulum). It is important to avoid abrasion between the two surfaces as small particles of debris can cause inflammation. The materials used must simulate the mechanical properties of bone to avoid uneven stresses which would weaken bones and induce reshaping.

SEE ALSO *Femur, Fractures, Joints, Osteoarthritis, Osteoporosis, Pelvis, Rheumatoid arthritis, Rickets, Skeletal system, Synovial fluid*

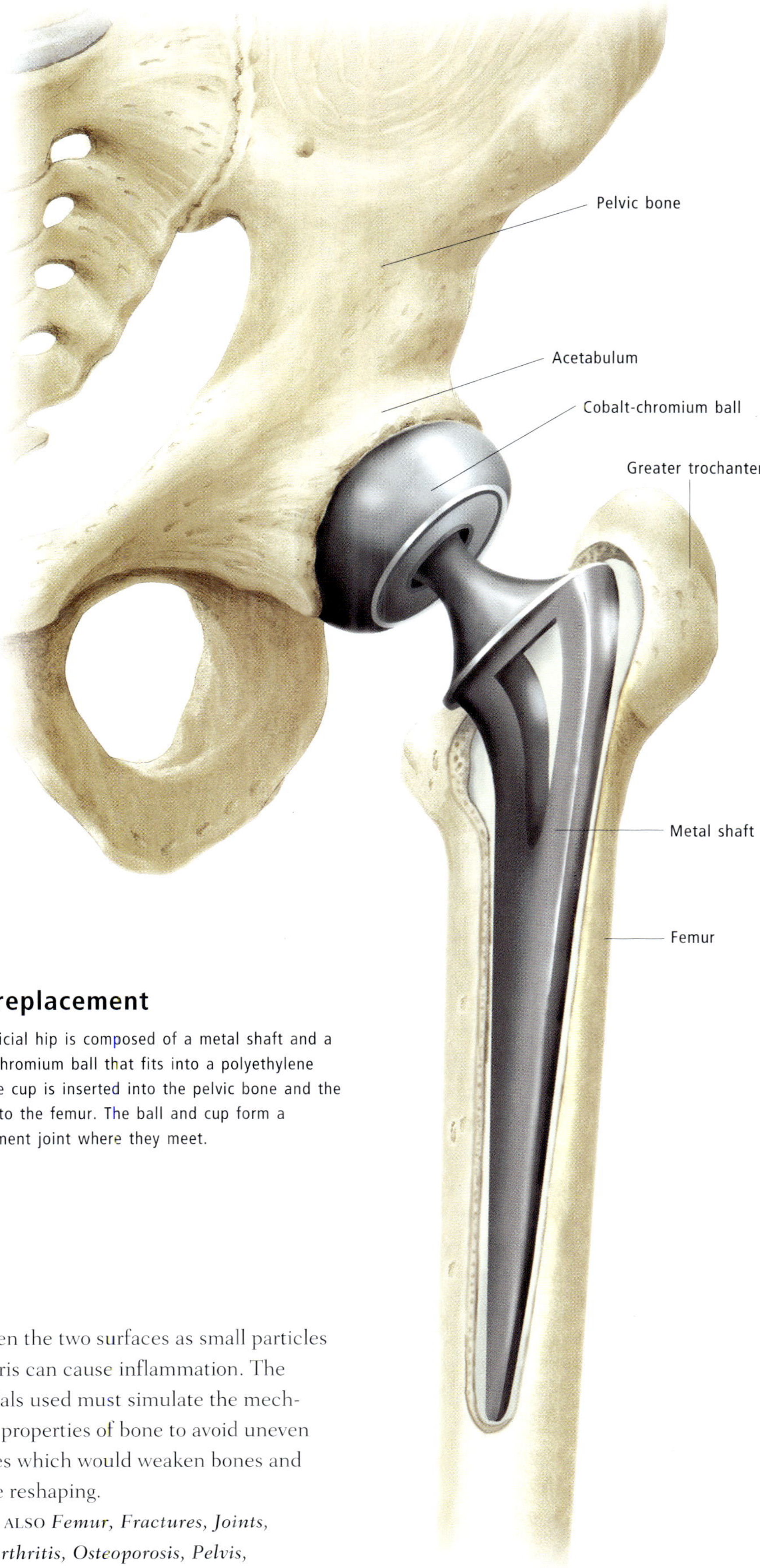

Hip replacement

An artificial hip is composed of a metal shaft and a cobalt-chromium ball that fits into a polyethylene cup. The cup is inserted into the pelvic bone and the shaft into the femur. The ball and cup form a replacement joint where they meet.

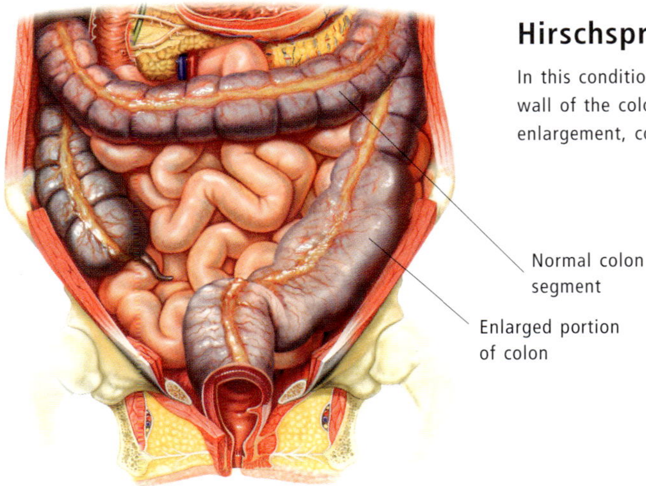

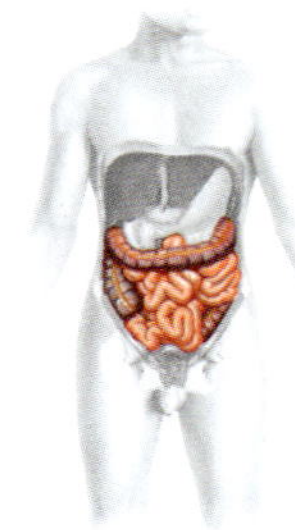

Hirschsprung's disease

In this condition, the nerve cells in the wall of the colon are absent, resulting in enlargement, constipation and obstruction.

HIRSCHSPRUNG'S DISEASE

Hirschsprung's disease is a congenital condition (present at or before birth). The basic abnormality is the absence of nerve cells in the wall of the lower large bowel. Without these nerve cells, the bowel is unable to make the peristaltic movements which propel the feces towards the anus. Consequently, the infant will have constipation, abdominal swelling, reluctance to feed and vomiting.

Temporary relief may be obtained by washing out the colon with a saline solution, but in the long term the child may need a colostomy to allow evacuation of the large bowel.

SEE ALSO *Bowel, Colon, Congenital abnormalities, Intestines*

HIRSUTISM

Hirsutism is the excessive growth of hair, or the presence of hair in areas that are not usually hairy. It is more common in women, when unwanted hair may appear on the face, chest, around the nipples, lower back and buttocks and inner thighs.

The cause is usually a hormonal disturbance, such as polycystic ovarian syndrome, or, less commonly, an ovarian tumor or a disorder of the adrenal gland. Drugs may also cause the condition, especially steroids, phenytoin, minoxidil and diazoxide. Mild hirsutism may occur naturally after menopause. Other signs of virilization (such as clitoral enlargement and baldness) are usually absent.

The treatment depends on the cause. Hormonal causes often respond to oral contraceptives or spironolactone, though it may take 3–6 months before an improvement is noticed. Meanwhile, unwanted hair can be removed by shaving, waxing, tweezing, use of depilatories, and/or electrolysis. Also, as obesity seems to worsen the condition, losing 10–15 percent of body weight may ease hirsutism in obese persons.

SEE ALSO *Adrenal glands, Hormones, Virilization*

HISTAMINE

Histamine is a chemical messenger found in all body tissues that reacts with histamine receptors on cell surfaces causing change in certain specific bodily functions. Histamine affects smooth muscles, such as those in the intestine, heart and lungs, causing them to contract; or can cause the smaller blood vessels to dilate resulting in a fall in blood pressure and release of lymphatic fluid into surrounding tissues, as when redness and swelling follows a sting or bite.

Overproduction of histamine can occur when the body comes into contact with something to which it is allergic, e.g. pollen in hay fever sufferers. Extreme cases can be life threatening.

SEE ALSO *Allergies, Anaphylaxis, Antihistamines, Hay fever*

HISTOPLASMOSIS

Histoplasmosis is infection caused by the fungus *Histoplasma capsulatum*, which grows in bat or bird droppings. Humans may inhale dust containing the spores; this causes no problems for most people but in people with damaged immune systems (such as AIDS sufferers) the fungus multiplies in the lungs and may spread to other organs. The disease can cause lung damage with weight loss, cough, and breathlessness, fever, fatigue and muscle pains. Treatment is with anti-fungal medications.

HIV

HIV (human immunodeficiency virus) is a retrovirus, one of a unique family of viruses consisting of RNA surrounded by a protein envelope. It attacks a type of white blood cell critical to the immune system known as helper T lymphocytes, or T4 helper cells. This may eventually cripple the immune system and leave the body vulnerable to a variety of life-threatening illnesses that are ordinarily harmless. Transmission of the virus can occur through sexual contact, via blood through transfusions or needle sharing, and from a pregnant woman to the fetus.

A person may be HIV-positive for many years before developing illnesses that indicate a serious deterioration of the immune system. At that stage, a person is said to have acquired immunodeficiency syndrome (AIDS). There is, at present, no cure for AIDS, but drugs have been developed that suppress replication of HIV virus in the body, and so effectively arrest or stop the progress of the disease.

SEE ALSO *AIDS, Viruses*

Histamine

When allergens (like pollen) enter the body, antibodies to the allergen trigger histamine release from circulating mast cells, causing symptoms such as runny nose and sneezing.

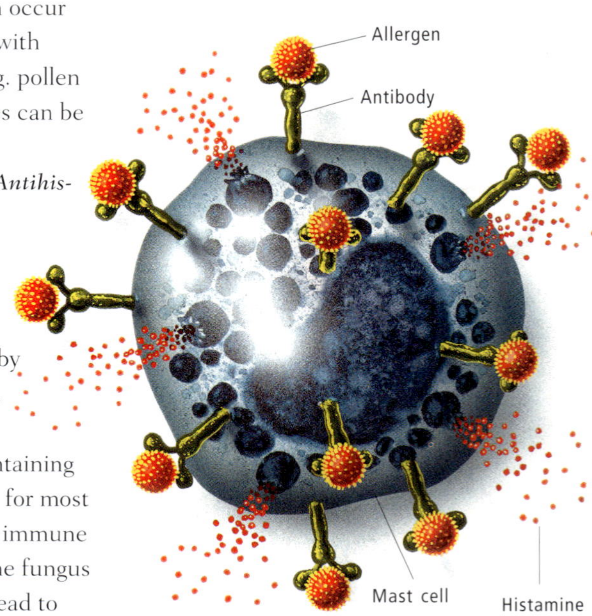

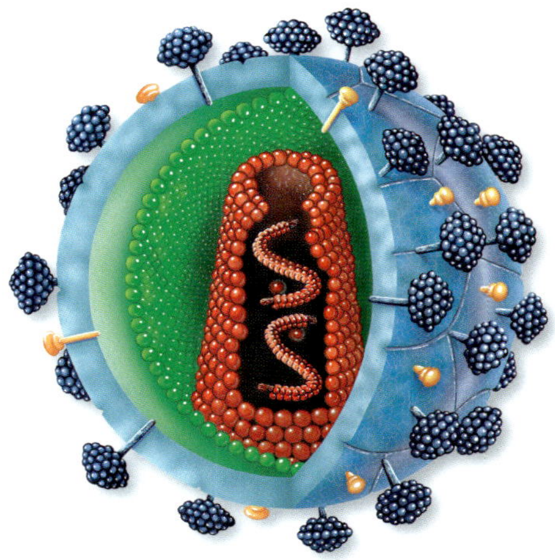

Human immunodeficiency virus (HIV)

HODGKIN'S DISEASE

Hodgkin's disease is a type of lymphoma (a cancer arising in lymph nodes), which was first described by Thomas Hodgkin in 1832. Lymphomas are a relatively common group of cancers (typically ranking fifth or sixth in frequency among both men and women) of which Hodgkin's disease makes up a variable proportion (approximately one-fifth in most economically developed nations). What makes Hodgkin's disease distinctive is that it usually develops in young to middle adult life, when most other types of cancer are rare.

Hodgkin's disease is more enigmatic than many other cancers. As is true for most tumors, the exact cause of its development remains unknown. There is a strong suspicion that certain viral infections may contribute to its emergence, at least in a proportion of cases, but the sequence of events by which this might occur is not clear. Even the specific cell type that gives rise to Hodgkin's disease remains uncertain and it appears quite likely that more than one type of cell is involved.

Hodgkin's disease typically produces enlargement of the lymph nodes early in the disease. The patient may notice a swelling, for example in the neck, but the nodes are usually not painful. Quite often, patients with Hodgkin's disease develop symptoms such as fever, weight loss and night sweats as part of their illness, which are triggered by chemical signals released by the cancer cells and by the patient's response to the tumor. In addition, some patients develop complicating infections, because Hodgkin's disease is associated with suppression of the immune response, although the reason for this is not entirely clear.

The microscopic appearance of Hodgkin's disease is quite distinct from other types of lymphoma, which allows it to be diagnosed by examination of a sample of involved tissue. Unlike most other lymphomas, it usually does not spread far and wide at an early stage, but instead extends progressively from one group of nodes to the next, with later involvement of the spleen and other tissues. This relatively slow and orderly progression may be one reason why Hodgkin's disease is more responsive to treatment with anti-cancer drugs than many other varieties of lymphoma.

The extent of spread at the time of diagnosis is the most important determinant of the patient's likely response to chemotherapy. Also relevant is the specific variety of Hodgkin's disease that the individual has developed. With modern combination chemotherapy, the disease is controlled in the great majority of patients with early stage disease, and a substantial proportion can expect to be cured.

SEE ALSO *Cancer, Chemotherapy, Lymph glands, Lymphatic/Immune system, Non-Hodgkin's lymphoma*

HOLTER MONITOR

Worn over one shoulder, the Holter monitor consists of electrodes (EKG wires) attached to the chest and a monitor which correlates heart rhythm disturbances with symptoms such as dizziness or palpitations. The patient is required to keep a diary for 24 to 48 hours and record any symptoms and activity taking place during moments of rhythm irregularities. The information gained is used to determine the pattern and severity of disturbance in heart rhythm.

SEE ALSO *Electrocardiogram, Heart*

HOME NURSING

Home nursing or home care can include nursing care; care by a physician, social worker, physical therapist, occupational therapist or speech therapist; and housework and other home help services. Community services may also be available.

Many types of care, which were originally undertaken by hospitals, are now often conducted in the home, with family members performing many of the duties of nursing and hospital staff. Apart from the rising costs of hospitalization, many patients also prefer home care to hospital care when given the choice.

Being cared for at home often helps patients to feel more comfortable and secure than they would in a hospital environment, particularly if education for the patient and family, as well as home health care services, is available. Transportation to appointments or services is often available using community or health resources for those who need the service. Home nursing is often an option for the elderly, cancer sufferers and those who have had a stroke.

SEE ALSO *Palliative care*

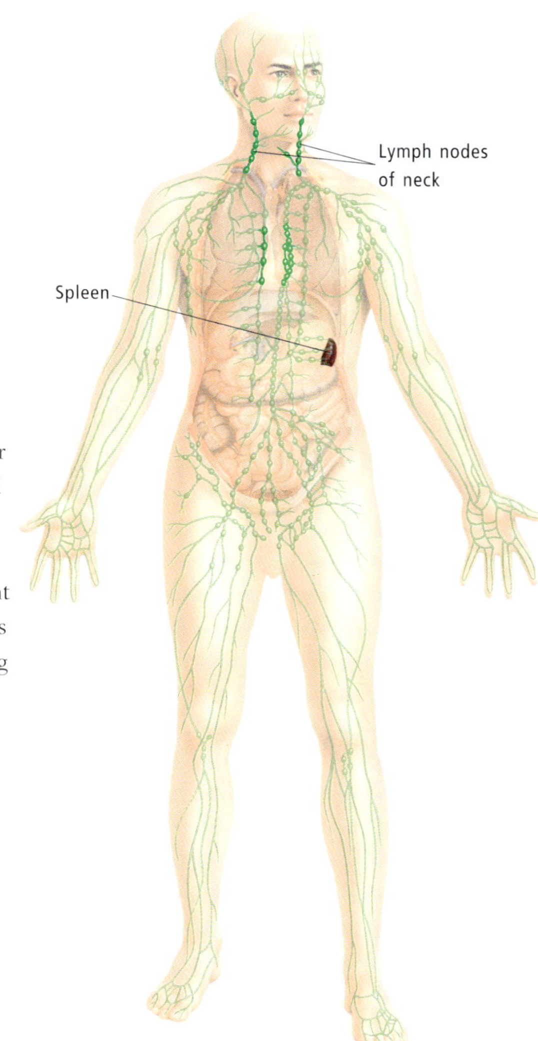

Hodgkin's disease

This type of lymphoma produces enlargement of the lymph nodes, often starting with the lymph nodes in the neck and spreading progressively to other nodes in the body, the spleen and other tissues. Symptoms include fever, night sweats and infections.

HOMEOPATHY

The pioneer of homeopathy was Samuel Hahnemann (1755–1843), a German physician. After working as an orthodox doctor, Hahnemann became dissatisfied with the medical practices of his day and turned to research.

For one of his experiments he dosed himself with Peruvian bark, or cinchona, a known remedy for malaria. To his surprise he found that he quickly developed malaria-like symptoms: drowsiness, trembling, heart palpitations, flushed cheeks, fever and thirst. This outcome suggested to him that substances which produced a specific set of symptoms in a healthy person could also cure the same set of symptoms in an ill person.

Hahnemann recognized the connection between his idea and the references made by the ancient Greek physician Hippocrates to a medicine of "similars": substances which could both cause and cure an illness. It was an idea utilized soon after by Edward Jenner in his development of a smallpox vaccine; Hahnemann supported Jenner, who was widely condemned as a quack.

Early developments

Hahnemann continued to experiment on himself and healthy colleagues, recording his observations rigorously. A range of plants, herbs, animal and mineral matter were tested in a process known as "proving". The provings produced remedy "pictures" which described the first line, or keynote symptoms, the second line or less common symptoms, and the third line or idiosyncratic symptoms of each substance.

Finding a cure

Homeopathy uses the principle of "like cures like"—the idea that the same substance can both cause and cure an illness. Edward Jenner's development of a vaccine against smallpox in the nineteenth century was based on a similar principle.

Smallpox virus

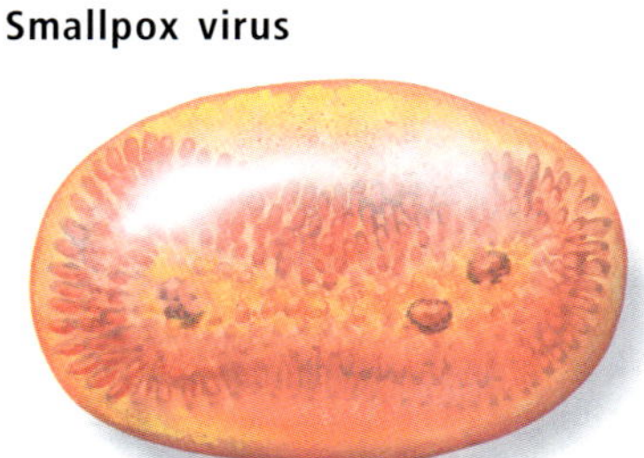

Next Hahnemann and his colleagues trialed the remedies in their clinics. Patients were physically examined and questioned closely about their symptoms, general health, way of life and attitudes. This process produced a "symptom picture" which was then matched with a "remedy picture", i.e. the symptoms of the patient were similar to those produced by the chosen remedy's "proving". These remedies worked.

Hahnemann concluded that from these trials that "like should be treated by like" according to a theory he called the "law of similars", naming his new form of medicine homeopathy from the Greek *homios* (similar) and *pathos* (suffering).

A further refinement to homeopathy was made when Hahnemann observed that in some patients there was a worsening of symptoms before an alleviation took place. To prevent this, he started to dilute his remedies by 1:100 and then to mix them by repeatedly banging (succussing) the vials against a hard surface, which he believed released the energy of the substance. Remedies prepared in this way, known as "potentization", proved to be even more successful. The complications produced by each remedy were reduced while at the same time the healing power of the remedy was increased.

Later developments

In the nineteenth century homeopathy quickly spread from Germany across Europe and to the Americas as well as Asia. Its reputation grew in Europe when Hahnemann's prescription of homeopathic doses of camphor proved successful in treating cholera.

By the early twentieth century two schools of homoeopathy had emerged. The classical homeopaths, following the work of American homeopath Dr James Tyler Kent, prescribed high-potency remedies according to the patient's emotional make-up and appearance, as well as their physical symptoms. Other homeopaths, following the English homeopath Dr Richard Hughes, prescribed lower potencies according to purely physical symptoms.

In recent times homeopathy has enjoyed a resurgence, and the practice of classical homeopathy in particular has gained popularity with both homeopaths and medical doctors. Self-treatment for minor physical ailments has also become popular as low potency remedies have become available commercially, e.g. arnica in 6x potency to treat physical shock and injury.

Homeopathic treatment

Homeopathy views illness as a unique manifestation of a specific disease in the patient. Symptoms are believed to be the body's way of trying to maintain an equilibrium as it instinctively seeks healing, and thus should not be suppressed. A homeopathic remedy prescribed in accordance with the patient's total symptoms, constitution, temperament and disease state will hasten recovery by stimulating the body's innate vital force.

Finding the right homeopathic remedy to treat a person is a complex procedure. It starts with the homeopath taking a lengthy personal history which covers medical history, emotional reactions, food preferences, reactions to weather, state of mind and personal beliefs. An understanding of the patient's unique physical and psychological make-up is crucial to the homeopath making a correct diagnosis and choice of remedy.

Homeopaths treat chronic illnesses and their symptoms by stages, giving progressive remedies to peel back ailments layer by layer. The homeopathic "Laws of Cure" state that symptoms will disappear first from the most important organs to the least important, and in reverse chronological order to the onset of symptoms. Thus homeopaths approach all the patient's physical and mental health problems as related, rather than treating any one ailment in isolation.

The homeopath chooses remedies that match the patient's basic constitution to unravel the underlying causative factors of an illness. For example, the constitutional remedy "Nat Mur" is often prescribed to serious, conscientious people who are inclined to suppress their emotions.

In the course of treatment the patient may experience an "aggravation", or brief worsening, of symptoms. This signals to the homeopath that the body is in the process of healing itself and that an improvement will soon follow. As well as prescribing remedies, homeopaths advocate that the body's vital force be supported with adequate sleep, regular exercise, proper hygiene and a nutritious diet.

The remedies

In today's homeopathic *Materia Medica* up to 3,000 remedies are listed, made from plants, minerals and animals, many of which would be poisonous in large doses. For example the deadly plant *Aconite napellus,* used throughout history as an arrow poison, is made up into homeopathic doses of aconite to treat sudden and acute onsets of fever, inflammation or fear.

Once the remedy is chosen, its potency has to be decided—ideally the minimum dose necessary to stimulate the patient's self-healing process. In homeopathy the greater the dilution the more potent the remedy. Homeopathic remedies are given either in liquid form as drops or as small pills, usually one to ten doses over a period of one to seven days.

HOMOSEXUALITY

Homosexuality is defined as sexual attraction between persons of the same sex. Homosexual or gay are the terms used for men; gay or lesbian are the terms used for women. Some people are neither totally homosexual nor heterosexual, but attracted to both sexes (bisexual).

Homosexuality is not considered a psychological disorder and does not need treatment. However individuals who are not happy with their sexuality can benefit from counseling. The outbreak of HIV (AIDS) has had a devastating effect on homosexual communities.

SEE ALSO *AIDS, Bisexuality, HIV, Sexuality*

HOOKWORM

The hookworm (*Ancyclostoma duodenale*) is a common parasitic roundworm found in tropical and subtropical climates, and flourishing in unsanitary conditions. The eggs are found in infected human feces, and hatch into infective larvae which can then infect another human, either by direct contact, usually through bare feet, or by swallowing contaminated soil—a common source of infection for children in areas with poor sanitation.

Where the hookworm enters the skin it creates an itchy patch, hence its other name, "ground itch". Upon entering the body, it travels to the intestines where it attaches to the intestinal wall and sucks blood from it for nourishment.

In severe cases, symptoms can include abdominal pain, diarrhea, loss of appetite and weight loss. A stool sample will determine if the infection is great enough to cause anemia or protein deficiency as a result of the blood loss. This can retard growth and mental development in children, and hookworm infection can be fatal in babies. Treatment is usually drugs over a one to three day period, sometimes with an iron supplement.

SEE ALSO *Worms*

HORMONAL THERAPY

Hormones are natural chemicals produced by the body to regulate various processes such as blood sugar metabolism, bone growth or milk production. Some cancers will only grow in the presence of certain hormones; for example, certain types of breast cancers need the female hormones estrogen and progesterone to grow. Hormonal therapy seeks to prevent these cancers from growing by altering the hormonal environment around them. It is usually used in conjunction with other cancer treatments such as surgery and radiation therapy.

Cancers that are stimulated by hormones have certain areas on their surface called receptor sites. By using a drug that blocks these receptor sites, the growth of the cancer can be slowed or even stopped. For example, many breast cancers have estrogen and progesterone receptors, and are stimulated by these hormones. This means they may respond to treatment with a drug such as Tamoxifen, which blocks the effects of estrogen on breast cancer. Treatment with Tamoxifen reduces cancer recurrence and is used after surgery or radiation therapy. Not all breast cancers respond to the drug; before commencing treatment with Tamoxifen a section of breast cancer must be tested in a pathology laboratory to see whether it will respond to the drug.

In males, prostate cancer grows more quickly when exposed to the male hormone testosterone. By reducing the amount of testosterone in the environment around the prostate, hormone therapy can be used to reduce the growth and spread of these cancers. This is done by surgically removing the testicles or treating the patient with drugs that block the action of testosterone on the prostate. Alternatively estrogens or luteinizing-hormone-releasing hormones may be given. The treatment is also effective in slwong the progress of prostate cancer metastases (secondaries). It is usually used in conjunction with surgery, radiation therapy, or chemotherapy.

Side effects associated with hormonal therapies include loss of libido, weight gain, diarrhea, tiredness, hot flashes, bone loss, and, in women, irregular menstrual periods and vaginal dryness or bleeding.

SEE ALSO *Breast cancer, Cancer, Hormones, Prostate cancer*

HORMONE REPLACEMENT THERAPY

At menopause, the ovaries start to regress and women produce less of their reproductive hormones, estrogen and progesterone. The decrease in the quantity of these hormones can cause a variety of symptoms, which include hot flashes (sudden feeling of heat, usually over the face and neck, often with redness and sweating), headaches, vaginal dryness, anxiety and sleep problems. The hot flashes are probably the result of sharp surges in pituitary hormones as a result of falling ovarian hormone levels while vaginal dryness is a direct result of estrogen withdrawal.

Estrogen loss also increases the risk for other health problems such as heart disease. Loss of bone substance also increases after menopause, and can lead to osteoporosis where the bones lose calcium and are easily fractured.

Most of the problems associated with menopause can be prevented by hormone replacement therapy (HRT). HRT involves supplementing the patient's hormone levels with doses of estrogen, often in combination with progesterone. HRT can be very effective in relieving symptoms such as hot flashes and vaginal dryness, while also aiding in reducing the risk of heart disease and osteoporosis.

In some cases HRT is taken cyclically to allow for monthly bleeding, much like a menstrual cycle, and in other cases it is taken without pause, which will cause regular bleeding to cease. The HRT regimen is tailored to suit each patient, depending on her symptoms and other health problems.

HRT can also be useful in some cases of incontinence, where there is a loss of bladder control leading to leakage of urine. This is known as "stress incontinence", where increases in abdominal pressure can force urine out, for instance when coughing or sneezing. This is common in postmenopausal women, due to a weakening of the pelvic floor muscles. Estrogen treatment may be helpful, as may pelvic muscle exercises and other medications. Changes in the lower urinary tract after menopause can also predispose a woman to cystitis (bladder infection). This causes frequent and sometimes painful urination and can be helped by HRT.

HRT can lead to a number of unwanted side effects. Women may experience breast tenderness and swelling, unwanted vaginal bleeding, nausea, fluid retention and a degree of weight gain.

The levels of estrogen and progesterone used in HRT are generally lower than those used in the oral contraceptive pill. Thus complications which have been associated with taking the pill (particularly the higher doses used in early pill preparations), such as increased blood pressure and increased risk of pulmonary embolism, are not considered to be problems with HRT. However HRT may not be considered appropriate in people who have already had these problems.

Estrogen given on its own has been shown to increase the risk of uterine (endometrial) cancer. Combination therapy (estrogen and progesterone) is not associated with an increased risk of uterine cancer, so it is the preferred treatment for women who have not had a hysterectomy. HRT is not recommended in certain conditions. For instance, many breast cancers are sensitive to estrogen, which stimulates their growth, so HRT should not be used in these cases. A full breast examination and mammogram is therefore recommended before HRT treatment begins.

SEE ALSO *Cystitis, Estrogens, Hormones, Menopause, Osteoporosis, Progesterone, Urinary incontinence*

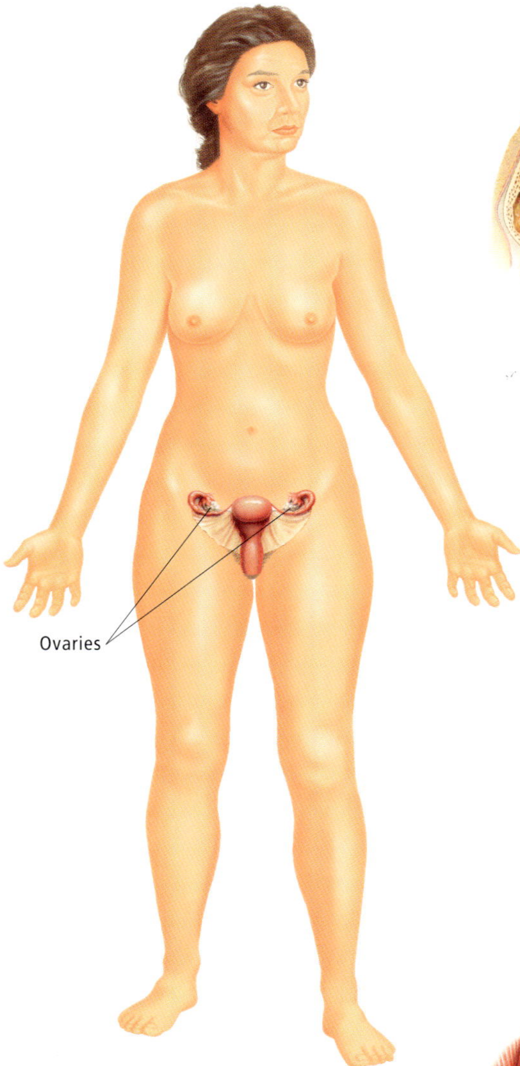

Hormone replacement therapy

At menopause, the ovaries produce less estrogen and progesterone. A woman may choose to supplement her hormone levels with hormone replacement therapy. HRT can reduce the risk of osteoporosis, heart disease and bladder problems such as incontinence.

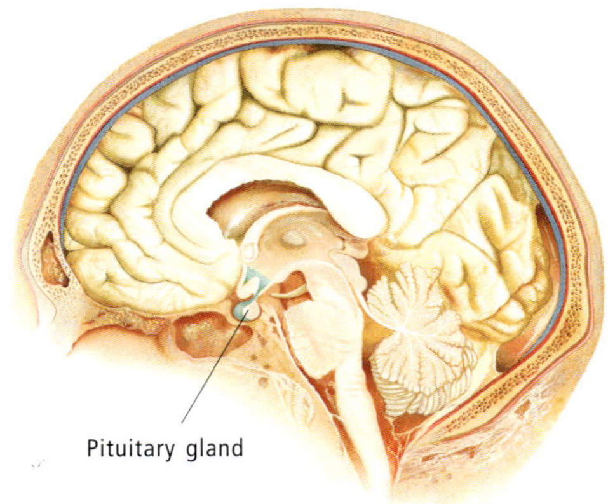

Pituitary hormones

Surges of pituitary hormones as a result of falling ovarian hormone levels cause the hot flashes often experienced during menopause.

Incontinence

Weakening of the pelvic floor muscles is common after menopause and may result in incontinence. Estrogen treatment can improve symptoms.

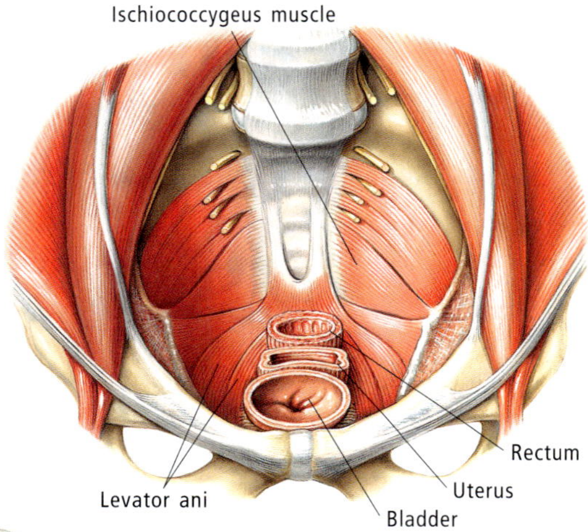

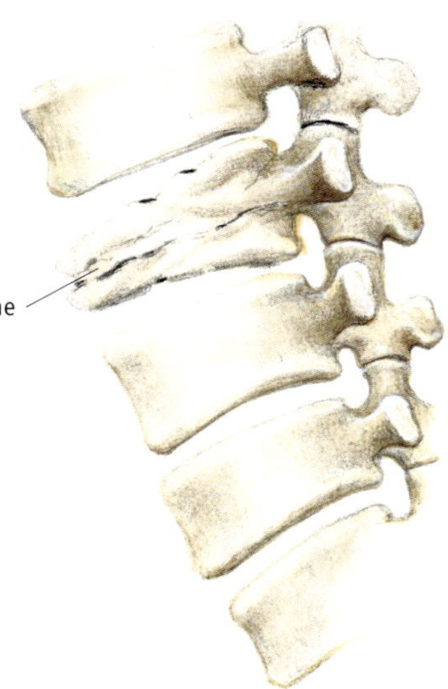

Osteoporosis and fracture

The risk of osteoporosis and resulting bone fractures increases greatly when estrogen levels fall after menopause. HRT can slow down calcium loss preventing loss of bone density.

Thyroid microstructure

The thyroid is the only endocrine gland that does not release its hormones straight into the body. It stores thyroid hormones (which control metabolism) in colloid fluid held in the follicles of the gland. The hormones are then secreted gradually into the blood when needed.

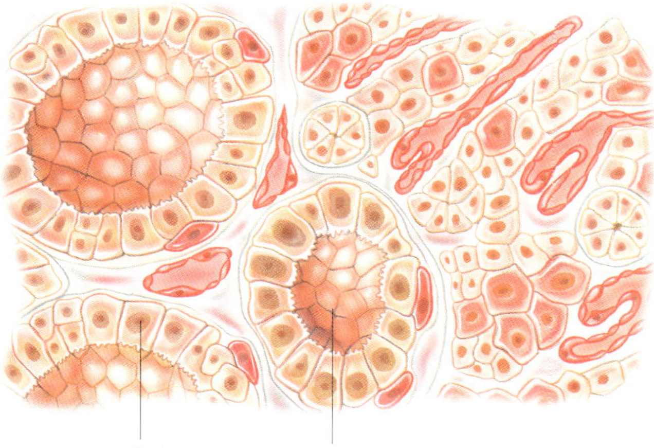

Pituitary gland

The pituitary gland is a small but very important gland in the base of the brain. It secretes hormones which control other endocrine glands elsewhere in the body. The pituitary gland itself is regulated by hormones secreted by the hypothalamus, which lies just above it.

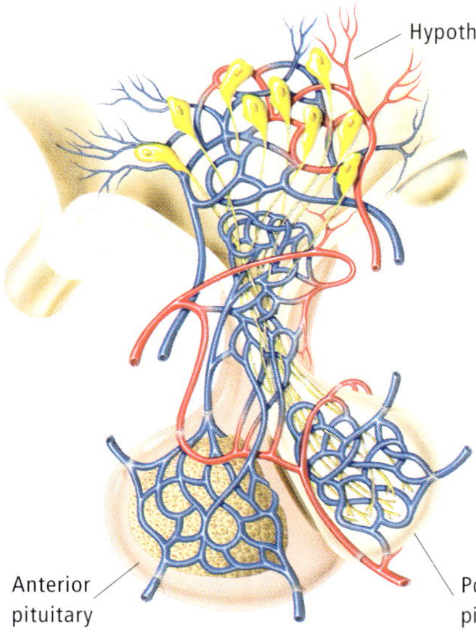

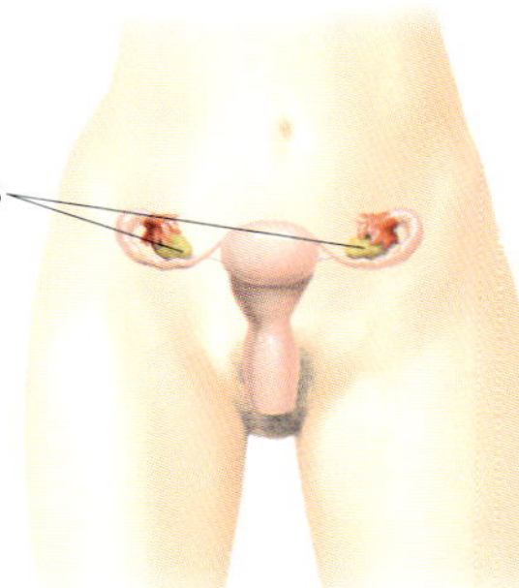

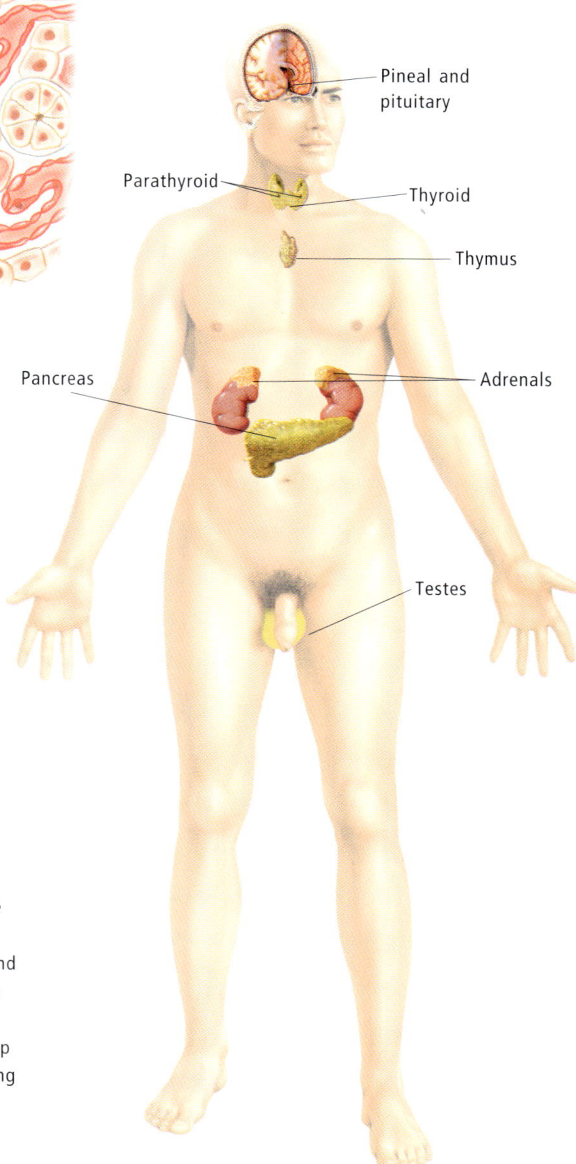

Endocrine system

Hormones are produced in the endocrine glands, specialized organs whose cells produce and release hormones directly into the bloodstream. The thyroid gland, for example, is made up of cells producing and secreting thyroid hormones.

HORMONES

Hormones are chemical substances that are produced by endocrine organs, including the pituitary, thyroid, parathyroid, adrenal, pancreas, gonads (the testes in males and the ovaries in females) and the placenta (during pregnancy). They are released into the bloodstream and carried to other regions called target organs, where they alter the activity of target cells.

Hormones control a whole range of body functions including growth, metabolism and reproductive activity. They are divided into three main classes, according to their chemical structure: peptide and protein hormones, such as growth hormone and insulin; hormones made from the amino acid tyrosine, such as epinephrine (adrenaline) and thyroxin; and steroid hormones, which include corticosteroids and the sex hormones.

The way hormones are produced depends on their type. Peptide and protein hormones are made from an mRNA (messenger RNA) sequence, like cellular proteins, and stored in the cell in membrane-bound vesicles until released. Thyroxin and epinephrine are made by specific chemical reactions within the thyroid and adrenal glands. Steroid hormones, such as estrogen and testosterone, are made from cholesterol; they are not stored in vesicles but are found free in the cell cytoplasm.

Hormones work by combining with specific receptors in the target cells. These receptors are usually proteins and may be in the cell membrane (for peptide hormones) or in the cell cytoplasm or nucleus (for steroid hormones). Having bound to the receptor, the hormone may stimulate or inhibit specific metabolic pathways in the cell, for example, they may change the activity of an enzyme, or stimulate production of a new protein. Receptors for some hormones (for example, thyroxin) are present on many body cells and hence the effects of the hormone are widespread. For other hormones (such as thyroid stimulating hormone) the receptors are only present

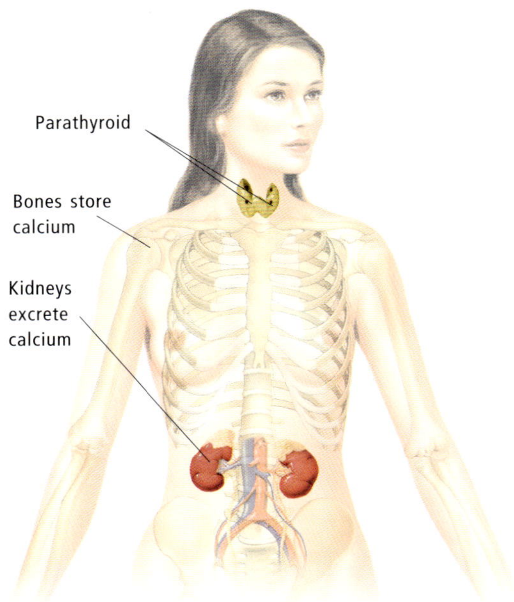

Negative feedback mechanism

The body uses the mechanism of the negative feedback loop to regulate hormone levels. In this system, an excess or deficit of a particular hormone triggers a response to normalize hormone levels. Calcium levels in the blood, for example, are controlled by parathyroid hormones which instruct the bones to store calcium or the kidneys to excrete it, depending on circulating levels. If levels fall too low, for example, the parathyroid registers the deficit and releases parathyroid hormone which tells the bones to release calcium, increasing blood calcium levels.

on specific tissues (the thyroid gland) and thus their effects are very localized.

While many hormones are carried in the blood, some cells are known to release secretions which act locally, generally referred to as paracrine secretions. Yet others, called autocrine secretions, can act on the same cell (that is, the secretory cell itself has receptors).

Hormones can have long-lasting effects, for instance growth hormone from the pituitary acts on a wide range of tissues to stimulate growth during childhood. Other hormones can cause very rapid changes, such as epinephrine (adrenaline). Produced in the adrenal medulla, it is important in the "fight or flight" response to stress and can cause an increase in heart rate, widening of the airways and release of glucose.

Besides regulating many body functions throughout our lives, some hormones are important at specific times, such as during pregnancy, childbirth and lactation. These include sex hormones like estrogen and progesterone, and hormones from the placenta (for example, chorionic gonadotropin) and pituitary (for example, prolactin).

Hormone levels, and thus their impact on the body, are controlled in different ways, depending on the hormone, but a common mechanism is called negative feedback. This is a system whereby either an excess or deficit of a hormone prompts a response that results in that hormone's return to normal levels. For example, calcium levels are controlled by parathyroid hormone from the parathyroid gland, which acts on tissues such as the bones and kidneys, to mobilize or excrete calcium. If calcium levels fall, this stimulates the parathyroid gland to increase the secretion of parathyroid hormone, which activates the bones to release calcium, thus increasing blood levels.

Conversely, if blood calcium rises, parathyroid hormone secretion is decreased, calcium in bones is retained and calcium excretion by the kidney is increased. Similar negative feedback loops operate for many hormones (such as the control of glucose by insulin), although several hormones often interact for the final outcome.

Hormone imbalance can occur when there is an excess or deficiency of one hormone, which can often affect the function of others. Imbalances can also occur when there is sufficient hormone produced, but the target tissue fails to respond properly, usually because of changes in the receptors. The effects of hormone imbalance will differ depending on the particular hormone and its target area.

During the menopause in women, when menstruation ceases, there are surges in pituitary hormones (FSH and LH) as a result of falling levels of ovarian hormones, due to the increasing unresponsiveness of the ovaries. These surges in pituitary hormones can result in hot flashes.

Female and male sex hormones

The development of the gonad into an ovary or testis occurs early in fetal life, and is dependent on the sex chromosomes (XX in females, XY in males).

During childhood, the ovaries and testes are relatively dormant. At puberty, the hypothalamus in the brain releases gonadotropin-releasing hormone (GnRH) which starts the changes leading to sexual maturity. This in turn stimulates the pituitary to release the gonadotropins, lutenising hormone (LH) and follicle stimulating hormone (FSH) in both men and women.

These hormones stimulate the ovaries in females for follicle maturation and ovulation, and the testes in males for sperm production and testosterone secretion. The ovary and testes secrete sex hormones; testosterone in males, and estrogen and progesterone in females.

At puberty, sex hormones are involved in the development of the external genitalia and secondary sexual characteristics. For the male this includes enlargement of the penis and testes, growth of body and facial hair, development of body musculature and growth of the larynx, causing a deepening of the voice. For the female the changes include development of the breasts, growth of body hair, and the beginning of menstruation (menarche).

After puberty has begun, the production of sex hormone is continuous in the male; in females, however, production occurs in cycles (menstrual cycles) which last until women reach menopause.

SEE ALSO *Adrenal glands, Endocrine glands, Endocrine system, Menopause, Ovaries, Parathyroid glands, Pituitary gland, Placenta, Puberty, Testes, Thyroid gland*

HORNER'S SYNDROME

Horner's syndrome is the result of damage to the sympathetic nerves which supply the face. It is characterized by a small pupil, drooping eyelid and loss of sweating on the face.

It may be a pointer to more serious disease. It is most commonly caused by Pancoast syndrome, when cancer in the apex of the lung invades the nerve.

SEE ALSO *Eye, Pupil of eye*

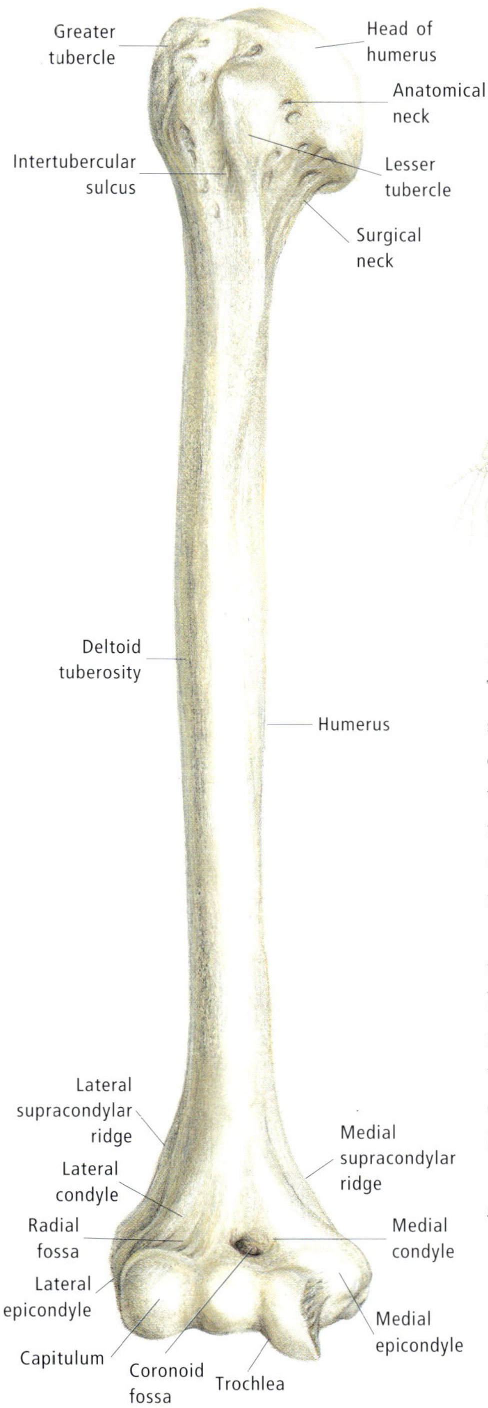

Humerus

Humerus

The humerus forms the skeleton of the upper arm. It is a long bone comprised of a cylindrical shaft and two enlarged extremities.

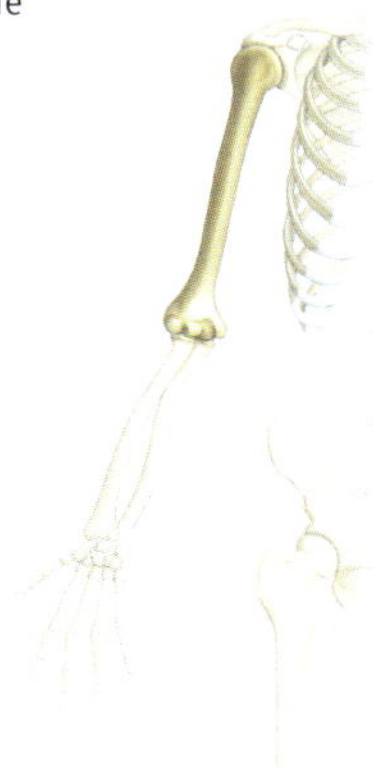

HUMERUS

The humerus is a long bone that forms the skeleton of the arm. It consists of a cylindrical shaft, a rounded head (upper end), which articulates with the scapula to form the shoulder joint, and paired condyles (lower end), which articulate with the radius and ulna to form the elbow joint.

Several major nerves lie in contact with the humerus and are at risk in fractures or blows to the bone. The familiar tingling sensation which we experience in our hand when we "hit our funny bone" is actually caused by hitting the ulnar nerve as it passes behind the humerus on its way to the hand.

SEE ALSO *Arm, Elbow, Radius, Skeletal system, Ulna, Ulnar nerve*

HUNTINGTON'S DISEASE

Also known as Huntington's chorea, Huntington's disease is a rare genetic disorder involving degeneration of nerve cells in the cerebrum (the largest portion of the brain). It is inherited as a dominant condition; this means that it is inherited from only one parent and there is a 50 percent chance that someone with the condition will transmit it to an offspring.

Some people with the disorder are affected more severely and earlier in life than others. Usually, however, it begins between the ages of 35–50 when the affected person notices the gradual onset of involuntary, jerky and contorted movements of the limbs ("chorea" refers to the tendency to writhe and twist in a constant, uncontrollable motion, similar to a dance). Mental deterioration and severe personality change follows. The affected person may eventually need institutionalized care.

There is no cure for Huntington's disease and it is usually fatal within 10–20 years. Treatment is aimed at maximizing the ability to function for as long as possible. Medications have been found to be only partially successful at reducing abnormal behaviors and movements. A blood test is available that can identify the defective gene before any symptoms appear. Genetic counseling may be advised if there is a family history of the disorder.

SEE ALSO *Brain, Congenital abnormalities, Genetic counseling, Nerves*

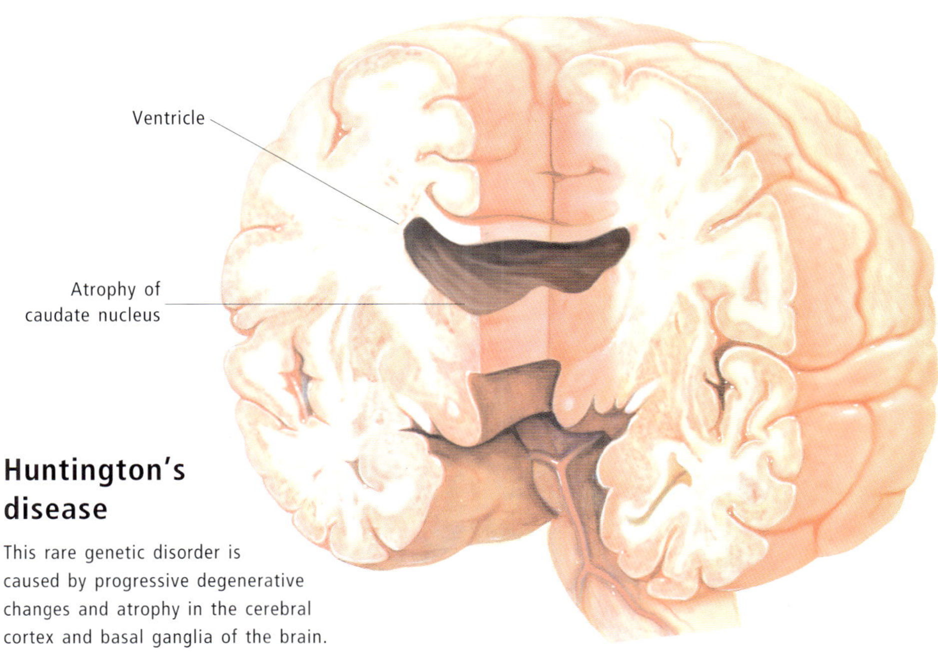

Huntington's disease

This rare genetic disorder is caused by progressive degenerative changes and atrophy in the cerebral cortex and basal ganglia of the brain.

HOUSEMAID'S KNEE

Housemaid's knee is one example of bursitis, inflammation of a bursa. A bursa is a fluid-filled sac that helps to protect ligaments, tendons, skin or muscle where they rub across bone. In this case, it is the prepatellar bursa in front of the patella that becomes inflamed. Bursitis may result from injury, pressure or overuse. The condition is painful and limits movement. It may be relieved by rest or anti-inflammatory drugs.

SEE ALSO *Bursitis, Knee*

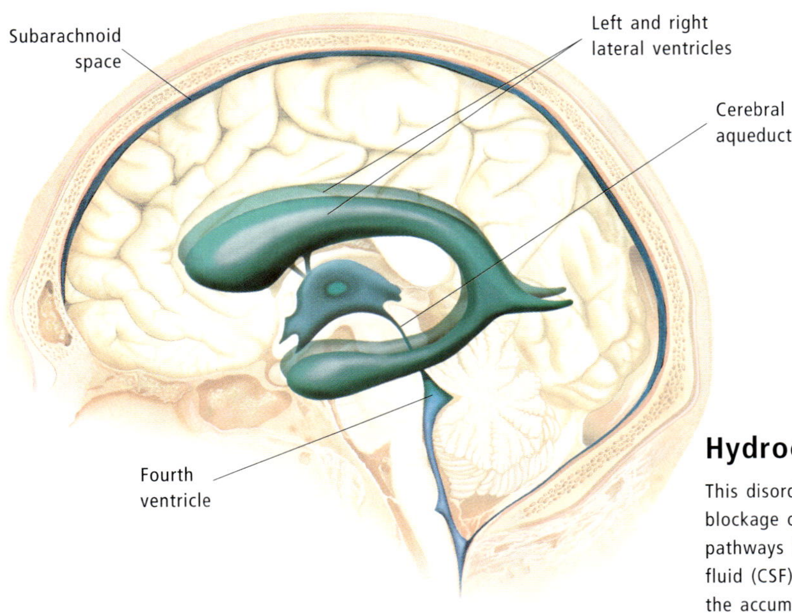

Hydrocephalus

This disorder is caused by blockage or narrowing of the pathways for cerebrospinal fluid (CSF). This results in the accumulation of CSF in the ventricles, which exerts pressure on the brain.

HYDATID DISEASE

Hydatid disease is an infection, usually of the liver, that is common in southern South America, the Mediterranean, the Middle East, central Asia and Africa. It is caused by the larvae of a type of tapeworm (*Echinococcus granulosus*), which can infest dogs, foxes, wolves, cattle and sheep.

Humans become infected when they swallow food contaminated with tapeworm eggs. The larvae lodge in the liver, where they form cysts which grow slowly for 10–20 years before producing symptoms of a lump and a dull ache on the right side of the abdomen. Occasionally other organs such as the lung, brain and bones are also affected. X-rays and CAT scans will highlight the cyst(s), which must be surgically removed.

SEE ALSO *Liver, Tapeworm*

HYDATIDIFORM MOLE

A hydatidiform mole is a benign (noncancerous) growth that develops within the uterus from a degenerating embryo. The abnormal growth produces multiple cysts, often resembling a bunch of grapes. The tumor usually causes bleeding similar to that from a threatened miscarriage. It may be spontaneously expelled from the uterus; if not, a dilation and curettage (scraping) is performed to surgically remove it. In some cases, a hydatidiform mole will progress to form a malignant tumor called a choriocarcinoma.

SEE ALSO *Dilation and curettage, Miscarriage, Pregnancy*

HYDROCELE

Hydrocele refers to an accumulation of fluid in the sac which covers the testes, the tunica vaginalis. It is a common cause of swelling in the scrotum and may be due to injury or inflammation in the testes, or obstruction of drainage. The fluid can be removed, but may reappear. Hydroceles are usually painless, but, if causing discomfort, they can be treated surgically.

SEE ALSO *Scrotum, Testes*

HYDROCEPHALUS

Hydrocephalus ("water on the brain") is a condition in which there is an excess of fluid within or surrounding the brain. This fluid, known as cerebrospinal fluid or CSF, is produced at a constant rate within the ventricles (cavities) of the brain. It circulates from the ventricles into the space surrounding the brain (subarachnoid space) and from there it drains into the venous system. The total volume of CSF is replaced about three times per day so, if CSF circulation is blocked (e.g. by a tumor) or its drainage is defective, the CSF accumulates and exerts pressure on the brain.

Occasionally, in some infants, the openings between the ventricles and the subarachnoid space fail to develop, and the resulting hydrocephalus causes the head to enlarge, because the skull bones have not yet fused. In adults, where the skull has fused and cannot expand further, nearby structures can become compressed and CSF pressure builds up inside the skull, which can affect consciousness and result in headache and vomiting.

Hydrocephalus is usually treated by placing a tube (shunt) into the ventricles, which enables the excess CSF to drain into the internal jugular vein in the neck.

SEE ALSO *Brain*

HYDROTHERAPY

The term hydrotherapy covers a broad range of health treatments involving the use of water. The use of hydrotherapy goes back to antiquity, with many cultures advocating bathing in hot mineral springs and sea water to restore health. Modern hydrotherapy spa treatments were pioneered in the nineteenth century by Father Sebastian Kneipp, a Bavarian monk.

Central to hydrotherapy is the idea that water is naturally healing because it is both essential to life and is the major component of our bodies. The temperature of the water is of crucial significance in many treatments. Hot water is used to encourage relaxation and sweating, and to draw blood to the surface of the skin. Cold water constricts the blood vessels, reduces surface inflammation and stimulates blood flow to the internal organs.

Different forms of hydrotherapy are used by a variety of health professionals. Physical therapists recommend gentle exercise in warm water or whirlpool baths in order to relax muscles, and recommend iced water compresses for physical trauma, such as tendinitis. Naturopaths prescribe sitz baths for pelvic problems, steam baths for congestion, foot or hand baths for insomnia, hot and cold water showers for menstrual problems and colonic irrigation to cleanse and tone the bowel. Aromatherapy treatment uses essential oils in baths or inhalations.

SEE ALSO *Aromatherapy, Naturopathy*

HYMEN

In a female infant the vaginal opening is closed by a thin membrane called the hymen. This membrane usually ruptures before puberty to allow menstrual blood to escape. An intact hymen used to be considered evidence of virginity but in fact in most cases the hymen commonly ruptures, at least in part, during physical exercise. Further rupture usually occurs during the first sexual intercourse.

After childbirth there is little of the hymen left in the mother. In rare cases the hymen will fail to rupture before puberty, causing menstrual blood to accumulate in the vagina. The hymen then must be cut surgically.

SEE ALSO *Reproductive systems, Vagina*

HYPERGLYCEMIA

Hyperglycemia is a condition in which the blood sugar level is higher than normal. It occurs in diabetics, in pancreatic disorders, as a complication of extensive burns and in cases of acute stress. People who find it difficult to control their diabetes probably have hyperglycemic periods every day. In diabetics, hyperglycemia is caused by missing or miscalculating doses of insulin or by overeating or drinking too much alcohol. If untreated, it can lead to coma.

Symptoms are thirst and blurred vision together with numbness and tingling. When diabetes mellitus is first diagnosed, the symptoms of hyperglycemia are likely to be present. These include increased urination, increased thirst, weight loss despite increased food intake, fatigue and increased susceptibility to yeast infections.

Once diabetes has been diagnosed, patients are taught how to test their own blood glucose levels at home so that they can control hyperglycemia with either insulin injections or oral medications.

SEE ALSO *Blood sugar tests, Diabetes, Insulin, Pancreas*

HYPERTENSION

Hypertension is the term for high pressure (tension) in the arteries (i.e. high blood pressure). The average normal blood pressure at rest is about 120/80 mm Hg, and is usually between 100/60 and 140/90. Systolic blood pressure (the upper number) represents the maximum pressure in the arteries as the heart contracts and ejects blood into the circulation. Diastolic pressure (the bottom number)

Hypertension

High blood pressure (hypertension) describes a condition in which the pressure of the blood in the arteries is too high. This can occur when the heart pumps blood too forcefully around the body, or when arterioles narrow, inhibiting blood flow. Hypertension causes a number of (often fatal) complications including arteriosclerosis, stroke and heart disease.

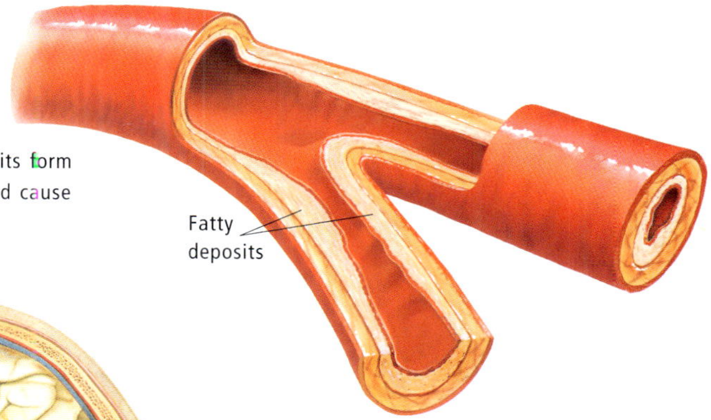

Arteriosclerosis
Hypertension may lead to the development of arteriosclerosis, a condition in which fatty deposits form beneath the lining of arteries and cause them to narrow.

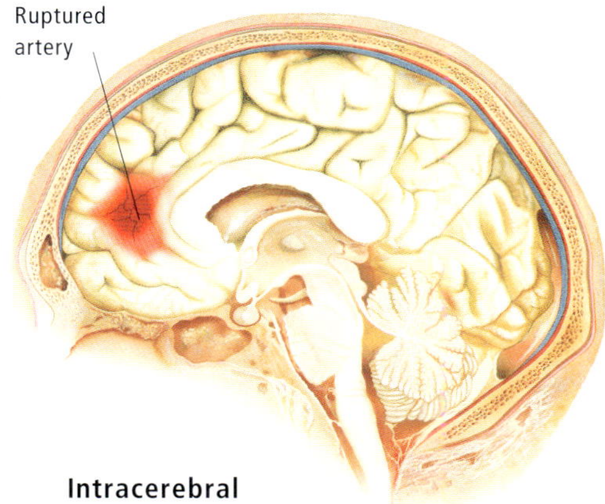

Intracerebral hemorrhage
Hypertension may cause an artery to rupture and bleed, especially if it is already affected by arteriosclerosis. A ruptured artery in the brain for example may cause an intracerebral hemorrhage.

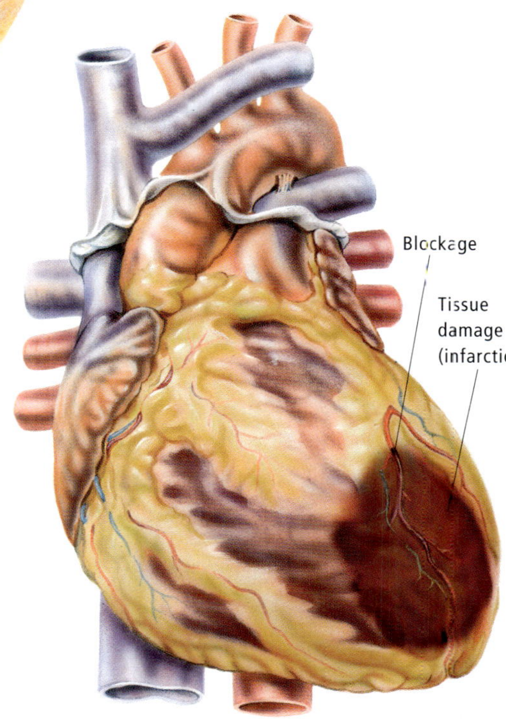

Ischemia/myocardial infarction
Hypertension is one of the causes of myocardial infarction. It causes the arteries to harden and narrow (arteriosclerosis) which obstructs the blood supply to the heart muscle.

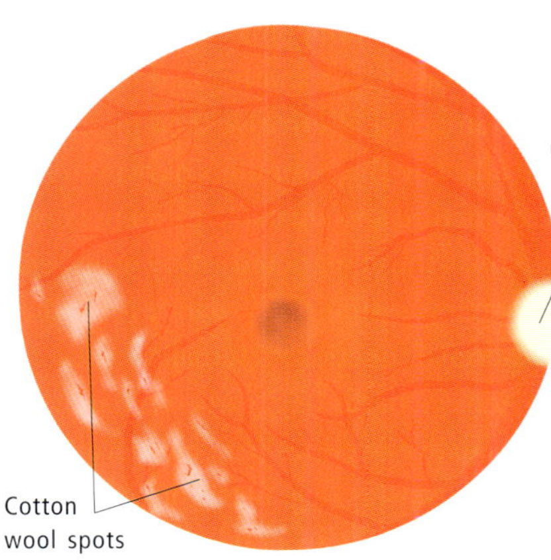

Retinopathy
After many years, hypertension can cause eye damage and even blindness. The arteries of the retina may narrow, small hemorrhages can occur and areas of damaged retina appear, seen here as pale-colored areas called "exudates" and "cotton wool spots".

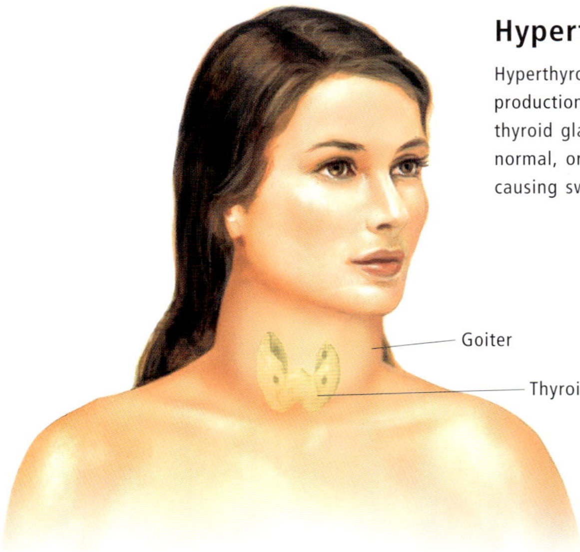

Hyperthyroidism

Hyperthyroidism is caused by an excess production of thyroid hormones from the thyroid gland. The gland may appear normal, or it may become enlarged, causing swelling in the neck (goiter).

represents the minimum blood pressure as the heart relaxes following a contraction.

Although blood pressure varies from person to person and from time to time, someone is said to have hypertension when the blood pressure is 140/90 or above. High blood pressure is one of the causes of arteriosclerosis which in turn can cause heart attack, stroke, intermittent claudication and kidney failure. Hypertension can exist silently for decades; by the time it is diagnosed, the damage has already occurred. Hence, hypertension is sometimes called "the silent killer".

In 90 percent of cases, no-one knows what causes hypertension. People with a family history of hypertension, who smoke, are overweight or obese, and consume a diet high in salt are at particular risk. Stress and excess alcohol consumption are also thought to be contributing factors. In 10 percent of cases there is a predisposing medical condition such as kidney disease or a tumor of the adrenal gland.

The diagnosis of hypertension can be made by a primary care physician (general practitioner) using simple blood pressure measurements, repeated to confirm the diagnosis. Additional tests may be required if the physician suspects an underlying disease is causing hypertension.

Because of its role in stroke, heart attack and kidney failure, it is important to bring hypertension under control. Preventive measures are the first line of treatment. Smoking and alcohol use should be stopped, or at least reduced, regular aerobic exercise and weight control introduced, and intake of salt and animal fats reduced. These measures can reduce blood pressure by about five points in 50 percent of sufferers. If this fails to control the hypertension, drug therapy is the next step. Drugs used for treating hypertension include diuretics, beta-blockers, alpha-adrenergic blockers, angiotensin-converting enzyme (ACE) inhibitors, and calcium channel blockers.

About 1 percent of people with hypertension have a severe form of the condition called accelerated or malignant hypertension. In these people, diastolic blood pressure exceeds 140 and is associated with headache, nausea and dizziness. This condition requires urgent hospital treatment to prevent stroke or brain hemorrhage.

High blood pressure in pregnancy can indicate preeclampsia, or toxemia of pregnancy. Other symptoms are fluid retention and albuminuria (protein in the urine). If the blood pressure is not quickly reduced to normal, there is an increased chance of the mother developing eclampsia, which can be fatal to both mother and fetus.

A number of alternative therapies may help alleviate the symptoms of hypertension. Acupuncture and shiatsu treatments may help relax the constricted artery walls, calm the nervous system and balance the kidney and adrenal functions. Herbalism prescribes hypotensive herbs (e.g. garlic or linden), with sedative nervines (e.g. motherwort), arterial cleansers (e.g. nettle or hawthorn) and diuretics (e.g. uva ursi or dandelion).

Naturopathy advises a vegetarian low-fat wholefood diet with restricted tea, coffee, alcohol, salt and sugar intake, and regular consumption of ginger and garlic. Supplements prescribed include vitamins B and C plus a range of minerals. Meditation, biofeedback or other relaxation techniques, as well as gentle exercise such as qigong, t'ai chi or yoga may help in the management of hypertension by relieving stress.

SEE ALSO *Arteriosclerosis, Blood pressure, Preeclampsia, Toxemia*

HYPERTHERMIA

Hyperthermia is the term for abnormally high body temperature. High temperatures are used as part of an experimental approach to controlling and eliminating cancer. This is a non-ionizing, non-invasive radiation therapy which kills cancer cells through the use of high temperatures. Hyperthermia during pregnancy may cause abnormal development of the fetus.

SEE ALSO *Body temperature*

HYPERTHYROIDISM

Hyperthyroidism (or thyrotoxicosis) occurs when overactive thyroid tissue secretes too much thyroid hormone into the bloodstream. The thyroid tissue may be overactive as a result of abnormal stimulation, as in Graves' disease; there may be an isolated overactive thyroid nodule or an entire overactive gland.

Symptoms of thyrotoxicosis include nervousness, increased appetite with weight loss, poor tolerance of hot weather, increased sweating, palpitations, increased frequency of bowel motions, menstrual problems, infertility and muscular weakness. An enlarged thyroid gland (goiter), increased heart rate, fine hair and warm, moist skin may also occur. Patients with Graves' disease will often have a wide-eyed staring appearance, due to the protrusion of the eyeballs (exophthalmos).

Blood tests usually reveal elevated levels of thyroid hormone and the absence of thyroid stimulating hormone (TSH), which is produced by the pituitary. If left untreated, hyperthyroidism can cause heart attacks, arrhythmias and heart failure, progressive weight loss and death.

Treatment is with antithyroid drugs to interfere with thyroid hormone production, radioactive iodine to destroy hyperactive thyroid tissue or surgery to remove excessively active thyroid tissue. The choice of treatment depends on the age and state of health of the patient and the size of the goiter.

SEE ALSO *Goiter, Graves' disease, Pituitary gland, Thyroid gland, Thyrotoxicosis*

HYPNOTHERAPY

The use of hypnotism in medicine began with the Austrian doctor Franz Anton Mesmer (1734–1815), a flamboyant character who put his patients into a light hypnotic trance . The word "mesmerize" is derived from the name of Dr Mesmer. His work was largely discredited, but some of his trance-inducing techniques were researched, most notably by James Braid, a Scottish surgeon who coined the term "hypnotism" in the mid-1800s. Braid performed some of his surgery using hypnosis but the development of quicker forms of anesthesia, such as chloroform, eclipsed his achievements.

The use of hypnotic states in treating psychological disorders was investigated by a few European doctors, most notably Jean-Martin Charcot and Sigmund Freud, in the latter part of the nineteenth century.

Widespread recognition of the therapeutic applications of hypnosis developed in the mid-twentieth century, when its use was endorsed by both the British and American Medical Associations. In recent times hypnotherapy has been used for a number of physical and psychological disorders including stress-related problems, addictions and phobias, as well as sleep disorders, respiratory conditions and pain management.

The word hypnotherapy is derived from the Greek *hypnos*, meaning "to sleep". This is somewhat misleading as the hypnotic state is actually an altered state of consciousness that falls somewhere between waking and sleeping, similar to when a person daydreams. To help induce this state in a patient the hypnotherapist uses a progressive relaxation technique, such as a step-by-step countdown procedure, or the patient is asked to focus on a particular object, image or light.

Hypnotherapists stress that a hypnotic state will only be achieved if the patient chooses to go along with the process, and that for this reason all hypnosis is in fact "self-hypnosis".

Once the patient reaches the hypnotic state the hypnotherapist guides their attention to a particular health issue such as reducing pain or anxiety. The patient's mind is both more focused and more receptive so that health problems are able to be approached from a fresh mental perspective. Phrases and images are given to the patient to focus on which generate feelings of mental and physical well-being. Suggestions for behavioral or attitudinal change made by either the patient or the hypnotherapist are more likely to be taken up and acted upon when received under hypnosis.

Hypnotherapy aims to combine a state of concentration with a state of relaxation so that patients can focus on something that would normally distress them and yet stay relaxed. This may help alleviate traumas, fears and anxieties in everyday life. During the course of treatment the hypnotherapist often teaches patients a method of self-hypnosis which they can practise when at home.

Hypnotherapy should only be practised by a fully qualified practitioner, as it can do harm when improperly used.

SEE ALSO *Relaxation techniques*

HYPNOTICS

Hypnotics are a group of drugs used to ease anxiety or to produce sleep. They function by depressing the central nervous system. Hypnotics are sometimes called sedatives or tranquilizers, though neither of these induces sleep, as hypnotics do.

In the past, barbiturates and chloral hydrate were often used as hypnotics, but they have been replaced with benzodiazepines, which are safer and have less likelihood of overdose.

Hypnotics can be useful in cases where sleep is important to recovery. Nevertheless, they are not without dangers.

While overdose is very rare with benzodiazepines, it may occur where benzodiazepines are taken in combination with alcohol or other drugs.

Because of possible side effects such as drowsiness, loss of co-ordination, and loss of judgement, these drugs should not be used with alcohol and other similar types of drug. The dose should be kept low when prescribed for the elderly. Warnings should also be given about driving and working with machinery.

SEE ALSO *Anxiety, Anxiolitics, Detoxification, Drug dependence, Insomnia, Sedatives, Sleeping pills, Tranquilizers, Withdrawal*

H

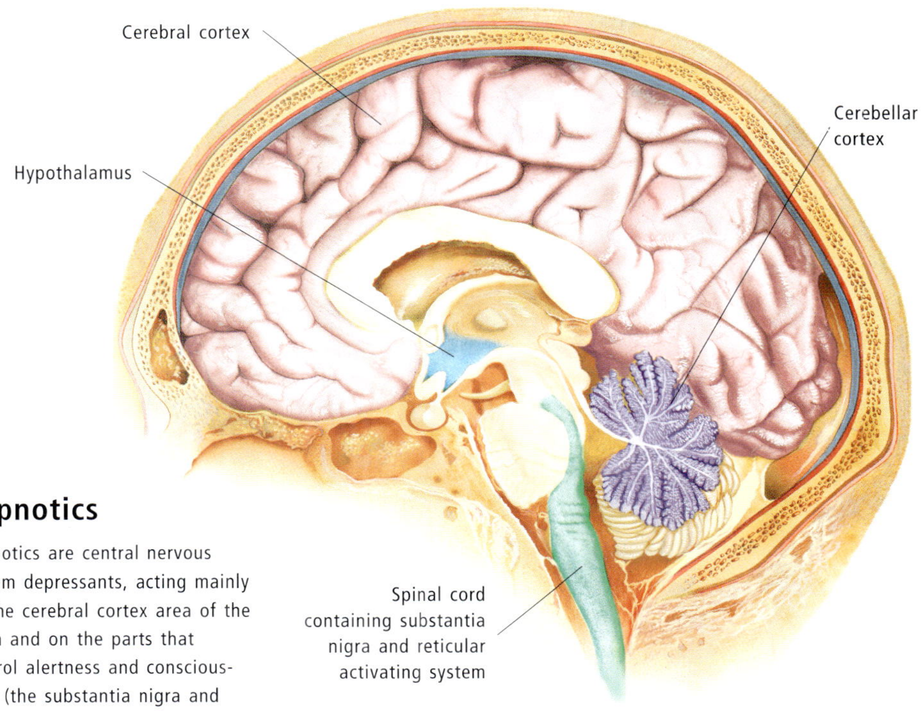

Hypnotics

Hypnotics are central nervous system depressants, acting mainly on the cerebral cortex area of the brain and on the parts that control alertness and consciousness (the substantia nigra and reticular activating system).

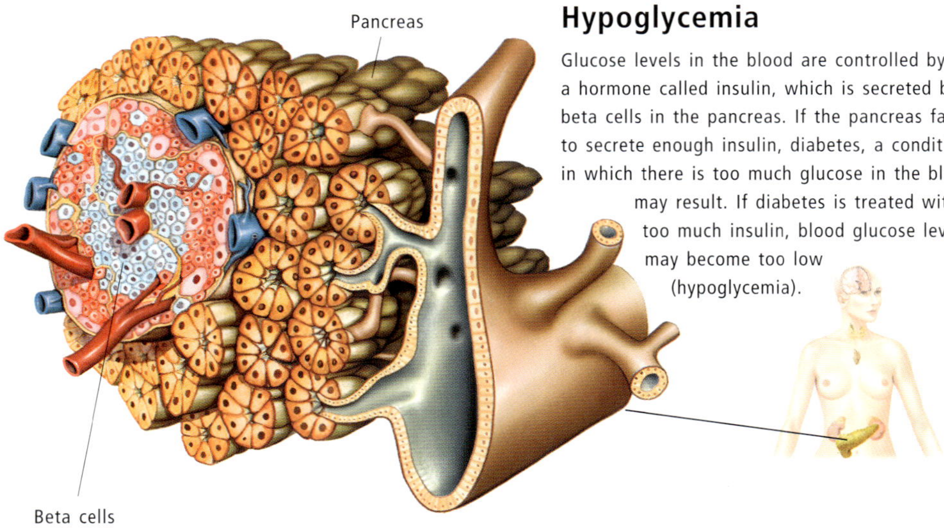

Hypoglycemia

Glucose levels in the blood are controlled by a hormone called insulin, which is secreted by beta cells in the pancreas. If the pancreas fails to secrete enough insulin, diabetes, a condition in which there is too much glucose in the blood, may result. If diabetes is treated with too much insulin, blood glucose levels may become too low (hypoglycemia).

HYPOCALCEMIA

Hypocalcemia is the medical term for abnormally low levels of calcium in the blood. It may be caused by underactivity of the parathyroid glands (hypoparathyroidism), or by vitamin D deficiency. Mild hypocalcemia causes no symptoms and may only be detected after a routine blood test. More severe hypocalcemia causes muscle twitching and seizures. Over time, chronic calcium deficiency contributes to poor mineralization of bones (osteoporosis), soft bones (osteomalacia) and rickets in children.

Treatment is with oral or intravenous calcium and oral vitamin D supplements.

SEE ALSO *Calcium, Osteomalacia, Osteoporosis, Rickets, Parathyroid glands, Vitamins*

HYPOGLYCEMIA

Hypoglycemia is a condition caused by abnormally low levels of glucose (sugar) in the blood. This may be due to glucose leaving the blood at an excessive rate, or to decreased secretion of glucose into the blood. It most often occurs in persons with diabetes mellitus. For example, the condition may occur if a diabetic taking insulin (or other diabetic medication) has not eaten enough or has increased their amount of exercise without increasing the intake of food, or it may occur if the dosage of their medication is too high. In rare cases, hypoglycemia may be caused by an insulinoma, a tumor in the pancreas which secretes insulin. Occasionally, hypoglycemia may occur without any apparent cause.

Hypoglycemia deprives the body's cells of nutrients necessary for normal metabolic functioning. It causes dizziness, weakness, sweating, hunger, mental confusion, and/or personality changes. Severe hypoglycemia, which may cause coma, brain damage or death, is a medical emergency.

A diabetic learns to recognize the symptoms of hypoglycemia and takes sugar by mouth (by sucking candy, for example). In more serious cases, such as a coma, an injection of glucose or glucagon (a hormone that raises blood glucose levels) may be needed. After recovery, the diabetic's medication and/or diet will need to be adjusted by the physician.

SEE ALSO *Blood sugar tests, Diabetes, Insulin, Pancreas*

HYPOKALEMIA

Potassium is crucial to the normal functioning of our cells. Classified medically as an electrolyte, it is involved in the maintenance of a normal heartbeat, regulation of the body's water balance and the activities of nerves and muscles. A deficiency of potassium in the blood and body tissues is known as hypokalemia, a dangerous and potentially life-threatening condition most often associated with chronic illness and ageing. It may also occur as a side effect of certain drugs.

Symptoms of a deficiency may include high blood pressure, abnormal heartbeat rhythms, depression, fatigue, slow reflexes, muscle weakness and paralysis. Depletion of the body's potassium can be caused by excessive vomiting, diarrhea or sweating, kidney disease or certain medications, such as digitalis (for heart problems) and diuretics.

Most people can obtain sufficient potassium through a balanced diet, and minor deficiencies can be treated by increasing your intake of potassium-rich foods, such as oranges, tomatoes, bananas, potatoes with their skins on, carrots, dried apricots and fish. More severe deficiencies may require oral or intravenous potassium supplements and hospitalization.

SEE ALSO *Electrolytes, Nutrition, Potassium*

HYPONATREMIA

Publicity about the dangers of high-salt diets has made many people aware of the health risks of too much sodium. But an abnormally low concentration of sodium in the blood—known as hyponatremia—can also cause some problems. Usually the condition occurs when too much water is consumed in relation to sodium, or the body fails to excrete excess water. Both situations can create an imbalance in the body.

People who are more likely to be susceptible to hyponatremia include the elderly, the very young and the mentally ill patients who may not be able to respond appropriately to their thirst, and people with certain kidney disorders.

Hyponatremia can also be a problem for athletes, particularly distance and marathon runners, who can develop the condition if they drink too much water without also replacing sodium lost in sweat during excessive physical exertion. The problem can be avoided by quenching thirst with sports drinks that contain electrolytes, rather than just water alone.

Symptoms of hyponatremia range from nausea, muscle cramps, weakness and fatigue to seizures and a loss of consciousness in severe deficiencies. In extreme cases the condition can be fatal.

SEE ALSO *Sodium*

HYPOPARATHYROIDISM

Hypoparathyroidism is a rare disorder in which production of parathyroid hormone—which helps regulate blood calcium levels—is either reduced or non-existent due to dysfunctional or absent parathyroid glands. It may be a congenital condition or, less commonly, acquired later in life (usually due to surgical damage to or removal of the parathyroids).

Hypoparathyroidism leads to abnormally low blood calcium levels (hypocalcemia) which can trigger a nerve disorder called tetany, characterized by painful muscle spasms and twitches. People born with hypoparathyroidism can also suffer from dry skin, hair loss and a susceptibility to yeast (*Candida*) infections.

Without treatment, hypoparathyroidism in children can lead to impaired physical and mental development. The condition is treated with calcium and vitamin D supplements, which need to be taken for life.

SEE ALSO *Parathyroid glands*

HYPOPHOSPHATASIA

Hypophosphatasia is an inherited metabolic disorder caused by abnormally low levels in the body of the enzyme serum alkaline phosphatase which is critical in the development of the bones. The severity of the condition can vary widely from patient to patient.

Symptoms of the mildest forms may not appear until late childhood or adulthood. In the most severe cases, newborns can suffer from impaired growth and eventually die. In all sufferers, the skeleton is affected in some way and the teeth are often involved. There is no known treatment for hypophosphatasia.

SEE ALSO *Congenital abnormalities, Enzyme deficiencies*

HYPOPLASIA

Incomplete or defective development of a body organ or tissue is known as hypoplasia. Potential causes are many and varied and may depend on the particular part of the body affected.

Cartilage-hair hypoplasia, in which the cartilage is affected leading to bone abnormalities, has a genetic cause. This condition is characterized by dwarfism. Enamel hypoplasia, which affects the teeth, can also be a genetic disorder. Pulmonary hypoplasia can occur when other organs have compressed the lungs during their development in the uterus. The cause of optic nerve hypoplasia remains unclear but it is sometimes blamed on substances taken by a mother during pregnancy. Sufferers of this disorder are missing 10–90 percent of the 1.2 million nerve fibers usually found in an optic nerve, impairing vision in the affected eye.

SEE ALSO *Congenital abnormalities*

HYPOSPADIAS

This is a relatively common male birth defect of unknown cause, in which the development of the penile urethra is abnormal. Instead of forming a tube that extends the full length of the shaft and opens at the tip of the glans penis, the urethral opening (the meatus) develops at some point on the underside of the penis, interfering with normal voiding of urine.

Hypospadias may be accompanied by a downward curve of the shaft of the penis, known as chordee. There is no associated abnormality of the testes, and the condition can be corrected surgically, usually with good results.

SEE ALSO *Penis, Reproductive systems, Urethra, Urinary systems*

HYPOTENSION

Hypotension, or low blood pressure, is a condition in which the blood pressure is below the average measurement of 120/80 mm Hg. Often a low blood pressure is of little significance, being a statistical variant from the average, and normal for a particular person (it may even indicate a prolonged life expectancy).

Sometimes hypotension may be caused by disease, such as vasovagal syncope, hypoaldosteronism, diabetes mellitus, tabes dorsalis or Parkinson's disease. Some drugs, especially antidepressants, may have hypotensive effects.

Often hypotension has no symptoms and is diagnosed during a visit to the doctor for a routine checkup or for some other reason. The sufferer may go to the doctor complaining of feeling dizzy and fainting, especially when standing up quickly. Most cases get better without treatment. If there is an underlying cause, treating it will reverse the condition. If hypotension is due to drug treatment, the drug(s) should be stopped if possible.

SEE ALSO *Blood pressure*

HYPOTHALAMUS

The hypothalamus is a small but vital region at the base of the brain, which is essential for the maintenance of life. It contains specialized receptor cells, which can detect changes in the properties of circulating blood (for example, temperature, hormone levels, osmotic pressure). The pituitary gland, or hypophysis, is attached to its exposed surface.

By regulating hormone production in the pituitary gland, and through neural connections with other parts of the brain and spinal

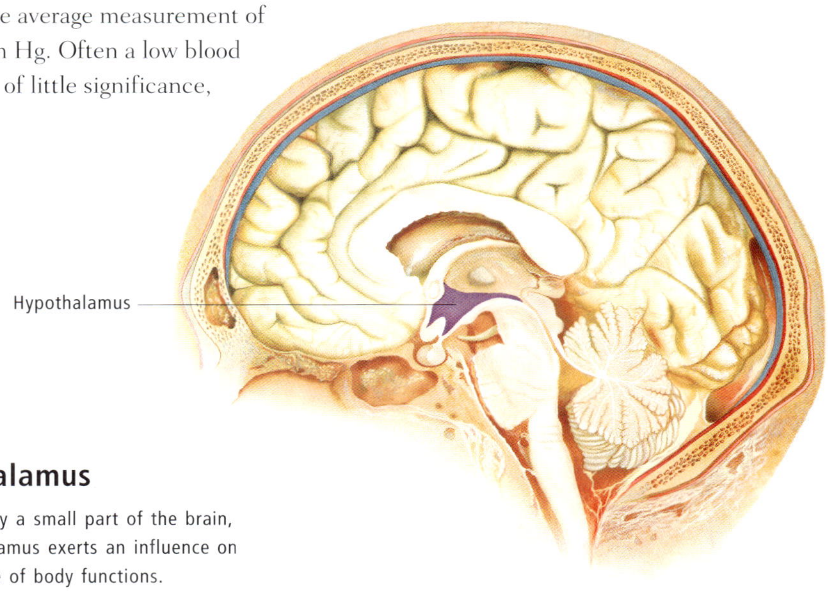

Hypothalamus

Although only a small part of the brain, the hypothalamus exerts an influence on a wide range of body functions.

cord, the hypothalamus provides overall control of the autonomic nervous system, which coordinates activity in the body's internal organs. It contains centers which regulate the heart and blood pressure, body temperature, water balance, food intake, growth and sexual reproduction. It is also important in the expression of emotions such as fear, anger and pleasure.

Activity in the hypothalamus may be disrupted by tumors, vascular disease or head injury. The most common disorder of the hypothalamus is diabetes insipidus, a condition in which there is excessive urine production, accompanied by constant drinking (up to 10 quarts or 10 liters per day). Inability to maintain a constant body temperature, eating disorders (such as obesity and bulimia), sleeping problems and memory loss may also associated with disorders of the hypothalamus.

SEE ALSO *Autonomic nervous system, Brain, Diabetes insipidus, Hormones, Pituitary gland*

HYPOTHERMIA

Hypothermia results from exposure (usually accidental) to cold. It occurs commonly in the elderly and children (who have difficulty shivering to keep warm), in ill or alcohol-dependent people. Healthy people, for example, mountaineers, caught out in the cold can also develop hypothermia especially when conditions also involve snow, wind and/or rain.

In hypothermia, the body's core temperature gradually drops below the normal level of 98.6°F (37°C) to as low as 80°F (27°C). When this happens, the body's metabolism, respiration and heartbeat all slow down and the person becomes mentally confused, with slurred speech and muscle cramps. If untreated, coma and death may follow.

Any wet and frozen clothing should be removed and the person's body needs to be gradually warmed in layers of dry, warm clothing. Hospitalization may be necessary.

SEE ALSO *Body temperature*

HYPOTHYROIDISM

This refers to the reduced secretion of hormones by the thyroid gland, principally involving the underproduction of thyroxine. It may be caused by insufficient thyroid tissue, inhibition of hormone synthesis or by decreased production of thyroid stimulating hormone by the pituitary gland. If untreated, infants develop a condition called cretinism, while in adults hypothyroidism leads to myxedema.

SEE ALSO *Cretinism, Myxedema, Pituitary gland, Thyroid gland*

HYPOXIA

Hypoxia is a shortage of oxygen in the cells and tissues. There are many potential causes. It can result from a variety of disorders or substances, such as carbon dioxide or carbon monoxide, which reduce the blood's ability to transport and circulate oxygen throughout the body. It can be caused by environmental factors, particularly high altitudes. Or it may be due to a disease or injury that affects a tissue's ability to use oxygen.

Hypoxia can be isolated to a particular organ or it may be widespread in the body. The tissues that are most sensitive to reduced oxygen levels are the heart, brain, liver and blood vessels to the lungs. In severe or protracted episodes of hypoxia, permanent tissue damage due to cell death can occur. The onset of the condition can often appear without warning. Early symptoms may include a rise in heart and respiration rates in response to falling oxygen levels in the blood. Another early symptom can be a sense of euphoria, or well-being—something like an alcohol-induced high. Dizziness and mental confusion may follow.

Treatment for hypoxia will depend on the cause. A patient may require mechanical ventilation, drugs to stimulate respiration, or oxygen therapy.

HYSTERECTOMY

Hysterectomy is the surgical removal of the uterus and it is the second most common operation on women in the industrialized world after dilation and curettage. It may be performed for a number of reasons. These include cancer of the uterus, the cervix or the ovaries; benign tumors, such as large fibroids; extreme cases of endometriosis; a severe prolapse of the uterus; excessive blood loss that is not responding to treatment; and, very rarely, after childbirth or gynecological surgery.

There are several forms of this operation. A total hysterectomy is the removal of the entire uterus plus the cervix. A subtotal hysterectomy removes the uterus but not the cervix. A radical hysterectomy removes the uterus and the associated lymph glands in the pelvis. A hysterosalpingo-oophorectomy removes the uterus, ovaries and tubes on both sides.

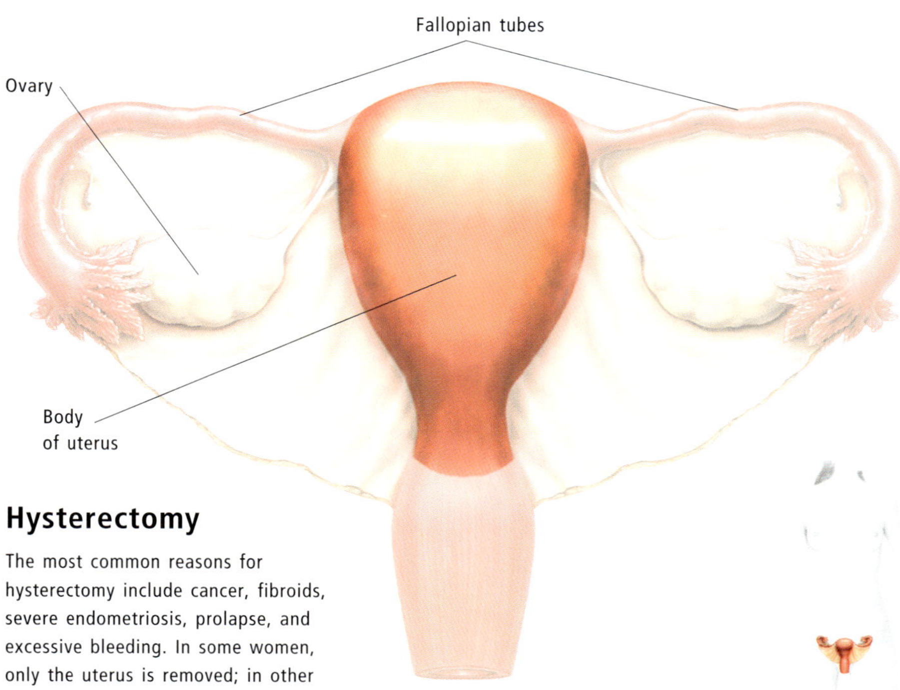

Hysterectomy

The most common reasons for hysterectomy include cancer, fibroids, severe endometriosis, prolapse, and excessive bleeding. In some women, only the uterus is removed; in other cases, the cervix, ovaries and fallopian tubes need to be removed as well.

The operation can be performed through an abdominal incision or through the vagina; the latter method is now more common. A laparoscope, a narrow tube with a fiber-optic light on one end, is often used in the operation. It is inserted through a small incision just below the navel and enables the surgeon to view the reproductive organs and to operate using small instruments guided by the laparoscope.

Risks include infections and damage to other organs. An abdominal hysterectomy is major surgery which will require post-operative painkillers and a convalescence period of around six weeks. Vaginal hysterectomy causes less post-operative pain and requires a shorter convalescence. Laparoscopic hysterectomy has more complications but a very short recovery time.

Once the woman has recovered from the operation, hysterectomy will not affect her ability to have sexual intercourse and, in many cases, will improve her quality of life. A serious operation, a woman may require adequate support and counseling, if necessary. Side effects include no more menstrual periods and no risk of pregnancy. A woman who must have a hysterectomy before she has reached menopause will need hormone replacement therapy, if her ovaries are not left in place.

Fewer hysterectomies are performed now than in the 1970s, when there was some controversy over unnecessary operations.

SEE ALSO *Endometriosis, Fibroids, Hormone replacement therapy, Hysterosalpingo-oophorectomy, Ovaries, Reproductive systems, Uterus*

HYSTEROSALPINGOGRAPHY

Hysterosalpingography is a medical x-ray investigation (*-graphy*) aimed at visualizing the uterus (*hystero-*) and fallopian tube (*salpingo-*). The investigation involves introducing a fluid which is opaque to x-rays into the uterine cervix, under gentle pressure.

This fluid fills the interior of the uterus and tube, making it possible, using x-rays, to detect tumors or obstructions which might cause infertility.

In most modern investigations of infertility, hysterosalpingography has largely been superseded by laparoscopic examination, where a fiberoptic instrument allows the practitioner to see the interior of the pelvis, combined with colored dye injection.

SEE ALSO *Fallopian tubes, Laparoscopy, Salpingitis, Uterus*

HYSTEROSALPINGO-OOPHORECTOMY

This is the surgical removal of the uterus, fallopian tube and ovaries. It may be used in combination with radiation and hormone therapy to treat advanced cases of carcinoma (cancer) of the cervix and uterus.

SEE ALSO *Cervix, Fallopian tubes, Hysterectomy, Ovaries, Uterus*

HYSTEROSCOPY

Hysteroscopy is the use of a hysteroscope, a uterine speculum with reflector, to remove by excision a fibroid tumor that is bulging into the uterine cavity. It is also used in visual examination of the canal of the uterine cervix and the uterus.

SEE ALSO *Cervix, Fibroids, Hysterectomy, Uterus*

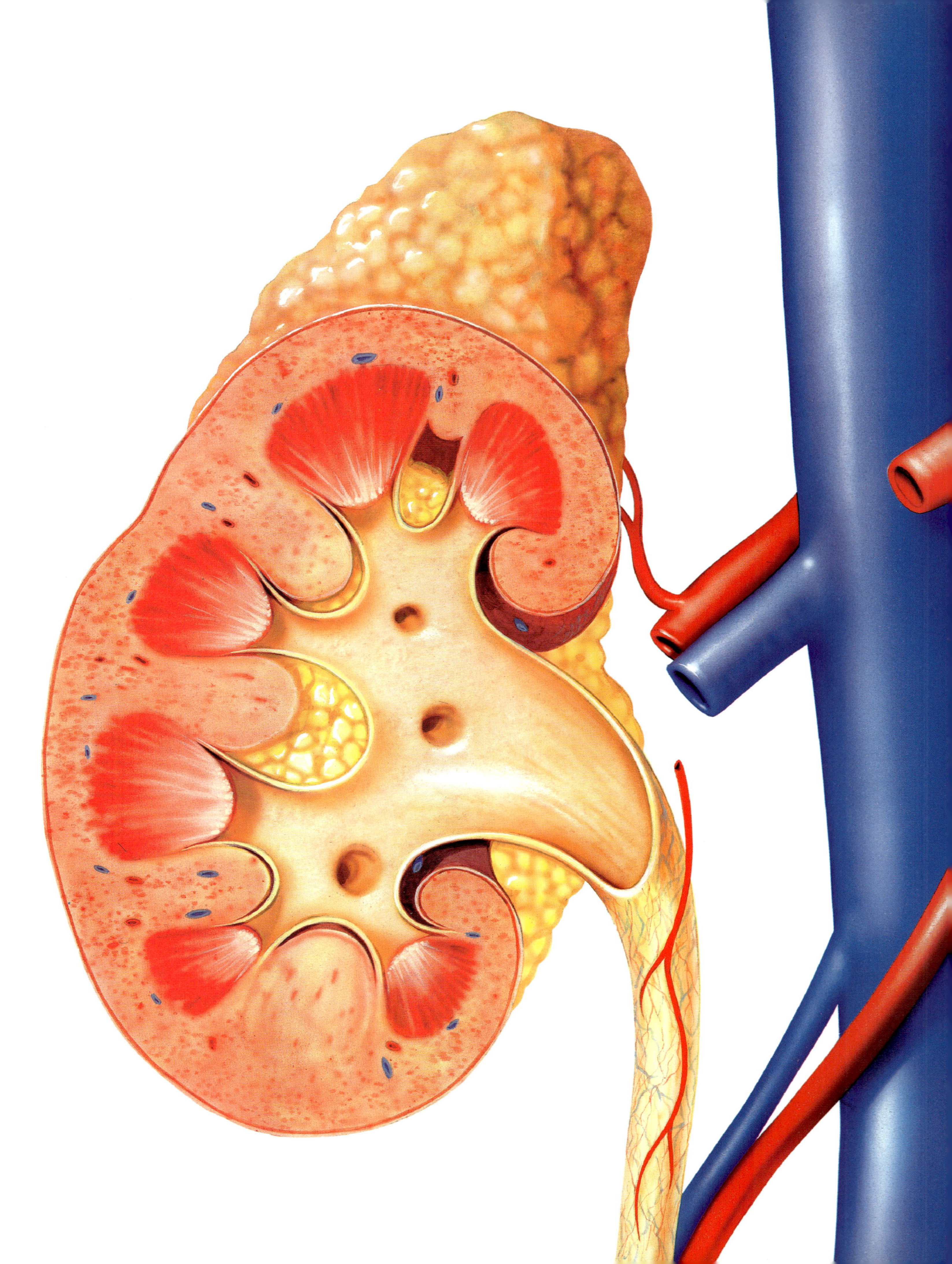

IJK

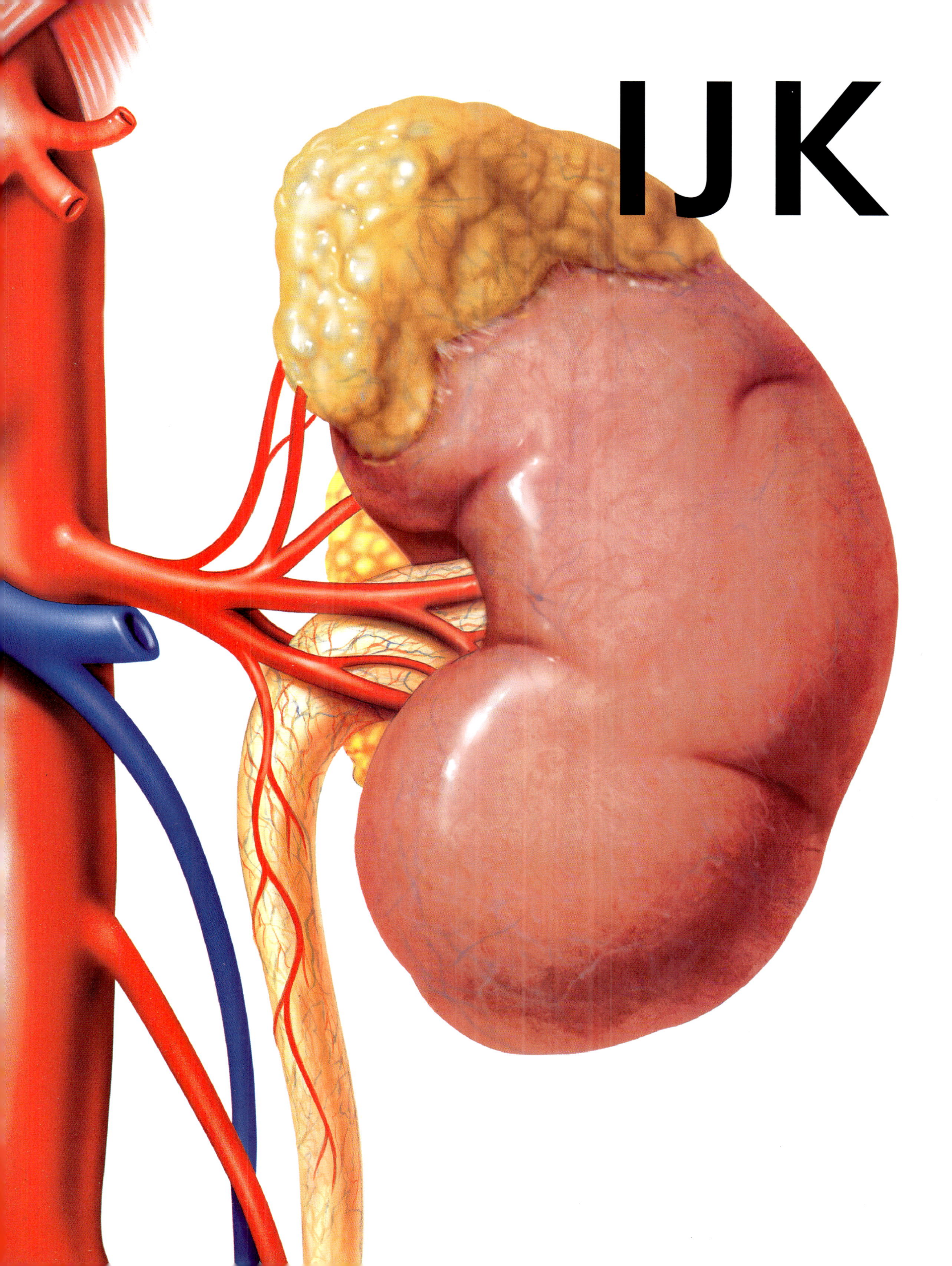

IATROGENIC DISEASE

Iatrogenic disease is disease caused by medical treatment or resulting from the effects of a doctor's words, treatments or actions on the patient. It may be an unavoidable side effect of the treatment or occur because the treatment was inappropriate.

The word iatrogenic comes from the Greek *iatros* ("physician") plus *genic* ("produced by"). Iatrogenic diseases are estimated to cause between two and four times as many fatalities annually as road accidents in developed countries. The elderly are twice as much at risk as young people. It can occur in orthodox and alternative medicine.

Prevention strategies include seeking treatment outside of hospital where appropriate, obtaining information about treatment options, reading consent forms carefully, obtaining a second opinion about a proposed treatment, and delegating a relative to liaise with staff in hospitals.

ICHTHYOSIS

Ichthyosis is an inherited disorder in which the skin becomes thickened, forming cracks and fissures, which give it a fish-scale appearance.

Legs, arms, hands and trunk are the areas most affected. The condition typically begins in childhood before the age of four and improves during adulthood; however, it may recur when a person becomes elderly. There are various types of ichthyosis, but most are inherited genetic traits. Some forms may be acquired or develop in association with other diseases.

There is no cure for ichthyosis, but the use of mild, non-drying soaps and moisturizing creams and ointments will help the condition. Ointments that contain catalytic agents, such as lactic acid and salicylic acid, are especially useful, as these chemicals help the skin to shed.

SEE ALSO *Skin*

ILEITIS

Ileitis is literally inflammation of the ileum, which is the furthest end of the small intestine. Inflammation can occur as the result of infection with viruses or bacteria, and includes common conditions such as viral gastroenteritis and rarer conditions such as tuberculosis of the intestine, which affects the ileum more commonly than other parts of the bowel.

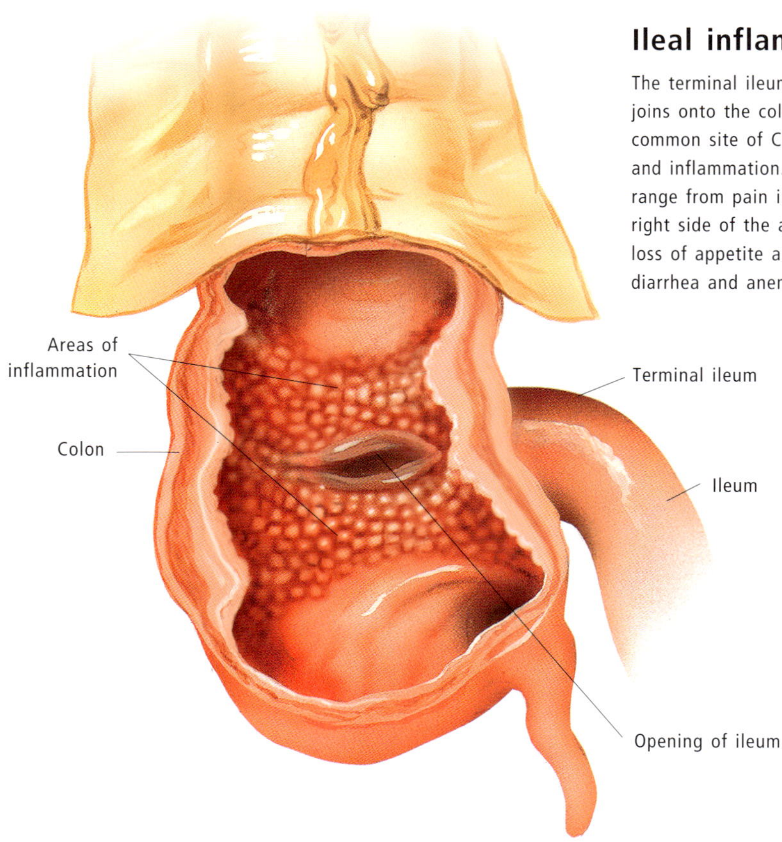

Ileal inflammation

The terminal ileum—where it joins onto the colon—is a common site of Crohn's disease and inflammation. Symptoms range from pain in the lower right side of the abdomen to loss of appetite and weight, diarrhea and anemia.

Crohn's disease is an inflammatory disease of the gastrointestinal tract, which most commonly affects the ileum. Its cause remains unknown, but appears to involve a combination of genetic and environmental factors.

Ileitis may also occur following radiation therapy of the abdominal organs. A person suffering from ileitis may experience pain in the abdomen and loss of appetite and weight. Treatment involves medication to remove the source of infection.

SEE ALSO *Crohn's disease, Ileum, Intestines*

ILEOSTOMY

Ileostomy is a surgical procedure in which the last part of the small intestine (the ileum) is permanently opened and brought to the surface of the abdomen. Fecal matter leaves the body through this opening which is called a "stoma". The stoma is located in the right lower quadrant of the abdomen. The procedure is usually performed after removal of the entire colon and rectum for the treatment of ulcerative colitis, Crohn's disease or familial polyposis coli.

Fecal matter will be more liquid and will pass more frequently than fecal matter from a colostomy. The procedure is performed under general anesthesia in a hospital. Full recovery takes about six weeks.

SEE ALSO *Colostomy, Ileum, Intestines*

ILEUM

The ileum is the last part of the small intestine. It leads on from the jejunum and empties into the cecum at the ileocecal junction. The ileum is about 10 feet (3 meters) long and, along with the jejunum, is suspended from the back abdominal wall by a fold of membrane called the mesentery.

While most nutrients (fats, sugars and amino acids) are absorbed from the duodenum and jejunum, there are important substances absorbed primarily from the ileum. These include bile acids, which are produced by the liver and secreted into the duodenum to break up fat globules. The bile acids are then recycled by being reabsorbed from the ileum and returned to the liver. The ileum is also important as the absorption site for vitamin B_{12} (cyanocobalamin).

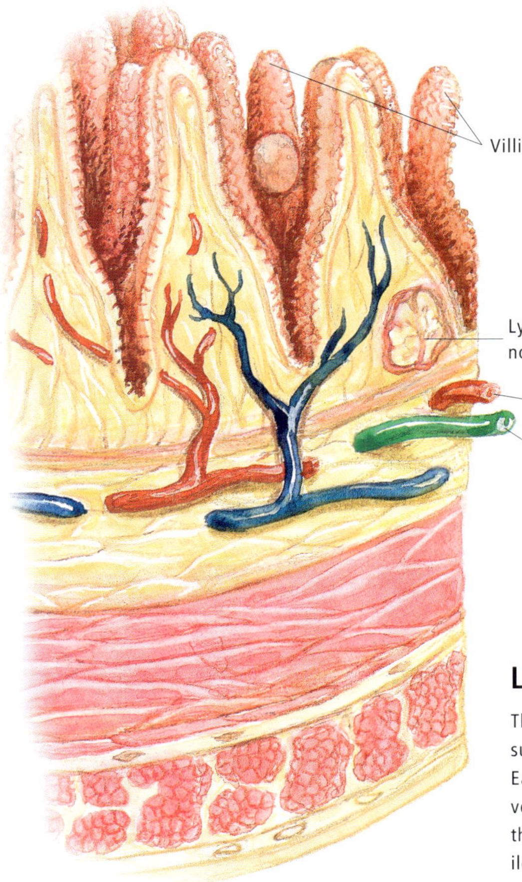

Lining of the ileum

The villi and microvilli increase the surface area of the small intestine. Each villus contains lymph and blood vessels and it is through these villi that bile acid is absorbed from the ileum and returned to the liver.

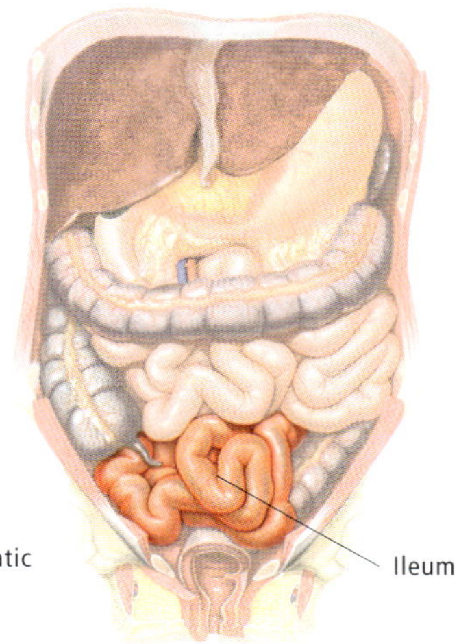

Ileum

The ileum is the last part of the small intestine, which absorbs bile acids and vitamin B_{12}. The working of the ileum can be affected by a number of illnesses, such as gastroenteritis and Crohn's disease.

The ileum can be affected by bowel obstruction, Crohn's disease and gastroenteritis. Crohn's disease is most common in the terminal ileum, with patients usually complaining of diarrhea, recurrent abdominal pain, weakness, weight loss and fever. Obstruction of blood vessels supplying the ileum may cause gangrene of the bowel, requiring immediate surgery.

Tumors are rare in the small intestine, comprising only 1–5 percent of all tumors of the gastrointestinal tract.

SEE ALSO *Crohn's disease, Digestive system, Duodenum, Gastroenteritis, Intestines, Jejunum*

ILEUS

Ileus refers to paralysis of bowel movement (a normal function known as peristalsis). It may arise in several different situations: after major abdominal surgery, infection in the abdomen, low output of blood from the heart, and even as a result of pneumonia. The abdomen is distended and bowel sounds are usually absent, although occasional faint or irregular bursts of bowel movement may be heard. When an x-ray is taken, the loops of bowel appear to be distended.

In newborn infants with cystic fibrosis, ileus may occur due to the presence of a thick plug of meconium (meconium ileus). In normal newborn infants the meconium, which is a paste filling the bowel before birth, is cleared from the bowel within a few days. Surgical intervention may be required to remove the blockage.

SEE ALSO *Bowel, Intestines, Peristalsis*

IMAGING TECHNIQUES

These are techniques used in the production of diagnostic images. Since the discovery of x-rays (electromagnetic radiation) in 1895, imaging techniques have played an important role in diagnosis.

Radiography uses x-rays to produce a negative photographic image of the internal bones and organs. The various parts of the body allow the x-rays through to differing degrees; the film creates an image by recording these variations in contrast. Often, to outline organs and tissues, opaque substances are used as well; for example, in a barium meal, the patient drinks a barium compound, which outlines the stomach and increases its contrast with surrounding tissue.

New technologies offer more precise images and are safer than x-rays. Ultrasound is a sonar technique that bounces sound waves off internal bodily structures and measures their density. The resulting picture can be used to visualize organs and body structures and detect movement. Ultrasound is especially useful in investigating pregnancy because it does not harm the fetus or the mother.

Computerized axial tomography (CAT) scanning is a technique in which a machine passes x-rays through a patient's body from various angles. A computer then creates a three-dimensional image of internal organs and structures inside the body. Using CAT scanning, a physician can tell the difference between a solid tumor, a fluid-filled cyst and a blood-filled hematoma in brain tissue.

Magnetic resonance imaging (MRI) uses an external magnetic field created by a series of powerful electromagnets in a scanner to excite hydrogen atoms in the body, which give off radio signals to the scanner. These signals are read by a computer and converted into a detailed image. By using magnetism instead of x-rays, MRI scanning avoids exposing people to radiation.

Nuclear scans are scans in which radioactive material such as thallium is injected into a vein. The isotope passes through the body, to be selectively taken up by organs such as the heart, bone and kidneys, depending on which isotope is used. A scintillation camera or scanner then detects radiation emitted from the isotope, converts them into images and displays them on a video screen for interpretation to help assess defects in the organ's structure and function. Nuclear scans are usually perfomed in the nuclear medicine department of a hospital.

SEE ALSO *Barium meal, CAT scan, Magnetic resonance imaging, Ultrasound, X-ray*

IMMUNITY

Immunity is the body's ability to protect itself from disease. It is achieved via the immune system, a complex network of organs, cells and proteins that recognizes foreign substances (such as viruses, bacteria, fungi and other pathogens) in the body and destroys them. This process is called the immune response.

There are two broad parts to the immune system. One part is called the humoral immune system, so called because the immune response takes place in the body fluids (humors). When a foreign body, or antigen, is identified, proteins called antibodies are produced by B lymphocytes (white blood cells) in the blood and body fluids which then attack the antigens or render them more easily attacked by other white blood cells.

The second component is the cell-mediated immune system, involving the different types of T lymphocytes. Some ingest and destroy invading pathogens while other T lymphocytes destroy them directly. Antibodies are not involved.

The first time an individual is exposed to a pathogen, or antigen, there is a delay while the immune system responds and overcomes the pathogen. The next time the individual is exposed to that same pathogen, the response is much faster, and the individual may not develop the disease. This is due to "memory" B and T cells, stored since the first encounter with that particular pathogen. The individual is then said to have immunity to that pathogen.

Immunity can be artificially induced by vaccination. A vaccine is a weakened or killed form of the pathogen. It causes the body to manufacture antibodies against the pathogen, so that if it is later exposed to the live form of the pathogen, the body can then launch a prompt and effective immune response.

Immunity is acquired through either active or passive means. Active immunity refers to those situations where the body itself has created the immunity, either as a result of past exposure to the disease, or because it has been vaccinated against it. In cases of passive immunity, the response has come from elsewhere, either from an injection of antibodies for example, or, in the case of the fetus, from the mother. Unlike active immunity, which has "memory" and can mount future responses to the same pathogen, passive immunity is usually only temporary.

Immunodeficiency

When the immune system fails to work properly and is deficient, a person is said to have an immunodeficiency. This can be due to a genetic disease or may be acquired—for example, in acquired immunodeficiency syndrome (AIDS) due to the human immunodeficiency virus (HIV). If the immune system is severely damaged, serious infections, called "opportunistic infections" may develop after exposure to pathogens that would not normally cause disease.

Allergy

An allergy is a condition in which the immune system reacts with unusual hypersensitivity to a substance or substances (called allergens). In the process, a compound

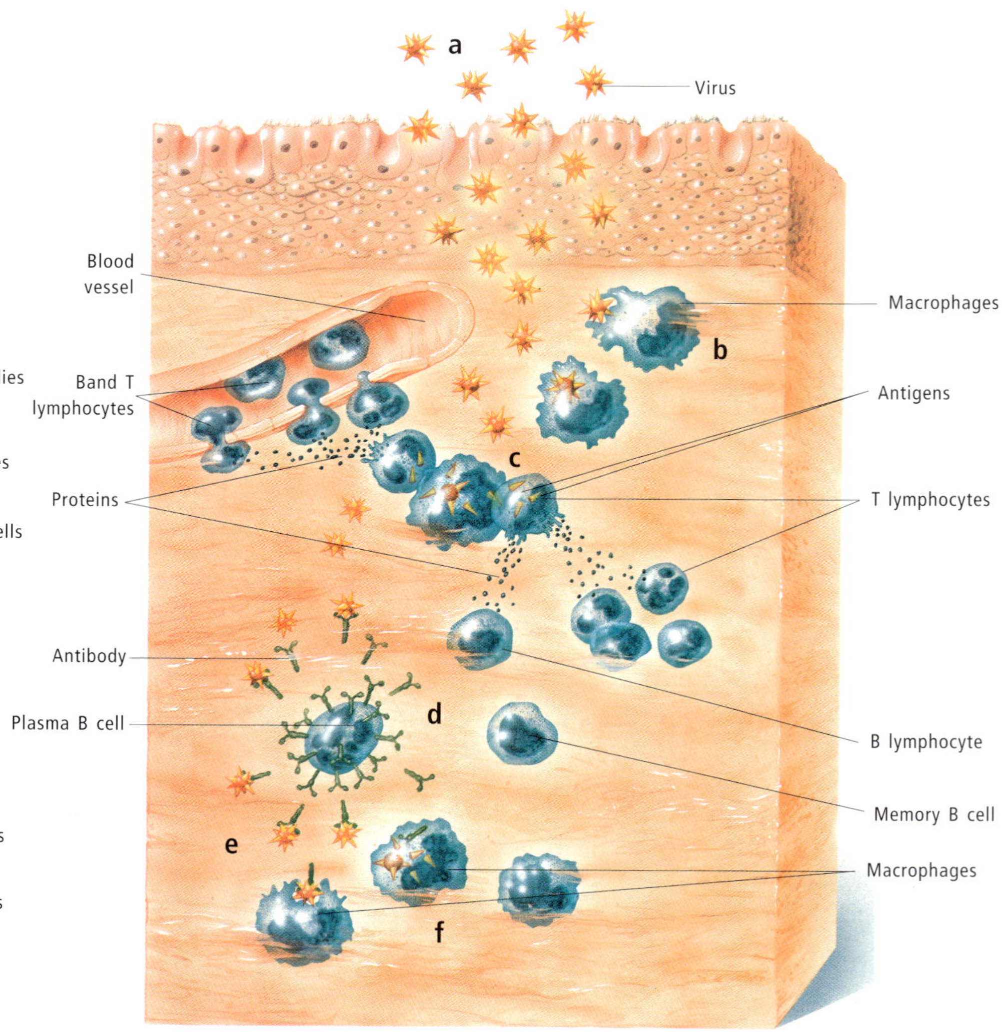

Humoral immune response

B lymphocytes (white blood cells) produce antibodies to help identify and eliminate invading antigens (carried by bacteria or viruses). They are helped in the body's defenses by circulating T lymphocytes and macrophages (scavenging white blood cells).

(a) Virus particles invade tissue through surface cells and multiply.

(b) Virus particles are consumed by macrophages.

(c) The macrophages break down the virus and present antigens to circulating T lymphocytes. These release proteins to recruit more T and B lymphocytes from nearby blood vessels and tissue to help defend the body.

(d) B lymphocytes divide into memory B cells (which remember the invading virus for future attacks) and plasma B cells which make antibodies specific to the invading virus.

(e) The circulating antibodies attach onto the virus particles.

(f) Macrophages primed to recognize the antibody consume the virus and break it down, saving the body from infection.

called histamine is released from special body cells called mast cells. This excess of histamine irritates the surrounding tissues and causes allergy symptoms, such as coughing, sneezing, wheezing and rash.

There are several common allergic conditions. Hay fever causes a runny nose and watering or itching eyes. In urticaria (hives) there is itching, redness and lumps in the skin. An allergy to antibiotics, especially penicillin, may cause a skin rash, while asthma causes a wheezing in the chest. An allergic person can undergo desensitization with injections of the allergen known to cause the symptoms, however, the results are very variable and may not last.

Autoimmune diseases

Autoimmune diseases develop when the body's immune system fails to recognize tissues belonging to the body and attacks and destroys them as though they were foreign. The cause is not fully understood, but in some cases it is thought to be triggered by exposure to microorganisms and drugs, especially in people with a genetic predisposition to these disorders.

Autoimmune disorders and the tissues they attack include: Hashimoto's thyroiditis (thyroid), pernicious anemia (blood), Addison's disease (adrenal cortex), diabetes mellitus (pancreas), rheumatoid arthritis (joints), systemic lupus erythematosus (connective tissues), and myasthenia gravis (muscles).

Organ rejection

After organ transplantation, the immune system of the body may not recognize the transplanted tissue as part of the recipient's body tissues and may mount an immune response against it. This is known as organ rejection, and is a common complication of transplantation. It is less likely if the donor is a close relative of the recipient.

SEE ALSO *AIDS, Allergies, Antibodies, Autoimmune disease, HIV, Immunization, Lymphatic/Immune system, Opportunistic infection, White blood cells*

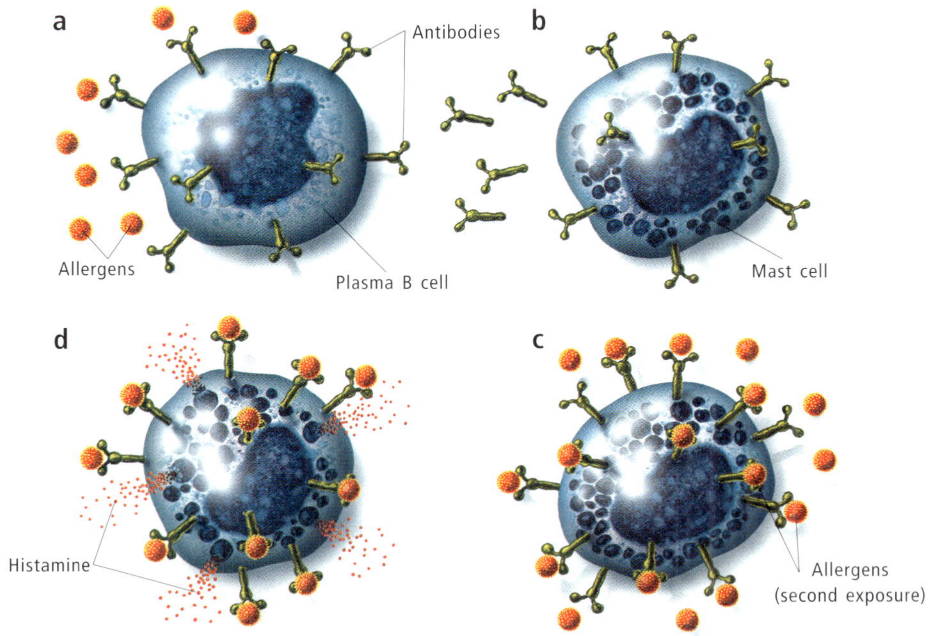

Allergic reaction

Exposure to invading allergens (that the body is sensitive to) leads to the release of histamine, which irritates tissues and causes sypmtoms such as sneezing and rash.

(a) On the body's first exposure to an allergen, plasma B cells produce antibodies.

(b) The antibodies attach to mast cells circulating in the body's tissues.

(c) The next time allergens enter the body they are captured by the antibodies on the mast cells.

(d) The mast cells respond by releasing histamine, a chemical that causes inflammation and the symptoms of allergy.

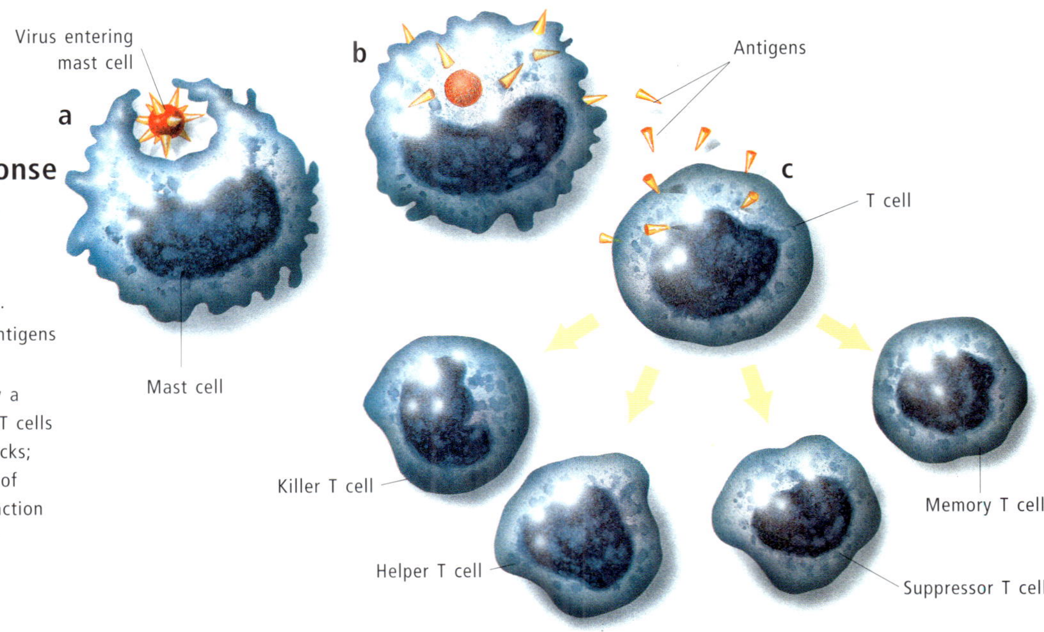

Cell-mediated immune response

T lymphocytes (a type of white blood cell) are responsible for the delayed action of the cell-mediated response.

(a) Circulating mast cells ingest invading virus.

(b) Mast cells process the virus and present antigens to T cells.

(c) The T cells produce clones which each play a special role in the immune response: memory T cells remember the invading antigen for future attacks; helper T cells recruit B and T cells to the site of antigen attack; suppressor T cells inhibit the action of B and T cells; and killer T cells attach onto invading antigens and destroy them.

IMMUNIZATION

Immunization uses a killed virus or bacterium, a weakened strain ("attenuated"), a deactivated toxin ("toxoid"), or sometimes a synthetically or genetically engineered vaccine to help the body build up its immunity to certain diseases. After being immunized, the body's immune system manufactures antibodies which are special proteins that can recognize and help destroy viruses and bacteria or foreign toxins when they invade the body. In addition, other parts of the immune system are also activated to combat an infection.

A single dose of some vaccines will give immunity for life, however others need to be given according to a specific schedule and need boosters or additional reinforcing doses to maintain immunity. When children are immunized against diphtheria, tetanus and pertussis (whooping cough) they are given a vaccine known as DTP. This has recently been replaced with a newer vaccine called DTaP, which contains a different form of pertussis vaccine called "acellular pertussis" vaccine and has fewer side effects than the older form. When children are immunized against measles, mumps and rubella, they are given a vaccine called MMR. A vaccine is available in some parts of the world for varicella (chickenpox), and a vaccine that against all four of these , called MMRV, is being developed. Vaccinations against *Haemophilus influenzae* type b and poliomyelitis are also part of the usual childhood immunization schedule in most countries. It is important that when children are being immunized, that they receive the full schedule of initial and booster vaccinations so that the immunization process is effective. The timing is also important in immunization. Schedules have been established by health authorities to achieve the most effective results.

There are other vaccines which are available or being developed, and many of these are also intended for travelers and people at high risk of infection such as the elderly or people with underlying diseases, who may have weakend immune systems. Some of these vaccines include hepatitis A, Japanese encephalitis, yellow fever, tuberculosis (BCG vaccine), pneumococcal infection, meningococcal infection, influenza, varicella-zoster (chickenpox and shingles), plague and typhoid. Some of these are not available in all countries, and there are other vaccines currently under development. There are as yet no effective vaccines for dengue fever, malaria or HIV (AIDS).

It is advisable for travelers to be aware of the schedule for certain immunizations when they are traveling to countries where vaccine-preventable diseases are a risk.

The vaccines used in immunization have been tested thoroughly and are safe and effective. Though minimal risks have been found with some vaccines, serious reactions are rare. The complications associated with the disease far outweigh the risks of complications from the vaccine.

Immunization against infectious diseases of all types has probably saved more lives than any other public health measure, apart from the provision of sanitation and clean water. Research into new vaccines is ongoing with a vaccine for infants against meningitis and blood poisoning being among the newest to become available.

SEE ALSO ***Antibodies, Chickenpox, Diphtheria, Hepatitis, Measles, Mumps, Poliomyelitis, Rubella, Smallpox, Tetanus, Whooping cough***

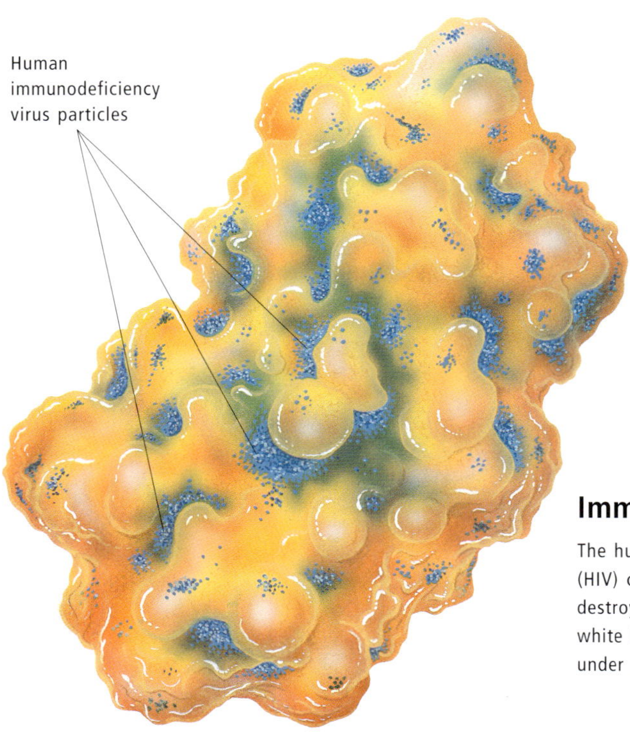

Immunodeficiency

The human immunodeficiency virus (HIV) compromises immunity by destroying T4 helper cells—a type of white blood cell. Here a T4 cell is under attack.

IMMUNODEFICIENCY

When an individual's immune system has been damaged and is deficient, that person is said to have an immunodeficiency. Immunodeficiency can be congenital (due to a genetic disease), or it can be acquired, as in cancer, leukemia or infection with the human immunodeficiency virus (HIV). Congenital immunodeficiency is relatively rare and involves inborn defects in the production of B and T lymphocytes.

If the immune system is severely damaged, exposure to pathogens that would not normally cause disease in healthy people may cause serious infections; these are called opportunistic infections. Examples include candidiasis (thrush); herpes simplex viruses, which can cause oral herpes (cold sores) or genital herpes; and *Pneumocystis carinii* pneumonia which can cause a fatal pneumonia. People with damaged immune systems are also prone to developing cancers such as Kaposi's sarcoma.

Immunodeficiency can be detected by measuring the levels of white blood cells in the blood. In HIV infection, for example, there is a fall in the number of white cells called T4 cells, which can be monitored. The T4 cell count gives an indication of how far the HIV infection is progressing.

SEE ALSO *AIDS, Cancer, HIV, Leukemia, Lymphatic/Immune system, Opportunistic infection*

IMMUNOSUPPRESSION

Immunosuppression is inhibition of the immune system. It may occur as a side effect of drugs used to treat cancer, or in radiation therapy, when the bone marrow or other tissues of the immune system are damaged. It may also occur as a rare side effect of commonly used drugs.

Immunosuppression also refers to the use of certain drugs to prevent the body's immune system destroying its own tissues. This may be necessary, for example, after transplantation of organs or in autoimmune diseases. Examples of immunosuppressant drugs are corticosteroids and azothiaprine.

SEE ALSO *Autoimmune disease, Corticosteroids, Radiation therapy*

Impetigo

This contagious bacterial infection of the skin involves blister-like spots that fill with pus, rupture and become itchy yellow crusts.

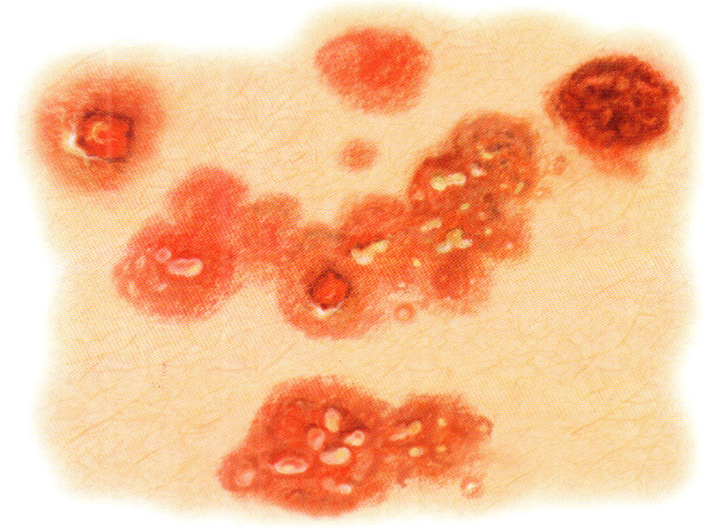

IMPETIGO

Also known as "school sores" in some parts of the world, impetigo is a bacterial skin infection which is highly contagious and occurs mainly in young children. It affects in general the mouth and nose area, but can also occur under diapers in babies, or anywhere else on the body. It is not painful, but it can be itchy and lead to scratching which will spread the infection. The surface of the skin is infected with bacteria, either *Streptococcus pyogines* or *Staphylococcus aureus*, which feed on a wound such as a cut or insect bite, or a skin condition such as eczema.

Appearing first as red blisters, the spots become filled with pus and form a scab. Impetigo is treated with a course of antibiotics and/or antibiotic ointment prescribed by a physician. If the sore is surrounded by red skin or the person is unwell, then further medical attention should be sought.

As impetigo is highly contagious, the sufferer needs to bathe or shower daily, keep linen and towels separate, be scrupulous about cleaning under fingernails and washing hands, and stay away from other people, at least outside the family, until the sores have healed.

SEE ALSO *Staphylococcal infections, Streptococcal infections*

IMPOTENCE

Impotence is a man's inability to produce or maintain an erection of the penis, so that he is unable to engage successfully in sexual intercourse. It can occur at any age, but is more common in older men. Impotence may be temporary, or long lasting.

Impotence often has a psychological origin, such as stress, anxiety, depression or marital conflict. There may be a physical cause, such as a stroke, atherosclerosis, diabetes mellitus or alcoholism. Brief bouts of impotence may follow illnesses such as influenza, or after taking drugs or alcohol. It may occur as a side effect of some medications or following surgery, or from a combination of factors.

If the condition has a psychological basis, discussion (together with the affected male's sexual partner) of the condition with a qualified sex therapist or relationship counselor may be of benefit. If the cause is a physical disorder, the underlying cause must be treated first. If this is not possible, there are several treatments available. A prosthesis (which may be inflatable) can be surgically inserted into the penis. Non-surgical treatments include needle injection therapy, vacuum cup devices and medications such as sildenafil (Viagra).

SEE ALSO *Erection, Penis, Sexual dysfunction*

IN VITRO FERTILIZATION

In vitro fertilization (IVF)—the fertilization of an ovum ("egg") in vitro ("in glass") and the return of the resulting embryo to the woman's uterus—is the pioneer procedure which produced what were originally called "test tube babies". This technique was first used in the 1970s to offer hope to women who were infertile because something interfered with the passage of the ovum from the ovary to the uterus via the fallopian tube. It is now available to treat infertility arising from most causes.

IVF begins when the woman takes ovary-stimulating drugs for about 10 days. Ultrasound checks determine the number and size of the ovarian follicles in which eggs are developing. The eggs are collected using a trans-vaginal probe when the woman is under local or general anesthetic.

The man will be required to masturbate to produce a semen sample. A small amount of this semen will be processed to remove debris and then added to the dish which holds an egg. Fertilization can take up to 18 hours, and one to five days later the embryos—which at this stage are technically known as blastocysts—will be ready for implanting into the woman's uterus.

Generally up to three fertilized eggs are transferred to the uterus to increase the chances of pregnancy, and most transfers are done on day two. The transfer is done using a fine catheter and the woman does not need to be sedated. The woman may be prescribed hormones to increase the chances that the fertilized eggs will successfully implant.

Only between 15 and 20 percent of embryos created in this artificial environment are truly viable—that is, have the potential to continue their development.

SEE ALSO *Embryo, Fertilization, Infertility, Ovum, Semen*

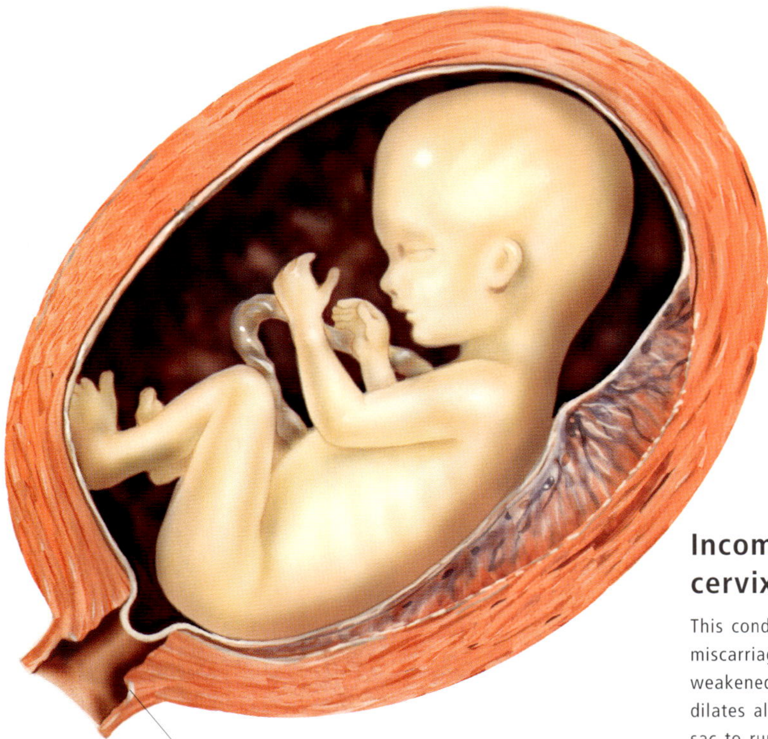

Incompetent cervix

This condition can cause miscarriage, as the weakened cervix prematurely dilates allowing the amniotic sac to rupture.

INCOMPETENT CERVIX

During pregnancy, the cervix (the entrance to the uterus) is sealed with a plug of mucus and remains tightly shut, keeping the fetus safely within the uterus, until labor begins. However, in some cases, especially where the cervix has been damaged by surgical procedure such as a cone biopsy, the cervix can be weakened and may open prematurely during the third or fourth month of pregnancy. When this happens, the amniotic sac may pass through the cervix into the vagina and may rupture, causing loss of amniotic fluid and miscarriage.

The condition is not usually diagnosed until a miscarriage has occurred; however, subsequent miscarriages can be prevented by a procedure in which the cervix is stitched closed with strong thread which tightens the cervix and keeps it from dilating prematurely. The stitches are removed at about 37 weeks to allow delivery of the fetus to take place.

SEE ALSO *Cervix, Childbirth, Miscarriage, Pregnancy, Reproductive systems, Uterus*

INCONTINENCE

In an infant, daytime control of the bladder is achieved around the age of two, and nighttime control some years later. Lack of voluntary control of the bladder beyond this age is called incontinence. It is a problem most common in the elderly.

There are several causes of incontinence in adults. Shortening of the urethra and loss of the normal muscular support for the bladder and floor of the pelvis, for example, may cause incontinence. This occurs during pregnancy, after childbirth (especially after multiple pregnancies) and as a consequence of ageing. Any neurological disorder affecting the bladder such as spina bifida, multiple sclerosis, and the nerve degeneration that occurs with conditions like diabetes mellitus can cause incontinence.

Stress incontinence is the involuntary leakage of urine during exercise, coughing, sneezing, laughing, lifting heavy objects, or during other body movements that put pressure on the bladder. Urge incontinence is the inability to hold urine back long enough to reach a toilet. It is a major complaint of patients with urinary tract infections. Overflow incontinence is the leakage of small amounts of urine from a bladder that is always full. In older men, this can occur when the flow of urine from the bladder is blocked, for example in enlargement of the prostate gland (prostatomegaly) or following surgery or cancer.

Most people with incontinence can be cured or helped. For mild incontinence, the use of a portable urinal or bedside commode, and wearing sanitary pads or panty liners may be sufficient to manage the disorder. Other treatments include strengthening of bladder muscles and pelvic floor muscles, and surgery to tighten relaxed or damaged bladder muscles, or to remove a blockage due to an enlarged prostate.

Incontinence of the bowels can also occur. In young children, lack of bowel control may simply be resistance to toilet training. In older children, it may occur because of stress or a psychological disorder. In adults it may be caused by chronic constipation, diarrhea or stress. It may follow childbirth (when the anal sphincter muscle may be torn), or an operation for anal fistula or fissure. In the elderly, it may be associated with senility, or with neurological disorders such as a stroke, multiple sclerosis or diabetes mellitus. Treatment options include rectal muscle strengthening and surgery to the rectal sphincter.

SEE ALSO *Bladder, Urinary incontinence, Urinary systems*

INDIGESTION

Indigestion is defined as abdominal discomfort experienced within a few hours of eating. It may be characterized by heartburn, cramps, flatulence and belching. It may be of no clinical significance (no more than a normal consequence of over-eating) or it may indicate serious disease (for example, upper abdominal pain following a meal may be a symptom of gastric ulcer or cancer).

The symptom of indigestion on its own is no clear indicator of the type of problem: it is the accompanying symptoms and signs and subsequent clinical investigations that will indicate the presence or absence of serious disease. Upper abdominal discomfort or pain following a meal may be the result of a wide variety of diseases involving the esophagus (reflux esophagitis), stomach, duodenum (duodenal ulcer) or gallbladder (chronic cholecystitis due to gallstones). Indigestion may also arise as a side effect of several common drugs, such as aspirin (acetylsalicylic acid), non-steroidal anti-inflammatory drugs and antibiotics.

SEE ALSO *Cholecystitis, Digestive system, Duodenal ulcer, Duodenum, Esophagus, Gallstones*

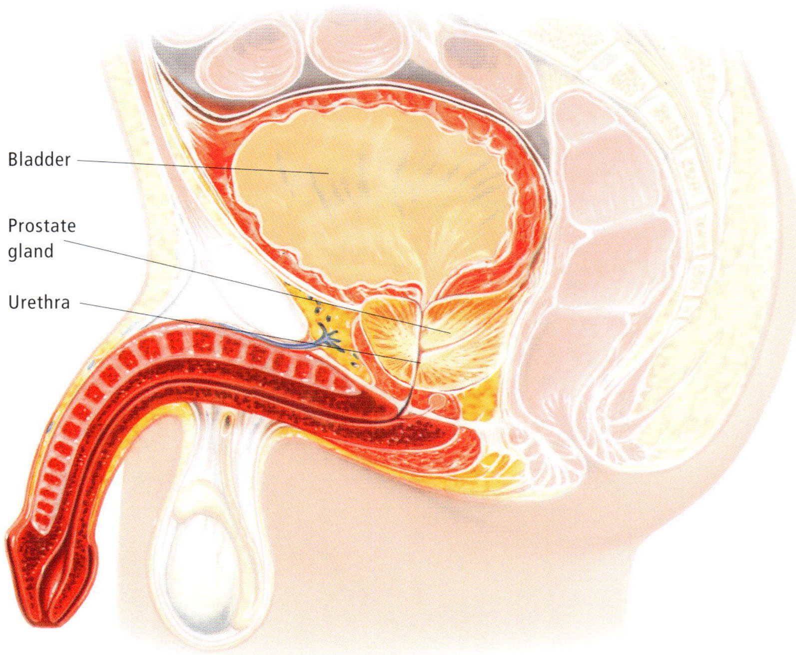

Female incontinence

Women may suffer incontinence during pregnancy and after childbirth due to a weakening of the muscles which support the bladder and the floor of the pelvis.

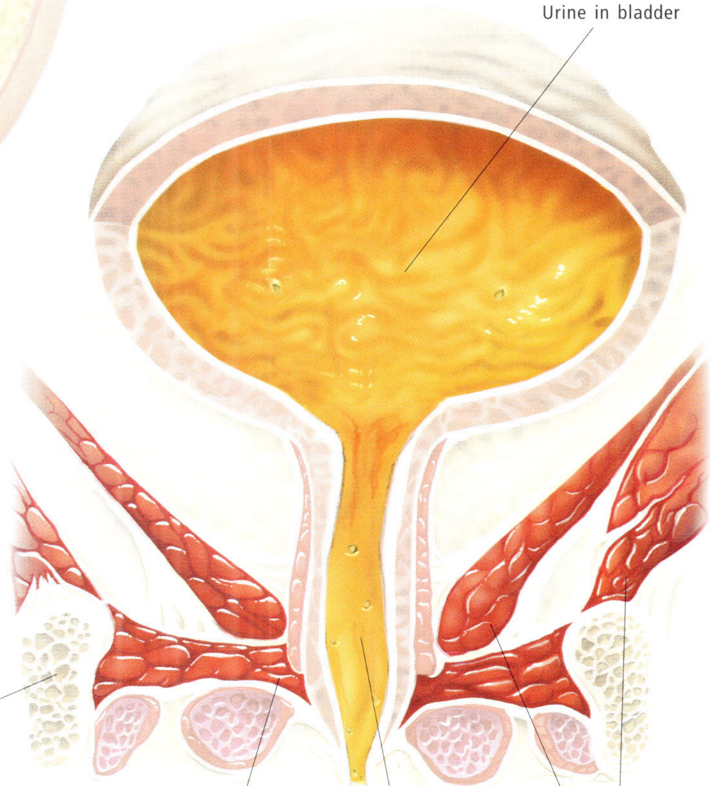

Male incontinence

Incontinence in men is often caused by an enlarged prostate gland which compresses the urethra, obstructing the flow of urine. Urine then collects in the bladder and eventually leaks out.

Incontinence

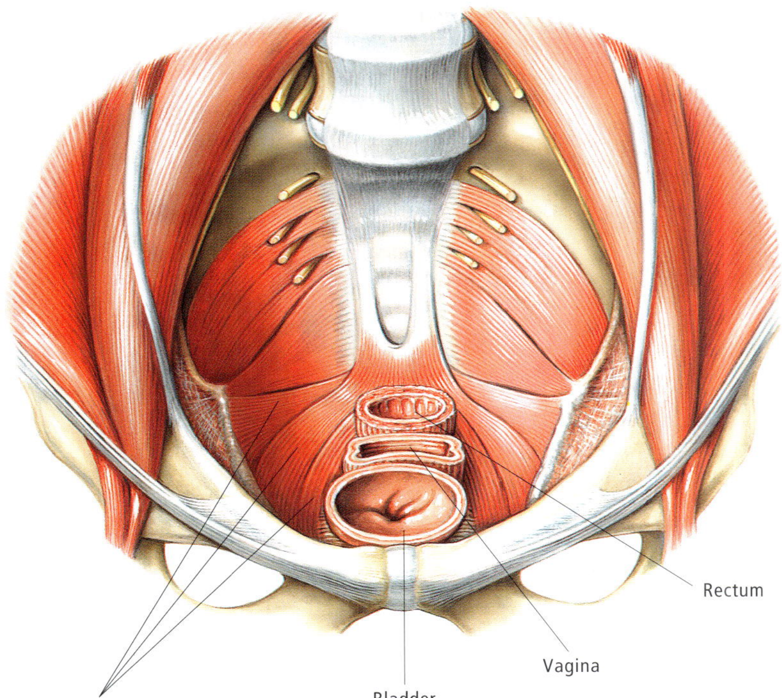

Muscle control in incontinence

Performing a series of appropriate exercises daily can strengthen pelvic floor muscles and help to avoid incontinence.

I

INFANCY

An infant, or baby, is a child of 12 months of age or less (although some authorities define this stage as 2 years or less). It is an important period, during which the child gains in weight and height, begins to walk and talk, begins teething, and develops sensory discrimination.

A baby grows and develops more rapidly in the first 12 months than at any other time. At birth, an average newborn infant weighs 7½ pounds (3.4 kg) and is about 20 inches (51 cm) long and gains weight at an average of 6 to 7 ounces (170 to 200 grams) per week for the first 3 months. After this the rate declines to an average of 2 ounces (60 grams) per week by 12 months.

A baby's skeleton includes a greater percentage of cartilage than an adult skeleton in that some parts are still made of cartilage and have not yet ossified. Some cartilagenous parts do not become bone until the child is almost an adult.

A baby's brain also grows at a remarkable rate in the first year, doubling in weight as the number of brain cells (glia) increases, together with increases in the number of connections between cells and parts of the brain.

Developmental stages

Babies develop individually. Some develop physically more quickly than others, others develop mental or social skills sooner than their peers. Skills develop in a particular order because of the way the body and the nervous system mature, but not every child will go through every stage.

The infant's means of exploring and understanding the world begins with reflex movements—sucking, grasping, throwing and kicking. By 4 months of age the infant can reach out and grasp an object, and can hold a small object between thumb and forefinger by the tenth month. At 4 months most babies are able to sit up for a short while without support, and can do so without support for 10 minutes or longer by the age of 9 months. Crawling begins between 7 and 10 months, and by 12 months most infants can stand up alone. With help, most babies can walk by 12 months and can walk by themselves at 14 months.

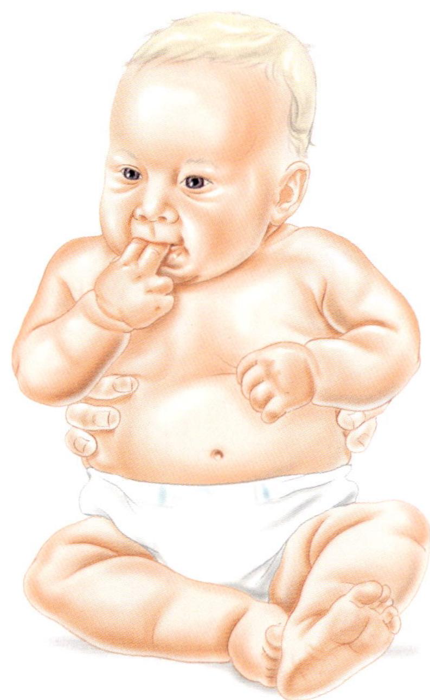

4 months

Infancy

Infants develop at their own rate, but there is a specific order of developmental changes. For example, babies must learn the muscular skill of head control before they learn to sit up.

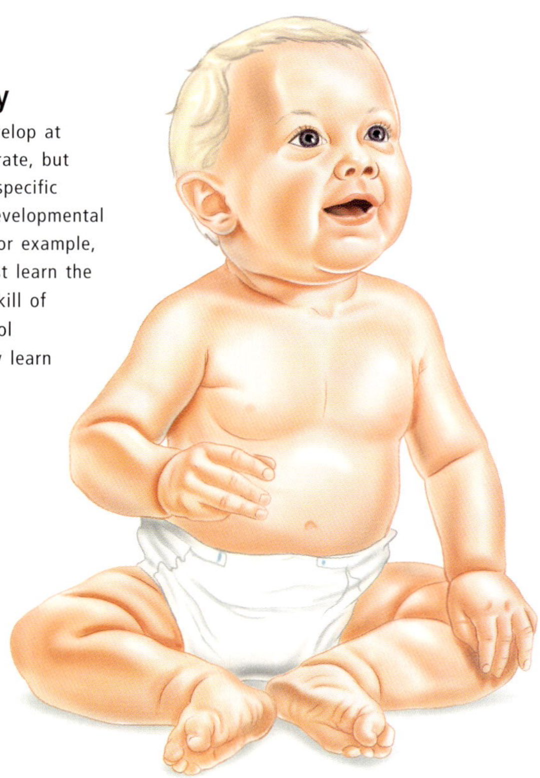

8 months

Infants

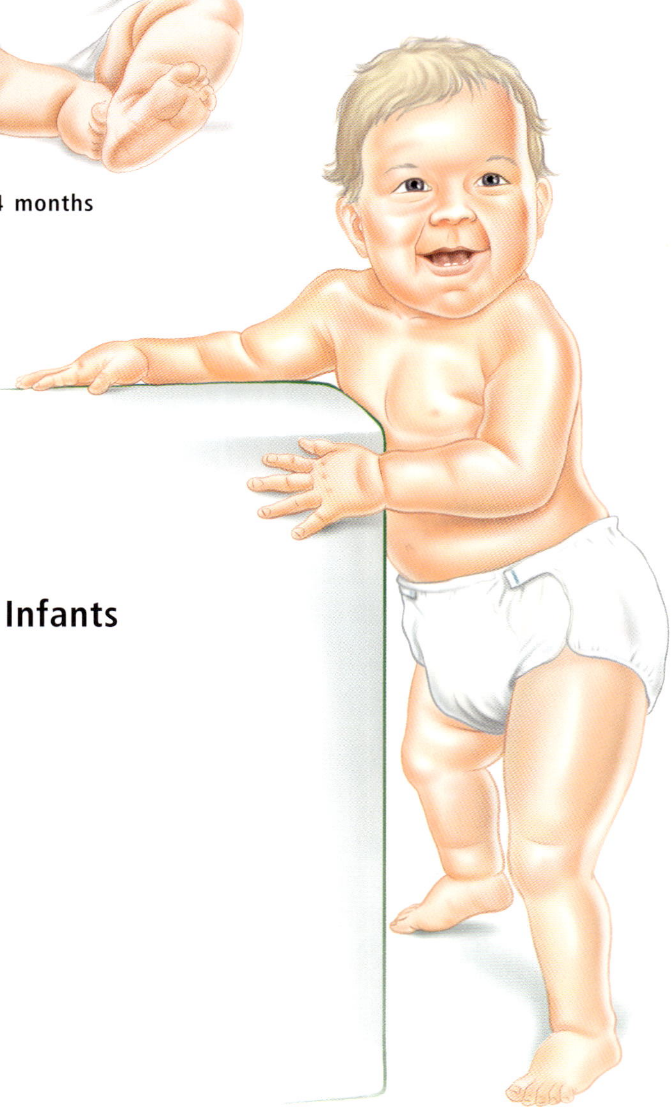

12 months

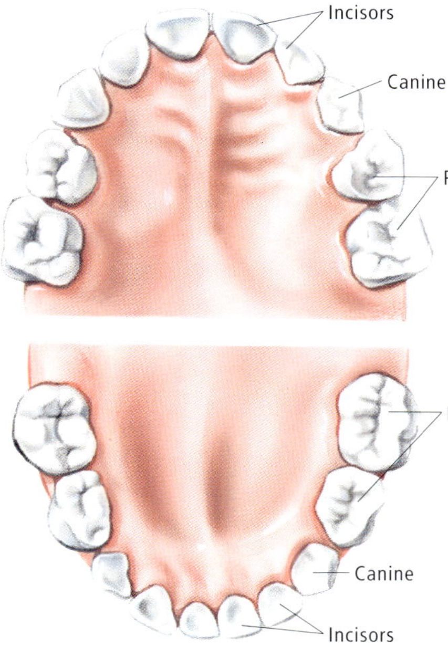

Infancy—teething

The first teeth usually appear when the infant is approximately 6–8 months of age; by the age of 3, a full set of "baby teeth" should be present.

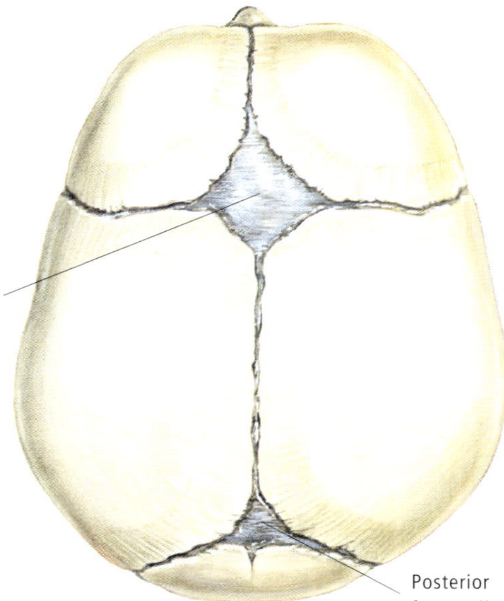

Fontanelle

The fontanelles are gaps between the bones in a baby's skull due to the normal delay in the joining together of several flat bones.

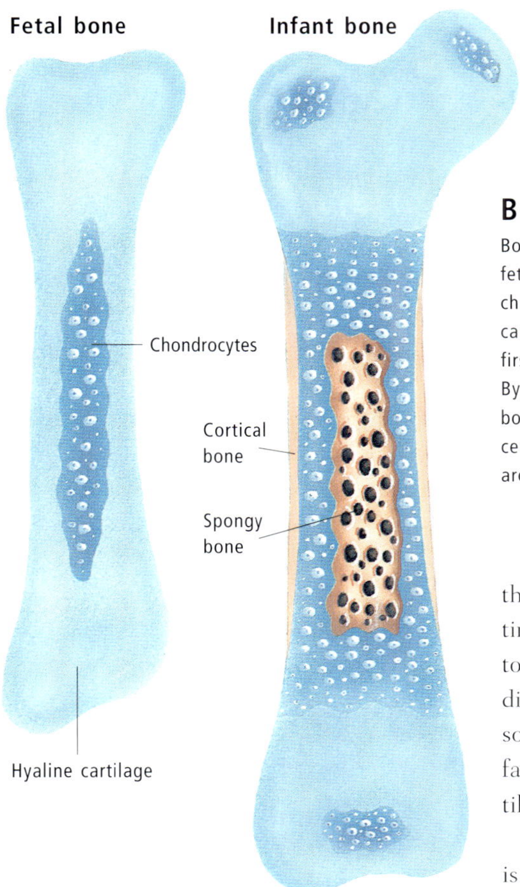

Bone development

Bone growth begins very early in fetal development. At 6 weeks, chondrocytes in the center of the cartilage begin to enlarge—the first stage in bone development. By the time the baby is born, bone has been laid down in the center of the shaft and in a collar around the middle of the shaft.

The senses also develop rapidly during the first 3 months of life. Newborns can distinguish between sounds and objects close to their face; within 3 months the infant can distinguish color and form. Mimicking of sounds begins soon after birth, but the infant's first full words will not be uttered until between 12–18 months.

A baby born before week 37 of pregnancy is classified as premature. Premature babies' development stages generally need to be corrected to the age the baby would be if born full term—thus a baby born 3 weeks early will be developmentally 3 weeks behind a full-term baby born at the same time.

Immunization and illnesses

Regular checkups to ensure that a baby is growing and developing normally will allow any problems to be detected and treated quickly if necessary. Checkups are also important to ensure that the baby is protected against a range of childhood diseases which can have serious repercussions, including death.

Immunization programs have been designed to protect children against a number of diseases, including diphtheria, measles, mumps, poliomyelitis, rubella (German measles), tetanus (which can cause lockjaw), whooping cough (pertussis), *Hemophilus influenzae* type B (which can result in meningitis) and hepatitis B.

Other common illnesses which babies can suffer in the first year include bronchiolitis, bronchitis, conjunctivitis (also known as pink eye), croup, ear infections, encephalitis, gastrointestinal upset, hand, foot and mouth disease, herpes simplex, hepatitis, influenza, pneumonia and roseola infantum.

Feeding

Problems can arise with breast feeding, often because the new mother has not received the right advice and information from those around her. Bottle feeding has its own set of problems, including the possibility of infection and under or over feeding, if correct procedures are not followed. Weaning onto family foods may not proceed as expected for numerous reasons, including allergy, too early introduction of food or unrealistic expectations on the part of the parents.

Breast milk is the ideal food for a human baby for the first 6 months of life, and for up to 12 months gives many benefits. Breast milk changes for each feed and within each feed to meet the individual baby's needs. It is a unique substance which has not been duplicated artificially. Breast milk contains antibodies, which provide immunity against infections, and many other important nutrients including choline, which aids in the development of the brain. The action of the baby's mouth during breast feeding facilitates the optimum development of the facial muscles.

Babies who are not breast fed need an infant formula (artificial baby milk) which is appropriate to their age and fortified with iron. These formulas are nutritionally complete, but do not contain the antibodies found in human breast milk.

Some time after the age of 4 months, and ideally around the age of 6 months, a baby should begin to eat family foods. A baby has to learn how to eat, and new tastes and textures (from puree to lumpy to mashed and chopped) need to be introduced quite quickly. Iron is very important in a baby's food intake after about 6 months. By the time children are a year old they need to be eating a wide variety of healthy foods.

Sleeping

Understanding *how* a baby sleeps (which is very different from the way adults sleep) and how *much* sleep is needed, is the second greatest problem faced by parents and care givers. Many sleep problems are really problems of adults' perceptions of a baby's sleep needs. A baby sleeps better in the presence of others and with some noise around; baby sleep is much more restless than adult sleep; a baby's brain is more alert during sleep than an adult's and in the first 3 months a baby will generally wake after an REM (rapid-eye-movement) stage of sleep. Not until the end of month 3 can a baby fall into a deep sleep. By 6 months a baby has the ability to sleep for longer periods, but will still need adult comfort and attention when awake.

Bedtime routines, including story reading, bathing and soft singing, work for some families; other families sleep together or in the same room and find that this gives everyone the required night sleep. There are many theories and methods to help parents come to terms with, and develop strategies for, getting the night's sleep they want.

Teething

Babies' first teeth usually appear between 6 and 8 months of age. Already formed inside the gums at birth, the teeth slowly push and twist their way through. Teething can be painful and may cause drooling, irritability, swollen gums, difficulty sleeping and a strong biting urge. Signs include rosy cheeks, frantic finger sucking and ear pulling. Recent research suggests that teething does not cause diarrhea or fever as was commonly thought.

Discomfort can be alleviated by rubbing the gums with a clean finger or offering rusks, teething rings, a cold wet washcloth, a cool spoon or slushy frozen fruit juice to chew on. Also available are teething salves containing anesthetic and non-prescription oral pain relievers. Alternatively, simply distracting the child with walks and new play activities can help.

By one year of age, up to 12 of the 20 "milk" teeth are usually in place. The two lower front teeth or central incisors are often first, followed by the upper central incisors, then the lower and upper lateral incisors either side of the front teeth. The large back molars and the sharp canine teeth either side of the incisors usually erupt between 12 and 30 months. There is no "normal" teething timetable, however—parents may find it starts as early as 3 months and end as late as 3 years.

Communicating

Babies are born with the ability to communicate with the adults responsible for their care. From day one, babies can gaze into the eyes of a person holding them at chest height (if drugs are used during labour it may take a little longer). They can imitate their carers' facial expressions and one day, some time in the first 6 weeks, will smile. In order to thrive, babies need the love and attention of those who care for them; this ability to smile and gaze at parents or carers is vital in establishing emotional bonds between baby and carer.

Crying is babies' other method of communication and the most important way they communicate in the first 12 months. Many adults have little experience of a baby's cries until they have responsibility for a baby for the first time. Some babies cry more than others and need more attention. This is normal, but crying can sometimes become a problem in itself and it is important that parents learn strategies to help them cope with their babies' needs without being overwhelmed.

Babies cry for one or more of the following reasons: they are hungry, they are too hot or too cold, they have a pain in the stomach, they need their diapers changed, they are feeling insecure or lonely, they are bored, or they have become over-excited and need to be calmed. Unfortunately, determining which of these problems it is can sometimes be difficult.

Over the age of 6 months one of the most common reasons for crying is boredom. A stimulating environment with changing patterns, shapes, sounds and colors will amuse a baby, as will the presence of an adult or older child who spends time interacting with the baby.

Parental concerns

Sudden infant death syndrome (SIDS) is an issue which frightens many parents. Understanding and taking heed of the risk factors are the best safeguards parents can have to protect their child.

Teething is often blamed for illnesses such as diarrhea, stomach upsets and infections, but these are not symptoms of this normal part of development. Teething can cause considerable discomfort and unhappiness but not illness.

Failure to thrive is another issue that often confronts parents. A baby who has not gained weight in accordance with standardized baby growth charts may be described as "failing to thrive". In many instances it can be explained that parents' expectations are unrealistic, but in some infants there can be feeding or malabsorption problems which are affecting growth rate.

Apart from feeding and sleeping, babies require a great deal of time. Their physical needs, including comfort and warmth, must be met. This means changing diapers up to ten times in a 24-hour period, as well as bathing once a day. On top of this, taking a baby out requires safety devices for car travel, a stroller for shopping trips and baby carriers for other outings. Parents are generally concerned to give the babies they bear the best possible beginning in life.

SEE ALSO *Breast feeding, Bottle feeding, Newborn, Reflexes, Sudden infant death syndrome*

INFECTIOUS DISEASES

An infectious disease is a disease caused by the invasion of and multiplication in the body's tissues of microorganisms that have been passed from one person (or animal) to another. These microorganisms include bacteria, viruses, fungi, protozoa or rickettsiae. Some diseases may be caused by the toxins (poisons) these microorganisms produce.

For infection to occur, a number of factors must be present: an infectious agent; an environment in which it can reproduce, such as contaminated food; a mode of transmission; and a susceptible host.

Transmission can occur in many ways. Infectious agents can be spread in droplets through the air when infected persons sneeze or cough. Whoever inhales the droplets can then become infected. Some diseases can be passed through contaminated eating or drinking utensils. Similarly, ingesting contaminated food or liquids exposes a healthy person to the disease. Other diseases can be spread through sexual activity. Common entry routes into a host are the skin (especially if it has been injured) and the mucosal surfaces of other body openings. A pregnant mother may also transmit infections from her blood supply to that of the fetus. Occasionally, infections can be spread in the course of medical or surgical treatment, or through using dirty injection equipment, as occurs with some drug users.

Every infectious disease has an incubation period. This is the length of time between the entry of the infectious agent into the body and the appearance of the first symptoms of the disease. It may be as short as a few days, as with the common cold, or it may be months or years, as in some slow viral diseases that affect the brain.

Not everyone who has an infectious agent contracts the disease. The virulence of the microorganism may be insufficient for the exposed person to develop the disease. However, this person (known as an asymptomatic carrier) may be harboring the disease and may spread it to another. Carriers may also include someone who is incubating the disease and is yet to develop it, or someone who may have recovered from the disease but is still capable of transmitting it to others.

A person whose immune system has been damaged by diseases of the immune system, leukemia and cancer is more likely to prove susceptible to disease. A disease which a normal person would fight off easily but which causes often serious illness in someone with a damaged immune system is called an opportunistic infection.

An infection may be local and confined to one area or it may be generalized. If it is localized it often produces characteristic symptoms of pain, swelling and reddening at the site of infection. This response is the body's way of fighting the infection and is known as inflammation. If the infection is generalized it will spread through the blood and affect the whole body, causing fever, chills, and a rapid pulse.

Different types of infectious agents (pathogens) cause different types of disease.

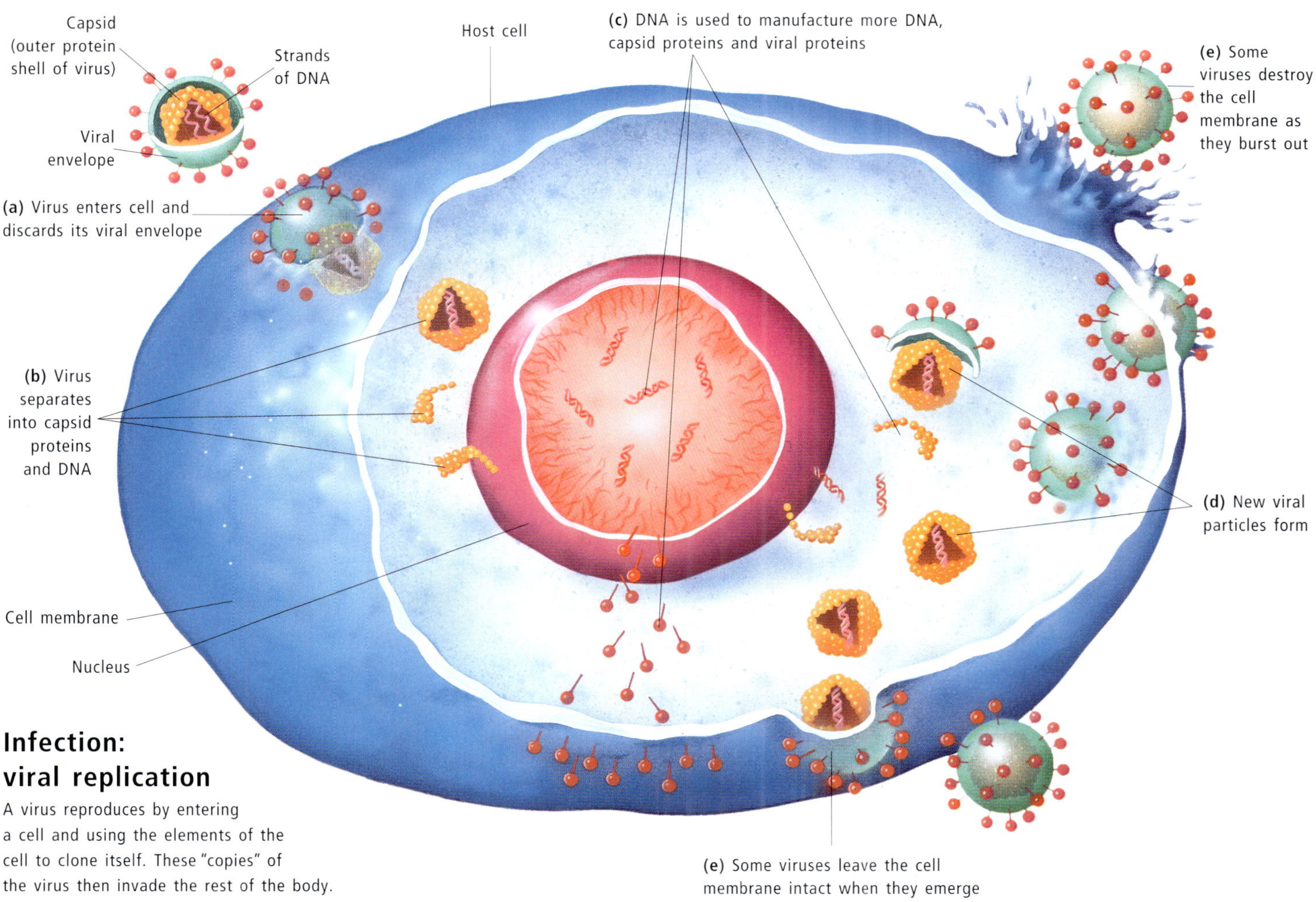

Infection: viral replication

A virus reproduces by entering a cell and using the elements of the cell to clone itself. These "copies" of the virus then invade the rest of the body.

Infectious mononucleosis

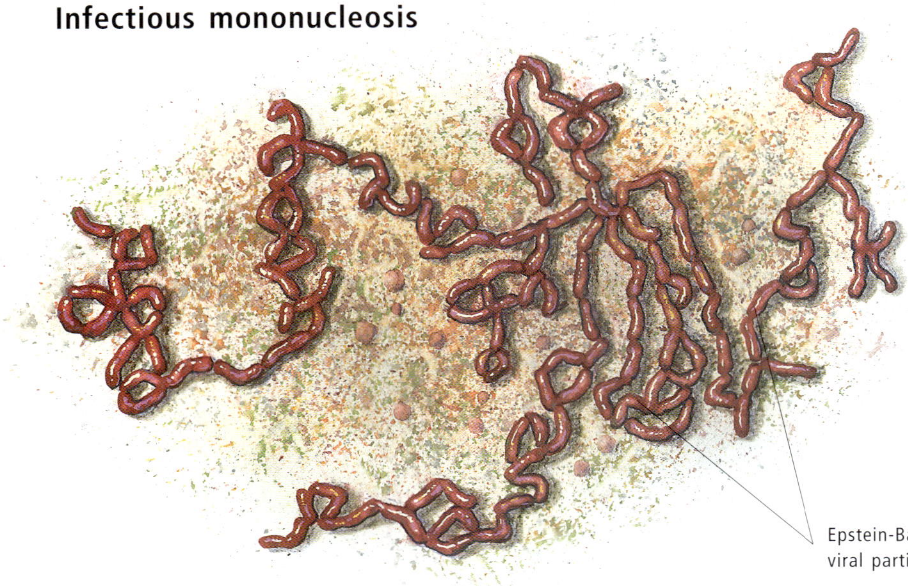

Bacteria

Bacteria are tiny, single-celled organisms with a cell wall but no nucleus. They may need oxygen to live (aerobic bacteria) or they may be able to live without oxygen (anaerobic bacteria). Some bacteria are spherical (*cocci*), corkscrew-shaped (*spirilla* or *spirochetes*) or rod-shaped (*bacilli*). They are also classified as gram-negative or gram-positive, according to whether their cell wall holds a special laboratory stain called Gram's stain.

Bacteria are responsible for many epidemic diseases, such as cholera, dysentery, plague, tuberculosis and typhoid fever. Many cause skin diseases, such as dermatitis, erysipelas, leprosy and yaws. They may also cause infections of other organs, such as gastroenteritis (infections of stomach and intestine), cystitis (bladder infection), pneumonia (lung infection), meningitis (infection of the meninges, the membranes that cover the brain), osteomyelitis (infection of bone), conjunctivitis (infection of the conjunctiva, the membrane that covers the eyeball) and many others. Some bacteria, especially *Staphylococcus*, may form a collection of pus, comprised of dead cells, bacteria and white blood cells, known as an abscess.

Most bacteria can be treated by antibiotics, which kill bacteria by interfering with their metabolism. Antibiotics can be injected or taken orally. Certain antibiotics work only against a certain type of bacteria, for example, they may work against gram-positive but not gram-negative bacteria. Bacteria tend to develop resistance to antibiotics over time.

Public health measures have led to much quality lengthening of life in industrialized countries. In many emerging countries these measures need to be introduced to control infectious diseases that continue to kill millions of people.

Viruses

Viruses are between 20 and 100 times smaller than bacteria. They contain either deoxyribonucleic acid (DNA) or ribonucleic acid (RNA). They are not considered to be alive, since they cannot reproduce outside a living cell. However, a virus can reproduce by entering a cell and using the cell's parts to make more copies of itself, which then leave the cell and spread elsewhere in the body, causing disease. These are called intracellular infections.

Common viral illnesses include hepatitis, influenza, the "common cold", measles, herpes and HIV (which causes AIDS). Many common childhood diseases are caused by viruses, including measles, mumps, rubella and chickenpox.

Viruses have also been implicated in causing some types of cancers. Antibiotics are ineffective against viruses, although antiviral drugs are available for some viral diseases. However, many viral diseases can be vaccinated against, including poliovirus, influenza, rabies, rubella, yellow fever, measles, mumps, and chickenpox.

Fungal infections

Fungal infections are diseases caused by the growth of fungi in or on the body. Fungal infections are usually mild, normally involving only the skin, hair, nails or other superficial sites, and they clear up spontaneously. Such infections include athlete's foot and ringworm. In someone with a damaged immune system, fungi may invade internal organs of the body and cause serious disease. Fungal disease can usually be treated with antifungal drugs, which are administered intravenously, orally, or applied to the skin.

SEE ALSO *Antibiotics, Bacteria, DNA, Inflammation, Lymphatic/Immune system, Opportunistic infection, Viruses*

INFECTIOUS MONONUCLEOSIS

Infectious mononucleosis (also known as glandular fever) is an illness commonly resulting in swollen lymph nodes (also known as lymph glands), fatigue, fever and a sore throat. Often referred to as "the kissing disease", infectious mononucleosis is thought to be spread through saliva, as well as through nasal secretions, sexual contact, blood transfusions and respiratory droplets. The disease is called mononucleosis as the blood of sufferers contains unusually large numbers of the white blood cells known as mononuclear leukocytes or monocytes, which are formed in the spleen and bone marrow.

The illness is caused by the Epstein-Barr herpes virus (EBV) which often produces no symptoms in young children and can stay in the body without effect for a long time before being activated by, for instance, a weakening of the immune system due to disease. EBV commonly results in mononucleosis in people aged 15–35 years.

Lethargy is often the first sign of illness. Other symptoms include muscular aches, loss of appetite, enlarged spleen and, occasionally, a faint pink rash. After about ten days acute symptoms subside, but fatigue, a general feeling of discomfort and sometimes depression may continue for up to about three months. Bed rest may cure the illness within six weeks, while painkillers and other non-prescription medications may be used to treat symptoms.

SEE ALSO *Spleen, Viruses, White blood cells*

Infertility

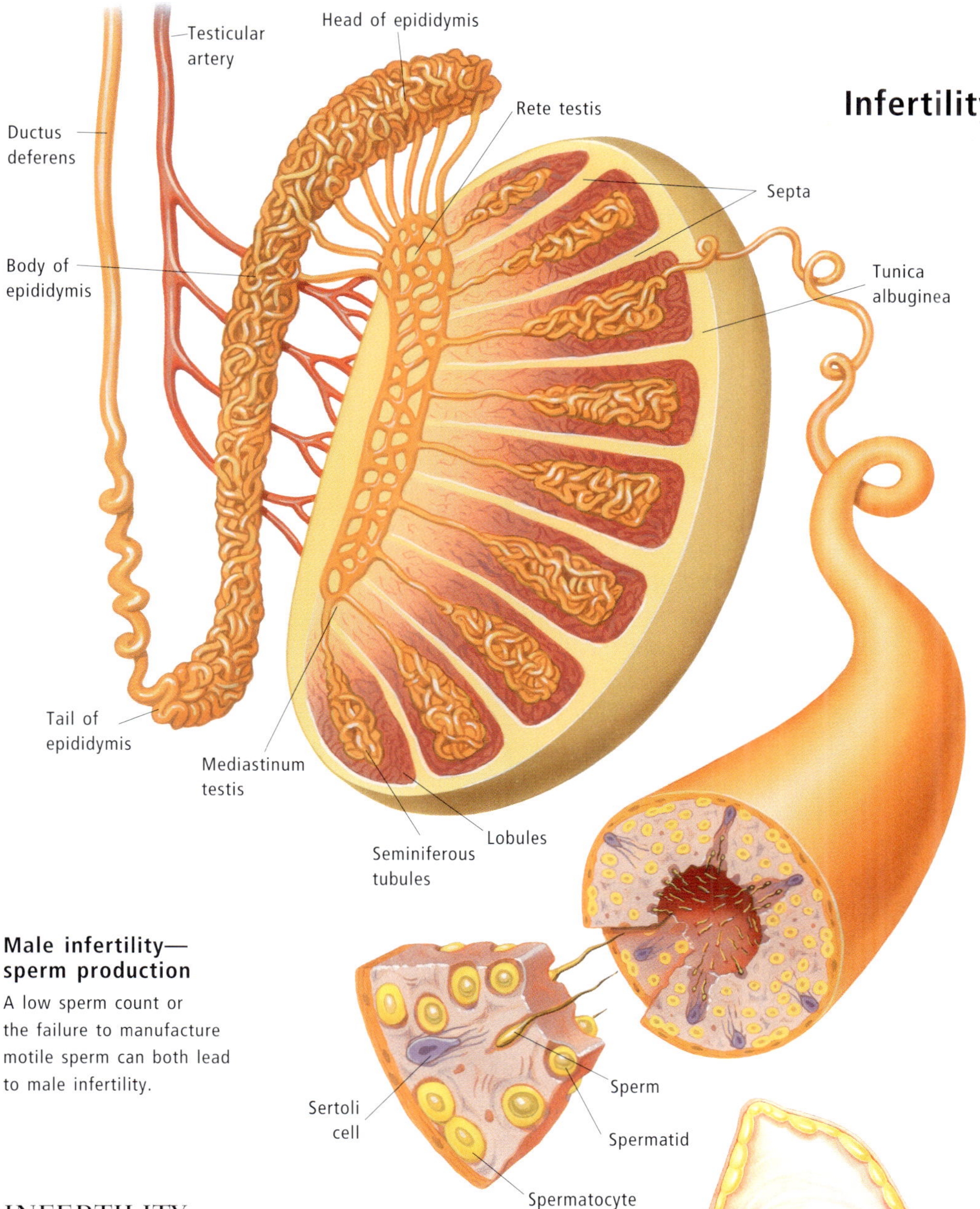

Male infertility—sperm production

A low sperm count or the failure to manufacture motile sperm can both lead to male infertility.

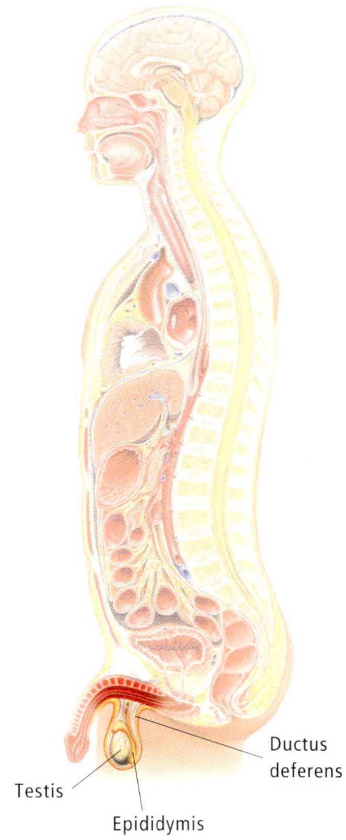

INFERTILITY

In a fertile couple having unprotected sexual intercourse two or more times a week, a pregnancy will result within 12 months in 90 percent of cases. Only after this time will the couple be considered for infertility treatment, unless there are unusual circumstances. The term used today is subfertility rather than infertility and it is used to describe failure to conceive after 12 months of regular sex without contraception.

Couples who have never had a baby are said to suffer from primary subfertility; those who have had one or more children are said to have secondary subfertility. After treatment, around half of these couples will achieve a pregnancy and in most cases this takes about 12 months—though it can take up to 10 years. In about 35 percent of cases

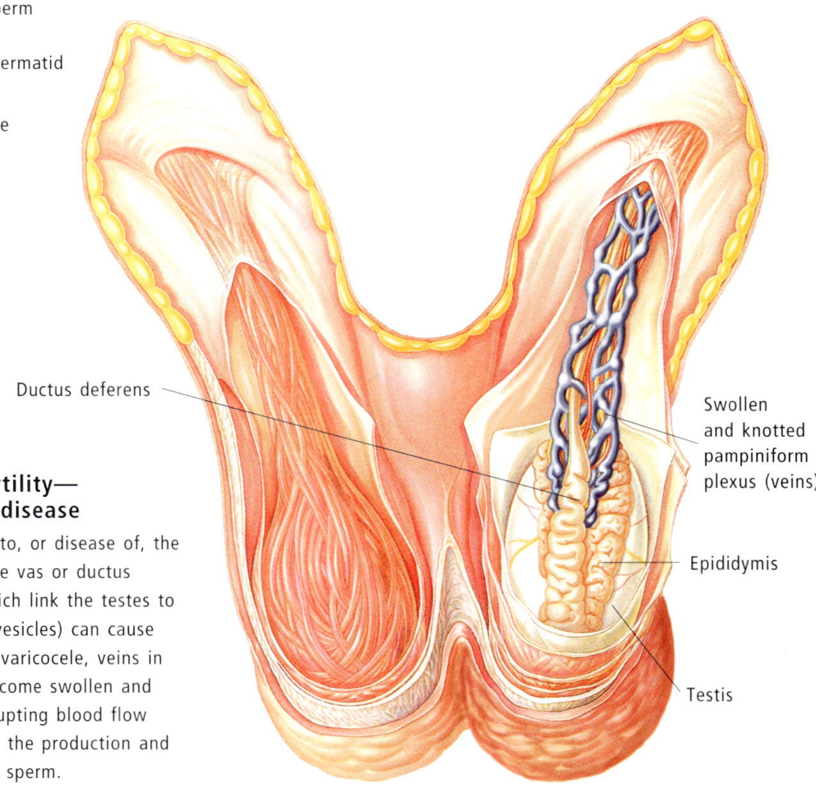

Male infertility—testicular disease

Any damage to, or disease of, the testes and the vas or ductus deferens (which link the testes to the seminal vesicles) can cause infertility. In varicocele, veins in the testes become swollen and knotted, disrupting blood flow and affecting the production and movement of sperm.

it is the man who has a fertility problem, in 35 percent it is the woman, while in the remaining 30 percent both have problems.

Subfertility rates in industrialized countries are rising alarmingly, mostly, it is thought, because women are delaying childbearing. Discovering that conception will need medical assistance and may even be impossible has a profound effect on the lives of couples who have planned a child. Counseling as well as medical assistance is important.

Causes

One of the causes of subfertility can be recurrent miscarriage or recurrent spontaneous abortion (RSA). The two main reasons for these are, firstly, a chromosomal abnormality that prevents normal development of the embryo or, secondly, something wrong with woman's reproductive system. Hormonal and anatomical problems, such as a structural abnormality of the uterus, can be responsible. For some, miscarriage is "unexplained", which may be due to immunological factors or could be due to environmental factors such as pollution or chemicals.

Male causes may be the failure to manufacture sperm (azoospermia); the sperm may be weak or few in number (oligospermia: fewer than 20 million per milliliter), or the tubes (vas deferens or ductus deferens) that link the testicles to the seminal vesicle where the sperm is stored may be damaged. Problems may be caused by testicular disease; a varicocele (a lump of varicose veins in the scrotum); occupational factors such as working with certain chemicals; general health disorders; mumps; treatment such as radiation therapy; excessive smoking or alcohol intake.

The woman may not produce an ovum; or the fallopian tube (oviduct) along which the sperm and fertilized ovum must travel may be blocked. In some cases it is thought that the cervical mucus is hostile to the sperm, thus preventing them from reaching the ovum.

Problems with sexual intercourse and disorders with the lining of the uterus (the endometrium) can also prevent conception.

Treatment

Before treatment can commence, tests must be done to establish the cause. Treatments include improving the sperm count, reducing antibodies to sperm, and stimulating ovulation. Fertility drugs which will stimulate ovulation in most women include gonadotrophin-releasing hormone (GnRH). Surgery to unblock the fallopian tubes (tuboplasty) is not guaranteed to be successful as scar tissue may form a barrier even if the tube can be opened.

Other treatments are assisted conception, such as artificial insemination or in vitro fertilization, used when the woman's reproductive system is functioning; semen from her partner or from a donor may be used. In vitro fertilization (IVF) involves uniting ova with sperm in a glass dish and then placing the fertilized ova in the uterus. Gamete intrafallopian transfer (GIFT) involves ova being taken from the ovary and being placed with sperm in the fallopian tube where fertilization may take place. It has a better success rate than IVF.

MIFT (microinjection fallopian transfer), PROST (pronuclear stage transfer), TEST (tubal embryo stage transfer), ZIFT (zygote intrafallopian transfer) are all acronyms for treatments which begin the same way as IVF but transfer the fertilized ova to the tube rather than to the uterus. The difference between these methods and GIFT is that the ovum is fertilized before transfer. In MIFT, using a microscope, sperm is injected into the ovum and when fertilized the ovum is transferred to the fallopian tube; in PROST the fertilized ovum is transferred as soon as the sperm has penetrated the ovum but before the ovum and sperm have united; in TEST the embryo is transferred when it reaches the two, four or eight cell stage; in ZIFT a single-cell embryo is transferred.

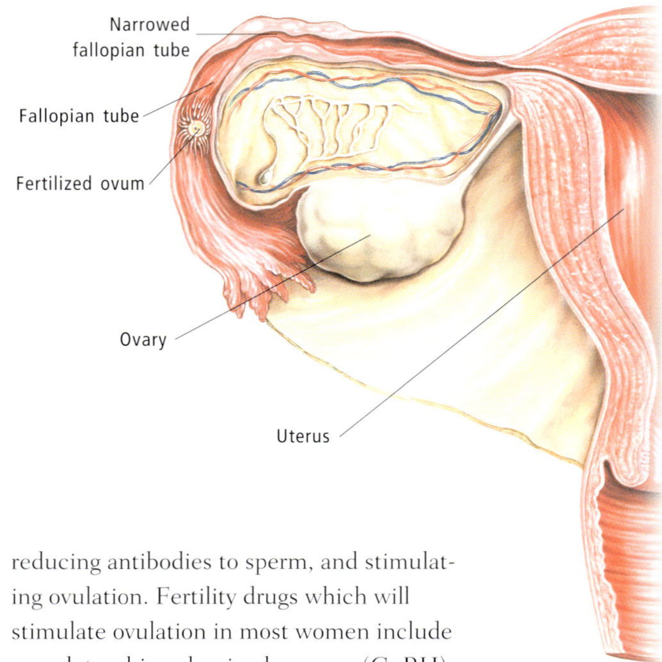

Female infertility

Women may suffer infertility if they cannot produce an ovum, or if one of the fallopian tubes is blocked or infected.

Future methods

Future methods of dealing with subfertility are likely to include the use of frozen ova which have been harvested from young women planning a career before a family, or women undergoing potential infertility-inducing treatment; ova would be thawed and fertilized at a later date. Another method is to use frozen ovaries, which will involve sections of ovaries containing immature ova being frozen, then thawed and matured when needed.

DNA transfer is a process which will bypass problems with older ova by swapping the nucleus of the older ovum with that of a younger one. Cytoplasmic donation, whereby cytoplasm from a younger ovum will be added to an older one, improves the chances that the older ovum will develop properly. A further method is to use improved growth media in which chemical solutions that mimic the female reproductive tract make it easier to implant embryos because they are more mature and hardier.

In order to cope with both the treatment itself and the chances of success or failure, counseling is vital for both partners. If a cause for infertility is found, this can result in feelings of guilt and blame which can be very destructive to a relationship and a person's emotional stability. Sex may be no longer pleasurable and this too can affect the relationship. If treatment fails and a pregnancy is not forthcoming, the

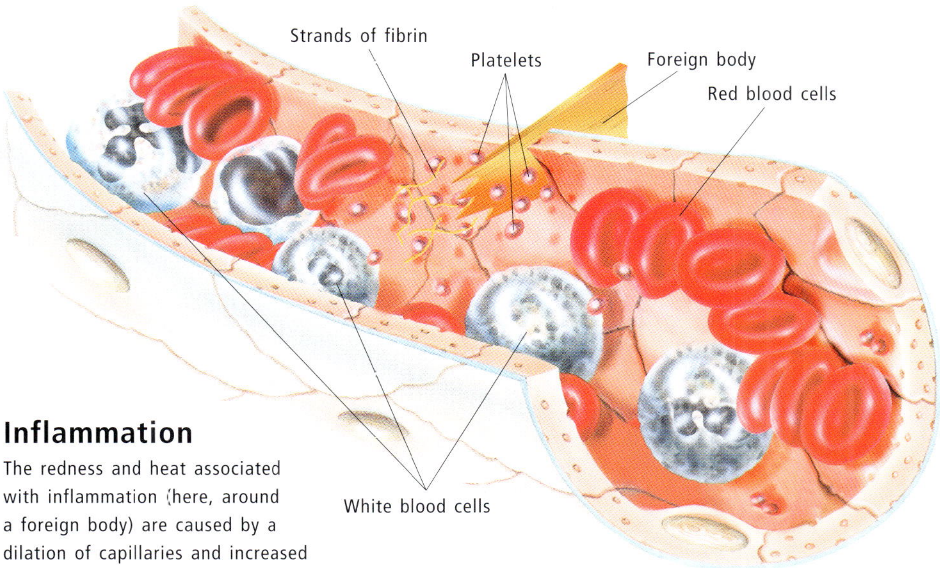

Inflammation

The redness and heat associated with inflammation (here, around a foreign body) are caused by a dilation of capillaries and increased blood flow to the affected area.

ouple will need to work through feelings of grief and loss.

SEE ALSO *Artificial insemination, Fertility, Fertilization, In vitro fertilization, Miscarriage, Pregnancy, Reproductive systems, Sperm*

INFLAMMATION

Inflammation is a reaction of body tissue to disease, injury or irritation, producing swelling, pain, redness and an increase in temperature of the affected area. Exposure to chemicals, allergens, radiation, heat and cold can cause inflammation, as well as physical trauma, surgery and diseases such as rheumatoid arthritis. It is part of the healing process and helps the body to rid itself of irritants and damaged tissue. A build-up of pus may occur and if severe can cause an abscess if not discharged through the skin during healing.

Inflammation may be acute or chronic. If acute it may happen suddenly, is often short-lived and produces characteristic redness, swelling, pain, increased temperature and loss of function. If chronic it may last months or years, beginning slowly and causing dull pain without visible symptoms.

Redness and increased temperature are caused by increased blood flow due to the dilation of blood vessels in the affected area. Swelling is brought about by fluid passing from capillaries into the fluid between cells and tissues. White blood cells also pass out of the capillaries into surrounding tissue to help fight infection or remove debris. They release chemicals which may also cause pain.

Treatment depends on the body part involved and the severity. For mild cases it may be sufficient to wash and rest the affected part; the use of aspirin or acetaminophen (paracetamol) may help.

SEE ALSO *Tissue*

INFLUENZA

This viral disease is quite distinct from the common cold and other upper respiratory infections that are often incorrectly referred to as "the flu", although the symptoms of influenza are varied and can resemble a severe common cold.

Influenza is usually transmitted by airborne droplet infection and occurs more commonly in winter. The virus is remarkable because of the frequency with which its outer coat proteins change. Since immunity to viral infections depends on the binding of antibodies to such proteins, the immune system of a previously infected person cannot recognize the influenza virus with a new outer coat and thus infection can recur.

Relatively minor variations in the recognizable surface proteins (antigens) of the influenza virus occur almost every year, producing new infective strains. Major antigenic shifts occur much less frequently, but effectively produce completely new viruses, leading to large-scale epidemics of influenza that can spread worldwide (known as pandemics).

Influenza typically causes acute onset of fever with chills, headaches, aching muscles and extreme tiredness. There may also be a dry cough, a sore throat and loss of appetite. Fever usually reaches 100–104°F (38–40°C) and persists for 3 or 4 days. Other symptoms last for 1 to 2 weeks. Although influenza is usually self-limiting, the patient usually feels most unwell and the illness is responsible for considerable time lost from work and school.

What makes influenza potentially dangerous are the major complications that are associated with this infection. Persons with pre-existing chronic lung disease may suffer exacerbations of their condition when they develop influenza. The virus itself can affect the lungs, producing a pneumonia with severe breathlessness, which may develop in patients of any age. A complicating bacterial infection, leading to typical pneumonia with cough and sputum production, is especially common in older persons. Pneumonia associated with influenza can cause death, especially during major outbreaks.

It is important for persons at high risk of developing influenza to be immunized. High-risk groups include individuals aged 65 or more, persons with chronic heart or lung disease, diabetics and immunosuppressed persons. Immunization is also recommended

Influenza virus

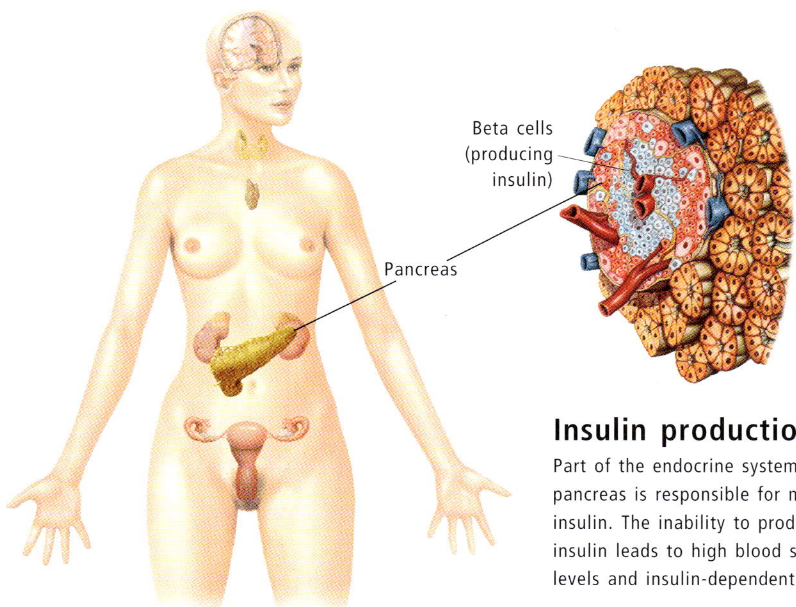

Insulin production

Part of the endocrine system, the pancreas is responsible for making insulin. The inability to produce insulin leads to high blood sugar levels and insulin-dependent diabetes.

for persons in nursing homes because of the likelihood of transmission of infection in such an environment. Killed influenza virus vaccines provide a high level of protection against development of influenza and its complications. Because of the constant antigenic variations that the virus undergoes, it is essential that individuals be reimmunized each year with the vaccine developed against the most recent infective strains.

The diagnosis of influenza is usually presumptive, based on the clinical features. Making a specific diagnosis of influenza used to be quite difficult, because of the need for complex laboratory tests which took several days to yield a result, but methods for rapid and precise diagnosis are now available. These are of particular interest because of the recent release of specific antiviral drugs that can treat influenza in its early stages. These drugs do not prevent the development of serious complications, so they are clearly not a substitute for immunization and should only be used where appropriate.

SEE ALSO *Common cold, Immunity, Immunization, Infectious diseases, Pneumonia, Respiratory system, Viruses*

INSOMNIA

Insomnia is defined as difficulty falling asleep or staying asleep—it is not the number of hours a person sleeps or how long it takes to fall asleep. When it occurs only occasionally it is not generally harmful and is described as transient insomnia, when it occurs more frequently it is called intermittent insomnia, and when it occurs night after night it is referred to as chronic insomnia.

There are many causes but the most common are stress, noise, extreme temperatures, change in the environment, changes in sleep/wake schedules such as those caused by jet travel and shift work, and side effects of medication. It can happen to both men and women but is more likely to occur in women who have reached menopause, the elderly (the ability rather than the need to sleep diminishes with age) and those with depression.

Diseases that can cause insomnia are arthritis, kidney disease, heart failure, asthma, sleep apnea, narcolepsy, restless legs syndrome, Parkinson's disease, hyperthyroidism and depression. Controllable influences include caffeine, alcohol, worrying about not sleeping, and sleeping too much during the day or early evening.

Chronic insomnia is often caused by a number of different factors. It needs treatment in order for the person to resume a normal life. Identifying and reducing behavior which aggravates the situation, sleeping pills and relaxation therapy are among the common forms of treatment.

A number of alternative therapies may help to alleviate the symptoms of insomnia. Acupuncture and shiatsu treatments may help break the cycle of insomnia by calming the mind. Treatments can be supported by Chinese herbs. Traditional Chinese Medicine advises going to bed before 11 p.m. to sleep well. Aromatherapy suggests massages and baths with relaxant oils such as lavender, ylang-ylang or sandalwood. Counseling or psychotherapy may be helpful where insomnia is due to emotional distress. Herbalists prescribe sedative nervines such as hops, linden, skullcap, chamomile, valerian or passiflora, usually to be taken as teas. Hypnotherapy may help with anxiety and teach specific self-hypnosis techniques to induce sleep. Light therapy may help to break cycles of insomnia or balance sleep patterns in shift workers. Naturopathy suggests regular exercise and bedtimes, avoiding tea, coffee, chocolate or alcohol at night, eating a low-protein dinner at least three hours before retiring, and having a relaxing warm bath with Epsom salts at night. One can also try relaxation techniques, such as autogenic training. Yoga teaches yoga nidra relaxation which may help insomnia, as may a few gentle yoga postures done in the evening.

SEE ALSO *Jet lag, Relaxation techniques, Sleep disturbances, Sleeping pills*

INSULIN

Insulin is a hormone produced in the pancreas that affects the body's ability to use sugars. Produced in either abnormally high or abnormally low quantities it can have a severe effect on the body's metabolism. Too much insulin leads to low blood sugar levels (hypoglycemia); too little causes high blood sugar levels (hyperglycemia).

Normally, when food is digested, carbohydrates are broken down into sugars such as glucose and absorbed into the bloodstream. This triggers the secretion of insulin into the blood by clusters of cells in the pancreas known as the islets of Langerhans. The pancreas is part of the body's endocrine system, a network of glands that secrete various hormones into the blood to chemically regulate body functions. Insulin aids the absorption of glucose into body cells, for immediate use or storing.

In insulin-dependent diabetes, the insulin-producing cells are destroyed, causing sugars to remain in the blood and pass out of the body in the urine. This causes weight loss, weakness, hunger and thirst, and insulin injections are needed for the body to function properly. The insulin for these injections may be synthetic or obtained from cattle or pig pancreases. It is injected under the skin at regular intervals daily.

SEE ALSO *Blood sugar tests, Diabetes, Endocrine system, Hyperglycemia, Hypoglycemia, Islets of Langerhans, Pancreas*

INTELLECTUAL DISABILITY

Formerly known as mental retardation, intellectual disability affects around 2 percent of the population. It can be defined as limited intelligence or cognitive potential. Those who have this condition have a reduced capacity to learn, to solve problems and possibly to perform other functions, depending on the degree of disability.

Intellectual disability is classified according to severity, and is usually measured by intelligence quotients (IQ) or scores.

In the general population the average intelligence quotient is 100. The upper range of intellectual disability, known as mildly disabled, falls in an IQ range of around the low 50s to high 60s. These people comprise the majority of intellectually disabled persons and they are able to learn basic academic skills with some difficulty and to be employed, usually in unskilled or semi-skilled jobs; they are also able to function independently.

Those who are classified from the high 30s to mid 50s are described as moderately disabled. They are able to care for themselves, to live in a sheltered workshop situation and to live in a home with supervision.

The severely disabled fall into the low 20s to high 30s, and have slow motor development and limited communication skills. They may also have physical disabilities but will be able to care for their basic needs and contribute to their own care in work and living situations.

The last and smallest group are the profoundly disabled, with IQs below the low 20s. These people need full-time care because they have poor motor development and communication skills and are unable to care for themselves or to work except in highly structured activities.

Caused by events before, during or after birth, intellectual disability can be found in those with genetic disorders, such as Down syndrome; infectious disease, for example meningitis; metabolic disorders; fetal alcohol syndrome; physical malformations; poisoning, for example lead poisoning; trauma or injuries to the head; and malnutrition.

Diagnosis

Children with the more severe disabilities will usually be diagnosed before they reach their first birthday, often as a result of parental concerns. Mildly intellectually disabled children are sometimes not diagnosed until they are attending preschool or school, when it is the abstract areas of reasoning, problem solving and use of language which indicate a problem.

A comprehensive evaluation is very important. Tests which are coordinated by a pediatrician or a child psychiatrist, in areas such as neurology, psychology, psychiatry, special education, hearing, speech, vision and physical therapy, may be necessary to determine the extent of intellectual disability.

Treatment

Intellectual disability cannot be cured, but early diagnosis may lead to early treatment and help the family to establish appropriate expectations for their child and to handle the stresses which this level of disability can bring to both child and family. Children diagnosed as intellectually disabled will benefit from an education that is tailored to their needs and from continued monitoring and evaluation.

In many countries it was believed that mental health problems could be solved by deinstitutionalizing and that the ordinary health care system could give the same or better care than that provided by institutions. However, recent research has found that governments need to address the problem of the stress a disability causes to a family and the decrease in the quality of life for both the family and the disabled person that this stress can bring. It has been found that the majority of mental health problems are not solved by deinstitutionalization and this is no substitute for professional assistance.

SEE ALSO *Down syndrome, Fetal alcohol syndrome, Learning disorders*

INTERTRIGO

Intertrigo is an inflammatory condition in which moisture and bacteria accumulate in a skin fold, causing the skin to become red and inflamed. Skin folds of the inner thighs, armpits and underside of the breasts are most often involved, especially in obese people. Treatment involves keeping the skin clean and dry, and dieting and exercise to lose weight.

INTESTINES

The intestines consist of two parts: the small intestine (duodenum, jejunum and ileum) and the large intestine (colon and rectum). The intestines occupy the lower two-thirds of the abdominal cavity. The small intestine (or small bowel) leads on from the stomach, and is mainly concerned with absorption of nutrients from food after digestion (simple sugars, amino acids from protein, fatty acids and glycerol from fats). Some vitamins are also absorbed here (for example, vitamin B_{12}, which is absorbed from the end of the ileum).

The large intestine leads on from the small intestine and is concerned with absorption of water and salts (electrolytes), thereby forming the stool or fecal mass by the time the rectum is reached. It is arranged like a picture frame around the margins of the abdomen and is composed of an initial part called the cecum, with the small vermiform appendix attached. It also includes the ascending colon, transverse colon, descending colon, sigmoid colon and rectum.

The small intestine occupies the central part of the frame provided by the large bowel. It contains about 3½ fluid ounces (100 milliliters) of gas, while the large intestine has considerably more. In fact the average person produces up to approximately 1 quart (about 1 liter) of gas per day as flatus. This gas is mainly nitrogen with some carbon dioxide, oxygen, hydrogen and methane. The last four are produced by bacteria in the large bowel, while nitrogen may enter the bowel from the bloodstream.

Diseases and disorders

Cancer of the large intestine arises when the cells forming the lining of the gut multiply out of control. Bowel cancer cells

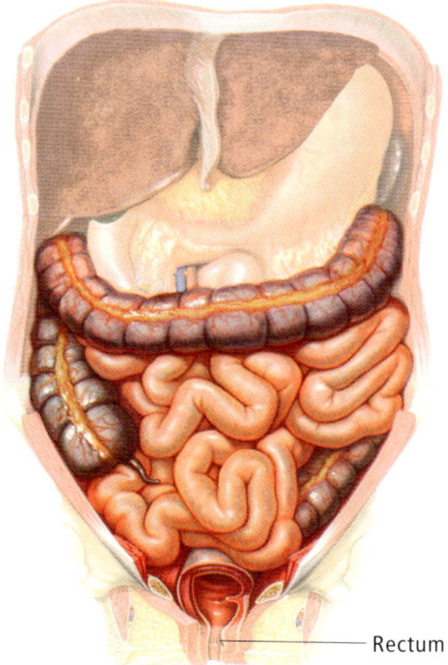

Intestines

The small and large intestines together measure approximately 25 feet (7.5 meters) in length, and lie folded up in the lower part of the abdominal cavity.

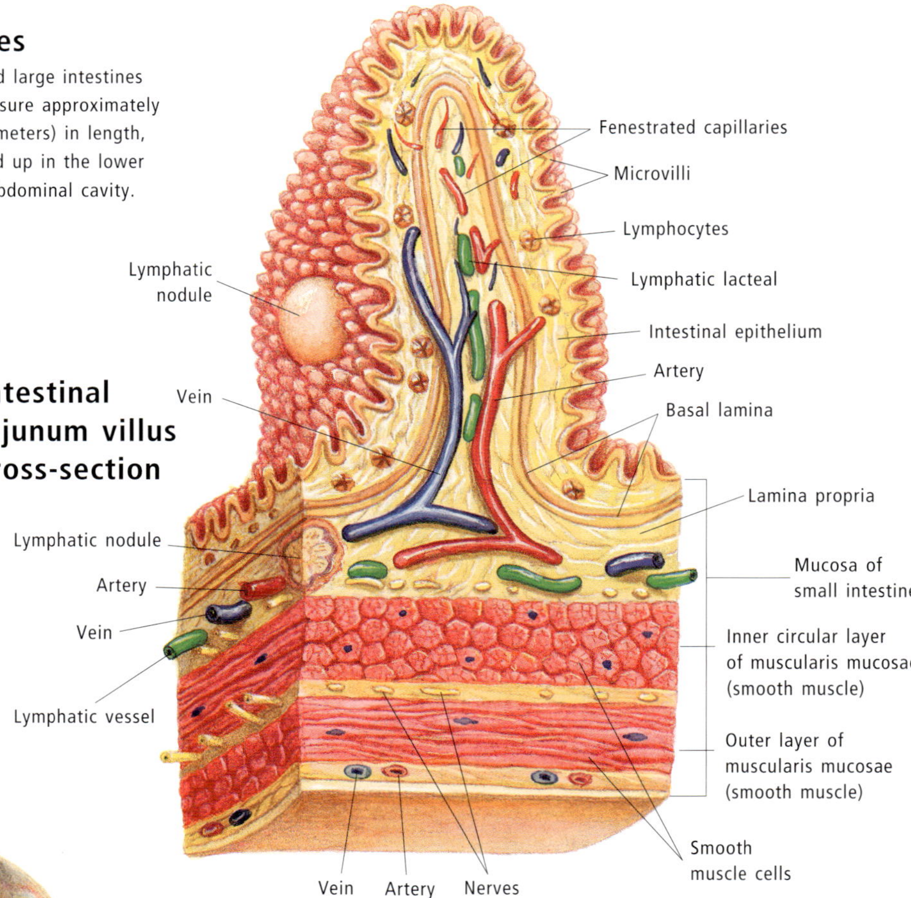

Intestinal jejunum villus cross-section

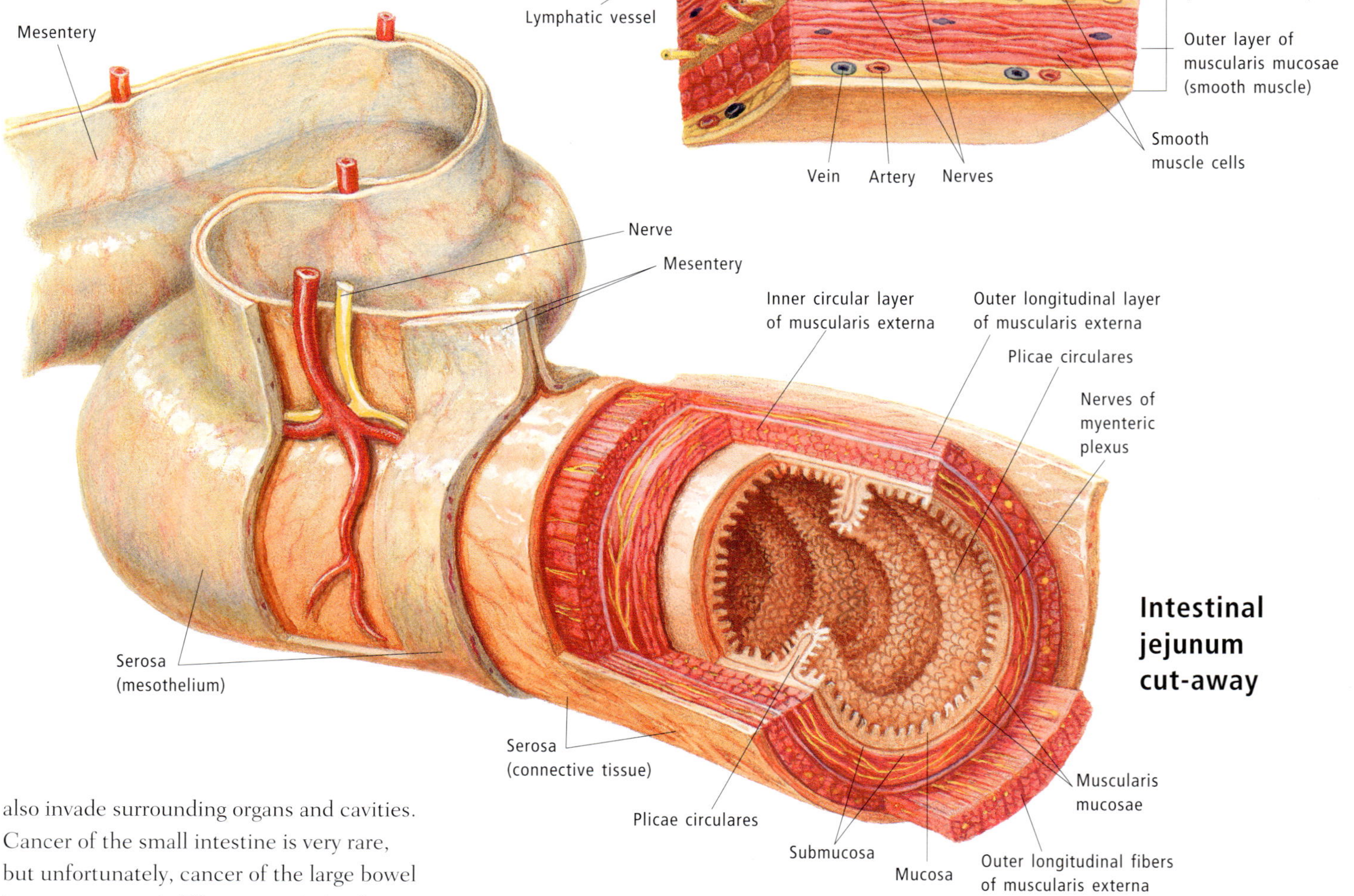

Intestinal jejunum cut-away

also invade surrounding organs and cavities. Cancer of the small intestine is very rare, but unfortunately, cancer of the large bowel is very common in Western societies. In fact, each year in the USA more than 100,000 new cases of bowel cancer are diagnosed and about half that number of people die from the disease each year. The causes may be genetic, with some families being particularly at risk, and/or dietary; diets high in protein and fat are shown to be contributing factors. Greater consumption of meat may change the type of bacteria present in the bowel, favoring bacterial species that turn bile acids and other chemicals into cancer-causing agents (carcinogens).

The most common site for cancer of the large intestine is in the rectum, which accounts for more than a third of cases. Symptoms and signs vary depending on the actual part of the bowel involved, but commonly patients complain of bleeding from the anus, change in bowel habit (i.e. less or more frequent), a feeling of incomplete emptying when a motion is passed, weakness and sometimes abdominal pain and discomfort.

Irritable bowel syndrome is a condition in which the patient experiences bloating, abdominal cramping, diarrhea and sometimes constipation. There are no obvious changes in the structure of the bowel, so it appears that the disease involves changes in the function of the colon, in particular the function of the smooth muscle and nerve cells in the bowel wall. Patients appear to have increased sensitivity to several factors, but the actual source of this increased sensitivity is so far unclear.

Obstruction may occur in either the small or large intestine. Small bowel obstruction leads to profuse vomiting, upper abdominal distension, often severe discomfort, and constipation. It is usually caused by adhesions between the small bowel and other structures within the abdominal cavity; involvement of a length of bowel in a hernia; twisting of a loop of bowel around itself (volvulus); or intussusception, the infolding of one length of bowel into another. Large bowel obstruction may be caused by twisting of the sigmoid colon (volvulus), bowel cancer, or adhesions to other organs. It gives rise to constipation, pain in the lower abdomen and eventually vomiting.

Fecal incontinence may result when there is a neurological problem with the anorectal region (such as lack of sensation or lack of control of muscles around the anus). It can also occur when there has been trauma or surgery to the area, or when the patient has constipation with obstruction and overflow incontinence around a hardened fecal mass. The latter may occur in children with poor bowel habit.

SEE ALSO *Anus, Bowel, Bowel cancer, Colon, Digestive system, Duodenum, Ileum, Incontinence, Intussusception, Irritable bowel syndrome, Rectum*

INTUSSUSCEPTION

Intussusception is a condition in which one part of the bowel telescopes inside an immediately adjacent segment (forming a tube within a tube). It is the most common cause of bowel obstruction in children under two and is more common in boys than girls. The disease can have serious consequences if left untreated, because gangrene may arise in the telescoped part of the bowel due to loss of blood supply.

Intussusception appears to be associated with previous viral infection which causes enlargement of clumps of immune system cells (Peyer's patches) in the bowel. Often the cause is not known, and the condition may only become apparent when an otherwise healthy infant experiences sudden and severe abdominal pain.

Treatment of the disease involves reversal of dehydration, therapeutic barium enema to distend the intussusception, or surgery if bowel perforation and/or peritonitis occur.

SEE ALSO *Bowel, Intestines*

IODINE DEFICIENCY

This is the cause of some types of goiter (a swelling of the thyroid gland), in particular the form that is widespread among people living in the foothills of the world's major mountain ranges (such as the Himalayas and the Andes). Leaching of iodine from the soils in these areas is the reason for deficiency of iodine in the diet. Iodine is essential for hormone production by the thyroid gland. When its availability is limited, the gland attempts to compensate for reduced hormone output by increasing in size.

If iodine deficiency persists for many years, the goiter may become nodular and massive. Extreme iodine deficiency may cause hypothyroidism and children may suffer significant mental impairment, referred to as cretinism. Dietary supplementation, for example by providing iodized salt, can eliminate these problems.

SEE ALSO *Cretinism, Goiter, Hypothyroidism, Thyroid gland*

IRIDOLOGY

Iridology, or iris analysis, is a diagnostic technique used by a range of natural therapists; it was pioneered in the late nineteenth century by Ignatz von Peczeley, a Hungarian doctor. In this technique, the pigmentation, texture, patterns and rings of the iris of the eye are closely examined to gain an indication of the overall constitution of the patient.

Iridology is based on the belief that different areas of the iris are linked to different organs of the body through the nervous system, so that markings in any particular part of the iris can give information about the past and present health of the linked organ.

IRIS

The iris is a colored ring positioned in front of the lens and behind the cornea of the eye. The center of the ring is the hole through which light is admitted into the interior of the eye, the pupil. By opening and closing, the iris controls the amount of light entering the eye through the pupil. In bright light, muscles of the iris make the pupil smaller, reducing the amount of light that passes through. In dim light, these muscles make the pupil larger to admit more light. The color of the eyes is determined by pigments in the iris; eye color is inherited. An albino person has no

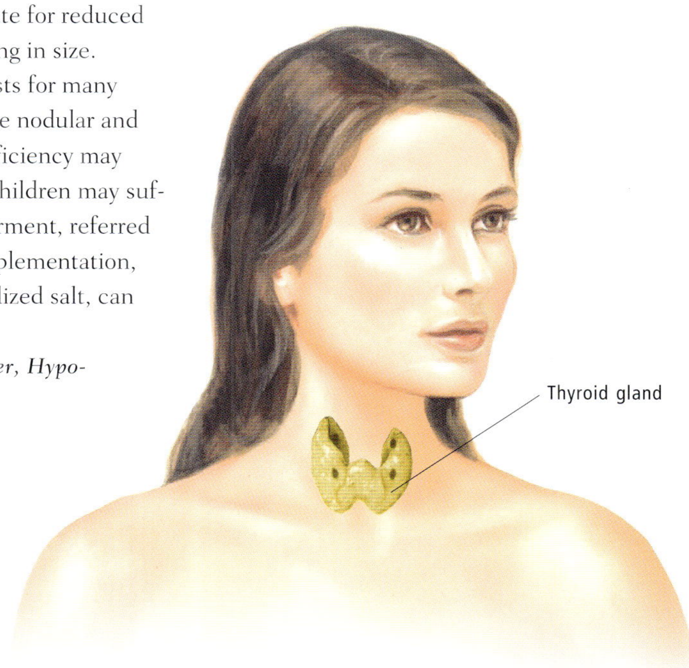

Iodine deficiency

Iodine is found in thyroid gland hormones. A deficiency of iodine can cause swelling of the thyroid gland (goiter) or physical and mental retardation in children (cretinism).

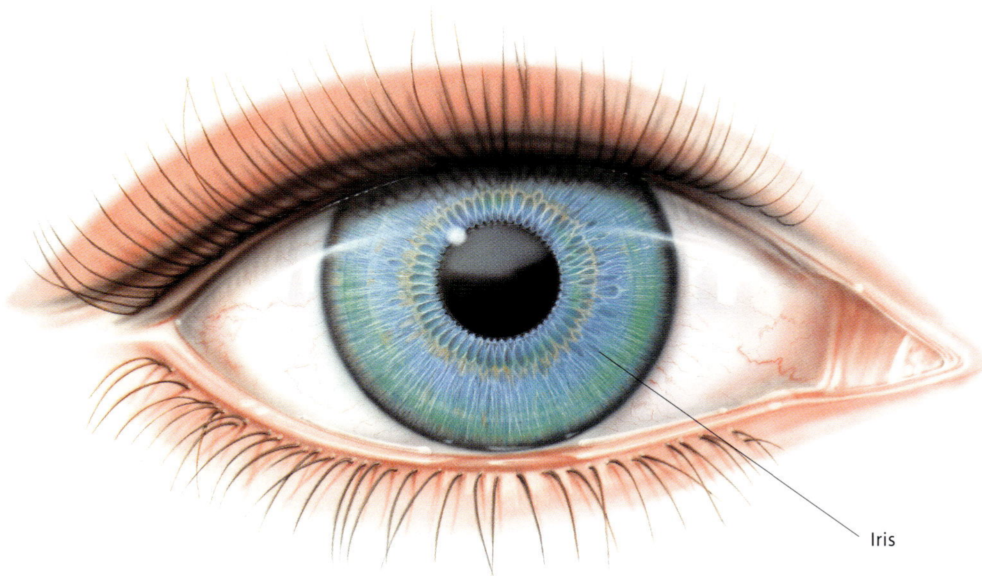

Iris
The iris is the colored part of the eye, encircling the black pupil.

pigmentation in the iris so the eyes look pink due to the small blood vessels in the retina.

The iris can become inflamed (iritis), producing pain, sensitivity to light (photophobia), and redness in the eye.

SEE ALSO *Cornea, Eye, Iritis, Pupil of eye*

IRITIS

Iritis is inflammation of the iris, the colored ring positioned in front of the lens and behind the cornea. Iritis causes pain, photophobia (intolerance to light), redness, blurred vision, and a small, irregular iris. A foggy-looking cornea may develop. It is associated with various illnesses, including ankylosing spondylitis, collagen disease and toxoplasmosis. Treatment is with eye drops that dilate the pupil, such as atropine sulfate and homatropine, and corticosteroid drops.

SEE ALSO *Cornea, Eye, Iris, Photophobia*

IRON

A chemical element, iron is a metal essential for the formation of hemoglobin, the component in red blood cells that transports oxygen and carbon dioxide to and from the body's cells. It is also required for the formation of myoglobin (a muscle protein) and certain enzymes needed in respiration.

The body needs a small but constant supply of iron, which it gets from foods. Foods rich in iron include liver, eggs, spinach, and lean meat. The average adult needs about 15 milligrams of iron a day; a female between puberty and menopause needs about twice that amount. Pregnant women and growing children also need additional iron.

Iron deficiency anemia is a condition that occurs when iron is being lost from the body, for example in a bleeding peptic ulcer, heavy menstrual bleeding, or bleeding caused by bowel cancer. Treatment is to cure the underlying condition and replace the body's depleted iron reserves by taking iron tablets regularly.

Too much iron can be toxic to the body; in a hereditary disease called hemochromatosis, excess absorption of iron by the body leads to damage to organs such as the pancreas, liver, and skin.

SEE ALSO *Anemia, Hemochromatosis, Hemoglobin, Red blood cells*

IRRITABLE BOWEL SYNDROME

Irritable bowel syndrome (IBS) is a common condition, affecting between 15 and 25 percent of people in Western societies. Symptoms include abdominal pain (especially cramps and spasms), bloating and abnormal function of the bowel. Some patients may have hard stools and difficulty in passing motions, whereas others may have loose stools and a feeling of urgency to pass motions. Patients with IBS appear to have a greater degree of pain sensitivity in the lower bowel compared with the general population. The cause remains obscure, but appears to involve some increased sensitivity of the bowel to the sensations of bowel function.

The diagnosis is usually made in the absence of other physical evidence of gut disease: the condition is thought to be a functional, rather than a structural or biochemical, change in the bowel.

Treatments which have been used include antidepressants and drugs which

Irritable bowel syndrome
Irritable bowel syndrome is characterized by cramping abdominal pain and spasms plus unusual diarrhea or constipation, but does not have the inflammation associated with other diseases of the intestinal tract.

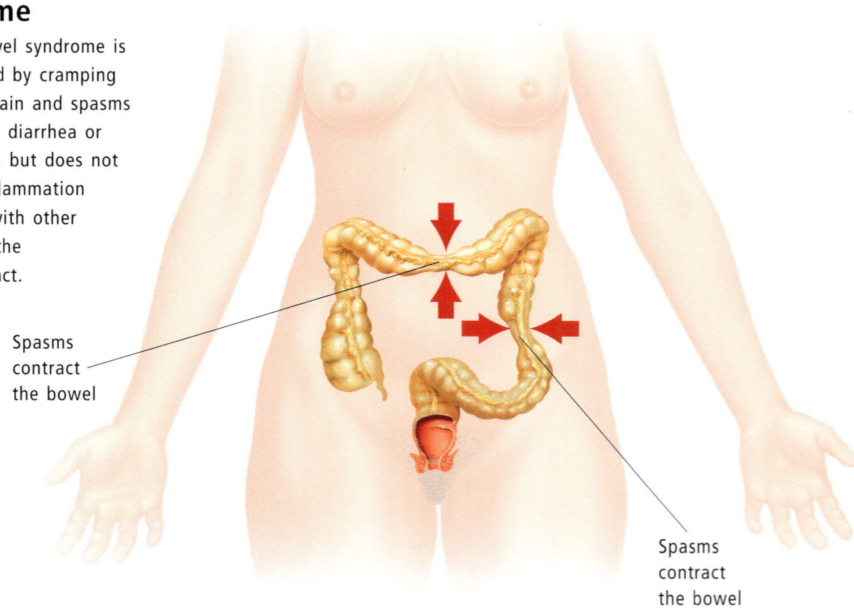

inhibit the function of a neurotransmitter known as serotonin.

There are a number of alternative therapies that may help to alleviate the symptoms of IBS. Acupuncture may relieve symptoms and help with anxiety levels. Chinese herbs can be given in support of treatment. Chiropractic or osteopathic treatment can be given where spinal maladjustment or a trapped spinal nerve is a contributing factor. Herbalism prescribes peppermint and chamomile teas and slippery elm powder. Homeopathy uses a number of remedies that address the specific symptoms of irritable bowel syndrome. Hypnotherapy or psychotherapy may help patients identify and deal with stress. Massage of the abdomen may relax the area, and can be self-administered. Reflexology massage works on colon zones. Shiatsu massage attempts to balance colon function. Any relaxing style of massage may help with anxiety levels. Naturopathy prescribes a wholefood diet to maintain bowel action, and fiber or bulk laxatives such as linseed or psyllium seeds. Relaxation techniques are also recommended. One should avoid irritants such as tea, coffee and alcohol, and check for possible allergies, particularly dairy or wheat.

SEE ALSO *Bowel, Digestive system, Intestines*

ISCHEMIA

Ischemia is the lack of supply of oxygenated blood to a particular part of the body. It is usually caused by disease in the blood vessels (most commonly arteriosclerosis), but it may also result from the blockage of an artery following an injury or a blood clot. If lower limb arteries are affected, ischemia produces leg cramps and intermittent claudication (pain on walking). If the heart is affected, angina pectoris or myocardial infarction can occur. In the brain, ischemia causes transient ischemic attack (TIA) or stroke.

SEE ALSO *Angina pectoris, Arteriosclerosis, Circulatory system, Myocardial infarction, Stroke, Transient ischemic attack*

ISCHEMIC HEART DISEASE

Ischemic heart disease refers to a group of conditions where there is insufficient blood supply to the heart muscle. This is usually due to partial or complete blockage of the coronary arteries supplying the heart by a disease called atherosclerosis. Atherosclerosis is a common condition in Western society and involves the accumulation of fatty and fibrous tissue in the vessel wall.

If coronary artery obstruction is only partial, the patient will experience pain in the center of the chest (angina pectoris) during exercise or emotional excitement. If coronary artery obstruction is complete, there may be death of heart muscle (myocardial infarction).

SEE ALSO *Angina pectoris, Arteriosclerosis, Atherosclerosis, Coronary arteries, Coronary artery disease, Heart, Myocardial infarction*

Ischemia

Ischemia results from a constriction or blockage of a blood vessel, so that oxygenated blood does not reach a particular part of the body. Obstruction of the arteries to the heart can lead to angina or a heart attack.

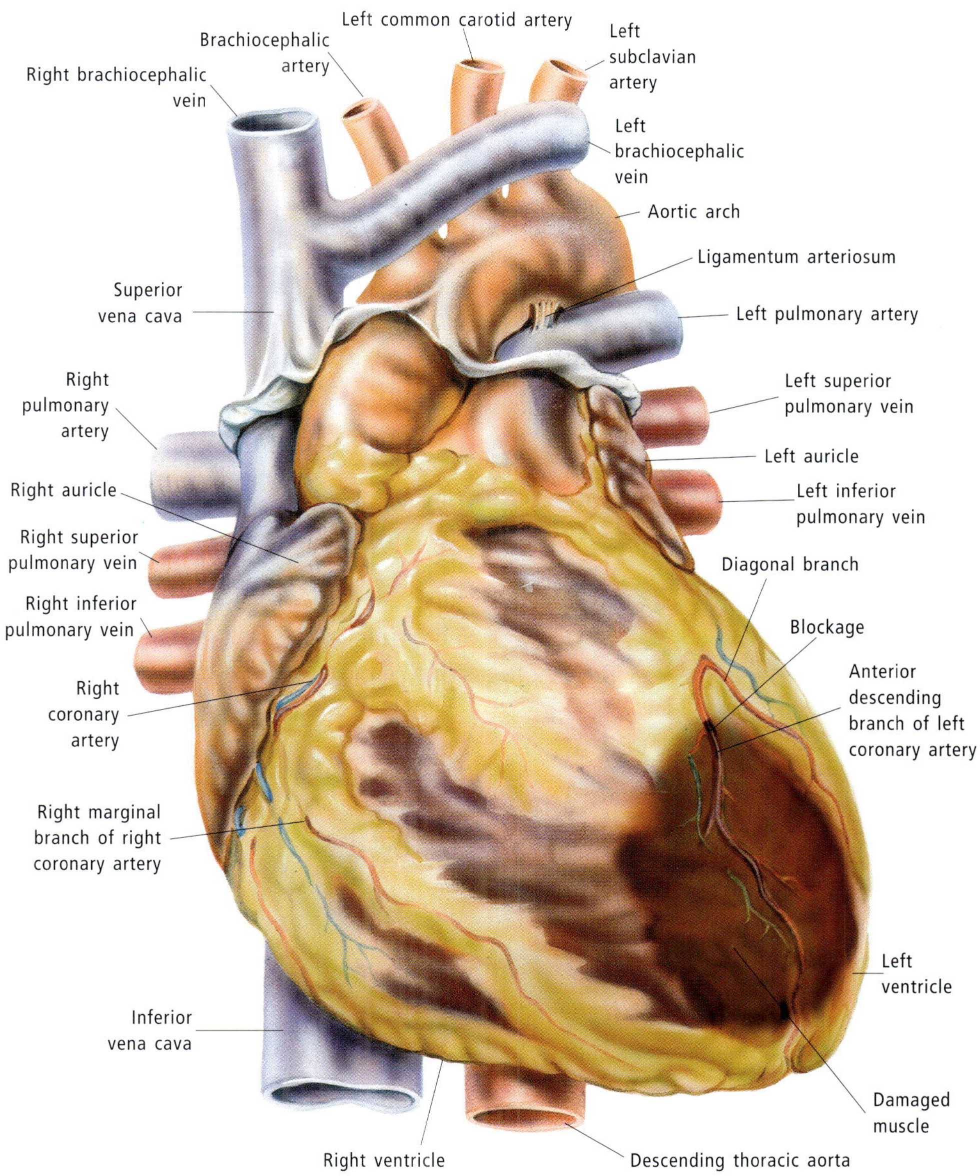

ISLETS OF LANGERHANS

These are many spherical clusters of specialized cells within the pancreas. They are a type of endocrine gland, i.e. a gland that secretes hormones directly into the bloodstream rather than onto the surface of the gut or skin. The islets are made up of several different types of cell. The first two types (alpha and beta cells) are involved in the control of blood sugar concentration and are responsive to changes in that concentration. The alpha cell type produces a

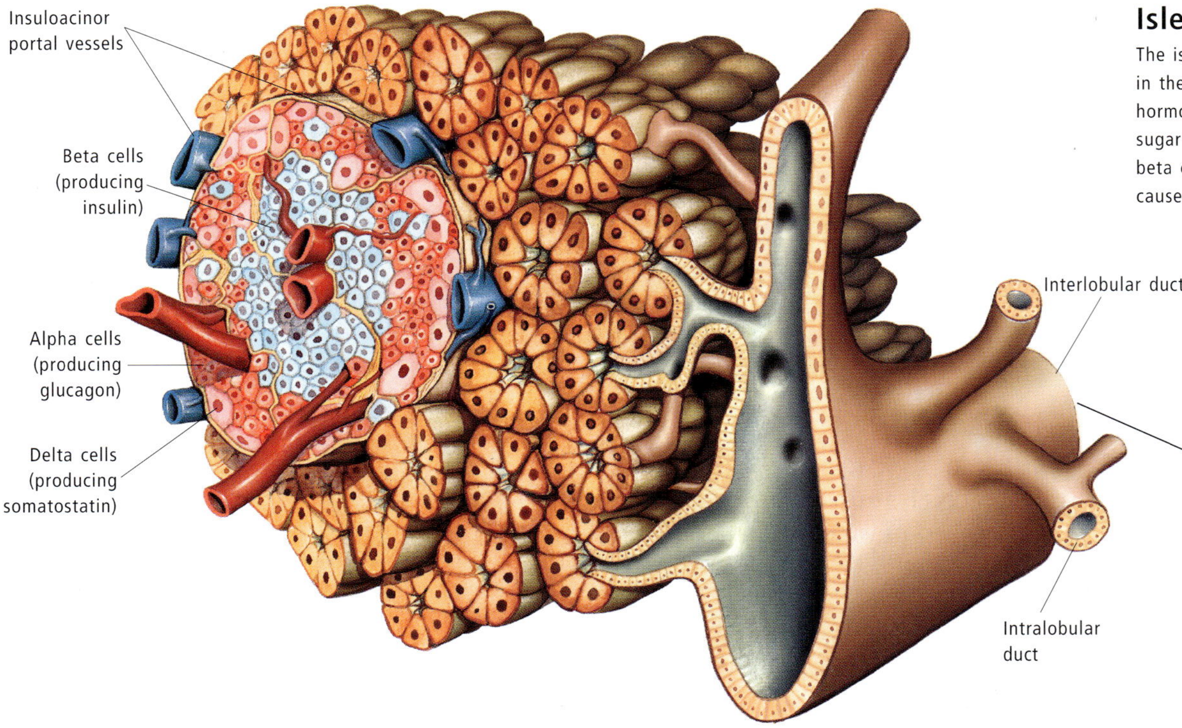

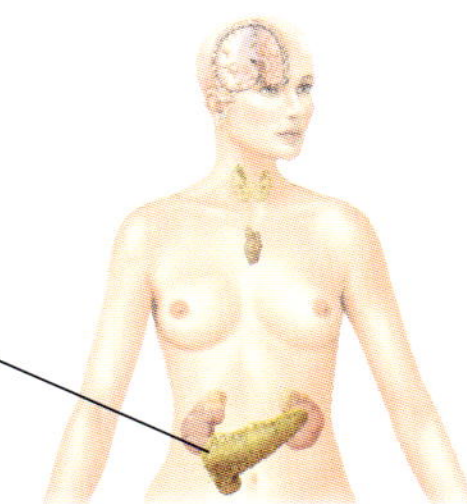

Islets of Langerhans

The islets of Langerhans are found in the pancreas; they produce hormones to raise or lower blood sugar levels. Abnormalities of the beta cells, which produce insulin, cause diabetes mellitus.

hormone known as glucagon, which acts to increase blood sugar level. The beta cell type produces the hormone insulin, which has the effect of reducing blood sugar level. A third type, the delta cell, secretes somatostatin, which inhibits the release of glucagon and insulin.

SEE ALSO *Endocrine glands, Endocrine system, Insulin, Pancreas*

JAUNDICE

Jaundice is a condition in which there is yellowing of the skin and eyes due to an increased concentration of bilirubin in the blood. The condition may be due to excessive breakdown of blood cells (hemolytic jaundice), excessive production of pigments (pigment overload), problems with liver cells (hepatocellular jaundice), or obstruction of the ducts leading from the liver to the gut (obstructive jaundice). In practice, many cases of jaundice present a mixture of these types.

Hemolytic or pigment overload jaundice is due to abnormalities of red blood cells or the metabolic pathways involved in the production of hemoglobin. Red blood cells are normally broken down and recycled, but patients with hemolytic jaundice have a higher than normal rate of destruction of blood cells. The excess hemoglobin is converted into excess amounts of bilirubin.

Hepatocellular jaundice is due to damage to liver cells, as seen in hepatitis and alcoholic cirrhosis, or a result of inherited problems with enzymes in the liver. In this type of jaundice the liver cells are unable to process bile pigments and excrete them into the bile duct system. Bilirubin builds up in the blood to produce jaundice. Destruction of liver cells releases enzymes, which can be detected in the patient's blood.

Obstructive jaundice is often due to the presence of gallstones in the biliary duct system, although tumors in the head of the pancreas, parasites in the bile duct, inflammation of the pancreas, drugs and pregnancy may also cause the condition. Patients develop pale stools and dark urine. The stools are pale because the pigments which normally pass down the bile duct to color the feces are no longer reaching the gut. The dark urine is due to excretion of bile salts by the kidney. Blood tests may show elevated concentrations of an enzyme called alkaline phosphatase. If the obstruction is caused by a gallstone, the gallbladder is unlikely to be enlarged; if it is due to a cancer in the head of the pancreas which is compressing the lower part of the bile duct, the gallbladder may be enlarged and easily felt just below the ribs on the right side of the abdomen. Patients with obstructive jaundice will often experience itching of the skin due to deposition of bile salts.

All normal newborn infants have a small degree of jaundice which is due to immature enzyme systems in the liver. This "physiological" jaundice, will usually disappear over a few days, but may become a serious problem in infants who are born prematurely or who have increased destruction of red blood cells due to other diseases. If the concentration of bilirubin in the blood rises too high, the brain may be damaged in a condition called kernicterus.

Jaundice may also be caused by drugs including phenacetin, paracetamol, sex steroids, anti-psychotic drugs, some anesthetics, selected antibiotics and anti-tuberculosis drugs. Some toxic chemicals like carbon tetrachloride can also damage the liver and cause jaundice.

SEE ALSO *Cirrhosis of the liver, Gallbladder, Gallstones, Hemoglobin, Hepatitis, Liver, Newborn, Red blood cells*

JAW

The jaw consists of two parts: a moveable lower jaw, formed by the mandible, and a fixed upper jaw, formed by the maxillae. The mandible is made up of a thickened body (which forms the lower border of the face); an alveolar part (which contains sockets for the lower teeth); and a ramus (which projects upwards from each end of the body). The top of each ramus has a small rounded head, which fits into a socket on the base of the skull to form the temporomandibular joint. This joint, which is reinforced by a capsule and strong ligaments, allows gliding (backwards, forwards and sideways) movements, as well as a hinge movement, which occurs during opening and closing of the jaw. Sometimes, when the jaw is opened too far, the mandible can be pulled forwards out of its socket, causing it to dislocate.

The movements of the temporomandibular joint are brought about by a group of muscles known as the muscles of mastication. These muscles include the medial and lateral pterygoid, masseter and temporalis muscles. The medial pterygoid and masseter muscles cover the medial (inner) and lateral (outer) surfaces respectively of the ramus of the mandible and, with the temporalis muscle, act to elevate (close) the mandible. They can all be palpated when the teeth are clenched. It is interesting to note that the masseter muscle is said to be the strongest muscle in the body (based on force per unit of mass). The lateral pterygoid muscle is the major depressor (opener) of the mandible.

The upper jaw is formed by the maxillae. It has an alveolar part (which contains sockets for the upper teeth); a palatine part (which forms the hard palate in the roof of the mouth); and a hollow body (which forms part of the cheek). The cavity in the body is known as the maxillary sinus, and is a frequent site of minor infections (sinusitis) which can spread to it from the nose, or in some cases from the upper teeth.

The alveolar parts of the maxilla and mandible contain sockets for the teeth (alveolar sockets). The base of each socket contains a hole through which branches of the superior and inferior alveolar nerves and blood vessels reach the inside (pulp cavity) of the teeth. In an adult, each jaw contains sockets for 16 teeth, including 4 incisors (for cutting), 1 pair of canines (for tearing), 2 pairs of premolars and 3 pairs of molars (for grinding). In many people the alveolar parts of the mandible and/or maxilla are not long enough to accommodate the third pair of molars (often called the wisdom teeth) causing them to become "impacted".

SEE ALSO *Face, Sinuses, Sinusitis, Teeth*

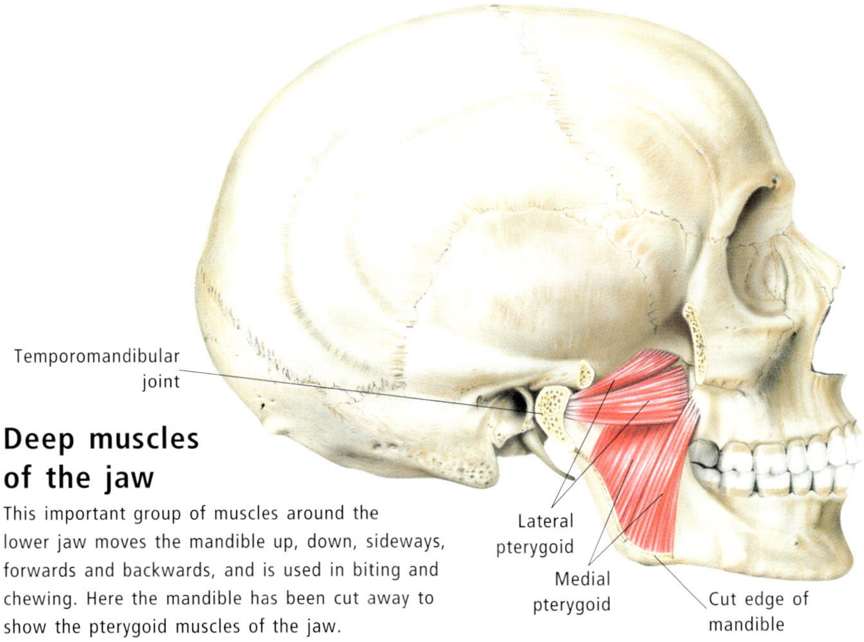

Deep muscles of the jaw

This important group of muscles around the lower jaw moves the mandible up, down, sideways, forwards and backwards, and is used in biting and chewing. Here the mandible has been cut away to show the pterygoid muscles of the jaw.

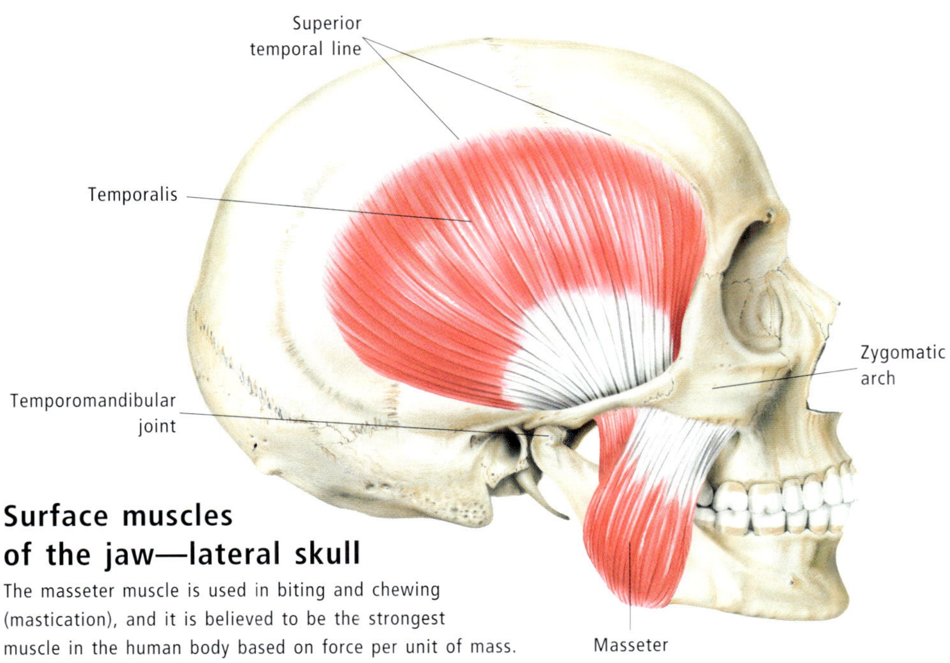

Surface muscles of the jaw—lateral skull

The masseter muscle is used in biting and chewing (mastication), and it is believed to be the strongest muscle in the human body based on force per unit of mass.

JEJUNUM

Located in the upper left part of the abdomen, the jejunum is the middle part of the small intestine, extending from the duodenum to the ileum. It is about 4 feet (1.2 meters) long and together with the duodenum, makes up about two-fifths of the length of the small intestine.

The jejunum, like the rest of the small intestine, is covered by smooth muscle with an inner, circular layer that is thicker than the outer, longitudinal layer. Food passes from the duodenum into the jejunum by a series of muscular contractions and relaxations known as peristalsis. In the jejunum, as in the duodenum, food is digested and absorbed, passing though the lining of the walls of the jejunum into the lymphatic vessels and the hepatic portal vein to the liver.

The jejunum is one part of the small intestine that is either partially or completely bypassed during gastric bypass operations, which are sometimes performed as a treatment for obesity.

Like the duodenum, the jejunum is suspended from the back of the abdominal wall by a fold of membrane called the mesentery. Blood vessels, nerves and lymphatic vessels travel through the mesentery and supply the jejunum.

Wall of the jejunum

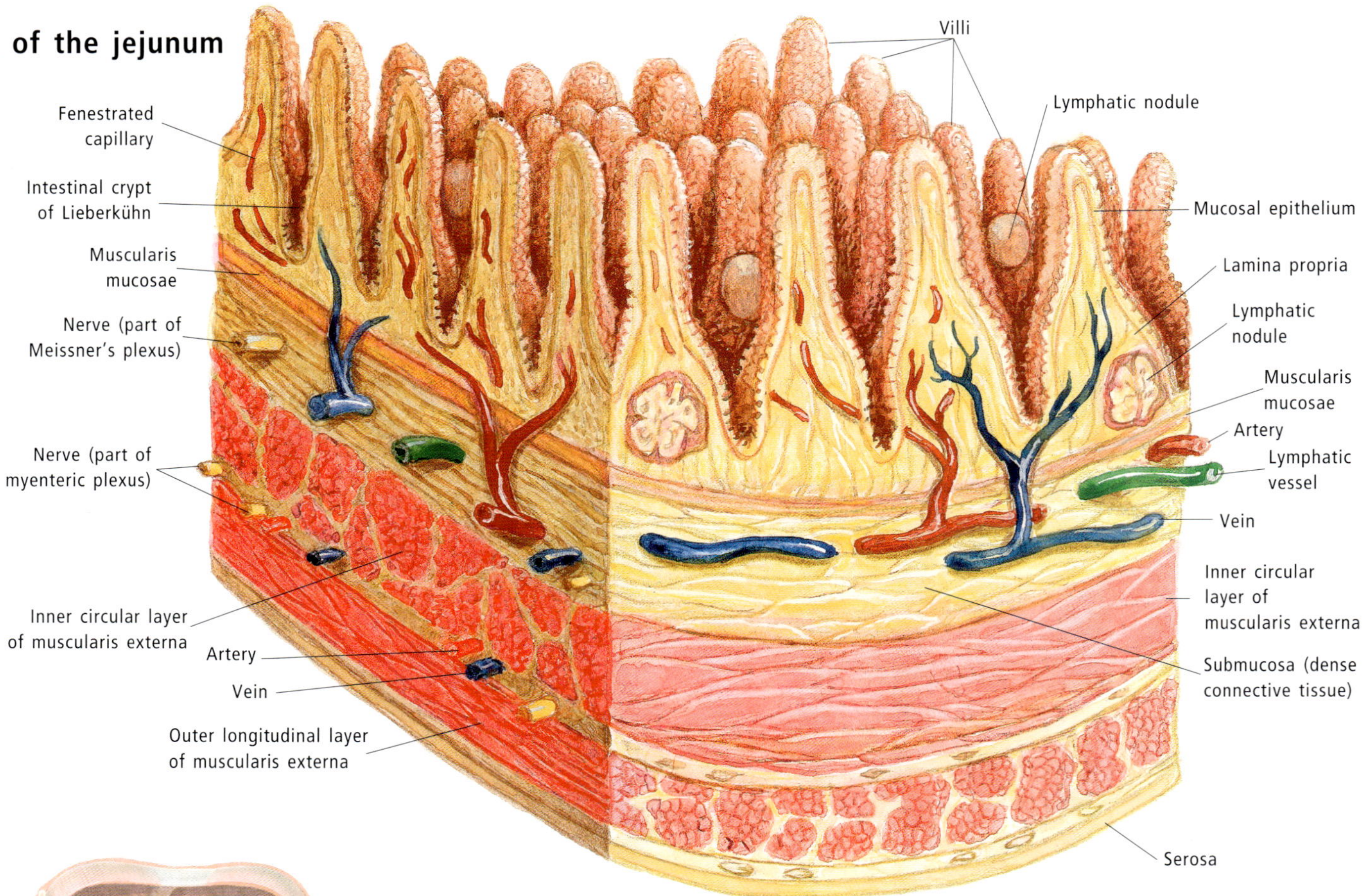

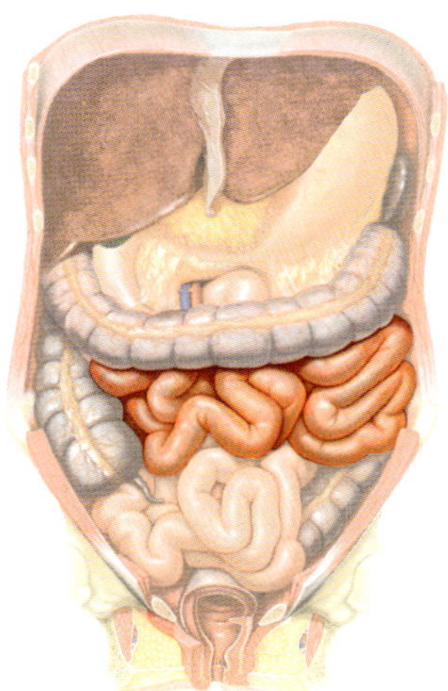

Jejunum

The jejunum is the part of the small intestine between the duodenum and the ileum. It digests and absorbs food, sending nutrients to the lymphatic vessels and liver.

The jejunum can be affected by several diseases, including bowel obstruction, gastroenteritis, celiac disease and Crohn's disease. Peptic ulcers, though occurring commonly in the duodenum, do not occur in the jejunum. Tumors are rare in the jejunum.

The jejunal button and jejunostomy tube (J-tube) are surgically installed feeding devices that deliver nutrients directly into the jejunum. They are used to assist patients with nutritional inadequacies or who are unable to eat due to illness.

SEE ALSO *Celiac disease, Crohn's disease, Digestive system, Duodenum, Gastroenteritis, Ileum, Intestines, Peristalsis*

JET LAG

Symptoms of jet lag are daytime drowsiness, fatigue, difficulty sleeping and a general feeling of vagueness. The person who travels across time zones in a jet plane will suffer varying degrees of jet lag. The person who travels from north to south will not experience jet lag, though they may be tired.

Many hormones change in level at approximately 24-hour intervals: these periodic changes are called circadian rhythms. Cortisol, the major steroid hormone secreted by the adrenal cortex, is at a low level during sleep, rising rapidly in the early morning hours and gradually descending during the day, with spurts during meal times. The rhythm of this hormone is dependent on night–day cycles and lasts for some days after jet travel into different time zones. The period when the body is adjusting to the change of these patterns is characterized by jet lag. One of the problems with jet lag is that all the body's rhythms are upset. After a few days (this differs from individual to individual) the body will have settled into the new time frame; heart rate will adjust ahead of body temperature.

There are dozens of theories on how to prevent or stave off the effects of jet lag. These include keeping to the same sleep hours you would normally follow in the new destination (this is only possible for short stays); taking melatonin, a human hormone available in tablet form (this is controversial) and taking sleeping pills (these result in their own form of grogginess).

Other ways to minimize jet lag are getting a good night's sleep before the trip; flying in the late afternoon and evening; anticipating the new time zone by trying to follow its eating and sleeping patterns while on the plane; not drinking alcohol or caffeine, but drinking plenty of water; immediately adopting the new time on arrival; keeping the room cool so you can sleep at night; making sure the morning is bright (if there's no sun turn on all the lights); exercising in the morning when you wake up and eating lightly for the first days after arrival.

SEE ALSO *Insomnia, Sleep disturbances*

JOINTS

A joint is an area in the body at which two bones articulate. The bones may be fixed and immobile, such as the connections between the bones of the skull. These joints, (which are also called synarthroses) occur where two bones are fused or fixed together before or shortly after birth. Joints may be slightly mobile, such as the junction of the bones making up the front of the pelvis. These joints (also called symphyses) have a layer of cartilage between them and are held together by strong fibrous ligaments. Joints may also be freely mobile, such as the bones of the limbs. These joints (also called diarthroses) are held together and moved by muscles, ligaments, and tendons.

The bony surfaces of movable joints are covered with smooth cartilage. A thin fluid called synovial fluid, which is produced by the synovial membrane which lines the joint capsule, lubricates the joints.

There are several different kinds of mobile joints. In a ball-and-socket joint, such as the hip and the shoulder, free movement occurs in all directions. The elbow and the knee are essentially hinge joints, allowing movement mainly in one plane only. A saddle joint, such as the base joint of the thumb, allows sliding movement in two directions. A plane (or gliding) joint, such as those found between the carpal bones of the wrist allows only slight sliding movements. Pivot joints allow rotation about a single axis and are found between the first two vertebrae.

A mobile joint may have more than one type of joint movement; the elbow, for example, includes a hinge joint and a pivot joint.

Diseases and disorders

Displacement of the bones at a joint is called dislocation, and is more common in some joints, such as the shoulder, than in others which are more stable, such as the elbow. In some cases the dislocation is present from birth; this is called a congenital dislocation. This is common at the hip joint ("clicky hip") and, if not treated, will prevent the joint from developing normally.

Inflammation in the joints is called arthritis. There are two common types of arthritis, with different causes. In osteoarthritis, long-term heavy use of a joint causes the cartilage to become rough

Gliding joint

Aided by synovial fluid, the bones in the joint slide across each other in a limited movement.

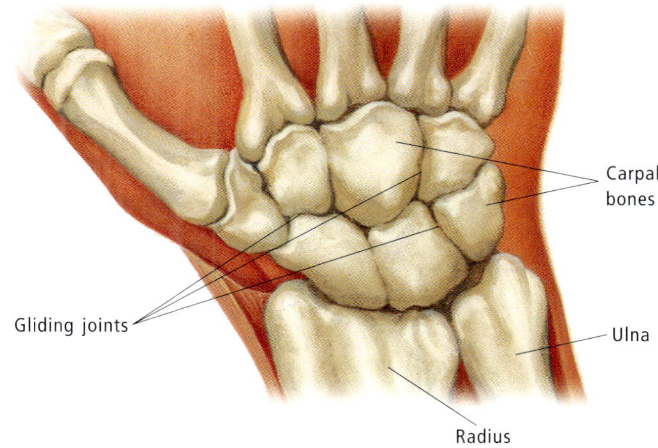

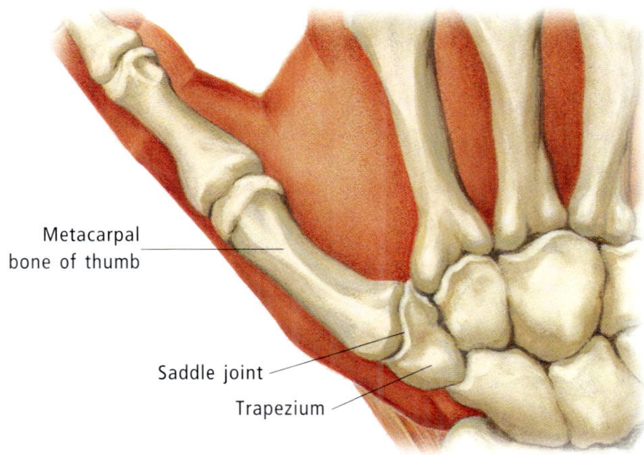

Saddle joint

A saddle joint allows almost as much movement as a ball-and-socket joint.

Ellipsoidal joint

This is a joint structure which allows movement in two directions, such as that which takes place at the wrist joint.

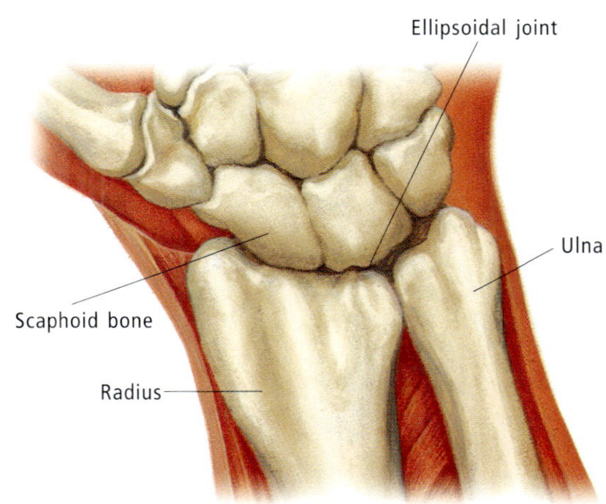

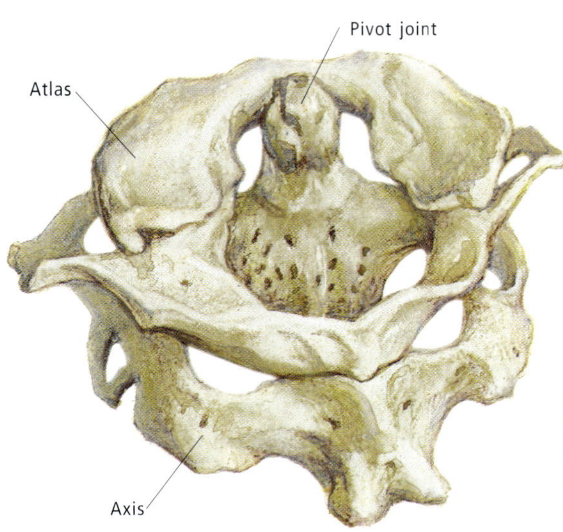

Pivot joint

The joint between the first and second cervical vertebrae rotates—this is known as a pivot joint.

Ball-and-socket joint

A bone with a cup-like socket rests on the lubricated ball-like end of another bone. This type of joint gives the greatest freedom of movement.

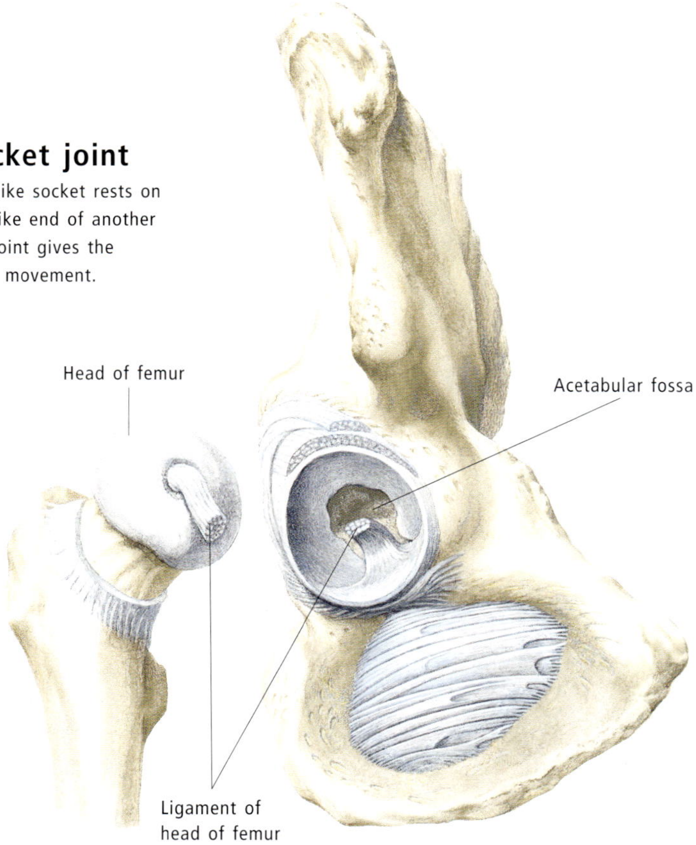

Hinge joint

As the name suggests, the joint can move in one plane only, such as the flexion (bending) and extension (straightening) of the elbow.

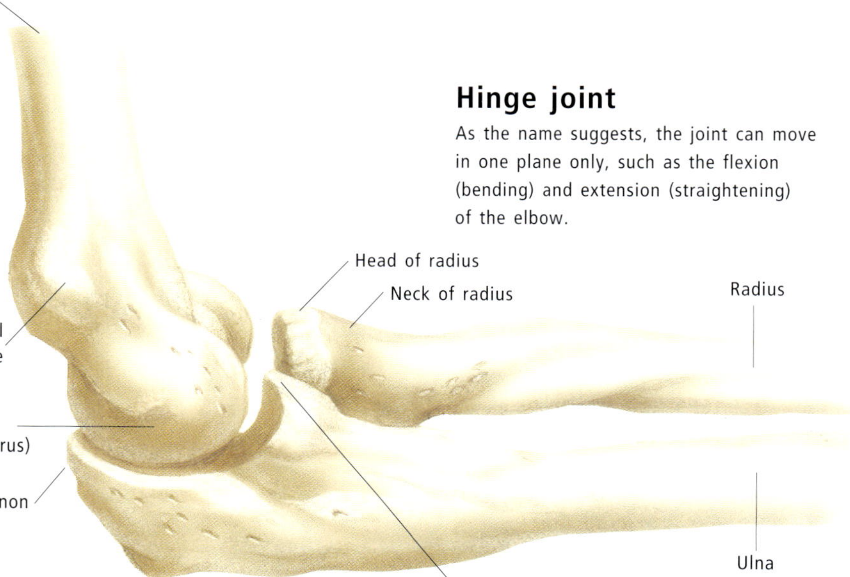

and frayed and gradually worn away. This is particularly common in the hip and knee joints, which get heavy use. It is usually seen in older people, but can also occur earlier in sportspeople such as football and netball players. The joint is painful to use and movement is limited. If damage is severe the joint can be replaced by an artificial hip or knee, which relieves the pain and restores movement.

The other type of joint inflammation is rheumatoid arthritis, an immune disorder which involves the synovial membrane and cartilage within the joint. It is particularly common in women, and usually affects the small joints in the wrists and fingers. The joints are very painful and gradually become deformed. Treatments include anti-inflammatory drugs, sometimes injected directly into the joint.

Besides developing rheumatoid arthritis and osteoarthritis, joints can also become infected, when an increase in synovial fluid in the joint makes it swell and become hot and painful. Joints also become swollen, hot and painful in gout, where crystals of uric acid precipitate within them. Excess fluid in a joint can be removed by aspiration, in which a needle is inserted into the joint cavity. This can relieve the pain. The fluid can be used to diagnose the infective agent or to confirm the presence of crystals.

Joints can also be investigated by arthroscopy, a technique in which a small tube is inserted into the joint to transmit images of the interior to a screen; arthroscopy can be used to guide surgical procedures within the joint, such as taking a biopsy of synovial membrane.

The disease ankylosing spondylitis particularly affects the joint between the spine and hip bone (sacroiliac joint) and the small joints of the spine. It can cause severe back pain and reduced movement. It is a long-term disease, most common in young men. Diagnosis is confirmed by x-rays and blood tests, and treatment includes anti-inflammatory medication and physical therapy.

Pain in the angle of the jaw may be due to excess tension in jaw muscles, often with tooth grinding, referred to as the temporomandibular joint syndrome. The pain is usually on one side and may spread to the ear, temples and back of the head. Treatment includes a dental visit to check tooth alignment, a soft diet and medication to relax muscles and relieve stress.

Many joints, such as the elbow and knee, have blind sacs, or bursae, which allow tendons or skin to move smoothly over the joint. Like the joint cavity itself, these sacs can become inflamed, swollen and painful. "Student's elbow" and "housemaid's knee" are common names for bursitis of the elbow and knee. The shoulder is also a frequent site for bursitis, leading to pain with certain movements (the painful arc).

The capsule of the shoulder joint can become inflamed and thickened, causing movements to gradually become more limited, a condition referred to as frozen shoulder. This requires pain relief; physical therapy can also be useful.

SEE ALSO *Ankylosing spondylitis, Arthritis, Bones, Bursitis, Gout, Housemaid's knee, Osteoarthritis, Rheumatoid arthritis, Skeletal system, Synovial fluid, Synovial membrane, Temporomandibular joint syndrome*

JUGULAR VEIN

A jugular vein is any one of the four large veins in the neck (two on either side) that drain venous blood from the brain, face and neck into larger veins that eventually drain into the heart. Sometimes the jugular veins are used to gain access for intravenous administration of fluids and drugs to a patient in hospital by insertion of an intravenous cannula. Jugular veins can be affected by thrombophlebitis (inflammation of the vein and clotting). If a jugular vein is severed, rapid loss of blood will occur and immediate action is required.

SEE ALSO *Thrombophlebitis, Veins*

KALA-AZAR

Kala-azar is a form of leishmaniasis, a protozoal infection spread by the bite of a bloodsucking sandfly found in tropical regions. The disease is transferred in the saliva of the fly after biting an infected animal. The symptoms include fever, weight loss, and enlargement of liver and spleen. It is usually fatal unless treated. Kala-azar is treated with amphotericin B (an antifungal medication) or pentamidine.

SEE ALSO *Leishmaniasis*

Kaposi's sarcoma

These cancerous growths on the skin first appear on the lower extremities and then spread up the body.

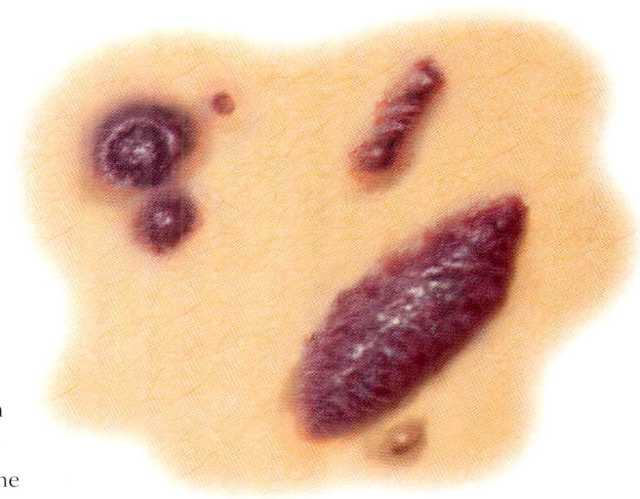

KAPOSI'S SARCOMA

A malignant skin tumor most often seen in late-stage AIDS, Kaposi's sarcoma is possibly caused by an unknown virus. It is the most common cancer seen in AIDS. Flat, reddish brown or purple patches appear first on the toes or feet and then slowly spread over the skin and in the mouth, developing into plaques or nodules. They may also occur in the digestive tract or lungs. Treatment is with radiation therapy and anti-cancer drugs.

SEE ALSO *AIDS*

KAWASAKI'S DISEASE

This disease, which is of unknown cause, usually affects children under five years. Typically there is fever; inflammation of the skin, producing a rash with prominent involvement of the palms and soles; and inflammation of mucous membranes, leading to conjunctivitis, a sore mouth and a red tongue. The child often develops enlarged lymph nodes (also known as lymph glands), especially in the neck. Less commonly, the inflammation affects the heart, damaging and weakening the walls of the coronary arteries or injuring the heart muscle itself.

Treatment with anti-inflammatory drugs such as aspirin helps to control the disease and the development of complications.

SEE ALSO *Inflammation*

Jugular vein

The jugular veins are responsible for transporting blood from the head and neck back to the heart. Severing a jugular vein will lead to rapid blood loss and death if the wound is not attended to immediately.

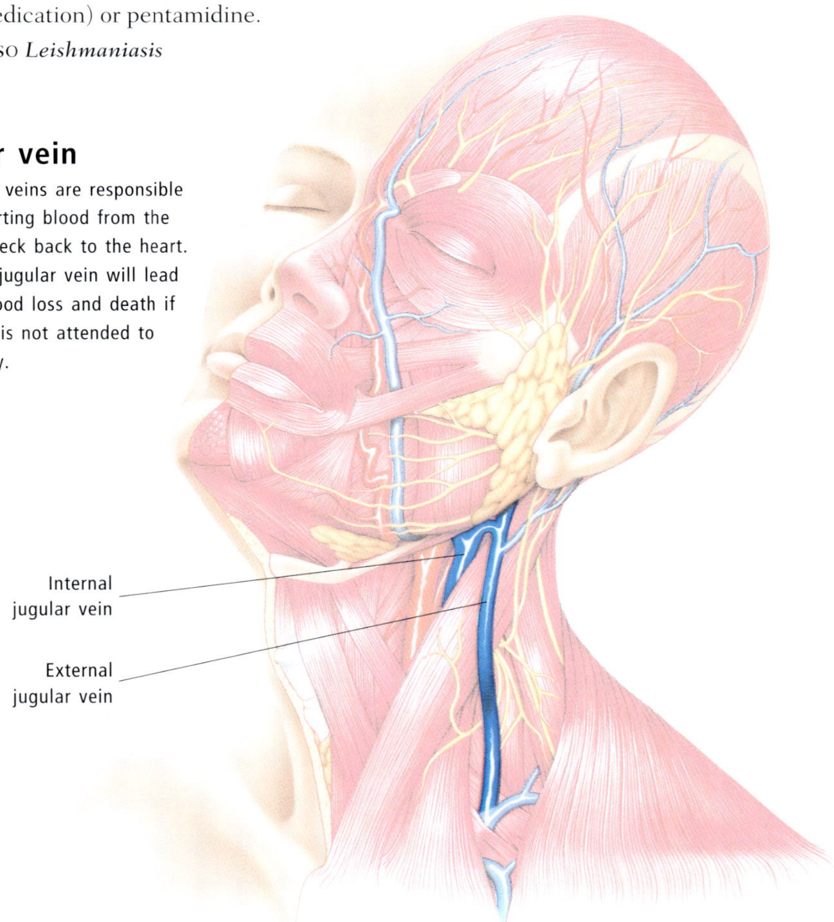

KELOID

Overproduction of collagen in scar tissue at the site of a wound creates a keloid, or keloid scar. People with darkly pigmented skin have a greater tendency than others to develop keloids. Firm, raised, hard and slightly pink, keloids usually arise following surgery or after a burn, but sometimes arise from a minor scratch. They may appear anywhere on the skin, but most commonly form on the breastbone, upper back and shoulder. They may itch, cause pain or be tender to the touch; although of cosmetic concern they are otherwise harmless. In some cases the keloid scar continues to grow and may develop claw-like projections into the surrounding skin.

Keloids can be treated by surgical excision, cryosurgery, or injection of corticosteroids into the keloid. Unfortunately they may recur.

SEE ALSO *Collagen, Scar, Skin*

Dendritic keratitis
This inflammation of the cornea is caused by the herpes simplex virus, which is also responsible for the formation of cold sores.

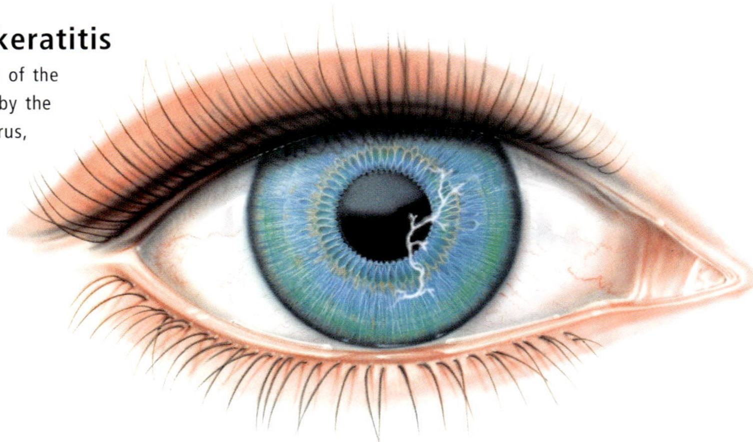

Diskiform keratitis
An opaque disk develops on the cornea. If this covers the pupil, light is restricted from entering the eyes and sight may be lost.

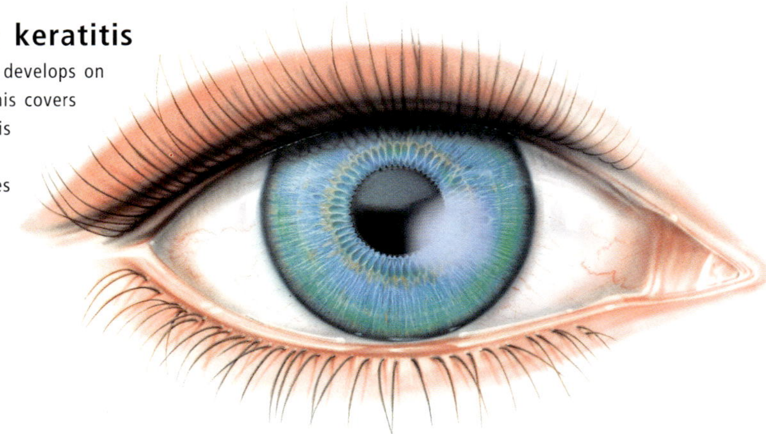

Punctate keratitis
Small lesions caused by foreign bodies on the surface of the cornea can result in painful inflammation.

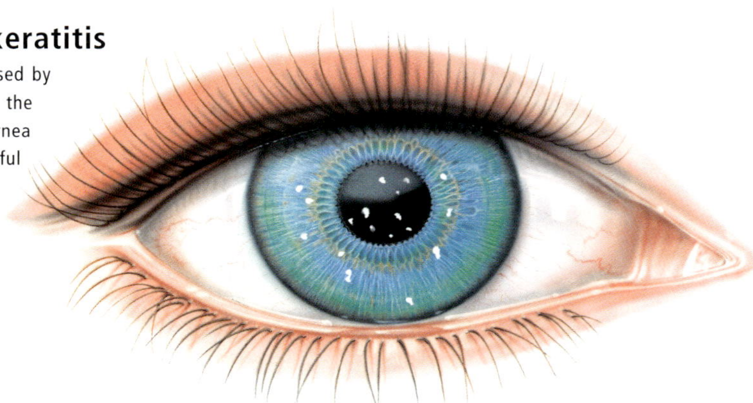

KERATIN

Keratin is a tough, highly fibrous, protein that is rich in sulfur. It is the main component of our hair, nails and tooth enamel, and forms part of our epidermis (the outermost layer of the skin).

Keratin is also found throughout the animal kingdom in feathers, beaks, horns and hooves.

In our skin, this protective substance helps prevent injury and microbial invasion and, because it is insoluble in water, provides waterproofing.

SEE ALSO *Epidermis, Skin*

KERATITIS

Inflammation of the corneal surface is known as keratitis. This may be caused by chemicals (acids or alkalis) splashed into the eye, ultraviolet radiation (arc welding, sun exposure or snow blindness), bacterial, viral or fungal infections (especially herpes simplex virus type 1), or sensitivity to cosmetics, air pollution, or allergens such as pollen. Symptoms vary, but pain and an inability to tolerate light are usual. Treatment depends on the original cause. A temporary eye patch is often needed. Antibiotic or antiviral eye drops and ointments may be indicated for infection. Non-prescription eye drops containing topical corticosteroids should not be used as they may worsen the condition or perforate the eyeball. With early treatment, most types of keratitis can be cured. Severe cases may cause corneal scarring, and corneal replacement may be necessary.

SEE ALSO *Cornea*

KERATOSIS

A keratosis is a thickened lesion of the outermost skin layers. There are several different forms. Small lumps on the upper arms, and less commonly the thighs, characterize a harmless condition known as keratosis pilaris. It tends to run in families and can be controlled but not cured.

Seborrheic keratoses—sometimes called "barnacles of ageing"—are harmless, slightly raised, dark spots that appear as the skin ages. Usually, they first appear after the age of 30. They may thicken and become wartlike in appearance but do not require treatment, although they can be cut or burned off. They only occasionally turn malignant.

Actinic or solar keratoses are precancerous lesions caused by sun exposure. Because they inevitably develop into skin cancer they should be removed.

SEE ALSO *Skin, Skin cancer*

KETOSIS

Ketosis is a condition in which there is a high concentration of a type of chemical called ketone bodies in the blood. Ketone bodies are produced during starvation, but ketosis is most often seen in the Western world in diabetics who have insufficient insulin to control their blood sugar concentration. This causes the blood to become dangerously acidic (ketoacidosis).

Common symptoms are thirst, frequent urination, nausea and weakness. The affected person is dehydrated, has rapid pulse and breathing, is confused or comatose, and has a fruity breath odor (indicating the presence of ketones). Ketoacidosis is a medical emergency requiring urgent treatment in hospital with intravenous insulin and fluid and electrolyte replacement. The condition has a 10 percent mortality rate.

SEE ALSO *Acidosis, Diabetes*

KIDNEY

The kidneys are a pair of bean-shaped, red-brown organs whose function is to dispose of the waste matter produced by the normal functioning of the body, and to keep the salts and water of the body in correct balance. They do this by filtering excess water and chemicals from the blood and excreting them as waste in the form of urine.

The kidneys are located at the back of the abdomen, one on each side of the spine, at the level of the lowest ribs. Because of the position of the liver, the right kidney in most people is located slightly lower than the left. Each kidney is about 4 inches (10 centimeters) long and 1 inch (2.5 centimeters) thick and weighs about 5 ounces (140 grams). Each has an outer layer (the cortex), an inner layer (the medulla), and a pelvis, a hollow inner structure that joins with the ureters, the tubes that conduct urine to the bladder.

At the center on one side of each kidney is an indentation known as the renal hilus, the exit point for the ureter and the location where nerves, blood and lymphatic vessels enter and exit. Enclosing each kidney is a protective membrane, the renal capsule. Surrounding each capsule is a cushion of fatty tissue and a layer of connective tissue which attaches the kidneys to the back wall of the abdomen. An adrenal gland sits on top of each kidney.

The renal medulla contains between 8 and 18 renal pyramids, triangular shaped as their name implies and with a striped appearance. The pyramids are positioned with their tips, the renal papillae, facing towards the renal hilus and their bases aligned with the edge of the renal cortex. The cortex continues in between each pyramid creating areas known as renal columns.

The functional units of the kidneys are microscopic structures called nephrons, of

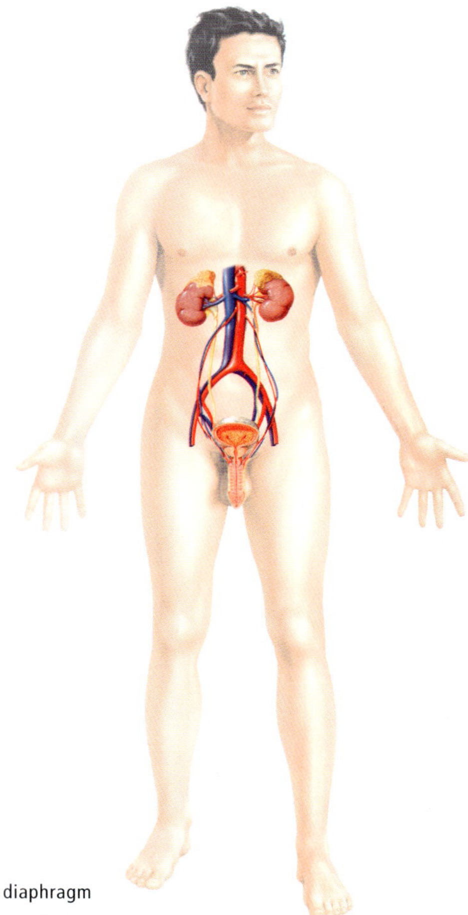

Kidney

The two kidneys filter the blood and send the waste products (as urine) to the bladder via the ureters. Kidney stones sometimes block one of the ureters, causing intense abdominal pain.

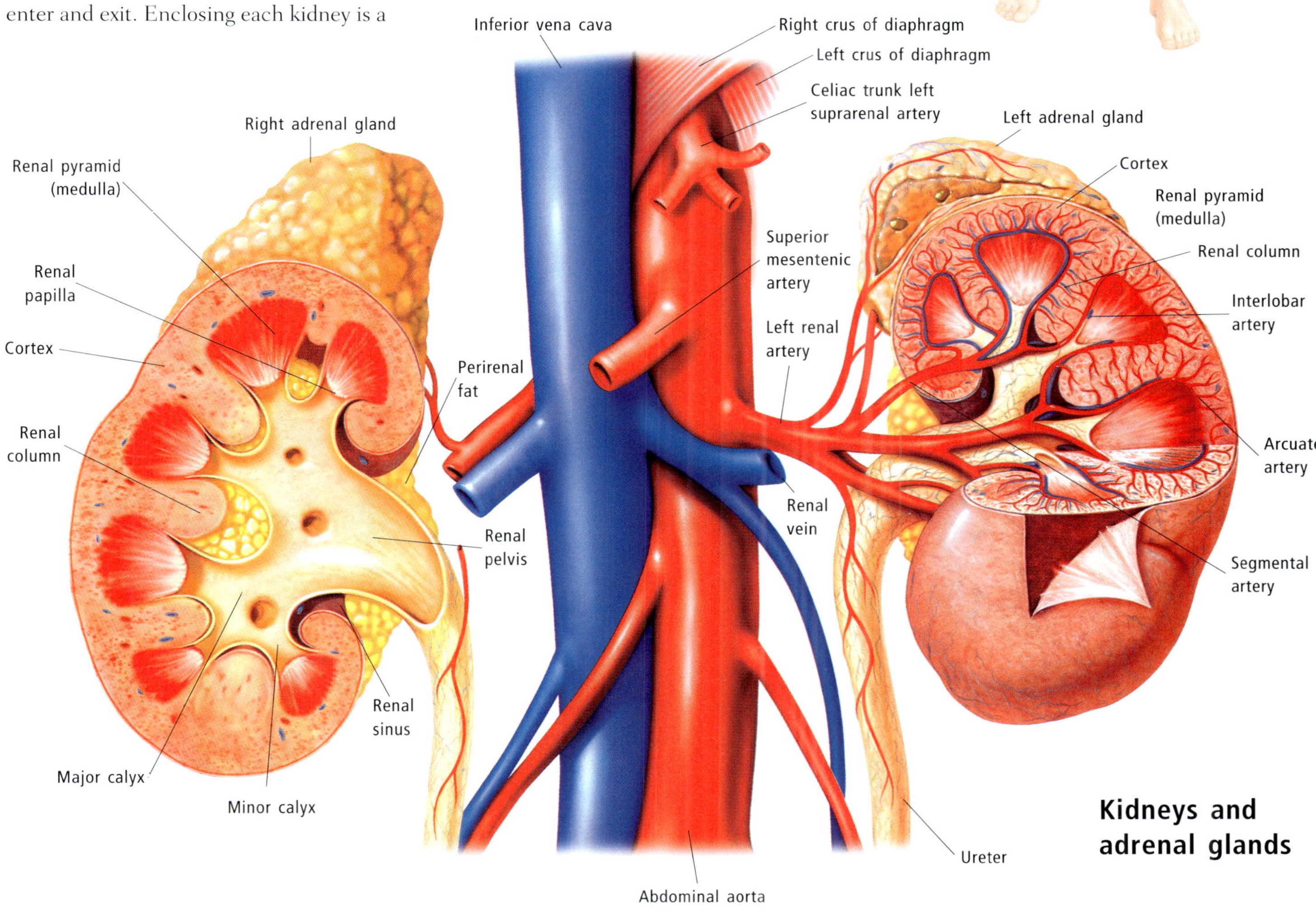

Kidneys and adrenal glands

which there are estimated to be about 1.2 million in each kidney. Each nephron has a renal corpuscle, which lies in the renal cortex, and a renal tubule which runs through a renal pyramid. The renal corpuscle is comprised of an extensive ball-shaped capillary network called the glomerulus surrounded by a double-walled cup of epithelial tissue—the glomerular or Bowman's capsule. Together, these structures filter the blood, producing a liquid (the filtrate) containing minerals, wastes and water.

The purified blood is returned to the body while the filtrate passes into the renal tubule, which comprises the proximal convoluted tubule, the descending limb of the loop of Henle, the ascending limb of the loop of Henle and the distal convoluted tubule. As the filtrate passes along the renal tubule, a network of tiny blood vessels called the peritubular capillaries reabsorbs useful substances from it and secretes additional wastes into it. About 99 percent of the filtrate is reabsorbed in this way and returned to the general circulation. The rest—1 percent, or about 1–1½ quarts or 1–1¼ liters a day—collects in the pelvis and is transported to the bladder as urine.

If the body needs to conserve water (or needs to dilute salt in the blood), the kidneys return more water to the capillaries. If the body has more water than it needs, more is excreted in the urine. In this way, the precise balance of salts and water in the body is maintained. Toxins, such as urea, are not reabsorbed but are excreted in the urine and in this way the body rids itself of the unwanted products of metabolism.

Kidney disease may be caused by many factors, such as injury, infection, cancer, or be part of a more generalized disease affecting other parts of the body. In some cases, there may be no obvious cause of kidney disease. Treatment depends on the cause and may involve the care of a nephrologist, a specialist in kidney diseases.

The symptoms of kidney disease vary and may be vague until the disease is well advanced. One common symptom is generalized edema (swelling of tissues such as ankle, abdomen and face), which is due to the accumulation of water in body tissues. The formation of either abnormally large quantities of urine (polyuria) or of diminished amounts of urine (oliguria) are also features of kidney disease. Blood may be found in the urine (hematuria), or there may be severe abdominal pain (colic).

If damage to the kidney is severe, toxic wastes build up and cause a range of ailments including hypertension, heart failure, anemia, disturbances of calcium metabolism, acidosis, nerve damage, bleeding, confusion, coma and death.

Several different types of diagnostic test will reveal the presence of kidney disease. Abnormal substances in the urine such as protein (proteinuria), sugar (glycosuria), blood (hematuria), or abnormal levels of white blood cells (which indicate infection) may be detected by examining a urine sample. A blood test may reveal excess levels of urea, creatinine, calcium and other biochemical abnormalities in someone with chronic renal failure.

Radiological examination may also be used to detect disease in the kidneys. For an intravenous pyelogram, dye is injected into the bloodstream. The kidneys concentrate and excrete the dye, which shows up the outlines of the kidney (and any stones or tumors) in an x-ray. For a retrograde pyelogram, the dye is injected via a tube that is passed into the urethra, bladder and ureters. Renal ultrasound, a less invasive test, shows the size and shape of the kidneys and may detect stones or obstructed ureters. Abdominal CAT scan, MRI examination, arteriogram and renal biopsy are other techniques used to diagnose kidney disease.

Diseases and disorders

Nephritis is a general term for any inflammation of the kidney. It may involve the glomeruli, the kidney's tiny filtration units (glomerulonephritis), the spaces within the kidney (interstitial nephritis), or the main tissue of the kidney and pelvis (pyelonephritis). Nephritis may be acute (sudden onset) or chronic (slow onset). Glomerulonephritis is inflammation of the glomeruli. Inflamed and scarred glomeruli are unable to filter the blood to make urine, which may lead to poor kidney function and kidney failure.

Pyelonephritis is an infection of the kidney and the renal pelvis. Acute pyelonephritis is usually the result of upstream spread of a bladder infection.

Chronic pyelonephritis is caused by destruction and scarring of the kidney tissue as a result of recurrent or untreated bacterial infection.

Stones may form in the kidneys (nephrolithiasis). They may be caused by an underlying metabolic disorder, or may form for no obvious reason. Stones may form in the tissue of the kidney and cause damage, or they may form in the kidney and pass into the ureter, causing severe colicky pain. Sometimes they may not cause pain at all, but instead silently obstruct the ureter, raising the pressure in the renal pelvis and producing distension of the pelvis (hydronephrosis) and progressive loss of kidney function.

Sometimes kidney stones may be passed spontaneously. If not, they need to be surgically removed. This may sometimes be done via cystoscopy. Lithotripsy is a new technique in which a machine called a lithotriptor sends sound waves into the body to break up stones which then pass out in the urine.

Cancer of the kidney may occur in the renal pelvis, or in the body of the kidney itself. Hypernephroma, or Grawitz's tumor, is the most common form of kidney cancer and occurs mainly in adults. Less common is nephroblastoma (also called Wilms' tumor) which usually occurs in children under the age of seven. Treatment of both malignant cancers is nephrectomy (surgical removal of the affected kidney) plus radiation treatment and anti-cancer drugs.

Polycystic kidney disease is an inherited condition in which cysts form in the kidney, enlarging the kidneys and reducing their function. It may appear soon after birth or, more commonly, in adulthood. Symptoms include blood in the urine (hematuria), hypertension (high blood pressure), kidney infection and pain in the lower back. The function of the kidneys gradually deteriorates until, after several years, chronic kidney failure occurs, and the patient requires dialysis or a kidney transplant.

Nephrosis, or nephrotic syndrome, is an abnormal kidney condition in which there is excess protein in the urine and edema (swelling of the body tissues). Other symptoms include fatigue, weakness and loss of appetite. The condition usually begins in children under the age of six.

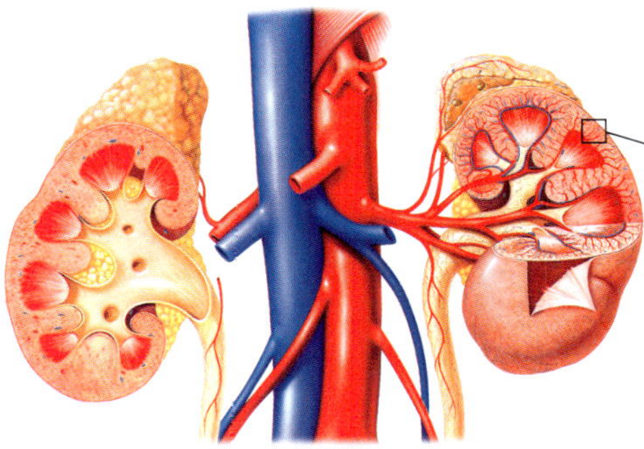

Disorders elsewhere in the body may affect the kidney. As well as producing excess sugar in the urine, diabetes mellitus can, over time, cause damage to the glomeruli or to the blood supply to the kidney. High blood pressure damages the small vessels of the glomeruli and can cause renal failure. Hormone disorders, such as Cushing's syndrome, hyperthyroidism and hyperparathyroidism, can affect the functioning of the kidneys.

Treatment

Early stage kidney failure can be controlled through the restriction in the diet of salt, fluid and protein. However, if the kidneys are unable to fulfil more than 10 percent of their normal function, this is considered end-stage kidney disease and dialysis is necessary. Dialysis is a method of removing toxic substances (impurities or wastes) from the blood when the kidneys cannot do so.

There are two types of dialysis: hemodialysis and peritoneal dialysis. Hemodialysis involves slowly filtering the blood through an artificial kidney machine called a dialyzer which removes specific soluble materials from the blood. The purified blood is then fed back into one of the patient's veins. Peritoneal dialysis uses the person's abdominal peritoneal membrane to act as the dialyzer. It involves filling the abdominal cavity via a catheter with a special solution that absorb toxins.

Usually, dialysis needs to be performed three times a week for periods of four to six hours. Dialysis may take place in a hospital, at a special dialysis center, or at the patient's home. In chronic renal failure, it will need to be performed for the rest of the person's life or until a kidney transplant is performed.

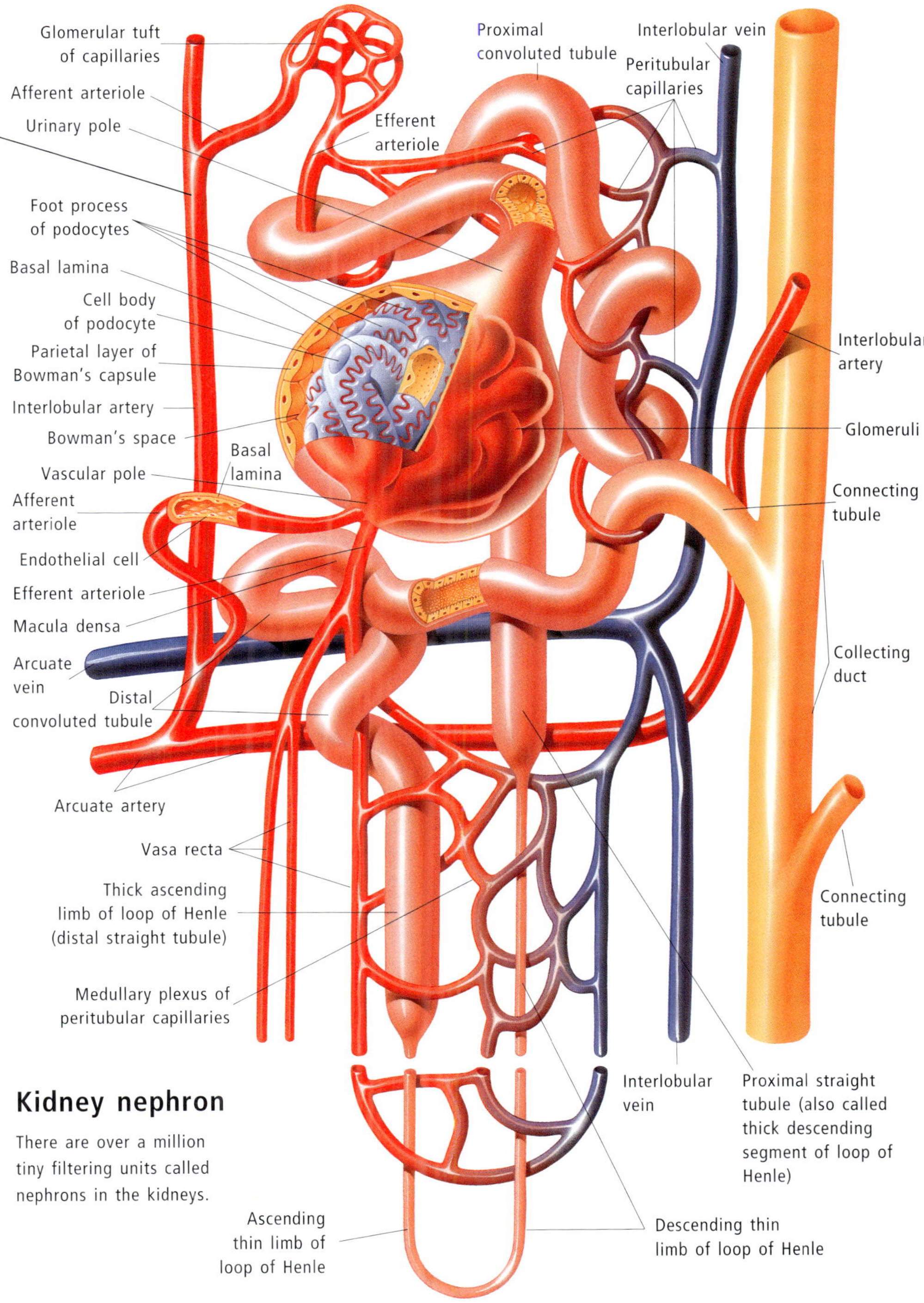

Kidney nephron

There are over a million tiny filtering units called nephrons in the kidneys.

Renal transplant is the surgical implantation of a healthy kidney into a patient with kidney disease or kidney failure. It allows a patient suffering from kidney disease to live a life without dialysis. Transplantation is usually preceded by a period of dialysis while a donor can be found. The donor may be living (usually a blood relative) or someone recently deceased. As with other transplants, the main problem with kidney transplantation is rejection of the new kidney by the recipient's immune system. Hence, the recipient needs life-long treatment with medications that suppress the immune response. Transplants from a blood-related living donor are slightly less likely to be rejected. Other problems include finding a donor, and the high expense.

SEE ALSO *Adrenal glands, Dialysis, Edema, Glomerulonephritis, Hemodialysis, Hypertension, Nephritis, Peritoneal dialysis, Polycystic kidney disease, Pyelonephritis, Pyelogram, Urinary systems*

K

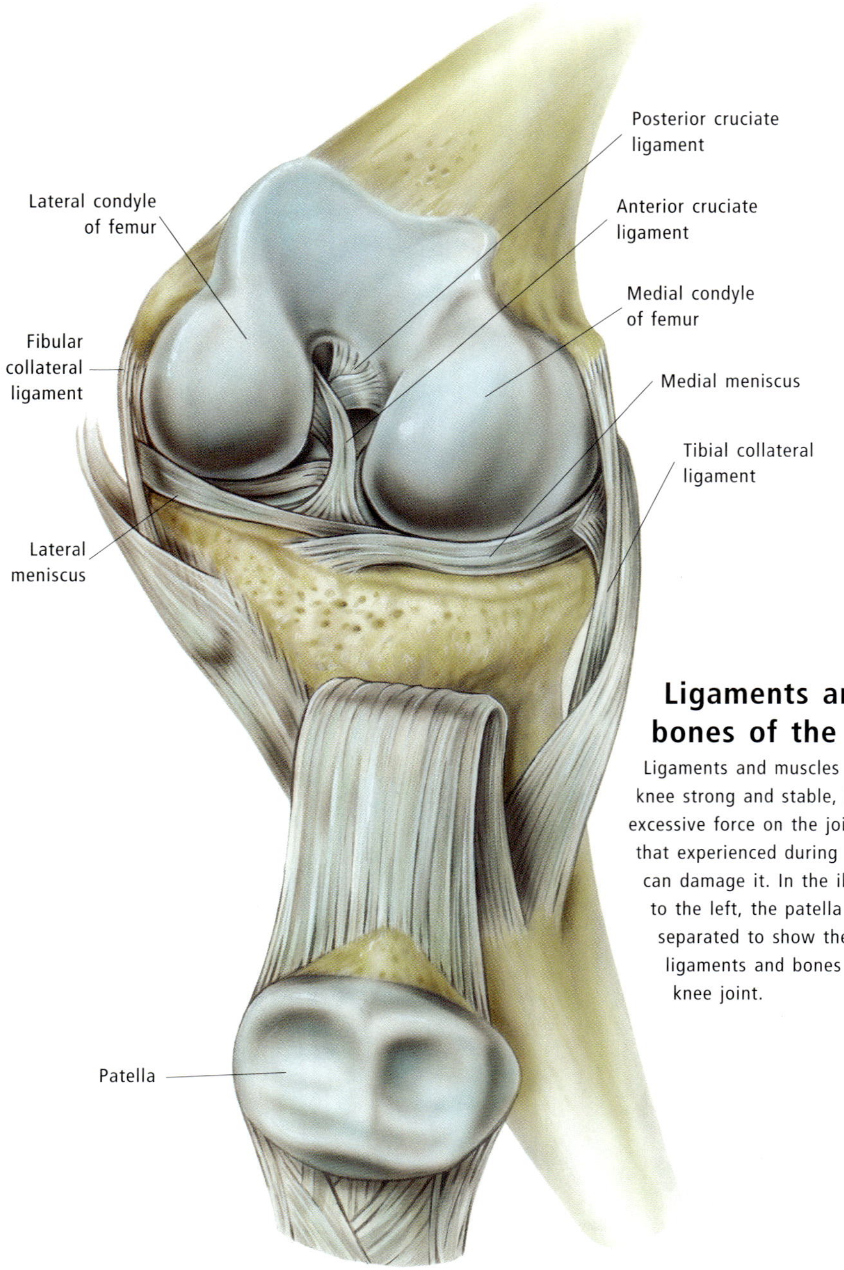

Ligaments and bones of the knee
Ligaments and muscles keep the knee strong and stable, but excessive force on the joint, like that experienced during sport, can damage it. In the illustration to the left, the patella has been separated to show the inner ligaments and bones of the knee joint.

KNEE

The knee joint, between the thigh and the lower leg, is one of the most important and complicated joints in the body. Because its adjacent surfaces do not fit closely together, it relies mainly on ligaments and muscles for stability. As a mobile but weight-bearing joint, the knee is under a great deal of strain and is vulnerable to injury when excessive force is put on it.

The knee is essentially a hinge type of joint with its main movements being flexion (bending) and extension (straightening), but some backward and forward gliding movements also occur in association with the hinge movements of flexion and extension. A small amount of rotation also occurs at the end of extension (to "lock" the knee) and at the beginning of flexion (to "unlock" the knee).

The knee joint is formed by three bones: the femur above, the patella (kneecap) in front and the tibia below. The lower end of the femur has a concave surface at the front, into which the back of the patella fits, and two rounded bulges at the bottom called condyles. The upper surface of the tibia has two rounded slightly concave areas (also

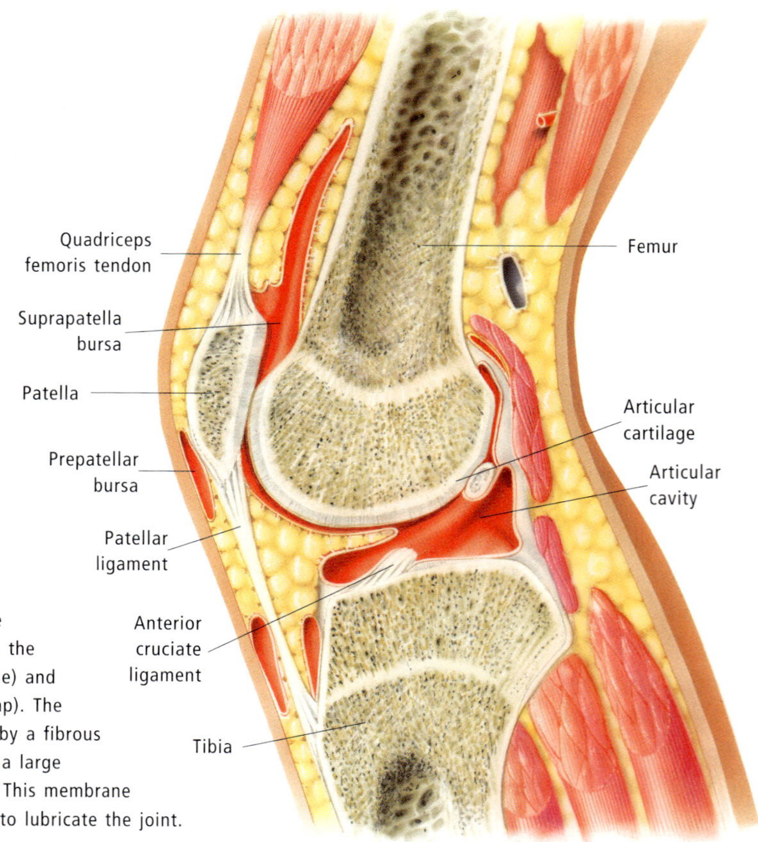

Knee joint
The knee is a complex hinge joint between the femur (upper leg bone), the tibia (the lower leg bone) and the patella (the knee cap). The three bones are united by a fibrous capsule which encloses a large membrane-filled cavity. This membrane produces synovial fluid to lubricate the joint.

KLINEFELTER'S SYNDROME

Klinefelter's syndrome is a genetic disease of males, caused by the presence of one or more extra X (female sex) chromosomes. An affected infant appears normal at birth, but at puberty the breasts may become enlarged and the testicles remain unusually small. The affected person remains infertile. Varying degrees of intellectual disability may also be present. There is no specific treatment for the disorder.

SEE ALSO *Chromosomal abnormalities, Chromosomes*

K

called condyles) separated by an intercondylar space. Each of the rounded condyles of the femur fits into the shallow sockets formed by the corresponding condyle of the tibia. The adjacent (contacting) surfaces are lined by cartilage.

The knee joint capsule

The three bones are united by a fibrous capsule (the knee joint capsule) which encloses a single, large joint cavity between the bones. The inside of the capsule is lined by a membrane, which produces an oily fluid called synovial fluid that acts to lubricate the joint surfaces to keep them friction-free. In some areas, pouches of synovial membrane extend beyond the confines of the joint capsule forming sacs known as bursae, and making the synovial membrane of the knee joint the most extensive of any joint in the body. Consequently, when the knee is traumatized, and the synovial membrane responds by producing more fluid to protect the joint, the swelling that occurs can be quite considerable.

Some bursae, which are not continuous with the synovial cavity of the knee, may become swollen due to friction on the overlying skin. These include one between the skin and the front of the kneecap, which becomes inflamed in a condition known as "housemaid's knee", and one between the skin and the upper surface (tuberosity) of the tibia, which becomes inflamed in "clergyman's knee".

The knee joint capsule is continued in front by the quadriceps tendon above, the kneecap and the patellar ligament below (attaching the kneecap to the tibia). The kneecap is incorporated into the joint, fitting into a concavity on the front of the femur. It glides up and down on the femur during contraction and relaxation of the quadriceps muscle and may be fractured in falls onto the front of the knee.

The knee joint cavity contains two circular fibrocartilaginous disks, or menisci, which are attached to the top of each tibial condyle. These are the "cartilages" often referred to in descriptions of injuries. Each disk is wedge-shaped in cross-section, with the thicker surface on the outside, so they act to deepen the sockets on top of the tibia and to allow a small amount of rotation to

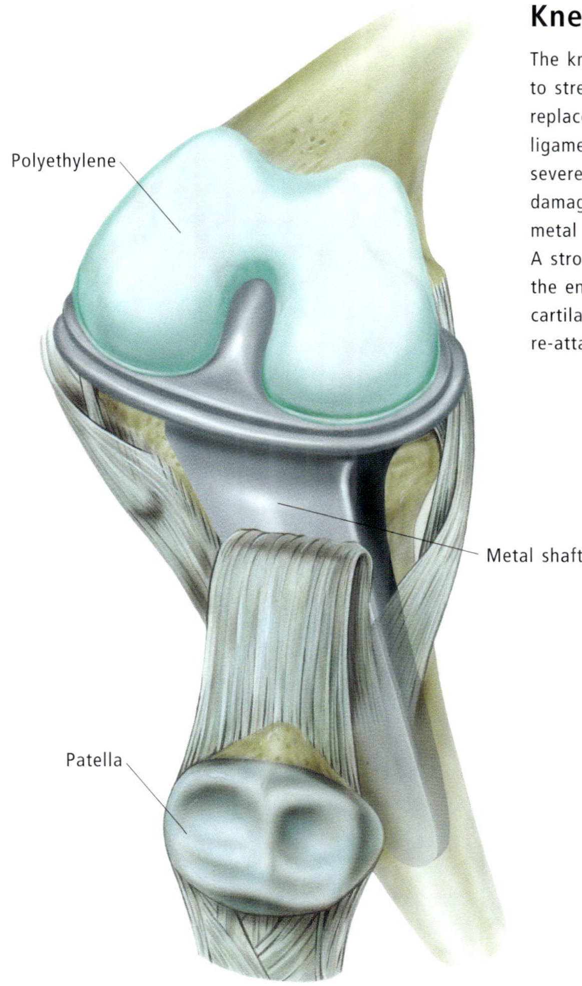

Knee replacement

The knee joint is particularly vulnerable to stress injuries, and reconstruction or replacement may be necessary if the ligaments have been badly torn or severed. In knee replacement the damaged joint is repaired by inserting metal shafts into the tibia and femur. A strong polyethylene coating covers the end of the shafts (in place of cartilage) and the knee ligaments are re-attached to hold the joint together.

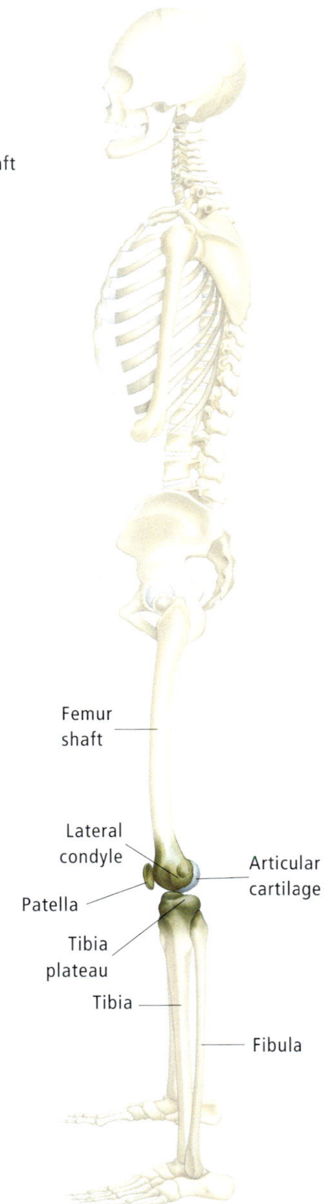

occur between the tibia and femur. The menisci may be torn if they get caught between the tibia and femur when the knee is forcibly rotated in the flexed (bent) or semiflexed position, as may occur when someone is tackled or tripped around the ankles or legs, and their thighs and body twist forward.

In osteoarthritis the cartilage that protects the bone surfaces from rubbing against each other degenerates and the joint may become so damaged and painful that it needs to be replaced with a prosthesis. A knee replacement may also be needed after damage from rheumatoid arthritis or injury. Although it will greatly reduce the pain and restore full mobility to the joint, a replacement joint is not as strong as a natural one. Extensive physical therapy will help rebuild muscle.

Ligaments

Because the sockets on the tibia are so shallow, the ligaments are important in strengthening the knee joint and limiting excessive or unwanted movements. The inner (medial) side is reinforced by the medial collateral ligament, which is a long flat band of fibers, about ½ inch (1 centimeter) wide and 4½ inches (10 centimeters) long, extending from the sides of the femoral condyle down onto the shaft of the tibia. As it passes the joint it is fused to the capsule and the medial meniscus. The medial ligament can be stretched and torn when the knee is struck forcefully from the outer (lateral) side. In serious injuries the medial meniscus, which is fused to the ligament, may also be damaged.

The outer (lateral) side is reinforced by the lateral collateral ligament, a narrow cord-like band about 1–1½ inches (2–3 centimeters) long, which extends from the lateral femoral condyle down to the head of the fibula. Damage to this ligament is much less common than to the medial ligament but can occur when the knee or leg is struck from the inner side.

Two important ligaments also exist internal to the joint capsule, in the space between the medial and lateral pairs of condyles. Because the two internal ligaments cross over each other in the form of an X they are known as the cruciate ligaments. The anterior cruciate ligament passes from the front of the tibia up and backwards to the back of the femur. The posterior cruciate ligament passes from the back of the tibia upwards and forwards to the front of the femur. The cruciate ligaments guide the tibia in its movement around the end of the femur and prevent excessive forward and backward gliding during flexion and extension of the knee. The anterior cruciate ligament may be damaged when the knee is hit from the front and overextended or in twisting injuries of the knee. The anterior cruciate ligament is only half as thick as the posterior cruciate ligament and so is more frequently damaged.

If the ligament is completely severed a "knee reconstruction" may be performed, in which parts of tendons surrounding the knee are used to replace the damaged ligament.

Muscles

The muscles that surround the knee joint are also important in maintaining its stability. The tendons of the hamstrings, which pass over the inner and outer sides of the joint, help to reinforce it, but the most important muscle is the quadriceps femoris muscle on the front of the thigh, whose tendon reinforces the front of the joint and ensures correct movement of the patella on the femur. Weakness in the inner side of the quadriceps muscle, which occurs when the knee has been inactive after previous injury, can cause the patella to dislocate to the outer side.

SEE ALSO *Bursitis, Hamstring muscles, Housemaid's knee, Joints, Knock-knee, Leg, Ligaments, Muscles, Synovial fluid, Synovial membrane*

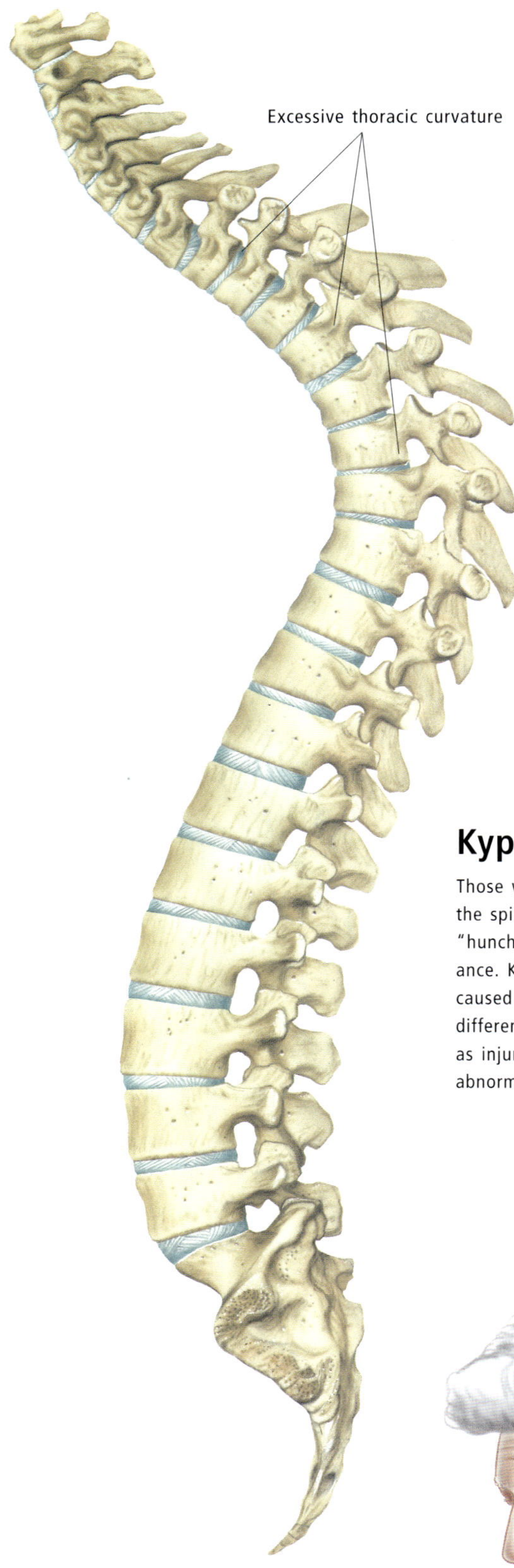

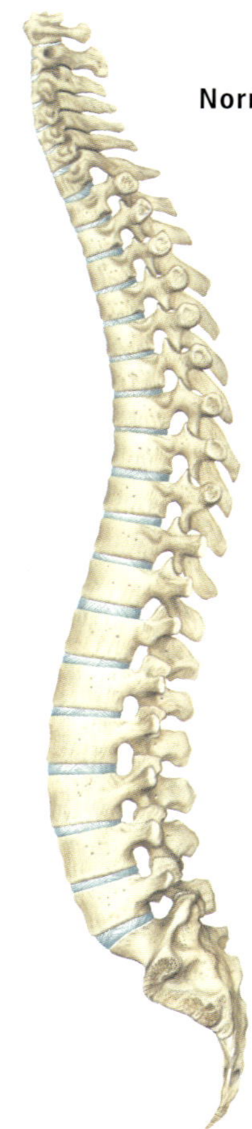

Normal spine

Kyphosis

Those with kyphosis of the spine have a "hunchbacked" appearance. Kyphosis can be caused by a number of different reasons, such as injury or a congenital abnormality.

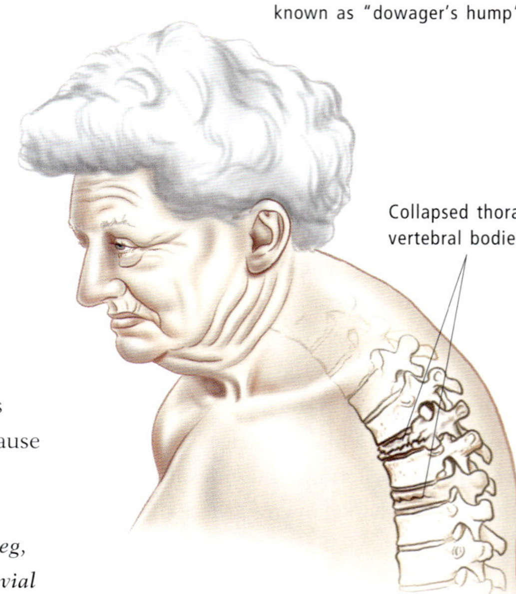

Dowager's hump

Kyphosis (curvature) of the spine in older women is often caused by osteoporosis. This is known as "dowager's hump".

KNOCK-KNEE

Knock-knee (genu valgum) is a condition in which there is a significant space between the ankles when the knees are touching in the normal stance position; it is commonly seen in childhood. This outward angulation of the lower legs causes the knees to knock together when walking.

Knock-knee often appears at about three years of age as a normal part of development and usually corrects itself by the time a child reaches puberty. The condition may also be symptomatic of disease, irregular bone growth or weak ligaments, however. It is rare that knock-knees cause difficulty walking, although they may lead to foot and back pain, and damage to the knees. Most problems are associated with low self-esteem due to the appearance of the legs.

While knock-knee is usually not treated, strengthening exercises or braces may be used to encourage correct bone alignment. Surgery may be considered in severe cases to prevent or correct excessive abnormal wear on the cartilage of the knee joint.

A procedure known as osteotomy may be performed, where a wedge of bone is taken from the inside of the upper leg bone just above the knee. The bone is then fixed with plates and screws.

SEE ALSO *Knee*

KWASHIORKOR

Kwashiorkor is a type of malnutrition affecting children fed diets high in starch and low in protein, particularly when weaned directly onto these foods. Common in rural areas of developing countries, the condition develops through starvation, or at times of rapid growth or recovery from illness when the body needs more protein.

Symptoms are a lack of energy, reddening of the hair and fluid retention causing a distended belly and a moon-shaped face. Diarrhea, anemia and skin rash are common, behavioral development is slowed and growth may be permanently retarded.

Kwashiorkor, in which the body accumulates fluid, is often combined with another form of low-protein malnutrition—marasmus—where the body breaks down its own tissues for energy and proteins. The condition is treated with protein supplements or a high-protein diet.

SEE ALSO *Malnutrition*

KYPHOSIS

Kyphosis is an abnormal curvature of the spine in an anterior or forward direction. It usually occurs in the upper part of the spine, causing a hunched back and shoulders, with back pain and stiffness. It may be a congenital condition, appearing in children or adolescents, but more commonly it develops later in life (in older women it is sometimes known as "dowager's hump").

Kyphosis is caused by compression fractures of the spine, due to osteoporosis, ankylosing spondylitis, infection, endocrine diseases, arthritis, Paget's disease, cancer or tuberculosis of the vertebrae. The curvature, along with any degenerative changes in the vertebrae, is easily seen in an x-ray of the spine.

Treatment aims to reverse the underlying cause; back pain and stiffness may be helped by exercises, a firm mattress for sleeping, and a back brace. Bed rest and sometimes traction are recommended for severe pain. Surgery can be used to correct the defect, but is not usually feasible if the condition is due to osteoporosis or other degenerative disease.

SEE ALSO *Lordosis, Scoliosis, Spine*

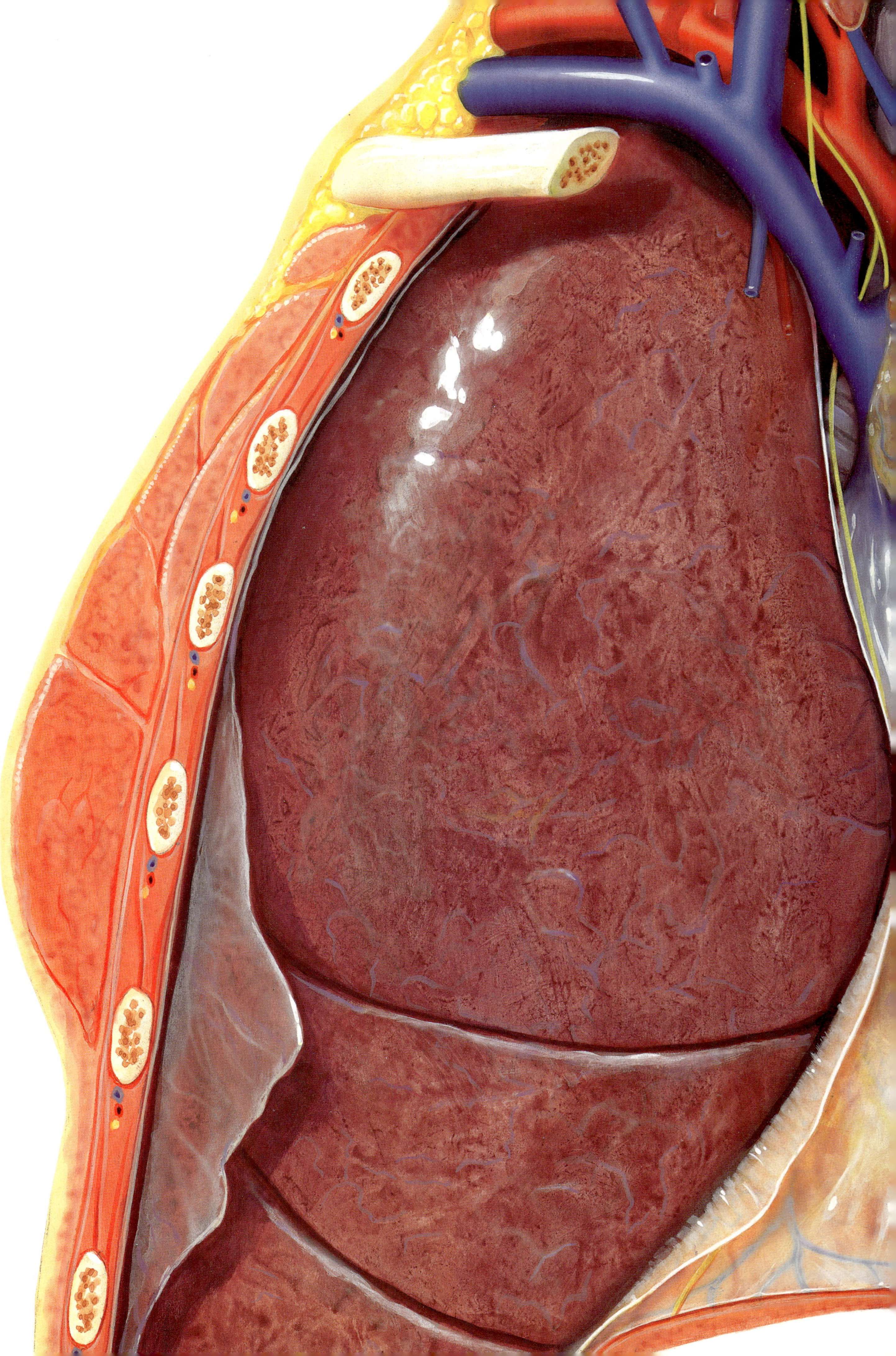

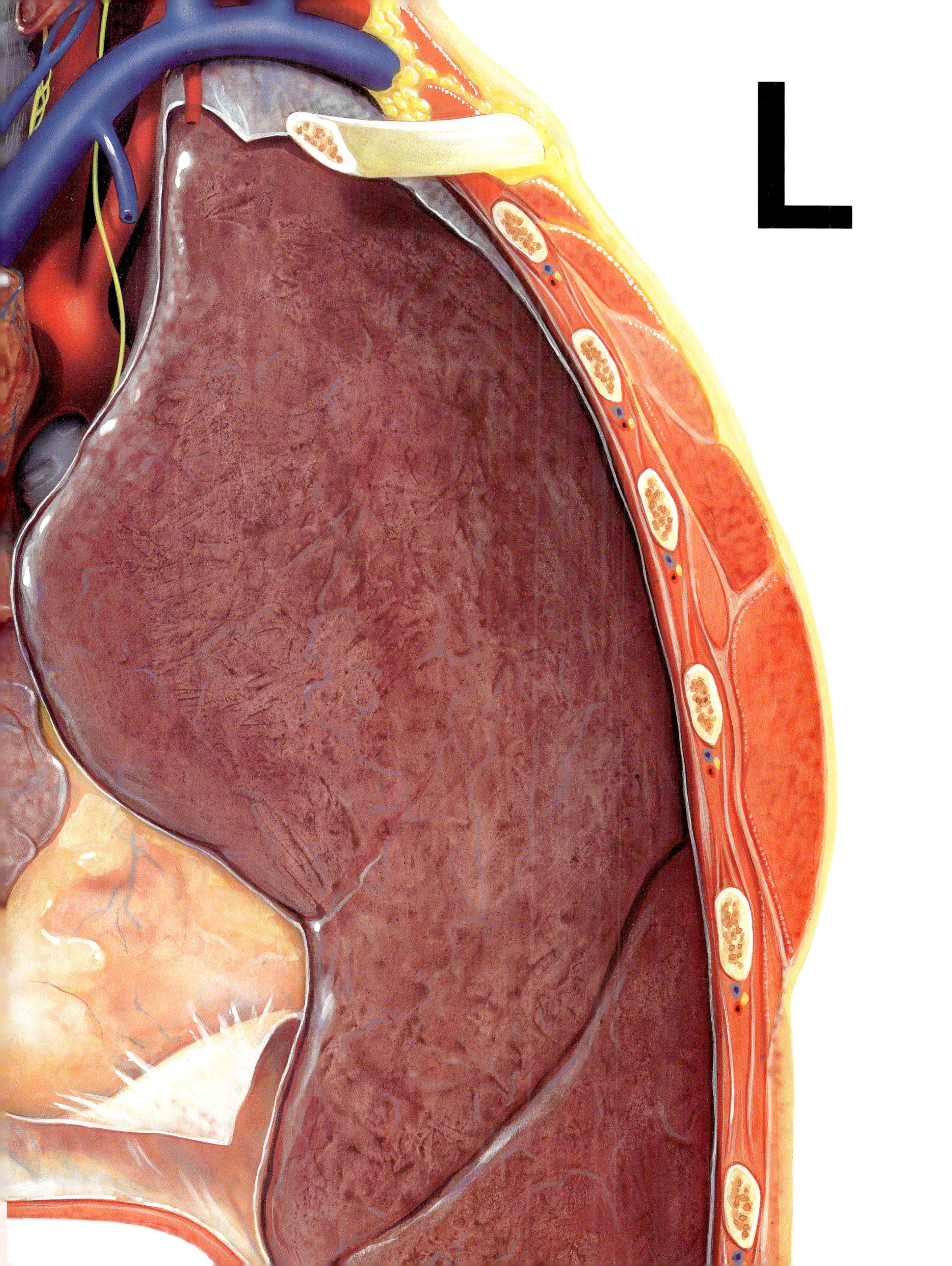
L

LABYRINTHITIS

Labyrinthitis is inflammation of the labyrinth, the network of fluid-filled semicircular canals in the inner ear that is responsible for monitoring the body's position and movement, and helping the brain to maintain equilibrium and balance. Labyrinthitis is usually caused by a virus, but may also be caused by bacteria spreading from a middle ear infection (otitis media), meningitis or following an ear operation.

Symptoms of labyrinthitis include vertigo (sensation that you or your surroundings are spinning around), dizziness, especially with head movement, loss of balance, nausea and vomiting, and sometimes temporary deafness and tinnitus (ringing in the ear).

Viral labyrinthitis is treated with anti-nausea (or anti-motion sickness) drugs and bed rest; recovery usually takes several weeks. Bacterial labyrinthitis is treated with antibiotics. Surgical drainage of the ear may be necessary if the condition is associated with serious otitis media ("glue ear").

SEE ALSO *Balance, Deafness, Ear, Semicircular canals, Tinnitus, Vertigo*

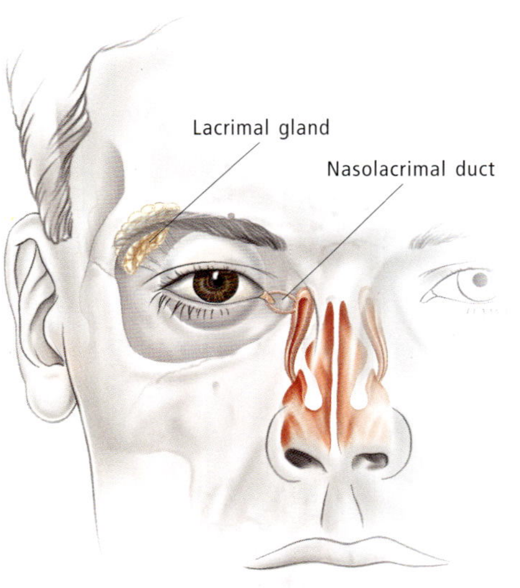

LACRIMAL GLANDS

The lacrimal glands, one above each eye, produce fluid (tears), which moves across the eye from the outer corner toward the nose, lubricating the eyeball. The tears eventually drain into the nose through the nasolacrimal duct and are swallowed or blown out with other nasal fluids. Tears keep the eye moist and clean and may be produced in response to irritation of the eye or emotion.

Sjögren's syndrome (also called dry eye syndrome) is a condition in which the lacrimal glands become inflamed and are unable to produce enough tears. It is an autoimmune disorder, which also affects the salivary glands. The treatment is to administer artificial eye drops frequently.

Dacryoadenitis is inflammation of the lacrimal gland or glands. It is most commonly seen in younger children, often due to bacterial infection. Antibiotic eye drops can help clear the condition.

SEE ALSO *Eye, Glands, Sjögren's syndrome*

LACTOSE INTOLERANCE

Lactase, the enzyme that helps break down lactose, the sugar in milk, is found in the brush border cells of the small intestine. If the enzyme is missing, the lactose cannot be digested and so produces increased gas, colic and sometimes violent, watery and acid diarrhea.

Lacrimal secretions

The lacrimal glands excrete a complex fluid (tears) to the eye surface. The fluid moves across the eye surface, lubricating the eyeball and keeping it moist.

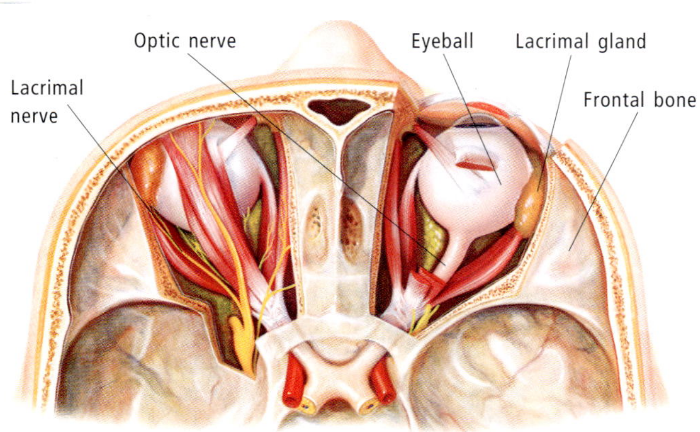

Lacrimal glands—orbital cavity

The lacrimal glands sit in the orbital cavity just above each eye. Their nerve supply comes from the lacrimal nerve.

There are several forms of lactose intolerance. Premature infants of under 30 weeks are often unable to cope even with breast milk because the lining of the intestine is immature. There is also a form of lactose intolerance that runs in families and can be extremely severe. It is usually associated with intractable vomiting from infancy.

Temporary damage to the lining of the small intestine often follows an episode of gastroenteritis in children, and results in temporary lactose intolerance. The lining heals in a week or so; until then, the child should avoid milk and dairy products.

The commonest form of lactose intolerance is genetic: up to 90 percent of Asians, 70 percent of African-Americans and up to 25 percent of Caucasians have lactase deficiency in varying degrees.

Diagnosis is made by the lactose tolerance test, when after ingesting lactose blood glucose does not rise, while the patient becomes flatulent and develops diarrhea.

Treatment means avoiding milk and milk products; soy milk is often used instead. In many instances of the genetic form, sufferers can tolerate up to a cup of milk each day.

SEE ALSO *Digestive system, Gastroenteritis, Intestines*

LANUGO

From the third month of pregnancy, the unborn child (fetus) develops hair follicles which initially produce very delicate hairs over much of the body, mainly on the forehead, cheeks, back and shoulders. These hairs are called lanugo (from the Latin *lana*, meaning wool). The lanugo is shed before birth except in the region of the eyebrows, eyelids and scalp, where it persists until it is replaced by stronger hairs a few months after birth. No more hair follicles are formed after birth.

The presence of a larger than usual amount of lanugo on a newborn infant may be an indication of prematurity.

SEE ALSO *Fetal development, Hair*

LAPAROSCOPY

Laparoscopy is a procedure for examining the abdomen internally, which is sometimes referred to as "keyhole" surgery.

Two rods inserted through small incisions in the abdominal wall below the navel, one for viewing and one with lighting, allow intricate operations and diagnostic surveillance to be undertaken. After the incision is made, carbon dioxide gas is pumped into the abdomen to elevate the abdominal wall. This makes it easier for the surgeon to see and manipulate organs in order to collect tissue samples. When the female reproductive organs are being examined a dye may be injected through the cervical canal so that the fallopian tubes are easier to see.

Through the same incision, surgical procedures can also be carried out. These include gallbladder removal, hernia repair, removal of ectopic pregnancies, sterilizing procedures and even removal of uterus, ovaries and fibroids. In vitro fertilization is also undertaken by this method.

The laparoscopy procedure is much less invasive than normal surgery and, depending on the severity of the medical problem involved, may be performed on an out-patient basis. The greater risk of perforation of organs than in conventional surgery is counterbalanced by far shorter convalescence.

SEE ALSO *Fibroids, Gallbladder, Hernia, Hysterectomy, In vitro fertilization, Sterilization*

LAPAROTOMY

Laparotomy is the exploration of the abdominal cavity by surgical means and is used in unexplained illness where a diagnosis remains obscure despite investigation with ultrasound and CAT scans. Laparotomy may also be used following trauma such as motor vehicle accidents, or puncture wounds from implements such as knives and bullets, to check for bowel perforation.

Laparotomy can detect conditions such as an inflamed appendix, various infections and cancer of the liver, ovary, colon and pancreas. It can be used to correct hernias in the abdominal wall and to remove diseased organs and abnormal tissue. During the procedure the surgeon may take samples of fluid in the abdominal cavity for laboratory examination. Where internal bleeding is suspected in ectopic pregnancies, laparatomy may also be carried out.

Laparotomy has now largely been superseded by laporoscopy.

LARYNGECTOMY

This operation involves the surgical removal of the voice box (larynx), and is most commonly performed when the larynx has been irretrievably damaged by injury or invaded by cancer. The patients most at risk of needing a laryngectomy include heavy smokers and drinkers.

Air travels past the vocal cords upon exhaling, causing them to vibrate, and it is this vibration that causes sounds. However, after a laryngectomy the passage of air between lungs and mouth cannot occur as the connection between the mouth and windpipe no longer exists.

The operation leaves an opening from the windpipe to the outside. This permanent opening, or stoma, allows air to pass directly into the trachea and on to the lungs. Sometimes a tracheostomy tube is inserted in the stoma temporarily to help it stay open during the healing process. It is important that the stoma does not become blocked as it is the only existing air passage.

In most cases the laryngectomy procedure does not affect the swallowing of food and liquid as the connection between mouth and esophagus remains.

After a laryngectomy, laryngeal speech is no longer possible. In the past, patients who underwent the procedure were taught to "speak" again by trapping air in the esophagus. Patients now often speak through the use of electronic devices that are held against the throat. Artificial vocal cords may also be surgically implanted.

SEE ALSO *Esophagus, Larynx*

LARYNGITIS

Laryngitis is usually an acute illness that is characterized by hoarseness due to an inflammation of the voice box (larynx). It is caused by a viral upper respiratory infection which normally lasts up to a week. During the acute phase talking should be limited. If a high temperature persists, a doctor should be consulted. Small children may develop croup (noisy difficult breathing) from swelling of the vocal cords and windpipe.

The most common form of laryngitis is an infectious condition caused by a virus. It may be associated with a bacterial infection or illnesses such as the common cold, influenza, bronchitis, pneumonia and upper respiratory infection.

Allergies, trauma, malignant tumors and laryngeal polyps are among other causes. Fever and upper respiratory infection may accompany the characteristic hoarseness or loss of voice.

Diphtheria-type laryngitis is a rarity nowadays but if undiagnosed, it can be fatal. Tubercular laryngitis is very painful, as is epiglottitis or bacterial inflammation of the epiglottis and larynx. The latter condition is a medical emergency; typically the patient isunable to swallow due to pain, and drooling and a high fever are other symptoms.

Chronic laryngitis can be caused by overuse of the voice, or the frequent inhalation of chemical fumes and other irritants. For all types of laryngitis, the initial treatment is rest. The use of a humidifier may offer some relief from the discomfort felt in the throat. Associated upper respiratory infection may be alleviated with the help of analgesic or decongestant medication. If the condition does not improve, medical advice should be sought.

SEE ALSO *Croup, Epiglottis, Larynx, Respiratory system, Throat, Trachea, Vocal cords*

LARYNGOSCOPY

Laryngoscopy is an examination of the interior of the larynx or voice box. Indirect laryngoscopy is the simplest type and involves holding a small mirror against the back of the palate, with the mirror angled down towards the larynx. This procedure may not be suitable for those with a strong gag reflex. Direct laryngoscopy is another option and, as the names suggests, is a way of looking directly at the larynx. It is usually performed under general anesthetic because of problems with the gag reflex, and involves the insertion of an instrument called a laryngoscope in the mouth. During this procedure a microscope can be used for a magnified view of the vocal cords and other parts of the larynx. Tissue biopsies can also be taken.

Other optical instruments can also be used to examine the larynx. A flexible nasopharyngoscope can be inserted through the nose to look at the vocal cords during normal speech. This may cause a little gagging and

Larynx

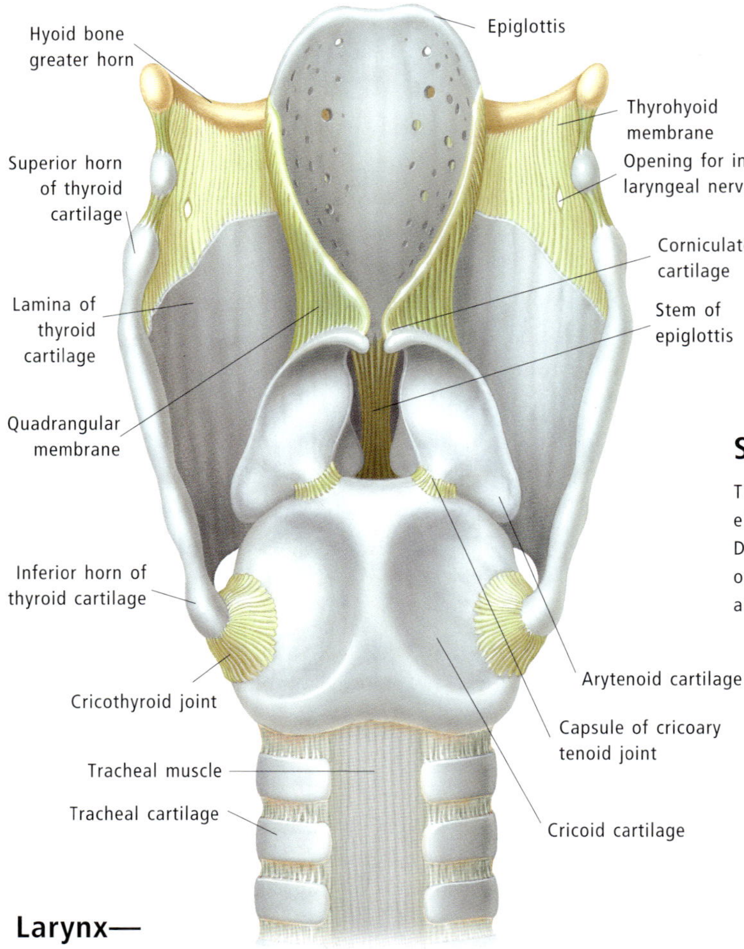

Larynx—posterior view

The larynx is a triangular box composed of nine cartilages that are joined by ligaments and controlled by skeletal muscles. It serves as a passageway for air between the pharynx and the trachea, and provides a framework for the vocal folds (vocal cords). Muscles in the larynx close the air passage while food is pushed into the esophagus.

Position of the larynx

This passageway lies in the middle of the neck below the hyoid bone and in front of the laryngopharynx.

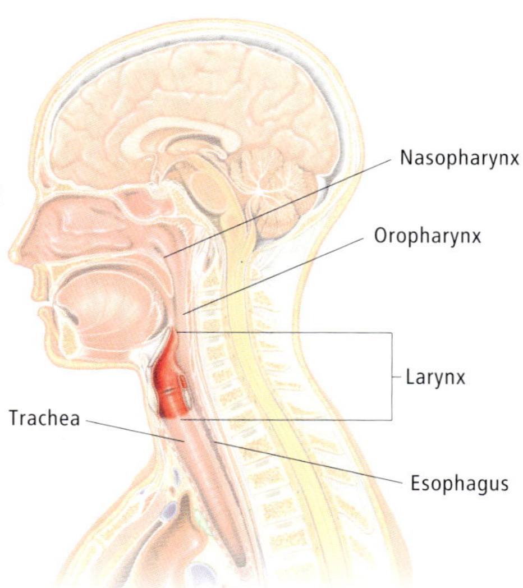

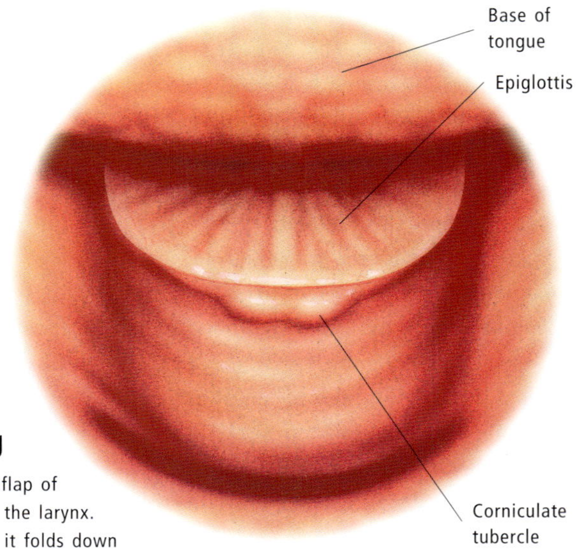

Swallowing

The epiglottis is a flap of elastic cartilage in the larynx. During swallowing it folds down over the glottis to prevent food and drink passing into the airway.

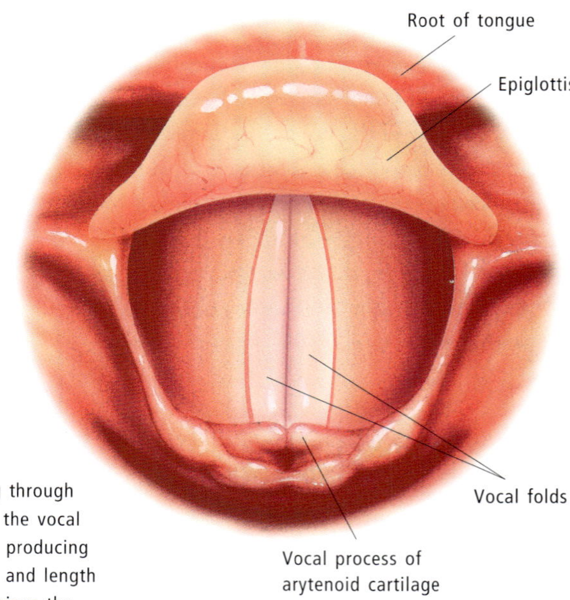

Speaking

Exhaled air flowing through the larynx vibrates the vocal folds (vocal cords), producing sound. The tension and length of the cords determines the pitch of the sound.

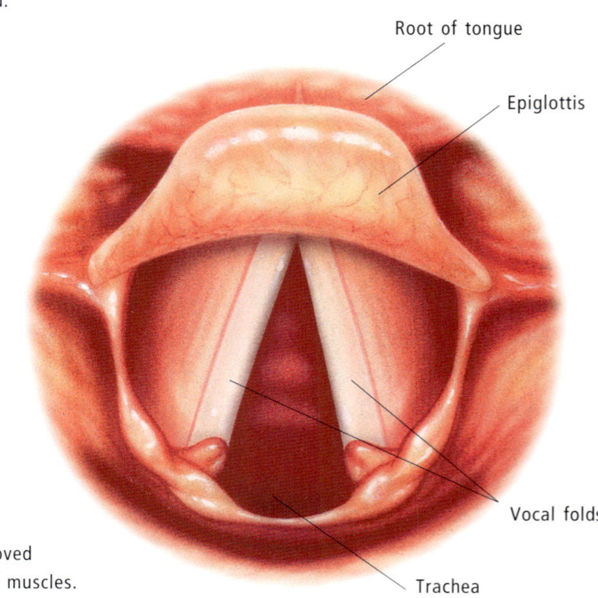

Breathing

In breathing, the vocal folds are moved apart by laryngeal muscles.

the image obtained is not as clear as when looking at the larynx directly. A rigid instrument called a 90 degree telescope may be placed at the back of the throat for a clear, magnified image of the vocal cords. A camera may be attached to these instruments to record information during the examination.

SEE ALSO *Larynx*

LARYNX

The larynx (or voice box) is the part of the throat that leads from the pharynx to the trachea (windpipe) and lungs. The larynx serves two main functions: to protect the airway to the lungs from inhalation of food and water; and to produce a source of air vibration for the voice. The larynx is composed of nine cartilages which provide strength for the airway and attachments for the various muscles, ligaments and membranes of the larynx.

The uppermost cartilage is the epiglottis, which lies immediately behind and below the tongue and can be bent downwards and backwards by muscles to close off the entrance to the larynx during swallowing. The largest cartilage of the larynx can be felt at the front of the throat and is called the thyroid cartilage, because the thyroid gland lies in front of its lower part. This cartilage consists of two slightly curved plates, which meet in the midline at a prominent ridge. Above the ridge lies a notch, called the thyroid notch.

In males, the thyroid cartilage grows rapidly after puberty, resulting in an increased prominence of the ridge and notch of the thyroid cartilage (the Adam's apple). This enlargement elongates the vocal ligament, which is attached to the back of the thyroid cartilage and vibrates to produce the sound of the voice. A longer vocal ligament vibrates with a lower frequency (pitch), thus making men's voices lower in pitch than those of women and children.

The other cartilages of the larynx include the cricoid, which lies below the thyroid cartilage and encircles the airway; the arytenoids, which are paired cartilages lying on top of the cricoid; and the tiny corniculate and cuneiform cartilages, which strengthen the folds of membrane around the laryngeal entrance.

The voice depends on several key elements for its production. The first is that the column of air above the larynx must be set vibrating. The larynx contains the vocal cords, which are the source of the sounds we produce. The vocal cords consist of a tent-shaped fold that extends upwards on each side from the cricoid cartilage to attach to the thyroid and arytenoid cartilages. The paired upper free edges of this membrane (vocal ligaments) are covered by mucous membranes to form paired vocal folds. When these folds are brought together across the larynx, they can be set vibrating by forcing exhaled air between them and thus producing sound waves.

In speech, sound is modified by the complex action of muscles in the throat, larynx and mouth. Vowels are usually produced by modifying the shape of the air column in the throat, mouth and nose, while consonants are produced by introducing noise into the pure tone of the vibrating column (for example, by touching the tongue to the back of the teeth or the roof of the mouth). The length and tension of the vocal ligaments can be adjusted to produce sounds of different pitch. Volume is determined by the force used when breathing air through the vocal cords.

Laryngitis is inflammation of the inner lining of the larynx, usually produced by viral infection. Cancer of the larynx is much more common in those who drink and smoke heavily. It may be treated, firstly, by surgery to remove both the actual tumor and any lymph nodes to which the cancer may have spread, and secondly, by irradiation of the throat.

SEE ALSO *Epiglottis, Laryngitis, Pharynx, Respiratory system, Trachea, Vocal cords*

LAXATIVES

A laxative is a drug that speeds the passage of stool or feces through the intestinal tract and causes a bowel movement. Laxatives are used to treat or prevent constipation (infrequent bowel movements), thereby relieving associated abdominal discomfort.

Some laxatives, such as senna and cascara, act by directly stimulating the nerves and muscle of the bowel. This starts a series of contractions known as peristalsis which encourage a bowel movement. Others, called hyperosmotics, work by attracting water into the bowel from surrounding tissues, increasing the bulk and volume of the stool, which speeds its passage through the bowel. These do not increase the number of bowel movements and are more for preventing constipation than treating it. They are recommended for people who need to avoid straining while defecating, such as those recovering from childbirth and certain types of abdominal surgery. Hyperosmotics include milk of magnesia, Epsom salts (magnesium sulfate) and Glauber's salts (sodium sulfate). Bulk laxatives such as bran, psyllium and vegetable fiber, and general roughage absorb water in the intestinal tract, swelling, and forming soft, bulky stool. They are the safest and most effective forms of laxatives and are available in powder form for mixing in a drink, or as wafers, granules or tablets containing bran. To be safe and effective, these must be taken with a least one glass of water, so are not suitable for people suffering from other conditions that demand a restricted fluid intake such as kidney failure.

Using natural measures, such as increasing the amount of fiber and fluid in the diet, is preferable to taking laxatives.

Laxatives should be a short-term treatment for constipation only, particularly harsh stimulant varieties which may be habit-forming and in large doses can cause side effects such as cramps, dehydration and malnutrition. If taken for too long, abnormalities of the bowel wall may occur. Laxatives should not be taken if constipation occurs with abdominal pain or fever as these symptoms may indicate a bowel obstruction.

SEE ALSO *Bowel, Constipation, Intestines*

LEAD POISONING

Lead is widely distributed in the earth's crust and is a "heavy metal", which accumulates in and is toxic to humans. Adults may be exposed to increased levels of lead through their work, and children through contamination of the home environment. Occupational exposure through inhalation of fumes or dusts occurs in mining of lead ore, smelting operations, soldering or oxy-cutting of lead alloys, lead-acid battery manufacture and the use of lead pigments. Children may be exposed to lead released from lead paints in pre-1950 houses during renovations. Paint fragments settle as a fine dust after sanding and may contaminate the house and soil for many years afterwards. Lead dust particles are so small that they can often pass through protective masks and filters.

Since the 1980s there has been a reduction in environmental lead exposure through the use of unleaded gasoline and the discontinuation of lead soldering of tin cans. Water is also safer, although the use of lead pipes or lead-lined galvanized tanks increases lead levels in the water supplies of some countries. Wine contains more lead than other beverages, probably due to the previous use of lead arsenate as an insecticide on vines.

The symptoms of lead poisoning generally occur late in the course of exposure. The earliest effects are on the nervous system and include impairment of memory and learning ability, and decreased attention and reaction time. Affected persons may exhibit fatigue, personality changes, pins and needles sensations, and muscle weakness. Later effects include abdominal pain, constipation or diarrhea, anemia and kidney failure.

Since these effects occur late, the current approach is preventive; for example by monitoring blood lead levels in workers at risk. During fetal life and the first 4 years of childhood, lead can affect the developing brain, resulting in intellectual impairment. It is important, therefore, for women to avoid occupational lead exposure during pregnancy and lactation. Environmental lead exposure should be minimized for young children. Infants aged 1–3 years who often put their hands in their mouth during play are particularly at risk. Some children may show no symptoms while others are obviously suffering from the effects of lead poisoning which can inhibit growth, impair hearing and damage the central nervous system, reproductive organs and kidneys. In severe cases of lead poisoning they may suffer from seizures or coma, and even die.

Lead gradually accumulates in the body with continued exposure and is carried in the blood on the surface of red blood cells. It inhibits several red blood cell enzymes, resulting in anemia. Over 90 percent of the total body lead is contained in the bones.

Treatment of lead poisoning is difficult, due to the large amount of lead that has accumulated by the time symptoms occur. Removal from the place of occupational exposure is essential. As lead leaves the body through the kidneys, this can be accelerated by the use of chemicals which bind to lead (chelation therapy). Patients must be well hydrated and their kidney function closely monitored during such treatment.

SEE ALSO *Poisoning*

LEARNING DISORDERS

A learning disorder affects a person's ability either to link the information within the brain or to interpret what they see and hear, resulting in the person learning differently from someone without a malfunction. This type of disorder can involve spoken and written language; memory and reasoning; coordination; social competence; or emotional maturation, including self-control or attention span.

Learning disorders affect around 15 percent of school children—more often boys than girls. The disorders may be caused by a problem in the nervous system that affects the receiving, communication and processing of information. Some children with learning disabilities also have a short attention span or are hyperactive. Children with reading problems are sometimes described as dyslexic though many professionals no longer use this term.

Some children may be developmentally delayed, intellectually disabled or suffering from a physical problem such as cerebral palsy. Others who have been, or are, chronically ill will be at risk of learning problems as they miss or drop behind in schoolwork.

Signs that a child has a learning disability are: difficulty following and understanding simple instructions; an inability to master reading, writing and/or mathematical skills (these children may have difficulty processing words as they hear them, or they may have difficulty with word-finding); a difficulty differentiating left from right; a lack of coordination which indicates difficulties with motor functions—using pens and scissors may pose a problem; an inability to understand the passage of time (these children have a visual memory problem which makes the understanding of sequential organization a difficulty); difficulty remembering what they have been told (these children may have suffered from recurrent ear infections which can mean their auditory memory is not intact and they find it difficult to work or sound out new words).

The longer a learning disability is left untreated, the worse it will become. Once it has been determined that a child has a learning disability and any underlying health problems have been treated, treatment by a remedial teacher or a psychiatrist trained in working with children suffering from learning disabilities may help the child to overcome the disability.

SEE ALSO *Attention deficit hyperactivity disorder, Autism, Dyslexia, Cerebral palsy, Memory, Speech*

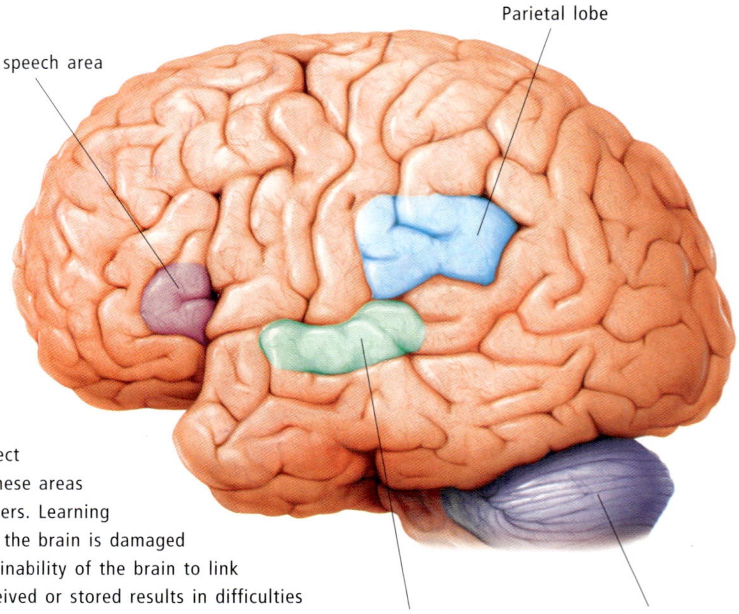

Learning disorders

The areas of the brain associated with learning activities include the Broca's area, parietal lobe, cerebellar cortex and auditory lobe. Problems in the nervous system that affect information processing by these areas can result in learning disorders. Learning difficulties may also arise if the brain is damaged by disease or accident. The inability of the brain to link or interpret information received or stored results in difficulties retaining or understanding language, calculations, or reason.

LEG

In anatomical terms, the leg refers only to the area between the knee and the ankle, while the term lower leg includes the thigh, leg and foot. However, in general usage "leg" refers to the whole limb, except for the foot. The leg is designed on a similar structural plan to the arm, but in humans is adapted to bipedal locomotion, that is, walking upright on two legs. The bones are long to increase the stride, the joints are large and bound by strong ligaments, and the muscles controlling locomotion are powerful.

Bones and joints

The two hip bones (the pelvic girdle) connect the lower limb to the vertebral column and join in front at the pubic symphysis. Together with the sacrum, they are known as the bony pelvis. Body weight is transferred from the vertebral column, through the relatively immobile sacroiliac joints to the hip bones, and from the socket of each hip bone to the femur.

The femur is the longest bone in the body. It has an almost spherical head and a long neck (a common site of fracture in the elderly), at the end of which are two enlargements (trochanters) for muscle attachment. The shaft angles inward, so that the knees come to lie together in the midline below the trunk. This arrangement reduces lateral body sway, and hence reduces energy expenditure in walking. The two femoral condyles at the lower end take part in the knee joint. The femur articulates with the kneecap (patella), a bone within the tendon of the quadriceps muscle. It also articulates with, and transfers weight to, the tibia.

The tibia is the second longest bone in the body. The tibia and fibula comprise the bones of the lower part of the leg. The tibia is the bone most commonly fractured, often breaking though the skin (compound fracture) as it is just below the skin (subcutaneous) through much of its length. The fibula is thin, and bears little weight. It serves as a structure for muscle attachment, and stabilizes the outside of the ankle joint.

The tibia and fibula articulate with the talus bone at the ankle joint. It is a mortice-like joint, with the tibia and fibula projecting down on either side of the talus to prevent sideways movement. The bones of the foot are the tarsals (7, including the talus

Bones of the leg

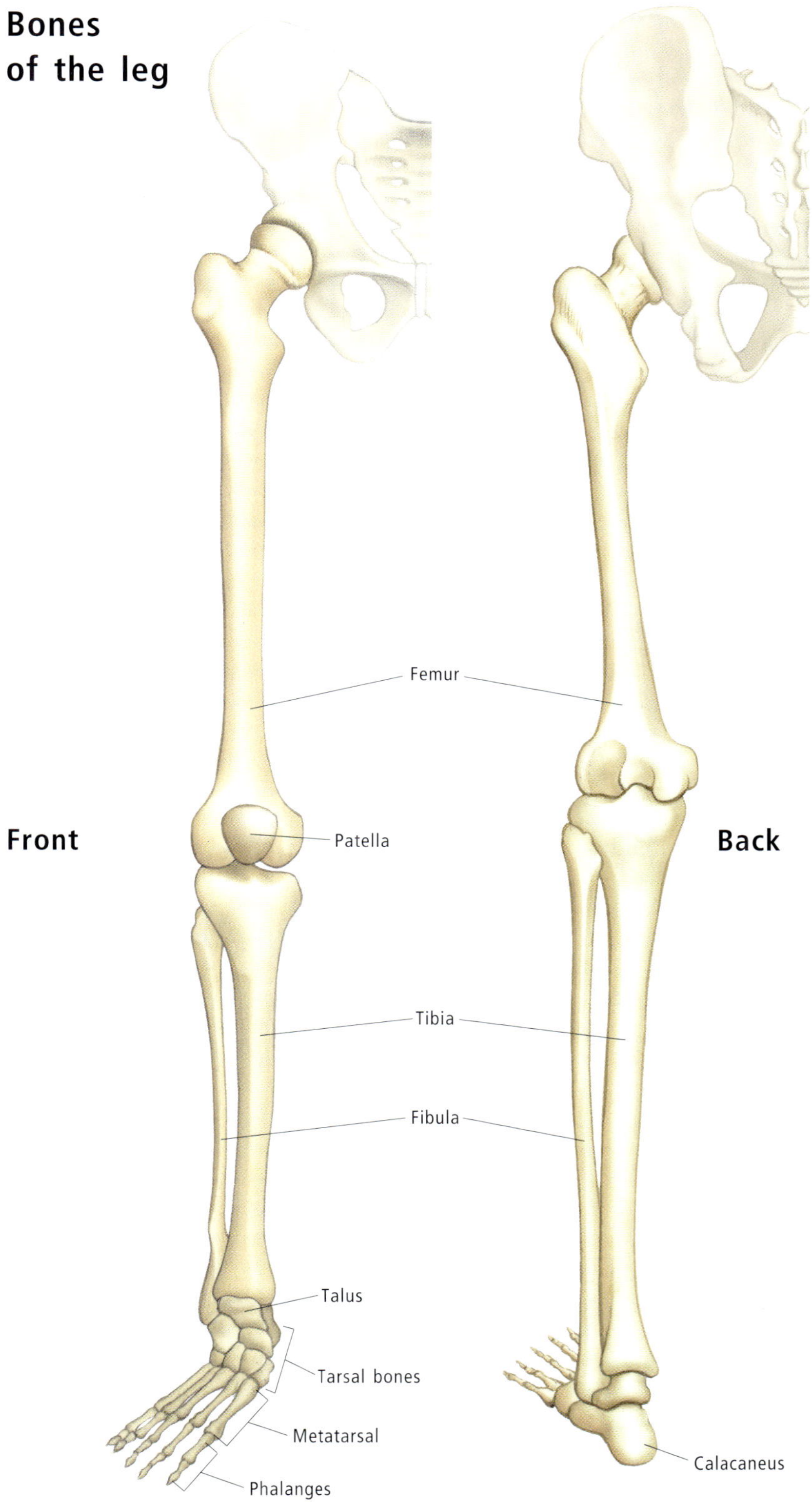

and the calacaneus), metatarsals (5) and phalanges (14 of these constitute the toes).

In bow legs, the lower part of the leg angles outward towards the knee. It may occur as a consequence of injury (such as a fracture) or disease (such as rickets, osteomalacia, Paget's disease, or osteomyelitis affecting growth plates in children).

Muscles

Powerful muscles surround and stabilize the hip region. The gluteal region is situated posteriorly and the characteristic shape of the buttocks in humans is a result of the gluteus maximus muscle.

This is the largest muscle in the body and powerfully extends the thigh when

Surface muscles of the leg

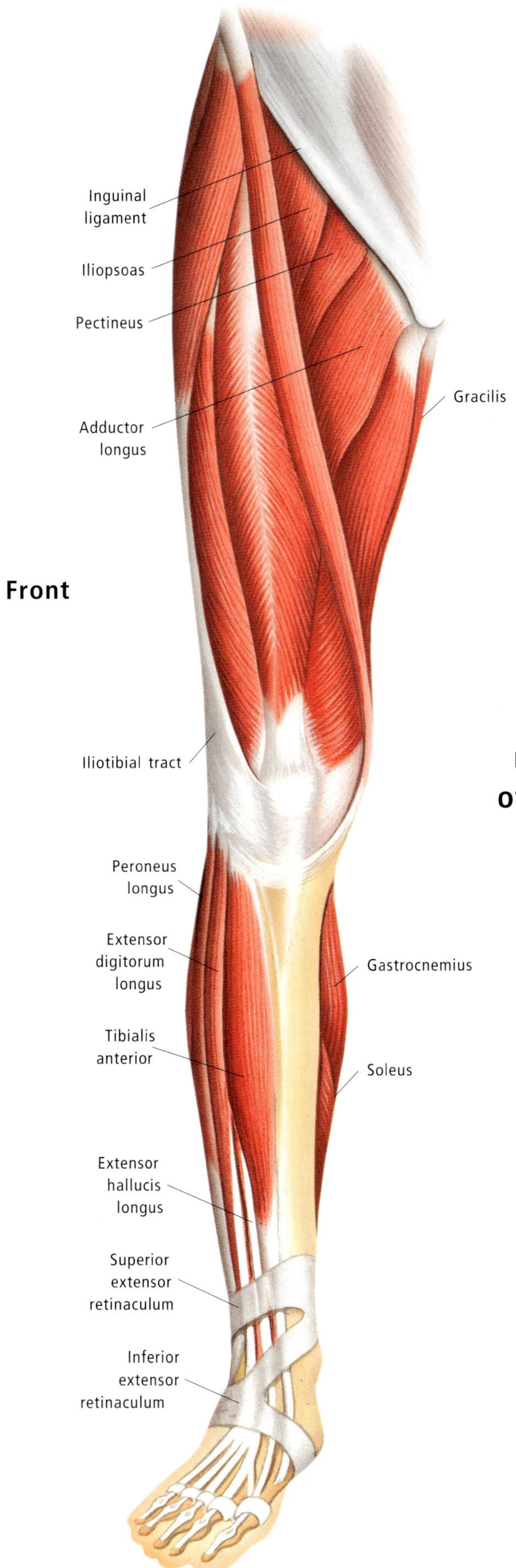

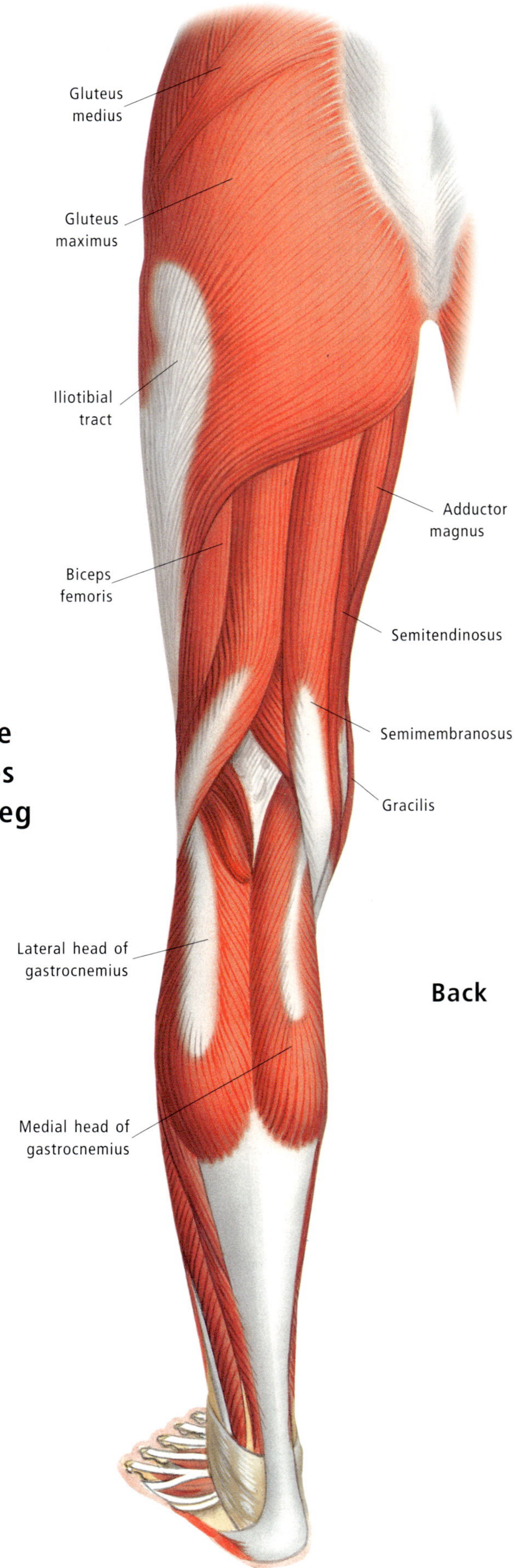

Deep muscles of the leg

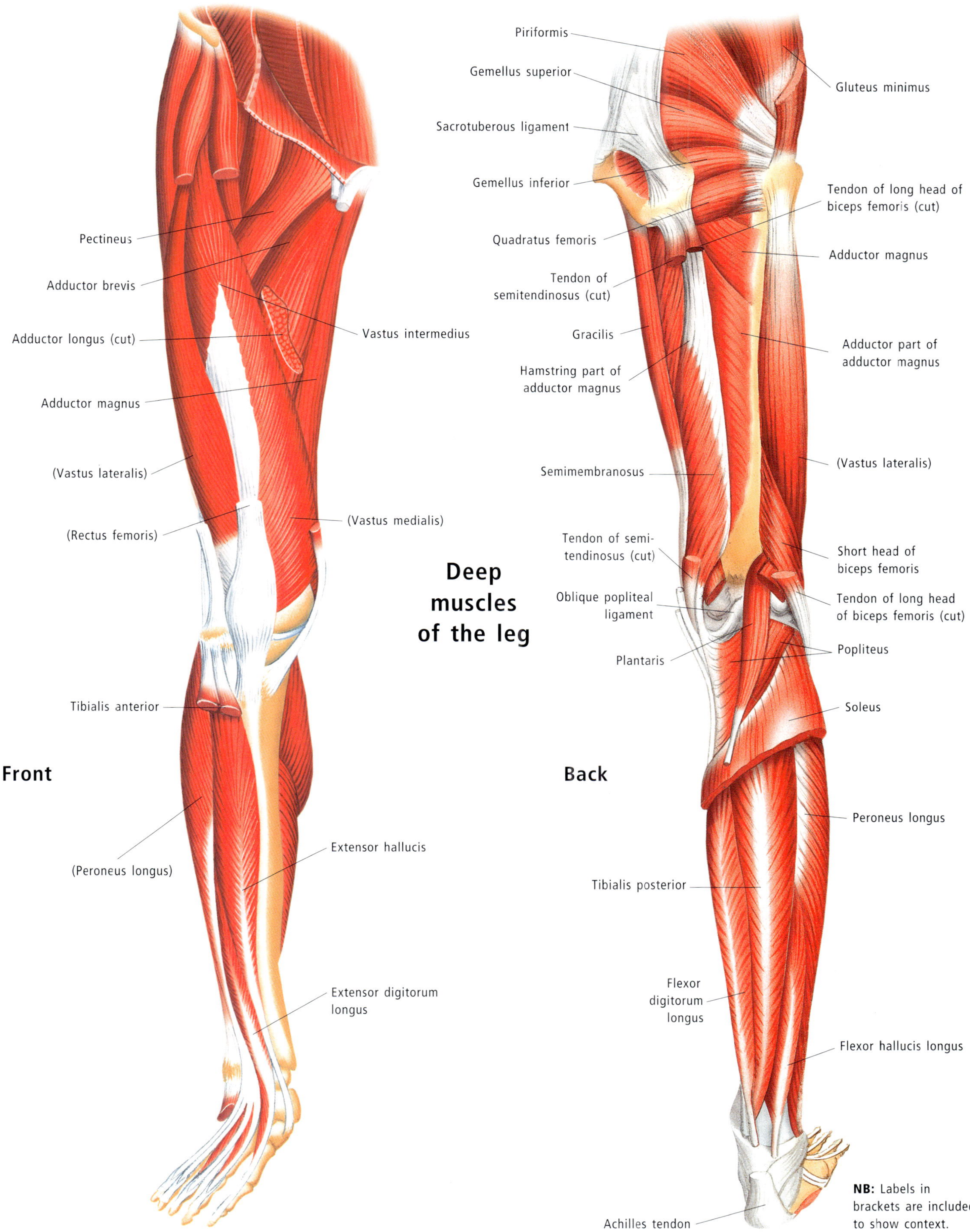

NB: Labels in brackets are included to show context.

L

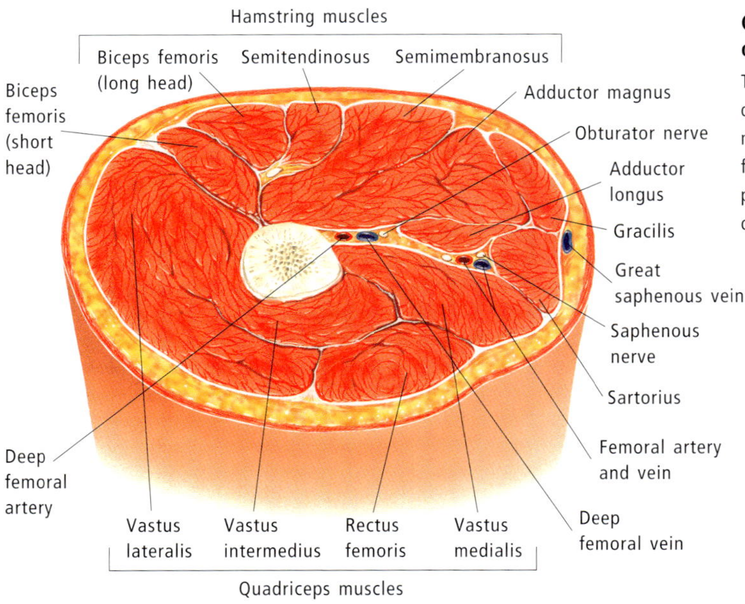

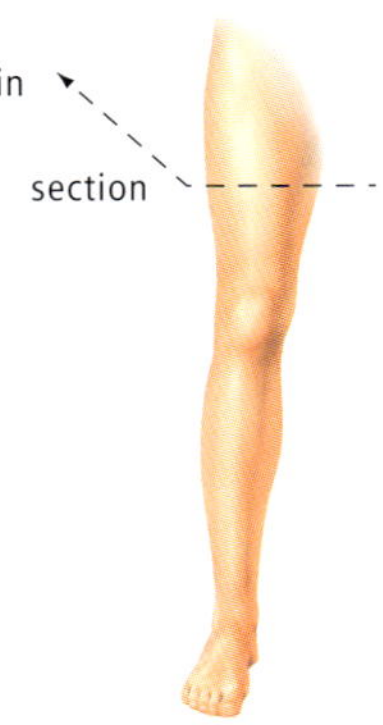

Cross-section of the thigh

The thigh contains the quadriceps and hamstring muscles as well as the femoral artery, the principal supplier of blood to the leg.

running or climbing. Gluteus medius and minimus muscles are laterally placed and are important in keeping the pelvis level, and swinging the opposite side forward, during walking.

The thigh has two distinct muscle compartments, separated by connective tissue (deep fascia). The quadriceps (Latin for "four heads") muscle lies in the anterior (front) compartment and extends the knee joint. The hamstring muscles lie in the posterior compartment (at the back). They extend the hip joint and flex the knee. The posterior compartment also contains the adductor muscles, which pull the leg toward the midline. They are important in counterbalancing the action of the gluteus medius and minimus muscles (adductors) when walking.

The lower part of the leg is divided into three compartments by deep fascia. The anterior (front) compartment contains muscles that move the foot upwards (dorsiflex the ankle), an action that is important in allowing the toes to clear the ground when swinging the leg forward in walking. The lateral compartment (on the outside of the lower leg) contains only two muscles, that turn the sole of the foot outwards (eversion). The calf region (posterior compartment) contains the greatest number of muscles, and is divided into two groups—those closest to the skin (superficial) and the deeper group. The superficial group contains the powerful gastrocnemius and soleus muscles, both critical to pushing off from the ground (plantarflexion of ankle joint—in which the foot moves downwards) during walking, running and jumping, and when standing on one's toes.

The deeper group of muscles pass behind the ankle joint and attach to bones of the foot. The largest of these, flexor hallux longus muscle, is critical to pushing off from the big toe during walking.

Due to the inelastic nature of the fascia bounding the compartments of the lower part of the leg, any swelling in a compartment results in pressure build-up, which can impair the blood supply. This is called compartment syndrome and may result from inflammation of muscles caused by excessive exercise in an unfit person, or trauma, such as fracture. With muscle overuse, it commonly involves the anterior, or deep posterior, compartments of the lower part of the leg and is characterized by shin pain (commonly known as shin splints) that increases during exercise and reduces at rest. Compartment syndrome may also be associated with pins and needles sensations and muscle weakness.

Nerve and blood supply

The femoral, obturator and sciatic nerves are the principal nerves of the leg, supplying the muscles and much of the skin. The sciatic nerve and its branches (tibial and common peroneal nerves) supply the hamstrings and all the muscles of the lower part of the leg and foot.

The femoral artery is the principal artery of supply to the leg. It descends in the front of the thigh. Two-thirds of the way down, it passes backward behind the knee and is renamed the popliteal artery. It then divides into anterior and posterior tibial branches that descend in the anterior and posterior compartments of the lower part of the leg. The femoral artery in the groin is easily exposed and is often used in cardiac catheterization (in coronary bypass surgery).

Veins are divided into two groups: the deep group and the superficial group. The deep group of lower limb veins travel with the arteries and are similarly named. The superficial veins (e.g. great and small saphenous) travel in the superficial tissue just below the skin. Lower limb veins have numerous valves directing blood toward the heart, and when muscles in the leg contract, the veins are squeezed and blood is forced upward. When the muscles relax, blood can flow from the superficial veins into deep veins via perforating or communicating veins. Faulty valves in the communicating veins can cause the superficial veins to become elongated, tortuous and enlarged (varicose veins).

Stasis of blood in veins may result in the formation of clots (thrombosis). When formed in the deep veins of the lower part of the leg it is called deep vein thrombosis (DVT). Increased risk is associated with advanced age, bed rest, immobilization and oral contraceptives. The greatest risk of thrombosis is that a piece of clot may dislodge and become lodged in the lung; this is called a pulmonary embolus, and is a major cause of death in the USA. Painful white leg ("milk leg") from venous thrombosis can also occur in the last three months of pregnancy or in the postdelivery period. Thrombophlebitis is the tenderness associated with a blood clot in a vein.

If blood in the skin of the lower part of the leg becomes stagnant (for example, from valve incompetence or venous thrombosis) even minor trauma to the poorly nourished skin can result in a varicose ulcer. It is especially common over the subcutaneous surface of the tibia. Leg ulcers can also result from arterial disease, underlying systemic disease (such as diabetes), neuropathy, malignant changes and infection.

SEE ALSO *Ankle, Compartment syndrome, Embolism, Foot, Hamstring muscles, Hip, Knee, Muscles, Pelvis, Thrombophlebitis, Thrombosis, Varicose veins, Veins*

LEGIONNAIRES' DISEASE

Named after an occasion when several members of the American Legion (ex-servicemen) became ill at a reunion in Philadelphia, USA in 1976, this disease has symptoms that are similar to pneumonia. More severe in heavy smokers with lung disease and in those who lack immunity, the disease is caused by a bacterium of the *Legionella* species. The strain identified in the original outbreak was *L. pneumophila*, but other strains can also cause the disease. It has been attributed to contaminated water, particularly in air-conditioning units and is contracted by breathing in fine water droplets or aerosols that contain bacteria. It cannot be acquired by drinking contaminated water and is not passed from person to person.

Legionella bacteria may also thrive in spa pools, humidifiers, garden potting mix and reticulated water systems where water temperature is kept between 20 and 45 degrees.

The flu-like symptoms of Legionnaires' disease usually appear 2–10 days after infection. These include headache, loss of appetite, muscle aches, a dry cough progressing to grey or blood-stained sputum, disorientation, fever, and sometimes stomach cramps and diarrhea. Diagnosis is confirmed by a sputum culture and many antibiotics appear to be effective. Untreated, the condition can be fatal.

SEE ALSO ***Lungs, Pneumonia, Sputum tests***

LEISHMANIASIS

Leishmaniasis is a parasitic disease caused by various protozoan parasites of the genus *Leishmania*, which live on dogs and rodents in many parts of world, especially tropical and subtropical countries. The parasites are transmitted from infected animals or people to new hosts by sandfly bites.

There are two main types. One is visceral leishmaniasis, also called kala-azar, which attacks the internal organs, and causes fever, enlargement of the spleen, anemia and skin darkening. Symptoms include cough, fever, weight loss, diarrhea, general abdominal discomfort, thinning hair and scaly, ashen skin. Not all symptoms appear at the same time, however, and as many of them are associated with other diseases it increases the difficulty of diagnosing leishmaniasis. After a sandfly bite the bone marrow, spleen and lymph nodes are invaded by parasites. In children there may be a sudden onset of vomiting, diarrhea, fever and cough, while adults may suffer fever for up to 2 months, as well as general fatigue, loss of appetite and weakness. As the disease progresses the immune system is damaged and death may occur within 2 years from complications such as infection. It can be fatal if untreated.

The other type is cutaneous leishmaniasis, also known as Delhi boil or oriental sore, which attacks the skin, causing skin lesions and ulcers. It can attack the mucous membranes, causing nasal congestion, nose bleeds, mouth and nose ulcers, and difficulty breathing and swallowing. The characteristic skin lesions may look like those of cancer, tuberculosis or leprosy. They can cause disfigurement requiring plastic surgery.

Treatment of both types is with antimony compounds or pentamidine. There is a good chance of a cure if the disease is diagnosed before the immune system is damaged. Some cases of cutaneous leishmaniasis heal spontaneously and do not require treatment.

Leishmaniasis has been reported in all continents except Australia. Travelers to endemic areas should avoid sandfly bites by using insect repellent, wearing appropriate clothing, and ensuring that windows and beds are screened with fine netting.

SEE ALSO ***Kala-azar***

LENTIGO

Lentigines ("lentigo" is the singular form) are flat, round, light-brown spots that appears mostly on sun-affected areas such as the face and hands, and are frequently found on Caucasians and Asiatics. Though often confused with freckles, they do not fade during the winter months. Liver spots (solar lentigines) on the back of the hands of people who have spent a lot of time outdoors rarely become malignant. Lentigines are occasionally up to an inch (2.5 centimeters) across, irregular in shape and staining. If they change in size or shape, indicating possible melanomas, they need immediate attention from a doctor. Sun protection such as a hat, long sleeves, sunglasses and sunscreen with at least SPF15 may reduce the occurrence of lentigines. Skin bleaching creams may help fade them.

SEE ALSO ***Melanoma***

LEPROSY

Leprosy is caused by a rod-shaped bacterium, *Mycobacterium leprae*, a relative of the tuberculosis bacillus. It is prevalent in Central and South America, in East Asia, and in the tropical countries of Asia and Africa. There are two main forms: tuberculoid leprosy and lepromatous leprosy.

Tuberculoid leprosy is an infection in the deep skin layers, which destroys the hair follicles, sweat glands and nerve endings at the site of infection. The skin above the site becomes dry and discolored and loses the ability to sense touch, heat and cold, and pain. Fingers and toes are easily injured and may become mutilated and fall off.

In lepromatous leprosy, the organism multiplies freely in the skin. Large, soft bumps, or nodules, appear over the body and face. The mucous membranes of the eyes, nose, and throat may be invaded. In extreme cases the voice may change drastically, blindness may occur, or the nose may be destroyed.

Both types of leprosy are only mildly contagious (via the respiratory tract) and the infection is very slow to develop, ranging from 6 months to 10 years. Typical early

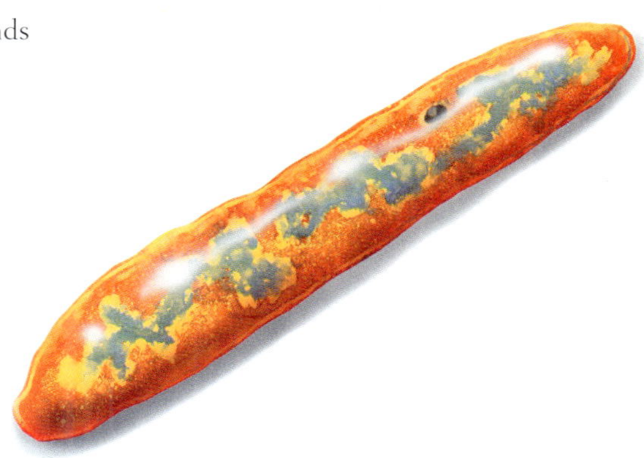

Legionnaires' disease

The bacteria *Legionella pneumophila* found in contaminated water (for example in air-conditioning cooling towers) causes Legionnaires' disease.

L

signs of the disease include one to three slightly raised patches on the skin which are non-itching, may be reddish in color and on which there is sensory loss. The diagnosis can be confirmed through a biopsy of the edge of an affected skin area or nerve.

Leprosy most commonly strikes people aged 10–20 years, and is seen more in men than women. It is thought to be transmitted through the inhalation of dust particles laden with bacilli. It is particularly prevalent in poorer countries where overcrowding and malnutrition make the spread of the disease easier.

Leprosy has existed for thousands of years and has a huge stigma attached to it because of the dreadful deformities that can result from infection. For this reason it is now often referred to by another name—Hansen's disease—in an effort to avoid fear and hysteria that may disadvantage efforts to treat the disease and reduce its incidence.

Early treatment is important in preventing deformities and other physical handicaps. Drugs such as dapsone, rifampin and clofazimine are used in combination to prevent drug resistance and may cure the disease within a year. Treatment usually needs to be continued for several years after the disease becomes inactive.

LEPTOSPIROSIS

Also called icterohemorrhagic fever, leptospirosis is a rare bacterial infection caused by *Leptospira*, a spiral-shaped microorganism (spirochete). It is contagious, being transmitted to humans mostly via liquids, soil, contaminated with the urine of infected wild or domestic animals—mainly rats, dogs, pigs and cattle. It may also be passed on by direct contact with the urine or tissue of an infected animal. The bacteria may enter the body through an open cut on the skin, through the intact mucous membrane of the mouth or when contaminated water is swallowed.

After an incubation period of 1–3 weeks, in a mild case the victim experiences a sudden onset of fever, shivering attacks (rigor), headache, muscle aches and pains (myalgia). These symptoms usually last 4–7 days, after which there may be a period where the sufferer feels well. The fever then recurs and 2 –4 weeks later may be accompanied by inflammation of the nerve to the eye, brain and spinal column (meningitis), and less commonly disease of the gallbladder, lungs and heart.

In about 10 percent of cases a severe form of the illness develops (known as Weil's syndrome), involving symptoms such as jaundice, mental confusion, kidney failure and bleeding abnormalities. The condition may be fatal, sometimes by drowning as the lungs fill with blood or fluid after the illness attacks the respiratory system.

Leptospirosis is diagnosed by testing of the blood, urine or spinal fluid. Treatment with antibiotics such as penicillin or doxycycline may be effective if commenced early in the illness.

LESION

This is a general term given to changes that occur in organs or tissues following injury or disease. An open wound is a lesion, as is the resulting scar. A birthmark or a mole is a superficial lesion, while a change from a mole to a melanoma produces a new lesion.

There are a number of ways of categorising lesions, one of which is size. A gross lesion is one that can be seen by the naked eye, and a microscopic or histologic lesion may only be viewed with the help of a microscope. Some lesions are known for their characteristic shape, such as bull's-eye or target lesions which are symptoms of a number of diseases and appear as well-demarcated raised red concentric circles. Round shadows that may appear on chest x-rays are sometimes referred to as coin lesions.

Some lesions are benign, while others are malignant. Inflammations or infections are not lesions, although lesions may be produced, such as the scar which can be seen on x-ray following an episode of tuberculosis. Other common examples of skin lesions are blisters, scabs, ulcers and boils.

SEE ALSO *Birthmarks, Melanoma, Moles, Scar*

LEUKEMIA

Leukemia is a progressive, malignant disease arising from the white cells in the blood. It occurs in both adults and children, and is the most common type of malignant disease in children. The disease is characterized by an increase in white cells in the blood and in the blood-forming organs, the bone marrow and spleen. The leukemic white cells do not perform the normal function of fighting infection, but rather they interfere with the function of the normal white cells. They also interfere with the development of red blood cells and platelet cells in the bone marrow.

There are many types of leukemia, but they can be grouped according to the following criteria: duration (acute or chronic); the type of proliferating white cell; and the fluctuations in the number of abnormal cells in the blood.

Acute leukemia is a form of leukemia that develops rapidly, over weeks, and is quickly fatal if not treated. Patients develop infections, which are persistent and fail to respond to usual antibiotic treatment. The infections are generally due to bacteria and result in fever with or without local symptoms. Common sites of infection are the throat, gums, chest and skin.

Acute leukemia also causes exceptional fatigue and shortness of breath, due to anemia from decreased production of red blood cells. Easy bruising and spontaneous bleeding, from the nose and gums or from cuts, results from the interference with the production of platelet cells. The rapid expansion of white cells in the bone marrow can cause severe bone pain in the ribs and spine.

No single cause has been identified for acute leukemias and the cause of most cases is unknown. Exposure to high doses of ionizing radiation, such as in nuclear accidents like Chernobyl, resulted in increased cases of leukemia. However, it is not known whether low-level exposure to ionizing or other forms of radiation also increases the risk. The use of some toxic chemicals increases the occurrence of leukemia; benzene and its derivatives have the strongest association. Acute leukemia can also occur after the use of certain chemotherapy drugs recommended for other cancers, or after the use of certain drugs designed to suppress the rejection of kidney and other transplants.

There is a possibility that some drugs or chemicals affecting a woman during pregnancy can increase the risk of acute leukemia later developing in the child; these include alcohol, cannabis, benzene and pesticides. There is increasing interest in the possible role of viruses in causing leukemias in humans. Hereditary leukemia is rare but there is an increased incidence in conjunction with some genetic diseases, such as trisomy 21 (Down syndrome).

Acute lymphoblastic leukemia is the common form of childhood leukemia. It is derived from the type of white blood cells called lymphocytes. Blast cells are the immature cells from which the different types of blood cells normally develop. In acute lymphoblastic leukemia the blast cells that normally develop into lymphocytes do not do so and accumulate instead. Specific chromosomal or genetic abnormalities have now been identified in 60–75 percent of patients with acute lymphoblastic leukemia, giving hope for improvements in the understanding and treatment of this disease.

Acute myeloid leukemia is the common form of adult leukemia, whose incidence increases with age. It arises from an increase in myeloblasts in the bone marrow. At least six types of acute myeloid leukemia are recognized. Many are associated with specific chromosomal abnormalities and almost all patients have some chromosomal abnormality in their leukemic cells. In one type, acute promyelocytic leukemia, this knowledge has led to a major breakthrough in treatment with the use of a form of vitamin A.

Treatment of acute leukemia involves combinations of chemotherapy drugs and supportive treatment to prevent infections and bleeding. The initial chemotherapy is administered by intravenous injection and in tablet form over several days. Often a plastic catheter is inserted into a large vein to make repeated injections more convenient. The purpose of the initial treatment is to achieve apparent eradication of the leukemic cells; this is known as a remission. Once remission has been achieved, it is followed by consolidation chemotherapy and, in the case of lymphoblastic leukemia, more prolonged maintenance chemotherapy.

The results of treatment have improved with the development of powerful antibiotics, platelet transfusions and the use of growth factors to stimulate recovery of the

Leukemia

This malignant disease involves the rapid and uncontrolled proliferation of leukocytes (white blood cells) in the blood-forming organs. The white cell count is greatly elevated and large numbers of immature cells are found in the circulating blood.

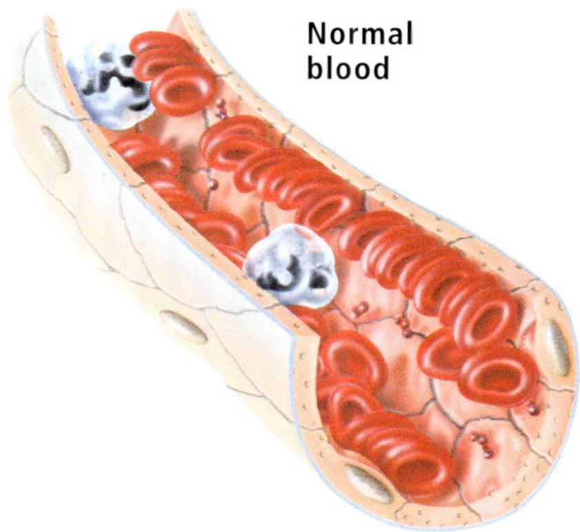

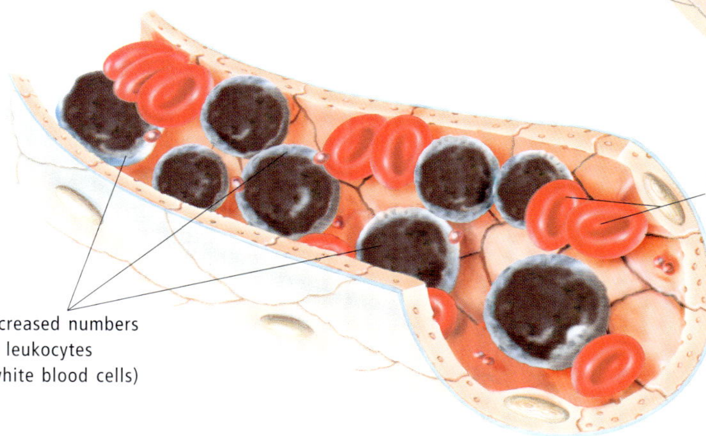

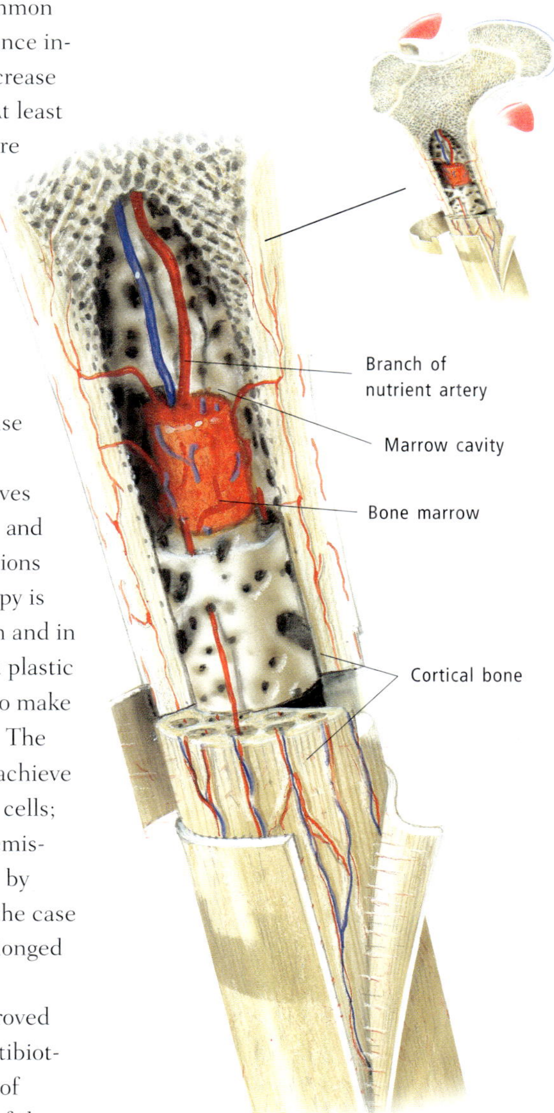

Leukemia—spleen

The spleen produces lymphocytes (one type of white blood cell) which are essential to the body's immune system. Overproduction of lymphocytes results in the most common form of leukemia—chronic lymphocytic leukemia. This can cause enlargement of the spleen.

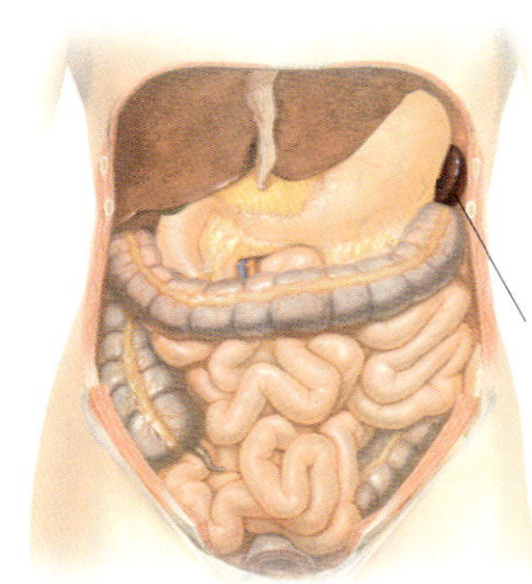

Leukemia—bone marrow

The bone marrow is the most important site for the storage and production of white blood cells (leukocytes) in the body. Leukocytes are produced mainly in the long bones, spine, skull, ribs, and sternum. In acute leukemia, the rapid expansion of white cells in the bone marrow can cause severe pain.

normal white cells. With current best methods of treatment, remission can now be achieved in 70–80 percent of adults up to 60 years of age and 97–99 percent of children. Bone marrow transplantation in remission can achieve cure rates of 50–60 percent in adults and 75–80 percent in children.

Chronic, as differentiated from acute, leukemias are leukemias which run a more gradual and prolonged course. They are often detected by chance, such as through a routine blood test, in which the raised white cell count appears. These leukemias involve an increase in mature white blood cells.

The most common leukemias is chronic lymphocytic leukemia, in which there is an increase in the number of lymphocytes. This occurs mainly in men over 50 years of age. It can cause enlargement of the lymph glands and spleen. Often there is an increased susceptibility to bacterial infections, due to reduced production of antibodies by normal lymphocytes. However, some patients may be completely asymptomatic and may not require treatment for years.

Chronic myeloid leukemia has its peak incidence at 20–40 years and involves an increase in mature myeloid cells, or granulocytes, in the blood and bone marrow. Enlargement of the spleen is an important feature of this condition, as is the association with a chromosomal abnormality in the bone marrow cells, called the Philadelphia chromosome, after the city in which it was first described. This form of leukemia generally requires treatment and can be cured in young patients with bone marrow transplantation. In those not suitable for this procedure, the use of injections of interferons (agents that inhibit cellular growth) can decrease the number of Philadelphia-positive cells and prolong patient survival.

SEE ALSO *Cancer, Lymphocytes, Spleen, White blood cells*

LEUKOPLAKIA

Leukoplakia refers to a whitish-looking patch on the mucous membrane of the cheeks, gums or tongue that cannot be removed by scraping. It is most often the result of thickening of the surface layer of cells (the epithelium), and is a response to injury or chronic irritation. This may be a result of friction caused by rough edges on teeth, fillings, and ill-fitting dentures and crowns. It occurs most often in smokers (especially pipe smokers) and in users of chewing tobacco, but other irritants can also trigger leukoplakia.

A white or gray colored lesion usually develops slowly over a period of weeks or months. This area may be sensitive to touch, heat and spicy foods. In a small proportion of patients, the change is either pre-cancerous or represents an early cancer of the mouth, both of which can only be excluded by microscopic examination of a biopsy sample.

Other forms of this condition include hairy leukoplakia, which involves fuzzy patches on the tongue and occasionally other parts of the mouth. It is a symptom of AIDS. A rare form of leukoplakia of unknown cause has also been reported on the external genital area (vulva) of women.

SEE ALSO *Mouth, Tongue*

LEUKORRHEA

It is natural for all women to have some relatively odorless vaginal mucus or leukorrhea (white fluid discharge). Most vaginal secretions come from the cervix with a lesser amount coming through the vaginal walls. Normally, the glands secrete a clear mucus which combines with bacteria, discarded vaginal cells and other secretions. The amount of leukorrhea secreted by the cervical glands fluctuates during the menstrual cycle and may vary in consistency from thick to pasty to thin. It may be clear, cloudy or colored and in some cases, perhaps where infection is present, may be malodorous.

The production is largely under hormonal control: an excess of estrogens produces too much. Women who take the contraceptive pill as well as those who are pregnant often have excessive moisture, as do women in an excited sexual state. The possible causes of significant changes in the color, smell, consistency and amount of vaginal discharge include yeast infection, sexually transmitted disease, the use of certain medications and irradiation of the reproductive tract. Itchiness can be associated with excessive mucus production.

If there is no infection present, reassurance is usually all that is needed.

SEE ALSO *Cervix, Estrogens, Vagina*

LICE

Lice are tiny parasites, about the size of sesame seeds, which live on the skin of the human body where they suck blood for food.

Head lice

Head lice (*Pediculus humanus capitis*) live in human hair. They hatch out from tiny eggs known as nits which are attached with a glue to the human hair, and can affect anyone. Contrary to popular belief, they do not thrive on dirty hair in unsanitary conditions; they prefer clean hair and are no respecters of social or economic status. Once laid the nits will stay attached to the hair shaft, unless dislodged, for 10 days, when they will hatch and reach maturity in about 2 weeks. A female louse can live for up to 30 days and lay about 6 eggs a day.

Lice are passed from one person to another by direct contact, which is why young children in constant contact with each other are most likely to spread them. They can be transmitted on combs, brushes, hats, pillowcases and towels. Scratching and occasionally small white specks are the signs.

More easily seen in sunlight and on dark hair than light, nits and lice can be difficult to eradicate. They are mostly found on the scalp behind the ears and near the neckline at the back. Eradication involves the use of a fine "nit" comb, insecticidal shampoo, a warm to hot hairdryer and disinfecting everything the head may have come in contact with—by washing in hot water and drying in hot air or strong sunlight. Head lice and nits on the eyelids need to be physically removed. Bed linen and stuffed toys that cannot be washed or dry cleaned should be placed in sealed plastic bags for 2 weeks. Carpet and furniture should be thoroughly vacuumed. It is important that other household members ensure they have not been infected.

Pubic lice

Pubic lice or crabs (*Phthirus pubis*) live in the hair in the pubic and thigh area. Crabs can be a problem in crowded living conditions. They are mainly contracted during sexual activity but can also contaminate bedding and clothing. Lice on toilet seats are usually injured and not likely to be looking for a new host. They can live in wet towels and be passed on in a gym or household.

Pubic lice can be easily visible attached to or moving in the pubic hairs, and look like a crab under magnification. They feed on blood and can live up to 30 days, mating frequently in that time. The most common symptom is an itch in the genital area; a rash, or tiny blue spots, may also be evident.

Treatment is with an insecticidal lotion or shampoo (often permethrin). The itching continues for some days after the lice have been killed and all bed linen and clothing must be disinfected in hot water and dried in hot conditions. Bathrooms, towels and linen need to be disinfected by washing with hot, soapy water and hot drying. Sexual contact should be avoided until the infection has been treated successfully so that the lice are not passed on to partners.

Body lice

Larger than head and pubic lice, body lice (*Pediculus humanis corpons*) usually live on people in unhygienic, crowded conditions.

These are the lice responsible for carrying diseases such as typhus, trench fever and relapsing fever (or tick fever). They too can be eradicated by hot washing of everything that has come into contact with the body and by the use of an insecticidal shampoo.

SEE ALSO ***Head lice, Relapsing fever, Scabies, Typhus***

LICHEN PLANUS

Lichen planus is a rare and recurrent skin inflammation characterized by small, slightly raised bumps that itch. It usually starts at the wrists or on the legs and may spread to the trunk. Lesions may also appear in the mouth, vulva or penis, and the nails may be affected.

The exact cause of the condition is unknown, but is thought to be a result of an allergic or immune reaction. Exposure to potential allergens such as certain medications, dyes and other chemical substances has been implicated. It has also been reported that symptoms worsen with emotional stress, which is thought to affect the immune system.

This disease is extremely rare in children, mostly affecting the middle-aged and elderly. The dark red-purple lesions may be almost 1½ inches (4 centimeters) long, with distinct borders and a shiny or scaly appearance. They may appear singly or in clusters. Other symptoms include a dry mouth with a metallic taste, ridges on the nails and hair loss.

Lichen planus
Small slightly raised bumps with an accompanying itch characterize this inflammation of the skin.

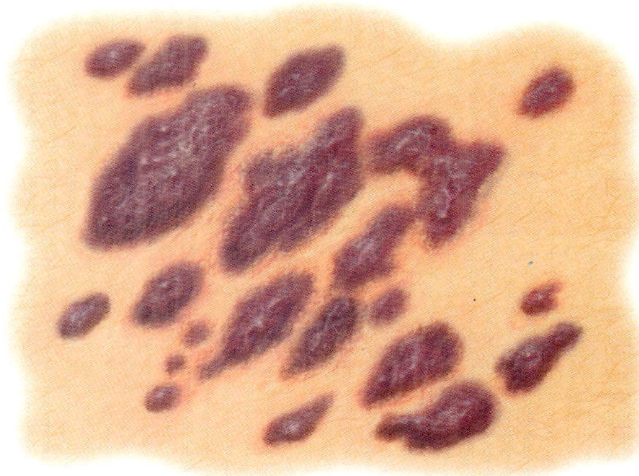

Creams or lotions containing corticosteroid drugs are used to control the condition, which may subside after a few months. However, symptoms may recur for years.

In some instances lichen planus may be a precursor to squamous cell cancer. Mouth ulcers that do not clear up may develop into oral cancer.

LIFE SUPPORT

Life support is the term generally given to the efforts to maintain vital body functions, such as respiration, circulation and fluid and nutrient intake, in patients who are comatose and cannot maintain these functions naturally. Life support involves the use of mechanical ventilation, intravenous fluids, physical therapy and round-the-clock nursing care in an intensive care unit in hospital.

Ethical questions have been raised regarding the quality of life of people kept alive by artificial life support. When the patient is unlikely to make any recovery, physicians—with the cooperation of the patient's relatives—may elect not to continue life support, especially where the patient has been declared brain dead. Some indivduals draw up what is known as a "living will" in which they specify how they wish to be treated if accident or illness leaves them in a vegetative state.

SEE ALSO *Death*

LIGAMENTS

Ligaments (from the Latin *ligamentum*, meaning a band or tie) are tough, white, fibrous, slightly elastic tissues. They support many internal organs, including the uterus, the bladder, the liver and the diaphragm, and they also help in shaping and supporting the breasts. Their main function is to support and strengthen joints, preventing excessive movement that might cause dislocation and breakage of the bones in the joint.

A ligament may be damaged or torn if a joint, through injury or accident, is moved into a position it was not designed for. The tear may be a complete tear of all the strands of the ligament or a partial tear, where only some of the ligament strands are torn. A tear in a ligament is sometimes called a sprain.

Sprains most often occur in the ankle and knee joints, but may also occur in the fingers, wrist, shoulder and the spine.

Sprains are treated with the application of cold compresses, immobilization of the joint, elevation of the joint to allow fluid around the joint to drain away, and the application of a bandage or splint. Nonsteroidal anti-inflammatory drugs (NSAIDs) may be given for pain relief and to aid healing.

Ligaments tend to heal very slowly because of their poor blood supply. Healing takes 7–10 days for mild sprains and 3–5 weeks for severe sprains. Surgery may be required if a ligament is completely torn or severed from its point of attachment to the bone.

An ankle sprain is a common injury and usually results when the ankle is twisted, or inverted. The foot turns inward, towards the other foot, causing the ligaments on the outside of the ankle (the lateral ligaments) to stretch and tear. The ankle swells and becomes painful and bruised. It is treated with ice, elevation, rest, painkillers, a bandage,

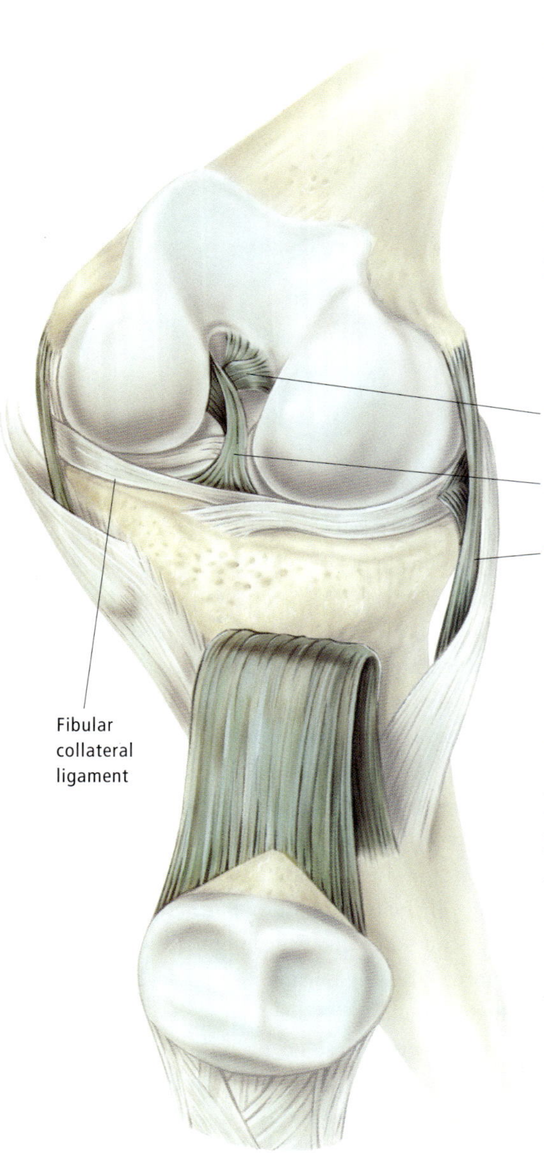

Ligaments

The main function of ligaments is to mobilize joints and prevent excessive movement. This strengthening and support system saves joints from fractures and dislocations.

Ligament microstructure

The direction of fibers within ligaments is related to the stress that is applied to them. The considerable interweaving increases structural stability and resilience.

and crutches, to keep the weight off the affected foot. Healing of the ligaments usually takes about 6 weeks.

The anterior cruciate ligament is a strong ligament that provides stability to the knee. It is often damaged during sporting activities. A sudden change in direction while running or jumping, as occurs in football and squash, for example, may result in a partial or complete tear, dislocation or stretch of the ligament.

Treatment involves rest, analgesics and physical therapy. In fit and active people, surgical repair is often performed with excellent results. This is often done via arthroscopy, involving a tube with a microscope inserted into the knee joint. Injury to the medial and to the lateral collateral ligaments of the knee may also occur.

SEE ALSO *Ankle, Joints, Knee, Sprain*

LIGHT THERAPY

Since 1981, intense artificial light therapy has been used in the USA and Europe, principally for the treatment of seasonal affective disorder (SAD) or winter depression. Light therapy affects the body's circadian rhythms by lengthening the day with bright light. Exposure to the light suppresses secretion of the night-time hormone melatonin and may enhance the effectiveness of serotonin and other neurotransmitters, producing an antidepressant effect in those whose depression is caused by a sensitivity to the reduction in sunlight.

The lamps used for this therapy produce a high intensity light, far brighter than normal lighting—at least eight times brighter than normal household lighting—and equal to standing outside on a sunny spring day. The individual with SAD sits in front of this lamp, usually for half an hour upon first waking. It is not necessary to stare at the lamp, but the patient may be advised to look at the lamp at regular intervals whilst carrying on with activities such as reading or watching television. Treatment for SAD commences in early autumn as the days begin to shorten and ends in spring when longer hours of daylight diminish the symptoms of SAD.

Light therapy is also used to treat sleep disorders, since exposure to light in the morning advances the circadian rhythm. This means that a person who is unable to fall asleep until very late at night can fall asleep earlier. Exposure to light at night delays the circadian rhythm, normalizing the sleep of those who are fatigued in the early evening and then wake early in the morning.

Light therapy can help shift workers and jet-lag sufferers to reset their body clocks. It may give SAD sufferers some relief from symptoms such as irritability, fatigue, low energy levels and weight gain. With regular light therapy treatment symptoms may disappear and the length of the sessions may be reduced.

SEE ALSO *Seasonal affective disorder, Sleep disturbances*

LIMBIC SYSTEM

The limbic system is a collective term for a group of interconnected brain structures that are involved in behaviors associated with survival, including the expression of emotion, feeding, drinking, defense and reproduction, as well as the formation of memory. The term "limbic system" comes from the fact that the earliest parts of this system to be identified were observed to form a ring or "limbus" around the central structures of the brain (cingulate, parahippocampal and hippocampal gyri), but later definitions include a number of other structures. The key components of this system are the hippocampus, amygdala, septal area and hypothalamus.

The hippocampus is located deep in the temporal lobe and is continuous with the cortex on the inner part of the lower surface of that lobe. It is connected to other parts of the cerebral cortex, thalamus and hypothalamus and is essential in the formation of new memories.

When the hippocampus is damaged, patients are able to recall old memories but are unable to remember what they did or said 5 minutes before. In other words, they cannot transform newly acquired knowledge into a memory, but old memories are intact—this condition is known as anterograde amnesia. This form of amnesia is seen in Alzheimer's disease, in which degeneration of the hippocampus is a characteristic feature. Because the hippocampus is very sensitive to oxygen deprivation, patients who recover from near-drowning or suffocation may suffer from anterograde amnesia for some time after the incident.

The amygdala is located in the temporal lobe, just in front of the hippocampus. It is strongly linked to the olfactory (smell) system, hippocampus, cerebral cortex and hypothalamus, and is an important center for the expression of emotions. People or animals in which the amygdala is removed fail to react to stimuli that would normally cause fear. In other words they are unable to recognize a fearful or threatening situation. Conversely, electrical stimulation of the amygdala in cats, for example, causes a full-blown defensive reaction. In humans it causes feelings of anxiety and irritability.

The septal area, a small region of the inner surface of the brain, beneath the front of the corpus callosum, is linked to the hippocampus, amygdala and hypothalamus. It is thought to be a pleasure or reward center and is a focus of some studies investigating addictive behavior.

The hypothalamus is a small but vital region that regulates the activity of the body's organs (viscera) through connections with other parts of the brain and through regulating the production of hormones. It is interconnected with all parts of the limbic system and is responsible for bringing about visceral changes associated with emotions, such as the increase in blood pressure, heart and breathing rate which occurs when scared or anxious, or blushing when embarrassed. The behavioral and cognitive changes associated with emotional expression are brought about mainly through projections from the various limbic structures (hypothalamus, amygdala, hippocampus) to the cortex of the frontal and temporal lobes.

SEE ALSO *Alzheimer's disease, Amnesia, Brain, Hypothalamus, Thalamus*

LIP

Part of the face, the lips are the muscular borders of the mouth. They are covered in front with skin, and at the back by a mucous membrane that forms part of the lining of the oral cavity. The free edges of the lips are covered by a type of very thin skin called the vermilion border which, due to its dense nerve supply and thinness, is extremely sensitive to touch. The vermilion border itself is

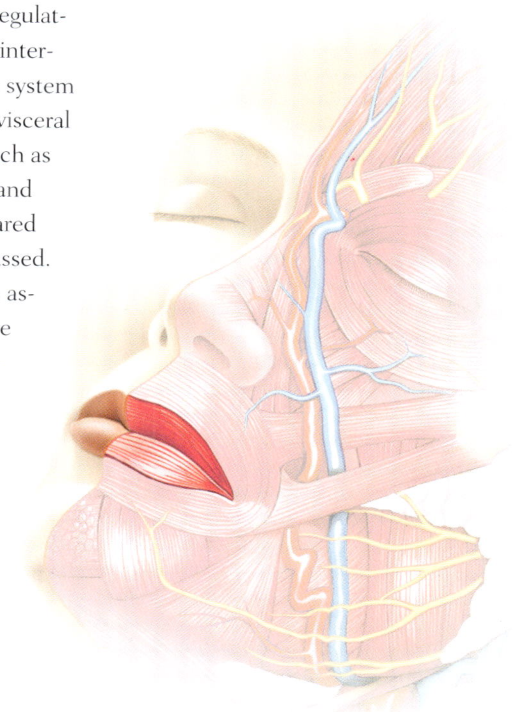

Lip
The lips play an essential role in speech by modulating sounds into recognizable words. They are an important part of the expressiveness of the face and contain many nerve endings, making them highly sensitive.

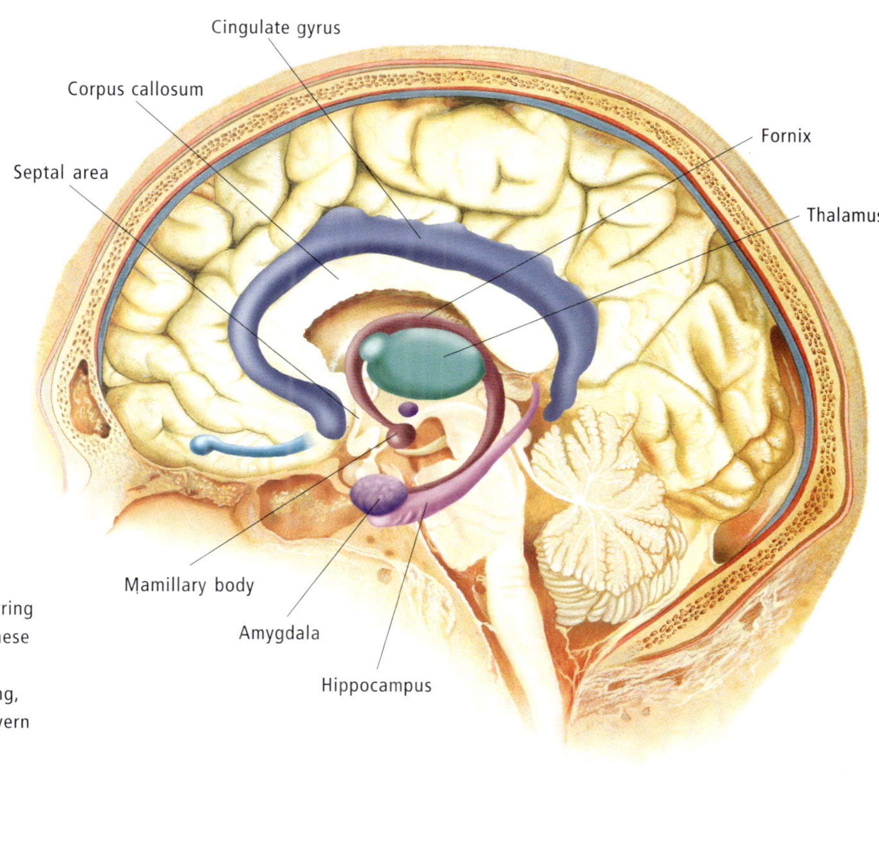

Limbic system
This "system" is a collective term referring to a group of elements in the brain. These structures are involved in behaviors associated with survival, such as feeding, defense and reproduction, and also govern emotional states and memory storage.

unpigmented, but blood from the blood vessels shows through it, giving the lips their characteristic red color.

The muscles of the lips are divided into two groups. The fibers of one group run concentrically around the mouth like purse strings and act to close it. The other muscles have fibers that run radially and are used to open the mouth. The lips serve to make a watertight and airtight closure of the mouth for drinking, swallowing and chewing. The muscular movements of the lips form an important part of the expressiveness of the face and, in infants, are essential for suckling on the breast. The lips and teeth form the embouchure (mouthpiece), by which musicians play wind instruments.

The delicate surface of the vermilion border is especially liable to injury. Lips may also require sunscreen and moisturizing preparations to protect against painful sunburn and chapping.

SEE ALSO *Face, Mouth, Mucous membranes*

L

LIPIDS

Lipids include fats and cholesterol. They are organic chemical substances of biological origin, and are usually esters (alcohol and acid compounds) of fatty acids. Lipids are characterized by not mixing with water. This gives them important physical properties, especially in the formation of cell membranes and the myelin sheaths of nerves. Lipids are widely distributed in the body, and form an important part of the diet.

SEE ALSO *Fats, Nutrition*

LIPODYSTROPHY

The lipodystrophies are a group of rare disorders causing loss of fat (adipose) tissue under the skin due to a disturbance of normal fat metabolism. Other metabolic disorders such as diabetes may be present. Lipodystrophy may be congenital (present at birth) or acquired, and may be generalized (affecting the whole body), partial or local, affecting just one area of the body.

One type of lipodystrophy is seen in people who are being treated with protease inhibitor drugs for AIDS-related illness. Their face, arms and legs become thin due to loss of fat, while fat builds up on the back of the neck, and the breasts and stomach become enlarged with tissue. Other symptoms include cracked lips, dry skin, weight loss and protruding veins. It is not known why these drugs have this effect.

Generalized lipodystrophy may be congenital or it may occur after an infectious illness, especially measles, chickenpox or whooping cough. The main feature is loss of fat; the affected person looks as though their skin is drawn tightly over their bones. There is also associated growth disorder; the affected person appears to be suffering from acromegaly, as they have coarse facial features and large feet and hands, and their internal organs are enlarged. Intellectual disability is common. There is no treatment and affected persons often die at an early age. Insulin may be needed to control the diabetes that is also associated with the condition.

Acquired partial lipodystrophy affects females in the first decade of life. The loss of fat usually affects only the upper half or, less commonly, one side of the body. This variation is not as severe as the generalized form and the outlook is better.

SEE ALSO *Acromegaly, Diabetes, Fats, Metabolism*

LIPOMA

A lipoma is a benign tumor composed of fatty tissue which is often found just under the skin. Lipomas manifest as soft swellings that can occur in multiples and are commonly seen in the back, thighs, buttocks and breasts. Lipomas in the breast are sometimes mistaken for malignant tumors if they are firmer than usual to the touch.

Lipomas are more prevalent in adults than children. As they are generally benign they do not invade nearby tissue and may be left untouched for many years. Medical advice should be sought, however, if they increase in size or shape in case they are malignant. Lipomas are usually easily removed by surgery to improve cosmetic appearance or reduce discomfort if they are inconveniently located.

Lipomas may also form inside the body. They may be found in muscle tissue, where they can grow quite large before detection. They may attach to the spinal cord, causing complications such as paralysis, and in rare instances may attach to the pancreas.

SEE ALSO *Tumors*

LIPOSUCTION

Liposuction (also known as lipolysis or suction lipectomy) is the surgical removal of fat from the body for cosmetic purposes using a suction apparatus inserted into the body through an incision.

The most common method is tumescent liposuction. In this procedure, several quarts (liters) of saline solution are pumped under

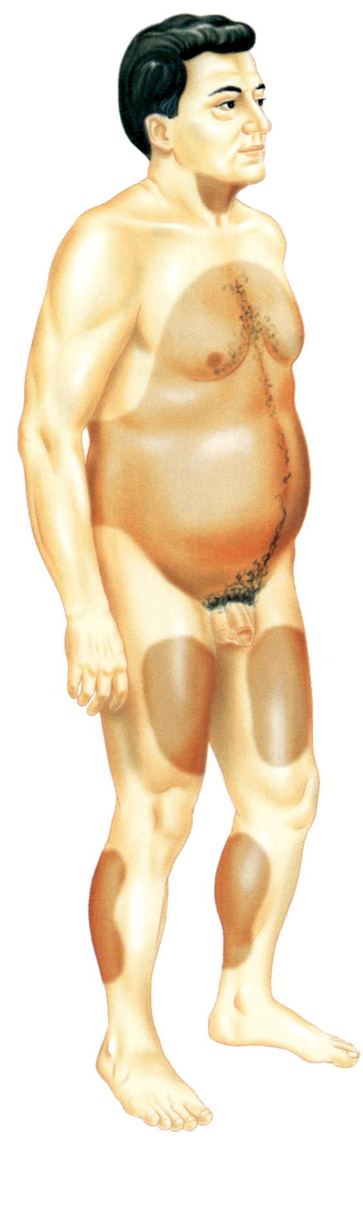

Liposuction

Liposuction involves the removal of unwanted fat from the body. The most commonly treated areas include the thighs, buttocks, hips, chin, and abdomen.

the skin, then the fat is sucked out using a tube, or cannula, to which a high-pressure vacuum is applied. The saline solution also includes a local anesthetic to numb the area being treated and a substance that constricts blood vessels to minimize bleeding. With ultrasonic-assisted liposuction, a wand-like instrument is energized with ultrasonic energy to liquefy fat. This method—known as lithotripsy—is often used to re-treat areas of the body that have already undergone liposuction. However, it may require longer incisions, takes more time to complete and be more expensive. It also carries a greater risk of burns to the skin or inside of the body.

The most commonly treated areas are the buttocks, thighs, hips, knees, abdomen, upper arms, back and chin. The procedure may also be used to "contour" the neck, calves and ankles. It is not used for breast reduction, for removing fatty tumors or as a treatment for obesity. Nor will it eliminate the dimpled appearance of skin caused by cellulite.

Serious and potentially fatal complications can occur while undergoing tumescent liposuction as a result of blood clots (thrombosis), fluid overload resulting in the collection of fluid in the lungs (pulmonary edema) and slowed heart rate in combination with lowered blood pressure.

SEE ALSO Cosmetic surgery

LISPING

Lisping is the term broadly used to describe a range of speech impediments, the most common of which is pronounciation of the sibilant sounds of "s" or "z" as "th". This happens when the tip of the tongue is positioned too far forward in the mouth, instead of against the hard palate. Lisping may be treated with speech therapy.

SEE ALSO *Speech*

LISTERIOSIS

Listeriosis is an infection caused by *Listeria monocytogenes*, a bacterium found in nature and in some foods. Infection is not common and there are usually few or no symptoms in healthy people though it can cause a flu-like illness. In pregnancy, however, listeriosis is dangerous to the fetus and can cause miscarriage, stillbirth or premature birth.

Lithotripsy

Stones that have formed in the gallbladder, kidneys or bladder can be shattered using shock waves. This avoids the need for invasive surgery. Once shattered, gallstone fragments pass out of the body via the bile duct and bowel; kidney and bladder stone fragments are passed with urine through the ureter.

Gallstones

Bladder stones

Stones shattered with lithotripsy

Stones no larger than $\frac{5}{8}$ of an inch (1.5 centimeters) are ideal candidates for lithotripsy.

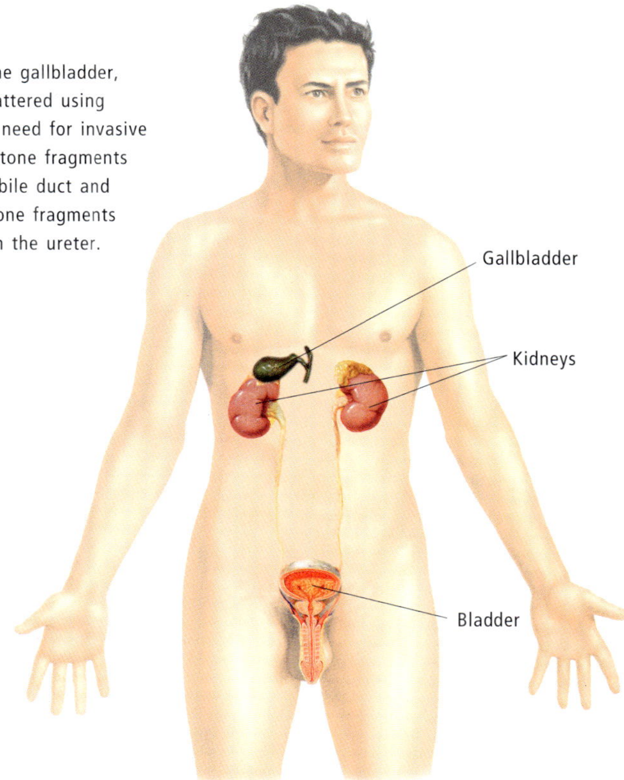

About half of the babies infected at or near birth will die. Signs that a newborn is infected include a red skin rash, whitish nodules on mucous membranes, respiratory distress, shock, vomiting, lethargy and jaundice. The condition often manifests as meningitis in babies aged 2 weeks or older.

In adults, the infection can take many forms depending on the body part affected. It may manifest as meningitis, septicemia, pneumonia, endocarditis or, in less severe cases, skin lesions, conjunctivitis or abscesses.

The organism can be found in such foods as soft cheese, cold cooked chicken, cold meats and paté, raw seafood, pre-prepared salads and smoked seafood. Observing good hygiene and avoiding these foods during pregnancy minimizes the risk of infection.

SEE ALSO *Bacteria, Food poisoning*

LITHOTRIPSY

The procedure known as lithotripsy is used to shatter stones (calculi) that have formed in the bladder, gallbladder, ureter or kidney. Extracorporeal shockwave lithotripsy is a common technique that involves the creation of shock waves outside the body which are targeted at the stone to break it up. This technique is generally used on stones no more than $\frac{5}{8}$ inch (1.5 centimeters) in diameter and some sort of anesthesia is given. The patient may be positioned in water during the procedure. X-rays or ultrasound are used to ensure the accurate location of the stone.

While surgical stone removal once required a lengthy stay in hospital, lithotripsy may take only 45 minutes and can sometimes be performed on an out-patient basis. Depending on the size of the stone and the strength and duration of the shock waves needed, anesthesia may be used to alleviate pain. It may take between 800 and 2000 shocks, for example, to break up a kidney stone. Stone fragments are sometimes passed from the body with the aid of a catheter inserted in the ureter.

Another type of lithotripsy involves the insertion of an instrument called a lithotrite through the ureter which shatters or crushes stones using an electrical spark.

Complications of lithotripsy include blood in the urine for a few days after treatment, bruising on the abdomen or back, and pain or discomfort as stones pass out of the body in the urine. More than one treatment may be required if the stone is not completely shattered the first time.

SEE ALSO *Bladder, Gallbladder, Kidney, Ureter*

LIVER

The liver is an organ associated with the digestive tract. It is the heaviest single organ in the body, weighing about 3½ pounds (1.5 kilograms) in an adult, and makes up about one-fiftieth of total body weight. The liver is normally reddish brown in color and lies under the cover and protection of the lower ribs on the right side of the upper abdomen.

The liver has an upper (diaphragmatic) surface, which is in contact with the diaphragm, and a lower (visceral) surface, which is in contact with organs in the abdominal cavity. The two surfaces are separated at the front by a sharp inferior border, which may sometimes be felt when the liver becomes enlarged and protrudes below the line of the ribs. The visceral surface of the liver is in contact with the gallbladder (which is usually attached to the liver by connective tissue), with the kidney, part of the duodenum, the esophagus, the stomach and a part of the large bowel.

The liver is attached to the diaphragm—the muscle which separates the chest and abdominal cavities—by a series of folds of membrane called the falciform, triangular and coronary ligaments.

The liver is also joined to the stomach and duodenum by folds of membrane called the gastrohepatic and hepatoduodenal ligaments respectively.

On the visceral surface of the liver lies a region known as the porta hepatis. This is the site at which vessels and ducts enter and leave the liver. Within the porta hepatis are the portal vein, which carries blood from the gut to the liver, the hepatic artery, which carries blood from the aorta to the liver, and the common hepatic, cystic and bile ducts, all of which are part of the biliary system of ducts concerned that store bile and deliver it to the duodenum.

Microscopic structure

Microscopically, the liver contains sheets of cells (hepatocytes) arranged in hexagonal prism-shaped lobules. Each hepatocyte is about one-thousandth of an inch (25 thousandths of a millimeter) across and they are piled up in sheets one cell thick, much like bricks in a wall. Hepatocytes contain a large amount of glycogen, which is an energy storage chemical made from glucose.

The space between the sheets of hepatocytes is filled with small blood vessels called liver sinusoids. In the walls of the liver sinusoids are special cells called macrophages (Kupffer cells) that are capable of engulfing debris. A system of bile ductules runs between the hepatocytes. These ductules carry bile, which is produced by the hepatocytes. The ductules eventually join together to form hepatic ducts, which in turn join together to form the bile duct.

At the corners of each hexagonal liver lobule lie branches of the portal vein, hepatic artery and hepatic ducts, while the center of each lobule is occupied by a central vein.

Venous blood from the gut flows past the sheets of liver cells on its way to the central vein. Nutrients, bile salts and toxic and waste substances are removed from the portal blood by hepatocytes and processed as necessary. The central veins of all the lobules join together and contribute blood to the hepatic veins. These in turn drain into the inferior vena cava, which carries blood back to the heart.

Metabolic functions

The liver serves many metabolic functions. It receives all the blood returning from the gastrointestinal tract, which is laden with glucose derived from the breakdown of food. The liver converts much of this glucose to a storage molecule called glycogen. Glycogen can be converted back to glucose for release into the blood whenever it is required. This means that the liver plays a key role in maintaining a relatively constant concentration of glucose in the blood, regardless of the time of day or the energy demands of the body. Two hormones released from the pancreas, insulin and glucagon, are important in the control of this function.

The liver also plays a key role in the metabolism of other sugars, as well as fats and proteins. Liver cells have much of the cellular machinery (granular endoplasmic reticulum) associated with making proteins and glycogen. Under the electron microscope, granules of glycogen with the appearance of berries are often visible in liver cells. Liver cells also contain many mitochondria—tiny chemical power houses whose presence indicates very high metabolic activity in the liver. The position of the liver in the flow of blood from the gut also allows it to remove and destroy any toxic substances that may be ingested along with food and water. These toxic substances include alcohol, drugs and the chemicals produced by microorganisms. Bacteria entering the body from the gut must also get past the defensive scavenger cells (Kupffer cells) of the small vessels of the liver before they can reach the body at large.

The liver makes and stores vitamin A, which is essential for the well-being of the surface-lining tissues of the body, and stores iron, used in the production of hemoglobin in the blood. Bile, which is used to aid the digestion of fats, is made in the liver and released into the duodenum through the biliary system of ducts. The liver also produces albumin, an important plasma protein in the blood, which helps to control fluid movement between the inside of blood vessels and the spaces between the cells throughout the body. Finally, the liver makes several important substances involved in the control of blood clotting, including the clotting factors prothrombin and fibrinogen.

Bile is a yellow-orange fluid produced and excreted in the liver. It consists of water, bile salts and a chemical called bilirubin. Bile is produced by the hepatocytes and flows along tiny channels (bile canaliculi) towards the bile duct branches at the corners of the lobules. Bile is also continually recycled, as it is reabsorbed from the gut once the digestion of fats has taken place. About 90 percent of bile secreted by the liver is actually recycled from the gut. The bile flows back to the liver in the portal vein blood, where it is transferred by hepatocytes to the bile duct branches for delivery back to the gut for further fat digestion.

Diseases and disorders

Several congenital diseases may affect the liver. These include congenital bile duct atresia, in which the bile ducts fail to develop, and problems with the enzymes responsible for bile metabolism. Children with these disorders develop jaundice, or yellowing of the skin, during the first few days to weeks of postnatal life. This should be distinguished from the normal mild jaundice that occurs to some extent in all infants shortly after birth, and which disappears within a few days.

The liver may be damaged by penetration or blunt injury. Laceration of the liver or its blood vessels by bullets or knives can cause dangerous blood loss. Blunt injury occurs when there is a direct blow to the upper abdomen, such as in a car accident. Treatment involves the surgical control of bleeding by repairing torn vessels and maintaining the patient's blood volume by blood transfusion.

Hepatitis is inflammation of the liver, which can be caused by viruses (such as hepatitis A, B, and C), bacteria, parasites, nematodes, drugs or alcohol. The different types of viral heptatitis are transmitted in different ways; for example, heptatitis A by

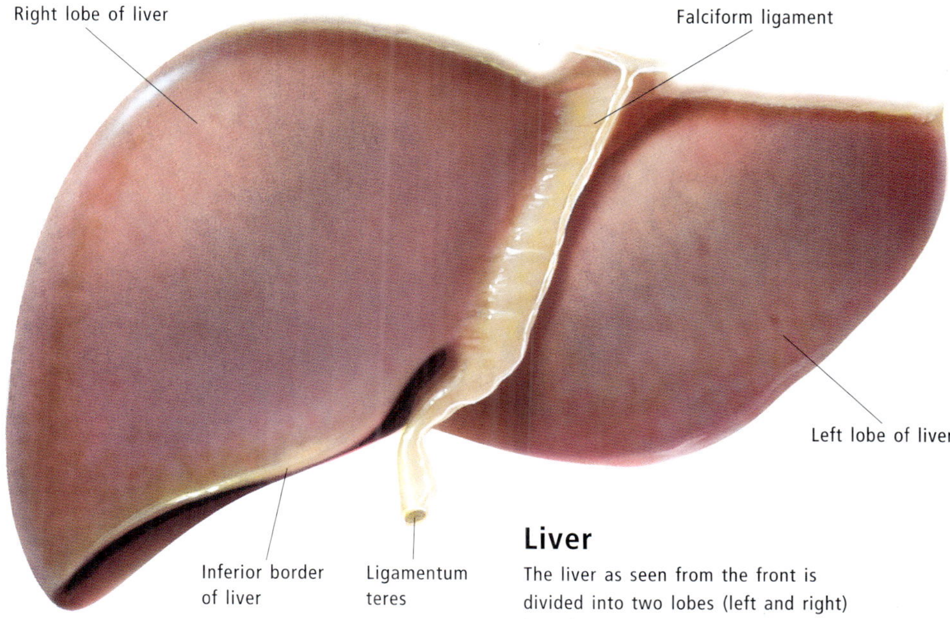

Liver

The liver as seen from the front is divided into two lobes (left and right) by a fold of peritoneum called the falciform ligament. The lower edge of the falciform ligament is called the ligamentum teres and is a remnant of a structure important before birth—the left umbilical vein. The left umbilical vein carries blood from the placenta back to the developing fetus and shuts down shortly after birth.

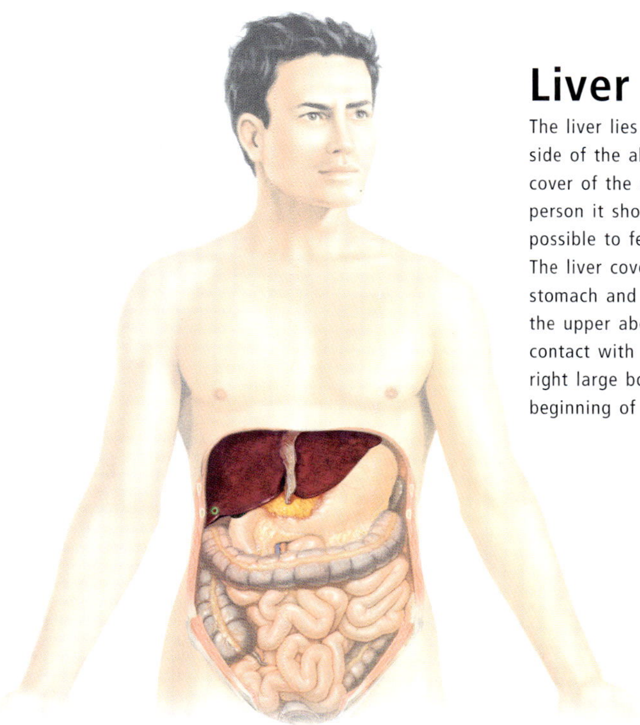

Liver

The liver lies in the upper right side of the abdomen under the cover of the ribs. In a healthy person it should not be possible to feel the liver. The liver covers part of the stomach and other organs of the upper abdomen and is in contact with the right kidney, right large bowel and the beginning of the duodenum.

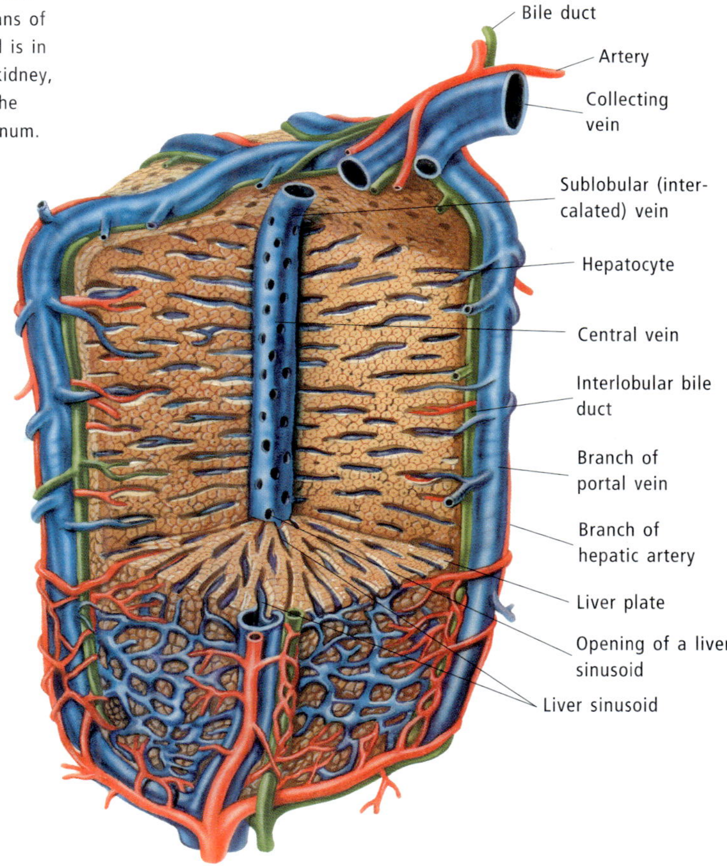

Liver lobule

The liver is made up of many hexagonal structures called liver lobules. Each liver lobule has a central vein at its core, which drains blood from the lobule to the hepatic veins that lead out of the liver. Blood arrives in the liver from the gut via the portal vein, which has branches at the corners of the liver lobule. More blood is brought into the liver by the hepatic artery and its branches. The bile produced by liver cells passes into the branches of the bile duct, which eventually drains towards the duodenum.

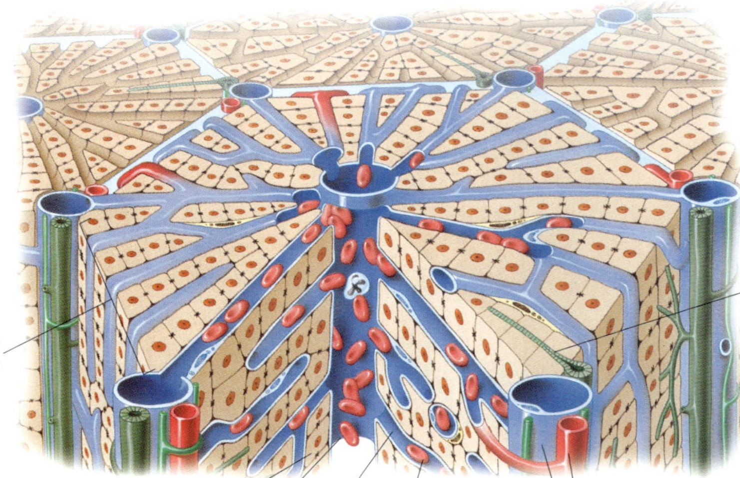

Liver—microstructure

Each liver lobule consists of radially arranged sheets of specialized epithelial cells interpenetrated and ensheathed by supporting connective tissue. Small blood vessels called liver sinusoids run past the sheets of liver cells. Branches of both the portal vein and hepatic artery feed into these sinusoids. Nutrients and toxic substances are drawn from the passing blood by liver cells and processed appropriately. Other fine tubular structures between the liver cells, called bile canaliculi, collect bile and carry this fluid towards the branches of the bile duct located at the corners of the liver lobule.

the gut through contaminated food or water and hepatitis B and C by blood, intravenous drug use with shared needles, or sexual intercourse. The incubation period for hepatitis A is 2–6 weeks, while type B and C have longer incubation periods of about 6 weeks to 6 months. Patients experience a period of feeling generally unwell, followed by nausea, vomiting and disinterest in eating. They may also develop fever, upper abdominal pain and yellowing of the skin and eyes (jaundice) due to high levels of a chemical called bilirubin in the blood. Sometimes, widespread destruction of liver cells occurs, with a progression to complete liver failure, coma and even death (though fortunately this is rare).

The liver can be infected by parasites, bacteria or fungi, resulting in the production of pus-filled cavities (abscesses). Liver abscesses may form in patients with diverticulitis of the bowel, or they may appear on their own. Patients with liver abscesses develop high fevers, up to 106°F (41°C), and chills. The liver is enlarged and may be tender. Treatment is by an appropriate antibiotic and surgical drainage of pus from the abscess.

Cirrhosis of the liver is a condition involving the death of liver cells, followed by fibrosis and regrowth of the liver cells in small lumps or nodules. Causes of cirrhosis include alcoholism; hemochromatosis, an iron storage disease; Wilson's disease, an inherited disease of copper metabolism; heart problems and immunological disorders.

Patients with cirrhosis often commonly develop jaundice. They may also experience swelling of the abdomen and ankles, breast enlargement and testicular wasting in men, mental confusion, disorientation and coma. The disordered regrowth of liver cells interferes with blood flow through the cirrhotic liver. This raises the pressure of blood in the portal vein, leading to a condition known as portal hypertension, which can have serious consequences because small veins in the lower esophagus swell (esophageal varices) and may rupture. Patients with cirrhosis can die from blood loss due to bleeding from esophageal varices, or they may develop low blood pressure, high levels of ammonia in the blood, coma and ultimately kidney failure.

Cancer in the liver may have spread from other parts of the body, including the large bowel, breast, lung, pancreas, stomach, kidney and uterus, or arise in the liver itself (primary cancer of the liver). In Western countries, cancer which has spread from other sites to the liver is about 20 times as common as primary liver cancer. Cancer may be spread to the liver by blood from the gut, along lymphatic vessels, or by arterial blood. Treatment may include surgery, if only an isolated nodule of tumor is present, or chemotherapy delivered directly to the liver. Life expectancy once a tumor has spread to the liver is very low.

Primary cancer of the liver is a very serious disease with a very low life expectancy after diagnosis. It is not common in Western countries, but has a high incidence in Africa and Asia, where the causes seem to be environmental and cultural rather than racial. The incidence of liver cancer among people from those regions living in Western countries is no different than in Caucasians.

Liver cancer commonly occurs in patients with previous cirrhosis of the liver. In developing countries, infestation with liver flukes or ingestion of a fungal toxin (aflatoxin) on grains and peanuts probably play important roles in its initiation. A particular type of liver cancer (angiosarcoma of the liver) is caused by industrial exposure to vinyl chloride. With primary liver cancer, removal of part or all of the liver is the only hope of a complete cure. Chemotherapy may also delay the advance of the tumor.

Diagnostic tests

Investigation of liver disease often involves taking blood specimens to test for liver enzymes, which are released from damaged liver cells. Removal of a small specimen of liver for examination (liver biopsy) may be performed to investigate jaundice, liver enlargement or suspected cirrhosis. Patients are given medication to calm nervousness, and a special biopsy needle is inserted between ribs 8 and 9 on the right side of the body below the nipple. The tissue is examined by a pathologist to assist in making a diagnosis. Other diagnostic tools for liver disease include ultrasonography, which uses sound waves to form images of internal organs; computerized tomography and magnetic resonance imaging techniques; and isotope scans to detect regions of high blood flow and metabolic activity.

SEE ALSO *Cirrhosis of the liver, Digestive system, Hemochromatosis, Hepatitis, Insulin, Jaundice, Liver function blood tests, Portal hypertension, Wilson's disease*

LIVER FUNCTION BLOOD TESTS

Liver function blood tests are tests on the blood which give information about the health of the liver. The liver performs many essential functions. It makes many important proteins, such as albumin and clotting factors. Albumin is the major protein in the blood, responsible for keeping fluid in the blood vessels and transporting chemicals.

Liver function blood tests will reveal levels of albumin in the blood. In severe liver disease, the albumin level decreases and fluid leaks into the limbs (edema) and abdominal cavity (ascites). A reduction in clotting factors also occurs, resulting in easy bruising and a tendency to bleed.

Other abnormalities may also be detected, such as abnormal enzyme levels. Liver cells contain enzymes which are released into the blood when they are damaged. An alcoholic binge will produce this, as well as damage by viruses or chemicals.

SEE ALSO *Liver*

LORDOSIS

Lordosis, often described as swayback, is one of a group of spinal deviations. It is an exaggeration of the normal forward or inward curvature of the lumbar (middle to lower) spine. It can be caused by diseases of the hip joint, obesity or abdominal enlargement. Physical therapy and exercises may be beneficial.

SEE ALSO *Kyphosis, Scoliosis, Spinal curvature, Spine*

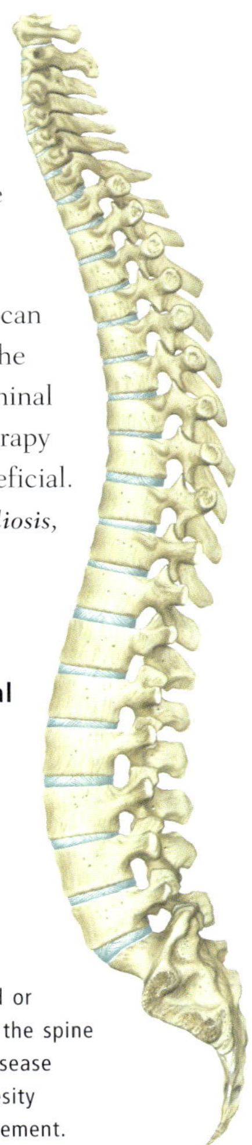

Normal spine

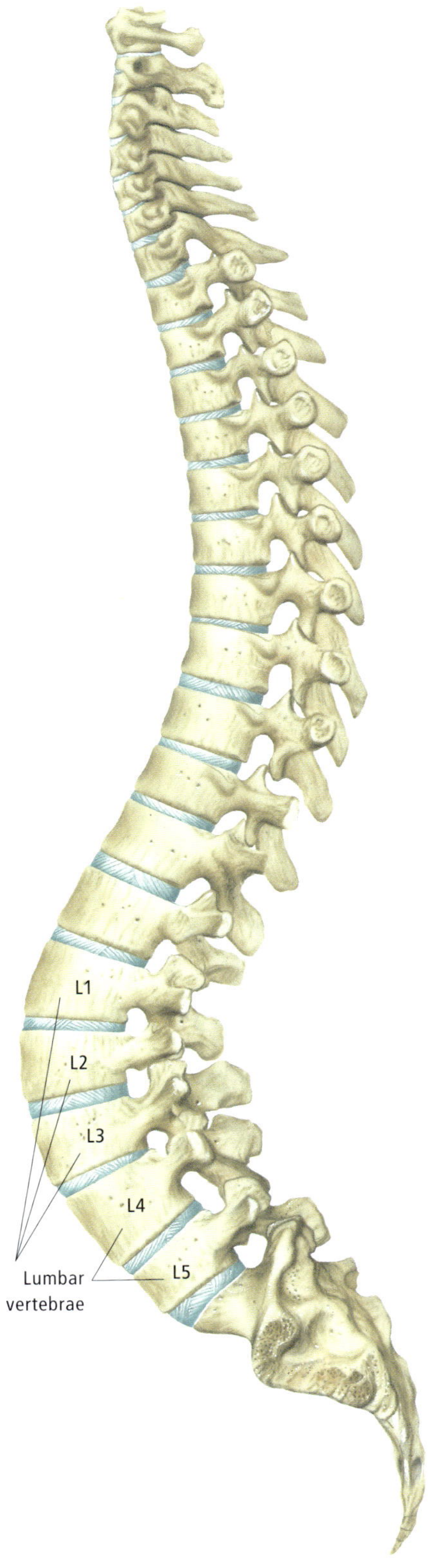

Lordosis

Exaggerated forward or inward curvature of the spine can be caused by disease of the hip joint, obesity or abdominal enlargement.

LUMBAGO

Although lumbago means simply "backache", it is usually applied to an ache in the lower portion of the back associated with spinal disk damage. When humans first stood upright, the spine became a weight-bearing organ, something for which it was not designed. As a consequence, awkward weight bearing and unusual strains can disrupt the disks between the vertebrae. When damaged disk tissue projects into the spinal canal, nerves are frequently comrpressed, producing neuralgia (such as sciatica). An operation to remove the displaced piece of disk or injections of an enzyme into the disk to make it shrink back into position may be required. Surgery is imperative if muscle weakness occurs.

Diagnosis depends largely upon the result of CAT scan, x-rays or MRI (magnetic resonance imaging). The patient may need advice on the best methods of lifting as well as back-strengthening exercises.

Lumbago may also be due to referred pain from pelvic organs, such as prostate inflammation and cancer, or associated with menstrual pains or uterine or ovarian disease.

SEE ALSO *Disk, intervertebral, Pain, Sciatica, Spine*

LUMBAR PUNCTURE

Lumbar puncture is a procedure that involves the insertion of a needle into the spinal cavity (usually below the third lumbar vertebra) to take a sample of cerebrospinal fluid or to administer drugs or an anesthetic. The five lumbar vertebrae are situated in what is known as the "small" of the back. The procedure is also known as a spinal tap.

SEE ALSO *Disk, intervertebral, Spine*

LUMPECTOMY

A lumpectomy is a surgical procedure to remove a small tumor or lump (benign or malignant) while disturbing as little of the surrounding tissue as possible. Lumpectomy is particularly associated with the treatment of breast cancer and is a more conservative form of surgery than a mastectomy where the whole breast may be removed.

A lumpectomy may be followed by radiation therapy and possibly chemotherapy to kill any remaining cancer cells. Depending on the type and development of the tumor, it may be the only treatment necessary. It may also act as a diagnostic tool through which physicians can decide whether more radical surgery is needed.

SEE ALSO *Breast cancer, Mastectomy*

LUNG CANCER

Lung cancer is a common cancer, ranked second in frequency in both men (after prostate cancer) and women (after breast cancer). It is usually more aggressive than other cancers and is thus the most common cause of cancer death in most countries.

Tobacco smoking plays a very important role in causing lung cancer. A variety of precancerous changes can be seen in the inner layer of cells (the epithelium) lining the major airways of smokers. Cigarette smoking is particularly incriminated, although pipe and cigar smoking also increase the risk of developing lung cancer. Long-term heavy smokers have at least a 20-fold higher risk of lung cancer than non-smokers.

The risk decreases for those who stop smoking, approaching that of non-smokers after 15 years, with a progressive disappearance of the abnormalities in the epithelium. Lung cancer can therefore be regarded as a preventable disease. Given that there is also a strong association between smoking and vascular disease, and increased risk of a number of other cancers in smokers, the implementation of public health strategies in this area is still only partially successful. Other risk factors for the development of lung cancer include exposure to asbestos, a variety of metal dusts, ionizing radiation and certain industrial chemicals.

Although most lung cancers develop in the epithelium of the airways, lung cancer is not a single type of tumor. Several different varieties can be recognized microscopically, of which one known as small cell cancer is of particular importance. As they grow, lung cancers usually invade through the airway wall, causing cough and sometimes the coughing up of blood. The cancer may also grow into the airway tube, which tends to cause obstruction leading to wheezing, repeated chest infections or breathlessness.

In a proportion of patients, the first evidence of lung cancer is the appearance of secondary growths, especially in the bones (causing pain), in the liver (causing enlargement) and in the brain (causing seizures and various other complications). This pattern is especially likely to occur in small cell lung cancer, which is spread quickly through the body via the blood. Unusual symptoms can also develop as as a result of hormone secretion by the tumor cells.

Early diagnosis is the key to effective treatment of cancers. In the case of lung cancers, however, few symptoms develop early in the course of the disease. There is as yet no available diagnostic test that is sensitive, easy to perform and inexpensive. While x-rays, examination for cancer cells in the sputum, biopsy via bronchoscope and other techniques allow a specific diagnosis to be made, these techniques are unsuitable for population screening. As a result, by the time symptoms become obvious and a diagnosis is made, the tumor is already quite large and has typically invaded into surrounding structures, spread via the lymphatics and the blood, or both. This is why the success rate for the treatment of lung cancer is still very poor.

Surgery and radiation therapy are used for most types of lung cancer, but early blood-borne spread of small cell cancers means that these tumors can only be treated with chemotherapy.

SEE ALSO *Cancer, Lungs, Smoking*

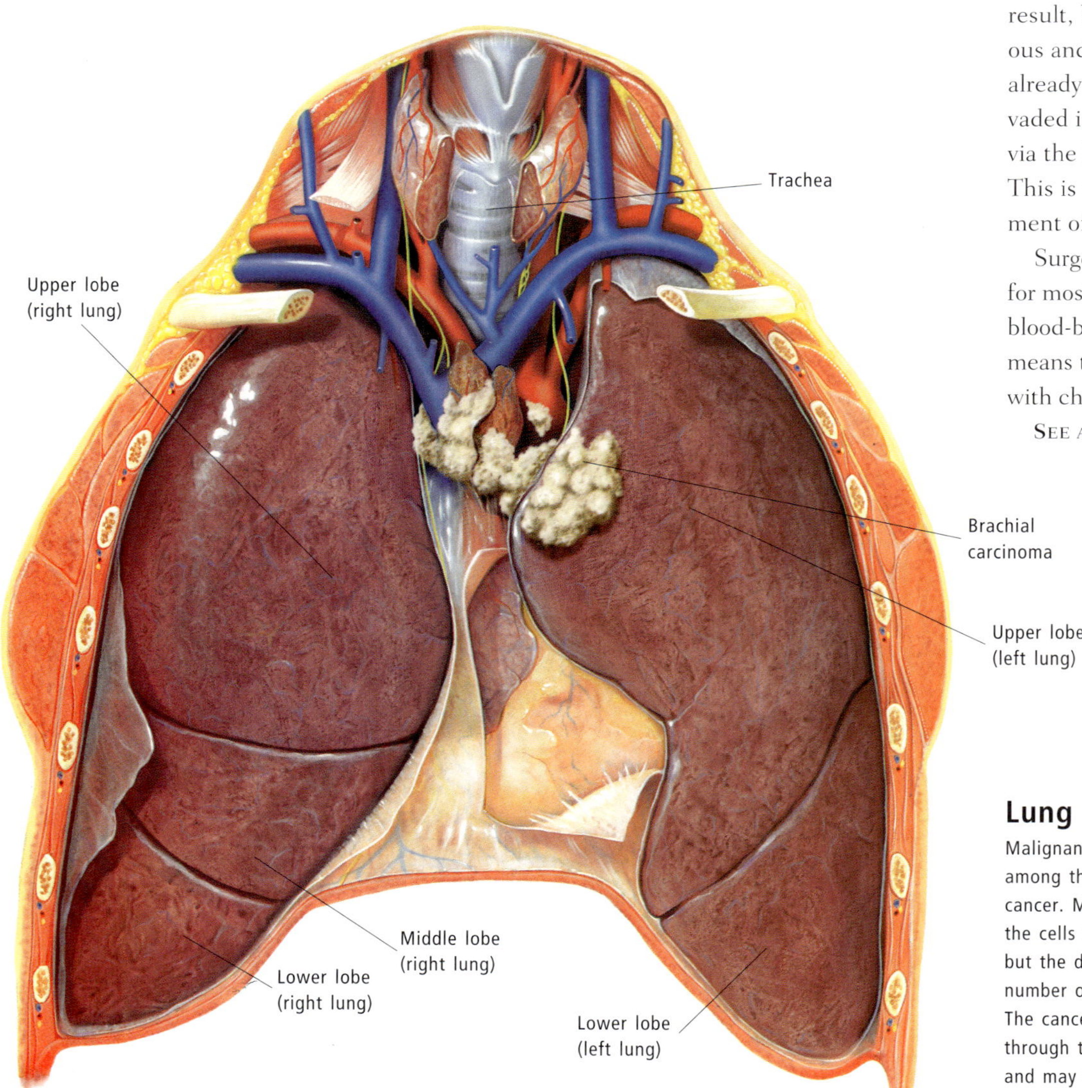

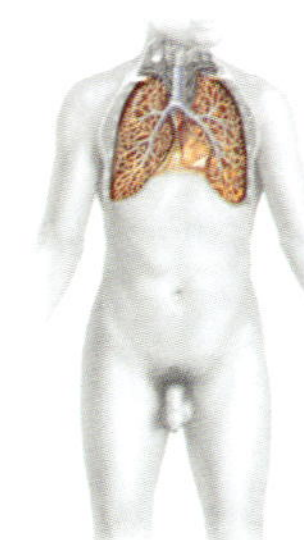

Lung cancer

Malignant growths of the lung are among the most common types of cancer. Most lung cancers arise in the cells that line the major airways, but the disease encompasses a number of different tumor types. The cancer usually progresses through the walls of the airway and may then spread through the blood to other organs.

LUNGS

The lungs are paired organs in the chest that are responsible for gas exchange between the atmosphere and the blood. Inhaled oxygen is supplied to the blood, and carbon dioxide is exhaled. The lungs are enclosed within pleural sacs, which provide a smooth, low friction surface so that the lungs can move freely inside the chest. Between the two pleural sacs, with their enclosed lungs, lies the mediastinum, a group of organs in the central part of the chest cavity. The mediastinum contains the heart, esophagus, trachea and major vessels and nerves.

Each lung has a roughly conical or pyramidal shape, with a base sitting on top of the diaphragm; sides in contact with the rib cage (costal surface), the mediastinum (mediastinal surface), and the backbone (vertebral surface); and an apex. The lung apex is encircled by the first rib and actually lies above the first rib in the hollow at the angle between the neck and the shoulder.

On the mediastinal surface of each lung is a region known as the lung hilum, where the large airways (left and right main bronchi) enter the lung and the major lung vessels (pulmonary arteries and veins) enter and leave, respectively. The bronchi subdivide into the bronchioles—smaller tubes which in turn subdivide into the alveoli (tiny clusters of air sacs). The lungs are divided into lobes, usually three in the right lung and two in the left lung, by a series of clefts or fissures (the horizontal fissure in the right lung and the oblique fissures in both the left and right lungs).

Inflation and deflation of the lungs

Most of the expansion of the lungs with each intake of breath, or inspiration, is due to the contraction of the diaphragm, the muscle separating the chest and abdominal cavities. Breathing out air from the lungs depends mainly on the passive recoil of elastic tension built up in the lungs and chest during inspiration. Some lung expansion is produced by the intercostal muscles, which lie in the space between the ribs and can actively raise or lower the ribs. As the lungs compress and expand, the pressure within also rises and falls in relation to the outside atmospheric pressure. The pleural sacs are at a pressure below that of the outside atmosphere. This ensures that when the chest expands or the diaphragm muscle descends, the lungs are also expanded as air flows in to equalize the pressure.

To reach the lungs, air must flow through the mouth or nose, pharynx, larynx, trachea and main bronchi. The walls of the windpipe (trachea), the main, lobar and smaller bronchi are strengthened by the presence of cartilage either as incomplete rings around the airway (as in the trachea and main bronchi) or as large plates (as in the finer divisions of the bronchi). Air reaches the lungs via the two main bronchi entering at the hilum of each lung. There the bronchi divide repeatedly, as many as 23 times, into finer and finer divisions (bronchioles), until the tiny air sacs known as alveoli are reached.

The inner surfaces of the larger airways are lined with special cell types. Some of these cells produce mucus to trap inhaled debris and bacteria, while others have fine hairs, called cilia, on their surfaces which beat rhythmically towards the larynx, thus wafting the debris towards the throat, where it may be swallowed or coughed up as sputum. In the air passages, particularly concentrated towards the alveoli, are scavenger cells called macrophages, which clean up debris and defend against invasion by bacteria. The inner surfaces of the alveoli are covered with a thin film of fluid, which contains a special chemical known as pulmonary surfactant. The surfactant helps to reduce the surface tension in the alveoli and thus prevent the tiny air sacs from collapsing when air is breathed out.

Gas exchange

The alveoli are the sites where gas exchange between blood and inhaled air occurs. The walls of the alveoli are extremely thin—less than a few ten-thousandths of an inch (hundredth of a millimeter) thick, and are richly supplied with thin-walled capillaries, filled with blood. Venous blood from the right side of the heart, which has relatively high levels of carbon dioxide and low levels of oxygen, flows through the lung's capillaries. As it does so, carbon dioxide in the blood diffuses into the air spaces of the alveoli, and oxygen diffuses from the air spaces to the blood.

Oxygen entering the blood is bound to a protein called hemoglobin in the red blood cells. Hemoglobin contains another type of chemical called the heme group. It also contains several bound iron atoms, each within a heme group, which assist with the transport of oxygen. Hemoglobin is the chemical that gives blood its red color.

Gas exchange in the lungs is most effective at sea level and is driven by the pressure difference for that particular gas between the alveolar air and the blood. At higher altitudes the partial pressure of oxygen in the air is lower, so that oxygen loading of hemoglobin may not be complete. People traveling from low to high altitude within a few hours will experience shortness of breath and be easily fatigued. In a healthy person, these symptoms will disappear after a few days to weeks as the body acclimatizes to the changed conditions.

Diseases of the lungs

Asthma is a very common lung disease characterized by recurrent attacks of wheezing due to obstruction of the airways. The airway obstruction arises because of a combination of spasms in the smooth muscle of the airway and excessive amounts of secretions in the airways. The underlying problem seems to be hyper-reactivity of the bronchial tree to a variety of inhaled stimuli. These stimuli include the house dust mite (*Dermatophagoides*), flower and grass pollens, feathers, animal dander, some drugs, foods, cold air, exercise, infection and wood dust.

Another important group of lung diseases in Western countries is chronic obstructive pulmonary disease (COPD). There are two serious diseases within this classification: chronic bronchitis and emphysema, which can occur together.

Chronic bronchitis is characterized by cough and sputum production, occurring on most days during at least three consecutive months for more than two successive years. The sputum may contain just mucus or may include some pus in it if additional infection is present. Chronic bronchitis is more likely to be found in people who smoke.

Emphysema often accompanies chronic bronchitis. Whereas chronic bronchitis mainly involves the larger airways, emphysema involves the destruction of very fine airways and alveoli. This is caused by a combination of repeated infection, tissue

Lungs

The lungs are divided into lobes. The left lung has only two lobes and is smaller than the right lung as the heart and its vessels take up more space in the left side of the chest. The trachea carries inhaled air down into the bronchial tree within the lungs, where oxygen and carbon dioxide are exchanged.

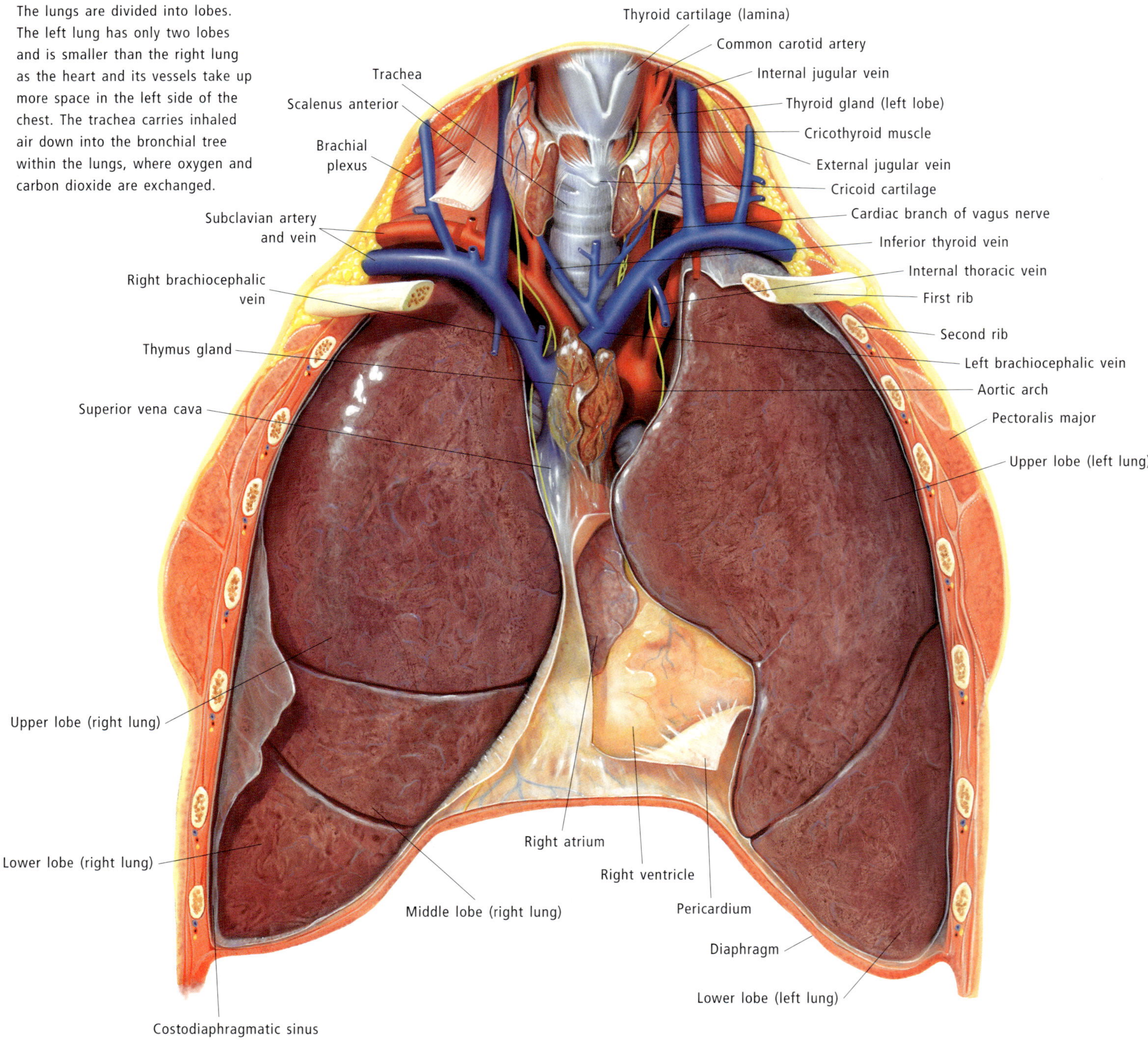

degeneration and over-distension of alveoli due to obstruction of the larger airways in chronic bronchitis.

Infections of the lung are of many different types and are named according to the lung sites affected. Bronchitis is infection of the large airways by bacteria and may follow viral infections of the upper respiratory tract. Bronchiolitis is infection of the finer airways (bronchioles) in infants and is usually due to respiratory syncytial virus. Bronchiectasis is the dilation of the large airways with the accumulation of secretions and chronic infection. The disease is usually seen in childhood. The incidence of bronchiectasis has declined considerably since the introduction of antibiotics, but is still seen in cystic fibrosis, congenital immune system deficiency, and after measles and whooping cough. Pulmonary tuberculosis is due to infection of the lung by mycobacteria. Tuberculosis is now much rarer than in the nineteenth century, but is still a serious public health problem.

Tumors or cancers of the lung most commonly arise from cells lining the large airways (bronchial carcinoma). There is little doubt that many bronchial carcinomas are caused by smoking. Nicotine does not by itself cause cancer, although it is very addictive and toxic to airway cells in other ways.

Lungs

The lungs are the two main organs of the respiratory system, lying on either side of the heart within the chest cavity. The trachea and a network of tubes (the bronchial tree) supply the lungs with air. Alveoli, tiny sacs at the end of the bronchioles, transfer oxygen from the air into the bloodstream.

NB: In this illustration the top two-thirds of the lungs and pleura have been cut away to show the heart and the bronchial tree.

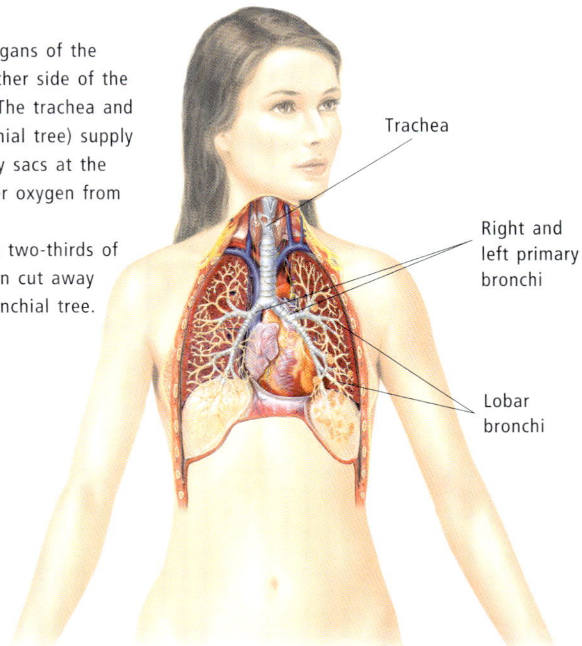

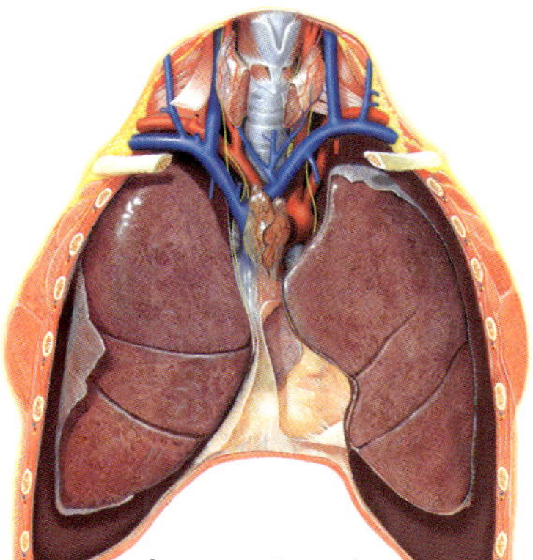
Lungs at rest

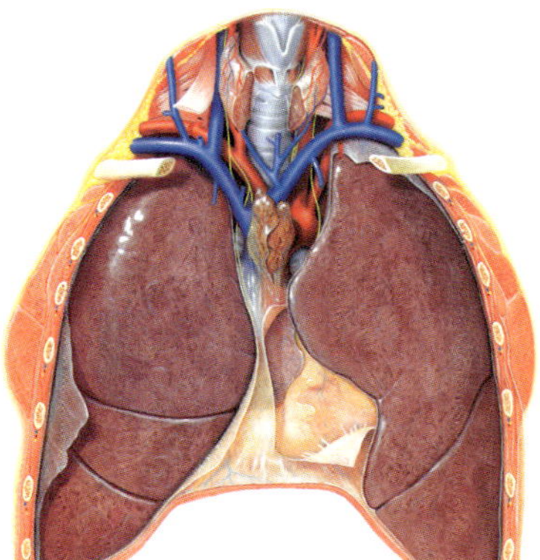
Inspiration

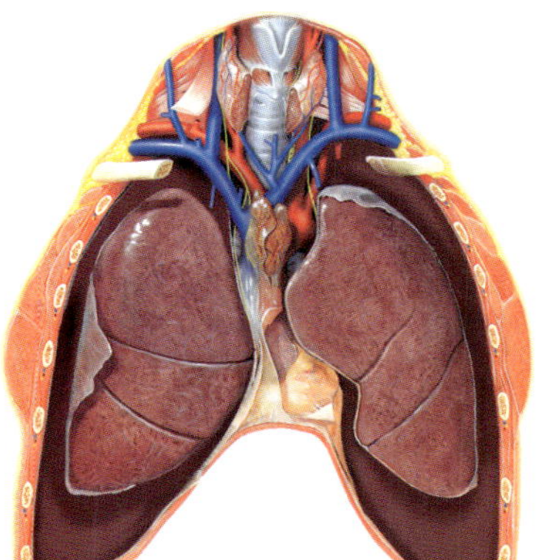
Expiration

Breathing

When we breathe in, the intercostal muscles move the ribs upwards and outwards and the diaphragm pushes downwards. This draws air into the expanded lungs.

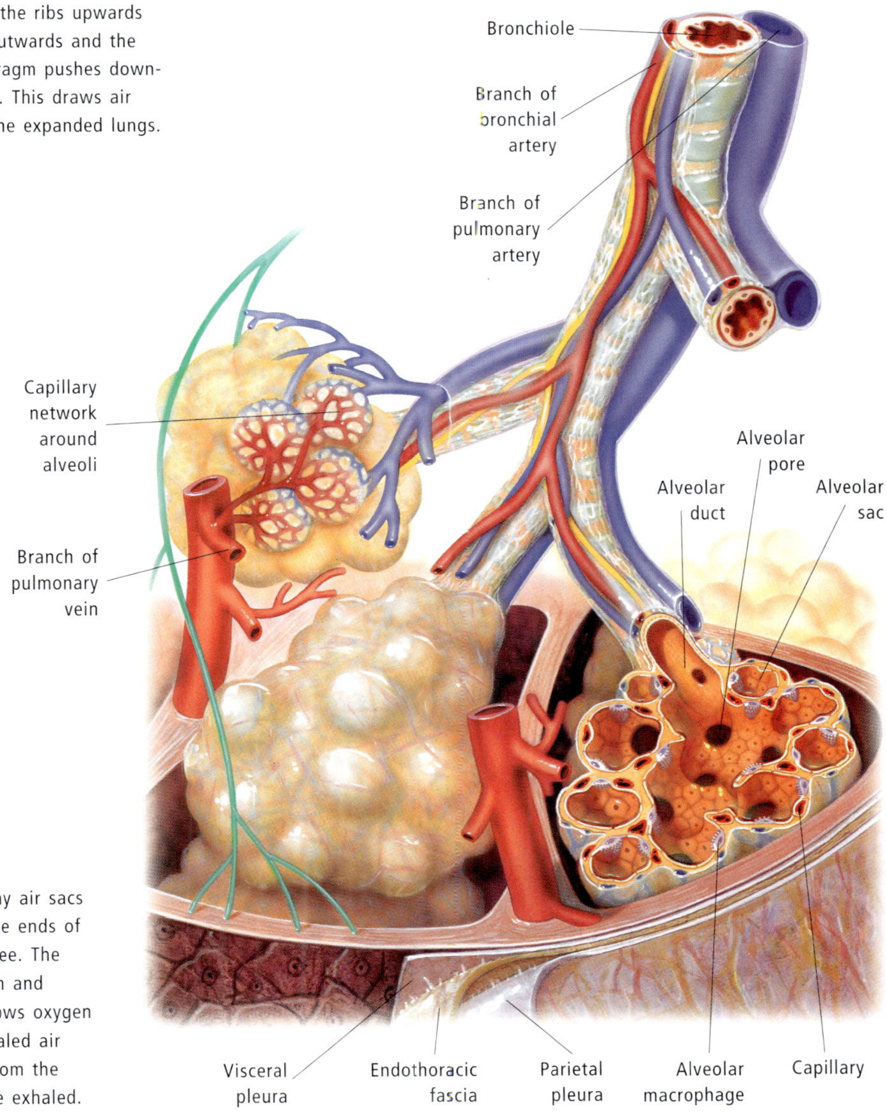

Lung function—gas exchange

The lungs contain millions of tiny air sacs (alveoli) which are located at the ends of the branches of the bronchial tree. The alveolar walls are extremely thin and coated with capillaries. This allows oxygen to pass into the blood from inhaled air and carbon monoxide to pass from the blood to the alveoli so it can be exhaled.

Other contributing factors are atmospheric pollution and the inhalation of uranium or asbestos during mining, although these are of small significance compared to smoking.

Occupational lung diseases are a varied group of disorders caused by exposure to dusts, gases or fumes. The largest group are the pneumoconioses, which are caused by prolonged inhalation of inorganic dusts such as coal dust, silica and asbestos. Asbestosis is a particularly serious form, because asbestos fibers can cause both fibrosis of the lung and cancer of the pleural sac (mesothelioma) and lung (bronchial carcinoma).

Another important occupational lung disease is extrinsic allergic alveolitis, caused by inhalation of organic dust which produces an allergic reaction in the lung (for example, "farmer's lung", due to moldy hay; "bird fancier's lung", due to pigeon and budgerigar droppings; and "malt worker's lung", due to moldy barley and malt).

Other occupational respiratory conditions include occupational asthma, in which dusts and fumes cause constriction of the airways within a few minutes to hours of exposure (for example, cedar dust asthma among carpenters), and toxic reactions to irritant gases like chlorine.

Trauma may also cause lung problems. Pneumothorax, where air at atmospheric pressure enters the normally airtight pleural cavity surrounding the lung, is one example. It may follow a penetrating injury to the chest or rupture of a lung airspace following blast injury. The lung of the affected side collapses, making lung ventilation impossible.

Some lung disorders are inherited. The best-known example is cystic fibrosis, a genetic disorder affecting one in every 2,500 live births.

Some lung problems arise because of disease of other organs. One example is pulmonary edema, which is the accumulation of fluid in the lower lungs due to failure of the heart to pump blood effectively.

SEE ALSO *Asbestosis, Asthma, Breathing, Bronchitis, Bronchoscopy, Cystic fibrosis, Emphysema, Farmer's lung, Lung cancer, Pneumothorax, Pulmonary function tests, Respiratory system, Smoking, Tuberculosis*

Lungs and heart

Pleural sacs around the lungs provide a smooth, low friction surface, allowing the lungs to inflate and deflate freely within the chest. Here the front of the lungs has been cut away to show the organs of the mediastinum—the heart, trachea and blood vessels.

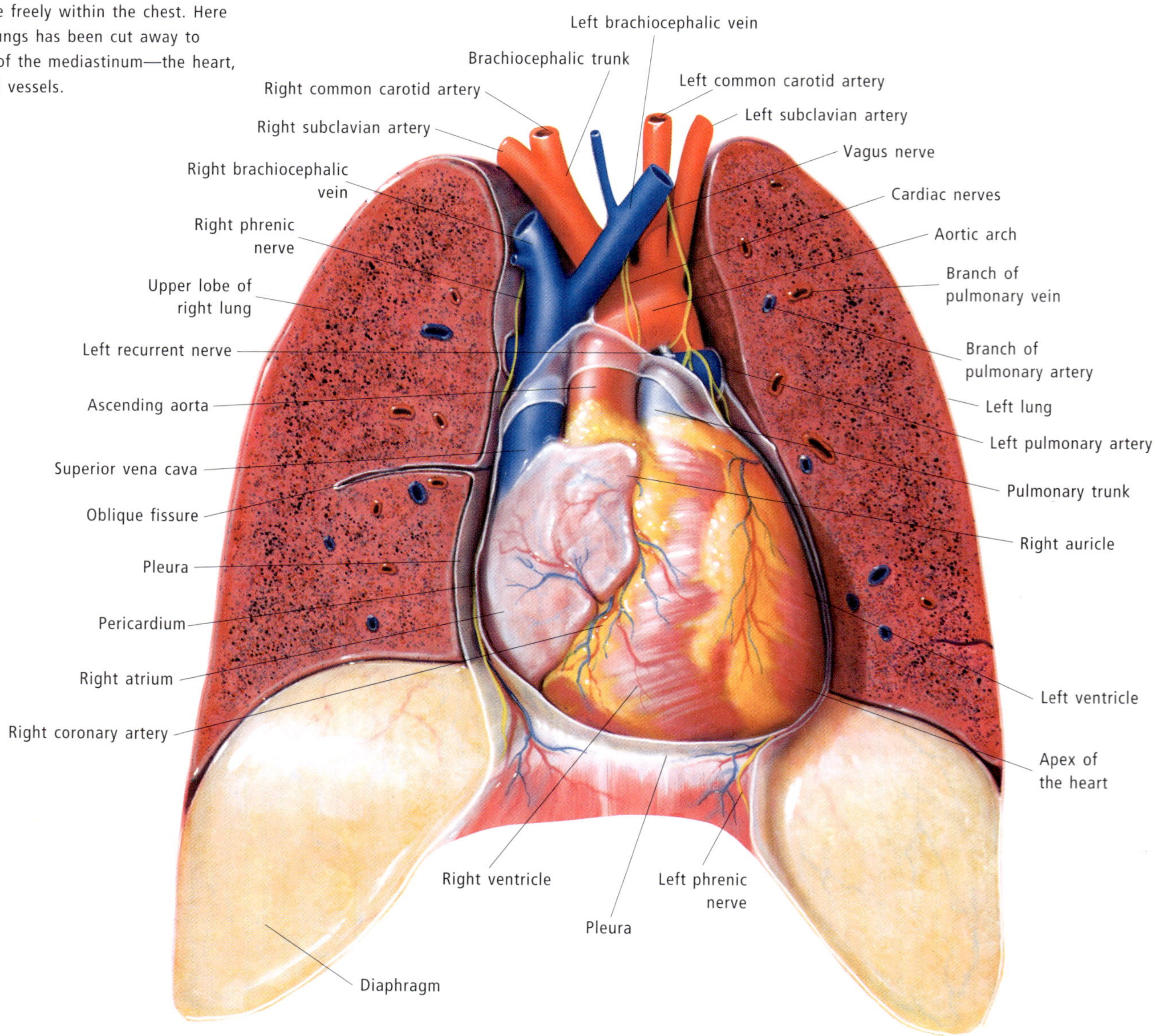

LUPUS ERYTHEMATOSUS

Lupus erythematosus is an autoimmune connective tissue disease in which the body's immune system attacks its own tissues. There are two forms: discoid lupus erythematosus (DLE), which affects only the skin, and systemic lupus erythematosus (SLE), which attacks joints and internal organs as well as the skin.

DLE is a chronic skin disorder that occurs most commonly in middle-aged women. It produces thickened, reddish patches on the face, cheeks and forehead. Sunlight makes the condition worse, so patients with DLE should wear hats and sunscreen to protect their skin. Corticosteroid skin creams are helpful. In severe cases, the antimalarial drug hydroxychloroquine may be beneficial.

In SLE, not only is the skin involved (in a similar way to DLE) but other organs are involved too. Generalized symptoms of fever, fatigue, weight loss and nausea are common. Arthritis usually develops in the fingers, hands, wrists and knees. A malar (butterfly-shaped) rash over the cheeks and bridge of the nose is a characteristic feature and may be made worse by sunlight. There may also be kidney, nervous system, blood, heart and lung damage.

No cure exists for SLE, but symptoms can be treated. Nonsteroidal anti-inflammatory medications (NSAIDs) are used in mild cases to treat arthritis. Corticosteroid creams are used to treat skin rashes. Antimalarial drugs (hydroxychloroquine) are sometimes prescribed for skin and arthritis symptoms. Severe or life-threatening cases may require the use of corticosteroid therapy, immunosuppressants (medications to suppress the immune system) or cytotoxic drugs, which block cell growth.

SEE ALSO *Autoimmune diseases*

LYME DISEASE

A multisystemic recurrent inflammatory disease, Lyme disease (also known as Lyme borreliosis or Lyme arthritis) is transmitted by tick bite, with symptoms ranging from skin lesions to chronic arthritis. It is caused by a corkscrew-shaped bacterium or spirochete called *Borrelia burgdorferi* which ticks, especially the *Ixodes* variety, collect from the bodies of white-footed field mice and other rodents. The ticks are dispersed by deer and migratory birds.

First documented in Europe in the 1880s as a skin rash, the full arthritic disease was named in the 1970s when a group of mothers from three towns in southeastern Connecticut—including Lyme and Old Lyme—became aware that their children all suffered from what was thought to be rheumatoid arthritis. The condition has now been reported in many other countries around the world.

Lyme disease is difficult to diagnose due to the variety of symptoms, which are similar to those seen in many other disorders, and to the fact that most sufferers do not recall the tick bite. The most recognizable symptom is a rash which may have concentric red rings and is accompanied by chills and fatigue. Days to weeks afterwards, there may be joint pain and problems with the nervous system or heart, and up to a year later skin disorders, arthritis and neurological problems such as facial palsy may appear.

Treatment with antibiotics in the early stages may prevent these later symptoms. However, if the disease has progressed, long-term treatment (including several weeks of intravenous antibiotics) may be necessary.

People living, traveling or working in tick-infested areas should wear light-colored long-sleeved shirts, long pants, socks, closed shoes, and a hat; tick repellent is also advisable.

SEE ALSO *Ticks*

LYMPH

The body's tissues are bathed in an almost-clear liquid called interstitial fluid, which filters out from blood vessels. It is collected (along with tissue and cellular wastes), drained away, cleaned in lymph nodes and

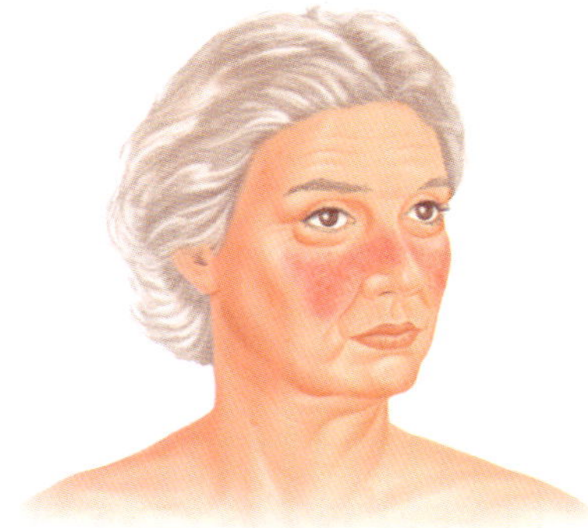

Lupus erythematosus

The body's immune system attacks its own tissues in this disease, producing a distinctive red rash on the face. Middle-aged women are most commonly affected.

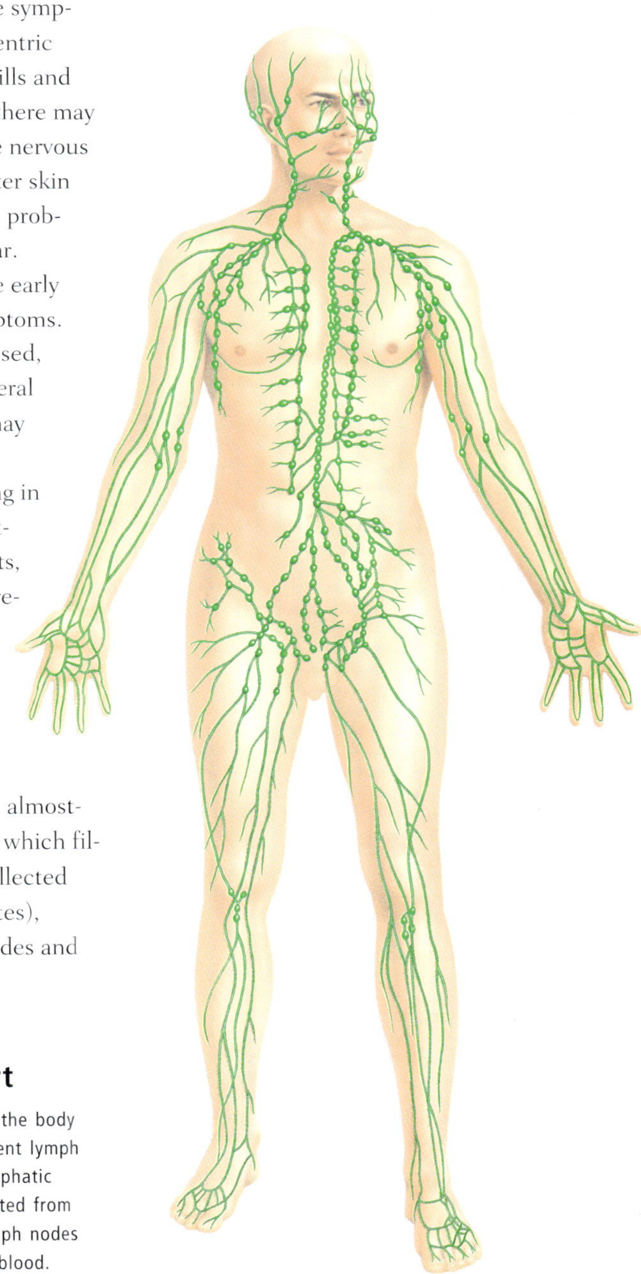

Lymph transport

Lymph fluid passes round the body via a network of transparent lymph vessels, known as the lymphatic system. Lymph is transported from tissues, filtered in the lymph nodes and then returned to the blood.

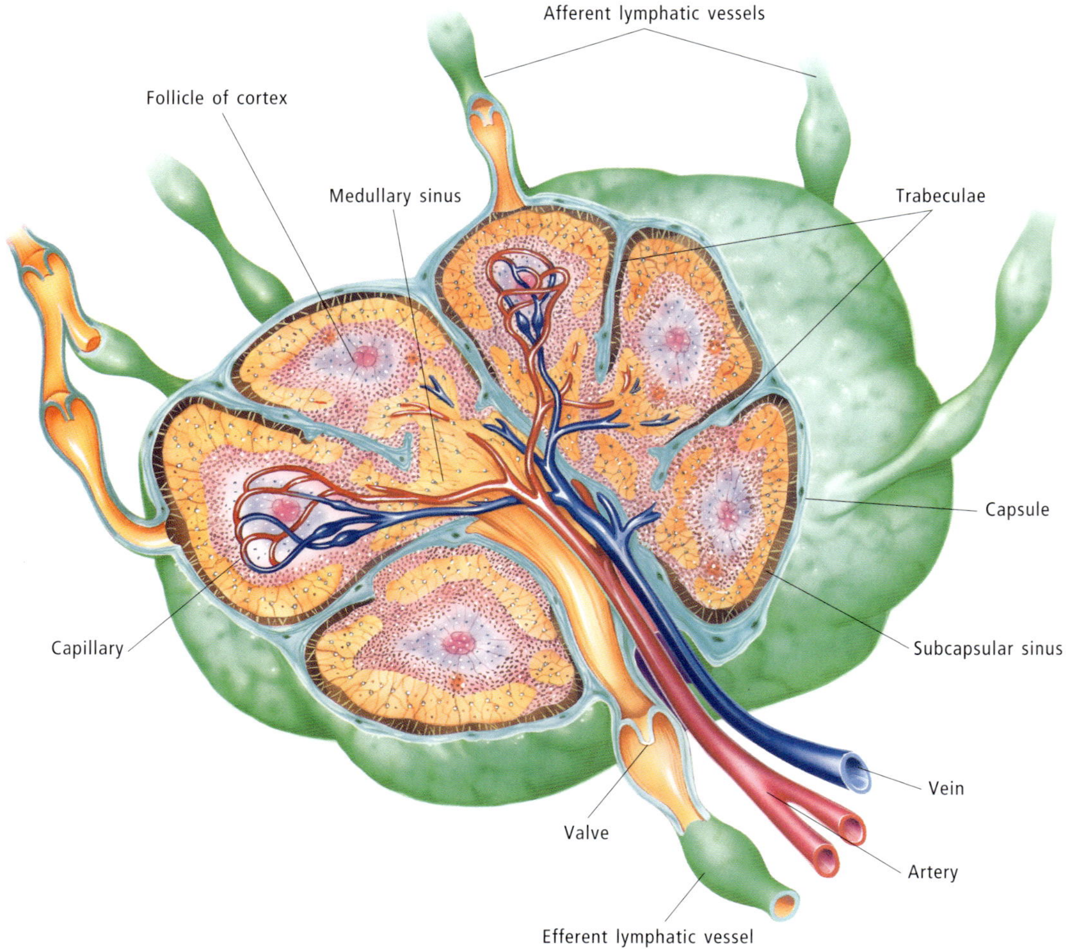

Lymph nodes

Lymph fluid is filtered and cleaned by white blood cells in the lymph nodes or glands. The nodes cluster in groups along the lymphatic vessels. Each node is enclosed in a fibrous capsule and has compartments divided by partitions of collagen fibers (trabeculae). Afferent lymphatic vessels bring lymph fluid to the node from surrounding tissues; efferent vessels transport lymph to the veins.

Lymphatic vessel

Numerous valves prevent the backflow of lymph as it passes through the lymphatic vessels. Blockage of the vessels can cause a buildup of lymph fluid, which may result in swelling of body parts.

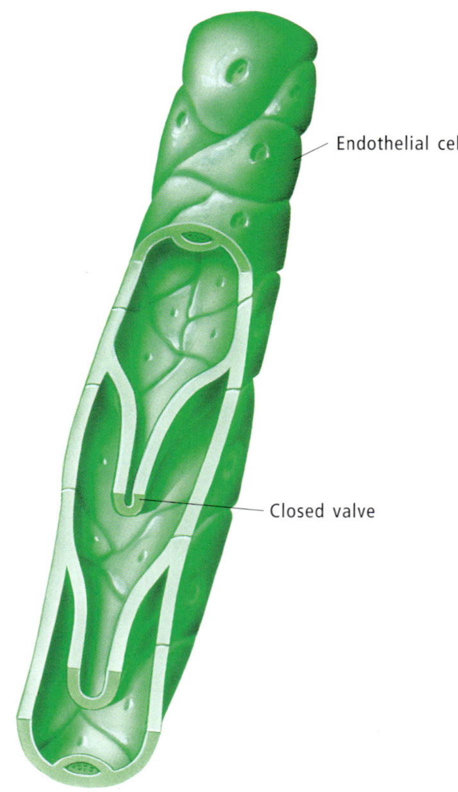

recycled back into the blood by the vessels of the lymphatic system. When this liquid is flowing through lymph vessels it is called lymph. It contains mainly water, protein molecules, salts, glucose, urea and disease-fighting white blood cells. Lymph also carries, en route to the blood, certain fats and fat-soluble vitamins collected from the digestive tract. The lymphatic system has no pump. The movement of lymph through the body is assisted by the actions of the skeletal muscle and breathing contractions and is slower than the movement of blood.

SEE ALSO *Lymphatic vessels, Lymphatic/Immune system, Lymph nodes*

LYMPH NODES

Lymph nodes, also called lymph glands, are nodular structures occurring along the course of the lymphatic vessels. They are composed of cells of the immune system, mainly lymphocytes. When foreign substances, such as bacteria, enter the body's tissues, they are conveyed via the lymphatic vessels to the regional lymph nodes. It is here that the body's immune system mounts the first defense against infection.

Normal lymph nodes are generally up to about ¾ inch (2 centimeters) in diameter, and can be felt under the skin in thin people. They are located on both sides of the neck, in the armpits and groin area, as well as in the internal body cavities. During a reaction to infection, the cells within a lymph node multiply and the node becomes enlarged and painful. Lymph nodes can also enlarge when tumor cells grow there. This occurs most often when cancers spread to regional nodes but may also occur in tumors arising in nodes—these are known as lymphomas.

If enlargement of the lymph nodes is detected and this persists without any apparent cause, a lymph node biopsy is performed to obtain cells for the pathologist to examine under the microscope. The biopsy can be performed either surgically or using a fine needle.

SEE ALSO *Lymphatic/Immune system, Lymphatic vessels, Lymphoma*

LYMPHATIC VESSELS

Lymphatic vessels form a parallel circulation to the veins and arteries throughout the body. Lymphatic capillaries drain fluid that has oozed out of capillaries into body tissues. The fluid, called lymph, is conveyed through larger lymphatics to regional lymph nodes. In the lymph nodes, the cells of the immune system can respond against invading bacteria or can ingest foreign particles, such as tattoo dyes. The protein-rich lymph is then channeled to the upper part of the chest cavity, where it passes through the thoracic duct to re-enter the venous circulation. Lymph from the intestinal tissues has a creamy color, due to absorbed fats.

The blockage or disruption of lymphatic vessels can result in the accumulation of lymph—this is known as lymphedema. Occasionally this occurs asthe result of hereditary underdevelopment of the lymphatic vessels. More often it is a consequence of repeated infection spreading to the lymphatics (lymphangitis), damage from tumors, or damage caused by the treatment of tumors. For example, surgery to remove lymph glands in the armpit involved by breast cancer can result in lymphedema of that arm.

Worldwide, blockage by filarial worms is the commonest cause of lymphedema, which may be so severe it results in elephantiasis. Treatment of lymphedema includes skin care, preventive antibiotics, elevation and compression of the affected limb and, more recently, microsurgery.

SEE ALSO *Elephantiasis, Filariasis, Lymph, Lymph glands*

LYMPHOCYTES

Lymphocytes are one of the major white cell types in the body and are the main cells responsible for our immunity. They circulate in the blood and are also found in the organs of the immune system—the lymph nodes and spleen. Several types of lymphocytes are now recognized. Most of the lymphocytes in the blood are T cells, which help the body fight certain difficult infections and also cancers. These are the cells ravaged by the AIDS virus, which leaves sufferers prone to opportunistic infections. The other main type of lymphocyte is the B cell, which produces antibodies to help fight bacteria and viruses.

SEE ALSO *Lymphatic/Immune system, Spleen, T cells, White blood cells*

LYMPHOGRANULOMA VENEREUM

Lymphogranuloma venereum (also called LGV, lymphogranuloma inguinale, climatic bubo or Nicolas-Favre disease) is a sexually transmitted disease common in tropical areas and spread by unprotected sexual intercourse. It is caused by the bacterium *Chlamydia trachomatis* and develops between 3–12 days after contact with the infection.

First symptoms are a small painless blister on the penis or in the vagina, which may become an ulcer and heal without being noticed. Lymph glands then become swollen and tender and may develop sinuses—openings to the skin surface which discharge fluid. Fever, headaches and joint pains may develop without treatment, which is normally the antibiotic tetracycline or, in pregnant women, erythromycin.

SEE ALSO *Granuloma inguinale, Sexually transmitted diseases*

Lymphocytes

Essential to the functioning of the body's immune system, lymphocytes are a type of white blood cell. Found in lymph, lymphatic tissue and the blood, they identify and destroy invading bacteria and viruses.

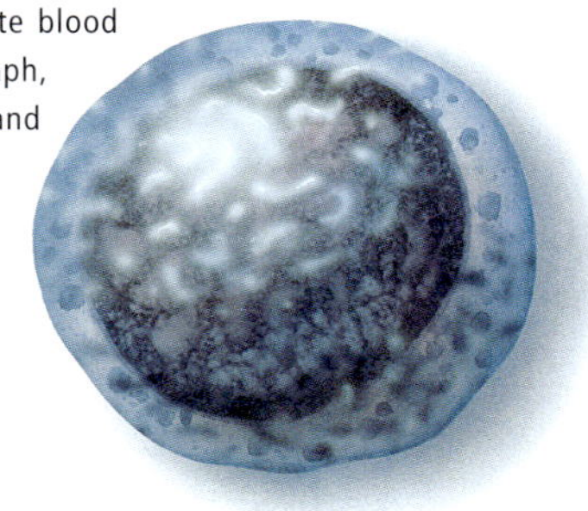

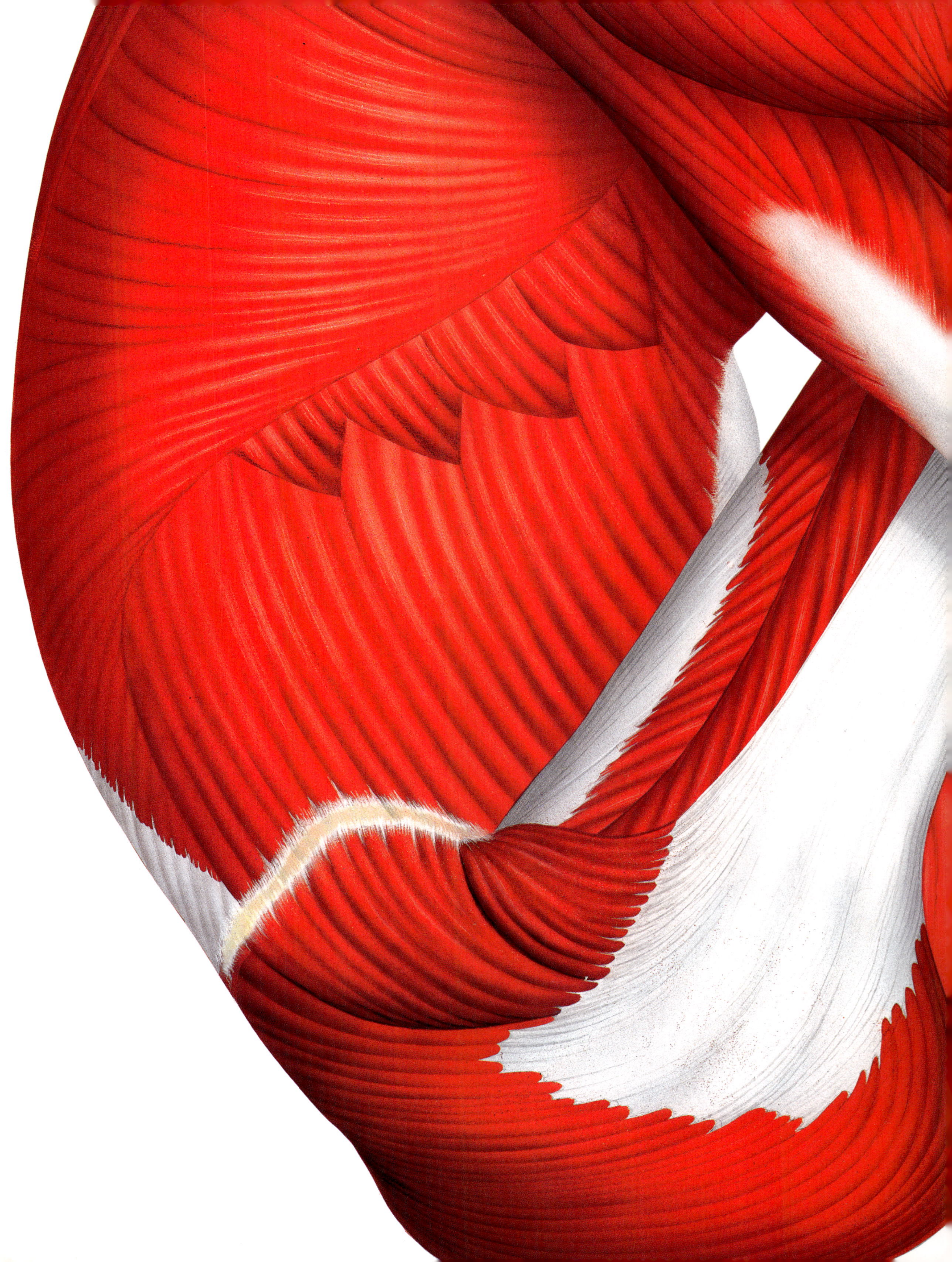

M

MACULAR DEGENERATION

A condition of the macula in which impaired blood supply causes gradual vision loss. The macula is the area on the retina that provides fine visual acuity, used in driving, reading, watching television or activities that require focusing on very small objects. The disorder results in the loss of central vision only; peripheral visual fields are always maintained. It usually develops over a long period, often going unnoticed in its early stages. The cause is often not known.

Macular degeneration is one of the leading causes of blindness in Western countries and is common in the elderly. There is no treatment; though laser surgery in some cases can slow the progression of the disease.

SEE ALSO *Blindness, Eye, Retina*

MAGNETIC RESONANCE IMAGING

Magnetic resonance imaging (MRI) is a non-invasive procedure used for imaging tissues that have a high water and fat content. MRI uses an external magnetic field created by a series of powerful electromagnets in a scanner to excite hydrogen atoms in the body, which give off radio signals to the scanner. These signals are read by a computer and converted into a detailed image. Because it uses a magnetic field instead of x-rays, MRI scanning does not expose people to radiation.

During an MRI, the patient lies on a table that slides into a cylindrically shaped machine, and must remain motionless for up to 90 minutes. The test is painless but noisy, and can cause claustrophobia in some people; a mild sedative can relieve the anxiety.

SEE ALSO *CAT scan, Imaging techniques, Ultrasound, X-ray*

MALARIA

Malaria is a tropical febrile illness caused by the protozoan parasite *Plasmodium*, transmitted to animals and humans by the *Anopheles* mosquito. There are four varieties of the parasite, the most common being *Plasmodium vivax*, followed by *P. falciparum* (which causes malignant or cerebral malaria), and then *P. malariae* and *P. ovale*. Usually two weeks after a bite by an infected mosquito, the patient develops violent chills and shivering, high fever and drenching sweats. Headache, muscle pains, cough and diarrhea may all occur. *P. falciparum* may also produce "blackwater" (dark urine) from the massive breakdown of red blood cells and the excretion in the urine of the blood pigment (hemoglobin).

Malaria causes over 1 million deaths yearly worldwide, especially from cerebral malaria due to *P. falciparum*. This type may progress rapidly, with confusion, convulsions and coma possibly leading to death within a day.

Diagnosis of malaria is made by the examination of blood films taken over three days. As malaria may not appear for between four weeks and several months after infection, tourists are advised to treat any unexplained fever on their return as potential malaria (or other possibile infections like dengue fever).

Many countries where malaria is common regularly spray insecticides to eliminate mosquitoes. As the mosquito needs water and animals to breed, malaria is not likely to be present in major cities and most holiday resorts. Even so, travellers should take precautions against being exposed to malaria and other diseases caused by mosquitoes. They should use mosquito repellent, especially at dawn and dusk, wear long sleeves and pants, wear light-colored clothing, avoid perfumes, perfumed soaps and deodorants, have mosquito nets on the beds, and use an insecticide coil in the room.

There are now kits for self-diagnosis and treatment. Travelers into malarial areas are advised to take prophylactic tablets such as doxycycline, chloroquine, primaquine or mefloquine. Unfortunately, resistance to these drugs is developing rapidly. For the treatment of an acute attack, quinine and artemisin-type drugs may be used together with combinations of the prophylactic drugs. Malaria, especially the *P. vivax* type, can become a chronic illness, recurring over many years.

SEE ALSO *Infectious diseases*

Macular degeneration

This condition involves the breakdown of the cells in the eye that allow the perception of detail. Those with macular degeneration can compensate for this partial loss of vision by using a magnifying glass.

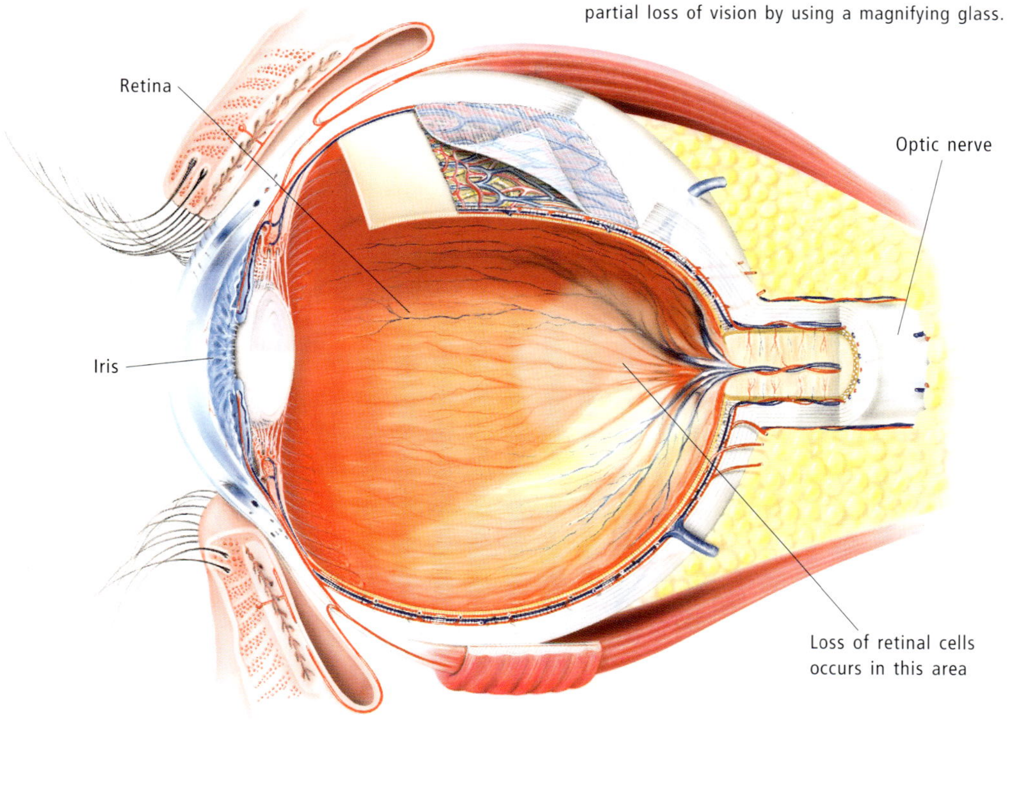

MALNUTRITION

Malnutrition is a condition caused by one of three types of dietary deficiency. Firstly, an inadequate intake of energy-producing food, such as carbohydrates, fats and proteins, which provide the calories needed for work. Secondly, inadequate intake of tissue-building food, particularly protein, especially in children and after illness. Thirdly, an inadequate intake of vitamins and minerals, needed for health.

Malnutrition is normally taken to refer to inadequate intake, but excessive intake is also a problem, leading to nutritional disorders such as obesity and heart disease.

Nutritional disorders can arise from, for example, defective intake of food (starvation); defective digestion and absorption (malabsorption syndrome); defective utilization of nutriment (such as cancer, which in later stages produces wasting); and loss of nutrients from the body (for example, nephrotic syndrome, where protein is lost in the urine).

Severe malnutrition is manifested by loss of body weight, particularly fat and muscle, together with the symptoms of associated vitamin deficiencies such as rickets and scurvy. Iron deficiency leads to anemia, and copper deficiency is believed to be an important contributory cause of heart disease.

Malnutrition is an economic and social problem affecting a large proportion of humanity. Even in regions where sufficient food is available for purchase, nutritional disorders may occur because of poverty, prejudice and ignorance. Malnutrition can also be associated with alcoholism.

SEE ALSO *Eating disorders, Minerals, Nutrition, Pellagra, Rickets, Scurvy, Vitamins*

MALOCCLUSION

Ideally, with the mouth closed, the middle lower teeth should abut against the back of the middle upper teeth. Any deviation of the teeth forwards, backwards or sideways will produce malocclusion. Although usually a problem with growing children—particularly if the teeth are too large for a small mouth—adults who have teeth removed from one side of the mouth may find that the remaining teeth drift sideways towards the gap and result in malocclusion. Other causes include unbalanced contractions of the muscles responsible for chewing, and prolonged thumb sucking. Tooth decay, inability to chew properly and tension headaches can all result.

Treatment is provided by orthodontists who, by bracing or banding the teeth and applying gentle but prolonged pressure, eventually straighten the teeth. In older children and adults, wisdom teeth must occasionally be removed to allow adequate room for the remaining teeth.

SEE ALSO *Braces, Orthodontics, Teeth*

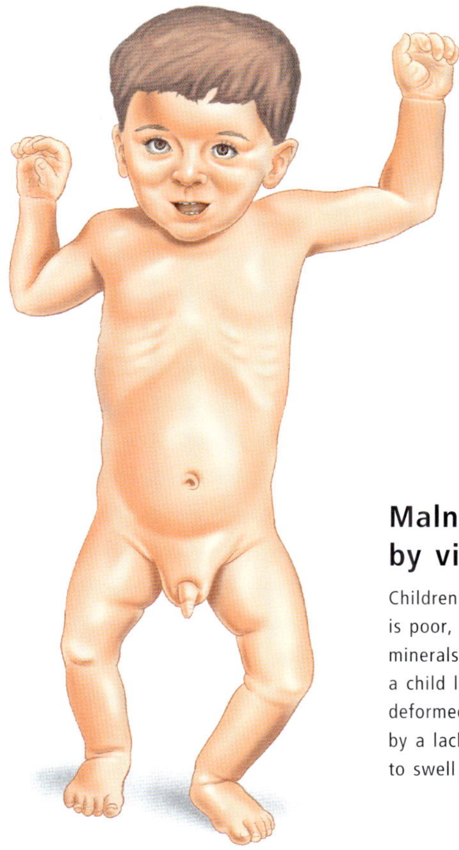

Rickets

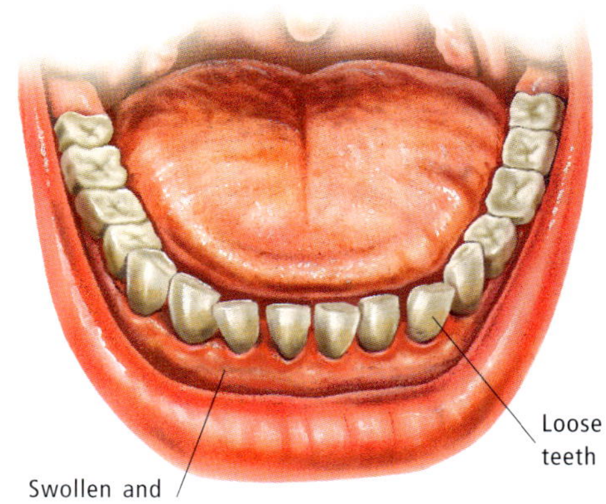

Scurvy

Malnutrition caused by vitamin deficiency

Children can easily become malnourished if their diet is poor, as they require a good supply of vitamins, minerals and proteins for growth. For example, a child lacking vitamin D may have weakened or deformed bones (rickets). Scurvy, which is caused by a lack of vitamin C in the body, can cause gums to swell and bleed, and teeth to become loose.

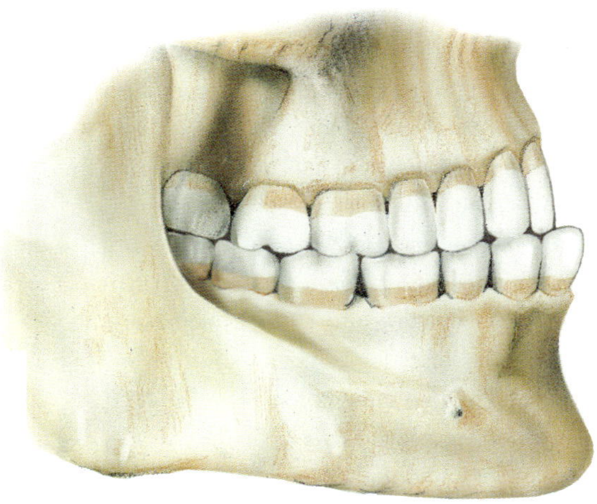

Malocclusion (underbite)
When the mandible (lower jaw) juts out further than it should, the teeth become misaligned and malocclusion occurs.

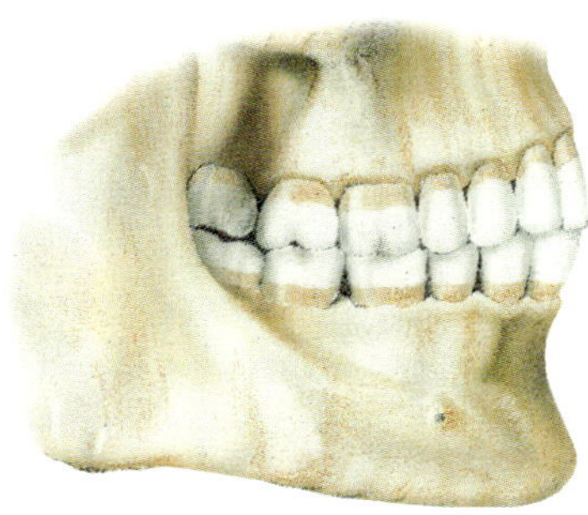

Normal bite
When teeth are correctly positioned, the middle lower teeth should abut against the back of the middle upper teeth.

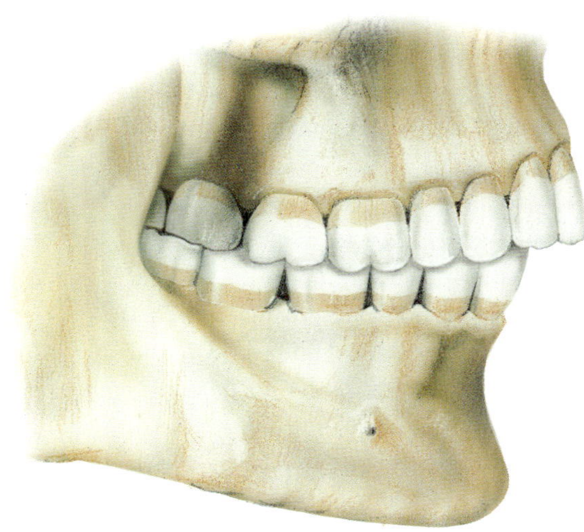

Malocclusion (overbite)
When the maxilla (upper jaw) protrudes over the mandible (lower jaw), or in some cases when the mandible is underdeveloped, an overbite malocclusion occurs.

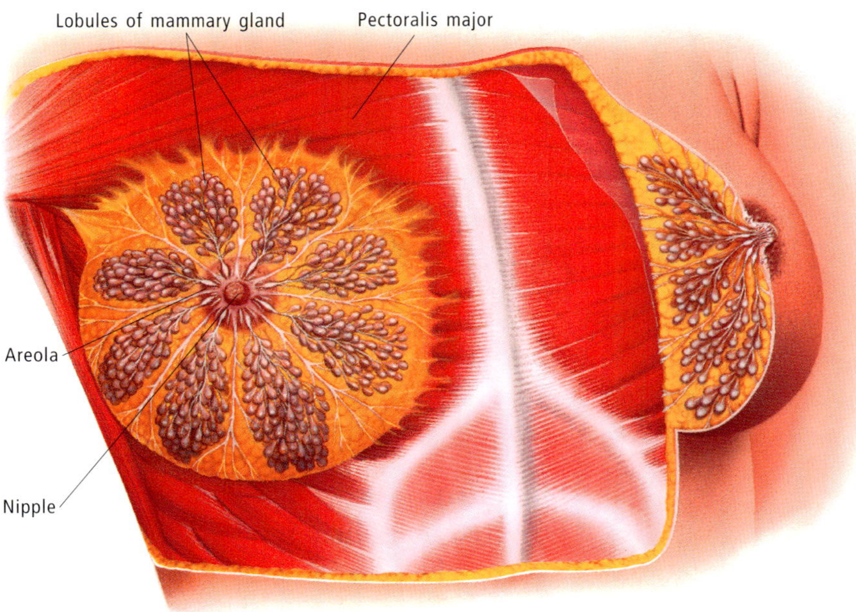

Mammary glands

In women, the hormones secreted during and after pregnancy stimulate the mammary glands to produce milk.

MAMMARY GLANDS

Mammary glands, or breasts, are modified sweat glands and are present in all mammals. They develop in the embryo along two narrow elongated regions (milk lines) extending from the armpit (axilla) to the groin. In humans a single pair of mammary glands develops under the skin of the upper chest although it is not uncommon for rudimentary extra mammary glands to develop elsewhere in the milk line.

Female mammary glands undergo considerable changes during the individual's life. At birth the mammary glands of both sexes are alike, consisting of a limited amount of glandular tissue leading into 15–20 openings in the nipple (some domestic animals have only one opening into the nipple). There is little fat or fibrous tissue. Some temporary secretory activity, traditionally known as witch's milk, may occur briefly just after birth under the influence of placental hormones.

After puberty, development involves elevation and pigmentation of the nipple and a considerable increase in fat and fibrous tissue. There is also some proliferation of the glandular tissue. Transient changes such as swelling may occur towards the end of each menstrual cycle.

During pregnancy, under the influence of placental hormones, there is a decrease in the amount of fat and fibrous tissue and an enormous increase in the amount and complexity of the glandular components. During the third trimester a liquid called colostrum is secreted. Colostrum contains milk fat and immunoglobulins but few nutrients. It continues to be secreted for the first few days after birth and then is followed by the production of true milk, induced by a lactation-stimulating hormone, prolactin.

Release of milk from the mammary glands is controlled by another pituitary hormone, oxytocin. Breast milk is rich in lactose, protein, calcium and fat, and also contains vitamins and immunoglobulins. Lactation can continue for several years if suckling is maintained. After weaning, most of the glandular tissue breaks down and is replaced by increased amounts of fat and fibrous tissue.

The glandular and fibrous components of mammary glands gradually decrease with age up to and after menopause, and there is an increased amount of fat. Fat is more translucent to x-rays which facilitates mammograms in older women.

The mammary glands in males have a similar structure throughout life to that of prepubescent females. Male mammary tissue is, however, sensitive to a variety of hormonal influences with temporary enlargement sometimes occurring at puberty and more permanent enlargement in ageing males. Considerable development may also accompany certain pituitary tumors which secrete excessive amounts of prolactin. Mammary enlargement in males or prepubescent girls is called gynecomastia.

SEE ALSO *Breast, Breast feeding, Colostrum, Estrogens, Menstruation, Oxytocin, Progesterone*

MAMMOGRAPHY

A mammogram is an x-ray picture of the breasts. It is used to detect tumors and cysts and help differentiate malignant (cancerous) tumors from benign (non-cancerous) ones. Any woman with breast symptoms such as a lump, nipple discharge, breast pain, dimpling of the skin on the breast, or a recent retraction of the nipple, should have a mammogram. Approximately 90–95 percent of breast cancers are detected with mammography. The test is also used to screen for breast cancer in women with no symptoms. The American Cancer Society recommends a screening mammogram around age 40; annually or every two years between the ages of 40 and 49; and every year thereafter.

SEE ALSO *Breast, Breast cancer*

MAMMOPLASTY

Mammoplasty is an operation to reconstruct a breast after removal of a tumor, or to change the size and shape of the breasts for cosmetic purposes.

Reduction mammoplasty involves reducing the size of the breasts and is commonly done to relieve pain and discomfort from enlarged breasts. A plastic surgeon removes some of the breast tissue together with excess skin under general anesthesia, and may relocate the nipples higher on the breasts. The operation can take up to six hours.

A breast uplift procedure is a shorter procedure in which skin is removed from a section of the breast; the areola, nipple, and underlying breast tissue are then moved up to a higher position.

Augmentation mammoplasty is an operation to increase breast size, shape and fullness. A plastic surgeon places breast implants—bags filled with saline or silicone gel—either above or below the pectoralis major muscle in the chest. The implant should last indefinitely, but if it leaks or ruptures, it can cause the formation of lumps in the breast. There is no evidence currently that breast implants cause autoimmune diseases.

Mammoplasty does not predispose a woman to breast cancer, and it should not interfere with normal breast feeding.

SEE ALSO *Breast, Cosmetic surgery, Plastic surgery*

MANIA

Mania is a form of mental disorder characterized by emotional excitement and lack of self-control and judgment, often resulting in impulsive, bizarre or violent behavior. Other symptoms include excessive euphoric feelings, a decreased need for sleep, an unrealistic belief in one's abilities and power, increased sexual drive and abuse of drugs (particularly cocaine, alcohol and sleeping medications).

Mania is one of the phases of bipolar disorder (manic-depressive illness), a psychiatric disorder characterized by severe swings in mood from mania to depression. An early sign of bipolar disorder may be hypomania, a mild form of mania in which the person shows a high energy level, excessive moodiness, and impulsive or reckless behavior.

Lithium-based drugs help to lessen the mood swings of bipolar disorder. They may be combined with an antidepressant. Certain anxiolytics or sedatives may be used where lithium therapy is not tolerated or effective.

SEE ALSO *Bipolar disorder, Depression*

MANTOUX TEST

The Mantoux test is a test for tuberculosis in which a solution made from dead tuberculosis bacteria is injected between the skin layers, usually on the forearm. If a slight swelling or redness develops at the site within two to three days, this indicates the presence of infection-fighting antibodies which in turn indicate a past or present infection with tuberculosis. Infections less than two weeks old may not show up with this test. Named after French physician Charles Mantoux, who developed the test in 1908, the Mantoux test is also known as a purified protein derivative (PPD) test.

SEE ALSO *Tuberculosis*

MANUAL LYMPH DRAINAGE

The technique of manual lymph drainage was pioneered in the 1930s by Danish therapists Astrid and Emil Vodder. This alternative therapy is a gentle pumping massage that claims to help the circulation of the lymph and its flow in the blood circulation. The massage rhythm is slow and only light pressure is used because the lymph vessels are close to the skin's surface.

The sequence of the massage through the body is crucial, since the therapist follows the flow of the lymphatic system. First the superficial lymphatic nodes are emptied with circular movements over the main lymph node of each section of the body (located in the neck, armpit, groin, knees and elbows). Then rhythmical pumping movements are performed up towards the nodes. The whole procedure takes around an hour.

Alternative therapists believe that manual lymphatic drainage will speed up the removal of waste products through the lymphatic system. They recommend it for the treatment of edema, acne, eczema and cellulitis, and to help reduce swelling and scarring resulting from injuries. This treatment may also be used for rheumatism or neurological disorders such as migraine or neuralgia. It is most commonly performed by massage therapists and naturopaths.

SEE ALSO *Lymph, Lymphatic/Immune system, Massage*

MARIJUANA

Marijuana (cannabis) is a drug derived from Indian hemp that is now in widespread—and mostly illegal—use in Western society. The dried leaves and flowers are used to make cigarettes, or the tarry resin (hashish) smoked in a pipe or eaten cooked in cakes or bread. Marijuana is a sedative-type drug which produces a euphoric or tranquilized state, and colors, sounds and pleasurable sensations may appear heightened. Motor abilities decrease, making driving unsafe. Early use during pre-adolescence may affect development of visual abilities and produce permanent attention disorders. Other effects may include arterial disease, even in adolescent users. Heavy or chronic use can lead to mental disorders and has been known to precipitate or worsen psychiatric conditions such as schizophrenia and panic attacks. Bronchitis is common in heavy smokers, and there is an increased risk of lung cancer as with cigarette smoking. Marijuana is used in some countries as a pain killer and anti-nausea drug, especially in cancer, where its use is strictly controlled.

SEE ALSO *Drug dependence*

MASSAGE

The practice of massage is as old as humankind, with many variations being found throughout the world. Chinese artifacts point to the practice of massage as far back as 3000 BC. An Indian Ayurvedic medical text written about 1800 BC describes how to rub and "shampoo" the body to aid its recovery after injury. In ancient Greece and Rome, massage was a principal method of medical treatment. The Greek physician Hippocrates wrote in 400 BC that "The physician must be experienced in many things, but assuredly in rubbing... for rubbing can bind a joint which is too loose and loosen a joint that is too hard".

After the collapse of the Roman Empire, massage fell out of favor in Europe as it was associated with the sinful pleasures of the flesh. It was not until the early nineteenth century that massage became more popular, due to the development of the Swedish massage technique by Per Henrik Ling, a medical professor and gymnastics instructor. Ling studied ancient Greek and Roman massage techniques as well as those from Asia where the use of massage was highly respected and well-developed. In Stockholm, massage studies were offered by a Western college for the first time in 1813. Massage was incorporated into other natural therapies that were being pioneered around this time, such as naturopathy, hydrotherapy and chiropractic.

Benefits of massage

Massage aims to work on both body and mind. On a physical level, massage generates a mechanical heat which has beneficial effects throughout the body. It is believed to relax the muscles and the central nervous system and stimulates sluggish body systems, aiding digestion and the elimination of waste products. Massage aims to reduce swelling, stimulate blood and lymph flow, soften skin and scar tissue and break down fibrous tissue around joints.

Emotionally, massage helps people to relax and feel "cared for", which relates back to the infant's instinctive need to be touched.

Techniques

Massage can vary from being a relaxing sensuous experience to a vigorous workout on the muscles. The more common forms of massage techniques include the following.

Stroking is used at the beginning of the massage to gently establish contact with the patient and to spread oil over the areas to be massaged.

Effleurage uses long, even strokes with steady pressure which increase warmth and circulation.

Massage

Massage—manipulation of parts of the body by rubbing, kneading or tapping—can relax muscles, stimulate blood flow, invigorate the skin and reduce stress.

Petrissage involves rolling and squeezing to loosen knotted muscle fibers; it may help to relieve muscle fatigue and release built-up toxins.

Kneading is used to relax and invigorate large areas of flesh not close to the bone.

Frictions are small circular movements made by the thumbs, fingers or heel of the hand which work on a deep level where there is a tension build-up.

Hacking is a light percussive chopping stroke, done with the side of the hands, that may increase circulation and stimulate the nerve endings.

Cupping is a percussive movement with a slightly cupped palm; it draws blood to the surface and is extremely invigorating.

Styles

There are a huge range of different massage styles available now throughout the world. The most common are the following.

Swedish massage

This is a system of soft tissue and muscle movement using stroking and pulling to relieve tension and relax bound muscle fibers. Swedish massage aims to loosen fibrous thickenings around the joints and to help the elimination of toxic and acidic deposits, and fatty accumulations. It is used in health spas and gyms to break up cellulite deposits before applying stronger stimulation using connective tissue massage and vibration. It is also often used by physical therapists, especially to restore blood circulation and limb movement to stroke patients or people confined to bed for long periods. In Swedish massage, fixed oils are used to reduce friction on the skin. Essential oils may also be used to give an aromatherapy massage.

Connective tissue massage

This is a vigorous massage involving strong upward stroking and pulling move

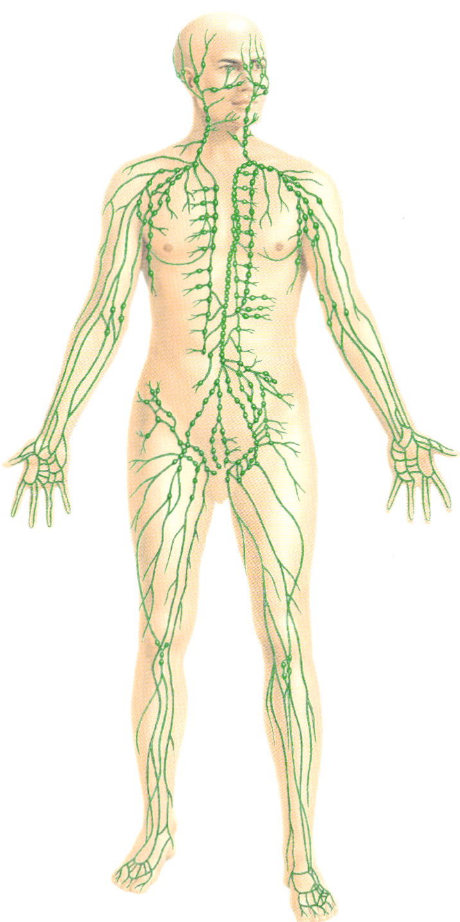

Lymphatic benefits

Massage can increase the flow of lymph in the body, improving circulation and reducing inflammation.

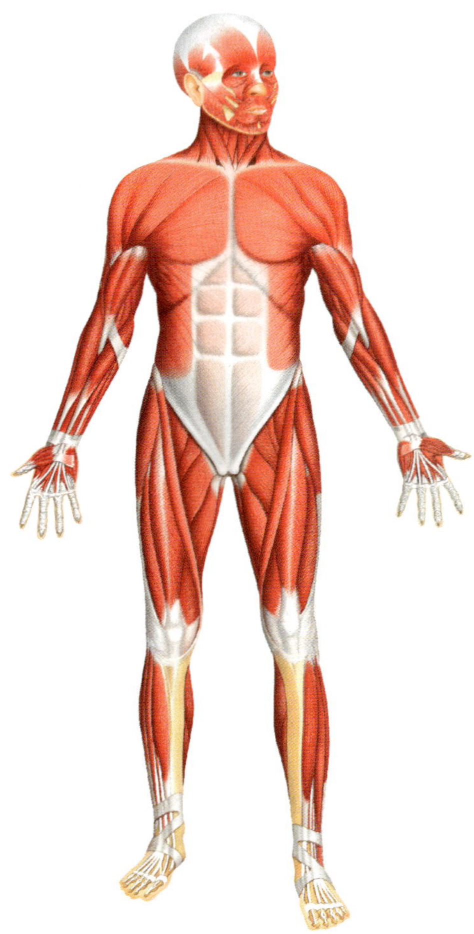

Muscular benefits

Tense or tight muscles all over the body can be relaxed, stretched and made more flexible with massage.

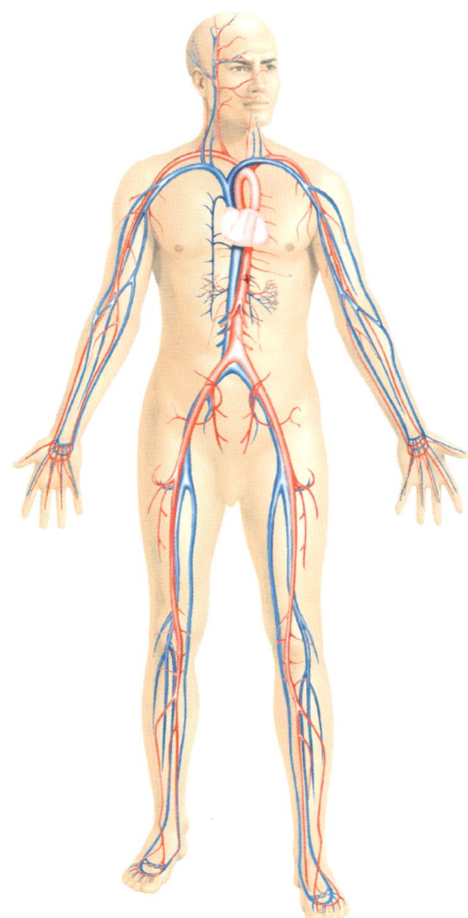

Circulatory benefits

The rubbing action of massage encourages blood to circulate around the body, increasing vitality and energy.

ments that may stimulate lymphatic drainage, decongest areas of fluid retention and break up localized fatty deposits. It is also used as a cellulite treatment.

Remedial massage
In remedial massage, Swedish massage techniques are combined with other remedial work such as stretches, exercises, acupressure or reflexology. It is used to treat muscular problems of the back and neck. Sports massage is a form of remedial massage which helps prepare the muscles for vigorous activity and aids their recovery after such activity.

Deep tissue massage
Deep pressure is used to help the body realign itself to regain its natural posture. Deep tissue massage works specifically on areas which have been injured or misused to reduce muscle pain and tightness and to improve flexibility.

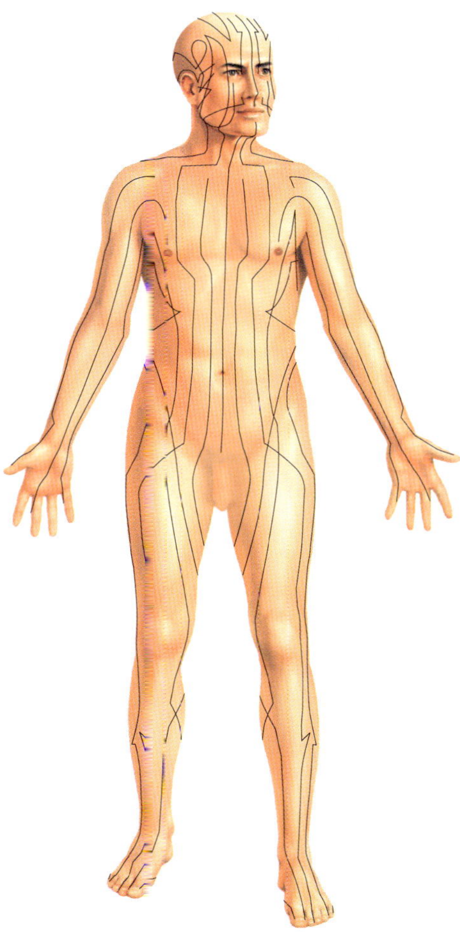

Eastern medicine

Practitioners of Eastern massage utilize the traditional Chinese meridian system, dividing the body into sections with a number of pressure points in each section.

Rolfing (also known as "structural integration" or "postural integration") and Hellerwork both utilize deep tissue massage in their treatment plans.

Polarity therapy
Developed by Randolph Stone, a chiropractor, osteopath and naturopath, polarity therapy uses manipulation and touch to balance the body's vital energy. Stone drew on the Eastern concept of "life energy" (known as *prana* or *ch'i*) and combined it with his studies of electromagnetic flows in the body. He mapped the body's positive, negative and neutral energies and devised hands-on techniques that he believed would stimulate their flow throughout the body to achieve an overall balance. Polarity therapy techniques can be integrated into other styles of massage.

Asian massage
Eastern massage styles are usually vigorous and deep. Pressure is applied on points mapped out by the meridian system of Traditional Chinese Medicine. Styles include Japanese *shiatsu* and Chinese *tui na*.

Ayurvedic massage
Ayurvedic massage is commonly practised at home in India, where there is a tradition of massaging babies every day for the first three years. Massage is done with essential oils to nourish the body internally and externally, and works through energy points in the body, known as *marmas*, using light, steady strokes.

Uses

Massage is believed to help relieve stress-related illnesses and muscular pain as well as aiding general preventive health care. In pregnancy, massage can be used to relieve insomnia and to ease back pain. Baby massage results in a calmer and more content baby while massage given to the elderly and sick provides both physical and emotional comfort.

SEE ALSO *Acupressure, Aromatherapy, Ayurvedic medicine, Manual lymph drainage, Shiatsu, Somatic therapies*

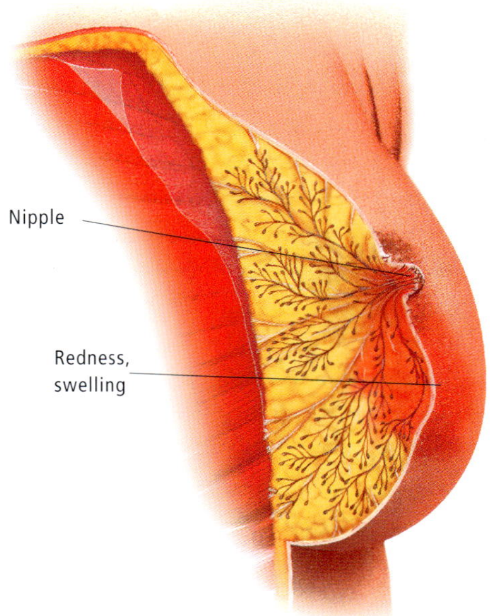

Mastitis

A sore and inflamed breast can result from a hormone imbalance or an infection of the tissues in the breast.

MASTECTOMY

Mastectomy is the surgical removal of the breast to treat diseased breast tissue, usually cancer. There are several approaches to removing diseased breast tissue, depending on the type of tumor present, its size, how fast it has grown, how widely the cancerous cells have spread, and the patient's general health. Lumpectomy is the surgical removal of a lump only. Simple mastectomy is the removal of the breast only. Radical mastectomy is the removal of the breast and the surrounding lymph nodes, muscles, fatty tissue and skin. Modified mastectomy is the removal of the breast and part of the muscles. A breast implant (prosthesis) can often be inserted at the time of the surgery (except in the case of radical mastectomy).

SEE ALSO *Breast, Breast cancer, Lumpectomy*

MASTITIS

Mastitis is inflammation of the breast. Acute mastitis is caused by an infection that enters the breast through a cracked nipple, most commonly while breast feeding. The breast becomes hot and swollen and there may be a fever. Mastitis is treated with antibiotic drugs, painkillers and bandaging of the breast. Breast feeding should be continued if possible. If an abscess forms, breast feeding should cease and the abscess must be incised and drained. Chronic mastitis is another name for fibrocystic disease of the breast.

SEE ALSO *Breast, Breast feeding, Fibrocystic disease of the breast*

MASTOIDITIS

Inflammation of the air-filled spaces encased in the mastoid part of the temporal bone behind the ear can follow inadequately treated inflammation of the middle ear (otitis media). The acute phase can often be reversed with antibiotics. However, should the infection become chronic, the patient will complain of severe pain behind the ear with associated fever, local redness and swelling. Appropriate antibiotics chosen on the basis of a culture from the inflamed middle ear may control the infection, but more often an operation to drain the area is necessary. Diagnosis is made both clinically and by confirmatory x-rays or CAT scans.

SEE ALSO *Ear, Otitis media*

MASTURBATION

Masturbation is the erotic stimulation of one's own, or a sexual partner's, genital organs for pleasure. It is a natural expression of human sexuality that begins in childhood and which can be an important part of self-discovery and satisfaction in a sexual relationship with a partner. Once the subject of taboos and superstitions, masturbation was said to cause numerous ill effects, ranging from hairy palms to insanity, none of which had any foundation in fact. Most people will masturbate at some time, some more often than others.

While children need to know the social etiquette of not masturbating in public, preventing them from masturbating can affect natural exploration of their own sexuality and lead to guilt and associated problems.

SEE ALSO *Sexual activity*

MEASLES

An extremely infectious viral disease, measles is spread by droplet infection. It is normally a childhood illness, but adults can also contract it. The incubation period is 10–14 days. Initially a high fever develops, accompanied by a runny nose and dry cough. Two days before the characteristic rash appears, small white spots, called Koplik's spots, may be seen inside the cheeks or in the region of the back teeth.

The spots fade within two or three days, by which time the rash will have appeared. The rash begins on the face and behind the ears, then spreads sequentially onto the body and limbs, including the palms and soles. The rash tends to be irregular and in patches. The lymph glands enlarge generally, while the eyes become inflamed, bleary and sensitive to light.

The eyes may discharge secretions. There is a dry cough, unproductive and exhausting. Within a week the patient begins to improve rapidly, though bronchitis, frequently appearing as a secondary infection, may persist. The rash fades but can leave temporary brown staining and may flake slightly.

Complications include middle ear infections, bronchitis, pneumonia and, most seriously, encephalitis or meningitis. If encephalitis occurs, usually three to seven days after the rash begins, the patient may sink into coma, have convulsions and vomit. Up to one in five people with measles encephalitis can die. Those who survive may remain epileptic or become retarded.

Beyond general nursing measures and controlling extreme fevers, little can be done to treat measles. Antibiotics may be of value if a middle ear infection or pneumonia occurs (as happens in 15 percent of cases). Vitamin A may be beneficial.

Since the introduction of immunization with an attenuated live measles virus in infancy (12–15 months), the periodic epidemics seen earlier are now rare. A booster dose is recommended at the age of 10–12, while people over 20 traveling into developing countries are advised to have a further booster. When immunized the child may develop a mild fever, slight cough and even a transient rash. However, this is not infectious. The measles vaccine is nowadays combined with mumps and rubella (German measles) vaccine (MMR). The vaccine, because it contains a live virus, should not be given in pregnancy or immune deficiency.

Measles has an average mortality rate in industrialized countries of about 1 in 1,000, more if contracted in infancy. In developing countries mortality is much higher because of coexisting malnutrition, other diseases and infections, and lack of access to medical care.

SEE ALSO *Immunization, Infectious diseases, Viruses*

Measles

Measles is usually a childhood disease. It begins with flu-like symptoms such as headache, fever, runny nose and cough, before a rash appears on the face and spreads to the rest of the body.

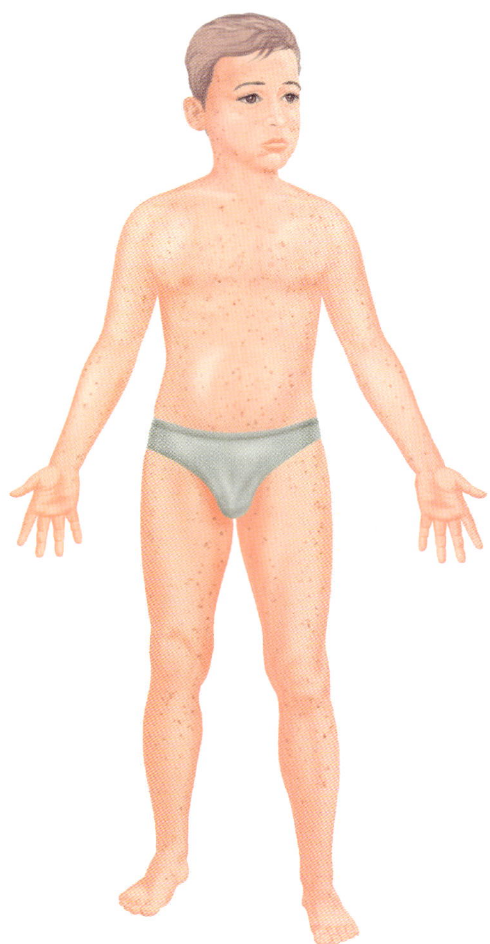

MEDITATION

While meditation is an integral part of many of the world's religions, it is not in itself a religion. It is a method of resting the mind from its habitual involvement in the "busyness" of thinking in order to achieve a state of relaxation and detached observation. This state may be seen as a prelude to experiences of self-realization, or it may be seen as an end in itself, bringing with it the benefits of inner peace and mental refreshment.

In the East, Traditional Chinese Medicine and Ayurvedic medicine have advocated meditation for thousands of years as an essential means of maintaining health of mind and body through its ability to bring about an emotional and mental equilibrium.

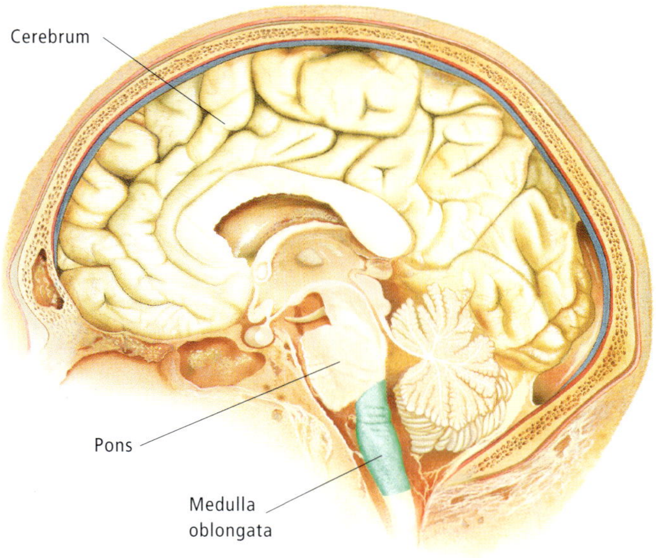

Medulla oblongata

The medulla oblongata sits above the spinal cord and below the pons. It is an important part of the brain, as it contains the nerve centers for vital functions such as breathing and heartbeat.

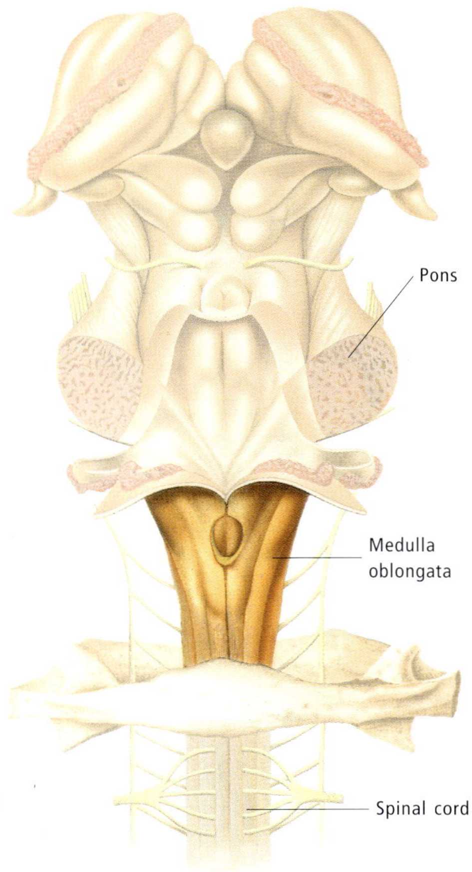

The health benefits of meditation began to be studied in the West in the 1960s when transcendental meditation (TM) started to become popular. In TM a personal secret phrase, called a mantra, is repeated, inducing a state of deep relaxation. Research showed this practise to lower blood pressure, protect against heart and circulation problems, and increase perceptual abilities.

TM is one of a range of meditation techniques which aims to achieve states of deep relaxation through the power of concentration, either by focusing on a mantra or an image such as a mandala or a flame, or on one's own pattern of breathing. Other forms of meditation, such as Vipassana, aim for a detached awareness by observing all that is going on outside and inside the meditator—sounds, thoughts, and sensations—without judging or getting involved in them.

The Vietnamese Buddhist monk Thic Nhat Hanh teaches a form of mindfulness meditation which can be done by bringing full attention to simple daily acts such as washing the dishes or answering the phone. In all cases meditation attempts to help the busy mind let go of all of its usual fretting over past and future concerns so as to become receptive and open to the present moment.

Meditation does not have to be done cross-legged on the floor. It can be done sitting in a chair or lying down, or in whatever position best supports the stillness of the body so that attention can then be directed to the relaxing of the mind. In some cases meditation teachers combine the deeply relaxed state of meditation with guided visualizations to induce feelings of peace and well-being.

One of the first doctors to study the positive effects of meditation on health was Australian psychiatrist Dr Ainslie Meares, who observed that it brought about a significant reduction of stress and discomfort in his cancer patients. Today doctors may suggest that their patients meditate as part of their health program, particularly those being treated for heart disease, cancer, AIDS and immune disorders, since the regular practise of meditation is believed to enhance immune function. Meditation is also taught in substance abuse recovery programs to build self-discipline as well as decrease anxiety.

MEDULLA OBLONGATA

The medulla oblongata is the upward continuation of the spinal cord which forms the lower part of the brain stem. It contains pathways taking information between the brain and spinal cord and gives rise to the hypoglossal, accessory, glossopharyngeal and vagus nerves. It contains a central core of gray matter called the reticular formation, which is involved in regulating sleep and arousal, and in pain perception. The reticular formation also includes vital centers that regulate breathing and heart activity. Trauma to the medulla oblongata may occur from a fracture of the skull base and is often fatal.

SEE ALSO *Brain, Skull, Spinal cord*

MEGALOMANIA

Megalomania, also known as delusions of grandeur, is an unrealistic and exaggerated belief or paranoia that one's self is of utmost importance. It is usually combined with the conviction that others do not recognize how important one is. Well-known megalomaniacs include the Roman emperor Caligula; the World War II Fascist dictator, Mussolini; and Shakespeare's fictional King Lear.

SEE ALSO *Paranoia, Personality disorders*

MELANIN

Melanin is responsible for the brown to black or golden coloring of the hair, skin and eyes. The melanins are a group of pigments found mainly in the skin, hair and the retina of the eye, and are also widely distributed in nature. There are two main types: eumelanin (dark) and pheomelanin (golden yellow). In the skin, the dark melanins serve to protect the skin against sunburn. Melanin is produced by cells called melanocytes, which pass the pigment on to the more numerous surrounding cells (keratinocytes, which produce keratin).

SEE ALSO *Keratin, Melanoma*

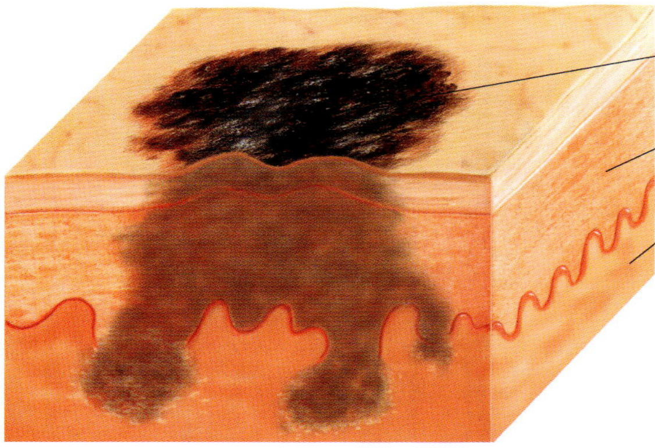

Melanoma
Melanomas are dark, cancerous growths found on the skin. They can begin as ordinary moles which become malignant.

MELANOMA

This is a dangerous form of cancer, which arises from pigment-producing cells (melanocytes), normally located in the deepest part of the surface layer of skin cells (the epithelium). The melanoma tumor is frequently referred to as malignant melanoma, which emphasizes its cancerous growth pattern (the term is now redundant because benign tumors of the melanocytes are no longer called melanomas, but are called "nevi"). Melanomas most commonly occur in the skin, but can also develop at other sites.

These tumors have the potential to spread via the lymphatic system and the blood, with a fatal outcome. On the other hand, melanoma can be cured if diagnosed early and treated appropriately by surgical removal. Thus it is most important for any individual who develops a pigmented area or lump on the skin to seek early medical attention.

Development of a melanoma of the skin is related to exposure to sunlight, especially in fair-skinned persons who lack protection against injury by ultraviolet rays. This is not the only predisposing factor, as a tumor may arise in a pre-existing mole (nevus) or in skin that has not been subjected to repeated or prolonged sun exposure. Heredity plays a role in a minority of cases.

Because melanomas arise from pigment-producing cells, they may have a dark color, but this is by no means necessary. Distinguishing a melanoma from a mole may not be easy, especially in children, in whom one variety of nevus used to be referred to as juvenile melanoma. In adults, recognition of an early melanoma is most effectively achieved by careful self-examination.

Development of an enlarging new mole in an adult, increase in size of an existing mole, changes in the surface or color, development of irregularity of the borders or additional pigmented areas around the edges, itching or pain, and bleeding are all important warning signs. The diagnosis can only be established by microscopic examination of a biopsy sample.

In the early stages of a melanoma, the tumor spreads radially, meaning that it grows outwards from its origin to form a larger but still superficially located collection of tumor cells. Later, it shows vertical growth, in that the tumor cells invade the deeper layers of the skin. If a melanoma is found microscopically to still be in the phase of radial growth, the likely outcome is much better than if it shows vertical growth. The greater the depth of invasion into deeper tissues, the higher the likelihood of spread to lymph nodes (lymph glands) or distant sites and the poorer the response to treatment.

SEE ALSO *Moles, Skin cancer, Sun exposure*

MELASMA

Light-skinned women who become pregnant frequently acquire dark tan staining of their cheeks or foreheads, called melasma or chloasma. After the birth of the baby the staining persists and darkens each summer if exposed to the sun. Though melasma occurs in darker skinned people, it is not as obvious. The estrogen-containing contraceptive pill has a similar side effect.

Other causes of this staining include menopausal changes, certain types of ovarian tumors, and endocrine disorders such as Addison's disease where changed pigmentation is also noted inside the mouth and in the creases of the palms.

It has been found that the use of sunscreen creams all year round before one ventures out will allow the staining to fade in time.

SEE ALSO *Addison's disease, Menopause, Pregnancy, Sun exposure*

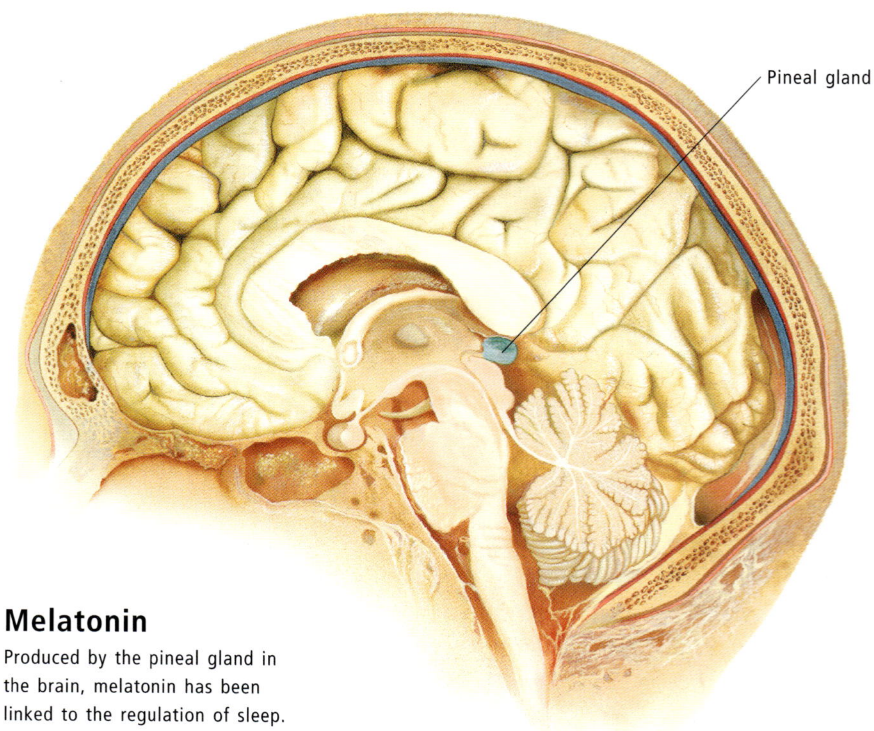

Melatonin
Produced by the pineal gland in the brain, melatonin has been linked to the regulation of sleep.

MELATONIN

Melatonin is a hormone secreted by the pineal gland, located deep inside the brain. Thought to be involved in regulating the body's sleep–wake "clock", melatonin production is highest during a person's normal sleeping hours and drops off as the body begins waking. There is evidence that melatonin supplements may help some forms of insomnia and ease the symptoms of jet lag by hastening the body's return to its usual sleep–wake cycle.

Research investigating a wide range of potential applications suggests melatonin supplements could also be useful in birth control, boosting the immune system, treating cancer and depression and in the management of many other disorders.

SEE ALSO *Insomnia, Jet lag*

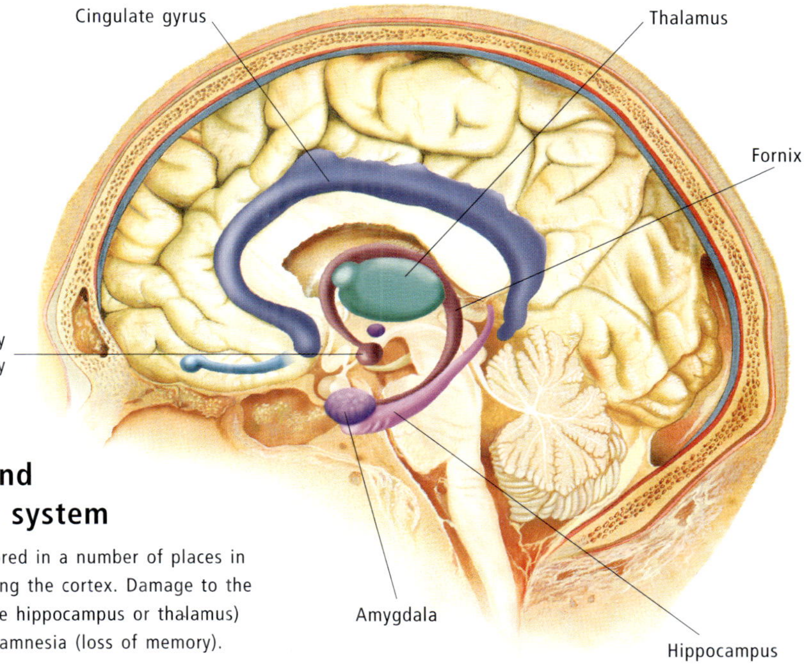

Memory and the limbic system

Memories are stored in a number of places in the brain, including the cortex. Damage to the limbic system (the hippocampus or thalamus) can also lead to amnesia (loss of memory).

MELIOIDOSIS

Melioidosis (Whitmore disease) is a predominantly tropical disease caused by the bacterium *Pseudomonas pseudomallei*, which is found in soil and stagnant water. Most cases occur in Southeast Asia and northern Australia. Symptoms range from headache and fever to chest pain, appetite loss and cough. Melioidosis commonly affects the lungs and can be fatal. Treatment is with antibiotics.

SEE ALSO *Bacteria*

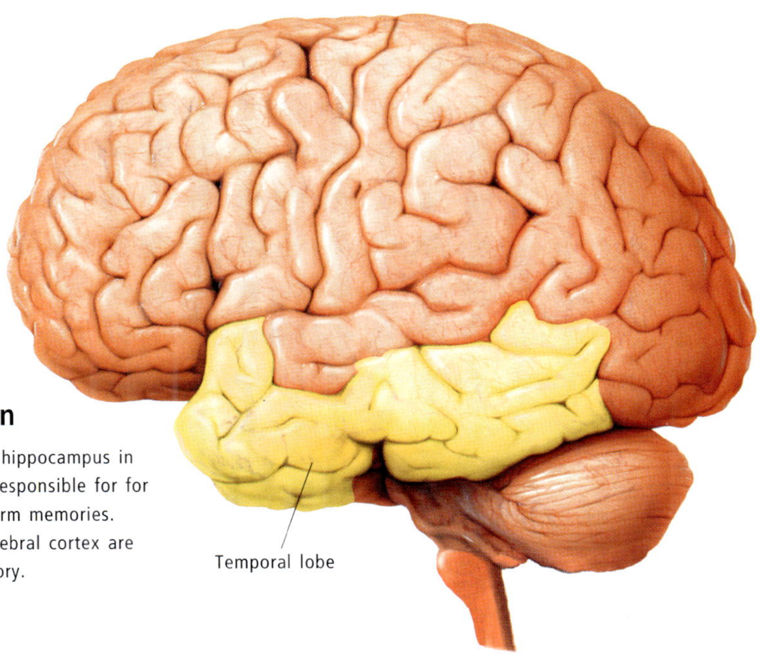

Memory and brain function

It is thought that the hippocampus in the temporal lobe is responsible for for the storage of long-term memories. Other parts of the cerebral cortex are also involved in memory.

MEMBRANE

Membranes are thin and flexible sheets of tissue that line surfaces or divide spaces in the body. Three of the four main types—mucous, serous and cutaneous membrane—are composed of an epithelial cell layer overlaying a connective tissue layer. In synovial membranes the epithelial layer is modified as a mesothelial layer.

SEE ALSO *Connective tissue, Mucous membranes*

MEMORY

Memory is a cognitive process which allows humans to retain and retrieve information about previously experienced events, impressions, sensations and ideas. Humans acquire knowledge and store it as memory.

The ability to learn or the ability to reason is largely dependent on the ability to remember. For example, the ability to perform a simple task, such as making a cup of coffee or crossing the street, is based on remembering earlier experiences. In solving a problem or even simply recognizing that a problem exists, one is depending on memory.

Although not exactly understood, neuroscientists describe the storing of memory in three ways: sensory memory, which lasts from milliseconds to seconds; short-term memory, which lasts seconds to minutes; and long-term memory, which lasts days to years.

Different storage mechanisms are said to exist for short-term and long-term memory. In short-term memory, a limited amount of information (from five to ten separate items) can be held for a few seconds, after which they must be transferred to long-term memory or they will be lost. For example, we use short-term memory to remember a phone number after looking it up in a directory, but only for as long as it takes to dial the number. The capacity of long-term memory is large—certain items, especially important events, can be stored for life.

Psychologists also divide memory into four different categories: recollection, recall, recognition and relearning. Recollection is the mental reconstruction of previous events from reminders that "jog" the memory. Recall is the unprompted active remembering of events or incidents from the past. Recognition is the identifying of a stimulus as being familiar from the past. Relearning is the ability to commit to memory with relative ease something that has been forgotten previously, the learning process being easier than the first time.

Memory is thought to be stored over wide areas of the brain rather than in any single location. However, the limbic system, notably the hippocampus on the medial side of the temporal lobe and some parts of the thalamus, are thought to be particularly important in the laying down of memories and in their recall when required. Injury to these areas of the brain results in amnesia, a disorder of memory.

Learning, and thus remembering, begins in the uterus. Ultrasound observations of twins have shown the development of gestures and habits as early as 20 weeks gestation, which continue into early childhood.

The fetus also becomes familiar with the native language of its mother; for example, in tests, French babies look to persons who are talking French. Taste is also learned in utero, as the baby becomes familiar with its mother's diet by inhaling and swallowing the amniotic fluid it lives in. Emotion too is learned; studies have found that babies whose mothers were depressed during pregnancy also exhibited symptoms of depression at birth.

Problems

Forgetting is normal, and apart from a rare few, everyone forgets. Over time something which is not practised will be forgotten. The ability to forget, however, is also important to the process of learning. One is continually adjusting the ability to learn with the ability to forget in order to adapt to new learning experiences and learn new skills. Those who are unable to forget have been found to be extremely confused.

Certain situations, conditions or illnesses can affect memory. Depression, if it includes agitation and psychomotor retardation,

Location of the meninges

The meninges (highlighted here in pale blue) are a set of three continuous membranes that cover and protect the brain and spinal cord.

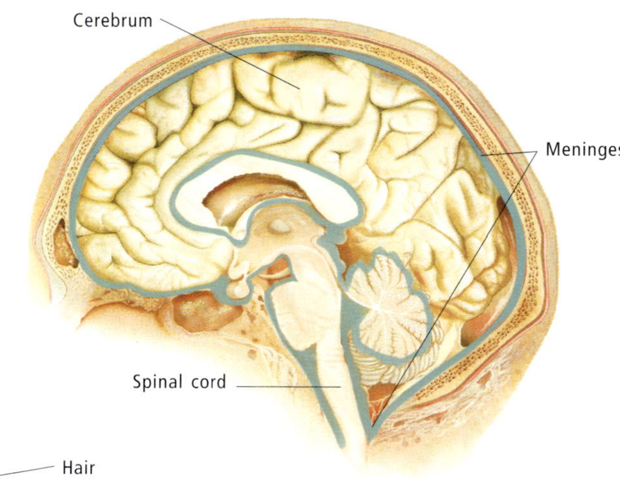

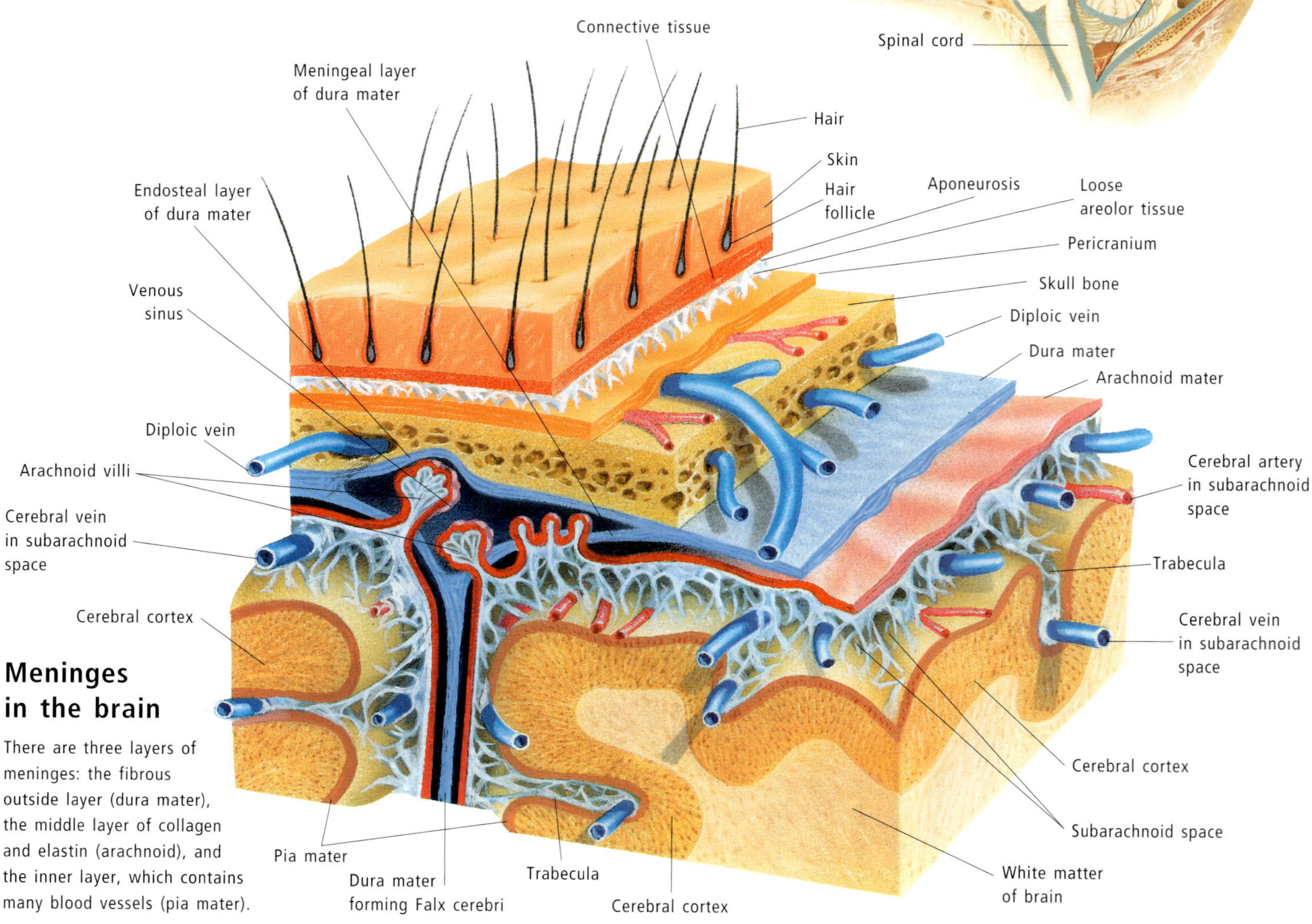

Meninges in the brain

There are three layers of meninges: the fibrous outside layer (dura mater), the middle layer of collagen and elastin (arachnoid), and the inner layer, which contains many blood vessels (pia mater).

makes it difficult for people to remember as well as they would normally, and such depression can lead to pseudo-dementia. Anxiety can reduce the ability to concentrate, for instance in an examination situation, and can affect memory. With age, the ability to learn new skills and to recall information from one's memory can diminish. This may be partly because the memory store is greater in the elderly than in younger persons, thus making recall more complicated. This has been described as age-associated memory impairment (AAMI). Boredom, tiredness, hearing and sight impairment, alcohol, drugs and pain can all reduce the ability to remember and thus learn.

Infections, particularly of the brain (such as meningitis), can cause memory problems, as can an under-active thyroid gland, which will slow down the body's processes. Severe heart or lung disease will affect memory by reducing the supply of oxygen to the brain, and untreated, or poorly treated, diabetes with high or low levels of sugar in the blood can affect the brain's workings.

The most serious cause of memory problems is dementia. Rarely a problem for people under 65 years of age (when it is usually associated with conditions such as Creutzfeld-Jakob disease), the risk of dementia increases with age. One in five people over the age of 80 will suffer from dementia, the most common cause being Alzheimer's disease.

Memory improvement

It is possible to assist memory by using certain strategies. There are many programs available aimed at teaching people to maximize the ability to remember and learn. Strategies include the following.

- Being selective: deciding what it is that one wants to learn. Taking notes, writing things down, and being organized are recognized memory aids.
- Learning by rote: repeating and memorizing important facts and formula is essential for some subjects.
- Reciting out loud: this has been found to be one of the most powerful tools in transferring knowledge from short-term to long-term memory.
- Having a good basic background: learning new skills depends a great deal on what a person already knows.
- Using memory aids such as mnemonic devices: for example, "homes", a word that contains the first letter of each of the Great Lakes (Huron, Ontario, Michigan, Erie and Superior).
- Applying and practising what has been learnt: for example, when the concepts are abstract, discussion will aid understanding; when it is a dance step, repetition will imprint the movements on one's memory.
- Keeping fit and healthy: healthy people who enjoy regular exercise, eat a nutritious diet, drink alcohol moderately and do not take unnecessary drugs help their minds to stay alert. Those who have hearing or sight defects need to ensure they have the correct aids to maximize their ability to experience and learn.
- Keeping the brain active: using the mind and continuing to exercise it by learning new skills, practising those already learnt, and including hobbies such as doing crosswords and playing word games helps to keep the brain working.

Well-educated people seem to experience fewer memory problems as they age than others, which may be because they have a better memory to begin with than those who are having problems, or it may be that because they continue to solve problems, study and learn, their brains remain active.

SEE ALSO *Alzheimer's disease, Creutzfeld-Jakob disease, Dementia, Wernicke-Korsakoff syndrome, Learning disorders*

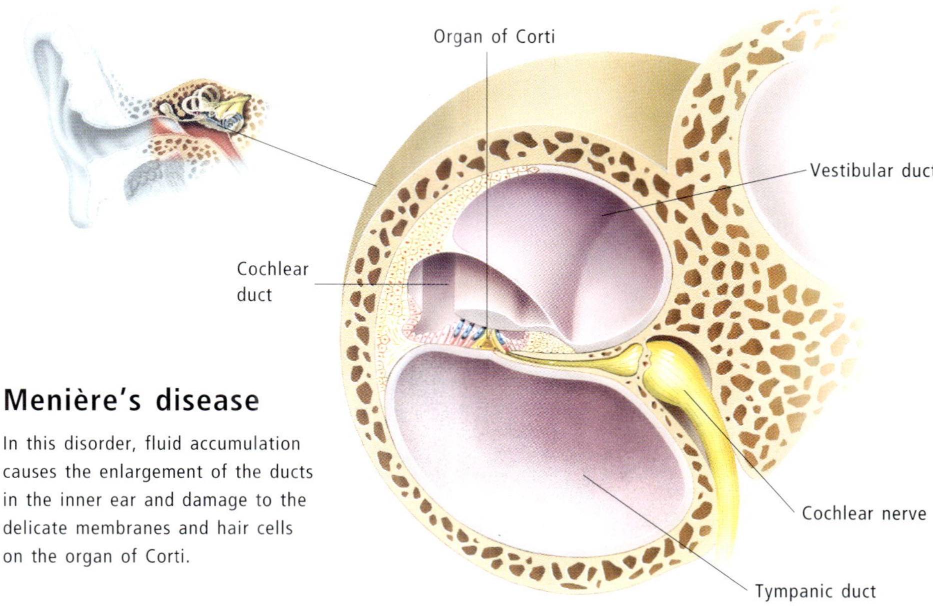

Menière's disease

In this disorder, fluid accumulation causes the enlargement of the ducts in the inner ear and damage to the delicate membranes and hair cells on the organ of Corti.

MENIÈRE'S DISEASE

Menière's disease is a disorder of unknown cause characterized by periodic attacks of vertigo and hearing loss. The first symptom can be a ringing or hissing sound in the ears, known as tinnitus. This is followed by debilitating vertigo, nausea and vomiting that may last up to 24 hours. There may be a feeling of pressure or fullness in the ears. There is progressive hearing loss over time. The vertigo can be treated temporarily with drugs or more permanently by surgically cutting the nerves of the semicircular canals, the organs of balance within the inner ear.

SEE ALSO *Deafness, Ear, Hearing, Semicircular canals, Tinnitus, Vertigo*

MENINGES

The meninges are three thin, protective, continuous membranes surrounding the brain and spinal cord. The outermost is a tough, fibrous layer called the dura mater. The middle membrane, the arachnoid, is a fragile network of collagen and elastin fibers with a cobweb appearance. The innermost membrane, the pia mater, is a layer of collagen and elastic fibers containing many blood vessels. Cerebrospinal fluid fills the space between the arachnoid and pia mater.

A meningioma is a tumor originating in the meninges. It is usually benign but may cause problems by placing pressure on the brain. Surgical removal is often successful.

SEE ALSO *Brain, Meningitis, Spinal cord*

Meningitis bacteria

Meningitis can be caused by a number of different agents, including fungi, viruses or bacteria. The condition causes inflammation of the tissues (meninges) which encase the brain and spinal cord.

MENINGITIS

Meningitis is an infection in the meninges, the membranes which cover the brain and spinal cord. It can be caused by fungi, protozoa, a virus or, in its most serious and potentially fatal forms, by a number of different bacteria.

Bacterial meningitis can be caused by *Meningococcus (Neisseria meningitidis), Haemophilus influenza* type B (HIB), *Pneumococcus, Streptococcus* or *Staphylococcus.*

Meningococcal meningitis is found in all countries and primarily affects adolescents and children under age 10, as does the type of meningitis produced by *Haemophilus influenzae.* In adults, the most common cause is *Streptococcus pneumoniae.* It is an infection which can be only a very mild disturbance and therefore difficult to diagnose, or can make the sufferer extremely ill.

Bacterial infections of the middle ear or of another region of the body can be carried to the meninges via the blood. The bacteria then multiply quickly, causing the first symptoms to appear very rapidly. The first symptom is usually vomiting, followed by a severe headache, which is due to inflammation of the meninges and increased pressure of the cerebrospinal fluid. The neck may be very stiff, even arched and drawn backwards in young children. Fluid may accumulate in the brain, causing coma and death unless relieved.

Other symptoms include moderate to high fever, headache, vomiting, collapse, convulsions, lethargy, inability to tolerate bright light, bulging fontanelle in children under two, and a purple rash all over the body. (This kind of purple rash is associated with *Meningococcus* infection, which is a very virulent form of meningitis.) In very young children, the fever may be the only sign until the child is suddenly critically ill.

The various forms of bacterial meningitis are spread through the secretions of the nose and throat, by coughing or kissing, but not by less intimate contact or in the air. Prolonged contact, such as between people sharing the same room or house, or children at the same daycare centers or school classroom, can cause infection and these people would be considered at risk in an outbreak.

A diagnosis is made by taking a sample of spinal fluid and testing for bacteria and abnormal chemical components. This is in order to differentiate between meningitis and encephalitis, and to establish which type of organism is responsible for the infection. Early diagnosis is vital in preventing death from the more serious bacterial forms of the disease.

Safe and effective vaccination is available against HIB, some strains of meningococcal meningitis (also known as *Neisseria meningitidis*) and forms of *Streptococcus pneumoniae.* HIB vaccines should be given routinely to infants with three doses before age 6 months, and a fourth between 12 and 18 months. Vaccines against meningococcal meningitis are not effective in children under 18 months. Available vaccines against pneumococcal meningitis were, until recently, not effective in children under the age of 2 years, the major group at risk. However, a vaccine developed and approved for use in the USA offers hope for a dramatic improvement in protection against brain damage, hearing loss and death rates—currently 10 percent of those infected—for babies and infants up to the age of 5 years.

Adults may be vaccinated during outbreaks of the disease and should consider vaccination prior to travel in infected areas.

SEE ALSO *Brain, Encephalitis, Immunization, Meninges, Spinal cord*

MENINGOCELE

The neural tube develops in the human embryo as the precursor of the spinal cord. Normally, the tube closes to produce the nervous system structures; if it does not, the membranes or meninges covering the nerve tissue of the cord may protrude through the skin in the form of a fluid-filled sac.

Meningocele is a term that encompasses any congenital abnormality involving inadequate closure of the spine.

Sometimes parts of the spinal cord also protrude into the hernia. This is known as a meningomyelocele, and is more common, and also more serious, than meningocele because the spinal cord and nerve roots may be damaged, causing weakness or paralysis below the defect.

Both conditions occur in the lower lumbar or sacral areas of the back, which are the last parts of the fetal spine to close. Other congenital disorders such as hydrocephalus or dislocated hip may also be present. Both types require surgical treatment shortly after birth to repair the defect. Any neurological damage is often irreversible and physical therapy will be needed to minimize future disability.

SEE ALSO *Congenital abnormalities, Hydrocephalus, Spinal cord*

MENINGOCOCCAL DISEASE

Meningococcal disease is a rapid, potentially fatal form of bacterial infection, due to *Neisseria meningitidis.* It is most commonly seen in children under 5 years of age, and its incidence has increased in recent years. As a general rule, meningococcal disease is a combination of meningitis and septicemia.

The illness develops rapidly, with a flu-like infection, headache, confusion, and the appearance of a blotchy, purplish rash. Early treatment with intravenous antibiotics can be lifesaving.

The infection occurs mainly in winter, is spread through respiratory secretions and can occur in epidemics. People who are in close contact with the patient require preventive antibiotics. Vaccination against meningococcal disease is advised for travelers to epidemic areas and those with reduced immunity.

SEE ALSO *Meningitis, Septicemia*

M

MENOPAUSE

Menopause literally means "pause in menstruation". Menopause does not accurately describe what is happening to a woman's body at the time when ovarian function and hormonal production decline and the body adjusts itself. Climacteric is a more accurate term because it describes a time of life, just as puberty describes the time after the menarche, the first menstruation.

During the climacteric period, which can last several years, the woman's body goes through three phases. The premenopause is the time before the menstrual cycle ceases; this term can also refer to most of a woman's fertile years, but more commonly to the years when the menstrual periods are irregular and heavy. The next phase, the perimenopause, are the years on either side of the menopause when a woman may experience some of the symptoms commonly associated with menopause, including hot flashes (also known as hot flushes), depression and loss of interest in sexual intercourse. The menopause is defined as starting after the final menstrual period, which can only be determined when 12 months have passed without a menstrual bleed. After the menopause comes the postmenopause, which extends to the end of the woman's life.

There are three important hormones produced by the ovaries: estrogen, progesterone and relaxin. Once a woman has passed the menopause, estrogen and progesterone will no longer be produced by the ovaries, though in some obese women estrogen may still be produced by fat tissue, thus reducing some of the symptoms. Estrogen is needed to maintain healthy body tissues and long term estrogen deficiency can result in stroke, dowager's hump, angina, genital degeneration and fractures, commonly of the hip, due to osteoporosis.

Physical effects

Around the time a woman reaches menopause she may experience some or all of the following symptoms: hot flashes, night sweats, palpitations and sleep problems (which are a result of changes in the normal working of the blood vessels), anxiety and depression, vaginal dryness, and decreased or no interest in sexual intercourse.

There are many physiological changes that accompany the climacteric and many women will be unaware of most of them. They include the following.

- Changes to the urogenital tissue. A reduction in the blood supply to the tissues leads to an alkaline environment, with the possibility of infections and itching.
- Changes to the reproductive organs. The ovaries, which produced eggs during the woman's reproductive years, no longer do so and, because it is the egg follicle which produces progesterone, production of this hormone ceases. The inner part of the ovary known as the stroma continues to produce hormones, most importantly, androstenedione and testosterone. Androstenedione converts to estrone, which is important in maintaining pelvic organs, the vagina, skin and hair. Testosterone, a male hormone, is important in maintaining energy levels; however, this hormone also increases the risk of heart disease.
- Poor bladder control. The pelvic floor muscles lose their elasticity and strength. This can result in continence problems, which can be combated by doing pelvic floor exercises.
- Changes to the menstrual cycle. Bleeding may become heavier, lighter, or more irregular for several years prior to the final menstrual period. This is a symptom of the alteration in the pattern of female and pituitary hormones at this time.
- Dry skin that is more prone to wrinkles. The skin will lose much of its elasticity and because of a decrease in collagen, wrinkles will appear. A loss of melanocytes, cells which manufacture melanin and give the skin a tanned appearance, means the skin is also more likely to burn under the sun's rays.
- Changes in hair growth patterns. Hair on the head loses its body and thickness and becomes finer. This hormonally-related hair loss occurs around 40 years and there is no known cure. It is not the same as alopecia (baldness). Hair on the body, on the other hand, can become thicker and darker as a result of the hormonal changes. This can lead to masculine-like hair growth on the face, arms and legs, which can be counteracted with estrogen therapy.
- Osteoporosis. This is a disease in which the amount of bone calcium in the skeleton reduces to the point that the bones are thin, brittle and prone to fracture. Osteoporosis can result after the menopause because insufficient estrogen leads to calcium loss. Hormone replacement therapy can prevent bones from deteriorating.
- Loss of muscle strength and mobility. Weak muscles lead to poor coordination. This, together with lack of exercise

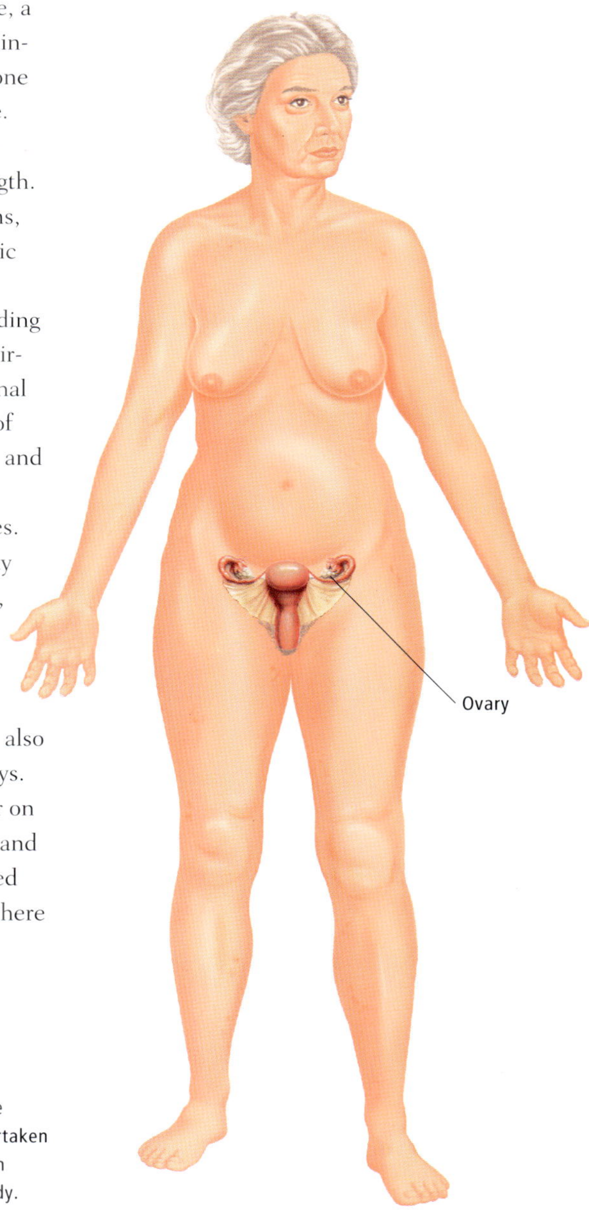

Menopause

At menopause, ova (eggs) are no longer produced by the ovaries, and menstruation ceases. Hormone replacement therapy may be undertaken to compensate for hormones which are no longer produced by the body.

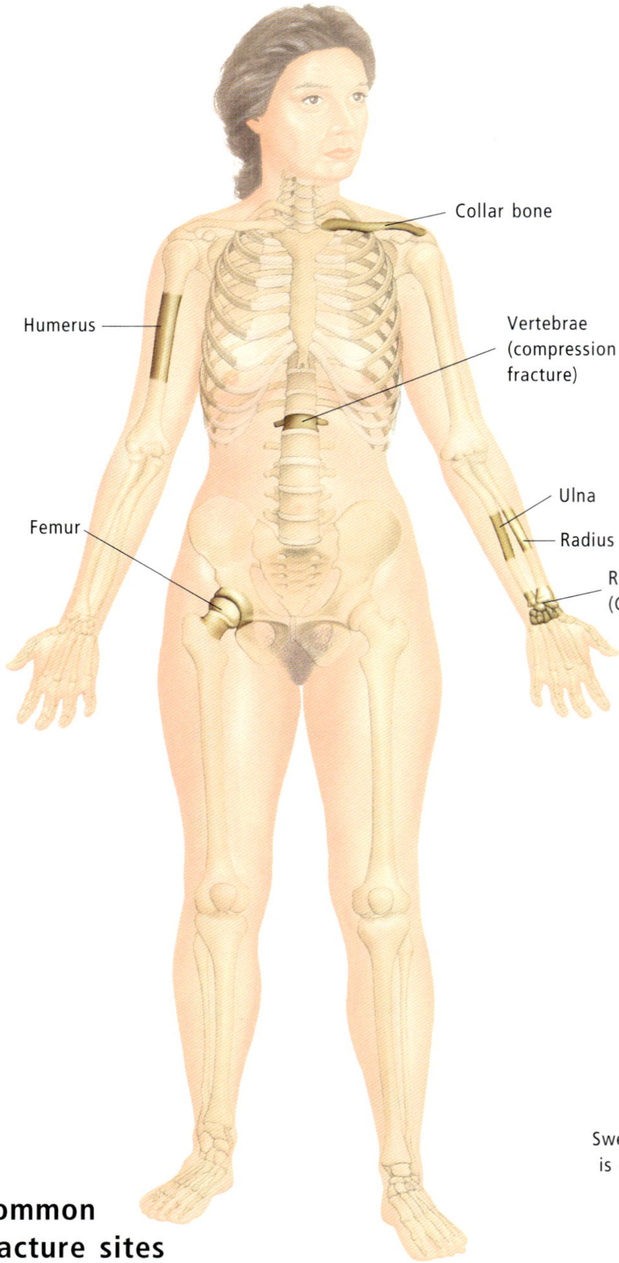

Common fracture sites

A reduction in the level of estrogen in the body during menopause can result in a loss of calcium and lead to brittle bones (osteoporosis). There is an increased risk of fractures during this period of life; the most common include fractures of the collar bone, upper and lower arm, radius (Colles' fracture), femur, and compression fractures of the spine.

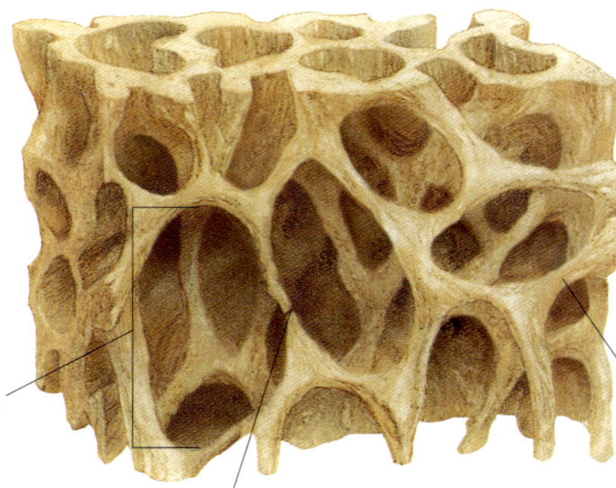

Osteoporosis

Women entering menopause are encouraged to take calcium and vitamin D supplements and to maintain exercise levels, to avoid bones becoming porous and weak.

During a hot flash

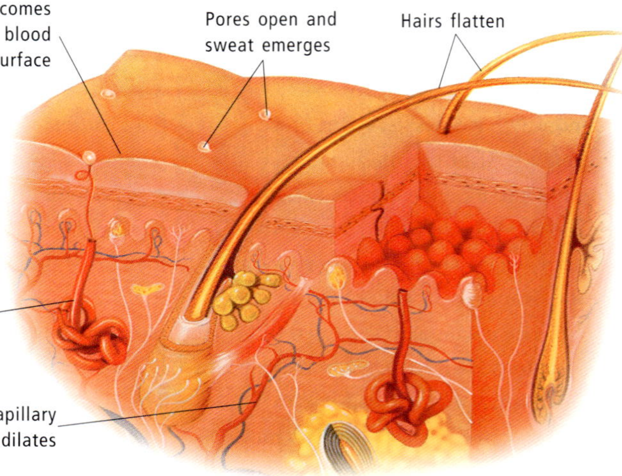

After a hot flash

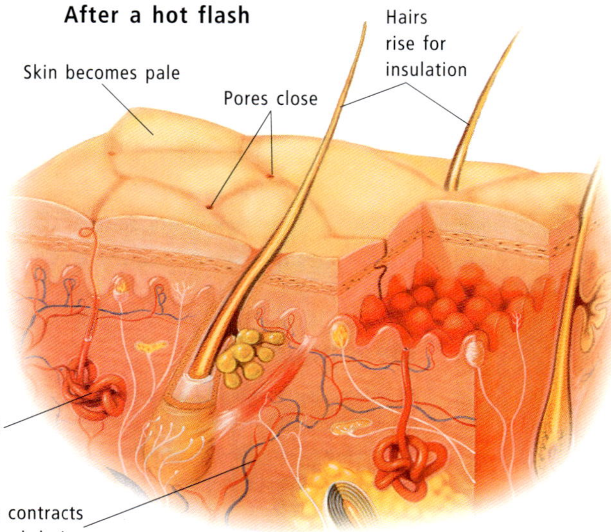

Hot flash

Hormone imbalances during menopause cause the capillaries of the skin to dilate, sending a sudden flood of warm blood to the surface. After the flash has passed, the capillaries rapidly constrict, the skin becomes pale and cold as blood drains away and hairs rise to provide insulation.

Menopausal fat distribution

Falling estrogen and progesterone levels during menopause affect fat distribution in women. Before menopause, most women have some fat deposits around the thighs, hips, breasts and upper arms. After menopause, fat tends to collect around the breasts, abdomen and waist.

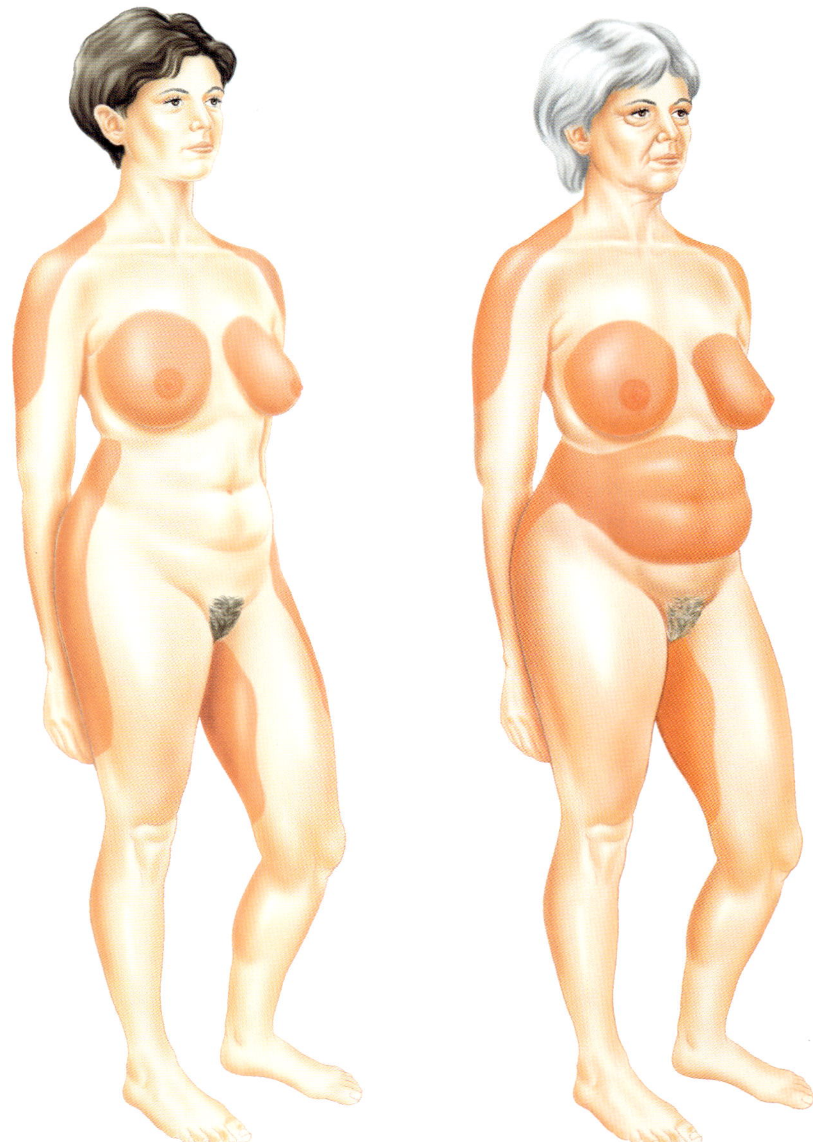

Fat distribution before menopause

Fat distribution after menopause

and the decline in estrogen and progesterone, can lead to a sedentary lifestyle which may bring its own set of problems and diseases.

- Increased chance of heart disease. Once a woman reaches menopause she is at much greater risk of cardiovascular disease than she was before, because her ovaries are no longer producing estrogen. Hormone replacement therapy (HRT) can reduce these risks.
- Breasts flattening and losing their fullness. This too can be prevented with the use of HRT. Breast cancer, however, is a concern with HRT and the risk factors need to be discussed with a medical practitioner when this therapy is considered.

Other effects

The menopause can produce many different responses in a woman. Some of the above symptoms, together with a decline in the male hormones, can be responsible for a loss of interest in a sexual relationship. For some women, male hormone replacement may be of benefit. However, if a woman maintains a healthy lifestyle and seeks help for any symptoms she encounters, she often finds the menopause brings a new lease of life in some ways, such as a sex life where contraceptive worries are removed.

Researchers have found that most women who had an enjoyable sex life before they reached the menopause continue to enjoy sex afterwards.

In some cultures, menopause confers new power and prestige on the woman, while in other societies it is seen as a decline in femininity and sexuality. An understanding of what to expect, and support and recognition of changes, can greatly help a woman feel at ease with what is an entirely natural phase of every woman's life.

The climacteric is a natural life event and the hormone deficiency state that accompanies it may, or may not, need medication.

Alternative therapies

There are a number of alternative therapies that may be helpful during menopause. Aromatherapy massage may help alleviate dry skin, anxiety and insomnia. Fennel, cypress and sage oils are recommended by aromatherapists for menopausal symptoms. Herbalism treats with herbs that may support liver function (dandelion, milk thistle), herbs that are high in plant estrogens and progesterone (red clover, wild yam, sage, agnus castus, dong quai) and sedative nervines (passiflora, skullcap, chamomile). Calendula ointment is prescribed for vaginal dryness. Naturopathy suggests a wholefood diet rich in calcium and phyto-estrogens (found primarily in soy products). Caffeine, alcohol and cigarettes should be avoided, as well as foods rich in oxalic acid (e.g. spinach and rhubarb), which bind with calcium in the body. A regular weight-bearing exercise program is suggested to counteract bone loss. Supplements of vitamins B, C and E, calcium, magnesium, flaxseed oil and fish oils may help. Various flower essences and remedies may help with emotional issues. Traditional Chinese Medicine uses acupuncture and Chinese herbal treatments to correct energy and hormonal imbalances.

SEE ALSO *Ageing, Angina, Breast, Estrogens, Hormone replacement therapy, Urinary incontinence, Menstruation, Osteoporosis, Progesterone, Reproductive systems, Testosterone*

MENSTRUATION

Cycle regulation

The hypothalamus and the pituitary gland in the brain regulate the menstrual cycle. At the start of the cycle they release luteinizing hormone (LH) and follicle stimulating hormone (FSH) which trigger follicles (egg sacs) in the ovaries to release estrogen and progesterone. The follicles then mature and finally release an egg.

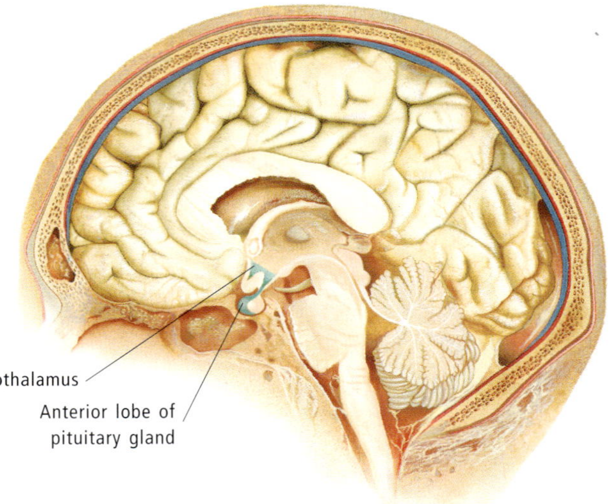

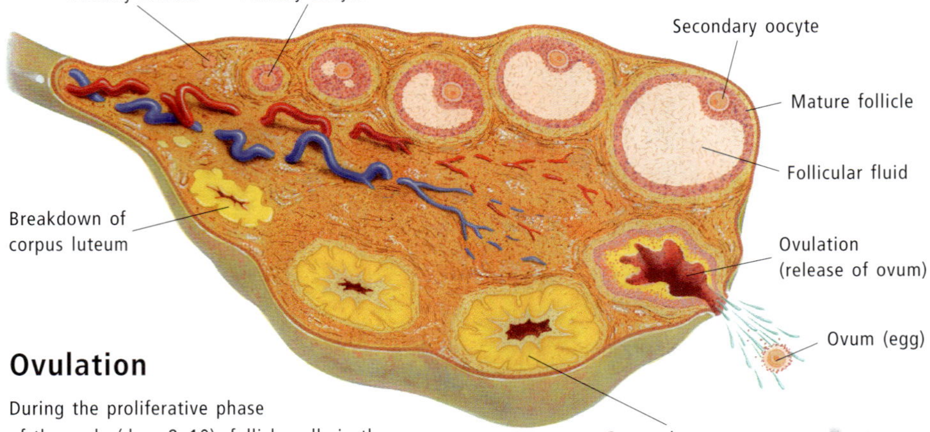

Ovulation

During the proliferative phase of the cycle (days 8–10), follicle cells in the ovary divide and increase in size, creating a sac that contains an oocyte (female sex cell). By days 10–14, a mature follicle holding a secondary oocyte (mature egg) has formed. A surge of hormone from the pituitary gland triggers ovulation—the follicle releases its ovum into the fallopian tube. The ruptured follicle then transforms into the corpus luteum, which secretes progesterone and estrogen. If the egg is not fertilized the corpus luteum breaks down, hormone levels fall and menstruation occurs.

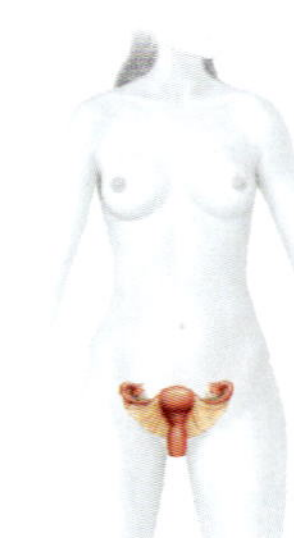

Menstruation is the cyclic vaginal discharge of blood and tissue debris derived from breakdown of the uterine lining. The menstrual cycle is considered to start with the onset of menstruation, which occupies approximately 5 days out of the complete cycle of about 28 days (both these figures can vary considerably from the average). Apart from menstruation, the cycle can be divided into two phases, the days before (proliferative phase) and the days after ovulation (secretory phase). The menstrual cycle is an unusual type of reproductive cycle found only in humans and a few other primates.

The most obvious changes during the menstrual cycle take place in the uterine lining (endometrium). Menstruation involves the degeneration and loss of a large amount of endometrium along with about 1–2 fluid ounces (35–50 milliliters) of blood from broken endometrial vessels. At the end, a small amount of the lining (about 1 millimeter thick) remains, which is essential for regeneration. Regeneration of the endometrium occurs under the influence of estrogen from follicles developing in the ovary during the proliferative phase, and proceeds until the lining is about $\frac{1}{10}$ inch (3 millimeters) thick. The fully formed endometrium is a richly vascular tissue that also contains glands.

Progesterone derived from the corpus luteum (the follicle that matured and released its egg) is the predominant hormone from just after ovulation to about 2 days before menstruation (approximately day 26). The main function of progesterone is to stimulate the endometrial glands to produce a secretion capable of nourishing the embryo for the first few days of pregnancy, before a functional placenta has formed. The secretion occurs regardless of whether pregnancy has taken place or not.

If the woman is not pregnant, the corpus luteum lasts until about day 26 of the cycle when it starts to degenerate and progesterone production decreases rapidly. The blood vessels in the uterine lining are sensitive to levels of circulating progesterone and respond to reduced levels by contracting and cutting off the blood supply to all but the deepest parts of the endometrium. This results in tissue breakdown and bleeding from the damaged blood vessels, which leads to the onset of the next menstruation. Menstrual flow is facilitated by muscular contractions and by substances produced in the endometrium which prevent clotting of menstrual blood.

Menstruation does not take place if the woman has become pregnant because the corpus luteum survives and continues to secrete progesterone under the influence of hormones derived from the early placenta. This is essential to maintain the pregnancy until the placenta is able to produce its own progesterone towards the end of the first trimester. Only then does the corpus luteum gradually cease to function.

Menarche

The first menstruation normally occurs between 10 and 16 years and is called the menarche. Puberty is a more general term describing both the onset of menstruation and the development of secondary sexual characteristics, which usually precedes menarche. This includes the growth of pubic hair, breast development and a spurt in body growth. The hormonal events leading up to puberty are not fully understood but changes in the pituitary a couple of years before puberty result in increased secretion of the sexual hormones, the gonadotropins.

The age of menarche appears to be related to a number of social factors. Menstruation tends to occur earlier in urban girls of higher socioeconomic status and also relates to heredity and better nutrition. It was widely believed in the past that menarche took place earlier in tropical climates, but this seems to be a racial rather than a climatic effect. The age of puberty has dropped by several years over the last hundred years but this trend now seems to have slowed down.

Puberty is considered to be precocious or abnormally early if it occurs before 8 or 9 years. This may be due to ovarian cysts or rare hormonal disorders, but in many cases there is no obvious cause.

Menstrual problems

The days preceding menstruation are a time of discomfort for some women; this is known as premenstrual tension or premenstrual syndrome and should be differentiated from dysmenorrhea, which is discomfort or pain during menstruation. Dysmenorrhea is usually most severe for the first 12 hours or so of the period. It is most prevalent in younger women and usually appears 2–4 years after the onset of menstruation and is uncommon after the thirtieth year. It is widely believed that childbirth will cure dysmenorrhea but this is not always the case.

The pain characterizing dysmenorrhea ranges from a dull ache to a severe ache with colic. It is usually located in the lower abdomen but may also be referred to the inside and front of the thighs. Nausea, vomiting, diarrhea and migraines sometimes accompany the pain. It is now generally accepted that the pain is the result of the actions of a group of substances produced in the endometrium, called prostaglandins. These are involved in both endometrial breakdown and control of excessive bleeding during menstruation. They also stimulate contractions of the uterine and cervical muscle during menstruation which may become painful (prostaglandins are involved in uterine contractions during labor). Oral administration of prostaglandin inhibitors for the first few days of the period help to alleviate the dysmenorrhea. Prostaglandin production does not occur without previous stimulation of the uterus by progesterone, so an alternative therapy is to use oral contraceptives which suppress ovulation.

Dysmenorrhea most commonly occurs in the absence of any recognizable abnormality, when it is called primary dysmenorrhea. It may also be a symptom of a number of gynecological disorders including endometriosis, a condition in which fragments of endometrium are relocated and become attached to other organs. These fragments remain functional and

Menstruation

(a) During menstruation (days 1–6) the lining of the uterus (endometrium) breaks down and is discharged.
(b) At the start of the proliferative phase (days 7–13), cells begin to repair the endometrium and
(c) Follicles in the ovary begin to form an ovum (egg).
(d) Ovulation takes place (around day 14) and the ovary releases its ovum into the fallopian tube.
(e) The secretory phase (days 15–28) follows ovulation. The ovum travels up the fallopian tube towards the uterus and hormones thicken the endometrium in readiness to support a fertilized ovum. If the ovum is not fertilized, hormone levels fall and blood vessels in the uterus constrict. This causes the unused endometrial blood and tissue to be discharged from the body and the menstrual cycle begins again.

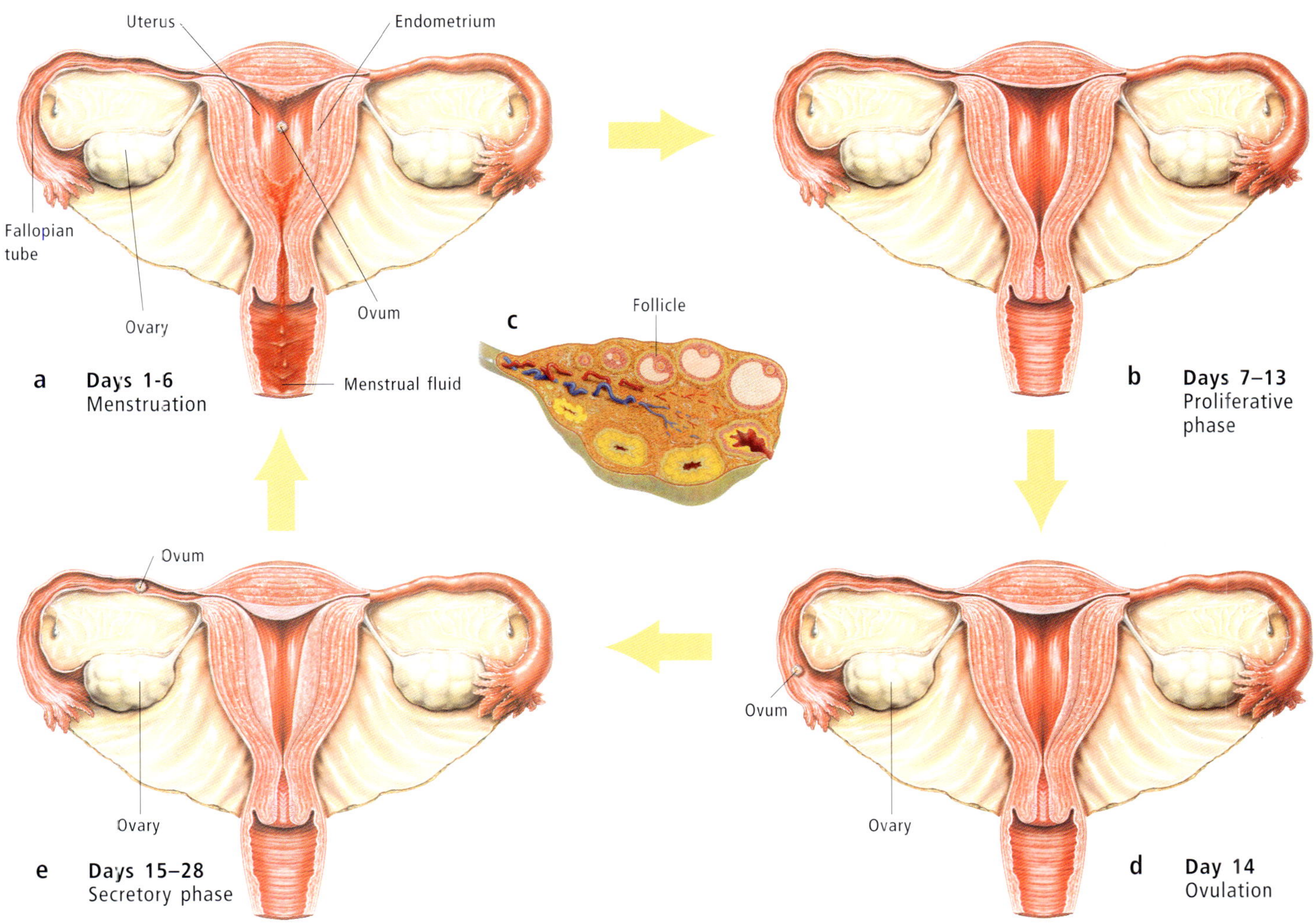

hormonally responsive and undergo variable amounts of hemorrhage at menstruation. The pain is due to build-up of blood in the displaced fragments and is thus usually worse at the end of the period than at the beginning, as with dysmenorrhea.

Amenorrhea is absence of menstruation, either primarily in women who have never menstruated or secondarily, when menstruation ceases after having occurred previously. Amenorrhea of either sort may be the result of pituitary malfunction due either to injury or to a tumor or, rarely, to the congenital inability of the pituitary to produce gonadotropins. Stress, excessive or heavy exercise or low body weight are also implicated. Primary amenorrhea may be the result of chromosomal or genital abnormalities or ovaries that are insensitive to gonadotropins.

Uterine bleeding

Uterine bleeding, similar to normal menstruation, may occur even if ovulation has not taken place. The hormonal environment prior to endometrial breakdown in an anovulatory cycle will clearly be different from that in a normal cycle. If ovulation does not occur, there is no corpus luteum to produce progesterone and so the bleeding is not the result of progesterone withdrawal. Instead the follicle which should have ovulated continues to secrete estrogen for a variable length of time until it degenerates and blood estrogen levels drop. The endometrial response is to undergo breakdown in a similar way to that which occurs under progesterone withdrawal, although often to a lesser extent, so that loss of blood and tissue debris is noticeably lighter than with a normal period. Withdrawal bleeding when an oral contraceptive is stopped for a few days occurs in a similar way.

Anovulatory cycles are normal for the few months after menarche and just before menopause. Anovulation may be established by biopsy of the uterine lining and looking for changes in the tissue which indicate the influence of progesterone.

Uterine bleeding is considered to be abnormal if menstruation is excessively heavy, of normal intensity but occurring too frequently, or if bleeding or spotting occurs consistently between normal periods. This can be the result of disturbances to the normal production of pituitary gonadotropins, ovarian hormones or prostaglandins. Other possible factors include cancer of the uterus, cervix, ovary or fallopian tube, retained fragments of placenta, an infection such as pelvic inflammatory disease, ectopic pregnancy, polycystic ovary syndrome and, occasionally, coagulation disorders which prevent normal blood clotting (e.g. von Willebrand's disease).

Irregular abnormal bleeding may be associated with the use of an intrauterine device for contraceptive purposes. Emotional disturbances affect bleeding in some women. Occasionally bleeding may be associated with ovulation. Benign tumors in the uterine muscle called fibroids or leiomyomas are found in perhaps 50 percent of all women over 40 years of age. Most are symptomless but they can also be a common cause of excessively heavy menstruation (sometimes called "flooding") in older women.

Irregular or heavy bleeding is frequently associated with menopause. In the absence of any abnormality this is a symptom of the alteration in the pattern of female and pituitary hormones at this time. Bleeding occurring after menopause should be investigated thoroughly as it may be a symptom of a malignant disease of the uterus.

Social and cultural aspects

Menstrual bleeding is a normal functional event but it is also a biological oddity, as bleeding is usually a sign of trauma. This may partly account for the numerous beliefs, customs and rituals that have been associated with menstruation since ancient times.

Almost all tribal cultures have restrictions and taboos on the activities of menstruating women. Most of these are based on the concept that either menstrual fluid or menstruating women are contaminating or harmful to others. Cultural practices may include the maintenance of special places of residence ("menstrual huts") to which women retire for the duration of their menstrual period. Other customs aimed to restrict the activities of menstruating women by preventing them from collecting or handling food, touching hunting equipment, planting crops or having sexual intercourse.

The early religious writings of Zoroastrianism, Judaism, Christianity and Islam provided rules for most aspects of living. These included codes of behavior for both the menstruating woman and the people with whom she came into contact, and were usually based on the concept that menstruation was unclean. Many of these rules are now either forgotten or disregarded.

The physiology of the menstrual cycle was described early in the twentieth century and the hormones responsible for the cyclic changes in the uterine lining were discovered and synthesized in the laboratory shortly afterwards. Despite this, prior to the introduction of the oral contraceptive in the late 1950s, numerous beliefs regarding the danger of menstruation prevailed. These beliefs perceived the danger as being directed towards the menstruating woman herself, rather than towards others. Bathing, swimming, washing hair or indulging in vigorous physical exercise were considered to be harmful at this delicate time. Even having the hair permed was to be avoided in case the perm did not "take". Menstruation was described as "the curse" or as being "unwell", a concept which persists, with some justification, up to the present time in the expectation that the premenstrual and menstrual phases of the female cycle will be uncomfortable or even incapacitating.

Attempts were also made during the early twentieth century to establish whether menstrual fluid was actually toxic. These scientific studies have since been discredited but, at the time, some claimed to have isolated a substance named menotoxin present in menstrual blood and sweat, tears, urine, saliva and other bodily secretions of menstruating females, which was responsible for the ancient belief of harm.

Despite the inconvenience and possible discomfort, menstruation is still accepted as a necessary part of female function, even for women who suppress their natural cycles by taking the contraceptive pill. The pill is almost always administered in an intermittent pattern which mimics the menstrual cycle, although there is little medical evidence to support this as being a better or healthier approach than continuous use which would exclude bleeding altogether.

SEE ALSO *Fibroids, Menopause, Mittelschmerz, Ovaries, Ovulation, Premenstrual syndrome, Progesterone, Prostaglandins, Puberty, Reproductive systems*

M

MERCURY POISONING

Mercury poisoning is caused by ingestion, inhalation or absorption through the skin of mercury compounds. Although it is a naturally occurring metal, mercury is used at potentially dangerous concentrations for a wide range of industrial purposes. Effects on the body depend on exposure levels. Acute poisoning occurs when large amounts are ingested in a short space of time. Symptoms include a burning sensation in the throat, a metallic taste in the mouth, abdominal pain, vomiting, excessive saliva production and blood-tinged diarrhea. Kidney failure may lead to death. Mercury can also cross the placental barrier and cause birth defects.

Mercury accumulates in body tissues, particularly the liver, kidney, brain and blood. Chronic poisoning results when small quantities are swallowed or absorbed gradually through persistent low-level exposure. Symptoms include red and swollen extremities ("pink disease"), irritability, fevers, hair loss, nail damage and eventually tremors, convulsions, personality changes and brain damage.

In one tragic incident of mass poisoning during the 1950s, many residents in the Japanese fishing village of Minamata died after eating seafood that had been contaminated by mercury-laden industrial waste. Workers making felt hats in the 1800s routinely used mercury and frequently suffered symptoms of chronic poisoning, leading to the expression "mad as a hatter". These days, however, mercury poisoning is rare although there is debate about the potential for mercury in teeth fillings to cause chronic poisoning.

SEE ALSO *Poisoning*

MESOTHELIOMA

Mesothelioma is a rare and malignant form of cancer of the membranes lining the lungs (the pleura), abdomen (the peritoneum) or heart (the pericardium). It is almost always caused by previous exposure to asbestos, which may have taken place 20 years or more before the symptoms of the disease appear. Those symptoms are cough, shortness of breath, weight loss and chest pain. There is often an accompanying pleural effusion (fluid in the pleural sac of the lung). A chest x-ray, thoracic CAT scan and a lung biopsy will confirm the diagnosis. The disease is usually incurable, though surgery, radiation therapy, and chemotherapy may control symptoms.

SEE ALSO *Asbestosis, Lung*

METABOLISM

Everything that happens in the human body is dependent upon chemical reactions in the cells. These complex biochemical events or pathways that drive all of the body's systems are collectively referred to as metabolism. There are two fundamental phases or processes involved in metabolism—one is constructive and uses energy, the other breaks down compounds and creates energy.

During the building-up phase, called anabolism, simple molecules are used to create more complex molecules and substances. For example, amino acids are bonded together to build proteins and simple sugars are packaged up to produce polysaccharides. Anabolic reactions require energy and occur during the growth, repair and maintenance of body cells and systems.

During the reverse process, catabolism, complex substances such as food are broken down into simpler compounds. Catabolic reactions produce energy, which is stored in a substance known as ATP until required for use in anabolic reactions. Chemical diges-

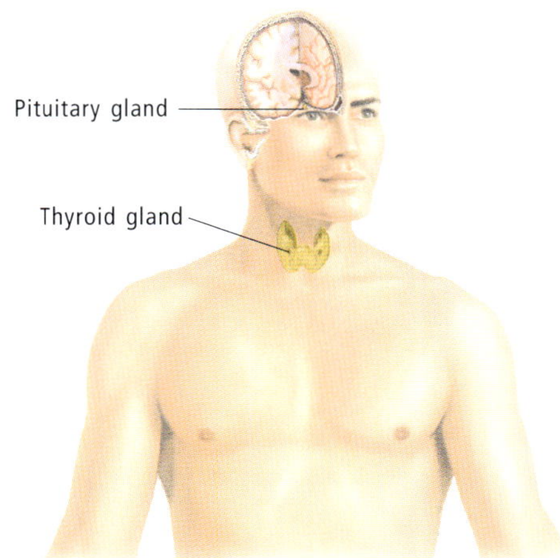

Metabolism—regulating mechanisms

Metabolism is the collective term for all the chemical processes that run our body. Thyroid hormones regulate the metabolic rate, so under- or over-activity of the thyroid can disrupt the body's metabolism. The pituitary gland controls the release of thyroid hormones.

Chemical metabolism

One of the most important chemical processes in the body is the breakdown of carbohydrates into glucose, and the subsequent conversion of glucose into energy. Chemicals in the pancreas, stomach and intestines break down carbohydrates and other nutrients to allow the body to run efficiently. The liver metabolizes food and stores glucose to provide energy for body cells and muscles.

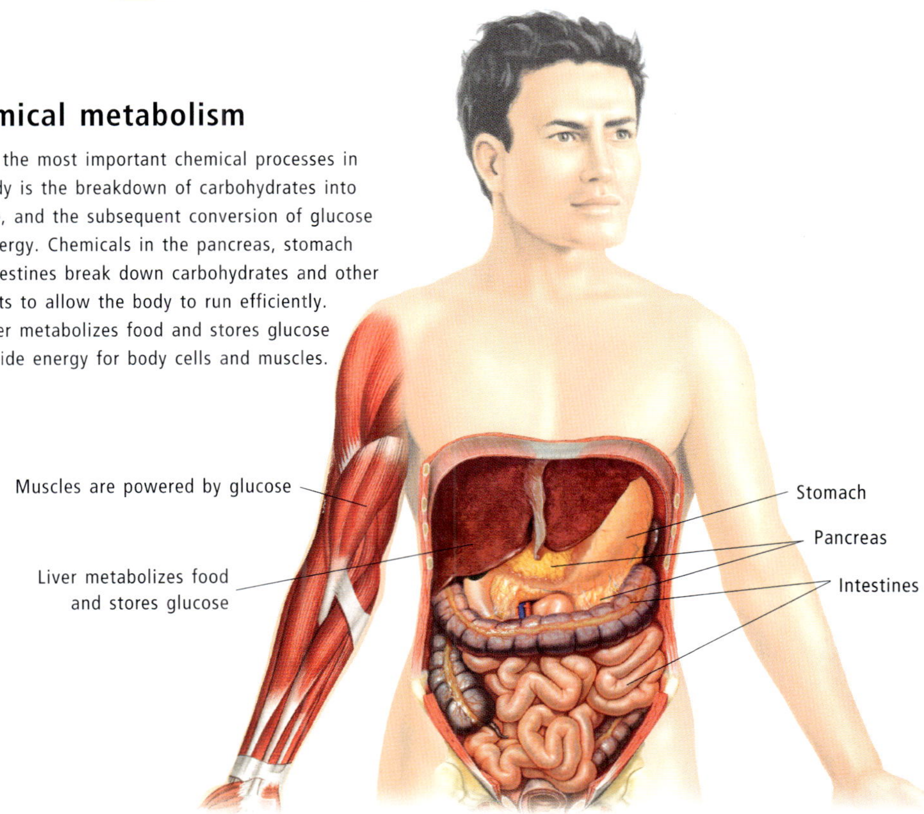

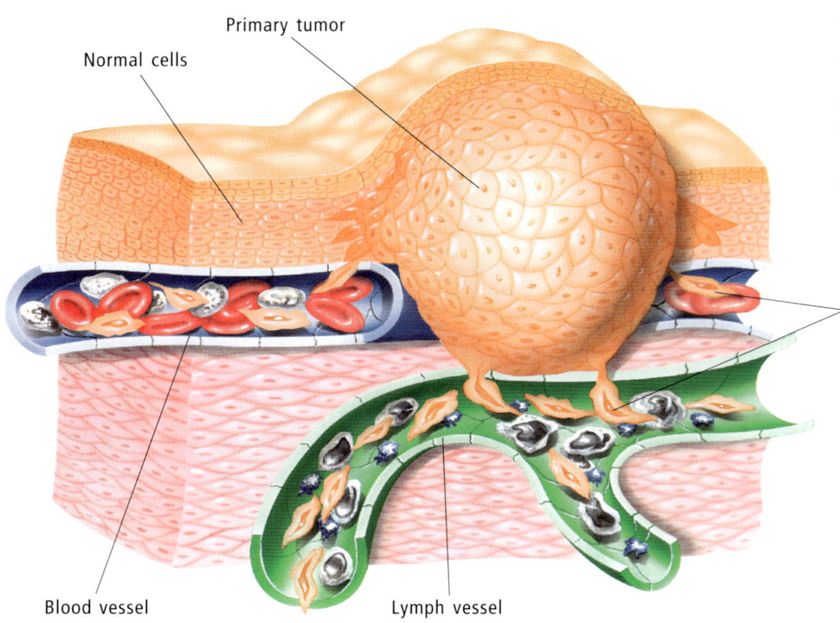

Metastasis

When diseases or cancerous cells spread from the primary source of infection or tumor to another part of the body, they are said to have metastasized. Metastasis can occur via the bloodstream or the lymphatic system.

tion, during which food molecules are broken down and energy released, is an example of a catabolic process.

Substances that are crucial to the chemical reactions that run our bodies include enzymes, which are produced by the body itself, and nutrients, which are extracted from the foods we eat. Nutrients include carbohydrates, lipids, proteins, minerals and vitamins. Many metabolic disorders involve an inability of the body to produce or use particular enzymes or to break down or use certain nutrients from foods.

Fortunately, most serious metabolic disorders are exceptionally rare. Many are congenital (present from birth). These include fructose intolerance, galactosemia, maple sugar urine disease and phenylketonuria (PKU). Early recognition of such diseases is crucial because their impacts on the body can often be controlled or limited by strict nutritional or dietary regimes.

Basal metabolic rate is the lowest rate of energy use required by the body to sustain its essential functions, including respiration, blood circulation and temperature maintenance. It is measured between 14–18 hours after the last meal, when the person is awake but at complete rest in a comfortable environment. The resulting measurement is known as the basal metabolic rate (BMR), which is ultimately an expression of the pace at which a particular person's body breaks down food. On average, a healthy human uses 1,500–2,000 kilocalories (6,000–8,000 kilojoules) per day in the maintenance of basic body functions.

A person's overall metabolism is regulated internally by hormones, particularly those secreted by the thyroid gland. Too much or too little of these can alter the metabolic rate and may cause serious health problems.

There are, however, many other factors that also affect metabolic rate. For example, our metabolism slows with age and increases with exercise. The metabolic rate of women tends to be lower than that of men, although it increases during pregnancy and lactation. Stress hormones raise the metabolic rate, as do other hormones such as testosterone. High temperatures, associated with illness, will also cause an increase in metabolic rate. The metabolic rate slows during sleep and when we are malnourished.

SEE ALSO *Amino acids, Diabetes, Enzyme deficiencies, Hormones, Phenylketonuria*

METASTASIS

Metastasis is the general term for the spread of cancer from one part of the body to another. A single tumor that has spread is called a metastasis (also called a "secondary"); more than one are referred to as metastases (or "secondaries"). Metastases are caused by cancer cells that have separated from a primary tumor, have spread through the veins or lymphatic system (less commonly via an artery) and have lodged in distant tissue and grown to form tumors themselves. Metastases are commonly found in the liver, lung, bones and brain. The cancer cells in a metastasis are the same as in the primary tumor.

A metastasis may also spread across the surface of a body cavity such as the peritoneum (the lining of the abdomen) or the pleura surrounding the lungs. Occasionally, metastases result from surgery and may be found in the scar of the wound through which a tumor has been removed. A metastasis usually indicates advancing spread of the cancer, and a generally poorer prognosis.

Treatments such as radiation therapy, surgery and chemotherapy are usually aimed at relieving the symptoms rather than curing the cancer. Occasionally it may be the metastasis rather than the primary tumor that causes the initial symptoms of cancer. Sometimes the primary tumor is never found.

SEE ALSO *Cancer*

METHADONE

Methadone is a synthetic narcotic painkiller (analgesic) similar to morphine. It blocks the effects of heroin withdrawal, and so is used primarily in the treatment of heroin users, though it may sometimes be used in the management of cancer pain. It can be given once a day as an oral preparation. Side effects are similar to those other narcotics and include nausea, constipation and urinary retention. Methadone is itself addictive but it is thought to be easier to withdraw from than heroin, though still not easy.

Though not a cure for drug dependence in itself, methadone gives people the opportunity to manage their lives and reduces their dependence on crime and the illegal drugs market, and therefore minimizes the social and legal consequences and the risks of transmission of infections such as HIV (AIDS), hepatitis B and C.

SEE ALSO *Drug dependence, Heroin*

MICROCEPHALY

Microcephaly is a rare disorder in which a child's head circumference is below the normal size range for age and sex. There are a variety of causes, including premature closing of the fontanelles, genetic abnormalities and disease. Microcephaly can be present at birth, or it may develop during a child's early years. Some degree of intellectual disability and impaired physical development are common. Life expectancy is often low.

MICROSURGERY

Microsurgery is a surgical technique in which a surgeon uses a microscope and specially adapted hand-held miniaturized instruments to operate on tiny structures, such as very small blood vessels and nerves. It is used for operations that require extreme delicacy, such as plastic surgery, reconstruction and transplantation. Microsurgery is frequently used in surgery of the ears, the eyes, or the brain.

MIDBRAIN

The midbrain is located deep inside the brain, below the cerebrum. It sits directly above the pons and, together with this structure and the medulla oblongata, forms the brain stem, the part of the brain attached to the spinal cord. The brain stem is the most primitive part of the brain and is involved in many basic body functions. The midbrain itself relays motor signals from the cerebral cortex to the pons, and sensory transmissions in the other direction, from the spinal cord to the thalamus. Cranial nerves III and IV, which service the eye muscles, start in the midbrain, making this area important in eyelid, eyeball, lens and pupil movements. The midbrain is also referred to as the mesencephalon.

SEE ALSO *Brain, Eye, Medulla oblongata, Spinal cord*

Midbrain

Also known as the mesencephalon, the midbrain relays information between the medulla oblongata and the cerebral hemispheres. It contains the nerve centers for the third and fourth cranial nerves, and includes the colliculi and cerebral peduncles.

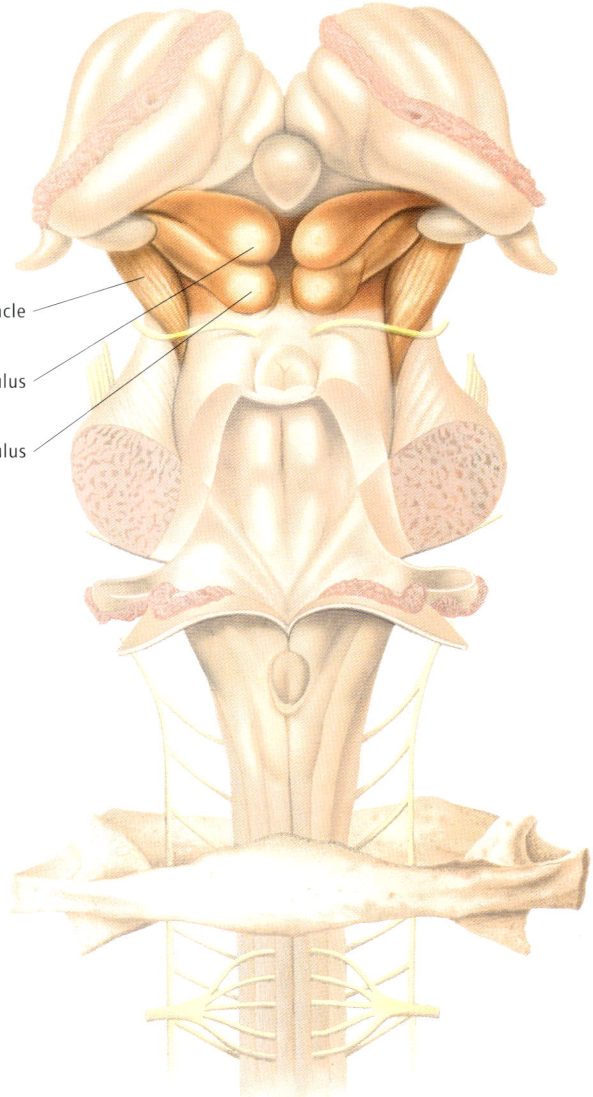

Midbrain

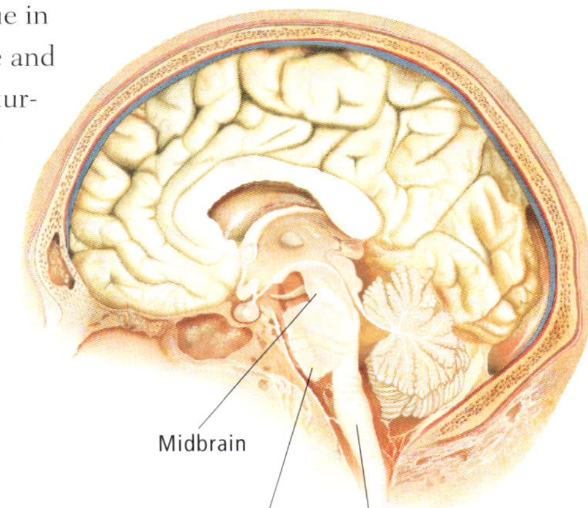

MIDDLE EAR

The middle ear is part of the mechanism for sensing sound. It is situated within the skull, adjacent to the outer ear. A thin tympanic membrane (eardrum), which vibrates under the influence of sound, covers the inner end of the ear canal. A sound wave striking the ear causes the membrane to vibrate. The vibrations are transmitted to a sensory region, the cochlea, from which the auditory nerve conveys the sensation of sound, now in the form of nerve impulses, to the brain.

SEE ALSO *Cochlea, Ear, Hearing, Otitis media*

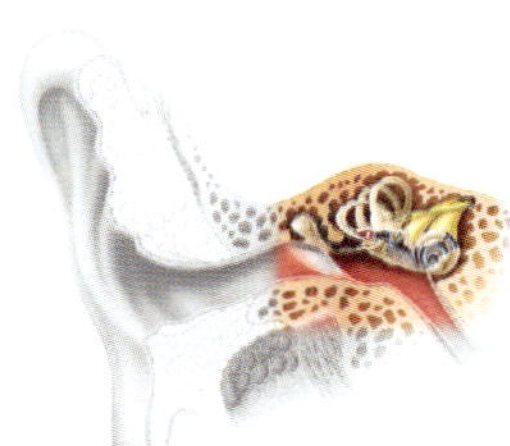

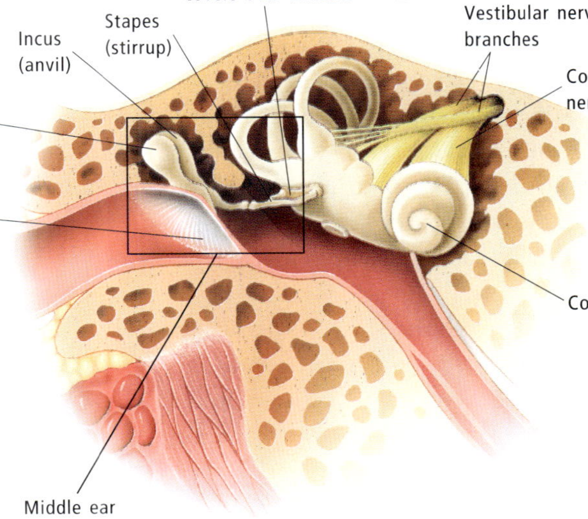

Middle ear

The middle ear is a short chamber between the eardrum and the oval window of the inner ear. It contains a chain of three small bones or ossicles (malleus, incus and stapes), which carry sound waves from the vibrating eardrum to the cochlea.

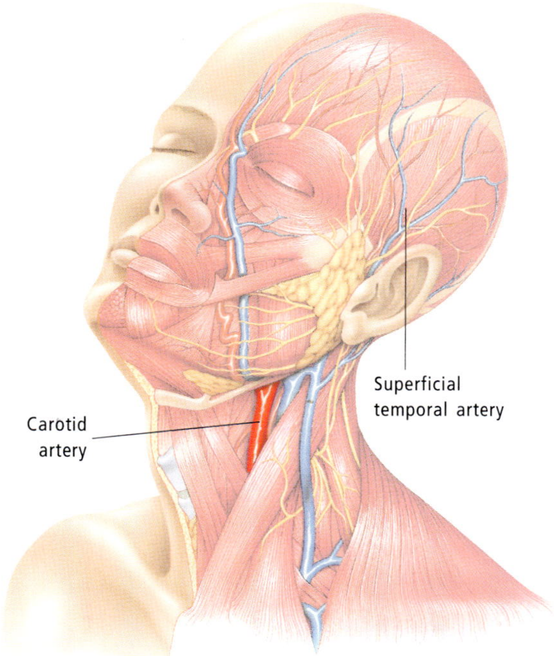

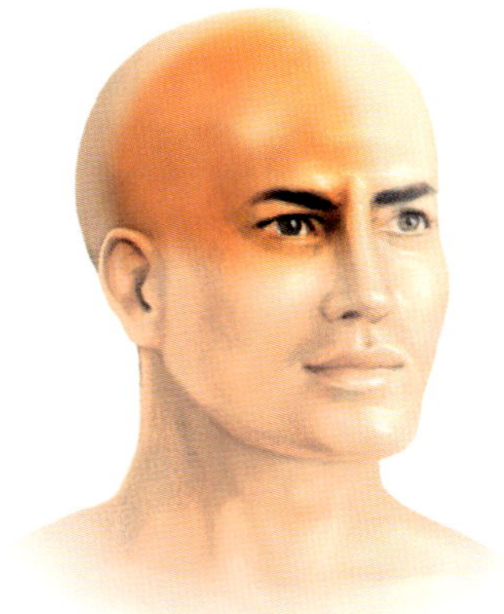

Migraine

Migraines have been linked to the dilation of cerebral blood vessels such as branches of the the carotid arteries. Pain relief may be obtained from drugs that stop the dilation of blood vessels, but only if taken in the early stages of the migraine.

MIGRAINE

Migraine headaches are the most common and serious variety of vascular headaches, estimated to affect over 10 percent of the population. They are associated with dilation of one or more branches of the carotid and vertebral arteries, which supply the scalp and structures within the skull. Migraine is not a single disease entity. Although most migraine headaches share a number of clinical features, several varieties of the migraine syndrome are recognized. The precise cause of migraine headaches remains unknown, as does the mechanism of development of the clinical features. Recent research indicates that abnormalities with serotonin (a neurotransmitter) or with serotonin receptors in the brain may be involved.

Migraine headaches typically cause severe, often throbbing pain that usually affects one half of the head or behind one eye (although sometimes it can be on both sides). The sufferer may wake up with a headache, which usually lasts several hours, sometimes a whole day or longer. There may be associated nausea and vomiting, as well as tenderness of the scalp (sometimes overlying the involved dilated arteries). After the headache subsides, the person is usually exhausted.

The common form of migraine affects women approximately three times more often than men. A tendency to develop migraine runs in families. Many precipitating factors have been identified, such as fatigue and stress, oversleeping or missing a meal; consumption of certain foods (especially chocolate, drinks containing caffeine, alcoholic drinks, especially red wine, and nuts, beans, lentils and cheeses); and various food additives (such as nitrates/nitrites in processed meats, monosodium glutamate in processed foods and some Asian foods, as well as certain food colorings.

Hormonal factors apparently play a very important role; migraine headaches are often related to menstrual periods, and may occur in the first trimester of pregnancy, during menopause and as a side effect of oral contraceptive therapy.

A less common variety of migraine is known as classic migraine or migraine with aura. In this form, the patient develops symptoms suggestive of interference with normal brain function, for periods of 5–30 minutes before the onset of the headache. The symptoms may include visual disturbances, such as seeing flashing lights or partial loss of vision; disruptions in hearing, taste or smell; or, rarely, speech disturbances, partial paralysis, dizziness or loss of balance. These abnormalities are temporary and reversible, usually disappearing as the headache worsens. The headache is otherwise similar to common migraine. Other variant forms of migraine are quite rare but may be associated with more severe neurological disturbances.

Migraine headaches are difficult to treat, although some effective drugs are available. Prevention is best, so, where possible, known precipitating factors should be avoided. If avoidance of dietary triggers and modifications of lifestyle do not help to reduce the frequency of headaches, a number of drugs can be used to prevent the onset of migraine, although their effectiveness is variable.

There are a number of alternative therapies that may be used to alleviate the symptoms of migrane. Acupuncture and shiatsu treat points to relieve the pain and correct imbalances of the liver and gallbladder meridians. Aromatherapy prescribes a 5-minute hot water foot bath with chamomile, melissa, lavender or rosemary, or regular massage as a preventive measure. Psychotherapy or somatic therapies may help to pinpoint and release underlying tensions. Herbalism prescribes chamomile, ginger and feverfew. Homeopathy treats migraine with constitutional remedies prescribed according to an overall patient "picture". Naturopathy eliminates possible food allergies or other triggers.

Low blood sugar levels or hormonal imbalances are treated with diet and supplements; emotional upsets are treated with flower essences. Qi gong, t'ai chi or yoga seek to prevent migraine by helping release accumulated stresses held within the body.

SEE ALSO *Headache*

MINERALOCORTICOIDS

Mineralocorticoids are a class of hormones produced by the adrenal gland. They are concerned with maintaining adequate fluid volume, blood pressure and heart output in the body. The main mineralocorticoid is aldosterone. A deficiency of mineralocorticoid, for example in Addison's disease, can cause reduced cardiac output and fatal shock.

SEE ALSO *Hormones*

MINERALS

Minerals, in the present context, are inorganic substances found in the body or diet. In general, minerals are required for the formation of bone, for use as electrolytes in intracellular and extracellular fluids, and for incorporation into the molecules of hemoglobin, enzymes and coenzymes.

Minerals important for health include calcium, chloride, magnesium, phosphorus, iron, potassium and sodium. Some minerals, such as those mentioned above, are required in relatively large quantities; others, generally known as trace elements, are required only in very small amounts and may be toxic if taken in large amounts. Many mineral substances are toxic in any dose, notably lead, mercury and all radioactive substances.

Electrolytes are chemical substances, which when dissolved in fluids, dissociate into electrically charged ions. They are so-called because in their ionic form they can conduct electricity. The main minerals required as electrolytes are sodium, potassium, magnesium, calcium and chloride.

Sodium is a major electrolyte of all fluids in the body. Potassium is an important electrolyte in intracellular fluid. Fruit juices are an important dietary source of potassium. Some medications cause loss of potassium, but overdose of potassium is serious and may be fatal. Magnesium is another important intracellular electrolyte. Calcium is an important intracellular electrolyte, playing a vital role in muscle action and nerve transmission. Chloride is a major anionic (negatively charged) electrolyte, occurring in all body fluids. Electrolytes are lost in sweat, vomiting and diarrhea. Excessive intake of salt (sodium chloride) may be harmful in heart disease and pregnancy.

Calcium, besides acting as an electrolyte, is a major constituent of bone, which is a hydroxyapatite (a mixture of calcium phosphate and calcium hydroxide) deposited in an organic matrix. The adult body typically contains about 42 ounces (1,200 grams) of calcium. Milk is an important source.

Iron is required for the synthesis of hemoglobin (the red pigment of the blood) and myoglobin (a similar pigment found in muscle). Iron deficiency, usually due to poor absorption of iron, leads to anemia. Paradoxically, excessive iron is also harmful. Phosphorus is required for bone, DNA,

Minerals—bone and muscle function

Minerals are important in the formation of bone, as well as in nerve transmission and in muscle action.

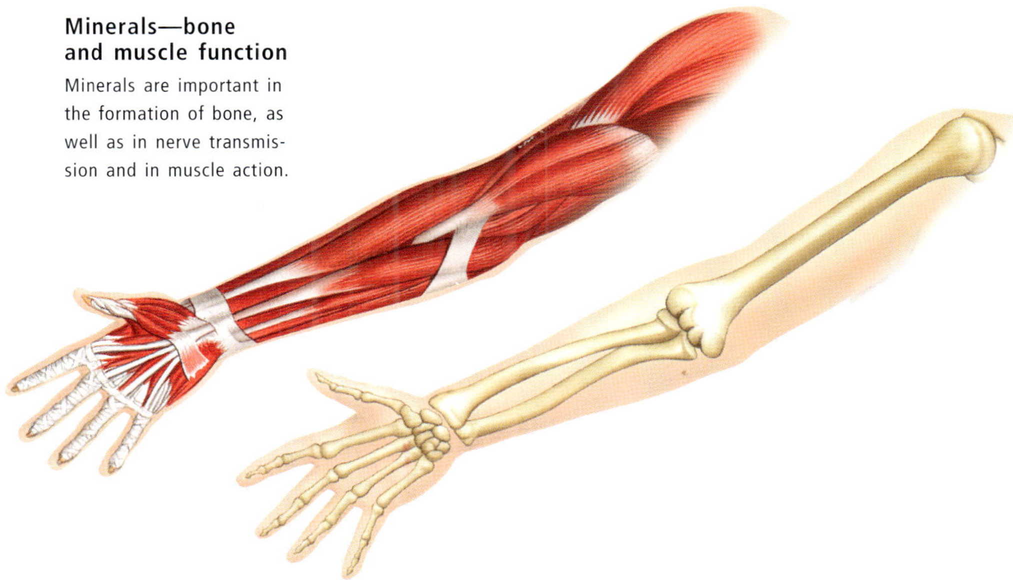

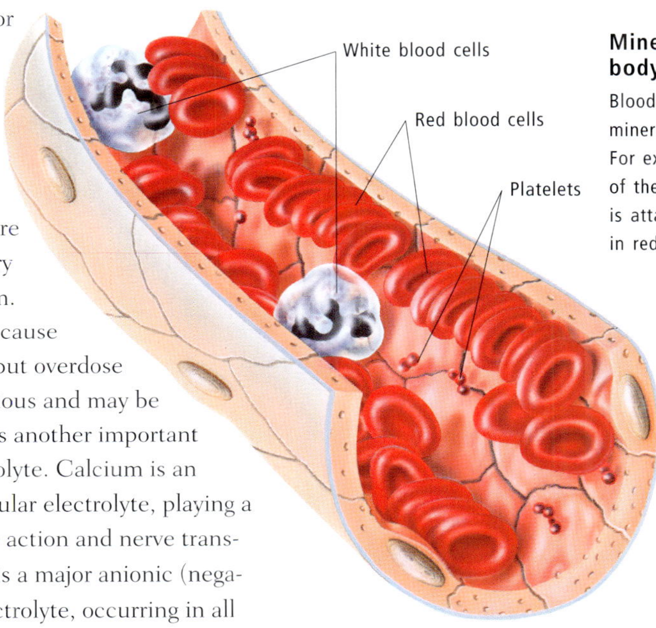

Minerals—body fluids

Blood carries the various minerals around the body. For example, two-thirds of the iron in the body is attached to hemoglobin in red blood cells.

Minerals

Minerals cannot be manufactured by the body and hence must be ingested. They perform three important functions: they play a role in physiological processes, such as the movement of muscles and skeletal development; they determine the concentration of fluids in body cells; and they are important for enzymatic reactions.

M

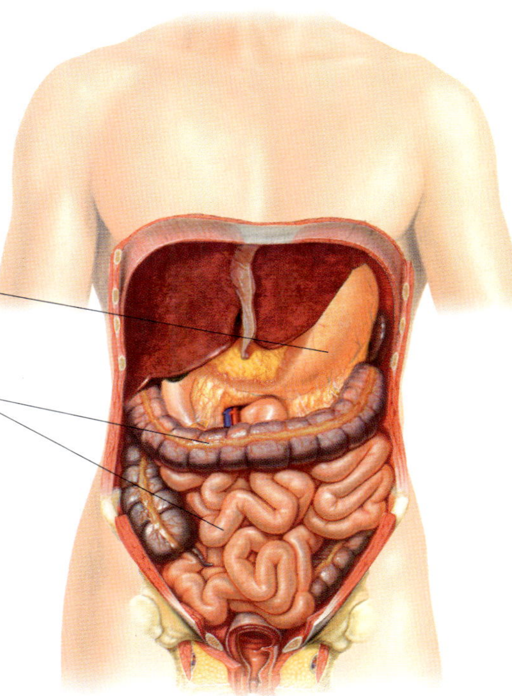

Minerals—enzyme reactions

Minerals are required for the body to produce enzymes. These are needed for food processing and absorption. Zinc, for example, is needed for the production of gastric acid.

RNA and some coenzymes, playing an important role in all metabolic processes. Sulfur is an essential constituent of proteins, such as the amino acids cysteine and methionine. It is found particularly in the hair.

There are several other minerals which are essential, but needed only in small quantities. Iodine is required for thyroid hormone. Its main dietary sources are seafood (for example, fish and seaweed), and artificially iodized salt. Deficiency causes goiter. Zinc is an essential component of some enzyme systems, required for important functions including wound healing, immune responses and reproduction. Copper deficiency is believed to be an important cause of heart disease. Cobalt is a component of vitamin B_{12}. Manganese is a component of several enzyme systems.

Fluorides are deposited in the enamel of the developing teeth of children, giving increased resistance to dental caries. Dietary sources are naturally or artificially fluoridated water, tea, and sea-fish.

Diet during pregnancy and lactation must include the additional minerals necessary for the needs of the growing fetus and baby, notably calcium, phosphorus and iodine.

SEE ALSO *Calcium, Electrolytes, Fluoridation, Iodine deficiency, Iron, Lead poisoning, Nutrition, Potassium, Sodium*

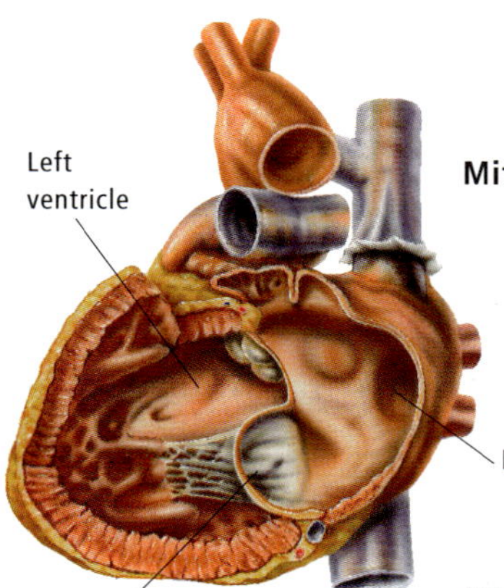

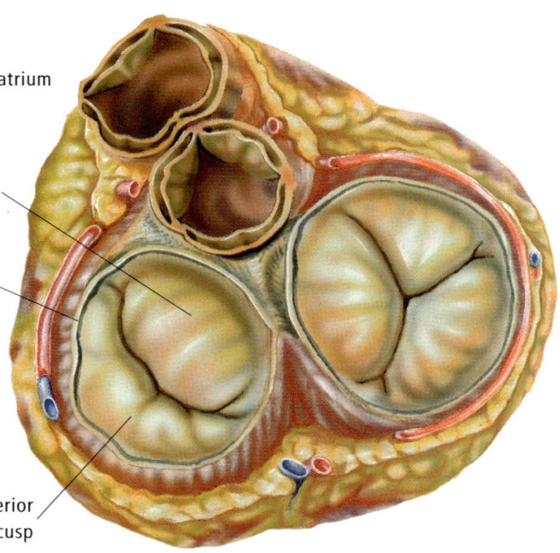

Mitral valve

The mitral valve, also known as the bicuspid valve, is located between the left atrium and left ventricle. Prolapse of the mitral valve may result in chest pain, dyspnea, palpitations, fatigue and fainting.

MISCARRIAGE

A miscarriage or spontaneous abortion generally occurs before week 12 of a pregnancy. Miscarriage occurs in one in every five pregnancies. Before week 20 of the pregnancy the loss of a fetus is a miscarriage; after that date it is a stillbirth.

Around 85 percent of miscarriages are related to fetal abnormalities. Of the remaining 15 percent, two-thirds are due to problems in the mother and one-third have an unknown cause. Miscarriage can follow a severe fever, particularly if it is caused by a virus. It can be due to some abnormality of the uterus. It is less common in women under 25, and more likely after the age of 35.

Bleeding, first spotting then a heavier discharge, is usually the first sign of a miscarriage, though some minor bleeding can also occur as part of a normal pregnancy. Cramping of the uterus follows. If an ultrasound detects a fetal heartbeat, then there is around a 90 percent chance that the pregnancy will proceed. Although some doctors still recommend bed rest there is no evidence that this is necessary. When the fetus is no longer viable, cramping will continue and pieces of tissue may be expelled. It is important to seek medical advice if miscarriage seems possible. Sometimes a curette may be suggested to scrape out any remaining contents of the uterus; however, ultrasound will usually indicate that this is not necessary.

Late miscarriage (between weeks 12 and 20) can be caused by a weak cervix (in approximately 20 percent of women). If this is found to be the cause, a stitch (cervical cerclage) may be used. After 20 weeks a miscarriage can be the result of placental insufficiency. Recurrent miscarriage (after a woman has had three or more miscarriages in succession) will need investigation by a specialist. The next pregnancy will need careful monitoring.

SEE ALSO *Abortion, Dilation and curettage, Placenta, Pregnancy*

MITRAL VALVE

The mitral valve is one of the valves in the heart; it prevents the backflow of blood from the left ventricle to the left atrium during systolic contraction of the heart. The mitral valve gets its name due to the distinctive shape of the valve, which resembles the miter worn by bishops. The mitral together with the tricuspid valves are called atrioventricular valves because they lie between the atria and ventricles. Both atrioventricular valves have parachute-like valve cusps, which have tough fibrous cords (chordae tendineae, the "heart strings") attached along the free edge.

The other ends of the chordae are attached to small tongue-shaped elevations of the heart muscle of the ventricle (papillary muscles) which are designed to pull down on the chordae and the valve cusps when the ventricle contracts, thus keeping the tricuspid and mitral valves shut as the ventricles rapidly decrease in size during contraction.

Mitral valve disease usually is divided into two types: mitral stenosis, where the valve opening is too narrow, and mitral insufficiency (or incompetence) where the mitral valve is unable to prevent backflow of blood from the left ventricle to the left atrium. Most mitral valve disease is due to rheumatic heart disease, but mitral insufficiency may be caused by ruptured or defective chordae tendineae or papillary muscles.

Patients with mitral stenosis usually present to their doctor with symptoms of failure of the left side of the heart, including shortness of breath, breathlessness while lying down, and coughing up blood. They may develop palpitations (the sensation of rapid heart beating in the chest) and chest pain. Patients may also develop atrial fibrillation (the chaotic and ineffectual contraction of the left atrium) which can have serious consequences if blood coagulates in the left atrium and throws off tiny fragments to block arteries in the brain, limbs or kidneys. There will be a murmur (a sound produced by abnormal blood flow through the heart) heard best on the lower left side of the chest.

Medical treatment for mitral stenosis is aimed at treating arrhythmias (abnormal rhythm) and usually includes digoxin, beta-adrenergic blocking drugs and maybe quinidine in various combinations, but would depend on the clinical circumstances. Anticoagulants like warfarin prevent formation of thrombosis in the atrium which can dislodge and block other arteries. Antibiotics are used to treat infections on valve surfaces.

Surgical treatment involves separating the valve cusps (valvotomy), which are often stuck together along their edges. In some cases, the entire valve may need to be replaced by an artificial valve (prosthesis), or a valve graft from pig heart.

Patients with mitral insufficiency often complain to their physician of fatigue, shortness of breath and episodic breathlessness at night. Symptoms may start suddenly if the condition is due to sudden rupture of the chordae tendineae. A murmur is also present, but the timing of the sound differs from that heard in mitral stenosis. Medical treatment may be similar to that used in mitral stenosis; surgical treatment involves replacing the damaged mitral valve with a prosthetic valve or graft.

Replacement of the mitral valve in either mitral stenosis or insufficiency will require open-heart surgery, in which the patient's body is cooled and the function of the heart is temporarily taken over by a heart–lung machine. This will allow the heart to be stopped and opened, so that the surgeon may reach the damaged valve.

SEE ALSO *Heart, Ventricle*

MITTELSCHMERZ

Of German origin, mittelschmerz is a term used to describe the pain experienced by women mid-way through the menstrual cycle, at around day fourteen. It is thought to be caused by the stretching of the nerves around the ovary as it increases in size. It is often accompanied by bloating, mood changes, headache, and fluid retention. Mittelschmerz can be treated if necessary with diuretics and painkillers, or, in severe cases, by suppressing ovulation through the use of oral contraceptives.

SEE ALSO *Menstruation, Ovulation*

MOLES

A mole is the common term for a nevus, a congenital pigmented skin marking. Moles are also known as birthmarks because they usually appear shortly after birth. Moles can also appear during childhood and early adolescence. They may be round and raised or flat. They range in color from brown or black to bluish or blue-gray. Most people have twenty to thirty—some people have several hundred. There are many varieties, including cafe-au-lait spots, congenital nevi, hairy nevi and sebaceous nevi.

Cafe-au-lait spots are light tan, the color of coffee with milk. Multiple cafe-au-lait are associated with neurofibromatosis, a genetic disorder causing abnormal growth of nerve tissues.

A mongolian spot (or mongolian blue spot) is usually bluish or bruised-looking. It appears most commonly over the lower back or buttocks, but may also occur in other areas such as the trunk or arms. Mongolian spots may persist for months or years but are benign and do not become cancerous.

Congenital nevi (those present at birth) have an increased risk of developing into malignant melanoma, a form of skin cancer. Those with a mixture of colors, those that are irregular in shape, and those that are large have the highest potential for malignancy. People living in areas with high levels of ultraviolet radiation such as Queensland in Australia are also at high risk, as are those with moles in trauma areas such as the palms of hands, soles of feet, under nails, on the genitals, inside the mouth, or belt and bra areas. All congenital nevi should be examined periodically; if there are changes in the size, color, or surface texture, or sudden ulceration, bleeding, or itching in the birthmark, a physician should be consulted and the mole should be removed.

Diagnosis of the type of mole is made by a physician based on the appearance of the mole, when it appeared, and any symptoms or pre-cancer type features. Usually the mole doesn't need to be treated; however, if it looks ungainly and is causing concern, it can be covered with cosmetics. Alternatively, it can be surgically removed.

If a mole has an increased risk of cancer, surgical removal is desirable. Usually, moles can be removed under local anesthesia in a physician's office. Alternatively a mole can be removed using liquid nitrogen, electrotherapy or radiation therapy.

A hydatidiform mole is a benign (noncancerous) growth that develops within the uterus from a degenerating embryo and causes bleeding similar to that from a threatened miscarriage. It may be spontaneously expelled from the uterus; if not, a dilation and curettage (scraping) is performed to surgically remove it. In some cases, a hydatidiform mole can become malignant, when it is called a choriocarcinoma.

SEE ALSO *Birthmarks, Choriocarcinoma, Hydatidiform mole, Melanoma, Sun exposure*

M

MOLLUSCUM CONTAGIOSUM

Characterized by multiple little blisters or blebs $\frac{1}{10}$ inch (2–3 millimeters) across with a central dimple, molluscum contagiosum is an acutely infectious disease transmitted by skin to skin contact.

Due to a pox-type virus, it is common to find the infection on the body and limbs of children where it is probably spread by skin contact with other children. In adults, it can be spread by sexual contact and is commonly found in the genital area in this case.

People with AIDS may develop florid molluscum all over the face, with the blebs being up to $\frac{1}{5}$ inch (5 millimeters) across. The incubation period is relatively long, ranging from a week to several months.

Treatment includes freezing with liquid nitrogen, using electric high-frequency currents (diathermy), or applying various chemicals injected into each spot with a sharpened sterile toothpick.

SEE ALSO *Sexually transmitted diseases, Viruses*

MORNING SICKNESS

Nausea and vomiting experienced generally in the first trimester of pregnancy are commonly referred to as morning sickness. At least 50 percent of pregnant women are affected by it to some degree, and many also experience headaches, dizziness and exhaustion. Symptoms may be more common in the morning but can be present at any time of day.

Although the exact cause is not known, major contributing factors are thought to be hormonal changes and lower blood sugar levels in early pregnancy. The condition may be aggravated by excess stomach acid, traveling, an enhanced sense of smell, fatigue, stress and some foods. Drinking small amounts of fluid between meals may prevent stomach distension which can cause vomiting, and eating dry toast or crackers before getting out of bed may settle the stomach.

In cases of excessive vomiting in pregnancy, known as hyperemesis gravidarum, anti-nausea drugs may be prescribed by a physician or fluids may be administered intravenously to prevent dehydration and malnutrition.

There are a number of alternative therapies that may be used to alleviate the symptoms of morning sickness. Acupuncture or acupressure treat specific points for morning sickness. Herbalism prescribes slippery elm bark, or ginger, lemon balm or chamomile teas. Homeopathy has a number of remedies for morning sickness prescribed according to specific symptoms. Naturopathy prescribes vitamin B complex and a diet of frequent small meals of plain food. Coffee, orange juice, and oily or fried foods should be avoided.

SEE ALSO *Nausea, Pregnancy*

MORPHINE

Morphine is a bitter-tasting crystalline alkaloid derived from the opium poppy and related to codeine and meperidine. It was discovered in 1803 and called morphine after Morpheus, the Greek god of dreams. A powerful narcotic painkiller (analgesic), it is usually prescribed for people in severe pain, such as the pain associated with terminal cancer. It is also used in the treatment of acute heart failure and shock.

Morphine may be taken orally, but because of its slow and poor absorption by the intestine, it is more usually injected or given via an infusion pump. If used for longer than a week or two, withdrawal symptoms may be experienced on ceasing the treatment.

Because morphine depresses respiration, it should be used with care in people with lung disease such as chronic bronchitis, and in the elderly or the very young (who are particularly sensitive to the drug's respiratory depressant effects). Constipation is another common side effect.

SEE ALSO *Narcotics*

MOTION SICKNESS

Most people experience motion sickness at some stage in their lives—on a boat or ship tossed on the ocean, in an aircraft struck by turbulence, in a long car or train trip or on an amusement park ride. Even astronauts in space get motion sickness. It begins with sweating, headaches and fatigue and culminates in nausea, dizziness and vomiting. In most cases, symptoms disappear rapidly when the motion stops. In some people, however, it can continue for days after.

Motion sickness is associated with the way the brain assesses the body's balance and movement, which relies on a stream of information from various nervous system components. Signals from the inner ears, the eyes and stretch receptors in the muscles allow the brain to establish where the body is in space. When the brain receives conflicting messages, the symptoms of motion sickness develop. For example, when a person reads in a moving car, the eyes signal no motion while the inner ears indicate movement.

A range of medications is available for motion sickness, from ginger tablets to antihistamines.

SEE ALSO *Balance, Sea sickness*

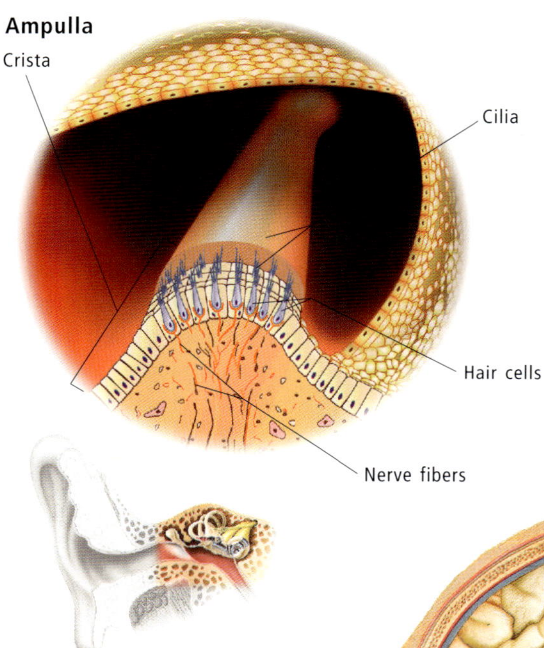

Motion sickness—balance

Changing the position of the head moves fluid in the inner ear, which stimulates hairs on the surface of the ampulla. These hairs send signals to the brain. When these signals are disrupted or confused, such as when traveling in a car, plane or boat, you may suffer from motion sickness.

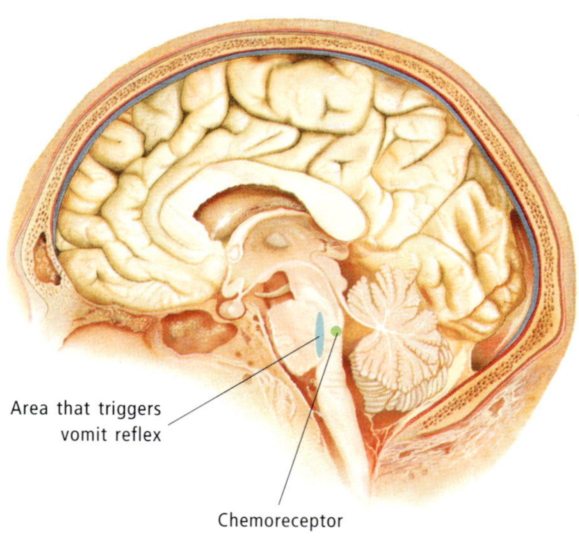

Vomiting and nausea centers

Two points in the brain instigate the nausea associated with motion sickness. The chemoreceptor triggers the vomit reflex when the brain receives conflicting messages about the position of the body in space and time.

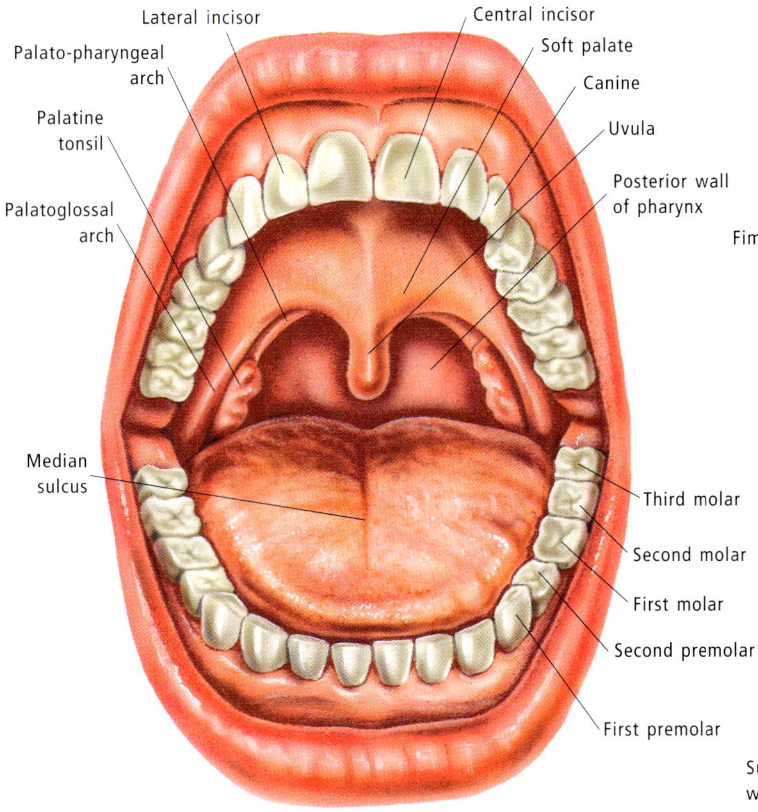

Structure of the mouth
(with tongue down)

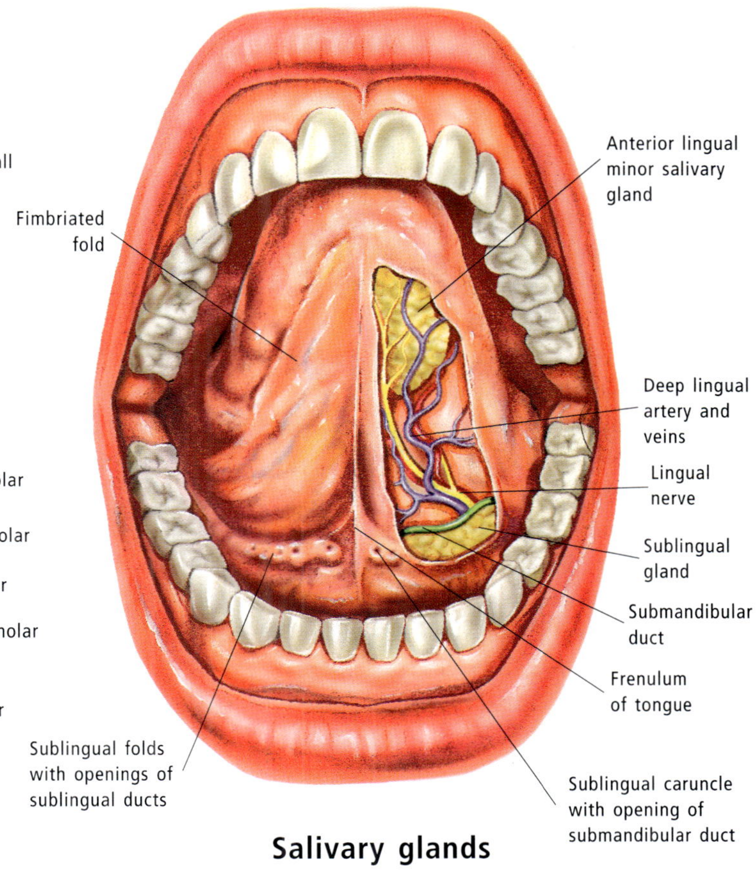

Salivary glands
(with tongue up)

MOUTH

The mouth is the first part of the digestive tract. It consists of an outer vestibule, which lies between the teeth and the cheeks or lips, and an inner true oral cavity within the arches formed by the teeth. The true oral cavity has a roof formed by the hard palate in the front and the soft palate at the back, which separate the mouth from the nasal cavity. The hard palate is bony; the soft palate is formed of muscle covered by mucous membrane. The prominent droplet-shaped fleshy structure which hangs from the rear edge of the soft palate is called the uvula. The floor of the oral cavity is made up of the tongue and the tissue between the tongue and the teeth. At the back, the oral cavity leads into the oropharynx, which is part of the throat. The external opening and the lips are encircled by a muscle called the orbicularis oris, which allows the lips to be pursed for whistling and sucking on straws. Each cheek is formed by another facial muscle, the buccinator, whose fibers run forward into the orbicularis oris.

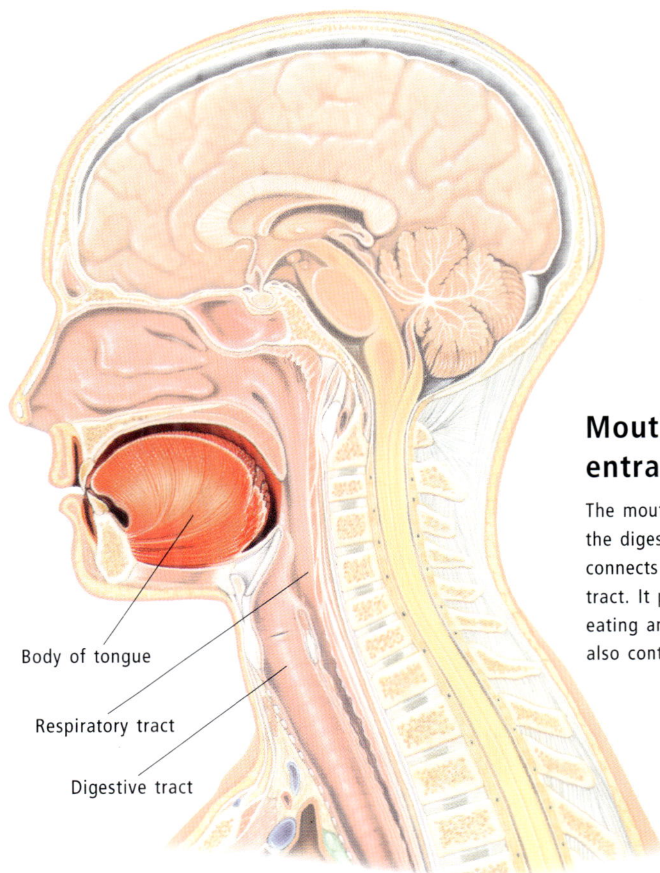

Mouth—entrance to body

The mouth is the entrance to the digestive tract and also connects to the respiratory tract. It plays a vital role in eating and speaking, and can also contribute to breathing.

Teeth and gums

In the adult, 32 permanent teeth are arranged in two arcades of 16 teeth. On each side of each jaw are 8 teeth, which fall into four types. At the front on each side lie 2 incisors, specialized chisel-shaped teeth for cutting food into segments. Further to the side lies the canine, a sharp dagger-tooth designed for gripping food. The canine ("dog" tooth) is not particularly large in humans, but can be very prominent in males of other primate species (e.g. baboons) and in carnivores. Behind the canine lie the 2 premolars or bicuspids and at the back are 3 molars. Premolars and molars are specialized for grinding food. The last molars, often called the wisdom teeth, emerge from the gum at about the eighteenth year of life.

During infancy a set of 20 deciduous or milk teeth is arranged as 5 teeth (2 incisors, 1 canine and 2 molars) in each jaw on each side. They emerge between 6 months and 2 years of age and are progressively replaced by permanent teeth between 6 and 18 years, in a rough sequence from front to back.

Each tooth consists of a central pulp cavity containing nerves and blood vessels. This is surrounded by dentine, which is in turn capped by enamel, the hardest substance in the body. Dentine is constantly exposed to intense physical wear during chewing. Dentine is similar to bone elsewhere in the body and is composed mainly of collagen and calcium. Enamel is 97 percent calcium salts and 3 percent organic material. The enamel does not cover the tooth below the gum line, where a bone-like structure called cementum covers the tooth. A periodontal membrane or ligament, a collagen-rich fibrous structure, surrounds the cementum of the root, and helps to fix the tooth firmly into the jaw.

Tongue

The tongue is a muscular organ which helps to move food around the mouth and assists in speech. Muscles of the tongue are arranged in three directions—vertical, horizontal and longitudinal. When the vertical fibers are activated the tongue becomes flat, when the longitudinal fibers contract the tongue becomes shorter, when the transverse fibers are contracted the tongue becomes narrower. Some people have a genetically determined ability to activate discrete sets of transverse muscle fibers and are able to curl their tongue.

The tongue is attached to the floor of the mouth and is divided into two main regions by a V-shaped groove (the sulcus terminalis). The front part consists of about two-thirds of the tongue and is covered with specialized projections and taste buds. The tongue is covered with projections called papillae, which come in three main types. The filiform papillae are elongated cone-shaped projections from the upper tongue surface, which are designed for gripping food. They are very prominent on the tongues of many animals and can be felt when a cat licks your hand. Fungiform papillae are mushroom shaped projections from the upper tongue surface, which contains taste buds. The circumvallate papillae are shaped like small castles, with a central bulge and a surrounding moat. The circumvallate papillae are arranged in a V in front of the sulcus terminalis and contain taste buds. The back one-third of the tongue is covered by lymphoid tissue called the lingual tonsil, which is important for the defence of the body from microorganisms. On each side the tongue is joined to the palate by arches of tissue (palatoglossal arches). Immediately behind these lie the palatine tonsils, which are lymphoid organs like the lingual tonsil.

Salivary glands

The mouth is kept moist by the secretions of two types of salivary glands. The minor salivary glands are either very small or microscopic while the major salivary glands (parotid, submandibular and sublingual) are large structures which drain into the mouth through relatively long ducts. The parotid glands lie in front of the ears and have ducts which drain forward to open opposite the upper second molar. The sublingual and submandibular glands lie below the floor of the mouth. The ducts of the submandibular glands open below the tongue, while the sublingual glands lie below paired ridges under the tongue and open by many shorter ducts into the oral cavity.

Diseases of the mouth

The oral cavity may be involved in a variety of infections, which may be due to viruses like herpes simplex and Coxsackie virus type A, or yeast. Infection with yeast can result in oral thrush or candidiasis, particularly in those people whose immune systems are functioning poorly due to chemotherapy for tumors or leukemia. Infection of the tooth pulp with pus-forming bacteria can result in abscesses of the jaw.

Mouth ulcers may result from herpes simplex or from diseases elsewhere in the body such as aplastic anemia, a condition where the bone marrow ceases to produce red and white blood cells. Mouth ulcers may also accompany leukemia, erythema multiforme and Stevens-Johnson syndrome. Erythema multiforme is a generalized disease of the whole body characterized by fever, sore throat, headache, gastroenteritis, joint pains and gastroenteritis. Stevens-Johnson erythema is a particularly severe form of erythema multiforme with lesions in the mouth, eyes and genital region.

Disease of the gums (gingivitis) may cause separation of the gum from the enamel, exposing the cementum and dentine of the tooth neck to plaque-forming bacteria and resulting in tooth decay (caries) and possibly tooth loss. Caries are partly (up to 60 percent) preventable by ensuring adequate levels of dietary fluoride during tooth development.

Cancer of the oral cavity often occurs between the ages of 45 and 85 in association with heavy smoking and high alcohol intake, or poor oral hygiene. Many cancers arise around the edge of the tongue or in the gutter between the tongue and the gums of the lower teeth (the "cancer gulch"). Often the cancers develop as ulcers which are found by dentists. Final diagnosis is made by taking a biopsy.

Oral cancer can be treated by surgery in combination with radiation therapy. All patients with oral cancer should be carefully examined for tumors of the nose, airways, esophagus and larynx. Cancer of the lip is more frequent in farmers, sailors and others exposed to sunlight over prolonged periods. Treatment of lip cancer is by surgery or radiation therapy. The chances of survival are quite good for lip cancer, with about 90 percent of patients still alive after five years. Survival rates are lower if the tumor has spread to local lymph nodes.

SEE ALSO ***Gingivitis, Gums, Jaw, Lip, Palate, Salivary glands, Teeth, Tongue***

M

MUCOUS MEMBRANES

Mucous membranes form the lining of many of the hollow internal cavities of the body, notably the nose and mouth, the larger respiratory passages and the gut. A mucous membrane (mucosa) consists of several layers of cells, and is kept moist by secretions (mainly mucus) from glands found in or underneath the mucous membrane. The cells on the surface are adapted to the functions of that particular organ. For example, the surface of the mucous membrane of the mouth has many layers of flattened cells which give some resistance to abrasion from food, whereas that of the respiratory passages carries hair-like cilia to sweep foreign particles away.

SEE ALSO *Mouth, Nose, Respiratory system*

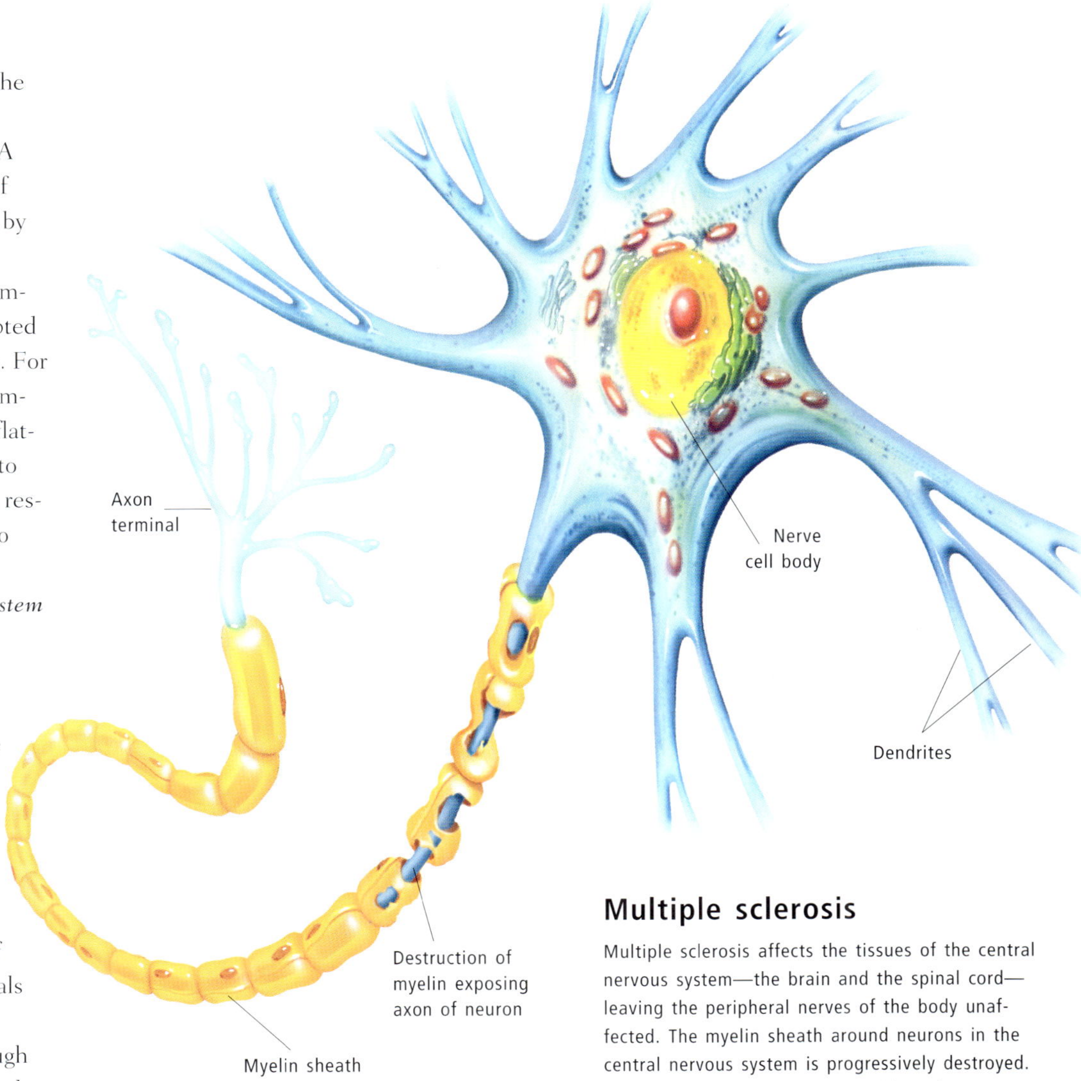

Multiple sclerosis

Multiple sclerosis affects the tissues of the central nervous system—the brain and the spinal cord—leaving the peripheral nerves of the body unaffected. The myelin sheath around neurons in the central nervous system is progressively destroyed. This leads to symptoms such as blurred vision, fatigue, poor coordination and tingling sensations.

MULTIPLE SCLEROSIS

Multiple sclerosis (MS) is a progressive and frequently debilitating disease of the central nervous system (CNS). It involves the ongoing destruction of the protective myelin sheaths around neurons in the brain and spinal cord. This interferes with the transmission of impulses by neurons, and disrupts signals sent throughout the CNS.

The cause of MS is unknown, although evidence suggests the trigger may be viral. Whatever the trigger, it is thought to stimulate an autoimmune response in which T cells mistakenly identify the myelin of the CNS as foreign. The T cells, which normally fight disease, then set up an immune response that leads to myelin destruction.

Just over 1 million people worldwide suffer from MS. Statistics reveal it to be far more prevalent in women than men, most common in people of northern European descent (particularly those with Scottish ancestry), extremely rare in people of Asian or African descent, and far less common in the tropics than in temperate areas. Aside from ethnicity and ancestry issues, there are other indications that genetics may predispose a person to developing MS. Children of a parent suffering from MS are 30 to 50 times more likely to develop the disease than the general population.

MS is not fatal, although the life span of sufferers is usually reduced by an average of six years due to complications of the disease, with lung and kidney infections being the principal life-threatening risks. MS can also have a debilitating impact on a person's quality of life. Because the symptoms and progression of the disease vary widely between sufferers, however, it is hard to predict how an individual will be affected.

At one end of the range, between 20 percent and 35 percent have such a mild form of the disease that they suffer little, if any, impact. Up to 12 percent of patients fall into the category at the other end of the spectrum and suffer from a serious and particularly aggressive form of the disease which may involve paralysis and dementia.

The first signs vary and do not always immediately suggest a serious disorder. They usually appear some time between the ages of fifteen and forty, but the disease most often strikes for the first time when the sufferer in the twenties or thirties. Blurred or double vision is frequently one of the earliest indicators. Pain and involuntary movements in the eyes are also common in people who later go on to develop MS. Extreme tiredness, clumsiness and tingling sensations are other early symptoms.

The disease usually takes years to progress, with sufferers often experiencing periods of remission when symptoms apparently disappear, followed by relapses. In advanced-stage MS, symptoms can include spasticity, poor coordination and vertigo, loss of bladder control, constipation, uncomfortable but short-lived sensations in the extremities, sexual problems including impotence in men, tremors in the arms or legs and mental dysfunction that can range from simple memory lapses to impaired problem-solving abilities.

There is no cure for MS and symptoms are often difficult to treat, although there is a range of therapies and medications available that can help make life more tolerable, including drugs which prevent muscle stiffness.

SEE ALSO *Brain, Neurons, Nervous system, Spinal cord*

MUMPS

In its simplest form, mumps is a viral illness of childhood due to a paramyxovirus which produces a mild febrile condition lasting a few days and characterized by painful swelling of the salivary glands that lie under and in front of the ears. After a 2–3 week incubation period, the patient becomes infectious a day or so before the swelling occurs and for 3 or 4 days thereafter. The illness is spread by droplets transmitted by coughing or breathing. Occasionally one side of the neck only will swell. The other side may swell up several days later. Adults usually suffer more than children. Occasionally the other salivary glands will also enlarge.

Complications are not uncommon, the most frequent being aseptic meningitis, which is usually mild and often not suspected unless an examination of the fluid around the brain and spinal cord (cerebrospinal fluid) is carried out. Twenty-five percent of adult males can develop swelling of one or both testes, occasionally leading to sterility. Similar painful swelling of the ovaries occurs in adult women. Inflammation of the pancreas in the abdomen can produce severe upper abdominal pain, sometimes with nausea and vomiting.

Far less common complications include encephalitis (often with high fever and disorientation), inflammation of the thyroid gland, inflammation of the heart muscle (myocarditis), arthritis, kidney inflammation (nephritis) and thrombocytopenia, a condition in which the platelet cells in the blood decrease in number, leading to otherwise unexplained bruising. Deafness can also be a complication.

As far as is known, the fetus is not affected. Mortality is minimal, most deaths resulting from encephalitis.

Diagnosis of mumps is largely clinical, the result of a physical examination. Isolating the virus from saliva is possible, especially if pancreatitis is present.

Other viral infections, including influenza type A, coxsackie infections and infectious mononucleosis (glandular fever), can produce swelling of the salivary glands. However, the general symptoms are sufficiently different to allow a proper diagnosis.

Treatment for mumps is largely simple nursing in bed. Testicular swelling (orchitis) may need surgical intervention, although high doses of hydrocortisone may help. The pain is often lessened if the scrotum is suspended in a scrotal support.

Live virus vaccine is available and usually given in conjunction with live measles and rubella vaccines, at the age of 12–15 months. Complications of immunization are rare but can include mild fever and minor swelling of one or both salivary glands. Even so the child is not infectious. A booster dose is recommended when the child is about 14 years old. It should not be given to people who lack immunity (HIV infected people or cancer patients undergoing treatment), or to pregnant women.

SEE ALSO *Immunization, Meningitis, Viruses*

Glands affected by mumps

Mumps most commonly causes swelling and tenderness in one or both of the parotid (salivary) glands that lie just under and in front of the ears. Occasionally the other salivary glands, testes and ovaries may also be affected.

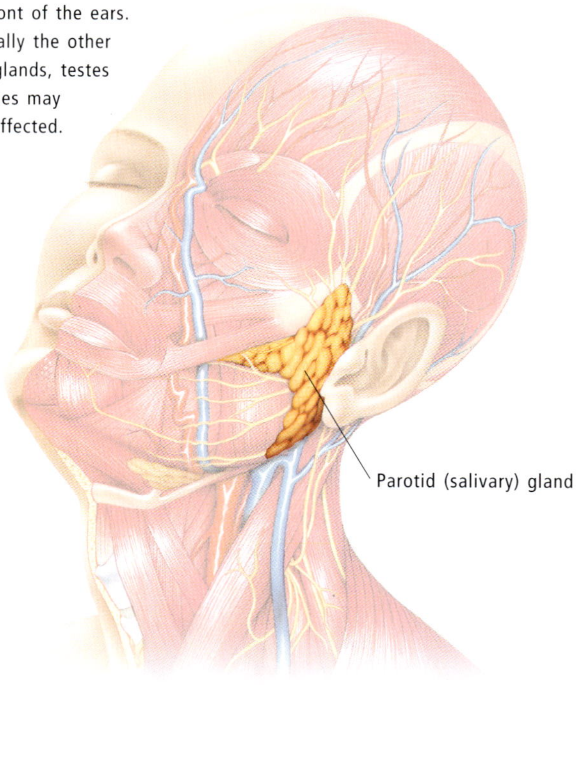

Mumps in childhood

Mumps is usually a childhood disease and symptoms are often more severe if it is contracted by adults. Immunization against mumps, measles and rubella is generally given at age 12–15 months.

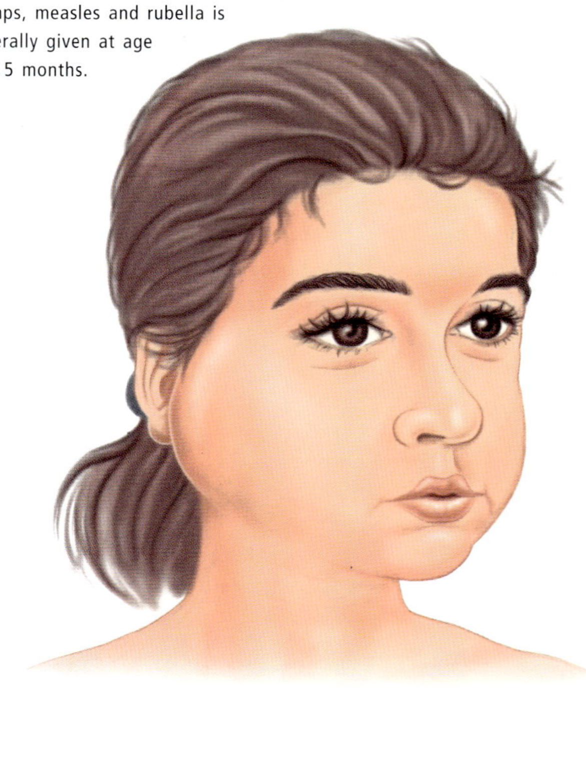

MUSCLE

Muscle is a type of body tissue responsible for the movement of the bones and joints. Muscle movement is normally controlled by the central nervous system (CNS). Smooth muscle is responsible for motility (movement) of some internal organs such as the intestine and blood vessels.

Muscles rear view

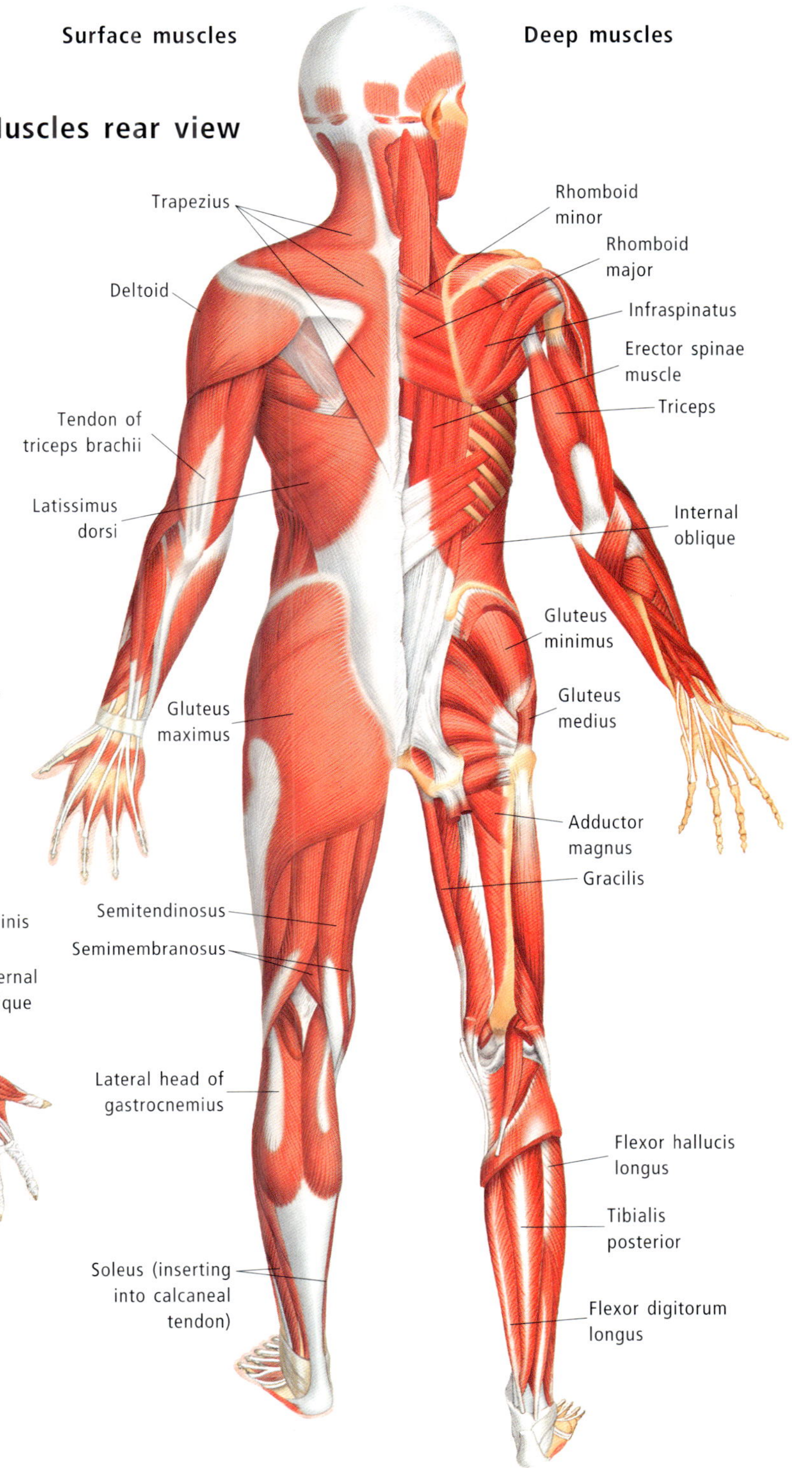

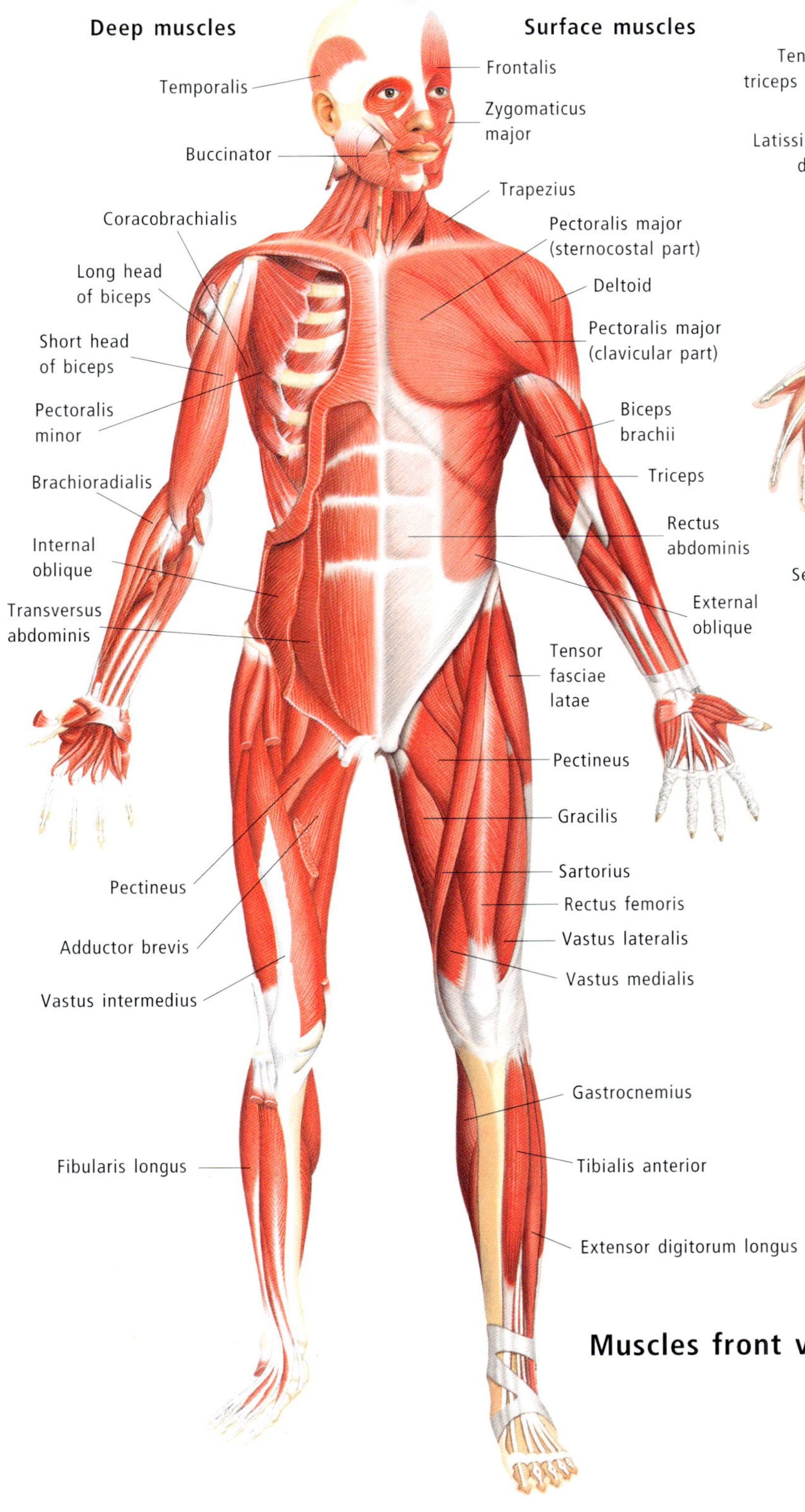

Muscles front view

Muscles have the property of being able to contract. They are composed of fibers, which are elongated cells containing tiny, threadlike structures made of complex proteins, myofibrils. Myofibrils consist of regularly arranged protein strands called myofilaments; the so-called "thick" myofilaments contain the protein myosin, while "thin" filaments contain the proteins actin, troponin and tropomysin. Thick and thin myofilaments lie side by side with their ends

Muscles

Muscles can be classified based on their general shape–some muscles have mainly parallel fibers and others have oblique fibers. Muscle fiber arrangements may be very complicated. The shape and arrangement of the muscle fibers reflects the function of the muscle. For example, if its function is to move bone, its fibers will be aligned in the same direction. If its function is to support organs or soft tissues, fibers will be criss-crossed. If its function is to open and close an entrance, for example in the bowel or urinary tract, fibers will be arranged in a circular pattern.

Unipennate

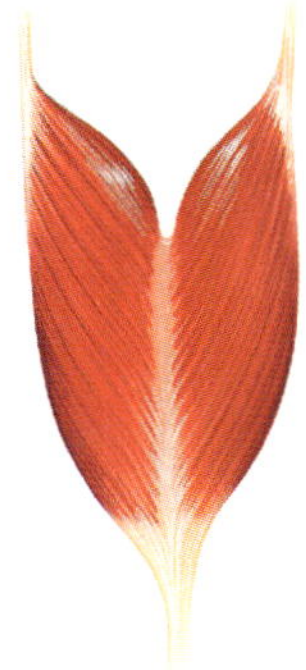

Bipennate

Multi-pennate

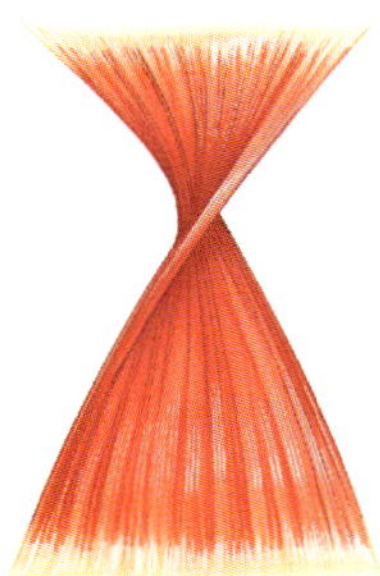

Spiral

Spiral

Radial

M

Quadrilateral

Strap

Strap
(with tendinous intersections)

Cruciate

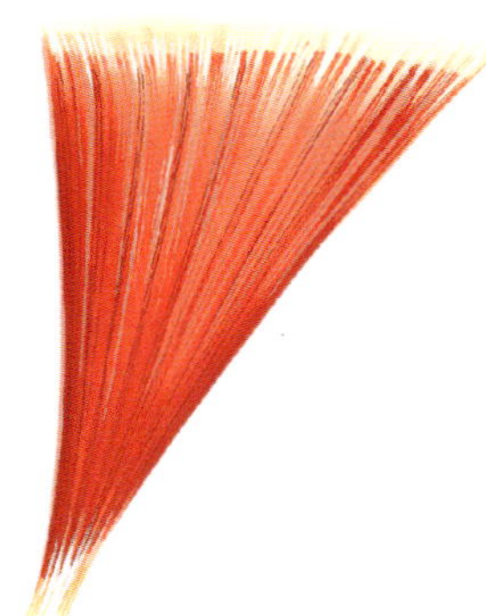

Triangular

Multicaudal

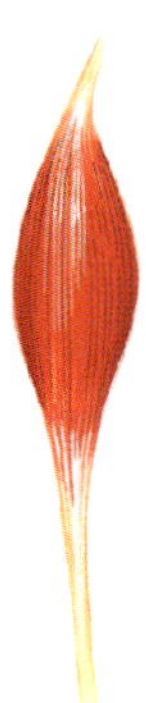

Fusiform

Bicipital

Tricipital

Quadricipital

Digastric

Circular

interlinked by chemical cross bridges. When stimulated, they slide along each other and the result is a muscle contraction.

If the force of a muscle contraction is greater than the force that is resisting the contraction, the contraction is said to be isotonic. If, however, the resistance to contraction is equal to the force generated in muscle tissues, the muscle will not contract. This is called an isometric contraction.

Types of muscles

The human body has three types of muscle: cardiac, smooth and skeletal. Each has different characteristics.

Cardiac muscle is found only in the heart and consists of a network of branches of muscle fibers that do not contract voluntarily and are not under the control of the central nervous system. A heart muscle contraction originates with an electrical impulse in a natural pacemaker called the sinoatrial node, located within the heart itself. This node and the electrical conducting system that runs through the muscle control the heart rate. The heart is, however, supplied with nerves from the autonomic nervous system, but these nerves speed or slow the heart rate rather than originate contractions.

Smooth muscle is found in the digestive system, reproductive system, major blood vessels, skin and some internal organs. Smooth muscle contraction is involuntary and not under the control of the central nervous system (CNS), being influenced by the autonomic nervous system. Peristalsis—the regular and rhythmic contraction of smooth muscle in the gastrointestinal tract which propels food along the tract—is an example of the autonomous contraction of smooth muscle.

Skeletal muscle is the most prominent type of muscle and may account for up to 60 percent of the mass of the body. It is attached to the bones of the skeleton at both ends by tendons. It acts voluntarily: nerve endings that carry electrical impulses from the CNS control its movement. These nerve endings terminate at the cell membrane of the muscle fibers. The contraction of a muscle cell is activated by the release of calcium from inside the cell in response to electrical changes at the cell's surface.

Muscle tissue

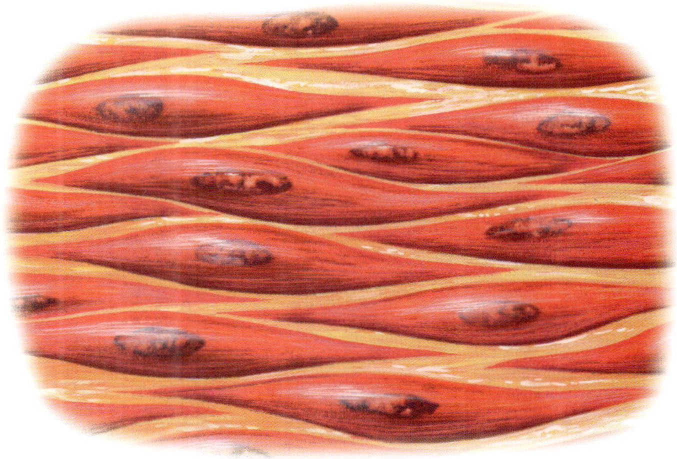

Smooth muscle tissue

Smooth muscle is controlled by the autonomic nervous system, and is found in the skin, the blood vessels, and the reproductive and digestive systems.

Skeletal muscle tissue

Skeletal muscles allow the body to move. They are voluntary muscles, controlled by the brain and spinal cord.

Cardiac muscle tissue

Cardiac muscle is the heart muscle, which contracts and relaxes rhythmically in an involuntary manner.

Skeletal muscle is usually found in bundles, forming characteristic shapes and sizes, depending on where it is located in the body and what bones and joints it moves. When skeletal muscle contracts, it usually thickens and shortens.

Most skeletal muscle is clearly visible below the surface of the skin and is responsible, together with the skeleton, for an individual's physique.

Skeletal muscles that are exercised regularly may hypertrophy, that is, increase in

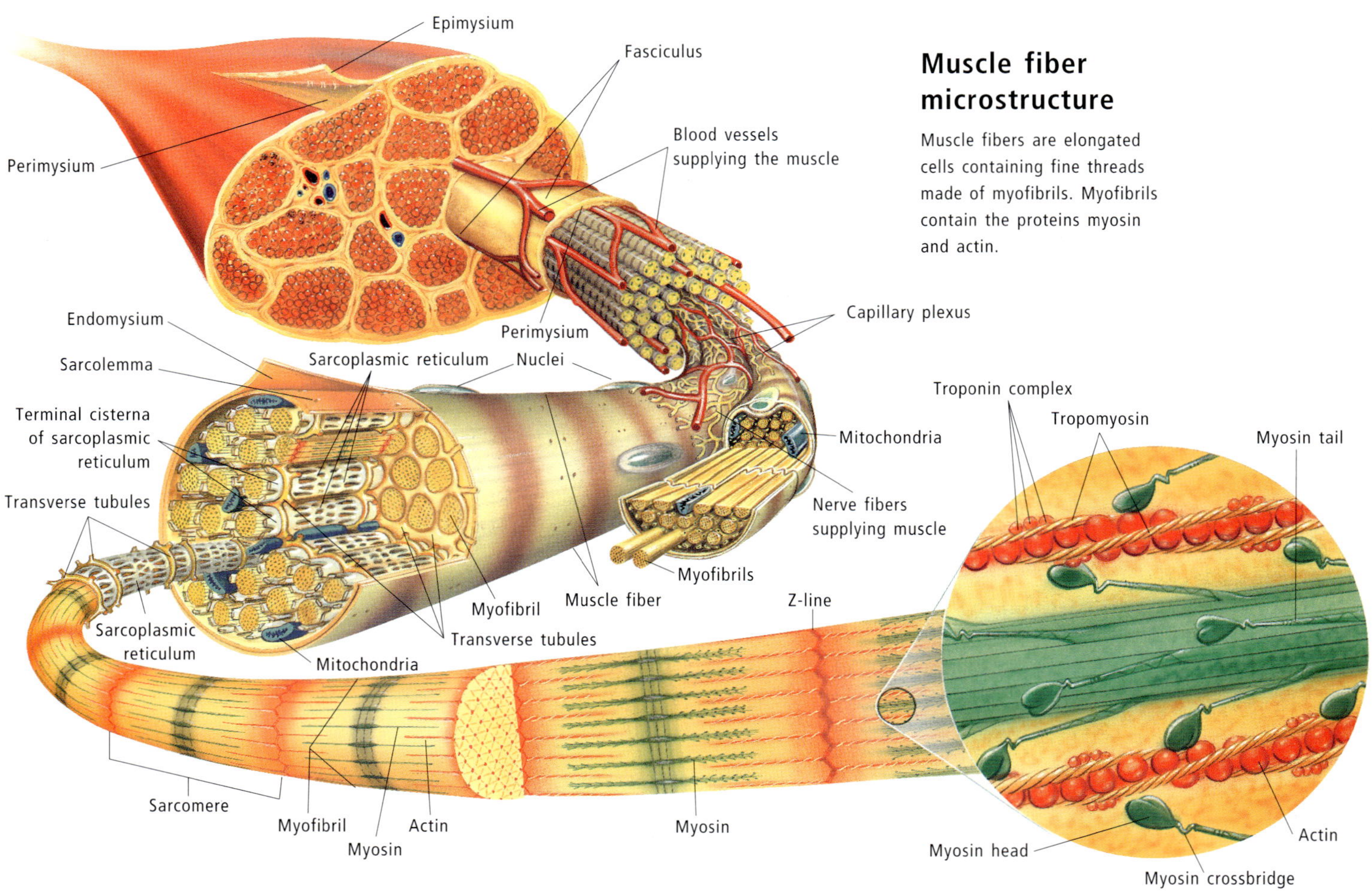

Muscle fiber microstructure

Muscle fibers are elongated cells containing fine threads made of myofibrils. Myofibrils contain the proteins myosin and actin.

size and strength. If these muscles are not used sufficiently (for example in paralysis or disease), they may atrophy, or diminish in size, and become weaker.

Muscle injuries and diseases

A pulled muscle, also known as a strained muscle, is a common term for a muscle that has been damaged by a sudden rupture of fibers within the muscle tissue. It is common in sporting and work-related injuries. The pulled muscle causes pain and stiffness that gradually improves over a number of days. It is treated with rest, ice packs and painkillers (analgesics).

Muscle cramps are painful, involuntary contractions of muscles experienced during exercise. They are caused by changes in the chemistry of muscle cells that occur during exercise brought on by lack of oxygen. They are treated with applications of ice or heat, gentle massage or physical therapy.

Muscles are subject to a variety of diseases. They may become inflamed, a condition known as myositis. The muscle becomes hot, tender, painful and there may be fever. Dermatomyositis is inflammation of muscle and skin; polymyositis refers to inflammation of multiple muscle groups.

Muscles may become infected with bacteria such as *Staphylococcus*. Disruption or damage to the blood supply may cause muscle tissue to die, a condition called gangrene. Muscles may become paralyzed by injury or disease. Poliomyelitis and polyneuritis are viral diseases that result in paralysis and muscular wasting. Muscular dystrophies are hereditary diseases characterized by progressive muscular weakness and wasting.

Myasthenia gravis is a condition in which transmission of nerve impulses is incomplete and paralysis follows. Sometimes individual muscles or muscle groups may be affected by injury or disease; Bell's palsy is paralysis of all the muscles on one side of the face, caused by acute malfunction of, or damage to, the facial nerve that supplies them.

Drug treatments

Muscle relaxant drugs relax skeletal muscles by blocking the transmission of nerve impulses that cause muscle contraction. They are used to relieve painful muscle spasms that sometimes occur in stroke, in some muscle and rheumatic disorders, and in some skeletal muscle disorders. Neuromuscular blocking drugs are drugs that paralyze skeletal muscles by blocking nerve impulses completely and are used in general anesthesia.

Muscles can gain greater bulk and strength through the use of anabolic steroids such as testosterone, methandrostenolone and nandrolone. These drugs are sometimes used by athletes to enhance performance. Over time, however, these drugs can be responsible for a range of side effects such as depression, arterial disease, liver cancer, reduced sperm count in males and masculinization in females.

SEE ALSO *Anabolic steroids, Bell's palsy, Bones, Cramp, Gangrene, Joints, Muscular dystrophy, Myasthenia gravis, Peristalsis, Poliomyelitis, Skeletal system*

MUSCULAR DYSTROPHY

Muscular dystrophy (MD) is the name of a group of chronic hereditary disorders, which cause a gradual deterioration of the body's muscles. Different types affect different areas of the body, such as shoulders, hips or face, and also differ in their type of inheritance (dominant genes, recessive genes and so on), and in the age when symptoms appear.

The affected person suffers gradual weakening of muscles and loss of muscle bulk, giving rise to walking and other movement difficulties. Muscle contractures are common, caused by shortening of the muscle fibers and fibrosis of the connective tissue. Some types of muscular dystrophy involve the heart muscle, causing cardiomyopathy or arrhythmias.

Muscular dystrophy affects males more than females, usually between 5–12 years of age. The condition is incurable and persons with the condition rarely reach adulthood. Physical therapy can maintain muscle strength and functioning and the use of orthopedic appliances, such as braces and wheelchairs, may improve mobility.

The most common and severe form is Duchenne muscular dystrophy, a rapidly progressive type. Other forms include limb-girdle, Becker, facioscapulohumeral and myotonic dystrophies. In these types, progression of the disease is generally slow.

Muscular dystrophy is a genetic abnormality. Carriers can be detected with medical testing. If there are relatives with the disorder, genetic counseling and prenatal testing in pregnancy are advisable.

SEE ALSO *Congenital abnormalities, Duchenne muscular dystrophy, Muscle*

MUSIC THERAPY

In traditional societies music is an important component of healing rites and ceremonies. In the West, music was introduced into hospitals for its therapeutic effects in the nineteenth century. Today music therapists treat people with mental illness, physical disabilities, learning disabilities and chronic illnesses such as Alzheimer's disease.

There are a number of ways in which music can be used therapeutically. It has been found that music stimulation can increase endorphin release which helps to relieve pain and anxiety. In neonatal intensive care units in the USA, lullaby tapes which echo the sound of a human heartbeat are played to calm the babies and help them sleep. Carefully selected music is also played to patients before, during and after surgery in many hospitals.

In vibroacoustic therapy, a form of music therapy popular in Europe, selected music is played to children with physical and mental disabilities to induce physical and mental relaxation. In India traditional ragas have been researched and found to be beneficial in the treatment of hypertension and mental illness.

Another form of music therapy involves encouraging patients to sing and play instruments in an improvised manner for free emotional expression. The therapist and patient relate to each other through their shared music making. Singing and playing may help the physically disabled to improve breath control and physical movement.

SEE ALSO *Dance movement therapy*

MYASTHENIA GRAVIS

Most often an autoimmune disorder, myasthenia gravis may also be due to a tumor of the thymus gland (thymoma). Characterized by fluctuating but progressive weakness of the voluntary muscles, early symptoms can include double vision (diplopia) and lid-droop after prolonged reading, fading of the voice during a speech, difficulty swallowing the latter part of a meal and tiredness of the legs and arms. The weakness is reversed by resting the affected muscles, but the condition is slowly progressive.

Diagnosis is made when there is a rapid reversal of the weakness after the administration of certain drugs.

Treatment may be continued with drugs but the removal of the thymus gland will produce the greatest improvement. The occasional patient may require steroids or other immunosuppressive drugs. Myasthenia gravis may be associated with other autoimmune disorders such as thyrotoxicosis (overactive thyroid), rheumatoid arthritis and lupus erythematosis. Small cell cancer of the lung and botulism can produce a somewhat similar myasthenia.

SEE ALSO *Autoimmune disease, Muscle, Thymus gland*

MYCOSIS FUNGOIDES

Mycosis fungoides can be mistaken initially for a simple fungal rash. It is, however, a rare and frequently fatal form of cancer of the immune system that often takes years to progress. The first outward indications are raised, scaly, red or brown, itchy skin lesions that tend to form open sores. As the disease

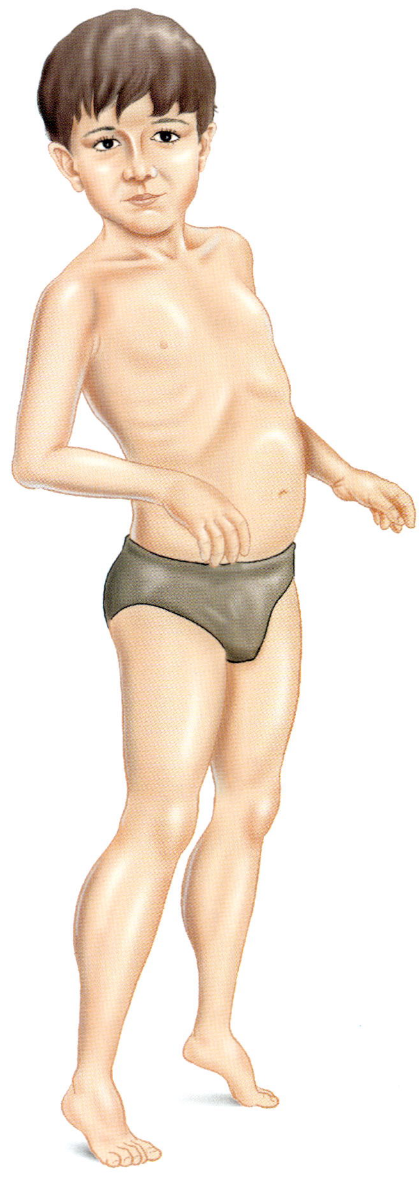

Muscular dystrophy

An early sign of muscular dystrophy in children is bulging calf muscles, which are caused by excessive fat rather than healthy muscles.

Mycosis fungoides
Mycosis fungoides generally develops over three stages commencing with itchy skin lesions, followed by large raised skin lesions and finally mushroom-like tumors which frequently ulcerate.

advances, the patient develops swollen lymph glands and then tumors on the skin. During the late stages, much of the skin reddens, peels and becomes scaly and extremely itchy. Eventually, cancer cells spread to the lymph glands and internal organs. If treated early enough, mycosis fungoides can sometimes be cured. Remission brought about by various cancer treatments is also possible in later stages.

SEE ALSO *Cancer, Lymphatic/Immune system*

M

MYELITIS

Myelitis is a general term for inflammation of the spinal cord. It involves the loss of fatty tissue (myelin) around the nerves. One of the most common types is acute transverse myelitis, a neurological syndrome that involves inflammation through one level of the spinal cord. This rapidly developing condition obstructs the path of motor nerve fibers, causing low back pain, muscle spasms, dysfunction of the spinal cord, headache, numbness and tingling in the legs. It can be brought on by viral infection, spinal cord injuries and immune system abnormalities in which the spinal cord is attacked.

SEE ALSO *Spinal cord*

MYELOGRAPHY

Myelography refers to x-ray photography of the spinal cord, as well as the biopsy examination of cells in bone marrow. The spinal x-rays are called myelograms and are used in the diagnosis of disorders such as herniated disks and spinal tumors. They are taken after injecting a radiopaque dye into the fluid around the spinal cord.

SEE ALSO *Spinal cord, X-ray*

MYELOMA

Myeloma is a tumor of plasma cells in the bone marrow, which results in pain and weakness of the bones, anemia and the production of an abnormal protein. It is the commonest tumor actually arising in bone, rather than spreading to bone as other cancers may do. It occurs most often in men over 65 years of age. There is an increased risk after exposure to high-dose ionizing radiation or pesticides. There have been recent reports of the possible role of a virus.

Myeloma may be detected by the finding of anemia and other blood abnormalities, or by the presence of severe, persistent bone pain. The pain is often in the spine or ribs and can be due to the myeloma itself or to fractures resulting from weakening of the bones. X-rays will typically show punched-out holes in the bones. If myeloma is suspected, testing of blood and urine is done to detect an abnormal protein produced by the malignant plasma cells. The diagnosis is confirmed by bone marrow biopsy.

The treatment of myeloma is initially pain control and treatment of complications, such as infection, high blood calcium or reduced kidney function. Then chemotherapy is given in the form of tablets or injections, usually as monthly cycles, for periods of up to 12 months. Myeloma is not curable but can be controlled for several years on average. Recent advances in treatment include bone marrow transplantation and the use of the drug, thalidomide.

SEE ALSO *Bone marrow biopsy, Bones*

MYOCARDIAL INFARCTION

The myocardium is the name for the muscle of the heart, while infarction is the death of tissue due to interference with its blood supply. Myocardial infarction is the death of heart muscle due to loss of arterial blood supply. This generally occurs as a result of blockage of the coronary arteries which supply the heart with blood, usually due to a disease known as atherosclerosis, which leads to the accumulation of fatty and fibrous tissue in the walls of arteries in discrete patches called plaques.

If plaques lose their surface layer, blood may coagulate on the rough surface of the vessel wall, causing sudden obstruction of the entire vessel. A patient with a myocardial infarction will experience a crushing pain centered mainly in the middle of the chest, but possibly spreading to the left arm, neck or upper abdomen. The pain will not be relieved by rest or prescription medication, and patients should immediately seek medical help.

With very early intervention it may be possible to dissolve the coagulated blood, but in most cases treatment is aimed at minimizing the amount of heart muscle lost, supporting the heart and providing pain relief. Patients may die if the loss of heart muscle is so great that heart function cannot be maintained, or if the electrical function of the heart is impaired.

SEE ALSO *Arrhythmia, Atherosclerosis, Coronary artery disease, Fibrillation, Heart*

MYOCARDITIS

Myocarditis is inflammation of the heart muscle, which usually accompanies a generalized disease of the body (such as diphtheria or toxoplasmosis)or a viral infection (such as poliomyelitis). Patients often experience rapid heart rate in mild cases. In more severe cases, as the heart fails, there may be shortness of breath, enlarged heart and murmurs.

SEE ALSO *Heart*

MYOMECTOMY

Myomectomy is an operation to remove a fibroid, or tumor, formed of muscle tissue in the uterus. It is performed instead of a hysterectomy when it is important to preserve the woman's fertility. About one-quarter of women who would formerly have had a hysterectomy now have a myomectomy, which leaves the uterus in place and is not a major operation. This operation can be done by vaginal incision, or abdominal incision, which may mean that a cesarean is necessary should the woman later decide to have children.

SEE ALSO *Fibroids, Hysterectomy, Hysteroscopy, Uterus*

MYOPIA

Myopia—also called nearsightedness or shortsightedness—is a condition in which close objects are clearly visible while distant objects are blurred. It is caused by an abnormality of the eye in which the image is focused in front of the retina rather than directly on it. This may happen because the eyeball is too long, or because the lens is focusing the image too strongly. The condition usually develops in school age and may run in families. Myopia is usually treated by wearing eyeglasses or contact lenses. Radial keratotomy, a surgical procedure performed on the cornea, improves or corrects the condition in many cases.

SEE ALSO *Contact lenses, Eye, Sight*

Myocardial infarction

Commonly called a heart attack, myocardial infarction occurs when the cardiac muscle and tissues are deprived of oxygen because the blood supply to the heart has been disrupted in some way.

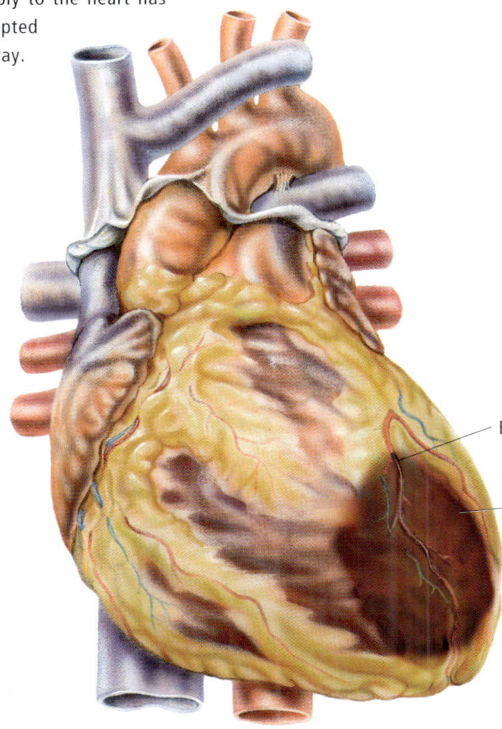

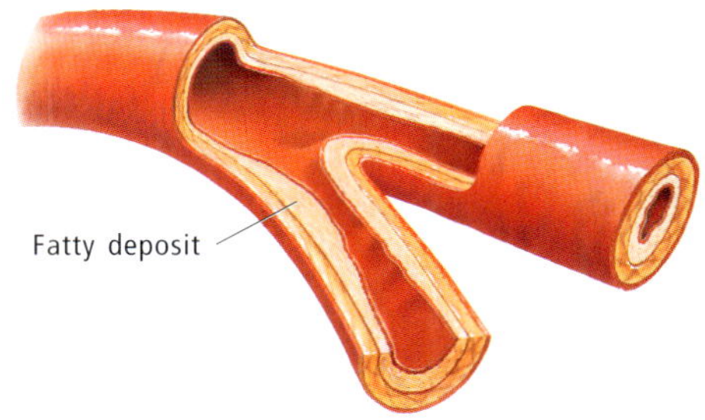

Blocked arteries

In atherosclerosis, fatty deposits on the inner layer of arteries cause narrowing and sometimes blockage of these vessels. If this happens to the coronary arteries, the tissues of the heart can be irreparably damaged—leading to myocardial infarction.

MYXEDEMA

Myxedema is a condition resulting from a reduced metabolic rate throughout the body, in turn a result of low thyroxine levels (hypothyroidism).

There is progressive slowing of mental and physical activity, and the disorder is characterized by a puffy face, coarse dry skin and hair, lethargy, sensitivity to cold, slowed heart rate and constipation. Causes include disease of the thyroid gland (such as Hashimoto's disease) or lack of stimulation (from the pituitary gland, for example). Treatment is by giving thyroid hormones to replace the low levels.

SEE ALSO *Hashimoto's disease, Hypothyroidism, Pituitary gland, Thyroid gland*

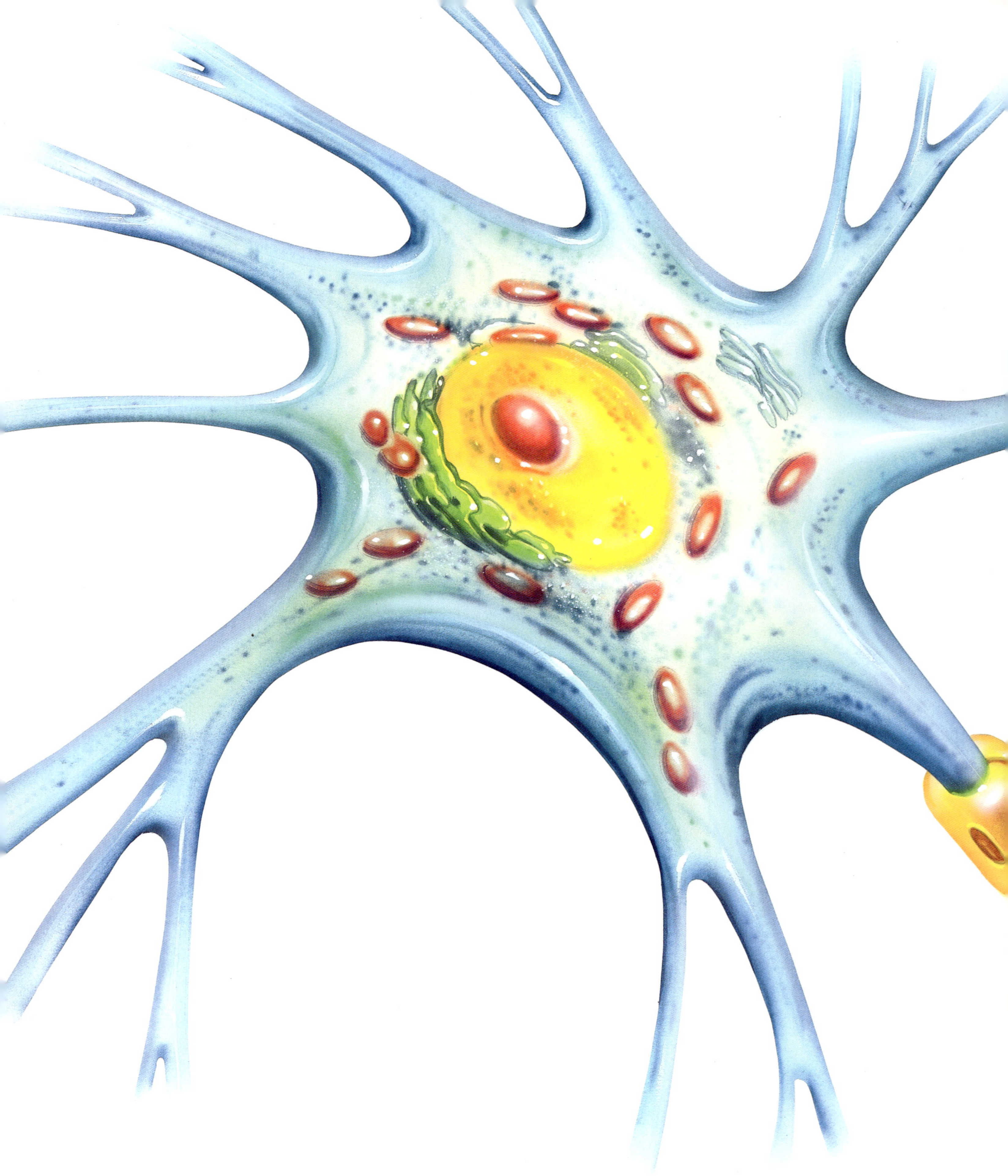

NO

NAILS

The primary function of our nails is to provide protection for the sensitive tips of our fingers and toes, and they are well-designed for the purpose. They are made mainly of the tough protein called keratin and most of what we can see of them is actually dead—attributes that make them reasonably resilient to everyday knocks.

The only living part of a nail is the root, where growth occurs. This is located under the flap of skin—the cuticle—at the nail's base. Beneath the nail is the nail bed, visibly pink through the nail in healthy circumstances due to a rich blood supply. If a nail becomes detached from the bed it is inevitably replaced. Because fingernails grow at an average rate of about 2 inches (5 centimeters) a year, it takes about 6 months for a nail to regrow fully. Toenails grow more slowly, taking 12–18 months to grow back.

Although most nail afflictions are minor and easily remedied, neglect or incorrect treatment can turn them into painful, lingering and unsightly problems. For example, tearing or biting a hangnail—a piece of partly detached skin at the side or base of a fingernail—is one way of damaging the skin near a nail and causing a tender and swollen bacterial infection, known as a paronychia. Hangnails should be cut off neatly with sharp scissors. A paronychia usually responds quickly to antibiotics.

A fungal infection in a nail—onychomycosis—is usually more persistent. This is most likely to occur on a toe, rather than a finger, and is often indicated by a discolored, brittle or peeling nail. Without treatment, onychomycosis can cause numbness or pain in the affected area. The nail may separate from the nail bed and eventually be destroyed. Treatment often includes taking an oral antifungal medication over several months.

Another normally minor problem that is far more likely to affect toes than fingers, particularly the big toe, is an ingrown nail. This occurs mostly when a nail is trimmed overly short or shoes are too tight, forcing the sharp corner of a growing nail to push into the skin. The result is a painful swelling and sometimes infection. Regular massage of the skin surrounding the ingrown corner often corrects the problem. Gently taping the skin back from the nail edge may also help, as can going barefoot for a while. In the unlikely event that the problem persists, several minor surgical procedures are available.

As well as suffering their own minor maladies, nails can also be excellent indicators of a person's more general state of health. For example, white bands running across a nail—Meet's lines—can be a sign of a particular protein deficiency caused by illness, some anti-cancer drugs or arsenic poisoning. A change in color from normally healthy pink can indicate a problem with a major organ. Hepatitis, which affects the liver, can give nails a yellow tinge. A brown discoloration can indicate kidney disease. Nails that look very white suggest anemia, a lack of iron in the blood. Small white flecks usually indicate minor injuries and normally disappear after a few weeks.

SEE ALSO *Cuticle, Finger, Keratin, Paronychia*

NARCOLEPSY

Narcolepsy is a rare sleep disorder characterized by uncontrollable episodes of falling asleep at any place or time. Attacks of sleep may last minutes or hours and may vary in frequency from an occasional episode to ten or more in a single day. On awakening, the person feels refreshed, but another attack may occur again quickly. The condition usually begins in adolescence or young adulthood and continues throughout life. There may be a family history of the disease.

The condition can be diagnosed by sleep studies (continuous recordings of brain waves, muscle movements, and pulse and breathing patterns during sleep). Narcolepsy cannot be cured, but symptoms can be controlled with regular planned naps, and antidepressant and stimulant drugs.

SEE ALSO *Sleep apnea*

NARCOTICS

Narcotics (or narcotic analgesics) are drugs that produce relief from pain, a state of stupor or sleep and often addiction or physical dependence.

Opium, produced from the opium poppy, has been in use for thousands of years; in 1803 the alkaloid compound morphine was discovered and in 1898, heroin (diacetylmorphine) was discovered and used as a treatment of morphine addiction (though it was later found to be even more addictive and dangerous than morphine).

Modern narcotics are either opium derivatives, such as morphine and codeine, or synthetic drugs known as meperidine and methadone. They are used primarily for controlling strong to severe pain, such as pain from kidney stones, cancer pain and post-operative pain.

Codeine is sometimes used in cough mixtures because it suppresses coughing and sometimes as a treatment for diarrhea. Methadone is sometimes used in the treatment of heroin addiction, though it is itself addictive. Side effects of narcotics can be problematic; they include constipation, nausea and vomiting and urinary retention.

SEE ALSO *Analgesics, Drug dependence, Methadone, Morphine*

NATUROPATHY

Ancient Greek physicians, such as Hippocrates, were among the earliest to articulate naturopathic philosophies in their belief that the body will naturally cure itself when given pure air, water, food and exercise. Naturopathic medicine was revived and developed in association with hydrotherapy in nineteenth-century Europe. It was introduced into the USA in the 1890s by Benedict Lust after he was treated successfully at the health spa of Father Sebastian Kneipp. Today naturopathy is well established in most Western countries.

The naturopathic view is that illness stems from a biochemical or metabolic imbalance that is due to physical or emotional stress over a prolonged period. Disease is not seen as the cause of illness but as the end result of an overworked body with a weakened immune system. Symptoms of illness such as fever or vomiting are believed to be the body's attempt to move itself back into a state of health. For this reason naturopaths encourage symptoms to come out, rather than to suppress them, as part of the body's self-healing process.

Naturopaths stress the importance of giving the body time to restore itself to health. In order to devise an ongoing individualized regime of treatment, they take a detailed

Naturopathy

The holistic approach adopted by naturopathic practitioners is based on adhering to a "triad of health": psychological, biological and structural factors should all be balanced. Illness is a sign of imbalance in the system, so analysis of individual parts—the eyes, nails and tongue, for example—may be used to identify problems elsewhere in the body.

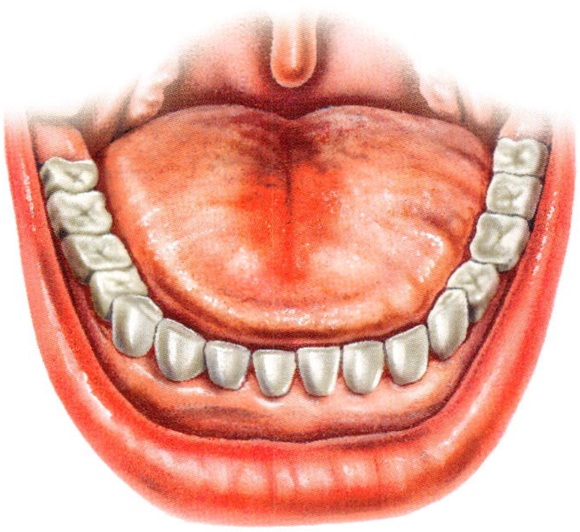

Tongue
The color and texture of the tongue is used by naturopaths to assess ill health. Red in the center of the tongue may indicate a stomach-related problem.

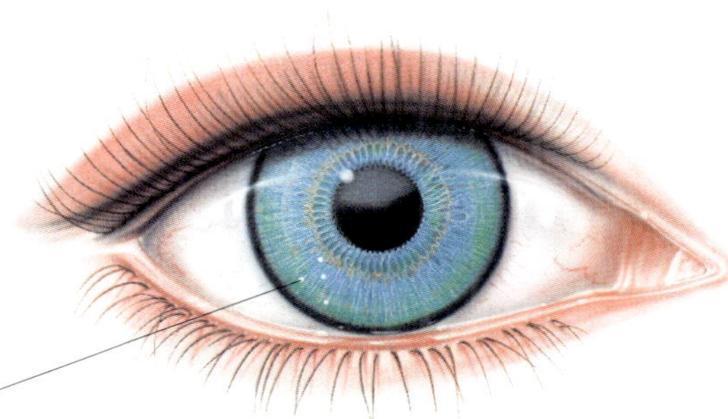

Iris
The iris is divided by naturopaths into sections that correspond to parts of the body. White spots in a particular section, for example, may indicate a disorder of the chest. A dark ring may indicate toxins.

Nails
White spots on nails may indicate low zinc levels.

medical history to identify the stresses carried by the patient. Diagnosis of the iris, nail and tongue may be used and pathology tests may be carried out.

A prime area of focus in naturopathy is diet, where there is an emphasis on highly nourishing "clean" food and water, free of pesticides and preservatives and as unprocessed as possible. Typically, naturopaths suggest a diet that is high in fresh vegetables, fruits, seeds, nuts and whole grains, and low in meat, coffee and alcohol.

To aid detoxification of the body, naturopaths may prescribe fasts. Special attention is paid to the health of the bowel as this is where nutrients are absorbed into the bloodstream. Diets are given to clear the gut of yeasts and bacteria that are seen to contribute to toxicity, allergy and poor immunity. Colonic irrigation may also be prescribed.

Many naturopaths warn patients of the possibility of some kind of "healing crisis" where symptoms briefly worsen soon after the commencement of detoxification as the body's organs become overloaded by the release of toxins into the bloodstream.

As well as nutrition, naturopathy emphasizes the importance of rest, relaxation, exercise, fresh air and bathing. Treatment for illnesses may also include hydrotherapy, massage, herbs, homeopathic remedies and nutritional supplements; the latter is viewed as necessary because of the depletion of the nutrient content of soils through modern agriculture. Flower essences, relaxation techniques or counseling are recommended for psychological stress.

Naturopathic medicine, especially in its use of nutrition to strengthen the body, is gaining widespread acceptance. It is becoming more common to find medical doctors adopting naturopathic practices or working in alliance with naturopaths, especially where patients are being weaned off pharmaceutical drugs. Naturopathy is particularly suited to treating stress-related chronic illnesses including asthma, arthritis, skin and digestive disorders.

SEE ALSO ***Counseling, Detoxification, Flower remedies and essences, Hydrotherapy, Massage, Relaxation techniques, Orthomolecular therapy***

NAUSEA

Nausea is the unpleasant sensation of feeling sick in the stomach and of being about to vomit. It is often followed by vomiting. It may be caused by conditions such as food poisoning and other gastrointestinal disorders, early pregnancy, or a physical or emotional shock. It may also be a side effect of medication.

The treatment of nausea depends on the cause. Lying down can often help. If vomiting accompanies the nausea, it is important to frequently drink fluids in small amounts to replace lost fluid. Antihistamines such as cyclizine or meclizine, that have an anti-nausea effect, may help. Scopolamine is also often used, but causes dry mouth, blurred vision and urinary retention.

Morning sickness is nausea and vomiting during pregnancy. It affects about 50 percent of women in pregnancy, usually from about the sixth to the twelfth week. The symptoms may be present at any time of day, not just the morning. Eating frequent, small, bland meals and avoiding an empty stomach may ease the symptoms. In severe cases, an anti-nausea drug may be required.

Motion sickness is caused by a disrupted sense of balance that occurs when the brain receives conflicting information about the body's orientation in space during movement. Air sickness, car sickness and sea sickness are all examples of motion sickness. It may be caused by amusement rides such as carousels and rollercoasters. Children are more prone to it than adults. Motion sickness is best avoided by prevention; while traveling, look at the horizon for a stable perspective rather than watching passing scenery. Anti-nausea drugs taken before a journey may help in severe cases.

SEE ALSO ***Morning sickness, Motion sickness, Sea sickness, Vomiting***

Neck cross-section

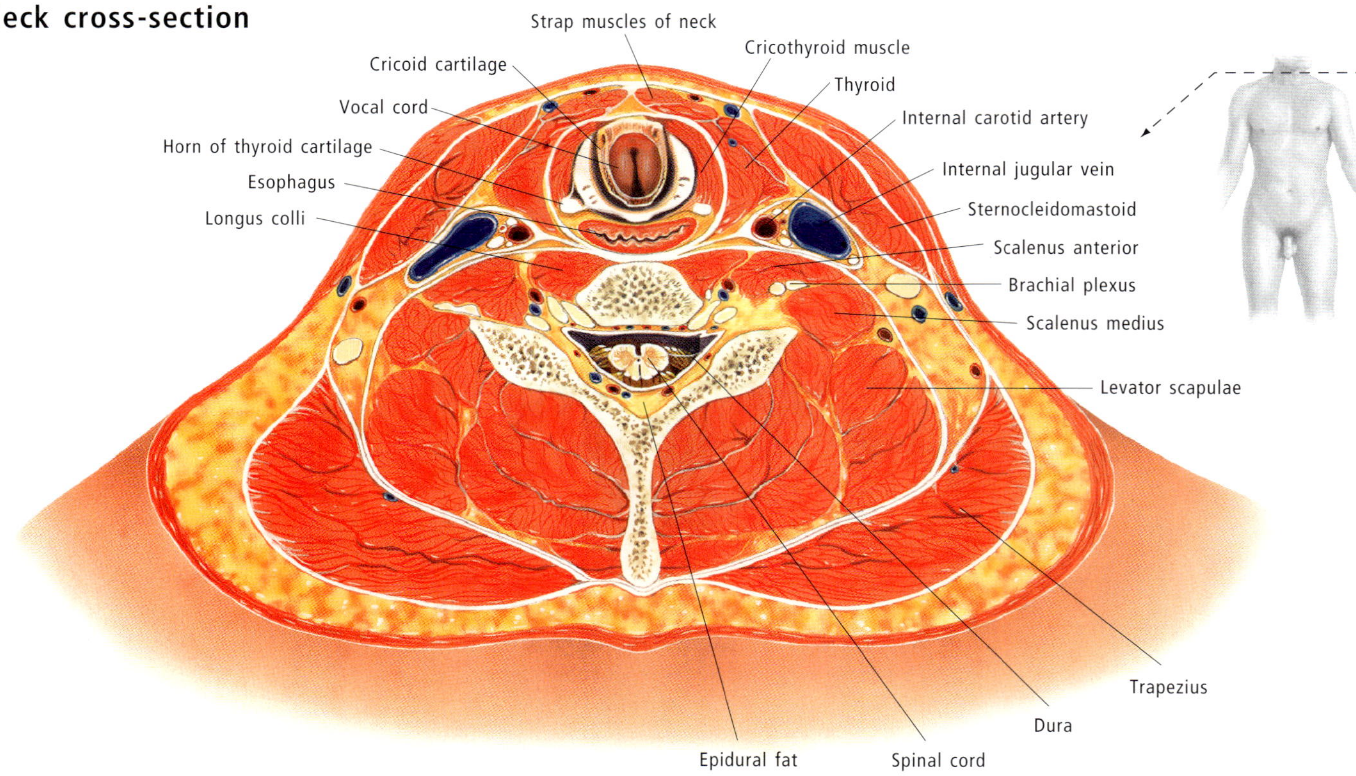

NECK

The neck supports and provides mobility for the head and contains a large number of important structures in a relatively confined space: the spinal cord, protected by the vertebrae; major blood vessels to the brain and face; and passageways for food and air. Important nerves course through the neck and some arise from the neck region.

The neck can be divided into two major columns. At the back, the nuchal region comprises the vertebrae of the neck (cervical vertebrae) and their supporting musculature. In front, it comprises a "visceral" column containing the larynx and trachea and behind them the pharynx and esophagus. On either side of these are major blood vessels.

The thyroid gland is attached to the front and sides of the trachea and larynx, and covering these structures at the front are thin strap-like muscles and skin. There are two large muscles, the sternocleidomastoid and trapezius.

Surrounding the muscles and visceral structures in the neck are a series of connective tissue sheaths that can affect the spread of infection.

Musculoskeletal column

The vertebrae in the neck are small (compared to those of the spine), since they carry very little weight, but the opening in the vertebrae for the spinal cord is relatively large. The two upper cervical vertebrae are specialized.

The first vertebra, the atlas, is a bony ring, and forms two joints (atlanto-occipital joints) with the base of the skull, allowing a nodding action.

The next vertebra, the axis, has an upward projecting bony element that forms a joint in the midline with the atlas. This, together with a joint on either side, allows a pivoting movement to occur, as in shaking the head when saying no. About 45 degrees of rotation in the neck occurs at these joints alone (the atlantoaxial joint).

The remaining vertebrae have a typical vertebral pattern with a body in front, a bony arch behind and spines projecting backward (spinous processes) and to the sides (transverse processes). The intervertebral disks that separate and cushion neighboring vertebrae from each other are relatively thick in the cervical region of the spine, permitting great freedom of movement.

Blood vessels

A feature of cervical vertebrae is that an artery (vertebral artery) passes through openings in the bony transverse processes. It ascends on the left and right, protected by the vertebrae, and supplies blood to the lower parts of the brain (cerebellum, brain stem and lower posterior part of the cerebral hemispheres).

Muscles

Muscles attach to the front, back and sides of the vertebrae, producing forward, backward and sideways movements. Those with an oblique orientation also produce rotation (turning). The largest musculature lies to the back. Some of these muscles are exclusively related to moving the head and neck (for example, splenius capitis and cervicis, semispinalis capitis and cervicis), while others are related to moving the shoulder (for example, trapezius, levator scapulae) or raising the upper two ribs (the scalene muscles).

Nerves

The spinal cord in the neck region gives origin to nerves (cervical nerves C1–C8) that pass to the skin and muscles of the neck (C1–C4) and upper limb (C5–C8). They

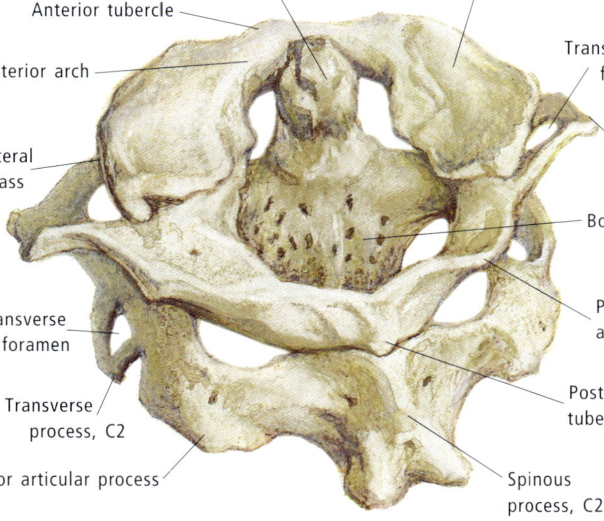

Atlas and axis

There are 7 vertebrae in the neck—the first 2 are more specialized than the others. C1, the atlas, supports the head and allows it to have a nodding movement. C2, the axis, articulates with the atlas and gives the head its ability to rotate.

Musculoskeletal column

The various muscles of the neck have fibers arranged in a number of different directions, giving the head and upper spine great freedom of movement.

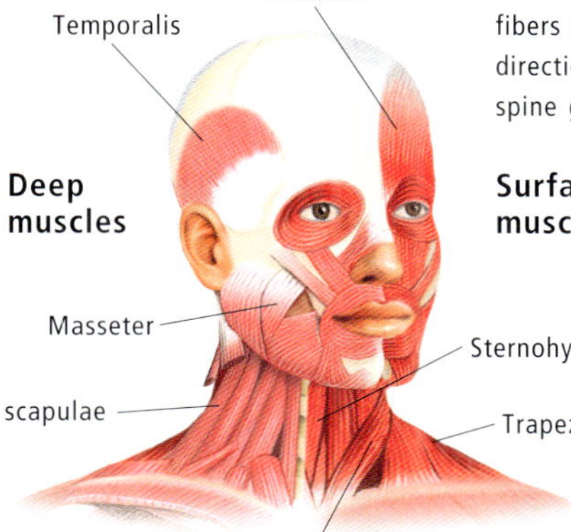

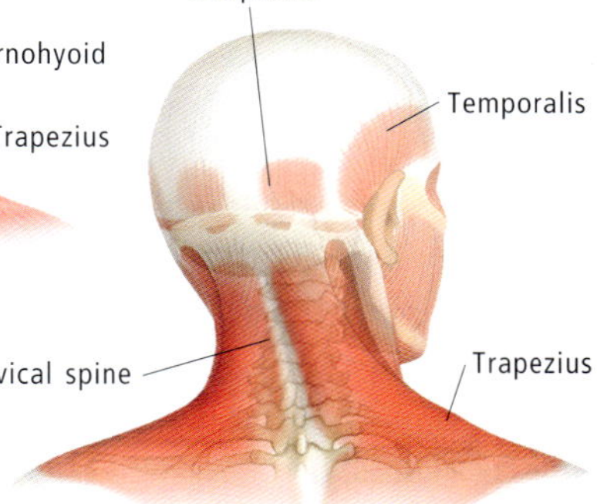

The neck

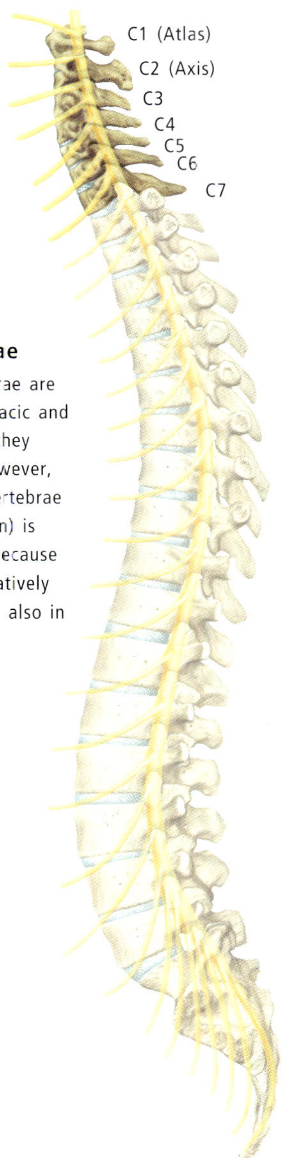

Cervical vertebrae

The 7 cervical vertebrae are smaller than the thoracic and lumbar vertebrae as they carry less weight. However, the opening in the vertebrae (the vertebral foramen) is comparatively large because the spinal cord is relatively thick at the neck and also in the lumbar regions.

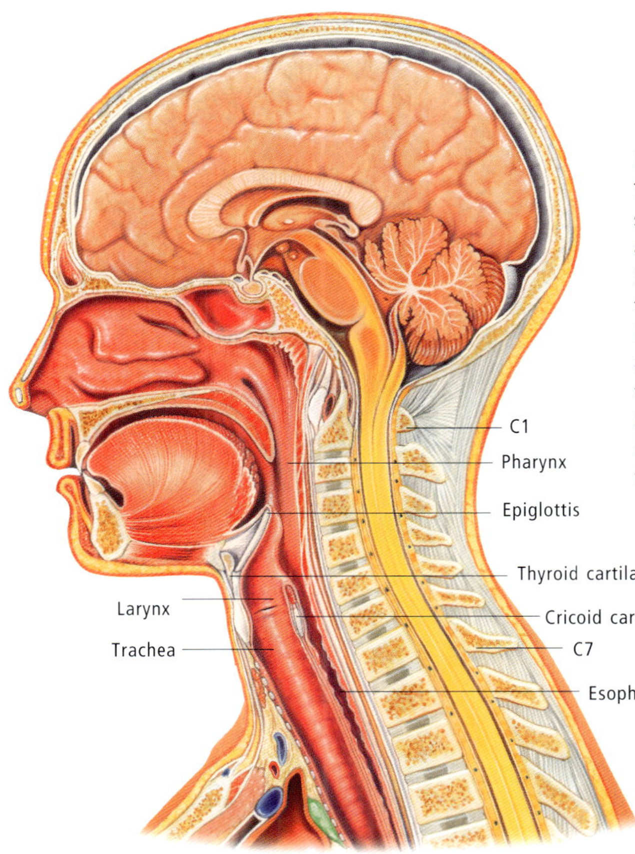

Neck column

The front of the neck houses several important structures in a relatively small area. These include the larynx (voice box), the upper part of the trachea (windpipe), the thyroid gland, and the pharynx (throat) which leads to the esophagus. Running beside these are large blood vessels, one of which is the carotid artery.

pass out through openings between the vertebrae (intervertebral foramen) and can be compressed here by bony outgrowths of the vertebrae (osteophytes), giving rise to symptoms such as tingling, numbness and weakness in the arm and hand.

The phrenic nerve is formed in the neck. It supplies the diaphragm, the muscle that contracts on inspiration. Damage to one or both phrenic nerves will affect breathing. Fracture of the cervical vertebrae may affect the spinal cord and/or cervical nerves. If damage occurs at spinal cord level C4 or higher it can be fatal, because the diaphragm is paralyzed.

Visceral column

At the angle in the upper part of the front of the neck is a small, U-shaped bone called the hyoid bone and, suspended from this, the voice box (larynx). The larynx is part of the upper respiratory tract, and a cartilaginous framework serves to keep the airway open. In males, the thyroid cartilage forms a distinct prominence called the laryngeal prominence or Adam's apple. The epiglottis, a piece of flexible cartilage at the inlet to the larynx, helps to prevent food and fluids from entering the airway when swallowing. The vocal cords, or vocal folds, are located within the larynx and control the size of the aperture between them (the rima glottidis). The folds lie close together and vibrate during speech, move wide apart in deep breathing, and may stop the flow of air completely (for example, when holding the breath).

The trachea commences at the lower end of the larynx and descends into the thoracic cavity to connect with the lungs. It can be felt, and moved from side to side, in the lower part of the neck. Wrapping around the upper trachea and extending onto the sides of the larynx and trachea is the thyroid gland. It has a narrow piece in front and expanded lobes on either side. It is bound to the larynx and trachea by connective tissue and so moves with them on swallowing, a feature that allows an enlargement of the thyroid gland to be distinguished from other swellings in the neck (such as an enlarged lymph node, which does not move with swallowing).

The pharynx lies behind the larynx. It is connected below to the esophagus, which lies directly behind the trachea, and empties into it when food is swallowed. The pharynx and esophagus have muscular walls that contract in a milking action to move food toward the stomach.

Blood vessels

On either side of the pharynx, larynx, trachea and esophagus are large blood vessels bound together by a connective tissue sheath (carotid sheath).

Within the sheath, in the lower part of the neck, is the common carotid artery, that divides into an internal and external carotid arteries at about the level of the laryngeal prominence. The internal carotid artery supplies the brain and the external carotid artery supplies the face and neck.

The pulse of the common carotid artery may be felt at the side of the larynx, and can be compressed against a bony outgrowth of the sixth cervical vertebrae (the carotid tubercle), stemming its flow. Carotid comes from the Greek word *karoo*, meaning "to put to sleep".

Within the carotid sheath, on the outer aspect of the internal and common carotid arteries, is the internal jugular vein, that drains the blood from the brain. Veins from the face and neck drain into it. At its lower end is a valve that prevents backflow of blood toward the brain. Behind and between the blood vessels and within the sheath is the vagus nerve, an important nerve supplying the larynx, trachea, pharynx, esophagus, heart, lungs and much of the gastrointestinal tract. Branches of the vagus (external laryngeal nerve and recurrent laryngeal nerve) pass to muscles controlling the vocal cords and may be damaged in thyroid surgery.

Muscles

In front of the visceral tubes and thyroid gland are thin strap-like muscles (infrahyoid muscles) that move the larynx and hyoid bones. Attaching to the skin of the neck is a wide, thin muscle, the platysma muscle, that is involved in facial expression, and tenses in anger. A large muscle that extends from the skull to the clavicle and sternum is the sternocleidomastoid muscle. It contracts when one lifts the head, and can be subject to spasm, as occurs in the condition torticollis or wryneck. The spinal nerves which supply the arm (C5 to T1) come together in the brachial plexus and separate into the nerves of the arm. They then pass obliquely down and outward, just below the skin, in the angle between this muscle and the clavicle. The outer margin of the neck is defined by the trapezius muscle, and the degree of development (bulk) of this muscle, can affect the shape and appearance of the neck.

Injuries

The neck is easily traumatized in whiplash injuries, where the muscles are not able to protect the neck from excessive movement. Damage to ligaments, muscles and joints may produce pain and instability. Following severe trauma, the neck needs to be immobilized and assessed for spinal cord damage, that can result in quadriplegia, or may be fatal if damage occurs to the highest part of the spinal cord.

Stiff neck is a condition of strained ligaments and muscles in the neck. It may be caused by a sudden twisting of the neck, by sleeping in an awkward position, or by stress or injury. The symptoms are neck pain and stiffness. Aspirin or non-steroidal anti-inflammatory drugs and physical therapy (heat, massage and exercise) will help relieve the symptoms.

Cervical osteoarthritis is a gradual deterioration of the cervical vertebrae. It affects mainly people over 50, developing slowly over many years. The symptoms are neck pain and stiffness. Sometimes a spinal nerve may be pinched by a damaged vertebra or herniated disk, causing numbness or pain that radiates down the neck and shoulders.

A neck x-ray usually shows the degenerative changes of osteoarthritis. Aspirin or non-steroidal anti-inflammatory drugs may help the symptoms. Physical therapy including heat and massage will also help. A neck collar that supports and immobilizes the neck may be needed intermittently, and traction may be required in severe cases. Surgery is sometimes an option, though the results are variable due to the poor condition of the vertebrae.

SEE ALSO *Carotid arteries, Disk, intervertebral, Epiglottis, Esophagus, Jugular vein, Larynx, Pharynx, Quadriplegia, Spinal cord, Thyroid gland, Torticollis, Trachea, Vagus nerve, Vertebrae, Vocal cords, Whiplash injury*

N

NEEDLE BIOPSY

A needle biopsy is a procedure to sample an abnormal lump or mass in the body. It may also be used to determine whether disease is present in normal tissue, for example in the lung or liver. A needle biopsy is usually performed by a radiologist.

During the procedure, the radiologist inserts a small needle into the abnormal area and removes a sample of the tissue, which is then sent to a pathologist. The pathologist then determines what the abnormal tissue is: cancer, non-cancerous tumor, infection or scar. The procedure is quicker and causes much less damage to normal tissue than an open biopsy, which leaves a surgical scar.

SEE ALSO *Biopsy*

NEPHRITIS

Nephritis is a general term for any inflammation of one or both kidneys and may be acute or chronic. It may involve the glomeruli (glomerulonephritis), the main tissue of the kidney and pelvis (pyelonephritis), or the spaces within the kidney (interstitial nephritis).

Nephritis—glomerulonephritis

This type of kidney disorder may begin with an infection, often of the throat. It can also be a result of the immune system not working properly. Treatment must be sought to avoid damage to the kidneys.

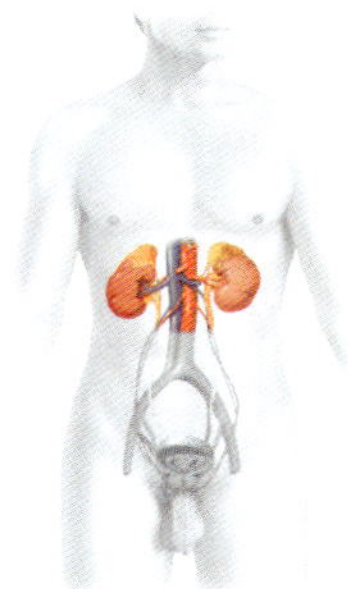

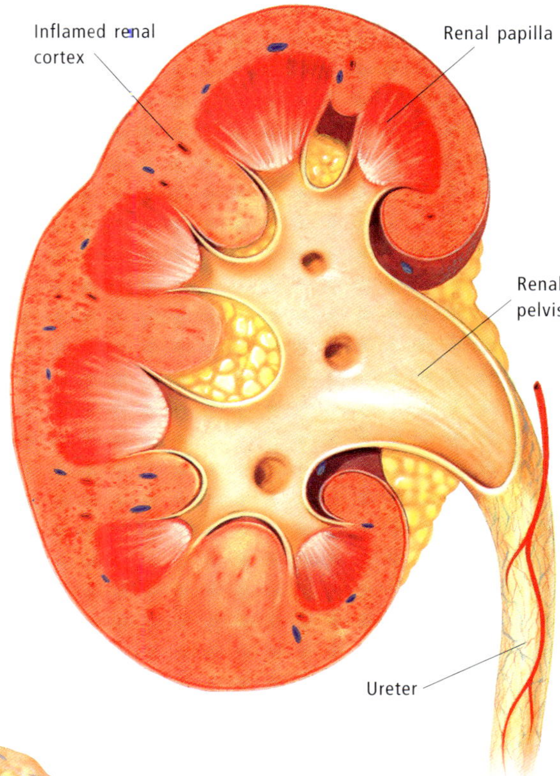

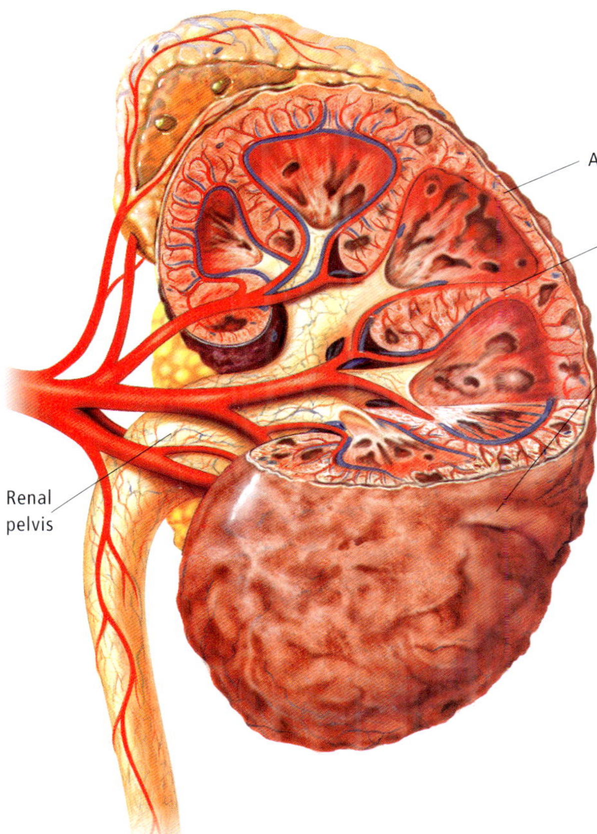

Nephritis—chronic pyelonephritis

This condition can be the result of a bacterial or viral infection of the renal pelvis. If untreated, severe kidney damage may occur. The main symptoms are high fever, intense pain, vomiting, diarrhea and blood in the urine.

Glomerulonephritis

Glomerulonephritis is inflammation of the glomeruli, which are clusters of renal capillaries. Damage to the glomeruli results in an inability to filter the blood properly, so that blood and protein pass out into the urine. This may lead to poor kidney function and kidney failure.

Acute (sudden) glomerulonephritis sometimes follows a throat infection or other streptococcal infection and is more common in children than in adults. There may be no symptoms but, usually, the affected person notices smoky or slightly red urine, puffy eyes and ankles, a general ill feeling, drowsiness, nausea or vomiting and headaches. Analysis of the urine reveals it to contain blood and proteins. Mild cases are treated by a carefully controlled diet and bed rest. Sometimes, and especially in adults, kidney dialysis is necessary until the kidneys recover. Recovery is usually complete.

Chronic (slow onset) glomerulonephritis may develop after a case of acute nephritis, even after a long interval, or the affected person may have never had the acute form. Symptoms vary greatly, but may include poor appetite, fatigue, anemia and high blood pressure. Treatment involves a strict diet low in proteins and sodium. High blood pressure may require treatment with antihypertensive drugs. In severe cases, cortisone or cytotoxic drugs, kidney dialysis and, eventually, kidney transplantation, may be necessary. There is no known cure for chronic glomerulonephritis, but the progress of the disease can be delayed.

Pyelonephritis

Pyelonephritis is an infection of the kidney and the renal pelvis. It develops from pyelitis, a less severe inflammation of the renal pelvis. Acute pyelonephritis is usually the result of a bladder infection that has spread to the kidney. It is characterized by the sudden onset of pain in the lower back, fever with chills, nausea and vomiting. A urine

Hydronephrosis

Hydronephrosis is caused by an obstruction or atrophy of the urinary tract resulting in distension of the renal pelvis and calyces. The condition begins with pain in the kidney region and blood in the urine.

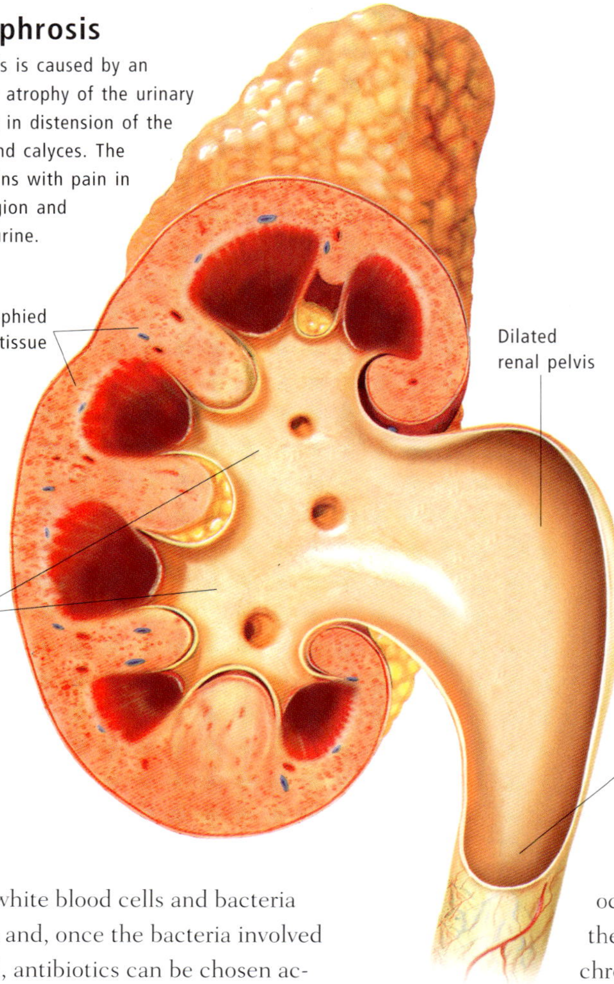

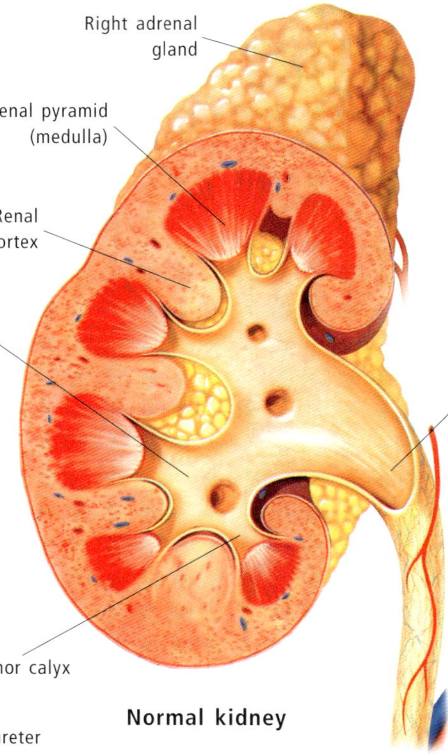

Normal kidney

test shows white blood cells and bacteria in the urine and, once the bacteria involved is identified, antibiotics can be chosen accordingly. Acute pyelonephritis generally responds to treatment with antibiotics given intravenously in hospital.

Chronic pyelonephritis is caused by destruction and scarring of the kidney tissue as a result of recurring or untreated bacterial infection. This may be due to an abnormality of the urinary tract, that leads to repeated infection. Treatment is via a course of antibiotics to treat the infection, and surgical correction of any underlying abnormality. If left untreated, renal failure may occur, requiring dialysis or transplantation.

Interstitial nephritis

Interstitial nephritis is inflammation of the spaces between the renal tubules and (sometimes) of the tubules themselves. It is usually a temporary, reversible condition, occurring as a side effect of certain drugs such as analgesics or antibiotics. Interstitial nephritis causes varying degrees of impaired kidney function; if severe, dialysis may be needed temporarily. Corticosteroids or anti-inflammatory medications may be of benefit in some cases.

Less commonly, occurring usually in the elderly, it may be chronic and progressive, when eventually long-term dialysis or renal transplantation may be necessary.

SEE ALSO *Dialysis, Glomerulonephritis, Kidney, Pyelitis, Pyelonephritis, Urinary systems*

NEPHROBLASTOMA

Nephroblastoma, which is also called Wilms' tumor, is a rapidly developing malignant tumor of the kidney. It occurs mainly in children under the age of seven and most often in children with congenital abnormalities.

Symptoms are an enlarged abdomen (a large, firm, smooth tumor can be felt in the child's abdomen), high blood pressure, blood in the urine, weight loss and, sometimes, abdominal pain. An ultrasound, CAT scan or MRI scan of the abdomen will show the tumor.

Treatment is with surgery, radiation therapy and anti-cancer drugs. In most cases the child can be cured, especially if the tumor is detected before it spreads to other organs.

SEE ALSO *Cancer, Kidney*

NEPHRON

Nephrons are the tiny filtering units found in the kidney. There are millions of tiny nephrons located within the cortex of both kidneys. Each is composed of a ball-shaped cluster of capillaries (the glomerulus) and a narrow, hairpin-shaped little tube (the tubule). An extension of the tubule forms a cup-shaped capsule part of the way around the glomerulus called Bowman's capsule.

From the arterial circulation, blood passes into the capillaries of the glomerulus. Because the capillary membranes are thin and permeable, a fluid composed of blood minus red and white blood cells and proteins filters readily through the glomerulus and capsule membranes into the tubule.

This filtrate passes along the tubule, which twists and turns, and contains a U-shaped section called Henle's loop. As the filtrate passes along the tubule, a network of capillaries reabsorbs water, glucose and salts from the filtrate, and secretes unwanted substances into the filtrate. The remaining filtrate, that contains the wastes such as urea that are toxic to the body, drains from the tubules into the renal pelvis and is then transported to the bladder via the ureters as urine.

SEE ALSO *Bladder, Kidney, Plasma, Ureter, Urinary systems*

NEPHROSIS

Also called nephrotic syndrome, nephrosis is any abnormal kidney condition in which damage to the glomeruli leads to high loss of protein in the urine. Other symptoms include edema (swelling of the body tissues), fatigue, weakness and loss of appetite. The condition usually begins in children under six years of age.

The leakage of protein, especially albumin, out of the glomeruli and into the urine lowers the concentration of protein in the blood, causing a shift in osmotic pressure. Because of this change in pressure, fluid then leaks out of the blood and into the tissues, causing puffy eyes and ankles, a swollen abdomen and other signs of edema.

Nephrosis can be caused by damage to the glomerulus in conditions such as glomerulonephritis, diabetes, systemic lupus erythematosus and other autoimmune disorders. It is likely that several, not just one, pathologic processes are involved, all of which affect the glomeruli. Nephrosis may also be caused by any condition that causes an increase in the pressure of blood in the vessels of the glomerulus, such as heart failure or following a thrombosis in the renal vein. Elevated pressure in the blood vessels of the kidney also forces protein out into the urine. In some cases there is no obvious cause.

The condition cannot be cured but the symptoms can be controlled with cortisone or immunosuppressive drugs, which reduce kidney inflammation; diuretics, which reduce fluid retention and edema; and a low salt diet. In severe cases dialysis or kidney transplant may be needed.

Hydronephrosis is a different condition that occurs when the kidney's pelvis and calyces become distended because urine is unable to drain into the bladder. This distension occurs because ureter is blocked, for example by a tumor or a stone in the ureter or bladder or by enlargement of the prostate gland. If the condition progresses unchecked, this distention destroys the tubules in the cortex of the kidney, which may become atrophied and scarred. Urinary tract infection is a common accompaniment, leading to further kidney damage. If both kidneys are affected, kidney failure may be the end result. The symptoms are recurrent back pain, pain on passing urine, fever and chills. The urine may be cloudy and may contain blood. Sometimes the condition presents no symptoms and is discovered only during investigations for something else. Diagnosis can be confirmed with a pyelogram (x-ray investigation in which the kidney is outlined with the use of dye), ultrasound, CAT scan of the kidneys or abdomen or abdominal magnetic resonance imaging. These tests will also reveal the underlying cause.

The treatment is to treat the underlying cause. It may be necessary to surgically drain the dilated renal pelvis and remove the cause of the blockage. If there is a urinary tract infection it must be treated with antibiotics.

SEE ALSO *Diabetes, Glomerulonephritis, Kidney, Lupus erythematosus, Urinary systems*

NERVE CONDUCTION TESTS

Nerve conduction tests evaluate the health of a nerve by recording how fast an electrical impulse travels through it. Two electrodes are placed on the skin at different points along the path of a nerve being tested. One electrode initiates a nerve impulse which travels along the nerve and the other records the impulse. The time between the stimulus and response is recorded to determine how quickly and thoroughly the impulse travels along the nerve.

In a number of nerve conditions, such as nerve entrapment syndromes or degenerative nerve diseases, the transmission of nerve impulses is slowed. Different nerve diseases will affect conduction in different ways, and the test can be used as a diagnostic aid. The person being tested feels a small electric shock, but most people tolerate the test well.

SEE ALSO *Nerves*

Nephron

A nephron is the tiny filtering unit in a kidney. Each kidney is made up of millions of nephrons.

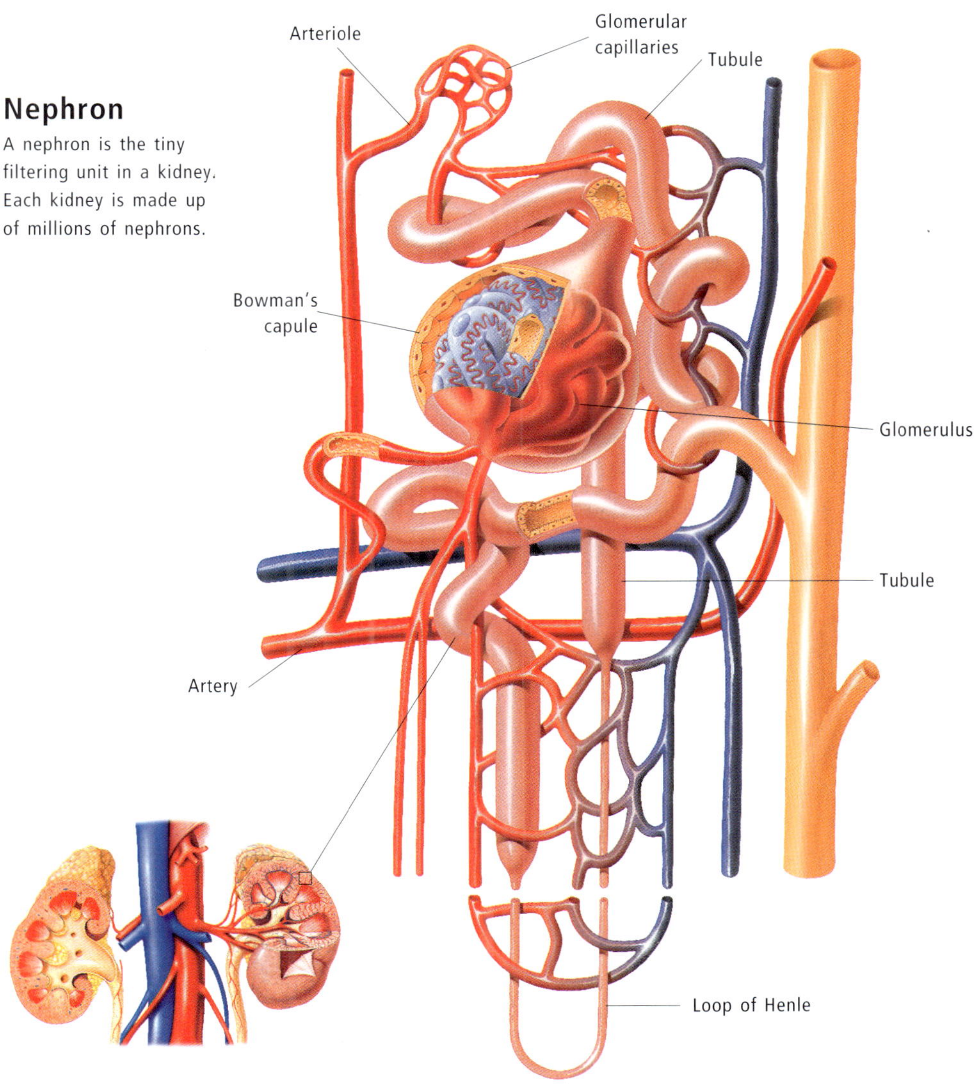

N

NERVES

Nerves connect the brain and spinal cord (central nervous system, CNS) with peripheral regions such as the muscles, skin and viscera. Their role is to carry signals which provide us with sensations or control our muscles. Twelve pairs of nerves arise from the brain and are called cranial nerves; they include the trigeminal and facial nerves and the vagus nerve. Nerves arising from the spinal cord, between the vertebrae, are known as spinal nerves. There are 31 pairs of spinal nerves, supplying the trunk and limbs.

A special branch of the peripheral nervous system, the autonomic nervous system, is concerned with controlling muscles in the viscera, such as the gut, bladder, heart and blood vessels. The autonomic nervous system has two parts, the sympathetic and parasympathetic. Some axons of the sympathetic system (e.g. those serving blood vessels in the limbs) travel with ordinary (somatic) nerves to reach their targets. Other autonomic, sympathetic and parasympathetic axons travel in special visceral nerves, such as the splanchnic nerves, to the gut and pelvic organs.

N

Nerve cells

Nerves contain the long processes of the nerve cells called axons, with one nerve containing many thousands of axons, running together in parallel bundles. Each axon extends all the way from the CNS to the tissue it supplies. Thus an axon can extend from the spinal cord to the hand or foot, a distance of over a meter, although others (e.g. to muscles and skin on the back) may be much shorter. There are two types of axons, sensory and motor. Sensory axons carry signals coming into the CNS from structures such as the skin, muscles, joints and viscera. They carry information about touch, temperature, pain, joint and muscle position. The nerve cell bodies of these axons (sensory neurons) lie in ganglia close to the CNS. Motor axons carry signals coming from the CNS to muscles in the body wall, limbs and viscera, to control our body movements. Their nerve cell bodies, known as motor neurons, lie in the CNS.

The signals carried by axons consist of short pulses of electrical activity, called action potentials, each about 0.1 volt and lasting about one-thousandth of a second. Action potentials in sensory axons start in the periphery (e.g. skin) with a stimulus (e.g. touch) which activates particular receptors (e.g. hair receptors). The action potentials then travel to the CNS where they activate other nerve cells, in sensory centers, to cause sensations. For motor outputs, action potentials start in motor cells in the CNS and travel out along the motor axons to muscles, causing the muscle to contract.

Most nerves contain both sensory and motor axons, with signals going both to and from the CNS in the different axons. Because each axon is like a separate insulated wire it does not interfere with its neighbors. A few nerves are purely motor in function, such as the hypoglossal nerve controlling muscles in the tongue. Similarly, a few nerves are purely sensory, such as the sural nerve to the skin on the lateral side of the foot. Activity in a nerve can be blocked by a local anesthetic, which prevents action potentials from passing through the block. This can be useful for stopping pain signals, for instance from the teeth during dental repairs.

Nerves also contain supporting cells called Schwann cells that envelop the axons. The combination of axon and Schwann cell is often referred to as a nerve fiber. A Schwann cell extends just a short distance along the axon, with the next cell looking after the next section of axon, from one end to the other. Larger axons are completely surrounded by the Schwann cells, that wrap their cell membranes around the axon, making a special layer known as myelin. This acts as an electrical insulator, and is important for increasing the speed at which action potentials can travel (conduction velocity). These axons are called myelinated axons. Smaller axons do not have any myelin (unmyelinated axons). They are still surrounded by Schwann cells which help to insulate them, but the cell does not wrap them in layers of membrane, and their signals travel more slowly.

In sensory axons there is a relationship between the size of an axon and the type of sensation it carries. Large myelinated axons carry information for fine tactile discrimination (e.g. texture of a surface), vibration and limb position. They can transmit signals at about 16–230 feet (5–70 meters) per second (e.g. it takes less than one-tenth of a second for action potentials to reach the spinal cord from the foot). Smaller unmyelinated axons carry signals about cold, warmth and pain, as well as a crude sense of touch. Being smaller and lacking a layer of myelin, their signals are carried more slowly, at about 3 feet (1 meter) per second. In these axons, action potentials from the foot, for example, take about 1 second to reach the spinal cord.

The activity traveling along a nerve can be recorded at certain sites by electrodes on the skin surface. Assessing the function of nerves in this way (nerve conduction testing) can be used to detect the slowing of conduction velocity which may occur when the nerve is injured or the myelin is damaged. This is similar to the evoked potential tests that can be used to detect slowing of conduction in central pathways, as with multiple sclerosis.

Connective tissue

Nerves also contain several layers of connective tissue, which protect the nerve and carry blood vessels. Connective tissue surrounds individual axons and groups them into bundles (fascicles) as well as surrounding the whole nerve. Blood vessels to nerves have a special barrier, the blood–nerve barrier, that is similar to the blood–brain barrier. The blood–nerve barrier prevents certain chemicals in the blood from entering the nerve, thus providing further protection for the axons. When the blood supply to a nerve is restricted or there is pressure on a nerve, strange sensations, usually called paresthesias, can be felt in the area supplied by the nerve. These include tingling sensations, "pins and needles" and numbness. If such a sensation is due to tight clothing or a particular posture (e.g. sitting in a squatting position), it usually disappears when the pressure is relieved. Other paresthesias may need treatment, e.g. pressure to the median nerve at the wrist can give pins and needles in the thumb, that may require surgery.

Nerve damage and disease

Nerves can be damaged by mechanical injuries, such as fractures or stab wounds. Some nerves are particularly vulnerable. For example, the radial nerve can be injured in fractures of the arm, where the nerve passes close to the bone; the median nerve can be injured when the wrist is cut, for instance in suicide attempts. Severing the nerve breaks the continuity of the axons and prevents them from transmitting signals to or from the periphery, thus loss of control of movement and loss of sensation occur in the affected area. The part of the axon separated from the nerve cell body in the CNS dies, but the part connected to the cell body is able to regenerate. As it grows at approximately $\frac{1}{25}$ inch (1 millimeter) per day, it may take many weeks to recover.

In order to grow back to the appropriate region, it is important for the separated ends of the nerve to be rejoined. Even very careful repair is not able to reconnect individual axons, however, so that regeneration is often rather inaccurate, and recovery may be limited. Other nerves, such as the sural nerve in the leg, can be used for a nerve graft if the damage is extensive or part of the nerve is missing. Crush injuries to nerves usually recover better than injuries where the nerve is cut because the nerve is left in continuity after crushing, which can improve the extent and accuracy of the regeneration.

If nerve continuity is not re-established, the growing axons form a tangled ball of sprouts (neuroma) at the cut end of the nerve. This can occur after amputations and may be painful or contribute to phantom sensations that the limb is still present.

Diseases of peripheral nerves are usually called neuropathies, although if they involve inflammation the term neuritis may be used. Another term, neuralgia, refers to pain along the course of a nerve. Nerve disorders may affect just one nerve, for instance in carpal tunnel syndrome and Bell's palsy. More often, neuropathies involve many nerves, often symmetrically on the two sides of the body. Guillain-Barré syndrome is an example of an acute inflammatory neuropathy. Other examples include nerve damage as a result of diabetes, that particularly involves sensory fibers, and alcoholic neuropathy, that affects both sensory and motor fibers.

The optic nerve is unusual in that it is actually an extension of the brain, and therefore part of the CNS rather than a peripheral nerve. Inflammation of the part of the nerve close to where it leaves the eye is called optic neuritis. It causes partial or complete loss of vision in the affected eye and is frequently associated with multiple sclerosis.

A disease that affects only motor pathways, but involves both the CNS and peripheral nerves, is amyotrophic lateral sclerosis (motor neuron disease). The cause is unknown, but the disease leads to a gradual loss of motor neurons and their axons, with associated weakness and paralysis.

SEE ALSO *Autonomic nervous system, Bell's palsy, Brain, Carpal tunnel syndrome, Guillain-Barré syndrome, Multiple sclerosis, Nerve conduction tests, Nervous system, Neuritis, Neuroma, Neuropathy, Radial nerve, Sciatic nerve, Spinal cord, Sympathetic nervous system, Trigeminal nerve, Ulnar nerve, Vagus nerve*

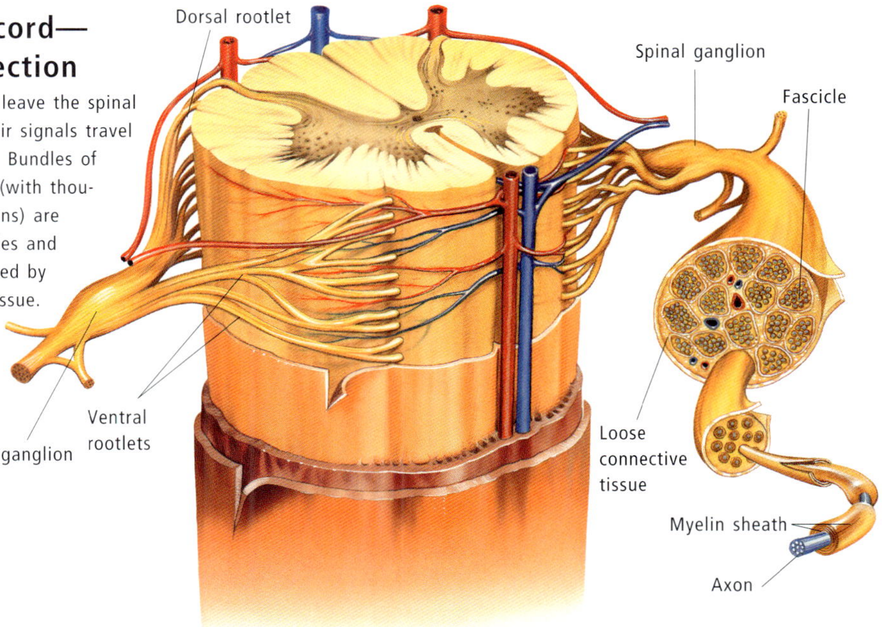

Spinal cord—cross-section

Nerve fibers leave the spinal cord and their signals travel along axons. Bundles of nerve fibers (with thousands of axons) are called fascicles and are surrounded by connective tissue.

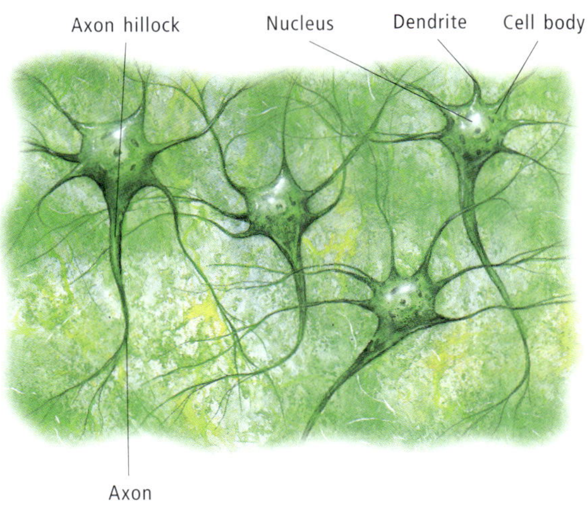

Neural tissue

Neural tissue processes neural data and conducts electrical impulses from one part of the body to another part. Ninety-eight percent of neural tissue is located in the brain and spinal cord.

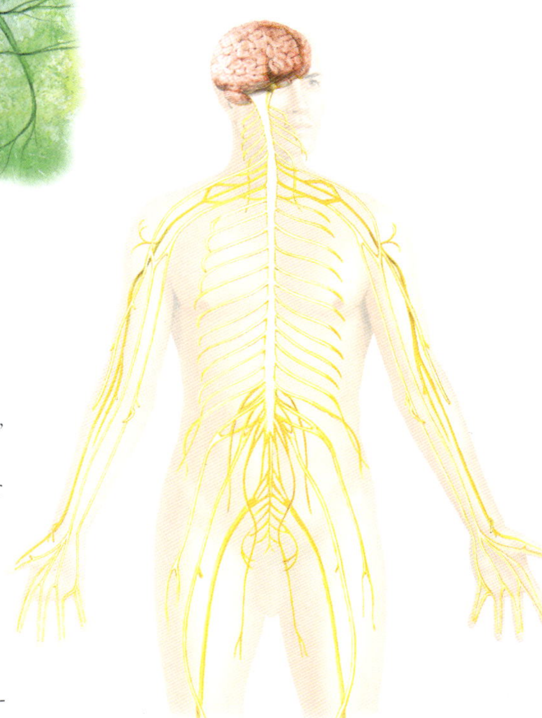

Peripheral nervous system

The peripheral nerves branch out from the central nervous system (the spinal cord) to carry messages to and from all parts of the body.

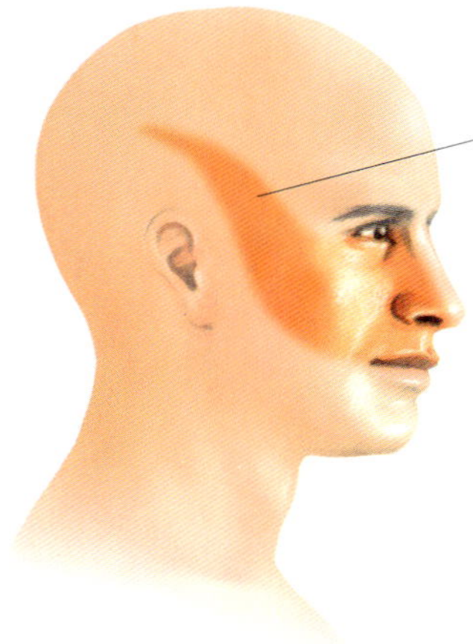

Neuralgia

Neuralgia is pain in or along the course of a sensory nerve. Trigeminal neuralgia causes severe pain in the face and cheek on one side of the face. The pain is often triggered by chewing, brushing the hair, washing the face, drinking cold liquids, and cold winds.

NEURAL TUBE DEFECT

Neural tube defects are disorders resulting in the abnormal development of the brain and spinal cord, and/or the membranes (meninges) surrounding them, in the embryo. In week 3 or 4 of pregnancy, a narrow sheath normally folds and closes to form what is known as the neural tube. This is the first stage of development of the central nervous system (brain and spinal cord); if the tube fails to close perfectly such defects as spina bifida, anencephaly and hydrocephalus can occur. Anencephaly is a condition in which a large part of the brain, skull and scalp are absent due to the incomplete closure of the end of the neural tube nearest the head. Incomplete closure of the bottom end of the tube results in spina bifida, a defect in which the spinal cord and its membranes are exposed and may protrude through a gap in the vertebrae.

Research has shown that ensuring a daily intake of 0.4 milligrams of folic acid (vitamin B_9) before and during pregnancy can halve the risk of neural tube defects. Folic acid occurs naturally in foods such as dark green leafy vegetables; supplements may be taken in tablet form. Neural tube defects can be detected by prenatal tests.

SEE ALSO *Brain, Fetal development, Hydrocephalus, Nervous system, Spinal cord, Spina bifida*

NEURALGIA

Pain in or along the route of a sensory nerve is known as neuralgia. The pain is often sudden, severe and stabbing. Although any part of the body may be affected, the most common sites are the face, arms and chest. An infection such as tooth decay can trigger neuralgia. So too can pinching or pressure on a nerve, as occurs briefly with a knock on the "funny bone" at the elbow. Carpal tunnel syndrome, in which there is inflammation of soft tissues in the forearm, produces a more sustained form of neuralgia. A nervous system disorder can be responsible or it may be associated with other conditions such as diabetes mellitus, some vitamin deficiencies and arthritis. In many cases, however, it is not always possible to identify an underlying cause for neuralgia.

One of the most common forms of neuralgia is trigeminal neuralgia, involving the trigeminal nerve that carries sensory impulses to the brain from the jaws, nose, mouth and eyes.

The sensations associated with this condition occur as very short but overwhelmingly painful repetitive stabs along the path of the trigeminal nerve on one side of the face. Pain may be short-lived, lasting only a few seconds, or can persist for minutes at a time. Trigeminal neuralgia also tends to occur in a series of episodes over several days, disappearing for a brief period and then returning.

Because the facial muscles often twitch in response to the pain, as if in a "nervous tic", trigeminal neuralgia is sometimes known by the French term *tic douloureux*. It usually occurs in the middle-aged and elderly and is also common in people who have advanced multiple sclerosis. Episodes of pain may be sparked by eating or by touching certain trigger zones on the face.

Glossopharyngeal neuralgia is another form of neuralgia affecting the head region. In this case, however, the pain occurs deep inside the throat, starting near the tonsils and extending into an ear. Chewing and swallowing are frequent triggers. The cause is usually a blood vessel pressing on the nerves involved in swallowing.

A form of neuralgia known as postherpetic neuralgia sometimes occurs following episodes of shingles, a condition caused by the chickenpox virus. After a bout of chickenpox, the virus responsible can hide in nerve roots along the spinal cord, later in life making its presence felt as shingles at times of physical or emotional stress. During an episode of shingles the virus multiplies and spreads along the nerve, causing the tissues it supplies to experience pain and sensitivity. Blisters and a rash form on the skin serviced by the affected nerve. In postherpetic neuralgia, pain along the nerve can persist for weeks or months after the shingles rash disappears.

Treatment for neuralgia depends on the cause, if one can be found. Sometimes the condition rights itself spontaneously. Analgesics such as aspirin and ibuprofen usually help to ease the pain. Pressure on affected nerves may be relieved by using anti-inflammatory drugs to reduce tissue swelling. In severe and persistent cases of neuralgia, when drug treatments fail to bring relief, various surgical options are available.

SEE ALSO *Carpal tunnel syndrome, Nerves, Shingles, Tic douloureux, Trigeminal nerve*

NEURITIS

Neuritis is an inflammation of a nerve or group of nerves. When more than one nerve is affected the disorder is sometimes referred to as polyneuritis. When the condition involves the root of a spinal nerve, it is termed radiculitis.

Symptoms of neuritis vary, depending on which nerves are affected and the severity of the condition. The impacts can range from strange but mild sensations, such as pins and needles, to the severe complications of paralysis. There may be pain (often in the form of a burning sensation), defective reflexes and either a loss of sensitivity or heightened sensitivity in the area supplied by the affected nerves.

The symptoms may not always, however, readily point to nervous system involvement. In some cases, for example, muscles served by inflamed and dysfunctional nerves may weaken and degenerate over time. Similarly, problems in joints may be caused by neuritis. Low blood pressure is a possible outcome when neuritis affects the autonomic nervous system; in this case abnormal nerve signals lead to the failure of veins and leg muscles

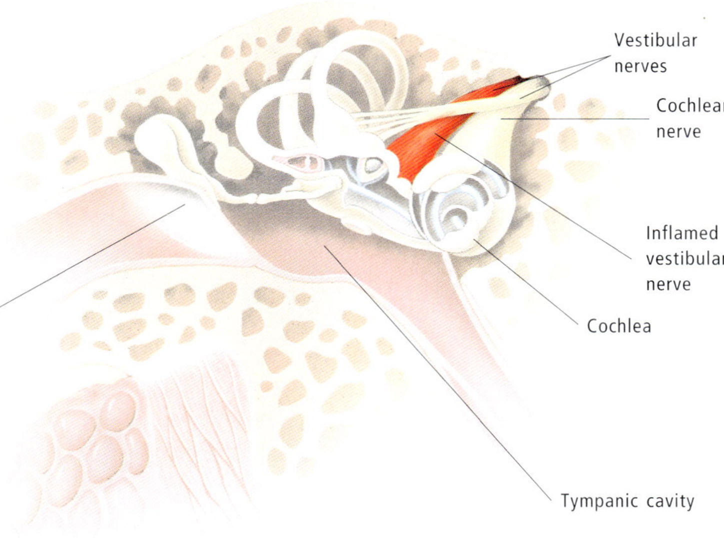

Neuritis
Neuritis is the inflammation of a nerve or a group of nerves. Vestibular neuritis affects the vestibular nerves in the ear and can cause dizziness.

to return venous blood to the heart. This causes pooling of blood in the legs.

There are many different potential causes for neuritis, including injury, nutritional deficiencies and disease. Toxins produced by the bacteria responsible for the diseases diphtheria and leprosy can cause neuritis. Vitamin B deficiencies, associated with diseases such as beriberi and alcoholism, commonly cause neuritis. Other factors that can underpin the condition include diabetes mellitus, lung cancer, industrial poisoning and autoimmune diseases such as multiple sclerosis (MS).

Optic neuritis, which involves inflammation of the optic nerve serving the eye, can affect a person's vision. It occurs more commonly in women than men and normally afflicts one eye rather than both (although it often occurs in both eyes simultaneously in children). Optic neuritis is also known as retrobulbar neuritis. It can be caused by encephalitis or an infection that has spread from the sinuses or may arise after an injury to the eye area. In adults, the condition is often an early sign of MS. Statistically, about 40 percent of people who develop optic neuritis later go on to develop MS.

The symptoms of optic neuritis usually appear over several days, often beginning with a blurring of vision in the affected eye, followed by a loss of color vision and the appearance of blind spots. Eye movements may be painful. Although effects on vision can be so extreme that a patient may be barely able to detect light with the affected eye, optic neuritis usually gets better and full vision is restored. Treatment commonly involves anti-inflammatory medications but the condition often improves on its own without intervention.

Vestibular neuritis is a condition involving inflammation of a vestibular nerve, which is integral to the sense of balance. The vestibular nerves convey messages about head movements from the inner ear to the brain. Neuritis in one of these nerves is usually caused by an infection due to a virus, possibly a member of the herpes family. The main symptom is dizziness. Hearing is not affected but a slight sensitivity to head movements can persist in some people for months, even years.

SEE ALSO *Multiple sclerosis, Nerves, Optic nerve*

NEUROBLASTOMA

Neuroblastoma is a cancer that affects fetal nerve cells, causing a tumor in early childhood. It often begins in the adrenal gland in the abdomen and may spread quickly to parts of the body such as the bone marrow and lymph nodes. Surgical removal of the tumor, radiation therapy, chemotherapy and bone marrow transplant are treatment options.

SEE ALSO *Cancer*

NEURODERMATITIS

Neurodermatitis is a general term used to describe an itchy skin disorder thought to have emotional or "nervous" causes. Disorders such as atopic dermatitis (a type of eczema) and lichen simplex chronicus, which leads to thickening of the skin, are often grouped under this heading although they may have other contributing causes.

SEE ALSO *Dermatitis, Eczema*

NEUROFIBROMATOSIS

Neurofibromatosis refers to a range of hereditary nervous system disorders caused by chromosomal abnormalities that result in multiple benign fibrous tumors (fibromas) on the peripheral nerves, internal organs, spine and skin. Type 1 neurofibromatosis (sometimes known as von Recklinghausen's disease) is also characterized by brown (café-au-lait) spots on the skin. Type 2 neurofibromatosis usually involves less spots and may include tumors of the acoustic nerves in the ear (acoustic neuromas). Learning disabilities may result from the disease. There is no specific treatment, although tumors that cause pain, affect the function of a body part or turn malignant are surgically removed if possible.

SEE ALSO *Chromosomal abnormalities, Nerves, Nervous system, Neuroma*

N

NEUROMA

Neuromas are benign tumors formed from nerve cells, sometimes referred to as schwannomas. They may occur singly, or in multiples, along with pigmented patches on the skin (neurofibromatosis or von Recklinghausen's disease).

Neuromas may occur between the bones in the ball of the foot (plantar or Morton's neuroma). This is due to compression of the nerves between the metatarsal bones where the toes join the foot, causing swelling, inflammation and a sharp burning sensation that may radiate to the toes. Surgery may be needed to remove severe tumors. Otherwise, rest, ice packs and anti-inflammatory medications should offer pain relief.

Painful neuromas sometimes form on the stumps of amputated limbs where severed nerves grow back abnormally.

Acoustic neuromas are benign tumors of unknown cause that grow on the acoustic nerve in the ear canal and are sometimes associated with hereditary neurofibromatosis

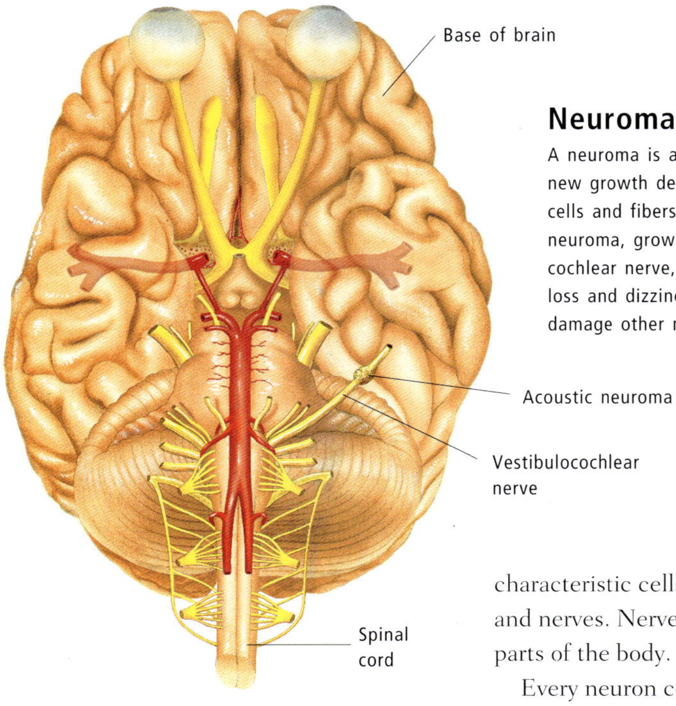

Neuroma

A neuroma is a benign tumor or new growth derived from nerve cells and fibers. An acoustic neuroma, growing on the vestibular cochlear nerve, can cause hearing loss and dizziness, and may damage other nerves close by.

Type 2. They may cause hearing loss and ringing (tinnitus) in the affected ear, loss of balance, dizziness, pain and numbness. Large acoustic neuromas may cause complications by pressing on the skull. Surgical removal may result in total hearing loss in the affected ear and paralysis of facial muscles.

SEE ALSO *Ear, Nerves, Neurofibromatosis, Tinnitus, Tumor*

NEURONS

Neurons, also known as nerve cells, are specialized cells involved in sensation, information processing and cognition, and control of muscle and gland activity. Neurons are the characteristic cells of the brain, spinal cord and nerves. Nerves penetrate virtually all parts of the body.

Every neuron consists of a cell body (perikaryon), a cell nucleus, contained within the cell body, and one or more narrow projections, known as processes. The processes, which radiate from the cell body, are of two types: dendrites, which convey impulses to the cell body; and axons, which normally convey impulses away from it. Neurons usually have a single axon, and a variable number of dendrites, depending on the cell's function.

The central nervous system (CNS) is composed of nerve cells whose axons are situated in the brain, eye and spinal cord. The peripheral nervous system is composed of nerve cells whose axons are situated outside the CNS. The brain consists of a mass of neurons of various types, together with supporting cells (glia) and blood vessels. Nerves consist of bundles of axons, together with supporting cells (Schwann cells) and connective tissue.

Some axons and dendrites are protected by a covering of Schwann or glial cells containing a fatty substance called myelin. Myelinated axons and dendrites carry impulses faster than unmyelinated ones.

Impulses are conveyed along dendrites and axons by the passage of a wave of chemical and electrical changes affecting the cell membrane of the dendrite or axon. The point at which an impulse is transmitted from one neuron to another is called a synapse: chemical transmitter agents, such as glutamate, norepinephrine (noradrenaline) and serotonin, convey impulses from one cell to another. There is no direct contact between the axon of one neuron and the dendrite of another.

Sensory neurons receive sensations from the outside environment and carry them to the spinal cord or brain. They generally have terminals specialized for the reception of specific sensations, such as touch, vibration, temperature, pain and movements.

Motor neurons carry impulses in the opposite direction: that is, away from the brain and spinal cord, and towards muscles. They function by stimulating muscles. In addition, they produce and control both voluntary and involuntary movements of muscles, and maintain muscle tone. Motor nerves connect to muscle cells by structures called motor end plates.

Intermediate neurons (interneurons), which are the most numerous in the brain,

Neuron

Neurons are specialized cells found in the nervous system which conduct nerve impulses. Each neuron has three main parts: the cell body, the branching projections (dendrites) that carry impulses to the cell body, and one elongated projection (the axon) that conveys impulses away from the cell body.

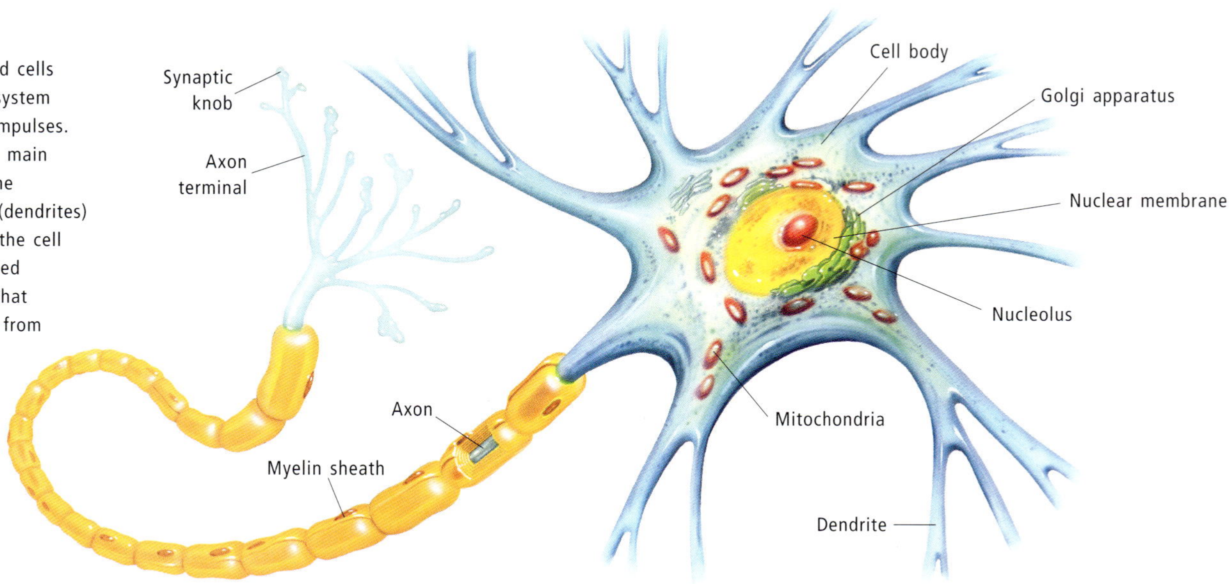

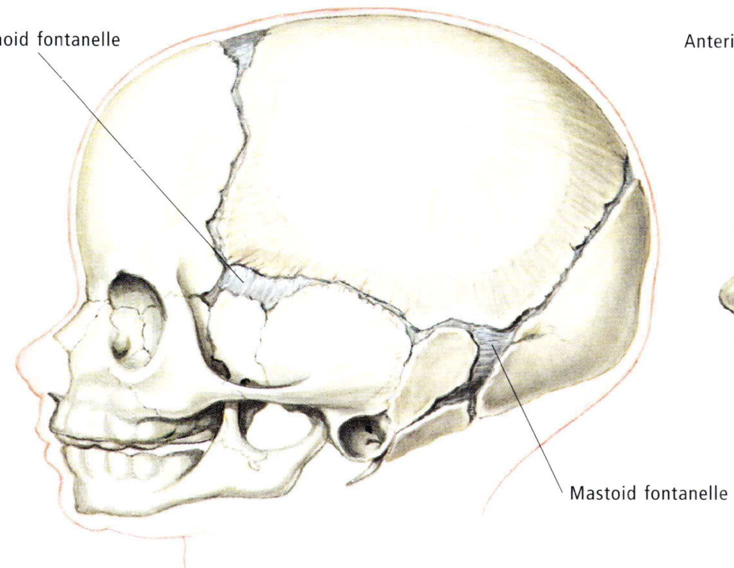

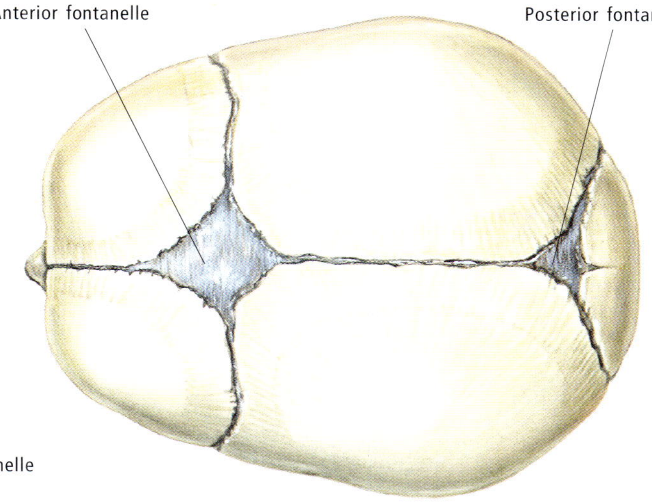

Newborn's skull

There are six "soft spots" on a baby's skull, which allow some compression of the skull during birth. These regions are called fontanelles. By a baby's second birthday these bones have joined together.

connect sensory and motor neurons either directly or by networks of cells. Cell networks are responsible for cognition and memory.

Reflexes, such as the knee jerk, involve a minimum of two neurons: a sensory neuron (which, in this case, detects stretching of the quadriceps muscle) and a motor neuron, which is stimulated by the sensory neuron and fires to initiate muscle contraction (in this case, contraction of the quadriceps muscle). Usually there is at least one intermediate neuron in between the sensory neuron and the motor neuron.

The total number of neurons is greatest before birth, and decreases during life. Once lost, neurons do not regenerate, but cut axons in damaged nerves may regenerate.

Disorders affecting neurons may include injury, congenital defects, cancer, infections, vitamin deficiency and degeneration. Epilepsy is due to the inappropriate generation of impulses by neurons in the cerebral cortex.

SEE ALSO *Brain, Epilepsy, Nervous system, Reflexes, Spinal cord*

NEUROPATHY

Neuropathy refers to disorders of the peripheral nerves. Causes include diabetes, lead poisoning, vascular disorders and damage due to penetrating injury, broken bones, mechanical pressure or exposure to cold or radiation. Weakness, numbness, tingling and pain in the feet, legs, hands or forearms are symptoms. Treatment depends on the cause.

SEE ALSO *Nerves, Peripheral nervous system*

NEWBORN

A newborn is a baby less than 6 weeks old. Healthy newborn babies begin to breathe almost as soon as they reach the outside world and before the umbilical cord, which attaches the navel to the placenta that has been their life support, has stopped pulsating. Usually the cord is left intact until it has stopped pulsating, then it is clamped, or in some countries it is bound.

The head of a newborn is disproportionately large in relation to the body, the hair, if present, is wet, the skin is peeling, wrinkly or furry, or all three, and the complexion may be red, pink or blue. The baby may be alert or crying, quiet or sleepy.

A newborn baby has more individual bones than an adult. (Many bones ossify and fuse together with growth.) A newborn baby's skull is made up of a number of individual bones held together by fontanelles, the most obvious being the soft spot (often called the fontanelle) in the top of its skull. A newborn has a low sloping forehead, a receding chin and often a slightly misshapen head which is from pressure and only temporary when the baby is born vaginally. The newborn's skin may be covered in a creamy substance known as vernix. The molding of the skull may be high and pointed if the baby was delivered in the posterior position (with its spine against the mother's); the face may be swollen and bruised if the baby was born face first. If the contractions of the uterus pushed the baby's head against a cervix that was not fully dilated, the baby may have a large bump on the head like a blister (called a caput).

Enlarged genitals, a slight menstrual-like bleeding in some girls, and "milk" in the breasts of both sexes are all caused by the presence of the mother's hormones in the baby's bloodstream, and disappear quite soon.

A baby born before week 37 is termed premature or pre-term. These babies are immature, smaller than full-term babies, and usually need special care. They are more likely than full-term babies to be covered in dark hair (lanugo). They are more likely to suffer from breathing and cardiovascular problems, anemia, jaundice and feeding problems, and to be unable to control their body temperature. Premature babies are also prone to infection.

A baby born after the normal length of gestation is described as postmature and may have dry, peeling skin and long finger and toe nails. Some postmature babies will be undernourished with disproportionately large heads, and may be described as "small-for-dates".

Immediately after birth a test called the Apgar test (named after Virginia Apgar, the US anesthesiologist who devised it) is performed on newborns in many industrialized countries. The Apgar test scores an aggregate of observations about the baby's vitality based on heart rate, breathing, skin color, muscle tone and reflex response. It is repeated 5 minutes after the first test.

Another test, the Neonatal Behavioral Assessment Scale, is now used in hospitals worldwide. Devised by American pediatrician T. Berry Brazelton, it assesses the baby's behavioral response to human and non-human stimuli.

Other checkups done on a newborn include measuring the diameter of the head and the length from head to foot, recording the weight, checking hips and jaws for dislocation and the mouth for cleft palate. Babies' reflexes are also tested.

A pH test may be done to test the blood in the umbilical cord artery for acidity. A low pH indicates that blood and tissues contain too many metabolic products and that the newborn's oxygen supply is lacking.

Vitamin K may be administered, either intravenously or orally, to prevent vitamin K deficiency bleeding (hemorrhagic disease of the newborn). Newborns have only minimal stores of vitamin K, which is essential to the clotting of blood. Bleeding from the umbilicus, intracranially, or from a circumcision, can occur up until week 26 after birth, and is most likely to occur between weeks 4 and 6 after birth in babies who are deficient in vitamin K.

SEE ALSO *Infancy, Reflexes, Sudden infant death syndrome, Umbilical cord*

NICOTINE

Nicotine is a poisonous alkaloid found in tobacco smoke and in other tobacco products. Like other alkaloids, such as cocaine and morphine, it is habit-forming and narcotic, producing physical and psychological dependence and tolerance.

If delivered via a cigarette, nicotine acts as a stimulant when inhaled in short puffs, but it acts as a tranquilizer when inhaled in deep drags. Hence, tobacco may be used by smokers for the relief of symptoms of depression, anxiety, attention deficit disorder or stress. However, studies have shown that nicotine does not enhance performance. Moreover, nicotine is known to constrict the blood vessels and raise blood pressure, and smoking is linked to some forms of cancer as well as to heart disease.

Nicotine withdrawal is characterized by feelings of stress, anger and irritability. Nicotine replacement therapies are frequently used in smoking cessation treatments. They include nicotine gum, nicotine patch, nicotine nasal spray and the nicotine inhaler.

Because nicotine depresses the appetite, people who give up smoking often find they are eating more and putting on weight. Chewing gum is recommended by some therapists.

SEE ALSO *Smoking, Withdrawal*

NIGHT BLINDNESS

Night blindness is a condition which can be caused by the disease retinitis pigmentosa. It can occur in people who have normal daytime vision but cannot see properly in reduced light. Some of the light-sensitive cells (rods) in the retina degenerate, and vision in low light gradually diminishes. The field of vision narrows, resulting in tunnel vision in the later stages of the disease. Deterioration progresses to total blindness. Ophthalmic examination may show early signs.

Night blindness is believed to be an inherited condition and at present there is no treatment to slow or reverse the damage to the retina.

SEE ALSO *Blindness, Eye, Retina, Retinitis pigmentosa*

NIPPLE

The nipple is the raised area in the center of a breast. It is surrounded by a disk-shaped pigmented area called the areola. The milk ducts of the breast empty into the nipple. The nipples, which contain some erectile tissue, can be an erogenous zone, common to both men and women.

Tenderness in the nipple may result from local trauma or friction or be a feature of lactation (breast feeding). A milky-looking nipple discharge may normally occur during or shortly after pregnancy, or during breast feeding. It may also be caused by endocrine (hormonal) disorders and some drugs. Less commonly, a discharge may indicate underlying breast cancer. Bleeding from the nipple may also indicate breast cancer and should be investigated by a physician. Treatment aims at correcting any underlying cause.

The nipples need extra care when a woman is breast feeding. Good breast hygiene and the use of breast pads will maintain dryness between feedings and relieve symptoms of tenderness and irritation. Breast creams may be used to help keep the nipple area lubricated and supple.

Occasionally the nipple and areola may be affected by a rash; most are benign and easily treated, but a rash (especially with a discharge) may indicate an underlying carcinoma known as Paget's disease of the breast.

SEE ALSO *Breast, Breast feeding, Paget's disease of the breast*

NON-HODGKIN'S LYMPHOMA

Non-Hodgkin's lymphoma is a tumor of the lymph glands, which is distinct from Hodgkin's lymphoma (also called Hodgkin's disease). It is a group of malignant diseases

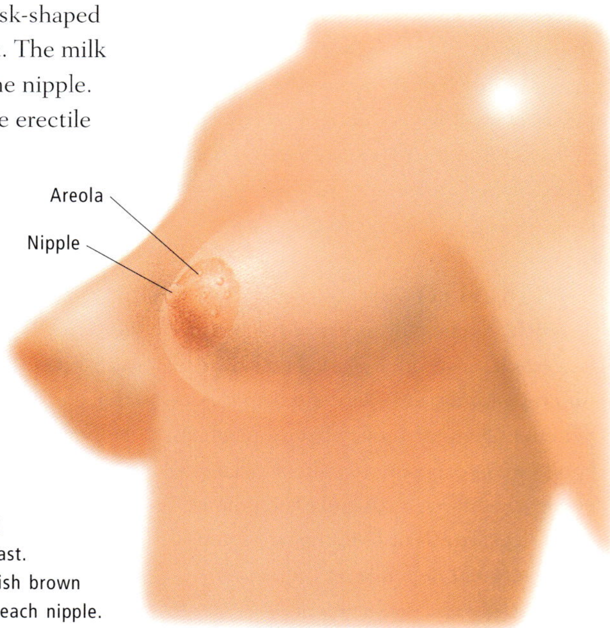

Nipple
The nipple is a conical projection of each breast. The areola is the reddish brown region of skin around each nipple.

arising in the lymph glands (also called lymph nodes) rather than spreading there, such as cancers do. Microscopic examination of a lymph gland by the pathologist accurately distinguishes between the two conditions.

Non-Hodgkin's lymphomas are more common than Hodgkin's disease, and the average age of patients is 50 years. The cause is generally unknown, although several possible causes have been identified. Exposure to high-dose ionizing radiation increases the risk, as do chemicals such as benzene and pesticides.

The risk of lymphoma is increased in certain occupations, such as farmers and forestry and timber workers, from exposure to herbicides. Chemotherapy drugs can lead to later development of lymphoma, which is also increased in patients with reduced immunity, either from medication or acquired immune deficiency syndrome (AIDS). Other viruses than HIV of AIDS have also been associated with lymphoma, including Epstein-Barr virus, the cause of infectious mononucleosis (glandular fever).

The main symptoms of lymphoma are persistent fever, drenching night sweats and severe unexplained weight loss. Patients may notice enlarged lymph glands in the neck, under the armpits or in the groin area and there may be enlargement of the spleen. The diagnosis is made by biopsy of an enlarged lymph gland, either using a fine needle or by a minor operation. Sometimes lymphoma causes a tumor that is not in the glands, such as lymphoma of the stomach or brain.

There is a variety of treatments for non-Hodgkin's lymphomas, depending on the particular type. Some lymphomas are very slow-growing and may not require treatment, particularly if the patient is elderly. If such a tumor causes symptoms, it can often be treated with mild chemotherapy tablets or radiation therapy to the affected area. Although such lymphomas are compatible with survival for years, they are not currently curable.

An important new development has been the production of antibodies directed against the cells causing lymphomas. These antibodies can kill the lymphoma cells without the side effects caused by most chemotherapy drugs. Other types of lymphoma are rapid-growing and require strong chemotherapy for treatment. The treatment consists of a combination of tablets and injections given on a cycle of three to four weeks for a total of six to nine treatments, generally given as an outpatient. Common side effects include nausea, hair loss and reduction of the normal white blood cells, leading to increased risk of infection. Injections are now available to stimulate the white cells to recover sooner, reducing the risk of infection. With such treatments, a proportion of aggressive lymphomas can be cured.

Currently, doctors are assessing higher doses of chemotherapy with the use of the patient's own (autologous) marrow or stem cell transplants. In this procedure the patient's normal cells are collected and stored in liquid nitrogen, so that they can be returned to "rescue" the patient following doses of chemotherapy so high that they destroy both lymphoma and healthy bone marrow cells.

SEE ALSO *Cancer, Hodgkin's disease, Lymph glands, Lymphatic/Immune system*

Non-Hodgkin's lymphoma

Non-Hodgkin's lymphoma is a group of malignant diseases that cause tumors of the lymph glands (nodes). The nodes of the neck, armpits, and groin area are most commonly affected. Enlargement of these nodes may be the first signs of disease.

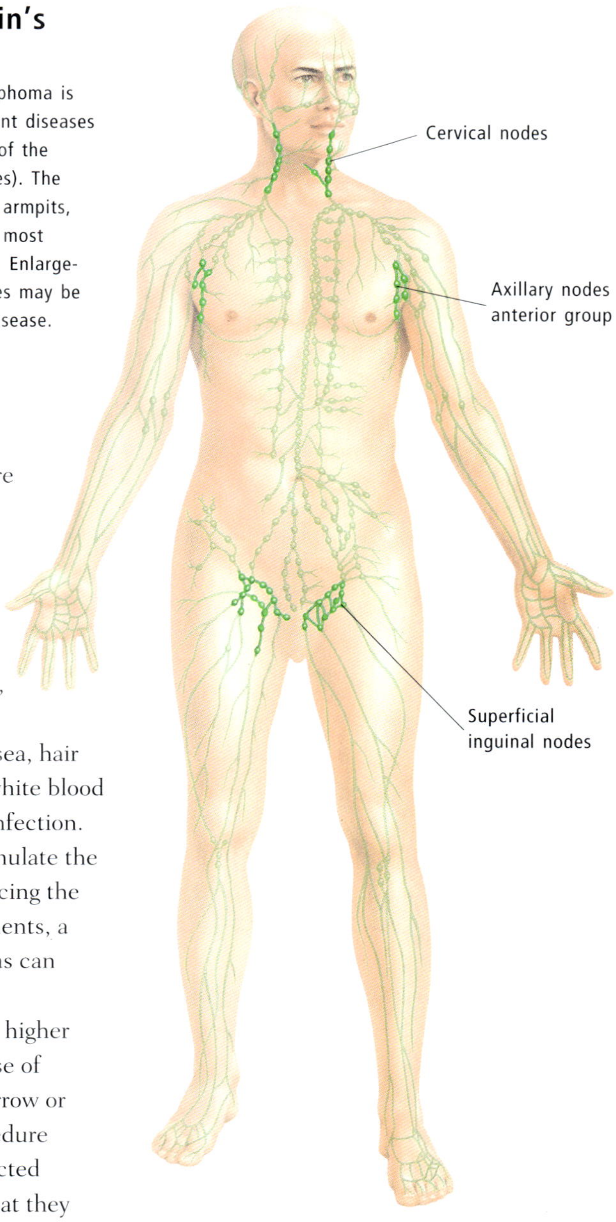

NONSTEROIDAL ANTI-INFLAMMATORY DRUGS

Along with aspirin and acetaminophen (paracetamol), nonsteroidal anti-inflammatory drugs (NSAIDs) are the drugs most commonly used to treat mild-to-moderate pain, fever and inflammation. NSAIDs work by inhibiting prostaglandin synthesis in body tissues, which in turn reduces pain, fever and inflammation. They are used in acute injuries and conditions such as rheumatoid arthritis, osteoarthritis, ankylosing spondylitis, menstrual cramps, tendinitis, bursitis and gout.

There are many NSAIDs on the market. Many are available over the counter, as well as on prescription from a physician. The most commonly used include ibuprofen, naproxen, indomethacin, mefanamic acid and phenylbutazone. They are non-habit forming and most are taken by mouth as a pill or liquid.

Side effects of NSAIDs include nausea and heartburn and, after long-term use, peptic ulcers. They can also cause clotting disorders and kidney disease. Anyone suffering from indigestion, stomach ulcer, kidney or blood diseases should consult a physician before taking NSAIDs.

SEE ALSO *Analgesics*

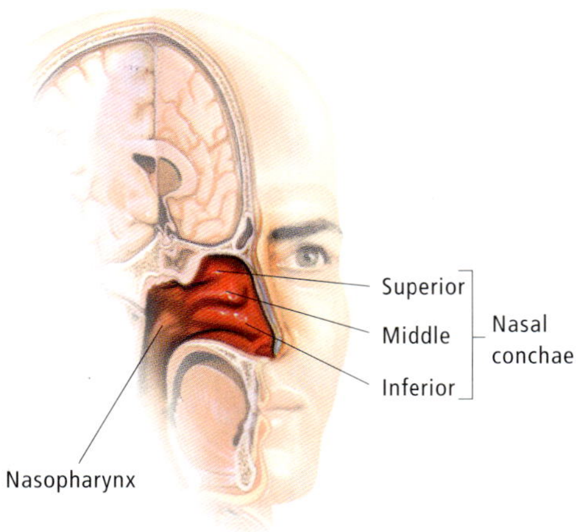

Nose

The main passageway for air entering the body is the nose. Air enters the nostrils and passes through the nasal cavities into the nasopharynx, trachea and down into the lungs.

NOSE

The nose is a part of the respiratory system. Its bony structure forms part of the skull. The bones of the external nose consist, on each side, of a nasal bone and the maxilla. The framework of the nostrils is made of cartilage, while the nasal septum, which separates the nostrils in the midline, is part bone and part cartilage.

Inside, the nose contains cavities which form part of the respiratory tract. The nose serves to warm and humidify inhaled air, and to filter out particles of dust. Air is normally breathed into and out of the body through the nose, via the nostrils. The nostrils are guarded by hairs (vibrissae) whose function is to prevent entry by insects and larger particles of dust. The nostrils lead to the nasal cavities, one on each side, which in turn lead to the pharynx and thence to the voice box (larynx) and windpipe (trachea). The nasal cavities are also connected to the paranasal sinuses and receive drainage of tear fluid through the nasolacrimal ducts; the eustachian tubes connect the ears to the pharynx.

In each nasal cavity, three curved plates, called the conchae (also known as turbinates), project from the side wall. These increase the surface area of the cavity, exposing inspired air to a greater amount of warm, moist surface due to a rich supply of blood vessels.

The bones surrounding the nasal cavities are the vomer and portions of the frontal, ethmoid, maxillary and sphenoid bones. The floor of the nasal cavities forms the roof of the palate. The two nasal cavities are separated by a partition called the nasal septum, which is commonly deviated to one side, thereby enlarging one nasal cavity at the expense of the other.

Most of each nasal cavity is lined by a specialized type of mucous membrane called respiratory mucosa. This is characterized by the presence of cilia, which are minute hairs that waft foreign particles on a sheet of mucus towards the nasopharynx. In the upper region of each nasal cavity, the mucous membrane changes to olfactory mucosa, containing specialized nerve cells for the reception of smell. Glands of the mucous membrane produce a watery secretion which both protects the walls of the nasal cavities and is evaporated to humidify the inspired air.

Problems affecting the nose include the common cold (a viral infection predominantly affecting the nasal mucosa), hay fever (an allergic reaction to pollen particles in inhaled air) and bleeding. Besides injury, nose bleeding may be associated with high blood pressure.

SEE ALSO *Common cold, Hay fever, Mucous membranes, Nosebleed, Olfactory system, Smell*

NOSEBLEED

A nosebleed (epistaxis) is a common occurrence, and is due to rupture of the delicate blood vessels just beneath the mucous membrane covering the nasal septum. In this position the blood vessels are susceptible to damage from fingers or trauma. Nosebleeds are common in childhood and are often related to upper respiratory infection, which results in sneezing or vigorous noseblowing. In children, the possibility of a foreign object in the nose needs to be considered.

Nosebleeds can also be due to more serious medical conditions. They can result from clotting disorders, similar to hemophilia, or a low number of platelet cells. Blood-thinning drugs, nasal polyps, tumors, or, occasionally, abnormally fragile blood vessels are other causes. Some believe that high blood pressure can cause nosebleeds. Most nosebleeds are minor and, although alarming and distressing, they are not harmful. The bleeding usually comes from the front part of the nose and can be controlled by firm finger pressure on the nostril against the nasal septum for several minutes. An icepack over the bridge of the nose can be helpful also. If the bleeding is severe or is not controlled with these simple measures, medical attention must be sought. Such bleeding is treated with nasal packing or special balloon catheters, and a cause is then investigated.

SEE ALSO *Blood, Nose, Platelets*

NUCLEIC ACID TESTING

Nucleic acids are present in body cells as well as in viruses, bacteria and other agents of infection. Tests exist that can detect the presence of foreign nucleic acids in the body, and are a very useful diagnostic tool.

NUMBNESS

Numbness is the absence of sensation in a part of the body. It is usually due to damage or degeneration of a peripheral nerve, though it may also be caused by injury to the central nervous system (brain and spinal cord).

Total loss of sensation means all of the nerve is damaged. But if the nerve is partly injured, there may be partial numbness, accompanied by tingling (also known as paresthesia).

Numbness may be temporary, as when the blood supply to a hand or foot is temporarily cut off because of the position a person is in, causing the hand or foot to fall asleep. When the blood supply is restored, normal sensation returns. Or the numbness may be permanent and irreversible. Conditions causing permanent nerve injury include diabetes, degenerative nerve diseases, local injury to the nerves under the skin, pressure on the nerves caused by a herniated disk, nerve damage from the effect of toxins (lead, alcohol or tobacco) or as the side effects of drugs.

It is necessary to treat the underlying condition where possible. A numb hand or foot is prone to accidental injury, so care must be taken to protect it from cuts, bumps or other injuries.

SEE ALSO *Nerves, Nervous system*

NUTRITION

Nutrition is the intake of food and its use by the body. Nutritional research extends into genetics, which examines how differences in genetic makeup can influence the body's reactions to food components; into psychology and eating disorders; into the influence of various foods on mental functions and physical performance; into the reasons why people eat what they do and their personal and cultural beliefs; and into the attitudes, habits and preferences which influence food intake.

Weight is affected by nutrition. If the diet supplies too little energy, body tissues are metabolized and weight generally falls. If too much energy is supplied by the diet, the excess is often stored as fatty tissue under the skin or around major organs, which may lead to high blood pressure and circulatory problems.

Nutritional standards

Good nutrition is fundamental to good health. Many diseases are directly related to either excessive or insufficient intake of certain foods or food types, or to identifiable patterns of food intake. Poor health and the onset of disease are costly to communities as health care services are funded in part or whole by taxes, thus many governments are concerned to raise nutritional standards which in turn will eventually improve the general health of the population. Laws which control the manufacture or supply of certain basic foods are one example of this involvement. The fluoridation of water is a public health measure which is practised in many countries, including the USA, UK and Australia.

The international bodies, the Food and Agricultural Organization (FAO) and the World Health Organization (WHO) jointly publish dietary guidelines in the form of RDAs (recommended dietary allowances) which set nutritional standards based on daily consumption of the basic food components. These figures are used by health professionals to compile or assess diets and may be found as consumer information on food labels or on diet sheets.

Government agencies in most industrialized countries have worked with nutrition scientists to specify the foods and quantities needed to make a healthy diet. These guidelines differ from country to country because they rely on using foods that are locally available and commonly eaten in that country. They all recognize the need to limit consumption of fats, oils and foods high in proteins and generally aim for a diet where around 70 percent of daily energy (calorie or kilojoule) needs are supplied by dietary carbohydrates, mainly from grain and cereal foods.

As developing nations turn away from agriculture to industry and grow in prosperity, their populations change their diets. They turn away from traditional eating habits, generally based on cereals and relatively little protein and fat, and abandon practices such as breast feeding, which ensures the best available nutrition for infants. They can afford to eat more of the foods they like and think of as luxuries, which generally means diets become higher in fat, higher in protein and correspondingly lower in carbohydrates. Infants are raised on breast milk substitutes, bottle feeding sometimes being mistakenly seen as more "advanced" than breast feeding. This inevitably has harmful effects on health, with a rise in dietary diseases caused by high intakes of protein and fat, rising infant malnutrition and higher death rates.

Because of the huge number of food products available in the industrialized nations, it is essential that consumers are aware of the ingredients. Labelling laws ensure that some details are given, including basic nutritional values and the presence of additives, synthetic and natural, which may trigger allergies in sensitized people. The increasing number of additives used to assist in marketing foods and food products has led to regulations intended to avoid potentially harmful consequences.

Energy

Energy derived from nutrients is measured in calories or kilojoules, one calorie being equal to 4.2 kilojoules. The human body at rest consumes energy at the rate of approximately 1.25 calories (5.25 kilojoules) per minute for males and 0.9 calories (3.78 kilojoules) per minute for females; this is known as the basal metabolic rate (BMR). Activity will increase consumption to approximately 5 calories (21 kilojoules) per minute for walking, and up to 15 calories (63 kilojoules) per minute for high-performance sports.

Daily energy needs vary according to lifestyle. A manual worker in a non-mechanized society may need as much as 5,000 calories (21,000 kilojoules) each day, and even more during periods of exceptionally heavy labor. In contrast, a worker in a sedentary occupation in an industrialized society may need as little as 2,000 calories (8,400 kilojoules). Women generally have lower requirements than men, but actual needs vary widely, depending upon body mass and daily activity.

While it is burning food for energy, the body must also replenish dead cells, grow new tissue and maintain all the chemical processes which sustain life. The nutrients in food which must supply all these needs must also include the chemicals and organic compounds which the body cannot manufacture for itself.

A balanced diet

The essence of good nutrition is variety, with expert advice suggesting people should eat up to 30 different foods in the course of a week to ensure they obtain a wide range of nutrients. The food we eat must supply certain basic nutrients which will be available after digestion in a form the body can use. Digestion begins as we chew food, generating saliva which contains enzymes, chemical substances that break down food. Digestion continues as the food enters the stomach where it is bathed in acids and other secretions, and as it passes through the small and large intestines. Nutrients pass through the walls of the intestines into the bloodstream which distributes them throughout the body. Unwanted or undigested food and waste products accumulate in the rectum and pass out of the body through the anus.

Good nutrition in youth lays a groundwork that is an investment in future health, particularly in middle and old age. It starts with a diet based on a wide variety of natural or basic, non-manufactured, foods including meats, fish, nuts, cereals, fruits, vegetables and water. A balanced diet means limiting the intake of fats, oils and protein-rich foods in favor of cereals, fruits and vegetables, and eating in moderate quantities. A modest

Digestion and absorption of nutrients

All the nutrients needed to maintain vital body functions are absorbed into the body via the gastrointestinal tract (or alimentary canal). As it travels along the tract, food is progressively broken down and the proteins, fats, carbohydrates, vitamins and minerals needed by the body are absorbed, leaving the remaining material to be excreted as waste. Many diseases of the digestive tract interfere with these processes and result in nutritional deficiencies.

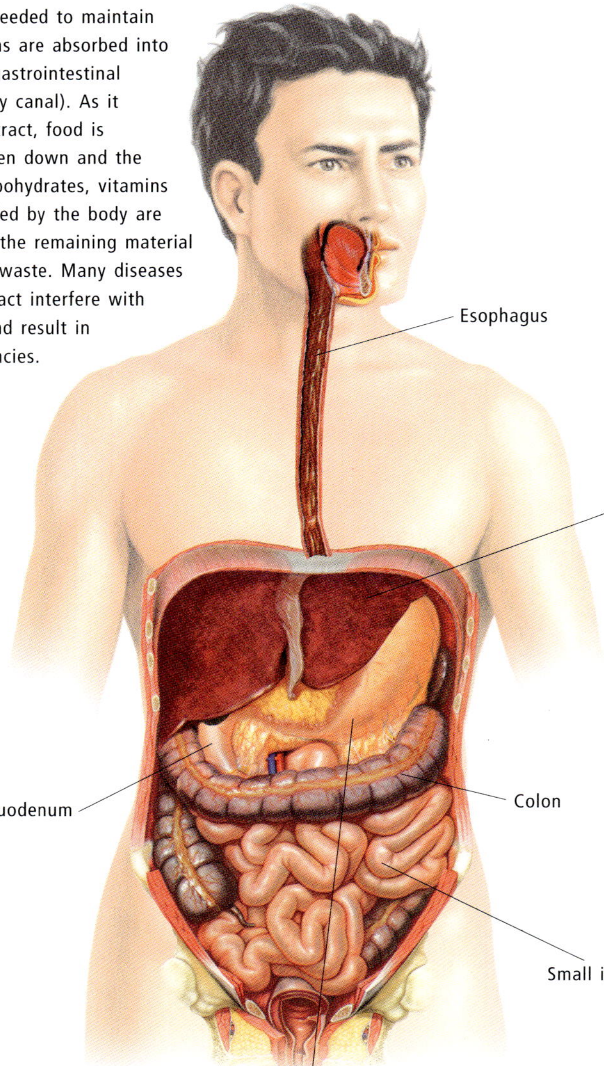

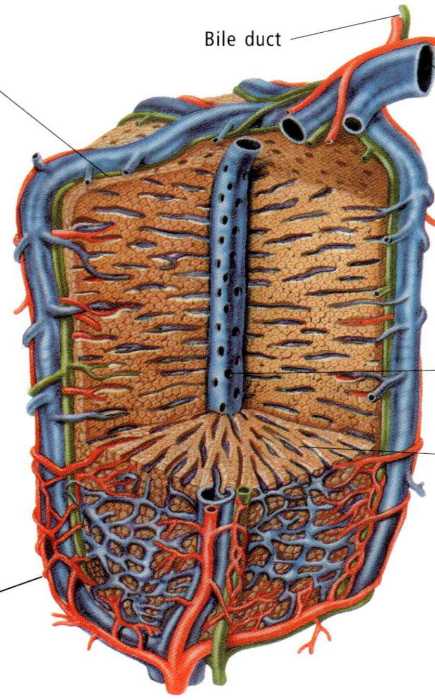

Liver

The absorbed nutrients pass from the small intestine via the bloodstream into the liver. A liver lobule is full of hepatic cells arranged around a vein. The hepatic cells extract nutrients from the blood that flows along the branches of this vein and extract oxygen and fat from the branches of the hepatic arteries. These nutrients are used for metabolism (energy supplies for the body) and to produce bile (for digestion).

Stomach

Food is swallowed via the mouth, travels down through the esophagus and enters the stomach, where it is mixed with acid and pepsin, an enzyme that breaks down proteins into amino acids.

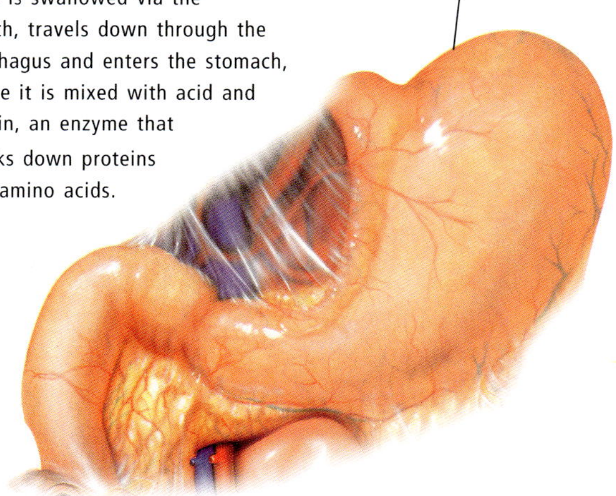

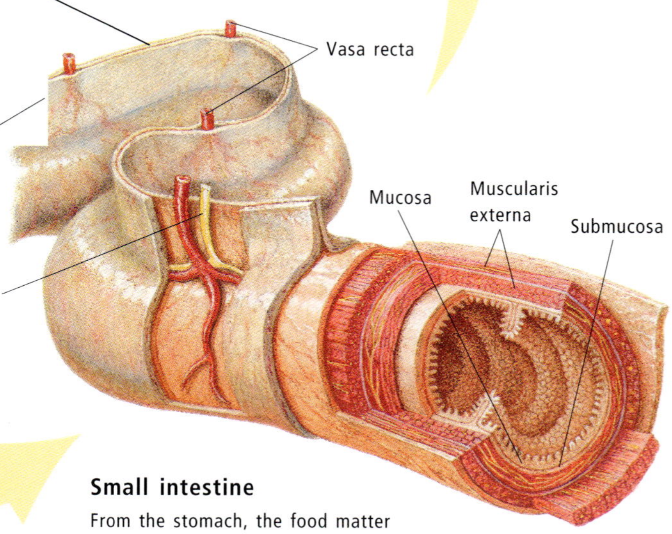

Small intestine

From the stomach, the food matter (now in a semiliquid form called chyme) passes into the small intestine where it mixes with enzymes from the pancreas and bile from the gallbladder. The chyme, containing carbohydrates, proteins and fats, is broken down into simple sugars, amino acids, and fatty acids, which are small enough to be absorbed through the lining of the small intestine. What is left over will pass along the colon (large intestine) and be excreted as feces.

amount of exercise each day is also considered essential in regulating the appetite, which helps to set correct levels for food intake. Exposure to sunlight is important in manufacturing vitamin D, essential for building strong bones.

Nutrients

The nutrients from food are categorized broadly as carbohydrates, fats and oils, cholesterol, proteins, water, minerals and vitamins.

Carbohydrates

Carbohydrates supply 4 calories (16.8 kilojoules) per gram and are the main sources of fuel energy for the body. They include sugars and starches, which are compounds of carbon, hydrogen and oxygen. These are easily and quickly digested, except for their cellulose or fiber content, which humans cannot digest but which is valuable in stimulating the muscular action of the intestine and in carrying waste products out of the body.

Carbohydrates are mainly supplied by plant foods such as fruits and vegetables, and cereals such as wheat, oats and corn, and come in company with many other nutrients of which the body needs only small quantities, like minerals and vitamins. Carbohydrates also come from sugars such as cane sugar, golden syrup and honey, which provide mainly energy for fuel. Sugars are sometimes called "empty calories" and may be a cause of overweight. Carbohydrates should supply about 65 percent of daily calorie intake.

Fats and oils

Fats and oils are necessary only in small quantities. Fats and oils are the most difficult food components to digest and have the highest energy rating by weight at 9 calories (37.8 kilojoules) per gram. They are a hidden component in many manufactured snack foods in which they can easily be eaten to excess, contributing to overweight. They contribute vitamin E but few other micronutrients. Fats and oils may be used as an energy source in very active people, but in others any excess is stored, contributing to overweight. Fats in food carry flavors and provide fatty acids which the body cannot manufacture, the most important of which is linoleic acid, used in building cell structure.

Fats, solid at room temperatures, and oils, liquid at room temperatures, are essentially similar substances which are classified according to their structure as saturated, monounsaturated or polyunsaturated. Fats or oils should supply between 15 and 30 percent of daily calorie needs.

Saturated fats are mostly animal fats, found in meat and dairy products. This group is believed to aid the deposition of cholesterol on arterial walls, impeding blood circulation and increasing the risk of heart attack.

Monounsaturated fats are found mainly in olive, canola and peanut (groundnut) oils. These fats are considered to have the most beneficial effect in lowering cholesterol levels in the bloodstream.

Polyunsaturated fats are found in sunflower, safflower, corn and soybean oils, and the oils used in making margarine. These also can have a beneficial effect on cholesterol levels, but only when their consumption accounts for 10 percent or less of the daily calorie intake. When eaten in excess they may contribute to raising blood cholesterol levels.

Cholesterol, a substance similar to fat, is manufactured by the liver from the breakdown of saturated fats ingested in the diet; it is also supplied in small quantities in eggs and animal foods. It is important in building and repairing cells, the production of sex hormones and the bile acids which aid digestion. Dietary fats provide the mechanism for transporting cholesterol in the bloodstream to cells, and to the liver for excretion.

Cholesterol is incorporated into compounds called lipoproteins for circulation in the bloodstream. There are two types, high-density lipoprotein (HDL) and low-density lipoprotein (LDL). HDL helps to excrete waste cholesterol from the body and is associated with a low risk of heart and circulatory disorders. LDL forms deposits on the walls of arteries, leading to atherosclerosis, which carries a high risk of heart disease. This condition may result from a diet too high in saturated fats.

Proteins

Proteins are complex substances made up of over 20 amino acids, many of which, the essential amino acids, cannot be synthesized inside the body and must be supplied by foods. Proteins are used to build and repair cells in every part of the body, from hair to internal organs, bones, muscle, skin and toenails; they also transport oxygen from lungs

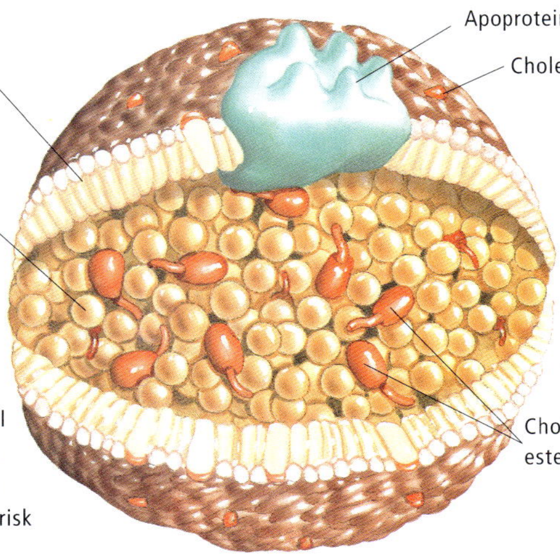

Cholesterol
Cholesterol travels round the body in lipoproteins and helps to build and repair cells. Excess cholesterol can be dangerous to health as high levels circulating in the blood can increase the risk of atherosclerosis.

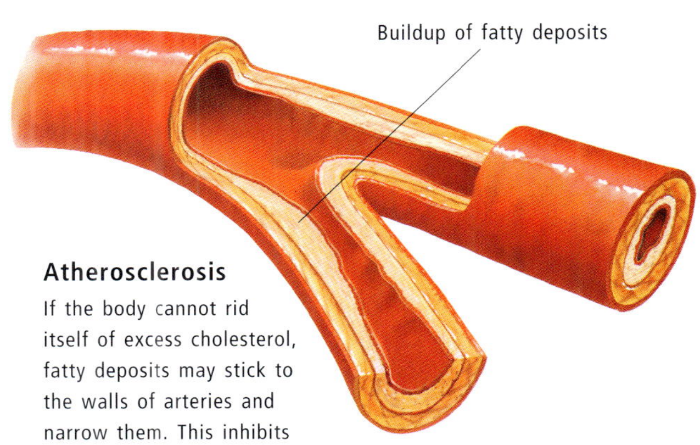

Atherosclerosis
If the body cannot rid itself of excess cholesterol, fatty deposits may stick to the walls of arteries and narrow them. This inhibits blood flow and may lead to a heart attack.

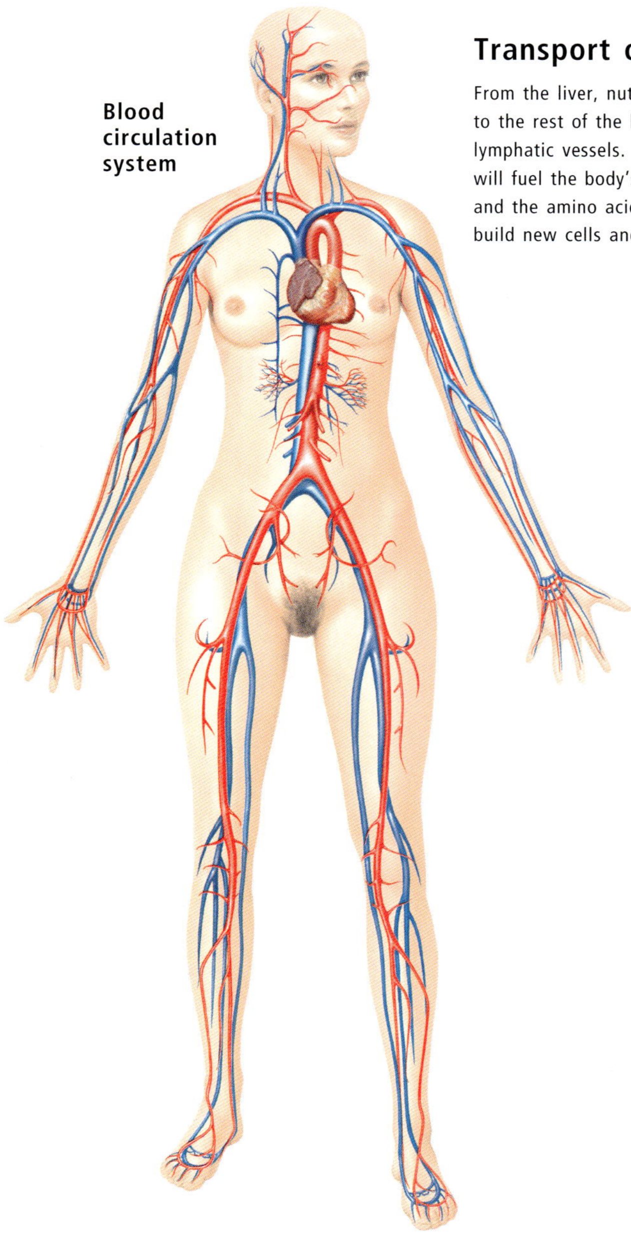

Transport of nutrients

From the liver, nutrients are transported to the rest of the body in the blood and lymphatic vessels. The sugars and fats will fuel the body's chemical reactions and the amino acids will be used to build new cells and body tissues.

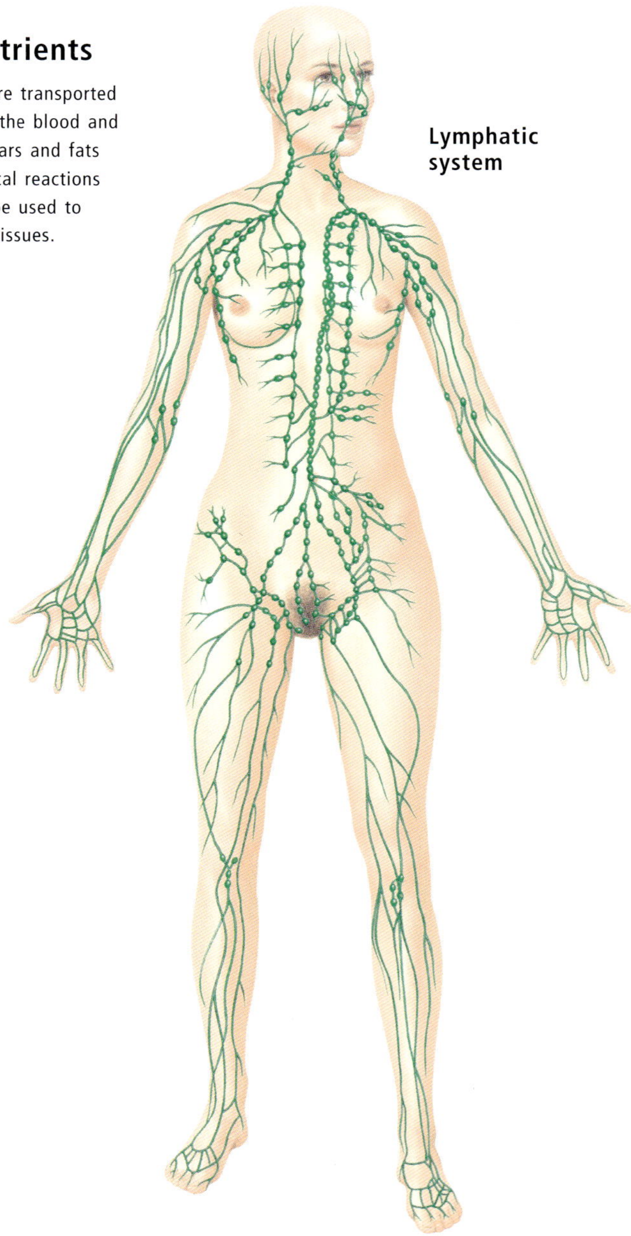

to cells and act as chemical messengers. Animal foods (meat, eggs, milk, fish and poultry) in the diet supply complete proteins containing all the amino acids that cannot be synthesized. Plant foods such as soybeans, cereals and nuts each lack one or more essential amino acid and thus must be eaten in combinations which supply all the amino acids to provide a complete source of protein. Excess protein can be burned as energy if required but is likely to be stored as excess weight in many individuals. Proteins should supply up to 20 percent of daily calorie needs.

Water

Water is essential for life. It forms part of every cell in the body and is a major component of blood. The human body is about two-thirds water, men's bodies containing a greater percentage of water than women's, and that level must be maintained for health. Loss of only 1 or 2 percent of bodyweight in fluids causes dehydration with headache, fatigue, loss of appetite, dizziness, dry mouth and eyes. Loss of 10 percent bodyweight brings severe illness and of 20 percent almost certain death. Chronic dehydration may cause permanent damage to internal organs.

One problem in maintaining fluid levels is that signals of thirst do not arise until after mild dehydration has begun. The body loses water constantly through sweat, urine, feces and respiration.

For proper hydration, males should drink about 3 quarts (3 liters) of water each day and females at least $2\frac{1}{4}$ quarts (2.5 liters); recent research in North America, however, has indicated that people drink only about half that amount.

Water aids efficient removal of the body's waste matter. Excretion of toxins from the bloodstream depends on the availability of water for production of urine. Water is a major component of foods, particularly vegetables and fruits, and has a nil calorie value. As food sources will not supply the body's needs, adults should aim to drink about eight glasses of plain water a day, regardless of any other fluids ingested.

Minerals

Minerals are inorganic chemical elements that occur in small amounts in most foods.

More than twenty are required for good nutrition and health and are better obtained from eating a wide variety of foods than taken as supplements.

Iron, supplied by meat, milk and some plant foods, is vital in binding oxygen to red blood cells. Blood loss increases the need for iron and extra amounts may also be needed in pregnancy and throughout breast feeding. Calcium is present in bones and blood plasma and its levels are maintained by hormones. Absorption of calcium is inefficient and the diet must contain more than is theoretically needed. Sodium is required in very limited amounts to maintain intracellular fluid volume. Too much causes edema or fluid retention and may contribute to high blood pressure. Iodine, magnesium, phosphorus, potassium, sulfur and selenium are other minerals vital to good nutrition.

Vitamins

Vitamins are organic compounds identified by the letters A through K, most of which cannot be synthesized within the body. When vitamins are not supplied by the diet, symptoms of deficiency will occur. A deficiency of vitamin C (a vitamin found only in fresh fruits and vegetables) often produced scurvy on early voyages of exploration, causing bleeding gums and general ill health; in 1754 orange or lemon juice was found to prevent it. A lack of vitamin D will prevent proper bone development in children, a condition known as rickets, with gross deformities in limbs. Night blindness is one effect of a vitamin A (retinol) deficiency, because it directly affects the adjustment of the eye to dim light.

Nutrition through life

Pregnancy is a time to give special attention to good nutrition as the developing fetus needs a rich supply of nutrients for proper growth. It is not necessary to eat more but much more important to eat foods of good nutritional value. Energy value from foods should be from 1,700 to 2,100 calories (7,140 to 8,820 kilojoules) per day. Nutrient deficiencies will be made up from the mother's body tissues before the fetus is deprived. Folic acid requirements increase in pregnancy when it is needed in forming hemoglobin, the oxygen-carrying component of red blood cells and for proper neural tube development. Folate deficiency can cause anemia, and in pregnancy can result in premature birth, low birth weight or neural tube defects in the baby.

Children's growth and mental development are strongly influenced by nutrition, from the moment of conception. Good nutrition is important in laying the foundation for healthy bones, muscles and teeth. Poor nutrition and an unbalanced diet can result in obesity very early in life, in abnormal cholesterol levels and high blood pressure. These disorders lay a poor foundation for health in adulthood. Children are particularly at risk of deficiency diseases as their reserves are low and their nutrient needs high. Deprivation of nutrients over a long period may cause permanent physical or mental damage. Hydration is also very important, as children's bodies lose fluid fast during episodes of vomiting and diarrhea.

Adolescence is also a time of rapid growth and high nutritional needs, and a time when good nutrition can suffer through outside influences such as fad diets. Eating disorders that restrict food intake, such as anorexia, can delay the onset of the menarche in girls and severely affect growth. Disorders which involve vomiting can deplete the body's reserves of fat and protein, producing all the symptoms and health risks of starvation.

Women going through menopause should pay particular attention to their calcium intake as estrogen levels decrease at this time, reducing calcium levels in the body and decreasing bone strength. Osteoporosis in older people is the eventual consequence of seriously depleted calcium levels; it can become evident earlier in life as a consequence of poor diet. Medical advice may prescribe hormone replacement therapy and calcium supplements at menopause.

Ageing does not necessarily bring special nutritional needs. Energy requirements at any age are regulated mostly by body weight and activity levels. Nutrients are required throughout life to replenish body tissues and rebuild cells. Illness or disability are likely to be factors affecting the desire to eat and the absorption of nutrients from foods, and may have more severe consequences in an older person than in a younger person with greater reserves. Attention to diet and daily exercise are important for men and women as age advances. It is important to eat a variety of foods to ensure a good supply of vitamins and minerals.

Vegetarianism

Vegetarianism is the practice of avoiding animal foods in the diet, eating only foods of plant origin. It is generally seen as a healthful alternative. Properly constructed vegetarian or vegan diets supply all the body's needs and contribute very little to overweight or dietary disease. Ovo-lacto vegetarians eat eggs, cheese, milk and milk products as well as plant foods. A vegan diet is more strictly vegetarian and adherents neither eat nor wear anything of animal origin.

A macrobiotic diet incorporates many Japanese foods into a diet based on beans, vegetables and whole-grain foods combined with a lifestyle philosophy that seeks harmony between body and mind. Foods are classed as *yin* or *yang* and these elements are balanced to achieve optimum health. The principles of food combinations used in vegetarianism are applied to ensure the diet provides complete proteins.

SEE ALSO *Breast feeding, Cholesterol, Digestive system, Eating disorders, Fats, Minerals, Obesity, Proteins, Vitamins, Weight*

N

NYSTAGMUS

Nystagmus is involuntary circular movement of the eyes. It may occur normally, for example, when a person is looking out the window of a moving vehicle: the slow phase of the nystagmus occurs as the eyes drift while maintaining the gaze at the object outside, the quick phase takes place when the eyes dart back to their original position.

Nystagmus may be horizontal (side to side movements), vertical (in an up and down direction) or rotary (in a circular pattern). It may occur without any underlying disorder and usually does not affect vision. Nystagmus may also be a symptom of disease; it can be the result of injury to the cerebellum in the brain, injury to the labyrinth of the inner ear, hereditary diseases or ingestion of toxins (poisons). The underlying condition will need to be treated.

SEE ALSO *Eye*

OBESITY

Obesity is the build-up of excess fat in the body, the simple cause being consistent overeating (consuming more calories in food than the body needs). The underlying reasons for obesity may be far more complex.

The presence of obesity is usually obvious overweight, but overweight and obesity are not synonymous. Athletes and body-builders and those who inherit a large skeletal frame can register weights well above average for their height. This may be due to development of muscle tissue rather than fat. When weight is 20 percent or more above the optimum, obesity is the most likely cause. Weight-for-height tables and calculation of the Body Mass Index (BMI) are not definitive but can be used as a guide to individual optimal weight, with a BMI greater than 30 indicating a need for treatment (normally BMI should be about 20–25).

Adipose or fatty tissue is present throughout the body, and is stored mainly at sites of the greatest numbers of fat cells—the hips, thighs, buttocks and abdomen. Fat also accumulates in a layer beneath the skin and in membranes coating internal organs and lining cavities such as the abdominal cavity, one of the body's main fat stores.

Obesity in childhood results in the creation of an abnormal number of fat cells, which do not disappear when weight is reduced. The fat cells lose only some of their fat content, but they retain their capacity for fat storage, giving the individual a tendency to overweight in adolescence and adult life.

An overweight child can be disinclined to take part in physical activities. Overweight can be worsened by the inactivity which results from spending time on sedentary leisure pursuits such as playing computer games and watching television. When activity levels are low, fewer calories are burned and more are stored as fat. The overweight child who is unable to keep up with peer-group sports and games may suffer low self-esteem, a factor which can lead to seeking comfort in food, aggravating the problem. Puberty and adolescence bring increasing body awareness and fast growth, which can turn mild obesity into a more serious problem.

Other factors in the development of obesity include the following.

Disorders of the hypothalamus, the part of the brain which regulates appetite, can result in obesity.

Genetic influences (inherited physical traits) can favor weight gain.

Hormonal disorders may upset hormone levels and cause weight gain.

Low levels of physical activity can be a problem at all ages, as walking and manual labor give way to car transport, sedentary occupations and leisure time spent in front of the television.

Side effects from drugs can cause weight gain; corticosteroid drugs, in particular, have been identified as having this effect.

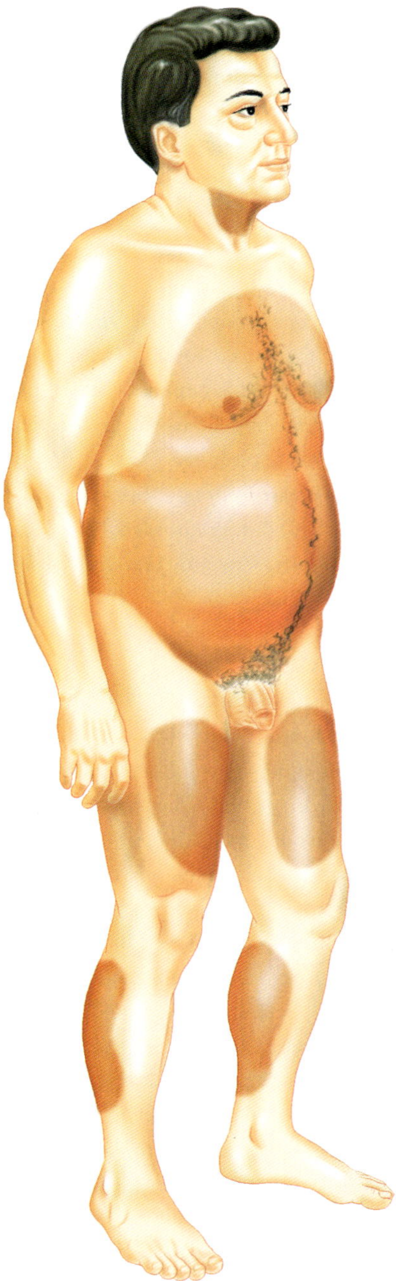

Obesity—male fat distribution

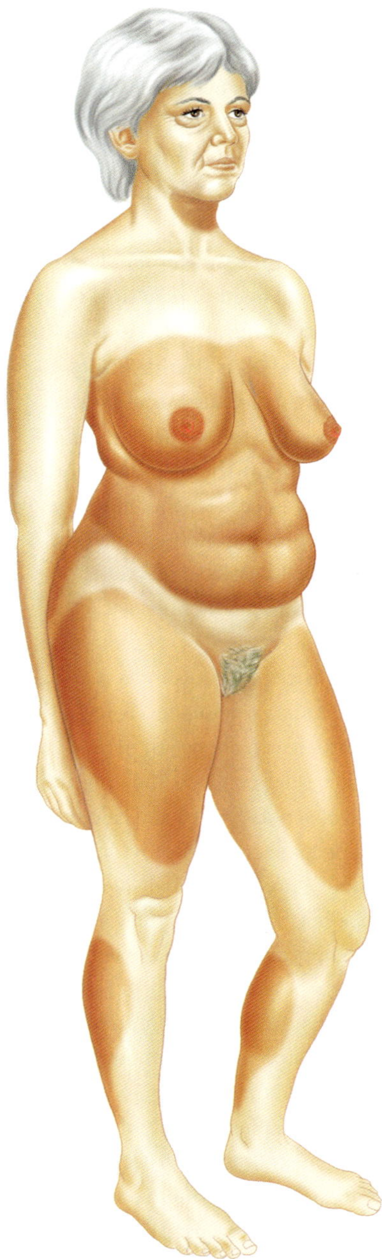

Obesity—female fat distribution

Obesity

Obesity is defined as an abnormal increase of the percentage of fat in the body. It may be a symptom of a physical or behavioral disorder, or the result of genetic influences. Fat tends to be mainly deposited around the abdomen and top of the legs.

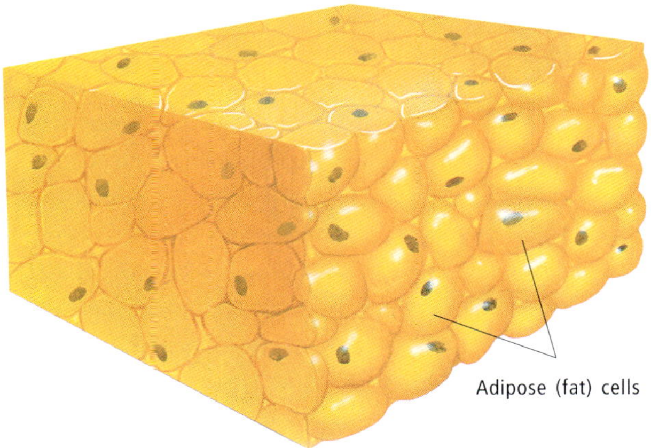

Fatty tissue
Adipose (fat) cells occur in greater numbers around the hips, thighs, buttocks and abdomen, creating deposits of fatty tissue. The number of fat cells in the body is determined during the first few years of childhood.

Obesity generally brings greater risk of cancer, gallbladder disease, menstrual disorders, adult-onset diabetes, high blood pressure and raised blood cholesterol levels which can lead to heart disease. Overweight increases the load on the heart, lungs, spine and all the weight-bearing joints. Upper body obesity, common in men, is a greater health risk than lower body obesity, more common in women. Paradoxically, women are 8 times more likely to seek help with weight reduction than are men. Treatment may involve both increasing physical activity and reducing weight.

Successful weight loss must be followed with a long-term regime to ensure that weight is maintained at optimal levels. Weight loss clinics, self-help groups and individual supervision by dietitians are common methods. Prescription drugs may be used to assist initial weight loss but must be combined with therapy and diet re-education for long-term success. Surgery, to reduce stomach size and eating capacity, is a more drastic choice, carrying risks of complication and death alongside the promise of a permanent solution to a distressing and life-threatening condition.

SEE ALSO *Body Mass Index, Eating disorders, Fats, Hypothalamus, Nutrition*

OBSESSIVE-COMPULSIVE DISORDER

Obsessive-compulsive disorder (OCD) is a psychiatric illness in which obsessive thoughts lead to compulsive actions such as repeated counting, cleaning or checking. Sufferers are plagued by persistent unwelcome thoughts or images that can sometimes be of a violent or sexual nature. Many are obsessed with germs or dirt and may continually wash their hands. Others spend hours rearranging objects. However, they derive little, if any, relief from their compulsive behavior.

The exact cause is not known. Once thought to have psychological origins, recent research suggests that OCD could be genetic and that damage to the basal ganglia, a part of the brain that controls automatic activities, could be a contributing factor. Streptococcal infection is also thought to trigger the disorder in some sufferers.

Symptoms fluctuate and may last for decades. OCD produces a high level of anxiety, interrupts the normal flow of life and may be accompanied by depression. It can also contribute to other problems, such as eating disorders.

Treatment is by a combination of antidepressant medication and behavioral therapy. One behavioral treatment is exposure and response prevention, where sufferers voluntarily expose themselves to the trigger of their disorder and are encouraged to avoid their compulsive action for as long as possible.

SEE ALSO *Antidepressants, Behavior therapy, Depression, Personality disorders*

OBSTRUCTIVE JAUNDICE

Jaundice is a condition in which there is yellowing of the skin and eyes due to an increased concentration in the blood of a

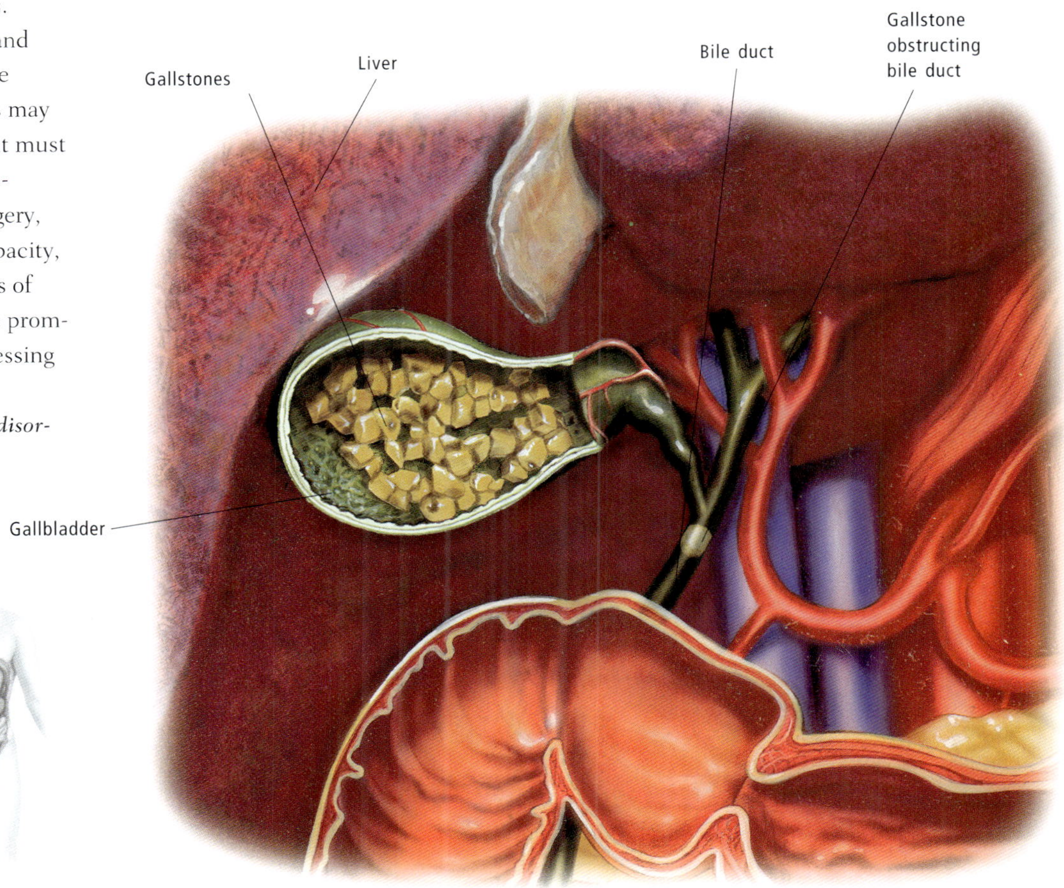

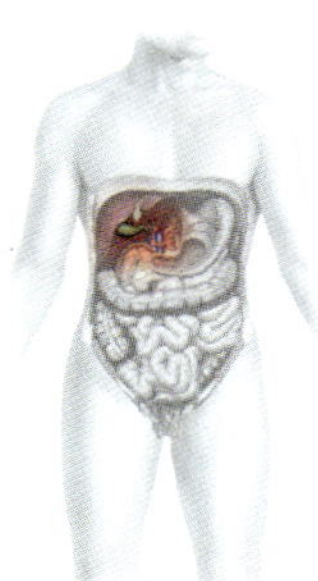

Obstructive jaundice
Obstructive jaundice results when bile is unable to be discharged through the bile ducts into the intestine. Causes include gallstones and cancer of the pancreas and bowel.

chemical called bilirubin. If the bilirubin gets into the blood because of obstruction of the ducts leading from the liver to the duodenum, the condition is known as obstructive jaundice. Common causes of obstruction of these ducts include gallstones, cancers of the gallbladder or pancreas, hepatitis, pregnancy, parasites and inflammation of the pancreas (pancreatitis). Patients with obstructive jaundice will experience itching of the skin due to accumulation of bile salts in the skin. Treatment will depend on the cause: gallstones should be removed, ducts obstructed by cancer should be dilated.

SEE ALSO *Duodenum, Gallstones, Hepatitis, Jaundice, Liver, Pancreas, Pancreatitis*

OLFACTORY SYSTEM

The olfactory system is concerned with the sense of smell, through the detection of airborne chemical substances in the nose. Odors are sensed by special nerve cells in the lining of the nose. Sensations of smell are conveyed by the olfactory nerves to a part of the brain, lying above the nose, referred to as the rhinencephalon or limbic lobe. The senses of smell and taste act together for the assessment of food.

In the roof of the nasal cavities, the mucous membrane contains nerve cells that are specialized for the reception of odors. This region of the mucous membrane is known as the olfactory epithelium or olfactory organ, and has a total area of about 1 square inch (5 square centimeters). The surface of the epithelium is kept moist, to dissolve odors from passing air. The olfactory receptor cells, of which there are about 100 million, are modified neurons. A dendrite extends from each cell body towards the surface of the epithelium, where it terminates as a swelling termed an olfactory vesicle. This vesicle is specialized for the reception of smell. The sensation is carried by an unmyelinated axon (nerve fiber) from each receptor cell into the connective tissue beneath the epithelium, where it joins with others to form bundles of olfactory nerve fibers, called the olfactory nerves. These, about 20 in number, pass through holes (foramina) in the cribriform plate of the ethmoid bone, to terminate in the brain at the olfactory bulbs.

The olfactory bulbs are ovoid structures forming forward extensions of the olfactory area of the brain. In the olfactory bulbs, axons from olfactory sensory cells converge and end (synapse) on dendrites of cells known as mitral cells because of their shape (conical). Each mitral cell receives approximately 1000 axons. These synapses between olfactory sensory cells and mitral cells are grouped to form conspicuous clusters known as glomeruli. The axons of the mitral cells run back (posteriorly) to terminate in the cerebral cortex and adjacent parts of the forebrain, providing a pathway for conscious perception of smell. The pathway from the olfactory receptors to the cerebral cortex therefore has only one synapse (in the olfactory bulb), a more direct connection than that for any other type of sensation. Other cells (interneurons) in the olfactory bulb link one glomerulus with another, and also link the two olfactory bulbs across the midline. Axons from mitral cells and other cells of the olfactory bulb travel through the

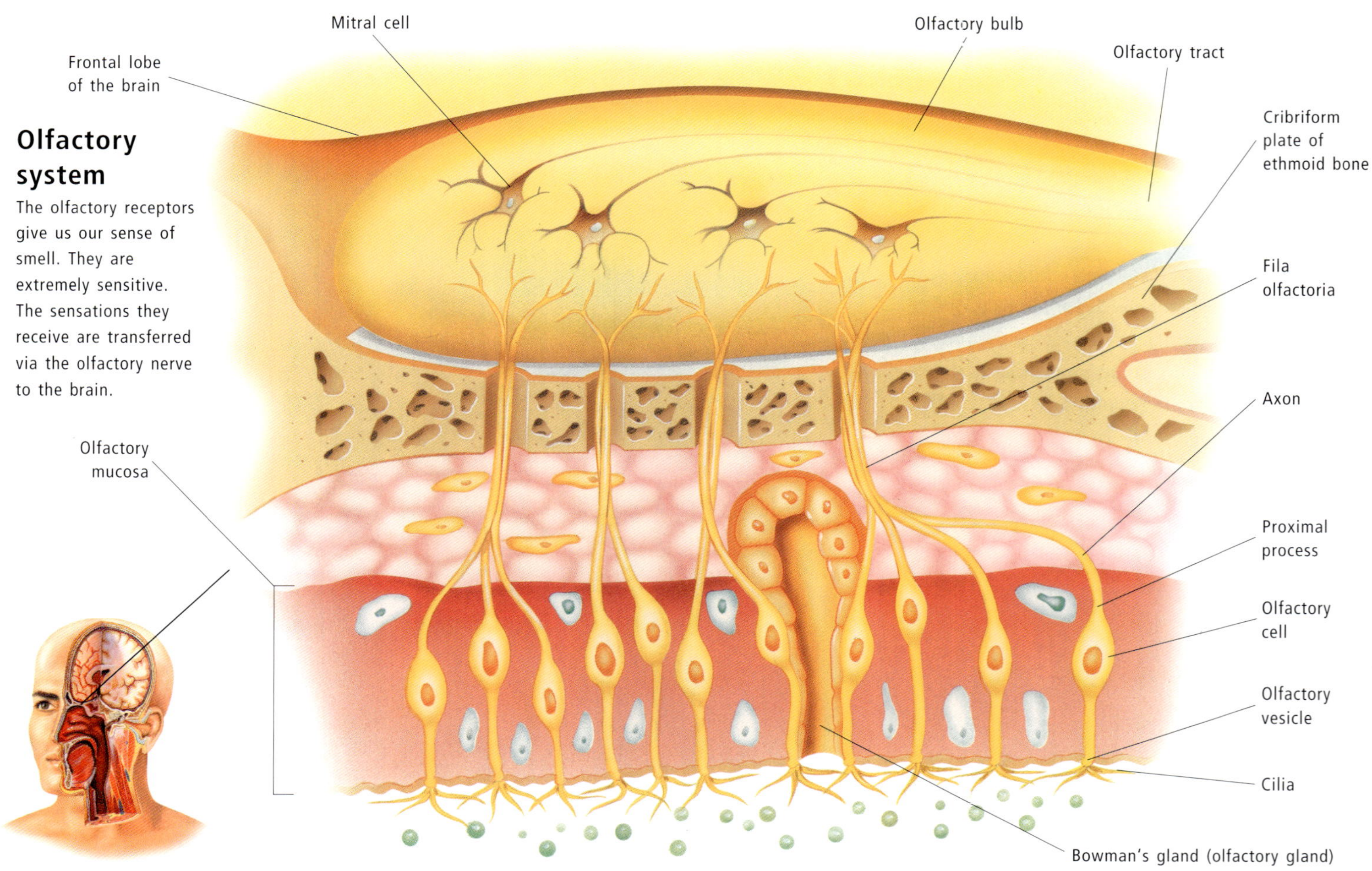

Olfactory system

The olfactory receptors give us our sense of smell. They are extremely sensitive. The sensations they receive are transferred via the olfactory nerve to the brain.

olfactory tract and terminate, either directly or through relay neurons, in two areas of the brain called the medial olfactory area and the lateral olfactory area.

Both medial and lateral olfactory areas have neural connections to the hypothalamus, hippocampus and brain stem nuclei. These latter areas control automatic responses to smells, particularly feeding activities (such as salivation) and also emotional responses (such as pleasure, fear, and sexual drives).

Loss of the sense of smell (anosmia) is most commonly due to blockage of the nose, for example, by a common cold. Hallucinations of smell may be due to physical or psychological causes, including tumors of the temporal lobe.

SEE ALSO *Neurons, Nose, Smell*

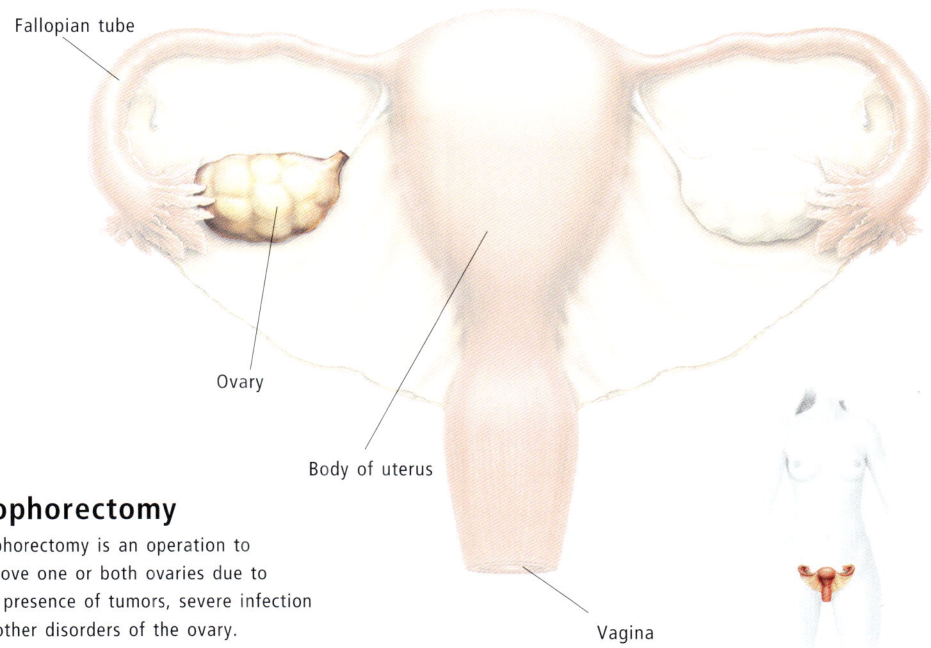

Oophorectomy

Oophorectomy is an operation to remove one or both ovaries due to the presence of tumors, severe infection or other disorders of the ovary.

OMPHALOCELE

An omphalocele is a congenital abnormality of the abdominal wall occurring in approximately one out of every 5,000 births. The normal layers of the abdominal wall are missing at the navel; only the thin peritoneal membrane lies between the intestines (which protrude through the opening) and the air. Urgent surgery is required to repair the defect so as to prevent peritonitis and dehydration of the intestines.Other birth defects that may be associated with the condition will require treatment.

SEE ALSO *Abdomen, Congenital abnormalities, Intestines*

OOPHORECTOMY

Oophorectomy means surgical removal of one or both ovaries (unilateral or bilateral oophorectomy). Ovaries are removed for a variety of reasons, including extensive or very large cysts, or ovarian cancer. Oophorectomy may sometimes accompany hysterectomy, even though the ovaries are not diseased. It has been argued that removing the ovaries avoids possible future problems of cysts or ovarian cancer. However, the advantage of leaving at least one ovary in premenopausal women is the avoidance of symptoms of premature menopause and the possible need for hormone replacement therapy.

SEE ALSO *Hysterectomy, Ovarian cysts, Ovaries*

OPHTHALMOSCOPY

Ophthalmoscopy is examination of the interior and the retina of the eye with an ophthalmoscope, an instrument about the size of a flashlight, which projects a beam of light through the pupil. The instrument allows the physician to view the interior and back portion of the eye, including the retina, optic disc and blood vessels, and to detect and evaluate symptoms of eye disease such as glaucoma, or the effect of other diseases such as diabetes, atherosclerosis or hypertension on the eye.

SEE ALSO *Eye*

OPPORTUNISTIC INFECTION

Infections that take advantage of a weakness in the immune defenses are called "opportunistic". They are common in HIV/AIDS, cancers, blood disease such as leukemia, bone marrow disease and aplastic anemia.

Examples of opportunistic infections include candidiasis (thrush)—a fungal infection of the mouth, throat, or vagina, cytomegalovirus, a viral infection that causes eye disease that can lead to blindness, herpes simplex, viruses which can cause oral herpes (cold sores) or genital herpes, *Pneumocystis carinii*, which can cause a fatal pneumonia, and toxoplasmosis, a brain infection.

Treatment involves correcting (if possible) the underlying condition and treating the invading organism with antibiotic, antifungal or antiviral medications—usually by intravenous injection in an isolation ward in hospital. In the absence of a normal immune system, opportunistic infections are often fatal.

SEE ALSO *AIDS, Candidiasis, Cold sores, Cytomegalovirus, Genital herpes, Herpes simplex, HIV, Pneumonia, Toxoplasmosis*

OPTIC ATROPHY

Optic atrophy is wasting or degeneration of the optic nerve, the nerve that transmits the impulses for the sense of sight. It can occur in one or both eyes, and is the end result of some type of injury or damage to the optic nerve, such as severe head injury or anoxia (lack of oxygen). It may also occur as a hereditary disorder appearing in childhood. Optic atrophy usually results in blindness and there is no cure.

SEE ALSO *Blindness, Eye, Optic nerve*

OPTIC NERVE

The optic nerve connects the eye to the brain and is the second of the 12 cranial nerves. It contains the long processes (axons) of ganglion cells in the retina, the light-sensitive layer at the back of the eye. The retina and optic nerve grow out from the brain and are actually part of the central nervous system. The axons of the ganglion cells converge at the optic disk (blind spot), where the optic nerve leaves the eye. The nerve continues to

O

Optic nerve

The optic nerve carries impulses for the sense of sight. Damage to the optic nerve may be the result of infections, metabolic or nutritional disorders, or an accident. Diabetes mellitus and anemia may affect the optic nerve and lead to loss of sight.

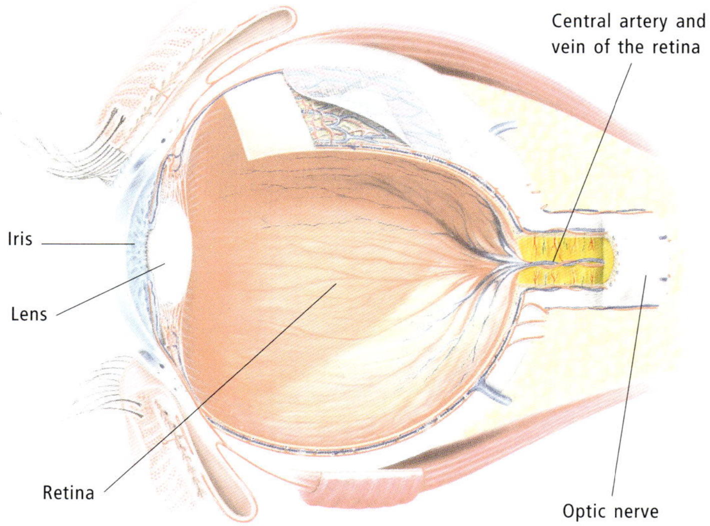

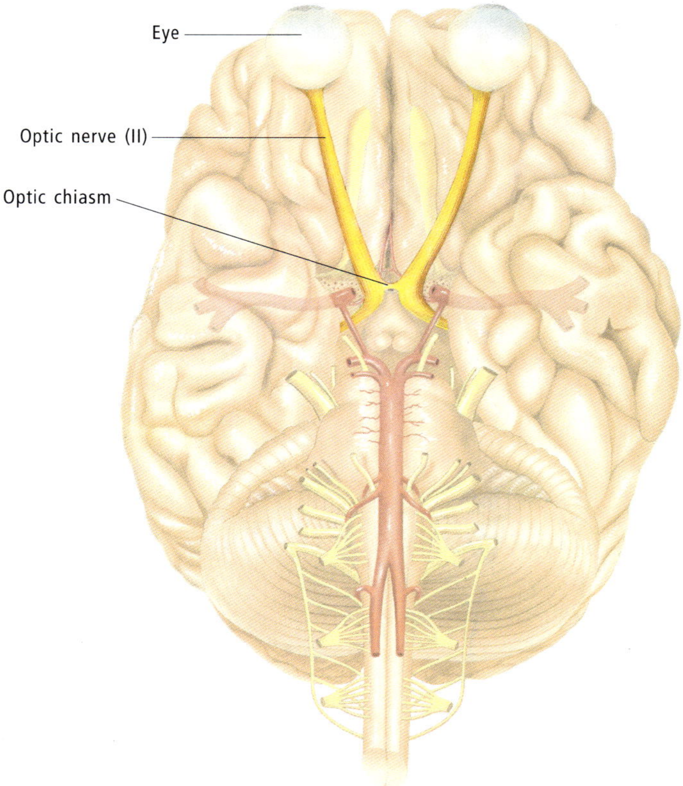

the optic chiasm, where it joins the nerve from the other eye. There are about a million axons in each optic nerve, as well as blood vessels supplying the retina. Action potentials in the nerve are transmitted to the brain to provide visual sensations.

Damage to the optic nerve can cause partial or complete blindness in the affected eye. The nerve can be inflamed at the optic disk where it leaves the eyeball (optic neuritis). This can occur in multiple sclerosis as well as in some diseases of blood vessels, such as temporal arteritis. When viewed through an ophthalmoscope, the normal optic disk looks like a cup, but in optic neuritis it appears swollen and red. Treatment to reduce the inflammation is important, to prevent blindness. The optic disk is also swollen (papilledema) when there are increases in pressure within the brain (increased intracranial pressure).

SEE ALSO *Cranial nerves, Eye, Nerves, Nervous system, Neuritis, Papilledema, Retina*

OPTIC NEURITIS

Optic neuritis is inflammation of the optic nerve, causing sudden partial blindness in the affected eye. It may occur as the result of a viral infection, an autoimmune process or in multiple sclerosis. The symptoms are a sudden loss of vision in one eye and pain on movement of the affected eye. Fortunately, vision often returns to normal in a few weeks. If intravenous steroids are given, visual acuity may return earlier than this. However, if the condition is due to herpes zoster or systemic lupus erythematosus (an autoimmune disease), then complete recovery is less likely.

SEE ALSO *Autoimmune disease, Eye, Lupus erythematosus, Multiple sclerosis, Neuritis, Sight*

ORAL CANCER

Oral cancer is a term that encompasses cancer of the lips, tongue, the floor of the mouth, the inside of the cheek, the gums and the palate. Oral cancers occur most commonly in older people, more commonly in men than in women, in people whose dental and oral hygiene is poor and who smoke cigarettes, cigars or pipes, or who are heavy users of alcohol. The cause is thought to be the irritant effect of these toxins.

Oral cancers are malignant squamous cell carcinomas. They begin as a small, painless lump or ulcer on the tongue, lips or elsewhere in the mouth. They grow and spread rapidly, ulcerating and bleeding, and as they become larger they cause difficulties in talking, chewing and swallowing.

The diagnosis is conformed by a biopsy of the cancer. Treatment is surgical removal, which may involve radical head and neck surgery if the cancer has spread to the lymph nodes in the neck. Surgery is sometimes combined with radiation therapy. Early detection gives the best hope of a cure, but unfortunately most cancers are advanced by the time of diagnosis. About 50 percent of people with oral cancer will survive longer than 5 years.

SEE ALSO *Cancer, Mouth, Smoking, Squamous cell carcinoma*

ORAL CONTRACEPTIVES

The most common oral contraceptive in current use is the low-dose combination pill containing both estrogen and progesterone. Progesterone-only pills are also available but tend to be used only when the combined pill is contraindicated. Some combination pills contain the same concentrations of estrogen and progesterone throughout the dose cycle, in others the relative amounts of the hormones are varied in pills to be taken at different times of the cycle. The rationale of these latter preparations is that variable hormone levels resemble the natural situation more closely.

Estrogen and progesterone in the oral contraceptive have to be in a form which can be taken by mouth and still remain active, which precludes use of natural hormones. If natural hormones are taken by mouth they are broken down in the liver before they enter the general blood circulation of the body.

Synthetic hormones resemble the natural ones closely but have a slight modification to their molecular structure which overcomes this problem. The estrogens are either ethinyl estradiol or mestranol. The most commonly used synthetic progesterones are levonorgestrel, norgestrel and norethindrone.

Oral contraceptives are usually taken for 21 days and then stopped for 7 days, during which time withdrawal bleeding occurs. This mimics but is not the same as a period. The regimen may be varied if it is desired to avoid withdrawal bleeding at a particularly inconvenient time. Anecdotal evidence also suggests that at least some women elect to take the pill continuously rather than cyclically and thus avoid the nuisance of withdrawal bleeding altogether. During a normal menstrual cycle, a few follicles develop in the ovaries during the first half of the cycle (the follicular phase) under the influence of follicle stimulating hormone (FSH) from the pituitary. These follicles produce increasing amounts of estrogen and this in turn stimulates a surge of luteinising hormone (LH) from the pituitary which induces ovulation. The amount of estrogen and progesterone in the pill is approximately the same as that present at the beginning of the follicular phase.

Estrogen levels in a normal cycle would rise by about six- to ten-fold during the natural follicular phase, but this does not occur with the contraceptive pill. Low levels of estrogen and progesterone result in decreased production of FSH and LH by the pituitary, which in turn suppresses ovarian function and prevents ovulation.

Oral contraceptives affect other parts of the reproductive tract besides the ovary. Progesterone makes the cervical mucus thick and impermeable to sperm, and both estrogen and progesterone affect the motility of the fallopian tube and thus may reduce gamete or zygote transport. Changes occur in the endometrium that render it hostile to implantation and it also becomes thin after prolonged contraceptive use. These changes are reversible when the pill is stopped and regular ovulations are restored in the vast majority of women within 3 to 6 months.

Progesterone-only pills often do not inhibit ovulation but instead function by causing changes in cervical mucus and the endometrium as described above. It is also thought that they may interfere with capacitation of sperm in the female tract.

The most obvious advantage of the pill is its almost 100 percent reliability and it is thought that the occasional failures are more often due to non-compliance than to method failure. The pill also offers many non-contraceptive benefits, including relief from a wide range of menstrual disorders and reduction in the incidence of ovarian cysts, rheumatoid arthritis, ectopic pregnancies and pelvic inflammatory disease. There is also decreased risk of endometrial and ovarian cancer. The most serious of the reported disadvantages are disorders of the cardiovascular system in some individuals. These include abnormal blood clots (thromboembolism), stroke and some elevation of blood pressure. Risks appear to increase slightly with age but are reduced considerably in non-smokers and with low-dose pills. Many of the other problems reported in the past have been shown to be due to other causes or of minimal significance with the low-dose pill. Some drugs, including certain antibiotics and anticonvulsants, may reduce the effectiveness of oral contraceptives to some extent.

SEE ALSO *Contraception, Estrogens, Follicle stimulating hormone, Hormones, Hypertension, Menstruation, Ovulation, Reproductive systems, Stroke, Thromboembolism*

ORCHITIS

Orchitis is an inflammation of one or both of the testicles. It is caused by viruses (especially mumps), bacteria and sexually transmitted organisms, such as those that cause gonorrhea or chlamydia. Orchitis often occurs with infection of the prostate (prostatitis), infection of the urethra (urethritis) and infection of the epididymis (epididymitis).

Symptoms of orchitis are pain in the groin and testicle, pain with urination (dysuria), pain with intercourse or ejaculation and, sometimes, a discharge from the penis. Lymph nodes in the groin may be tender and enlarged and, when a rectal examination is performed, the prostate gland may be tender and enlarged as well.

Urinalysis and blood tests will confirm the diagnosis and isolate the organism responsible. The condition is treated with analgesics and antibiotics (if caused by bacteria). If the condition is sexually transmitted, sexual partners must also be treated. A full recovery is usual, though sterility may follow mumps orchitis.

SEE ALSO *Chlamydia, Epididymis, Gonorrhea, Mumps, Prostatitis, Testes, Urethritis*

ORTHODONTICS

Orthodontics is a branch of dentistry concerned with the diagnosis, prevention and correction of misaligned teeth and jaws. This involves the fitting of braces, plates, retainers

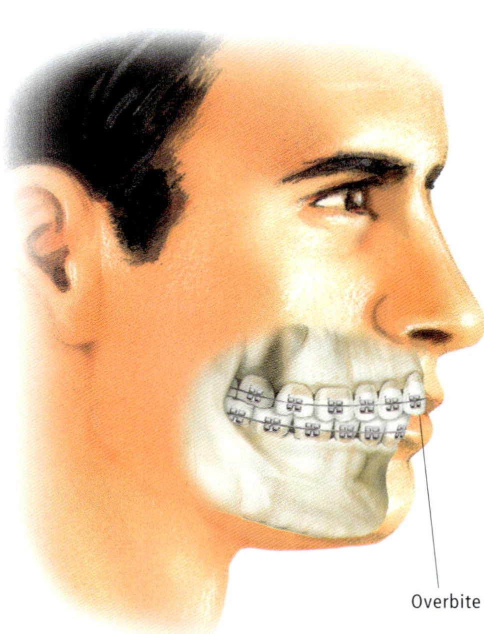

Orthodontics

The misalignment of teeth and jaws can be corrected by orthodontic appliances. Many teenagers are fitted with braces to rearrange the position of their teeth within the jaw to obtain a more favorable even line of teeth.

and other dental appliances to reposition and straighten teeth. The result is improved appearance, function and dental health.

Most orthodontic procedures are performed on children whose jaws, unlike those of adults, are not fully developed. This early treatment makes it easier to manipulate the teeth and jaw and prevent malocclusion, or a bad bite, from developing or worsening.

When upper and lower teeth do not meet correctly, problems with biting and chewing can arise. Teeth may wear unevenly or excessively due to grinding or clenching. They may also become overcrowded, making cleaning difficult and increasing the risk of inflammation, gum disease and tooth loss. In severe cases, where the teeth and/or jaw develop incorrectly, or where they have suffered trauma, results can be infection, difficulty with speech and poor nutrition. Aside from the physical aspects of poor dental development, many orthodontic procedures are carried out for cosmetic reasons as a means of improving self-confidence.

Common orthodontic problems

A common type of malocclusion is overbite, where the upper jaw juts out past the bottom jaw, making teeth more prone to damage. An underbite is where the lower jaw protrudes further than the upper jaw and can wear down the front teeth. With a normal bite, the top teeth close over the bottom teeth slightly. In some instances the top teeth may completely cover the bottom teeth. This is known as a deep bite and can damage the gum behind the top front teeth. Cross-bite is when the upper jaw is too narrow, causing the bottom jaw to swing to one side so that the teeth can meet. An open bite occurs when some teeth don't meet and is a common cause of eating and speech problems. Orthodontic procedures may also be recommended in order to fill gaps made by missing teeth or where teeth or jaw are crooked or misshapen due to such things as thumb sucking in infancy.

Treatment

The orthodontist assesses each dental problem with the help of x-rays to decide how the teeth and bone can be manipulated. Treatment may involve the extraction of some teeth or surgical manipulation of the jaw. With children, assessment usually takes place at 8–10 years of age when most adult teeth have appeared. Treatment, usually involving braces, is a slow process during which teeth are gradually moved over a period of about 18–24 months. It is slower and perhaps a little more painful for adults as the fully developed adult jaw is more difficult to manipulate.

Braces usually consist of brackets fitted over individual teeth and connected by wires. Rubber bands attached to the braces, or an appliance fitted to the head, may also be needed. Every 4–8 weeks the orthodontist adjusts the wires. Traditional designs are made of stainless steel, though less conspicuous clear ceramic types are now available. When the braces are taken off, a removable appliance called a retainer, or plate, is worn for a certain period to help keep the teeth in the correct position.

SEE ALSO *Braces, Malocclusion, Teeth*

ORTHOMOLECULAR THERAPY

The term orthomolecular, referring to a system of medicine which treats with vitamin, mineral and amino acid supplements, was coined in the 1960s by American biochemist Dr Linus Pauling. The Greek word *ortho* meaning "to correct", refers in this case to the body's restoration of good health through achieving the right balance of nutrients.

In Pauling's view, individual requirements for nutrients vary widely and can be a good deal higher than the minimum recommended doses for good health. He became famous for advocating very high doses of vitamin C to counter infections and to strengthen the immune system, views which provoked considerable controversy in the medical community. His view has been upheld to some extent by later research into the use of all the antioxidant vitamins for the prevention and treatment of degenerative diseases.

Another American researcher into megavitamin doses, Dr Abram Hoffer, advocated the use of high doses of vitamin B_3 in the treatment of schizophrenia. His work has led to the subfield of orthomolecular psychiatry, where B group vitamins in particular have been used for the treatment of certain kinds of depression and also for drug dependencies.

Orthomolecular therapy should only be used under professional guidance as some nutritional supplements are toxic in high doses. They may be prescribed by either doctors or naturopaths.

SEE ALSO *Amino acids, Antioxidants, Minerals, Vitamins*

OSGOOD-SCHLATTER DISEASE

Osgood-Schlatter disease is a relatively common, minor ailment of late childhood and early adolescence. It is characterized by pain, tenderness and often swelling at the attachment of the quadriceps tendon just below the knee on the front of the shin (the tibial tuberocity) and usually affects both legs. The disease is more common in boys than girls and usually occurs in highly active or athletic children. It is caused by excessive use of the quadriceps muscles and inflammation in the quadriceps tendon where it inserts into the front of the tibia. Avoidance of strenuous exercise, particularly jumping, usually corrects the problem although, in severe cases, the affected limb may need to be immobilized in a cast for several weeks.

SEE ALSO *Knee, Tibia*

OSTEOARTHRITIS

Osteoarthritis is the most common form of joint disease, where progressive deterioration of cartilage is accompanied by the formation of bony spurs and growth of dense bone at the margins of the joint. This condition does not necessarily involve the inflammation common in other forms of arthritis, many of which occur as a result of infection or accident trauma.

Symptoms of osteoarthritis have been found in skeletons of Neanderthal man and are consistently found in humans over the age of 70, but can occur much earlier. It is a condition common in all vertebrate animals, including birds and fish and all mammals except bats and sloths, which spend their lives hanging upsidedown placing little weight on their joints. Estimates are that over 40 percent of the adult population of the USA and the UK have symptoms which show under x-ray, and a considerable number of children also suffer the condition.

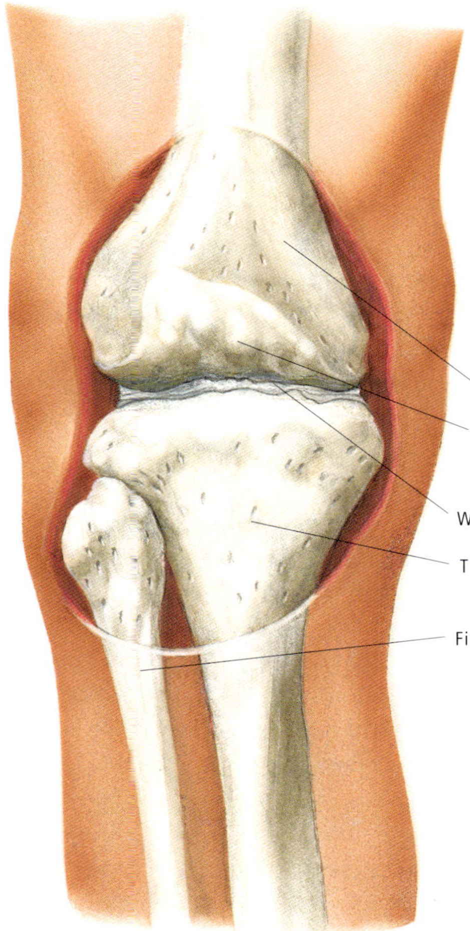

Osteoarthritis

The cause of osteoarthritis is disintegration of the cartilage that covers the ends of the bones. This will occur as part of the normal ageing process and frequently affects the knees, hips, joints of the big toes and lower sections of the spine. When symptoms are severe, movement can be restricted and part of the affected bone may wear away.

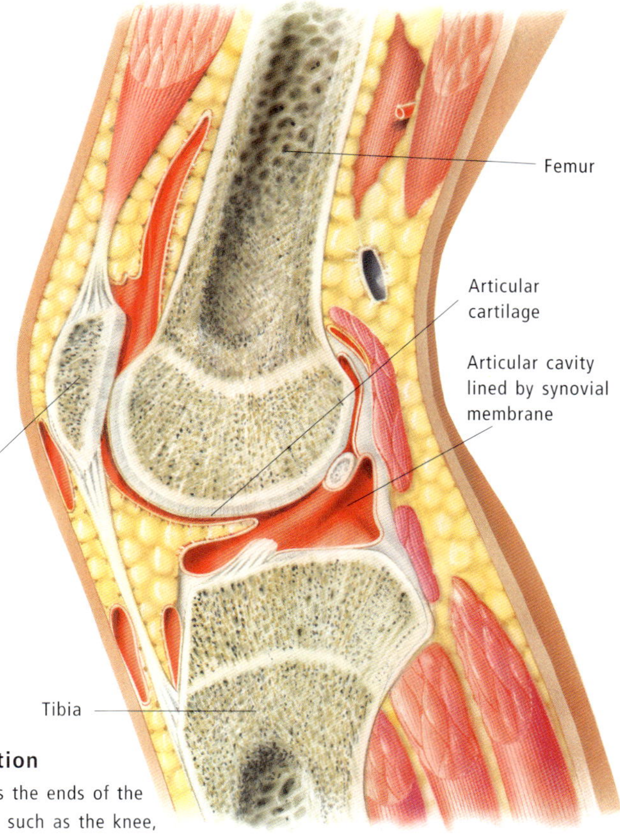

Synovial deterioration

The cartilage that covers the ends of the bones in synovial joints, such as the knee, is lubricated by a fluid that is similar to blood plasma. It is produced by the synovial membrane and is essential to proper lubrication and function of the normal joint. There may be some deterioration of the synovial membrane in osteoarthritis.

Joints are formed where two bones meet. Synovial joints have cartilage on the adjacent surfaces that cushions the adjoining surface of each bone, reducing friction on movement and protecting from shock. Synovial joints are lubricated by synovial fluid and enclosed within a fibrous capsule. Heavy use and the passage of time causes wear and tear on the cartilage coating bone ends, sometimes eroding it completely together with the underlying bone surface.

Ageing of the cartilage normally begins in early adult life and most commonly affects joints of the hip, knee, spine and hands. This degenerative damage is irreversible. Gradually the cartilage becomes less well lubricated and less effective as a shock absorber, with increased friction and pain on movement. There may be increasing stiffness and discomfort, particularly on rising.

Osteoarthritis in older individuals most commonly affects the major weight-bearing joints, such as the hips and knees. The degree of pain and stiffness involved can vary widely from person to person.

Although osteoarthritis is a more common ailment in older age groups, factors other than age are the primary cause. Sites of sports injuries in youth, an injured knee for example, often become the first reported site of osteoarthritic effects such as limited mobility, pain and stiffness. Such damage can occur to weight-bearing joints of large-framed or overweight people early in life, yet go unnoticed until distinct symptoms are felt. Genetic factors may also be involved and twice as many women suffer as men.

Symptoms include swelling and pain at the joint in response to activity or a change in position, limited flexibility, and a condition known as Heberden's nodes, which are bony lumps, particularly noticeable at the joints nearest the ends of the fingers, and are thought to be genetic in origin. There may be tenderness at joints, and x-rays may show a change in shape and a reduction in the thickness of cartilage in the joint. Diagnosis may include blood tests.

Sufferers often complain of a deep ache in the center of the joint, worsened by use and relieved by rest. This pain may become constant and severe enough to interfere with sleep. Pain and discomfort may respond to analgesics and to corticosteroids if there is accompanying inflammation. Pain-relieving therapies include application of heat by taking hot baths or applying heat pads, or the application of cold by the use of ice packs. Further damage to the joint may be preventable through exercise to strengthen supporting muscles and improve flexibility and range of movement. Excess weight should be reduced where this is a contributing factor. A common and increasingly successful solution is joint replacement, with artificial hip, knee and finger joints being recommended in some cases.

SEE ALSO *Arthritis, Hip, Inflammation, Joints, Knee*

OSTEOCHONDRITIS DISSECANS

Osteochondritis dissecans is a disorder that usually affects young adults, who have recurrent attacks of mild pain and "locking" of a joint, usually the knee but sometimes the elbow. The symptoms are caused by a loose fragment of cartilage and underlying bone breaking off and moving about freely in the joint. It is thought that a disruption to the blood supply of the bone causes the fragment to break off. The fragment usually needs to be removed by an orthopedic surgeon under general anesthesia, followed by physical therapy to restore the movement of the joint.

SEE ALSO *Elbow, Joints, Knee*

OSTEOCHONDROSIS

Osteochondrosis is an abnormal condition of bone and cartilage formation in children, affecting growth plates at the ends of bones. It may occur at areas where tendons or ligaments attach to bones, or in areas that receive a lot of impact stress. This may be the hip (Perthes' disease), the tibial tuberosity (Osgood-Schlatter disease), or the calcaneus, the bone in the heel of the foot (Sever's disease).

In all cases, degeneration of bone and cartilage occurs; this is thought to be caused by an interruption to the blood supply of the bone, which is followed by spontaneous regeneration. The child feels pain and sometimes a lump at the site where the degeneration has occurred.

Treatment is aimed at protecting the bone and joint while spontaneous healing takes place, through bed rest and the use of appliances such as a brace, cast or splint. In most cases the bone heals without any resulting deformity.

SEE ALSO *Bones, Cartilage, Osgood-Schlatter disease, Perthes' disease*

OSTEOGENESIS IMPERFECTA

Osteogenesis imperfecta, also called brittle bones, is a rare inherited condition in which the bones are abnormally brittle. It is usually present at birth. Bone fractures and deformities occur easily, especially once the child begins to walk. There may be deafness and the whites of the eyes can appear bluish. There is no specific treatment; when bones fracture they must be repaired quickly to avoid deformities.

There are four separate genetic types, each with different manifestations and a prognosis. The disorder is fatal in some types, in others there is a normal life expectancy.

SEE ALSO *Bones, Fractures*

OSTEOMALACIA

Osteomalacia is softening of the bones caused by lack of vitamin D. It can be caused by poor dietary intake of vitamin D, poor absorption of vitamin D from the intestine, or too little exposure to sunlight, which is necessary for the formation of vitamin D in the body. Other causes include hereditary or acquired disorders of vitamin D metabolism, and kidney failure. In children, the condition is called rickets.

Common symptoms are aching bones, fractures and deformities, muscle weakness and spasms. The condition is diagnosed with x-rays of the bones, and blood tests for calcium, vitamin D and phosphorus. Treatment depends on the cause and may include vitamin D, calcium and phosphorus supplements.

SEE ALSO *Bones, Rickets*

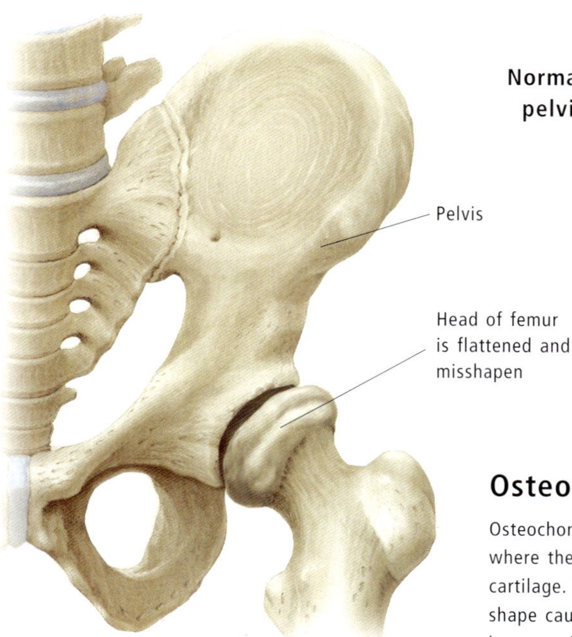

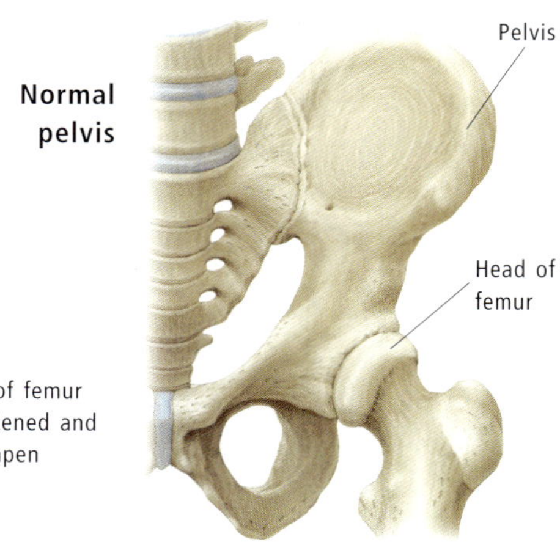

Osteochondrosis

Osteochondrosis occurs mainly in children, where there is degeneration of bone and cartilage. The bone may be moved out of shape causing a deformity. The most likely bones to be affected are the hip and shin.

OSTEOMYELITIS

Osteomyelitis is an infection of bone. Acute (sudden onset) osteomyelitis occurs most often in children, is usually caused by a bacterium or fungus which has traveled from an infection elsewhere in the body—a boil, or an ear infection, for example—to the bone. In children, the long bones are usually affected. In adults, the vertebrae and the pelvis are most commonly affected. It can also follow injury, such as an open fracture.

Symptoms are fever and general illness followed a few days later by pain, swelling, redness, warmth and tenderness in the area over the infected bone. X-rays of the bone are normal in the early stages, but the infection will show up in a bone scan. A bone biopsy and culture will grow the organism causing the infection and thus determine what antibiotic to use. Treatment is with intravenous antibiotics in massive doses for at least six weeks. If an abscess has formed, surgery will be needed to remove the abscess and drain any pus.

Slow onset (chronic) osteomyelitis results when bone tissue has died (become necrotic) following an acute infection. An opening to the skin (sinus) may form and drain pus, which may persist intermittently for years. Chronic osteomyelitis is treated by surgical removal of dead bone tissue, which is replaced with bone graft or other material, which promotes the growth of new bone tissue. In some cases amputation is required.

SEE ALSO *Bones*

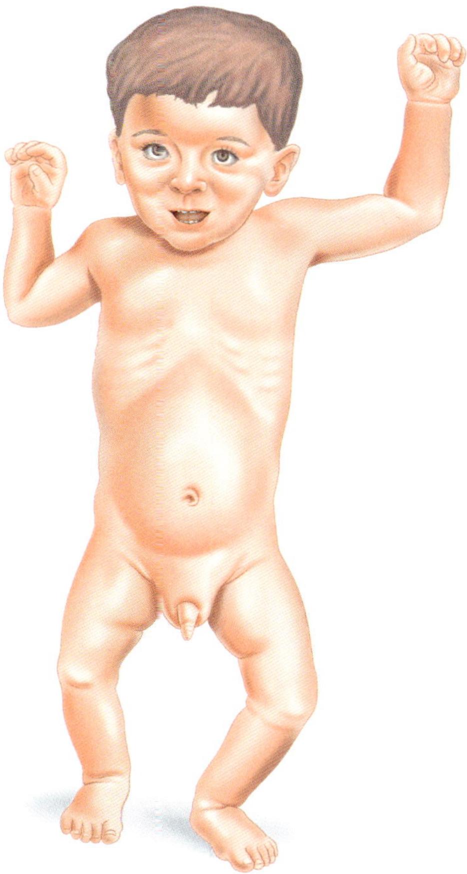

Osteomalacia

Osteomalacia is the result of insufficient vitamin D, either due to an inadequate diet or poor absorption by the individual. The condition inhibits the uptake of calcium by the body and this causes pain in the bones and sometimes also muscle weakness.

OSTEOPATHY

The term osteopathy derives from the Greek words *osteo*, meaning "bone", and *pathos*, meaning "suffering". Osteopathy was pioneered as a form of medical treatment in the late nineteenth century by the American Dr Andrew Taylor Still. A deeply religious man, he believed that the body was created in perfect harmony, with a capacity to self-heal when correctly adjusted and balanced.

Dr Still believed that dysfunctions in the body structure (that is, the muscles, joints and skeleton) affected the health of the body's organ systems by disrupting the nerve and blood supply. He diagnosed various health conditions by touching parts of the body, and assessing the speed and quality of blood flow to that area while noting the changes in position and movement of the musculoskeletal system. Through massage and manipulation he corrected the body's dysfunction and set up the right conditions for self-healing.

Osteopathic treatment is largely done with the hands. Practitioners use a combination of gentle techniques including soft tissue stretching, joint articulation and manipulation, and deep pressure. Minimum force is used in line with the tensions found within the body itself.

Osteopathy is similar to chiropractic treatment in its use of manipulation of the body to correct postural misalignments, but differs in its philosophy and treatment approaches. Whereas chiropractic focuses on the spine and nerve supply in the body, osteopathy focuses on the full musculoskeletal system and improvement of blood and lymph circulation.

Osteopaths make their diagnosis through taking a detailed medical history and assessing the patient's current lifestyle, including diet and exercise. They closely examine body structure and posture by observing the patient standing, sitting, lying and walking. By palpating different parts of the body the osteopath observes muscle tone and joint movement while also noting the skin's health.

As well as treating through the gentle pulling and pushing of bones and muscles, osteopaths often advise on diet, exercise, posture and lifestyle. Osteopaths commonly treat back pain, headaches, arthritis, sciatica and cartilage injuries, as well as digestive problems and chronic respiratory ailments accompanied by chronic muscular tension.

Osteopathy is widely accepted within the USA where it is practised by medical practitioners. Outside the USA osteopaths train in colleges or universities which teach

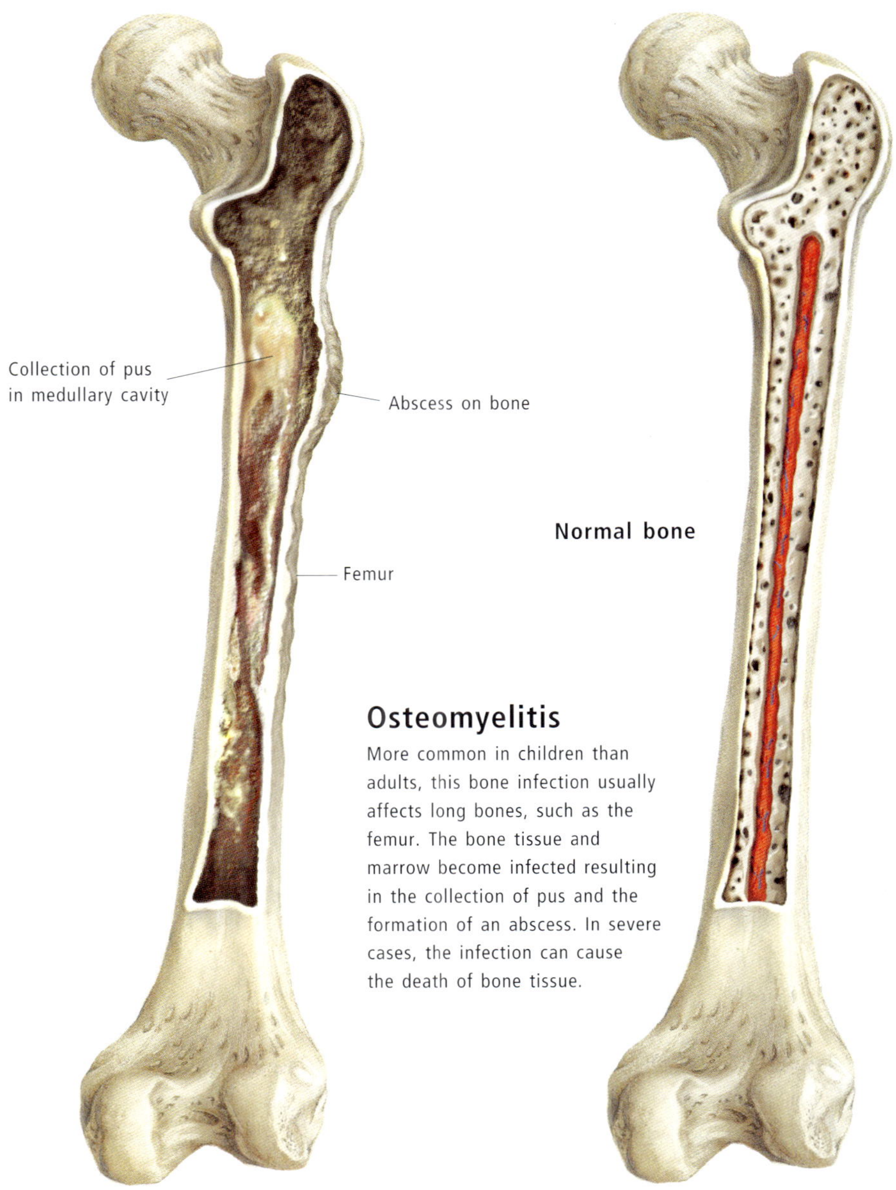

Osteomyelitis

More common in children than adults, this bone infection usually affects long bones, such as the femur. The bone tissue and marrow become infected resulting in the collection of pus and the formation of an abscess. In severe cases, the infection can cause the death of bone tissue.

Osteoporosis

Osteoporosis occurs in both older men and women, however the incidence is higher for women. The condition occurs when bone mass is severely reduced, resulting in porous, weak and brittle bones which break easily.

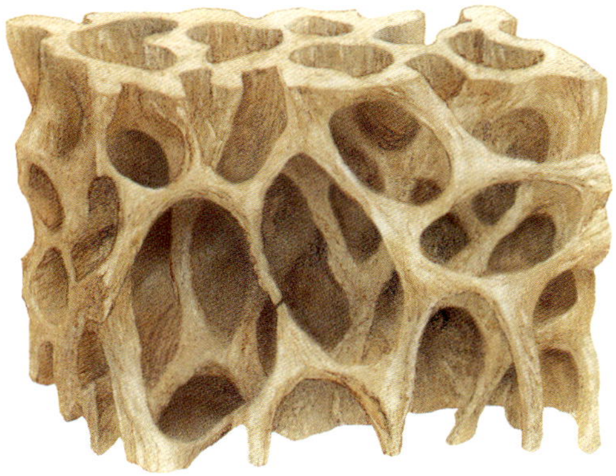

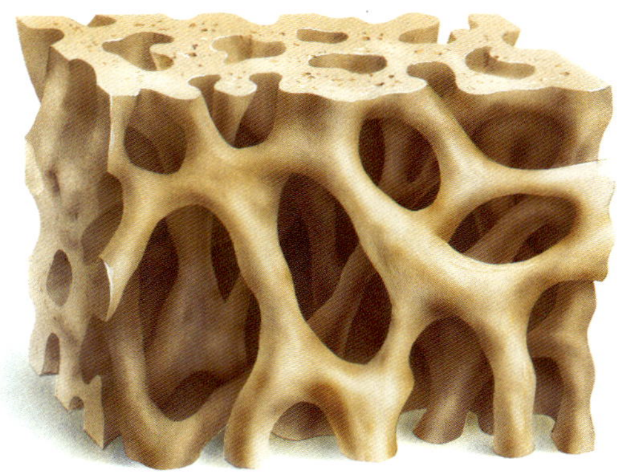

Normal bone

osteopathy in conjunction with naturopathic techniques and orthodox medical diagnosis.

Cranial osteopathy and its latest variant, cranio-sacral osteopathy, are methods of balancing the body through very slight movements of the bones of the skull and spinal column. This form of osteopathy was pioneered by Dr William Garner Sutherland, who believed that the bones in the skull are designed to allow very little movement, being interlocking and held together by dense connective tissue. The inside of the skull bones is lined by the dura mater, one of the membranes surrounding the brain and containing the cerebrospinal fluid. Sutherland's belief was that if the flow of cerebrospinal fluid becomes interrupted or distorted for any reason, an imbalance leading to disease can result. The cranial osteopath gently releases any tensions between the skull bones to allow the cerebrospinal fluid to pump correctly.

This treatment is particularly recommended for children and babies, especially where there has been birth trauma. It can also be helpful for treating both old and recent injuries to the head, neck or back, recurring ear or sinus infections and headaches.

SEE ALSO *Chiropractic*

Dowager's hump

Dowager's hump develops in older women with severe osteoporosis. The vertebrae in the spine may compress, so that the normal curve of the spine is exaggerated. This condition may progressively worsen.

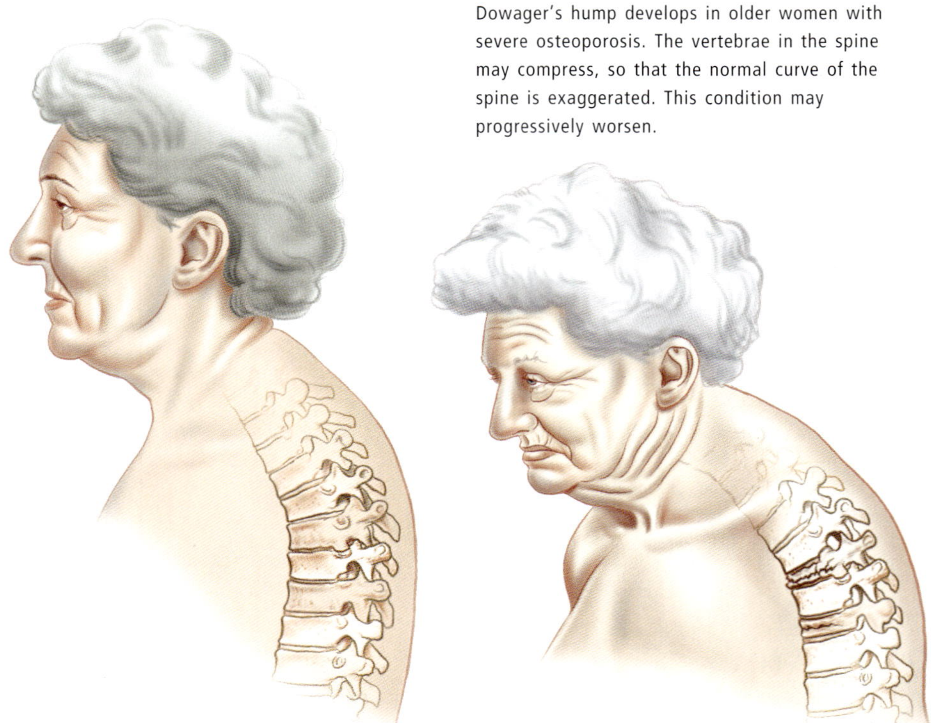

OSTEOPOROSIS

Osteoporosis is a disorder in which bones lose their density and become weak and brittle. The condition gets worse with age and is seen most commonly in postmenopausal women. The bone loss is greatest in bones containing a large percentage of spongy (trabecular) bone, found in the vertebral column, the hips and the wrist. The bones lose calcium and phosphate, as well as the connective tissue that is the matrix of the bone. Consequently they become brittle and prone to fracture. Osteoporosis is different from osteomalacia, which is caused by vitamin D deficiency, and in which only calcium, but not the matrix, is lost from the bone.

The cause of osteoporosis is unknown. However, some factors are known to accelerate the condition; they include a diet low in calcium, lack of exercise, cigarette smoking, excessive alcohol consumption and prolonged bed rest. In women, estrogen appears to protect against osteoporosis, but levels of estrogen fall after menopause and so from the age of 50 or so, osteoporosis is more common in women than men.

Some diseases can cause or accelerate osteoporosis. They include Cushing's syndrome (overactivity of the adrenal glands) and hyperparathyroidism (overactivity of the parathyroid glands). Liver, kidney or heart disorders can also accelerate osteoporosis. Other possible causes include eating disorders, such as anorexia, and some drugs, such as thyroid hormones and corticosteroid medication taken over a long period.

Typically the sufferer has no symptoms but gradually loses height over the years, finally becoming stooped with forward curvature of the thoracic spine (also known as dowager's hump, or kyphosis). Back pain can be severe and a back brace may be needed for support. Fractures, especially of the hip and wrist, are common in the elderly, and can happen without warning. Compression fractures of the vertebrae may compress the surrounding nerves and cause severe pain.

The diagnosis can be confirmed with x-rays and photodensitometry (a scanning technique that measures bone density). These tests show bones with diminished density, and may be used to predict future fractures. There is no treatment for osteoporosis. Instead, management is directed at preventing further bone loss, and treating fractures and other complications. Calcium and vitamin D supplements and adequate protein will prevent further bone loss.

In postmenopausal women, hormone replacement therapy is often used. Estrogen taken orally halts bone demineralization, as well as protecting against heart disease and stroke, and relieving the hot flashes and mood swings of menopause. To prevent the possibility of cancer of the endometrium (the lining of the uterus), estrogen is usually given along with the hormone progesterone.

There are several drugs available, including the hormone calcitonin, which prevent loss of bone mineral and allow the bone to gain density. Calcitonin must be given daily by injection.

The best approach to the problem of osteoporosis is prevention. Adequate calcium in the diet (at least three to four glasses of milk per day or the equivalent), regular exercise, giving up tobacco and reducing alcohol consumption will prevent or slow the progression of the disease. Women should begin these measures in their teens.

SEE ALSO *Bones, Calcium, Estrogens, Hormone replacement therapy, Kyphosis*

OTITIS EXTERNA

Otitis externa is inflammation of the outer ear, that is, the skin of the ear canal extending from the eardrum to the outside of the ear. Symptoms of otitis externa include itching, ear pain that worsens when the earlobe is pulled, a slight discharge and (sometimes) deafness. The cause is usually a bacterial or fungal infection resulting from a number of causes, including swimming in dirty, polluted water (the condition is also known as swimmer's ear), scratching the ear, the use of ear plugs for prolonged periods, or excessive sweating. It may also occur in people with eczema (an inflammation of the skin) or diabetes mellitus.

Treatment is with ear drops that contain antibiotics to fight infection and cortisone drugs to control inflammation. Oral antibiotics may be needed in severe infection. Any dead skin, pus or wax should be removed by a physician.

SEE ALSO *Ear*

OTITIS MEDIA

Otitis media is inflammation of the middle ear. It is most commonly caused by the spread of bacteria from the throat into the middle ear via the eustachian tube. Usually there is an associated infection of the throat, such as the common cold or tonsillitis.

The sufferer, usually a child, develops fever, deafness in the affected ear, and severe earache, due to an accumulation of pus in the middle ear which can build up until it ruptures the eardrum, releasing the pus and relieving the earache. Diarrhea, abdominal pain, and vomiting accompany the symptoms—in infants they may be more obvious than the earache.

Treatment is with painkillers and antibiotics. If the eardrum has ruptured or been surgically opened and is discharging pus, the ear should be kept clean and dry until the eardrum has healed. Sometimes, pus under pressure may need to be released surgically via an incision in the eardrum (myringotomy). In some children, otitis media becomes recurrent and may become chronic (glue ear), when the insertion of a drainage tube becomes necessary. If untreated, chronic otitis media can cause deafness.

SEE ALSO *Deafness, Ear*

OTOSCLEROSIS

Otosclerosis is a disorder of the middle ear that leads to progressive deafness. It is caused by the gradual build-up of abnormal spongy bone tissue around one of the small bones (the stapes) in the middle ear. The abnormal bone prevents the stapes from vibrating, thereby preventing the transmission of sound vibrations from the eardrum to the inner ear. The result is progressive deafness in the affected ear and, sometimes, ringing in the ear (tinnitus). Eventually both ears become affected. Otosclerosis is most commonly seen in women between the ages of 15–30 and may be triggered by pregnancy. A family history of otosclerosis is common.

The condition is treated by a surgical procedure called a stapedectomy, in which

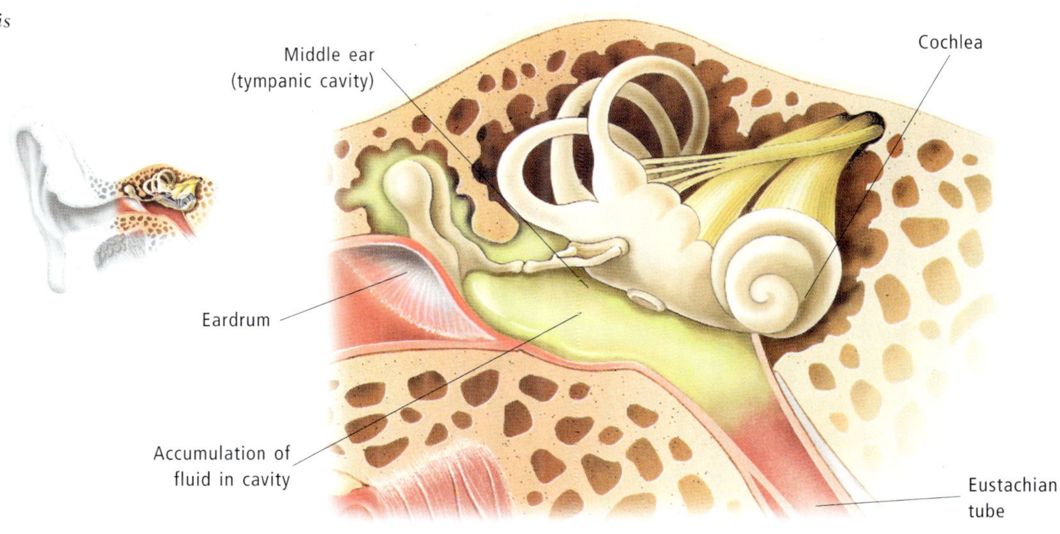

Otitis media

Otitis media is inflammation of the middle ear, which occurs frequently in infants and young children. Fluid accumulates in the ear behind the tympanic membrane. There is hearing loss, which ceases after treatment.

the diseased stapes bone is replaced with a prosthesis, which restores hearing in most cases. A hearing aid may be used as an alternative to surgery.

SEE ALSO *Deafness, Ear, Hearing*

OVARIAN CYSTS

Ovarian cysts are relatively common and can occur in females of all ages, including both newborns (neonates) and those who have been through menopause. They are hollow, fluid-filled structures which may be derived from abnormal development of ovarian follicles or of a corpus luteum (an ovarian follicle that has matured and released its egg).

Ovarian cysts are usually multiple and affect both ovaries. They contain a watery or bloody fluid and are usually quite small although some may be as large as 2 inches (5 centimeters) or more in diameter. They are often symptomless and ovulation may occur in their presence; however, complications are not uncommon. These include pain, disturbances to the menstrual cycle and to ovulation with resulting infertility, excessive hair growth, rupture of one or more of the cysts and degeneration of adjacent normal ovarian tissue. Larger cysts may damage the ovarian blood supply with possible loss of the entire ovary.

The cause of ovarian cysts of this type is complex but has been linked to imbalances in the production of certain pituitary hormones, collectively called gonadotropins, which are involved in the control of ovarian function. In women of childbearing age some of the complications of ovarian cysts may be reduced with weight loss. Estrogen and/or progesterone or fertility drugs are other possible treatments. In some instances, drainage or surgical removal of the larger cysts or even of the whole ovary may be necessary.

Certain types of cystic ovaries may be inherited. One of the best known is polycystic ovary syndrome or Stein-Leventhal syndrome, which is characterized by numerous small cysts and excessive thickening of the tissues forming the covering of the ovary. There are also higher than normal amounts of male sex hormones in circulation (ovaries produce these hormones normally but they are generally converted to estrogens).

Certain ovarian cysts are frequently associated with endometriosis (a condition in which tissue-like uterine lining is found outside the uterus). These cysts are lined with fragments of displaced uterine lining (endometrium) and are known as chocolate or tarry cysts because they contain a viscous brown material, arising from bleeding into cavities of the cysts during menstruation. Chocolate cysts are commonly multiple, large and affect both ovaries. These can be treated by giving hormones for the endometriosis, removing the cysts surgically or by using laser treatment.

Several forms of cystic tumors also exist and, unlike other types of ovarian cyst, may become malignant. One of the most common is multilocular cystadenoma. Usually only one ovary is affected, with a mass of tiny, mucus-filled cysts surrounding a single very large cyst. This can grow to enormous size, 44 pounds (20 kilograms) or more, which will distend the abdomen. The cyst may either be drained, or surgically removed. Sometimes the whole ovary will need to be removed. Other types of cystic tumor do not reach the considerable size of an untreated multilocular cystadenoma.

SEE ALSO *Endometriosis, Endometrium, Ovaries, Stein-Leventhal syndrome*

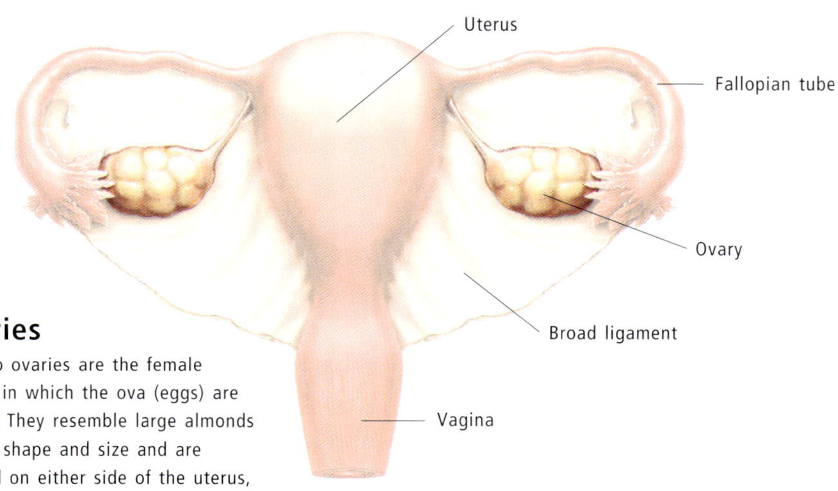

Ovaries

The two ovaries are the female gonads in which the ova (eggs) are formed. They resemble large almonds in both shape and size and are situated on either side of the uterus, supported by the broad ligament. The ovaries produce the female hormones estrogen and progesterone.

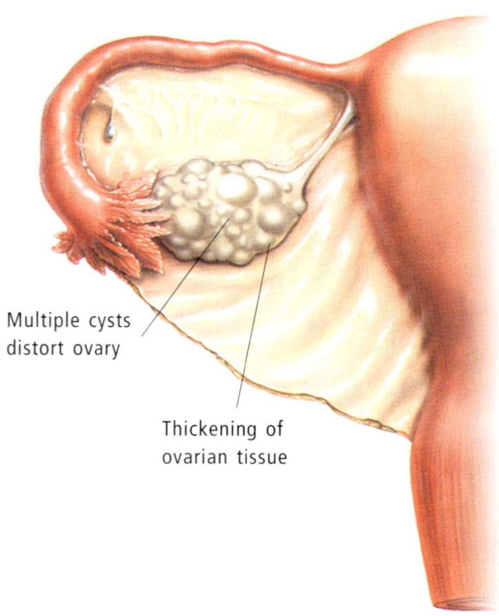

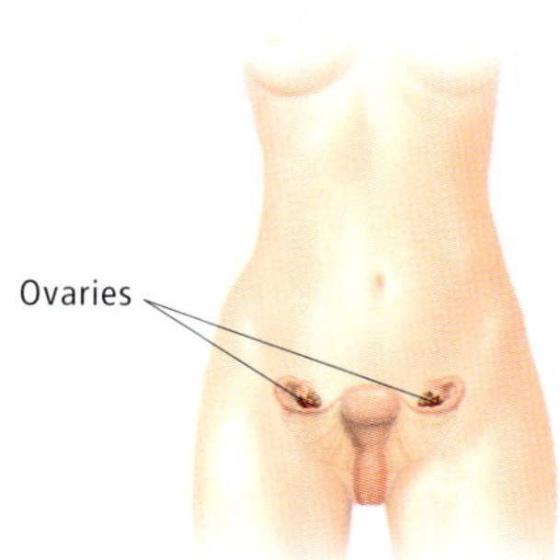

Ovarian cysts

In polycystic ovary syndrome multiple fluid-filled cysts form in the ovaries from follicles that fail to rupture and release eggs.

OVARIES

The ovaries are elliptical organs roughly $1\frac{1}{2}$ inches (3 centimeters) long and $\frac{1}{2}$ inch (1 centimeter) wide. They are situated close to the side walls of the pelvis and are sup-

Ovary cross-section

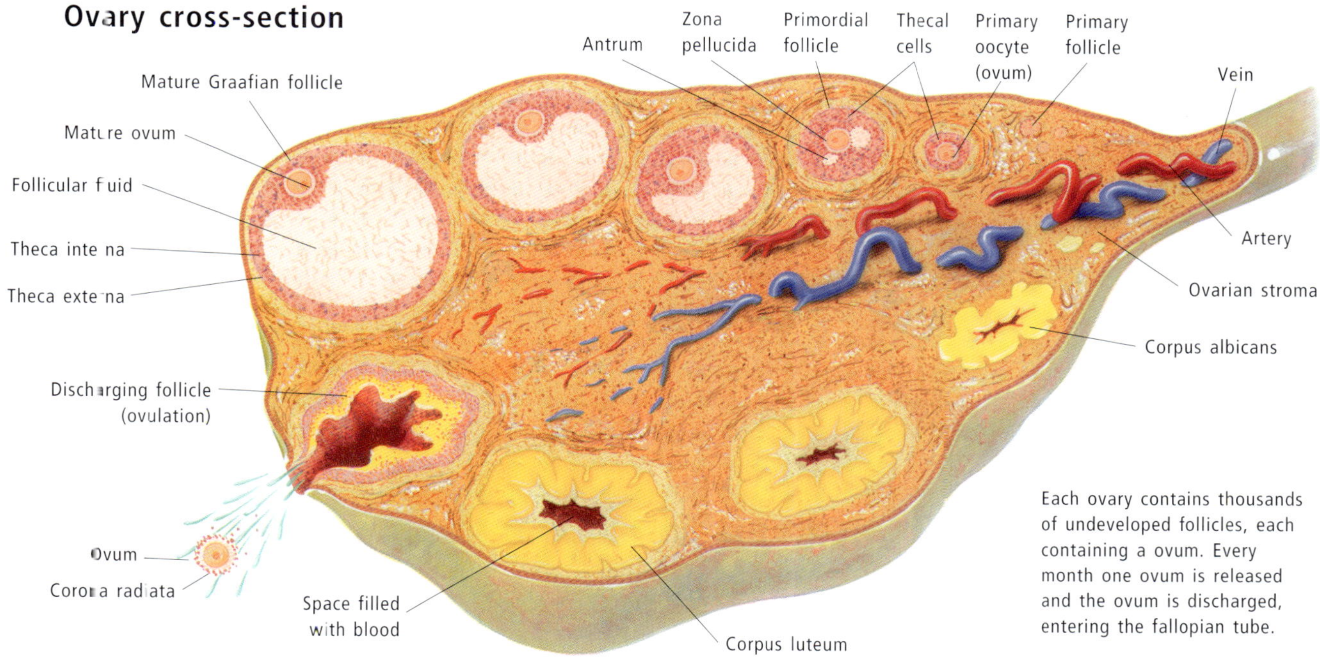

Each ovary contains thousands of undeveloped follicles, each containing a ovum. Every month one ovum is released and the ovum is discharged, entering the fallopian tube.

ported by the broad ligament of the uterus.

Ovaries contain thousands of small undeveloped follicles, each of which consists of an ovum surrounded by specialized secretory cells that produce female hormones. Ovaries in women of reproductive age also contain a few follicles undergoing enlargement and development prior to each ovulation. Most of these developing follicles will degenerate so that only a single ovum from one of the ovaries will finally be ovulated.

After ovulation, a corpus luteum is formed from the remains of the ovulated follicle. About two days before the start of the next menstrual cycle it will begin to degenerate. Degenerating follicles and corpora lutea persist for a number of cycles and in some women continue to produce small amounts of estrogen and progesterone.

There are changes in the normal structure and function of the ovaries associated with age. Several years prior to menopause the number of follicles (both undeveloped and developing) begins to decrease, there is a decline in the overall amount of estrogen in circulation and loss of other ovarian tissue, resulting in an overall decrease in size of the ovaries.

Ovarian abnormalities are likely to cause infertility, for example if the ovary is unable to respond normally to the stimulating gonad hormones (gonadotropins) from the pituitary. This occurs in the polycystic ovary syndrome (Stein-Leventhal syndrome). Individuals with this syndrome have infrequent or absent menstruation, infertility, excessive facial and body hair and are usually obese. Both ovaries are smooth and enlarged with numerous small cysts. The condition is caused by a congenital inability to produce normal amounts of estrogen. Instead testosterone-like substances, which precede estrogen, are released into the blood. Decreased estrogen secretion is involved in the failure to ovulate and menstruate normally. Other types of ovarian cysts may also affect ovulation.

In some individuals, ovaries do not develop normally (gonadal dysgenesis). This occurs in certain genetic disorders, for example Turner's syndrome, where the ovaries are often fibrous streaks without follicles. No estrogens are produced, resulting in total amenorrhea and absence of secondary sex characteristics, including breast development and axillary and pubic hair.

Ovarian malignancies are the commonest cause of death from gynecological cancers and can occur at any age, although they are rare in childhood. Ovarian cancers are often diagnosed late because they are relatively asymptomatic until well developed or have spread to other organs. It is common for ovarian cancer to be described as if it were a single entity but there are many different types with different rates of spread and response to therapy. There is even a particular type of tumor called a teratoma, usually benign but sometimes malignant, in which fragments of skin, hair, cartilage, thyroid-like tissue and even teeth develop. Some types of cancer are more common after menopause and they can cause postmenopausal bleeding. Ovaries are also a fairly common site for secondary cancers arising from other organs.

SEE ALSO *Estrogens, Menstruation, Ovarian cysts, Ovulation, Progesterone, Reproductive systems, Stein-Leventhal syndrome, Turner's syndrome*

OVERDOSE

Excessive doses of medication or drugs, taken either by accident or deliberately, usually constitute an overdose. Accidental overdoses are generally taken by curious children and confused elderly people, or as a result of doctor, pharmacist or patient error; deliberate overdoses are often attempted suicide or even homicide.

If there are several equally effective drugs to treat a particular condition, doctors will generally prescribe the one with the lowest risk of toxicity should an overdose occur.

Substances which people can and do overdose on include the following.

Amphetamines, also known as speed because these drugs seem to speed up the central nervous system, have severe effects in overdose including brain hemorrhage, heart attack, coma and occasionally death.

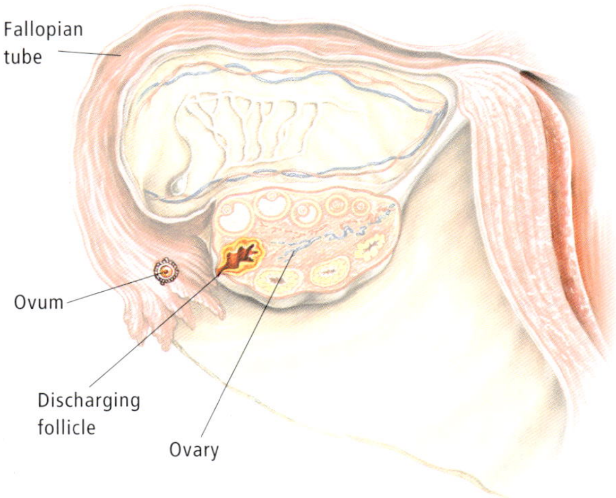

Ovulation

The release of an ovum (egg) from the ovary is known as ovulation and takes place on about day 14 of the menstrual cycle. A surge of hormone encourages the follicle that carries the mature ovum to burst open. The ovum is discharged and is swept up into the fallopian tube.

Barbiturates, which are drugs classed as sedative hypnotics, are used to manage seizures or sometimes as a sedative. Intoxication with barbiturates slows a person's movements and breathing and can cause coma and loss of most reflexes.

Cocaine is a stimulant drug produced from the leaves of the coca plant. Overdose can happen to anyone and very small amounts can have an overdose effect on susceptible persons. Death can result.

Heroin, a drug made from the opium poppy and originally used as a painkiller, is very easy to overdose on. Even small amounts can result in an overdose for some people, and the longer the drug is used the more likely it is that an overdose will be taken. Symptoms of overdose include a slowing of breathing, a very low pulse rate or blood pressure, and drowsiness or unconsciousness. Coma and death can result.

Methadone is an opioid painkiller used to treat people dependent on heroin. Overdose to methadone happens when more than the prescribed dose is taken or when the substance is injected or taken with alcohol or minor tranquilizers.

MethyleneDioxyMethAmphetamine (MDMA), commonly known as Ecstasy, is a synthetic drug used as a stimulant. Overdose can result in death.

Minor tranquilizers, drugs in the benzodiazepine group, including diazepam, tempazepam and clonazepam, can cause overdose. Many sleeping pills fall into this category.

It is also possible to overdose on some substances that are generally considered safe, such as vitamin supplements.

Vitamin A is a fat-soluble vitamin found pre-formed in animal foods such as egg yolk, fatty fish and full-fat dairy foods. Excess vitamin A is toxic. Overdosing on supplements can cause headache, joint pain and itchy skin and can be fatal to the developing fetus. Vitamin B_6 in large quantities is also dangerous. Vitamin D is the most toxic vitamin and large doses as supplements lead to loss of appetite, nausea, vomiting and even death.

Prescription and over-the-counter medicines can also be taken in overdose; some are far more dangerous than others.

Acetaminophen (paracetamol) is a common cause of accidental poisoning in children, but such overdoses also occur in other age groups and need immediate medical treatment. Ibuprofen can also be taken in overdose and medical attention must be sought if this occurs.

SEE ALSO *Amphetamines, Barbiturates, Cocaine, Detoxification, Drug dependence, Heroin, Methadone, Poisoning, Sleeping pills, Stimulants, Tranquilizers, Vitamins*

OVULATION

Ovulation is the release of an ovum from the ovary on about day 14 of an average menstrual cycle. It can take place from either ovary; the selection of left or right ovary seems to be a random process.

Prior to ovulation, during the first half of each menstrual cycle, a few follicles, each consisting of an ovum and the secretory cells which surround it, start to develop. Most of these follicles will degenerate at various stages of maturity until usually just one is left to undergo ovulation. Development of the follicles is stimulated by the follicle stimulating hormone (FSH), a gonadotropin, released by the pituitary gland.

As the follicles develop, the secretory cells produce increasing quantities of estrogen which is released into the blood. When blood estrogen reaches a particular concentration, the pituitary is stimulated to produce a surge of another gonadotropin called luteinising hormone (LH). This induces ovulation through a temporary break in the surface of the ovary. The open end of the fallopian tube adjacent to the ovary draws the ovum inside the tube. The ovum is either fertilized here or degenerates within the next few days. Transport into the uterus occurs if fertilization has taken place. Occasionally the fallopian tube may fail to collect the ovum, which then falls into the peritoneal cavity. If fertilization then occurs, ectopic implantation may result on one of the pelvic or peritoneal organs.

After ovulation, the secretory cells remaining in the ovary become a corpus luteum which will produce progesterone and small amounts of estrogen until day 26 of a non-pregnant cycle. The corpus luteum degenerates at this time with a rapid decline in concentrations of progesterone in the blood resulting in menstruation.

Determining whether and when ovulation has taken place is important in establishing the cause of infertility and also in "natural" methods of birth control and in timing intercourse to maximize the possibility of conception. Tests should be made over a number of cycles in order to establish a pattern of ovulation. The simplest method is to take daily body temperature readings and to record these on a temperature chart. Temperatures should be lower during the first half of the cycle and there may be a further drop at the time of ovulation. Alternatively, cervical mucus may be sampled throughout the cycle. This dries in a characteristic fern-like pattern around the time of ovulation, a pattern not seen during the rest of the cycle.

Other techniques rely on the fact that a functional corpus luteum and progesterone production can only occur if ovulation has taken place. These can be established either by measuring blood progesterone levels

O

during the second half of the cycle or by biopsy of the uterine lining in order to see if changes consistent with progesterone production have occurred. Monitoring of the developing follicles with ultrasound is sometimes used. In some women pelvic pain ("mittelschmerz"), possibly accompanied by bleeding, may be associated with ovulation.

An anovulatory cycle is one in which ovulation does not occur and therefore a corpus luteum does not form. Uterine bleeding may still take place but is the result of the withdrawal of estrogen rather than of progesterone and is often irregular. Ovulation failure in women of reproductive age may be caused by a malfunction of organs, such as the pituitary, which produce hormones affecting the ovaries. It can also be the result of certain therapeutic drugs, obesity, starvation or may have a psychological basis. In some cases ovulation may be restored by fertility drugs such as clomiphene citrate. Doses are kept low in order to avoid multiple ovulations. Oral contraceptives are used to deliberately introduce anovulatory (not related to ovulation) cycles.

Anovulatory cycles are common for the first few months after menstruation first occurs (menarche), before a mature hormone pattern is established. They also occur in increasing frequency prior to menopause as a result of normal hormone changes at that time. Occasionally ovulation can occur several years after assumed menopause.

SEE ALSO *Estrogens, Fertility, Fertilization, Follicle stimulating hormone, Infertility, Menstruation, Mittelschmerz, Ovaries, Ovum, Progesterone, Reproductive systems*

OVUM

The ovum is the mature female germ cell. The ovaries of women of reproductive age contain about 800,000 immature ova (oocytes), each surrounded by a covering of specialized cells which secrete female hormones. Only about 400 of these will be ovulated. The rest degenerate sometime during the reproductive years or just after menopause.

Normal body cells are diploid, that is, they contain 23 pairs of chromosomes and divide by mitosis to produce daughter cells which also have 23 pairs of chromosomes. Germ cells (oocytes and sperm) are haploid, that is, they contain only one of each pair of chromosomes (23 single chromosomes). This is possible because oocytes are produced in the embryo by a special form of cell division called meiosis (reduction or division) which halves the number of chromosomes. Sperm are also produced by meiosis. When fertilization takes place and ovum and sperm join together, the chromosome number in the new individual is restored to the normal 23 pairs (46 single chromosomes).

The development of normal ovaries and oocytes takes place only if the individual is a normal female and two conditions are fulfilled: the individual does not have a Y chromosome (carrying the normal gene for maleness), and there are two normal X chromosomes. If one X chromosome is missing, as is the case in Turner's syndrome, the oocytes degenerate and the ovaries do not develop in the embryo.

SEE ALSO *Cells, Chromosomes, Embryo, Fertilization, Hormones, Ovaries, Reproductive systems, Sperm, Turner's syndrome, X chromosome, Y chromosome*

OXYTOCIN

Oxytocin is a hormone secreted by the pituitary gland and also by the ovary and placenta. Secretion of this hormone results from stimulation of nerves in the nipple during suckling. Oxytocin is responsible for the release of milk during breast feeding (lactation), whereas the manufacture of milk by the glandular tissue is under the control of a different pituitary hormone, prolactin.

It is also thought that oxytocin is important in maximizing uterine contractions during the later stages of labor. It may also help to reduce bleeding after delivery by causing mild uterine contractions which compress damaged blood vessels. However, oxytocin does not seem to be involved in the initiation of labor.

SEE ALSO *Breast feeding, Childbirth, Hormones, Mammary glands, Pituitary gland*

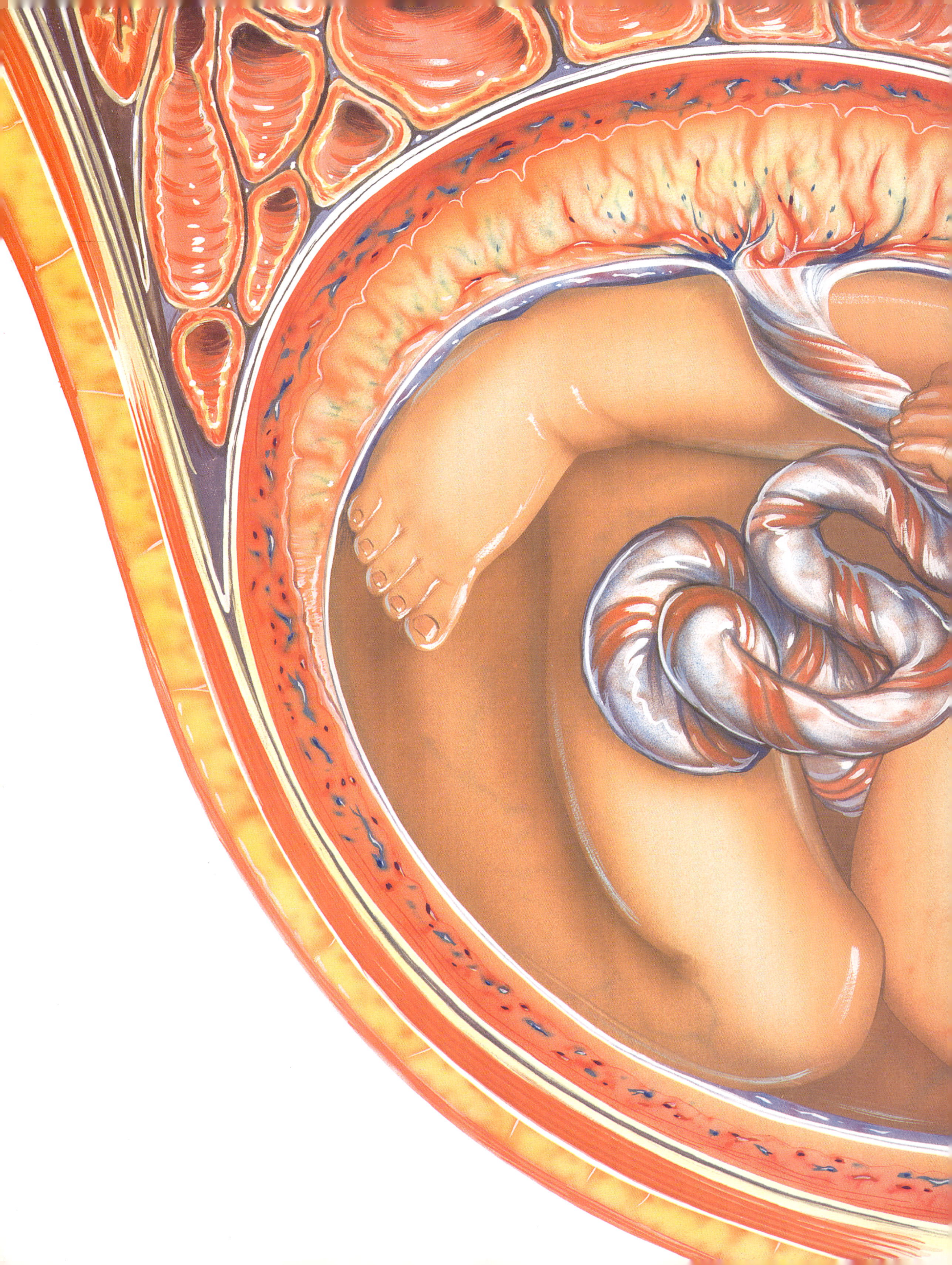

P

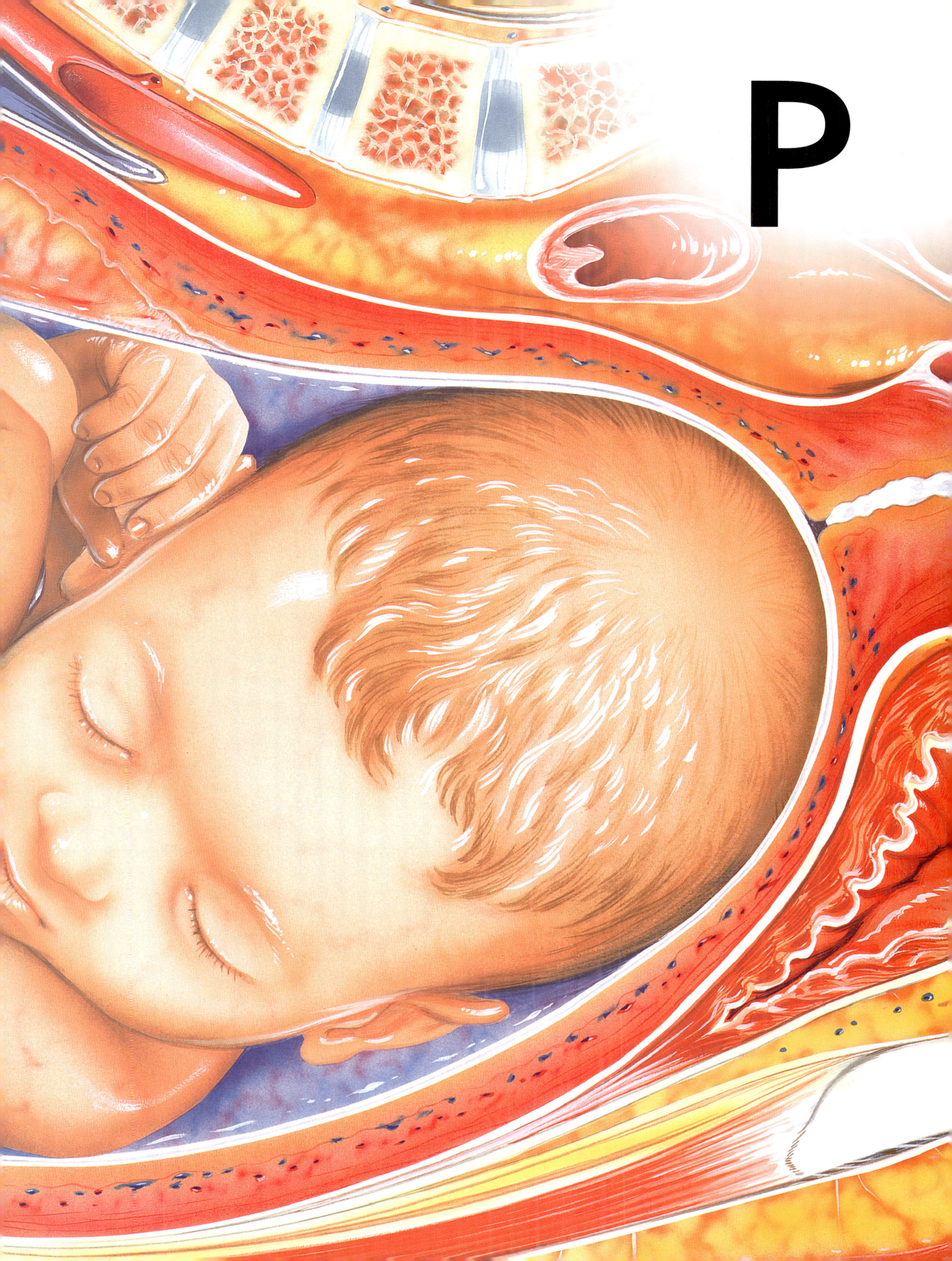

PACEMAKER

This term is usually used in reference to the heart, although other organs (such as the uterus and bowel) may also have specialized tissue which controls rhythmic contraction. There is a naturally occurring pacemaker, called the sinoatrial node, which directly controls the rhythmic contraction of the heart.

The sinoatrial node is located in the wall of the right atrium near the superior vena cava and has its own rhythmic cycle of electrical activity. This activity is transmitted to surrounding heart muscle and through specialized conducting cells to all parts of the heart, thus initiating heart muscle contraction. The electrical rhythm of the sinoatrial node may be slowed by the vagus nerve, or quickened by the sympathetic cardiac nerves and circulating hormones such as epinephrine (adrenaline).

If the heart is unable to maintain an adequate rhythm due to disease, then artificial pacemakers may be used. They give the heart small stimulant shocks by delivering electrical impulses at a pre-determined rate. These impulses trigger contractions of the heart muscle which cause blood to pump through the heart.

Artificial pacemakers usually consist of two main components: a transducer for generating electrical impulses and tiny wires, or electrodes, which are fed into veins and make contact with the heart muscle. The transducer is a small device weighing about 1 ounce (28 grams) and powered by a lithium battery that may not need changing for at least five years. The transducer is usually implanted beneath the skin just below the collar bone via a small incision. This is a relatively minor procedure carried out using mild sedation and local anesthetic. Transducers are often encased in titanium, which usually does not irritate the body. Alternatively, the transducer may be worn externally on a belt around the body.

Electrical impulses from the transducer travel along the electrodes to the heart muscle at a rate that may be preset or controlled externally by a remote switch. Depending on the heart condition involved, the transducer may monitor the heart's rate of contraction and send out electrical impulses only when it beats abnormally. In this way, pacemakers can be used to stimulate a heart that beats too slowly due to such problems as blocked arteries, metabolic abnormalities or the side effects of certain medications. They can also help to stabilize a heart that beats too fast or to re-establish the heart's rhythm after cardiac arrest.

SEE ALSO *Heart*

PACHYDERMOPERIOSTOSIS

Pachydermoperiostosis is a rare condition marked by thickening of the skin and enlargement, or clubbing, of the fingers and toes due to the build-up of a fibrous covering on the bones. Thought to be hereditary, it usually develops during childhood or adolescence and progresses slowly over about 10 years.

Symptoms include the formation of skin folds or furrows on the scalp, coarsening of facial features and excessive sweating of feet and hands. The nails of the fingers and toes may become increasingly curved. Despite the apparent severity of the condition, there is usually little associated pain.

SEE ALSO *Skin*

PACHYONYCHIA

Pachyonychia (literally "elephant nails" and also known as nail-bed hypertrophy) is a rare condition involving the overgrowth and excessive thickening of the nails. It is often a congenital disorder and may be combined with other disorders of the skin and mucous membrane.

Jadassohn-Lewandowski syndrome is a type of pachyonychia in which abnormally curved and thickened nails are accompanied by other symptoms such as white plaques in the mouth, thickening of the skin on the elbows, palms, soles and knees, and excessive sweating of feet and hands.

SEE ALSO *Nails*

P

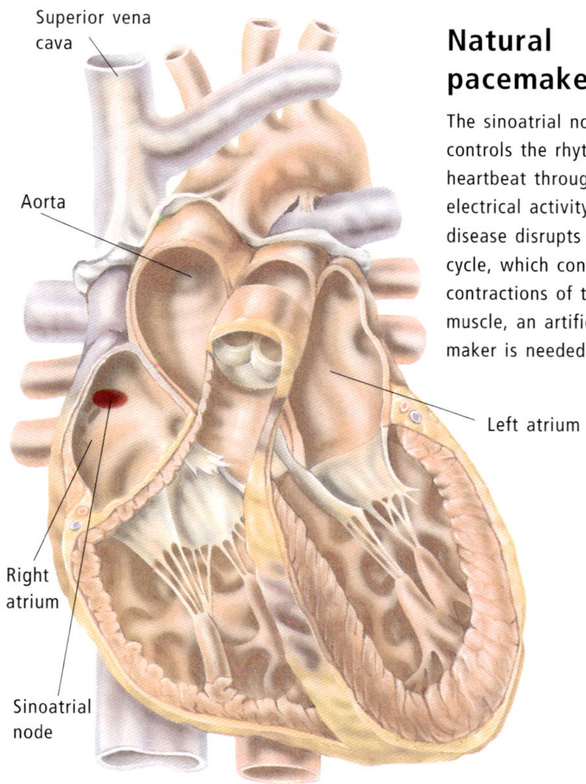

Natural pacemaker

The sinoatrial node usually controls the rhythm of heartbeat through its own electrical activity. When disease disrupts this electrical cycle, which controls contractions of the heart muscle, an artificial pacemaker is needed.

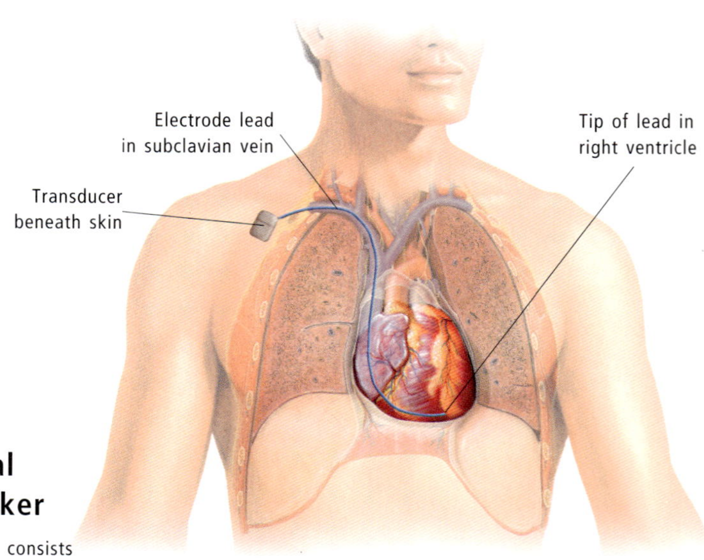

Artificial pacemaker

A pacemaker consists of two main components: a transducer to generate electrical impulses, and electrodes (tiny wires) to make contact with the heart muscle.

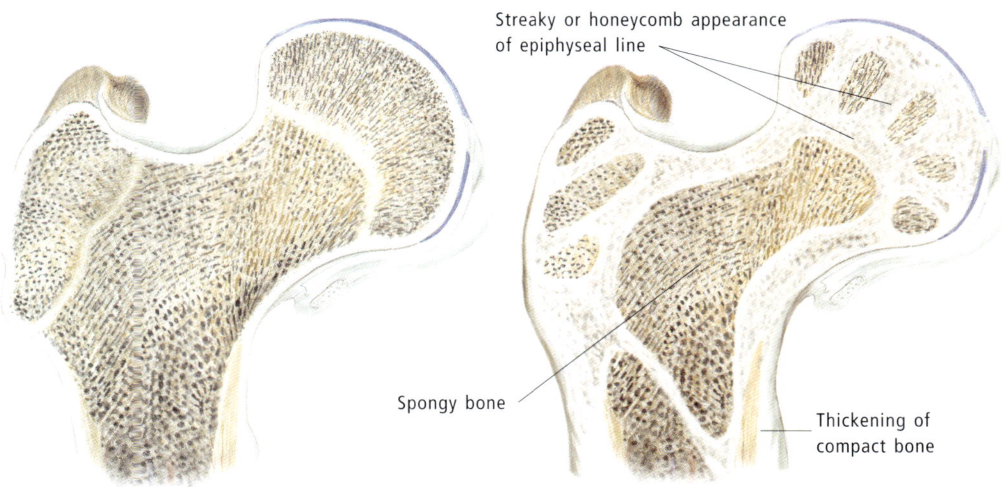

Normal bone

Paget's disease of bone

In Paget's disease, the growth of new bone tissue is disrupted, resulting in bones becoming coarse and soft.

PAGET'S DISEASE OF BONE

Paget's disease of bone, or osteitis deformans, is a disorder in which several bones, most often the pelvis, the lower limbs and the skull, gradually thicken. The disease involves abnormally fast bone destruction and reformation where the new bone matter is structurally abnormal and fragile. This is a chronic, slowly progressive disease that mostly affects elderly people. It may be localized in one or two parts of the body or become widespread. The cause of the disorder is unknown, though recent research points to genetic causes or viral infection. It is known to be common in Europe, Australia and New Zealand.

The disorder (which has no connection with Paget's disease of the breast) often has no symptoms, and is generally discovered during examination or x-ray for some other complaint. In advanced cases, it can cause thickening of the skull, spinal curvature, barrel-shaped chest, bowing of the legs and leg pain. When the skull is affected the head may become enlarged, and hearing loss and blindness may occur if bone growth damages cranial nerves. Radiating sciatic pain in the lower extremities may be felt if the bones of the lumbar spine thicken. Bones affected by Paget's disease fracture more easily than normal bones. Osteosarcoma, a cancer of bone, may sometimes arise from the affected bones.

X-rays and bone scans help diagnose the condition, showing increased bone density and thickening. Blood tests show normal serum calcium with raised serum levels of the bone enzyme alkaline phosphatase. If treatment is required, anti-inflammatory drugs such as aspirin and ibuprofen may be used to relieve pain. Drugs such as calcitonin which suppress bone loss and relieve pain may be prescribed if symptoms persist. If there is extensive damage to the hip, a total hip replacement may be needed.

SEE ALSO *Bones, Paget's disease of the breast*

PAGET'S DISEASE OF THE BREAST

Paget's disease of the breast is an uncommon form of breast cancer, characterized by a lesion on the skin of the nipple similar to moist eczema. Paget's disease does not respond to standard treatments for eczema and is distinguished pathologically by the presence of large pale cells (Paget's cells) never seen in healthy nipple tissue. Since these cells may accumulate pigment, the disease is sometimes mistaken for melanoma.

The affected nipple may be slightly firmer than usual. Other symptoms include nipple discharge, redness or itching around the nipple and a lump or thickening under or near the nipple or areola.

Paget's disease is almost invariably accompanied by or is a precursor to malignant growth (carcinoma) in the underlying breast. It usually affects only one nipple. Rare cases have been reported in male breast cancer.

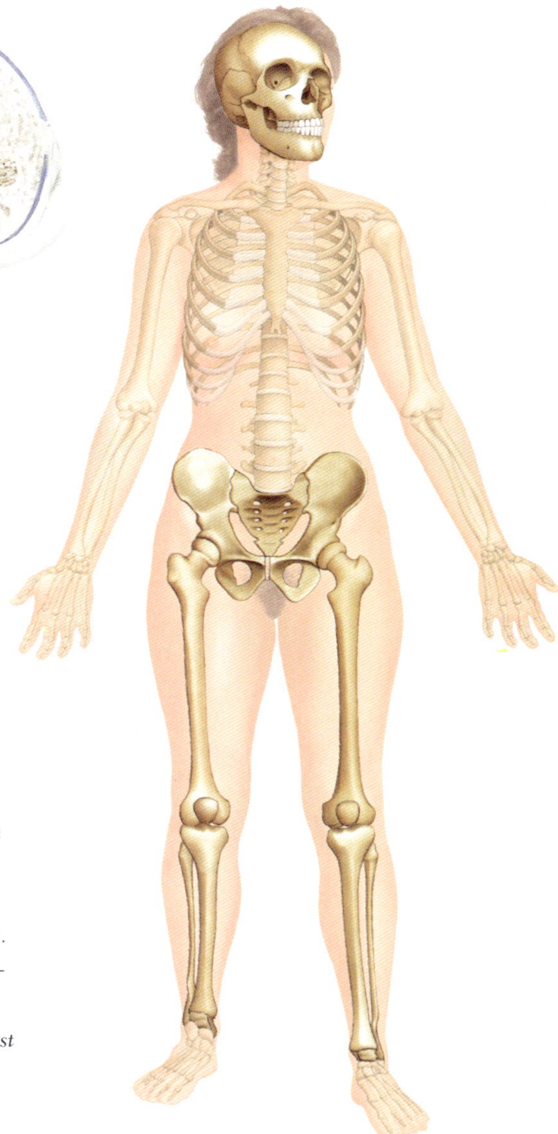

Bones affected by Paget's disease

In the advanced stages of this disease, the bone may be so weakened that even a light blow may cause a fracture. Paget's disease most often affects the pelvis, the lower limbs, and the skull.

Treatment is similar to that for breast cancer without Paget's disease. This may include surgery to remove at least the nipple, areola and some underlying tissue. Alternatively, a mastectomy may be performed as there is a risk that the disease may have spread to other parts of the breast. The risk of this occurring is higher if there is a lump in the nipple area. This disease has been known to occur in the skin areas of the anus and genitals, where it is called extramammary Paget's disease.

SEE ALSO *Breast, Breast cancer, Melanoma, Nipple*

PAIN

Pain is an unpleasant experience associated with real or potential damage to the body. Pain usually serves as a signal that tissues are being damaged, and that the sufferer needs to move away from the painful stimulus as quickly as possible. It also urges rest and recovery from any damage that has been done, to allow healing to take place.

There are two main types of pain. If pain does not outlast its cause, such as a burn or cut, then it is often referred to as acute pain. Such pain serves a useful warning function. For example, there are some rare people born without a sense of pain. While this might seem to be a blessing, such people die relatively young because they do not receive warning of potential damage, and may experience burns, fractures and joint damage.

Unfortunately, however, pain does not always serve a purpose. It may outlast the initial injury and the healing process. It may have a cause which cannot be removed, such as cancer or a malfunction of nerve cells. This is chronic pain and may involve hyperalgesia (increased sensitivity to painful stimuli), allodynia (pain caused by stimuli which would not normally be painful) and spontaneous pain, which has no obvious cause. Chronic pain is debilitating and difficult to treat.

Pain receptors and stimuli

The sensory neurons that mediate pain sensation are known as nociceptors. They have endings or receptors in skin, muscles, joints and internal organs. These nerve endings are connected to the spinal cord or brain stem by nerve fibers which generally lack the myelin sheath which insulates most other sensory nerve fibers.

Nociceptors are activated by a range of potentially damaging (noxious) stimuli which may be mechanical (such as a pinch or cut), thermal (such as a burn) or chemical (such as exposure to acid). Once nociceptors have been activated, signals are conducted along their nerve fibers to the spinal cord or brain stem, and from there to parts of the brain such as the thalamus and cerebral cortex.

Nociceptors have properties which depend on the tissue in which they are located. Nociceptors in the skin are readily activated by pinching or cutting, but internal organs, such as the liver or appendix, can be pinched with forceps without causing pain. This does not mean that the internal organs are entirely insensitive to pain. It is more likely that many of the nociceptors in the viscera are so-called "sleeping" nociceptors. These are only activated by mechanical stimuli when they have already been stimulated by chemicals produced when tissue is inflamed. Sensitization of nociceptors in this way contributes to the increased pain sensitivity felt following tissue damage.

Most of us are familiar, for example, with increased sensitivity of the skin due to sunburn, or how ordinary movement becomes painful following a joint injury. Many analgesics, such as aspirin or acetaminophen (paracetamol), help relieve pain in damaged or inflamed tissues by preventing the production of chemicals which sensitize nociceptors.

Transmission and recognition of pain

Nociceptors form only part of a complex network of nerve cells that give rise to the sensation of pain. Nociceptors send signals to neurons in the spinal cord or brain stem. These neurons receive information not only from nociceptors, but also from mechanoreceptors. These sensory receptors transmit information about muscle length, skin pressure or joint angle—information which normally has nothing to do with pain. Signals from mechanoreceptors do not normally activate spinal neurons which deal with pain. However, in chronic pain, the spinal neurons which deal with painful stimuli receive excessive input from nociceptors. This sensitizes the spinal neurons, which now overreact to inputs from nociceptors or even from mechanoreceptors. The body can therefore become more sensitive to painful stimuli, and can often perceive harmless stimuli as painful as well. The changes in spinal neurons which contribute to chronic pain are often long-lasting and difficult to reverse.

Drugs that have proven useful for acute pain relief include non-narcotic analgesics such as aspirin and acetaminophen (paracetamol), and for more severe pain, narcotic (opioid) drugs such as morphine, codeine and pethidine. There is a common misconception that using opioids for pain relief carries a risk of addiction, but this risk is negligible when they are used purely for the relief of pain in prescribed doses. Chronic pain is often more difficult to relieve than acute pain, but may be treated with anti-epileptics and tricyclic antidepressants as well as non-steroidal anti-inflammatory drugs and opioids such as morphine and methadone.

Once pain signals have been processed in the spinal cord, they are transmitted to the thalamus and cerebral cortex. Relatively little is known about the role of the cortex in pain perception, but recent techniques of brain imaging have been very useful in showing that several areas of the cortex are involved, probably dealing with different aspects of pain. Objective aspects of a painful stimulus (intensity and location) appear to be represented in the somatosensory cortex, while emotional aspects (unpleasantness, associations with other events) are represented in other parts of the cortex, such as the anterior cingulate cortex. Decisions about what sort of action to take in order to avoid the pain may involve the motor cortex.

People (including many doctors) tend to think that the pain they experience depends simply on the intensity of the painful stimulus. This is often not the case. While the nociceptors themselves are very simple, their connections within the spinal cord and brain are complex, and include circuitry which can suppress or even enhance pain sensation. Some people are very sensitive to painful stimuli, while others are quite insensitive. It is also often thought that there are significant cultural differences in pain sensitivity, but such differences are probably more to do with the expression of pain rather than the sensation itself.

Pain sensation can also depend on circumstance. For example, someone injured in a football game or in the heat of battle may hardly notice even a severe injury; conversely pain may be exaggerated by fear or anticipation—an injection may be more painful if there is time to worry about it in advance. Some of these differences in pain perception are due to the control that parts of the brain can exert on pain sensation.

Treatment of pain

Drugs are perhaps the most common measure employed to relieve pain. However, these are not always effective, particularly for chronic pain, and many people turn to alternative therapies, such as chiropractic or acupuncture, for the relief of pain which conventional medical treatment has not been able to alleviate. People may be helped by these alternative treatments, although there is little firm clinical evidence to prove their efficacy.

SEE ALSO *Analgesics, Brain, Narcotics, Neurons, Nerves, Nervous system, Spinal cord*

Processing pain

The brain controls our perception of pain in a number of different areas. Pain signals are relayed to the brain via the thalamus. The sensation and location of pain is registered in the sensory cortex and emotional responses are governed by the limbic system.

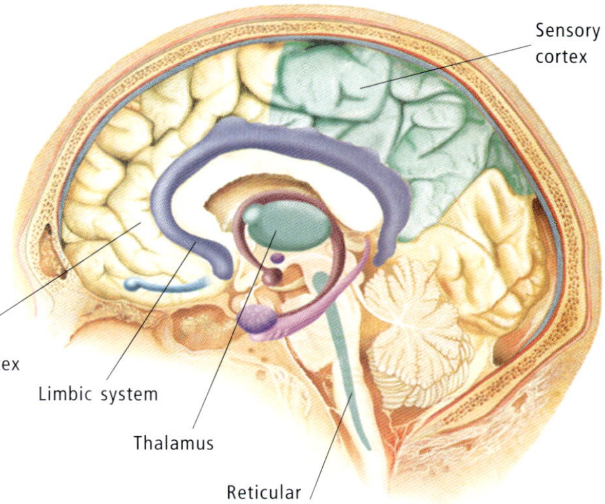

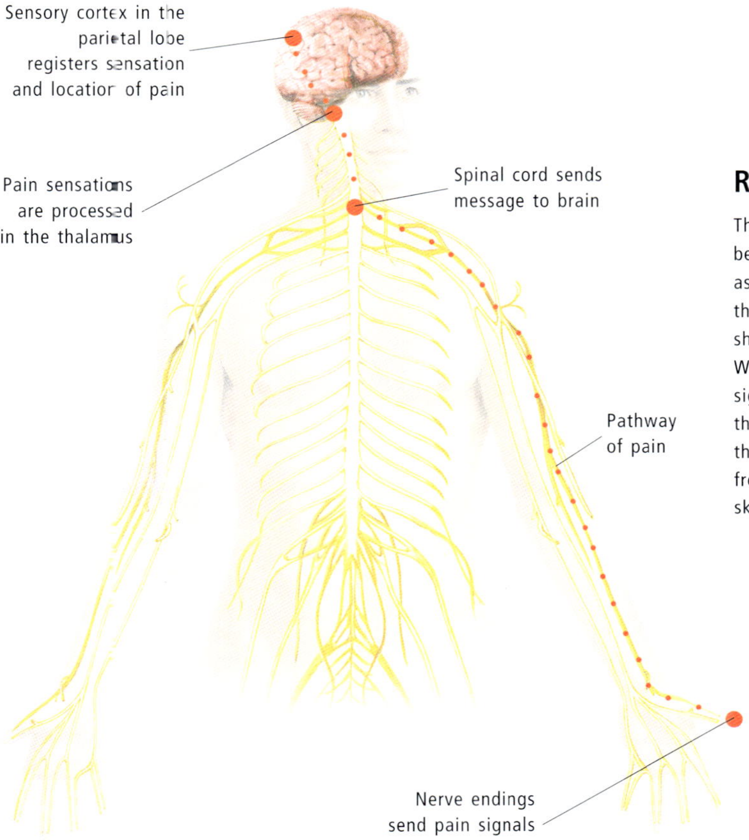

Referred pain

The pain from internal organs may be felt on the surface of the skin as well as internally. This is because the skin and internal organs may share the same pain pathways. When an organ sends pain signals to the spinal cord, the brian may perceive the signal as coming from an area of the skin.

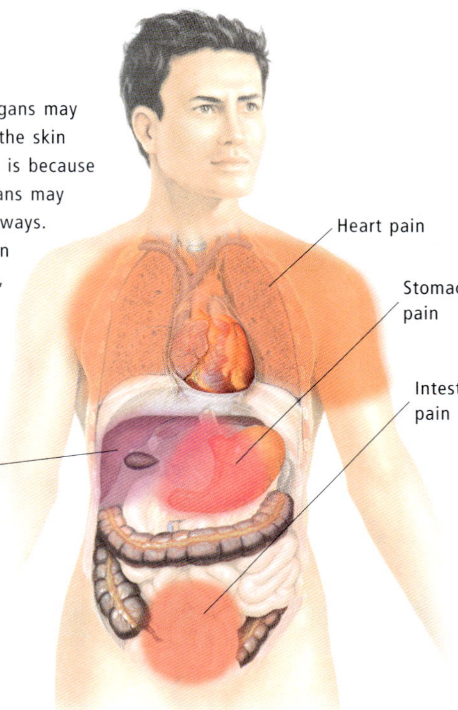

Pain pathways

When sensory neurons (nociceptors) in skin, muscles, joints or internal organs are activated by pain they send signals along nerve fibers to the spinal cord. From there the signals pass up the spinal cord to the brain stem and on to the thalamus and cerebral cortex where the sensation of pain is registered.

Spinal cord

When stimulated, nociceptors (pain receptors) send messages to the spinal cord and then to the brain. These messages are interpreted as pain.

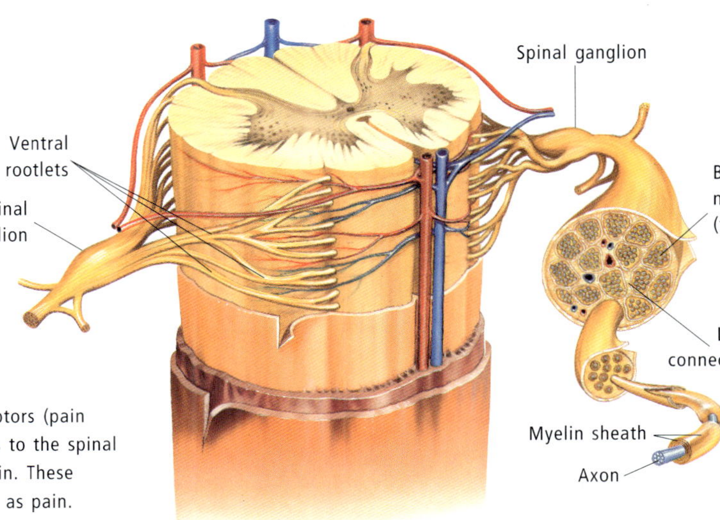

P

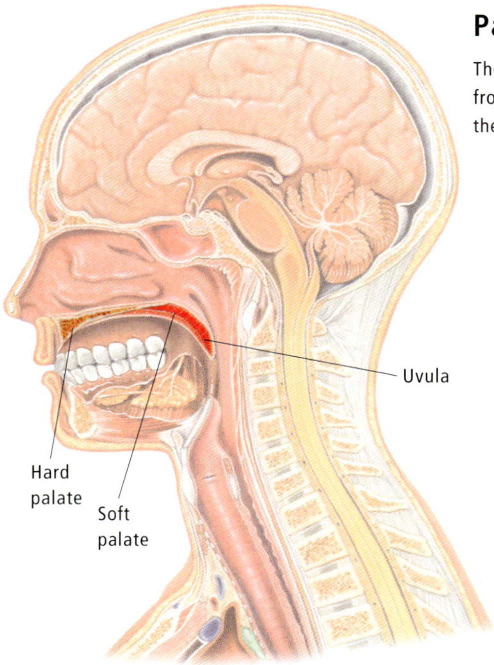

Palate

The hard palate extends back from the top teeth, separating the oral and nasal cavities.

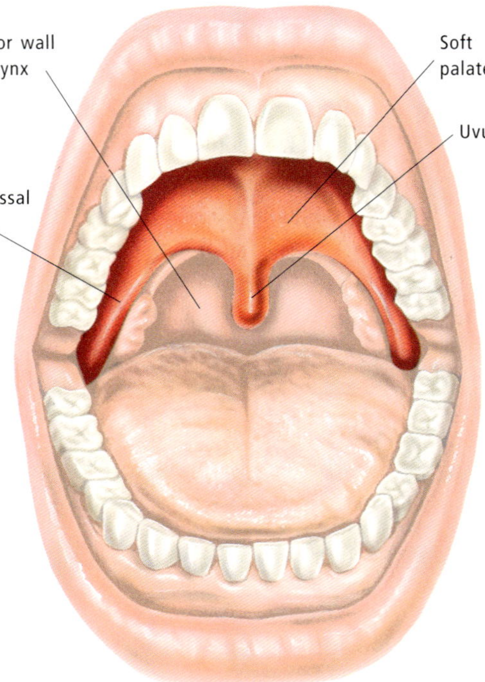

Palate—front view

The soft palate is mainly composed of muscle fibers and mucous membrane. The uvula is its most prominent feature.

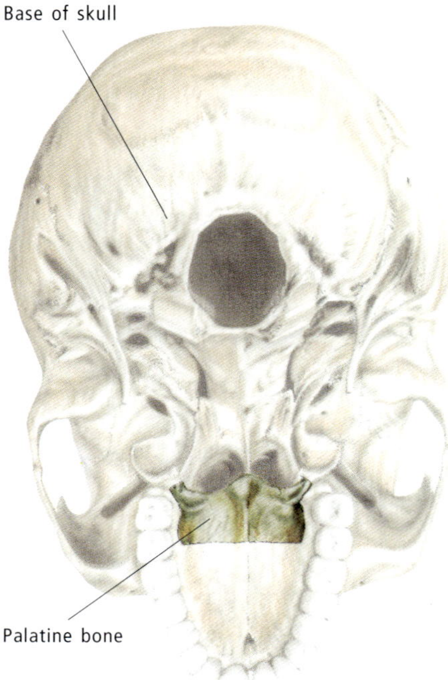

Palatine bone

Situated at the back of the nasal cavity, the palatine bone forms part of the hard palate.

PALATE

The roof of the mouth, separating the oral and nasal cavities, is called the palate. It comprises two sections—one hard, the other soft. Both are covered by mucous membrane containing numerous lubricating glands that keep the mouth and throat moist.

Much of the hard palate, extending from directly behind the top teeth, is formed by parts of the upper jaw bones, or maxillae. These normally fuse at the midline during fetal development. If this fails to occur, it leaves an opening or cleft along the midline which may extend from the teeth to the nasal cavity. This is known as cleft palate and is usually surgically repaired during early childhood. The posterior section of the hard palate is formed by the two L-shaped palatine bones of the skull. Ridges on the hard palate help with maneuvering food in the mouth during chewing and swallowing. When the mouth is closed, the tongue rests on the hard palate.

The soft palate is the fleshy structure that extends from the edge of the hard palate at the back of the mouth. Its own edge is like an incomplete curtain suspended between the back of the mouth and the beginning of the throat (pharynx). The soft palate is composed of muscle fibers and mucous membrane. A small cone-shaped projection, the uvula, hangs from the middle of the soft palate. Both the soft palate and uvula move up during swallowing or sucking to stop food entering the nasal cavity.

SEE ALSO *Jaw, Mouth, Teeth*

PALATINE BONE

The palatine bone is an irregularly shaped bone at the back of the nasal cavity that forms part of the hard palate. It consists of a horizontal plate in the bony palate and a vertical plate that has three projections, or processes, which help form the floor of the eye socket, the outer wall of the nasal cavity and other adjoining parts of the skull.

SEE ALSO *Nose, Palate, Skull*

PALLIATIVE CARE

Palliative care is defined by the World Health Organization as "the active total care of a person whose disease is not responsive to curative treatment". The aim of palliative care is to meet the needs of the whole person—their physical, psychosocial and spiritual needs—as well as those of their family in order to give them the best quality and quantity of life possible under the circumstances. Palliative treatments relieve but do not cure.

Many treatments and therapies for terminal illnesses can prolong the life of the patient for many years, which makes palliative care a complex mix of managing symptoms and therapies, and providing emotional support to prepare the patient and their family for the inevitability of death.

To be effective, palliative care must provide for the needs of the patient coping with the rigors of therapy as well as maintain, as much as possible, a level of physical, mental and social functioning which is satisfactory to the patient. Palliative care has become a subspeciality of medicine in many countries.

When a person is dying, the most important goal is comfort. Forms of comfort include: pain medication which is tailored to the needs of the individual patient; drugs, oxygen therapy and emotional support to relieve shortness of breath; the management of incontinence with drugs, catheters or disposable products; products to relieve dry mouth, such as fluids, humidified air, ice to suck on, or medication; the support and care needed in order to sleep as much as necessary; and an understanding that a patient's appetite may alter or fluctuate.

Other factors that can enhance comfort and dignity are personal grooming—a daily bath, change of sheets or clothes, hair styling or manicure if that is important to the patient; attention to skin care to ensure the avoidance of bed sores; and proper care of teeth, mouth and dentures.

Emotional and spiritual support is also very important. Family, friends and community and health care professionals who can offer honest, compassionate communication about the treatment as well as arranging personal affairs and helping the person to prepare for death are paramount. Patients benefit from being involved in treatment decisions for as long as possible. Working through any unresolved issues is also important for both the patient and their family and carers. People with religious or spiritual beliefs may find they receive support and comfort from priests or counselors. It is common for a person who is dying to feel depressed and this can be alleviated with counseling and medication. The patient and family may need help talking about their needs, wants and expectations and may also need assistance getting any necessary documents, such as a will, finalized.

SEE ALSO *Death*

PALLIDOTOMY

Pallidotomy is a surgical procedure used in the treatment of nervous system disorders such as Parkinson's disease, during which a part of the globus pallidus in the brain is destroyed. It is used to reduce symptoms such as involuntary movements, tremors, slow movement and rigidity.

A wire probe is inserted into the globus pallidus, which lies deep within the brain in the corpus striatum. Radio waves are transmitted via the probe, causing surrounding tissue to heat up, destroying cells in a precisely targeted area of the sensorimotor section of the globus pallidus.

Pallidotomy may be used when medication fails. Possible side effects include impaired vision.

SEE ALSO *Brain, Nervous system, Parkinson's disease*

PALPITATIONS

Usually, a person is not aware of the beating of their heart. However, when the heart beats rapidly or irregularly, there may be an awareness of the heartbeat, and these noticeable beats are referred to as palpitations.

Palpitations are often a normal response to anxiety, fear, exertion, excitement, excessive smoking, or drinking too much coffee. They may also be a symptom of abnormal heart rhythms (arrhythmias), such as fibrillation or tachycardia.

These may be caused by disease of the heart, such as coronary artery disease, or by other diseases, such as anemia or thyrotoxicosis. Palpitations may be accompanied by other symptoms such as chest pain, shortness of breath, or feelings of lightheadedness or dizziness.

Some arrhythmias, such as atrial fibrillation and ectopic beats, are usually not life threatening. Others, such as ventricular fibrillation and ventricular tachycardia, can cause cardiac arrest, a severe decrease in blood flow to tissues and organs, and death. Anyone with palpitations should therefore seek medical advice.

A physician or cardiologist may perform tests such as an electrocardiogram (EKG) and 24-hour Holter monitoring to determine the cause of palpitations. Drugs such as digitalis, quinidine, beta-blockers, calcium antagonists or disopyramide may need to be taken to control an arrhythmia.

SEE ALSO *Arrhythmia, Fibrillation, Heart, Heartbeat, Tachycardia*

PANCOAST'S SYNDROME

Pancoast's syndrome is a complex of symptoms stemming from a malignant tumor known as Pancoast's tumor in the upper part of the lung. It is brought about as neural structures in the lung are invaded and destroyed by the cancer.

Symptoms includes nerve pain (neuralgia) in the arm due to pressure on the brachial plexus, a network of nerves supplying the shoulder and arm. This pain is usually felt in the shoulder area.

Often associated with Pancoast's syndrome is another complex of symptoms known as Horner's syndrome, which includes drooping eyelids, narrowed pupils and facial dryness. Symptoms are relieved by treatment of the underlying cancer.

SEE ALSO *Cancer, Horner's syndrome, Lungs*

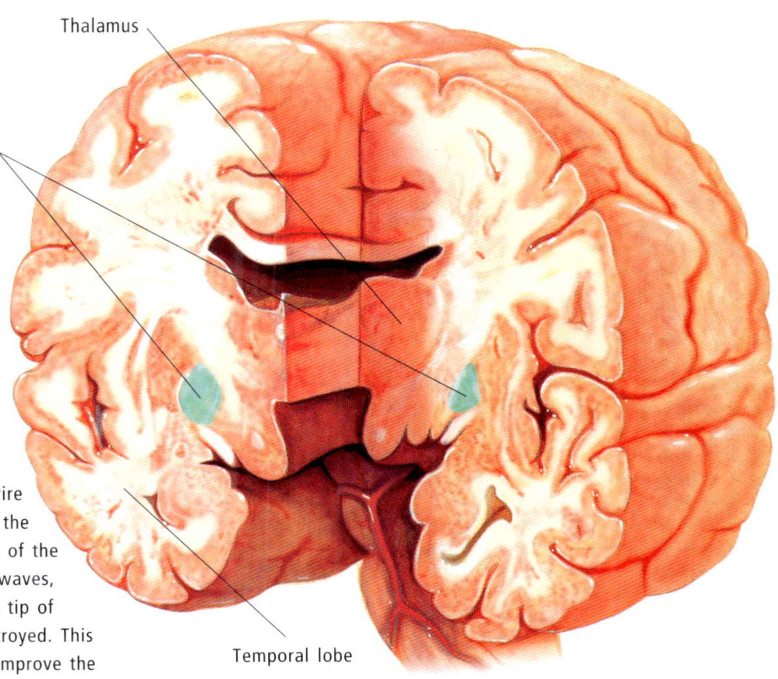

Pallidotomy

In this procedure, a wire probe is inserted into the globus pallidus region of the brain; by using radio waves, the region around the tip of the probe can be destroyed. This procedure is used to improve the symptoms of Parkinson's disease.

PANCREAS

The pancreas is a mixed gland, which has some cells which secrete enzymes into the gut (exocrine pancreas) and other cells which produce hormones which enter the bloodstream (endocrine pancreas). In other words, the pancreas is part of both the digestive and endocrine systems of the body.

The pancreas lies within the abdominal cavity, behind the stomach and in front of the large artery and vein which pass down the center of the abdomen (the aorta and inferior vena cava respectively). The pancreas has a head region which is encircled by the four parts of the duodenum. Leading off to the left from the head region are the neck, body and tail of the pancreas. The tail meets the spleen on the left of the abdomen.

The pancreas has a series of ducts within it which allow digestive enzymes to flow into the interior of the duodenum. The point at which the larger of these ducts enters the duodenum is called the ampulla of Vater. The exocrine secretions of the pancreas are slightly alkaline to neutralize the acid juices coming into the duodenum from the stomach. Enzymes in the pancreatic juices help to digest protein, fat and starch in the food.

Under normal circumstances, the enzymes of the pancreas are prevented from digesting the pancreas itself by three mechanisms. Firstly, the enzymes are stored within cells of the pancreas in separate compartments from the other cell proteins. Secondly, the enzymes are secreted in an inactive form. Thirdly, there are chemical inhibitors of the enzymes present within the pancreatic ducts and tissue.

The endocrine function of the pancreas is concerned with both foodstuff storage after meals and foodstuff release during fasting. The two pancreatic hormones responsible for these functions are respectively insulin and glucagon, which are produced in special cell types within many tiny spherical clumps of pancreatic tissue—these are known as the pancreatic islets, or the islets of Langerhans.

The pancreatic islets are a type of endocrine gland, that is, a gland that secretes products directly into the bloodstream rather than onto the surface of the gut or skin. Insulin release is stimulated by rising blood levels of glucose and amino acids. The hormone in turn stimulates the uptake of sugars, protein and nucleic acids by the body's cells. Glucagon is released in response to low blood glucose and amino acid concentration. It, in turn, stimulates release of glucose, amino acids and fats from body stores.

Damage to the endocrine part of the pancreas by viruses or unknown agents may be one cause of diabetes mellitus, a condition of inadequate control of blood sugar level. In fact, some patients with chronic pancreatitis may develop diabetes mellitus as a complication.

Diseases of the pancreas

Some congenital conditions involve the pancreas. One of these is annular pancreas, in which a ring of pancreatic tissue surrounds the descending duodenum, causing upper gut obstruction in infants and adults. These patients present with vomiting after meals and x-rays often show a dilated stomach and upper duodenum. Surgery to bypass the obstructed segment will correct the problem.

Cancer of the pancreas is a very serious disease, which is a significant cause of death among men aged between 35 and 60 years. It appears to be more frequent in cigarette smokers and diabetics. It is particularly serious because early spread of the disease to nearby structures, lymph nodes and the liver is common, thus making complete surgical removal of the cancer impossible. Cancer in the head of the pancreas may obstruct the duct system of the pancreas, causing weight loss and jaundice from build-up of bile salts.

Other pancreatic cancers located in the tail of the pancreas, away from the pancreatic duct system, will produce weight loss and abdominal pain as the initial symptoms. The prognosis for pancreatic cancer is poor, with most patients dying within a year of diagnosis. Only about 10 percent of patients will survive 5 years, and complete cures are extremely rare.

Occasionally tumors may arise from the islet cells of the pancreas. Insulinomas, for example, arise from the beta cells of the islets. They produce insulin in excess amounts, which gives rise to symptoms of low blood sugar level. Patients show bizarre behavior, memory lapses, palpitations, sweating and unconsciousness. Some may even be mistakenly treated for psychiatric illness. Symptoms are relieved by food, so patients often gain weight from overeating. Treatment may be by drugs, which suppress release of insulin from the tumor, or by surgical removal if the tumor can be located.

Very rarely, gastrin-producing tumors may arise in the pancreas or duodenum. Gastrin is a hormone which controls the amount of stomach acid produced, and it is usually released in response to distension of the stomach by food. These gastrin-producing tumors are often cancers of pancreatic islet cells. They cause a condition known as Zollinger-Ellison syndrome, in which the patient develops peptic ulcers from increased gastric acid secretion, abdominal pain and diarrhea. Treatment should ideally involve locating and removing the gastrin-producing tumor, although removal of the stomach may be necessary if the tumor cannot be found.

The pancreas may be involved in a non-infective inflammatory disease known as pancreatitis. This disease may be short-term or chronic and is often due to gallstones or excessive alcohol intake. The precise sequence of events leading to the disease is poorly understood, but damage to the pancreas is known to be due to release of pancreatic enzymes into pancreatic tissue, with digestion of the pancreas by the patient's own digestive enzymes. Patients will experience nausea, vomiting and upper abdominal pain which may radiate through to the back.

Complications of the disease include the formation of pus-filled abscesses, and cysts filled with digestive enzymes. Treatment is usually medical for acute cases, and is aimed at relieving pain, correcting fluid imbalance and reducing the production of digestive enzymes by the pancreas. Surgery may be necessary for chronic cases.

SEE ALSO *Amino acids, Diabetes, Digestive system, Endocrine system, Islets of Langerhans, Insulin, Pancreatitis, Zollinger-Ellison syndrome*

P

Pancreas

The pancreas plays two different roles in the body. Most of its cells (the exocrine acinar cells) secrete enzymes into the gut and are part of the digestive system. Other cells (in the islets of Langerhans) produce hormones which enter the bloodstream and are part of the endocrine system.

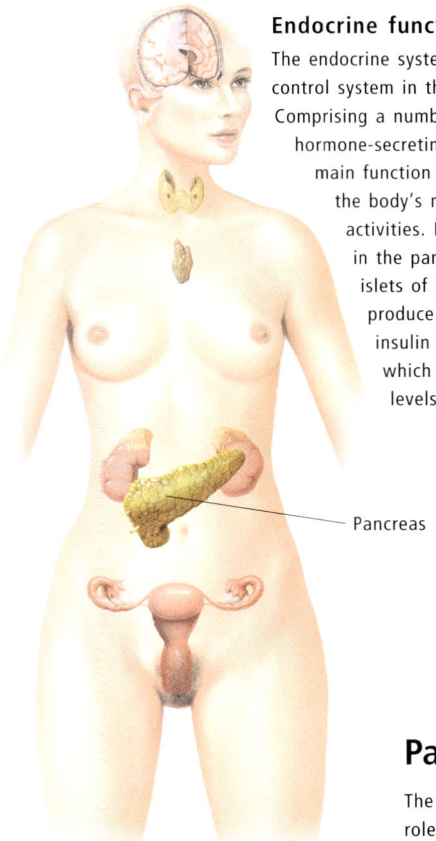

Endocrine function

The endocrine system is a major control system in the body. Comprising a number of hormone-secreting glands, its main function is regulating the body's metabolic activities. Endocrine cells in the pancreas—the islets of Langerhans—produce the hormones insulin and glucagon which control sugar levels in the body.

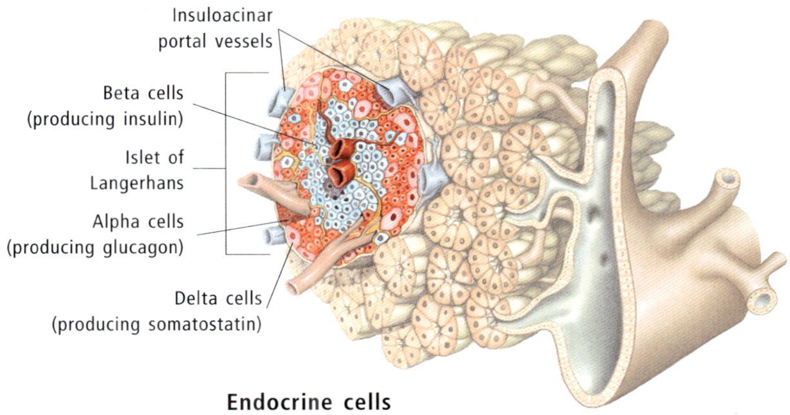

Endocrine cells

Clusters of hormone-producing endocrine cells—the islets of Langerhans—are scattered throughout the pancreas. Alpha cells secrete glucagon which elevates blood sugar. Beta cells secrete insulin which affects the metabolism of fats, proteins and carbohydrates. Delta cells secrete somatostatin which can inhibit the release of both glucagon and insulin.

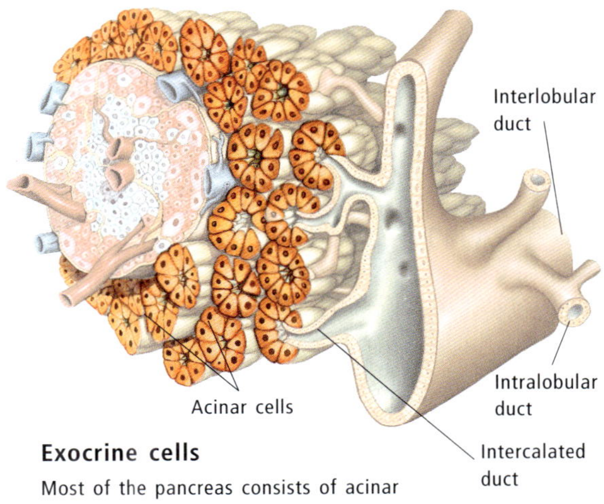

Exocrine cells

Most of the pancreas consists of acinar cells which secrete digestive enzymes that aid in food processing. The enzymes flow from the cells into the small intestine along a network of attached ducts.

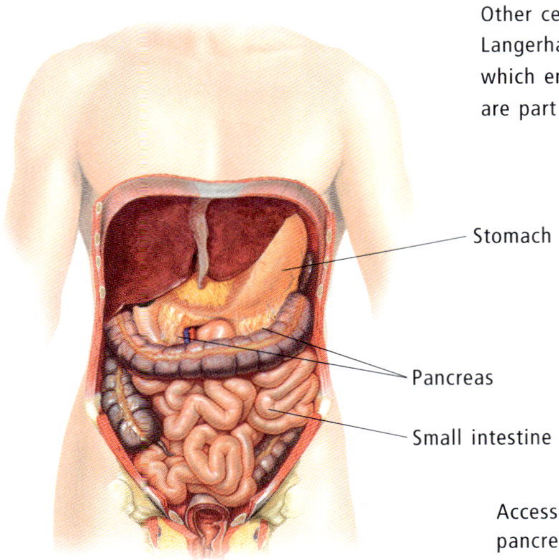

Pancreas—digestive function

The pancreas lies in the abdominal cavity just behind the stomach. The exocrine part of the pancreas secretes enzymes which flow into the small intestine and help the body break down food and extract nutrients.

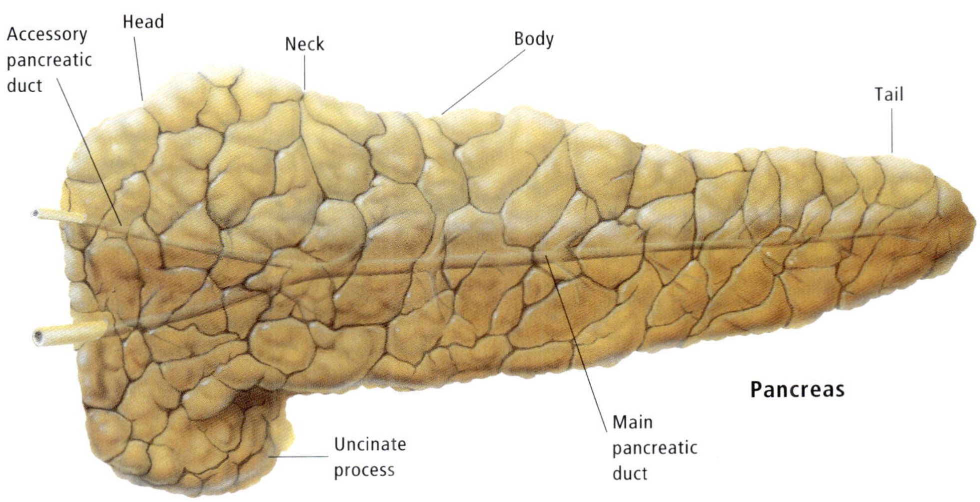

Pancreas

P

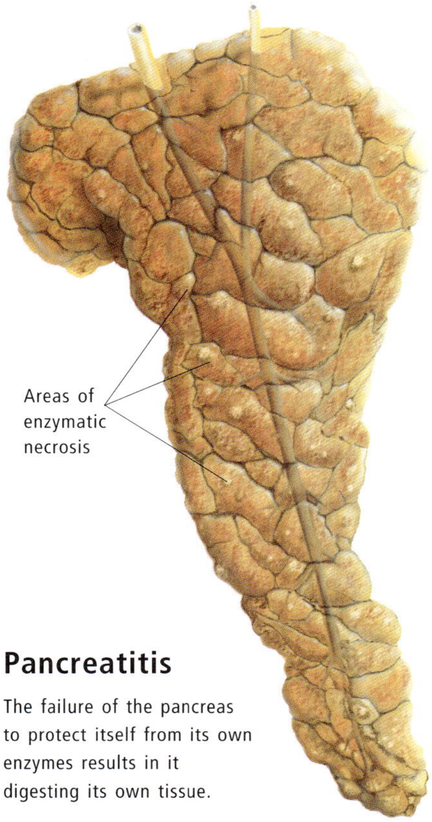

Pancreatitis

The failure of the pancreas to protect itself from its own enzymes results in it digesting its own tissue.

PANCREATITIS

Pancreatitis is a non-bacterial inflammation of the pancreas. It is caused by the digestion of the tissue of the pancreas by its own enzymes. Pancreatitis may be acute, with a sudden onset and relatively short duration, or chronic, lasting for weeks to months with frequent relapses.

Individuals suffering acute pancreatitis experience a sudden onset of pain in the upper abdomen, nausea and vomiting, and have increased concentrations of the digestive enzyme amylase in their blood. Acute pancreatitis may be caused by gallstones (about 40 percent of cases), excessive alcohol intake (a further 40 percent of cases), increased levels of calcium or fats in the blood, surgery or drugs, such as corticosteroids, diuretics and oral contraceptives.

Complications of acute pancreatitis include the formation in the pancreas of abscesses, or pus-filled cavities, and a pancreatic pseudocyst (a cavity filled with fluid rich in digestive enzymes). Treatment does not usually involve surgery unless complications are experienced. Medical treatment can include fluid replacement, pain relief, gastric suction and the control of blood calcium levels.

Chronic pancreatitis is often caused by alcoholism. Patients with chronic pancreatitis suffer recurrent bouts of abdominal pain and problems with absorbing food, and frequently develop diabetes mellitus. Treatment may be medical, as described for acute pancreatitis, or involve surgery to relieve chronic pain.

SEE ALSO *Alcoholism, Diabetes, Gallstones, Pancreas*

PANIC ATTACKS

Panic attacks are a form of anxiety disorder. They can occur in people who also suffer agoraphobia but may happen without warning to people with no previous history or symptoms of such disorders.

A panic attack is characterized by all the physical and emotional signs of a body in danger. The nervous system is activated where no obvious danger exists; there may be chest pain, shortness of breath, irregular or accelerated heartbeat, sweating, dizziness, trembling, weakness, nausea and feelings of fear and a desire to escape. With no apparent reason for the attack, there is no obvious means of escape, and fear of further attacks can lead to staying only in safe areas. The sufferer may stay home through fear of having an attack in a public place, or may only leave home if accompanied. There is a loss of confidence and inability to cope.

Specialist treatment is readily available and should be sought before the disorder creates further problems. Treatment may involve drugs in combination with behavior therapy to help the sufferer understand what causes the attacks and to control the fear of having them.

SEE ALSO *Agoraphobia, Anxiety, Anxiolytics, Behavior therapy*

PAP SMEAR

The Pap smear (or Papanicolaou smear) is a cervical cell sample prepared for viewing under a microscope.

It can reveal the presence of precancerous and cancerous cells in the cervix and is regarded as a crucial screening test that should be performed regularly throughout a woman's life, starting from the time she becomes sexually active.

Since its introduction in the 1940s, the Pap smear has contributed to a massive worldwide reduction in deaths due to cervical cancer.

Taking the smear is a simple and painless procedure that can be performed in a doctor's office. Medical advice should be sought on the frequency with which Pap smears need to be taken because it may vary according to a patient's personal history.

SEE ALSO *Cervix, Reproductive systems*

PAPILLEDEMA

A serious eye disorder, papilledema involves inflammation and swelling of the optic disk, at the point where the optic nerve joins the eye. It is caused by increased pressure inside the brain, often due to a tumor, infections such as meningitis, or cerebral hemorrhage. Symptoms may include blurred or double vision, headaches and nausea. Partial blindness can develop quickly. Papilledema requires immediate medical attention.

SEE ALSO *Eye, Optic nerve*

PAPILLOMA

A papilloma is a non-cancerous growth or tumor on the skin or a mucous membrane. Usually, it is covered by a thickened outer skin layer (epidermis). Warts are among the best known papillomas and are caused by viruses (human papilloma virus, or HPV). Corns, which develop with repeated rubbing of the skin, are also regarded as papillomas.

SEE ALSO *Epidermis, Warts*

Papilloma

Warts and corns are two types of papilloma—a non-cancerous growth on the skin or a mucous membrane.

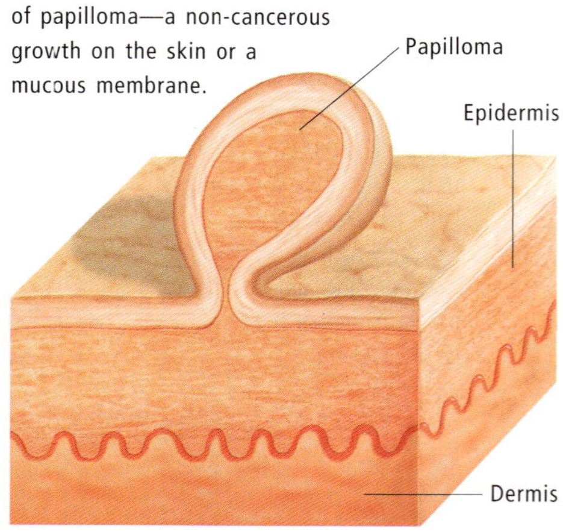

PARACENTESIS

Paracentesis (also known as abdominal tap or peritoneal tap) is a medical procedure which involves removing fluid from a body cavity, usually from within the abdomen. It can be performed in a doctor's treatment room or a hospital. A specialized needle is inserted through the body wall, after the area has first been numbed with a local anesthetic, and fluid is then drawn off. An incision may be needed to assist insertion of the needle.

Paracentesis is commonly used to sample excessive abdominal fluid (ascites) to test for its cause, check for internal bleeding or relieve the effects of fluid build-up.

SEE ALSO *Abdomen, Ascites*

Paralysis

The disruption of nerve pathways by disease or injury, especially in the brain and spinal cord, can result in the paralysis of body parts.

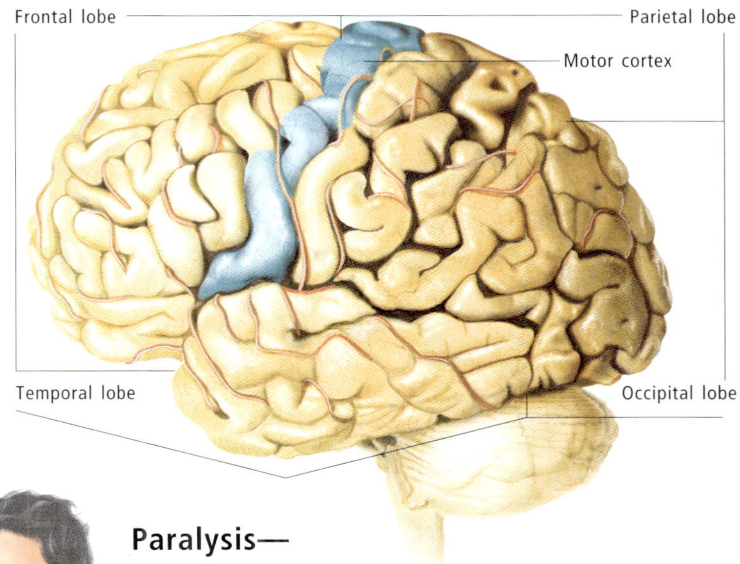

PARALYSIS

Paralysis is the loss of the ability to move a part of the body. It is caused by the inability to contract one or more muscles and usually results from injury to the brain, the spinal cord, a nerve or a muscle. It may be partial or full, and is usually accompanied by a loss of sensation.

There are many causes leading to paralysis; all of them involve an injury or disruption to the nerve pathway through which signals are sent from the brain to the muscles to instruct them to move. The disruption may be in the brain, for example, as a result of stroke (the most common cause), brain tumor, hemorrhage or infection (encephalitis). It may be in the spinal cord, for example, due to injury from trauma (also very common), or pressure on the spinal cord from disk prolapse (herniation) or from spondylosis.

Diseases of the spinal cord, such as multiple sclerosis, poliomyelitis, motor neuron disorders of the peripheral nervous system (neuropathies) and muscle disorders, such as muscular dystrophy, are less common causes of paralysis.

The kind and degree of paralysis differs according to whether the damage is to a peripheral nerve or to the central nervous system (brain and spinal cord). Damage to a peripheral nerve can cause loss of the ability to move a particular muscle or muscles, and a consequent wasting away of those muscles. Damage to the central nervous system, by comparison, produces weakness or loss of the use of a group of muscles, frequently affecting an entire limb. The muscles are stiff when moved (spasticity) but there is no wasting.

Paralysis of the cranial nerves in the head and neck causes paralysis of the facial, throat and eye muscles, causing difficulty speaking and swallowing, and blurred or double vision.

If there is partial or complete paralysis of both legs (and sometimes the trunk), the condition is known as paraplegia. If the arms are also affected, it is called quadriplegia (also called tetraplegia). These conditions are caused by damage to the spinal cord, usually from trauma (most commonly road accidents and sporting injuries), but may also be caused by spinal cord tumors or birth defects. An injury to the neck results in quadriplegia, while an injury to the chest or lower back can result in paraplegia. Hemiplegia is paralysis of the limbs on the same side of the body, often the result of a brain tumor or stroke. The weakness or paralysis occurs on the side of the body opposite to the side of the brain which has been affected.

When the spinal cord is damaged, other disabilities usually occur, such as loss of

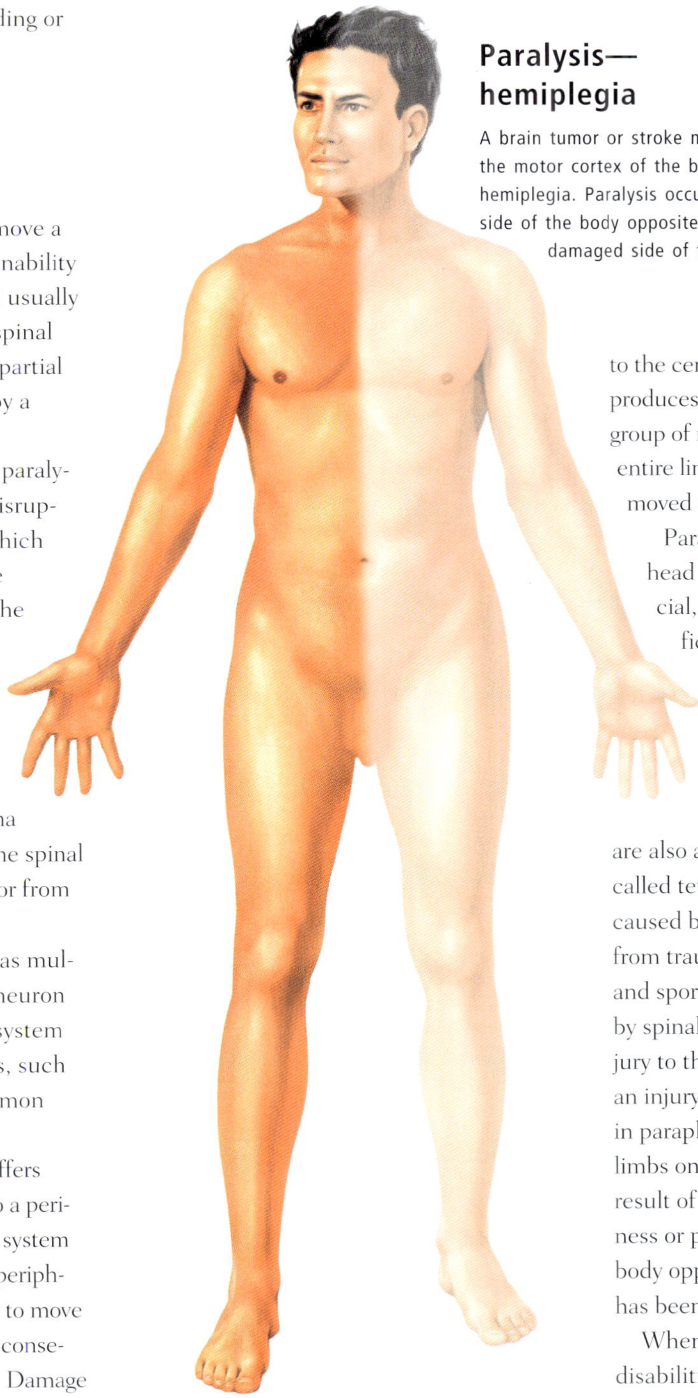

Paralysis—hemiplegia

A brain tumor or stroke may damage the motor cortex of the brain, causing hemiplegia. Paralysis occurs on the side of the body opposite to the damaged side of the brain.

urinary and bowel control, impaired sexual function, loss of normal blood pressure, loss of control of body-temperature, constipation, and breathing difficulties.

Treatment of paralysis requires treating the underlying cause, where possible. Immediate treatment may mean hospitalization, which may take place in intensive care with artificial ventilation if breathing muscles are affected.

Surgery may be possible to limit further spinal-cord damage or to remove bone fragments or a tumor if necessary. Peripheral nerve injuries can be helped by nerve transplants, orthopedic operations to immobilize a joint (arthrodesis), or the transplant of the tendon of a working muscle to aid paralyzed muscles.

Physical therapy and rehabilitation play an important part in the treatment of paralysis. With rehabilitation, many lost functions can be compensated for or restored. Passive exercises for paralyzed muscles will help prevent contractures. Physical therapy will prevent joint stiffness.

Someone who has been in an accident and has neck pain or possible spinal cord injury should not be moved unless absolutely necessary. The injured person's neck should be immobilized with splints or pillows to prevent movement until an ambulance or other emergency service arrives.

SEE ALSO *Brain, Hemiplegia, Nerves, Nervous system, Paraplegia, Quadriplegia, Rehabilitation, Spinal cord*

PARANOIA

Paranoia, or paranoid disorders, are usually classified as personality disorders. People with psychotic disorders, such as schizophrenia or bipolar disorder, may also suffer from paranoid delusions.

Individuals with paranoia suffer from delusions of persecution and are always searching for evidence to support their suspicions. Hostility towards others and angry reactions to perceived insults are also characteristic of paranoia.

In some cases, delusions of grandeur may accompany the feelings of persecution.

SEE ALSO *Personality disorders, Psychosis*

PARAPLEGIA

Paraplegia is partial or full paralysis of the body below the chest or waist, involving the trunk and lower limbs. If all four limbs are affected the condition is known as quadriplegia or tetraplegia.

Paraplegia is caused by damage to the spinal cord, usually from trauma (most commonly the result of road accidents or sports injuries), which disrupts the nerve pathways that connect the brain and muscles. Males between 15 and 35 years old are the group most commonly affected. Less frequently, paraplegia is caused by spinal cord tumors or birth defects.

In paraplegia, all body parts below the level at which the spinal cord is damaged are affected. In addition to paralysis, this may mean constipation, problems with blood pressure and sexual function, as well as the inability to control body temperature or bowel and urinary movements. Treatment as soon as possible

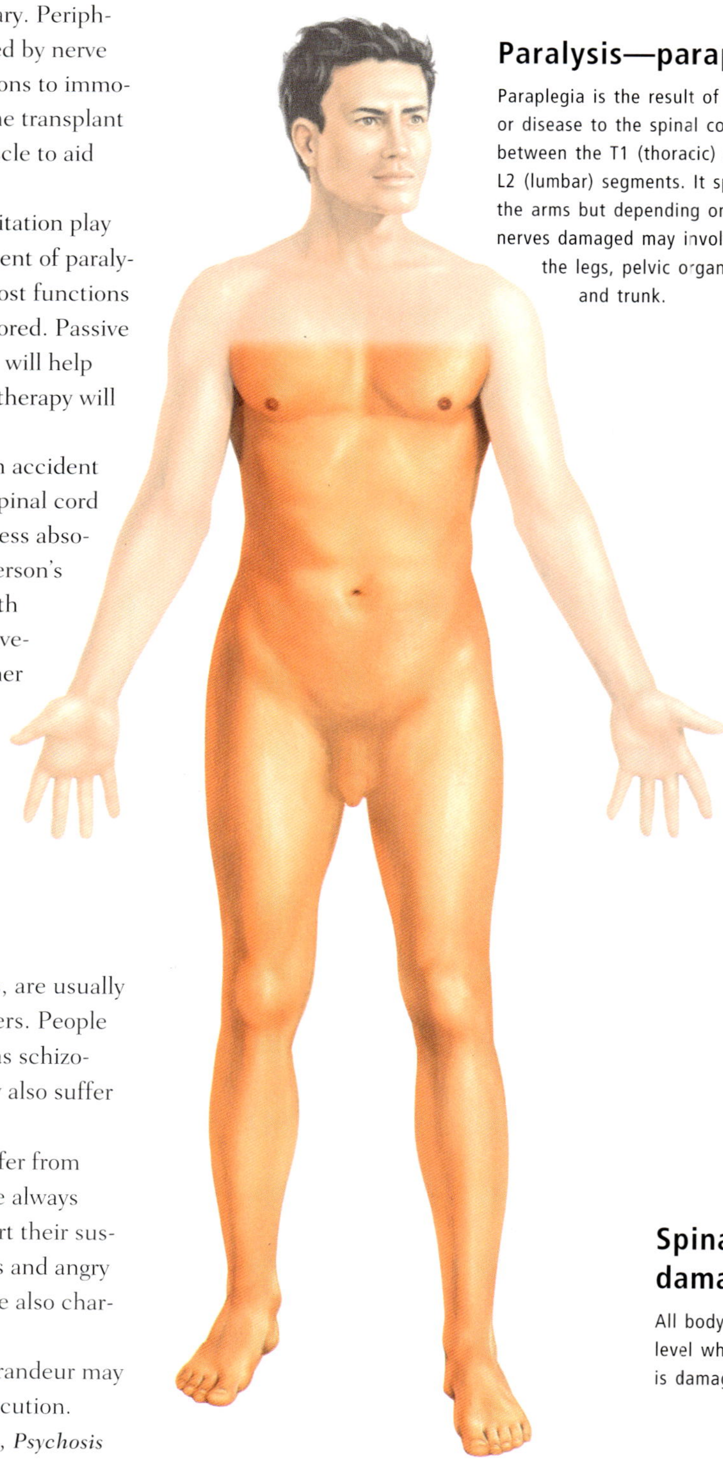

Paralysis—paraplegia

Paraplegia is the result of injury or disease to the spinal cord between the T1 (thoracic) and L2 (lumbar) segments. It spares the arms but depending on the nerves damaged may involve the legs, pelvic organs and trunk.

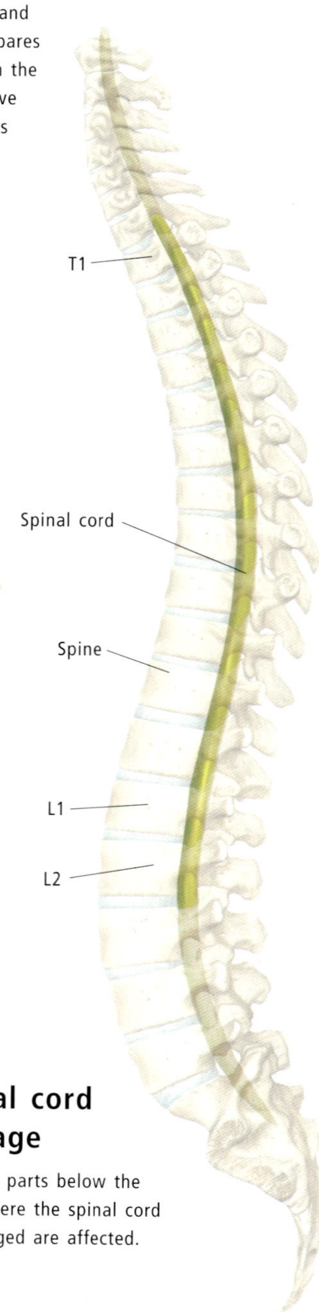

Spinal cord damage

All body parts below the level where the spinal cord is damaged are affected.

after the injury will provide the injured person with the greatest chance of recovering some function. Treatment may include surgery in order to remove fluid or tissue that presses on the spinal cord (decompression laminectomy), to remove bone fragments or foreign objects, or to stabilize fractured vertebrae by fusion of the bones or insertion of hardware. Bed rest and spinal traction (which immobilizes the spine and reduces dislocation) will promote healing.

If movement or sensation return within 1 week after the injury, then most function will eventually be recovered (although this may take 6 months or more). Losses that remain after 6 months are likely to be permanent. Approximately one-third of sufferers remain permanently wheelchair-bound.

Most treatment for paraplegia is therefore centered around rehabilitation. Passive exercises for paralyzed muscles will help prevent contractures. Physical therapy will prevent joint stiffness. Occupational therapy and psychotherapy or counseling may help depression or sexual problems. Prolonged immobility can cause serious complications; for this reason, frequent position changes and good skin care are very important. Complications such as bed sores, kidney stones, muscle spasms and leg ulcers need to be treated immediately.

Paraplegics will need to come to terms with permanently reduced mobility and may require help with accommodation, employment, transport, access to buildings, and in dealing with the financial costs and isolation. Life expectancy for a paraplegic is on average 90 percent of that expected by the able-bodied population.

In many cases, paraplegia can be prevented. Paraplegia often results from road accidents, so drinking alcohol or using mind-altering drugs before or during driving should always be avoided. Seat belts should be worn in cars. In the case of sporting accidents, it is advisable to wear protective headgear for contact sports or while riding a bicycle or motorcycle. Do not dive into shallow swimming pools or into water of unknown depth.

SEE ALSO *Nervous system, Paralysis, Quadriplegia, Rehabilitation, Spinal cord*

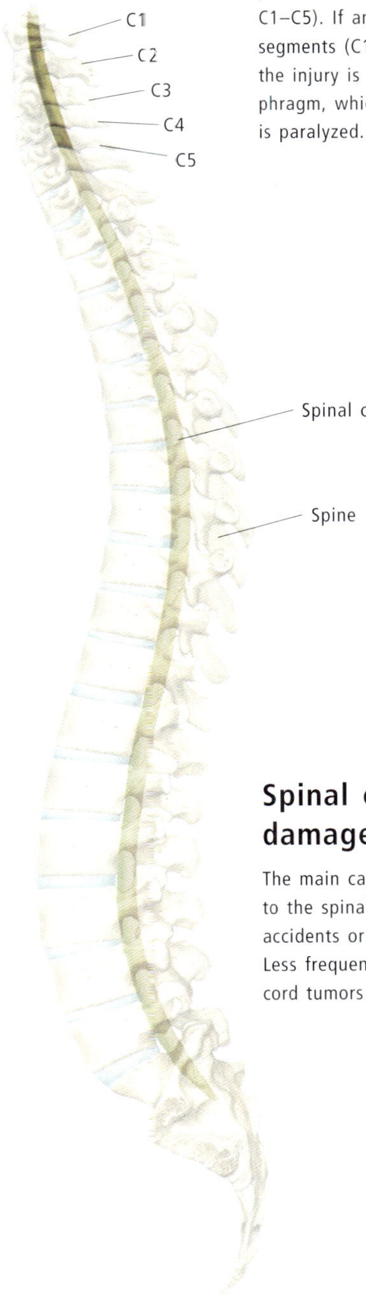

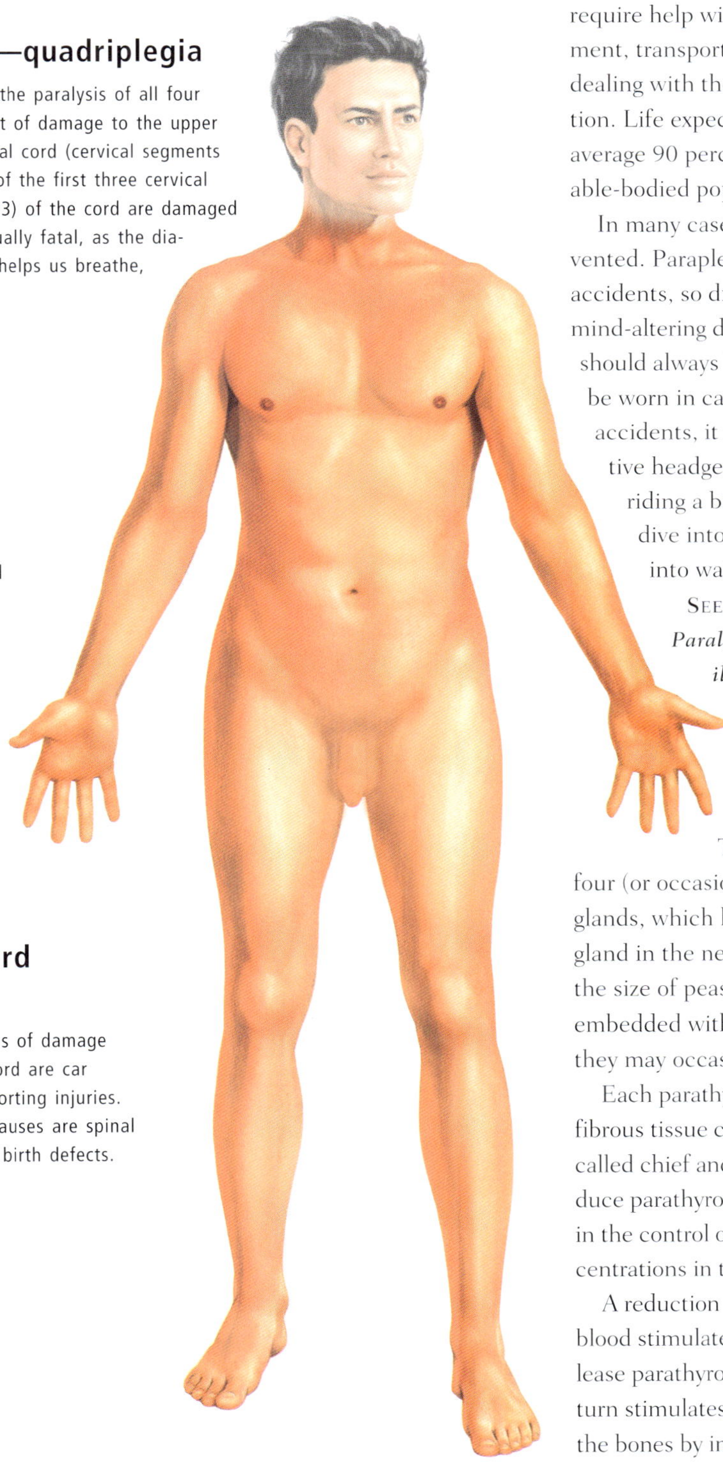

Paralysis—quadriplegia

Quadriplegia is the paralysis of all four limbs as a result of damage to the upper part of the spinal cord (cervical segments C1–C5). If any of the first three cervical segments (C1–C3) of the cord are damaged the injury is usually fatal, as the diaphragm, which helps us breathe, is paralyzed.

Spinal cord damage

The main causes of damage to the spinal cord are car accidents or sporting injuries. Less frequent causes are spinal cord tumors or birth defects.

PARATHYROID GLANDS

The parathyroid glands are four (or occasionally three) small endocrine glands, which lie just behind the thyroid gland in the neck. The glands are only about the size of peas. Sometimes these glands are embedded within the thyroid gland itself; they may occasionally be found in the chest.

Each parathyroid gland comprises a fibrous tissue capsule and two types of cell called chief and oxyphil cells. Chief cells produce parathyroid hormone, which is involved in the control of calcium and phosphate concentrations in the blood.

A reduction in the levels of calcium in the blood stimulates the parathyroid gland to release parathyroid hormone. This hormone in turn stimulates the release of calcium from the bones by increasing the activity of cells

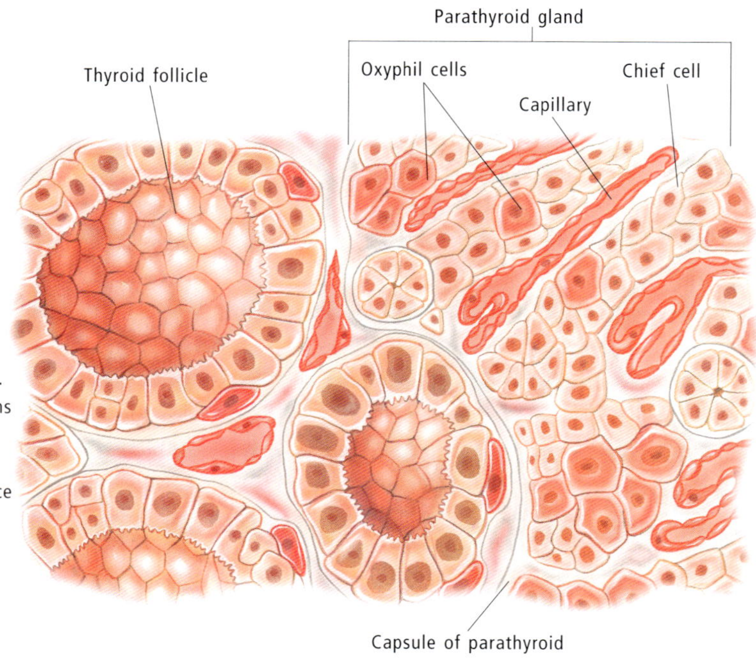

Parathyroid gland microstructure

The cells of the parathyroid are separated from thyroid cells by a dense capsule of fibers. The parathyroid contains two different cells: chief cells and oxyphil cells. Chief cells produce parathyroid hormone when blood levels of calcium fall.

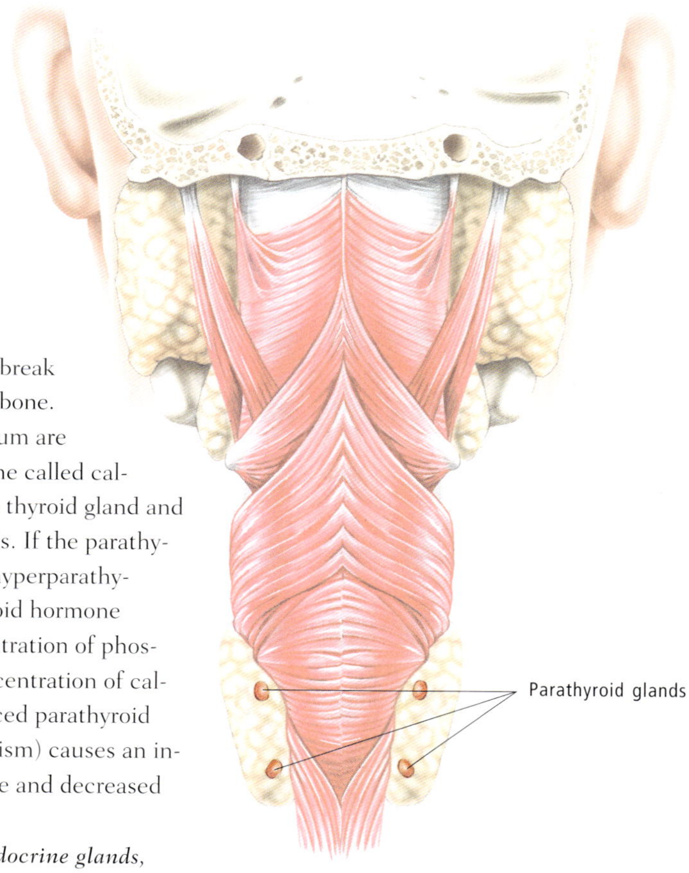

Parathyroid glands

These tiny glands lie behind the thyroid gland at the base of the neck. They secrete parathyroid hormone which controls calcium levels in the blood.

called osteoclasts, which break down the mineral part of bone.

If levels of blood calcium are too high, another hormone called calcitonin is released by the thyroid gland and acts to decrease the levels. If the parathyroid gland is too active (hyperparathyroidism) excess parathyroid hormone causes decreased concentration of phosphate and increased concentration of calcium in the blood. Reduced parathyroid activity (hypoparathyroidism) causes an increase in blood phosphate and decreased blood calcium.

SEE ALSO *Calcium, Endocrine glands, Glands, Hormones, Thyroid gland*

PARATYPHOID

Paratyphoid is a gastrointestinal disease caused by certain forms of *Salmonella* bacteria. It occurs throughout the world but, because it is spread via food or water contaminated by feces or urine from an infected person, outbreaks occur mainly where sewerage and sanitation systems are inadequate. Symptoms, similar to but usually less severe than those of typhoid, appear between one and ten days after consuming a contaminated product. They include headaches, watery diarrhea, a rosy chest and abdominal rash, and dry cough. In severe cases, the disease can cause intestinal bleeding, mental fogginess and minor deafness. Death is rare when medical attention is provided. Treatment commonly involves antibiotics.

SEE ALSO *Gastroenteritis, Typhoid*

PARKINSON'S DISEASE

First described in 1817 by the British physician James Parkinson, Parkinson's disease is a disease of the central nervous system, characterized by gradual, progressive muscle rigidity, tremors and clumsiness.

The affected person suffers muscle stiffness and slowness, has a mask-like expression and an awkward or shuffling walk with a stooped posture, and talks in a slow, monotonous voice. Walking, talking, or completing other simple tasks becomes progressively more difficult. The symptoms are made worse by tiredness or stress. Some people with Parkinson's disease become severely depressed. In the later stages of the disease, mental deterioration and dementia may occur.

Parkinson's disease affects approximately two out of 1,000 people, and most often develops after age 50; it is one of the most common neurologic disorders of the elderly. The exact cause is unknown, but common to all is a progressive deterioration of the nerve cells in the part of the brain that controls muscle movement. As a result, there is a deficiency of a neurotransmitter (a chemical that relays messages across the nerve pathways) called dopamine that is normally found in this area of the brain. Without dopamine, the nerve cells cannot properly transmit messages, and this results in abnormal firing of neurons and consequently, abnormal muscle movement. The disorder may affect one or both sides of the body, with varying degrees of loss of function.

Parkinsonism refers to those cases where Parkinson's disease occurs as a result of another disorder. It can be caused by medications (especially the phenothiazine tranquilizers), and brain disorders such as post-influenza encephalitis and some slow virus infections.

Parkinson's disease is incurable. However, symptoms can be relieved or controlled by medications, which work by increasing levels of dopamine in the brain. They include levodopa, which is converted by the body to dopamine, and carbidopa, which reduces the side effects of levodopa. These drugs are successful in decreasing tremors and reducing muscle rigidity, but they often have significant side effects. These may be controlled with antihistamines, antidepressants, bromocriptine, monoamine oxidase inhibitors, and other drugs.

Most people respond to medications, but to a variable degree. The therapeutic effect of the medications tends to wear off after a few years. Surgery to destroy parts of the nerve pathways in the brain responsible for tremors may reduce symptoms in some people. A new technique involves surgical grafting of dopamine-secreting neurons into the brains of Parkinson's sufferers. The long-term success of this technique is not yet established.

Regular rest periods and avoidance of stress will help symptoms such as tremor. Physical therapy, speech therapy, occupational therapy, social work and other counseling services help the affected person to function as normally as possible.

SEE ALSO *Nerves, Nervous system, Neurons, Palliodotomy*

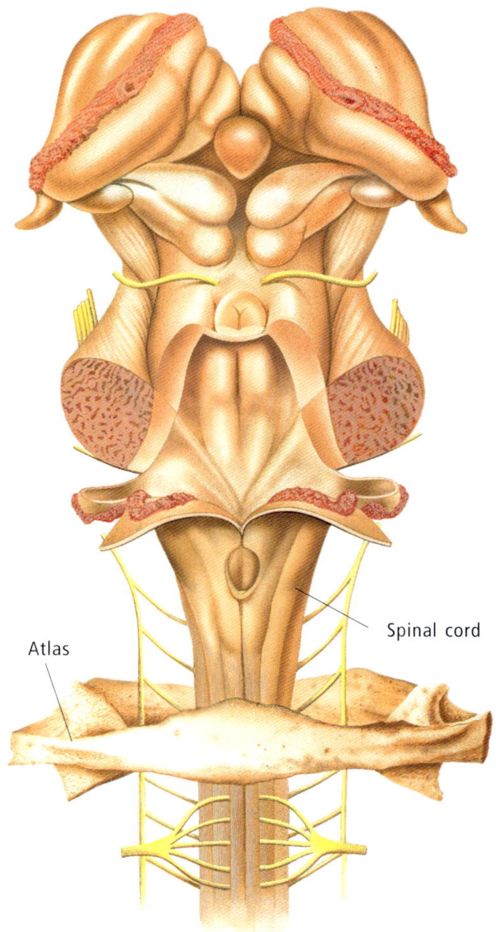

Parkinson's disease

Nerve cells in the substantia nigra (part of the brain stem) control muscle tone and movement. The progressive deterioration of these cells is the most common cause of Parkinson's disease, which causes muscle rigidity and tremors.

PARONYCHIA

Paronychia is an infection of the skin around a nail. It is caused by bacteria, fungi (especially candida) or both. Usually the infected skin is already damaged, from biting, picking or trimming nails or from immersing hands in water for long periods, for example. The skin around the nail becomes red and swollen, and in the case of bacterial paronychia, there may be tiny abscesses. The nail is often infected as well, becoming discolored and misshapen. Treatment is with antibiotic or antifungal creams or ointments. Fungal paronychia may take some months to clear.

Paronychia is best prevented by caring for nails and the skin around them. Protective gloves should be worn to prevent exposure to detergents and chemicals. Nails should be kept smooth and should be trimmed regularly. Biting or picking at the nails, trimming the cuticles and the use of cuticle removers may worsen the condition. Diabetics are especially prone to paronychia and need to take special care.

SEE ALSO *Nails*

PATENT DUCTUS ARTERIOSUS

Normally the fetus receives oxygen from the placenta via the umbilical cord, so the lungs are not needed. Hence, there is a channel between the pulmonary artery and the aorta called the ductus arteriosis. The function of this duct is to allow the blood flowing through the fetal heart to bypass the lungs and be pumped straight into the systemic circulation and around the body.

Shortly after birth the duct normally closes, and the heart commences pumping blood into the lungs as well as the rest of the body. In about 60 out of 100,000 infants, the duct doesn't close properly—this condition is known as patent ductus arteriosus. It is similar to atrial septal defect except that in that condition, the hole that fails to close is between the two upper chambers of the heart (the atria). The cause is unknown, but it is more common in premature infants. Patent ductus arteriosus causes mild shortness of breath and failure to thrive, which may progress over time to heart failure.

The condition is diagnosed by a physician using a stethoscope (usually a heart murmur is audible) and an echocardiogram (ultrasound of the heart). Surgical ligation of the patent ductus corrects the condition and is usually done between 6 months and 3 years of age, earlier if heart failure develops.

SEE ALSO *Atrial septal defect, Fetal development, Heart, Lungs, Placenta*

PECTORAL MUSCLES

The pectoral muscles lie in the front of the chest, under the breasts. There are two on each side: the pectoralis major and pectoralis minor. They arise mainly from the collar bone (clavicle), sternum and rib cage, and are attached to the humerus in the upper arm and the

Pectoral muscles

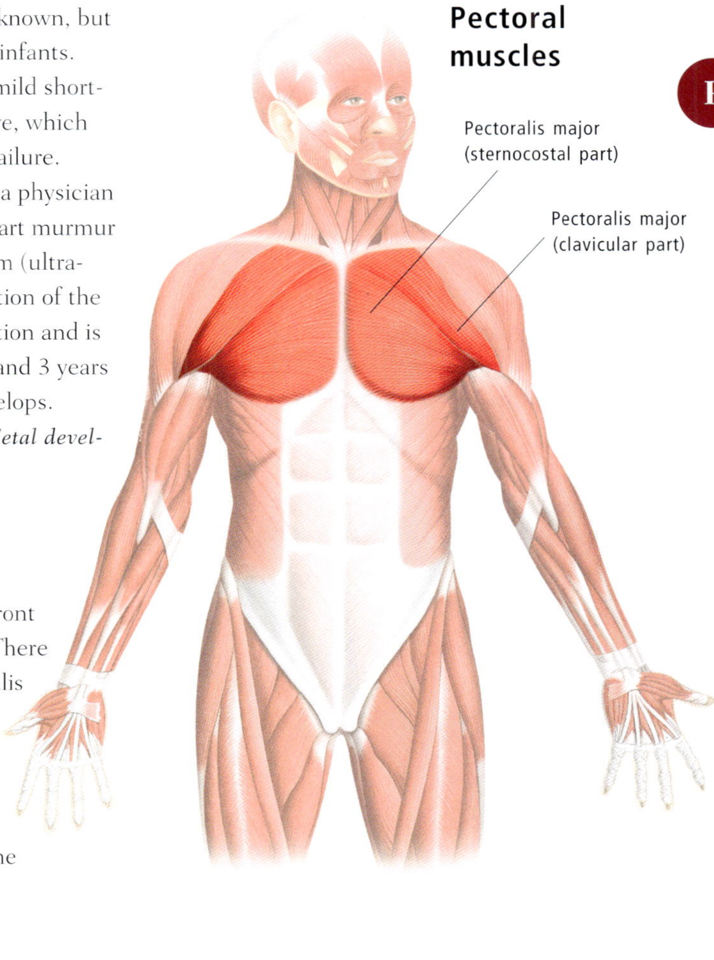

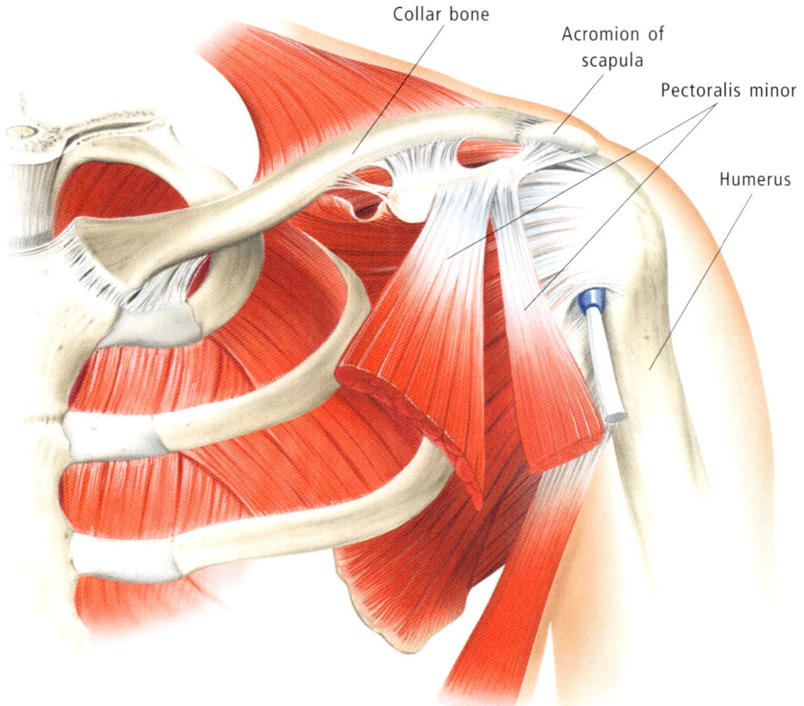

Pectoral muscles

The pectoral muscles cover the front of the chest and are attached to the shoulder and humerus. They work in combination with the scapula to control the movement of the humerus (the upper arm bone).

coracoid process of the shoulder blade (scapula). The pectoralis major can be felt under the breast when the muscle is tensed by attempting to pull a fixed object sideways towards one's midline.

SEE ALSO *Chest, Collar bone, Muscle, Ribs, Scapula, Sternum*

PELLAGRA

Due to the progressive nature of its symptoms, pellagra is sometimes called the disease of the four Ds: dermatitis, diarrhea, dementia and death. It is caused by a deficiency in niacin (one of the B group vitamins) or the amino acid tryptophan, which is used by the body to make niacin. It usually stems from poor diet and can develop rapidly—within 8 weeks in people with severe deficiencies.

Loss of appetite, falling weight, irritability and lack of energy are early signs. A scaly, sun-sensitive skin rash and diarrhea follow. Mental disturbances, including depression, delirium and ultimately dementia, appear in chronic cases. Without treatment, death is inevitable. Oral vitamin B supplements, however, are a simple and effective remedy, usually evoking a rapid turnaround of symptoms within 24 hours.

These days pellagra is rare in industrialized countries, although it is occasionally seen in alcoholics. It is more common in poor nations where people have inadequate nutrition. African populations that rely on a diet of corn, and little else, are particularly susceptible because this grain, unlike wheat, contains virtually no tryptophan. Foods rich in niacin or tryptophan include liver, eggs, milk, red meat, fish, wholegrain products, yeast, peas, beans and nuts.

SEE ALSO *Amino acids, Vitamins*

PELVIC FLOOR MUSCLES

The pelvic floor muscles form a "floor" or diaphragm across the pelvis, running from the back to the front and in from the sides. Strung like a hammock between the sacrum at the back and the hip bones at the front and sides, these muscles support the bladder and bowel and, in women, the uterus.

The pelvic floor muscles have openings for the urethra (the tube that connects the bladder to the outside of the body), the anus (anal canal) and, in women, the vagina.

In some conditions, the pelvic floor muscles can become overstretched and weakened. These conditions include pregnancy (especially repeated pregnancy), advanced age, and menopause; disorders that increase pressure in the abdomen, such as tumors, chronic coughing and chronic constipation; or activities such as continuous lifting. Stretched and weak pelvic floor muscles can have several consequences: uterine prolapse (a disorder in which the uterus moves down, out of its normal position); urinary incontinence (the leaking of urine during coughing, straining or physical exertion); rectal prolapse; and in women, difficulty keeping tampons in place.

The treatment of weakened pelvic floor muscles involves exercises to strengthen and tighten them. The exercises should be performed daily and may need to be continued indefinitely. These exercises include tightening one at a time, the openings from front to back, or back to front, or interrupting urination in mid-stream. The exercises should be practised during and after each pregnancy. An exercise program can be obtained from a physician, a physical therapist or from a childbirth clinic.

SEE ALSO *Bladder, Bowel, Hip, Intestines, Pelvis, Prolapse, Sacrum, Urinary incontinence, Uterus*

PELVIC INFLAMMATORY DISEASE

Pelvic inflammatory disease involves infection of the female reproductive organs above the level of the uterine cervix. This type of infection is serious for several reasons. Firstly, infection may spread throughout the abdominal cavity, giving rise to peritonitis. Secondly, infection may spread to nearby pelvic organs to create an abscess. Thirdly, pelvic inflammatory disease is a common cause of infertility because the fallopian tubes may become blocked by scar tissue during healing.

Most pelvic infections are caused by bacteria. They may occur after childbirth or termination of pregnancy, in which case invasion of the tissues by bacteria (*Clostridium, E. coli, Streptococcus*) is rapid and the patient may be at great risk of dying from septicemia. Where the infection is due to the bacteria *Neisseria gonocccus* (gonorrhea), the progress is usually slower, with the patient complaining of vaginal discharge, fever, burning when passing urine, and pelvic pain.

Long-term pelvic infection may cause abnormal periods, menstrual pain, painful intercourse and infertility. Treatment for pelvic inflammatory disease includes the appropriate antibiotic and pain relief, although surgery may be required for complications of chronic infection.

Pelvic inflammatory disease is an important social problem because of its link to sexually transmitted diseases such as gonorrhea, and the increasing incidence of infection with drug-resistant bacteria.

SEE ALSO *Cervix, Fallopian tubes, Gonorrhea, Infertility, Peritonitis, Reproductive systems*

PELVIS

The term pelvis (from the Latin meaning "basin") encompasses a number of structures. It can refer to the bony pelvis, a ring of bone between the trunk and thigh. It can refer to the lesser or true pelvis, the part of the bony pelvis below the pelvic inlet, or may refer to the pelvic cavity, a funnel-shaped region within the lesser or true pelvis that contains pelvic organs, including the bladder, rectum and internal genitalia. Usually the term refers to the lesser pelvis.

Bony pelvis

The bony pelvis forms the skeletal framework for the pelvis and is mostly covered by muscles. It functions to transfer weight from the vertebral column to the lower limbs as well as to provide protection for the pelvic and lower abdominal organs. It comprises the hip bones, sacrum and coccyx. Each hip bone is made up of three bones (ilium, ischium and pubis) that are separate in a child, but later fuse. Each hip bone unites in front at the pubic symphysis and joins the sacrum behind at the sacroiliac joints. The coccyx (tail bone) forms a joint with the lower end of the sacrum.

The pelvic inlet demarcates a region called the greater or false pelvis above (part of the abdominal cavity) and the lesser or true pelvis below. The lower borders of the bony pelvis form the pelvic outlet.

Lesser pelvis

The lesser pelvis (or true pelvis) is bounded behind and above by the sacrum and coccyx. Muscles of the wall include the piriformis muscle toward the back, and the obturator internus muscle on the side wall. The pubic bones and pubic symphysis lie in front and below, and the floor is formed by the pelvic diaphragm; below this is the urogenital diaphragm. The lesser pelvis is open above to the abdominal cavity.

Pelvic cavity

Within the lesser pelvis is a funnel-shaped cavity or region, known as the pelvic cavity. It is defined as the area between the pelvic inlet above and the thin, sheet-like muscle of the pelvic diaphragm below. It contains and protects the pelvic organs: the bladder and rectum in both sexes; the uterus and vagina in the female; and the prostate and seminal vesicles in the male.

The bladder lies in the front of the pelvic cavity and rests partly on the pubic bones. The rectum lies to the back against the curve of the sacrum and coccyx.

The uterus and vagina lie between the bladder and the rectum in the female, and in the male, the prostate lies below the bladder while the seminal vesicles and vas deferens can be found behind the bladder. Abdominal organs (small and large intestines) hang down into the pelvic cavity, and expansile pelvic organs, such as the full bladder and pregnant uterus, are able to rise up through the pelvic inlet and extend into the abdominal cavity.

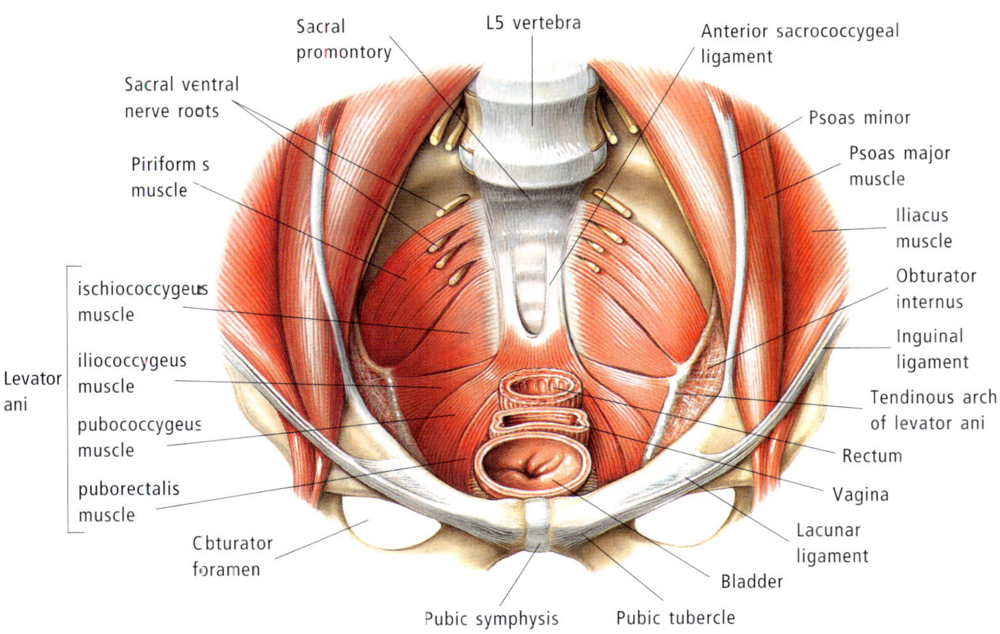

Pelvic floor muscles

Stretching from the sacrum at the back to the hip bones at the front, the pelvic floor muscles form a muscular floor across the pelvis.

Pelvic diaphragm

The pelvic diaphragm (pelvic floor) is important in supporting the pelvic organs. It is formed by the coccygeus and the levator ani muscles, and has a sphincteric (constrictive) action on the rectum and vagina, and assists in increasing intra-abdominal pressure. The puborectalis part of the pelvic diaphragm is important in fecal and urinary continence.

The pelvic diaphragm reflexly contracts when coughing, sneezing, laughing and straining. Poor muscle tone can lead to urinary incontinence when intra-abdominal pressure rises suddenly.

Damage to the pelvic diaphragm or to the perineal body (for example during childbirth) may lead to prolapse (herniation) of pelvic organs such as the bladder, uterus or rectum. The perineal body is a fibrous and muscular structure into which many muscles of the region attach, including the pelvic diaphragm, urogenital diaphragm and anal sphincter.

The integrity of the structure of the perineal body is therefore critical in pelvic support.

Male and female pelvis

In women, the pelvis is constructed to accommodate the fetus during childbirth. Therefore, the pelvic inlet and outlet are larger than in the male pelvis, the length of the canal is shorter and its walls are more parallel than those of the male.

In men, the pelvis has a smaller, heart-shaped inlet, a small pelvic outlet and a more cone-shaped, longer cavity. In addition, the male pelvis is distinguished by its larger bones, more defined muscle markings and larger joint surfaces, reflecting the generally stronger build and heavier weight of men.

A quick reference for differentiating between the male and female bony pelvis is the subpubic angle (angle below the pubis). This is at about 80–85° in the female, and 50–60° in the male.

One example of how knowledge of these differences is used, is that bicycle seat design reflects the difference in the size of the pelvic outlet in men and women. The sitting bones (ischial tuberosities), which form part of the pelvic outlet, are closer together in the male pelvis and further apart in the female.

The dimensions of the lesser pelvis, particularly the inlet and outlet, are very important in women as they must be large enough for the infant's head to pass through during childbirth.

These dimensions are usually measured carefully by the obstetrician. The greatest dimension of a baby's head is front to back. The typical "gynecoid" female pelvic inlet is slightly wider than it is deep, hence the infant's head will pass through this opening transversely (face directed to the side). The outlet is normally deeper than it is wide, so that the baby's head rotates within the pelvic cavity so that the back of the infant's neck lies against the pubic bones, and the face is directed backward at birth.

Not all women have a gynecoid pelvic inlet, however. Some have an android shape (heartshape, similar to the male), anthropoid shape (narrow from side to side, and deep front to back) and, less commonly, a platypelloid shape (excessively wide, and shortened front to back). Awareness of these differences in shape is essential for anticipating any possible complications during labor.

Injuries

A direct blow or compression injury may cause the pelvic bones to fracture and/or the joints to dislocate. Falls on the feet may fracture the part of the hip bone associated with the hip joint—this is called fracture of the acetabulum.

Soft tissue injury must be considered in pelvic fractures, as there is potential for damage to bladder, urethra, rectum, blood vessels and nerves.

SEE ALSO *Coccyx, Hip, Prolapse, Sacrum, Skeletal system*

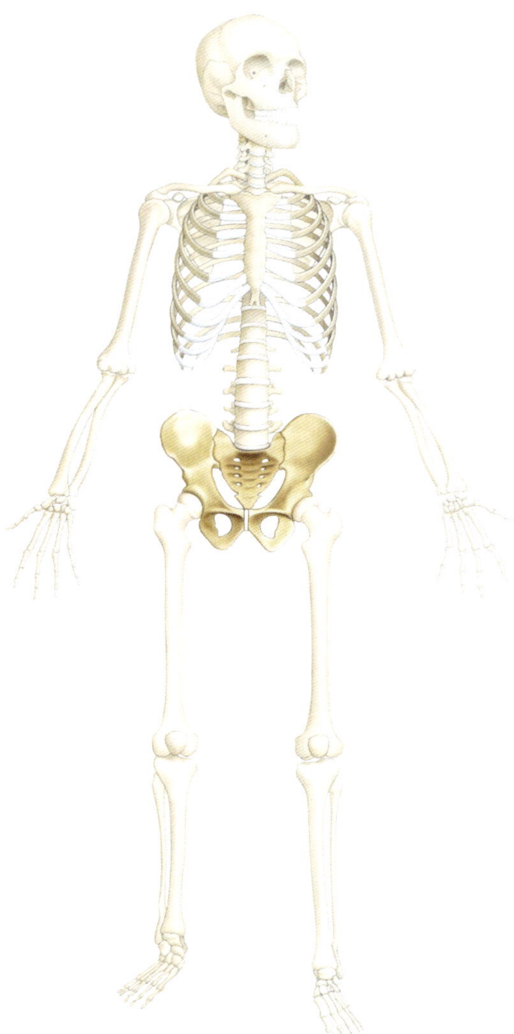

Pelvis

The pelvis helps protect the lower abdominal organs and transfers weight from the vertebral column to the lower limbs.

PEMPHIGOID

In the autoimmune disease pemphigoid (or bullous pemphigoid), large blisters appear on the skin. Uncomfortable, but rarely fatal, the condition can be controlled by strong drug treatments. It is incurable, but sometimes disappears after several years. Pemphigoid usually occurs in the over-50s, and more often in women than in men. The cause is unknown but it is not contagious.

SEE ALSO *Autoimmune disease*

PEMPHIGUS

Formerly, the rare and incurable autoimmune disease pemphigus was invariably fatal. These days, treatment with steroids and immunosuppressive drugs make it possible for sufferers to lead a near-normal life. Characterized by large blisters on the skin and mucous membranes, pemphigus may initially appear similar to the disease pemphigoid but it is not related.

People of all ages and both sexes can develop pemphigus although it is rarely seen in children. The blisters are extremely painful and tend to appear mostly on the scalp, face, chest, armpits, groin, navel area, nose, mouth, throat and, in women, the vagina. The cause is unknown.

SEE ALSO *Autoimmune disease*

PENICILLINS

First discovered by British physician Alexander Fleming in 1938, penicillins are a class of antibiotics used to kill bacteria. They were originally extracted from molds of the genus *Penicillium*, but are now synthesized. They work by preventing bacterial cells from forming a cell wall, killing them in the process. Penicillins can be given orally via tablet, syrup or capsule, or by injection. In some people, they may cause allergic reactions such as skin rashes, swelling of the joints, and in rare instances, anaphylaxis, which may be fatal.

Excessive use of penicillins has resulted in the development of bacterial strains that are resistant to them. Newer penicillins such as amoxycillin, methicillin, oxacillin and dicloxacillin have been developed that are effective against many resistant strains.

SEE ALSO *Antibiotics, Bacteria*

Pelvis—female

Unlike its male counterpart, the female pelvis is designed to support the fetus during pregnancy. The inlet and the outlet are larger than the male, while the canal is shorter.

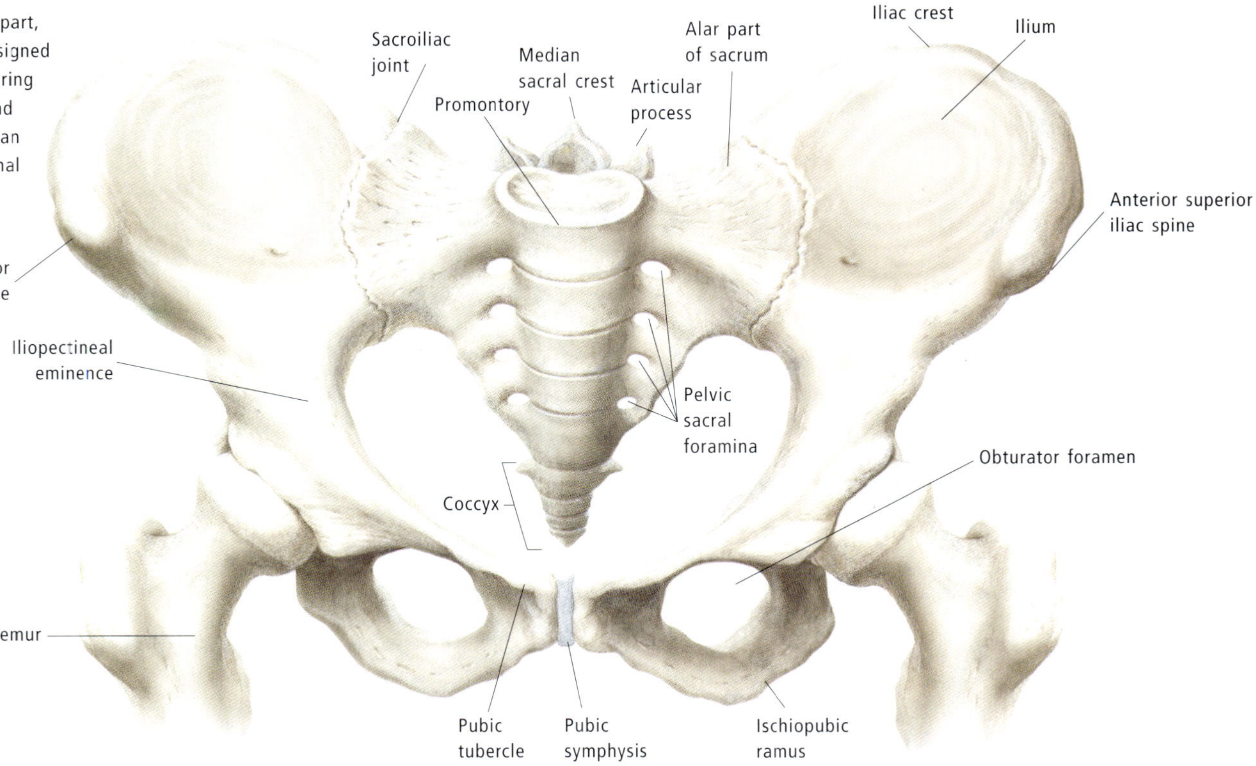

Pelvis—male

The male pelvis is easily distinguished from the female by the presence of stronger bone and larger joint surfaces.

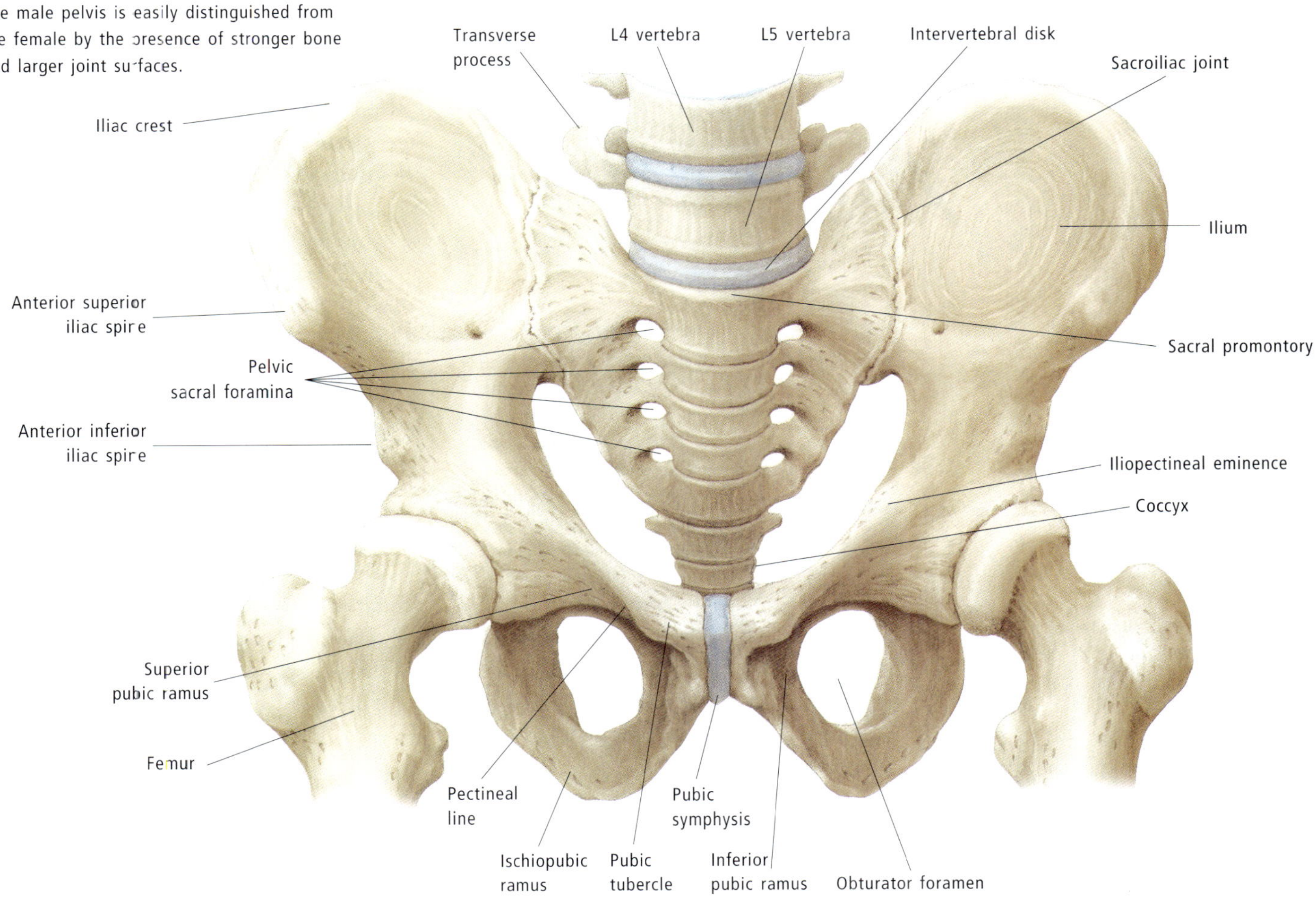

P

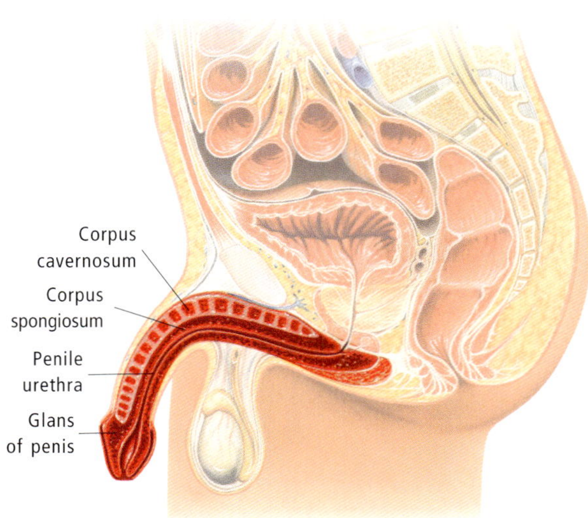

Penis

The penis is the male urinary and reproductive organ comprising three cylinders. Two cylinders (the corpus cavernosum and corpus spongiosum) are composed of sponge-like vascular tissue which allow erection; and the third cylinder contains the urethra—part of the urinary system.

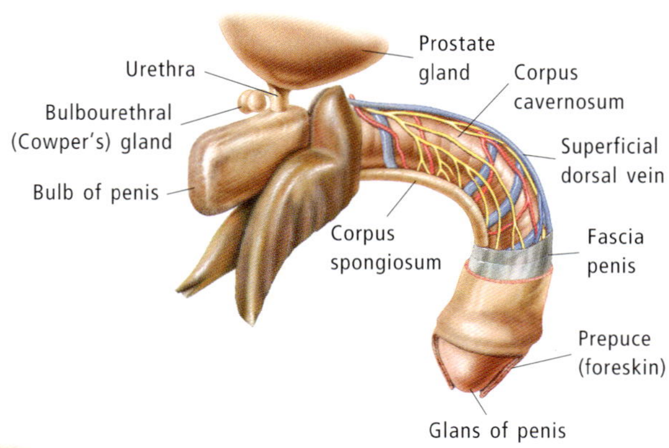

Penis—reproductive system

The penis is attached to the pelvic bone by connective tissue, and usually hangs flaccid unless sexually stimulated. Stimulation increases the blood flow in the network of vessels that surround the spongy cylinders of the corpus cavernosum, allowing erection.

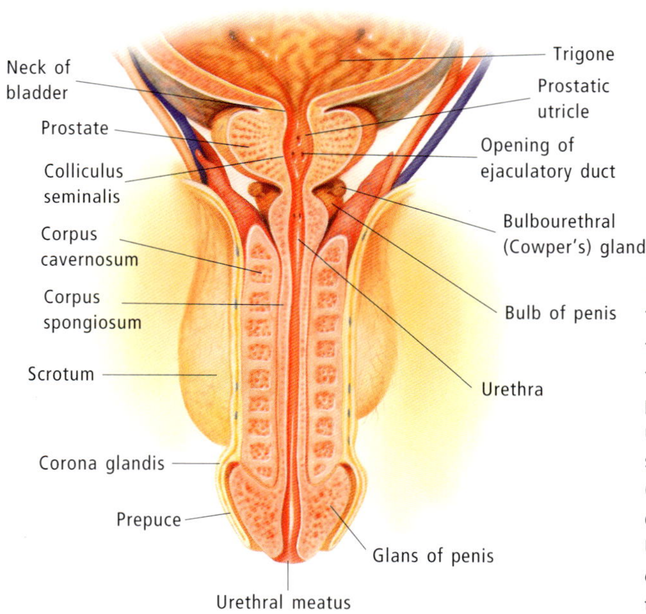

Penis—urinary system

The largest part of the urethra—the tube that carries urine from the bladder out of the body—passes through the penis. The urethra ends in an external swelling at the tip of the penis (the glans) where urine passes out through the urethral meatus. Urinary tract infections may cause discharge or pain in the penis.

PENIS

The penis is the external male reproductive and urinary organ, through which semen and urine leave the body. It is attached at its base to the pelvic bone by connective tissues. It is comprised primarily of two cylinders of sponge-like vascular tissue (corpora cavernosa). A third cylinder contains the urethra, a tube that carries the urine and the ejaculate. The urethra ends in an external swelling at the tip of the penis, the glans. The glans is particularly sensitive and, in an uncircumcised penis, is covered by a protective foreskin (prepuce).

After physical or psychological sexual stimulation, the two spongy cylinders become engorged with blood and the penis becomes erect and hard. This enables the male to insert the erect penis into the female's vagina during sexual intercourse. The blood is unable to drain out through the veins in the penis because they are temporarily closed by pressure from arterial blood in the corpora cavernosa. An erection ceases when the veins open, allowing the blood to flow back into the body's circulation. Sildenafil (Viagra) works by closing these same veins.

Circumcision is the surgical removal of all or part of the foreskin of the penis. In infancy it is usually performed (often without anesthetic) for social or cultural reasons, as there are no medical reasons for routine circumcision of newborn boys. In adults, it may be performed for medical reasons, for example for phimosis or paraphimosis.

Diseases and disorders

Balanitis is inflammation of the glans of the penis. It is usually caused by a yeast such as candida (thrush), and is more common in males who have not been circumcised, and who have not been keeping the glans clean. Symptoms are a red, shiny glans with itchiness and a slight discharge. It is treated with antifungal creams or ointments and by keeping the glans washed and clean.

The penis is often affected by venereal (sexually transmitted) diseases. Syphilis or chancroid form ulcers (chancres), on the skin of the penis; other venereal diseases, such as gonorrhea, cause infections of the urethra (urethritis). Symptoms of urethritis are pain on urinating (dysuria) and a discharge from the penis. Treatment is with an antibiotic appropriate for the particular microorganism causing the disease.

Cancer of the penis occurs most commonly in elderly, uncircumcised males who have had chronic balanitis (infection of the glans). It manifests as a small ulcer that bleeds easily and does not heal. It is treated either by amputating the end of the penis or by radiation therapy.

Phimosis is a condition in which the foreskin of the penis is so tight that it cannot be easily pulled back over the tip (the glans). Balanitis may accompany it. Circumcision is the usual treatment. Paraphimosis is a condition in which the foreskin of the penis is retracted and "stuck" and cannot be returned to its normal position. As a result, the glans becomes swollen and painful. Circumcision under general anesthetic is the usual treatment.

Peyronie's disease (curvature of the penis due to a band of fibrous tissue) is a bend in the penis that occurs during erection. It cannot be cured but it can be minimized with corticosteroid injections into the penis.

Epispadias is a congenital defect in which the urethra, the duct connecting the bladder to the tip of the penis, opens abnormally on the top of the penis, either in the head or along the entire length. In hypospadias, another congenital defect, the urethral opening appears on the underside of the penis. Both conditions cause abnormal leakage of urine (incontinence) and sexual dysfunction in adulthood. Reconstructive surgery usually cures both defects.

Priapism is a condition where the penis remains persistently and painfully erect without any sexual arousal or desire. It may be caused by excessive sexual stimulation or by certain drugs, including corticosteroids, anticoagulants and antihypertensives. Injuries to the spinal cord or to the penis may also result in priapism. Treatment options include surgery, spinal anesthesia, and aspiration of blood from the penis.

Impotence is an inability to produce or maintain an erection of the penis sufficient for successful sexual intercourse. It is more common in older men and often has a psychological origin, such as stress, anxiety, depression or relationship problems. Brief bouts of impotence may follow illnesses such as influenza, or after taking drugs or alcohol. There may be a physical cause, such as a stroke, atherosclerosis, diabetes mellitus or alcoholism. In other cases, it may occur as a side effect of certain medications or following surgery.

If the cause of impotence is a physical disorder, the underlying cause must be treated first. If not, sex therapy with a qualified sex therapist may be of benefit. Possible treatments include a prosthesis surgically inserted into the penis, needle injection therapy, vacuum cup devices and medications such as sildenafil.

SEE ALSO *Circumcision, Epispadias, Erection, Glans, Gonorrhea, Impotence, Peyronie's disease, Priapism, Reproductive systems, Sexual intercourse, Sexually transmitted diseases, Syphilis, Urethra, Urethritis, Urinary systems*

PEPTIC ULCER

Peptic ulcers result from the damaging action of acidic stomach juices on the vulnerable mucosal lining of the esophagus, stomach or duodenum. They affect men three times more often than women. Among patients under 50 years of age, duodenal ulcers are ten times more common than stomach (gastric) ulcers.

A patient with peptic ulcer will experience pain in the upper abdomen, which may be relieved by food or antacid preparations. In some patients, the ulcer may erode through a blood vessel, leading to the vomiting of large amounts of blood. If left untreated, the ulcer may perforate the gut wall, spilling stomach or duodenal juices into the abdominal cavity and causing painful chemical peritonitis. Swelling and scarring of the gut wall, which may cause obstruction of the gut, may arise with ulcers in the lower esophagus and pyloric sphincter.

At one time it was thought that peptic ulcers arose from excessive acid secretion as a result of psychological stress. It is now recognized that infection of the upper gut with acid-resistant bacteria and use of nonsteroidal anti-inflammatory drugs play a major role in their initiation. Treatment of peptic ulcers makes use of antacid preparations, antibiotics and drugs to control acid secretion (triple therapy).

There are a number of alternative therapies that may help to alleviate the symptoms of peptic ulcers. Acupuncture treats ulcers along points said to improve gastrointestinal function, relieve pain and reduce feelings of stress and anxiety. Herbalism treats with demulcent herbs (marshmallow, for example), antibacterial herbs (such as echinacea), astringent herbs (like golden seal) and herbs which may aid tissue healing (such as calendula). Hypnotherapy, meditation and other relaxation therapies treat anxiety and stress

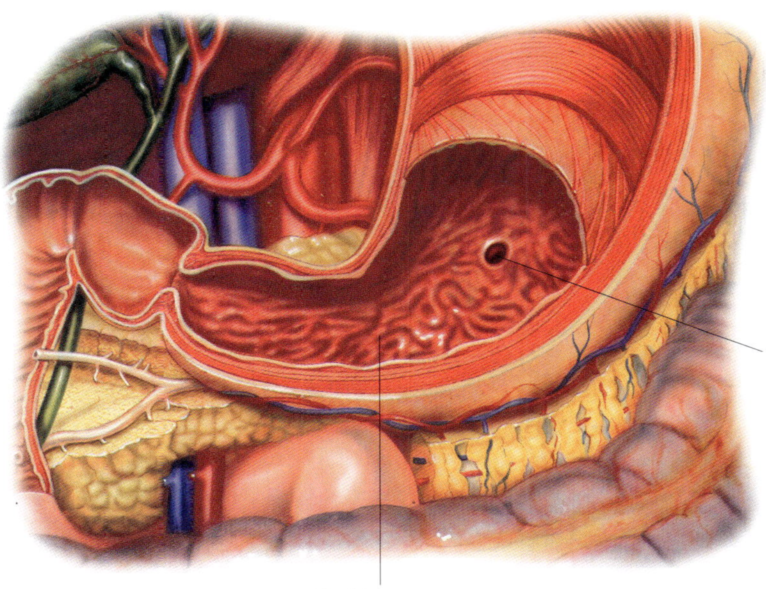

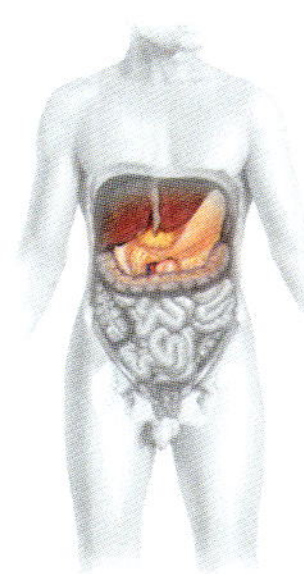

Peptic ulcer

Damage to the mucous membrane can result in the formation of a peptic ulcer. Ulcers can form in the lining of the stomach, esophagus and duodenum.

Ulcer-causing bacteria

The presence of an acid-resistant bacteria *(Helicobacter pylori)* in the upper intestine plays a major role in the formation of peptic ulcers.

associated with ulcers. Psychotherapy is also thought to be beneficial. Naturopathy suggests a low-fat wholefood diet of small meals that are thoroughly chewed. Smoking, coffee, tea, sugar, citrus and alcohol should be avoided. Cow's milk should be substituted with soy or rice milks. Possible food allergies such as wheat need to be eliminated. Supplements prescribed include vitamins A, C and E, zinc, *Lactobacillus acidophilus*, digestive enzymes and slippery elm. Reflexology massage aims to relax the nervous and gastrointestinal systems while stimulating the stomach and duodenal zones.

SEE ALSO *Digestive system, Duodenum, Esophagus, Stomach*

PERICARDITIS

The pericardium is the tissue sac that surrounds the heart. The sac consists of an inner double-layered part and an outer tough fibrous part. Pericarditis is literally inflammation of the pericardium and may be the result of infection (viruses, tuberculosis or pus-forming bacteria), invasion by cancer cells (leukemic infiltration), connective tissue diseases (rheumatoid arthritis, systemic lupus erythematosus) or changes in blood chemistry (kidney failure and gout). Patients complain of sharp, strong pain in the center of the chest. Unlike myocardial infarction, the pain is made worse by breathing in, moving and lying flat on the back. Patients also commonly have fever and an audible friction rub, heard when a stethoscope is applied to the chest; they may develop failure of the right ventricle.

SEE ALSO *Heart, Pericardium*

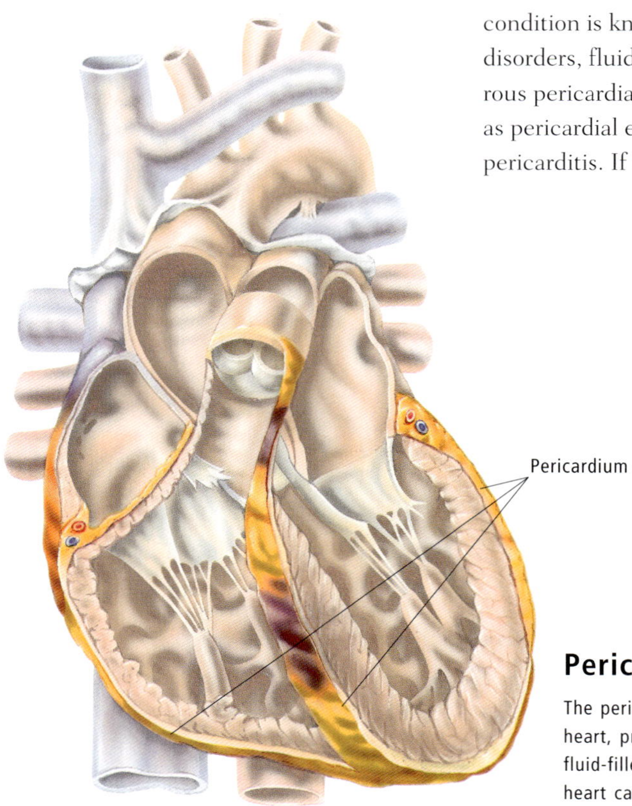

Pericardium

The pericardium surrounds the heart, providing a low-friction fluid-filled space in which the heart can beat freely.

PERICARDIUM

The pericardium is a series of sacs that enclose the heart. The inner set of sacs is called the serous pericardium and provides a low-friction, fluid-filled space to permit the beating heart to move freely. The serous pericardium has an inner visceral layer and an outer parietal layer, separated by a thin film of fluid. Outside the parietal layer of the serous pericardium lies the fibrous pericardium. This is a tough layer of connective tissue that is attached at the top around the great vessels entering and leaving the heart, and is fused below with the central part of the diaphragm. The fibrous pericardium provides a strong mechanical support to maintain the position of the heart within the center of the chest.

The pericardium may be involved in disease. When it becomes inflamed the condition is known as pericarditis. In some disorders, fluid may accumulate in the serous pericardial sac. This condition is known as pericardial effusion and may accompany pericarditis. If a large volume of fluid accumulates in the pericardial space, then the normal distension of the ventricle during the rest phase of the cardiac cycle may be impaired. This is known as cardiac tamponade and may be fatal unless the excess fluid is drained urgently.

SEE ALSO *Cardiac tamponade, Heart, Pericarditis*

PERINEUM

The perineum encloses the base of the pelvis in both men and women. It consists of a sheet of fibrous tissue and muscle and provides support for the pelvic floor muscles immediately above. It also contains the urethral and anal sphincters. Tears in the perineum are not uncommon during childbirth and may result in prolapse of the vagina.

SEE ALSO *Anus, Childbirth, Pelvic floor muscles, Prolapse, Urethra*

PERIODONTITIS

Periodontitis is inflammation of the gums that leads to the infection of the ligaments and bone supporting the teeth. The condition is usually caused by a build-up of plaque on the teeth due to poor dental hygiene. If untreated, the teeth become loose and fall out. Warning signs include swelling and a red-purple coloring of the gums, blood on the toothbrush, tenderness and bad breath. Bone structure can be damaged before the condition is realized as there is usually little or no pain.

Treatment involves thorough cleaning by a dentist and perhaps surgical trimming of scar tissue and reshaping of bone. In severe cases, some teeth may need to be removed to stop the spread of infection.

SEE ALSO *Gums, Teeth*

PERIOSTEUM

Periosteum is a thin, fibrous membrane that covers all bone surfaces, except those that are involved in joints (which are covered by cartilage).

Periosteum is made up of two layers. The inner layer comprises osteoblasts or bone-producing cells) which produce bone when a fetus or child is growing. Following a fracture, they produce new bone in order to

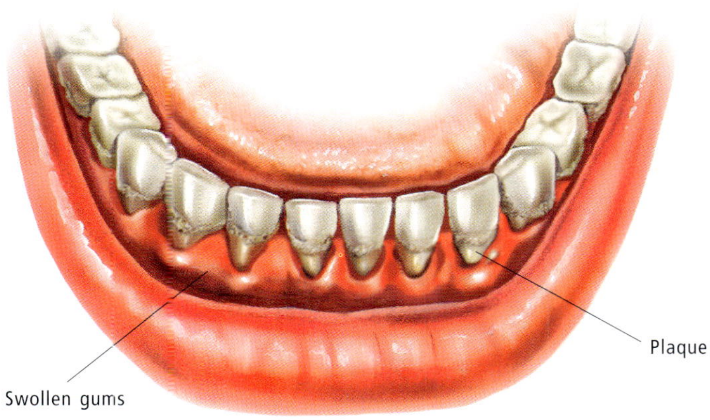

Periodontitis

In this condition, a painful inflammation of the tissues supporting the teeth is caused by bacteria, food particles and calcium deposits collecting in the spaces between the teeth and gum.

mend the two ends of the broken bone together. Fibers from this inner layer also penetrate the underlying bone and help bind the periosteum to the bone. The dense outer layer contains nerves and blood vessels. Branches of these blood vessels penetrate the bone to supply the cells with nutrients.

Periostitis is inflammation of the periosteum. It usually occurs along with infection of bone (osteomyelitis). A periosteoma (also called a periostoma) is a benign tumor arising from the periosteum.

SEE ALSO *Bones, Joints, Osteomyelitis, Periostitis*

PERIOSTITIS

Periostitis is inflammation of the periosteum, the thin, fibrous membrane that covers bone surfaces. It may occur from overuse, especially along the medial side of the shin bone (a form of "shin splints"), in people who are physically active. Treatment involves rest and anti-inflammatory drugs. Periostitis may also occur with infection of bone (osteomyelitis) when it is caused by bacteria. In these cases, treatment is with intravenous antibiotics.

SEE ALSO *Bones, Joints, Osteomyelitis, Periosteum*

PERIPHERAL NERVOUS SYSTEM

The peripheral nervous system (PNS) is one of the two main divisions of the nervous system, the other being the central nervous system (CNS). The PNS is the network that collects signals from sensory receptors throughout the body's periphery and carries them back into the CNS (spinal cord and brain), that interprets the data and formulates a response. The instructions from the CNS are then carried to the muscles and glands by the PNS. The nerve cells of the PNS that transmit messages into the CNS are known as sensory (afferent) neurons. The nerve cells that carry messages out from the CNS are called motor (efferent) neurons.

The PNS includes peripheral parts of two systems, called the somatic nervous system (SNS) and the autonomic nervous system (ANS).

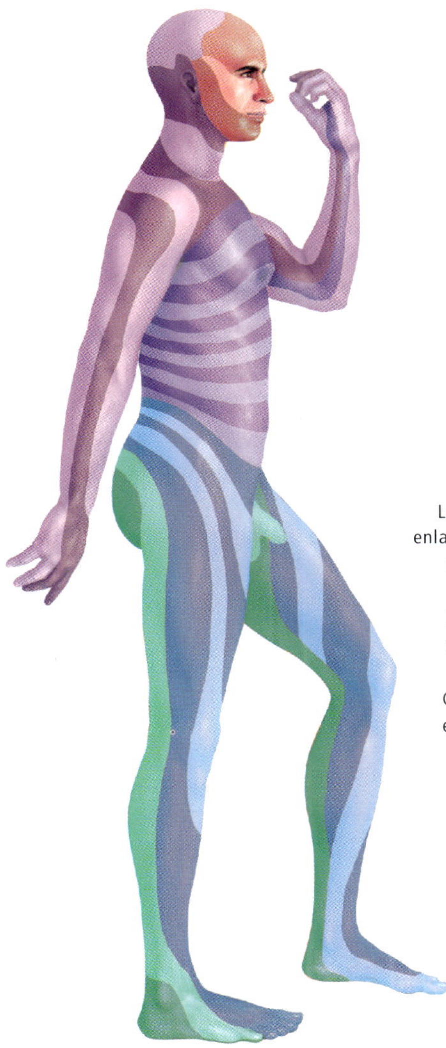

Peripheral innervation

The nerves from the spinal cord (part of the central nervous system) branch out along a network of peripheral nerves that serve different parts of the body. The area of skin supplied by a given spinal nerve is called a dermatome.

Peripheral nervous system

The peripheral nervous system is a network of nerves that transports signals between sensory receptors in the peripheral areas of the body (skin and muscles, for example) and the central nervous system (brain and spinal cord).

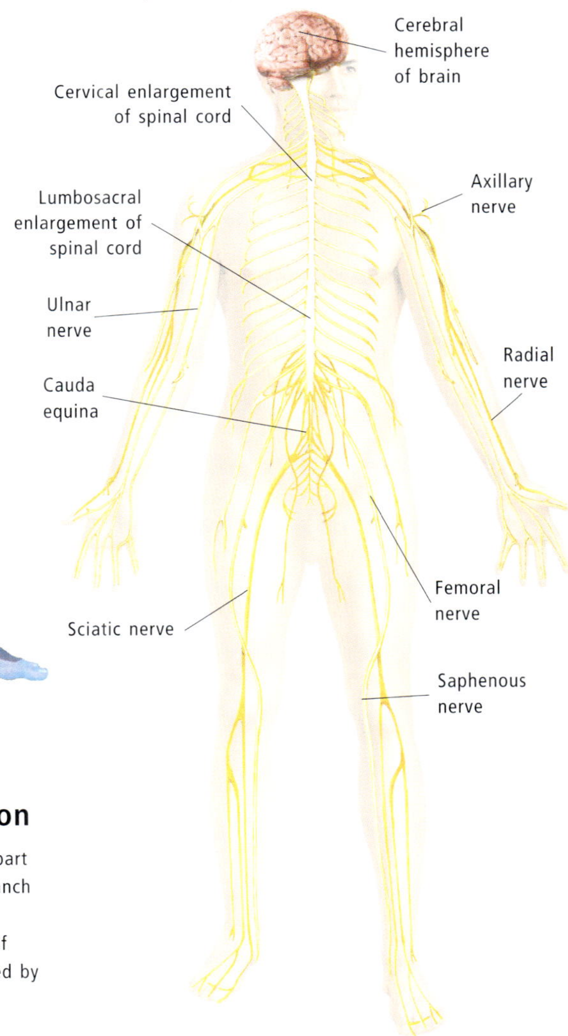

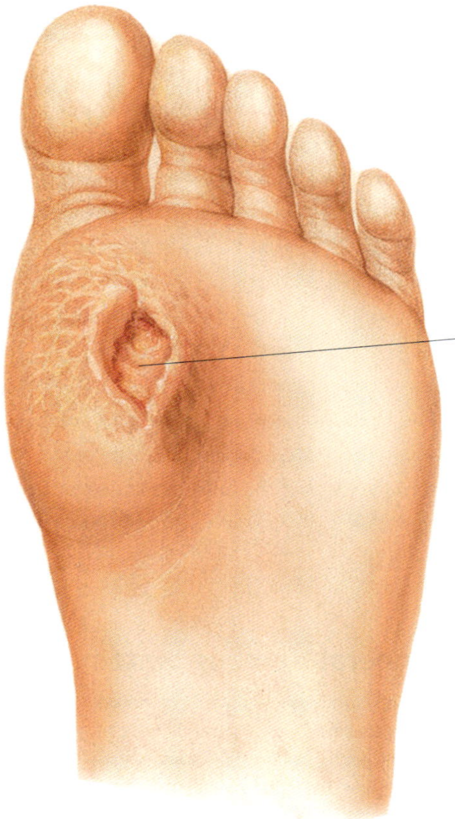

Peripheral vascular disease

The deterioration of arteries can cause disruption to the flow of blood to arms and legs. Reduced blood supply can cause pain in the limbs and, in severe cases, ulcers can develop.

Somatic nervous system (SNS)

The motor neurons of the SNS transmit signals directly to the skeletal muscles. These are the muscles people can normally move and control consciously or voluntarily, such as those attached to the bones in the arms and legs. For this reason, the SNS is also known as the voluntary nervous system. It stimulates the muscle activity needed to run, jump, flick a switch to turn on a light and perform the many other movements that people choose deliberately to make.

Autonomic nervous system (ANS)

In contrast, the ANS transmits messages to the glands and cardiac (heart) and smooth muscle. Smooth muscle is found in the walls of internal organs such as the stomach and intestines, around blood vessels, in the skin around hair follicles and in the eye. The actions of cardiac and smooth muscle are mostly out of a person's conscious control and so the ANS is also often referred to as as the involuntary nervous system. It maintains and controls heartbeat, blood pressure, breathing, digestion and the many other fundamental functions of the body necessary to maintain life.

The ANS consists of two components, the sympathetic nervous system and the parasympathetic nervous system, which essentially create complementary but opposite actions. The sympathetic components mostly stimulate activities that use energy. The parasympathetic side of the system switches the same activities down and conserves energy. For example, when faced by a sudden threat the body responds instinctively with a range of reactions that together are known as the "fight or flight" response, the sympathetic nervous system automatically preparing the body to confront or run from danger. The pupils dilate. Heart rate and blood pressure rise. The hairs on the back of the neck stand up. Digestion slows as blood is diverted from the intestines and made available for use by the skeletal muscles. The adrenal glands are stimulated to produce hormones that accelerate all of these activities.

When the danger has passed, the parasympathetic nervous system calms the body down and switches on what are sometimes called "rest and digest" activities. Most of these are directly opposite to those of the "fight or flight" responses. Heart rate and blood pressure fall, the pupils constrict and digestive processes restart.

SEE ALSO *Adrenal glands, Brain, Nerves, Nervous system, Neurons, Spinal cord, Sympathetic nervous system*

PERIPHERAL VASCULAR DISEASE

Peripheral vascular disease refers to deterioration of the arteries supplying blood to the arms and legs. This is almost always due to atherosclerosis and tends to affect the legs and feet most severely.

Atherosclerosis, commonly referred to as hardening of the arteries, results from deposition of fatty material, such as cholesterol, in the arterial wall. This causes gradual narrowing of the artery and weakening of its wall, decreased blood flow to the legs and, sometimes, an enlargement of the weakened part of the artery, called an aneurysm. Narrowing of the arteries causes pain in the affected leg muscles supplied by that artery, due to insufficient oxygen supply for their metabolism. This type of pain is called intermittent claudication, since it occurs only upon commencing walking and is relieved by stopping. Reduced blood supply to the legs can make them look pale and feel cool to the touch. The skin becomes shiny and there is hair loss and thickening of the nails. In severe cases ulcers develop and gangrene may occur.

Atherosclerosis is caused by a combination of factors, including high cholesterol, high blood pressure, diabetes and smoking. It is most common in men over the age of 40 but is also common among women who smoke. Smoking is a most important factor in the development of peripheral vascular disease. Once it develops, the continuation of smoking will lead to gangrene of the affected limb. Medical treatment is unsatisfactory and surgical by-pass grafting is required if symptoms worsen. Gangrene is treated by amputation and the fitting of prosthetic limbs.

SEE ALSO *Aneurysm, Arteries, Atherosclerosis, Cholesterol, Diabetes, Gangrene, Hypertension, Smoking*

PERISTALSIS

Peristalsis consists of wave-like contractions in the muscular walls of the esophagus, stomach, intestines, ureters and fallopian tubes that propel the contents of the tube along. The walls of many tubular structures in the body are composed of smooth muscle whose contractions, like those of the heart muscle, are involuntary, that is, controlled by the autonomic nervous system. When food is swallowed, muscular contractions in the esophagus push the food downwards into the stomach. There, peristalsis in the stomach mixes the chewed food with gastric juices and moves it through the pyloric sphincter to the small intestine, where peristalsis continues to move gut contents into the large intestine.

Esophageal spasm is a disorder in which muscle spasm affects normal swallowing, causing chest pain, with the potential for achalasia to develop. Ileus is failure of intestinal peristalsis caused by blockage, surgery, drugs or trauma.

SEE ALSO *Achalasia, Digestive system, Esophagus, Fallopian tubes, Ileus, Intestines, Muscle, Ureter*

PERITONEAL DIALYSIS

Peritoneal dialysis is a technique in which the abdominal peritoneal membrane is used as a dialysis mechanism to remove toxic substances from the blood. The abdominal cavity is filled (via a catheter) with a special solution that absorbs toxins, using the peritoneal membrane inside the abdomen as the semipermeable membrane. The solution is allowed to absorb wastes for several hours, and then the waste-filled fluid is exchanged for a fresh batch of solution.

SEE ALSO *Abdomen, Dialysis*

PERITONITIS

Inflammation of the peritoneum (the membrane that lines the wall of the abdomen and covers the organs) is known as peritonitis. It can result from infection (such an abdominal abscess), injury or occasionally other diseases. Symptoms include abdominal pain, distension and tenderness, fever, nausea and vomiting. The cause must be quickly identified and treated, for example with intravenous antibiotics in the case of bacterial peritonitis. Untreated, the mortality rate is high.

SEE ALSO *Abdomen*

PERSONALITY DISORDERS

A personality disorder is not easy to define because there is no clear line between what is and is not a disorder. However, behavior that significantly deviates from societal or cultural expectations, or behavior that is an extreme variant of normal behavior and thus hampers an individual's ability to function in society, may be defined as characteristic of a personality disorder. In many instances, a person with a personality disorder does not seek treatment unless ordered by a court or pressured by relatives. It is estimated that about 20 percent of people in the general population has one, or more than one, personality disorder.

In medical practice, there are ten defined personality disorders.

Antisocial personality disorder People with this disorder disregard the feelings and rights of others. They often break the law, lie, act impulsively and get into violent fights. Their behavior towards others, including their partners and children, may be violent. They can also be called sociopaths or psychopaths. People with this disorder may be a major danger to society and often die a violent death themselves.

Avoidant personality disorder is often seen as intense shyness, coupled with anxiety. Sufferers avoid occupations or activities that bring them into contact with others and see themselves as socially inadequate.

Borderline personality disorder is a condition characterized by intense emotional instability. Those who suffer from this disorder are thought of as unstable and are unable to maintain relationships. They may attempt suicide or self-mutilation. Alcoholism, depression, drug dependence and eating disorders are common among people with this disorder.

Dependent personality disorder People with this disorder allow others to make most of their important life decisions and are severely emotionally dependent on others. They are not comfortable with themselves and are often preoccupied with thoughts of being abandoned.

Histrionic personality disorder This state is characterized by the need to be the center of attention. Sufferers often display inappropriate sexual behavior, and they are easily influenced.

Narcissistic personality disorder is characterized by a grandiose sense of self-importance. Sufferers of this disorder seek and expect excessive attention from others. They believe they are special and often have very fragile self-esteem.

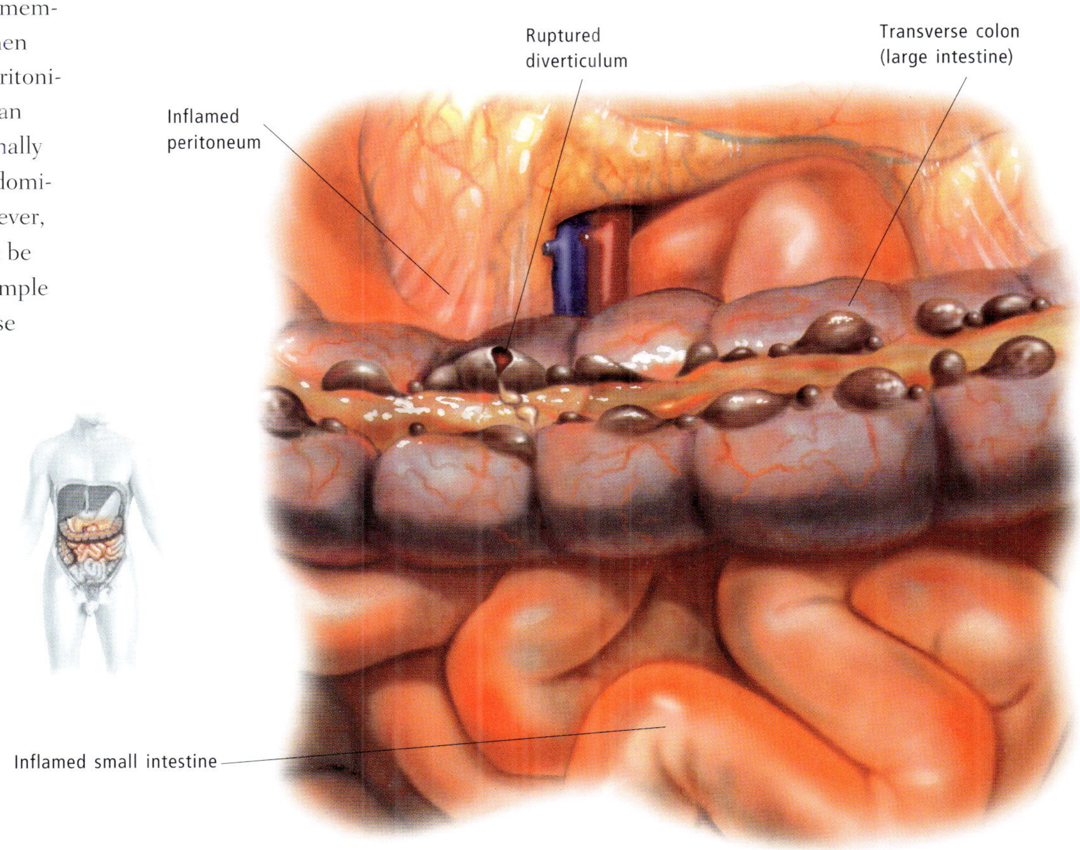

Peritonitis

An infection in the abdomen, if untreated, can lead to inflammation of the peritoneum—peritonitis—as in this example of a ruptured diverticulum.

P

Obsessive-compulsive personality disorder is marked by a preoccupation with details, rules, lists, order, organization or schedules to the point where the purpose is lost. These people are rigid, formal and serious and their behavior is often marked by strange rituals.

Paranoid personality disorder is a state of constant suspicion and distrust of others. A person suffering from such a disorder is always on the lookout for evidence to support their suspicions and believes that everyone is against them.

Schizoid personality disorder involves a lack of desire for close relationships, including sexual relationships, and an emotional detachment resulting in social isolation.

Schizotypal personality disorder is marked by odd thinking and behavior. People with this disorder speak in a disjointed fashion and sometimes believe they have magical powers. Close relationships make them uncomfortable. It is thought this form of personality disorder could be a less severe form of schizophrenia.

Other personality disorders exist, sometimes described as depressive personality disorder and passive-aggressive personality disorder. A sufferer may exhibit traits of more than one disorder, making diagnosis difficult.

Personality disorders are the result of a combination of life experience and inherited characteristics. They are often the result of unresolved conflicts, which may date back to childhood. Because patients often refuse to admit that there is anything wrong, such disorders are difficult to treat and therapists will often try a range of methods including psychoactive drugs and psychotherapy.

SEE ALSO *Obsessive-compulsive disorder, Paranoia, Schizophrenia*

PERTHES' DISEASE

Perthes' disease is a chronic disorder that affects children, in which the head of the femur (the ball part of the ball-and-socket hip joint) becomes inflamed and flattened, due to an interruption in its blood supply. The cause of the condition is unknown. Movement of the affected joint becomes limited, resulting in a limp, with pain in the thigh and groin. The condition occurs most frequently in boys aged 4–10 years and tends to run in families. In most cases, the bone heals itself without any resulting deformity. Treatment is aimed at protecting the bone and joint while healing takes place. Bed rest and the use of appliances such as a brace, cast or splint is usually recommended. Osteoarthritis of the affected hip may develop in adulthood.

SEE ALSO *Femur, Hip, Osteoarthritis*

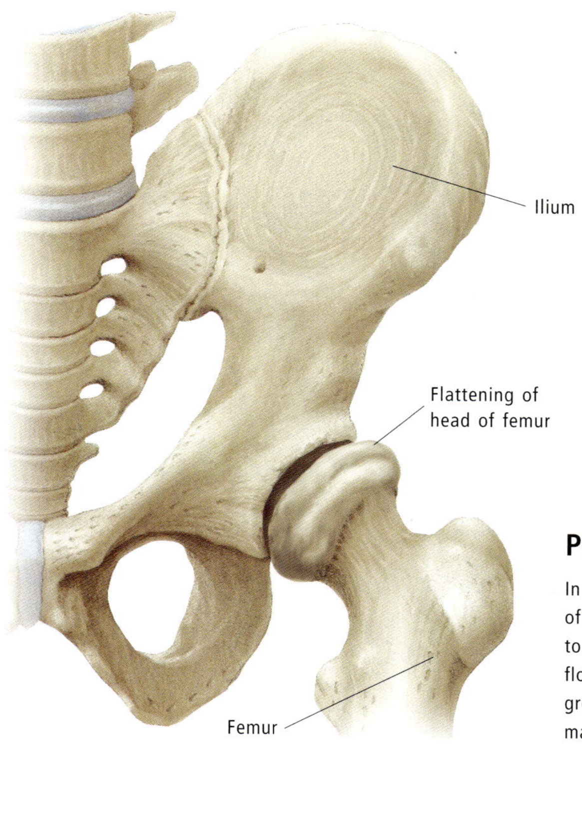

Perthes' disease

In this condition, the ball part of the femur degenerates due to an interruption to the blood flow, resulting in pain in the groin and thigh. Osteoarthritis may occur in affected adults.

PEYRONIE'S DISEASE

Peyronie's disease (curvature of the penis) is a bend in the penis that occurs during erection. It is caused by the abnormal presence of fibrous tissue in the vascular sheath that runs the length of the penis (corpora cavernosa). The obstruction causes the bend in the penis to form during erection which is painful and interferes with intercourse.

The condition is uncommon, affects older males and is sometimes associated with Dupuytren's contracture. It cannot be cured but can be alleviated somewhat with radiation therapy or the injection of hormones (corticosteroids) into the fibrous tissue in the corpora cavernosa.

SEE ALSO *Dupuytren's contracture, Erection, Penis*

PHARYNGITIS

Pharyngitis is an inflammation of the throat (pharynx). The symptoms of pharyngitis include a sore throat and discomfort or pain on swallowing. Acute pharyngitis may be caused by the viruses which cause such conditions as the common cold, laryngitis, infectious mononucleosis (glandular fever), tonsillitis and sinusitis. It may also be caused by the streptococcal bacterium, when the infection is known as strep throat. Other bacterial causes of acute pharyngitis include gonorrhea and mycoplasma.

When a physician examines the affected throat, it is seen to be red and swollen. The lymph nodes in the neck may be enlarged and tender and there may be a fever. If the cause is bacterial, antibiotics will cure the condition (antibiotics are ineffective in viral pharyngitis). Painkillers and decongestants will help the symptoms, which clear up in a week or so.

Chronic pharyngitis may be caused by smoking cigarettes or drinking too much alcohol. It may also be caused by postnasal drip resulting from chronic nasal or sinus inflammation. Treatment involves improving oral hygiene, giving up smoking and alcohol, and using antiseptic gargles.

SEE ALSO *Common cold, Infectious mononucleosis, Laryngitis, Pharynx, Sinusitis, Throat, Tonsils*

Pharynx

The pharynx is the common passageway for air, fluids and food entering the body. It comprises the nasopharynx (behind the nose), the oropharynx (behind the mouth) and the laryngopharynx (the voice box). The muscles that surround the pharynx are used in speech and swallowing.

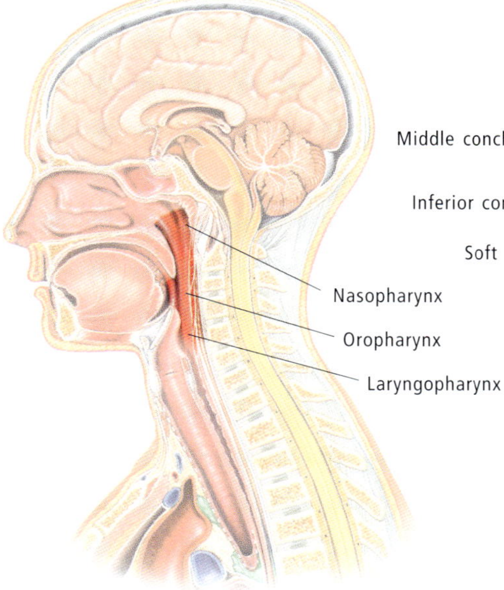

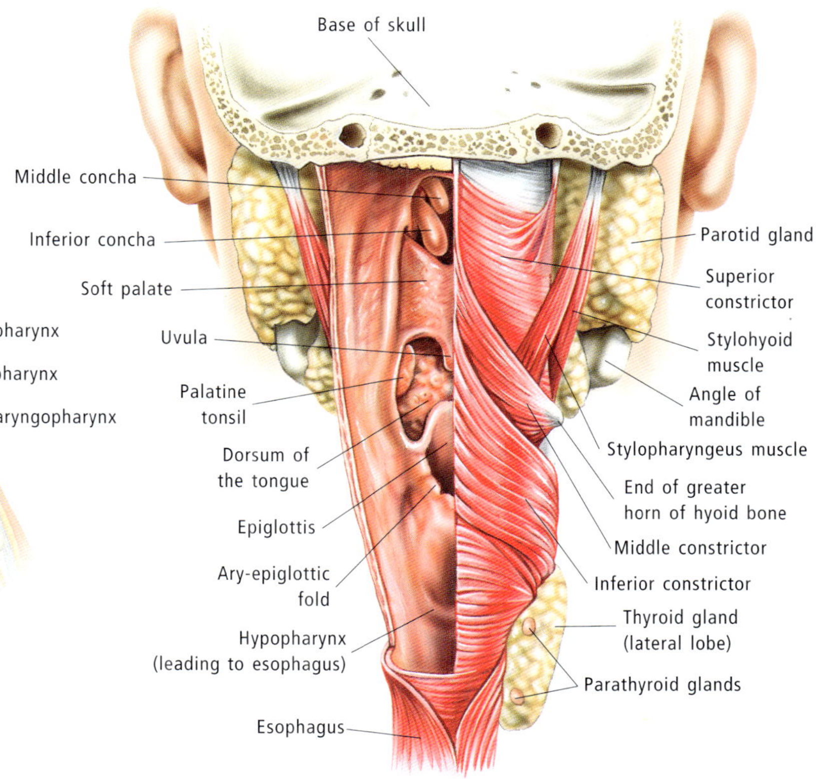

PHARYNX

The pharynx is a vertically elongated tube that lies behind the nose, mouth and voice box (larynx). The pharynx has openings to all three of these regions and is a common passage for air, water and food. The pharynx is divided into three parts. From the top down, these are the nasopharynx, the oropharynx and the laryngopharynx.

Nasopharynx

The nasopharynx lies immediately beneath the base of the skull and behind the nose. Air from the nose passes through the nasopharynx on its way down to the lungs. In the side walls of the nasopharynx lie the openings of the auditory (eustachian) tubes, which connect the pharynx with the middle ear. These tubes allow air pressure in the middle ear to be equalized with the outside environment, thus allowing the eardrum to move freely in response to air vibrations.

The auditory tubes are particularly important when one is changing altitude, as in an aircraft flight, or ascending in an elevator to the top of a tall building. If the auditory tube becomes blocked by mucus, as in a head cold, discomfort or pain will be felt in the ear and hearing may be temporarily impaired.

The nasopharynx also contains tonsillar tissue in the form of the nasopharyngeal tonsils or adenoids. These tissues of the immune system protect the body from any disease-causing organisms that may enter the body via the nose.

Oropharynx

The oropharynx lies behind the mouth and provides a passage for air, water and food. It is separated from the mouth by paired arches of tissue on each side. The entrance from the mouth to the pharynx is guarded by the palatine tonsils, which lie in a ditch (fossa) between the paired arches on each side and serve a similar function to the tonsillar tissue in the nasopharynx. The oropharynx receives air and nasal mucus from the nasopharynx above and opens into the laryngopharynx and laryngeal inlet below.

Laryngopharynx

The laryngopharynx, or hypopharynx, is the lowest part of the pharynx and extends from the tip of the epiglottic cartilage to the lower edge of the larynx. The laryngopharynx has an opening into the larynx in front, and air may pass through the upper laryngopharynx on its way to the larynx. Food from the oropharynx passes through the laryngopharynx on its way to the esophagus and stomach. Chicken and fish bones sometimes become lodged in pockets in the sides of the laryngopharynx. These pockets are called the piriform recesses and have an important nerve, the internal laryngeal nerve, lying in their floor. The internal laryngeal nerve supplies sensation to the upper larynx.

Cancer of the pharynx

Cancer may arise in the pharynx and, like mouth and tongue cancers, is usually associated with heavy smoking and drinking. These cancers need to be treated early and aggressively, with surgery and irradiation, for the patient to have a good chance of survival. Spread of the cancer to nearby lymph nodes is often present at diagnosis.

SEE ALSO *Adenoids, Ear, Larynx, Mouth, Nose, Pharyngitis, Respiratory system, Tonsils*

PHENYLKETONURIA

In most Western countries, 1 in every 10,000 to 20,000 children is born with the hereditary genetic disorder phenylketonuria (PKU). Despite its rare occurrence, all newborns are routinely tested for PKU using a simple blood analysis, the Guthrie test. This is because PKU can produce devastating affects without early intervention. People with PKU produce little or none of the enzyme phenylalanine hydroxylase, which breaks down the amino acid phenylalanine found in many foods. As a result, phenylalanine, which is toxic to brain tissue, accumulates in the body. The most serious impact is progressive mental retardation. This can be avoided, however, by a strict diet and regular monitoring.

SEE ALSO *Enzyme deficiencies*

P

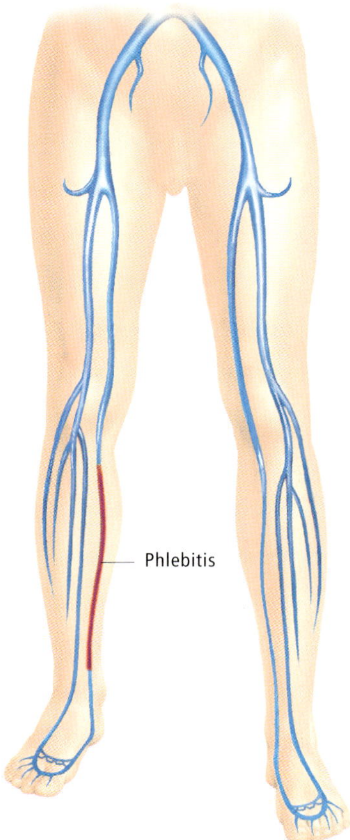

Phlebitis

Phlebitis is an inflammation of the veins, occurring mainly in the legs. The inflamed area swells and can become red and warm, and the blood flow may slow or stop.

PHLEBITIS

Phlebitis, or inflammation of the veins, is most commonly seen in the superficial veins of the legs. It results in pain and redness at the sites of inflammation, along the course of the vein. Inflammation of the vein wall causes the blood to clot at that point, and a lump can be felt under the skin. This condition is known as thrombophlebitis.

Phlebitis is most often a complication of varicose veins and may occur after prolonged standing or during pregnancy. Sometimes it occurs due to trauma to the vein or a reaction to a plastic cannula inserted for intravenous therapy.

Generally phlebitis is resolved with simple measures, such as rest and elevation of the leg, pain relief and anti-inflammatory medication. Sometimes it may extend to the deep venous system or be a sign of underlying malignant disease.

SEE ALSO *Thrombophlebitis, Varicose veins, Veins*

PHLEBOTOMUS FEVER

A virus transmitted by the bite of a female sandfly is responsible for phlebotomus fever. Symptoms appear suddenly, between three and six days after the bite, and include a general feeling of weariness, stomach pain, fever, headaches, muscle aches and sensitivity to light. Phlebotomus fever is prevalent throughout hot dry areas of the tropics and sub-tropics, where sandflies occur. The recommended treatment is simply bed rest and plenty of fluids. The disease runs its course after a few days and has never been known to have resulted in a fatality. Other names for phlebotomus fever include sandfly fever, pappataci fever and three-day fever.

SEE ALSO *Viruses*

PHOBIA

A phobia is a persistent, irrational fear, often recognized as such by the sufferer. A phobia may be triggered by specific objects, activities or situations and produces feelings of anxiety which can be overwhelming, often interfering with the sufferer's capacity to cope with everyday life. Typically, the anxiety is out of proportion to reality, but the fear is real and the person may be unable to control their feelings, even in cases where they are aware that they are overreacting.

Phobias are a form of anxiety disorder specific to physical objects or circumstances, and they produce all the symptoms characteristic of fear in other situations. Symptoms may involve heart palpitations, sweaty palms and breathing difficulties, and the sufferer may faint or feel dizzy.

There are various known phobias, for example, acrophobia is a fear of heights, arachnophobia is fear of spiders, claustrophobia is fear of enclosed spaces, agoraphobia is fear of open spaces—chronic agoraphobics may fear to leave their own homes—and social phobia causes a dread of being embarrassed in front of others.

Development of a phobia may result from a spontaneous panic attack, and the situation where that first attack was experienced may become the focus of phobic fear in the future. Behavioral therapy is successful in treating many phobias and involves gradual confrontation, under controlled conditions, with the fear and the objects or circumstances which produce it. After continued increasing exposure, the sufferer may become accustomed to the cause and lose their fear.

SEE ALSO *Acrophobia, Agoraphobia, Anxiety, Behavior therapy, Claustrophobia, Panic attack*

PHOTOCOAGULATION

Photocoagulation is a form of laser surgery used to correct certain eye disorders. It involves an intense beam of light directed into the eye to destroy damaged blood vessels and seal off leaking ones. Photocoagulation usually takes about 30 minutes, is relatively painless and is performed in a medical center or doctor's office by a specially trained ophthalmologist.

SEE ALSO *Eye*

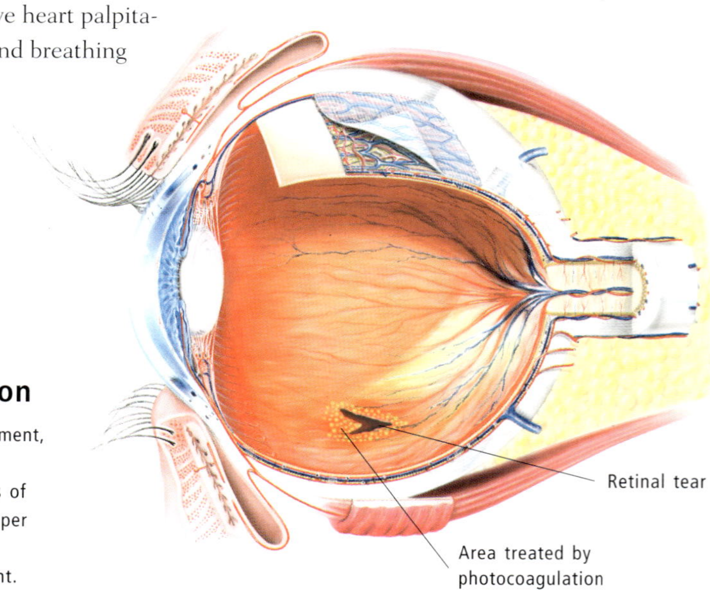

Photocoagulation

In cases of retinal detachment, photocoagulation can be used to "weld" the edges of the torn retina to the deeper layers of the eyeball and prevent further detachment.

PHOTOPHOBIA

Photophobia is an abnormal fear of or intolerance to light. It may develop as a result of infection, such as iritis, which causes pain and extreme sensitivity to light.

SEE ALSO *Iritis, Phobia*

PHOTOSENSITIVITY

Photosensitivity is a reaction to sunlight or ultraviolet light. It can be the cause of some skin conditions such as solar urticaria where itching wheals appear. Photosensitivity can cause blistering in people diagnosed with the enzyme deficiency disease porphyria cutanea tarda. It can also cause rosacea, a type of acne sometimes related to long-term exposure to sunlight. Light can be a source of pain and discomfort to migraine sufferers. Certain chemicals or drugs, such as some antibiotics, can produce photosensitivity.

SEE ALSO *Porphyria, Rosacea, Sun exposure, Urticaria*

PHYSICAL THERAPY

Physical therapy (physical medicine or physiotherapy) involves the use of physical modes of treatment—such as heat, massage, exercise and electrical currents—in the treatment of people physically disabled by pain or disease

Physical therapy is an important part of the treatment of many conditions, including fractures, back pain, stroke, nerve and spinal cord injuries, and arthritis. The physical therapist (physiatrist or physiotherapist) is one of a team of health professionals involved in the rehabilitation of patients suffering from these illnesses; such a team may also include speech and occupational therapists, psychologists and counselors.

The objectives of physical therapy are to relieve pain and/or improve functions such as muscle strength, joint mobility, muscular coordination and breathing capacity. Heat may be used to stimulate circulation and to relieve pain. Heat may be applied by infrared lamps, short-wave radiation, high-frequency electrical currents (diathermy), immersion in hot water (hydrotherapy), application of hot moist compresses or by ultrasound. Exercise is used to increase the range of motion of a joint, to increase the strength in a muscle, or to improve muscle coordination. Breathing exercises may be used to improve the breathing of patients with lung disorders and correct faulty posture. Massage to an injured or diseased area aids circulation and relieves local pain or muscle spasm.

SEE ALSO *Hydrotherapy, Massage, Rehabilitation*

PICA

People with pica crave and eat non-food substances, such as clay, dirt, gravel, glue, ice, plaster and hair. The disorder occurs mostly in pregnant women, children aged between one and six years, people afflicted with certain forms of mental illness, and some people with intellectual disability. The cause may be an underlying nutritional problem. For example, an iron deficiency may prompt a person to crave and eat clay, or there may be psychological reasons. Treatment depends on the cause. Psychological or psychiatric counseling may help. In the case of a nutritional deficiency, the cravings may be dispelled by dietary adjustments or nutritional supplements.

PIGEON TOES

The condition known as pigeon toes or intoeing is characterized by feet that turn in during walking or running. It is seen commonly in toddlers and sometimes older children and is due to a temporary twist in a leg or foot bone, usually caused by the way a child lay in the uterus. It is uncommon in adults. In the past, the condition was often treated with corrective bracing or special footwear. These days this is rarely done as it is understood that, in all but a few cases, pigeon toes gradually improve by exercising the foot, and the condition usually disappears by the time a child starts school.

SEE ALSO *Foot*

PILATES METHOD

The Pilates method of exercise was devised by Joseph Pilates in the 1920s to aid in the rehabilitation of people injured in World War I. It is based on developing an awareness of the positioning of the body during exercise to achieve better muscle control, and aims to achieve pelvic stability, improve posture and safeguard the back from injury.

In Pilates exercises muscle groups are isolated to achieve maximum performance with minimal expenditure of energy. By strengthening and elongating muscles the exercises can help treat back injuries or pain.

SEE ALSO *Alexander technique, Feldenkrais method*

PILONIDAL SINUS

Pilonidal sinus (or cyst) is a common disorder that occurs most frequently in hairy young males. The affected person has a minor congenital abnormality, a small skin sac (sinus) at the base of the spine in the cleft between the buttocks. It causes no problems, unless it is infected (pilonidal abscess), causing pain and swelling in the area and a discharge of pus. The condition is treated with antibiotics, surgical drainage, and later, when the infection has subsided, surgical removal of the sinus.

SEE ALSO *Cyst*

PIMPLES

A pimple is an eruption in the skin, most commonly of the face, chest or upper back, which shows as a white spot (pustule), possibly surrounded by a reddened and inflamed area. Pimples form where skin pores are

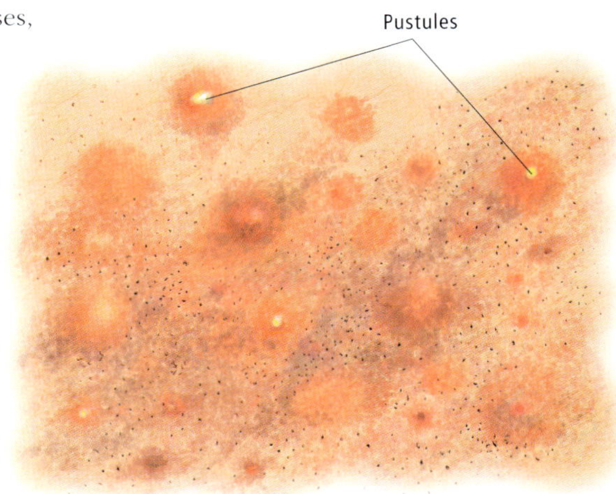

Pimples

Pimples form when skin pores become blocked by dried sebum from the sebaceous glands.

clogged by dried sebum (the oil from the sebaceous glands), flaked skin and bacteria. Bacterial growth in the blocked pore irritates the skin and a white head of pus forms from debris, largely white blood cells. A blackhead may form from dead skin cells if there is no bacterial infection in the pore.

Drugs such as anabolic steroids, corticosteroids, iodides, bromides and phenytoin can cause acne and eruptions of pimples. Keratosis pilaris is a disorder causing small pointed pimples on upper arms, thighs and buttocks.

SEE ALSO *Acne, Acne rosacea*

Pituitary function

The pituitary gland controls all the other endocrine glands in the body. It has two parts: the neurohypophysis (posterior pituitary), which secretes two hormones (vasopressin and oxytocin), and the adenohypophysis (anterior pituitary), which secretes hormones that control the thyroid and adrenal glands, and the follicles and corpus luteum in the ovaries.

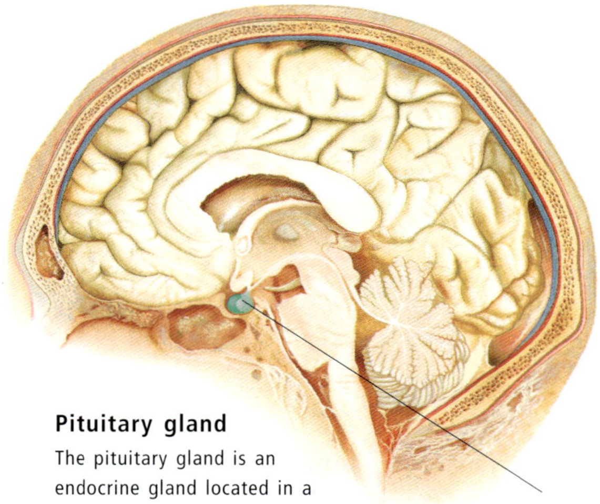

Pituitary gland
The pituitary gland is an endocrine gland located in a recess of the sphenoid bone at the base of the brain.

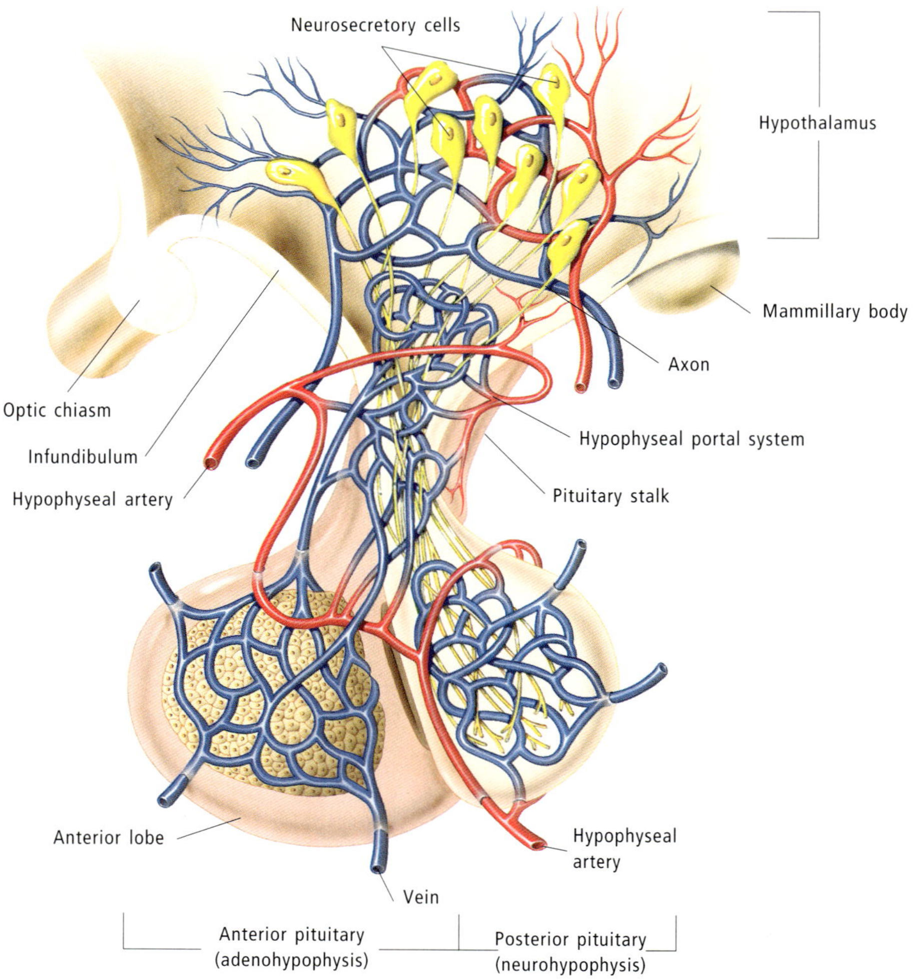

PINS AND NEEDLES

Pins and needles (parasthesia) is the sensation of tingling and pricking felt in the skin, usually in the hands and feet. It is due to a problem with the peripheral nerve supplying that region of the skin. Often the problem is pressure on the nerve, and will disappear when body position is changed and the pressure is relieved. Sometimes the pressure may be due to the nerve being trapped in a confined space, as in carpal tunnel syndrome, which causes pins and needles in the thumb, index and middle finger. Pins and needles also occur in diseases like diabetes and kidney failure which affect the nerves.

SEE ALSO *Carpal tunnel syndrome, Diabetes, Nerves*

PINWORMS

Pinworms (*Enterobius vermicularis*) are common gut parasites which usually cause only mild symptoms such as itching around the anus, and minor diarrhea. They infect people when their eggs are swallowed and hatch inside the colon. Adult pinworms, which look like white threads up to $\frac{1}{2}$ inch (1 centimeter) long, lay their eggs in the rectum. Poor personal hygiene, particularly among children, is responsible for their spread—typically, an infected person scratches their anus, picks up the eggs on their fingers and reinfects themselves or passes the parasite on.

Effective medications are available but, even without treatment, infections usually disappear within weeks if strict personal hygiene measures are taken. Other names include seatworm and threadworm.

SEE ALSO *Worms*

PITUITARY GLAND

The pituitary gland (hypophysis) is a small organ lying immediately below the hypothalamus of the brain. It weighs only about $\frac{1}{60}$ of an ounce (0.5 gram), but plays a very important role in the control of endocrine gland function throughout the body. Endocrine glands are those glands that secrete special chemicals called hormones into the bloodstream or body cavities.

The pituitary gland is divided into two basic parts, each of which has a different origin during embryonic life. The part towards the back of the gland is derived from the embryonic brain and is called the neurohypophysis (posterior pituitary). It is connected to the brain by a stalk called the infundibulum. The other part of the gland towards the front is derived from a pouch in the roof of the developing mouth (Rathke's pouch) and is called the adenohypophysis (anterior pituitary).

Neurohypophysis

The neurohypophysis is responsible for the release of two hormones: vasopressin (antidiuretic hormone—ADH) and oxytocin. Both hormones are polypeptides (chains of amino acids) that are made in the hypothalamus, a part of the brain immediately above the pituitary. Vasopressin increases water reabsorption from the urine as that fluid is being formed by the kidneys, thus making the urine more concentrated. The ultimate effect of this is to dilute the blood. Not surprisingly, vasopressin release is regulated in response to blood concentration, with special parts of the hypothalamus detecting changes in that concentration. Oxytocin causes contraction of smooth muscle cells in the uterus during childbirth and in the breasts during milk release (the milk ejection reflex).

Adenohypophysis

The adenohypophysis is also under the control of the hypothalamus, but is regulated by the release of hormones which flow in a special blood vessel system from the hypothalamus to the pituitary. The adenohypophysis releases many important hormones, with functions implied by their names. Growth hormone (GH) is important in the control of cartilage growth in long bones. Thyroid stimulating hormone (TSH) stimulates the production of thyroid hormone. Prolactin (lactogenic hormone) triggers the secretion of milk by the breasts (lactation). Adrenocorticotrophic hormone (ACTH or corticotropin) stimulates the production of hormones (corticosteroids and sex hormones) from the outer part of the adrenal glands (adrenal cortex). Follicle stimulating hormone (FSH) stimulates the development of egg follicles in a woman's ovaries and sperm cells in a man's testes. Luteinizing hormone (LH) stimulates the rupture of egg follicles in the ovary, and the formation of a corpus luteum in the ovary to produce progesterone during the latter half of a woman's menstrual cycle. The proper functioning of many of these hormones is essential to the correct growth, maturation and reproduction of an individual.

Tumors of the adenohypophysis usually grow slowly, but may damage nearby structures such as the visual pathways, causing partial blindness in the outer parts of the visual fields for each eye. Some endocrine diseases may arise due to abnormalities in hypothalamic/pituitary function (for example, failure to reach sexual maturity, some types of infertility, gigantism and acromegaly). Hypophysectomy is the surgical removal of all or part of the pituitary gland. It is sometimes necessary in the treatment of a pituitary tumor.

SEE ALSO *Adrenal glands, Endocrine system, Follicle stimulating hormone, Glands, Growth disorders, Hormones, Hypothalamus, Oxytocin*

PITYRIASIS ROSEA

A common and harmless skin disorder, pityriasis rosea is of unknown cause. It occurs mostly in adolescents and young adults, is slightly more common in females than males, and is more prevalent in spring and autumn.

The condition is characterized by a skin rash that follows a distinctive pattern. It begins on the trunk, upper arms, neck or thighs with a single, raised, oval-shaped, scaly, dark-red "herald patch" which can be mistaken for ringworm. Within three weeks many similar but smaller lesions appear, mainly in lines following the ribs, creating a Christmas-tree pattern. The rash may spread to other parts of the body but is rarely seen on the face, palms or soles of the feet. Treatment is not necessary although calamine lotion, cortisone creams and oral antihistamines should provide relief for people who experience itching from the rash.

Pityriasis rosea always clears by itself, usually after four to eight weeks, although the rash can persist for up to three months. It leaves no scars but darkly pigmented skin may bear discolored spots for several months. People rarely contract pityriasis rosea more than once. Although it is a minor affliction, a doctor should be consulted to rule out more serious conditions.

PLACEBO

A placebo is a "medicine" with no pharmacological action, sometimes given as make-believe medicine. Placebos are occasionally used in clinical trials of new medicines: consenting patients are divided into two groups, one of which is given the medicine, and the other group a placebo. The placebo will resemble the real medicine in appearance and taste but lack its pharmacological action. The trial is successful if patients taking the new medicine do significantly better than those taking the placebo.

PLACENTA

An organ of pregnancy, the placenta joins the mother and offspring, providing for selective exchange of substances through its membrane.

Formation

At conception, the ovum and sperm combine to form a single-celled embryo, the zygote. This divides rapidly and forms a hollow structure called a blastocyst upon reaching the uterus on day 4 of gestation. Some of the cells inside the blastocyst will become the embryo and fetal membranes, the outer cells will form the placenta.

On about day 6 the blastocyst adheres to the lining of the uterus (the endometrium). The outer cell mass undergoes changes which make it highly invasive and the entire blastocyst burrows its way into the endometrium which heals over it. That part of the outer cell mass which will form the placenta becomes elaborately folded and, as further erosion into the endometrium occurs, maternal blood vessels are broken down and maternal blood seeps into the spaces between the folds. Gradually a circulation is set up with maternal blood flowing in from the ends of arteries and out via the veins. Fetal blood vessels develop within the folds of the placenta and these connect with the blood vessels in the body of the embryo via the umbilical cord.

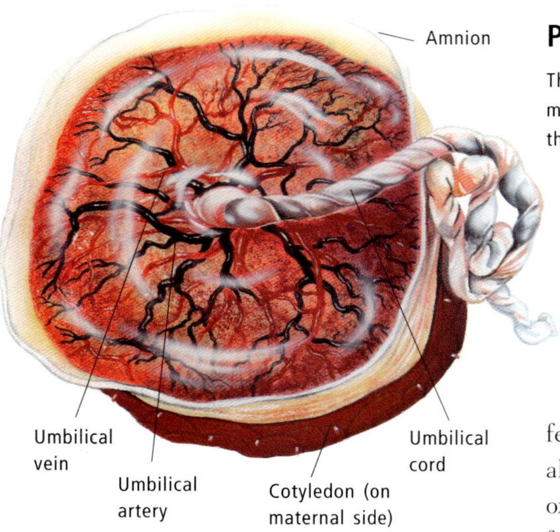

Placenta

The placenta connects the baby to the mother via the umbilical cord. It keeps the baby in position and ensures the baby receives adequate nutrients and oxygen. The placenta also acts as an endocrine organ, producing hormones such as placental prolactin, estrogen, and human chorionic gonadotropin during the pregnancy.

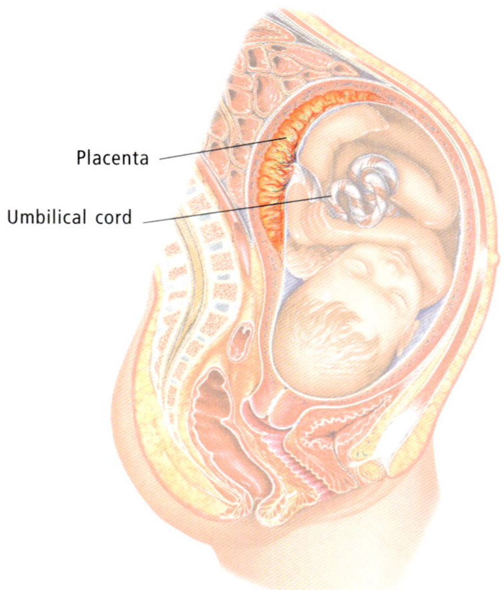

The parts of the placenta overlying the fetal capillaries become very thin in order to allow for diffusion of nutrients and oxygen from the maternal blood into the fetal blood and for fetal wastes to pass back to the mother's blood. Despite their close proximity, the two bloodstreams never actually have direct contact. As pregnancy proceeds, the fetus and the amnion enlarge so much that the cavity of the uterus is totally filled.

The blastocyst can implant anywhere in the uterus but most commonly in the upper posterior wall. Implantation near the opening of the cervix results in a placenta previa which partly or wholly covers the cervical opening. This forms a physical barrier at birth between the fetus and the birth canal; a placenta previa may also prematurely separate from the uterine wall. This can cause severe or fatal hemorrhaging of the mother's blood, either before or just after birth.

Other functions

The placenta produces many hormones including human chorionic gonadotropin (HCG), estrogen, progesterone, growth hormone and placental prolactin. HCG is the earliest placental hormone to be produced and is first secreted on day 6 of gestation. HCG maintains the corpus luteum (the ovarian follicle from which the ovum burst) and ensures that it continues to manufacture progesterone and estrogen until the placenta is able to produce adequate amounts of both, usually by the third month of gestation, when HCG levels decline. Progesterone is secreted by the placenta in increasing amounts during the last two trimesters and is necessary for the maintenance of pregnancy. HCG crosses the placenta into the maternal blood and is the basis for many of the tests for pregnancy.

The placenta forms a protective barrier between the maternal and fetal blood although certain noxious agents can travel across it and infect the fetus. These include many (though not all) viruses, notably rubella and HIV, anti-Rhesus factor antibodies, alcohol, pesticides, drugs such as thalidomide, and hormones such as diethylstilbestrol. Microbes larger than viruses usually cannot cross the placenta but exceptions include the bacterium of syphilis and the protozoan parasite which causes toxoplasmosis.

Tumors

Hydatidiform mole and choriocarcinoma are tumors arising from the placenta. Hydatidiform moles are characterized by some, or all, of the placental folds undergoing abnormal proliferation to form a mass of watery cysts. The embryo is usually missing, especially when the mole affects the whole placenta. These tumors grow rapidly and can cause severe hemorrhage if they invade deep into the uterine wall or the adjacent pelvic vessels. They produce large amounts of HCG which is used to diagnose the condition. Choriocarcinoma is a rare, highly malignant tumor formed from placental tissue; it may follow a hydatidiform mole or occur after a spontaneous abortion or normal pregnancy.

SEE ALSO *Embryo, Estrogens, Fetal development, Hydatidiform mole, Pregnancy, Progesterone, Reproductive systems, Toxoplasmosis*

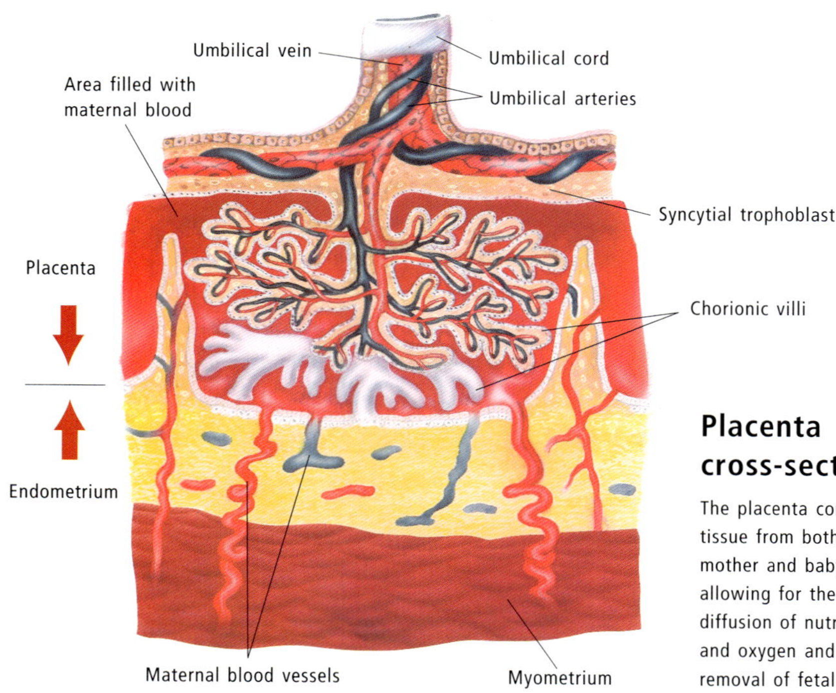

Placenta cross-section

The placenta contains tissue from both the mother and baby, allowing for the diffusion of nutrients and oxygen and the removal of fetal waste.

PLANTAR FASCIITIS

A common cause of heel pain, plantar fasciitis often occurs in athletes and people who walk a lot on hard surfaces. It is an inflammation of the thick band of fibrous tissue on the bottom of the foot—the plantar fascia—and can persist for months. Treatment includes anti-inflammatory medications and resting the affected foot.

SEE ALSO *Foot*

PLASMA

Plasma refers to the fluid component of the blood. It consists of water, salts and proteins and contains all the chemicals which circulate between body tissues, including glucose, hormones, enzymes and growth factors. Plasma generally contributes approximately half the blood volume, the rest being due to red and white blood cells.

The major plasma protein is albumin, synthesized by the liver and important in maintaining the blood's osmotic pressure. The liver also makes some of the blood clotting proteins, which are found in the plasma. Another group of plasma proteins are the globulins, which include immunoglobulins produced by the immune system and are responsible for fighting infection.

Plasma is lost together with red and white cells during bleeding and may need to be replaced if loss is severe. Initial replacement can be with plasma substitutes, followed by the infusion of fresh frozen plasma. This is produced from donated blood, the plasma being separated by centrifugation and frozen until required.

In some diseases the patient's plasma may be exchanged with normal plasma or albumin solution as part of the treatment. The procedure is known as plasmapheresis and is performed using an apheresis machine.

SEE ALSO *Blood, Globulins, Liver, Lymphatic/Immune system, Plasmapheresis*

PLASMAPHERESIS

Plasmapheresis is a technique in which plasma is passed through a filtration device that removes certain antibodies and abnormal protein elements and returns the plasma, free of antibodies and these protein elements, to the patient. It is used in the treatment of certain autoimmune diseases (caused by antibodies attacking the body's own tissue), such as systemic lupus erythematosus (SLE), myasthenia gravis and multiple myeloma.

SEE ALSO *Antibodies, Autoimmune disease, Plasma*

PLASTIC SURGERY

Plastic or reconstructive surgery is a versatile specialty which includes the correction of disfigurement, restoring impaired function and improving physical appearance (cosmetic surgery). Reconstructive surgery is performed on abnormalities caused by congenital defects, developmental abnormalities, trauma, infection, tumors or disease. One of the possible sources of the term is the Greek word *plastikos*, which means "to mold or give form".

The driving force behind most developments in plastic surgery was war. World War I (1914–18) resulted in outstanding developments in plastic surgery. At this time doctors were required to treat many extensive facial and head injuries, ranging from shattered jaws and blown-off noses to gaping skull wounds. At first this specialty had no formal training. Then in the 1930s the American Society of Plastic and Reconstructive Surgeons was launched. In the 1940s, during World War II, the skills of plastic surgeons were again in great demand.

In the 1960s silicone emerged as a tool for plastic surgeons. Initially it was used to treat skin imperfections. However, in 1962 it was first used by an American surgeon, Thomas Cronin, in a breast implant device. It was not until 1990 that concerns about silicone implants came to a head and patients began to sue manufacturers, leading to the ban of silicone breast implants in the USA in 1992.

Plastic surgery repairs or reshapes tissue structures, removes tissues and grafts or transfers tissue. Grafting is used to treat cases of trauma such as severe burns, injuries from automobile accidents and gunshot wounds. If the circumstances are favorable, plastic surgeons may also reattach a severed body part. Congenital deformities—commonly cleft lip and palate—can also be corrected by plastic surgery.

SEE ALSO *Cosmetic surgery, Mammoplasty*

PLATELETS

Platelets are small cell fragments in the blood that prevent bruising and bleeding. They adhere to small breaks in blood vessels and form a plug, which blocks the defect. Platelets release chemicals which attract more platelets to the affected area and trigger the clotting system to form a clot, or thrombus.

Thrombocytopenia is a condition in which there are too few platelets, and results in a tendency to bleed. Having too many platelets, a condition known as thrombocytosis, increases the risk of thrombosis, which can cause heart attack or stroke.

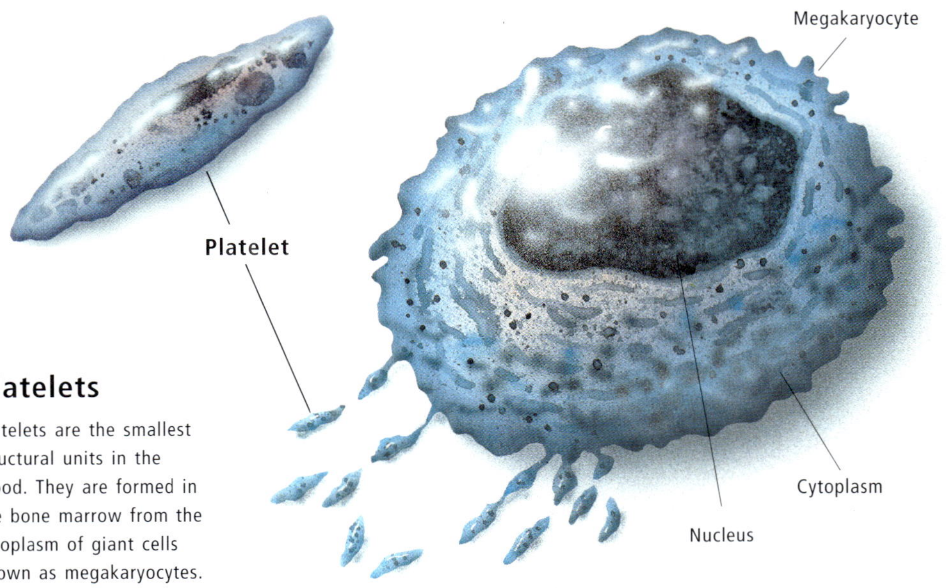

Platelets

Platelets are the smallest structural units in the blood. They are formed in the bone marrow from the cytoplasm of giant cells known as megakaryocytes.

P

Aspirin blocks the release of chemicals by platelets and can cause easy bruising in some people. It is widely used to reduce the risk of thrombosis as it makes platelets less sticky or adherent.

SEE ALSO *Blood, Thrombocytopenia, Thrombocytosis, Thrombosis, Thrombus*

PLAY THERAPY

Play therapy was recognized in the 1930s as a valuable way of helping troubled children. Through play children develop, integrate and communicate their emotions, thoughts and sense of self. In play therapy, children are encouraged to play freely in the safe environment provided by a psychotherapist. The therapist learns about the children's concerns by observing their play.

Discussion between the child and the therapist about the play allows the therapist to support the child and understand the child's feelings. Play also helps the therapist make diagnoses, and establish rapport with the child. Play therapy is helpful for children with emotional, behavioral and learning difficulties.

SEE ALSO *Counseling, Psychotherapy*

Viral pneumonia

The influenza virus is one of several viruses that can cause pneumonia.

Bacterial pneumonia

Culture of the sputum of pneumonia sufferers will reveal bacteria. These need to be tested for sensitivity to antibiotics before treatment.

Pneumonia

In pneumonia, air spaces in the lungs fill with fluid and cellular debris preventing gas exchange. This can result in respiratory or cardiac failure.

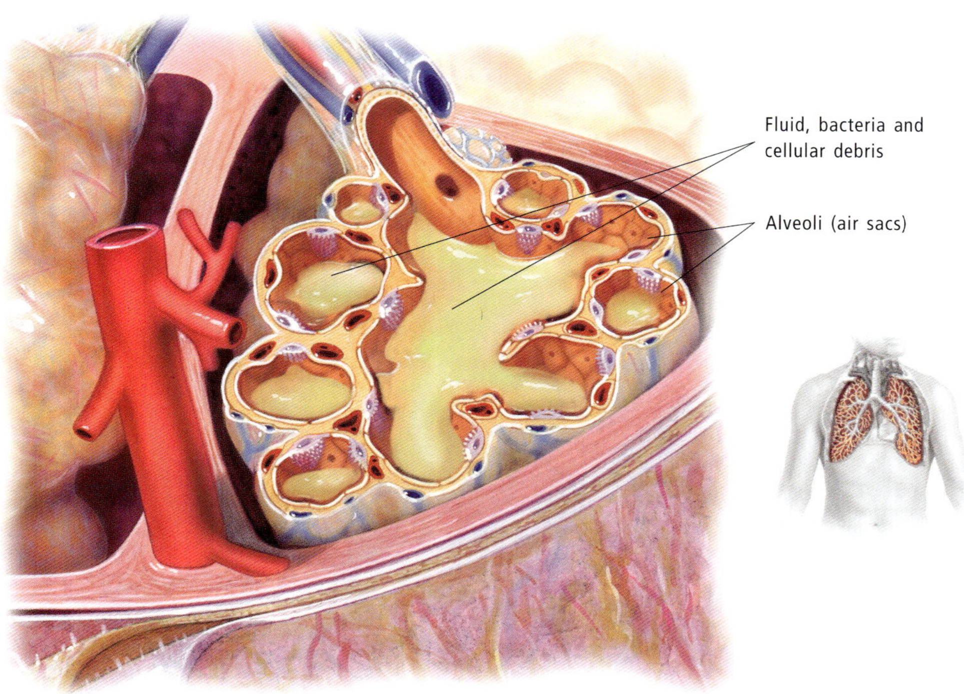

PLEURISY

Pleurisy is inflammation of the pleura, a thin, two-layered membrane that lines the lung and chest cavity and enables the lungs to move smoothly against the chest wall during breathing. Pleurisy is a consequence of other lung conditions rather than a disease in itself. Conditions that may lead to the development of pleurisy include bronchitis, pneumonia, a blood clot in the lung, lung cancer, collagen vascular diseases (such as systemic lupus erythematosus or rheumatoid arthritis), congestive heart failure or kidney and liver disorders.

The symptoms of pleurisy are sudden chest pain that worsens with breathing, and coughing. Other symptoms of the underlying disease may also be present; for example, chest pain, cough and fever.

Depending on the cause, pleurisy may occur with a pleural effusion (fluid that has collected in the pleural cavity). A pleural effusion may show up on a chest x-ray, which may also show evidence of the disorder causing the pleurisy—pneumonia or lung cancer, for example. Other investigations may be ordered by the physician, depending on the cause. Treatment is directed toward the underlying cause and may include painkillers, anti-inflammatory drugs and antibiotics.

SEE ALSO *Breathing, Lungs, Respiratory system*

PLEURODYNIA

Also known as Bornholm disease or epidemic myalgia, pleurodynia is a temporary inflammation of the pleura, the tissue lining the lungs, occurring most often in children. The condition is caused by the Group B coxsackie viruses. The patient suffers severe pain in the lower chest (worsened by breathing and coughing), muscle pain, fever, sore throat, and headaches. Symptoms usually clear up in 2–4 days without treatment, though relapses may occur. Acetaminophen (paracetamol) may help relieve pain and fever .

SEE ALSO *Lungs*

PNEUMOCONIOSIS

Pneumoconiosis is a group of diseases caused by prolonged inhalation of inorganic dusts, which collect in the lungs. These dusts (coal, silica or asbestos) are usually inhaled in the course of particular occupations, such as coal mining, sand blasting, pottery, stone dressing or asbestos mining. Symptoms vary slightly according to the type of dust, but all patients with pneumoconiosis experience breathlessness.

SEE ALSO *Lungs*

PNEUMONIA

Pneumonia is a serious lung disease in which inflammation, caused by bacteria and/or viruses, results in the accumulation of fluid and cellular debris in the air spaces of the lungs. This prevents the exchange of carbon dioxide and oxygen in the lungs. Pneumonia is very common, affecting about 1 percent of the population every year. It is most common in winter and spring because of sudden drops in air temperature, overcrowding in poorly ventilated rooms and the prevalence of bacteria and viruses. Smoking, alcoholism, a poor immune system and air pollution are associated with an increased risk of pneumonia. As many as 5–10 percent of those developing pneumonia may die from the disease, usually the very young or the elderly. Bedridden patients with dementia, hip fractures or chronic heart disease are particularly prone to developing pneumonia, which is often the ultimate cause of death.

Depending on the site involved, different types of pneumonia may be described: lobar pneumonia affects an entire lobe of the lung; lobular pneumonia affects lung tissue around the major airway branches; bronchopneumonia is lobular pneumonia affecting both lungs.

The microorganisms responsible for pneumonia include bacteria, such as *Streptococcus pneumoniae*, *Staphylococcus aureus*, *Klebsiella pneumoniae* and *Haemophilus influenzae*, and viruses, such as influenza, adenovirus and respiratory syncytial virus. Occasionally pneumonia may be caused by unusual microorganisms such as fungi, rickettsiae and mycoplasma. Unusual microorganisms like fungi and mycoplasma are more likely to be found to be responsible when the patient's immune system is functioning poorly, as in those with AIDS.

Patients with pneumonia may at first complain of cough and sputum (coughed-up lung fluid), breathlessness, sharp chest pain aggravated by coughing or by taking a deep breath, fever and a general feeling of being unwell. The sputum is usually yellow or green and may occasionally contain blood, particularly if vessels in the lung have been ruptured by vigorous coughing. A chest x-ray will show loss of the normal air-filled spaces, so that the lung fields appear white, either uniformly, within a lobe of the lung (lobar pneumonia) or in patches (bronchopneumonia). Culture of the sputum will reveal bacteria, which may be the actual causative organism or present as secondary bacterial infection of a pneumonia caused by a virus. The bacteria need to be tested for sensitivity to antibiotics, because in recent years many bacteria have developed resistance to some of the available antibiotics (such as the penicillin family). The concentration of oxygen in the arterial blood may be reduced, and in the severely ill the concentration of carbon dioxide in the blood may rise.

Treatment of pneumonia involves prescribing the appropriate antibiotic for the causative microorganism. The patient should be supported by inhaled oxygen, receive physical therapy to clear the airways and analgesics to relieve pain. Complications which may arise include respiratory failure, cardiac failure, abscesses (pus-filled cavities) in the lung and fluid in the pleural sacs around the lung (pleural effusion). Occasionally pus may collect in the pleural sacs around the lung (pleural empyema).

SEE ALSO *Bacteria, Lungs, Sputum tests, Viruses*

Pneumothorax

In this condition, air enters one or both of the pleural sacs which enclose the lungs. This may occur if the chest wall is pierced. When air is trapped in the chest cavity, increased pressure can result in the collapse of the lungs.

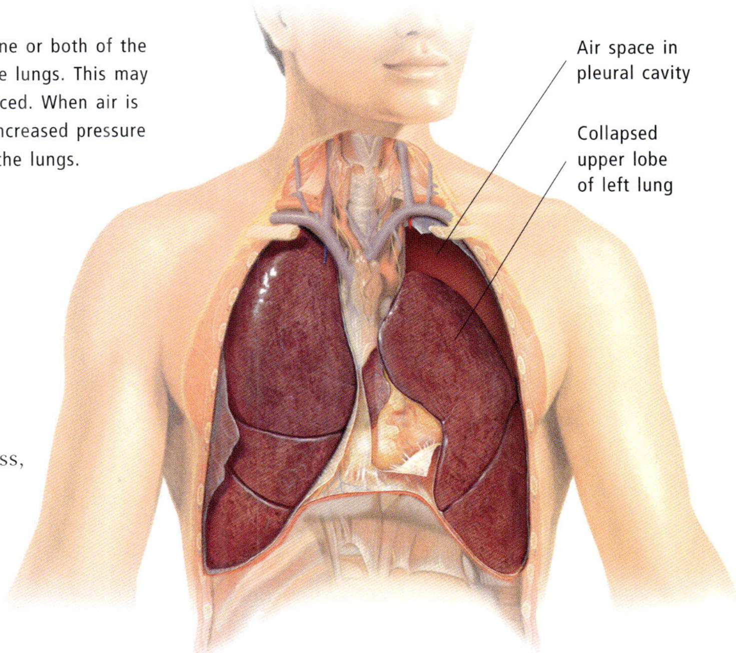

PNEUMOTHORAX

Pneumothorax literally means "air in the chest". It occurs when air enters one or both of the pleural sacs which enclose the lungs. Pneumothorax may occur spontaneously, due to rupture of an air space in the outer part of the lung, or as a result of injury, which leads to perforation of the chest wall. Traumatic pneumothorax may follow penetrating chest wall injuries, blast injuries and diving accidents.

A particularly dangerous type of pneumothorax is tension pneumothorax, which occurs when a flap-valve effect in the damaged pleural membrane allows air to enter the pleural sac, but not escape. Pressure in the pleural sac rises rapidly, causing complete collapse of the lung on the affected side and a movement of the organs in the center of the chest to the opposite side of the chest, thus compressing the other lung. Both heart and lung function may be seriously affected, and rapid reduction of the air pressure in the pleural sac may be required.

Pneumothorax is treated by insertion of a tube into the affected side of the chest. This tube is connected to a drain and water valve mechanism, which allows air to leave the pleural sac but prevents re-entry. Often pneumothorax is accompanied by bleeding into the pleural sac (hemothorax), which may require drainage if a large amount of bleeding has occurred.

SEE ALSO *Lungs*

POISONING

Any substance that can cause illness or death is a potential poison. Poisons can be swallowed, inhaled, injected, absorbed through the skin or developed within the body. Some substances are more toxic than others and only a small quantity may be needed in order to poison a person; other poisons may need to be ingested in large quantities before they produce an effect.

Different poisons operate in different ways and will affect different parts of the body. Some poisons will act immediately, other substances are only poisonous once they reach certain levels in the body—lead poisoning is a good example of this.

For some substances, how they enter the body can also determine whether they will be poisonous or not; some are harmless when eaten but deadly if injected into a vein. In other cases, a substance which is harmless to an adult may poison a baby or child, for example, a dose of aspirin or alcohol. Listeria (listeriosis), not usually noticeable in adults, is particularly dangerous to an unborn child if the mother should be infected.

Food poisoning

One of the most common types of accidental poisoning is food poisoning. Symptoms of vomiting, diarrhea, abdominal cramps and general nausea result from consumption of foods which are contaminated by bacteria (*Salmonella, Shigella, Staphylococci, Clostridium* and *E. coli*) or their toxic products. Cooking destroys salmonella but cooked foods can be recontaminated if they come in contact with raw foods.

Strict personal hygiene standards when preparing and serving foods are essential, because bacteria can be transferred through the oral-fecal route—for example, by not washing hands after defecating or urinating and then working with food. It is also important to keep hot food very hot and to refrigerate food immediately at temperatures of 41°F (5°C) or lower after cooking, if it is not being eaten. Utensils and equipment used for preparing food needs to be kept scrupulously clean.

Food poisoning can also be caused by toxins from plants and animals or chemical poisons. Healthy adults usually recover quickly from food poisoning, though it can lead to chronic illness such as Reiter's syndrome and reactive arthritis. In young children, the elderly and those with a compromised immune system, food poisoning demands immediate treatment.

Mussels, clams, certain other shellfish and some fish can be poisonous when ingested by humans. Examples include tetraodon poisoning (which is poisoning from certain puffer-like fish) and scombroid poisoning (from fish in the mackerel family, such as tuna and bonito, which have lost their freshness). Mussels and clams can become poisonous, particularly in the Pacific Ocean, feeding on microorganisms that appear in the warmer months of the year.

Other foodstuffs which can poison, if taken in large quantities, include dietary supplements such as iron tablets and the vitamins D and A.

Environmental poisoning

Carbon monoxide poisoning is the most common cause of poison-related deaths in the USA. Carbon monoxide is a tasteless, colorless, odorless gas produced by the incomplete burning of fuel containing carbon—automobile exhaust, coal gas and furnace gas are all sources of carbon monoxide.

Lead poisoning—contamination from lead paints, dust, contaminated soil, and automobile gases—affects the blood, nervous system and digestive system. A blood test will reveal a person's lead level, although simple precautions, plus a diet which is low in fat and includes sufficient iron, are effective methods of minimizing the risks.

Other sources of environmental poisoning are pesticides and herbicides, often ingested through their accidental contact with foodstuffs. Toxic chemicals used around the home include soap and detergents, mothballs, bleaches and cleaners, rat or mouse bait, cosmetics, eucalyptus and tea-tree oil. Any of these can poison children who ingest them accidentally.

Poisonous plants, while sometimes attractive to children, are not considered to be a major cause of poisoning. Poisoning can result from eating any of several species of mushroom or toadstool. Plant poisoning can also occur from eating green or sprouting underground roots which contain solanine, sometimes found in green potatoes.

Treatment

First aid for poisoning varies depending on the poison ingested. The best course for the untrained person is to call a Poison Information Hotline or Control Center. A knowledge of first aid including cardiopulmonary resuscitation may be helpful. Inducing vomiting can worsen the damage and should only be done on the advice of a medical practitioner. Victims of an inhaled poison should be removed to fresh air, and when poisoning is via the skin, the area affected should be repeatedly rinsed with water.

SEE ALSO *Listeriosis, Overdose, Reiter's syndrome*

POLIOMYELITIS

Poliomyelitis (commonly known as polio) is a viral illness, usually affecting young children. It is spread from the infected individual to others by fecal-oral infection (which may occur if hands are not washed properly after defecating or urinating) or droplet infection (such as with sneezing). It is usually a mild illness; symptoms are slight fever, malaise, headache, sore throat, and vomiting 3–5 days after exposure. Complete recovery normally occurs in 24–72 hours. In about 10 percent of cases, however, it causes inflammation of the spinal cord and the brain stem.

Symptoms are fever, severe headache, stiff neck and muscle pain. In some cases, this may progress to weakness or paralysis of muscle groups, causing difficulty swallowing and breathing, and paralysis of the muscles of the legs and lower torso.

The condition is diagnosed by identifying the virus in cerebrospinal fluid, in the throat or in feces. Treatment involves physical therapy to aid muscle function. In severe cases, a tracheostomy (cutting an opening in the windpipe to insert a breathing tube) and an artificial respirator may be necessary.

The disease can be prevented by immunization. Polio vaccine may be given by injection, or (more usually) by mouth, at the ages of 2 months, 4 months, 6–18 months and 4–6 years. The development of polio vaccines has almost eliminated the disease in industrialized countries.

SEE ALSO *Immunization, Paralysis, Spinal cord, Viruses*

Poliomyelitis

The success of vaccines against the polio virus has greatly reduced the incidence of poliomyelitis. Jonas Salk developed the first effective vaccine, which has been largely superseded by an oral vaccine developed by Albert Sabin.

POLYCYSTIC KIDNEY DISEASE

The most commonly inherited disorder in the USA, polycystic kidney disease (PKD), is characterized by pain in the back and side of the body, frequent kidney infections, blood in the urine and high blood pressure. In this condition, cysts grow in the kidneys causing symptoms and damaging the kidneys. There is no treatment for the cysts themselves, but the symptoms of the disease can be treated. Over half of those suffering from PKD will suffer from kidney failure at some time in their life.

Genetic counseling is generally available for couples with a family history of PKD, and tests such as chorionic villus sampling and amniocentesis can determine whether a fetus will have the disease.

SEE ALSO *Amniocentesis, Chorionic villus sampling, Kidney*

POLYCYTHEMIA

Polycythemia, literally "many blood cells", refers to a group of blood conditions in which the numbers of cells in the blood increases. This may involve the red cells, white cells and/or the platelets. The most common and important form is an increase in the red cells, causing facial redness and increased viscosity of the blood. The affected person may have a sensation of fullness in the head and of itching, particularly after a hot bath or shower, which releases histamine from the white cells. The increased red cells and platelets result in a greater tendency to clotting in the veins and arteries, leading to deep venous thrombosis, heart attack or stroke.

Treatment is based on reducing blood viscosity through regular venesection, which is removal of blood from a vein—a needle is inserted into a large vein at the front of the elbow. Sometimes medication is required to control the increased cell production by the bone marrow.

SEE ALSO *Blood, Platelets, Red blood cells, White blood cells*

POLYMYOSITIS

Polymyositis is an autoimmune inflammatory disease of muscle. It causes muscle weakness, especially around the shoulders and hips. The muscles ache and may be tender to the touch. Fatigue, weight loss and a low-grade fever are common. The cause is unknown. The condition is treated with physical therapy and corticosteroids or immunosuppressant drugs.

SEE ALSO *Autoimmune disease*

POLYPS

A polyp is a growth or tumor protruding from a mucous membrane. It may be shaped like a grape on a stalk or may be a small lump. While polyps are usually benign (non-cancerous), they may lead to complications. They are most commonly found in the colon (large intestine), the nasal passages, the cervix of the uterus and within the uterine cavity.

Intestinal polyps are found most often in the rectum and sigmoid colon. They usually cause no symptoms, though in some cases there may be bleeding from the rectum. They should be removed, as they may become malignant. Surgery to remove a polyp is usually done via a proctoscope or

Polycystic kidney disease

In this inherited disease, cysts damage the kidneys resulting in blood in the urine and frequent kidney infections. Kidney failure and high blood pressure may also occur.

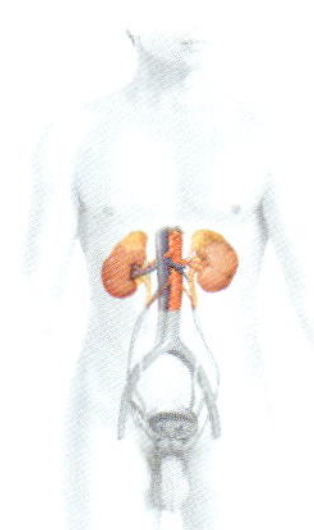

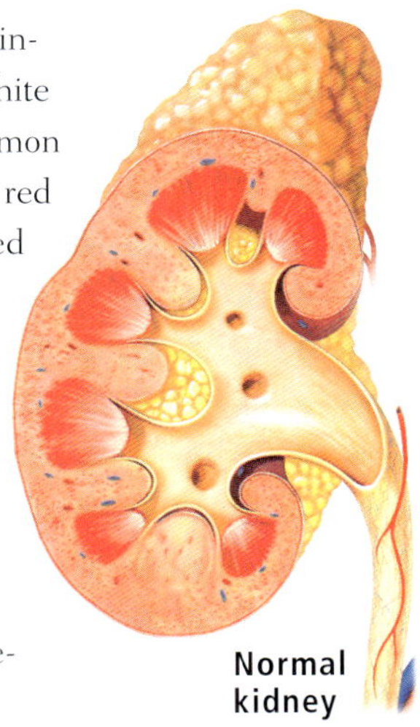

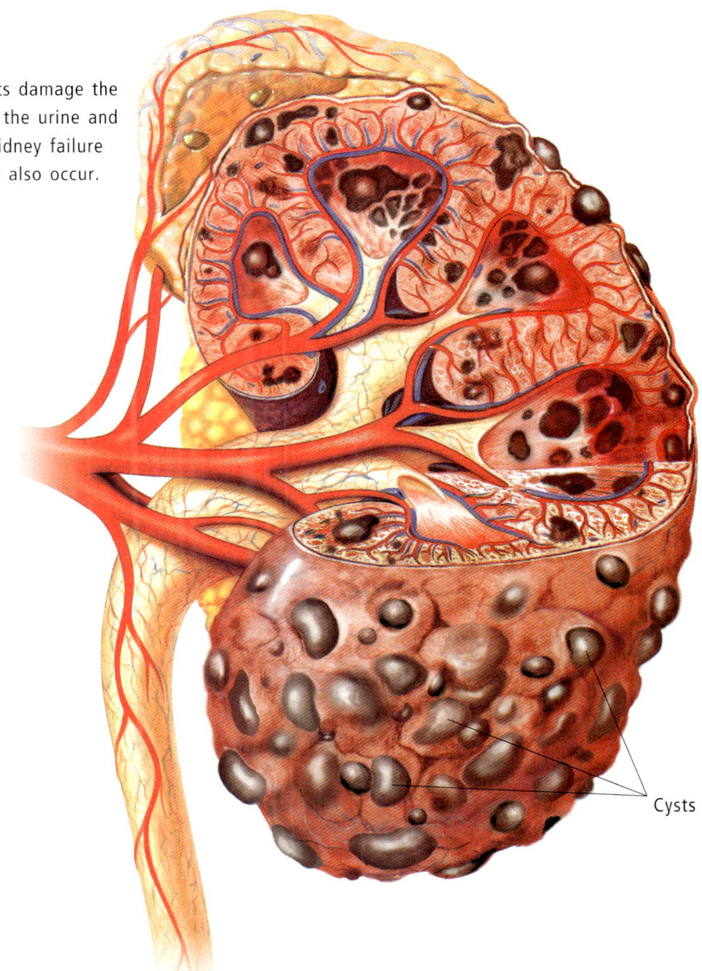

P

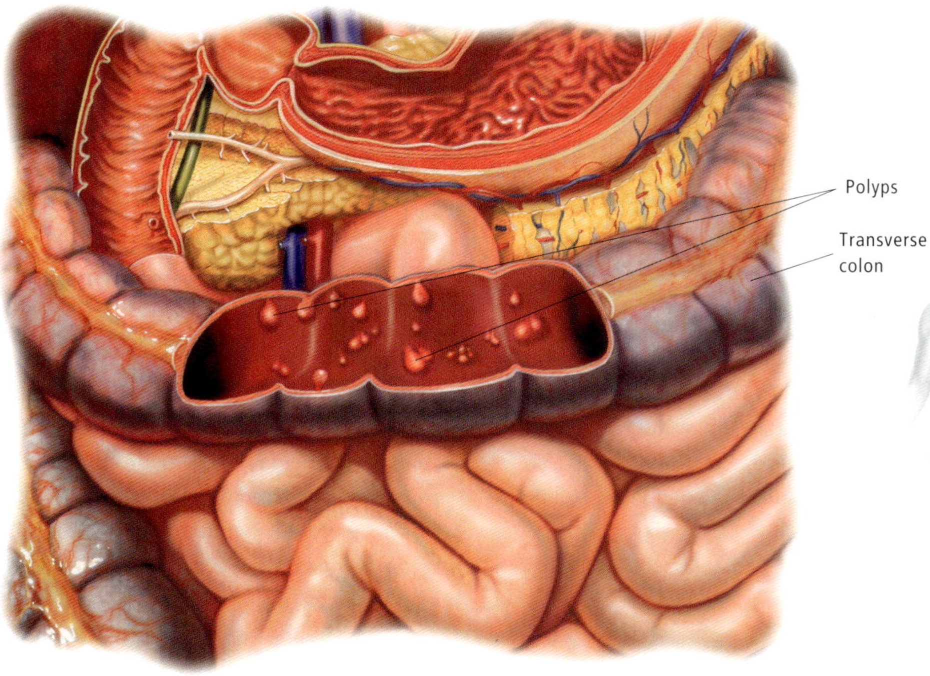

Polyps

Most commonly found in the colon, polyps are growths or tumors which protrude from the mucous membrane. A polyp may be a small lump, or shaped like a grape with a stalk.

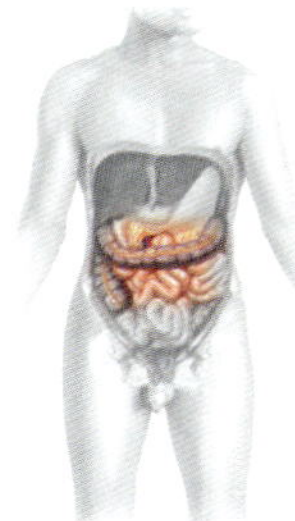

sigmoidoscope inserted via the rectum; the polyps are snipped off or destroyed by electric cauterization. Anyone with a personal or family history of polyps should have regular sigmoidoscopic examinations.

Familial polyposis is a rare hereditary condition in which multiple polyps cover the colon and rectum. It usually develops into cancer, so the rectum and colon must be removed surgically. Relatives should have periodic sigmoidoscopic examinations.

Nasal polyps are caused by chronic infection or allergy in the nose (allergic rhinitis). They cause a nasal discharge and chronic stuffiness. They are easily removed with minor surgery under local anesthesia.

SEE ALSO *Colon, Nose, Proctoscopy*

PORPHYRIA

Porphyria is a rare group of disorders resulting from defects in the production of heme, the oxygen-carrying portion of hemoglobin. An accumulation of chemicals called porphyrins results in attacks of abdominal pain and mental disturbance in one type of porphyria (King George III was thought to suffer from this), and blistering of the fingers in another. Symptoms can be triggered by a variety of factors including alcohol, certain drugs, hormonal irregularities and exposure to the sun. There is no cure—sufferers should avoid the offending substance, wherever possible.

SEE ALSO *Blood, Hemoglobin*

PORTAL HYPERTENSION

Portal hypertension is an increase in the pressure of the blood in the portal venous system. This is the system of veins that drains blood from the intestines to the liver.

The most common cause of this condition is chronic liver disease leading to cirrhosis, which obstructs blood flowing through the liver. This causes life-threatening bleeding into the lower esophagus and stomach. The patient may vomit copious amounts of blood (hematemesis) or pass black, tar-like feces containing altered blood (melena). The associated swelling of the abdomen is due to the accumulation of fluid in the abdominal cavity (ascites). Fluid collects in the abdomen and lower legs because the diseased liver is unable to produce a protein called albumin which helps to control fluid movement between the tissues of the body and the bloodstream.

SEE ALSO *Cirrhosis of the liver, Liver, Portal vein*

PORTAL VEIN

The portal vein is a wide but short vein that collects nutrient-rich blood from the veins leading from the large and small intestines, the stomach, the spleen, the pancreas and the gallbladder. It then transports this collected blood to the liver. The portal vein enters the liver through a slit called the porta hepatis (Latin for "door to the liver") and ends as a network of capillaries in the liver called sinusoids, which permeate the entire liver. There, ageing red cells, bacteria and other debris are removed from the blood, and nutrients are added to the blood or removed from it for storage. The blood then leaves the liver via the hepatic veins, which empty into the inferior vena cava.

Portal hypertension is increased pressure in the portal vein, and the veins that supply it, resulting from increased resistance to the blood flow into the liver, usually from scarring due to cirrhosis. A portacaval shunt is a surgically produced junction between the hepatic portal vein and the inferior vena cava, bypassing the liver. It is performed in cases of severe portal hypertension to improve the flow of blood through the portal vein to the inferior vena cava.

SEE ALSO *Portal hypertension*

POSITRON EMISSION TOMOGRAPHY

Commonly referred to as a PET scan, positron emission tomography is an imaging technique for monitoring body processes such as blood flow and metabolism. Chemical compounds containing radioactive isotopes are injected into an organ, and the body is scanned using a special machine. Positrons (positively charged electrons) emitted by the isotopes collide with electrons within the body, creating gamma radiation that is detected by the scanner. The resulting information is converted to computer images to give a cross-sectional view of the organ being studied. This technique is used to assess such things as muscle damage after a heart attack and the effects of chemotherapy drugs on body tissue.

SEE ALSO *Imaging techniques*

POSTNATAL DEPRESSION

Postnatal depression, also known as postpartum depression, is experienced by some women after giving birth. It is characterized by mood swings, insomnia, despondency, feelings of hopelessness and an inability to cope with normal situations. The condition is thought to result from extreme hormonal changes after birth, combined with the stress of looking after a new baby. It affects about 3 percent of mothers, even those with no history of psychological illness.

Many mothers suffer from a milder, short-lived depression known as "baby blues" in the week following a delivery, during which they may cry and feel anxious and moody. About 10 percent of mothers develop full-blown symptoms of postnatal depression, sometimes up to a year after the birth. They may have a preoccupation with their baby's health, feel guilty about not loving the child enough and appear detached from the baby. There may also be physical symptoms, such as headaches, chest pain, lethargy, heart palpitations and hyperventilation. Behavior can be extreme and hostile, and may include having nightmares, hallucinations and panic attacks. The condition usually lasts anywhere from 3–6 months.

Family problems or stressful events can put a woman at greater risk of suffering from postnatal depression. In some cases, the condition may resolve itself spontaneously. Where necessary, treatment is with a combination of counseling and medication (although some drugs can affect the baby via breast milk).

SEE ALSO *Childbirth, Depression, Infancy, Newborn*

POSTPOLIO SYNDROME

Postpolio syndrome is a condition that occasionally affects individuals who have previously had poliomyelitis. Sufferers experience weakness, fatigue and muscle twitches, as late as 20–30 years after the initial illness. The symptoms develop gradually; muscle groups that were not originally affected may become involved. In most cases, symptoms of the disease reach a plateau and do not deteriorate further.

Postpolio syndrome is not a recurrent bout of polio, but is thought to be due to death of nerve cells (neurons) that survived the original disease. There is no specific treatment but physical therapy may help manage the symptoms.

SEE ALSO *Poliomyelitis*

POST-TRAUMATIC STRESS DISORDER

Post-traumatic stress disorder (PTSD) is a debilitating condition that follows a terrifying event. First recognized as a condition of war veterans, called "shell shock" or "battle fatigue", it can be caused by any traumatic incident, such as car or train wrecks, natural disasters such as floods or earthquakes, or violent attacks against a person.

Symptoms usually begin within 3 months of the trauma, and may include recurrent, intrusive and distressing recollections of the event, flashbacks and dreams of the event, difficulty in concentrating, and memory impairment. The disorder can be accompanied by chronic anxiety, insomnia, depression and substance abuse. Not everyone who experiences a traumatic event suffers from PTSD, and many who do experience such an event may display these symptoms for only a short time. The diagnosis of PTSD is usually only made if the symptoms last longer than 1 month.

The recommended treatment is psychotherapy and counseling on an individual or group basis, as needed. Several different methods of therapy are available, including behavior therapy, desensitization, and hypnotherapy. The earlier the therapy takes place after the incident, the better the outcome. Psychiatric hospitalization may be needed for a suicidal patient or one who is severely dysfunctional.

The prognosis of PTSD is variable; some sufferers recover within six months, while in others symptoms last much longer. In some cases the condition may be ongoing.

SEE ALSO *Anxiety, Behavior therapy, Counseling, Depression, Psychotherapy, Trauma*

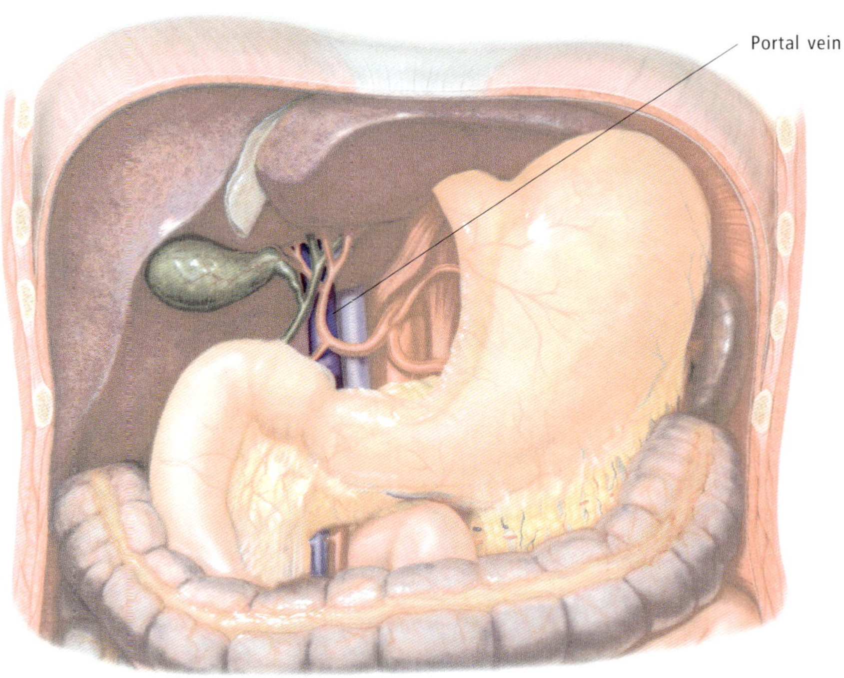

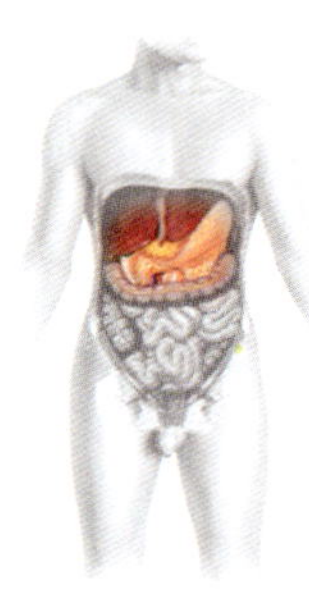

Portal vein

The portal vein collects blood from the veins that lead from the digestive tract. It transports this collected blood into the liver, where sugars and amino acids are removed.

NB: In this illustration the liver has been lifted up to show the portal vein.

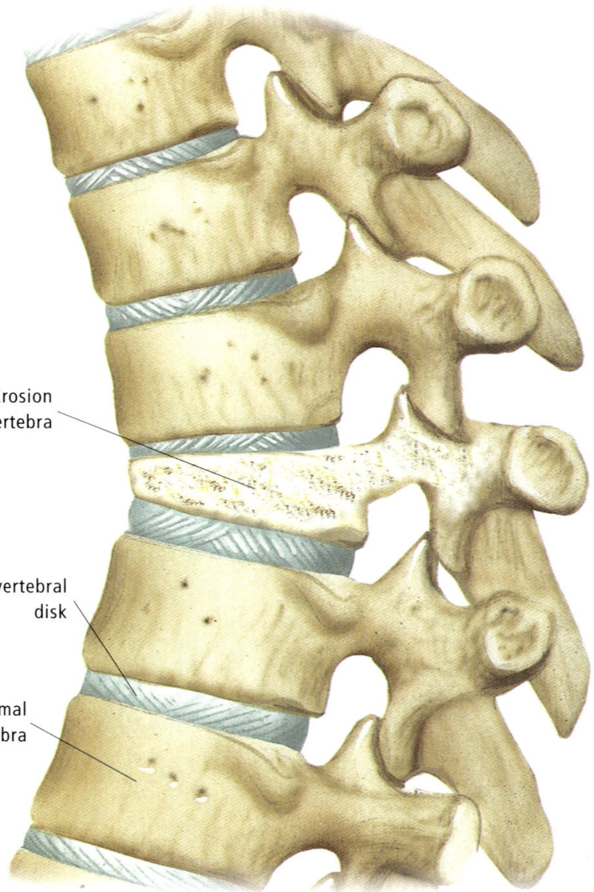

Tuberculosis bacteria

Pott's disease

Caused by the tuberculosis bacteria, Mycobacterium tuberculosis, this disease of the spine first affects the vertebrae, then attacks the intervertebral disks. Spinal curvature may result if the disease is left untreated.

POTASSIUM

Potassium occurs in the body in the form of the positively charged ion (K^+). A small amount of potassium is essential in the diet. It plays an important role in metabolic processes, including those involved in changing food into the energy used for repairing body cells and tissues.

Together with sodium, potassium works inside cells to regulate the balance of acidity and water in the blood. This action is controlled by the kidneys. As potassium is found in vegetables, fruit, meat, chicken, dairy and grain foods, potassium deficiency does not generally occur in healthy individuals eating a varied diet.

Potassium deficiency can occur as a result of diarrhea, vomiting, taking laxatives or diuretics, or from fasting. A diet that is higher in sodium than potassium can draw water out of muscle cells and lead to high blood pressure. A low intake of potassium can also alter heart rhythm. People who exercise more than normal, such as those who play competitive sport, should increase their potassium intake.

Foods which are high in potassium, such as chickpeas, lean steak, baked beans, fish, potatoes, sweet corn, spinach and prunes, can be eaten in order to balance the high levels of sodium which are often difficult to avoid.

SEE ALSO *Kidney, Minerals, Nutrition, Sodium*

POTT'S DISEASE

Pott's disease is a form of tuberculosis of the spine which affects the vertebrae and may progress to include damage to the intervertebral disks. If untreated, it may cause a hunchback curvature of the spine, pain on motion, and pain and swelling of a knee or hip, usually resulting in a limp.

Diagnosis of Pott's disease is confirmed by the presence of the tubercle bacillus (*Mycobacterium tuberculii*) and treatment is with antibiotics.

Surgery may be required to correct any damaged to the spine, for example, if kyphosis results.

SEE ALSO *Spine, Tuberculosis*

PREECLAMPSIA

A condition that may develop in the second half of pregnancy, preeclampsia is characterized by edema, high blood pressure, and protein in the urine. It occurs in about 5 percent of pregnancies and the exact cause is unknown, although poor nutrition is possibly involved.

Particularly at risk are first-time mothers, those carrying multiple babies, women in their teens or over 40 years of age, those with high blood pressure or chronic nephritis (kidney inflammation or infection), and those who have had preeclampsia before.

There are no symptoms in the early stages so it is important that women in these risk categories have regular antenatal check-ups to screen for the condition.

Initial signs include a sudden increase in edema (some swelling is normal in pregnancy), sudden weight gain, nausea and dizziness. Then there may be abdominal pain and vomiting, severe headaches and disturbed vision. If left untreated it may develop into eclampsia, a condition that can trigger life-threatening seizures.

Preeclampsia is potentially fatal for the fetus as it restricts the blood supply to the placenta, causing the baby to grow more slowly. The only cure is the birth of the baby. If the pregnancy is not far enough advanced for the baby to be delivered, bed rest or hospitalization may be recommended. Preeclampsia is also known as toxemia or pregnancy-induced hypertension.

SEE ALSO *Blood pressure, Eclampsia, Fetal development, Hypertension, Kidney, Nephritis, Placenta, Pregnancy, Toxemia*

PREGNANCY

Pregnancy is the state of having a developing fetus in the uterus, which, in the human female and other mammals, extends from conception (union of an ovum and spermatozoon) to labor (parturition).

In the human female a pregnancy takes approximately 283 days (10 lunar months) from the first day of the last menstrual period or approximately 267 days from conception. Only 5 percent of babies whose mothers go into labor and give birth naturally are born on their estimated date of delivery—in the majority of cases, the baby will born within the 10 days either side of this date.

There are about 24 hours in every menstrual cycle when a woman is fertile, and sperm can survive for up to 5 days in the woman's reproductive system; this means that for about 5 days in every 28 sexual activity could result in pregnancy. Approximately 1 in 4 women who are planning pregnancy will conceive in the first 3 months. When a couple is fertile and have unprotected sexual intercourse at least 2 or 3 times a week, a pregnancy will result within 12 months in 90 percent of cases. If fertilization does take place, within 5–6 days the fertilized egg will have implanted itself into the womb's lining (the endometrium) and the placenta will have begun to develop and to produce hormones.

A pregnancy that ends prematurely with the loss of the embryo or fetus either spontaneously or by artificial induction is an abortion. A spontaneous abortion is also known as a miscarriage.

Tests and signs of pregnancy

Blood tests can confirm a pregnancy from the ninth day after ovulation, or 4 or 5 days before the monthly period is due. Urine tests can confirm a pregnancy from the eleventh day after ovulation. Generally, tests are conducted when the period is missed; this is often the first indication of the pregnancy.

Many women, however, may notice changes in their body at or before this time that indicate they are pregnant. These can include enlarged and tender breasts, enlarged nipples, nausea (which can occur in the morning or any other time), increased frequency of urination, tiredness, dizziness, moodiness and skin changes—acne can either break out or clear up as a result of the pregnancy hormones.

In medical terminology, a pregnancy is divided into three trimesters (periods of 3 months) and many of the symptoms described above have usually passed by the second trimester. During this trimester, the woman generally feels fit and well, and it is often now that it becomes more obvious to others that she is pregnant. Sometime between weeks 18 and 22 she will feel the fetus move for the first time, and a woman may have an ultrasound to determine whether the fetus is developing according to the dates calculated.

In the last two months of the pregnancy new symptoms of discomfort may appear or worsen. These include practise contractions of the uterus (known as Braxton Hicks contractions), which can be quite painful; constipation, which can be alleviated by increasing the intake of fiber and water in the diet; hemorrhoids, which may need a cream prescribed; varicose veins, which, like hemorrhoids, are due to the relaxing or softening of the vein walls by the pregnancy hormones and are best relieved with rest and support hosiery; edema or swelling of the ankles, which also responds to rest; increased frequency of urination; leg cramps, particularly at night; itchy skin; stretch marks due to breaks in tissue deep below the skin (not removable by massage or creams); backache, which can be the result of poor posture; skin changes, including the linea nigra (a brown line down the middle of the abdomen); and chloasma, or pregnancy mask, which is a brown patch on the face.

Antenatal care

This includes regular checkups by qualified health care providers and information about a healthy lifestyle, and has reduced many of the problems which women previously encountered during pregnancy. With modern obstetrics the risks to both mother and baby have been greatly reduced.

Medical checks

There are many tests which can be conducted during a pregnancy. Tests to monitor the health of mother and baby include urine tests for the presence of protein, to exclude the possibility of abnormal kidney function, and for sugar, to test for diabetes. Blood tests may also be carried out to determine blood group, to screen for blood group antibodies, and to test for anemia and rubella.

Tests which are available but not routinely performed are the alpha-fetoprotein test, which can detect a multiple pregnancy and spina bifida, and screening for syphilis, a disease which can cause malformations in the fetus. An HIV antibody test for AIDS can also be performed. Other tests that are performed on women whose fetuses are at risk of abnormalities include chorionic villus sampling and amniocentesis.

Complications can arise during pregnancy and regular antenatal checks will often detect these and treatment can be prescribed. Vaginal bleeding during pregnancy, depending on the severity and timing, can be a breakthrough bleed caused by hormonal changes; in late pregnancy it can be a sign that labor is about to begin; or it can be a hemorrhage or a placental abruption in which the placenta has separated from the lining of the womb—the last two eventualities are both medical emergencies. Urinary tract infections are common and can lead to premature birth and low birth-weight babies so antibiotic treatment is generally prescribed. Diabetes can be caused by the pregnancy and needs dietary monitoring. Preeclampsia, which occurs in 5–10 percent of pregnancies, can lead to life-threatening eclampsia if not treated. Preeclampsia is dangerous to the unborn baby and can cause the placenta to fail and labor to begin prematurely. Hypertension (high blood pressure) will occur in 1 in 6 women and is defined as blood pressure of 190/140, or more, that persists or increases—the normal value is 120/80.

Most Caucasians (about 85 percent) have red blood cells which are Rhesus positive (Rh+). The remaining 15 percent are Rhesus negative (Rh-). This incidence of Rh- is higher than in any other human group—Southeast Asians have the lowest incidence of Rh- blood, at 1 percent. Rhesus factor incompatibility may become a problem if the woman is Rhesus negative and the baby is Rhesus positive. The woman's body manufactures antibodies against the blood of the new baby, which can become a

Pregnancy—early stages

Once fertilized, an ovum (egg) is called a zygote and begins to divide immediately. This developing mass moves along the fallopian tube and reaches the cavity of the uterus 5–6 days after fertilization. The mass of cells (now called a blastocyst) implants in the wall of the uterus and begins to develop into an embryo.

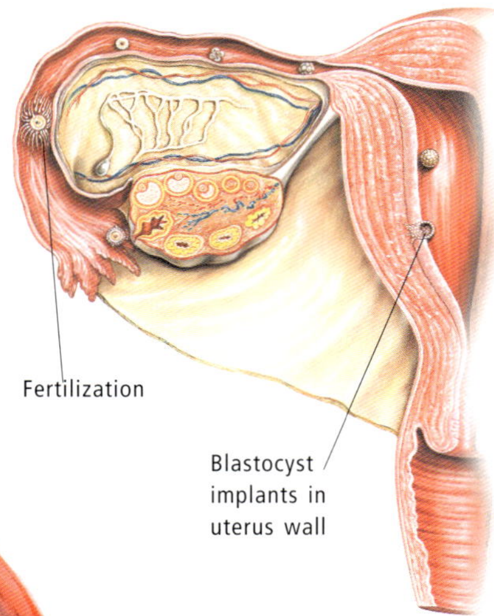

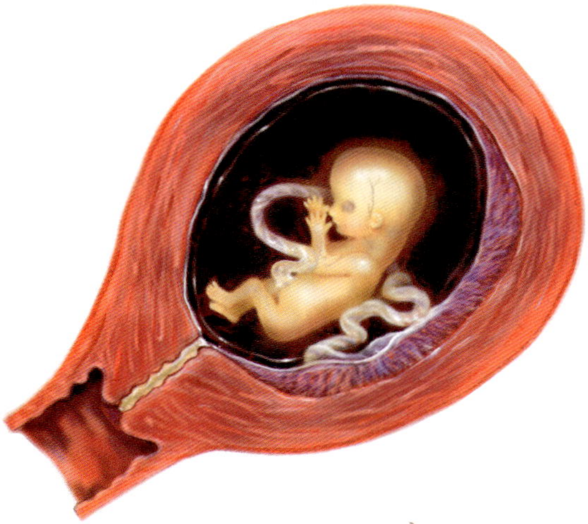

Fetus

By the eleventh week, the fetus is distinguishable as a human.

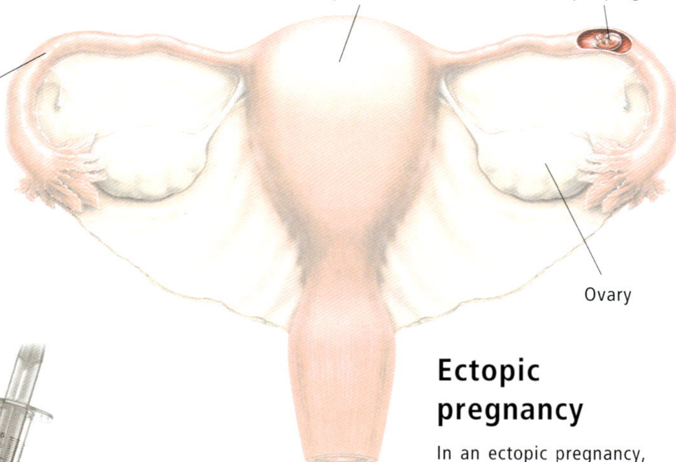

Ectopic pregnancy

In an ectopic pregnancy, the embryo develops in a site other than the uterus, usually in the fallopian tube. If the pregnancy is not terminated, serious complications can occur.

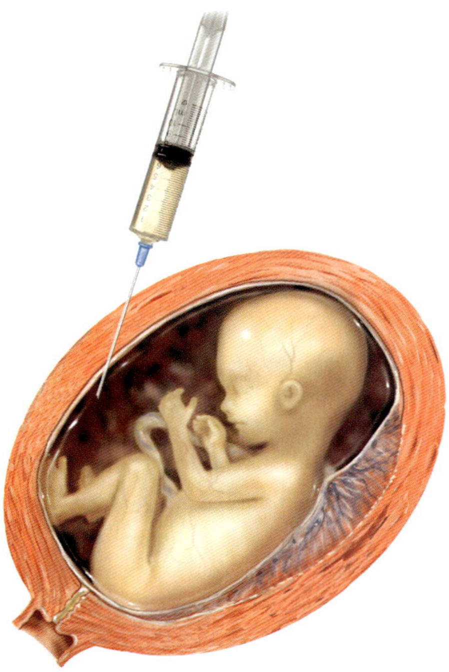

Amniocentesis

In this procedure, amniotic fluid is extracted and tested for fetal abnormalities.

problem in later pregnancies when the antibodies attack the "foreign" cells of the baby. Future Rhesus factor problems can be prevented with an injection of anti-D immunoglobulin to the mother within about 72 hours of the birth of the first baby or after a spontaneous miscarriage or termination of a pregnancy.

A pelvic ultrasound is a common test that can predict the length of the pregnancy and also detect multiple pregnancy suspected ectopic pregnancy and some fetal abnormalities. Because pelvic ultrasound itself has not been found to improve the outcome for either mother or baby, it is not recommended as routine. Ectopic pregnancy (ectopic literally means "out of place"), is a pregnancy that implants itself in the fallopian tubes or occasionally on the ovary or in the abdominal cavity. It is dangerous to the mother and is treated as a medical emergency. It is extremely rare for an ectopic pregnancy to be viable.

The chance of a multiple pregnancy increases with the age of the mother and the number of children she has already borne. Heredity and race are also factors. A multiple pregnancy is more likely when the woman has received treatment for subfertility that involves stimulation of ovulation. Without medical assistance, the chance of having twins is 1 in 90; of triplets, 1 in around 8,000; and of quadruplets, 1 in 750,000. With a multiple pregnancy the woman is at increased risk of pregnancy-induced hypertension, premature labor, abnormal presentation—the baby not presenting for birth head-first and facing the mother's spine—difficult labor and birth, and low birthweight babies.

Antenatal care also monitors the position of the baby. Labor and birth are extremely painful for many women, though perception of pain depends on the woman's preparation for and education about the processes as well as her pain threshold. A baby who is not presenting head first, facing towards the mother's spine and with the head tucked in, will cause a more painful and often a more difficult delivery. The most common abnormal presentation is breech or bottom first. Because the baby's soft bottom rather than its firm head is pressing against the cervix, the first stage of labor can be prolonged. Some obstetricians and midwives will turn breech babies if they do not turn of their own accord. In many instances, a cesarean delivery will be advised.

Other abnormal presentations are face or brow first, or posterior presentation with the baby facing outwards and its spine against the mother's spine. Both these positions can cause a long, painful labor. Shoulder presentation, which is rare, and transverse lie (the baby lying across the uterus) necessitate a cesarean delivery in both cases.

Healthy lifestyle

Though a pregnant woman does not need to eat twice as much food as she would normally, she does need a daily intake of between 1,700 and 2,100 calories (7,000–9,000 kilojoules). This should consist of a minimum of four servings of bread and cereals; a minimum of four servings of vegetables and fruit; one or two servings of lean meat, eggs, fish, chicken or nuts; approximately three servings of dairy foods, but no more than the equivalent of four tablespoons of fats (butter, oil, spreads); six to eight glasses of water and no more than two cups of tea and coffee. Foods high in fat or sugar should be reduced or eliminated. While excess weight during pregnancy can be a problem being underweight can also lead to fetal and maternal complications.

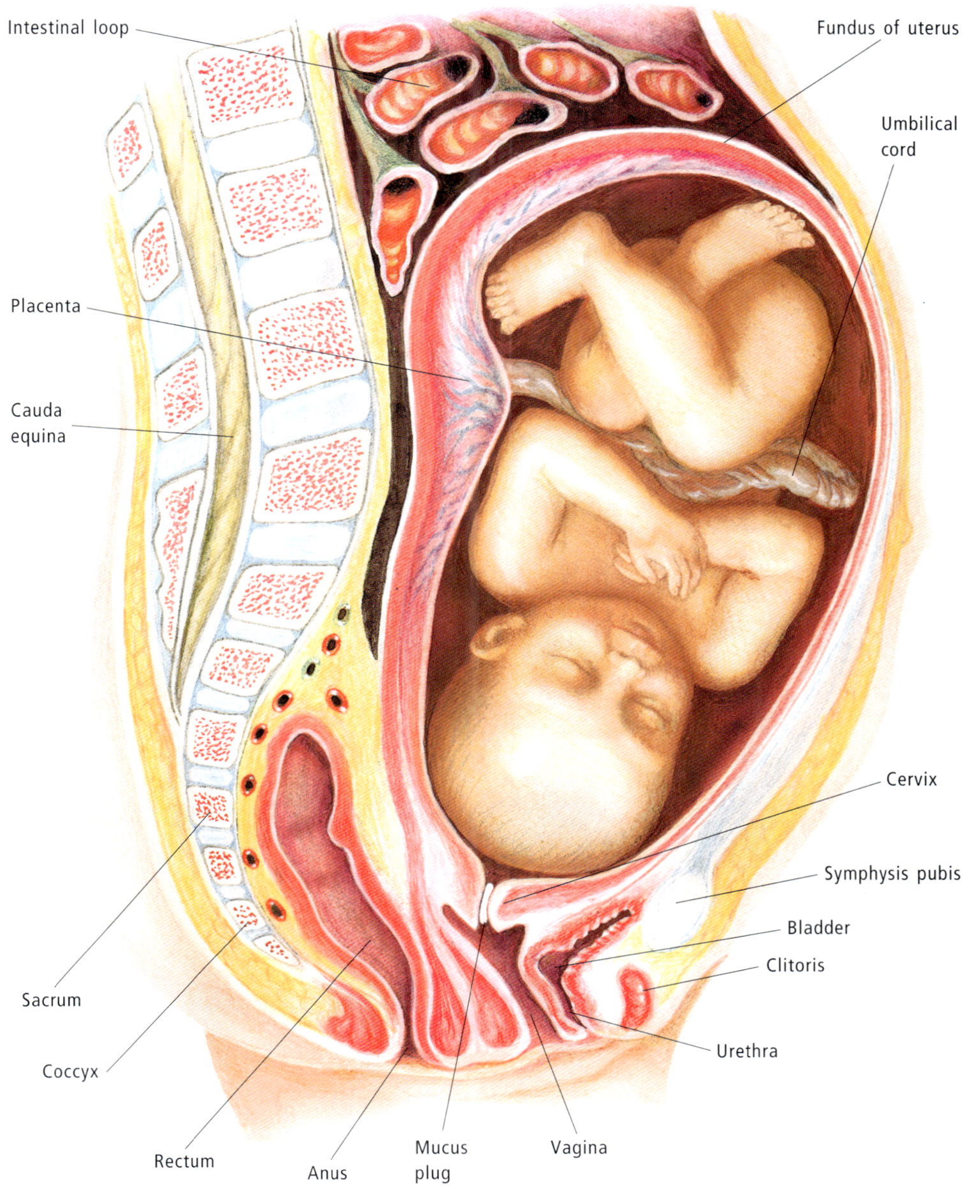

Pregnancy—full term

A full-term pregnancy lasts about 40 weeks. At the end of the pregnancy, waves of rhythmic contractions sweep through the uterus, moving the baby through the cervical canal.

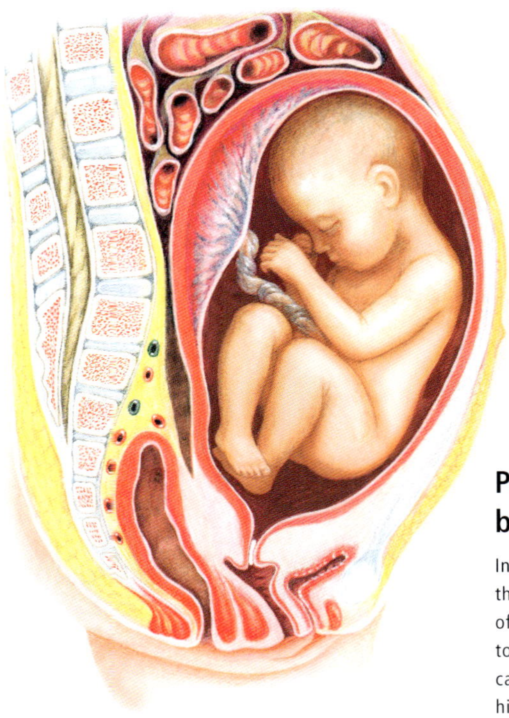

Pregnancy—breech

In a breech presentation the baby's bottom, instead of its head, faces down towards the uterus. This can cause prolonged labor and a higher risk of complications.

Drugs, including tobacco, alcohol, over-the-counter preparations and herbal and alternative remedies, are best avoided, except on the advice of a health care provider who is aware that the woman is pregnant. Alcohol, if not avoided completely, should be limited to no more than one drink a day. Abnormalities in the developing fetus have been linked with regular consumption of just two standard drinks per day.

Fitness and exercise also need to be maintained during pregnancy. Most forms of exercise, if carried out before the pregnancy, can continue throughout, though confirmation of this with a doctor, midwife or physical therapist is essential. Sports which are generally advised against include both high-impact sports such as strenuous aerobics and competitive contact sports such as basketball

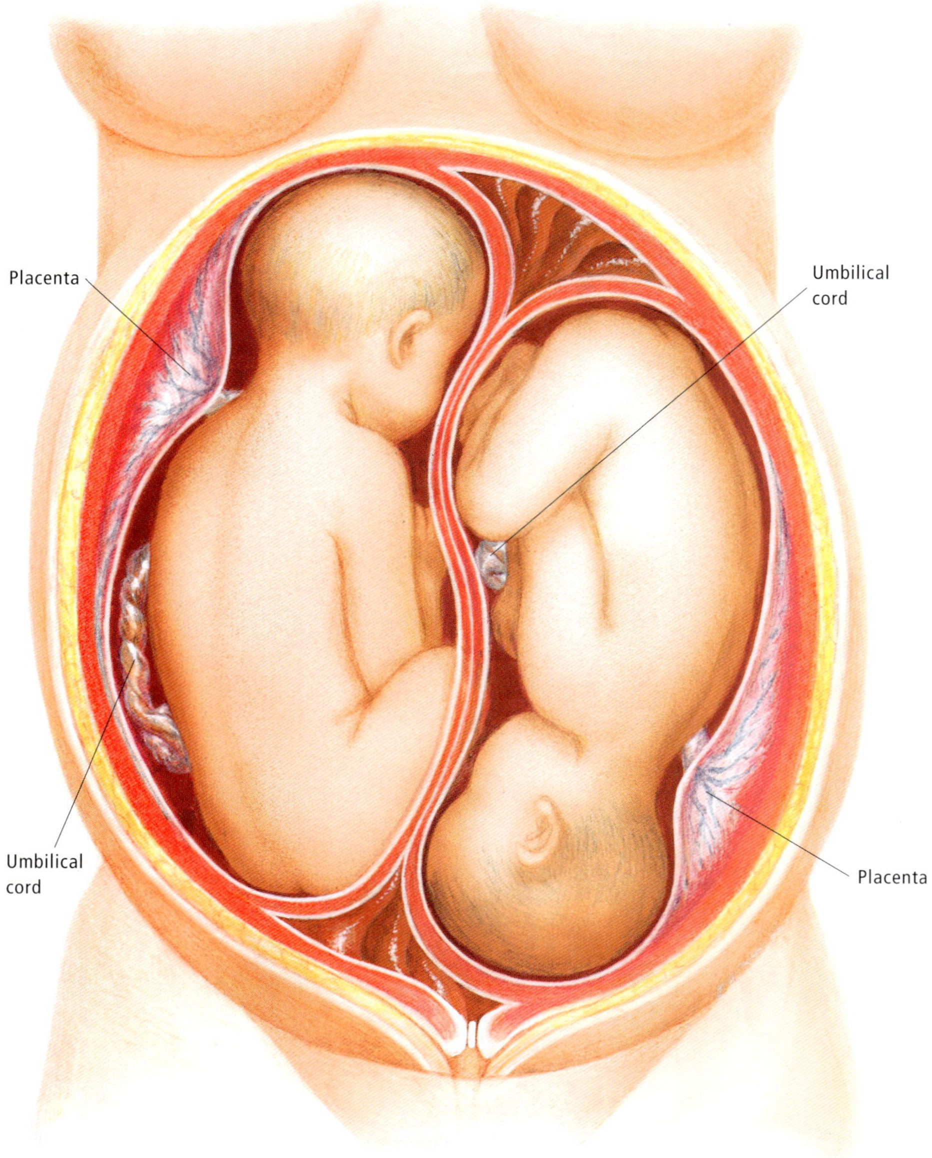

Pregnancy—twins

Fraternal (non-identical or dizygotic) twins develop when two eggs are fertilized independently by two different sperm. Unlike identical (monozygotic) twins, who come from the same egg and share a placenta, fraternal twins have separate placentas.

and netball, horse-riding, skiing and competitive tennis. Taking precautions against overheating, over-exertion and back strain is also recommended. Swimming, t'ai chi, yoga, belly dancing and walking are generally considered to be suitable during pregnancy.

In a healthy pregnancy, prohibition of sexual activity is quite inappropriate and many women find that their libido increases due to the hormones active throughout pregnancy. Others find that it diminishes—that too is normal. Sex during pregnancy can be fun, carefree (no worries about contraception) and a chance to experiment as the woman's growing abdomen means trying out different ways to sexually satisfy both partners. Sex can also be beneficial in inducing an overdue baby. The woman's orgasm coupled with the prostaglandins in the man's sperm can induce a birth when the cervix is beginning to dilate and labor is imminent.

Pregnancy is a state of wellness, not an illness. While it is important for the woman and her health care providers to monitor any problems, the medicalization of pregnancy, labor and birth can lead to its own set of problems. A woman and her partner who plan their pregnancy and prepare themselves mentally and physically by abstaining from alcohol, giving up smoking, having medical checkups and adopting a healthy lifestyle give themselves the best possible chance of conceiving a healthy baby.

SEE ALSO *Abortion, AIDS, Amniocentesis, Chorionic villus sampling, Contraception, Eclampsia, Embryo, Fertilization, Fetal alcohol syndrome, Fetal development, Hemorrhoids, Infertility, Miscarriage, Newborn, Placenta, Preeclampsia, Reproductive systems, Rhesus (Rh) factor, Rubella, Twins, Ultrasound*

PREMATURE DELIVERY

The birth of a live baby or babies at less than 37 weeks gestation is described as a premature (or preterm) birth; prematurity is not defined by birth weight. Around 5 percent of babies are born prematurely and usually the cause is unknown. Nearly half of all multiple births will occur prematurely. Other causes of prematurity are: maternal illness; placental problems such as placenta previa; premature rupture of the membranes, often with no explanation; cervical problems such as cervical incompetence; health problems in the mother such as diabetes, smoking, anxiety, distress or poor nutrition; health problems in the baby; maternal age—for those over 40 and under 17 years the risk is greater; and a previous low birth weight baby. Around 6 percent of all babies are born underweight, the majority of these being premature—the rest are termed small-for-dates.

A pregnancy that ends prematurely with the loss of the embryo or fetus either spontaneously or by artificial induction is an abortion. A spontaneous abortion is also known as a miscarriage.

There is little that can be done to prevent premature delivery. Drinking plenty of fluids, particularly water (about 8 glasses a day), has been found to prevent premature labor in some instances. A woman who lives in an industrialized country and who goes into premature labor will be closely monitored in a hospital environment. Attempts will be made to continue pregnancy and if that is not possible, then the baby will be cared for after birth in a neonatal intensive care unit.

SEE ALSO *Abortion, Childbirth, Miscarriage, Placenta, Pregnancy*

PREMATURE EJACULATION

Premature ejaculation is a condition in which male orgasm and ejaculation occurs too quickly for satisfactory intercourse—often happening before penetration has taken place. It is the most common sexual complaint, and is especially common in younger men and adolescents for whom sex is a new experience. It may cause feelings of self-doubt, inadequacy and guilt in the man and may lead to sexual dissatisfaction and tensions in the relationship for both members of the couple.

Often an explanation of the condition from a sympathetic physician is enough to solve the problem. If the problem persists, therapy from a qualified sex counselor may be needed.

There are several techniques that can be used to help the man delay ejaculation. One common approach is the "stop and start" method, in which the man recognizes that he is about to ejaculate; the couple simply ceases stimulation for about 30 seconds, after which time stimulation can begin again. These steps are repeated until the woman is ready to achieve orgasm, at which point stimulation is allowed to end in ejaculation.

The "squeeze" method is a similar technique whereby, after recognizing that he is about to ejaculate, the man (or his partner) gently squeezes the end of the penis (where the glans meets the shaft) for several seconds, withholds further sexual stimulation for about 30 seconds, and then resumes stimulation again.

SEE ALSO *Erection, Penis, Sex therapy, Sexual dysfunction, Sexual intercourse*

PREMENSTRUAL SYNDROME

Premenstrual syndrome (PMS) describes a range of physical and psychological symptoms which usually occur for a few days prior to menstruation. About 80–90 percent of women experience PMS at some time during their reproductive lives, although only about 5 percent report severe symptoms. In some cases PMS may extend as far back as ovulation; a few women may experience PMS-like symptoms only around the time of ovulation and not later in the cycle. PMS is most common in women over 30, especially those who have had years of natural menstrual cycles uninterrupted by pregnancies or oral contraception.

It has been suggested that PMS is less common in non-Western societies but this is probably related to more frequent pregnancy and lactation than to any other social factors. Behavior characteristic of PMS has also been reported in non-human primates (rhesus monkeys and baboons) which also have menstrual cycles.

Physical disturbances commonly associated with the syndrome may include weight gain, fluid retention, a sensation of pelvic heaviness or bloating, breast tenderness or enlargement, skin blemishes, headaches, constipation, frequency of urination, gingival bleeding and mouth ulcers. Preexisting conditions such as varicose veins, migraine and acne may become worse. The thyroid gland may be enlarged and blood sugar slightly elevated.

Psychological or behavioral changes may include an inability to concentrate, tiredness, mood swings, irritability and depression. PMS has been taken as a mitigating circumstance in certain criminal trials but this also undermines female responsibility in other spheres. Suicide or suicidal thoughts and accidental death have been reported as being more common in the latter part of the menstrual cycle. Symptoms should be classified as due to PMS only where they occur between ovulation and menstruation and are resolved within a few hours of the onset of menstruation.

Many theories have been put forward to explain PMS. Possible psychological causes include negative social or cultural attitudes towards menstruation and the unconscious association of menstruation with preexisting psychological or psychiatric problems. It has been hypothesized that endocrine imbalances involving prolactin, insulin, cortisone and androgens may be the cause.

Many practitioners believe that a simple explanation can be found in progesterone deficiency or in altered progesterone-to-estrogen ratios. However, studies of hormone levels of women suffering from PMS have failed to conclusively confirm these theories, although the occurrence of PMS at times of hormonal fluctuations, such as at puberty or after pregnancy, indicates at least some involvement of endocrine factors.

The wide range of symptoms and the uncertainty regarding their cause makes effective treatment of PMS difficult. Keeping a daily chart of physical and psychological symptoms may help in deciding which symptoms should be considered for treatment. Vitamin B_6, fluid tablets, prostaglandin inhibitors, antidepressants and low doses of progesterone have all been tried but, although they give relief in some women, are not uni-

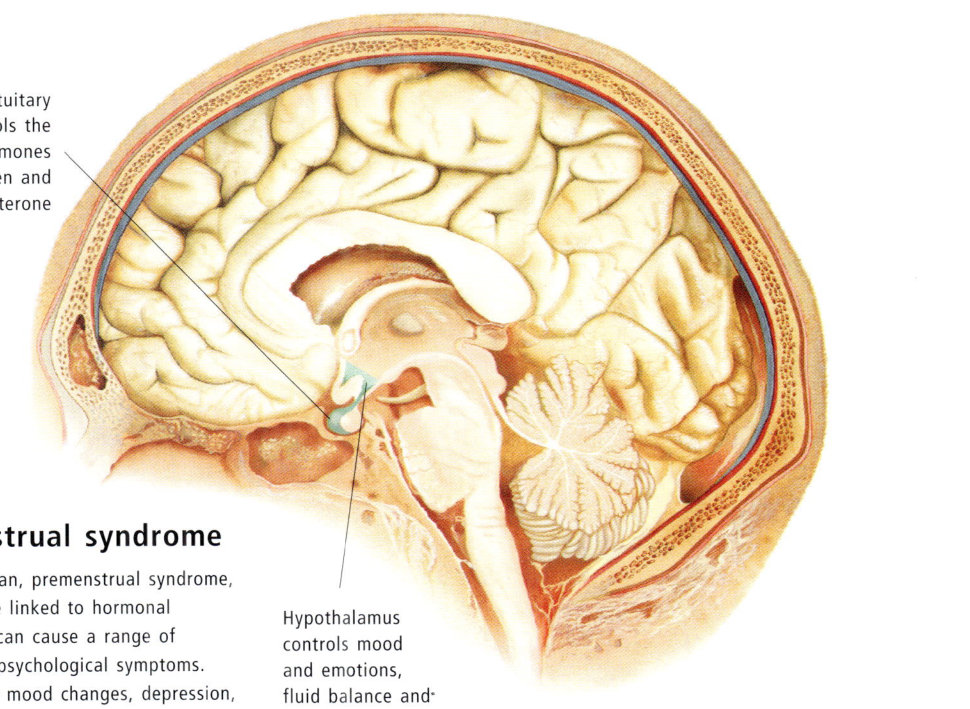

Premenstrual syndrome

In some woman, premenstrual syndrome, which may be linked to hormonal fluctuations, can cause a range of physical and psychological symptoms. These include mood changes, depression, irritability and lack of concentration.

versally successful. Altering the hormonal pattern of a normal menstrual cycle with oral contraceptives may alleviate PMS in some women but others report aggravation of symptoms. Some success has also been reported with dietary changes, including reduction in caffeine or salt intake, and with increased exercise. Surgical removal of the ovaries (oophorectomy, also known as ovariectomy) has occasionally been used as a last resort in severe cases. There is little evidence that pregnancy or tubal ligation have any effect on PMS.

There are a number of alternative therapies that may help to alleviate premenstrual symptoms. Acupuncture, shiatsu and Chinese herbal treatment given regularly are said to reduce premenstrual tension by regulating blood and energy flows, especially through spleen and liver meridians. Chinese medicine advises women with menstrual disorders to avoid exposure to cold or eating too much cold or raw food. Aromatherapy suggests massage or baths with oils such as clary sage, lavender, juniper or rose.

Herbalism prescribes agnus castus for hormonal balance, and diuretics (horsetail, dandelion). Estrogenic herbs (sage, parsley, dong quai) are prescribed for those with a tendency towards premenstrual depression, confusion or memory loss. Naturopathy suggests a wholefood diet with increased soy products, reduced salt and dairy intake and avoidance of caffeine, sugar, animal fats and alcohol. Supplements prescribed include vitamin B with additional B_6, vitamin E, zinc, calcium, magnesium and evening primrose oil. Regular aerobic exercise is also suggested.

SEE ALSO *Estrogens, Hormones, Menstruation, Ovulation, Progesterone, Prostaglandins, Reproductive systems*

PRIAPISM

Priapism is a condition in which the penis remains persistently and painfully erect without any sexual arousal or desire. It is caused by a blockage of the veins that carry blood from the penis, trapping blood in the penis and causing its engorgement. It may be brought on by excessive sexual stimulation or by certain drugs, including corticosteroids, anticoagulants and antihypertensives.

Treatment options include surgery, the injection of anesthesia into the spinal cord, and the draining (aspiration) of blood from the penis. Without treatment the penis may be permanently damaged, making normal erections impossible.

SEE ALSO *Erection, Penis, Sexual dysfunction*

PROCTITIS

Proctitis is inflammation of the rectum. It can occur as part of ulcerative colitis. It may also be due to bacterial infection, as is sometimes seen in male homosexuals with gonorrhea of the rectum from anal intercourse. These patients will complain of rectal irritation, itching, pain and pus-containing (purulent) discharge. Gonorrhea of the rectum is treated with the appropriate antibiotic (penicillin and/or tetracyclines).

Occasionally proctitis may be due to physical factors, as seen in radiation proctitis, a side effect of radiation therapy of tumors in the uterine cervix, bladder, uterus or prostate. In those patients the inflammation may be reduced with steroids.

SEE ALSO *Gonorrhea, Radiation therapy, Rectum, Ulcerative colitis*

PROCTOSCOPY

Proctoscopy is an internal examination of the anal canal and rectum using a short rigid speculum (proctoscope); sometimes, to include an examination of the colon, a flexible or fiberoptic tube (sigmoidoscope) is used. This painless procedure allows the bowel lining to be examined, biopsies to be taken and other medical procedures to take place. It is used to aid in the diagnosis of such diseases as rectal cancer and diverticulosis.

SEE ALSO *Colon, Diverticulosis, Rectum*

PROGESTERONE

Progesterone is a steroid sex hormone produced in the corpus luteum (ruptured follicle) in the ovaries during the second half of the menstrual cycle. Progesterone is one of the main hormones of pregnancy (or gestation). It stimulates the endometrium to secrete a fluid which protects and nourishes the fertilized ovum in the uterus before implantation. It also fosters placental growth.

If pregnancy does not occur, then the corpus luteum only functions until about day 26 of an average cycle, after which progesterone production decreases rapidly; this causes changes in the lining of the uterus which lead to menstruation. If the woman becomes pregnant, the placenta secretes human chorionic gonadotropin (HCG), which prolongs the production of ovarian progesterone until the end of the first trimester, after which progesterone is secreted by the placenta.

Progesterone drops to very low levels a few hours after birth. The pituitary gland during lactation produces large amounts of prolactin and this often disrupts development of follicles in the ovary and suppresses ovulation. Even when menstruation is restored, which can be as early as three months after birth, the first few cycles are often anovulatory. Anovulatory cycles do not produce a corpus luteum. Diminished secretions of progesterone can lead to spontaneous abortion (miscarriage) in pregnant women.

Synthetic progesterone is used as an oral contraceptive, most commonly in combination with estrogen but sometimes on its own if use of estrogen is inadvisable.

SEE ALSO *Estrogens, Hormones, Menstruation, Oral contraceptives, Ovulation, Pituitary gland, Placenta, Pregnancy*

PROGESTOGENS

Progestogens are a group of natural and synthetic steroid hormones derived from cholesterol. Natural progestogen is progesterone produced by the ovary which is inactive if given by mouth and only slightly active if injected and is thus unsuitable for therapeutic use. Slight modifications of the natural molecule can be made, which produces a range of hormones which can either be taken by mouth or injected.

Synthetic progestogens, including levonorgestrel, norgestrel and norethindrone are used in oral contraceptives, either alone or in conjunction with a synthetic estrogen. Contraception with oral contraceptives is due to anovulation (prevention of ovulation). Synthetic progestogens are also used, along with estrogen, in hormone replacement

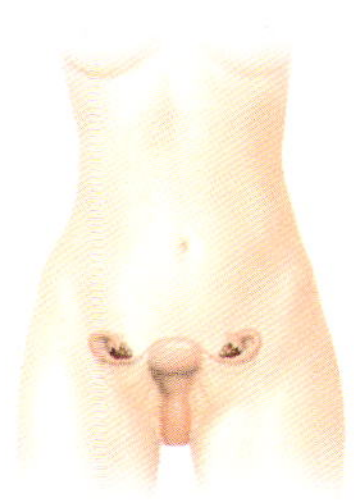

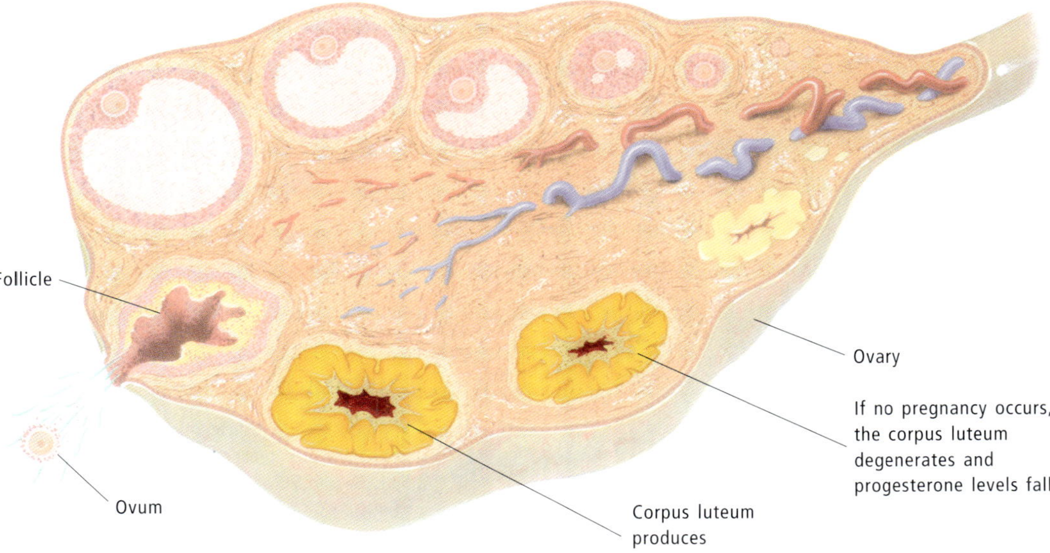

Progesterone

After releasing its ovum (egg), an ovarian follicle turns into a gland-like structure, the corpus luteum. This produces progesterone which prepares the uterus for pregnancy.

therapy (commonly referred to as HRT). HRT consisting of estrogen alone has been linked to an increased risk of endometrial carcinoma. This increased risk is removed if a progestogen is added to the HRT.

SEE ALSO *Cholesterol, Estrogens, Hormone replacement therapy, Hormones, Oral contraceptives, Progesterone*

PROLAPSE

A prolapse is the outward movement, or slipping, of any one of a number of body parts from its normal position.

Prolapsed intervertebral disk

A prolapsed intervertebral disk (also known as slipped disk or herniated nucleus pulposus) occurs when the soft center of a disk (nucleus pulposus) ruptures through a tear or fracture in the fibrous tissue of the disk. This can happen in the lumbar (lower back) or cervical (neck) regions, putting pressure on spinal nerves (radiculopathy).

Lumbar radiculopathy (sciatica) is characterized by severe lower back pain that radiates to the buttocks, legs and feet, and may be combined with tingling in the legs, muscle weakness, muscle spasms and groin pain. Cervical radiculopathy brings pain in the sides and back of the neck, down the shoulders and arms and sometimes the hands and fingers.

The natural ageing and degeneration of the spine cause most prolapsed disks. Middle-aged and older men are most at risk, especially those who undertake strenuous physical activity. Bed rest on a firm mattress, medication and perhaps physical therapy are usually prescribed to reduce inflammation; surgery may be needed in extreme cases.

Prolapsed rectum

A prolapsed rectum is an abnormal movement of the internal mucous membranes of the rectum, the end section of the large intestine, down to or through the anus. It appears as a red mass up to several inches (about 10 centimeters) long, which may bleed. Prolapsed rectums are most common in children under the age of 6 years. The condition usually corrects itself in young children—a physician may gently push the protruding mass back inside. Surgery is often needed when the condition occurs in adults and may involve attaching the rectum to surrounding muscle for support. Alternatively, the anus may be tightened via the insertion of a circle of wire or nylon.

Prolapsed rectum may be associated with conditions such as cystic fibrosis, constipation, malnutrition and infestation with pinworm or whipworm.

Prolapsed uterus

A prolapsed uterus is the displacement of the uterus into the vaginal canal as a result of weakness in the supporting ligaments. Slackening of the ligaments may be due to the normal ageing process or the result of stretching during childbirth, particularly with large babies or rapid deliveries. Hormonal changes during menopause are also thought to be a cause and, rarely, a pelvic tumor. Obesity, chronic bronchitis, excessive coughing, chronic constipation and asthma may increase the risk of developing the condition. Sufferers may experience feelings of pressure or pulling in the pelvis, pain in the anus or lower abdomen, urinary tract infections, excessive vaginal discharge and difficulty having sexual intercourse. They may also urinate when coughing, laughing, or straining to lift heavy objects. In severe cases the neck of the uterus (cervix) protrudes from the vagina. A pelvic examination will determine the severity of the prolapse. Treatment may be via vaginal pessary, a ring-shaped object that is inserted into the vagina, or by surgery.

SEE ALSO *Anus, Disk, intervertebral, Hernia, Intestines, Pelvic floor muscles, Rectum, Spine, Uterus*

PROPRIOCEPTION

Proprioception is perception of one's own body, which is of vital importance for everyday activities. Activities such as standing, walking, and picking up objects require information on the position and movement of each part of the body and of muscle activity, which is provided by sensors in joints and muscles. The sense of balance is provided by the semicircular canals and otolith organs of the inner ear. Visceral sensations include hunger, thirst, the feeling of food being swallowed, and the necessity to defecate or

P

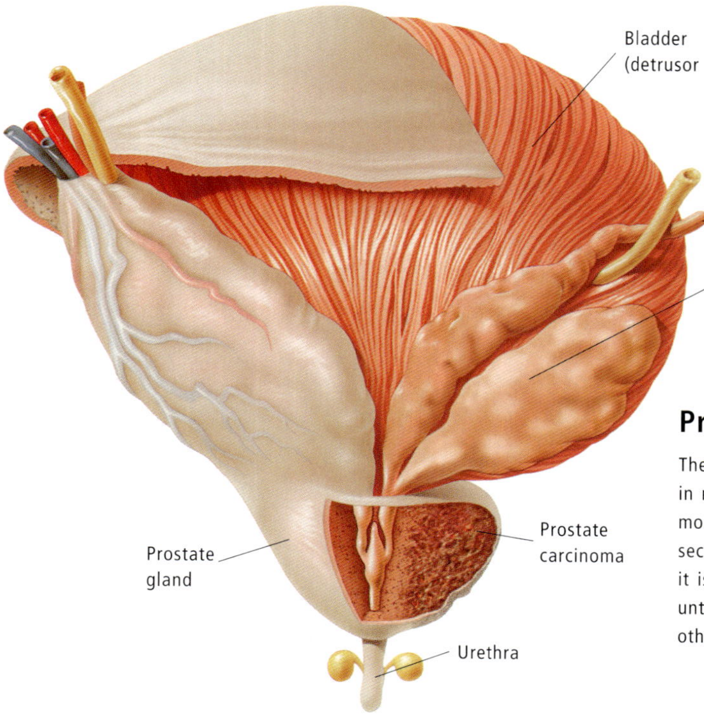

Prostate cancer

The most common cancer in men, prostate cancer mostly arises in the outer section of the prostate and it is seldom diagnosed until it has spread to other organs.

urinate. Other proprioceptive sensations include palpitations (awareness of the beating of the heart), and (on occasion) the necessity to breathe.

SEE ALSO *Balance, Breathing, Palpitations, Semicircular canals*

PROSTAGLANDINS

Prostaglandins are an important group of chemicals produced in many tissues of the body, including platelet cells, blood vessels, the uterus and stomach. They play an important role in inflammation and pain.

Prostaglandins produce contractions of the uterine muscle, which can induce labor, abortion or painful menstrual periods (dysmenorrhea). Anti-inflammatory medication is a common treatment prescribed to inhibit the painful uterine contractions which cause dysmenorrhea. Prostaglandins in platelets cause them to clump together, resulting in the formation of blood clots, as in a heart attack or stroke. Aspirin inhibits prostaglandin production in platelets, making them less sticky.

SEE ALSO *Anti-inflammatory drugs, Platelets, Prostate gland, Uterus*

PROSTATE CANCER

Prostate cancer is the most common cancer in men, typically occurring in individuals aged over 60 years. It is also one of the most common causes of death from cancer in men. Despite its frequency, almost nothing is known about the causes of prostate cancer, although genetic factors may play a role.

Development of prostate cancer appears to be age-related and latent tumors (tumors which are demonstrable by microscopic examination of the prostate but do not produce any clinical effects) are present in more than 50 percent of men aged over 80 years.

The growth of prostate cancer cells depends at least in part on stimulation by testosterone, but the exact role of hormones in the development of this cancer remains poorly understood.

Prostate cancer commonly produces discomfort during urination or symptoms suggesting obstruction of urine flow. Because the cancer usually arises in the outer part of the prostate gland, whereas the urethra runs through the central portion, symptoms relating to urinary outflow may not develop until quite late in the course of the disease. In some patients, prostate cancer first becomes apparent as a result of spread to other organs, in which case the outcome is less favorable.

A major site of spread of prostate cancer is into bone, especially the spine and pelvis, producing pain. Unlike most other tumors, prostate cancer that has spread to bone is typically associated with new bone formation around the secondary deposits, making these easily visible on x-rays.

Benign (non-cancerous) enlargement of the prostate is very common among men in the same age group (much more common than cancer of the prostate) and causes similar urinary obstruction. This makes it quite difficult to distinguish the two conditions, a situation that is complicated by the fact that they often co-exist. However, much as is the case for other cancers, early diagnosis is critically important in achieving a good response to treatment.

One way of demonstrating the possible presence of a cancer of the prostate is by digital rectal examination (DRE), because many cancers can be felt directly by the medical practitioner by examination through the rectum. Specific diagnosis usually requires needle biopsy of the gland under ultrasound guidance.

Unfortunately there is no effective screening test that allows an early diagnosis of prostate cancer to be made easily and cheaply. A blood test for prostate-specific antigen (PSA), an antigen produced by prostate cells, is available but is not considered to be sufficiently sensitive or specific for use as a screening test for early prostate cancer. The PSA test is still valuable in following the progress of prostatic cancer after a person has had treatment for the cancer.

The extent of spread at the time of diagnosis has an important bearing on the approach to treatment of prostate cancer. Surgical removal or radiation therapy may be the initial treatment of choice. Because tumor cell growth is partly controlled by testosterone, treatments that reduce the levels of testosterone or block its activity are also valuable. Patients with early cancers often have an excellent response to therapy but those with late-stage disease have a poor outcome.

SEE ALSO *Cancer, Prostate gland, Testosterone, Urethra*

PROSTATE GLAND

The prostate gland is a part of the male sex organs. About the size of a walnut, it surrounds the neck of the bladder and the urethra, the tube which carries urine from the bladder to the tip of the penis, and is composed of both glandular and muscle tissue.

Secretions from the prostate and the seminal vesicles make up the seminal fluid ejaculated during sexual orgasm that contains the glucose and enzymes which provide the energy spermatozoa need for their journey toward the ovum. Secretions from the prostate can also be tested to reveal the presence of infections that may affect sperm count and quality.

By the age of 50, it is common for the prostate to show some signs of enlargement. It may increase in weight from less than an ounce (20 grams) to five or six times this. Known as benign prostatic hypertrophy, this enlargement may eventually obstruct flow of urine from the bladder, and if uncorrected, can cause bladder and kidney damage.

Symptoms of urethral obstruction include nocturia (the need to empty the bladder often at night); dysuria (pain or difficulty with urination); and the sudden urgency for urination. Usually, the bladder will not empty completely and urine may stagnate, causing infection or the formation of stones. Straining to pass urine may make things worse and can cause bleeding and abdominal pain. A catheter may be inserted to drain the bladder.

Diagnostic procedures to confirm abnormality include excretory urography, which is an x-ray of the urinary tract, and cystourethroscopy, an internal visual examination of the bladder.

Prostatic cancer is more common as age advances but it is generally slow-growing and may be well advanced before producing detectable symptoms. Some prostate cancers, however, can grow aggressively and cells often spread to nearby lymph nodes and then to bone, kidneys or the brain. Early detection increases the chances of a cure. Older patients with slow-growing cancers may opt for "watchful waiting" to avoid the negative effects of treatment.

Surgical removal of part or all of the prostate is common to correct hypertrophy and for treating cancer. In serious cases, the entire prostate, seminal vesicles and ejaculatory ducts are removed. Surgical techniques aim as far as possible to retain sexual function and normal urinary control and success rates are constantly improving. Cancers that have spread are not usually curable but their growth may be slowed by blocking the effects of testosterone. Side effects include loss of sexual drive, impotence and breast enlargement.

Testing for prostate cancer can include the prostate-specific antigen test (PSA) and digital rectal examination (DRE). The PSA tests for antigens which are produced by prostate cells at higher than normal levels in benign enlargement of the prostate, and at much higher levels in prostatic cancer. Neither method is totally effective at detecting cancer of the prostate, but men aged over 50 are advised to have PSA and DRE regularly.

There are a number of alternative therapies that may help to alleviate the symptoms of enlarged prostate. Herbalism prescribes saw palmetto, nettle root and epilobium to treat enlargement, couch grass and horsetail to ease symptoms. Naturopathy advises hot and cold compresses or sitz baths and regular exercise; vitamin E, evening primrose oil and zinc supplements, and a low-fat wholefood diet eliminating tea, coffee and alcohol are also prescribed. Reflexology advises the massaging of the "prostate zone", located on the inner (medial) side of the foot beneath the ankle. Yoga suggests a number of traditional hatha yoga poses, particularly the thunderbolt or kneeling pose. Acupunture and shiatsu treatments are also said to ease symptoms.

SEE ALSO *Bladder, Penis, Prostate cancer, Prostatitis, Reproductive systems, Urethra, Urinary systems*

PROSTATITIS

Prostatitis is inflammation of the prostate gland, the walnut-sized organ that encircles the urethra at the base of the bladder. It is caused by bacteria such as *E. coli* (transmitted from the bowel) or gonorrhea, chlamydia or trichomoniasis (transmitted through sexual contact with an infected partner). Prostatitis commonly occurs along with urethritis (inflammation of the urethra), epididymitis (inflammation of the epididymis), and/or orchitis (inflammation of the testis).

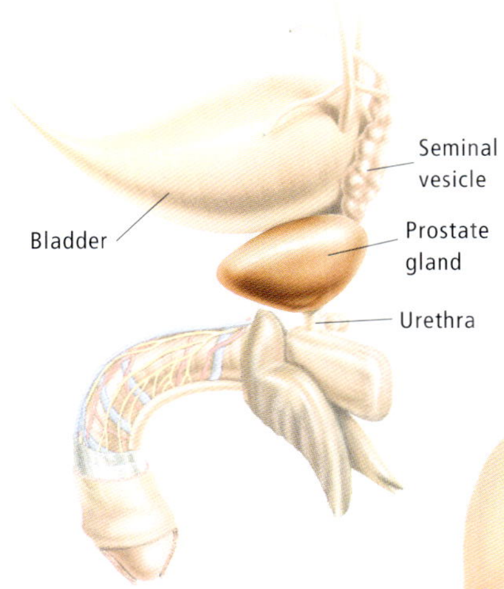

Prostate gland

The prostate gland is a structure about the size of a walnut. It secretes some of the fluid present in semen.

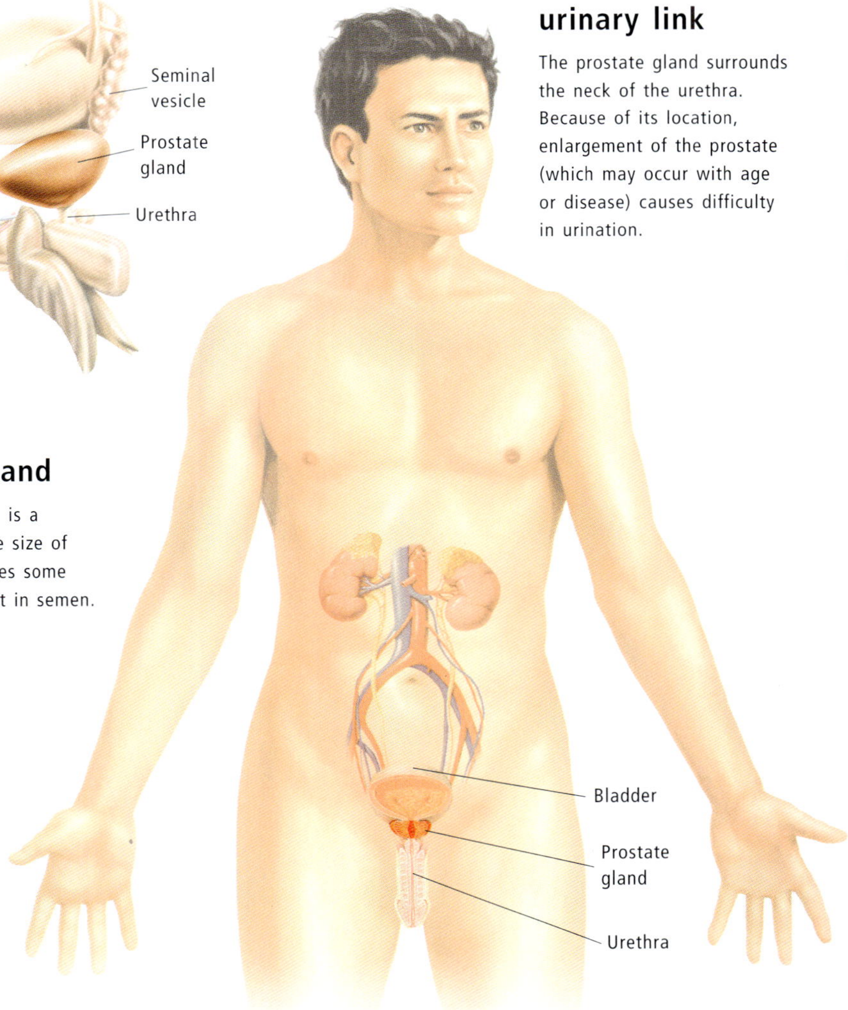

Prostate–urinary link

The prostate gland surrounds the neck of the urethra. Because of its location, enlargement of the prostate (which may occur with age or disease) causes difficulty in urination.

The symptoms of prostatitis are a burning pain on urination, a diminished urine stream and pain on ejaculating. There may be fever, chills and low back pain. Blood may be found in the urine or the semen, and there may be a frequent desire to urinate urgently. The testes may be painful.

A physician will diagnose the condition after finding an enlarged and tender prostate on rectal examination. A urethral swab and a urine sample are taken to determine which bacteria are involved, and their sensitivity to antibiotics. Oral antibiotic therapy will need to be continued for 6–8 weeks. Most cases are successfully treated, but recurrence is common and in some men the condition becomes chronic.

SEE ALSO *Prostate gland*

PSITTACOSIS

Psittacosis is a common infectious disease of many bird species that is sometimes contracted by humans. It is caused by the bacterium *Chlamydia psittaci*. Psittacosis can be aquired by inhaling dust from dried infected bird droppings or from handling affected birds. Symptoms usually appear within 10 days of contact and include fever, headache, fatigue, chills, muscle aches, chest pains and a cough.

A severe form of pneumonia can develop that, if left untreated, may be fatal, particularly among the elderly. The disease is, however, treatable with tetracycline antibiotics. Psittacosis is also known as ornithosis and parrot fever.

SEE ALSO *Pneumonia*

PSORIASIS

With up to 3 percent of the world's adult population suffering from psoriasis, this mostly mild but frequently distressing skin disorder is considered common. Its exact cause remains a medical mystery, although it is known to involve an abnormal reaction by the body's immune system against the skin.

Genetic factors influence the likelihood of developing the disorder. A person with a father suffering from psoriasis has about a 30 percent chance of developing the disease. The child of a mother with psoriasis has a 20 percent chance. The disease is rarely seen during childhood years, often making its first appearance with the onset of puberty.

The impact of the disease varies widely between sufferers. Typically, it causes a rash of sensitive red patches covered by silvery-white scales on the elbows, knees, lower back and scalp. The outer layer of skin at the sites of these flaking sores grows approximately seven times faster and thicker than normal. These areas can range in diameter from a few millimeters to several centimeters. In severe cases they may join to form very large "plaques" that can cover large areas of skin, such as a person's entire back.

Psoriasis does not normally affect the face, is not contagious, does not cause scars and rarely leads to hair loss. It does, however, often affect the nails, causing pitting, discoloration and separation from the nail bed. About 10 percent of sufferers develop a form of arthritis that causes swollen and painful joints and can become debilitating. A very rare, but potentially fatal, form of the disease is erythrodermic psoriasis, in which the skin becomes inflamed and red all over and sufferers have problems regulating body temperature.

Contrary to popular belief, psoriasis is not an allergic reaction and avoidance of certain foodstuffs will not control the disease. It is, however, aggravated by excessive alcohol intake. It also has a tendency to repeatedly appear and disappear, with possible triggers including stress, streptococcal throat infections, certain medications and skin wounds.

Although the condition is incurable and difficult to treat, there is a great array of therapies and medications available to help control symptoms. Complete remission is rare.

Sufferers usually need to experiment to find the treatment that works best for them. Careful exposure to ultraviolet light may help some people. Soaking in warm water with bath oil or a coal tar solution can soften and loosen the scale. Special shampoos can control a scaly scalp, and simple moisturizing creams, such as sorbolene, can also help keep the scales soft and prevent the skin from cracking.

A variety of creams and ointments, intended to reduce the scaling, is available, ranging from simple products based on coal tar preparations to high-strength steroid preparations so strong that they can only be used for short periods of time. Oral medications for psoriasis are normally prescribed in only the most serious cases because they often have dangerous or unpleasant side effects.

SEE ALSO *Lymphatic/Immune system, Skin*

PSYCHOSIS

Psychosis is a severe mental illness in which a person loses contact with reality. Psychotic people suffer from poor judgment and insight and a disordered thinking process. They may experience acute distress, confusion, hallucinations and delusions, which may include the belief that someone will harm them or their family. Usually they do not realize they have the condition.

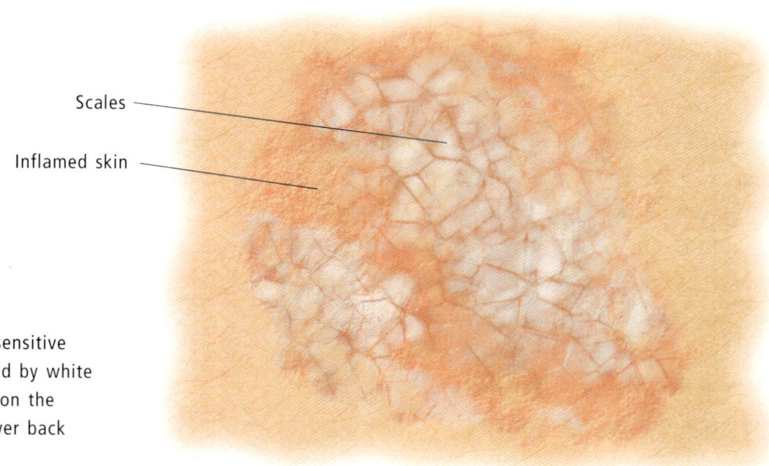

Psoriasis

In this condition, sensitive red patches covered by white scales can appear on the elbows, knees, lower back and scalp.

Psychoses may be organic or functional. Organic psychoses are those with a physical cause such as dementia, a brain tumor, alcoholism, poisoning or a head injury. The symptoms improve if the underlying condition can be treated.

Functional psychoses are those with no organic cause. Schizophrenia is the most common, and involves a withdrawal from reality, hallucinations, delusions and an inability to feel normal emotions. The onset is usually in the teens and there may be only one episode, or there may be recurrent episodes. In some individuals the illness is chronic and they may need to be hospitalized permanently. The cause of schizophrenia is unknown, although there is a genetic predisposition to develop the disease. Schizophrenia cannot be cured but the symptoms can be controlled with antipsychotic drugs. Psychotherapy may be useful in some cases.

Other psychiatric disorders such as depression and bipolar disorder (manic depression) may have a psychotic element to them, especially if they are accompanied by delusions, hallucinations or paranoia. Psychosis can be caused by certain drugs such as LSD and cannabis. Usually the symptoms disappear when the effects of the drug wear off. A brief psychosis lasting from several hours to a week may occur in an otherwise normal person after an extremely stressful event, such as a death in the family.

SEE ALSO *Bipolar disorder, Depression, Hallucinations, Paranoia, Schizophrenia*

PSYCHOTHERAPY

The term psychotherapy describes a broad range of treatments for mental or emotional disorders that use psychological methods to focus on a person's thoughts, behavior and emotions.

Central to this practice is the theory that the mind is comprised of conscious and unconscious components, and the unconscious state of mind affects conscious thoughts and behavior. Psychotherapy works to bring unconscious thoughts, behaviors and emotions into consciousness to allow the patient greater choice.

Psychotherapy may use the analysis of fantasies and dreams to uncover unconscious thoughts and feelings. The building of trust and rapport between the psychotherapist and the patient is crucial.

Common psychotherapeutic approaches include the following.

Psychoanalysis was pioneered by the Viennese psychiatrist Sigmund Freud (1856–1939). This approach focuses on the repressed material found in the unconscious which expresses itself in disguised forms known as defense mechanisms. Psychoanalysis aims at freeing the patient from repeating past conflicts. Techniques used include free association, dream interpretation and the interpretation of the relationship between analyst and patient. This form of therapy is sometimes used for chronic neurosis, traumatic pasts or relationship difficulties.

Analytical psychotherapy, based upon the work of the Swiss psychiatrist Carl Jung (1875–1961), views the unconscious as the container of all conscious life. The therapy works with the theory of archetypes (such as the "mother" or the "hero") contained within the "collective unconscious". It utilizes dream work, active imagination and the relationship between patient and therapist to free the patient from being driven by either unconscious forces or the expectations of external environments. It can help with non-clinical depression and adjustment to midlife crisis and the ageing process.

Existential therapy focuses on the fundamental questions of what it means to be alive and how to address the issues of self and life with openness. This psychotherapy seeks to understand the patient's experience and process and its aim is personal authenticity. The main technique is reflection. It can help with life dissatisfaction.

Cognitive behavioral therapy (CBT) aims at changing the patient's negative thinking and behavior patterns. Patients are helped to identify the link between the assumptions they make about themselves and their lives, and the outcomes in their life. The therapy helps the patient to achieve greater self-esteem and self-care through adopting positive thought and action. The therapist takes an active role, teaching strategies and setting homework assignments. This form of therapy can help phobias, obsessive-compulsive disorder, post-traumatic stress disorder, and depression and anxiety states.

Humanistic psychotherapy is based on belief in the individual's innate capacity to realize their true self and become fully functioning. The main focus is on current problems and the patient's feelings towards themselves and their lives. The patient is encouraged to develop self-knowledge, communicate thoughts and feelings honestly and to achieve a positive self-esteem and view of the world. The therapist aims to create a safe place for the patient that is free of judgmental criticism, probing for hidden motives or personality interpretation. Humanistic psychotherapy can help address issues arising from traumatic pasts, relationship difficulties, bereavement or other major life changes.

SEE ALSO *Art therapy, Behavior therapy, Counseling, Dance movement therapy, Music therapy*

PSYCHOTROPIC DRUGS

Medications that affect the mind and behavior are called psychotropic drugs. They include antidepressants, neuroleptics, mood stabilizers, and benzodiazepines. These drugs may be prescribed by a psychiatrist to treat conditions such as depression, anxiety, phobias and insomnia. They may be used in conjunction with psychotherapy.

Determining the right medication(s) and doses that work best for a particular person is usually a matter of trial and error. The drugs do not always work, but when they do the effect may be dramatic, allowing a sufferer to function in day-to-day living. However, in many cases people may become dependent on them, or use them after they are no longer needed. Also, withdrawal from psychotropic drugs may cause unpleasant symptoms. (On the other hand, some drugs must be continued indefinitely.) It is important to seek medical advice before coming off these drugs.

Medication alone can not solve a psychological problem and will not substitute for learning the coping skills necessary to adapt to and enjoy life.

SEE ALSO *Antidepressants, Anxiety, Anxiolytics, Depression, Detoxification, Drug dependence, Insomnia, Phobias, Psychotherapy, Tranquilizers, Withdrawal*

PUBERTY

Puberty is the 2–6 year period between childhood and adolescence when hormonal changes cause a rapid increase in body size, changes in the shape and composition of the body, and rapid development of the reproductive organs and the secondary sexual characteristics.

In females, this process includes the development of the breasts, widening of the hips, rapid growth of the uterus, and the appearance of hair on the underarms and around the vulva. Menstruation, a monthly discharge of blood and uterine tissue, begins about 2 years after the onset of puberty and continues to be irregular for 2 years or so before becoming more regular. The changes are caused by the actions of the sex hormones, estrogen and progesterone, released by the ovaries under the control of hormones from the pituitary gland.

In males, secondary sexual characteristics include rapid growth in the size of the testes and the penis; an increase in the size of the larynx, which deepens the voice and gives the "Adam's apple" look to the front of the neck; and the appearance of facial, underarm, pubic and body hair. Height increases rapidly and the first ejaculation occurs, usually about a year or so after the penis begins enlarging. These changes are governed by the male sex hormone testosterone.

In both females and males, there is also increased glandular activity. The apocrine glands, located in the underarms, the anus, the genitals and the breasts, become active at this time, giving off their characteristic odors. The sebaceous glands increase their production of sebum—an oily substance that lubricates the skin. This may lead to the familiar problem of acne in adolescence.

Although girls undergo greater physical change during puberty than boys, they tend to reach puberty earlier and take less time to reach maturity. Puberty in girls begins around age 11 and continues until about age 16. In boys, the corresponding period begins about age 13 and continues until about age 18. Differences in the times and rates of growth and sexual maturity are caused by a combination of inherited tendencies, nutrition, and the environment.

Emotional and behavioral changes accompany these physical changes. Hormonal

Puberty

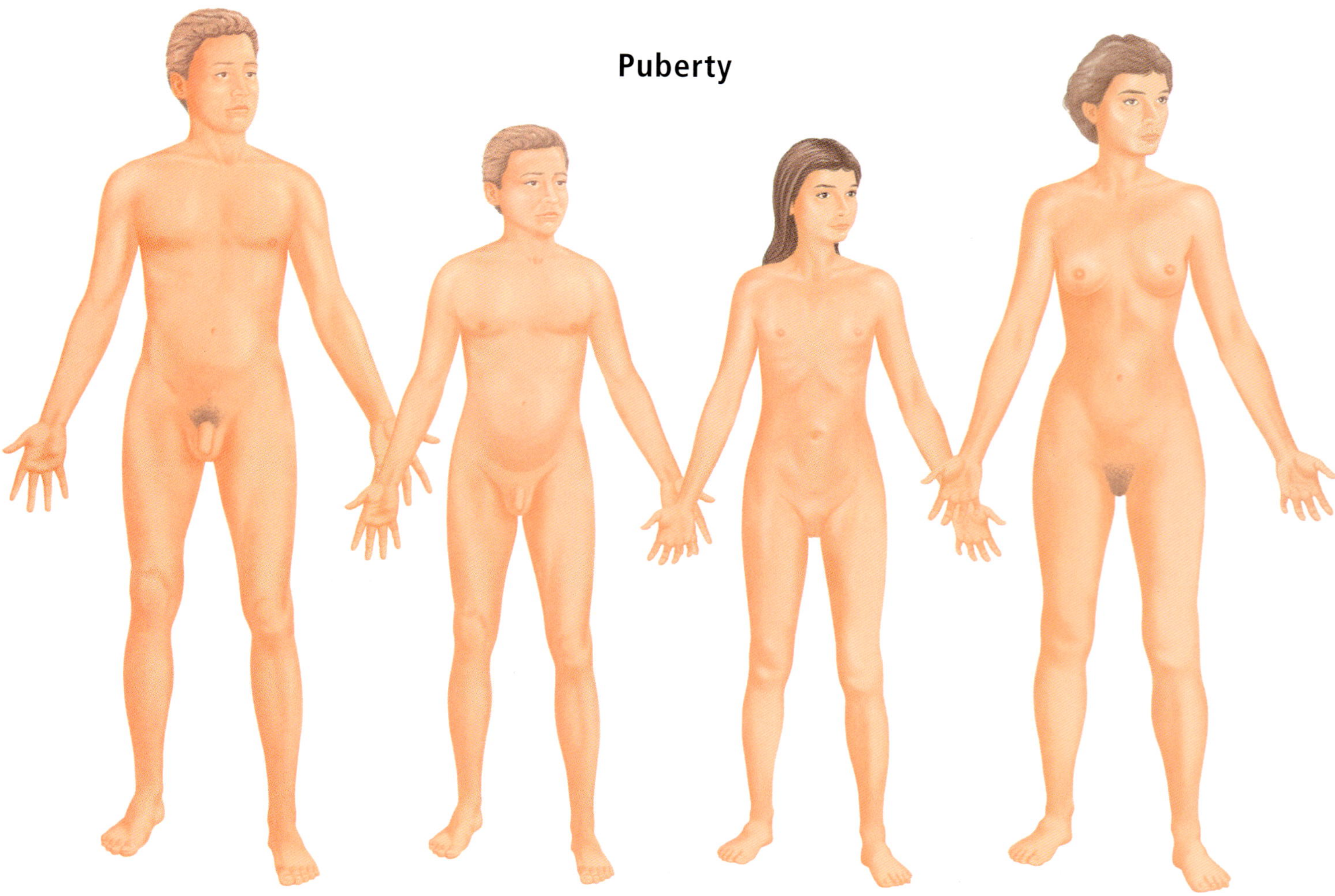

17-year-old male
Appearance of facial hair along with body and pubic hair, and increase in the size of the testes and penis are the predominant signs of male puberty. The larynx also increases in size creating the "Adam's apple" look at the front of the neck.

12-year-old male
Puberty in males occurs about 2 years later than in females. At age 12, a boy has little or no body hair, a small penis and testes, and still appears childlike.

10-year-old female
There is little or no breast development, no pubic hair and an almost boyish appearance at this age.

17-year-old female
Fully developed breasts, hair growth around the vulva and widening of the hips are the outward signs of female puberty.

changes awaken sexual feelings, and many adolescents have some sexual experience. Dating normally begins during puberty.

In some cases puberty occurs later than usual or does not occur at all. Sexual development can be retarded by many different factors, including metabolic defects, hereditary conditions, hormonal disorders and poor nutrition.

SEE ALSO *Acne, Adolescence, Hormones, Menstruation, Reproductive systems*

PULMONARY ARTERY

The pulmonary trunk or pulmonary artery is the large vessel which carries relatively deoxygenated blood from the right side of the heart into the lungs. Blood from the right ventricle of the heart is expelled into the pulmonary trunk through the pulmonary valve, which prevents regurgitation of the blood back into the ventricle when the heart muscle relaxes.

The pulmonary trunk is quite short, about 1 inch (2–3 centimeters) long. It divides into the left and right pulmonary arteries to enter each lung. During fetal life, the pulmonary trunk is joined to the aorta by a duct (ductus arteriosus) which allows blood to flow from the right side of the heart to the aorta, bypassing the uninflated lungs. After birth, the duct closes up, leaving a ligament called the ligamentum arteriosum.

SEE ALSO *Aorta, Circulatory system, Fetal development, Heart, Lungs*

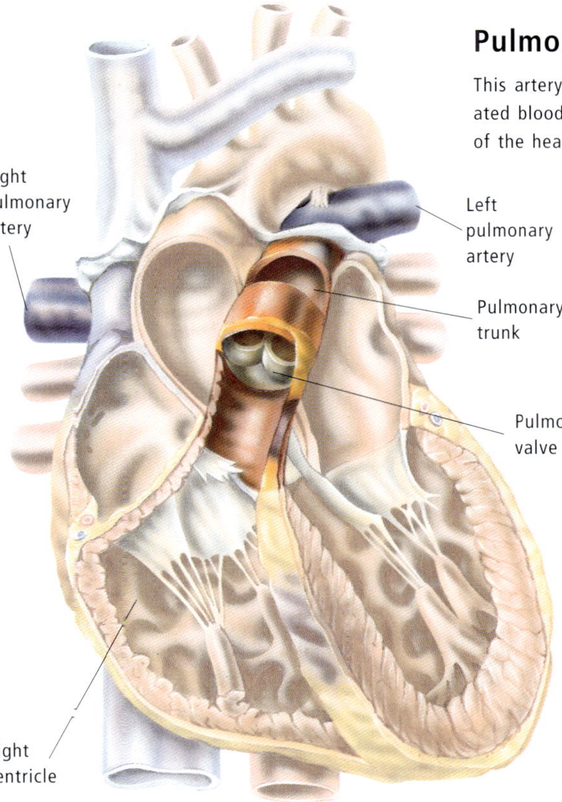

Pulmonary artery

This artery carries the deoxygenated blood from the right side of the heart to the lungs.

PULMONARY CIRCULATION

In the human body, blood passes through the heart twice during each complete passage of the circulatory system. In this so-called "double circulation" system, found in all mammals, the blood follows two complementary but separate routes from the heart. Systemic circulation takes the blood around the body and back; pulmonary circulation transports the blood to the lungs and back.

The purpose of pulmonary circulation is to pass the blood close to the thin-walled air sacs (alveoli) of the lungs so that the blood can exchange carbon dioxide collected from the body for oxygen. Before being sent into the pulmonary blood vessels, the blood returns, deoxygenated and dark red, from the head, limbs and internal organs, to the heart. The oxygen-depleted blood enters the right atrium then passes, via the tricuspid valve, to the right ventricle located immediately below. From there the blood is pumped out along the route of the pulmonary circulation.

The right ventricle sends the blood through the pulmonary valve and on to the lungs via the pulmonary arteries, the only arteries that carry deoxygenated blood after birth. The right pulmonary artery runs to the right lung and the left goes to the left lung. Each pulmonary artery divides repeatedly to culminate in a network of tiny, thin-walled capillaries around the air sacs of a lung. Here, carbon dioxide diffuses out of the blood into the lungs, from where it is exhaled. At the same time, oxygen contained in air breathed into the lungs diffuses into the blood.

From each lung the oxygenated blood (now bright red) flows from the capillaries to venules and eventually into the two pulmonary veins. Most veins after birth carry deoxygenated blood but the pulmonary veins, transporting oxygenated blood from the lungs back to the heart, are the exception.

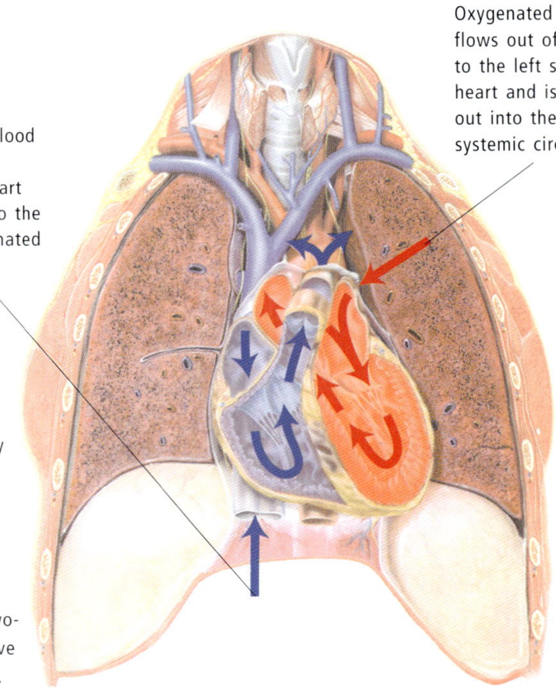

Pulmonary circulation

The primary purpose of pulmonary circulation is to offload carbon dioxide, which the blood has collected from the body, and pick up oxygen through the thin-walled air sacs of the lungs.

NB: In this illustration the top two-thirds of the lungs and pleura have been cut away to show the heart.

The pulmonary circulation is completed when blood is delivered back to the heart at the left atrium. From there the oxygenated blood passes through the mitral valve to the muscular left ventricle and then on to the rest of the body via the systemic circulation.

Pulmonary circulation comes "on-line" in humans only after birth. Before that, the lungs (along with the gastrointestinal tract) do not function. Instead, the fetal blood collects oxygen from and dumps carbon dioxide into the mother's circulation through the placenta.

Pulmonary hypertension and pulmonary embolism are two of the most commonly encountered serious disorders of the pulmonary circulation. Pulmonary hypertension is abnormally high blood pressure in the lungs. It is not necessarily related to high blood pressure in the systemic circulation and can interfere with oxygen levels in the blood. Possible causes include tissue damage in the lungs due to disease or the inflammation of blood vessels in the lungs.

In pulmonary embolism, a condition requiring urgent medical attention, a pulmonary artery becomes blocked by fat, an air bubble, tumor or blood clot (which will usually have arisen in the deep leg veins). Symptoms include breathing discomfort, sudden chest pain, shock and a blue discoloration to the skin caused by an excess of deoxygenated blood in the body. Very large pulmonary embolisms are often fatal.

SEE ALSO *Circulatory system, Deep venous thrombosis, Lungs, Mitral valve, Placenta, Pulmonary embolism, Veins, Ventricle*

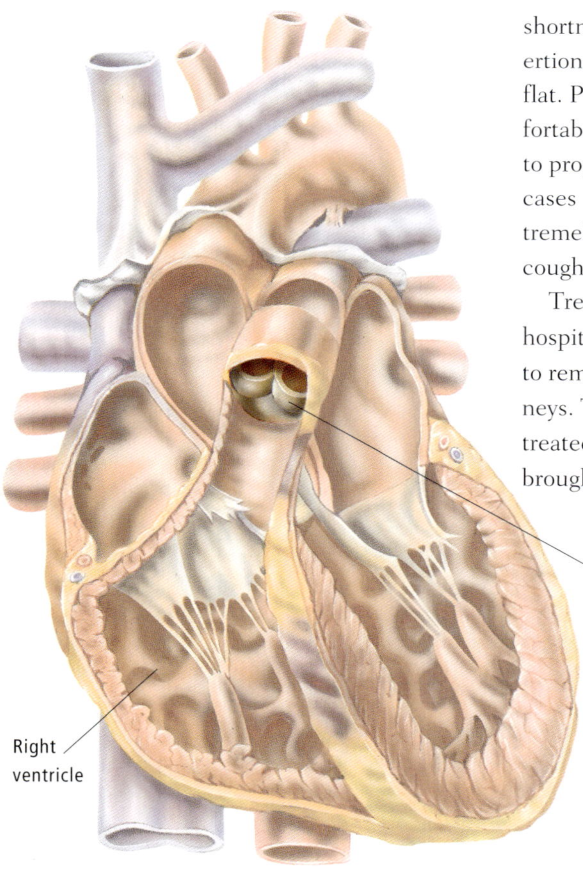

Pulmonary valve

This valve prevents the backflow of blood into the ventricle when the heart muscle relaxes.

PULMONARY EDEMA

Pulmonary edema is a build-up of fluid in the lungs, most often due to heart failure, which may be a complication of a myocardial infarction (heart attack), myocarditis (disease of the heart muscle), mitral or aortic valve disease, or other heart disorders.

Pulmonary edema may also occur in cases of fluid overload, for example, in someone who has been given too much intravenous fluid in hospital. It may result from a major allergic reaction such as anaphylactic shock. As the heart muscle weakens, it becomes less able to pump blood forward into the arterial system and thus pressure rises in the veins of the lungs, the pulmonary veins. This results in leakage of fluid into the air spaces in the lungs.

The symptoms of pulmonary edema are shortness of breath, occurring initially on exertion and later at rest, especially when lying flat. People with heart failure are more comfortable sitting up and may use extra pillows to prop themselves up at night. In severe cases they may wake during the night extremely short of breath, gasping for air and coughing frothy pink fluid.

Treatment requires urgent admission to hospital for intravenous diuretic medication to remove fluid from the lungs via the kidneys. The patient is given oxygen, and is treated for any underlying condition that has brought on the heart failure, such as infection, irregular heartbeat or heart attack. Medication may be given to increase the pumping ability of the heart.

SEE ALSO *Circulatory system, Edema, Heart, Lungs*

PULMONARY EMBOLISM

Pulmonary embolism is obstruction of the pulmonary circulation by solid or cellular material that has traveled from the venous circulation through the right side of the heart and lodged in an artery of the lungs, blocking the blood supply. It is usually caused by a blood clot from a vein in the lower leg (a deep vein thrombosis). Less commonly the embolus may be air, fat, or bone marrow.

Not only does the embolus cut off the blood supply to the lungs, but just as importantly, it disrupts the flow of blood through the left side of the heart and the rest of the body. If the blockage is large enough, the cardiac output falls and the body tissues die.

The risk of a pulmonary embolus is greatest in people with deep vein thrombosis or those with a propensity to clotting—that is, those who are immobile, bedridden, pregnant, taking oral contraceptives, or who have had recent surgery, especially pelvic surgery.

The symptoms of pulmonary embolism are sudden chest pain (as the heart is deprived of oxygenated blood), difficulty in breathing, a pale skin, a rapid heart rate, and faintness. The condition is a medical emergency and must be treated in hospital. Pulmonary embolism will be confirmed by a lung scan; blood tests should be done to measure the levels of oxygen in the blood. Angiography (an x-ray test in which dye is injected into the veins) or Doppler ultrasound studies of the veins can confirm whether there is a deep vein thrombosis.

The treatment is with intravenous drugs that dissolve the clot (thrombolytic drugs). Further clotting is prevented with intravenous anticoagulant drugs. In the meantime the patient is given oxygen by mask. With adequate treatment, the death rate is low.

After surgery the condition is best prevented by patients walking around as soon as possible, combined with the use of elastic support stockings. Heparin (an anticoagulant) can be given in small doses under the skin to patients requiring prolonged bed rest.

SEE ALSO *Anticoagulants, Circulatory system, Lungs, Thrombosis*

PULMONARY FUNCTION TESTS

Pulmonary function tests (also known as lung capacity tests) measure the effectiveness of ventilation. They are used in lung diseases such as asthma, bronchitis, emphysema and fibrosis of the lung to determine the severity of the disease.

Spirometry is a test using an instrument called a spirometer, which measures how well the lungs take in air, how much air they hold, and how well the lungs exhale air. A peak flow meter is a smaller device that measures how quickly the lungs can expel air. Both tests can be performed in the physician's office.

SEE ALSO *Asthma, Bronchitis, Emphysema, Lungs*

PULMONARY VALVE

The pulmonary valve is situated where the blood from the right ventricle of the heart flows out into the large artery to the lungs, the pulmonary trunk. The pulmonary valve prevents backflow of blood from the pulmonary trunk into the right ventricle when the heart muscle relaxes. Both the pulmonary valve and the aortic valve are said to be semilunar valves, because they each consist of three half-moon shaped valve cusps.

Disease may affect the pulmonary valve, resulting in either pulmonary stenosis or pulmonary insufficiency (incompetence). Pulmonary stenosis is usually a congenital disease in which the cusps of the pulmonary valve are fused in the form of a membrane or diaphragm with a narrow central opening, rather than the normal semilunar (half-moon) shaped cusps.

Pulmonary insufficiency means that the pulmonary valve is unable to prevent the backflow of blood from the pulmonary trunk into the right ventricle when the ventricle stops contracting. It most often arises in individuals who have had rheumatic heart disease, in which the valve cusps become contracted and fused with the wall of the artery, or in cases of increased blood pressure in the lung circulation.

SEE ALSO *Circulatory system, Heart, Lungs*

Pulse points

The pressure created by a beat of the heart can be felt quite easily where arteries are close to the skin.

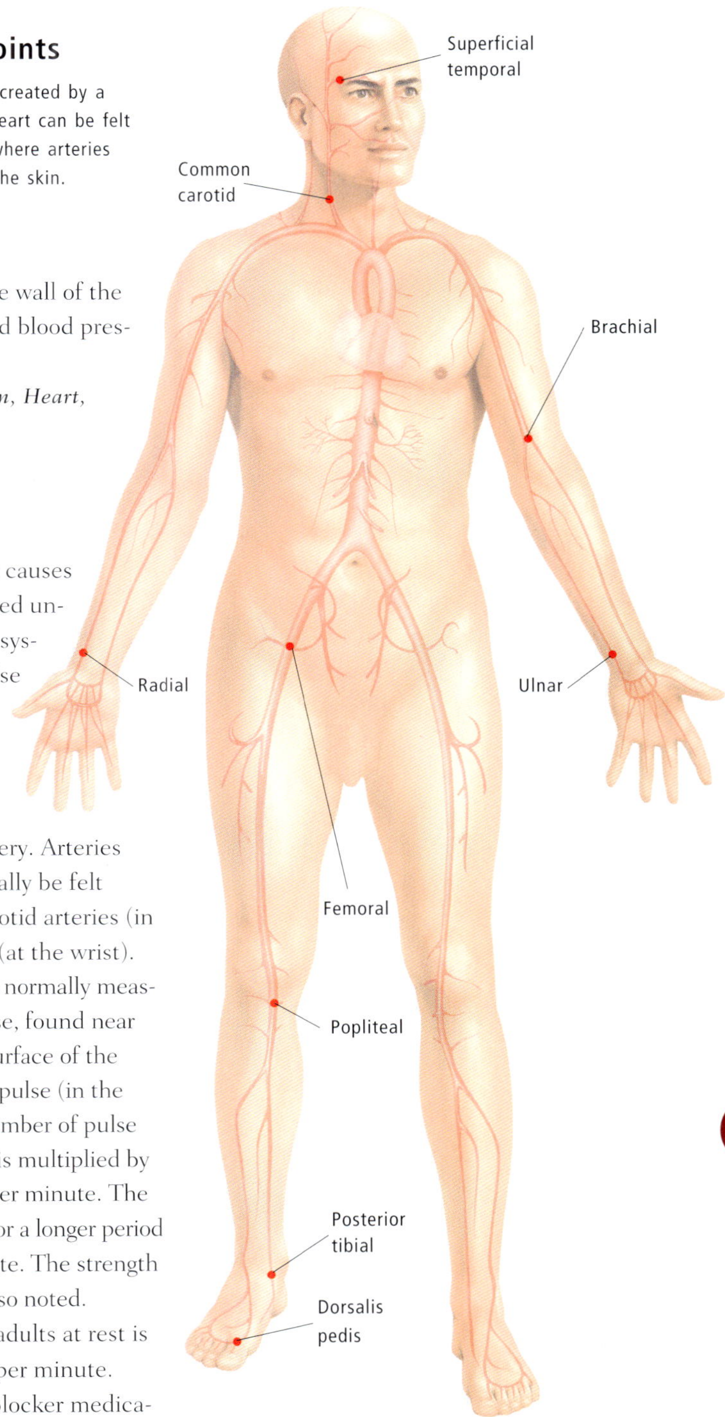

PULSE

As the heart beats, each beat causes a quantity of blood to be forced under pressure into the arterial system. These beats cause a pulse or shock wave that travels along the walls of the arteries. This pulse can be felt in several parts of the body by placing the finger over an artery. Arteries in which the pulse can normally be felt particularly easily are the carotid arteries (in the neck) and radial arteries (at the wrist).

Clinically, the pulse rate is normally measured by feeling the radial pulse, found near the thumb side of the front surface of the wrist. Sometimes the carotid pulse (in the neck) is used instead. The number of pulse beats counted in 10 seconds is multiplied by 6 to obtain the rate in beats per minute. The pulse must, however, be felt for a longer period to check for irregular pulse rate. The strength or weakness of the pulse is also noted.

The pulse rate in healthy adults at rest is typically about 60–70 beats per minute. Athletes and those on beta-blocker medication may have slower pulse rates, while children and babies have faster pulse rates. The pulse rate increases during exercise to increase the output of blood from the heart. The rate is also increased by excitement.

SEE ALSO *Carotid arteries, Heart, Palpitations, Radial artery*

PUPIL OF EYE

The pupil of the eye is the central hole in the iris through which light enters the eye. Tiny muscles in the iris control the size of the pupil. In daylight, the pupil is typically about $\frac{1}{10}$ inch (3 millimeters) in diameter. In dark conditions, it opens to about $\frac{1}{3}$ inch (7 millimeters) in diameter to allow more light to enter the eye. Adaptation to dark also involves adaptation in the retina. When using an optical instrument, such as a telescope or binoculars, the diameter of the exit hole of the instrument should be matched to that of the pupil. For this reason, binoculars intended for night use have a larger exit hole than those intended for daylight use.

SEE ALSO *Eye, Iris, Retina*

P

PURPURA

Purpura is a disease in which hemorrhages occur in the skin and mucous membranes. It manifests itself as small red spots on the skin. There are two main types: thrombocytopenic purpura, involving a decrease in platelet count in the blood; and nonthrombocytopenic purpura, which does not involve any such decrease.

Causes of purpura include exposure to drugs or chemical agents; cancerous diseases such as leukemia; and infectious diseases such as rubella.

Schönlein's purpura is a nonthrombocytopenic purpura characterized by pain and tenderness in the joints and often accompanied by mild fever and hive-like skin eruptions. Henoch's purpura is an allergic nonthrombocytopenic purpura marked by attacks of gastrointestinal pain, bleeding and hive-like skin eruptions.

Allergic purpura, also known as Schönlein-Henoch purpura, is an uncommon allergic disorder manifesting itself as an inflammation of blood vessels in the skin, joints, gastrointestinal tract or kidneys. It mainly affects young children and is more common in boys (from 2–8 years) than in girls. It usually develops as the result of an infection but may be drug related. Treatment depends on the cause.

SEE ALSO *Hemorrhage, Thrombocytopenia*

PYELITIS

Pyelitis is an inflammation of the pelvis of the kidney. It is most often caused by bacteria that make their way to the kidney via the blood or the bladder.

Pyelitis is reasonably common, particularly in children. It is easily treated but requires prompt attention to ensure that it does not lead to the development of the more serious kidney infection known as pyelonephritis.

SEE ALSO *Bladder, Kidney, Pyelonephritis, Urinary systems*

PYELOGRAM

A pyelogram is the film produced by a radiology technique (pyelography) in which a contrast medium (iodine-containing radiopaque dye) is introduced into the kidneys and the urinary collecting system, after which an x-ray is taken. There are two main types; intravenous pyelography (IVP) and retrograde pyelography.

In intravenous pyelography, dye is injected into the bloodstream at designated intervals. As the kidneys excrete the dye, a series of x-rays are taken which reveal the rate of excretion; detail the outlines of the kidney and ureters, showing their shape and size, and highlight any abnormalities, such as stones, tumors, scarring, or hydronephrosis, for example.

In retrograde pyelography, the dye is injected via a tube that is passed through the urethra and bladder and into the ureters where the dye is injected. The dye is then forced along the tube to the kidneys. Retrograde pyelography has been found to be most suitable for highlighting specific parts of the urinary tract, such as the ureters and the renal pelvis. Both procedures are performed in a radiology department of a hospital or in a radiology clinic.

SEE ALSO *Bladder, Kidney, Ureters, Urethra, Urinary systems*

PYELONEPHRITIS

Pyelonephritis is an infection of the kidney and the renal pelvis. Acute (sudden onset) pyelonephritis is usually the result of the

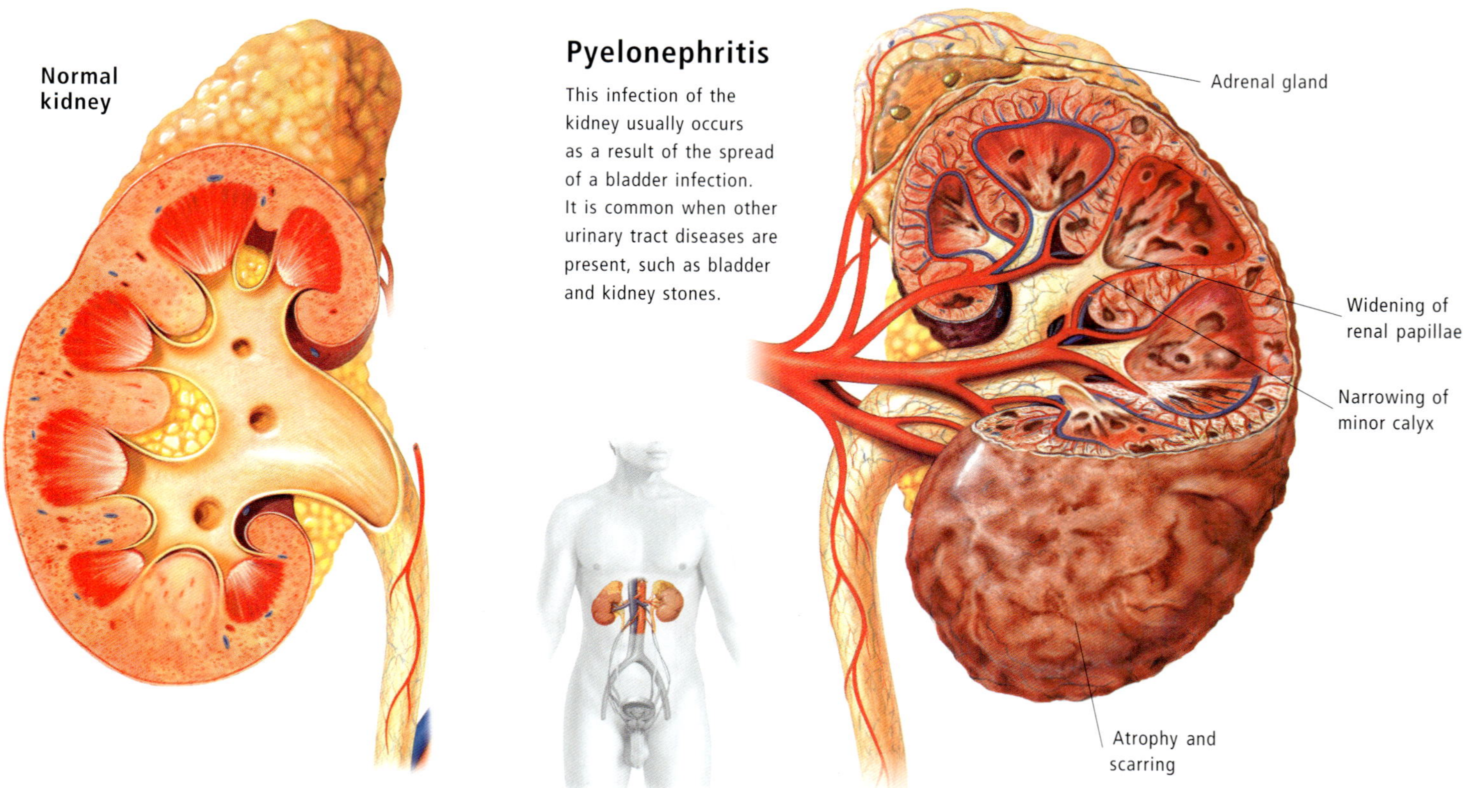

upstream spread of a bladder infection (cystitis). It is more common if there is preexisting urinary tract disease, such as kidney or bladder stones. It is characterized by the sudden onset of pain in the lower back, fever with chills, nausea, and vomiting, pain passing urine (dysuria) and frequent urination. In children, the symptoms may be milder and less obvious. A urine test shows white blood cells and bacteria in the urine, while a culture of the urine will show the specific bacteria that is causing the infection (most commonly *E. coli*), and also its antibiotic sensitivity. Acute pyelonephritis generally responds to treatment with antibiotics given intravenously in hospital. The infection usually clears in 10–14 days.

Chronic pyelonephritis is caused by destruction and scarring of the kidney tissue as a result of recurrent or untreated bacterial infection. There is often an associated abnormality of the urinary tract, which leads to repeated infection. Treatment is surgical correction of any abnormality and a prolonged course of antibiotics. Eventually there may be renal failure requiring dialysis or transplantation.

SEE ALSO *Bladder, Cystitis, Dysuria, Kidneys, Ureter, Urinary systems, Urinary tract*

Pylorus

This ring of muscle prevents the contents of the intestines re-entering the stomach.

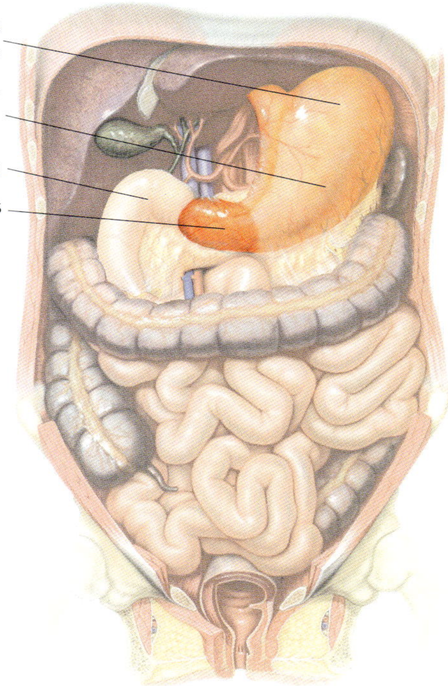

PYLORIC STENOSIS

Pyloric stenosis is a disease which usually affects only newborn infants. It is more common in boys than girls and results from the thickening of the muscle (pyloric sphincter) surrounding the exit from the stomach to the duodenum. Infants with pyloric stenosis are usually born at full term and feed and grow well for the first two weeks of life. After this time they begin to regurgitate milk with increasing force over the next few days until the vomiting becomes projectile. Unless the problem is corrected, the infant may become dehydrated, lose weight and die.

Treatment may be by antispasmodic drugs and rehydration with intravenous fluids, but usually surgery to sever the fibers of the enlarged pyloric sphincter will be required.

SEE ALSO *Newborn, Pylorus*

PYLORUS

The pylorus is a cone-shaped gate of muscle between the stomach and the small intestine (duodenum). Its role is to prevent the contents of the intestine from re-entering the stomach and also to prevent large food particles and undigested food from entering the small intestine prematurely.

SEE ALSO *Duodenum, Intestines, Stomach*

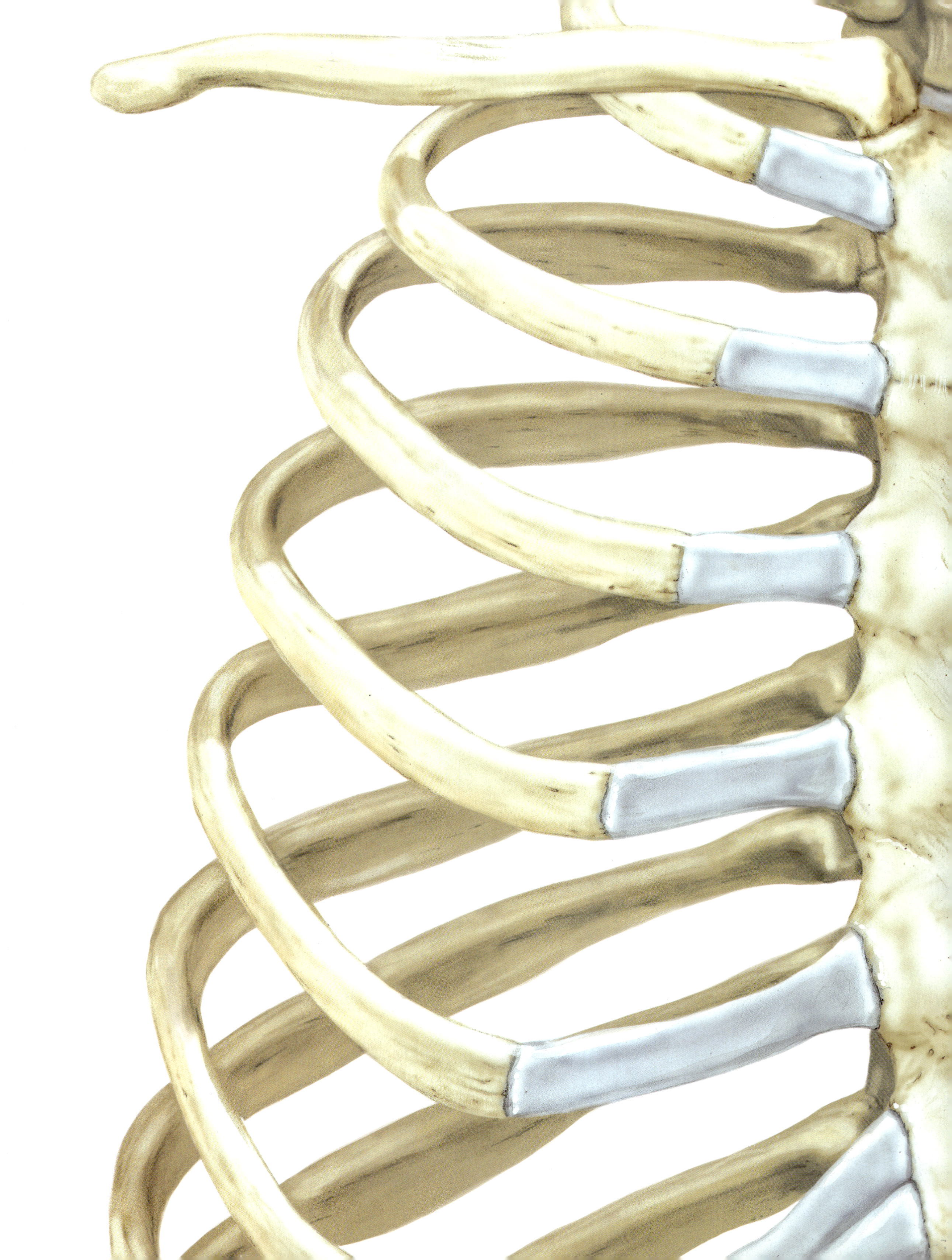

QR

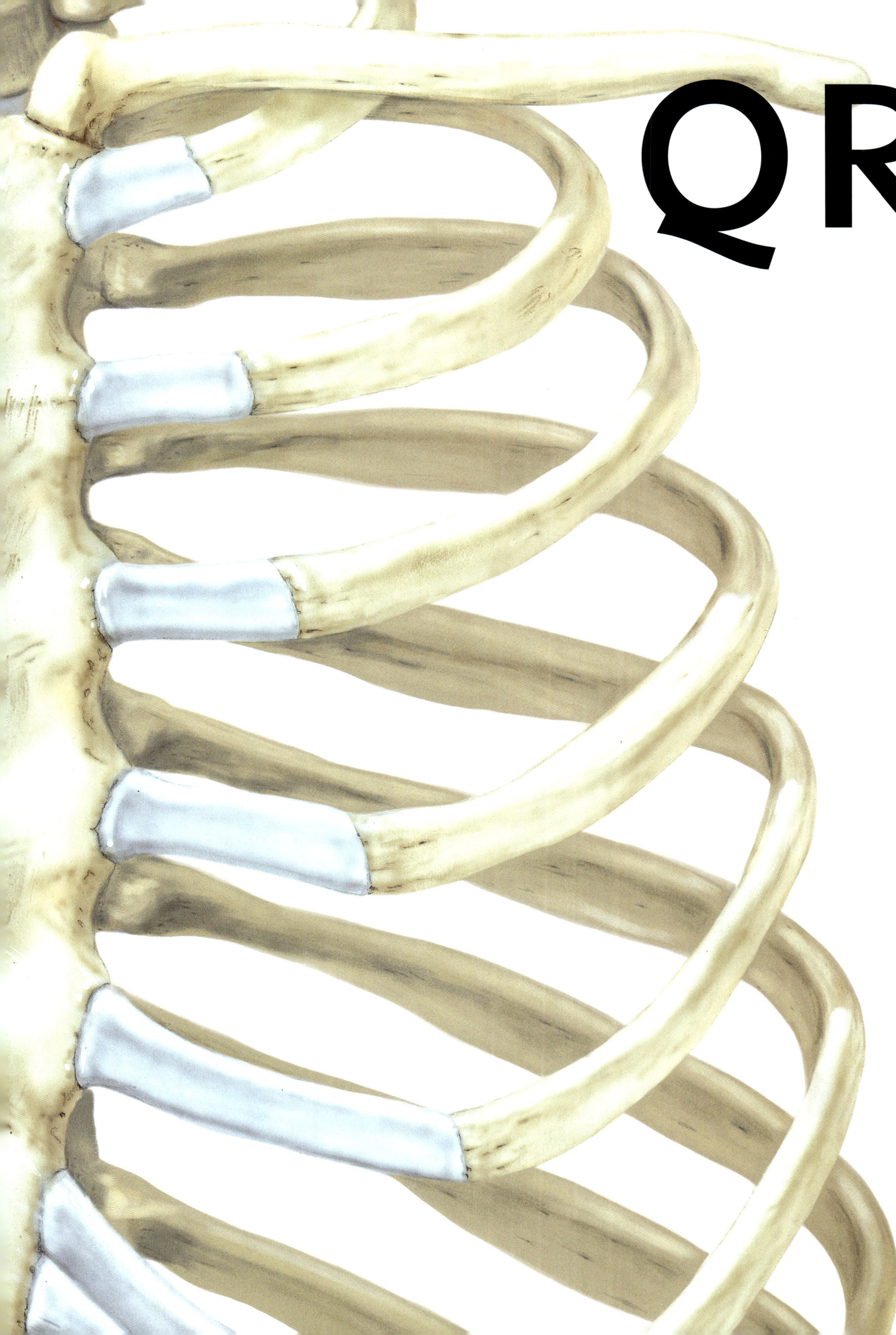

Q FEVER

Q fever is an infectious disease acquired from animals; it causes fever, chills and muscular pains and sometimes more serious illnesses such as pneumonia, chronic hepatitis and encephalitis. It is caused by the micro-organism *Coxiella burnetii*, which is found in domestic animals such as cattle, sheep, goats and cats, as well as in wild animals and ticks. The disease may be passed to humans when they inhale contaminated dust or droplets, consume contaminated food or unpasteurized milk or come into contact with materials, such as soil, which are contaminated with infected blood or feces.

The incubation period is 9–28 days after which a fever suddenly occurs, accompanied by symptoms resembling influenza, such as severe headaches, shivering, muscle pain and sometimes chest pain. After a week a dry cough may develop and the fever may continue for up to 3 weeks. This early form of the disease is known as Q fever (early) and may include complications such as pneumonia and hepatitis. Q fever (late) is a rare relapse of the illness that may cause problems with the aortic heart valve.

People who work with animals, such as farmers and veterinarians, are most at risk. Q fever rarely causes death and is treated with antibiotics. It is widely found in Europe, North America and parts of Africa.

SEE ALSO *Encephalitis, Hepatitis, Infectious diseases, Pneumonia*

Q

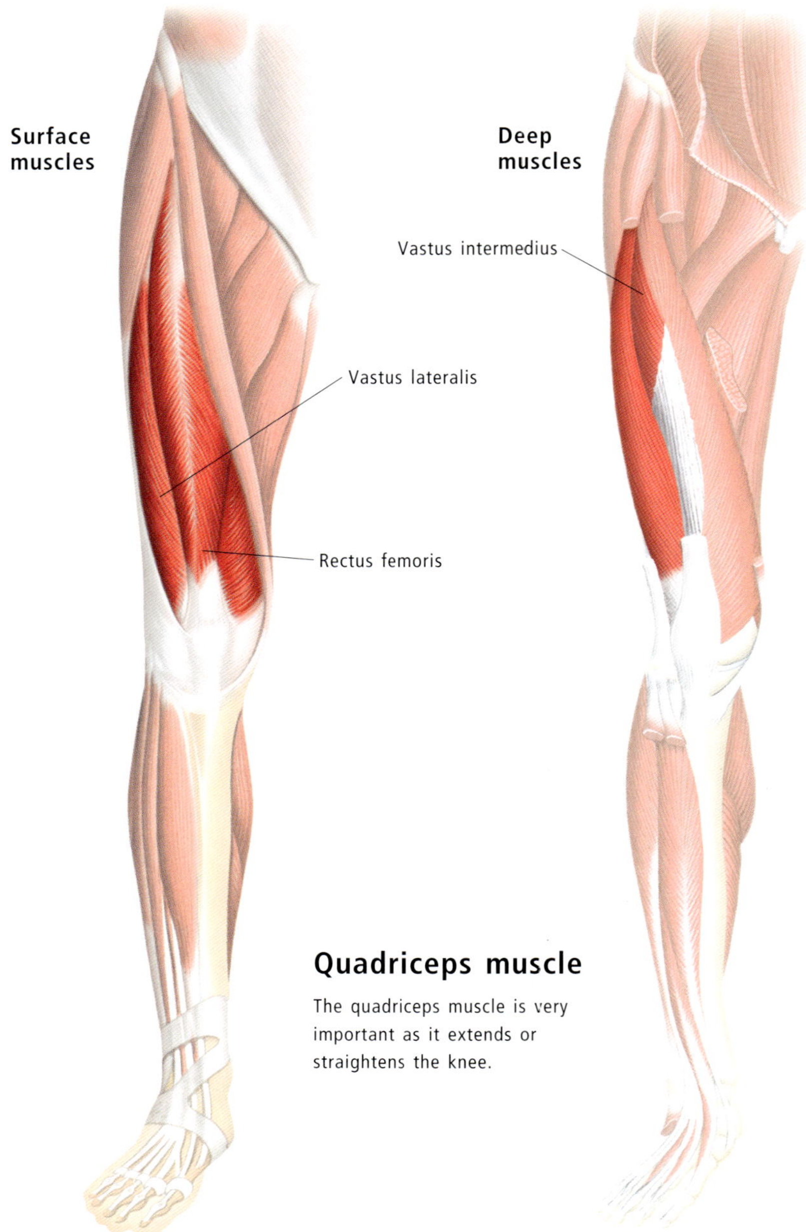

Quadriceps muscle

The quadriceps muscle is very important as it extends or straightens the knee.

QI GONG

Qi gong, also known as chi kung, is an ancient Chinese healing technique which combines movement, meditation and breath regulation to improve the flow of *qi (ch'i)* or life energy throughout the body. Practitioners trace the acupuncture meridians through the body with their hands, using visualization and breath control to cleanse and activate the vital organs, and to facilitate the flow of blood, lymph and energy.

Qi gong is widely practised in China, where it is combined with conventional medical treatments, and it is also used in Western countries. It is considered to be particularly beneficial for stress-related disorders and respiratory and circulatory problems.

SEE ALSO *Acupuncture, Meditation*

QUADRICEPS MUSCLE

The quadriceps muscle forms the major muscle mass of the front and outer side of the thigh, covering most of the front and sides of the thigh bone (femur). The muscle is properly known as the quadriceps femoris muscle, so called because it has four parts, each with separate names. These are the rectus femoris, vastus lateralis, vastus medialis and vastus intermedius.

The quadriceps muscle arises mainly from the upper two-thirds of the thigh bone, and also from the bony pelvis. At its lower end, the tendons of the component muscles blend together to form a single tendon, which is attached to the upper surface of the kneecap (patella). The tendon extends below the patella as the "patellar ligament", which is attached to the tubercle of the shin bone (tibia) and is spread out on both sides to strengthen the capsule of the knee joint.

The quadriceps serves to straighten the knee. It also flexes the thigh on the pelvis. Both of these actions can be produced simultaneously. The quadriceps is also involved in the knee jerk reflex.

The quadriceps and hamstring muscles contribute to the stability of the knee joint, and recovery from knee injuries is assisted by strengthening these muscles.

SEE ALSO *Knee, Leg, Muscle*

QUADRIPLEGIA

Quadriplegia (also referred to as tetraplegia) is partial or full paralysis and loss of sensation below the neck, involving all four limbs and the trunk of the body. (If only the lower limbs and trunk are affected, the condition is called paraplegia.)

Quadriplegia is caused by damage to the spinal cord in the neck, usually at the level of the fourth and fifth cervical vertebrae (if injuries occur above this level the diaphragm is often paralyzed and the victim may die). The injury is usually from trauma, most commonly road accidents and sporting injuries. Males between 15 and 35 years old make up the group most likely to be affected.

Less frequently, quadriplegia may be caused by spinal-cord tumors or birth defects. As well as muscle paralysis, quadriplegia leads to dysfunction of other organs and body systems whose nerve supply from the spinal cord has been disrupted. There may be loss of urinary and bowel control, impaired sexual function, loss of normal blood pressure, loss of body-temperature control, poor healing of tissues, and constipation.

Treatment as soon as possible after the injury gives the injured person the greatest chance of minimizing the extent of the damage and of recovering some function. Surgery may be performed to remove fluid or tissue that is pressing on the spinal cord (decompression laminectomy); to remove bone fragments or foreign objects; or to stabilize fractured vertebrae by fusion of the bones or insertion of hardware. Bed rest and spinal traction (which immobilizes the spine and reduces dislocation) promotes healing.

If movement or sensation return within a week after the injury, then most function will eventually be recovered (although it may take 6 months or more). Losses of function that remain after 6 months are likely to be permanent. Approximately one-third of sufferers will be permanently wheelchair-bound.

Thus, rehabilitation remains the mainstay of treatment. Physical therapy can help joint stiffness, and passive exercises will help prevent contractures.

Prolonged immobility can give rise to complications such as constipation, pressure sores and ulcers, so frequent position changes and good skin care are important. Other complications, such as bladder and lung infections and kidney stones, will also need to be treated. Psychotherapy or counseling may relieve depression and sexual problems.

With rehabilitation, some lost functions can be restored or compensated for. However, quadriplegics will have permanently reduced mobility and will require help with many facets of their lives, including accommodation, employment, transport, and access to buildings.

The condition can often be prevented by following commonsense safety precautions such as the wearing of seat belts in cars and of protective headgear for contact sports.

SEE ALSO *Paralysis, Paraplegia, Rehabilitation, Spinal cord*

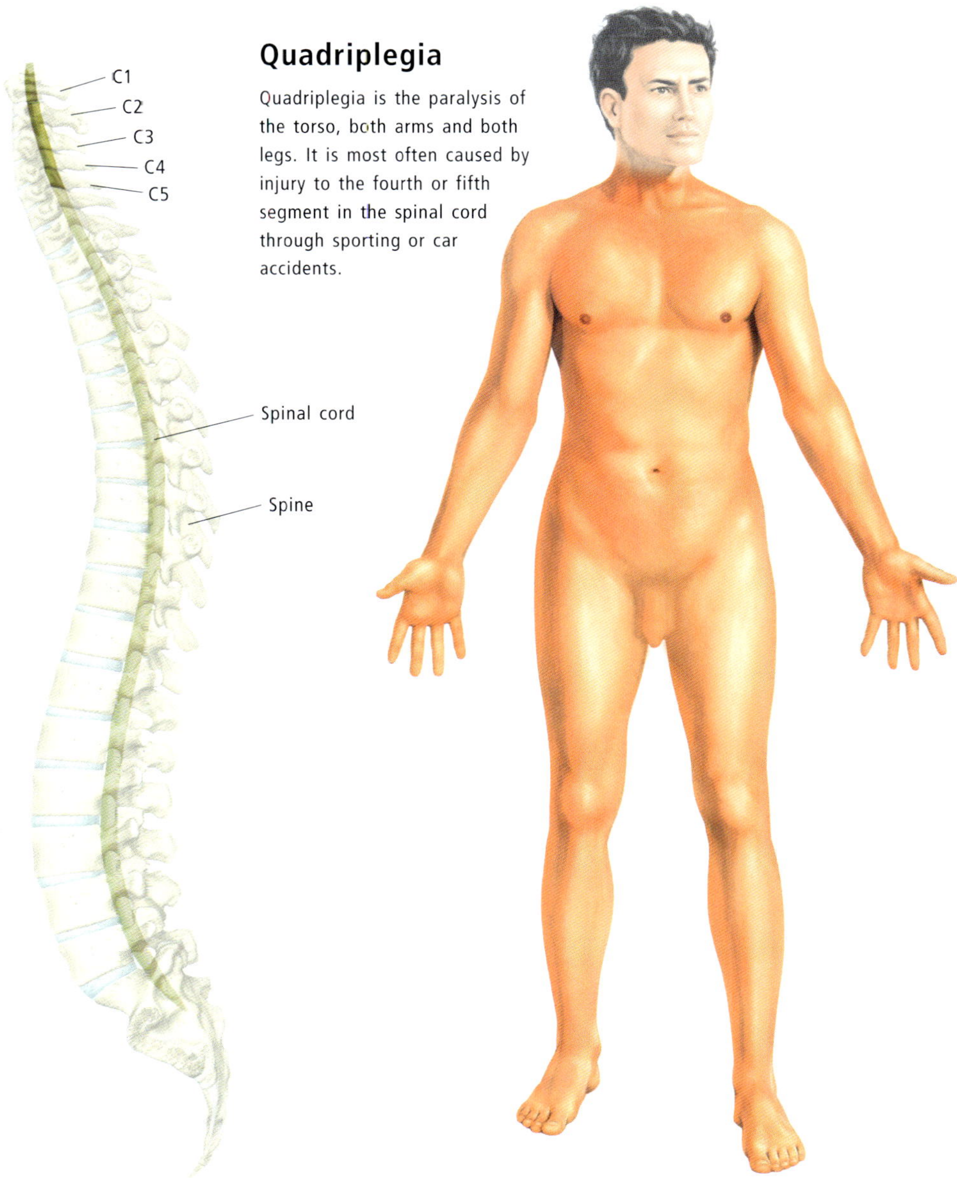

Quadriplegia

Quadriplegia is the paralysis of the torso, both arms and both legs. It is most often caused by injury to the fourth or fifth segment in the spinal cord through sporting or car accidents.

QUINSY

Quinsy, also known as peritonsillar abscess, is a relatively uncommon infection of the tissue surrounding the tonsils that results in an abscess or collection of pus. Often caused by spreading infection from tonsillitis, its symptoms include fever, severe pain when swallowing, and difficulty opening the mouth. It may be treated with antibiotics if caught in the early stages.

More severe conditions may require draining of the pus via a surgical incision. The infection can recur and if left untreated may spread to the mouth, neck, chest and lungs, causing life-threatening tissue swelling that can block airways. Quinsy is most common in older children, teenagers and young adults.

SEE ALSO *Abscess, Tonsils*

RABIES

Rabies is an acute viral disease that affects the nervous system of animals and is transmitted to humans via saliva, commonly after being bitten or licked on broken skin by a rabid animal, such as a bat, dog or cat. The average incubation time is 1–2 months, though it may occasionally be more than a year. It starts with fever, depression, nausea and vomiting. In "furious" rabies the victim becomes highly agitated, with uncontrollable behavior, spasms of the throat muscles, excessive saliva and frothing at the mouth which makes them unable to drink water. For this reason, rabies was once known as hydrophobia, which means "fear of water". "Dumb" rabies is characterized by sluggishness, weakness and paralysis. Once symptoms appear death is inevitable, usually within a week.

Vaccination soon after exposure to infection offers protection. An injection of rabies immune globulin is followed by a course of rabies vaccine over 28 days. Vaccination does not cancel out the risk of infection but reduces the intensity of the disease in those infected. Possible side effects of vaccination include headache, dizziness, nausea, muscle aches and, less commonly, neurological disorders and paralysis. Family pets should also be vaccinated.

SEE ALSO *Immunization, Viruses*

RADIAL ARTERY

The radial artery is a medium-sized artery which conveys blood through the forearm to the hand. It is one of two major arteries of the forearm, the other being the ulnar artery. It runs superficially through the muscular part of the forearm towards the thumb. The radial artery provides blood to muscles of the forearm and, together with the ulnar artery, contributes to the palmar arches in the hand, from which the digital arteries arise to supply the fingers.

The superficial course of the radial artery makes it easily accessible to the clinician taking the pulse during assessment of a patient. The examiner's fingers are placed over the radial artery at the wrist, just beside the tendon of flexor carpi radialis. Information can be obtained this way regarding the pulse rate and rhythm, whether it is strong or weak, and about the firmness of the arterial wall. With the ageing process the arterial wall hardens (arteriosclerosis) and this can be felt in the radial artery. The radial artery's superficial position also makes it vulnerable to injury at the wrist, before it descends into the space between the radius bone and the base of the thumb.

SEE ALSO *Arms, Arteries, Arteriosclerosis, Hand, Radius*

RADIAL NERVE

The radial nerve is one of the major nerves in the arm. It starts in the armpit (axilla) from a network of nerves (the brachial plexus). It supplies extensor muscles in the back of the arm, such as the triceps and extensors for the wrist, fingers and thumb. It also supplies skin over the back of the arm and hand, on the thumb side.

The radial nerve can be compressed in the armpit, for instance by the arm being draped over the back of a chair in sleep or when one is intoxicated, causing pins and needles or even temporary paralysis ("Saturday night palsy"). It can also be damaged by fractures of the humerus or injuries in the forearm. These injuries can lead to wrist-drop, in which the hand and fingers cannot be extended.

SEE ALSO *Arm, Hand, Nerves, Radius, Wrist*

RADIATION

Radiation is the emission or transfer of radiant energy as a stream of ions (electrically charged atoms), subatomic particles or electromagnetic energy waves. Heat, sound, light, radio waves and microwaves all come under the banner of radiation and are known as nonionizing radiation.

Ionizing radiation, including x-rays and gamma rays, is so named because it can cause substances such as human tissue to break into ions. It is used in medicine to treat cancers by damaging the cancerous cells so they are unable to grow and divide. This practice, known as radiation therapy or radiotherapy, may involve radiation created by a machine outside the body or by radioactive material, such as radium, implanted in the body. Radiosensitive cancers include leukemias and lymphomas.

Ultraviolet radiation from the sun, or ultraviolet light, has a wavelength shorter than the violet end of the visible spectrum of light, making it invisible to the eye. It is now known that prolonged exposure to ultraviolet radiation, especially over a lifetime, can be harmful to the skin and is associated with

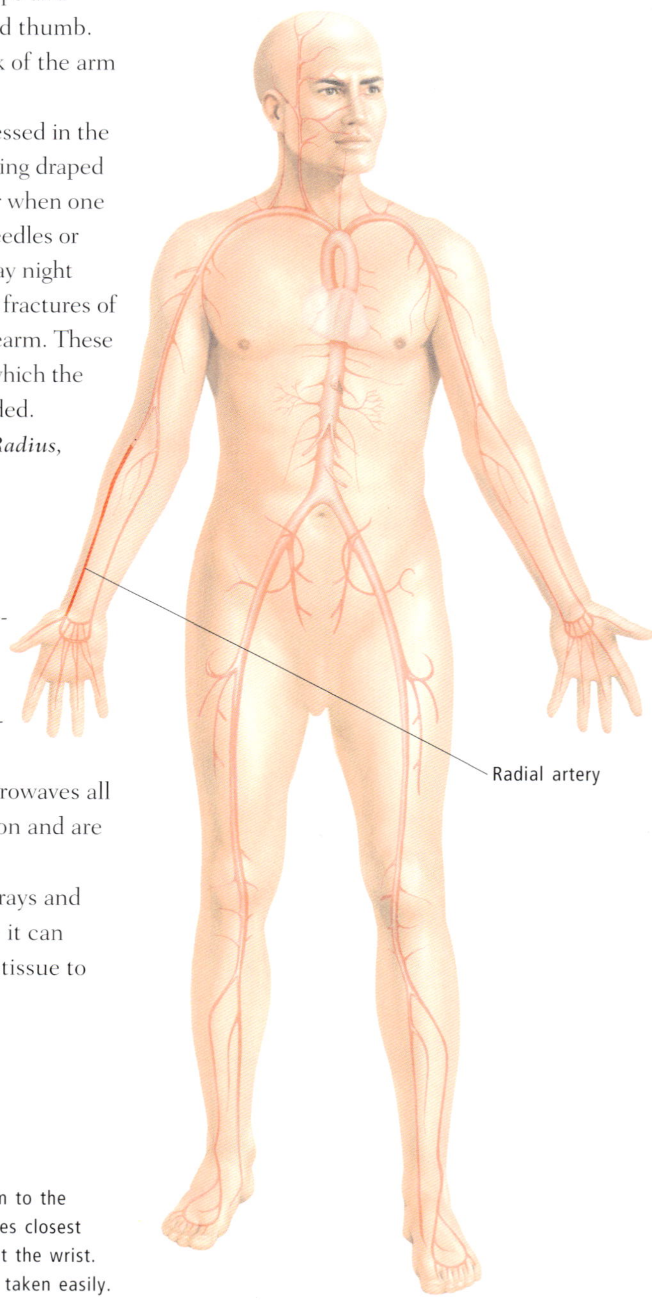

Radial artery

Passing through the forearm to the hand, the radial artery comes closest to the surface of the skin at the wrist. This allows the pulse to be taken easily.

solar keratoses ("sun spots"), skin cancer, melanoma and cataracts of the eye. Ultraviolet light is classified as UVA, UVB, or UVC depending on the wavelength. These different wavelengths are also be used in the treatment of skin diseases (phototherapy) such as acne vulgaris and psoriasis.

SEE ALSO *Cancer, Radiation therapy, Skin cancer, Ultraviolet therapy, X-ray*

Radiation therapy

In this treatment, high energy rays are directed towards a specific area of the body (such as a cancerous tumor) in order to target damaged cancer cells. Applying localized radiation in this way minimizes damage to normal tissues.

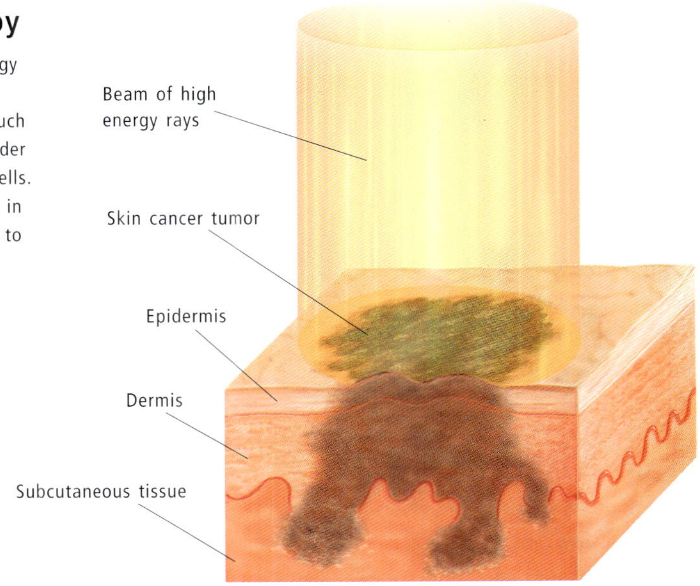

RADIATION SICKNESS

Accidental or intentional overexposure to ionizing radiation, either from x-rays or contact with radioactive substances can cause radiation sickness. Symptoms depend on the type of radiation, the length of exposure, the amount of radiation received and the parts of the body exposed.

Symptoms usually begin with fatigue, nausea, vomiting, diarrhea and burns. The victim may then suffer from the loss of hair and teeth, conjunctivitis, an unsteady gait, convulsions and open sores. In extreme cases, blood-forming tissue can be damaged, causing anemia and bleeding; inflammation of the stomach and intestinal lining (gastroenteritis) may also develop.

Radiation sickness affects the body's immune system, leaving the sufferer vulnerable to infection. It can cause miscarriage in pregnant women or result in damage to the fetus.

Exposure to low doses of radiation over an extended period may cause what is known as delayed radiation sickness. This is characterized by cataracts, a reduction in fertility, premature ageing and an increased risk of developing cancer or leukemia. It is also known as radiation poisoning or radiation syndrome.

SEE ALSO *Radiation, X-ray*

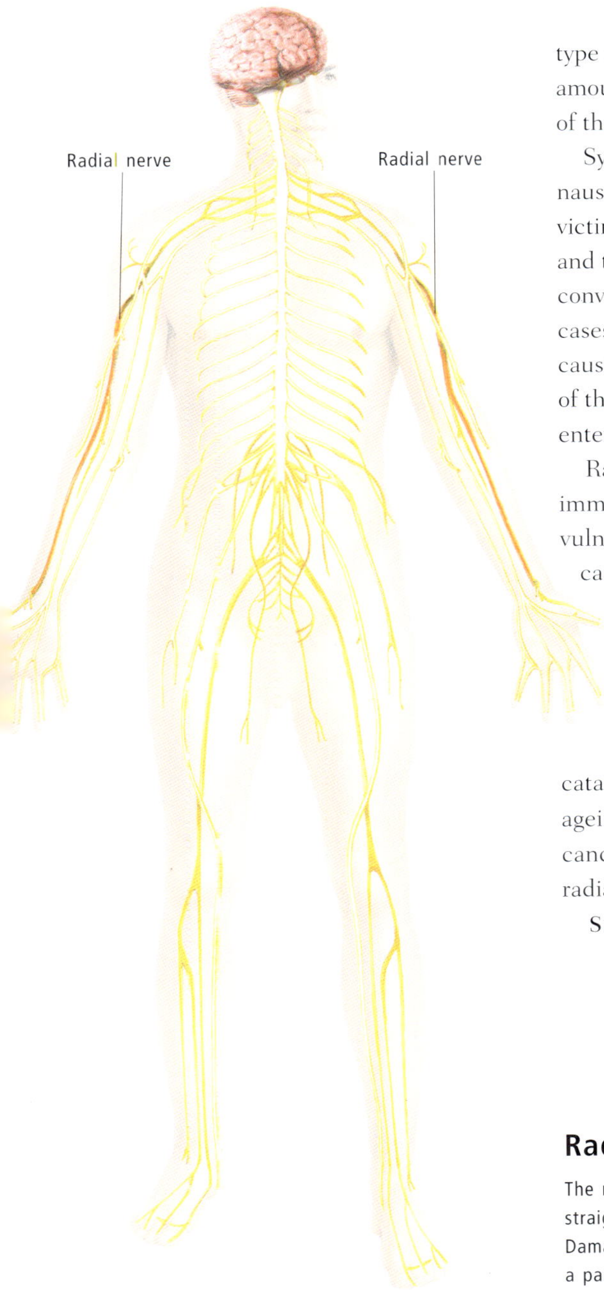

Radial nerve

The radial nerve controls the muscles that straighten the elbow and extend the wrist. Damage to this nerve can lead to wrist-drop, a paralysis of the extensor muscles of the hand.

RADIATION THERAPY

Radiation therapy (or radiotherapy) is the treatment of disorders using radiation. It is most widely used in the treatment of many different types of cancer. High-energy rays are used to damage cancer cells and stop them from growing and dividing. Like surgery, radiation therapy is a local treatment; it affects cancer cells only in the treated area. It may be used with other forms of treatment, like chemotherapy and surgery. Often it is used to shrink a tumor, which is then removed during surgery. It may also be used to provide temporary relief of symptoms, or to treat malignancies not accessible to surgery.

The machinery used is similar to x-ray equipment, but it contains a source of high-energy radiation, such as radium or a radioactive isotope of cobalt. Treatment is usually given on an outpatient basis in a hospital over several weeks. Patients are not radioactive during or after the treatment. Alternatively, the radiation can be administered via an implant, a small container of radioactive material placed directly into or near the tumor. Some patients receive both kinds of radiation therapy.

Radioimmunotherapy is a form of radiation therapy in which radioactive particles (radionuclides) are attached to antibodies. These antibodies are introduced into the body, travel to tumor cells, attach to them and kill them. The technique has the advantage of other types of radiation therapy in that normal (non-cancer) cells are unaffected.

R

The side effects depend on the treatment dose and the part of the body that is treated. Tiredness, skin reactions (such as a rash or redness) in the treated area, and loss of appetite are the most common side effects. Sometimes the production of white blood cells may be suppressed. The side effects of radiation therapy can usually be treated or controlled and are not permanent.

SEE ALSO *Cancer, Chemotherapy, Radiation, X-ray*

RADICULOPATHY

Radiculopathy is the name given to any disorder of the radicular nerves (spinal nerve roots). Spinal tumors and abscesses may cause radiculopathy, but by far the most common cause is a slipped or herniated intervertebral disk which compresses one or more of the roots; some people incorrectly take the term radiculopathy to refer to this condition alone.

In old age, the gelatinous material in the interior of the disk between the vertebra may degenerate. Under strain, such as when bending and lifting, it may herniate or rupture, becoming displaced from its normal position. In the process it tends to impinge on a nearby spinal nerve root, causing pain, numbness in the skin and weakness in the muscles supplied by that nerve root. Any part of the spine may be affected, but it is most common in the lumbar region, followed by the cervical region of the spine.

It occurs most often in the disk between the fifth lumbar vertebra and the sacrum, causing severe low back pain (which radiates to the buttocks, legs, and feet), tingling or numbness in legs or feet and, if severe, muscle weakness in the legs. The treatment is bed rest, analgesics and anti-inflammatory drugs, and physical therapy. If the condition persists, back surgery may be needed.

SEE ALSO *Disk, intervertebral, Sacrum, Spine, Vertebrae*

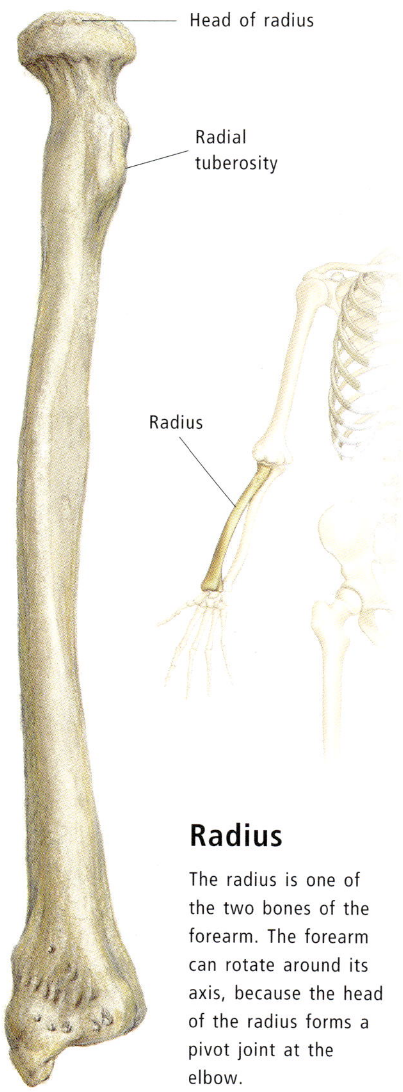

Radius

The radius is one of the two bones of the forearm. The forearm can rotate around its axis, because the head of the radius forms a pivot joint at the elbow.

RADIOLOGY

Radiology is a branch of medicine that uses various imaging techniques to generate pictures of the body that can detect a huge range of diseases and conditions. Originally, radiology involved the use of x-rays, a form of electromagnetic radiation that penetrates the body to form an image on film. Later, contrast materials such as barium were introduced to give a clearer picture of blood vessels and organs. In more recent years, other forms of diagnostic imaging have been utilized. These include: computerized axial tomography (CAT) scanning, which uses x-rays to give a three-dimensional view of the body; ultrasound, which uses sound waves; radioisotope scanning; nuclear magnetic resonance imaging (MRI); and positron emission tomography (PET) scanning.

SEE ALSO *CAT scan, Imaging techniques, Magnetic resonance imaging, Positron emission tomography, Ultrasound, X-ray*

RADIOISOTOPE SCAN

Also known as a nuclear scan, a radioisotope scan uses radioactive isotopes in the diagnosis of disorders of the bones, the heart, the lungs, thyroid gland and kidney. It can measure the size, shape, position and function of an organ, and can detect abnormalities such as cysts, abscesses, tumors or other diseases in these organs.

During the test, the radioactive isotope is introduced into the body in one of two ways: either it is swallowed and concentrated by the organ being examined, or it is introduced into the organ via a catheter that is inserted into a vein or artery and guided to that organ. A camera, which can detect the gamma rays emitted by the isotope, then takes an image of the organ, and a physician interprets this picture.

The patient is exposed to a small amount of radiation, but this is outweighed by the benefits of the scan; the dose is not considered dangerous. The test takes a few hours and usually takes place in a physician's office or hospital radiology clinic.

SEE ALSO *Imaging techniques, Radiation, X-ray*

RADIUS

The radius is one of the two bones of the forearm. Located on the thumb side, it lies parallel to and rotates around the other forearm bone, the ulna. Near the uppermost end of the radius, which forms part of the elbow, is a raised and roughened area called the radial tuberosity. This is an attachment point for the biceps brachii (commonly called the biceps), the long muscle of the upper arm. At its other, larger end, the radius forms part of the wrist. A fracture of the radius just above this joint, known as a Colles' fracture, forces the wrist into an unnatural upwards position.

SEE ALSO *Arm, Ulna, Wrist*

RASH

Rash is a general term used to describe the temporary occurrence of raised or differently colored spots or patches on the skin. Rashes have a variety of causes and will vary in appearance depending on how severely the person is affected. Detailed information on the various rashes illustrated on the page opposite will be found under the specific entries for the various conditions.

Rashes

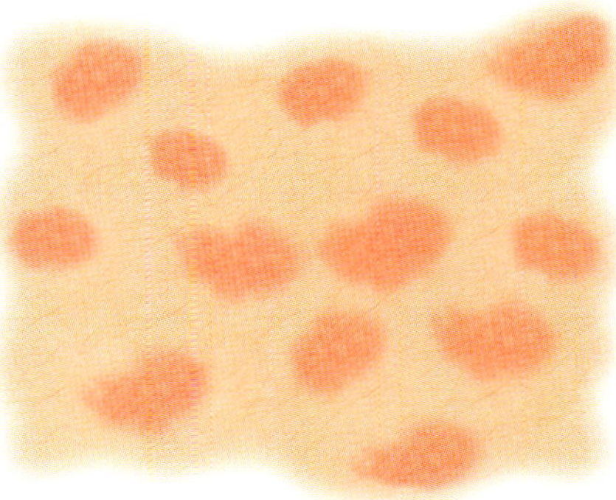

Measles
Small, white spots in the mouth, followed by reddish spots on the face and then the rest of body.

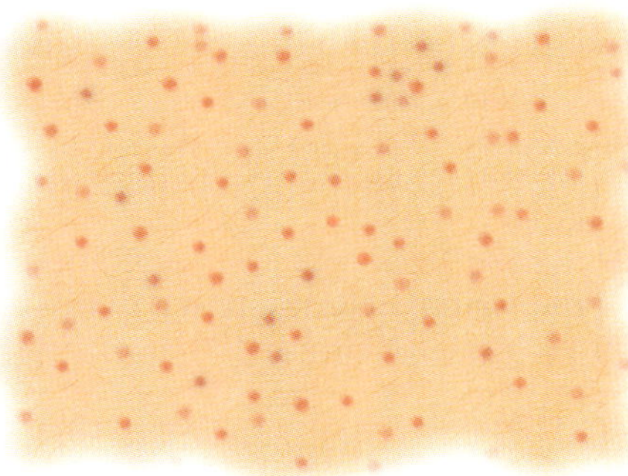

Rubella (German measles)
Like measles, but a fainter pink rash, spreading from the face to the rest of the body.

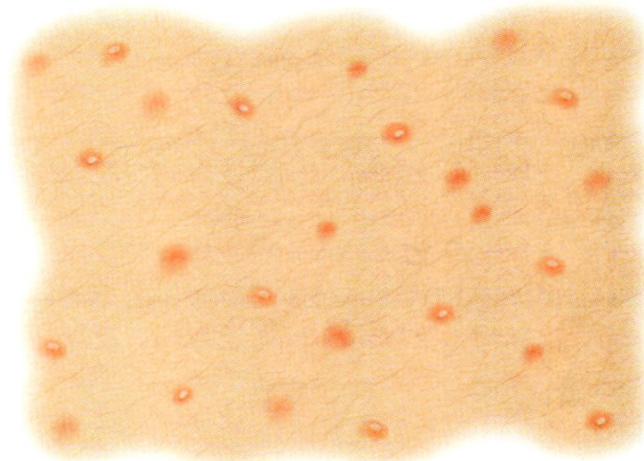

Chickenpox
Small itchy fluid-filled blisters appear on the chest and back, then spread to the rest of the body.

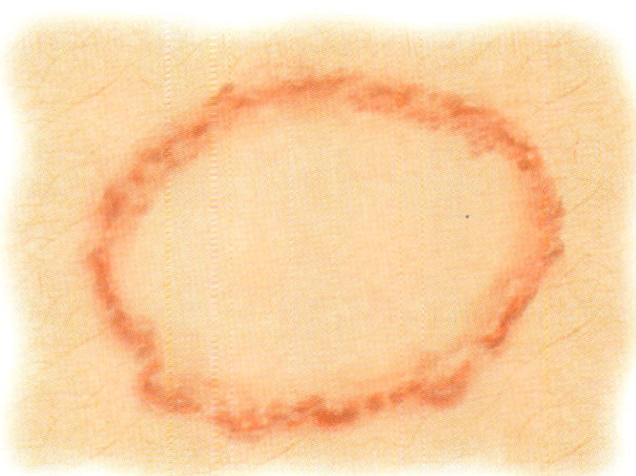

Ringworm
Reddish, ring-shaped patches of blisters or scales on the skin, caused by fungi.

Scabies
A rash of tiny red lumps around a wavy line caused by mites burrowing under the skin.

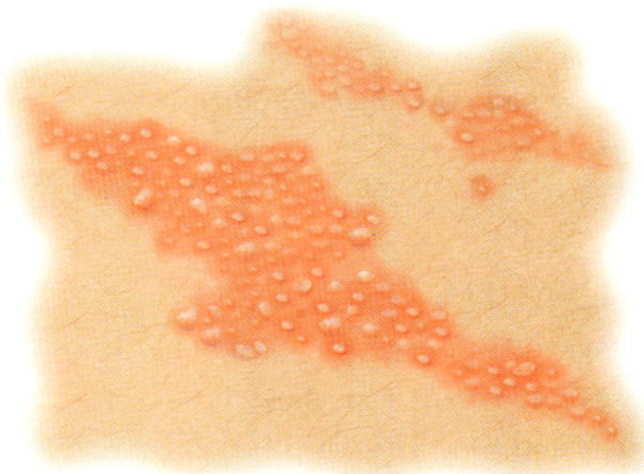

Shingles
Itchy blisters form on a part of the body, on one side, breaking down into a painful ulcerative rash.

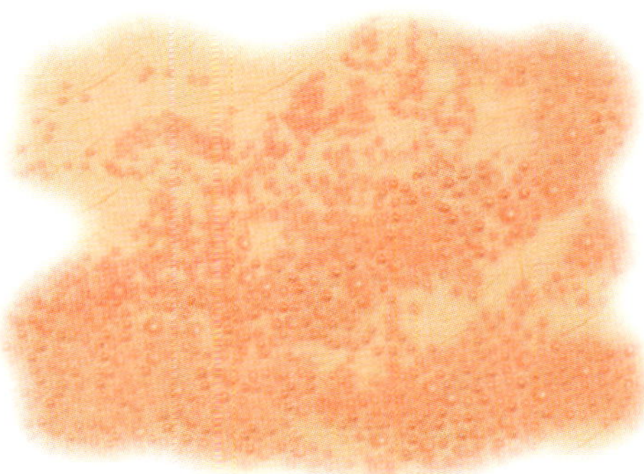

Atopic dermatitis
Itchy and dry inflammation of the skin, usually on the face, neck, arms and legs.

Seborrheic dermatitis
Itchy red scaly patches, usually seen on the scalp as dandruff, and on the face, forehead and chest.

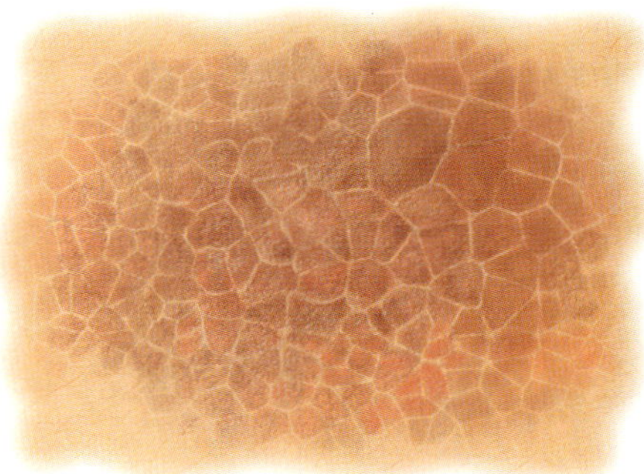

Ichthyosis
Inherited disorder resulting in skin that appears dry, rough, thick and scaly.

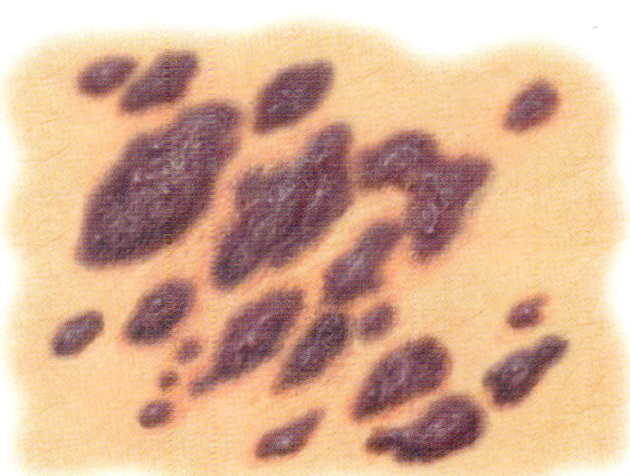

Lichen planus
Raised shiny pink or purple itchy spots, which may become scaly and spread to join together.

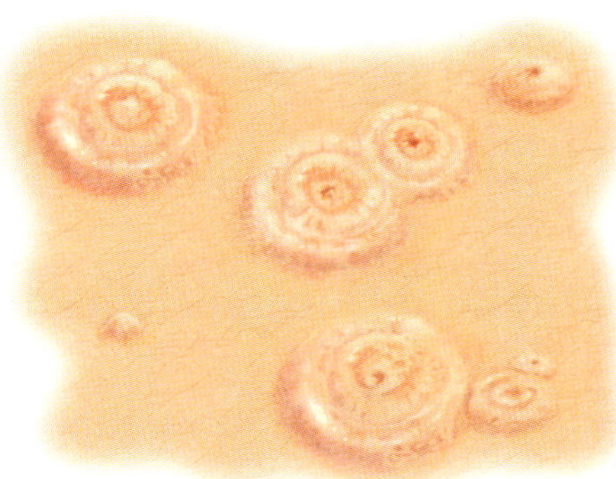

Erythema multiforme
Characterized by the reddening of the skin in circles around a central lesion.

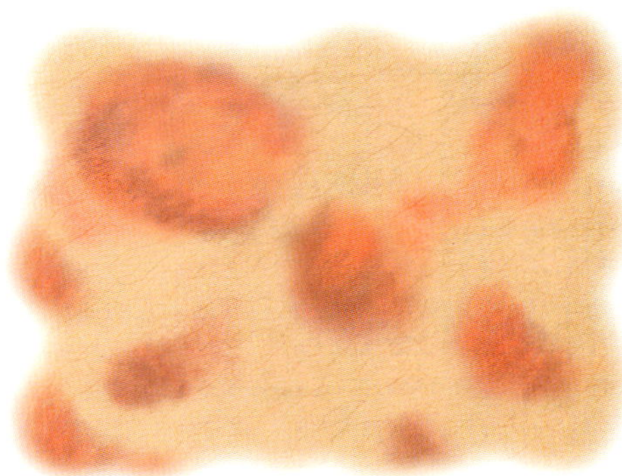

Erythema nodosum
Tender, red nodules which commonly appear on the shins; in time they become bruise-like patches.

RATBITE FEVER

Ratbite fever is a rare infectious disease carried by rats (and other rodents such as mice and squirrels), which is transmitted to humans via a bite, a scratch or the ingestion of food or water contaminated by the animal's feces. The infection may take the form of septicemia, with symptoms including rashes on the hands and feet, headaches, relapsing fever, weakness, muscular pain and arthritis. Alternatively, it may be marked by swollen lymph glands, muscular pain and an open sore on the bite mark. The disease is treated with antibiotics and can sometimes be fatal. Potential complications include pneumonia and heart problems.

SEE ALSO *Fever, Infectious diseases, Septicemia*

RAYNAUD'S DISEASE

In Raynaud's disease, the smaller blood vessels go into spasm, especially those of the fingers and toes. The digits become progressively cold and white, then blue, and then turn red as they warm up again. Attacks may last from a few minutes to several hours and are usually set off by cold or emotional upset. In severe cases, ulcers and gangrene of the fingers or toes may develop. The cause is usually unknown, though it may occur as a complication of other conditions such as connective tissue disease, vascular disease, or trauma.

Treatment involves giving up smoking if the sufferer is a smoker, and avoiding the trigger factors of cold and emotional stress. The extremities,especially the hands and feet, should be kept warm and covered in winter. Any underlying cause should be treated. Vasodilators (arterial muscle relaxants) and sympathectomy (surgical excision of the sympathetic nerves supplying the arteries) may be tried in severe cases.

The symptoms that are associated with Raynaud's disease are also known as Raynaud's phenomenon.

SEE ALSO *Blood vessels*

RECTUM

The rectum is the second last part of the digestive tract and leads into the last part, the anus. The rectum receives fecal material from the sigmoid colon and stores it for a short time until it is convenient to expel the stool. It also receives gas, which is passed as flatus. The upper rectum has a series of folds in its wall called the rectal valves. At the lower end of the rectum are longitudinally running folds called anal (or rectal) columns. The lower ends of these columns are joined together by anal valves to form the pectinate line. Immediately above each valve lies an anal sinus, into which open the anal glands. These glands may become sites of infection to form anorectal abscesses. Below the pectinate line is the anal canal, which leads to the external environment.

The exterior anus and rectum are common sites of disease and can be involved in hemorrhoids (dilated veins of the anorectal junction), cancer and inflammatory disease (proctitis). In rectal prolapse, the rectum may be turned inside out through the anal canal. This may occur as a congenital problem in babies or in adults whose pelvic muscles are weakened, injured or paralyzed.

SEE ALSO *Anus, Colon, Digestive system, Hemorrhoids, Proctitis, Prolapse*

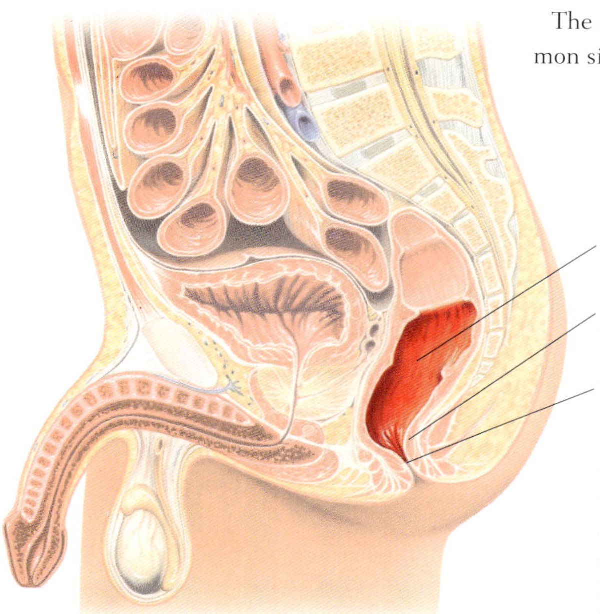

Rectum

The rectum and the anal canal measure 6–8 inches (15–20 centimeters). Rings of muscle called the anal sphincters keep the anus closed when fecal matter is not being expelled.

RED BLOOD CELLS

Red blood cells are the most numerous cells in the blood and their production rate by the bone marrow the highest in the body. They are highly specialized cells, devoted to the carriage of oxygen to the tissues and the removal of carbon dioxide. This allows the tissues to perform the metabolic processes required for the body to function.

Red cells are produced from early stem cells in the bone marrow, which multiply rapidly. The more mature red cells accumulate a red pigment, hemoglobin, which has special properties that ensure the efficient binding and release of oxygen. The fully mature red cell extrudes its nucleus and appears in the circulation full of hemoglobin. Its shape is that of a biconcave disk, which allows it to deform and squeeze through narrow spaces, such as in the small capillaries. Red cells are stored in the spleen which discharges them as needed. In emergencies, such as hemorrhage, some of the stored cells are released. After an average lifespan of 120 days the ageing red cell loses its ability to change shape and is destroyed in the spleen.

The number of red blood cells normally remains fairly stable, despite their constant production and destruction. The normal red cell count ranges between 4,000,000 and 6,000,000 per cubic millimeter, with the amount of hemoglobin in blood ranging between 14 and 18 grams per 100 milliliters in normal adults.

A deficiency of red cells results in anemia. There are many causes of anemia, which may result from diseases of the bone marrow, vitamin or mineral deficiencies affecting red cell production, diseases causing increased breakdown of red cells, or simple bleeding.

Red blood cells

Red blood cells

The flat, plate-like shape of red blood cells enables them to bend and squeeze through small capillaries and also to stack together for ease of blood flow.

Cell content

Red blood cells contain hemoglobin, which carries oxygen to the tissues of the body. Hemoglobin contains the protein heme—a pigment that gives blood its color—and iron ions which bind with oxygen molecules.

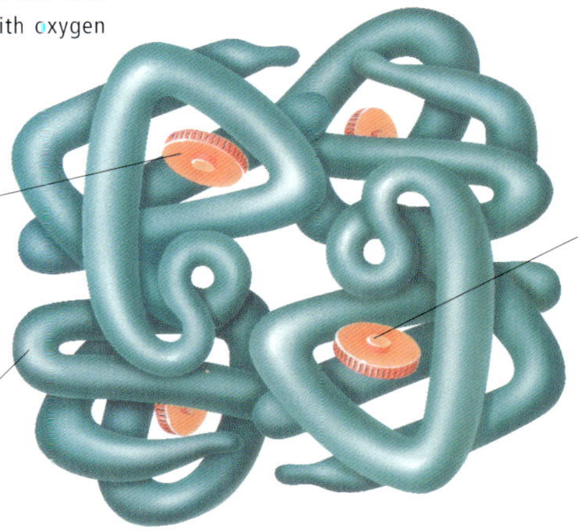

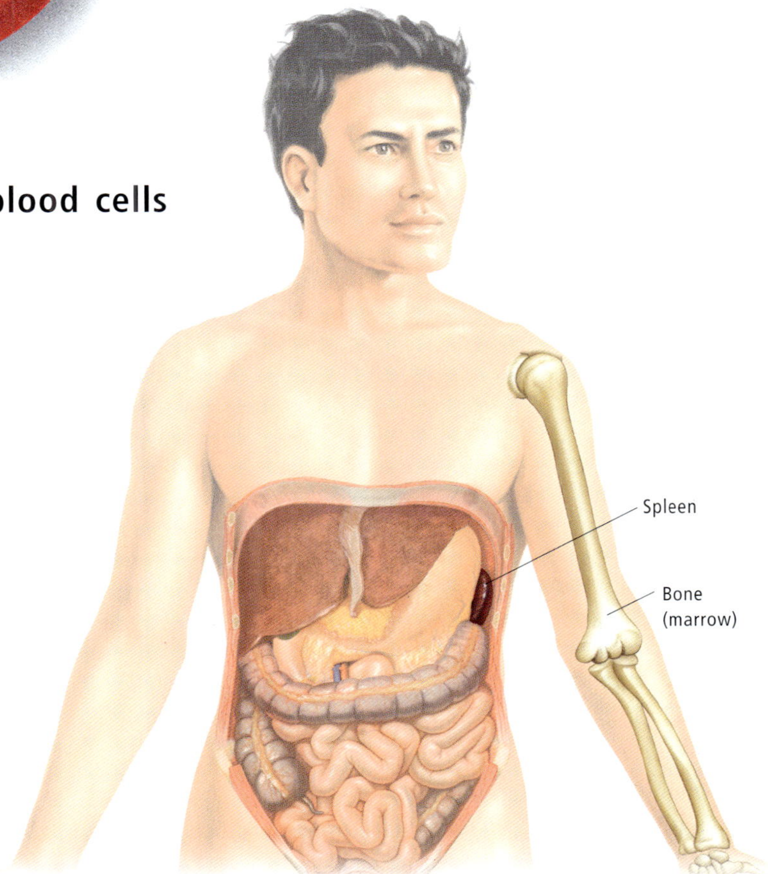

Red blood cell production

Red cells are formed in the bone marrow and pass into the body's circulatory system. The spleen filters out any old and damaged red blood cells and stores healthy cells until they are needed.

The most common cause of anemia is iron deficiency. Iron is a central part of the hemoglobin molecule, responsible for the binding of oxygen. It is obtained from the diet, red meat being especially rich in iron. Iron deficiencies in developing countries are mainly due to a combination of poor diet and chronic blood loss from hookworm infection. In industrialized countries, iron deficiency may result from heavy periods in menstruating women, or from chronic gastrointestinal bleeding.

Another cause of anemia is decreased production of the globin molecules which make up hemoglobin. This form of anemia is known as thalassemia, of which the major forms are alpha- and beta-thalassemia, corresponding to the globin chain affected. Thalassemia is an inherited disorder that involves mutations in the globin chain genes. It is most prevalent in the Mediterranean and Southeast Asia. The minor forms of this condition do not result in physical symptoms but the major forms of thalassemia can cause severe anemia and even the death of a fetus.

Sickle cell disease is another inherited abnormality of the globin gene, which results in abnormal sickle-shaped red cells. As well as causing anemia, sickle cell disease can result in the blockage of small blood vessels, causing severe, painful secondary conditions.

An increase in the rate of breakdown of red cells occurs in various conditions and is termed hemolytic anemia. Released hemoglobin is converted in the liver to bilirubin; a more rapid rate of red cell destruction can result in abnormally high levels of bilirubin. This may result in yellow coloration of the skin and eyes, called hemolytic jaundice. Increased breakdown of red cells in the spleen results in enlargement of the spleen.

The most common cause of hemolytic anemia worldwide is malaria, caused by a group of parasites which infect red blood cells and destroy them. The malaria parasites breed in certain mosquitoes and are transmitted to humans by the bite of the mosquito. The occurrence of malaria throughout the equatorial parts of the world is due to the presence of these mosquitoes. It is thought that thalassemia and sickle cell disease may have evolved as adaptations to malaria in those regions, since they make the red cell relatively resistant to infection by the parasite.

SEE ALSO *Anemia, Blood, Hemoglobin, Hemolytic anemia, Iron, Malaria, Sickle cell disease, Thalassemia*

R

Reflexes

Reflexes are quick and automatic responses to stimuli, whereby a nerve impulse travels to a nerve center in the spinal cord. The nerve center then sends a message outward to a muscle or gland to effect a response without the person being consciously aware of it.

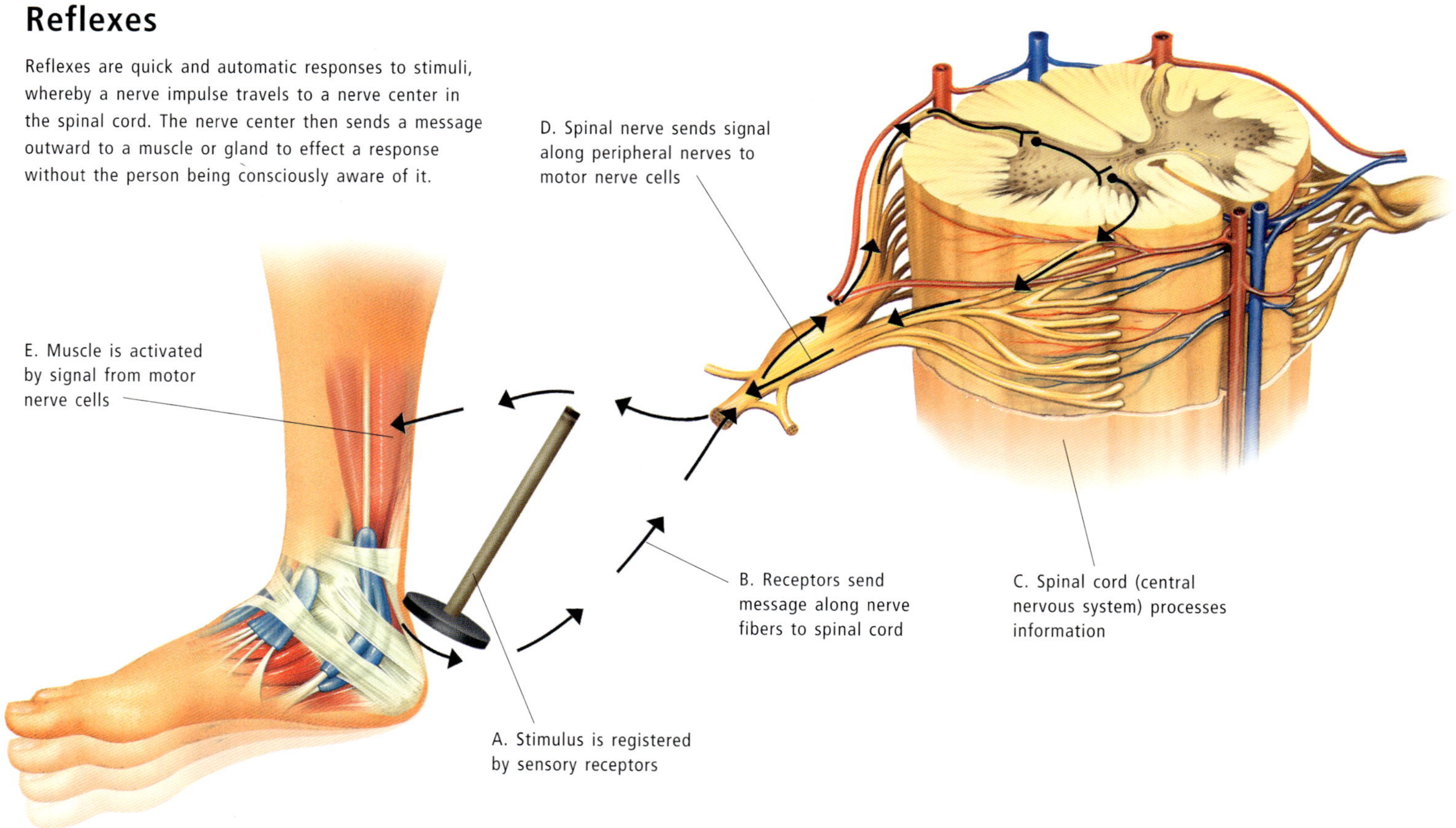

REFLEXES

A reflex is an involuntary immediate movement or other response to an appropriate stimulus, which occurs unconsciously (without being willed). If you touch a sharp spike or a hot surface you will pull your hand away in a reflex action. There are many everyday reflexes that we take for granted.

When a bright light is shone into a person's eyes the pupils will contract; a blink is a reflex action that protects the eye; a cough or a sneeze protects the lungs and the respiratory system, and there are many other reflexes. Four things happen when a reflex acts—reception, conduction, transmission and response—and all of these involve the nervous system.

The well-known knee-jerk or patellar reflex is the sudden kicking out of the lower leg when the patellar tendon, just below the knee, is tapped sharply. This reflex is used to test for damage to the central nervous system and the peripheral nerves and in recognizing thyroid disease. Many other reflexes can also be tested to evaluate the nervous system.

The concept of the conditioned reflex is attributed to the Russian physiologist Ivan Pavlov, who won the Nobel Prize in 1904 for his work. After noting that a hungry dog salivated at the sight of food, he rang a bell when the food appeared. After some time the dog would salivate at the sound of the bell when no food was present—thus the "conditioned" reflex.

There are three groups of reflexes found in a newborn. The first group, which are vital for survival, include the rooting reflex—when a baby's cheek is gently stroked it will turn its head and open its mouth on that side; the sucking reflex, which is triggered by pressure on the upper palate of the baby's mouth; the swallowing reflex; the gagging reflex, which is triggered if the baby swallows too much fluid; and the labyrinthine reflex, which makes the baby raise its head when lying on the stomach. Newborns also have protective reflexes. For example, if a cloth is held over a baby's face the baby will brush the cloth away. Medication during labor, brain damage and prematurity can affect these survival reflexes and these will be tested if there is any doubt about the newborn's state of health.

The second group of reflexes are found in the newborn. The stepping reflex, activated when a baby's foot touches the ground, is usually gone by the time a baby is two months old. The crawling reflex is displayed when a newborn is placed in a face-down position. The Babinski reflex comes into play when the sole of the foot is stroked from heel to toe, resulting in the toes curling up and the foot turning in. It will generally last until the baby is around 2 years old. In older age groups, the Babinski reflex may also be used as a diagnostic tool to determine disorders of the central nervous system.

The third group of reflexes are behavior patterns that no longer appear to serve a function. These include the grasp reflex, which can also be found in the baby's foot; the Moro or startle reflex, which is used by doctors to test muscle tone; and the galant reflex, which is tested by gently stroking a finger along one side of the baby's back while the baby is being held under the stomach. The baby's body will bend like a bow, pulling the pelvis towards the side stroked. It indicates the development of the spinal nerves and will last until the baby is about 9 months old.

SEE ALSO *Nervous system, Newborn*

REFLEXOLOGY

Modern reflexology, also known as reflex zone therapy, was developed by American ear, nose and throat specialist Dr William Fitzgerald in the early twentieth century. In a system known as zone therapy he divided the body into 10 vertical zones through which he believed vital energy flowed. He found when he applied pressure to a point in the hand or foot of one zone that an analgesic response occurred in other body parts that lay within that same zone.

Fitzgerald's work was developed further by Eunice Ingham, an American masseur, who devised the Ingham reflex method of compression massage, in which points on the feet are massaged, using an alternating pressure, with the aim of stimulating the related organ or body system (for example, massaging the toes helps to clear the sinuses).

Reflexology massage aims to stimulate nerve endings and energy flow while also breaking up lactic acid, uric acid and calcium crystals accumulated beneath the skin's surface. A particularly tender point on the foot is believed to be an indication that the related organ is in some kind of difficulty. Reflexologists believe that their system increases the body's overall state of relaxation and helps improve circulation; it may also be used in the treatment of minor pain and stress-related disorders.

REHABILITATION

Rehabilitation is a branch of medicine concerned with helping people recover as fully as possible from a physical disability, and then helping them to live with physical challenges that do remain. It is integral to the treatment of many conditions, including stroke, neurological conditions, accidents, heart attacks, and drug and alcohol dependence.

Successful rehabilitation involves health professionals from a number of disciplines: family physicians, social workers, physical therapists, occupational therapists, rehabilitation nurses, speech pathologists, psychologists and vocational counselors.

Physical therapies include exercise, heat and ultrasound, massage, diathermy (the use of high-frequency electrical current) and hydrotherapy. Physical therapy also involves teaching the use of such aids as braces, artificial limbs and wheelchairs.

Occupational therapy involves activities to increase independent function and prevent disability. The therapist may help adapt the home or work environment to maintain function and independence as much as possible. The occupational therapy departments of many hospitals have facilities in which the patient may be trained to use tools for trades and light industrial work, or for clerical duties.

Speech therapists treat speech disorders caused by physical malformations, diseases, injuries, or psychological disorders, and work with the patient to develop or improve communication skills: speaking, reading, and writing techniques.

In some disorders, rehabilitation is an essential part of the treatment, without which recovery cannot hope to take place. For example, rehabilitation is a necessary part of recovery from disorders of the musculoskeletal system, such as back pain, whiplash, tennis elbow, on-the-job or sports injuries, and fractures. Rehabilitation should start immediately after the initial treatment. Programs with a multidisciplinary approach using physical therapy together with physical and mental training yield the best results. If the injury is not serious, the individual may be encouraged to participate in an alternative sport to maintain overall conditioning.

Patients with spinal cord injuries may never fully recover, but rehabilitation will allow them to adapt physically and psychologically to their disability. Passive exercises for paralyzed muscles will help prevent contractures. Physical therapy will prevent joint stiffness. Occupational therapy and psychotherapy or counseling may help depression or sexual problems.

Children with spina bifida and cerebral palsy learn to take care of themselves and their bodily needs; many are able to attend school and achieve vocational goals with the use of crutches and wheelchairs.

In stroke victims, rehabilitation therapy is crucial; the goal is to teach the patient to make the best use of remaining skills and to compensate for those lost. Further strokes can sometimes be prevented and there will be recovery as other areas of the brain take over functioning for the damaged areas. Patients with stroke may learn to walk and perform daily activities using mainly their remaining abilities. Speech therapy, occupational therapy, physical therapy and other interventions may be used.

Many medical centers now offer cardiac rehabilitation programs for heart attack survivors and people who have undergone heart surgery. These programs help patients make the necessary changes in their daily

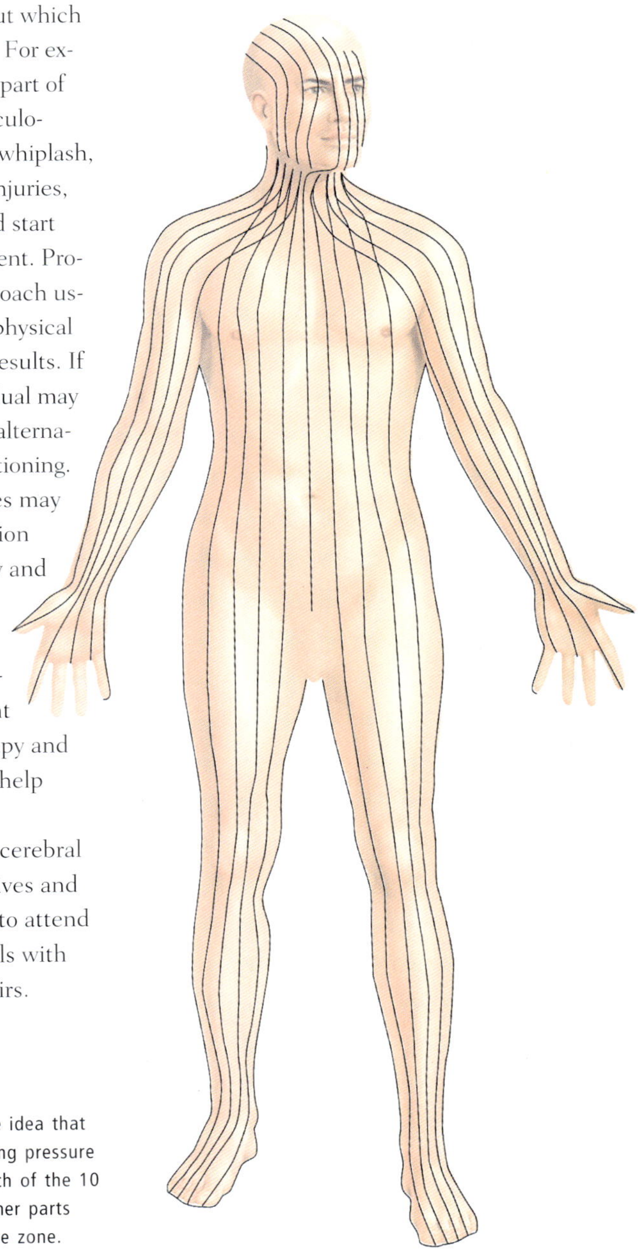

Reflexology

Reflexology is based on the idea that massaging or simply applying pressure to certain points within each of the 10 energy zones stimulates other parts of the body within the same zone.

Rehabilitation

Rehabilitation aims to help those who are sick or injured to regain physical and psychological strength in order to return to their normal lives, or to deal with any permanent disabilities. Rehabilitation may include education about healthy eating for a heart attack victim, teaching a paraplegic how to be independent, or physical therapy for someone recovering from a hip replacement operation.

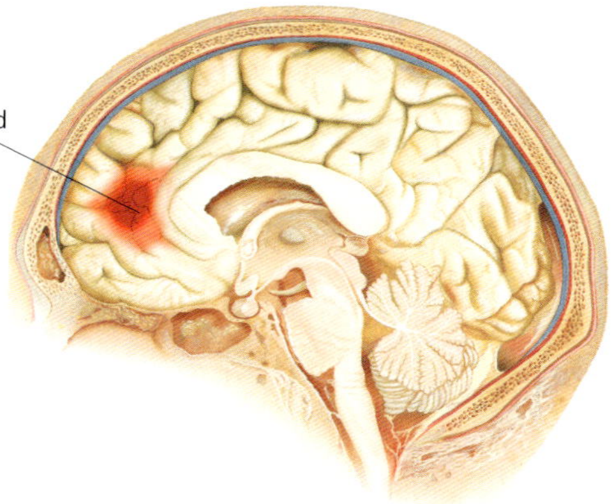

Stroke

Rehabilitation allows stroke patients to make the best use of their remaining skills and to compensate for those lost. It may include physical therapy, occupational therapy, speech therapy and psychotherapy.

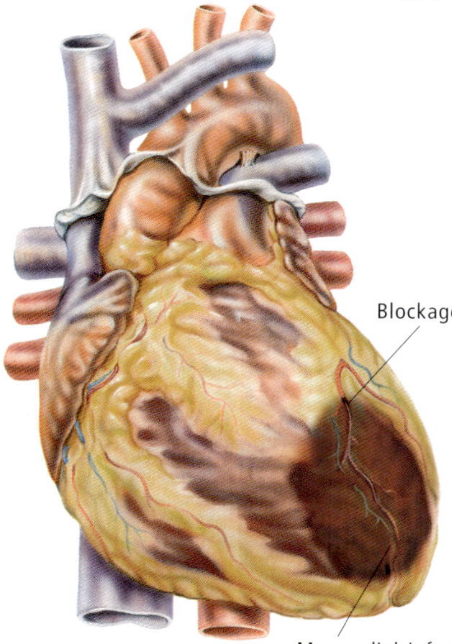

Heart attack

Rehabilitation is an important part of treatment after a myocardial infarction (heart attack). It usually includes exercise, the modification of diet to eliminate fat, cholesterol and salt, and the cessation of smoking.

Whiplash

Physical therapy, such as exercise, heat and electrical current therapy, plays an important role in the treatment of soft tissue injuries such as whiplash, although many resolve naturally over time.

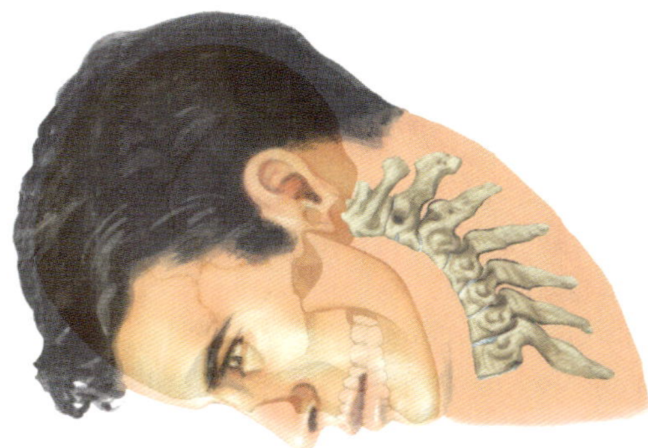

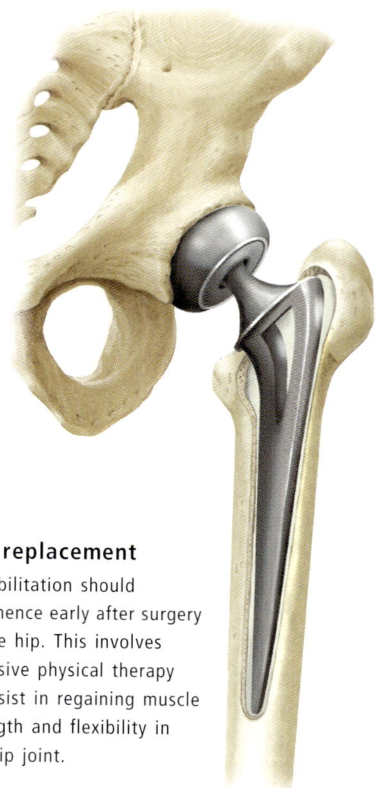

Hip replacement

Rehabilitation should commence early after surgery to the hip. This involves intensive physical therapy to assist in regaining muscle strength and flexibility in the hip joint.

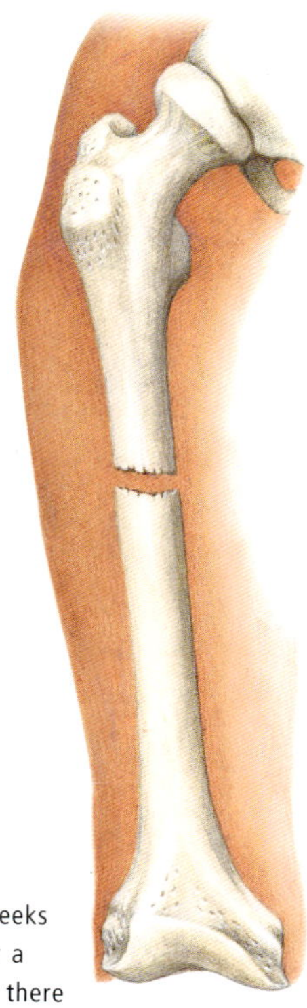

Fracture

Over the 6–8 weeks that it takes for a fracture to heal there is a danger that muscles will atrophy and joints will stiffen, especially if the joint is immobilized. Once the bone has healed, exercises to strengthen muscles and maintain joint movements should begin as soon as possible.

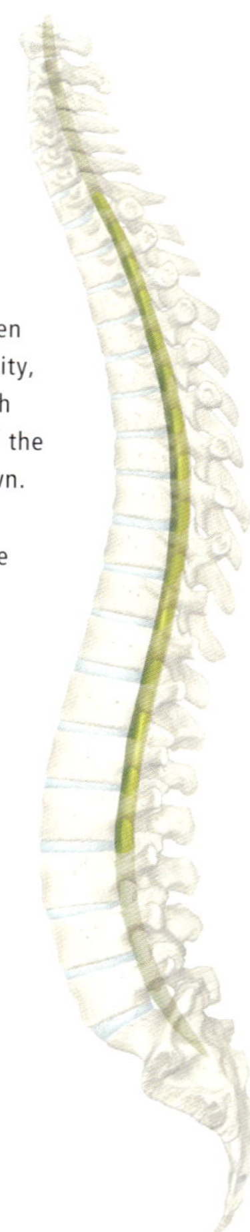

Paralysis

Injuries to the spine often result in physical disability, such as paraplegia which may involve paralysis of the body from the arms down. The degree of physical disability depends on the part of the spine that is damaged. Long-term rehabilitation is necessary and usually involves a team of professionals including a physical therapist, an occupational therapist, a rehabilitation engineer and a psychological counselor.

lives and improve recovery. Rehabilitation begins in the hospital and can continue for weeks to months after returning home. Most programs offer group therapy. Cardiac rehabilitation improves the quality of life and extends the life expectancy of heart patients, but lifelong follow-up is usually necessary.

SEE ALSO *Alcoholism, Drug dependence, Paraplegia, Quadriplegia, Spinal cord, Sports medicine, Stroke*

REIKI

The word *reiki* means "universal life force". It describes a form of healing founded early in the twentieth century by Dr Mikao Usui, a Japanese Christian minister, from his studies of an ancient Tibetan healing technique. Reiki practitioners are taught through a series of initiations by Reiki masters to draw in *ki,* or life force, and to redirect it to the patient through their hands. A higher power is believed to direct the life force to wherever it is needed in the patient's body to remove blockages to the energy flow and to rebalance it. Reiki practitioners claim that their treatment relaxes and energizes the patient, without promising specific cures.

REITER'S SYNDROME

Reiter's syndrome is a potentially chronic disease marked by arthritis, conjunctivitis and urethritis (inflammation of the urethra), along with lesions of the skin and mucous membranes. The exact cause is not known, although it is thought that certain people are genetically predisposed. The syndrome often occurs after severe diarrhea or a sexually transmitted infection, such as chlamydia. It is most common in men under the age of 40. Arthritic symptoms tend to dominate and may recur over several years. The infection is treated with antibiotics, anti-inflammatory medications and pain relievers.

SEE ALSO *Arthritis, Chlamydia, Conjunctivitis, Urethritis*

RELAPSING FEVER

Relapsing fever, also known as recurrent fever or tick fever, is a bacterial infection transmitted by ticks and lice that causes repeated bouts of fever. Symptoms include vomiting, headache, chest pain, muscle aches and rapid heartbeat, which set in after an incubation period of about 7 days. These may be accompanied by a rash, nosebleeds, and blood in the urine and vomit. After about a week the fever passes, causing blood pressure and body temperature to drop, accompanied by excessive sweating and extreme weakness. Symptoms recur within a week and keep recurring in a progressively milder form until immunity is built up.

The disease often has severe effects on the central nervous system of children, causing seizures and neuritis. It may also cause inflammation of the heart muscle and liver.

The bacteria that causes relapsing fever are usually carried by the *Ornithodorus* tick, which is common in the western USA. The disease is also found in West Africa and tropical regions of the world. Preventive measures include avoiding wooded areas where ticks live, covering exposed skin and using insect repellent. Antibiotics will cure most cases of relapsing fever, although the condition can sometimes be fatal.

SEE ALSO *Fever, Lice, Ticks*

RELATIONSHIP COUNSELING

At some time almost anyone in a relationship may find they need assistance to help deal with problems; to learn how to improve a relationship or even how to form one; to cope with a relationship which is in crisis or to change a relationship when there is violence involved. Everyone in a relationship experiences problems. It is the people who know how to deal with these problems and meet the challenges who have successful relationships.

It can often strengthen a relationship to talk about it. Relationship counselors, formerly called marriage guidance counselors in many places, are trained to help people sort out problems, to learn to understand and accept the differences in people and to handle conflict.

SEE ALSO *Counseling*

RELAXATION TECHNIQUES

Modern research has shown that learning how to consciously relax can have a powerful healing effect on body and mind. When a person relaxes in this way, heart and respiratory rates slow, blood pressure drops, muscle tension decreases, blood flow to skin and internal organs increases and brain wave patterns alter, leading to mental and emotional peace. The body's nervous, endocrine and immune systems, which all feel the direct impact of stress, are rested. It has been found that even a short period of relaxation can increase mental clarity, emotional stability and physical energy.

Relaxation techniques are highly valued and well developed in many ancient Eastern spiritual and healing traditions, where deep

Reiter's syndrome

Arthritis (such as in the sacroiliac joint) is the most obvious symptom of Reiter's syndrome; it is accompanied by conjunctivitis, urethritis and lesions. Young men are most commonly affected.

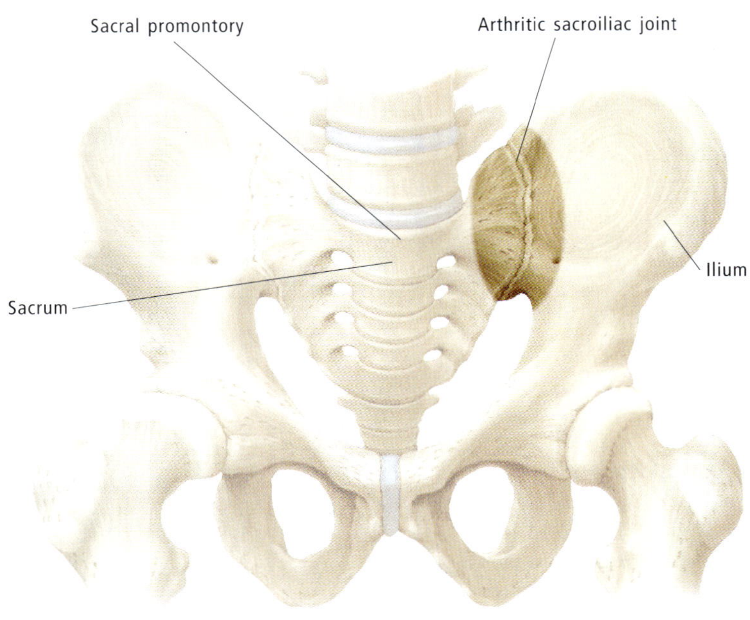

states of relaxation are achieved through a variety of practices including meditation, yoga, t'ai chi, shiatsu and acupuncture. In the West, relaxation therapies developed during the twentieth century often incorporated the more accessible of the Eastern techniques.

In his book *The Relaxation Response*, Herbert Benson, an American physician, identified four basic components he found common to a range of traditional and modern relaxation techniques—quiet environment; a mental device, such as a repeated word, sound or phrase, to help avoid distracting thoughts; a passive attitude, which disengages from distracting thoughts as they arise; and a physically comfortable position.

In the 1920s Dr Johannes Schultz, a German neuropsychologist, developed a relaxation therapy known as autogenic training, sometimes also called Western meditation. This technique resulted from his quest to find an alternative to hypnotism which would equal its results. It has elements in common with meditation and yoga as well as with self-hypnosis.

Autogenic training uses a sequence of six standard exercises that involve focusing the mind on the body while silently repeating a series of statements to oneself (for example, "my right arm is heavy"). This form of relaxation consists of becoming progressively aware of sensations of heaviness in different parts the body, such as arms, legs, neck; feelings of warmth in the limbs; the calmness and regularity of the heartbeat; the calmness and regularity of breathing; feelings of warmth in the abdomen; and a coolness in the forehead.

Response to relaxation

Relaxation techniques such as meditation and massage may help to reduce tension, anxiety, stress and chronic pain. When a person relaxes, heart and respiratory rates slow, blood pressure drops, muscle tension decreases, and blood flow to the skin and organs increases. Much of this effect is coordinated by the parasympathetic nervous system, the part of the autonomic nervous system that promotes physiological relaxation.

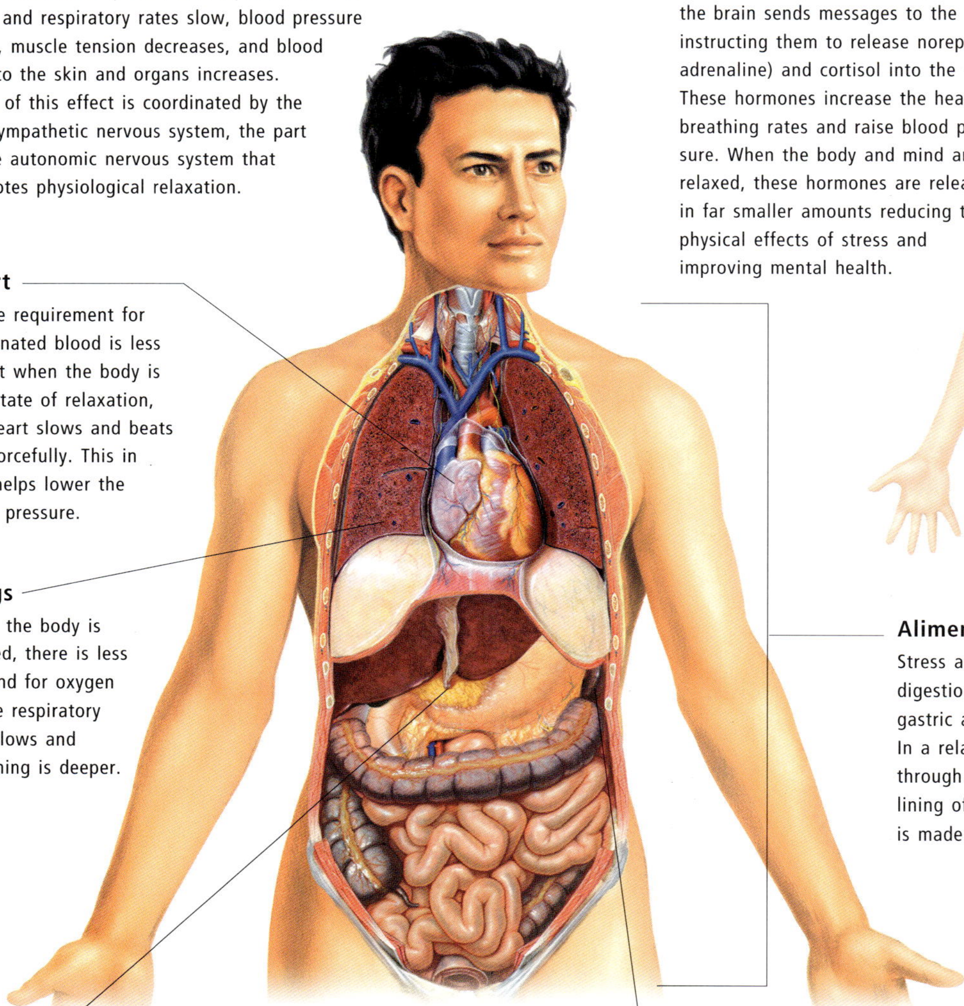

Heart

As the requirement for oxygenated blood is less urgent when the body is in a state of relaxation, the heart slows and beats less forcefully. This in turn helps lower the blood pressure.

Lungs

When the body is relaxed, there is less demand for oxygen so the respiratory rate slows and breathing is deeper.

Blood glucose

Less glucose is needed in the bloodstream when the body is relaxed. Hence, the pancreas secretes more insulin and the liver releases less glucose than normal, both of which act to lower glucose levels in the blood.

Relaxing the brain

Stress affects the body's endocrine system, which produces the hormones that control many body functions. Under stress, the pituitary gland in the brain sends messages to the adrenal glands instructing them to release norepinephrine (noradrenaline) and cortisol into the bloodstream. These hormones increase the heart and breathing rates and raise blood pressure. When the body and mind are relaxed, these hormones are released in far smaller amounts reducing the physical effects of stress and improving mental health.

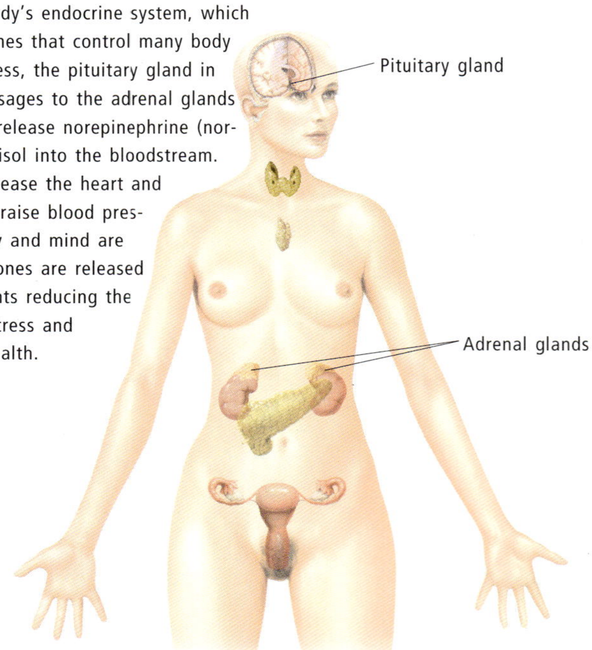

Alimentary tract

Stress and anxiety can interfere with digestion and increase the production of gastric acid, which may cause stomach pain. In a relaxed state, food moves more slowly through the bowel. Blood flow through the lining of the bowel increases, and digestion is made more efficient.

Immunity

Stress leads to higher circulating levels of the hormone cortisol, which compromises the immune system. When the body is relaxed, the immune system functions more efficiently increasing the body's ability to fight off infection.

Relaxation

NB: In the main illustration the top two-thirds of the lungs and pleura have been peeled away to show the heart.

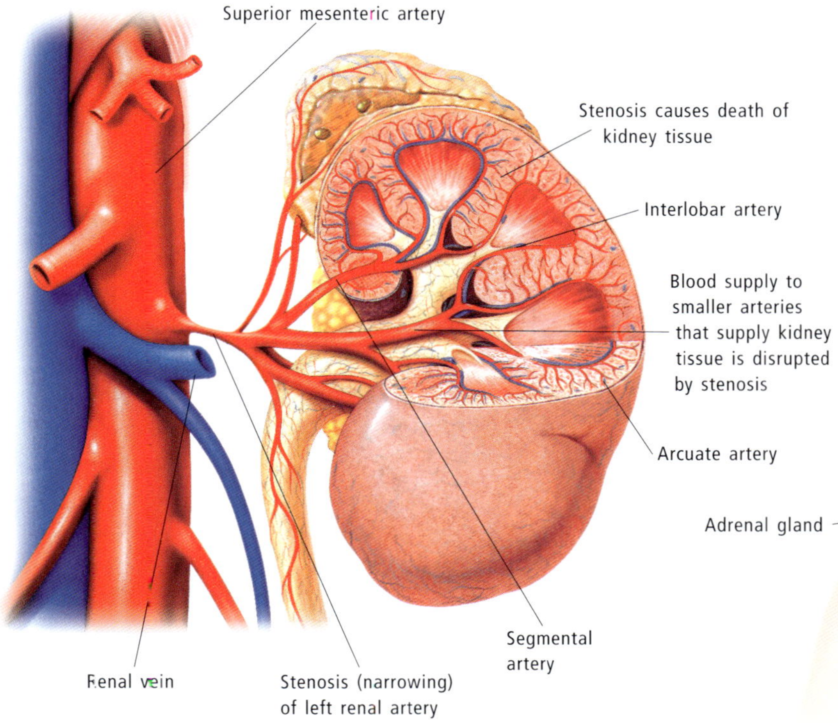

Renal artery

There are two renal arteries, supplying blood and oxygen to the kidneys. Branches of the renal artery supply the adrenal gland and ureter. In people suffering from stenosis, the arteries have narrowed, restricting blood flow. If the blood supply is completely disrupted, death of kidney tissue will occur and the kidneys will cease to function.

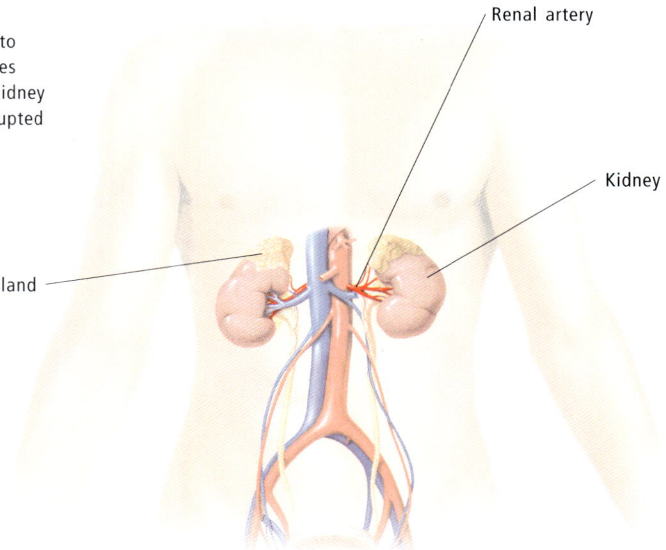

Autogenic training is usually taught by trained practitioners in weekly sessions. It is recommended that it be practised three times a day after eating. This form of relaxation is useful for those wishing to reduce or stop tranquilizer medication as well as for all stress-related disorders. It may be also be helpful in the management of chronic pain.

The technique of focusing on breathing to induce a state of relaxation is well known from meditation and yoga practice. Breathing exercises which encourage deep rhythmic breathing are known as diaphragmatic breathing. In this type of breathing an individual focuses on the rib muscles and their role in expanding the diaphragm while breathing deeply and slowly. This helps avoid the panting or shallow breathing from the upper chest which accompanies states of tension or anxiety.

SEE ALSO *Meditation, Stress, T'ai chi ch'uan, Yoga*

REMISSION

Remission is the disappearance or reduction of symptoms during the course of an illness. When this happens, the illness is said to be "in remission". This condition may be permanent or temporary, sometimes lasting for years before symptoms recur.

RENAL ARTERY

The renal arteries are two large blood vessels that branch off either side of the abdominal aorta to supply the two kidneys. They pass through the hilum, or entrance, of the kidney, where each artery gives off small branches to the adrenal gland and ureter and then divides into two large branches, which are called the anterior and posterior divisions of the artery.

Each branch divides into smaller and smaller branches, eventually forming the capillaries which supply oxygen to the kidney tissue and take part in kidney filtration via their role in the nephrons.

The renal arteries can be affected by arteriosclerosis, which may cause clots (thrombi), or a narrowing (stenosis). Blockage of the arteries can disrupt the blood supply to the kidneys, causing death of kidney tissue and loss of function. Treatment is by angioplasty (for example balloon angioplasty) or bypass surgery.

Less commonly, arteriosclerosis may cause an aneurysm in the artery, which may rupture, causing abdominal pain and sometimes death. Treatment is by surgical repair of the aneurysm.

Renal angiography is a radiological test designed to show abnormalities in the structure and function of the renal arteries and the kidneys. It is routinely undertaken prior to angioplasty or other renal artery surgery. Under local anesthesia, a catheter is inserted through an artery in an arm or a leg, passed through the aorta and into the renal artery. A dye which is opaque to x-rays is injected via the catheter, and as the dye passes through the renal artery and its divisions, a series of x-rays is taken. Any blockages or clots are highlighted by the dye.

SEE ALSO *Aneurysm, Angiography, Angioplasty, Arteries, Arteriosclerosis, Kidney*

RESTLESS LEGS SYNDROME

This is a neurological disorder marked by unpleasant sensations in the lower legs which compel the sufferer to move their legs, sometimes involuntarily. The exact cause is not known but conditions such as iron-deficiency anemia, arthritis and pregnancy may play a part. There is no specific treatment but treatment of any suspected underlying cause may alleviate discomfort.

SEE ALSO *Legs, Nerves*

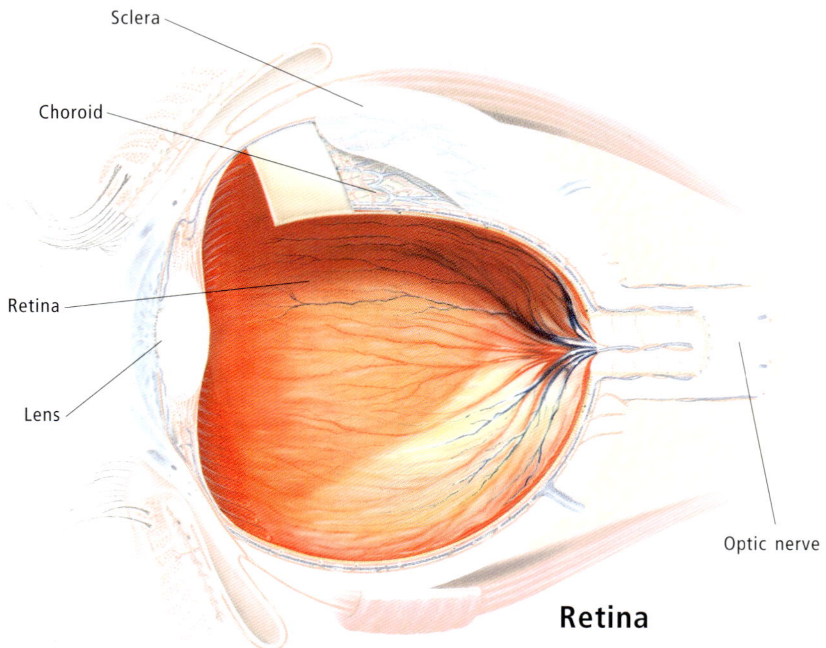

Retina

The retina is a light-sensitive layer at the back of the eye. It transforms the image formed by the lens into nerve impulses which are sent to the brain via the optic nerve. Detachment of the retina from the choroid, either by disease or injury, can lead to blindness.

RETINA

The retina is a light-sensitive layer at the back of the eye; it has photoreceptors that send visual information to the brain via the optic nerve. Light reaches the retina after passing through the cornea into the pupil, then through the optic lens and vitreous humor. The retina contains light-sensitive cells called rods and cones, which specialize in perceiving light intensity and color vision.

Disorders of the retina

The retina draws a rich blood supply from a vascular layer called the choroid. A hole or tear in the retina may lead to partial or total detachment from the choroid. Vision in the eye may be lost completely if the retina cannot be reattached. The hole may be caused by natural degeneration of the retina, disease or a blow to the eye. Symptoms include specks in the field of vision, flashes of light, blind spots and blurred vision. Laser surgery may be used to close the hole.

Retinoblastoma is a potentially fatal malignant tumor on the retina, usually found in children under the age of five. It may strike one or both eyes, giving the pupil a whitish glow and leading to impaired vision, pain and inflammation. Removal of the eye may be necessary in severe cases, though the disease may still return in the other eye. Other treatment options include laser surgery, and a combination of radiation therapy and chemotherapy.

Retinopathy is a non-inflammatory disease of the retina which manifests in a number of ways. Retinopathy of prematurity affects premature infants, causing extreme vision impairment or blindness due to rapid tissue production and retinal detachment. The exact cause is unknown and symptoms include white spots in the pupil, cross eyes, and cataracts. The condition is treated by surgical reattachment of the retina, or by reducing unwanted tissue via laser therapy or cryotherapy (a treatment involving the application of extreme cold).

Diabetic retinopathy involves damage to the blood vessels nourishing the retina, causing cloudy vision and possibly blindness. It usually strikes diabetics aged 25 years or older, and is marked by the sudden onset of blurred vision, loss of vision in either eye, decreased color perception and flashing lights or black spots. Laser surgery may be used to seal or destroy abnormal or bleeding blood vessels, though this may not improve vision.

Hypertensive retinopathy is caused by high blood pressure and may result in hemorrhaging, lesions, permanently impaired vision or blindness. Blood pressure needs to be controlled to arrest progression of the disease.

Diagnosis

In order to diagnose retinal disorders and diseases, a bright beam of light is shone through the pupil using an instrument called an ophthalmoscope. It gives a magnified view of the retina to help check for conditions such as retinal or macular degeneration and cataracts. During an eye examination, a procedure called retinoscopy may also be used to determine how light is refracted in the eye. A retinoscope measures how a projected beam moves over the surface of the retina, helping to detect refractive errors such as near- and farsightedness (or short- and longsightedness). This also determines the prescription for glasses or contact lenses to correct or neutralize refractive errors.

SEE ALSO *Blindness, Cataracts, Diabetes, Eye, Ophthalmoscopy, Retinitis pigmentosa, Sight*

RETINITIS PIGMENTOSA

This is a rare degenerative disease of the retina in which the progressive breakdown of pigment stops the eye from responding to light and color in the usual way. Night blindness is usually the first indication of the disease, followed by the loss of peripheral vision, a reduction in color sensitivity, deterioration of daytime vision and narrowing of the field of vision from the edges inward, or tunnel vision. In some instances the disease may result in blindness.

Retinitis pigmentosa is thought to be hereditary and there is currently no definitive treatment or cure.

SEE ALSO *Blindness, Eye, Night blindness, Retina, Sight*

RETROVERSION OF THE UTERUS

The uterus is usually tilted forward in the pelvis (anteverted). Retroversion, where the uterus is tilted backwards, exists in about 20 percent of women. The condition may be present from puberty but, providing the uterus remains mobile and is able to expand during pregnancy, no symptoms or complications are likely to occur.

In some instances retroversion may occur later in life because the pressure of either a tumor or adhesions fixes the uterus in an abnormal position. In such cases symptoms such as backache and pelvic pain may be experienced and there may be difficulties in conception and pregnancy. These symptoms can arise from a variety of other conditions, however, which must be eliminated before surgery is considered.

There is little evidence to support the idea that retroversion may cause prolapse of the uterus.

SEE ALSO *Uterus*

REYE'S SYNDROME

Reye's syndrome (RS) is a disease that occurs mostly in children; it most seriously affects the brain and the liver, but also affects all other body organs. In its most serious form it can be fatal.

The syndrome was first reported by Australian pathologist R. D. K. Reye in 1963. It causes an acute increase of pressure within the brain, together with massive accumulations of fat in the liver and other organs. It can develop in children following or during influenza, chickenpox or other viral infections.

Reye's syndrome has been misdiagnosed as encephalitis, meningitis, diabetes, poisoning, drug overdose, sudden infant death syndrome or a psychiatric illness. This is because the symptoms include nausea, vomiting (though babies do not always have this symptom), lethargy, drowsiness, disorientation, seizures, respiratory arrest and coma.

The precise cause of the illness is still unknown, although studies have found that aspirin or medications which contain salicylate can increase the risk of the disease developing. A decline in the incidence of the illness in the 1980s was attributed to the reduction in the use of these drugs in children.

RS does not have a cure. Early diagnosis is important to survival and complete recovery, and treatment is aimed at protecting the brain against irreversible damage. Not all sufferers will recover completely; some may suffer brain damage because of the severity of the swelling of the brain.

SEE ALSO *Diabetes, Encephalitis, Meningitis, Non-steroidal anti-inflammatory drugs, Overdose, Poisoning, Sudden infant death syndrome*

RHESUS (Rh) FACTOR

Rhesus (Rh) factor is named after an antibody produced in 1940 in the blood of a rabbit after immunizing it with red blood cells from a rhesus monkey. This antibody was shown to be the same as one found the previous year in the blood of a woman who had a stillborn child. The child was born with hydrops fetalis, or generalized swelling, due to severe anemia.

What had been discovered was a new blood group system, separate from the ABO system already known. Eighty-five percent of Caucasians are now known to have the Rh antigen on the cell membrane of their red blood cells and are Rh positive; the other 15 percent lack this antigen and are Rh negative. The presence or absence of an Rh factor is important when considering the compatability of blood types, especially in pregnancy and blood transfusions.

When an Rh negative woman and Rh positive man have a baby, there is a possibility that the baby will be Rh positive and that its red cells will be destroyed by Rh antibodies. The Rh positive cells of the baby are introduced into an Rh negative woman via the placenta. This Rh incompatibility stimulates the woman's immune system to produce antibodies, a process called isoimmunization, which destroy the foreign, introduced cells, or antigens. Of real concern is that the antibodies then travel from the mother to the baby, where they continue to attack the Rh positive red cells. This may result in increased physiological jaundice of the newborn, in neonatal anemia or, if severe, in hydrops fetalis.

Immunization to Rh antigens can also result from the transfusion of Rh positive blood to an Rh negative recipient, leading to destruction of the transfused cells in a blood transfusion reaction.

The discovery of the Rh blood group system has resulted in safer blood transfusion, through testing for the Rh factor during crossmatching of blood. It has also led to measures to prevent Rh isoimmunization in pregnancy. Before the development of DNA sequence analysis, the Rh system contributed to the identification of blood or body fluids at the scene of crimes or accidents and was also used in testing for disputed parentage.

The Rh system consists of six major antigens, the most important being the D antigen, which results in the most severe isoimmunization. Initial exposure to the D antigen results in sensitization of the immune system; a second exposure produces a strong antibody response. It is now routine practice to test women during pregnancy for the Rh antigen. If a woman is Rh negative and her partner Rh positive, there is a possibility of isoimmunization. If this is the woman's first pregnancy, it is unlikely that she will become sensitized until delivery, when small numbers of fetal red cells enter the maternal circulation.

If she delivers an Rh negative baby, she will receive an injection of anti-D globulin to prevent her immune system reacting and

R

Retroverted uterus

One-fifth of all women have a retroverted uterus, in which the uterus is tilted backwards in the pelvis.

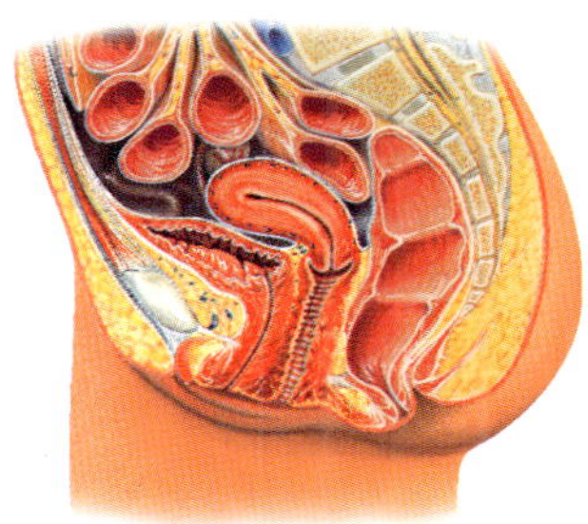

Normal uterus

A normal uterus is tilted forward in the pelvis.

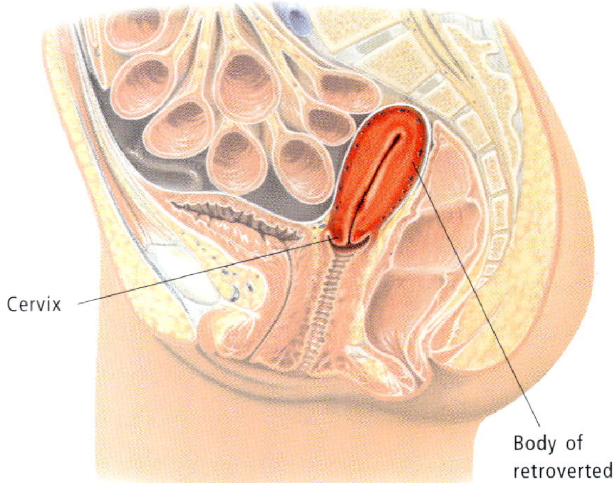

Rhesus (Rh) factor

In pregnancy, problems may occur if the mother is Rh negative and the fetus is Rh positive. The red blood cells of the fetus may be destroyed by the mother's Rh antibodies, which can lead to hydrops fetalis (swelling in the fetus due to excessive fluid).

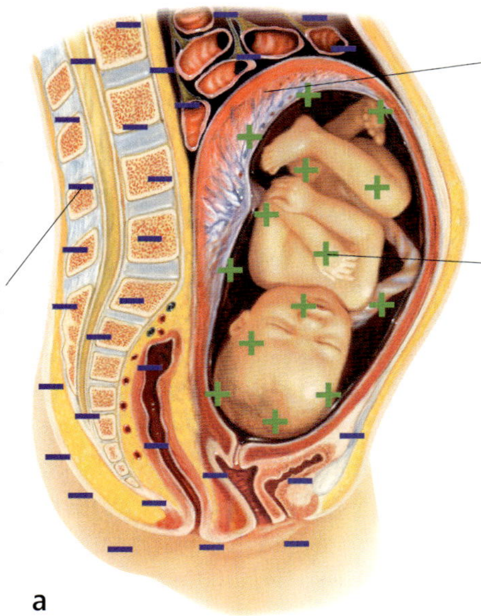

First pregnancy
Problems rarely occur during the course of the pregnancy, as the bloodstreams of the mother and the fetus do not mix.

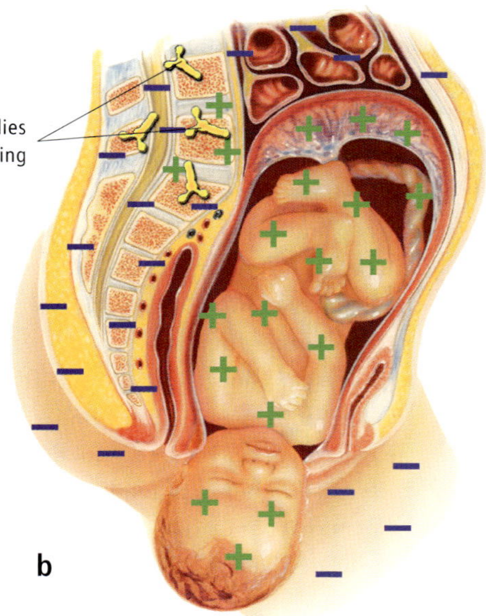

First pregnancy—delivery
During delivery, the baby's blood can leak into the maternal bloodstream; this causes the Rhesus-negative mother to develop antibodies which destroy Rhesus-positive blood cells.

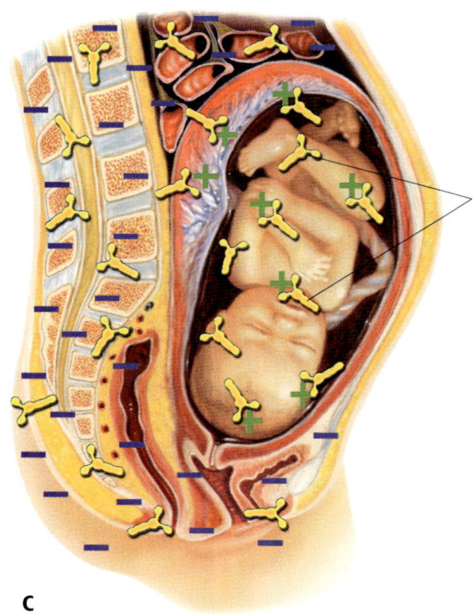

Second and subsequent pregnancies
If the mother does not receive an Anti-D globulin injection following the first pregnancy (to halt the production of antibodies), her antibodies may attack the blood cells of subsequent Rhesus-positive babies.

forming Rh antibodies that could affect future pregnancies. Anti-D is also given to Rh negative women following an abortion, miscarriage or amniocentesis. The other means of preventing Rh isoimmunization is through the transfusion of Rh negative blood to Rh negative women of childbearing age.

These precautions have resulted in a marked decrease in the incidence of Rh immunization and its effects on the newborn. Hemolytic disease of the newborn (anemia caused by excessive destruction of red blood cells) does still occur, either due to episodes of sensitization not treated by anti-D globulin or due to other Rh or ABO antibodies. However, it is unusual now to see increasingly severe cases in successive pregnancies, as in the past, resulting in fetal death.

SEE ALSO *Anemia, Antibodies, Blood groups, Hemolytic disease of the newborn, Newborn, Pregnancy*

RHEUMATIC FEVER

In some children between the ages of 5 and 15, streptococcal infection of the tonsils or throat may be followed 2 weeks later by an immune reaction called rheumatic fever. It manifests as fever and arthritis; the joints become tender, swollen and red. It can also damage the tissues of the heart, central nervous system and skin.

With bed rest, treatment with aspirin (and sometimes corticosteroid drugs), the symptoms usually resolve in a matter of weeks. However, the endocardium (the internal lining of the heart) may be permanently scarred, resulting in heart murmurs and valvular heart disease.

People with rheumatic heart disease should take antibiotics before undergoing medical and dental procedures to prevent bacterial endocarditis (infection of the internal lining of the heart).

SEE ALSO *Arthritis, Endocarditis, Fever, Heart, Streptococcal infections*

RHEUMATISM

Rheumatism is a name given to several conditions which involve inflammation of connective tissues in joints and muscles, causing pain and stiffness. The term includes degenerative disorders such as

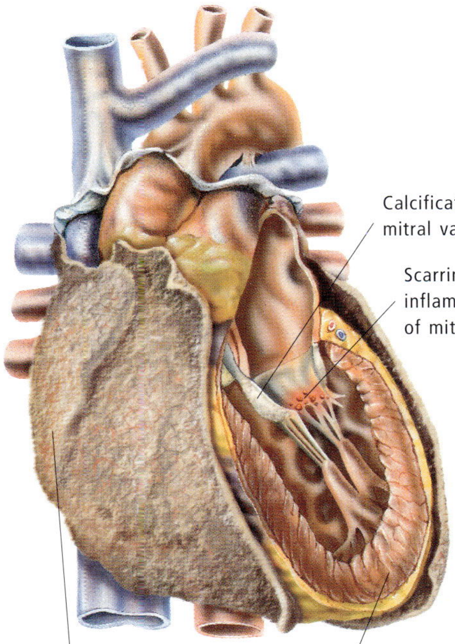

Rheumatic fever

Symptoms of rheumatic fever include fever, lethargy, painful swelling of the joints, and the formation of nodules under the skin and in the heart. Permanent heart damage may result from inflammation of the lining, valves and muscles of the heart, scarring of the valves and the development of a fibrous, thickened layer around the pericardium.

rheumatoid arthritis and osteoarthritis, septic or infectious arthritis resulting from tuberculosis, and bacterial, viral or fungal infections of the synovial fluid in joints.

Desert rheumatism is a condition involving inflammation of the eye surface and joints, as well as formation of skin nodules. It develops with coccidioidomycosis, a lung infection caused by inhalation of fungal spores found in soil. The disease has a mild form, which usually clears up without treatment, and a progressive form, which may be fatal and often requires lifelong treatment.

SEE ALSO *Connective tissue, Joints, Muscle, Osteoarthritis, Rheumatoid arthritis, Synovial fluid*

RHEUMATOID ARTHRITIS

Rheumatoid arthritis (RA) is a chronic and progressive condition which inflames connective tissue throughout the body. It most commonly affects both sides of the body simultaneously and involves the small joints of fingers, wrists, toes, ankles and elbows where the adjoining bone ends are enclosed in a membrane containing fluid for lubrication to ease movement.

Lungs and kidneys may also be affected; the spleen may enlarge; heart membranes, conjunctiva and sclera of the eyes or arteries may become inflamed; anemia, dry eyes and reduced secretion of saliva are also possible effects. RA is one of many forms of arthritis, a group of around 100 disorders which may affect up to 20 percent of people in industrialized society, making it possibly the most common chronic cause of continuing or permanent disability.

Symptoms of RA most commonly arise in women between ages 35 and 55 and in men between ages 40 and 60, but children and the elderly can suffer attacks. A minority recover after only one attack, but for others the disease is progressive, needing continual treatment. The major effects are aching and stiff joints, fatigue and anemia, weight loss and wasting muscles, with the onset of the disease marked by inflammation and redness around the affected areas.

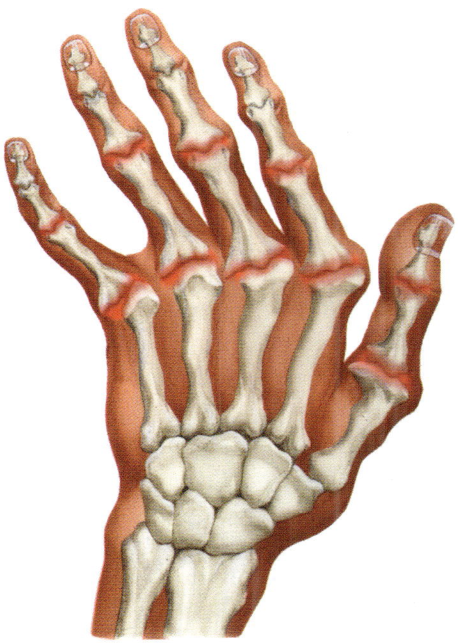

Rheumatoid arthritis

One of the most common areas of the body to suffer rheumatoid arthritis is the hands. The joints become stiff, painful, inflamed and swollen, making even the most simple of tasks such as picking up an object—difficult or impossible to do.

Repeated attacks may produce problems such as carpal tunnel syndrome, with pain and numbness in the hand and wrist; permanent swelling of finger joints, knuckles and wrist; inflamed tendons; tenosynovitis; and nodules under the skin of the arms. When attacks subside, joints may become excessively loose and mobile, and it is in this state that they are most susceptible to further damage through overuse.

Diagnosis involves a blood test used to distinguish RA from similar conditions such as rheumatic fever, infectious arthritis and gout, and to detect the presence of a distinctive antibody called rheumatoid factor, carried by about 70 percent of people, some of whom will never suffer the disease.

The exact cause of the disease is unknown, but since the rheumatoid factor antibody is found in most sufferers, RA is thought to have an autoimmune mechanism, a reaction which causes the body's defense system to attack its own tissues. It is also thought that susceptibility to RA is a genetically inherited trait, with the disease being triggered by infection or possibly by environmental factors.

Treatment can involve rest, diet therapy, drugs and surgery, depending on individual symptoms. Rest may relieve pain and is recommended during attacks because movement aggravates the inflamed joints. Supports and splints can be used to immobilize joints for limited periods but regular use

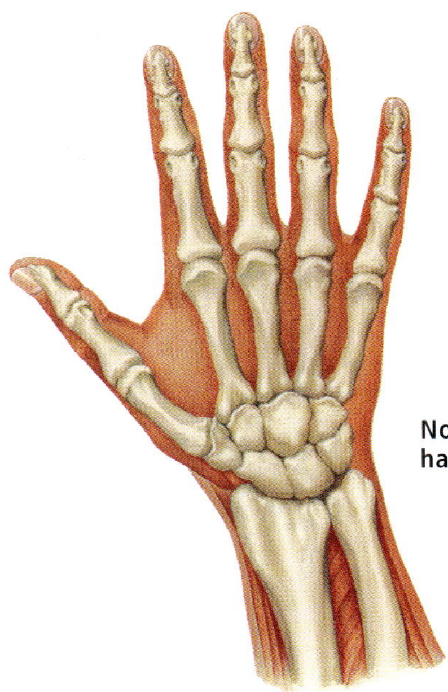

and movement of the joints is essential to prevent stiffness and preserve mobility. Certain foods can cause attacks in some people and paying careful attention to a balanced diet may help.

The drugs prescribed for the relief of rheumatoid arthritis are mainly non-steroidal anti-inflammatories (NSAIDs), including aspirin and ibuprofen. These should not be taken by those with gastric ulcers, however, as side effects may include digestive upsets as well as headaches, increased blood pressure and edema. There are also specific antirheumatoid drugs including steroids, penicillamine, gold preparations and methotrexate, but most of these have potentially severe side effects.

Lack of movement in joints and muscle weakness can create difficulties in walking and accomplishing everyday tasks. A range of aids is available, from orthopedic shoes to specially designed household appliances and hand tools. Fusion of small joints or replacement of hips or knees are options of last resort where other treatments have failed.

SEE ALSO *Arthritis, Autoimmune disease, Connective tissue, Osteoarthritis, Rheumatism, Synovial joints, Tenosynovitis*

RHINITIS

Rhinitis is the inflammation of the mucous membranes lining the nose and is usually accompanied by an excessive production of mucus, which may be watery or thick. There may be difficulty breathing through airways restricted by swelling and mucus.

Infection with the common cold or other viruses, bacterial infections, irritation by smoke or airborne pollutants, and allergic reactions can all produce similar symptoms.

Symptoms can be treated with nasal sprays or orally administered drugs which constrict the blood vessels in the swollen membranes and return them to near normal size, freeing up the airways. These drugs should be used for a few days only as their prolonged use may actually produce symptoms of congestion. If the mucous membrane itself is infected, nasal mucus may be yellow and pus-like and the nose will bleed easily. Antibiotics may be prescribed, depending on the cause.

Allergic rhinitis results from inhaling a substance to which the individual has been sensitized, whether or not there has been a previous allergic reaction. There is increased production of mucus, and there may also be redness and irritation of the eyes. Severe reactions can bring feelings of tightness in the chest and difficulty breathing. These changes are caused by the body's production of histamine, a substance used to help fight invading organisms.

The main culprit is pollen, rye grass pollen in particular, and symptoms can arise very quickly following contact. Seasonal allergic rhinitis is an almost permanent affliction for many allergy sufferers from spring through summer as airborne pollen levels rise in the growing season. Animal hair and skin flakes, mold, dust and the feces of the household dust mite are also known causes.

Medication with antihistamines may counter the immediate symptoms; for more serious reactions, corticosteroids may be prescribed. Identification of the allergenic substance is important to therapy which aims to desensitize chronic sufferers.

SEE ALSO *Allergies, Antihistamines, Histamines, Nose*

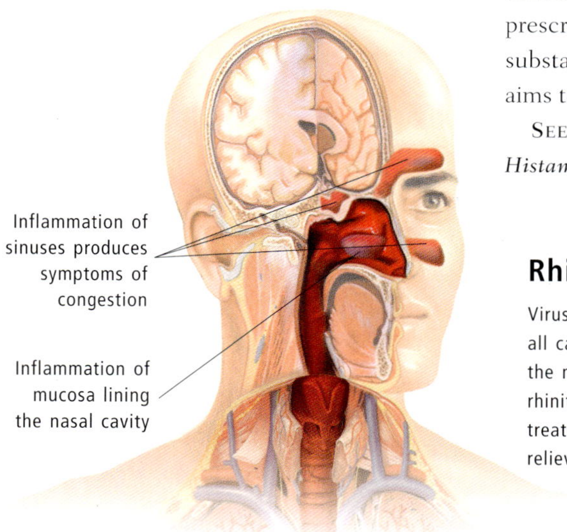

Rhinitis

Viruses, bacteria and allergens can all cause the mucous membranes of the nose to become inflamed. Acute rhinitis (or the common cold) is treated with decongestants to relieve nasal congestion.

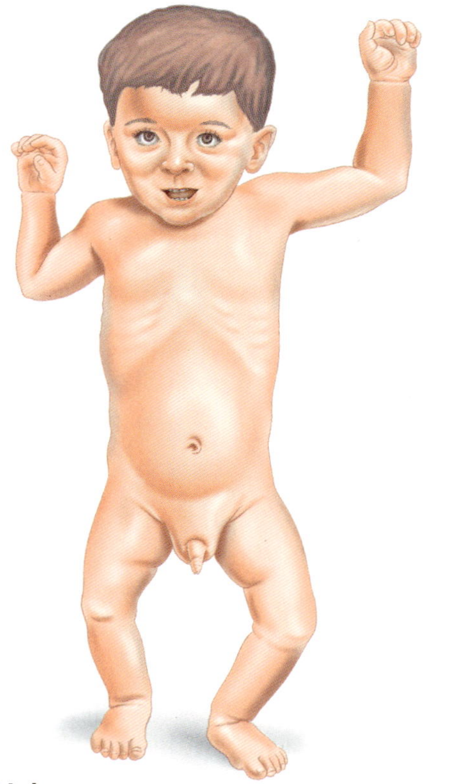

Rickets

A lack of vitamin D in children can cause soft and deformed bones, as without this vitamin, calcium and phosphorus cannot be utilized by the body's cells.

RHINOPHYMA

Rhinophyma is a rare condition in which the nose becomes enlarged and red, with thickened skin and the appearance of veins near the surface. The nose takes on a bulb-like shape and oil-producing glands become enlarged. Once thought to be the result of excessive alcohol consumption, rhinophyma strikes just as many non-drinkers. It usually only affects men and is associated with the skin disease, acne rosacea. While antibiotics may be successful in reducing symptoms in the early stages, surgical reshaping of the nose is the only other treatment.

SEE ALSO *Acne rosacea, Nose*

RIBS

The rib cage helps shield the heart and lungs from injury. Movement of the rib cage also assists the diaphragm in controlling the intake and expulsion of air during breathing.

Typically, the human skeleton has 24 ribs, arranged in 12 pairs. At the back, they join the thoracic vertebrae in the spine. At the front, each of the upper seven pairs connects to the sternum (or breastbone) directly by a costal cartilage. Pairs 8, 9 and 10 also connect to costal cartilages but these join with each other and then join the cartilage of the seventh rib. As they are not directly attached to the sternum, they are termed false ribs. The top seven pairs are directly attached to the sternum, and so are called true ribs. Pairs 11 and 12 are not attached at all at the front and are called floating ribs.

Occasionally a person may have a small additional rib, joined only at the back to a vertebra in the neck, usually the seventh cervical vertebrae. This so-called cervical rib may often go unnoticed but if it comes to place pressure on nerves and blood vessels it may need to be removed surgically.

SEE ALSO *Cervical rib syndrome, Skeletal system*

RICKETS

Rickets is a bone disease of infants and children that is caused by a lack of vitamin D from either insufficient sunlight or inadequate diet. Occasionally, it may be caused by disorders of the kidney, liver or biliary system. The lack of vitamin D causes progressive softening and weakening of the bone structure which can result in deformity.

Infants with rickets grow more slowly than normal, and take longer to begin crawling or walking. When the infant does start to walk, the legs may bend, resulting in either bowlegs or knock-knees. The chest may also be deformed, producing a pigeon chest, and small knobs may develop on the ends of the ribs.

Rickets is treated by giving the child a concentrated supply of vitamin D, calcium and phosphorus; an adequate diet is essential. Deformities usually disappear if the condition is treated in the early stages.

SEE ALSO *Bones, Vitamins*

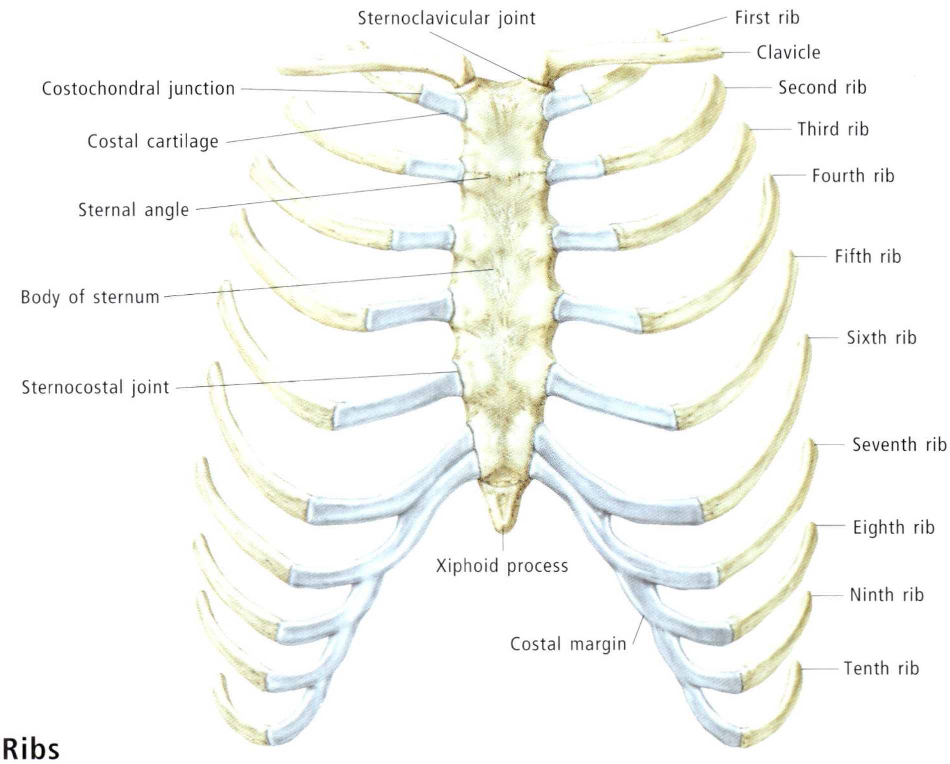

Ribs

The 24 ribs are arranged in 12 pairs. The first 7 pairs are referred to as "the true ribs" because they are directly attached to the breastbone (sternum). Pairs 8–10 are known as "false ribs" because they are not attached to the sternum. the lowest two pairs (11 and 12) are not attached at the front and are called "floating ribs".

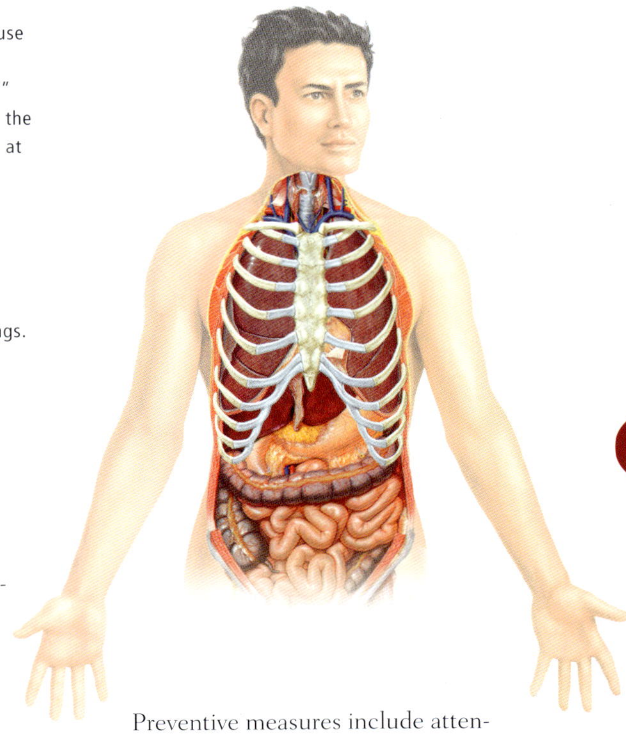

Rib cage

The rib cage is designed to protect the organs within the chest, particularly the heart and lungs. Damage to the rib cage may lead to serious problems, such as a punctured lung.

RINGWORM

Ringworm is a skin infection caused by various fungi, which results in a characteristic red, ring-shaped rash. The fungi, called dermatophytes, invade the top layer of skin and affect the tissue underneath. Ringworm is particularly common among children and is usually treated with non-prescription antifungal creams and powders. Oral medications and stronger topical creams may be used for more severe and persistent cases.

Preventive measures include attention to personal hygiene and keeping the skin clean and dry.

Because the infection is highly contagious, hairbrushes, clothing and other personal items should be cleaned and dried after use. The complications of ringworm include secondary skin infections and spread of tinea to other parts of the body. Tinea is ringworm of the feet (athlete's foot), scalp, groin and nails.

SEE ALSO *Antifungals, Tinea*

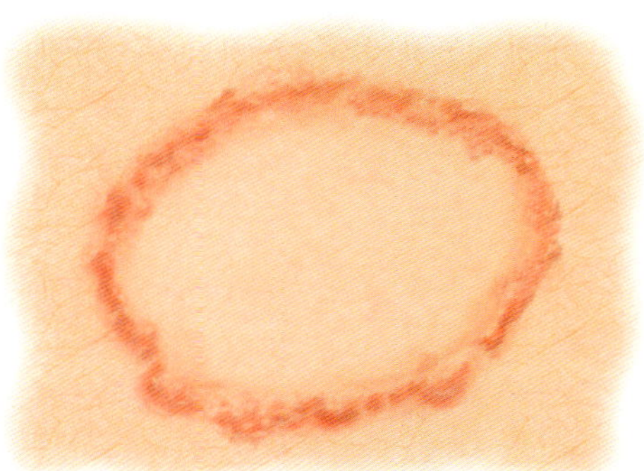

Ringworm

Also called tinea, this disease is caused by a fungus, not a worm as the name suggests.

ROOT CANAL THERAPY

Root canal therapy is a dental procedure in which the center, or pulp, of a dead or infected tooth is removed. The pulp includes nerves, blood vessels and lymphatic tissue which pass through the root canal. Root canal therapy is usually needed to avoid severe toothache and abscesses that can result from infection or trauma such as a blow to the mouth. It may save a tooth that would otherwise be extracted. The empty tooth is usually filled with a plastic substance. A crown may be fitted to improve the strength of the tooth, which may become weak as a result of the treatment.

SEE ALSO *Crown and bridge, Teeth*

ROSEOLA INFANTUM

A common infection of early childhood, roseola infantum is caused by a type of herpes virus and marked by a temperature which rises rapidly to a high fever of 39–40°C (102–104°F). This fever lasts 3–4 days and then suddenly disappears. Other symptoms may include febrile convulsions, mild diarrhea, a cough, enlarged lymph glands (lymph nodes) in the neck and earache. The fever is followed by a rash which is mildly itchy and spreads from the trunk and neck to behind the ears and lasts for about 2 days. Roseola infantum is highly contagious and can incubate for 5–15 days.

Treatment is aimed at relieving the symptoms, particularly the high fever; it is important to seek medical attention when a child's temperature rises to this level. This disease is sometimes confused with measles, the difference being the height and duration of the fever which precedes the appearance of the rash. A child who has a suppressed immune system may develop hepatitis or pneumonia. Recovery is generally rapid, however, and once the rash has disappeared the child will return to normal.

SEE ALSO *Convulsions, Fever, Hepatitis, Herpes simplex, Pneumonia*

ROTATOR CUFF MUSCLES

The rotator cuff muscles are dynamic stabilizers of the shoulder joint. They hold the head of the humerus securely in its shallow socket, while muscles attaching further from the joint powerfully move the arm. The subscapularis muscle forms the anterior part of the cuff, the infraspinatus and teres minor form the posterior part, and the supraspinatus the superior part. All four cuff muscles arise from the shoulder blade (scapula) and attach to bony elevations (tubercles) close to the head of the humerus.

The subscapularis muscle rotates the front of the arm inward, as in a forehand stroke in tennis. The infraspinatus and teres minor muscles rotate it outward, as in a backhand stroke. The supraspinatus muscle assists the deltoid muscle in raising the arm (abduction). The tendon of the supraspinatus passes under a bony and ligamentous arch (coracoacromial arch) and is separated from it by a bursa that allows the structures to glide easily against each other. Sometimes the tendon and bursa become inflamed, causing pain when the arm is raised.

SEE ALSO *Humerus, Shoulder*

ROUNDWORMS

Roundworms belong to the class Nematoda, a group containing over 10,000 species, many of which are parasites. Roundworms infecting humans live mostly in the intestine, range in length from a millimeter to many centimeters, and include hookworms, pinworms and whipworms. The most common roundworm is a long pale yellow worm with the scientific name of *Ascaris lumbricoides*, which infects the human gastrointestinal tract and lungs.

Root canal therapy

A damaged tooth may be saved by root canal therapy. First the tooth is opened up to allow access to the abscess and all pulp is removed (a). Then the abscess and canal is cleaned and sterilized (b). Finally the canals are sealed with filling (c).

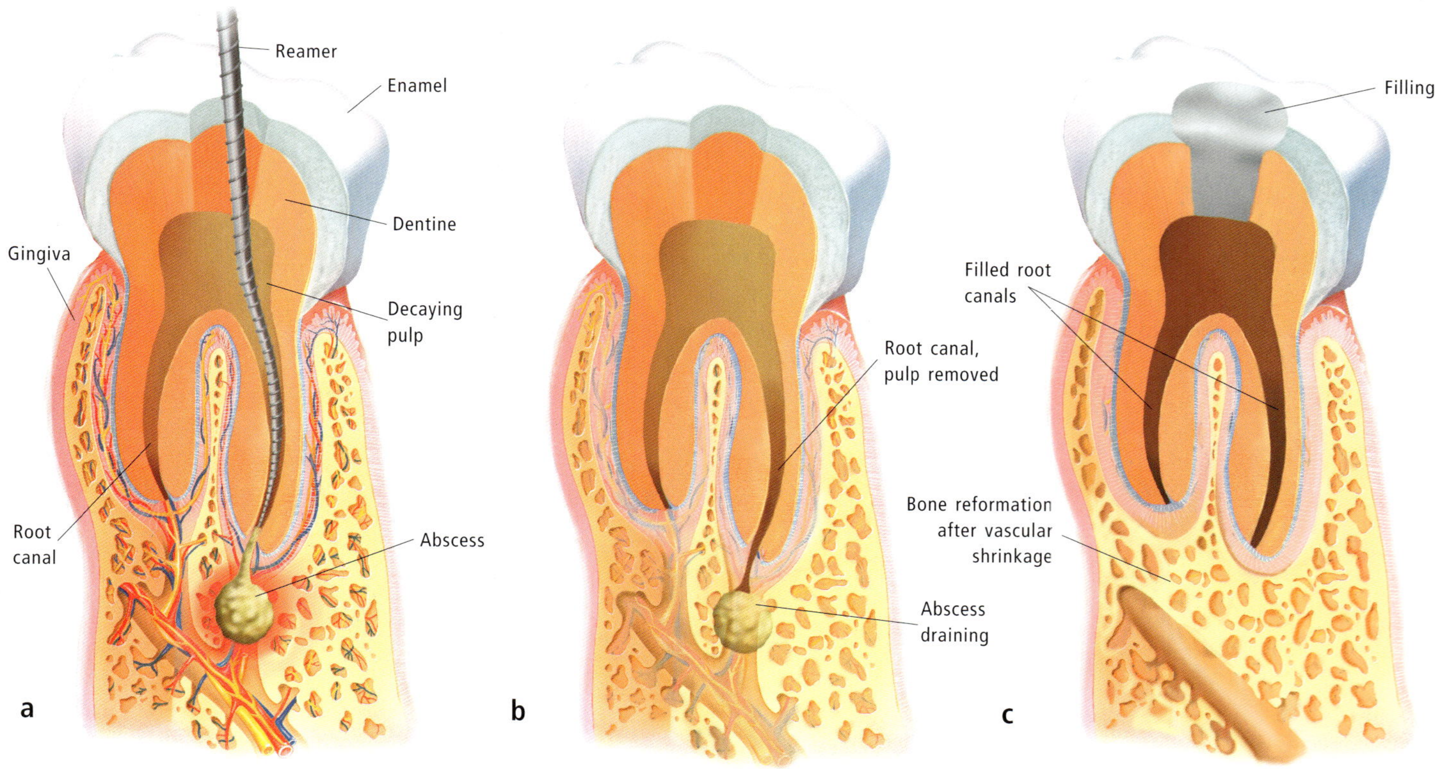

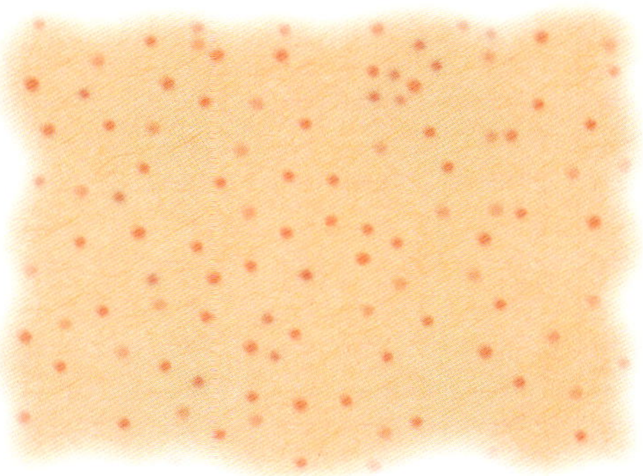

Rubella

Also known as German measles, rubella is similar to but less contagious than measles. The rash begins on the face and scalp, and then quickly spreads to the body and arms.

Ascariasis infection affects an estimated 1 billion people worldwide, mainly in developing nations where untreated human sewage is used to fertilize food crops. It develops when people consume food, water or soil traces contaminated with roundworm eggs.

In heavy infestations, adult worms can cause intestinal obstructions or malnutrition, and larvae can irritate the lungs. Oral medications are usually effective in eradicating infections although surgery may be needed to clear blockages.

SEE ALSO *Hookworm, Strongyloidiasis, Threadworms, Whipworm, Worms*

RUBELLA

Rubella (German measles) is caused by a virus which is transmitted by droplet inhalation. The incubation period for rubella is 2–3 weeks. Highly infectious, rubella is usually a mild illness lasting days only, but may be occasionally complicated by arthritis. If an expectant mother develops rubella during early pregnancy there is a high risk of congenital abnormalities developing in the fetus.

In childhood the condition usually begins with slight irritability and minor but tender enlargement of lymph glands in the back of the neck and head. A transient spotty rash will usually appear initially on the face and behind the ears, and then spread rapidly over the body. Occasionally the rash is noted when a child is being bathed in warm water, yet will have faded by the time the child is seen by the doctor and not recur. A few spots may be seen on the palate at the same time. There may be mild fever but the child is usually only minimally ill, with a runny nose. Adults often, and children rarely, develop various painful joints, particularly in the fingers. Occasionally it is noted that a child develops bruising due to a transient shortage of platelet cells in the blood. A very low percentage of patients develop an encephalopathy where there is inflammation and damage to the brain. Mortality in that instance may be 20 percent but recovery otherwise is usually complete.

If a woman is planning a pregnancy she is advised to have her rubella antibody level checked well beforehand. If there are adequate antibodies present, then there is no problem; if antibodies are absent, she is advised to be vaccinated at least three months before starting on a pregnancy.

If the embryo is infected before 14 weeks, a variety of different problems can occur, ranging from miscarriage to congenital heart defects, cataracts, glaucoma and deafness. The brain may not develop adequately and retardation can occur, even if the developing infant is past 14 weeks.

Rubella vaccination, usually combined with measles and mumps vaccines, is given initially at the age of 12–15 months. A second vaccination may be given in the early teens. Arthritis is an occasional complication with older children and women but otherwise there are few complications following immunization.

SEE ALSO *Congenital abnormalities, Infectious diseases, Immunization*

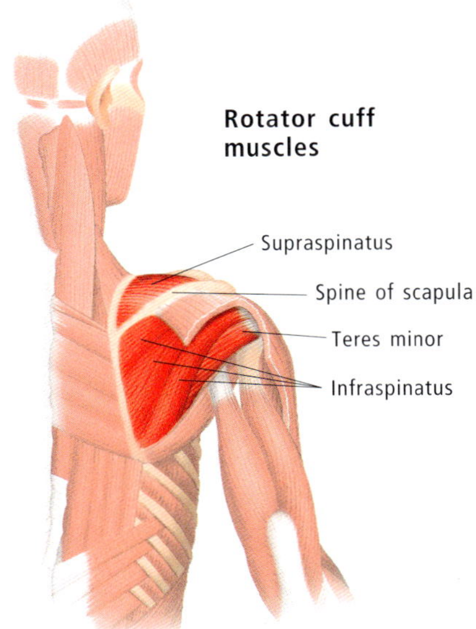

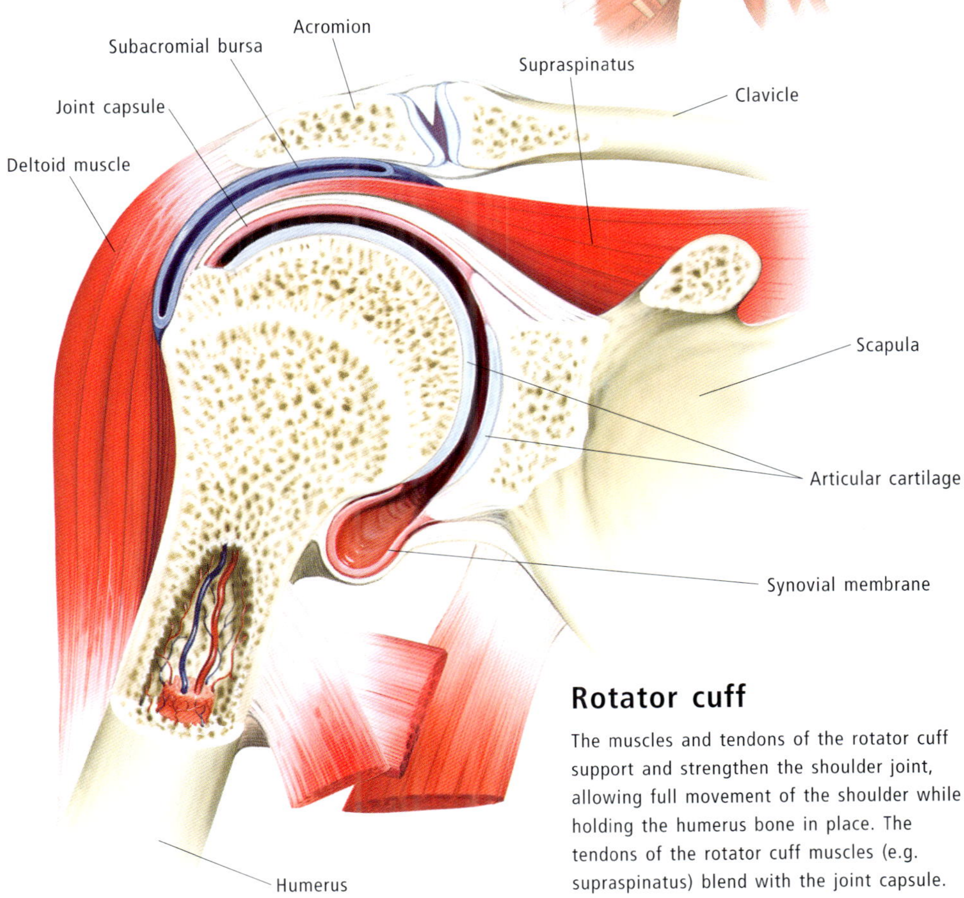

Rotator cuff

The muscles and tendons of the rotator cuff support and strengthen the shoulder joint, allowing full movement of the shoulder while holding the humerus bone in place. The tendons of the rotator cuff muscles (e.g. supraspinatus) blend with the joint capsule.

R

S

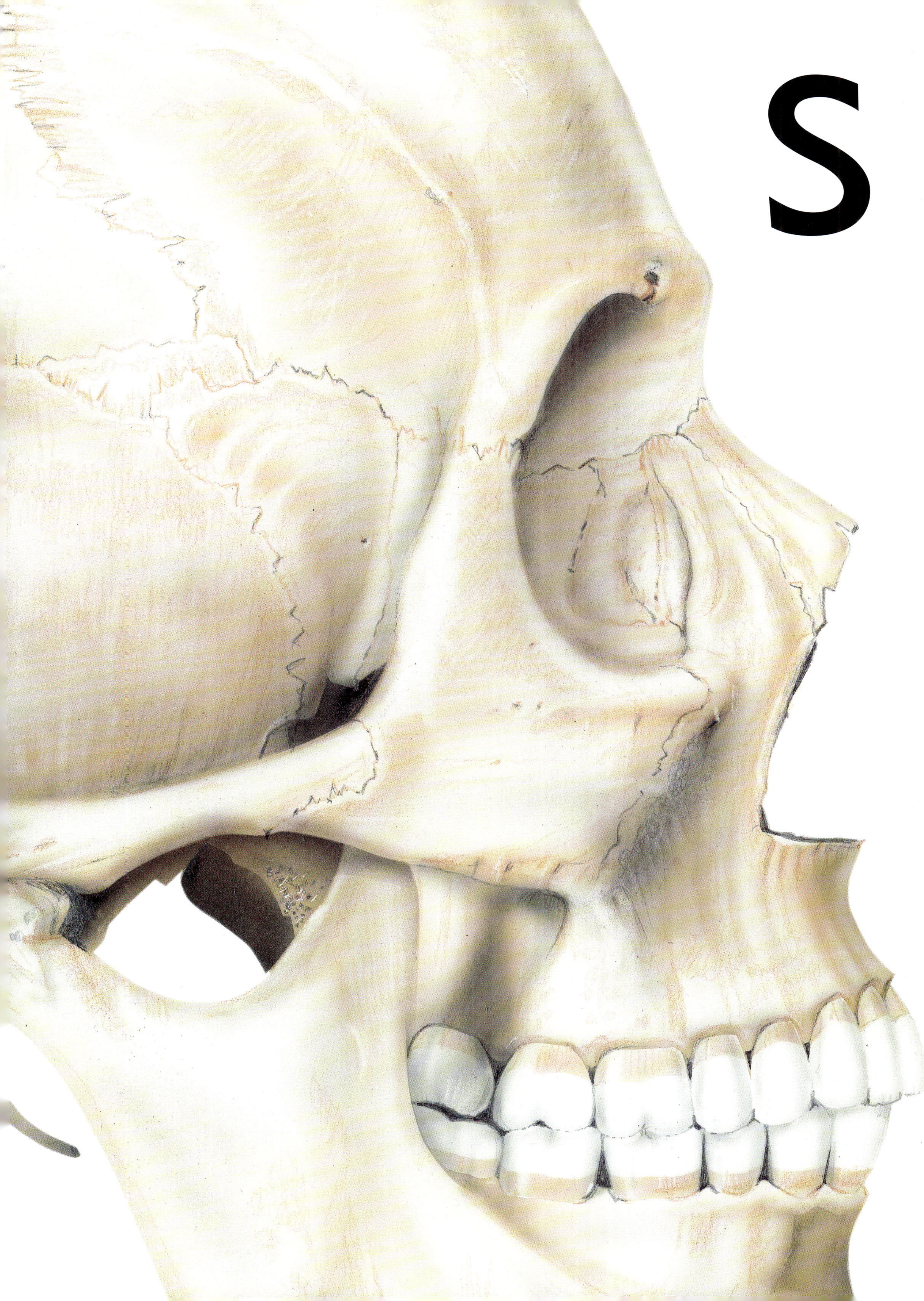

SACROILIAC JOINT

The sacroiliac joint is located where the ilium of the hip bone and the sacrum at the base of the spine meet. Because the weight of the trunk passes through this joint, powerful interosseous ligaments are required to unite the bones. At the front, the joint is synovial and at the back it is fibrous.

The synovial part of the joint has an L-shaped surface, which is usually related to the first three fused segments of the sacrum in the male and the first two segments in the female. The sacral and iliac articular surfaces are reciprocally ridged and furrowed to increase stability.

The interosseous sacroiliac ligament is strong and unites the roughened areas of bone behind the synovial part of the joint. The weight of the body tends to drive the upper end of the sacrum downward, tightening this ligament and drawing the joint surfaces together. This same force tends to tilt the lower end of the sacrum upward, which is resisted by the powerful sacrotuberous and sacrospinous ligaments.

The sacroiliac joint is capable of only a small amount of movement and is subject to great stress, from the downward pressure of the body's weight and the upward thrust of the legs and pelvis. It must also be able to cope with the movements of the body, for example as it turns, twists, pulls and pushes. Movement of the sacroiliac joint increases during pregnancy. An excess motion can cause a strain on the joint. With increasing age, the joint cavity may become partially or completely obliterated by fibrous tissue or fibrocartilage, and may even show bony fusion in the very old.

SEE ALSO *Hip, Joints, Sacrum, Skeletal system, Spine*

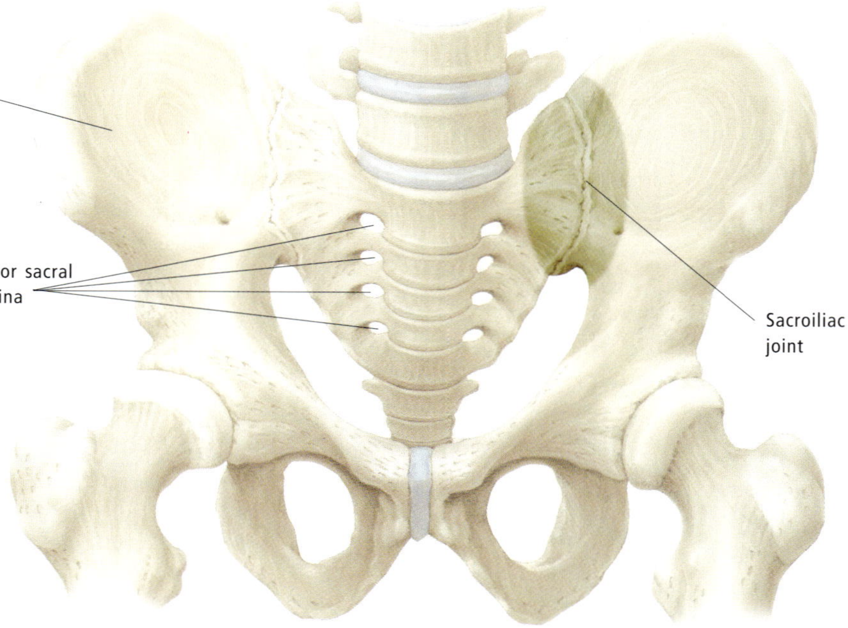

Sacroiliac joint

The sacroiliac joint articulates between the sacrum and ilium bone of the hip. It transfers body weight to the pelvis. The range of movement is relatively small.

SACRUM

The sacrum and coccyx form the lower end of the spine. The sacrum is formed by fusion of the five sacral vertebrae. The sacrum forms a part of the bony pelvis, being joined to the hip bones at the sacroiliac joints. Above, it articulates with the fifth lumbar vertebra, and below with the coccyx. Passing through the sacrum from top to bottom is the sacral canal, which is a continuation of the spinal canal of the rest of the vertebral column. The spinal roots (cauda equina) of the spinal cord pass through the sacral canal, giving off sacral spinal nerves which leave through pelvic and dorsal passages in the bone (sacral foramina).

SEE ALSO *Skeletal system, Spine, Vertebrae*

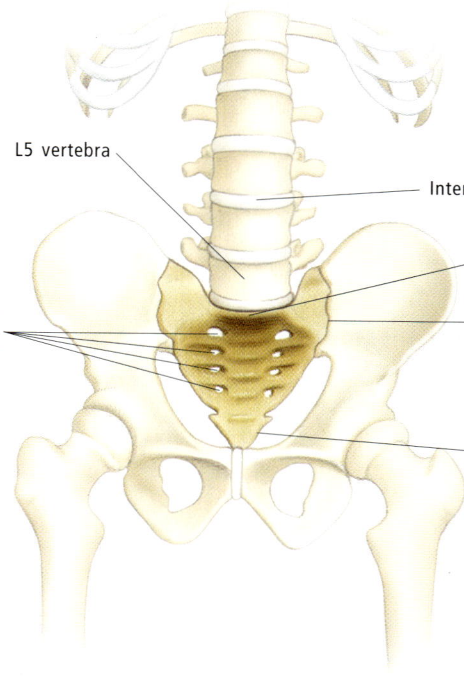

Sacrum

The sacrum is located at the base of the spine above the coccyx, and consists of five fused vertebrae.

SALIVA

Saliva is an alkaline fluid secreted by salivary glands that helps soften food, moistens the mouth and aids in digestion. Saliva is composed of mucus, water, mineral salts, proteins and amylase. The mucus helps in swallowing the food, the water dissolves some of the components of food and helps in tasting, and the amylase begins the digestion of carbohydrates. Saliva helps keep the mouth moist and clean. It is also important in helping the body to retain control of its water balance and, in its role of removing food debris, reducing tooth decay.

SEE ALSO *Mouth, Salivary glands*

S

SALIVARY GLANDS

The salivary glands are located around the beginning of the digestive tract. They produce saliva, a fluid that moistens food and enables food to be bound together into a mass called a bolus, thereby making chewing and swallowing easier. The moisture of saliva allows chemicals in the food to be dissolved and delivered to the taste buds for tasting. Saliva is also rich in digestive enzymes—chemicals that initiate the breakdown of food into simpler substances. The main enzyme in saliva is amylase, which begins the breakdown of starches into their constituent chemicals. This process will continue until the food bolus reaches the stomach and the acid of that region reduces the activity of amylase. Human saliva also contains substances such as lysozyme, and antibodies that control bacteria, thereby protecting the body against invasion by potentially disease-causing bacteria.

The salivary glands are divided into two groups. The major salivary glands are large structures that are easily seen with the naked eye. They consist of three pairs of glands: the parotid, submandibular and sublingual glands. The minor salivary glands are microscopic and are scattered around the mouth, palate and throat. Human saliva is made up mainly of secretions of the

Salivary glands microstructure

There are three distinctive pairs of salivary glands—the parotid, sublingual and submandibular glands. Each pair has a unique cellular organization and produces saliva with slightly different properties.

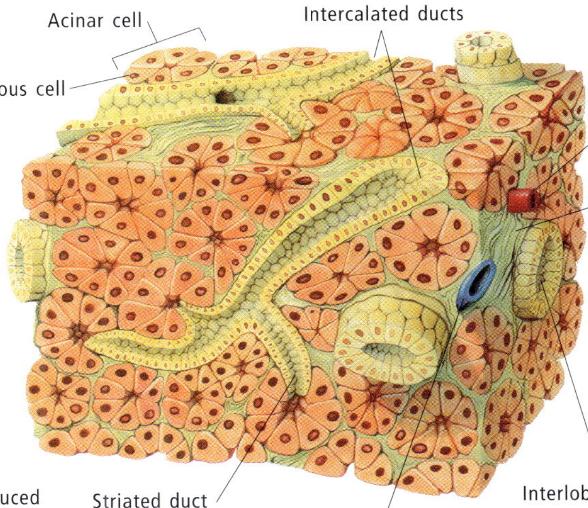

Parotid microstructure

The thin saliva produced by the parotids contains enzymes specially designed to break down starch.

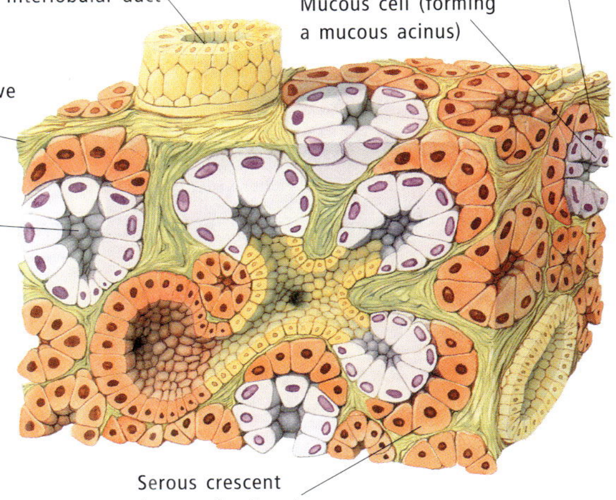

Submandibular microstructure

The submandibular gland is comprised of a mixture of enzyme-producing serous cells and mucus-producing cells. Its saliva is predominantly water.

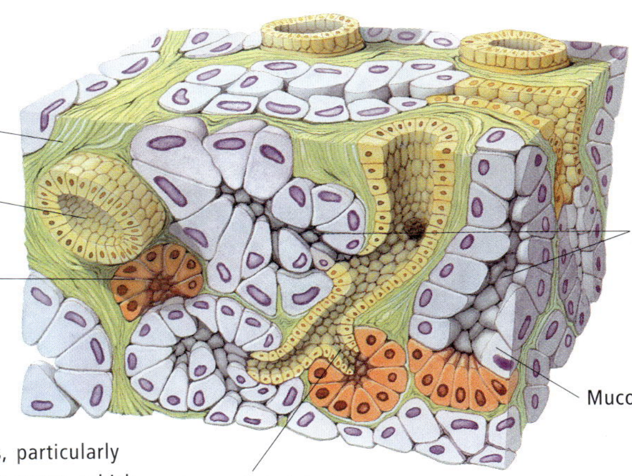

Sublingual microstructure

This gland produces thicker, watery mucus, particularly in response to milk or cream, which helps to lubricate the mouth.

Salivary glands

The salivary glands secrete saliva into the mouth. This fluid is needed to moisten food to ease swallowing and begins food breakdown in the preliminary stage of digestion. Infection of the salivary glands can cause swelling and pain.

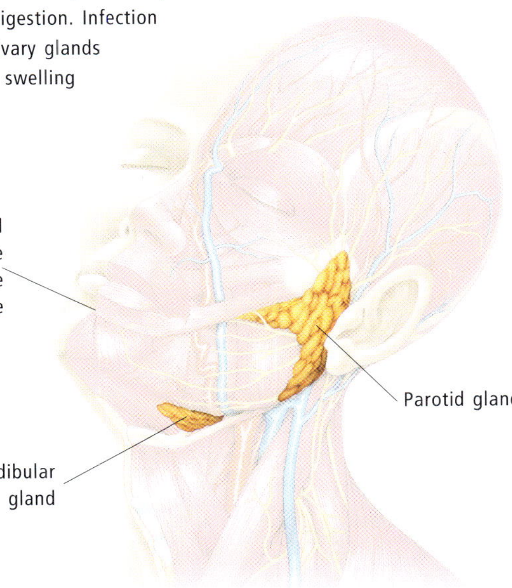

S

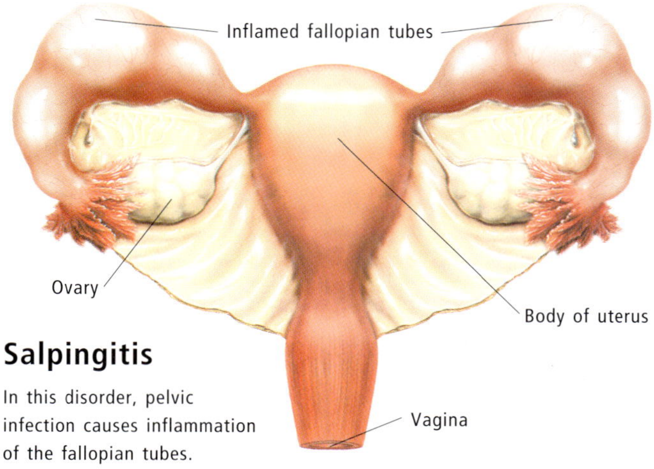

Salpingitis

In this disorder, pelvic infection causes inflammation of the fallopian tubes.

submandibular gland, with contributions from the parotid, sublingual and minor salivary glands in decreasing order of importance.

The parotid gland is located in front of the ear. It gives rise to a duct that runs forward to open into the mouth opposite the second molar of the upper teeth on each side. A flap of mucosa is present at the point where the duct opens into the mouth, and may be felt with the tip of the tongue. The submandibular gland is located below the jaw on each side, about 1 inch (2–3 centimeters) in front of the angle of the jaw. It gives rise to a duct which runs forward a short distance to open into the floor of the mouth under the tongue. The sublingual glands are small, and lie within ridges on the floor of the mouth beneath the tongue. They open by many small ducts into the floor of the mouth.

Salivary glands are mainly under the control of the nervous system, although some hormones may affect their function. The two parts of the autonomic nervous system, the parasympathetic and sympathetic divisions, both contribute nerves to the salivary glands. The parasympathetic nerves are probably most important, because they provide the stimulus to release copious amounts of saliva which is rich in digestive enzyme. This occurs in response to the smell and sight of food, as well as to the presence of food in the mouth. Sympathetic stimulation of salivary glands tends to produce a dry mouth (such as during states of anxiety or fear) with very little enzyme content in the saliva.

The salivary glands may be involved in disease. Infection with the mumps virus produces a characteristic enlargement of the parotid gland, which causes painful swelling in the face and cheek. Tumors may also arise in the salivary glands. Most tumors arise in the parotid gland, and about 80 percent of these are benign (non-invasive and less dangerous). About half of the tumors arising from the submandibular gland are benign, while the others are malignant (invasive and potentially fatal). Cancers of the salivary gland may be treated by surgical removal or radiation therapy.

SEE ALSO *Autonomic nervous system, Digestive system, Mouth, Mumps, Saliva, Sympathetic nervous system, Tongue*

SALPINGITIS

Salpingitis is inflammation of the fallopian (uterine) tubes, usually due to pelvic infection. Prolonged infection can lead to infertility due to obstruction of the tubes so that either sperm cells cannot reach the eggs, or fertilized eggs cannot reach the uterus.

SEE ALSO *Fallopian tubes, Pelvic inflammatory disease, Reproductive systems*

SAPHENOUS VEINS

The saphenous veins are the major superficial veins of the leg. The great saphenous vein returns blood from the foot and leg to the femoral vein below the groin, and the small saphenous vein returns blood from the calf to the popliteal vein behind the knee. The location of these veins requires them to return blood towards the heart against the action of gravity. Most of the venous blood in the calf is returned to the heart by the deep veins, assisted by the increased pressure applied by contraction of the calf muscles.

The deep veins receive blood from the great saphenous vein via "perforating" veins;

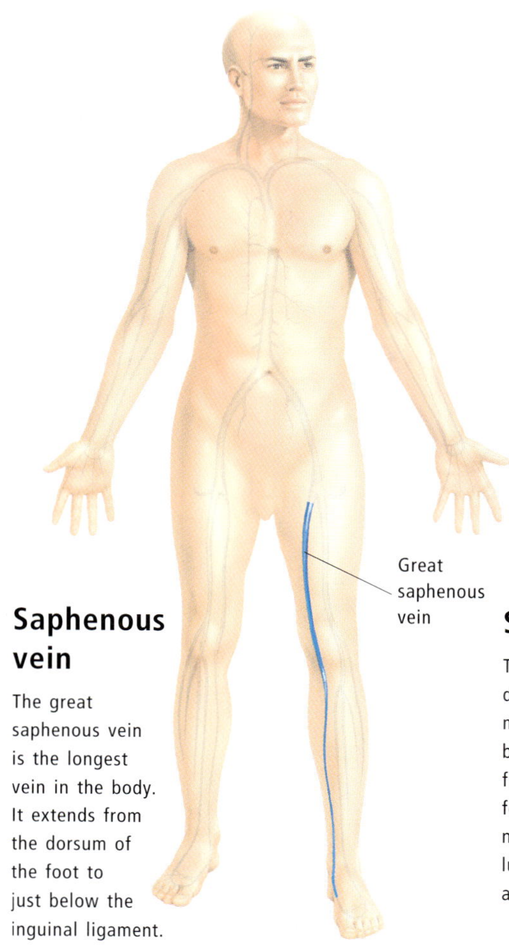

Saphenous vein

The great saphenous vein is the longest vein in the body. It extends from the dorsum of the foot to just below the inguinal ligament.

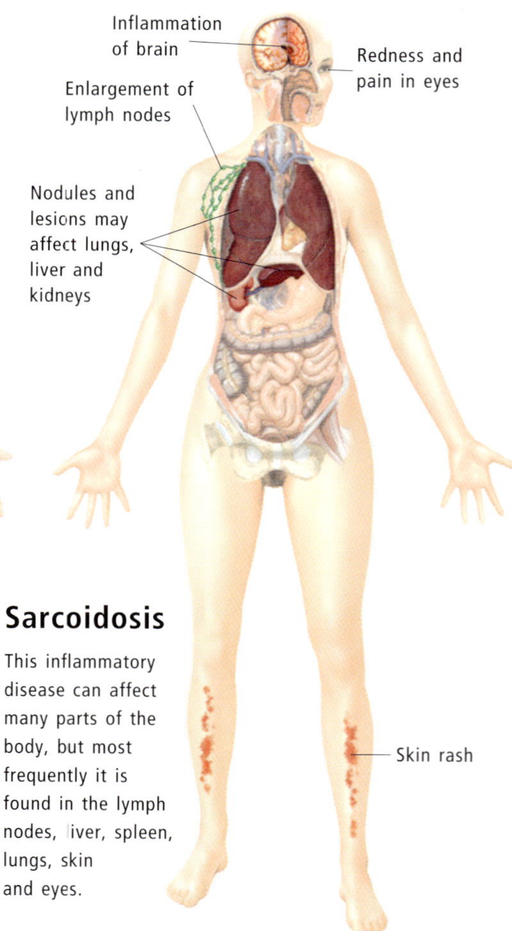

Sarcoidosis

This inflammatory disease can affect many parts of the body, but most frequently it is found in the lymph nodes, liver, spleen, lungs, skin and eyes.

these contain valves preventing backflow of blood from deep veins to the great saphenous vein. If the valves fail, blood is squeezed into the superficial veins by the muscle pump, distending the veins, which become varicose.

SEE ALSO *Leg, Phlebitis, Thrombosis, Varicose veins*

SARCOIDOSIS

Sarcoidosis is a systemic inflammatory disease of unknown origin, which may affect a variety of body organs. Most often it is detected as an incidental finding on a chest x-ray. It causes enlargement of lymph nodes in the chest and may cause shadows in the lungs. Later, symptoms such as persistent dry cough or shortness of breath may develop. Other symptoms may include a painful red rash on the shins and redness and pain of the eyes. Less commonly, sarcoidosis may affect the kidneys, heart or brain. The inflammatory cells involved can produce an increased level of calcium in the blood and urine. Young women are most often affected.

Sarcoidosis is diagnosed by x-rays, blood tests and tissue biopsy. It needs to be distinguished from other causes of enlarged lymph glands, such as lymphoma and tuberculosis. The physician will often assess the function of various organs with further tests, such as an electrocardiograph or detailed lung function studies. Often the condition is mild and may improve without treatment, especially in children. In other cases treatment is required with anti-inflammatory medication. This can range from mild drugs, such as aspirin, to cortisone or powerful immunosuppressants in severe cases.

SEE ALSO *Lungs, Lymph nodes*

Scabies

Scabies is caused by female parasitic mites burrowing under the skin to lay their eggs. An allergic reaction to the mites' feces causes an itchy rash to appear.

SCABIES

Tiny mites (*Sarcoptes scabiei*) cause the highly contagious skin condition scabies. It is spread by close personal contact with an infected person, by sharing their bed or wearing their clothes. Female mites burrow under the skin—favoring hands, toes, groin and bends of elbows and knees—to lay eggs. It takes about 10 days for the mites to mature and continue the cycle. Within weeks, the skin develops an allergic reaction and itches intensely. An eczema-like rash often develops and the mite burrows may be visible.

Treatment includes chemical washes, but the itching may persist for weeks.

SEE ALSO *Sexually transmitted diseases, Skin*

SCALP

The scalp is the skin and connective tissue covering the skull. The hair that grows from it protects against heat loss, minor abrasions and ultraviolet light. The adult human scalp contains around 100,000 hair follicles. Hair may disappear because the follicles are

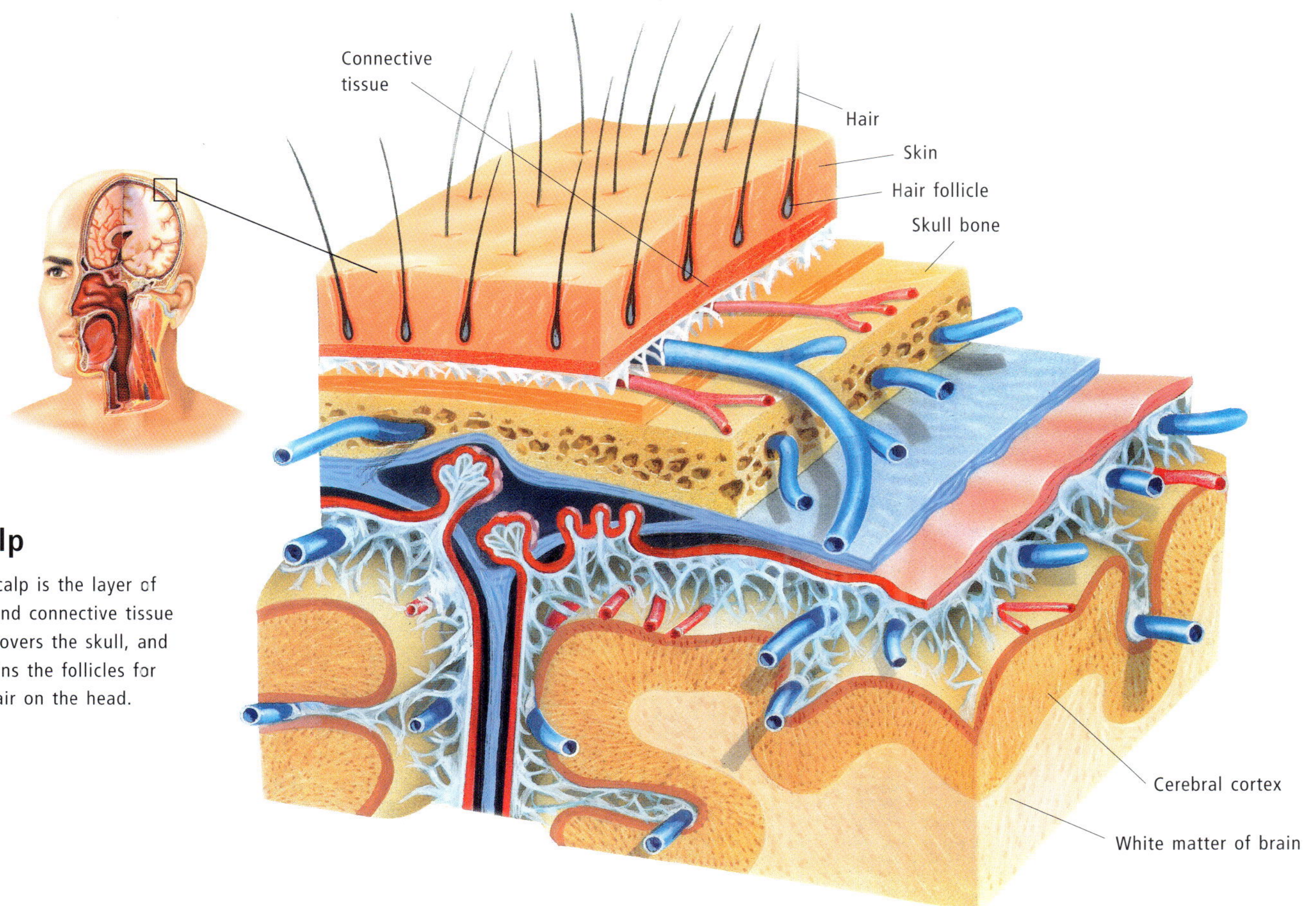

Scalp

The scalp is the layer of skin and connective tissue that covers the skull, and contains the follicles for the hair on the head.

damaged, either permanently or temporarily; because the person is going bald for reasons of heredity or hormonal imbalance; or because it has been voluntarily removed.

Conditions that can cause itchiness of the scalp include dandruff, scalp psoriasis and head lice. Dandruff is a mild form of seborrheic dermatitis, cause unknown, and is more of a cosmetic problem than a medical one. It can usually be controlled by a medicated shampoo. Scalp psoriasis, also cause unknown, produces scaly lesions that can be treated with shampoos and other preparations, including topical corticosteroids. Infestations of head lice require diligent fine combing, the use of an insecticidal shampoo and sometimes washing the hair with hot soapy water to remove the lice and eggs.

Cradle cap, common in babies, is a scalp condition created when sebum from the sebaceous glands forms layers on the scalp. It is generally a yellow color and feels greasy. It is not dirty. Rubbing olive oil into the crusts the night before and washing with a gentle shampoo will often remove it, though sometimes a doctor may prescribe a lotion for stubborn cases. The actual cause is unknown and older children may also suffer from it.

SEE ALSO *Cradle cap, Dandruff, Hair, Head lice, Psoriasis*

Scapula—back view

Each scapula is connected to the humerus bone and clavicle (collar bone).

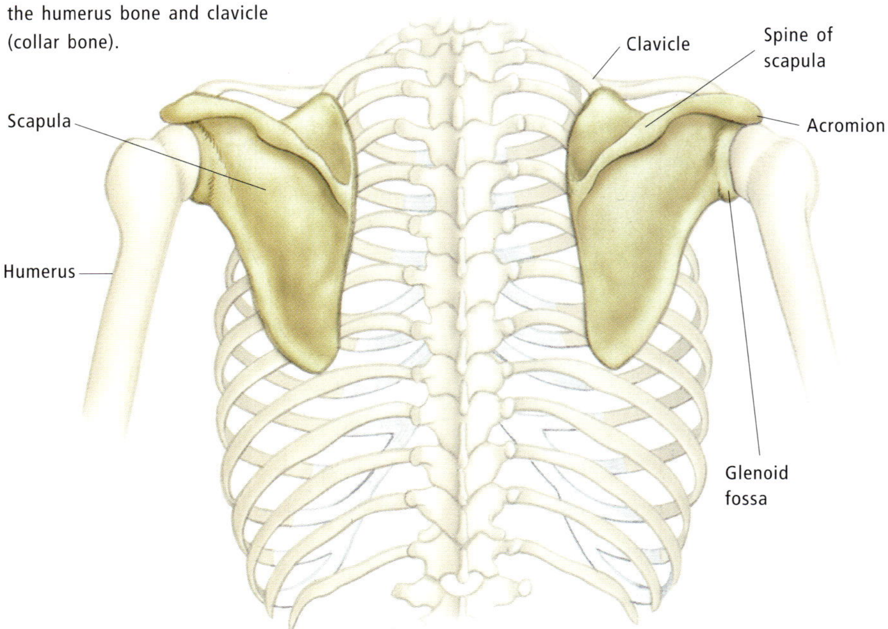

SCAPULA

The scapula (shoulder blade) forms part of the shoulder, at the back. It is a triangular, flattened bone, with several projections. The scapula is attached to the outer end of the collar bone (clavicle) at the acromioclavicular joint. Its outer end provides a socket for the head of the upper arm bone (humerus), forming the bony articulation of the shoulder joint. The scapula is held in place by strong muscles, which can move it in relation to the chest wall. It provides attachment for many of the muscles of the shoulder and upper arm, including the biceps.

SEE ALSO *Collar bone, Humerus, Shoulder*

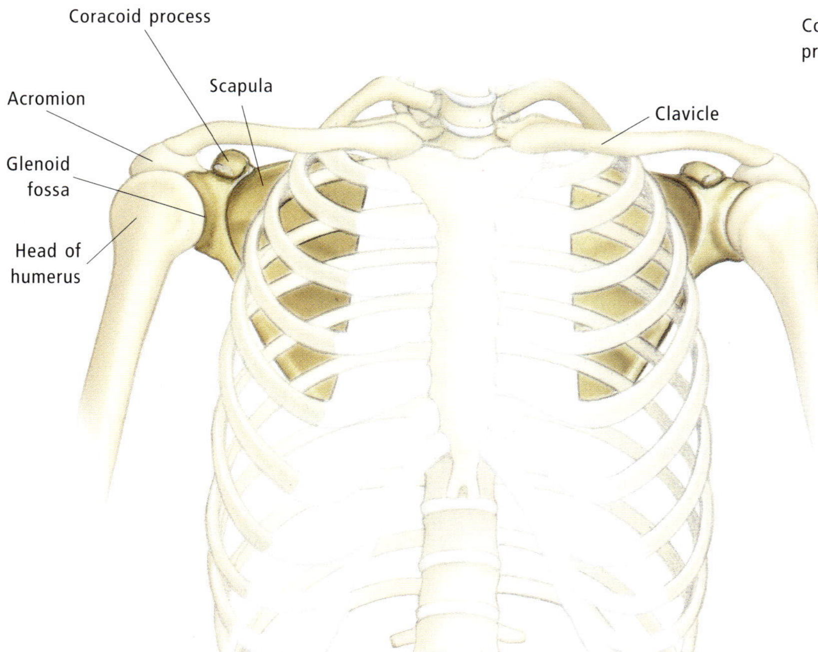

Scapula—front view

The connection between the scapula and the head of the humerus forms the shoulder joint.

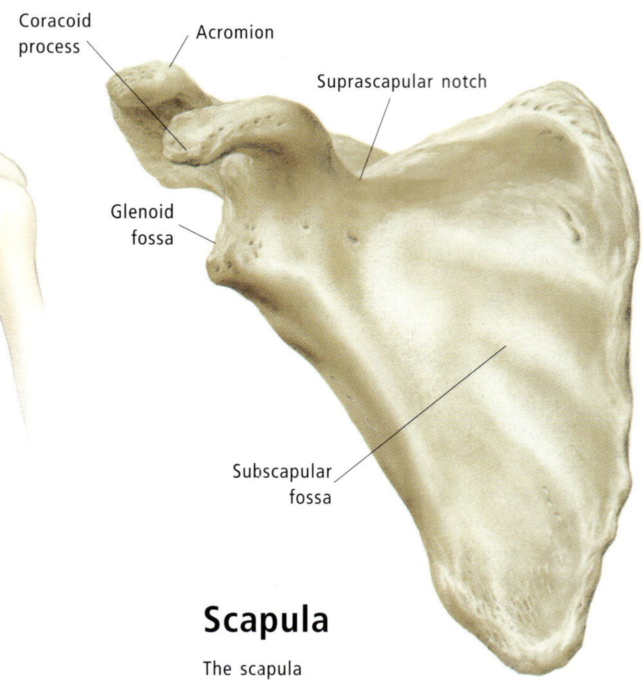

Scapula

The scapula (shoulder blade) is a flat triangular bone located in the back of the shoulder.

SCAR

A scar, or cicatrix, is toughened fibrous tissue that develops while a burn, wound or surgical incision heals. A scar helps knit the wound together. Inside the body, scars rarely cause problems. People are more commonly concerned about scars on the skin. The extent to which an injury will leave a scar depends on where it occurs on the body, its size and depth. Scarring will also vary with a person's age, genetic predisposition to scarring, and skin characteristics.

A range of treatments is available to minimize scarring, including dermabrasion, during which the surface of the skin is frozen with an aerosol spray and then abraded by mechanical means.

SEE ALSO *Keloid*

SCARLET FEVER

Scarlet fever is caused by bacteria known as Group A beta-hemolytic streptococci. Thanks largely to the advent of antibiotics, which offer quick and effective treatment, this once common disease is no longer the deeply feared scourge it was during the 1800s and early 1900s.

As immunity usually develops after one bout of scarlet fever, the disease tends to occur mainly in children. It begins suddenly with a fever and sore throat within two days of contact with an infected person. Shivering, headaches and vomiting may follow. Within two days of the first symptoms, a small bright red rash begins appearing, first on the neck and chest but eventually spreading to the rest of the body. The rash, which feels like sandpaper, is a reaction to a toxin released by the bacteria. It may last up to a week, after which the skin peels as if it has been sunburnt. During the early stages of scarlet fever, the tongue is coated in white and the taste buds are red and swollen—known as a "strawberry tongue". Later, the white coating disappears to leave a "raspberry tongue", which is red all over.

Before antibiotics were developed, scarlet fever was often followed by meningitis or rheumatic fever. These are now rare as complications of streptococcal infection.

SEE ALSO *Antibiotics, Bacteria, Infectious diseases*

Scar

The growth of granulation tissue during wound healing may leave a mark or scar on the skin.

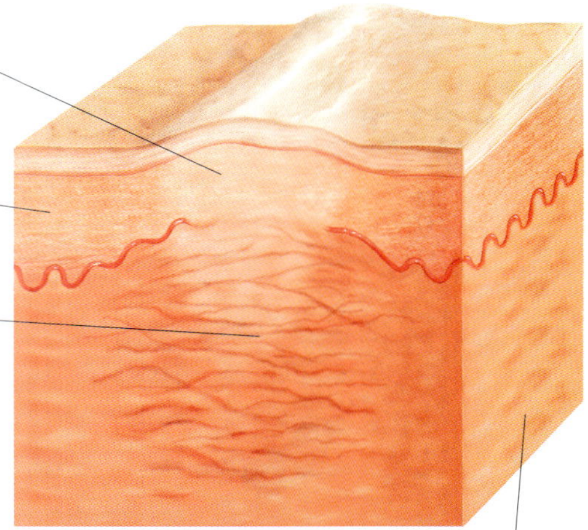

SCHISTOSOMIASIS

Schistosomiasis is an infection caused by the *Schistosoma* genus of trematode worms, and is second only to malaria in prevalence worldwide. The worms develop in snails and are released into fresh water where their larvae penetrate the skin to infect humans. The most common form of the disease occurs in South America, Africa and the Middle East, while another form occurs in the Far East.

Local inhabitants may not develop symptoms of initial infection, whereas visitors may develop intense itching (swimmer's itch). Weeks later a febrile illness occurs with cough and diarrhea, due to an immune reaction to the developing worms and their eggs in the intestines. Prolonged exposure to the worm infection can result in scarring of the liver (cirrhosis) and enlargement of the liver and spleen.

Infection is diagnosed by increased blood eosinophils, antibody tests and microscopic stool examination for eggs. Drugs are available which are active against the infection.

SEE ALSO *Swimmer's itch, Worms*

SCHIZOPHRENIA

Schizophrenia is a serious and incurable mental illness that profoundly disrupts thought patterns, thinking processes and emotions. The disorder is difficult to describe accurately because it produces a broad range of symptoms which can affect every attribute of character and personality. Language and thought, perception and response, and the individual's sense of self may all be upset; it may be impossible for sufferers to respond properly to people or events and to differentiate between what is real and what is imagined.

Schizophrenics may hold delusions or invest everyday events or actions with strange meanings. They may experience hallucinations, both visual and auditory. Their speech may be incoherent and disorganized. They may show no emotion or respond to others in a very limited emotional manner, or they may grossly exaggerate their responses. They may withdraw from all interaction with others or become deeply depressed. The effects of schizophrenia have a marked impact on the ability to carry on everyday activities.

One popular analogy to explain what is happening in schizophrenia is to liken the normal brain to a telephone switchboard where incoming perceptions are sent to the correct part of the brain, which produces an appropriate response—an action, thought, feeling or verbal reply. In the schizophrenic brain it is as if the incoming signals get jammed or sent to the wrong place and the response generated is inappropriate or nonexistent. There is a foundation for this analogy, as the brains of some schizophrenia sufferers have been found to have altered levels of chemicals called neurotransmitters which are responsible for carrying nerve impulses. This disturbance in the levels of neurotransmitters can be treated by medication under supervision.

Schizophrenia most often appears in early adulthood, in the mid to late twenties; it is found in men and women of all cultures, races and social groupings, occurring in about 1 percent of the population of industrialized societies. Onset may be gradual or quite sudden, with one or a series of psychotic episodes, and the course of the disease varies widely from person to person.

The exact cause of schizophrenia is still largely unknown but is believed to be

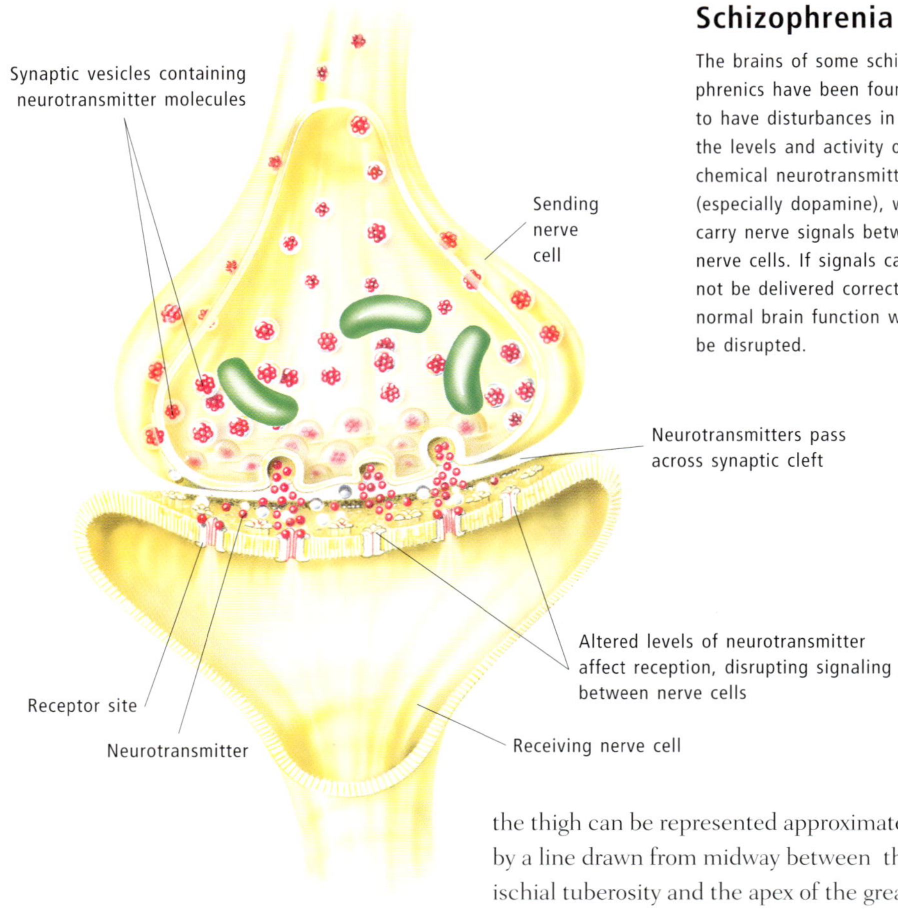

Schizophrenia

The brains of some schizophrenics have been found to have disturbances in the levels and activity of chemical neurotransmitters (especially dopamine), which carry nerve signals between nerve cells. If signals cannot be delivered correctly, normal brain function will be disrupted.

genetic or a chemical imbalance in the brain. Gradual signs of onset are usually observed by immediate family as a marked change in behavior, often believed to be temporary. Eventually it becomes obvious that something is seriously wrong, and professional help is sought.

While schizophrenia is neither preventable nor curable, an appropriate medication regime can do much to ameliorate its symptoms. People need to be encouraged to continue medication even when they feel well.

SEE ALSO *Antipsychotics*

SCIATIC NERVE

The sciatic nerve is the major nerve of the back of the thigh. At its commencement, it is the thickness of a little finger in diameter—the thickest nerve in the body. It arises from the lumbar and sacral plexus at the base of the spine. It leaves the pelvis through the greater sciatic foramen, passes under the gluteus maximus muscle and runs down the back of the thigh. In the lower third of the thigh, it divides into two branches, the tibial and common peroneal nerves. Its course in the thigh can be represented approximately by a line drawn from midway between the ischial tuberosity and the apex of the greater trochanter (both of which can be felt in the hip area), to the apex of the popliteal fossa, located behind the knee.

The sciatic nerve sends branches to supply several muscles, namely the biceps femoris, semitendinosus, semimembranosus, and the ischial head of the adductor magnus. The sciatic nerve also provides sensation for the hip joint.

Injections into the buttocks must be placed to avoid the sciatic nerve as injury or inflammation to it may cause pain that can travel down the length of the leg. Sciatica is pain experienced in the region supplied by the sciatic nerve. It is usually due either to a slipped, or herniated, intervertebral disk or to osteophytes—bony outgrowths affecting the roots of the nerve in the sacral foramina.

SEE ALSO *Nerves, Sciatica, Spine*

Sciatic nerve

This is the widest nerve of the body. It extends from the base of the spine down the thigh, then branches out through the lower leg and foot.

SCIATICA

Each leg is served by a sciatic nerve which begins at the base of the spine, travels through the hip and buttock, then down the length of the limb. Pain along it or its branches is called sciatica.

Sciatica is usually caused by stress on the nerve around the point where it emerges from the vertebral column.

Sciatica occurs most commonly when the nerve becomes pinched by a herniated disk between vertebrae or is placed under pressure around the base of the spine due to arthritis or pregnancy.

Occasionally, sciatica may be due to more serious conditions such as a tumor, blood clot or abscess in the spine. The severity and type of pain varies, from pins and needles in the toes to excruciating pains that run the

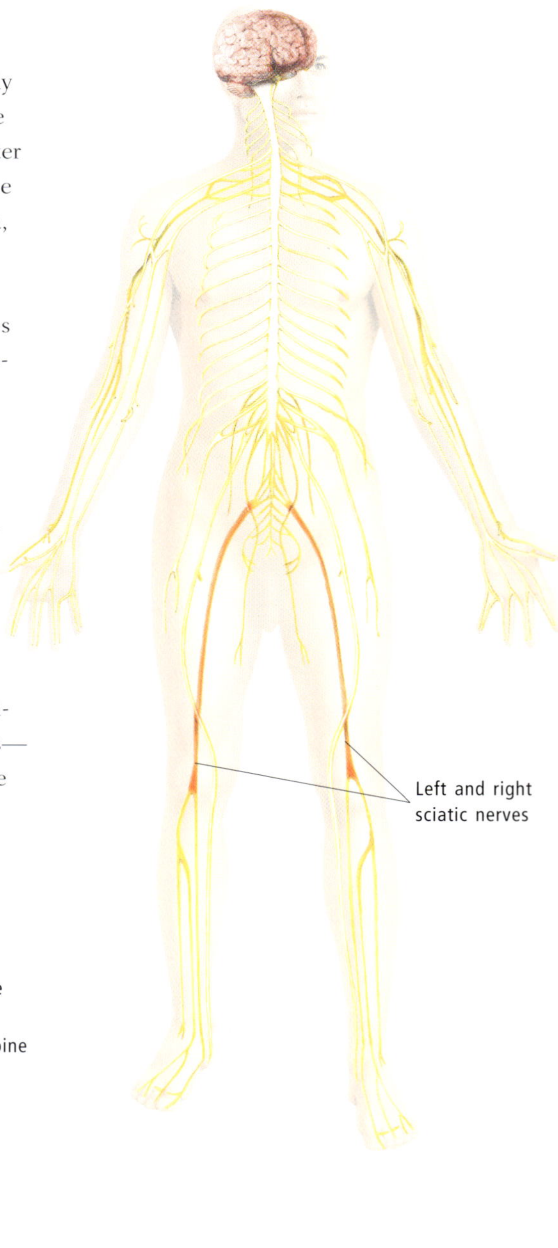

length of the limb. Weakness in the lower leg muscles can result; in severe cases, it may be difficult to bend the knee or even move the foot, making standing near-impossible.

Sciatica usually gets better with simple treatments, often within a few days, although very occasionally surgery may be necessary. In most cases, over-the-counter pain killers and anti-inflammatory drugs ease the pain.

SEE ALSO *Nerves, Sciatic nerve, Spine*

SCLERA

The sclera and the cornea together form the outside of the eyeball. Part of the sclera is visible, the so-called white of the eye. It is composed of dense, tough fibrous tissue.

Besides containing and protecting the optical parts of the eye, the sclera provides attachment for the muscles which move the eye.

SEE ALSO *Cornea, Eye*

SCLERITIS

Scleritis is inflammation of the sclera, the dense white fibrous covering of the eye beneath the transparent conjunctiva.

A relatively mild nodular scleritis sometimes occurs in the superficial layers of the sclera; it is thought to be an allergy and it generally responds to treatment with corticosteroid eye drops.

A more severe and often painful form of scleritis is often associated with autoimmune diseases such as Crohn's disease, rheumatoid arthritis or other connective-tissue disorders. However, in some cases, no cause is found.

The symptoms are severe eye pain, blurred vision, and sensitivity to light. Purple-red, inflamed areas may appear in areas of the white of the eye.

Scleritis may affect one or both eyes. The condition usually responds to treatment with corticosteroid eye drops or oral corticosteroids, but may recur. If the underlying disease can be treated, the condition will improve. In some cases it is chronic and progressive. If there is any vision loss, it is usually permanent.

SEE ALSO *Eye, Sclera*

Sclera

Commonly called the "white" of the eye, the sclera is composed of dense, tough, fibrous tissue.

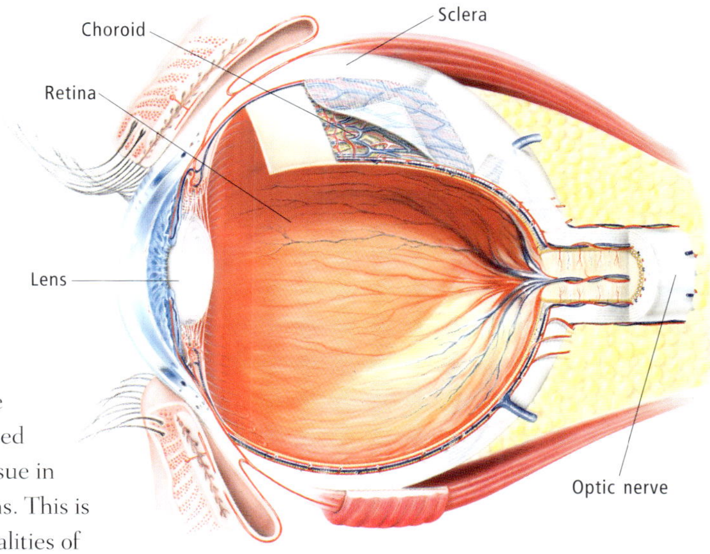

SCLERODERMA

Scleroderma is a disease characterized by increased deposition of fibrous tissue in the skin and other organs. This is associated with abnormalities of blood vessels, such as spasm precipitated by the cold, resulting in color change in the extremities (Raynaud's phenomenon). The fingers become swollen and small blood vessels may be prominent; gradually the skin over the fingers and face becomes thickened and tight. In severe cases the lungs, heart and kidneys can be affected.

Diagnosis is aided by the presence of autoantibodies in the blood. Treatment of scleroderma is difficult and the condition tends to progress gradually.

SEE ALSO *Raynaud's disease, Sclerosis*

SCLEROSIS

Sclerosis is the hardening or thickening of body tissue. Possible causes range from inflammation to the deposition of mineral salts to scarring. It is usually an abnormal and undesirable condition, often associated with disease. For example, the incurable and chronic illness known as progressive systemic sclerosis (also called scleroderma) is characterized by a thickening of the connective tissue causing debilitating changes to the skin, blood vessels and internal organs. In arteriosclerosis, the walls of the arteries thicken, calcify and lose their elasticity.

SEE ALSO *Arteriosclerosis, Scleroderma*

SCOLIOSIS

Scoliosis is an abnormal sideways deviation of the vertebral column (spine). It affects the muscles and ligaments connected to the spine and if left untreated can lead to

Scoliosis

Scoliosis is lateral curvature of the spine. The first visible sign is likely to be unevenness of the hips or shoulders.

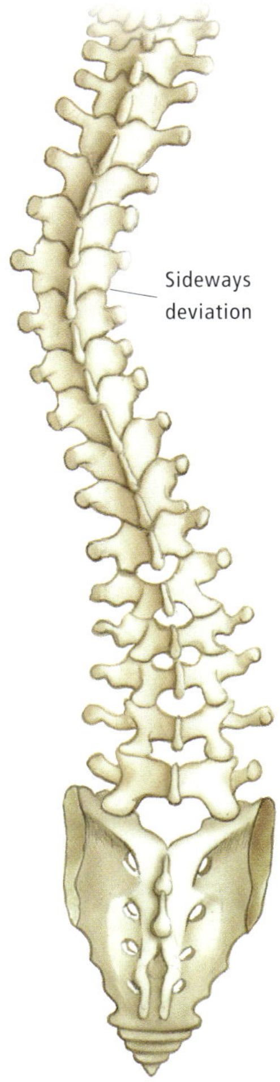

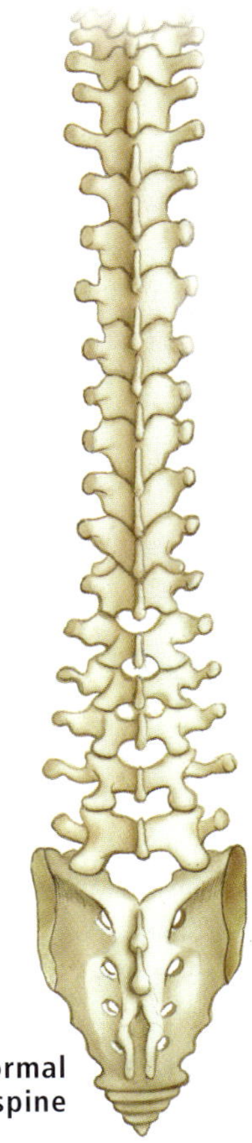

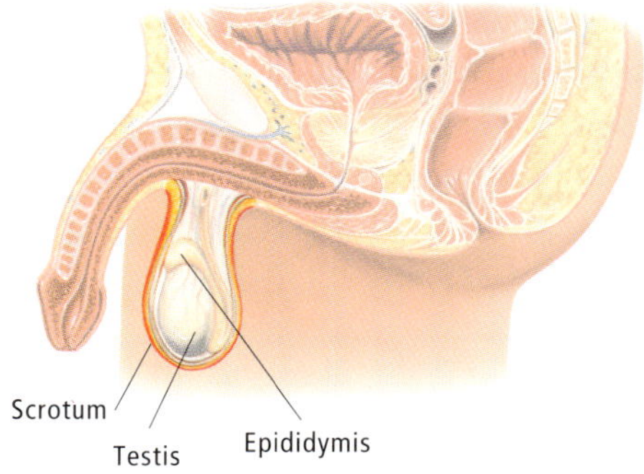

Scrotum

The scrotum is a bag of skin which hangs just behind the penis and contains the testes. The cremaster muscle adjusts the tension of the skin of the scrotum, moving the testes towards or away from the body in response to changes in temperature.

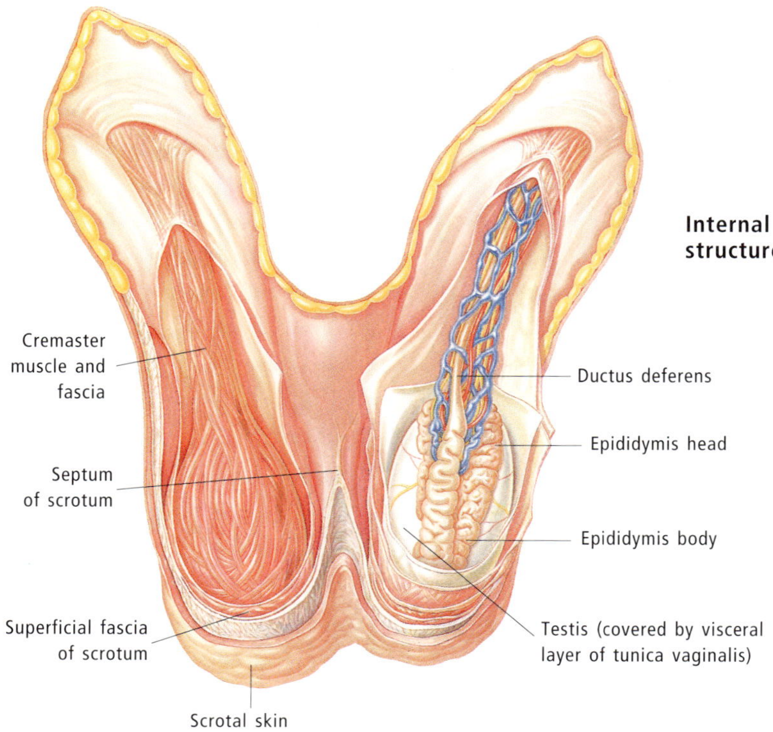

deformities of the rib cage, which in turn can result in heart and lung problems. Treatment may involve wearing a corrective back brace, the use of traction, exercise, a plaster cast or, in more severe cases, orthopedic surgery, in which a metal rod is inserted to support the spine.

SEE ALSO *Lordosis, Kyphosis, Spine*

SCROTUM

The scrotum is the bag of skin and soft tissue attached to the perineum in the male, hanging between the thighs. It contains the testes and the lower parts of the spermatic cords. Under the skin of the scrotum is a thin layer of muscle (dartos muscle), whose contractions make the skin of the scrotum wrinkle. The testes normally descend before or just after birth from the abdominal cavity, along the inguinal canal, and into the scrotum. In rare cases, the testes fail to descend into the scrotum. An inguinal hernia, particularly the indirect type, will often descend into the scrotum along the route taken by the testis and will need to be surgically corrected.

Several other conditions cause a lump in the scrotum besides an inguinal hernia. They include epididymitis (inflammation of the epididymis), tumors such as carcinoma of the testes, varicocele (a group of varicose veins in the scrotum), hematocele (a collection of blood within the scrotum) and a spermatocele (a cyst-like mass within the scrotum containing fluid and dead sperm cells).

A physician will often diagnose the lump with the help of an ultrasound of the scrotum, or a biopsy performed during surgery.

Treatment depends on the cause; most conditions can be easily treated and some such as hematoceles and spermatoceles do not need treatment. A scrotal support (jockstrap) may be worn to help relieve pain and discomfort.

It is a good idea for males to regularly self-examine each testis and the scrotum and consult a physician if a lump is found. A lump that is accompanied by sudden severe pain in a testis may be a sign of torsion of the testis, indicating that it has become twisted in the scrotum and is losing its blood supply. Urgent medical attention should be sought or the testicle may be damaged permanently.

SEE ALSO *Hernia, Reproductive systems, Testes*

SCRUB TYPHUS

Scrub typhus is an infectious disease which is caused by a microorganism called *Rickettsia tsutsugamushi*. It is transmitted from rodents to humans via the bite of mite larvae. The disease is most prevalent in eastern Asia, northern Australia and the western Pacific.

Symptoms occur suddenly between 1–3 weeks after a bite and can include severe headaches, fever, swollen and tender lymph nodes, muscle aches, eye pain and a rash. Often a dark-colored ulcer appears where the mite has attached to the skin.

There is no effective vaccine, however broad-spectrum antibiotics are effective against scrub typhus. In severe cases, serious complications such as pneumonia may occur if left untreated. Death from scrub typhus is rare.

SEE ALSO *Infectious diseases*

SCURVY

Scurvy is an illness caused by inadequate intake of vitamin C. This essential vitamin is needed by the body to make collagen, the connective tissue that helps form healthy bones, teeth and capillaries, and which is used also for wound healing.

In the late eighteenth century it was noted that scurvy in sailors was due to a dietary deficiency and could be cured by eating citrus fruits and vegetables. The disease now occurs mostly in infants or elderly people whose diets are poor, or in people following fad diets that do not include fruits and vegetables.

over-the-counter anti-dandruff lotions containing salicylic acid, coal tar, zinc, or selenium. The hair should be shampooed vigorously and frequently (once a day). Loosen scales with the fingers, scrub for at least 5 minutes, and rinse thoroughly.

More severe cases require treatment with shampoos or lotions containing selenium or ketaconazole, or corticosteroid creams or ointments applied directly to the scalp.

In newborns and small children up to the age of 3 years, seborrheic dermatitis appears as cradle cap. Thick, crusty, yellow scales appear over the child's scalp, on the eyelids and ears, around the nose, or in the groin.

Cradle cap can be treated with massaging of the scalp to loosen the scales, daily shampoos with mild soap, and brushing the hair several times a day. If cradle cap persists, consult a physician who may prescribe a cream or lotion to be applied to the scalp.

SEE ALSO *Cradle cap, Dandruff, Dermatitis, Skin*

SEDATIVES

Sedatives are drugs which are prescribed to calm anxiety or mental disturbance, induce sleep or drowsiness and reduce the body's functional activity. Sedatives may also be prescribed for insomnia and epilepsy. They can be taken as tablets or by injection. Anxiety is often treated with sedative drugs because they relax muscles, thus reducing tension and allowing sleep to provide a temporary relief from symptoms. Travelers with a fear of flying or who suffer claustrophobia may use sedatives to reduce anxiety before and during a flight.

Common side effects include drowsiness, impaired judgement, lack of coordination, lowered heart rate and blood pressure, nausea and diarrhea, and dependence. More rarely sedatives produce memory defects, hallucinations, constipation, vomiting and headaches, and loss of consciousness. Sedatives should be taken only on prescription and under medical supervision, used only intermittently, and not taken in pregnancy.

Long-term use can lead to dependence, and stopping use should be a gradual process under medical supervision. All sedatives may interact with other similar drugs, such as anti-epilepsy, antidepressant and antipsychotic drugs, and especially alcohol, which increases the risk of side effects and overdose.

SEE ALSO *Anxiety, Anxiolytics, Barbiturates, Drug dependence, Overdose, Sleeping pills*

Semicircular canals

Located in the inner ear, the semicircular canals contain the fluid-filled semicircular ducts, which provide our sense of balance.

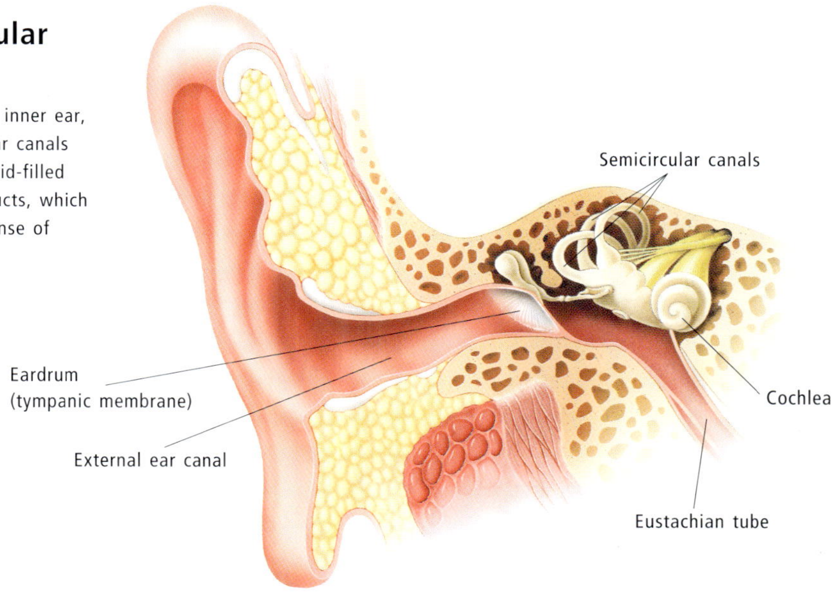

SEMEN

Also called seminal fluid, semen is a liquid that is emitted from the male reproductive tract. It comprises sperm cells and the fluids that nourish and support them. The fluids are produced and secreted by the various tubules and glands of the reproductive system, including the prostate gland and seminal vesicles. These ensure that the semen contains the correct concentration of nutrients and electrolytes needed to keep the sperm healthy. These nutrients include sugars, amino acids, phosphorus, potassium, and prostaglandin hormones. A small amount of mucus is also secreted into the semen by the bulbourethral and urethral glands. The secretions of the testes and other glands are controlled by the male hormone testosterone.

Semen contains millions of sperm cells, needed to fertilize female ova (eggs). Sperm cells are produced by the testes, stored in the epididymis, then transported down a muscular tube called the ductus deferens (or vas deferens).

During ejaculation, muscles around the epididymis and ductus deferens contract, forcing semen into the urethra. The fluid is then expelled out of the body by spasmodic contractions of the bulbocavernosus muscle in the penis.

When a man ejaculates, at the height of sexual excitation, he will normally discharge about $\frac{1}{20}$–$\frac{1}{5}$ ounce (1.5–5 milliliters) of semen from his urethra. Each ejaculation normally contains between 200 and 300 million sperm which comprise only about 2–5 percent of the ejaculate.

Semen analysis is usually carried out to assess a man's fertility—about one-third of infertility problems seen in couples are due to male problems. The semen must be tested within 2 hours of collection for a valid result. Low sperm counts or insufficient semen production may be the cause of infertility.

SEE ALSO *Fertility, Infertility, Reproductive systems, Sperm*

SEMICIRCULAR CANALS

As well as being fundamental to hearing, the ears are also organs of balance. Head movements are detected deep inside the inner ear (labyrinth) by the semicircular ducts—three liquid-filled looped tubes in the bony semicircular canals arranged at right angles to each other. The end of each has a bulge (ampulla), containing sensory hairs which bend as the liquid in the canals moves. Nerve cells at the base of the hairs send signals to the brain about the head's movement. Each canal registers a slightly different movement: one detects the head nodding, another senses side-to-side shaking and the third perceives tilting.

SEE ALSO *Balance, Ear*

SENSES

The senses are the faculties that enable individuals to perceive changes in their external and internal environments. These changes are detected by sense organs—specialized organs in the body consisting of receptors that can detect physical stimuli, such as light, heat, touch and sound. The organs change physical stimuli into nerve impulses

Sensory pathways

Sensory receptors provide information on conditions inside and outside of the body. When stimulated, they pass information along the peripheral nerves to the central nervous system, where the signals are recognized as a sensation.

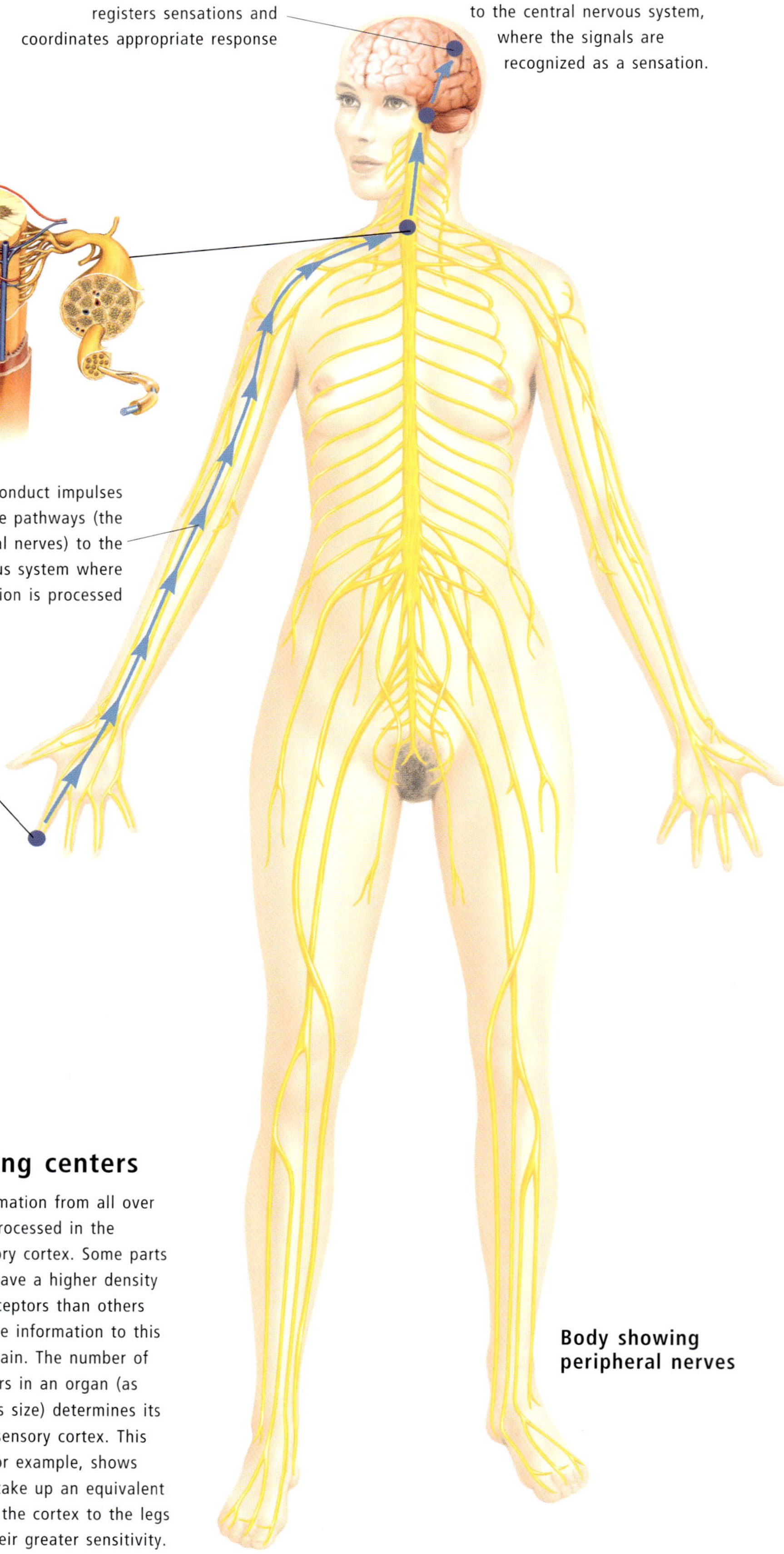

Body showing peripheral nerves

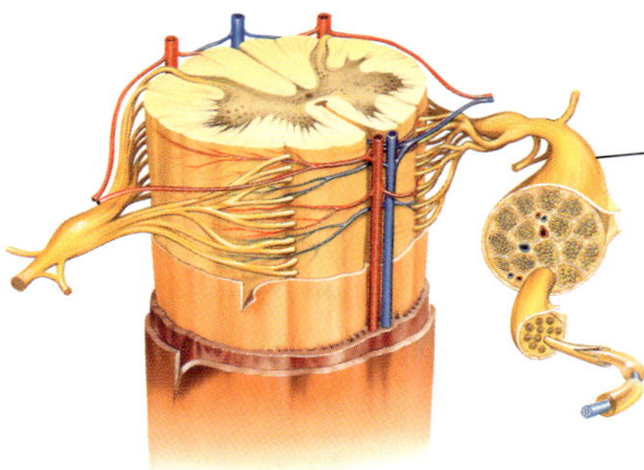

Spinal cord

Peripheral nerves pass sensations on to the central nervous system via the spinal cord.

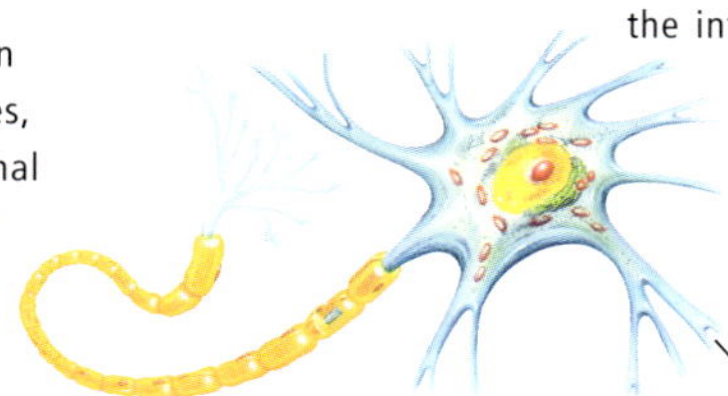

Neuron

Nerve endings in the skin, muscles, joints and internal organs transmit signals of pain, temperature or pressure along peripheral nerves.

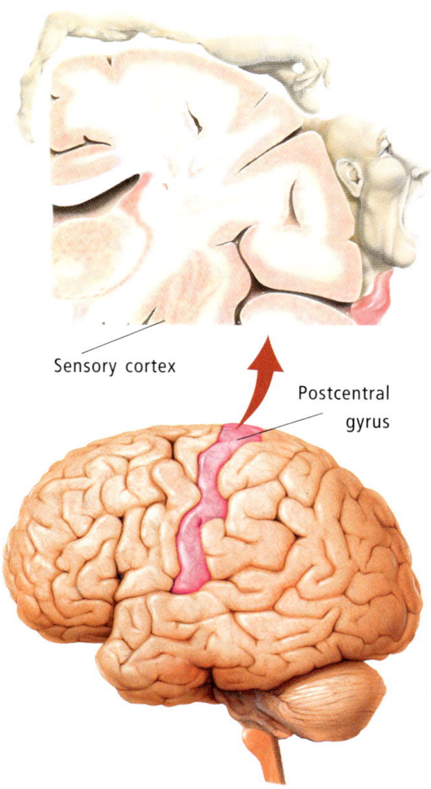

Processing centers

Sensory information from all over the body is processed in the somatic sensory cortex. Some parts of the body have a higher density of sensory receptors than others and send more information to this part of the brain. The number of nerve receptors in an organ (as opposed to its size) determines its share of the sensory cortex. This illustration, for example, shows that the lips take up an equivalent proportion of the cortex to the legs because of their greater sensitivity.

S

General senses

The general senses include temperature, pain, pressure, proprioception and vibration. The receptors for these sensations are distributed throughout the body. Some receptors provide information about the environment outside the body, some detect sensations in internal organs and tissues, others monitor the position and movement of joints, muscles and tendons.

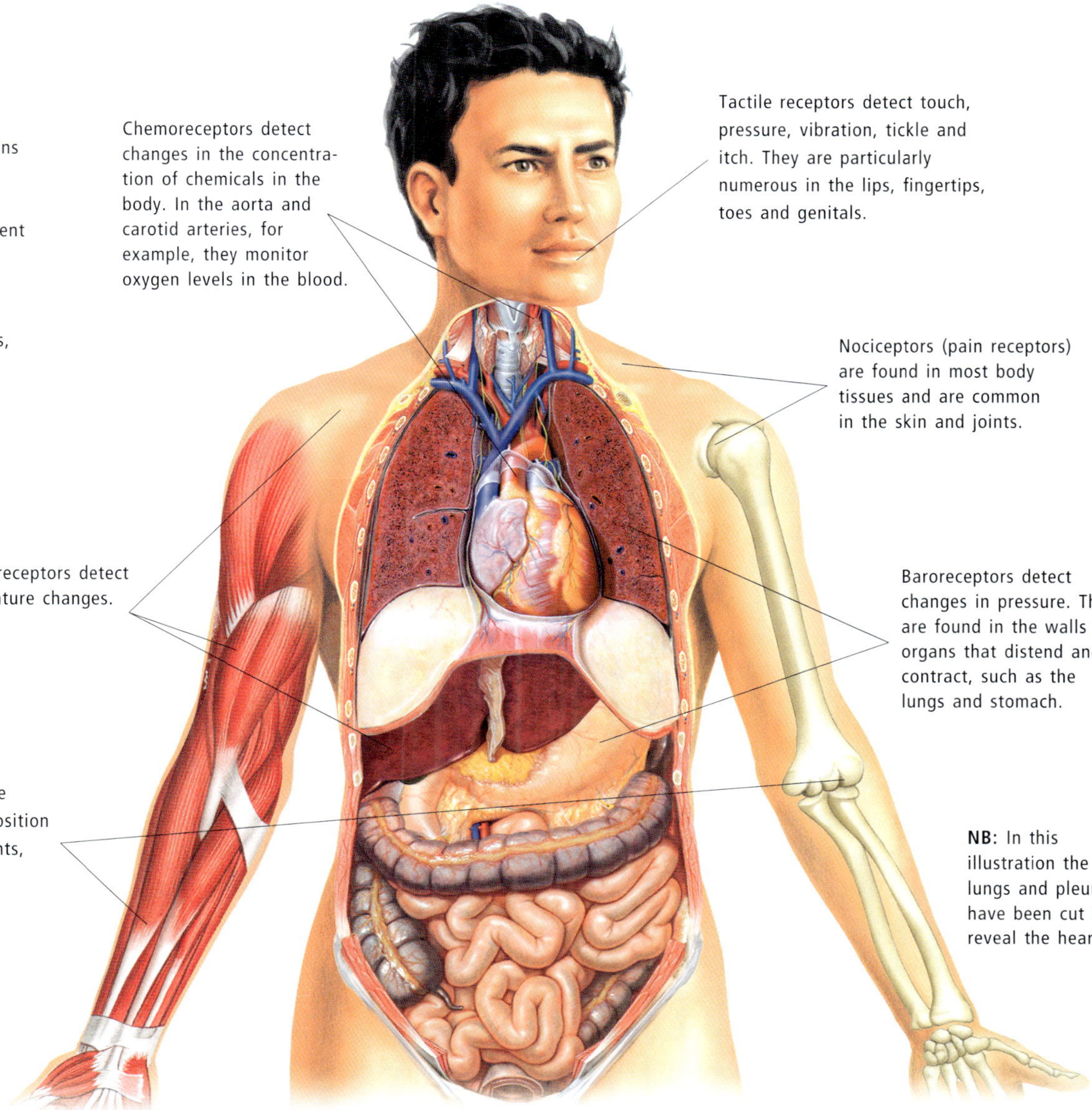

Senses

Special senses

The special senses are smell, taste, hearing, sight, and equilibrium (balance). All the special sense organs are found in the head and nerve impulses from these organs travel to the brain via the cranial nerves.

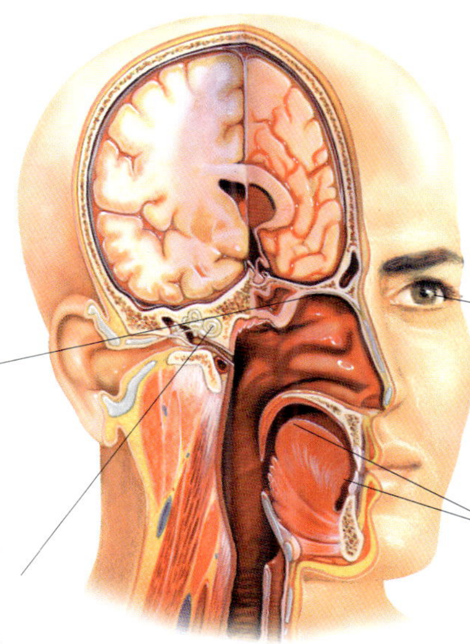

and send these impulses along sensory nerve pathways to the brain where they are interpreted as sensations.

The senses are commonly divided into general senses and special senses.

General senses include touch, pressure, vibration, proprioception, stretch, pain, heat and cold. The receptors for these senses are distributed widely throughout the body. They are nerve endings, most of which are covered by a capsule of connective tissue.

The special senses include olfaction (smell), vision, taste, hearing and equilibrium (balance). The receptors for these senses are found in very localized areas of the body and are more complex.

Receptors are often classified according to the type of stimulus they can detect. For example, sight is detected by photoreceptors; touch, sound and equilibrium are detected by mechanoreceptors; smell and taste by chemoreceptors; heat and cold by thermoreceptors; and pain by nociceptors.

General senses

Many of the receptors of the general senses are found in the skin. Tactile receptors are mechanoreceptors, which can detect touch, pressure, vibration, tickle and itch. There are at least six different types of tactile receptors found in the skin, including Ruffini endings, Meissner's corpuscles, Krause's end bulbs, Pacinian corpuscles, and Merkel's disks.

Tactile receptors are particularly numerous in certain areas such as lips, fingertips, palms, toes, nipples, the glans of the penis and the clitoris. When a stimulus, such as a pinprick or vibration, is applied to one of these receptors, it generates a nerve impulse, which then travels along a sensory (or afferent) nerve to the spinal cord. The stimulus then travels up the spinal cord along special pathways through the thalamus to the cerebral cortex, where it reaches consciousness as a vibration, pinprick or other sensation according to the nature of the original stimulus and the brain's general level of consciousness at the time.

Other types of receptors found in skin include thermoreceptors and nociceptors.

Other general sensory receptors are found deep in the tissues of muscles, tendons and joints.

Proprioceptors give rise to sensations of weight, position of the body, movements of body parts such as limbs, and the position of various joints. Proprioceptors include muscle spindles, Golgi tendon organs and joint receptors. These receptors provide the body with the sensory information needed to coordinate muscle movements and maintain body position. Most of the information from proprioceptors does not reach consciousness.

Thermoreceptors (receptors that detect changes in temperature) are widely distributed in the body. Separate thermoreceptors detect heat and cold and can detect wide variations in temperature, ranging from freezing cold to burning hot. They are especially numerous in the skin around the lips, mouth and anus.

Nociceptors (pain receptors) are also found in most tissues of the body. They may detect somatic pain (from the skin, muscles, tendons or joints) or visceral pain (from the internal organs of the body).

These receptors respond to chemicals released by damaged cells, by high temperatures, by stretched muscle fibers and other stimuli.

The nerves carrying the impulses from visceral nociceptors may enter the spinal cord at the same place as nerves from a different and separate area of skin on the surface of the body. Pain is often felt in the skin area rather than in the affected organ; this is known as referred pain. Some nociceptors, known as "silent" nociceptors, do not respond to intense stimuli unless they are sensitized by chemicals released by cells in inflamed tissue.

Special senses

The special senses are smell, vision, taste, hearing and equilibrium (balance). The special sense organs are all found in the head and the impulses from these organs travel to the brain via the cranial nerves.

The receptors for smell are found in the nasal cavity. Substances suspended in air enter the nasal cavity and react with tiny receptors on olfactory hairs in the nasal cavity. The receptors generate impulses that are transmitted via the olfactory nerve to specialized areas at the base of the brain where they are interpreted as odors. The olfactory receptors can detect thousands of different odors.

On the tongue and parts of the palate and throat are the taste buds, located in cuplike structures called papillae on the tongue, palate and throat. Receptors on the tongue are more sensitive to sweet and salty stimuli, while those on the palate and throat respond more readily to sour and bitter ones. When combined with substances dissolved in saliva, the taste buds generate impulses that travel along the facial, glossopharyngeal and vagus nerves and eventually to the cerebral cortex. The sensation of taste is complemented by that of smell; about 80 percent of the sensation of taste is actually due to smell.

The sense organs for vision are the eyes. Light enters the eye and strikes the retina at the back of the eyeball, where special photoreceptors called cones and rods convert the image to electrical impulses. These travel via the optic nerves to the occipital cortex and other parts of the brain where they are experienced as vision.

The sense organs for hearing are the ears, a pair of complex organs housed in the temporal bones of the skull. In the cochlea, the ear converts sound waves into mechanical waves and then into electrical impulses. These impulses travel via the cochlear part of the vestibular-cochlear nerve to the brain's cerebral cortex to be interpreted as sound.

Also in the ear are the organs concerned with the sense of balance, or equilibrium. These organs are known as the vestibular system and consist of the semicircular canals and the utricle and saccule of the vestibule of the inner ear. They detect changes in the body's position and relay this information via the vestibular part of the vestibulocochlear nerve to the brain.

If a person is deprived of one or more special senses, other senses will often become sharper. For example, if people lose their sight their sense of hearing may become more acute, or they may develop a heightened sense of touch.

SEE ALSO *Balance, Ear, Eye, Hearing, Mouth, Nervous system, Nose, Olfactory system, Pain, Proprioception, Sight, Skin, Smell, Spinal cord, Taste, Temperature, Tongue, Touch*

S

SEPARATION ANXIETY

Separation anxiety, the feeling of distress that comes from being separated from a loved one, most often occurs in children. From about the age of 8–9 months, many babies become upset when their parents or important carers go out of sight. This is particularly common in children who spend their time with one primary carer. It can also be a problem with babies who have been left to "cry it out". At 12 months of age many children will be able to wave goodbye but still may become distressed or miserable until distracted or occupied in play.

When children are older they learn that their carers will come back eventually. Separation can create unhappiness at any age, but for most people is a short-lived source of anxiety.

If a deeper sense of insecurity exists, children will display symptoms even after the apparent causes are resolved. These can include persistent crying or irritability, poor appetite, sleeplessness, pains or compulsive behavior. These signs should not be ignored, particularly if there is an obvious possible trigger for the distress.

Support and reassurance can help to resolve the problem. It is important to recognize the anxiety and remove any obvious causes. If the problem cannot be resolved quickly, seek expert advice.

SEE ALSO *Infancy, Childhood*

SEPTICEMIA

Septicemia (commonly called blood poisoning) is an infection of the bloodstream, which can occur directly or as a complication of infection at another site. It is a serious illness resulting in high fever and often violent shaking, called rigors. Infective organisms are more likely to gain access to the blood in people with decreased immunity or in hospitalized patients with intravenous catheters or undergoing invasive procedures. The effects of septicemia are due to the combination of bacterial toxins and the body's immune response to the infection. The elderly may fail to mount a high fever.

Treatment is with prompt introduction of intravenous antibiotics and supportive therapy in hospital.

SEE ALSO *Bacteria, Infectious diseases*

Serotonin

Serotonin is one of the key neurotransmitters in the limbic system, a collection of neural centers and tracts in the cerebrum, thalamus and hypothalamus that are involved in regulating mood and alertness levels. Low levels of serotonin have been linked to depression.

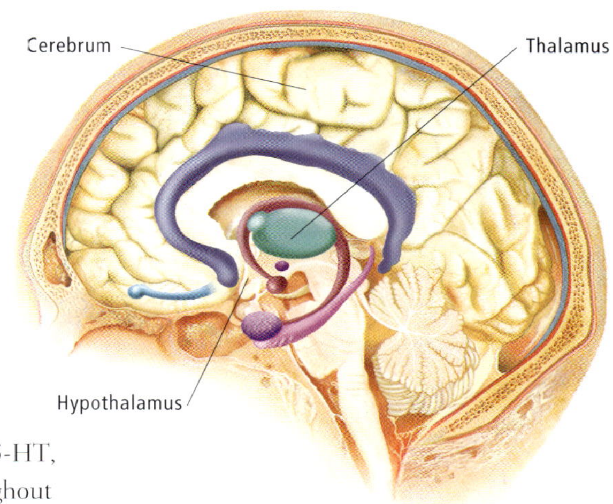

SEROTONIN

Also called 5-hydroxytryptamine or 5-HT, serotonin is a chemical found throughout the plant and animal kingdoms. In the human body it is synthesized from the amino acid tryptophan (found in many foods) and has various roles. It stimulates muscle contractions in the intestine and blood clotting at the site of wounds. Blood vessels constrict when serotonin levels rise and dilate when levels fall.

Migraine pain is thought to be caused partly by blood vessels in the brain dilating due to low serotonin levels.

Serotonin also works in the brain as a neurotransmitter responsible for regulating moods. Low levels are thought to trigger depression. The serotonin-specific reuptake inhibitor group of antidepressants help the brain optimize limited amounts of serotonin.

SEE ALSO *Amino acids, Antidepressants, Depression, Migraine*

SERUM SICKNESS

Serum is the part of the blood that contains antibodies. If you are exposed to a dangerous toxin or microorganism against which you have no antibodies, treatment sometimes involves an antiserum injection. This is produced from the serum of another person or animal already exposed to the offending toxin or microorganism; the serum contains the relevant antibodies to temporarily boost your immunity until you can develop your own antibodies.

Serum sickness is a type of allergic reaction to antiserum that can develop 2–3 weeks after having an antiserum injection. Symptoms include an itchy skin rash, joint stiffness and fever. Patients usually recover fully within weeks. Treatment often involves antihistamines and corticosteroids.

SEE ALSO *Allergies, Antibodies*

SEX

Sex is the sum of anatomical and physiological features which divides the members of a species into two groups that complement each other—male and female. In humans the two sexes, sexuality and sexual intercourse are all interwoven with the propagation and survival of the species, although each can also stand apart.

Sex is determined genetically at conception when the X chromosome from the ovum is paired with an X or Y chromosome from the sperm. An XX pairing leads to a genetic female, an XY pairing to a genetic male. Other genetic elements, as yet poorly understood, may modify the expression of the basic genetic coding.

SEE ALSO *Chromosomes, Genes, Sexual intercourse, Sexuality*

SEX EDUCATION

Sexual feelings are present from birth and sex education begins in the family situation from that moment. Baby boys can have erections and both girls and boys will get pleasure from their sexual organs. Some time before their first birthday children have usually discovered their genitals and may enjoy playing with them—it is quite natural.

By the time children reach the age of 3 or 4 they will be aware that the other sex has different genitals and be interested in looking at the human body, usually without any feelings of coyness. By this age most children are also curious about where babies come from, and are interested in body processes, but do not usually understand sexual intercourse. They will ask questions which need to be answered at their level of understanding.

Sexual organs

During sex, the man's penis penetrates the vagina, delivering sperm which travel up the cervical canal to the fallopian tubes. Eggs released by the ovaries are fertilized by incoming sperm.

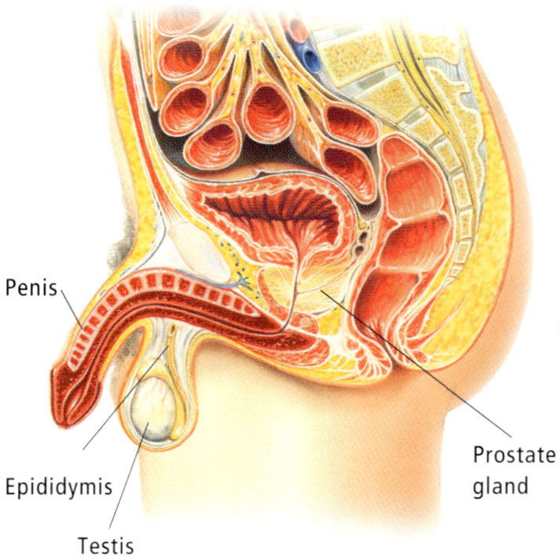

Male reproductive organs
The organs and glands of the male reproductive system are specially designed to produce sperm and deliver them to a woman's reproductive organs through sexual intercourse. Sperm are produced and mature in the testes. During sex they are ejaculated by the penis.

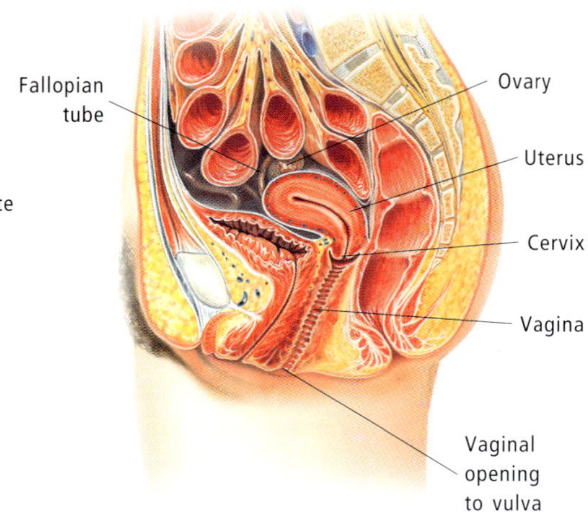

Female reproductive organs
The female reproductive system consists of the the outer genitals—the vulva—and internal parts—the ovaries, fallopian tubes, uterus and vagina.

Sex hormones and behavior

The hypothalamus and pituitary gland in the brain, together with the adrenal glands, stimulate the gonads—testes in men and ovaries in women—to produce testosterone and estrogen. The release of these hormones modulates sexual appetite and activity.

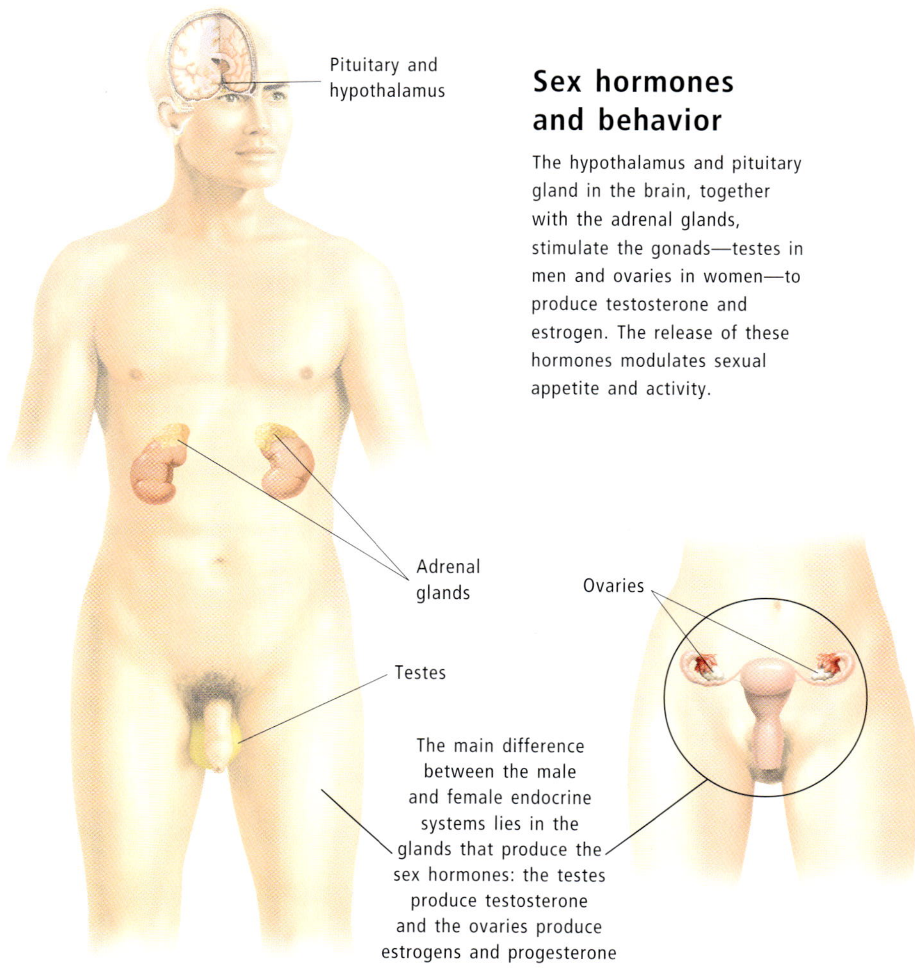

The main difference between the male and female endocrine systems lies in the glands that produce the sex hormones: the testes produce testosterone and the ovaries produce estrogens and progesterone

By the age of about 5 or 6, children become more aware of sexuality and social restraints. Children who can talk to their parents or carers about their bodies, who know the right names for the sexual parts, and who are in a loving environment, will generally grow up with a healthy attitude to sex.

Inappropriate attitudes to sex may indicate sexual abuse. Children who know more about sex than you would expect for their age, have unexplained injuries to the genitals, force other children to play sex games, talk about sex a great deal, draw sexual parts frequently, and show signs of stress or anxiety, may have been abused.

Knowledge about sexual behavior, about sexually transmitted diseases and pregnancy is important as adolescents reach the age when they are ready for a sexual relationship. Societies which provide medically accurate sex education as part of the education of their children, encourage adolescents to make responsible decisions about their sexual relationships, and provide easy access to contraception and reproductive health care, have lower rates of teenage pregnancy.

Formal sex education includes scientific information on human sexual physiology, reproduction and cultural attitudes.

SEE ALSO *Sexual behavior, Sexual intercourse, Sexuality*

SEX THERAPY

Sex therapy is a form of behavior modification or psychotherapy which endeavors to solve difficulties with sexual relationships, based on techniques pioneered by William Masters and Virginia Johnson in the 1960s. It may be done individually, as a couple or in a group. A trained counselor may use exercises and therapy to treat impotence (erectile dysfunction), rapid or inhibited ejaculation, orgasmic difficulties in women and men (anorgasmia), problems with sexual desire or dissatisfaction with sex.

Both physical and psychological issues must be addressed. If a physical problem is suspected, treatment from the appropriate specialist, such as a urologist, gynecologist or endocrinologist, is important.

SEE ALSO *Behavior therapy, Impotence, Premature ejaculation, Psychotherapy, Sexual dysfunction*

SEXUAL BEHAVIOR

Sexual behavior is any activity that leads to sexual arousal; it may be solo, between two people or in a group. The sexual appetite begins in the brain in the hypothalamus which, together with the adrenal glands, is responsible for stimulating the gonads to produce estrogen and testosterone. These hormones combine with other factors to initiate sexual activity. In many societies, romantic love is associated with the sexual act.

The contraceptive pill and the freedom it brought from the risk of an unwanted pregnancy led to a revolution in sexual behavior in many societies in the 1960s, leading to sex being seen as a recreational activity. Greater freedom has resulted in a wider knowledge and understanding of sexuality and sexual intercourse.

Women's role in these changes has been crucial, though there are still marked differences between cultures. In many industrialized societies women's attitudes have become more permissive over the past 40 years, and many girls are experimenting with sex earlier in life. Many women are also taking control of their own fertility and planning their families to fit in with other life goals.

Human sexual behavior can be divided into heterosexuality (a sexual relationship between a man and woman), homosexuality (a sexual relationship between people of the same sex) and bisexuality (sexual relationships with both sexes).

Heterosexuality is everywhere accepted as the norm, and other forms of sexuality are not accepted in many societies.

Male-to-male sexual techniques include voyeurism, mutual masturbation, kissing, body rubbing to orgasm, fellatio (oral–penile sex) and sodomy (penile–anal sex).

Female-to-female relationships (also known as lesbianism) involve sexual techniques including foreplay, body rubbing, kissing, licking, clitoral stimulation, oral sex, digital vaginal penetration, the use of both vibrators and dildos (artificial penises).

Heterosexual relationships may involve any of these practices, as well as penile–vaginal penetration.

Bisexuality is more prevalent in some cultures than others and is thought to be more prevalent in men than women. Transsexualism is seen in people who are biologically one gender but identify with the opposite.

Social taboos have made the study of sexual behavior in industrialized countries difficult. Much of the recent information available comes from the Institute for Sex Research (also known as the Kinsey Institute) and from research in Sweden.

SEE ALSO *Bisexuality, Brain, Contraception, Homosexuality, Hypothalamus, Masturbation, Sexuality, Transsexualism*

SEXUAL DISORDERS

Sexual disorders or paraphilias, a preference for unusual sexual practices, include hypersexuality, divided into satyriasis, an uncontrollable, obsessive craving by men for sex, and nymphomania, an abnormally high sex drive in women.

Other sexual disorders include exhibitionism, that is, exposing genitals to unsuspecting strangers; fetishism, sexual fantasies involving material objects; masochism, abuse or humiliation used to raise sexual excitement; necrophilia, sexual arousal induced by contact with dead bodies; pedophilia, sexual activities with children; sadism, sexual excitement achieved by physical or psychological acts of cruelty; voyeurism, observing unsuspecting people in sexual acts; and zoophilia, using an animal for sex.

SEXUAL DYSFUNCTION

Not easy to define, a sexual dysfunction could be said to be any condition which results in dissatisfaction with performance, sensation or satisfaction during any part of a sexual interaction. Men and women perceive sexual dysfunction differently, men tending to see it as associated with physical problems whereas women understand it as associated with relationship problems. Sexual dysfunctions include the following.

Anorgasmia is the inability to experience orgasm, either during sexual intercourse or sexual activity with a partner or during masturbation; this is mostly a female problem, although men may also suffer. It was originally termed frigidity. Sex therapists have discovered that the problem is mostly due to a lack of sexual knowledge or to religious or social prohibitions that have prevented the development of a sexual awareness through masturbation.

Dyspareunia or painful or difficult sexual intercourse in women is most commonly caused by insufficient arousal and lubrication of the vagina prior to penetration. Spending time in foreplay and ensuring that the woman is aroused will usually resolve the problem. Inflammation or irritation of the vulva can also cause dyspareunia and intercourse is best avoided until the condition is resolved. Pain during deep penile thrusting can be due to endometriosis; cervical infections or other infections surrounding the uterus, tubes or pelvic organs; or abdominal surgery. Vaginal dryness, often a problem for women after menopause, can usually be solved by hormone replacement therapy.

Impotence or problems with erection is one of the most common worries for men. Where impotence is due to lack of libido, the solution is often the same as for women who suffer anorgasmia (see above). Damage to the blood vessels to the penis may cause impotence; heart problems, smoking, diabetes, trauma and radiation may also cause impotence, as may the drugs used to treat these conditions.

Libido problems include the absence, temporary loss or reduction of libido and can cause sexual difficulties. Natural differences in libido can create tensions in relationships, despite romantic love. Stress, fatigue and negative feelings about a partner can be the cause of temporary loss of libido which will return when, and if, the problems are solved. (As with anorgasmia, this was previously called frigidity in women.) Some medications can also be responsible for reduced libido.

Male "menopause" is considered by some medical authorities to be an emotionally triggered mid-life crisis, while others believe it is a physical condition resulting from changing hormone levels, in particular of testosterone.

Orgasm problems. Orgasm may not always be reached during sexual intercourse, a source of concern for many women. It should be remembered, however, that orgasm can result from any sexual activity—it does not have to be sparked by sexual intercourse. Understanding and wanting sexual intercourse, a sympathetic and caring partner

Sexuality

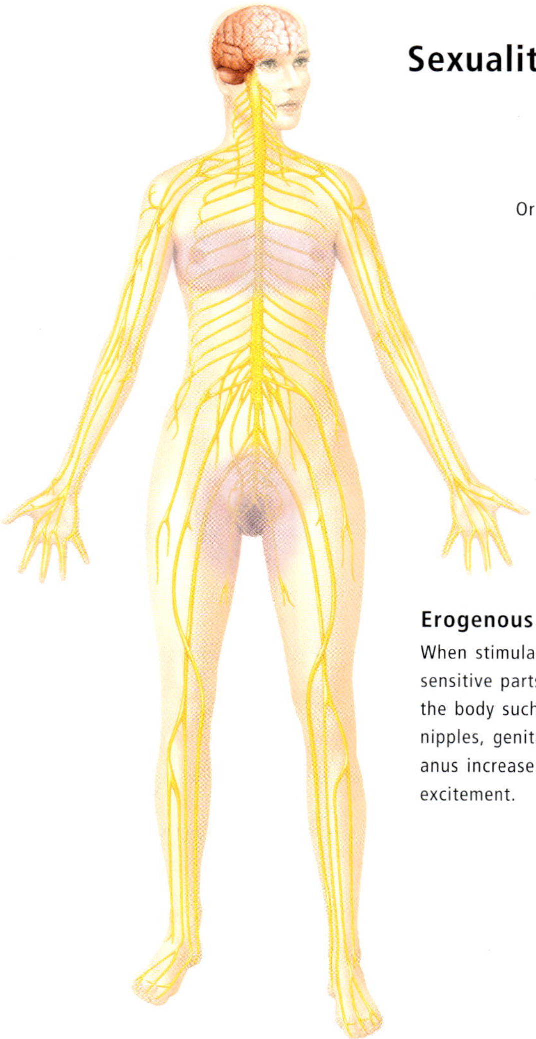

Erogenous zones
When stimulated, sensitive parts of the body such as the nipples, genitalia and anus increase sexual excitement.

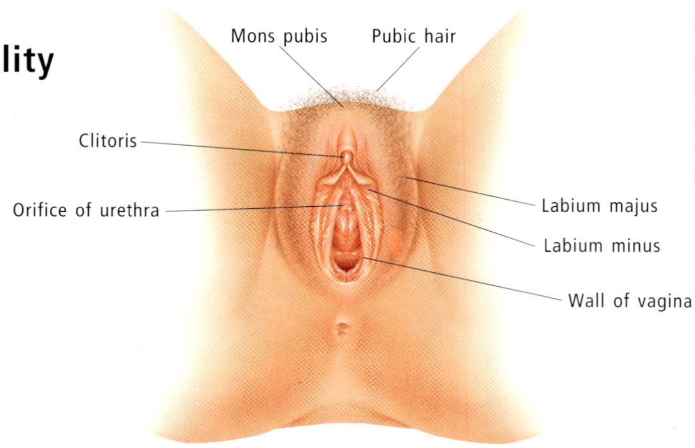

Female sexual arousal
When sexually aroused, blood flows to the woman's vulva and the clitoris becomes firm. Continued stimulation of the clitoris can lead to orgasm.

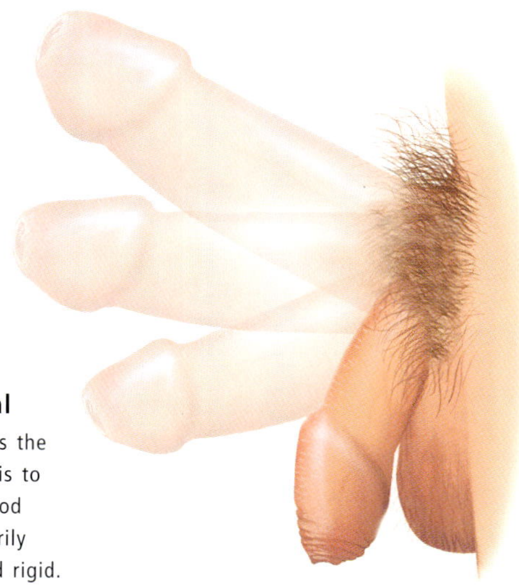

Male sexual arousal
Sexual stimulation causes the blood vessels of the penis to dilate. The increased blood supply makes the ordinarily flaccid penis swollen and rigid.

who understands the need for foreplay, and experimenting with positions can help to solve this concern. Men can also have problems with orgasm, for similar reasons.

Premature ejaculation occurs when a man cannot delay orgasm or has a partial orgasm and ejaculation before he and his partner are ready. The cause can be any one of a number of psychological and physical reasons. Premature ejaculation can usually be solved with sexual therapy and a cooperative partner.

Retarded ejaculation occurs when a man cannot achieve orgasm. Similarly to premature ejaculation, it is accompanied by emotional and physical frustration, discomfort and loss of interest in sexual intercourse. Consultation with a sex therapist and an understanding partner will usually solve the problem.

Sexual headache is a relatively rare but extremely painful phenomenon. It affects four times as many men as women. It usually starts at the beginning of sexual intercourse and intensifies during orgasm and is thought to be related to tension in the head, face and neck muscles. About one in four sufferers also suffer from migraines. Drug therapy is available.

Vaginismus is involuntary spasm of the muscles round the entrance of the vagina which causes pain as soon as sex begins. A vaginal examination can also trigger this problem. An overwhelming fear of sex, often after a traumatic or violent sexual experience, is usually the cause. Sex therapy can help, although treatment is often long term.

SEE ALSO *Hormone replacement therapy, Hormones, Impotence, Menopause, Premature ejaculation, Sexual behavior, Sexual intercourse, Vaginismus*

SEXUAL INTERCOURSE

Sexual intercourse, or coitus, is the union between a male and female whereby the woman is penetrated by the man's penis, usually resulting in ejaculation. It may also be defined more widely as any sexual contact between two individuals involving stimulation of the genitals of at least one of them. Using the first definition, sexual intercourse is an integral part of the reproductive process and basic to the existence of the human species (forgetting the development of technologies that allow reproduction without sexual intercourse).

Normal sexual intercourse begins with foreplay, when a couple arouse each other sexually by caressing, kissing and stimulation, preparing their bodies for sexual intercourse. Arousal increases blood supply into the penis, causing it to extend and become erect. It also increases blood flow to the woman's vulva and vagina, which becomes coated with a lubricating mucus; the clitoris becomes erect and the nipples more sensitive.

When the woman is ready for penetration the penis enters the vagina. The man, and often the woman, will usually experience orgasm during intercourse, not necessarily at the same time. The man usually experiences orgasm as he ejaculates. After ejaculation the penis becomes limp. After intercourse the bodies of both man and woman will return to normal, although it usually takes the woman's body longer.

Anal intercourse, in which the penis is inserted via the anus into the rectum of the other person, is occasionally used by heterosexual couples, but more frequently in homosexual relationships. As the anus is not designed to accommodate a thrusting penis, damage is more likely than in vaginal sex. There is also the possibility of infectious bacteria adhering to the penis after anal intercourse, thus hygiene is important. As autoimmune deficiency syndrome (AIDS) can be transmitted by unprotected anal intercourse (among other ways), a condom should always be used.

Oral sex is the term used to describe mouth and genital contact. It has been part of sexual activity for centuries, being depicted in ancient Indian and carvings and in the *Kama Sutra*, a famous Hindu love and sex manual from the second century BC.

Contraceptives can be used to prevent unwanted pregnancy and to protect both parties against sexually transmitted diseases.

SEE ALSO *Contraception, Reproductive systems, Sexual behavior, Sexually transmitted diseases*

SEXUALITY

A person's sexuality results from the combination of sexual attributes, behavior and tendencies. Sexual feelings are present from birth, and continue right through life.

Sexual desire is influenced by many factors and its intensity may fluctuate greatly over a lifetime. For women, sexual desire may be influenced by changes in hormone levels at different life stages (such as menopause), changes in roles and responsibilities, whether child-rearing or work outside the home, and economic and relationship factors. Men experience less fluctuation in hormone levels, but sexual desire and arousal is affected by many factors including economic problems, stress, work pressure and family situation.

Sexual feelings continue to be present as people age. Although sexual arousal may occur less often and men may find that erections are not as strong or as frequent, and women may suffer problems such as vaginal dryness, the need for, and the rewards from, an active sex life continues for many people to the end of their lives. Passing the menopause gives many women a greater sense of sexual freedom.

Sexual feelings are also important to people who suffer from physical and mental disabilities. Physically disabled or challenged people have a normal need for sexual expression and often the ability to participate in a sexual relationship is only limited by the nature of their disability. Paraplegia, however, can affect sexual function severely. While a woman's fertility is often restored when menstruation returns after spinal cord injury, anorgasmia is common. Men may suffer impotence, which can be solved with the use of external mechanical devices, but orgasm, ejaculation and the quality of sperm are usually affected and involuntary muscle spasms may be a problem.

Sexual relationships in the emotionally or intellectually disabled pose a problem for society when people are not capable of caring for a child without support. There is no easy solution to the ethical dilemmas created by such situations and the issues continue to be debated in most societies.

SEE ALSO *Sexual behavior, Sexual dysfunction, Sexual intercourse*

SEXUALLY TRANSMITTED DISEASES

A sexually transmitted disease (STD) is any disease transmitted from one person to another through sexual contact. Such diseases may also be transferred from mother to child before, during, or immediately after birth, or through kissing, tainted blood transfusions or the use of unsterilized hypodermic syringes. The diseases may be bacterial, viral or parasitic in origin. STDs have been around for all of recorded history and up until the end of the twentieth century they were known as venereal diseases.

The annual rates of reported new cases of STDs in the USA are the highest of any country in the industrialised world, higher than in some developing countries. *Chlamydia* is the most frequently reported infectious disease in the country.

Bacterial diseases

Bacterial STDs include the following.

Chlamydia is caused by the bacterial parasite *Chlamydia trachomatis*. It has been linked with pelvic inflammatory disease, ectopic pregnancy, premature birth, and infections causing conjunctivitis or pneumonia in babies.

Sexually transmitted diseases

Bacterial disease
Chlamydia is a bacterial infection that can be treated with antibiotics. If it is not treated, it can cause sterility in both men and women.

Viral disease
Herpes is a viral disease, and as such cannot be cured. Therefore, individuals infected with herpes often suffer repeat attacks of symptoms, such as blisters on the genital area, throughout their lives.

Chancroid (or soft chancre) is an STD most common in tropical regions and often associated with HIV transmission. Shallow painful ulcers appear in the infected area, usually the genitals, 3–5 days after exposure by sexual contact. They are caused by the bacterium *Haemophilus ducreyi* and can be mistaken for the first symptoms of syphilis; localized swelling and inflammation of lymph glands follow the ulcers.

Gonorrhea is caused by the bacterium *Neisseria gonorrhoeae*. It mainly affects people aged 15–30 and is highly contagious. Many people have no symptoms. Men may have a pus-like discharge from the penis and pain on urinating. In women there may be a yellowish, smelly vaginal discharge and pain on urinating. The infection can spread into the body, causing arthritic pains and high temperatures; untreated, it can result in infertility, miscarriage or premature birth.

Granuloma inguinale (also known as donovaniasis) is characterized by deep, purulent ulcers on or near the genitals. Common in subtropical and tropical areas, and often occurring with syphilis or gonorrhea, it is not as infectious as some of the other STDs.

Lymphogranuloma venereum (LGV) is an infection of the lymph vessels and lymph nodes, caused by the same organism as chlamydia. Swollen lymph nodes, ulcers, enlargement of the genitals and rectal stricture are symptoms of the disease, relatively common in subtropical and tropical areas. Fevers and joint pains often occur.

Syphilis, a serious disease caused by the spirochete *Treponoma pallidum*, progresses through three stages, each separated by months and even years. It begins with a lesion—a painless, circular chancre which may appear on the lips, mouth, tongue, nipple, rectum or genitalia; nearby lymph nodes may enlarge but are not painful. The chancre heals and weeks or months later the secondary symptoms appear, caused by microbes spreading to every organ and tissue in the body. Non-painful skin rashes appear and disappear, sometimes in association with fever, headache and hair loss. Tertiary lesions, appearing years later, can destroy normal skin, bone and joints by ulceration. Tertiary syphilis also attacks the nervous system.

Viral diseases

Viral STDs include the following.

AIDS, caused by the human immunodeficiency virus (HIV), is transferred via body fluids and blood. The virus invades and multiplies within the lymphocytes (cells essential to the immune system) until it eventually destroys them. The body fluids that can pass the virus to another person are blood (including menstrual blood), semen, fluid from the vagina and cervix, and breast milk. HIV can also be spread by intravenous (IV) drug use with shared needles.

Hepatitis B (HBV) is spread through blood transfusions, IV drug use with shared needles, unprotected sexual intercourse or sharp instruments which break the skin. The virus remains in the body for many years. It can become chronic and lead to permanent liver damage through cirrhosis or cancer. Symptoms appear between 40 days to 6 months after exposure, and include fatigue, abdominal pain, loss of appetite, nausea, diarrhea, dark urine and jaundice. Treatment is bed rest. Babies born to a mother with HBV have up to a 95 percent chance of being infected. A vaccine that provides protection for at least 5 years is available.

Genital herpes is caused by one of the family of herpes viruses—Type II mainly affects the genital area. It can be spread to the mouth via oral sex. A temperature, mild headache, swollen lymph glands, small blisters on the genitals and vaginal discharge are common symptoms.

Molluscum contagiosum, contagious lumps caused by a type of pox virus, usually have a tiny dimple in the middle, are pinkish and itchy but not painful. They can be spread by close skin contact but in adults are usually transmitted sexually.

Genital warts are caused by the human papilloma virus (HPV). Reddish soft swellings that grow rapidly, they flourish in the genital area, the foreskin, the cervix and vulva being common sites. Warts can be painful during sexual intercourse. Women with genital warts should have regular gynecological checkups, including a Pap smear.

Parasitic diseases

Parasitic STDs include the following.

Pediculosis pubis (pubic lice or crabs) can be a problem in crowded living conditions. They are mainly acquired during sexual activity but can also be transmitted from contaminated bedding and clothing. Small white specks, which under a microscope look like a crab, pubic lice feed on blood. They can live up to 30 days, mating frequently in that time. The most common symptom is an itch in the genital area; a rash or tiny blue spots may also be evident.

Scabies is caused by a tiny mite known as *Sarcoptes scabiei*. It burrows under the skin, making a wavy line and causing a severe itch. It is usually spread in adults by sexual contact. The rash, which appears on the wrist, between the fingers, in the armpits or on the penis or thighs, is treated with lotions which kill the mites and their eggs.

Trichomoniasis vaginalis (TV) is another STD that causes genital ulcers. It infects the vagina, urethra, bladder and sometimes glands. Up to 90 percent of men who are infected have no symptoms, though it may cause pain on urination and itchiness.

When a test is carried out for a particular STD, it is wise to have tests for others which may have been contracted at the same time. While the female condom will provide protection from STDs, including HIV/AIDS, any person with an STD should avoid sexual intercourse while symptoms are present or until a medical practitioner advises that it is safe.

SEE ALSO *AIDS, Chancroid, Chlamydia, Genital herpes, Genital warts, Gonorrhea, Granuloma inguinale, Hepatitis, Lice, Lymphogranuloma venereum, Molluscum contagiosum, Scabies*

SHIATSU

The Japanese word *shiatsu* means "finger pressure". It is the name of a therapy developed in Japan based on traditional massage, stretching and breathing techniques. Shiatsu therapists use the meridian system of traditional Chinese medicine to help them determine on which points in the body to apply pressure to rebalance the body's energy flow or *ki* (*ch'i* or *qi* in Chinese medicine). Shiatsu therapists use their fingers, knees, elbows, knuckles, palms and feet to release blockages of *ki*, applying a pressure which comes from body weight.

Diagnosis is done by palpating the abdomen (or *hara*), which is considered central

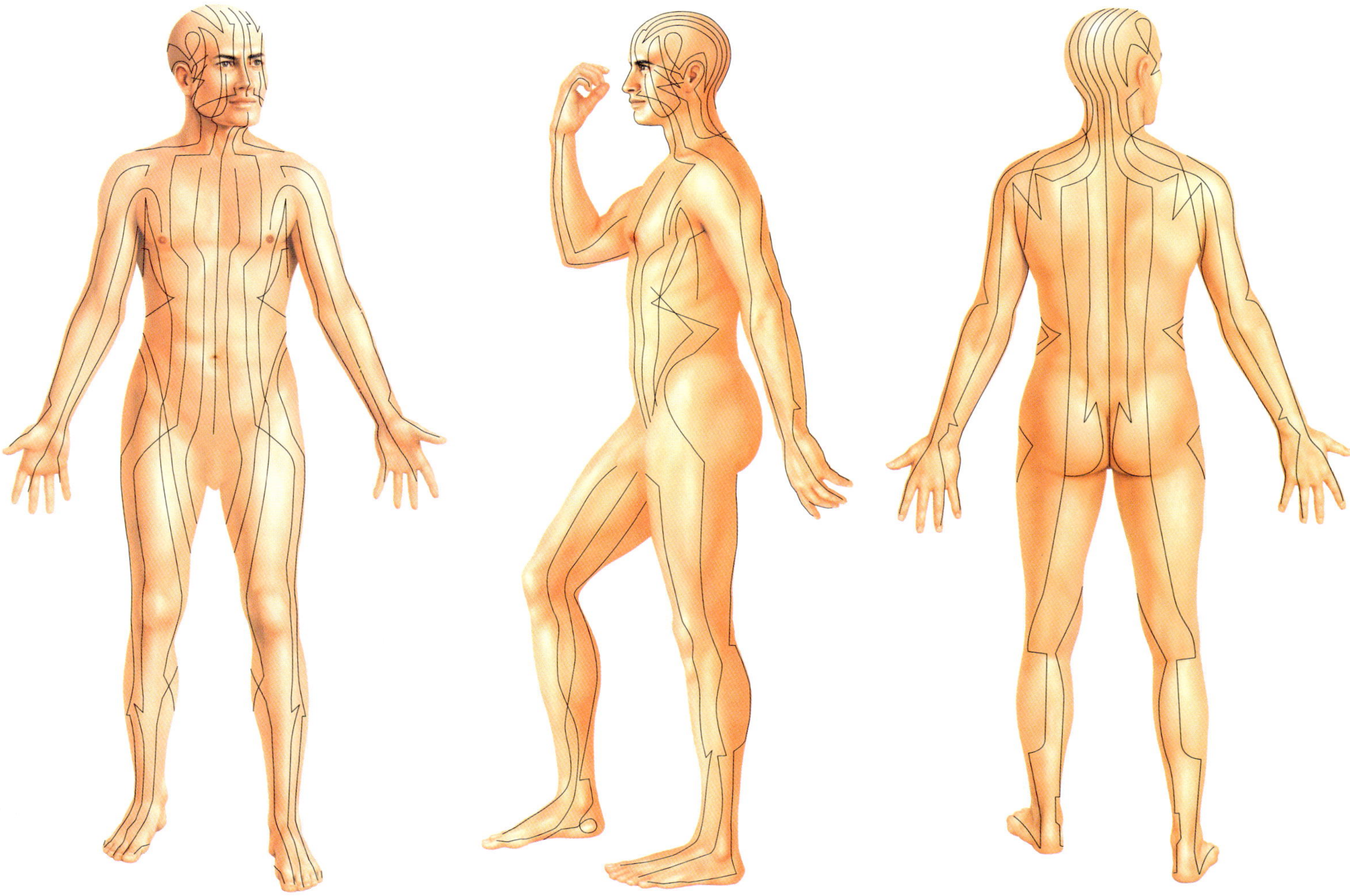

Shiatsu

In this Eastern therapy, pressure is applied to points along the body's meridian pathways to stimulate and balance the body's energy flow. The meridian system is thought to indicate the path of energy through different organs in the body. Disturbance or blockage of this flow can lead to illness.

to overall health and vitality as all the meridian pathways connect to this area. Pulses in the wrist are also read, as well as facial signs. Once the diagnosis is made the shiatsu therapist works in a series of sequences through the body to tonify and disperse *ki*, using pressure and gentle stretches combined with breathing techniques. Shiatsu is done on a clothed patient lying on a floor mat. Dietary advice according to macrobiotic principles is also often given.

Shiatsu is a holistic treatment considered to benefit body and mind. It is said to be particularly effective in treating chronic pain, digestive and respiratory problems and stress-related illnesses.

SEE ALSO *Acupuncture, Massage*

SHIN SPLINTS

"Shin splints" is a common term that is used to refer to a variety of different conditions, all of which cause pain in the lower leg. To most medical practitioners, however, shin splints are more accurately referred to as medial tibial stress syndrome, an inflammation of soft tissues associated with the tibia which causes aching or tenderness along the shin. This is one of the most common injuries affecting joggers and is often caused by excessive walking or running, particularly on hard surfaces. Inadequate training is often blamed and susceptibility to shin splints can be reduced by improving the strength and flexibility of the lower leg. Rest is the usual treatment.

SEE ALSO *Leg, Tibia*

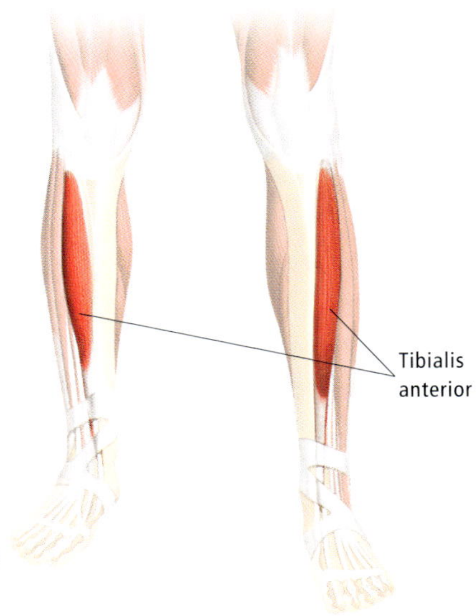

Shin splints

Running on hard surfaces such as bitumen or concrete for extended periods can cause inflammation of the tissues that join the muscles and bones of the lower leg. The soft tissues linked to the tibia (such as the tibialis anterior muscle) are most commonly affected.

S

Shock

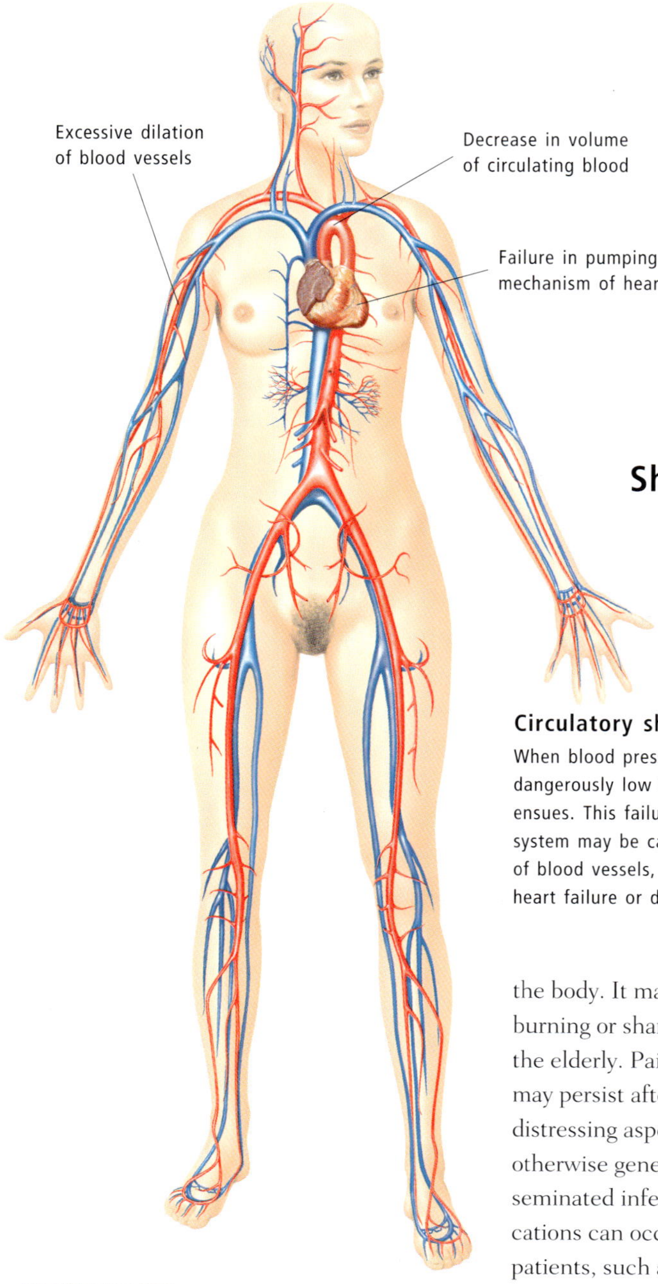

Circulatory shock

When blood pressure falls to dangerously low levels, shock ensues. This failure of the circulatory system may be caused by dilation of blood vessels, severe blood loss, heart failure or dehydration.

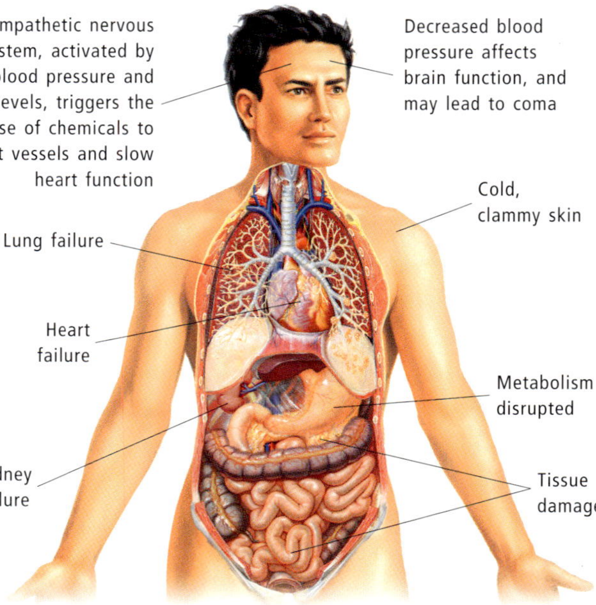

Shock—organ failure

To compensate for falling blood pressure and fluid levels, a body in shock releases chemicals to constrict vessels and slow body processes. This can lead to oxygen deprivation and damage to vital organs such as the kidneys, stomach and lungs. The effects can be fatal if not attended to immediately. **NB:** In this image part of the lungs, pleura, and liver have been cut to show the heart and kidney.

SHINGLES

Shingles is the common term for herpes zoster infection, a reactivation of the varicella-zoster virus that causes chickenpox. Following chickenpox infection the virus remains dormant in the body and reactivation can occur years later, particularly if the body's immunity decreases. This occurs most commonly with age.

While dormant the virus is located in spinal ganglia beside the spinal cord; on activation it migrates along a sensory nerve to the area of skin it supplies (its dermatome). It is here that the infection appears as a rash composed of small blisters with surrounding inflammation. The rash is therefore localized, and usually strictly confined to one side of the body. It may be associated with severe burning or sharp nerve pain, particularly in the elderly. Pain may precede the rash and may persist afterwards. This is often the most distressing aspect of the infection, since it is otherwise generally benign. More severe disseminated infection and neurological complications can occur in immunocompromised patients, such as those with lymphoma or following bone marrow transplantation.

More effective antiviral medications have been developed in recent years to treat shingles, including oral medications. When commenced soon after the rash appears, these can reduce the duration of infection and the pain during and after it.

SEE ALSO *Chickenpox, Nerves, Viruses*

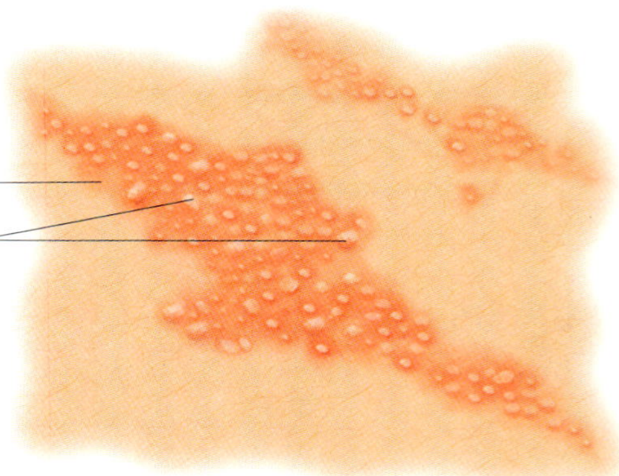

Shingles

Caused by the herpes zoster virus, shingles is characterized by painful blisters on the skin.

SHOCK

Shock is a term used in the medical sense to describe a complex sequence of events resulting in collapse of the circulatory system. Although an emotional component of fear or anxiety may also be present, it is only part of a severe body response. The most important feature of shock is failure of the circulation to maintain an adequate blood pressure to allow vital organs to continue to function.

Causes

Shock may result from a failure of the pumping ability of the heart, from a reduction in the circulating blood volume or from excessive dilatation of the blood vessels. The most common cause of shock is reduction in the blood volume, due to hemorrhage or severe dehydration. Another important cause of shock is septicemia, in which severe infection results in the release of chemicals called endotoxins, causing dilation of blood vessels. They may also impair the function of the heart. Heart diseases themselves can result in shock, particularly in the case of a major heart attack (myocardial infarction) which damages a large proportion of the heart muscle.

A number of conditions can cause dilation of blood vessels resulting in shock, including anaphylaxis and poisonings. Anaphylaxis is a severe immediate allergic reaction resulting in the release of histamine, a chemical which causes the dilation of blood vessels. Poisoning by a variety of drugs and chemicals may result in depression of cardiac function and dilation of blood vessels. Drugs include those used for the treatment of cardiovascular diseases or depression, as well as non-prescription drugs including alcohol. Exposure to high-voltage electricity can cause shock through cardiac arrest and severe electrical burns, resulting in fluid loss.

Symptoms

The symptoms of shock depend initially on the precipitating factor. They may be dramatic, such as a heart attack or an electric shock. Sometimes shock develops more gradually as a result of progressive dehydration or infection. Anaphylactic shock is associated with swelling of the lips and throat, wheezing and difficulty breathing, and the rapid appearance of an itchy raised rash.

Regardless of the initial symptoms, a common sequence of events then ensues. Decrease in the blood pressure affects brain function, resulting in confusion and even coma. The body mounts a protective defense of the circulation by releasing chemicals from the adrenal glands and activating the sympathetic nervous system. Chemicals such as epinephrine (adrenaline) increase the pumping action of the heart and constrict blood vessels. These chemicals are also responsible for symptoms of tremor and anxiety that accompany the shock syndrome.

The body's response may result in the person appearing pale, cold and clammy. While it is beneficial in maintaining the blood pressure, the compensatory response is only a temporary measure before organ function is compromised further. Constriction of blood vessels can reduce blood flow to vital organs, especially the kidneys. Also, the lack of blood supply to body tissues results in anaerobic metabolism with the accumulation of lactic acid. Ultimately shock can result in an irreversible situation, in which tissue damage has become so great that the condition becomes fatal.

Treatment

Treatment of shock relies on its early detection and institution of emergency measures, such as oxygen and epinephrine (adrenaline) in anaphylaxis. The maintenance of circulatory volume by intravenous fluids is essential and is combined with infusion of drugs to maintain blood pressure. Specific treatment, such as antibiotics for septicemia or antidotes for poisoning, is also given.

SEE ALSO ***Anaphylaxis, Circulatory system, Epinephrine, Myocardial infarction, Poisoning, Septicemia, Toxic shock syndrome***

SHOULDER

The shoulder includes three bones—the clavicle (collar bone), the scapula (shoulder blade) and the humerus—and their associated joints and muscles, as well as major nerves and blood vessels passing to and from the arm.

The arm is attached to the trunk by the pectoral girdle, which consists of the clavicle and the scapula. The clavicle acts as a strut to hold the arm away from the center of the body. It forms joints with the sternum (breastbone) at one end and with the scapula at the other end. The scapula is a flat triangular-shaped bone which covers part of the upper back. It is largely enclosed by muscle but has a prominent spine, which can be felt extending across the back towards the shoulder, where it expands to form the acromion.

Joints

The joints of the shoulder region include the following.

Acromioclavicular joint

The inner surface of the acromion meets the clavicle to form the acromioclavicular joint, which can be felt at the top of the shoulder. This joint allows a small amount of gliding movement to occur between the two bones in conjunction with movements of the arm. The acromioclavicular joint is supported by a capsule and several ligaments, the most important of which is the coracoclavicular ligament. These ligaments, which pass down from the under surface of the clavicle to the coracoid process (a part of the scapula which protrudes forward under the clavicle) also help to support the weight of the arm.

Heavy falls on to the back of the shoulder (as may occur when someone is thrown from a motorcycle) cause the scapula to be driven forwards under the clavicle and may result in rupture of the conoid and trapezoid ligaments. When this occurs, the arm is pulled down by its own weight and the affected shoulder appears lower than the shoulder on the other side, a condition known as shoulder separation. This is a serious injury and usually requires a surgical prodecure in order to repair the damaged ligaments.

Shoulder joint

The outer (lateral) angle of the triangular scapula is flattened to form a shallow cavity, in which the head of the humerus (the long bone of the upper arm) sits, forming the glenohumeral or shoulder joint. The shoulder joint is a ball and socket joint, allowing movement of the arm to occur in almost any direction. The socket, which is formed by the glenoid cavity of the scapula, is very shallow and has a small contact area, relative to the head of the humerus, which forms the ball.

Only a small part of the head of the humerus is in contact with the glenoid cavity at any time, making the joint extremely mobile but also making it relatively unstable (easy to dislocate). A ring of fibrocartilage, the glenoid labrum, which encircles the edge of the glenoid cavity, deepens the socket slightly and increases the contact area.

The joint surfaces are covered by smooth, glassy cartilage and the two bones are held together by a relatively loose capsule. The

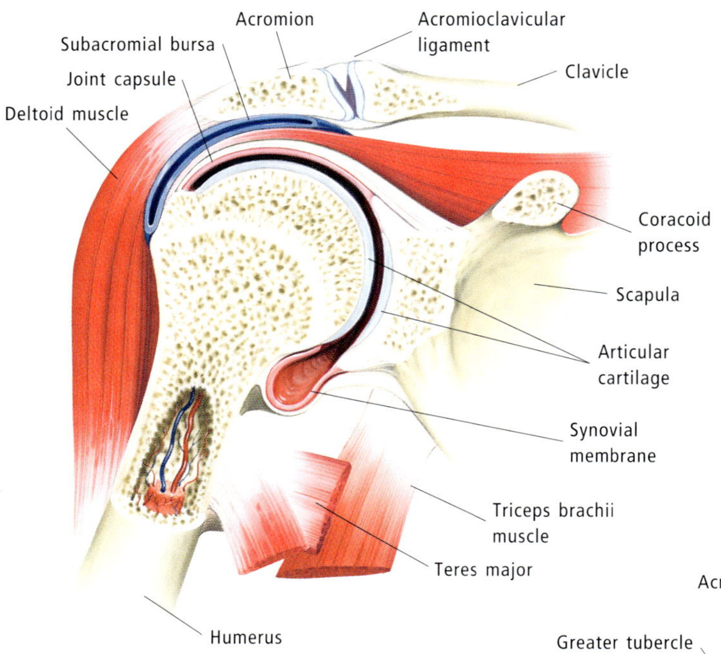

Shoulder cross-section

A loose capsule lined with a synovial membrane joins the humerus bone to the scapula. The synovial membrane secretes a fluid which lubricates the joint, reducing friction and easing movement. Damage to the synovial membrane or cartilage that cushions the joint may cause pain and stiffness in the shoulder.

Shoulder

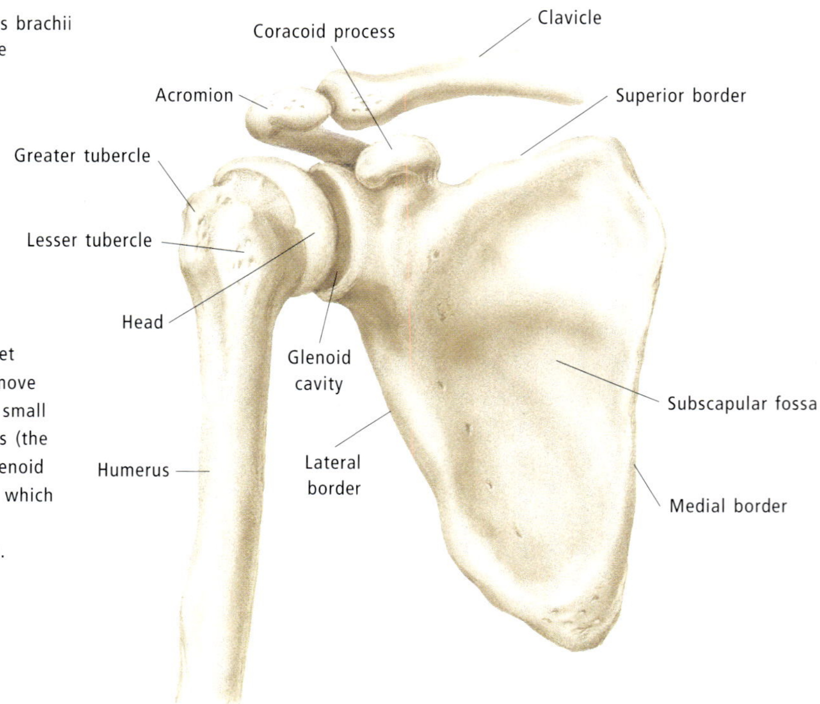

Shoulder joint

The shoulder is a ball and socket joint which allows the arm to move in almost any direction. Only a small part of the head of the humerus (the ball) makes contact with the glenoid cavity (the socket) at any time, which provides maximum mobility but increases the risk of dislocation.

Pectoral girdle

The bones and muscles of the pectoral girdle provide a support network for the shoulder joint. One set of muscles attaches the humerus bone of the arm to the shoulder girdle, another set attaches the shoulder girdle to the trunk of the body.

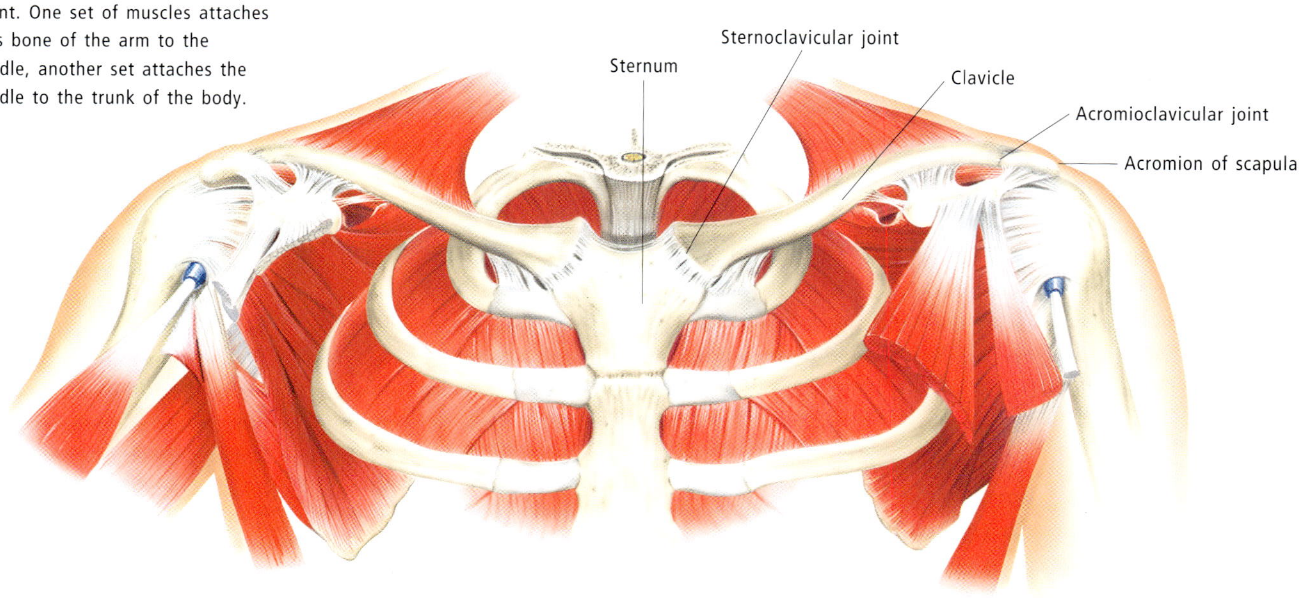

inside of the capsule is lined by a synovial membrane, which produces an oily synovial fluid that is released into the joint cavity to lubricate the cartilage surface and reduce friction. The capsule is reinforced on the top, front and back by a group of muscles known as the rotator cuff muscles, whose tendons blend with the capsule as they pass over it. In addition to enabling certain movements at the joint, these muscles are said to act as "dynamic ligaments", holding the head of the humerus in the socket during movement. The rotator cuff muscles, subscapularis covering the front, infraspinatus and teres minor covering the back and supraspinatus covering the top of the capsule, are the most important factors preventing dislocation of the head of the humerus from the socket when force is placed on the joint.

Dislocation of the shoulder is a relatively common occurrence and usually occurs as a result of a sudden force being transmitted along the arm when it is in the elevated (abducted) position. In this position, the force from the head of the humerus is transmitted to the lower part of the capsule where it is weakest and not reinforced by tendons, forcing the head to pop out of the lower part of the socket. Although the humerus can be placed back into the socket with the assistance of local anesthetic and muscle relaxants, the damage that is usually sustained by the capsule and labrum in the dislocation makes the joint vulnerable to dislocation in the future, and surgery may be required to overcome the problem.

The shoulder joint is bridged and protected above by a structure known as the coracoacromial arch, which consists of the acromion behind, the coracoid process in front and the coracoacromial ligament passing between them. A cushion of synovial fluid enclosed by a synovial membrane, and known as the subacromial bursa, lies between the supraspinatus tendon (which blends with the joint capsule) below and the coracoacromial arch above. It functions to reduce friction between the greater tubercle of the humerus and the arch when the arm is elevated.

Stress on the supraspinatus tendon in some people may cause degeneration of the tendon with age, resulting in the formation of crystalline calcium deposits in the tendon (tendinitis) which cause friction and consequent swelling of the bursa. When this occurs the person experiences pain on elevating the arm because of pressure on the swollen bursa as the humerus impinges on the acromion, a condition known as "painful arc syndrome". The syndrome is usually treated with heat, physical therapy and anti-inflammatory medication.

Frozen shoulder (adhesive capsulitis) is caused by inflammation of all the rotator cuff tendons causing generalized thickening of the shoulder capsule, which may adhere (stick) to the humerus. It may or may not be preceded by trauma to the joint. Frozen shoulder is characterized by increasing pain and stiffness of the shoulder. Over time the pain subsides but the stiffness continues to increase. The stiffness usually outlasts the pain by a few months before movement gradually returns to normal. The course of the disease may take 1–2 years, but a good recovery can usually be expected.

Movements

The shoulder is a multi-axial ball and socket joint, which allows movement in almost any direction. The arm (humerus) can be drawn forwards (flexed), drawn backwards (extended), elevated (abducted), drawn downwards (adducted) and rotated (around its own axis). Movements of the shoulder joint are always accompanied by movements of the pectoral girdle (clavicle and scapula), which increase the range of movement. For example, the arm cannot be elevated above the level of the shoulder without rotation of the scapula. This can be verified by observing someone from behind (with their shirt removed) as they lift the arm above the head—the lower angle of the scapula can be seen to move up and outwards as the arm is raised.

Muscles

The muscles associated with the shoulder and pectoral girdle fall into two groups, those attaching the humerus to the shoulder girdle and trunk wall, and those attaching the shoulder girdle to the trunk.

The first group includes the rotator cuff muscles: the deltoid (covers the shoulder and gives it its rounded contour); the pectoralis major (covering the front of the chest); the latissimus dorsi (large flat muscle covering the lower back and converging on a tendon which attaches to the humerus); and the teres major (a small bulky muscle passing from the scapula to the humerus).

The second group includes the rhomboids and levator scapulae, which pass from the inner (medial) side of the scapula to the vertebral column; the trapezius (a large triangular muscle extending from the skull and vertebral column across to the spine of the scapula and the clavicle); the latissimus dorsi (covering the lower back and converging on a tendon which attaches to the humerus); and the serratus anterior and pectoralis minor (both extending from the scapula to the front of the chest wall).

As a general rule, muscles which pass in front of the shoulder joint act to flex or rotate the humerus, those passing behind the joint extend and or rotate the humerus, and those passing above abduct the humerus. Because the large deltoid muscle passes over three sides of the joint (front, back and top), it is involved in most shoulder movements. Muscles which are most important for flexion of the shoulder joint are the pectoralis major and deltoid muscles. Muscles which are important for extension include the teres major, latissimus dorsi and deltoid muscles.

Abduction is brought about by the deltoid assisted by supraspinatus; medial rotation by subscapularis, latissimus dorsi, teres major, pectoralis major and part of the deltoid muscle. Lateral rotation is brought about by infraspinatus and teres minor; and adduction mainly by latissimus dorsi at the back and pectoralis major at the front and teres major; although teres major only adducts when the movement is resisted. The trapezius muscle has fibers passing up to the skull and across to the vertebral column and is important in shrugging the shoulders and in rotating the scapula upwards (when lifting the arm above the head). The serratus anterior is also essential for scapular rotation.

Weakness or paralysis of any of these muscles will impair shoulder movement.

Nerves and blood vessels

Most of the nerves and blood vessels supplying the arm pass through the armpit (axilla), just below the front of the shoulder joint as they travel to and from their target structures in the shoulder region and arm. They include the large axillary artery and vein and their branches, and the axillary, radial, musculocutaneous, median and ulnar nerves. In this area these structures are held together by loose connective tissue (axillary sheath). The nerves arise from a complex known as the brachial plexus, located on the side of the neck, where it can be felt as cords passing towards the arm, just above the clavicle.

The axillary nerve is of particular importance to the shoulder because it supplies the deltoid muscle from its deep surface by encircling the surgical neck of the humerus. It is vulnerable to injury in shoulder dislocations (when it is stretched) and in fractures of the surgical neck of the humerus. When injury of this nature occurs the muscle quickly atrophies due to lack of use, and the shoulder becomes angular and bony. The person experiences weakness of most shoulder movements, but particularly in elevation (abduction) of the arm. Damaged peripheral nerves will repair themselves over time, although recovery may not be complete.

SEE ALSO *Adduction and abduction, Arm, Collar bone, Deltoid muscle, Humerus, Joints, Muscle, Nerves, Rotator cuff muscles, Scapula, Skeletal system, Tendinitis, Trapezius*

Sickle cell disease

In this blood disorder, red blood cells form curved or sickle shapes, resulting in the blockage of small blood vessels. This causes tissue damage and pain can be severe.

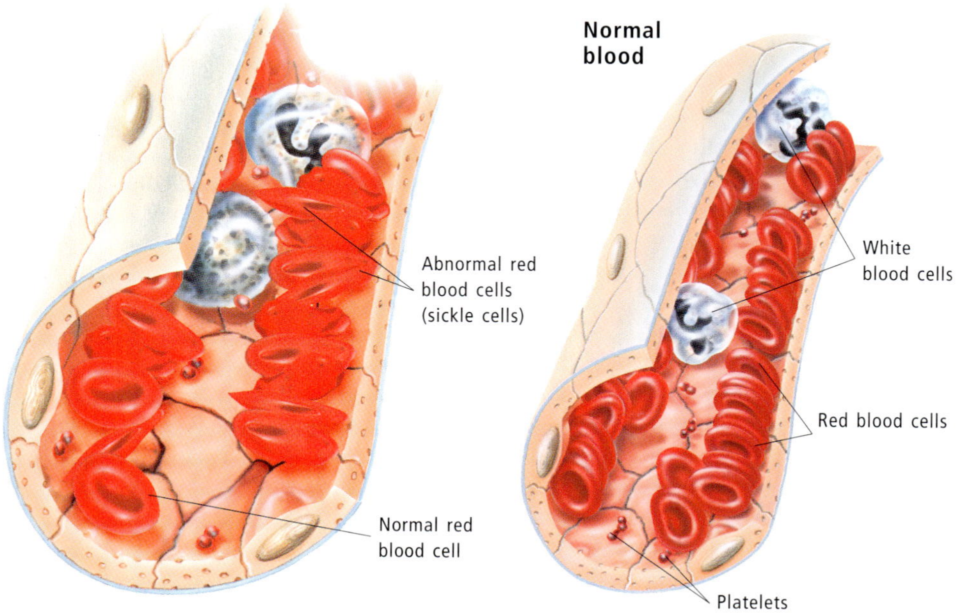

SHOULDER-HAND SYNDROME

Shoulder-hand syndrome is a condition marked by stiffness and pain in the shoulder, as well as stiffening and swelling of the hand and fingers. It is a type of reflex sympathetic dystrophy, a nervous system disorder affecting extremities which often results from an injury. The condition may also stem from myocardial infarction.

SEE ALSO *Hand, Myocardial infarction, Shoulder*

SIAMESE TWINS

Siamese (conjoined) twins are identical twins formed from a single fertilized ovum, joined together by a part, or parts, of their bodies at birth. Many are joined at the hip, head or chest, and some share limbs and internal organs such as the liver and heart. Most are delivered by cesarean section and less than half survive after birth. Siamese twins joined only by superficial tissue may be easy to separate surgically. This procedure becomes more risky and sometimes impossible, when organs and arteries are shared; in such cases, one twin may not survive.

The condition results from the failure of a zygote to fully separate into two after fertilization. Despite the difficulties of facing life joined to another person, some Siamese twins marry and have children.

SEE ALSO *Fertilization, Twins*

SICK SINUS SYNDROME

Sick sinus syndrome is a relatively rare malfunction of the heart's natural pacemaker, the sinus node, that results in abnormal heartbeat rhythms. It can be caused by a variety of diseases.

Sufferers often experience lethargy, weakness, dizziness and fainting. The only long-term treatment is implantation of an artificial pacemaker.

SEE ALSO *Heart, Pacemaker*

SICKLE CELL DISEASE

Sickle cell disease is due to the inheritance of a variant gene for the protein globin, which results in altered physical properties of the hemoglobin in red blood cells. It is the commonest variant of hemoglobin occurring worldwide.

The gene is most prevalent in equatorial regions of Africa, the Middle East and in North America in those of African descent. It is thought that the sickle gene has undergone selection by providing resistance to infection of the red cells by malarial parasites. Inheritance of one sickle gene results in the carrier state and two genes cause the disease to manifest.

Sickle hemoglobin undergoes aggregation under conditions of decreased oxygen, which causes the red cells to form a curved or sickle shape. This results in blockage of small blood vessels, causing the characteristic painful crises of the disease and resulting in tissue damage. The pain is severe and affects the bones, chest and abdomen.

Sickle cell disease may result in painful swelling of fingers and toes, leading to arthritis. Other organs can also be damaged, including the kidneys, lungs and brain. Renal complications are common.

The severity of the symptoms of sickle cell disease varies between affected individuals and can be reduced by avoiding cold conditions and by early treatment of infections.

Regular blood transfusions can reduce complications during pregnancy. In severe cases bone marrow transplantation has been used as curative treatment.

SEE ALSO *Congenital abnormalities, Genes, Hemoglobin*

SIGHT

Sight is a process in which light received by the eye triggers nerve impulses in the brain to enable the perception of the shape, size, color, movement and position of objects. The ability to see clearly defined images with the correct color and intensity depends on the way in which rays of light pass through the eye and the resulting chain of physical, chemical and electrical reactions.

The amount of light entering the eye is controlled by the iris, the colored part of the eye which lies behind the transparent curved cornea at the front of the eye. The cornea focuses light rays through the pupil to the lens, another transparent structure responsible for the fine focusing of light. As the light rays travel through the eyeball they are refracted, or bent. The degree of refraction depends on the shape of the cornea and the lens; the shape of the lens can be altered by surrounding muscles to allow the eye to focus on objects both nearby and far away.

The light rays then pass through a jelly (vitreous humor) in the center of the eye to the retina, a highly sensitive layer of cells at the back of the eye. It is here that nerve impulses are generated for transmission to the brain via the optic nerve.

Color and intensity

The retina is made up of millions of light-receptor cells known as rods and cones. The cone cells are responsible for color vision while the rod cells specialize in the perception of light intensity, enabling vision in dim light. As rod cells cannot provide color vision, objects seen in semidarkness are perceived in shades of gray. The rod cells contain a red photosensitive pigment called rhodopsin (visual purple) and the cone cells contain opsin. When light is focused on the rods and cones a chemical reaction takes place and the pigments are broken down, triggering the electrical impulses that travel to the brain.

A deficiency of rhodopsin in the rod cells can lead to a condition known as night blindness, in which vision is impaired when light intensity drops below a certain level. The deficiency is sometimes due to a lack of vitamin A in the diet but more commonly follows the disorder retinitis pigmentosa, a degenerative disease of the retina. Absent or abnormal pigments in the cone cells lead to either partial or total color blindness.

In color blindness the perception of colors is not normal, making it difficult to distinguish between them. Color perception is a result of the stimulation of three pigments in the cone cells, which react to red, green and blue. Partial color blindness usually involves the inability to distinguish between red and green, sometimes with both appearing as shades of yellow. Total color blindness or achromatism results in everything being seen as shades of gray.

The optic nerve

The rods and cones of the retina send nerve impulses to the optic nerve via a network of nerve fibers. Nerve impulses concerning the left field of vision of each eye are sent to one part of the brain's cerebral cortex, and the impulses concerning the right part of the field of vision of each eye are sent to another. When interpreting this information, the brain combines the two messages to form one image. The brain also inverts images which are focused on the retina upside down. It is not known how this occurs.

The optic nerve can become inflamed (optic neuritis) causing sudden loss of vision in the affected eye, impaired color vision and painful eye movement. The cause of this condition is uncertain but it may be due to deterioration of a fatty layer of cells known as the myelin sheath, which aids in the transfer of nerve impulses.

Binocular vision

Normal human vision is binocular, that is, the images from each eye are fused into one focused image. Each eye sees the same scene or object in a slightly different way because each sees it from a slightly different angle. Binocular vision is the ability to maintain focus on a scene or object with both eyes, blending the two pictures to create one image that is seen with depth. A person without perfect binocular vision may have difficulty visually estimating distance due to problems with the perception of depth.

The condition in which two images of an object are perceived instead of one is known as double vision (diplopia). This may be a side effect of a disorder known as astigmatism in which the curved shape of the cornea is not symmetrical, or it may be caused by the muscles of one eye being stronger or weaker than those of the other. Double vision may be a symptom of a squint (strabismus) where pairs of muscles surrounding the eyeball do not work in unison, causing abnormal movement of the eye. The result can be cross-eye, where one or both eyes turn inward toward the nose, walleye, where the eyes turn outward, or the need to peer at scenes or objects with eyes partially closed to aid focusing. The brain receives two different images, distorting depth perception.

Refractive errors

For an object to be seen clearly, light rays must focus at a precise point on the retina. When this does not happen, due to the shape of the eyeball, it leads to problems with vision known as refractive errors. These include shortsightedness (nearsightedness or myopia), longsightedness (farsightedness or hyperopia), presbyopia and astigmatism. Rather than being caused by disease or trauma, these focusing errors are due to the natural physical characteristics of the eye.

In longsightedness the eye has difficulty focusing on nearby objects but no problems with objects far away. Light rays from nearby objects focus on a point beyond the retina instead of directly on it, because the eyeball is not deep enough, or because the lens is weak. The blurred vision associated with longsightedness may lead to eyestrain and headaches.

Longsightedness caused by a decrease in the elasticity of the lens due to the normal ageing process is known as presbyopia. This makes it difficult to adjust focus for viewing close objects. Everybody suffers from presbyopia to some degree, mostly after the age of 45. Sometimes known as "old man's eyes", this condition cannot be prevented.

In shortsightedness the eye has difficulty focusing on objects far away but has no problem with those close up. This is because the eyeball is too deep or the lens too curved, causing light rays to bend too much so that visual images are focused in front of the retina instead of on it. This focusing error, like longsightedness, may be hereditary or may develop later in life as the lens becomes less elastic. An irregularly curved cornea or lens results in a condition known as

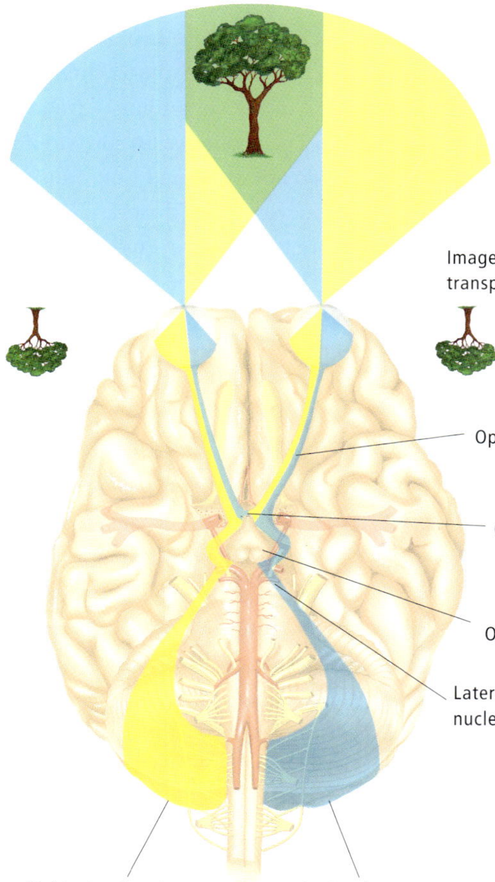

Visual pathways

The left and right eyes have slightly different, but overlapping fields of vision. The discrepancy between the images in the binocular field allows us to judge how far away an object is and its 3-D structure. Images are inverted, transposed and converted into nerve impulses. The impulses pass down nerve fibers to the optic nerves and through the optic chiasm to the lateral geniculate nuclei of the thalamus. These nuclei carry out some processing of the visual information and then send it to the visual cortex in the occipital lobes of the brain. Images are combined and interpreted in the visual cortex.

Field of vision

The structure of the eye is specially designed to bend and concentrate light rays to form a tiny image of a seen object on the back of the eye. This is then transported to the brain in the form of nerve impulses. Light rays entering the eye strike the cornea, which bends (refracts) the rays bringing them closer together. The rays then pass through the lens which focuses the rays on the back of the retina. The retina consists of a layer of light-sensitive cells—rods and cones. When stimulated by light, the rods and cones send electrical signals along the cells of the optic nerve.

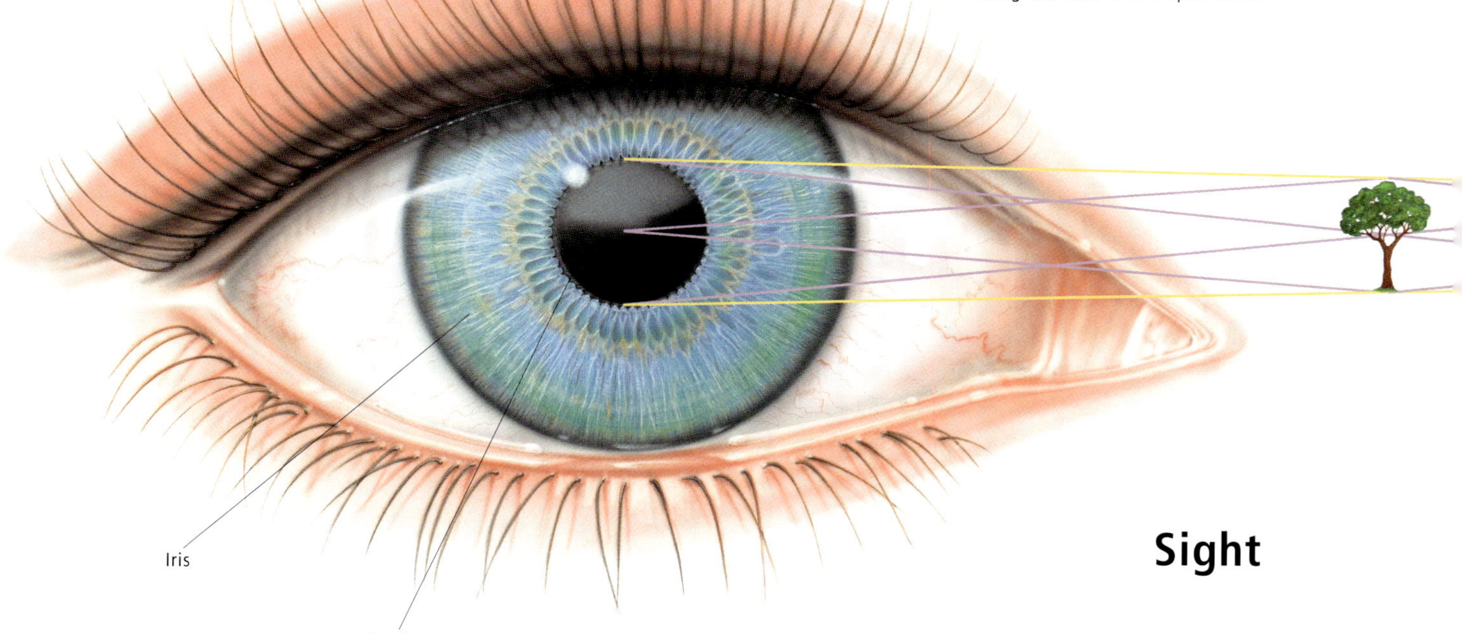

Sight

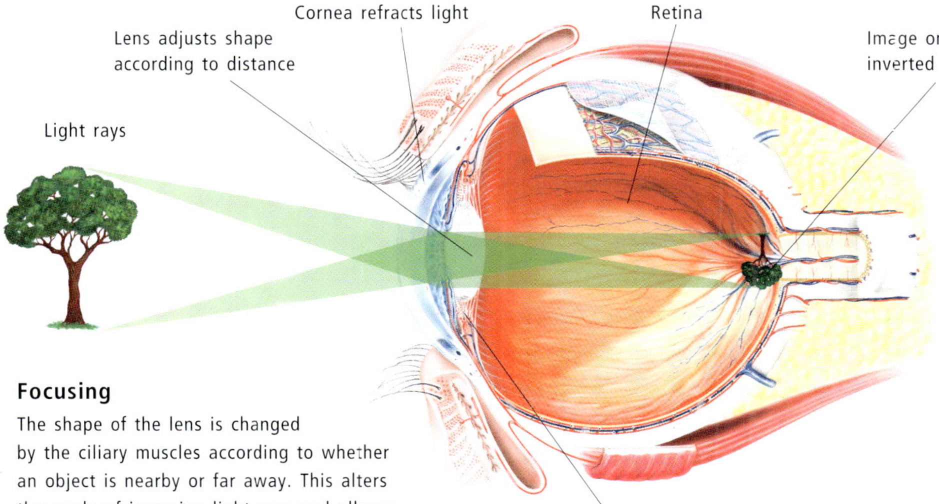

Focusing

The shape of the lens is changed by the ciliary muscles according to whether an object is nearby or far away. This alters the angle of incoming light rays and allows the retina to focus. The cornea refracts light rays as they enter the eye. The rays are brought together for focusing and cross over, creating an upside down image on the back of the retina.

Color blindness

Color perception is the result of the stimulation of three groups of cone cells in the retina which react to red, green and blue. Color blindness occurs when one group of cones is missing or not functioning. Inability to distinguish between red and green (one of the most common forms of color blindness) occurs when red cones are missing. Tests can reveal difficulties in distinguishing between colors—anyone with red–green color blindness will not be able to see the number in this image.

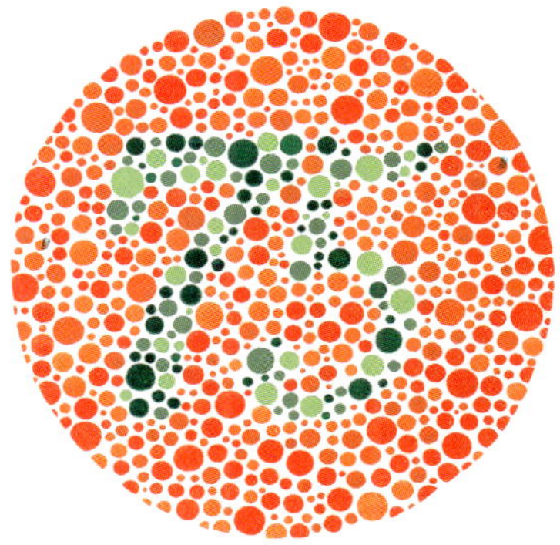

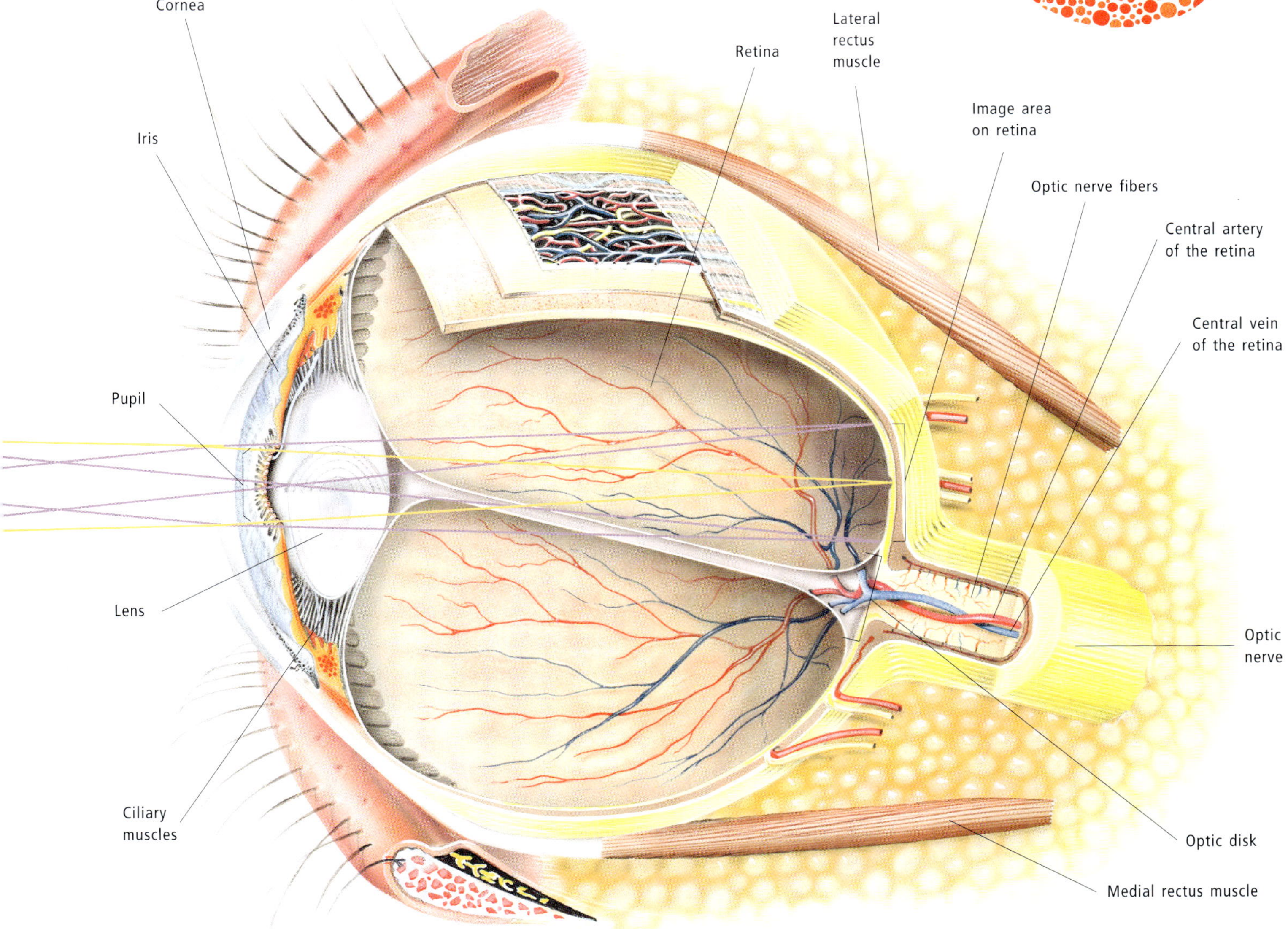

S

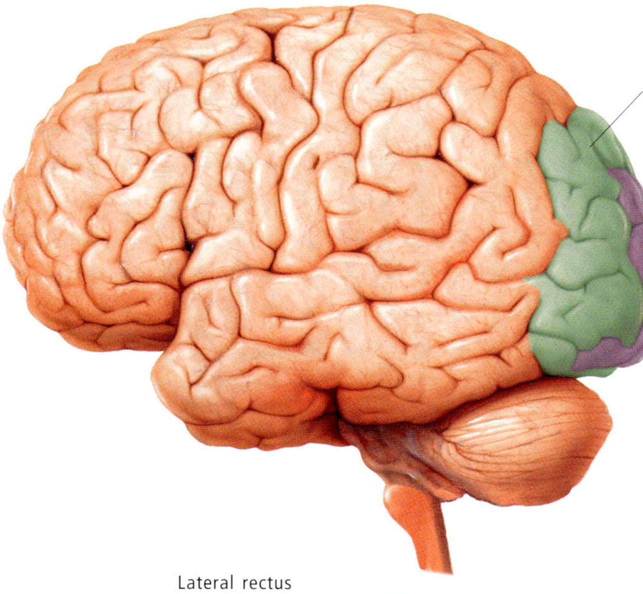

Visual cortex and visual association cortex

The visual cortex interprets and makes sense of the nerve impulses sent from the eyes via the optic nerves and thalamus. This is where objects are recognized and given meaning. The visual association cortex process more complex features of the visual stimulus such as color and movement.

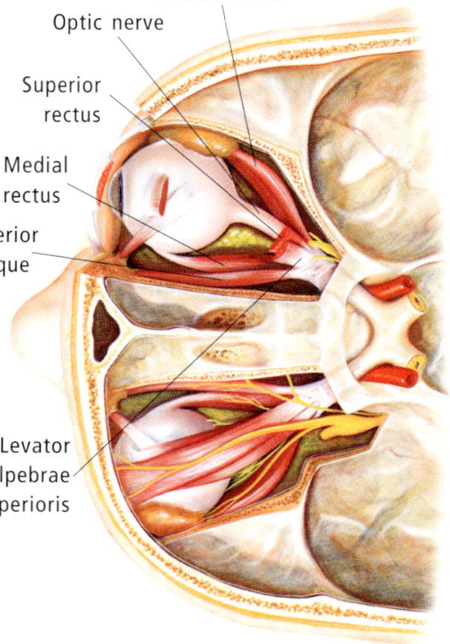

Eye movement and innervation

The movement of the eyeball is controlled by six muscles, allowing the eye to look down, up, left and right. This provides a wide field of vision. The optic nerve carries sensory information, in the form of nerve impulses, from the eyes to the brain for processing.

astigmatism, where light also focuses in front of or behind the retina instead of on it. This can be hereditary or due to injury or disease and causes blurred or distorted vision.

Field of vision

Sight defects often affect the size or shape of the field of vision, the total area perceived by the eye. They include a condition called macular degeneration in which the central part of the retina (macula) deteriorates, causing blurring and a gradual loss of central vision. Peripheral vision is usually not affected by this condition. A large number of the eye's nerve endings are concentrated in the macula, the part of the eye where vision is sharpest. Macular degeneration may be a natural part of the ageing process or be due to disease or environmental factors.

Severe narrowing of the peripheral field of vision (the outside edges of the visual field), as if looking through a tube, is called tunnel vision. It often develops as a complication of the disease glaucoma, when the pressure of excess fluid in the eye damages the optic nerve. It is also a symptom of advanced retinitis pigmentosa, a degenerative disease of the retina. As a result of the restricted visual field, a person suffering tunnel vision may not see someone standing right alongside. The condition often causes night blindness, resulting in difficulty functioning normally in light below a certain level.

Hemianopia is the loss of vision or blindness in one half of the normal visual field in one or both eyes. Loss of vision usually occurs in the left or right half of the visual field, but may also manifest in the upper or lower half. The disorder often goes undetected in the early stages as the vision loss is equal in both eyes. Hemianopia is caused by a brain disorder in which images transmitted by the eyes are not received and processed properly. It often appears in people who have suffered a brain injury.

Treatment options

Glasses and contact lenses, which change the refractive power of the eye, are the most common forms of treatment for refractive errors.

Laser surgery may be used to correct or improve nearsightedness, longsightedness and astigmatism in some cases. The most common form of laser therapy for treatment of refractive errors is known as laser in-situ keratomileusis (LASIK), in which a thin flap of the cornea is surgically peeled back and a laser beam used to remove some of the cornea by heating tissue cells to bursting point. This changes the shape of the cornea according to the refractive error being treated, allowing the correct movement of light through the eye for focusing on the retina.

There is a chance, however, that best corrected vision—with the use of glasses or contact lenses—may be worse after laser surgery than it was before. Laser surgery may also be used to rid the eye of scar tissue and excess blood vessels caused by certain diseases and injuries.

Vision which is below the normal range and which cannot be corrected by the use of glasses, contact lenses, surgery or other medical treatment is referred to as partial sight or low vision. It is often caused by damage to the macula, as well as by diseases and disorders such as diabetic retinopathy, glaucoma, cataracts and retinitis pigmentosa. Many people with partial sight may appear to be blind but have some usable vision. Activities such as reading may still be possible with the aid of such things as large-print books and magnifiers.

SEE ALSO *Astigmatism, Blindness, Cataracts, Color blindness, Contact lenses, Cornea, Eye, Glaucoma, Iris, Macular degeneration, Myopia, Neuritis, Optic nerve, Retina, Retinitis pigmentosa, Squint*

S

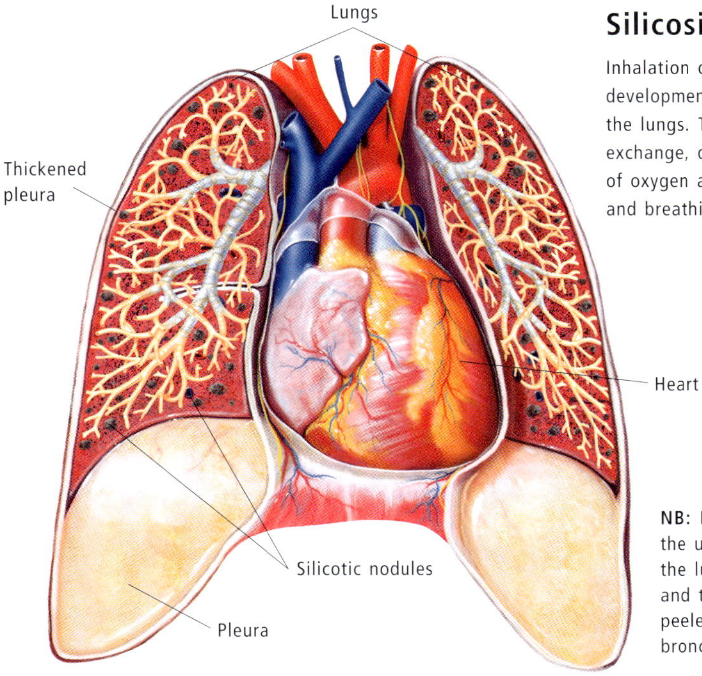

Silicosis

Inhalation of silica dust causes the development of hard nodules in the lungs. The nodules impede air exchange, depriving body tissues of oxygen and causing coughing and breathing difficulties.

NB: In this illustration the upper two-thirds of the lungs have been cut and the pleura has been peeled back to reveal the bronchial tree and heart.

SILICOSIS

Known also as grinder's disease, miner's phthisis and potter's asthma, silicosis is a respiratory disorder caused by inhaling silica, mainly in industrial situations. Occupations at risk include those involving close contact with stone, sand or ceramics such as mining, quarrying, tunneling and the manufacture of ceramics and pottery. The most serious effect of the inhaled silica dust is impaired gas exchange associated with the development of small hard nodules and fibrosis in the lungs.

The severity of the disease depends on the level and length of time of exposure. Chronic or simple silicosis develops after more than 10 years of low-level exposure. Higher levels over 5–10 years cause accelerated or complicated silicosis. Acute silicosis results from highly concentrated exposure over a short period of time.

Symptoms range from shortness of breath and a dry cough in mild forms to lethargy, restless sleep, appetite loss, chest pain, a cough that produces blood, and hypoxia (lack of oxygen in the blood) which shows as blueness of the lips and skin. There is no cure for silicosis and it commonly reduces life expectancy and quality of life. Records of the disease date back two thousand years. It was prevalent in the nineteenth and early twentieth centuries but is becoming rarer due to improved occupational health and safety standards.

SEE ALSO *Lungs, Respiratory system*

SINUSES

A sinus is, in general terms, a small passage or cavity relatively wide in relation to its length. The term is commonly applied to a cavity containing air (the paranasal sinuses) or blood (particularly the venous sinuses). A sinusoid is a small sinus: sinusoids containing blood occur in many organs, including liver, spleen and bone marrow, where they serve to facilitate contact between blood and the cells of the particular organ.

The paranasal sinuses are air-containing cavities within the frontal, ethmoid, maxillary and sphenoid bones of the skull, which are connected by passages to the nose. They lighten the bones in which they occur, assist in cushioning blows to the head, and add resonance to the voice. These sinuses are rudimentary at birth, and develop rapidly at the age of puberty. In women, the sinuses are relatively small. Because of the narrowness of the connecting passages to the nose, and their orientation, the paranasal sinuses do not always drain properly. This may lead to acute or chronic infection (sinusitis).

The venous sinuses of the dura mater (a tough membrane covering the brain and spinal cord) are channels which collect venous blood from the brain and the bones of the cranium. They are situated inside the skull, between the two layers of the dura mater.

SEE ALSO *Nose, Sinusitis, Skull*

SINUSITIS

The paranasal sinuses are cavities lined with mucous membrane in bones around the nose and eyes. Under normal conditions mucus moves steadily from the sinuses into the nose. In sinusitis, the sinuses become inflamed and fill with mucus or pus, causing headaches, facial tenderness and minor breathing difficulties. There are two types of this disorder, which affects 35 million people in the USA alone. Acute sinusitis is caused by a disorder that causes swelling of the membranes of the nose, such as a viral respiratory infection or allergic rhinitis. The swelling prevents fluid from draining out of the sinus normally, and infection with bacteria, viruses or fungi then follows. Swimming

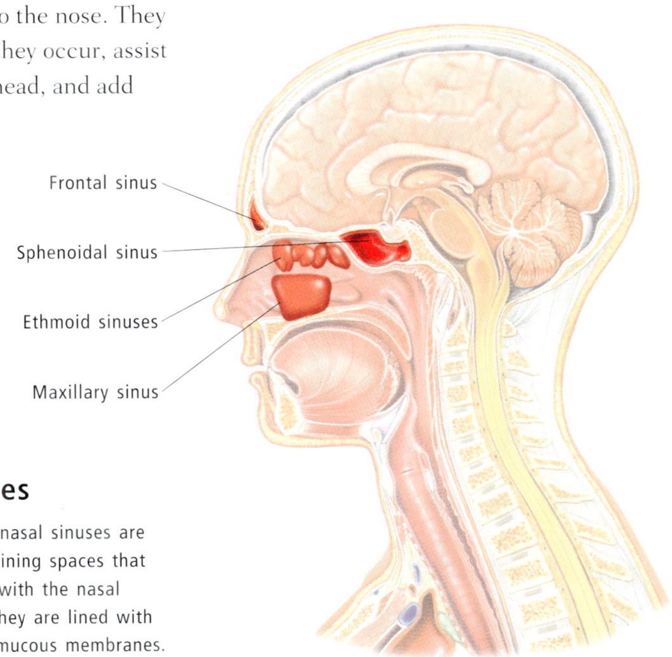

Sinuses

The paranasal sinuses are air-containing spaces that connect with the nasal cavity. They are lined with ciliated mucous membranes.

S

or immersion of the head in water may allow water and bacteria to enter the sinus, causing irritation and infection. Less commonly, dental infections such as a tooth abscess may spread into the sinus and infect it directly.

One of the symptoms of sinusitis is headache, the location of which depends on the sinus(es) involved. There may also be pain in the front of the head or around the eyes, the forehead or cheeks, or in the roof of the mouth or teeth. The pain results from the accumulation of undrained fluid which causes pressure within the sinus. There is often a thick yellow or yellow green nasal discharge and there may be fever and chills.

If the condition is due to bacterial infection, sinusitis is treated with antibiotics. Oral or nasal decongestants may help the sinuses to drain, although the use of nasal drops or sprays should be temporary, since long-term use can cause damage to the nasal lining. If sinusitis is persistent or recurrent the condition is known as chronic sinusitis. It is less common than acute sinusitis and may be caused by a deviated nasal septum or other obstruction of the nose. Chronic sinusitis can also be treated with antibiotics (if infection) and steroid or cromoglycate nasal sprays (if allergic).

If the condition is severe, surgery may be required to control it. This may involve unblocking the sinus, or repairing a deviated septum or nasal obstruction.

There are a number of alternative therapies that are used in chronic sinusitis. Acupuncture treatment is said to stimulate circulation and drainage in blocked sinuses. Aromatherapy uses hot water inhalations with added essential oils of tea tree, pine or eucalyptus. Herbalism uses horseradish, chilli, eyebright, goldenseal, garlic or olive leaf. Externally, poke root (*Phytolacca*) ointment can be rubbed over the blocked sinus region. Naturopathy suggests a light dairy-free wholefood diet, vitamin A and C supplements and exercise in fresh air. Reflexology massage is said to stimulate sinus zones located on each of the toes. Yoga practitioners use a Neti pot to pour weak salty water through the nasal passages to clear and cleanse. Pranayama or breathing exercises are also said to aid nasal decongestion.

SEE ALSO *Allergies, Common cold, Sinuses*

SJÖGREN'S SYNDROME

The second most common autoimmune rheumatic disorder after rheumatoid arthritis, Sjögren's syndrome is a syndrome of dryness of the eyes and mouth. It is caused by a failure of the lacrimal glands, which produce tears, and the parotid glands, which produce saliva. In Sjögren's syndrome (for reasons that are not yet understood) these glands are attacked by the body's own immune system which produces antibodies against the gland tissues. The syndrome may occur on its own, or may be associated with other connective tissue disorders such as rheumatoid arthritis, scleroderma, or systemic lupus erythematous.

The symptoms of Sjögren's syndrome are dryness and grittiness of the eyes (sufferers complain of the sensation of "something in the eye", redness and burning of the eyes and sensitivity to light. Dryness of the mouth causes difficulty in swallowing and talking, abnormal taste or smell, mouth ulcers and dental cavities. A physician will confirm the condition with a special test called Schirmer's test which measures the quantity of tears produced in 5 minutes. Salivary flow studies may also be performed.

The disorder cannot be cured, but the symptoms can be managed by using artificial tears for eye dryness, and methylcellulose or saline sprays for mouth dryness. In cases of severe underlying disease corticosteroid and immunosuppressive drugs may be prescribed.

SEE ALSO *Lacrimal glands, Salivary glands*

SKIN

The skin is a protective organ that covers the body, merging with mucous membranes at the openings of the body such as the mouth and anus. It is loosely attached to underlying tissues, and varies in thickness from 0.5 millimeter on the eyelids to $\frac{1}{7}$ inch (4 millimeters) or more on the palms and soles.

The function of skin is to protect the body from damaging external agents, extremes of temperature and invading organisms such as viruses, bacteria, fungi and parasites. Specialized nerve receptors in the skin also allow the body to sense pain, hot and cold, touch and pressure. Skin plays a role in temperature regulation, protection from ultraviolet light, in the manufacture of vitamin D and in attracting the opposite sex.

Structure

Skin is composed of two layers. The outer layer, called the epidermis or epithelium, is several cells thick. The deepest layers of the epidermis are called the basal and spinous layers and are made up of living cells. They produce cells called keratinocytes, which contain a tough insoluble protein called keratin. The hard dead outer layer of the skin, called the stratum corneum or horny layer, is made up of dead keratinocytes. This layer has a protective function and is particularly thick in the soles of the feet and the palms of the hand. Cells of the horny layer are continuously being shed and replaced by new keratinocytes from the deeper layers. In some areas, keratinocytes form specialized keratin-containing appendages such as the hair and the nails. The basal layer of the epidermis also contains melanocytes, which make the pigment melanin.

The dermis is the inner layer of the skin. It is composed of a network of fibers made from the proteins collagen and elastin, which provide strength and support to the skin. Among them are networks of blood vessels, nerves and fat lobules. The junction of the dermis and epidermis is irregular, with finger-like projections of dermis called papillae running up into the epidermis and causing elevations in the surface in the palms of the hands and the soles of the feet. In the fingers they create fingerprints.

Among the layers of the epidermis and the dermis are the specialized structures—the hair follicles, the sweat glands and the sebaceous glands. These develop from the epidermis and extend into the dermis. Beneath the dermis is a layer of fat cells arranged in lobules, which serves to insulate the body against extremes of temperature and provides a storage site for fat. The thickness of this layer varies greatly.

Specialized functions

The skin has several specialized functions. It plays a major role in temperature regulation. Tiny glands in the skin secrete sweat, a salty, watery fluid. As the sweat evaporates it cools the body surface and helps prevent overheating. Tiny hairs embedded in the skin have the ability to become erect in cold conditions, forming a fine blanket that helps insulate the skin from the cold. The skin contains fine blood vessels. In hot conditions the blood vessels dilate, allowing heat to escape from the skin. This also happens when body temperature is abnormally high, as in a fever. When outside conditions are cold, the blood vessels in the skin contract, diverting blood flow away from the skin to minimize loss of heat.

The skin contains varying amounts of a dark pigment called melanin, which protects the underlying tissues from harmful ultraviolet light by absorbing it. The amount of melanin in the skin varies according to a person's racial origins and is passed on as a genetic trait. The amount of melanin in the skin can be temporarily increased following periods of exposure to sunlight (suntanning). Sunlight also leads to the production of vitamin D in the skin—essential for the absorption of calcium from the gut and the maintenance of bone density.

Sebaceous glands in the skin open into hair follicles and secrete a material called sebum. Sebum is responsible for the waxy feel of skin; its function is to lubricate and soften the skin and to protect it from damage by water, chemicals and microorganisms.

Skin also contains specialized nerve endings that can sense hot and cold, touch, pain and pressure. Nerve impulses travel to the brain via nerves and pathways in the spinal cord, allowing the brain to experience these sensations and take appropriate action.

As the body ages, the features of skin change. In infancy the skin is soft, dry and free of wrinkles. At adolescence, pigmentation increases and body hair becomes longer and thicker, especially in the male. Exposure to the elements, along with physiological changes, result in ageing skin becoming dry, wrinkled and flaccid.

Skin may be destroyed by injury, burns or disease. In most cases regeneration takes

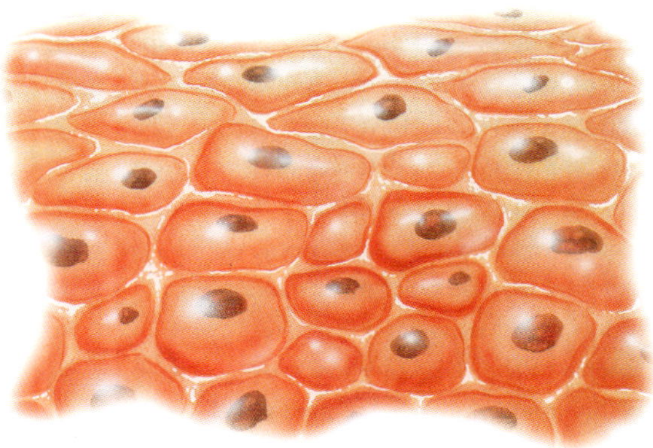

Stratified squamous skin cells

Near the surface of the skin (the horny layer), cells are flattened. The arrangement of cell layers provides a protective shield and prevents dehydration.

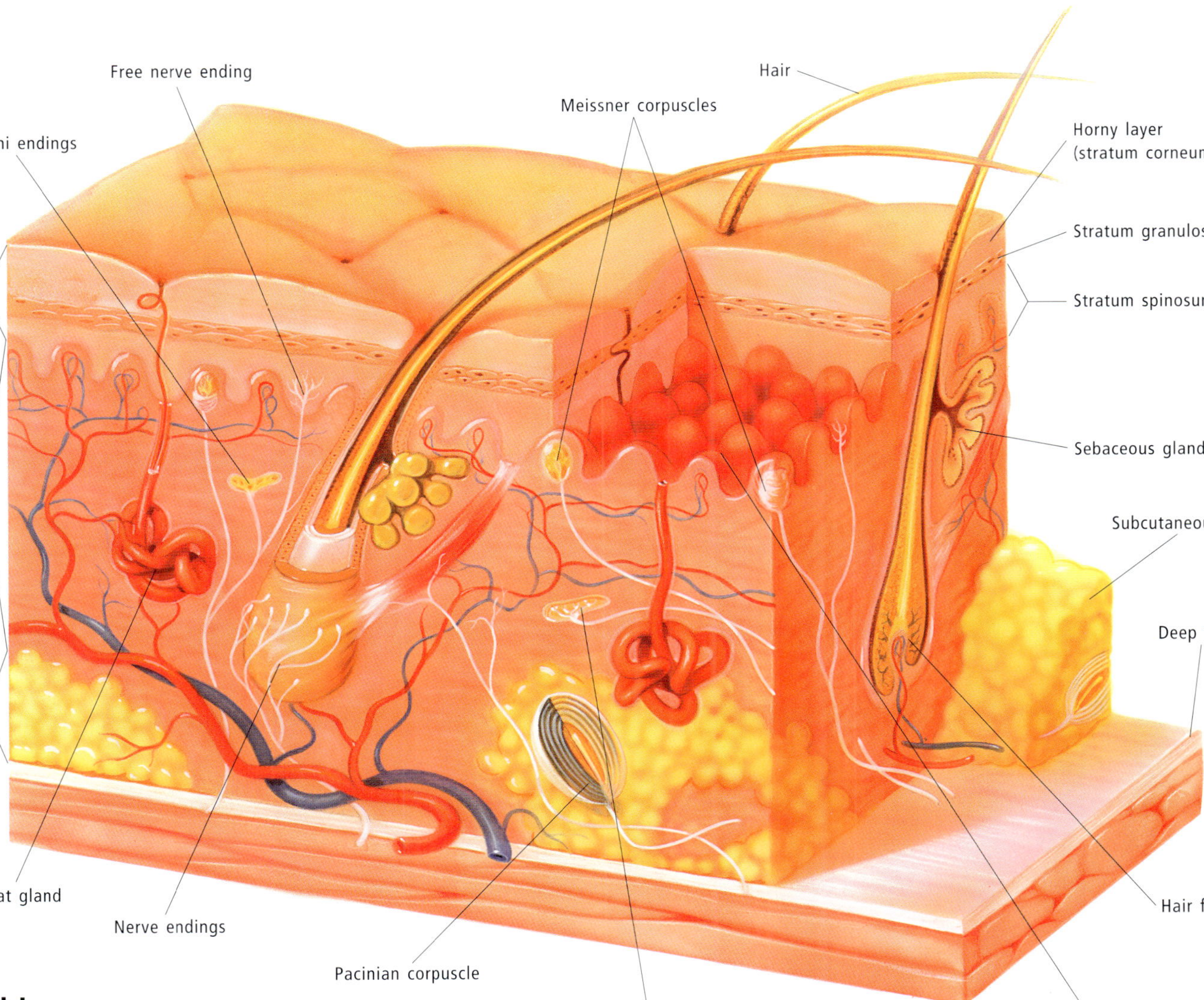

Skin

place from normal skin at the margins of the injured area. If the injury is severe enough, scar tissue forms, over which skin cannot regrow. The damaged area can be covered in skin taken from another site in the body. This is known as skin grafting.

Diseases and disorders

Skin can be affected by a number of diseases and conditions. Bacteria, viruses and fungi can cause infections such as acne, impetigo, herpes blisters and ringworm. Inflammation of the skin, dermatitis, may be caused by infection, a foreign irritant, or an allergic reaction. Many systemic diseases involve the skin, such as the so-called "childhood" diseases of measles and chickenpox. Other skin disorders include benign and malignant tumors, cysts, ulcers and frostbite. In certain conditions the skin color can change due to the presence of abnormal pigments; for example, it may appear yellow in jaundice because of high levels of the pigment bilirubin. Skin disorders are frequently treated by a primary-care physician; more difficult conditions are treated by a specialist dermatologist.

SEE ALSO *Acne, Blood vessels, Dermatitis, Hair, Herpes, Impetigo, Jaundice, Keratin, Melanin, Nails, Nerves, Ringworm, Scar, Sebaceous glands, Senses, Skin cancer, Sun exposure, Sweat glands, Temperature regulation*

SKIN CANCER

There are several different types of skin cancers. Collectively, they are among the most common cancers, especially in fair-skinned people. Exposure to the sun is the most important risk factor for development of skin cancer. In dark-skinned individuals, the skin pigment melanin provides some protection against damage by ultraviolet rays. Persons who lack this protection and/or those whose exposure to the sun is excessive may develop premature ageing of the skin, pre-cancerous skin changes such as scaly spots, and eventually cancers.

Other factors that can contribute to the development of skin cancers include exposure to certain industrial chemicals, exposure to x-rays, and certain hereditary disorders.

The three major varieties of skin cancer, known as basal cell carcinoma, squamous cell carcinoma and melanoma, arise from the surface layer of cells (the epidermis).

Basal cell carcinoma is the most common and most often develops on the upper part of the face, producing a lump or ulcer. This tumor invades locally but very rarely spreads beyond the site of origin. However, its invasive growth can destroy nearby tissues to a considerable extent.

Squamous cell carcinoma is the next most common and may develop anywhere on sun-exposed skin, including the face, neck and back of the hands. It usually appears as a scaly patch which may be red or ulcerated. Unlike basal cell carcinoma, squamous cell carcinoma of the skin will eventually spread to nearby lymph nodes or other body organs. An early (pre-invasive) form of squamous cell carcinoma is known as Bowen's disease, which looks similar but is easier to treat.

By far the most dangerous form of skin cancer is melanoma, a cancer of the pigment-producing cells of the skin. The tumor may have a dark color, but this is by no means necessary. Although the development of a melanoma is related to damage by ultraviolet rays, it may also arise in pre-existing moles or in skin that has not been subjected to repeated or prolonged sun exposure. Heredity plays a role in some cases. If untreated, this aggressive cancer spreads to lymph nodes and other organs of the body, and can cause death.

For all skin cancers—as is the case for cancers at almost all sites—the best outcomes are achieved if the diagnosis is made at an early clinical stage and treatment is begun promptly. Because the development of skin cancers is clearly related to sun exposure, minimizing ultraviolet-induced injury is the most effective approach to reducing the risk of these tumors. Wearing protective clothing and using suitable sunscreens are two obvious methods of limiting such injury to the skin. Less simple, but perhaps more important, is the changing of lifestyle and behavior to reduce risk.

Uncommonly, the skin can also be affected by a tumor known as mycosis fungoides, a variety of lymphoma that arises from T lymphocytes. This produces raised, scaly, itchy areas of skin that vary in color from bluish to brown and may develop ulcers. Mycosis fungoides can be controlled and may even be cured by treatment such as radiation therapy or chemotherapy.

SEE ALSO *Basal cell carcinoma, Melanoma, Mycosis fungoides, Squamous cell carcinoma*

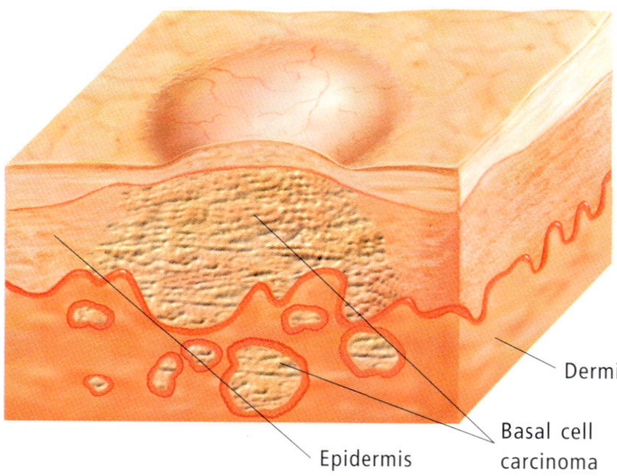

Skin cancer

Basal cell carcinoma is the most common form of skin cancer. It usually forms a localized tumor and very rarely spreads.

SKIN GRAFT

Skin grafting is a procedure in which healthy skin is taken from one area of the body and applied to area where no skin exists. It is part of the treatment of extensive wounds or burns, or in other surgery, for example, removal of large skin lesions.

The procedure is performed by a general surgeon or a plastic and reconstructive surgeon in hospital. During the procedure, healthy skin is removed using a skin-cutting instrument called a dermatome under local or general anesthesia. This healthy skin is spread on the area to be covered and held in place by a dressing or by stitches. The raw donor area is covered with a sterile dressing for a few days to prevent infection. If all goes well, new blood vessels will begin growing from the recipient area into the transplanted skin within 36 hours, though complete recovery takes 6 weeks or so. In some cases the graft does not "take" and the procedure will need to be performed again.

SEE ALSO *Grafting, Skin*

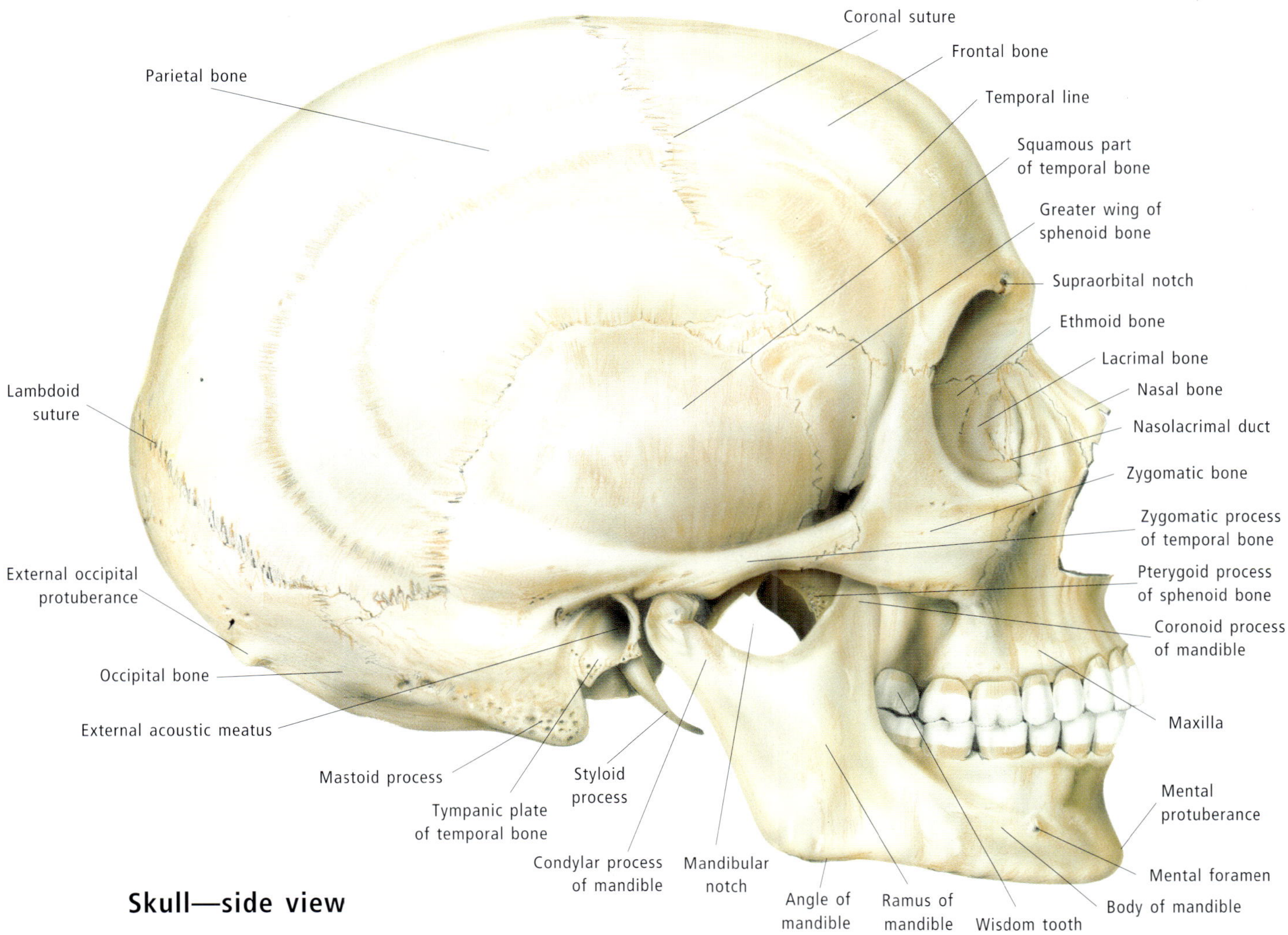

Skull—side view

SKULL

The skull forms the skeleton of the head, and is a part of the axial skeleton. It serves to protect the brain, eyes and inner ears; forms the upper and lower jaws; and provides attachment for muscles of the face, eyes, tongue, pharynx and neck.

The skull provides a strong protective case for the brain and the sensory organs for sight, hearing, balance and smell. This protective value is based on several factors, including the convex shape of the part enclosing the brain, the strength of the interlocking arches of the face, the hardness of the outer bones, and the presence of spongy bone within to absorb impact.

The skull consists of a number of small, irregular-shaped bones. There are seven unpaired, midline bones: the ethmoid, frontal, hyoid, occipital and sphenoid bones and the mandible and vomer. There are 10 pairs of paired bones, one on each side: the lacrimal, maxillary, nasal, palatine, parietal and zygomatic bones, and the temporal bone and middle ear bones (stapes, incus, malleus). There is also a variable number of sutural bones.

The forehead is formed by the frontal bone. Below that are the two nasal bones, with an opening below each. On either side are cavities for the eyes, called the orbits, so named because the eyes rotate in them. An arch of bone, the zygomatic arch, forms the skeleton of the cheek. The roof or vault of the cranium is formed by the frontal, parietal and occipital bones. The rear view of the skull is dominated by the occipital bone in the midline below, with the parietal bones above on each side. At the sides of the skull, the temporal bones contain the middle and inner ears, with the special sense organs for hearing and balance. The middle ear is unique in containing a chain of three tiny bones (ossicles) which relay sound vibrations from the tympanic membrane.

A woman typically has a smaller, lighter skull with relatively smaller paranasal sinuses and other small differences, but it is often impossible to say whether a given skull is male or female. Minor differences in the shape of the frontal, ethmoid, maxillary and sphenoid bones occur between different races.

Strictly, the skull consists of the cranium and the mandible (lower jawbone) plus the hyoid bone at the base of the tongue, but the term "skull" is often applied loosely to the cranium only.

Cranium

The cranium consists of two regions, one accommodating the brain and the other forming the skeleton of the face. The first part consists of a strong box, approximately ovoid in shape, supported by the spine. To this box is attached a series of arches, which form the skeleton of the face. From the side, the division of the skull into the larger, ovoid brain-case and the smaller, approximately triangular skeleton of the face, is clear.

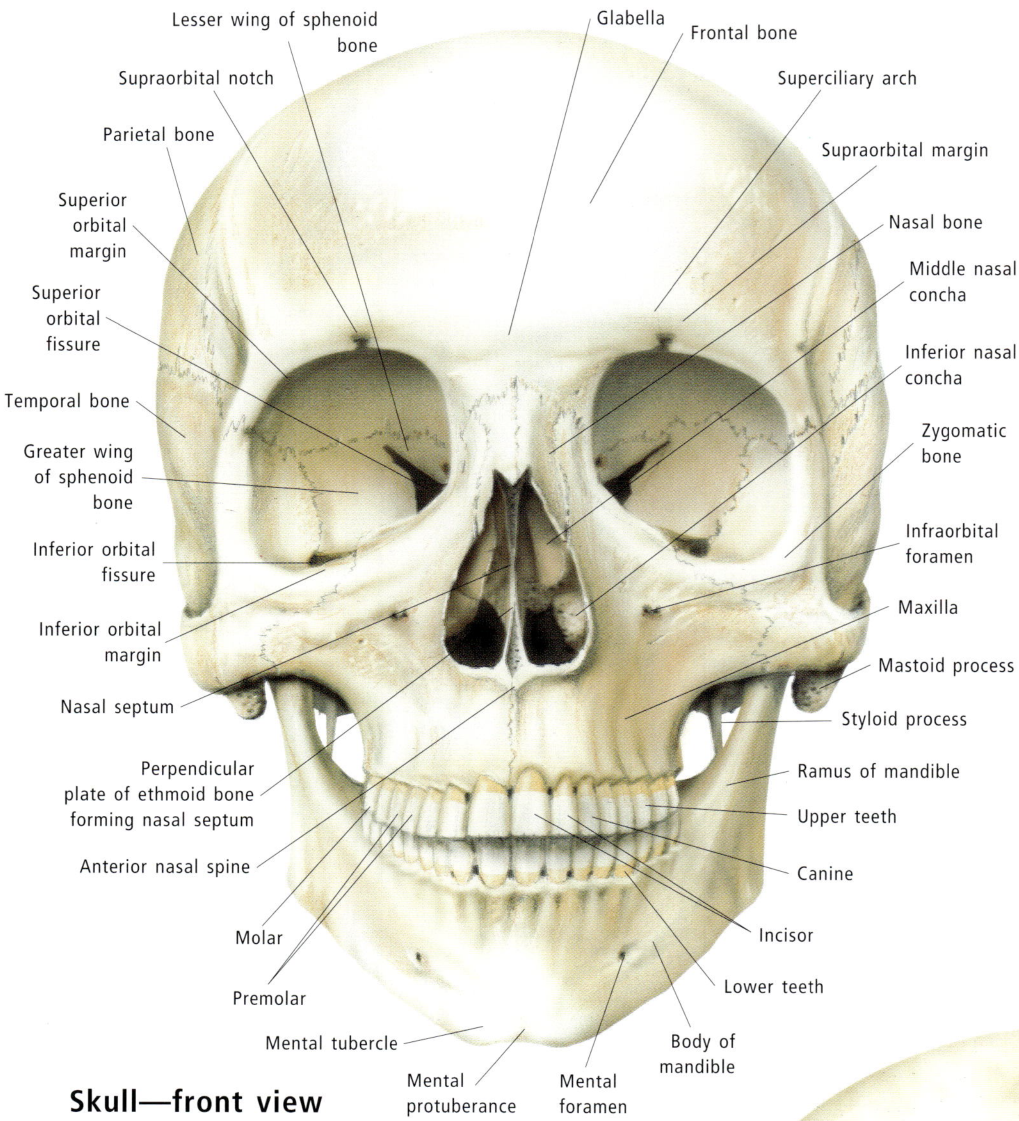

Skull—front view

The bones of the cranium are linked together by "joints" known as sutures, found only in the skull. No active movement occurs. The adjacent bones have irregular, interlocking edges (rather like a jigsaw puzzle) bound together by fibrous connective tissue. Sometimes there are small sutural bones interpolated in sutures between the bigger bones.

At birth, the cranium is relatively large and the face is small. The teeth are not fully formed and the paranasal sinuses are rudimentary. There is no mastoid process. Between some bones of the vault, ossification is incomplete, leaving gaps containing fibrous connective tissue, particularly at the angles of the parietal bones. These gaps are called fontanelles. The anterior fontanelle, easily felt in the newborn child, lies between the separate halves of the frontal bone and the two parietal bones; about 1½ inches (3 centimeters) long and 1 inch (2 centimeters) wide, it closes during the second year. The posterior fontanelle at the apex of the occipital bone, between the two parietal bones, is closed at 2 months. There are several smaller fontanelles. Growth of the skull is rapid for the first 7 years, then slows until puberty, when there is another period of rapid growth.

Base of the skull

The base of the skull is supported by joints between the occipital bone and the uppermost bone of the spine (the atlas or first cervical vertebra). The joint with the atlas permits the head a nodding motion. There is a large hole in the occipital bone, the foramen magnum, above the spinal canal of the atlas vertebra, for the passage of the medulla oblongata and meninges.

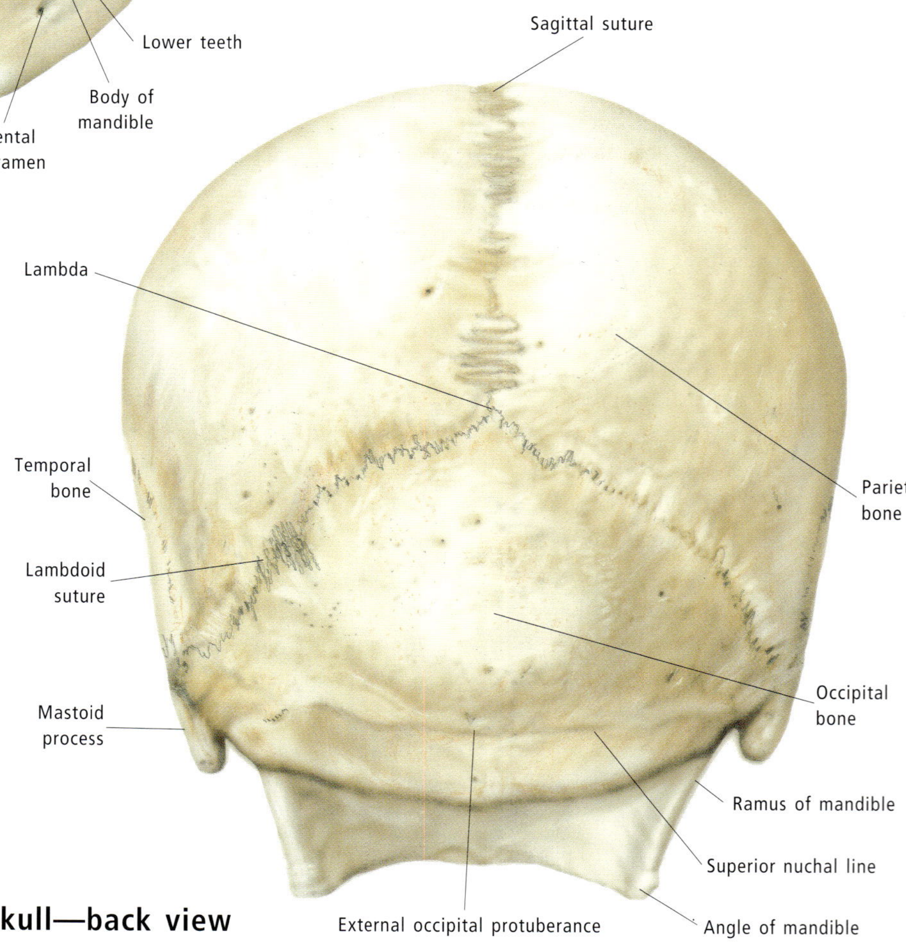

Skull—back view

Jaw

The upper jaw and the bony roof of the mouth are formed by the maxillary and palatine bones. The mandible, the skeleton of the lower jaw, articulates with the temporal bones on each side at the temporomandibular joints. These joints are condylar synovial joints, enabling the mandible to be elevated and depressed, protruded, retracted and moved side to side. The hyoid bone lies in the root of the tongue, where it gives attachment to muscles of the tongue, floor of the mouth and neck.

The teeth are bony structures attached to the upper and lower jaws, projecting through the mucous membrane of the mouth into the mouth cavity. Their free surfaces are covered with a very hard mineral substance called dental enamel. The other end of each tooth has one or more roots embedded in sockets in the maxilla or mandible.

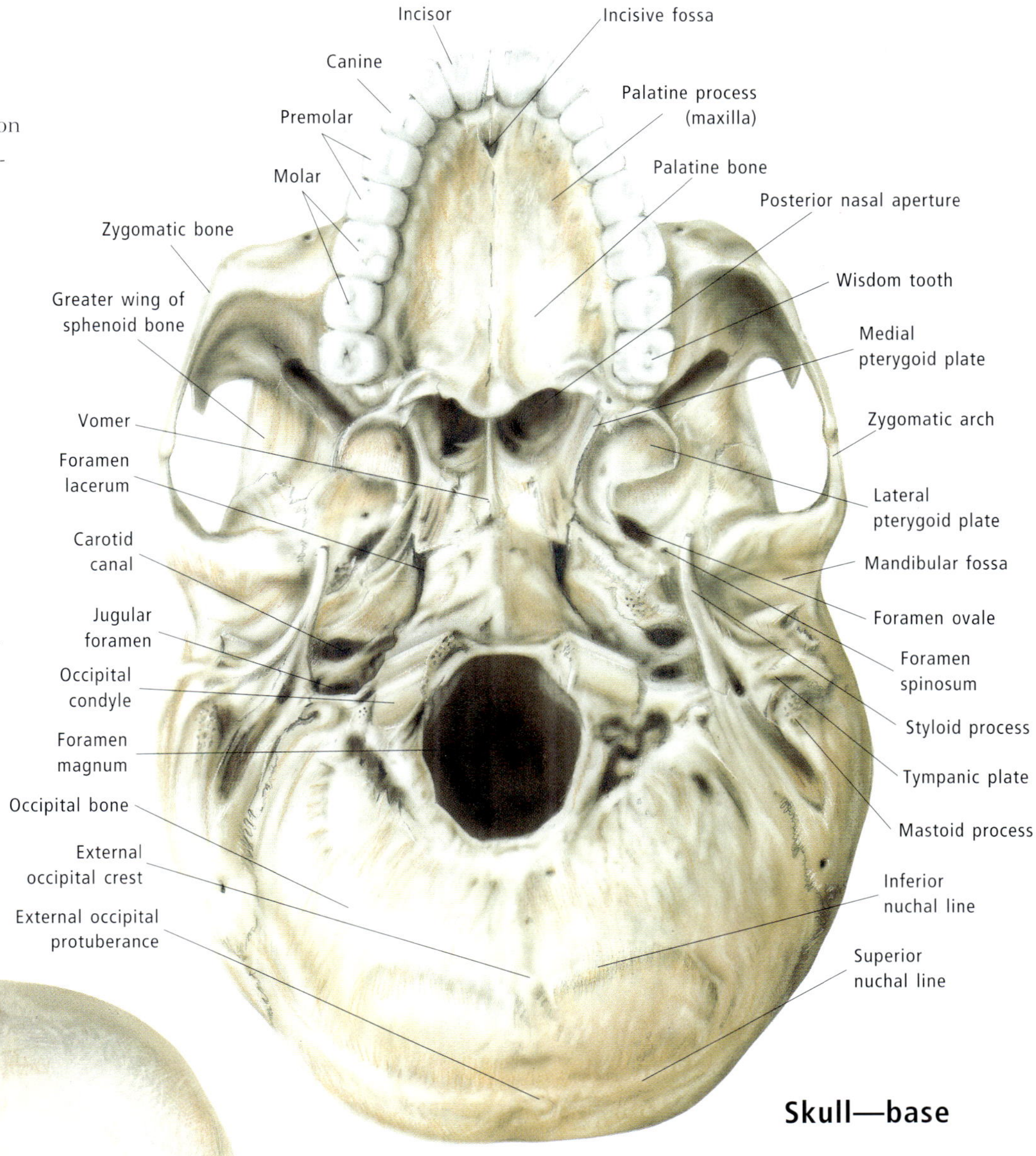

Skull—base

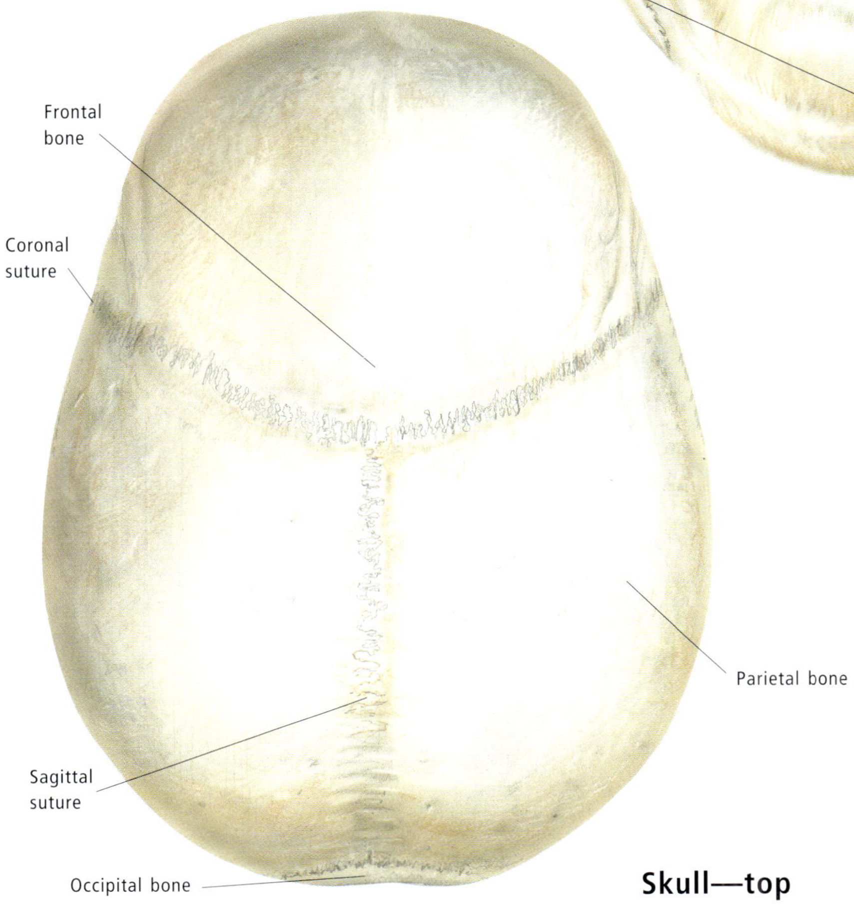

Skull—top

Cavities of the skull

The bones of the skull enclose several spaces. The largest cavity accommodates the brain; this is usually described as three contiguous regions, the anterior, middle and posterior cranial fossae. The orbits are pyramidal spaces (tapering backwards) on either side of the face. The nasal cavities are flattened ducts, into which protrude curved plates called conchae or turbinates, which increase the surface area of the nasal cavities. The nasal cavities are connected to paranasal sinuses in the frontal, ethmoid, maxillary and sphenoid bones.

The skull has openings to the exterior for the eyes, nostrils, ears, and mouth, as well as the foramen magnum already mentioned. There are numerous small apertures for nerves and blood vessels.

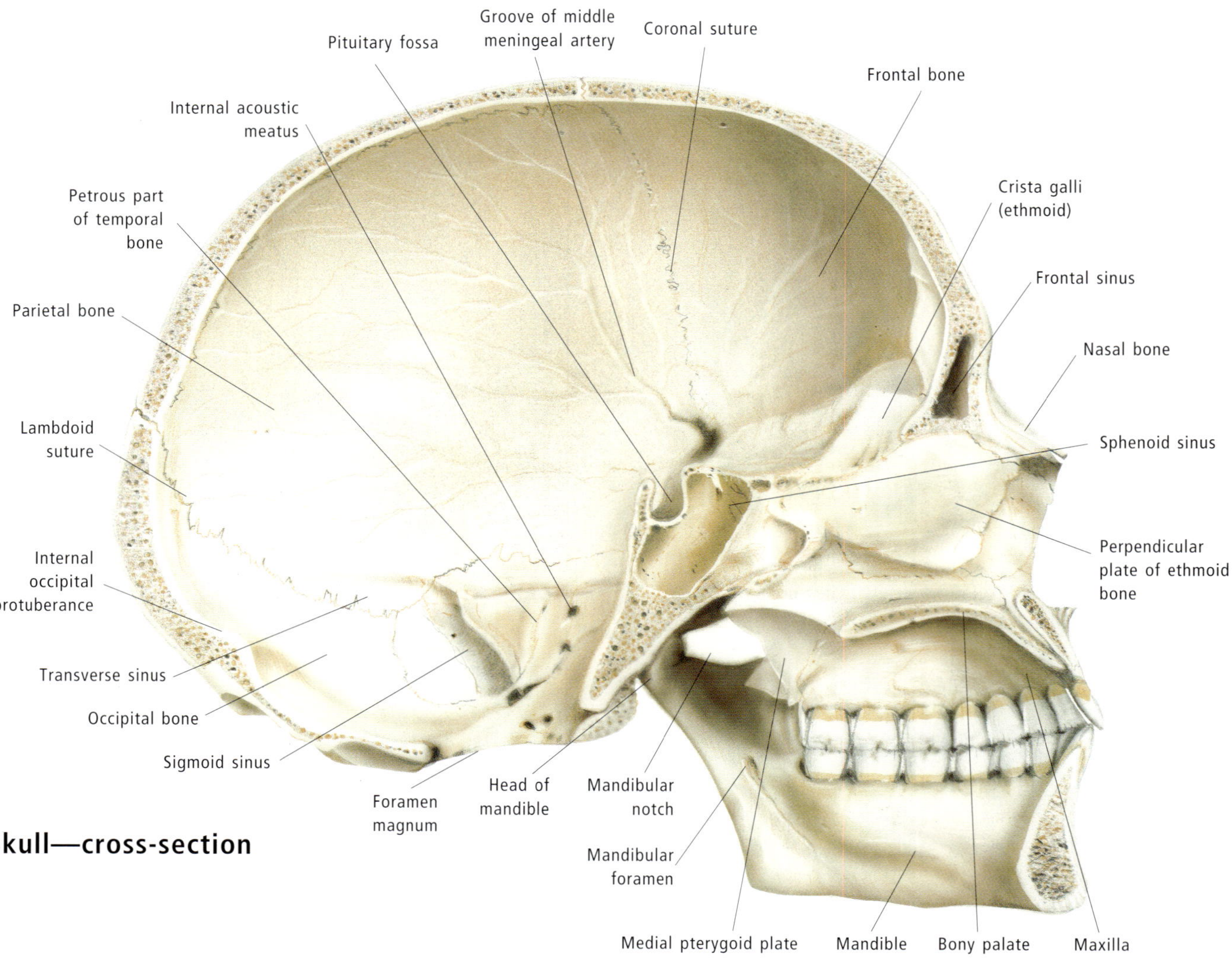

Skull—cross-section

Fetal skulls

The fontanelles are of great importance during the birth of a baby as they give the baby's head the capacity to change shape as it passes through the narrow birth canal.

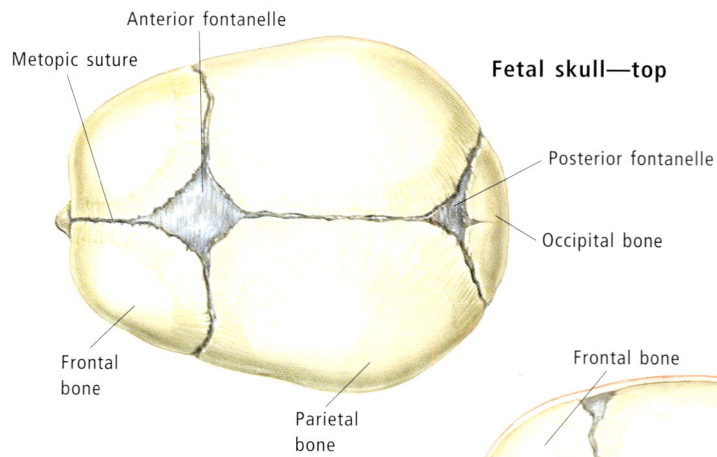

Fetal skull—top

Skull injuries

Fractures of the bones of the skull can be associated with serious injury to the brain, meninges and the sensory organs for sight, hearing, balance and smell. A particular risk with skull fractures is intracranial hemorrhage, which may cause pressure damage to the brain. The most frequently fractured bones are the lower jaw and the nasal bones. The skulls of children are more elastic than those of the adult; blows to the head may produce serious injury to the underlying brain and meninges without fracturing bones.

SEE ALSO *Bones, Ear, Fontanelle, Head, Nose, Sinuses, Skeletal system, Teeth*

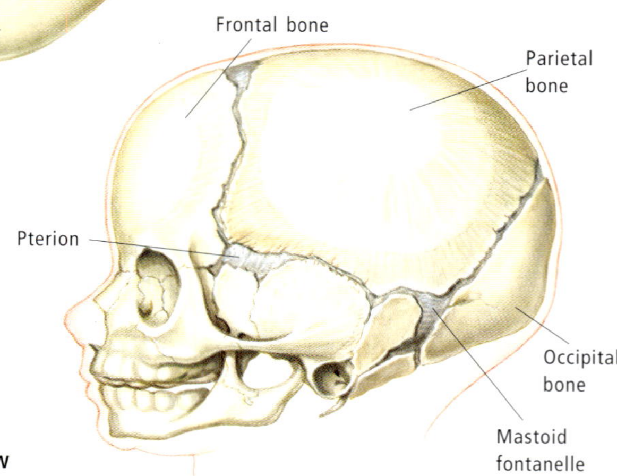

Fetal skull—side view

SLEEP

Sleep has a number of functions in keeping the human body running smoothly. A "biological clock" located in the brain regulates circadian (daily) sleeping and waking patterns. Sleep researchers have defined four stages in the way human adults sleep.

The first is the transition from wakefulness through drowsiness to real sleep. Stage two is real (but light) sleep—the sleeper can usually be aroused. Stages three and four are deep slow-wave (referring to brain-wave patterns) sleep, stage four being the deepest. A sleeper is difficult to wake during this time.

An adult sleeps in 90-minute cycles at night, starting with light sleep (about 50 percent of sleep time), going to deep sleep (about 20 percent of sleep time) and back to light sleep, with dreams (about 30 percent of sleep time). There are two distinct sleep states—rapid eye movement (REM), when the eyeballs move rapidly back and forth under the eyelids, which is associated with dreaming, and non-REM (when the body shuts down to vital functions only).

Babies sleep very differently from adults. They sleep better in a noisy environment than a quiet one; their sleep is more restless and characterized by a variety of facial expressions. REM and non-REM sleep are almost identical for a newborn baby; not until around 3–4 months does a baby fall into a deep sleep, which lasts only half the time it does in an adult. Around the first birthday a child's sleep–wake pattern begins to approximate that of an adult. Babies must learn the difference between night and day as their circadian rhythms are not naturally "tuned" at birth. Research suggesting that babies dream, beginning at 25 weeks' gestation, has led to the conclusion that dreaming is necessary to stimulate and activate the development of the brain. Research has still to establish the purpose of dreaming in older people.

Babies are unable to manage on nighttime sleep alone. Most need to nap in 1–2 hour periods during the day, usually until they are aged about 2–3 years. By this time most babies will have fewer or no night wakings.

Children sleep more deeply than adults. They are not at all responsive to stimuli such as sound, light, touch or heat. Adolescents also sleep differently from adults and in most instances, because of their lifestyle, are probably sleep-deprived. Adolescents who are allowed to sleep until they wake naturally usually sleep for 10–11 hours; it has been found that their circadian rhythms shift so that they naturally go to sleep later at night, and wake later in the morning.

How much sleep people need differs among individuals. It is generally thought, however, that babies need between 9–18 hours in a 24-hour period, children and adolescents between 9–12 hours, and adults between 8–9 hours.

When humans do not get enough sleep on a regular basis they establish a "sleep debt" and are unable to perform at their best throughout the day. This applies to children as well as adults. Both children and adults are getting enough sleep when they wake up of their own accord.

SEE ALSO *Infancy, Insomnia, Sleep apnea, Sleep disturbances, Snoring*

Sleep

Neurons in the reticular formation of the brain stem are important in regulating sleep. Distinct groups of neurons trigger REM and non-REM sleep. A "biological clock" located in the hypothalamus regulates daily sleeping and waking patterns (circadian rhythm).

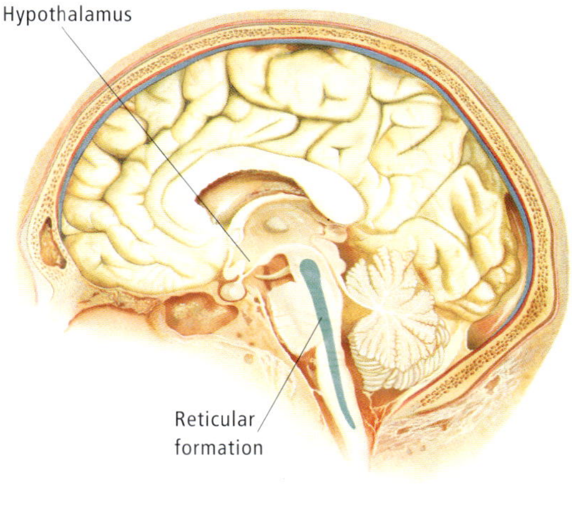

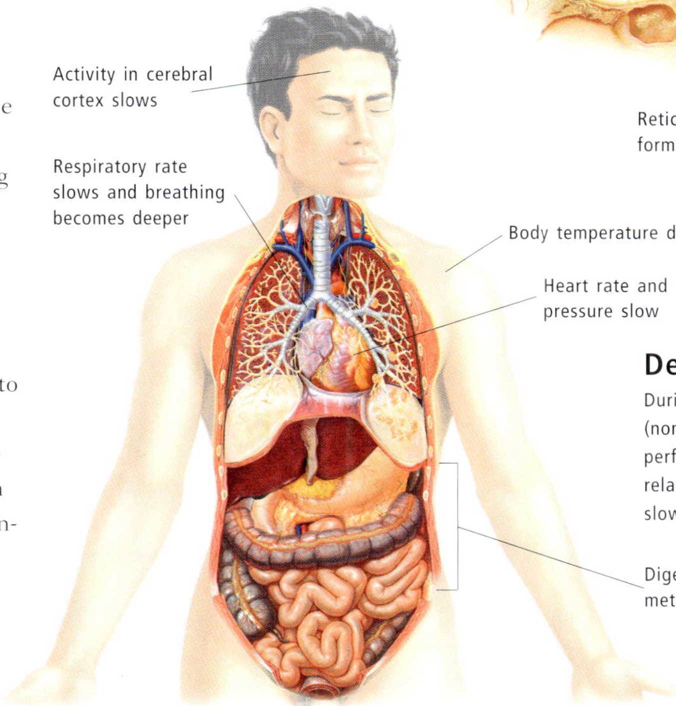

Deep sleep

During deep non-rapid eye movement (non-REM) sleep, the body slows down to perform only vital functions. The muscles relax, the rate of breathing and heartbeat slows and blood pressure decreases.

NB: In this illustration the top two-thirds of the lungs and pleura have been cut away to show the heart and bronchial tree.

SLEEP APNEA

Sleep apnea is one of the most common and dangerous types of sleep disorder, characterized by repeated episodes of the cessation of breathing during sleep. It can cause drowsiness, fatigue and loss of concentration in the day and has also been linked to hypertension and heart disease. Snoring, not in itself a sign of sleep apnea, often accompanies it.

Sleep apnea sufferers will have difficulty breathing while asleep because the airflow is blocked. The reason may be over-relaxation of the throat muscles and tongue, often a problem in people with receding chins, or those with fatty tissue in the airway (often linked to obesity). Other causes may be central sleep apnea (a dysfunction in the brain that controls breathing), smoking and excessive alcohol. Sleep apnea affects about 9 percent of men and 4 percent of women.

Treatment for sleep apnea is nasal continuous positive airway pressure (CPAP). The sufferer wears a soft plastic mask over the nose during sleep; this provides

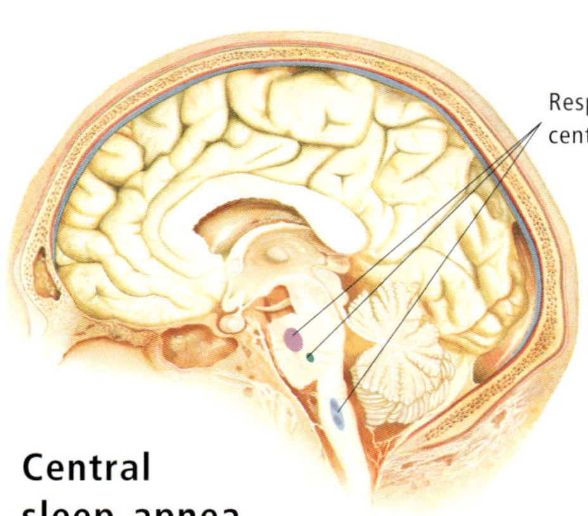

Central sleep apnea

During sleep, respiratory centers in the brain stem automatically control the breathing muscles. A dysfunction in this part of the brain causes central sleep apnea.

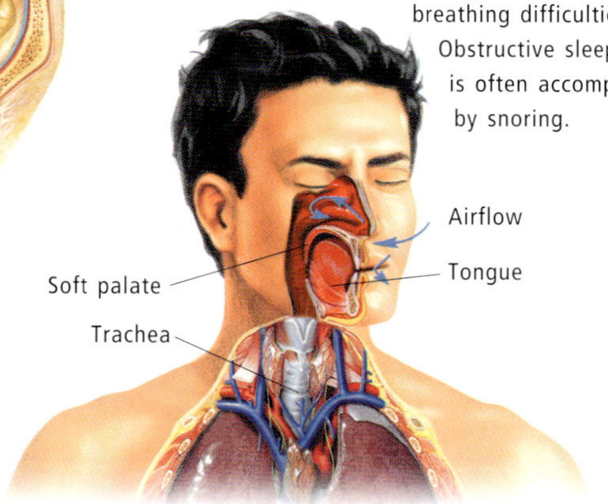

Obstructive sleep apnea

In this condition, over-relaxation of the throat muscles and tongue during sleep obstructs the flow of air to the trachea, causing breathing difficulties. Obstructive sleep apnea is often accompanied by snoring.

pressurized room air to prevent the airways from collapsing. Surgery is an option in extreme cases, and in children the removal of adenoids and tonsils may be recommended.

SEE ALSO *Insomnia, Sleep, Sleep disturbances, Snoring*

SLEEP DISTURBANCES

Sleep disturbances include insomnia, narcolepsy, restless legs syndrome (akathisia), night terrors, nightmares, teeth-grinding (bruxism), sleeptalking (somniloquy), sleepwalking (somnambulism), snoring, sleep apnea and bed-wetting (enuresis).

Those who describe themselves as poor sleepers are usually found, upon investigation, to sleep better than they imagine, although they usually have disturbed sleep with frequent body movements, less REM sleep than other people, and some wakeful periods. Poor sleepers are treated either with medication or behavioral programs.

Nightmares are vivid, frightening dreams which can happen at any time of life. They occur in the last third of the sleep period and can usually be recalled. They usually reflect current difficulties or anxieties. Anxiety dreams which happen occasionally to many people are often precursors to nightmares.

Night terrors (pavor nocturnus) usually occur in children, occasionally in young adults, and are quite different from nightmares. The child sits upright in bed and screams or shouts, is sometimes coherent, sometimes incoherent, and usually inconsolable. Waking the child during the terror is not recommended as it may cause confusion and distress. The episode will be forgotten in the morning. No treatment is needed unless episodes are frequent or there is some other cause for concern, in which case medical advice should be sought.

Restless legs syndrome is fairly common and occurs just before falling asleep. It is found mostly in the over-50s, in pregnant women and in people suffering from stress. In severe cases the movement of the legs may be uncontrollable; it may be treated by benzodiazepines (but not in pregnancy).

Sleeptalking is usually incoherent mumbling rather than intelligible sentences. It is common and occurs at all ages. Sometimes sleeptalking is associated with night terrors, sleepwalking or confusional arousals, but mostly it is of little consequence.

Sleepwalking happens mostly in childhood and adolescence and is a complex set of automatic behaviors. It generally lasts for less than 15 minutes and takes place in the first third of the sleep period. Sleepwalkers get out of bed and walk slowly in an automatic way. They may engage in activities such as eating or getting dressed, but their actions are automatic and uncoordinated. Sleepwalking may be associated with stress, anxiety, sleep deprivation, a full bladder, noise or medication. There is often a family history. The best action is to safeguard the sleepwalker from any accidents.

Teeth-grinding is not associated with a particular sleep stage and does not affect sleep. Other sleep problems include poor sleep hygiene, a common problem among adolescents who do not get enough sleep at the right time and so have difficulty falling asleep and staying asleep, and may also have difficulty staying awake during the day; environmental sleep disturbance, which is directly related to too much light or too much noise or both; obstructive sleep apnea, which is difficulty breathing during sleep; bed-wetting; hyposomnia (too little sleep); and hypersomnia (an increase in sleep of around 25 percent more than normal, and which may indicate a more serious problem in the individual).

SEE ALSO *Bed-wetting, Insomnia, Narcolepsy, Restless legs syndrome, Sleep, Sleep apnea, Sleeping pills, Snoring, Teeth-grinding*

SLEEPING PILLS

Drugs administered to induce sleep are usually potentially addictive and therefore dangerous over long periods. As the mechanism of sleep is understood more thoroughly, so also are the effects of medications used to induce sleep. Some drugs affect REM (rapid eye movement) sleep, and research suggests this may have far-reaching consequences. Alternative remedies such as Bach flower essences, acupuncture, aromatherapy, massage and relaxation techniques are said to be just as effective with fewer unpleasant consequences.

SEE ALSO *Acupuncture, Aromatherapy, Drug dependence, Massage, Sedatives, Sleep, Sleep disturbances*

SLEEPING SICKNESS

In tropical Africa, the bites of the tsetse fly can pass parasites called trypanosomes to humans, causing the frequently fatal sleeping sickness or African trypanosomiasis. The first sign is sometimes a red sore at the site of the bite. Other symptoms, which may not follow for weeks or even months, include headaches, fever, extreme fatigue, swollen lymph nodes and aching muscles and joints. As the parasites invade the central nervous system, confusion, seizures and impaired walking and talking occur.

There is no vaccine or preventive medication available. With drug treatment and hospitalization, patients normally recover, although it may take years to be completely free of the disease.

SEE ALSO *Infectious diseases*

SMALLPOX

Smallpox was an acute and contagious viral infection that was eradicated worldwide by a vaccination campaign launched by the World Health Organization. The program began in 1967, when smallpox caused about 2 million deaths. The last known naturally occurring case of the disease was reported in 1977.

Smallpox was spread by contact, the virus being exhaled or expelled in saliva by the infected person. The infection could cause death before the characteristic skin pustules appeared, or be so minor that symptoms went unnoticed; in those cases the virus could continue to be spread. The virus could also live in bedding, clothing or dust for up to 18 months, although it would not replicate outside the human body. The vaccination program was so successful that it has now generally been discontinued.

SEE ALSO *Immunization, Viruses*

SMELL

The sense of smell is one of the major senses, along with sight, hearing, taste and balance, and the senses of touch, proprioception (sense of movement and body position), pain and temperature. It responds to the chemical nature of airborne substances breathed into the nose, and also to odors from food and drink that reach the nose from the mouth and pharynx. It is extraordinarily sensitive to some volatile substances, such as methyl mercaptan, which is added to natural gas to give it an odor. The receptors for the sense of smell are situated in the olfactory mucosa that line the upper part of the cavities of the nose. Sensations are carried by the olfactory nerves to a part of the brain above the nose which is specialized for receiving and interpreting sensations of smell.

SEE ALSO *Nose, Olfactory system*

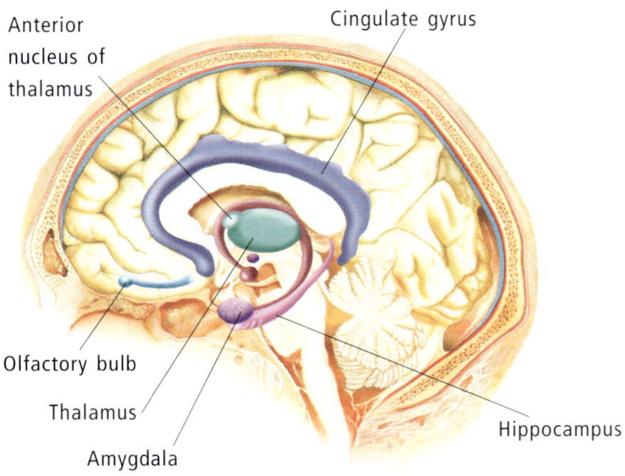

Smell and the limbic system

The olfactory bulbs are directly connected to the hippocampus and the amygdala in the limbic system, which is important for memory and emotion. This is why smells are evocative of past places and feelings. Some smells stimulate the limbic system to activate the hypothalamus and pituitary gland,which triggers the release of hor-mones associated with appetite and emotional responses including pleasure, fear, and sexual drive.

Olfactory path

Odor molecules enter the nostrils and pass into the nasal cavity where they dissolve in olfactory mucosa in the nasal lining. They stimulate olfactory receptors which send signals to the olfactory bulb. From here, nerve signals travel along the olfactory tract to reach the olfactory cortex, the limbic system and the hypothalamus in the brain. This is where smells are identified and the body's response coordinated. Smell has the most direct pathway to the brain of all the senses.

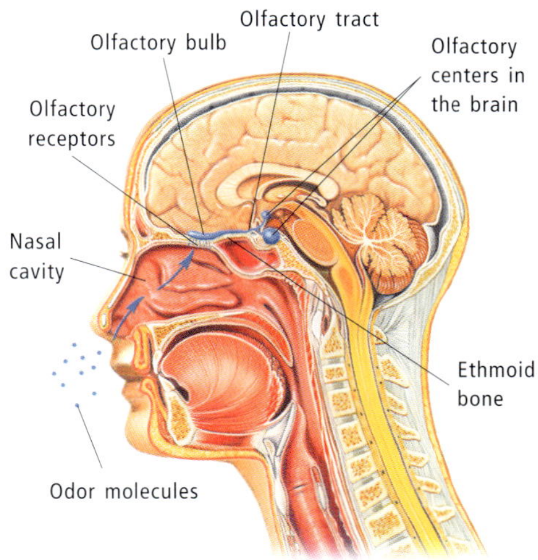

Smell

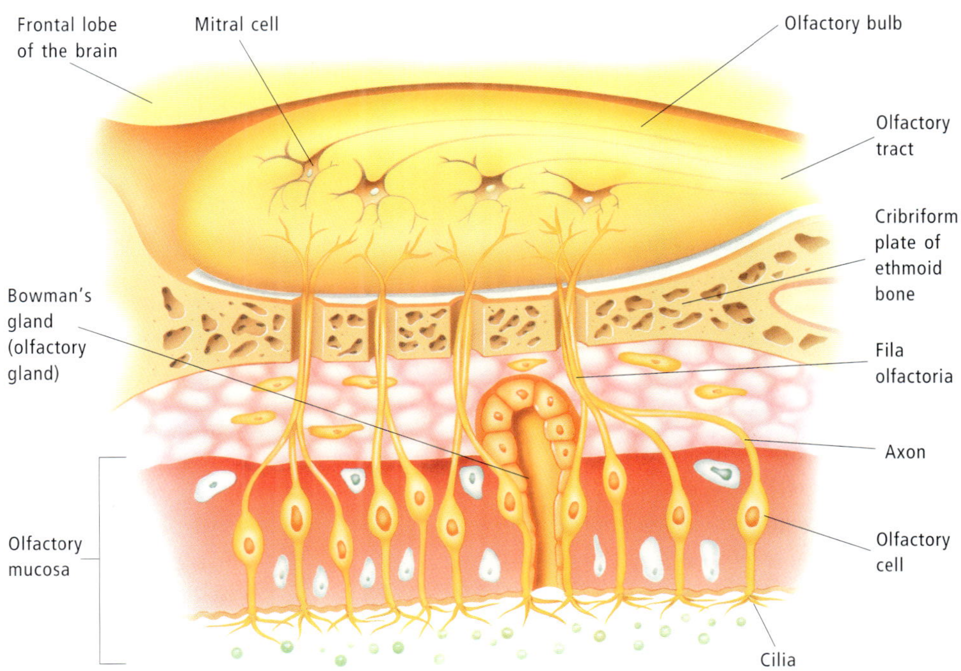

Olfactory apparatus

The olfactory receptors are located in the roof of the nasal cavity. A small area of mucous membrane (the olfactory epithelium) contains millions of nerve cells bearing cilia. When odor molecules are dissolved on the moist surface of the epithelium, they stimulate the nerve cells. Nerve impulses are transmitted along the nerve fibers through holes in the cribriform plate to the olfactory bulb under the frontal lobe of the brain.

SMOKING

Smoking is the drawing into the mouth, and inhalation, of smoke from burning tobacco or other plant material. Cigarettes are the most common form of smoking, with pipes and cigars in a minority. Tobacco is the substance most commonly smoked, but the use of cannabis, also smoked in cigarettes and pipes, is also widespread although it is illegal in many parts of the world.

Smoking was introduced into European society by explorers who observed its use by the peoples of Asia and the Americas, who believed it had medicinal properties. Current use of tobacco is likely to be habitual for reasons of pleasure and relaxation and to relieve the craving for nicotine, a chemical component of tobacco on which smokers become dependent.

Throughout the twentieth century evidence accumulated that smoking had harmful, even deadly, effects on health and that it delivered no physical benefits other than to relieve the cravings of those addicted. The strength of this addiction can be such that in times of economic and currency instability, or in special situations such as in the huge prison camps set up in Europe during World War II, cigarettes are used as a form of currency.

In 1964 the Surgeon General of the United States of America gave the first official warning of the health hazards of smoking. Since then the percentages of the populations of Australia, UK and the USA who smoke have declined, but current trends show an increase in women as a proportion of all smokers as more women than men take up the habit.

Smoking is now actively discouraged in many countries, both by private regulation, including organizations creating no-smoking areas, and by legislation, enforcing health warnings on product packs, prohibiting sale of tobacco products to minors and banning smoking in areas such as designated public places or on public transport. Health and life insurance premiums are generally lower for non-smokers.

That about a quarter of most populations continue to smoke illustrates just how difficult it is to overcome nicotine addiction and the aggressive marketing strategies used by cigarette companies.

Heart disease

By causing disease of the arteries that supply oxygen to the heart, smoking increases the risk of a range of heart conditions including angina, myocardial infarction, cardiomyopathy, heart failure and cardiac arrest. Cessation of smoking is an essential part of the treatment for individuals with heart disease.

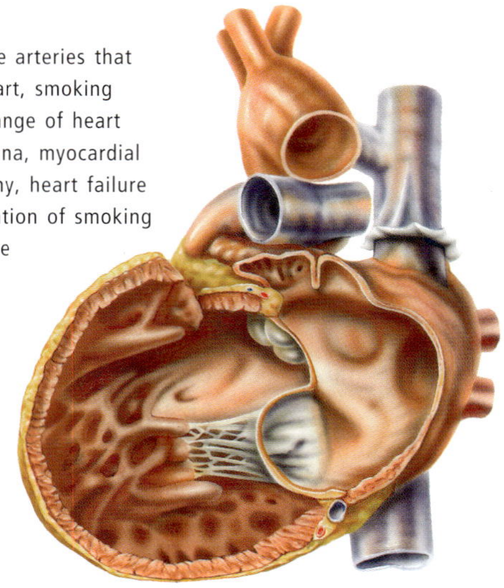

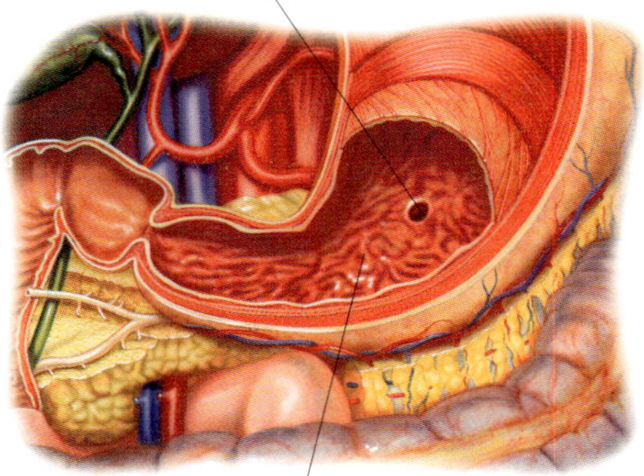

Gastric ulcers

Smokers are at increased risk of developing gastric ulcers. When tobacco smoke is inhaled it stimulates acid production by the stomach. Over time, this acid attacks the mucous membrane in the walls of the stomach causing ulceration.

Stroke and cerebral hemorrhage

When the walls of blood vessels thicken and deteriorate as a result of smoking, the arteries in the brain may narrow, blocking off the blood supply and causing a stroke. Diseased vessels may develop aneurysms and burst, causing a cerebral hemorrhage. Either condition may result in death or severe neurological disability.

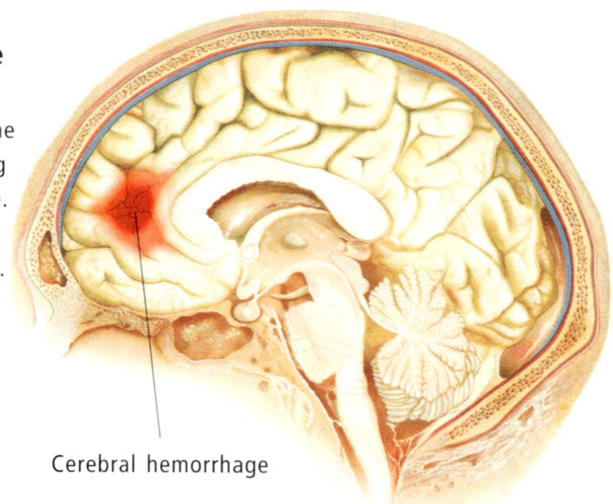

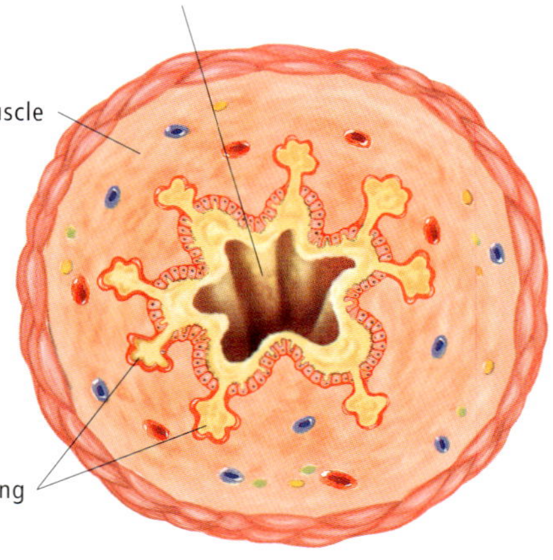

Asthma

Cigarette smoke irritates the smooth muscles of the bronchi (airways) and increases mucus secretion from the glands in the bronchi. It aggravates the symptoms of asthma including breathing difficulties, and may precipitate an asthma attack.

The effects of smoking

The immediate effects of inhaling tobacco—increased heart rate, raised blood pressure and stimulation of the nervous system—are reversible. However, the long-term effects of years of smoking are often not reversible, making smoking one of the leading causes of death and disease.

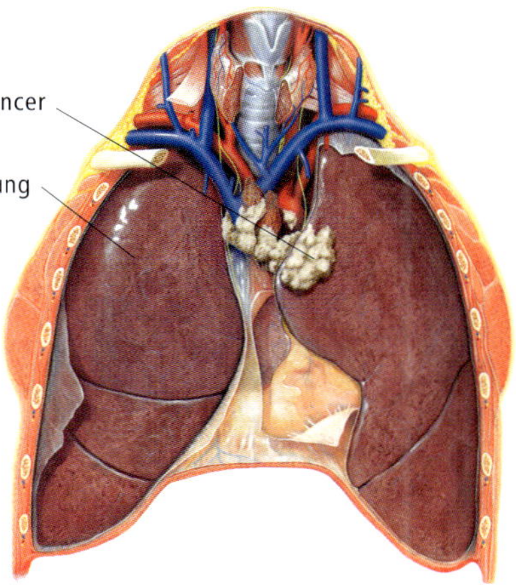

Cancers

Cigarette smoke contains 43 known carcinogens (cancer-causing agents). It can cause cancers in the tissues of the lungs, mouth, pharynx and esophagus through direct contact, as well as cancers at more distant sites, such as the bladder, kidney, pancreas and cervix. Smoking causes almost 90 percent of lung cancers.

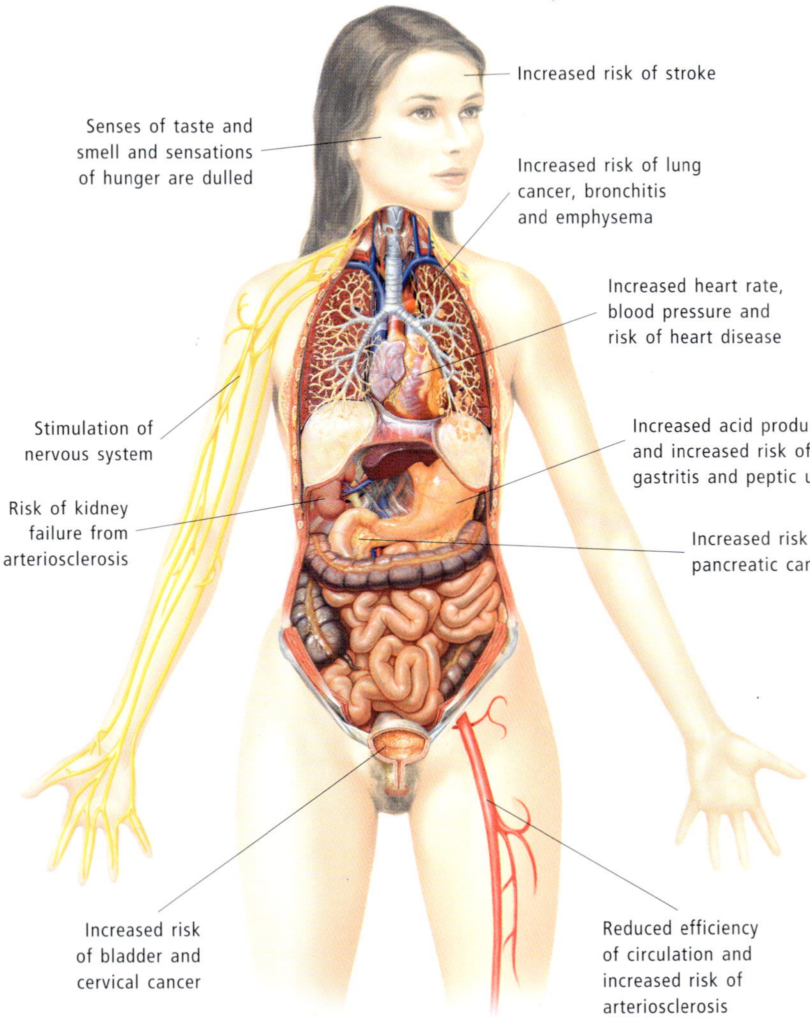

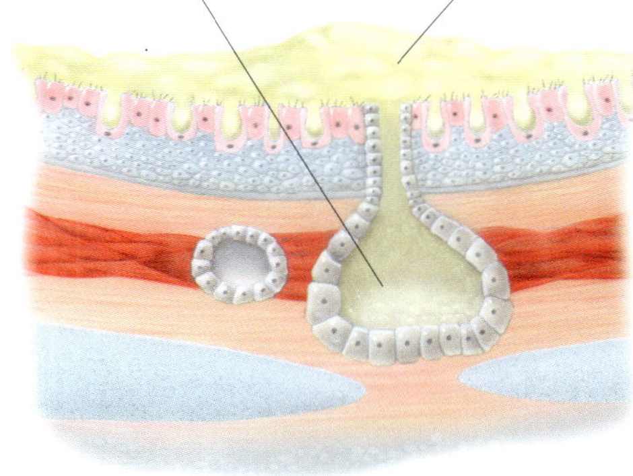

Bronchitis

Cigarette smoke damages the airways of the lungs, increasing the risk and frequency of chest infections such as acute bronchitis. Many heavy smokers develop chronic bronchitis (repeated and prolonged episodes of bronchitis) in which excess mucus secretion in the airways causes cough and sputum production.

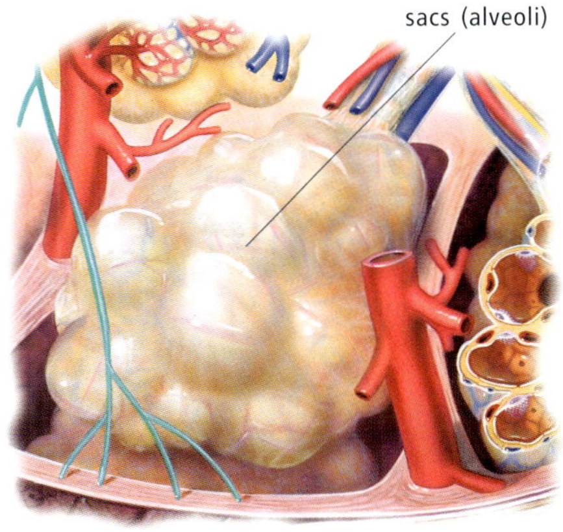

Emphysema

Cigarette smoke destroys the delicate structure of the air sacs (alveoli) in the lungs, preventing the efficient exchange of oxygen and carbon dioxide. When advanced, this condition is called emphysema and is characterized by severe shortness of breath.

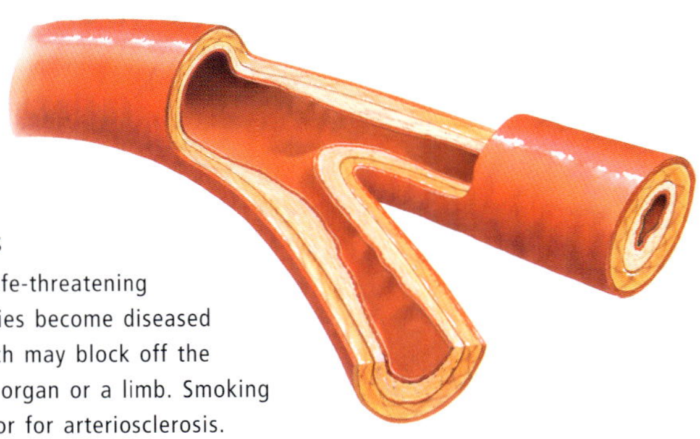

Arteriosclerosis

In this potentially life-threatening condition, the arteries become diseased and narrowed, which may block off the blood supply to an organ or a limb. Smoking is a major risk factor for arteriosclerosis.

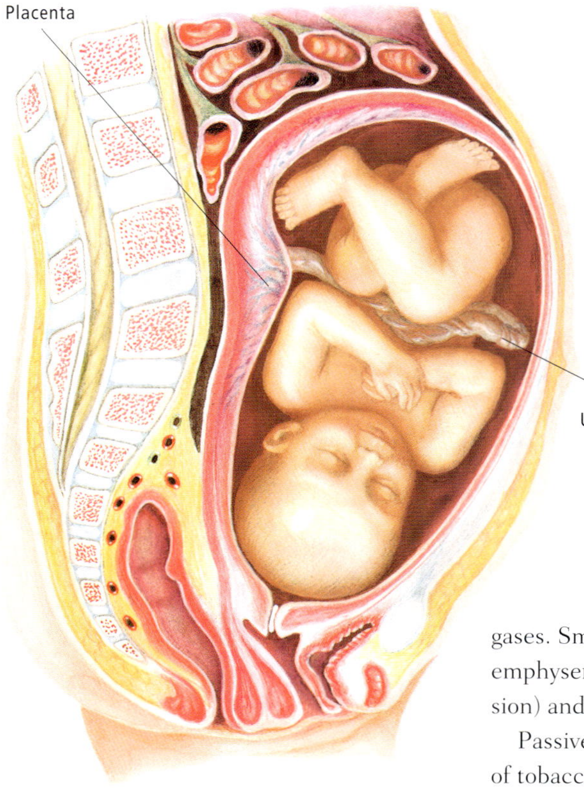

Smoking during pregnancy
Pregnant women who smoke are more likely to suffer a miscarriage, have a complicated delivery, or have a baby who is underweight, than women who do not smoke. Carbon monoxide from tobacco smoke passes into the mother's bloodstream and through the umbilical cord to the baby. This affects the amount of oxygen and blood flow to the baby, inhibiting healthy development.

Effects of smoking

Inhaling tobacco smoke immediately increases the heart rate, raises blood pressure, excites the nervous system and slows down the cilia, tiny hairs in the airways to the lungs which act as filters to clean incoming air. Other short-term effects of smoking are to increase acid production in the stomach, reduce urine produced by the kidneys, dull the senses of taste and smell and sensations of hunger, thus reducing appetite, and to reduce the efficiency of blood circulation.

Long-term smoking has been proven to increase the risks of developing cancer in those areas of the body in direct contact with inhaled smoke. Cancers of the lung, mouth, pharynx and esophagus affect more smokers than non-smokers, as do cancers of the bladder, kidney, pancreas and cervix. Smoking also increases the risks of dying from these disorders. The culprits are nicotine and the various tars which leave deposits seen as stains on teeth and fingers and on the internal surfaces of the lungs, where they reduce the flow of oxygen into the blood. Inhaled smoke contains less oxygen than normal air and more carbon monoxide, a deadly poison also found in car exhaust gases. Smokers are also more susceptible to emphysema, high blood pressure (hypertension) and heart disease.

Passive smoking is the term for inhalation of tobacco smoke by those around the smoker. This sidestream smoke has adverse effects on health that can significantly increase risks of disease in non-smokers.

Smoking in pregnancy is to be avoided. Carbon monoxide from tobacco smoke passes into the mother's bloodstream and through the umbilical cord to the baby, reducing the oxygen intake and increasing the baby's heart rate. The blood vessels in the cord narrow, reducing blood flow to the baby. Nicotine also passes to the baby, affecting the development of proper breathing movements. Pregnant women who smoke are more likely to miscarry, to have complications at birth, and to deliver a low birthweight baby, or to lose the baby shortly after birth. Smoking in pregnancy may be a factor in SIDS (crib or cot death), and the later development of asthma and respiratory infections in the baby. Quitting at any stage in the pregnancy is statistically better than smoking to full term.

Smoking while breast feeding passes inhaled poisons to the baby through the milk. Smoking near a baby may result in the development of a sensitivity to smoke which leads to asthma and breathing problems, poor lung function, frequent coughs, and chest infections, including bronchitis and pneumonia.

Smokers develop a tolerance to nicotine which produces a need to smoke more tobacco to allay cravings, the level varying with the individual. The development of serious diseases related to smoking is affected by the quantity of tobacco smoked: the more tobacco is smoked over a given period, the faster related health disorders develop. Increased intake deepens an individual's dependence and results in stronger symptoms of withdrawal when the effects of the last intake diminish.

Withdrawal symptoms make it extremely difficult to quit smoking. They include coughing, difficulty concentrating, headaches, irritability, nervous tension, and changes in taste and smell. There are psychological difficulties in withdrawing from tobacco, as many daily activities or habits trigger the desire to smoke, such as smoking after eating or lighting up immediately on rising each morning. A successful program to quit smoking must address all the factors creating dependency.

Quitting smoking

The immediate benefits of stopping tobacco use may go unnoticed under the accompanying withdrawal symptoms but they are important and significant. Only 6 hours after the last cigarette, heart rate slows to normal and blood pressure reduces. After 12 hours, nicotine has been eliminated from the body. After 24 hours, carbon monoxide has been cleared from the lungs, and there may be increased coughing as wastes are expelled. In two days many other chemicals from smoking are also expelled. After a year, the risk of heart disease falls. After 10 years, the risk of smoking-related illness is reduced to the same level as in non-smokers.

Quitting smoking is difficult and first time efforts may not be successful. Therapies include clinics and self-help groups supplemented by aids such as nicotine replacement therapy to overcome physical cravings. Hypnotherapy has also been used to reinforce the willpower needed to successfully overcome a pernicious habit, which has been called the most health-damaging single activity an individual can undertake.

SEE ALSO *Cancer, Emphysema, Heart, Hypertension, Lung cancer, Lungs, Nicotine, Pregnancy, Respiratory system, Withdrawal*

S

SNEEZING

Sneezing is a sudden, noisy and spasmic exhalation of air through the nose and mouth. A sneeze is an involuntary reflex action triggered by stimulation of nerves in the mucous membranes of the nose or by overstimulation of the optic nerve by very bright light. Sneezing often accompanies respiratory infections such as the common cold where nasal membranes become swollen and inflamed. Inhaling tiny foreign particles, such as specks of ground pepper or talcum powder, can also lead to the sort of nasal irritation that elicits sneezing.

Allergens, such as mold or pollen, are among the most common causes of persistent sneezing. For people suffering from protracted allergy-related sneezing, there are several over-the-counter medications that may offer relief. These include antihistamines, decongestants and nasal sprays.

Interrupting or suppressing a sneeze is dangerous and can result in damage to abdominal muscles or to the middle ear as air is forced up the eustachian tube. Trying to suppress a sneeze can also propel mucus into the middle ear or sinuses which may then promote the development of infections in these areas. Very occasionally, the pressure that results from stifling a sneeze can cause an eardrum to rupture.

A sneeze is sometimes also called a sternutation.

SEE ALSO *Common cold, Mucous membranes, Reflexes, Rhinitis*

SNORING

It is estimated that between 30–50 percent of people will be snoring during sleep by the time they have reached their 50s. Snoring is defined as breathing during sleep in a way that causes a vibration of the soft palate and produces a rough audible sound. It generally occurs when people sleep on their back with the mouth open. In this position, the mouth tends to fall open and the tongue comes to rest in the back of the mouth, partly obstructing the airway. This causes passing air to make the snoring sounds. In most cases, people who snore are unaware that they do so.

Usually there is nothing dangerous about snoring, but it may be annoying for a sleeping partner or others in the vicinity. Sometimes snoring can be caused by anatomical characteristics such as a small chin, by enlarged tonsils or by obesity. It can run in families, or be related to an underactive thyroid gland or sleep apnea, allergy or respiratory infection. Smoking, excessive alcohol and sedatives can cause or aggravate snoring.

There are many other simple remedies that may alleviate mild snoring and the right solutions will usually depend on the cause. Often a light snorer will cease making noise if they are rolled from their back onto their side during sleep. Increasing the humidity in your bedroom can help if snoring is caused or exacerbated by dry and swollen mucous membranes.

When obesity is a contributing factor, exercise and healthy eating can make a difference by improving muscle tone and promoting weight loss. Other people may find that modifying pre-bedtime behaviour and habits improves the situation. Avoiding meals, alcohol and medications that induce deep drug-induced sleeping (such as tranquilizers and some antihistamines) during the 2–3 hours preceding bedtime may, for example, have a beneficial effect. Some light snorers may also be able to reduce or eliminate the problem by raising their bedhead slightly. Other people have success with oral anti-snoring devices, of which there are now many different forms available, usually through pharmacies.

Although snoring is usually innocuous, adults who are heavy and persistent snorers may occasionally suffer from or develop a serious health problem. Because of this, it is usually recommended that they seek the opinion of a medical specialist to identify and treat the causes and any potentially unhealthy consequences of their snoring. In severe cases, where a person's health is affected by snoring or when snoring indicates certain underlying physical or medical conditions, there are a number of surgical procedures that may prove helpful.

Persistent heavy snoring in children or adolescents usually warrants investigation by a medical professional as it often indicates tonsil or adenoid problems that may require treatment.

SEE ALSO *Insomnia, Sleep, Sleep apnea, Sleep disturbances*

SNOW BLINDNESS

Snow blindness is sunburn on the cornea—part of the lens of the eye. It is a temporary condition caused by exposure of the eyes to ultraviolet rays reflected from snow or ice. These rays can damage the outer layers of the cornea, causing intolerance to light, temporary blindness, and/or inflammation and pain in the eye. The condition affects mostly skiers, as well as people walking or driving in snow-covered areas. A similar condition can also result in people whose unprotected eyes have been exposed to high-voltage electric sparks, the flames of arc welding or light emitted by sun or tanning lamps. Affected people should rest in a dark room. Sometimes an antibiotic ointment, eye patches or over-the-counter pain relief medications may be necessary. With proper rest, a full recovery with no lasting ill effects usually takes only 24 hours. In cases of severe or extended exposure of unprotected eyes to intense ultraviolet light, however, there may be permanent damage that irreversibly affects vision. Snow blindness can be avoided by wearing dark glasses when going out in the snow.

SEE ALSO *Blindness, Eye*

SODIUM

Sodium is a mineral element important in small quantities for proper nutrition. It helps maintain the proper water balance in the body. Sodium ions are a component of common salt, sodium chloride, which is often added to food during processing, or in domestic cooking.

The quantities ingested often add up to amounts well in excess of the body's needs and long term this can cause fluid retention (edema) and may contribute to high blood pressure, leading to strokes, heart disease and kidney failure. Conversely, an inadequate sodium intake can lower blood pressure and can lead to diuresis, or excessive excretion of fluids from the body, which causes a degree of dehydration by reducing cell fluids below healthy levels.

Disease or illness involving diarrhea or vomiting, or other massive loss of fluids, may lead to sodium depletion, which causes blood pressure to fall, the heart to beat faster and symptoms of exhaustion to occur.

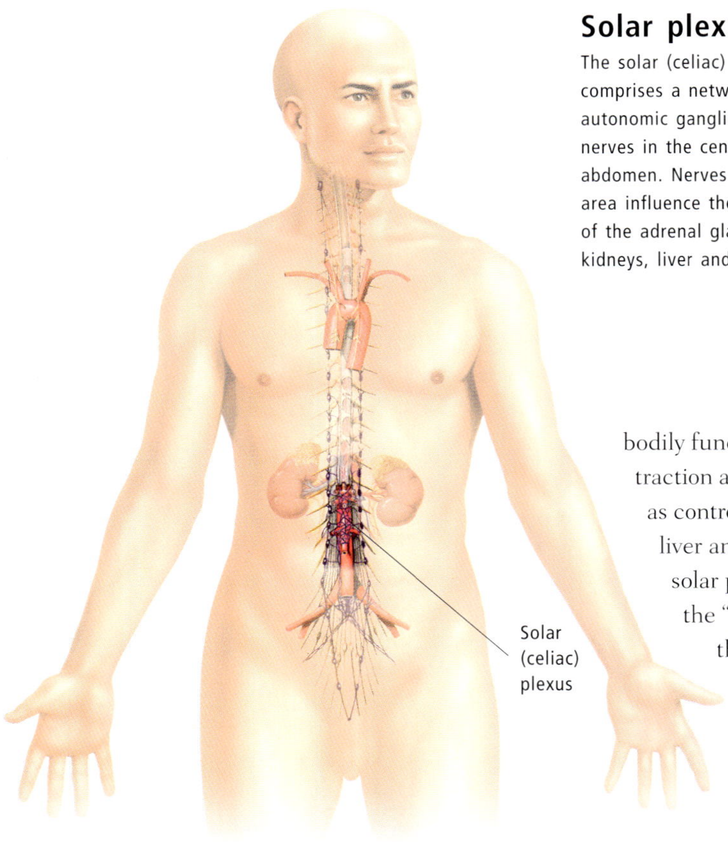

Solar plexus
The solar (celiac) plexus comprises a network of autonomic ganglia and nerves in the center of the abdomen. Nerves in this area influence the function of the adrenal glands, kidneys, liver and stomach.

Adequate amounts of sodium can be obtained from basic foods. Adding salt in cooking or at the table is a choice made largely from habit and a tolerance to salty tastes that is built up over time. Large amounts of salt added to manufactured food products and prepared meals are often hard to detect or to calculate from detailed information found on labels.

Drinking sufficient water, around eight glasses each day, is one way to assist the body in ridding itself of any excess sodium.

SEE ALSO *Dehydration, Edema, Hypertension, Hyponatremia, Hypotension, Minerals, Nutrition, Stroke*

SOLAR PLEXUS

The solar plexus is a dense network of nerve cells on the abdominal aorta behind the stomach. The solar plexus is known anatomically as the celiac plexus due to the fact that it is situated around the celiac artery just below the diaphragm.

The solar plexus is part of the autonomic nervous system and nerve fibers branch out from it to all the abdominal viscera. Through these, the solar plexus helps to regulate vital bodily functions such as intestinal contraction and adrenal secretion, as well as controlling the kidneys, spleen, liver and pancreas. The region of the solar plexus is often referred to as the "pit of the stomach." A blow to the solar plexus can cause severe pain and difficulty in breathing. This is because there is temporary paralysis of the diaphragm and chest and abdominal muscles.

A celiac plexus block (known also as a neurolytic celiac plexus block or NCPB) is a form of long-term pain relief used occasionally in the palliative care of patients terminally ill with certain forms of abdominal cancer, particularly those affecting the pancreas. The block involves a procedure during which a chemical is injected into the solar plexus, leaving it paralyzed so that the transmission of pain signals from the abdomen to the brain is impeded. This form of treatment is usually applied in conjunction with other methods of alleviating pain and discomfort in dying patients.

SEE ALSO *Autonomic nervous system, Abdomen, Diaphragm, Kidney, Nerves, Stomach*

SOLVENT SNIFFING

Solvent sniffing is a form of drug abuse in which the fumes of a volatile substance are inhaled. The act is not illegal and the substances used for sniffing are mostly legally available—gasoline (petrol), butane gas, glues, cleaning fluids, aerosol pain relief sprays, paint removers, lighter fluid and correcting fluid. Effects are felt almost immediately after inhalation because substances enter the lungs and pass directly into the bloodstream.

Solvents contain central nervous system depressants, which lower inhibitions and bring feelings of disorientation and lack of coordination, giving way to headaches and hangovers as effects wear off.

Physical damage from short-term use may be reversible. Accidents related to sniffing in hazardous situations pose greater dangers. Long-term use can damage kidneys, liver and brain, as the chemicals bind with lipids (fats) and are carried to these organs before being broken down and eliminated. Sniffing leaded gasoline can in the long term cause leukemia and other cancers as the lead cannot be broken down but accumulates in the body. Gasoline sniffing can also lead to anorexia, seizures involving spasms and loss of consciousness, and death by heart failure.

SEE ALSO *Drug dependence, Withdrawal*

SOMATIC THERAPIES

Somatic therapies explore the interface between mind and body, combining psychotherapy with techniques such as massage, breathing exercises, physical movement and postural awareness. In the somatic therapist's view emotional or psychological distress always has a bodily expression, which when worked with therapeutically has a corresponding positive effect on the psyche.

The foundations of somatic therapy were laid by the psychiatrist Wilhelm Reich (1897–1957). A follower of Freud, Reich developed his own theories and methods which primarily focused on the accumulation in the body of physical tensions resulting from psychological trauma and emotional inhibitions. In Reichian therapy the patient is asked to observe their breathing patterns, muscular tension and habitual postures while the therapist works with exercises and massages to release the "character armoring" of the body.

Reich's work was further developed and refined by his pupil Dr Alexander Lowen in the 1960s. Lowen's bioenergetic therapy focuses awareness on habitual postures and body movements, which are seen to be associated with chronic psychological states such as depression or anger. Exercises, stress positions and emotional release are used to help "unlock" the armoring, thereby mobilizing energy. Bioenergetics is said to help those with sexual dysfunction, psychosomatic or stress-related illnesses, postural difficulties or poor self-image.

Rolfing, also known as structural integration, is another somatic therapy, a form of massage pioneered by American biochemist Ida Rolf, in which the therapist's hands, elbows and knees are used with the aim of relaxing tension and softening hardened connective tissue (or fascia), resulting from incorrect posture and prolonged stress. Rolf believed that loosening the fascia helps release early memories of trauma, which in turn helps the body to regain its natural alignment. Patients are encouraged to talk about early trauma, although this is not the primary focus of the therapy. Rolf believed that realigning the body restored physical and psychological well-being. Rolfing is done over ten sessions, with each session focusing on a different area of the body.

Hellerwork, an offshoot of Rolfing, was devised in the late 1970s by Joseph Heller, an American aerospace engineer. Consisting of a series of sessions which work systematically through the body, it is recommended by its practitioners for poor posture, musculoskeletal injuries or other physical disabilities. Hellerwork combines three strands—bodywork, in which the practitioner manipulates and releases the tension in the fascia; movement education, which supports supple and tension-free movement; and dialogue, which explores links between mental attitudes and emotions and their affect on the body.

The gentle, non-invasive somatic therapy known as the Traeger approach was developed by Dr Milton Traeger. There are two aspects to this therapy, which aims to relax muscles and dissolve unconscious patterns of muscle tension. In the passive state the patient lies on a table and is gently rocked and moved by the practitioner to release holding and tension patterns. In the active state (known as pentastichs), the patient learns to make movements while releasing muscle tension. Originally developed to help those suffering from paralysis or neuromuscular disorders, the Traeger approach is also recommended by its practitioners for stress-related disorders.

SEE ALSO *Alexander technique; Feldenkrais method, Massage, Pilates method, Psychotherapy*

Producing sound

Producing sound, and turning it into speech, is a three-step process. First, the lungs expel air. Second, the vocal cords open and close to alter the air flow and cause vibrations, making a sound. Third, this sound is modified by muscles in the mouth and tongue—involving movement of the soft palate, tongue and lips.

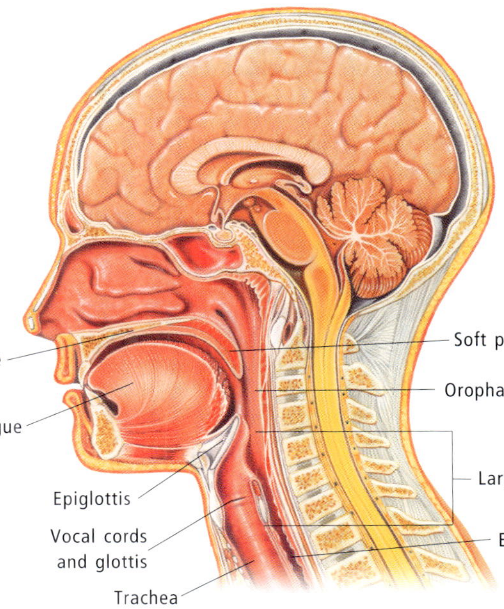

Speech

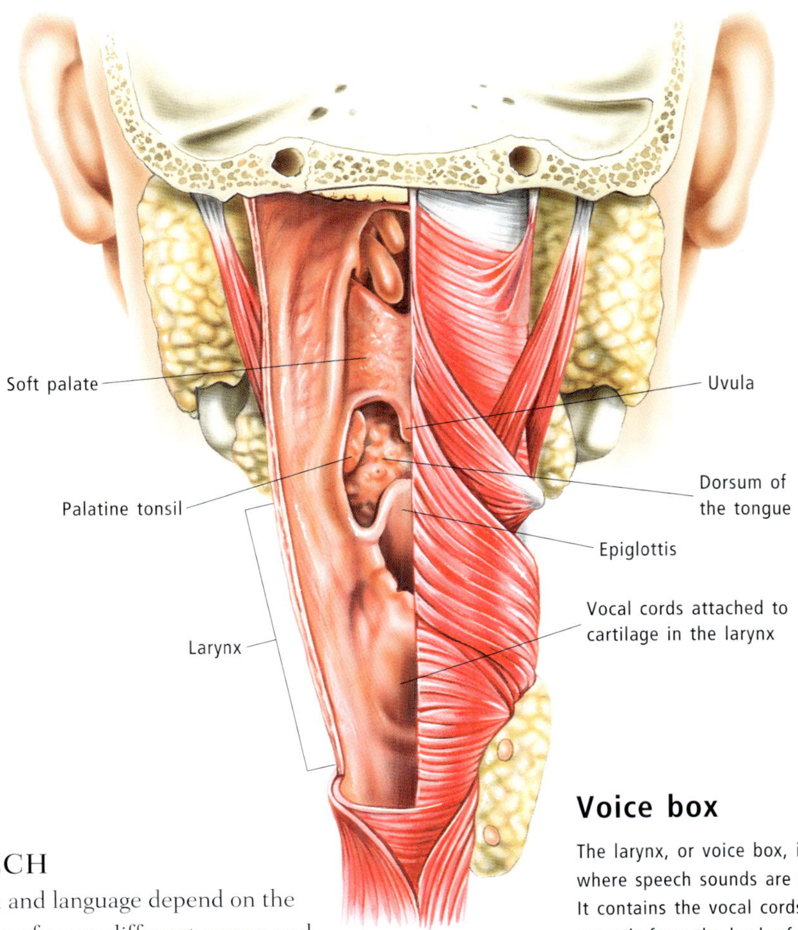

Voice box

The larynx, or voice box, is where speech sounds are made. It contains the vocal cords and extends from the back of the tongue down to the trachea. Air from the lungs passes up the trachea and through the larynx vibrating the cords. The force of the airflow determines the loudness of the voice.

SPEECH

Speech and language depend on the function of many different organs and structures within the body. These can be divided into: nervous system elements, for planning language production and control of muscles; parts of the respiratory system and larynx, for the production of the raw sound (phonation); and the mouth area, for the modification of this raw sound to produce the vowels and consonants of speech (articulation).

Within the brain, usually in the left hemisphere, there are two specialized language regions known as Broca's area and Wernicke's area. Wernicke's area is concerned with the comprehension of language, while Broca's area is involved in the expressive aspects of language. These areas act through the cerebral cortex to control the activities of neurons in the brain stem and so to produce phonation and articulation. The cerebellum at the back of the brain also plays an important role in articulation.

Raw sound is produced by expelling air from the lungs through the larynx. Within the larynx are the two vocal cords, which can be separated during intake of breath and brought close together during speech. When the vocal cords are close together, and air is forced between them, they begin to vibrate, in the same way that two leaves held close together will vibrate when air is forced between them. This raw sound can be altered by increasing or decreasing the tension or length of the vocal cords.

Vowel sounds (such as "ah" or "ooh") are produced by modifying the shape of the expelled air above the vibrating vocal cords. This is done by moving the soft palate, tongue and lips in a precisely coordinated fashion. Most consonants are produced by temporarily stopping the flow of air. Consonants are often named according to the part of the airway involved. Thus, labial consonants ("b", "p") are produced by bringing the lips (labia) together; dental consonants ("d", "t") involve the tongue touching the teeth; nasal consonants ("m", "n") involve passing air through the nose; and glottal consonants ("q", "g", "k") involve the temporary closing of the back of the tongue (the epiglottis) against the soft palate.

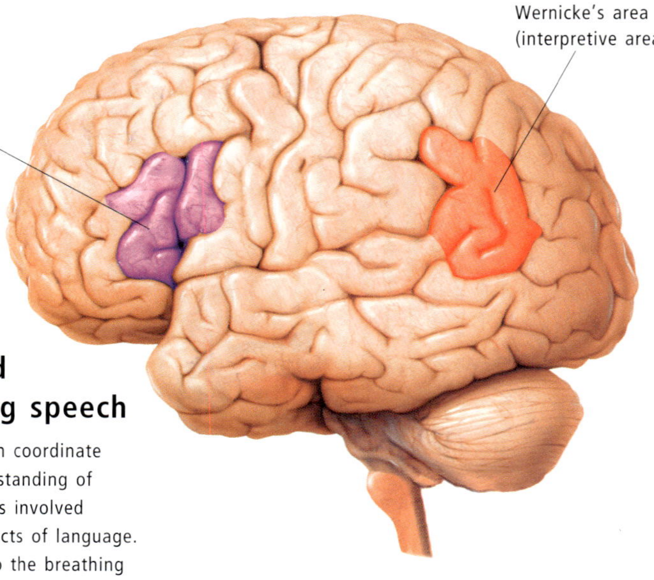

Speaking and understanding speech

Two areas in the brain coordinate speech and our understanding of speech. Broca's area is involved in the expressive aspects of language. It gives instructions to the breathing muscles, the muscles of the larynx, pharynx, tongue and lips to regulate the airflow and vocalization needed for speech. Wernicke's area is involved in understanding and interpreting speech.

Speech

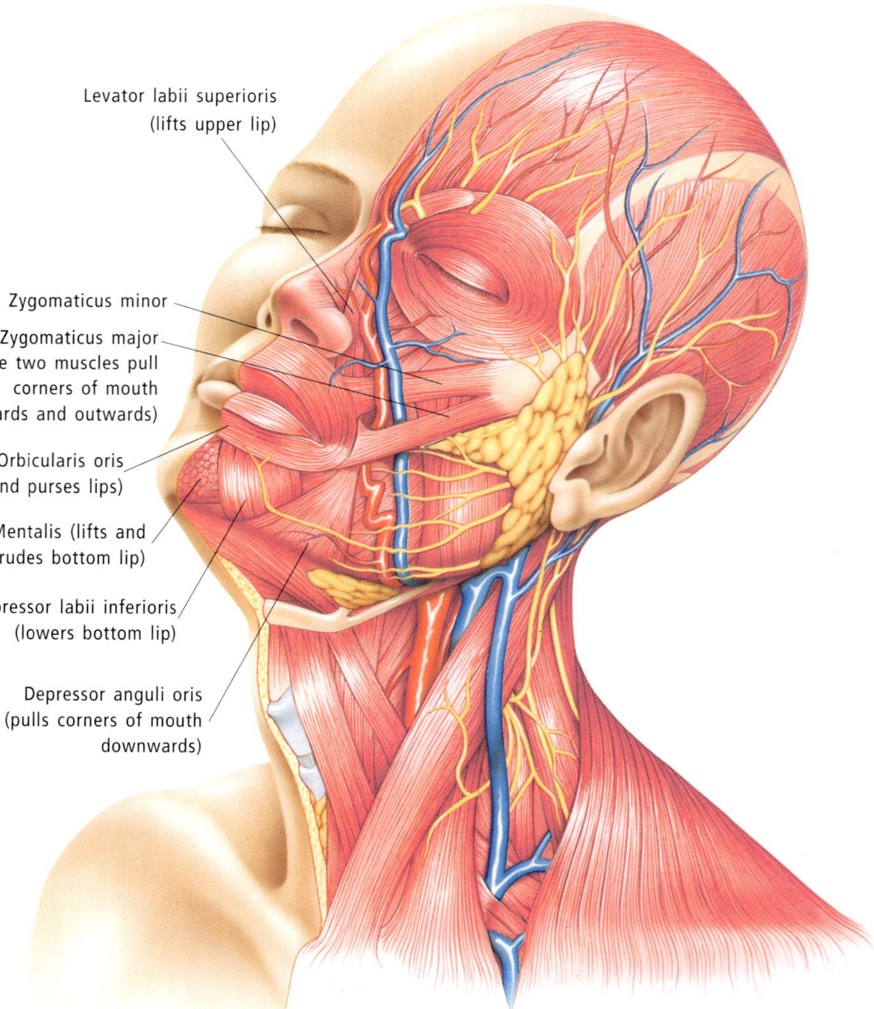

Lip movement for speech

The movement of the lips modifies the sounds that come from the larynx and vocal cords into speech. The lips need to join to make the sound "m", for example, need to touch the teeth (with the bottom lip) to make "f", and round to make "o". The accurate movements that speech requires are made possible by a complex arrangement of muscles around the mouth and cheek areas.

Vocal cords

The vocal cords, or vocal folds, are two folds of mucous membrane that vibrate to make sound when we speak. One end of each vocal cord attaches to cartilage at the front of the larynx. The other ends of the cords are attached to cartilages that can move freely, allowing the cords to vibrate and make sound. The folds are also very flexible—relaxing them will make low-pitched sounds and making them taut will produce high-pitched sounds

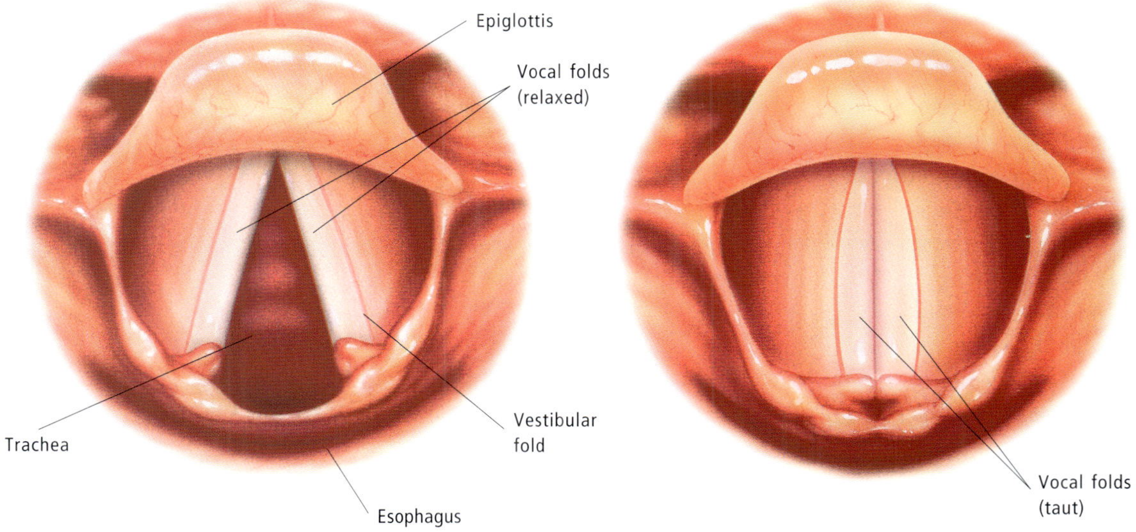

Speech development

From the time they are born, babies are listening, watching and attempting to copy actions and expressions of those around them. The human face, or any clear, large, face-shaped object, will fascinate. Babies begin by making little noises and by as early as four weeks may be squealing; by around six weeks familiar voices, particular the mother's, will bring a response. Cooing type sounds slowly develop, first one syllable, then two syllables. Around 7 months most babies will be making a sound that resembles "dada" or "papa". By 12 months the average child will normally be able to say at least one word.

Understanding precedes speech, so that in the early years children will understand much more than they can articulate. By 18 months of age a vocabulary of around 10 words is considered average. Gradually language skills develop, until some time between the age of 30 and 42 months the child begins to talk in sentences.

Speech disorders

Speech disorders have been a concern since the beginning of recorded history. It has been estimated that around 10 million Americans have a speech disorder of some kind. The major types include voice disorders (dysphonias), which can be caused by paralysis of the larynx, injury or a disease of the endocrine glands; and speech disorders, the most common being those that disrupt a child's ability to learn a language. These include an absence of speech, unintelligible speech and lisping, and may be caused by genetic factors or by damage some time before, during or shortly after birth. Poor language skills within the family, parental neglect or prolonged illness can also play a part.

It is perfectly normal for some children, particularly boys, not to talk until they are 3 years of age, when they will often talk in sentences; however, such a delay may also be caused by the factors just mentioned. Delay in language development may also be the result of intellectual disability or a delay in learning to read and write, sometimes described as dyslexia.

Difficulties in articulation come in different forms. Cluttering (tachyphemia) is mumbled, fast, sloppy speech that is difficult to understand and is hereditary. Lisping has a number of different forms and can be caused either by physical factors, such as abnormal position of the teeth or hearing loss, or by behavioral factors such as imitation of other lispers. It is not easy to outgrow and often persists into adult life. Stuttering or stammering (dysphemia) is the most common and obvious type of disturbed speech. Experts are still undecided about the causes, however it is found more in males than females and is often hereditary. Treatment is difficult and often combines psychotherapy with behavioral therapy. Emotional problems are often part of this disorder.

Physical problems can also affect speech. Injury to the part of the brain related to language results in dysphasia; it may be the result of stroke or head injury. Aphasia (speechlessness) happens when the left side of the brain is damaged. It involves the loss of memory for the meaning of language and how it is produced. Sufferers may know what they want to say but be unable to say or write it. Together with treatment for the cause of the problem, the sufferer must also re-educate the parts of the brain that still function normally.

Tongue-tie (ankyloglossia) is easy corrected with surgery, but major defects of the tongue will reduce the ability to articulate. Sufferers can be taught to speak despite these defects. Hypernasal speech, where increased nasal resonance results in a person "talking through the nose", can be caused by paralysis, congenital malformation, injury or palate defects. Treatment needs a thorough understanding of the causes. A cleft in the palate, lip or other part of the mouth is a congenital malformation which can be corrected by surgery; speech therapy will help to correct speech defects.

Symptomatic speech disorders, caused by lesions in the nervous system, are known as dysarthria. When speech development is limited by mental disorders, it is known as dyslogia.

Hearing loss in early childhood will result in distorted speech known as audiogenic dyslalia; speech problems caused by defects to the lips, teeth or mouth are known as dysglossia. Cerebral palsy, chorea, Parkinson's disease and other nervous disorders can also affect the production of speech.

SEE ALSO *Aphasia, Cleft palate, Dyslexia, Larynx, Lisping, Mouth, Stuttering, Vocal cords*

SPERM

Sperm are the mature male reproductive cells which combine with the ovum, the female reproductive cell, to begin the process leading to pregnancy and the development of a baby. Sperm are produced at the rate of about 50,000 every minute of every hour from puberty until late in life. They are made in the testes (or testicles) which hang outside the body in a sac of skin—the cooler scrotum (sperm do not develop properly at full body temperature).

Newly produced sperm pass into the epididymis, a tube at the back of each testis, where they mature and wait to be ejaculated. During ejaculation, muscle contractions squeeze the sperm along the sperm duct and into the urethra. Along the way, the seminal vesicles and prostate gland add seminal fluids, which mix with the sperm and mobilize them. Semen contains 90 percent seminal fluids and 10 percent sperm and epididymal fluid. On average, between 80 million and 300 million sperm are ejaculated each time a man has an orgasm.

Although sperm can live up to 72 hours in the female reproductive tract, their death rate is high; assuming ejaculation occurs when the woman is fertile, generally only

Sperm production

Sperm are produced in the seminiferous tubules—tightly coiled tubes in the testes. Sperm cells (spermatocytes) divide and produce spermatids, which mature into spermatozoa. Each tubule contains sperm cells at different stages of development and a number of Sertoli cells which support the developing sperm. Spermatozoa move through the testes and into the epididymis, a tube at the back of the testes. Here they mature and wait to be ejaculated.

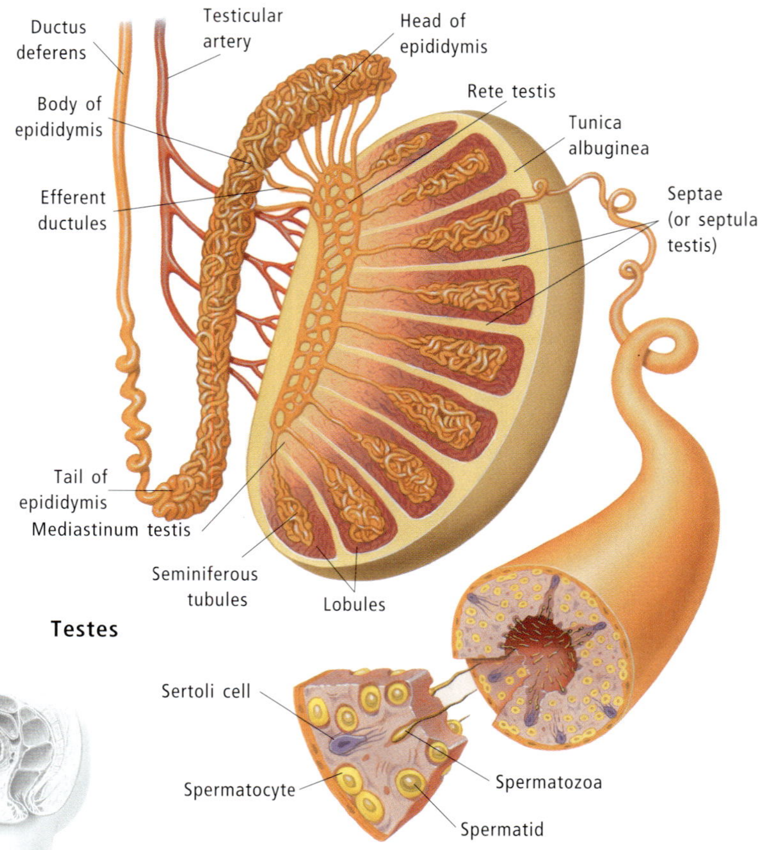

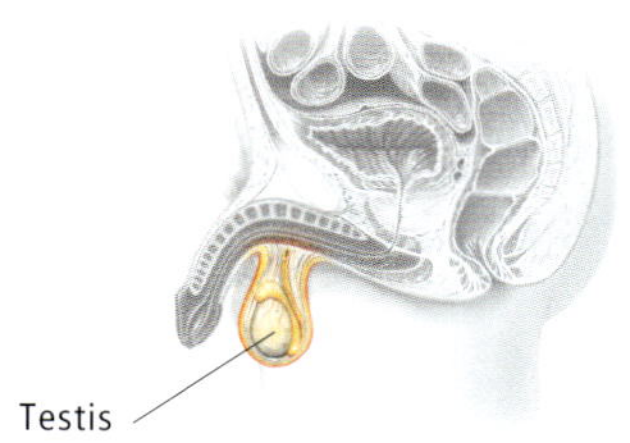

Sperm structure

The head of each sperm has a nucleus, containing chromosomes, and an acrosomal membrane which holds enzymes needed for fertilization. The tail of the sperm helps it move in a corkscrew action on its journey from the testes to the female reproductive organs.

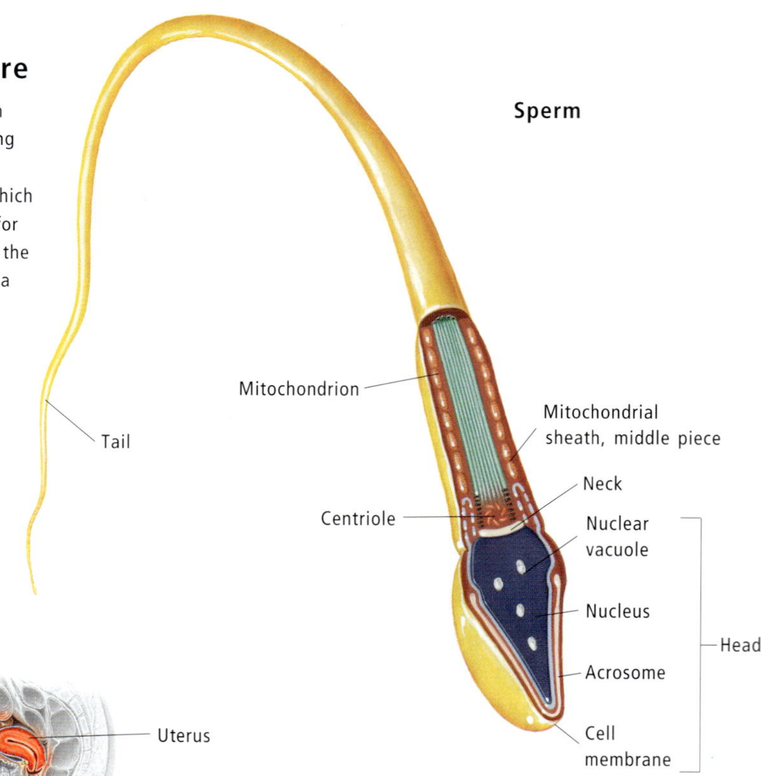

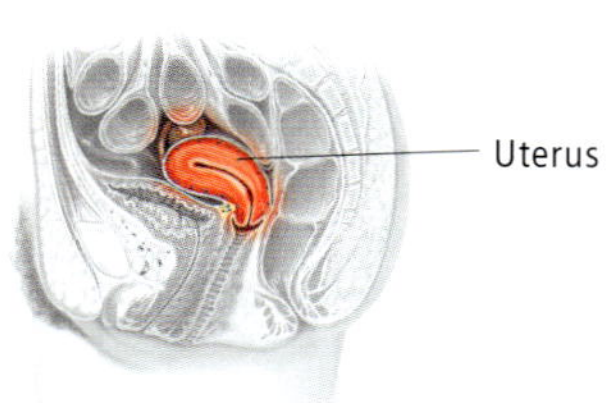

Fertilization

Millions of sperm are ejaculated into the woman's reproductive tract, but only one successfully fuses with the ovum. When the sperm reach the ovum, enzymes released from the acrosomes help to break down the shell. This allows one sperm to penetrate the ovum and fertilization to occur.

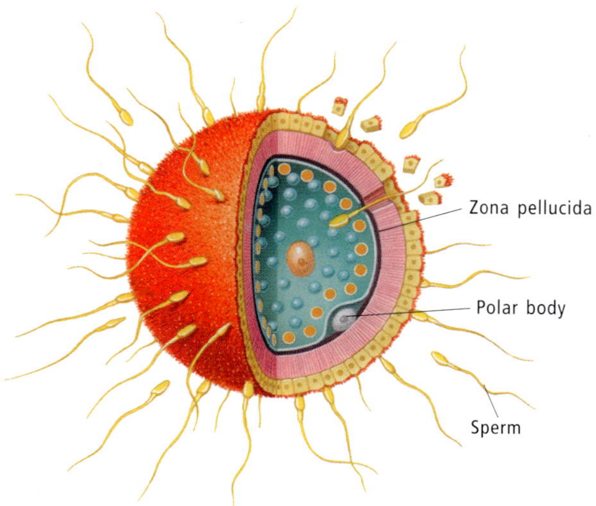

one sperm will penetrate the ovum. Sperm which are not ejaculated are reabsorbed into the man's lymph glands over a period of time.

Sperm carry the man's genetic potential. One half of the chromosomes which carry the genetic makeup of a new human being are to be found in the head of the sperm, the other half coming from the mother's ovum. The sperm decides the sex of the baby; one half of sperm cells contain the Y chromosome which produces a male child, the other half contain the X chromosome which produces a female child.

The microscopic sperm, often likened to a tadpole in shape, has a tail which enables it to "swim" from the vagina, through the cervix and uterus and into the fallopian tube to meet the ovum. In each sperm is a cap (acrosome) containing enzymes which can penetrate the coating around the ovum.

In the sterilization procedure known as vasectomy, a portion of the ductus deferens (or vas deferens), the tube leading from the testicles to the seminal vesicle where the sperm is stored, is removed to prevent sperm traveling from the testes and into the semen, thus rendering the man infertile. A vasectomy does not affect the production of semen, nor does it affect libido—it simply means that when the man ejaculates his semen contains no sperm. After this operation it takes about 16 ejaculations for all sperm to disappear from the semen. This means that normal contraception methods should be continued for up 2 months after a vasectomy is performed.

Where subfertility (infertility) is a problem, tests are carried out on both partners to determine the reason. A man may fail to manufacture sperm (azoospermia); sperm may be weak or few in number (oligospermia: fewer than 20 million per milliliter) or there may be damage to the ductus deferens.

SEE ALSO *Epididymitis, Fertilization, Infertility, Reproductive systems, Scrotum, Semen, Testes, Vasectomy*

SPINA BIFIDA

Spina bifida is a congenital defect of the spinal column resulting from the abnormal formation of the neural tube very early in embryonic development (usually during weeks 3–4 of fetal life). It can appear in several forms. In its most benign form, spina bifida occulta, neither the spinal cord nor the meninges (the covering of the spinal cord) protrudes through the opening left in the vertebrae.

In its most severe form, meningomyelocele, the spinal cord and nerves are exposed. Weakness in the feet (sometimes paralysis), problems with reflexes, and spinal defects indicate spina bifida. A soft fatty deposit on the skin covering the defect, or a cyst protruding over the spine, may also be present. Babies born with meningomyelocele usually undergo surgery soon after birth. Early surgical correction of the defect is important to minimize the risk of meningitis and further neurological damage. Although surgery will improve quality of life for the child, disorders such as limb paralysis and bladder and bowel problems may still occur.

During pregnancy it is important that the mother's diet contains adequate folic acid to reduce the risk of spina bifida in the baby. Many foods are now fortified with this compound and it is also available in tablet form if prescribed.

Women of childbearing age should aim to ingest 400 micrograms of folic acid a day. It is recommended that folic acid supplementation should begin 3–4 months prior to conception and should continue for the first 3 months of the pregnancy.

Spina bifida can be screened for in pregnancy with the alpha-fetoprotein (AFP) test, ultrasound and amniocentesis.

SEE ALSO *Amniocentesis, Congenital abnormalities, Folate, Neural tube defect, Spinal cord, Ultrasound*

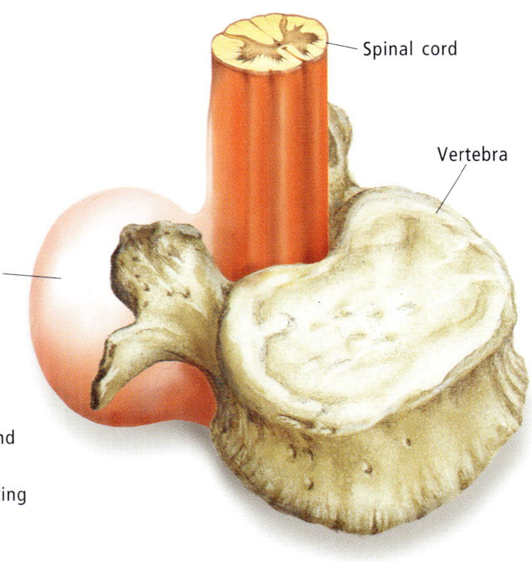

Spina bifida

Spina bifida occurs when the bony column that surrounds the spinal cord does not fuse properly during embryonic development. The spinal cord and its covering (the meninges) may then protrude through the opening between the vertebrae, creating a cystic swelling filled with cerebrospinal fluid.

SPINAL CORD

The spinal cord is a cylindrical nervous structure which occupies the vertebral canal, a cavity extending the length of the vertebral column. A series of rootlets (made up of nerve cell fibers) attaches in a line along the front and back of each side of the cord. Those attaching to the front (ventral rootlets) and to the back (dorsal rootlets) group together to form 31 pairs of spinal nerves, giving the cord a segmented appearance. These nerves supply skin, bone, muscles and joints of the limbs and trunk.

The spinal cord is usually $16\frac{1}{2}$–$17\frac{3}{4}$ inches (42–45 centimeters) long and does not extend the full length of the vertebral column. In the adult its lower end (conus medullaris) is usually located at the level of the L1 or L2 vertebra. Below this, the vertebral canal is occupied largely by the elongated rootlets of the lumbar and sacral spinal nerves (cauda equina, which is Latin for "horse's tail") traveling down to lower levels before they exit from the canal.

The spinal cord is made primarily of nerve cell bodies and their associated fibers that function to process and transmit sensory information to the brain and motor information from the brain. The cell bodies group together in the center of the cord to form a column of gray matter, which is H-shaped in cross-section, the H being formed by pairs of dorsal "horns" at the back and ventral horns at the front, separated by an inter-

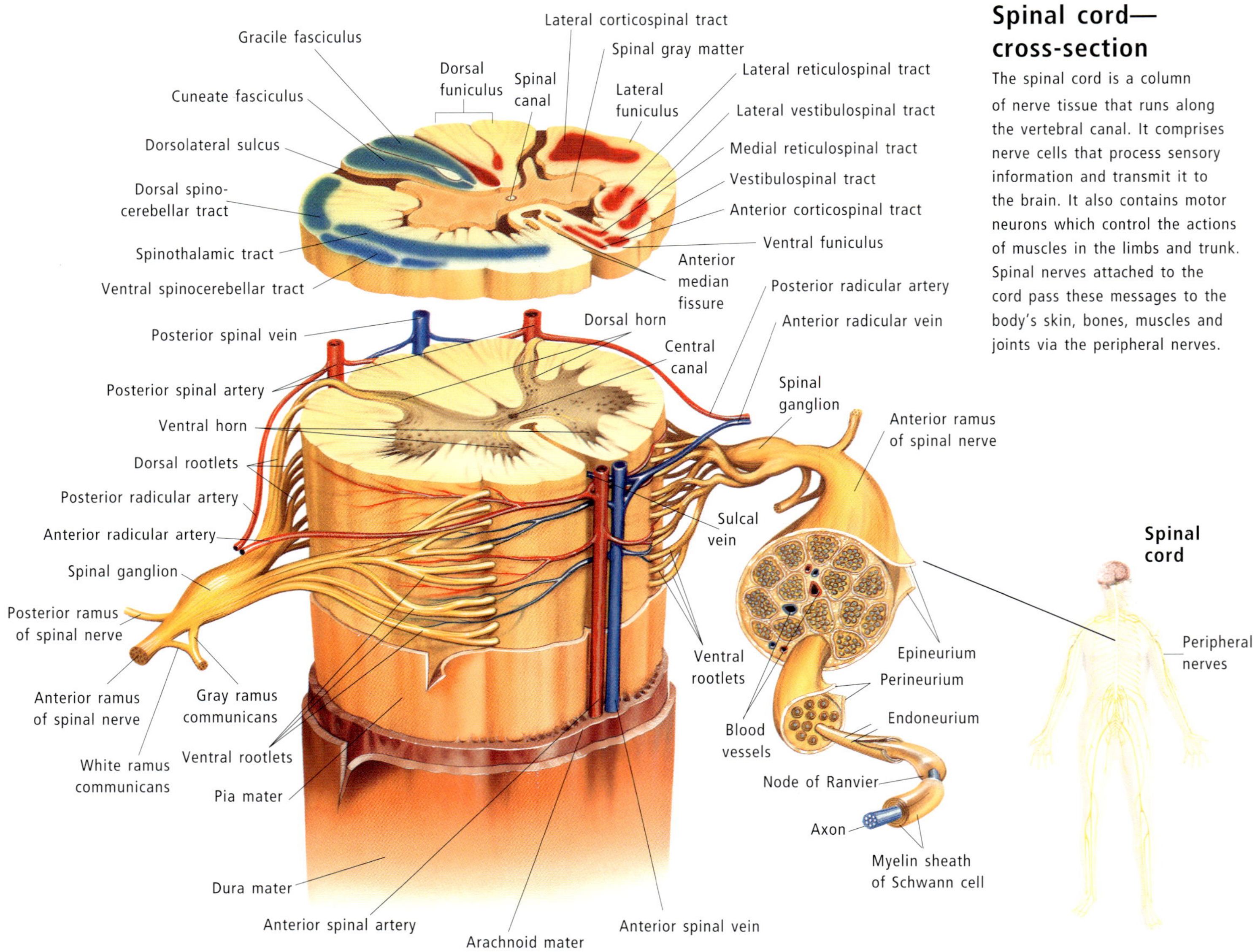

Spinal cord—cross-section

The spinal cord is a column of nerve tissue that runs along the vertebral canal. It comprises nerve cells that process sensory information and transmit it to the brain. It also contains motor neurons which control the actions of muscles in the limbs and trunk. Spinal nerves attached to the cord pass these messages to the body's skin, bones, muscles and joints via the peripheral nerves.

mediate zone. The dorsal horns are specialized to process sensory information (for example, touch, pain, temperature, joint sensation) and to relay this information up to the brain. The ventral horns contain motor neurons, which transmit messages out to the muscles via spinal nerves. The intermediate zone contains many interneurons involved in linking incoming sensory neurons with outgoing motor neurons to bring about automated (reflex) responses which do not involve the brain. Simple spinal reflexes include the stretch reflex such as the knee jerk, in which tapping the patellar ligament below the kneecap brings about contraction of the quadriceps muscle of the thigh; and the withdrawal reflex, in which a pain stimulus to the skin (such as touching a hot iron) causes a reflex withdrawal from the stimulus.

The gray matter of the spinal cord is surrounded by white matter (nerve fibers), transmitting information to and from the brain. Fibers carrying similar types of information tend to group together into bundles known as tracts. When the spinal cord is cut or damaged these tracts may be severed, meaning motor commands cannot get to levels below the damage and sensory information from these levels cannot get past the damage to the brain. If only the lower limbs are affected the person is said to be paraplegic, and if all limbs are affected they are said to be quadriplegic. Injured neurons in the spinal cord regenerate or repair themselves, so the effects are usually permanent.

SEE ALSO *Nerves, Nervous system, Neurons, Paralysis, Paraplegia, Quadriplegia, Reflexes, Spinal nerves, Spine*

SPINAL CURVATURE

The human spinal column is normally curved, but abnormal curvature is also a common condition. It can be caused by weak ligaments, poor posture, disease, injury or congenital abnormalities.

Hunchback (kyphosis) is an exaggeration of the normal curvature of the thoracic spine; swayback (lordosis) is an exaggerated forward or inward curvature of the lumbar (middle to lower) spine. Pott's disease is a form of tuberculosis which affects the vertebrae and causes deformities; a sideways deviation of the spine is called scoliosis (humpback). Treatment may include plaster jackets, traction, pads, electrical stimulation, exercise and surgery.

SEE ALSO *Lordosis, Kyphosis, Pott's disease, Scoliosis, Spine*

SPINAL NERVES

Spinal nerves emerge from the sides of the vertebral column and function to transmit information in both directions between the spinal cord and the peripheral structures of the body. Each nerve is made up of sensory fibers (transmitting information from skin, muscles, bones and joints to the spinal cord) and motor fibers (transmitting messages away from the spinal cord towards the skeletal muscles). Some spinal nerves also carry sympathetic (autonomic) fibers (transmitting messages to sweat glands and blood vessels) and parasympathetic fibers to mucous membrane and smooth muscle in the pelvis.

Each nerve is formed within the vertebral canal by the union of its dorsal and ventral roots. The dorsal roots, made up of sensory fibers, emerge in a line along each side of the back of the spinal cord. The ventral roots, made up mainly of motor fibers, emerge in a line along each side of the front of the cord. Once the two roots unite, the spinal nerve leaves the vertebral canal through a space on each side between each pair of adjacent vertebrae. Soon after it leaves these vertebrae, the spinal nerve divides into a small branch, which supplies structures in the back, and a large branch, which supplies the limbs and the remainder of the trunk.

The 31 pairs of spinal nerves are named according to the level that they exit from the vertebral column. There are eight cervical spinal nerves (C1–C8), twelve thoracic (T1–T12), five lumbar (L1–L5), five sacral (S1–S5) and one coccygeal nerve. Each nerve supplies a circumscribed area of skin (dermatome) and a specific group of muscles. The thoracic nerves supply skin and muscles of most of the trunk wall, whereas the ventral rami of cervical, lumbar and sacral nerves form complex networks, known as plexuses, from which branches emerge to supply the motor and sensory needs of the limbs.

Spinal nerves and dermatomes

There are 31 pairs of spinal nerves which emerge from the sides of the vertebral column. Each spinal nerve supplies a specific group of muscles and a circumscribed area of skin (dermatome).

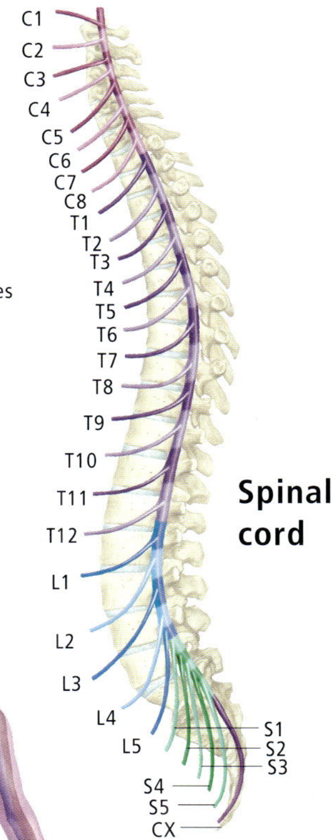

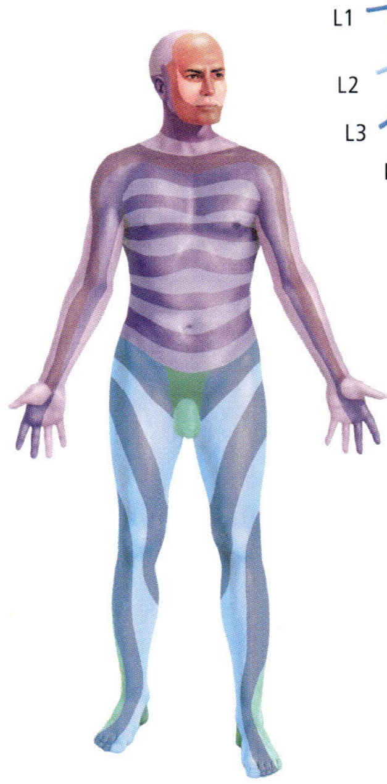

Spinal curvature

The spinal column is normally curved, but abnormal or excessive curvature (as in kyphosis or lordosis) may be caused by disease, injury or congenital disease.

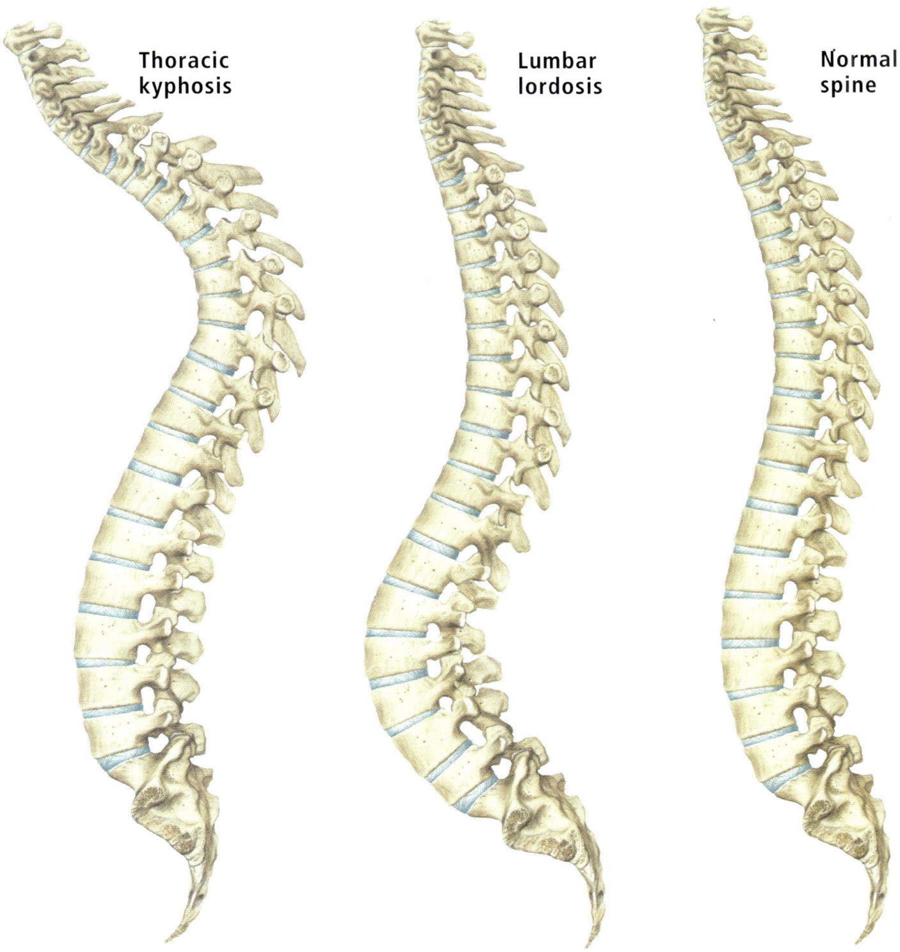

A spinal nerve may be torn due to excessive tension, such as a heavy fall on the shoulder, rupturing the C5 and/or the C6 nerves. When a spinal nerve is torn the person will experience a loss of sensation in the skin area and weakness in the muscles it supplies. The level at which the nerve is damaged will determine whether recovery can be expected.

One common disease which affects spinal nerves is shingles, in which the varicella-zoster virus that causes chickenpox infects the cells of the sensory roots of one or more spinal (or cranial) nerves. Painful blisters appear in the skin area supplied by the infected nerve. In recent years antiviral medications have been developed, which can alleviate the symptoms when an attack occurs.

SEE ALSO *Dermatomes, Nerves, Nervous system, Shingles, Spinal cord, Spine*

S

SPINE

The spine, or vertebral column, extends down the midline of the back, from the base of the skull to the pelvis, and forms the central axis of the skeleton. It also functions to protect the spinal cord, a nervous structure located in a hollow canal (the vertebral or spinal canal) which runs down the center of the vertebral column. The spine must be firm enough to support the body weight but it also requires flexibility to allow bending of the trunk. These requirements are satisfied by its curved, segmented structure made up of 26 bones (vertebrae), which are separated from each other by pads of cartilage (intervertebral disks). These disks make up 25 percent of the length of the vertebral column in a young adult.

The spine is divided into five regions—cervical, thoracic, lumbar, sacral and coccygeal. The cervical region is formed by seven vertebrae, numbered 1–7 from the top down (C1–C7). The thoracic region is formed by twelve vertebrae (T1–T12), all of which have ribs attaching to their sides. The lumbar (lower back) region has five vertebrae (L1–L5). The sacrum, a single curved bone in the adult, actually develops as five separate vertebrae (S1–S5), which fuse to each other during early development to form a single bone. Similarly, the four vertebrae of the tail region fuse during development to form the coccyx, a rudimentary bone attached to the lower end of the sacrum.

Viewed from side on, the vertical column is not straight, but curved into an S-shape. At birth the vertebral column is bent forward into a C-shape, this forward curvature remaining in the adult in the thoracic and sacral regions (primary curvatures). During childhood two reverse curves appear, in the cervical and lumbar regions, to better balance the weight of the head and body. The cervical curvature appears when the child begins to lift the head and the lumbar curvature appears as the child learns to sit, stand and walk. Because the cervical and lumbar curvatures appear after birth they are said to be secondary curvatures.

Developmental factors, poor posture or pathological changes can cause the curvatures to become abnormal. An exaggerated thoracic curvature (hunchback) known as kyphosis commonly develops in the elderly as a result of degenerative changes in the vertebrae due to osteoporosis. An exaggerated lumbar curvature (sway back) known as lordosis is commonly seen in pregnant women. Bending of the vertebral column to one side is known as scoliosis. This is quite common and may result from asymmetry in the back muscles as can occur in athletes who play predominantly one-handed sports, for example, baseball pitchers and tennis players.

Structure of vertebrae

All vertebrae have a similar structural pattern, although the size and shape of the individual features varies in different regions. Each vertebra consists of the following.

- A body at the front, which gets progressively larger from the top to the bottom of the column, because it is the weight-bearing part of the vertebra.
- An arch of bone, known as the vertebral arch, which attaches to the back of the body and surrounds a hole in the center called the vertebral foramen. The arch is divided on each side into a pedicle attaching to the body and a lamina at the back.

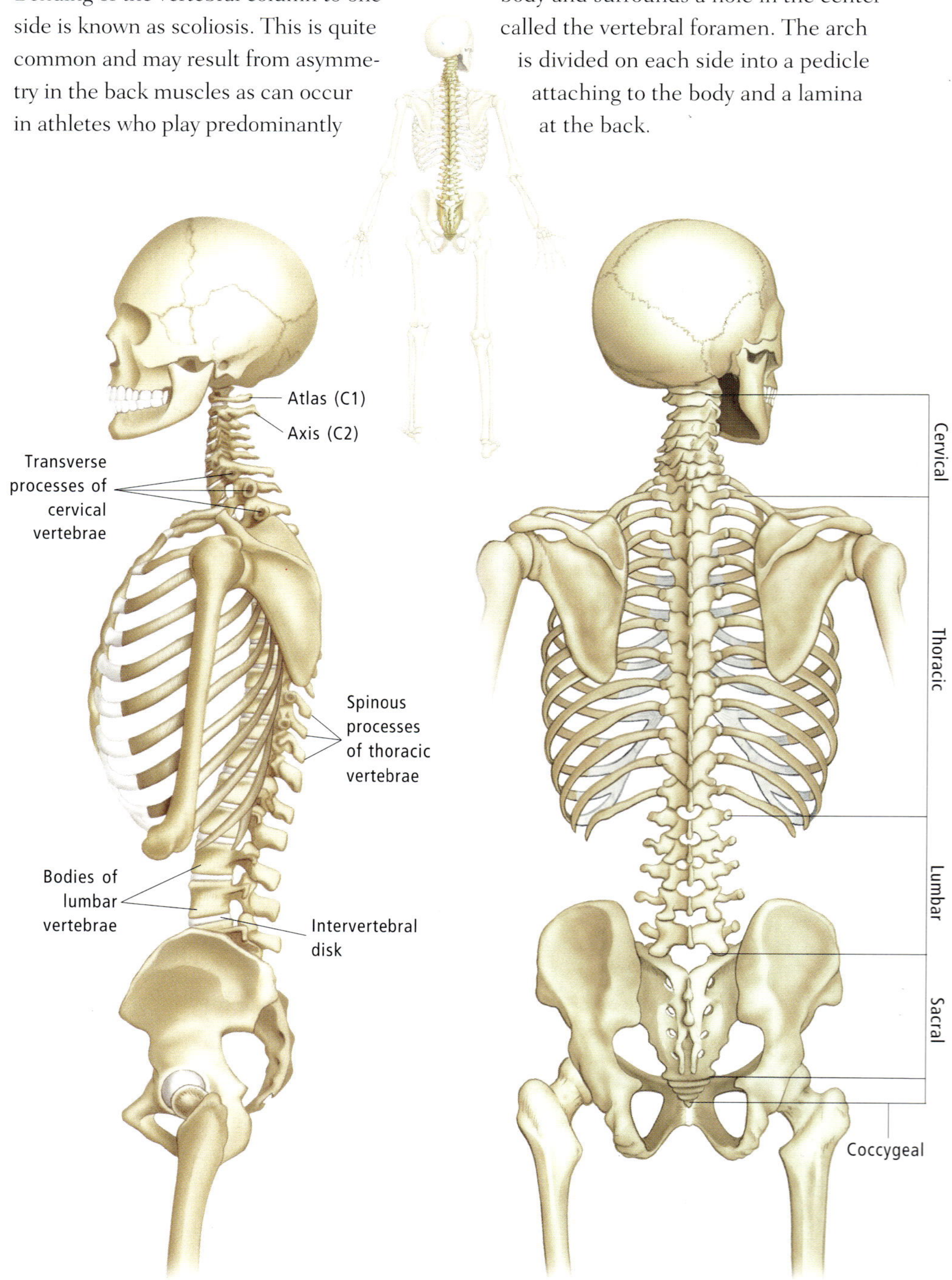

Spine

The spine forms the central axis of the skeleton and supports the weight of the head, neck and trunk. Its segmented structure provides flexibility, allowing the trunk to bend and twist.

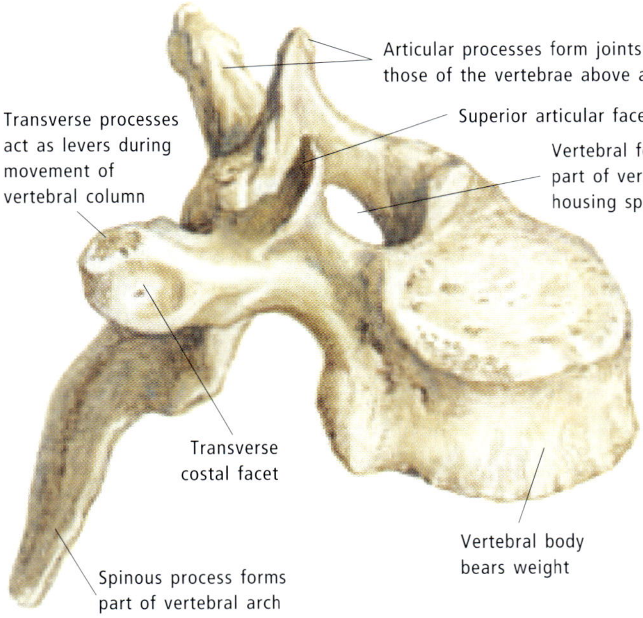

- A spinous process (spine), which extends backwards from the arch. The spinous processes can be easily felt extending down the midline of the back. That of the C7 vertebra (the "vertebra prominens") is particularly prominent at the base of the neck and can be used as a landmark for counting other vertebrae.
- A pair of transverse processes, which extend outwards from each side of the arch. The spinous and transverse processes act as levers during movements of the vertebral column.
- Two pairs of articular processes, extending from the upper and lower surfaces of each side of the arch. These processes form joints with those of the vertebrae above and below.

The atlas (C1) is atypical in that it does not have a body or spinal process.

The upper and lower surfaces of the pedicles of each vertebral arch are notched, so that when two vertebrae sit together, the adjacent notches form an incomplete ring, which is known as an intervertebral foramen. The spinal nerves enter and exit through these holes from each side of the vertebral canal.

Movements of the vertebral column

The vertebral column is a flexible structure that acts as a single unit, in which large movements result from the sum of the many small movements occurring at the joints between the vertebrae. Movements of the vertebral column are flexion (to bend

Vertebrae

The vertebra is the basic unit of the spine. All vertebrae have a similar structural pattern, but the size and shape of their features varies according to their location in the spine.

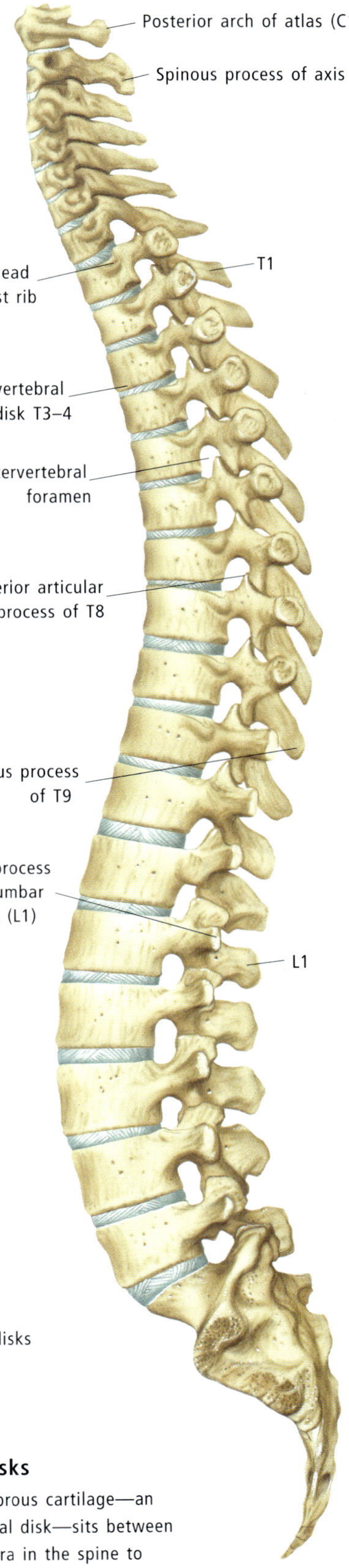

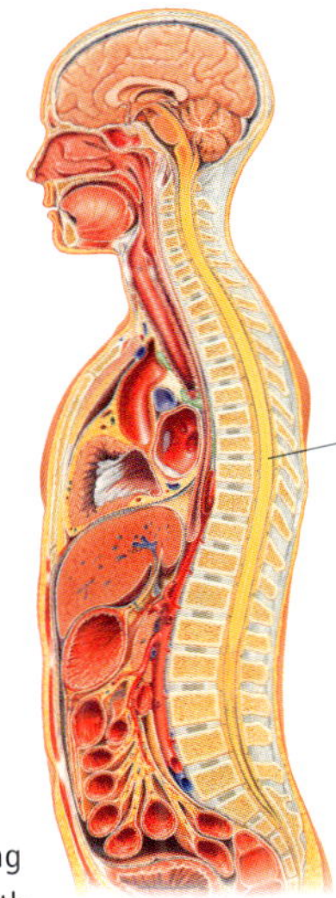

Spinal canal

The vertebral column provides a protective casing for the spinal cord, a length of nervous tissue that runs from the brain to the level of the first or second lumbar vertebrae. Cerebrospinal fluid and a layer of membrane fill the space between the vertebral canal and cord to provide additional cushioning.

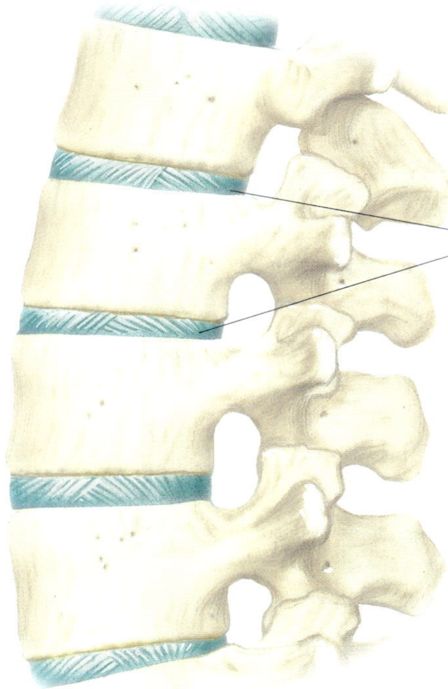

Spinal disks

A pad of fibrous cartilage—an intervertebral disk—sits between each vertebra in the spine to provide mobility and shock absorption. Each disk has a pulpy central nucleus that allows the disk to change shape under pressure (as the spine bends or turns) and a tough, fibrous outer layer that holds the nucleus in position and attaches the disk to the vertebrae.

forwards), lateral flexion (to bend sideways), extension (to bend backwards), rotation (around its own axis) and circumduction (a combination of all these movements). The range of movement varies in different regions—the cervical and lumbar regions are the most mobile, with less movement possible in the thoracic region because of the presence of the ribs.

Joints

Each vertebra forms three separate joints with the vertebra above or below—a pair of facet joints and a single anterior intervertebral joint. A facet joint is formed on each side between the articular processes of the two vertebrae. The facet joints are synovial joints so they have a fluid-filled cavity between the bones, which are held together by a joint capsule. The adjacent cartilage-covered surfaces are able to glide on each other during movements of the vertebral column. The direction of orientation of the joint surfaces determines the type of movements that are permitted in different regions. For example, pure rotation of the vertebral column can only occur in the thoracic region. The facet joints are vulnerable to osteoarthritic changes in the elderly, particularly in the lumbar region, where they are one of the most common causes of localized low back pain. In some cases surgery may be required (known as a laminectomy) to relieve pain caused by bony deposits which form around the joint, compressing a nearby spinal nerve.

The anterior intervertebral joints, between the bodies of the vertebrae, are designed for strength and involve a pad of strong fibrous cartilage called the intervertebral disk. The disk sits between each pair of vertebral bodies and serves to both unite the vertebrae and permit movement between them. The disks may be relatively thin and flat in shape (as in the thoracic region) or wedge-shaped and thicker, as in the lumbar and cervical regions.

The intervertebral disks are reinforced in front and behind by the anterior and posterior longitudinal ligaments. These are bands of ligamentous fibers, which attach to the bodies of the vertebrae and extend along the length of the vertebral column. The anterior longitudinal ligament prevents excessive extension, and is commonly injured in automobile accidents, when a car is struck from behind and the head is suddenly and forcibly thrown backwards. This type of injury is known as whiplash.

Each intervertebral disk consists of two parts, a central region known as the nucleus pulposus, and a surrounding region called the annulus fibrosus. As its name suggests, the nucleus has a pulpy or gelatinous texture, and is easily able to change shape when pressure is placed upon it. The annulus is tough and fibrous, and is firmly attached to the vertebrae above and below. It consists of concentric rings of strong fibers, which pass in an oblique direction from one vertebra to the next. The fibers in adjacent rings are oriented at right angles to each other, allowing some movement to occur between the bones but also providing a strong bond between them. It also serves to hold the nucleus in position. The nucleus pulposus does not sit exactly in the center of the disk. It is located more towards the back, so the annulus is thinner behind than in front.

The fibers of the annulus become more fragile with age and can be torn during sudden, forceful movements of the joint, causing the nucleus to bulge into the damaged area of the annulus, a condition commonly known as a slipped disk. The fibers in the outer back part of the annulus are most vulnerable to injury because the annulus here is thinnest and not protected by the longitudinal ligaments. When this occurs, the bulging disk may compress a spinal nerve as it passes out of the vertebral column. This happens most commonly in the lumbar region, when nerves supplying the lower limb can be compressed, causing a type of pain known as sciatica. Sciatica can also result from osteoarthritic changes in the facet joints.

The vertebral canal

The vertebral canal is a hollow cavity that extends the length of the vertebral column and contains the spinal cord and the roots of the spinal nerves. It is surrounded at the front by the vertebral body and at the sides and back by the vertebral arch. The vertebral canal is lined by a membrane known as the dural sheath. The dural sheath consists of an outer fibrous layer called the dura mater and a thin, inner layer called the arachnoid mater. A fluid-filled space, the subarachnoid space, exists between the dural sheath and the spinal cord. It contains cerebrospinal fluid and is continuous with a similar space surrounding the brain. The spinal cord usually ends at the level of the first or second lumbar vertebrae and below this level the canal is occupied only by spinal nerve roots, passing along its sides. It is therefore reasonably safe to place a needle between the spines of the fourth and fifth lumbar vertebrae to take samples of cerebrospinal fluid for neurological examination. This procedure is known as a spinal tap or lumbar puncture.

The dural sheath is separated from the bone surrounding the canal by a narrow epidural space, which is filled with fat and some veins. The sacral spinal nerves, which supply the organs of the pelvis, can be anesthetized by placing anesthetic into the epidural space of the sacrum. This type of anesthesia, known as epidural anesthesia, is commonly used when babies are born by cesarean section, allowing the mother to remain conscious during the birth.

SEE ALSO ***Coccyx, Disk, intervertebral, Epidural anesthesia, Joints, Kyphosis, Lordosis, Lumbar puncture, Neck, Osteoarthritis, Sacrum, Sciatica, Scoliosis, Skeletal system, Spinal cord, Vertebrae, Whiplash injury***

SPLEEN

The spleen is an organ about the size of a fist, which is situated high in the left side of the abdomen, beneath the diaphragm. It is an important blood-forming organ during fetal life but is not essential to life in the adult. The spleen receives a disproportionately large blood supply for its size, which it filters through channels called sinuses. Red blood cells squeeze through narrow pores in the sinuses and older, more rigid cells are destroyed there. The part of the spleen that forms blood cells in fetal life and filters the blood through the sinuses is called the red pulp. The other portion functions as part of the body's immune system and is called the white pulp.

The spleen is part of the immune system and contains large numbers of lymphocytes. It assists the body in fighting certain infections, especially pneumonia and meningitis.

S

If the spleen is removed (splenectomy), vaccinations are given to boost the body's immunity against such infections. Even so, a small risk remains of severe infection and people who have undergone splenectomy are advised to carry a medical alert card or necklace to alert medical staff of the fact in the event of a sudden febrile illness.

The spleen is a soft organ and is easily ruptured by injuries to the upper abdomen, such as occur in car collisions or contact sports, or with certain infections, such as malaria. If the spleen is enlarged, for example by glandular fever, it is even more susceptible to rupture. Rupture results in severe pain and internal bleeding and is a medical emergency. Splenectomy may need to be performed as a life-saving procedure. Sometimes it is possible for the surgeon to repair the damage and preserve part of the spleen, so that it can continue to function.

Enlargement of the spleen

There are many problems that can affect the spleen, causing enlargement.

Hemolysis

In conditions in which there is increased destruction of red blood cells, called hemolysis, the spleen becomes enlarged (splenomegaly) and can be felt below the rib cage. Hemolysis can result from a variety of disorders—some inherited, some developing during adult life. The treatment for a number of these conditions may include splenectomy.

The most common cause of hemolysis is malaria, in which there is an infection of the red blood cells by parasites transmitted by *Anopheles* mosquitoes. This results in high fevers, shaking, chills, anemia and jaundice. The damaged red cells are removed by the spleen, which becomes enlarged and painful. In countries where malaria is endemic, the spleen may eventually become very large in people exposed to repeated infections.

Other infections

Other infections can cause enlargement of the spleen, in particular infection by the Epstein-Barr virus, which causes infectious mononucleosis (glandular fever). This disease generally causes painful enlargement of the spleen, which gradually subsides as recovery occurs.

Lymphomas

Due to its link with the lymphatic system, the spleen may be affected by the same sorts of diseases that affect the lymph nodes. For example, lymphomas or tumors of the lymph nodes may cause enlargement of the spleen. Generally this does not cause pain but is detected during abdominal examination. The physician may confirm that the spleen is enlarged by ultrasound study, isotope scan or

Spleen

The spleen is designed to filter blood and also functions as part of the body's immune system. Its red color and pulpy texture are due to its high blood content. The organs that surround the spleen (the stomach, colon and kidney) leave impressions on its soft surface. An enlarged spleen may indicate a disease or disorder elsewhere in the body.

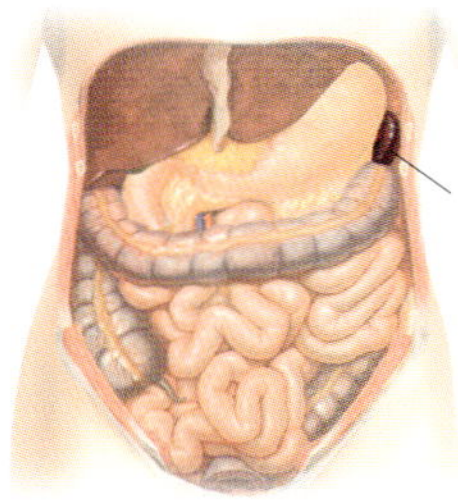

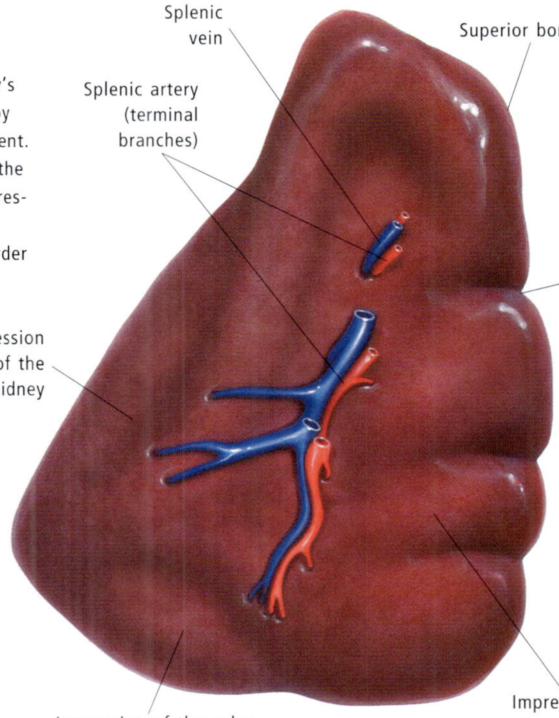

Spleen—microstructure

Red blood cells are filtered through channels, called sinuses, in the spleen which remove old and abnormal cells. The capillaries in the spleen are surrounded by lymphatic tissue.

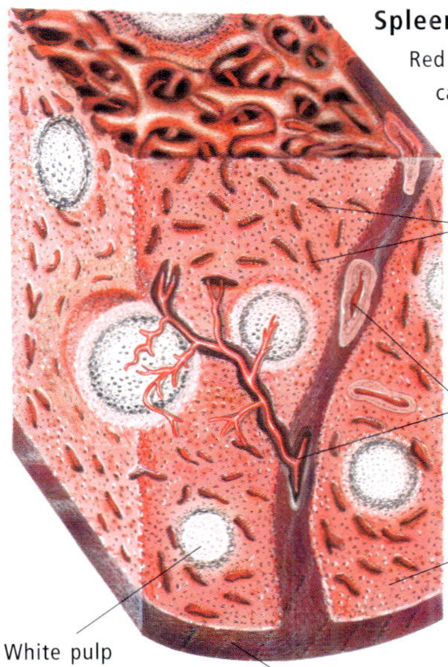

Spleen—immune function

The spleen is the largest unit of lymphatic tissue in the body. It plays a vital role in the body's immune system by producing and storing lymphocytes, a type of white blood cell. These cells attack invading bacteria and viruses and make antibodies against them.

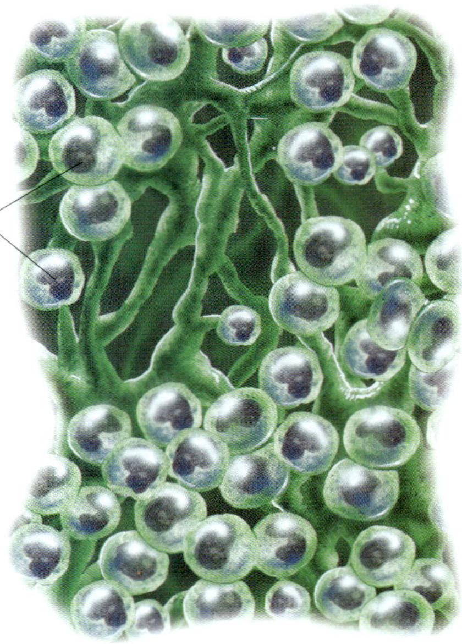

CAT scan. The spleen may be involved by Hodgkin's or non-Hodgkin's lymphomas. Splenectomy is only usually performed for the diagnosis of non-Hodgkin's lymphomas that affect the spleen alone.

Leukemia

Leukemias can also cause enlargement of the spleen, which may be massive in the case of chronic myeloid leukemia. Other disorders of the blood cells that cause enlargement need to be distinguished from leukemias. In particular, a myeloproliferative disease—myelofibrosis (also called agnogenic myeloid metaplasia), can cause massive splenic enlargement. In this disease, while the adult spleen regains the capacity for blood cell formation, its massive enlargement results in a net decrease in circulating red blood cells.

Other diseases

The spleen can also enlarge due to a buildup of pressure in the splenic vein—the result of portal hypertension complicating cirrhosis of the liver. Other causes of splenomegaly include autoimmune diseases such as rheumatoid arthritis and systemic lupus erythematosus (SLE), and storage diseases such as amyloidosis and Gaucher's disease.

Whenever the spleen is markedly enlarged, a reduction in circulating red blood cell counts may occur because of the destruction or pooling of blood cells in the spleen. This condition is called hypersplenism and can result in anemia, leukopenia and thrombocytopenia.

Treatment

If the spleen is enlarged because of a blood disorder it may cause pain or hypersplenism needing treatment. In some cases the spleen can be shrunk using medication or chemotherapy. Sometimes a small dose of radiation therapy can be directed over the spleen to relieve the patient's symptoms. Otherwise splenectomy may be recommended.

It is now possible to perform splenectomy laparoscopically, through a very small incision in the abdominal wall. This allows for much quicker post-operative recovery as well as a more acceptable cosmetic result.

Following removal of the spleen, red blood cells containing small nuclear remnants (which are usually removed from the circulation by the spleen) appear in the blood. Sometimes this characteristic is found in the blood of a person whose spleen has not been removed. Occasionally this may be due to absence of the spleen from birth, but it is generally a sign of an underlying disease resulting in atrophy of the spleen. Such diseases include celiac disease (which results from an allergy to gluten protein) and autoimmune diseases such as hyperthyroidism.

Splenic atrophy is also a feature of sickle cell disease, as repeated episodes of vascular occlusion by misshapen red blood cells may damage the microstructure of the spleen. People with splenic atrophy require the same vaccinations as those whose spleens have been surgically removed.

Occasionally following splenectomy, an accessory spleen will develop from residual splenic tissue left behind at the time of surgery. This may result in a recurrence of the disease for which the spleen was removed and may require a second operation.

SEE ALSO *Anemia, Autoimmune disease, Celiac disease, Hodgkin's disease, Immunity, Infectious mononucleosis, Lymphatic immune system, Leukemia, Malaria, Non-Hodgkin's lymphoma, Red blood cells, Thrombocytopenia*

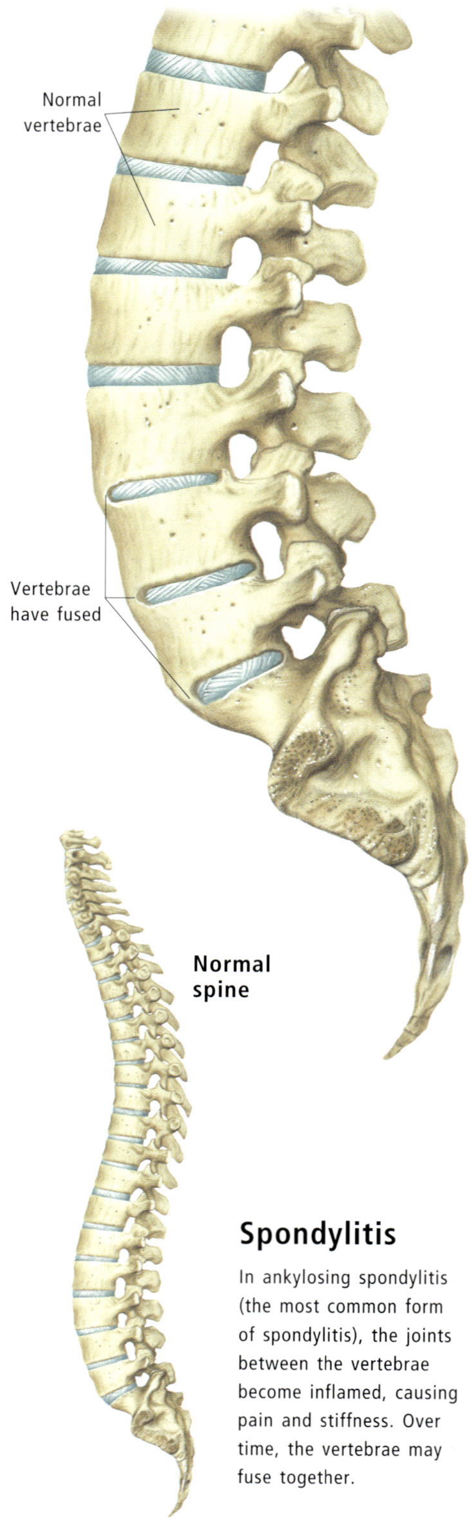

Spondylitis

In ankylosing spondylitis (the most common form of spondylitis), the joints between the vertebrae become inflamed, causing pain and stiffness. Over time, the vertebrae may fuse together.

SPONDYLITIS

Spondylitis is the inflammation of one or more vertebrae in the spine. The most common form is ankylosing spondylitis, a rheumatic disorder in which the joints between the vertebrae become inflamed and the spine becomes increasingly stiff until the vertebrae fuse together.

Initial symptoms include lower back pain and/or hip pain and stiffness. There may be joint pain and swelling in the shoulders, knees and ankles, heel pain, stooping, fever and limited chest expansion as the disease spreads upwards from the lower back. About a quarter of spondylitis sufferers experience eye inflammation. In fact, this may be an early symptom of the disease, sometimes appearing years before any spinal inflammation occurs.

Spondylitis may also be associated with inflammatory bowel disease or tuberculosis of the vertebrae. About 10 percent of people who suffer from psoriasis—a condition marked by a scaly rash on the elbows, knees and scalp—also suffer from spondylitis, often years after the rash appears.

Anti-inflammatory drugs, physical therapy and exercise are used to treat spondylitis. Ensuring good posture may also help.

SEE ALSO *Ankylosing spondylitis, Spine, Vertebrae*

SPONDYLOSIS

Spondylosis is osteoarthritis of the spine, due to natural ageing. It is also known as osteoarthritis. It often occurs in the neck (cervical) region of the spine and is caused by the degeneration of the disks located between the vertebrae. The condition can be aggravated by excessive activity or repeated injury. Abnormal bone growths (spurs) may occur, leading to compression of nerve roots and spinal cord. This can cause severe neck pain, radiating to the arms and shoulders, as well as loss of movement, function and sensation in parts of the body below the compression. There may be difficulty moving the head, buzzing in the ears, muscle weakness and loss of balance.

Treatment, if any, may include exercises to strengthen the neck and maintain good head movement, plus anti-inflammatory medication, and hospitalization and traction for severe cases.

SEE ALSO *Neck, Osteoarthritis, Spine*

SPORTS MEDICINE

Sports medicine is a field of health care focused on the prevention and treatment of sports injuries. It is primarily concerned with minimizing risk factors involved in any sport or physical activity, and offering effective treatment when injuries occur. Specialist doctors, trainers, physiologists and researchers are all involved in finding ways to improve the safety of sporting practice and in the formulation of training regimes to help athletes perform to the highest standard. Part of this doctrine is the gradual increase in stamina and strength through working muscles progressively harder over a set period, particularly after an injury.

Traumatic injuries

Most sports injuries are "traumatic". These happen suddenly and may involve immediate pain, swelling or bruising, or an open wound. Most are minor injuries to soft tissue, muscles, tendons or ligaments, such as strains and sprains. They may be due to a sudden wrenching or twisting of a body part, or have no obvious cause.

Ensuring a safe environment in which the physical activity takes place can minimize the risk of suffering from traumatic injury. For example, slippery floors are highly dangerous in basketball. Using safety gear such as mouthguards, helmets and padding where appropriate, is a priority and all equipment used must be in good condition.

Overuse injuries

These are products of particular physical activities, especially repetitive ones, and are characterized by a gradual increase in pain and discomfort. An example is tennis elbow. These types of injuries can be avoided by building a progressive training regime that allows the body to get used to potentially damaging physical activity. For example, weight lifters start with light weights and build their bodies up so that they can cope with heavy lifting. Sudden changes in training routines may also put stress on a part of the body. Rest and recovery days are recommended if pain is experienced.

Warming up and cooling down before and after physical activity is essential to avoid muscle stiffness. Warm-ups might include stretching muscles, bouncing movements for the joints and sprints to get the heart beating. A healthy diet with energy-giving carbohydrates and plenty of fluids is also important to help avoid fatigue and dehydration.

Treating an injury

Once an injury is sustained it is important not to add extra stress by keeping up the physical activity that caused it. Treatment will depend on the type and extent of the injury. A strained muscle may require gentle stretching exercises to regain flexibility, then strengthening exercises to help avoid a recurrence of the injury. Joint injuries may also respond to exercises that strengthen surrounding muscles. This will help stabilize the joint, after which a training regime can be formulated aimed at regaining mobility and function. Training programs must be progressive to avoid risk of further injury.

There is a simple way of remembering how to give immediate treatment to acute injuries on the sports field: Rest, Ice, Compression and Elevation (RICE). Rest minimizes hemorrhage and swelling, applying ice reduces pain and inflammation, and compression and elevation limit bruising.

SEE ALSO *Exercise, Joints, Muscle, Tennis elbow, Trauma*

Sprain

The ankle and wrist are particularly susceptible to sprains—the tearing or severe stretching of the tendons, muscles and ligaments that support the joint.

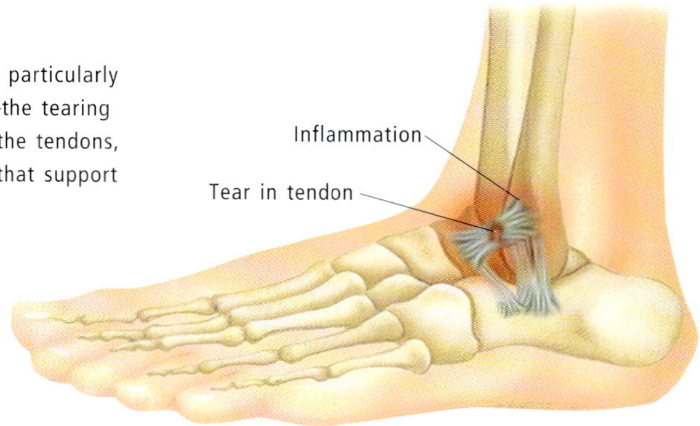

SPRAIN

Sprain is severe stretching or tearing of the tendons, muscles or ligaments surrounding a joint such as the ankle or wrist. This may be caused by a sudden twisting or wrenching movement and results in joint or muscle pain, swelling and sometimes bruising. Joint movement may also be impaired.

Applying cold compresses immediately after the injury and keeping the injured joint elevated above the heart will help reduce swelling. Severe cases may require bandaging and splinting. Resting the joint is the main treatment—depending on the severity of the sprain, it may be four or five weeks before normal use should be resumed.

SEE ALSO *Joints, Ligaments, Muscle, Tendons*

SPRUE

Sprue is a disorder of the small intestine marked by impaired absorption of food, especially fats. It is most common in the tropics where it is thought to be caused by infection. In other regions it can result from any illness or medical treatment that interrupts normal intestinal cell activity, such as celiac disease, pancreatitis, radiation treatment, worm infection or the surgical removal of part of the stomach or small intestine.

Symptoms include dry skin, weight loss, soreness in the corners of the mouth, a red tongue (due to vitamin B deficiency), flatulence, and foul-smelling bowel movements. Swollen ankles and abdomen and clubbing of the fingers may occur, along with weakness, fatigue, diarrhea and muscle cramps. Treatment depends on the underlying cause.

SEE ALSO *Celiac disease, Intestines, Pancreatitis, Radiation therapy*

Squint

Three pairs of muscles control eye movement. A squint (misalignment of the eyes) occurs when any of the pairs does not function correctly. With a squint, one or both of the eyes may look inward (cross-eyed) or outward (wall-eyed).

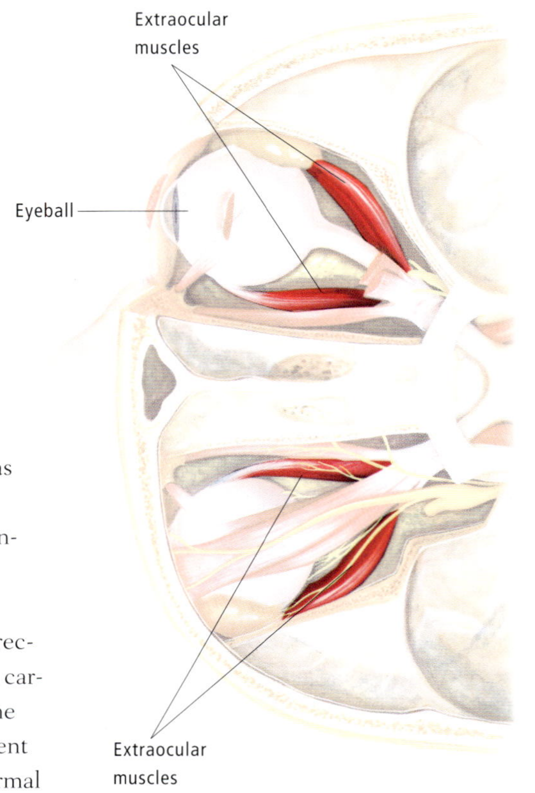

SPUTUM TEST

Sputum is the fluid that patients cough up from their lungs, usually during infective or allergic lung conditions, or after inhaling dust. Sputum may contain a lot of clear thick mucus, as seen in asthma or chronic bronchitis; pus, as in pneumonia; frothy fluid tinged with blood, as in heart failure with pulmonary edema; or black material, found in coal-miner's lung and heavy air pollution. Sputum may be analyzed for the presence of bacteria, which can be cultured and tested for antibiotic resistance; pus cells, indicating infection; malignant cells, which indicate cancer; or asbestos bodies, seen in asbestosis.

SEE ALSO *Asbestosis, Asthma, Bronchitis, Lungs, Pneumonia, Pulmonary edema*

SQUAMOUS CELL CARCINOMA

This term describes a large group of cancers. Multiple layers of squamous (flat) cells form the normal covering epithelium (surface cell layer) in many parts of the body, including the skin, the mucous membranes of the mouth, anal canal, vagina and cervix, and the lining of the esophagus and larynx. Irritation of other mucous membranes can lead to a change in cell type from glandular epithelium to squamous epithelium, such as in the lung as a result of smoking.

When squamous epithelium turns cancerous, the resulting tumor is called a squamous cell carcinoma (SCC). It has microscopic features that allow it to be recognized by a pathologist. Squamous cell carcinomas do not all grow and spread at the same rate. The site of origin and the extent of microscopic change (compared to normal epithelium) may indicate likely behavior.

SEE ALSO *Cancer, Mucous membranes, Smoking*

SQUINT

A squint (also known as strabismus) is a condition in which a person looks with partially closed or crossed eyes, primarily due to misalignment of the eyes. There are six muscles attached to each eye that work in pairs to allow movement; if muscle coordination is affected the eyes have trouble working in unison and can point in different directions. One eye may turn inward (cross-eye) or outward (wall-eye) while the other looks straight ahead. This sends two different pictures to the brain, which may ignore one image or allow two images to be seen, resulting in double vision. When one eye is favored over the other, vision in the nondominant eye can be lost as a consequence and the sense of depth perception distorted.

A squint may be a congenital condition, or the result of a neurological disorder, cranial nerve and eye diseases, eye trauma or cerebral palsy. Farsightedness can be a contributing factor. The condition can usually not be prevented, but exercises to strengthen muscles around the eye often improve symptoms. In severe cases, the muscles of one or both eyes may be repositioned and shortened by surgery.

This may not totally cure the condition, but the squint will be significantly reduced. Squinting generally appears at a young age and early treatment is important to avoid permanent loss of vision in one eye.

SEE ALSO *Eye, Sight*

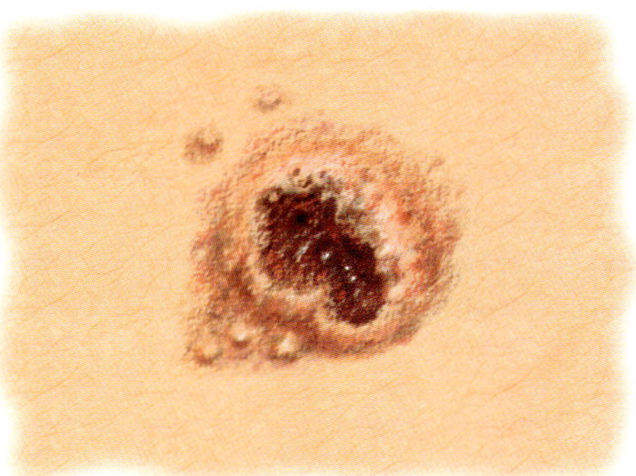

Squamous cell carcinoma

Malignant changes in the squamous cells that form the skin's surface layer can result in the formation of a cancerous tumor called a squamous cell carcinoma.

STAPHYLOCOCCAL INFECTION

Staphylococci are bacteria responsible for a wide range of human infections. Several species exist including *Staphylococcus epidermidis,* which is part of the normal bacterial flora of the skin, and *S. aureus,* commonly known as "golden staph", which has a greater potential to cause infection.

Staphylococcal infection most commonly involves the skin, in the form of abscesses, but the bacteria may spread to deeper tissues to cause deep abscesses, osteomyelitis or septicemia. Some strains of *S. aureus* produce a toxin that results in toxic shock syndrome—high fever, a red rash, low blood pressure and organ dysfunctions. Staphylococci are very common causes of infections in hospitals: *S. epidermidis* causes infection of intravenous cannulas and *S. aureus* can cause severe infections in diabetics, patients with renal (kidney) failure and intravenous drug users. Treatment of staphylococcal infection is with antibiotics and surgical drainage of abscesses when required. The widespread use of antibiotics in hospitals has led to the emergence of multi-resistant staphylococci, which are important pathogens in surgical and intensive care units. Prevention of cross-infection by the use of handwashing is important for reducing staphylococcal infections.

SEE ALSO *Abscess, Bacteria, Osteomyelitis, Septicemia, Toxic shock syndrome*

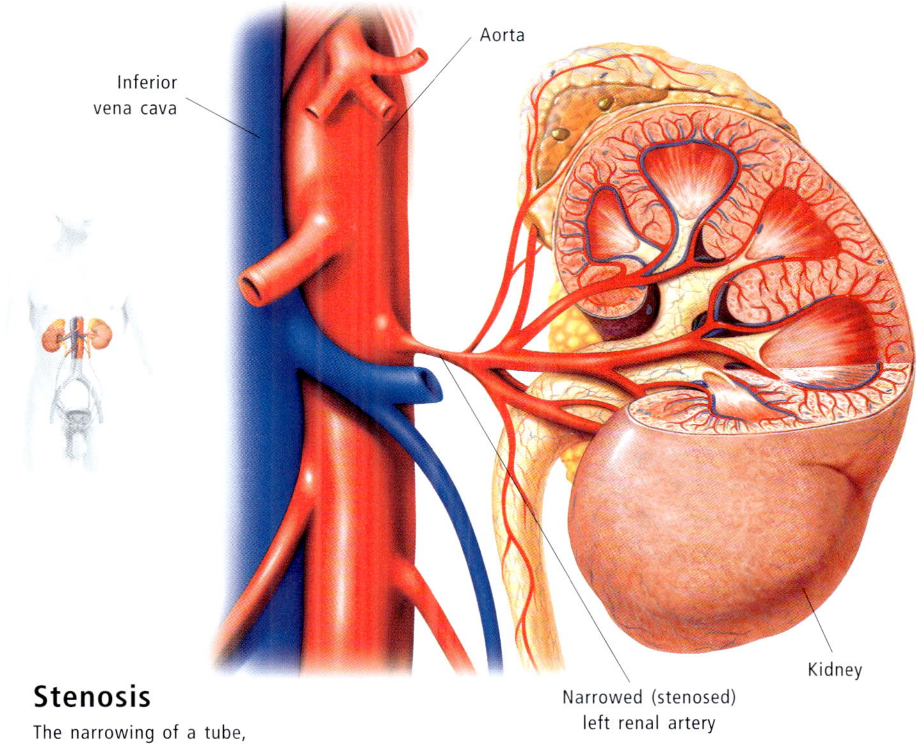

Stenosis

The narrowing of a tube, such as an artery, or duct is known as stenosis. In renal artery stenosis, constriction of the artery disrupts blood flow to the kidney and affects kidney function.

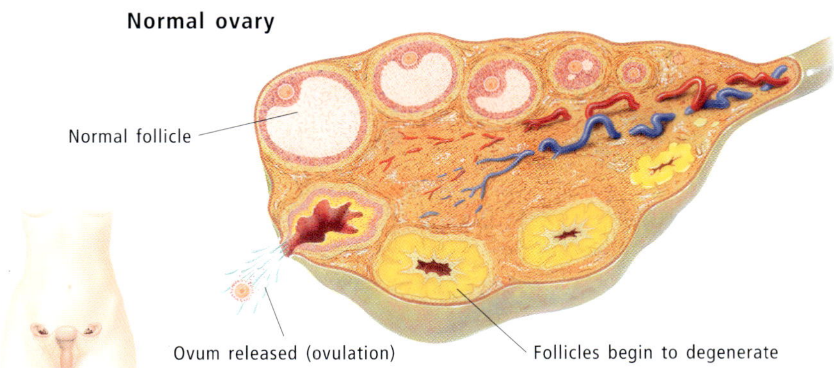

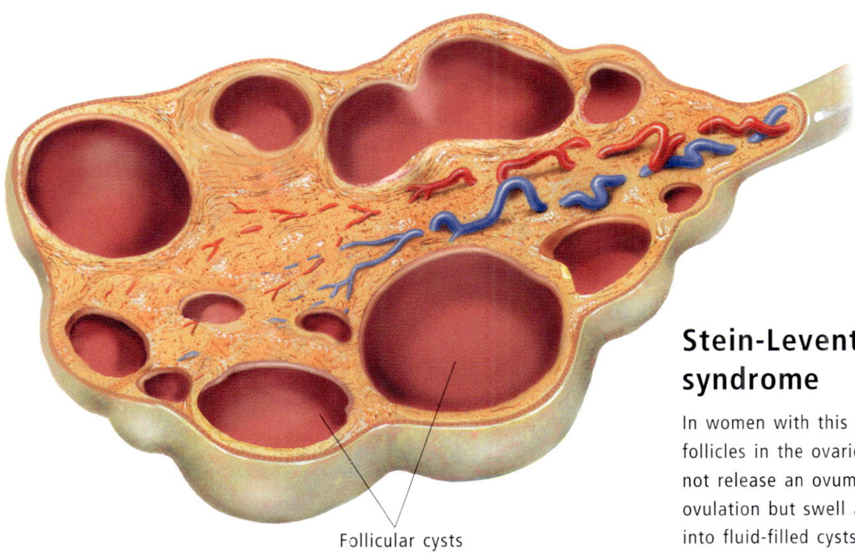

Stein-Leventhal syndrome

In women with this disorder, follicles in the ovaries do not release an ovum at ovulation but swell and turn into fluid-filled cysts.

STEIN-LEVENTHAL SYNDROME

Stein-Leventhal syndrome, also known as polycystic ovarian syndrome, is a disorder of the follicles in the ovaries characterized by multiple cysts, the absence of menstruation, obesity, infertility and increased hair growth on the face and body. Instead of releasing ova, the swollen follicles fill with fluid and turn into cysts. The ovaries can consequently become two to five times larger than normal. Abnormal hormone levels are thought to cause the condition, which commonly occurs just after puberty and appears to a have a hereditary link.

Oral contraceptives are one of the medications used to treat the disorder. Pregnancy may be possible with medical help.

SEE ALSO *Hormones, Oral contraceptives, Ovarian cysts, Ovaries*

STENOSIS

Stenosis is the constriction of a tube or duct in any one of a number of locations inside the body. One type is spinal stenosis, a condition that usually affects middle-aged and elderly people in which the spinal canal narrows due to degenerative bony overgrowth. Pyloric stenosis occurs at the exit to the stomach and in adults is commonly caused by muscle spasms. Babies may suffer from a congenital form of pyloric stenosis, in which

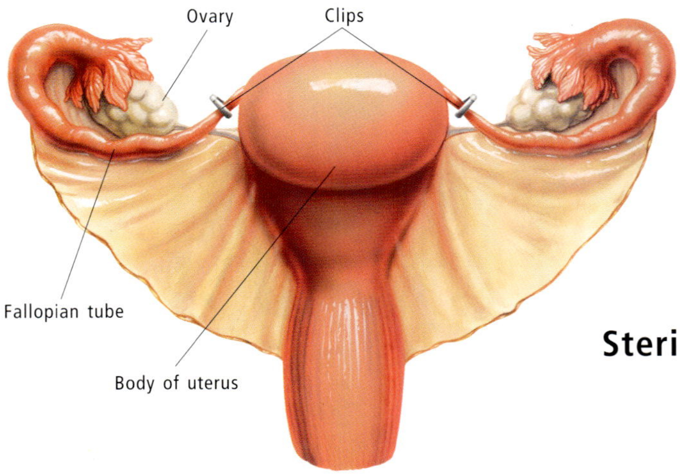

Female sterilization
Female sterilization is achieved by blocking the fallopian tubes. The tubes may be severed or clips applied to block the movement of ova from the ovaries to the uterus.

Sterilization

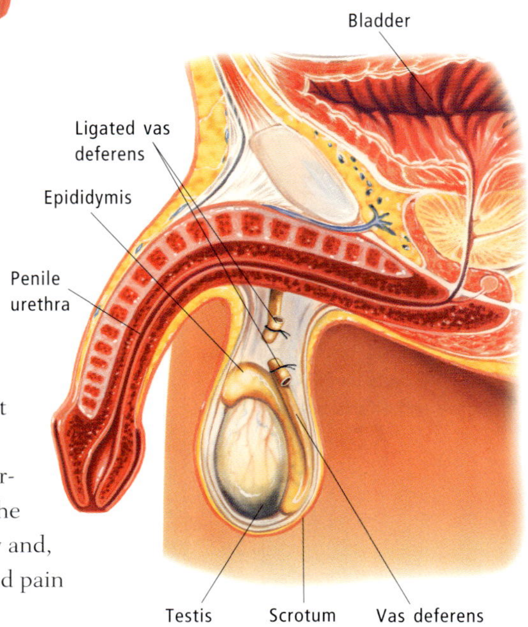

Male sterilization
Usually performed under local anesthetic, a vasectomy involves cutting the vas deferens tube that carries sperm from the testes to the urethra. Sterilization can be reversed if the tubes are rejoined.

case an operation may be performed to cut the muscle and thereby prevent spasms from occurring.

Stenosis may also occur in the arteries of the leg or the carotid artery in the neck. This causes reduced blood flow and, when the leg is affected, cramping and pain in the calf muscle.

Other parts of the body that may be affected by stenosis include the heart valves and salivary glands. Treatment for these and other forms of stenosis includes medication and/or surgery.

SEE ALSO *Spine, Heart, Pyloric stenosis*

S

STERILIZATION

Sterilization is a permanent surgical form of contraception involving a vasectomy in men and tubal ligation or tubal sterilization in women, the latter often referred to as tying the tubes. These procedures are commonly chosen by couples who don't want to have more or any children, and who prefer to avoid drug-based forms of birth control or those that carry a higher risk of pregnancy. It is estimated that as many as 100 million couples worldwide have opted for sterilization as a method of birth control. More female sterilizations have been performed than male, but demand is high for both.

The advantages of permanent protection against pregnancy, no effect on sexual pleasure and no lasting side effects, may outweigh any costs or the possibility of later regrets. As both of these operations should be regarded as permanent, it is a good idea for anyone contemplating sterilization to receive some counseling.

Vasectomy

Vasectomy is the quicker, simpler operation. Usually performed under local anesthetic it involves the cutting of the vas deferens (or ductus deferens), the tube that carries the sperm to the urethra from the testicles. A small opening is usually made in the front of the scrotum allowing each vas deferens to be cut and sealed. The operation takes around 20 minutes and is not effective until all the sperm in the tubes have been ejaculated, which can take up to 16 ejaculations. Samples of semen need to be tested some months after the operation to ensure that it has been successful.

The most common side effects are a slight soreness, swelling and bruising which last for a few days. A few men suffer bleeding or infection. About one in 300–500 vasectomies will fail to sterilize, usually because the tubes were not completely blocked off, the surgery healed itself or there was a third undetected vas deferens.

Tubal sterilization

Female sterilization is a more serious operation in which the fallopian tubes are blocked. Surgery can be performed by using a laparoscope (an optical instrument) inserted through an incision near the navel and into the abdominal cavity, or through the vaginal vault. The tubes, once found, are blocked by rings or clips, or by burning with diathermy or laser. A mini-laparotomy involves a small incision just below the pubic hairline.

After sterilization, the ovaries will continue to release ova, but sperm will not be able to reach them. The menstrual cycle is not affected by the procedure, with periods and menopause still occurring. There are usually no side effects after recovery from the operation, although some women have reported heavier than usual periods, strong cramps, recurrent abdominal pain and pelvic infections.

The failure rate of tubal ligation is around two per 1,000. This may be due to tubes joining themselves back together and, on rare occasions, may result in a potentially dangerous ectopic pregnancy where a fertilized ovum embeds in a fallopian tube or somewhere else outside the uterus.

While reversal of these operations is possible, the success rates differ. Although microsurgery is improving all the time, sterilization is not a procedure which should be undertaken if the person has any thoughts of producing children later in life.

SEE ALSO *Contraception, Reproductive systems, Tubal sterilization, Vasectomy*

STERNUM

The sternum (or breastbone) forms part of the skeleton of the thorax. It is situated in the front wall of the chest, in the midline. It consists of three parts, from top to

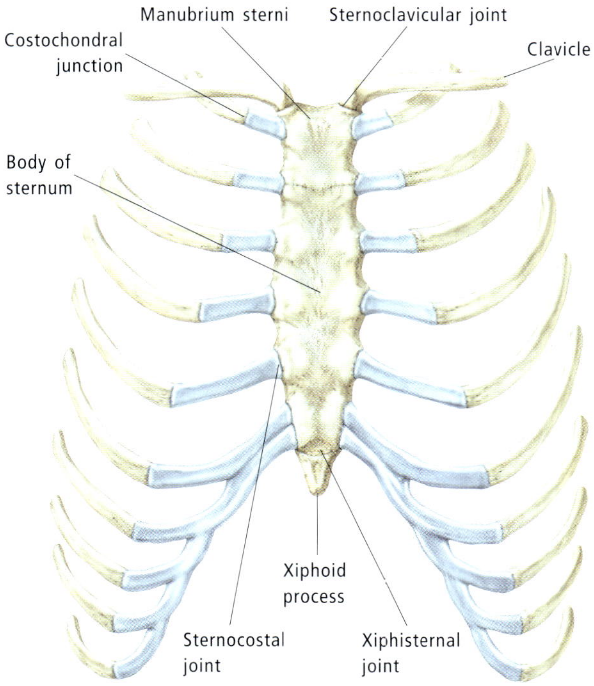

Sternum

Forming part of the anterior wall of the thorax, the sternum consists of three parts: the manubrium, the body and the xiphoid process.

bottom: the manubrium; the body of the sternum; and the xiphoid process (pronounced "ziffoid"). The manubrium articulates with the clavicles (collar bones), thereby assisting in stabilizing the shoulders. The ribs are connected to the sides of the manubrium and body of the sternum by their costal cartilages. The pectoralis major muscle is attached in part to the sternum. The sternum contains a marrow cavity, which is a convenient site for bone marrow biopsy.

SEE ALSO *Collar bone, Ribs, Shoulder*

STEROIDS

Steroids are a group of chemicals that comprise a large number of the body's hormones. They are synthesized from cholesterol mainly in the adrenal glands and gonads, and regulate a number of important body processes.

There are three main groups of steroids: glucocorticoids, mineralocorticoids and sex steroids (androgens and estrogens). The major glucocorticoid is cortisol, which is also known as the "stress hormone". It is released from the adrenal gland in response to physiological stresses such as exercise, injury or infection, or psychological stresses, such as fear or depression. Cortisol acts on many cells in the body, regulating their metabolism and activity. It prepares the body for action by mobilizing glucose stores and preventing excessive tissue reaction to injury. This anti-inflammatory action is used when cortisol-type medication is prescribed for the treatment of autoimmune diseases.

These synthetic steroid medications have a similar chemical make-up to steroids that occur naturally in the body and are designed to have the same effect. Corticosteroids were first used in the 1940s for the treatment of rheumatoid arthritis and today there are many more types prescribed by physicians to provide relief from conditions such as allergies, asthma and skin inflammation.

The wide range of effects explains the potential for many side effects from cortisol treatment. In large doses it may increase blood sugar and blood pressure, affect mood, accelerate osteoporosis, and reduce wound healing and response to infection. Patients with Cushing's syndrome, in which there is increased cortisol production from an adrenal tumor, show similar symptoms.

Mineralocorticoids help the body control salt and water balance. Androgens are produced by the adrenal glands; however, they require conversion in the testes to the main male hormone testosterone. The main female sex hormone, estradiol, is made from cholesterol by cells in the ovaries.

Synthetic anabolic steroids are different to other steroid medications. Chemically similar to the male sex hormone testosterone, they increase muscle growth and lean body mass, and they have been abused by body builders and athletes who often use dangerously high amounts in order to boost their physical performance. This overuse creates a severe imbalance in the secretion of natural hormones by the body and if the synthetic steroids are suddenly withdrawn may lead to side effects such as weakness, nausea, vomiting, weight loss and abdominal pain.

SEE ALSO *Adrenal glands, Autoimmune disease, Cholesterol, Cushing's syndrome, Hormones*

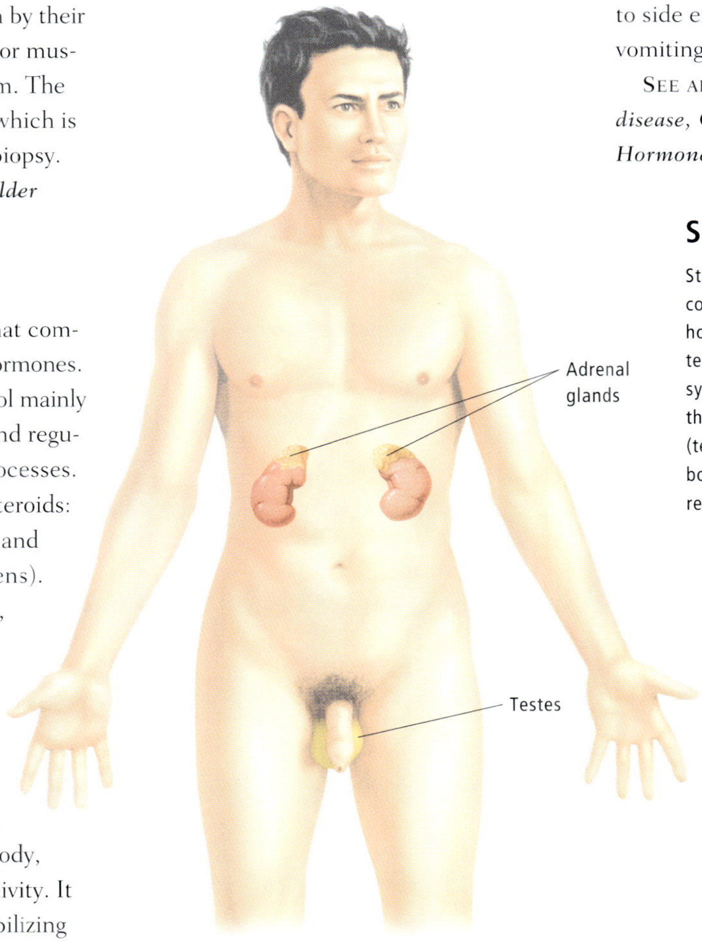

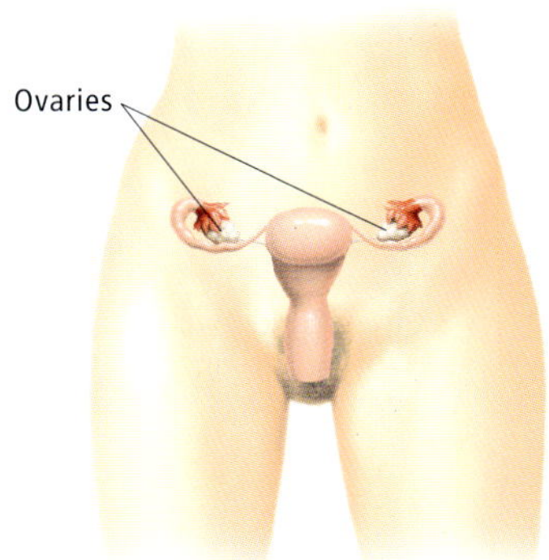

Steroids

Steroids are a group of chemicals that comprise a large number of the body's hormones, including the sex hormones testosterone and estrogen. Many are synthesized from cholesterol, mainly in the adrenal glands and in the gonads (testes and ovaries). Steroids regulate body processes, such as growth, and the repair of body tissue.

STEVENS-JOHNSON SYNDROME

Stevens-Johnson syndrome, a type of erythema multiforme, is a rare and potentially fatal skin condition marked by blisters in the mouth, throat, anal region and the mucous membranes lining the eyelid. It usually occurs after other illnesses and infections, or in response to certain medications. Ring-shaped lesions appear on the palms, hands, arms, legs and feet. These are often accompanied by fever, aching joints and itching, and sometimes mouth sores, bloodshot eyes and abnormal vision. Blisters in the throat may be extremely painful, making swallowing very difficult.

Some relief may be experienced by applying moist compresses to skin lesions. Antihistamine medications can be used to control itching and topical anesthetics applied to mouth sores to reduce pain and discomfort.

Hospitalization is often necessary, with the use of antibiotics and other medications to control inflammation and secondary infections. Skin grafts may be performed when lesions affect large areas.

Due to the severity of Stevens-Johnson Syndrome there is a high risk of death. Complications may include shock due to the loss of body fluids, systemic infection and scarring.

SEE ALSO *Erythema*

STILL'S DISEASE

Still's disease, or juvenile rheumatoid arthritis (JRA), is a form of rheumatoid arthritis that affects children under 16 years of age. As with adult rheumatoid arthritis, the cause is unknown, but it is thought to be an autoimmune connective tissue disease, as it affects not only the joints of the body, but also other organs such as the heart and pericardium (the lining around the heart), the lungs and pleura (the lining around the lungs), the eyes and the skin.

There are various forms of the illness. In one form, arthritis is the prominent feature; the joints are swollen, painful and tender to touch and may be hot and red. In another form, the joints are not affected but fever, chills and a rash are present, and the spleen may be enlarged (splenomegaly). In this type, uveitis (inflammation of the inner lining of the eyes and iris muscle) may occur, leading to visual problems or blindness.

The diagnosis of Still's disease is usually made by a specialist pediatrician or rheumatologist. Blood tests, which may reveal the presence of certain proteins such as rheumatoid factor and antinuclear antibody, help make the diagnosis easier.

Treatment is with drugs such as corticosteroids and nonsteroidal anti-inflammatory agents (NSAIDs) and in some cases gold and chloroquine. Physical therapy and exercise programs are often recommended; in severe cases, joint replacement may be needed. However, most of the time the disease burns itself out (often at puberty) without leaving any permanent loss or deformity.

SEE ALSO *Autoimmune disease, Connective tissue, Joints, Rheumatoid arthritis*

STIMULANTS

Stimulants are drugs that accelerate (excite) mental or bodily functions. Laxatives, for example, are stimulants used to overcome constipation or lack of motility in bowel functions, which work by stimulating the intestines to contract.

There are many mild stimulants readily and legally available which act on the nervous system. These include caffeine, found in coffee, tea, cola drinks, maté and guarana, and theobromine, found in cocoa. Nicotine, found in cigarettes and other tobacco products, is regarded as a stimulant as its immediate effects on inhalation of tobacco smoke are to increase heart rate, raise blood pressure and excite the nervous system.

Stronger stimulants include illegal substances (street drugs), such as cocaine, and drugs such as methylxanthines, amphetamines (also known as speed), or methylated purines, which are available on prescription.

Amphetamines stimulate the central nervous system, elevating alertness and well-being, increasing energy and self-confidence and at the same time reducing appetite. They can also induce anxiety, increased heart rate and palpitations; high intake of these drugs may result in feelings of hostility and aggression. Long-term use brings dependency and can cause hallucinations, delusions (including hearing voices) and feelings of persecution. Overdose can cause brain hemorrhage, heart attack, coma and death. Amphetamines were first prescribed for depression, narcolepsy and, because they reduce appetite, for obesity.

More recently amphetamines have been prescribed for children with some types of hyperactivity. Use without a prescription is generally illegal.

SEE ALSO *Amphetamines, Attention deficit hyperactivity disorder, Cocaine, Drug dependence, Drugs, Laxatives, Nicotine, Overdose*

STITCH

A stitch is a sharp abdominal pain usually experienced during physical exertion. It is commonly felt under the rib cage on one side of the body due to muscle cramps in the abdominal wall.

People with low fitness levels are more likely to get a stitch. The pain disappears without treatment but gently rubbing the affected area may help. Ceasing physical activity for 15 minutes or so is also recommended.

SEE ALSO *Abdomen, Cramp*

STOKES-ADAMS SYNDROME

Stokes-Adams syndrome is a form of heart block. The normal electrical impulses that regulate the heartbeat are blocked as they pass from the upper chambers of the heart to the lower chambers—usually because the heart muscle is damaged. This slows the heartbeat temporarily, reducing blood flow to the brain and causing fainting.

The condition is most common in the elderly and is associated with coronary heart disease. It results from transient or permanent heart problems and is characterized by episodes of loss of consciousness, sometimes referred to as Stokes-Adams attacks.

These attacks may last from a few seconds to a few minutes. When consciousness is regained, sufferers may experience spells of nausea, dizziness and faintness when they try to sit or stand. The heart rate may return to normal spontaneously or a complete heart block may persist.

Stokes-Adams syndrome is best treated with an artificial pacemaker. Alternatively, drug treatment may be used. The condition is also called Adams-Stokes syndrome.

SEE ALSO *Heart, Heartbeat, Pacemaker*

STOMACH

The stomach receives food from the esophagus and continues the process of digestion. It acts as a reservoir, permitting the intake of large amounts of food every few hours. When empty of food, the stomach contains only about one-twelfth of a pint (50 milliliters) of liquid, but can expand to accommodate up to 2 pints (1,200 milliliters) after a large meal is eaten. The stomach mixes the food with the acidic gastric juices, which digest protein and carbohydrates, and delivers semi-digested food to the next part of the gut, the duodenum. The stomach is also the site of absorption of some drugs such as aspirin.

Structure and function

The stomach has many parts. The cardia is located at the entrance of the esophagus into the stomach (cardioesophageal junction). The fundus lies to the left of the cardia, while the body of the stomach is the large central part which extends from the fundus to the pylorus. The pylorus is the final part of the stomach and consists of a pyloric antrum, which leads to the pyloric canal. The pyloric canal is encircled by a ring of muscle known as the pyloric sphincter, which controls the passage of stomach juices and food into the duodenum.

The inner lining of the stomach has many types of specialized cells. Some, such as the mucous cells, produce a thick layer of mucus to protect the stomach from its own acid juices. Another group, the parietal or oxyntic cells, produces the hydrochloric acid to keep the stomach interior at the optimal acidity level for protein digestion, while another group, the zymogen cells, produces the enzymes to digest protein and fat. There are also several cell types in the stomach which produce hormones for controlling acid secretion and regulating nutrient levels in the blood.

The stomach is a very muscular organ and can churn the partially digested food it receives to break it up into more easily digested fragments. Waves of muscular contraction, called peristalsis, move down the stomach from the body to the pylorus. When the food is ready to be moved on down the digestive tract, these waves propel the food into the pyloric canal and on to the duodenum.

The secretion of stomach acid is controlled in several phases or stages. The sight, smell, taste and even the thought of food act upon the brain to stimulate acid secretion. The nerve impulses which control this are carried from the brain stem by the vagus nerve. When the food reaches the stomach, local mechanical and chemical stimulation leads to the release of gastrin, a hormone which controls gastric juice secretion.

Diseases and disorders

There are many problems that can affect the stomach, including the following.

Cancer

Stomach cancer is fortunately becoming rarer in Western countries. The incidence of stomach cancer is higher in Japan and in eastern and central European countries, compared to the USA. Cancer of the stomach, rare in people aged under 40, is about twice as common in men as in women.

There are several different types of stomach cancers. About one-quarter of cancers produce ulcers and can be mistaken for peptic ulcers. A further quarter produce bulky bulbous growths in the interior of the stomach, while about 15 percent spread superficially through the surface lining of the stomach. Unfortunately, many stomach cancers are advanced at the time of diagnosis and are found to be both partly within and partly outside the stomach. Most tumors arise in the pyloric region, the bulk of the remainder developing in the stomach body.

Most patients with stomach cancer will initially note a vague feeling of heaviness after meals. Weight loss will follow and may be

Stomach

The walls of the stomach serve several purposes. The mucosa and submucosa, which form the stomach's inner lining, secrete gastric juices and other substances to aid digestion. The layers of muscle contract and expand in order to mix and expel the stomach contents. The outer coating of the wall is smooth and slippery, easing movement of the stomach.

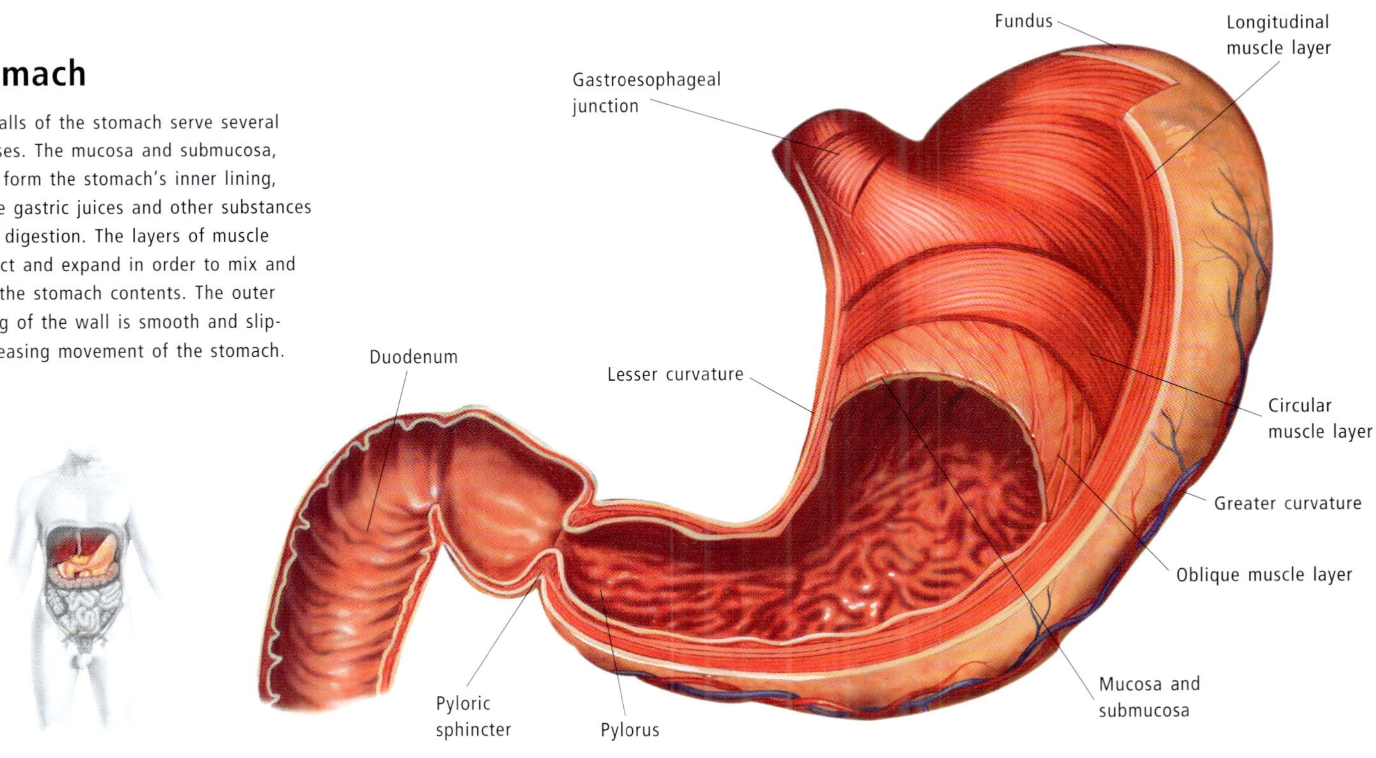

accompanied by vomiting of a coffee-ground colored material. A palpable lump may be present in the upper abdomen and the liver may be enlarged if the tumor has spread to that organ.

The diagnosis may be made by barium meal x-ray and examination with a fiberoptic instrument (gastroscopy). The only curative treatment is the surgical removal of the tumor (gastrectomy), any local lymph nodes and portions of surrounding organs if necessary. The long-term prospects for patients with this disease are poor. Of all patients with stomach cancer only about 12–15 percent will survive 5 years; of those patients where the tumor is localized at the time of diagnosis, 40–50 percent may survive for 5 years.

Ulcers

Peptic ulcers result from the action of stomach juices on the vulnerable surface lining of the stomach, duodenum or esophagus. Peptic ulcers in the stomach are usually located along the lesser curvature and most are within a few inches of the pylorus. Patients will experience pain in the upper abdomen, which is relieved by food and antacids. Complications arising from peptic ulcers include bleeding, obstruction and perforation of the stomach, duodenum or esophagus.

Ulceration of the lining of the stomach may also occur as a result of stressful illnesses such as acute blood loss, serious infection, burns, brain injury and brain tumors. Patients with stress ulcers from burns or infection typically develop bleeding from the stomach and duodenum, and some patients may have perforation of the stomach or duodenum wall. Ulcers developing in patients with brain injury or tumors are usually due to increased gastrin production and excessive stomach acid secretion. Alcohol and drugs such as aspirin, steroids and anti-inflammatories can also cause irritation and ulceration of the stomach lining. Treatment may include the eradication of any infection.

Hiatus hernia

Parts of the stomach may protrude (herniate) through the diaphragm in a condition called hiatus (hiatal) hernia. Hiatus hernia can be of two types. The paraesophageal or rolling hiatal hernia involves the herniation of the stomach fundus through the esophageal opening. Sliding hiatus hernia is more common than the rolling type and involves the movement of the cardioesophageal junction through the diaphragm into the chest cavity. Rolling hiatus hernia may may not be accompanied by any symptoms, while patients with sliding hiatus hernia usually experience heartburn, particularly on lying down, and a feeling of regurgitation.

Gastroenteritis

Infection of the stomach and intestines may occur as a result of ingesting disease-causing viruses and bacteria (food poisoning). This causes an inflammatory condition called gastroenteritis. The sufferer experiences nausea, vomiting and upper abdominal discomfort if the infection involves the upper gastrointestinal tract.

SEE ALSO *Cancer, Digestive system, Esophagus, Gastrectomy, Gastritis, Gastroenteritis, Hiatus hernia, Peptic ulcer, Peristalsis, Pylorus*

Stomach function

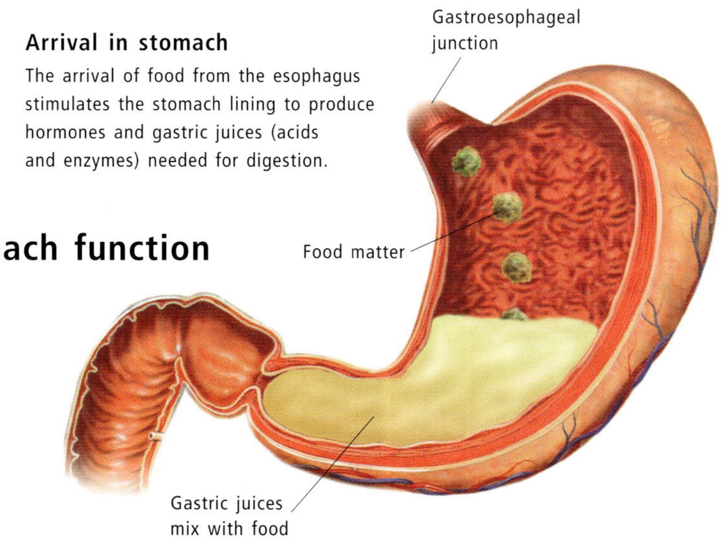

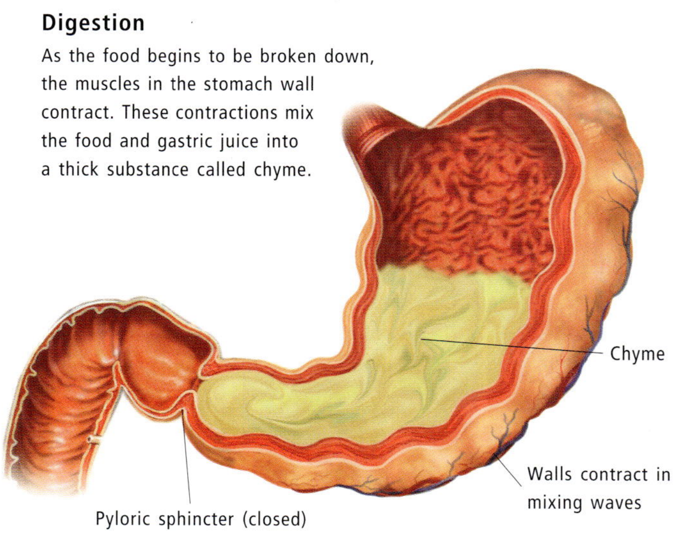

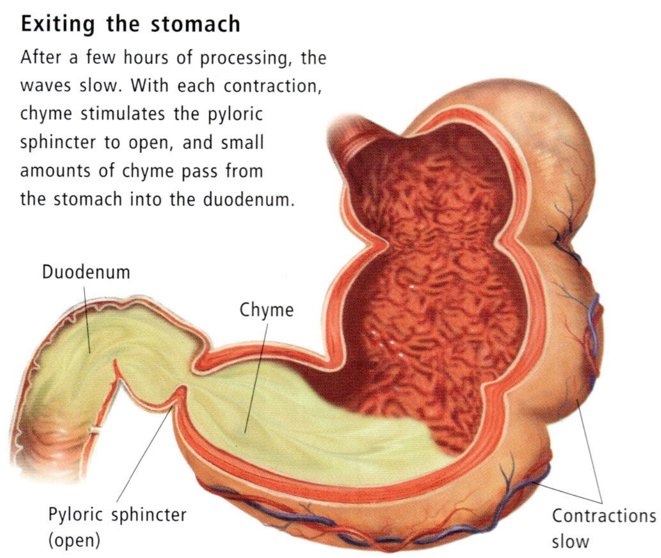

STREPTOCOCCAL INFECTIONS

Streptococcal infections are caused by perhaps the most common human bacterial pathogen, *Streptococcus*. Streptococci are classified into several groups and cause a spectrum of disease, ranging from minor to life-threatening. The same groups of streptococci that cause minor infections can occasionally cause severe disease.

The commonest streptococcal infection is streptococcal pharyngitis, or "strep throat". This is generally due to infection by Group A streptococci, which most often causes sore throat and fever in childhood. Although most cases of throat infection are viral and associated with the common cold, throat swabs should be taken if streptococcal infection is suspected, particularly in children aged 5–15 years. Antibiotic treatment can prevent the development of possible serious long-term complications. Apart from otitis media, sinusitis and abscess formation, there may be occasional immune-mediated complications. These are acute rheumatic fever and post-streptococcal glomerulonephritis. The former can be prevented by a full 10-day course of penicillin, avoiding possible later damage to the heart valves.

Another common form of superficial Group A streptococcal infection is impetigo. This causes crusted pustules, mainly on the legs, of young children in tropical climates. Occasionally Group A streptococci cause severe invasive infections, such as streptococcal toxic shock syndrome or necrotizing fasciitis ("flesh-eating bacteria").

Group B streptococci are the commonest cause of infection of the uterus after childbirth and neonatal infection. Group D streptococci are major causes of pneumonia and endocarditis (infection of the heart valves).

Streptococci

While usually causing only mild infections such as "strep throat", streptococci bacteria are also responsible for more severe disorders such as streptococcal toxic shock syndrome and necrotizing fasciitis.

STRESS

Stress is difficult to define, but it can be thought of as the body's response to a threatening or dangerous situation, or to demands arising from a new or changing situation. These stimuli may be physical, emotional or mental, internal or external.

Under these conditions, physiological changes take place. The sympathetic nervous system is activated and the body produces hormones such as epinephrine (adrenaline). Together, these increase blood supply to the muscles, raise the heart rate, increase respiration, and increase the blood sugar supply. These changes, sometimes called the "fight-or-flight" response, allow a person to cope with the threat or the demand. If the stressful situation is resolved, the symptoms disappear. If the stressful situation continues, however, its long-term effects may prove harmful.

Health can be damaged by stress in several ways. Stress can cause sleep problems, weight gain or weight loss. It may encourage unhealthy lifestyle practices. It can weaken the immune system, making a person more vulnerable to colds and other diseases. It is also an important contributing factor in diseases such as high blood pressure, cardiovascular disease, arthritis and other inflammatory diseases, asthma, sleep disturbances, and anorexia nervosa and other eating disorders. Stress is also related to migraine headaches, ulcers, respiratory or lung diseases, and skin conditions. Although the relationship between health and stress is not fully understood, medical researchers estimate stress may play a part in between half and two-thirds of all illnesses.

Everyone's tolerance of stress is different, and individuals handle various types of stress in different ways. Researchers have divided human behavior into two broad types according to how people handle stress. Type A individuals react with aggressive and competitive behavior. Type B people are more patient, easygoing, and relaxed. Type A individuals are more likely to develop heart disease and other illnesses than Type B individuals. Some experts believe there is a third group, Type C individuals, who are prone to cancer as a result of chronic stress.

Stress can be beneficial in some circumstances, as it enhances performance; an athlete in a race, for example, may perform better because of the stress of the event. However, once stress reaches a certain limit, additional stress will detract from performance levels. Stress or nervousness before a big presentation may help a speaker perform better or think with more clarity and precision; conversely, excessively high levels of stress and anxiety may cause confusion and forgetfulness. Doctors recommend recognizing individual limits and adjusting the circumstances so that the amount of stress involved in a situation will benefit, rather than hinder, an individual.

Moderate stress may be relieved by exercise and self-relaxation techniques such as deep breathing, muscle relaxation and meditation. A change of job, environment or living situation may reduce stress. Severe stress may require psychotherapy to uncover and work through the underlying causes. A form of behavior therapy known as biofeedback enables the patient to become more aware of internal processes and thereby gain some control over bodily reactions to stress.

SEE ALSO *Biofeedback, Epinephrine, Meditation, Psychotherapy, Relaxation techniques*

STRETCH MARKS

Stretch marks are streaks or lines which appear on the skin as a result of rapid growth, or as reactions to certain diseases and topical medications. They are commonly seen on the abdomen and breasts of pregnant women, but can also occur on the buttocks, hips, thighs and sides, wherever the elastic fibers in the skin stretch and rupture. Hormonal changes and the rapid growth of puberty cause them in both males and females. They appear as soft, red-purple glossy streaks and generally can't be prevented or cured by applying moisturizers. However, they often fade or disappear with time, especially when the initial cause of the skin stretching has passed.

SEE ALSO *Pregnancy*

S

STROKE

Stroke is loss of brain function as a result of cérebral infarction (lack of oxygen and death of tissue in some part of the brain) as a consequence of interruption to the blood supply to the brain. It is a common condition, particularly in the elderly, affecting about one in 500 people. Stroke is the third largest cause of death in industrialized countries after heart disease and cancer.

Causes

There are several causes of cerebral brain infarction. Most commonly, a blood clot forms in one of the carotid arteries (the major arteries in the neck) and obstructs blood flow to the brain. The clot usually forms in a part of the artery that has been damaged by atherosclerosis (hardening of the arteries).

A blood clot may also form in the carotids, then dislodge and travel via the bloodstream to the brain, where it causes the infarction. Similar blockages may occur in any of the multiple branches of the carotid or vertebral arteries, which supply blood to specific areas of the brain.

Less commonly, stroke is caused by bleeding (hemorrhaging) from a diseased artery. This may occur in an artery affected by atherosclerosis or one with a congenital berry aneurysm, either of which may rupture. Bleeding into surrounding brain tissue damages the tissue and causes stroke.

Symptoms

The symptoms of stroke vary according to the part of the brain affected. Common symptoms are loss of movement (paralysis) of a body area, weakness, decreased sensation, numbness, loss of coordination, vision problems and difficulty speaking. Symptoms may occur suddenly, or develop over a period of days, fluctuating in severity. With hemorrhage there may be a sudden severe headache and discomfort with bright light.

A precursor to a stroke is often a transient ischemic attack (TIA), a "mini stroke" in which the deprivation of blood is not sufficient to cause permanent damage. The symptoms are the same as those of a stroke, but are temporary, and the affected person makes a full recovery, usually within 24 hours. The episode serves as a warning of the possibility of a complete stroke in the future.

Treatment

Suffers of stroke are usually treated in hospital, and may require intensive care. The sooner the patient is taken to hospital the better the chances of effective treatment. A CAT (computed axial tomography) scan or MRI (magnetic resonance imaging) of the head may be used to rule out bleeding (hemorrhage) or other lesions and to define the location and extent of the stroke.

If there is bleeding or a blood clot, surgical removal of blood or blood clots from the brain cavity, or repair work at the source of the bleeding, may be possible. Usually, however, there is no cure for stroke; treatment is centered around rehabilitation. Programs of speech therapy, occupational therapy, physical therapy and other measures are designed to recover as much function as possible.

Part of treatment involves minimizing the risk of future strokes. This includes reducing risk factors for atherosclerosis, such as smoking, high blood pressure, high levels of lipids in the blood and diabetes. Carotid endarterectomy (removal of plaque from the carotid arteries) may be performed in some cases.

About a quarter of stroke sufferers recover most or all impaired functions, a quarter die of the stroke or its complications, and half experience long-term disabilities.

SEE ALSO *Arteries, Arteriosclerosis, Atherosclerosis, Brain, Carotid arteries, Transient ischemic attack*

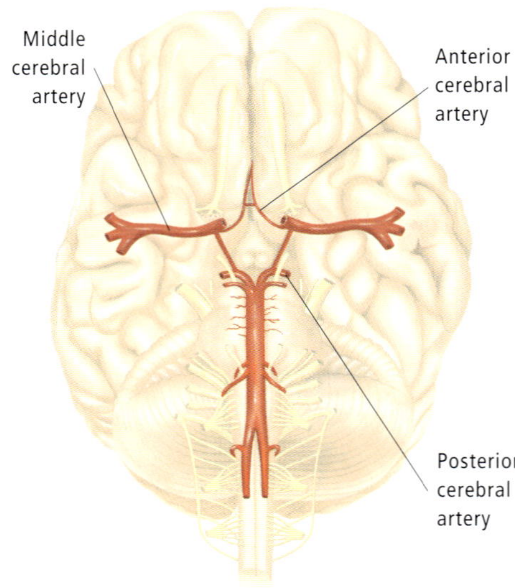

Cerebral thrombosis

Blockage of the cerebral arteries by a thrombus (blood clot) is a common cause of stroke. The clot may form in the cerebral arteries due to high blood pressure or arterial disease, or may form elsewhere and travel to arteries in the brain before blocking the blood supply.

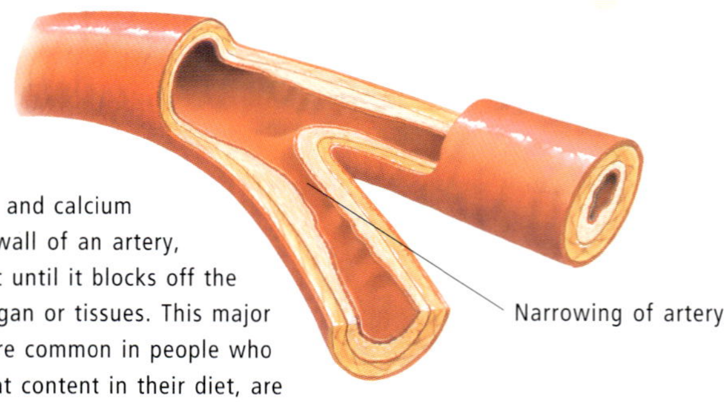

Arteriosclerosis

In arteriosclerosis, fat and calcium deposits form in the wall of an artery, gradually narrowing it until it blocks off the blood supply to an organ or tissues. This major cause of stroke is more common in people who smoke, have a high fat content in their diet, are overweight, who have a family history of stroke or heart disease, or have high blood pressure.

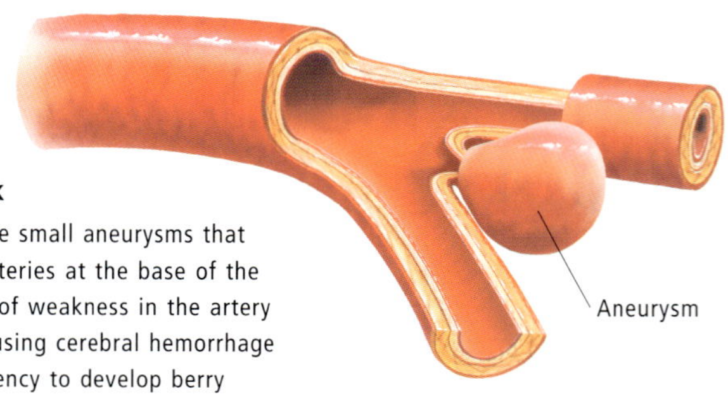

Congenital risk

Berry aneurysms are small aneurysms that can occur in the arteries at the base of the brain. These areas of weakness in the artery wall may burst, causing cerebral hemorrhage and stroke. A tendency to develop berry aneurysms may be inherited and people who have them may suffer a stroke at a relatively early age.

Cerebral infarction

Cerebral infarction is the death of brain tissue. This occurs when the brain is deprived of sufficient oxygen to keep the tissue alive and functioning normally. All the cerebral tissue may be affected if there is insufficient oxygen in the blood, for example following cardiac arrest. When localized, as in this illustration, infarction is usually due to the disease of a cerebral artery, which has blocked off the blood supply to that area.

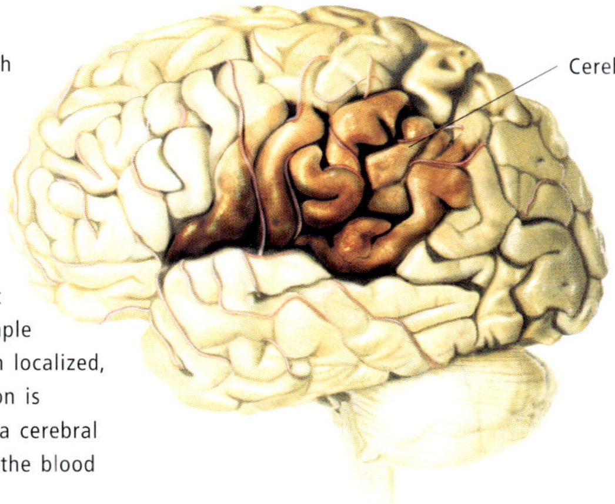

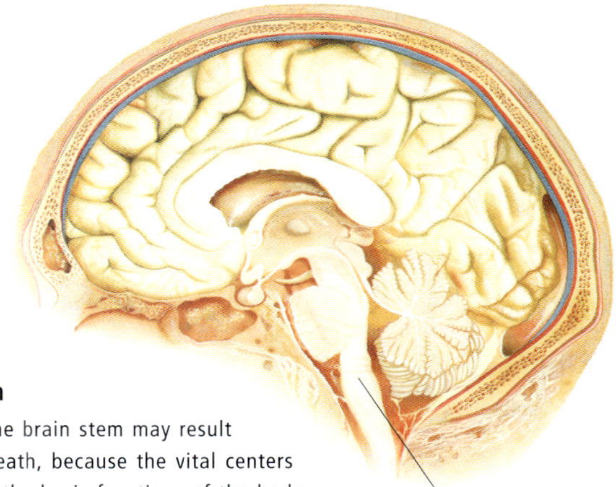

Brain stem

A stroke in the brain stem may result in coma or death, because the vital centers that regulate the basic functions of the body, such as breathing and blood pressure, are located here.

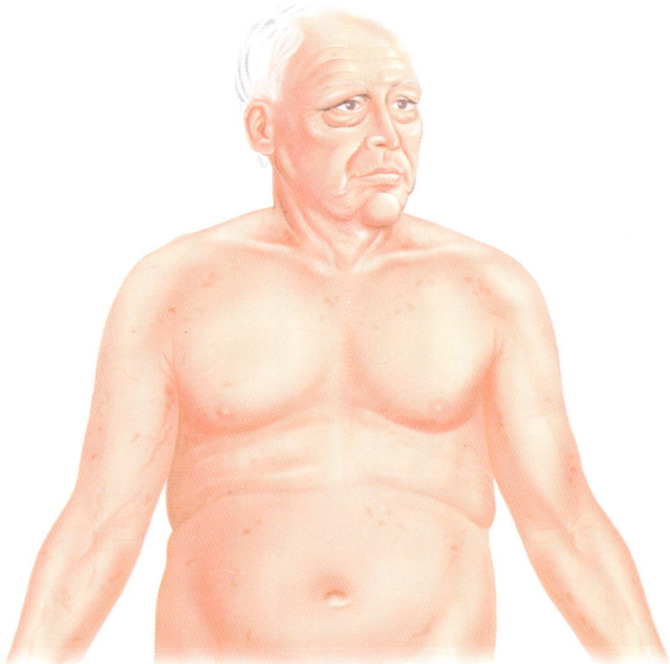

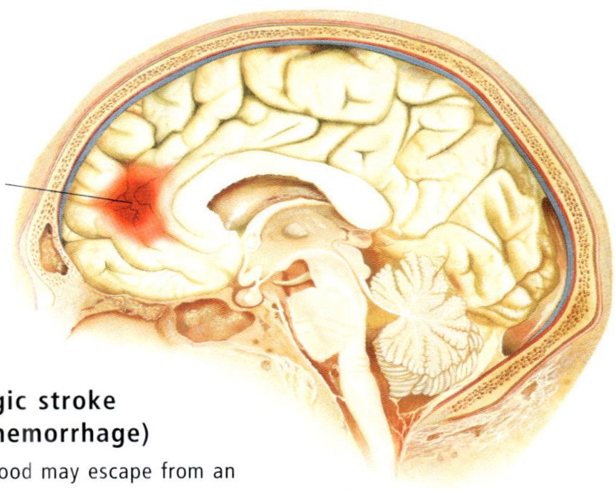

Hemorrhagic stroke (cerebral hemorrhage)

Sometimes blood may escape from an artery into the brain tissue (cerebral hemorrhage). The pressure of this bleeding destroys surrounding brain tissue, causing a stroke. Bleeding usually occurs at a section of artery that is damaged by arteriosclerosis. The diseased artery may weaken and balloon out, forming an aneurysm, which may burst. The risk of an aneurysm bursting is higher in people who suffer from hypertension (high blood pressure).

Stroke

Stroke is the term for loss of brain function arising from the death of brain tissue usually caused by arterial disease. It is one of the leading causes of death and illness in industrialized countries and particularly affects the elderly. Stroke usually cannot be cured, but preventive measures can be taken and, in some people, rehabilitation after a stroke may restore much of their former function.

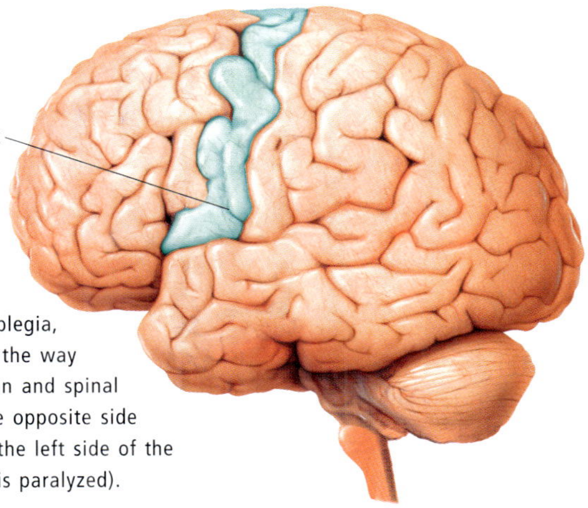

Hemiplegia

When a stroke damages the motor part of the cerebral cortex, the result is often hemiplegia, or paralysis of half of the body. Because of the way the nerve pathways are arranged in the brain and spinal cord, the part of the body affected is on the opposite side to the damaged part of the brain (i.e when the left side of the brain is affected, the right side of the body is paralyzed).

S

STRONGYLOIDIASIS

Strongyloidiasis is a widespread infection of humans by worms, occurring in the tropics. Microscopic worm larvae penetrate the skin and migrate through the lungs, where they may cause cough and shortness of breath. On reaching the intestine they multiply and are excreted in the stools. Diagnosis is suspected by blood eosinophilia and confirmed by microscopic examination of the stool.

SEE ALSO *Worms*

STUTTERING

Stuttering or stammering (dysphemia) is the most common and obvious type of disturbed speech. Every child will stutter at some time, as will many adults. The condition is characterized by hesitant or jerky speech and an inability to pronounce or join syllables. While experts are uncertain of the causes, it is found more in males than females and may be caused by a combination of genetic and emotional problems. In young children, stuttering can be a mechanism for the child to hold a place in the conversation while thinking of what to say and how to say it.

The time to seek help is when the child is embarrassed or worried about speaking, when the stuttering is pronounced and the child is getting stuck on words, or when there are physical signs of speech difficulty, such as tension in the neck or blinking. Parental support and cooperation are important. Some research suggests that stuttering is not really a problem and that those who stutter should seek occupations which allow them to stutter without feeling shame.

Treatment for stuttering may include medication, aimed at blocking excess dopamine activity in the brain, or behavioral therapy focusing on changing speech mechanisms.

SEE ALSO *Speech*

Subarachnoid hemorrhage

An aneurysm or the dilation of an intercranial artery may cause bleeding (hemorrhage) into the subarachnoid space.

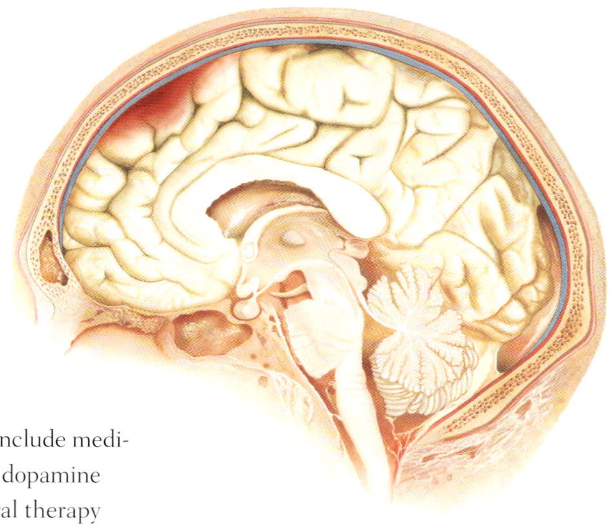

STYE

A stye is the inflammation of one or more sebaceous glands on or under the eyelid due to bacterial infection.

Styes occur near the roots of eyelashes and look like pimples or boils. These red, swollen lumps fill with pus over 1–2 days, causing pain, watering eyes and blurred vision. They are best left to burst on their own.

In the meantime, applying a warm, wet cloth for 10 minutes a few times each day may offer some relief. Antibiotics are used to treat persistent styes. Styes can be prevented by washing the hands before touching the eye area, particularly after treating acne and skin infections.

SEE ALSO *Eye, Eyelashes, Eyelid, Sebaceous glands*

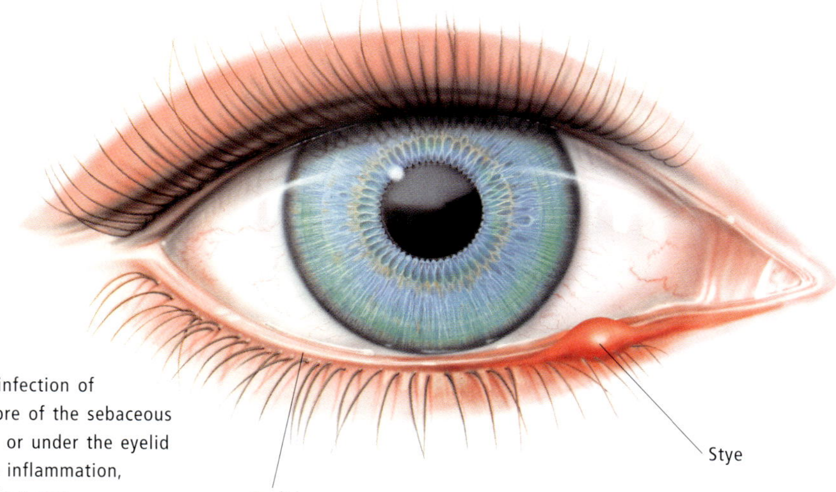

Stye

Bacterial infection of one or more of the sebaceous glands on or under the eyelid can cause inflammation, resulting in a stye.

SUBACUTE SCLEROSING PANENCEPHALITIS

A rare progressive disease, subacute sclerosing panencephalitis develops months or years after measles infection in childhood. It is thought to result from persistent infection of the central nervous system by altered forms of the measles virus. There is damage to nerve cells and to the protective covering (the myelin sheaths) of nerves, as well as inflammation in the brain. The sufferer develops seizures, spasticity and impaired mental function. Treatment can include physical therapy, occupational therapy, and drugs such as anticonvulsants and muscle relaxants.

SEE ALSO *Measles, Nerves, Nervous system*

SUBARACHNOID HEMORRHAGE

Subarachnoid hemorrhage is bleeding into the subarachnoid space over the surface of the brain. This occurs mostly from an aneurysm of an intracranial artery which weakens its wall. The bleeding results in sudden severe headache with vomiting and temporary unconsciousness. It is a surgical emergency which can have serious consequences such as coma or death.

SEE ALSO *Brain*

SUBCLAVIAN VEIN

The subclavian vein is a major vein draining the arm. It is a continuation of the axillary vein. It lies beneath the collar bone (clavicle), where it may be injured by fracture of that bone, or compressed by backwards pressure on the shoulder. It joins with the external and internal jugular veins, draining the superficial and deep tissues of the head and neck respectively, to form the brachiocephalic vein. Prior to its termination is the last valve which blood passes before reaching the heart.

SEE ALSO *Collar bone, Veins*

SUBDURAL HEMATOMA

Subdural hematoma is a blood clot on the surface of the brain, beneath its covering layer, the dura. It results from head injury, either from a direct blow or from sudden acceleration, as in whiplash injury. It may develop immediately (acute) or gradually (chronic), after injury.

The main sign of acute subdural hematoma is rapidly decreasing consciousness following head injury, together with enlargement of the pupil on the same side as the injury. This is a surgical emergency requiring immediate drainage of the hematoma. If drowsiness is more gradual, a CAT scan of the brain is performed to confirm diagnosis.

Chronic subdural hematoma is more likely to occur in the elderly or alcoholic person following minor head trauma. It may cause rapidly developing dementia associated with headache. Surgery is not always required for the chronic forms.

SEE ALSO *Brain*

SUDDEN INFANT DEATH SYNDROME

Sudden infant death sydrome (SIDS) is the unexpected and unexplained death of a baby while sleeping—it is also known as crib death or cot death. There are no symptoms or warning signs—the child is usually thought to be sleeping peacefully when death occurs and no struggle is evident. It is thought that respiratory and cardiac function are at the root of the syndrome, which generally affects infants between 2 weeks and 1 year of age, with most deaths occuring from 2–4 months.

While the exact cause has not been pinpointed, certain risk factors have been identified from research into the health, environment and family background of infants who have died from SIDS. For instance, it has been established that more male babies succumb to SIDS than females, and that most SIDS deaths occur in autumn and winter. Children with a greater risk of dying from SIDS include the following.

- Premature babies with low birth weight
- Children from multiple births
- Siblings of babies who have died from SIDS
- Babies with mothers who smoke or are drug dependent
- Babies with mothers under 20 years of age
- Children from pregnancies that are close together
- Children who live in overcrowded conditions
- Those whose mothers have had late, little or no prenatal care

Scientists have been researching a theory that brain abnormalities present at birth mean some children have an increased chance of dying from SIDS. A part of the brain is involved known as the arcuate nucleus of the medulla, which helps control breathing and waking during sleep. These abnormalities may stem from a lack of oxygen during pregnancy or exposure to toxic substances. Other theories have focussed on events after birth, such as excessive intake of carbon dioxide as a result of rebreathing exhaled air trapped in bedding. A metabolic disorder which prevents the proper processing of fatty acids is also thought to be a contributing factor.

Reducing the risk of SIDS

There is no definite prevention, though the following measures have been found to reduce the incidence of SIDS.

- Lying the baby on its back to sleep rather than its front. The side is also better than the front, with a rolled blanket placed near the front to stop the baby rolling forward.
- Placing the baby to sleep on a firm mattress without fluffy pillows, blankets or coverings, or soft surfaces such as sheepskins. Stuffed toys should be kept out of the crib.
- Ensuring that overheating does not occur; this may allow the baby to slip into too deep a sleep, and it may be difficult to arouse the baby. The room temperature should be comfortable and the baby should not be overdressed.
- Providing a smoke-free environment. Exposure to passive smoking is thought to double the risk of SIDS, and smoking during pregnancy to triple it by reducing the amount of oxygen available to the fetus.
- Breast feeding the baby, as this is thought to offer protection from infections.

If a baby is found to be not moving or breathing, cardiopulmonary resuscitation (CPR) should be started and an ambulance called immediately.

SEE ALSO *Infancy, Pregnancy, Smoking*

Subclavian vein

One of the major veins in the upper body, the subclavian vein lies beneath the collar bone. It carries blood from the arms towards to heart.

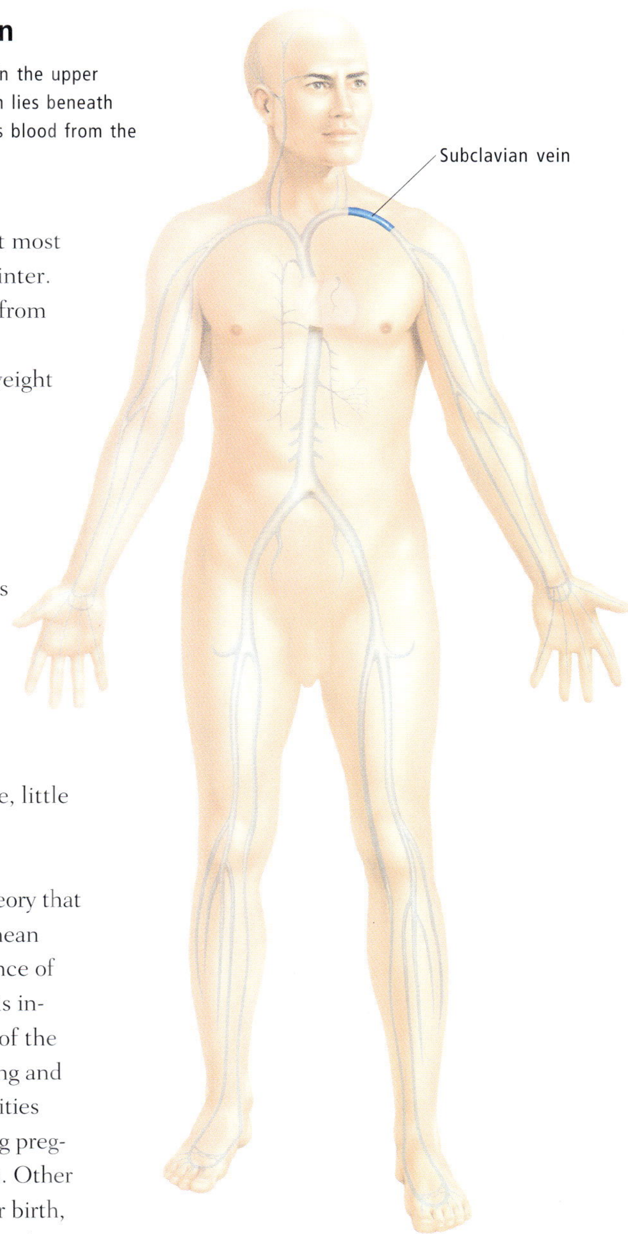

SUGAR

Sugar is a general term for simple sugars, organic compounds which, along with complex carbohydrates, are the main constituents of foods of plant origin. The main sources of the refined sugar (sucrose), used throughout the world as a sweetener, are sugar cane and sugar beet.

There are two kinds of sugars: monosaccharides, the simplest forms of carbohydrate, which include glucose, fructose and galactose; and disaccharides, made up of two monosaccharides, which include sucrose, lactose (found in milk) and maltose (formed from starch).

Digestion converts carbohydrates, except plant fiber or cellulose which humans cannot metabolize, into glucose to provide energy to cells. Any surplus becomes glycogen and is stored in the liver and muscles, for later use in metabolic processes; large oversupplies are stored as excess weight. Blood glucose levels, which normally rise after eating, are maintained at proper levels by the hormone insulin produced in the pancreas.

Diabetes is a disease caused by lack of insulin, leading to inability to control blood sugar levels. Hypoglycemia, or a low blood sugar level, can result in coma or death. Gluconeogenesis, the synthesis of blood sugar from the liver and kidneys, is an important part of recovery after strong physical exertion. There are several types of glycogen-storage diseases which interfere with the normal production of glycogen and result in enlarged liver and spleen.

SEE ALSO *Blood sugar tests, Diabetes, Hypoglycemia, Insulin, Nutrition, Pancreas*

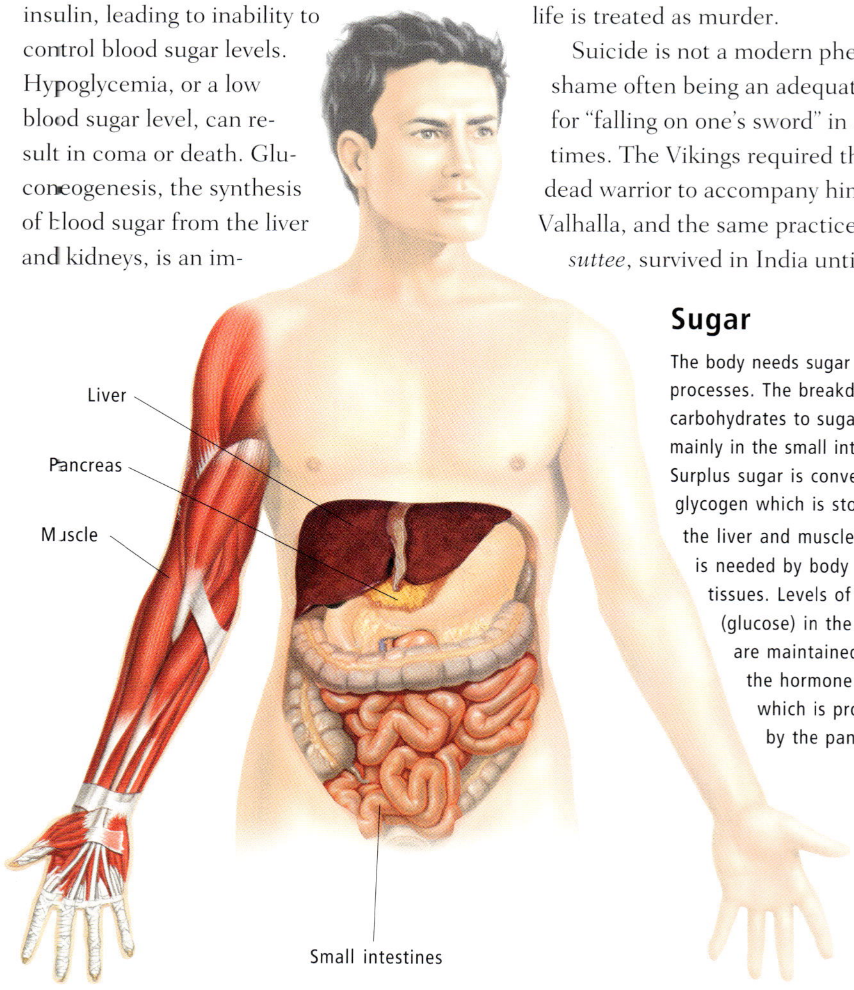

Sugar

The body needs sugar for metabolic processes. The breakdown of carbohydrates to sugars occurs mainly in the small intestine. Surplus sugar is converted to glycogen which is stored in the liver and muscles until it is needed by body cells and tissues. Levels of sugar (glucose) in the blood are maintained by the hormone insulin, which is produced by the pancreas.

SUICIDE

Suicide (literally "self-murder"), is the act of intentionally ending one's own life. Until the mid-twentieth century it was illegal in some countries, being seen as a crime against Church and State, a view formed in medieval times when laws were passed to deny suicides church services at burial. The Koran also forbids suicide. In more recent times, the stigma of an illegal act was often circumvented by sympathetic clergy, while coroners gave verdicts of death as "suicide, while of unsound mind", a way of sidestepping the issue by granting the deceased the indulgence of supposed insanity. Although in most countries suicide itself is no longer a crime, aiding a person to end his or her own life is treated as murder.

Suicide is not a modern phenomenon, shame often being an adequate reason for "falling on one's sword" in ancient times. The Vikings required the wife of a dead warrior to accompany him to Valhalla, and the same practice, known as *suttee*, survived in India until the early twentieth century. Japanese warriors practised *hara-kiri* or ritual self-disembowelment to avoid the humiliation of defeat or failure. Suicide has also been used as a protest, as seen in the self-immolation of Buddhist monks in Vietnam in the civil war prior to reunification, and as an act of defiance.

It is generally true that more men succeed in suicide than women, and that more women attempt suicide than men. In many industrialized nations, suicide ranks among the top 10 causes of death. In the USA, rates for suicide in late adolescence and early adulthood rose significantly over the last 50 years, the causes being cited as increased use of drugs, availability of guns, and a rising incidence of mental illness in that age group.

In everyday life, despair or extreme emotional suffering, mental illness, depression, hopelessness, the misery of a debilitating disease, stress and feelings of inability to cope can trigger a suicide attempt.

Depression is usually seen prior to suicide, as is a feeling of hopelessness, suicide becoming the alternative to an unbearable life. Social isolation is very common among suicide victims, who commonly live alone or lack the emotional support of family or close friends. The impact of a fatal suicide attempt is very great, often adding guilt and shame to the natural feelings of grief felt by relatives and friends at the death.

An unsuccessful suicide attempt may be seen as a cry for help, and may lead to an improvement in the situation, a result which may unconsciously have been hoped for and influenced the attempt.

People who are considering suicide often give warning signs. They may talk about dying, or express a wish to die. They may write about death in letters or essays, or depict it in drawings. There may be changes in behavior and attempts to tidy up affairs before death, such as giving away favorite things. If these signs are acted upon, by asking the person if they are thinking of suicide, the help of a trained counselor may prevent the suicide.

Suicide-prevention programs take the form of counseling, usually through phone-in services run by health-oriented charities and welfare organizations or through resident counselors in colleges and universities. But these services can help only when they are called, and the evidence is that women call more often than men, who are more at risk.

SEE ALSO *Death, Depression*

SUN EXPOSURE

Exposure to the sun is essential to human growth and development, but it can also have harmful effects. Exposure to sunlight in infancy and childhood aids production of vitamin D, vital for bone formation and growth, and prevents the development of rickets, a deficiency disease marked by soft and deformed bones. The harmful effects of over-exposure to sunlight include sunburn, premature ageing of the skin and formation of skin cancers.

Ultraviolet light

The sun emits ultraviolet radiation, which is classified by wavelength from the longest, UVA radiation, to UVB radiation, to UVC radiation. UVA penetrates the most through the atmosphere and causes long-term subcutaneous damage. UVB is partially blocked by the Earth's ozone layer and causes sunburn. UVC kills living organisms and is produced artificially for sterilization and, fortunately for life on Earth, is completely blocked by the ozone layer.

Seasonal affective disorder, or SAD, is a form of depression caused by lack of sunshine that commonly occurs in winter in the northern hemisphere and is treated with artificial light. Medical use of sunlight or natural ultraviolet light includes treatments for the chronic skin conditions psoriasis and vitiligo, which combine drug therapy with controlled sun exposure.

Sun damage

Exposure to sunlight stimulates cells called melanocytes to increase production of melanin, a dark pigment that colors the skin and protects deeper tissues from UV light. Exposure to direct sunlight for more than an hour or so will bring risks of sunburn, real tissue damage similar to any other burn.

Severe or frequent sunburn in childhood increases the risks of developing skin cancers (especially melanoma). Outdoor workers and others with a lifetime of sun exposure commonly develop squamous or basal cell carcinomas, most of which are treated by removal. Fair-skinned people or those with a history of severe childhood sunburn are at considerably higher risk of melanoma, an aggressive cancer which can spread very quickly through the body.

Sun exposure

Exposure to sunlight makes skin cells called melanocytes produce pigment (melanin), resulting in a suntan. Repeated exposure may make melanocytes produce pigment uncontrollably, which can lead to melanoma, a potentially life-threatening cancer.

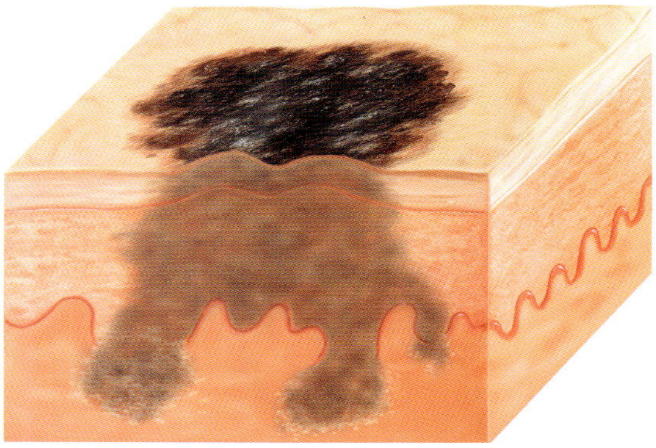

Symptoms of sunburn often appear as redness and pain, later with swelling or blistering and subsequent peeling of dead skin cells. A cool bath or applying cool compresses to the skin may soothe symptoms. Severe sunburn may require medical assistance. Sunstroke is a form of heatstroke brought on by sun exposure and caused by the inability to sweat sufficiently to reduce internal body temperature. Developing quickly, the condition causes heart rate and breathing to speed up; internal temperature may rise markedly, bringing disorientation and loss of consciousness and a risk of death. Looking directly into sunlight can harm the eyes, producing an inflammatory condition called flash keratoconjunctivitis. Extreme sensitivity to sunlight (photosensitivity), with a reaction after very brief exposure, affects sufferers of systemic lupus erythematosus and porphyria; it can also be a side effect of certain drugs, notably isotretinoin, used to treat acne. Sun spots are smooth dark brown spots on exposed skin formed from a concentration of melanocytes that commonly appear in middle and later life.

Sun protection

Sun protection is a sensible precaution for everyone and is particularly important for children. The most effective defense against sun exposure is to stay out of direct sunlight, particularly from late morning to early afternoon when the sun is at its strongest. Reflected sunlight from water or snow can also burn skin and cause eye damage. Protective clothing is a good second line of defense. Exposure to sun should be gradual, allowing the body time to produce melanin, a process which is fast for some and almost nonexistent in very fair-skinned people.

Sunscreen creams and lotions have a part to play in sun protection but are far less effective than shade or clothing because they may not be applied evenly or thickly enough to give their full potential protection, and they degrade with time and exposure to air and water.

SEE ALSO *Basal cell carcinoma, Melanoma, Photosensitivity, Seasonal affective disorder, Skin, Skin cancer, Squamous cell carcinoma, Ultraviolet therapy*

SWEAT GLANDS

Sweat glands are of two types: eccrine and apocrine. Both secrete a watery fluid—perspiration—onto the surface of the skin.

The eccrine sweat glands are distributed over the body, except on the lips and some parts of the genital regions. They are small tubular glands, opening at pores onto the surface of the skin. They can secrete large quantities of sweat, which cools the body by evaporation. The sweat glands are activated when the body becomes overheated (due to environmental conditions or exercise), and occasionally by emotions such as fear ("cold sweat").

The apocrine sweat glands are special sweat glands found in the axillary and pubic regions and in the areolae of the breasts. These tubular glands have a particularly wide lumen (internal cavity), which opens into hair follicles rather than directly onto the skin surface. They secrete an odorifer-

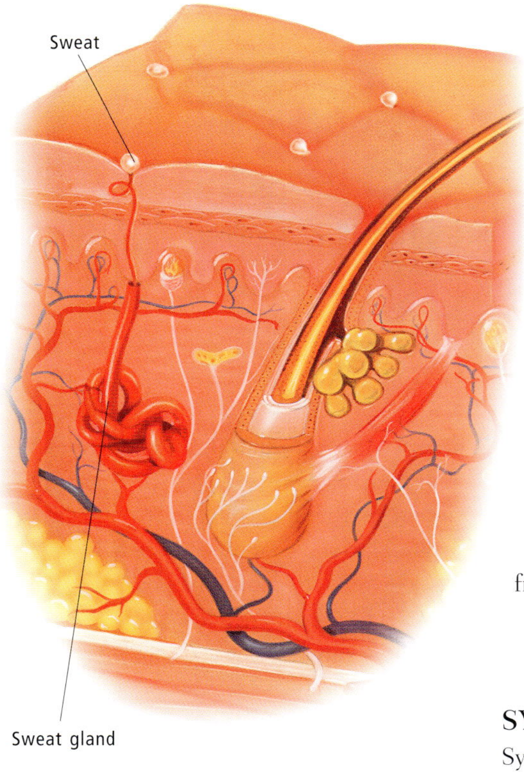

Sweat gland

Sweat glands are small tubular glands that open onto the surface of the skin. They secrete sweat (perspiration) to promote cooling.

ous secretion which probably acts as a pheromone for sexual attraction.

Body odor is determined primarily by sweat from both types of glands, and by interactions between bacteria and sweat, particularly the sweat produced by the apocrine glands.

SEE ALSO *Glands*

SWIMMER'S ITCH

Penetration of the skin by larvae of trematode worms of the *Schistosoma* genus (nonhuman schistosome cercariae) causes the skin infection swimmer's itch (also known as swamp itch, cutaneous schistosomiasis or schistosome dermatitis). The disease is contracted when swimming, as the worms are found in freshwater lakes in the USA, Canada, Europe and Asia.

SEE ALSO *Schistosomiasis, Worms*

SYDENHAM'S CHOREA

Chorea is a neurological disorder characterized by involuntary, purposeless, spasmodic movements of the body. The most common types of this disorder are Sydenham's (or rheumatic) chorea, once known as Saint Vitus' dance, and Huntington's disease. Sydenham's chorea occurs in 50 percent of children aged 5–15 who have had rheumatic fever and is more common in girls.

Triggered by emotional upset and episodes of crying, the spasms can range from mild to completely incapacitating. Attacks can last for several weeks and recurrence is frequent. Bed rest in a pleasant environment is the best treatment; some patients benefit from sedation and tranquilizers.

SEE ALSO *Huntington's disease*

SYMPATHOMIMETIC DRUGS

Sympathomimetic drugs are medications whose actions are similar to those of the hormone epinephrine (adrenaline). They work by mimicking the effects or stimulating the release of epinephrine or norepinephrine (noradrenaline). They are often used in the treatment of conditions such as asthma, shock and cardiac arrest. They are also used in over-the-counter preparations to relieve nasal congestion and allergic disorders, and to suppress appetite.

Side effects include rapid heart rate (tachycardia), high blood pressure, increased body temperature, agitation, cardiac arrhythmias and seizures. Amphetamines and ephedrine are both sympathomimetic drugs. An overdose can be fatal.

SEE ALSO *Amphetamines, Epinephrine, Nervous system*

SYNAPSES

Synapses are junctions between nerve cells (neurons), where impulses are passed from one cell to another, or from one cell to an effector organ. Synapses usually occur between the axon terminal of one cell and a dendrite or cell body of another. The neural impulse is carried across the synapse, in one direction only, by chemical molecules known as a neurotransmitters. Common neurotransmitters include glutamate and serotonin. Low levels of neurotransmitters or disruption of their action can cause neurological disorders.

SEE ALSO *Nerves, Nervous system, Neurons*

SYNOVIAL FLUID

The fluid contained within synovial joints lubricates the joint surfaces, helps to reduce friction and provides nourishment for the joint cartilage. It is normally a clear, pale yellow, viscous fluid, and is only present in small amounts. Its composition is similar to blood plasma except that it contains hyaluronate and lubricin, which are essential for viscosity and lubrication. Monocytes, lymphocytes and macrophages are also found in low numbers in the synovial fluid.

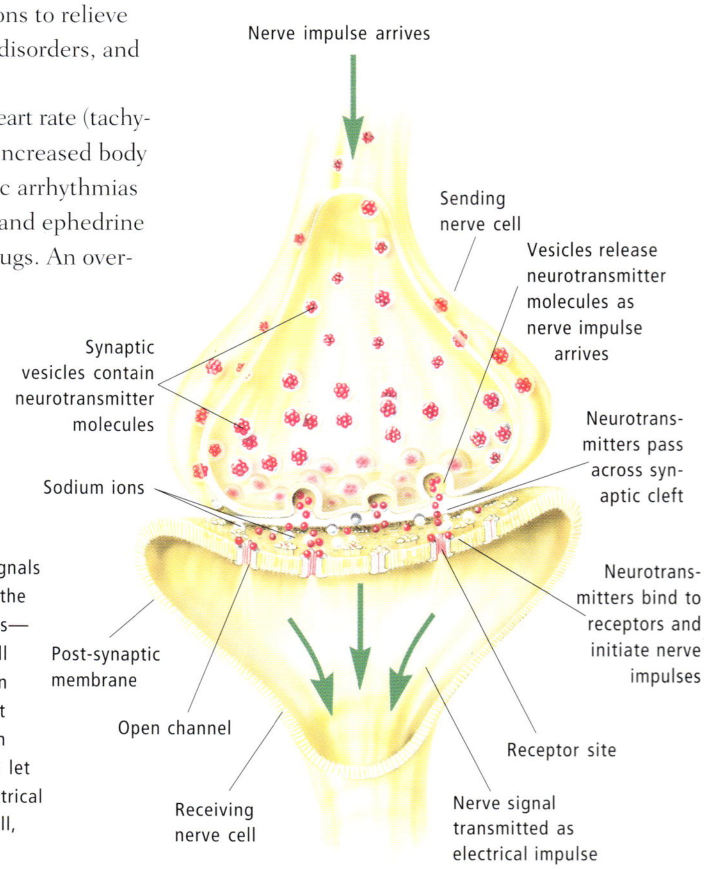

Synapses

A synapse is the junction between two nerve cells (neurons). Nerve signals are passed from cell to cell across the synaptic cleft by chemical molecules—neurotransmitters. The receiving cell has receptor sites specific to certain neurotransmitters. When the correct transmitters lock in place they open channels in the nerve membrane to let in sodium ions. This causes an electrical change which fires the receiving cell, passing on the nerve signal.

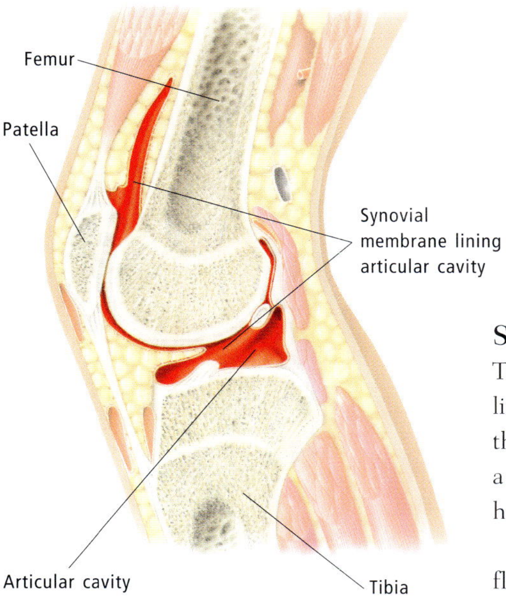

Synovial membrane

This type of membrane lines the non-cartilage areas of synovial joints such as the knee. Specialized cells in the membrane produce fluid that is critical for the lubrication of joint surfaces and the nourishment of cartilage.

Synovial fluid may be aspirated from a joint and checked for the presence of red blood cells, inflammatory cells, infectious agents and crystals (for example, gout).

SEE ALSO *Joints*

SYNOVIAL MEMBRANE

Synovial membrane is found in synovial joints, bursae and tendon sheaths. It lines the non-cartilage areas of synovial joints, such as the joint capsule and exposed bony surfaces. The membrane is very vascular. It appears pink, smooth and shiny and may exhibit folds and fringes. Accumulations of fat are found in the membrane in some joints (for example, fat pads in the knee and elbow joints).

Specialized cells of the membrane (synoviocytes) both produce and reabsorb synovial fluid, a fluid that is critical to the lubrication of joint surfaces, and nourishment of the cartilage. These cells also remove debris from the joint cavity and may initiate an immune response to foreign material in the joint.

SEE ALSO *Joints, Synovial fluid*

SYNOVITIS

The cavities of freely movable joints are lined with synovial membranes, smooth, thin sheets of connective tissue that secrete a nourishing lubricant (synovial fluid) which helps bones move freely over other bones.

When a synovial membrane becomes inflamed, the condition is called synovitis. It can often cause an entire joint to become swollen and tender. Synovitis can occur with a bacterial infection, follow an irritation or trauma to the site such as a sprain or fracture, or be a complication of diseases such as gout and rheumatoid arthritis.

Treatment depends on the cause. In many cases time and rest are sufficient but severe or chronic synovitis may need treatment with analgesics or anti-inflammatory drugs.

SEE ALSO *Joints, Synovial fluid, Synovial membrane*

SYPHILIS

Syphilis is a serious, sexually transmitted diseased caused by the organism *Treponema pallidum*. Clinically it can resemble many other diseases, including gonorrhea. A disease that progresses through three stages, each separated by months and even years, cases of infection are currently on the rise in many parts of the world, including the USA.

Syphilis begins with a lesion, a painless, circular chancre that may appear on the lips, mouth, tongue, nipple, rectum or genitalia; nearby lymph nodes may enlarge but are not painful. The chancre heals and weeks, or even months later, the secondary symptoms appear when microbes spread to organs and tissues in the body. Non-painful skin rashes appear and disappear, sometimes in association with fever, headache and hair loss. Tertiary lesions, which can appear years later, may destroy normal skin, bone and joints by ulceration.

Tertiary syphilis also affects the nervous system. It can take three forms: cardiovascular syphilis, which affects the heart severely; neurosyphilis, which affects the brain and the nervous system; and benign late syphilis.

Difficult to diagnose (a series of blood tests is often necessary), syphilis can be treated with penicillin, or an alternative for those allergic to this drug. Anyone who has sex with a person known to have syphilis, or someone known to have another sexually transmitted disease, should be tested for syphilis. It can pass into the fetus at any stage of pregnancy and cause growth deformities in the baby or stillbirth; this can be prevented by treatment early in the pregnancy.

SEE ALSO *Sexually transmitted diseases*

Syphilis

A serious sexually transmitted disease caused by the bacteria *Treponema pallidum*, syphilis may take years to develop fully. In its final stages, the disease affects the nervous system.

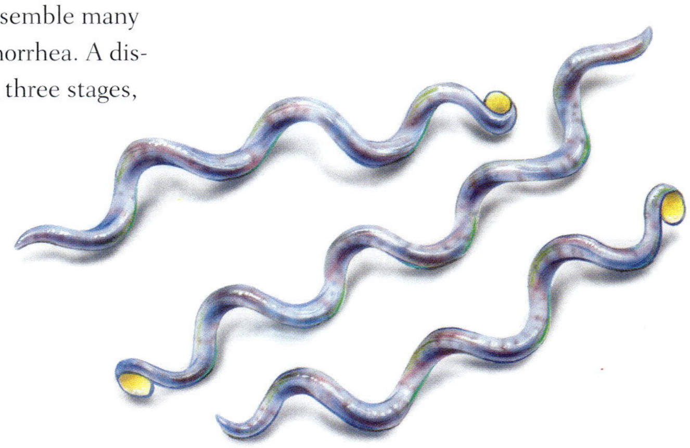

S

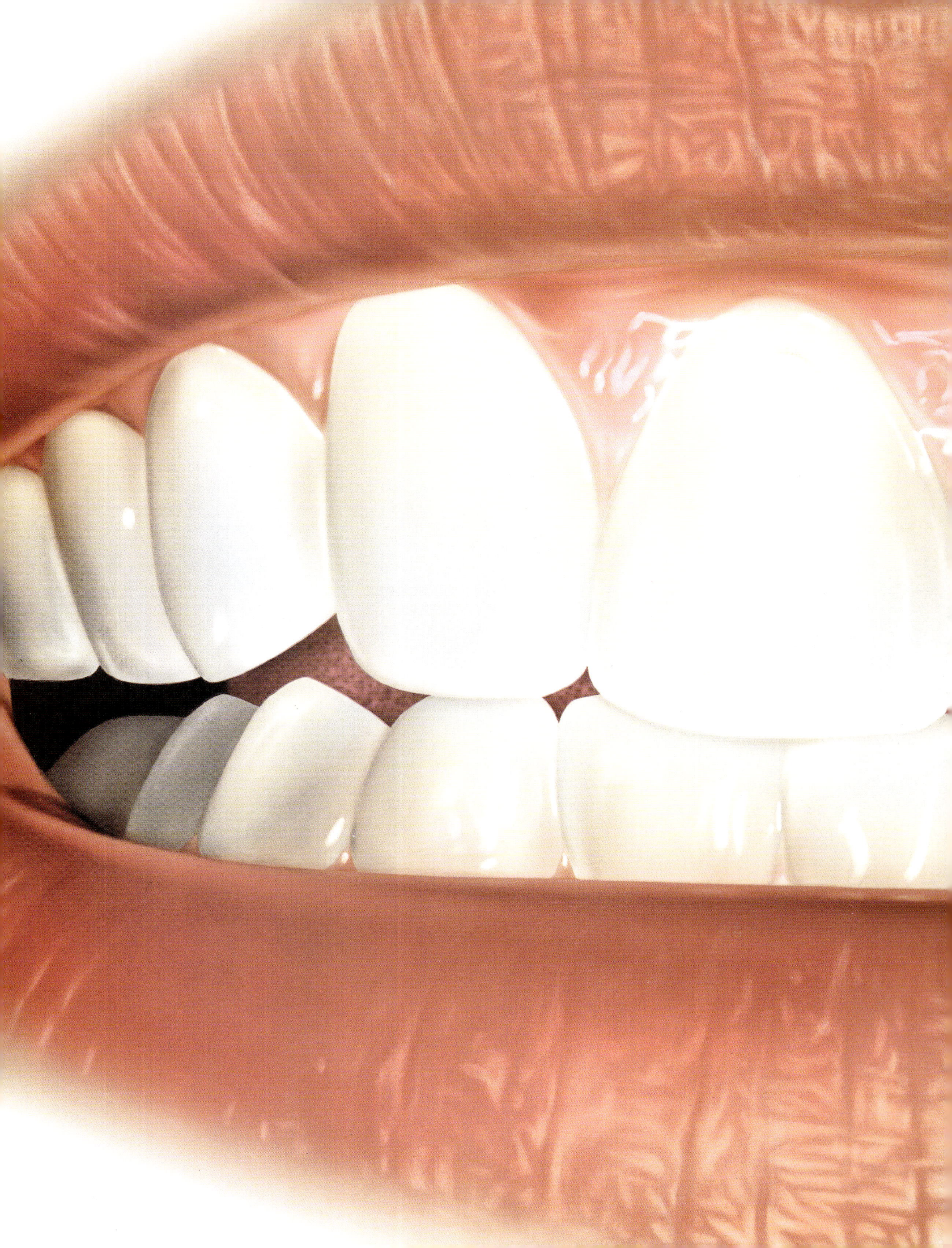

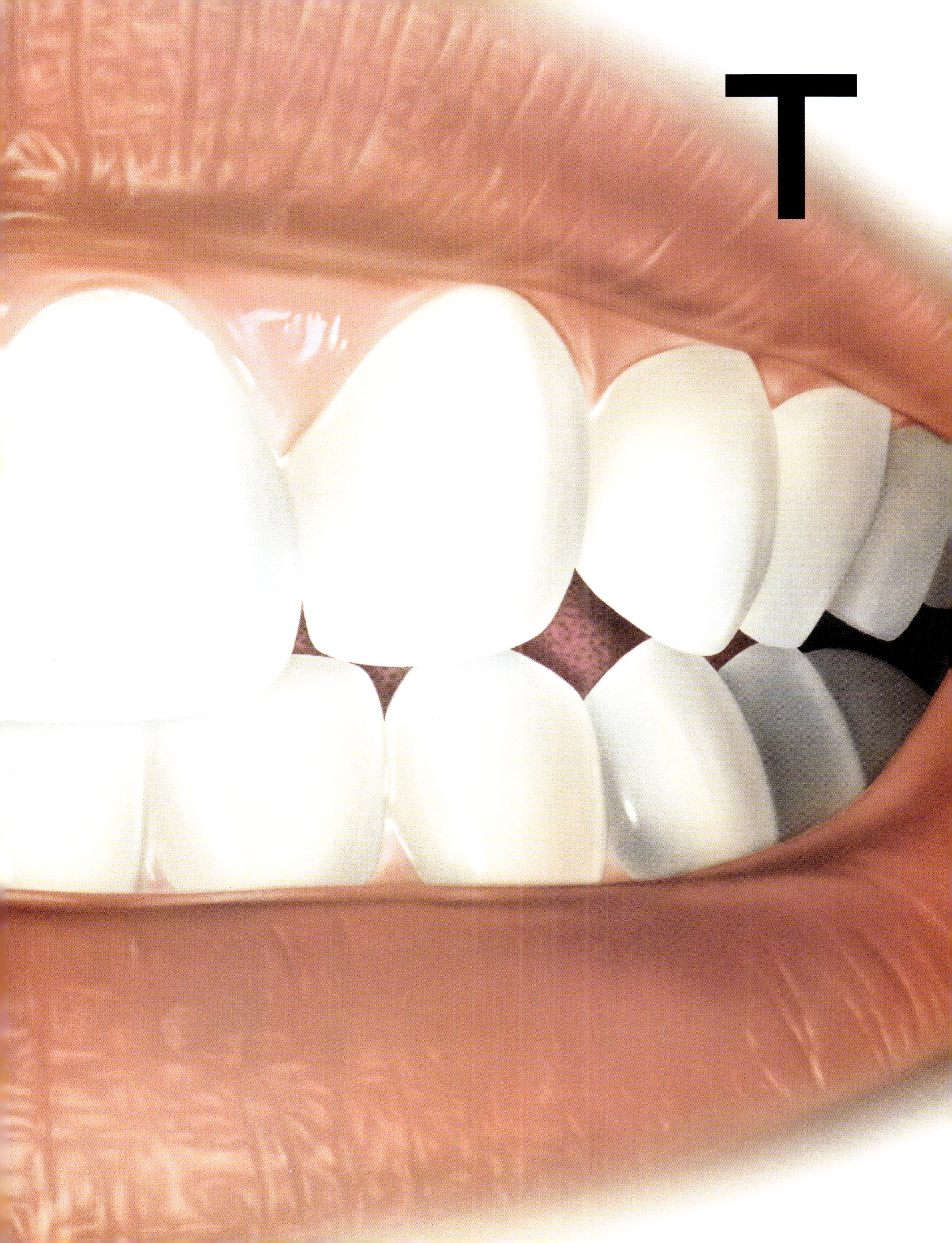
T

T CELLS

Lymphocytes are the white blood cells responsible for the body's ability to distinguish and react to foreign substances, such as bacteria, viruses and other microbes. They are part of the body's line of defense against invaders.

Lymphocytes are small rounded cells that originate in the bone marrow from primordial cells (called stem cells). Once they have matured, they pass into the bloodstream where they travel to areas of lymphoid tissue, such as the spleen, lymph nodes, tonsils, and the lining of the intestines.

Some lymphocytes enter the thymus gland, where they multiply and turn into special types of lymphocytes called thymus-derived, or "T", cells. These T cells rejoin the bloodstream and circulate to lymph tissue around the body. There, their function is to patrol the body for bacterial or viral invaders by means of receptors on their cell surfaces which recognize foreign molecules. Once identified, the T cells multiply, attack and destroy the foreign cells. This process is known as "cell-mediated" immunity. T cells are also involved in regulating B lymphocytes. These are another type of white blood cell which produce antibodies to foreign molecules in the immune process known as "humoral" immunity.

Progress of HIV (human immmunodeficiency virus) infection can be monitored by measuring the sufferer's T cell count (more specifically the T4 cell count) in the blood at regular intervals. T4 cells (also known as CD4 or T helper cells) play a specific role in the body's fight against infection and cancer.

In HIV infection, T4 cells are invaded and destroyed; a fall in blood T4 numbers gives an indication of how far the infection has progressed. The T4 cell count usually drops sharply in the late stages of AIDS; serious opportunistic infections develop at counts of below 200 cells per mm^3.

SEE ALSO *AIDS, HIV, Immunity, Thymus*

T cell production

T cells take about 3 weeks to develop in the thymus and are then released into the bloodstream.

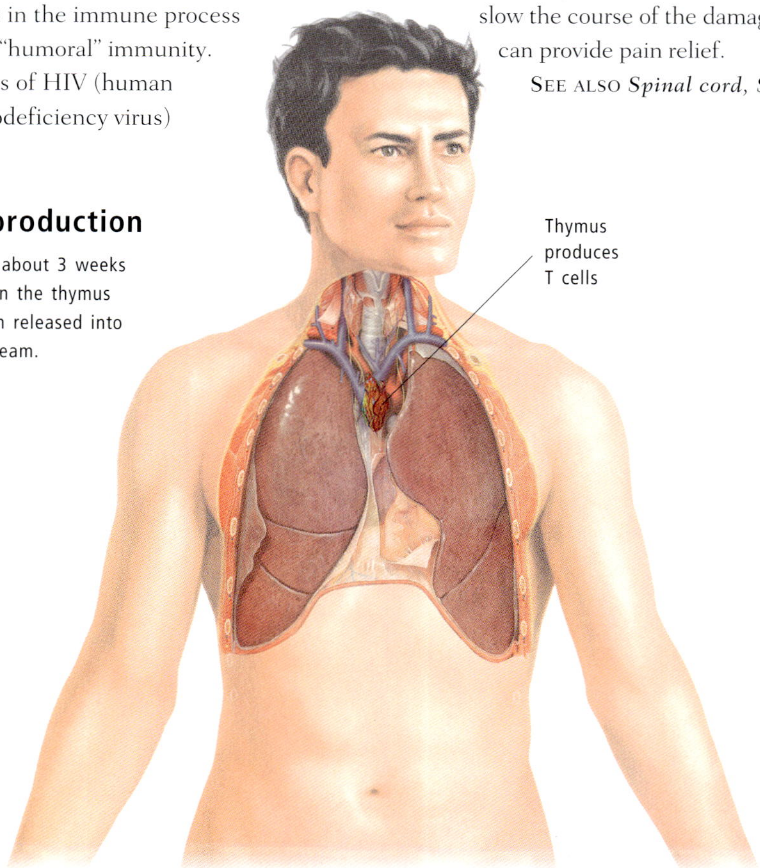

TABES DORSALIS

Tabes dorsalis is one of the later effects of syphilis, occurring 20–30 years after the initial infection. It involves damage to the part of the spinal cord involved in sensory inputs—the posterior (dorsal) roots and columns. The damage causes sudden sharp pains, usually starting in the legs. The sense of limb position is affected so that there is difficulty walking, especially in the dark. Tendon reflexes are also lost and there may be bladder and bowel incontinence, and impotence. There is no cure, but medication may slow the course of the damage and can provide pain relief.

SEE ALSO *Spinal cord, Syphilis*

TACHYCARDIA, PAROXYSMAL

Paroxysmal tachycardia refers to episodes of rapid heart rate (140–220 beats per minute). It may arise from problems with either the atria or ventricles in the heart. In both types the patient complains of palpitations, the sensation of a rapidly beating heart fluttering in the chest. The ventricular type is more serious, and is often a complication of severe heart disease. Ventricular tachycardia often causes chest pain and breathlessness: these symptoms are less common in atrial tachycardia. The two types can be distinguished by an electrocardiogram (EKG) and treated with appropriate antiarrhythmic medication.

SEE ALSO *Heart, Palpitations, Ventricle*

T'AI CHI CHU'AN

T'ai chi chu'an, which translates as "supreme ultimate power", is a traditional Chinese form of moving meditation which grew out of its predecessor *qi gong*. Combining elements of Chinese martial arts with Taoist breathing practices, t'ai chi's exercises incorporate mental discipline and creative visualization with a focus on deep, rhythmic breathing.

T'ai chi works through a choreographed sequence of movements, where every motion is coordinated with the breath. The movements often draw inspiration from nature with names like "embrace tiger, return to mountain", and practitioners are encouraged to visualize themselves embodying

T cell

T cells are a type of white blood cell that play an important role in the body's immune system. In healthy people they circulate around the body, identifying and destroying invading bacteria and viruses.

these images. Each sequence of movements is known as a "form", and can vary from 5–60 minutes in length.

There are a number of different forms and styles of t'ai chi which are taught throughout China and increasingly in the West. The main aims of t'ai chi are to develop the *chi* (life force) in the body, relax the mind, restore balance, strengthen muscles, slow down the ageing process and reconnect the body with mind and nature. It can be learnt by people of all ages and levels of fitness and is thought to be useful in treating stress-related illnesses, as well as back pain and digestive and respiratory disorders.

SEE ALSO *Qi gong*

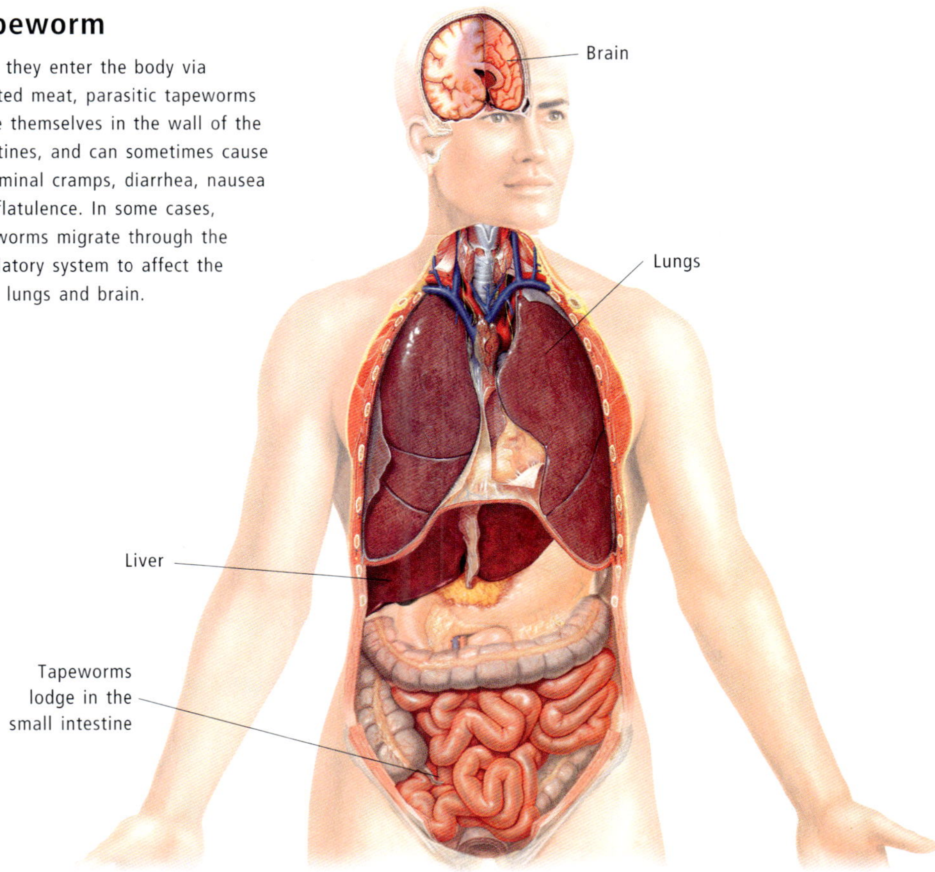

Tapeworm

After they enter the body via infested meat, parasitic tapeworms lodge themselves in the wall of the intestines, and can sometimes cause abdominal cramps, diarrhea, nausea and flatulence. In some cases, tapeworms migrate through the circulatory system to affect the liver, lungs and brain.

TAPEWORM

Parasitic tapeworms, members of a group of parasitic flatworms, can infect the intestinal tract. The condition is not contagious. Most sufferers have no symptoms; some people, however, may experience pain in the upper abdomen, diarrhea, unexplained weight loss or symptoms of anemia. Bowel movements will contain worms and worm eggs.

Tapeworm infestation results from eating infected or improperly cooked beef, pork or fish containing encysted larvae. It is most common in Africa, the Middle East, Eastern Europe and South America. A drug may be prescribed to kill the parasite. Hygiene before eating is important, as well as avoiding food which could be infected. Proper cooking provides the most certain protection.

SEE ALSO *Worms*

TARDIVE DYSKINESIA

Tardive dyskinesia is a side effect of antipsychotic drugs (neuroleptics), such as those used in the treatment of schizophrenia. The symptoms are involuntary and abnormal movements of the mouth and tongue, such as lip smacking and grimacing, which interfere with talking and swallowing, as well as writhing movements, which may continue during sleep. This neurological disorder may subside when drugs are withdrawn or may continue indefinitely. Prevention is best achieved by minimizing dosage and duration of drug intake, and close observation for early detection of symptoms.

SEE ALSO *Antipsychotics, Schizophrenia*

TARTAR

Tartar (dental calculus or dental plaque) is a hard yellowish film composed of calcium and food particles which is deposited on the teeth by the saliva. Found mostly at the line where the gum and tooth meet, and behind the lower front teeth and sides of the back teeth, it is not in itself responsible for tooth decay; rather it is the bacteria which lodge behind it that cause both decay and gum disease. Thorough brushing, preferably with an electric toothbrush, is essential to prevent build-up of tartar. Deposits should be removed regularly by a dentist.

SEE ALSO *Gums, Teeth*

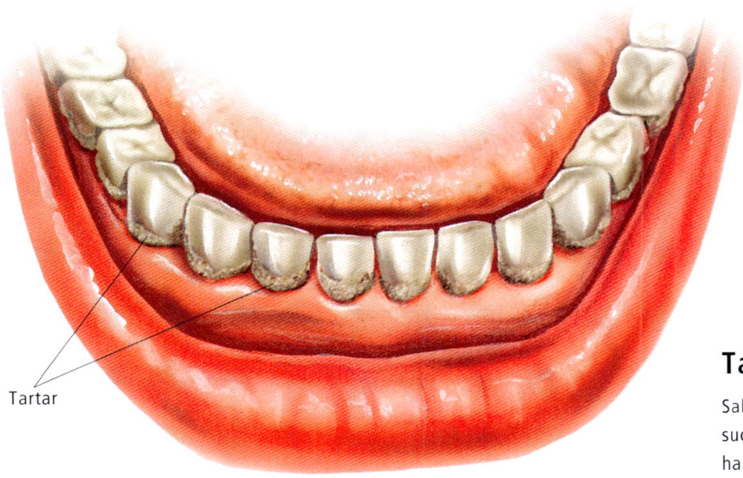

Tartar

Saliva, scraps of food and other material such as calcium carbonate form tartar, a hard, yellow deposit on the teeth.

TASTE

Taste, also known as gustation, is one of the five special senses. The organs of taste are the taste buds, specialized receptors made up of small clusters of cells called papillae, which are located on the surface and sides of the tongue, the roof of the mouth, and the entrance to the pharynx. At the top of each taste bud there is an opening called the taste pore. In order for food to be tasted it must be dissolved in a watery solution like saliva so that it can activate the receptors. Each person has 2,000–5,000 individual taste buds (with women having more than men). The taste buds are capable of discerning among the four basic taste sensations: sweetness, sourness, saltiness and bitterness.

Historically, it was believed that each bud could only taste one type of taste—for example, those at the tip of the tongue were thought to detect sweetness, whereas those on the sides of the tongue would detect saltiness and sourness. Researchers now believe, however, that all taste buds are capable of detecting multiple combinations of the four basic taste types. Nevertheless, different areas of the tongue are not equally sensitive to all four tastes. The back of the tongue is more sensitive to bitter, the sides of the tongue to sour, the tip to sweet, and the tip and the sides to salt. Taste can be tested by applying a salty or sweet solution to the front two-thirds of the tongue.

The exact mechanism whereby a taste bud detects a particular taste is poorly understood. However, it is thought that when a food particle is dissolved in saliva and comes into contact with the taste bud, it causes a chemical reaction within the bud. The taste bud then sends a nerve impulse via a nerve fiber attached to the base of the bud, which joins nerve impulses from other taste buds and travels via the cranial nerves to the brain.

Three different cranial nerves are involved in relaying taste: the facial nerve relays taste impulses from the front two-thirds of the tongue, the glossopharyngeal nerve supplies the back of the tongue and the vagus nerve supplies taste buds in the throat. These impulses are then relayed through nerve pathways in the brain stem and the thalamus and thence to a taste-receiving area in the anterior cerebral cortex where they are experienced as a particular taste.

The taste fibers follow a complicated route. The taste fibers of the facial nerve are distibuted to taste buds in the front two-thirds of the tongue, predominantly along the lateral borders. The taste fibers travel with the lingual nerve but cross to the facial nerve in the chorda tympani, so that taste is impaired if the facial nerve is damaged above this junction with the chorda tympani (as is often the case in Bell's palsy). These fibers enter the brain stem in the sensory root of the facial nerve (nervus intermedius). The fibers are joined by taste fibers from the glossopharyngeal and vagus nerves and terminate in the nucleus of the tractus solitarius. The part of this nucleus that receives taste fibers is often called the gustatory nucleus. Fibers ascend from here to reach the thalamus. Fibers then ascend from the thalamus to the cortical area for taste which is located at the lower end of the sensory cortex in the parietal lobe. The taste area is adjacent to the sensory area of the cortex for the tongue and pharynx.

The taste fibers of the glossopharyngeal nerve are distributed to taste buds in the back third of the tongue and the pharynx while the taste fibers of the vagus only supply the epiglottis. The vagal taste fibers are relatively unimportant because few persist into adult life. The vagal and glossopharyngeal fibers terminate in the gustatory nucleus. The fibers then ascend to the cortex from the gustatory nucleus in the same way as described above for the facial nerve.

Our state of consciousness, our cultural conditioning, our past experiences of taste and, in particular, the sense of smell, are all important in how we finally perceive a particular taste. About 80 percent of what we experience as taste is actually due to smell.

Taste abnormalities can be caused by conditions that affect the tongue and throat, the nasal passages, or the nerve pathways and brain. Conditions that can attenuate the sense of taste include the common cold, nasal infections, influenza, viral pharyngitis, mouth dryness, ageing (taste buds tend to diminish in number with age) and heavy smoking (which tends to dry the mouth).

SEE ALSO *Nervous system, Saliva, Senses, Smell, Tongue*

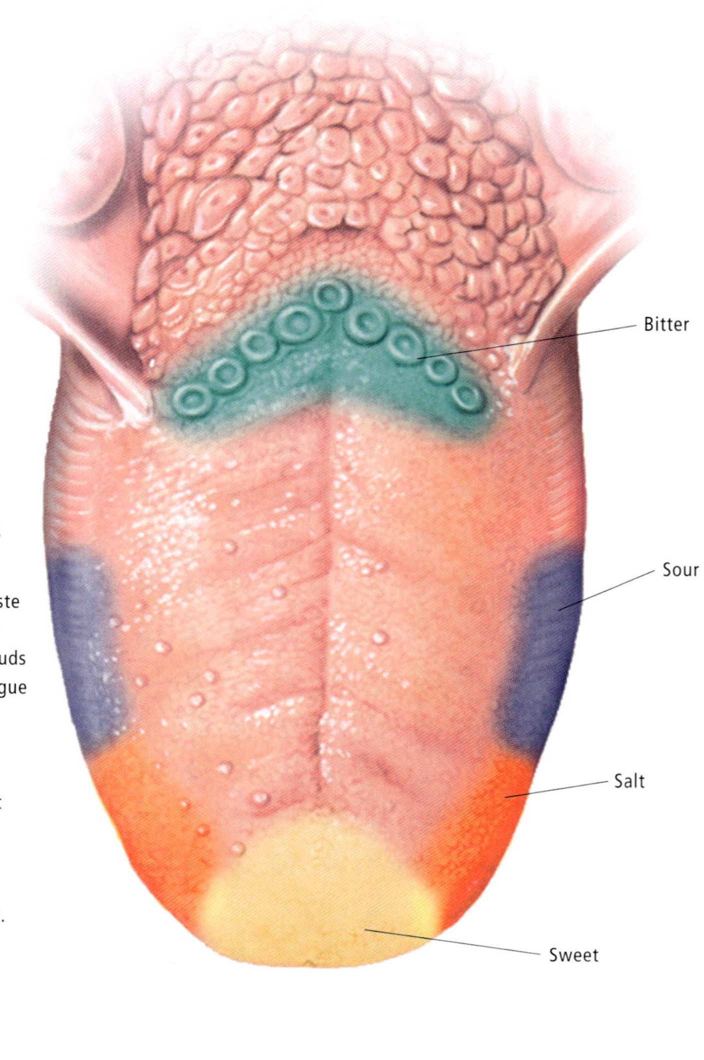

Tongue zones

There are four distinct tastes registered by taste buds: sweet, salt, sour and bitter. The taste buds at the front of the tongue are most sensitive to sweet and salty foods, the ones at the sides of the tongue are most sensitive to any sour taste, and bitterness is best registered at the back of the tongue.

T

Taste

Nerve stimulation

Three cranial nerves that lead directly to the brain from different parts of the head and neck are involved in our sense of taste.

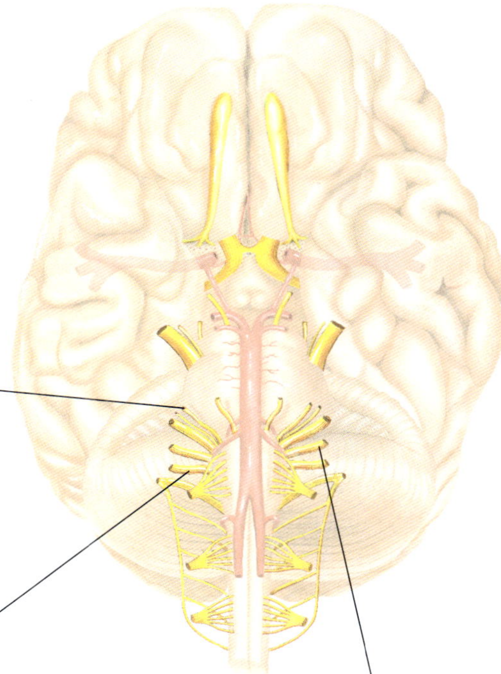

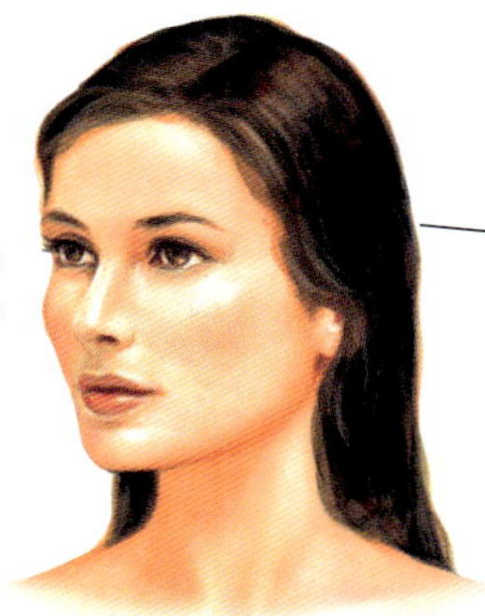

The facial nerve (cranial nerve VII) is responsible for the sensation of taste in the front part of the tongue

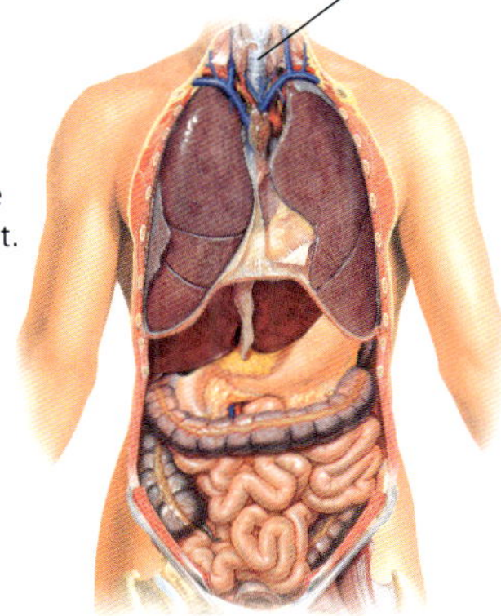

The vagus nerve (cranial nerve X) supplies the taste buds in the throat.

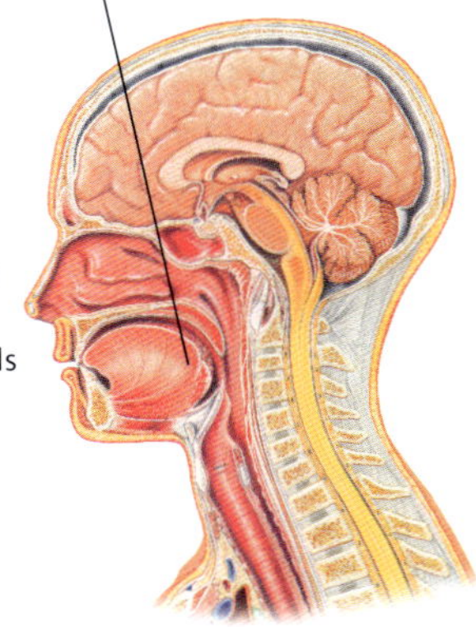

The glossopharyngeal nerve (cranial nerve IX) relays taste signals from the back part of the tongue

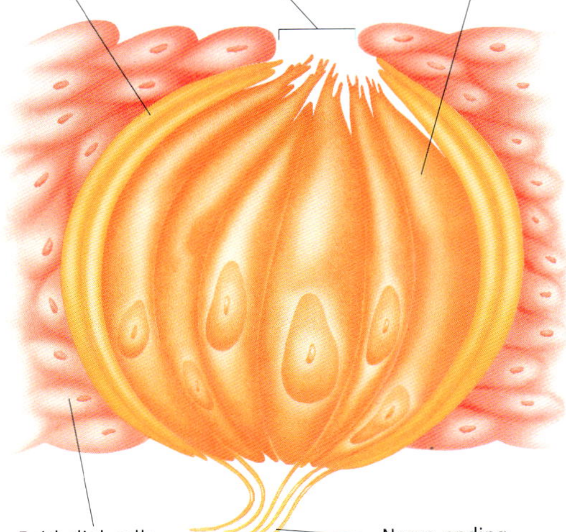

Taste buds

Taste buds are packed together in groups at various places on the tongue. These bundles of cells are sensitive to sweet, salty, bitter and sour flavors. Substances must be dissolved in a watery solution like saliva in order to activate the taste buds.

Taste pathways

Taste buds at the front and back of the tongue and in the throat send nerve impulses via the cranial nerves to the medulla in the brain stem. From here, the information passes to the thalamus and on to taste-receiving areas in the parietal lobe of the cerebral cortex where the taste is identified. The olfactory organs provide additional information vital for interpreting and appreciating different tastes.

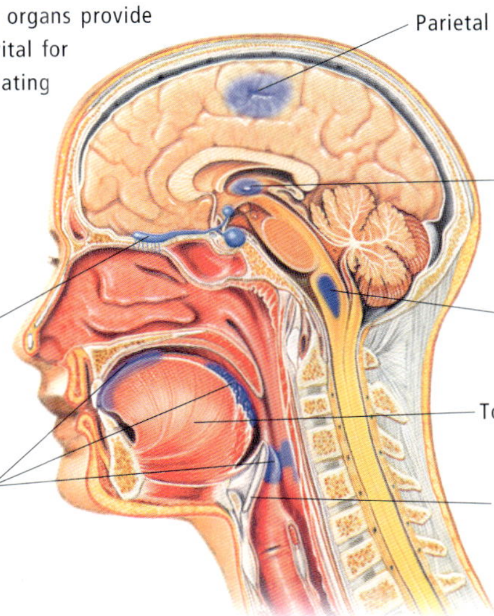

TATTOOING

A tattoo is a permanent pattern made on the body by introducing pigment into the dermis layer of the skin. Practised in most parts of the world for many centuries, tattooing is thought by some societies to provide protection against misfortune, and in others is seen as an indication of status or as signifying membership of a group. Tattoos may also be thought of as works of art. They have also been used to brand slaves and criminals and to identify prisoners.

It is important that tattooing be done under sterile conditions, as non-sterile needles can transmit HIV and hepatitis. Some people develop allergies to the dyes used.

Removing a tattoo is not a simple procedure; it is best to consult an experienced plastic surgeon. Every method of removal leaves at least a faint blemish on the skin, the amount of scarring depending on the age, size and depth of the tattoo and the colors used to make it. Covering one tattoo with another has been found to increase the risk of scarring when removal is attempted. Surgical removal, by cutting out the tattoo, works best with small tattoos. Dermabrasion, literally "sanding off" the tattoo, generally causes more bleeding than other methods. Lasers can also be used, but this method usually requires a number of treatments.

SEE ALSO *Hepatitis, HIV, Skin*

TAY-SACHS DISEASE

Tay-Sachs disease (TSD) is a rare genetic disorder affecting chiefly Ashkenazi Jews, Cajun communities and French Canadians. It produces progressive deterioration of the brain and central nervous system.

Afflicted babies initially appear normal, but start to decline mentally and physically at about 6 months, rapidly becoming lethargic and unresponsive. They are unable to produce the enzyme hexosaminidase A (hex A) whose function is to break down a certain type of lipid (fat); this fat accumulates in the brain cells, causing cell death and a gradual failure of the central nervous system. A variant of the disease occurs when the enzyme deficiency appears around 2 years of age.

Both forms of TSD are untreatable and invariably fatal; most of those afflicted die before the age of 5. The presence of the defective gene can be detected by a blood test measuring the level of the enzyme hex A, allowing screening and genetic counseling of potential carriers.

SEE ALSO *Congenital abnormalities, Genes, Genetic counseling*

TEETH

Teeth are calcified bonelike structures in both jaws whose role is to chew food, aid with speech and influence the shape of the face. The crown of the tooth, that part above the gum line, is covered with enamel, which is the hardest substance in the body. Under the enamel is dentine, slightly softer, which makes up the main part of the tooth. The dentine below the gum line is covered with cementum, a hard bony substance covering the roots of the teeth. Dentine is a sensitive tissue, with millions of tubules running into the central pulp or nerve, which runs from the tip of the root into the center of the tooth. The cementum is surrounded by the periodontal ligament, which contains the fibers that anchor the tooth in the bone of the gum.

Humans develop two sets of teeth in a normal lifetime. The first set, 20 in number, are known as the deciduous, primary or baby teeth. The secondary or permanent set, containing 32 teeth, begins to replace the first set around the age of 7 years; there are 16 teeth in each jaw.

There are different types of teeth. The incisors, with sharp edges for biting, are at the front of the mouth; next to them, the canines have sharp points to tear food; at the back of the mouth the molars, together with the premolars which only appear in the second set of teeth, are used to grind food.

A baby is born with the teeth already developing in the jaws. Occasionally a baby is born with some teeth already apparent. In most babies the teeth begin to erupt between the ages of 5 months and 1 year; the average age for the appearance of the first four front teeth is 7 months. It takes nearly 20 years for the complete set of permanent teeth to be established, the final set of molars (often called "wisdom teeth") erupting usually in late adolescence.

Care of the teeth

Good nutrition helps to ensure healthy teeth. Reducing the number of snacks consumed between meals reduces the amount of tooth decay (dental caries). Every time food is consumed the teeth are attacked by lactic acid, formed by the action of bacteria on carbohydrates. Other factors which lead to the development of tooth decay are inherited susceptibility (genetic make-up is partly responsible for tooth structure); the amount and frequency of consumption of fermentable sugars (carbohydrates); the presence of oral microorganisms; the flow of saliva; dental hygiene; factors in food working against decay; and fluoride.

Tooth care can help to prevent problems. From the time the first teeth appear they need to be cleaned, at first with a clean wet cloth, later with a soft baby toothbrush. A baby should never fall asleep with milk or any other fluid except water in the mouth; once the child is eating family foods, sticky, chewy foods should be avoided.

By the time a child reaches adolescence, teeth should be cleaned twice a day with fluoride toothpaste, flossed at least once a day, smoking and chewing tobacco should be avoided, the correct headgear, including mouthguards, should be used while playing sport and there should be regular dental check-ups. Adults need to continue these habits and to seek professional help when teeth problems arise.

It is better to keep natural teeth than replace them with artificial teeth. Fluoride is one of the most important weapons against decay, protecting teeth by increasing the tooth's resistance to acid attack, helping the tooth to repair and inhibiting the growth of bacteria. Fluoride in the water supply is the most efficient way of reducing dental caries in a population.

Cosmetic dentistry

Cosmetic dentistry involves repairing or improving the appearance of teeth. Teeth can be bonded with a tooth-colored plastic when the problem is chipped, stained or heavily filled front teeth or gaps that need closing up. Porcelain veneers can also be used to improve the appearance of the teeth and teeth can be whitened with bleach. A missing front tooth can be replaced with a partial

Teeth—structure

Although it looks like a solid piece of bone, a tooth contains a network of nerves, veins and arteries which enter the tooth through the root canal.

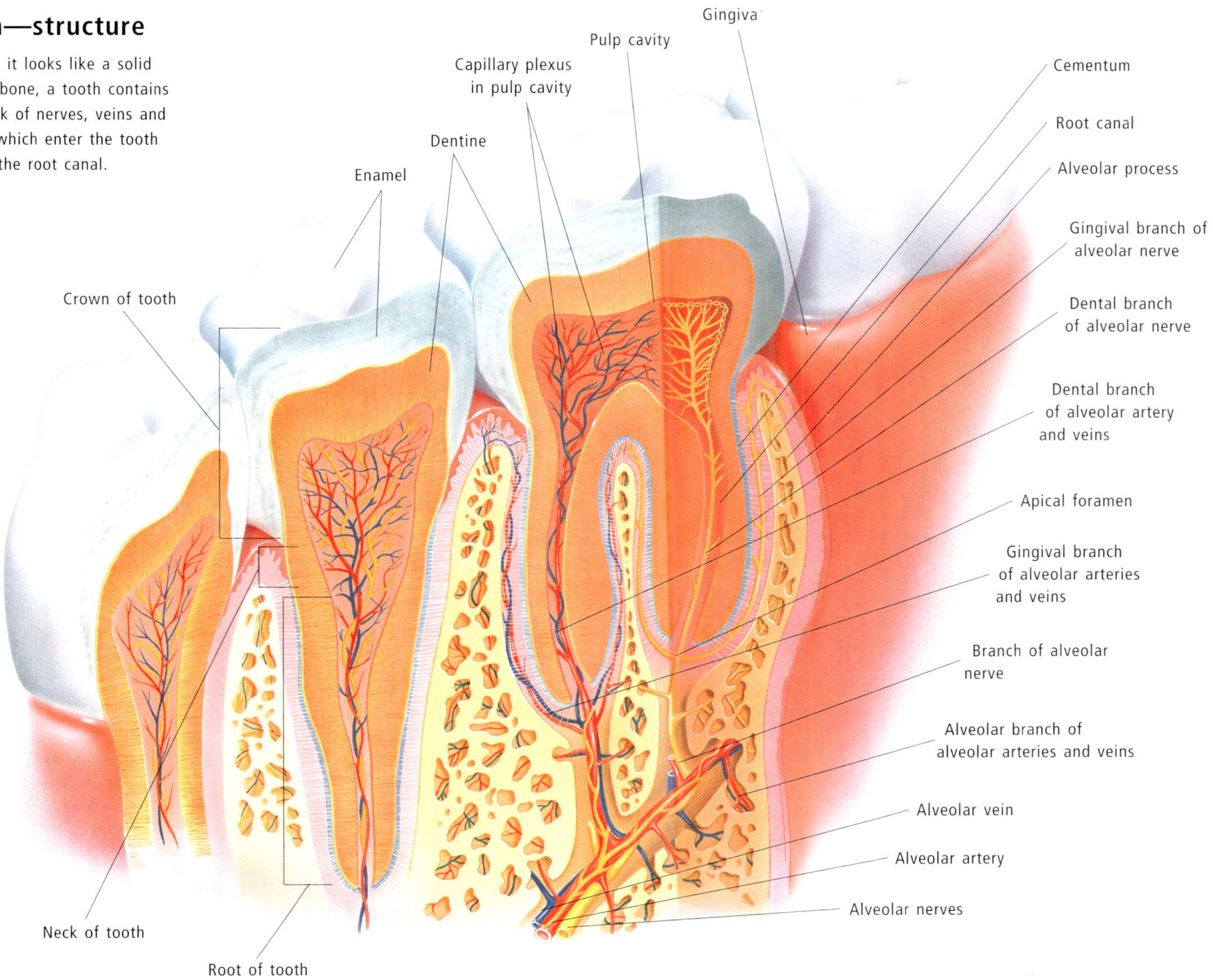

denture, bridgework or an implant. One or more missing teeth elsewhere may be replaced by a partial denture, either removable or fixed. Implants are artificial teeth, requiring surgery which can only be performed on people with healthy gums and adequate bone; implants require a commitment to meticulous ongoing hygiene.

Teeth problems

The most common problems experienced with teeth include the following.

Abscess When the pulp of a tooth becomes infected the infection can spread into the tissues near the root tip, and a pocket of pus (an abscess) can form in the gum. Treatment begins with antibiotics.

Bad breath Poor oral hygiene, gum disease, a dry mouth (xerostomia), tobacco products, various foods and medical problems are the main causes of bad breath. Once the cause has been determined, improving oral hygiene is the best method of keeping bad breath at bay.

Crooked or large teeth Orthodontic treatment will help to correct malocclusion ("bad bite") caused by overlarge, crowded or crooked teeth. Adjustable or removable appliances will help the teeth of younger children to develop in the proper positions; once all the permanent teeth have erupted fixed appliances may be used.

Decay (caries) Decay can be stopped or reversed in the early stages by appropriate use of fluoride and proper cleaning. More advanced decay can be repaired by removing damaged tissue and filling the tooth with amalgam or composite resin, which is tooth-colored. Other materials that can be used are glass ionomer cement, porcelain and gold. Crowns, which cap teeth, are usually made from porcelain and metal.

Discoloration There are many causes of unattractive blemishes on the teeth. Smoking, inherited conditions, childhood illnesses, inappropriate antibiotic treatment, injury and fluorosis, which is a superficial blemish, are some of the most common.

Fissures These are grooves on the chewing surface of the molars which are very susceptible to decay. They can be sealed.

Gum disease Periodontal or gum disease affects three out of four adults at some time. Gums that bleed, are sore, have pulled away from the teeth, persistent bad breath, loose teeth or a change in the bite are all indications of gum disease. Removing plaque or tartar is the first remedial step. Antibiotics may be necessary, as may surgery in severe cases.

Severely damaged teeth Root canal therapy may be necessary to save a tooth damaged by fracture or a deep cavity,

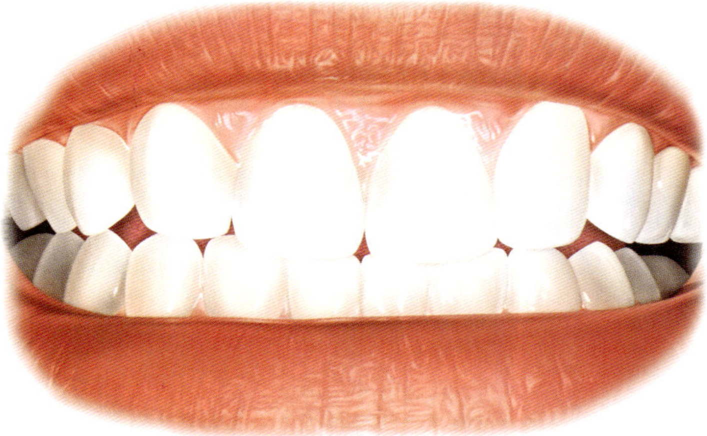

Teeth

Adults have 16 teeth in each jaw. The enamel that covers the teeth is the hardest substance in the human body.

which may cause the pulp to die. If the problem is discovered in time this treatment will save the tooth.

Wisdom teeth These are the last of the back molars to erupt and play a valuable role if they are healthy and properly positioned. If the jaw is not large enough for proper eruption (partial eruption), the wisdom teeth may damage adjacent teeth, or a cyst may form, destroying surrounding structures, and they should be surgically removed.

Yellowing As people age, teeth often become yellow, the result of plaque build-up and changes in the dentine. Gum disease and bad breath can become problems. Every effort should be made to preserve teeth.

SEE ALSO *Braces, Crown and bridge, Dentures, Fluoridation, Gums, Mouth, Orthodontics, Saliva, Teeth-grinding, Teething*

TEETH-GRINDING

Teeth-grinding (bruxism) is the act of grinding or clenching the teeth, usually during sleep. It is not associated with any particular stage of sleep and does not affect sleep—though it can damage teeth and cause face pain or headache. It seems to run in families and can occur at all ages. The most important treatment is to protect teeth and for this a mouth guard, as prescribed by a dentist, may be necessary.

SEE ALSO *Sleep disturbances, Teeth*

TEETHING

Teething is the term used to refer to the eruption of the first teeth in a baby. A baby's first tooth will generally erupt anytime between the fifth and twelfth month of the first year of life; a few babies will get their teeth earlier or later. A very small number, about 1 in 2,000, will be born with one or more teeth. The last tooth usually erupts around the age of 3 years. There are 20 primary teeth (also called deciduous or milk teeth), which are smaller and usually whiter than the permanent set of teeth.

In general, the lower central teeth (incisors) arrive first, followed by the central upper incisors, the lateral incisors (lower and upper), the first molars, the canines and the second molars, though not all children get their teeth in this order. These first teeth guide the permanent teeth into place and aid in the growth of the jawbone. It is important that they are kept healthy and clean—they are not dispensable.

A baby's first teeth can be cleaned with a clean wet cloth, sitting the baby on an adult's lap and gently rubbing the teeth. Once the child is accustomed to this routine twice a day, a very soft toothbrush can be used. Children will need assistance cleaning their teeth until middle childhood.

Signs that a tooth is about to erupt can include dribbling and a need to chew on anything and everything. A baby who is teething may also be unhappy and pull on the ear, because the ear canal is connected to the same nerve as the lower jaw. There is much folklore surrounding teething, inaccurately blaming it for fever, diarrhea, constipation, loss of appetite, diaper rash and convulsions. All these symptoms require medical attention—they are not symptoms of teething and indicate other conditions. The canines and the molars tend to cause the most distress.

The best treatment for sore gums due to teething is a cool (not cold), hard, clean teething ring or similar. The dribbling which naturally accompanies teething results in some fluid loss and babies are generally more thirsty when they are teething. Many babies wake at night while they are teething and need to drink.

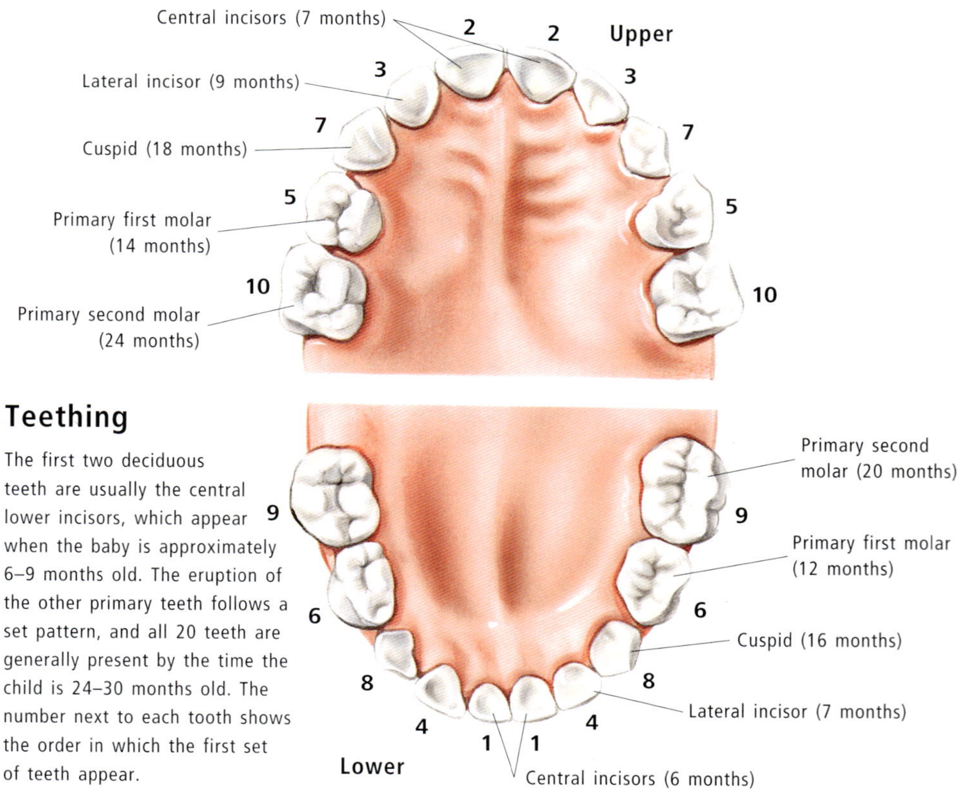

Teething

The first two deciduous teeth are usually the central lower incisors, which appear when the baby is approximately 6–9 months old. The eruption of the other primary teeth follows a set pattern, and all 20 teeth are generally present by the time the child is 24–30 months old. The number next to each tooth shows the order in which the first set of teeth appear.

The arrival of teeth is not a reason to stop breast feeding as babies do not usually bite the nipple, except occasionally in an attempt to relieve teething pains. The baby's tongue normally protrudes over the bottom teeth while sucking, thus protecting the nipple.

Teething gels that contain anesthetics can cause allergies and must be treated with caution; acetaminophen (paracetamol) may be used to relieve discomfort.

SEE ALSO *Infancy, Teeth*

TEMPERATURE

The temperature of the normal healthy human body is generally assumed to be 98.6°F (37°C), but may range from 97.2–100°F (36.2–37.8°C); temperatures ranging from 95.9–101.2°F (35.5–38.4°C) have also been recorded in healthy individuals. Temperature can only be taken accurately by using a thermometer (holding the hand to the forehead is not an accurate method of measurement). A person may sometimes appear to be hot when the core body temperature is actually normal.

The temperature can be taken in the mouth (orally) by placing a thermometer under the tongue; rectally, by inserting the thermometer a short distance into the rectum; or under the armpit (axilla). The rectal temperature is usually 1°F (0.5°C) higher than the oral temperature; the axillary temperature is usually 1°F (0.5°C) lower than the oral temperature. The temperature should always be taken by the same route for purposes of comparison in illness.

A child with a high fever, over 101°F (38.2°C), needs treatment to reduce their temperature in order to avoid the possibility of convulsions. This can be done by removing clothing, and bed clothes if necessary, and cooling the child with a tepid sponge. A tepid bath may also be used. Shivering is not the aim as this will raise the body's temperature. A fan may also help. Acetaminophen (paracetamol) or ibuprofen may be given to children to help reduce fever, but never aspirin, as it may cause Reye's syndrome. Aspirin is appropriate only for adults.

SEE ALSO *Convulsions, Fever, Reye's Syndrome, Temperature regulation*

TEMPERATURE REGULATION

Most organisms, humans included, are not able to maintain a body temperature that is significantly different from that of their environment for any length of time. Two categories of animals employ physiological mechanisms to maintain body temperature: warm-blooded creatures (endotherms), including mammals and birds, generate heat internally, while cold-blooded creatures (ectotherms), which include reptiles, use external heat to regulate body temperature.

Temperature regulation

The body has an in-built mechanism for maintaining a stable temperature. This mechanism is regulated by the hypothalamus in the brain. A change in external temperature is relayed to the hypothalamus by nerve endings in the surface of the skin. If the hypothalamus receives messages that the body is cold, it increases heat production in the body by increasing the metabolic rate. If the body is hot, the hypothalamus sends blood to the skin where heat can be lost through radiation, conduction, convection and evaporation.

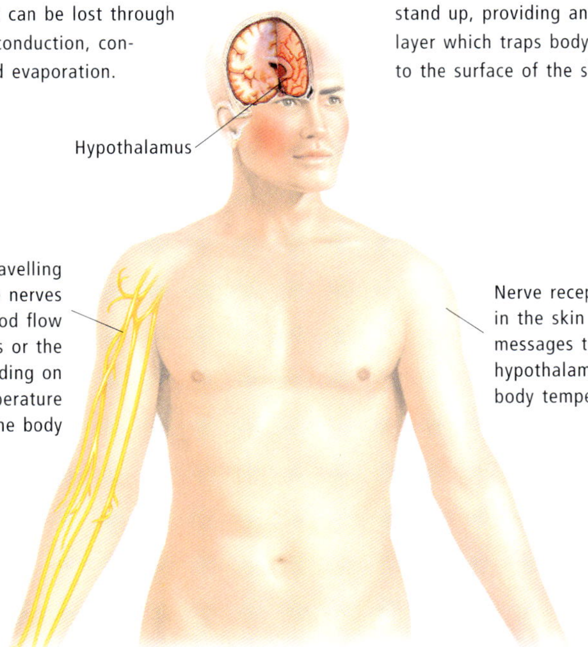

Skin and temperature

Both the dermal and epidermal layers of the skin are involved in regulating body temperature. When the body is hot, arteries dilate and blood flow to the skin increases, maximizing heat loss. The sweat glands are stimulated and release fluid, which evaporates and reduces the body's temperature. When the body is cold, the pores and arteries contract and the hairs of the skin stand up, providing an insulating layer which traps body heat close to the surface of the skin.

Skin reaction to cold

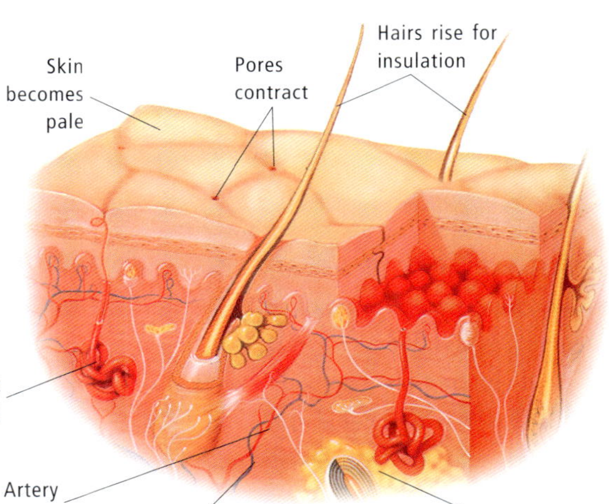

Skin reaction to heat

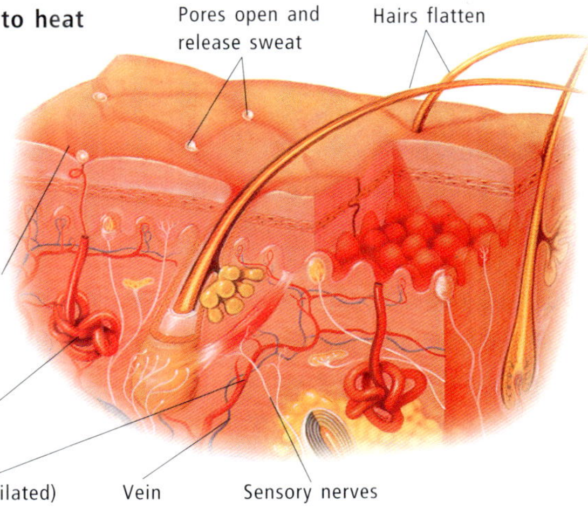

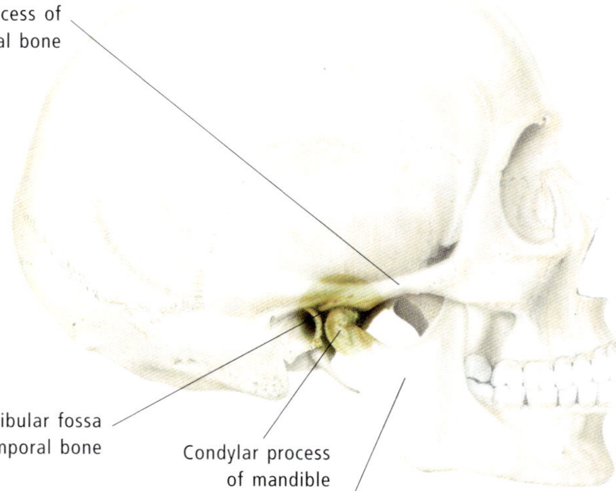

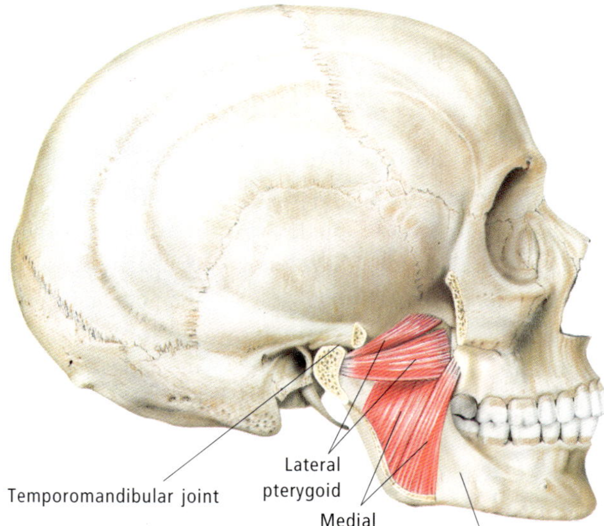

Temporomandibular joint syndrome

The temporomandibular joint has a complex action that allows movement up and down, side to side and backwards and forwards. Damage to cartilage in the joint or to the supporting muscles can result in temporomandibular joint syndrome. This may limit the action of the joint, cause clicking noises, or pain in the jaw muscles, neck or head.

The human body's usual core temperature ranges from 97.2–100°F (36.2–37.8°C). The core body temperature varies according to the time of day and is also affected by the environment, physical activity, food intake and emotions. Typically temperature is lowest early in the morning and highest in late afternoon, a normal part of the body's circadian rhythm.

Body temperature is the result of the balance between heat loss and heat production. Body heat is lost through radiation, which is affected by the rate of blood flow to the skin's surface; evaporation (the sweat glands can dissipate as many as 1,700 kilocalories (7,100 kilojoules) an hour; convection and conduction. The body's fat provides the insulation which helps to maintain the body temperature when exposed to hot or cold environments.

The part of the brain which regulates body temperature is the hypothalamus. When the body is heated, heat loss is initiated by messages sent to the hypothalamus; the blood vessels dilate and the body sweats. If the body temperature is too high (hyperthermia) the skin may become dry, deep, fast breathing will follow, and the patient may experience headaches, nausea and unconsciousness. When the body is exposed to cold stress, the first symptom of hypothermia is pain. This is followed by numbness, mental confusion, lethargy and irregular heartbeat.

A sharp rise in body temperature (hyperthermia) can trigger heat-related illnesses such as heat cramps, heat exhaustion and heatstroke. Hypothermia is a dangerous lowering of the body's temperature to below 95°F (35°C); there is a recorded case of survival after body temperature sunk to 57°F (13.9°C). Chilling is the first stage of cold injury; from this point body temperature can lower rapidly, leading to more serious cold injury. Frostnip is the next stage, when the skin blanches or loses its color. There may be numbness and as the area is rewarmed tingling may be felt. If the situation is not remedied frostbite may follow and crystals of ice may form in the tissues.

Babies and children are vulnerable to extremes of temperature, particularly cold, because they have a greater body surface compared to their weight than adults. However, babies and children do not need to be dressed differently than an adult in a similar environment. It is possible for babies to overheat when they are overdressed for the temperature. It is also possible for insufficient warm clothing to cause distress; this can happen where parents are overly concerned about sudden infant death syndrome and do not dress a baby warmly enough for sleep. The room temperature for a sleeping child should be kept around 68°F (20°C).

Fever occurs when the body's temperature is raised as a defense mechanism against infection or injury. As white blood cells are drawn toward the areas of the body where the infection is situated, chemicals are released into the bloodstream, causing the fever. Fever in itself is rarely harmful. As the temperature rises, fever and chills may be experienced together with mild dehydration. Very occasionally a child may suffer convulsions with a fever.

SEE ALSO *Convulsions, Fever, Heatstroke, Hyperthermia, Hypothermia, Skin, Sudden infant death syndrome, Sun exposure, Temperature*

TEMPORAL ARTERITIS

Temporal arteritis is a serious progressive disorder that involves inflammation of the arteries of the scalp, particularly those supplying blood to the temples and eyes. It is also known as giant cell arteritis and cranial arteritis. The swelling narrows the arteries and impedes blood flow, which can lead to severe headaches, sudden and permanent loss of sight in an eye, or a stroke. Temporal arteritis occurs almost exclusively in the over-50s, and most commonly in women aged 70-plus. The exact cause is unknown but, because it tends to afflict older people, it is thought likely that it is associated with the ageing process. Steroid medications and aspirin are commonly used in treatment.

SEE ALSO *Arteries*

TEMPOROMANDIBULAR JOINT SYNDROME

Temporomandibular joint (TMJ) syndrome is a term for a range of problems in the joint and surrounding muscles of the jaw that may produce pain, discomfort, clicking noises, aching or tender muscles, locking or restricted movement of the joint, neck pain, apparent toothache and headaches.

The action of the temporomandibular joints is complicated, allowing movements in three directions—hinging to open and close, sliding backward and forward, and moving from side to side. Between the jawbone (mandible) and the temporal bone of the skull is a cartilaginous disk which cushions the joint and can sometimes be displaced, as it is subject to great pressure during chewing.

Teeth-grinding (bruxism) during sleep can wear away biting surfaces, causing the teeth to meet unevenly ("bad bite"). This can cause jaw muscles (which must work together in a smooth and balanced way) to spasm, producing pain and headaches; the jaw may be displaced or lock in an abnormal position. Displaced disks rarely need surgery; teeth-grinding can be stopped by wearing a custom-made bite plate at night.

Osteoarthritis and rheumatoid arthritis can affect the joint and it is important to maintain mobility to avoid calcification of ligaments or fusion (ankylosis), which requires surgical correction.

In the absence of injury or other clear causes, muscular tension is often found to be the cause of TMJ syndrome. Rest and avoiding opening the jaw wide, even when yawning, may cure the problem, and reducing stress levels should also help.

SEE ALSO *Arthritis, Jaw, Joints, Teeth-grinding*

TENDINITIS

Tendinitis is inflammation of a tendon, the connective tissue which joins muscles to bones, commonly at the point of attachment. Tendons are liable to injury through repetitive action, as in manual occupations like typing; through hard use in vigorous sports; through trauma; or by degeneration. The tendons may suffer small tears or ruptures which accumulate gradually, over time becoming inflamed, painful and restricting movement.

A common cause of shoulder pain in middle age is painful arc syndrome, where pain is felt on raising the arm away from the body. It may begin after excessive use, after injury, or where there is calcification of the supraspinatus tendon in the joint. Dislocation of the shoulder will often tear the muscles or tendons of the rotator cuff. Biceps tendinitis can happen at any age, when repeated lifting of the arm damages tendons of the biceps muscle where they pass over the head of the humerus or upper arm bone. Pain is felt on raising the arm above shoulder level. Biceps tendinitis is a common cause of shoulder pain in throwing sports, when the tendon becomes irritated and inflamed; it may make a crackling sound (crepitus) on movement.

Elbow tendinitis or lateral epicondylitis ("tennis elbow") produces pain on opening a door or lifting a cup; it is caused by damage to the tendons joining the forearm extensor muscles to the elbow.

The Achilles tendon at the back of the heel can suffer tendinitis from running or jumping or repetitive movement. Swelling and tenderness may prevent walking. If the foot cannot be moved the tendon may have ruptured and will need surgical repair.

Regardless of where it occurs, the treatment of tendinitis is the same. The affected tendon must be rested—immobilized with a bandage, splint or temporary brace if necessary—to allow the inflammation and swelling to subside. Nonsteroidal anti-inflammatory medications taken by mouth, and heat or cold applied to the affected area will help reduce the pain and inflammation. Sometimes an injection of corticosteroid into the tendon may be needed. Occasionally surgery is indicated—if the condition does not improve or if the tendon has ruptured. The affected limb or extremity should not be used until completely pain free. Then physical therapy in the form of limb exercises can retain and improve the range of movement and help prevent freezing or stiffening of the joint. If the condition was caused by overuse, the contributing activity should be modified. Avoiding repetitive motion and overuse of that part of the body, and warming up by exercising at a relaxed pace before vigorous activity can help prevent the reoccurrence of tendinitis.

SEE ALSO *Achilles tendon, Ankle, Elbow, Rotator cuff muscle, Shoulder, Tendons, Tennis elbow, Tenosynovitis*

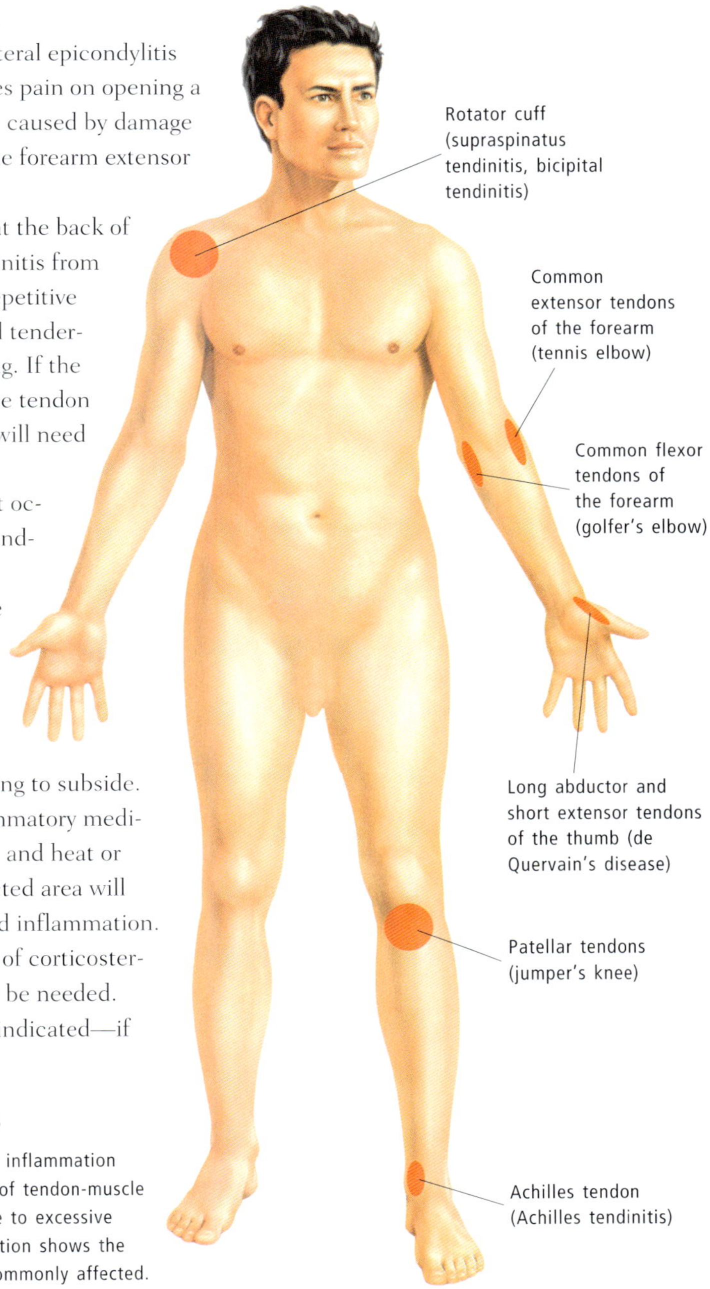

Tendinitis

Tendinitis is the inflammation of tendons and of tendon-muscle attachments due to excessive use. The illustration shows the tendons most commonly affected.

TENDONS

A tendon is a glistening white cord of connective tissue that attaches muscle to bone. It is similar in structure to a ligament, which connects bone to bone. Tendons play a critical role in the movement of the human body by transmitting the force created by muscles to move bones. In this way, they allow muscles to control movement from a distance. The fingers, for example, are moved by tendons with force supplied by the forearm muscles.

Like ropes, tendons are tough, fibrous and flexible. They are not, however, particularly elastic. If they were, much of the muscular force tendons are intended to carry would have dissipated before it had a chance to reach, let alone move, the bones.

Tendons are formed from the same components that make up other kinds of connective tissue, such as cartilage, ligament and bone. These components are collagen fibers, ground substance, and cells, which in the tendon are called fibrocytes. At the point where a tendon touches bone, the tendon fibers gradually pass into the substance of the bone and meld with it.

Some tendons run inside a fibrous sheath. Between the sheath and the tendon is a thin film of lubricant called synovial fluid. This arrangement helps tendons glide smoothly over surrounding parts.

Diseases and disorders

Inflammation of the tendon sheath is a painful condition known as tenosynovitis. Strain or trauma to a tendon sheath through repeated use, calcium deposits and high blood cholesterol levels are all potential causes. So too are diseases such as rheumatoid arthritis, gout or gonorrhea. Sometimes, during movement, a crackling noise occurs around the area of an inflamed tendon sheath.

Tenosynovitis is the underlying cause of two relatively common disorders responsible for pain in the hands and wrists—trigger finger and de Quervain's disease. In the case of trigger finger, the sheath through which the finger tendons run becomes swollen, restricting the movements of the tendons within and leading to a finger (or less commonly a thumb) becoming locked in a bent position. Trigger finger often affects people such as musicians, industrial workers and

Tendon microstructure

Tendons are constructed primarily of collagenic fibers arranged in a regular formation. This structure provides the strength needed to attach muscles to bones.

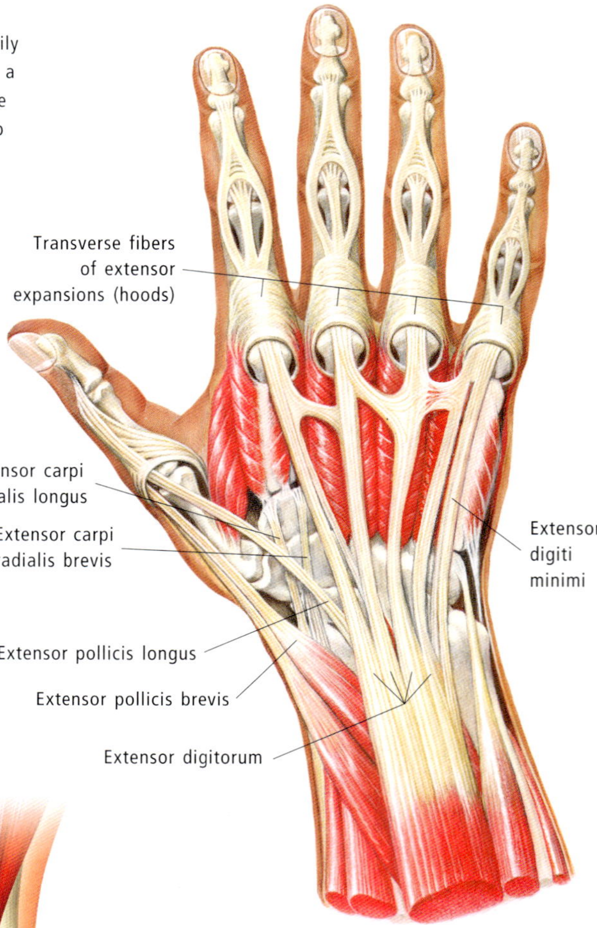

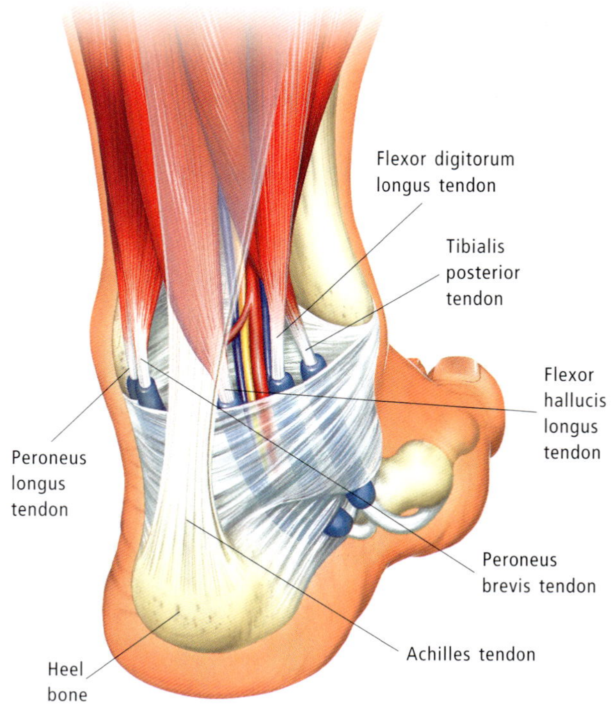

Tendon

Tendons are tough, fibrous tissues that join muscles to bones. In the hand, tendons link the fingers with the forearm muscles, allowing a full range of movement; while in the foot, the calf muscle is connected to the heel bone by the Achilles tendon.

T

farmers who use their fingers or thumbs in repetitive movements. The condition may also be caused by degenerative tissue changes associated with diseases such as rheumatoid arthritis and diabetes.

In de Quervain's disease, thickening of the sheath containing the specific tendons to the thumbs leads to pain in the wrists and along the back or base of the thumbs. A direct knock to the thumb or repetitive grasping with the thumb in situations such as gardening and racquet sports can provoke the condition. So too can the presence of inflammatory diseases such as rheumatoid arthritis.

Inflammation of a tendon itself leads to a condition known as tendinitis. It is most commonly caused by overuse or a sudden overstretching of a tendon. Both situations can lead to small tears or ruptures in a tendon. As tendons undergo a gradual process of degeneration with age, they weaken as people get older and become more prone to tendinitis. This may be why tendinitis in the rotator cuff tendons, in particular, is more common with age. These tendons help create the flexibility and huge range of movement normally permitted in the shoulders. Catching a heavy object with the arm extended or carrying out repetitive overhead activities with the arms can lead to rotator cuff tendinitis.

Tendinitis is often an underlying cause of repetitive strain injury (RSI), a painful disorder involving the hands, wrists or arms, produced by excessive or repetitive motion, such as typing on a keyboard.

The elbow is commonly afflicted by two types of tendinitis—"golfer's elbow" or medial epicondylitis, and "tennis elbow" or lateral epicondylitis.

Swinging a golf club, chopping wood with an axe, pitching a baseball and any other activity that requires repetitive gripping, grasping and turning of the hand and bending of the wrist can cause golfer's elbow. This condition is characterized by pain on the inside of the elbow.

With tennis elbow, the pain occurs in the upper forearm on the outer side of the elbow. It is caused by repetitive grasping and twisting actions such as those involved in swinging a tennis racquet, painting a house or using certain tools common in the carpentry trade. Over the last few years, tennis elbow has also started to appear in children who spend a lot of time playing hand-held computer games. Sufferers of tennis elbow not only experience pain, they can sometimes have difficulty actually straightening the forearm fully.

Another common form of tendinitis, known as "jumper's knee", affects the patellar tendon of the knee. As its name suggests, it often occurs in people playing jumping sports such as basketball and netball and is caused by the repeated impact of the force on the knee tendon that occurs when the foot hits the ground after jumping.

There are other sites in the legs where tendinitis can develop and about which sportspeople should be particularly careful. Achilles tendinitis—an inflammation of the large Achilles tendon that stretches from the calf muscles to the back of the heel—is common in runners, particularly sprinters. Long-distance runners tend to be more inclined to develop a form of tendinitis called iliotibial band syndrome, which produces pain along the outside of the knee. It is also a common affliction of dancers, cyclists and football players.

Treatment

Complete rupture of a tendon is rare and requires immediate medical attention and usually surgery. In the vast majority of cases, however, damage to tendons, or the sheaths surrounding them, responds well to ice treatments, elevation of the injury and rest, including immobilization of the affected area by strapping or even plaster, in severe cases. Non-steroidal anti-inflammatory drugs can help to reduce pain and swelling, and physical therapy will usually assist and accelerate the healing process. Steroid injections may sometimes be used in order to reduce severe pain and stiffness.

Occasionally, if tendinitis is failing to heal, surgery may be required. The extent of damage to soft tissues such as tendons can be assessed using the modern scanning technique known as magnetic resonance imaging (MRI).

SEE ALSO *Achilles tendon, Bones, Connective tissue, Elbow, Muscle, Tendinitis, Tenosynovitis, Tennis elbow, Trigger finger*

TENNIS ELBOW

"Tennis elbow" (lateral epicondylitis) refers to a strain of the muscles and tendons on the lateral side (outer or thumb side) of the forearm, near the elbow. These muscles are used for extending the wrist, as can occur in backhand strokes in tennis. Excess use can lead to tearing of the muscles or tendons and inflammation. Pain is felt at a point on the outer side of the elbow (near the lateral epicondyle) and may extend down the arm. It is aggravated by use. Although known as tennis elbow, this condition can also occur in people who never play sport.

Treatment includes resting the elbow and wrist, avoiding the movements which cause pain. Strapping the arm just below the elbow, ice packs and physiotherapy may help. Steroid injections can be used and surgery to the tendon may also be considered.

A similar condition, known as "golfer's elbow" (medial epicondylitis), can occur on the inner (medial) side of the elbow. It is due to strain in muscles used for flexing the wrist and hand, as can occur in playing golf. Like tennis elbow, the condition may occur in non-golfers. Treatment is similar to that outlined for tennis elbow.

SEE ALSO *Elbow, Muscle, Tendons*

TENOSYNOVITIS

Tenosynovitis is inflammation of a tendon and its tendon sheath, producing pain and restricting movement. Tendons, the strong connective tissues which attach muscles to bones, are often encased in fine protective sheaths through which they slide as joints are moved. The interior lining of the sheath produces a lubricating fluid to ease the tendon and allow free movement.

Inflammation reduces this lubrication and may also constrict the sheath around the tendon.

Overuse of joints and muscles, and repetitious practice of the same movement, as occurs in many sports, can cause irritation in tendon sheaths. Infections can produce inflammation and reduce the production of lubricating fluid. Certain occupations, such as keyboard operator, dentist and violinist, which involve repetitious movements of the hand, commonly produce tenosynovitis in the wrist.

When the wrist is affected, the condition may develop into carpal tunnel syndrome. Hands and shoulders are other areas that may be affected, although it can occur at any tendon site.

The symptoms of tenosynovitis are joint pain, stiffness and tenderness around the joint, pain on movement of a joint and difficulty straightening a joint. There may be swelling of the affected area.

The treatment is to rest or immobilize the tendon, as further use while the inflammation persists can lead to further damage, including a permanent thickening of the sheath and restricted motion of the affected muscle. The tendon can be immobilized by splinting the joint, or by means of a temporary brace. Nonsteroidal anti-inflammatory medications taken by mouth, and the application of heat or cold to the affected area will help reduce inflammation and pain. Sometimes corticosteroid drugs may be injected into the area to relieve inflammation. In severe cases, surgical release of the tendon may be needed.

Once the inflammation and pain has subsided, physical therapy in the form of limb exercises will strengthen muscles, prevent joint stiffness and help prevent recurrence. The condition is best prevented by making sure the tendon is not subjected to overuse, injury, strain, or excessive exercise.

SEE ALSO *Carpal tunnel syndrome, Ganglion, Joints, Tendinitis, Tendons*

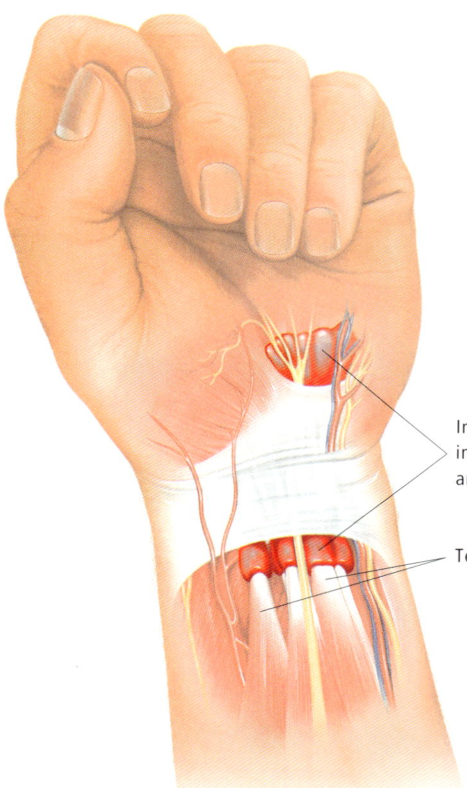

Tenosynovitis

Intense and continuous use of a tendon may result in tenosynovitis—the inflammation of a tendon and its sheath. This condition occurs mainly in the hands, wrists, feet and ankles.

TENSION HEADACHE

One of the most common type of headache, especially in adults and adolescents, tension headache is a result of the contraction of the neck and scalp muscles, which stretches the blood vessels, muscles and nerves in the skin and scalp, causing pain. Tension headaches often arise during an activity that causes the head to be held in one position for extended periods, such as when working at a computer keyboard or using industrial equipment over a long time. Sleeping with the neck in an abnormal position can also cause tension headache. People who suffer stress, depression, or anxiety are more susceptible to tension headaches than others.

The symptoms of tension headache are a dull ache, usually on both sides of the head, and worse in the scalp, temples, or back of the neck. Muscle stiffness also occurs in the neck or scalp. There are usually no other symptoms—a headache accompanied by visual disturbances, or an aura (an unusual sensation) is more likely to be a migraine.

General measures such as regular exercise and rest periods during work will help prevent tension headaches. Some people find meditation or relaxation exercises helpful. Mild analgesics such as acetaminophen or aspirin will help relieve pain, as will massage of the shoulders, neck, jaw and scalp. If a headache persists for longer than 24 hours a physician should be consulted.

SEE ALSO *Headaache, Migraine*

TERATOGEN

A condition, event or material substance that can cause physical defects in the developing fetus is called a teratogen. By altering the genetic makeup of cells during vital stages in the development of the embryo or fetus, teratogens produce congenital malformations, cancer, and other illnesses, depending upon the stage of pregnancy and the teratogen involved. There are over 2,000 known teratogenic agents. The more common ones include social drugs such as alcohol, cocaine and nicotine; medications, especially anticonvulsant drugs; environmental agents such as organic solvents, pesticides, lead and anesthetic gases; infectious diseases, especially rubella, cytomegalovirus, genital herpes, toxoplasmosis and chickenpox (varicella).

Avoiding exposure to teratogens is not always possible. For example, it has been estimated that there are more than 50,000 chemicals in common use in industrialized Western countries, and it has been estimated that as many as 20 percent of these may be teratogenic. However, there are some teratogens that can be avoided. Alcohol is a common cause of teratogenic disorders, affecting up to one in every 750 births. If consumed in excessive amounts, alcohol may cause growth retardation and low birth weight, slow development, learning disabilities and hyperactivity. Binge drinking may result in the baby having a small head circumference (microcephaly), intellectual disability and congenital heart disease, a syndrome known as fetal alcohol syndrome. Cigarette smoking during pregnancy also slows fetal growth and increases the risks of premature delivery and stillbirth.

All women should ensure they are protected against rubella (German measles) by vaccination if they have not already had the disease before becoming pregnant. Rubella is a viral infection which can lead to miscarriage if contracted in the first trimester, and to serious defects in the baby at any stage.

Because most drugs, alcohol and cigarettes are potential teratogens, complete abstinence during pregnancy is safest. Significantly elevated body temperature and radiation are also potential teratogens.

SEE ALSO *Fetal alcohol syndrome, Pregnancy, Rubella, Smoking*

T

TESTES

The testes, or testicles, are the major organs of reproduction in the male. They are two ovoid organs contained in the scrotum, a sac which lies directly behind the penis. In this location they are kept cooler by about 3.5°F (2°C) than within the body, functioning better at this lower temperature. The testes produce male sex hormones (primarily testosterone) and manufacture sperm, the microscopic cells which carry the man's genetic material to combine with that of the woman after fertilization of her ovum. The testes produce sperm continually from puberty to old age.

Testes develop from undifferentiated gonads in the fetus at about 6 weeks if a Y chromosome is present—the chromosome needed for the development of a male. When there is no Y chromosome, the gonads become ovaries. The testes at 8 weeks produce male hormones (androgens) which stimulate the growth of all the male sexual organs and inhibit the development of female organs. In rare cases organs of both sexes develop, resulting in a hermaphrodite.

In the fetus, the testes are located within the abdominal cavity close to the kidneys until the seventh or eighth month, when they descend through the inguinal canal (an opening in the abdominal wall) to the scrotum. Undescended testicles, a condition

Testes—posterior view

Contained in the scrotum, the testes are the main organs of reproduction in the male. They produce both sperm and the male sex hormones, including testosterone.

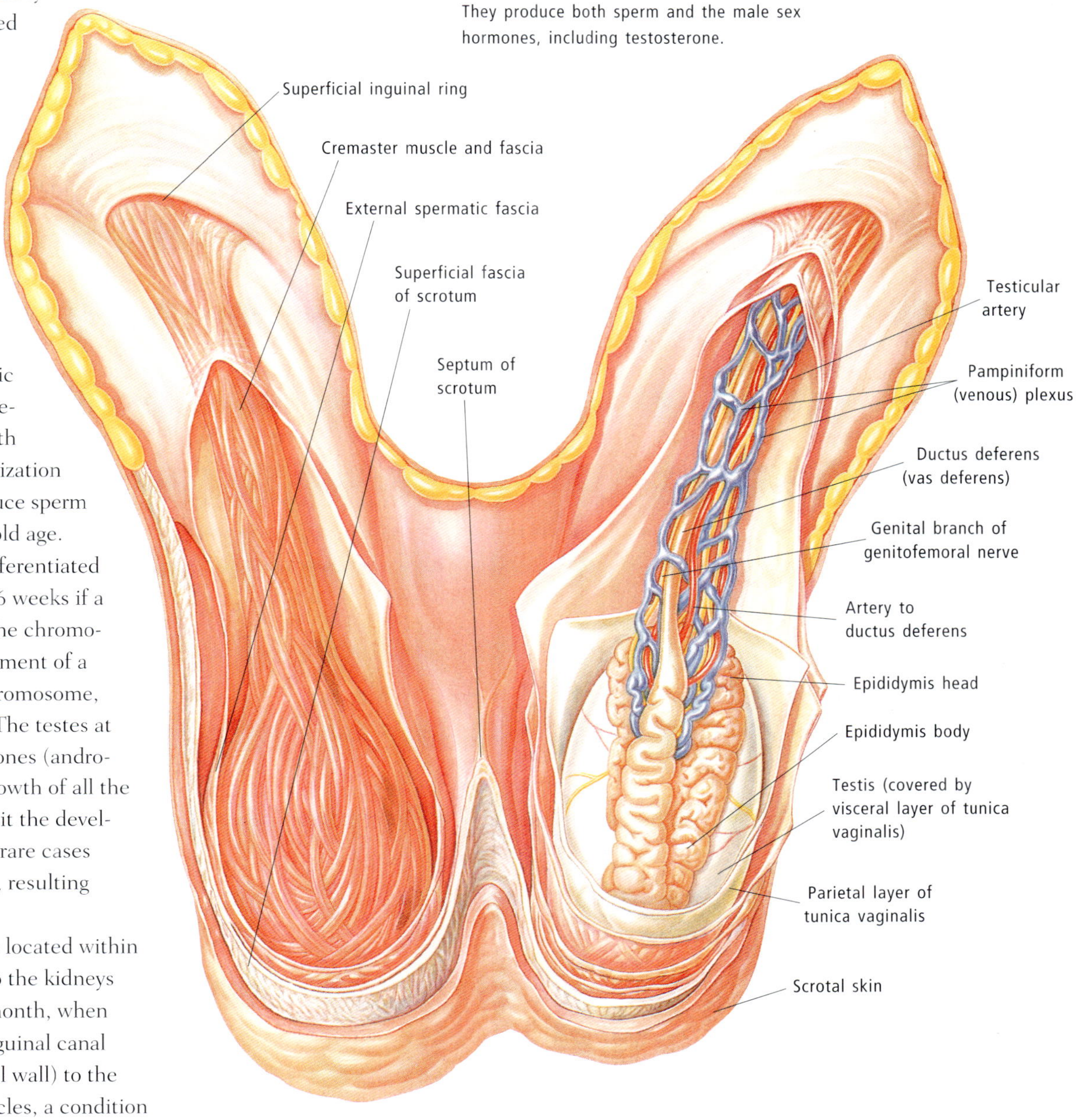

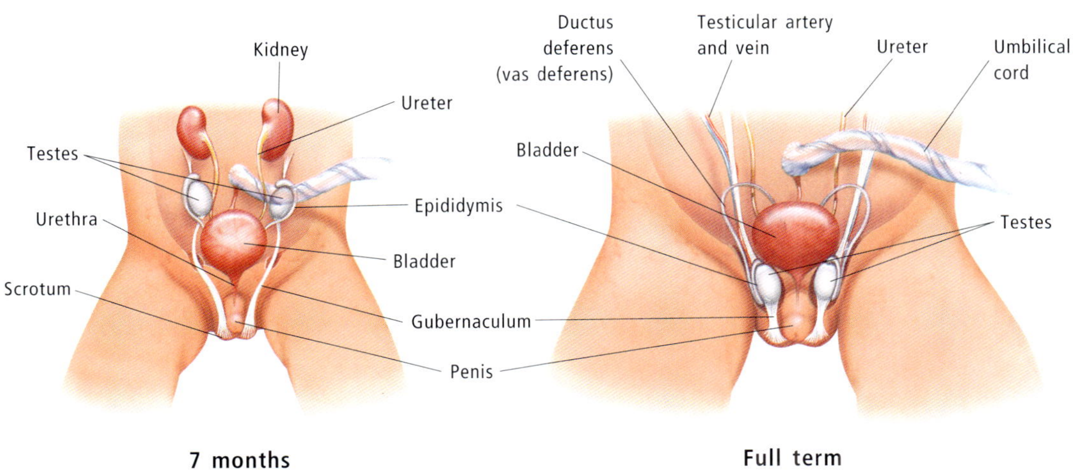

Development and descent of the testes

In the developing male fetus, the testes are located in the abdominal cavity near the kidneys until the seventh or eighth month. They then descend through the abdominal wall at the groin and enter the scrotum. They are accompanied by ducts, nerves, and blood vessels, all of which are contained in the spermatic cord.

known as cryptorchidism, can be corrected by surgery or by hormone injections. An inguinal hernia occurs when a loop of intestine passes through the inguinal canal with the testis.

At puberty the reproductive organs mature to become fully functional. This change is triggered by hormones released from the pituitary gland which enable the testes to start producing sperm and testosterone. The testes and penis grow larger at this time. Sperm are produced continually from puberty to old age at a rate of about 50,000 per minute, but taking about two and a half months to develop. Mature sperm leave the testicles through small ducts that lead into the epididymis. From here, they move into the seminal vesicles where they are stored until expulsion by ejaculation during orgasm. Sperm not expelled in ejaculations are reabsorbed by the body.

Diseases and disorders

A hydrocele is a usually painless, soft swelling due to fluid accumulation around a testicle which can be present at birth and if large may be corrected by surgery. A hematocele is a mass of blood that collects around a testicle, usually as a result of an injury; if large it may be removed surgically. Mumps, a viral disease that usually affects the salivary glands in the neck, can also cause pain and swelling in the testes (orchitis). If contracted after puberty it may permanently impair the ability to produce sperm. A varicocele is a mass of veins in the scrotum, like varicose veins, which can impair the production of healthy sperm by raising the temperature of the testes; the condition can be corrected by surgery. Testicular torsion, the twisting of one testicle and its spermatic cord, can be a congenital defect or result from injury or exertion; symptoms are pain and swelling, nausea and vomiting. Ultrasound may be used for diagnosis and the condition must be resolved within 24 hours as blood flow to the testicle is cut off, causing tissue death.

Testicular cancer is rare but is most often found in men between 15 and 35 years of age. It is not caused by injury but is often found on inspection after trauma. Generally painless, it often begins as a noticeable lump which can be detected by self-examination. Treatment is to remove the testicle (orchiectomy), which can be replaced by a cosmetic prosthesis if required; the other testicle will produce a normal amount of sperm and hormones. In prostate cancer, a complete orchiectomy may be performed to stop the production of testosterone, which some tumors need for growth.

Self-checking monthly by feeling each testicle between the thumb and forefinger can reveal early changes. Normal testicles are slightly soft but firm and smooth to the touch. Any hardness or lumpiness, or marked differences between testicles should be a signal for a medical check-up.

SEE ALSO *Hernia, Hormones, Hydrocele, Orchiectomy, Orchitis, Reproductive systems, Scrotum, Sperm, Testosterone*

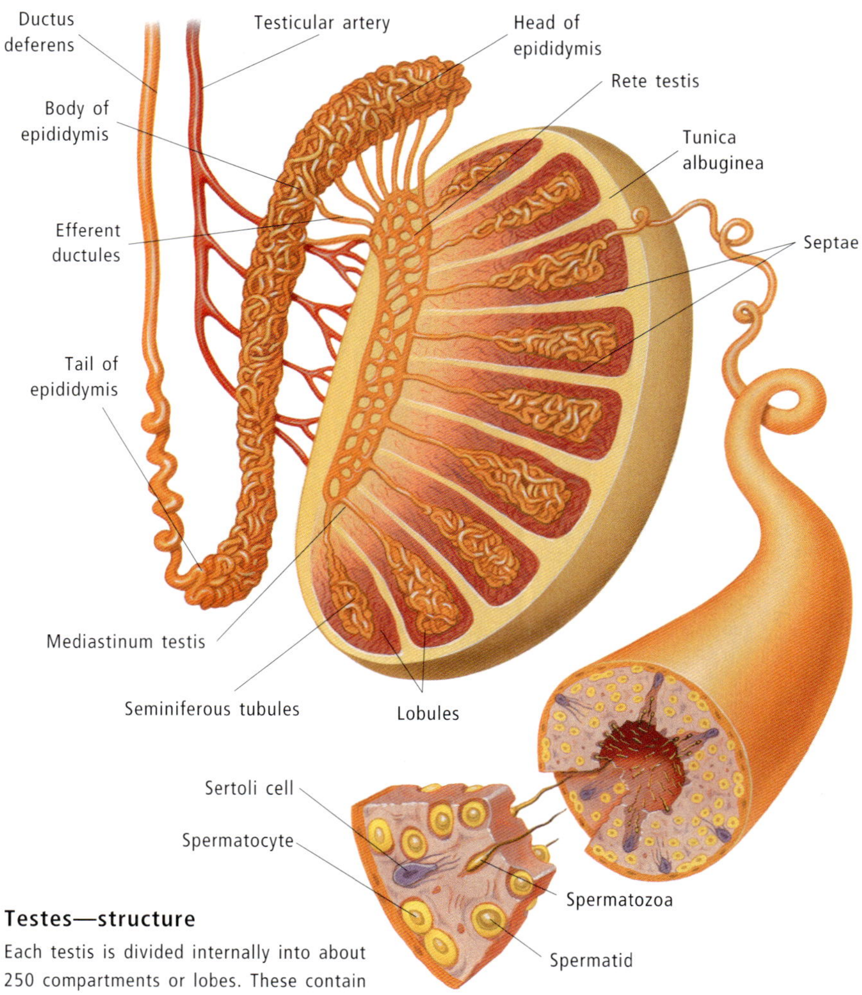

Testes—structure

Each testis is divided internally into about 250 compartments or lobes. These contain one to three very small convoluted tubules within which spermatozoa (sperm) are produced.

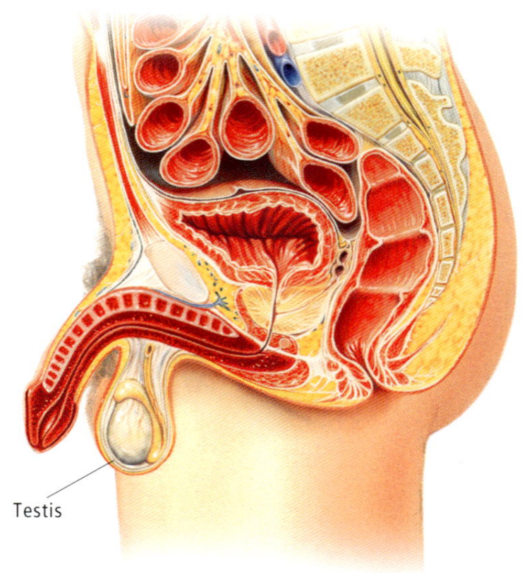

Location of the testes

Situated outside the body in the scrotum, the testes lie directly behind the penis.

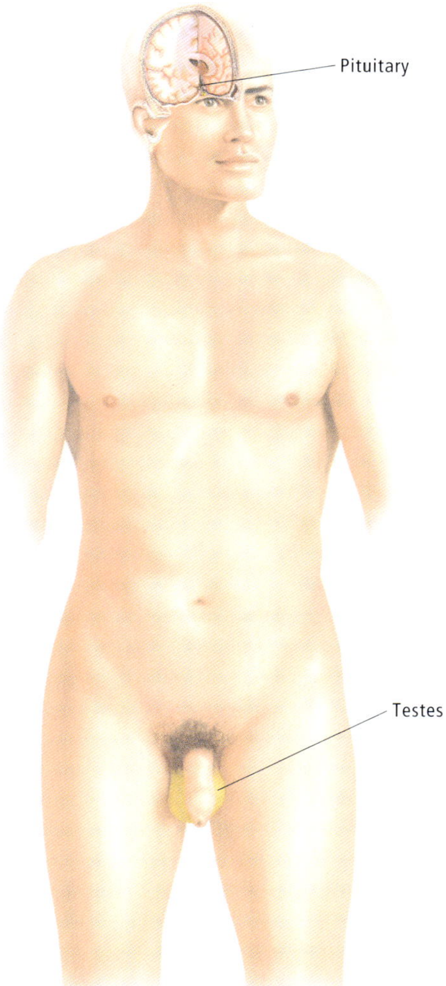

Testosterone

The hormone testosterone is produced by the testes under the control of the pituitary gland. Testosterone controls the development of male characteristics, such as facial hair and sperm production, and also plays a role in muscle growth and the body's metabolism.

TESTOSTERONE

Testosterone is the hormone responsible for the development of secondary sexual characteristics in the male. Secreted by the testes, it stimulates growth of facial and pubic hair, enlargement of the larynx and deepening of the voice, enlargement of the penis and testes, and an increase in muscle strength. Earlier in life, testosterone plays an important part in the development of external genitalia in the male fetus.

Testosterone production is controlled by the follicle stimulating hormone (FSH) and luteinizing hormone (LH). Both of these hormones are secreted by the front lobe of the pituitary gland. Small amounts of testosterone are also synthesized from cholesterol in the adrenal glands, ovaries and placenta.

Synthetic steroids similar to testosterone are used by athletes to promote muscle growth and improve performance, often with adverse side effects. Drugs based on synthetic testosterone have clinical uses such as the suppression of milk supply in lactating women and the treatment of female frigidity, breast cancer and testicular disorders.

SEE ALSO *Follicle stimulating hormone, Hormones, Pituitary gland*

TETANUS

Tetanus is an acute infectious disease, which occurs in both humans and animals, produced by the bacillus *Clostridium tetani* entering the body through a dirty wound, particularly a puncture wound. Symptoms include muscle stiffness and cramps, which appear first around the mouth and jaw (hence the disease's previous common name, lockjaw), a sore throat and difficulty breathing and swallowing, proceeding to severe muscle spasms and convulsions.

Tetanus can incubate for between 2 days and 2 weeks, but sometimes as long as 3 months; the longer the incubation period the milder the disease.

The severity of the symptoms is related to the amount of toxin produced by the bacterial infection and the resistance of the person to the disease. Of those who contract tetanus, 30–40 percent will die if they are not treated. In nearly half of tetanus cases no puncture wound is evident; any wound can serve as the entry point for tetanus germs, even a superficial abrasion. The spores of *Clostridium tetani* are most commonly found in topsoil and are spread by animal feces. They may also live on anything lying on the ground.

Tetanus is more prevalent in older people and agricultural workers who regularly come into contact with animal manure. Many incidences are caused by puncture wounds from rusty metal objects such as nails.

Wounds should be thoroughly cleaned and any dead tissue removed. Recovery from a tetanus attack does not guarantee immunity from the disease. Complications include hypertension, fractures of the spine or long bones, abnormal heartbeat, coma, general infection, blood clots in the lungs, pneumonia and death.

Immunization against tetanus is available as part of immunization programs in most industrialized countries, starting with babies from 6 weeks of age. It consists of a series of injections, the number depending on which type of tetanus toxoid is used; it is important that the immunization be repeated every 10 years. Redness and a hard lump are the most common side effects of the vaccine; if other side effects are noticed a medical check-up is a wise precaution. Accident victims are usually routinely administered with the vaccine. Treatment of tetanus includes antibiotics, sedatives and muscle relaxants.

SEE ALSO *Immunization, Infectious diseases*

TETANY

Tetany is a muscular spasm in the hands, feet and face, which is a symptom of a metabolic imbalance. This potentially life-threatening disease can be caused by abnormally low levels of calcium, potassium or magnesium in the blood or by an over-acid or over-alkaline condition of the body.

It is a painful condition in which the muscles of hands and feet cramp rhythmically and the larynx spasms, causing difficulty in

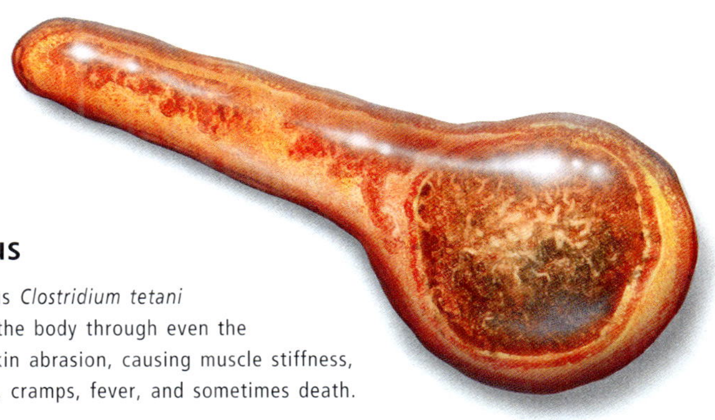

Tetanus

The bacillus *Clostridium tetani* can enter the body through even the smallest skin abrasion, causing muscle stiffness, headaches, cramps, fever, and sometimes death.

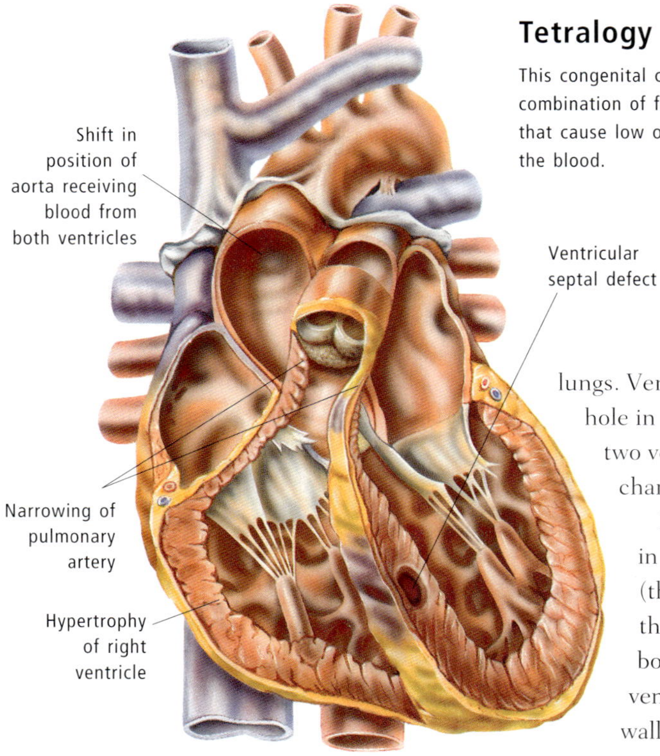

Tetralogy of Fallot

This congenital condition is a combination of four heart defects that cause low oxygen levels in the blood.

breathing, nausea, vomiting and convulsions. There may also be sensory abnormalities such as an odd feeling in the lips, tongue, fingers and feet, general muscle aches and spasms of the facial muscles.

The condition may accompany poorly controlled hypoparathyroidism, hypophosphatemia, osteomalacia, renal disorders or malabsorption syndromes. If caused by abnormal calcium levels, tetany may be associated with a vitamin D deficiency.

The aim of treatment is to restore metabolic balance, for example by intravenous administration of calcium in cases of calcium deficiency (hypocalcemia).

SEE ALSO *Acidosis, Alkalosis, Calcium, Potassium*

TETRALOGY OF FALLOT

Tetralogy of Fallot is a congenital disease of the heart; in other words, the basic disorder is present before the time of birth. The word tetralogy implies that there are four main abnormalities comprising the disease.

The two most important disorders are pulmonary stenosis and ventricular septal defect. Pulmonary stenosis is a severe narrowing of the pulmonary artery that leads from the right side of the heart to the lungs. Ventricular septal defect is a hole in the wall that separates the two ventricles, or main pumping chambers, of the heart.

In addition, there is a shift in the position of the aorta (the main artery passing from the heart to the rest of the body) so that it lies over the ventricular septal defect. The wall of the right ventricle thickens as a consequence of the narrowed pulmonary artery. The result of these disorders is that insufficiently oxygenated blood is pumped from the heart to the body. Blood flow to the lungs is decreased, which compounds the cyanotic effects. Children with this disease usually develop a blue tinge to the lips and mouth (cyanosis) within the first year of life. Breathlessness and fainting will become increasingly more severe and frequent. These episodes of fainting are referred to as "Tet spells".

It is estimated that about 50 in 100,000 infants develop tetralogy of Fallot, with a higher than normal incidence in children with Down syndrome. As with most congenital heart defects, the cause of this group of disorders is unknown, but prenatal occurrences thought to be associated with such conditions include viral illnesses, alcohol abuse, insufficient nutrition and diabetes. Treatment is by corrective surgery.

SEE ALSO *Congenital abnormalities, Cyanosis, Heart, Ventricular septal defect*

THALAMUS

The thalamus is an ovoid structure composed of a group of nerve cells lying deep within the brain. There are two thalami, lying on either side of the third ventricle, a fluid-filled space in the midline of the brain. A large bundle of nerve fibers, known as the internal capsule, lies to the side of each thalamus.

There are several parts of the thalamus, which serve as sensory relay centers between so-called "lower" parts of the central nervous system and the surface of the brain, the cerebral cortex. For example, sensory information from the retina in the eye is relayed through the thalamus to the visual cortex at the back of the brain. However, the thalamus is not a passive relay station—some of the information processing necessary for sensory perception must occur within the thalamus.

Other parts of the thalamus are motor, or muscle control, relay centers. The thalamus is involved in two "motor loops", circuits by which nerve impulses are transmitted from the motor parts of the cortex to nerve cells in the lower parts of the brain, back up to the thalamus and thence returned to the cortex. One of these loops involves the brain stem and cerebellum; the other involves the basal ganglia, which are large groups of nerve cells lying to the side and in front of each thalamus.

There are also parts of the thalamus that are said to be "non-specific" and have connections with the cortex, for which no clear functional significance is available at present.

SEE ALSO *Brain, Cerebral cortex, Nervous system*

THALASSEMIA

Also known as Cooley's anemia, Mediterranean anemia or hereditary leptocytosis, thalassemia is a group of hereditary diseases characterized by a deficiency of normal hemoglobin, the protein that transports oxygen to the tissues. The illness is caused by an imbalance in the alpha and beta protein globin chains which are needed for the production of hemoglobin.

Thalassemia major (homozygous thalassemia) may be diagnosed in the first year of life with symptoms of anemia and enlarged spleen and liver; by the age of 4, growth is stunted and bone deformities may be evident.

Thalassemia minor (heterozygous thalassemia) is characterized by mild anemia, often with no other symptoms.

Thalamus

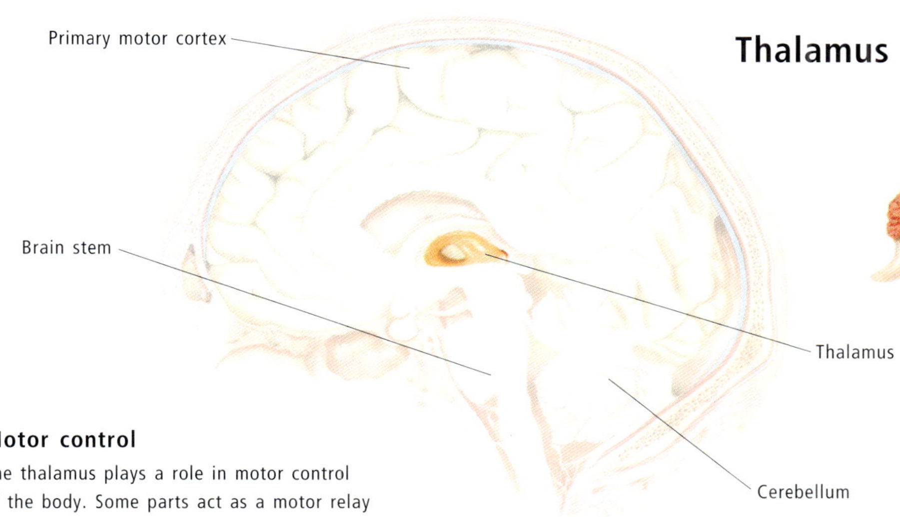

Motor control
The thalamus plays a role in motor control of the body. Some parts act as a motor relay center, sending information to the cerebellum and the motor cortex in the brain.

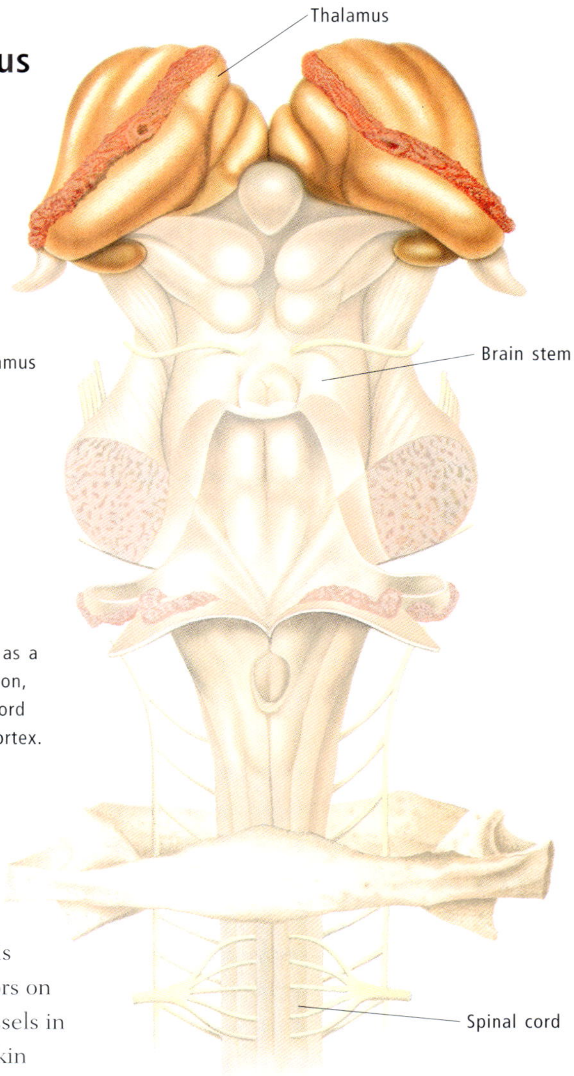

Sensory relay center
The thalamus functions primarily as a relay center for sensory information, passing signals from the spinal cord and brain stem to the cerebral cortex.

For people to suffer from the symptoms of thalassemia they must inherit defective genes from both parents. If they inherit only one gene they will become carriers of the disease, without exhibiting any symptoms. In its most severe form the disease may cause an infant to be stillborn.

Transfusions may be required when the anemia is severe. However, close monitoring is required as too much iron from the transfusions may cause damage to the liver, heart and endocrine systems. There is no cure for these diseases.

SEE ALSO *Anemia, Hemoglobin*

THERMOGRAPHY

Thermography is a technique involving measuring the temperature in different parts of the body by scanning with a heat-sensitive infrared camera. It is especially known for its use in the diagnosis of breast cancer by measuring skin temperature—a tumor is marginally hotter than surrounding tissue. Before the scan the skin is exposed to the air for 10 minutes to stabilize its temperature and increase the accuracy of the test.

The scanning procedure results in an infrared photo of the body's surface temperature, called a thermogram, which may show up such things as disease-causing plaque on the arteries of the heart, various cancers and infection. The procedure has also been used in the diagnosis and treatment of pain, such as in the back and in the wrists where carpal tunnel syndrome is suspected. Pain shows up as cool colors on the thermogram as it causes blood vessels in the skin to constrict, which reduces skin temperature. It is estimated that about a quarter of thermographic tests bring false positive responses, making the technique unreliable for the screening of serious disease such as cancer.

SEE ALSO *Atherosclerosis, Breast cancer*

THROAT

The throat is the front portion of the neck. Within it are the fauces, the opening that leads from the back of the mouth into the pharynx, and the pharynx itself, the cavity that connects the mouth, nose and larynx, which is situated behind the arch at the back of the mouth.

The nasal part of the pharynx, or nasopharynx, is the space just above the soft palate that joins with the back of the nose. It contains the adenoids and the openings of the eustachian tubes on each side (which lead to the middle ear). The oropharynx lies at the back of the mouth and contains the tonsils (one on each side) and the back of the tongue. The laryngeal pharynx connects the back of the throat to the voice box, or larynx, and the esophagus (gullet). At the top of the laryngeal pharynx is the epiglottis, a flap of tissue that lies just behind the base of the tongue. From the epiglottis the laryngeal pharynx leads downward to the esophagus. A separate passageway leads to the larynx.

During the action of swallowing, muscles in the walls of the throat lift the pharynx, pushing food down to the esophagus, and closing the epiglottis over the trachea so food and liquids do not pass into the trachea.

A sore throat is a symptom of many disorders, including colds, diphtheria, influenza, laryngitis, measles, infectious mononucleosis (glandular fever), pharyngitis and tonsillitis. Sore throats may be caused by bacteria such as *Streptococcus*, but most are caused

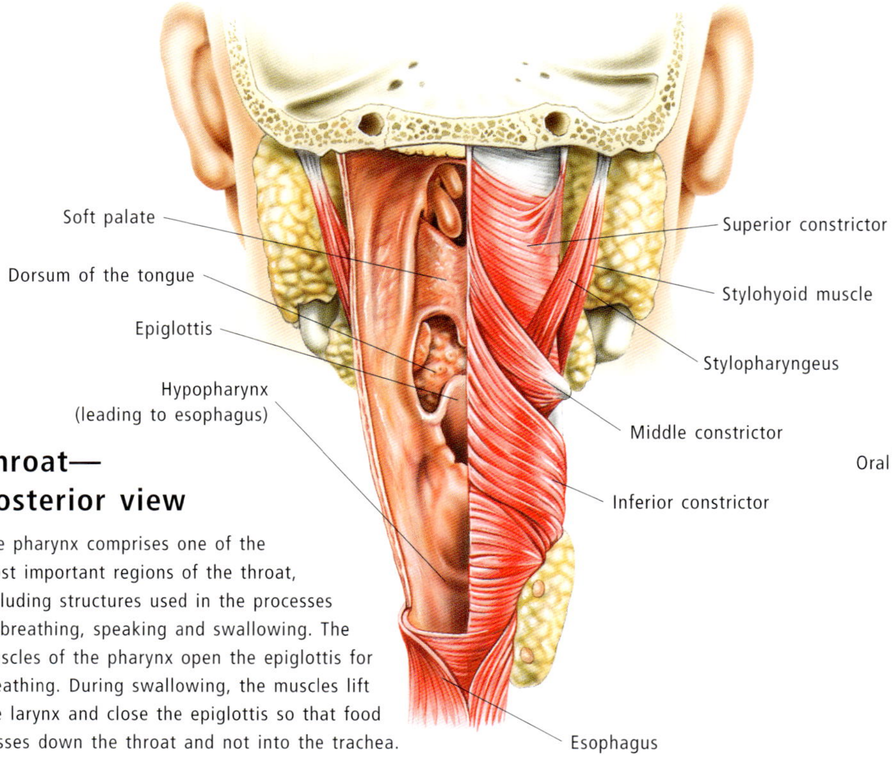

Throat—posterior view

The pharynx comprises one of the most important regions of the throat, including structures used in the processes of breathing, speaking and swallowing. The muscles of the pharynx open the epiglottis for breathing. During swallowing, the muscles lift the larynx and close the epiglottis so that food passes down the throat and not into the trachea.

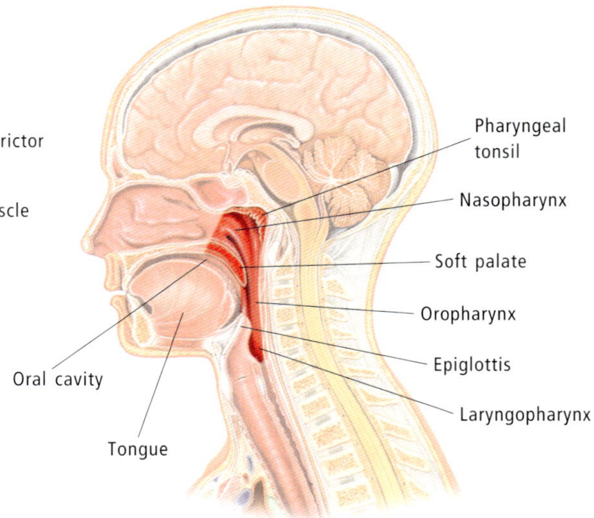

Throat

The throat is the common passageway that links the nose and mouth with the respiratory and digestive systems.

by viruses; therefore, treating all sore throats with antibiotics (which do not cure viral infections) is inappropriate.

SEE ALSO *Adenoids, Digestive system, Epiglottis, Esophagus, Larynx, Pharynx, Trachea*

THROMBOANGIITIS OBLITERANS

In thromboangiitis obliterans, also known as Buerger's disease, clots and inflammation in the lining of blood vessels cause them to become constricted or blocked. The small and medium-sized arteries of the feet and legs are most commonly affected, although the hands may also be involved. Intermittent pain, blueness and eventual tissue damage and destruction result from reduced blood supply to affected areas. Painful ulcers, other infections and eventually gangrene requiring amputation can occur.

Pain in the hands and feet may be severe and accompanied by tenderness, tingling and burning sensations, which tend to be felt more during rest than when active. Foot pain is often felt in the arch. Other symptoms include skin changes or ulcers on the feet and hands. These extremities may feel cold or may be pale, red or a bluish color, with prominent cord-like veins. Symptoms of the disease may worsen if the sufferer is exposed to cold temperatures or experiences emotional stress.

The cause of thromboangiitis obliterans is unknown, but smoking is considered to be a trigger because the disease is most prevalent in cigarette-smoking men aged between 20 and 40 and rarely affects non-smokers. Stopping smoking also generally results in the partial healing of the affected area.

People with autoimmune diseases also have more risk of suffering from the disease. There is no cure and the goal of treatment is to control and reduce symptoms. As well as stopping smoking, it is helpful to avoid anything that restricts blood circulation, such as the cold. Staying warm and undertaking gentle exercise may help to increase circulation. In some cases, surgically cutting the nerves to the worst affected areas (sympathectomy) may offer pain control.

SEE ALSO *Arteries, Blood vessels, Smoking*

THROMBOCYTOPENIA

Thrombocytopenia is a reduction in the number of platelets circulating in the blood. Because platelets are essential for clotting, the main symptom of this disorder is abnormal bleeding, particularly into the skin where the blood forms bruises and small hemorrhages called petechiae, which appear as round purple-red spots. Mouth and nosebleeds are also common.

There is a range of possible causes of thrombocytopenia. One of the most frequent is an autoimmune disease called idiopathic thrombocytopenic purpura. This involves the production of antibodies against platelets by spleen and lymph tissue, resulting in the destruction of platelets in the spleen. As well as the characteristic bruising and skin hemorrhaging, this type of thrombocytopenia may also cause abnormal menstrual bleeding and sudden loss of blood in the intestinal tract. More children are affected than adults, mostly after viral infection, and often treatment is not necessary. In adults idiopathic thrombocytopenic purpura may develop into a chronic condition and does not usually follow viral infection.

Drug-induced non-immune thrombocytopenia is a reaction to certain drugs, some of which can damage bone marrow and slow the production of platelets. This is potentially fatal if it leads to bleeding in the brain or another vital organ. Other drugs may not affect the production of platelets but rather render them useless by ensuring that they cannot adhere to one another, a property

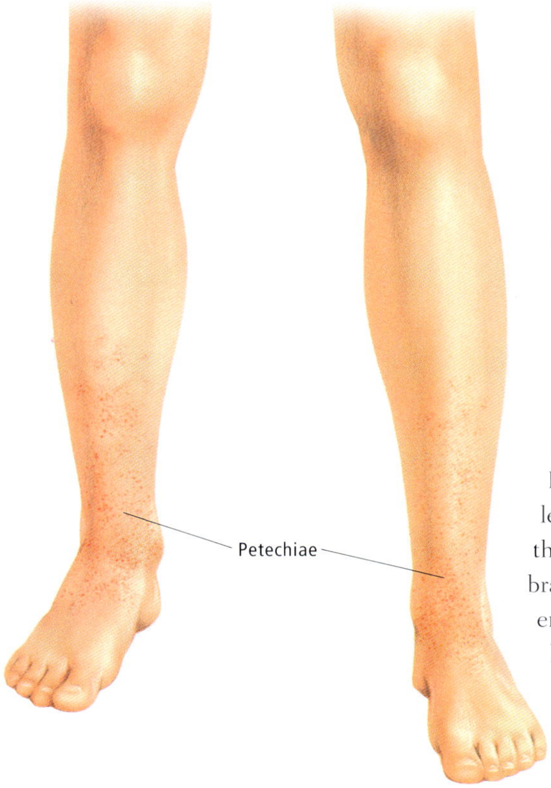

Thrombocytopenia

In this condition, reduced numbers of platelets in the blood inhibit clotting. This results in a distinctive rash of small red spots—usually on the legs—caused by abnormal bleeding into the skin. These spots are known as petechiae.

that is required for blood clotting. Drug-induced immune thrombocytopenia is the development of antibodies to blood platelets, either as a result of the direct use of certain drugs or, in the case of an affected fetus, due to drugs taken by the mother during pregnancy.

The condition may also occur with certain other diseases or infections, such as leukemia or AIDS, or as a reaction to particular drugs. Treatment depends on the cause.

Some forms of the illness will resolve themselves over time. Others may require treatments such as a transfusion of platelets. Complications can include bloody stools and vomiting blood.

SEE ALSO *AIDS, Autoimmune disease, Blood, Leukemia, Nosebleed, Platelets*

THROMBOEMBOLISM

Thromboembolism is the process of clot formation in a blood vessel (thrombosis) and its subsequent dislodgment and travel to another part of the circulation (embolism). When the thrombosis occurs in an artery, the dislodged fragment (embolus) travels to a more distant part of the arterial circulation until it obstructs a smaller branch. The blockage deprives the tissues in that area of their normal blood flow, cutting off their oxygen supply and causing death of the tissues in that organ or body part. Emboli from deep vein thrombosis in the legs or, occasionally, the arms travel to the right side of the heart and lodge in a branch of the pulmonary artery (pulmonary embolism). Alternatively an embolus may lodge in an artery in the extremities (especially in the legs and feet), the brain, the heart, or (less commonly) the bowel or kidney.

Thromboembolism is often associated with other conditions such as atherosclerosis (where a thrombus may form in the diseased area of an artery). It is more likely to affect people with blood diseases, those who are immobilized for long periods, and people with major illnesses such as cancer.

The symptoms of thromboembolism depend on where the embolus has lodged. In a limb or extremity it may cause pain and numbness; the limb will be cold and pale, lacking a pulse. Foot or leg ulcers and gangrene (death of tissue) may develop. In an internal organ the embolus usually causes pain and the loss of function of that organ—for example, stroke in the brain (causing paralysis); angina or myocardial infarction in the heart (which may cause heart failure or sudden death); and breathlessness and collapse in the lung.

Thromboembolism requires emergency treatment in hospital. Intravenous drugs are given—thrombolytic drugs such as streptokinase to break up the clot and anticoagulant medications such as heparin to prevent the development of new clots. Sometimes surgery is undertaken to remove the clot.

After recovery, oral anticoagulant drugs such as warfarin may need to be taken indefinitely.

SEE ALSO *Arteries, Blood vessels, Embolism, Pulmonary embolism, Thrombosis, Veins*

THROMBOLYTIC DRUGS

Thrombolytic therapy is treatment used to dissolve, or lyse, a clot. The drugs employed to dissolve clots act by enhancing the body's own anti-clotting mechanism, the fibrinolytic system. This is a series of proteins whose actions result in the breakdown of fibrin, the hard clot formed when the coagulation system is activated.

Thrombolytic therapy has been used mainly to treat coronary artery thrombosis which can cause heart attack. Studies have shown that thrombolytic therapy can significantly reduce the resulting damage to heart muscle and the risk of death from heart attack. However, the treatment must be given within hours of onset to be effective.

SEE ALSO *Coronary artery disease, Coronary thrombosis, Heart, Myocardial infarction, Thrombosis*

THROMBOSIS

Thrombosis is the formation of a clot, or thrombus, in a blood vessel. The blood is normally maintained in a liquid state within the circulation. However, a hemostatic system exists to allow the blood to clot in response to injury to a blood vessel. In disease states abnormal clotting may occur, leading to organ damage.

Disease may affect various aspects of the hemostatic system, which comprises the vessel wall and its lining endothelial cells, the platelet cells and the coagulation system. It may also affect the body's protective anti-clotting system, the fibrinolytic system.

Thrombosis may occur in arteries or veins, or in small vessels such as capillaries. The causes of these various forms of thrombosis vary.

Arterial thrombosis is generally caused by disease of the arterial wall, mostly due to atherosclerosis. This results in the irregular narrowing of blood vessels (plaque formation) and a later breakdown or ulceration of the smooth lining of the artery. Exposure of the raw surface of the artery causes platelet cells to adhere as a protective response. Eventually a clot will form and totally obstruct the vessel cavity (lumen). This deprives the organ supplied by the obstructed artery of oxygen and nutrients, and tissue death (infarction) occurs.

THROMBUS

A thrombus is a blood clot inside a vein or artery. It can be dangerous if it severely impedes or stops the flow of blood, leading to a condition known as thrombosis. In cerebral thrombosis, a thrombus develops in an artery to the brain and can cause a stroke. A thrombus in an artery leading to cardiac muscle can lead to a heart attack. Certain factors predispose people to developing blood clots. These include slow blood circulation, the disease arteriosclerosis, prolonged use of the contraceptive pill,

Thrombosis

Thrombosis is the formation of a blood clot (thrombus) inside an artery or vein which impedes blood flow. The total blockage of a blood vessel by thrombi can deprive organs of vital oxygen and nutrients and lead to the death of tissue (infarction).

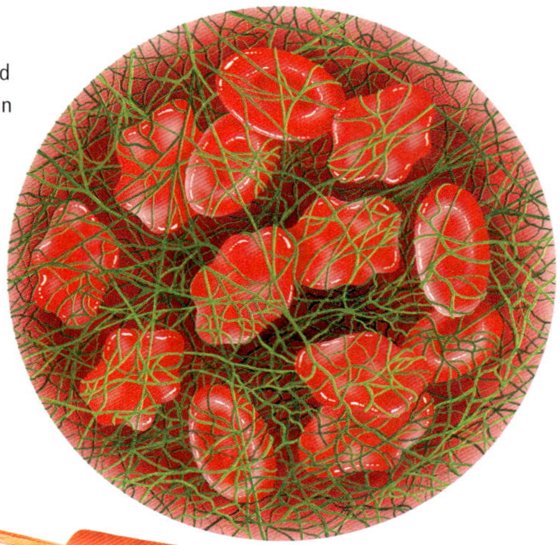

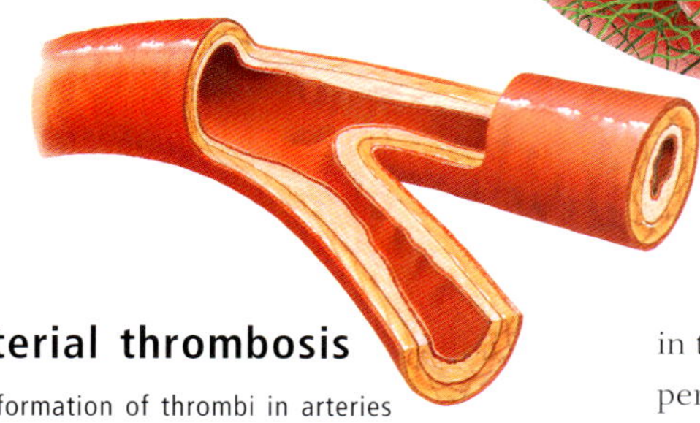

Arterial thrombosis

The formation of thrombi in arteries is most commonly caused by atherosclerosis—a disease in which the blood vessels narrow and the lining of the vessel walls deteriorates.

The most common forms of serious infarction are myocardial infarction (heart attack), cerebral infarction (stroke) and peripheral arterial thrombosis leading to gangrene. Prevention of these forms of thrombosis includes treating the risk factors for atherosclerosis, such as hypertension and high cholesterol; anti-platelet drugs such as aspirin are often prescribed.

Venous thrombosis occurs most commonly in the deep veins of the legs, resulting in pain and swelling due to blockages in the blood leaving the legs. More serious consequences can occur if the clot detaches from the vein wall and travels to the lungs (pulmonary embolism). Venous thrombosis can occasionally occur in the brain or the intestines, with serious effects. Thrombosis in the veins may be related to disease of the vein wall, such as varicose veins. However, there are generally other contributory factors, such as sluggish circulation (stasis) or an alteration in the composition of the blood, making it clot more readily. This is generally due to an increase in proteins of the coagulation system and/or a decrease in the protective antifibrinolytic system.

Deep vein thrombosis is most likely to occur during periods of immobility, such as after an operation. Apart from the resulting venous stasis, there are changes in the blood during surgery which make a person less likely to bleed and more likely to clot. Similar changes occur during pregnancy, also increasing the risk of venous thrombosis.

It is increasingly recognized that some people inherit genes making them more susceptible to clotting. This tendency is known as thrombophilia and often explains why there is an increased incidence of clotting in some families, or why some pregnant women or some women taking the oral contraceptive develop thrombosis and others do not. The risk of venous thrombosis can be reduced by early mobilization after surgery and preventive treatment with anticoagulant drugs, such as heparin or warfarin.

SEE ALSO *Arteries, Atherosclerosis, Blood, Blood vessels, Capillaries, Cholesterol, Circulatory system, Gangrene, Hypertension, Myocardial infarction, Platelets, Pulmonary embolism, Stroke, Veins*

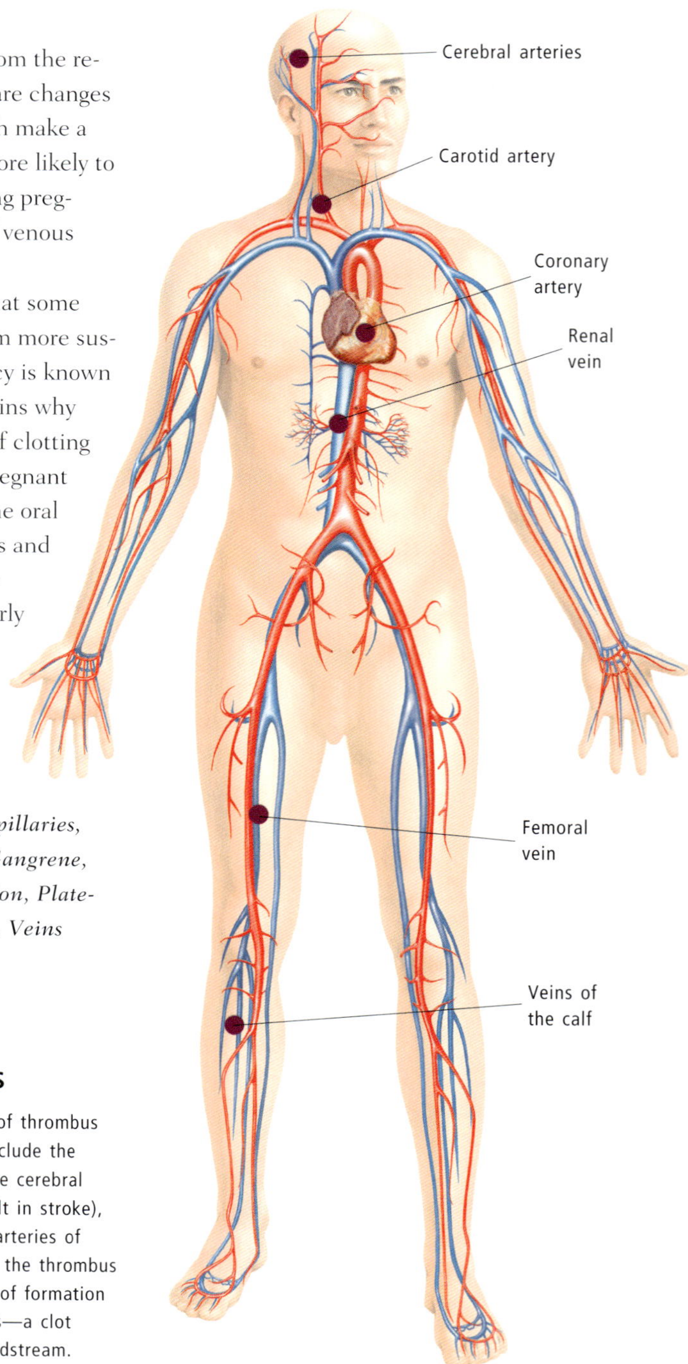

Thrombus sites

The most common sites of thrombus (blood clot) formation include the deep veins of the leg, the cerebral arteries (which may result in stroke), the renal veins and the arteries of the heart. In some cases the thrombus breaks free from its site of formation and becomes an embolus—a clot carried along in the bloodstream.

smoking and a serious injury. A thrombus that breaks away from the site where it formed is called an embolus.

SEE ALSO *Arteriosclerosis, Myocardial infarction, Stroke*

THUMBSUCKING

Many babies suck their thumbs while still in the uterus and can be born with blisters on the top lip, commonly referred to as sucking blisters. Although frowned upon in some societies, sucking the thumb (occasionally the fingers or some other part of the hand) is a comfort mechanism used by many babies and small children which is both emotionally comforting and physically harmless.

Children who continue to suck their thumbs into the school years, however, may be in need of emotional support or counseling, as such long-term sucking is often a replacement activity for some need. By this age the action of sucking may also damage the alignment of the teeth, a problem which can usually be rectified quite easily with orthodontic treatment if it does not right itself with time. The other result may be calluses on thumbs or fingers, but these too will disappear when the habit ceases. In most cases no treatment is needed.

SEE ALSO *Orthodontics, Teeth*

THYMUS GLAND

The thymus gland is found beneath the sternum, at about the level of the large vessels leaving the heart. It is much more obvious in children and adolescents, when it is active, than in adults, when it has shriveled to a fatty, fibrous remnant. At birth the thymus weighs about ½ ounce (14 grams) and reaches about 1 ounce (28 grams) by puberty. In adults the gland reduces in weight again to only ½ ounce (14 grams).

Although it is called a gland, the thymus is actually a lymph organ, producing T lymphocytes (a type of white blood cell) for distribution to the rest of the body. T lymphocytes are involved in the defense of the body against viruses and cancer cells, in delayed-type hypersensitivity reactions and in graft rejection.

If the thymus is removed from a newborn rat, other lymphoid organs in the body fail to develop and there is a decrease in the number of T lymphocytes in the blood. The animal is unable to make an adequate defense against viruses or to reject transplanted foreign tissue. Animals subsequently become weak, lose weight and die about 3–4 months after birth, due to widespread and overwhelming infections occurring throughout the body. Removal of the thymus in adults (sometimes advised for the treatment of the disease myasthenia gravis) does not have such serious effects because T lymphocytes have already been distributed throughout the body. In humans there are some diseases where T lymphocytes fail to develop. Children so affected will die soon after birth if untreated.

SEE ALSO *Lymphatic/Immune system, T cells*

Thymus

Part of the endocrine system, the thymus is a ductless gland located just under the sternum in the chest. It is a lymph organ and uses the hormones it produces to manufacture mature T lymphocytes, which play an important role in the body's immune defenses.

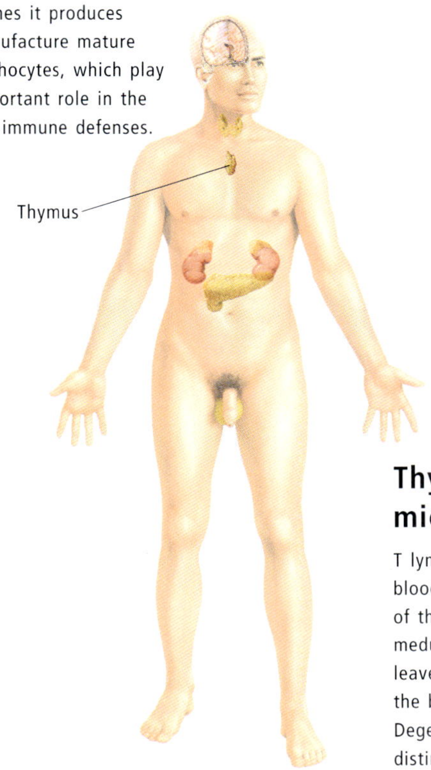

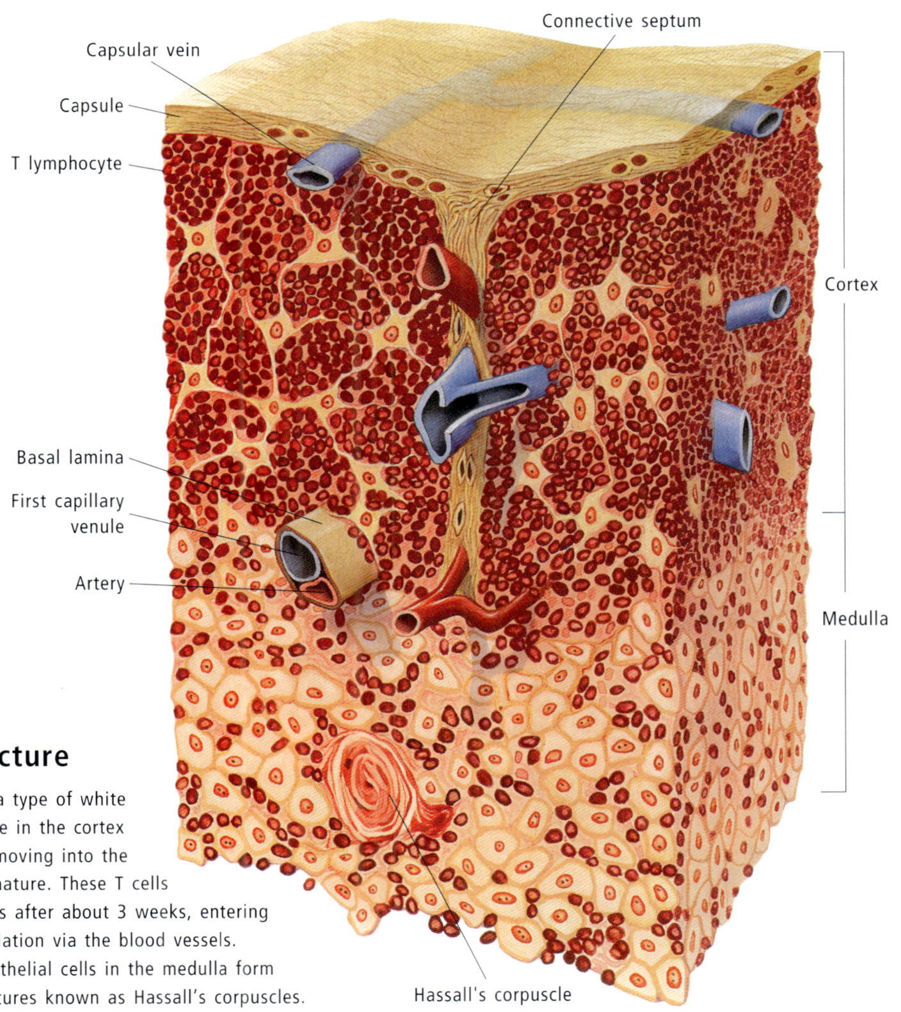

Thymus microstructure

T lymphocytes (a type of white blood cell) divide in the cortex of the thymus, moving into the medulla when mature. These T cells leave the thymus after about 3 weeks, entering the body's circulation via the blood vessels. Degenerated epithelial cells in the medulla form distinctive structures known as Hassall's corpuscles.

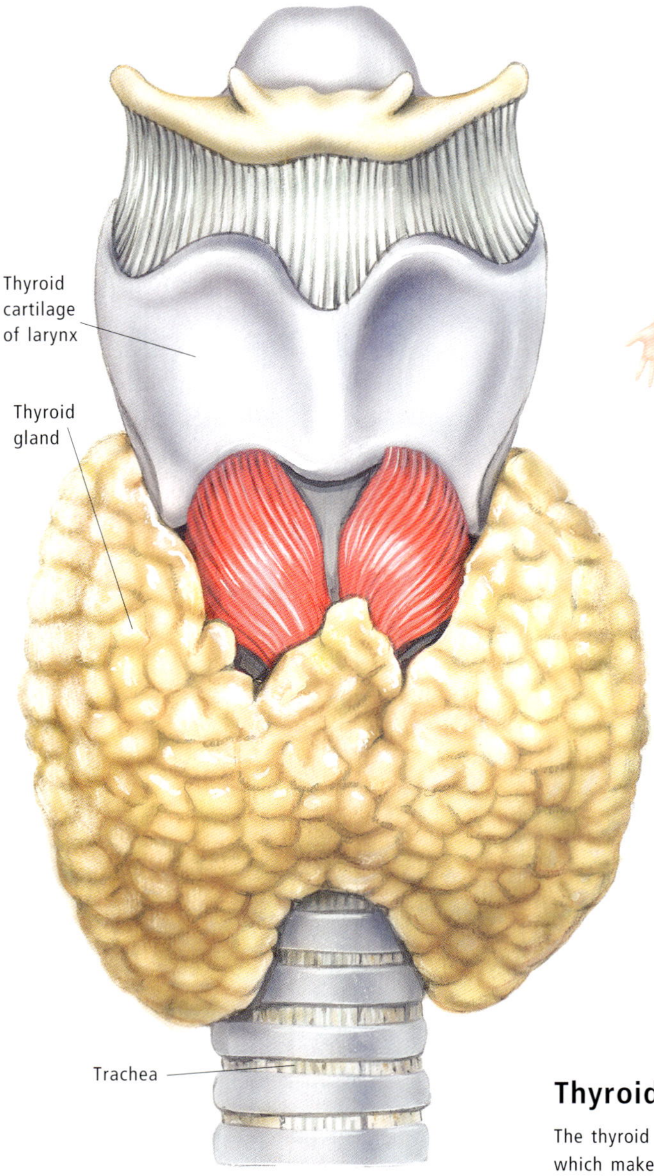

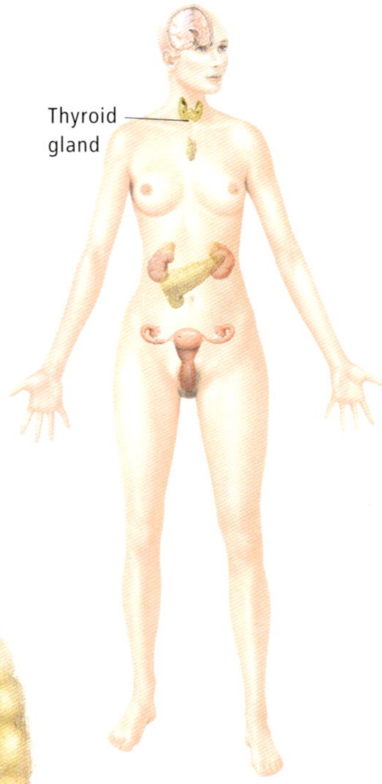

Thyroid

The largest of the endocrine glands, the thyroid is situated at the front of the trachea in the neck. The two lobes of the gland are joined by a narrow bridge (or isthmus).

Thyroid microstructure

The thyroid gland comprises many follicles which make thyroid hormone and secrete it into the bloodstream. Each follicle consists of thyroid epithelial cells arranged around a cavity (or lumen) filled with colloid, a gelatinous substance. Thyroid hormones are stored within the colloid.

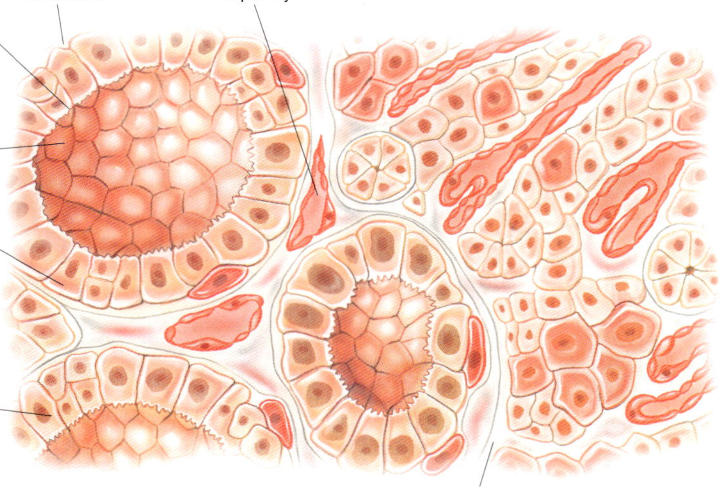

THYROID GLAND

The thyroid gland is one of the endocrine glands, which secrete hormones directly into the bloodstream or body cavities. The thyroid gland consists of two lobes joined together in the midline by a narrow bridge or isthmus. It is located in the neck immediately below and in front of the voice box (larynx). The thyroid gland is very well supplied with blood by a series of arteries and lies in close proximity to several important nerves which supply the larynx. These nerves must be carefully identified and protected during surgery on the thyroid. Enlargement of the thyroid gland is known as a goiter. This may occur with either increased or decreased thyroid hormone production.

The thyroid gland is made up of many follicles, which are spherical or polygonal structures consisting of cells arranged around a cavity filled with a gelatinous substance called colloid.

The follicles of the thyroid gland make thyroid hormone and secrete it into the bloodstream. Thyroid hormone is composed of two different substances: thyroxine (also called T4, or tetraiodothyronine) and triiodothyronine (T3). Most thyroid hormone is made up of thyroxine. An essential component of both substances is iodine, found in the diet.

Thyroid hormone has several functions, the main one being to determine the metabolic rate of the body tissues, that is, how fast the tissues of the body will use up oxygen and produce waste materials. An excess of thyroid hormone will speed up metabolism and a deficiency will slow it down. Thyroid hormone is also necessary for the normal growth and development of children—too little thyroid hormone will produce short stature and mental retardation. The production of thyroid hormone is under the control of thyroid stimulating hormone (TSH), which is released from the pituitary gland. The presence of thyroid hormone in the bloodstream inhibits the production of TSH in a feedback loop control system. Between the thyroid follicles are parafollicular cells (C cells) which are responsible for the production and secretion of another hormone, calcitonin, which acts to reduce the concentration of calcium in the blood.

Diagnostic tests

Tests of the thyroid gland and its function include blood tests to determine the concentrations of thyroid hormone and thyroid-stimulating hormone in the blood, and isotope scans to determine the presence of "cold" or "hot" spots in the thyroid gland. Thyroid hormone concentration will be elevated in hyperthyroidism, while levels will be reduced in hypothyroidism or myxedema. Reduced levels of both TSH and thyroid hormone indicate a problem with the pituitary gland's production of TSH.

Diseases and disorders

Many diseases and disorders can affect the thyroid gland.

Hyperthyroidism

In hyperthyroidism (thyrotoxicosis), there is an increased level of thyroid hormone circulating in the blood. It may be due to a solitary hypersecretory thyroid nodule (Plummer's disease), a multinodular goiter with increased secretion, or excessive stimulation of the thyroid gland by factors circulating in the bloodstream, as seen in Graves' disease.

Patients experience symptoms reflecting the effects of excess circulating thyroid hormone, including nervousness, increased sweating, increased appetite, weight loss, muscular weakness, increased frequency of bowel movements, menstrual problems and intolerance to heat.

If blood levels of thyroid hormone reach dangerous heights during thyrotoxicosis, the patient may develop a condition known as thyroid storm. In this situation the patient will experience accentuated thyrotoxic symptoms, heart failure, grossly elevated fever and delirium.

Hyperthyroidism may be treated with the use of antithyroid drugs, radioactive iodine tablets, or surgery, depending on the patient's age, state of health and the size of the goiter.

Hypothyroidism

In hypothyroidism (also called myxedema) there is a reduced level of thyroid hormone in the blood. In this condition the patient will experience a puffy thickening of the skin below the eyes, and in the skin of the lips, fingers and legs. The patient will also complain of lethargy, the slowing of thought processes, weight gain and the loss of hair. Hypothyroidism in adults is most commonly seen in Hashimoto's disease and in endemic goiter, where iodine levels in the diet are low.

Graves' disease

Named after the Irish physician Robert James Graves, Graves' disease is the most common (though not the only) cause of hyperthyroidism (thyrotoxicosis). Also known as toxic diffuse goiter, it is an autoimmune disease, in which the body's own immune system attacks and inflames the thyroid gland. Antibodies to their own thyroid gland can be detected in the blood of people who have Graves' disease.

In this condition, the thyroid gland swells in size (develops into a goiter) and secretes excessive amounts of thyroid hormone into the bloodstream, causing thyrotoxicosis. The affected person experiences rapid heartbeat, tremor, increased sweating, weight loss (despite increased appetite), and weakness and fatigue.

A condition called exophthalmos often develops, in which the eyeballs protrude and the eyelids retract. This is caused by edema (fluid accumulation) in the tissues surrounding the eyeball in its socket. This eye protrusion usually responds to treatment of the excessive thyroid activity, but may cause loss of vision if not treated promptly.

Graves' disease is more common in women than in men and tends to run in families.

The condition is diagnosed by blood tests which show excess thyroid hormone in the blood, and a radioactive thyroid scan. There are several treatment options, including treatment with drugs such as propylthiouracil, and for severe cases the surgical removal of part of the thyroid gland, or oral administration of radioactive iodine.

Hashimoto's disease

Hashimoto's disease, also known as Hashimoto's thyroiditis or chronic lymphocytic thyroiditis, is a slowly developing persistent inflammation of the thyroid gland. Patients experience enlargement of the neck with pain and tenderness in the region of the thyroid. The enlargement of the thyroid gland may cause compression of the windpipe (trachea) and esophagus, resulting in difficulty in breathing and swallowing.

Like Graves' disease, it is an autoimmune disorder, affecting woman more often than men, and tends to run in families, but unlike Graves' disease, the inflammation may result in the undersecretion of thyroid hormone into the bloodstream, or hypothyroidism, the symptoms of which are intolerance to cold, weight gain, fatigue, constipation, joint stiffness and facial swelling.

Hashimoto's thyroiditis is often slow to develop, and is often associated with other autoimmune endocrine disorders such as diabetes mellitus or Addison's disease. High levels of thyroid autoantibodies are almost always present. Diagnosis can be made by a needle biopsy of the thyroid gland, with subsequent examination with a microscope.

Treatment may involve surgery to remove excess thyroid tissue which is compressing nearby structures. In mild cases, there may be no treatment required. Replacement therapy with thyroid hormone will be needed if there is hypothyroidism. In some patients, however, replacement therapy is associated with progression of the goiter.

Because Hashimoto's disease is slow to progress and often remains stable for many years, prospects for recovery are usually good.

Cretinism

Thyroid hormone is essential for brain development, and iodine is necessary for synthesis of thyroid hormone. In areas of the world where dietary iodine is inadequate, the fetus and neonate may not make sufficient thyroid hormone for normal brain maturation. In this condition, known as cretinism, the child will be intellectually disabled and have stunted growth. The face will be broad, emergence of the teeth will be delayed, and the tongue and mouth will be large. Parts of the world where this may occur are usually mountainous. Fortunately, supplementation of the diet with small amounts of iodine can completely prevent the problem.

Cretinism may also arise in children with congenital absence of the thyroid gland or in those who have a genetic defect in the enzymes that make thyroid hormone. In these children the condition may be remedied by thyroid hormone supplementation. Early diagnosis and treatment are essential.

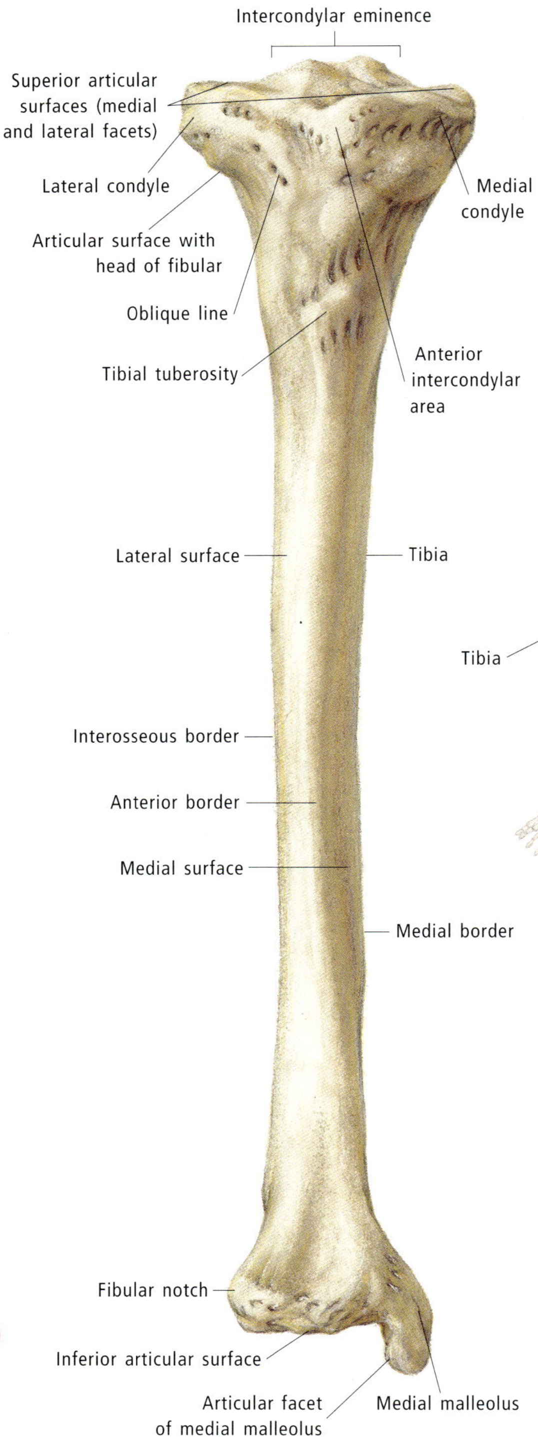

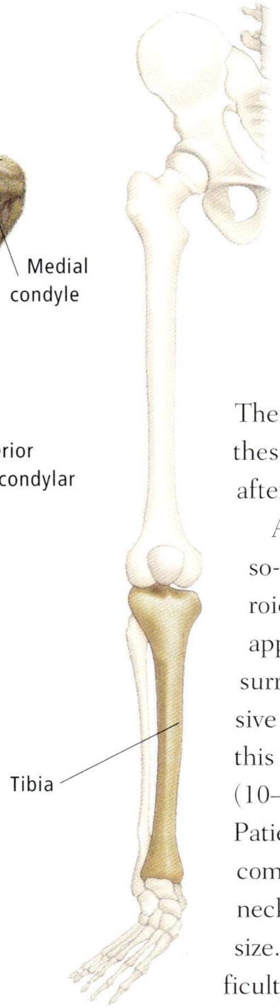

Tibia

The tibia or "shinbone" is the second-longest bone in the body. Joining with the femur, it helps form the knee joint, and combines with the fibula and the talus to form the ankle joint.

Cancer

Cancers may arise from the thyroid gland, and are more common if there has been irradiation of the head and neck earlier in life. Thyroid cancers are of several different types. Those found in young patients (papillary adenocarcinoma) are usually slow-growing and spread outside the gland relatively late in the course of the disease. There are good survival rates for these tumors (over 80 percent after 10 years).

At the other extreme are the so-called undifferentiated thyroid cancers, which usually appear later in life and invade surrounding tissue in an aggressive manner. Survival rates with this kind of cancer are quite low (10–15 percent after 10 years). Patients with thyroid cancers complain of a painless lump in the neck, which gradually increases in size. They may also experience difficulty in swallowing and hoarseness of the voice, particularly if the nerves to the larynx have been damaged. Treatment is by surgery to remove the tumor and any involved lymph nodes, accompanied by radioactive iodine therapy. Aggressive tumors may need to be treated with chemotherapeutic agents. Tumors from the kidney, breast and lung sometimes spread to the thyroid gland, but they usually produce multiple lumps rather than one.

SEE ALSO *Cretinism, Endocrine glands, Glands, Goiter, Graves' disease, Hashimoto's disease, Hyperthyroidism, Hypothyroidism, Myxedema, Pituitary gland, Thyrotoxicosis*

THYROTOXICOSIS

Thyrotoxicosis or hyperthyroidism is caused by increased secretion of thyroid hormone into the bloodstream from the thyroid gland. The increased activity of the thyroid gland may be the result of an enlarged and hyperactive gland arising on its own, or to stimulation of the thyroid gland by antibodies in autoimmune disease (Graves' disease).

Patients complain of symptoms such as nervousness, weight loss with increased appetite, increased sweating, increased bowel movements, menstrual problems, rapid heart rate and a swelling in the neck (goiter).

In severe cases the condition may result in collapse and, if untreated, death—a condition sometimes called "thyroid storm".

Treatment is with drugs such as propylthiouracil, which block the production of thyroid hormone by the thyroid gland. Alternatives are the oral administration of radioactive iodine, which is taken up by the thyroid and destroys the gland's hormone-producing cells, or surgical removal of part of the gland.

SEE ALSO *Goiter, Graves' disease, Hyperthyroidism, Thyroid gland*

TIBIA

The tibia, or shin bone, is the inner and thicker of the two bones of the lower leg, the other being the fibula. It is also the second longest bone in the body, after the thighbone (femur). At its upper end, the tibia meets the femur to form the knee joint. At its lower end it meets with the fibula and a small bone called the talus to form the ankle joint. The small bump felt protruding on the inside of the ankle is part of the tibia that articulates with the talus. It is known as the medial malleolus. Pain along the tibia is often caused by shin splints (strain of the long flexor muscles of the toes).

A fracture of the tibia is a common injury, especially in childhood. It is usually caused by a direct blow to the child's leg, most often during a contact sport. In adults it may occur after weakening of the bone from repeated stress during jogging running or walking.

After the injury, there is severe pain in the leg at the fracture site, swelling of the tissue surrounding the fracture and, if the fracture is complete (that is, broken all the way through), the leg is deformed.

The fracture must be set under general anesthesia in hospital. X-rays of the tibia will confirm that the ends of the bone have been correctly aligned. The bone is held in place with a cast which extends above the knee and below the ankle. Healing usually takes 6–8 weeks. Then physical therapy is needed to restore muscle strength and eliminate stiffness in the ankle and knee.

SEE ALSO *Ankle, Femur, Fibula, Fractures, Knee, Leg, Shin splints*

TIC

A tic is the involuntary production of a movement or sound that occurs suddenly, rapidly, without conscious control, and may recur many times within a short period.

Movements are generally purposeless and may take the form of throat clearing, squinting, facial spasms, shrugs or jerks of the neck. More complex actions such as jumping or hopping are also tics. Vocal tics can involve repeated uttering of obscenities or generally unacceptable words, or of meaningless sounds.

Tics may be more frequent under stress or anxiety. They can be linked to emotional disturbance, obsessive behavior or developmental delays. Tics can range from mild to severe, and the affliction can be brief or long-lasting. Children, boys more than girls, often suffer transient tics which generally disappear without treatment. If the tics persist, the possibility of Tourette's syndrome must be considered.

Obsessive-compulsive disorder may produce behaviors similar to tics which are not classified as tics because they involve purposeful and conscious repetition; tics are purposeless and not the product of any identifiable abnormality.

SEE ALSO ***Neuralgia, Obsessive-compulsive disorder, Tourette's syndrome***

TIC DOULOUREUX

Tic douloureux, or trigeminal neuralgia, is a disease of the trigeminal nerve, the principal sensory nerve in the face. The condition is marked by flashes of excruciating pain, which can be set off by touching a sensitive area of the face or by movements of the jaw. It can occur many times in a day and is usually felt in the cheek near the nose or above the temporomandibular joint.

This disorder is sometimes associated with compression of a nerve by an artery, and may be relieved by surgery, but generally the cause is unknown.

Normal pain relief does not work because of the spasmodic nature of the attacks, although antidepressant drugs may sometimes give temporary pain relief. Surgical destruction of the nerves is a possible treatment as a last resort.

SEE ALSO ***Neuralgia***

TICKS

Ticks are small eight-legged arachnids related to mites and spiders. They feed by attaching themselves to the skin of humans and animals and sucking their blood. Although some people may experience a reaction to a tick, serious disease arises not so much from the tick itself but from diseases it transmits. Ticks can be the source of several diseases, including Lyme disease, Rocky Mountain spotted fever and Colorado tick fever.

Lyme disease is also known as Lyme arthritis. It is caused by the bacterium *Borrelia burgdorferi* and is transmitted by the bite of ticks carried on the bodies of animals, especially deer, field mice and other small rodents. It causes lethargy, muscle weakness, loss of coordination, and paralysis, which may affect the respiratory muscles. If diagnosed and treated early with antibiotics, the condition is usually curable.

Rocky Mountain spotted fever is caused by infection with microscopic parasites known as rickettsiae. Symptoms include a spotted rash, fever, muscle and joint pain, as well as nausea, vomiting and hallucinations. Treatment is with antibiotics. If left untreated, the disease can lead to heart failure, kidney failure, or death.

Colorado tick fever is a viral infection causing a flu-like illness, severe headache, sensitivity to light, and a rash. The symptoms last for about a week, and return after a few days of remission. Treatment is with rest, fluids and painkillers.

In tick-infested areas, it is best to wear protective clothing and use an insect repellent containing DEET (diethyltoluamide). To remove an attached tick, grasp it behind its head as close to the skin as possible, using fine-point tweezers or a tick remover. Gently pull the tick out sideways with a sharp twisting action. Hands should be washed with hot, soapy water, and the tweezers and bite disinfected. Do not attempt to kill the tick with alcohol, petroleum jelly, methylated spirits or any other substance as this causes the tick to inject more bacteria and toxins. Mass infestations of tiny (larval stage) ticks are best removed by soaking for 20 minutes in a deep, warm bath with one cup of bicarbonate of soda added.

SEE ALSO ***Lyme disease, Rocky Mountain spotted fever***

TINEA

Tinea is a fungal infection caused by various species of either *Trichophyton* or *Microsporum*, which can grow on the skin, in the hair or the nails, creating visible signs such as dry, scaly, red or cracked skin, but no permanent damage. Ringworm, an infection of the skin causing reddish circular marks, is caused by a tinea fungus—despite the name, no worm is involved.

Tinea has become increasingly common in recent times because the spores can survive for long periods in flaked-off skin cells, which may be picked up on the bare feet from floor coverings. This is an easy method of transporting infection between users of hotel rooms and sports clubs, and between residents in private homes.

Tinea grows fast in warm moist areas of the body, particularly in skin folds. The skin rash is quite characteristic, appearing as a slightly raised patch with sharp borders, which, as it expands and spreads, leaves a dry or scaly clearing in the center. Between the toes it may cause painful itchy cracks in the skin and a characteristic unpleasant smell. Effects can vary from redness to blisters, which can become sites of secondary bacterial infection, particularly if blood circulation is poor.

Tinea infections are named after the part of the body where they are found and are as follows.

Tinea capitis affects the scalp, creating itchy red areas and hair loss.

Tinea corporis is tinea found on any part of the trunk, arms or legs, particularly in skin folds, where it will create red spots which spread as the fungus grows.

Tinea cruris, also called jock itch, is tinea in the groin. It affects men more than women and is often associated with wearing groin protectors.

Tinea pedis, or athlete's foot, is probably the most common form of this fungal infection, and usually presents as a patch of white scaly skin under the little toe; it may not be evident elsewhere.

Tinea unguium infects toenails and fingernails (onychomycosis), appearing as white or powdery patches, thickening the nail or causing it to fall off.

Tinea versicolor, an infection caused by the yeast *Pityrosporum orbiculare*, changes the color of skin and prevents tanning. People with dark skin may develop light patches, and those with light skin dark patches. There may be scaliness and irritation, but usually there is no pain or itching. Treatment is with antidandruff (selenium) shampoos, which may cause skin irritation. Pigmentation takes some time to return after clearing the infection, which may recur whenever conditions are favorable.

In most cases, tinea is easily recognizable by the physician. If there is doubt, a skin lesion biopsy (most commonly, scraping of the skin) can be performed followed by microscopic examination or culture, which shows the fungus responsible.

Most tinea infections are mild and can be treated with antifungal creams or powders, such as those that contain miconazole or clotrimazole. In some cases, topical corticosteroids may be added as well. In cases of severe or chronic infection, oral antifungal medications containing ketoconazole or sulconazole or another antifungal agent may be needed. Antibiotics may be needed to treat secondary bacterial infections. The condition may take up to 4–6 weeks to completely clear.

As the fungal spores are so hardy, it is important to eradicate them from shoes, socks and floor surfaces to avoid continual reinfection. Preventive measures are to ensure feet and toes are completely dry before dressing, to go without shoes and socks when indoors, to avoid skin contact with areas in common use at pools or gyms and to clean home floor coverings; it may also be wise to throw away shoes that have been worn for some time.

SEE ALSO *Antifungals, Ringworm*

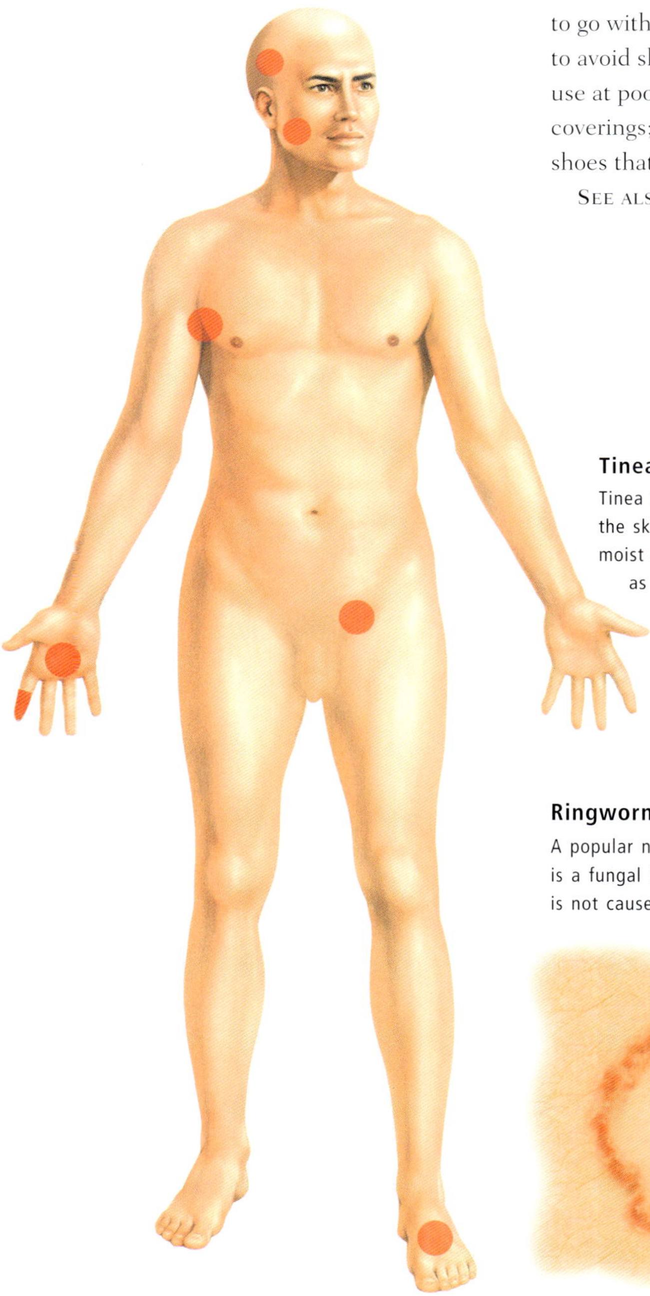

Tinea sites

Tinea is a fungal infection of the skin, especially in warm moist areas of the body, such as between the toes and in the groin area.

Tinea

Ringworm

A popular name for tinea, ringworm is a fungal infection of the skin and is not caused by a worm.

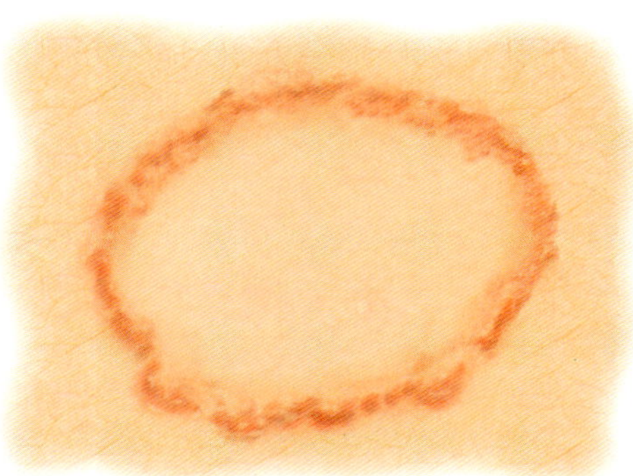

TINNITUS

Tinnitus is the sensation of hearing a sound in one or both ears when there is no external noise from the environment. The sound may be a buzzing or ringing, a high pitched hiss or whine, or more complex sounds, and may be continuous or intermittent.

Tinnitus is a symptom of a number of possible conditions. It is generally associated with ear damage from exposure to loud noise, or with age-related hearing loss, and can also follow a middle ear infection. A rushing noise may indicate vascular problems. Certain drugs, after long periods of use, can affect the inner ear.

Tinnitus can also be caused by tumors on, or injury to, the vestibulocochlear nerve; problems with the temporomandibular joint; otosclerosis, a stiffening of the bones (ossicles) of the middle ear; head and neck injury; and Menière's disease. Sometimes tinnitus may arise with no identifiable cause. It may be so severe as to interfere with concentration or sleep.

There is no cure, but to prevent the condition worsening, loud noise and drug use should be avoided. The noise can sometimes be masked by "filling silence" with more pleasant sounds such as a radio or softly ticking clock; users of hearing aids often report that this makes the tinnitus less intrusive. Some people find that the symptoms are worse when they are anxious or stessed.

There are a number of alternative therapies that may help to alleviate the symptoms of tinnitus. Herbalism practitioners prescribe ginkgo biloba, a stimulant for peripheral circulation, or black cohosh, an antispasmodic of the small blood vessels. Homeopathy suggests a number of specific remedies to treat various noises in the ear.

Hypnotherapists aim to either remove ringing in the ear or to lessen the patient's awareness of and reactions to the tinnitus if the sounds cannot be eliminated. Naturopathy suggests vitamin B complex, calcium, magnesium and potassium supplements. Traditional Chinese Medicine views an imbalance of the kidney energy as one possible cause of tinnitus. Acupuncture and Chinese herbs may bring relief in some cases.

SEE ALSO *Ear, Hearing, Menière's disease, Otosclerosis*

T

TISSUE

A tissue is a group or layer of cells of a similar kind, plus the material packaged between them, all of which function together for the same specialized purpose. There are four major types of tissue in the human body: epithelial, connective, muscular and nervous.

Epithelial tissue

Epithelial tissue, also known simply as epithelium, is made up of cells that are packaged so closely together there is virtually no room between them for any extra material. The cells are also arranged in continuous sheets in either single or multiple layers. Epithelial tissue has a wide range of roles including protection, excretion, absorption, sensory reception, secretion and reproduction. Compared to other tissue types, it is often exposed to a high degree of wear but has the capacity to renew itself relatively efficiently and quickly. Epithelium has a nerve supply but no direct blood supply. Vessels in neighboring tissue provide nutrients and carry out the removal of wastes.

Epithelial tissue is classified broadly into two main types. Glandular epithelium has a secretory function and forms both exocrine and endocrine glands. The second type, covering and lining epithelium, is more widespread. It forms the outermost layer of the skin and of some internal organs. It also lines the digestive, respiratory, reproductive and urinary systems as well as ducts, blood vessels and body cavities. Covering and lining epithelial tissue comes in either single or multiple layers and contains one of a number of different cell types, depending on the specific function of the tissue.

For example, simple squamous epithelium is a thin single-layered film that lines the air sacs of the lungs and allows for the diffusion of respiratory gases (oxygen and carbon dioxide) across its surface. In contrast, stratified squamous epithelium, which has a predominantly protective role, is a multi-layered variation which covers the tongue and forms tough moist surfaces such as the linings of the vagina, esophagus and mouth.

Connective tissue

Connective tissue is widespread in the body. The principal roles of connective tissue are to bind, support or strengthen organs or other tissues. It also functions inside the body to divide and compartmentalize other tissues and organ structures.

Structurally, connective tissue consists of cells linked together and supported by a matrix composed of protein fibers in a medium known as "ground substance". The ground substance can be in fluid, gel or solid form and is normally secreted by the cells of the connective tissue. The protein fibers come in three forms—collagen, elastin and reticular fibers—the proportions of which vary depending on the function of the tissue in which they are found. Each, however, provides support and strength along with flexibility. The molecules that form the protein fibers and ground substance are secreted by specialized connective tissue cells.

Other cells commonly found in connective tissue include disease-fighting macrophages, antibody-secreting plasma cells and mast cells, which produce histamine to stimulate the dilation of blood vessels at inflammation sites.

Humans have five main types of connective tissue: loose connective tissue, dense connective tissue, cartilage, bone and blood. Loose connective tissue includes adipose tissue, which is specialized for fat storage. One type of dense connective tissue, known as dense regular connective tissue, forms tendons and cartilage. Another, elastic connective tissue, is specialized for stretching and is found in the lungs, some artery walls and the vocal cords.

Cartilage comes in three forms: hyaline, fibrocartilage and elastic cartilage. Hyaline cartilage is the weakest and most abundant cartilage in the body. It covers the bones where they form synovial joints. Fibrocartilage forms a component of some other joints, which usually have a limited range of movement. Elastic cartilage is the hard material which can be felt in the external ear.

Muscle tissue

Muscle tissue accounts for up to 50 percent of total body weight in a healthy person, and comprises cells that are purpose-built for contraction. Muscle tissue equips the body for movement, helps transport substances around the body and produces as much as 85 percent of body heat. Through sustained contractions, muscle tissue also helps stabilize the body's posture and regulates the volume of internal organs such as the bladder.

There are three main forms of muscle tissue: skeletal, cardiac and smooth. The muscle fibers, or myofibers, of skeletal muscle are long, cylindrical, arranged parallel to each other and have a striped appearance under the microscope. This is the sort of muscle tissue that produces movements inside the limbs. It is usually attached to bones and is termed voluntary because one normally has conscious control over it.

Cardiac muscle cells are similar in that they too have a striped appearance. They are, however, branched and operate outside of conscious control. For this reason, cardiac muscle is known as involuntary. This is the muscle found in the heart; it cannot regenerate after being destroyed.

Smooth muscle tissue is also involuntary but it has no striations. This is the type of muscle found in the walls of blood vessels, in airways and inside the eye. Compared to the other muscle tissue types, it has reasonably good powers of regeneration.

Nervous tissue

Nervous tissue functions to sense changes both inside and outside the body, to analyze and interpret these sensory stimuli and to initiate a response. Nervous tissue forms the nervous system, which comprises the central nervous system (CNS) and the peripheral nervous system (PNS). The CNS includes the brain and spinal cord and is responsible for sorting and responding to stimuli, generating thoughts and emotions and forming and storing memories. All other nervous tissue in the body is included in the PNS, which collects sensory stimuli and transports it into the CNS, and then transports messages controlling the body's response out to the muscles, glands and sense organs.

Nervous tissue is composed of two main types of cells: neuroglia and neurons. Impulses travel around the body via the neurons. The glial cells, which are usually smaller and far more abundant, provide support and protection for the neurons. Types of neuroglia include astrocytes, oligodendrocytes, Schwann cells, microglia, ependymal cells and satellite cells. The glial cells function to maintain the proper biochemical environment required by neurons, fight invading microbes and produce material that physically supports and protects the neurons.

It is thought that, from about the age of 6 months, most human neurons lose the ability to reproduce themselves. As a result, when a neuron is destroyed completely it cannot be replaced. Some types of damage can, however, be repaired. Under certain conditions, nerve fibers in the PNS can regenerate after injury—but not in the case of the brain or the spinal cord. Damage to nervous tissue in these locations usually has some sort of permanent impact.

SEE ALSO *Cells, Collagen, Connective tissue, Muscle, Nervous system, Neurons*

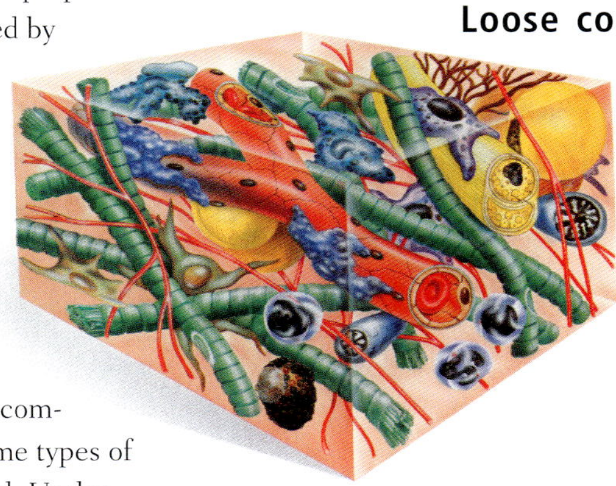

Loose connective tissue

Lymphatic tissue

Neural tissue

Muscle tissue

Skeletal muscle

Smooth muscle

Cardiac muscle

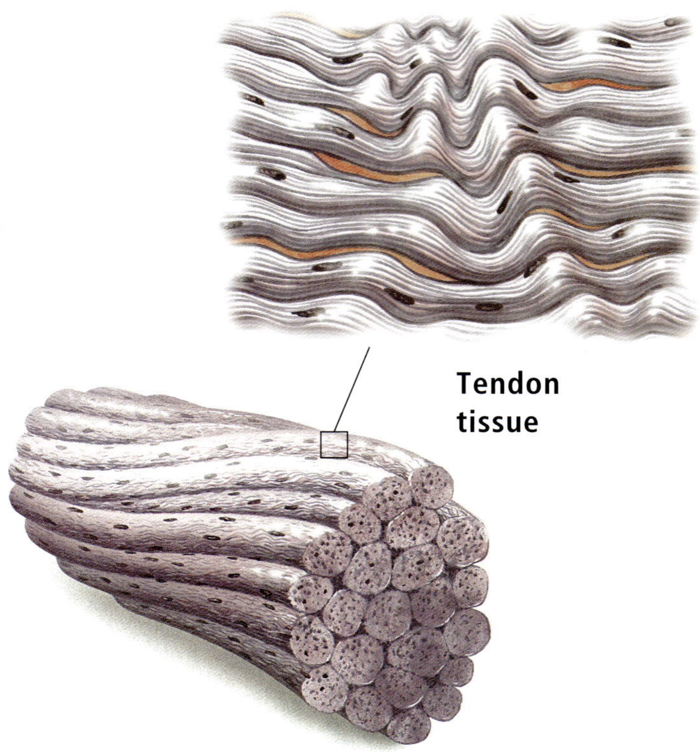

Tendon tissue

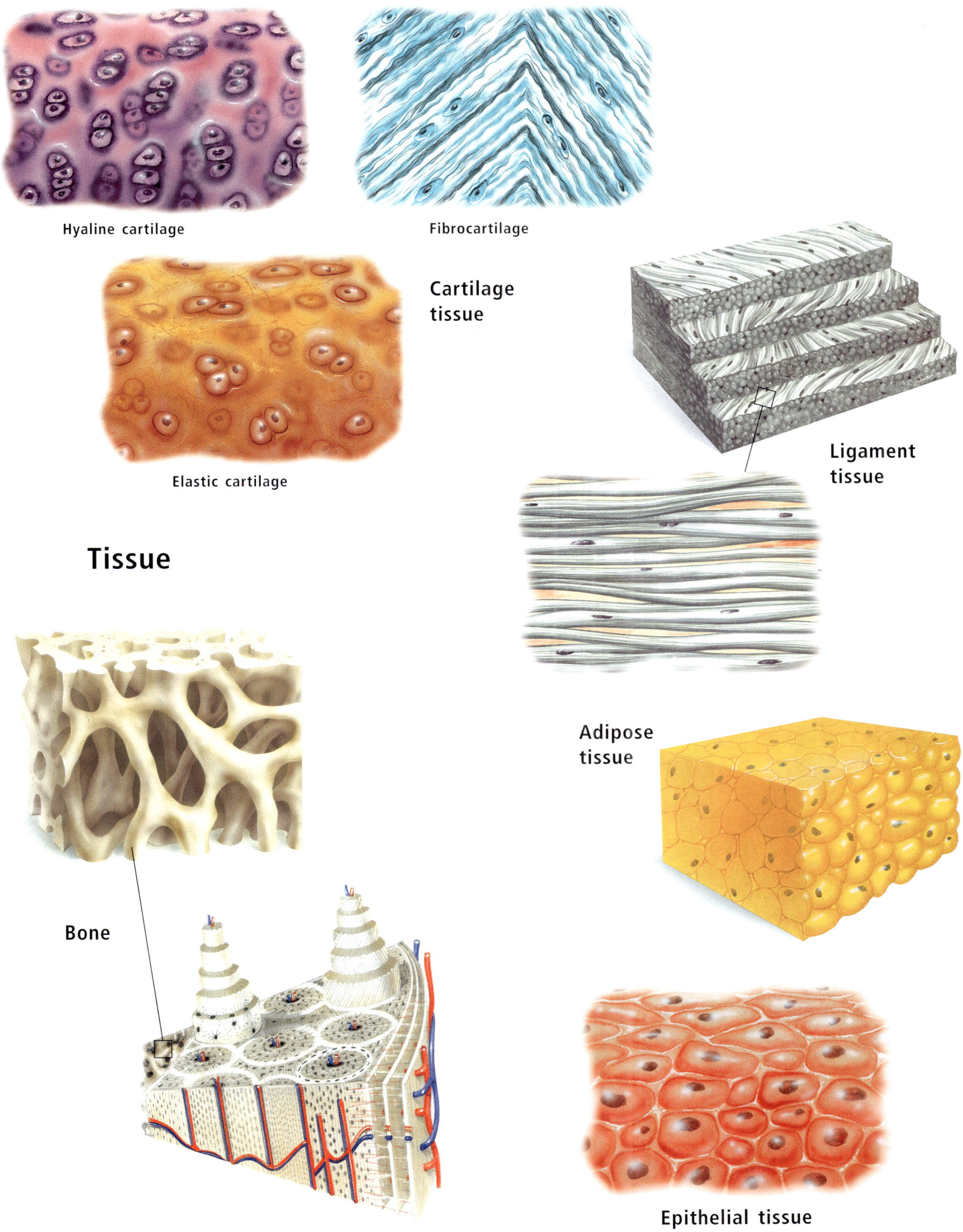
Hyaline cartilage
Fibrocartilage
Cartilage tissue
Elastic cartilage
Ligament tissue
Tissue
Adipose tissue
Bone
Epithelial tissue

TOILET TRAINING

There is no specific age when a child is ready to use a toilet. Up until the age of 15 months a child does not have the muscle control necessary to hold in the contents of the bladder or bowel until an appropriate moment. Emotional readiness is also an important element of toilet training; this sometimes does not develop until the end of the third year. Once children are aware of their bodily functions and of what society expects of them, by observing others, they will usually begin to use a toilet without much "training". Emotional stress or distress, anxiety over performance and fear of failure can all hinder the process.

It is advisable for parents to let children take their time in learning to use a toilet and to allow the child to proceed gradually at their own pace. In some societies a "potty" (chamberpot) is introduced before the toilet; children will usually progress naturally from this to a toilet before they reach school age. It is very important that children are also taught the importance of hygiene when they empty their bladder or bowels.

SEE ALSO *Bed-wetting*

TONGUE

The tongue is a muscular and sensory organ that is attached to the floor of the mouth. It has a dorsum or upper surface, a base attached to the floor of the mouth, a soft lower surface and a tip.

Structure and function

The tongue plays an important role in tasting, chewing and swallowing food, and in speech. Taste is sensed through the many taste receptors (taste buds) that are located on the dorsum of the tongue. The tongue's role during chewing is to move food around the mouth, pushing partially chewed food into position between the back teeth (molars). In swallowing, the tongue helps form a ball or bolus of food, which is gripped between the back of the tongue and the soft palate and squeezed backwards into the oropharynx.

During speech, the tongue makes contact with other structures in the mouth to help form consonants. Some consonants are formed by the tongue meeting the teeth (dental consonants like d, t), the soft palate (glottal consonants like g, k) or the hard palate (palatal consonants like n).

The dorsum of the tongue is studded with small projections called papillae, which come in three types. Filiform papillae are tiny cone-shaped elevations, which do not contain taste buds. Their role is to grip food and they are particularly well-developed in animals like cats which groom their fur with the tongue. Fungiform papillae are mushroom-shaped projections. They are less numerous than the filiform papillae, often contain taste buds and have a red appearance.

About two-thirds of the way back from the tongue's tip lies a V-shaped group of 7–12 vallate (also called circumvallae) papillae. These papillae have a central elevation, which is surrounded by a deep groove, much like a moat surrounding a castle. Taste buds located in the walls of the moat are continuously bathed in fluid, which clears food from the taste buds so that new taste stimuli can be tested. Other taste buds are located in nearby regions such as the palate, epiglottis and pharynx.

The pharyngeal part of the tongue behind the vallate papillae contains a lymphoid organ called the lingual tonsil. The lingual tonsil is involved in defending the body from microorganisms entering by the mouth.

The bulk of the tongue is made up of muscle, which can be divided into two main groups. The first group is called the intrinsic tongue muscles. They lie within the tongue itself and are responsible for changing its shape. Their fibers are arranged in three directions: vertical, longitudinal and horizontal. When vertical fibers contract they make the tongue thinner. When longitudinal fibers, which run the length of the tongue, contract, they make the tongue shorter. Horizontal fibers make the tongue narrower when they contract. Some people have a genetically determined ability to curl the tongue either upwards or downwards by controlling different groups of horizontal fibers separately.

Extrinsic tongue muscles, attached to the jaw, skull, palate and hyoid bones, are responsible for changing the position of the tongue. The hyoid bone is a small bone in the neck immediately below the jaw, which protects the airway from being crushed. The extrinsic muscles can move the tongue forward (genioglossus muscle), backward (styloglossus muscle), upward (palatoglossus muscle) and downward (hyoglossus muscle). Most of the tongue muscles are supplied by the hypoglossal nerve, which is one of the cranial nerves relaying messages to the brain.

The underside of the tongue is soft and kept very moist by salivary gland secretions. Beneath the tongue lie the openings of the ducts from the sublingual and submandibular salivary glands. The sublingual glands raise a ridge on the floor of the mouth on each side of the tongue's base. There is a midline ridge on the lower surface of the tongue called the frenulum. On each side of this ridge lie paired deep veins of the tongue, which are visible through the thin surface layer.

Diseases and disorders

Cancer of the tongue usually occurs in men aged between 40 and 80. It is often associated with heavy smoking, heavy drinking and poor oral hygiene. Most tongue cancers develop in the front two-thirds, particularly on the lateral border adjacent to the teeth. Tumors of the tongue often invade the floor of the mouth and may have spread to lymph nodes of the neck by the time diagnosis is made. The best form of treatment is surgical removal, including the removal of lymph nodes, and irradiation to kill cancer cells which may have spread to other neck structures. The chances of survival depend on the site of the cancer and whether spread to lymph nodes has occurred.

Those patients with cancers on the tip of the tongue have excellent rates of survival (greater than 80 percent after 5 years), while patients with cancers that have spread to the neck lymph nodes by the time of diagnosis have a very poor prognosis (less than 20 percent survive after 5 years).

Inflammation of the tongue (glossitis) may be due to many different causes. The tongue may be involved in oral yeast infections (oral thrush or candidiasis). In individuals who smoke and drink alcohol to excess, there may be degeneration of the tissues of the mouth, including the tongue, which may appear as flat white patches

Tongue—cross-section

The tongue is a muscular organ which is used in chewing, swallowing and speech. Taste buds are located in the papillae, which are projections on the upper surface of the tongue.

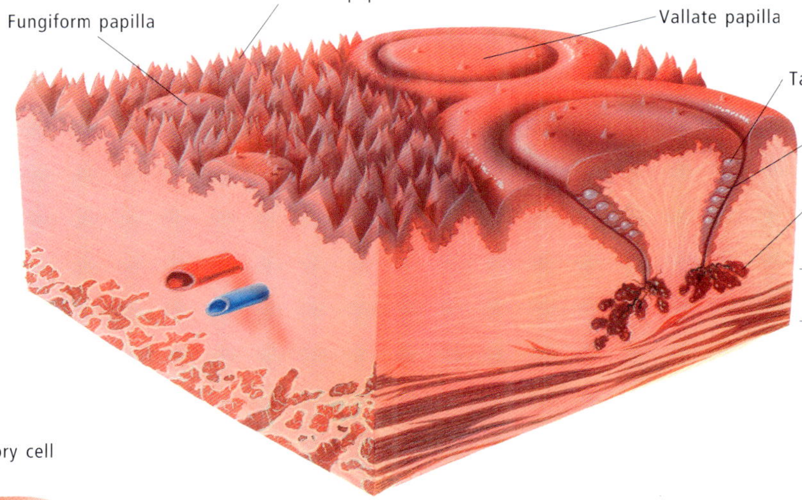

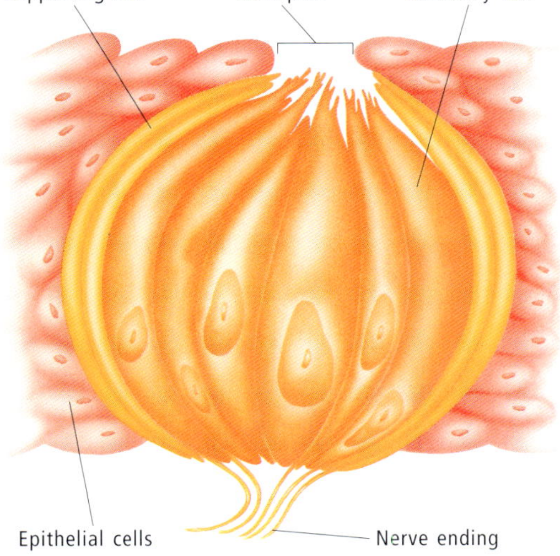

Tongue—taste

Taste buds are packed together in groups at various places on the tongue. These bundles of slender cells with hair-like branches are sensitive to sweet, salty, bitter and sour flavors.

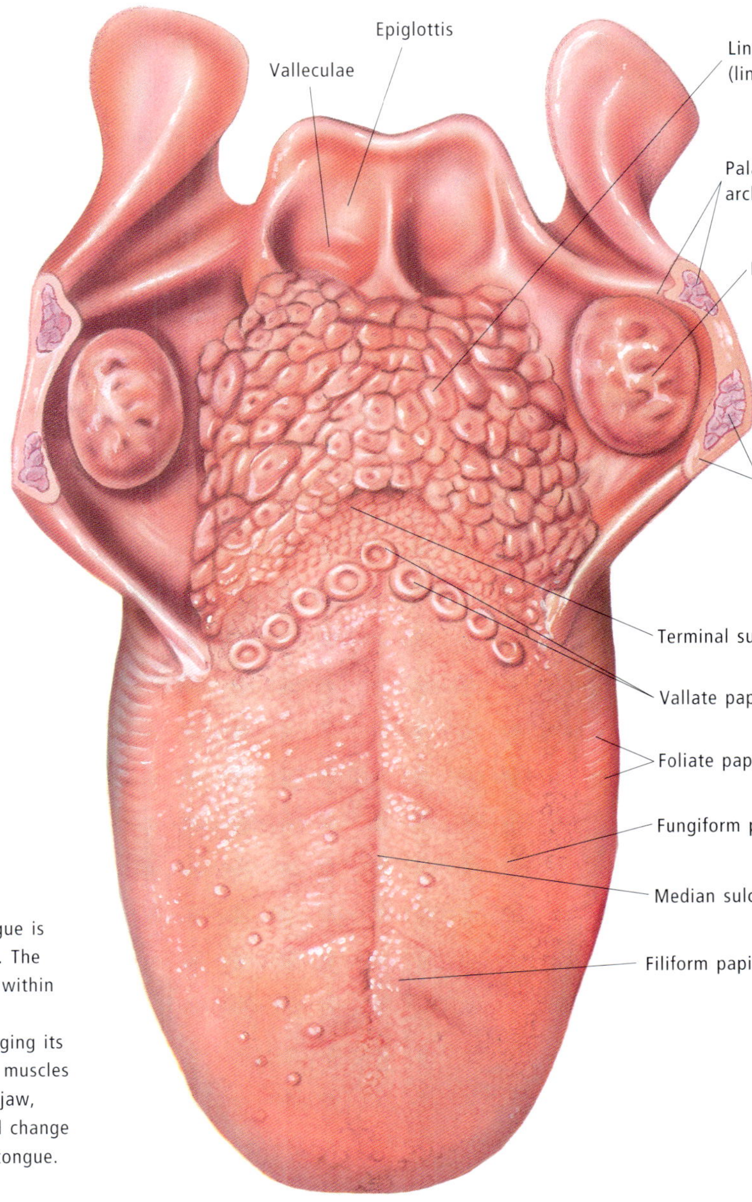

Tongue

The bulk of the tongue is made up of muscles. The intrinsic muscles lie within the tongue and are responsible for changing its shape. The extrinsic muscles are attached to the jaw, skull and palate and change the position of the tongue.

T

(leukoplakia) or as areas of redness (erythroplasia). The patient may experience a burning sensation in the affected areas, although many will have no symptoms at all. Patients with this type of degeneration should be advised to change their personal habits before cancer develops in the mouth tissues.

SEE ALSO *Glossitis, Mouth, Palate, Saliva, Speech, Taste*

TONOMETRY

Tonometry is the measurement of intraocular pressure (pressure within the eye), which is typically elevated in people with glaucoma. Various techniques are available, but applanation tonometry is considered to be the most accurate. This procedure involves bringing the measuring instrument into contact with the anesthetized cornea.

SEE ALSO *Cornea, Eye, Glaucoma*

TONSILS

The tonsils are lymphoid organs which lie under the surface lining of the mouth and throat. There are three sets of tonsils, named according to their position. The lingual tonsil lies on the back third of the tongue; the palatine tonsils lie on either side of the back of the tongue, between pillars of tissue which join the soft palate to the tongue; the pharyngeal or nasopharyngeal tonsils (adenoids) lie in the space behind the nose.

The tonsils are arranged around the entrance to the respiratory and digestive tracts to protect the body from bacteria and viruses which may enter from the mouth and nose. Tonsils produce lymphocytes, which cross into the mouth and throat.

Tonsillitis is inflammation of the tonsils, usually due to bacterial infection of the tonsillar tissue. The palatine tonsils have deep clefts, penetrating into their interior, which appear as pus-filled spots in tonsillitis. Patients with chronic tonsillitis will suffer from severe recurrent sore throats with fever. Frequent attacks of tonsillitis will require surgical removal of the tonsil, known as tonsillectomy. If the infection spreads from the palatine tonsil to the space around the soft palate, a pus-filled peritonsillar abscess will form. This disease is known as quinsy and requires high-dose intravenous antibiotics and surgical drainage.

SEE ALSO *Adenoids, Lymphocytes, Quinsy, Respiratory system, Throat*

Tonsils

Tonsils are part of the lymphatic system and filter the circulating lymph of bacteria that may enter the body through the nose and the mouth.

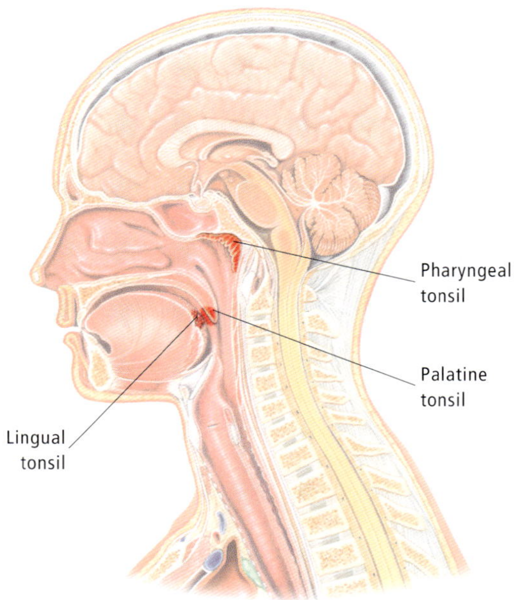

Tonsillitis

Bacterial infection of the tonsils can cause inflammation (tonsillitis). The tonsils may need to be removed if infection recurs frequently.

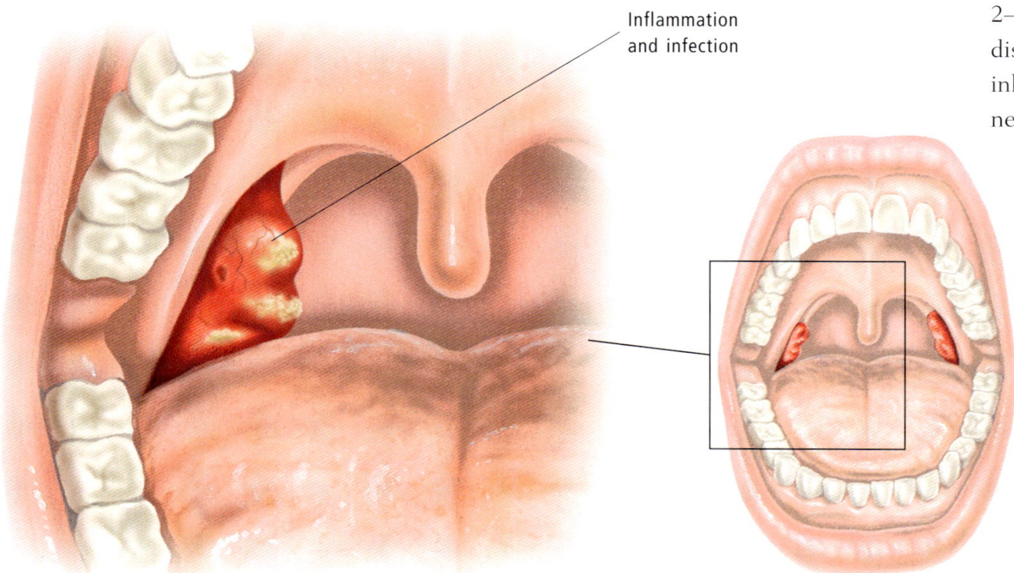

Palatine tonsils

The palatine tonsils are a pair of oval-shaped structures partially embedded in the mucous membrane on each side of the back of the throat.

TORTICOLLIS

Torticollis (or spasmodic torticollis) is a condition in which involuntary muscle spasms lead to prolonged contraction of the neck muscles. This causes the head to turn to one side, lean toward one shoulder or forward or backward, or to shake. Neck pain and headache may also occur. Symptoms increase gradually and usually plateau in 2–5 years. They may also spontaneously disappear in this time. Torticollis may be inherited or may result from neck trauma or nervous system damage.

Torticollis

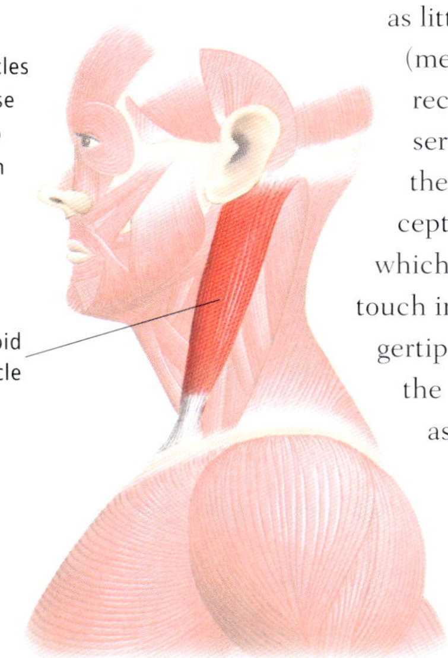

Torticollis affects the muscles of the neck. Spasm of these muscles twists the neck so that the head is held in an abnormal position.

Babies may suffer from torticollis at birth due to the positioning of the head and neck in the uterus. Treatment involves stretching exercises, massage, traction or surgery, depending on the cause.

SEE ALSO *Neck*

TOUCH

The sense of touch, that is the perception of the skin coming in contact with an object, is also called the tactile sense. The surface of the skin has thousands of sensory nerve endings known as cutaneous receptors, which can detect different levels of pain, pressure and vibration, and temperatures ranging up to 113°F (45°C) and down to 50°F (10°C). The degreee of sensitivity to touch varies greatly over the body, as nerve endings are concentrated in particular parts of the body, such as the fingertips, lips and tongue. The fingertips can distinguish between objects which are barely 1/12 inch (2 millimeters) apart, whereas on the back of the hand, which has fewer receptors, the objects must be 2 inches (50 millimetres) apart before they can be defined as more than one object. Fingertips can also detect vibration of as little as one 10-millionth of a yard (meter). The whole body is usually receptive to touch. The area of skin served by one nerve fiber is called the receptive field of that fiber; receptive fields overlap. Body parts which are particularly sensitive to touch include the tongue, lips and fingertips. The tongue has roughly twice the concentration of pressure spots as a fingertip.

Touch is important to a newborn baby because it provides comfort and reassurance—the first skin to skin contact between a mother and her new baby is known to help in bonding their relationship. It is recognized that even babies in intensive care need to be touched in order to achieve optimal development. The sense of touch is also vital to the development and learning experiences of a baby. A baby uses touch to help learn about and understand the environment around it. The experience of different textures helps the baby to relate visual perceptions to touch. Touch continues to be an important part of communication, both good and bad, between humans throughout their lives.

A person touching a sharp spike or a hot surface will pull the hand away in a reflex action. There are other reflex actions which occur as a result of touch. In a newborn baby these include: the grasp reflex, which can also be found in the baby's foot; the Moro or startle reflex, which is used by doctors to test muscle tone; and the galant reflex, which is tested by gently stroking a finger along one side of a baby's back while supporting the baby under the abdomen. The baby's body will bend like a bow, pulling the pelvis towards the side stroked. This reflex indicates the state of development of the spinal nerves and will last until the baby is about 9 months old.

Certain medicines, injuries to the nervous system and illnesses can damage the peripheral nerves and impair the sense of touch. A lessening sense of pain, vibration, cold, heat, pressure and touch occurs with ageing.

Therapeutic touch is a school of alternative practice which believes that people who are ill have disturbed energy fields and that the hands of a trained person can move over the patient's body without touching to detect malalignments and re-pattern energy fields. There is no scientific evidence that this works, although it may have psychological benefits. Massage, however, the actual

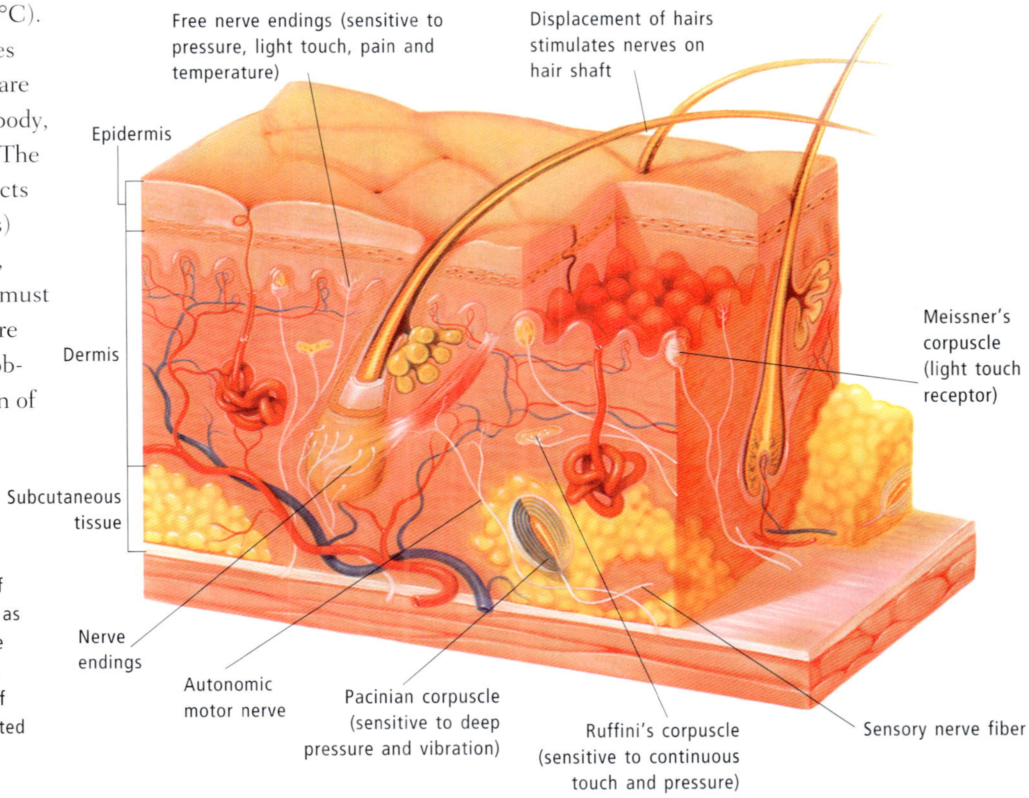

Touch receptors

The skin contains thousands of sensory nerve endings, known as cutaneous receptors, which are sensitive to temperature, pain, vibration and pressure. Each of the receptors is specially adapted to provide different types of sensory information.

T

touching of the body, is recognized as having a therapeutic effect on both the nervous and muscular systems and on the body's systemic circulation.

Massage is known to have been in use 3,000 years ago in China; it can relieve pain and reduce swelling, relax muscles and speed the healing process of sprain and strain injuries. Studies have found that massage improves the functioning of the nervous system and lowers stress hormone levels. It has also been found to be of benefit in a wide variety of maladies including asthma and migraine.

SEE ALSO *Hyperthermia, Hypothermia, Massage, Reflexes, Skin, Tongue*

Touch

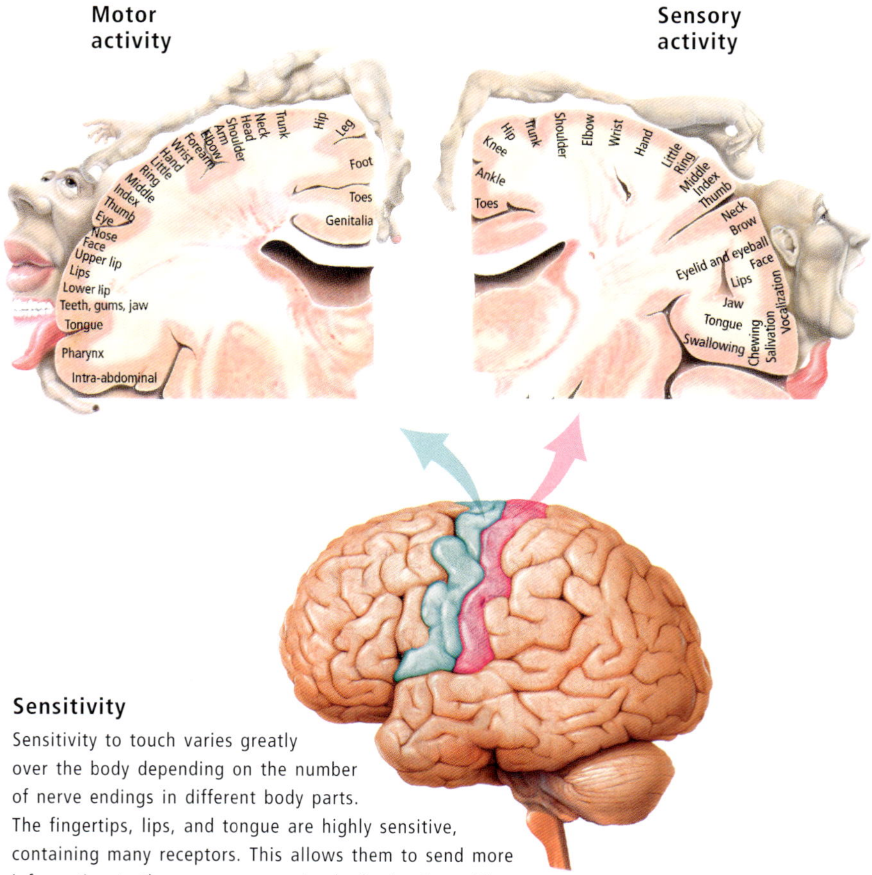

Sensitivity

Sensitivity to touch varies greatly over the body depending on the number of nerve endings in different body parts. The fingertips, lips, and tongue are highly sensitive, containing many receptors. This allows them to send more information to the sensory cortex in the brain. Once this information has been processed, the motor part of the cortex coordinates an appropriate response, such as moving the hand away from a hot object.

Touch pathways

Touch receptors in the surface of the skin pass on their sensory information via the peripheral nervous system. Nerve impulses pass from the skin to peripheral nerves, then to the spinal nerve that innervates that region of the body. From here, the message is relayed up the spinal cord to processing centers in the brain stem and then to the cerebral cortex in the brain.

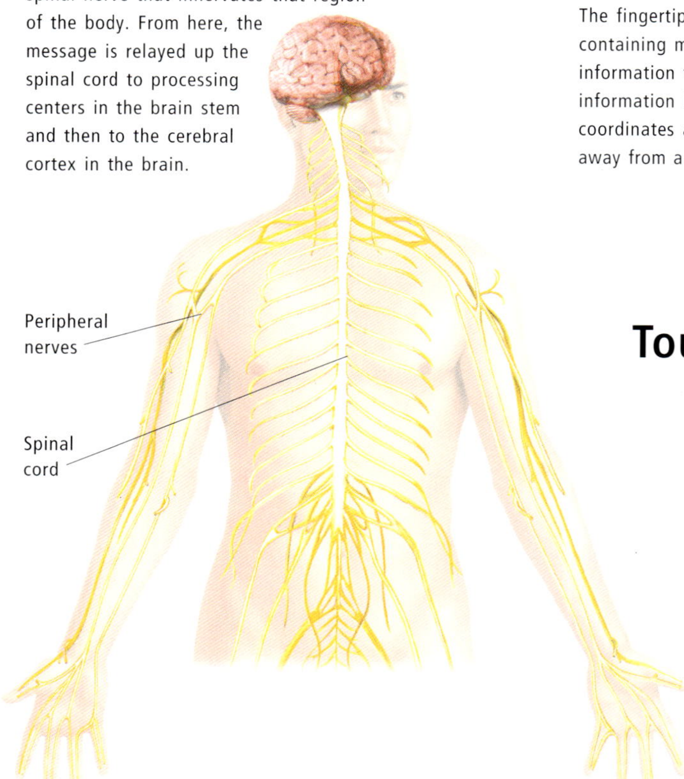

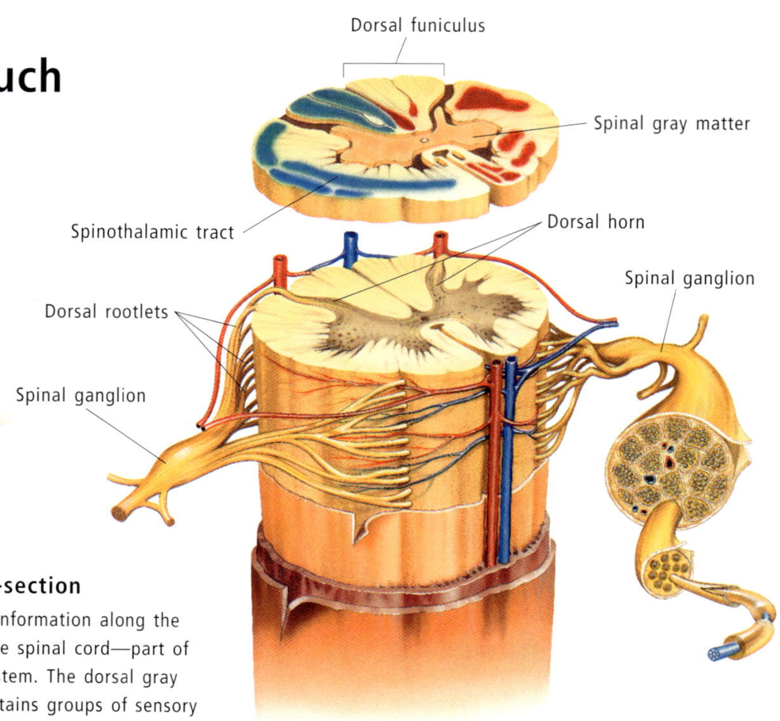

Spinal cord cross-section

Touch receptors relay information along the peripheral nerves to the spinal cord—part of the central nervous system. The dorsal gray matter of the cord contains groups of sensory cells that receive this information and pass the signals on to the brain.

TOURETTE'S SYNDROME

Tourette's syndrome, a disorder of the central nervous system, involves the involuntary production of sudden sounds and movements, the results of multiple motor and vocal tics. The movements are purposeless and generally recur many times in a day but they subside during sleep. Sometimes there is meaningless repetition of swearwords as part of this syndrome.

The symptoms may change frequently and vary in intensity, being worsened by stress and anxiety. In children the symptoms can even disappear just before a medical examination.

The condition generally starts in childhood or adolescence and affects three times as many males as females. It can sometimes be associated with learning difficulties or with hyperactivity.

Children can sometimes suffer transient tics, which last for a relatively short period and disappear spontaneously; diagnosis of Tourette's syndrome relies partly on the presence of tics for a period of time longer than one year.

SEE ALSO *Tics*

TOXEMIA

Toxemia is a type of blood poisoning caused by toxins, or poisons. Many bacterial infections, such as bacterial dysentery, diphtheria, food poisoning and tetanus, cause toxemia. It is possible to immunize against some diseases that cause toxemia, such as tetanus or diphtheria.

Toxemia of pregnancy (also known as eclampsia or preeclampsia) is a serious disturbance in blood pressure, kidney function and the central nervous system, which may occur in late pregnancy.

SEE ALSO *Eclampsia, Preeclampsia, Septicemia*

TOXIC SHOCK SYNDROME

Toxic shock syndrome is a potentially fatal bacterial infection commonly associated with the use of highly absorbent tampons by menstruating women. A toxin produced by the *Staphylococcus aureus* bacterium causes fever, chills, headaches, rash and diarrhea about 5 days into a menstrual period.

This is accompanied by rapidly falling blood pressure and loss of body fluids, which induces shock. Other symptoms may include hallucinations, confusion, muscle pain, a sore throat and dry mouth, eyes and vagina. Women who have recently given birth, had surgery, used barrier type contraceptives or had a prior toxic shock infection have a greater risk of being infected.

It is not known exactly why the infection occurs. It is estimated that about 1 percent of menstruating women have the bacteria in their vaginas during a period. Changing tampons frequently or alternating them with sanitary pads is recommended as a means of reducing the risk of infection.

Hospitalization may be required, with the administration of antibiotics for the infection and intravenous fluids for the shock. Though rare, toxic shock syndrome also affects babies, young children and men, often as a result of *Staphylococcus aureus* bacterium entering the body via such things as skin wounds and boils.

SEE ALSO *Shock, Staphylococcal infections*

TOXOCARIASIS

Toxocariasis is an infection by nematode worms of the genus *Toxocara*, parasites found in the gut of the dog and the cat. Infection by *T. canis* (found in dogs) is more common than infection by *T. cati* (found in cats). Eggs from the feces of dogs and cats, found in the soil, can be transferred directly to the mouth via the hands.

This infection may have no obvious symptoms, or quite mild symptoms, and can only be detected by a blood test to check the levels of eosinophils or a liver biopsy. The infection may disappear without treatment after 6–18 months.

If symptoms such as skin rash, enlarged spleen, recurring pneumonia or an eye lesion are present, treatment will be necessary, together with the worming of animals and the adoption of hygienic practices, such as washing hands more frequently.

SEE ALSO *Infectious diseases, Worms*

TOXOPLASMOSIS

Toxoplasmosis is an infection caused by the parasite *Toxoplasma gondii*. It is usually acquired after eating raw or undercooked meat, raw eggs or unpasteurized milk containing infective cysts. The organism spreads from the intestines throughout the body, even crossing the placenta and infecting a fetus if a woman is pregnant.

Handling cat feces or soil contaminated with cat feces can also cause an infection. Most people have no symptoms, although sometimes there may be flu-like symptoms or a lymph gland may enlarge.

The main concern is infection during pregnancy, as the disease can seriously harm the developing fetus; people with weakened immune systems are also at greater risk of suffering serious illness. A month-long course of medication is the only effective cure for the condition.

SEE ALSO *Food poisoning*

TRACHEA

The windpipe (trachea) is a $3\frac{1}{2}$–5 inch (9–12 centimeter) long and $\frac{3}{5}$ inch (1.5 centimeter) wide tube for the passage of air, beginning at the lower end of the voice box (larynx), and passing into the thoracic cavity where it terminates by dividing into the left and right main bronchi.

It is a fibro-elastic and muscular structure, reinforced by U-shaped cartilages. The cartilages prevent collapse of the airway, and the elastic fibers allow it to stretch and recoil with the movements of the larynx (which is used in swallowing and speech) and diaphragm (used in breathing). The back of the trachea is flat. Here, the ends of the cartilage are bridged by transversely oriented muscle (trachealis muscle), whose contractions reduce the diameter of the airway. The esophagus lies against this surface and expands into the gap in the cartilage when food is swallowed.

A tracheo-esophageal fistula is an abnormal opening between the esophagus and trachea. It can occur during development *in utero* or may be secondary to cancer, infection or trauma. It needs surgical correction.

The mucous membrane lining the trachea traps dust particles. Hair-like projections on the membrane (cilia), move the dust-laden mucus toward the throat where it may be swallowed or spat out. This clearing activity of the cilia is inhibited by smoking.

T

Since the larynx and trachea are the only air passage to the lungs, obstruction of the larynx (due to an allergic reaction, for example) may require surgical opening of the trachea (tracheostomy). The cavity, or lumen, of the trachea is very small in infants and inflammation of the trachea (tracheitis) can cause severe breathing difficulties.

SEE ALSO *Esophagus, Larynx, Pharynx, Tracheostomy*

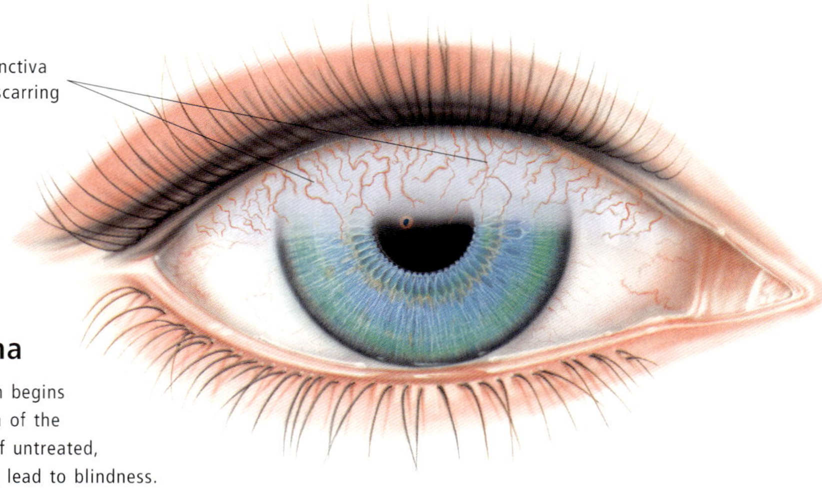

Trachoma

This condition begins with infection of the conjunctiva. If untreated, trachoma can lead to blindness.

TRACHEITIS

Tracheitis is inflammation of the trachea, or windpipe. It may be viral or bacterial, and is usually a mild condition in an adult. In young children, however, it can be a serious medical emergency. This is because in children the diameter of the trachea is much smaller than in adults, so the swelling of the lining of the trachea as a result of tracheitis may block the passage of air, causing severe difficulty in breathing, and ultimately even death.

The inflammation is usually caused by bacterium such as *Staphylococcus*, and usually follows a viral upper respiratory tract infection. The child has a high fever, looks very ill, and develops a high-pitched crowing sound when breathing in, called stridor.

A child with this condition must be taken to hospital immediately. An endotracheal tube (a breathing tube placed in the trachea) will need to be inserted to keep the airway open and allow oxygen to be administered. Intravenous antibiotics such as penicillins or cephalosporins are administered intravenously. If treatment is prompt, the child will recover fully.

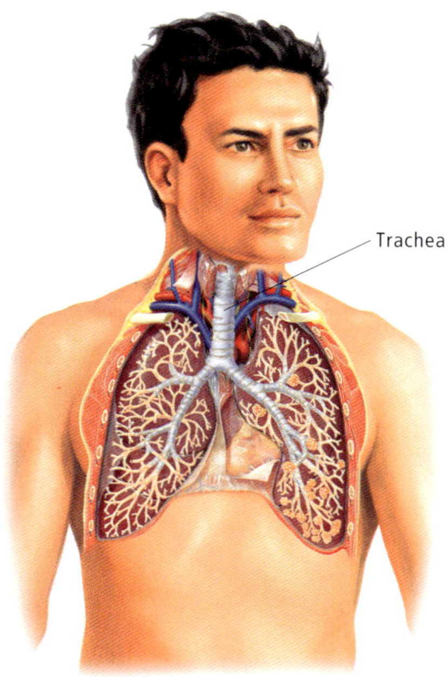

Trachea

The trachea is reinforced at the front and sides by a series of C-shaped rings of cartilage, which keep the passageway open. Gaps between the rings are occupied by muscle.

TRACHEOSTOMY

Tracheostomy is a surgical procedure in which an opening in the front of the windpipe (the trachea) is created to maintain a clear airway. A silicon tracheostomy tube is then placed in the opening. A tracheostomy is performed on someone who has had a mouth or chest injury or who has undergone a major operation, such as lung surgery. It is also performed on someone who needs to be on a mechanical ventilator for an extended period of time.

An emergency tracheostomy may need to be performed after an accident or injury if the normal airway is blocked by swelling or by blood.

SEE ALSO *Trachea*

Trachea

The trachea (windpipe) is the air passage that connects the larynx (voice box) and the two bronchi.

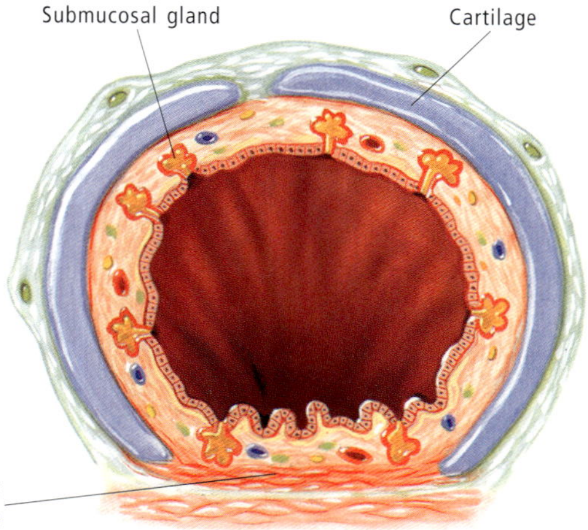

TRACHOMA

Also called granular conjunctivitis, trachoma is a disease of the eye caused by infection with the organism *Chlamydia trachomatis.* It is the world's most common cause of blindness, with as many as 500 million people affected around the world. The people affected are mainly in developing countries (as inadequate supply of running water often being a factor). The disease is spread by direct contact from person to person.

The condition begins slowly as a mild conjunctivitis which develops into a severe infection with copious amount of eye discharge. Erosions form in the cornea of the eye, which becomes infiltrated by blood vessels and scarred, causing blindness.

Trachoma is easily treated with antibiotics such as oral erythromycin. If treated early, the eye will recover completely. However, once scarring and blindness have occurred, vision usually cannot be restored. The condition is best prevented by improving sanitation and overcrowding in at-risk communities and educating them about the disease.

SEE ALSO *Blindness, Cornea, Eye, Eyelids*

TRACTION

Traction is the application of a pulling force to a part of the body, a technique used to align fractured bones to allow proper healing, and also used in physical therapy to overcome muscle tension, or to relieve pressure on bulging or herniated disks of the spine. Traction is generally applied by using weights to exert a sustained pull in one direction for a set period of time.

If applied to the spine (lumbar traction), the therapist may recline the patient and attach a fixed harness to restrain the upper body. A second harness is fitted around the hips or upper thighs and weights or a machine used to exert a carefully calculated degree of pull which is intended to straighten the spine and relieve pressure from the vertebrae on the disks.

In fractures of major bones such as the femur or pelvis, the patient may be similarly restrained in bed, with traction being applied by weights attached to the limb or a cast to ensure the bones knit in exact alignment. Traction may be applied for periods ranging from half an hour in physical therapy treatments to several months in the case of broken bones.

Some forms of exercise, notably yoga, use postures which place muscles under traction to properly align the spine and extend the range of available joint movement.

SEE ALSO *Physical therapy, Yoga*

TRANQUILIZERS

Tranquilizers, drugs which calm nervous activity, are of two types—antipsychotics and antianxiety drugs. The most commonly prescribed types of antianxiety drugs are the benzodiazepines, which are usually prescribed for anxiety states, panic or sleep problems, to control epileptic fits or the symptoms of alcohol withdrawal. Tranquilizers are absorbed into the bloodstream and affect the central nervous system, slowing down physical, mental and emotional responses. They can affect judgment, memory and the ability to concentrate, and cause drowsiness, dizziness, confusion and mood swings. In the long term they can be responsible for nausea, loss of libido, increased appetite and weight gain and lethargy. Taken at the same time as alcohol, painkillers or antihistamines (even cold remedies) they can cause unconsciousness and failure to breathe.

It is important to take tranquilizers only in the manner prescribed. Tranquilizers can easily become a drug of dependence when they are important to a person's daily life, even within 4–6 weeks of regular usage. Withdrawal creates its own set of symptoms—sleep problems, tension, muscle pain, panic attacks and depression—and must be undertaken carefully under medical supervision.

SEE ALSO *Antipsychotics, Drug dependence, Sedatives, Sleeping pills*

TRANSCUTANEOUS ELECTRICAL NERVE STIMULATION

Transcutaneous electrical nerve stimulation (TENS) is a pain-relieving treatment using a device that sends out electrical impulses to the nerves from electrodes attached to the surface of the skin. It works on the principle of counter-irritation—the electrical impulses suppress the original pain sensations by inhibiting the messages of the pain pathway to the brain.

The electrodes are usually placed on or near the site of the ache or pain, or on acupuncture points, in a technique known as electroacupuncture. TENS devices are used to relieve both acute and chronic pain, reducing the need for analgesic drugs.

SEE ALSO *Acupuncture, Pain*

TRANSIENT ISCHEMIC ATTACK

Transient ischemic attacks (commonly known as TIAs) are short episodes that result from the temporary obstruction of one of the small blood vessels carrying oxygen and other nutrients to the brain. The blockage is usually caused by a floating body (embolus) which gets lodged in one of these arteries, but frees itself after seconds or minutes. While the artery is blocked the brain tissue supplied by branches arising beyond the blockage is affected but, because it is only deprived of oxygen for a short time, function returns to normal once the floating body is freed and the blood supply to the tissue is restored.

The effects of a TIA usually last from a few seconds up to 10 minutes, but they can last as long as 24 hours. The effects will depend on which artery has been blocked, and may include temporary disturbances of vision or speech, dizziness, and numbness and/or weakness of one or more of the limbs or the face.

People who are suffering from heart disease, hardening of the arteries (atherosclerosis) or high blood pressure (hypertension) are the most at risk of having a TIA, which often precedes or accompanies the development of a stroke. Treatment usually involves the use of blood-thinning (anticoagulant) medications.

SEE ALSO *Arteries, Atherosclerosis, Blood vessels, Coronary artery disease, Hypertension, Stroke, Thrombus*

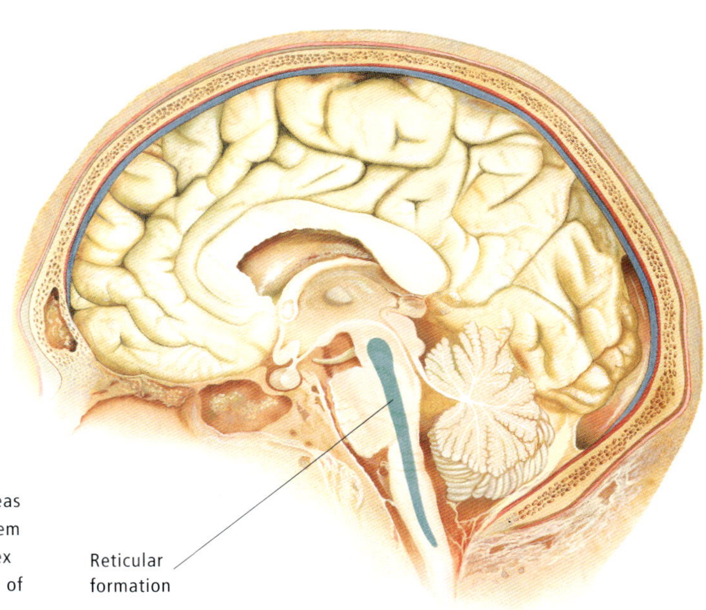

Tranquilizers

These drugs calm nervous activity and affect wide areas of the central nervous system including the cerebral cortex and the reticular formation of the brain.

T

TRANSPLANT SURGERY

Organ, tissue and limb transplant surgery, or grafts, means permanently transferring a tissue or organ from one part of the body to another, or from one person to another. The first records come from the sixth century BC, when Hindu doctors used skin flaps from the patient's own arm to repair damage to the nose. Kidneys were the first organs used in person-to-person transplants and are now the organ most commonly transplanted.

Current surgical techniques also make it possible to graft corneas, teeth, heart, lungs, liver, pancreas, cartilage, bone marrow, brain tissue, blood and skin to one person from another. More recently hip and knee joints have been transplanted, and even hands. Transplants of animal donor tissues to humans (xenotransplants) have also been made, and have included chimpanzee and baboon hearts, and heart valves and fetal brain cells from pigs. Some of these are highly experimental and are very contentious, largely due to the possibility of serious viral infections.

Autografts, where donor and host are the same person, pose no threat of tissue rejection, nor do grafts from one identical twin to another. A graft from any other source will stimulate rejection by the host because of the differences in histocompatibility antigens on the cell surfaces of donor and host tissues, which can quickly kill the implant. Immunosuppressive drugs are used to counter this reaction. Organ grafts are usually a long-term solution undertaken to sustain life in a chronically ill patient. Skin grafts may be short-term measures to prevent fluid loss and infection at burn sites while host tissue regenerates.

People who have decided that in the event of their death their organs can be used as transplants are referred to as organ donors. This information may be recorded on a card or driver's license. Organs are removed after death and transported to hosts, patients on a waiting list in priority of need. Transplant organs go to the patient on the waiting list who is nearest death, priority being given to those in whom earlier transplants have failed.

Transplant surgery is a very costly and uncertain procedure not funded by many private health insurers, and ethical questions stimulate much debate about the procedure. A black market in organs exists in some developing countries.

SEE ALSO *Bones, Eye, Grafting, Heart, Kidney*

TRANSSEXUALISM

Transsexualism is a condition in which a person sees himself or herself as a member of the opposite sex. Transsexualism occurs more frequently among men than in women. Transsexuals dislike their own sexual anatomy, feeling a strong need to act like and be treated like a member of the opposite sex. Some transsexuals undergo reassignment surgery to change their external anatomy to that of the opposite sex, in conjunction with hormone therapy to alter their sexual characteristics.

SEE ALSO *Sexual behavior, Sexuality*

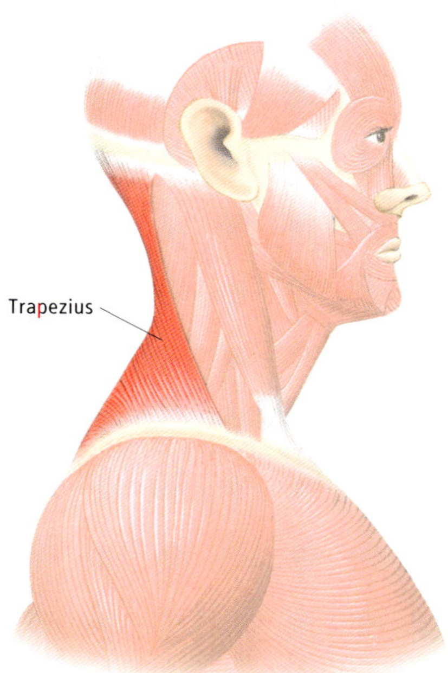

Trapezius muscle

The trapezius muscle acts to steady the shoulder during arm movement. This muscle is flat and is situated at the back of the neck and upper chest.

TRAPEZIUS MUSCLE

The trapezius muscle is a flat, triangular muscle, lying under the skin of the back of the neck and upper part of the back of the chest. The triangular muscles on each side of the back meet in the midline, forming a trapezoidal (four-sided) shape.

The trapezius muscle arises, directly or through ligaments, from the spines of the vertebrae of the thorax and neck, and from the occipital bone of the cranium. The muscle fibers converge upon the shoulder, where they are attached to the collar bone (clavicle) and shoulder blade (scapula). The trapezius muscle acts mainly in steadying the shoulder during arm movements; it also assists in movements of the scapula.

SEE ALSO *Collar bone, Muscle, Scapula*

TRAUMA

Trauma is any injury, whether physical or psychological. A traumatic wound is an injury resulting from violence or external force. A broken bone, a burn, or a knocked-out tooth are all defined as trauma.

Trauma emergencies include dislocation and other serious bone and joint injuries. Extreme fear and apprehension, grief, witnessing or undergoing extremely disturbing experiences can cause psychological trauma, with long-lasting effects which may require counseling, medication and in some cases hospitalization.

SEE ALSO *Post-traumatic stress disorder*

TREMOR

A tremor is an involuntary shaking of the body or part of the body, caused by a neurological disease that interferes with the nerve supply of certain muscles. Tremors are seen in a range of neurological diseases, such as Parkinson's disease or alcoholic brain damage, or as a side effect of drugs such as antipsychotics. If there is no discernible cause, the condition is known as essential tremor.

A tremor may affect the whole body, or just certain areas such as the head, hands, arms or eyelids. A tremor may occur sporadically, or at regular intervals. Often a tremor worsens with voluntary movement or emotional stress and disappears during sleep. It may improve after consuming alcohol.

Treatment is directed at the underlying condition where possible. If the tremor prevents essential activities such as speaking or writing, drugs such as beta blockers, anticonvulsants or mild tranquilizers will help.

SEE ALSO *Parkinson's disease*

TRICHINOSIS

Trichinosis is a roundworm infection in which the parasite migrates through the body causing cystlike growths in the muscle fibers. The infection commonly occurs due to eating undercooked pork infected with larvae of the *Trichinella spiralis* roundworm. Pigs pick up the parasite by eating uncooked garbage. High temperatures kill the larvae; undercooking pork allows them to survive. The larvae mature and reproduce in the intestine, sending new larvae through the circulatory system to the muscles. In most cases there is little or no pain, but severe infection may result in muscular rheumatism. Treatment is by antiparasitic medication. Infection can be prevented by cooking meat thoroughly at 150°F (65°C) or more, or freezing it for 2 days at –16°F (–26°C).

SEE ALSO *Food poisoning, Worms*

TRICHURIASIS

Trichuriasis is an intestinal infection with the roundworm *Trichuris trichiura*, caused by eating the worm's eggs in contaminated food. The infection is common in tropical areas with poor sanitation, where soil is contaminated with feces. The larvae mature in the intestine and migrate to the colon where they multiply. It may produce no symptoms, but with heavy infestations can cause bloody diarrhea, weight loss, stomach pain and nausea. Extreme cases can result in dehydration and anemia. Treatment is by antiparasitic medication and prevention can be achieved by improving sanitary and waste disposal systems.

SEE ALSO *Roundworms, Worms*

TRICUSPID VALVE

The tricuspid valve is one of four valves that control the direction of blood flow through the heart. Comprising three triangular flaps of tissue, called cusps or leaflets, it is an opening between the right atrium and right ventricle of the heart. The closing of the tricuspid and other valves creates the heartbeat sound.

Blood flows from the veins into the right atrium and passes through the tricuspid valve into the right ventricle. The right ventricle then contracts and sends the blood through the pulmonary valve to the lungs. The tricuspid valve closes as the right ventricle contracts in order to prevent bloodflow back into the right atrium (regurgitation).

A disease-damaged tricuspid valve may cause regurgitation from ventricle to atrium to veins, reducing bloodflow to the lungs where fresh supplies of oxygen are gathered and transported back to the heart. The valve may be too narrow (stenotic), causing turbulence as blood passes through the constricted passage. This is heard as a rumbling murmur. The tricuspid valve may also be blocked or even absent due to congenital heart disease. Depending on the heart condition, an artificial valve may be surgically inserted to replace a damaged or abnormal one.

SEE ALSO *Circulatory system, Heart, Lungs, Ventricle*

TRIGEMINAL NERVE

The trigeminal nerve is the fifth cranial nerve that arises from the brain stem and passes to the face to supply skin on the face and scalp, the teeth, mucous membranes in the nose, mouth and eye, and the muscles responsible for chewing (muscles of mastication). It mainly contains sensory fibers which are involved in touch, pain and temperature. As its name implies, it has three components: ophthalmic, maxillary and mandibular.

The nerve divides not far from the brain stem, while still in the cranial cavity, and the three divisions pass out of the cranial cavity

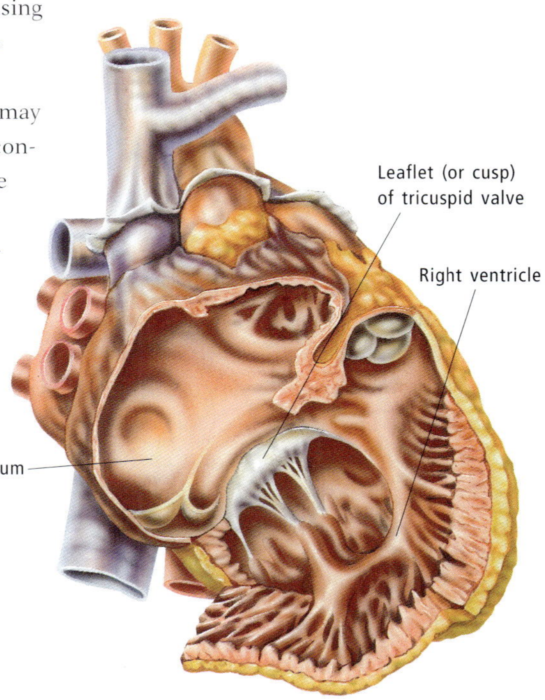

Tricuspid valve

This valve helps to control the direction of blood flow between the right atrium and right ventricle of the heart. Damage to the tricuspid valve may affect blood flow to the lungs.

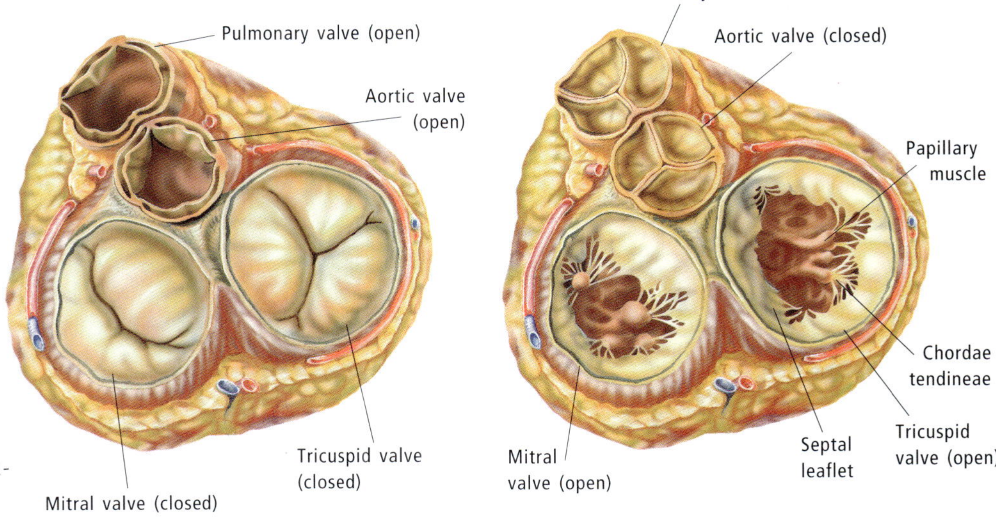

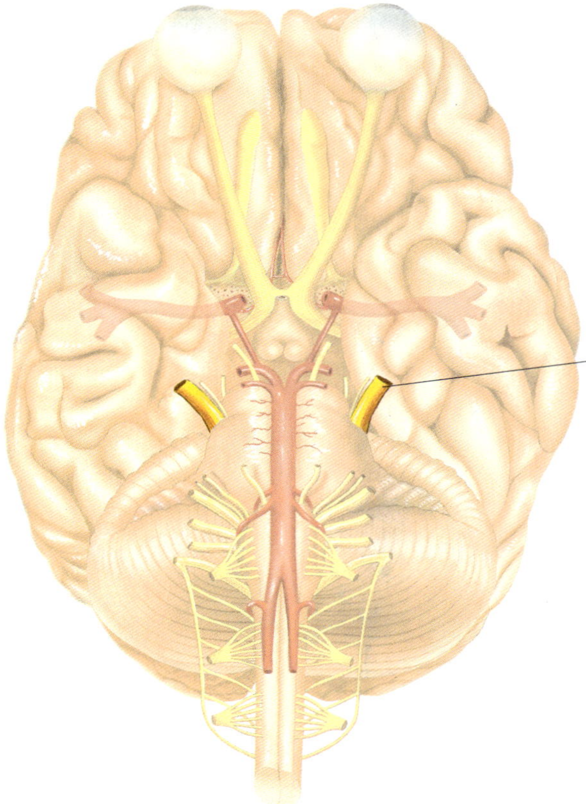

Trigeminal nerve

The fifth cranial nerve (trigeminal nerve) supplies sensory fibers to areas of the face including the eyelids, tongue and jaw.

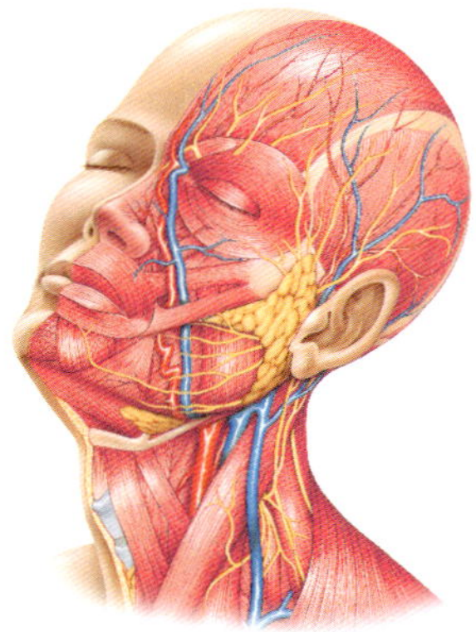

through separate openings. The ophthalmic nerve supplies the skin of the upper eyelid, forehead and scalp as far back as the top of the head (vertex), part of the nose and the cornea. The maxillary nerve supplies skin on the temple and on the face from the lower eyelid to the upper lip. It also supplies the upper teeth, mucous membrane of the nose, hard and soft palate, and cheek. The largest branch, the mandibular nerve, supplies skin on the jaw, temple and ear, the lower teeth, mucous membrane of the floor of the mouth and the anterior two-thirds of the tongue. It is the only branch that supplies muscles, primarily the four muscles of mastication.

Trigeminal neuralgia (otherwise known as tic douloureux) is a disorder of the trigeminal nerve, the main sensory nerve in the face. It causes sudden, severe pain on one side of the face, in one of the areas supplied by the trigeminal nerve—usually along the second and third nerve divisions, which supply the lower face and jaw. The pain can be set off by touching a sensitive area of the face or by certain movements of the jaw whilst speaking, chewing or swallowing. The condition usually affects older women and over time the attacks may become more frequent. The cause is often unknown but it may be caused by a blood vessel or small tumor pressing on the nerve (which can be cured by surgery). In most cases however, there is no known cure for the disorder, so treatment is aimed at control of the pain. Unfortunatly this is not easy to achieve because of the spasmodic nature of the attacks. Mild over-the-counter analgesics such as aspirin or narcotic analgesics such as codeine may bring some relief. Anticonvulsants or antidepressants may also help. Surgical destruction of the nerve is a possible treatment as a last resort.

SEE ALSO *Nerves, Nervous system, Neuralgia, Tic douloureux*

TRIGGER FINGER

"Trigger finger" is a finger locked in the flexed or bent position, often a result of tenosynovitis, where the finger tendon is inflamed and swollen. As the finger is bent, the swollen tendon moves out of its sheath but does not slide back in to allow the finger to straighten. However, the finger can be straightened with additional effort or with pressure from the other hand, often with a snap (hence "trigger finger"). Treatment is usually rest or anti-inflammatory drugs.

SEE ALSO *Finger, Tendinitis, Tenosynovitis*

TUBAL STERILIZATION

Tubal sterilization, also called tubal ligation, is the surgical closing of the fallopian tubes to prevent future pregnancies. The fallopian (uterine) tubes allow passage of sperm cells to the ovum and movement of the fertilized ovum to the body of the uterus for implantation and development into a baby. Removal of a length of the tube, combined with clipping or tying of the cut ends, will prevent sperm reaching the ovum, thus sterilizing the woman. The procedure is performed in a hospital under general anesthesia by an gynecologist usually via a laparoscope (a telescopic tube). Recovery is quick, allowing the patient to return home the same day as the procedure. Strenuous exercise is best avoided for a few days, after which time work may be resumed. Normal sexual activity can be resumed when the woman feels ready, normally within a week. In a small number of cases—one out of 400 women—there is faulty closure of the tubes and the

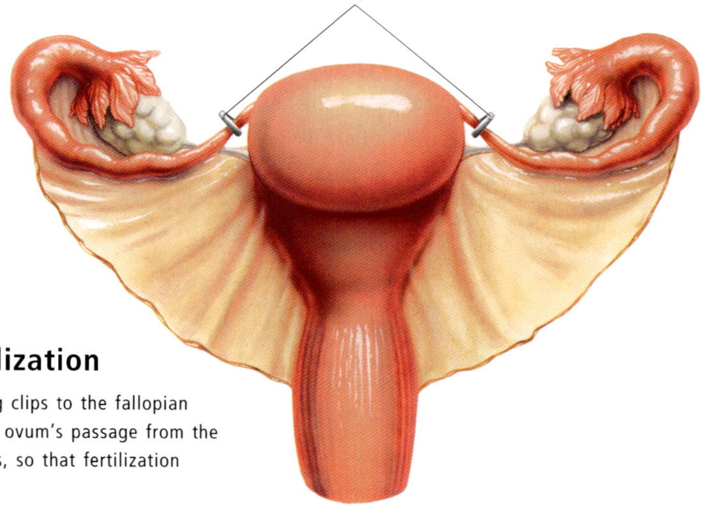

Tubal sterilization

Cutting or applying clips to the fallopian tubes prevents the ovum's passage from the ovary to the uterus, so that fertilization cannot take place.

chance of becoming pregnant again. This procedure may be reversed (with difficulty) by reparative microsurgery so it is suitable only for women who are certain that they wish to permanently prevent future pregnancies. It is not suitable as a temporary contraceptive measure.

SEE ALSO *Fallopian tubes, Sterilization*

TUBERCULOSIS

Tuberculosis is an infectious, inflammatory disease caused by bacteria belonging to the *Mycobacterium* group (usually *M. tuberculosis*). Infection of humans by *M. bovis* from cattle is now rare in industrialized nations, due to the eradication of this bacterium from cattle in these countries. Tuberculosis is primarily a disease of the lungs, but it may spread to other parts of the body, particularly in patients whose immune systems have been weakened and are in the last stages of the disease.

Tuberculosis was a common disease in Europe during the nineteenth century, but its prevalence began to decline when living conditions improved. At present in industrialized countries, tuberculosis is largely confined to people living in overcrowded and/or impoverished conditions, such as the very poor and homeless.

About 10–20 new cases per 100,000 population are diagnosed each year in industrialized nations, so it is still a very important public health problem. AIDS sufferers are at risk of contracting the disease, and it is becoming resistant to drug treatment. Another concern is that the disease may once again spread to the wider community if the quality of living conditions declines.

There are several predisposing factors to tuberculosis. Particular racial groups such as native North Americans and Inuits are more susceptible to the disease than people of European ancestry. Poor living conditions with overcrowding and malnutrition are major contributing factors, while smoking and other diseases such as alcoholism, diabetes mellitus and occupational lung diseases (silicosis) increase individual susceptibility to tuberculosis. A weakened immune system, due to AIDS or immunosuppressive drugs, may also increase the likelihood of the disease developing and advancing.

Initial infection with tuberculosis usually occurs in childhood. The bacteria are inhaled and cause a small patch of pneumonia in the middle or lower areas of the lung. The initial site develops a tubercle (hence the name of the disease), which is a clump of immune system and other cells surrounding a cavity filled with cheeselike material derived from dead lung tissue. The infection also spreads to lymph nodes in the center of the chest, but may not spread further at this stage. Children infected in this manner may have no symptoms at all, or complain only of a mild fever, cough and feeling unwell.

If the initial infection occurs in adults, the tubercle usually develops in the upper parts of the lung. In most cases this initial infection is halted and the bacteria are walled-off inside the tubercle. The bacillus can then lie dormant in the body for some years, with the possibility of it becoming active again at a later date. This secondary tuberculosis is common in people with a generally lowered resistance to disease.

The serious complications of tuberculosis arise when the bacteria escape from the initial site of infection and spread through the lung or the rest of the body. Widespread infection of the lung may cause the collapse of lung lobes and further infection of the pleural sacs around the lung. The bacteria may also spread via the bloodstream to the spleen, liver, kidneys, testes, fallopian tubes and brain membranes, with consequences ranging from sterility to death from overwhelming infection.

Treatment of tuberculosis is by the appropriate combination of antibiotics. The tuberculosis bacteria are likely to develop drug resistance if only a single drug

Tuberculosis

In this bacterial infection, inflammation of the passageways of the lungs results in the development of lesions and nodules or tubercles in the lungs. From here the infection may spread to the lymph nodes in the chest and to other organs in the body.

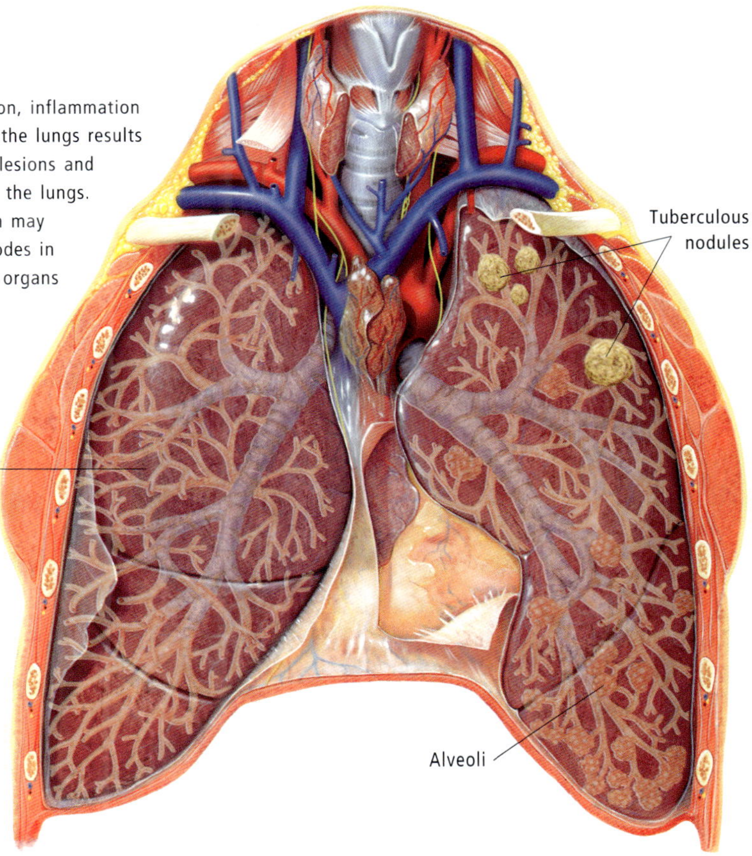

Tuberculosis bacteria

Tuberculosis is usually acquired by breathing in air which has tiny droplets of water containing the bacillus *Mycobacterium tuberculosis*.

is used, so a combination of three drugs is usually given. Treatment must also continue for long periods to avoid recurrence. In those patients with extensive disease, up to 2 years of antibiotic treatment may be required.

SEE ALSO *Infectious diseases, Lungs*

TUMORS

A tumor (or neoplasm) is an abnormal growth or swelling of tissue. It may be cancerous (malignant) or noncancerous (benign). A malignant tumor is a neoplasm that grows and spreads throughout the body.

Malignant tumors can spread by extension into surrounding tissues, or beyond. They may spread to nearby lymph nodes via the lymphatic vessels, or to distant sites via blood vessels. This process is called metastasizing—an area of tumor that has derived from elsewhere in the body is called a metastasis, or a secondary (the original tumor is called a primary).

A benign tumor is a neoplasm that, if it grows, does so slowly, and does not spread or infiltrate other tissues of the body. The cells in benign tumors are similar under a microscope to the cells in the tissue they grow from. Cells in malignant tumors may look quite different. Not all cancers are tumors, however—cancers of the blood cells such as leukemia, for example, do not form growths.

Malignant tumors are more likely to be fatal (though in some circumstances benign tumors can cause death where their expansion destroys surrounding tissue, for example in the brain). On the other hand, some malignant tumors, such as some skin cancers, are treatable, especially if diagnosed early. Others grow so slowly that the affected person may die of some other condition—this is true of many men with prostate cancer. Much depends on the site of the tumor—cancer of the colon, for example, may be slow growing but is often fatal because it only causes symptoms at a late stage and is often not detected until it has grown and spread. Some benign tumors may eventually turn malignant and need to be treated.

The aim of treatment of a tumor is to destroy as much of it as possible without destroying normal tissue. This can be achieved by surgery, chemotherapy, radiation therapy or combinations of all of these.

SEE ALSO *Cancer*

TURNER'S SYNDROME

Turner's syndrome is a chromosome anomaly of females in which one of the two X chromosomes normally present in a female is absent. The disorder inhibits sexual development and causes infertility. A person with Turner's syndrome has short stature, a broad chest with widely spaced nipples, multiple birthmarks, coarctation (narrowing) of the aorta, and abnormalities of the eyes and bones. At puberty, the breasts fail to develop normally, and menstruation does not occur.

Although there is no cure for Turner's syndrome, after puberty, treatment with synthetic estrogen and progesterone can be given to replace the missing natural ovarian hormones. Normal secondary sexual characteristics should then develop and menstruation may occur. The affected person will remain infertile.

SEE ALSO *Chromosomal abnormalities, Chromosomes, Hormones*

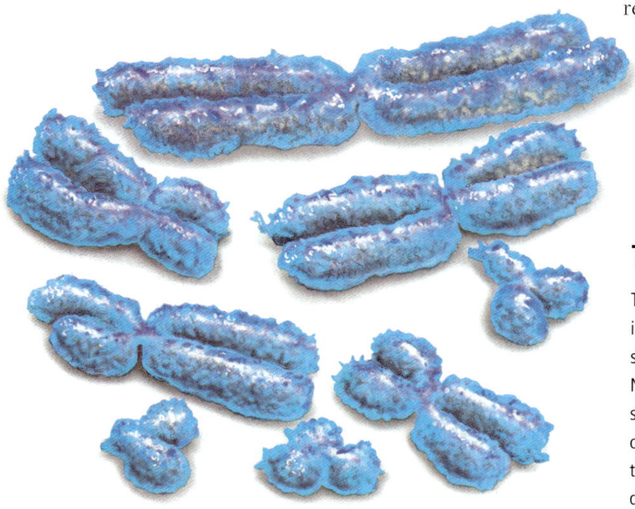

Turner's syndrome

The chromosomes carry the body's genetic information, with the X and Y chromosomes determining a person's sex. Normally a woman has two X chromosomes, but in Turner's syndrome there is only one X chromosome. Because some of the genetic information is missing, sexual development is impaired.

TWINS

The chance of a natural pregnancy being a multiple pregnancy varies according to heredity, age, race and the number of children a woman has already conceived.

Twins occur in approximately one out of every 86 natural pregnancies; the rate is higher in pregnancies resulting from infertility treatments. Seven out of ten pairs of twins are the result of two eggs being released by the woman's ovaries and fertilized at the same time, producing fraternal (dizygotic or non-identical) twins. Fraternal twins may be of different sex and develop with separate placentas (occasionally these may fuse into one). Identical (monozygotic) twins are produced after, rather than at the time of, conception, often after the fertilized egg has implanted itself into the uterine lining, when it splits into two. In this instance the twins will share a placenta and be of the same sex. Multiple births involving three or more babies, which are less common, occur through similar processes.

Twins, or a greater number of babies, fill the available space in the uterus more quickly than a singleton; the mother is at greater risk of hemorrhoids, heartburn, backache and premature (preterm) labor. The babies are also at greater risk of prematurity, poor fetal growth, perinatal death and, in the long term, cerebral palsy. Multiple pregnancies require additional support, though there is no medical evidence for the common belief that hospitalization for bed rest is beneficial.

SEE ALSO *Fertilization, Pregnancy*

TYPHOID

Also known as enteric fever, typhoid is a debilitating intestinal disease caused by infection with the bacterium *Salmonella typhi*. It is rare in the industralized countries. The disease incubates for between 1 and 2 weeks. Symptoms include headache, loss of appetite, fatigue and constipation, followed by abdominal pain and rosy spots on the abdomen and chest which last for 3–4 days, and diarrhea, which is the main problem; pneumonia may be a complication in severe cases. A blood test will determine if typhoid has been contracted. The disease can be treated with antibiotics.

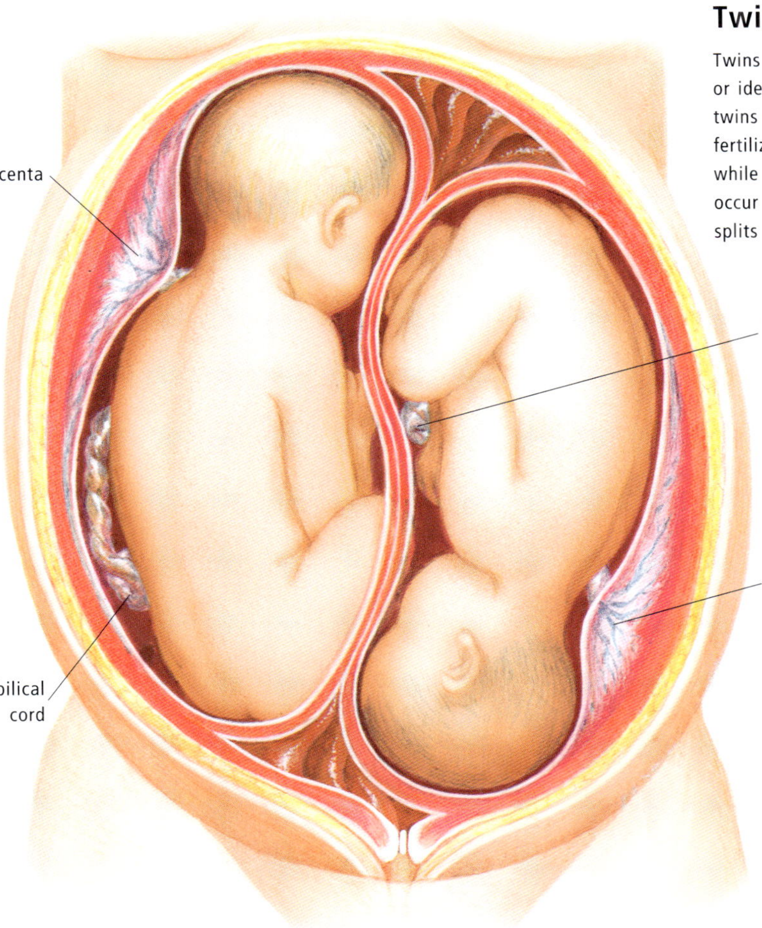

Twins

Twins can be fraternal or identical; fraternal twins result from the fertilization of two eggs, while identical twins occur when a single egg splits into two.

Typhoid vaccines give partial protection and the risk of the disease can be reduced by proper sanitation, good hygiene, by boiling or purifying all drinking water, pasteurizing milk and washing fruit and vegetables. People who have had typhoid may become carriers.

SEE ALSO *Gastroenteritis, Infectious diseases*

TYPHUS

Typhus is a general term for any of several related diseases caused by species of the microorganism *Rickettsia*, which are transmitted by a louse or a flea from infected rats or mice. They include epidemic typhus, endemic typhus and scrub typhus. Symptoms are fever, headache and the appearance of pink spots on all parts of the body except the face, hands and feet. Vomiting and delirium may occur. Antibiotics usually eradicate the infection.

Vaccines are available against epidemic and endemic typhus, but not scrub typhus. Insecticides, mite-repellent creams and clothing covering arms and legs are recommended in places where typhus is common.

SEE ALSO *Infectious diseases*

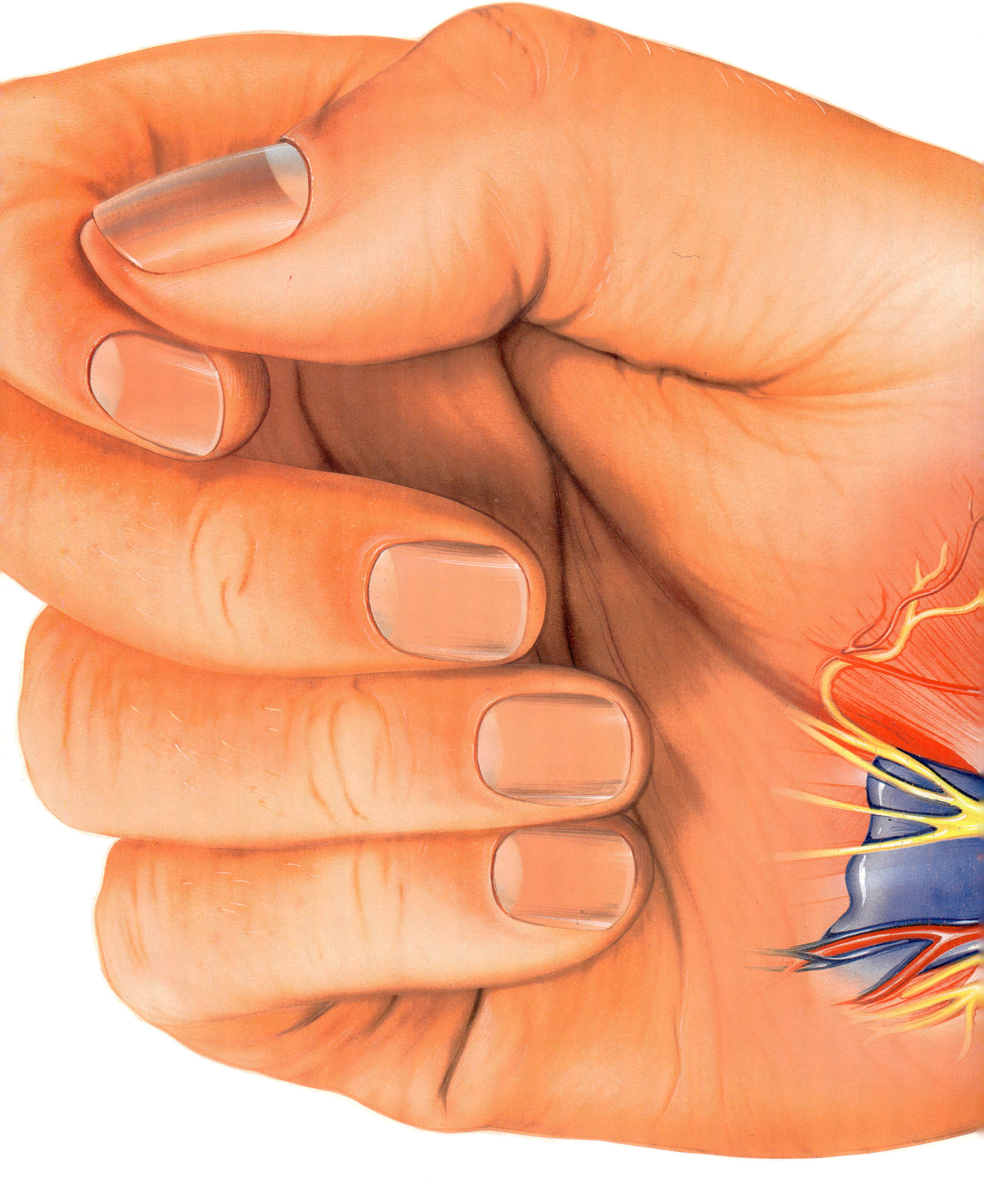

UVWXYZ

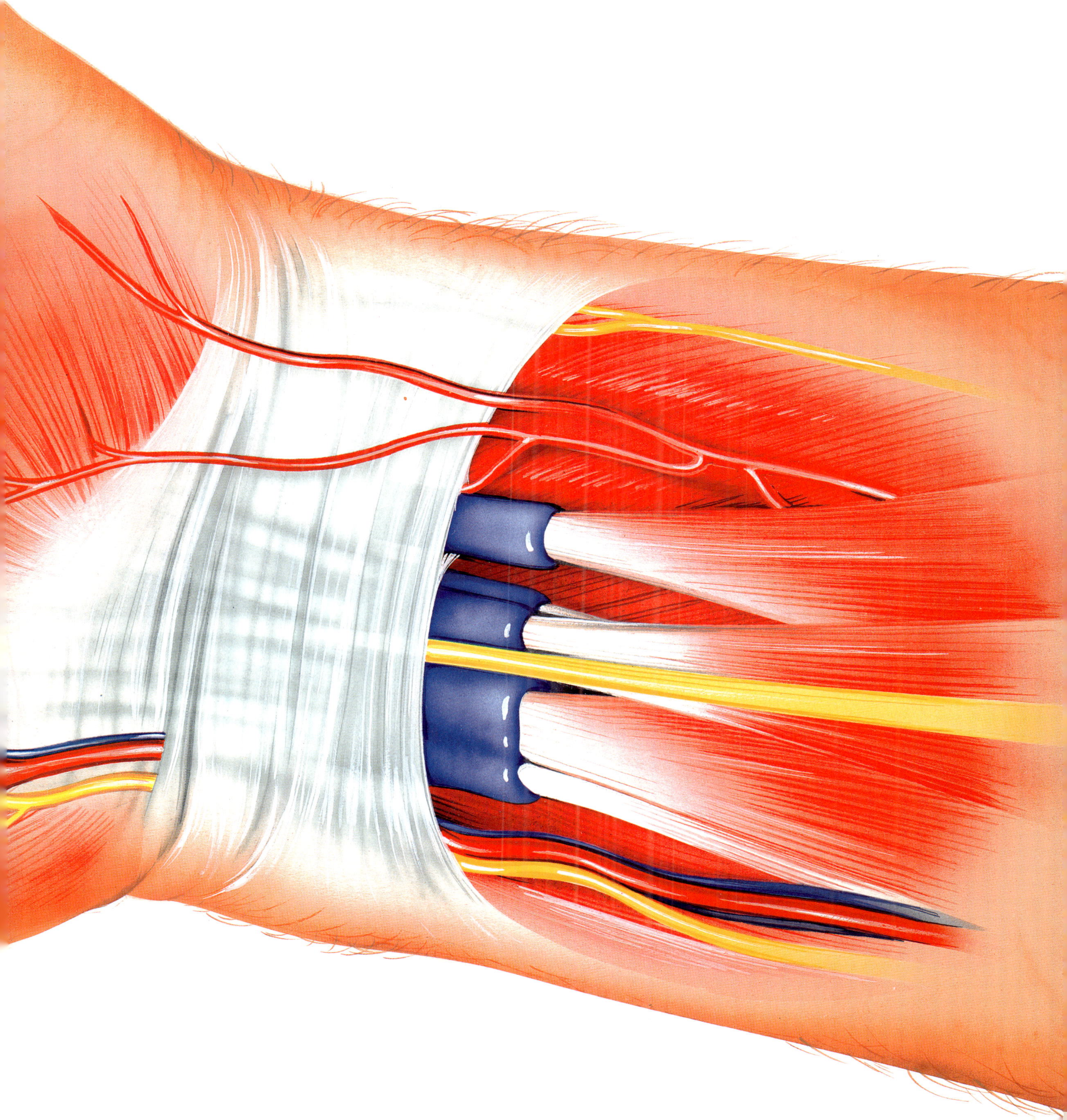

ULCER

An ulcer is a region where the surface layer of the skin, or the lining of an internal organ such as the gut or airway, has been lost. There is often loss of underlying tissue, so that the region has a punched-out appearance, as if a cookie-cutter has been used.

Ulcers may occur in many areas of the body. On the skin, decubitus ulcers (bedsores) can occur following prolonged and unrelieved pressure on the skin, sometimes associated with poor circulation. Some skin cancers may develop ulcers in their central regions, as seen with rodent ulcers (basal cell carcinomas). Varicose ulcers develop around the ankles, due to problems with drainage of venous blood from the skin of the leg. The cornea at the front of the eye may become ulcerated, with serious consequences for vision. Inside the mouth, aphthous ulcers may develop due to poor dentition, poor oral hygiene, excessive alcohol intake or cigarette smoking. Peptic ulcers develop in the upper gut, usually after the *Helicobacter pylori* bacterium has weakened and damaged the protective lining of the stomach or duodenum, allowing penetration by corrosive digestive juices. Multiple ulcers may occur in the colon and rectum in the condition known as ulcerative colitis.

SEE ALSO *Basal cell carcinoma, Cornea, Peptic ulcer, Ulcerative colitis*

ULCERATIVE COLITIS

Ulcerative colitis is predominantly a disease of the large bowel, although it may also involve the end of the small bowel. The disease usually arises between 15 and 20 years of age, although some patients develop the disease in their sixties. The disease involves loss of the surface lining of the bowel (ulceration) with bleeding. Patients complain of rectal bleeding and diarrhea, frequent discharges of watery stool mixed with blood, pus and mucus. Many patients have cramping abdominal pain, with fever, vomiting, weight loss and dehydration.

The complications of ulcerative colitis are very serious. About 30–40 percent of patients will develop cancer in the affected bowel within 20 years of onset. Other complications include a life-threatening dilation of the colon (toxic megacolon), which occurs in about 3 percent of patients; and perforation of the bowel in a further 3 percent.

Treatment may involve anti-inflammatory drugs, or surgery, particularly if chronic symptoms or cancer develop. Due to better treatment, the mortality rate is much lower now than 30 years ago.

SEE ALSO *Bowel cancer, Intestines, Rectum, Ulcer*

ULNA

The ulna and radius are the two bones of the forearm. The ulna lies on the medial (inner) side of the forearm, extending from the el-

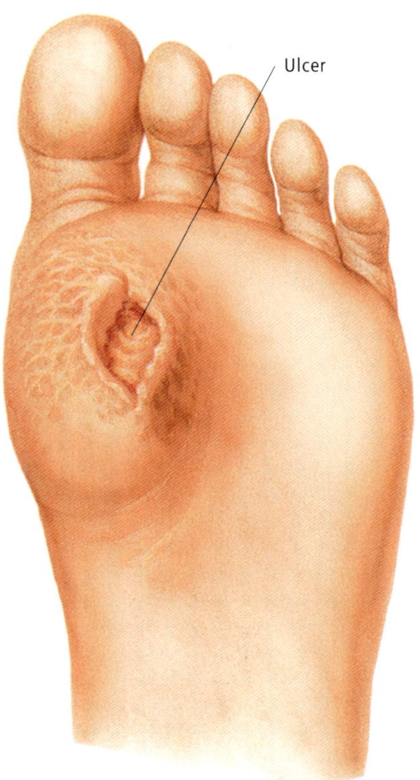

Foot ulcer
Diabetics often have poor circulation to the legs and feet and may develop ulcers in these areas. These ulcers often take a long time to heal.

Ulcerative colitis
This condition is characterized by patches of ulceration on the mucous membranes.

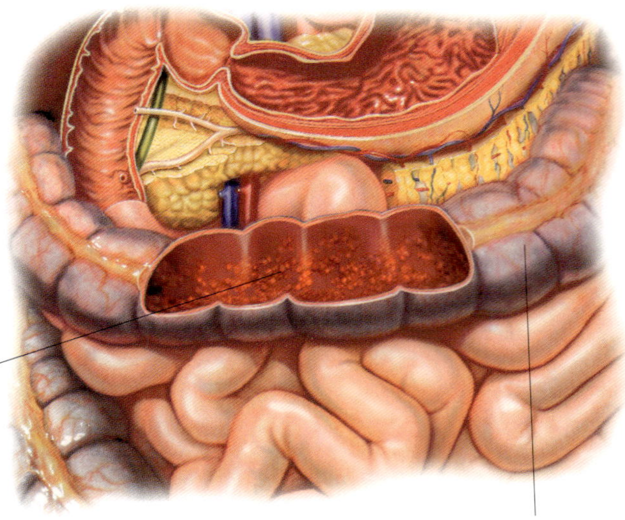

Ulcer
An ulcer forms when small parts of tissues or organs die, leaving painful, inflamed holes.

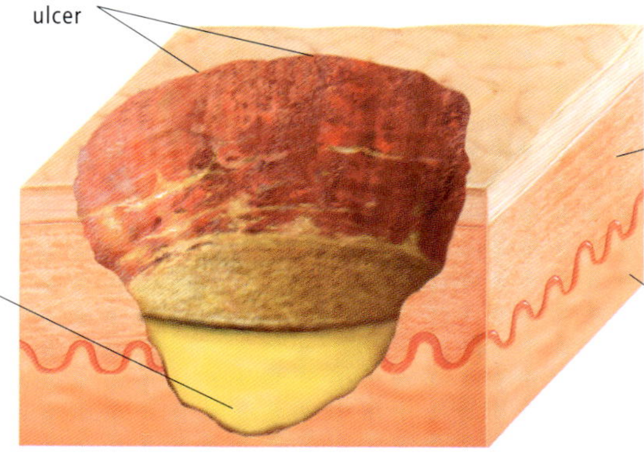

bow to the wrist. The ulna is a long bone of irregular cross-section, thickest at the elbow end and tapering towards the wrist. It projects above and behind the elbow. At the elbow, the ulna forms a hinge joint with the humerus. The radius articulates with the ulna at both ends, and is firmly bound to it along most of its length by a fibrous membrane which permits the radius to swing around the ulna, carrying the wrist with it. The ulna is not involved in the wrist joint. The ulna and radius are often fractured (resulting in a broken forearm).

SEE ALSO *Arm, Elbow, Humerus, Radius*

ULNAR NERVE

The ulnar nerve is one of the major nerves of the upper limb arising from the brachial plexus in the shoulder. It runs down the inner side of the upper arm, initially accompanying the brachial artery, winds around the inner side of the elbow joint to enter the forearm, and runs along the inner side of the forearm to enter the hand on the little-finger side. In the forearm, its position can be mapped by a line from the medial epicondyle of the humerus to the inner edge of the pisiform bone.

Branches of the ulnar nerve activate the flexor carpi ulnaris muscle and half of the flexor digitorum profundus muscle, and small muscles of the hand. The ulnar nerve provides sensation for the skin on the little-finger side of the hand. At the elbow, the ulnar nerve lies in a groove on the upper surface of the medial epicondyle, where it is liable to injury.

SEE ALSO *Arm, Elbow, Humerus, Ulna*

ULTRASOUND

Also known as ultrasonography or sonography, ultrasound is a diagnostic procedure that uses sound waves above 20,000 cycles per second to create an image. It produces excellent images of soft organs or organs filled with fluid; it is used to detect both cysts and solid tumors, to investigate the cause of abdominal pain and to guide the insertion of a needle during a needle biopsy or a test such as amniocentesis. During pregnancy ultrasound is used to confirm the age of the fetus, the position and/or health of the placenta, the number of babies and the physical development of the baby.

Ultrasound is usually performed as an outpatient procedure. A small amount of gel is applied to the skin over the area to be scanned, which improves the transmission of sound waves. The ultrasound transducer is moved backwards and forwards over the

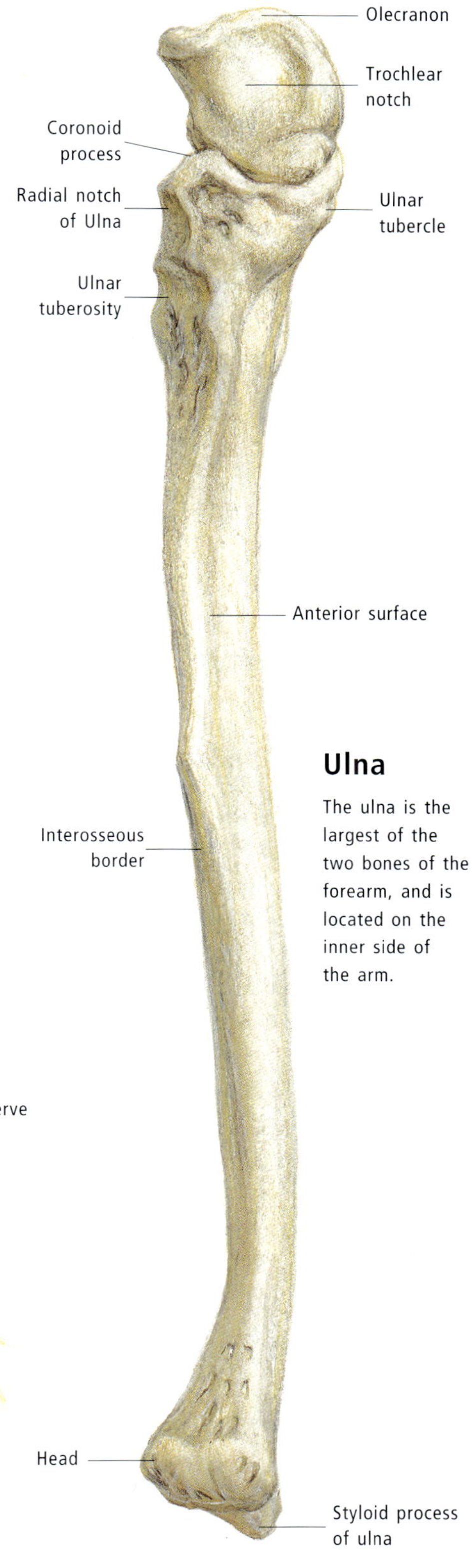

Ulna

The ulna is the largest of the two bones of the forearm, and is located on the inner side of the arm.

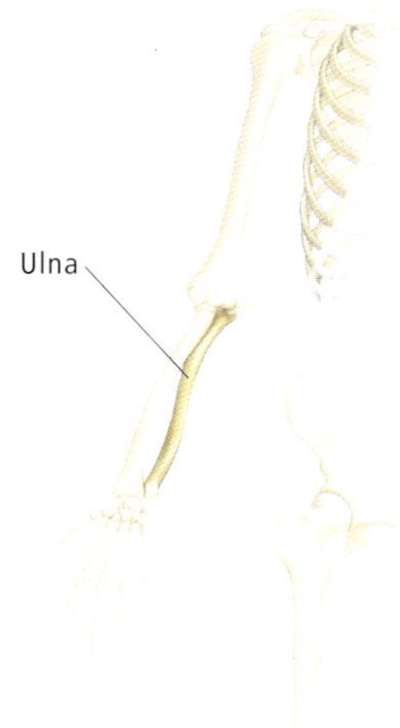

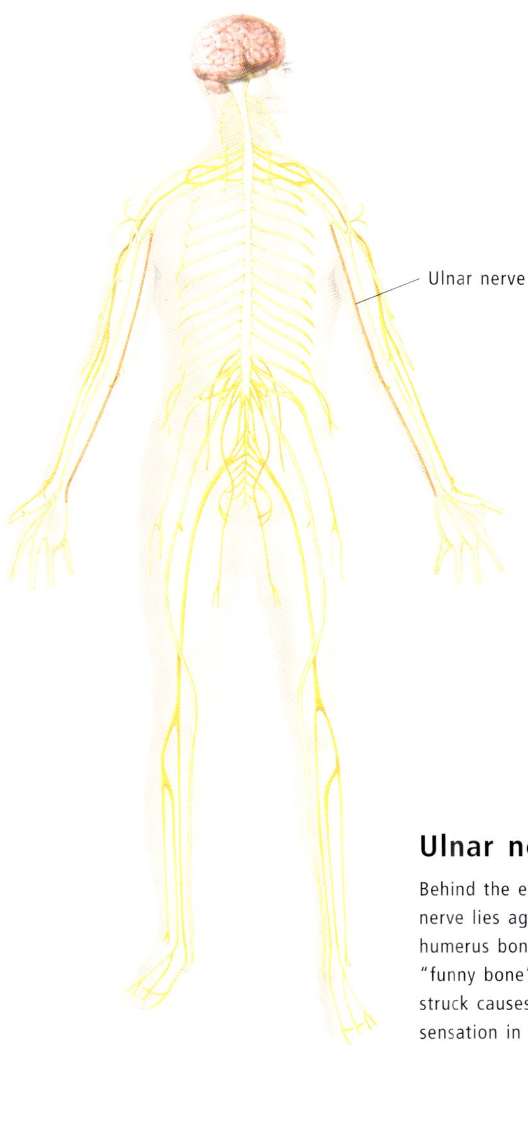

Ulnar nerve

Behind the elbow, the ulnar nerve lies against the humerus bone—this is the "funny bone", which when struck causes an odd sensation in the elbow area.

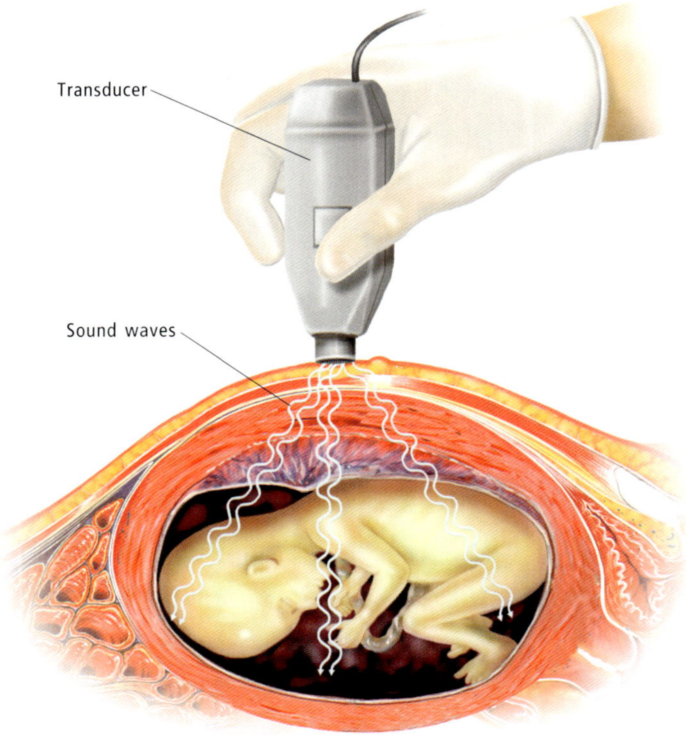

Ultrasound

This procedure uses sound waves to form a two-dimensional image of internal organs. It is commonly used in antenatal care to determine the health and development of the fetus. The transducer transmits reflections of the sound waves to a computer which converts them into an image on a screen.

area, transmitting the reflections of the sound waves to a computer, which converts them to an image on a screen.

Doppler ultrasonography is a specialized type of ultrasound used to investigate the flow of blood through blood vessels, and to look at the movement of parts of organs such as heart valves. Very high energy ultrasound produces a heating effect that is used in sports physical therapy to treat soft tissue injury. Ultrasound is also used in one form of lithotripsy, using the sound waves to shatter kidney stones.

In many industrialized societies ultrasound is treated as an expected part of antenatal care. It has many advantages over other methods of imaging, including the fact that the transmission of sound makes it safer than x-rays, which use ionizing radiation.

SEE ALSO *Amniocentesis, Biopsy, Doppler ultrasonography, Fetal development, Imaging techniques, Lithotripsy*

ULTRAVIOLET THERAPY

Ultraviolet (UV) therapy is a form of light therapy (or phototherapy) used to treat skin disorders. The patient stands undressed in a specially designed cabinet containing fluorescent light tubes. Ultraviolet light is administered as either longwave UV light energy (UVA) or shortwave UV light energy (UVB). One form of this treatment, known as PUVA, combines UVA light with psoralen medication, which renders the skin more responsive to the therapy. Ultraviolet therapy is principally used in the treatment of psoriasis, as well as for dermatitis, vitiligo and cutaneous T cell lymphoma.

SEE ALSO *Dermatitis, Psoriasis, Vitiligo*

UMBILICAL CORD

The umbilical cord serves to join the unborn baby (fetus) to the afterbirth (placenta), by which the fetus obtains nourishment from its mother. The fully developed cord is ½–1 inch (1–2 centimeters) in diameter and about 20 inches (50 centimeters) long, but its length is very variable: 8–48 inches (20–120 centimeters). It contains two umbilical arteries and one umbilical vein, embedded in a mucoid connective tissue known as Wharton's jelly. It is covered by a thin layer of epithelium. Nourishment and oxygen pass from the placenta to the baby; waste products pass in the other direction.

Immediately after birth, blood from the placenta and umbilical cord passes into the baby. After delivery, the umbilical cord is tied in two places and cut between the ties (the ties prevent loss of blood). The remnants of the cord initially remain attached to the navel (umbilicus), then shrivel up and fall off after 3–4 days.

SEE ALSO *Childbirth, Placenta, Pregnancy*

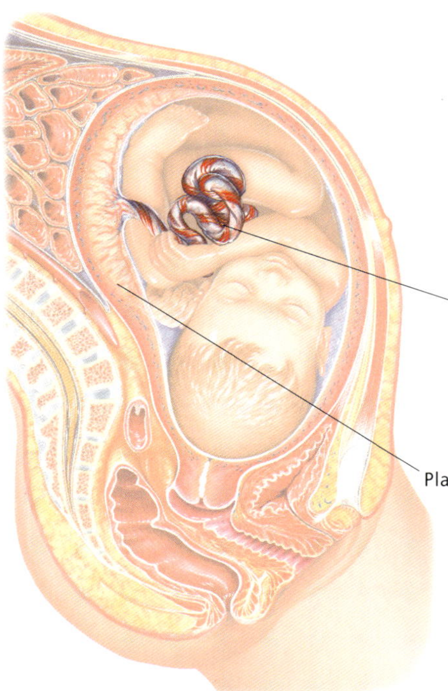

Umbilical cord

The umbilical cord is the "lifeline" that connects the fetus to the placenta. It has two arteries that carry oxygenated blood to the fetus and one vein that carries deoxygenated blood away.

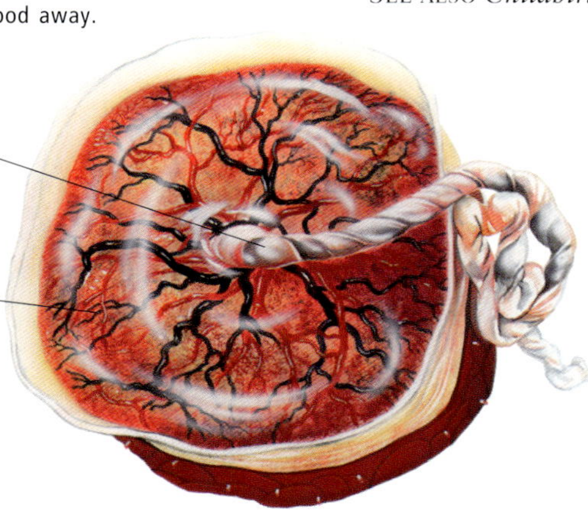

UNCONSCIOUSNESS

An unconscious person is one who is hard to rouse or is unaware of their surroundings. Unconsciousness is caused by illness, injury or emotional shock. It may be temporary, as in fainting or blacking out, or it can be prolonged, as in coma. Depending on the cause, someone in a coma may never recover.

Unconsciousness has many causes; some of the more common include stroke, epilepsy, diabetic coma, drug overdose, concussion, low blood sugar (hypoglycemia) and heart attack. People who suffer from a medical condition that can cause unconsciousness should wear an identification bracelet or pendant, carry a card in a wallet, or have a special sticker on the back of their driver's license.

First aid is vital in the treatment of unconsciousness. Do not give an unconscious person food or drink. Do not leave an unconscious person alone. If the victim has stopped breathing, give artificial respiration and if the victim's heart has stopped, give external cardiac compression. Stop any bleeding with bandages and pressure, and call emergency medical services.

Anyone who has been unconscious for a period should see a physician even if they have apparently recovered, as it may signify an underlying illness or head injury.

SEE ALSO *Coma*

UREMIA

Uremia is the medical term for retention in the blood of urinary substances, normally caused by severe kidney failure. It occurs when the diseased kidney is no longer able to clear the blood of waste products such as creatinine, urea and ammonia. The term uremia has been used for over a century. It was originally used because it was presumed that the symptoms of renal failure were due to retention of abnormal amounts of urea in the blood. However, it is now clear that the symptoms of renal failure are attributable not so much to the accumulation of urea but to disturbances of water and electrolyte balance and the accumulation of many other endproducts of metabolism.

Uremia can cause a wide range of clinical symptoms. Symptoms vary from patient to patient, depending on the degree of reduction in renal function and the rapidity with which renal function is lost. At an early stage patients will often have no symptoms, but as renal function deteriorates, symptoms develop. Loss of appetite, nausea, hiccups and vomiting are the common initial symptoms of uremia. Stomach ulcers occur in one-quarter of uremic patients. The patient's skin often develops a sallow complexion (a yellow-brown appearance). This is due to the combined effect of impaired excretion of urinary pigments (urochromes) combined with anemia. High blood pressure (hypertension) is the most common complication of uremia. Fluid retention may result in congestive heart failure and/ or pulmonary edema (fluid in the lungs). Pericarditis (inflammation of the lining of the heart) may occur. The patient may experience disturbances of the nervous system that can include loss of concentration, memory loss and minor behavioral changes. A peripheral sensory neuropathy is common and results in loss of sensation, typically in the legs. Other symptoms include muscle cramps and muscle twitching. In terminal uremia patients become drowsy and finally sink into a coma.

Diabetes and high blood pressure are the commonest causes of uremia. Other causes include glomerulonephritis (inflammation of the kidney), analgesic nephropathy (due to long-term ingestion of large quantities of analgesics), systemic vascular disease (e.g. systemic lupus erythematosus), obstruction of the urinary tract (by congenital defect, kidney stones or tumors) and polycystic kidneys (a congenital abnormality).

The treatment is to correct the underlying kidney disease if possible. A diet low in protein, salts and water will help minimize the production of wastes by the body and alleviate symptoms. Eventually, kidney dialysis or a kidney transplant may be necessary.

SEE ALSO *Dialysis, Kidney, Transplant surgery*

Ureter

The muscular walls of the ureters propel urine from the kidneys to the bladder.

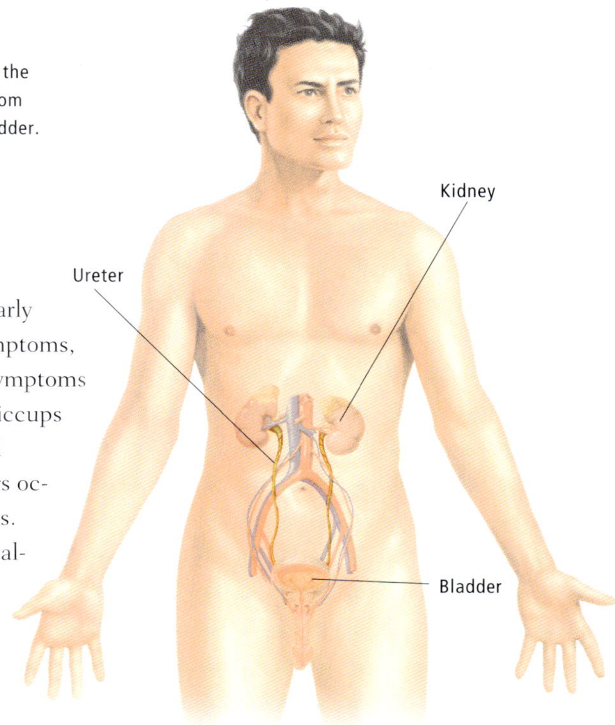

URETER

The ureters are two thin, muscular tubes that pass urine from the kidneys to the bladder. The walls of the ureters contain smooth muscles, which contract and propel urine in waves to the bladder.

The ureter may become blocked by a stone or a tumor. It may become inflamed, along with the rest of the urinary tract, in pyelonephritis.

Disorders of the ureter can be identified by a pyelogram, an x-ray taken after dye has been injected, showing the outline of the ureter and the other organs in the urinary tract.

SEE ALSO *Bladder, Kidney, Pyelonephritis, Urinary systems*

URETHRA

The urethra is the tube through which urine travels from the bladder to the outside of the body. In women, the urethra is short; it opens between the vagina and clitoris. The urethra is longer in men and also serves as the passage for semen. It passes through the prostate gland, where it is joined by the sperm ducts, and opens at the tip of the penis.

Various disorders may affect the urethra. It may become infected and inflamed (urethritis). Symptoms include pain on urinating (dysuria) and in men, a discharge from the

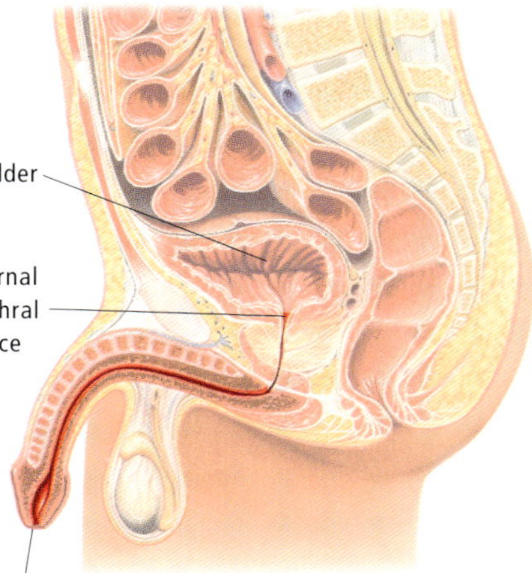

Male urethra

In men, the long urethral tube (usually 8 inches or 20 centimeters long) passes from the bladder through the prostate gland and penis. It transports urine and semen out of the body.

Female urethra

The female urethra is relatively short. As a result, invading bacteria can pass more easily into the body, leading to frequent bladder infections such as cystitis.

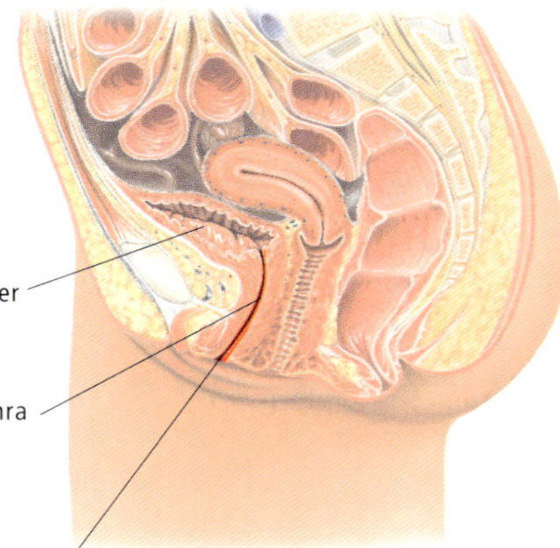

penis. Treatment is with an antibiotic appropriate for the particular microorganism causing the disease. Urethritis may result in scarring and narrowing of the urethra in men.

Epispadias is a congenital defect in which the urethra opens abnormally on the top of the penis, either in the head of, or along the entire length of, the penis. In hypospadias, the urethral opening appears on the underside of the penis. Both conditions cause urinary incontinence and sexual dysfunction in adulthood. Reconstructive surgery usually cures the defects.

SEE ALSO *Bladder, Epispadias, Hypospadias, Urethritis, Urinary incontinence*

URETHRITIS

Urethritis is inflammation of the urethra—the tube through which urine travels from the bladder to the outside of the body. It often occurs with cystitis (inflammation of the bladder), prostatitis (inflammation of the prostate) or epididymitis (inflammation of the epididymis). Urethritis is often sexually transmitted, as in the case of gonorrhea and nonspecific or nongonococcal urethritis.

Symptoms are painful or burning urination, a frequent urge to urinate even when there is not much urine in the bladder, and a discharge that may be thick and yellow, or watery and white. A swab and culture of the discharge will identify the organism and help the physician to prescribe the correct antibiotic which usually cures the condition. Urethritis may result in scarring and narrowing of the urethra in men.

SEE ALSO *Bladder, Cystitis, Epididymitis, Gonorrhea, Prostatitis, Urethra*

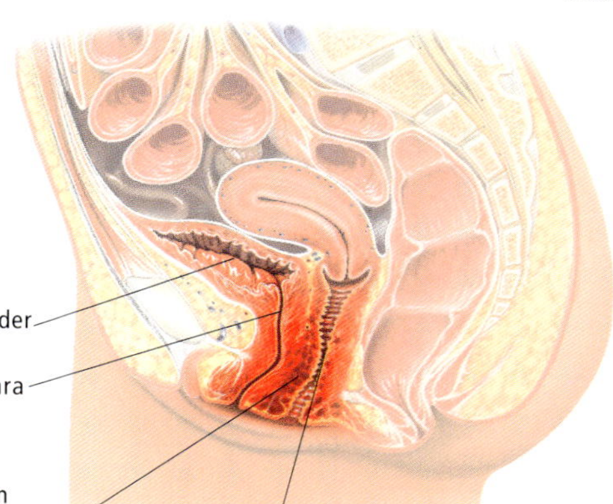

Urethrocele

A weakness in the vaginal wall can result in urethrocele, in which the urethral tube bulges against the vagina.

URETHROCELE

A urethrocele is a bulge of the urethra (the tube that carries urine from the bladder to the outside of the body) along the front wall of the vagina. It is caused by a weakness in the vaginal wall, usually following childbirth. A minor urethrocele doesn't produce symptoms, but a larger one causes a lump inside the vaginal opening and may cause urinary incontinence. Surgery, performed through the vagina, will repair the weakness in the vaginal wall and the bulging urethra.

SEE ALSO *Bladder, Urethra, Urinary incontinence, Vagina*

URINALYSIS

Urinalysis is a test performed to analyze cells, proteins and other chemicals in the urine. It is used to detect disease, especially of the kidney and urinary tract. For example, the presence of blood in the urine (hematuria) may be due to a urinary tract infection, a stone, a polyp or cancer. Pus cells and bacteria may indicate urinary infection, while protein in the urine (proteinuria) may indicate nephritis or myeloma. Bilirubin in the urine may be a sign of jaundice, and glucose in the urine is usually caused by diabetes mellitus.

The sample of urine may be cultured for 24–48 hours. If bacterial colonies form in the culture it may be a sign of infection in the urinary tract. The culture will show the specific organism causing the infection and further tests can determine which antibiotics will kill it.

SEE ALSO *Cystitis, Kidney, Nephritis, Urinary systems, Urinary tract*

URINARY INCONTINENCE

The abnormal lack of voluntary control of the bladder in older children and adults is called incontinence. It may be caused by a neurological disorder or a disorder interfering with control of the sphincter muscle that normally closes the bladder—for example after pelvic surgery. In males, it may result from partial obstruction caused by enlargement of the prostate gland (prostatomegaly). Some women with prolapse (displacement) of the uterus develop stress incontinence as the uterus presses on the bladder and allows urine to escape when the woman coughs or laughs. It is important that the underlying cause of incontinence is treated. Leakage of urine can be managed by the use of waterproof undergarments with absorbent pads.

SEE ALSO *Bladder, Prolapse, Prostate gland*

URINARY TRACT

The urinary tract is a specialized filtering and recycling system that excretes certain fluid wastes produced by the body in the process of metabolism, such as urea, creatinine and ammonia. These wastes, along with excess water, are removed from the blood as urine by the two kidneys. Urine then passes through tubes called ureters into the bladder. From the bladder the urine passes out of the body through another tube called the urethra.

The urinary tract is subject to various disorders. Urinary tract infection is an infection of one or more parts of the urinary system, usually caused by bacteria. Urinary tract obstruction occurs when there is a blockage in the urethra, bladder or ureters. The condition may be congenital (existing from birth) or it may be caused by tumors or mineral deposits that form stones.

Diseases of the kidneys can lead to an accumulation of wastes in the blood, a condition called uremia. Cancers may form in the bladder or kidney. Diseases of the urinary tract are investigated by x-rays, pyelograms (x-rays taken after radiopaque dye has been injected, which show the outline of the urinary tract), cystoscopy (a tube inserted into the bladder through which the bladder can be viewed), CAT scans and ultrasound.

SEE ALSO *Bladder, Kidney, Urethra, Urinary systems*

URTICARIA

Urticaria (hives or nettle rash) is a skin rash in the form of wheals that are red, itchy and raised. It appears suddenly and may disappear just as quickly, leaving no trace or permanent damage. It can affect either sex and appear at any age. Urticaria of pregnancy may appear in the last two or three weeks and disappears after delivery. Urticaria can occur after illness, as a result of skin infection, or as the result of an allergic response when the chemical histamine is produced within the body. The rash may disappear as the allergic reaction subsides.

Urticaria

More commonly known as hives, urticaria is a rash of itchy red wheals that can be caused by an allergic reaction to food or plants, illness or emotional stress.

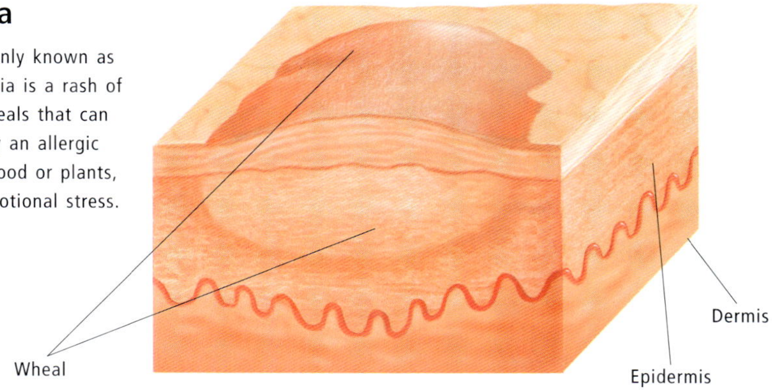

Occasionally urticaria may cause swellings in the throat and restrict breathing. If the rash appears to be below the skin surface and there is burning or pain rather than itching, a medical examination may be needed to establish whether it is urticaria or angioedema, a more serious condition.

Visible symptoms and the torment of itching can be relieved by taking a lukewarm bath with soothing additives, or by applying cool compresses to the rash. Medical advice should be sought in all cases where urticaria is persistent or is causing distress or discomfort. Drugs used in treatment include corticosteroid creams, antihistamines and, where there are breathing difficulties, epinephrine (adrenaline).

SEE ALSO *Allergies, Angioedema, Antihistamines*

UTERUS

The uterus (womb), the organ of gestation, is located in the pelvis, between the bladder and the rectum. It undergoes regular changes during the menstrual cycle. The non-pregnant uterus is pear shaped and flattened from front to back. It communicates with the vagina below. The two fallopian tubes open into its upper part, one on each side. In about 80 percent of women the uterus is anteverted (tilted forward); in the remaining 20 percent it is retroverted (tilted backwards). The uterus should be somewhat mobile and can be displaced vertically by a very distended bladder. This displacement is used to allow a clearer view of a non-pregnant uterus during ultrasound examination.

The uterus consists of the fundus (top), body and cervix. The wall of the body consists of an endometrium or inner lining adjacent to the central cavity; a thick muscular myometrium; and an outer layer of peritoneum or perimetrium. The endometrium contains large numbers of glands and blood vessels. It undergoes proliferation and secretion during much of the menstrual cycle, followed by sloughing of all but the deepest parts at menstruation. The remaining tissue forms the basis for regeneration of a new endometrium during the next cycle. The myometrium undergoes mild contractions during menstruation.

The uterus enlarges enormously in pregnancy and its hollow center is obliterated during the third month. It reaches the top of the pubic bone by about 12 weeks, the level of the umbilicus at about 20 weeks and the diaphragm at 36 weeks. The pregnant uterus also displaces or compresses adjacent abdominal organs.

The uterus is attached to the lateral walls of the pelvis by the broad ligament. Further support is provided by ligaments attached to the cervix, which cross the pelvic floor and attach to the walls of the pelvis. Pelvic floor muscles are also important in maintaining the uterus in its correct position. Damage or weakening of these supports can lead to a prolapsed uterus. In this condition the uterus and cervix become inverted and descend into the vagina or in extreme cases

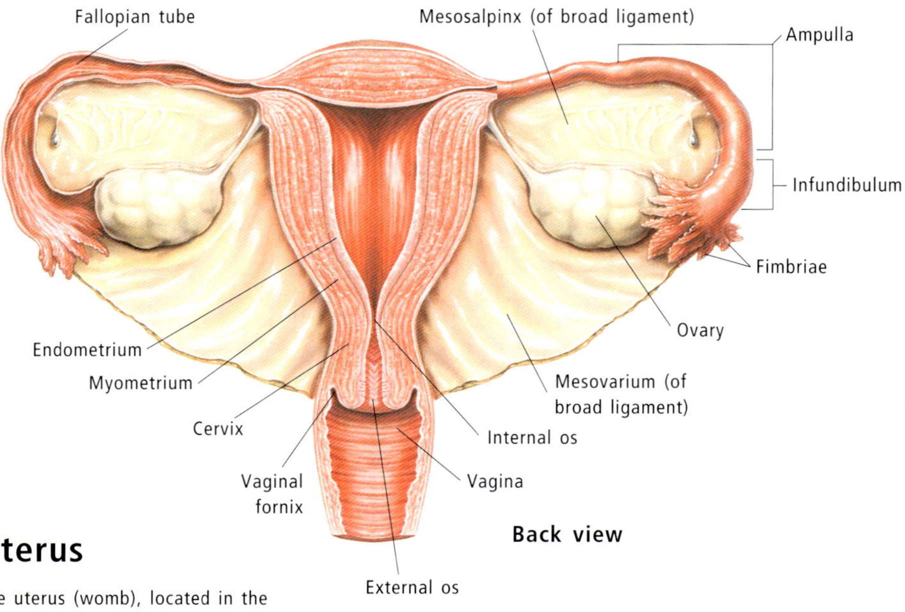

Back view

Uterus

The uterus (womb), located in the pelvis between the bladder and rectum, is where the fertilized ovum develops into an embryo and fetus.

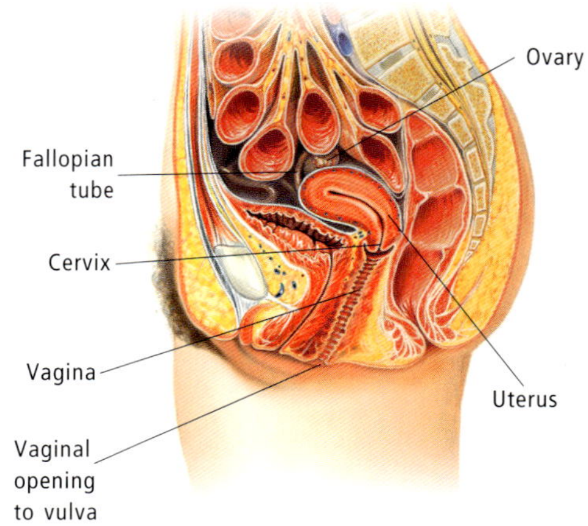

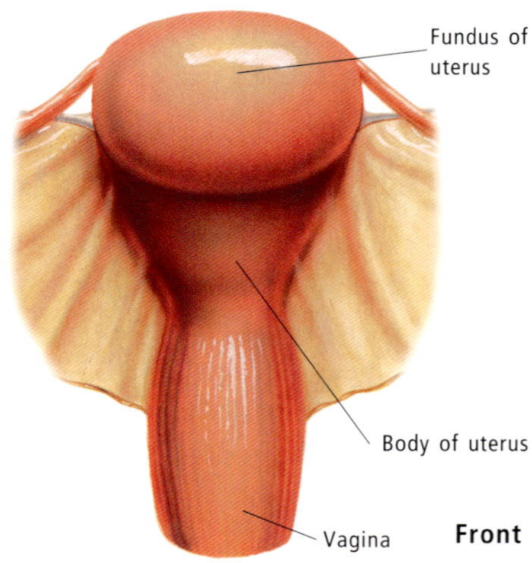

Front view

may protrude, along with the vagina, outside the body. The bladder and ureters (tubes connecting the kidneys to the bladder) may be inverted as well and this often causes acute urinary retention. The rectum and loops of intestine can also be involved.

The cervix has a thick muscular wall and a mucus-secreting lining which is not sloughed at menstruation. The mucus is usually thick and fills the cervical canal to form a protective plug and a barrier to sperm penetration. The mucus becomes thinner around the time of ovulation. Some of the mucus glands may become blocked and enlarged to form cysts. The layer of cells adjacent to the cervical canal, which connects the vagina to the uterus, is thin but becomes thicker just above the opening of the cervix with the vagina. This is where the majority of cervical carcinomas develop and, for this reason, pap smears are taken from this region. The cervical canal is comparatively narrow and has to be expanded under either local or general anesthetic in order to obtain a biopsy of the endometrium. A tissue sample is taken via curettage. Curettage can also be used as a treatment for abnormal uterine bleeding.

The internal structure of the uterus may be observed by passing a fiberoptic telescope through the cervix into the uterine cavity which has previously been inflated with gas or fluid. Alternatively, radiopaque contrast medium may be introduced into the uterus and the outline of the cavity observed. The fallopian tubes can be checked at the same time for patency (the condition of being wide open) or abnormalities.

Diseases and disorders

Cervical mucus resists the penetration of pathogens from the vagina. However, this protection is only partial, and the microbes responsible for pelvic inflammatory disease (PID) usually ascend from the vagina, although they may arise from an abdominal infection. Oral contraceptive users have a lower incidence of PID, apparently due to changes in the cervical mucus which render it more impervious to bacterial penetration.

The uterus is particularly vulnerable to infection after childbirth when there is an incomplete endometrial surface and possible damage to the cervix or when there are retained fragments of placenta. Infection may spread to adjacent organs or the bloodstream, leading to blood poisoning (septicemia) or puerperal fever. Permanent damage may follow, including chronic inflammation, adhesions and uterine displacement. Puerperal sepsis or fever is now uncommon due to improved obstetric care and antibiotics.

Fibroids (myomas or leiomyomas) commonly occur in the myometrium. These are benign tumors, consisting of spherical masses of muscle and fibrous tissue and ranging in size from minute to occasionally enormous. They are more frequent and likely to cause abnormal uterine bleeding in women over 35 years of age. Treatment involves the use of progestins, removal of the myoma, or hysterectomy.

The junction of the endometrium and myometrium is usually clearcut. In a sizeable minority of women, however, there is some growth of the endometrium into the myometrium, a condition known as adenomyosis. This is sometimes associated with endometriosis, fibroids or abnormal endometrial thickening. The tissue forming the adenomyosis may or may not respond to ovarian hormones. Adenomyosis may be symptomless or associated with menstrual discomfort or dysfunction. Treatment can be either surgical or hormonal. Adenomyosis may sometimes be associated with malignant changes.

Hysterectomy is surgical removal of the uterus. This is described as subtotal when only the uterus is excised and total if both the uterus and cervix are removed. A radical hysterectomy involves removal of uterus, cervix, fallopian tubes, ovaries, the upper third of the vagina and at least some of the adjacent lymph nodes. Hysterectomy may be carried out via an abdominal incision or via an incision around the cervical opening (vaginal hysterectomy).

Complete absence of the uterus is rare but deformities resulting in either a bicornate (double) uterus or a single uterus divided by an internal septum can occur. These reflect the embryological origin of the uterus, which starts as two separate tubes which fuse during fetal life. A double or septate vagina may accompany bicornate uterus. The external genitalia, which have a separate embryological origin, are usually normal.

SEE ALSO *Cervix, Endometrium, Hysterectomy, Menstruation, Pap smear, Pelvic floor muscles, Pelvic inflammatory disease, Pregnancy, Reproductive systems, Retroversion of uterus*

VAGINA

The vagina is the passage connecting the uterus to the outside of the body. It is situated in the lower pelvis and pelvic floor and is located between the bladder and the rectum. The lower opening in virgin women is partly closed by a thin membrane called the hymen. The vaginal wall consists of a thick external muscle, an inner mucosa, and a cavity with the inner surfaces in direct contact. The cavity tilts slightly backwards and is at about 90° to the cervical canal, which connects the vagina with the cavity of the uterus. The vagina contains fluid consisting of cervical mucus and plasma from capillaries in the mucosa. The external opening of the cervix protrudes into the upper part of the vagina and is surrounded by a groove or fornix. The vagina is supported by the cervical ligaments and pelvic floor muscles.

The vagina and external cervix can be observed by expanding the vaginal cavity with the aid of a vaginal speculum.

The mucosa is lined with a thick layer of cells containing glycogen. The superficial cells are sloughed into the vaginal fluid and replaced by cell divisions deeper in the lining. The sloughed cells are broken down by bacteria (*Lactobacillus*), which are normal vaginal flora. The lactic acid thus produced discourages invasion by pathogens. If the *Lactobacilli* are destroyed, for example when antibiotics are administered, then yeast (candida) may proliferate and cause thrush. Symptoms are a white discharge (leukorrhea) and vulval itching.

There is little glycogen in the lining cells before puberty and vaginal infections are correspondingly more common. Glycogen also decreases after menopause and the vaginal mucosa becomes thin and prone to infection and irritation, leading to postmenopausal or atrophic vaginitis. Treatment is by topical or oral estrogens.

Diseases and disorders

Benign vaginal tumors can arise in the fibrous tissue of the vaginal wall or from remnants of embryonic tissue. These may be removed surgically if causing bleeding, discharge or local irritation. Vaginal malignancies are often the result of secondary spread from growths elsewhere. Primary vaginal carcinomas are more common in postmenopausal women. Treatment is either by irradiation, or by removal of the carcinoma or the entire vagina and possibly adjacent organs. Primary vaginal adenocarcinoma may occur in women under 25 who were exposed *in utero* to diethylstilboestrol (a non-steroidal synthetic estrogen) administered to their mothers early in pregnancy.

Vaginal prolapse can include a part of the bladder, which is pulled downwards through a weakness in the vaginal wall. This is termed a cystocele and can cause difficulties in urination. Surgical repair is usually the best treatment.

Fistulas are abnormal canals formed as a result of injury or occasionally as developmental abnormalities. Vaginal fistulas are the result of obstetric, surgical or accidental trauma or heavy irradiation. Fistulas connecting the vagina with the bladder cause continuous leakage of urine, causing physical damage and social embarrassment. Surgical closure is the most common treatment. Sometimes recent fistulas may close of their own accord if the bladder is drained continuously while the woman is maintained in a prone position. Fistulas can also connect the vagina to parts of the intestine, particularly the rectum (recto-vaginal fistula).

SEE ALSO *Candidiasis, Cystocele, Estrogens, Fistula, Prolapse, Reproductive systems, Vaginitis*

VAGINISMUS

Vaginismus is a condition in which spasm of the muscles at the entrance to the vagina precludes normal intercourse or renders it impossibly painful. It is usually psychological in origin and can arise from a fear of intercourse or of ensuing pregnancy. It can also follow traumas such as rape, painful childbirth, painful initial attempts at intercourse or intercourse too soon after gynecological surgery. It may occur even though sexual desire is quite strong. The woman may be sexually responsive to non-penetrative stimuli or capable of clitoral orgasm.

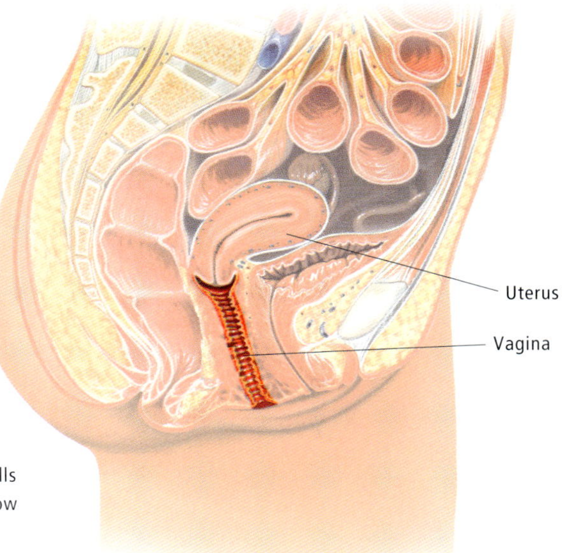

Vagina

The vagina is the passage that links the uterus to the exterior of the body. Its muscular walls are flexible enough to allow the passage of the baby during childbirth.

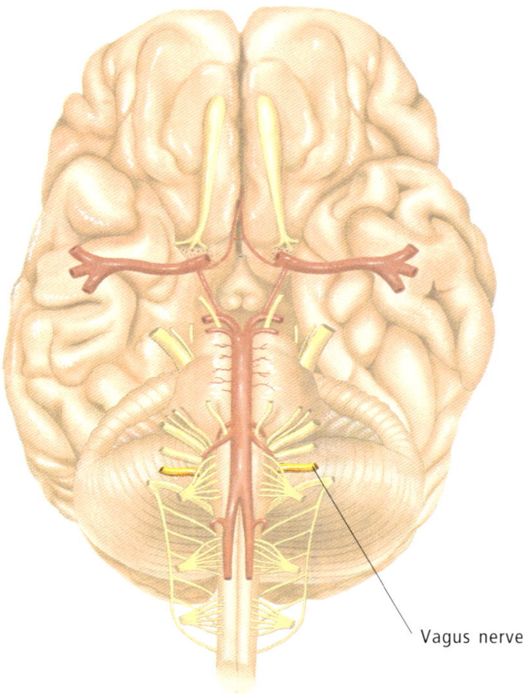

Vagus nerve

The tenth cranial nerve (vagus nerve) is involved in a variety of functions, such as sneezing, swallowing, coughing, speech, heartbeat, and the secretion of stomach acid.

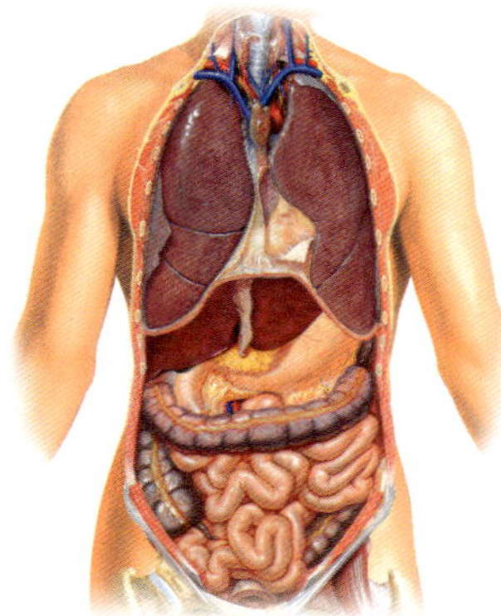

In the absence of organic problems, treatment for vaginismus is usually psychotherapy aimed at treating the fears underlying the condition. Gentle gradual dilation of the vaginal opening may also help.

SEE ALSO *Sexual intercourse, Vagina*

VAGINITIS

Vaginitis is a common gynecological complaint characterized by a discolored discharge and vaginal irritation and redness. Vaginitis is specific if it can be attributed to a particular irritative agent or bacterium. This is usually the case with vaginitis in women of reproductive age. Pre- and postmenopausal women have low levels of estrogen and the vaginal lining is very susceptible to a wide range of noxious agents. It is often impossible to pinpoint the cause of this type of vaginitis and it is described as non-specific.

One of the most common causes of vaginitis in young women is thrush resulting from infection with candida (yeast). Candida infections are not usually transmitted sexually and are due, in some cases, to loss of *Lactobacillus* as a result of antibiotic administration. Candida infections are especially prevalent in diabetes or pregnancy. Treatment is with fungicides. Vaginitis can also be the result of bacterial and protozoal infections, spread primarily by sexual contact.

The vaginal mucosa atrophies after menopause, with little glycogen produced to maintain an acid environment. This renders the vagina prone to infection or irritation leading to postmenopausal or atrophic vaginitis. This is characterized by tiny ulcers, often with a blood-stained discharge accompanied by itching or soreness. Ulceration may cause adhesions between the walls which partly obliterate the vaginal cavity. The condition is treated with estrogen pessaries or oral estrogens. These can cause uterine bleeding so are used only for a limited time.

SEE ALSO *Candidiasis, Estrogens, Menopause, Sexually transmitted diseases, Vagina*

VAGUS NERVE

The vagus or tenth cranial nerve is one of 12 cranial nerves which extend in pairs directly from the brain stem. The vagus nerve contains autonomic nerve fibers, which regulate functions in the body which operate without conscious control. It runs through the neck and thorax to the abdominal cavity and controls breathing, swallowing, speaking, heartbeat, the constriction of blood vessels and bronchial tubes, and digestion. It also conveys the sensation of taste to the brain from the throat.

The vagus nerve is only rarely damaged. One of its branches, the recurrent laryngeal nerve, may be damaged during surgery of the thyroid gland; this will paralyse muscles of the larynx, leading to hoarseness.

In vagotomy, the vagus nerve is cut adjacent to the esophagus to reduce secretion of hydrochloric acid as part of the treatment of stomach ulcer. While the vagus normally

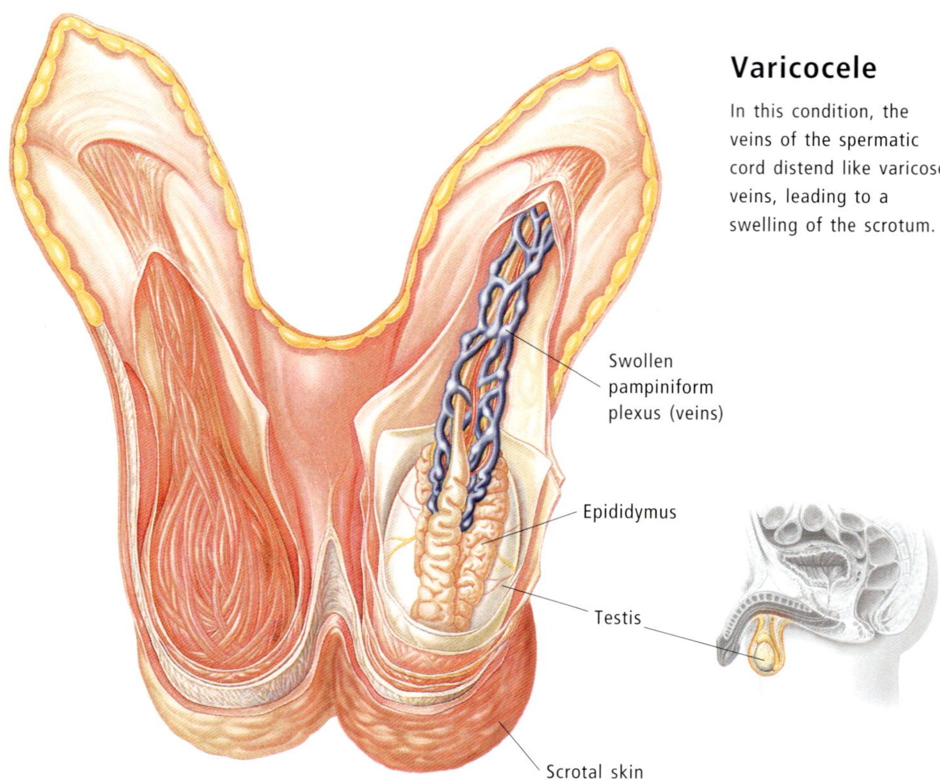

Varicocele

In this condition, the veins of the spermatic cord distend like varicose veins, leading to a swelling of the scrotum.

V

controls the stimulation of the stomach walls and lower sphincter, normal peristaltic action can continue without it. Vasovagal syncope is fainting caused by slowing of the heartbeat in response to signals from the vagus which arise during severe stomach cramps, through pain, fear or apprehension. The vagal response can, in cases of severe injury, completely inhibit normal movement of food through the bowels for several days. Heart arrhythmia, where the heart rate speeds up for no apparent reason, can sometimes be stopped by stimulation of the vagus nerve. In epilepsy, experiments using an implanted electronic device similar to a heart pacemaker are being used to stimulate the vagus nerve to stop or weaken seizures.

SEE ALSO *Arrythmia, Autonomic nervous system, Epilepsy, Nerves, Nervous system, Spinal cord*

VARICOCELE

A varicocele is a mass of enlarged and distended veins, similar to varicose veins, arising from the spermatic cord, which feels like a "mass of worms" on the testicle. The mass is more obvious when standing and often disappears on lying down, as blood pressure to it decreases. A varicocele more commonly develops on the left side and can result from defective valves in the testicular vein or by problems with the renal or kidney vein. A varicocele may produce an ache but is usually painless. If it prevents proper drainage of blood from the testes it may raise their temperature and reduce sperm production.

SEE ALSO *Fertility, Testes, Veins*

VARICOSE ULCER

Varicose ulcers, or venous stasis ulcers, occur on the leg just above the ankle. They are caused by problems with circulation in the leg. In the normal leg there is a set of valves which prevents backflow of venous blood from deep veins to surface veins when the calf muscles contract. If these valves become damaged or weakened, the surface veins are subjected to higher than normal internal pressure. This in turn interferes with the flow of blood through the small vessels supplying the skin around the ankle. The poor blood flow means that the skin becomes starved of nutrients and overloaded with waste products. Portions of the skin may die and ulcers result.

SEE ALSO *Circulatory system, Veins*

Varicose veins

Faults in the walls or valves of the veins, or the formation of blood clots, can disrupt blood flow in the veins of the legs causing swollen and knotted (varicose) veins. Faulty valves allow blood to pool, swelling and distending the veins.

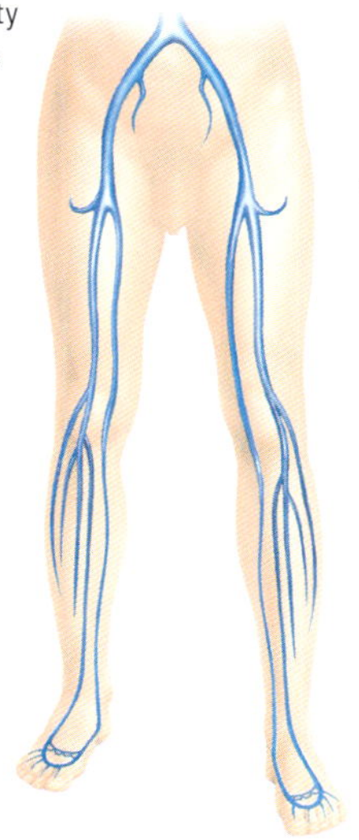

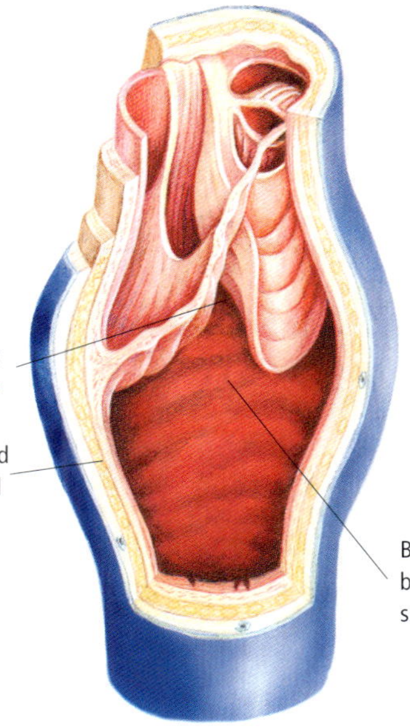

VARICOSE VEINS

Varicose veins are dilated, elongated, tortuous veins. They arise in the superficial veins of the leg—the great and small saphenous veins and their tributaries. Saphenous comes from the Greek word *saphenes*, meaning "obvious".

Varicose veins are defined as primary when they arise as a result of problems in the superficial veins themselves (many sufferers have a family history). Alternatively they may be secondary to the formation of clots (venous thrombosis) in the deep leg veins (deep vein thrombosis, DVT), or secondary to faulty valves in the veins that normally direct blood from the superficial veins into the deep leg veins. In the latter two cases, pressure in the superficial veins increases, either because blood cannot flow into the blocked deep veins, or because faulty valves in the communicating veins result in backflow into superficial veins when the leg muscles contract.

Valves in the veins may become incompetent when veins are overstretched by excessive pressure for long periods (weeks to months), for example when standing for prolonged periods or in pregnancy. The pressure causes the veins to become dilated but the valves do not increase in size, therefore affecting the efficiency of the valves. Elevating the legs and external compression with elastic support stockings can relieve varicose veins and relieve the swelling or edema in the lower leg that accompanies them.

Sluggish flow (stasis) of blood in varicose veins can affect the nourishment of the skin in the area, and even minor trauma can lead to the formation of a varicose ulcer. This is especially common over the subcutaneous surface of the tibia.

SEE ALSO *Circulatory system, Thrombosis, Varicose ulcer, Veins*

VASCULITIS

Vasculitis (angiitis) is a general term for a group of uncommon diseases causing inflammation of the blood vessels. Examples of vasculitis include Kawasaki disease, Behçet's disease, polyarteritis nodosa, Wegener's granulomatosis, Takayasu's arteritis, Churg-Strauss syndrome, giant cell arteritis (temporal arteritis) and Henoch Schönlein purpura. There is no known cure, but corticosteroids and immunosuppressants can help control the symptoms.

SEE ALSO *Autoimmune disease, Blood vessels*

VASECTOMY

Vasectomy is a surgical operation which involves cutting the two tubes (each called the ductus deferens or vas deferens) which run from the testes to the urethra. This prevents sperm reaching the seminal vesicles where they are held prior to ejaculation through the urethra during orgasm.

Vasectomy is a simple procedure that usually requires only a local anesthetic. There is some local bruising and discomfort but recovery takes only a few days. Sperm continue to be produced by the testes but they die and degenerate in the ductus deferens or in the epididymis. The other secretions which make up the seminal fluid are still produced and thus the man continues to ejaculate. After the operation it will take from 16–20 ejaculations to expel all the stored sperm and for the man to be declared infertile.

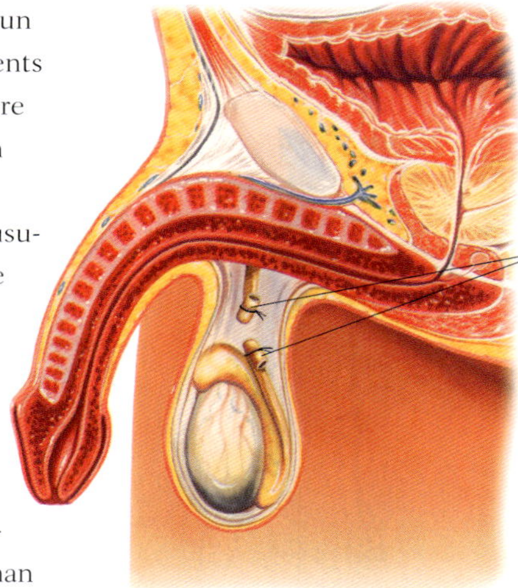

Vasectomy

A vasectomy involves severing the vas deferens tubes between the testes (where sperm is produced) and the urethra, so that sperm cannot leave the body.

Reversal of the operation is possible. It requires a general anesthetic and takes up to 2 hours, with recovery time related to the period spent anesthetized. About 60 percent of reversals succeed, enabling their subjects to father children. The best chances of success come with reversals performed less than 5 years after the original vasectomy and where the female partner is under 30 years of age and normally fertile.

Factors mitigating against success include the growth of fibrous tissue in the spermatic tubes and the production of antibodies to sperm after the vasectomy. Sperm may be frozen prior to vasectomy, for future use.

Vasectomy is the most effective form of contraception for men and may be done voluntarily for this purpose. It may also be done for prophylactic reasons where there is infection of the epididymis or testes.

SEE ALSO *Contraception, Reproductive systems, Sterilization, Testes*

VASODILATORS

Vasodilators are drugs that dilate small blood vessels, such as arterioles (small arteries) and venules (small veins). They increase blood flow to the tissues, lower the blood pressure of the circulation, and make the work load of the heart easier. Some, like nitroprusside and nitroglycerine, are used in ischemic heart disease and congestive heart failure, while others like hydralazine (a smooth muscle relaxant), diltiazem (a calcium channel blocker) and enalapril maleate (an ACE inhibitor) are used in the treatment of hypertension, often in combination with other hypertensive drugs such as diuretics and beta-blockers.

SEE ALSO *Arteries, Beta-blockers, Blood vessels, Calcium channel blockers, Hypertension*

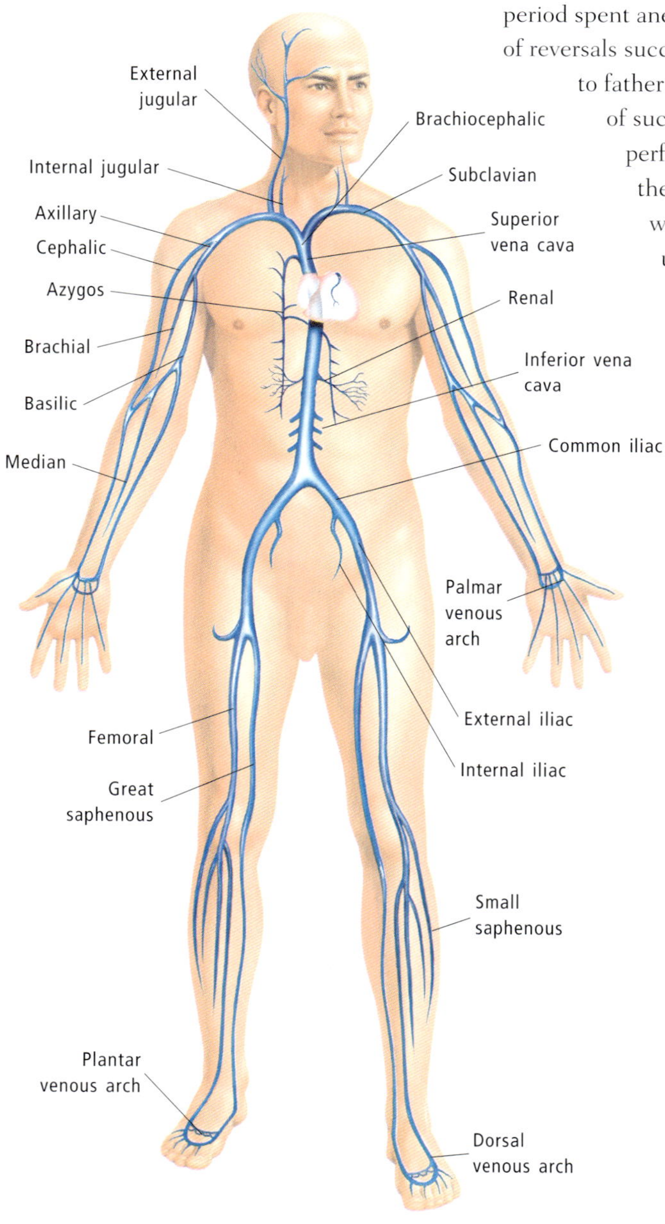

Veins

Deoxygenated blood travels back to the heart via a network of veins. Valves stop the blood from pooling in the veins, particularly where blood flow is fighting gravity (such as in the arms and legs).

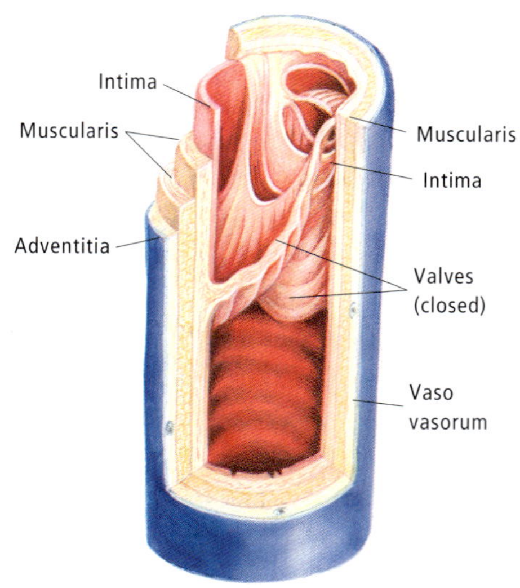

V

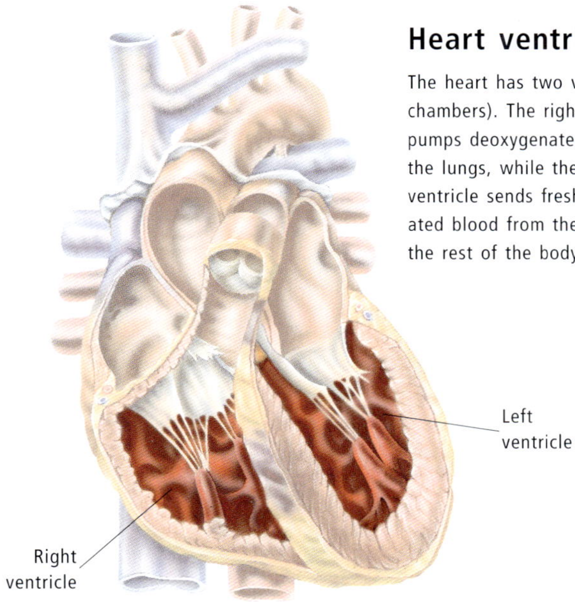

Heart ventricles

The heart has two ventricles (or chambers). The right ventricle pumps deoxygenated blood to the lungs, while the left ventricle sends freshly oxygenated blood from the lungs to the rest of the body.

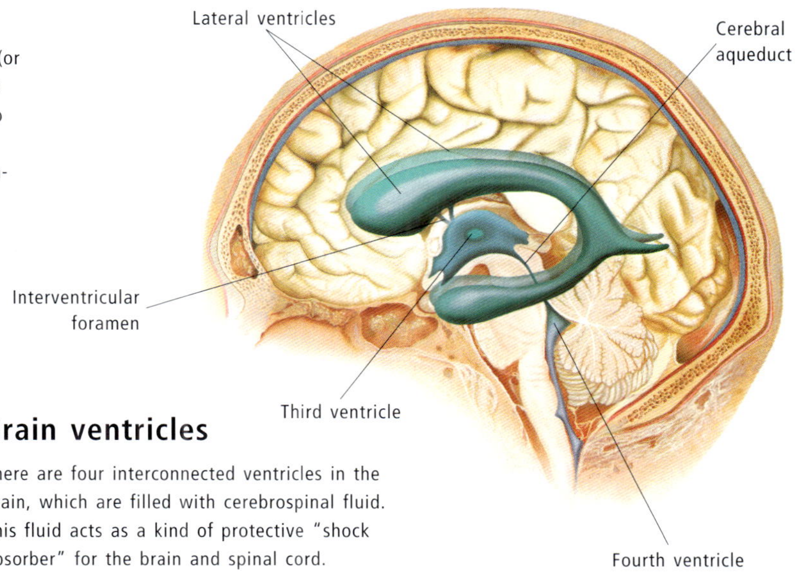

Brain ventricles

There are four interconnected ventricles in the brain, which are filled with cerebrospinal fluid. This fluid acts as a kind of protective "shock absorber" for the brain and spinal cord.

VEINS

Veins are thin-walled, low-pressure blood vessels that return blood to the heart. The smallest veins are the venules, which commence at the venous end of capillaries. Veins receive tributaries from other veins and progressively increase in size as they approach the heart. Many, but not all, veins contain one-way valves.

The two largest veins in the body are the superior and inferior vena cavae, which drain into the heart from above and below respectively. The brachial, basilic and cephalic veins drain the upper limbs. They drain in turn into the axillary vein, which becomes the subclavian vein. The internal jugular vein, which drains the head and neck, joins the subclavian vein to form the brachiocephalic vein. The left and right brachiocephalic veins join to form the superior vena cava, which drains into the heart. The azygos vein, which drains the thoracic cavity, joins the superior vena cava just before it enters the heart.

The femoral vein drains the lower limb. It becomes the external iliac vein as it enters the trunk and is joined by the internal iliac vein from the pelvis to become the common iliac vein. The two common iliac veins join to form the inferior vena cava, which passes up the posterior abdominal wall. It is joined here by veins from the kidneys, gonads and back region, and just below the diaphragm by large veins from the liver. It passes through the diaphragm and almost immediately enters the heart.

Only a small number of veins in the trunk have valves; most are valveless. Blood in the trunk therefore flows according to pressure differences, making respiratory movements important in venous return. Inspiration creates a negative pressure within the thoracic cavity that not only draws air into the lungs but assists venous return to the heart.

Valves are common in veins within the limbs, where they assist the return of blood against the effect of gravity. They are particularly numerous in the lower limb. A large valve is also present in the lower end of the internal jugular vein, preventing the flow of blood back up toward the head and neck.

In the upper limb, most venous blood returns by the superficial veins which travel in the tissue just below the skin. In the lower limb, most venous blood returns by the deep veins which lie in compartments which contain muscles.

The contraction of nearby muscles compresses the veins and blood is forced by the valves in the direction of the heart. Blood then flows from superficial leg veins to the now empty deep veins, thus reducing pressure in the superficial veins.

Faulty valves in the veins communicating between the superficial and deep veins can lead to backflow of blood into the superficial veins when muscles contract. This results in the superficial veins becoming dilated and tortuous, otherwise known as varicose veins. Two of the superficial veins of the lower limb are named saphenous after the Greek word *saphenes*, meaning "obvious".

Stagnation of blood in veins can lead to the formation of blood clots (venous thrombosis). This most commonly occurs in the calves, and can be exacerbated by prolonged inactivity, such as bed rest or a long journey without exercise. Activation of the calf muscles can help to prevent pooling and stagnation of blood by assisting venous return from the area. The radiographic imaging of veins in the body is known as venography.

SEE ALSO *Circulatory system, Thrombosis, Varicose veins, Venography*

VENOGRAPHY

Venography is the x-ray examination of veins, usually to check for blood clots. Veins do not show up in an x-ray under normal conditions as the waves of electromagnetic radiation pass right through them. Instead, they need to be injected with a radiopaque dye that absorbs the x-rays, enabling the veins to be easily seen on the x-ray picture, or venogram. The injection is given under local anesthetic via a catheter that is inserted into a vein in the area of the body to be x-rayed.

SEE ALSO *Veins*

VENTRICLE

A ventricle is the term used for a small cavity or chamber in the brain and heart. The two lowest of the four chambers of the heart are called the right and left ventricles. The right ventricle pumps oxygen-depleted blood to the lungs via the pulmonary artery.

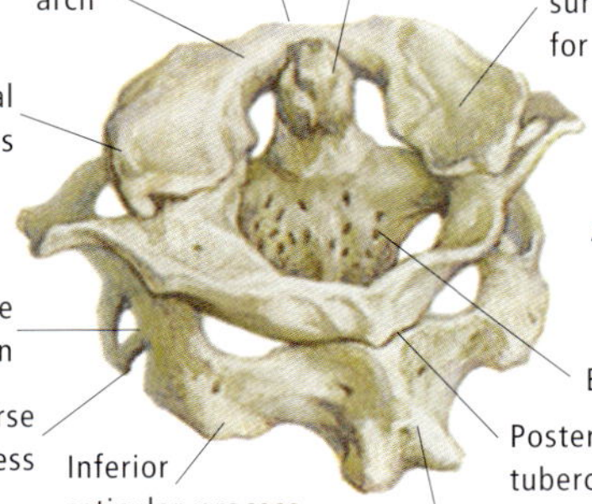

Axis and atlas

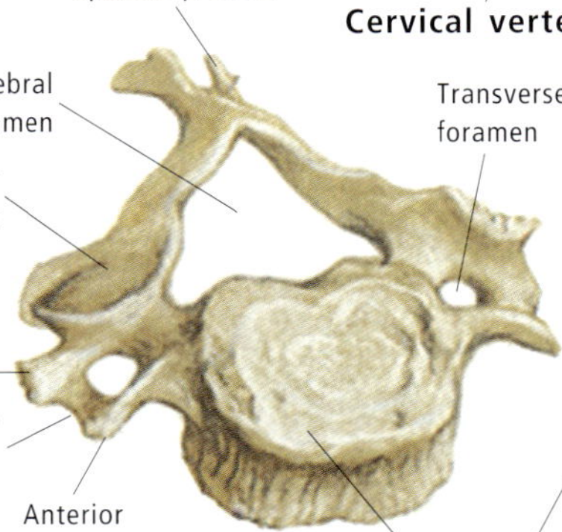

Cervical vertebra

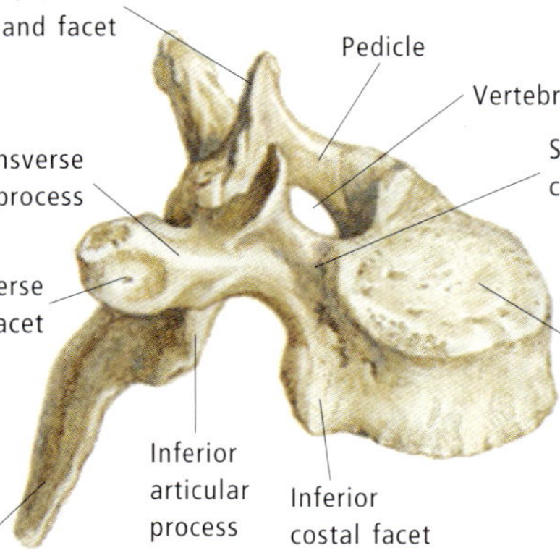

Thoracic vertebra

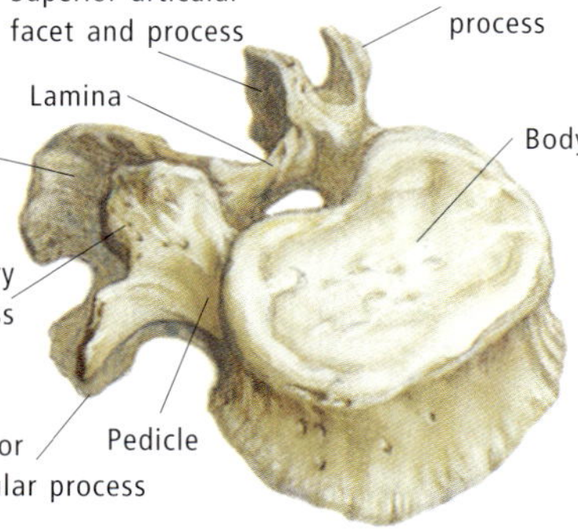

Lumbar vertebra

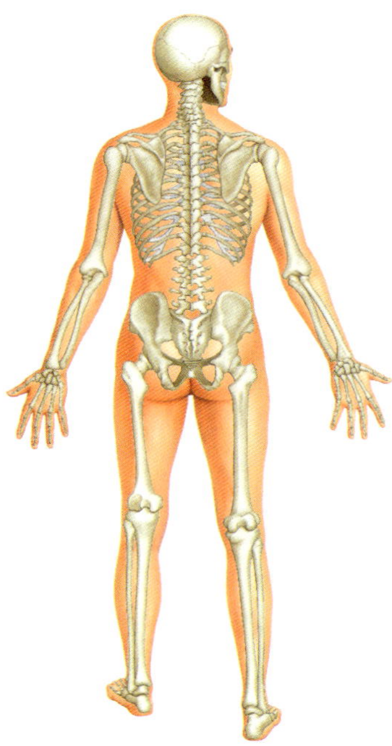

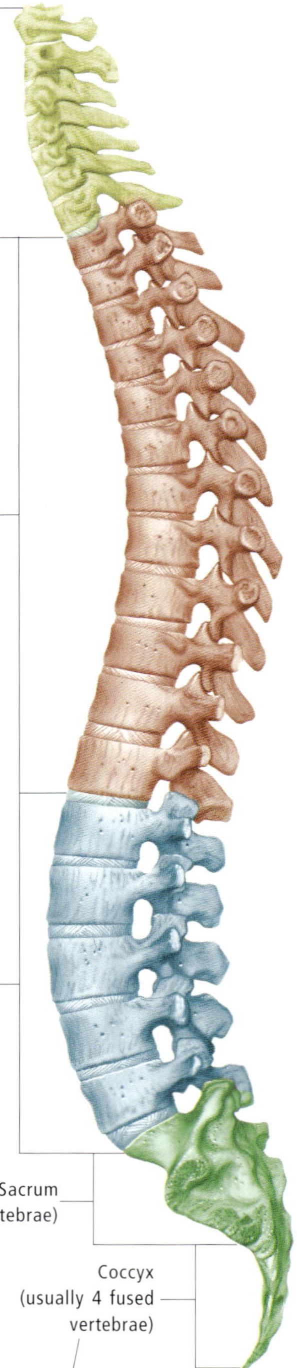

Vertebrae

The spine is made up of 33 vertebrae, which form a strong yet flexible housing for the spinal cord.

Coccyx

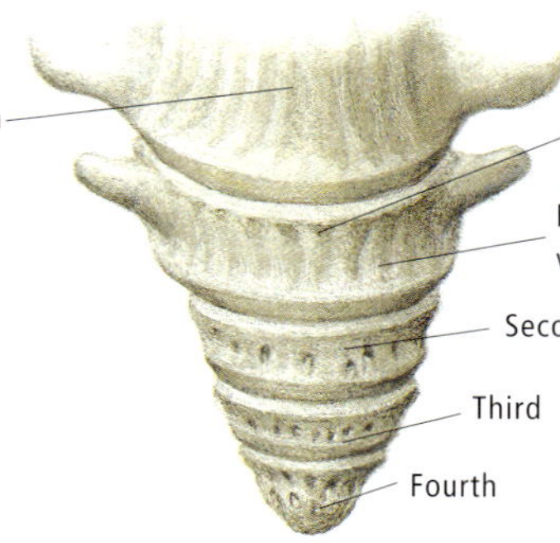

V

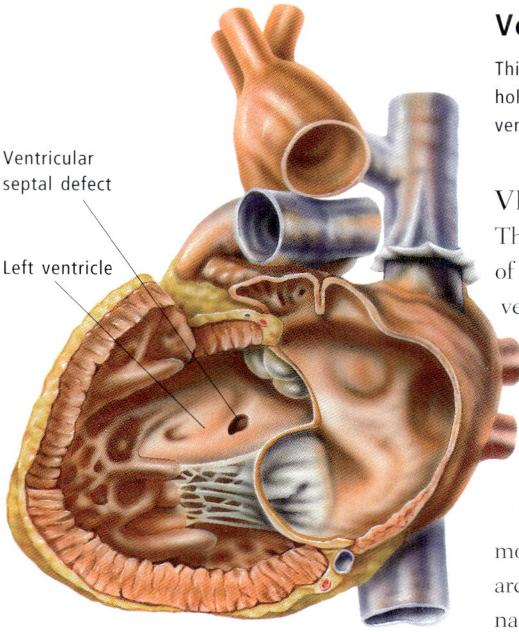

Ventricular septal defect

This congenital heart defect occurs when a hole forms in the membrane dividing the two ventricles of the heart.

The more muscular left ventricle pumps oxygen-rich blood through the aorta to the rest of the body.

In the brain, there are four ventricles. These connect with each other, the central canal of the spinal cord, and the subarachnoid space surrounding the brain.

Specialized capillaries called choroid plexuses in the ventricles of the brain produce cerebrospinal fluid. This clear liquid fills the ventricles and the other cavities with which they are connected to create a protective cushion for the central nervous system.

SEE ALSO *Brain, Heart, Spinal cord*

VENTRICULAR SEPTAL DEFECT

A ventricular septal defect (VSD) is a hole in the wall separating the two ventricles, or lower chambers, of the heart. Because of pressure differences between the two ventricles, blood passes through the hole from left to right. Blood in the left ventricle then leaks into the right ventricle with the result that more blood than normal is pumped to the lungs. This often produces chest infections and breathing difficulties. A large opening in a very small child can also cause symptoms of heart failure. Although small and medium-sized ventricular septal defects often close by themselves, surgery is usually needed to repair larger holes.

SEE ALSO *Heart, Ventricle*

VERTEBRAE

The vertebrae are the bony building blocks of the vertebral column (or spine). Individual vertebrae, separated by intervertebral disks, give the vertebral column both strength and flexibility. The vertebral column is comprised of seven cervical, twelve thoracic, five lumbar, five fused sacral and three to five fused coccygeal vertebrae.

The same basic elements are found in most vertebrae: a vertebral body; a vertebral arch comprising two pedicles and two laminae; and processes that project away from the arch. The bodies lie in front and are weight bearing. They increase in size as they progress down the spine. The body and vertebral arch form a bony housing for the vertebral canal, which protects the spinal cord and spinal nerve roots. The pedicles form the side walls of the foramen and the two laminae form the back walls. During fetal development the laminae fuse in the midline at the back; failure of fusion is known as spina bifida.

The backward-projecting spinous process and the two side-projecting transverse processes provide leverage for muscles that move the vertebral column. The articular processes project up and down from the left and right sides of the vertebral arch and form joints with the articular processes of adjacent vertebrae. The orientation of these joint surfaces affects the direction of movement between vertebrae.

Vertebrae may fracture as a result of trauma. Fracture or displacement may affect the spinal cord and associated nerves, and produce temporary or permanent loss of sensation and movement.

SEE ALSO *Intervertebral disks, Skeletal system, Spine*

VERTIGO

Vertigo is a hallucination of movement, usually a feeling that the person or their surroundings is revolving. It may produce feelings of dizziness and confusion; intense vertigo may cause nausea and vomiting.

Vertigo may be caused by disorders of the inner ear, such as a blockage of the fluid in the semicircular canals, which regulate balance and detect movements of the head, or by disorders of the central nervous system. Vertigo is dangerous if experienced in high places and is an occupational hazard for divers and pilots, who are frequently in situations where there are no visual reference points. They may suffer spatial disorientation, becoming unable to properly judge their direction or speed of movement.

SEE ALSO *Acrophobia, Dizziness, Semicircular canals*

VIRILIZATION

Normal virilization or masculinization is the appearance of male secondary sexual characteristics in the male. Virilization occurring in adult females or children usually indicates a serious underlying condition. It may be associated with hirsutism (abnormal male pattern hair growth) which is also a signal of an underlying disorder. In boys, the changes of puberty may appear early due to abnormal production of testosterone, the male sex hormone. This abnormal production of testosterone first accelerates bone growth and then stops it earlier than normal, resulting in lower final height. Treatment with synthetic hormones can achieve normal growth.

Virilization can occur in females (when it is also called virilism) when ovarian tumors produce the hormones testosterone and progesterone. If unchecked, the presence of these hormones will affect body shape, causing increasing muscularity and growth of facial and body hair. In addition, the breasts may atrophy or fail to develop, the voice deepens and the clitoris enlarges. Menstruation and ovulation both cease. Disorders of the adrenal gland in females, causing production of excessive quantities of androgens (male hormones), will create the same symptoms of virilization.

Girls who are deficient in adrenal hormones will appear normal at birth but may fail to undergo puberty or to menstruate. Urine tests can detect abnormal hormone levels and aid diagnosis of tumors or adrenal problems. Drug medication with dexamethasone can prevent adrenal production of androgens. Surgical removal of tumors or of the adrenal gland is sometimes necessary.

Viruses

Influenza virus

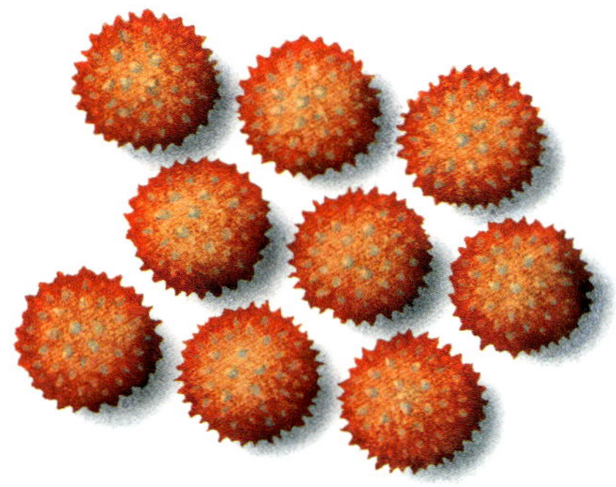

Rotavirus

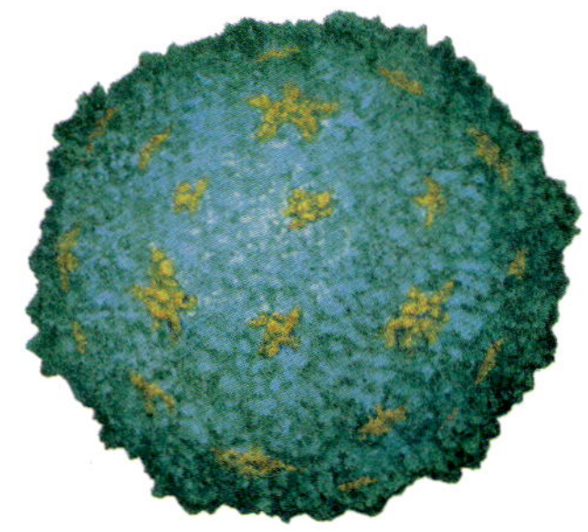

Cold virus

Polio virus

Herpes virus

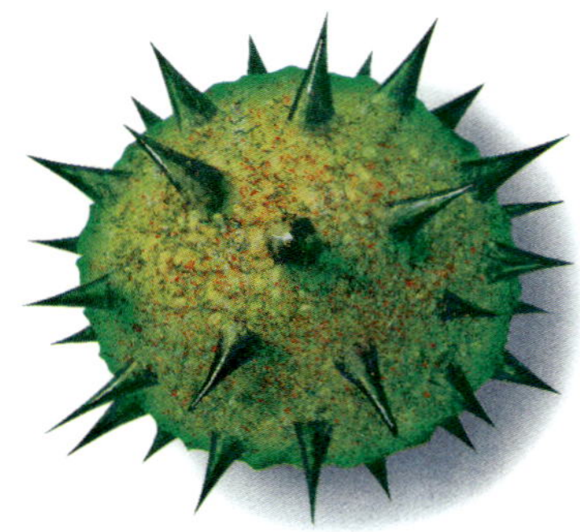

Wart virus

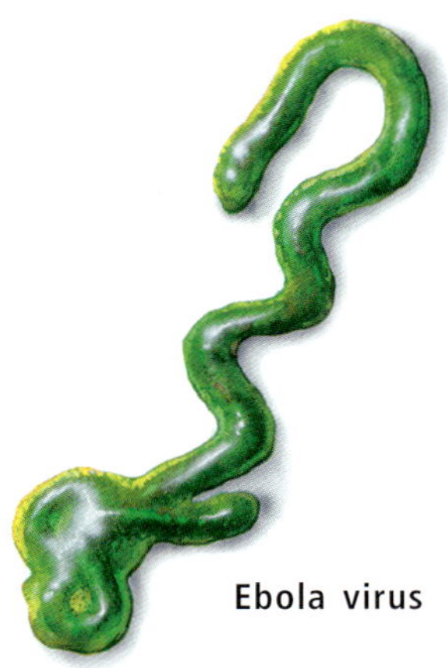

Ebola virus

The exposure of a female fetus to high levels of androgens (sex hormones) early in pregnancy, through drugs prescribed to prevent a miscarriage or the presence of a hormone-producing tumor in the mother, may result in genital abnormalities, with the external genitals developing a male appearance. This may include a greatly enlarged clitoris and absence of a vaginal opening, while the internal reproductive organs develop normally. This condition is known as female pseudohermaphroditism. Surgical reconstruction may be necessary to correct the genital abnormalities.

SEE ALSO *Adrenal glands, Hormones, Progesterone, Puberty, Testosterone*

Viruses

These tiny infectious organisms are much smaller than bacteria and vary considerably in shape and structure. In order to survive they must invade another cell, taking over their host's cellular machinery and using it to reproduce. Each virus has a preference for a different part of the body—the wart virus, for example, infects the skin; the polio virus attacks the nervous system.

VIRUSES

Viruses are a group of infectious organisms so small that they are only visible through electron microscopes. Just about all they contain is enough genetic material to duplicate themselves. They are much smaller than bacteria and cannot provide their own energy, nor can they replicate themselves outside living cells. They rely on invading another organism to survive, taking over its cellular machinery and using it to reproduce. Viruses infect all body tissues, but individual viruses show a preference for particular parts; for example, the poliomyelitis virus only infects part of the nervous system, the herpes virus infects the skin.

Some viruses cause acute disease lasting for only a short time and others cause recurring or chronic disease, while others do not cause any disease. The acute viral infections are of two types, local and systemic, as the result of the effect of the invading virus on the host.

Local infections occur at the site of the viral infection, such as the common cold, which infects the area around the nose, or enteritis, which causes bowel inflammation. Many viruses enter the body via the nose or mouth and begin their cycle of infection in the nose and throat. They then enter the bloodstream where they are spread to other parts of the body as in, for example, measles, mumps and chickenpox.

Other viral diseases are transmitted by the bites of insects, ticks and mites. These diseases begin in the skin or lymph nodes and spread rapidly into the bloodstream. Many viruses have an affinity for specific organs, for example, encephalitis and meningitis viruses affect the brain.

Some viruses remain in the tissues after the initial infection even though there are specific antibodies for them circulating in the blood and tissues. It is thought that these viruses reside inside cells where they are protected from antibodies, which are unable to penetrate the cell membrane. Measles and herpes viruses fit into this category.

Other viruses can remain in the body for a number of years before producing any symptoms.

Once a virus has entered the body it will find little resistance, apart from the presence of lymphocytes, a type of white blood cell that produces antibodies, and a small amount of interferon, which also helps to destroy viruses. After a few days the body begins to produce antibodies and greater amounts of interferon. Because viruses are so intimately involved in the vital processes of cells they are difficult to eradicate with medication without damaging the cells, although there are a few antiviral drugs. Antibiotics are ineffective against viruses because they work on elements found in bacteria which are not found in viruses.

Many viral diseases can be prevented by good hygiene. This means efficient sanitation and waste disposal combined with personal cleanliness and clean water. Immunization by vaccine can prevent epidemics caused by certain acutely infectious viruses and has been particularly effective against viruses such as smallpox and poliomyelitis. Some viruses are easier to immunize against than others. The common cold, which is caused by rhinoviruses, may prove impossible to immunize against because there are at least 100 antigenic types of the virus.

SEE ALSO *Antibodies, Bacteria, Chickenpox, Common cold, Encephalitis, Hepatitis, Herpes simplex, Infectious diseases, Measles, Meningitis, Multiple sclerosis, Mumps, Poliomyelitis, Ticks*

VISUALIZATION

Also known as creative visualization, this alternative therapy technique combines self-hypnosis, relaxation and the use of imagery to utilize the power of the mind to influence the body and emotions.

The use of visualization to support healing has become known through the work of American doctors Carl and Stephanie Simonton and Bernie Siegel. In their practices they encourage patients with cancer to visualize the tumor or cancer in their bodies and then to imagine it being eradicated or cured by specific images such as an attacking army of healthy blood cell soldiers or a healing waterfall.

Proponents of visualization believe it is effective for relaxation and pain relief. For example, patients might be asked to imagine themselves resting in a place of peace or being bathed in a succession of colors. In other cases patients might be encouraged to picture themselves full of energy or free from anxiety.

To practise visualization, patients sit or lie in a comfortable position, close their eyes, relax their muscles and slow their breathing before being guided into their visualization. Sometimes it is suggested they visualize a television screen which shows what they want to see.

Visualization may be used by holistic health practitioners, psychotherapists and hypnotherapists. It may also be practised alone with the aid of audiotapes.

SEE ALSO *Hypnotherapy, Meditation, Relaxation techniques*

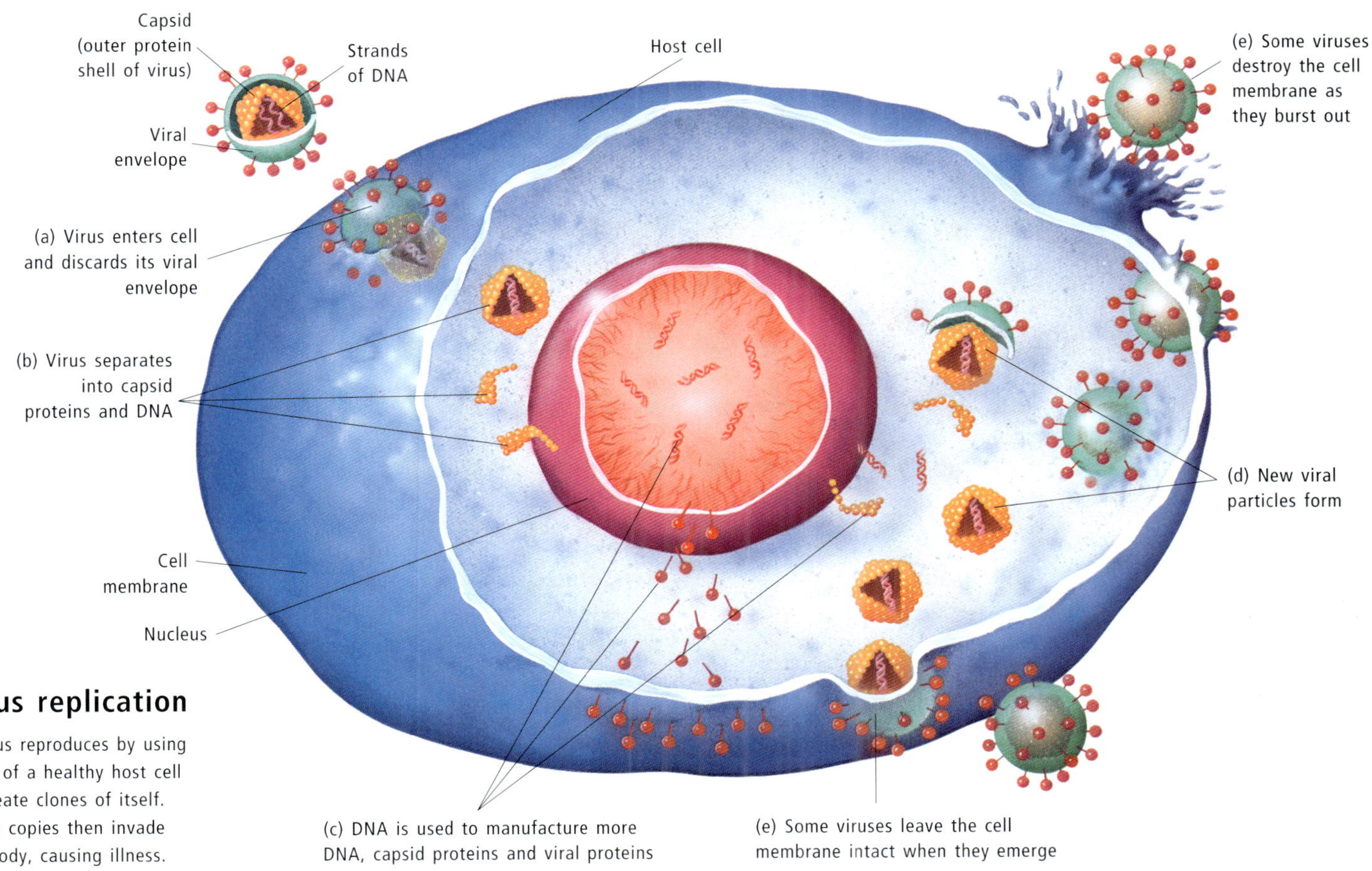

Virus replication

A virus reproduces by using parts of a healthy host cell to create clones of itself. These copies then invade the body, causing illness.

V

VITAMINS

Vitamins are micronutrients, organic substances found in foods which are essential to the body but only in very small amounts, acting as catalysts in various chemical reactions. They may be either water-soluble or fat-soluble. Water-soluble vitamins are easily destroyed in cooking, not stored in the body for long periods, and any excess is usually excreted in the urine. They must be eaten regularly as deficiencies can develop relatively quickly. Vitamins of the B complex and vitamin C are water-soluble.

Fat-soluble vitamins are less easily destroyed in cooking and can be stored for long periods in body fat, making deficiencies slow to develop in adults. Deficiencies are still dangerous and may develop very quickly in babies and children. Vitamins A, D, E and K are fat-soluble.

Good nutrition, preferably involving breast feeding for at least the first year of life and eating a wide variety of foods from all food groups, should ensure adequate intake of all vitamins, in which case no benefits will be derived from vitamin or mineral supplements. A restricted diet with a very limited range or very small quantities of foods can result in a deficiency of one or several vitamins which may produce readily identifiable symptoms.

Self-dosing with vitamin supplements is unwise as some vitamins become toxic when taken in excess. The recommended daily allowances (RDAs) published by national health authorities are calculated as reference guides useful in planning the vitamin content of diets to avoid deficiencies. Excessive intakes usually arise from self-administration of supplements or from abnormally high consumption of highly concentrated food sources.

Vitamin A is obtained directly from food as retinol, retinal or retinoic acid, and indirectly as substances which are converted to vitamin A in the body (carotenoids and beta-carotene). It is important to the formation of visual purple in the eyes for normal vision and night vision, to growth and reproduction and nourishment of the epithelial cells, which line the mouth and airways, and for defence against infection.

Sources include liver, dairy products, and some fish oils. Beta-carotene is found in yellow and green vegetables such as pumpkin, carrots and spinach and fruits such as apricots, peaches and cantaloupe.

Deficiency comes only after several months when the body's stores are exhausted but is serious, causing susceptibility to infection and damage to the eyes with loss of night vision, dryness and ulceration of the whites and cornea (xerophthalmia), which can result in blindness. Excess vitamin A is toxic (early Arctic explorers died from excess vitamin A after eating polar bear liver), causing enlargement of the spleen and kidneys, headache, peeling skin, thickening bones and joint pain. Drinking excessive amounts of carrot juice may yellow the skin and the whites of the eyes.

Vitamin B₁ (thiamine) aids metabolization of carbohydrates and alcohol. Sources include wholegrain cereals, nuts, yeast and meats. The body stores only small quantities and a deficiency will appear in about a month where diet is inadequate.

Deficiency causes the tropical disease beriberi. Alcoholics are prone to thiamine deficiency and may develop Wernicke-Korsakoff syndrome. The symptoms are confusion, double vision, nystagmus (rapid uncontrolled eye movements) and lack of muscular coordination. Prompt treatment with direct injection of thiamine is indi-

Vitamin B1

The body can only store small quantities of this vitamin, which is needed to maintain nervous system function and for the metabolism of carbohydrates and alcohol.

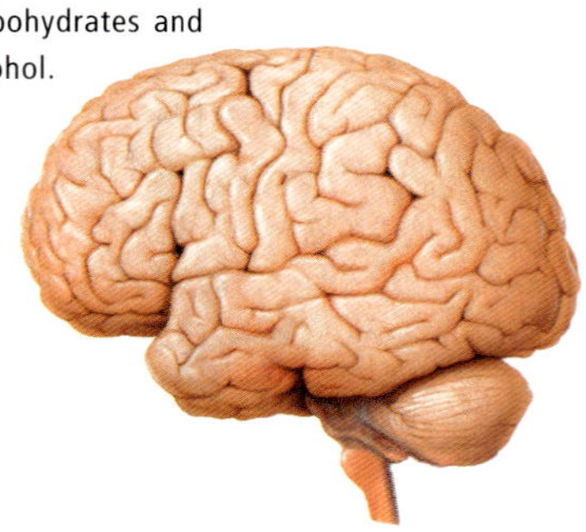

Vitamin B2

This vitamin helps to repair skin and body tissues; deficiency can cause dermatitis. It is also important for metabolic processes.

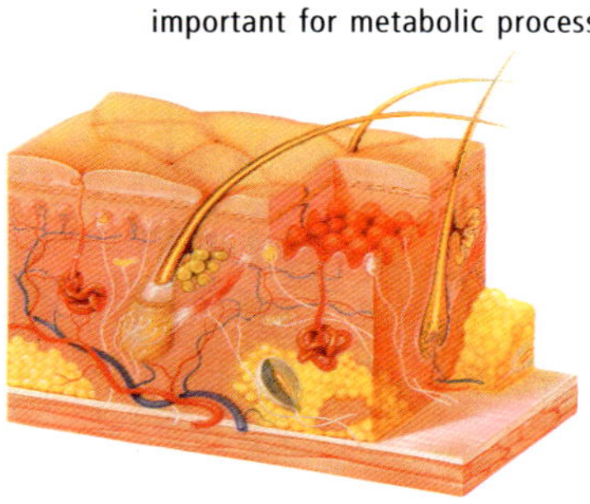

Vitamin B3

Absorbed from food or made in the body, vitamin B3 contributes to the health of the digestive organs, skin and nerves. It aids metabolism, helping the body break down food for energy.

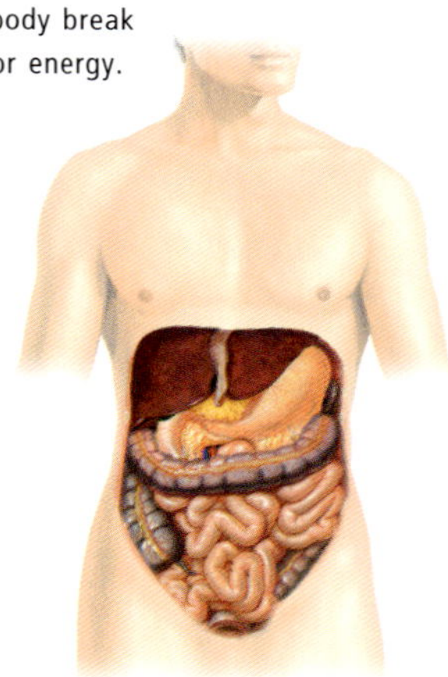

Vitamin B5

Vitamin B5 is essential for the formation of hemoglobin, fatty acids and cholesterol, and for the transmission of nerve impulses.

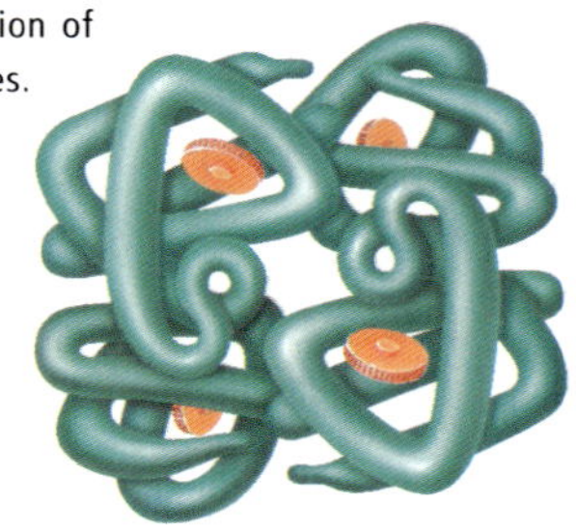

Vitamin A

Important for the formation of pigments needed for night and normal vision, this vitamin is also used for the growth and replication of epithelial cells and helps defend the body against infection.

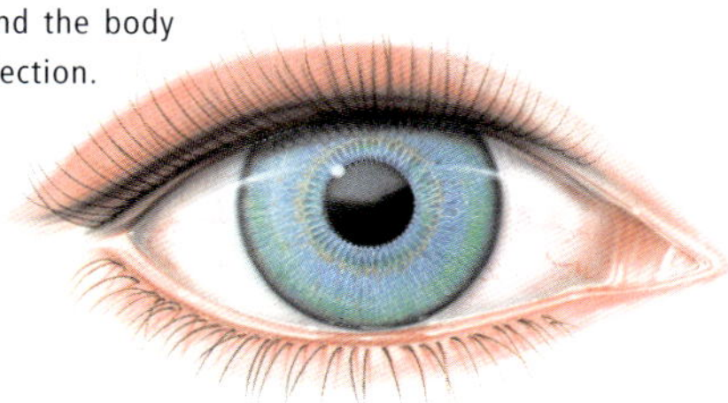

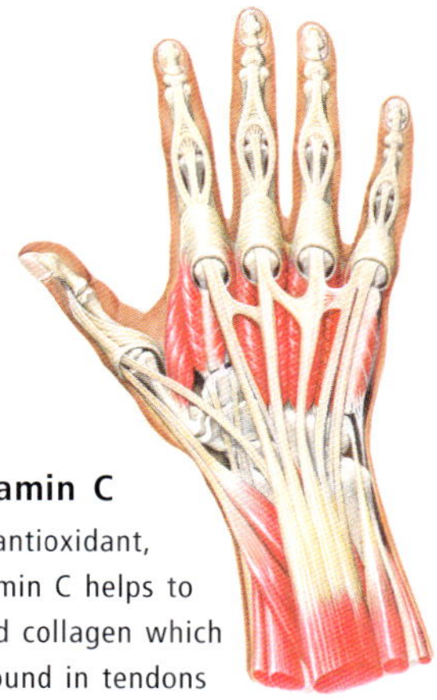

Vitamin C

An antioxidant, vitamin C helps to build collagen which is found in tendons and cartilage. Deficiencies in this vitamin cause the disease scurvy.

Vitamin D

Needed for the formation and growth of bones and teeth, vitamin D helps the body absorb calcium and phosphate. Deficiency causes skeletal problems, such as rickets in children and osteomalacia in adults.

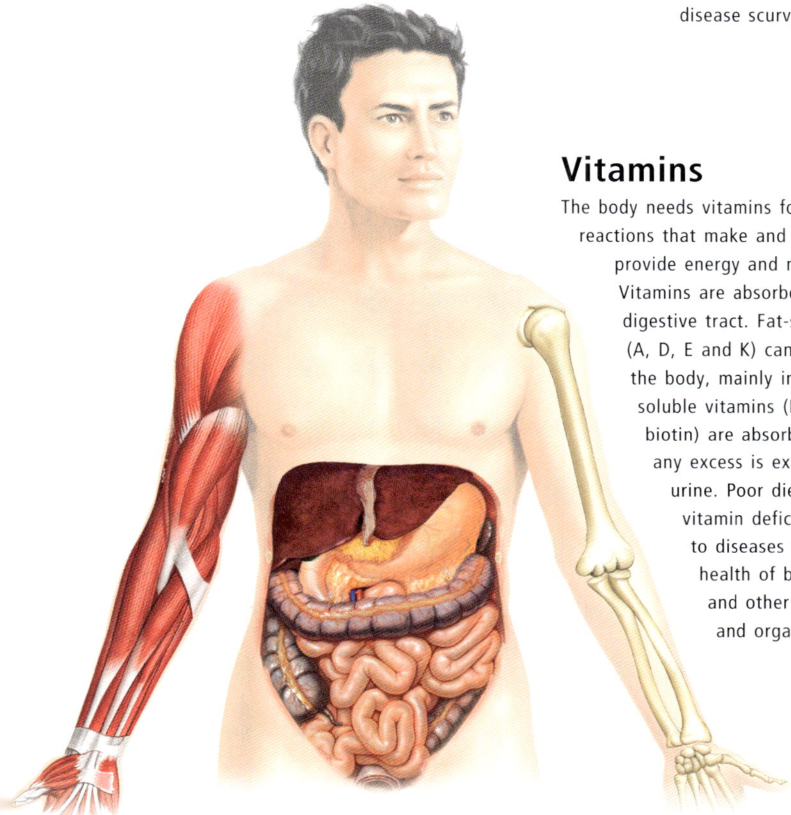

Vitamins

The body needs vitamins for the chemical reactions that make and repair cells, provide energy and maintain health. Vitamins are absorbed in the digestive tract. Fat-soluble vitamins (A, D, E and K) can be stored by the body, mainly in the liver. Water soluble vitamins (B, C, folacin and biotin) are absorbed quickly, but any excess is excreted in the urine. Poor diet can result in vitamin deficiencies, leading to diseases that affect the health of bones, muscles and other body tissues and organs.

Vitamin E

An important antioxidant, vitamin E prevents cell damage and extends the life of red blood cells.

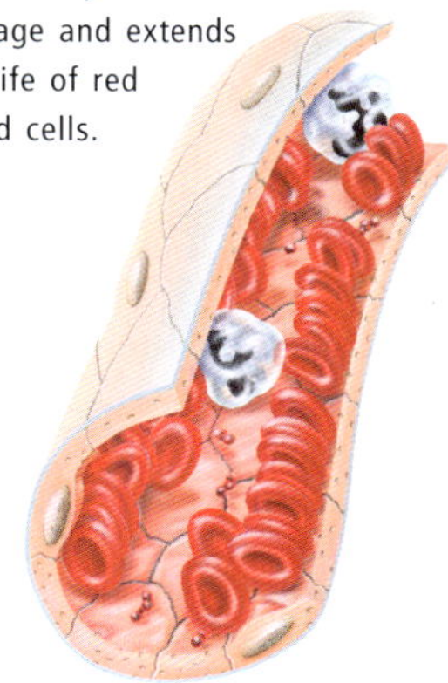

Vitamin K

Vitamin K makes proteins needed for blood clotting, and for the bones and kidneys.

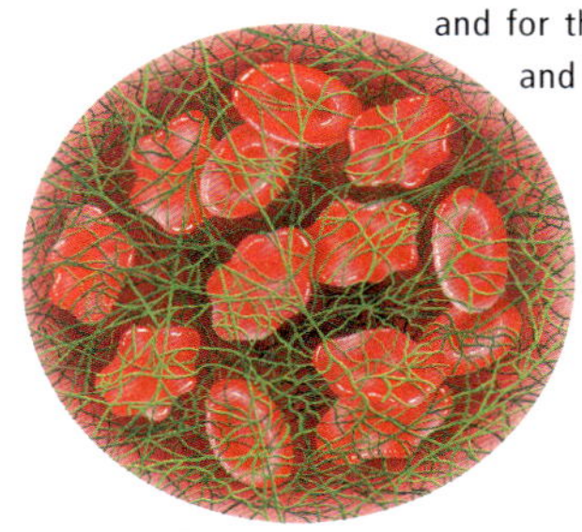

Vitamin B6

Vitamin B6 is important for the health of nerve cells and tissue and aids in the formation of red blood cells and proteins in the body.

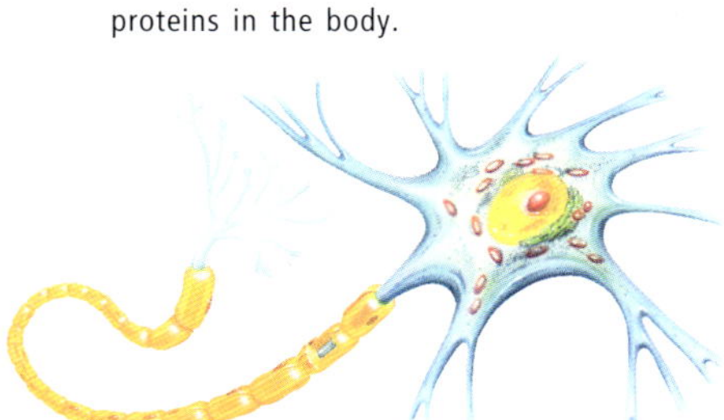

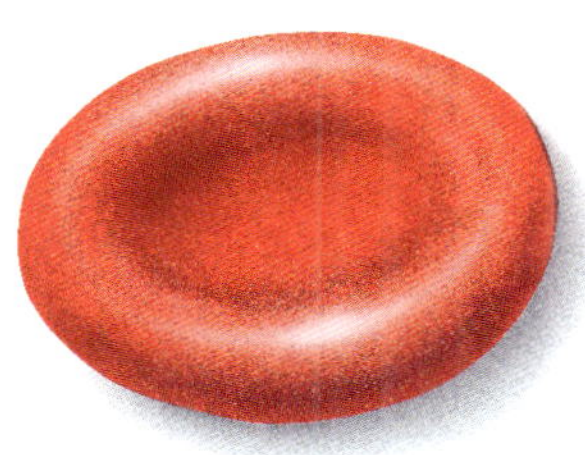

Vitamin B12

Deficiency in B12 causes anemia as this vitamin is essential for the production of red blood cells.

Folacin (folic acid)

Important for the formation of new body cells, folic acid is particularly important during the first 3 months of pregnancy as it helps prevent developmental defects in the fetus.

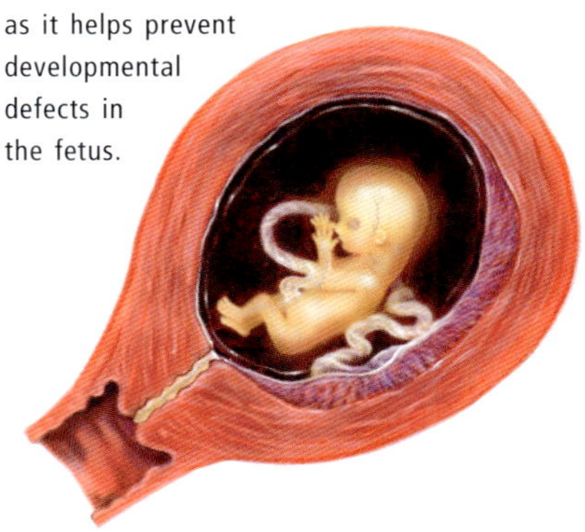

cated, although this may not prevent permanent brain damage.

Vitamin B₂ (riboflavin) is important for repairing skin and other body tissues. Sources include yeast, almonds, dairy foods, fish, meat and kidney. Riboflavin is easily destroyed by sunlight, which is why some countries have black milk bottles. Deficiency leads to cracked lips, dermatitis and susceptibility to infection. Excess is not toxic, as the excess is excreted in the urine.

Vitamin B_3 (niacin) can be made in the body from the aminoacid tryptophan or absorbed directly from food. It aids reactions within the body which break down foods to release energy. It is needed for the health of skin, digestive organs and nerves. Sources include cereals, flour, wholegrains, organ meats and poultry.

Deficiency causes pellagra, common in the southern USA early last century, where corn was the staple food. Symptoms are lack of appetite and muscular weakness, followed by diarrhea, dermatitis and dementia. These diseases have now been largely eradicated by changes in processing methods which retain essential nutrients and by widening the range of foods available. Excess intake, above 1,000 milligrams per day, causes unpleasant skin rashes and can lead to diabetes and gout.

Vitamin B_5 (pantothenic acid) is important to formation of hemoglobin, fatty acids and cholesterol, and transmission of nerve impulses. Sources include wholegrain foods, liver, kidney, beans, meat and poultry. Deficiency is rare but produces vomiting, pain, cramps, poor circulation and personality changes. Excess intake is also rare, but large doses can cause diarrhea.

Vitamin B_6 (pyridoxine, pyridoxamine, pyridoxal) helps digest protein and to build protein structures including antibodies, red blood cells and nerve tissue. Sources include some breakfast cereals, wheat germ, pork, fish, peanuts, potatoes, avocados, lentils and legumes. Deficiency brings mouth sores, fatigue, nausea, dizziness and muscle spasms. Excess intake, taking multiples of the RDA over a long period, can cause nerve damage.

Vitamin B_{12} (cyanocobalamin, cobalamin) is important in the manufacture of DNA and red blood cells, of tissue for nerve sheaths and in digestion of nutrients. Sources include animal foods, particularly liver, kidney and mushrooms. It also occurs in some fermented foods, where it occurs as a product of bacterial action (this is also thought to occur in the human intestine). Deficiency is very rare as body stores can last 5 years. Vegans, particularly babies and children, are most at risk of deficiency. An inability to absorb vitamin B_{12} causes pernicious anemia. Treatment is to give the vitamin by injection. Excess is not toxic even at high doses.

Folacin (folic acid) acts with vitamin B_{12} in many processes, including passing instructions from genes to cells to convey hereditary characteristics, making red blood cells and using fats in the body. Sources include chicken livers, yeast and yeast extracts, and leafy green vegetables.

As folacin is easily destroyed in cooking, deficiency is very common worldwide and can cause anemia, particularly in pregnancy, greatly increasing the risk of spina bifida and other neural tube defects in the fetus. This type of deficiency can be cured using yeast extract. Excess causes minimal toxic effects.

Biotin, originally known as vitamin H, is now recognized as a member of the B complex. Sources include liver, nuts and eggs, yeasts and bacteria in the intestine. Deficiency is rare since biotin is manufactured internally. Stores may be depleted by taking antibiotics. Symptoms are dermatitis, loss of appetite, nausea and high blood cholesterol. Excess causes no known toxic effects.

Vitamin C (ascorbic acid) helps to build collagen, the fibrous tissues of tendons and cartilage, maintains healthy bones and blood vessels, helps absorption of iron, prevents infection, is an antioxidant, may prevent development of cancer-causing substances, and helps the liver excrete waste products.

Sources include fresh vegetables and fruits. Vitamin C is stored for only 3 weeks in the body and should be replenished daily; in past times, sailors on long voyages were at risk of developing scurvy from lack of vitamin C. Babies get vitamin C from breast milk. Deficiency leads to scurvy, sometimes seen in alcoholics and drug-dependent people whose diets are grossly deficient, with weakness, bleeding gums, ulcers, joint pains and bruising. Excess intake is dangerous as it interferes with fertility, blood glucose levels and the effects of drugs, including aspirin, and can cause diarrhea, kidney stones and scurvy when excess intake ceases.

Vitamin D is vital for absorption of calcium and phosphate by bones. It can be made in the skin through exposure to sunlight and obtained in the diet from oily fish, dairy foods and as an ingredient of margarine.

Deficiency leads to rickets in children and osteomalacia in adults, with bone deformation and brittleness. Rare in the industrialized countries, vitamin D deficiency may occur in newborn babies in cultures where they are totally protected from exposure to sunlight for long periods. Excess intake is dangerous. Vitamin D is the most toxic vitamin in excess, causing stunted growth and weight loss, and depositing calcium in soft tissues such as heart, kidney and lungs. Sun exposure does not result in excess. Supplementing the diet is dangerous without medical supervision.

Vitamin E is an important antioxidant, preventing cell damage, ensuring normal life span of red blood cells and protecting against toxic chemicals. Despite claims it will prolong life and increase virility, there is no significant evidence for this. Sources include seeds, nuts and other plant foods, and seafood. Deficiency is rare but may cause anemia in newborn babies. Excess intake, at 20 times the RDA, causes nausea and indigestion.

Vitamin K (phylloquinone) makes proteins important for blood clotting and is used to make proteins in bones and kidneys. Sources include leafy green vegetables, cabbage, sprouts, liver, milk and eggs. Vitamin K is also made by bacteria in the human intestine.

Deficiency is rare, but occurs in adults because of inability to absorb it and in newborns whose intestines do not contain the bacteria that manufacture it. Deficiency in babies causes bleeding (hemorrhagic disease of the newborn), which is prevented by an injection given at birth. It is associated with diseases of the pancreas in alcoholics. Excess is not toxic, but very large doses may cause anemia.

SEE ALSO ***Anemia, Breast feeding, Diet, Minerals, Nutrition, Osteomalacia, Rickets, Scurvy, Sun exposure, Wernicke-Korsakoff syndrome***

VITILIGO

Up to 2 percent of the world's population, or some 50 million people, suffer from vitiligo. This disorder involves destruction of pigment-producing cells (melanocytes), which occur in the skin, linings of the mouth, nose, genital and rectal areas, and in the retinas. The result is white (pigment-free) patches on the skin. Hair growing at affected sites also turns white. The cause of vitiligo is unknown, although it is most prevalent in people with certain autoimmune disorders. One of the most beneficial treatments is psoralen photochemotherapy, which involves careful, controlled and long-term use of certain drugs combined with ultraviolet light exposure.

SEE ALSO *Autoimmune disease, Ultraviolet therapy*

Vitiligo

In this condition white patches develop on various parts of the body, such as the skin, as a result of damage to pigment-producing cells.

VOCAL CORDS

The vocal cords are a part of the voice box (larynx), situated in the neck, and are involved in breathing, speech and singing. The production of sound is generally due to vibration of the vocal cords. Each vocal cord consists of a ledge of elastic tissue extending across the cavity of the larynx. The term glottis is normally applied to the gap between the two vocal cords, or (sometimes) collectively to the gap, the vocal cords and the associated muscles.

The positions and tensions of the vocal cords are delicately controlled by laryngeal muscles. Air passes through the larynx and the glottis on its way to and from the lungs. During normal breathing, the vocal cords are separated by a moderate opening for unobstructed passage of air. During deep or forced breathing, the gap widens. For the production of shrill tones of speech or singing, the gap narrows and the cords are tensed. When air is forced through them, the cords vibrate, producing sound waves. The glottis can be fully closed to interrupt the passage of air.

Hoarseness is usually due to inflammation of, or damage to, the vocal cords. Another cause is accidental damage to the recurrent laryngeal nerve during thyroidectomy. Singers, who put the vocal cords under strain, are liable to develop nodules and cancer on the vocal cords.

SEE ALSO *Speech, Larynx*

Vocal cords

The two pairs of mucous membranes that form the vocal cords sit in the larynx, on either side of the glottis.

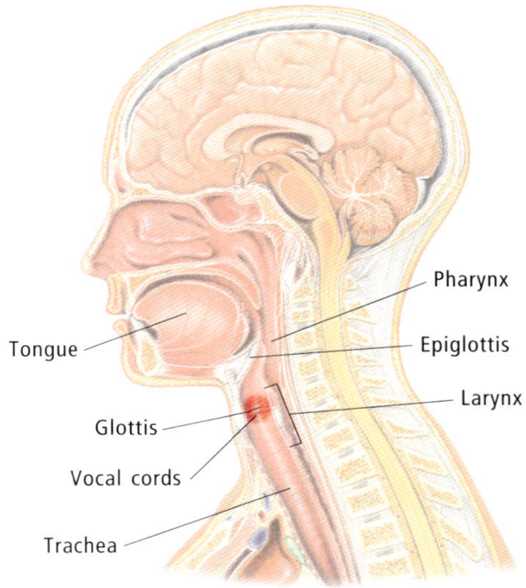

VOLVULUS

A volvulus is a twisting of the intestine around itself, most commonly towards the lower end of the digestive tract—in the ileum, cecum or sigmoid colon of the bowel. It blocks the intestine and constricts the blood vessels serving the intestine. Abdominal pain and swelling, vomiting and constipation result. Surgery to untwist the volvulus is usually necessary. If gangrene has set in, the affected portion of the intestine must be removed. A volvulus in a very small child may relate to an intestinal malformation during fetal development. In older people, the twisting may be due to scar tissue caused by surgery or infection.

SEE ALSO *Digestive system, Intestines*

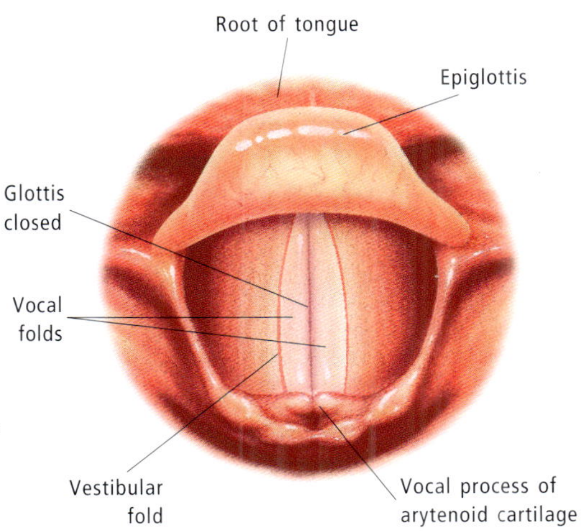

Vocal cords taut

When the gap between the vocal cords is almost closed, air passing through them makes them vibrate and creates sound waves.

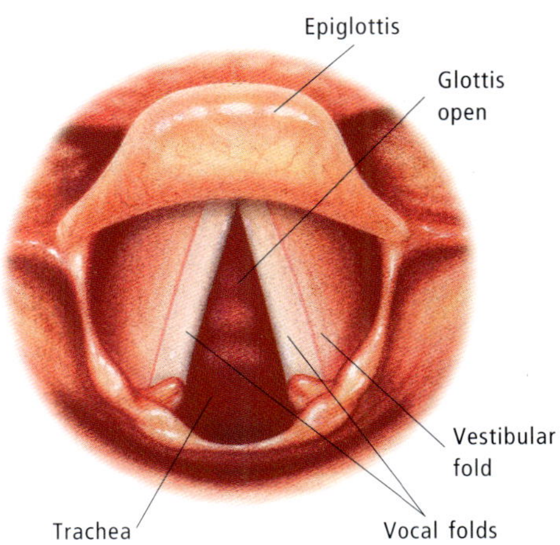

Vocal cords relaxed

During breathing the vocal cords are separated. Air passes freely past them without making them vibrate, and so no sound is made.

VOMITING

Vomiting, or emesis, is the forceful ejection of the stomach contents from the mouth by reversal of peristalsis, the normal muscular contractions of the digestive system. Nausea may or may not occur at the same time.

Vomiting may be caused by motion sickness, the use of certain drugs, an obstruction in the intestine, acute gastritis, injury to the head, appendicitis and pregnancy. The most common cause is the presence of a toxin, such as occurs in food poisoning, irritating the gut. Overindulgence in food and alcohol is another cause. Vomiting may be self-induced, particularly in people suffering from anorexia nervosa or bulimia.

Many babies posset (bring up a small amount after each feed), but this is not vomiting. True vomiting in a baby may be the symptom of a serious problem such as pyloric stenosis or a gastric illness, both of which require immediate medical help, or it may be the result of gastroesophageal reflux, which is common and not life-threatening. Because babies can dehydrate much more quickly than adults it is always important to seek medical reassurance.

Vomiting on an occasional basis during pregnancy is common; pregnancy nausea is even more common. Severe vomiting, or hyperemesis gravidarum, may require hospitalization; it disappears after the baby is born.

Vomiting blood (hematemesis) is very serious at any time and needs immediate evaluation by an expert. It can be caused by acute gastritis, a peptic ulcer, bleeding esophagal varices, or, more rarely, hemophilia, leukemia and other blood disorders.

An antiemetic is a drug that prevents vomiting. The three main types are phenothiazines, antihistamines and anticholinergics. Care should be taken if taking any of these medications as the side effects (especially drowsiness) can be quite severe.

SEE ALSO *Digestive system, Eating disorders, Food poisoning, Gastritis, Gastroesophageal reflux, Peristalsis, Pregnancy, Stomach*

VON WILLEBRAND'S DISEASE

Von Willebrand's disease is the most common inherited defect of the coagulation system. It results in a bleeding disorder similar to but generally milder than hemophilia. Unlike hemophilia, however, it affects males and females equally. It is due to a deficiency of von Willebrand factor, a protein involved in the interaction between platelet cells and a damaged blood vessel wall. Von Willebrand factor is present in the circulation complexed to Factor VIII, the clotting factor that is deficient in hemophilia. In severe von Willebrand's disease the Factor VIII level is low.

SEE ALSO *Blood vessels, Hemophilia, Platelets*

VULVA

The female external genitalia are collectively known as the vulva. They consist of paired folds, the labia majora, which are covered by skin and pubic hair and have a moist internal lining. The labia minora are fleshy folds within the labia majora which lie on either side of the vestibule containing the vaginal and urinary openings and mucus-secreting glands. The clitoris is erectile tissue like the penis and has erotic functions. The upper ends of the labia minora join around the clitoris. In some cultures, female genital mutilation is carried out. This usually involves dividing the clitoris and removing the labia.

Inflammation and irritation of the vulval skin can be the direct result of local irritants or be secondary to vaginal or urinary tract infection. Carcinoma of the vulva accounts for about 5 percent of all genital cancers and is usually treated with irradiation or surgery.

SEE ALSO *Clitoris, Penis, Vagina*

VULVITIS

The female external genitalia are collectively known as the vulva. Vulvitis describes any inflammation or irritation of this area with a variety of causes including local infections, allergic reactions or skin irritation resulting from vaginal discharges or urinary disorders. Vulvitis may also arise from changes in the skin of the vulva associated with a decline in circulating estrogens at menopause.

SEE ALSO *Menopause, Vagina, Vulva*

VULVOVAGINITIS

Vulvovaginitis is the result of a discharge from a vaginal inflammation or infection which produces a secondary irritation of the vulva (the external genitalia). In women of reproductive age, a common cause of vulvovaginitis is the vaginal discharge from thrush. Vulvovaginitis in childhood may be caused by infection or irritation from a foreign body in the vagina.

SEE ALSO *Vaginitis, Vulvitis*

Vulva

The vulva is the collective term for the external parts of a woman's genitals, including the labia majora, labia minora, mons pubis and clitoris.

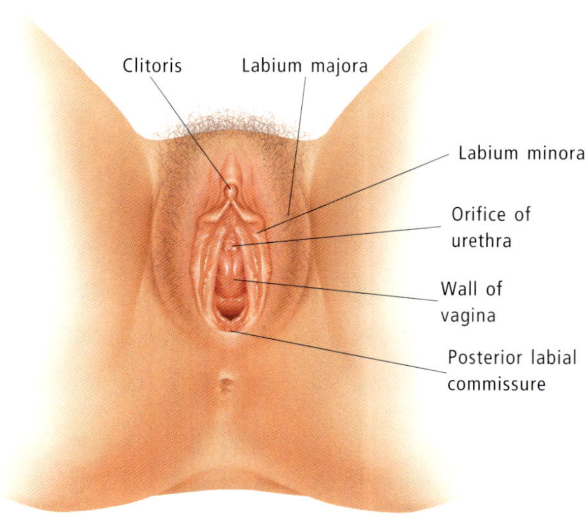

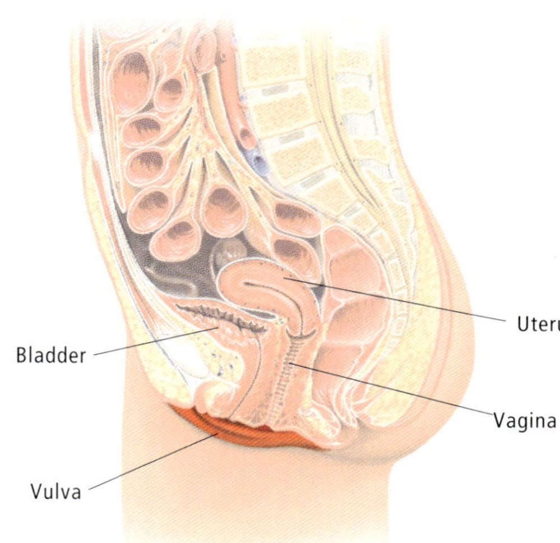

WARTS

Warts are benign tumors that occur in the outer layers of the skin. Typically, they appear as a raised, rough, round or oval lump that may be skin-colored, or lighter or darker than surrounding normal skin. Caused by the papillomavirus, they are mildly contagious and occur most often on the hands, feet, and face, though they may occur elsewhere.

Warts are often named for where they occur; plantar warts occur on the soles of the feet, genital warts in the skin on or around the genitalia. If they occur on the hands, arms or legs they are called common warts, or verrucae vulgaris. Multiple pinhead-sized warts occurring in children are called verrucae planae juveniles.

Warts usually cause no symptoms (though plantar warts may be painful) and disappear spontaneously within 2–3 years. If unsightly or painful they may be treated with an over-the-counter paint containing a mildly corrosive agent such as salicylic acid and/or lactic acid, which is applied daily for several weeks. They can be surgically removed with cryotherapy (freezing), electrocautery (burning), or laser treatment. Recurrence is common.

SEE ALSO *Genital warts, Skin, Viruses*

Warts

Caused by a virus, warts are small benign tumors that most commonly occur on the skin of the hands, feet and face.

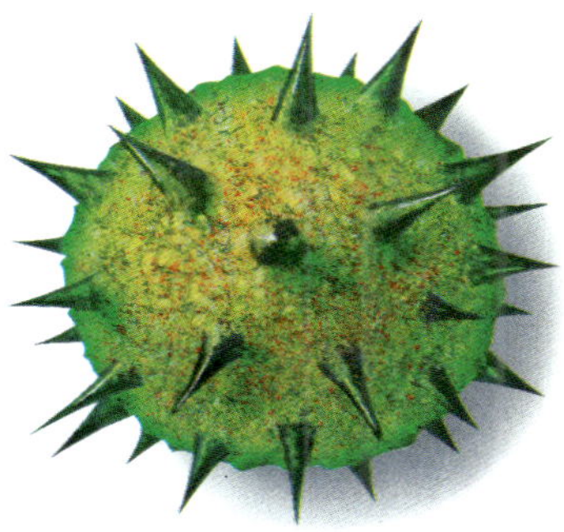

Wart virus

The papillomavirus is contagious and can be spread by scratching or rubbing infected skin.

WEIGHT

By definition, weight is the force with which a mass is attracted to the earth by gravity. When a person consumes more calories (or kilojoules) than is used through activity, body mass, and therefore weight, increases.

Pregnancy

During pregnancy the average weight gain in Western countries is around 26 pounds (12 kilograms); from 22–28½ pounds (10 to 13 kilograms) is thought to be ideal. One-third of this weight is made up of baby, placenta and amniotic fluid, one-third comprises an increase in breast tissue, other tissues and extra blood, and the remainder is body fat and retained water.

Babies and children

Growth and weight gain are important measures of healthy development in babies, and weight is among the first measurements taken of a newborn. When assessing a baby's weight it is important to take into account the baby's genetic inheritance and degree of prematurity, and the mother's health during pregnancy.

The growth charts used to assess a baby's growth are a valuable tool but need to be carefully interpreted, remembering that they show the range of weight of babies and children at various ages. The expected growth rate of children in industrialized countries is very different to that of children in less developed nations.

Weight charts need to be interpreted in conjunction with height charts to assess whether the baby or child is underweight or overweight. Not every child grows or gains weight at the same rate, so the overall pattern is necessary for a proper assessment. When a child is consistently overweight or underweight the cause needs to be investigated.

Failure to thrive means failure to gain weight, and in children up to the age of 2 is an indicator of serious illness or emotional or nutritional deprivation. Inadequate energy input, intestinal disease, heart and lung disease, metabolic conditions, congenital defects and emotional issues should all be investigated.

In many affluent countries childhood obesity is a growing problem. Obesity results in the creation of an abnormal number of fat cells, which may not disappear when weight is reduced, only losing some of their fat content. The cells retain a capacity for fat storage which gives the individual a tendency to become overweight in adolescence and adulthood. An overweight child can be disinclined to take part in physical activities. Obesity caused by poor eating habits can be worsened by the inactivity that results from sedentary leisure pursuits. The risk of becoming obese is greatest in children who have two obese parents; recent research indicates that genetic factors are important in determining obesity in adults.

Adults

Many women gain weight around the time of the menopause. In 90 percent of cases, this weight gain is the result of changes in lifestyle, not hormonal changes as is often thought. Women who remain physically active are less likely to increase their weight.

Weight-loss medicines, taken under medical supervision, and combined with a diet which reduces the daily calorie (kilojoule) intake, will help most obese people to lose weight. The best course is prevention; failing that, taking control of the amount of food consumed and exercise taken will help prevent health and lifestyle problems. Recent research suggests that metabolic and genetic disorders may cause obesity in some people.

SEE ALSO *Body Mass Index, Body shape, Diet, Nutrition, Obesity*

Wernicke-Korsakoff syndrome

Caused by a deficiency of thiamine, Wernicke-Korsakoff syndrome involves inflammation of the cerebellum, fourth ventricle and thalamus. This results in loss of motor skills, failing memory and general mental confusion.

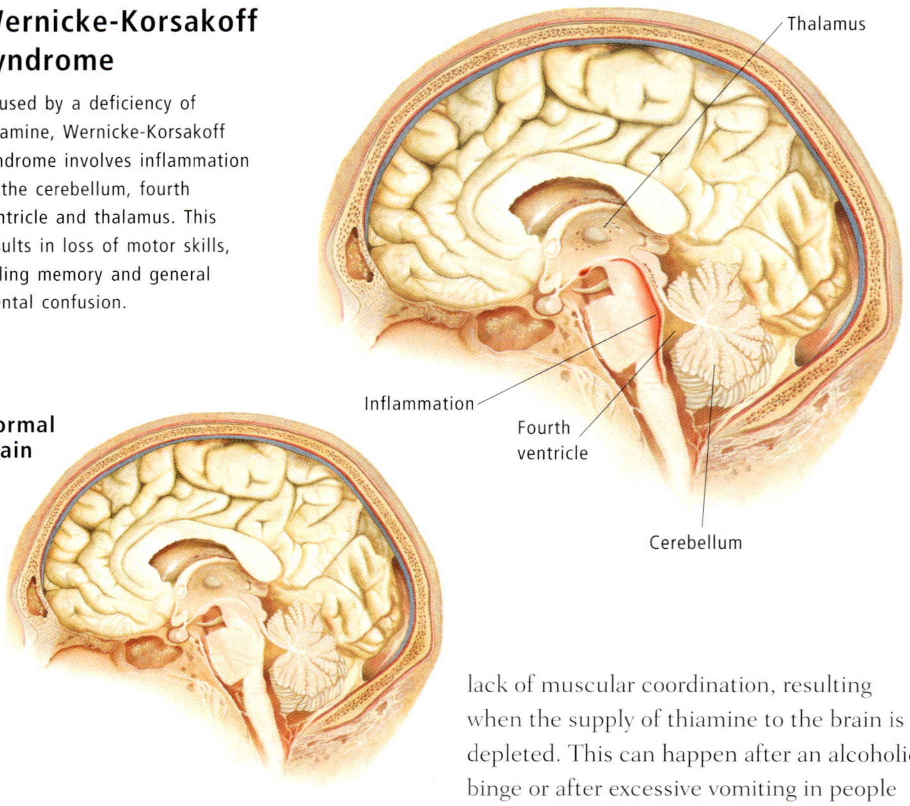

WERNICKE-KORSAKOFF SYNDROME

This syndrome is a combination of two disorders of the brain, Wernicke's encephalopathy and Korsakoff's amnesia, resulting from a deficiency in vitamin B_1 (thiamine). Long-term thiamine deficiency may become severe enough to affect the brain.

Wernicke's encephalopathy is an acute state involving confusion, memory loss and lack of muscular coordination, resulting when the supply of thiamine to the brain is depleted. This can happen after an alcoholic binge or after excessive vomiting in people who are generally undernourished. Thiamine deficiency is associated with alcoholism because alcoholics substitute alcohol for food and become generally malnourished.

The characteristics of Wernicke's encephalopathy are double vision, very rapid movements or paralysis of the eyes, mental confusion, drowsiness and uncoordinated walking. Emergency treatment is by direct injection of thiamine, but this may not prevent permanent brain damage.

People who recover from Wernicke's encephalopathy may suffer Korsakoff's amnesia or psychosis. Symptoms are mental confusion, loss of memory, apathy and delirium.

SEE ALSO *Alcoholism, Amnesia*

WHEEZING

Wheezing is a whistling sound heard in the chest when air passes through obstructed airways while breathing, especially when exhaling. It is one of the main symptoms of asthma. The sound is caused by the air passing through airways narrowed by muscle spasm, inflammation and the mucous secretion that occurs during asthma. Wheezing disappears when the asthma is treated. In severe asthma there may be no wheezing, as the bronchi may become so obstructed that no air can pass through.

SEE ALSO *Asthma, Breathing*

WHIPLASH

Whiplash is a term often applied to trauma to the cervical spine and tissues caused by rapid movement of the head and forceful flexion of the neck, causing pain, muscle spasm and limited motion. Treatment is usually protective support for the neck and back and sometimes the use of weights attached to head or legs to stretch the injured muscles and relieve pressure on the nerves.

SEE ALSO *Neck*

Whiplash

People involved in car accidents often suffer whiplash, as the sudden impact makes the head snap forward and then backwards, damaging the muscles and tissues of the neck and overstretching the cervical vertebrae.

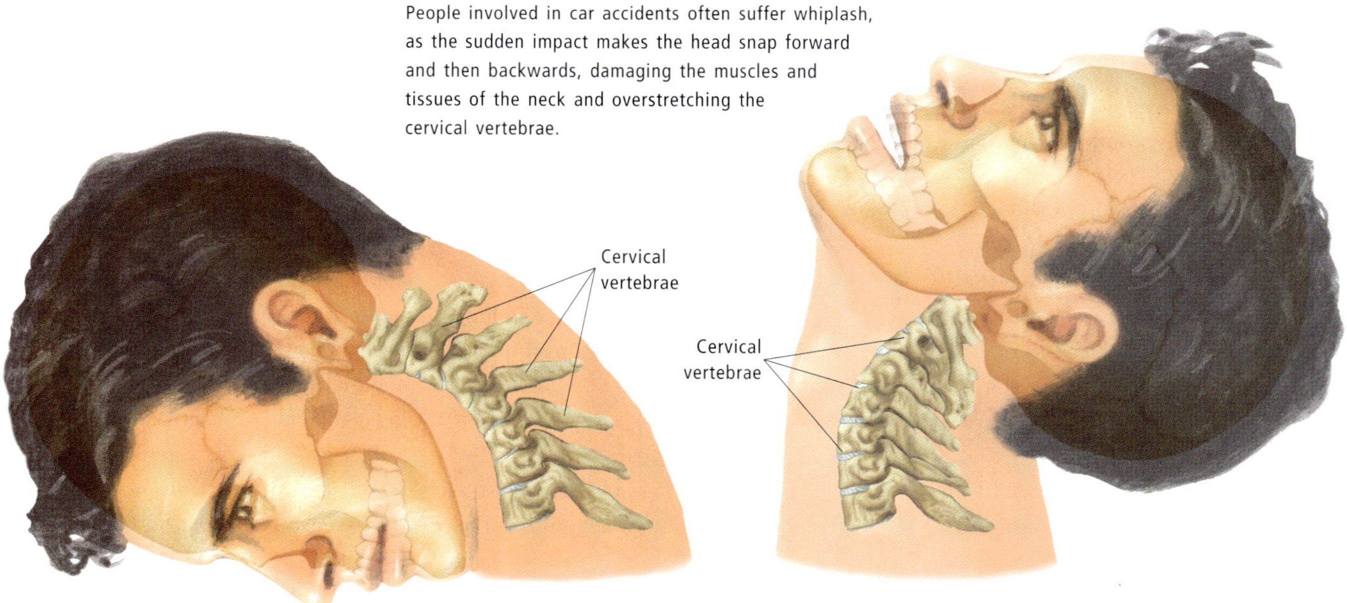

W

WHIPWORM

The whipworm (*Trichuris trichiura*) is a parasitic roundworm. Humans become the hosts for these worms when they eat uncooked food from crops grown in soil fertilized with sewage that has not been treated properly, or eat food prepared by infected handlers. The infection is known as trichuriasis and symptoms are abdominal pain and diarrhea; in small children complications such as intestinal blockage can result. Treatment with mebendazole is usually effective.

SEE ALSO *Trichuriasis, Worms*

WHITE BLOOD CELLS

Throughout life the body faces ongoing assault from thousands of different viruses, bacteria and other microbes, as well as a range of invertebrate parasites. The first lines of defense, the skin and mucous membranes, keep most of these potential invaders out. The comparative few that make it through to deeper tissues to cause disease face a barrage of attacks from the white blood cells (WBCs). Known also as leukocytes, WBCs are produced in red bone marrow and lymphatic tissue. There are five major types: neutrophils, eosinophils, basophils, monocytes and lymphocytes.

Most WBCs can "squeeze" through very small spaces to sites of infection in the body, a process referred to as emigration. These spaces include those between the cells of capillary walls. Neutrophils are the first to arrive at the site of an invasion. There they release bacteria-killing enzymes and ingest microorganisms and foreign particles by a process called phagocytosis. The monocytes arrive a little later but in much larger numbers, becoming macrophages once they migrate from the blood into tissues. They kill offending organisms and clean up debris associated with infection. Eosinophils also consume and engulf foreign material; in addition they release enzymes associated with allergic reactions which kill certain parasitic worms and protozoa. Basophils are also involved in inflammation and allergic reactions. Once they enter infected tissue they become mast cells, which release substances such as histamine that intensify the body's inflammatory response to foreign matter, producing hypersensitivity reactions.

White blood cells

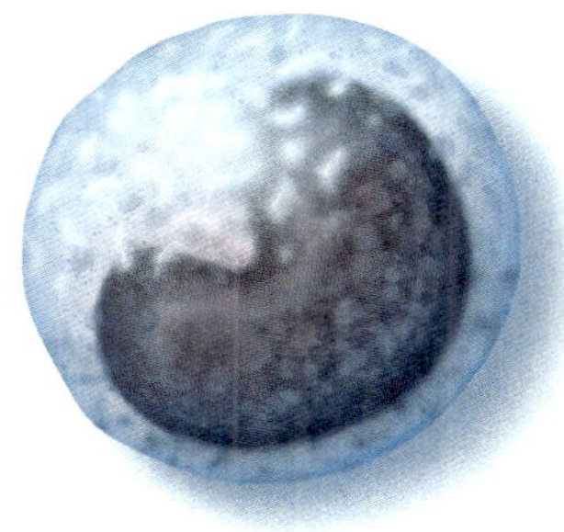

Monocyte
Monocytes circulate in the blood for 1–2 days before entering the body tissues to become macrophages.

Macrophage
Macrophages fight infection by engulfing foreign organisms and debris.

Neutrophil
The front-line defense against bacterial invasions, neutrophils engulf and destroy microorganisms.

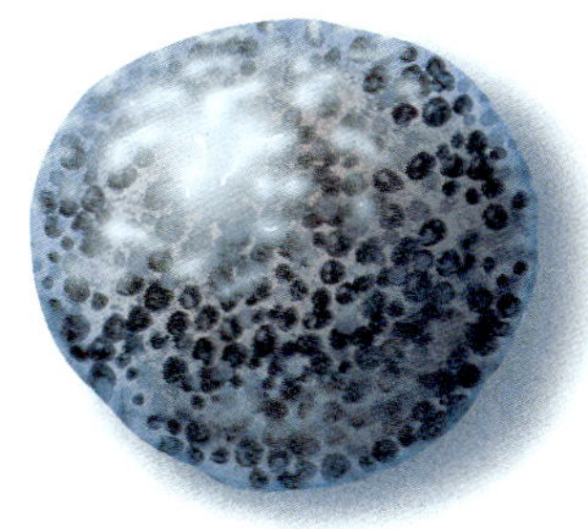

Basophil
These cells release substances that increase the body's response to invading allergens.

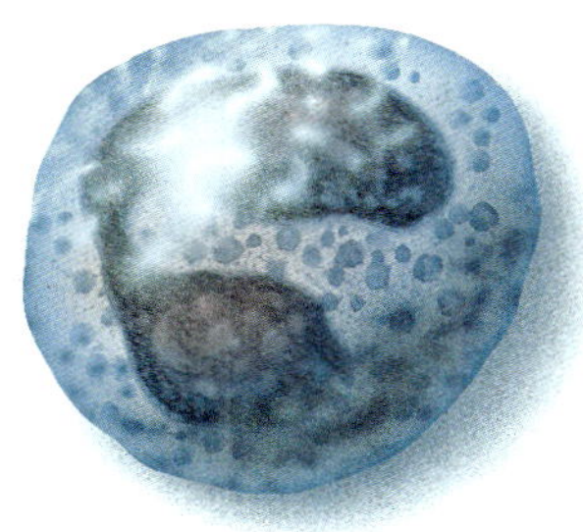

Eosinophil
Eosinophils release enzymes which cause allergic reactions and kill some parasites.

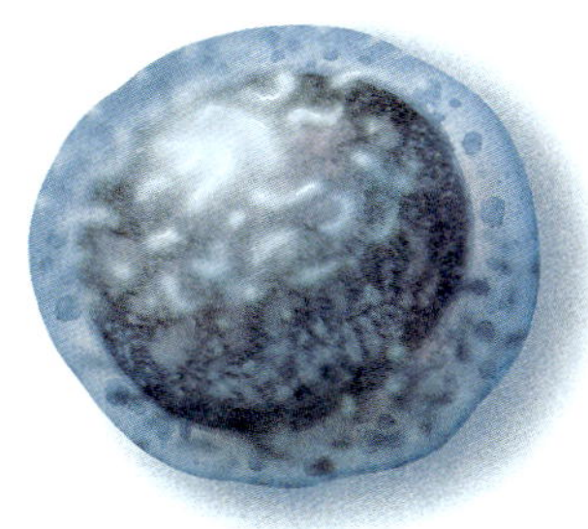

Lymphocyte
There are three types of lymphocyte. Natural killer cells and T cells attack foreign invaders directly; B cells make antibodies.

There are three types of lymphocytes: natural killer cells, T cells and B cells. Natural killer cells attack a wide variety of microorganisms and certain tumor cells. The T and B cells are directly involved in the body's immune responses. T cells combat viruses, fungi and cancer cells, and attack foreign tissue in organ transplants.

Before they can respond, T cells must become sensitized to a foreign invader. Different T cells learn to "recognize" different pathogens or harmful substances—there are literally millions of different T cells circulating in a healthy body. The situation is similar with B cells, which deal particularly well with bacteria and are highly effective at deactivating their toxins. Unlike T cells, B cells do not directly attack foreign material. Instead, they develop into plasma cells which secrete antibodies to do the work.

T and B cells can circulate in the body for years. The other WBCs are, like suicidal soldiers, eventually killed by their combat efforts—particularly by the toxic material they engulf. Their life spans are usually only a few days but during times of infection they may survive for only a matter of hours.

An increase in the number of WBCs in the blood usually indicates inflammation or infection. Because each WBC type plays a different role, the percentage of each type present in the blood helps diagnose disease. For example, a high eosinophil count suggests an allergic reaction or a parasitic worm infection. Normally, WBCs number between 5,000 and 10,000 per cubic milliliter of blood; over 10,000 suggests infection. An elevated WBC count is called leukocytosis and an abnormally low count is called leukopenia.

SEE ALSO *Blood, T cells*

WHITLOW

A pus-filled inflammation on the end of a finger or toe may be termed a whitlow. A herpetic whitlow is a swollen painful fingertip caused by the herpes simplex virus entering through a wound after exposure to infected oral or respiratory secretions; it may also occur as the result of nail-biting. Treatment may include the release of pus.

SEE ALSO *Herpes simplex*

WHOOPING COUGH

Whooping cough, also known as pertussis, is caused by the organism *Bordetella pertussis*. It is a serious, common and highly infectious illness in young children, particularly children under two years. It is spread by coughing, sneezing and close personal contact. Whooping cough incubates for between one and two weeks and can last for as long as three months. The affected person remains infectious for up to a month after the onset of the cough.

Beginning like a cold, whooping cough turns into exhausting coughing bouts with a characteristic whooping sound. Pneumonia is the most common complication and middle ear infections, nosebleeds, hemorrhages inside the eye, loss of appetite and dehydration are other possible complications.

Adults and older children who contract the disease are not likely to suffer as severely, but can still spread the disease. For those under two years, hospitalization is often necessary. Full immunization is the most sensible precaution.

SEE ALSO *Immunization, Infectious diseases*

Wilson's disease

When the body cannot metabolize copper, dangerously high levels of the metal accumulate in the liver, brain, kidneys, bones and eyes. The appearance of brown or green rings in the eyes (Kayser-Fleischer rings) are the most obvious symptom of the disease.

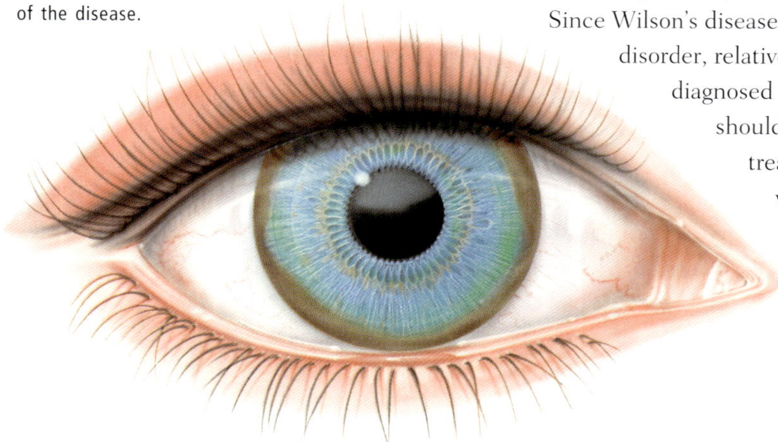

WILSON'S DISEASE

A rare condition also known as hepatolenticular degeneration, Wilson's disease is a hereditary defect characterized by the accumulation of copper in organs such as the liver, brain, eyes, kidneys and bones, caused by a deficiency in the circulation of the copper-binding protein ceruloplasmin. This can lead to chronic hepatitis and cirrhosis. The eyes may develop a brown or green ring in the outer margin of the cornea, known as the Kayser-Fleischer ring. Wilson's disease usually appears in the second or third decade of life. Early diagnosis and treatment has the potential to reverse the effects of the disorder and prevent permanent damage.

Since Wilson's disease is an inherited disorder, relatives of a person diagnosed with the disease should be screened and treated early to prevent or minimize organ damage.

Whitlow

Small fluid-filled blisters are a feature of herpetic whitlows, caused by the highly contagious herpes simplex virus.

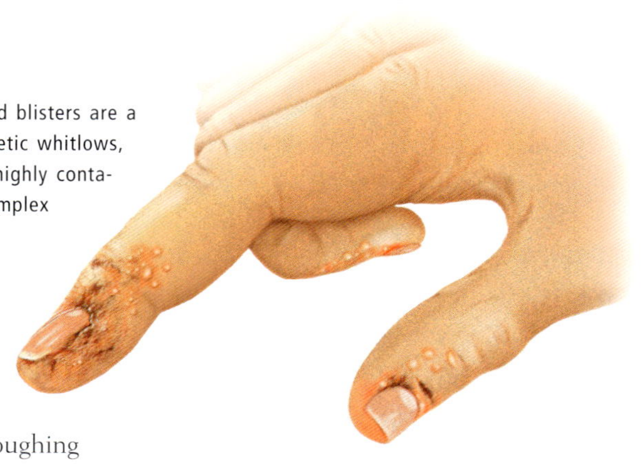

WITHDRAWAL

Withdrawal is the reaction of the body and mind in a drug-dependent person when the effect of the substance of dependence wears off. It also refers to the period in which these effects are felt, typically when dependence is first being treated. Dependence on any substance involves craving; uncontrolled intake; physical or mental dependence; repeated use and increasing tolerance.

Repeated use causes the level of toxic substances in body tissues and bloodstream to rise. When use stops, these toxins are excreted and levels fall in the process of detoxification, which is the body's natural process of breakdown and excretion of waste. In the substance-dependent person, this fall in toxin levels triggers the craving and often results in harrowing physical and psychological withdrawal symptoms, including depression, suicidal impulses and life-threatening physical disorders, varying in degree with the particular substance (alcohol, street drugs, amphetamines or tranquilizers).

Withdrawal from alcohol and many drugs is characterized by trembling, restlessness, watery eyes and running nose, hallucinations, delusions, fever, dilated pupils, sweating, inability to sleep and excessively rapid heartbeat. Withdrawal from anti-anxiety drugs may cause panic attacks, deep depression, itching, muscle pain and sensitivity to light. Without medical attention, withdrawal symptoms may be serious enough to cause death.

Withdrawal because of failure of supply can provoke irrational or desperate behavior. Crime statistics in many industrialized nations show a high incidence of violations triggered by the need for money to obtain illegal drugs.

Withdrawal as a consequence of treatment for drug dependency is usually managed by physicians or counselors. They may use tranquilizers to relieve distress and replace illegal drugs with legal substances as a step toward breaking dependency.

Delirium tremens is a state of confusion and mental disorder induced by the withdrawal of alcohol. Alcohol withdrawal is sometimes treated with naltrexone to ease the cravings, or disulfiram, which causes nausea when alcohol is taken.

Heroin addiction is often treated with methadone, which is itself a potential substance of dependence. It can also be treated with naltrexone. Counseling often plays a vital part in managing the process of withdrawal.

SEE ALSO *Alcoholism, Delirium tremens, Detoxification, Drug dependence, Stimulants*

WORMS

A worm is an invertebrate animal with a soft slender body and no limbs. Four main groups cause parasitic infections in humans: flatworms (Platyhelminthes) such as the tapeworm, roundworms (Nematoda), ribbon worms (Nemertea) and segmented worms (Annelida). Infection is caused by ingestion of eggs or penetration of the skin by larvae.

The diseases caused by worms include the following.

Ankylostomiasis is an intestinal infection caused by the roundworms *Ancylostoma duodenale* and *Necator americanus*.

Ascariasis is an infection caused by *Ascaris lumbridoides*, an intestinal roundworm.

Elephantiasis is a chronic condition caused by the filiarial worms *Wuchereria bancrofti* or *Brugia malayi*, which enter the body through an infected mosquito.

Enterobiasis is a pinworm infection (threadworm, seatworm). It is caused by *Enterobius vermicularis* and spreads by transfer on the fingers after scratching the seat of infection, the anus. Eggs can also be inhaled as they drift in air.

Flukes of various kinds (Trematoda) can cause serious infections of the blood, liver, intestines and lungs. Intestinal flukes are transmitted from vegetation or freshwater fish; sheep liver flukes come from watercress containing cysts; clonorchiasis is caused by freshwater fish flukes; lung fluke infestations are transmitted from crabs and crayfish; schistosomiasis is caused by blood flukes entering the body from infested water.

Onchocerciasis is a serious infestation by the parasitic worm *Onchocerca volvulus*.

Strongyloidiasis is an intestinal infection by the threadworm *Strongyloides stercoralis*.

Tapeworm infections include intestinal infections by *Taenia saginata* (beef tapeworm) and *T. solium* (pork tapeworm). They may also include cysticercosis, infection by species of dwarf tapeworms, and, in sheepraising areas, echinococcosis, caused by the tapeworm *Echinococcus granulosus*, producing hydatid cysts.

Toxocariasis is an infection caused by *Toxocara canis* or *T. cati*, nematodes found in the dog and cat.

Trichinosis is an infection caused by the *Trichinella spiralis* worm, usually ingested from cysts in undercooked pork.

Trichuriasis is an infection caused by *Trichuris trichiura*, an intestinal roundworm also known as the whipworm.

SEE ALSO *Hookworm, Hydatid disease, Pinworms, Roundworm, Tapeworm, Trichinosis, Trichuriasis, Whipworm*

WRINKLES

Wrinkles are tiny ridges or furrows on the surface of the skin, associated with aging. They are caused by the gradual loss of elasticity in the skin that accompanies ageing. The elasticity of skin is due to the presence of fibers of the proteins elastin and collagen. In old age, there is a gradual reduction in the amount of elastin, and in the elastic properties of collagen, which lead to the appearance of wrinkles.

While the wrinkling of skin is a natural process which cannot be avoided, there are some environmental factors that will increase the rate at which they form, and these can be avoided. These include frequent exposure to sunshine and smoking. To minimize skin wrinkling, it is advisable to stop smoking, stay out of the sun as much as possible, wear protective clothing when outside, and use sunscreen. In some cases, the appearance of someone with early onset wrinkles can be improved with plastic surgery such as a facelift or browlift.

Wrinkle creams may be tried but their value is questionable and some, for example those containing female sex hormone (which stimulates regeneration of skin and improve its elastic properties), may have side effects if used frequently.

WRIST

The wrist (carpus) contains a group of eight bones, known as the carpal bones, which join the radius and ulna to the hand. This complex joint allows a wide range of movement, in which the hand can be bent forward (flexion) or backward (extension) or moved from side to side. Two of the carpal bones are particularly prone to injury. The scaphoid, which lies on the thumb side of the wrist and forms the floor of a region known as the "snuff box", can be fractured in a fall on an outstretched hand. The adjacent bone, the lunate, can dislocate fairly easily, and may cause a painful click during wrist movements.

The shape of the carpal bones forms a concavity or U-shape. The roof of this concavity is closed over by a dense band of connective tissue, forming the carpal tunnel. Long flexor tendons to the fingers and thumb pass through this tunnel, as well as the median nerve. Swelling within the tunnel can cause the median nerve to be compressed, and lead to carpal tunnel syndrome.

As well as the long flexor tendons that cross in front of the wrist through the carpal tunnel, long tendons associated with extension of the fingers and thumb pass across the back of the wrist. All these tendons are surrounded by synovial sheaths that lubricate them. These sheaths can get inflamed and painful, for example with overuse or in association with arthritis. Inflammation of two tendons to the thumb, a condition known as de Quervain's disease, causes pain which is exacerbated by gripping and twisting movements, as in wringing clothes. Resting the tendons by avoiding the painful movements usually helps, and anti-inflammatory medication may be recommended. The tendon sheaths can also form a small swelling or ganglion, usually on the back of the wrist. The ganglion may not be painful, but if necessary it can be removed surgically.

Three nerves cross the wrist to supply the skin and muscles of the hand—the median,

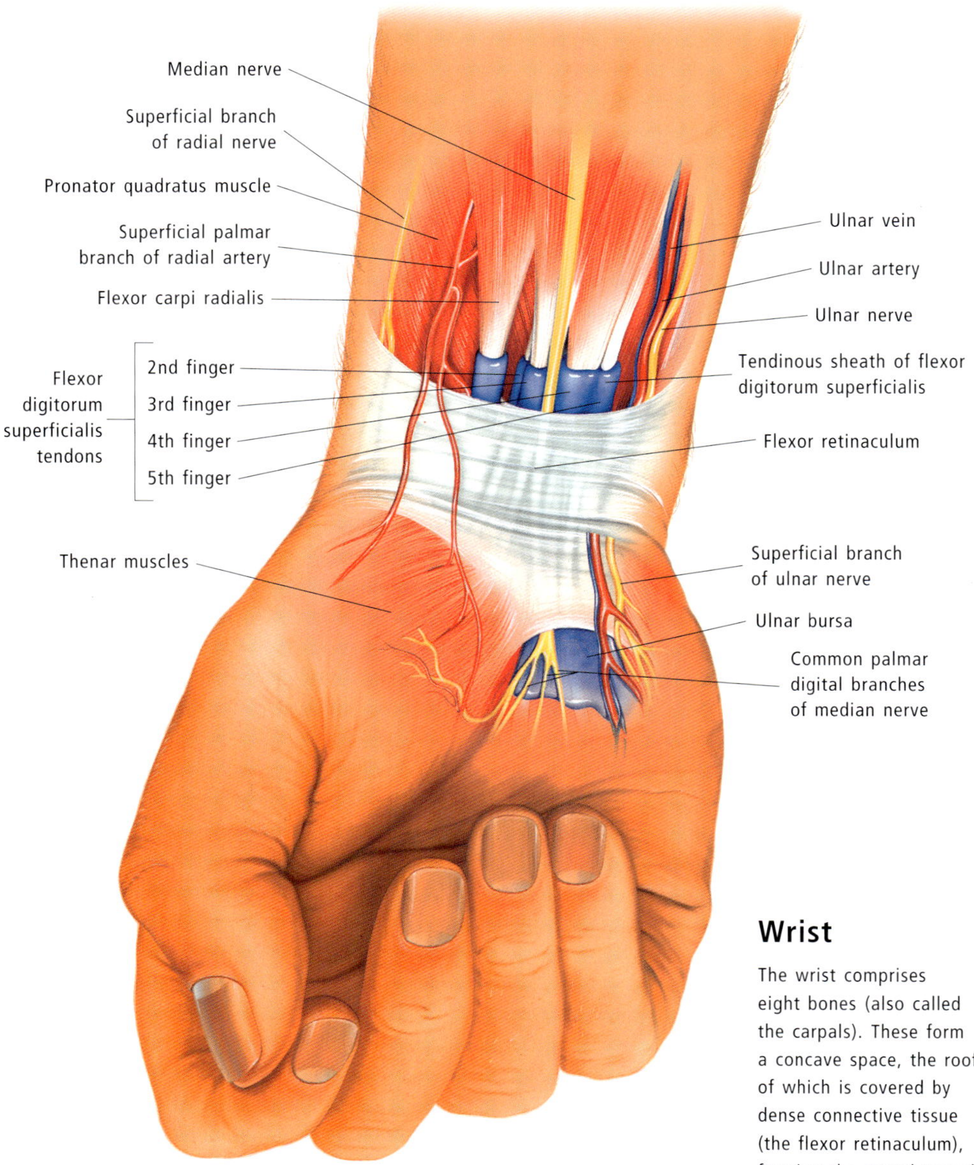

Wrist

The wrist comprises eight bones (also called the carpals). These form a concave space, the roof of which is covered by dense connective tissue (the flexor retinaculum), forming the carpal tunnel.

ulnar and radial nerves. Like the median nerve, the ulnar nerve can be compressed in a connective tissue tunnel (tunnel of Guyon) at the wrist. The ulnar nerve is particularly important for fine finger movements. The wrist is also crossed by two arteries, the ulnar and radial arteries. The pulse from the radial artery can be felt at the wrist, near the base of the thumb, while that for the ulnar artery is felt against the ulnar bone near the wrist.

The wrist is one of the joints commonly involved in rheumatoid arthritis. There is pain, joint stiffness and reduced movement, with joint deformity and swelling which may lead to carpal tunnel syndrome.

Osteoarthritis can occur in the wrist, especially if there has been a previous injury. Osteoarthritis is also common in the joint between the wrist and first metacarpal bone, which is involved in thumb movements (carpometacarpal joint). Arthritis in this joint can be the result of a common fracture of the metacarpal bone called Bennett's fracture. There is pain at the base of the thumb, aggravated by thumb movements. Treatment includes resting the joint, anti-inflammatory medication and steroid injections.

SEE ALSO *Carpal tunnel syndrome, Connective tissue, Ganglion, Hand, Joints, Osteoarthritis, Radial nerve, Radius, Rheumatoid arthritis, Tendons, Ulna, Ulnar nerve*

X CHROMOSOME

The cells of the human body each contain 23 pairs of chromosomes; one pair determines the sex of the individual, and consists of two X chromosomes (female) or one X and one Y chromosome (male). The sperm cell and the egg cell each have only 23 single chromosomes (one from each pair). When these cells unite the chromosomes pair up so the newly fertilized cell has 46 chromosomes (23 pairs).

At conception, there is one X chromosome present in the ovum, while the sperm may contain an X chromosome or a Y chromosome. If the united cell has two X chromosomes, the baby will be female, if there is an X and a Y chromosome the baby will be male.

SEE ALSO *Chromosomes, Fragile X syndrome, Y Chromosome*

X-RAY

X-rays are a form of electromagnetic radiation, similar to light but of a much shorter wavelength. They can penetrate soft tissue such as skin and muscle rather easily, but are absorbed by bones and other objects containing heavy atoms.

X-rays, or their penetration, are recorded or observed by use of photographic film or fluorescent screens, so they can therefore be used to study the internal structure of the body, particularly bones. Also observable are the presence and location of foreign objects, such as swallowed coins, and surgically-inserted needles and metal plates. Cavities, such as those of the gut, bladder, heart and blood vessels, can be studied by filling them with substances which are either radiopaque (for example, barium) or radiolucent (for example, carbon dioxide). The radiopaque substances offer resistance to x-rays, and appear as light areas on exposed film; the radiolucent substances permit their passage and appear as dark areas on exposed film.

Because x-rays are a form of ionizing radiation, they are potentially damaging to tissue. Excessive exposure to x-rays must be avoided. Exposure is normally minimized by employing a narrow beam of x-rays, covering sensitive parts of the body with lead-containing rubber shields, and using sensitive recording devices which require only low x-ray dosage. The damaging effects of x-rays can be of therapeutic value in the treatment of cancer and other tumors.

Cross-sectional pictures of body structures are obtained by computed axial tomography (CAT scanning), in which a series of x-ray images focused on different planes are analyzed by computer and presented as sections. CAT scans show soft tissue in more detail than plain x-rays.

SEE ALSO *Barium enema, Barium meal, CAT scan, Contrast x-rays, Imaging techniques*

XANTHELASMA

Xanthomas—flat, fatty, yellow deposits in the skin—are known as xanthelasmas when they affect the eyelids and surrounding area. In about half the number of people with this characteristic there is an association with high blood cholesterol and hyperlipidemia, and the appearance of xanthomas elsewhere on the body.

Seen most commonly in the elderly, xanthomas do not cause discomfort or disease. There is no treatment, though the spots may be removed for cosmetic reasons.

SEE ALSO *Cholesterol, Eyelids, Xanthoma*

XANTHOMA

A xanthoma is a small, firm, yellow to red-brown raised lesion that develops just beneath the skin and appears on the skin's surface as a nodule, papule, plaque or benign tumor. It is a painless deposit from the bloodstream of excess fats (lipids) such as cholesterol and triglycerides. Xanthomas can occur anywhere on the body but tend to be seen particularly on the elbows, knees, hands, feet, buttocks, joints and tendons.

Although they can be unsightly, xanthomas in themselves cause few problems. They may be indicators of a range of underlying metabolic disorders characterized by undesirable elevated blood lipid levels. For example, xanthomas can appear when the disease diabetes mellitus is poorly controlled.

Clustered around the joints in a condition known as xanthoma tuberosum, these nodules can suggest cirrhosis of the liver or certain thyroid disorders. In xanthoma tendinosum, xanthomas occur in clumps on the tendons and indicate a hereditary lipid storage disease. When they occur on the eyelids, xanthomas frequently indicate high cholesterol levels. The sudden appearance of large clusters on the legs, arms, buttocks or trunk indicate dangerously elevated triglyceride levels in the blood.

Most xanthomas disappear eventually, if the underlying cause is treated successfully.

SEE ALSO *Cholesterol, Fats, Xanthelasma*

Y CHROMOSOME

Chromosomes are the thread-like structures in cell nuclei that carry coded hereditary information. Normal humans have 46 chromosomes, arranged in 23 pairs, in each of their body cells. However, the sex cells (sperm and ova) each have only 23 single chromosomes. The sex chromosomes are labeled X and Y, the latter being responsible for the development of male characteristics. Sperm contain either an X or Y chromosome, but ova only ever contain the X chromosome. When a sperm fertilizes an ovum, the chromosomes combine to form the normal complement of 23 pairs. Only if the sperm carries a Y chromosome will the fertilized egg develop into a male.

The Y chromosome is roughly a third the length of the X chromosome, and apart from its role in determining maleness, is otherwise genetically inactive. This confers a biological advantage on the female, because if a male inherits a recessive gene on the X chromosome, for example the gene causing hemophilia, there is no second X chromosome with a dominant gene to counteract it. By contrast, a female who inherits the recessive disease-causing gene on the X chromosome from one parent, will probably inherit the normal, dominant gene from the other parent, and so probably will not develop the disease. The condition therefore is usually only seen in men (but is carried by women) and is termed sex-linked. Other examples of sex-linked conditions are red-green color blindness and night blindness.

SEE ALSO *Chromosomes, X chromosome*

YAWNING

In yawning, the mouth is opened very wide and a long deep breath is taken. Sometimes, the upper limbs are stretched, which may promote venous return. An involuntary act, a yawn is believed to be triggered by a need to get rid of accumulated carbon dioxide. Yawning typically occurs on waking from sleep, or when tired, but it may be of psychological origin.

SEE ALSO *Sleep*

YAWS

An infectious and debilitating disease of the skin and bones, yaws is also known as frambesia. Found in moist tropical regions of the world, it is most common in children aged 2–5 who wear few clothes, and live in areas where hygiene is poor. It is caused by the spirochete (spiral microorganism) *Treponema pertenue*, which enters the body through a break in the skin. Yaws is similar to syphilis but is not sexually transmitted.

Yaws has three stages, the first a single bump on the skin which gradually grows larger and is characterized by a wart-like thickening; this becomes fibrous and ulcerates, with a discharge. After about a month this will disappear and multiple eruptions of the same type develop. These lesions look similar to a raspberry. At this stage the disease may also affect the bones and joints. The third stage, which develops in 10 percent of sufferers, causes deformities which can resemble leprosy, and can also affect the spleen, brain and blood vessels.

Penicillin or another antibiotic may be used as a preventive measure as well as a treatment and is usually successful. Yaws is rarely fatal.

SEE ALSO *Infectious diseases*

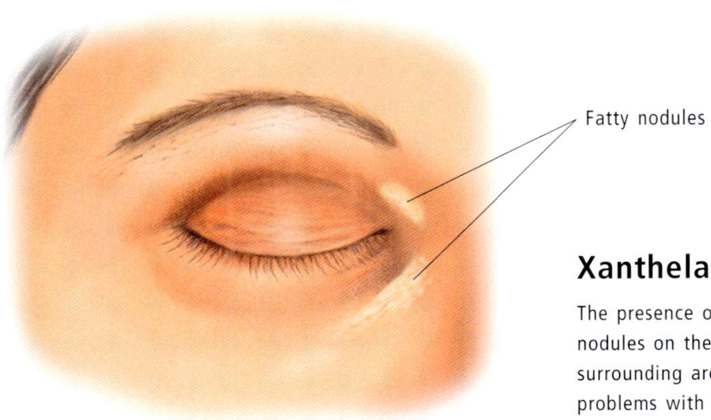

Xanthelasma

The presence of these fatty nodules on the eyelids and surrounding areas indicates problems with high cholesterol.

YELLOW FEVER

The bite of the mosquito *Aedes aegypti* can transmit the virus infection yellow fever to humans. Common in tropical climates, particularly Africa and South America, yellow fever is an acute infectious disease. There are two different patterns of transmission of the disease—either from person to person via the mosquito or from a mammalian host, often a monkey, to a forest mosquito and from there to a human.

Symptoms appear abruptly. Shivering, a high fever, severe headache, bone pains, dizziness, backache, nausea and vomiting strike suddenly, within three to six days of being infected. The virus destroys liver cells, and jaundice (yellowing of the skin) is common. While the majority of sufferers recover completely, others may become delirious and go into a coma, with death often the result. Those who recover have lifelong immunity. There is no cure and the only treatment is administration of intravenous fluids, anti-nausea medication, kidney dialysis and skilled medical care.

Immunization with an extremely mild yellow fever virus will give protection for 10 years. This vaccine cannot be given to children under the age of one.

SEE ALSO *Immunization, Viruses*

YOGA

The term yoga comes from the Sanskrit word *yuj*, which means "to bind together" or "union". In yoga this refers both to finding union between mind and body and to the experience of oneness that lies beyond the dualistic nature of the material world and the mind. Yoga was developed in India some four thousand years ago.

At first yoga was practised only by small numbers of spiritual disciples, who lived as recluses. They developed many of the postures of yoga from studying animals, which were seen to be healthier and more relaxed than humans.

The basic philosophies and practice of yoga were first written about in the second century BC by Patanjali in his yoga sutras, which summarize the eight limbs of yoga—*yamma*: moral codes of a universal nature; *niyama*: personal conduct; *asanas*: the practice of postures; *pranayama*: breath control; *pratyhara*: control of the senses; *dharana*: the power of concentration; *dhyana*: the stillness of meditation; and *samadhi*: contemplation and reflection.

The rise in popularity and spread of yoga throughout the world has taken place over the last 200 years. In the West, yoga is particularly popular for the physical effects of its postures, which promote flexibility and good health, and its relaxation and meditation practices, which help to reduce stress.

Yoga is particularly recommended for all stress-related illnesses, sciatica, back pain, emphysema, asthma, rheumatism, arthritis, digestive ailments and menstrual pain.

Techniques

Yoga utilizes an awareness of breath, body and mind. The major techniques, in the order they are practised in a typical hatha yoga class, are: physical postures (asanas), which are said to heal and maintain the physical body by increasing flexibility, strengthening the muscles and detoxifying and toning all the body systems; breathing exercises (pranayama), which are said to stimulate and increase the vital energy in the body and are also seen as helpful in calming the emotions and sharpening the mind; meditation (dhyana), which is believed to bring awareness of the inner reality, helping to transcend the illusions and stresses of external life; and total relaxation (yoga nidra), which achieves a deeply relaxed state by systematically guiding awareness through all the parts of the body.

Styles

There are a number of different yoga styles, some concentrating more on postures, others spending more time on relaxation and meditation. There is also a wide variation on the pace and degree of challenge involved in the practice of postures.

The three most common schools of yoga are Hatha yoga, Iyengar yoga and Oki yoga. In Hatha yoga, traditional postures are practised gently and slowly with breathing exercises, meditation and relaxation. They aim for a balance between energizing and relaxing practices to support overall well-being.

In Iyengar yoga, and its offshoot Astanga, the emphasis is on strengthening and maintaining the body through various postures, many of which are quite challenging.

Oki yoga is a Japanese version of yoga which focuses on the movement of *ch'i* (life energy) through the acupuncture meridians and which uses different postures in different seasons.

SEE ALSO *Exercise, Meditation, Relaxation techniques*

Yoga

The health benefits of yoga are achieved by exploiting the links between body and mind. Meditation and relaxation act on the hypothalamus and limbic system in the brain (which control autonomic functions such as breathing and heart rates, muscle tension and emotional state) to deliver physical benefits.

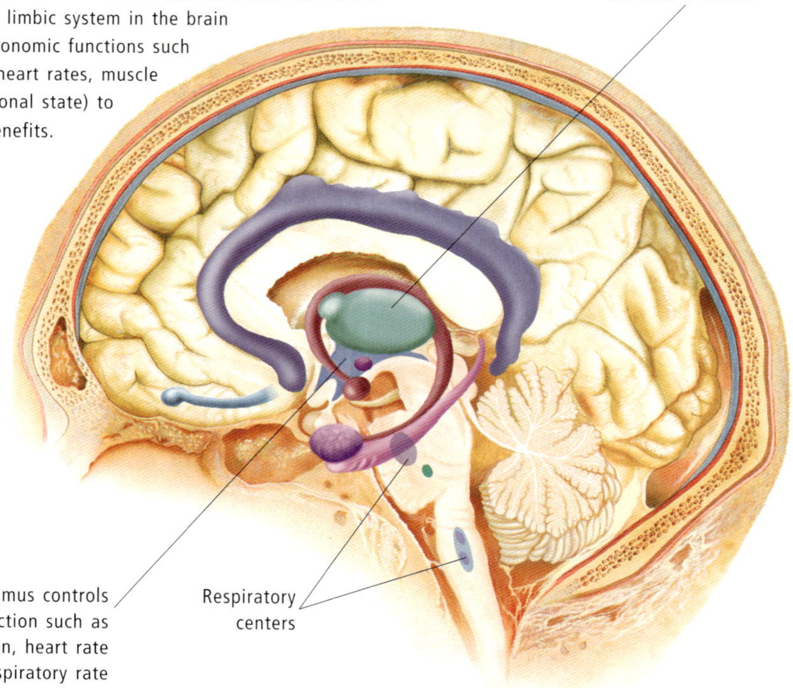

Y

ZOLLINGER-ELLISON SYNDROME

This is an unusual disease caused by secretion of excess amounts of the hormone gastrin by tumors called gastrinomas. Gastrinomas most often arise from certain cells in the pancreas, although they may arise elsewhere in the duodenum or abdomen. The tumor may be small and very difficult to find. The gastrin produced by the tumor increases the secretion of acid by the stomach, causing stomach ulcers and problems with digestion. Patients may complain of upper abdominal pain and diarrhea.

Unlike other peptic ulcers, the pain is not easily relieved by antacids or milk. Treatment should ideally be to remove the gastrinoma if it can be found, or control the acid secretion with H_2 receptor blockers such as cimetidine.

SEE ALSO *Peptic ulcer, Stomach*

ZYGOTE

In a normal pregnancy, the ovum (egg) will be fertilized in the fallopian tube within 48 hours of intercourse.

This fertilized ovum, known as the zygote, begins to divide rapidly, first into two cells, then four, then eight, as it journeys down the fallopian tube, becoming a cluster of cells known as the blastocyst. About six days after fertilization the blastocyst implants itself into the uterine wall, where it will develop into the embryo.

SEE ALSO *Fertilization, Pregnancy, Reproductive systems*

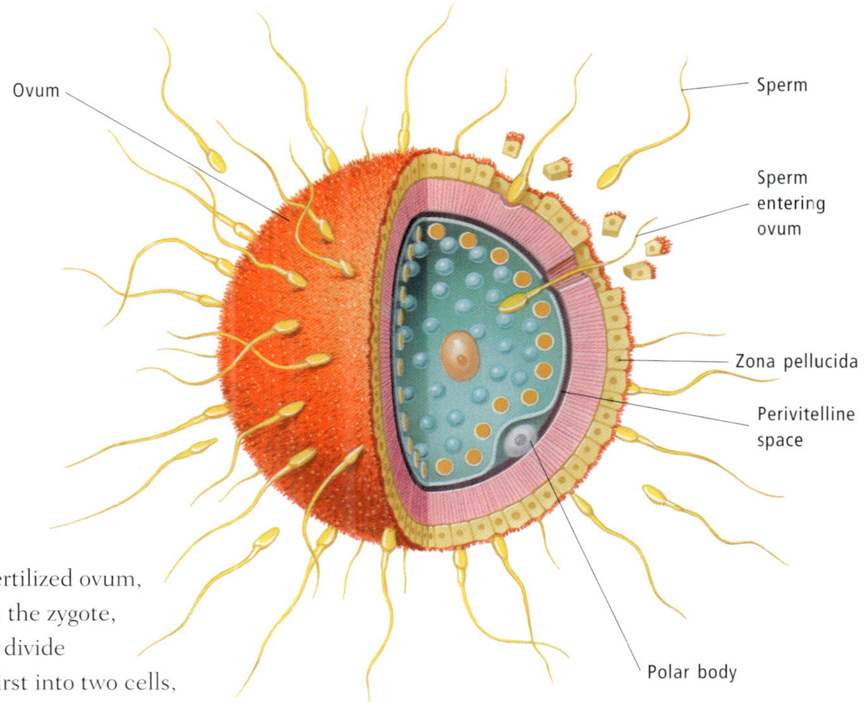

Zygote

A zygote is the cell created when a sperm enters and fertilizes an ovum, before it begins the process of division that will ultimately lead to the development of an embryo.

First Aid Emergency Guide

What is First Aid?

First aid is the initial care of the ill or injured. At any time, you may find yourself in a situation where someone has had an accident or is suffering from a sudden illness and needs help until a qualified health care professional, such as a doctor, registered nurse or ambulance officer, arrives.

The aims of first aid:

- promote a safe environment
- preserve life
- prevent injury or illness from becoming worse
- help promote recovery
- provide comfort to the ill or injured.

What a first aider should do:

- assess the situation quickly
- identify the nature of the injury or illness as far as possible
- manage the casualty promptly and appropriately
- arrange for Emergency Services to attend
- stay with the casualty until able to hand over to a health care professional
- give further help if necessary.

Other first aiders

The first aider who arrives first at the scene of an incident takes charge and stays in charge until handing over control. Any other first aider who arrives should offer to help the original first aider without trying to take over control.

If you feel another first aider at the scene is more qualified to handle the situation, ask that person to take control. However, the most qualified person does not need to be in control, especially if another first aider already has matters well in hand.

Remember:

It must be stressed that reading this book, without attending a first aid course with its practical components, does not constitute a complete first aid education.

Emergency First Aid—The DRABC action plan

1 Check for DANGER—to you, to others and to the casualty.

2 Check for RESPONSE—shout and gently shake the shoulders. Is the casualty conscious or unconscious? If no response, go to 3. If responsive, go to 9.

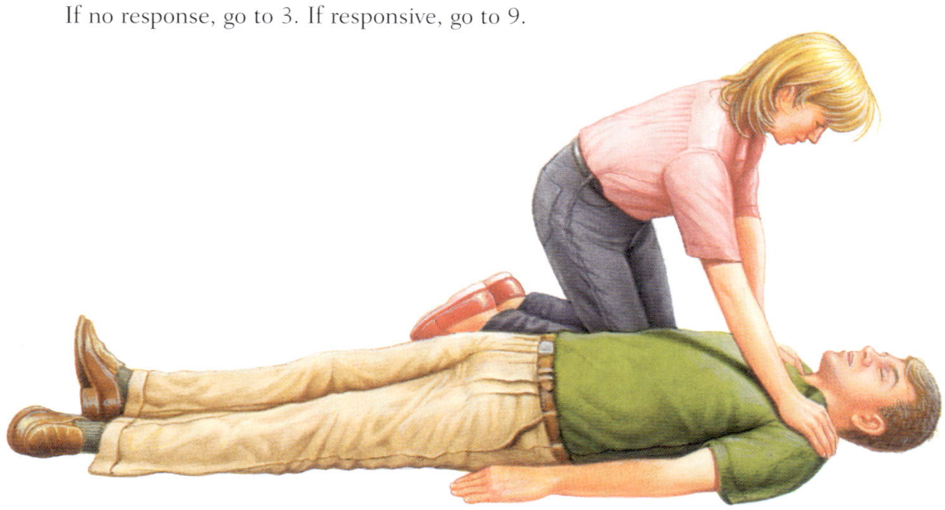

3 If no response, place the casualty in the recovery position.

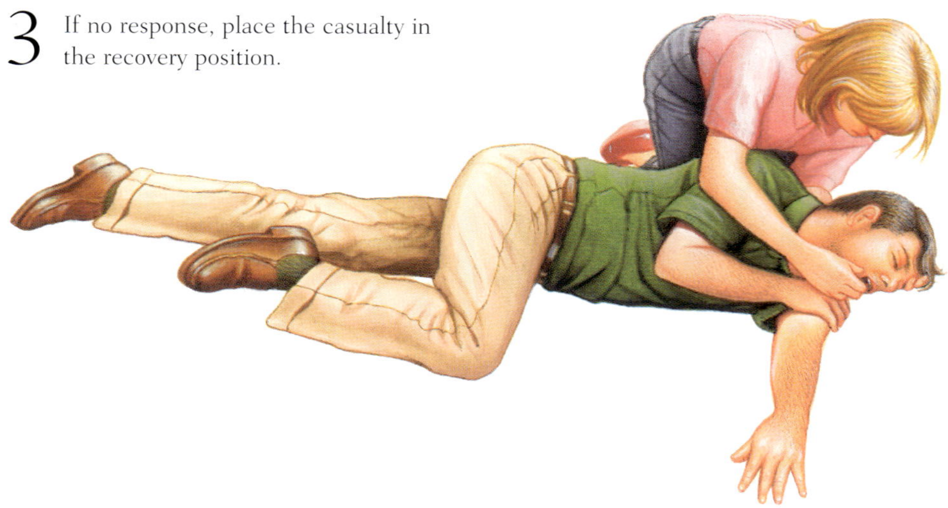

4 Check the AIRWAY—clear the mouth, tilt the head back to open the airway. Is the airway clear of objects? Is the airway open?

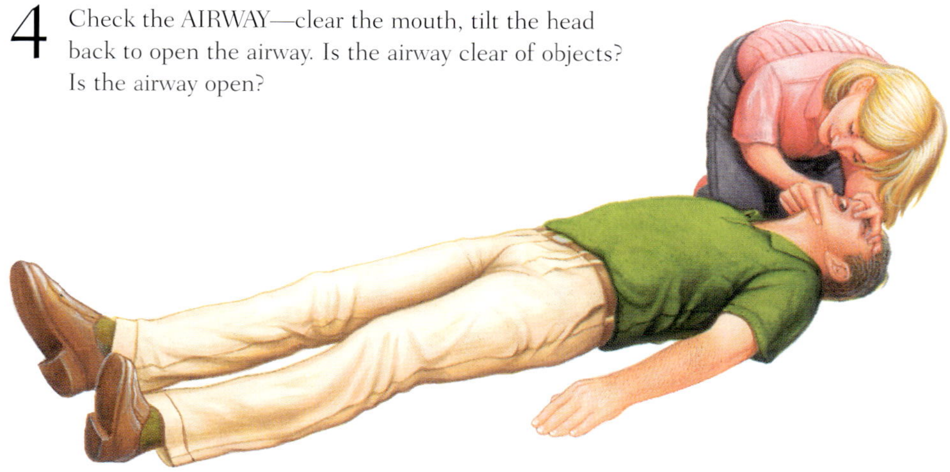

5 Check for BREATHING—look, listen and feel for breath. Is the chest rising and falling? Can you hear the casualty's breathing? Can you feel the breath on your cheek?
If the casualty is not breathing, go to 6.
If breathing, go to 10.

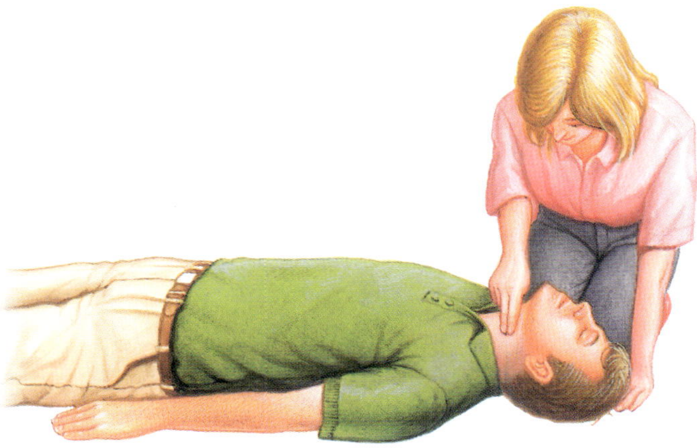

6 If not breathing—call the Emergency Services number for your area, then give two effective breaths.

7 Check for CIRCULATION—check the pulse at the neck. Can you feel a pulse? Can you see any obvious signs of life? If there is no pulse, go to 8. If the pulse is present, go to 11.

8 If there is no pulse, commence Cardiopulmonary Resuscitation (CPR):

- at a ratio of 15 compressions to 2 breaths in 15 seconds—4 cycles per minute for adults
- at a ratio of 5 compressions to 1 breath in 5 seconds—12 cycles per minute for children
- for both adults and children, check the pulse about every minute until medical aid arrives.

9 If responsive—manage any bleeding or injuries, monitor breathing and pulse, seek medical aid.

10 If breathing—leave casualty in the recovery position. Manage any bleeding or injuries, and seek medical aid. Check breathing and pulse regularly until medical aid arrives.

11 If the pulse is present but the casualty isn't breathing, continue Expired Air Resuscitation (EAR):

- at a ratio of 1 breath every 4 seconds for adults
- at a ratio of 1 breath every 3 seconds for children
- for both adults and children, check the pulse about every minute until medical aid arrives.

The Recovery Position

Adults and children (from age 1)

1 **Position casualty's legs:**

- kneel beside the casualty
- straighten the casualty's limbs
- lift the nearer leg at the knee so it is fully bent upwards.

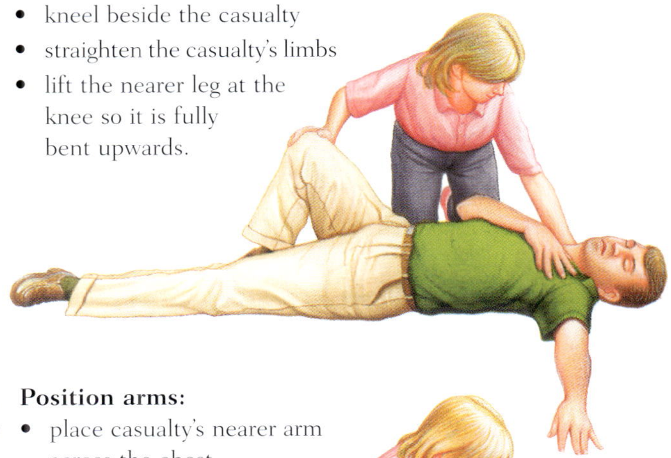

2 **Position arms:**

- place casualty's nearer arm across the chest
- place the farther arm at right angles to the body.

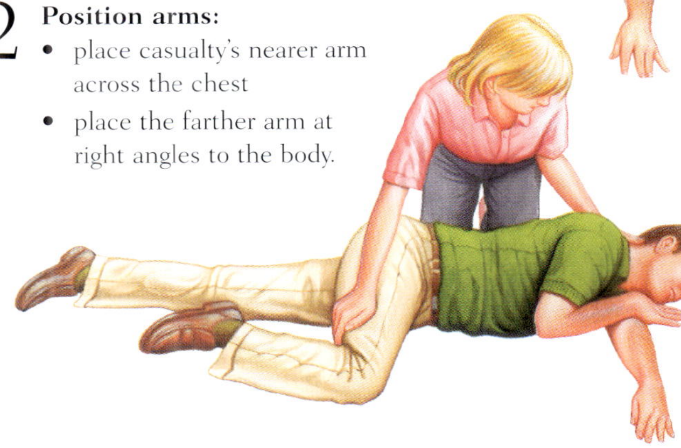

3 **Roll casualty into position:**

- roll casualty away from you onto their side
- keep the bent leg at right angles, with knee touching the ground to prevent casualty rolling onto their face.

4 **Make casualty steady:**

- make any adjustments necessary to ensure casualty does not roll.

5 **Ensure the airway is open.**

Infants (under 1 year)

- lay the infant face down on your forearm
- support the infant's head with your hand
- check the infant does not choke on their tongue or inhale vomit.

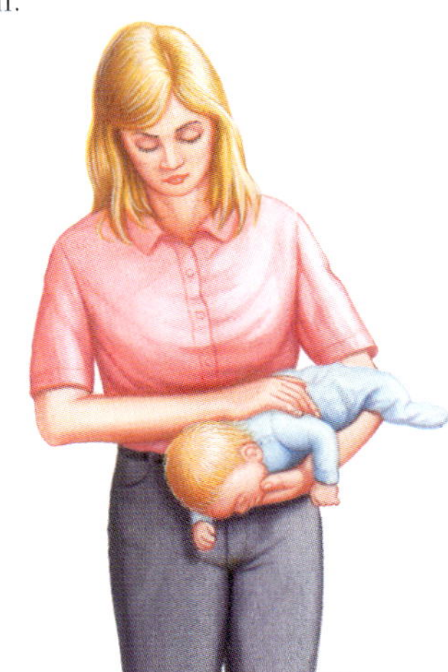

WARNING

If the casualty has head or neck injuries:

- ensure the head and neck are supported at all times
- do not allow rotation between the head and spine
- do not tilt the head back if neck injury is suspected.

Expired Air Resuscitation (EAR) for adults

If breathing:

1 **Clear the airway:**

- place casualty in recovery position
- lift chin and open mouth
- use finger to remove any obvious obstruction
- tilt head back gently
- check breathing for up to 10 seconds.

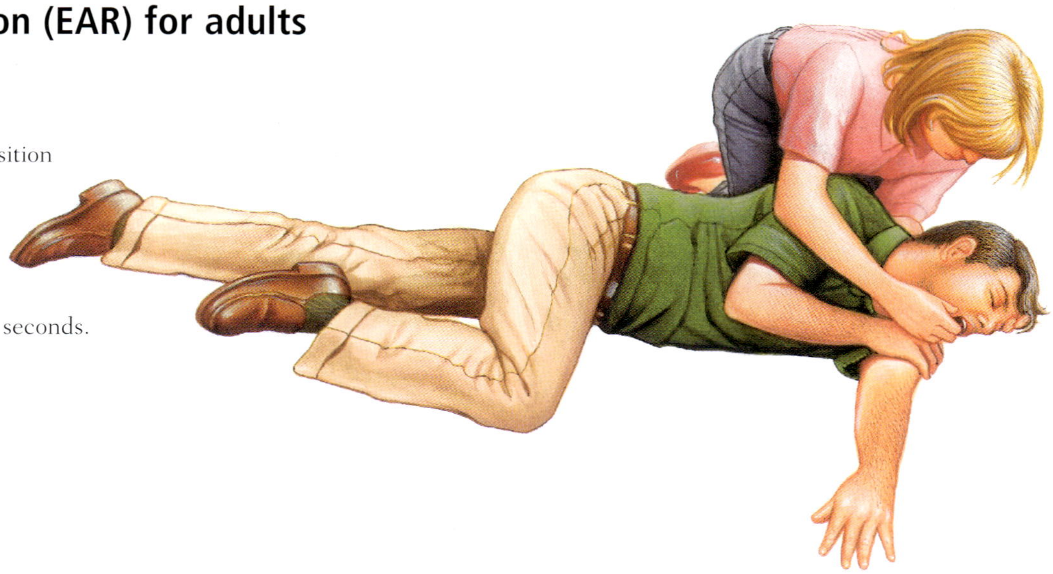

If not breathing:

2 **Open airway:**

- turn casualty onto their back
- gently tilt the head back
- pinch the nose closed (use thumb and index finger)
- open mouth and maintain chin lift.

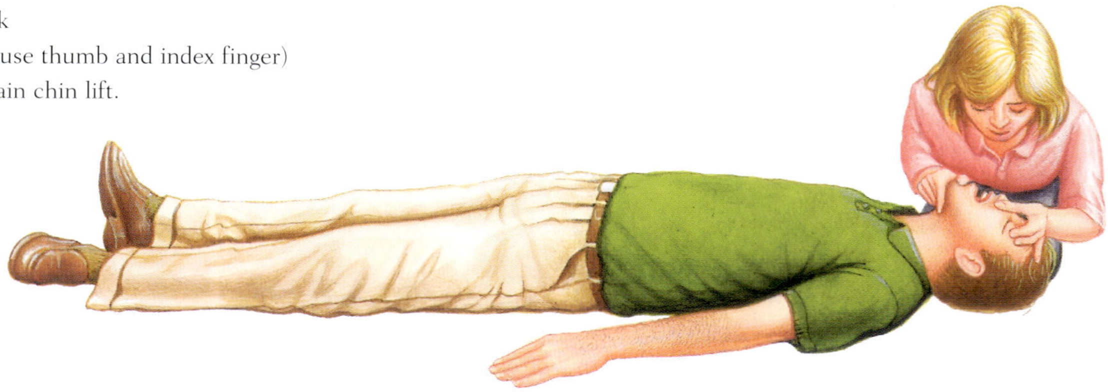

3 **Give EAR (mouth-to-mouth resuscitation):**

- take a full breath and place the lips on casualty's mouth (ensure a good seal)
- blow steadily into the mouth for 1–2 seconds
- watch for the chest to rise
- take mouth away and watch for the chest to fall
- take another breath and repeat the sequence, giving two effective breaths.

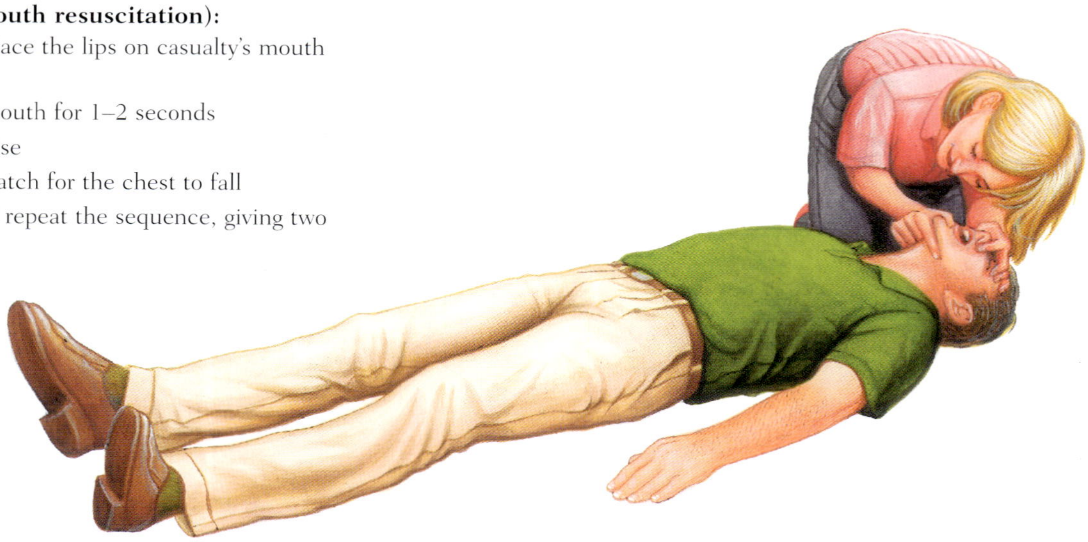

4 **Check for pulse:**

- check the pulse at the neck or wrist
- if pulse is absent, commence CPR
- if pulse is present, continue EAR at 15 breaths per minute
- recheck the pulse and look for other signs of recovery about every minute.

5 **Place in recovery position when breathing returns.**

Cardiopulmonary Resuscitation (CPR) for adults

1 **Position hands for CPR:**
- place casualty on their back
- find the groove at the neck between the collar bones
- find the lower end of the breast bone by running a finger along the last rib to the center of the body
- extend the thumb of each hand equal distances to meet in the middle of the breast bone

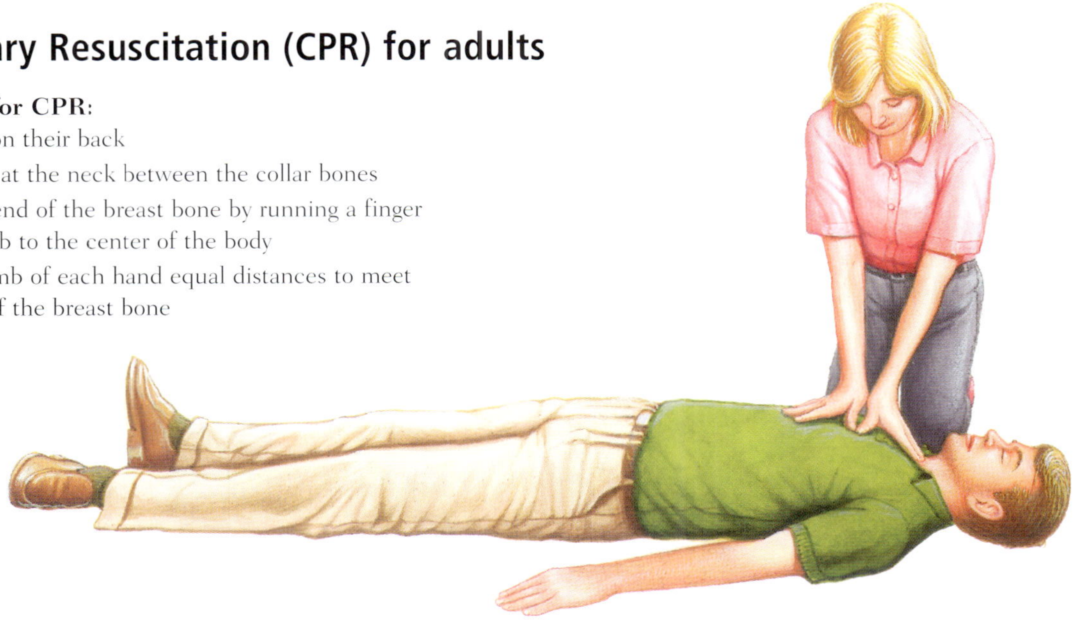

- keep the thumb of the left hand in position and place the heel of the right hand below it
- place the heel of the left hand on top of the right and interlock fingers of both hands.

2 **Commence chest compressions:**
- position yourself vertically above the casualty's chest
- with your arms straight, press down on the breast bone to depress it about 2 inches (4–5 centimeters)
- release the pressure.

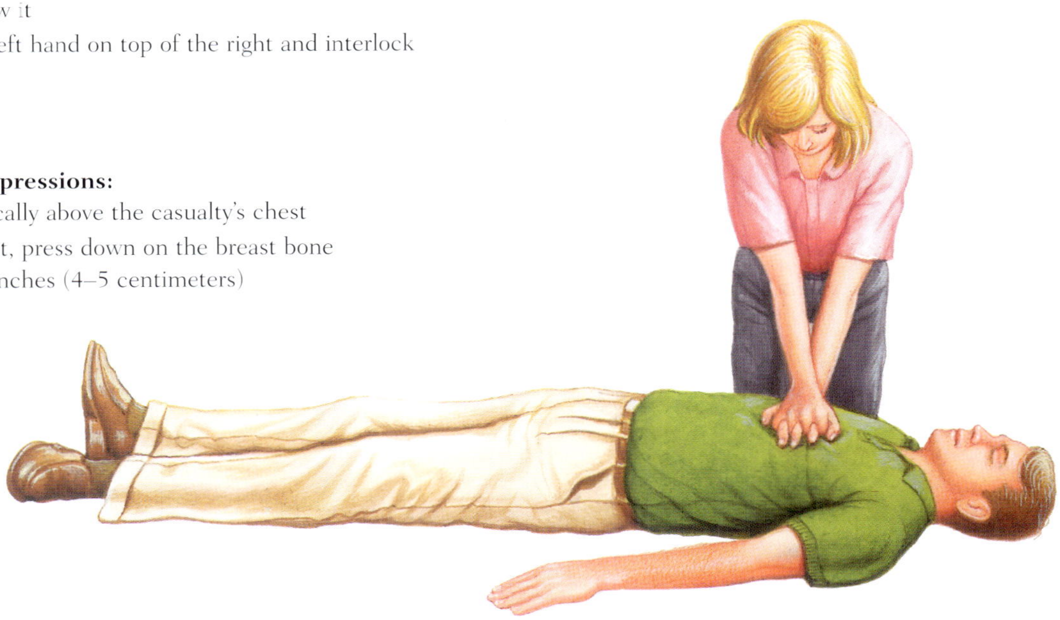

3 **Continue CPR:**
- complete 15 compressions
- give two effective breaths (EAR)
- continue compressions and breaths in a ratio of 15:2 at a rate of 4 cycles per minute
- check the pulse about every minute.

NOTE

CPR combines chest compressions with expired air resuscitation (EAR).

CPR is given when the casualty is not breathing and has no pulse.

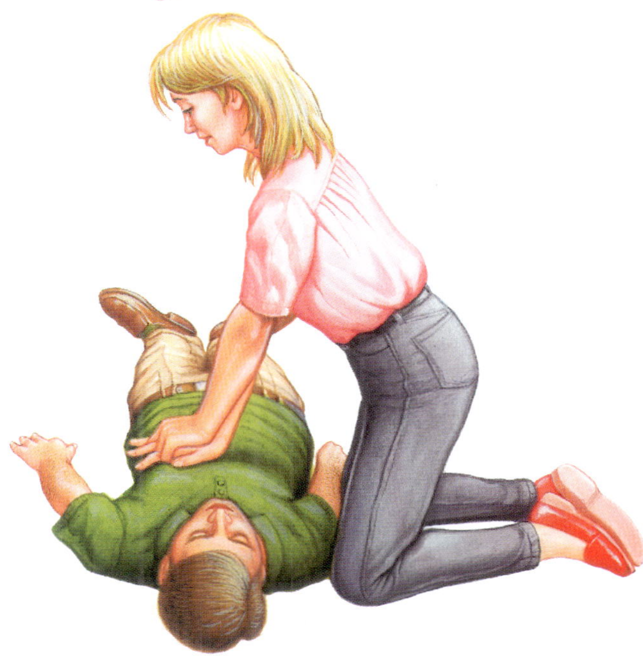

Expired Air Resuscitation for children and infants

EAR for children (aged 1–8) and infants (under 1 year)

If breathing:

1 **Clear the airway:**
- place the infant/child in the recovery position
- tilt the head back very gently
- lift chin and open the mouth
- use a finger to remove any obvious obstruction
- check breathing for up to 10 seconds.

If not breathing:

2 **Open airway:**
- turn casualty onto back
- gently tilt head back slightly
- open mouth and lift chin.

3 **Give EAR (mouth-to-mouth resuscitation):**
- cover the mouth and nose with your mouth
- give two gentle breaths/puffs into the child or infant's mouth and nose
- check for the pulse—for an infant, on the inside upper arm; a child at the neck or wrist
- if pulse is absent, commence CPR
- if pulse is present, continue EAR at 20 breaths per minute
- recheck the pulse and look for other signs of recovery about every minute.

4 **Place in the recovery position when breathing returns.**

Cardiopulmonary Resuscitation for children and infants

CPR for children (aged 1–8)

- use the heel of one hand placed over the lower half of the breast bone to give chest compressions
- compress the chest approximately one-third the depth of the chest
- give 5 chest compressions in 3 seconds
- give one effective breath (EAR)
- continue compressions and breaths in a ratio of 5:1 at a rate of 12 cycles per minute
- check the pulse about every minute.

CPR for infants (under 1 year)

- place the tips of two fingers (index and middle) on the lower half of the breast bone
- compress the chest approximately one-third the depth of the chest
- give 5 chest compressions in 3 seconds
- give one effective breath (EAR)
- continue compressions and breaths in a ratio of 5:1 at a rate of 12 cycles per minute
- check the pulse about every minute.

NOTE

Adult EAR and CPR resuscitation techniques can be safely used on children over the age of 8 years.

For a newborn baby, chest compressions should not be attempted by anyone untrained in neonatal resuscitation.

Handling an emergency

Putting together a First Aid Kit:

A first aid kit should be kept in the home, car and workplace. It is important to ensure that you regularly check the contents of your first aid kit to make sure they are clean, packets are properly sealed, expiry dates have not been exceeded, and that you have replaced any previously used items.

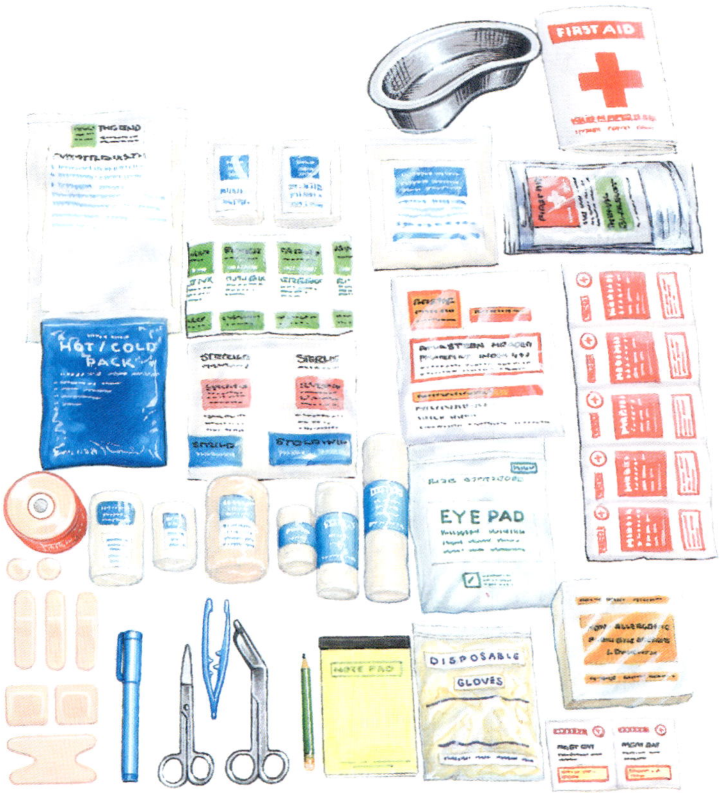

Although it is safer to use sterile bandages and dressings, there will be emergencies when you will not have a first aid kit immediately to hand. You will then have to use whatever materials you can find.

A basic first aid kit may contain:

Bandages

- two triangular bandages
- various crepe or conforming bandages of different sizes

Dressings

- non-adherent dressings
- various wound dressings
- adhesive shapes

Pads

- combine pads
- eye pads

Swabs

- gauze swabs
- alcohol swabs

Other

- adhesive tape
- disposable hand towels
- stainless steel scissors
- saline eyewash
- safety pins
- insect bite and sting lotion
- plastic bags
- stainless steel tweezers
- thermo blanket
- note pad and pencil
- disposable gloves.

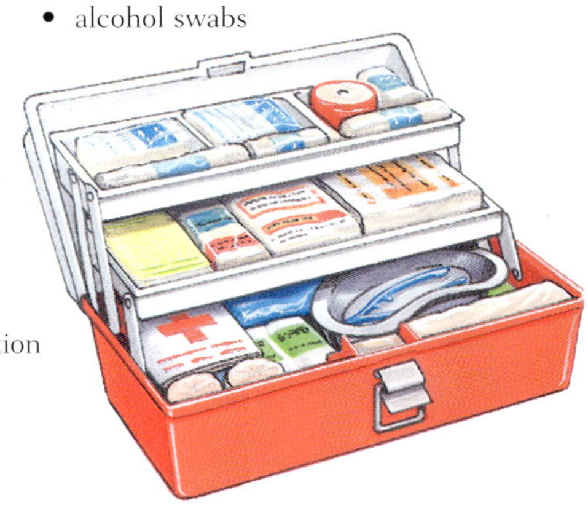

Lifting and moving casualties

Always try to give first aid where the casualty is found, as moving can result in further injury or make existing injuries worse. A casualty should only be moved if there is immediate danger—such as from a collapsing structure, traffic hazards, fire or poisonous fumes.

Moving a casualty

Use the quickest means available. Then make sure:

- there is no further danger
- the casualty has a clear airway and is able to breathe
- bleeding is controlled.

Before moving, consider:

- whether you can handle the size and weight of the person without injury to either of you
- what other help is available
- the type and seriousness of the injuries
- the terrain to be crossed
- the distance the casualty has to be moved
- whether a neck stabilizing collar should be applied before movement
- if travel or motion sickness may make the casualty worse.

WHEN LIFTING A CASUALTY, REMEMBER TO:

- bend at the knees
- keep your back straight and head up
- keep in a balance position
- keep your center of gravity low
- hold the weight close to your body for stability
- take small steps
- work as a team—someone must take the role of leader.

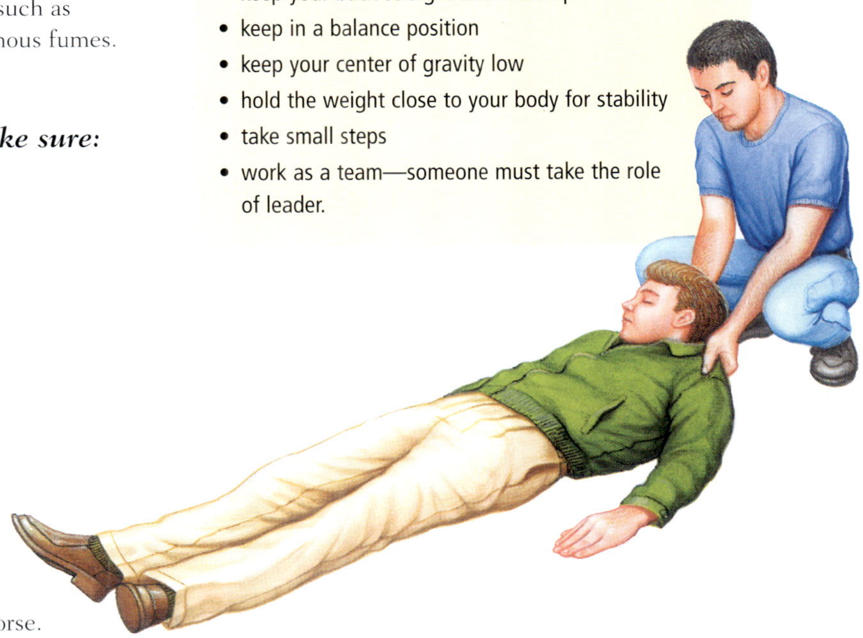

Asthma attack

If casualty is unconscious:

- follow DRABC
- seek medical aid urgently—call the Emergency Services number for your area.

If casualty is conscious:

1 **Make the casualty comfortable:**
- help the casualty into a comfortable position—usually sitting upright and leaning forward
- ensure adequate fresh air
- tell casualty to take slow, deep breaths.

2 **Help with administration of casualty's medication:**
- give 4 puffs of a reliever inhaler—casualty takes a breath with each puff
- if a spacer is available give 4 puffs, one at a time – casualty takes 4 breaths after each puff
- wait 4 minutes
- if no improvement, give another 4 puffs.

3 **If the attack continues:**
- call the Emergency Services number for your area
- in a severe attack, keep giving children 4 puffs every 4 minutes and adults 6–8 puffs every 5 minutes, until an ambulance arrives.

NOTE

If necessary, and where permitted under local legislation/regulations:

- use another person's reliever inhaler or use one from a first aid kit to assist a casualty with a severe asthma attack
- if someone is exhibiting difficulty breathing, but has not previously had an asthma attack, assist in giving 4 puffs of a reliever and continue with 4 puffs every 4 minutes if required, until an ambulance arrives.

Bleeding

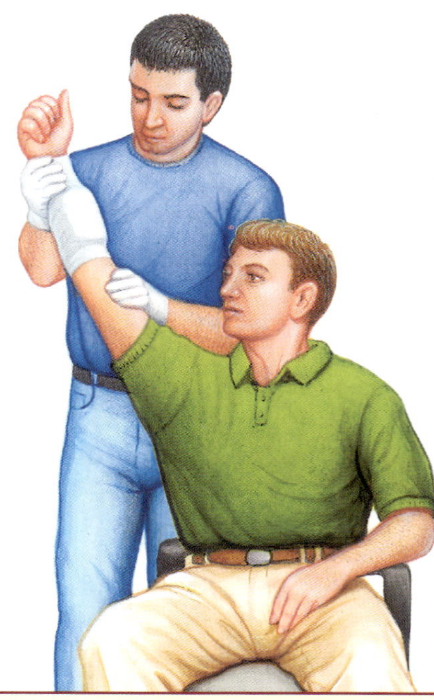

Major wounds

1 **Apply pressure to the wound:**
- remove or cut the casualty's clothing to expose the wound
- apply direct pressure over wound
- cover wound with sterile dressing
- apply a pad.

2 **Raise and support injured part:**
- lie the casualty down
- raise the injured part above the level of the heart
- handle gently if you suspect a fracture.

3 **Bandage wound:**
- apply bandage firmly in place
- apply another dressing or pad if bleeding continues.

4 **Check circulation below the wound.**

5 **Seek medical aid if severe bleeding persists—call the Emergency Services number for your area.**

6 **Treat for shock.**

Minor wounds

- clean the wound thoroughly with gauze soaked in sterile or cooled boiled water, or under running tap water
- apply a non-stick dressing.

WARNING

Do not apply a tourniquet.

If bleeding from a limb does not stop, apply pressure with hand to pressure point.

If there is an embedded object in the wound, apply pressure either side of the wound and place pad around it before bandaging.

Wear gloves, if possible, to guard against infection.

If casualty becomes unconscious, follow DRABC action plan.

Dirty, penetrating or open wounds should be examined by a doctor, as tetanus or other serious infections may result.

Burns

1 **Remove casualty from danger:**
- follow DRABC
- if clothing is on fire STOP, DROP AND ROLL
- pull casualty to the ground
- wrap in blanket or similar
- roll casualty along ground until flames are extinguished.

2 **Cool the burnt area:**
- hold burnt area under cold running water for at least 10 minutes
- if a chemical burn, run cold water over burnt area for at least 20 minutes
- if a bitumen burn, run cold water over burnt area for 30 minutes
- if the burn is to the eye, flush the eye with water for 20 minutes.

3 **Remove any constrictions:**
- remove clothing and jewelry from burnt area (unless sticking to the burn).

4 **Cover the burn:**
- place sterile, non-stick dressing over the burn.

5 **Calm the casualty.**

6 **Seek medical aid urgently—call the Emergency Services number for your area.**

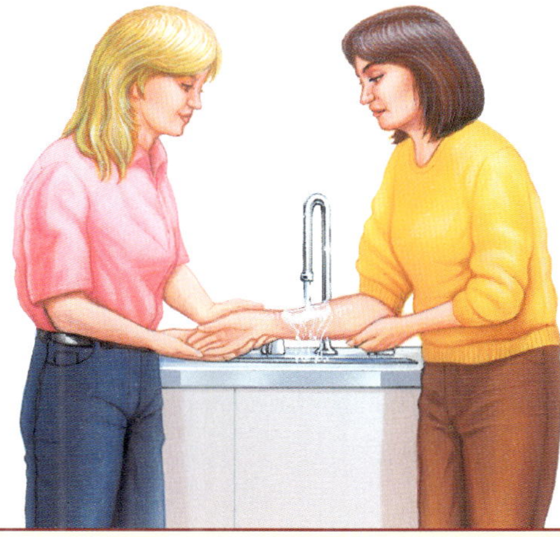

WARNING

Do not apply lotions, ointment or fat to burn.

Do not touch the injured areas or burst any blisters.

Do not remove anything sticking to the burn.

If the burn is large or deep, manage the casualty for shock.

Chest pain or discomfort

1 **Advise casualty to rest:**
- advise the casualty to stop any activity, and sit or lie down and rest.

2 **Casualty to take medication:**
- if casualty has medication for angina, get it and assist casualty in taking it.

3 **Seek urgent medical attention:**
- if unconscious, follow DRABC
- call the Emergency Services number for your area immediately
- do not drive the casualty to hospital, in case of cardiac arrest.

4 **Give aspirin:**
- give 300 milligrams (one tablet) of aspirin in water if ambulance help is delayed for more than 30 minutes
- no aspirin is given to those allergic to it, to asthmatics or to those on anti-coagulant medication (for example warfarin).

5 **Monitor vital signs:**
- monitor pulse, breathing, consciousness and skin color
- be prepared to give CPR.

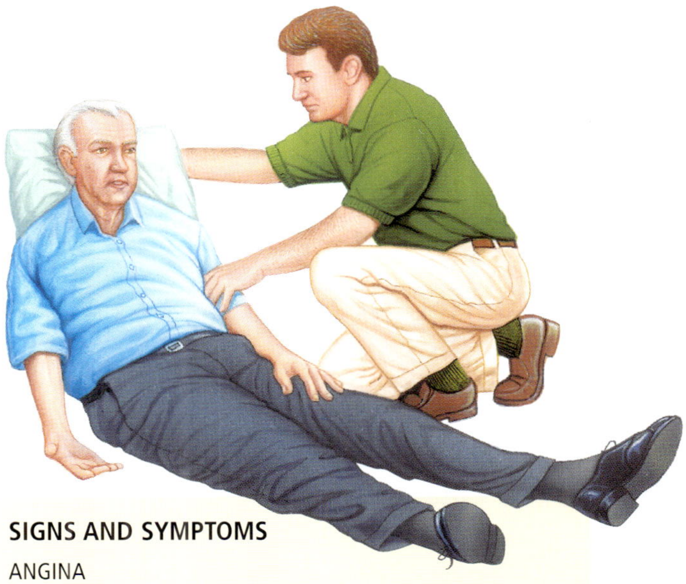

SIGNS AND SYMPTOMS

ANGINA
- pain or discomfort in the center of the chest
- pain radiating to neck and arms
- onset with exercise or emotional stress
- pain relieved by rest or medication.

HEART ATTACK

Signs and symptoms are similar to angina, and may include:
- severe, vise-like chest pain
- anxiety/confusion
- shortness of breath
- nausea/vomiting
- irregular pulse
- sometimes immediate collapse.

NOTE

Always treat chest pain or discomfort as a life-threatening situation

Choking

Adults and children (9 years and over)

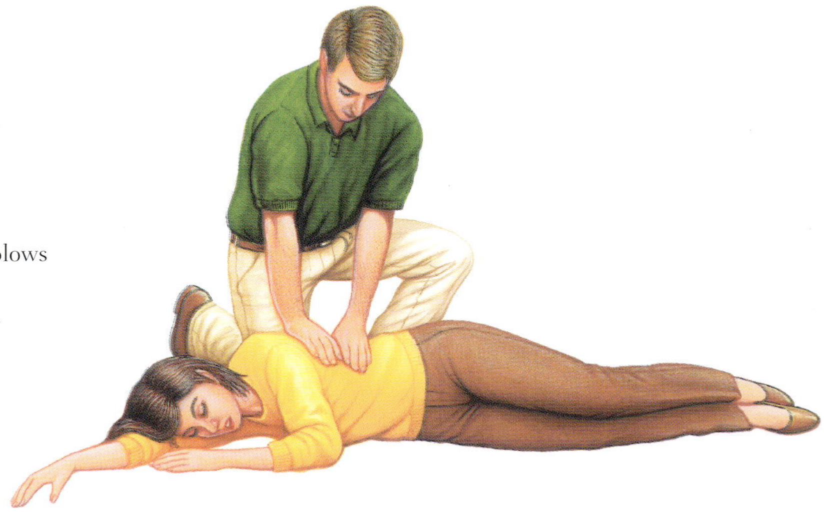

Partial blockage:

- encourage casualty to relax and breathe deeply
- ask casualty to cough
- if unsuccessful, bend casualty well forward and give 4 sharp blows between shoulder blades
- if unsuccessful, place the casualty on their side on the floor—call the Emergency Services number for your area.

Total blockage:

- lie casualty on their side on the floor
- give 4 sharp blows between the shoulder blades
- if unsuccessful, give 4 quick downward lateral chest thrusts (place your hands on the side of the chest, below the casualty's armpit)
- if unsuccessful—call the Emergency Services number for your area
- repeat steps until help arrives or blockage clears
- follow DRABC.

Child (1–8 years)

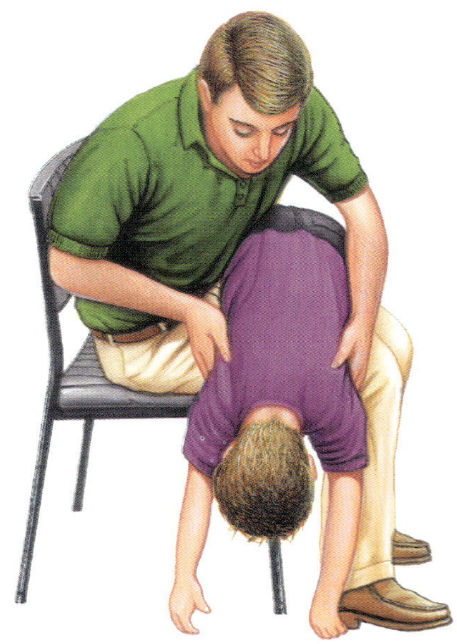

Partial blockage:

- ask the child to try to cough up the obstruction
- if unsuccessful, place child with head low and face down
- give 4 sharp blows between the shoulder blades.

Total blockage:

- place child face down on the floor or across your lap
- give 4 sharp blows between the shoulder blades
- if not breathing, give up to 4 quick, squeezing lateral chest thrusts on both sides simultaneously (place your hands below the child's armpits)
- if unsuccessful—call the Emergency Services number for your area
- repeat above steps until help arrives or blockage clears
- if not breathing, follow DRABC.

Infant (up to 1 year)

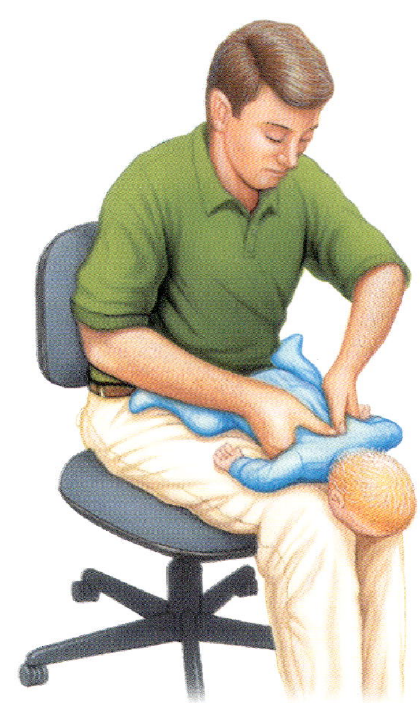

Partial blockage:

- lie infant face down on your forearm with their head low
- support the infant's head and shoulders on your hand
- give 4 sharp slaps between the shoulders
- check in the infant's mouth and remove any obstruction that has come loose
- if unsuccessful—call the Emergency Services number for your area.

Total blockage:

- place the infant face down on your lap
- give 4 sharp slaps between the shoulders and check for signs of breathing
- if not breathing, give 4 quick squeezing lateral chest thrusts on both sides simultaneously (place your hands below infant's armpits)
- check in infant's mouth and remove any obstruction that has come loose
- if unsuccessful—call the Emergency Services number for your area
- repeat above steps until help arrives or blockage clears
- follow DRABC.

Convulsions

Infantile convulsions

1 **During convulsions:**
- place the child on the floor for safety
- do not restrain the child.

2 **After convulsions:**
- follow DRABC
- turn the child onto their side
- remove excessive clothing or wrapping
- get medical aid urgently—call the Emergency Services number for your area.

SIGNS AND SYMPTOMS
- fever
- twitching of face or limbs
- eyes rolling up
- congestion of face and neck
- blue face and lips
- stiffness of body with arched back
- unconsciousness.

WARNING
Do not cool the child by sponging or bathing.

Epileptic seizure

1 **Check breathing and pulse:**
- follow DRABC.

2 **Protect casualty:**
- protect from injury
- do not restrict movement
- do not place anything in the mouth.

3 **Manage injuries:**
- place on side as soon as possible
- manage injuries resulting from seizure
- do not disturb if casualty falls asleep
- continue to check airway, breathing and pulse.

4 **Seek medical aid if:**
- the seizure continues for more than 5 minutes
- another seizure quickly follows
- the person has been injured.

SIGNS AND SYMPTOMS
THE CASUALTY MAY:
- suddenly cry out
- fall to the ground
- have a congested and blue face and neck
- have jerky, spasmodic muscular movements
- froth at the mouth
- bite the tongue
- lose control of bladder and bowel.

Diabetic emergency

If casualty is unconscious:
- follow DRABC
- get medical aid urgently—call the Emergency Services number for your area.

If casualty is conscious, and signs suggest low blood sugar:
- give sweet food or drink (not diet, diabetic or sugar-free drinks) every 15 minutes until casualty recovers or medical aid arrives
- get medical aid urgently—call the Emergency Services number for your area.

If casualty is conscious, and signs suggest high blood sugar:
- allow casualty to self-administer insulin—do not administer but assist if required
- get medical aid urgently—call the Emergency Services number for your area
- give casualty sugar-free fluids to drink, if help is delayed.

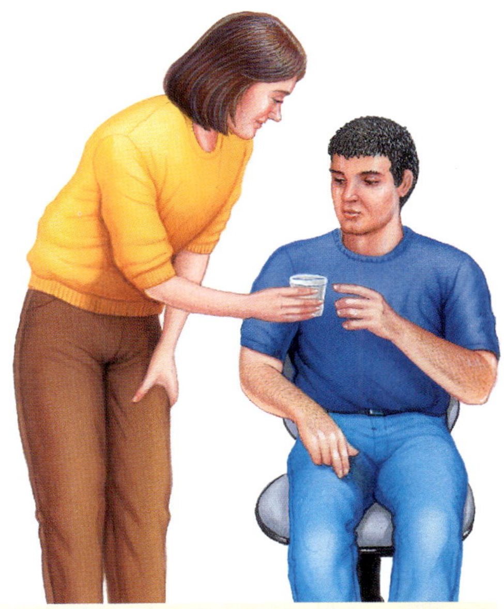

SIGNS AND SYMPTOMS

LOW BLOOD SUGAR
- pale
- hungry
- sweating
- weak
- confused
- aggressive

HIGH BLOOD SUGAR LEVELS
- thirsty
- needs to urinate
- hot dry skin
- smell of acetone on breath

NOTE
If you are not sure which form of diabetic emergency the casualty has, give a sweet drink. If the casualty has a high blood sugar emergency, then giving a sweet drink will not do undue harm.

FIRST AID

Drug overdose

Persons who are under the influence of drugs or alcohol may be at risk of harming themselves or others through dangerous or violent behavior. In such a situation DO NOT put yourself at risk. If there is any risk to yourself call for assistance from Emergency Services. If the casualty collapses, check and maintain their airway. If the casualty becomes unconscious, perform EAR or CPR if required.

Fractures, dislocations, sprains and strains

Fractures and dislocations

1 **Follow DRABC.**

2 **Control any bleeding and cover any wounds.**

3 **Check for fractures:**
- open, closed or complicated.

4 **Ask casualty not to move the injured part.**

5 **Immobilize the fracture:**
- use broad bandages (where possible) to prevent movement at joints above and below the fracture
- support the limb, carefully passing bandages under the natural hollows of the body
- place a padded splint along the injured limb (under the leg for fractured kneecap)
- place padding between the splint and the natural contours of the body and secure tightly
- check that bandages are not too tight (or too loose) every 15 minutes.

6 **For a leg fracture, immobilize the foot and ankle:**
- use figure of eight bandage.

7 **Watch for signs of loss of circulation to foot or hand.**

8 **Seek medical aid**—call the Emergency Services number for your area.

Electric shock

If a person has been electrocuted, check they are not still in contact with the electrical supply or you may also become a casualty.

1 **Switch off power if possible.**

2 **Remove casualty from the electrical supply without directly touching the casualty by using something that will not conduct electricity.**

3 **Follow DRABC.**

4 **Treat casualty as for a burn.**

NOTE

If the collar bone is fractured, support arm on injured side in a sling that goes under the elbow to support the arm against the chest with the fingers pointing up towards the opposite shoulder. If dislocation of a joint is suspected, rest, elevate and apply ice to the joint. It can be difficult for a first aider to tell whether the injury is a fracture, sprain or strain. If in doubt, always treat as a fracture.

SIGNS AND SYMPTOMS

Fracture and dislocation:
- pain at or near the site of the injury
- difficult or impossible normal movement
- loss of power
- deformity or abnormal mobility
- tenderness
- swelling
- discoloration and bruising.

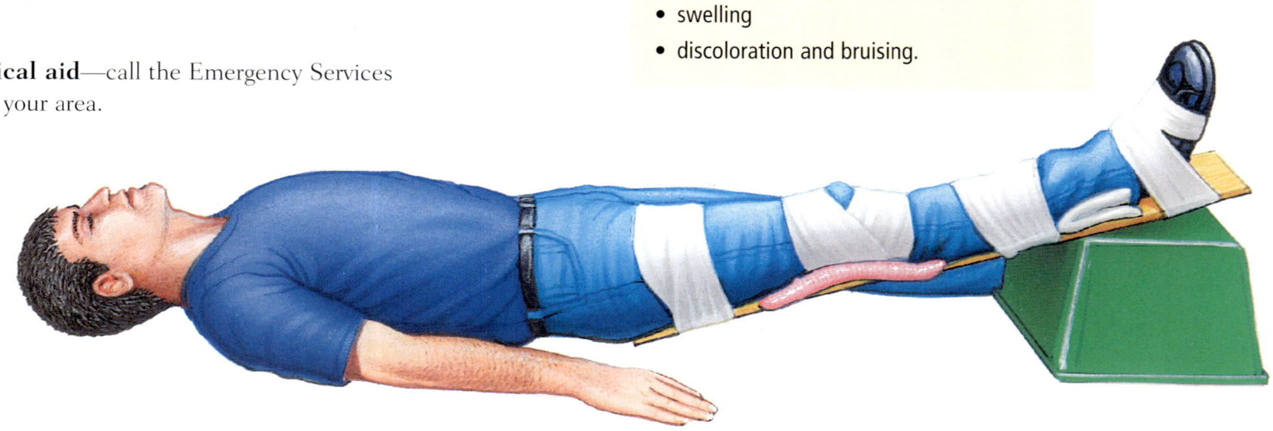

Sprains and strains

1 **Follow DRABC.**

2 **Follow RICE management plan:**
- R—rest casualty
- I—ice pack applied to injury for 15 minutes every 2 hours
- C—compression bandage over the injury
- E—elevate limb.

3 **Seek medical aid**—call the Emergency Services number for your area.

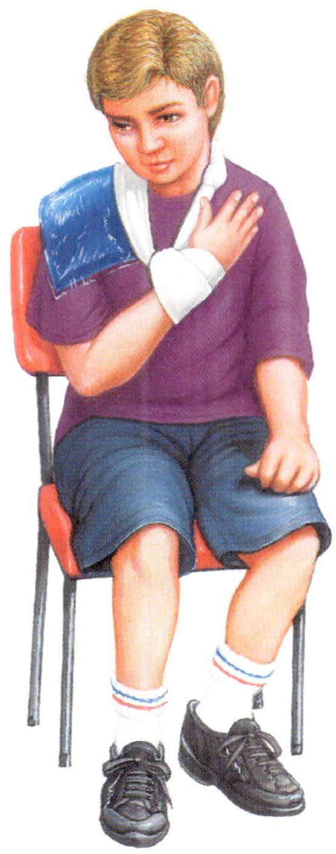

Head, eye and ear injuries

Head injuries

1 **Monitor breathing and pulse:**
- if casualty is unconscious, follow DRABC
- keep casualty's airway open with your fingers (if face badly injured).

2 **Support the head and neck:**
- support the casualty's head and neck during movement in case the spine is injured.

3 **Control bleeding:**
- place a sterile pad or dressing over the wound
- apply direct pressure to the wound unless you suspect a skull fracture
- if blood or fluid comes from ear, secure a sterile dressing lightly in place and allow to drain.

SIGNS AND SYMPTOMS
- altered or abnormal responses to commands and touch
- wounds to the scalp or face
- blood or clear fluid escaping from nose or ears
- pupils becoming unequal in size
- blurred vision
- loss of memory.

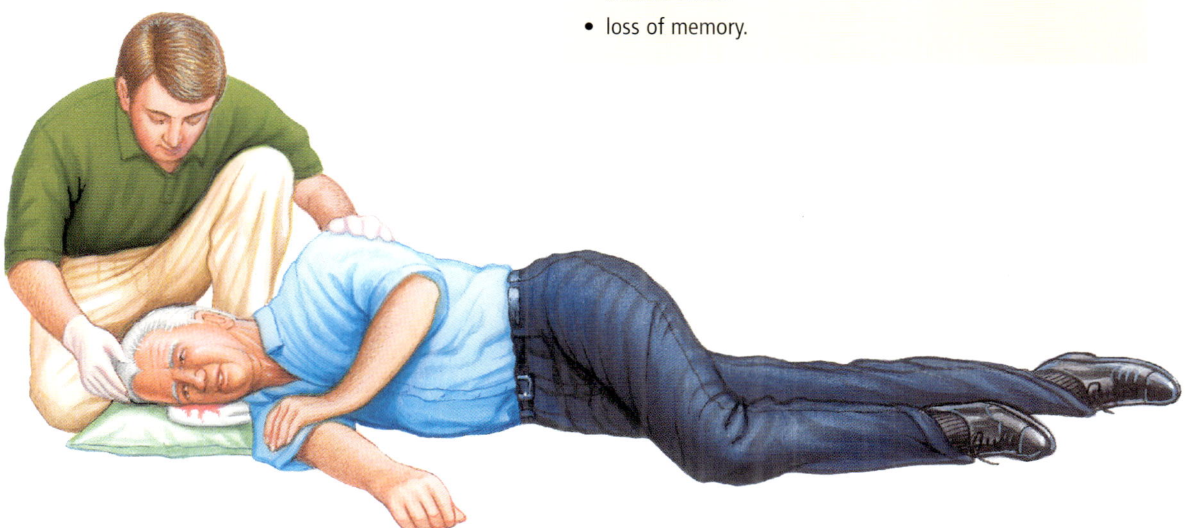

4 **Lie casualty down:**
- place casualty in a comfortable position with head and shoulders slightly raised
- be prepared to turn casualty onto their side if they vomit
- clear the airway quickly after vomiting.

5 **Seek medical aid urgently**—call the Emergency Services number for your area.

WARNING

Wear gloves, if possible, to protect against infection. If bleeding does not stop, reapply pressure to the wound and use another pad on top of the first.

Ear injuries

Ear injuries are common. Sport injuries and falls can damage the outer soft tissue. A direct blow to the head or pushing something into the ear may result in internal injury to the eardrum. Foreign objects—beads, stones, grass seeds—can become lodged in the canal. These can sometimes be removed by tilting the head to the side, pulling down on the earlobe and gently shaking the head.

Bleeding from within the ear:

- follow DRABC
- do not plug the ear canal
- do not administer drops of any kind
- allow fluid to drain freely
- place casualty on their side with the affected ear down
- place a sterile pad between the ear and the ground
- call the Emergency Services number in your area.

> **WARNING**
> Do not put anything in the ear to try and remove an object.

Eye injuries

1 **Support casualty's head:**
- support the casualty's head to keep it as still as possible
- ask casualty to try not to move their eyes.

2 **Flush eye with cool, flowing water:**
- if a chemical or heat burn, or there is smoke in the eyes, flush with water.

3 **Place dressing over eye:**
- place a sterile pad or dressing over the injured eye
- ask casualty to hold this in place
- bandage the dressing in place, covering the injured eye
- if there is an embedded object in the eye, lie casualty on their back, place pad around object and bandage in place.

4 **Seek urgent medical aid**—call the Emergency Services number for your area.

> **WARNING**
> Do not touch the eye or any contact lens.
> Do not allow casualty to rub the eye.
> Do not try to remove any object embedded in the eye.
> Do not apply pressure when bandaging the eye.

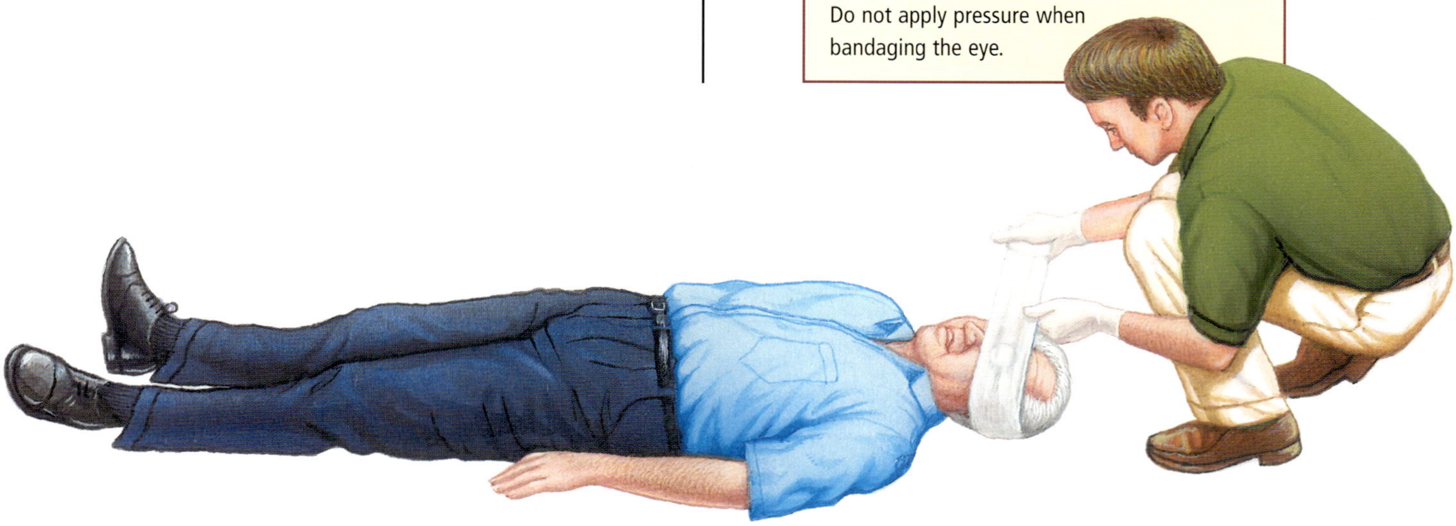

Gassing

Poisoning by inhalation occurs when a person breathes toxic fumes from a gas or substance. Such fumes usually cause breathing problems and can cause unconsciousness.

1 **Move casualty to fresh air being careful not to succumb to the gases or fumes yourself.**

2 **Loosen tight clothing.**

3 **If casualty is unconscious, perform EAR or CPR if required.**

Heat induced conditions

Heat exhaustion:

1 **Lie casualty down:**
- move casualty to lie down in a cool place with circulating air.

2 **Loosen tight clothing:**
- remove unnecessary garments.

3 **Sponge with cold water.**

4 **Give fluids to drink.**

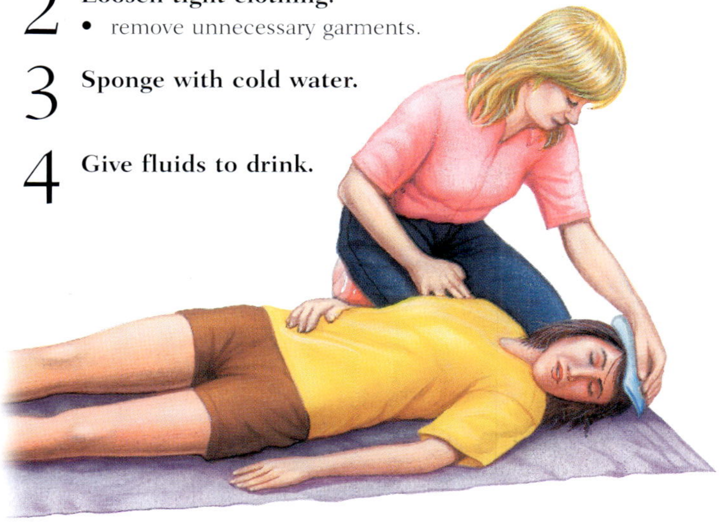

5 **Seek medical aid:**
- if casualty vomits
- if casualty does not recover promptly.

SIGNS AND SYMPTOMS
- feeling hot, exhausted and weak
- persistent headache
- thirst and nausea
- giddiness and faintness
- fatigue
- rapid breathing and shortness of breath
- pale, cool, clammy skin
- rapid, weak pulse.

Heatstroke

1 **Follow DRABC.**

2 **Apply cold packs or ice:**
- apply to neck, groin and armpits.

3 **Cover with a wet sheet.**

ADDITIONAL SYMPTOMS FOR HEATSTROKE:
- high body temperature
- flushed skin
- irritability and mental confusion may progress to seizure and unconsciousness.

Hypothermia

1 **Follow DRABC.**

2 **Remove the casualty to a warm, dry place.**

3 **Protect casualty:**
- protect the casualty and yourself from wind, rain, sleet, cold, as well as wet ground.

4 **Avoid excess activity or movement.**

5 **Maintain casualty in horizontal position.**

6 **Remove wet clothing.**

7 **Warm casualty:**
- place between blankets, in a sleeping bag, or wrap in a space blanket.

8 **Cover the head to maintain body heat.**

9 **Give warm drinks if conscious:**
- do not give alcohol.

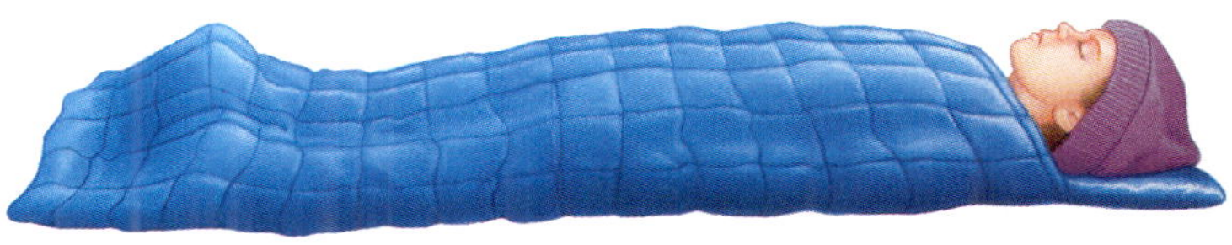

SIGNS AND SYMPTOMS

When body temperature falls, early warning signs may include:
- feeling cold
- shivering
- clumsiness and slurred speech
- apathy and irrational behavior
- heart rate may slow.

WARNING

Call the Emergency Services number for your area if the level of consciousness declines, shivering stops and the pulse is difficult to find. Use any other available forms of warming except direct radiant heat.

FIRST AID

Poisons, bites and stings

Poisoning

Poisons can be ingested, inhaled, absorbed or injected into the body. Most people are aware of potentially lethal venomous snakes or spiders in their area, and that poisonous fumes can be inhaled from a car exhaust or other toxic substance. However, many are not aware that some substances used in the home—cleaning products, pesticides, alcohol and medication—can also cause poisoning.

1 **Determine the type of poisoning:**
- if casualty is conscious, try to determine the type of poison taken.

2 **Seek medical advice urgently**—call the Emergency Services number for your area.

3 **Call the fire department if the area is contaminated with smoke, gases or fumes.**

4 **Monitor airway and breathing:**
- if casualty loses consciousness, follow DRABC.

SIGNS AND SYMPTOMS
- abdominal pain
- drowsiness
- nausea/vomiting
- burning pains from mouth to stomach
- difficulty in breathing
- tight chest
- blurred vision
- odors on breath
- change of skin color with blueness around lips
- sudden collapse.

WARNING

Do not attempt to induce vomiting unless advised to by the Emergency Services in your area.

Do not perform EAR on a casualty poisoned with cyanide.

Spider bites

For funnel-web spider, black widow and brown recluse spider bites follow the steps outlined for snakebites. For red-back spider bites apply an ice pack to the bitten area and seek medical aid.

SIGNS AND SYMPTOMS
- sharp pain
- profuse sweating
- nausea, vomiting, diarrhea.

ADDITIONAL SYMPTOMS FOR FUNNEL-WEB SPIDER BITE
- copious saliva
- confusion leading to coma
- muscular twitching
- breathing difficulty.

ADDITIONAL SYMPTOMS FOR RED-BACK SPIDER BITE
- intense pain, spreading
- small hairs stand on end.

Insect stings

While insect stings can be very painful, they are rarely fatal. They can, however, be dangerous for those who have an allergic reaction.

Management of insect stings:

1 **Follow DRABC.**

2 **If a severe allergic reaction, call the Emergency Services number in your area.**

3 **In cases of bee sting:**
- remove the sting by scraping sideways with your fingernail or the side of a sharp object, such as a knife.

4 **In cases of ticks:**
- if you can see an attached tick, grasp it behind its head as close to the skin as possible, using fine point tweezers or a tick remover
- gently pull the tick straight out with steady pressure
- wash your hands with hot, soapy water and disinfect the tweezers and the bite
- do not attempt to kill the tick with alcohol, petroleum jelly, methylated spirits or any other substance as this causes the tick to inject more bacteria and toxins
- mass infestations of tiny (larval stage) ticks are best removed by soaking for 20 minutes in a deep, warm bath with one cup of bicarbonate of soda added.

5 **Apply a cold compress to relieve pain if necessary.**

6 **Monitor airway, breathing and circulation, as in the DRABC action plan—give CPR if necessary.**

Snakebite

The following is based on the current guidelines on first aid for snakebite as agreed by the World Health Organisation Working Group on Natural Toxins:

1 **Check breathing and pulse:**
- if casualty is unconscious, follow DRABC.

2 **Calm casualty.**

3 **Apply pressure immobilization bandage:**
- apply a firm roller bandage starting just above the fingers or toes and moving up the limb as far as can be reached
- the bandage needs to be firm, as for a sprain, but not too tight.

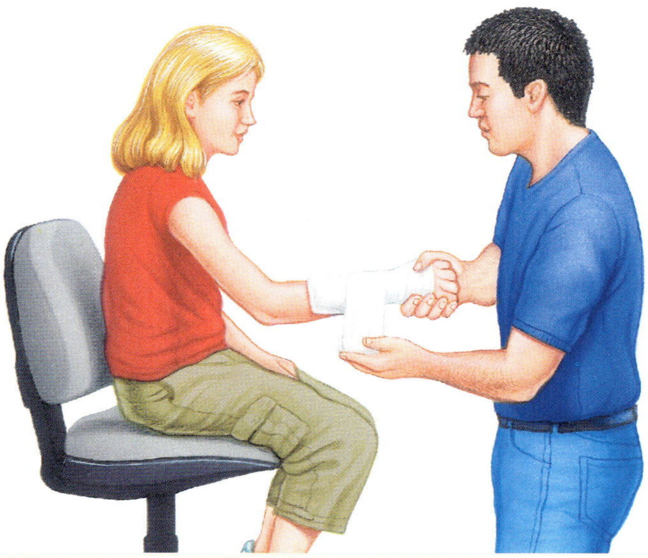

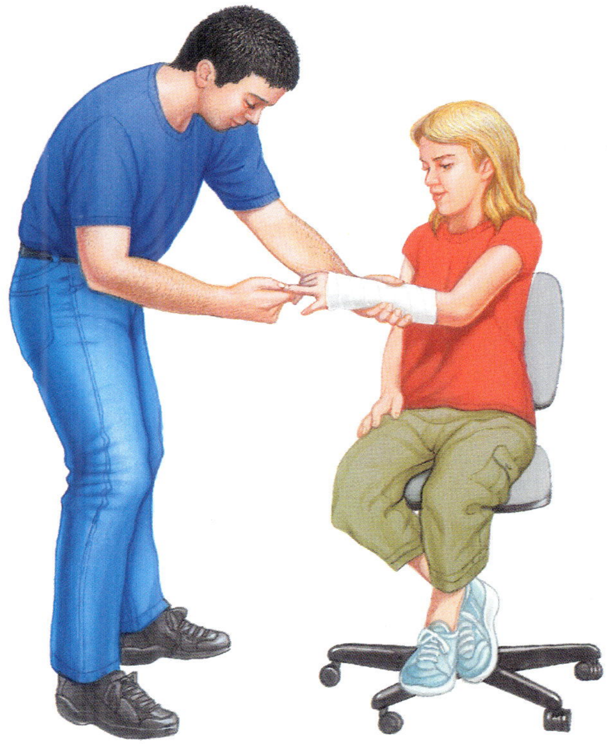

4 **Immobilize casualty:**
- apply a splint to immobilize the bitten limb
- check circulation in fingers or toes
- if possible, ensure the casualty does not move.

5 **Seek medical aid urgently—call the Emergency Services number for your area.**

NOTE

Applying a pressure immobilization bandage and splinting of the limb is recommended for managing snakebites which are not known to cause local tissue damage. These include all Australian snakes, and in other countries, the sea snakes, coral snakes, kraits, non-necrotic snakes, mambas and colubrids.

For bites by snakes that are known to cause local tissue damage, the pressure immobilization method is unlikely to do much harm with the exception of the viper and necrotic cobras. In these cases the management should only be to splint the limb.

NOTE

All snakebites must be treated as potentially lethal. The impact of the venom will be more rapid if one or more of the following cases exists:

- if the casualty is a child
- if the casualty has been physically active immediately following the bite
- if there have been multiple bites
- some species, such as the taipan and Russell's viper, are more likely than others to inject a lethal dose of venom.

SIGNS AND SYMPTOMS

- puncture marks
- nausea, vomiting, diarrhea
- headache
- double or blurred vision
- breathing difficulties
- drowsiness, giddiness
- pain or tightness in chest or abdomen
- respiratory weakness or arrest
- local tissue damage caused by snakes (e.g. some cobra venoms, many of the viper venoms and a few of the elapid venoms); Australian snakes do not cause tissue damage.

WARNING

Do not cut bitten area or try to suck venom out of wound.

Do not use a constrictive bandage (i.e. arterial tourniquet).

Do not try to catch the snake.

Do not wash venom off the skin as retained venom will assist identification (for Australian snakes venom only).

Shock

1 **Lie casualty down:**
- protect the casualty from cold ground
- calm the casualty.

2 **Assess casualty:**
- follow DRABC.

3 **Seek medical aid urgently**—call the Emergency Services number for your area.

4 **Manage any injuries:**
- control any bleeding
- raise the legs (unless fractured) above heart level
- dress any wounds or burns
- immobilize fractures.

5 **Ensure comfort:**
- loosen any tight clothing around neck, chest or waist
- maintain body warmth (do not heat)
- if thirsty, moisten lips (but give nothing to drink or eat).

6 **Monitor breathing and pulse:**
- maintain a clear and open airway.

7 **Place casualty in recovery position:**
- place in recovery position if casualty has difficulty breathing, is likely to vomit, or becomes unconscious.

SIGNS AND SYMPTOMS
- weak, rapid pulse
- cold, clammy skin
- rapid breathing
- faintness/dizziness
- nausea
- pale face, fingernails, lips.

Spinal injury

1 **Do not move casualty unless they are in danger.**

2 **Check breathing and pulse:**
- if casualty is unconscious, follow DRABC.

3 **Support the casualty's head and neck at all times:**
- place hands on the side of the head until other support is arranged
- apply a cervical or improvised collar to minimize neck movement.

4 **Give reassurance:**
- calm casualty.

5 **Seek medical aid urgently—call the Emergency Services number for your area.**

SIGNS AND SYMPTOMS
- pain at or below site of injury
- loss of sensation, or abnormal sensation, such as tingling, in hands or feet
- loss of movement or impaired movement below site of injury.

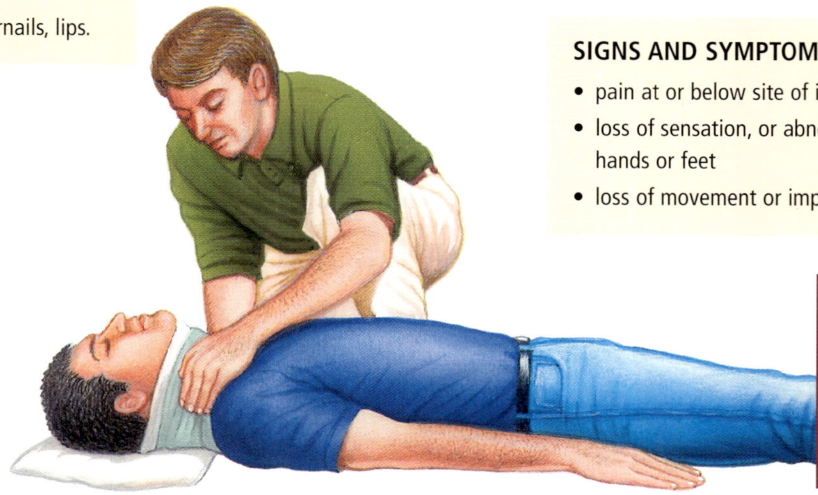

WARNING

If casualty is unconscious, place in recovery position.

If casualty is conscious, do not move, but support head.

Symptoms guide

This section provides information on common symptoms and associated diseases. You may find it useful to refer to this symptom guide if you would like to find out more information on a particular symptom, and what it may mean.

This symptoms guide **does not** replace your doctor, and should not be used as a guide to diagnosing medical conditions in yourself or a family member. Refer to your doctor or other appropriately qualified health professionals if you believe you or another person may have one of the diseases described.

LIST OF SYMPTOM ENTRIES

Abdominal distension
Abdominal pain
Arm and shoulder problems
Back deformity
Back pain
Bad breath (halitosis)
Blackouts, including fainting
Bones, fracture/brittleness
Bowel, bleeding from
Breast Lump
Breathing problems
Bruising
Chest pain
Constipation
Cough
Cramp
Diarrhea
Dizziness
Ear pain (earache)
Eye problems
Eyelid problems
Eyesight problems
Facial pain
Fatigue
Fever
Flatulence
Foot and ankle problems
Genital itching
Genital pain
"Glands", swollen
Gums, bleeding
Hair problems
Hallucinations
Hand and wrist problems
Headache
Hearing loss (deafness)
Heartburn
Hip problems
Hot flashes/flushes
Jaundice
Knee problems
Leg problems
Memory loss
Menstrual problems
Nail abnormalities
Nausea and vomiting
Neck problems
Nosebleed
Numbness and tingling
Palpitations
Seizures (known as "fits", including convulsions)
Sexual function problems
Skin problems
Sleep disturbances
Snoring
Speech problems
Swallowing problems
Throat problems
Tongue problems
Toothache
Tremor
Urination, difficult
Urination, frequent
Urination, painful
Vaginal problems
Voice problems
Weakness and paralysis
Weight gain
Weight loss
Wounds or sores, non-healing

How to use this guide

Symptoms are listed alphabetically, and usually contain the name of the affected body part. For example, if you would like information on pain in the eye, refer to *Eye problems* to find entries on pain and other problems relating to the eye.

Each entry includes a list of descriptions of various ways in which the symptom may be experienced. Look down the *Symptom characteristics* column until you find a description that best matches the symptom in which you are interested.

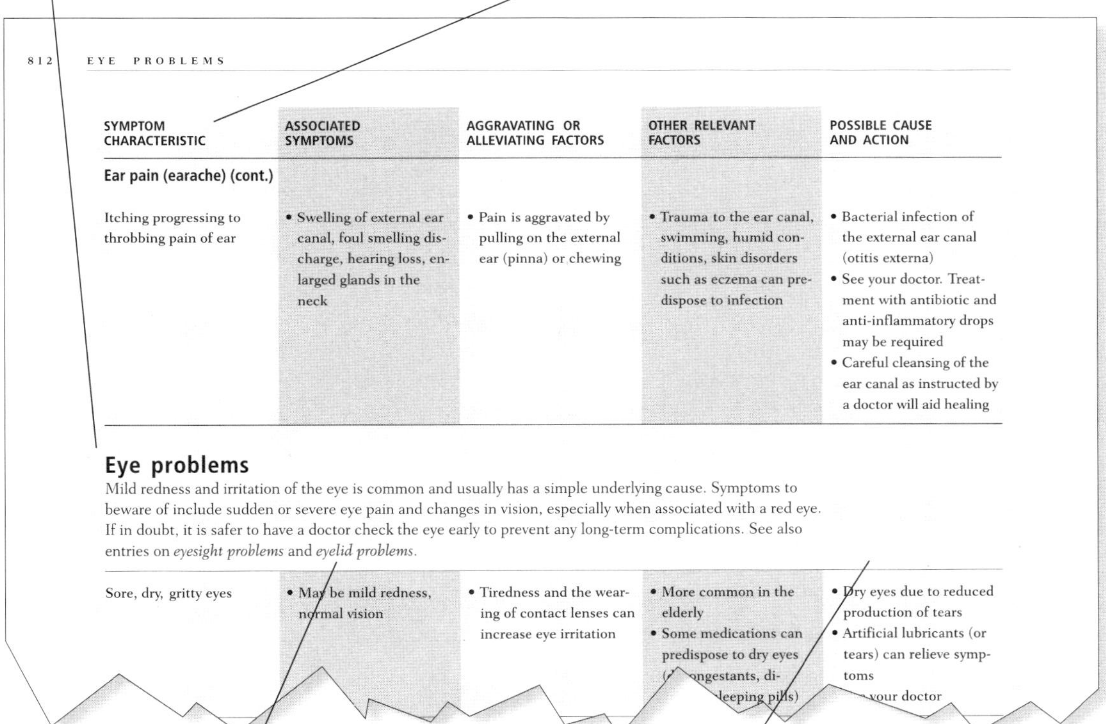

812 EYE PROBLEMS

SYMPTOM CHARACTERISTIC	ASSOCIATED SYMPTOMS	AGGRAVATING OR ALLEVIATING FACTORS	OTHER RELEVANT FACTORS	POSSIBLE CAUSE AND ACTION
Ear pain (earache) (cont.)				
Itching progressing to throbbing pain of ear	• Swelling of external ear canal, foul smelling discharge, hearing loss, enlarged glands in the neck	• Pain is aggravated by pulling on the external ear (pinna) or chewing	• Trauma to the ear canal, swimming, humid conditions, skin disorders such as eczema can predispose to infection	• Bacterial infection of the external ear canal (otitis externa) • See your doctor. Treatment with antibiotic and anti-inflammatory drops may be required • Careful cleansing of the ear canal as instructed by a doctor will aid healing

Eye problems
Mild redness and irritation of the eye is common and usually has a simple underlying cause. Symptoms to beware of include sudden or severe eye pain and changes in vision, especially when associated with a red eye. If in doubt, it is safer to have a doctor check the eye early to prevent any long-term complications. See also entries on *eyesight problems* and *eyelid problems*.

Sore, dry, gritty eyes	• May be mild redness, normal vision	• Tiredness and the wearing of contact lenses can increase eye irritation	• More common in the elderly • Some medications can predispose to dry eyes (decongestants, di... sleeping pills)	• Dry eyes due to reduced production of tears • Artificial lubricants (or tears) can relieve symptoms ... your doctor

There is also a list of other symptoms that may be associated with the main symptom. Symptoms listed in the *Associated symptoms* column may not all occur at once, and not all of them must be present for the medical problem suggested under *possible cause* to be a likely explanation for the symptoms.

Diseases mentioned in the *possible cause* column suggest problems that may cause the symptoms described, but do not represent definitive diagnoses. Not all disease possibilities are listed, especially those that are less common.

You can read more about many of these symptoms, diseases and illnesses in the main A-Z section of this book.

The symptoms appear in alphabetical order and are listed above.

Abdominal distension

A wide variety of conditions may cause distension of the abdomen—causes range from pregnancy to conditions such as obstruction of the bowel that require urgent medical attention. More than one cause may be present at the same time. See also entries on *abdominal pain* and *flatulence*.

SYMPTOM CHARACTERISTIC	ASSOCIATED SYMPTOMS	AGGRAVATING OR ALLEVIATING FACTORS	OTHER RELEVANT FACTORS	POSSIBLE CAUSE AND ACTION
Mild distension, possibly with bloated sensation	• Flatulence, increased "rumbling" noises from the gut, abdominal discomfort	• Symptoms may be worsened by eating foods that ferment (e.g. the non-sugar sweetener sorbitol, milk, ice cream, fruit juices, onions, beans, celery, carrots, bananas, raisins, pretzels, bagels, wheat germ)	• Occasionally symptoms may occur in people with a history of malabsorption (inability to absorb foods properly in the gut) • A diet low in indigestible carbohydrates and lactose is less prone to fermentation and may alleviate the symptoms	• Increased gas in the stomach, small bowel or colon (flatulence) due to another disease or in a healthy person due to excessive fermentation of food by bacteria in the gut • See your doctor if you are worried or if symptoms persist
Generalized distension of the abdomen, with fullness in the flanks; may develop over days or weeks	• Shortness of breath and diminishing exercise tolerance (if heart disease is the cause) • Loss of appetite, nausea and tiredness (if liver disease is the cause) • Loss of appetite, weight loss and a general feeling of being unwell (if a tumor is the cause)		• Symptoms are more likely in a person with a history of heart problems, liver disease, heavy alcohol use, which can cause liver damage, or cancer	• Increased build up of fluid in the abdomen (ascites) • Causes include tumors, cirrhosis of the liver, heart failure • See your doctor at once
Rapidly developing generalized distension of the abdomen	• Rapid onset of abdominal pain that comes and goes in waves • Total constipation (inability to pass solids or gas) • Vomiting		• Bowel obstruction occurs more commonly in people who have had abdominal surgery, a hernia or other bowel problems	• Bowel obstruction • See your doctor at once
Distension in the lower area of the abdomen or pelvic area	• Difficulty passing urine, vague abdominal pain		• Ovarian cancer is more common with age and occasionally occurs in women under 35 years of age	• Pregnancy, ovarian cyst, tumor of the ovary or uterus, bladder distension due to retention of urine • See your doctor at once
Lump next to the umbilicus, near a surgical scar, or (in men) in the groin	• Painless	• Appears when straining or coughing or when you stand up (i.e. when pressure in the abdomen rises); lump then disappears spontaneously or can be pushed back	• Weakness in the abdominal wall may be caused by a congenital defect in the abdominal wall, a surgical incision, or muscle weakness due to obesity, pregnancy or wasting	• Hernia or inguinal hernia See your doctor

SYMPTOM CHARACTERISTIC	ASSOCIATED SYMPTOMS	AGGRAVATING OR ALLEVIATING FACTORS	OTHER RELEVANT FACTORS	POSSIBLE CAUSE AND ACTION
Lump that remains visible whether or not you are straining, coughing or standing	• Associated symptoms, if present, will depend on the cause			• Enlargement of an abdominal organ (e.g. liver or spleen), tumor, hernia that has become trapped • See your doctor at once

Abdominal pain

Abdominal pain may be related to any abdominal organ, and the type of pain will vary widely, depending on the cause. It is important to see your doctor or emergency room immediately if abdominal pain is severe or of sudden onset, since many common causes require immediate surgical intervention. See also entry on *abdominal distension*.

SYMPTOM CHARACTERISTIC	ASSOCIATED SYMPTOMS	AGGRAVATING OR ALLEVIATING FACTORS	OTHER RELEVANT FACTORS	POSSIBLE CAUSE AND ACTION
Episodes of pain in the upper abdomen, typically central and characterized as a burning sensation or heartburn	• Bitter fluid may return into the mouth from the stomach	• Symptoms may be aggravated by lying down • May be alleviated by antacids	• Symptoms may be brought on by stooping, straining or lying down	• Esophagitis caused by reflux • See your doctor
Episodes of pain in the upper abdomen, typically central but may also be on the right or left; may be characterized as a burning or gnawing sensation		• Pain is typically related to food, and may either occur before meals and be relieved by eating, antacids or vomiting, or may occur shortly after meals, sometimes making the person feel reluctant to eat	• The incidence of peptic ulcer is highest among people aged 30–50 years; may occur in teenagers and rarely in children • Ulcers are most frequently caused by a *Helicobacter pylori* infection or by the use of non-steroidal anti-inflammatory drugs	• Peptic ulcer • See your doctor
Episodes of colicky or constant pain in the upper abdomen, typically central or on the right side and of rapid onset; pain may radiate around the right side of the body into the shoulder and typically lasts for hours at a time	• Nausea • Sometimes vomiting • Sometimes yellowness of the skin may ensue (jaundice), possibly with darkened urine and pale stools	• This pain is not relieved by vomiting or antacids	• An episode may follow eating a fatty meal • Occurs in adults; women on oral contraceptives are at higher risk • May have a family history of gallstones	• Gallstones • See your doctor
Upper abdominal pain, gradually worsening and typically constant over hours or days before subsiding; pain may radiate directly through to the back	• Nausea, vomiting	• May be aggravated by food, drink or vomiting • Typically aggravated by lying down and alleviated by sitting up and leaning forward	• Symptoms may follow a bout of heavy drinking • May have background of alcohol use or gallstones	• Sudden-onset (acute) pancreatitis • See your doctor at once
Persistent upper abdominal pain, typically characterized as a constant background pain; pain may radiate directly through to the back	• May later develop weight loss or pale stools	• Pain may be aggravated by lying down and alleviated by sitting up and leaning forward	• May have background of alcohol use or gallstones	• Long-term (chronic) pancreatitis or pancreatic tumor • See your doctor

SYMPTOM CHARACTERISTIC	ASSOCIATED SYMPTOMS	AGGRAVATING OR ALLEVIATING FACTORS	OTHER RELEVANT FACTORS	POSSIBLE CAUSE AND ACTION
Abdominal pain (cont.)				
Constant discomfort on the right side of upper abdomen, typically felt as a dull ache	• Nausea, loss of appetite, tiredness, fever, eventually jaundice • Other symptoms depend on the cause • Shortness of breath, diminishing exercise tolerance and ankle swelling may occur with a heart problem • Loss of appetite, weight loss and a general feeling of being unwell may occur with a tumor		• Liver symptoms are more likely to occur in people with a history of heart disease, heavy alcohol users, cancer, recent intravenous drug use or blood transfusion, overseas travel, recent contact with a person with a similar illness	• Liver pain due to heart failure (causing swelling of the liver), viral hepatitis, hepatitis caused by heavy alcohol use, liver tumor • See your doctor
Rapid onset of diffuse cramping pains, typically centered around the central abdomen	• Diarrhea, nausea, vomiting, fever		• Symptoms may follow overseas travel or eating carelessly prepared food	• Gastroenteritis or food poisoning • Drink plenty of fluids • See your doctor if you are worried or if symptoms persist
Rapid onset of pain on the right side of the lower abdomen; the pain may either be constant or occur in waves; pain typically starts around the middle of the abdomen, then moves to the right lower abdomen	• Loss of appetite, nausea, vomiting, low fever		• Most common in children or young adults	• Appendicitis • This is a medical emergency • Go to the emergency room or call an ambulance immediately
Pains in the lower abdomen that may be cramping, occur in waves, or vague discomfort	• Change in bowel habit • May have blood or mucus in the stools	• Pain may be worse before defecation and alleviated by defecation or passing wind	• Cancer is a common cause in patients over 50, but can also occur in younger people • In older patients (> 70 years of age), bowel obstruction is one of the most common causes of abdominal pain requiring surgical intervention	• Inflammatory bowel disease or tumor of the colon • See your doctor • If severe pain, abdominal distension and total constipation (inability to pass solids or gas) occurs, this is a medical emergency • Go to the emergency room or call an ambulance immediately
Sudden severe pain on one flank, typically radiating from the loins around to the front of the abdomen and down to the groin	• May have a change in the color of your urine or blood in the urine • May be associated with nausea	• Passing a stone in the urine may cause severe pain	• May have a predisposing factor such as gout	• Kidney stone • This is a medical emergency • Go to the emergency room or call an ambulance immediately

SYMPTOM CHARACTERISTIC	ASSOCIATED SYMPTOMS	AGGRAVATING OR ALLEVIATING FACTORS	OTHER RELEVANT FACTORS	POSSIBLE CAUSE AND ACTION
Loin pain, typically a dull ache	• Fever • Passing urine more frequently • Painful urination		• May be a predisposing condition like an abnormality in the urinary tract or a disorder that impairs immune defenses • In women and infants, may occur without a predisposing factor	• Pyelonephritis (kidney infection) • See your doctor at once
Lower abdomen or pelvic pains in women	• Associated symptoms will depend on the underlying cause; there may be menstrual changes or difficulties or vaginal discharge		• Pain may be related to the menstrual cycle • Onset and severity will depend on underlying cause	• Problem of uterus or ovaries (e.g. endometriosis) • See your doctor
Severe, sharp, well localized abdominal pain; pain may be of abrupt onset, but sometimes is more gradual		• Pain aggravated by movement or coughing	• Predisposing conditions include peptic ulcer, abdominal aneurysm, hernia	• Peritonitis caused by appendicitis, perforation of a peptic ulcer, complication of abdominal aneurysm, strangulation or twisting of the bowel • This is a medical emergency. Go to the emergency room or call an ambulance immediately
Bouts of severe abdominal pain in an infant	• Screaming and drawing up the legs during the bouts of pain, vomiting, red stools		• Intussusception is most common during the first two years of life	• Intussusception • This is a medical emergency. Go to the emergency room or call an ambulance immediately

Arm and shoulder problems

Symptoms in the arm or shoulder often result from overuse, injury, and falls. Sporting activities and occupational tasks are common causes of problems in this area. Pain in the arm can also be a symptom of a heart attack, so see your doctor immediately if you experience unexplained pain. See also entry on *chest pain*.

SYMPTOM CHARACTERISTIC	ASSOCIATED SYMPTOMS	AGGRAVATING OR ALLEVIATING FACTORS	OTHER RELEVANT FACTORS	POSSIBLE CAUSE AND ACTION
Pain in the shoulder with movement, especially lifting the arm over the head; may occur following an injury or activity involving repetitive movements	• Tenderness and swelling in the area, weakness of the arm	• Symptoms are aggravated by further movement • Pushing and twisting movements (e.g. reaching behind the back, dressing) are often painful	• Lifting, twisting and sporting activities often cause these problems	• Tendinitis • Rest and apply ice • See your doctor if you are worried or if pain persists
Sharp pain in the arm or shoulder following vigorous activity	• Swelling, stiffness, tenderness	• Symptoms may be aggravated by movement of the arm	• Often occurs when sudden or unfamiliar stresses are placed on the arm (e.g. falls, lifting heavy objects, new exercise)	• Muscle strain or ligament sprain • Rest and apply ice • See your doctor if you are worried or if symptoms persist

SYMPTOM CHARACTERISTIC	ASSOCIATED SYMPTOMS	AGGRAVATING OR ALLEVIATING FACTORS	OTHER RELEVANT FACTORS	POSSIBLE CAUSE AND ACTION
Arm and shoulder problems (cont.)				
Sudden pain on the top of the shoulder; may be worse upon waking	• May be some redness and tenderness, limited movement	• Symptoms are usually aggravated by raising arm out to the side or twisting movement	• Can occur with overuse, infections, arthritis, injuries	• Bursitis • See your doctor for advice
Gradually worsening elbow pain that occurs with repeated movements	• Pain may spread down into the muscles in the forearm • May be tender to touch	• Symptoms are aggravated by further movement and alleviated by rest	• More likely to occur in those with weak wrist and arm muscles, and in tennis players using an incorrect backhand stroke	• Tennis elbow • Rest and apply ice • See your doctor if you are worried or if pain persists
Increasing shoulder pain and stiffness that has worsened over several weeks	• Limited movement in all directions	• Symptoms are aggravated by movement in most directions, especially away from the body	• Often occurs in older people, especially following an injury or shoulder/chest surgery	• Frozen shoulder • See your doctor
Intense arm pain following a fall or direct blow to the arm	• Arm or shoulder may be deformed	• Symptoms are aggravated by any attempt at movement		• Fracture or dislocation • See your doctor at once
Persistent, severe pain radiating from the chest down the left arm	• Shortness of breath, nausea, sweating • Feeling of chest being squeezed	• Pain does not change with arm movements	• Increased likelihood in a person who has previously had a heart attack or with a history of coronary heart disease	• Myocardial infarction (heart attack) • This is a medical emergency. Go to the emergency room or call an ambulance immediately

Back deformity

Abnormalities of the spine may occur due to an acquired disease, as a developmental problem in growing children, or as part of one of the syndromes of multiple anatomical abnormalities that are caused by genetic defects. Any unusual appearance of the spine should be checked by a doctor.

SYMPTOM CHARACTERISTIC	ASSOCIATED SYMPTOMS	AGGRAVATING OR ALLEVIATING FACTORS	OTHER RELEVANT FACTORS	POSSIBLE CAUSE AND ACTION
Sideways curvature of the spine (scoliosis) in an adolescent, visible while sitting erect and straight; spine is S-shaped or corkscrew shaped	• Postural problems, pain, fatigue of back muscles, visible disfigurement in severe cases		• The cause of idiopathic scoliosis unknown, but it is thought to be due to complex inherited causes • The condition is twice as common in females as males, and usually appears at around puberty	• Idiopathic scoliosis
Exaggeration of the normal outward curve of the spine at the level of the rib cage (kyphosis)	• Poor posture, fatigue or pain in back muscles		• Abnormal curvature may first appear in a young growing child	• Exaggerated kyphosis ("hunchback"), due to injury or a developmental abnormality • See your doctor
Exaggeration of the normal inward curve of the spine at the lower back (lordosis)	• Poor posture, fatigue or pain in back muscles		• Abnormal curvature may first appear in a young growing child	• Exaggerated lordosis ("swayback"), due to injury or a developmental abnormality • See your doctor

SYMPTOM CHARACTERISTIC	ASSOCIATED SYMPTOMS	AGGRAVATING OR ALLEVIATING FACTORS	OTHER RELEVANT FACTORS	POSSIBLE CAUSE AND ACTION
Sideways curvature of the spine (scoliosis) which worsens over time	• Difficulty running, jumping, hopping, muscle weakness, enlarged calf muscles, breathing problems • Children use their arms to pull themselves up from the ground after sitting or lying down • Spinal curvature may become painful over time		• Duchenne muscular dystrophy is a genetic disorder affecting only boys • The condition is present at birth, but signs only appear between 3–5 years of age	• Duchenne muscular dystrophy • See your doctor
Gradual development of a exaggerated outwards curvature (kyphosis) or sideways curvature of the spine (scoliosis) in an elderly person	• Multiple fractures of the vertebrae may result in "dowager's hump" • New vertebral fractures may be very painful, but pain usually subsides within weeks to months		• Osteoporosis is more common in women than men	• Osteoporosis • See your doctor
Exaggeration of the outward curve of the spine at the rib cage level (kyphosis), with flattening of the normal inward curve of the lower back in a young person with pain and stiffness	• Back stiffness and pain, chest pain arthritis and pain in other joints (e.g. knee, hip, heel), iritis, cardiovascular problems, bowel problems • Occasionally fatigue, fever, night sweats or loss of appetite may occur	• Stiffness may be worse in the morning	• Ankylosing spondylitis runs in families and is more common in men than women • The condition is relatively common in children in developing countries, but tends to occur in young adults in industrialized countries	• Ankylosing spondylitis • See your doctor

Back pain

The majority of cases of backache relate to the lower back. Low back pain is one of the most common symptoms that people experience. In adults, a majority of cases are based on a mechanical problem relating to posture, muscle strain, arthritis or disk problems. Sometimes, no physical cause is found.

In some circumstances, prompt and adequate early treatment of acute mechanical back pain may help to avoid progression to ongoing long-term pain, so do not hesitate to see your doctor. Back pain which is progressive, severe, persistent or associated with neurological symptoms such as weakness, numbness or tingling sensations always warrants a visit to a doctor. See also entry on *numbness and tingling*.

SYMPTOM CHARACTERISTIC	ASSOCIATED SYMPTOMS	AGGRAVATING OR ALLEVIATING FACTORS	OTHER RELEVANT FACTORS	POSSIBLE CAUSE AND ACTION
Vague back ache in an adult		• Tends to worsen as the day progresses	• More common with obesity, late pregnancy, or in people who are inactive or unfit	• Postural backache • If symptoms are mild, try gentle physical activity (e.g. swimming), maintain good posture when sitting and standing, avoid remaining in one position for long periods when sitting • See your doctor or a physical therapist if you are worried or if symptoms persist

SYMPTOM CHARACTERISTIC	ASSOCIATED SYMPTOMS	AGGRAVATING OR ALLEVIATING FACTORS	OTHER RELEVANT FACTORS	POSSIBLE CAUSE AND ACTION
Back pain (cont.)				
Steady ache not confined to a specific place, most often in the lower back; may begin suddenly during straining, twisting or unusual physical activity, or may start after such activities	• Stiffness	• Aggravated by movement but not by coughing or straining • May be relieved by lying still	• Adults or children • Commonly occurs as a sporting or occupational injury • Sometimes follows trauma, e.g. motor vehicle accident	• Acute muscle or ligament strain • Minor strains usually settle quickly and do not require medical attention • See your doctor or a physical therapist if you are worried or if symptoms persist
Sudden episodes of pain, usually in the lower back; often described as sharp and/or shooting in character; often radiates down into the buttock and leg	• Neurological symptoms may develop, such as tingling or some loss of sensation in the buttock or part of the leg	• Pain aggravated by bending (especially to the side), coughing/sneezing, laughing • May be alleviated by lying in the fetal position	• Pain may have been precipitated by trauma or an unusual movement • The pain may spontaneously go away for a time	• Intervertebral disk problem (e.g. herniated disk or disk protrusion) • See your doctor at once
Gradual onset of pain, usually in the lower back	• Similar symptoms in other joints, stiffness in the mornings	• Stiffness tends to gradually ease as the day progresses, pain tends to be worse with activity and eased by resting	• Not precipitated by physical activity or trauma • Osteoarthritis is more common with age; other forms of arthritis may occur in younger people	• Arthritis (e.g. osteoarthritis or rheumatoid arthritis) • See your doctor
Dull aching pain; may radiate to one side; most commonly in the middle or lower spine		• Worse with exertion, posture, movement, coughing	• May result from severe trauma, or minor or unnoticed trauma in a person with osteoporosis or a bone abnormality	• Vertebral fracture • See your doctor at once
Lower back ache, sometimes throbbing in nature	• May have stiffness, rash, other joints affected, or symptoms from the gastrointestinal, urinary or genital tract	• Characterized by being worse with rest, and alleviated by activity; this contrasts with mechanical causes of back pain	• Often in young adults or people with inflammatory disease of the bowel	• An inflammatory joint disorder • See your doctor
Unremitting continuous and possibly progressive pain, usually of gradual onset; may be deep, boring pain	• Weight loss, loss of appetite, malaise, fever, chills, nervous system problems	• Posture or motion typically have little effect on the pain	• Pathological lesions are rarely the cause of low back pain in adults; they are a more common underlying cause of pain higher up in the spine or low back pain in a child	• Cancer metastasis, cancer of the blood (e.g. leukemia), inflammation or infection • See your doctor at once

Bad breath (halitosis)

Most people have slightly bad breath when they first wake in the morning, because the normally physiological mechanisms that clean the mouth are inactive while sleeping. Transient bad breath may be of no particular significance or associated with an obvious short-term problem in the mouth or throat. Occasionally, persistent and genuinely bad breath results from serious underlying disorders of major bodily systems.

SYMPTOM CHARACTERISTIC	ASSOCIATED SYMPTOMS	AGGRAVATING OR ALLEVIATING FACTORS	OTHER RELEVANT FACTORS	POSSIBLE CAUSE AND ACTION
Transient, bad breath usually of easily recognizable attribution			• These causes are common and generally well recognized	• Lifestyle factors (e.g. smoking, drinking, eating certain foods such as garlic or onions) • See your doctor or dentist if you are worried or if symptoms persist
Persistent bad breath, may have a putrid odor			• These are the most common causes of halitosis	• Poor dental hygiene, rotten teeth, gingivitis, infections in the mouth or throat • See your doctor or dentist
Persistent bad breath; may have a putrid odor	• Cough, sputum, fever, headache (sinusitis)		• Sinusitis is the most common out of this group of conditions	• Respiratory infections resulting in build-up of stagnant secretions in the respiratory tract, sinusitis, lung diseases (e.g. lung abscess, lung cancer) • See your doctor at once
Characteristically, a sweet, fruity acetone smell on the breath	• Excessive thirst, increased urine volume, mental confusion, apathy, reduced awareness, which may progress to coma		• This type of diabetes typically begins before 40 years of age	• Uncontrolled Type I diabetes (insulin-dependent diabetes of juvenile-onset) • See your doctor at once • If drowsiness or coma is present, this is a medical emergency. Go to the emergency room or call an ambulance immediately
Persistent bad breath; characteristically, an ammonia or urinary smell on the breath	• Often associated with an unpleasant taste sensation • Many other symptoms may be associated including loss of appetite, weight loss, itchiness, headache, restlessness, hiccough, bruising, bleeding from the nose, drowsiness, nausea and vomiting, convulsions, muscle twitching		• Typically will have a known history of kidney disease and failure	• Chronic kidney failure • See your doctor • If drowsiness or coma is present, this is a medical emergency • Go to the emergency room or call an ambulance immediately

SYMPTOM CHARACTERISTIC	ASSOCIATED SYMPTOMS	AGGRAVATING OR ALLEVIATING FACTORS	OTHER RELEVANT FACTORS	POSSIBLE CAUSE AND ACTION
Bad breath (halitosis) (cont.)				
Persistent bad breath; variously described as a fishy, musty or mousy smell on the breath	• Fatigue, weight loss, fluid retention, general deterioration in health, yellowness of skin (jaundice) • There may be drowsiness, which may progress to coma		• May develop either as an rapidly progressive acute condition or due to liver problem	• Liver failure • See your doctor • If drowsiness or coma is present, this is a medical emergency. Go to the emergency room or call an ambulance at once

Blackouts, including fainting

Fainting results from a transient loss of consciousness. Lapses in awareness or falling to the ground suddenly without warning may also occur without loss of consciousness. Faints are more common in elderly people, who are also at greatest risk of injury from the resulting falls. In about 50 percent of cases, no cause is found.

SYMPTOM CHARACTERISTIC	ASSOCIATED SYMPTOMS	AGGRAVATING OR ALLEVIATING FACTORS	OTHER RELEVANT FACTORS	POSSIBLE CAUSE AND ACTION
Transient loss of consciousness with awareness that you are about to lose consciousness; occurs when upright, causing the person to fall to the ground	• Before losing consciousness, may have a feeling of weakness or lightheadedness, or dimness of vision • On waking, usually well oriented • May have milder episodes without loss of unconsciousness	• Episodes are transient because falling to the ground restores blood flow to the brain	• Fainting may be caused by pregnancy, standing in the sun for a long time, standing up while on medication for high blood pressure, sudden severe emotional stress, after a long bout of violent coughing, or as a response to pain, fear, injections, or the sight of blood	• Fainting • See your doctor if you are worried or if symptoms persist
Transient loss of consciousness often without warning; may occur when upright or when lying down	• Lightheadedness, palpitations, chest pain, or breathlessness preceding loss of consciousness • While unconscious, the person may be noticeably pale • On waking, the person is usually well oriented and quickly feels well again		• In some cases, fainting is precipitated by exercise • The risk is increased if the person is also dehydrated	• Heart disease • See your doctor at once
Transient lapse of consciousness—normal activity and awareness ceases briefly with or without falling or prior warning; may occur when upright or when lying down	• During the attack, may have fluttering of eyelids, rolling up of eyes, or there may be some jerking of the limbs or repeated simple muscle actions • May be confused for a period on waking		• Young person, or known history of epilepsy • Begins in childhood • May also experience other forms of epileptic seizure	• Epilepsy that does not involve convulsive movements • See your doctor
Falling to the ground suddenly without warning; may occur with or without loss of consciousness	• Sudden onset of persistent nervous system problems (e.g. blindness, weakness, pins and needles, numbness, difficulties with speech, lack of muscle coordination)		• More common with advancing age • Risk increased in people with hypertension, lipid abnormalities (e.g. high cholesterol), diabetes	• Stroke • This is a medical emergency • Go to the emergency room or call an ambulance at once

SYMPTOM CHARACTERISTIC	ASSOCIATED SYMPTOMS	AGGRAVATING OR ALLEVIATING FACTORS	OTHER RELEVANT FACTORS	POSSIBLE CAUSE AND ACTION
Sudden transient loss of consciousness, or falling to the ground, without warning	• There may be a sudden onset of transient neurological problems such as loss of vision, weakness, pins and needles, numbness, difficulties with speech, lack of muscle coordination, vertigo • These symptoms spontaneously resolve		• May have a history of cardiovascular disease or osteoarthritis of the neck • May have been precipitated by a particular movement of the head • More common with advancing age • Risk increased in people with hypertension, lipid abnormalities (e.g. high cholesterol), diabetes	• Transient ischemic attack • This is a medical emergency • Go to the emergency room or call an ambulance at once
Loss of consciousness, generally prolonged	• Before losing consciousness may experience confusion, sweating, possibly headache, faintness and weakness	• Loss of consciousness can usually be prevented by eating glucose candy or jelly beans and taking sugary drinks (e.g. fruit juice) as soon as the attack is recognized	• Person on medication to treat diabetes • May have missed a meal, exercised more than anticipated, or recently altered their diabetic medication	• Hypoglycemia (low blood sugar) • This is a medical emergency • Go to the emergency room or call an ambulance at once

Bones, fracture/brittleness

Suspected fractures always require immediate medical attention, especially when there is substantial blood loss, symptoms of nerve damage or any suggestion of damage to internal organs. If the injury may affect the spinal column—for example following a direct blow to the neck or back, falls from a height or high-speed accidents—great care must be taken to immobilize the spine until an ambulance arrives to transport the person to hospital.

SYMPTOM CHARACTERISTIC	ASSOCIATED SYMPTOMS	AGGRAVATING OR ALLEVIATING FACTORS	OTHER RELEVANT FACTORS	POSSIBLE CAUSE AND ACTION
Pain with loss of limb function and possibly also change in shape	• The skin overlying the fracture may be broken (open fracture) or intact (closed fracture) • There may be substantial blood loss, or damage to nerves or internal organs	• Pain is aggravated by any movement of the affected part	• Fractures may be caused by a heavy blow hitting or crushing a bone (direct force) or twisting, bending or compressing a bone (indirect force) • In adults, the break is usually through the full thickness of the bone • In children, the bones are more springy and incomplete fractures are common ("greenstick" fractures)	• Fracture • See your doctor at once • First aid involves controlling bleeding, covering any open wounds and supporting the limb in its most comfortable position
Broken bone following repeated activity that stresses a particular site (usually a limb)	• The most characteristic pattern of symptoms is pain that initially starts after the exercise or activity, then begins to occur during the activity and later is present at other times as well • There is no deformity and the limb functions normally		• Usually occurs in otherwise healthy active people	• Stress fracture • See your doctor at once

SYMPTOM CHARACTERISTIC	ASSOCIATED SYMPTOMS	AGGRAVATING OR ALLEVIATING FACTORS	OTHER RELEVANT FACTORS	POSSIBLE CAUSE AND ACTION
Bones, fracture/brittleness (cont.)				
Broken bone following slight trauma	• Pain with loss of limb function and possible deformity • Elderly women with long-term multiple fractures of the vertebrae may develop a hump at the top of the back	• Pain is aggravated by any movement of the affected part	• Pain or deformity of the bone before the fracture occurred suggests the cause may be a pre-existing abnormality of the bone • There may have been previous episodes of fracture • Fractures of the hip, wrist and vertebrae are most commonly associated with osteoporosis • Osteoporosis is more common in women than men • Factors that increase risk of developing osteoporosis include inherited factors (family history, ethnicity), hormonal factors (menopause, ovarian problems, disease of thyroid gland), calcium deficiency, alcohol abuse, smoking, lack of exercise, or drug treatment	• Fracture due to an abnormality making the bone more fragile (pathological fracture) • Causes include osteoporosis, cancer with metastasis, blood cell abnormalities • See your doctor at once

Bowel, bleeding from

Bleeding from the bowel always warrants a visit to the doctor to determine the cause and, if blood loss has been substantial, to support the circulation. The most common cause is hemorrhoids, but more serious conditions such as bowel cancer are common and may be responsible for a bleed of any description. Serious pathologies need to be excluded by a doctor even if a minor ailment such as hemorrhoids is present. Some of the important causes in adults, such as hemorrhoids and rectal cancer, do not occur in children.

This table deals with bleeding through the rectum. Bleeding from the upper gastrointestinal tract (esophagus, stomach, duodenum) often causes vomiting of blood, which may either be fresh blood or darkened blood resembling coffee grounds.

SYMPTOM CHARACTERISTIC	ASSOCIATED SYMPTOMS	AGGRAVATING OR ALLEVIATING FACTORS	OTHER RELEVANT FACTORS	POSSIBLE CAUSE AND ACTION
Squirt or drip of fresh blood in toilet or on toilet paper after defecation	• Hemorrhoids are usually painless unless there are complications • A sensation of unsatisfied defecation or urgency signals a problem inside the rectum		• Straining to defecate predisposes to hemorrhoids	• Hemorrhoids, polyps, tumors • See your doctor
Small amount of fresh blood on toilet paper after defecation with sharp pain in the anus during or after defecating			• Straining to defecate may predispose to anal injuries	• Anal tear or break in tissue (fissure), tumor • See your doctor

SYMPTOM CHARACTERISTIC	ASSOCIATED SYMPTOMS	AGGRAVATING OR ALLEVIATING FACTORS	OTHER RELEVANT FACTORS	POSSIBLE CAUSE AND ACTION
Fresh blood mixed with stool or dark blood in stool, with or without blood clots	• No other symptoms or there may be diarrhea, constipation, abdominal pain, abdominal distension, weight loss, loss of appetite, general feeling of being unwell, symptoms of anemia (tiredness, lack of energy, breathlessness on exertion, pallor of skin or gums, fingernails) • Mucus may be passed with stools		• More likely in a person with personal or family history of polyps or bowel cancer • Conditions that predispose to bowel cancer include benign polyps, ulcerative colitis	• Bowel tumor, polyp, other problems of rectum or bowel • See your doctor
Episodes of bloody diarrhea	• Abdominal pain, aches, general feeling of being unwell, weight loss, fever, symptoms of anemia (tiredness, lack of energy, breathlessness on exertion, pallor of skin or gums, fingernails) • Mucus may be passed in stool		• Inflammatory bowel disease is most common in Jewish people (3–6 times higher than for non-Jewish racial or ethnic groups), and is higher among white racial groups than in black people or Asians • It commences most commonly at age 15–35 • The cause of inflammatory bowel disease is unknown	• An inflammatory bowel disease such as Crohn's disease or ulcerative colitis • See your doctor at once
Sudden onset of watery, bloody diarrhea or of smaller stools with blood, mucus and pus	• Abdominal pain, fever, aches, general feeling of being unwell • In children, high fever may develop so rapidly as to cause febrile seizures		• Dysentery is highly contagious, and is most common following travel or contact with others who have similar symptoms • Outbreaks are usually relatively mild in industrialized countries and most frequently occur in institutions such as schools • Outbreaks occurring in developing countries (or infections originating with a traveler to these countries) are more severe and sometimes fatal	• Dysentery, infection of the bowel • See your doctor at once • Dysentery is highly contagious, so contact the doctor's office or emergency department first to advise of symptoms
Bloody diarrhea of sudden onset	• Abdominal pain		• Most common in elderly people with a history of other cardiovascular disease, but no contact with dysentery	• Loss of blood supply to a portion of the bowel (ischemic colitis) • This is a medical emergency • Go to the emergency room or call an ambulance at once

SYMPTOM CHARACTERISTIC	ASSOCIATED SYMPTOMS	AGGRAVATING OR ALLEVIATING FACTORS	OTHER RELEVANT FACTORS	POSSIBLE CAUSE AND ACTION
Bowel, bleeding from (cont.)				
Heavy bleeding from the rectum	• Lightheadedness or fainting, confusion, severe thirst, feeling cold and clammy, pallor of skin, gums and nails		• Diverticulitis is more common in men than in women • Heavy bleeding is a rare complication of diverticulitis, which is usually associated with invisible or light bleeding	• Diverticulitis • This is a medical emergency • Go to the emergency room or call an ambulance at once
Melena (black tarry stools)	• May also vomit blood, either as fresh blood or darkened blood resembling coffee grounds		• Peptic ulcer can occur in any age group, but is relatively common in elderly people taking non-steroidal anti-inflammatory drugs for painful inflammatory conditions such as osteoarthritis or rheumatoid arthritis	• Bleeding from the esophagus, stomach, or duodenum, caused by a peptic ulcer, or gastritis, or dilated veins in the esophagus • This is a medical emergency • Go to the emergency room or call an ambulance at once
Blood in feces or red-colored stool in an infant	• Unwell with vomiting and bouts of abdominal pain and screaming		• Most common in children under 2 years	• Intussusception • This is a medical emergency • Go to the emergency room or call an ambulance at once

Breast lump

Most women will detect a lump in their breast at some time in their life. Most of these lumps are found to be benign on further assessment. Breast cancer has been found responsible for up to 25 percent of breast lumps and remains the most common cancer in women.

SYMPTOM CHARACTERISTIC	ASSOCIATED SYMPTOMS	AGGRAVATING OR ALLEVIATING FACTORS	OTHER RELEVANT FACTORS	POSSIBLE CAUSE AND ACTION
General breast lumpiness, tender breast lumps usually affecting both breasts, but occasionally a single lump only; lumps are soft, round and smooth; pain and tenderness may occur during menstrual cycles, usually of both breasts; lumps may come and go with menstrual cycles		• Pain and tenderness worse premenstrually • Sometimes symptoms may be alleviated by reducing intake of coffee, tea and chocolate	• Usually affects premenopausal women • Symptoms usually diminish or disappear after menopause	• Fibrocystic disease of the breast • See your doctor • If fibrocystic disease is diagnosed a well-fitted bra may help provide adequate support • Vitamin E supplementation may reduce symptoms
Firm, elastic breast lump that moves freely; usually a single smooth lump approximately 1½ inches (3–4 centimeters) in diameter	• Usually painless	• Lump may enlarge during adolescence or pregnancy	• Usually occurs in women 20–40 years of age	• Fibroadenoma • See your doctor

SYMPTOM CHARACTERISTIC	ASSOCIATED SYMPTOMS	AGGRAVATING OR ALLEVIATING FACTORS	OTHER RELEVANT FACTORS	POSSIBLE CAUSE AND ACTION
Hard or irregular breast lump which may be fixed in one position or attached to nearby tissues; usually only one breast is affected	• No other symptoms or pain (5 percent of patients), bloody or non-milky discharge from nipple, dimpling of the skin, tenderness or lumps under the armpit		• More common in women than in men • Most common after 40 years of age but may occur much earlier in women with a genetic predisposition	• Breast cancer • See your doctor at once
Firm single irregular lump, which may be attached to the skin	• Lump is painful and tender		• Gradual onset (over months) after breast trauma; the trauma involved may be subtle	• Abnormality in fat tissue • See your doctor
Single, tender breast lump that develops rapidly in a women who is breast feeding	• Pain and tenderness of lump, redness of the overlying skin, fever, chills		• Occurs during lactation	• Breast abscess • See your doctor

Breathing problems

Shortness of breath can be a gradually developing phenomenon or may be rapidly developing and life-threatening. Some of the more prominent causes of each are described in this section.

SYMPTOM CHARACTERISTIC	ASSOCIATED SYMPTOMS	AGGRAVATING OR ALLEVIATING FACTORS	OTHER RELEVANT FACTORS	POSSIBLE CAUSE AND ACTION
Long-term or repeated shortness of breath on exertion; onset gradual	• Shortness of breath on lying flat, waking up at night with shortness of breath which is relieved by sitting up, swelling of the legs, cough, wheeze may be present, gradual decline in exercise capacity, shortness of breath at rest	• Symptoms may be aggravated by lying down	• Chronic heart failure is most common in the middle-aged and elderly, and rarely occurs in younger people • Heart failure may follow rheumatic fever, heart attack/coronary artery disease, hypertension, arrhythmia, or heart valve abnormalities	• Chronic heart failure • See your doctor at once
Long-term or repeated shortness of breath on exertion; may progress gradually over many years	• Wheezing • Cough with sputum, often worse in the morning • Gradual decline in exercise capacity	• Sometimes alleviated by leaning forward or lying on stomach with head down	• Chronic obstructive lung disease is very much more common in smokers and in the elderly	• Chronic obstructive lung disease, bronchitis, emphysema • See your doctor
Long-term or repeated shortness of breath on exertion, occurring in episodes with no symptoms at other times	• Wheezing, persistent cough, usually without sputum	• Symptoms may be triggered by exposure to cigarette smoke or air pollution, exposure to pollens, cold air, exercise, respiratory infections	• History of hay fever or eczema; family history of asthma, eczema or allergies • Usually more frequent in winter, following a common cold or when pollen levels are high • May be exacerbated by exposure to pets or cigarette smoke	• Asthma • See your doctor • If breathing is difficult, or you suspect oxygen shortage, this is a medical emergency • Go to the emergency room or call an ambulance at once

SYMPTOM CHARACTERISTIC	ASSOCIATED SYMPTOMS	AGGRAVATING OR ALLEVIATING FACTORS	OTHER RELEVANT FACTORS	POSSIBLE CAUSE AND ACTION
Breathing problems (cont.)				
Long-term or repeated shortness of breath on exertion in a person working in a dusty environment; gradually progressive over a long period	• Cough		• Occupational exposure to coal, silica, asbestos	• Occupational lung disease • See your doctor
Acute shortness of breath at rest; onset may be sudden	• Chest pain if the episode is precipitated by a heart attack • May have a background history or recent worsening of shortness of breath on exertion and/or when lying flat, and/or waking up short of breath at night	• Breathlessness aggravated by lying down	• Pulmonary edema is more likely in a person with a history of this problem • May be caused by cardiac disease, lung infections, shock (e.g. cardiac surgery, serious infections, inhaled toxins)	• Pulmonary edema • This is a medical emergency • Go to the emergency room or call an ambulance at once
Sudden onset shortness of breath at rest	• Fever, chills, pain around the chest which is aggravated by breathing in		• Pneumonia is a relatively common condition in all age groups, but may be more likely with an inhaled foreign body, pre-existing lung diseases, immune suppression (e.g. other disease, medications)	• Pneumonia • See your doctor at once
Acute shortness of breath at rest; sudden onset	• Chest pain		• May occur spontaneously or as a result of chest trauma • Most often occurs in young healthy people without a prior lung problem • Predisposing factors include cystic fibrosis, chronic obstructive lung disease	• Pneumothorax • This is a medical emergency • Go to the emergency room or call an ambulance at once
Acute shortness of breath at rest	• Chest pain, dizziness, faintness, loss of consciousness, rapidly turning blue		• Predisposing factors to an embolus include the use of oral contraceptives in young women, recent surgery, recent childbirth, a long period of bed rest or immobility, history of a blood clot in the leg, abnormal heart rhythms	• Pulmonary embolism • This is a medical emergency • Go to the emergency room or call an ambulance at once

SYMPTOM CHARACTERISTIC	ASSOCIATED SYMPTOMS	AGGRAVATING OR ALLEVIATING FACTORS	OTHER RELEVANT FACTORS	POSSIBLE CAUSE AND ACTION
Very sudden shortness of breath at rest with choking; occurring while eating or where there is a high probability of a toddler inhaling a small object	• Severe distress with inability to take in air despite desperate efforts, collapse, blue skin and gums, loss of consciousness (in complete obstruction) • Rapid labored breathing with loud harsh noise while breathing in, gagging (in partial blockage of the airway)		• Inhalation is probable if onset while eating • In adults, this is more likely to occur if a person is intoxicated or has a reduced level of consciousness/awareness • Toddlers commonly inhale other objects	• Upper airway obstruction due to inhaled foreign body such as a piece of food • This is a medical emergency • Go to the emergency room or call an ambulance at once
Sudden shortness of breath at rest with choking; occurring when inhalation of food or a small object is unlikely	• Severe distress with inability to take in air despite desperate efforts, collapse, blue skin and gums, loss of consciousness (in complete obstruction) • Rapid labored breathing with loud harsh noise while breathing in, gagging (in partial blockage of the airway)		• Inflammation of the airways may be caused by an insect bite or sting, an allergic reaction to food or a new medication, inhalation of hot gases or other toxins • Eating peanuts is a relatively common cause of severe reaction, which may occur in a person without a known history of peanut allergy	• Upper airway obstruction due to swelling of structures in the throat • This is a medical emergency • Go to the emergency room or call an ambulance at once

Bruising

Bruising is a normal reaction to injury and is caused by blood leaking from damaged blood vessels under the skin. Bruises start off as a red mark, quickly turn blue then fade into a green or yellow color as they heal. Frequent or severe bruising after a minor injury could be a sign of an underlying disorder of the blood vessels or the ability of the blood to clot. Any unusual bruising should be checked by a doctor.

SYMPTOM CHARACTERISTIC	ASSOCIATED SYMPTOMS	AGGRAVATING OR ALLEVIATING FACTORS	OTHER RELEVANT FACTORS	POSSIBLE CAUSE AND ACTION
Bruise confined to a single area	• Pain, tenderness, may be a lump under the bruise if severe	• Cold compresses can reduce the bruising	• Bruising occurs in healthy people, usually after injury • Women tend to bruise more easily then men • Bruising is often more extensive in the elderly	• Bruise resulting from minor injury • Placing an ice pack over the injured site may reduce bruising • See your doctor if you are worried or if symptoms persist
Extensive dark purple bruises in an elderly person, often on arms or legs	• Pain, tenderness, may be a lump under the bruise if severe	• Cold compresses can reduce the bruising	• Usually a history of minor injury • Occurs in the elderly due to weakening of the blood vessels and skin	• Senile purpura (bruising due to old age) • Creams available from your pharmacist can speed healing of the bruise • See your doctor if you are worried or if symptoms persist

SYMPTOM CHARACTERISTIC	ASSOCIATED SYMPTOMS	AGGRAVATING OR ALLEVIATING FACTORS	OTHER RELEVANT FACTORS	POSSIBLE CAUSE AND ACTION
Bruising (cont.)				
Slow healing bruises	• Slow healing wounds, frequent infections, tingling and numbness in the hands or feet	• Improving blood sugar control can minimize complications of the disease	• May occur in people with a history of poorly controlled diabetes	• Diabetes • See your doctor
Bruising following minor injuries	• May be prolonged bleeding after cuts	• Cold compresses can reduce the bruising	• Medications that may be associated with increased bruising include aspirin, cortisone-type drugs (corticosteroids), non-steroidal anti-inflammatory drugs, blood thinning drugs (anticoagulants)	• Medication-related bruising • See your doctor
Development of bruising and tiny red dots on the skin	• Nosebleeds or bleeding from gums in severe cases • Heavy menstrual bleeding in young women	• Bruising settles as disorder resolves and clotting returns to normal	• Most common in children from 2– 4 years of age and young women • Illness may be prolonged in adults but is usually self-limiting in children without treatment	• Thrombocytopenia • See your doctor
Scattered bruises of varying ages, appearing over a period of weeks	• Severe fatigue, loss of appetite, pallor, episodes of fever, bone pain	• Treatment of underlying condition will improve the function of bone marrow and blood clotting	• May be a history of frequent infections	• Leukemia • See your doctor at once
Frequent, often severe bruising without significant injury; bruises may be firm and hard due to blood clotting under the skin	• Other signs of bleeding may be also present such as painful or swollen joints, excessive bleeding following cuts or dental extractions, blood in the urine • Symptoms of brain hemorrhage include irritability, drowsiness, headache, confusion, nausea, vomiting and double vision • Other internal bleeding may result in breathing problems, weakness, pallor or loss of consciousness	• Visible or internal bleeding may occur without any obvious trauma • Signs of bleeding (e.g. brain hemorrhage) may occur several days after an injury	• Hemophilia occurs only in males • The worldwide incidence is one in 10,000 males • Hemophilia is an inherited disorder, so there may be family history of a bleeding tendency	• Hemophilia or other bleeding disorder • See your doctor • If the person is bleeding or shows signs of internal bleeding, this is a medical emergency • Go to the emergency room or call an ambulance at once

Chest pain

Chest pain typically arises from the heart, lungs, chest wall or esophagus. Occasionally, chest pain is due to disease of upper abdominal structures such as the stomach or gallbladder. Any chest pain warrants full examination by a doctor.

SYMPTOM CHARACTERISTIC	ASSOCIATED SYMPTOMS	AGGRAVATING OR ALLEVIATING FACTORS	OTHER RELEVANT FACTORS	POSSIBLE CAUSE AND ACTION
Repeated episodes of central chest heaviness, pressure, tightness or discomfort occurring on exertion and relieved by rest; often the pain radiates into the neck and/or left arm, or the arm may feel numb or tingly; attacks usually last a few minutes, sometimes up to 15 minutes	• Shortness of breath or anxiety may be present	• Alleviated by rest or nitrate tablet taken under the tongue	• Angina pectoris occurs most frequently in the middle-aged or elderly • Rarely occurs in children with congenital heart problems	• Angina pectoris • See your doctor
Central burning pain radiating up the throat	• Bitter taste in the mouth or return of bitter fluids into the mouth from the stomach	• Relieved by antacids	• Heartburn occurs in adults and children and is a symptoms of gastroesophageal reflux • Attacks are often provoked by lying flat in bed at night, or bending over	• Heartburn • Avoid large meals, eating within a few hours of bedtime and any specific foods which provoke symptoms • See your doctor
Dull cramp-like central chest pain which occurs only after swallowing; the pain can be quite severe	• Difficulty swallowing		• Esophageal spasm may occur as a result of gastroesophageal reflux	• Esophageal spasm (a disturbance of the contractions of the esophagus which usually push food through to the stomach) • See your doctor
Severe central chest heaviness, pressure, tightness or discomfort which usually lasts more than 30 minutes; often the pain radiates into the neck and/or left arm; onset at rest or on exercise but without relief after resting	• Shortness of breath, sweating, cold, faintness, nausea or vomiting, palpitations • Symptoms may be relatively mild in a person with a past history of heart disease		• Myocardial infarction most commonly occurs in middle-aged or older people	• Myocardial infarction (heart attack) • This is a medical emergency • Go to the emergency room or call an ambulance at once
Sharp stabbing chest pain within a well-defined area, occurring on or worsened by breathing in	• Fever, cough with sputum that may contain pus, shortness of breath	• Pain is aggravated by taking a deep breath, or by coughing	• Pneumonia may result from a bacterial infection in previously healthy people, or due to lowering of resistance resulting from another illness (e.g. chronic obstructive pulmonary disease or cancer)	• Pneumonia • See your doctor at once

SYMPTOM CHARACTERISTIC	ASSOCIATED SYMPTOMS	AGGRAVATING OR ALLEVIATING FACTORS	OTHER RELEVANT FACTORS	POSSIBLE CAUSE AND ACTION
Chest pain (cont.)				
Sharp stabbing chest pain within a well-defined area, worse on breathing in; may affect one or both sides of the chest	• Shortness of breath • Coughing up blood	• Pain is aggravated by taking a deep breath, or by coughing	• Predisposing factors include a period of immobilization or bed rest, recent surgical procedure, recent childbirth, history of a blood clot in the leg, the use of oral contraceptives	• Loss of blood supply to an area of lung tissue (pulmonary infarct), usually due to blockage of blood vessels by a clot • See your doctor at once
Sudden onset of sharp localized pain on one side of the chest, worse on breathing in	• Shortness of breath	• Pain is aggravated by taking a deep breath, or by coughing	• Pneumothorax may occur in adults and children, either spontaneously or as a result of injury to the chest • Most often occurs in young healthy people without a prior lung problem • Predisposing factors include cystic fibrosis chronic obstructive lung disease	• Pneumothorax • See your doctor at once
Dull aching localized pain, usually on one side, and worse with movement (turning, twisting, bending), straining (e.g. lifting), possibly by coughing or deep breathing in	• Tenderness of the chest wall	• Aggravated by movement	• May follow trauma or unusual exertion	• Injury to the chest wall • See your doctor
Constant burning pain on one side of the chest followed by rash	• Painful blistering rash appears in the painful area a few days after the initial pain	• The pain is not affected by breathing, posture or exertion	• Shingles mainly occurs in adults over 60 years, and is due to reactivation of the same virus responsible for chickenpox • In children, chickenpox frequently causes a painful blistering rash on the chest	• Shingles • See your doctor at once
Sudden severe central chest pain	• Severe shortness of breath, fainting • Skin may be cold, clammy, pale		• Predisposing factors include a period of immobilization or bed rest, recent surgical procedure, recent childbirth, history of a blood clot in the leg, use of oral contraceptives	• Pulmonary embolism • This is a medical emergency • Go to the emergency room or call an ambulance at once

SYMPTOM CHARACTERISTIC	ASSOCIATED SYMPTOMS	AGGRAVATING OR ALLEVIATING FACTORS	OTHER RELEVANT FACTORS	POSSIBLE CAUSE AND ACTION
Sudden onset of severe tearing pain of the front or back of the chest which moves as time progresses; the pain often radiates through to the back or may be felt predominantly in the back of the chest; pain may also involve the arms, neck, trunk or legs	• Shortness of breath, fainting • Complications may cause symptoms in other bodily systems (e.g. paralysis of the legs, mental disturbances, bloody diarrhea)		• Most often occurs in middle-aged or elderly men with hypertension	• Tearing along the inside wall of the aorta (dissecting aneurysm) • This is a medical emergency • Go to the emergency room or call an ambulance at once
Central chest tightness or discomfort	• Shortness of breath, wheezing	• Symptoms may be triggered by exposure to cigarette smoke or air pollution, exposure to pollens, cold air, exercise, respiratory infections	• Asthma occurs more commonly in adults or children with a history of hay fever or eczema, or a family history of asthma, eczema or allergies • Usually more frequent in winter, following a common cold or when pollen levels are high • May be exacerbated by exposure to pets or cigarette smoke	• Asthma • See your doctor at once

Constipation

Constipation is the most common symptom relating to the gastrointestinal tract. Different people have different normal bowel habits—for a particular person it may be usual to pass anywhere between three stools per week and three per day. In most cases, constipation can be thought of in terms of a change away from an individual's usual pattern. Sometimes a person may by troubled by very hard stools or difficulty in expelling stools rather than a reduction in frequency.

Frequently the cause of constipation relates to lifestyle factors. Laxatives are not usually needed and can themselves cause constipation if used inappropriately, so it is preferable to seek medical advice before taking them. Occasionally serious underlying pathology is responsible, or constipation is a manifestation of disease in another bodily system. Prescription and over-the-counter medicines commonly cause or aggravate constipation.

SYMPTOM CHARACTERISTIC	ASSOCIATED SYMPTOMS	AGGRAVATING OR ALLEVIATING FACTORS	OTHER RELEVANT FACTORS	POSSIBLE CAUSE AND ACTION
Stools are dry and hard and may require straining to expel; the condition may be long-standing	• Vague discomfort in the abdomen • Children may also have a sense of bloating, irritability, soiling of underwear	• Can be alleviated by increasing your dietary fiber intake, which tends to increase the weight and water content of the stools and speed up their transit through the gut	• Most common in adults; may occur in children • Simple constipation is commonly due to a low-fiber diet, inadequate fluid intake, lack of exercise • May be triggered by any upset of eating or bowel routine (e.g. travel, recent bed rest or immobilization, recent dietary changes), ignoring the urge to have a bowel movement, recently toilet-trained children	• Simple constipation • Increase your dietary fiber intake from vegetables, fruits, and whole grains, avoid excessive intake of fatty or sugary foods, engage in some form of physical activity • See your doctor if you are worried or if symptoms persist, or if constipation occurs in a child

SYMPTOM CHARACTERISTIC	ASSOCIATED SYMPTOMS	AGGRAVATING OR ALLEVIATING FACTORS	OTHER RELEVANT FACTORS	POSSIBLE CAUSE AND ACTION
Constipation (cont.)				
Inconsistent frequency and/or character of stools; may be long-standing	• May have a sense of bloating or vague abdominal discomfort	• May be aggravated by stress	• Most commonly young adults, but may occur at any age	• Irritable bowel syndrome • See your doctor
Recent change from usual bowel habit or worsening of any pre-existing problem; may experience an early morning rush to go to the toilet	• Vague abdominal discomfort or crampy abdominal pains, blood or mucus in the stools, weight loss, loss of appetite, general feeling of being unwell • Laxative use less effective than previously		• More common with advancing age • Usually occurs after 40 years of age, but occasionally may occur at younger age • Predisposing conditions for bowel cancer include benign polyps, familial polyposis (an inherited condition in which many polyps form in the bowel at puberty), ulcerative colitis	• Bowel tumor • See your doctor
Passage of stools causes pain, so is consciously avoided by the person	• May be associated with urgent or painful desire to pass stools or fresh blood on the toilet paper		• May occur at any age • If an urgent or painful desire to pass stools is present, this points toward a potentially serious rectal lesion	• Anal tear/fissure, hemorrhoids, tumor of the anus or rectum • See your doctor
Stools are small, hard and are passed infrequently (e.g. once every few days); may be a recurrent problem	• Soiling of underwear		• Most likely in the elderly person • May be triggered by periods of bed rest or immobilization, poor fluid intake	• Feces wedged firmly in the rectum • See your doctor

Cough

Coughing is the body's way of clearing the airways of secretions or foreign material. A cough may be caused by any irritation or inflammation of the airways or lungs. Any persistent cough should be assessed by a doctor.

SYMPTOM CHARACTERISTIC	ASSOCIATED SYMPTOMS	AGGRAVATING OR ALLEVIATING FACTORS	OTHER RELEVANT FACTORS	POSSIBLE CAUSE AND ACTION
Rapid onset of cough that is dry or productive (produces phlegm)	• Runny nose, sore throat, fever, fatigue • If sputum is present it is usually clear or white	• Cough may be aggravated by cold air	• May follow recent contact with person with cough or cold • Often occurs in winter	• Infectious cough, often caused by a virus which causes irritation of the lining of the windpipe and the production of mucus • Usually self-limiting without treatment • See your doctor if you are worried or if symptoms persist

SYMPTOM CHARACTERISTIC	ASSOCIATED SYMPTOMS	AGGRAVATING OR ALLEVIATING FACTORS	OTHER RELEVANT FACTORS	POSSIBLE CAUSE AND ACTION
Acute onset of moist cough productive of phlegm	• Fever, shortness of breath, fatigue, sharp chest pain on breathing in due to inflammation of the pleura (pleurisy) • Sputum produced is yellow or green and may contain some blood	• Cough may be aggravated by cold air, smoky environment or exercise	• May follow recent cold or flu • More common in smokers	• Bronchitis or pneumonia caused by an infection • If the cause is bacterial, you may require treatment with antibiotics • See your doctor
Episodic dry cough with tight feeling in chest, often occurring at night or after exercise	• Wheeze, shortness of breath	• Usually more frequent in winter, following a common cold or when pollen levels are high • May be exacerbated by exposure to pets or cigarette smoke	• History of hay fever or eczema • Family history of asthma, eczema or allergies	• Asthma • Any episodic cough, especially if associated with wheeze should be assessed by a doctor • Management of acute episodes of asthma usually requires inhaled medications to open the airways (bronchodilator or "reliever" medication) • Continuous preventative medication may be required even when cough is not present • See your doctor if having difficulty breathing
Sudden onset of cough which persists, without other explanation (e.g. signs of a cold infection)	• Occasional wheeze		• History of choking • More common in children • Small objects such as peanuts or beads are commonly responsible	• Inhalation of a foreign body • See your doctor at once
Chronic cough, often productive of phlegm	• Shortness of breath on exertion, wheezing		• History of smoking or exposure to cigarette smoke	• Chronic bronchitis or chronic lung disease • See your doctor • Any change in the nature of a chronic "smoker's cough" should be checked by a doctor at once to rule out cancer of the airways (lung cancer)

Cramp

A cramp is a sudden, prolonged and painful contraction of one or a group of muscles. Although the term "cramp" is often used to describe abdominal pain (abdominal cramps) and period pain (menstrual cramps), this table will focus on cramps of voluntary muscles of the body. Muscular cramps occur very commonly and are usually benign. Occasionally they may indicate a serious underlying disease process so it is important to have any frequent or persistent cramps assessed by a doctor.

SYMPTOM CHARACTERISTIC	ASSOCIATED SYMPTOMS	AGGRAVATING OR ALLEVIATING FACTORS	OTHER RELEVANT FACTORS	POSSIBLE CAUSE AND ACTION
Sudden, prolonged and painful contraction of a small group of muscles	• If severe, tenderness and weakness may remain after the cramp has resolved	• Usually worse at night	• Most common in the elderly, often occurs in the calves	• Benign cramps • See your doctor

SYMPTOM CHARACTERISTIC	ASSOCIATED SYMPTOMS	AGGRAVATING OR ALLEVIATING FACTORS	OTHER RELEVANT FACTORS	POSSIBLE CAUSE AND ACTION
Cramp (cont.)				
Sudden, prolonged and painful contraction of muscles		• Occurs during or following strenuous exercise • Rest and gentle stretching of muscles can ease the spasm	• May occur after insufficient warm-up before strenuous exercise	• Benign cramps induced by exercise • Thorough warm-up and stretching before exercise can help prevent cramps • See your doctor if you are worried or if symptoms persist
Very prolonged painful contraction of muscles, usually in the extremities	• Occur during strenuous exercise involving excessive sweating	• Excessive sweating, heavy clothes, dehydration	• Sometimes known as "miner's cramps" or "stoker's cramps"	• Heat cramps • Replacement of depleted salts and water by consuming electrolyte enriched drinks may relieve symptoms • See your doctor if you are worried or if symptoms persist
Spasms of muscles in a particular position, usually the hands		• Aggravated by long periods of repetition of the same position or movements	• Common in writers using a pen, or musicians using repetitive fine hand movements	• Writers' cramp • Usually settles with rest • See a physical therapist or your doctor if cramps persist
Frequent generalized cramps in muscle groups anywhere in the body		• If electrolyte imbalance is present, correction of this (e.g. by hospital treatment) will alleviate cramps	• May be a sign of underlying neurological disease or electrolyte imbalance • Motor neuron disease is relatively rare, occurring in less than 0.01percent of people; more common in men than women, and occurs most often at around 60 years of age	• Motor neuron disease • See your doctor

Diarrhea

Diarrhea refers to the passing of frequent and abnormally loose or watery bowel actions. Diarrhea is often the result of gastrointestinal infection and lasts only a few days. Sometimes diarrhea can be caused by a more serious disease process. The consistency, color and frequency of the diarrhea will give valuable clues with regard to the underlying cause. Any prolonged or unusual diarrhea should be assessed by a doctor to rule out an underlying medical condition.

SYMPTOM CHARACTERISTIC	ASSOCIATED SYMPTOMS	AGGRAVATING OR ALLEVIATING FACTORS	OTHER RELEVANT FACTORS	POSSIBLE CAUSE AND ACTION
Abrupt onset of watery diarrhea; mucus often present but rarely blood; lasts 1–3 days	• Vomiting, mild abdominal pain, low-grade fever • May follow an upper respiratory tract infection	• Eating and drinking may aggravate diarrhea	• Very common in children, especially in winter • Highly contagious, spread by fecal–oral transmission	• Viral gastroenteritis • Oral rehydration is usually sufficient treatment • Medications to reduce nausea and vomiting, and acetaminophen (paracetamol) can be helpful • Contact your doctor for advice

SYMPTOM CHARACTERISTIC	ASSOCIATED SYMPTOMS	AGGRAVATING OR ALLEVIATING FACTORS	OTHER RELEVANT FACTORS	POSSIBLE CAUSE AND ACTION
Abrupt onset of watery diarrhea, moderate in quantity, lasting 1–3 days	• Generally painless, although mild abdominal cramps may be present • Low-grade fever or vomiting may be present	• Eating and drinking may aggravate diarrhea	• May be history of ingesting poorly prepared food or travel to South America, Africa or Asia	• A bacterial infection • See your doctor at once
Abrupt onset of watery diarrhea, copious in quantity, lasting 2–7 days	• Effortless vomiting usually follows the onset of diarrhea, nausea usually absent • Dehydration, muscle cramps • May cause serious, possibly fatal dehydration within hours		• Most common in developing countries including India, Bangladesh, African and Latin American countries • Often occurs in epidemics • Usually spread by drinking contaminated water • More common and serious in children	• Cholera • This is a medical emergency • Go to the emergency room or call an ambulance at once • Where medical help is unavailable, dehydration may be alleviated by maintaining fluid intake with solutions containing glucose and salt, or by breast feeding in babies
Abrupt onset of diarrhea containing blood or mucus, with an offensive odor	• High fever, aches and pains, nausea and vomiting, moderate to severe abdominal cramps, frequent urge to pass stool with little result	• Eating and drinking may aggravate diarrhea	• May be a history of travel to a developing country or simultaneous illness in people who have shared contaminated food	• Food poisoning • Antidiarrheal agents are not recommended for this type of diarrhea • See your doctor at once
Abrupt onset of watery diarrhea; symptoms may persist for weeks	• Mild abdominal pain, bloating, flatulence, malabsorption (passage of larger volume stools than normal due to inability to absorb food), low-grade fever	• Eating and drinking may aggravate diarrhea	• Often a history of travel • Common in children	• Infection with protozoal organism called giardia (giardiasis) • See your doctor
Abrupt onset of diarrhea while taking antibiotic medication	• Range from mild abdominal pain and bloating to severe abdominal cramps, fever and bloody diarrhea	• Cessation of antibiotics will generally relieve the symptoms	• May be simply a side effect caused by overgrowth of gastrointestinal flora or due to colitis caused by overgrowth of the bacteria *Clostridium difficile*	• Antibiotic-related diarrhea • See your doctor
Chronic intermittent diarrhea with mucus, sometimes alternating with constipation	• Abdominal pain, flatulence, bloating	• Emotional stress can aggravate symptoms • Increasing dietary fiber can improve symptoms	• Most common in young to middle-aged women	• Irritable bowel syndrome • See your doctor
Watery diarrhea; no mucus or blood	• Recent constipation, bloating and abdominal discomfort • No fever or other signs of infection • Fecal incontinence may occur	• Diet lacking in fiber can aggravate condition	• May be a history of chronic constipation • Watery stool leaks around the compacted feces	• Chronic constipation with overflow diarrhea • See your doctor

SYMPTOM CHARACTERISTIC	ASSOCIATED SYMPTOMS	AGGRAVATING OR ALLEVIATING FACTORS	OTHER RELEVANT FACTORS	POSSIBLE CAUSE AND ACTION
Diarrhea (cont.)				
Loose, bulky, offensively smelling stools	• Abdominal bloating and discomfort, flatulence, weight loss, signs of malnutrition or poor growth	• Worse with certain types of food such as dairy products or wheat products	• May be a history of gallbladder disease, disorders of the pancreas	• Poor absorption of food from the bowel due to lactose intolerance or celiac disease • Malabsorption • See your doctor
Gradual onset of frequent, loose stools containing blood and mucus	• Abdominal pain, weight loss, abdominal tenderness, bloating and passage of larger volume stools than normal due to inability to absorb food • May be associated arthritis or skin lesions	• Anti-inflammatory medication can relieve symptoms	• There may be a family history of inflammatory bowel disease	• Inflammatory bowel disease • Ulcerative colitis and Crohn's disease are the most common of these • See your doctor

Dizziness

Dizziness is a commonly reported symptom. The term "dizziness" is used to describe a variety of sensations such as lightheadedness, faintness, spinning or giddiness. Dizziness usually means either faintness (the feeling that precedes a faint) or vertigo (a false sense of movement). It is often a brief sensation, however persistent or frequent episodes of dizziness occasionally herald a serious medical condition so it is important to have these assessed by a doctor.

SYMPTOM CHARACTERISTIC	ASSOCIATED SYMPTOMS	AGGRAVATING OR ALLEVIATING FACTORS	OTHER RELEVANT FACTORS	POSSIBLE CAUSE AND ACTION
Faintness	• Lightheadedness, visual blurring, loss of vision, heaviness of limbs, loss of consciousness	• Raising legs may improve blood supply to the brain and alleviate the dizziness	• Usually a brief episode	• Faint caused by reduced blood supply to the brain • Causes include low blood pressure on standing, disturbance in heartbeat rhythm, dehydration • See your doctor at once
Sensation of movement or spinning	• Nausea	• Unfamiliar head movements or motion	• Commonly occurs while traveling in cars or on boats	• Motion sickness • Medication to relieve nausea and vomiting can relieve symptoms • See your doctor if you are worried or if symptoms persist
Sudden feeling of dizziness or spinning lasting a few seconds	• Nausea	• Occurs on changes to the position of the head such as rolling in bed	• Related to the blockage of fluid in the balance centers of the inner ear sometimes by tiny "stones"	• Benign paroxysmal positional vertigo • Your doctor can show you simple head movements to unblock the inner ear • Antiemetic medication can relieve symptoms • See your doctor

SYMPTOM CHARACTERISTIC	ASSOCIATED SYMPTOMS	AGGRAVATING OR ALLEVIATING FACTORS	OTHER RELEVANT FACTORS	POSSIBLE CAUSE AND ACTION
Severe episodes of dizziness with a sensation of spinning or linear movement	• Nausea, tendency to fall toward the side of the abnormality, rapid involuntary movements of the eyes	• Aggravated by movement of the head	• May occur only once or lead to recurrent episodes of vertigo	• Acute labyrinthitis caused by infection, poor blood supply to the inner ear or toxicity (drugs or alcohol) • See your doctor
Recurrent episodes of dizziness lasting 20 minutes to 2 hours	• Ringing in the ears (tinnitus), feeling of fullness of the ears, balance problems, nausea, hearing loss	• Reducing dietary salt, caffeine, alcohol may help control episodes	• May be caused by fluid in the canals of the inner ear	• Menière's disease • Full medical assessment is required • Investigations to rule out other causes of symptoms such as acoustic neuroma may be required • Diuretics can help prevent attacks, antiemetics can provide symptomatic relief • See your doctor

Ear pain (earache)

Ear pain is usually due to increased pressure in the middle ear or infection of the ear or surrounding structures. In addition to significant distress and discomfort, ear infections can lead to serious complications such as perforation of the eardrum or spread of an infection to the covering of the brain (meningitis). It is important to seek a doctor's advice, since antibiotic therapy may be needed.

SYMPTOM CHARACTERISTIC	ASSOCIATED SYMPTOMS	AGGRAVATING OR ALLEVIATING FACTORS	OTHER RELEVANT FACTORS	POSSIBLE CAUSE AND ACTION
Dull deep ear pain, feeling of fullness or pressure	• Nasal and sinus congestion, sore throat	• Swallowing can relieve the pressure in the middle ear	• Swelling and blockage of the tubes draining the middle ear results in increased pressure	• Fluid and pressure build-up in the middle ear • Treatment with decongestant medication may help improve the drainage from the middle ear • See your doctor if you are worried or if symptoms persist
Rapid onset of severe deep ear pain	• Fever, hearing loss, feeling of pressure in the ear, discharge if perforation of eardrum occurs, dizziness may occur if inner ear is involved	• Pulling on the external ear does not increase pain • Spontaneous perforation of the eardrum will relieve pain but prolong hearing loss	• Fever may be the only symptom in young children	• Infection of the middle ear (otitis media) caused by a virus or bacteria • See your doctor
Rapid onset of severe pain behind the ear	• Fever, swelling and tenderness over the mastoid (bony process behind the ear containing air cells that are linked to the middle ear)	• Pressure applied over the mastoid process increases the discomfort	• May be a history of otitis media as infection can spread from the middle ear to the mastoid • Meningitis is a complication of mastoid infection	• Bacterial infection of the mastoid air cells (mastoiditis) • See your doctor at once

SYMPTOM CHARACTERISTIC	ASSOCIATED SYMPTOMS	AGGRAVATING OR ALLEVIATING FACTORS	OTHER RELEVANT FACTORS	POSSIBLE CAUSE AND ACTION
Ear pain (earache) (cont.)				
Itching progressing to throbbing pain of ear	• Swelling of external ear canal, foul smelling discharge, hearing loss, enlarged glands in the neck	• Pain is aggravated by pulling on the external ear (pinna) or chewing	• Trauma to the ear canal, swimming, humid conditions, skin disorders such as eczema can predispose to infection	• Bacterial infection of the external ear canal (otitis externa) • See your doctor. Treatment with antibiotic and anti-inflammatory drops may be required • Careful cleansing of the ear canal as instructed by a doctor will aid healing

Eye problems

Mild redness and irritation of the eye is common and usually has a simple underlying cause. Symptoms to beware of include sudden or severe eye pain and changes in vision, especially when associated with a red eye. If in doubt, it is safer to have a doctor check the eye early to prevent any long-term complications. See also entries on *eyesight problems* and *eyelid problems*.

SYMPTOM CHARACTERISTIC	ASSOCIATED SYMPTOMS	AGGRAVATING OR ALLEVIATING FACTORS	OTHER RELEVANT FACTORS	POSSIBLE CAUSE AND ACTION
Sore, dry, gritty eyes	• May be mild redness, normal vision	• Tiredness and the wearing of contact lenses can increase eye irritation	• More common in the elderly • Some medications can predispose to dry eyes (decongestants, diuretics, sleeping pills)	• Dry eyes due to reduced production of tears • Artificial lubricants (or tears) can relieve symptoms • See your doctor
Sore, red eye, yellow sticky discharge, affecting one or both eyes	• Sensitivity to light, itching, burning, gritty feeling on moving the eyes, normal vision	• Rubbing eyes increases itching and discharge	• Highly contagious, often spreads from one eye to the other	• Conjunctivitis caused by a bacteria or virus • Gently cleanse eyes with cool water and avoid wearing contact lenses • See your doctor if you are worried or if symptoms persist
Rapid onset of red, painful eye	• Blurred vision, sensitivity to light, increased tear production, small pupil		• More common in people with joint diseases such as ankylosing spondylitis or Behçet's disease or other autoimmune diseases	• Iritis • See your doctor at once
Rapid onset of red, extremely painful eye on one side	• Nausea, vomiting and blurred vision, cornea may be hazy due to swelling, pupil becomes fixed and dilated in severe cases • Episode may be preceded by vision disturbances such as halos around lights	• Symptoms worsen at night when the pupil dilates • Some medications can make glaucoma worse such as some antidepressants or steroids	• May be a family history of glaucoma • More common in older people with diabetes or hypertension	• Glaucoma • See your doctor at once
Rapid onset of eye pain, oversensitivity to light and blurred vision on one side	• May be a visible white spot on the clear surface of the eye	• Movement of the eye aggravates pain	• May be a history of trauma to the eye such as a scratch	• Corneal ulceration due to infection, exposure or trauma • See your doctor at once

Eyelid problems

The eyelids protect the delicate surface of the eye, so any abnormality of the lid can affect the eye. Most problems of the eyelid are due to infection or structural weakening. See also entries on *eye problems* and *eyesight problems*.

SYMPTOM CHARACTERISTIC	ASSOCIATED SYMPTOMS	AGGRAVATING OR ALLEVIATING FACTORS	OTHER RELEVANT FACTORS	POSSIBLE CAUSE AND ACTION
In-turning of the eyelids	• Eyelashes rub the eye's surface causing irritation	• Worsens with age	• Lower lid affected more than the upper lid	• Entropion • See your doctor
Lower eyelid drooping outwards	• Watering of eye, irritation of eye, ulceration of the eye	• Cold wind and dust can cause irritation to eye due to exposure	• More common in the elderly and people with facial nerve damage	• Ectropion • See your doctor
Drooping of the upper eyelid	• Obstruction of visual field if pupil is obscured, brow ache, tired expression	• Worsens with age and when tired	• Can be a sign of nerve damage or muscular diseases such as muscular dystrophy or myasthenia gravis; occasionally present from birth (congenital ptosis)	• Ptosis • See your doctor
Firm, tender, red lump in or on the edge of the eyelid	• May point like a pimple, vision normal	• Rubbing the eye will aggravate the lump	• Inflammation or cysts in the glands within the eyelid margin (meibomian gland) may result in swelling that remains after healing	• Infection in a hair follicle or gland of the eyelid (stye) • Apply warm compresses and take mild analgesics • See your doctor if you are worried or if symptoms persist
Redness, soreness and scaling of the edge of the eyelid	• Itchiness of eyelid, vision normal • Eyelids may appear greasy, ulcerated or crusted	• Rubbing eyes can spread the infection	• Blepharitis most commonly occurs with acne rosacea or dandruff (seborrheic dermatitis)	• Inflammation of the eyelid (blepharitis) • Cleanse eyes gently with saline • Wash hands after touching eyes and use a clean tissue or cloth on each eye to avoid spreading infection from one eye to the other • See your doctor if you are worried or if symptoms persist
Redness, swelling and tenderness of the eyelid and surrounding face	• Fever, difficulty moving the eye or protrusion of the eyeball is a sign of severe infection	• Rubbing eyes will increase redness and swelling	• Common in children • Severe infection can lead to abscess of the eye-socket (orbit) or spread via the blood to the covering of the brain (meningitis)	• Inflammation within the tissue around the eye (periorbital cellulitis) • See your doctor at once

Eyesight problems

Disturbances of vision are very common. Whether vision is just blurred or there is complete or partial loss of eyesight, visual disturbance is a very distressing and disabling symptom. The eyes are extremely delicate organs and can be damaged by many diseases involving other parts of the body. This section will concentrate on conditions localized to the eye. See also entries on *eye problems* and *eyelid problems*.

SYMPTOM CHARACTERISTIC	ASSOCIATED SYMPTOMS	AGGRAVATING OR ALLEVIATING FACTORS	OTHER RELEVANT FACTORS	POSSIBLE CAUSE AND ACTION
Gradual onset of distorted vision, blurred vision especially when reading	• Central vision is affected but peripheral vision remains intact	• Tends to get worse with age	• Most common cause of loss of vision in the elderly	• Macular degeneration • Have your vision tested as you may need glasses • See your doctor if you are worried or if symptoms persist
Gradual onset of cloudy, foggy vision, distorted color, halos around lights	• Pupil of the eye may appear milky instead of black • Frequent changes in eyeglass prescription	• Vision is worse at night with glare from bright lights	• Cataracts are frequently a complication of diabetes	• Cataracts • See your doctor
Loss of parts of peripheral vision (visual field defects)	• Vision loss is the first symptom	• Early detection and treatment is the only way to prevent permanent vision loss • Those people at risk should be tested for glaucoma	• Risk factors include older age, black race, diabetes, hypertension, nearsightedness and a family history of glaucoma	• Glaucoma • See your doctor at once
Rapid development of hazy vision in one or both eyes lasting days to weeks	• Distortion of color, eye movements may be painful • Pupil is less reactive to light on the affected side	• Symptoms resolve without treatment	• Leads to an increased risk of developing multiple sclerosis	• Inflammation of the optic nerve (optic neuritis) • See your doctor at once
Rapid loss of vision in one eye	• Recent vision disturbances such as "floaters" (dark spots or shapes floating in the field of vision) due to previous small bleeds	• Symptoms depend of the size of the bleed into the vitreous humor (gel-like substance within the eye)	• Common in diabetics with disease of the blood vessels of the retina	• Hemorrhage into the fluid in the eye (vitreous hemorrhage) • See your doctor at once
Sudden loss of vision on one side	• Headache, tenderness of the temple area, pain in the jaw on chewing, fever • May be associated with muscle and joint pains and fatigue	• Anti-inflammatory drugs may relieve symptoms	• Rare disease occurring in the elderly • More common in women	• Temporal arteritis • See your doctor at once
Sudden, painless deterioration of vision in one eye	• Vision loss may be moderate to severe (unable to count fingers)	• Symptoms usually resolve over several months without treatment	• More common in people with glaucoma, atherosclerosis and high blood pressure	• Blockage of the central retinal vein • See your doctor at once

SYMPTOM CHARACTERISTIC	ASSOCIATED SYMPTOMS	AGGRAVATING OR ALLEVIATING FACTORS	OTHER RELEVANT FACTORS	POSSIBLE CAUSE AND ACTION
Sudden, complete, painless loss of vision in one eye	• Pupil does not react to light on one side	• Firm pressure on the eye may dislodge the obstruction	• More common in people with carotid artery atherosclerosis • Vision loss is often permanent	• Blockage of the central retinal artery • This is a medical emergency • Go to the emergency room or call an ambulance at once
Sudden painless loss of vision in one eye, like a curtain falling down	• Recent visual disturbances such as flashing lights or spots before the eyes	• Pressure on eye may aggravate vision loss	• May be a history of trauma, glaucoma, cataract surgery or nearsightedness	• Detached retina • This is a medical emergency • Go to the emergency room or call an ambulance at once

Facial pain

Facial pain can be a severe and distressing symptom. Facial neuralgia (recurrent stabbing, burning facial pain in a particular area of the face) may be severe, and do not respond well to simple painkillers. Any worrying facial pain should be assessed by a doctor.

SYMPTOM CHARACTERISTIC	ASSOCIATED SYMPTOMS	AGGRAVATING OR ALLEVIATING FACTORS	OTHER RELEVANT FACTORS	POSSIBLE CAUSE AND ACTION
Aching pain in the forehead, cheeks and upper jaw	• Feeling of pressure, nasal discharge, discharge from the back of the nose into throat, fever, tenderness of the forehead and facial bones	• Leaning forward can worsen pain	• May be a history of upper respiratory tract infection	• Sinus congestion or sinus infection (sinusitis) • Try decongestant medications from your pharmacist • See your doctor if you are worried or if symptoms persist
Episodes of sudden excruciating pain in the lips, gum, cheek or chin on one side of the face, lasting seconds to minutes	• Episodes occur regularly, day or night for several weeks	• Touching face, chewing, smiling, talking, blowing nose can trigger pain	• Usually occurs in the elderly • More common in women than men • There is usually no known cause	• Tic douloureux (trigeminal neuralgia) • See your doctor at once
Episodes of aching or burning pain on one side of the face	• Numbness, tingling in the same area	• Touching or moving the face can trigger an episode of pain	• May be a history of shingles	• Pain following shingles (post-zoster neuralgia) • See your doctor at once
Episodes of burning, stabbing pain, usually on one side of the face lasting up to an hour	• Numbness or tingling, may be followed by a headache	• Painkillers may relieve the pain	• May be a history of migraine • More common in women	• Migrainous neuralgia • See your doctor at once
Severe aching pain from the side of the face, in front of the ear on one side	• Tenderness over upper jaw joint (temporomandibular joint), malocclusion of teeth	• Chewing makes pain worse	• Usually occurs in elderly women • May be a history of rheumatoid arthritis	• Arthritis of the temporomandibular joint • See your doctor
Ache in the upper or lower jaw on one side	• Teeth sensitive to hot or cold, pain on chewing, feeling of pressure in jaw, may be fever	• Painkillers should relieve the pain	• May be a history of previous problems with teeth or fillings	• Tooth decay or abscess • Painkillers will ease the pain • See your dentist as soon as possible

SYMPTOM CHARACTERISTIC	ASSOCIATED SYMPTOMS	AGGRAVATING OR ALLEVIATING FACTORS	OTHER RELEVANT FACTORS	POSSIBLE CAUSE AND ACTION

Fatigue

Fatigue, or tiredness, is a common symptom that can occur after periods of exertion or following a poor night's sleep. However, in conjunction with other symptoms, it can also signal more serious medical problems.

SYMPTOM CHARACTERISTIC	ASSOCIATED SYMPTOMS	AGGRAVATING OR ALLEVIATING FACTORS	OTHER RELEVANT FACTORS	POSSIBLE CAUSE AND ACTION
Daytime fatigue and drowsiness	• Trouble falling asleep at night and/or difficulty sleeping through the night	• Stress and anxiety about inability to fall asleep or about personal problems	• Mild insomnia is common during pregnancy	• Insomnia • Try relaxation strategies before bed (e.g. taking a warm bath, reading for pleasure (not work-related reading), relaxation exercises) • Self-help information may be available at your pharmacy or hospital • See your doctor if you are worried or if symptoms persist
General leathargy that may limit daily activities	• Tendency to feel stressed or anxious		• Fatigue is common in those who try to do too much, or fit too much into their daily routine at the expense of rest and relaxation	• Lifestyle problems (e.g. overwork, lack of regular exercise, obesity, lack of sleep time) can contribute to fatigue • Try to change elements of lifestyle (e.g. exercise more, lose excess weight, cut down on excess workload where possible) • See your doctor if you are worried or if symptoms persist
Weakness and fatigue	• Dizziness, faintness, pale skin, loss of appetite, heart palpitations		• Commonly occurs with blood loss (e.g. after surgery or with repeated heavy periods) • Anemia may develop in pregnancy due to the increased demands placed on the mother's iron supplies	• Iron deficiency anemia • See your doctor
Debilitating fatigue that lasts for several months or longer, and becomes worse over time	• Persistent low-grade fever, aches and pains, weakness, swollen lymph nodes, joint pain, sore throat	• Fatigue is not from exertion and is not relieved by rest; however it can worsen following physical exertion	• This condition primarily affects young, urban professionals • The cause of this illness is not clear, but viruses, allergies, and hormonal imbalances may play some role • It may last for several months or years, but the majority or sufferers do recuperate	• Chronic fatigue syndrome • See your doctor

SYMPTOM CHARACTERISTIC	ASSOCIATED SYMPTOMS	AGGRAVATING OR ALLEVIATING FACTORS	OTHER RELEVANT FACTORS	POSSIBLE CAUSE AND ACTION
Fatigue that develops after starting new medication		• Not affected by physical activity or rest	• Medications that can cause fatigue include sleeping pills, cough and cold preparations, and blood pressure medication	• Medication side effect • See your doctor
Fatigue and lack of energy	• Persistent sadness and pessimism, change in appetite, difficulty sleeping or tendency to oversleep • May have thoughts of death or suicide	• May follow stressful life-changing events (e.g. death of a family member, loss of job, diagnosis of serious illness)	• Depression affects 25 percent of women, 10 percent of men, and 5 percent of adolescents at some time in their lives	• Depression • See your doctor at once
Extreme fatigue that develops quickly	• Sore throat, fever, chills headache, body aches, cough, nasal congestion		• Flu vaccination is recommended for those at risk or over 65 years of age	• Influenza • Rest as much as possible, drink plenty of fluids, take fever-reducing medication • See your doctor if you are worried or if symptoms persist
Fatigue, faintness, weakness	• Excessive thirst, frequent urination, increased appetite, weight loss, nausea, blurred vision • In women, frequent vaginal infections; in men, impotence • Recurring yeast infections in both sexes			• Diabetes • See your doctor at once
Fatigue that may progressively worsen	• Weight loss, cough (sometimes with bloody sputum), slight fever, night sweats, pain in the chest or back		• Lung cancer is most common among cigarette smokers • Tuberculosis occurs most frequently in Asia, Africa, the Middle East and Latin America	• Tuberculosis or lung cancer • See your doctor at once
Fatigue and weakness	• Shortness of breath, coughing, swelling of the abdomen or legs, rapid heartbeat	• Symptoms may worsen with exertion	• The risk of developing congestive heart failure is elevated in people with a history of cardiovascular disease, including hypertension or arrhythmia • Congestive heart failure may be triggered by infection, anemia, pregnancy or rheumatic fever	• Congestive heart failure • This is a medical emergency • Go to the emergency room or call an ambulance at once

SYMPTOM CHARACTERISTIC	ASSOCIATED SYMPTOMS	AGGRAVATING OR ALLEVIATING FACTORS	OTHER RELEVANT FACTORS	POSSIBLE CAUSE AND ACTION

Fever

Fever is defined as a body temperature higher than the normal 98.6°F (37°C) taken orally. Mild or short-term temperature rises are common with minor infections, but high or sustained fever can signal a potentially dangerous and serious infection. Fever is often accompanied by other symptoms, as outlined below, which may help identify the cause.

The first table that follows applies to fever in adults and children of all ages. The second table deals with some additional symptoms specific to infants and children.

Fever in adults and children of all ages

SYMPTOM CHARACTERISTIC	ASSOCIATED SYMPTOMS	AGGRAVATING OR ALLEVIATING FACTORS	OTHER RELEVANT FACTORS	POSSIBLE CAUSE AND ACTION
Fever—body temperature above 98.6°F (37°C)	• Flushed face, hot skin, sore throat, mild headache		• May follow exposure to people with similar symptoms	• Viral infection (e.g. cold or flu) • Take decongestant and fever-reducing medication • For any fever it is advisable to: – remove excess layers of clothing – drink plenty of fluids – take fever-reducing medication – have a lukewarm bath – check temperature every 4–6 hours • See your doctor if: – temperature remains at 102.2°F (39°C) or above in adults or 101.3°F (38.5°C) in children – fever lasts longer than 48 hours – the patient is pregnant – the patient is a child • In children, use a non-aspirin fever-reducing medication formulated for children • See your doctor if the fever does not respond quickly to medication or if the child has a sore throat or painful ear

SYMPTOM CHARACTERISTIC	ASSOCIATED SYMPTOMS	AGGRAVATING OR ALLEVIATING FACTORS	OTHER RELEVANT FACTORS	POSSIBLE CAUSE AND ACTION
Fever	• Aches, chills, nausea, vomiting, cramping, diarrhea		• Affects all age groups, but may cause life-threatening dehydration in the very young, the very ill and the elderly	• Gastroenteritis or other viral infection • Rest and follow standard advice for any fever: – remove excess layers of clothing – drink plenty of fluids – take a fever-reducing medication – have a lukewarm bath – check temperature every 4–6 hours • Use anti-diarrhea and anti-vomiting medications as advised by your pharmacist or doctor • See your doctor if vomiting lasts longer than 12 hours or if there is bloody diarrhea • See your doctor if you are worried or if symptoms persist
Fever	• Cough that is producing yellow or green mucus, rapid, light breathing, fatigue			• Respiratory infection (e.g. bronchitis or pneumonia) • See your doctor to assess the degree of lung congestion • Antibiotics may be required
Fever	• Severe headache, neck stiffness, drowsiness, vomiting, sensitivity to light		• May be confused and unable to respond well to questioning	• An infection in the area around the brain (meningitis) • This is a medical emergency • See your doctor or emergency department
Fevers that come and go over a period of weeks	• Sore throat, tiredness		• Infectious mononucleosis (glandular fever) with symptoms is most common in adolescents and adults • Although the infection is common in children, symptoms are generally milder and resemble a common cold, so the diagnosis is rarely made	• Prolonged viral illness such as infectious mononucleosis (glandular fever), other infection, or sign of another medical condition • See your doctor

SYMPTOM CHARACTERISTIC	ASSOCIATED SYMPTOMS	AGGRAVATING OR ALLEVIATING FACTORS	OTHER RELEVANT FACTORS	POSSIBLE CAUSE AND ACTION
Fever (cont.)				
Sudden onset of fever with simultaneous sore throat	• Headache		• Tends to occur during the colder months and can be precipitated by stress, overwork, exhaustion and when the body's immune system is fighting other infections	• Strep throat (streptococcal infection) • Rest and follow standard advice for any fever: – remove excess layers of clothing – drink plenty of fluids – take a fever-reducing medication – have a lukewarm bath – check temperature every 4–6 hours • See your doctor
High fever over 107.6°F (42°C)	• Flushed, dry, hot skin, rapid pulse, confusion, constricted pupils, seizures or fainting		• Follows exposure to hot weather or strenuous exercise in high temperatures, and dehydration	• Heatstroke, including sunstroke • Quickly move person to a cool place and cover body with cool, wet clothes • This is a medical emergency • Go to the emergency room or call an ambulance at once
Fever in a person taking medications for another medical condition			• May occur with anticancer chemotherapy (due to temporary immune system suppression), drugs used to treat invasive fungal infections, anticoagulants used in cardiovascular disease	• Fever can occur as a side effect of some medications • See your doctor—medication may be changed or dose altered
Fever	• Ear pain, hearing loss, feeling of fullness or fluid in the ear		• Fever may be the predominant sign in a child too young to indicate other symptoms	• Middle ear infection (otitis media) or outer ear infection (otitis externa) • Ear infections can lead to more serious problems if not treated, so see your doctor for assessment • Antibiotic treatment may be required • See your doctor
Fever	• Pain with urination or low back pain, tenderness on both sides of the lower back			• Kidney infection • You may require treatment with antibiotics • See your doctor at once

SYMPTOM CHARACTERISTIC	ASSOCIATED SYMPTOMS	AGGRAVATING OR ALLEVIATING FACTORS	OTHER RELEVANT FACTORS	POSSIBLE CAUSE AND ACTION
Fever	• Open sore or wound that is red • Red streaking on the arms or legs originating near the wound • Surrounding skin may be tender and hot; there may also be localized swelling			• Blood poisoning as a result of infection of the skin or lymphatic system • See your doctor at once

Fever in infants and children

SYMPTOM CHARACTERISTIC	ASSOCIATED SYMPTOMS	AGGRAVATING OR ALLEVIATING FACTORS	OTHER RELEVANT FACTORS	POSSIBLE CAUSE AND ACTION
Fever in a child aged under 3 months	• Lethargy, pale skin, irritability			• Fever in a baby should always be investigated to rule out serious infection • See your doctor at once
High fever over 101.3°F (38.5°C)	• Barking cough			• Croup • See a doctor as soon as possible • For any fever it is advisable to: – remove excess layers of clothing – drink plenty of fluids – take a fever-reducing medication – have a lukewarm bath – check temperature every 4–6 hours • See your doctor at once
Fever	• Blisters over face, back, neck and chest		• Occurs most commonly in children • May occur in adult not previously infected • Follows recent contact with person with chickenpox • Highly infectious, so common among childcare and hospital workers • Vaccination to prevent is now available in some countries	• Chickenpox • Chickenpox infection may be severe in adults, so ask medical advice at once • Take children with suspected chickenpox for assessment by a doctor, and keep child away from others who have not been infected • See your doctor • Chickenpox is highly contagious, so warn the doctor's office of the possibility of infection before attending

SYMPTOM CHARACTERISTIC	ASSOCIATED SYMPTOMS	AGGRAVATING OR ALLEVIATING FACTORS	OTHER RELEVANT FACTORS	POSSIBLE CAUSE AND ACTION
Fever (cont.)				
High fever, above 102°F (39°C)	• Seizure or convulsion may be triggered by high fever		• Three percent of children have at least one febrile convulsion • Cooling a feverish child in a lukewarm bath can help prevent a convulsion • A rapid rise in body temperature is more likely to cause seizures than a slow rise to the same temperature	• Febrile seizure • This requires immediate action • Ensure the airway is clear and turn child on to the side • Remove clothing and bathe or sponge with lukewarm water after the seizure has finished • See your doctor as soon as possible

Flatulence

Flatulence is the feeling or presence of gas in the stomach and intestines. A build-up of gas can cause a sensation of fullness or discomfort in the abdomen, which can lead to the passing of flatus (gas) through the anus or belching through the mouth. It is usually not harmful but can be a source of embarrassment for some people. See also entry on *abdominal distension*.

SYMPTOM CHARACTERISTIC	ASSOCIATED SYMPTOMS	AGGRAVATING OR ALLEVIATING FACTORS	OTHER RELEVANT FACTORS	POSSIBLE CAUSE AND ACTION
An uncomfortable, bloated feeling in the abdomen	• Bloating of abdomen, frequent passing of gas from the anus, abdominal pain	• Constipation may cause or worsen gas build-up in the bowel, by slowing the passage of food and increasing the chance of fermentation	• Flatulence may be caused by eating foods that ferment in the intestines and produce gas including beans, peas, wheat, oats, bran, cabbage, corn, brussels sprouts	• Dietary imbalance • Eat less of those foods likely to cause flatulence • This may require eliminating one food group at a time to see what leads to the flatulence • Anti-flatulent medications (e.g. charcoal tablets, simethicone) may also be useful • For constipation, eat foods rich in fiber and drink plenty of fluids • See your doctor if you are worried or if symptoms persist • See your doctor at once if abdominal pain is constant
Frequent passing of flatus, bloating of the abdomen following consumption of dairy foods	• Abdominal cramps, frothy diarrhea, vomiting	• Worsens after eating dairy products, disappears when these are eliminated from the diet	• More common in people from Asia, Africa and the subtropics, due to their low consumption of dairy products after infancy which leads to an underproduction of lactase, the enzyme that is necessary for digestion of lactose	• Lactose intolerance • See your doctor • Do not attempt to treat yourself or a child for lactose intolerance without medical advice • If lactose intolerance is confirmed, restrict consumption of dairy products, or take a lactase supplement to aid the digestion of lactose

SYMPTOM CHARACTERISTIC	ASSOCIATED SYMPTOMS	AGGRAVATING OR ALLEVIATING FACTORS	OTHER RELEVANT FACTORS	POSSIBLE CAUSE AND ACTION
Frequent belching (burping)		• Hurried eating or gulping, talking while eating, chewing gum, drinking carbonated (fizzy) drinks	• Dental problems and nose or mouth deformities may lead to belching due to an increase in swallowed air	• Too much air swallowed • Don't talk while eating, eat slowly and take small mouthfuls of food • Minimize chewing gum • Drink less carbonated drinks • See your doctor if you are worried or if symptoms persist
Increased passing of flatus, abdominal pain, bloating	• Constipation or diarrhea shortly after meals	• Abdominal pain usually relieved after passage of wind or bowel movement	• Overeating, bingeing or too much fat in the diet can bring on an episode	• Irritable bowel syndrome • Cause is unknown but may be related to stress, food sensitivities, eating irregularly • See your doctor

Foot and ankle problems

Most people experience occasional problems with the foot or ankle. Ankle sprains are one of the most common musculoskeletal injuries, while degenerative disorders such as gout and heel spurs may often affect people as they age.

SYMPTOM CHARACTERISTIC	ASSOCIATED SYMPTOMS	AGGRAVATING OR ALLEVIATING FACTORS	OTHER RELEVANT FACTORS	POSSIBLE CAUSE AND ACTION
Pain and swelling, usually on one side of the ankle, following twisting injury or fall	• Bruising, warmth	• May be aggravated by walking, but pain does not stop walking	• Most commonly affects the outer side of the ankle	• Injury to the ligaments in the ankle (ankle sprain) • Rest, apply ice, elevate the foot, use a compression bandage • See your doctor
Severe pain around the ankle following a fall, twisting injury, or direct blow to the ankle	• Swelling of the ankle and possibly foot and toes, throbbing, warmth, bruising, inability to walk	• Aggravated by walking or movement of the ankle		• Fracture or severe ligament sprain • Elevate the leg, apply ice • See your doctor at once
Pain under the heel and arch of the foot	• Maybe stiffness in the heel	• Prolonged walking or running	• Can lead to development of a heel spur (see directly below)	• Plantar fasciitis • See your doctor
Sharp pain under the heel	• May be some swelling	• Aggravated by walking, pressing on the heel	• May be more common in those with flat feet	• Excess growth of bone at the heel (spur) • See your doctor
Sudden onset of severe pain in the big toe, foot or ankle; pain often begins at night and may last for several days	• Swelling, skin over the affected area is usually red, hot, shiny and very tender to touch • May be fever and chills	• Aggravated by walking, anything pressing on the area (e.g. shoes, socks)	• Most commonly affects the big toe, but can affect many other joints in the body • Usually affects one or two joints at a time, and attacks recur	• Gout • See your doctor

SYMPTOM CHARACTERISTIC	ASSOCIATED SYMPTOMS	AGGRAVATING OR ALLEVIATING FACTORS	OTHER RELEVANT FACTORS	POSSIBLE CAUSE AND ACTION
Foot and ankle problems (cont.)				
Dull ache or pain at the back of the heel which travels up the back of the ankle and lower calf	• Mild swelling, tenderness, warmth at the back of the ankle	• Aggravated by running, jumping, walking, bicycling especially when first begin the activity	• More common in those with flat feet or tight muscles in the calf	• Inflammation of the Achilles tendon at the back of the ankle (tendinitis) • Avoid activities that cause pain • See your doctor for advice
Pain in the front part of the foot, usually during prolonged running or walking, or athletic activity	• May be some swelling, tenderness to touch	• Continuous, repeated activity especially running, walking	• More common in people whose feet have high arches	• Stress fracture • See your doctor

Genital itching

Genital itching is usually a symptom of infection or irritation of the genitals. It may occur in conjunction with genital pain (see following entry) and can be a symptom of some sexually transmitted diseases. See also entries on *genital pain* and *vaginal problems*.

SYMPTOM CHARACTERISTIC	ASSOCIATED SYMPTOMS	AGGRAVATING OR ALLEVIATING FACTORS	OTHER RELEVANT FACTORS	POSSIBLE CAUSE AND ACTION
Mildly itchy, raised growths on the vulva, penis or anus, which may develop a cauliflower-like appearance	• Mild pain, increased dampness or moisture in the area of the growths, increased discharge from the vagina or penis		• Although human papillomavirus infections are associated with some cancers (e.g. cervical cancer), most genital warts are caused by a different strain of human papillomavirus which does not cause cancer	• Genital warts • See your doctor
Itchy, painful rash around the vagina or on the penis	• In women, the vulva may be swollen and red, and there may be a thick, white discharge	• Sexual intercourse may increase discomfort	• Yeast infections can be a side effect of taking antibiotics, or may be triggered by stress, pregnancy, or use of the contraceptive pill • Candidiasis is most likely in women with diabetes or as a side effect of some antibiotics	• Candidiasis ("thrush") • or moniliasis infection • Wear cotton underwear and loose clothing • See your doctor
In females, itching, dryness and irritation of the vagina		• Sexual intercourse may be difficult and painful	• May occur in women following menopause, because a lack of estrogen causes dryness of the vagina	• Hormonal deficiency • Dryness can be relieved with vaginal lubricants • See your doctor if you are worried or if symptoms persist
Itching and burning of the genitals after sexual intercourse	• Redness or rash	• Symptoms may be aggravated by sexual intercourse	• Spermicides or other products used directly on the genitals may cause allergic reactions in susceptible people	• Allergic reaction • Discontinue use of spermicides • See your doctor

SYMPTOM CHARACTERISTIC	ASSOCIATED SYMPTOMS	AGGRAVATING OR ALLEVIATING FACTORS	OTHER RELEVANT FACTORS	POSSIBLE CAUSE AND ACTION
In females, irritation and itching inside and outside the vagina	• Inflammation or swelling, vaginal discharge, foul or fishy vaginal odor, dryness or discomfort during sexual intercourse, discomfort or burning with urination	• Symptoms may be aggravated by sexual intercourse		• Vaginitis • Vaginitis has a range of causes, including infections with bacteria, fungus, viruses • See your doctor

Genital pain

Pain in the genital area is usually the result of an infection, or may occur following injury. Sexually transmitted diseases are a common cause of infection, so it is important to practice safe sex to prevent further spread of these conditions, and consult your doctor for treatment. Any pain with sexual intercourse should be investigated by a doctor. See also entries on *genital itching* and *vaginal problems*.

SYMPTOM CHARACTERISTIC	ASSOCIATED SYMPTOMS	AGGRAVATING OR ALLEVIATING FACTORS	OTHER RELEVANT FACTORS	POSSIBLE CAUSE AND ACTION
Painful blisters on the genitals, which may break, weep and form sores; the first occurrence of blisters may last from 5 days to several weeks; further episodes are usually shorter and less severe, and usually occur less frequently	• Itchy, tingling sensation, swollen and tender lymph nodes in the groin, pain on urination, discharge from the urethra in men and vagina in women • Weakness or constipation may occur • Erectile dysfunction may occur in men	• Pain may be aggravated when urine comes into contact with the blisters	• Triggers for an episode may be stress, illness, sexual intercourse, menstruation • If a pregnant woman has an attack of genital herpes towards the end of her pregnancy, there is a risk of passing it on to the baby and causing serious problems such as brain damage; cesarean section may overcome this problem	• Genital herpes • Wear cotton underwear and loose clothing • See your doctor at once • Avoid sexual contact until medical advice is obtained
In women, tender swelling of the vaginal opening or swelling of one labia	• May be hot and painful to touch	• Sexual contact may aggravate pain		• Infection or abscess in a Bartholin's gland, or an infection of the labia • See your doctor at once
Burning sensation or pain with urination	• Frequent urge to urinate, even when bladder is empty • Urinating only small amounts • Burning sensation in lower abdomen, urine with a strong odor	• Lack of adequate fluid intake may prolong symptoms • Sexual contact may aggravate pain	• Cystitis is more common in women than in men • Infection may be triggered by sexual contact, use of diaphragm for birth control or use of urinary catheters	• Cystitis • Drink plenty of water • See your doctor
In men, tender and swollen tip of the penis		• Symptoms may be aggravated by sexual contact, pressure from tight clothing		• Infection of the head of the penis (balanitis) • See your doctor at once
In men, pain with ejaculation	• Blood in the semen, tenderness with bowel movements, or pain behind the penis or scrotum		• Sudden-onset prostatitis caused by a bacterial infection is most frequent in young men • Prostatitis may be triggered by the use of urinary catheters	• Prostatitis • See your doctor at once

SYMPTOM CHARACTERISTIC	ASSOCIATED SYMPTOMS	AGGRAVATING OR ALLEVIATING FACTORS	OTHER RELEVANT FACTORS	POSSIBLE CAUSE AND ACTION
Genital pain (cont.)				
In women, mild pain or discomfort while urinating	• Vaginal discharge, abdominal pain, rectal pain, sore throat		• Chlamydia is one of the most common sexually transmitted infections, and is most common in young, sexually active people • Most chlamydial infections do not cause any symptoms, so transmission is very common and easy	• Chlamydia • See your doctor at once • Avoid sexual contact until medical advice is obtained
In men, pain during urination	• Pus or mucus may be visible in urine		• Urethritis is the most common form of sexually transmitted disease • Occurs most frequently in sexually active young men	• Urethritis, caused by sexually transmitted infection • See your doctor at once
Painful urination in men or women	• Inflamed genitals after sexual intercourse • In males, discharge of pus from the penis • In females, vaginal discharge, urge to urinate frequently, abnormal menstrual bleeding • The infection may spread from the genitals to the urethra, rectum, conjunctiva, pharynx or cervix		• The incidence of gonorrhea is much higher in the USA than in other industrialized countries • Potential complications include inflammation of reproductive organs, peritonitis, inflammation around the liver, inflammation of the Bartholin's gland in women and epididymitis or abscess around the urethra in men, arthritis, dermatitis, endocarditis, meningitis, myocarditis or hepatitis	• Gonorrhea • See your doctor at once
Pain and tenderness in the genital area	• Bruising, possibly some discharge, urinary tract infection • Person may appear irritable or fearful	• Symptoms are aggravated by walking or sitting		• Sexual abuse or rape • See your doctor at once
Pain with sexual intercourse in women	• Bleeding after sexual intercourse, watery discharge from vagina, painful bowel movements, frequent urge to urinate		• Vaginal tumors are rare	• Tumor of the vagina • See your doctor at once

SYMPTOM CHARACTERISTIC	ASSOCIATED SYMPTOMS	AGGRAVATING OR ALLEVIATING FACTORS	OTHER RELEVANT FACTORS	POSSIBLE CAUSE AND ACTION

"Glands", swollen

The term "swollen glands" usually refers to swelling of the lymph nodes (also known as lymph glands) in the neck, armpit or groin. There are many causes of swollen lymph nodes, ranging from mild infections to serious disorders such as cancer. Swelling often goes down as the infection resolves, but if your glands stay swollen for more than two weeks consult your doctor.

SYMPTOM CHARACTERISTIC	ASSOCIATED SYMPTOMS	AGGRAVATING OR ALLEVIATING FACTORS	OTHER RELEVANT FACTORS	POSSIBLE CAUSE AND ACTION
Swollen, tender lymph nodes ("glands") in the neck, armpit or groin	• Skin over the nodes may be hot and red • There is usually an obvious site of infection nearby (e.g. an infected cut or sore, or a tooth, eye or ear infection) • Red lines may radiate from the site of infection towards the lymph nodes		• Inflammation of the lymph nodes (lymphadenitis) may occur with bacterial, viral or fungal infections	• Lymphadenitis • See your doctor
Swollen, lymph nodes in the neck	• Fever, fatigue, sore throat, headache		• Infectious mononucleosis occurs most commonly in young adults • The virus is contagious and is passed via kissing, coughing and sneezing; sometimes known as "the kissing disease"	• Infectious mononucleosis (glandular fever) • See your doctor
Swollen, tender lymph nodes in the neck	• Sore throat, headache, fever, bad breath, white spots on the tonsils	• Symptoms may be aggravated by moving the neck, swallowing or speaking		• Streptococcal infection ("strep throat") • See your doctor
Enlarged, non-tender lymph nodes throughout the body	• Fatigue, night sweats, weight loss, fever, severe itching all over the body • Lymph nodes enlarge slowly and are usually painless		• Non-Hodgkin's lymphoma is a relatively common cancer, and occurs most frequently in children and young adults • Hodgkin's disease occurs most commonly in young adults or in people over 50 years, and is more prevalent in men then women	• Cancer of the lymphatic system (lymphoma) (e.g. Hodgkin's lymphoma or non-Hodgkin's lymphoma) • See your doctor at once
Swollen lymph nodes in the neck, groin or armpit	• Weight loss, fatigue, tendency to bruise or bleed easily, loss of appetite • Anemia is common during the early stages of leukemia		• Leukemia may increase susceptibility to infections (e.g. tonsillitis, pneumonia) • Leukemia is most common in children and young adults	• Leukemia • See your doctor at once

SYMPTOM CHARACTERISTIC	ASSOCIATED SYMPTOMS	AGGRAVATING OR ALLEVIATING FACTORS	OTHER RELEVANT FACTORS	POSSIBLE CAUSE AND ACTION
"Glands", swollen (cont.)				
Swollen, inflamed lymph nodes just above the angle of the jaw, on one or both sides of the face	• Fever, fatigue, swelling of the lymph nodes under the tongue, testicular swelling in males, or abdominal pain	• Pain with chewing or swallowing	• Mumps is contagious, but less so than other infections such as measles or chickenpox • It is a preventable through immunization • In countries where mumps vaccination is widely practiced, mumps occurs most frequently in adults • Prior to routine vaccination it occurred most commonly in children • Mumps is spread by close contact	• Mumps • See your doctor

Gums, bleeding

Bleeding gums are usually a sign of gum disease, most often caused by poor oral hygiene. Smokers are more than twice as likely as non-smokers to develop gum disease, while other at-risk groups include people with diabetes, leukemia, and Crohn's disease.

SYMPTOM CHARACTERISTIC	ASSOCIATED SYMPTOMS	AGGRAVATING OR ALLEVIATING FACTORS	OTHER RELEVANT FACTORS	POSSIBLE CAUSE AND ACTION
Swollen, red gums that bleed easily, e.g. with brushing of the teeth or with eating	• Gums are tender when touched or when chewing food	• Eating can aggravate symptoms	• The hormonal changes of pregnancy can worsen the condition • Gingivitis is most commonly caused by poor oral hygiene, including inadequate brushing and flossing of the teeth	• Gingivitis • See your doctor or dentist
Bleeding, red gums	• Pus around the teeth, bad taste in the mouth, halitosis (bad breath) • Periodontitis may lead eventually to deepening of the pockets around the teeth, loose teeth, and loss of teeth	• Symptoms may be aggravated by eating	• Periodontitis occurs when gingivitis extends to the supporting structures of the teeth	• Periodontitis • See your dentist
Sudden onset of painful gums that bleed easily	• Fatigue, bad breath, excess saliva, appearance of gray-white mucus covering the gums	• Eating and swallowing may aggravate symptoms	• Poor oral hygiene predisposes to this condition, known as trench mouth; the term comes from World War I when many soldiers in the trenches developed the infection	• Bacterial infection of the mouth (Vincent's angina, Vincent's disease known as trench mouth) • See your dentist

SYMPTOM CHARACTERISTIC	ASSOCIATED SYMPTOMS	AGGRAVATING OR ALLEVIATING FACTORS	OTHER RELEVANT FACTORS	POSSIBLE CAUSE AND ACTION
Tendency to bleed easily from the gums and nose	• Swollen lymph nodes in the neck, groin or armpit, weight loss, fatigue, tendency to bruise easily, loss of appetite		• Increased susceptibility to infections (e.g. tonsillitis, pneumonia)	• Leukemia or serious infection (e.g. AIDS) • See your doctor at once
Extremely sore, swollen gums that bleed easily	• Earaches, symptoms similar to those of sinusitis, nosebleeds, fever, weight loss, cough, fatigue		• Wegener's granulomatosis is a rare disease occurring most commonly in white people • It occurs at any age, most common around 40 years	• Wegener's granulomatosis, a rare, serious disease • See your doctor at once

Hair problems

Hair loss or the growth of excessive hair can be a distressing symptom. While this may be a normal part of ageing, sometimes abnormal hair loss or growth can herald an underlying disorder. If your loss or gain of hair is worrying you, seek advice from your doctor. Many types of hair problems can be treated.

SYMPTOM CHARACTERISTIC	ASSOCIATED SYMPTOMS	AGGRAVATING OR ALLEVIATING FACTORS	OTHER RELEVANT FACTORS	POSSIBLE CAUSE AND ACTION
Gradual hair loss in the front or on the top of the head in men	• Affects middle-aged to elderly men		• May be a history of similar hair loss in male family members	• Male-pattern baldness • See your doctor
Gradual thinning or loss of hair all over the head, in a person taking medication	• Hair may fall out in clumps	• Hair loss will stop and new hair grow when medication ceased	• Person is taking a medication such as chemotherapy or steroids • Occasionally hair loss is a side effect of some anti-ulcer drugs, blood thinners or drugs to control blood pressure	• Medication-related hair loss • See your doctor
Gradual thinning or loss of hair all over the head in older adult women	• Hot flashes (flushes), mood swings, absentmindedness, irregular menstruation	• Gentle hair-care may prolong the life of ageing hair follicles	• Usually occurs in women over 50 years of age who may be undergoing menopause	• Hormonal changes related to ageing in women, or anemia (e.g. pernicious anemia or iron deficiency anemia) • See your doctor
Rapid thinning or loss of hair all over head	• Emotional or physical stress	• Rest and relaxation may reduce hair loss	• History of major surgery, childbirth or emotional stress	• Stress-related hair loss • Reduce stress • See your doctor if you are worried or symptoms persist
Small patches of hair falling out on the head	• Coin-shaped areas of baldness, healthy scalp and remaining hair is healthy	• No obvious cause or pattern to hair loss	• Usually resolves spontaneously • Occasionally can result in hair loss from the whole body	• Alopecia • See your doctor

SYMPTOM CHARACTERISTIC	ASSOCIATED SYMPTOMS	AGGRAVATING OR ALLEVIATING FACTORS	OTHER RELEVANT FACTORS	POSSIBLE CAUSE AND ACTION
Hair problems (cont.)				
Small patches of hair falling out on the head	• Oily, red or purple patches on scalp • May be similar lesion elsewhere on the body	• Scratching area can increase hair loss and increase inflammation	• Usually resolves over time but treatment may be necessary	• Dandruff (seborrheic dermatitis) or other skin diseases (e.g. fungal infection, lichen planus) • See your doctor at once
Excessive growth of dark coarse hair on face or body in a female	• May have deep voice or irregular periods	• Weight loss in the overweight can reduce the level of male hormone, reducing hair growth	• Person may be taking birth control pills, hormone supplements or anabolic steroids • Rarely, a tumor or the adrenal glands may produce excess male hormones	• Hirsutism due to excess male hormone (androgen) • See your doctor

Hallucinations

Hallucinations—hearing, seeing or feeling things that are not really there—are usually a symptom of mental illness, but may also occur in response to certain drugs, infections or as a result of alcohol withdrawal.

SYMPTOM CHARACTERISTIC	ASSOCIATED SYMPTOMS	AGGRAVATING OR ALLEVIATING FACTORS	OTHER RELEVANT FACTORS	POSSIBLE CAUSE AND ACTION
Hearing or seeing things that are not really there	• Excess physical activity and elation, irritability, hostility, easily distracted, impatient, false convictions of personal power, wealth and importance, paranoia, decreased need for sleep, increased sexual desire and risk-taking behavior (e.g. gambling) • Episodes usually emerge over a period of days to weeks, but may occur within a few hours (often morning)	• Symptoms may be aggravated by stress	• Symptoms usually develop rapidly, over a period of several days; while the collection of symptoms usually makes the diagnosis of mania straightforward, the person suffering from the disorder frequently denies there is anything wrong, so doctors usually have to obtain information from family members • Alcohol abuse or substance abuse often occur with bipolar disorder • Among patients with bipolar disorder, women are more prone to depressive episodes and men to manic episodes	• Mania • Mania most frequently occurs as a symptom of bipolar disorder ("manic-depression") • See your doctor

SYMPTOM CHARACTERISTIC	ASSOCIATED SYMPTOMS	AGGRAVATING OR ALLEVIATING FACTORS	OTHER RELEVANT FACTORS	POSSIBLE CAUSE AND ACTION
Hearing voices telling you what to do or saying things about you	• Visual hallucinations, delusions, disorganized speech, irrational behavior, stupor, rigidity or floppiness of limbs (catatonic behavior), lack of emotion, social withdrawal, lack of energy	• Symptoms may be aggravated by stress	• Schizophrenia is a relatively common psychotic disorder, affecting up to one in every 200 people at some time in their life • The likelihood of developing schizophrenia is greater if a family member has the disease • In males it most often develops in the teenage years to early 20s, and in females during their late 20s to mid-40s • Schizophrenia can be difficult to diagnose and usually requires assessment over several months	• Schizophrenia • This is a medical emergency • Go to the emergency room or call an ambulance at once
Seeing things that do not exist	• Sudden onset of symptoms such as confusion about the current time, date, location or identity, difficulty paying attention, loss of recent memory, inability to think logically, fever or other signs of infection, tremors, evidence of recent drug use		• If hallucinations occur with delirium they are usually visual • Delirium is not a mental disease, but can be caused by many disorders or conditions including dehydration, drug-intoxication, stroke or serious infections	• Delirium • See your doctor at once
Hearing things that are not really there, in a person with memory loss	• Gradual onset of symptoms such as forgetfulness of recent events, loss of memory, confusion, difficulty finding the right word to use, loss of ability to recognize people, places and objects, depression, fears, anxiety, wandering away		• If hallucinations occur with dementia, they are usually related to hearing voices or noises • Dementia can be an early sign of Alzheimer's disease, or occur in people with AIDS	• Dementia • See your doctor
Hearing voices that are accusing or threatening, causing fear and terror in a person with alcoholism; may last for several days	• Tremor, weakness, sweating, nausea • Symptoms of delirium tremens (high fever, confusion, sleeplessness, anxiousness, nightmares, profound depression, tremors, poor coordination)		• Symptoms usually begin 12–24 hours after a person with alcoholism stops drinking alcohol; if untreated, the person may develop delirium tremens (DTs) 2–10 days after cessation	• Hallucinations as a result of alcohol withdrawal in a person with alcoholism • See your doctor at once

SYMPTOM CHARACTERISTIC	ASSOCIATED SYMPTOMS	AGGRAVATING OR ALLEVIATING FACTORS	OTHER RELEVANT FACTORS	POSSIBLE CAUSE AND ACTION
Hallucinations (cont.)				
False hallucinations such as visual and auditory hallucinations that the sufferer understands are not real; sensations may be related (e.g. listening to music may cause colors to appear and move in time to the music)	• Impaired judgment, leading to dangerous decision making or accidents, panic, delusions, dilated pupils		• The ability to cope with the hallucinations depends on the user's experience and feelings of fear before taking the drug • An inexperienced user who is afraid is less able to cope and more likely to experience unpleasant hallucinations ("a bad trip") • Bad trips may cause temporary psychosis (a loss of contact with reality)	• Substance abuse involving hallucinogens such as LSD • See your doctor • Most users of hallucinogens do not seek medical treatment • A calm, dark room and quiet talk may help a user having a bad trip • If a user has prolonged psychosis, psychiatric treatment may be required

Hand and wrist problems

Problems in the wrist or hand can be caused by a variety of conditions, including overuse, injury and falls. The hands are also a common site for developing arthritis.

SYMPTOM CHARACTERISTIC	ASSOCIATED SYMPTOMS	AGGRAVATING OR ALLEVIATING FACTORS	OTHER RELEVANT FACTORS	POSSIBLE CAUSE AND ACTION
Pain in the wrist or hand following repeated movements	• May be some mild swelling, tingling	• Aggravated by continuing the repeated movements; alleviated by rest	• Inflammation of the tendons in the wrist or hand (tendinitis) may be caused by overuse • Healing is often delayed in people with arthritis, diabetes or gout	• Tendinitis • Try anti-inflammatory medication as advised by your pharmacist • See your doctor
Numbness, tingling, burning in the hand, wrist pain that shoots into the palm of the hand; may be worse at night	• Weakness, may be mild swelling	• Flexing the wrist, making a fist	• More common in women • Associated with occupations that involve repeated forceful movements of the wrist (e.g. using a screwdriver)	• Carpal tunnel syndrome • See your doctor
Pain and swelling following a fall or twisting injury	• Stiffness, bruising, limitation of movement	• May be aggravated by certain wrist movements		• Wrist sprain • See your doctor
Intense pain and swelling in the wrist following a fall, commonly onto an outstretched hand	• Hand may appear deformed (e.g. bent to the side)	• Aggravated by movement		• Fracture • See your doctor at once
Pain, swelling, stiffness in the wrist and/or finger joints, often worse after periods of inactivity	• Affected joints may feel hot, possible chills or fever • Can progress to cause deformities of the hand	• May be aggravated by movement	• Usually affects both hands/wrists at the same time • May have other joints that are affected • Affects more women than men	• Rheumatoid arthritis • See your doctor at once

SYMPTOM CHARACTERISTIC	ASSOCIATED SYMPTOMS	AGGRAVATING OR ALLEVIATING FACTORS	OTHER RELEVANT FACTORS	POSSIBLE CAUSE AND ACTION
Temporary patchy red and white discoloration of the fingers, usually following exposure to cold, may last for minutes or hours	• May be associated numbness, tingling, burning, feeling of pins and needles	• Alleviated by warming the hands	• Can also affect the feet • Most common in young women • More likely in smokers	• Raynaud's disease • See your doctor

Headache

Headache is the term used to describe any form of pain or discomfort in the head. It is an extremely common problem and one that most people have experienced. While most headaches are minor and easily treated with pain relievers, some warrant further medical investigation, and occasionally signal a more serious problem.

SYMPTOM CHARACTERISTIC	ASSOCIATED SYMPTOMS	AGGRAVATING OR ALLEVIATING FACTORS	OTHER RELEVANT FACTORS	POSSIBLE CAUSE AND ACTION
Dull, non-throbbing pain that feels like a vise around the head, squeezing both temples, extending into the neck	• Scalp or neck tenderness, tight or tender neck and shoulder muscles	• Symptoms may start after working in one position for several hours, or after driving; may be related to stress or anxiety		• Tension headache • Try relaxation techniques • Heat may help to relax neck and shoulder muscles, and analgesics may help the pain • See your doctor if you are worried or if symptoms persist
Mild-to-moderate headache generalized over the whole head, and may be throbbing	• Fever, aches, chills, nasal congestion, cough, nausea, vomiting or diarrhea		• Recent contact with infected person	• Viral infection such as a cold, flu or stomach virus • Ask your pharmacist for advice about medications to relieve symptoms • See your doctor if you are worried or if symptoms persist
Intense, throbbing, one-sided headache, may be centered around the eye; pain may last from a few hours to several days	• Vomiting and nausea may occur • In some people, the headache is preceded by a warning sign (aura), which may include visual disturbances such as flashing lights or spots • Oversensitivity to light, odors or sound may be experienced	• May be aggravated by bending forward, climbing stairs, or lying down (initially)	• Migraine may be triggered by certain foods (e.g. cheese, strawberries, chocolate) • In women, migraine may be associated with the menstrual cycle	• Migraine • Take analgesics such as acetaminophen (paracetamol) at once on onset of symptoms, and lie down • See your doctor if you are worried or if symptoms persist
Throbbing pain in the front of the head and around the eyes	• Feeling of pressure around the eyes and nose, thick nasal discharge	• May worsen with bending forward; may follow a recent cold or episode of hay fever	• Occurs with viral infections, allergies, deep sea diving or dental infections	• Sinusitis • Decongestants may be helpful to relieve symptoms • See your doctor if you are worried or if symptoms persist

SYMPTOM CHARACTERISTIC	ASSOCIATED SYMPTOMS	AGGRAVATING OR ALLEVIATING FACTORS	OTHER RELEVANT FACTORS	POSSIBLE CAUSE AND ACTION
Headache (cont.)				
Severe headache	• Stiff neck, vomiting, fever, drowsiness, delirium, unconscious, or have convulsions	• May be worsened by exposure to bright lights	• A child may be difficult to wake and have an unusual high-pitched moaning cry	• Meningitis • This is a medical emergency • Go to the emergency room or call an ambulance at once
Headache following recent injury to the head or after recently being knocked out	• Confusion, dizziness, memory loss • Worsening headaches, confusion, and increasing sleepiness over days or hours after injury		• History of trauma to the head	• Concussion or subdural hematoma • This is a medical emergency • Go to the emergency room or call an ambulance at once
Severe, piercing pain in and around one eye, lasting 30 minutes to several hours; headaches may occur one or more times a day for a period of weeks or months	• The affected eye may be bloodshot and watery • There may be associated nasal congestion and facial flushing	• Pain often occurs at night	• Occurs much more frequently in men than in women	• Cluster headache • See your doctor
Generalized headache in a person taking regular medication			• Occurs with regular or continuous use of medication	• Rebound headache • These headaches may occur with continuous use of certain medications such as nitrates (used to treat angina), or with overuse of analgesics or tranquilizers • See your doctor
Persistent, throbbing headache that begins first thing in the morning, and may lessen during the day	• Vomiting, nausea, fatigue, blurred vision, weakness • Headache may be unlike any other headache the person has had before	• May be worsened by changing positions (e.g. moving from lying down to standing)	• Hypertension causing these symptoms is relatively rare • Brain tumors are rare, and may be inherited or associated with exposure to ionizing radiation	• Severe hypertension or brain tumor • This is a medical emergency • Go to the emergency room or call an ambulance at once
Severe headache that begins suddenly	• Vomiting, limb weakness, double vision, slurred speech, difficulty swallowing, loss of consciousness			• Cerebral hemorrhage or aneurysm • This is a medical emergency • Go to the emergency room or call an ambulance at once

Hearing loss (deafness)

Significant loss of hearing is common, and can result from damage to the ear, disease of the ear or changes with age that damage the delicate structures enabling us to hear. Hearing loss is due to disturbances in the external or middle ear or abnormalities in the inner ear or neuronal (nerve) pathways. Any persistent loss of hearing should be assessed by a doctor to determine the type of hearing loss, possible causes and whether treatment is available which will restore hearing.

SYMPTOM CHARACTERISTIC	ASSOCIATED SYMPTOMS	AGGRAVATING OR ALLEVIATING FACTORS	OTHER RELEVANT FACTORS	POSSIBLE CAUSE AND ACTION
Intermittent hearing loss in one or both ears	• Usually no associated symptoms or pain	• Wax-softening drops may relieve hearing loss	• May have history of ear wax blockage	• Ear wax blockage (ceruminosis) • See your doctor • Do not try to remove the blockage yourself • You may damage the eardrum or small bones in the ear • Your doctor has special instruments to do this safely
Sudden-onset hearing loss in a child, without any history of ear infections	• Usually no other symptoms • May be itching or discomfort around the ear	• Pressure on the outside of the ear may increase discomfort	• Occurs most commonly in toddlers, who are likely to place small objects (e.g. buttons, beads, food) in their ear • Foreign bodies may be visible to the eye	• Foreign body in the ear canal • See your doctor • Do not try to remove the blockage yourself • You may damage the eardrum or small bones in the ear • Your doctor has special instruments to do this safely
Sudden hearing loss in one or both ears	• Fever, symptoms of a cold, discomfort ranging from a feeling of pressure in the ear to persistent, severe ache in one or both ears • Nausea and vomiting, dizziness or ringing in the ears	• Decongestants can aid drainage from the inner ear	• Most commonly occurs following a cold • Most common in children aged 3 months to 3 years, due to narrow eustachian tubes (tubes that allows pressure between the mouth or nose and ears to be equalized) • Eustachian tubes that are not fully developed may block easily with inflammation of the nose or throat, or with allergies	• Otitis media (viral or bacterial ear infection) commonly caused by a cold virus • Symptoms are caused by build-up of fluid • Perforation of the eardrum is a potential complication • This can lead to more prolonged but usually temporary hearing loss • See your doctor • See you doctor at once if the patient is a child
Gradual onset of hearing loss, usually in both ears	• High pitched sounds become hard to hear first followed by low pitched if deterioration continues	• Unprotected exposure to loud noise will cause further deterioration	• Commonly occurs in industrial workers exposed to loud noises, when correct ear-protection is not used • Can occur following just a few exposures to very loud sound	• Noise-induced hearing loss or occupational hearing loss • See your doctor

SYMPTOM CHARACTERISTIC	ASSOCIATED SYMPTOMS	AGGRAVATING OR ALLEVIATING FACTORS	OTHER RELEVANT FACTORS	POSSIBLE CAUSE AND ACTION
Hearing loss (deafness) (cont.)				
Gradual loss of hearing with age	• Initial reduction in ability to hear higher pitched noises, gradually affects whole hearing range		• Age-related hearing loss occurs in men more commonly than in women • Usually begins between ages 40–50 years	• Ageing-associated hearing loss (presbycusis) • See your doctor
Recurrent episodes of hearing loss, mainly low tone sounds, usually lasting 20 minutes to several hours	• Dizziness, ringing, rushing or buzzing sound in the ears (tinnitus), nausea, feeling of movement or dizziness (vertigo) • Occurs intermittently	• Reducing dietary salt, caffeine, alcohol may help control episodes	• Affects only one ear in the majority of people with the disease • May be caused by fluid in the canals of the inner ear	• Menière's disease • See your doctor • Antiemetics may provide symptomatic relief
Gradual onset of hearing loss on one side	• May have facial weakness on the same side		• Acoustic neuromas grow slowly and are more common in older people	• Acoustic neuroma (a benign tumor of nerve cells) • Tumors may grow large enough to put pressure on other structures (e.g. nerves in the face, jaw or mouth) • See your doctor
Gradual loss of hearing with age, usually in both ears	• May be associated with tinnitus and vertigo		• An inherited condition affecting approximately 1 percent of people	• Otosclerosis • See your doctor
Recent onset inability to hear high-pitched noise, in a person taking medication for another medical problem	• Ringing in the ears, dizziness		• Occurs mainly with antibiotics, particularly those used to treat serious infections in hospital	• Drug-induced ear damage • Check the consumer information on all the medications you take • See your doctor at once • Medications may be altered or stopped and blood tests may be required
Hearing loss in childhood	• Delayed language development		• Infection during pregnancy (e.g. rubella or cytomegalovirus) can cause congenital hearing loss in children • Repeated ear infections may cause deafness in children • Meningitis can lead to hearing loss in one or both ears • Any child with suspected hearing loss or delayed language development should have their hearing tested	• Congenital deafness, meningitis or otitis media • See your doctor

Heartburn

Heartburn does not involve the heart, but is a traditional name given to a symptom of a digestive problem that can often be relieved by indigestion medications. However, it is important to make sure the chest pain is not caused by angina or a heart attack.

SYMPTOM CHARACTERISTIC	ASSOCIATED SYMPTOMS	AGGRAVATING OR ALLEVIATING FACTORS	OTHER RELEVANT FACTORS	POSSIBLE CAUSE AND ACTION
Painful burning sensation in the chest, behind the breast bone, which may rise up to the throat	• Bitter taste in the mouth	• Large meals, fatty or spicy foods may cause symptoms • Lying down or bending may worsen symptoms • Smoking or alcohol may aggravate symptoms • Tight clothing or belts may make symptoms worse	• Typically occurs after food • Heartburn may occur during pregnancy but usually resolves after the baby is born	• Back-washing of food and stomach acid upwards into the esophagus (gastroesophageal reflux) • Take an antacid as advised by your pharmacist or doctor • Avoid foods that seem to cause the symptoms, and do not eat within 2 hours of going to bed • Quit smoking and reduce alcohol intake • Raise the head end of the bed 4 inches (10 centimeters) • Lose weight if you are overweight • See your doctor if you are worried or if symptoms persist
Intermittent pain behind the breast bone, which at first may not be easily distinguished from heartburn		• Worse with exercise, relieved by resting or rapidly acting nitrate drugs	• Most common in those with previous history of coronary heart disease	• Angina pectoris, a form of coronary heart disease • See your doctor at once • Failure to treat the cause of angina may result in a heart attack
Intense chest pain, which may at first be mistaken for severe heartburn	• Pain spreading to left arm or both arms; pain in jaw; feeling of chest being squeezed		• Increased likelihood in a person who has previously had a heart attack or with a history of coronary heart disease	• Heart attack (myocardial infarction) due to sudden loss of blood supply to a section of the heart muscle due to blockage of the coronary arteries supplying the heart muscle • This is a medical emergency • Go to the emergency room or call an ambulance at once

Hip problems

Hip problems often occur following a fall, especially in the elderly, or because of arthritis. Other causes of hip pain and stiffness include frequent running or problems with the cartilage in the hip joint.

SYMPTOM CHARACTERISTIC	ASSOCIATED SYMPTOMS	AGGRAVATING OR ALLEVIATING FACTORS	OTHER RELEVANT FACTORS	POSSIBLE CAUSE AND ACTION
Intense hip pain following a fall	• Leg may be held in an abnormal position, may develop swelling	• Standing, straightening the leg, lifting the leg	• More likely to occur in the elderly	• Hip fracture • See your doctor at once
Pain or clicking on the outside of the hip	• May be some tenderness or swelling	• Aggravated by activities involving repeated hip movement (e.g. running, bicycling, walking, climbing stairs)	• Often related to sporting activities	• Muscle strain, irritation of the sheath covering the muscles on the outer side of the thigh, or bursitis • Rest • See your doctor if you are worried or if symptoms persist
Stiffness and pain in one or both hips	• May have swelling and redness around the joints, stiffness and pain in other joints	• Stiffness often aggravated by long periods in one position • Pain aggravated by lots of walking or standing	• More likely in older people	• Arthritis • See your doctor for advice
In infants, clicking of the hip	• May be some pain when the hip is stretched, movement may be limited		• More common in girls than boys, also more common in babies born breech (buttocks first) or in those with a relative who has the same disorder	• Congenital dislocation of the hip • See your doctor
In teenagers, stiffness in the hip, pain and limping	• May also have pain in the knee or thigh • Affected leg may be twisted outward	• Aggravated by walking	• More common in overweight teens • Affects boys more than girls	• Dislocation of the top of the thigh bone (slipped capital femoral epiphysis) • See your doctor at once
In children, gradual onset of hip pain and stiffness; symptoms progress slowly	• Limping, wasting of thigh muscles, limited movements	• Aggravated by walking	• Most common in 5–10 year olds • Affects boys more than girls	• Degeneration of the top of the thigh bone (Perthes disease) • See your doctor
Shooting or burning pain in the back of one hip or buttock; pain may travel down the back of one leg	• May also have low back pain, numbness or tingling in the foot	• Aggravated by coughing, sneezing, bending, lifting	• More common in people with stiff backs or past back injury	• Sciatica • See your doctor

Hot flashes/flushes

Hot flashes/flushes is a classic symptom of menopause. Often symptoms are not severe enough to require treatment, but it is still worthwhile visiting your doctor to talk about the effects of menopause and possible strategies to prevent unnecessary discomfort. Certain conditions become much more common in women after menopause, especially heart disease and osteoporosis. See also entry on *skin problems* for other causes of flushing.

SYMPTOM CHARACTERISTIC	ASSOCIATED SYMPTOMS	AGGRAVATING OR ALLEVIATING FACTORS	OTHER RELEVANT FACTORS	POSSIBLE CAUSE AND ACTION
Episodes of sudden transient warmth and redness of the face, neck and upper chest in women	• Menstrual irregularities, nervousness, anxiety, irritability, fatigue, depression, urinary problems, vaginal dryness and irritation		• Frequency and severity varies greatly between individuals, usually begins in late 40s or early 50s	• Onset of menopause • See your doctor
Episodes of sudden transient warmth and redness of the face, neck and upper chest in a person taking hormonal medication		• Usually worst at commencement of course of medication and settles over time	• Hot flushes related to sex hormone changes may be associated with some medications (e.g. treatment for endometriosis or breast cancer in women, prostate cancer in men)	• Medication-related estrogen deficiency (women) or androgen deficiency (men) • See your doctor
Flushing of face and neck in a person taking medication			• Hot flushes may occur as a side effect of some medications (e.g. medications used in hypertension, Alzheimer's disease) or as an unusual reaction to a wide range of drugs	• Adverse effect of medication • See your doctor

Jaundice

Jaundice is a yellow discoloration of the skin and eyes due to excessive bile pigment (bilirubin) in the blood. Jaundice may be caused by abnormal breakdown of red blood cells releasing pigment into the blood (hemolytic anemia), inflammation or disease of the liver preventing excretion of bilirubin or obstruction of the flow of bile into the bowel. Jaundice always warrants a thorough medical assessment to determine the underlying cause.

SYMPTOM CHARACTERISTIC	ASSOCIATED SYMPTOMS	AGGRAVATING OR ALLEVIATING FACTORS	OTHER RELEVANT FACTORS	POSSIBLE CAUSE AND ACTION
Jaundice in a baby within the first 24 hours of life	• Sleepiness, poor feeding	• Dehydration may make the jaundice worse	• May be a history of jaundice in previous babies • Jaundice in the first 24 hours of life is always abnormal and is usually due to a mismatch of mother and baby's blood groups • High levels of jaundice can be dangerous to young babies	• Hemolytic anemia • See your doctor at once
Mild jaundice in a baby in the first few days of life	• Baby is otherwise well	• Dehydration may make the jaundice worse	• More common in breast fed babies and babies bruised during delivery	• Physiological jaundice • See your doctor

SYMPTOM CHARACTERISTIC	ASSOCIATED SYMPTOMS	AGGRAVATING OR ALLEVIATING FACTORS	OTHER RELEVANT FACTORS	POSSIBLE CAUSE AND ACTION
Jaundice (cont.)				
Gradual onset of jaundice or recurrent episodes of jaundice	• Color of urine and bowel movements are normal, spleen may be enlarged • Sickle cell disease can lead to sudden episodes of severe chest, abdominal or limb pain known as a sickle cell crisis	• Jaundice is more severe if underlying liver disease is present	• Pigment from red blood cells is released into the blood faster than the liver can excrete it; may be a history family history of abnormal red blood cells • Hemolytic anemia occurs in sickle cell disease, a genetic disorder of platelets which is more common among black racial groups	• Hemolytic anemia • See your doctor at once
Episode of jaundice lasting weeks to months	• Headache, fever, nausea, vomiting, abdominal pain, fatigue • Bowel movements may be pale, urine may be dark	• Jaundice fades as inflammation of the liver resolves	• Hepatitis A infection may result from eating contaminated food and is common with travel to a developing country • Intravenous drug use, unprotected sex and healthcare work involving the usage of needles increase a person's risk of contracting hepatitis B or C	• Viral hepatitis • See your doctor at once
Gradual onset of jaundice which is progressive	• Itchiness, loss of appetite, fatigue, weakness and muscle wasting, red palms, abdominal distension, vomiting blood or black sticky bowel movements, memory loss and confusion	• Excess alcohol or drugs that can damage the liver can increase the jaundice	• May be a history of hepatitis B or C infection, alcohol abuse or other liver disease	• Cirrhosis of the liver • See your doctor at once
Gradual onset of jaundice or recurrent episodes of jaundice	• Dark urine and pale bowel movements, itchiness, may be fever, abdominal pain or chills	• Jaundice fades once obstruction of the bile ducts is resolved	• Due to obstruction of the flow of bile from the liver to the bowel • May be a history of gallstones, liver disease or a family history of jaundice	• Obstructive jaundice • See your doctor at once
Gradual onset of jaundice in a person taking medications	• Itchiness	• Jaundice fades when medication is ceased	• Some antibiotics, anticonvulsant drugs, oral contraceptive pills and anesthetic agents can cause jaundice	• Medication-induced jaundice • See your doctor at once

Knee problems

Knee pain is a common symptom in all age groups. Problems range from mild pain under the kneecap to ligament tears requiring surgery. The knee is also a common site for developing arthritis.

SYMPTOM CHARACTERISTIC	ASSOCIATED SYMPTOMS	AGGRAVATING OR ALLEVIATING FACTORS	OTHER RELEVANT FACTORS	POSSIBLE CAUSE AND ACTION
Intermittent pain under the kneecap	• May be some tenderness when the kneecap is pushed down on the thigh bone (femur), may be some grating under the kneecap	• Aggravated by walking up and, particularly, down stairs or hills, aching when sitting for long periods of time, running, jumping	• Most common in people involved in sports or who have jobs requiring a lot of knee bending or walking up and down stairs	• Patellofemoral pain syndrome ("runner's knee") • Try to avoid activities that make the pain worse • See your doctor if you are worried or if symptoms persist
Intermittent pain inside the knee or along one side of the knee, often starts following a twisting injury	• Knee may lock, may feel blocked and unable to straighten it fully, may have clicking of the knee; some swelling may be present	• Aggravated by squatting or twisting	• More commonly occurs on the medial (inside) part of the knee	• Tearing of the cartilage in the knee (meniscus) • Apply ice and rest • See your doctor
Knee pain following a fall, twisting injury, hyperextension (knee forced straight) injury, or direct blow to the knee	• Popping sound at the time of injury, swelling that develops soon after the injury, giving way of the knee	• Giving way is aggravated by twisting movements or change of direction	• Common sporting injury and one of the most serious, often requiring surgery and extensive rehabilitation	• Tearing of one of the ligaments running through the knee joint from front to back (anterior cruciate ligament) • See your doctor
Long-term aching and stiffness in the knee which has become worse over a period of months	• Limited movement; the person may be unable to bend or straighten fully	• Pain is alleviated by rest, aggravated by a lot of activity • Stiffness is often worse in the morning	• More common in people over 50 years	• Osteoarthritis • See your doctor
Pain along the inner or outer knee, usually following a direct force to one side of the knee while the foot remains planted on the ground	• Tenderness on one side of the knee	• Twisting the leg while the foot stays on the ground	• Often occurs during sports such as soccer, football, skiing	• Damage to one or more of the ligaments on the inside or outside of the knee (collateral ligaments) • See your doctor
Pain, warmth and stiffness just below the kneecap	• Swelling and tenderness below the kneecap	• Bending, kneeling	• More common in people whose occupation requires frequent or prolonged kneeling	• Bursitis ("housemaid's knee") • See your doctor
Red, swollen knee	• Constant ache, swelling, fever, generally feeling unwell	• May be aggravated by movement	• Infection may spread through the blood, through a penetrating injury	• Osteomyelitis or joint infection (septic arthritis) • See your doctor at once

Leg problems

Leg problems can arise from a variety of conditions, from simple muscle strains to fractures and serious circulation disorders. See also entries on *knee problems, hip problems*, and *foot and ankle problems*.

SYMPTOM CHARACTERISTIC	ASSOCIATED SYMPTOMS	AGGRAVATING OR ALLEVIATING FACTORS	OTHER RELEVANT FACTORS	POSSIBLE CAUSE AND ACTION
Sudden pain in the leg associated with quick movement of the leg (e.g. kicking, sprinting, change of direction)	• Swelling, bruising	• Stretching or bending the leg but can still move it	• Common sporting injury, often affects hamstrings (muscles at back of thigh), quadriceps (muscles on the front of thigh) and calf muscles	• Muscle strain or tear • Rest and apply ice to the area • See your doctor
Severe, constant leg pain following an injury, fall or direct blow to the leg	• Swelling, may be some deformity of the leg	• Aggravated by attempts to walk or move the leg		• Fracture • This is a medical emergency • Go to the emergency room or call an ambulance at once
Intermittent pain over the front of the shin	• Maybe some pain when the shin is pressed	• Repetitive motion (e.g. running, bicycling, jumping, walking up and down hills)	• More common in those with flat feet, bow legs, knock knees	• Shin splints • See your doctor
Prominent veins in the legs	• Aching in the legs, foot swelling, itching	• Aggravated by standing for long periods of time • Alleviated by elevating the legs while lying down	• More common in women than men • Can worsen during pregnancy	• Varicose veins • Wear support stockings • See your doctor
Cramping pain in the calves, feet or hips while walking	• May develop numbness or tingling in the feet	• Aggravated by walking, especially quickly or up hills, usually alleviated by rest	• Risk is increased in people with abnormal cholesterol or triglyceride levels, diabetes, hypertension, men over 55 years old, women over 65 years old, those with a family history of cardiovascular disease, cigarette smokers, and those with obesity or little physical activity	• Peripheral vascular disease • See your doctor
Shooting or burning pain in the buttock and down the back of one leg	• May also have low back pain, numbness or tingling in the foot	• Aggravated by coughing, sneezing, bending, lifting	• More common in people with stiff backs or past back injury	• Sciatica • See your doctor
Pain and swelling in the back of the calf	• Warmth, pain when touched		• Most common following surgery or following long air flights or bus trips	• Deep venous thrombosis • This is a medical emergency • Go to the emergency room or call an ambulance at once

Memory loss

Among elderly people, memory loss is a common complaint. A family member may be the first to notice the problem. Dementia is a common cause of significant memory impairment in this age group, but correctable conditions or other causes may be discovered on medical assessment. Certain medications, such as sedatives, can precipitate sudden memory impairment.

SYMPTOM CHARACTERISTIC	ASSOCIATED SYMPTOMS	AGGRAVATING OR ALLEVIATING FACTORS	OTHER RELEVANT FACTORS	POSSIBLE CAUSE AND ACTION
Gradual onset of forgetfulness in everyday affairs, (e.g. misplacing things, difficulty remembering names, difficulty remembering things to be done)			• Typically occurs in an otherwise healthy person over 50 years	• Benign forgetfulness associated with age • Use memory aids such as lists and mnemonics • See your doctor if you are worried or if symptoms persist
Memory loss, usually developing gradually over months or years; memory progressively declines; ability to remember recent events is affected more than events that happened long ago	• Gradual relentless decline in thinking skills and overall mental function • Unusual behavior • Decline in standards of personal care		• Usually elderly people • Sometimes a correctable cause may be identified • Dementia may occur as a result of other diseases (e.g. AIDS)	• Dementia • See your doctor
Memory loss, usually of gradual onset over days or weeks	• Loss of concentration • Sadness • Lack of enjoyment in life • Difficulty sleeping • Low self-esteem		• May occur in any age group • Depression is a probable explanation if forgetfulness occurs in a young or middle-aged person • May have been precipitated by a personal loss	• Depression • See your doctor
Memory loss usually of rapid onset			• Any age group • A likely possibility if forgetfulness occurs in a young person or in middle age	• Alcohol (alcoholism) or drug abuse (drug dependence) • See your doctor
Sudden memory loss	• Headaches, vomiting, fever		• The risk of stroke is increased in people with a history of coronary heart disease, hypertension or other cardiovascular disease, abnormal cholesterol levels, and cigarette smokers • Professional fighters (e.g. boxers) are prone to trauma-related memory loss	• Brain tumor, infection (e.g. meningitis, encephalitis), stroke, severe or repeated trauma • See your doctor

Menstrual problems

Most menstrual problems warrant a full medical investigation, since they may indicate the presence of a disease that requires treatment. Although period pain or premenstrual syndrome may respond to simple self-treatment, it is important to ask your doctor's advice if symptoms persist or worsen.

SYMPTOM CHARACTERISTIC	ASSOCIATED SYMPTOMS	AGGRAVATING OR ALLEVIATING FACTORS	OTHER RELEVANT FACTORS	POSSIBLE CAUSE AND ACTION
Temporary emotional instability just prior to menstrual period	• Bloating or discomfort in lower abdomen, irritability, depression, tearfulness, inability to concentrate, sleep disturbances, fatigue, lethargy	• Symptoms usually disappear when menstruation begins • Caffeine may worsen irritability	• Approximately one-third of fertile women experience some premenstrual symptoms • The full premenstrual syndrome occurs in about 3–10 percent	• Premenstrual syndrome (PMS) • There is no standard treatment • Ask your pharmacist's advice on over-the-counter medication for bloating or pain • Vitamin B_6 supplements may help ease the symptoms • See your doctor if you are worried or if symptoms persist
Mild to moderate cramping pain during menstrual period		• Pain may be aggravated by flatulence or constipation • Pain may be alleviated by heat applied to the lower abdomen (e.g. a hot water bottle or bath)	• Period pain sufficiently severe to cause missed school or work days is common in teenagers and young women • Severe symptoms may suggest endometriosis	• Period pain (menstruation) • Try analgesic or non-steroidal anti-inflammatory drugs as recommended by your pharmacist • See your doctor if you are worried or if symptoms persist
Gradual onset of more pain than usual during and just before menstrual period	• Low back pain, period pain lasting more than 2–3 days and starting before the onset of bleeding • Spotting of small amounts of blood for 1–3 days prior to onset of period • Menstrual bleeding may be heavier than usual	• Pain in pelvic area may worsen during sexual contact • Pregnancy may temporarily resolve the problem, though symptoms may recur months or years later	• Endometriosis occurs in approximately 5–10 percent of women, and is more likely in women with a mother or sister with the disease, and in women who have never become pregnant • Endometriosis may result in infertility	• Endometriosis • See your doctor
More pain than usual during and just before menstrual period	• Fever, vaginal discharge with offensive odor, abnormal vaginal bleeding, abdominal pain, pain during urination • Onset of symptoms is usually gradual when caused by an intrauterine device (IUD)		• Pelvic inflammatory disease occurs almost exclusively in sexually active women • Pelvic inflammatory disease may result from infections (usually sexually transmitted infections), uterine surgery (e.g. dilation and curettage, insertion of IUD, cesarean section) or childbirth	• Pelvic inflammatory disease • See your doctor at once

SYMPTOM CHARACTERISTIC	ASSOCIATED SYMPTOMS	AGGRAVATING OR ALLEVIATING FACTORS	OTHER RELEVANT FACTORS	POSSIBLE CAUSE AND ACTION
Increased volume and length of menstrual bleeding in women with an intrauterine device (IUD)	• Spotting of blood between menstrual periods, increased pain during periods		• IUD may change the pattern of menstrual bleeding	IUD related adverse effect See your doctor
Excessive menstrual bleeding	• Pain during menstrual bleeding, longer than usual menstrual periods		• Fibroids are most common in women over 35 years old or who have had several pregnancies	• Uterine fibroids • See your doctor
Irregularity or cessation of menstrual periods in a woman who is not pregnant	• Fatigue or lethargy may occur with thyroid disease		• A menstrual period may occasional be missed in some women during the use of oral contraceptives • Excessive exercise or weight loss (e.g. during athletic training or anorexia nervosa) may cause cessation of menstrual periods	• Hormonal abnormality due to an ovarian problem, oral contraceptive use or a thyroid problem • See your doctor
Cessation of menstrual periods in sexually active women	• Breast tenderness, abdominal bloating or feeling of fullness, nausea		• All methods of contraception carry a slight chance of failure leading to pregnancy	• Pregnancy • Use pregnancy test kit—if positive, see your doctor • See your doctor if you are worried or if symptoms persist
Cessation of menstrual periods in women aged over 35 years	• Irritability, hot flushes (flashes)	• Estrogen supplements, plant estrogens or diets high in soy may relieve symptoms of menopause	• The onset of menopause most commonly occurs between the ages of 40–55 • Early menopause may occur from 35 years, or younger in rare cases	• Menopause • See your doctor
Recommencement of menstrual bleeding in a woman who has already gone through menopause	• Abdominal swelling or discomfort, vaginal discharge		• Some hormonal medications may cause uterine bleeding	• Uterine tumor or vaginal infection • See your doctor

SYMPTOM CHARACTERISTIC	ASSOCIATED SYMPTOMS	AGGRAVATING OR ALLEVIATING FACTORS	OTHER RELEVANT FACTORS	POSSIBLE CAUSE AND ACTION

Nail abnormalities

Injury and fungal infections are the most common causes of nail changes. Since some causes may indicate other conditions or permanently damage the nail bed, it is advisable to ask your doctor's advice on any nail abnormalities that does not heal quickly. If there is a build-up of skin crusts under the nail, do not attempt to remove debris from under the nail with manicure instruments until the condition has been checked by a doctor.

SYMPTOM CHARACTERISTIC	ASSOCIATED SYMPTOMS	AGGRAVATING OR ALLEVIATING FACTORS	OTHER RELEVANT FACTORS	POSSIBLE CAUSE AND ACTION
Crusty light-colored build-up under the nails	• Light-colored band at the end of the nail, vertical light-colored lines running from the nail tip towards the cuticle, lifting of nail, pain, crusty white skin between the fingers or toes	• Recent use of public showers or direct skin contact with a person with a fungal infection	• Toenails are more commonly affected than fingernails	• Fungal infection of the nail (onychomycosis) • These symptoms may also occur with psoriasis • See your doctor
Uneven ridges in the nail	• Bruising under the nail may have occurred some weeks before the nail begins to grow unevenly		• History of injury to the nail	• Nail bed injury • Nails may become misshapen due to trauma ranging from mild unnoticed stubbing of finger or toe, to an obvious cause like slamming the fingernail in a door • See your doctor if you are worried or if symptoms persist
Lifting of the hard part of the nail (the nail plate) from the soft tissue underneath (the nail bed)	• Pain, build-up of debris	• May be due to damage to the quick caused by scraping too deeply when cleaning under nails	• Fingernails are more commonly affected	• Psoriasis, fungal infections or nail injury • These symptoms may also occur for no known reason • Keep the nail area dry, keep the nail short, avoid scraping debris from under the nail and use only mild soap and shampoos • See your doctor if you are worried or if symptoms persist
Discoloration of nail plate (green)	• Moisture may be present under the nail	• Attempts to clean under the nail may cause spreading	• Commonly occurs with long fingernails	• Infection under the nail • See your doctor
Discoloration of the nail (red to black)	• Pain (feeling of uncomfortable pressure to severe throbbing pain)		• May follow known injury	• Bruise under the nail • Black discoloration may also follow the use of the antibiotic minocycline, or may indicate melanoma • See your doctor

SYMPTOM CHARACTERISTIC	ASSOCIATED SYMPTOMS	AGGRAVATING OR ALLEVIATING FACTORS	OTHER RELEVANT FACTORS	POSSIBLE CAUSE AND ACTION
Discoloration (blue, yellow, white)			• May be associated with medications or other medical conditions	• Nail discoloration may occur with the use of medications such as antimalarial drugs (blue) or antibiotics (white, black) • It also occurs with cirrhosis of the liver (white) or renal failure (red) • See your doctor
Thinning and roughening of all nails of toes and fingers	• Non-painful		• Occurs in pre-adolescent children	• "Twenty nail" dystrophy • Although it usually heals without treatment, it may indicate the onset of other skin diseases • See your doctor
Abnormal spoon-shaped concavity of nails (koilonychia)	• Fatigue, pallor (if anemia is cause) • Fatigue, joint pain (if hemochromatosis is the cause)		• This type of curvature may occur in children without any other condition • Hemochromatosis is an inherited condition that is most common in Caucasians	• Koilonychia may occur for no discernible reason, with iron deficiency anemia or with hemochromatosis • See your doctor
Exaggerated lengthwise curvature of nail (clubbing)	• Symptoms of underlying disease; caused by another medical condition • May also be boggy feeling around nail		• Parents or other relatives may have similar-shaped nails	• Clubbing may simply be hereditary, or can occur with liver, lung or heart diseases • See your doctor
Exaggerated curve of nails (over-curvature)	• There may be pain in the soft tissue at the sides of the nail		• Parents or other relatives may have similar-shaped nails	• May be due to ingrown toenail, or simply hereditary ("pincer" nail) • Avoid trimming outer edges of nail • See your doctor if you are worried or if symptoms persist
Swelling of the skin around the edges of the nail	• Pain	• Swelling may worsen following damage by rough manicure or injury to nail	• Manicure may cause damage to cuticle	• May follow injury or may occur with infections such as herpes, candidiasis ("thrush") • Keep the area clean and dry • See your doctor

Nausea and vomiting

Nausea and vomiting occur with many medical conditions, and the cause is not always obvious. Since some conditions that may cause these symptoms are potentially serious, it is advisable to consult a doctor if the problem does not resolve quickly. If symptoms recur, and/or are accompanied by any other unusual symptoms, you may need medical tests to find the problem. When a person vomits blood or has severe pain, the situation should be treated as an emergency and a doctor consulted at once.

SYMPTOM CHARACTERISTIC	ASSOCIATED SYMPTOMS	AGGRAVATING OR ALLEVIATING FACTORS	OTHER RELEVANT FACTORS	POSSIBLE CAUSE AND ACTION
Nausea and vomiting that does not occur within a short time of eating and seems unrelated to food eaten, in a person taking medication	• Unusual taste or general feeling of slight nausea between episodes	• There may be no distinct pattern	• Recent commencement of a new medication or combination	• Reaction to a medication • See your doctor if you are worried or if symptoms persist
Persistent nausea and vomiting over more than a week in women of child-bearing age	• Missed menstrual period	• Certain foods or smells may worsen symptoms • Symptoms may be consistently worse at certain times of day	• Non-predictable; a woman may experience morning sickness with one pregnancy but not a subsequent pregnancy	• "Morning sickness" of pregnancy • See your doctor • Avoid an empty stomach by eating frequent small meals • Nibbling dry crackers between meals and before getting out of bed may help
Nausea and vomiting after eating	• Diarrhea may follow	• Unable to tolerate food or liquids	• Symptoms occur after eating food that may have been kept too long or at incorrect temperature such as hot food kept warm several hours, or cold food that has been kept at room temperature or uncovered for several hours	• Bacterial contamination of food (food poisoning) • Take frequent small amounts of fluid, if tolerated • Typical cases of food poisoning will usually pass in under 12 hours • See your doctor if the person is severely ill and unable to drink fluids, if you are worried or if symptoms persist
Intermittent nausea and vomiting	• Burning pain high in the abdomen	• Worse after eating, especially spicy foods • Bland foods may relieve pain	• Use of anti-inflammatory medications for pain (prescription or non-prescription) may damage stomach lining • Ulcers are commonly caused by a bacterial infection and require antibiotics	• Gastritis, or ulcer of stomach or esophagus • If symptoms are mild and not persistent, use an antacid (your pharmacist may advise you on a suitable choice) • See your doctor

SYMPTOM CHARACTERISTIC	ASSOCIATED SYMPTOMS	AGGRAVATING OR ALLEVIATING FACTORS	OTHER RELEVANT FACTORS	POSSIBLE CAUSE AND ACTION
Recent onset nausea and vomiting	• Fever and cold or flu symptoms, diarrhea	• Inability to tolerate food or liquids		• Viral gastroenteritis • Rest and take frequent small amounts of fluids if tolerated (e.g. diluted soft drink or an electrolyte sachet from your pharmacist) • Your doctor or pharmacist may advise you further about treating specific symptoms • See your doctor if the person is unable to tolerate fluids, if you are worried or if symptoms persist
Nausea and vomiting with intermittent severe pain	• Pain in the upper right abdomen, fever	• Pain may worsen after eating greasy foods		• Gallbladder inflammation or gallstones • See your doctor if you are worried or if symptoms persist
Nausea and vomiting with steady worsening pain	• Recent onset abdominal pain in middle or lower right, fever		• Pain may begin as dull discomfort centrally and become more severe and localized to the right side	• Appendicitis or a bowel obstruction • This is a medical emergency • Go to the emergency room or call an ambulance at once
Nausea and vomiting in a person with diabetes			• High blood sugar on blood test using home monitoring kit and ketones on urine strip test	• Ketoacidosis, a complication of diabetes • This is a medical emergency • Go to the emergency room or call an ambulance at once
Vomiting in a baby or young child	• Crying, irritability or quietness, inability to become interested in toys		• Child under 2 vomiting for more than 6 hours, or child over 2 vomiting for more than 12 hours	• Viral infections are a common cause • Children may rapidly become dehydrated • See your doctor • If you suspect severe dehydration, go to the emergency room or call an ambulance at once
Vomiting in a baby or young child	• Uncontrollable crying, dark red diarrhea, unable to keep down any fluids		• Obstruction is relatively rare	• Intestinal obstruction • This is an emergency • Visit your doctor or the emergency room at once

SYMPTOM CHARACTERISTIC	ASSOCIATED SYMPTOMS	AGGRAVATING OR ALLEVIATING FACTORS	OTHER RELEVANT FACTORS	POSSIBLE CAUSE AND ACTION
Nausea and vomiting (cont.)				
Vomiting in a baby	• Forceful expulsion of stomach contents, persistent vomiting		• 20 percent of healthy babies vomit or regurgitate frequently enough to worry parents and cause them to seek medical advice • Approximately 7 percent of babies show more severe symptoms suggesting gastroesophageal reflux disease	• Stomach obstruction or reflux • Ask your doctor's advice to confirm the cause

Neck problems

Symptoms involving the neck may result from a wide variety of conditions. Infections in the body will often lead to swelling of the neck glands, while poor posture and arthritis can cause neck pain and stiffness.

SYMPTOM CHARACTERISTIC	ASSOCIATED SYMPTOMS	AGGRAVATING OR ALLEVIATING FACTORS	OTHER RELEVANT FACTORS	POSSIBLE CAUSE AND ACTION
Dull ache in the neck that comes on gradually, often when sitting or standing in one position for prolonged periods of time	• Tightness and ache across the shoulders and back of the head, headache	• May be aggravated by sitting in a slumped position, prolonged forward head posture (e.g. when typing or reading) • May also be aggravated by stress and anxiety • May be alleviated by moving the head and neck and changing positions frequently	• Common in those who have poor posture (e.g. rounded shoulders, slouched sitting, and in those whose work involves sitting at a desk or computer)	• Muscle fatigue or strain • Avoid prolonged neck positions and improve posture • See your doctor if you are worried or if symptoms persist
Neck stiffness that is present after sleep or periods of inactivity, gradually worsens over time	• Pain and limitation of movement, spine may be tender to touch	• Aggravated by periods of inactivity or following exercise • May be alleviated by moving the neck gently	• Most common in those aged over 40	• Osteoarthritis • See your doctor
Neck pain that develops after a jolt to the neck (e.g. a car stopping suddenly)	• Muscle spasm, stiffness, dizziness, headache • Severe injury can cause numbness and tingling in the arms and legs, weakness, difficulty walking	• May be aggravated by movements of the neck	• Most commonly develops after a car accident	• Whiplash injury • See your doctor at once • If there are severe symptoms (numbness, tingling, weakness, difficulty walking), this is a medical emergency • Go to the emergency room or call an ambulance at once
Swelling or a lump at the side or back of the neck	• Pain, fever, general feeling of illness	• Aggravated by touching the area, sometimes by neck movement	• There may be an infection near the area (e.g. strep (streptococcal) throat, scalp infection, ear infection)	• Enlarged lymph nodes caused by bacterial or viral infection • See your doctor

SYMPTOM CHARACTERISTIC	ASSOCIATED SYMPTOMS	AGGRAVATING OR ALLEVIATING FACTORS	OTHER RELEVANT FACTORS	POSSIBLE CAUSE AND ACTION
Intense neck pain that radiates into the shoulders and possibly down the arms	• Tingling or numbness in the hands, arm weakness	• Aggravated by neck movements, especially bending the head forward • May be aggravated by sneezing or coughing	• May follow an injury or begin after regular daily activities	• Vertebral disk injury causing pressure on a spinal nerve • See your doctor
Lumps in the neck that have been growing, or have been in the neck for more than 2 weeks	• Fatigue, fever, night sweats, weight loss		• Lumps are usually painless	• Tumor (e.g. lymphoma or leukemia) • See your doctor at once
Neck stiffness with a severe headache	• Vomiting, fever, drowsiness, may become delirious, unconscious or have convulsions	• Exposure to bright lights increases the pain	• A child may be difficult to wake or have a high-pitched cry	• Meningitis • This is a medical emergency • Go to the emergency room or call an ambulance at once

Nosebleed

Nosebleeds occur very commonly and are usually harmless. They usually happen infrequently and simple pressure to the nose is enough to control the bleeding. Sometimes bleeding can be severe and requires treatment by a doctor to prevent major blood loss. Any frequent or severe nosebleeds should be assessed by a doctor.

SYMPTOM CHARACTERISTIC	ASSOCIATED SYMPTOMS	AGGRAVATING OR ALLEVIATING FACTORS	OTHER RELEVANT FACTORS	POSSIBLE CAUSE AND ACTION
Spontaneous bleeding from the nose of mild to moderate severity	• Person is otherwise well	• Blowing the nose may increase bleeding	• No history of injury • Common in winter when cold dry air dries out the lining of the nose	• Nosebleed of unknown cause (idiopathic epistaxis) • Apply pressure by pinching the nose • See your doctor if you are worried or if symptoms persist
Mild to severe bleeding from the nose	• Nasal pain, swelling, nasal deformity	• Blowing the nose may increase bleeding	• History of injury	• Injury to the lining of the nose • Apply pressure by pinching the nose • See your doctor if you are worried or if symptoms persist
Recurrent episodes of mild to severe bleeding from the nose	• Red spidery spots on the skin and mucous membranes which become pale on pressure	• Irritation of the lining of the nose can increase bleeding	• May be a family history of blood vessel disorders	• Abnormality of the blood vessels of the nose (hereditary telangiectasia) • See your doctor
Recurrent episodes of mild to severe bleeding from the nose	• Headache, throbbing	• Stress or exertion may precipitate a bleed	• More common in the elderly • May be a history of hypertension	• Hypertension • Apply pressure by pinching the nose • See your doctor

SYMPTOM CHARACTERISTIC	ASSOCIATED SYMPTOMS	AGGRAVATING OR ALLEVIATING FACTORS	OTHER RELEVANT FACTORS	POSSIBLE CAUSE AND ACTION
Nosebleed (cont.)				
Sudden onset of moderate to severe bleeding from the nose	• No pain, easy bruising, prolonged bleeding after minor cuts	• Blowing the nose may increase bleeding	• May be a family history of bleeding problems such as hemophilia • Person may be taking blood thinners	• Bleeding disorder • Apply pressure by pinching the nose • See your doctor
Episodes of mild to severe bleeding from the nose	• Gradual onset of nasal obstruction, deafness (build up of fluid in the middle ear)	• Symptoms resolve when underlying condition is treated	• Vascular tumors of the nose usually occur in young men under the age of 25 years • Malignant tumors of the nose are common in Southeast Asia representing 20 percent of all malignant tumors	• Nasal tumor • See your doctor at once

Numbness and tingling

A feeling of numbness or tingling usually results from a malfunction in part of the body's nervous system. The symptoms may be caused by an isolated problem in one nerve, or may be part of a more serious degenerative disease. See also entry on *weakness and paralysis*.

SYMPTOM CHARACTERISTIC	ASSOCIATED SYMPTOMS	AGGRAVATING OR ALLEVIATING FACTORS	OTHER RELEVANT FACTORS	POSSIBLE CAUSE AND ACTION
Numbness or tingling in the hand, foot, arm or leg after being in one position	• May feel some mild stiffness when start to move	• Further aggravated by remaining in the same position • Alleviated by moving around		• Nerve compression • See your doctor if you are worried or if symptoms persist
Numbness or tingling in one arm or one leg	• Neck or back pain, weakness of the affected limb • In serious cases, may have difficulty urinating	• Aggravated by sitting, bending forward, sneezing, coughing	• The precise location of the symtoms defines which part of the back or neck is affected	• Pressure on a nerve caused by swelling of a ruptured or bulging vertebral disk in the spine • See your doctor at once
Numbness and tingling in the palm of the hand and wrist; may be worse at night	• Shooting pain into the hand, weakness, maybe mild swelling	• Flexing the wrist, making a fist	• More common in women • Also occurs in people who have to perform repeated forceful movements of the wrist (e.g. using a screwdriver)	• Carpal tunnel syndrome • See your doctor
Numbness or tingling in the hands and face, especially around the lips	• Palpitations, shaking, fear, anxiety	• Aggravated by stress, and fear of another attack	• Women are 2–3 times more likely to have an attack than men	• Panic attack • See your doctor if you are worried or if symptoms persist

SYMPTOM CHARACTERISTIC	ASSOCIATED SYMPTOMS	AGGRAVATING OR ALLEVIATING FACTORS	OTHER RELEVANT FACTORS	POSSIBLE CAUSE AND ACTION
Tingling or numbness in the arms, legs, trunk or face	• Loss of strength or dexterity, vision disturbances, dizziness, unusual tiredness, difficulty walking, trembling, loss of bladder control	• Aggravated by very warm weather, hot bath, fever	• More common among people who have lived in a temperate climate up to age 10 • Occurs much less commonly in those whose childhood was spent in a tropical climate, and extremely rare at the equator	• Multiple sclerosis • See your doctor at once
Numbness or tingling on one side of the body; symptoms usually start suddenly	• Weakness in hands or feet, confusion, dizziness, partial loss of vision or hearing, slurred speech, inability to recognize parts of the body, unusual movements, fainting		• More common with advancing age • Risk increased in people with cardiovascular disease (e.g. hypertension, coronary heart disease) lipid abnormalities (e.g. high cholesterol), diabetes	• Transient ischemic attack or stroke • This is a medical emergency • Go to the emergency room or call an ambulance at once

Palpitations

Palpitations is the term used to describe an uncomfortable awareness of your heartbeat. The palpitations may take the form of fluttering, throbbing, pounding or racing in the chest. The heart may feel as though it is beating irregularly. Palpitations may be harmless, but in certain cases they signal underlying heart disease.

SYMPTOM CHARACTERISTIC	ASSOCIATED SYMPTOMS	AGGRAVATING OR ALLEVIATING FACTORS	OTHER RELEVANT FACTORS	POSSIBLE CAUSE AND ACTION
Recurrent fluttering, racing, pounding, thumping in the chest; may have feeling of a strong pulse in the neck	• Chest discomfort, weakness, dizziness, shortness of breath		• There are many types of variation from normal heartbeat rhythm, some of which are serious • Arrhythmia is most commonly caused by heart disease, but may also occur with caffeine use, excessive alcohol, vigorous exercise	• Arrhythmia • See your doctor at once
Temporary racing, pounding, thumping in the chest; usually lasts for 10–20 minutes	• Trembling, dizziness, shortness of breath, feeling of choking, nausea, diarrhea, an out-of-body sensation, tingling in the hands, chills, fear of dying	• May be aggravated by stress, and the fear of further attacks	• Women are 2–3 times more likely than men to have these attacks	• Panic attack • See your doctor if you are worried or if symptoms persist
Racing heartbeat	• Shortness of breath on exertion, tiring easily, swelling in the legs and abdomen • May be sudden fever and flu-like symptoms	• May be aggravated by exertion	• Can occur as the result of infection, or in association with many diseases, or may have no identifiable cause	• Cardiomyopathy (disease of the heart muscle) • See your doctor at once

SYMPTOM CHARACTERISTIC	ASSOCIATED SYMPTOMS	AGGRAVATING OR ALLEVIATING FACTORS	OTHER RELEVANT FACTORS	POSSIBLE CAUSE AND ACTION
Palpitations (cont.)				
Awareness of forceful heartbeats, especially when lying on the left side	• Shortness of breath on exertion, swelling of the legs, chest pain, dizziness		• More common in those who have had rheumatic fever	• Heart valve disorder • See your doctor for advice
Sudden heavy pounding or thumping in the chest	• Pain in the middle of the chest that may spread down the left arm, sweating, shortness of breath, faintness, anxiousness, sense of impending doom	• Symptoms are not alleviated by rest	• Increased likelihood in a person who has previously had a heart attack or with a history of coronary heart disease	• Myocardial infarction (heart attack) • This is a medical emergency • Go to the emergency room or call an ambulance at once

Seizures (known as "fits", including convulsions)

Seizures result from an abrupt episode of abnormal electrical activity within the brain. There are many different types of seizures and many possible causes. Seizures may be generalized (generalized tonic-clonic convulsion also known as grand mal seizure) or localized to a particular part of the body (focal convulsion). Some seizures manifest as a brief aura followed by loss of awareness of surroundings. Any seizure warrants assessment by a doctor and often full medical investigation.

SYMPTOM CHARACTERISTIC	ASSOCIATED SYMPTOMS	AGGRAVATING OR ALLEVIATING FACTORS	OTHER RELEVANT FACTORS	POSSIBLE CAUSE AND ACTION
Repeated episodes of a generalized tonic-clonic seizure (grand mal seizure); begins with stiffness of limbs and jaw locking (tonic phase) followed by jerking of limbs (clonic phase) then a period of drowsiness and confusion (postictal phase)	• Urinary incontinence during fit	• Sleep deprivation, flickering lights, hyperventilation	• No fever or current illness	• Epilepsy • See your doctor at once
Repeated episodes of seizures that involve disturbances in the senses (sensory seizures)	• May have preceding aura involving visual and auditory hallucinations or distortions of taste and smell, followed by period of altered awareness sometimes associated with lipsmacking or repetitive movements (automatisms)	• May be brought on by sleep deprivation, flickering lights, hyperventilation		• Temporal lobe epilepsy • See your doctor at once
Brief generalized seizure in child under 5 years	• Fever • No signs of infection of the brain (encephalitis) or covering of the brain (meningitis), no history of epilepsy	• Rapid rise in temperature	• 3 percent of children have at least one febrile convulsion	• Simple febrile seizure of childhood • See your doctor at once

SYMPTOM CHARACTERISTIC	ASSOCIATED SYMPTOMS	AGGRAVATING OR ALLEVIATING FACTORS	OTHER RELEVANT FACTORS	POSSIBLE CAUSE AND ACTION
Repeated episodes of focal seizures (localized to a particular part of the body)	• Involuntary movements may occur in a single limb, one side of the body or involve eyes deviating to one side		• Indicates a localized lesion within the brain triggering the seizures	• Head injury is the most common cause in young adults, while cerebrovascular accidents (strokes) are the most common cause in the elderly • Congenital malformations of the brain, early meningitis or perinatal brain damage are common causes in children • This is a medical emergency • Go to the emergency room or call an ambulance at once
Generalized or focal convulsion	• Headache, drowsiness, neck stiffness, oversensitivity to light, fever	• May have preceding febrile illness	• May occur in previously healthy person	• Meningitis or encephalitis • This is a medical emergency • Go to the emergency room or call an ambulance at once
Isolated generalized or focal convulsion	• Headache, nervous system abnormalities, decreased consciousness, newly developed squint	• May follow head injury	• May indicate raised pressure within the confined space of the skull	• Brain tumor, abscess or cerebral hemorrhage • This is a medical emergency • Go to the emergency room or call an ambulance at once

Sexual function problems

Several problems limit sexual pleasure or the proper function of sex organs. See your doctor, since many problems affecting sexual function may be treated. Untreated sex problems can lead to relationship problems, depression and anxiety. See also entries on *genital pain* and *vaginal problems*.

SYMPTOM CHARACTERISTIC	ASSOCIATED SYMPTOMS	AGGRAVATING OR ALLEVIATING FACTORS	OTHER RELEVANT FACTORS	POSSIBLE CAUSE AND ACTION
In males, ejaculation before or immediately after intercourse begins	• Anxiety, frustration, depression	• May be aggravated by further worry about it happening	• More common in young men • Physical causes are rare, and most cases have a psychological cause	• Premature ejaculation • See your doctor if you are worried or if symptoms persist
In males, inability to have or keep an erection sufficient for sexual intercourse	• Anxiety, frustration, depression		• More likely as men get older • Physical disorders are the main cause, especially in men aged over 50	• Erectile dysfunction (impotence) • See your doctor
In males, pain during sexual contact	• May be redness or rash, or other symptoms of infection such as fever	• Symptoms are aggravated by continued sexual contact		• Infection (e.g. prostate, testes or urethra), allergic reaction to spermicide • See your doctor

SYMPTOM CHARACTERISTIC	ASSOCIATED SYMPTOMS	AGGRAVATING OR ALLEVIATING FACTORS	OTHER RELEVANT FACTORS	POSSIBLE CAUSE AND ACTION
Sexual function problems (cont.)				
Lack of sexual desire or inability to experience sexual pleasure	• Anxiety, frustration	• May be aggravated by stress, fatigue, anxiety, relationship problems	• More common in women than men • Physical and psychological causes can lead to this problem	• Arousal dysfunction • See your doctor
In females, pain during intercourse; pain may be in the vaginal area or deeper in the pelvis	• Vaginal discharge, itching, dryness	• May be aggravated by continued sexual contact	• Pelvic inflammatory disease and infections are most common among young, sexually active women • Endometriosis is most common among women with a family history of the disease, and in women who have never been pregnant • Hormonal imbalances causing vaginal dryness are more common following menopause	• Pelvic inflammatory disease, infections, hormonal imbalance, endometriosis • See your doctor
In females, inability to have intercourse due to contraction of the vaginal muscles	• Fear, anxiety, pain	• Fear of intercourse, pain, memories of unpleasant sexual experiences	• This is an involuntary response, outside the woman's control	• Vaginismus • See your doctor

SYMPTOM CHARACTERISTIC	ASSOCIATED SYMPTOMS	AGGRAVATING OR ALLEVIATING FACTORS	OTHER RELEVANT FACTORS	POSSIBLE CAUSE AND ACTION

Skin problems

The skin can show a very wide range of noticeable changes. It is important to check your skin regularly and report any changes to your doctor, since it is often difficult to tell the difference between significant changes (e.g. early skin cancers or eruptions due to other diseases) and unimportant ones, by appearance alone.

Changes in skin color

SYMPTOM CHARACTERISTIC	ASSOCIATED SYMPTOMS	AGGRAVATING OR ALLEVIATING FACTORS	OTHER RELEVANT FACTORS	POSSIBLE CAUSE AND ACTION
A longstanding spot that is brown (and a different color from the rest of the skin), unchanging in size or appearance; usually smooth and well defined; may be slightly raised or hairy	• None		• Moles commonly appear in childhood, during pregnancy or during treatment with medications containing estrogen • The pigment indicates that the lesion contains cells which produce melanin, a brown pigment present in the skin • Any change in a mole (e.g. itching, growing or spreading, becoming darker or lighter in color, changing shape, developing an irregular border, bleeding, becoming inflamed or ulcerated) may be a sign of cancer	• Mole • See your doctor • Although moles are harmless, any skin spot with this appearance should be examined by an expert to confirm that it is not a skin cancer
A new, growing or changing brown or blue-black pigmented lesion, usually irregular or asymmetric in shape and color; often over ¼ inch (0.5 centimeter) in diameter; may be bleeding or ulcerated	• Usually painless • May be itchy • Surrounding skin may be inflamed		• Melanoma occurs in all adult age groups but is rare in pre-pubescent children • Risk is increased in people with fair skin or hair, many freckles or moles, or moles of unusual appearance • Up to 50 percent of melanomas develop from moles • Sun exposure, especially before age 10, may predispose to melanoma	• Melanoma • See your doctor at once
Sharply defined white (depigmented) patches of skin			• Vitiligo may occur in people with a family history of the disease or in those with immune disorders	• Vitiligo • See your doctor

Changes in shape of skin surface

SYMPTOM CHARACTERISTIC	ASSOCIATED SYMPTOMS	AGGRAVATING OR ALLEVIATING FACTORS	OTHER RELEVANT FACTORS	POSSIBLE CAUSE AND ACTION
Rash of pimples and pustules on face, chest and back	• Inflamed raised red spots, excessive oiliness, blocked pores (whiteheads, blackheads), scarring	• May be exacerbated by some foods or medications	• Acne is most common in teenagers but also occurs in 10–20 percent of adults	• Acne (acne vulgaris) • See your doctor
Unusual growth or ulcerated raised lump on the face	• May be itchy or painful		• Incidence increases with age • Skin cancers are most common on the face, but can develop on other sun-exposed areas of the body • Growth rate depends on the type of cancer; the growth may develop over a month or so, or slowly over many months	• Skin cancer • See your doctor
A well-defined, round swelling just under the skin of the scalp or back of the neck; typically the swelling feels smooth to firm and the surface is smooth and shiny; the swelling is attached to the skin and may have a central hole	• The swelling is painless and the overlying skin normal		• Cysts may occur at any age, but rarely before adolescence • Cysts grow slowly • There may be one or several cysts	• Sebaceous cyst • See your doctor
Small (pinpoint or pin head size) raised round pink or pearly shiny bumps with pits in the center			• Molluscum contagiosum is most common in children • Contacts (e.g. family members or friends) may also be affected • Commonly occurs on the face, eyelids or genital, but may develop on any area	• Molluscum contagiosum • See your doctor

SYMPTOM CHARACTERISTIC	ASSOCIATED SYMPTOMS	AGGRAVATING OR ALLEVIATING FACTORS	OTHER RELEVANT FACTORS	POSSIBLE CAUSE AND ACTION
Small red, warm, tender bump around a hair follicle, that develops suddenly	• Painful		• Boils may occur singly, or several may appear at the same time • Occasionally multiple boils in the same area result in inflammation of the whole area • Conditions that may predispose to boils include scratching of the skin, which allows bacteria to enter, illnesses which lower the body's resistance (e.g. diabetes)	• Boil • See your doctor
One or more small red bumps that appear suddenly and are randomly distributed, in a person exposed to insects	• Bumps are itchy	• Scratching may worsen inflammation and may cause open weeping sores	• May occur after spending time gardening or outdoors	• Insect bites • Calamine or other soothing lotions available from your pharmacist may relieve itching • See your doctor if you are worried or if symptoms persist
Red bumps or elevated red patches that appear suddenly, each of which lasts from a few hours to 2 days; may be white in the center	• Itching and tingling or a pricking sensation • Swelling around the mouth or throat, difficulty breathing	• Scratching may worsen inflammation and may cause open weeping sores	• Hives most often appear on the arms, legs or waist, but any part of the body may be affected • Common causes include food allergies, exposure to dusts, medicines, infections, heat or cold	• Hives (urticaria) • If needed, calamine or other soothing lotions as recommended by your pharmacist may relieve itching • See your doctor at once
Sudden appearance of bright red or dark red-blue tender deep-seated bumps or raised areas about 1–2 inches (2–5 centimeters) in diameter; usually on the front of both legs, occasionally on the outer forearms	• Lumps are painful • Fever, feeling of being generally unwell, joint pains, sore throat		• Most often affects 20–30 year olds, more commonly females • Erythema nodosum may occurs as a symptom of infection, drug reaction, or an underlying illness	• Skin eruption caused by inflammation within the skin (erythema nodosum) • See your doctor

Rashes

SYMPTOM CHARACTERISTIC	ASSOCIATED SYMPTOMS	AGGRAVATING OR ALLEVIATING FACTORS	OTHER RELEVANT FACTORS	POSSIBLE CAUSE AND ACTION
A tender, red, warm, swollen area of skin with an undefined border	• Fever		• May occur where skin is broken (e.g. a cut or scratch)	• Cellulitis • See your doctor

SYMPTOM CHARACTERISTIC	ASSOCIATED SYMPTOMS	AGGRAVATING OR ALLEVIATING FACTORS	OTHER RELEVANT FACTORS	POSSIBLE CAUSE AND ACTION
Skin problems–rashes (cont.)				
Small purplish-red bruise-like spots, may be flat or slightly raised	• Associated symptoms, if present, will depend on the underlying cause		• Purpura may be due to bruising, inflammation of capillaries, the use of cortisone-type medications (e.g. ointments or oral medications), diseases affecting the platelets, or serious infections	• Bleeding into the skin (purpura) due to medical condition affecting the blood or blood vessels • See your doctor at once
Red rash with tiny fluid-filled blisters; lesions tend to be dry and fragmented; may be swollen, scaly or develop painful cracks; the margins of the rash are often ill defined	• Severe itching • Skin may be dry in general • Other symptoms of allergies	• Itching is exacerbated by changes in temperature, mood and contact with irritating materials	• Symptoms may commence at any age, may occur intermittently or long-term, and may fluctuate in severity • Allergic dermatitis is most common in people with a family history of allergic diseases • May occur with other allergic conditions (e.g. asthma or hay fever)	• Eczema or dermatitis • See your doctor
Red rash with tiny fluid-filled blisters (vesicles) in an area exposed to an irritating substance; may be swollen or scaly	• May be itchy or sore	• Scratching may worsen inflammation and may cause open weeping sores	• Contact dermatitis)may occur following exposure to clothing, cosmetics, household detergents, occupational exposure to petroleum-based products, oils, solvents, paint, cement, rubber, resins, plants, or medicines which are applied directly to the skin • Contact dermatitis may occur on the shoulders, neck and scalp if the irritant is in the form of dust	• Contact dermatitis • Try to identify the cause by eliminating suspected substances • Avoid contact with the substance by wearing protective clothing • See your doctor if you are worried or if symptoms persist
Red rash or ring-like area; may be scaly	• Itchy • If the area affected is the scalp, hairs within the affected area tend to be broken		• May affect the nails, feet, hands, groin, trunk or scalp • Ringworm may follow contact with pets (e.g. dogs, cats or horses)	• Fungal infection (e.g. ringworm) • See your doctor
Reddish plaques covered with silvery scales; the margins are well defined	• Usually not itchy • Arthritis may occur	• Trauma, infections or emotional upsets may predispose to symptoms	• May affect any age group, but uncommon before 10 years of age and most common at 15–30 years of age • Usually develops gradually • Usually chronic	• Psoriasis • See your doctor

SYMPTOM CHARACTERISTIC	ASSOCIATED SYMPTOMS	AGGRAVATING OR ALLEVIATING FACTORS	OTHER RELEVANT FACTORS	POSSIBLE CAUSE AND ACTION
Rapid onset of well defined reddish, slightly scaly patches on the trunk; usually a single patch precedes the development of others by a week or so	• Patches may be slightly itchy • May also affect the arms and legs		• The cause of pityriasis rosea is unknown • Symptoms occur most commonly in spring and autumn • Any age group may be affected, most commonly young adults	• Pityriasis rosea • See your doctor
Sudden development of small round red target-like patches and bumps which are darker in the center than the outside of the lesion; may have blistering	• Feeling of being generally unwell, fever, sore throat, diarrhea		• Attacks may be triggered by medications, infections, cancer, pregnancy • Most commonly affects the back of the hands and forearms in a symmetrical fashion; may affect other areas	• Erythema multiforme, an inflammatory disease of the skin, which is usually a reaction to infection or medication • See your doctor
Flat blotchy red rashes, which begin 4 days after symptoms of a cold in a child; rashes may join up to form one larger red area	• Before the rash develops there may be a general feeling of being unwell, loss of appetite, fever, cough, runny nose, red watering eyes		• Measles is preventable by vaccination • Measles tends to be more severe in adults than in children	• Measles • Rest in bed and avoid contact with others, especially pregnant women • See your doctor • Measles is highly contagious, so warn the doctor's office of symptoms before you attend
Long-term redness of the cheeks, chin and central forehead, often with small round circumscribed bumps which may contain pus		• Before permanent redness develops, flushing may occur with heat, emotional reactions, alcohol, hot drinks or spicy foods	• Gradual onset • Begins after 30 years of age, typically in middle age • More common in women • More likely to develop in people who experience frequent pronounced flushing; flushing persists longer with repeated episodes until the condition becomes permanent	• Acne rosacea • See your doctor
Scaly rash across the nose and cheeks or forehead; spots are butterfly-shaped or round, with well defined margins	• Arthritis, joint pain, fever, hair loss, kidney problems		• Usually long-term • Onset is gradual • Women are twice as likely as males to develop lupus erythematosus • More common in African races (e.g. Afro-Americans) than white races	• Lupus erythematosus • See your doctor

SYMPTOM CHARACTERISTIC	ASSOCIATED SYMPTOMS	AGGRAVATING OR ALLEVIATING FACTORS	OTHER RELEVANT FACTORS	POSSIBLE CAUSE AND ACTION
Skin problems–rashes (cont.)				
Bright red rash on the cheeks ("slapped cheek"); after a day or two, rash typically also appears on the forearms and thighs	• Fever, general feeling of being unwell • Arthritis may occur in adults		• Most common in children aged 3–12 • Infection during pregnancy may cause fetal damage	• Fifth disease (erythema infectiosum), an infectious viral disease • Avoid contact with other people, especially pregnant women • See your doctor • Fifth disease is infectious, so warn the doctor's office of symptoms before you attend
Greasy, scaly round dirty-yellow or gray colored patches in hairy areas of the body such as the scalp; the patches may be pinhead to coin sized	• May be itchy or burning	• Scratching may cause open, inflamed or weeping sores	• Onset is gradual • Symptoms may occur in episodes or become long-term • Commonly affected areas include the scalp, eyelids, eyebrows, ears, chest, groin or between the buttocks • May occur in babies ("cradle cap")	• Dandruff (seborrheic dermatitis) • See your doctor

Blistering conditions

SYMPTOM CHARACTERISTIC	ASSOCIATED SYMPTOMS	AGGRAVATING OR ALLEVIATING FACTORS	OTHER RELEVANT FACTORS	POSSIBLE CAUSE AND ACTION
Groups of bright red tiny fluid-filled blisters, which rupture and form crusts	• Rash is itchy • Fever (before blisters appear), feeling of being generally unwell • Adults may also experience aches and pains, headaches, serious nerve damage (rare)		• Rash mostly affects the trunk and face • Children are most often affected, especially between 2–8 years of age; condition is usually mild, but occasionally can be fatal • A person may be affected at any age if they have not previously had the condition • Severe illness occurs more often in adults	• Chickenpox • Rest, use calamine lotion or other medications recommended by your doctor or pharmacist to relieve itching, acetaminophen (paracetamol) for fever, daily bathing • Avoid scratching spots • See your doctor • Chickenpox is highly contagious, so warn the doctor's office of symptoms before you attend
Groups of tiny fluid-filled blisters in a band-like distribution on one side of the body; the vesicles usually rupture and crust over	• Severe pain in the area of the rash usually begins 1–2 days before the skin lesions		• Mostly occurs in adults • May recur	• Shingles • See your doctor at once

SYMPTOM CHARACTERISTIC	ASSOCIATED SYMPTOMS	AGGRAVATING OR ALLEVIATING FACTORS	OTHER RELEVANT FACTORS	POSSIBLE CAUSE AND ACTION
Small and larger blisters around the face and ears in a child	• Often itchy • Scratching can lead to further spread of the lesions		• May affect adults but more common in children	• Impetigo • Highly contagious • Other members of the household should avoid unnecessary contact with toweling or napkins that come into contact with the lesions • See your doctor
Multiple large blisters of the skin	• Not itchy, tender when the blister ruptures • After healing, area may remain darker than surrounding skin		• Pemphigus is a long-term disorder • Occurs mainly in the elderly; rarely occurs in people under 40 years of age	• Pemphigus/pemphigoid • See your doctor

Itching

SYMPTOM CHARACTERISTIC	ASSOCIATED SYMPTOMS	AGGRAVATING OR ALLEVIATING FACTORS	OTHER RELEVANT FACTORS	POSSIBLE CAUSE AND ACTION
Itching without other evidence of skin disease	• Associated symptoms will vary greatly depending on the specific cause			• No definable cause or liver disease, kidney disease, blood abnormalities, thyroid disease, human immunodeficiency virus (HIV) infection, tumors • See your doctor
Itchy, painful rash or raised red spots occurring during sea bathing	• Generalized inflamed rash or rash only in areas covered by clothing while swimming	• Thimble jellyfish reactions are exacerbated by clothing that traps the tiny creatures against the skin e.g. wearing T-shirts while swimming	• Causes vary with region e.g. thimble jellyfish reactions are common in Florida, USA and tend to occur in certain years, reactions to stinger tentacles are common in northeast Australia • Other creatures also known as "sea lice" cause tiny bites that may be painful rather than itchy	• Reaction to various marine irritants known as "sea lice" (e.g. thimble jellyfish, particles of broken stinging tentacles of marine stingers) • See your doctor
Intense itching that worsens at night; affects same areas on both sides of body in symmetrical pattern	• Dark wavy lines visible on skin of wrists, fingers, elbows, penis • Blisters, rash or pustules in skin folds (e.g. under breasts) • Face, scalp, neck or palms unaffected in adults but may be affected in infants	• Itching aggravated by hot showers • Scratching causes sores	• Scabies is contagious and is spread through personal contact • Outbreaks in developed countries tend to occur in institutions (e.g. nursing homes) • Symptoms begin 4–6 weeks after contact with an infected person	• Infestation by human itch mite (scabies) • See your doctor

SYMPTOM CHARACTERISTIC	ASSOCIATED SYMPTOMS	AGGRAVATING OR ALLEVIATING FACTORS	OTHER RELEVANT FACTORS	POSSIBLE CAUSE AND ACTION
Skin problems–itching (cont.)				
Extremely itchy areas ¾ inch (2 centimeters) diameter, followed by itching, burning for weeks; mostly on ankles or at areas where tight clothing is worn	• Blistering and bleeding		• Occurs in bushy, scrubby areas in tropics and sub-tropics, and occasionally temperate areas in warm weather • Other parasites (e.g. mites) may cause intense itching	• Infestation by harvest mite larvae (chiggers) • See your doctor
Itchy open weeping areas on head, neck, shoulders	• Oozing, crusting, matting of hair, infections, swollen painful "glands" (lymph nodes) • "Nits" (louse eggs) may be visible stuck to hairs		• Lice infestation is most common among preschool and primary school-aged children	• Head lice infestation • See your doctor
Itching areas around neck or pubic area, armpits, eyelashes	• Thickened and darkened skin follows long-term infestations • "Nits" (louse eggs) may be visible stuck to hairs or clothing		• Body lice infestations occur mainly in the homeless and in people living in extreme poverty • Pubic lice are spread through direct contact or clothing	• Body lice or pubic lice • See your doctor

Sleep disturbances

Sleep problems are not uncommon in normal healthy people, but sleep disturbances can become extremely troubling and sometimes dangerous. Inappropriate use of sleeping pills can aggravate sleeping problems, so it is important to consult your doctor before using them.

SYMPTOM CHARACTERISTIC	ASSOCIATED SYMPTOMS	AGGRAVATING OR ALLEVIATING FACTORS	OTHER RELEVANT FACTORS	POSSIBLE CAUSE AND ACTION
Difficulty initiating or maintaining sleep	• Daytime fatigue • Depression may cause early morning waking • Drug and alcohol use may result in frequent waking during the night	• May be aggravated by irregular daytime naps or performing anxiety-producing tasks (e.g. work or non-relaxing chores) immediately before bedtime	• Insomnia may be caused by a change in the body clock, anxiety, depression, drug or alcohol use (e.g. inappropriate use of sedatives), psychiatric illness, physical discomfort due to medical disorders	• Insomnia • Undertake regular physical activity • Avoid heavy meals, alcohol or stimulants (e.g. coffee) at night • Avoid napping during the day • Go to bed and get up at the same time every day • Avoid lying in bed without sleeping for lengthy periods • If you haven't fallen asleep within 30 minutes, get up, do something relaxing, and try again later • See your doctor if you are worried or if symptoms persist

SYMPTOM CHARACTERISTIC	ASSOCIATED SYMPTOMS	AGGRAVATING OR ALLEVIATING FACTORS	OTHER RELEVANT FACTORS	POSSIBLE CAUSE AND ACTION
Excessive daytime sleepiness; falling asleep when not stimulated	• Snoring	• Symptoms may be exacerbated by alcohol	• Sleepiness may occur in healthy people if they feel bored or tired or have slept poorly at night • Sleep apnea is most common among obese people, and in middle-aged and older adult men	• Sleep apnea • See your doctor
Brief irresistible attacks of sleep during the day in inappropriate situations or while active, e.g. while eating or talking; attacks are often frequent; usually the sleep attacks are refreshing and the person is easily woken from them	• Episodes of physical weakness set off by surprise or emotions, frightening hallucinations occurring during the transition to sleep or on waking, inability to move for a short period on waking		• Typically starts at 15–25 years of age	• Narcolepsy • See your doctor
Walking or talking during sleep; usually not recalled afterwards			• Sleepwalking commonly occurs in healthy children and occasionally in adults	• Sleepwalking • Ensure sleep is taken in a secure environment to reduce the risk of injuries/accidents while sleepwalking • Avoid drinking alcohol or coffee at night • See your doctor if you are worried or if symptoms persist
Waking from a frightening dream in a frightened or agitated state; usually able to remember the episode			• Nightmares commonly occur during the rapid eye movement phase of sleep in healthy adults and children • Some medications may cause nightmares	• Nightmares • See your doctor if you are worried or if symptoms persist
Waking suddenly in a very agitated and frightened state; the episodes are usually more severe and prolonged than with nightmares; usually unable to remember the episode	• Loud screaming on waking, rapid heartbeat and breathing, heavy sweating		• Most common in children around 5 or 6 years old; usually settles in adolescence • Sometimes, an epileptic disorder can cause sudden waking with agitation	• Night terrors • See your doctor
Hallucinations occurring during the transition to sleep or on waking			• Occurs in healthy people • More common in people with narcolepsy	• Hypnagogic hallucinations • See your doctor if you are worried or if symptoms persist

SYMPTOM CHARACTERISTIC	ASSOCIATED SYMPTOMS	AGGRAVATING OR ALLEVIATING FACTORS	OTHER RELEVANT FACTORS	POSSIBLE CAUSE AND ACTION
Sleep disturbances (cont.)				
Inability to move for a short period on waking			• Occurs in healthy people	• Sleep paralysis • See your doctor if you are worried or if symptoms persist

Snoring

Heavy snoring is a signal which may indicate an underlying problem, usually temporary obstruction of the windpipe (trachea) during sleep. Diagnosis and treatment are important for quality of life and long-term health, so consult your doctor for an assessment. See also entry on *sleep disturbances*.

SYMPTOM CHARACTERISTIC	ASSOCIATED SYMPTOMS	AGGRAVATING OR ALLEVIATING FACTORS	OTHER RELEVANT FACTORS	POSSIBLE CAUSE AND ACTION
Snoring during sleep, usually noticed by another person	• Daytime fatigue	• Aggravated when the person sleeps on the back • Alcohol and some medications may worsen snoring by relaxing the parts of the throat that cause snoring • Snoring may occur only during nasal congestion with hay fever or a cold	• Snoring is the sound of partially obstructed flow of air due the soft parts of the throat and mouth • 45 percent of adults snore at least occasionally, and 25 percent snore regularly • Heavy snoring is more common in overweight men and increases with age	• See your doctor if you are worried or if symptoms persist
Very loud snoring punctuated by long pauses in breathing, may be observed by sufferer's partner or room-mate	• Excessive daytime sleepiness due to poor quality of sleep • Tiredness, irritability, difficulty concentrating, loss of libido, morning headache, frequent waking during the night		• Most common in overweight middle-aged men • Predisposing factors include obesity, enlarged tonsils (especially in children), use of alcohol, sedatives/sleeping pills, neurological problems affecting the muscles around the windpipe	• Sleep apnea • Sleep on your side, lose weight if you are overweight, avoid drinking alcohol or using sedatives/sleeping pills • See your doctor

SYMPTOM CHARACTERISTIC	ASSOCIATED SYMPTOMS	AGGRAVATING OR ALLEVIATING FACTORS	OTHER RELEVANT FACTORS	POSSIBLE CAUSE AND ACTION

Speech problems

Speech or language problems are quite common in children. Have an audiologist check your child's hearing and if you are still concerned see a speech pathologist. The sudden onset of speech and/or language problems in adulthood are often indicative of an underlying medical problem. Therefore it is advisable to see your doctor and have the symptoms investigated.

SYMPTOM CHARACTERISTIC	ASSOCIATED SYMPTOMS	AGGRAVATING OR ALLEVIATING FACTORS	OTHER RELEVANT FACTORS	POSSIBLE CAUSE AND ACTION
The frequent repetition of sounds, usually at the beginning of words and sentences	• Eye blinking, head nodding or facial tension during speech	• Stressful situations or talking to unfamiliar people can make symptoms worse	• Often other members in the family have the same problem • More common in boys	• Stuttering • Children of any age who display signs of stuttering, particularly if it occurs with the associated symptoms, need to see a speech pathologist as soon as possible • Stuttering will not disappear if ignored • See your doctor if you are worried or if symptoms persist
A child with minimal speech	• Pointing or gesturing rather than talking	• Poor hearing	• Speech or language difficulties can run in families	• Language delay. If the child is not making babbling sounds by 12 months or producing some single words by 24 months see a speech pathologist • See your doctor if you are worried or if symptoms persist
Sudden onset of slurred speech	• Sudden difficulty thinking of words, getting words muddled up; knowing what you want to say but being unable to say it • Weakness on one side of the face or body • Difficulty understanding people		• More common with increasing age	• Transient ischemic attack or stroke • This is a medical emergency • Go to the emergency room or call an ambulance at once

Swallowing problems

Swallowing problems can occur in the mouth, throat or gullet (esophagus). The likelihood of swallowing difficulties increases with age. If symptoms occur see your doctor, as undetected swallowing problems can result in other health complications.

SYMPTOM CHARACTERISTIC	ASSOCIATED SYMPTOMS	AGGRAVATING OR ALLEVIATING FACTORS	OTHER RELEVANT FACTORS	POSSIBLE CAUSE AND ACTION
Food or drink keeps "going down the wrong way"; coughing or throat clearing during meals and/or when drinking	• Taking a longer time to eat and drink • Chest infections • Gradual loss of weight	• Fatigue usually makes swallowing more difficult • Some food or fluid may be more difficult to swallow than others	• Most likely in diseases of the nervous system	• Neurogenic dysphagia (nerve problem preventing normal use and coordination of swallowing muscles) • See your doctor

SYMPTOM CHARACTERISTIC	ASSOCIATED SYMPTOMS	AGGRAVATING OR ALLEVIATING FACTORS	OTHER RELEVANT FACTORS	POSSIBLE CAUSE AND ACTION
Swallowing problems (cont.)				
Food sticking in the throat		• Dry food tends to stick more often; drinking water often alleviates the problem	• May occur following damage caused by esophageal ulcers	• Narrowing of the esophagus • See your doctor
Indigestion/ heartburn	• Pain on swallowing • Coughing or choking on food after you have swallowed it • Coughing during the night • Husky voice	• Sleeping in a more upright position may help • Spicy foods can exacerbate the symptoms	• Typically occurs after food • Heartburn may occur during pregnancy but usually resolves after the baby is born	• Gastroesophageal reflux • See your doctor

Throat problems

Sore throats or discomfort when swallowing are common symptoms that often occur with viral infections and usually resolve without treatment. However, throat problems may sometimes indicate a more serious cause, so any persistent problem should always be checked by your doctor. See also the entry on *cough*.

SYMPTOM CHARACTERISTIC	ASSOCIATED SYMPTOMS	AGGRAVATING OR ALLEVIATING FACTORS	OTHER RELEVANT FACTORS	POSSIBLE CAUSE AND ACTION
Itchiness in the back of the mouth	• Dry or irritated feeling when swallowing • Urge to sneeze when attempt to rub area using the tongue • Watery discharge from nose or eyes	• Commonly occurs in spring or in dusty environment	• Common with other signs of allergy	• Allergic reaction (allergies) to airborne allergens (e.g. pollens) • Wait a few days to ensure the symptoms are not due to a respiratory viral infection like cold or flu • Ask your pharmacist or doctor for advice • Symptoms are usually readily relieved by medications such as oral anti-allergy tablets or nasal sprays • See your doctor if you are worried or if symptoms persist
Pain or discomfort on swallowing	• Sneeze, cough, headaches, swollen lymph nodes ("glands") under the jaw • Nasal discharge • Fever	• Worse on waking up		• Cold or flu (viral infection) • Rest, and see your pharmacist for advice on simple cough and cold remedies • See your doctor if you are worried or if symptoms persist

SYMPTOM CHARACTERISTIC	ASSOCIATED SYMPTOMS	AGGRAVATING OR ALLEVIATING FACTORS	OTHER RELEVANT FACTORS	POSSIBLE CAUSE AND ACTION
Pain or discomfort on swallowing	• Headache, swollen lymph nodes ("glands") under the jaw, fever, nausea, vomiting, diarrhea			• Viral gastroenteritis • Rest and drink plenty of fluids • Ask your doctor or pharmacist for advice on relieving symptoms • See your doctor if you are worried or if symptoms persist
Very sore throat, with white patches on the tonsils				• Bacterial streptococcal infection ("strep throat") or infectious mononucleosis (glandular fever) • See your doctor
Sore throat with cough	• Coughing mucus			• Bronchitis from cold or flu (viral infection) • See your doctor if you are worried or if symptoms persist
Sore throat with harsh barking cough in a child	• Fever			• Croup or epiglottitis • See your doctor at once
Sore throat	• Peeling skin within the mouth, inflammation and swelling of the tongue and gums		• Some medications may cause a strong inflammatory reaction in the mouth • Good oral hygiene, including brushing teeth and flossing gums may help prevent some oral infections	• Bacterial infection in the mouth (trench mouth) or reaction to prescription drugs • See your doctor or dentist

Tongue problems

Most problems affecting the tongue will resolve within a few days without treatment. However, it is important to have a medical assessment if symptoms recur or persist, since changes to the tongue may indicate other diseases.

SYMPTOM CHARACTERISTIC	ASSOCIATED SYMPTOMS	AGGRAVATING OR ALLEVIATING FACTORS	OTHER RELEVANT FACTORS	POSSIBLE CAUSE AND ACTION
Red, raw areas on tongue		• Discomfort may be increased by eating, drinking or use of mouthwashes	• Ulcers due to trauma; usually heal within a few days	• Ulcers due to trauma (e.g. false teeth or orthodontic braces) • See your doctor or dentist if you are worried or if symptoms persist

SYMPTOM CHARACTERISTIC	ASSOCIATED SYMPTOMS	AGGRAVATING OR ALLEVIATING FACTORS	OTHER RELEVANT FACTORS	POSSIBLE CAUSE AND ACTION
Tongue problems (cont.)				
Painful raw-looking white areas on or under tongue in an otherwise healthy person			• May occur with Crohn's disease or celiac disease	• Aphthous ulcers • Ulcers commonly occur in healthy people, and may be caused by herpes virus • See your doctor or dentist if you are worried or if symptoms persist
White spots surrounded by red area	• May be present on sides of mouth		• Most common in young children and babies, elderly people, or people with a suppressed immune system (e.g. diabetes, AIDS, taking cortisone-type drugs or chemotherapy for cancer)	• Oral candidiasis (thrush), a yeast infection • See your doctor
Enlarged tongue			• Occurs in developmental conditions such as Down syndrome	• Tumor or sign of another disease • See your doctor
Patchy pattern of raised light areas and flat red areas			• Patterns change over time	• "Geographic tongue" • A harmless inflammatory condition of the tongue • See your doctor
"Bald" or smooth appearance of tongue (loss of normal rough surface)	• May be painful			• Inflammation of tongue (glossitis), iron deficiency, vitamin deficiency or anemia • See your doctor
Inflammation and swelling of the tongue and gums	• Peeling skin within the mouth		• Some medications may cause a strong inflammatory reaction in the mouth • Good oral hygiene, including brushing teeth and flossing gums may help prevent some oral infections	• Bacterial infection in the mouth ("trench mouth") or reaction to prescription drugs • See your doctor or dentist
Bright or dark red tongue	• Fever		• Most common in young children	• Scarlet fever • See your doctor at once
Hairy appearance				• Overgrowth of normal projections on surface of tongue • See your doctor

SYMPTOM CHARACTERISTIC	ASSOCIATED SYMPTOMS	AGGRAVATING OR ALLEVIATING FACTORS	OTHER RELEVANT FACTORS	POSSIBLE CAUSE AND ACTION
Black or brown appearance			• Tobacco smoking or chewing may discolor the tongue	• Color changes due to antibiotics • See your doctor
Raised ulcer on edge of tongue with thickness or firmness of edges and surrounding areas			• Does not heal within a few days like common ulcers	• Cancer of the tongue • See your doctor at once

Toothache

Toothache warrants prompt attention, to maximize the chance of preserving the tooth. While problems involving pain in a tooth should generally be referred to a dentist, go immediately to the emergency room if a tooth is lost through injury outside your dentist's office hours.

SYMPTOM CHARACTERISTIC	ASSOCIATED SYMPTOMS	AGGRAVATING OR ALLEVIATING FACTORS	OTHER RELEVANT FACTORS	POSSIBLE CAUSE AND ACTION
Tooth knocked out by trauma to the mouth	• Pain in surrounding areas in the mouth		• In some circumstances, an otherwise healthy tooth that is accidentally knocked out may be saved	• This is a dental emergency • If a tooth has been completely knocked out, put it in a moist cool cloth or in your mouth to preserve it until you get to a dentist or emergency room • See your dentist or go to the emergency room at once
Pain in a specific tooth that is broken or chipped or a loose tooth				• If the chip has just occurred, keep chipped or broken off parts of tooth in a moist cool cloth • See your dentist at once
Pain in a specific tooth; initially pain occurs on exposure to hot and/or cold or when eating; may progress to continuous throbbing pain	• Pain may be continuous if there is inflammation or infection		• Poor dental hygiene increases the risk of tooth decay and cavities	• Tooth cavity or decay • See your dentist
Redness, swelling, tenderness and severe pain around a tooth and/or section of the gums	• May be swelling in the face		• May be preceded by other symptoms of tooth decay or periodontal disease, particularly if left untreated	• Dental abscess • See your dentist at once
Pain not necessarily related to a specific tooth	• Perhaps tenderness, gums may bleed easily on brushing or chewing, gums may be red and swollen, eventually loosening of the teeth may occur		• Usually starts with inflammation of the gums (gingivitis)	• Periodontal disease, most commonly inflammation of the supporting tissue around the teeth • See your dentist

Tremor

Tremor is a non-deliberate, rhythmic oscillation usually of the hands or head. It is relatively common in elderly people, or as a side effect of certain medications.

SYMPTOM CHARACTERISTIC	ASSOCIATED SYMPTOMS	AGGRAVATING OR ALLEVIATING FACTORS	OTHER RELEVANT FACTORS	POSSIBLE CAUSE AND ACTION
Coarse and rhythmical tremor of the hands at rest, sometimes the thumb moves over the fingers in a pill-rolling action	• Insidious onset of symptoms including slowness in initiating and performing movements, unusual shuffling or freezing up when walking and difficulties with balance and control of walking	• Tremor may disappear when actively using the hands and may be aggravated by emotion	• Most common among adults over 50 years of age	• Parkinson's disease • See your doctor
Fine trembling when using hands		• Aggravated when actively using the hands	• A normal tremor that is usually very subtle may be exaggerated by emotion, fatigue, cocaine, caffeine, advancing age, other medical conditions (e.g. thyroid disease), medications (e.g. drugs used in asthma), depression or other mood disturbances, epilepsy, psychiatric illness, withdrawal from alcohol dependency	• Physiological tremor—exaggeration of a slight tremor that is normally present in healthy people • See your doctor if you are worried or if symptoms persist
Trembling when using hands		• Alleviated by alcohol	• The tremor runs in the family	• Essential tremor • See your doctor
Coarse tremor when using hands		• Aggravated by actively using the hands in careful or precise movements	• Cerebellar disease may be due to biochemical, metabolic or toxic causes, problems of the immune system, tumors, abscess, loss of blood supply, hemorrhage, or bruising	• Cerebellar disease (disease or damage involving the part of the brain responsible for muscle tone, balance and coordination) • See your doctor
Coarse tremor of the head	• Difficulty maintaining balance, staggering when walking, jerkiness of movements, slurring of speech		• Genetically inherited tremors are relatively rare	• Age-related tremor, inherited condition, or a brain disease • See your doctor

Urination, difficult

The most common cause of difficulty on urinating is benign enlargement of the prostate, which frequently occurs in elderly men. However, any experience of difficulty urinating should be fully investigated by a doctor to ensure the cause is not serious and to determine whether your symptoms, or the condition responsible, may be treated. See also entries on *urination, painful* and *urination, frequent*.

SYMPTOM CHARACTERISTIC	ASSOCIATED SYMPTOMS	AGGRAVATING OR ALLEVIATING FACTORS	OTHER RELEVANT FACTORS	POSSIBLE CAUSE AND ACTION
In men, difficulty starting a urine stream	• Urine dribbling after urinating • Weak urine stream		• More common with ageing	• Prostate problems (e.g. enlargement, prostatitis or prostate cancer) • See your doctor at once
Feeling of incomplete emptying of bladder or difficulty in emptying	• Painful urination • Increase or decrease in urine volume		• History of urinary tract infections or other urinary problems • Genital injury (including childbirth)	• Urinary obstruction caused by a variety of conditions • See your doctor

Urination, frequent

Increase in the production or frequency of urination should be assessed by a doctor to ensure the cause is not potentially serious. Most common causes for these symptoms can be overcome or controlled, so there is no need to tolerate these symptoms without asking medical advice. See also entries on *urination, painful* and *urination, difficult*.

SYMPTOM CHARACTERISTIC	ASSOCIATED SYMPTOMS	AGGRAVATING OR ALLEVIATING FACTORS	OTHER RELEVANT FACTORS	POSSIBLE CAUSE AND ACTION
Frequent urge to urinate in a pregnant woman	• Less than usual volume in bladder	• Worse as pregnancy advances	• Common in pregnant women • Since other problems (e.g. diabetes) may be triggered by pregnancy, these symptoms should be assessed by a doctor	• The baby is pressing on the bladder • The problem should be resolved after birth • See your doctor
Involuntary leaking of urine		• Occurs with coughing, sneezing or exercise • May be worse during a bladder infection (cystitis), after drinking more fluids than usual or in cold weather	• Common in women after childbirth or with ageing	• Stress incontinence (weakness of bladder muscles causing leakage of urine) • See your doctor • Exercises may help strengthen the surrounding muscles • Severe cases may require surgery
Involuntary leaking of urine		• In elderly people with physical debility, difficulty moving about may exacerbate other causes of incontinence	• Some medications may cause bladder problems • Neurological disorders such as partial paralysis may result in incontinence	• Incontinence (other causes) • See your doctor
Producing more urine than usual			• Some medications cause increased urine production	• If you are taking medications, ask your pharmacist or doctor whether increased urine output is expected • See your doctor

SYMPTOM CHARACTERISTIC	ASSOCIATED SYMPTOMS	AGGRAVATING OR ALLEVIATING FACTORS	OTHER RELEVANT FACTORS	POSSIBLE CAUSE AND ACTION
Urination, frequent (cont.)				
Producing more urine than usual	• Discolored urine • Waking at night to urinate • Puffy swelling of extremities • Generally feeling unwell		• May occur with high blood pressure	• Kidney disease • See your doctor at once
Producing more urine than usual	• Excessive thirst, frequent urination, increased appetite, weight loss, nausea, blurred vision • In women, frequent vaginal infections; in men, impotence; recurring yeast infections in both sexes		• Diabetes is more common in people with obesity, hypertension, or a family history of diabetes	• Diabetes • See your doctor at once
In men, waking several times during the night to urinate	• Difficulty starting a urine stream • Urine dribbling after urinating		• More common with ageing	• Prostate problems (e.g. enlargement, prostatitis or prostate cancer) • See your doctor at once

Urination, painful

Any new occurrence of pain when urinating should be fully investigated by a doctor. For intermittent problems with which you are already familiar, like cystitis or genital herpes, your doctor or pharmacist can give advice on how to manage the problem when you recognize a new episode. See also entries on *urination, difficult* and *urination, frequent*.

SYMPTOM CHARACTERISTIC	ASSOCIATED SYMPTOMS	AGGRAVATING OR ALLEVIATING FACTORS	OTHER RELEVANT FACTORS	POSSIBLE CAUSE AND ACTION
Burning pain on urination	• Frequent urge to urinate, even when bladder is empty • Urinating only small amounts • Burning sensation in lower abdomen, urine with a strong odor	• Lack of adequate fluid intake may prolong symptoms • Sexual contact may aggravate pain	• Cystitis is more common in women than in men; infection may be triggered by sexual contact, use of diaphragm for birth control, or use of urinary catheters	• Cystitis • Drink plenty of water • See your doctor
Discomfort or burning pain on urination	• Cloudy urine, ache or stabbing pain in lower back, fever			• Kidney infection or kidney stones • See your doctor at once
Painful urination	• Pain under scrotum, difficulty urinating		• More common with ageing	• Prostate problems (e.g. prostatitis or prostate cancer) • See your doctor at once
Painful urination in sexually active men	• Discharge from tip of penis		• May follow recent sexual contact with a new partner	• Sexually transmitted infection of urinary tract (e.g. gonorrhea) • See your doctor at once • Avoid sexual contact until you obtain medical advice

SYMPTOM CHARACTERISTIC	ASSOCIATED SYMPTOMS	AGGRAVATING OR ALLEVIATING FACTORS	OTHER RELEVANT FACTORS	POSSIBLE CAUSE AND ACTION
Burning pain on urination	• Blisters or sores on external genital areas (may later become scabby) • Sore raw-feeling area inside vagina or on labia (women) • Vaginal discharge (women) • Discharge from infected sores • Burning pain in lower abdomen	• Urinating in a warm bath may alleviate scalding sensation • Outbreaks may be triggered by other viruses or stress	• New sores after others heal • Sores may become infected • First infection may cause flu-like symptoms	• Genital herpes • Wear cotton underwear and loose clothing • See your doctor at once • Avoid sexual contact until you obtain medical advice
In females, pain with sexual intercourse	• Bleeding after sexual intercourse, watery discharge from vagina, painful bowel movements, frequent urge to urinate		• Vaginal tumors are rare	• Tumor of the vagina • See your doctor at once

Vaginal problems

Some vaginal problems may be successfully treated with medications available from pharmacists. If you are unsure of the cause or if symptoms persist, see your doctor or sexual health clinic for a full sexual health check-up and to ensure possible infections do not result in fertility problems or other complications. See also entries on *genital pain* and *genital itching*.

SYMPTOM CHARACTERISTIC	ASSOCIATED SYMPTOMS	AGGRAVATING OR ALLEVIATING FACTORS	OTHER RELEVANT FACTORS	POSSIBLE CAUSE AND ACTION
Increased amount of discharge with normal light color, consistency and smell			• May be related to hormonal changes or new oral contraceptive	• Normal hormonal changes • See your doctor if the discharge changes or worries you
Thick white discharge forming clumps	• In women, the vulva may be swollen and red, and there may be a thick, white discharge	• Sexual intercourse may increase discomfort • Wearing tight clothing or synthetic underwear may worsen symptoms	• Yeast infections can be a side effect of taking antibiotics, or may be triggered by stress, pregnancy, or use of the contraceptive pill • Candidiasis is most likely in women with diabetes or as a side effect of some antibiotics	• Yeast infection (candidiasis) • Wear cotton underwear and loose clothing to allow air to the area • See your doctor
Greenish-yellow discharge with unpleasant smell			• Intense odor with only moderate amount of discharge	• Foreign object in vagina causing overgrowth of bacteria or yeasts that are naturally present • There may be an old tampon or contraceptive device in the vagina—check and remove • See your doctor if the discharge persists or if you cannot find a cause

SYMPTOM CHARACTERISTIC	ASSOCIATED SYMPTOMS	AGGRAVATING OR ALLEVIATING FACTORS	OTHER RELEVANT FACTORS	POSSIBLE CAUSE AND ACTION
Vaginal problems (cont.)				
Greenish-yellow discharge with unpleasant smell			• Recent sexual contact or new sexual partner in the last month	• Infection such as bacterial vaginosis or trichomoniasis (a parasitic infection) • See your doctor
Greenish-yellow discharge with unpleasant smell	• Pain in the lower abdomen, fever			• Pelvic inflammatory disease • See your doctor at once
Vaginal dryness	• Itching, irritation of vaginal lining		• No other symptoms	• Hormonal deficiency or undiagnosed infection • Lubricants to relieve itchiness or during sexual contact • See your doctor
Yellow discharge, may be thick like mucus	• Cervix bleeds when touched or scraped, abnormal menstrual bleeding, abdominal pain, fever, pain when urinating and pain and swelling of one or both labia		• May follow recent sexual contact with a new partner • The incidence of gonorrhea is much higher in the USA than in other industrialized countries • Potential complications include inflammation of reproductive organs, peritonitis, inflammation around the liver, inflammation of the Bartholin's gland in women and epididymitis or abscess around the urethra in men; arthritis, dermatitis, endocarditis, meningitis, myocarditis or hepatitis	• Gonorrhea • See your doctor or a sexual health clinic as soon as possible • Antibiotic treatment is important to prevent serious complications

Voice problems

Voice problems can occur for a number of different reasons. See your doctor if symptoms persist for more than two weeks. You may need to see an ear nose and throat doctor and speech pathologist who are the specialists in the diagnosis and management of voice disorders.

SYMPTOM CHARACTERISTIC	ASSOCIATED SYMPTOMS	AGGRAVATING OR ALLEVIATING FACTORS	OTHER RELEVANT FACTORS	POSSIBLE CAUSE AND ACTION
Husky voice, lasting longer than 2 weeks	• Throat pain • Upper respiratory tract infections (e.g. a cold) • Dry throat and the need to frequently throat clear	• Prolonged voice use, talking loudly and talking when tired exacerbates symptoms • Voice improves with voice rest, drinking water and avoiding smoking/ smoky environments	• People in occupations or lifestyles that involve constant voice use are predisposed to voice difficulties	• Functional voice loss • See your doctor

SYMPTOM CHARACTERISTIC	ASSOCIATED SYMPTOMS	AGGRAVATING OR ALLEVIATING FACTORS	OTHER RELEVANT FACTORS	POSSIBLE CAUSE AND ACTION
Sudden loss of voice	• May still be able to laugh and cough	• Stress		• Voice loss due to psychological causes (psychogenic voice loss) • See your doctor
Voice has a strangled, strained quality; voice breaks up during speech	• Can only speak with much effort	• Stressful situations can worsen voice quality but it can improve with laughing, singing and whispering		• Spasmodic dysphonia (spasm of vocal cords) • See your doctor

Weakness and paralysis

Weakness and paralysis are usually caused by disorders in the nervous system. Symptoms may involve the entire body, or be limited to one part such as an arm or leg. Paralysis (loss of muscle function) is a serious symptom and should be investigated by a doctor. See also entry on *numbness and tingling*.

SYMPTOM CHARACTERISTIC	ASSOCIATED SYMPTOMS	AGGRAVATING OR ALLEVIATING FACTORS	OTHER RELEVANT FACTORS	POSSIBLE CAUSE AND ACTION
Weakness or paralysis of the arms or legs	• Progressive numbness in the arms or legs, back or neck pain • Bladder, bowel and sexual functions may be affected	• May be aggravated by moving the neck or back	• Can occur following injury (e.g. broken neck or back), or due to a tumor, disease or infection	• Spinal cord damage • See your doctor at once
Weakness in one arm or one leg	• Neck or back pain, numbness and tingling of the affected limb	• Aggravated by bending, sitting, coughing, sneezing	• The precise location of the symptoms defines which part of the neck or back is affected	• Ruptured vertebral disk causing nerve compression • See your doctor at once
Weakness or paralysis on one side of the body, usually starts suddenly	• Tingling, confusion, dizziness, partial loss of hearing, slurred speech, inability to recognize parts of the body, unusual movements, fainting		• More common with advancing age • Risk increased in people with cardiovascular disease (e.g. hypertension, coronary heart disease) lipid abnormalities (e.g. high cholesterol), diabetes	• Transient ischemic attack or stroke • See your doctor at once
Weakness or paralysis in one part of the arm or leg, often after being in one position or following prolonged pressure to an area	• Numbness or tingling in the same area	• Aggravated by remaining in one position or continued pressure to an area • May be alleviated by moving around	• Can occur from prolonged postures such as sitting with legs crossed, sleeping on one arm • More likely in people who are unable to move around freely because of disability	• Single nerve injury • See your doctor
Profound weakness in both legs, then progresses upwards to both arms	• Tingling, numbness		• In the majority of cases, symptoms begin 3–21 days after a mild infection or surgery	• Guillain-Barré syndrome • This is a medical emergency • Go to the emergency room or call an ambulance at once

SYMPTOM CHARACTERISTIC	ASSOCIATED SYMPTOMS	AGGRAVATING OR ALLEVIATING FACTORS	OTHER RELEVANT FACTORS	POSSIBLE CAUSE AND ACTION
Weakness and paralysis (cont.)				
In males, progressive muscle weakness throughout the body, usually beginning in the muscles of the pelvis	• Muscles often enlarge • May also have trouble climbing stairs or getting out of a chair, frequent falls		• Usually first occurs in boys aged 3–7 years	• Muscular dystrophy • See your doctor at once
Weakness or paralysis on one side of the body	• Constant headache, poor balance and coordination, dizziness, double vision, loss of sensation, loss of hearing		• Most common in people with cancer in another part of the body	• Brain tumor • See your doctor at once

Weight gain

Weight gain usually relates to a mismatch between the intake and expenditure of calories. Sometimes, but infrequently, there is an underlying pathology of the brain and/or hormonal system. In children with obesity and short stature, congenital abnormalities must also be excluded. Weight gain due to fluid retention must be distinguished from that due to increased body fat so that appropriate treatment can be given.

SYMPTOM CHARACTERISTIC	ASSOCIATED SYMPTOMS	AGGRAVATING OR ALLEVIATING FACTORS	OTHER RELEVANT FACTORS	POSSIBLE CAUSE AND ACTION
Gradually progressive weight gain, usually generalized			• This is the most common cause of weight gain	• Overweight/obesity due to increased energy calorie intake or reduced physical activity • See your doctor
Recent weight gain in a woman of child-bearing age			• Commonly occurs in premenstrual phase and resolves after the period	• Normal weight fluctuation with menstrual cycle • See your doctor if you are worried or if symptoms persist
Weight gain after commencing a new medication	• May or may not have increased appetite		• The medication may either be increasing or restoring appetite, or causing retention of more fluid in the body • Drugs that may cause weight gain include corticosteroids, oral medications used in diabetes, the oral contraceptive pill, medications used in depression or schizophrenia	• Medication-induced weight gain • See your doctor if you are worried or if symptoms persist
Recent and rapid increase in weight over a day or two	• Deterioration in overall health, swollen legs, distended abdomen, swollen face, shortness of breath, waking up short of breath at night	• Symptoms may be aggravated or triggered by lying flat	• Diseases that may cause edema include heart failure, liver failure, kidney disease	• Edema • See your doctor

SYMPTOM CHARACTERISTIC	ASSOCIATED SYMPTOMS	AGGRAVATING OR ALLEVIATING FACTORS	OTHER RELEVANT FACTORS	POSSIBLE CAUSE AND ACTION
Weight gain that cannot be explained by excess calorie intake relative to physical activity	• An unusual distribution of the weight, unexplained increase in appetite, symptoms from other bodily systems, (e.g. headache, visual disturbances, excessive thirst, increased urine volume, inability to lose the weight using previously effective strategies, failure to gain height normally in a child)		• These causes are uncommon to rare	• Hormonal disorders, damage to the part of the brain which regulates appetite, congenital disorders • See your doctor

Weight loss

Unintentional weight loss is usually caused by serious underlying conditions. Cancer, gastrointestinal disease and depression are the most prominent causes. As with many other symptoms, a variety of medications can cause weight loss, so contact your doctor for advice if symptoms begin shortly after you start on a new medication. In about 25 percent of cases, no cause is identified.

SYMPTOM CHARACTERISTIC	ASSOCIATED SYMPTOMS	AGGRAVATING OR ALLEVIATING FACTORS	OTHER RELEVANT FACTORS	POSSIBLE CAUSE AND ACTION
Weight loss with reduced food intake; a substantial reduction in weight may occur rapidly	• Loss of weight and appetite may be the only early symptom, or there may be symptoms related to the specific bodily systems affected by the tumor		• Reduced food intake may be related to decreased appetite, a disturbed sense of taste, or nausea; energy requirements appear to increase	• Cancer • See your doctor at once
Weight loss with reduced food intake	• Other symptoms relate to the specific cause		• Reduction in eating may be due to pain, discomfort or nausea related to eating, or swallowing problems	• Inability to eat normally due to a peptic ulcer; disturbance of the contractions of the esophagus which usually push food through to the stomach; gallstones; problems with the mouth or teeth • See your doctor
Weight loss with reduced food intake	• Loss of concentration, sadness, lack of enjoyment in life, difficulty sleeping, low self-esteem, suicidal thoughts or feelings		• May affect any age group	• Depression • See your doctor
Weight loss with reduced food intake in teenage girls; extreme weight loss is typical	• Obsession with becoming thin through extremely strict dieting and exercise; exaggerated fear of becoming fat; distorted body image • Menstrual periods cease (or do not begin) because of starvation		• Girls and women are 10–20 times more likely to develop symptoms than boys or men	• Anorexia nervosa • See your doctor

SYMPTOM CHARACTERISTIC	ASSOCIATED SYMPTOMS	AGGRAVATING OR ALLEVIATING FACTORS	OTHER RELEVANT FACTORS	POSSIBLE CAUSE AND ACTION
Weight loss (cont.)				
Weight loss with reduced food intake	• Otherwise unwell • Other symptoms will depend on the particular cause			• Long-term or severe illnesses or infections • See your doctor
Weight loss despite normal appetite and adequate food intake	• Frequent stools, which may be pale and bulky, float in the toilet bowl and are difficult to flush, or have an unusually unpleasant smell		• Malabsorption may be due to liver disease, reduced stomach area after surgery to remove a tumor, or bowel surgery	• Malabsorption (inability to absorb digested nutrients through the bowel) • See your doctor
Weight loss despite normal appetite and adequate food intake	• Excessive thirst • Passing large amounts of urine		• This type of diabetes typically begins before 40 years of age	• Diabetes • See your doctor
Weight loss despite normal appetite and adequate food intake	• Intolerance of hot weather, increased anxiety, palpitations, excess sweating, itching		• May affect adults or children, females more often the males • The onset of symptoms is usually insidious over many months	• Thyrotoxicosis • See your doctor
Weight loss despite normal appetite and adequate food intake	• Fatigue, general feeling of being unwell, fever, diarrhea		• History of repeated infections • Risk of infection increased by unprotected sexual contact, sharing needles used for intravenous drug use, blood transfusion in a country without a system of routine screening for HIV	• Human immunodeficiency virus (HIV) infection • See your doctor

Wounds or sores, non-healing

Any wound that takes longer than normal to heal warrants investigation by your doctor, as slow-healing wounds may indicate an infection or significant problem affecting the whole body.

SYMPTOM CHARACTERISTIC	ASSOCIATED SYMPTOMS	AGGRAVATING OR ALLEVIATING FACTORS	OTHER RELEVANT FACTORS	POSSIBLE CAUSE AND ACTION
Area where normal skin surface has been lost and fails to heal (ulcer), especially if overgrown or sealed-looking at the edges	• May be itchy and/or painful		• Typically occurs in sun-exposed areas of the skin	• Skin cancer • See your doctor at once
Area where normal skin surface has been lost and fails to heal (ulcer) on the lower leg	• Long history of discomfort, swelling and skin changes of the lower leg		• History of disease of the leg veins (e.g. abnormal clotting or deep venous thrombosis) • Affects women more often than men	• Persistent ulcer that does not heal due to long-term abnormally high pressure in the leg veins (venous ulcer) • See your doctor at once

SYMPTOM CHARACTERISTIC	ASSOCIATED SYMPTOMS	AGGRAVATING OR ALLEVIATING FACTORS	OTHER RELEVANT FACTORS	POSSIBLE CAUSE AND ACTION
Area where normal skin surface has been lost and fails to heal (ulcer) on the tips of the toes or fingers or in areas subject to pressure	• Painful	• Discomfort is aggravated by pressure to the area	• History of disease in the arteries supplying blood to the affected area, or an injury affecting blood supply to the area	• Persistent ulcer that does not heal due to severe reduction of blood supply to the area (ischemic ulcer) • See your doctor at once
Area where normal skin surface has been lost and fails to heal (ulcer) in an area which suffers repeated trauma or pressure	• Painless • Numbness of the surrounding skin		• History of injury or disorder of the nerves supplying the affected area • The most common underlying cause is diabetes	• Persistent ulcer caused by repeated trauma to an area where the individual is unable to sense pain (neuropathic ulcer) • See your doctor at once
Area where normal skin surface has been lost and fails to heal (ulcer) in an area subjected to prolonged pressure while immobile in bed			• People who are elderly or physically incapacitated and unable to shift their weight are at risk • People with numbness who may not sense the need to shift their weight	• Bedsore • See your doctor at once
Persistent discharge from an unusual opening onto the skin	• Surrounding area may be painful or discolored		• May develop after a surgical procedure, after a traumatic injury which penetrates the skin, when a collection of pus (abscess) has drained through the skin, or when there is underlying tumor	• An infection or other problem below the surface of the skin • See your doctor at once
Failure in healing of a surgical wound	• Pain and discomfort of the operation site • Redness, tenderness, discharge from the wound		• The risk of wound infection is increased by contamination of a wound, damage to the surrounding skin or underlying tissues • More likely in people who are obese or poorly nourished, have reduced immune system function or chronic illness	• Wound infection • See your doctor at once
Area where normal skin surface has been lost and fails to heal (ulcer) on foot or lower leg in a person with diabetes			• Embedded foreign bodies of which the patient was unaware are commonly found in people with diabetic ulcers • Close control of blood sugar may help minimize the risk of foot ulcers	• Diabetic ulcer • See your doctor at once • Keep feet clean and dry at all times and wear properly fitted shoes • Inspect feet daily for callus, infection, abrasions or blisters

The Time of Your Life

DEVELOPMENTAL MILESTONES AND PREVENTIVE HEALTH ISSUES FOR WOMEN

WORLD HEALTH ORGANIZATION RECOMMENDED IMMUNIZATION SCHEDULE

This table shows a typical immunization schedule. While it highlights the main immunization recommendations for many regions, the schedule will vary from country to country, and dosing intervals and frequencies may be different. Furthermore, some high-risk areas will require additional vaccinations not listed here. Please consult your local health authority for the appropriate immunization schedule for your country. Certain immunizations are effective for a limited time and booster shots are required throughout life to maintain immunity.

DISEASE	Birth	2 months	4 months	6 months	12 months	12–18 months	4 years	10–13 years	15–19 years	50 years	65 + years
Hepatitis B	•	•	•	•				•*			
Diphtheria		•	•			•	•				
Tetanus		•	•			•	•		•	•	
Pertussis (whooping cough)		•	•			•	•				
Hemophilus influenzae B		•	•		•						
Polio		•	•	•			•		•		
Measles					•		•				
Mumps					•		•				
Rubella (German measles)					•		•				
Chickenpox (optional)						•**					
Pneumococcal infection											•***
Influenza											•****

* give 3 doses if not given as an infant. Second dose 1 month after first, third dose 5 months after second dose.

** can be given anytime after 12 months of age

*** give every 5 years from age 65

**** give every year from age 65

Birth–6 months

- At birth, babies have the ability to see about 8–12 inches (20–30 centimeters) in front of them and have fully developed hearing. The labia may be swollen.
- Within a few days of birth, babies develop a sense of taste and respond to their mother's voice and smell.
- First smile at 4–6 weeks.
- By 6 months, most babies can hold objects placed in their hand, focus in all directions, roll over and lift head and shoulders when lying on their stomach.

HEALTH CHECK

- Apgar score at 1 minute and 5 minutes after birth to assess color, heart rate, breathing, responsiveness, muscle tone. Length, weight and head circumference measured, plus thorough physical examination in first 12 hours after birth.
- Screening test at 4–5 days of age to detect presence of any rare metabolic diseases and some inherited diseases.
- Thorough physical examination at 6–8 weeks.
- Immunization at birth, 2 and 4 months. (See Schedule)

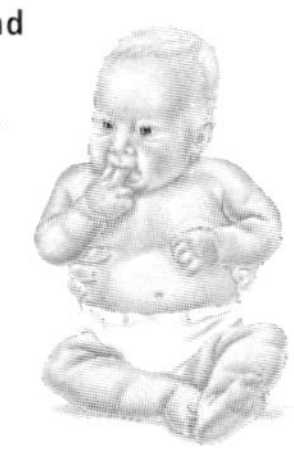

6–12 months

- First teeth usually appear by 6–8 months. Most babies can now sit with some support.
- By 9 months, babies are usually crawling, and may wave and clap hands. They may imitate sounds and will respond to own name.
- By 12 months of age, many babies will be walking by holding on to furniture, standing alone for a few seconds at a time and saying 1 or 2 single words.

HEALTH CHECK

- Immunization at 6 months and 12 months. (See Schedule)
- Physical and developmental examination may be done at 6–8 months.

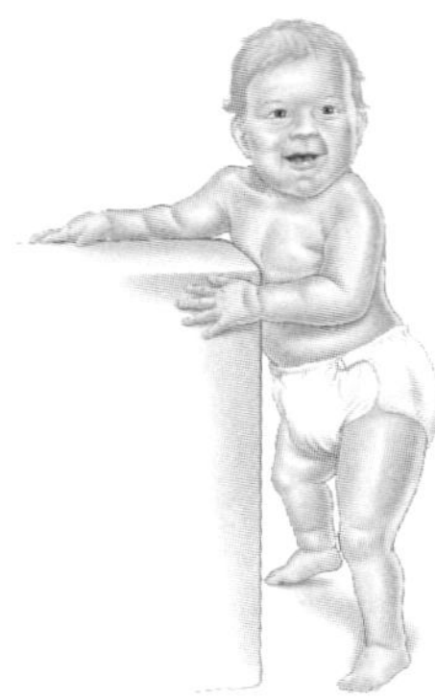

20–30 years

- Fertility peaks in the mid-20s, and this decade is the most likely time for childbearing to begin.
- Awareness of sexually transmitted diseases (STDs) and use of contraception is essential in all sexually active females.

HEALTH CHECK

- Physical examination every 2 years, including blood pressure, height and weight. From age 18, all women should have a Pap smear every 2 years.
- Breast self-examination should be done every month for life.
- Certain immunization boosters are necessary every 10 years. (See Schedule)

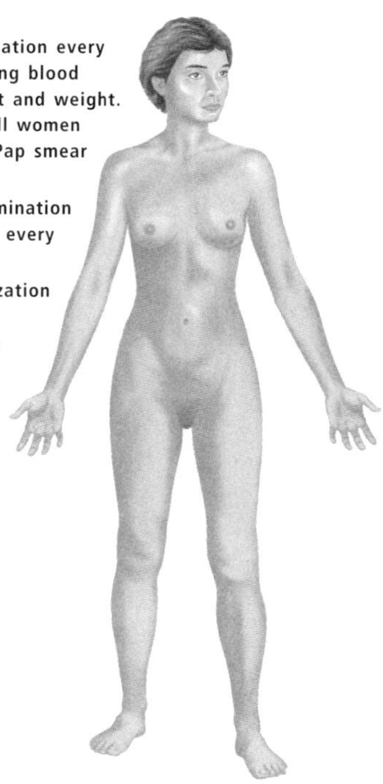

30–40 years

- Fertility declines, and risk of fetal abnormalities in the pregnant woman increases.
- Bone density starts to decline.

HEALTH CHECK

- Physical examination every 2 years, including blood pressure, height and weight. Pap smears continue every 2 years.
- Breast self-examination should be done every month.
- Cholesterol should be checked every 5 years.

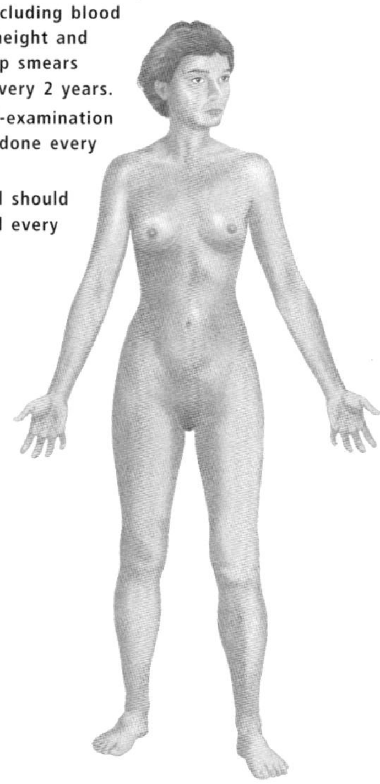

40–50 years

- Menopause usually commences, signifying the end of menstruation and fertility. Women may suffer hot flashes/flushes and other symptoms due to the decline in estrogen levels.
- Calcium and mineral content of bones decreases significantly.

HEALTH CHECK

- Physical examination every year, including blood pressure, height and weight, and clinical examination of breasts. Gynecological exam, including internal pelvic assessment every year. Pap smears, rectal examination and urine tests every year.
- Breast self-examination should be done every month.
- Mammograms may be done every 2 years.
- Eye test, including glaucoma screen, every 2 years.

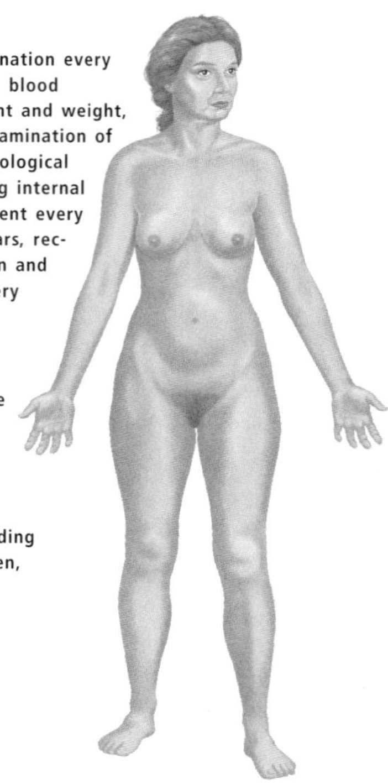

1–5 years

- The preschool years are a time of rapid development, and a time when a child's individuality becomes noticeable.
- At 18 months, she can walk well, stack blocks, throw a ball and push toys around the room.
- By her second birthday, she can run, walk up and down stairs and feed herself with a spoon. 2 year olds are easily frustrated and liable to throw temper tantrums. Vocabulary is expanding dramatically.
- 3–4 year olds learn to use simple sentences, and play involves more interaction with playmates. Girls are usually fully toilet-trained by this age.
- By age 4, girls have grown taller and appear slimmer, due to losing fat and gaining muscle. Most height increase involves the legs.

HEALTH CHECK

- Immunization at 12–18 months, and 4–5 years prior to school entry. (See Schedule)
- Development will be continually monitored at doctor's visits.

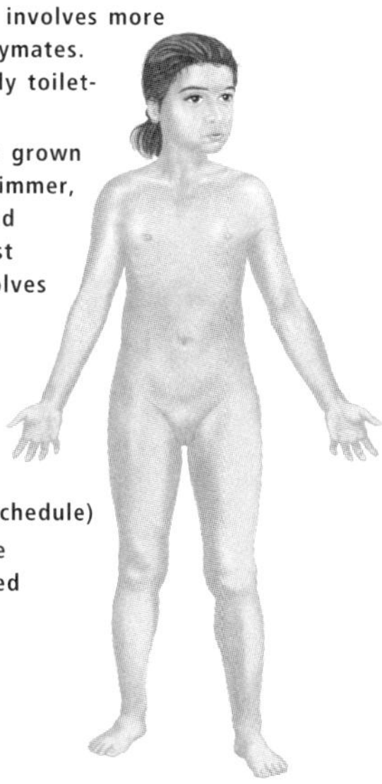

6–11 years

- These years are a time of rapid physical, intellectual and psychological growth.
- School begins at age 5–6, and girls start to develop close friendships, usually with other girls.
- Baby teeth begin to fall out around the sixth year.
- Reading and writing skills are developed and refined.
- For most girls, puberty begins after the age of 10. Signs of puberty include development of breasts and pubic hair, and a marked increase in physical size (growth spurt).
- Children of this age usually have the coordination and balance of an adult.

HEALTH CHECK

- Children who experience difficulties with schoolwork may be tested for attention deficit disorder (ADD) or learning problems such as dyslexia.
- Immunization boosters may be necessary. (See Schedule)

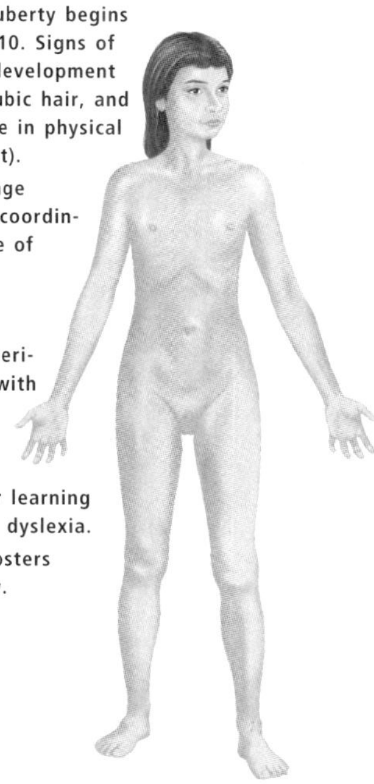

12–19 years

- Menstruation usually begins at 11–14 years of age, after which growth may slow down. Body fat increases around the hips and thighs, sweat glands develop further, and hormonal changes can start to cause skin problems.
- Eating disorders sometimes affect young women in this age group.

HEALTH CHECK

- Immunization at 10–13 years and 15–19 years. (See Schedule)
- Scoliosis screening is carried out at many schools. More girls than boys develop scoliosis—a sideways curvature of the spine.

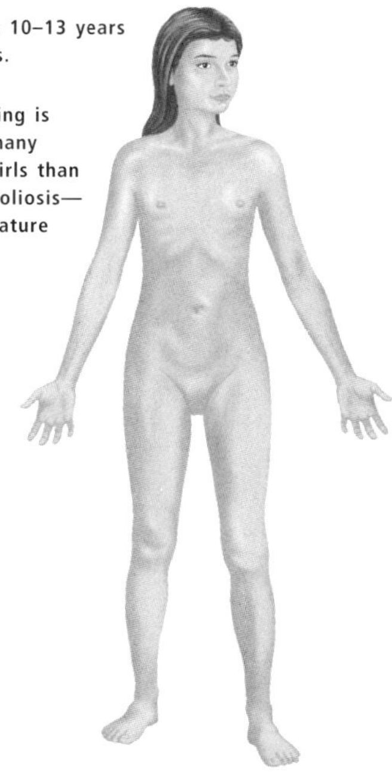

50–65 years

- Following menopause, bone density falls significantly. Lean body mass declines, and the metabolic rate decreases.

HEALTH CHECK

- Yearly screening continues, including blood pressure, height and weight, and clinical examination of breasts. Gynecological exam, including internal pelvic assessment and Pap smear every year. Rectal examination, urine tests and skin checks yearly. Eye test, including glaucoma screen, every 2 years.
- Additional annual screening following menopause is also necessary, including assessment of heart function, bone density and stools.
- Mammograms are recommended yearly.
- Sigmoidoscopy (visual examination of the rectum and lower colon) every 3–5 years is advised, and cholesterol screening every 5 years.

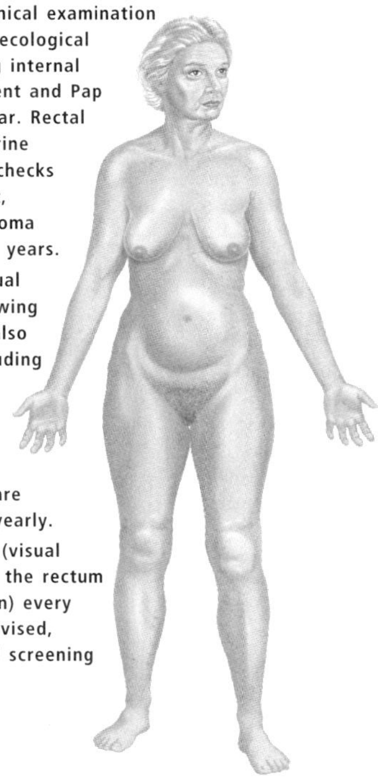

65–85 years

- By 65–70 years of age, a woman has half the bone density she had at age 30.
- There may be a decline in organ function, including the brain. Many older women will continue to be very active, but physical capabilities may become limited or more difficult.

HEALTH CHECK

- Yearly screening continues. Physical examination should include blood pressure, height and weight, and clinical examination of breasts. A gynecological examination, including internal pelvic exam and Pap smear, and rectal examination and urine tests are also advised. Yearly mammograms, as well as heart, bone, stool and cholesterol tests are recommended. Eye test, including glaucoma screen, every 2 years.
- Monthly breast self-examination should continue.
- Annual vaccination against influenza is advised.
- Pneumococcal immunization every 5 years.

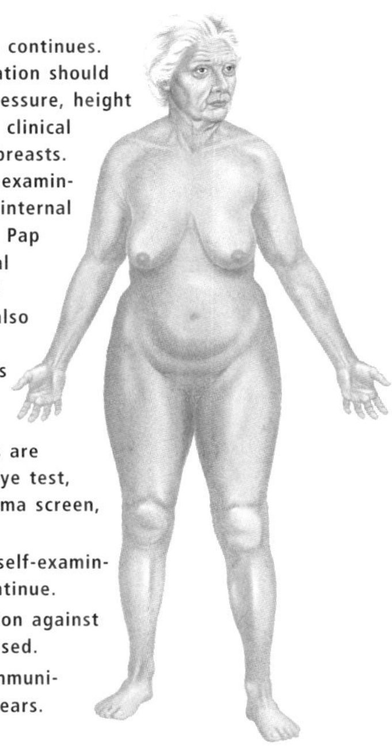

85+ years

- Loss of bone density continues. About 30 percent of all women reaching 90 years of age will suffer a hip fracture due to weakened bones.
- The incidence of dementia continues to increase. Lapses of memory and difficulty learning new information are noticed in those affected.

HEALTH CHECK

- Yearly screening continues. Physical examination should include full gynecological examination, including Pap smear, rectal examination, blood pressure, height and weight, skin checks and clinical examination of breasts and urine tests.
- Blood tests for cholesterol and sugar.
- Yearly mammograms, as well as heart, bone density and stool tests are recommended.
- Pneumococcal and influenza immunizations continue.
- Eye test, including glaucoma screen, every 2 years.
- Monthly breast self-examination should continue.

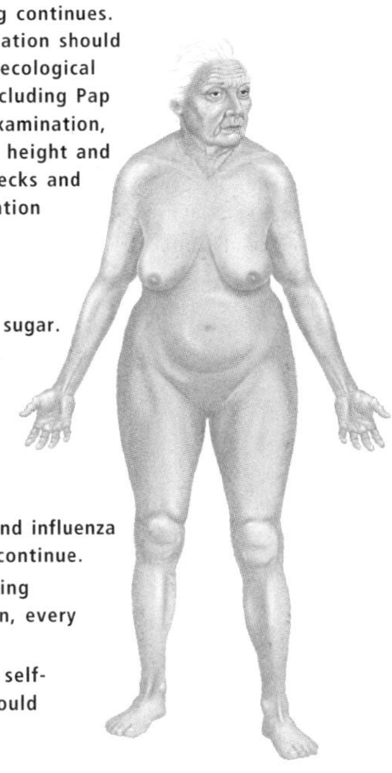

The Time of Your Life

DEVELOPMENTAL MILESTONES AND PREVENTIVE HEALTH ISSUES FOR MEN

WORLD HEALTH ORGANIZATION RECOMMENDED IMMUNIZATION SCHEDULE

This table shows a typical immunization schedule. While it highlights the main immunization recommendations for many regions, the schedule will vary from country to country, and dosing intervals and frequencies may be different. Furthermore, some high-risk areas will require additional vaccinations not listed here. Please consult your local health authority for the appropriate immunization schedule for your country. Certain immunizations are effective for a limited time and booster shots are required throughout life to maintain immunity.

DISEASE	Birth	2 months	4 months	6 months	12 months	12–18 months	4 years	10–13 years	15–19 years	50 years	65 + years
Hepatitis B	•	•	•	•				•*			
Diphtheria		•	•			•	•				
Tetanus		•	•			•	•		•	•	
Pertussis (whooping cough)		•	•			•	•				
Hemophilus influenzae B		•	•		•						
Polio		•	•	•			•		•		
Measles					•		•				
Mumps					•		•				
Rubella (German measles)					•		•				
Chickenpox (optional)						•**					
Pneumococcal infection											•***
Influenza											•****

* give 3 doses if not given as an infant. Second dose 1 month after first, third dose 5 months after second dose.

** can be given anytime after 12 months of age

*** give every 5 years from age 65

**** give every year from age 65

Birth–6 months

- At birth, babies have the ability to see about 8–12 inches (20–30 centimeters) in front of them and have fully developed hearing. Both testes should be present in the scrotum.
- Within a few days of birth, babies develop sense of taste and respond to their mother's voice and smell.
- First smile is usually at 4–6 weeks.
- By 6 months, most babies can hold objects placed in their hand, focus in all directions, roll over and lift head and shoulders when lying on their stomach.

HEALTH CHECK

- Apgar score at 1 minute and 5 minutes after birth to assess color, heart rate, breathing, responsiveness, muscle tone. Length, weight and head circumference measured, plus thorough physical examination in first 12 hours after birth.
- Screening test at 4–5 days of age to detect presence of any rare metabolic diseases and some inherited diseases.
- Thorough physical examination at 6–8 weeks.
- Immunization at birth, 2 and 4 months. (See Schedule)

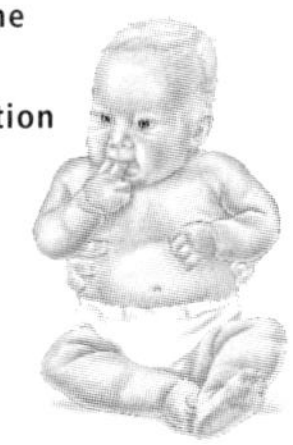

6–12 months

- First teeth usually appear by 6–8 months. Most babies can now sit with some support.
- By 9 months, babies are usually crawling, and may wave and clap hands. They may imitate sounds and will respond to own name.
- By 12 months of age, most babies have tripled their birth weight. Many babies will be walking by holding on to furniture, standing alone for a few seconds at a time and saying 1 or 2 single words.

HEALTH CHECK

- Immunization at 6 months and 12 months. (See Schedule)
- Detailed physical and developmental examination may be done at 6–8 months.

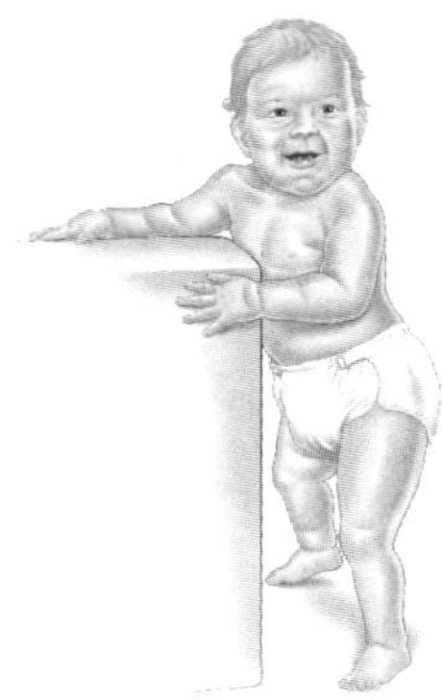

20–30 years

- Bones continue to broaden until the age of 20 in most males.
- Awareness of sexually transmitted diseases (STDs) and use of contraception is essential in all sexually active males.

HEALTH CHECK

- Regular physical examinations are recommended every 2 years, including height, weight, and blood pressure assessment.
- Testes should be clinically examined every 2 years, and self-examination is recommended every month.
- Certain immunization boosters are necessary every 10 years. (See Schedule)

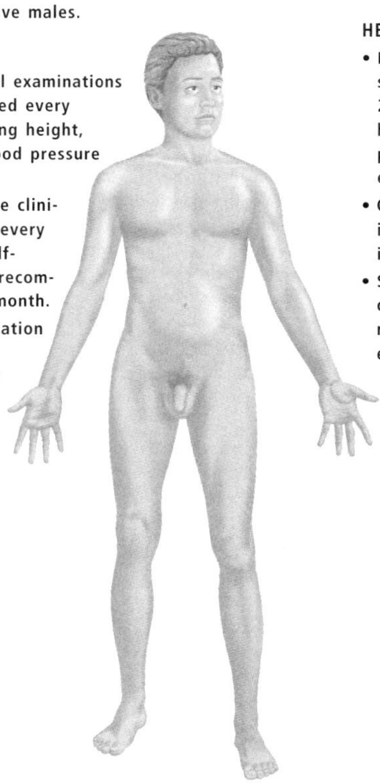

30–40 years

- Distribution of body fat may begin to change, becoming more prevalent around the abdomen.
- 30 percent of males in their 30s notice some hair loss.

HEALTH CHECK

- Regular physical exams should continue every 2 years, including height, weight, blood pressure, testicular examination.
- Cholesterol screening every 5 years is advised.
- Self-examination of testes is recommended every month.

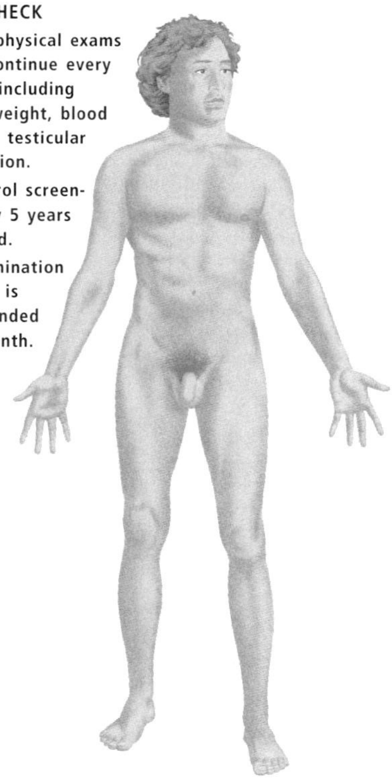

40–50 years

- Metabolism may slow, causing a tendency to gain weight.
- Prostate enlargement usually begins around age 45.

HEALTH CHECK

- Physical examination every year, including height, weight, blood pressure, and clinical examination of testes. Rectal examination and urine tests yearly.
- Cholesterol screening should become more frequent, and may be tested every 1–2 years.
- Self-examination of testes is recommended every month.
- Eye exam, including glaucoma screening, is recommended every 2 years.

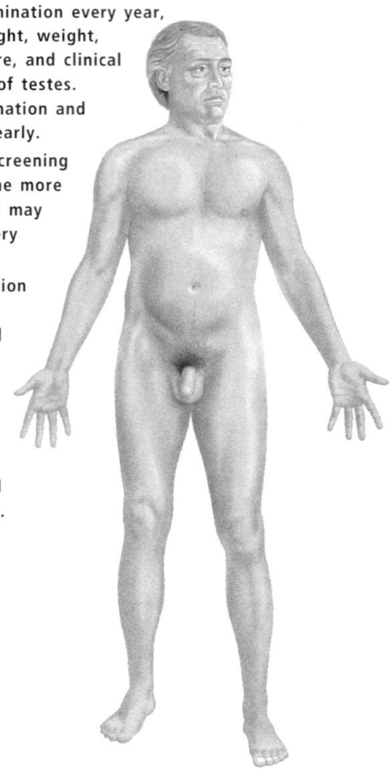

1–5 years

- The preschool years are a time of rapid development, and a time when a child's individuality becomes noticeable.
- At 18 months, he can walk well, stack blocks, throw a ball and push toys around the room.
- By his second birthday, he can run, walk up and down stairs, and feed himself with a spoon. 2 year olds are easily frustrated and liable to throw temper tantrums. Vocabulary is expanding dramatically.
- 3–4 year olds learn to use simple sentences, and play involves more interaction with playmates. Toilet-training in boys is usually complete by this time, although some boys may continue to have problems particularly at night.
- By age 4, boys have grown taller and appear slimmer, due to losing fat and gaining muscle. Most height increase involves the legs.

HEALTH CHECK

- Immunization at 18 months, and 4–5 years prior to school entry. (See Schedule)
- Development will be continually monitored at doctor's visits.

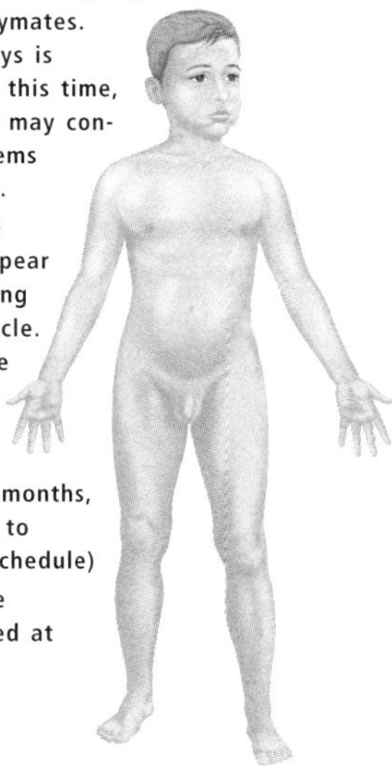

6–11 years

- These years are a time of rapid physical, intellectual and psychological growth.
- School begins at age 5–6, and boys start to develop close friendships, usually with other boys.
- Baby teeth begin to fall out around the sixth year.
- Reading and writing skills are developed and refined.
- Children of this age usually have the coordination and balance of an adult.

HEALTH CHECK

- Children who experience difficulties with schoolwork may be tested for attention deficit disorder (ADD) or learning problems such as dyslexia.
- Immunization boosters may be necessary. (See Schedule)

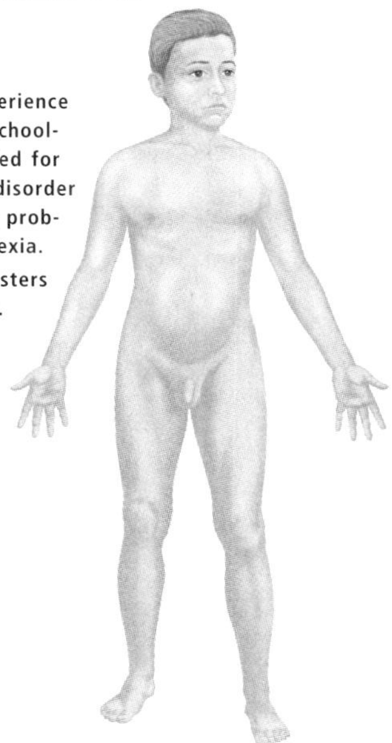

12–19 years

- Puberty in boys begins around 11–12 years. The testes and penis grow larger and the skin of the scrotum darkens. Pubic hair begins to appear.
- At the age of 12–13, boys have a growth spurt, growing rapidly in weight and height. The chest and shoulders become broader.
- At 13 or 14 the voice box begins to grow and the voice starts change. Many boys are able to ejaculate by this age.
- Underarm and facial hair, as well as sweat glands, typically begin to appear between 13 and 15 years of age.
- Height continues to increase until around 17–18 years of age.

HEALTH CHECK

- Immunization at 10–13 years and 15–19 years. (See Schedule)
- Screening for scoliosis (sideways curvature of the spine) is carried out at many schools.

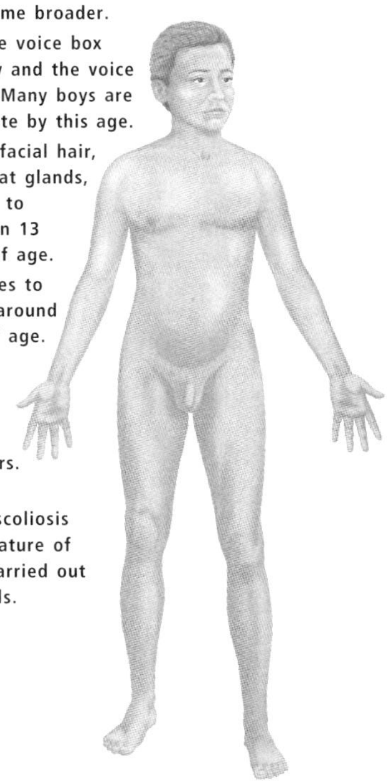

50–65 years

- Prostate enlargement continues. Bone density falls.
- Hair loss is evident in 50 percent of men aged over 50.

HEALTH CHECK

- Yearly screening continues, including height, weight, blood pressure, clinical examination of testes, urine tests, skin checks and stool test. Self-examination of testes is recommended every month.
- Annual rectal examination and blood tests for prostate-specific antigen (a marker of prostate cancer).
- Sigmoidoscopy (visual study of the rectum and lower colon) every 3–5 years is advised.
- Eye exam, including glaucoma screening, is recommended every 2 years.
- Stress test and electrocardiogram (EKG) may be necessary, depending on overall health and family history of heart disease.

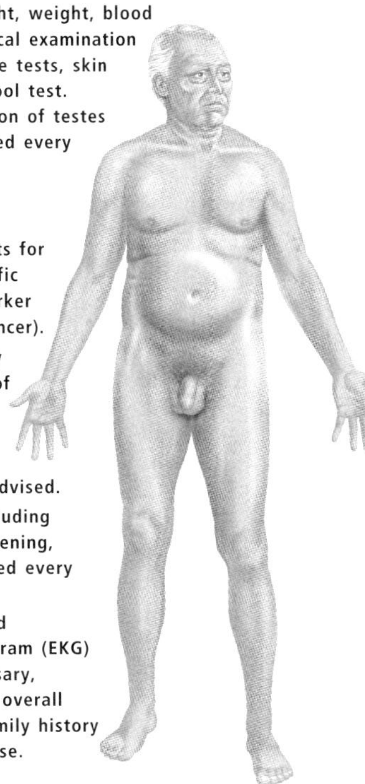

65–85 years

- Many older men will continue to be very active, but physical capabilities may become limited or more difficult. There may be a decline in organ function, including the brain.

HEALTH CHECK

- Yearly screening continues. Physical examination should include clinical examination of the testes and prostate, cholesterol measurements, height, weight, blood pressure, skin checks, heart tests and urine tests.
- Annual rectal examination, blood tests for prostate-specific antigen, and annual stool tests are necessary.
- Eye exam, including glaucoma screening, is recommended every 2 years.
- Yearly vaccination against influenza is advised.
- Pneumococcal immunization every 5 years.
- Self-examination of testes is recommended every month.

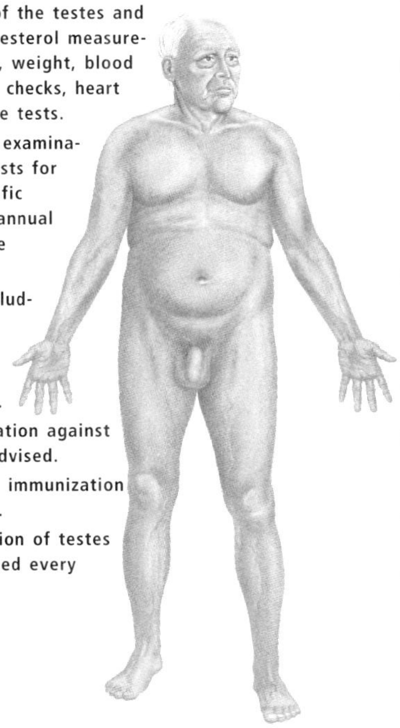

85+ years

- The incidence of dementia increases with age, affecting about 1 in 5 men over 85 years.
- Although age-related loss of bone density begins earlier and proceeds more rapidly in women, it is also a significant health problem in elderly men.
- Most elderly men remain independent.

HEALTH CHECK

- Yearly screening continues. Physical examination should include blood pressure check, rectal examination, height, weight, skin checks, heart tests and urine tests.
- Blood tests for cholesterol, sugar and prostate-specific antigen.
- Annual stool test for blood.
- Pneumococcal and influenza vaccinations continue.
- Tests for bone density are recommended.
- Self-examination of testes continues every month.

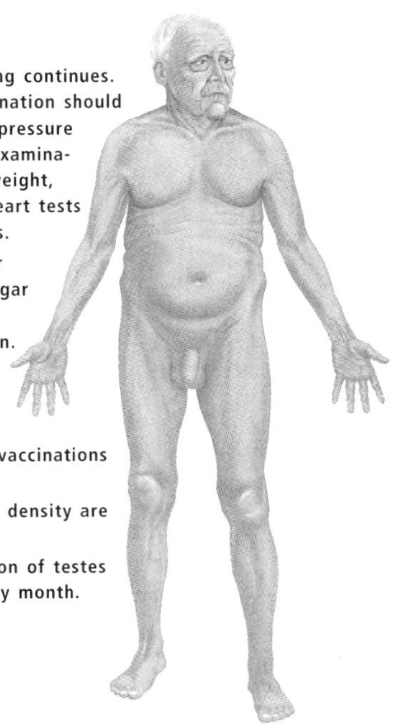

Index

Bold text denotes the main entry for a topic.

A

AA *see* Alcoholics Anonymous 235
AAMI *see* age-associated memory impairment 463
abdomen 52
see also bladder 124, gallbladder 308, intestines 399, kidneys 411, liver 438, ovaries 526, pancreas 538, stomach 679, ureter 741, uterus 743
abdominal aorta 95
abdominal cavity 52
abdominal cramp 199
abdominal hysterectomy 379
abdominal tap 541
abdominopelvic cavity 52
abduction, adduction and 61
abortion 53–54
see also congenital abnormalities 192, contraception 194, dilation and evacuation 228, miscarriage 476, pregnancy 571
abscess 54–55, 341
tooth 697
see also bacteria 117, boil 132
accelerated hypertension 374
accessory nerve 459
accessory respiratory muscles 38
ACE *see* angiotensin converting enzyme inhibitors 92, 235
acetabulum 362–363
acetaminophen 83
achalasia 55, 270
Achilles tendinitis 55–56, 701, 703
Achilles tendon 55–56
see also ankle 88, foot 303, leg 425, tendinitis 701
achondroplasia 56, 239
see also dwarfism 239, growth disorders 328
achromatic vision 188
acidosis 56
see also alkalosis 77, metabolism 471
acne 56–57
acne rosacea 57
acne vulgaris 56
acoustic neuroma 503–504
acoustic reflex 342
acquired immune deficiency syndrome *see* AIDS 70
acquired immunodeficiency 386
acquired partial lipodystrophy 436
acrocyanosis 57
see also arteries 102
acromegaly 57–58
see also gigantism 319, growth disorders 328
acromioclavicular joint 618, 637
acromion 637, 639
acrophobia 58
see also anxiety 94, panic attacks 540, phobia 558
acrosome 46, 665
ACTH *see* adrenocorticotropic hormone 64
actin filaments 22
actinic keratoses 410
action potentials 25
active immunity 384
acupressure 58
acupuncture 58–60
in anesthesia 86
acute respiratory distress syndrome 60
see also blood vessels 131, cyanosis 203, lungs 443, pulmonary edema 584
acyclovir 72, 93
Adam's apple 423, 496
Adams-Stokes syndrome *see* Stokes-Adams syndrome 678
ADD *see* attention deficit disorder 109
addiction 233
Addison's disease 60–61
see also adrenal glands 64
adduction and abduction 61
see also muscles 483, muscular system 20–23
adductor muscles 428
adenine 232
adenocarcinoma 61, 137
adenohypophysis 561
adenoids 61
see also otitis media 525, rhinitis 608, sinusitis 645, tonsils 724
adenoma 61–62
see also acromegaly 57, Cushing's syndrome 202, endocrine glands 260
adenomatosis 62
adenomyosis 744
adenovirus 62
see also conjunctivitis 193, DNA 231, pneumonia 565, viruses 752
ADH *see* antidiuretic hormone 224
ADHD *see* attention deficit hyperactivity disorder 109
adhesions 62
adhesive capsulitis 639
adipose tissue 721
adolescence 62–63, 66
see also acne 56, eating disorders 248, puberty 582
adrenal cortex 60, 64
adrenal glands 64, 320, 474
see also Addison's disease 60, androgens 83, Cushing's syndrome 202, endocrine glands 260, hormones 369, pituitary gland 560
adrenal hyperplasia 64
adrenal medulla 64
adrenaline *see* epinephrine 266
adrenocorticotropic hormone 48, 64
adrenogenital syndrome 64
see also adrenal glands 64, androgens 83, congenital abnormalities 192, feminization 287, genetic counseling 315, hormones 369, pituitary gland 560, steroids 677, virilization 753
adult asthma 106
adult respiratory distress syndrome 60
adult type diabetes 222
adulthood 67
aflatoxin 440
African trypanosomiasis 654
age spots 67
age-associated memory impairment 463
ageing 66–68
see also adolescence 62, childhood 174, geriatric medicine 316, infancy 390, menopause 465, puberty 582
aggression, in children 174
agonist muscle 22
agoraphobia 69
see also anxiety 94, panic attacks 540, phobia 558
agranulocyte 162
agranulocytosis 69
see also bone marrow biopsy 132, opportunistic infection 517, white blood cells 761
AIDS 70–72
see also HIV 364, Kaposi's sarcoma 409, T cells 692
air embolus 254
akathisia 239
albino 401
albumin 441, 563
albuminuria 374
alcohol consumption during pregnancy 289
alcohol tolerance 215
alcohol withdrawal 220
alcoholic cirrhosis 183, 354
alcoholic dependency 215
alcoholic hepatitis 354, 356
alcoholic rehabilitation 215
Alcoholics Anonymous 74, 221
alcoholism 73–75, 453
see also cirrhosis of the liver 183, delirium tremens 215, dementia 215, detoxification 220, drug dependence 233, fetal alcohol syndrome 289, pancreatitis 540, Wernicke-Korsakoff syndrome 760
aldosterone 198, 474
Alexander technique 76
alimentary canal 76–77
see also colon 187, digestive system 42–43, endoscopy 262, intestines 399, liver 438, pancreas 538, peristalsis 554, stomach 679
alkalosis 77
see also acidosis 56, metabolism 471
allergens 32, 77
allergic bronchial asthma 106
allergic conjunctivitis 193, 278
allergic purpura 586
allergic reaction 78, 385
to drugs 236
allergic rhinitis 336, 608
allergies 77–79
see also anaphylaxis 83, antibodies 90, antigen tests 92, antihistamines 92, asthma 106, autoimmune disease 110, conjunctivitis 193, dermatitis 218, desensitization 220, eczema 250, hay fever 336, photosensitivity 559, serum sickness 629, sinusitis 645, urticaria 743
allodynia 534
allograft 326
alopecia 118, 332
alpha cells 403
alpha globulins 322
alpha interferon 354
alpha-adrenergic blockers 92, 374
ALS see amyotrophic lateral sclerosis 82
alternative medicines 235
alveolar sacs 79
alveolar sockets 405
alveolar wall 37
alveolus 79
Alzheimer's disease 79–80
see also dementia 215, memory 461
amebic dysentery 239, 312
amenorrhea 470
amino acids 80
see also Kwashiorkor 417, malnutrition 452
ammonia 285, 353, 743
ammonium chloride 273
amnesia 80–81
see also alcoholism 73, Alzheimer's disease 79, convulsions 196, dementia 215, electroconvulsive therapy 252, memory 461, psychotropic drugs 581, stroke 682, trauma 730, Wernicke-Korsakoff syndrome 760
amniocentesis 82, 180, 255, 572
see also chromosomal abnormalities 180, congenital abnormalities 192, pregnancy 571
amnion 255
amniotic fluid 82, 291
amniotic membrane 255
amniotic sac 82, 255
amniotomy 172
amphetamine withdrawal 221
see also attention deficit hyperactivity disorder 109, drug dependence 233, stimulants 678
ampulla 288
ampulla of Vater 538
amygdala 434–435
amylase 615
amyotrophic lateral sclerosis 82
see also muscles 483, rehabilitation 599, spinal cord 666
anabolic reaction 471
anabolic steroids 82, 486, 677
see also testosterone 707
anabolism 471
anal columns 596
anal fissure 94, 297
anal itching 94
anal sphincter 94
analgesics 82–83
see also morphine 478, narcotics 492, pain 534, Reye's syndrome 605
analytical psychotherapy 581
anaphylactic shock 83, 637
anaphylaxis 32, **83**
see also allergies 77, antihistamines 92, epinephrine 266, steroids 677
androgens 64, **83–84**, 677
see also pituitary gland 560, puberty 582, testes 705, testosterone 707, virilization 253

androsterone 83
anemia 84–85
see also hemoglobin 350, hemolytic anemia 351, iron 402, red blood cells 596, sickle cell disease 640, thalassemia 708
anencephaly 256, 502
anesthesia 85–86
see also acupuncture 58, cocaine 183, epidural anesthesia 264, hypnotherapy 375, pain 534, synapses 688
aneurysm 86
see also aorta 95, arteries 102, arteriosclerosis 103, blood vessels 131, subarachnoid hemorrhage 684
anger 258
angiitis 747
angina pectoris 86, 344
see also arteriosclerosis 103, beta-blockers 121, electrocardiogram 252, heart 344
angioedema 86
see also allergies 77, urticaria 743
angiography 86–87
see also angioplasty 88, arteries 102, arteriosclerosis 103
angioma 87
see also anemia 84, blood vessels 131, stroke 682, subarachnoid hemorrhage 684
angioplasty 88
see also arteries 102, atherosclerosis 108, blood vessels 131
angiotensin 40
angiotensin converting enzyme inhibitors 92, 235, 374
angiotensinogen 40
anionic electrolyte 475
ankle 88–89, 303
damage to 304
see also foot 303, fractures (leg) 425, sprain 673
ankylosing spondylitis 89–90
see also arthritis 103
ankylostomiasis 763
annulus fibrosus 228–229, 670
anorectal fistula 298
anorexia nervosa 248
anorgasmia 631
anoscope 353
anosmia 517
anovulatory cycle 529
ANS see autonomic nervous system 27, 554
antacids 349, 361
antagonist muscle 22
anterior chamber of the eye 276
anterior cranial fossa 651
anterior cruciate ligament 416
anterior fossa 337
anterior intevertebral joint 670
anterior longitudinal ligament 670
anterograde amnesia 81
anteverted uterus 743
anthrax 90
anthroposophical medicine 90
anti-anxiety drugs 221, 729
antiarrhythmic drugs 90
see also heartbeat 348
antibiotics 90
see also bacteria 117, penicillins 548
antibodies 32, **90**
see also immunization 386
anticholinergics 92, 107
anticoagulants 91, 477
see also blood 128
anticonvulsants 91, 455
see also convulsions 196, epilepsy 266
anti-D globin 605
antidepressants 91, 94, 455
see also depression 217, psychotropic drugs 581
antidiarrheals 91–92
see also diarrhea 226
antidiuretic hormone 48, 224
antiemetic drugs 92
see also antihistamines 92, nausea 493, vomiting 758
antifungals 92
see also candidiasis 157, ringworm 609, tinea 717
antigen tests 79, **92**
see also allergies 77
antigens 32, 83, 90
antihistamines 92, 250, 336
see also allergies 77
antihypertensives 92–93
see also beta-blockers 121, hypertension 373
anti-inflammatory drugs 93
see also arthritis 103, corticosteroids 198, Reye's syndrome 605
antioxidants 93, 302
see also atherosclerosis 108, nutrition 509, vitamins 754
antipsychotics 93, 239
see also schizophrenia 619, tranquilizers 729
antipyretics 268
antiserum 629
antisocial personality disorder 555
antitrypsin 259
antivirals 93
see also chickenpox 168, genital herpes 315, herpes simplex 360, shingles 636, viruses 752
anus 94
see also hemorrhoids 353
anvil 339
anxiety 94, 258
see also agoraphobia 69, biofeedback 122, depression 217, panic attacks 540, phobia 558, psychotherapy 581, relaxation techniques 601, tranquilizers 729
anxiolytics 94
see also anxiety 94, barbiturates 119, drug dependence 233, psychotropic drugs 581, tranquilizers 729
aorta 95, 287
see also aneurysm 86, arteries 102, heart 344
aortic aneurysm 86, 95
aortic stenosis 34, 95
apex beat 348
apex of the lung 443
Apgar test 505
aphasia 96, 241, 663
aplastic anemia 85
apnea, sleep 653
apocrine sweat glands 687
appendectomy 96
appendicitis 96
appendicular skeleton 18
appendix 96
see also peritonitis 555
appetite 96
see also diet 227, nutrition 509, obesity 514
aqueous humor 276
arachnoid 463
arachnoid mater 670
arbovirus 217
ARC *see* AIDS-related complex 70
arcuate nucleus 685
ARDS *see* acute respiratory distress syndrome 60
areola 506
arm 97–100
see also bursitis 150, elbow 251, humerus 371
armpit 100, 454
aromatherapy 101–102
arrhythmia 102, 348, 487
see also angiography 86, antiarrhythmic drugs 90, echocardiogram 249, electrocardiogram 252, fibrillation 295, heart 344, tachycardia, paroxysmal 692
art therapy 102
arterial thrombosis 711
arteries 102–103
see also angiography 86, angioplasty 88, aorta 95, arteriosclerosis 103, blood vessels 131, hypertension 373, ischemia 403, Raynaud's disease 596, stroke 682, vasculitis 747
arteriosclerosis 103, 373
from smoking 657
see also angioplasty 88, arteries 102, atherosclerosis 108, cholesterol 179, hypertension 373, myocardial infarction 488, stroke 682
arthralgia 104
arthritis 103–105
see also anti-inflammatory drugs 93, autoimmune disease 110, connective tissue 193, corticosteroids 198, non-steroidal anti-inflammatory drugs 507, osteoarthritis 520, rheumatoid arthritis 607
arthroscopy 105
articular process of vertebrae 669
articulation 662
artificial baby milk 136
artificial hip 363
artificial induction 53
artificial insemination 105
see also infertility 395
artificial pacemaker 347, 532
artificial respiration 146
artificial valve 477
arytenoid cartilage 36
arytenoids 423
asbestos 105
asbestosis 105
see also cancer 154, mesothelioma 471
ascariasis 105–106, 611, 763
see also roundworms 367
ascending colon 187
ascites 106
see also paracentesis 541
ascorbic acid 302, 756
ASD *see* atrial septal defect 108
aseptic meningitis 482
Asian massage 457
aspirin 82, 93
asthma 106–107
and smoking 656
drugs 235
see also allergies 77, bronchitis 148, bronchodilators 148, corticosteroids 198, emphysema 258, lungs 443
astigmatism 107–108, 274
see also cornea 197, eye 274
asymptomatic carrier 393
atelectasis 108
see also bronchoscopy 148, lungs 443, pneumonia 565, respiratory system 36–38
atherosclerosis 108, 223, 286, 344
see also angioplasty 88, arteries 102, arteriosclerosis 103
atherosclerotic plaque 88
athetosis 108
athlete's foot 717
atlas bone 494–495
atopic dermatitis 218, 250, 595
atria 344
atrial fibrillation 295, 345, 348, 477
atrial septal defect 108–109
see also endocarditis 259, heart 344
atrial tachycardia 345, 692
atrioventricular bundle 344
atrioventricular node 344
atrioventricular orifice 34
atrioventricular valve 34, 344, 476
atrophic vaginitis 109
see also vaginitis 746, vulvitis 758
attention deficit disorder (ADD) 109
attention deficit hyperactivity disorder 109
see also amphetamines 82, behavioral and emotional problems 121, learning disorders 424
audiogram 109
audiologists 211
audiometer 109
audiometry 109, 211
see also ear 244, hearing 342
auditory canal 342
auditory ossicles 343
augmentation mammoplasty 454
auricle 244
autism 110
autocrine secretions 370
autogenic training 602
autograft 326

autoimmune disease 110–111
see also Addison's disease 60, connective tissue 193, dermatomyositis 220, diabetes 222, Hashimoto's disease 336, lupus erythematosus 447, myasthenia gravis 487, rheumatoid arthritis 607, vasculitis 747
autoimmune response, multiple sclerosis 481
automated external defibrillator 213
autonomic fibers 667
autonomic nervous system 27–29, 554
autopsy 212
AV (arteriovenous) fistula 225
AV block 348
avoidant personality disorder 555
axial skeleton 16
axillary vein 749
axis bone 494–495
axons 25, 500, 504
Ayurvedic massage 457
Ayurvedic medicine 111
azathioprine 220
azoospermia 396
AZT 72
azygos vein 749

B

B cell lymphoma 150
B cell 761
B lymphocyte 32, 384
baby blues 173, 217, 569
baby rash 225
Bach flower remedies 299
back 114
see also ankylosing spondylitis 89, coccyx 184, epidural anesthesia 264, exercise 271, kyphosis 417, lordosis 441, lumbago 441, osteoarthritis 520, osteoporosis 524, Paget's disease of bone 533, sciatica 620, scoliosis 621, skeletal system 15–19, spina bifida 665, vertebrae 751, whiplash 760
bacteremia 129
bacteria 117
see also antibiotics 90, immunization 386
bacterial conjunctivitis 193, 278
bacterial dysentery 239
bacterial labyrinthitis 420
bacterial meningitis 464
bacterial STDs 633
bactericidal antibiotics 90
bacteriostatic antibiotics 90
bad bite 697, 701
bad breath 697
balance 117, 244, 246
see also ear 244, Menière's disease 463, motion sickness 478, otitis media 525, semicircular canals 625, vertigo 751
balanced diet 509
balanitis 550
baldness 118, 332
see also androgens 83, anemia 84, autoimmune disease 110, hair 332, hormones 369, thyroid gland 714
ball-and-socket joint 407–408
balloon angioplasty 88
barbiturates 119, 375
see also anticonvulsants 91, anxiolytics 94, drug dependence 233, epilepsy 265, psychotropic drugs 581
barbituric acid 119
barium enema 119
see also colon 187, contrast x-ray 196, intestines 399
barium meal 119
see also contrast x-ray 196, endoscopy 262, esophagus 269, hiatus hernia 361
barium sulfate 119
barnacles of ageing 410
baroreceptors 627
barrel-chest 258
Bartholin's abscess 119
Bartholin's cyst 119
Bartholin's gland 119
see also vagina 745
basal cell carcinoma 120
see also skin cancer 648
basal ganglia 139
basal layer of epidermis 264, 646
basal metabolic rate 472, 509
basilic vein 749
basophil 761
battle fatigue 569
BCC *see* basal cell carcinoma 120
beard rash 284
Becker dystrophy 487
bedsore 738
bed-wetting 120
see also behavior therapy 120, bladder 124, kidneys 411
behavior therapy 120–121
see also counseling 199, psychotherapy 581
behavioral and emotional problems 121
in childhood 174
see also alcoholism 73, anxiety 94, bed-wetting 120, bipolar disorder 123, counseling 199, depression 217, drug dependence 233, eating disorders 248, obsessive-compulsive disorder 515, panic attacks 540, personality disorders 555, phobia 558, post-traumatic stress disorder 569, schizophrenia 619, seasonal affective disorder 624, smoking 656
Bell's palsy 121
see also paralysis 541
bends, the 212
benign non-nephropathic cystinosis 204
benign prostatic hypertrophy 579
benign tumor 734
Bennett's fracture 764
benzodiazepines 375, 729
benzoyl peroxide 56
berry aneurysm 86, 682
beta agonists 107
beta-blockers 92, 121, 374
see also angina pectoris 86, arrythmia 102, glaucoma 322, heart 344, hypertension 373, hyperthyroidism 374, migraine 474
beta cells 403
beta globulins 322
bicarbonate 253
biceps femoris 333
biceps muscle 97, 594
biceps tendinitis 701
bilateral oophorectomy 517
bile 308, 438
bile acids, reabsorption of 382
bile ducts 122
see also duodenum 237, gallbladder 308, gallstones 308, liver 438
biliary colic 309
biliary tree 122
bilirubin 352, 404
Billings, method of contraception 194
binaural hearing 342
binocular vision 641
biochemic tissue salts 122
see also homeopathy 366
bioenergetics 660
biofeedback 122
biological clock 653
biopsy 123
bone marrow 132
endometrial 260
see also tumors 734
biorhythms 123
biotin 756
bipolar disorder 123–124
see also anticonvulsants 91, antidepressants 91, attention deficit hyperactivity disorder 109, depression 217, electroconvulsive therapy 252, mania 455
bird fancier's lung 446
birth, position of fetus 172
birthmarks 124, 477
see also hemangioma 350
bisexuality 124
see also homosexuality 367, sexuality 633
biting, in children 176
bitterness 694
blackhead 56
blackwater 452
bladder 124–127
control 120
diverticulum 127
transitional cell carcinoma 127
see also biopsy 123, cystitis 204, kidney 411, prostate gland 578, urinary systems 39–41
bladder stones, treatment with lithotripsy 437
blastocyst 291
bleeding *see* hemorrhage 352
blepharitis 279
blepharoplasty 284
blind spot 276–277
blindness 127
see also cataracts 161, color blindness 188, diabetes 222, macular degeneration 452, night blindness 506
blocked arteries 489
blood 128–129
see also anemia 84, arteriosclerosis 103, embolism 254, hemoglobin 350, hemophilia 352, ischemia 403, lymphocytes 449, plasma 563, platelets 563, red blood cells 596, septicemia 629, thrombus 712, white blood cells 761
blood clot 91, 129, 198, 712
stroke 682
subdural hematoma 685
blood count 130
see also blood 128, hemoglobin 350, platelets 563, red blood cells 596, white blood cells 761
blood gas analysis 130
see also acidosis 56, alkalosis 77
blood groups 130
see also blood transfusion 130, rhesus factor 605
blood-nerve barrier 500
blood poisoning 129, 629, 727
blood pressure 130
see also hypertension 373, hypotension 377
blood sugar tests 130
see also diabetes 222, hyperglycemia 373
blood thinners 235
blood transfusion 130–131
see also blood 128
blood vessels 131
development of 256
see also aorta 95, arteries 102, blood 128, capillaries 157, heart 344, kidney 411, veins 748
blurred vision 220
BMI *see* body mass index 132
BMR *see* basal metabolic rate 472, 509
body, ageing process 67
body clock 123, 461
body language 131–132
body lice 432
body mass index 132
see also nutrition 509, obesity 514
body odor 688
body rhythms 406
body shape 132
see also cosmetic surgery 198, eating disorders 248, obesity 514
body temperature 132
see also fever 295, heatstroke 349
boil 132
bolus 615
bone conduction 211
bone fractures 305
bone marrow biopsy 132
see also anemia 84, biopsy 123, leukemia 430
bones 134–136
development in children 174, 175
fibula 296–297
healing 341
in infancy 391
of the hand 334
see also bone marrow biopsy 132, calcium 154, fractures 304, muscles 483, osteomyelitis 522, osteoporosis 524, skeletal system 15–19
bony pelvis 547
borderline personality disorder 555
Bornholm disease 564

bottle feeding 136
see also breast feeding 144, infancy 390, newborn 505
botulism 302
bow legs 425
bowel 136
see also colon 187, duodenum 237, ileum 382, intestines 399, jejunum 405, rectum 596
bowel cancer 136–137
see also anemia 84, barium enema 119, bowel 136, cancer 154, colon 187, Crohn's disease 201, intestines 399, rectum 596, ulcerative colitis 738
Bowman's capsule 412, 498
braces 137
see also teeth 696
brachial artery 100, 251
brachial vein 749
brain 138–140
development of 256, 291–292
see also brain wave activity 140, cerebellum 164, cerebral palsy 166, hydrocephalus 372, neurons 504, Parkinson's disease 544, stroke 682, thalamus 708, transient ischemic attack 729
brain stem 139, 473
brain stem death 212
brain wave activity 140–141
see also brain 138
branchial cyst 142
Braxton-Hicks contractions 571
breakbone fever 217
breast 142–143
cysts 295
lumps 143, 295
see also breast cancer 143, breast feeding 144, estrogens 270, fibroadenoma 295, fibrocystic disease 295, mammary glands 454, mastectomy 457, mastitis 457, nipple 506, pregnancy 571, puberty 582
breast cancer 143
see also biopsy 123, breast 142, cancer 154, mammography 454, mastectomy 457
breast enlargement 454
breast feeding 144–145
as contraception 195
see also breast 142, bottle feeding 136, infancy 390, mastitis 457, newborn 505, nipple 506, nutrition 509
breast implants 143, 455, 457, 563
breast milk 145, 454
breast reduction 454
breast uplift procedure 454
breastbone 676
breathing 146–147
see also asthma 106, bronchitis 148, dyspnea 241, lungs 443, tracheostomy 728
breathing apparatus 282
breech birth 173, 572–573
bridge 202
bridgework 697
brittle bones 522
broad spectrum antibiotics 90
Broca's area 241, 662
bronchial asthma 443
bronchial carcinoma 444
bronchial tree 38
bronchiectasis 444
bronchiolitis 62, 444
bronchitis 148, 458
see also asthma 106, bronchus 148, cough 199, emphysema 258, pneumonia 565, smoking 656
bronchodilators 107, **148**
see also anti-inflammatory drugs 93, asthma 106
bronchopneumonia 565
bronchoscope 148
bronchoscopy 148
see also lungs 443
bronchus 148
see also bronchitis 148, lungs 443, trachea 727
brucellosis 149
bruise 149
bruxism 698, 701
buccinator 479
Buerger's disease 710
bulbocavernosus muscle 625
bulimia nervosa 248
bullous emphysema 259
bullying, in children 176
bundle branch block 344
bunion 150, 304, 333
see also foot 303
Burkitt's lymphoma 150
see also biopsy 123, infectious mononucleosis 394, lymph nodes 448, lymphocytes 449, white blood cells 761
burping 361
bursa 150, 371
bursitis 150, 350, 371
see also joints 407
Buteyko breathing technique 150
see also asthma 106, breathing 146

C

cafe au lait spots 124, 477
caffeine 154, 678
see also stimulants 678, withdrawal 762
caisson disease 212
calcaneus 88
calcium 154
see also bones 135, hypocalcemia 376, kidney 411, nutrition 509, osteomalacia 522, osteoporosis 524, parathyroid glands 543, rickets 609, teeth 696, thyroid gland 714
calcium channel blockers 92, **154**, 374
see also arrhythmia 102, arteries 102, blood vessels 131, heart 344, hypertension 373, migraine 474
calculi, in bladder 124
calf 428
callus 341
cancer 154–156
Ewing's sarcoma 271
from smoking 657
Hodgkin's disease 365
hormone replacement therapy 368
in females 155
in males 155
rectal 298
see also bowel cancer 136, breast cancer 143, chemotherapy 168, leukemia 430, lung cancer 442, melanoma 460, metastasis 472, prostate cancer 578, radiation therapy 472, skin cancer 648
candidiasis 157, 270
see also antifungals 92, diaper rash 225, opportunistic infection 517, vaginitis 746
canines 696
cannabis 85, 656
cap, contraceptive 195
capacitation 289
capillaries 157
see also arteries 102, blood vessels 131, circulatory system 33–35, veins 748
capillary hemangioma 350
capsid 393
car sickness 478
carbohydrates 511
carbon monoxide poisoning 566
carbuncle 132
carcinoma 154
hepatocellular 354
cardia 679
cardiac arrest 213
cardiac arrhythmia 344
cardiac defibrillation 213
cardiac hypertrophy 158
see also angina pectoris 86, calcium channel blockers 154, cardiomyopathy 158, heart 344, hypertension 373, myocardial infarction 488
cardiac muscle 485
cardiac muscle tissue 485, 720
cardiac rehabilitation 599
cardiac tamponade 158
see also heart 344, pericarditis 552, pericardium 552
cardiac vein 344
cardioesophageal junction 361, 679
cardiomyopathy 158, 487
alcoholism 74
see also cardiac hypertrophy 158, heart 344
cardiopulmonary resuscitation 213, 347–348
cardiovascular disease 216, 271
cardiovascular isotope scanning 159
see also heart 344
cardioversion 345, 348
carotid artery 159, 496
see also arteries 102, cerebrovascular accidents 166, stroke 682, transient ischemic attack 730
carotid pulse 585
carotid sheath 496
carpal bones 159, 763
carpal tunnel syndrome 159, 709
see also wrist 763
carpometacarpal joint 764
carpus 763
cartilage 160–161
see also connective tissue 193, joints 407, knee 414, osteoarthritis 520
cartilage-hair hypoplasia 377
cascara 423
CAT scan 161, 266
see also contrast x-ray 196, magnetic resonance imaging 452, x-ray 764
catabolic reaction 471
catabolism 471
cataracts 161, 278, 316
see also eye 274
catarrh 162
see also common cold 189, hay fever 336, laryngitis 421, rhinitis 608
catatonia 162
see also schizophrenia 619
catatonic motor behavior 162
catatonic schizophrenia 162
catheter 162
catheterization 162
see also bladder 124, heart 344
cat-scratch fever 161
cauda equina 614, 665
cavernous hemangioma 350
CBT *see* cognitive behavioral therapy 581
CCBs *see* calcium channel blockers 154
CD4 70, 692
cecum 187
celiac disease 162
see also anemia 84, baldness 118, intestines 399, osteoporosis 524, sprue 673
celiac plexus 660
cell body 504
cell division 162
cell nucleus 504
cell-mediated immune system 384, 692
cells 162–164
ageing of 68
see also blood 128, DNA 231, skin 646, tissues 719
cellulite 164
see also cosmetic surgery 198
cellulitis 164
see also streptococcal infections 681
cementum 696
central artery of the retina 276
central cyanosis 203
central diabetes insipidus 224
central nervous system 25, 483, 500
development of 256
multiple sclerosis 481
central sleep apnea 653
central tendon 225
centrioles 162
cephalic vein 749
cerebellum 139, **164**
muscle control 22
see also brain 138
cerebral arteries 165
see also blood vessels 131, brain 138, cerebral cortex 165
cerebral cortex 138, **165**, 215–216
see also brain 138, neurons 504
cerebral edema 259
cerebral hemorrhage 165
from smoking 656
see also brain 138, stroke 682
cerebral infarction 683, 712

cerebral malaria 452
cerebral palsy 166
cerebral thrombosis, causing stroke 682
cerebrospinal fluid 372
cerebrovascular accidents 166
see also brain 138, ischemia 403, stroke 682, subarachnoid hemorrhage 684, transient ischemic attack 730
cerebrum 138
cervical canal 167, 744
cervical incompetence 167
cervical muscle 469
cervical osteoarthritis 496, 673
cervical polyps 167
cervical region, of the spine 668
cervical rib syndrome 166
see also neck 494, vertebrae 751
cervical spinal nerves 667
cervical vertebrae 114, 495, 751
cervix 166–167
see also miscarriage 476, Pap smear 540, reproductive systems, female 44–45
cesarean section 172–173, 265
CFS *see* chronic fatigue syndrome 181
chalazion 167, 277
see also eyelids 279
chambers of the heart 344
chancroid 167
see also sexually transmitted diseases 633, syphilis 689
cheeks 282
chemical peritonitis 551
chemoreceptors 627–628
chemotherapy 168, 472, 488
see also cancer 154, radiation therapy 472
cherry angioma 87
cherry plum 299
chest x-ray 168
see also x-ray 764
Cheyne-Stokes respiration 146
chi 693
chi kung 590
chickenpox 168, 595
see also infectious diseases 393, Reye's syndrome 605, shingles 636
chilblain 168
child abuse 169
childbirth 170–173
hemorrhage during 352
see also bottle feeding 136, breast feeding 144, cesarean section 172, epidural anesthesia 264, infancy 390, newborn 505, placenta 561, postnatal depression 569, pregnancy 571
childhood 66, **174–176**
see also behavioral and emotional problems 121
Chinese herbalism 176
Chinese medicine 58, 176
chiropractic 177–178, 523
see also massage 455, nervous system 24–26, skeletal system 15–19, spine 668, vertebrae 751
chlamydia 178
see also pelvic inflammatory disease 546, pneumonia 565, psittacosis 580, trachoma 728, urethritis 742
chloasma 460, 571
chloral hydrate 375
chloride 253
chloroform 85
chocolate cysts 526
cholangiogram 178
cholangiography 178–179
see also endoscopy 262, gallbladder 308, gallstones 308
cholangitis 179
see also cirrhosis of the liver 183, gallbladder 308, gallstones 308, liver 438, pancreas 538
cholecystectomy 179, 308
see also cholecystitis 179, gallbladder 308, gallstones 308, laparoscopy 420
cholecystitis 179, 308
see also cholecystectomy 179, gallbladder 308, gallstones 308
choledocholithiasis 309
cholelithiasis 308
cholera 179
see also dehydration 214, diarrhea 226, infectious diseases 393, intestines 399
cholesterol 179–180, 286
see also arteries 102, diet 227, fats 286, heart 344, myocardial infarction 488, nutrition 509
chondroblasts 160
chondrocytes 160
chondrosarcoma 161
chordae tendineae 476
chordee 377
choriocarcinoma 180, 372, 562
see also cancer 154, hydatidiform mole 372, tumors 734
chorion 180
chorionic gonadotrophin 370
chorionic villus sampling 180
see also amniocentesis 82, chromosomal abnormalities 180, congenital abnormalities 192
choroid 220, 274–275, 604
choroid plexus 751
chromosomal abnormalities 180–181
see also amniocentesis 82, chorionic villus sampling 180, chromosomes 181, Down syndrome 233, genetic counseling 315
chromosomes 181, 289, 291, 358
see also cells 162, chromosomal abnormalities 180, DNA 231, Down syndrome 233
chronic bronchitis 148, 443
chronic cholecystitis 309
chronic fatigue syndrome 181
chronic gastritis 311
chronic gingivitis 319
chronic glomerulonephritis 323
chronic glossitis 323
chronic insomnia 398
chronic laryngitis 421
chronic leukemia 432
chronic lymphocytic leukemia 432
chronic myeloid leukemia 432
chronic obstructive bronchitis 148
chronic obstructive pulmonary disease 443
chronic osteomyelitis 522
chronic pancreatitis 540
chronic pharyngitis 556
chronic pyelonephritis 587
chronic sinusitis 646
chronic subdural hematoma 685
chyle 31
cicatrix 619
cilia 291
cilia, in the trachea 727
ciliary body 274–276
cingulate gyrus 434
circadian rhythm 406, 653
circle of Willis 87
circulation, effect of massage 456
circulatory shock 636
circulatory system 33–35
circumcision 181–182
see also clitoris 183, glans 321, penis 550
circumvallate papillae 722
cirrhosis 356
cirrhosis of the liver 183, 250, 270
see also alcoholism 73, Dupuytren's contracture 238, hemochromatosis 350, liver 438, Wilson's disease 762
cisterna chyli 31
citric acid 302
classic migraine 474
claudication 403
claustrophobia 183
see also anxiety 94, anxiolytics 94, phobia 558
clavicle 186
clear layer of epidermis 264
cleft lip 183
cleft palate 183, 536
see also lip 435, mouth 479
clematis 299
clergyman's knee 415
clicky hip 407
climacteric 465
climatic bubo 449
clinical depression 217
clitoridectomy 181
clitoris 183
see also reproductive system, female 44–45, vulva 758
closed-angle glaucoma 322
clostridium botulinum 302
clotting 129
clubfoot 304
cluster headache 341
cluttering 663
CNS *see* central nervous system 256, 500
coagulation 129
coal tar 218
coarctation of the aorta 347
cobalt 476
cocaine 183
see also anesthesia 85, drug dependence 233, stimulants 678
coccidioidomycosis 607
coccygeal nerve 667
coccygeal vertebrae 751
coccygodynia 184
see also coccyx 184, spine 668
coccyx 184
see also coccygodynia 184, spine 668
cochlea 184, 246, 343
see also ear 244, hearing 342
cochlear implant 211, 248
codeine 83, 478
coffee 154
cognitive behavioral therapy 581
cognitive therapy 184–185
see also anxiety 94, behavior therapy 120, counseling 199, depression 217, psychotherapy 581
coitus 632
coitus interruptus 195
cold 628
cold sore 185, 360
see also genital herpes 315, herpes simplex 360
cold sweat 687
cold virus 752
colic 185, 412
see also breast feeding 144, infancy 390, newborn 505
colitis 186
see also barium enema 119, bowel 136, colon 187, Crohn's disease 201, intestines 399, irritable bowel syndrome 402, ulcerative colitis 738
collagen 186, 193
see also autoimmune disease 110, connective tissue 193
collagen disease 186
collapsed lung 108
collar bone 186–187
see also ribs 608, scapula 618, shoulder 637
Colles' fracture 100
colloid 714
colon 187
see also barium enema 119, colitis 186, Hirschsprung's disease 364, intestines 399
colonic irrigation 187
see also bowel 136, colon 187, intestines 399
colonic polyps 353
color blindness 188, 643
color vision 188
Colorado tick fever 717
colorectal polyps 137
coloring, food 302
colostomy 188, 364
see also bowel 136, colon 187, intestines 399
colostrum 144, 454
colposcopy 167
coma 188, 212
see also unconsciousness 741
comminuted fracture 304–305
common bile duct 122
common carotid artery pulse 348
common cold 189–190
see also asthma 106, respiratory system 36–38, Reye's syndrome 605, viruses 752
common peroneal nerve 428, 620
compartment syndrome 191, 428
see also muscle 483
complete denture 217
compound fracture 305

compression fracture 305
computerized axial tomography *see* CAT scan 161
conchae 508
concussion 191
see also amnesia 80, unconsciousness 741
condom 195
conductive deafness 210
conductive hearing 342
conductive hearing loss 209
condyles 415
cone cells 641
in the eye 188, 276
confusion 191–192, 215
see also delirium 215, dementia 215, memory 461
congenital abnormalities 192–193
see also achondroplasia 56, amniocentesis 82, chromosomal abnormalities 180, cleft palate 183, Down syndrome 233, genetic counseling 315, hemolytic disease of the newborn 352, Huntington's disease 371, phenylketonuria 557, sickle cell disease 640
congenital anomalies 294
congenital cataract 257
congenital dwarfism 239
congenital heart disease 347
congenital immunodeficiency 386
congenital nerve deafness 247
congenital nevi 477
congenital pigmented nevi 124
congestive cardiac failure 230, 344
conjoined twins 640
conjunctiva 277
conjunctivitis 193, 277
see also allergies 77, eye 274, eyelids 279, trachoma 728
connective tissue 193–194
see also autoimmune disease 110, collagen 186, dermatomyositis 220, lupus erythematosus 447, polymyositis 567, rheumatoid arthritis 607, scleroderma 621, scurvy 622
connective tissue disease 186, 193
connective tissue massage 456
consonants, making sounds of 662
constipation 194
see also bowel 136, intestines 399, irritable bowel syndrome 402, laxatives 423
contact dermatitis 218
contact lenses 194
see also astigmatism 107, cornea 197, eye 274, myopia 489, sight 641
contamination, food 302
continuous positive airway pressure 653
contraception 194–196
see also breast feeding 144, oral contraceptives 518, sterilization 676, tubal sterilization 732, vasectomy 747
contraceptive pill 195
contraceptives 518
contraction of muscles 22
contrast x-ray 196
see also barium enema 119, barium meal 119, CAT scan 161
contusion 149
conus medullaris 665
convulsions 196
in children 295
see also electroencephalogram 252, epilepsy 265, fever 295
Cooley's anemia 708
copper 476
copper deficiency 453
cor pulmonale 196–197
see also bronchitis 148, circulatory system 33–35, emphysema 258, heart 344, hypertension 373, lungs 443
coracoacromial arch 639
coracoacromial ligament 639
coracoid process 637, 639
cornea 197, 274–275
see also eye 274, sight 641
corneal ulcer 197, 278
corniculate cartilage 423
corns 304, 540
coronary arteries 102, **197**, 344
see also arteriosclerosis 103, coronary artery disease 197, heart 344
coronary artery angiography 197
see also coronary arteries 197, coronary artery disease 197
coronary artery bypass graft 344
coronary artery disease 197–198, 344
see also angina pectoris 86, arrythmia 102, arteriosclerosis 103, cholesterol 179, coronary arteries 197, heart 344, hypertension 373, myocardial infarction 488, obesity 514, smoking 656
coronary, heart attack 344
coronary thrombosis 198, 344
see also arteries 102, coronary arteries 197, heart 344, myocardial infarction 488, veins 748
coronaviruses 189
corpus albicans 44
corpus callosum 138
corpus cavernosum 47
corpus luteum 44, 468, 528
corpus spongiosum 46
corrosive esophagitis 269, 270
corticoid 198
corticosteroids 198, 369
for asthma 107
see also Addison's disease 60, adrenal glands 64, Cushing's syndrome 202, pituitary gland 560
corticotrophin releasing hormone 64
cortisol 198, 677
cortisone 218
cosmetic dentistry 696
cosmetic surgery 198–199, 284
see also plastic surgery 563
costochondritis 161
cough 199
see also bronchitis 148, common cold 189, emphysema 258, lungs 443
counseling 199
genetic 315
relationship 601
see also behavior therapy 120, psychotherapy 581
covering and lining epithelial tissue 719
coxal bone 362
coxiella burnetii 590
coxsackie viruses 564
CPAP *see* continuous positive airway pressure 653
CPR *see* cardiopulmonary resuscitation 347
crabs 432
crack, cocaine 183
cradle cap 199, 218
see also seborrheic dermatitis 624
cramp 199
muscle 486
see also muscle 483
cranial arteritis 341
cranial nerves 200–201, 500
ear 246
midbrain 473
see also brain 138, facial nerves 284, nerves 500, optic nerve 517, trigeminal nerve 731, vagus nerve 747
cranial osteopathy 524
cranio-sacral osteopathy 524
craniosynostosis 301
cranium 337, 649
creatinine 743
creative visualization 753
cremasteric muscle 46
crepitus 701
cretinism 201
see also iodine deficiency 401, thyroid gland 714
Creutzfeldt-Jakob disease 201, 463
see also Alzheimer's disease 79
CRH *see* corticotrophin releasing hormone 64
cricoid cartilage 36, 423
Crohn's disease 201
see also anemia 84, autoimmune disease 110, bowel 136, intestines 399
cross bite 520
cross-bridges 22
cross-eye 674
croup 201
crown and bridge 202
crown, tooth 202
see also teeth 696
cruciate ligaments 416
crying, in infancy 392
cryosurgery 202
cryptorchidism 294, 706
cryptosporidiosis 202
CSF *see* cerebrospinal fluid 372
CT scan *see* CAT scan 161
cuneiform cartilage 423
cupping, massage technique 456
curette 54
Cushing's syndrome 202
see also adrenal glands 64, pituitary gland 560
cutaneous leishmaniasis 429
cutaneous membrane 461
cutaneous schistosomiasis 688
cuticle 202
see also nails 492
CVS *see* chorionic villus sampling 180
cyanosis 203
cyst 203
breast 142
kidney 203
see also fibrocystic disease 295, hyadatid disease 372, ovarian cysts 526, tumors 734
cystic acne 56
cystic duct 122
cystic fibrosis 203
see also genetic counseling 315, liver 438, lungs 443, malnutrition 452, pancreas 538
cystic fibrosis, meconium ileus 383
cystinosis 204
see also amino acids 80, kidney 411
cystitis 204, 264
see also bladder 124, pyelonephritis 586, urinary systems 39–41
cystocele 204
see also bladder 124, urinary incontinence 742, urinary systems 39–41
cystogram 204
cystography 204
see also bladder 124, kidney 411
cystometography 204
see also bladder 124, urethra 741
cystoscopy 205
see also bladder 124, urethra 741
cytomegalovirus 205
see also immunity 384, viruses 752
cytoplasmic donation 396
cytosine 232
cytotoxic drugs 205
see also cancer 154, cells 162

D

D antigen 605
D & C *see* dilation and curettage 228
dacryoadenitis 208, 420
dacryocystitis 208
see also eye 274, lacrimal glands 420
dacryostenosis 208
dance movement therapy 208
see also Alexander technique 76, music therapy 487
dandruff 209, 218
see also cradle cap 199, dermatitis 218, scalp 617
dandy fever 217
dartos muscle 622
de Quervain's disease 701, 703, 763
deafness 209–211
see also cochlea 184, ear 244, hearing 342, Menière's disease 463, newborn 505, speech 661, tinnitus 718
death 212
decibels 342
decomposition 212
decompression laminectomy 591
decompression sickness 212–213
decongestants 213, 235
see also allergies 77, common cold 189, sinusitis 645
decubitus ulcer 738
deep bite 520

deep fascia 428
deep muscles 483
leg 427
deep tissue massage 457
deep venous thrombosis 213, 584, 711, 712
see also anticoagulants 91, embolism 254, thrombosis 711, veins 748
defibrillation 213, 345, 348
see also coronary artery disease 197, fibrillation 295, heart 344, ventricle 751
degenerate neurons 216
dehydration 214–215
see also Addison's disease 60, diarrhea 226, diabetes 222, diuretics 230, gastroenteritis 312, heatstroke 349, kidney 411
Delhi boil 429
delirium 191–192, **215**
see also alcoholism 73, delirium tremens 215, drug dependence 233
delirium tremens 73, **215**
see also alcoholism 73, delirium 215
delta agent 354
delta cell 404
deltoid ligaments 88
deltoid muscle 97, **215**, 639
see also arm 97, collar bone 186, muscle 483, shoulder 637
delusions 215
see also paranoia 542, psychosis 580, schizophrenia 619
delusions of grandeur 459
dementia 68, **215–216**, 463
see also alcoholism 73, Alzheimer's disease 79, memory 461, stroke 682
dendrites 25, 504
dendritic keratitis 278, 410
dengue 217
see *also* viruses 752
dental calculus 693
dental caries 697
dental plaque 693
dentine 696
dentures 217
see also gums 329, teeth 696
deoxygenated blood 344
deoxyribonucleic acid *see* DNA 231
deoxyribrose 231
dependence 233
dependent personality disorder 555
depressants 234
depression 217
see also antidepressants 91, bipolar disorder 123, counseling 199, electroconvulsive therapy 252, emotions 258, postnatal depression 569, psychotherapy 581, seasonal affective disorder 624
depressive personality disorder 556
dermabrasion 696
dermalophytes 609
dermatitis 218, 284
see also cradle cap 199, dandruff 209, eczema 250, seborrheic dermatitis 624, skin 646, varicose veins 747
dermatomes 218–219
see also nervous system 24–26, spinal cord 665, spinal nerves 667
dermatomyositis 220, 486
see also autoimmune disease 110, connective tissue 193
dermis 263, 646
descending colon 187
desensitization 220
see also allergies 77, antigen test 92
desert rheumatism 607
detached retina 220, 299
see also blindness 127, eye 274, retina 276, sight 641
detoxification 74, 215, **220–221**
see also alcoholism 73, anxiolytics 94, barbiturates 119, cocaine 183, drug dependence 233, hallucinogens 333, heroin 360, hypnotics 375, marijuana 455, methadone 472, morphine 478, narcotics 492, nicotine 506, psychosis 580, psychotropic drugs 581, sedatives 625, stimulants 678, tranquilizers 729, withdrawal 762
detoxification, natural health 221
see also Ayurvedic medicine 111, colonic irrigation 187, hydrotherapy 372, naturopathy 492
developmental delay 424
DHF *see* dengue hemorrhagic fever 217
diabetes 222–224
Dupuytren's contracture 238
hypoglycemia 376
see also blood sugar tests 130, hyperglycemia 373, hypoglycemia 376, insulin 398, pancreas 538
diabetes insipidus 224–225
see also diuretics 230, hypothalamus 377, kidney 411
diabetes mellitus 222
diabetic coma 222
diabetic retinopathy 224, 604
diacetylmorphine 360, 492
dialysis 225
see also hemodialysis 350, kidney 411, peritoneal dialysis 555
dialyzer 225
diaper rash 225
see also candidiasis 157, staphylococcal infections 674, streptococcal infections 681
diaphragm, contraceptive 195
diaphragm 225–226
see also abdomen 52, aorta 95, breathing 146, esophagus 269, gastroesophageal reflux 313, hiatus hernia 361, lungs 443, ribs 608, spinal cord 665, spine 668, stomach 679
diaphysis 135
diarrhea 226–227
see also celiac disease 162, cholera 179, colitis 186, constipation 194, dehydration 214, dysentery 239, gastroenteritis 312, giardiasis 319, irritable bowel syndrome 402, lactose intolerance 420, malnutrition 452
diarthroses 407
diastole 344, 347
diastolic blood pressure 130, 373
diathermy 477
diencephalon 139
diet 227–228
see also allergies 77, appetite 96, celiac disease 162, constipation 194, diabetes 222, nutrition 509, obesity 514
digestion and absorption 510
digestive organs 43
digestive system 42–43
development of 257
digestive tract 76
mouth 479
digital artery 335
digitalis 90, 213
digitoxin 90
digoxin 90
dilation and curettage 228
see also abortion 53, dilation and evacuation 228, miscarriage 476
dilation and evacuation 228
see also abortion 53, dilation and curettage 228
diphtheria 228, 488
see also immunization 386, infectious disease 393, larynx 423, throat 709, tonsils 724
diphtheria-type laryngitis 421
diploid cell 529
diplopia 233, 487, 641
direct laryngoscopy 421
disaccharides 686
discoid lupus erythematosus 447
disease, carriers of 393
disk, intervertebral 228–229
see also back 114, sciatica 620, spine 668, vertebrae 751
diskiform keratitis 278, 410
dislocation, of the hip 362
of joints 407
of the shoulder 639
disorientation 215
distal convoluted tubule 40, 412
distal phalanx 334
diuretic drugs 300
diuretics 230, 374
see also edema 250, glaucoma 322, hypertension 373, kidney 411, potassium 570
diverticulitis 230
see also bowel 136, colon 187, diverticulosis 230, peritonitis 555
diverticulosis 230
see also bowel 136, colon 187
diverticulum 230
see also esophagus 269, pharynx 557
dizziness 230–231
DLE *see* discoid lupus erythematosus 447
see also hypotension 377, Menière's disease 463, vertigo 751
DNA 231–232, 313
analysis 313
fingerprinting 313
mapping 358
transfer 396
virus 62
see also cells 162, chromosomes 181
domestic violence 232
see also child abuse 169
dominant genes 359
dopamine 544
Doppler ultrasonography 232, 740
see also ultrasound 739
dorsal horns 666
dorsal rootlets 665
dorsiflexion 88
dorsum of the tongue 722
double helix 231
double vision 233, 641
see also eye 274, sight 641
doulas 171
dowager's hump 316, 417–418, 524
Down syndrome 233, 255, 294
deafness 210
see also amniocentesis 82, chorionic villus sampling 180, chromosomal abnormalities 180, chromosomes 181, genetic counseling 315, intellectual disability 399
drug abuse 233
drug dependence 233–235
see also alcoholism 73, anxiolytics 94, barbiturates 119, cocaine 183, detoxification 220, hallucinogens 333, heroin 360, marijuana 455, methadone 472, morphine 478, narcotics 492, nicotine 506, psychosis 580, psychotropic drugs 581, sedatives 625, solvent sniffing 660, stimulants 678, tranquilizers 729, withdrawal 762
drug interactions 235–236
see also antibiotics 90, anticoagulants 91, anticonvulsants 91, antidepressants 91, antihistamines 92, beta-blockers 121, diuretics 230, sedatives 625
drug-induced non-immune thrombocytopenia 710
drugs 236
during pregnancy 294
in adolescence 63
see also allergies 77, analgesics 82, anesthesia 85, antihistamines 92, corticosteroids 198, diuretics 230, hormones 369, hypnotics 375, immunization 386, insulin 398, sedatives 625, vitamins 754
Duchenne muscular dystrophy 237
see also congenital abnormalities 192, genetic counseling 315, muscle 483, muscular dystrophy 487
ductus deferens 625
dumb rabies 592
dumping syndrome 237
see also digestive system 42–43, intestines 399, stomach 679

duodenal ulcers 237
see also duodenum 237, peptic ulcer 551, stomach 679
duodenum 237–238
see also duodenal ulcers 237, gallbladder 308, ileum 382, intestines 399, liver 438, pancreas 538
Dupuytren's contracture 238
see also connective tissue 193, finger 297, hand 334
dura mater 463, 670
dural sheath 670
dwarfism 56, **239**, 377
see also achondroplasia 56, growth disorders 328, pituitary gland 560
dysarthria 239
dysentery 239
see also bacteria 117, bowel 136, dehydration 214, diarrhea 226, intestines 399
dyskinesia 239
dyslexia 239–240
dyslogia 663
dysmenorrhea 469
dyspareunia 631
dysphagia 240–241, 269
see also esophagus 269, throat 709
dysphasia 241
see also aphasia 96, speech 661, stroke 682
dysphemia 684
dysphonia 663
dyspnea 241
see also breathing 146, lungs 443
dysrhythmia 102
dysuria 241, 579, 741
see also bladder 124, cystitis 204, prostate 578, urethritis 742, urinary systems 39–41

E

E. coli 302
ear 244–248, 339
development of 257
surgery 284
see also audiometry 109, balance 117, cochlea 184, deafness 209, hearing 342, labyrinthitis 420, mastoiditis 458, Menière's disease 463, otitis externa 525, otitis media 525, otosclerosis 525, semicircular canals 625, tinnitus 718, vertigo 751
ear damage, tinnitus 718
eardrum 244, 246, 473
earwax 342
eating disorders 248–249
see also diet 227, laxatives 423, malnutrition 452, nutrition 509
Ebola virus 752
EBV *see* Epstein–Barr virus 394
eccrine sweat glands 687
echocardiogram 249
see also heart 344
eclampsia 249, 374
see also hypertension 373, preeclampsia 570, pregnancy 571
ECT *see* electroconvulsive therapy 252
ectoderm 291
ectomorph 132
ectopic pregnancy 286, 572
ectotherms 699
ectropion 279
eczema 250
see also allergies 77, dermatitis 218
edema 250–251
pulmonary 584
see also diuretics 230, pulmonary edema 584
effleurage, massage technique 456
egg 285
Ehlers-Danlos syndrome 193
ejaculation 289, 625
EKG wires 365
EKG *see* electrocardiogram 252
elastic cartilage 160–161, 721
elastin 193
elbow 251–252
see also arm 97, radius 251, tennis elbow 703, ulna 738
elbow tendinitis 701
electro-acupuncture 60
electrocardiogram 252
see also arrythmia 102, heart 344
electroconvulsive therapy 252
for depression 217
see also bipolar disorder 123, depression 217, psychosis 580
electroencephalogram 252
see also brain wave activity 140, coma 188, epilepsy 265
electrolysis 364
electrolytes 253
see also adrenal glands 64, calcium 154, kidney 411, potassium 570, sodium 659
electromyogram 254
electromyography 254
see also muscles 483
electrosurgery 254
elephantiasis 254, 763
see also filariasis 297
elimination diet 228
ELISA *see* enzyme-linked immunosorbent assay 263
ellipsoidal joint 407
embolism 254, 711
see also anticoagulants 91, ischemia 403, myocardial infarction 488, stroke 682
embolus 254, 711
embryo 255–257
see also amniocentesis 82, fertilization 288, fetal development 291, placenta 561, pregnancy 571
embryofetoscopy 258
embryonic brain 256
embryoscopy 258
see also embryo 255, fetoscopy 295
emesis 758
emotions 258
see also anxiety 94, body language 131, depression 217, grief 327, mania 455
emphysema 258–259, 443
from smoking 657
see also asthma 106, breathing 146, bronchitis 148, lungs 443, respiratory system 36–38, smoking 656, wheezing 760
enamel 696
enamel hypoplasia 377
encephalitis 259, 458
mumps 482
see also brain 138, lumbar puncture 441, viruses 752
encephalomyelitis 259
see also brain 138, encephalitis 259, spinal cord 665
endemic typhus 735
endocarditis 259–260
see also heart 344
endocardium 259
endocrine function of the kidney 40
endocrine glands 260, 319–321
see also adrenal glands 64, endocrine system 48–49, hormones 369, ovaries 526, pancreas 538, pituitary gland 560, testes 705, thyroid gland 714
endocrine organs 369
endocrine pancreas 538
endocrine system 48–49, 369
endoderm 291
endolymph 339
endometrial biopsy 260
see also biopsy 123, dilation and curettage 228, endometrium 261
endometrial gland 468
endometrial vessel 468
endometriosis 261
see also adhesions 62, endometrium 261, hysterectomy 378, menstruation 468, reproductive system, female 44–45, uterus 743
endometrium 261–262, 291, 468, 743
cancer of 262
see also endometriosis 261, hormone replacement therapy 367, menopause 465, menstruation 468, oral contraceptives 518, placenta 561, pregnancy 571, reproductive system, female 44–45, uterus 743
endomorph 132
endorphins 262
see also acupuncture 58, exercise 271, heroin 360, morphine 478, narcotics 492
endoscope 262
endoscopic retrograde cholangiography 179
endoscopic retrograde cholangio-pancreatography 122
endoscopy 262–263
see also barium enema 119, bronchoscopy 148
endotherms 699
endotracheal tube 728
enema 263
see also barium enema 119, colonic irrigation 187, constipation 194
energy cycles, biorhythms 123
energy, daily needs 509
enkephalins 262
enteric fever 734
enteritis 263
see also dehydration 214, diarrhea 226, gastroenteritis 312, intestines 399
enterobiasis 763
enterocolitis 263
enterohepatic biliary circulation 308
enterokinase 42
entropion 279
enuresis 120
enzyme deficiencies 263
see also lactose intolerance 420, phenylketonuria 557
enzyme-linked immunosorbent assay 263
see also antibodies 90
eosinophil 761
epicondylitis 252
epidemic myalgia 564
epidemic typhus 735
epidermal cyst 624
epidermis 263–264, 646
see also dermatitis 218, keratin 410, sebaceous cyst 624, skin 646
epididymal fluid 664
epididymis 264–625
epididymitis 264
see also cystitis 204, sexually transmitted diseases 633, testes 705, urinary systems 39–41
epidural anesthesia 172, **264–265**
see also anesthesia 85, childbirth 170
epiglottis 265
see also esophagus 269, larynx 423, trachea 727
epilepsy 265–266
Dupuytren's contracture 238
see also anticonvulsants 91, brain 138, cerebral palsy 166, encephalitis 259, meningitis 464
epileptic attacks 196
epileptic fit 285
epinephrine 27, **266–267**, 369
see also adrenal glands 64, allergies 77, anaphylaxis 83, asthma 106
epiphyses 135
episclera 267
episcleritis 267
see also eye 274, rheumatoid arthritis 607, Sjögren's syndrome 646
episiotomy 172
epispadias 267
see also bladder 124, hypospadias 377, incontinence 388, penis 550, urethra 741, urinary systems 39–41
epistaxis 508
epithelial lining 269
epithelial tissue 341, 719, 721
epithelium 646, 719
eponychium 202
Epstein–Barr virus 394
equilibrium 628
ERCP *see* endoscopic retrograde cholangio-pancreatography 122
erection 267
priapism 576
see also impotence 387, penis 550, reproductive system, male 46–47

erector pili 332
erogenous zones 267–268, 632
see also sexuality 633
erysipelas 268
see also septicemia 629
erythema 268
see also corticosteroids 198, herpes simplex 360, Stevens-Johnson syndrome 678, tuberculosis 733, ulcerative colitis 738
erythema multiforme 268, 595, 678
erythema nodosum 268, 595
erythrasma 269
see also intertrigo 399
erythroblastosis fetalis 352
erythrocyte sedimentation rate 269
see also red blood cells 596
erythroplasia 724
esophageal atresia 269
esophageal disorders, alcoholism 75
esophageal diverticulum 270
esophageal spasm 555
esophageal varices 270
esophagitis 269
see also esophagus 269, hiatus hernia 361
esophagoscopy 262
esophagus 269–270
see also achalasia 55, candidiasis 157, cirrhosis of the liver 183, diaphragm 225, digestive system 42–43, dysphagia 240, gastroesophageal reflux 313, hiatus hernia 361, pharynx 557, stomach 680
essential amino acids 80
essential oils 101
estradiol 270
estrogens 270–271, 465
see also adrenal glands 64, cholesterol 179, fibroids 295, hormone replacement therapy 367, hormones 369, menopause 465, oral contraceptives 518, ovaries 526, pregnancy 571, testosterone 707
estrone 270
ether 85
ethmoid bone 282, 649
eumelanin 459
eustachian tube 244
euthanasia 212
Ewing's sarcoma 271
see also cancer 154, metastasis 472
exchange transfusion 131
excretion, kidneys 39
exercise 271–273
aerobic 273
anaerobic 273
Kegel 272
pelvic floor 272
see also heart 344, muscles 483, muscular system 20–23, obesity 514, osteoporosis 524, Pilates method 559, respiratory system 36–38, sports medicine 673, t'ai chi ch'uan 692, yoga 766
exhibitionism 631
existential therapy 581
exocrine glands 319, 321
exocrine pancreas 538
exophthalmos 273
see also eye 274, hyperthyroidism 374
expectorants 273
see also cough 199
expiration 146–147, 225
expressing milk 145
extensor muscle 100
extracellular fluid 39
extracorporeal shockwave lithotripsy 437
extradural hemorrhage 337
extra-mammary Paget's disease 533
extraocular muscle 233, 276
extrinsic allergic alveolitis 446
extrinsic tongue muscles 722
exudates 299
eye 274–279, 282
arteries of 277
development of 257
floaters 299
see also autonomic nervous system 27–29, cataracts 161, chalazion 167, color blindness 188, conjunctivitis 193, cornea 197, eyelashes 279, eyelids 279, glaucoma 322, iris 401, keratitis 410, lacrimal glands 420, myopia 489, pupil of eye 585, retina 604, sclera 621, sight 641, Sjögren's syndrome 646, squint 674, stye 684
eyeball 274–276
eyelashes 279
see also cornea 197, eyelids 279
eyelids 276–277, **279**
see also chalazion 167, conjunctivitis 193, eye 274, stye 684

F

F fibers *see* fast twitch fibers 22
face 282–284, 337
development of 257
see also acne 56, acromegaly 57, basal cell carcinoma 120, Bell's palsy 121, brain 138, cellulitis 164, cosmetic surgery 198, Cushing's syndrome 202, dermatitis 218, eye 274, facial nerves 284, folliculitis 301, Graves' disease 326, head 337, headache 340, herpes simplex 360, hypothyroidism 378, impetigo 387, jaw 404, lacrimal glands 420, leprosy 429, lip 435, melanoma 460, migraine 474, mouth 479, myasthenia gravis 487, nose 508, Parkinson's disease 544, plastic surgery 563, shingles 636, sinusitis 645, squamous cell carcinoma 674, teeth 696, tuberculosis 733
face lift 198, 284
facet joints, of vertebrae 670
facial nerves 200, **284**
tasting 694
see also Bell's palsy 121, cranial nerves 201, face 282
facioscapulohumeral dystrophy 487
factor VIII 352, 758
factor IX 352
fainting 284–285
see also blood pressure 130, hypotension 377, unconsciousness 741
fallopian tubes 285–286, 291
sterilization 676
see also embryo 255, fertilization 288, ovaries 526, ovum 529, reproductive system, female 44–45, pregnancy 571, salpingitis 616, sperm 664
false teeth 217
familial polyposis 568
family history 286
see also genetic counseling 315
farmer's lung 286, 446
see also lung 443
farsightedness 274, 641
FAS *see* fetal alcohol syndrome 289
fast twitch fibers 22
fat embolus 254
fats 286
see also atherosclerosis 108, cholesterol 179, lipids 436, lipoma 436
fauces 709
fear 258
febrile convulsions 196, 295
fecal impaction 263
feelings 258
Feldenkrais method 287
see also Alexander technique 76
female circumcision 181
female genital mutilation 181
female incontinence 389
female reproductive system 44–45
female reproductive tract 289
female sexual arousal 632
female sterilization 195, 676
feminization 287
see also estrogen 270, hormones 369, Turner's syndrome 734
femoral artery 287, 362, 428
see also aorta 95, arteries 102
femoral artery pulse 348
femoral condyle 415, 425
femoral hernia 360
femoral nerve 428
femoral vein 749
femur 287–288, 425, 590
fractures of 287
see also hip 362, knee 414, tibia 716
fertility 288
see also cervix 166, embryo 255, fallopian tubes 285, hormones 369, ovum 529, pelvic inflammatory disease 546, reproductive system, female 44–45, reproductive system, male 46–47, semen 625, sperm 664, uterus 743, vagina 745
fertility drugs 396
fertility test 288
fertilization 286, **288–289**
see also embryo 255, fallopian tubes 285, genes 313, ovaries 526, ovum 529, reproductive system, female 44–45, reproductive system, male 46–47, sperm 664, uterus 743
fetal abnormalities 294
miscarriage 476
fetal alcohol syndrome 289
see also alcoholism 73, fetal development 291
fetal development 291–294
see also amniocentesis 82, chorionic villus sampling 180, congenital abnormalities 192, embryo 255, fertilization 288, genetic counseling 315, lanugo 420, miscarriage 476, ovum 529, placenta 561, sperm 664, ultrasound 739, uterus 743
fetal development cycle 290
fetal movement 294
fetal skull 652
fetishism 631
fetoscopy 295
see also embryoscopy 258, fetal development 291
fever 295
see also body temperature 132, viruses 752
fibrillation 213, **295**, 344
see also arteries 102, defibrillation 213, heart 344, mitral valve 476, myocardial infarction 488, ventricle 751
fibrin 129
fibrinolytic system 711
fibroadenoma 142, **295**
see also breast 142, tumors 734
fibrocartilage 160–161, 721
fibrocystic disease 295
see also breast 142, menopause 465, menstruation 468, oral contraceptives 518
fibroids 271, **295–296**, 744
see also anemia 84, hysterectomy 378, menstruation 468, tumors 734, uterus 743
fibromyalgia 296
see also antidepressants 91, anti-inflammatory drugs 93, massage 455, muscles 483, rheumatism 606
fibrosis 296
see also adhesions 62, cirrhosis of the liver 183, hepatitis 354, keloid 409, peritonitis 555
fibula 296–297
see also ankle 88, knee 414, leg 425, tibia 716
field of vision 642, 644
fight-or-flight response 370, 554, 681
filariasis 297
see also elephantitis 254, lymphatic vessels 448
filiform papillae 722
fillings 297
see also teeth 696
fimbriae 44
finger 297
see also hand 334
fingertips 725
fissure 297–298
see also anus 94
fistula 298
see also anus 94, bladder 124, Crohn's disease 201, diverticulitis 230, rectum 596

fits 196
5-HT *see* serotonin 629
5-hydroxytryptamine *see* serotonin 629
flash keratoconjunctivitis 687
flat feet 298
see also foot 303
flatworms 693, 763
flatulence 298–299
see also colon 187, digestive system 42–43, intestines 399, lactose intolerance 420
flexion 334
flexor carpi ulnaris muscle 739
flexor digitorum profundus muscle 739
flexor muscle 100
flexor retinaculum 159
flexor tendons 334, 763
floaters 299
see also eye 274
flooding, during menstruation 470
flotation therapy 299
see also relaxation techniques 601
flower remedies and essences 299
flu *see* influenza 397
fluid balance 214
fluid retention 300, 374
see also angioedema 86, edema 250, hypothyroidism 378, myxedema 489, papilledema 540, preeclampsia 570, pulmonary edema 584, varicose veins 747
flukes 763
fluoridation 300
see also minerals 474, teeth 696
FMRI gene *see* fragile X syndrome 305
focusing 643
folic acid 502, 755–756
for reducing risk of spina bifida 665
folicin 755–756
follicle, hair 332
follicle stimulating hormone 48, **300**, 370
see also hormones 369, ovulation 528, pituitary gland 560
follicles, of thyroid gland 714
follicular cyst 301
see also menstruation 468, ovaries 526, ovum 529, Stein-Leventhal syndrome 675
folliculitis 284, **301**
see also hair 332
fontanelle 301
see also cretinism 201, newborn 505, skull 649
food additives 301
see also food poisoning 302, nutrition 509
food allergies 78
food coloring additives 302
food intolerance 78
food poisoning 302, 566
see also diarrhea 226, gastroenteritis 312
food preservatives 301
foot 303–304
see also Achilles tendon 55, ankle 88, bunion 150, flat feet 298, heel spur 349, joints 407
foot ulcer, diabetes 222
foramen magnum 650
forebrain 25
forceps, in birth 172
forehead 649
fornix, in the uterus 745
fractures 304
in old people 317
types of 305
see also bones 134
fragile X syndrome 305
see also chromosomes 181, congenital abnormalities 192, genes 313, genetic counseling 315, intellectual disability 399
frambesia 765
fraternal twins 734
frenulum 722
frequency response 211
friction, massage technique 456
frigidity 631
frontal bone 649
frontal lobe 25, 138
frozen shoulder 639
frozen sperm 105
fructose 686
fructose intolerance 472
FSH *see* follicle stimulating hormone 300
fugue amnesia 81
fundus 679
fungal infection 92, 394
fungal spores 336
fungiform papillae 722
furious rabies 592
furuncle 132

G

galactose 308, 686
galactosemia 308, 472
see also genetic counseling 315
galant reflex 725
gallbladder 308
removal 179
inflammation of 179
see also bile duct 122, cholangiography 178, cholecystography 179, gallstones 308, intestines 399, jaundice 404, liver 438, pancreas 538
gallstones 308–310
treatment with lithotripsy 437
see also cholelithiasis 308, gallbladder 308, liver 438, pancreas 538, pancreatitis 540
gamete intrafallopian transfer 396
gamma globulins 322, 352
ganglion 310
see also nerves 500, nervous system 24–26, spinal cord 665
gangrene 310
see also bacteria 117, circulatory system 33–35
gas exchange 443, 445
gas gangrene 310
see also bacteria 117, food poisoning 302, gangrene 310
gastrectomy 310
see also gastric ulcer 310, stomach 679
gastric reflux 55
gastric ulcer 310–311
alcoholism 75
from smoking 656
see also duodenal ulcer 237, stomach 679
gastrinoma 767
gastritis 311–312
see also anemia 84, autoimmune disease 110, biopsy 123, digestive system 42–43, endoscopy 262, stomach 679
gastroenteritis 302, **312**
stomach 680
see also cholera 179, dehydration 214, dysentery 239, food poisoning 302, giardiasis 319
gastroesophageal junction 361
gastroesophageal reflux 270, **313**, 348
see also esophagus 269, heartburn 348, hiatus hernia 361, stomach 679
gastrohepatic ligament 438
gastroscopy 313
see also endoscopy 262
gender difference 256
gene mapping 314
gene sequencing 314
gene therapy 314
general anesthesia 86
general senses 627–628
generalized lipodystrophy 436
generic drugs 236
genes 313, 359
see also chromosomes 181, congenital abnormalities 192, DNA 231, Down syndrome 233, genetic counseling 315, heredity 358, sickle cell disease 640
genetic code 314
genetic counseling 315
see also chromosomes 181, genes 313
genetic defects 358
genetic disorders 294
genetic dwarfism 239
genetic engineering 314
genioglossus muscle 722
genital herpes 315
see also herpes simplex 360, sexually transmitted diseases 633
genital organs, development of 292
genital tubercle 292
genital warts 315, 759
see also sexually transmitted diseases 633, warts 759
genu valgum 417
GERD see gastroesophageal reflux disease 348
geriatric medicine 316
see also ageing 66, cataracts 161, diabetes 222, glaucoma 322, incontinence 388, kidney 411, osteoarthritis 520, osteoporosis 524, palliative care 536, Parkinson's disease 544, shingles 635
geriatrics 316
germ cell 529
German measles *see* rubella 611
gestalt therapy 199
gestational, diabetes 224
GH *see* growth hormone 48, 57, 561
giardia 319
giardiasis 319
see also diarrhea 226, intestines 399
GIFT *see* gamete intrafallopian transfer 396
gigantism 319
see also acromegaly 57, growth disorders 328, pituitary gland 320
gingivae 329
gingivitis 319, 480
see also gums 329, periodontitis 552, teeth 696
glands 319–321
see also adrenal glands 64, endocrine glands 260, estrogens 270, hypothalamus 377, mammary glands 454, ovaries 526, parathyroid glands 543, pituitary gland 320, sebaceous glands 624, sweat glands 687, testes 705, testosterone 707, thymus 713, thyroid gland 714
glandular epithelium 719
glandular fever 394
glans 321, 550
see also clitoris 183, penis 550, urethra 741
glans clitoris 321
glans penis 321
glaucoma 276, **322**
diabetes 222
see also cornea 197, eye 274, iris 401, retina 604, sight 641, tonometry 724
glenohumeral joint 637
glenoid cavity 637
glenoid labrum 637
glia 504
gliding joint 407
globin 350, 640
globulins 322, 563
see also immunity 384, plasma 563
globus pallidus 537
glomerular capsule 412
glomerulonephritis 322–323, 497
see also dialysis 225, hypertension 373, kidney 411, urinary systems 39–41
glomerulosclerosis, diabetes 223
glomerulus 412
glossitis 323, 722
see also gingivitis 319, tongue 722
glossopharyngeal nerve 200, 459
tasting 694
glossopharyngeal neuralgia 502
glottis 757
glucagon 48, 222, 404
glucocorticoids 48, 64, 677
gluconeogenesis 686
glucose 686
glucose tolerance test 222
glue ear 61, 525
glue sniffing 660
gluten, celiac disease 162
gluteus maximus 362, 425
gluteus medius 362, 428
gluteus minimus 428
glycogen 271, 438, 686
glycosuria 412
goiter 323–324
see also Graves' disease 327, myxedema 489, thyroid gland 714, thyrotoxicosis 716
golden staph 674

golfer's elbow 100, 252, 701, 703
Golgi apparatus 162
Golgi tendon organs 628
gonadal dysgenesis 527
gonadotropic hormones 300
gonadotropin releasing hormone 370
gonadotropins 300
gonads 705
gonococcus 117
gonorrhea 324–325
see also pelvic inflammatory disease 546, sexually transmitted diseases 633
Goodpasture's syndrome 325
see also autoimmune disease 110, glomerulonephritis 322, kidney 411
goose bumps 27
gout 325
see also arthritis 103, joints 407
Graafian follicle 301, **325–326**
see also fertilization 288, menstruation 468, ovaries 526, ovulation 528, ovum 529, pregnancy 571, reproductive system, female 44–45
grafting 326, 563, 730
skin 648
see also immunosuppression 387, lymphatic/immune system 30–32, transplant surgery 730
grainy layer of epidermis 264
granular conjunctivitis 728
granulation tissue 341
granulocyte 162
granuloma inguinale 326
see also sexually transmitted diseases 633
grasp reflex 725
Graves' disease 327–328
see also exophthalmos 273, goiter 323, pituitary gland 320, thyroid gland 714
Grawitz's tumor 412
gray matter 138, 139
great saphenous vein 428, 616
greater trochanter 620
greenstick fracture 304–305
grief 258, **327**
grinder's disease 645
groin 327
see also hernia 360, lymph nodes 448
grommet 247
gross lesion 430
ground itch 367
group A streptococci 347
growth 327–328
see also dwarfism 239, gigantism 319, growth disorders 328, hormones 369, infancy 390, pituitary gland 320, puberty 469
growth deficiencies 289
growth disorders 328
see also achondroplasia 56, acromegaly 57, dwarfism 239, gigantism 319
growth hormone 48, 57, 58, 369
guanine 232
guarana 678
Guillain-Barré syndrome 328–329
see also nerves 500, neuropathy 505
gums 329
disease 697
see also gingivitis 319, teeth 696
gustation 694
Guthrie test 263, 557
gynecomastia 143, 271, 454

H

hacking, massage technique 456
Haemophilus influenzae type B 464
hair 332
hair follicles, infection of 301
hairy nevi 477
halitosis 333
see also gingivitis 319, gums 329, teeth 696
hallucinations 215, **333**
see also alcoholism 73, delirium 215, hallucinogens 333, schizophrenia 619
hallucinogens 234, **333**
see also drug dependence 233
hammer 339
hammer toe 304, **333**
see also foot 303
hamstring muscles 333, 428
see also fibula 296, hip 362, knee 414, tibia 716
hand 334–335
see also adduction and abduction 61, arteries 102, carpal tunnel syndrome 159, finger 297, muscles 483, nerves 500, radial nerve 593, skeletal system 15–19, tenosynovitis 703, ulnar nerve 739, wrist 763
hangnail 492
Hansen's disease 430
haploid cell 529
hard palate 479, 536
hardening of the arteries 103, 108
hare lip 183
Hashimoto's disease 336
see also autoimmune disease 110, hypothyroidism 378, thyroid gland 714
hashish 455
hatha yoga 766
HAV *see* hepatitis 354
hay fever 336
see also allergies 77, antigen tests 92, antihistamines 92, asthma 106, desensitization 220, respiratory system 36–38, rhinitis 78
HBV *see* hepatitis 354
HCG *see* human chorionic gonadotropin 180, 62
HCV *see* hepatitis 354
HDL *see* high-density lipoprotein 286
HDV *see* hepatitis 354
head 337–339
see also brain 138, ear 244, esophagus 269, eye 274, face 282, lacrimal glands 420, mouth 479, nose 508, pharynx 557, sinuses 645, sinusitis 645, skull 649, subarachnoid hemorrhage 684, teeth 696, throat 709, tinnitus 718, tongue 722, trachea 727
head lice 340
see also lice 432
headache 340–341
tension 704
see also brain 138, depression 217, hypertension 373, meningitis 464, migraine 474, osteoarthritis 520, sinusitis 645
healing 341
hearing 244, **342**, 627–628
aids 211, 248
damage 248
loss 209
tests 211, 248
see also deafness 209, ear 244
heart 344–347
development of 256, 291
fibrillation 295
see also angina pectoris, aorta 95, arrythmia 102, arteries 102, atherosclerosis 103, atrial septal defect 108, cardiomyopathy 158, circulatory system 33–35, coronary arteries 197, coronary artery disease 197, coronary thrombosis 198, endocarditis 259, fibrillation 295, hypertension 373, myocardial infarction 488, myocarditis 488, pacemaker 532, pericarditis 552, rheumatic fever 606, stenosis 675, ventricle 751, ventricular septal defect 751
heart attack 344
heartbeat 348
see also antiarrythmic drugs 90, arrythmia 102, beta-blockers 121, fibrillation 295, heart 344, mitral valve 476, pacemaker 532, pulse 585
heart block 344
heart cycle 346
heart disease 286, 344
from smoking 656
heart failure 250
heart muscle 485, 488
heart rate, rapid 692
heart strings 476
heart valves, mitral 476
heartburn 348–349
see also esophagus 269, gastroesophageal reflux 313, hiatus hernia 361, intestines 399, pregnancy 571
heat 628
heat rash 349
see also newborn 505, rash 594, skin 646
heatstroke 349
see also body temperature 132, fever 295
Heberden's nodes 521
heel pain 563
heel spur 349–350
see also bursitis 150, foot 303, fractures 304
Hellerwork 661
helper T cell 385
hemangioma 350
see also birthmarks 124
hematemesis 270, 758
hematocele 706
hematuria 412, 742
heme 350
hemianopia 644
hemiplegia 350, 541
due to stroke 683
see also paralysis 541, stroke 682
hemochromatosis 350
see also iron 402
hemodialysis 225, **350**
see also dialysis 225, kidney 411
hemoglobin 350–351, 475
see also anemia 84, red blood cells 596, sickle cell disease 640
hemoglobinuria 412
hemolysis 351, 671
hemolytic anemia 351
see also red blood cells 596, sickle cell disease 640, spleen 670, thalassemia 708
hemolytic anemia 85
hemolytic disease of the newborn 352
see also antibodies 90, rhesus factor 605
hemolytic jaundice 404
hemophilia 352
see also chromosomes 181, congenital abnormalities 192, genes 313
hemorrhage 352
see also blood vessels 131, bronchitis 148, cystitis 204, hemorrhoids 353, peptic ulcer 551, platelets 563, subarachnoid hemorrhage 684, vasculitis 747
hemorrhagic stroke 683
hemorrhoids 353
see also anus 94, constipation 194, rectum 596, thrombosis 711, veins 748
hemostatic system 711
hemothorax 565
Henle's loop 498
Henoch's purpura 586
heparin 91
hepatic artery 353
see also liver 438
hepatic ducts 122
hepatic encephalopathy 353
see also cirrhosis of the liver 182, hepatitis 354, liver 438, nervous system 24–26
hepatic liver 355
hepatitis 354, 360
see also alcoholism 73, cirrhosis of the liver 182, jaundice 404, liver 438, viruses 752, Wilson's disease 762
hepatocellular carcinoma 354
hepatocellular jaundice 404
hepatocytes 438
hepatoduodenal ligament 438
hepatolenticular degeneration 762
hepatoma 354
see also cancer 154, cirrhosis of the liver 182, hepatitis 354, liver 438
hepatorenal syndrome 356
see also cirrhosis of the liver 182, hepatitis 354, kidney 411, liver 438
herald patch 561

herbal medicine 356
herbalism 356–357
see also Ayurvedic medicine 111, Chinese herbalism 176, naturopathy 492
hereditary spherocytosis 351
heredity 358–359
see also chromosomes 181, congenital abnormalities 192, DNA 231, genes 313, genetic counseling 315
hernia 360
see also abdomen 52, groin 327, hiatus hernia 361
herniated disk 229
herniated nucleus pulposus 577
heroin 360, 492
withdrawal using methadone 472
see also detoxification 220, drug dependence 233, hepatitis 354, morphine 478, narcotics 492
herpes 210
genital 315
herpes simplex 185, **360–361**
see also chickenpox 168, infectious mononucleosis 394, viruses 752
herpes virus 752
herpes zoster 284, 636
heterosexuality 631
heterozygous thalassemia 708
HEV see hepatitis 354
hexosaminidase 696
HFV *see* hepatitis 354
HGH *see* human growth hormone 328
HGV *see* hepatitis 354
hiatal hernia *see* hiatus hernia 361
hiatus hernia 270, 349, 360, **361**
stomach 680
see also diaphragm 225, esophagitis 269, esophagus 269, heartburn 348, hernia 360, stomach 679
HIB *see* ***Haemophilus influenzae*** type B 464
hiccups 361
see also breathing 146, diaphragm 225
high blood pressure 92, 373
medications 235
hindbrain 25
hinge joint 407–408
hip 362–363
bones 425
fractures of 287
replacement 363
see also femur 287, fractures 304, joints 407, osteoarthritis 520, osteoporosis 524, pelvis 547, rheumatoid arthritis 607, rickets 609, skeletal system 15–19, synovial fluid 688
hippocampal gyrus 434
hippocampus 434–435, 462
Hirschsprung's disease 233, **364**
see also bowel 136, colon 187, congenital abnormalities 192, intestines 399
hirsutism 364
see also adrenal glands 64, hormones 369, virilization 751
histamine 336, **364**
see also allergies 77, anaphylaxis 83, antihistamines 92, hay fever 336
histocompatibility 730
histologic lesion 430
histoplasma capsulatum 364
histoplasmosis 364
histrionic personality disorder 555
HIV 364
see also AIDS 70, viruses 752
hives 743
Hodgkin's disease 365
see also cancer 154, chemotherapy 168, lymph nodes 448, lymphatic/immune system 30–32, non-Hodgkin's lymphoma 506
hole in the heart *see* septal defect 108, 256
Holter monitor 365
see also electrocardiogram 252, heart 344
home birth 170
home care 318, 365
home nursing 365
see also palliative care 536
home remedies 365
homeopathy 366
homeostasis 27
homograft 326
homosexuality 367
see also AIDS 70, bisexuality 124, HIV 364, sexuality 633
homozygous thalassemia 708
hookworm 367
see also worms 763
hordoleum 277
horehound 273
hormonal headache 340
hormonal therapy 367
hormone replacement therapy 367–368
see also cystitis 204, estrogen 270, hormones 369, menopause 465, osteoporosis 524, progesterone 576, urinary incontinence 742
hormones 48, **369–370**
see also adrenal glands 64, endocrine gland 260, endocrine system 48–49, menopause 465, ovaries 526, parathyroid glands 543, pituitary gland 560, placenta 561, puberty 582, testes 705, thyroid gland 714
Horner's syndrome 370
see also eye 274, pupil of eye 585
hot flashes (hot flushes) 465–466
housemaid's knee 371, 415
see also bursitis 150, knee 414
HRT *see* hormone replacement therapy 367
HSV-1 *see* herpes simplex 360
HSV-2 *see* herpes simplex 360
human chorionic gonadotropin 180, 562, 576
Human Genome Project 232
human growth hormone 328
human immunodeficiency virus *see* **HIV 364**
human papilloma virus 315
humanistic psychotherapy 581
humerus 371
see also arm 97, elbow 251, radius 100, skeletal system 15–19, ulna 738, ulnar nerve 739
humoral immune system 384, 692
Huntington's disease 294
see also brain 138, congenital abnormalities 192, genetic counseling 315, nerves 500
hyaline cartilage 160–161, 721
hydatid cyst 203
hydatid disease 372
see also liver 438, tapeworm 693
hydatidiform mole 372, 477
see also dilation and curettage 228, miscarriage 476, pregnancy 571
hydrocele 372
see also scrotum 622, testes 705
hydrocephalus 372
see also brain 138
hydrocortisone 60
hydrocortisone cream 250
hydrocortisone hormones 61
hydronephrosis 412, 498–499
hydrops fetalis 352, 605
hydrotherapy 372
see also aromatherapy 101, naturopathy 492
hydroxyapatite 475
hymen 372–373, 745
see also reproductive system, female 44–45, vagina 745
hyoglossus muscle 722
hyoid bone 496, 649, 651
hyperactivity 109
hyperalgesia 534
hypercalcemia 154
hyperemesis gravidarum 478
hyperglycemia 222, **373**
see also blood sugar tests 130, diabetes 222, insulin 398, pancreas 538
hypernasal speech 663
hypernephroma 412
hyperopia 641
hyperosmotics 423
hyperparathyroidism 544
hypersexuality 631
hypersomnia 654
hypersplenism 672
hypertension 213, **373–374**
see also arteriosclerosis 103, blood pressure 130, preeclampsia 570, toxemia 727
hypertensive retinopathy 604
hyperthermia 374
see also body temperature 132
hyperthyroidism 374–375, 716
see also goiter 323, Graves' disease 327, pituitary gland 560, thyroid gland 714, thyrotoxicosis 716
hypertrophic cardiomyopathy 158
hypertrophic gastritis 312
hypertrophic subaortic stenosis 158
hypertrophy, cardiac 158
hyperventilation 146
hypnosis 375
hypnotherapy 375
see also relaxation techniques 601
hypnotics 375
see also drug dependence 233, sedatives 625, sleeping pills 654, tranquilizers 729
hypocalcemia 376–377
see also calcium 154, osteomalacia 522, osteoporosis 524, parathyroid glands 543, rickets 609, vitamins 754
hypoglossal nerve 459, 500
hypoglycemia 222, **376**
see also blood sugar tests 130, diabetes 222, insulin 398, pancreas 538
hypokalemia 376
see also electrolytes 253, nutrition 509, potassium 570
hypomania 455
hyponatremia 376
see also sodium 659
hypoparathyroidism 376, **377**, 544
see also parathyroid glands 543
hypopharynx 557
hypophosphatasia 377
see also congenital abnormalities 192, enzyme deficiencies 263
hypophysis 377, 560
hypopituitarism 287
hypoplasia 377
see also congenital abnormalities 192
hyposomnia 654
hypospadias 377
see also penis 550, reproductive system, male 46–47, urethra 741, urinary systems 39–41
hypotension 377
see also blood pressure 130
hypothalamus 139, 267, **377–378**, 434–435
regulation of fluid 300
role in fertility 288
temperature control 700
see also autonomic nervous system 27–29, brain 138, diabetes 222, hormones 369, pituitary gland 560
hypothenar muscle 334
hypothermia 378
see also body temperature 132
hypothyroidism 378
see also cretinism 201, myxedema 489, pituitary gland 560, thyroid gland 714
hypoxia 378
hysterectomy 296, **378–379**, 488
see also endometriosis 261, fibroids 295, hormone replacement therapy 367, hysterosalpingo-oophrectomy 379, ovaries 526, reproductive system, female 44–45, uterus 743
hysterical amnesia 81
hysterosalpingogram 288, 379
hysterosalpingography 379
see also fallopian tubes 285, laparoscopy 420, salpingitis 616, uterus 743
hysterosalpingo-oophorectomy 379
see also cervix 166, fallopian tubes 285, hysterectomy 378, ovaries 526, uterus 743
hysteroscopy 379
see also cervix 166, fibroids 295, hysterectomy 378, uterus 743
hysterotomy 54

I

iatrogenic disease 382
IBS *see* irritable bowel syndrome 402
ibuprofen 507
ichthyosis 382, 595
see also skin 646
icterohemorrhagic fever 430
identical twins 734
idiopathic thrombocytopenic purpura 710
idoxuridine 93
Ig *see* immunoglobulin 32
ileitis 382
see also Crohn's disease 201, ileum 382, intestines 399
ileocecal junction 382
ileocecal valve 42
ileostomy 382
see also colostomy 188, ileum 382, intestines 399
ileum 382–383
see also Crohn's disease 201, digestive system 42–43, duodenum 237, gastroenteritis 312, intestines 399, jejenum 405
ileus 383
see also bowel 136, intestines 399, peristalsis 554
iliac arteries 102, 287
iliac veins 749
ilium 287, 362
imaging techniques 383
see also barium meal 119, CAT scan 161, magnetic resonance imaging 452, ultrasound 739, x-ray 764
immune disorders 32
immune response 32
immune system 92, 384
immunity 384–385
see also AIDS 70, allergies 77, antibodies 90, autoimmune disease 110, HIV 364, immunization 386, lymphatic/immune system 30–32, opportunistic infection 517, white blood cells 761
immunization 386
see also antibodies 90, diphtheria 228, hepatitis 354, measles 458, mumps 482, poliomyelitis 566, rubella 611, smallpox 655, tetanus 707, whooping cough 762
immunodeficiency 384, **386**
see also AIDS 70, cancer 154, HIV 364, leukemia 430, lymphatic/immune system 30–32, opportunistic infection 517
immunodeficiency diseases 32
immunogloblin 32
immunosuppression 387
see also autoimmune disease 110, corticosteroids 198, radiation therapy 472
impatiens 299
impetigo 284, **387**, 681
see also staphylococcal infections 674, streptococcal infections 681
implant, tooth 697
implantable cardiac defibrillator 213
impotence 387
see also erection 267, penis 550, sexual dysfunction 631
in vitro fertilization 387
see also embryo 255, fertilization 288, infertility 395, ovum 529, semen 625
incisional hernia 360
incisors 696, 698
incompetent cervix 388
see also cervix 166, childbirth 170, miscarriage 476, pregnancy 571, reproductive system, female 44–45, uterus 743
incomplete fracture 304
incontinence 317, **388**
urinary 742
see also bladder 124, urinary incontinence 742, urinary systems 39–41
incus 244, 649
indigestion 388
see also cholecystitis 179, digestive system 42–43, duodenal ulcer 237, duodenum 237, esophagus 269, gallstones 308
indirect laryngoscopy 421
indomethacin 507
infancy 390–392
see also breast feeding 136, bottle feeding 136, newborn 505, reflexes 598, sudden infant death syndrome 685
infant formula 136
infantile nephropathic cystinosis 204
infectious diseases 393–394
see also antibiotics 90, bacteria 117, DNA 231, inflammation 397, lymphatic/immune system 30–32, opportunistic infection 517, viruses 752
infectious mononucleosis 394
see also spleen 670, viruses 752, white blood cells 761
inferior turbinates 282
inferior vena cava 225, 749
infertility 395–397
see also artificial insemination 105, fertility 288, fertilization 288, in vitro fertilization 387, miscarriage 476, pregnancy 571, reproductive systems 44–47, sperm 664
inflammation 397
in mumps 482
healing role 341
see also tissue 719
inflammatory disease 296
influenza 397–398, 488
virus 752
see also common cold 189, immunity 384, immunization 386, infectious diseases 393, pneumonia 565, respiratory system 36–38, viruses 752
infrahyoid muscle 496
infrapatellar bursitis 150
infraspinatus muscle 610, 639
infundibulum 561
infusion, herbal 356
ingrown nail 492
inguinal canal 705
inguinal hernia 360, 622
inguinal ligament 287
inguinal region 327
inhalation 147
inherited congenital anomalies 192
inner ear 244
innominate bone 362
insomnia 398
see also jet lag 406, relaxation techniques 601, sleep disturbances 654, sleeping pills 654
inspiration 146, 225
insulin 49, 369, 370, **398–399**
see also blood sugar tests 130, diabetes 222, endocrine system 48–49, hyperglycemia 373, hypoglycemia 376, islets of Langerhans 403, pancreas 538
insulin-dependent diabetes 222, 398
insulinomas 376, 538
intellectual disability 289, **399**, 424
see also Down syndrome 233, fetal alcohol syndrome 289, learning disorders 289
intelligence quotient 399
interalveolar septa 37
intercerebral hemorrhage 165
intercondylar space 415
intercourse, sexual 632
intermediate neurons 504
internal capsule of thalamus 708
interosseous sacroiliac ligament 614
interosseus muscle 334
interstitial cells 46
interstitial lung disorders 296
interstitial nephritis 498
intertrigo 399
intervertebral disk 228
intestines 399–401
see also anus 94, bowel 136, bowel cancer 136, colon 187, digestive system 42–43, duodenum 237, ileum 382, incontinence 388, intussusception 401, irritable bowel syndrome 402, rectum 596
intoeing 559
intracellular electrolyte 475
intracellular fluid 39
intracellular infections 394
intracerebral hemorrhage 259, 373
intracranial hemorrhage 652
intraocular pressure 276, 724
intrathoracic pressure 38
intrauterine device 195
intravenous cholangiogram 179
intravenous pyelography 586
intrinsic tongue muscles 722
intussusception 401
see also bowel 136, intestines 399
invertebral disks 114
involuntary functions 122
involuntary muscles 20
involuntary nervous system 27
iodine deficiency 401
see also cretinism 201, goiter 323, hypothyroidism 378, thyroid gland 714
iodopsin 641
ionizing radiation 592
IQ *see* intelligence quotient 399
iridology 401
see also iris analysis 401
iris 274–275, **401–402**
see also cornea 197, eye 274, iritis 402, pupil of eye 585
iris analysis 401
iritis 402
see also cornea 197, eye 274, iris 401, photophobia 559
iron 402
see also anemia 84, hemochromatosis 350, hemoglobin 350, red blood cells 596
iron deficiency 453, 475, 597
iron deficiency anemia 402
irritable bowel syndrome 402–403
see also bowel 136, digestive system 42–43, intestines 399
ischemia 373, **403**
diabetes 223
see also angina pectoris 86, arteriosclerosis 103, circulatory system 33–35, myocardial infarction 488, stroke 682, transient ischemic attack 730
ischemic heart disease 403
see also angina pectoris 86, arteriosclerosis 103, coronary arteries 197, coronary artery disease 197, heart 344, myocardial infarction 488
ischium 333, 362
islets of Langerhans 403–404
see also endocrine glands 260, endocrine system 48–49, insulin 398, pancreas 538
isometric contraction 22
isotretinoin 57
IUD *see* intrauterine device 195
IVF *see* in vitro fertilization 387
IVP *see* intravenous pyelography 586
Iyengar yoga 766

J

Jadassohn-Lewandowski syndrome 532
jaundice 404
see also cirrhosis of the liver 182, gallstones 308, hemoglobin 350, hepatitis 354, liver 438, newborn 505, red blood cells 596
jaw 404–405, 651
see also face 282, sinuses 645, sinusitis 645, teeth 696
jaws, development of 257
jejunal button 406
jejunostomy tube 406
jejunum 405–406
see also celiac disease 162, Crohn's disease 201, digestive system 42–43, duodenum 237, gastroenteritis 312, ileum 382, intestines 399, peristalsis 554
jet lag 406
see also insomnia 398, sleep disturbances 654
jock itch 717
joint receptors 628

joints 407–408
see also ankylosing spondylitis 89, arthritis 103, bones 134, bursitis 150, gout 325, housemaid's knee 371, osteoarthritis 520, rheumatoid arthritis 607, skeletal system 15–19, synovial fluid 688, temporomandibular joint syndrome 699
JRA *see* juvenile rheumatoid arthritis 678
jugolodigastric nodes 31
jugular vein 409
see also veins 748
jugular vein 749
jumper's knee 703
juvenile melanoma 460
juvenile rheumatoid arthritis 678
juvenile-type diabetes 222
juxtaglomerular apparatus 40

K

kala-azar 409, 429
see also leishmaniasis 429
Kaposi's sarcoma 409
see also AIDS 70
Kawasaki's disease 409
see also inflammation 397
Kayser-Fleischer ring 762
keloid 409
see also collagen 186, scar 619, skin 646
keratin 332, **410**, 646
see also epidermis 263, skin 646
keratinocytes 459, 646
keratitis 410
see also cornea 197
keratosis 410
see also skin 646, skin cancer 648
kernicterus 352
ketoacidosis 222, 410
ketone bodies 410
ketosis 410
see also acidosis 56, diabetes 222
keyhole surgery 420
kidney 411–413
see also adrenal glands 64, dialysis 225, edema 250, glomerulonephritis 322, hemodialysis 350, hypertension 373, nephritis 497, peritoneal dialysis 225, pyelogram 586, pyelonephritis 497, urinary systems 39–41
kidney disease 412
kidney failure, mercury poisoning 471
kidney inflammation, mumps 482
kidney nephron 413
kidneys, development of 257
kidneys, regulation of electrolytes 253
killer T cell 72, 385
kissing disease 394
Klinefelter's syndrome 414
see also chromosomal abnormalities 180, chromosomes 181
kneading, massage technique 456
knee 414–416
see also bursitis 150, hamstring muscles 333, housemaid's knee 371, joints 407, knock-knee 417, leg 425, ligaments 433, muscles 483, synovial fluid 688
knee joint capsule 415
knee replacement 415
kneecap 287
knock-knee 417
see also knee 414
Korsakoff's amnesia 760
Krause's end bulbs 628
Kupffer cells 438
kwashiorkor 417
see also malnutrition 452
kyphosis 417
see also dowager's hump 417, lordosis 441, scoliosis 621, spine 668

L

labia majora 758
labia minora 183, 758
labor 171
labyrinth 420
labyrinthitis 420
see also balance 117, deafness 209, ear 244, semicircular canals 625, tinnitis 718, vertigo 751
lacrimal apparatus 276, 278
lacrimal bone 282, 649
lacrimal duct 208
lacrimal glands 282, **420**
see also eye 274, glands 319, Sjögren's syndrome 646
lacrimal sac 208, 278
lactase 263, 420
lactation 454
lactation-stimulating hormone 454
lactic acid 271
lacteals 31, 42
lactogenic hormone *see* prolactin 48
lactose 263, 454, 686
lactose intolerance 420
see also digestive system 42–43, gastroenteritis 312, intestines 399
lamina propria 261
laminae 751
laminectomy 670
lanugo 294, **420**
see also fetal development 291, hair 332
laparoscope 379
laparoscopy 288, **420–421**
see also fibroids 295, gallbladder 308, hernia 360, hysterectomy 378, in vitro fertilization 387, sterilization 676
laparotomy 421
large bowel 399
large intestine 399
laryngectomy 421
see also esophagus 269, larynx 423
laryngitis 421
see also croup 201, epiglottis 265, larynx 423, respiratory system 36–38, throat 709, trachea 727, vocal cords 757
laryngopharynx 557
laryngoscopy 421–423
larynx 422, **423**
see also epiglottis 265, pharynx 557, respiratory system 36–38, trachea 727, vocal cords 757
laser acupuncture 60
laser angioplasty 88
laser in-situ keratomileusis 644
laser, tattoo removal 696
late miscarriage 476
late-onset nephropathic cystinosis 204
lateral collateral ligament 416
lateral compartment 428
lateral epicondyle 703
lateral epicondylitis 701, 703
lateral femoral condyle 416
lateral malleolus 88
lateral pterygoid 405
latissimus dorsi 639
Laws of Cure, homeopathic 367
laxatives 423
see also bowel 136, constipation 194, intestines 399
LDL *see* low-density lipoprotein 179, 286
lead poisoning 423–424, 566
see also poisoning 566
learning disability 424
learning disorders 424
see also attention deficit hyperactivity disorder 109, autism 110, cerebral palsy 166, dyslexia 239, memory 461, speech 661
left atrium 344
left primary bronchus 148
left ventricle 344, 751
leg 425–428
see also ankle 88, compartment syndrome 191, embolism 254, foot 303, hamstring muscles 333, hip 362, knee 414, muscles 483, pelvis 547, thrombosis 711, varicose veins 747, veins 748
Legionella bacillus 117
Legionnaire's disease 429
see also lung 443, pneumonia 565, sputum tests 674
leiomyomas 470, 744
leiomyomata uteri 295
leishmaniasis 429
see also kala-azar 409
lens 274
lentigo 429
see also melanoma 460
lepromatous leprosy 429
leprosy 429–430
leptospirosis 430
lesbian 367
lesion 430
see also birthmarks 124, melanoma 460, moles 477, scar 619
lesser pelvis 547
leukemia 233, **430–432**
see also cancer 154, lymphocytes 449, spleen 670, white blood cells 761
leukocytes 341, 761
leukoplakia 432, 724
see also mouth 479, tongue 722
leukorrhea 432, 745
see also cervix 166, estrogens 270, vagina 745
levator scapulae 639
Leydig cells 46
LGV *see* lymphogranuloma venereum 449
LH *see* luteinising hormone 301, 528
libido 631
lice 432–433
see also relapsing fever 601, scabies 617, typhus 735
lichen planus 433, 595
lichen simplex chronicus 503
lid-droop 487
life support 433
see also death 212
ligaments 433–434, 721
see also ankle 88, joints 407, sprain 673
light therapy 434, 740
see also seasonal affective disorder 624, sleep disturbances 654
light-receptor cells 641
limbgirdle dystrophy 487
limbic system 138, **434–435**, 462
see also Alzheimer's disease 79, amnesia 80, brain 138, hypothalamus 377, thalamus 708
lingual tonsil 724
lip 435–436
see also face 282, mouth 479, mucous membranes 481
lipases 286
lipids 286, **436**
see also fats 286, nutrition 509
lipodystrophy 436
see also acromegaly 57, diabetes 222, fats 286, metabolism 471
lipolysis *see* liposuction 436–437
lipoma 436
see also tumors 734
lipoproteins 286
liposuction 436–437
see also cosmetic surgery 198
lisping 437, 663
see also speech 661
listeriosis 437
see also bacteria 117, food poisoning 302
lithium carbonate 123, 455
lithium citrate 455
lithotripsy 437
see also bladder 124, gallbladder 308, kidney 411, ureter 741
liver 438–440
see also cirrhosis of the liver 182–183, digestive system 42–43, hemochromatosis 350, hepatitis 354, insulin 398, jaundice 404, liver function blood tests 441, portal hypertension 568, Wilson's disease 762
liver biopsy 354, 440
liver cirrhosis, alcoholism 75
liver damage, alcoholism 73
liver failure 356
liver flukes 440
liver function blood tests 441
see also liver 438
liver lobule 439
liver sinusoids 438
liver spots 429
liver/gallbladder flushes 221
lobar bronchi 149
lobes, brain 140
lobular pneumonia 565
lobules, breast 142, 144
local anesthesia 86
lockjaw 707

longsightedness 641
long-term memory 461
loop of Henle 412
loose connective tissue 720
lordosis 441
see also kyphosis 417, scoliosis 621, spine 668
Lou Gehrig's disease 82
low-density lipoprotein 179
LSD see lysergic acid diethylamide 333
lumbago 441
see also disk, intervertebral 228, sciatica 620, spine 668
lumbar disk, damage 229
lumbar puncture 441
see also disk, intervertebral 228, spine 668
lumbar radiculopathy 577
lumbar region of the spine 668
lumbar spinal nerves 667
lumbar traction 729
lumbar vertebrae 114, 751
lumbricals 335
lump 142
lumpectomy 143, **441**
see also breast cancer 143, mastectomy 457
lung cancer 442
see also cancer 154, lungs 443, smoking 656
lung capacity test 585
lung hilum 443
lungs 443–446
see also asbestosis 105, asthma 106, breathing 146, bronchitis 148, bronchoscopy 148, emphysema 258, farmer's lung 286, lung cancer 442, pneumothorax 565, pulmonary function tests 585, respiratory system 36–38, smoking 656, tuberculosis 733
lungs, regulation of electrolytes 253
lupus erythematosus 447, 487
see also autoimmune disease 110
luteal phase, of menstrual cycle 261
luteinising hormone 48, 301, 370, 528, 707
lying, in children 176
Lyme arthritis 447
Lyme borreliosis 447
Lyme disease 447
see also ticks 717
lymph 447–448
see also lymph nodes 448, lymphatic/immune system 30–32, lymphatic vessels 448
lymph nodes 320, **448**, 460
effect of massage 456
see also lymphatic vessels 448, lymphatic/immune system 30–32
lymph node biopsy 448
lymph glands *see* lymph nodes 320, 448, 460
lymphadenopathy 31
lymphangiography 31
lymphangitis 31, 448
lymphatic capillaries 448
lymphatic/immune system 30–32, 448
lymphatic tissue 720
lymphatic vessels 448–449
see also elephantitis 254, filariasis 297, lymph 447, lymph nodes 448
lymphatics 341
lymphedema 448
lymphocytes 448, **449**, 761
see also lymphatic/immune system 30–32, spleen 670, T cells 692, white blood cells 761
lymphogranuloma inguinale 449
lymphogranuloma venereum 449
see also granuloma inguinale 326, lymphogranuloma inguinale 449, sexually transmitted diseases 633
lymphoid organs 31
lymphoid tissue 201
lymphoma 154, 365, 507
lysergic acid diethylamide 333
lysozyme 615

M

macrophages 162, 384, 761
macula 452
macular degeneration 452
see also eye 274, retina 604
magnesium 475
magnetic resonance imaging 452
see also CAT scan 161, imaging techniques 383, ultrasound 739, x-ray 764
major tranquilizers 93
malaria 452
see also infectious diseases 393
male incontinence 389
male menopause 631
male pattern baldness 118
male reproductive system 46–47
male sexual arousal 632
male sterilization 676
malignant hypertension 374
malignant melanoma 460
malignant tumor 734
mallet finger 297
mallet toe 304
malleus 244, 649
malnutrition 250, **452–453**
see also eating disorders 248, minerals 474, nutrition 509, pellagra 546, rickets 609, scurvy 622
malocclusion 453, 697
see also braces 137, orthodontics 519, teeth 696
malt worker's lung 446
maltose 686
mammary glands 142, 319, 321, **454**
see also breast 142, breast feeding 144, estrogens 270, menstruation 468, oxytocin 529, progesterone 576
mammogram 454
mammography 144, **454**
see also breast 142, breast cancer 144
mammoplasty 454–455
see also breast 142, cosmetic surgery 198, plastic surgery 563
mandible 282, 284, 404, 649, 651
mandibular nerve 732
manganese 476
mania 455
see also bipolar disorder 123, depression 217
manic-depressive illness 123
manipulation, chiropractic 178
Mantoux test 455
see also tuberculosis 733
mantra 459
manual defibrillator 213
manual lymph drainage 455
see also lymph 447, lymphatic/immune system 30–32, massage 455
manubrium 677
MAO *see* monamine-oxidase 91
maple sugar urine disease 472
Marfan's syndrome 193
marijuana 333, **455**
see also drug dependence 233
marriage counseling *see* relationship counseling 601
masculinization 751
masochism 631
massage 455–457
see also aromatherapy 101, Ayurvedic medicine 111, manual lymph drainage 455, shiatsu 634, somatic therapies 660
massage, reflexology 599
masseter muscle 405
mast cell 385
mastectomy 457
see also breast 142, breast cancer 143
mastitis 143, **457**
see also breast 142, breast feeding 144, fibrocystic disease 295
mastoid bone 247
mastoiditis 458
see also ear 244, otitis media 525
masturbation 63, 458
maté 678
maturity onset diabetes 222
maxillae 404, 508
maxillary bone 282, 284, 649
maxillary nerve 732
maxillary sinus 405
MCP joints *see* metacarpophalangeal joints 334
MD *see* muscular dystrophy 487
ME *see* myalgic encephalomyelitis 181
measles 458, 595
see also immunization 386, infectious diseases 393, viruses 752
measles vaccine 458
mechanoreceptors 534, 628
medial collateral ligament 415
medial epicondyle 739
medial epicondylitis 703
medial malleolus 89, 716
medial pterygoid 405
medial tibial stress syndrome 635
median nerve 763
mediastinum 443
medication 236
meditation 458–459
Mediterranean anemia 708
medulla oblongata 64, 139, **459**
see also brain 138, skull 649, spinal cord 665
Meet's lines 492
mefanamic acid 507
megalomania 459
see also paranoia 542, personality disorders 555
meibomian gland 167, 279
meiosis 289
Meissner's corpuscles 628
melancholia 217
melanin 264, 332, **459**, 687
see also keratin 410, melanoma 460
melanocytes 459–460, 687
melanoma 460
see also moles 477, skin cancer 648, sun exposure 687
melasma 460
see also Addison's disease 60, menopause 465, pregnancy 571, sun exposure 687
melatonin 461
see also insomnia 398, jet lag 406
melioidosis 461
see also bacteria 117, Whitmore disease 461
membrane 461
see also connective tissue 193, mucous membranes 481
membrane, cell 162
memory 461–463
see also Alzheimer's disease 79, Creutzfeld-Jakob disease 201, dementia 215, learning disorders 424, Wernicke-Korsakoff syndrome 760
memory B cell 384
memory improvement 463
memory T cell 72, 385
menarche 468
Menière's disease 463
see also deafness 209, ear 244, hearing 342, semicircular canals 625, tinnitus 718, vertigo 751
meninges 337, 462, **463**
see also brain 138, meningitis 464, spinal cord 665
meningioma 463
meningitis 463, **464**
see also brain 138, encephalitis 259, immunization 386, meninges 463, spinal cord 665
meningocele 464
see also congential abnormalities 192, hydrocephalus 372, spinal cord 665
meningococcal disease 464
see also meningitis 464, septicemia 629
meningococcus 117, 464
meningomyelocele 464, 665
menopause 262, **465–467**
see also ageing 66, angina 86, breast 142, estrogens 270, hormone replacement therapy 367, menstruation 468, osteoporosis 524, progesterone 576, reproductive system, female 44–45, testosterone 707, urinary incontinence 742
menstrual phase, of menstrual cycle 261
menstrual problems 469

menstruation 62, **468–470**
see also fibroids 295, menopause 465, ovaries 526, ovulation 528, premenstrual syndrome 575, progesterone 576, prostaglandins 578, puberty 582, reproductive system, female 44–45
mental illness 580
psychosis 580
schizophrenia 619
mental retardation 399
meperidine 478
mercury poisoning 471
see also poisoning 566
mercy killing 212
meridians 59
Merkel's disks 628
mescaline 333
mesencephalon 473
mesenteries 52
mesoderm 291
mesomorph 132
mesothelioma 471
see also asbestosis 105, lungs 443
messenger RNA 369
metabolic rate 472
metabolism 36, **471–472**
see also amino acids 80, diabetes 222, enzyme deficiencies 263, hormones 369, phenylketonuria 557
metacarpal bone 334
metacarpophalangeal joint 334
metastasis 472
see also cancer 154
metatarsals 304
methadone 472
see also drug dependence 233, heroin 360
methandrostenolone 486
methotrexate 220
microangiopathy 157
microcephaly 233, **473**
microfilariae 297
micronutrients 754
microscopic lesion 430
microsurgery 473
mid-inguinal point 287
midbrain 25, 139, **473**
see also brain 138, eye 274, medulla oblongata 459, spinal cord 665
middle ear 473
damage 210
infection 458
see also cochlea 184, ear 244, hearing 342, otitis media 525, mifepristone 54
MIFT *see* microinjection fallopian transfer 396
migraine 474
see also headache 340
migraine headache 340
migraine with aura 474
mild tranquilizers 94
miliaria 225, 349
milk glands 144
milk leg 428
milk lines 454
miner's phthisis 645
mineralocorticoids 49, 64, 474, 677
see also hormones 369
minerals 474–476
see also calcium 154, electrolytes 253, flouridation 300, iodine deficiency 401, iron 402, lead poisoning 423, nutrition 509, potassium 570, sodium 659
mini-stroke 216
minoxidil 333
miscarriage 53, 289, **476**
see also abortion 53, dilation and curettage 228, placenta 561, pregnancy 571
mitochondria 162
mitosis 162, 291
mitral insufficiency 476
mitral stenosis 38, 476
mitral valve 344, **476–477**
incompetence 34
see also heart 344, ventricle 751
mittelschmerz 477, 528
see also menstruation 468
mobilization, chiropractic 178
modified mastectomy 457
molars 696, 698
molds 336
mole 460
moles 477
see also choriocarcinoma 180, melanoma 460, sun exposure 687
molluscum contagiosum 477
see also viruses 752
monamine-oxidase 91
Mongolian blue spots 124
Mongolian slant 233
Mongolian spot 477
mono diets 221
monoamines 217
monocyte 761
monosaccharides 686
monozygotic twins 734
mons pubis 45
mood 258
mood swings 217
moon face, Cushing's syndrome 202
morning sickness 478
see also nausea 493, pregnancy 571
morning-after pill 54, 195
moro reflex 725
morphine 478
see also narcotics 492
Morton's neuroma 503
morula 291
motion sickness 478
see also balance 117, sea sickness 623
motor activity, brain areas 141
motor axons 500
motor fibers 667
motor neurons 504
motor systems 25
mouth 338, **479–480**
see also gingivitis 319, gums 329, jaw 404, lip 435, palate 536, salivary glands 615, teeth 696, tongue 722
mouth-to-mouth resuscitation 146
mouth ulcers 480
MRI scan 266
MRI *see* magnetic resonance imaging 452
mRNA *see* messenger RNA 369
MS *see* multiple sclerosis 481
mucopurulent bronchitis 148
mucosa 481
mucous membranes 481
see also mouth 479, nose 508, respiratory system 36–38
multi-infarct dementia 216
multilocular cystadenoma 526
multiple sclerosis 481–482
see also brain 138, neurons 504, nervous system 24–26, spinal cord 665
mumps 482
see also immunization 386, meningitis 464, viruses 752
muscae volitantes 299
muscle relaxant drugs 486
muscle spindles 628
muscle tissue 485, 720
muscle 483–486
branchial cyst 142
effect of massage 456
leg 426
of the hand 335
types of 484–485
see also anabolic steroids 82, Bell's palsy 121, bones 135, cramp 199, gangrene 310, joints 407, muscular dystrophy 487, myasthenia gravis 487, peristalsis 554, poliomyelitis 566, skeletal system 15–19
muscular dystrophy 487
see also congenital abnormalities 192, Duchenne muscular dystrophy 237, muscle 483
muscular system 20–23
music therapy 487
see also dance movement therapy 208
mutation 232
during fetal stage 294
of genes 313
myalgic encephalomyelitis 181
myasthenia gravis 487
see also autoimmune disease 110, muscles 483, thymus gland 713
mycosis fungoides 487–488, 648
see also cancer 154, lymphatic/immune system 30–32
myelin 488, 500
myelin sheath 481
myelinated axons 500
myelitis 488
see also spinal cord 665
myelograms 488
myelography 488
see also spinal cord 665, x-ray 764
myeloma 488
see also bone marrow biopsy 132, bones 134
myocardial infarction 373, **488**
see also arrhythmia 102, atherosclerosis 108, coronary artery disease 197, fibrillation 295, heart 344
myocarditis 347, **488**
see also heart 344
myocardium 488
myofibrils 22, 483
myoglobin 402, 475
myomas, in the uterus 744
myomectomy 296, **488–489**
see also fibroids 295, hysterectomy 378, hysteroscopy 379, uterus 743
myometrium 743
myopia 274, **489,** 641
see also contact lenses 194, eye 274, sight 641
myosin filaments 22
myositis, muscle 486
myotonic dystrophy 487
myringotomy 525
myxedema 489
see also Hashimoto's disease 336, hypothyroidism 378, pituitary gland 560, thyroid gland 714

N

NA *see* Narcotics Anonymous 221, 235
nail bed 492
nail bed hypertrophy 532
nails 492
see also cuticle 202, finger 297, keratin 410
nandrolone 486
nappy rash 225
naproxen 507
narcissistic personality disorder 555
narcolepsy 492
see also sleep apnea 653
narcotic analgesics 492
Narcotics Anonymous 221, 235
narcotics 492
see also analgesics 82, drug dependence 233, methadone 472, morphine 478
nasal allergies 213
nasal bone 282, 508, 649
nasal polyps 568
nasal septum 282, 508
nasolacrimal duct 278
nasopharyngeal tonsils 724
nasopharyngoscope 421
nasopharynx 557
natural killer cells 32, 761
naturopathic medicine 492
naturopathy 492–493
see also counseling 199, detoxification 220, flower remedies and essences 299, hydrotherapy 372, massage 455, orthmolecular therapy 520, relaxation techniques 601
nausea 493
see also morning sickness 478, motion sickness 478, sea sickness 623, vomiting 758
navicular 88
NCPB *see* neurolytic celiac plexus block 660
nearsightedness 274, 489, 641
neck 494–496
see also carotid artery 159, disk, intervertebral 228, epiglottis 265, esophagus 269, jugular vein 409, larynx 423, pharynx 557, quadriplegia 591, spinal cord 665, thyroid gland 714, torticollis 724, trachea 727, vagus nerve 747, vertebrae 751, vocal cords 757, whiplash 760

necrophilia 631
necrotizing fasciitis 681
needle biopsy 497
see also biopsy 123
negative feedback mechanism 370
nematode worms, toxocariasis 727
Neonatal Behavioral Assessment Scale 506
neonatal anemia 605
neoplasm 734
nephrectomy 412
nephritis 250, **497–498**
see also dialysis 225, glomerulonephritis 322, kidney 411, pyelitis 486, pyelonephritis 586, urinary systems 39–41
nephroblastoma 412, **498**
see also cancer 154, kidney 411
nephrogenic diabetes insipidus 225
nephrolithiasis 412
nephron 411, **498**
see also bladder 124, kidney 411, ureter 741, urinary systems 39–41
nephrosis 412, **499**
see also diabetes 222, glomerulonephritis 322, kidney 411, lupus erythematosus 447, urinary systems 39–41
nephrotic syndrome 412, 499
nerve cells 504
nerve conduction test 499
see also nerves 500
nerve stimulation, tasting 695
nerves 500–501
see also autonomic nervous system 27–29, Bell's palsy 121, brain 138, carpal tunnel syndrome 159, Guillain-Barré syndrome 328, multiple sclerosis 481, nerve conduction test 499, nervous system 24–26, neuritis 502, neuroma 503, neuropathy 505, radial nerve 592, sciatic nerve 620, spinal cord 665, trigeminal nerve 731, ulnar nerve 739, vagus nerve 747
nervous system 24–26, 85
nervous tissue 719
nettle rash 743
neural signals 276
neural tissue 501, 720
neural tube 291, 464
neural tube defect 502
see also brain 138, fetal development 291, hydrocephalus 372, nervous system 24–26, spina bifida 665, spinal cord 665
neuralgia 502
see also carpal tunnel syndrome 159, nerves 500, shingles 636, tic douloureux 717, trigeminal nerve 731
neuritis 502–503
see also multiple sclerosis 481, nerves 500, optic nerve 517
neuritis, alcoholism 74
neuroblastoma 503
see also cancer 154
neurodermatitis 503
see also dermatitis 218, eczema 250
neurofibromatosis 477, **503**
see also chromosomal abnormalities 180, nerves 500, nervous system 24–26
neuroglia 719
neurohypophysis 561
neuroleptics 93
neurolytic celiac plexus block 660
neuroma 503–504
see also ear 244, nerves 500, tinnitus 718, tumor 734
neuromuscular blocking drugs 486
neurons 26, **504–505**, 719
see also brain 138, epilepsy 265, nervous system 24–26, reflexes 598, spinal cord 665
neuropathy 505
see also nerves 500, peripheral nervous system 553
neutrophil 69, 761
nevus flammeus 350
newborn 505–506
see also infancy 390, reflexes 598, sudden infant death syndrome 685, umbilical cord 740
niacin 756
Nicolas-Favre disease 449
nicotine 506, 678
see also smoking 656, withdrawal 762
night terrors 654
night blindness 506
see also eye 274, retina 604, retinitis pigmentosa 604
nightmares 654
nipple 506
see also breast 142, breast feeding 144, Paget's disease of the breast 533
nitrogen gas bubbles 212
nitrous oxide gas, during birth 172
nits 340, 432
NK cells *see natural killer cells* 32
nociceptors 534, 627–628
nocturia 579
non-A hepatitis 354
non-B hepatitis 354
non-essential amino acids 80
non-Hodgkin's lymphoma 506–507
see also cancer 154, Hodgkin's disease 365, lymph nodes 448, lymphatic/immune system 30–32
non-insulin dependent diabetes 222
non-ionizing radiation 592
non-REM sleep 653
non-steroidal anti-inflammatory drugs 93, **507**
see also analgesics 82
nontropical sprue 162
norepinephrine 27
nose 282, 337, **508**
see also common cold 189, hay fever 336, mucous membranes 481, nosebleed 508, olfactory system 516, smell 655
nose surgery 284
nosebleed 508
see also blood 128, nose 508, platelets 563
nostrils 508
NSAIDs *see* non-steroidal anti-inflammatory drugs 93, 507
nuchal region 494
nuclear scan 383
nucleic acid testing 508
nucleotides 313
nucleous pulposus 228, 670
numbness 508
see also nerves 500, nervous system 24–26
nutrients 511
nutrition 509–513
during pregnancy 573
see also breast feeding 144, cholesterol 179, digestive system 42–43, eating disorders 248, fats 286, minerals 474, obesity 514, vitamins 754, weight 759
nutritional deficiency 215
nutritional disorders 453
nymphomania 631
nystagmus 513
see also eye 274

O

obesity 272, **514–515**
see also body mass index 132, eating disorders 248, fats 286, hypothalamus 377, nutrition 509
oblique fracture 305
obsessive-compulsive disorder 515
see also antidepressants 91, behavior therapy 120, depression 217, personality disorders 555
obstruction, bowel 401
obstructive jaundice 404, **515–516**
see also duodenum 237, gallstones 308, hepatitis 354, jaundice 404, liver 438, pancreas 538, pancreatitis 540
obturator nerve 428
occipital bone 649–650
occipital lobe 26, 138
occupational lung disease 446
occupational therapy 599
OCD *see* obsessive compulsive disorder 515
oils 511
Oki yoga 766
olecranon bursitis 150
olfactory apparatus 655
olfactory nerve 200
olfactory path 655
olfactory receptors 628
olfactory system 516–517
see also neurons 504, nose 508, smell 655
oligospermia 396
oliguria 412
omenta 52
omphalocele 517
see also abdomen 52, congenital abnormalities 192, intestines 399
onchocerciasis 763
onychomycosis 492, 717
oocyte 44, 529
oophorectomy 517
see also hysterectomy 378, ovarian cysts 526, ovaries 526
open-angle glaucoma 322
ophthalmoscope 517
ophthalmoscopy 517
see also eye 274
opium 492
opportunistic infection 517
see also candidiasis 157, cold sores 185, genital herpes 315, herpes simplex 360, pneumonia 565, toxoplasmosis 727
opthalmic nerve 732
optic atrophy 517
see also blindness 127, eye 274, optic nerve 517
optic disk 276
optic nerve 200, 276, **517–518**
see also cranial nerve 200, eye 274, nerves 500, nervous system 24–26, neuritis 502, papilledema 540, retina 604
optic neuritis 503, **518**
see also autoimmune disease 110, eye 274, lupus erythematosus 447, multiple sclerosis 481, neuritis 502, sight 641
optic system 276
optical axis 276
oral cancer 480, **518**
see also cancer 154, mouth 479, smoking 656
oral cavity 479
oral contraceptives 518–519
see also contraception 194, estrogens 270, follicle stimulating hormone 300, hormones 369, hypertension 373, menstruation 468, reproductive systems 44–47, stroke 682, thromboembolism 711
orbicularis oris 479
orbit 337
orchiectomy 706
orchitis 482, **519**, 706
see also chlamydia 178, gonorrhea 324, mumps 482, prostatitis 579, testes 705, urethritis 742
organ of Corti 209, 246, 343
organ rejection 385
organelles 162
organs, development of 256
orgasm 633
orgasm problems 631
oriental sore 429
ornithosis 580
oropharynx 479, 557
orthodontics 519–520
see also braces 137, malocclusion 453, teeth 696
orthomolecular therapy 520
see also amino acids 80, antioxidants 93, minerals 474, vitamins 754
orthostatic hypotension 231
Osgood-Schlatter disease 520
see also knee 414, tibia 716
ossicles 244, 339, 343, 649
ossification 66
osteitis deformans 533
osteoarthritis 317, 341, **520–521**
of the hip joint 362–363
see also arthritis 103, hip 362, inflammation 397, joints 407, knee 414
osteoblasts 135, 341
osteochondritis dissecans 522
see also elbow 251, joints 407, knee 414

osteochondrosis 522
see also bones 134, cartilage 160, Osgood-Schlatter disease 520, Perthes' disease 556
osteoclasts 135, 544
osteocytes 135
osteogenesis imperfecta 522
see also bones 134, fractures 304
osteomalacia 376, **522**
see *also* bones 134
osteomyelitis 522
see *also* bones 134
osteopathy 523–524
see also chiropractic 177
osteoporosis 271, 287, 317, 376, 466, **524–525**
see also bones 134, calcium 154, estrogens 270, hormone replacement therapy 367, kyphosis 417
osteoprogenitor cells 135
osteotomy 417
otitis externa 525
see also ear 244
otitis media 525
see also deafness 209, ear 244
otolaryngologist 211
otoliths 246
otoplasty 284
otosclerosis 525–526
see also deafness 209, ear 244, hearing 342
outer ear 244
oval window 244
ovarian cysts 526
see also endometriosis 261, endometrium 261, ovaries 526, Stein-Leventhal syndrome 565
ovarian hormone levels 367
ovarian tumor 364
ovaries 526–527
see also estrogens 270, menstruation 468, ovarian cysts 526, ovulation 528, progesterone 576, reproductive system, female 44–45, Stein-Leventhal syndrome 675, Turner's syndrome 734
overbite 453, 520
overdose 527–528
see also barbiturates 119, cocaine 183, detoxification 220, drug dependence 233, heroin 360, methadone 472, poisoning 566, sleeping pills 654, stimulants 678, tranquilizers 729, vitamins 754
overdue birth 173
overflow incontinence 388
ovulation 528–529
see also estrogens 270, fertility 288, fertilization 288, follicle stimulating hormone 300, infertility 395, menstruation 468, mittelschmerz 477, ovaries 526, ovum 529, progesterone 576, reproductive system, female 44–45
ovum 529
cysts 301
see also cells 162, chromosomes 181, embryo 255, fertilization 288, hormones 369, ovaries 526, reproductive system, female 44–45, sperm 664, Turner's syndrome 734, X chromosome 764, Y chromosome 765
oxyhemoglobin 350
oxyntic cells 679
oxytocin 48, 454, **529**
see also breast feeding 144, childbirth 170, hormones 369, mammary glands 454, pituitary gland 320
ozone layer 687

P

pacemaker 344, **532**
see also heart 344
pachydermoperiostosis 532
see also skin 646
pachyonychia 532
see also nails 492
Pacinian corpuscles 628
Paget's cells 533
Paget's disease of bone 533
see also bones 134, Paget's disease of the breast 533
Paget's disease of the breast 533
see also breast 142, breast cancer 143, melanoma 460, nipple 506
pain 534–535, 628
see also analgesics 82, brain 138, narcotics 492, nerves 500, nervous system 24–26, neurons 504, spinal cord 665
pain receptors 534
painful arc syndrome 639, 701
palate 536
see also jaw 404, mouth 479, teeth 696
palatine bone 282, **536**, 649
see also nose 508, palate 536, skull 649
palatine tonsil 724
palliative care 536
see also death 212
pallidotomy 537
see also brain 138, nervous system 24–26, Parkinson's disease 544
palpitations 537
see also arrhythmia 102, fibrillation 295, heart 344, tachycardia 692
palsy, cerebral 166
Pancoast's syndrome **370,** 537
see also cancer 154, Horner's syndrome 370, lungs 443
Pancoast's tumor 537
pancreas 538–539
see also amino acids 80, diabetes 222, digestive system 42–43, endocrine system 48–49, islets of Langerhans 403, insulin 398, pancreatitis 540, Zollinger-Ellison syndrome 767
pancreatic islets 538
pancreatitis 540
see also alcoholism 73, diabetes 222, gallstones 308, pancreas 538
pancytopenia 69
panic attacks 540
see also agoraphobia 69, anxiety 94, anxiolytics 94, behavior therapy 120
pantothenic acid 756
Pap smear 540
see also cervix 166, reproductive system, female 44–45
Papanicolaou smear *see* Pap smear 540
papillae 628, 722
on the tongue 694
papillary adenocarcinoma 716
papillary muscle 476
papilledema 540
see also eye 274, optic nerve 517
papilloma 540
see also epidermis 263, warts 759
papillomavirus 759
pappataci fever 558
paracentesis 541
see also abdomen 52, ascites 106
paracetamol 83
paraesophageal hiatus hernia 361
parafollicular cells 48, 714
parahippocampal gyrus 434
paralysis 541–542
see also brain 138, hemiplegia 350, nerves 500, nervous system 24–26, paraplegia 542, quadriplegia 591, rehabilitation 599, spinal cord 665
paranasal sinuses 338, 508, 645
paranoia 542
see also personality disorders 555
paranoid disorder 542
paranoid personality disorder 556
paraphilia 631
paraphimosis 551
paraplegia 542–543
see also nervous system 24–26, paralysis 541, quadriplegia 591, rehabilitation 599, spinal cord 665
parasympathetic nerve 348
parasympathetic nervous system 28, 554
parathyroid glands 260, 320, **543–544**
see also calcium 154, endocrine glands 260, glands 319, hormones 369, thyroid gland 714
parathyroid hormone 48, 377
paratyphoid 544
see also gastroenteritis 312, typhoid 734
paresthesia 508
parietal bone 649
parietal cells 679
parietal lobe 26, 138
Parkinson's disease 544–545
see also nerves 500, nervous system 24–26, neurons 504
Parkinsonian syndrome 239
paronychia 492, **545**
see also nails 492
parotid glands 616, 646
paroxysmal tachycardia 692
parrot fever 580
parthenogenesis 289
partial blindness 127
partial denture 217
passive-aggressive personality disorder 556
passive immunity 384
passive smoking 658
patella 287, 414
patellar ligament 590
patellar tendinitis 701
patent ductus arteriosus 294, 347, **545**
see also atrial septal defect 108, fetal development 291, heart 344, lungs 443, placenta 561
pathologic fracture 304–305
PDD *see* autism 110
peak flow meter 146, 585
pectinate line 596
pectoral girdle 637–638
pectoral muscles 545–546
see also collar bone 186, muscle 483, ribs 608, scapula 618, sternum 676
pectoralis major muscle 545, 639, 677
pectoralis minor 545, 639
pedicles 751
pediculosis pubis 634
pedophilia 631
pellagra 546
see also amino acids 80, vitamins 754
pelvic cavity 547
pelvic diaphragm 547
pelvic floor 547
pelvic floor muscles 546, 547
see also bladder 124, bowel 136, hip 362, intestines 399, pelvis 547, prolapse 577, sacrum 614, urinary incontinence 742, uterus 743
pelvic girdle 425
pelvic harness 362
pelvic inflammatory disease 546–547
see also cervix 166, fallopian tubes 285, gonorrhea 324, infertility 395, peritonitis 555, reproductive system, female 44–45
pelvic inlet 547
pelvic socket 362
pelvis 547–548
see also coccyx 184, hip 362, prolapse 577, sacrum 614, skeletal system 15–19
pemphigoid 548
see also autoimmune disease 110
pemphigus 548
see also autoimmune disease 110
penicillin 548
see also antibiotics 90, bacteria 117
penis 550–551
see also circumcision 181, epispadias 267, glans 321, gonorrhea 324, impotence 387, Peyronie's disease 556, priapism 576, reproductive system, male 46–47, sexual intercourse 632, sexually transmitted diseases 633, syphilis 689, urethra 741, urethritis 742, urinary systems 39–41
pennate muscles 20
peptic ulcer 551–552
see also digestive system 42–43, duodenum 237, esophagus 269, stomach 679

peptide hormones 369
perennial rhinitis 336
pericardial effusion 552
pericardial sac 225
pericardial tamponade 158
pericarditis 552, 741
see also heart 344, pericardium 552
pericardium 552
see also cardiac tamponade 158, heart 344, pericarditis 552
perichondrium 160
perimetrium 743
perineum 552
see also anus 94, childbirth 170, pelvic floor muscles 546, prolapse 577, urethra 741
periodontitis 552
see also gums 329, teeth 696
periosteoma 553
periosteum 552–553
see also bones 134, joints 407, osteomyelitis 522, periostitis 553
periostitis 553
see also bones 134, joints 407, osteomyelitis 522, periosteum 552
peripheral arterial thrombosis 712
peripheral nerves 501
peripheral nervous system 26, **553–554**
see also adrenal glands 64, autonomic nervous system 27–29, brain 138, nerves 500, nervous system 24–26, neurons 504, spinal cord 665
peripheral vascular disease 554
see also aneurysm 86, arteries 102, atherosclerosis 108, cholesterol 179, diabetes 222, gangrene 310, hypertension 373, smoking 656
peristalsis 554–555
see also achalasia 55, digestive system 42–43, esophagus 269, fallopian tubes 285, ileus 383, intestines 399, muscle 483, ureter 741
peritoneal dialysis 225, **555**
see also abdomen 52, dialysis 225
peritoneal tap 541
peritoneum 52, 472
peritonitis 555
see also abdomen 52
peritonsillar abscess 591, 724
pernicious anemia 84
personal space, body language 131
personality disorders 555–556
see also obsessive-compulsive disorder 515, paranoia 542, schizophrenia 619
Perthes' disease 556
see also femur 287, hip 362, osteoarthritis 520
pertussis 762
pertussis and tetanus immunization 228
pervasive developmental disorder 110
PET scan *see* positron emission tomography 568, 594
petechiae 710
pethidine, during birth 172
petrissage, massage technique 456
Peyer's patches 401
peyote 333
Peyronie's disease 267, **556**
see also Dupuytren's contracture 238, erection 267, penis 550
pH 56, 77
phagocytic, cell 162
phagocytosis 761
phalanges 297, 304, 334
pharmaceutical 236
pharyngeal tonsils 724
pharyngitis 556
see also common cold 189, infectious mononucleosis 394, pharynx 557, sinusitis 645, throat 709, tonsils 724
pharyngoconjunctivitis 62
pharynx 339, **557**
see also adenoids 61, ear 244, larynx 423, mouth 479, nose 508, pharyngitis 556, respiratory system 36–38, tonsils 724
phenothiazines 92
phenylalanine 263
phenylbutazone 507
phenylketonuria 472, **557**
see also enzyme deficiencies 263
pheochromocytoma 64, 266
pheomelanin 459
phimosis 47, 550
phlebitis 558
see also varicose veins 747, veins 748
phlebotomus fever 558
see also viruses 752
phobia 558
see also acrophobia 58, agoraphobia 69, anxiety 94, behavior therapy 120, claustrophobia 183, panic attack 540, photophobia 559
phonation 662
phonemes, dyslexia 240
phosphate 231, 253
photocoagulation 558
see also eye 274
photodensitometry 525
photophobia 559
see also iritis 402, phobia 558
photoreceptors 628
photosensitivity 559
see also porphyria 568, acne rosacea 57, sun exposure 687, urticaria 743
phototherapy 740
phrenic nerve 225, 496
phylloquinone 756
physical medicine 559
physical therapy 487, **559**
see also hydrotherapy 372, massage 455, rehabilitation 599
physiotherapy 559
phytotherapy 356
pia mater 463
pica 559
pigeon toes 559
see also foot 303
pigment overload jaundice 404
pigment-producing cells 460
PIH *see* pregnancy-induced hypertension 249, 570
pilar cyst 624
Pilates method 559
see also Alexander technique 76, Feldenkrais method 287
piles 353
pill, contraceptive 518
pilonidal cyst 559
pilonidal sinus 559
see also cyst 203
pimpiniform plexus 46
pimples 56, **559–560**
see also acne 56, acne rosacea 57
pine tar 273
pineal gland 461
pink disease 471
pinkeye 193
pinna 244
pins and needles 502, **560**
see also carpal tunnel syndrome 159, diabetes 222, nerves 500
pinworms 560
see also worms 763
pituitary gland 320–321, 369, 377, **560–561**
see also adrenal glands 64, endocrine system 48–49, follicle stimulating hormone 300, glands 319, growth disorders 328, hormones 369, hypothalamus 377, oxytocin 529
pituitary hormones 367
pityriasis rosea 561
pivot joint 407
PKD *see* polycystic kidney disease 567
PKU *see* phenylketonuria 557
placebo 561
placenta 561–562
see also embryo 255, estrogens 270, fetal development 291, hydatidiform mole 372, pregnancy 571, progesterone 576, reproductive system, female 44–45, toxoplasmosis 727
placenta previa, amniocentesis 82
plane joint 407
plantar fascia 304, 563
plantar fasciitis 563
see also foot 303
plantar neuroma 503
plantar wart 759
plantarflexion 88
plaque 693
plaques 103, 108, 216, 344
plasma 563
see also blood 128, globulins 322, lymphatic/immune system 30–32, liver 438, plasmapheresis 563
plasma B cell 384
plasmapheresis 563
see also antibodies 90, autoimmune disease 110, plasma 563
plasmodium 452
plastic surgery 563
see also cosmetic surgery 198, mammoplasty 454
platelets 563–564
see also blood 128, thrombosis 711, thrombus 712
plates 217
play therapy 564
see also counseling 199, psychotherapy 581
pleura 37, 472, 564
pleural effusion 471, 564
pleural sacs 443
pleurisy 564
see also breathing 146, lungs 443, respiratory system 36–38
pleurodynia 564
see also lungs 443
plexuses 667
plicae circulares 42
PMS *see* premenstrual syndrome 575
pneumococcal meningitis 464
pneumococcus 464
pneumoconiosis 446, **564–565**
see also lungs 443
pneumonia 62, 458, **565**
see also bacteria 117, lungs 443, sputum test 674, viruses 752
pneumonitis 286
pneumothorax 565
see also lungs 443
PNS *see* peripheral nervous system 553
poisoning 566
causing shock 637
see also listeriosis 437, overdose 527, Reiter's syndrome 601
polarity therapy 457
polio 566
polio virus 752
poliomyelitis 488, **566**
see also immunization 386, paralysis 541, spinal cord 665, viruses 752
pollen 336
pollinosis 336
polycystic kidney disease 567
see also amniocentesis 82, kidney 411
polycystic ovarian syndrome 364, 675
polycythemia 567
see also blood 128, platelets 563, red blood cells 596, white blood cells 761
polymyositis 486, **567**
see also autoimmune disease 110
polyneuritis 486, 502
polyposis of the colon 187
polyps 567–568
see also colon 187, nose 508, proctoscopy 576
polyuria 412
pons 139
popliteal artery 428
popliteal artery pulse 348
popliteal fossa 620
porcelain veneers 696
porphyria 568
see also blood 128, hemoglobin 350
port wine stain 350
porta hepatis 438, 568
portacaval shunt 568
portal hypertension 568
see also cirrhosis of the liver 182, liver 438, portal vein 568
portal vein 353, 438, **568**
see also portal hypertension 568
positron emission tomography 568–569
see also imaging techniques 383
post ganglionic nerve cells 27
post-streptococcal glomerulonephritis 681

post-traumatic stress disorder 569
see also anxiety 94, behavior therapy 120, counseling 199, depression 217, psychotherapy 581, trauma 730
posterior chamber of the eye 276
posterior compartment 428
posterior cranial fossa 651
posterior cruciate ligament 416
postherpetic neuralgia 502
postmenopause 465
postmortem examination 212
postnatal depression 173, **569**
see also childbirth 170, depression 217, infancy 390, newborn 505
postpartum depression 569
postpolio syndrome 569
see also poliomyelitis 566
postural hypotension 231
potassium 376, **570**
see also kidney 411, minerals 474, nutrition 509
Pott's disease 570
see also spine 668, tuberculosis 733
Pott's fracture 88
potter's asthma 645
power grip 335
precision grip 335
prednisone 220
preeclampsia 250, **570**
see also blood pressure 130, eclampsia 249, fetal development 291, hypertension 373, kidney 411, nephritis 497, placenta 561, pregnancy 571, toxemia 727
preganglionic nerve cells 27
pregnancy 571–574
diabetes 224
effects of smoking 658
fluid retention 300
mask 571
weight gain 759
see also abortion 53, AIDS 70, amniocentesis 82, chorionic villus sampling 180, contraception 194, eclampsia 249, embryo 255, fertilization 288, fetal alcohol syndrome 289, fetal development 291, hemorrhoids 353, infertility 395, miscarriage 476, newborn 505, placenta 561, preeclampsia 570, rhesus factor 605, reproductive system, female 44–45, rubella 611, twins 734, ultrasound 739
pregnancy-induced hypertension 249, 570
premature birth 173
premature delivery 574
see also abortion 53, childbirth 170, miscarriage 476, placenta 561, pregnancy 571
premature ejaculation 575
see also erection 267, penis 550, sex therapy 630, sexual dysfunction 631, sexual intercourse 632
premenopause 465
premenstrual syndrome 469, **575–576**
see also estrogens 270, hormones 369, menstruation 468, ovulation 528, progesterone 576, prostaglandins 578, reproductive system, female 44–45
premenstrual tension 469
premolars 696
premotor cortex 26
prepatellar bursa 371
prepuce 550
of the clitoris 183
presbyopia 274
preservatives 301
pressure 628
pressure, blood 130
preterm birth 574
priapism 576
see also erection 267, penis 550, sexual dysfunction 631
prickly heat 349
primary curvatures of the spine 668
primary intention 341
primary motor cortex 26
primary tumor 472
primary vaginal adenocarcinoma 745
prion 201
processes, nerve 504
proctitis 576
see also gonorrhea 324, radiation therapy 593, rectum 596, ulcerative colitis 738
proctoscope 353, 576
proctoscopy 576
see also colon 187, diverticulosis 230, rectum 596
progesterone 287, 368, 465, 468, **576**
see also estrogens 270, hormones 369, menstruation 468, oral contraceptives 518, ovulation 528, placenta 561, pituitary gland 560, pregnancy 571
progestin 195
progestogens 576–577
see also cholesterol 179, estrogens 270, hormone replacement therapy 367, hormones 369, oral contraceptives 518, progesterone 576
programmed cell death 68
prolactin 48, 370, 454
prolapse 577
see also anus 94, disk, intervertebral 228, hernia 360, intestines 399, pelvic floor muscles 546, rectum 596, spine 668, uterus 743
prolapsed uterus 743
proliferative phase, of menstruation 468
pronation 100
proprioception 577–578
see also balance 117, breathing 146, palpitations 537, semicircular canals 625
proprioceptors 627–628
PROST *see* pronuclear stage transfer 396
prostaglandins 54, 469, **578**
see also anti-inflammatory drugs 93, platelets 563, prostate gland 578, uterus 743
prostate cancer 317
see also cancer 154, prostate gland 578, testosterone 707, urethra 741
prostate gland 578–579
see also bladder 124, penis 550, prostate cancer 317, prostatitis 579, reproductive system, male 46–47, urethra 741, urinary systems 39–41
protatitis 579–580
see also prostate gland 578
proteins 80, 511
proteinuria 412, 742
proximal convoluted tubule 412
proximal phalanx 334
Prozac 91
pseudo-dementia 463
pseudo-ephedrine 213
pseudo-pregnancy 261
pseudomonas pseudomallei 461
psittacosis 580
see also pneumonia 62
psoriasis 580
see also lymphatic/immune system 30–32, skin 646
psychedelics 333
psychoanalysis 581
psychosis 580–581
see also bipolar disorder 123, depression 217, hallucinations 333, paranoia 542, schizophrenia 619
psychotherapy 581
see also art therapy 102, behavior therapy 120, counseling 199, dance movement therapy 208, music therapy 487, sex therapy 630
psychotropic drugs 581
see also antidepressants 91, anxiety 94, anxiolytics 94, depression 217, detoxification 220, drug dependence 233, insomnia 398, phobias 558, psychotherapy 581, tranquilizers 729, withdrawal 762
PTSD *see* post-traumatic stress disorder 569
puberty 469, **582–583**
see also acne 56, adolescence 62, hormones 291, menstruation 468, reproductive systems 44–47
pubic lice 432
pubic symphysis 287
pubis 362
pulmonary alveolus 79
pulmonary artery 344, **583**
see also aorta 95, circulatory system 33–35, fetal development 291, heart 344, lungs 443
pulmonary circulation 33, **583–584**
see also circulatory system 33–35, deep venous thrombosis 213, lungs 443, mitral valve 476, placenta 561, veins 748, ventricle 751
pulmonary edema 251, **584**
see also circulatory system 33–35, edema 250, heart 344, lungs 443
pulmonary embolism 584
see also anticoagulants 91, circulatory system 33–35, lungs 443, thrombosis 711
pulmonary emphysema 258
pulmonary function tests 585
see also asthma 106, bronchitis 148, emphysema 258, lungs 443
pulmonary hypertension 584
pulmonary hypoplasia 377
pulmonary insufficiency 585
pulmonary stenosis 347, 585, 708
pulmonary trunk 344
pulmonary tuberculosis 444
pulmonary valve 344, 585
see also circulatory system 33–35, heart 344, lungs 443
pulp cavity 405
pulse 287, 348, **585**
see also carotid artery 159, heart 344, palpitations 537, radial artery 592
pump lung 60
punctate keratitis 278, 410
pupil of eye 585
see also eye 274, iris 401, retina 604
purpura 586
see also hemorrhage 352, thrombocytopenia 710
pus 54
PUVA 740
pyelitis 586
see also bladder 124, kidney 411, pyelonephritis 586, urinary systems 39–41
pyelogram 412, **586**
see also bladder 124, kidney 411, ureter 741, urethra 741, urinary systems 39–41
pyelography 586
pyelonephritis 497, **586–587**
see also bladder 124, cystitis 204, dysuria 241, kidneys 411, ureter 741, urinary systems 39–41, urinary tract 743
pyloric sphincter 679
pyloric stenosis 587, 675
see also newborn 505, pylorus 587
pylorus 587
see also duodenum 237, intestines 399, stomach 679
pyridoxal 756
pyridoxamine 756
pyridoxine 756

Q

Q fever 590
see also encephalitis 259, hepatitis 354, infectious diseases 393, pneumonia 565
qi gong 590
see also acupuncture 58, meditation 458
quadriceps femoris muscle 416
quadriceps muscle 428, **590**
see also knee 414, leg 414, muscle 483
quadriplegia 591
see also paralysis 541, paraplegia 542, rehabilitation 599, spinal cord 665

quinidine 90
quinsy 591
see also abscess 54, tonsils 724

R

RA *see* rheumatoid arthritis 607
rabies 592
see also immunization 386, viruses 752
radial artery 251, 335, **592**
see also arm 97, arteries 102, arteriosclerosis 103, hand 334, radius 594
radial artery pulse 348, 585
radial keratotomy 489
radial nerve 592, 593
see also arm 97, hand 334, nerves 500, radius 594, wrist 763
radiation 592–593
see also cancer 154, radiation therapy 593, ultraviolet therapy 740, x-ray 764
radiation sickness 593
see also radiation 592, x-ray 764
radiation therapy 472, **593–594**
see also cancer 154, chemotherapy 168, radiation 592, x-ray 764
radical hysterectomy 378
radical mastectomy 457
radiculitis 502
radiculopathy 594
see also disk intervertebral 228, sacrum 614, spine 668, vertebrae 751
radioactive isotope 594
radiography 383
radioimmunotherapy 593
radioisotope scan 594
see also imaging techniques 383, radiation 592, x-ray 764
radiology 594
see also CAT scan 161, imaging techniques 383, magnetic resonance imaging 452, position emission tomography 568, ultrasound 739, x-ray 764
radiolucent 764
radionuclides 593
radiopaque 764
radiotherapy 593
radium 593
radius 100, 251, **594**
see also arm 97, ulna 738, wrist 763
ramus 404
rapid eye movement sleep 653
rash 594–595
see also chickenpox 168, dermatitis 218, erythema 268, German measles 611, ichthyosis 382, lichen planus 433, measles 458, ringworm 609, rubella 611, scabies 617, shingles 636
raspberry tongue 619
ratbite fever 596
see also fever 295, infectious diseases 393, septicemia 629
Rathke's pouch 561
Raynaud's disease 596
see also blood vessels 131
RDA *see* recommended daily allowance 509
recall 462
recessive genes 359
recognition 462
recollection 462
recommended dietary allowance 509
reconstructive surgery 563
breast 143
rectal columns 596
rectal polyps 353
rectal prolapse 596
rectal valves 596
rectum 596
see also anus 94, colon 187, digestive system 42–43, hemorrhoids 353, proctitis 576, prolapse 577
rectus femoris 362
recurrent fever 601
recurrent miscarriage 396
recurrent spontaneous abortion 396
red blood cells 596–597
see also anemia 84, blood 128, hemoglobin 350, hemolytic anemia 351, iron 402, malaria 452, sickle cell disease 640, thalassemia 708
red blood count 596
red pulp 670
reduction mammoplasty 454
referred pain 535
reflex zone therapy 599
reflexes 598
see also nervous system 24–26, newborn 505
reflexology 599
reflux 348
reflux esophagitis 269, 361
refraction 641
regional anesthesia 86
rehabilitation 599–601
see also alcoholism 73, drug dependence 233, paraplegia 542, quadriplegia 591, spinal cord 665, sports medicine 673, stroke 682
rehydration 215
reiki 601
Reiter's syndrome 601
see also arthritis 103, chlamydia 178, conjunctivitis 193, urethritis 742
relapsing fever 601
see also fever 295, lice 432, ticks 717
relationship counseling 601
see also counseling 199
relaxation techniques 601–603
see also meditation 458, stress 681, t'ai chi ch'uan 692, yoga 766
relearning 462
REM sleep *see* rapid eye movement sleep 653
remedial massage 457
remission 603
renal angiography 603
renal artery 603
see also aneurysm 86, angiography 86, angioplasty 88, arteries 102, arteriosclerosis 103, kidney 411
renal capsule 411
renal colic 40
renal corpuscle 412
renal cortex 411–412
renal hilus 411
renal medulla 411
renal papillae 411
renal pelvis 411
renal pyramids 411
renal transplant 413
renal tubule 412
renin 40
repetitive strain injury 334, 703
reproductive organs 630
reproductive system, development of 257
reproductive system, female 44–45
reproductive system, male 46–47
reproductive tract, cancer of 262
rescue remedy 299
resistance to drugs 236
respiration 146
respiratory system 36–38
development of 257
rest and digest activities 554
REST *see* restricted environmental stimulation therapy 299
restless legs syndrome 603
see also leg 425, nerves 500
resuscitation 146
retarded ejaculation 631
reticular formation 459
retina 276, **604**
see also blindness 127, cataracts 161, diabetes 222, eye 274, ophthalmoscopy 517, retinitis pigmentosa 604, sight 641
retinal detachment 276
retinitis pigmentosa 506, **604**
see also blindness 127, eye 274, night blindness 506, retina 604, sight 641
retinoblastoma 604
retinopathy 373, 604
diabetes 223
retrobulbar neuritis 503
retrocalcaneal bursitis 150
retrograde amnesia 81
retrograde pyelography 586
retroversion of the uterus 604–605, 743
see also uterus 743
retrovirus 364
Reye's syndrome 605
see also diabetes 222, encephalitis 259, meningitis 464, non-steroidal anti-inflammatory drugs 507, overdose 527, poisoning 566, sudden infant death syndrome 685
Rh disease 209
Rh factor *see* Rhesus factor 605–606
Rh negative 605
Rhesus factor 605–606
see also anemia 84, antibodies 90, blood groups 130, hemolytic disease of the newborn 352, newborn 505, pregnancy 571
rheumatic chorea 688
rheumatic fever 606
see also arthritis 103, endocarditis 259, fever 295, heart 344, streptococcal infections 681
rheumatic heart disease 347
rheumatism 606–607
see also connective tissue 193, joints 407, muscle 483, osteoarthritis 520, rheumatoid arthritis 607, synovial fluid 688
rheumatoid arthritis 487, **607–608**
see also arthritis 103, autoimmune disease 110, carpal tunnel syndrome 159, connective tissue 193, rheumatism 606, tenosynovitis 703, osteoarthritis 520
rheumatoid factor 607
rhinitis 78, 336, **608**
see also allergies 77, antihistamines 92, histamines 364, nose 508
rhinophyma 608
see also nose 508
rhinoplasty 198, 284
rhinoviruses 189
rhodopsin 276, 641
rhomboids 639
rhytidectomy 198
rib cage 609
ribbon worms 763
ribonucleic acid 394
ribosomes 232
ribs 608–609
see also skeletal system 15–19
RICE 673
rickets 362, 376, **609**
see also bones 135, vitamins 754
right atrium 344
right primary bronchus 148
right ventricle 344, 751
rigor mortis 212
riluzole 82
ringworm 595, **609**
see also antifungals 92, tinea 717
rock rose 299
rod cells 641
rodent ulcer 738
rods, in the eye 276
Rolfing 661
rolling hiatus hernia 361
root canal therapy 610, 697
see also crown and bridge 202, teeth 696
rootlets 665
rosacea 57
roseola infantum 610
see also convulsions 196, fever 295, hepatitis 354, herpes simplex 360, pneumonia 565
rotator cuff muscles 97, **610–611**
see also humerus 371, shoulder 637
rotavirus 227, 752
rough endoplasmic reticulum 162
roundworms 367, **610–611**
trichinosis 731
trichuriasis 731
see also hookworm 367, strongyloidiasis 684, whipworm 761, worms 763
RS *see* Reye's syndrome 605
RSA *see* recurrent spontaneous abortion 396
RSI *see* repetitive strain injury 703
rubella 294, 347, 595, **611**
see also congenital abnormalities 192, immunization 386, infectious diseases 393
Ruffini endings 628

S

S fibers *see* slow twitch fibers 22
saccule 246, 339
sacral canal 614
sacral foramina 614
sacral spinal nerves 667
sacral vertebrae 751
sacroiliac joint 614
see also hip 362, joints 407, sacrum 614, skeletal system 15–19, spine 668
sacrospinous ligament 614
sacrotuberous ligament 614
sacrum 614
see also skeletal system 15–19, spine 668, vertebrae 751
SAD *see* seasonal affective disorder 624
saddle joint 407
sadism 631
sadness 258
Saint Vitus' dance 688
saliva 614
see also mouth 479, salivary glands 615
salivary glands 319, 479, **615–616**
see also mouth 479, mumps 482, saliva 614, Sjögren's syndrome 646
salmon patches 124
Salmonella bacteria 302, 544
salpingitis 616
see also fallopian tubes 285, pelvic inflammatory disease 546, reproductive system, female 44–45
salt, dehydration 215
salt, hyponatremia 376
saltiness 694
sanatostatin 404
sandfly fever 558
saphenous veins 616–617
see also leg 425, phlebitis 558, thrombosis 711, varicose veins 747
sarcoidosis 617
see also lungs 443, lymph nodes 448
sarcoma 154
saturation response 211
Saturday night palsy 592
satyriasis 631
scabies 595, **617**
see also sexually transmitted diseases 633, skin 646
scalp 617–618
see also cradle cap 199, dandruff 209, hair 332, head lice 340, psoriasis 580
scalp psoriasis 618
scaphoid 763
scapula 97, **618**, 637
see also collar bone 186, humerus 371, shoulder 637
scar 619
see also keloid 409
scar tissue 62, 341
scarlet fever 619
see also antibiotics 90, bacteria 117, infectious diseases 393
scavenger, cell 162
SCC *see* **squamous cell carcinoma 674**
Schirmer's test 646
schistosome dermatitis 688
schistosomiasis 619
see also swimmer's itch 688, worms 763
schizoid personality disorder 556
schizophrenia 619
see also antipsychotics 93
schizotypal personality disorder 556
Schlemm's canal 276
Schönlein-Henoch purpura 586
Schönlein's purpura 586
school sores 387
Schwann cells 500, 504
schwannoma 503
sciatic nerve 428, **620**
see also nerves 500, sciatica 620, spine 668
sciatica 620–621
see also nerves 500, sciatic nerve 620, spine 668
sclera 267, 274, **621**
see also cornea 197, eye 274
scleritis 621
scleroderma 621
see also Raynaud's disease 596, sclerosis 621
sclerosis 621
see also amyotrophic lateral sclerosis 82, multiple sclerosis 481, scleroderma 621
scoliosis 621–622
see also kyphosis 417, lordosis 441, spine 668
scrotum 622
see also hernia 360, reproductive system, male 46–47, testes 705
scrub typhus 622, 735
see also infectious diseases 393
scurvy 622–623
see also diet 227, nutrition 509, vitamins 754
sea sickness 623
see also balance 117, motion sickness 748
seasonal affective disorder 624
see also depression 217, emotions 258, light therapy 434, sun exposure 687
sebaceous cyst 624
see also keratin 410
sebaceous glands 56, 319, 321, **624**
see also acne 56, fats 286, glands 319, hormones 369
sebaceous nevi 477
seborrhea 624
see also acne 56, sebaceous glands 624, skin 646
seborrheic dermatitis 218, 595, 618, **624–625**
see also cradle cap 199, dandruff 209, dermatitis 218, skin 646
seborrheic keratoses 410
sebum 624
secondary bronchi 149
secondary intention 341
secondary sexual characteristics 62
secondary tumor 472
secretory phase, of menstrual cycle 261, 468
sedative drugs 119
sedatives 375, **625**
see also anxiety 94, anxiolytics 94, barbiturates 119, drug dependence 233, overdose 527, sleeping pills 654
segmented worms 763
seizures 196
complex partial 266
epilepsy 265
focal 266
grand mal 266
partial 266
petit mal 266
tonic-clonic 266
selenium sulfide 209, 218
semen 625
volume of 288
see also fertility 288, infertility 395, reproductive system, male 46–47, sperm 664
semi-tendinosus 333
semicircular canals 246, **625**
see also balance 117, ear 244
semilunar valve 344
semimembranosus 333
seminal fluid 625, 664
senescence 67
senile dementia 216
senile plaques 80
senna 423
senses 626–628
see also balance 117, ear 244, eye 274, hearing 342, mouth 479, nervous system 24–26, nose 508, olfactory system 516, pain 534, proprioception 577, sight 641, skin 646, smell 655, spinal cord 665, taste 694, temperature 699, tongue 722, touch 725
sensitization 220
sensorineural hearing loss 209
sensory activity, brain areas 141
sensory axons 500
sensory fibers 667
sensory memory 461
sensory neurons 504
sensory pathways 626
sensory systems 25
separation anxiety 629
see also childhood 174, infancy 390
septa 334
septal area 434–435
septal cartilage 36
septal defect 256
septal deviation 36
septicemia 268, **629**
see also bacteria 117, infectious diseases 393
serotonin 474, **629**
see also amino acids 80, antidepressants 91, depression 217, migraine 474
serotonin-specific reuptake inhibitors 91, 629
serous membrane 461
serratus anteroir 639
serum 629
serum sickness 629
see also allergies 77, antibodies 90
sex 629
see also chromosomes 181, genes 313, sexual intercourse 632, sexuality 633
sex cells 358
sex differentiation, fetal 293
sex education 629–630
see also sexual behavior 631, sexual intercourse 632, sexuality 633
sex hormones 287, 369, 370, 630
sex life, effect of menopause 467
sex steroids 49
sex therapy 630
see also behavior therapy 120, impotence 387, premature ejaculation 575, psychotherapy 581, sexual dysfunction 631
sexual abuse, signs of 630
sexual arousal 632
sexual behavior 631
see also bisexuality 124, contraception 194, homosexuality 367, masturbation 458, sexuality 633, transsexualism 730
sexual changes, adolescence 62
sexual disorders 631
sexual dysfunction 631–632
see also hormone replacement therapy 367, hormones 369, impotence 387, menopause 465, premature ejaculation 575, sexual behavior 631, sexual intercourse 632, vaginismus 745
sexual headache 632
sexual intercourse 632–633
see also contraception 194, reproductive systems 44–47, sexual behavior 631, sexually transmitted diseases 633
sexuality 633
see also sexual behavior 631, sexual dysfunction 631, sexual intercourse 632
sexually transmitted disease 633–634
see also AIDS 70, chancroid 167, chlamydia 178, genital herpes 315, genital warts 315, gonorrhea 324, granuloma inguinale 326, hepatitis 354, lice 432, lymphogranuloma venereum 449, molloscum contagiosum 477, scabies 617, syphilis 689
shell shock 569
shiatsu 634–635
see also acupuncture 58, massage 455
shigella 302, 312
shin splints 635, 716
see also leg 425, tibia 425
shinbone 287, 716
shingles 595, **635**
see also chickenpox 168, nerves 500, viruses 752
shock 636–637
see also anaphylaxis 83, circulatory system 33–35, epinephrine 266, myocardial infarction 488, poisoning 566, septicemia 629, toxic shock syndrome 727
short-term memory 461
shortsightedness 641

shoulder 637–640
see also adduction and abduction 61, arm 97, collar bone 186, deltoid muscle 215, humerus 371, joints 407, muscle 483, rotator cuff muscles 610, scapula 618, skeletal system 15–19, tendinitis 701, trapezius muscle 730
shoulder blade 97, 618
shoulder joint 97, 637
shoulder-hand syndrome 640
see also hand 334, myocardial infarction 488, shoulder 637
Shprintzen syndrome 183
shunt 372
Siamese twins 640
see also fertilization 288, twins 734
sick sinus syndrome 640
see also heart 344, pacemaker 532
sickle cell disease 640
see also congenital abnormalities 192, genes 313, hemoglobin 350
sickle gene 640
sickle hemoglobin 640
side effects, of drugs 236
SIDS *see* sudden infant death syndrome 685
sight 627, **641–644**
see also astigmatism 107, cataracts 161, color blindness 188, contact lenses 194, cornea 197, eye 274, glaucoma 322, iris 401, macular degeneration 452, myopia 489, neuritis 502, optic nerve 517, retina 604, retinitis pigmentosa 604, squint 674
sigmoid colon 187
sigmoidoscopy 263
sign language 211
sildenafil 267
silent nociceptors 628
silica 645
silicone, in plastic surgery 563
silicosis 645
see also lungs 443, respiratory system 36–38
simian crease 233
simple fracture 305
simple squamous epithelium 719
single palmar crease 233
sinoatrial node 35, 344, 348, 532
sinus arrhythmia 102
sinus node, malfunction 640
sinuses 338, **645**
spleen 670
see also nose 508, sinusitis 645, skull 649
sinusitis 213, 338, **645–646**
see also allergies 77, common cold 189, sinuses 645
sinusoids 645, 568
Sjögren's syndrome 646
see also lacrimal glands 420, salivary glands 615
skeletal muscle 485, 720
skeletal system 16–19
skeleton, development of 292
skin 646–648
see also acne 56, blood vessels 131, dermatitis 218, epidermis 263, hair 332, herpes simplex 360, impetigo 387, jaundice 404, keratin 410, melanin 459, nails 492, nerves 500, ringworm 609, scar 619, sebaceous glands 624, senses 626, skin cancer 648, sun exposure 687, sweat glands 687, temperature regulation 699
skin cancer 648
see also basal cell carcinoma 120, melanoma 460, mycosis fungoides 487, squamous cell carcinoma 674, sun exposure 687
skin, cancers of 284
skin care 56
skin graft 648
skin layer 263
skull 337, 338, **649–652**
development of 291
fetal 652
of newborn 505
see also bones 135, ear 244, fontanelle 301, head 337, nose 508, sinuses 645, skeletal system 15–19, teeth 696
SLE *see* systemic lupus erythematosus 447
sleep 653
see also infancy 390, insomnia 398, sleep apnea 653, sleep disturbances 654, snoring 659
sleep apnea 653–654
see also insomnia 398, sleep 653, sleep disturbances 654, snoring 659
sleep disorders, light therapy 434
sleep disturbances 654
see also bed-wetting 120, insomnia 398, narcolepsy 492, restless legs syndrome 603, sleep 653, sleep apnea 653, sleeping pills 654, snoring 659, teeth-grinding 698
sleeping pills 654
see also acupuncture 58, aromatherapy 101, drug dependence 233, massage 455, sedatives 625, sleep 653, sleep disturbances 654
sleeping sickness 654–655
see also infectious diseases 393
sleeping, in infancy 392
sleeptalking 654
sleepwalking 654
sliding hiatus hernia 270, 361
slipped disk 229, 577
slipped epiphysis of the femur 362
slow twitch fibers 22
small bowel 399
small intestine 399
small saphenous vein 428, 616
smallpox 655
see also immunization 386, viruses 752
smell 516, 627–628, **655**
see also nose 508, olfactory system 516
smoker's cough 258
smoking 656–658
see also cancer 154, emphysema 258, heart 344, hypertension 373, lung cancer 442, lungs 443, nicotine 506, pregnancy 571, respiratory system 36–38, withdrawal 762
smooth muscle 483, 485, 720
sneezing 659
see also common cold 189, mucous membranes 481, reflexes 598, rhinitis 608
sniffing, solvent 660
snoring 659
see also insomnia 398, sleep 653, sleep apnea 653, sleep disturbances 654
snow blindness 659
see also eye 274
SNS *see* somatic nervous system 27, 554
social phobia 558
sodium 659–660
see also dehydration 214, edema 250, hypertension 373, hyponatremia 376, hypotension 377, minerals 474, nutrition 509, stroke 682
soft chancre 167
soft palate 479, 536
soft spot *see* fontanelle 301
solar keratoses 410
solar lentigines 429
solar plexus 660
see also abdomen 52, diaphragm 225, nerves 500, stomach 679
solvent sniffing 660
see also drug dependence 233
somatic nervous system 27, 554
somatic therapies 660–661
see also Alexander technique 76, Feldenkrais method 287, massage 455, Pilates method 559, psychotherapy 581
somatotypes 132
sonography 739
sore throat 709
sound 342
sourness 694
spa, used in hydrotherapy 372
special senses 627, 628
speech 661–663
see also aphasia 96, cleft palate and cleft lip 183, dyslexia 239, larynx 423, lisping 437, mouth 479, stuttering 684, vocal cords 757
speech processor 211
speech therapy 599
sperm 291, **664–665**
see also epididymitis 264, fertilization 288, infertility 395, reproductive system, male 46–47, scrotum 622, semen 625, testes 705, vasectomy 747
spermatic cord 46
spermatid 46
spermatogonia 46
spermicide 195
sphenoid bone 649
sphygmomanometer 130
spider angioma 87
spina bifida 255, 256, **665**
see also amniocentesis 82, congenital abnormalities 192, neural tube defect 502, spinal cord 665, ultrasound 739
spinal accessory nerve 200
spinal cord 114, **665–666**
development of 256
see also nerves 500, nervous system 24–26, neurons 504, paralysis 541, paraplegia 542, quadriplegia 591, reflexes 598, spinal nerves 567, spine 668
spinal curvature 666
see also lordosis 441, kyphosis 417, Pott's disease 570, scoliosis 621, spine 668
spinal disks 669
spinal nerves 114, 500, **667**
see also dermatomes 218, nerves 500, nervous system 24–26, shingles 636, spinal cord 665, spine 668
spinal stenosis 675
spinal tap 441
spine 668–670
see also coccyx 184, disk, intervertebral 228, epidural anesthesia 264, joints 407, kyphosis 417, lordosis 441, lumbar puncture 441, neck 494, osteoarthritis 520, sacrum 614, sciatica 620, scoliosis 621, skeletal system 15–19, spinal cord 665, vertebrae 751, vertebral column 114, whiplash injury 760
spinous process, of vertebrae 669
spiral fracture 305
spirometry 146, 585
spleen 670–673
see also anemia 84, autoimmune disease 110, celiac disease 162, Hodgkin's disease 365, immunity 384, infectious mononucleosis 394, leukemia 430, lymphatic/immune system 30–32, malaria 452, non-Hodgkin's lymphoma 506, red blood cells 596, thrombocytopenia 710
splenectomy 671
splenic atrophy 672
splenomegaly 671
spondylitis 672
see also ankylosing spondylitis 89, spine 668, verebrae 750
spondylosis 673
see also neck 494, osteoarthritis 520, spine 668
spontaneous abortion 53, 289
spontaneous mutation 294
sports medicine 673
see also exercise 271, joints 407, muscle 483, tennis elbow 703, trauma 730
spots before the eyes 299
sprain 673
see also joints 407, ligaments 433, muscle 483, tendons 702
sprue 673–674
see also celiac disease 162, intestines 399, pancreatitis 540, radiation therapy 593
sprue, nontropical 162
sputum test 674
see also asbestosis 105, asthma 106, bronchitis 148, lungs 443, pneumonia 565, pulmonary edema 584

squamous cell carcinoma 648, 674
see also cancer 154, mucous membranes 481, smoking 656
squint 674
see also eye 274, sight 641
SSRI *see* serotonin-specific reuptake inhibitors 91
stammering 663, 684
stapedectomy 247, 525
stapes 244, 649
staphylococcal infection 674
see also abscess 54, bacteria 117, osteomyelitis 522, septicemia 629, toxic shock syndrome 727
staphylococci 674
Staphylococcus bacteria 284, 302, 464, 486
star of Bethlehem 299
startle reflex 725
statis dermatitis 218
STD *see* sexually transmitted disease 633
Stein-Leventhal syndrome 675
see also hormones 369, oral contraceptives 518, ovarian cysts 526, ovaries 526
stem cells 692
stenosis 675–676
see also heart 344, pyloric stenosis 587, spine 668
stent 88
sterilization 676
see also contraception 194, tubal sterilization 732, vasectomy 747
sternocleidomastoid muscle 142, 494, 496
sternum 676–677
see also collar bone 186, ribs 608, shoulder 637
sternutation 659
steroid hormones 369
steroids 64, **677**
see also adrenal glands 64, autoimmune disease 110, cholesterol 179, Cushing's syndrome 202, hormones 369
Stevens-Johnson syndrome 678
see also erythema 268
stiff lung 60
stiff neck 496
Still's disease 678
see also autoimmune disease 110, connective tissue 193, joints 407, rheumatoid arthritis 607
stimulants 234, 678
see also amphetamines 82, cocaine 183, drug dependence 233, drugs 236, laxatives 423, nicotine 506, overdose 527
stirrup 339
stitch 678
see also abdomen 52, cramp 199
Stokes-Adams syndrome 678
see also heart 344, heartbeat 348, pacemaker 532
stoma 382
stomach 679–680
see also cancer 154, digestive system 42–43, esophagus 269, gastrectomy 310, gastroenteritis 312, hiatus hernia 361, peptic ulcer 551, peristalsis 554, pylorus 587, ulcers 738
stomach cancer 679
stonecutter's disease 645
stones, in bladder 124, 127
strabismus 674
stratified squamous epithelium 719
stratum corneum 264, 646
strawberry angioma 87
strawberry tongue 619
strep throat 556, 681
streptococcal infections 681
streptococcal pharyngitis 681
streptococci 681
Streptococcus 117, 464
stress 681
see also biofeedback 122, epinephrine 266, meditation 458, psychotherapy 581, relaxation techniques 601
stress fractures 350
stress hormones 472, 677
stress incontinence 368, 388
stress test 86
stretch 628
stretch marks 681
stridor 201
stroke 166, 350, **682–683**
from smoking 656
see also arteries 102, arteriosclerosis 103, atherosclerosis 108, brain 138, carotid artery 159, transient ischemic attack 241
stroking, massage technique 456
strongyloidiasis 684, 763
structural integration 661
stuttering 663, **684**
see also speech 661
stye 277–279, **684**
see also eyelashes 279, eyelid 279, sebaceous glands 624
styloglossus muscle 722
stylomastoid foramen 284
subacromial bursa 639
subacute sclerosing panencephalitis 684
see also measles 458, nerves 500, nervous system 24–26
subarachnoid hemorrhage 165, **684**
subarachnoid space 670
subclavian arteries 102
subclavian vein 684, 749
subcutaneous tissue 263
subdural hematoma 685
subdural hemorrhage 337
subfertility 288, 396
sublingual gland 616, 722
submandibular gland 616
subscapularis muscle 610, 639
sucrose 686
suction aspiration 54
suction curetting 54
suction lipectomy 437
sudden infant death syndrome 685
see also infancy 390, pregnancy 571, smoking 656
sugar 686
see also blood sugar tests 130, diabetes 222, hypoglycemia 376, insulin 398, nutrition 509, pancreas 538
suicide 686
see also death 212, depression 217
suicide genes 68
sulfite compounds 302
sun exposure 687
see also basal cell carcinoma 120, melanoma 460, photosensitivity 559, seasonal affective disorder 624, skin 646, skin cancer 648, squamous cell carcinoma 674, ultraviolet therapy 740
sun spots 687
sunburn 687
sunstroke 349
superior vena cava 749
supination 100
suppressor T cell 72, 385
suprarenal 64
supraspinatus tendinitis 701
supraspinatus tendon 100, 610, 639
sural nerve 500
surgical angioplasty 88
surgical evacuation 54
sutures, in the skull 650
swamp itch 688
swayback 441
sweat glands 319, 321, **687**
see also glands 319
Swedish massage 456
sweeteners 302
sweetness 694
swelling *see* edema 250
swimmer's itch 525, 619, **688**
see also schistosomiasis 619, worms 763
Sydenham's chorea 688
see also Huntington's disease 371
sympathetic fibers 667
sympathetic nerve 348, 370
sympathetic trunk 27
sympathomimetic drugs 688
see also amphetamines 82, epinephrine 266, nervous system 24–26
symphyses 407
synapses 688
see also nerves 500, nervous system 24–26, neurons 504
synarthroses 407
syncope 284, 747
synovial deterioration 521
synovial fluid 688
see also joints 407
synovial joint 19
synovial membrane 461, **689**
see also joints 407, synovial fluid 688
synoviocytes 689
synovitis 689
see also joints 407, synovial fluid 688, synovial membrane 689
syphilis 634, **689**
see also sexually transmitted diseases 633
syphilis spirochete 117
systemic circulation 33
systemic lupus erythematosus 448
systole 344, 347
systolic blood pressure 130, 373

T

T cells 385, 481, **692**
T helper cells 32, 692
T helper lymphocytes 70
T lymphocytes 32, 364, 384, 385
T suppressor cells 32
T3 714
T4 714
T4 cell count 70, 692
T4 helper cells 364
T4 lymphocytes 70, 72
tabes dorsalis 692
tachycardia, paroxysmal 692
tactile receptors 627–628
tactile sense 725
t'ai chi chu'an 692–693
tailbone 184
talus 88
tamponade, cardiac 158
tangles 80, 216
tantrums, in children 176
Tapanui flu 181
tapeworm 372, **693**, 763
tardive dyskinesia 93, 239, **693**
tarsal bone 88
tarsal cyst 167, 279
tarsus 303
tartar 693
taste 627–628, **694–695**
buds 694–695
fibers 694
pathways 695
pore 694
see also saliva 614, smell 655, tongue 722
tattoo 696
tattooing 696
see also hepatitis 354, HIV 364, skin 646
Tay-Sachs disease 696
see also congenital abnormalities 192, genes 313, genetic counseling 315
tears, function of 278
teeth 338, 696–698
fillings 297
in infancy 391
see also braces 137, crown and bridge 202, dentures 217, fluoridation 300, gums 329, mouth 479, orthodontics 519, saliva 614, teeth-grinding 698, teething 392
teeth-grinding 698, 701
see also sleep disturbances 654, teeth 696
teething 392, 698–699
see also infancy 390, teeth 696
temperature 699
see also convulsions 196, fever 295, Reye's syndrome 605, temperature regulation 699
temperature, body 132
temperature regulation 699–700
see also convulsions 196, fever 295, heatstroke 349, hyperthermia 374, skin 646, sudden infant death syndrome 685, sun exposure 687, temperature 699
temporal arteritis 341, 700
temporal bone 649, 651
temporal lobe 26, 138
temporalis muscle 405
temporomandibular joint 284, 337, 405, 651

temporomandibular joint syndrome 699, 701
see also arthritis 103, jaw 404, joints 407, teeth-grinding 698
tendinitis 701
see also Achilles tendon 55, ankle 88, elbow 251, rotator cuff muscle 610, shoulder 637, tendons 702, tennis elbow 703, tenosynovitis 703
tendons 702–703
of the hand 335
tissue 720
see also Achilles tendon 55, bones 134, connective tissue 193, elbow 251, muscle 483, tendinitis 701, tenosynovitis 703, tennis elbow 703, trigger finger 732
tennis elbow 100, 252, 701, **703**
see also elbow 251, muscle 483, tendons 702
tenosynovitis. 334, 703–704
see also ganglion 310, joints 407, tendinitis 701, tendons 702
TENS *see* transcutaneous electrical nerve stimulation 86, 729
tension headache 340, **704**
tension pneumothorax 565
teratogen 704
see also fetal alcohol syndrome 289, pregnancy 571, rubella 611, smoking 656
teres major muscle 639
teres minor muscle 610, 639
terminal disease 212
termination 53
tertiary bronchi 149
TEST see tubal embryo stage transfer 396
test tube babies 387
testes 705–706
descent during fetal stage 293
development of 705
see also hernia 360, hormones 369, hydrocele 372, orchitis 519, reproductive system, male 46–47, scrotum 622, sperm 664, testosterone 465
testicles 705
testicular cancer 706
testicular torsion 706
testicular vein 46
testosterone 83, 465, 472, 486, **707**
see also follicle stimulating hormone 300, hormones 369, pituitary gland 560
Tet spells 708
tetanus 707
see also immunization 386, infectious diseases 393
tetany 707–708
see also acidosis 56, alkalosis 77, calcium 154, potassium 376
tetracyclines 56–57
tetraiodothyronine 714
tetralogy of fallot 708
see also congenital abnormalities 192, Down syndrome 233, heart 344
tetraplegia 591
TGA *see* transient global amnesia 81
thalamus 462, **708**
see *also* brain 138, hypothalamus 377, limbic system 434, nerves 500, Parkinson's disease 544, schizophrenia 619, spinal cord 665
thalassemia 351, **708–709**
see also anemia 84, hemoglobin 350
thalidomide 347
thenar muscle 334
theobromine 678
therapeutic touch 725
thermogram 709
thermography 709
see also atherosclerosis 108, breast cancer 143
thermoreceptors 627–628
thiamine 754
thiamine deficiency 215, 760
thiazide diuretics 92, 230
thick myofilaments 483
thigh bone 287, 590
thin myofilaments 483
thoracic aorta 95
thoracic cage 18
thoracic duct 31
thoracic region, of the spine 668
thoracic spinal nerves 667
thoracic vertebrae 114, 751
three-day fever 558
throat 709–710
see also adenoids 61, digestive system 42–43, epiglottis 265, esophagus 269, larynx 423, pharynx 557, trachea 727
thromboangiitis obliterans 710
see also arteries 102, blood vessels 131, smoking 656
thrombocytopenia 563, 710–711
see also AIDS 70, autoimmune disease 110, blood 128, leukemia 430, nosebleed 508, platelets 563
thrombocytopenia, mumps 482
thromboembolism 711
see also arteries 102, blood vessels 131, embolism 254, pulmonary embolism 584, thrombosis 711, veins 748
thrombolytic drugs 711
see also coronary thrombosis 198, heart 344, myocardial infarction 488, thrombosis 711
thrombolytic therapy 711
thrombophilia 712
thrombosis 91, 711–712
see also arteries 102, atherosclerosis 108, blood 128, blood vessels 131, capillaries 157, cholesterol 179, circulatory system 33–35, gangrene 310, hypertension 373, myocardial infarction 488, platelets 563, pulmonary embolism 584, stroke 682, veins 748
thrombosis, coronary 198
thrombotic emboli 348
thrombus 129, 344, 712–713
see also arteriosclerosis 103, myocardial infarction 488, stroke 682, thrombosis 711
thumbsucking 713
see also orthodontics 519, teeth 696
thymine 232
thymoma 487
thymus derived cells 692
thymus gland 713
see also lymphatic/immune system 30–32, T cells 692
thyroid cancer 716
thyroid cartilage 36, 423
thyroid gland 320, 369, **714–716**
see also cretinism 201, endocrine glands 260, glands 319, goiter 323, Graves' disease 327, Hashimoto's disease 336, hyperthyroidism 374, myxedema 489, pituitary gland 560, thyrotoxicosis 716
thyroid gland deficiency 301
thyroid hormone 714
thyroid notch 423
thyroid-stimulating hormone 48, 323, 326, 327, 369, 374, 714
thyrotoxicosis 374, 487, **716**
see also goiter 323, Graves' disease 327, hyperthyroidism 374, thyroid gland 714
thyroxine 369, 378, 714
thyroxine, goiter 323
TIA *see* transient ischemic attack 241, 730
tibia 287, 425, **716**
see also ankle 88, femur 287, fibula 296, knee 414, leg 425
tibial nerve 428, 620
tic 717
see also neuralgia 502, obsessive-compulsive disorder 515, tic douloureux, Tourette's syndrome 727
tic douloureux 717
see also neuralgia 502
tick fever 601
ticks 717
see also Lyme disease 447
tied tubes 676
tinea 717–718
see also antifungals 92, ringworm 609
tinnitus 718
see also ear 244, hearing 342, Menière's disease 463, otosclerosis 525
tissue 719–721
see also cells 162, collagen 186, connective tissue 193, muscle 483, nervous system 24–26, neurons 504
tissue regeneration 341
titanium implants, teeth 217
TM see transcendental meditation 459
tobacco 506
toilet training 722
see also bed-wetting 120
tongue 339, **722–724**
see also glossitis 323, mouth 479, palate 536, saliva 614, speech 661, taste 694
tongue zones, for taste 694
tongue-tied 663
tonometry 724
see also cornea 197, eye 274, glaucoma 322
tonsils 724
see also adenoids 61, lymphocytes 449, quinsy 591, respiratory system 36–38, throat 709
tooth decay 697
tophi 325
torn cartilage 161
torsion of the testis 46
torticollis 496, 724–725
see also neck 494
total blindness 127
touch 628, 725–726
see also hyperthermia 374, hypothermia 378, massage 455, reflexes 598, skin 646, tongue 722
Tourette's syndrome 727
see also tic 717
toxemia 727
see also eclampsia 249, preeclampsia 570, septicemia 629
toxic megacolon 738
toxic shock syndrome 727
see also shock 636, staphylococcal infections 674
toxins 220
toxocariasis 727, 763
see also infectious diseases 393, worms 763
toxoplasmosis 488, **727**
see also food poisoning 302
trabecula 18–19
trachea 336, **727–728**
see also esophagus 269, larynx 423, pharynx 557, tracheostomy 728
trachealis muscle 37
tracheitis 728
tracheo-esophageal fistula 727
tracheostomy 728
see also trachea 727
trachoma 728
see also blindness 127, cornea 197, eye 274, eyelids 279
traction 729
see also physical therapy 559, yoga 766
Traditional Chinese Medicine 58
Traeger approach, somatic therapy 661
tranquilizers 375, 729
see also antipsychotics 93, drug dependence 233, sedatives 625, sleeping pills 654
transactional analysis 199
transcendental meditation 459
transcutaneous electrical nerve stimulation 729
see also acupuncture 58, pain 534
transducer, part of artificial pacemaker 532
transfusion 130
transhepatic cholangiogram 179
transient global amnesia 81
transient ischemic attack 241, **729**
see also arteries 102, atherosclerosis 103, blood vessels 131, coronary artery disease 197, hypertension 373, stroke 682, thrombus 712

transplant 326
transplant surgery 730
see also bones 134, eye 274, grafting 326, heart 344, kidney 411
transsexualism 730
see also sexual behavior 631, sexuality 633
transurethral resection 126
of the prostate 46
transverse colon 187
transverse fracture 305
transverse process, of vertebrae 669
trapezius muscle 494, 496, 639, **730**
see also collar bone 186, muscle 483, scapula 618
trauma 730
see also post-traumatic stress disorder 569
traumatic pneumothorax 565
trematode worms 619
tremor 730
trichiasis 279
trichinosis 731
see also food poisoning 302, worms 763
trichomoniasis vaginalis 634
trichuriasis 731
see also roundworms 610, worms 763
tricuspid valve 344, 476, **731**
see also circulatory system 33–35, heart 344, lungs 443, ventricle 751
tricyclic antidepressants 91
trigeminal nerve 200, **731–732**
see also nerves 500, nervous system 24–26, neuralgia 502, tic douloureux 717
trigeminal neuralgia 502, 717
trigger finger 732
see also finger 297, tendinitis 701, tenosynovitis 703
triglycerides 286
triiodothyronine 714
trimesters, of pregnancy 571
trisomy 21, 233
trochanters 425
trochlear nerve 200
trophoblast 291
true pelvis 547
trypsin 259
tryptophan 629
TSD *see* Tay-Sachs disease 696
tsetse fly, sleeping sickness 654
TSH, Graves' disease 327
TSH *see* thyroid stimulating hormone 323, 374
tubal embryo stage transfer 396
tubal ligation 195, 676, 732
tubal sterilization 732–733
see also fallopian tubes 285, sterilization 676
tubercular laryngitis 421
tuberculoid leprosy 429
tuberculosis 733–734
test for 455
see also infectious diseases 393, lungs 443
tui na 58
tumescent liposuction 436
tumors 734
see also cancer 154
tunica albuginea 46
tunica vaginalis 46
tuning fork, for hearing tests 211
tunnel of Guyon 764
tunnel vision 644
TUR see transurethral resection 126
turbinates 508
Turner's syndrome 287, **734**
see also chromosomal abnormalities 180, chromosomes 181, hormones 369
TURP *see* transurethral resection of the prostate 46
turpentine 273
twins 574, **734**
see also fertilization 288, pregnancy 571
tympanic membrane 244
tympanometry 109
type 1 herpes simplex 185
Type I diabetes 222
Type II diabetes 222
typhoid 734–735
see also gastroenteritis 312, infectious diseases 393
typhus 735
see also infectious diseases 393
tyrosine 263

U

ulcer 738
see also basal cell carcinoma 120, cornea 197, peptic ulcer 551, ulcerative colitis 738
ulcer, foot 304
ulcerative colitis 187, **738**
see also bowel cancer 136, intestines 399, rectum 596, ulcer 738
ulna 100, 251, **738–739**
see also arm 97, elbow 251, humerus 251
ulnar artery 251, 335
ulnar nerve 739
see also arm 97, elbow 251, humerus 251, ulna 738
ultrasonic-assisted liposuction 437
ultrasonography 739
ultrasound 739–740
during pregnancy 572
see also amniocentesis 82, biopsy 123, Doppler ultrasonography 232, fetal development 291, imaging techniques 383, lithotripsy 437
ultraviolet light 687
ultraviolet radiation 592
ultraviolet therapy 740
see also dermatitis 218, light therapy 434, psoriasis 580, vitiligo 757
umbilical arteries 257, 740
umbilical cord 740
see also childbirth 170, placenta 561, pregnancy 571
umbilical hernia 257, 360
umbilical vein 740
unconsciousness 741
see also coma 188
underbite 453, 520
undernourishment 248, 452
undescended testicles 705
undulant fever 149
unilateral oophorectomy 517
unstable angina 86
upper gastrointestinal endoscopy 263
urate, gout 325
urea 743
uremia 741
see also dialysis 225, kidney 411, transplant surgery 730
ureter 40, 741
see *also* bladder 124, kidney 411, pyelonephritis 586, urinary systems 39–41
urethra 741–742
see also bladder 124, epispadias 267, hypospadias 377, urethritis 743, urinary incontinence 742
urethritis 742
see also bladder 124, cystitis 204, epididymitis 264, gonorrhea 324, prostatitis 579, urethra 741
urethrocele 742
see also bladder 124, urethra 741, urinary incontinence 742, vagina 745
urge incontinence 388
uric acid, gout 325
urinalysis 742
see also cystitis 204, kidney 411, nephritis 497, urinary systems 39–41
urinary system 39–41
urinary incontinence 742–743
see also bladder 124, prolapse 577, prostate gland 578
urinary tract 743
see also bladder 124, kidney 411, urethra 741, urinary systems 39–41
urogenital diaphragm 40
urogenital folds 292
urticaria 78, **743**
see also allergies 77, angioedema 86, antihistamines 92, hives 743
uterine bleeding 470
uterine cancer 368
uterine muscle 469
uterine tube 285
uterus 743–745
tumors 295
see also cervix 166, endometrium 261, hysterectomy 378, menstruation 468, pelvic floor muscles 546, pelvic inflammatory disease 546, pregnancy 571, reproductive system, female 44–45
utricle 246, 339
UV therapy 740
UVA radiation 687
UVB radiation 687
UVC radiation 687
uvea 274–275
uveitis 90
uvula 479, 536

V

vaccine 384
vacuum extraction, in birth 172
vagina 745
see also candidiasis 157, cystocele 204, estrogens 270, fistula 298, prolapse 577, reproductive system, female 44–45, vaginismus 745, vaginitis 746
vaginal dryness 367
vaginal hysterectomy 379
vaginismus 632, **745–746**
see also sexual intercourse 632, vagina 745
vaginitis 746
see also candidiasis 157, estrogens 270, menopause 465, sexually transmitted diseases 633, vagina 745
vagotomy 746
vagus nerve 200, 459, 496, **746–747**
tasting 694
see also arrythmia 102, autonomic nervous system 27–29, epilepsy 265, nerves 500, nervous system 24–26, spinal cord 665
vallate papillae 722
valvotomy 477
valvular incompetence 347
valvular stenosis 347
varicella 168
varicocele 747
see also fertility 288, testes 705, veins 748
varicose ulcer 738, **747**
see also circulatory system 33–35, veins 748
varicose veins 747
see *also* circulatory system 33–35, thrombosis 711, veins 748
vas deferens 625
vascular headaches 340, 474
vasculitis 352, **747**
see also autoimmune disease 110, blood vessels 131
vasectomy 747–748
see also contraception 194, reproductive system, male 46–47, sterilization 676, testes 705
vasodilators 748
see also arteries 102, beta-blockers 121, blood vessels 131, calcium channel blockers 154, hypertension 373
vasopressin 224
vasovagal syncope 747
vegetarianism 513
veins 749
see *also* circulatory system 33–35, thrombosis 711, varicose veins 747, venography 749
venography 749
see also veins 749
venous sinuses 645
venous stasis ulcer 747
venous thrombosis 712, 749
ventilation 146
ventral rootlets 665
ventricle 344, 751
see also brain 138, heart 344, spinal cord 665
ventricles, brain 138
ventricular ectopic beat 348
ventricular extrasystole 348
ventricular fibrillation 295, 344–345

ventricular septal defect 751
see also heart 344, ventricle 751
ventricular tachycardia 345, 348, 692
vernix 294
verrucae planae juveniles 759
vertebrae 114, 669, **751**
see also disk, intervertebral 228, skeletal system 15–19, spine 668
vertebral arch 668, 751
vertebral body 751
vertebral canal 670
vertebral column 114, 668
vertigo 210, **751**
see also acrophobia 58, dizziness 230, semicircular canals 625
vestibular folds 36
vestibular neuritis 503
vestibular organs 246
vestibulocochlear nerve 200
veto-cardio-facial syndrome 183
vibration 628
vibrio cholerae 117
vibrissae 508
vibroacoustic therapy 487
Vipassana 459
viral diarrhea 227
viral envelope 393
viral infection 393
viral labyrinthitis 420
viral pinkeye 193
virginity 373
virilism 751
virilization 751–752
see also adrenal glands 64, hormones 369, progesterone 576, puberty 582, testosterone 707
viruses 752–753
see also antibodies 90, bacteria 117, chickenpox 168, common cold 189, encephalitis 259, hepatitis 354, herpes simplex 360, infectious diseases 393, measles 458, meningitis 464, multiple sclerosis 471, mumps 482, poliomyelitis 566, ticks 717
visceral column 494, 496
visceral fat 272
visceral leishmaniasis 429
visceral nociceptors 628
vision 628
visual pathways 642
visual tracing 254
visualization 753
see also creative visualization 753, hypnotherapy 375, meditation 458, relaxation techniques 601
vitamin A 754–755
vitamin B_1 754
vitamin B_2 754, 756
vitamin B_3 754, 756
vitamin B_5 754, 756
vitamin B_6 755–756
vitamin B12 755–756
absorption of 382
vitamin C 755–756
deficiency 622
for colds 189
scurvy 622
vitamin D 755–756
deficiency 376
vitamin E 755–756
vitamin H 756
vitamin K 755–756
in newborns 506
vitamins 754–756
deficiency 453
see also anemia 84, breast feeding 144, diet 227, minerals 474, nutrition 509, osteomalacia 522, rickets 608, scurvy 622, sun exposure 687, Wernicke-Korsakoff syndrome 760
vitiligo 757
see also autoimmune disease 110, ultraviolet therapy 740
vitreous body 276
vitreous humor 299
vocal cords 663, **757**
see also larynx 423, speech 661
vocal ligaments 423
vocal tics 717
voice box 423
voluntary muscles 20
voluntary nervous system 27
volvulus 401, **757**
see also digestive system 42–43, intestines 399
vomer 282, 649
vomiting 758
see also digestive system 42–43, eating disorders 248, food poisoning 302, gastritis 311, gastroesophageal reflux 313, peristalsis 554, pregnancy 571, stomach 679
von Recklinghausen's disease 503
von Willebrand's disease 758
see also blood vessels 131, hemophilia 352, platelets 563
vowel sounds 662
voyeurism 631
VSD *see* ventricular septal defect 751
vulva 758
see also clitoris 183, vagina 745
vulvitis 271, **758**
see also menopause 465, vagina 745, vulva 758
vulvovaginitis 758
see also vaginitis 746, vulvitis 758

W

walleye 674
warfarin 91, 477
wart virus 752
warts 759
genital 315
see also gential warts 315, skin 646, viruses 752
water birth 171
water on the brain 372
water pills 230
water, fluoridation of 300
water, in the body 512
waterbrash 361
WBCs see white blood cells 761
weight 759
see a*lso* body mass index 132, body shape 132, diet 227, nutrition 509, obesity 514
weight loss medicines 759
weightlifting 273
Wernicke's area 241, 662
Wernicke's encephalopathy 760
Wernicke's encephalopathy, alcoholism 75
Wernicke-Korsakoff syndrome 760
see also alcoholism 73, amnesia 80
Wharton's jelly 740
wheezing 760
see also asthma 106, breathing 146
whining, in children 176
whiplash 760
see also neck 494
whipworm 761
see also roundworm 610, trichuriasis 731, worms 763
white blood cells 761–762
see also, blood 128, leukocytes 341, lymphocytes 449, T cells 692
white lung 60
white matter 138–139
white of the eye 621
white pulp 670
whitehead 56
whitlow 762
see also herpes simplex 360
Whitmore disease 461
whooping cough 762
see also immunization 386, infectious diseases 393
Wilm's tumor 412, 498
Wilson's disease 354, 762
windpipe 727
winter depression 624
wisdom teeth 696, 698
witch's milk 454
withdrawal 762–763
see also alcoholism 73, delirium tremens 215, detoxification 220, drug dependence 233, stimulants 678
withdrawal symptoms, of smoking 658
womb 743
World Health Organization 70
worms 763
see also hookworm 367, hydatid disease 372, pinworm 560, roundworm 610, tapeworm 693, trichinosis 731, whipworm 761
wound, healing 341
wrinkles 763
wrist 763–764
see also carpal tunnel syndrome 159, connective tissue 193, ganglion 310, hand 334, joints 407, osteoarthritis 520, radial nerve 593, radius 594, rheumatoid arthritis 487, tendons 702, ulna 738, ulnar nerve 739
wryneck 496, 724

X

X chromosome 764
see also chromosomes 181, fragile X syndrome 305, Y chromosome 765
x-ray 764–765
chest 168
see also barium enema 119, barium meal 119, CAT scan 161, contrast x-rays 196
xanthelasma 765
see also cholesterol 179, eyelids 279, xanthoma 765
xanthoma 765
see also cholesterol 179, fats 286, xanthelasma 765
xanthoma tuberosum 765
xenotransplant 730
xiphoid process 677

Y

Y chromosome 765
see also chromosomes 181
yawning 765
yaws 765
see also infectious diseases 393
yellow fever 766
see also immunization 386, viruses 752
yin and yang 58
yoga 766
see also exercise 271, meditation 458, relaxation techniques 601
yuppie flu 181

Z

Zenker's diverticulum 230
ZIFT *see* zygote intrafallopian transfer 396
zinc 476
zinc oxide 225
zinc pyrithione 209, 218
Zollinger-Ellison syndrome 767
see also peptic ulcer 551, stomach 679
zona pellucida 289
zonule 275
zoophilia 631
zygomatic arch 649
zygomatic bone 649
zygote 255, 288–289, 291, **767**
see also fertilization 288, pregnancy 571, reproductive systems 44–47
zymogen cells 679